THE ROUGH GUIDE TO

Jazz

Written by

Ian Carr, Digby Fairweather, Brian Priestley

With contributions from

Charles Alexander, Roger Bardon, Gracie Cole, John Corbett, Ian Crosbie, Chris Ingham, Jeff Kallis, Matt Milton, Peter Moyse, Chris Parker, Richard Plant

Photographs by

Raffaella Cavalieri, Jak Kilby, Herman Leonard, Redferns, Roberto Serra

NEW YORK • LONDON • DELHI

www.roughguides.com

Introduction

The Rough Guide to Jazz is the most searching and up-to-the-minute guide to an area of music that gets more complex with each year. The only jazz dictionary written by musicians, it's a handbook that gives the facts, clarifies and defines the crucial issues, and gives straight answers to fundamental questions of value.

Jazz has grown so rapidly and in so many different directions that a newcomer might well feel bewildered. The music has moved from the simple structures and harmonies of its beginnings, through the developing sophistication of the 1920s and 1930s, the complexities of bebop and post-bop in the 1940s and 1950s, outright abstraction in the 1960s, jazz-rock-fusion in the 1970s, and into the pluralism that is its only constant in the 21st century. And even when a phase or movement has passed its peak, it is rarely over and done with. Virtually all styles and approaches continue to exist simultaneously, and any radical innovation is often accompanied by a reassertion of earlier styles: with the advent of bebop there was also a revival of traditional New Orleans, Chicago and Dixieland jazz; and with the experimentations that followed free jazz and jazz-rock came a revival of bebop. The very notion of what constitutes jazz is nowadays highly problematic – and doubtless this book will add to the controversy, both by what it omits and by what it includes.

The major part of the book is an A–Z of musicians – over two thousand of them. For a fuller understanding of these biographies, the book closes with a glossary that explains various terms (whether "swing" or "circular breathing"), and features concise essays on movements and styles, putting each in clear historical and musical perspective. All the major innovators and leading players are included – the extraordinary achievements of Louis Armstrong, John Coltrane, Miles Davis, Duke Ellington, Bill Evans, Dizzy Gillespie, Billie Holiday, and Charlie Parker, to name but a few, are covered incisively and comprehensively. There are detailed entries on hundreds of present-day musicians, giving not just their career outlines but also showing how each generation subtly shifts the balance of the existing order, often utterly changing how we hear the musicians that came before them. Entries on American musicians predominate, of course, but jazz has now become a world phenomenon and is now part of the culture of countries as diverse as Argentina and India: this guide has more of a global perspective than any other. And this book, uniquely, does justice to the less conspicuous figures of jazz – the sidemen, singers, accompanists and arrangers too often overlooked in jazz literature.

This is also a highly practical buyer's guide to jazz: discographies and pithy reviews lead you to the best and most representative recordings on CD (with a few essential LP listings to fill the gaps). To make sense of the immense amount of music available, we've selected the best of each artist – if you hear only a tenth of the recordings listed in this book, you'll have experienced jazz in its every aspect, and enjoyed some of the best music ever made.

A note on recordings

Each record listing is preceded by a symbol: ⊙ for an album on CD, ● for vinyl. The discs are listed in order of their recording dates, and the title of each disc is followed, in brackets, by the date of the original recording (when known) and the current label. Most of the recordings listed should be available both in Europe and in North America, on the label listed (sometimes as an import). However, record companies are forever deleting and reissuing CDs, and a recording will often re-emerge under a different label, either from the same major company stable or under license to an independent company. With recording contracts becoming increasingly scarce, many jazz artists have founded their own labels in order to issue material. In some instances the only (or best) recordings of a particular musician are deleted LPs – our reviews indicate whenever a search of the jazz stores might be in order. The rise of the internet means that many deleted LPs and CDs – as well as the obscurer independent labels – can be tracked down with relative ease.

Finally, where an artist has made an outstanding contribution to an album reviewed elsewhere, the symbol ››, at the end of the entry, directs you to the entry where you'll find it reviewed.

Ahmed Abdul-Malik

Bass, oud.

b. New York, 30 Jan 1927; d. 2 Oct 1993.

Born of a Sudanese father, Abdul-Malik was brought up in the Arab section of Brooklyn. Contrary to assertions in other sources, his name was not adopted in the mid-1950s by fellow Brooklyn bassist Sam Gill. A teenage friend of Randy Weston, Ahmed worked on bass with him and with others such as Art Blakey, Don Byas, Sam "The Man" Taylor, Thelonious Monk (in 1957–8), Herbie Mann in 1961 and Earl Hines in 1964. He also specialized in the oud (a type of lute), using it on record with Coltrane in 1961 and Hamiet Bluiett in 1977 and making several albums under his own name between 1958 and 1964, albums which promoted the introduction of Arabic music into jazz. [BP]

⊙ **Jazz Sahara** (1958; Riverside/OJC). Abdul-Malik's first album finds him surrounded by players on *darabeka*, *duf*, *kanoon* and violin, with the jazz element secured by Johnny Griffin and drummer Al Harewood.

John Abercrombie

Guitar, guitar synthesizers, electric 12-string guitar, mandolin guitar.

b. Port Chester, New York, 16 Dec 1944.

Abercrombie started on guitar at fourteen with lessons from a local teacher and played in rock bands while at school. At the Berklee School of Music from 1962–6 he studied guitar with Jack Petersen. He stayed in Boston from 1967–8, working with organist Johnny "Hammond" Smith, and in New York in 1969 he played briefly with Mike and Randy Brecker in the band Dreams. He spent a year and a half with Chico Hamilton in 1970–71, making his first trip to Europe with him and playing the Montreux festival. He worked with Jeremy Steig, Gil Evans and Gato Barbieri until 1973, then spent the next two years recording with Dave Liebman twice, playing with Billy Cobham, touring Europe with Jack DeJohnette, and leading his own trio and quartet. In 1974 he recorded his first album as leader for ECM, *Timeless*, with Jan Hammer on keyboards and Jack DeJohnette on drums, thus beginning his long and fruitful association with the label. Since then he has led a series of fine trios and quartets.

He was a member of Jack DeJohnette's New Directions band in the late 1970s, and from then into the 1980s he toured and recorded with fellow guitarist Ralph Towner, always with very fine artistic results. In 1988 he toured with a magnificent quintet led by trumpeter Kenny Wheeler, which included bassist Dave Holland, pianist John Taylor and Abercrombie's current trio drummer, Peter Erskine. Abercrombie also recorded with Wheeler's quintet and large orchestra in 1990, and toured America (in 1991) and Europe (in 1992) with the trumpeter. In November 1993, he toured again with Kenny Wheeler's Quintet, but this time bassist Palle Danielsson replaced Dave Holland. He also played with the huge orchestra under Gunther Schuller's direction which performed and recorded, posthumously, Charles Mingus's *Epitaph*. Over the years he has led Gateway, an occasional trio with Jack DeJohnette and Dave Holland. However, in the early 1990s, he returned to one of his first loves, the organ trio with Dan Wall (org) and drummer Adam Nussbaum; the three were together throughout the decade. In October 1998, this trio recorded for ECM with three guest stars, Wheeler, Joe Lovano and Mark Feldman. In 1997, Abercrombie had also played on composer/arranger Vince Mendoza's recording, along with Wheeler, John Taylor, Michael Brecker, Joe Lovano, Peter Erskine, Marc Johnson and the London Philharmonic Orchestra. In 2000 he recorded The Hudson Project with Erskine, John Pattatucci and Bob Mintzer.

Abercrombie is a guitarist for all contexts – jazz or rock, electric or acoustic, precomposed structures or free improvisation, small groups or larger ensembles – though he seems to favour the former. His melodic lines have great eloquence, he swings beautifully, and his emotional palette encompasses everything from the most exquisite shades of melancholy to unbridled exultation. His is one of the most highly individual voices of the post-Coltrane era and he is also an excellent composer. Abercrombie's early influences were Jim Hall, Barney Kessel and Tal Farlow; later ones were Pat Martino, George Benson, Larry Coryell and John McLaughlin. [IC]

John Abercrombie

⊙ **Timeless** (1974; ECM). Abercrombie's brilliant debut trio album with empathy and intensity sustained throughout.

Gateway (1975; ECM). Another superb trio with DeJohnette again and, this time, bassist Dave Holland. It's acoustic and a little more reticent, but highly focused and with plenty of absorbing incident.

John Abercrombie and Ralph Towner

Sargasso Sea (1976; ECM). With Towner on guitars and piano, the music is impressionistic and pastel-shaded but more sinewy than its surface suggests.

John Abercrombie

Characters (1977; ECM). This is a contemplative solo guitar album with great lyricism in the writing and playing. Abercrombie makes every note and phrase tell in this quietly impassioned personal statement.

Getting There (1987; ECM). This was a quartet outing with Michael Brecker (tenor) and another excellent rhythm-section – Marc Johnson (bass) and Peter Erskine (drums) – who had already been working with Abercrombie for two years. The presence of Brecker makes him raise his game, and the sparks fly in this dynamic set.

Animato (1989; ECM). Yet another superb trio with Vince Mendoza (synths) and the great Norwegian drummer, Jon Christensen. Several excellent compositions by Mendoza plus Christensen's brilliance spark Abercrombie, and the creative excitement is almost palpable. The electronics are also deployed to fine orchestral effect.

While We're Young (1992; ECM). Abercrombie had begun his career working with an organist and was now updating his roots and looking for "a really visceral sense of power and a heavy rhythmic aspect". Organist Dan Wall's power is leavened with subtlety and his four compositions are perfect vehicles for Abercrombie. Nussbaum's drumming is a crucial element, providing colour and definition in this compelling session.

November (1992; ECM). This is basically the old trio with Johnson and Erskine, but augmented by John Surman (soprano, baritone, bass clarinet) on four tracks out of twelve. The results are exquisite – moving from ballads and other composed pieces through different grades of abstraction to total collective improvisation. Surman's highly charged lyricism adds a vital extra dimension.

Speak Of The Devil (1993; ECM). The Abercrombie, Wall, Nussbaum trio again, but with more emphasis on atmospheric and poetic colours and textures, though the irrepressible Nussbaum frequently raises the temperature. There are two trio collective compositions, and the other seven pieces are by individual members of the group.

➤➤ **Jack DeJohnette** *(New Directions)*; **Kenny Wheeler** *(Music For Large & Small Ensembles; The Widow In The Window)*.

Brian Abrahams

Drums, percussion, vocals.

b. Cape Town, 26 June 1947.

Abrahams began making music at thirteen with local Cape bands, and was mostly noted for his singing. He developed as a drummer by backing singers and dancers in the early 1970s, and then played with a trio in Swaziland where he accompanied Sarah Vaughan and Nancy Wilson. He moved to the UK in 1975 and since then has worked with the John Taylor quartet, Ronnie Scott quintet, Chris Hunter band, Jazz Afrika, Dudu Pukwana's Zila, Johnny Dyani's Witchdoctor's Son and The Brotherhood of Breath. In the 1980s he began leading his own group, District 6. In 1988 he joined Abdullah Ibrahim's band, Ekaya, for a two year stint. Abrahams also collaborated with the late Jim Pepper (who had American Indian ancestry) between 1988 and the saxophonist's premature death in 1992. Abrahams has also worked in recent years with many leading musicians, including Dewey Redman, Mal Waldron, Archie Shepp, Annie Ross and Courtney Pine, and he has conducted drum clinics as well as running workshops for African choral music in Europe and Scandinavia. In America, Abrahams has recorded with Howard Johnson, Robin Eubanks and Buster Williams. He also toured Europe extensively with Ekaya, which included Delfayo Marsalis and Craig Handy. Other Americans he has performed with include Sonny Fortune, Arthur Blythe, Gary Bartz, Jimmy Witherspoon, David Murray and Don Cherry. Abrahams has played on many albums and appeared in numerous TV and radio broadcasts with some of the above-mentioned musicians, and also with his band District Six (who are still playing together today) and the Grand Union Orchestra. In 1998, he revisited his roots when he played on the debut album of the young South African alto saxophonist Ntshuks Bonga, *Abo Bhayi*. Bonga plays with a dazzling fervour reminiscent of the late Dudu Pukwana, and he also wrote the all-original material for the album, mostly in the exuberant spirit of the erstwhile Chris McGregor's Blue Notes. In 2002 he contributed to a radio tribute to the late British saxophonist Mike Osbourne, led by trumpeter Dave Holdsworth. Abrahams has been a professor of Jazz Studies at London's Guildhall School of Music since 1985, and is one of the most important and influential UK drummers. He admires Max Roach, Art Blakey and Jack DeJohnette, and has also been inspired by Ellington, Monk and Chris McGregor. [IC]

Brian Abrahams's District Six

Imgoma Yabantwana (1989; D6 Records). This quintet album mixes acoustic and electric instruments and the music, which ranges from lilting African rhythms and themes to Albert Aylerish free-playing, is magnificently realized. The compositions – three by trumpeter Jim Dvorak, three by the leader, and one by keyboardist Steve Lodder – show real imagination and melodic flair, and the performances "breathe" with considerable artistry.

➤➤ **Abdullah Ibrahim** *(African River)*.

Muhal Richard Abrams

Piano, composer, educator; also clarinet.

b. Chicago, 19 Sept 1930.

Abrams studied piano from the age of seventeen and spent four years at Chicago Music College. He began playing professionally in 1948 and was soon composing and arranging for bands. In 1961 he formed the Experimental Band, which included Eddie Harris, Donald Garrett, Victor Sproles and Roscoe Mitchell and was a rehearsal group for the city's improvisers. This grew into a more comprehensive organization

THE ROUGH GUIDE TO

Jazz

Other Rough Guide music titles:

Classical Music • Country Music • Cuban Music • Cult Pop • Elvis
Irish Music • Music USA • Opera • Reggae • Rock • The Beatles
World Music (2 volumes)

Acknowledgements

Ian Carr thanks all the musicians who returned their questionnaires, and Charles Alexander; Derek Bailey (Incus); Tom Callaghan; Phil Cassese (Arabesque); John Chilton; George Cole; John Crosby (Original Jazz Classics); John Cummings; Caroline Donockley (CDS Records); John Elson; George Foster; Mike Gibbs; Florence Haflon (Warners/WEA); Sharon Kelly (Sony Jazz); Jo Kennedy (RCA); Volker Kriegel; Steve Lake (ECM); Claire Logue (Linn); Trevor Manwaring (Harmonia Mundi); Tony Middleton; Hazel Miller (Cadillac Distribution); Mood Records (Germany); Alun Morgan; Wolf Mügler and Nathan Graves (Universal); all at Naxos; Eva Pakula and Jo Pratt (EMI/Blue Note); Chris Parker; Karen Pitchford (Koch International); Polly at Mac2; Enrico Rava; Ray's Jazz Shop; Steve Sanderson and Kerstan Mackness (New Note); Becky Stevenson (Polygram); Trevor Timmers (That Record Shop); Allan Titmuss; Steve Voce; Oliver Weindling (Babel); Sian Williams (Hush Hush); Valerie Wilmer.

Digby Fairweather thanks James Asman; John Barnes; Dave Bennett; Acker Bilk Agency; Lawrence Brown; Campbell Burnap; Mick Burns; John Chilton; Dave Claridge; Graham Colombe; Richard Cook; Eddie Cooke (Jazz Journal International, for generously opening his files); Bruce Crowther; Bix Curtis; Chris Ellis; Ena Fairweather; Jack Fallon; Jim Godbolt; Pat Hawes; Clarrie Henley; C. Hillman; C.J.B. Holme; Fred and Brenda Hunt; Keith Ingham; Ken Jones; Max Jones; Floyd Levin; Liza Lincoln; Adrian Macintosh; Dennis H. Matthews (Crescendo and Jazz Music); Tony Middleton; Brian Morton; Alan Morgan; Mike Murtagh (Just Jazz); David Nathan (Curator, National Jazz Archive); Keith Nichols; Paul Oliver; Len Page; Brian Peerless; Ed Polcer; Martin Richards; Brian Rust; Dave Shepherd; Jim Shepherd; Nevill Sherburn; Andrew Simons; Jim Simpson (The Jazz Rag); Michael Sisley; Nevil Skrimshire; Pete Strange; Maurice Summerfield; Warren Vaché Sr; Warren Vaché Jr; Peter Vacher; all at Verve Records; Jack Wallace (Jersey Jazz); Chris Wellard; Valerie Wilmer; Tiny Winters; Stan Woolley; Denny Wright.

Brian Priestley thanks Filippo Bianchi; John Chilton; Alex Dutilh (Jazzman); Louise Gibbs; Ira Gitler; Stephen Graham (Jazzwise); Andrew Homzy; Bill Kirchner; Joe Locke; Kerstan Mackness (New Note); Susan Mingus; Mole Jazz; Dan Morgenstern (Institute of Jazz Studies); Chris Parker; John Priestley (Sirocco Jazz); Peter Pullman; Ray's Jazz Shop; Lotte Scheffner (Bielefelder Katalog); Don Sickler; Simon Williams; Danielle Bias (Jazz At Lincoln Center); Tony Hall; Ron Horton; Frank Kimbrough; Suzy Melhuish (Caber); Lewis Porter; Yvette Shea; Peggy Sutton (PPR).

The Editors would like to thank Ken Bell for his more than conscientious proofreading; Katie Pringle for her customary patience and reliability; Matt Milton and Peter Buckley for invaluable editorial help; and Mchelle Pestana and David Guest for sorting out the pictures.

Rough Guide credits

Text editors: Joe Staines and Andy Dickson
Series editor: Mark Ellingham
Design and layout: Katie Pringle
Picture research: Michelle Pestana and David Guest
Proofreading: Ken Bell
Production: John McKay

Publishing Information

This third edition published May 2004 by Rough Guides Ltd,
80 Strand, London WC2R 0RL.

Distributed by the Penguin Group:
Penguin Books Ltd, 80 Strand, London WC2R 0RL
Penguin Books USA Inc., Hudson Street, New York 10014, USA
Penguin Books Australia Ltd, 487 Maroondah Highway, PO Box 257, Ringwood, Victoria 3134, Australia
Penguin Books Canada Ltd, 10 Alcorn Avenue, Toronto, Ontario, Canada M4V 1E4
Penguin Books (NZ) Ltd, 182–190 Wairau Road, Auckland 10, New Zealand
Typeset in Bembo, Helvetica and Kabel to an original design by Henry Iles.
Printed in Italy by LegoPrint S.p.A

944pp
A catalogue record of this book is available from the British Library.
ISBN 1-84353-256-5

called the Association for the Advancement of Creative Music (AACM). It began as a cooperative to help Chicago musicians promote and present music that could not be heard through established channels, but it rapidly developed into a social force serving the black community through music. As well as organizing festivals and concerts, Abrams and the AACM set up a school for young musicians, thus giving direction and structure to a hitherto haphazard and amorphous scene. In this, Abrams was the moral as well as the musical influence; he encouraged trombonist George Lewis to take up extra-musical studies – in this case, German philosophy. Saxophonist Joseph Jarman described, in an often-quoted statement, how he was helped: "Until I had the first meeting with Richard Abrams, I was like all the rest of the 'hip' ghetto niggers; I was cool, I took dope, I smoked pot, etc ... In having the chance to work in the Experimental Band with Richard and the other musicians there, I found something with meaning/reason for doing."

Several important groups and many leading musicians have emerged from the AACM, including the Art Ensemble Of Chicago, Air, Leroy Jenkins, Anthony Braxton, Chico Freeman and Ray Anderson. Abrams remained an *éminence grise* in Chicago throughout the 1960s and early 1970s, teaching, working as a pianist and often accompanying visiting soloists. In 1973 he toured with his group in Europe, and in 1976 left Chicago, moving to New York. He appeared at the Montreux festival in 1978, and at last began to get some international recognition as a pianist. There were more international appearances in the 1980s, and in 1994 his octet played six concerts in the UK for the Arts Council's Contemporary Music network. His important contribution to music has perhaps had the most substantial recognition in Scandinavia. In 1988, the Finnish UMO Jazz Orchestra recorded an album of Abrams' compositions, under his supervision, entitled *UMO Plays The Music Of Muhal Richard Abrams*, and in 1990 he was the very first recipient of The Danish Jazzpar Prize, the most substantial and prestigious jazz award in the world.

His music has almost always been variable in quality because the process of playing seems more important to him than the end product; spontaneous (abstract) improvisation is usually a major part of his performance, whether he's leading a group or playing solo. This attitude may derive partly from his experiences as an educationalist, because music was the medium through which self-discovery, self-help and a sense of community were achieved during the early days in Chicago.

His piano style incorporates the entire black tradition from ragtime, boogie-woogie and the stride school to bebop and free, totally abstract, improvisation. His influences range from James P. Johnson, Willie "The Lion" Smith and Art Tatum to Nat "King" Cole and Bud Powell. But he is also aware of the European classical tradition, and his compositions reflect all the disparate elements of his musical heritage. He composed *Novi* for symphony orchestra and jazz quartet, and his *String Quartet No. 2* has been performed by the Kronos Quartet. He continues to teach, tour and compose. [IC]

Jak Kilby

Muhal Richard Abrams

⊙ **Levels And Degrees Of Light** (1967; Delmark). Abrams leads an eight-piece band plus a vocalist, with mixed results.

⊙ **Young At Heart/Wise In Time** (1968; Delmark). Side one has Abrams in quintet formation with Leo Smith (trumpet) and Henry Threadgill (alto sax), plus bass and drums. Side two features Abrams playing solo piano.

⊙ **Sightsong** (1975; Black Saint). Abrams and Malachi Favors (bass and voice) in duo, creating a series of poetic tributes to fellow musicians.

⊙ **Spihumonesty** (1979; Black Saint). A well-disciplined septet album using electronic as well as acoustic instruments and including trombonist George Lewis, saxophonist Roscoe Mitchell and singer Jay Clayton.

⊙ **Colors In Thirty-Third** (1986; Black Saint). A sextet with Dave Holland, John Purcell, Andrew Cyrille, Fred Hopkins, John Blake. Abrams uses the personnel in trio, quartet, quintet and sextet formation, in a series of compelling performances.

⊙ **Blu Blu Blu** (1990; Black Saint). A fourteen-piece band including brass, reeds, two basses, percussion, and the maverick talents of virtuoso whistler Joel Brandon and rising guitar star Dave Fiuczinski. A thoughtful, forceful and varied orchestral album.

⊙ **One Line, Two Views** (1995; New World). Abrams with a ten-piece ensemble, including Marty Ehrlich (reeds), Mark Feldman (violin), Tony Cedras (accordion), Bryan Carrott (vibes), plus everyone on vocals when required, on this, one of the most focused and meaty albums in the Abrams discography.

⊙ **The Open Air Meeting** (1996; New World). This is a lively duo by Abrams (piano) and Marty Ehrlich (alto sax/clarinet), two old friends who first collaborated in the late 1970s. Their summer concert took place outside the Brooklyn Museum.

>> **Anthony Braxton** *(Three Compositions Of New Jazz)*; **Eddie Harris** *(Artist's Choice: The Eddie Harris Anthology)*.

Alex Acuña

Drums, percussion.

b. Pativilca, Peru, 12 Dec 1944.

Born into a highly musical family, Alejandro Neciosup Acuña (known as Alex) started on the drums at the age of four and was already playing in local bands by the time he was ten. Moving to Lima in his teens, he quickly established a reputation as one of Peru's outstanding drummers, and was snapped up by the great Latin band leader Perez Prado, travelling with his band to the USA in 1964. Three years later he arrived in Puerto Rico where he worked as a studio musician and freelance while studying classical percussion at the Puerto Rico Conservatory of Music.

In 1974, Acuña moved to Las Vegas, playing at various Hilton Hotels for such artists as Elvis Presley and Diana Ross. The following year he joined the great jazz fusion group, Weather Report, first as percussionist (1975–6), and then on drums (1976–7). This version of the group – with Joe Zawinul, Wayne Shorter, Jaco Pastorius, Acuña, and Badrena – was the group's finest and most successful incarnation. Acuña recorded two Weather Report albums: *Black Market* (1976), on which he was the percussionist, and *Heavy Weather* (1977) on which he played drums. The latter, which was one of the best sellers of the jazz-fusion era, included such tracks as "Birdland", "Havona" and the elegaic "A Remark You Made".

In 1978 Acuña moved to Los Angeles and became a studio musician, working with famous rock, pop, soul and jazz stars as well as film composers such as Michel Legrand, Dave Grusin and Michel Colombier. In 1989, he recorded his first solo record *Alex Acuña & the Unknowns* for JVC. A second solo album *Rhythms For A New Millennium*, with his Acuareles de Tambores, included varying styles of Latin, South American and African percussion. Hailed by the *Los Angeles Times* as "...the epitome of the world music percussionist, to whom no style is a stranger", Acuña has been named best Latin/Brazilian Percussionist by the readers' poll of *Modern Drummers* for five consecutive years. As well as running his own record company, Nido Entertainment, with his son Javier, this energetic and enterprising man is also a gifted teacher who also designs his own patented cymbals and sticks. [IC]

>> **Joe Zawinul** *(Heavy Weather)*.

Bruce Adams

Trumpet, flugelhorn; also guitar.

b. Birkenhead, UK, 3 July 1951.

Adams took up trumpet at eleven in Glasgow where his tutor was Maurice Deans. In 1965, with sponsorship from Nat Gonella, he won Opportunity Knocks, turning professional a year later. Between 1966–73 he played clubs, theatres and cruise liners (early on with his father, guitarist Bob Adams) and then returned to Glasgow to develop his jazz activities, co-leading small groups and a big band with Bill Fanning. In 1983 Adams won the "outstanding musician" award in Holsten's Big Band competition and in 1984 the BBC's soloist award in their rehearsal band competition. In 1986 Adams worked with Dick Hyman at the Edinburgh jazz festival, and other American collaborators from this same period included Benny Carter, Ray Bryant, and Scott Hamilton. In the 1990s his national reputation continued to develop as one of the prestigious players promoted by Big Bear Music, with a solo album release in 1992, a regular quintet with Alan Barnes (from 1993) the lead-trumpet chair with Kenny Baker's re-formed Dozen, work with the 'Echoes of Ellington' orchestra and regular backing to singer Elaine Delmar along with a great deal of solo activity at Ronnie Scott's London club and countrywide.

Adams is a player of formidable technique and range whose style, though all-embracing, leans naturally towards Swing inflections. His principal influences include Berigan, Armstrong, Butterfield and Roy Eldridge (whose range he can duplicate), as well as Lee Morgan and Clifford Brown. [DF]

⊙ **One Foot In The Gutter** (1992; Big Bear Records). Adams's debut album as a soloist-leader, demonstrating his strength, phenomenal range and stylistic versatility – from Louis Armstrong to Clark Terry – amid a tasteful quartet completed by John Clarke, Len Skeat and Bobby Orr.

⊙ **Let's Face The Music...** (1995; Big Bear Records). Featuring his quintet co-led with Alan Barnes, this collection is fine accessible bebop with the accent on swing, fire and communication. An outstanding feature for Adams is his leisurely, but muscular, exploration of Armstrong's "When It's Sleepy Time Down South".

George Adams

Tenor saxophone, flute, bass-clarinet.

b. Covington, Georgia, 29 April 1940; d. 14 Nov 1992.

Adams started on piano at eleven, and was soon accompanying the church choir; he then took up the sax and played with the high-school band and then R&B funk in a nightclub where he heard blues singers such as Howlin' Wolf and Lightnin' Hopkins. He won a scholarship to Clark College and graduated in music. In 1961 he spent the summer vacation touring with blues singer Sam Cooke. In 1963 Adams moved to Ohio, working with organ groups, and in 1966 toured Europe with organist Hank Marr's band, which included guitarist James "Blood" Ulmer. 1968 found Adams in New York working with Roy Haynes, Gil Evans and Art Blakey. He continued to collaborate and record with Evans in the later 1970s, but also played with Charles Mingus from 1973–6, commenting: "My association with Mingus as a musician and as a person – I consider that as one of the mainsprings of my musical life." After Mingus he freelanced for a while in New York, then played with McCoy Tyner. In the late 1970s and 80s he led his own groups, appearing at the New York jazz festival in 1979 and touring internationally with a fine quartet that included pianist Don Pullen, drummer Dannie Richmond and bassist Cameron Brown. On many occasions in the early 1980s he even treated the audience to a vocal blues.

Adams's playing had the vocal inflexions and power of his blues and gospel roots, as well as the harmonic and linear freedom of the leading post-Coltrane saxophonists. His huge sound harked back to Coleman Hawkins and Ben Webster, but he invested it with a flexibility of line and timbre which was all his own.

When Mingus's vast orchestral work *Epitaph* was given its posthumous premiere in 1989, Adams was one of the main soloists. His health began to decline the following year and he had breathing difficulties, but he continued to perform regularly with Mingus Dynasty until July 1992, and last played with it a month before his death. [IC]

City Gates (1983; Timeless). This is by the Adams-Pullen quartet, one of the most potent small groups of the 1980s, and it gives some idea of their scope – the homage to Mingus and Monk, their love affair with the blues and roots of jazz, their risqué affair with freedom.

Live At The Village Vanguard (1983; Soul Note). The Adams quartet again, and the whole session is available on two separate CDs giving a wonderful view of a working band in full cry, as the music moves dynamically from written structures to freedom and back.

>> **Gil Evans** *(Priestess)*; **Charles Mingus** *(Changes One)*.

Pepper Adams

Baritone saxophone.

b. Highland Park, Illinois, 8 Oct 1930; d. 10 Sept 1986.

Born Park Adams III, Pepper Adams played in early adolescence in Rochester, New York, then in Detroit with Lucky Thompson at the age of sixteen, when he also toured with Lionel Hampton. Before and after army service (1951–3), he performed regularly with fellow Detroit youngsters Donald Byrd, Kenny Burrell, Tommy Flanagan and Elvin Jones. Working with Stan Kenton, Maynard Ferguson and Chet Baker, he made the first albums under his own name on the West Coast in 1957. Based in New York from 1958, he played with Benny Goodman in 1958 and 1959 and was an occasional member of Charles Mingus groups in 1959, 1962 and 1963. After co-leading a quintet with Donald Byrd from 1958–62, he did some studio work before becoming a founder member of the Thad Jones-Mel Lewis band, with which he worked from 1965–78, including European tours. He also recorded under his own name while in Europe (1973, 1976) and undertook solo tours in the USA, Europe and Japan in the 1980s. A typical product of the post-bop era, Adams was one of very few players to attempt this style on the baritone. His hard, dry-sounding tone enhanced the razor-edged precision of his timing and his unstoppable steamroller lines. [BP]

Conjuration (1983; Reservoir). One of Adams's last featured recordings, this live set includes some original material by frontline partner Kenny Wheeler, as well as Adams's uncompromising improvisations.

Cannonball Adderley

Alto and soprano saxophones.

b. Tampa, Florida, 15 Sept 1928; d. 8 Aug 1975.

Cannonball (Julian Edwin) Adderley was a school music instructor in Fort Lauderdale both before and after army service, leading his own groups part-time. Encouraged by Eddie Vinson and others to move to New York, Cannonball did so in 1955 (shortly after the death of Charlie Parker) and made an immediate impact. He formed a touring quintet which included his brother Nat Adderley in 1956–7, then joined Miles Davis from 1957–9. In late 1959 Cannonball re-formed a quintet with Nat, a partnership which, with changing rhythm-sections, remained popular until his death from a stroke.

Adderley's solo playing was initially much influenced by Charlie Parker, although his less emphatic accents and rounded tone revealed an appreciation of Benny Carter; rhythmically, the strutting phraseology of Vinson and Louis Jordan left its mark, as on many of Cannonball's generation. He made all this into a homogeneous style, capable in the late 1950s of absorbing further influences such as aspects of John Coltrane's and even Ornette Coleman's work. In different ways, both of these latter approaches accorded with Adderley's penchant for melody and highly dif-

HERMAN LEONARD

Cannonball Adderley

fused decoration, which sometimes left his lines devoid of breathing spaces for the listener.

Leading his own group, he showed that he had also learned much from Davis. Cannonball's use of the rhythm-section, in particular, gave musical substance to the 1960s' style of "soul jazz", with which he was especially identified. Many observers were inclined to write off this development as being motivated purely by commercial zeal, but much of Adderley's work stands up better than other contemporary offerings. Although most of the popular tunes played by the quintet were written by band members, his own "Sermonette" and "Sack o' Woe" were widely used by other groups. [BP]

⊙ **Somethin' Else** (1958; Blue Note). The session owes much to Cannon's "sideman" Miles Davis (whose last small-group record under someone else's leadership this was), but the altoist is in top form on tracks such as "One For Daddy-O" and "Autumn Leaves".

⊙ **Quintet In Chicago** (1959; Verve). Though it features five-sixths of the current Davis sextet (ie without Miles), this is really just a standard "blowing session" which just happens to have a splendidly compatible cast of characters headed by Cannonball and Coltrane.

⊙ **Them Dirty Blues** (1960; Capitol). Perhaps superior to the salesworthy live album that preceded it, this session contained the hit versions of "Dat Dere" and "Work Song", along with Duke Pearson's "Jeannine". As well as Nat Adderley, this regular quintet briefly featured Bobby Timmons, replaced on nearly half the tracks by Barry Harris, and the excellent rhythm team of Sam Jones and Louis Hayes.

⊙ **The Best Of...The Capitol Years** (1962–9; Capitol). A shortlist of hits, many recorded live, with brother Nat and Joe Zawinul, who provides material such as "Mercy, Mercy, Mercy" and "Country Preacher".

Nat Adderley

Cornet, trumpet.

b. Tampa, Florida, 25 Nov 1931; d. 2 Jan 2000

Nat Adderley's work with Lionel Hampton in 1954–5, J.J. Johnson in 1957–8 and Woody Herman (1959) is overshadowed by the time spent in his elder brother's group (1955–7 and 1959–75). In the years after Cannonball's death, Nat continued the spirit of their collaboration, either as a guest soloist or as leader of his own group, which in later years included altoists Vincent Herring and Antonio Hart. Except when working in big bands, Nat preferred the mellower sound of the cornet to that of trumpet, and produced an interesting amalgam of Dizzy Gillespie, Clark Terry and Miles Davis, sounding at his best when not following any one of these too closely. He was also the composer of "Work Song" and "Jive Samba", frequently attributed to Cannonball; his son Nat Adderley Jnr (b. 22 May 1955) is a keyboard player who has worked with singer Luther Vandross. [BP]

⊙ **The Old Country** (1990; Enja). Nat revisited the territory of his brother's band via such numbers as "Jeannine" and "Nippon Soul", with his reliable quintet featuring the Cannonballesque alto of Vincent Herring.

Bernard Addison

Guitar.

b. Annapolis, Maryland, 15 April 1905; d. 22 Dec 1990.

Known principally for his reliable talents as a rhythm guitarist, Addison began on violin and mandolin, and, after early work with Claude Hopkins and others, specialized on acoustic guitar from 1928. Over the ensuing twelve years he worked in the best jazz company, including Louis Armstrong, Art Tatum, Fletcher Henderson's orchestra (1933–4), the Mills Brothers (1936–8), Stuff Smith and Sidney Bechet. After military service he played with Snub Mosley (among others), freelanced in Canada, and in the late 50s teamed with vocal group the Ink Spots, continuing to freelance throughout the 1960s and to work as a guitar teacher. [DF]

Jamey Aebersold

Alto and tenor saxophones, piano, educator.

b. New Albany, Indiana, 21 July 1939.

Principally known for his educational activities, Aebersold studied at Indiana University (1958–62) and later taught there and at the University of Louisville, while playing locally. Taking a leaf from the book of David Baker, he systematized previously scattered information on methods of bop and post-bop improvisation and, from 1967, started producing a continuing series of "minus-one" play-along albums, which have been a significant – and frequently acknowledged – influence on younger musicians. In 1971 he instituted his summer jazz courses in the USA, Europe and, from 1984, the UK. Aebersold also releases stylistically compatible recordings of finished performances through Double-Time Records, which in addition distributes educational material from other companies. [BP]

➤➤ **Bobby Shew** *(Tribute To The Masters)*.

Sylvester Ahola

Cornet, trumpet.

b. Gloucester, Massachusetts, 24 May 1902; d. 1995.

In Pee Wee Erwin's words "one hell of a trumpet player", Sylvester Ahola was easily combining the virtues of lead trumpeter and outstanding jazz soloist by 1925 in New York. He worked with Frank E. Ward's orchestra, Peter van Steeden and the California Ramblers, among many others, and also replaced the great Frank Guarente with Paul Specht's orchestra, which featured the ground-breaking small group the Georgians. After a period in 1927 with the legendary and short-lived Adrian Rollini New Yorkers (featuring Bix Beiderbecke, Frankie Trumbauer and Joe Venuti), he came to England to join first the Savoy Orpheans and later Ambrose. British records of the time are, in the words of Warren Vaché Snr, "saturated with his work" – he recorded more than 3000 (mostly unlisted) sides in the UK between 1927 and 1931. Finally a petition circulated by British trumpeters barred him, as an American, from recording other than with his band-leader Ambrose. "Hooley" returned home and picked up the threads with Ray Noble, Peter van Steeden (for NBC's new Bing Crosby radio show) and a full book of session work. Ahola made his last broadcast (with Van Steeden) in 1942, and by the end of the war was leading his own locally based group, "Sylvester's Music". In later years he worked with the Cape Ann Civic Symphony Orchestra, gave solo recitals and enjoyed retirement in his home community amid his collection of brass instruments. Ahola recorded more than four thousand sides in his career, which is the subject of a comprehensive bio-discography by Dick Hill. [DF]

Spike Hughes

His Decca-Dents And His Dance Orchestra 1930 Vol. 1 (Retrieval). This set has four fine titles featuring Ahola, including the very hot "It's Unanimous Now".

Toshiko Akiyoshi

Piano, composer.

b. Dairen, Manchuria, 12 Dec 1929.

Akiyoshi moved to Japan in 1946, becoming involved in jazz with various groups and leading her own group from 1951. Encouraged by Oscar Peterson to move to the USA, she studied at the Berklee School from 1956–9 and with the mother of Serge Chaloff. She formed the Toshiko-Mariano quartet, co-led by Charlie Mariano, whom she married. After spending a year with Mariano in Japan, she worked several months with Charles Mingus in 1962 (including his Town Hall concert), then returned to Japan for three years. In New York again, she did a radio series, wrote material for a specially assembled big band and formed a new quartet with second husband Lew Tabackin in 1970. Moving to Los Angeles two years later, she ran a big band of top studio musicians, making occasional live appearances and several albums. She returned to New York in 1983, forming a new big band co-led by Tabackin. She performed a Carnegie Hall concert in 1991 to celebrate her 35th anniversary in the USA, and from the late 1990s her band held a weekly residency at the new Birdland club. During the same period, Monday Michiru, her daughter by Mariano, earned an international reputation as a popular vocalist. Among her recent compositions, the major work *Hiroshima; Rising From The Abyss* was premiered in that city in 2001.

Although her piano work is extremely competent and clearly inspired by Bud Powell and later stylists, her big-band writing is far more individual. Here the influence of Gil Evans can be detected but the atmosphere is by no means the same, in part because of specifically oriental textures, especially in the use of woodwind and percussion. However, her background is reflected more profoundly and less self-consciously in the spaciousness and melodic grace of her best material. [BP]

David Redfern

Toshiko Akiyoshi

Toshiko Akiyoshi-Lew Tabackin Big Band (1974-6; Novus). With albums such as *Kogun* and *Sumi-e* unavailable except in Japan, this compilation gives a brief taste of Akiyoshi's piano and a larger helping of her original and atmospheric writing.

Manny Albam

Arranger, composer; also baritone saxophone.

b. Samaná, Dominican Republic, 24 June 1922; d. 2 Oct 2001.

Raised in New York, Albam studied clarinet in school and played professionally from 1940, soon specializing on baritone with a variety of big bands including Georgie Auld, Boyd Raeburn and Charlie Barnet. Already busy with arranging for these, and bands such as Herman, Kenton and Charlie Ventura, he stopped playing in 1950 and became a prolific freelance. In the LP boom of the late 1950s he recorded ten albums with his own studio bands; other album assignments included Coleman Hawkins (1956 and 1962), Joe Morello (1961) and Curtis Fuller (1962). From the mid-60s, as well as writing for TV, film, chamber groups and the Buddy Rich band, he began to teach arranging at the Eastman School and Glassboro State College, and from 1988 he and Bob Brookmeyer directed a weekly BMI Jazz Composers Workshop which led to founding a BMI/New York Jazz Orchestra in 1996. Still active as a writer, the enormously skilful Albam was chosen by Joe Lovano to score his 1996 *Celebrating Sinatra*. [BP]

The Jazz Workshop (1955; RCA Victor). Albam's first (and only available) session under his own name reflects the stylistic consolidations of the era, with his originals sounding not out of place beside updated tunes from the 20s. The six-horn octet features solos by Brookmeyer, Al Cohn, Joe Newman and others.

Joe Albany

Piano.

b. Atlantic City, 24 Jan 1924; d. 11 Jan 1988.

Italian-American Albany (Albani) was a post-war associate of Charlie Parker and Lester Young, with whom he can be heard on one airshot and one studio session respectively. He also worked with Benny Carter in 1944, Georgie Auld in 1945 and Stan Getz in 1947. Following an almost unbroken absence of 25 years from the jazz scene, Albany emerged again in the 1970s to forge a solo career. Still in many respects an unreconstructed bopper, he had the clarity of thought typical of keyboard players influenced by saxophonists such as Parker and Young. The brilliant touch and rhythmic vitality of his right-hand work were highlighted by a number of albums and a documentary film (Carole Langer's *Joe Albany ... A Jazz Life*), and attained a peak only hinted at in his mid-1940s work. [BP]

⊙ **Bird Lives!** (1979; Storyville). This collection of Parker lines, five out of eight being 12-bar blues, finds Albany in his element with Roy Haynes and bassist Art Davis.

Alvin Alcorn

Trumpet.

b. New Orleans, 7 Sept 1912; d.10 July 2003.

One of the most famous (and technically-able) of New Orleans trumpeters, Alcorn was taught trumpet by George McCullum Junior and worked early on with Henry Allen Senior, Armand J. Piron's society orchestra, and Clarence Desdune before spending eight years (1932-40) with trumpeter Don Albert's Ellington-style New Orleans-based swing band – a sensational Southern success which recorded for Vocalion in 1936. Thereafter Alcorn worked with Sidney Desvigne's swing orchestra and after military service rejoined Desvigne, by which time the New Orleans Revival was under way.

Alcorn then joined Papa Celestin, recorded with George Lewis, and worked for Alphonse Picou and others. In 1954 he joined Kid Ory in California, replacing Teddy Buckner, for a spell of club and concert appearances and fine recordings which established his name world-wide. He also appeared with Ory in *The Benny Goodman Story* in 1955, toured Europe with Ory again in 1956, and continued to work regularly (including recording with George Lewis in 1958) until the early 1960s by which time he was appearing regularly on Bourbon Street with his own groups and others. In 1966, he toured Europe with Keith Smith's New Orleans All Stars (subsequently with Mike Casimir in 1976 and later Chris Barber) and in 1969 was making guest appearances in New York. In 1973 he appeared as the trumpet-playing assassin in the opening scene of the James Bond classic *Live And Let Die* and from 1974 onwards was resident in New Orleans, at the Marriott Hotel on Canal Street ("the best session in New Orleans", said Owen Bryce in 1982).

In the 80s Alcorn also led a trio playing in restaurants (including the 'Commander's Palace' in New Orleans' up-market Garden district) and recorded with it for Sandcastle Records; he retired in 1990 and sadly died in 2003. [DF]

⊙ **Sounds Of New Orleans Vol. 6** (1952–3; Storyville). Representative example of Alcorn's controlled lead and solo work on two live dates and one studio session with Raymond Burke, "Slow Drag" Pavageau and others.

Howard Alden

Guitar, banjo.

b. Newport Beach, California, 17 Oct 1958.

Alden took up the banjo early and at the start of his teens was already playing in South Californian pizza parlours. Then he acquired a guitar and taught himself to play before taking lessons from Jimmy Wyble, and later Howard Roberts. By the age of eighteen he was working at Disneyland and in 1978 joined Red Norvo in Atlantic City for four months. Following a brief return to LA, Alden joined Dick Sudhalter's band in New York and moved there permanently in 1982, working at Eddie Condon's and the Rainbow Room with Woody Herman, as well as semi-regularly with Ruby Braff. From 1987 Alden joined Frank Tate in Braff's trio and continued moving into the best company, working with Kenny Davern, Flip Phillips, Buck Clayton's orchestra and Warren Vaché amongst others, as well as co-leading a highly respected quintet with trombonist Dan Barrett. In the mid-1980s Alden signed with Concord Records for a series of solo and group recordings, amongst others with Braff's trio and – perhaps most notably – with guitar-master George Van Eps for a set of leisurely and technically flawless duets. By the 1990s he was firmly established as the leading guitarist amongst America's new-generation swing revivalists, playing internationally as a soloist, starring at festivals, and working with select groups of fellow masters, including Ed Polcer's "Salute to Eddie Condon" band in 1993; following a period of ill-health he was fully back in action by 2003. [DF]

Howard Alden and Monty Alexander

⊙ **Snowy Morning Blues** (1990; Concord). A muscular exhibition of Alden's talents in the company of Monty Alexander, one of the most energized of contemporary pianists; programming ranges from Monk's "Bye-ya" to James P. Johnson's title track.

Ruby Braff Trio

⊙ **Bravura Elegance** (1990; Concord). Alden's unassuming musicality made him a more suitable partner for Braff than the brilliant but occasionally ostentatious George Barnes. The sound here recalls the Braff-Barnes quartet but Ruby is allowed to soar more naturally against Alden's discreet backings.

⊙ **Take Your Pick** (1996; Concord). With Lew Tabackin and Renée Rosnes, a later example of Alden's immaculate overview of Jazz's tradition and compositional history; intensity combined with flawless performance.

HOWARD ALDEN AND GEORGE VAN EPS

⊙ **13 Strings** (1991; Concord). Beautiful duets with seven-string maestro Van Eps, Alden's regular partner and professor, plus Dave Stone (bass) and Jake Hanna (drums).

⊙ **Seven And Seven** (1992; Concord). Following the *13 Strings* set, Alden determined to master the seven-string guitar and did; the results are here.

Oscar Alemán

Guitar.

b. Resistencia, Argentina, 20 Feb 1909; d. 10 Oct 1980.

The son of a guitarist who led an Argentinian folk troupe, Oscar was already a skilled professional, playing tangos, foxtrots and waltzes, when he first heard jazz while living in Brazil in the early 1920s. At the end of a two-year tour of Europe, backing American dancer Harry Flemming, Alemán stayed on, and in 1932 joined cabaret artiste Josephine Baker's accompanying band at the Casino de Paris. Alemán was a virtuoso guitarist with a hard-swinging jazz style, characterized by punchy chordal statements and incisive single-string runs. Although well regarded by Paris-based jazz musicians, including expatriate Americans such as Bill Coleman and Danny Polo, he remained in the shadow of Django Reinhardt and returned to Argentina on the German occupation of France. [CA]

⊙ **Special Guitars Vol.1** (1937–45; Jazz Time). This multi-artist compilation features Alemán's outstanding 1938 solo tracks "Nobody's Sweetheart" and "Whispering", together with 1939 trios plus quintet and septet tracks recorded back home in Argentina in 1942–5.

Eric Alexander

Tenor sax.

b. Galesburg, Illinois, 4 Aug 1968.

After moving with his family to the North-West, Alexander took piano lessons from the age of 7 and saxophone at 14, subsequently studying at Indiana University (1986–7) and William Paterson College in New Jersey (1987–90). During two years in Chicago, he worked with Von Freeman and began a long association with Charles Earland, with whom he made his first recordings. He also came second in the Thelonious Monk Competition in 1991 (the year it was won by Joshua Redman). Based in New York from 1992, he had further lessons with George Coleman and performed, among others, with Cecil Payne, Eddie Henderson, the Vanguard Jazz Orchestra and his former college teacher Harold Mabern. He co-founded the groups Tenor Triangle (with Ralph Lalama and Tad Shull) and One For All (with pianist David Hazeltine, trumpeter Jim Rotondi and others). His playing is rooted in post-bop but with pleasing allusions to more blues-based saxophone traditions. [BP]

⊙ **Alexander The Great** (1999; High Note). Whether producing hard-swinging, totally unpretentious Blakey-like jazz or showcasing his warm balladeer style, Alexander has a flawless tone, which is perfectly complemented by Charles Earland's organ, Jim Rotondi's sparky trumpet and Peter Bernstein's fluent guitar.

Gill Alexander

Double bass, vocals.

b. Hampton, Middlesex, 25 April 1935.

Alexander moved to Chelsea, London, in 1940, took up the guitar in 1944, and was performing in London concerts at the age of eleven. She studied harpsichord at Trinity College of Music from 1947 to 1950, and after that was at Chelsea School of Art where she was a founder-member and banjo player of the Temperance Seven – a 1920s revival band. In 1960 she took up double bass professionally, using her maiden name Gill Levin. Subsequently she has played with the Dick Williams band (1961–63), Pat Evans Quintet (c.1961–71), Keith Tippett (1968) and in Tippett's Centipede ensemble (1970), as well as with Harry Gold (1972–5). Alexander was also a member of the Morley College Jazz Orchestra (1964–9) and thereafter formed her own sixteen-piece jazz orchestra (1969–81). In 1981 she moved to Norfolk but carried on playing full-time and running her educational organization Jazzangles which continues to flourish. Alexander is a gifted bassist who runs her own quartet and has backed many leading soloists, both American and British. [DF]

➤➤ **Keith Tippett** *(Septober Energy)*.

Monty Alexander

Piano.

b. Kingston, Jamaica, 6 June 1944.

Montgomery Bernard Alexander did session work as a teenager with Ernest Ranglin and made an early mark in the 1960s when he relocated first to Miami and then New York. Recording under his own name since 1965, he made half a dozen albums with Milt Jackson in 1969, 1977 and 1982, all except one recorded live and co-featuring Ray Brown, who employed Monty in his trio from 1979 on. Since 1974 he has sometimes augmented his group with fellow Caribbean musicians, including steel-pan players, touring under the banner "Ivory And Steel" in the 1980s/early 90s and "Yard Movement" in the late 90s. The strong influence of Oscar Peterson's fluent technique is noticeable in Alexander's style and, as often with unpretentious players steeped in swing, the results can be highly compelling in person. [BP]

⊙ **Facets** (1979; Concord). The first of a series of sessions with Ray Brown as sideman, this includes jazz versions of the calypso "Hold 'Em Joe" and the Fats Domino-associated "I'm Walkin' " alongside more conventional material.

Stir It Up (1998; Telarc). The all-Bob Marley concept weighs a bit heavily, but there's some good playing here from Alexander, backed alternately by a "jazz" rhythm trio (plus guest Steve Turré on two tracks) and a reggae "ridim" section named The Gumption Band.

➤➤ **Milt Jackson** *(Soul Fusion)*; **Ernest Ranglin** *(Now Is The Time; Below The Bassline).*

Ray Alexander

Vibraphone, drums.

b. Lynbrook, Long Island, 7 Feb 1925; d. 8 June 2002.

Ray Alexander first studied the piano and later moving on to harmonica, trumpet and drums. Growing up amid the New York jazz scene of the 1940s he worked as a drummer with Stuff Smith, Joe Venuti, Chubby Jackson, Bobby Byrne, Mel Tormé, Claude Thornhill and the Dorsey Brothers. By the mid-1950s he was playing vibraphone more extensively with, among others, Charlie Barnet, Bill Evans, Stan Getz, Coleman Hawkins, Mel Lewis and Anita O'Day. He is also, reputedly, the vibraphonist on Peggy Lee and George Shearing's classic *Beauty And The Beat.* Alexander continued playing both vibes and drums (he played percussion on Martin Denny's *Quiet Village* album) and from the early 1960s was co-owner of a jazz restaurant in Westchester County. He also teamed up with drummer Mousey Alexander to form the quartet Alexanders The Great, and for the next fifteen years worked in and around New York. The good reviews for his first album, *Cloud Patterns* (1983), led to a second, *Rain In June,* and widespread solo visits to Europe. As well as touring, Alexander continued playing and teaching around New York until cancer curtailed his activities in December 2001. [DF]

Vigorous Vibes (1997; Cats Paw). Supported by a sympathetic trio, led by pianist Mac Chrupcala, Alexander's sonorous vibes are heard on a programme that includes standards, jazz standards (including RandyWeston's "Hi-Fly") and ballads. An enjoyable showcase for Alexander's seldom-heard talents.

Lorez Alexandria

Vocals.

b. Chicago, Illinois, 14 August 1929; d. 22 May 2001.

One of the most gifted and underrated jazz singers of the twentieth century, Alexandria sang first in gospel groups and church choirs before performing around Chicago in clubs including the "Brass Rail". Born Delorez Alexandria Turner, she began recording with pianist/arranger King Fleming for King Records, and later teamed up with pianist Ramsey Lewis. One of her earliest recordings, "Lorez Sings Pres", with trumpeters Paul Serrano and Cy Touff, achieved widespread popularity, and is well worth looking out for. In the early 1960s Alexandria moved to Los Angeles in search of wider recognition, singing at city clubs and appearing on TV. She recorded widely (with Toots Camarata among others) until the mid-60s when the burgeoning rock scene left her without a regular recording contract. Resuming recording in the later 1970s, she made several excellent albums for Discovery, Sony, Trend and Muse; three of them devoted to the songs of Johnny Mercer and all worthy of reissue on CD. Following a stroke in the mid-90s Lorez Alexandria retired from performing. [DF]

A Woman Knows (1978; Discovery). Critic Bruce Crowther calls Alexandria's performance of "I Can't Get Started" on this album "truly outstanding". There are several other high points, including "Trouble Is A Man" and the art-song "Something Cool".

Rashied Ali

Drums, congas.

b. Philadelphia, 1 July 1935.

Ali (whose mother sang with Jimmie Lunceford) first worked with local groups and R&B bands, and in 1953 played his first jazz gigs with his own group. In 1963 he moved to New York, working with Pharoah Sanders, Don Cherry, Paul Bley, Bill Dixon, Archie Shepp, Earl Hines, Marion Brown and Sun Ra. In 1965 he became second percussionist in John Coltrane's group, and when Elvin Jones left the group in 1966, Ali was the sole drummer. After Trane's death, Ali worked with the Alice Coltrane trio. In 1968 he toured in Europe with his own quartet and also worked with Sonny Rollins. He played with Jackie McLean in 1969 and continued leading his own groups. By 1972 he had formed Survival Records and organized a New York jazz musicians' festival. He opened his own loft, Ali's Alley/Studio 77, and continued workshops, concerts and occasional lectures throughout the 1970s. In the later 1980s he worked with James "Blood" Ulmer's band Phalanx, and in 1991 he played in duo with saxophonist Evan Parker at the Total Music Meeting in Berlin. Now in his late-60s he continues to perform and record with the likes of Sonny Fortune, and is credited with being one of the most technically adept pioneers of free percussion. [IC]

John Coltrane

Interstellar Space (1967; Impulse). This series of planetary-inspired pieces takes the freer rhythmic implications of Coltrane's last group to its stripped-down conclusion, in the saxophonist's only duo recording. Despite the intensity of the performance, Ali is never less than a sympathetic and interactive partner.

Don Alias

Percussion, drums; also guitar, bass.

b. New York, 25 Dec 1939.

Charles Don Alias was basically self-taught in the streets of New York and became part of Eartha

Kitt's backing group in 1957. While studying medicine in Boston and earning a degree in biochemistry, he began playing in clubs with such as Chick Corea and Tony Williams, then spent a few months at Berklee College and took private lessons. Moving back to New York, he joined Nina Simone and became involved in session work. He recorded with, among many others, Weather Report, Elvin Jones, Mongo Santamaria (on drums). He was heard on *Bitches Brew*, playing both percussion and drumkit (the latter notably on "Miles Runs The Voodoo Down"), and toured with Davis in 1971, returning to record *On The Corner* (1972) and *Amandla* (1989). In addition to these albums, he feels his best work to be on Jaco Pastorius's debut, Joni Mitchell's *Shadows And Light*, and *Heads Up* by Stone Alliance, the group he formed in the mid-70s with bassist Gene Perla. His favourite percussionists are Patato Valdes, Tata Güines and Giovanni Hidalgo, while particular inspirations are Miles, Dizzy and Herbie Hancock, with whom he toured in 1997. [BP]

➤➤ **Miles Davis** *(Bitches Brew, Amandla).*

Thomas Alkier

Drums.

b. Recklinghausen, Germany, 11 Aug 1965.

A professional drummer since 1985, Thomas Alkier is best known for his associations with larger ensembles – he has been a member of the Vienna Art Orchestra (VAO) since 1990 and plays regularly with the Nord Deutscher Rundfunk (NDR) Big Band – but he also contributes to smaller ensembles led by the likes of tenor player Christof Lauer, trumpeter Markus Stockhausen and alto player Wolfgang Puschnig. For both the NDR Big Band and the VAO, Alkier needs to be versatile: the repertoire of the former embraces everything from Monk to Mike Gibbs and from Hendrix to Lauer; the latter are equally at home with Eric Dolphy and Erik Satie. Accordingly, Alkier's personal taste ranges from Coltrane and Prince to Mozart, an eclecticism stretched on the VAO's *20th Anniversary*. Bowing out from the VAO in the late 90s, Alkier has recently played with various European small groups and has also been heard with divas Eartha Kitt and Jocelyn B. Smith. [CP/CI]

Christof Lauer

⊙ **Bluebells** (1992; CMP). An intriguing line-up – Lauer's tenor, Wolfgang Puschnig's alto, plus Bob Stewart on tuba and Alkier – that produces fiercely interactive original music with Stewart holding down the bass end of things while the saxophones duel above him and Alkier is assertively propulsive.

Vienna Art Orchestra

⊙ **20th Anniversary** (1997; Amadeo). Three-CD set roughly representative of VAO's many musical concerns over their twenty-year history. Alkier is best heard on *Powerful Ways: Nine Immortal Evergreens* for Eric Dolphy, which ranges from "Out There" and "Hat And Beard" to "Straight Up And Down" and the immortal "Jitterbug Waltz".

Geri Allen

Piano, keyboards.

b. Pontiac, Michigan, 12 June 1957.

After studying the piano from the age of seven, Allen's earliest jazz experience was in Detroit's Jazz Development Workshop, and she later played with Wallace Roney while teaching at Howard University, Washington, DC, in 1979. She then moved to New York and worked with Oliver Lake, Joseph Jarman and Lester Bowie, making her debut recording in 1983. An early member of the M-Base collective, she appeared on the first three albums of Steve Coleman in 1985–6, but then moved on to work with a wide variety of musicians, including Ralph Peterson and Dewey Redman, and in a trio with Charlie Haden and Paul Motian, touring Britain in 1991. Allen performed as a duo with Betty Carter and visited Europe with her in 1993. She wrote the suite "Sister Leola, An American Portrait", commissioned by Jazz At Lincoln Center (1993). She also toured with the new acoustic quartet of Ornette Coleman in 1994, and he appeared as a guest duettist on her 1996 album *Eyes...In The Back Of Your Head*. In the same year she was awarded the Jazzpar prize, and wrote the suite "Some Aspects Of Water" for the prizegiving concert. As well as her own projects, she has performed live and on record with her husband Wallace Roney and, despite lacking major-label support in recent years, has gone from strength to strength musically.

It was obvious early on that Allen's independent mind and complete command of her instrument would create excellent music that could not easily be categorized. She is interested in Monk and Herbie Nichols, yet plays on completely open forms just as enticingly as on jazz standards, and is equally compelling as a leader or when backing others. Like many musicians of her generation, she has been heard in a wide variety of contexts, from solo and trio set-ups to Oliver Lake's reggae-jazz. [BP]

Charlie Haden, Paul Motian and Geri Allen

⊙ **Etudes** (1987; Soul Note). Despite the billing, this is very much a piano trio, with unfailingly inventive work from Allen. Repertoire includes Ornette Coleman's "Lonely Woman" and Herbie Nichols's "Shuffle Montgomery" as well as original material.

Geri Allen

⊙ **The Nurturer** (1990; Blue Note). Allen assembles a quintet featuring her Detroit mentor, ex-Ray Charles trumpeter Marcus Belgrave, and other Belgrave students Kenny Garrett and Robert Hurst. She conjures moods as varied as the neo-bop of "Batista's Groove" and the dreamy spaciousness of the title track.

Harry Allen

Tenor saxophone.

b. Washington, DC, 12 Oct 1966.

The most gifted new-generation swing tenorist to emerge since Scott Hamilton, Allen began on accordion at the age of seven, and changed to clarinet and tenor sax in a Los Angeles high school, where his first major influence was Paul Gonsalves. Later living in Rhode Island, Allen was influenced by Hamilton, Lester Young and Ben Webster. He graduated from Rutgers University in New Jersey after initial work with Bucky Pizzarelli, amongst others. In 1991 he appeared in the "Swing Under 40" concert at the New York JVC jazz festival, and by then had begun recording with pianist John Colliani, as well as with the gifted expatriate British pianist Keith Ingham. As the 1990s progressed, Allen moved comfortably onto the international touring circuit, and his rounded talents, though different from Hamilton's, seem set for the same level of artistic success and recognition. [DF]

⊙ **Someone To Light Up My Life** (1991; Mastermix). Recorded with an Anglo-American alliance of Oliver Jackson (drums), John Horler (piano) and Pete Morgan (bass), this is an assured exposition of Allen's swing talents.

⊙ **I Know That You Know** (1992; Mastermix). Similarly recommended, this set teams Allen with two regular American colleagues, pianist John Colliani (MD for Mel Tormé) and great bassist Michael Moore; lack of drums gives attractive breathing space to Allen's relaxed style.

⊙ **Harry Allen Meets The John Pizzarelli Trio** (1995; BMG). Allen's (regular) partnership with the charismatic Pizzarelli and his drummer-less trio produces perfectly matched swing music in which every note is in place but never too groomed for comfort.

Henry "Red" Allen

Trumpet, vocals, composer.

b. New Orleans, 7 Jan 1908; d. 17 April 1967.

One of the best and brightest young trumpeters in New Orleans by the early 1920s (his father ran a famous brass band in the city from 1907 to 1940), Allen first moved north to join King Oliver's Dixie Syncopators in 1927. He moved back to New Orleans to work with pianist Walter "Fats" Pichon and Fate Marable, but Loren Watson, a Victor talent scout, signed him as the label's much-needed answer to Louis Armstrong.

Allen travelled to New York and recorded with Luis Russell's orchestra, which he then joined full-time. The orchestra, with old friends like Paul Barbarin, Greely Walton and Russell himself, felt like home. "It was the happiest band I ever worked in", Allen remembered later. "It was also the most swinging band in New York – it put the musicians in an uproar!" So did their young trumpet star, whose unique "modern style" – all slurs, atonal twists and growls – was a real Armstrong alternative, showing up dramatically in Russell classics like "Jersey Lightning" and on Allen's solo sides with his New Yorkers.

In 1933, tempted by money and prestige, Allen joined Fletcher Henderson. The stay, which involved great exchanges with Coleman Hawkins, lasted a year, then came three years with Lucky Millinder (during which Allen recorded his hit "Ride Red Ride", originally a poorly reviewed B-side). In 1937 he moved back to Russell as featured artist and warm-up man for Louis Armstrong, who by now was fronting Russell's band. Each night Allen was allowed a set spotlighting himself before Armstrong took the stand, but he kept busy as a freelance too, recording solo for Perfect and Vocalion, working with Joe Marsala in a mixed group, and playing up and down 52nd Street.

In 1940 Russell's band was sacked *en bloc* by Armstrong's manager Joe Glaser, and for the last 27 years of his life Allen led his own bands and worked solo. His sextet, formed that year (including, among others, Ed Hall, J.C. Higginbotham and Ken Kersey), quickly became successful and worked steadily for 14 years, commuting among Boston, Chicago, San Francisco and New York. By 1954, Allen found himself working regularly at the Metropole, New York, a noisy musicians' bar which featured two or more jazz bands at one time, in all styles. Allen's group – featuring Coleman Hawkins, Buster Bailey and J.C. Higginbotham – entertained most nights, and perceptive listeners noted that Allen's approach, amid the noise, was refining itself into something wonderful: a collage of blues phrases, rocket-flares, subterranean rumbles, growls and flutters, often delivered in a determined whisper.

The 1960s signalled a great "Red" Allen revival. With a quartet (the most popular format for swing trumpeters since Jonah Jones's) he recorded for Prestige, was featured in *Down Beat* in a complimentary session-commentary ("Condition Red – Allen, that is") and reviewed with five stars soon after. A second album, *Feelin' Good*, quickly turned into a

William Gottlieb

Henry "Red" Allen

classic and was given the seal of approval by modern trumpeter Don Ellis – "'Red' Allen is the most avant-garde trumpet player in New York." He continued his New York club work, and made visits to England in 1964, 1966 and 1967 (his first had been with Kid Ory in 1959), trips that produced as much love for his gentle personality and humour as respect for his music. His last visit to England, in tandem with Sammy Price, came in 1967, when it was plain that Allen was playing at reduced power: he died later that year of cancer. [DF]

Ride Red Ride (1930–34; ASV). Excellent cross-section of Allen's formative work, incuding sides with Luis Russell, Fletcher Henderson, Billy Banks et al, and including important classics such as "Queer Notions" and "Patrol Wagon Blues".

Henry "Red" Allen And His Orchestra 1929–33 (Classics). Allen's earliest sides as a leader, revealing his oblique, entirely original reinterpretation of the Armstrong canon in magnificent classics including "Biff'ly Blues", "Feeling Drowsy" and "Swing Out".

The Henry Allen Collection' 1932–46 (Collectors' Classics). The definitive Allen chronology; magnificent transfers by John R.T. Davies beginning with Billy Banks's Rhythmakers and moving on from there, incomplete takes included.

World On A String (1957; RCA Bluebird). Legendary sessions, with Higginbotham, Bailey and Hawkins gloriously displaying the subtle side of Allen's solos in tracks like "I Cover The Waterfront" and "Let Me Miss You Baby".

Mr Allen (1962; Prestige Swingville). The quartet recording praised by Martin Williams in *Down Beat*, a write-up that led to renewed critical acclaim for Allen in the 1960s.

Feelin' Good (1965; CBS). Perhaps Allen's greatest album, recorded live with a quartet at the Blue Spruce Inn, Long Island.

>> **Kid Ory** *(Henry "Red" Allen And The Kid).*

Pete Allen

Clarinet, alto and soprano saxophones, leader, vocals.

b. nr Newbury, Berkshire, UK, 23 Nov 1954.

Son of banjoist Bernie Allen, Pete Allen set up his Dixieland band after formative years in the West Country, when he played with trumpeter Rod Mason. Equipped with a hard-driving clarinet style that's sometimes reminiscent of Ed Hall, Allen presents a show of classic jazz repertoire which, by virtue of sound marketing as well as flair, has steadily attained the pulling-power of senior men such as Kenny Ball and Terry Lightfoot. Regular professional colleagues on the road include entertainers such as Beryl Bryden and Tommy Burton; fine players who have worked with him include Ian Hunter-Randall, Chris Hodgkins (trumpet), Mick Cooke (trombone), John Armatage (drums). Since his line-up stabilized, around 1983, Allen's band has achieved a new cohesion; by the mid-1990s he was combining band and solo appearances with running a jazz club and restaurant in Bath. Later in the 90s he reverted to fulltime bandleading amid strict Traditional format and (from 2003) more regular solo appearances, this time with pre-recorded rhythm. [DF]

Beau Séjour (1990; P.A.R.). A solo set that represents the best of Allen's extensive self-produced discography – brisk, efficient and good-humoured jazz.

Ben Allison

Bass, composer.

b. New Haven, Connecticut, 17 Nov 1966.

Allison, whose mother sang in amateur choirs, started on guitar when he was 9 and studied double-bass at Yale University and New York University. He was already an active sideman with Lee Konitz, when he co-founded with Frank Kimbrough the Jazz Composers Collective in 1992. Two years later the two also started one of the Collective's regular bands, The Herbie Nichols Project, which researched and performed the music of the pianist-composer of that name. A follower of funk bassist Chuck Rainey as well as Wilber Ware, Charles Mingus and Milt Hinton, Allison's wider inspirations include Donny Hathaway, Boubacar Troare and Alban Berg. In addition to leading his own groups Medicine Wheel (from 1996) and Peace Pipe (2001), he has composed music for National Public Radio and playwright Donald Margulies. [BP]

⊙ **Riding The Nuclear Tiger** (2000; Palmetto). One of several albums with a similar personnel, this features his JCC colleagues Ron Horton, Michael Blake, Ted Nash and Frank Kimbrough. Described by Allison as "the full realization of my Medicine Wheel project", it has absorbing original compositions including a Mingus tribute, "Love Chant Remix".

Herbie Nichols Project

⊙ **Strange City** (2001; Palmetto). With the musicians mentioned above, Matt Wilson and Wycliffe Gordon make up a septet that is far more than an average "repertory band", presenting previously undocumented Nichols material lodged at the Library of Congress.

➤➤ **Frank Kimbrough** *(Quickening).*

Mose Allison

Piano, vocals, composer; also trumpet.

b. Tippo, Mississippi, 11 Nov 1927.

Allison had piano lessons from the age of five and played trumpet with a Dixieland band in high school. He was steeped in the blues and black music of the Mississippi area, but also listened to Nat "King" Cole's trio and the beboppers. After college (Louisiana State University) he played all over the South until 1956, when he moved to New York. During the next three years he worked with Stan Getz, Gerry Mulligan, Al Cohn and Zoot Sims. He also led his own trios around New York and played with local rhythm-sections in Paris, Stockholm and Copenhagen. From the 1960s to the 1990s he continued to work with his trio in clubs in the USA and occasionally in Europe.

His favourites include blues singers such as Sonny Boy Williamson and Tampa Red, as well as Ellington and Monk, and his singing and playing blend all these influences. Everything he does is understated, with a superbly swinging time-feel. His soft voice has the rhythms, the throwaway (half-spoken) words and the inflexions of the country blues, but he projects a sophisticated and wry form of self-communion in the setting of his inherently "modern" trio. His piano-playing is also spare and epigrammatic, and Allison has a casual wholeness of vision which is unique. The music and lyrics of his own songs encapsulate his gently ironic view of the world, but he also brings the same manner and mood to all the standard songs and blues in his extensive repertoire. Some of his best-known compositions are: "Parchman Farm"; "If You Live"; "Everybody Cryin' Mercy"; "Look What You Made Me Do"; "I Don't Worry About A Thing"; and "Your Mind Is On Vacation". [IC]

⊙ **Sings And Plays** (1957–9; Prestige). This is a rich compilation with thirteen vocals (including several classic tracks) and ten instrumental numbers.

⊙ **Creek Bank** (1958; Prestige). This two-CD set is a pairing of the titular album with *Young Man Mose*, and features the trio with Addison Farmer on bass and Nick Stabulas or Ronnie Free on drums. This covers the gamut of Allison territory – original songs, standards and blues.

⊙ **I Don't Worry About A Thing** (1962; Rhino/Atlantic). A very fine album, with Addison Farmer again and Osie Johnson on drums. There are more classic vocals including the title track, and three instrumental pieces.

➤➤ **Al Cohn** *(You 'N' Me).*

Laurindo Almeida

Guitar.

b. São Paulo, 2 Sept 1917; d. Los Angeles, 26 July 1995.

After working as a studio musician on Brazilian radio, where he had his own group, Almeida joined Stan Kenton from 1947–9, playing on "Peanut Vendor" and guesting on some later sessions. He then did regular studio work on the US West Coast, specializing in acoustic guitar and also composing for films. His infrequent small-group recordings included famous quartet sessions featuring Bud Shank made in 1953 and 1958, which were highly influential in Brazil. In 1964 he also recorded and toured Europe as a guest with the MJQ, and in the following decade formed a more permanent quartet with Shank called the L.A.4. At a time when African-Cuban musicians were becoming involved with bebop, Almeida was one of the first to bring a more gentle Brazilian influence into the jazz context. [BP]

⊙ **Brazilliance Vol. 1** (1953; World Pacific). This series of recordings, first issued on two LPs, has Bud Shank plus bass and drums going Latin, on Almeida's mixture of Brazilian standards, originals and versions of songs such as "Speak Low". This "cool jazz" was crucial to the creation of the bossa nova in the late 1950s.

Barry Altschul

Drums.

b. Bronx, New York, 6 Jan 1943.

Altschul began on drums at eleven and studied with Charlie Persip. He worked with Paul Bley from 1964–70, going deeply into the free improvisation of the day, and was also involved with the Jazz Composers' Guild from 1964–8. In 1968 he went to Europe, playing bebop and working with Carmell Jones, Leo Wright and Johnny Griffin. Back in the USA he studied with Sam Ulano for nine months and in 1969 worked with Sonny Criss and Hampton

Hawes in California and Tony Scott in New York. Then he was with Circle from 1970–72, a group led by Chick Corea and including Dave Holland and Anthony Braxton, which toured the USA and Europe, recording a live double album in Paris. In 1972 Corea left the group, and the remaining three members with Sam Rivers recorded *Conference Of The Birds*, an album of Dave Holland's compositions.

From 1974–6 Altschul and Holland worked in the Braxton quartet (with Kenny Wheeler); they also graced the Sam Rivers trio until Altschul left in 1978. In 1975 he taught a great deal and wrote a conceptual study book for the drums. At around the same time he and Rivers had been leading a quartet with Ray Anderson (trombone), Brian Smith (bass) and Anthony Davis (piano), but soon after this Altschul's attentions turned to leading a new trio with Anderson and bassist Mark Helias. This trio toured extensively in the early-80s, though Altschul still found time to play with Art Pepper in 1981.

Altschul has studied African, Indian, Brazilian and Caribbean music, incorporating elements from them into his work. Although he began in the 1960s avant-garde, he eventually (like so many others from that period) re-examined the entire spectrum of jazz history, going back into bebop, hard bop and swing. He told Lee Jeske: "The avant-garde was a period that was necessary to extend the vocabulary of the musicians themselves. ... After a while the avant-gardists become the contemporary, then they become the mainstream." As a member of this so-called avant-garde mainstream, he remains a committed and active musician to this day. [IC]

Virtuosi (1967; Improvising Artists Inc). Altschul leads pianist Paul Bley and bassist Gary Peacock for this all-star session (on 2 CDs) which includes much free improvisation.

That's Nice (1985; Soul Note). This is mainly a quartet album with trombone (Glenn Ferris), reeds (Sean Bergin) and bass (Andy McKee), but pianist Mike Melillo plays on a couple of tracks. There are some good moments but the album lacks focus.

» **Chick Corea** *(The Song Of Singing).*

Franco Ambrosetti

Trumpet, flugelhorn, composer.

b. Lugano, Switzerland, 10 Dec 1941.

Franco Ambrosetti's father, Flavio, was a saxophonist who played opposite Charlie Parker at the 1949 Paris jazz festival. Franco had classical piano lessons until he was sixteen, and then taught himself to play the trumpet. In 1962 he began playing at Zurich's African Club and also commenced a long musical association with his father, George Gruntz and Daniel Humair. By 1972 this union had developed into the George Gruntz Concert Jazz Band. Since the 1960s he has continued to play in his father's quintet and to lead his own groups.

Ambrosetti is a brilliantly assured player in the neo-bop mould. His main influence in terms of sound, articulation and phrasing seems to be Freddie Hubbard, but with a harmon mute the spirit of Miles Davis (mid-1960s vintage) imbues his work. He often has leading Americans as well as Europeans in his groups and on his records, and his 1983 album *Wings*, with Mike Brecker, Kenny Kirkland, Humair, John Clark and Buster Williams, shows him at his best, as both player and small-group composer. In 1985 he led an all-star band at the Berlin festival which included Humair, Dave Holland, Gordon Beck and Dave Liebman.

Ambrosetti has a degree in economics from the University of Basel, and also works an eight-hour day as an executive of his family's firm, Ettore Ambrosetti & Sons, which produces steel wheels for cars and industrial and agricultural vehicles. He can also stay the pace in very fast jazz company; as he explains, "I am not able to play only music or to be only an industrialist. I need both." [IC]

Heartbop (1981; Enja). Ambrosetti on flugelhorn leading a quintet comprising Phil Woods (clarinet and alto sax), Hal Galper (piano), Mike Richmond (bass) and Billy Hart (drums). There are three compositions by Ambrosetti, including the aptly named title track, one by Galper and the Rogers & Hart ballad "My Funny Valentine". These are consummate performances of neo-bop, and Ambrosetti plays with real imagination and passion.

Gin And Pentatonic (1983 & 1985; Enja). This combines the best of two albums – *Wings* and *Tentets* – and includes trumpeters Lew Soloff and Mike Mossman, and other Americans. Ambrosetti and the bands play, as usual, with total conviction.

Live At The Blue Note (1992; Enja). This quintet outing is exceptional even by Ambrosetti's standards. The rhythm-section of Ira Coleman (bass) and Victor Lewis (drums) is outstanding whether playing a rock feel or straight jazz-time, and tenor saxophonist Seamus Blake has much to say. The pianist is Kenny Barron, and he and Ambrosetti (on flugelhorn throughout) are on top form.

Light Breeze (1997; Enja). Ambrosetti, on flugelhorn throughout, leads a superb quintet with John Abercrombie, Miroslav Vitous, Billy Drummond, and pianist Antonio Farao.

Albert Ammons

Piano.

b. Chicago, 23 Sept 1907; d. 2 Dec 1949.

One of the fathers of boogie-woogie, Ammons was a brilliantly versatile pianist who worked in Chicago clubs as a soloist in the 1920s and later on, around the turn of the decade, with territory bands and orchestras, including Louis Banks's. From1934–8 he led his own band in Chicago (including a residency at the Club DeLisa) and made his first records for Decca in 1936, featuring Guy Kelly (trumpet), Israel Crosby (bass) and others. Ammons's powerful "shouting" style and his gift for boogie were ideal for the dawning eight-to-the-bar commercial era, and in 1938 he moved to New York to appear at Carnegie Hall and regularly at Café Society, often with Pete Johnson and sometimes in trio with Meade "Lux" Lewis. Despite temporary hand paralysis in mid-decade, he remained successful all through the 1940s, and he continued touring (with residencies in Hollywood and Chicago), and recording (his last sides, with Crosby again, were made for Mercury in 1949), until he became seriously ill. [DF]

⊙ **Albert Ammons 1936–9** (Classics). This contains eighteen of Ammons's best solos, including "Shout For Joy" and "Boogie Woogie Stomp", plus two Decca sessions by his Rhythm Kings.

⊙ **Boogie Woogie Man** (1936–44;Topaz). A superb set assembling piano solos, duos and trios (including the mighty "Boogie Woogie Prayer" parts 1 and 2 with Meade "Lux" Lewis and Pete Johnson) plus famous sides with Harry James, the Port of Harlem Jazzmen and Ammons's 1944 Rhythm Kings including Hot Lips Page, Dickenson, Byas et al.

⊙ **Boogie Woogie Man** (1936–46; ASV) Similarly fine sampler, duplicating much of the above material but with excellent transfers and notes by the ever-reliable Vic Bellerby. You takes your money...

Gene Ammons

Tenor saxophone.

b. Chicago, 14 April 1925; d. 23 July 1974.

Gene Ammons, "Jug" to his friends, played with the Billy Eckstine band from 1944–7, then worked in Chicago recording under his own name and with his father, Albert. He was featured in the Woody Herman band in 1949, then co-led a two-tenor septet with Sonny Stitt in 1952. After continued appearances with his own group or as visiting soloist, and recording with all-star line-ups, he was imprisoned for drug offences (1958–60 and 1964–9). He made his only European trip to the 1973 Montreux festival and was working steadily until shortly before his death from pneumonia.

Ammons's approach derives from both Lester Young and Ben Webster, with something of the latter's tone applied to the lines of the former. The underlying simplicity and directness of Young and Webster fed a style which soon took on a life of its own and became very popular. His ballad playing was especially emotive but, although his melodies were in some senses obvious, they were never short of subtleties that appealed to the more jazz-minded audience. While Ammons's career ended before he had gained favour outside the USA, he founded a "Chicago school" of tenor which influenced numerous players, such as Johnny Griffin and Clifford Jordan, before becoming an unrecognized part of the international language of jazz – as, indeed, did his 1950 tune "Gravy", which was the basis for the standard "Walkin' ", copyrighted by his manager Richard Carpenter. [BP]

⊙ **All Star Sessions** (1950–5; Prestige/OJC). A combination of duos, or duels, with Sonny Stitt and an early-model "blowing session" with Art Farmer and Lou Donaldson, this gives some idea of Ammons's authority among his contemporaries.

⊙ **Gentle Jug** (1961–2; Prestige). Two LPs from an enormously prolific period, showing Ammons emoting on a programme of standards.

David Amram

French horn, composer; also guitar, piano, flutes, percussion.

b. Philadelphia, 17 Nov 1930.

After composition studies at Oberlin College and army service in Europe, Amram played and recorded in Paris in 1955. Based in New York from the end of that year, he worked briefly with both Charles Mingus and Oscar Pettiford, and led a long-standing quintet with saxophonist George Barrow from 1957–65. Mainly active in the symphonic field and as a composer of film music, he was an early champion of "third stream" and of world music, and accompanied Dizzy Gillespie and others on their historic first visit to Cuba in 1977. In the 80s and 90s, he conducted orchestral concerts featuring singer Betty Carter. [BP]

⊙ **Havana/New York** (1977; Flying Fish). This includes extended jamming with Arturo Sandoval and Paquito D'Rivera, plus New York tracks featuring exiled Cuban musicians with the likes of Thad Jones and Pepper Adams.

Arild Andersen

Double bass, electric bass, composer.

b. Oslo, Norway, 27 Oct 1945.

At college Andersen specialized in electronic engineering but studied music privately with George Russell. From 1967–73 he played with Jan Garbarek's quartet and trio, and at the same time worked with singer Karin Krog. He worked in the USA with Sam Rivers and Paul Bley in 1973–4, then formed his own group with Scandinavian musicians Pal Thowsen, Jon Balke, Juhani Aaltonen and Knut Riisnes. In 1979 he was a member of a quartet with Kenny Wheeler, Paul Motian and pianist Steve Dobrogosz, and in 1981 was part of another all-star quartet with Bill Frisell, John Taylor and Alphonse Mouzon. With his fellow-countryman drummer Jon Christensen, Andersen co-led a quintet in the mid-1980s called Masqualero with sidemen pianist Jon Balke, saxophonist Tore Brunborg and trumpeter Nils Petter Molvaer. The group toured Europe and the UK, performed in 1986 at the Village Vanguard in New York, and recorded albums in 1983 and 85. In 1975 the European magazine *Jazz Forum* voted him top European bass player. His main influences are Miles Davis, Don Cherry and Paul Bley. [IC]

⊙ **A Molde Concert** (1981; ECM). This is a brilliant live concert by the group with Taylor, Frisell and Mouzon. All nine superb compositions are by Andersen, and this is one of the great group performances of the decade, with major contributions from Frisell and Taylor. Andersen and Christensen are as usual faultless.

⊙ **If You Look Far Enough** (1988–92; ECM). This time the group is a quartet with Ralph Towner (guitar), Nana Vasconcelos and Audun Kleive (snare drum). Again, the folk/ethnic strain predominates, and the music has a quiet intensity and depth. Andersen and Towner have a perfect understanding, and the bass is employed both rhythmically and melodically to great effect.

Sagn (1990; ECM). A moody, folk/ethnic album recorded by a sextet including Nana Vasconcelos (percussion and vocals), three Scandinavian musicians – saxophones, guitar and keyboards – and a vocalist, Kirsten Braten Berg.

Hyperborean (1996; ECM). Andersen, with an ensemble comprising saxophonists Brunborg and Bendik Hofseth, keyboardist Kenneth Knudsen, drummer Paolo Vinaccia, plus the Cikada String Quartet, achieved this, perhaps his most focused and successfully realized album to date.

>> **Jan Garbarek** *(Afric Pepperbird); Karin Krog (Gershwin With Karin Krog).*

Cat Anderson

Trumpet.

b. Greenville, South Carolina, 12 Sept 1916; d. 29 April 1981.

Taught to play in Jenkins Orphanage, South Carolina, Cat (William Alonzo) Anderson soon after toured with a small Orphanage-based group, the Carolina Cotton Pickers. Other early professional engagements came from guitarist Hartley Toots, Claude Hopkins, Lucky Millinder, Erskine Hawkins (who was jealous of Anderson's stratospheric range, and fired him) and Lionel Hampton.

In 1944 Anderson succumbed to Ellington's persuasion and joined him at the Earle Theater in Philadelphia. Capable of playing more than five octaves, his trumpet became a vital part of Ellington's musical palette, ready to double a lead line two octaves up or simply supply altissimo colour to Ellington's tone poems. Like Maynard Ferguson some years later, Anderson saw playing in the trumpet's super-register as a mental exercise which any good player could acquire, but, like Ferguson again, he was much more than just a high-note man; he possessed a huge, beautiful sound all the way through the trumpet's register and – more than Ferguson ever did – had mastered the arts of half-valve and plunger-mute playing to perfect Ellingtonian level. It was a noise that Ellington delighted in and used to fantastic effect on trumpet showpieces such as "El Gato", "Trumpet No End" and "Jam With Sam".

For most of his life with Ellington, Anderson, a highly strung man of unbendable standards, played the lead book, to the apparent disapproval of Cootie Williams at the other end of the trumpet section. After Ellington's death he continued to work in studios and often made solo appearances where his talents were heard in a wider variety of roles, always to magnificent effect. [DF]

Duke Ellington Orchestra

The English Concerts (1969–1971; Sequel Jazz). The best way to hear Cat Anderson is on top of Duke Ellington's orchestra, and "El Gato" on this set is a perfect example of his spectacular contribution to Ellington's sound.

Cat Anderson

Plays W.C. Handy (1977–8; Black & Blue). Anderson in a small group setting again (with Norris Turney and Harold Ashby plus French musicians), and once again he shows off his all-round mastery of jazz trumpet, proving he was more than just the greatest "screech-trumpeter" of all.

Old Folks (1979; All Life). A rare chance to hear Anderson in a quartet setting, recorded in Paris, with Anderson playing superbly.

Chris Anderson

Piano.

b. Chicago, 26 Feb 1926.

A self-taught pianist, Anderson played in Chicago clubs from his teenage years onwards, and is present on a couple of live Charlie Parker recordings. After working for some years with Von Freeman, he briefly taught Herbie Hancock (c. 1961) and toured for a few weeks with Dinah Washington. Staying in New York, he recorded under his own name but, blind from his late teens and crippled (like Michel Petrucciani) as a result of the bone disease osteogenesis imperfecta, he never developed a steady career. He appeared on disc with Clifford Jordan in the mid-1970s and, encouraged by Jordan and Barry Harris, worked either solo or in duo with bassists such as Victor Sproles. His distinctive harmonic sense thrives in such spare surroundings, and Hancock has said that Anderson has "a whole other facet of tools of expression and harmonies that I hadn't heard in Bill Evans". [BP]

Charlie Haden & Chris Anderson

None But The Lonely Heart (1997; Naim). A couple of earlier recordings are slightly disappointing compared to his live performances, but this low-key album shows Anderson to perfection. Playing ballads and blues, he has a relaxed approach to time but his gently astringent chord-voicings, almost as unpredictable as Monk's, indicate what was of interest to Herbie Hancock.

Ernestine Anderson

Vocals.

b. Houston, Texas, 11 Nov 1928.

Anderson began her career with R&B bands in the 1940s, and recorded first in 1947 with Shifty Henry's orchestra for Black and White. Six years later she recorded with trumpeter Russell Jacquet's group for Network. Her appearance on Gigi Gryce's 1955 album *Nica's Tempo* led to a partnership with trumpeter Rolf Ericson for a three-month Scandinavian tour and an album with Harry Arnold's orchestra (*Hot Cargo*), which established her reputation in the USA. In 1959 Anderson won the Down Beat "New Star" Award and recorded for Mercury to more acclaim, before dividing her time from the mid-60s between America and Europe. Her re-emergence in the mid-1970s (at which time Ray Brown was her manager) came as a result of a sensational appearance at the 1976 Concord jazz festival – a string of albums for Concord followed, including the Grammy-nominated *Never Make Your Move Too Soon*. Anderson has continued her career revival into the 1990s, working with the Clayton-Hamilton Jazz Orchestra, amongst others. [DF]

⊙ **Live from Concord to London** (1978; Concord). This set has tracks from Anderson's legendary appearance at the Concord jazz festival as well as tracks recorded a year later at Ronnie Scott's London, with John Horler's trio.

⊙ **Never Make Your Move Too Soon** (1981; Concord). Anderson's blues-inflected style shows up well on the title track of this album, with a rhythm-section of Monty Alexander, Ray Brown and drummer Frank Gant.

⊙ **Boogie Down** (1990; Concord). A powerful singer, well used to shouting the blues in front of a big band, Anderson here does her stuff with the Clayton-Hamilton Jazz Orchestra, as well as gently reapproaching connoisseurs' songs like "Wait Till You See Him" and "Only Trust Your Heart".

Fred Anderson

Tenor saxophone.

b. Monroe, Louisiana, 22 March 1929.

Anderson played piano as a child, switching to tenor at age twelve, around the time he settled in Chicago. He started working professionally at a relatively advanced age in the 1960s, his thick tenor tone and linear melodicism influenced by Charlie Parker, Lester Young, Coleman Hawkins and Chu Berry. One of the original founding members of the Association for the Advancement of Creative Musicians (AACM) in 1964, he performed with most of Chicago's post-free-jazz generation; his group with saxophonist Joseph Jarman recorded under Jarman's name on the seminal *Song For* (Delmark), an album which includes Anderson's composition "Little Fox Run". Though he remained an under-acknowledged player into the 80s, recording infrequently and quietly running his venue the Velvet Lounge, Anderson has recorded and performed much more since, both at home and abroad. Recent records include the double-disc *Fred: Chicago Chamber Music* (Southport), duets with longterm partner drummer Hamid Drake (one featuring pianist Marilyn Crispell and another with bassist Peter Kowald, both on Okka Disk), and a quartet session *Birdhouse* (Okka Disk) with pianist Jim Baker. Anderson's elder statesman status in Chicago – working with younger improvisers such as the "post-rock" group Tortoise – has prompted many old recordings of his to be released since 2000, including blistering live performances with George Lewis and Roscoe Mitchell on *Dark Day/Live in Verona 1979* (Atavistic) and focused, moving duets with Sun Ra's drummer Robert Barry on *Duets 2001* (Thrill Jockey). [JC]

⊙ **Fred Anderson/DKV Trio** (1997; Okka Disk). A superb outing, Anderson's most concise and concentrated to date, matching the elder statesman's lithe linearity against the hot tenor and clarinet work of younger Ken Vandermark, supported by Kent Kessler on bass and Drake on drums. Six original Anderson compositions, most unrecorded since they were written in the 60s and 70s.

Ivie Anderson

Vocals.

b. Gilroy, California, 10 July 1905; d. 28 Dec 1949.

From the early 1920s Ivie Marie Anderson appeared as a soubrette at the Cotton Club, in reviews such as Sissle and Blake's Shuffle Along, as a band singer with leaders such as Anson Weeks and Curtis Mosby, and with Paul Howard's Quality Serenaders. The night she joined Duke Ellington, a lucky 13 February 1931 at the Paramount Theater, New York, the band broke every attendance record and from then on, in Ellington's words, "Ivie was our good-luck charm." Slim, beautiful and dignified, always dressed in white on stage, she sang with surprising strength and, said Helen Dance, "her voice became as much a part of the Ellington band as did the saxes of Carney and Hodges". Her part in a 1930s Ellington show included a crosstalk act with drummer Sonny Greer (which he refused to carry on with anyone else after she left), Ellington hits such as "A Lonely Co-Ed" and "I'm Checkin' Out, Goombye!" and a moving version of "Stormy Weather" (borrowed from Ethel Waters at the Cotton Club), which Ellington said "stopped the show cold" in London and France (1933). Harry Carney said of her, "She looked very angelic and above it all, yet backstage and on the bus, in hotels, restaurants, everywhere, she was always regular 100 percent! There was no side to her." She left Ellington in 1942 to open a Los Angeles restaurant, and continued singing for a while, despite chronic asthma, but died much too young. [DF]

⊙ **Ivie & Duke Vol. 1: Raisin' The Rent** (1932–7; Hep); **Vol. 2: All God's Chillun…!** (1937–40; Hep). The best CD collection of Anderson's work; 51 tracks superbly remastered with fine notes by Sally-Ann Worsfold.

⊙ **It Don't Mean A Thing** (1932–46; ASV). Though a less thorough survey than the above, an excellent collection nonetheless, with Ellington/Anderson classics including "It don't mean a thing", "Rocks in my bed" and one late 1946 track with Phil Morre, "Empty Bed Blues".

Jay Anderson

Double bass.

b. Ontario, California, 24 Oct 1955.

Jay Anderson's mother is a gifted pianist with perfect pitch who plays primarily by ear. Anderson began playing bass at the age of twelve, and studied classical and jazz bass throughout his schooling, until, in 1978, he graduated with a BM degree in Bass Performance from the California State University at Long Beach. In his teens he became principal bassist with the All Southern California Honor Orchestra, and won numerous awards. A month after graduating he was on the road with Woody Herman's band and he has been travelling, recording and performing incessantly ever since.

A versatile and intensely musical bassist, he is consistently in demand as a sideman for other leaders. He worked with Carmen McRae (1979–81), Red Rodney (1981–92), Ira Sullivan (1981–6), Michael Brecker (1989–91), Toots Thielemans (1992–6), and Joe Sample (1992 to the present). But during this twenty-year period, he has also performed and/or recorded with innumerable other leading musicians including Paul Bley, Mike Stern, Bob Berg, Lee Konitz, Tiger Okoshi, Toshiko Akiyoshi, Joe Lovano and Tom Waits. Anderson has been featured on more than one hundred and thirty albums, and has recorded two under his own name, *Local Color* and *Next Exit* (both DMP). He also plays on three albums with Paul Bley, two with Michael Brecker and one with Maria Schneider. His favourite bassists include Ray Brown, Paul Chambers, Charles Mingus, Scott LaFaro, Dave Holland and Charlie Haden. Other inspirations include Wayne Shorter, Kenny Wheeler, Keith Jarrett, Herbie Hancock, Miles Davis, Sting and Peter Gabriel.

In 1990, Anderson received a grant from the National Endowment of the Arts. He teaches bass at the Manhattan School of Music, and he is currently writing a bass method book, dealing primarily with finding one's own voice on the instrument. [IC]

⊙ **Next Exit** (1992; DMP). Anderson proves himself a fascinating and adventurous composer as well as a virtuoso bassist in this superlative album. The pieces range from funky, gospel and hoedown outings (the title track), to heartfelt tone poems, and his all-star sextet line-up which includes Randy Brecker and Wayne Krantz all sparkle in this context.

➤➤ **Tiger Okoshi** (*Echoes Of A Note*).

Ray Anderson

Trombone, alto trombone, slide trumpet, cornet, tuba, percussion, vocals.

b. Chicago, 16 Oct 1952.

Anderson took up trombone at the age of eight, playing in school bands with fellow pupil and trombonist George Lewis. He had classical lessons, but listened to mainstreamers such as Vic Dickenson and Trummy Young on record. Eventually he began attending concerts of the AACM, but also immersed himself in Chicago blues. During a year at Macalester College, St Paul, he played in funk bands after hours, then went to California, continuing to play funk but also working with, among others, drummer Charles Moffett. In 1972 he arrived in New York, where he sat in with Mingus, studied and freelanced. In 1977 he began working with both Barry Altschul's and Anthony Braxton's groups, but still freelanced, largely on the New York Latin scene. He led his own group at the 1979 Moers festival in West Germany and in 1980 toured and played festivals in Europe alongside Altschul. Anderson won the *Down Beat* critics' poll on trombone in 1981, as a "Talent Deserving Wider Recognition". Later in the decade, the humour and theatricality of his funk band, Slickaphonics, brought him to a wider audience, and he achieved some financial success.

Ever restless, in 1994 Anderson started his Alligatory band which was a descendant of his Slickaphonics in terms of vocals and wackiness, but with a greater underlying musical seriousness – despite his description of alligatory music as the expression of "swamp infested rug-cutters from the bayous of the mind with allegorical twists and an aleatoric *joie de vivre*". The Alligatory band was a sextet comprising trumpeter Lew Soloff, guitarist Jerome Harris, bassist Gregory Jones, drummer Tommy Campbell and percussionist Frank Colon. The band made a couple of albums, *Don't Mow Your Lawn* in 1994, and the following year *Heads And Tales*, both on Enja. By 1998, Anderson had formed yet another group, his Lapis Lazuli Band, in which he retained Harris and Campbell, and brought in Amina Claudine Myers on Hammond B-3 organ, piano and vocals, and bassist Lonnie Plaxico. Their album, *Funkorific*, was released early in 1999. Another of his concerns continues to be the Pocket Brass Band, which also features Bob Stewart (tuba); they released *Where Home Is* in 1998.

Although steeped in the whole jazz trombone tradition, Anderson is a radical exponent of the instrument, taking all its expressive potential to the limits. His range in the upper register is phenomenal, rivalling that of the trumpet, and he is a master of multiphonics (playing several notes at once by singing as he blows) and all the growls, slides and tonal distortions possible on the instrument. He is an exemplary new pluralist: a player with tremendous stamina and great technical ability who is equally at home with music ranging from Braxton's totally scored pieces to free improvisation, Latin music for dancers, neo-bop and funk bands. [IC]

⊙ **Slickaphonics** (1982; Enja). This is Anderson's irrepressibly energetic and good-humoured entertainment band. It's a quintet with reeds, bass, guitar and drums, but everyone also sings, and virtuosity heightens the wackiness.

⊙ **You Be** (1985; Minor Music). Anderson in trio formation with bassist Mark Helias and drummer Gerry Hemingway, delivering a virtuoso performance. Risks are taken, but Anderson comes home safely.

⊙ **Blues Bred In The Bone** (1988; Enja). Anderson humorously explores his blues roots with a quintet which includes blues master-guitarist John Scofield, pianist Anthony Davis, bassist Mark Dresser and drummer Johnny Vidacovich.

⊙ **Every One Of Us** (1992; Gramavision). Here leading a quartet with pianist Simon Nabatov and the famously classy rhythm-section of Charlie Haden and Ed Blackwell, Anderson is not only exhilarating, but sometimes profoundly moving, too.

⊙ **Big Band Record** (1993; Gramavision). This features Anderson with the George Gruntz Concert Jazz Band, and could well be the trombonist's masterpiece. The ensemble's discipline contains Anderson's most volatile adventures, and he in turn shows he can wax lyrical on a ballad. He also treats us to one of his comic funk vocals.

⊙ **Funkorific** (1998; Enja) There's something almost schizophrenic about the natural eloquence of Anderson's trombone playing and the self-indulgence of his often cod vocals and hammy behaviour. The music only just saves the day here, and makes one feel that this approach is moribund.

➤➤ **Lew Soloff** (*Little Wing*).

Wessell Anderson

Alto and sopranino saxophones.

b. Brooklyn, New York, 27 Nov 1964.

The son of drummer Wessell L. Anderson, Wessell Anderson received saxophone tuition from Nat Shapiro and piano lessons from Loyce Williams, but also learned about jazz from hearing his father play with the likes of Sonny Stitt, and from a family record collection that centred on the work of Coltrane, Ellington and Monk. After a number of workshops at the Bromley School of Music, and some experience sitting in with his father's bands, Anderson joined the Jazz Mobile Workshop in Harlem, where the baritone saxophonist Charles Davis introduced him to the complexities of improvisation and to the big-band class, run by Frank Foster. At Southern University in Baton Rouge, Louisiana, he met Wynton Marsalis (on tour with Art Blakey), who encouraged him to study under clarinettist Alvin Batiste before accepting him into his own band in 1988. He has become a regular fixture there since, appearing on nearly a dozen of the trumpeter's albums, including *Standard Time*, *Citi Movement*, *In This House*, *On This Morning* and *Blood On The Fields*, and his luxurious sweet-molasses sound has earned him the nickname "Warmdaddy". In addition to albums with Marsalis sidemen such as pianist Eric Reed, Anderson has also recorded with the Lincoln Center Jazz Orchestra, Branford Marsalis and Batiste, appearing alongside his erstwhile teacher on the 1993 Columbia recording *Late*. He has also made albums under his own name: *Warmdaddy In The Garden Of Swing* (1994; Atlantic), featuring Reed, and *The Ways Of Warmdaddy*, while a vivacious third album as leader, *Live At The Village Vanguard* (1997; Leaning House), caught Anderson at his swinging best. He continues with his Jazz At the Lincoln Centre activities and recently joined the faculty of the Juilliard Institute for Jazz Studies, New York. [CP/CI]

⦿ **The Ways Of Warmdaddy** (1995; Atlantic). Sharing front-line duties with trumpeter Antoine Drye, and with Ellis Marsalis on piano in the larger-ensemble tracks, Anderson swings sweetly through a pleasantly varied selection of material, including "Rockin' in Rhythm".

Peter Apfelbaum

Tenor saxophone, piano, drums, composer.

b. Berkeley, California, 21 Aug 1960.

Apfelbaum studied music in elementary and high school in Berkeley, and played drums with rock and jazz groups as a teenager, forming the Berkeley Arts Company and, in 1977, the Hieroglyphics Ensemble, which included fellow youngsters such as Benny Green, Craig Handy and Joshua Redman. In New York from 1978–82, he played with Carla Bley and the workshop orchestras of Warren Smith and Karl Berger, with whom he toured Europe. Back in San Francisco, he wrote a suite for the Hieroglyphics and Don Cherry in 1988, then played saxophone and piano on tour and record with Cherry's Multikulti group in 1990. After recording two now-unavailable Hieroglyphics Ensemble albums in the 1990s, Apfelbaum formed a sextet in 1995.

Inspired by Ornette Coleman, Roland Kirk, Pharoah Sanders, the Art Ensemble Of Chicago, Cecil Taylor and West African and other world music, Apfelbaum has written for the Kronos Quartet and for Cherry. But his favoured vehicle is the Hieroglyphics, which has at times included Craig Handy and Benny Green, as well as players versed in various ethnic musics. [BP]

⦿ **Luminous Charms** (1996; Gramavision). Fronting his sextet which includes some former members of the Hieroglyphics, Apfelbaum features himself far more than with the Ensemble. He dedicates this album to Don Cherry, and comes a bit closer to free-blowing conventions.

Peter Appleyard

Vibraphone.

b. Cleethorpes, Lincolnshire, UK, 26 Aug 1928.

Appleyard played drums in a boys' brigade band in Cleethorpes before working first with local dance bands then with the nationally established Felix Mendelssohn. In 1951 he moved to Toronto (via Bermuda), took up the vibraphone and worked with Calvin Jackson, before leading groups of his own in both Canada and the USA. A respected professional and a dynamic soloist, Appleyard continued to tour and record in the 1980s and 90s in a variety of contexts, both solo and with the likes of Peanuts Hucko (with whom he had earlier toured in the Pied Piper Quintet). Appleyard's Canadian-based activities (he even hosted his own TV show in the late 70s) have occasionally masked his status as one of Britain's international-level jazz talents, on a par with George Shearing or Victor Feldman. [DF]

⦿ **Barbados Heat/Barbados Cool** (1990; Concord). Recommended double-CD set recorded live in concert, featuring Rick Wilkins (tenor) plus Bucky Pizzarelli, Major Holley and Butch Miles.

Jimmy Archey

Trombone.

b. Norfolk, Virginia, 12 Oct 1902; d. 16 Nov 1967.

Archey made his debut in New York in 1927, with Edgar Hayes's orchestra, and worked with Fletcher Henderson's second band, Henderson's Rainbow Orchestra, as featured soloist. His first notable records, with James P. Johnson's orchestra (featuring King Oliver and Fats Waller) and Oliver's studio bands, revealed a strong, consistently shouting player, with technique to spare and progressive ideas. From 1930–37 Archey worked with Luis Russell's orchestra, and moved on to a star-studded selection of aristocratic big bands, including those of Benny Carter, Claude Hopkins, Coleman Hawkins, Duke Ellington (depping for Tricky Sam Nanton) and Cab Calloway.

By the late 1940s, after marvellous recordings with Mutt Carey's New Yorkers, a residency on Rudi Blesh's *This Is Jazz* radio show and an appearance with Mezz Mezzrow's band in Nice, he was increasingly regarded as a New Orleans revivalist, rather than the sophisticated big-band player he could be. In 1948 he joined young Bob Wilber's revivalist band, two years later took over the group for work in the USA and abroad, then for seven years from 1955 worked with Earl Hines's Dixieland-based band in San Francisco (including a long spell at Club Hangover, one of the city's two big jazz centres).

In the early 1960s Archey suffered a long illness, but re-emerged to tour the USA and Canada with Dixieland bands, including a European tour for the New Orleans All Stars, during which he was still a dominant feature. "Although his notes are produced in a manner worthy of the bop machine-gunners," wrote J.C. Hillman in *Jazz Journal* in 1966, "his style is surprisingly close to Jim Robinson, though neater and more accurate. His solos were powerful and inventive, and the ensembles really brought out the best in him." [DF]

⊙ **Jimmy Archey's Band From Jimmy Ryans** (1952; Storyville). A strong session of broadcast transcriptions from WMGM Radio NYC, also featuring trumpeter Henry Goodwin and Benny Waters on clarinet and soprano sax.

Neil Ardley

Composer, keyboards.

b. Carshalton, Surrey, UK, 26 May 1937; d. 23 Feb 2004.

In 1959 Ardley gained a BSc at Bristol University, then in 1960–61 studied arranging and composition with Ray Premru. From 1964–70 he was director of the New Jazz Orchestra (NJO), for which he wrote several arrangements and compositions. From 1969 he composed music for his own groups formed for recordings, broadcasts and tours. During the 1970s he also built up an electronic studio, and composed music mainly for television. Ardley has almost always earned his living apart from music, as a writer of scores of books on science, computers, natural history and music.

His *Greek Variations* (1969) was a composition in six parts for a nine-piece jazz group and string quartet, based on a motif from a Greek folk song. *A Symphony Of Amaranths* (1971), deploying a 25-piece band with strings, received the first Arts Council of Great Britain award for a jazz recording. Then came two compositions which are a fascinating melange of acoustic instruments and electronics: *Kaleidoscope Of Rainbows* (1975), which was based on Balinese scales and written for a thirteen-piece ensemble, and *The Harmony Of The Spheres* (1978), for a nine-piece ensemble plus the voices of Pepi Lemer and Norma Winstone. In 1988 he formed the band Zyklus with fellow composers John L. Walters and Warren Greveson (the latter also a computer expert), with the aim of exploring the boundaries of composition and improvisation by developing a semi-improvised electronic sound world which could accommodate an acoustic, improvising soloist. In 1993 he arranged "Barbara Song" for a Kurt Weill album by Barbara Thompson and the Medici string quartet, and in 1994 composed "On The Four Winds" for New Perspectives, a twelve-piece ensemble of jazz and classical musicians led by saxophonist John Williams. In 1998 and 1999, Ardley conducted four concerts of *Kaleidoscope Of Rainbows* with most of the original personnel, as part of the Millennium Concert Series, "The Music Of The 1970s"; the last two concerts were recorded. Much of his last years was taken up with writing and composing choral works. [IC]

Neil Ardley

⊙ **Kaleidoscope Of Rainbows** (1976; Line). This is a benign and glittering icon of the 1970s, and perhaps Ardley's masterpiece. It's an early example of world music, with jazz rock elements leavened by Balinese disciplines. A few years later, a Balinese dance troupe touring Australia were dancing to this very album.

Zyklus

⊙ **Virtual Realities** (1991; AMP). Using Zyklus computers, which can be "played" in live performance, the three composers create fascinating edifices of sound. Ian Carr, the only conventional instrumentalist on this stimulating album, excels on muted trumpet in a challenging electronic-music framework as Zyklus affectionately reconstruct the Monk classic "Round Midnight". [CA]

Julian Argüelles

Soprano, alto, tenor and baritone saxophones, various woodwinds, composer.

b. Birmingham, UK, 28 Jan 1966.

One of the most versatile players to have emerged from the 21-piece UK big band Loose Tubes, Julian Argüelles is as adept at big-band section work as he is in leading his own quartet. A thoroughly proficient player, he is adept in areas ranging from freely improvised jazz through straightahead to world-music-influenced styles. He began playing with various regional youth orchestras before studying briefly at Trinity College of Music in London. He joined Loose Tubes in 1985, recording two albums with them, and since their demise has collaborated with fellow Tubes alumni pianist Django Bates – working and recording with his band Delightful Precipice – and drummer Steve Argüelles (his brother) in his quartet. He has also played in larger groups led by trumpeter Kenny Wheeler, trombonist Mike Gibbs and US pianist Carla Bley.

Provocateur Records

Julian Argüelles

Argüelles made his recording debut as a leader in 1990 with the quartet album *Phaedrus*, featuring pianist John Taylor, but really hit his stride with 1995's *Home Truths*, another quartet recording, on which frontline duties were shared with guitarist Mike Walker and featuring Steve Swallow on bass. The following year saw the release of *Scapes*, a highly acclaimed duo album with brother Steve, and in 1997 a BBC Radio 3 commission resulted in an octet recording, *Skull View*. Whether as leader/composer of his own projects, or as multi-reed playing sideman with the likes of Colin Towns, Argüelles, like many other former Loose Tubes (Iain Ballamy, Mark Lockheart et al) is now a firmly established and highly productive member of the international jazz scene. [CP]

⊙ **Home Truths** (1995; Babel). Alternately bustling and lyrical originals vigorously performed by a fiercely interactive quartet, spearheaded by Argüelles on saxophones and bass-clarinet and Mike Walker on guitar, but driven by the subtly propulsive bass of Steve Swallow and the drums of Martin France.

⊙ **Skull View** (1997; Babel). Octet featuring the limpid piano of Mario Laginha, Django Bates on tenor horn, Mark Bassey on trombone and Iain Dixon on reeds. Punchy and cogent music, with occasional flashes of humour.

➤➤ **Loose Tubes** *(Open Letter)*; **Tommy Smith** *(Misty Morning And No Time)*.

Steve Argüelles

Drums.

b. Crowborough, Sussex, UK, 16 Nov 1963.

Like his younger brother Julian, Steve Argüelles came to prominence in Loose Tubes, and his various subsequent musical projects share the interest in so-called "world" musics and the painterly quality he brought to the band. Always an active collaborator rather than simply a hired accompanist, he has lent his attractively supple, exuberant drumming to the work of two players he considers important influences – pianist John Taylor and the late saxophonist Dudu Pukwana – as well as to visiting Americans such as Jimmy Giuffre, Steve Lacy, Mose Allison and George Coleman. Although a vital component of UK bands Human Chain and Argüelles (co-led with brother Julian), he is currently resident in Paris where he is part of The Recyclers, a trio featuring Parisian pianist Benoît Delbecq and guitarist Noël Akchoté. In addition to his work in film, theatre and dance music, he continues to make witty but cogent recordings under his own name.

Circuit (1997) further extended his regular quintet's range, while his work with the Recyclers was memorably caught by their second album, *Visit* (1997), recorded two years earlier in locations ranging from Paris to Vancouver and London. Dedicated to "aurally recycling the sounds and ideas of musicians we like ... reassembling our previous experiences", The Recyclers' music, courtesy of its knowing yet sparky eclecticism, places Argüelles – who also leads an experimental electric/acoustic band, Ambitroniques – at the heart of contemporary European jazz and related music. [CP]

⊙ **Steve Argüelles** (1990; Ah Um). Debut recording as a leader, containing sly quotations from and humorous references to everything from calypso through fairground music to country and western.

⊙ **Blue Moon In A Function Room** (1994; Babel). Oddly askew versions of family-function favourites such as "Blues in The Night", "Ruby" and "Bye Bye Blackbird" performed by Billy Jenkins, Stuart Hall and Steve Watts in addition to the leader.

⊙ **Busy Listening** (1994; Babel). Covers similar ground to that of debut album, but with Huw Warren on accordion, and repertoire enlivened by Mingus's "Jelly Roll" and Bill Frisell's "Rag".

Recyclers

⊙ **Visit** (1997; Babel). Taking its name from various "visits" to homes of musical friends (guitarist Billy Jenkins, Dutch trombonist Wolter Wierbos, etc), this is a wide-ranging album drawing as much on pianist Benoît Delbecq's free-improvising experience with Alan Silva's Celestial Communication Orchestra and Noël Akchoté's admiration for the work of fellow guitarists Eugene Chadbourne and Derek Bailey as on Argüelles's more structured eccentricities.

John Armatage

Drums.

b. Newcastle upon Tyne, UK, 5 Aug 1929.

Armatage turned professional in 1957 with John Chilton and soon after joined Bruce Turner's Jump Band, with whom he recorded, made a film, Living Jazz (1962), and toured until the band's break-up. Armatage then worked with Alan Elsdon's band, freelanced busily, toured abroad and continued – quite unobtrusively – to make a living from jazz. He played regularly in the 1970s and 80s with Pete Allen's band and with Terry Lightfoot (an old colleague), while all too occasionally parading his second skill, as a band arranger. One of Britain's best swing drummers, he plays in the loose, lithe idiom of Sid Catlett and Dave Tough. [DF]

Lil Armstrong

Piano, vocals.

b. Memphis, 3 Feb 1898 (or 1902); d. 27 Aug 1971.

Born Lillian Hardin, Lil Armstrong worked in Chicago as a classically trained piano demonstrator for Jones's Store on 35th and State. An ultra-modern jazz pianist who had left ragtime behind, she worked early on with Sugar Johnny's Creole Orchestra, the toast of Chicago, for $55 a week (Jones's had paid $3) and then with Freddie Keppard's sensational Original Creole Orchestra, where she was in her element at last – "Lil always had a grin a mile wide as she bent over the keyboard", remembers Mezz Mezzrow.

Hardin met the young and diffident Louis Armstrong when she played piano in King Oliver's Creole Jazz Band – he played second trumpet. After Oliver let fall that "as long as Louis's in my band I'm still King!" she encouraged the reluctant Armstrong to make the break – "I don't want to be married to no second trumpet player." They married on 5 February 1924; a year later Louis was back from a spell with Fletcher Henderson in New York, and a banner appeared in front of the Dreamland in Chicago advertising "Louis Armstrong – the world's greatest jazz cornetist" – with Lil Hardin's band. Armstrong had swapped one leader for another.

Hardin kept a loving and watchful eye on her husband's career: when a rival trumpeter featured top Es at a nearby cabaret, Hardin had Armstrong "make top Fs at home". But he was ribbed by his fellow bandsmen because he worked for his wife, and this led to on-stage confrontations: by 1931 relations were strained and by 1938 they were divorced. Lil sued Louis for royalties on tunes co-composed while they were married (and won), billed his successor, Jonah Jones, as "Louis Armstrong the Second" at the Lafayette Theater in New York, and relentlessly advertised herself as "Mrs Louis Armstrong" for future projects. Armstrong took it well. Lil's career – following a postgraduate degree in music – included an all-male band, an all-female band and a post as house pianist for Decca from 1936. In 1940 she opened a restaurant in Chicago, the Swing Shack, and for the last 30 years of her life was a celebrated club pianist around the city, and a likeable raconteuse. She died of a heart attack while taking part in a Chicago memorial concert to her late husband. [DF]

Louis Armstrong

⊙ **Louis Armstrong And His Hot Five, 1925–6** (Classics); **Louis Armstrong And His Hot Five And Hot Seven, 1926–7** (Classics). These two sets present Lil Armstrong in her classic and best-remembered setting, as the rumbustious elemental piano-thumper with the greatest small group in jazz history. Essential listening.

Lil Armstrong

⊙ **Lil Hardin Armstrong And Her Swing Orchestra 1936–40** (Classics). With a star-studded swing band (Higginbotham, Buster Bailey, Chu Berry and others), this set has Lil Armstrong singing an up-to-date selection of swing songs; she can be heard back at the keyboard on tracks from 1940.

Louis Armstrong

Trumpet, vocals, composer.

b. New Orleans, 4 Aug 1901; d. 6 July 1971.

Born in August 1901 (not Independence Day 1900, as he was always told and believed), Louis Armstrong sang on the New Orleans streets in a boyhood quartet and in 1913 was admitted to the Colored Waifs' home for firing a gun into the air. In the home he learned the trumpet, and within four years was challenging every trumpet king in his home town, from Freddie Keppard to Joe Oliver, his first father figure, whom he replaced in Kid Ory's band in 1919. In 1922 Oliver (by now King Oliver) invited Louis to join him in Chicago to play second trumpet. Tempting as it is to echo Nat Gonella's incredulous comment, "I can't imagine Louis playing second trumpet to anyone", Oliver was able to teach Armstrong a little. The regular harmonic experience of playing second (his ear, even then, was faultless) and, above all, the importance of playing straight lead in "whole notes", as Oliver did, were lessons that Armstrong was to remember for life.

Experience was by now, however imperceptibly, toughening the young man up. His second wife Lil Hardin helped to focus his streak of ambition and he was learning that people could be devious – Oliver, it transpired, was creaming his sidemen's wages. Although he loved Oliver until the end, by 1924 Armstrong had made the jump to New York and Fletcher Henderson's orchestra. It was hot city company for a country boy, but he had the humour and talent to counter mockery ("I thought that meant 'pound plenty'!", he quipped, when the stern Henderson ticked him off for a missed "pp" dynamic); somewhere along the way he decided he was the best, and got ready to defend his title if nec-

BETTMAN/CORBIS

Louis Armstrong's Hot Five (left to right) Armstrong, Johnny St. Cyr, Johnny Dodds, Kid Ory and Lil Armstrong

essary. "Louis played the Regal Theater in Chicago," remembers Danny Barker, "and they had this fantastic trumpeter Reuben Reeves in the pit. So in the overture they put Reuben Reeves on stage doing some of Louis's tunes. Louis listened – then when he came on he said, 'Tiger Rag'. Played about thirty choruses! The next show? No overture!"

In 1925 Armstrong, already a recording star, began OKeh dates with his Hot Five and Seven (featuring Johnny Dodds, Kid Ory and Lil Armstrong, until Earl Hines replaced her). The music on masterpieces such as "Cornet Chop Suey", "Potato Head Blues", "S.O.L. Blues" and "West End Blues" turned jazz into a soloist's art form and set new standards for trumpeters worldwide. At the peak of his young form, Armstrong peeled off top Cs as easily as breathing (previously they were rare) and pulled out technical tours de force which never degenerated into notes for their own sake. His singing introduced individuality to popular vocals and, just for good measure, he also invented scat singing, when he allegedly dropped the music one day at a recording session. Best of all was his melodic inspiration: his creations were still being analyzed, harmonized and celebrated half a century later. Rather than playing ever higher and harder, Armstrong simplified his music, polishing each phrase to perfection, while keeping his strength for the knockout punch.

By 1930 he was a New York star, with imitators all around him, but his business life was at a temporary impasse. Then he found his Godfather figure, a powerful, often ruthless Mafia operator called Joe Glaser, who was to steer his client's fortunes for 35 years. In 1935, with Glaser's approval, Louis teamed with Luis Russell's orchestra, an aggregation of old New Orleans friends, and for five years he was to tour and record with them: the records are classics and helped to get Armstrong into films such as *Pennies From Heaven* (1936) and *Artists And Models* (1937).

In 1940, Glaser's office brusquely sacked the band and Louis put together another containing younger "modernists" such as John Brown (alto), Dexter Gordon (tenor) and Arvell Shaw (bass), a long Louis associate, with Velma Middleton sharing the singing. It lasted until summer 1947, but big bands were on a downward slide and Armstrong found leading a headache.

In 1947 promoter Ernie Anderson presented him with a small band (directed by Bobby Hackett) at New York's Town Hall. The acclaim that greeted the move signalled the end of his big-band career, and for the last 24 years of his life, Louis led his All Stars, a six-piece band which featured, to begin with, a heady mixture of real stars ("too many make bad friends", said Armstrong ruefully later), including Jack

Teagarden and Earl Hines. It developed into a more controllable and supportive team featuring, at various times, Barney Bigard and Ed Hall (clarinet) and a strong right arm, Trummy Young (trombone). With his All Stars, Armstrong presented a tightly arranged show which, right down to repertoire and solos, seldom varied in later years, a policy which was sometimes criticized. But great records made with the All Stars, such as *Plays W.C. Handy*, *Plays Fats* and *At The Crescendo*, became jazz anthems, and solos such as *Louis And The Good Book* and its superior follow-up *Louis And The Angels* revealed Armstrong at a wonderful late peak.

At his own wish the All Stars maintained a crippling touring schedule and in 1959 he had his first heart attack. For his last ten years, amid hit-parade successes, unabated touring and recurring illness, Armstrong gradually slowed down: by 1969, when he visited Britain for the last time, it was noticeable that his playing was rationed (though still painfully beautiful) and that he was looking older. He died in bed (smiling) on 6 July 1971; his records have all remained in catalogue ever since and in 1994 a late Armstrong single, "We Have All The Time In The World", rose high in the pop charts.

It's impossible to discuss "Satchmo" without remembering the man: "He was a very joyous host," said Ruby Braff, "even in his dressing room with fifty people standing round." It is time to kill off the legend that Armstrong's big-heartedness was a pose: said Barney Bigard, "There never was any hidden side to him. He came 'as is'." Another legend deserves demolition: that Louis was simply the lucky one of countless talents in and around New Orleans (Jabbo Smith and Punch Miller are two cited contenders): the records prove otherwise. More recently it's been suggested that recurrent lip trouble (which Armstrong certainly suffered) caused a musical decline from the 1930s on: again, his performances demonstrate a continuing achievement. Finally, the old accusation that Louis Armstrong was an Uncle Tom: as Joe Muranyi, his later clarinettist, says, "Louis Armstrong was nobody's nigger!"

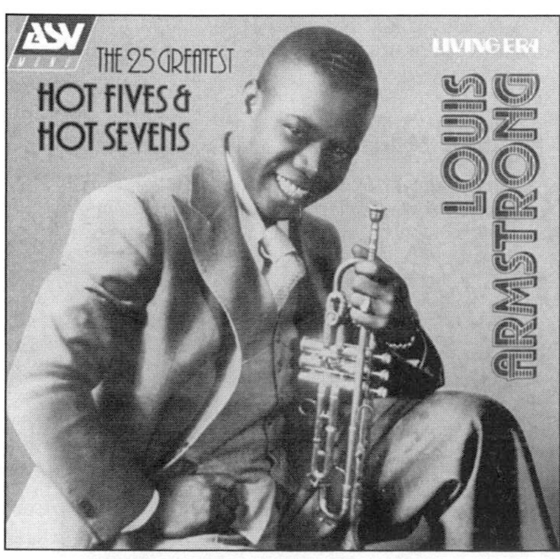

"He left an undying testimony to the human condition in the America of his time": Wynton Marsalis's way of saying, in 1985, that Louis was simply the greatest jazz trumpeter ever and, with Charlie Parker and Duke Ellington, the most influential jazzman of the classic era. [DF]

⊙ **Louis With Fletcher Henderson** (1924–5; FRP). Triple-CD set produced by Jeff Healey including all Louis's sides with Henderson, with alternate takes.

⊙ **Louis Armstrong Vol. 1 1925–1932** (Classics); **Louis Armstrong Vol. 2 1932–40** (Classics). Available separately or as two six-disc boxed sets, these superb surveys begin with "My Heart", made with the Hot Five in 1925, and go on to cover (in Vol. 2) his great big-band period, from "Medley of Armstrong Hits" (1932) to "You Run Your Mouth I'll Run My Business Brother" (May 1940).

⊙ **Louis Armstrong: The Complete RCA Victor Recordings (1932–1956).** Armstrong's long association with Victor produced numerous landmarks: 1930s classics including "That's My Home", "Hobo You Can't Ride This Train" and the unique "Laughin' Louis", his 1947 Town Hall concert, and many other recordings of importance, though some failed to place him in the best surroundings or present him with the most admirable material. Louis rides it all though, and this set is essential.

⊙ **Louis Armstrong: The Ultimate Collection** (1932–70; RCA Bluebird). This album – the recipient of a justifiable publicity drive by RCA in 1994 – has many of Armstrong's best-known classics, including "What A Wonderful World".

⊙ **Pops: The 1940s Small Band Sides** (RCA Bluebird). From his post-big-band period, definitive recordings including music from the film *New Orleans*, from the Town Hall concert of 1947 which created the All Stars, and early recordings by the All Stars with Jack Teagarden, Dick Cary, Barney Bigard and others.

⊙ **Satchmo Meets Big T** (1944–58; Giants of Jazz). Mainly Louis's and Jack Teagarden's great collaborations with the All Stars, but with one or two rarities thrown in for good measure.

⊙ **Satchmo Sings; Satchmo Serenades** (1945–55; MCA). Two well-loved albums containing a selection of Armstrong singles with a variety of orchestras – Gordon Jenkins, Sonny Burke, Sy Oliver, Jack Pleis et al. Not the most essential Armstrong but magic moments to spare including his trumpet on "Congratulations To Someone" and other songs which stayed in his act for years including "La Vie En Rose" and "C'est Si Bon".

⊙ **The Wonderful Duets** (1946–51; Avid). Armstrong's duets are a favourite area of his discography: here he is with Crosby, Louis Jordan, Fitzgerald, Holiday, Teagarden and Velma Middleton. Along with most of the best studio recordings, the sets have studio cuts from Crosby's radio shows including a live "Gone Fishin'". Admirable sound by Dave Bennett.

⊙ **The Complete Town Hall Concert 1947** (Fresh Sound Records). The ground-breaking concert promoted by Ernie Anderson which gave birth to Armstrong's All-Stars. Regrettably low-quality sound, but essential listening nevertheless with Teagarden, Hackett, Dick Cary et al.

⊙ **Louis Armstrong And The All Stars At Symphony Hall** (1947; Giants of Jazz). Classic concert with Jack Teagarden, Barney Bigard, Dick Cary and Sid Catlett. Catlett's "Steak Face" solo is one of the great drum events in jazz history.

⊙ **Louis Armstrong: The New And Revised Musical Autobiography Vols. 1–3** (1947–57; Jazz Unlimited). The complete *Autobiography* sessions (with additions), this time including Louis's likeable and valuable commentary.

The Complete Decca Studio Recordings Of Louis Armstrong And The All Stars (1950–8; Mosaic). This lavish six-CD boxed set is attractive but slightly flawed for completists – it covers all recordings by Armstrong under the All Stars banner, but not those featuring Louis in an orchestral setting. It also includes his *Autobiography* sessions (see above), unfortunately minus commentary.

The Happy 50s (1950–9; Ambassador). Part of a limited-edition (and marvellous) chronology of Armstrong's work, this set has Armstrong's l950s singles and the complete *Angels* album as a bonus. Well worth searching for.

The California Concerts (1951 & 1955; MCA). This four-CD set combines the essential All Stars concert at Pasadena Civic Auditorium in January 1951 with everything from Louis's 1955 appearance at the Crescendo Club; much previously unissued material included.

Louis Armstrong Plays W.C. Handy (1954; Columbia). Proudly restored by George Avakian to its original format in l996 (after needless meddling on earlier reissues), plus fascinating rehearsal takes and Avakian's interview with W.C. Handy; a definitive Armstrong classic, lovingly re-produced.

The Complete Ella Fitzgerald and Louis Armstrong On Verve (1957). Lavishly re-presented, all of their warm-hearted collaborations with Oscar Peterson's quartet including regular highlights ("Stomping At The Savoy"), the superb "Porgy And Bess" with Russell Garcia and two tracks with Louis's All Stars from the Hollywood Bowl concert l956.

Louis And The Angels/Louis And The Good Book (1957–8; Universal). Excellent pairing of two underrated Armstrong beauties; "Good Book" is delightful and the under-reissued "Angels" is arguably superior, with Louis's declamatory "And The Angels Sing" one highlight; others include the appealing "You're A Heavenly Thing", "A Sinner Kissed An Angel" and more.

Louis Armstrong And Duke Ellington: The Complete Collaborations (1961; EMI/Roulette). Ellington joining Armstrong's All Stars on piano for sessions that only occasionally reveal the differences between them; an essential disc from two jazz grandmasters.

Hello Dolly (1964; Kapp). Featuring the title-track hit single that established Armstrong with a new generation of fans.

Louis Armstrong And His Friends (1970; Flying Dutchman). A late Armstrong album including tunes by Pharoah Sanders and Lennon & McCartney, and arrangements by Oliver Nelson.

Lynne Arriale

Piano.

b. Milwaukee, Wisconsin, 29 May 1957.

Arriale learned classical piano from age four, and later gained her master's degree at Wisconsin Conservatory. She only became seriously involved in jazz playing in her twenties, and moved to New York in the mid-80s to study with a long list of leading jazz pianists. She did considerable freelance work while establishing her trio, eventually playing regularly with drummer Steve Davis and several excellent bassists. The winner of the 1993 Great American Jazz Piano Competition, she toured Japan with the "100 Golden Fingers" package featuring ten pianists from Hank Jones to Cedar Walton, and in 1996 performed at the first Women In Jazz festival at Washington's Kennedy Center. Involved in many educational workshops, she has visited the UK regularly and toured throughout Europe with her trio, which has recorded several albums. She names Keith Jarrett and Herbie Hancock as her favourites, and there is a delicate strength about her work which directly recalls Bill Evans. [BP]

Lynne Arriale

Melody (1998; TCB). Aptly titled, this features an eclectic programme from the folk-song "Hush-A-Bye" via a reworked "It Ain't Necessarily So" to a couple of captivating originals, and displays Arriale's clear touch and considered approach in conjunction with Steve Davis and the equally melodic bass of Scott Colley.

Inspiration (2000; TCB). Arriale gets a lot of mileage from standards – fairly straightforward except for the hard-hitting "America" by Bernstein – while pieces by Monk and Ellington receive surprising treatments, fuelled by Steve Davis's percussion work.

Art Ensemble Of Chicago

Saxophonist Roscoe Mitchell had been involved with the AACM since its inception in the mid-60s; in 1966 Lester Bowie (trumpet) moved to Chicago, gravitated to the AACM and joined Mitchell's band. With bassist Malachi Favors and saxophonist Joseph Jarman, Mitchell and Bowie formed the Art Ensemble Of Chicago in 1969. They moved to Paris, which in 1969 had a flourishing jazz scene and was a haven for black US musicians, and there they found their drummer, Don Moye. They stayed in Paris for eighteen months, recorded twelve albums, appeared individually on LPs with several other expatriates and when they returned to the USA at the end of 1971 the AEC and its members had laid the foundations of a solid international reputation.

The Ensemble showed a way out of the cul-de-sac of abstraction and became one of the key groups of the 1970s and 80s. Its inclusive, pluralistic music fused elements from free jazz and from the whole jazz tradition going right back to New Orleans, and there were also strong ethnic – particularly African – ingredients. Their performances also presented the music with brilliant theatricality; the stage crammed with both conventional instruments and all kinds of percussion and ethnic instruments including gongs, whistles and log drums. The musicians, with their faces painted in African ceremonial designs, wore outlandish hats and colourful African robes. David Spitzer wrote: "The members of the group produce musical sounds which run the gamut from the traditional to the absurd and the surreal. They also include valid, humorous, vocal discourses and cries, as well as atypical sounds produced on traditional instruments."

Since 1971 the group has toured and played major festivals all over the world, making a great impact and gaining a large international following. They have recorded for major labels including Atlantic and ECM, on which they have three superb albums; during the mid-1970s they ran their own AECO record label for a while. The AEC continued to perform and record fitfully during the 1980s, but their musical vision seemed less focused, less inspired; a series of collaborations, with musicians ranging from Cecil Taylor to the African vocal group Amabutho, failed to counteract the impression that they were tailing off – albeit with occasional flashes of their old form.

One way of renewing creativity is to go back to some area of the jazz tradition and look for a fresh visionary synthesis with the roots of the music, and in 1990 the Ensemble recorded two albums attempting just that: *Dreaming Of The Masters Suite* and *Dreaming Of The Masters Vol. 2: Thelonius Monk*, both on DIW. But no new vision was achieved, and the band's thirty-plus years of life seemed to be over. In 1993, Joseph Jarman, who had become a Buddhist priest, left the Ensemble, in order to run a Brooklyn dojo (a room for the practice of judo). A few years later the remaining members – Bowie, Mitchell, Favors and Moye – went to the Caribbean to record another effort, *Coming Home Jamaica* (1998; Atlantic), but failed to find new dynamism. Sadly, Lester Bowie died in November, 1999. The exciting formative stages of the Art Ensemble have been released as a five-CD box-set, *Art Ensemble 1967–68* (Nessa), while the remaining trio released the self-explanatory *Tribute To Lester* in 2003. [IC]

⊙ **People In Sorrow** (1969; EMI Jazztime). The group in their initial stage of self-discovery (before drummer Famoudou Don Moye had joined) creating one long, focused performance which grows organically.

⊙ **Nice Guys** (1978; ECM). By now, Moye was a regular member and there are some very good moments on this album. However, it tends to see-saw schizophrenically between modish free improvisation and either blatantly obvious popular song forms, such as the ska rhythm with vocal on Bowie's "JA", or conventionally swinging jazz rhythms. Either way, the free sections often seem to outstay their welcome.

⊙ **Full Force** (1980; ECM). The spacey free sections show much greater imagination and emotional resonance here and seem more organically connected to the in-time sections. Bowie and the two saxophonists play well, and the title track, which is a collective improvisation, seems mercifully devoid of the usual free-jazz clichés.

⊙ **Urban Bushmen** (1980; ECM). This is a very impressive two-CD album which shows an even greater sureness of touch – perhaps because it is a recording of a concert, and the group engage the audience very directly. Longueurs are few, the energy runs high and there is much fine improvised music, with a huge variety of textures and timbres and a range of styles from the freely improvised to marches. Mitchell and Jarman between them play all the saxes from bass to soprano, and as well as all the percussion toys employed by the five musicians, vibraphone and glockenspiel are also part of the soundscape.

⊙ **The Alternate Express** (1989; DIW). One of the most vital of the later albums – here feeling, energy and imagination are one, so focused is the group, and the music ranges from seething collectives to spare impressionist passages where even the silences bristle.

Georges Arvanitas

Piano, organ.

b. Marseilles, 13 June 1931.

Born to Greek parents, Arvanitas studied piano from age four and was soon drawn to improvisation. After military service, he moved to Paris in 1954 and began backing both residents and US visitors. His first two albums (now both reissued) were recorded in 1958–9 with Art Taylor and Louis Hayes respectively, and he led his own quintet from 1959–62. Married to American singer Barbara Belgrave, he made two working visits to the USA (1964–5 and 1966), touring with the Ted Curson, Yusef Lateef and Slide Hampton groups and singer Lloyd Price. Returning to Paris, he concentrated on studio work (for Michel Legrand, amongst others) and formed his own trio, backing visiting musicians such as Dexter Gordon and Johnny Griffin, both live and occasionally on record. With bassist Jacky Samson and drummer Charles Saudrais, the trio remained in existence until the death of Saudrais in 1992. Since then Arvanitas has continued to work internationally, appearing in Japan and on two visits to the UK. He was honoured by the French government as first a Chevalier (1985) and then an Officer (1990) of Arts and Letters. Known chiefly for his driving accompaniments, Arvanitas is an excellent post-bop soloist with an attack recalling Kenny Drew. [BP]

⊙ **Rencontre** (1997; Columbia). Recorded with a trio including Joe Chambers and bassist Ira Coleman, this has a strong list of jazz standards such as "Off Minor", "Footprints" and Cedar Walton's "Bolivia". The pianist's approach energizes everything, while the unaccompanied closer "In A Sentimental Mood" makes a pleasant contrast.

Dorothy Ashby

Harp.

b. Detroit, 6 Aug 1932; d. 13 April 1986.

Ashby appeared on the jazz scene in 1957, working mainly with her own groups, then hosting her own Detroit radio show in the early 1960s. Finding small-group appearances in limited supply, she turned toward studio work and moved to the West Coast, recording in the 1970s with Sonny Criss and Stanley Turrentine. Revered by other harpists, even of more avant-garde orientation, Ashby accomplished the seemingly impossible task of playing convincing bebop on her instrument. [BP]

⊙ **Jazz Harpist** (1957; Savoy). Preferable to a recently reissued late-1960s fusion album, this first session and other early albums find Ashby in a quartet setting, here with flautist Frank Wess and Ed Thigpen.

Harold Ashby

Tenor saxophone.

b. Kansas City, Missouri, 21 March 1925; d. 13 June 2003.

Harold Ashby was often associated with the style of Ben Webster: his two brothers (Herbert and Alec) both worked with Webster, as a youngster he listened to Webster in Chicago clubs, and Webster later sat in regularly with Ashby's quartet in Kansas City. By that time Ashby had worked with Walter Johnson's band and was doing the rounds with R&B groups. In 1957 he moved to New York, into a room adjacent to Webster, and began a regular working association with him. The next year Webster introduced him to Duke Ellington; two years later Ashby began depping in the orchestra, recording with Ellington alumni such as Webster, Johnny Hodges and Lawrence Brown, and working in specific Ellington projects (including the *My People* show). He joined Ellington permanently on 5 July 1968, staying until the leader's death in 1974. Freelance work followed, with Benny Goodman, Sy Oliver and others, and he played as a soloist in New York jazz rooms. In the mid-80s Ashby was making the rounds of jazz festivals, including Nice, where he scored a monumental hit in 1986 playing driving, Webster-inspired tenor. "Harold must surely rank among the great unsung masters of jazz," says Eddie Cook. [DF]

⊙ **What Am I Here For** (1990; Criss Cross Jazz). A programme of Ellington material featuring Ashby's aged-in-the-wood Websterian tenor; part of a grand and once endangered tradition.

Svend Asmussen

Violin, viola, vocals.

b. Copenhagen, 16 Feb 1916.

After studying the violin as a child, Asmussen turned professional with his own group in 1933, playing with the Mills Brothers (1937) and Fats Waller (1938) in Denmark. Like Django Reinhardt in France he enjoyed increased fame during the Nazi occupation, and later worked with Alice Babs and guitarist Ulrik Neumann in a group called Swe-Danes from 1958–63, achieving success in Europe and appearing in the USA. Though he recorded with John Lewis in 1962, Duke Ellington in 1963 and Stephane Grappelli in 1965, Asmussen's harmonically intelligent and emotionally cool playing has remained largely a secret outside his own country. [BP]

⊙ **Fit As A Fiddle** (1996; Dacapo). Recorded at live appearances in his 81st year, Asmussen's quartet (including guitarist Jacob Fischer) reveals his modernist tendencies even within a repertoire that goes from "Runnin' Wild" to "Night In Tunisia" via "Groove Merchant", played with octave pedal and a touch of wah-wah.

Dominic Ashworth

Guitar.

b. Ontario, Canada, 16 Dec 1959.

Ashworth studied guitar at the University of Toronto (where he played with clarinettist Phil Nimmons' big band) and then in Spain before moving to Britain to study and play full time in clubs. Over the last decade he has played, toured and recorded with singer Carol Kidd, Michael Garrick's big band and quartet (with violinist Christian Garrick), Julian Marc Stringle's Dream Band with whom he has toured (2001-present), and also leads his own acoustic trio and teaches at London's Trinity College of Music. He also joined Digby

Fairweather's Half Dozen (1998–present) after an informal sit-in at the Clacton Jazz Festival. A talented and versatile guitarist, Ashworth can play Charlie Christian as easily as Hendrix; his long unbroken lines mark him out as a melodic improviser of rare ability. [DF]

CAROL KIDD

⊙ **Crazy for Gershwin** (1994/Linn). In a classy compilation of Gershwin selections, Ashworth's acoustic guitar is gracefully featured on ballads including "Drifting" and "Someone To Watch Over Me".

Gilad Atzmon

Saxophones, clarinet, and various Arabic flutes.
b. Israel, 9 June 1963.

Atzmon is a unique figure on the British Jazz scene: a man of many parts, whose passion and restlessness make him a major force in the music. Having studied composition and jazz at Jerusalem's Rubin Academy of Music for one year, he began touring in Israel and Europe with the "Gilad Atzmon Quartet" and "Spiel Acid Jazz Band", playing at several prestigious festivals. He also composed for modern dance and films, as well as doing some producing and arranging for various Israeli dance and rock projects, and also played Jewish soul music in Europe and the USA.

As a secular Jew living in Jerusalem, Atzmon sympathized with the sufferings of the Palestinians and became increasingly critical of Zionism. Opting for voluntary exile, he first moved to Germany where he began recording for the Enja label, before settling in London. Here, he worked extensively with Ian Dury and the Blockheads, touring with them from 1996–8, as well as working with Robbie Williams, Sinéad O'Connor and Paul McCartney.

Although a virtuoso and charismatic performer of bebop and contemporary jazz, Atzmon is currently reinvestigating his roots in the music of the Middle East, North Africa and Eastern Europe. To this end, he founded the Orient House Ensemble (OHE) whose line-up includes the fine Israeli drummer, Asaf Sirkis, the English pianist, Frank Harrison, and talented bassist Yaron Stavi. The Tunisian vocalist and oud player, Dhafer Youssef, and the Palestinian singer Reem Kelani have also performed with the OHE. In its fusion of Jazz with Jewish and Arabic traditions and performers, Atzmon views the OHE as having an important political dimension. The first OHE album, *Nostalgico*, which included guitar, trombone and trumpet in its line-up, was an affectionate and sometimes tongue-in-cheek tribute to the jazz tradition and Atzmon's own past. His second OHE album was more overtly political and attempted to tell the story of 20th century Palestine through music that melded jazz with strong middle eastern influences. These two albums reveal Atzmon as a very gifted composer/arranger and a superlative performer on tenor and soprano saxophones. But arguably he is still struggling to reconcile the extremely disparate elements of his experience into a fully coherent musical vision.

Atzmon has also written and published a dynamic, raunchy and often hilarious semi-autobiographical novel entitled *A Guide to the Perplexed*. [IC]

JAK KILBY

Gilad Atzmon

Gilad Atzmon and the Orient House Ensemble

⊙ **Nostalgico** (2002; Enja). This is Atzmon's playful tribute to the past with deeply felt excerpts from "Singing In The Rain" and affectionate tributes to Ellington. Atzmon's own beautiful ballad "Then & There" features his ecstatic soprano and a gloriously lyrical Frank Harrison piano solo.

⊙ **Exile** (2003; Enja). A rich and highly focused album whose line-up includes violin, accordion, Romanian flute and three vocalists – including the Palestinian singer Reem Kelani. Atzmon composed six of the nine pieces which include deconstructed political anthems and deeply elegaic pieces which clutch at the heart strings.

Georgie Auld

Saxophones, clarinet.

b. Toronto, 19 May 1919; d. 7 Jan 1990.

Born John Altwerger, Georgie Auld came to prominence with Bunny Berigan's orchestra in 1937, playing swing saxophone that recalled two major influences, Coleman Hawkins and Ben Pollack's underrated Larry Binyon. In 1939 he joined Artie Shaw, taking over leadership for three months after Shaw's abdication, before moving to Benny Goodman in 1940; he recorded classic sides with Goodman's sextet that year. After another short spell with Shaw he joined the army briefly in 1943 but came out to form his own band (1943–6), which significantly included young modern jazzmen, including Erroll Garner, Dizzy Gillespie and Al Porcino. Auld aligned himself firmly with the bebop movement, playing modern jazz at the Three Deuces and running his own Troubadour Club on 52nd Street before joining Billy Eckstine's magnificent big band. After a role on Broadway in *The Rat Race* (1949), Auld worked busily with his own quintet (1950–51), featuring Frank Rosolino and Tiny Kahn, then, because of lung trouble, moved to the sunnier climate of California to open his own club, the Melody Room. For the rest of the 1950s studio work, bigband and solo appearances kept him busy.

A regular flow of solo albums, including *Georgie Auld Plays The Winners* and its follow-up *One For The Losers*, charted his musical course throughout the first half of the 1960s, and by 1967 he was musical director for Tony Martin. In the 1970s he became a star in Japan, undertaking over a dozen tours and recording sixteen albums by 1975; two years later he took a leading soundtrack and on-screen role in the Scorsese movie *New York, New York* (1977). During the 1980s he visited Japan and Europe before finally succumbing to cancer. [DF]

➤➤ **Charlie Christian** *(Genius Of The Electric Guitar).*

Lovie Austin

Piano, arranger.

b. Chattanooga, Tennessee, 19 Sept 1887; d. 10 July 1972.

A pioneer jazzwoman, Lovie Austin (née Cora Calhoun) received a thorough music education at Roger Williams College, Nashville, and then at Knoxville College, before touring vaudeville circuits backing her husband's act and directing her own shows, including Lovie Austin's Revue, which had a long run at New York's Club Alabam. She then settled in Chicago, working as house pianist for Paramount Records, playing piano for Ma Rainey, Ida Cox and Ethel Waters, and composing hits such as "Graveyard Blues" for Bessie Smith. For over twenty years she was leader of the pit orchestra at Chicago's Monogram Theater, and Mary Lou Williams remembers "seeing this great woman in the pit conducting a group of five or six men, a cigarette in her mouth and her legs crossed playing the show with her left hand and writing music for the next act with her right". Austin's many rampaging New Orleans-style records (featuring men such as Tommy Ladnier, Johnny Dodds and Jimmy O'Bryant) are classics, but she found herself out of fashion by the early 1930s, with very little copyright protection to ensure royalties on her compositions. During World War II she had to work in a war factory, and after that became a dance school pianist. Her last records were made in Chicago in 1961. [DF]

⊙ **Lovie Austin 1924–6** (Classics). The complete Austin with her Blues Serenaders, a variety of singers and a trio with Tommy Ladnier and Jimmy O'Bryant. Despite variable sound quality this is an invaluable document of a significant jazz pioneer.

Herman Autrey

Trumpet, vocals.

b. Evergreen, Alabama, 4 Dec 1904; d. 14 June 1980.

Autrey had enjoyed a very successful career for ten years with shows, dance bands and his own group in Florida, and was working at Smalls' Paradise with Charlie Johnson's orchestra, when Fats Waller came talent-spotting in 1934 with his new Victor recording contract. He hired Autrey on the spot, and there followed five glorious years of "House Full" signs, films, touring and recording sessions – often of unfamiliar material, taken care of in a take or two. "Fats was awful good to me", remembered Autrey. "He treated me like a son." Waller treated all his men well, and on one occasion he bought Autrey an expensive trumpet which he kept for more than thirty years. Autrey regularly doubled with other bands while Fats appeared solo and after Waller died he worked with Stuff Smith, played up and down 52nd Street, and became well known as a bandleader in Canada. In 1954 he was badly hurt in a car crash, but came back triumphantly and in the 1960s played with the immensely successful Saints and Sinners, a neat swing band featuring Rudy Powell and the great Vic Dickenson: their records are a delight. In the 1970s Autrey was busy as ever in New York, but most listeners will remember him for the commanding, rough-edged and occasionally wild trumpet that enlivened so many Waller creations. [DF]

➤➤ **Fats Waller** *(The Middle Years Part I).*

Avon Cities Jazz Band

Formed in 1949 by trumpeter Geoff Nichols and clarinettist Ray Bush, the Bristol-based Avon Cities Jazz Band grew from a capable West Country revivalist band into a nationally recognized unit capable of moving from authentic New Orleans style to R&B or soul-influenced music using a variety of instrumentations, including a powerful electric rhythm-section. Regularly to be heard all over the West Country, the Avon Cities made regular trips to London jazz bases like the 100 Club, and attracted a huge following; the band's numerous vinyl albums are worth searching out for their challenging repertoire, ingenious arranging and high level of performance. [DF]

Tempo Fugit (1997; ACCD). Excellent representation of the group's eclecticism in a recent session; Basie to Van Morrison with veteran leader Geoff Nichols leading on trumpet. Their older work deserves CD reissue.

Roy Ayers

Vibraphone.

b. Los Angeles, 10 Sept 1940.

With a piano-playing mother and a trombonist father, Roy Ayers was playing boogie-woogie piano at five, steel guitar at nine, and in his teens experimented with flute, trumpet and drums before settling on vibes at eighteen. Although he started musical life as a straightahead West Coast jazz musician with the likes of Gerald Wilson, Teddy Edwards and Chico Hamilton in the 1960s, Ayers is a great popularizer, mixing a fluent jazz improvising talent with a variety of commercially acceptable styles ranging from R&B through Latin music to smoochy funk and dance music. He formed the group Ubiquity in 1970, touching most of these bases and producing twenty albums in twelve years, veered towards disco in the late 1970s, and currently dispenses a crowd-pleasing amalgam of jazz and smooth, danceable funk. Although a popular singer, a great showman and a firm believer in audience participation, he never quite allows commercial considerations to stifle his jazz virtuosity and, along with Johnny Lytle, has been in the vanguard of those bringing jazz vibes to a wider public, particularly in the UK, continental Europe and Japan.

In the 1990s, Ayers become something of an icon for the "acid jazz" generation, his work sampled by the likes of A Tribe Called Quest, X-Clan, Big Daddy Kane and Arrested Development. He also contributed to recordings by Galliano and pop singer Vanessa Williams, toured with GangStarr's Guru, and – usefully for festival promoters worldwide – continued to attract large crowds of non-jazz fans to jazz events. He describes his music as "a combination of styles – pop, jazz, blues and soul – fused into one". [CP]

Ubiquity

He's Coming (1971; Polydor). Fusion album featuring bassist Ron Carter and drummer Billy Cobham.

Roy Ayers

Hot: Live At Ronnie Scott's (1993; Jazz House). Perfect introduction to immediately accessible current Ayers live sound.

Albert Ayler

Tenor, soprano and alto saxophones, composer; also vocals, bagpipes.

b. Cleveland, Ohio, 13 July 1936; d. New York, 25 Nov 1970.

Ayler's father Edward played sax and violin and sang, and his brother Donald is a trumpet player. Albert began on alto sax at the age of seven; at ten he began a seven-year study period at the Academy of Music with Benny Miller, who had once played with Charlie Parker and Dizzy Gillespie. As a teenager he began playing with R&B bands including Lloyd Pearson's Counts Of Rhythm and Little Walter. His early influences were Lester Young, Sidney Bechet, Wardell Gray and Charlie Parker, and in Cleveland he was nicknamed "Little Bird". He did army service (1958–61), playing in a Special Services band, and during this period he switched to tenor sax. After demobilization he found little sympathy for his unconventional musical ideas in the USA, and in 1962 left for Sweden where he worked with a commercial band and played his own music after hours. He made his first recordings there in October, and in January 1963 recorded in Copenhagen the album *My Name Is Albert Ayler*, which has been called "one of the classics of the new music". He met Cecil Taylor in Scandinavia and began playing with him in New York.

Ayler's reputation, which had been made in Europe, followed him back to the USA, and he began to record regularly. He was a member of the Jazz Composers' Guild, and in 1964, with Don Cherry, Gary Peacock (bass) and Sunny Murray (drums), he toured in Holland, Sweden and Denmark. In 1965 he formed a new group in the USA, with his brother Donald, saxophonist Charles Tyler, bassist Lewis Worrell and Murray again on drums, which recorded one of his most influential albums, *Bells*, live at a Town Hall concert. By this time controversy was raging about Ayler, ranging from assertions that he couldn't play and was a charlatan, to claims that he was the new Messiah of jazz.

Until about 1967 Ayler's music was a mixture of uncompromising abstraction and elements from traditional forms such as folk dances, marches, folk songs, and the dirges of old New Orleans funeral processions. As a saxophonist his true innovations were timbral and textural and in the climate of feeling that he engendered. He had a huge, emotive sound with a strong vibrato, and could move with rippling ease from gruff, honking low notes to hoarse screams in

DAVID REDFERN

Albert Ayler

the extreme upper register – all the characteristics of R&B tenor sax-playing abstracted and taken to their ultimate expression. In his work there is always a sense of violence barely under control, and he himself said in the early 1960s: "It's not about notes any more. It's about feelings." His tonal distortions and wild expressiveness spawned many imitators and disciples on the free-jazz scene, particularly in Europe. It has been said that he was in many ways closer to Bubber Miley and Tricky Sam Nanton (both of whom used tonal distortion expressively) than he was to Charlie Parker, Miles Davis or Sonny Rollins. Ayler's music, however, always seems unfinished and incomplete, as if it is perhaps the raw material out of which an art might be made. It lacks the necessary self-editing process, and much of it is too long and monotonous.

Like several other leading players on the free-jazz scene, Ayler began to turn away from abstraction in the later 1960s, and re-examined his musical roots. His work began to show strong elements from gospel music and R&B, and on his 1968 album *New Grass* he both talks preaching religion and sings with a nice little blues/gospel backing band which includes electric bass, Joe Newman on trumpet and Pretty Purdie on drums. He was accused by his old colleagues of "selling out", but it is highly unlikely that he was capable of such shallowness. Ayler was a driven man, deeply religious, with a powerful premonition of his own imminent death and the sincerity of one who can do only what he does. He died in mysterious circumstances: in November 1970 he went missing for twenty days, then his body was found floating in the East River, New York. He had died by drowning.

Ayler has had a considerable influence, particularly on saxophonists. He certainly influenced John Coltrane, who admired him, and who, after he had recorded his album *Ascension* in 1965, told Ayler, "I found I was playing just like you." Through Coltrane, Ayler's spirit and sound have touched countless subsequent musicians. [IC]

Witches And Devils (1964; Freedom). Originally released under the title "Spirits", this album caused a sensation in the 1960s. The wild, demonic atmosphere was worlds away from the already familiar freedom of Ornette Coleman.

Spiritual Unity (1964; ESP Disk). This has Ayler in trio formation with bassist Gary Peacock and drummer Sunny Murray.

Spirits Rejoice (1965; ESP Disk). The above trio is here augmented with Ayler's brother Donald on trumpet, Call Cobbs on harpsichord and second bassist Henry Grimes. The group take Ayler's anthemic themes and blow them, with eyewatering intensity, to the edge of chaos. The results demonstrate why Ayler's influence, for good or ill, was once so pervasive, though few could match the purposefulness and savage beauty found on this disc.

In Greenwich Village (1967; Impulse). For these two live sesssions recorded in February and December, Ayler plays alto and tenor sax, with Donald on trumpet and Beaver Harris on drums. The line-ups also include cello, violin and double basses.

Azimuth

➤➤ *see entry for* **John Taylor**.

Azymuth

A popular Brazilian fusion band, Azymuth began life as a trio consisting of José Roberto Bertrami (keyboard), Alex Malheiros (bass) and Ivan Conti (drums, all b. 1946). Enjoying success on the US West Coast in the 1970s, they expanded their personnel and tailored their sound to the dance market. By the 1990s Bertrami had been replaced by Marinho Boffa, but the recent renewed interest in fusion music has led to an increased reputation for their early work. [BP]

The Best Of Azymuth (1980–4; Milestone). This concentrates on original material despite the inclusion of Chick Corea's "500 Miles High" and, despite guest instrumentalists on each of the albums excerpted, the focus is always on the tight rhythm trio.

B

Roy Babbington

Bass, bass guitar.

b. Kempston, Bedfordshire, UK, 8 July 1940.

A versatile bassist equally adept on both acoustic and electric instruments, Roy Babbington is self-taught, having learned his trade in clubs and ballrooms before moving to London in 1969. In the 1970s, he worked as a session musician, playing with pop and blues figures such as Mike D'Abo and Alexis Korner as well as with musicians then at the forefront of the jazz-rock style: Mike Gibbs, Ian Carr and Mike Westbrook. He joined Soft Machine in 1973, appearing on the band's *Soft Machine 7* (1973) and *Bundles* (1974). He also worked regularly at the National Theatre, and recorded, in the late 1970s, with trumpeter Harry Beckett, composer Graham Collier and saxophonist Barbara Thompson. In the 1980s, he became a regular sideman with Stan Tracey, appearing both in the pianist's larger ensembles and in his quartets and trios. He also played with the BBC Radio Orchestra, and continues to back visiting Americans such as Mose Allison and singer Marlene VerPlanck, leading the trio that plays behind her on her frequent trips to the UK. Performing sideman duties for the likes of Alan Skidmore, Bob Koral and Sue Hawker, the Don Weller/Brian Spring Quartet and the Geoff Eales Trio, he is one of Britain's foremost bassists. [CP/CI]

Mike Gibbs

Just Ahead (1972; Polydor). Live recording of Mike Gibbs's thirteen-piece jazz-rock band performing live at Ronnie Scott's, featuring Babbington on bass guitar.

Stan Tracey

Genesis (1987; Steam). Suite about the creation composed by Tracey and performed by a fifteen-piece band; Babbington is featured on "The Firmament".

Playin' In The Yard (1987; Steam). Babbington shares bass duties with Dave Green on album featuring the Tracey quartet with Charlie Rouse guesting.

Marlene VerPlanck

I Like To Sing (1999; Audiophile). Although the album is divided between early 1980s material and songs recorded in London in 1998, Babbington's playing is magisterial in its skilful interaction with the US singer.

Geoff Eales

Red Letter Days (2001; Black Box). Top-notch post-bop piano jazz featuring the under-rated Eales and guest guitarist Jim Mullen.

Alice Babs

Vocals.

b. Kalmar, Sweden, 26 Jan 1924.

Born Alice Nilsson, Babs adopted her stage name as a teenage star in radio, records and film. She continued to be a successful singer of popular hits through the following decades, also leaning towards jazz in small-group work with the Swe-Danes from 1958–63. Her talent was recognized by Duke Ellington, who recorded her in Paris in 1963 and then used her in his Sacred Concerts in 1968 and 1973; though officially retired, she hosted the 1994 International Ellington Conference in Stockholm.

Babs's voice, equally at home in the alto range and a high soprano register, has a rhythmic grace and tonal purity which frequently recall her favourite instrumentalist, Johnny Hodges. [BP]

Duke Ellington

Second Sacred Concert (1968; Fantasy/OJC). Babs has four exceptional features in this Duke Ellington set, including "Heaven" and the wordless "T.G.T.T. (Too Good To Title)".

Benny Bailey

Trumpet.

b. Cleveland, Ohio, 13 Aug 1925.

Benny (Ernest Harold) Bailey worked as a teenager in R&B bands before joining Jay McShann in 1947, later moving to the Dizzy Gillespie big band (1947–8) and Lionel Hampton (1949–53). He remained in Europe after the Hampton tour of 1953, working in radio studio bands, then joined Quincy Jones's outfit which debuted in Paris and toured the USA in 1959–61. He returned to Europe and completed many years of studio work in Sweden, Germany and Switzerland; during this period, he played on all the engagements of the Kenny Clarke-Francy Boland band. More recently, he has made occasional small-group records and has worked in the USA again.

In big-band circles Bailey is revered for his section-leading ability, but his solo improvising has been vastly underrated. From a bebop-inspired approach he has fashioned a very individual style full of long lines and angular melodies, and his mannerism of dropping two octaves in the space of one note is instantly recognizable, even in the most uninspiring studio bands. [BP]

⊙ **For Heaven's Sake** (1988; Hothouse). This London session teams Bailey to excellent effect with fellow Clarke-Boland sideman Tony Coe and the expatriate rhythm-section of Horace Parlan, Jimmy Woode and Idris Muhammad.

➤➤ **Kenny Clarke** *(Two Originals)*; **Sahib Shihab** *(And All Those Cats)*.

Buster Bailey

Clarinet, saxophones.

b. Memphis, l9 July 1902; d. 12 April 1967.

Buster (William C.) Bailey acquired his legendary lightning technique from a classical teacher, Franz Schoepp, who taught at Chicago Music College (Benny Goodman was a pupil two or three years later), and by 1917 was touring with W.C. Handy's famous showband. Work with Erskine Tate and King Oliver followed and then in October 1924 Bailey joined Fletcher Henderson, one week after Louis Armstrong. In Henderson's technically demanding orchestra his speed and near-classical accuracy of execution became a byword, and he moved into the A-team of Henderson soloists headed by Coleman Hawkins. With short breaks he remained there until 1937, when he found another showcase in the perfectly polished and phenomenally successful John Kirby band. With Kirby came a starry round of cabaret work, hit records and weekly radio exposure. Once again, amid Charlie Shavers's intricate creations for Kirby's band, Bailey's woody, occasionally reedy and always precise playing found the perfect setting.

After the war he led his own band again on 52nd Street, spent two years with Wilbur de Paris and struck up a regular relationship with trumpeter Henry "Red" Allen, as well as lending his technique to the Sauter-Finegan orchestra, pitwork with the Ziegfeld Theater orchestra, and symphony concerts. From 1954 he was a regular member of "Red" Allen's band at New York's fast and furious Metropole sessions, and took part in definitive mainstream recordings with Allen and Taft Jordan, Pee Wee Erwin and Coleman Hawkins. After more freelancing with Wild Bill Davison, the Saints and Sinners, and others, the prosperous, elegant, and stately Bailey ended his career with Louis Armstrong, with whom he had joined Fletcher Henderson forty years before, playing his supporting role as perfectly as ever. [DF]

⊙ **Buster Bailey 1925–40** (Classics). Good start to CD representation of Bailey on record. Regularly he's teamed with Kirby colleagues; there's a good session with Henry "Red" Allen, and aficionados' treats including "Man With A Horn Goes Berserk" – an extraordinary display of Bailey's technical mastery. The best is yet to come.

⊙ **John Kirby Sextet** (1939–41; Columbia). Double-CD set showing Bailey in his element with Kirby's "biggest little band in the land", an ensemble which matched to perfection his classically academic approach mixed with swing. Classics in this chronology include "Royal Garden Blues", "It Feels So Good" and "Opus Five" as well as pastiches such as "Bounce Of The Sugar-Plum Fairy", "Sextet From Lucia" and more.

Derek Bailey

Guitar.

b. Sheffield, Yorkshire, UK, 29 Jan 1930.

Bailey studied music for eleven years (1941–52) with C.H.C. Biltcliffe and guitar with John Duarte. From 1952–65 he worked as a guitar soloist, accompanist or with orchestras in every kind of musical context: clubs, concert halls, dance halls, theatres, radio, TV and recording studios. However, from 1963 onwards he became increasingly interested in the possibilities of the freely improvised music to which he has since devoted himself. As he has said, "I have had the good fortune to work with most of the leading German blasters, American groovers, Dutch acrobats and English kaleidoscopists in this field."

In the 1960s he worked with the Spontaneous Music Ensemble, but since then has gradually withdrawn from group music, preferring to play solo electric guitar and only occasionally performing in duos with people to whom he feels a strong affinity, including Evan Parker, Tony Coe and a series of percussionists. Since 1965 he has performed solo concerts in all the major cities of Europe, Japan and the USA. In 1970 he formed, jointly with Evan Parker and Tony Oxley, Incus Records, the first independent, musician-owned record company in Britain. From 1974–6 he wrote his book, *Improvisation: Its Nature and Practice in Music*, then in 1976 formed Company, a changing ensemble of improvising musicians featuring players from Europe, North and South America, Africa and Japan. In 1977 he inaugurated Company Week, an annual event in London to which all kinds of improvisers from around the world are invited for five days of improvisational music-making.

He has pursued the austere path of total improvisation and abstraction with monolithic integrity, becoming one of the masters in that field. Yet, despite the severity of his approach, his music is often

alive with drama, intelligence and anarchic humour; ironically, his album *View from 6 Windows* (1982) was nominated for a Grammy award. Bailey's book on improvisation examines it in all its manifestations, from the European classical tradition to vernacular music of all kinds – ethnic, rock, jazz and free improvisation. Bailey spent two years (1989–91) with director Jeremy Marre, preparing a series of TV programmes based on his book. The series, entitled *On The Edge*, was screened by Channel 4 in Britain and shown in a number of other countries in 1993 and 1994.

Since 1995, Bailey's activities seem to have been centred on recording, primarily in the USA, and this has resulted in between thirty and forty CDs. His collaborators have ranged hugely from free-bop alto saxist John Zorn and bassist William Parker on the album *Harras* (1995; Tzadik), and drummer Tony Williams, plus bassist Bill Laswell on *Arcana* (1995; DIW), to Pat Metheny on *Sign Of 4* (1996; Knitting Factory) and The Ruins (a Japanese bass and drums rock duo) on *Saisoro* (1996; Tzadik). Bailey has also worked with Min XiaoFen, a Chinese pipa player, resulting in the album *Viper* (1996; Avant). He even tried some recordings with DJs, including *Guitar Drums & Bass* (1996; Avant) with DJ Ninj, and *Playbacks* (1998; Bingo). On his own label, Incus, he put out a solo CD, *Takes, Fakes & Dead She Dances*, and a double CD with Tony Oxley, *Soho Suites*, one recording from 1977 and one from 1996. At this time a bit of history was repeated and developed. From 1963–6, Bailey had played in a trio with Tony Oxley and Gavin Bryers who was then a bass player, and the trio called themselves Joseph Holbrooke. In October 1998, they played together again, for the first time in thirty-two years. The occasion was Oxley's sixtieth birthday and German Radio (Köln) honoured him with two days of concerts, one of which was by the J. Holbrooke trio, and one month later the trio recorded an album for Californian label, Cortical Foundation. Bailey is still busily performing concerts and has also enjoyed working with tap-dancer Will Gaines. On record he has recently turned up with the likes of Ingar Zach, Tony Bevan and Alex Ward. [IC]

⊙ **Han** (1986; Incus). Bailey and Dutch percussionist Han Bennink in duo – both men revealing their latent Dadaism.

⊙ **Figuring** (1987 & '88; Incus). Duo with elegant bass player Barre Phillips. In their abstract hands, double bass and guitar work eloquently together with rich sonorities, textures and harmonics.

⊙ **Solo Guitar: Vol. 2** (1991; Incus). Austere Bailey caught in the cold snows of his dreams.

⊙ **Village Life** (1991; Incus). Bailey in trio with the African percussionists (and vocalists) Thebe Lipere and Louis Moholo who flesh out the music. This was a live session at the Vortex in London, and distant voices and sounds enrich the textures.

⊙ **Playing** (1992; Incus). Bailey re-examines his roots in duo with drummer John Stevens. The two were closely associated in the Spontaneous Music Ensemble in the 1960s and this dialogue after a long silence fired them both.

⊙ **The Sign Of 4** (1996; Knitting Factory). Two apparent opposites, Bailey and Pat Metheny meet here with some help from two percussionists, Gregg Bendian and Paul Wertico. The two guitarists spent a week or ten days playing together before they went into the studio to record, and their rapport then seemed absolute.

⊙ **No Waiting** (1997; Potlatch). This is a live recording from a duo concert Bailey played in Paris with French bassist Joëlle Léandre. She comes from the classical tradition but is deeply involved with improvisation and had played with Bailey on several previous occasions. Bailey's innate courtesy to women enhances the subtlety and sonority of their interplay with delightful results.

Mildred Bailey

Vocals.

b. Tekoa, Washington, 27 Feb 1907; d. 12 Dec 1951.

Mildred Bailey (née Mildred Rinker) and her brother Al went to school in Spokane (where Bing Crosby attended a Jesuit college). Later she sang in local cabarets and on local radio before sending a demonstration record to Paul Whiteman, who was persuaded to hire her by what he heard and by his newly hired "Rhythm Boys" – Rinker, Crosby and Harry Barris. Beautifully featured (she signed early photographs "Face Bailey") and very fat, she had, said Crosby, a "heart as big as Yankee Stadium". For four years from 1929 she sang with Whiteman; a 1932 hit, "Rockin' Chair", led to her being dubbed "The Rockin' Chair Lady", scarcely the most attractive image for a young woman. In 1933 she married the diminutive Red Norvo (publicity shots of the mismatched couple are determinedly comic) and with him she was to achieve more fame with hits like "Weekend of a Private Secretary". She was Norvo's featured band singer from 1936–9, but it was an insecure marriage, as Bailey blamed any lack of success on her appearance and treated everyone to displays of deep affection alternating with towering outbursts of blackmouthed rage. The retiring, eager-to-please Norvo once confided to cornettist Rex Stewart that "Mildred was really two people: one, a warm solicitous wife, the other a moody and excitable artist."

Bailey, the first prominent female band singer, was a big star for most of the 1930s. Her records outsold most other female singers of the period apart from Billie Holiday, a singer for whom she had the highest musical (if not personal) respect. She had radio series of her own, a distinguished list of recorded accompanists and more money than she could spend. By 1939, though, her partnership with Norvo showed signs of cracking. She had cut short a 1938 tour to return to New York amid nervous strain and bad feeling among her accompanists, and late that year she appeared solo as a featured star on Benny Goodman's Camel Caravan programme. Her divorce was finalized in 1943.

Despite continuing club work around New York (at Café Society, the Blue Angel and elsewhere) her career was on a downhill swing, complicated by a liver complaint and a hint of heart trouble. By 1948 she was living with her beloved dogs in a ground-floor apartment on East 31st Street, NY, lonely, ill, and still unpredictably kind or angry. In 1949 she was taken to hospital near death (Bing Crosby and Frank Sinatra made arrangements for her care and paid the bills), and though she returned to work with Joe Marsala and Ralph Burns she never really got better. She died penniless, in 1951, of liver and heart failure. [DF]

Squeeze Me 1935–7 (1991; Charley Records). Good collection of vintage Bailey including four superb tracks with her Alley Cats (Bunny Berigan and Johnny Hodges 1935) and sixteen more of comparable quality.

The Rockin' Chair Lady 1931–50 (1994; GRP). Classily produced reissue ranging from 1931 sides with the Casa Loma Orchestra, classics with her Alley Cats, The Delta Rhythm Boys and more, and including her last two 1950 recordings with Vic Schoen.

Mrs Swing (2003; Properbox). Undoubtedly the best all-round survey of Bailey's best recordings in an economical four-CD boxed set. Excellent value.

Pearl Bailey

Vocals.

b. Newport News, Virginia, 29 March 1918; d. 17 Aug 1990.

The daughter of dancer Bill Bailey, Pearl Bailey began her long career winning amateur-night contests and working as a dancer in the mining towns of Pennsylvania (at $15 a week); she then joined Noble Sissle's band in the mid-30s before singing with Edgar Hayes, Cootie Williams and Don Redman. Her high-profile debut at New York's Strand Theater, substituting for Sister Rosetta Tharpe, led to rapid stardom – after cabaret work at the Village Vanguard, plus collaborations with Cab Calloway, she starred in the Arlen-Mercer musical *St. Louis Woman*, and appeared in films from 1947 (her first hit, "Tired", came from her first film, *Variety Girl*). A naturally humorous performer, with a uniquely wry and dry-sounding timbre, Bailey was a powerful personality and continued to do well in films, including starring roles in *Carmen Jones* (1954) and *St. Louis Blues* with Nat "King" Cole (1958), as well as on Broadway, notably in Harold Arlen's *House of Flowers* (1954) and later the all-black cast of *Hello Dolly* (1967). She also appeared internationally as a cabaret artist and on television.

In 1952 she married drummer Louie Bellson (her third marriage) and she worked regularly with him for the rest of her life, despite announcing her retirement in 1976 to serve as a member of the American Delegation to the United Nations. Hits like "Takes Two To Tango" established her primarily as a cabaret performer, but many recordings show this unmistakable vocal stylist to have been totally at home in the company of great jazz musicians, including Charlie Shavers. [DF]

Sixteen Most Requested Songs (1945–50; Columbia). A fine representative selection of Bailey's hits, including "Legalize My Name"and "A Woman's Prerogative", plus duets with Hot Lips Page, Jackie "Moms" Mabley and others.

Best of the Roulette Years (1957–63; Roulette). A typical mix of standards and old-style (and usually hilarious) vaudeville material like "Since I Became A Hussey For My Husband" and "Pushin' 40".

Chet Baker

Trumpet, flugelhorn, vocals.

b. Yale, Oklahoma, 23 Dec 1929; d. Amsterdam, 13 May 1988.

The uncharismatically named Chesney Henry Baker played briefly with Charlie Parker in 1952 after musical study and army service, then spent a year with the first Gerry Mulligan quartet. With Mulligan out of commission in 1953, Baker formed his own quartet, which lasted three years. His career was intermittent in the late 1950s and 60s owing to drug problems, and most of his last three decades were spent in Europe, although he continued to visit the

HERMAN LEONARD

Chet Baker

USA. An addict to the last, he died falling from a hotel window.

Baker was acclaimed as a "great white hope" at the tender age of 23, a burden from which his image never recovered. Not one of nature's bandleaders, he seldom asserted his authority and took part in some highly unsatisfying performances and albums. In the same way that his solo style remained in thrall to early Miles Davis, much of his favourite repertoire was selected from tunes recorded by Miles. Fragile to the point of transparency, like his singing, Baker's trumpet work treads a tightrope between affirmation and apathy but, when the surroundings are right, his lyrical playing can overcome all reservations. [BP]

Chet Baker

⊙ **Chet Baker Sings** (1954–6; Blue Note). Anyone drawn to Baker's singing should avoid the later efforts, including the album which is the soundtrack of Bruce Weber's documentary, *Let's Get Lost*. Here is the fresh-faced original style, sounding much like Mel Tormé's pre-teenage brother.

Chet Baker and Art Pepper

⊙ **Playboys** (1956; Pacific Jazz). Along with the early Gerry Mulligan albums, this is the best demonstration of Baker's intuitive approach to jazz, and benefits from the rhythm-section of Carl Perkins, Curtis Counce and Larance Marable.

Chet Baker

⊙ **Daybreak** (1979; Steeplechase). Outstanding among the multitude of often inferior albums recorded in his last decade, this is a fine example of a favourite format featuring just trumpet, guitar (Doug Raney) and bass (N.-H. Ørsted Pedersen).

David Baker

Trombone, cello, composer.
b. Indianapolis, Indiana, 21 Dec 1931.

Baker played with Indianapolis natives Wes Montgomery and Slide Hampton, and toured on trombone with Buddy Johnson, Stan Kenton in 1956, Maynard Ferguson in 1957, Lionel Hampton and Quincy Jones in 1961. From 1960 he was a member of the George Russell sextet until a muscular problem forced him in 1962 to concentrate on cello. He then became an enormously energetic teacher/theoretician as author of numerous textbooks and solo transcriptions, and as chairman of the jazz department of Indiana University from 1966 to the present. He has been a member of the National Arts Council from 1987–92 and, since 1991, has directed the Smithsonian Jazz Masterworks Orchestra.

Probably the first musician with a high-level performing reputation to move full-time into jazz education, Baker had compositions such as "LeRoi" and "Honesty" recorded by other musicians. Especially while with Russell, he displayed a brilliant technique and was one of the first trombonists to incorporate avant-garde effects such as slides, smears, rips and fall-offs. [BP]

➤➤ **George Russell** *(Ezz-thetics).*

Fred Thelonious Baker

Electric fretless bass, electric and acoustic guitars.
b. Tibshelf, Derbyshire, UK, 4 June 1960.

Although he began musical life as a guitarist, playing both jazz and classical music, Fred T. Baker took up electric bass in his mid-teens. He first came to public attention in the early 1980s with guitarist John Etheridge's band Second Vision, but established himself with his regular work for trumpeter/flugelhorn player Harry Beckett, with whom he has made three albums and toured extensively in Europe. In 1993 Baker recorded *A Moon of Roses* with pianist Horace Parlan in Germany and, the following year, as a guitar player, an eponymous Fred Thelonious Baker Group album featuring drummer Brian Abrahams, percussionist Mamadi Kamara, bassist Matt Rooke and saxophonist Shell Baker. With Phil Miller's In Cahoots, Baker has toured and made half a dozen albums, and he also works frequently in a folk/jazz context with Ric Sanders and Vicki Clay, his projects with them including a tribute album to Sandy Denny, *It Suits Me Well*, and various live performances involving multi-instrumentalist Chris Conway and ex-Jethro Tull drummer Clive Bunker. Baker also works with Elton Dean in two quartets, one featuring pianist Alex Maguire and drummer Liam Genocky, the other with guitarist Mark Hewins and drummer Mark Sanders. His association with Harry Beckett also continues – with saxophonist Chris Biscoe, keyboard player Alistair Gavin and drummer Tony Marsh, Baker has toured the UK performing tributes to Charles Mingus. Still a key member of In Cahoots, he also teaches jazz and progressive music at the Birmingham Conservatoire of Music. [CP/CI]

Harry Beckett

⊙ **All Four One** (1991; Spotlite). Unusual four-flugelhorn front line in album composed almost entirely of Beckett material, and featuring duo with Baker on "One For All".

Fred Thelonious Baker

⊙ **The Missing Link** (1999; Blueprint). Long-awaited solo album, featuring Baker on both bass and guitar, performing mostly self-penned material, but also including the odd Monk tune.

➤➤ **Harry Beckett** *(Live: Vol. 2).*

Ginger Baker

Drums.
b. London, 19 Aug 1940.

Baker began on trumpet and had lessons in theory and notation, but switched to drums when he became interested in blues and jazz while at school.

He played first with traditional jazz bands, and then with modern jazz groups, in one of which he met bassist Jack Bruce. Baker and Bruce had high reputations as up-and-coming young jazz musicians in the early 1960s, but after working with Alexis Korner's Blues Incorporated, then Graham Bond's Organisation, they joined forces with guitarist Eric Clapton and formed Cream in 1966. This trio of electric guitar, electric bass and amplified drums combined heavy rock rhythms and riffs with jazz and blues-based improvisation which made it one of the very first jazz-rock groups. Bruce's excellent songwriting and singing were the icing on the cake, and Cream became immensely popular in the USA. They disbanded at the height of their success in 1969; Baker and Clapton, with Stevie Winwood and Rick Grech, went on to form Blind Faith, touring in the UK and USA. After that group broke up, Baker formed Air Force, which played Afro-jazz flavoured music and featured some leading jazz musicians including saxophonist Harold McNair and legendary British drummer Phil Seaman. When that too folded, Baker dropped out of the scene, went to Africa and opened a recording studio in Nigeria. He worked and recorded with African musicians including Fela Kuti and the Nigerian band Salt, but in the early 1970s was back in the UK fitfully leading his own groups or working with other rock bands.

By the 1980s Baker was living in semi-retirement on a farm in Italy, but mid-decade he returned to music, working and recording with African and/or American and British musicians with generally uneven results. However, in the 1990s he recorded a magnificent trio album with bassist Charlie Haden and guitarist Bill Frisell, and also attempted to reinvestigate Cream territory with BBM, a trio consisting of Baker, Bruce and guitarist Gary Moore in place of Clapton.

In the mid-1990s, Baker moved to the USA, settling in Denver, Colorado, where he met trumpeter Ron Miles. The latter began to work with Baker in 1996, and the following year made a major contribution to Baker's album, *Coward Of The County*, not only playing on it, but co-producing it with Baker, and writing six of the eight pieces. The remaining tracks were written by Baker, and the album featured his group, The DJQ2O (The Denver Jazz Quintet To Octet). In 1999 Baker left America to settle in South Africa where he now owns a ranch and breeds polo ponies. [IC]

⊙ **The Album (1968–87; ITM).** This is a series of tracks showing Baker's musical odyssey from Cream through his various groups up to 1987.

⊙ **Palanquin's Pole** (1987; ITM). Baker leads five African percussionists, two of whom also sing and chant.

⊙ **Going Back Home** (1994; Atlantic). Baker sometimes seems all circumference and no centre, but here with Bill Frisell and Charlie Haden he sustains a highly focused series of performances. The music has a raw energy, it swings mightily, rocks hard, the empathy is constant and the whole thing shot through with feeling.

⊙ **Falling Off The Roof** (1996; Atlantic). The group is the same as for *Going Back Home* except that banjoist Bela Fleck is added for Charlie Parker's "Au Privave", and guitarist Jerry Hahn is added for Haden's "Sunday At The Hillcrest". Baker is a congenital jazzman and rocker – he revels in this company and the band takes off.

⊙ **Coward Of The County** (1997; Atlantic). The Denver Jazz Quintet seems to consist of Baker, Ron Miles, tenor saxophonist Fred Hess, pianist Eric Gunnison and bassist Artie Moore. Guitarist Todd Ayers is added on some tracks, and organist Shamie Royston is added on the title track. Baker's drumming never fails to swing and rock passionately throughout, and his compositions, "Cyril Davis", a 6/4 tribute to the late harmonica player, and "Dangle The Carrot", a tricky bebop-type theme, are deft and to the point. This is an excellent album.

Harold "Shorty" Baker

Trumpet.

b. St Louis, Missouri, 26 May 1913; d. 8 Nov 1966.

Harold "Shorty" Baker belongs to the great line of St Louis trumpeters which begins with Charlie Creath in the 1920s and goes on to Miles Davis in the 1980s. His main influences were Louis Armstrong and Joe Smith, and Baker began his career working in their image, playing on riverboats with Fate Marable and on the road with Erskine Tate, Don Redman, Teddy Wilson and Andy Kirk (he later married Mary Lou Williams, Kirk's pianist). "He was an excellent section man," says Clark Terry, "and they all loved having him around, he was such a happy humorous man." The first of countless stays with Duke Ellington began in 1942, and Baker was one of the most popular figures in the orchestra. His glassy-clear tone (which he achieved with a rare Hein mouthpiece – deep, thin and hard to handle) was often featured in Ellington niceties like "Mr Gentle and Mr Cool" (with Ray Nance, his close friend), "All Heart" and Hoagy Carmichael's "Stardust". Perhaps it was Baker's long association with Ellington that regularly gave him the courage to leave, however. "When you leave Duke's organization," he told Stanley Dance, "you feel very confident playing in any other band." Some of his freelance years were spent with Ben Webster, Teddy Wilson and Johnny Hodges' small band. In 1964, while Baker was at the Embers with a quartet, throat trouble put him in hospital. He was cheerful to visitors and busy planning a future, but cancer had taken hold. [DF]

⊙ **Shorty And Doc** (1961; Prestige Swingville). Despite the "modern" tendencies of the rhythm-section, this is a delightful quintet combining Baker with fellow trumpeter Doc Cheatham. Shorty is featured on "I Didn't Know What Time It Was".

Kenny Baker

Trumpet, cornet, flugelhorn, composer, leader.

b. Withernsea, Yorkshire, UK, 1 March 1921; d. 7 Dec 1999.

Baker was first heard on record in a public jam session of 1941 and quickly established an unbeatable reputation in London clubs. Brass band trained, with faultless technical command, the young Baker was lead trumpeter with Ted Heath's post-war orchestra (such *tours de force* as "Bakerloo Non-Stop" are still well remembered), and in the 1950s led his own Baker's Dozen. By the 1950s he was regularly in the studios, and his numerous recordings are world-class, a confident replay of Bunny Berigan without the errors and with range to spare. So good was Baker that when the Musicians' Union were trying to justify their ban on American players working in Britain, they were able to ask, "While we have Kenny Baker who needs Louis?"

In the 1960s and 70s he was on call for film and studio work (a famous appearance was a long hot-trumpet solo mimed by Kay Kendall in the film *Genevieve*, 1954), but he regularly emerged to play jazz clubs, sometimes with fellow trumpeters John McLevey and Tommy McQuater. With Betty Smith (later, Don Lusher and Roy Willox), he formed "The Best Of British Jazz", a show which toured regularly from 1976, and after the death of Harry James in 1983 he was asked by the James Foundation to take over their orchestra – an offer he declined. Later in the 1980s and into the 90s Baker continued to perform at premier level, re-recording all the solos of Louis Armstrong for a multi-volume digital collection, playing the cornet for Yorkshire Television's *Beiderbecke Tapes* and *The Beiderbecke Affair,* appearing regularly as star soloist alone and with the reformed Ted Heath Orchestra. A small fighting-cock of a man (he once elbowed Benny Goodman out of the way for persistently misjudging the tempo of a trumpet feature), Baker was a world-class lead trumpeter, solo performer and improviser, and – for many listeners and musicians – Britain's best-ever jazz trumpeter. [DF]

⊙ **Birth Of A Legend 1941–6** (Hep). Outstanding collection of formative Baker, from the "First English Public Jam Session" (1941) up to "Bakerloo Non-Stop" with Ted Heath (1946) and in between ever-excellent tracks from him with George Shearing, Harry Hayes, George Chisholm and more.

⊙ **The Half-Dozen – After Hours 1955–57** (Lake). Baker's swaggeringly accomplished small group (with Chisholm, Derek Collins, Harry Smith et al) plus quartet titles and one track with Bruce Turner; all demonstrate his supremacy as Britain's best swing trumpeter.

⊙ **Tribute To The Great Trumpeters** (1993; Horatio Nelson). An opulent big-band set of eighteen titles featuring Baker's tributes to inspirations from Red Nichols to Harry James; immaculate Baker with an orchestra of premier British sessionmen.

⊙ **The Boss Is Home** (1994; Big Bear). An overdue return of Baker's Dozen, fronted by Baker for a short season at Ronnie Scott's in Birmingham. Excitement is electric, the Boss is in top form, and there are worthy contributions from Alan Barnes, Brian Dee, Richard Edwards and Bruce Adams.

Burt Bales

Piano.

b. Stevensville, Montana, 20 March 1916.

One of the grand names of revivalist piano, Bales began his San Francisco-based career with Turk Murphy's band (1942) and Lu Watters (1943), after which he led his own bands, as well as working periodically with Murphy and Bob Scobey, before rejoining Watters in 1949. In the same year he began recording solo for the Good Time Jazz label, and was soon regularly working in San Francisco saloons as a soloist. Over his long career he also recorded with Bunk Johnson and the Yerba Buena Jazz Band (1943–4), Darnell Howard (1950), Scobey and Murphy, and he was still active in the 1980s in the San Francisco area, playing as well as ever. [DF]

➤➤ **Bunk Johnson** *(Bunk And Lu).*

Kenny Ball

Trumpet, vocals, bandleader.

b. Ilford, Essex, UK, 22 May 1930.

Kenny Ball started his career in bands led by Charlie Galbraith, Sid Phillips and Eric Delaney, before forming his own in 1958. It quickly set a new standard for British Dixieland of the period: sidemen such as Dave Jones (clarinet), John Bennett (trombone) and Ron Weatherburn (piano) seemed to come from nowhere and easily equalled the red-hot trumpet of their leader, who sounded as technically assured as the players he loved – Louis Armstrong, Kenny Baker and Clifford Brown (a highly eclectic set of influences for the period). Signed to Jack Fallon's Cana agency, the band quickly produced a hit single, "I Love You Samantha" (from *High Society*). More followed (including "Midnight In Moscow", "March Of The Siamese Children" and "So Do I"), and Ball's band rapidly became the most successful act of the trad boom.

After a period in cabaret and a worrying spell of lip trouble, he was back to full form by 1968, supporting Louis Armstrong at London concerts. Changes in his personnel during the 1960s brought in Andy Cooper (replacing Jones) and Johnny Parker (replacing Weatherburn). In the 1970s he continued to tour jazz clubs and theatres in Britain and Europe: peak spots on TV shows such as *Morecambe and Wise* and *Saturday Night At The Mill* and regular appearances on Royal Variety Shows kept him in the public eye, and by the 1980s the trumpeter had become a much-loved household name. In 1985 Kenny Ball's was the first British band to tour in the Soviet Union, where he was received with rapture. In the later 80s and into the 90s he continued to tour with his Jazzmen to sell-out crowds, and to record regularly. After a brief period of illness, he was back to full performing strength in 2003. [DF]

⊙ **Kenny Ball And His Jazzmen** (1960–1; Lake). Ball's first ground-breaking album *Invitation To The Ball*, plus six tracks from his second, *Kenny Ball And His Jazzmen*. Definitive music from his golden years and top-class traditional jazz by any standards.

⊙ **Strictly Jazz** (1961–5; Kaz Records). A return to the classic jazz repertoire, featuring Ball specialities like "Ostrich Walk" and "High Society" from his early days, as well as the attractive Ball original "Fleet Street Lightning".

The Very Best Of Kenny Ball (1991–4; Timeless). Ball's later dependable team (Andy Cooper, John Benson, plus founder members John Bennett and Ron Bowden) demonstrating undiminished power three and a half decades later.

Iain Ballamy

Soprano, alto and tenor saxophones, flute, piano.
b. Guildford, Surrey, UK, 20 Feb 1964.

Ballamy began on piano at the age of six, switching to alto sax at fourteen. Apart from a couple of saxophone lessons, he was largely self-taught on the instrument. In 1983 he started his own quartet, the Iains, which included Django Bates on keyboards, and he was also a founder member of the big band Loose Tubes. Bush Sense, a second quartet he led, included saxophonist Dale Barlow, bassist Mario Castronari and drummer Steve Argüelles. Ballamy has played with several other leaders including Gordon Beck, John Taylor, Stan Sulzmann, Gil Evans, Jim Mullen and John Stevens, and since 1985 he has been a member of Billy Jenkins's Voice Of God Collective. He was also a founder member of Bill Bruford's Earthworks, which has recorded four albums to date. The Iains toured the UK and Germany in 1985 and Morocco in 1986; Ballamy also toured Japan with Bruford. Collaborations with Gil Evans, George Coleman and Dewey Redman boosted his growing international reputation, and led him to work with vocalists Claire Martin and Ian Shaw. In 1994 he was a member of the eighteen-piece British band which augmented Hermeto Pascoal's group for a UK tour. He is also a member of Django Bates's Delightful Precipice orchestra, and of Bates's quartet Human Chain.

In the later 1990s Ballamy continued to pursue his interest in world music, playing concerts in India and Europe with the Karnataka College of Percussion, and appearing at the annual Grenzüberschreitungen/ Bordercrossings Global music encounter hosted by Iwalewa Baus in Bayreuth, Germany. He also toured with Sankalpam (the contemporary Indian Dance group) and played the part of Steve the Prat in Simon Black's stage play, *Out There*, which toured Britain in 1995 and 1996. His distinctive saxophone voice graced the BBC Radio 3 play *Signal To Noise*, by Neil Gaiman and Dave McKean, the film *Legend*, and a documentary *Joseph Losey – The Man With Four Names*.

Ballamy has a sound and approach all of his own, with hardly a trace of Parker, Sanborn or Coltrane, and his airy phrasing is often exquisitely melodic. He can also compose excellent themes. In 1985 he was awarded the John Dankworth cup for the most promising Young Musician soloist.

1998 saw Ballamy showcase a new quartet, Food, featuring himself and a Norwegian trio. Throwing both electronics and acoustic instruments into their stew, Food have now released two delectable live CDs: *Food* (1998) and *Organic And GM Free* (2001).[IC]

Balloon Man (1989; Editions EG). This is an impressive recording debut as leader of a magnificent quartet with Django Bates, bassist Steve Watts and drummer Martin France. The playing is exemplary, the music shot through with feeling, and Ballamy's compositions are often very fine. The intense personal statement of some of the pieces recalls Keith Jarrett's European quartet, but three of the pieces sound schizophrenically out of character – "Rahsaan", "Albert" and "Jumble Sale" seem more public than personal and are jokey and theatrical performances.

All Men Amen (1994; B&W Music). This rich album (with the same quartet) is packed with incident and feeling. There are seven excellent compositions by Ballamy, one for solo saxophone by Bates, and they all have interesting structures. The spirit of Jarrett still looms fitfully, but the schizophrenic aspect has disappeared and though "Serendipity" features some strangely satiric "stride" piano, "Haunted Swing" is very theatrical and "Meadow" is a kind of Afro-English kwela. These three pieces have a strong inner logic which makes them homogeneous with the other performances.

Acme (1996; B&W). Ballamy's quartet for this fine album comprises guitarist John Parricelli, bassist Michael Mondesir and his brother Mark on drums. All four musicians are virtuosi, and all are in almost permanent demand on the London scene. Ballamy has already proved himself an excellent composer, and does it all over again. The rhythm-section is superlative by any standards and Parricelli, comping and soloing, has an unerring sense of fittingness and adventure.

≫ **Django Bates** *(Quiet Nights).*

Phil Bancroft

Tenor and soprano saxophones, composer.
b. Lambeth, London, 29 Jan 1967.

His father played piano, while twin brother Tom (see below) is a drummer and sister Sophie a singer. Moving to Scotland when the brothers were aged 9, they performed in a trio with their father. After widespread gigging on the Edinburgh scene, Phil's musical identity was first apparent when he became musical director of the John Rae Collective in the late 1980s. In 1994 he and his brother, and guitarist Kevin MacKenzie, formed the group Trio AAB, which toured Hungary the following year. One of three equal contributors to the sound and repertoire of the group, he has seen their first album (*Cold Fusion*) named one of the best albums of 1999 and its follow-up (*Wherever I Lay My Home That's My Hat*) earning the same honour in 2001. He has also worked with musicians as diverse as Sun Ra (in 1992), Kenny Wheeler and the Scottish National Jazz Orchestra under Tommy Smith. [BP]

Trio AAB

Stranger Things Happen At C (2002; Caber). To be sure, the basic instrumentation is the same as Paul Motian's trio, but the mix includes Celtic music rather than Americana. That connection is emphasized in this third album, by the inclusion on half the tracks of folk-flautist Brian Finnegan.

≫ **John Rae** *(Beware The Feet).*

Tom Bancroft

Drums, bodhran, composer, arranger.
b. Lambeth, London, 29 Jan 1967.

A few minutes younger than twin brother Phil (see above), Tom has shared much of his history and musical experience. Taking up drums at 7, he studied composition with Jo Sullivan in Montreal (1988–89), visiting New York to take lessons with Joe Morello and Joey Baron. He formed his Orange Ear Ensemble in Montreal (1989) and an Edinburgh-based big-band (1990), which received commissions from both Scottish and English festivals, subsequently founding the Caber record-label in 1998 to issue a compilation of the big-band's recordings. He played regularly with Tommy Smith in the early 1990s, also working with Sun Ra, Nikki Yeoh, Sheila Jordan, Nguyên Lê (as a duo in 2000) and several musicians on the Scottish folk scene – an important influence on his jazz work. He organized the Clandemonium projects for the Glasgow Jazz Festival, and has played for dance and multimedia groups, as well as co-founding the important Trio AAB with his brother. [BP]

⊙ **Pieology** (1993-7; Caber). An impressive range of approaches to modernizing the big-band sound, occasionally recalling Mike Westbrook, is heard on three sets of recordings featuring such soloists as Phil Bancroft, Claude Deppa, Brian Kellock and Dutch altoist Jorrit Dykstra.

➤➤ **Phil Bancroft/Trio AAB** *(Stranger Things Happen At C).*

Billy Bang

Violin.
b. Mobile, Alabama, 20 Sept 1947.

New York violinist Billy Bang (born William Walker Vincent) studied classical violin in his youth, then gave it up until his return from Vietnam in 1968. Bang took lessons from fellow free violinist Leroy Jenkins, and his folkish, rough approach bears a distinct resemblance. Venturing out on a professional music career in the 70s, he recorded solo performances for the Hat Hut label and with various small groups as a leader for Soul Note. He was a founder member of the String Trio of New York with guitarist James Emery and bassist John Lindberg, composing and performing pieces that mixed open improvisation and chamber composition for acoustic instruments between 1977–86, recording five albums with them. He recorded with Bill Laswell's Material, and Bang's own album of the time, *Rainbow Gladiator* (1981), does contain traces of some of the angular funk of early 80s downtown New York amongst the Monkish melodies and sprawling neo-African grooves reminiscent of Sun Ra in "trad" mode. Bang led various quartets, quintets and sextets throughout the 80s. He sat in with Sun Ra's Arkestra (he also made a rather disastrous record, *A Tribute To Stuff Smith* (Soul Note), with pianist Sun Ra late in Ra's life) and recorded several albums with Chicago per-

Justin-Time Records

Billy Bang

cussionist Kahil El Zabar. Bang has frequently played with William Parker, Andrew Cyrille, Ronald Shannon Jackson and Marilyn Crispell. Thankfully his strong 1982 duet with drummer Dennis Charles, *Bangception* (hatOLOGY), has finally been reissued, and he continues to record surprisingly various albums such as his *Vietnam – The Aftermath* (2001) and two companionable trio albums in 2003 (one with William Parker and Hamid Drake; and one with Barry Altschul and Joe Fonda). [JC]

Kahil El Zabar's The Ritual

⊙ **Another Kind Of Groove** (1987; Sound Aspects). Bang's playing is at its funkiest and most exhilarating on this trio with El Zabar and bassist Malachi Favors. He fills space with manic glissandos and often dives for the woody deep end of the fiddle with palpably successful results.

Billy Banks

Vocals.
b. Alton, Illinois, c. 1908; d. Tokyo, 19 Oct 1967.

A protégé of Irving Mills, who heard him in Cleveland and brought him to New York to open at Connie's Inn in 1932, Banks is remembered best as head of the Rhythmakers, a legendary studio group starring Henry "Red" Allen and Fats Waller, which recorded for Mills that year. From 1934–8, after a brief return to Cleveland to run his parents' shoe shop, he toured with bandleader Noble Sissle. From 1938 for twelve years he was featured cabaret star at Billy Rose's legendary Diamond Horseshoe bar and by 1952 was touring Europe, including Holland, France and Britain (where he appeared and recorded with Freddy Randall's band, among others). After more touring, including Asia and Australia, he settled in Japan. [DF]

Billy Banks And His Rhythmakers (1932; Classics). Banks contributes high-pitched intense vocals (he was a part-time female impersonator) to sessions that are often cited as "the hottest jazz ever recorded".

Denys Baptiste

Tenor and soprano saxophones.

b. London, 14 Sept 1969.

Denys Baptiste is one of the most dynamic musicians on the London jazz scene. He had clarinet lessons at school at the age of thirteen but, inspired by Courtney Pine, changed to tenor saxophone at fourteen. He spent two years, 1990–2, studying music at the West London Institute (Brunel University), then attended the postgraduate jazz year (1992–3) at London's Guildhall School of Music. Throughout his period of study, Baptiste took part in workshops directed by tenor saxophonist Tim Whitehead, who took a personal interest in his progress. Since 1992, Baptiste has worked with bassist Gary Crosby's Nu Troop, one of the most important UK bands. In July 1998, Nu Troop played at the jazz festival in the French town Vienne, and won first prize as Best Ensemble, with Baptiste coming third in the Best Soloist category. He has also worked with Crosby's Jazz Jamaica group, and played with many other bands and leaders including The Jazz Warriors (1993–4), the American drummer Marvin "Smitty" Smith, saxophonist Courtney Pine, pianists Jason Rebello and Julian Joseph, vibraphonist Orphy Robinson, and singer Cleveland Watkins. Since 1995, he has also led his own Denys Baptiste Quartet, and made one album as leader. In 1999 he released a successful solo album, *Be Where You Are*, and followed on by winning a Mobo award. Another set, *Let Freedom Ring*, was released in 2003; it melted free-jazz, Afro-Cuban, and gospel tones into an intoxicating stew, all topped with words from Ben Okri.

Baptiste has a beautiful singing tenor sound, and he combines great swing and rhythmic drive with the most subtle artistry, making every note and phrase tell, and always projecting the most intense human feeling. He is also a superb composer of small group pieces. [IC]

Be Where You Are (1998; Dune Records). Baptiste's recording debut as leader is magnificent. Seven of the ten compositions were written by him, and they cover a wide spectrum of music and feeling, from the quiet distilled lyricism of the title track, to the headlong passion of "State Of Flux". Baptiste and his young rhythm-section – Andrew McCormack (piano), Larry Bartley (double bass), Daniel Crosby or Tom Skinner (drums) – handle the material with terrific panache, and gospel singer Juliet Roberts is added for Baptiste's uninhibitedly raunchy and funky arrangement of Stevie Wonder's "Have A Talk With God".

➤➤ **Gary Crosby** *(Nu Troop Migrations).*

JANINE IRONS

Denys Baptiste

Paul Barbarin

Drums, leader, composer.

b. New Orleans, 5 May 1899; d. 10 Feb 1969.

By his teens New Orleans's most famous drummer was already a familiar figure in the Young Olympia Brass Band, and in 1917 he struck out for Chicago to work its clubs and cabarets with, among others, Freddie Keppard and Jimmie Noone. Then it was back to New Orleans, to Chicago again to work with King Oliver's Dixie Syncopators, home again, and to New York to join Luis Russell's newly formed band with Henry "Red" Allen. Records with Russell such as "Panama" and "Jersey Lightning" illustrate Barbarin's driving New Orleans-based approach, as do classics like "Knockin' a Jug" and "Mahogany Hall Stomp", in which Louis Armstrong sounds particularly happy. From 1929–32, and again in 1935 (with Louis once more), Barbarin provided Russell with the "good old New Orleans up-and-down" beloved of Jimmie Lunceford, but then returned home again to lead his own band. From then on, with regular trips north to play with Bechet and Allen, guest spots with Art Hodes in Chicago (1953), and bandleading enterprises for clubs such as Child's in New York, Barbarin was happy to base himself in home-town New Orleans. There he led parades, formed his own successful band and played clubs, though he also regularly toured the US state capitals as a billtopper.

In 1955 he formed his own Onward Brass Band: it became his mission to see his band march in the whites-only Proteus procession that precedes Mardi Gras. The year they finally did, 1969, Barbarin collapsed on parade and died. [DF]

⦿ **Paul Barbarin And His Band** (1951; Storyville). A fine example of Barbarin's band at its best, with Albert Burbank, Ernie Cagnolatti and Lester Santiago all playing at full tilt.

Chris Barber

Trombone, bass trumpet, bass, vocals, composer, arranger.

b. Welwyn Garden City, Herts, UK, 17 April 1930.

Barber formed his first band in 1948, and by 1951 it featured two fine trumpeters, Ben Cohen and Dick Hawdon. After a brief attempt to team up with Ken Colyer in 1953 ("the whole band was sacked or sacked Ken, depending on who was telling the story," says George Melly), Barber brought in trumpeter Pat Halcox, a strong and versatile player. From that day his band, featuring blues singer Ottilie Patterson, clarinettist Monty Sunshine, Barber's own bucolic trombone and banjoist-singer Lonnie Donegan (replaced by Eddie Smith after "Rock Island Line", recorded for a Barber album, turned Donegan into a star), was set fair for success. It featured a broadly based adventurous repertoire

(reminiscent of the policy Wilbur de Paris operated in the USA), and quickly produced turntable hits like "Whistling Rufus", "Bobbie Shafto" and two for Monty Sunshine, "Hushabye" and "Petite Fleur", which did much to launch the trad boom of the late 1950s and ensured Sunshine a successful bandleading career of his own. All through the boom years, Barber's band (now with Ian Wheeler on clarinet) remained at the top of the popularity polls, and after the rise of the Beatles in 1962, it was Barber who most cleverly coped with the switch in fashion.

While other bands resigned themselves to cabaret-style reruns of old glories, Barber quickly re-formed as Chris Barber's Jazz and Blues Band, brought in an electric rhythm-section (featuring a fine blues guitarist, John Slaughter) and proceeded to combine his previous repertoire with contemporary blues-based material. The band's performances of the period are remarkable for their eclecticism: *Battersea Rain Dance*, which contained tunes by John Handy, a contemporary alto-saxophonist, and *Drat That Fratle Rat*, which corralled rock players such as Tony Ashton alongside Barber's regular band members. By now these included an outstanding Nottingham-based reedman, John Crocker, and Pete York, a versatile rock drummer who had worked with Spencer Davis. In the 1970s and 80s Barber continued to work on new jazz projects: a six-volume autobiographical set for Black Lion, regular new tours including *Echoes of Ellington* (a collaboration with Ellingtonians Russell Procope and Wild Bill Davis), and a stimulating teaming of Trummy Young with pianist John Lewis (who wrote a suite for the Barber band which back in the 1950s would have been dismissed as impossible). In the 1980s came the highly successful *Take Me Back To New Orleans* package with singer/pianist Dr John, which received comprehensive radio, TV and record coverage.

Later in the 80s he continued to enlarge his musical horizons to include (on record) a *New Orleans Overture* and *Concerto For Jazz Trombone And Orchestra*, and a solo trombone album with the

London Gabrieli Brass Ensemble. Following a serious but temporary illness for trumpeter Pat Halcox early in the 90s, the band was back to full strength in 1994 for a fortieth anniversary tour, and by 2003 had been augmented to include trumpeter Mike Henry, trombonist Bob Hunt and saxophonist Trevor Whiting.

Barber's career has been unflaggingly successful, thanks to his canny business sense, American-style bandleading policy, which keeps an eye on fashion without bowing to it too extravagantly, and all-round "entertainment without compromise" standards. While created in the image of the great American masters, his music is an important jazz oeuvre in its own right. [DF]

Forty Years Jubilee (1954–6; Timeless). Excellent live recording of Barber's first great band, with Patterson and Donegan's skiffle group.

In Concert: Vol. 1 (1956 & 1958; Dormouse). Fine concerts from Royal Festival Hall and Birmingham Town Hall.

The Great Reunion Concert (1975; Timeless). Celebrating the 21st anniversary of Barber's band, this set has both his original ensemble and latterday Blues and Jazz Band on best form.

Echoes Of Ellington Volumes 1 & 2 (1976; Timeless). Live concert recording of one of Barber's important American collaborations, with ex-Ellingtonians Russell Procope and organist Wild Bill Davis.

New Orleans Symphony (1989; Jazz Zounds). An impressive collaboration with the Berlin Rundfunk orchestra, conducted by Robert Hanell.

Under The Influence Of Jazz (1989; Timeless). Co-composed by Barber and Richard Hill, "Jazz Colours" and "Magnolia Suite" are highly effective marriages of jazz trombone with the classical ensemble of the London Gabrieli Brass.

He's Got The Whole World In His Hands (2000; Timeless). Excellent set of studio recordings including "Mabel's Dream", "Just A Little While To Stay Here" and other standards including the ever-excellent Crocker, Halcox and Wheeler.

Gato Barbieri

Tenor saxophone, flute, percussion, vocals, composer.

b. Rosario, Argentina, 28 Nov 1934.

Barbieri took up the clarinet at twelve after hearing a recording of Charlie Parker's "Now's The Time". He had private lessons for five years, also studying alto sax and composition, then at twenty he took up the tenor sax. He rejected the music of his homeland, and soon became Argentina's leading jazz musician, playing in Lalo Schifrin's orchestra, leading bands of his own and working with visiting American stars. After seven months in Brazil he and his Italian-born wife went in 1962 to Europe, living in Rome. His reputation grew and in 1963 he met Don Cherry and worked with him for some years. With Cherry, Barbieri went deeply into the avant-garde music of the time – free improvisation heavily influenced by Ornette Coleman – and the recordings he made then with Cherry were described as being "among the

Jak Kilby

Gato Barbieri

seminal works of the 'new music' ". In 1967, after recording the album *In Search Of Mystery* under his own name, Barbieri played with Mike Mantler's Jazz Composers' Orchestra until he began to move away from abstraction in order to explore his own neglected cultural roots. He said, "I felt something was wrong and I had to make a choice. I always liked to play melody and improvisation and rhythm ... in Argentina I played everything: tango, mambo, Brazilian music, guaracha, etc. ... So slowly, slowly, I changed."

He began incorporating the rhythms, harmonies and melodic flavour of South American music into his work, forging a new and more powerful identity in the process. His tenor sound became even warmer and more resonant, giving his driving, impassioned style a lyrical, more human dimension, and his music was enriched by a greater range of textures, colours and rhythms. In 1969 he recorded his first important album, *The Third World*; he then returned to Argentina to go more deeply into his roots. He composed and played the music for Bernardo Bertolucci's film *Last Tango In Paris*, in 1972, and the album won him a Grammy award. The film music changed him overnight from a cult figure into an international star, and he returned to South America to make a series of albums with local musicians and native instruments in Buenos Aires and Rio de Janeiro. Since then he has recorded and toured largely with musicians from South America, playing festivals there and in the USA and Europe. Barbieri's music must be seen as part of the post-abstraction phase of jazz and as one of the first examples of the new and beneficial influence of Latin American musicians – an influence which grew rapidly during the later 1970s and still shows no sign of diminishing. **[IC]**

⊙ **In Search Of Mystery** (1967; ESP). Barbieri leads a quartet comprising Calo Scott (cello), Sirone (bass) and Robert Kapp (drums). The music is uncompromisingly abstract, but this album was a turning point, and afterwards Barbieri slowly turned away from total abstraction and back to his South American roots.

⊙ **Confluence** (1968; Affinity). Barbieri is here in duo with pianist Abdullah Ibrahim (then still using his original name – Dollar Brand). The latter was also at a turning point and about to return to his African roots, but only the short, beatifically simple "Hamba Khale" gives any hint of the coming volte-face – the rest of the music is pretty wild and free.

⊙ **Chapter Three: Viva Emiliano Zapata** (1974; Impulse! GRP). This is the third in a quartet of albums which chart Barbieri's re-exploration of his Latin and jazz roots, and it is a very fine big-band album with French horns and tuba and a personnel of South American and jazz luminaries – including Randy Brecker, Ron Carter and Grady Tate. Perhaps the most famous track is a performance of an old Latin piece called "Cuando Vuelva A Tu Lado", known to English-speaking audiences as "What A Difference A Day Makes".

⊙ **Que Pasa** (1997; Columbia). Barbieri heads what is basically a small group here, but he adds trumpet, trombone and alto sax on occasion. His tenor sound is still broad, resonant and sensuous, but suffers at times from the (over) production. The stand-out track is "The Woman I Remember", a tribute to his recently deceased wife. It's an engaging album, but basically more of the same.

➤➤ **Charlie Haden** *(Liberation Music Orchestra).*

Eddie Barefield

Saxophones, clarinet, arranger.
b. Scandia, Iowa, 12 Dec 1909; d. 4 Jan 1991.

Barefield worked first in territory bands in the late 1920s and was with Bernie Young's band by 1930, when he first heard Lester Young and Art Tatum, two primary influences. In 1932 he travelled to New York with Bennie Moten, then with the Cotton Pickers (at the time including Roy Eldridge and young brother Joe), and the following year joined Cab Calloway for three years. For the rest of the 1930s Barefield was constantly to be found in the best company, including Fletcher Henderson, Don Redman and Coleman Hawkins, and for much of the 1940s he worked in studios and for Broadway shows as musical director. Throughout the 1950s he was MD for Cab Calloway, played in studios and freelanced with a variety of top bands (including the Dukes of Dixieland) and remained very busy with Sammy Price, the *Jazz Train* production, film work and leading bands of his own. By the late 1970s Barefield was appearing in the New York production of *One Mo' Time* and producing fine new albums, one appropriately titled *The Indestructible Eddie Barefield*. A lifelong friend of Ben Webster, Barefield later concentrated exclusively on tenor and, like another Webster associate, Budd Johnson, deserves to be much better known. **[DF]**

Dave Bargeron

Trombone, bass trombone, euphonium, tuba.
b. Athol, Massachusetts, 6 Sept 1942.

David Bargeron's father came from a family of entertainers who earned their living during the early 1930s as the "Musical Bargerons". The young Bargeron developed rapidly as a soloist and section leader and after gaining his Bachelor of Music from Boston University in 1964, he took his first job as lead trombonist with Clark Terry's big band. Then from 1968–70, he played bass trombone and tuba with Doc Severinson's band. In 1970, he joined Blood, Sweat & Tears, touring worldwide and recording eleven albums with them. A break in the band's schedule in 1972 enabled him to join the Gil Evans Orchestra and he has remained a member up to the present. In 1972, Bargeron was also a member of the George Russell Orchestra which recorded the album *Living Time* (Columbia), featuring pianist Bill Evans.

After leaving BS&T at the beginning of 1978, Bargeron was much in demand in the New York recording studios, and his career as an international artist also blossomed. He was a member of Jaco Pastorius's Word Of Mouth band in the early 1980s, and also recorded with rock stars Paul Simon, Mick Jagger and Eric Clapton. Bargeron is a featured soloist on the 1989 Grammy Award winning Gil Evans album *Bud + Bird*, and this won for him the 1989 NARAS (National Academy of Recording Arts and Sciences) Most Valuable Player Award on trombone. In 1991, he was a member of the orchestra that recorded *Live At Montreux* (Warner Bros) with Miles Davis and Quincy Jones, and the following year he recorded *Rebirth Of The Cool* (GRP) with Gerry Mulligan. He also recorded albums with Pat Metheny, David Sanborn and Johnny Griffin, and in 1995 was featured soloist with Howard Johnson's band Gravity on its eponymous CD for Verve. That year he also released his acclaimed first solo album *Barge Burns…Slide Flies.*

Bargeron is an extraordinary trombone virtuoso soloist with a glorious sound and a range that encompasses everything from basso profundo to bat squeak. He has spent ten years perfecting the "Bargeron Rapid Articulating Valve Option" (BRAVO) – a valve set into the mouthpiece which gives his slide trombone the fleetness of a trumpet or saxophone. He joined George Russell's Living Time Orchestra in 1991 and currently records and tours with it, and also with the George Gruntz Concert Jazz Band. Bargeron is also a demon on the tuba, which he continues to play live; his TubaTuba Tour will be sweeping across Europe from autumn 2003 through 2004. **[IC]**

Blood, Sweat & Tears

⊙ **Blood, Sweat & Tears Live** (1976; Columbia). Bargeron has a featured tuba solo on Laura Nyro's "And When I die".

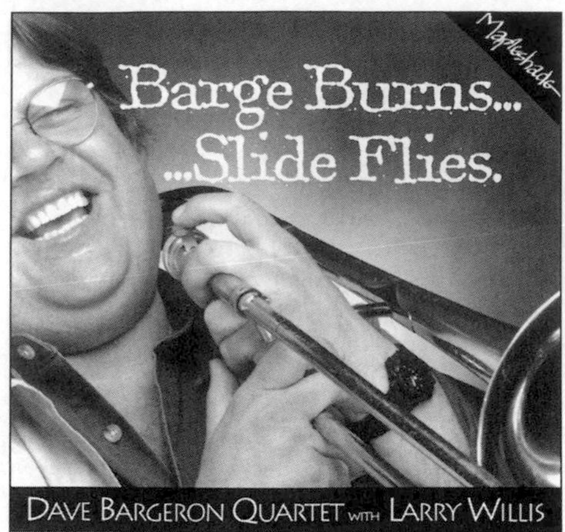

Dave Bargeron

DAVE BARGERON

Barge Burns...Slide Flies (1995; Mapleshade). Bargeron plays trombone with an excellent rhythm-section of piano, bass and drums in seven of the eight pieces. The eighth, "Blue Autumn", is performed as a trombone duet with pianist Larry Willis who composed it, and it brings out Bargeron's superlative lyricism. Bargeron composed six of the pieces, each presenting a different aspect of his playing; "BRAVO" is a bravura performance showcasing his articulating valve invention. The only standard, "There Is No Greater Love", is given a wild, dramatic reading.

>>**Howard Johnson** *(Gravity).*

Danny Barker

Guitar, banjo, composer.

b. New Orleans, 13 Jan 1909; d. 13 March 1994.

By 1930 Danny Barker was in New York after a New Orleans apprenticeship and some time in Chicago with – among others – "Li'l' Brother" Montgomery. He was busy with club work, but apart from a contract with Mae West's show ("the first chance I had to make a little loot in the Depression", he remembered later) he was often working for a few cents a night in the hard years. From this slow start, Barker moved into the big bands: Benny Carter, Lucky Millinder and in 1939 Cab Calloway, who called him "a fabulous player" and with whom Barker stayed for seven years. Then came a further spell accompanying Blue Lu, his singer wife, and regular work with fellow New Orleans men such as his uncle Paul Barbarin, Albert Nicholas and Wilbur de Paris. In the early 1960s he was a full-time bandleader at Jimmy Ryan's, then in 1965 he moved back to New Orleans, where he led parades (he was Grand Marshal for the Congo Square Brass Band), coached the Fairview Baptist Youth Band, and fronted his French Market Jazz Band in Tradition Hall. Barker continued playing until shortly before his death, making a guest appearance on the Dirty Dozen Brass Band's *Jelly* collection in 1993.

Just as important as his performing career, he was a devoted researcher and author who saw jazz as a discipline to be valued and studied and its people as creators of often neglected importance. In this second role, Barker was for many years assistant curator of the New Orleans jazz museum, a seasoned commentator for TV, radio and educational outlets, and co-author (with Jack Buerkle) of the best study of New Orleans music, *Bourbon Street Black*. "A fine teacher of the unwritten history of colour and of music," said Studs Terkel. [DF]

>> **Cab Calloway** *(The King Of Hi-De-Ho).*

Guy Barker

Trumpet, composer.

b. Chiswick, London, 26 Dec 1957.

Although coming to public attention chiefly as a pure-toned, virtuosic but utterly dependable sideman for the likes of Stan and Clark Tracey, Guy Barker is now fast establishing himself as a leading European jazzman and composer. Barker took up trumpet at twelve, joined the National Youth Jazz Orchestra at thirteen and had lessons from Clark Terry at seventeen. In the 1980s, he worked with John Dankworth and toured and recorded with the Gil Evans Orchestra (1983), Lena Horne (1984) and Bobby Watson's Young Lions in 1985. He was a member of the Clark Tracey Quintet 1984–92, though he continues to play with both the drummer-leader and his pianist father in his various bands. In addition to sideman work with everyone from Ornette Coleman, Carla Bley and Georgie Fame to Frank Sinatra and Cleo Laine, Barker has established himself as a fine leader/composer since winning a recording contract with Verve in the mid-1990s, with a string of fiery but increasingly elegant albums to his credit. His working band of the period had an international line-up – Spanish alto player Perico Sambeat, Portuguese pianist Bernardo Sassetti, British bassist Geoff Gascoyne and American drummer Gene Calderazzo – and was most impressive. His celebrated debut release on Provocateur marked yet another new phase of development for this gifted musician. [CP/CI]

Isn't It? (1993; Spotlite). Poised but fiery music from core band of Barker, pianist Julian Joseph, Alec Dankworth and Clark Tracey, augmented by other UK stalwarts such as saxophonist Nigel Hitchcock.

Into The Blue (1994; Verve). Assured and accessible post-bop, with earlier version of Barker's international band, featuring Icelandic alto player Sigurdur Flosason.

What Love Is (1998; Emarcy). With strings arranged by Colin Towns, this is a lush, but adventurous, album reworking everything from Ellington to Monk, and featuring Sting on vocals for "You Don't Know What Love Is".

Soundtrack (2001; Provocateur). A series of ingenious *film noir* pastiches for small big band, it was nominated for 2002's Mercury Music Prize and was regarded by many as the best British jazz album of the year.

>> **Stan Tracey** *(Portraits Plus).*

Stan Barker

Piano.

b. Clitheroe, Lancashire, UK, 24 May 1926, d. 30 June 1997.

A fine eclectic jazz pianist, Stan Barker was founder and also co-director of an educational organization, Jazz College, which operates in schools, colleges and universities. His activities included regular teaching for the Royal Northern College of Music (for whom he was on-staff Jazz Director) as well as for Merseyside Arts, South Wales Arts Association, Belfast School of Music and Southport Arts Centre, where he was Artist in Residence 1979–87. Barker combined his educational activities with regular appearances on the club circuit with his trio, backing American visitors such as Billy Butterfield, Al Grey and Buddy Tate, and solo work for radio and TV; in late 1994, following illness, he returned to full-time activities but died of a stroke in 1997. **[DF]**

Stan Barker and Digby Fairweather

Something To Remember Us By (1984; Jazzology). Barker's able and regularly romantic piano in duets with Digby Fairweather recorded during their Southport residency, live and in studio. This double CD includes their vinyl album *Let's Duet*.

Dale Barlow

Tenor and soprano saxophones, composer.

b. Sydney, Australia, 25 Dec 1959.

Barlow started to play the piano at an early age, then studied classical flute and clarinet. He played alto sax until he was sixteen, then switched to tenor. He played at the Monterey jazz festival in 1979 as a featured soloist with a young Australian band, and has since recorded and played with many leading Australian jazz groups. From 1982–3 he studied and played in New York, eventually touring Europe and the USA extensively with various groups. A concert he played with Sonny Stitt and Richie Cole was recorded, and he has also played and recorded with Cedar Walton and Billy Higgins. He then led his own groups in the UK and Europe. More recently Barlow has toured with Billy Cobham's band and is something of a media favourite in Australia. He is a consummate saxophonist in the hard-bop tradition, and with diverse influences: John Coltrane, Sonny Rollins, Wayne Shorter, Miles Davis, as well as Stravinsky, Bartok, Hancock, Bach, African and South American music, have all made their mark on his sound. **[IC]**

Hipnotation (1990; Spiral Scratch). Vintage Barlow with an American rhythm-section and aided and abetted by the marvellous, ever-improving trumpeter Eddie Henderson.

Windmills On Mars (2002; Hipnotation records). A stunning exploratory duet featuring the flute and sax of Barlow alongside the adept lines of pianist Walter Lampe.

Bob Barnard

Trumpet, cornet.

b. Melbourne, Australia, 24 Nov 1933.

Barnard played with his brother Len in a family band when young, and then worked semi-professionally in Melbourne before moving to Sydney in 1957 to join banjoist Ray Price's Trio for one year. After this he returned to Melbourne to work in a music store for four years before joining the Graeme Bell All Stars (Sydney, Queensland, 1962–4). He then returned to Sydney to work in theatres and as a sessionman for radio, TV and records. Following the success of two EMI Dixieland albums (1971), Barnard formed his own band in 1974 which included key sidemen John Costelloe (trombone), John McCarthy (reeds), and Chris Taperell (piano). Thereafter, he began to build an international reputation, recording widely with all of Australia's best, and touring Australia, Europe, India and Southeast Asia, as well as the USA from 1976. From 1973 until the end of the decade, Barnard also formed an indelible recording relationship with the brilliant and eclectic Australian arranger John Sangster; central to their collaborations are *The Hobbit Suite* (1973), *Lord Of The Rings* (1976/7) and the equally superb *For Leon Bismarck* [sic] (1977). In the 1980s Barnard continued to consolidate his reputation as a world-class soloist with appearances in Britain (including Soho's Jazz Festivals 1986/7 and in the 1990s at Ronnie Scott's) and via recordings with American giants such as Ralph Sutton. By the 1990s he was recognized as a talent worthy of comparison with American cornet giants Ruby Braff, Bobby Hackett and Warren Vaché Jnr.

A cornettist equally capable of filigree delicacy and challenging power, Barnard's contribution to jazz is considerable. His work on record (some of it still confined to Australian issues) deserves detailed reassessment. His son, resident in Britain since 1996, is guitarist Tony Barnard. **[DF]**

Count 'em (1975; Swaggie). With his own band, plus Errol Buddle (alto) and Tony Buchanan (baritone), this is a wide-ranging and finely recorded collection ranging from "Days Of Wine And Roses" to Barnard's good-natured and beautifully judged duo on "Wild Man Blues" with Chris Taperell.

Partners In Crime (1983; Dialogue). John Chilton called this "One of the finest trumpet-led quartet recordings ever made" (with Ralph Sutton).

Big Bob, Little Ben! (1986; Fly Records). Barnard in top British company (including Kenny Baker, George Chisholm, Ronnie Ross, Bruce Turner, Mitch Dalton et al) and making the grade amid fine arrangements by Max Harris, as well as more informal small-group settings featuring the great Bruce Turner.

New York Notes (1995; Sackville). Barnard in a quartet setting devised and led by the excellent Keith Ingham. Fine tunes skilfully located by Ingham and beautifully played by Barnard.

Alan Barnes

Saxophones, clarinet, bass-clarinet.

b. Altrincham, Cheshire, UK, 23 July 1959.

One of the most versatile reedsmen currently working in the UK, Alan Barnes has contributed both fine section work and blistering solos to all manner of bands playing everything from nostalgia-oriented music through sinewy hard bop and mainstream to cutting-edge modern jazz. After gaining a Diploma in Jazz and Light Music from the Leeds College of Music in 1980, he moved to London, playing with the Pasadena Roof Orchestra – specializing in light-hearted re-creations of 1920s music – from 1981 until 1983, when he joined the hard-bop band, the Tommy Chase Quartet. Between 1986–8, he co-led the Jazz Renegades, subsequently joining mainstream bandleader Humphrey Lyttelton's band. In 1992, he was voted Jazz Express Musician of the Year, and gained the British Jazz Awards for top alto player in 1993, 1995 and 1997, and for top clarinettist in 1994, 1996 and 1998. He was also voted top baritone player in 1998. He was a regular in the Pizza Express Modern Jazz Sextet 1989–98, and leads both his own groups and an award-winning quintet with Scottish trumpeter Bruce Adams.

Between 1997–8, he recorded eleven albums for the UK mainstream label Zephyr in everything from duo to octet formats, many featuring his own arrangements, and performed sideman duties in the big bands of Dick Walter, Kenny Baker, Don Weller, Stan Tracey and Mike Westbrook. Although he has recently concentrated on lower-register instruments (baritone saxophone and bass-clarinet), Barnes is a cogent but protean improviser on all his horns, citing Coleman Hawkins and Johnny Hodges as his main saxophone influences, along with Benny Carter, Sonny Criss, Jackie McLean and Art Pepper; his clarinet influences are Jimmy Hamilton and Barney Bigard. [CP]

Bruce Adams-Alan Barnes Quintet

⊙ **Side-Steppin'** (1993; Big Bear). Airy, instantly accessible but surprisingly subtle music covering ground between modern mainstream and bebop and featuring Barnes alongside trumpeter Adams.

Alan Barnes

⊙ **Thirsty Work** (1995; Fret). In a variety of settings – quartets, quintets and sextets – alongside a number of the UK's top studio/jazz musicians, Barnes applies his strident alto and mellow baritone to a highly enjoyable variety of modern-mainstream pieces, original and classic.

⊙ **Here Comes Trouble** (1996; Fret). Quartet album featuring Barnes on alto and baritone, playing originals and material by Hank Mobley, Charlie Parker etc, with a first-class rhythm-section – Scottish pianist Steve Hamilton, bassist Mick Hutton, drummer Bryan Spring.

>> **Bruce Adams** *(Let's Face The Music...)*.

George Barnes

Guitar.

b. Chicago Heights, Illinois, 17 July 1921; d. 5 Sept 1977.

George Barnes won a Tommy Dorsey Amateur Swing Contest when he was sixteen, but by that time had been on the road for three years with his own quartet. In 1938 he recorded with blues singers Washboard Sam, Big Bill Broonzy and Jazz Gillum while working as a staffman for NBC in Chicago, then carried on with staffwork (plus a stint with Bud Freeman) until 1942, when he was called up. After demobilization he went back to the broadcast studios with his nifty progressive octet and played each week on the *Plantation Party Show*. By 1951 he had graduated to New York, working for TV and radio and recording with Yank Lawson, Ernie Royal, Kai Winding, Bobby Hackett and Louis Armstrong (whose *Autobiography* set features him). Barnes's clipped electric guitar, with its blues-based phrasing, would have fitted rock and roll perfectly but he stayed faithful to his jazz roots (in public at least) and in the early 1960s formed a guitar duo for concerts and clubs with veteran master Carl Kress. After Kress's death in 1965 Barnes carried on with a younger partner, Bucky Pizzarelli. Their spectacular break-up after a quarrel was bemusedly reported by Whitney Balliett in *New York Notes* (1972) – "The guitarists' swan set at the tiny St Regis room was played not on their instruments but on each other." In 1973 Barnes teamed with Ruby Braff in a dazzling quartet, one of the great small groups in all jazz. By 1975, however, the finely honed sensibilities of the co-leaders had drawn sparks (Barnes's spectacular gifts as co-equal accompanist sometimes ran up against Braff's free-flow of inspiration), and the group ended. Barnes died soon after of a heart attack. [DF]

⊙ **The Best I've Heard: The Braff-Barnes Quartet** (1974; Chiaroscuro). Double CD showing the Braff-Barnes partnership at its zenith, with Barnes's guitar witticisms at their spectacular best.

John Barnes

Saxophones, clarinet.

b. Manchester, UK, 15 May 1932.

A "strict" New Orleans-style clarinettist in his early years, John Barnes began his career with the Manchester-based Zenith Six in 1952 and played with them for three years before joining Mike Daniels's Delta Jazzmen (1955–61). After that he played with Alan Elsdon, with whom he turned professional. By this time it was plain that Barnes's talents were developing and expanding, and they found their full showcase after he joined Alex Welsh's band, replacing Archie Semple in 1964. Welsh's first album with his new line-up (*Strike One*, 1966) dramatically revealed Barnes as not just a vibrant clarinettist but a fiery alto saxophonist with strong overtones of Willie

Smith, and (perhaps best of all) a world-class baritone saxophonist whose dark-toned fluency combined the best of Mulligan and Carney without aping either of them. For more than a decade he was a focal point of Welsh's finest-ever band, playing with it at the Newport jazz festival, touring Britain and Europe, and producing a string of fine recordings. He also formed a strong partnership with Roy Williams, just as capable of speeding through the Gerry Mulligan repertoire as playing "Muskrat Ramble". In 1977 he left Welsh to rejoin Alan Elsdon and Keith Nichols's newly formed Midnite Follies Orchestra, and in 1979 joined Humphrey Lyttelton's band for a twelve-year stay. Since leaving Lyttelton, Barnes has continued to freelance and to work with a variety of groups, including Keith Nichols, the Alex Welsh Reunion Band and the Great British Jazz Band. [DF]

Alex Welsh Band

Classic Concert (1971; Black Lion). Thought by many to be Welsh's greatest recording (some accolade!), this set features Barnes on clarinet, alto and baritone, plus vocal on "If I Had A Talking Picture Of You".

John Barnes

Fancy Our Meeting (1988; Calligraph). Barnes's only solo album and a worthy showcase, including all his instruments set in the company of Collin Bates's trio; arrangements include the multi-tracked "Boko's Bounce", arranged and composed by Pete Strange.

Charlie Barnet

Saxophones, vocals.

b. New York, 26 Oct 1913; d. 4 Sept 1991.

Charlie Barnet walks into jazz history around 1930 as the prototype Goodtime Charlie, making the rounds of Harlem, touring with trumpeter Jack Purvis – a wild and kindred spirit – and assembling bands for projects in and out of New York. "A happy-go-lucky millionaire", said Billie Holiday appreciatively, "living it up, and making money talk." It was typical of Barnet that at his first meeting with Holiday he insisted on breaking colour-bar restrictions by drinking with her and Teddy Wilson in the whites-only area of their club, and for the rest of his career he was to remain a committed supporter of good music, black or white. For much of the 1930s Barnet, a saxophonist who loved Hawkins, Armstrong and Ellington, found his career moving slowly: his most notable venture was to play the Apollo, previously reserved for black bands, in 1934. "That engagement opened up a whole new area, one no other white band had", he recalled later. "[And] after our record of 'Cherokee' came out in 1939 we began playing the whole of the black theatre circuit." His band also played on tour and for collegiate strongholds such as Glen Island Casino, where in 1935, with a mixed personnel featuring John Kirby and Frankie Newton, he played to a cool reception. For four more years that was the pattern. "I was with Charlie in the spring of 1939," recalls Billy May, "and business was terrible. Glenn Miller was getting all of it down at Glen Island Casino. Charlie used to say half-kiddingly, 'Let's run Miller out of business.' And so we did crazy musical things like playing 'Sunrise Serenade', one of Glenn's big numbers, and Charlie would blow the melody and the rest of the band would be playing Duke Ellington's 'Azure'."

Later in 1939 Barnet's band had the chance to replace Count Basie at New York's Famous Door; they caused a sensation (Bluebird records issued a new Barnet single every week at this period, including his big hit "Cherokee"), and later that year the band moved triumphantly back into the Apollo. He was soon established as a hitmaker with other best sellers like "Redskin Rhumba", "Wings Over Manhattan", "It's A Wonderful World" and his famous "Skyliner", featuring a soprano-led saxophone section, an unusual voicing in its day. In what he called the "chaotic Forties" Barnet was still discovering and signing new talent – from singer/dancer Bunny Briggs and Lena Horne to young bebop men like Dodo Marmarosa and Buddy DeFranco – and playing more or less as he pleased. But the US draft had a debilitating effect on his band: musicians were constantly called up and the generation that replaced them were often happier to play in a style that Barnet found rather too contrived. "I held out against the bebop influence until 1949," he wrote later, "but had to go along with it then because none of the newer musicians knew how to approach big-band playing except in that idiom. But I had a horror of ending up in Stan Kenton's bag." That was what Capitol Records thought he should do (they had lost Kenton's services in 1948), but Barnet's reaction was exactly what could be expected from a Johnny Hodges lover who didn't need the money. He broke up his band at the end of a two-week engagement at the Apollo in 1949, to regret on all sides, and moved into management, bought a chain of hotels and played what he wanted to. Charlie Barnet's occasional returns to bandleading in the 1960s and 70s were few but worth watching for. His autobiography (along with George Melly's *Owning Up*) is the most irresistible book ever written by a jazzman. [DF]

Charlie Barnet And His Orchestra 1933–36 (Le Jazz). Early examples of Barnet's output, with soloists including Red Norvo, Chris Griffin, Benny Carter and Toots Camarata.

Cherokee (1939–41; RCA Bluebird). A definitive selection, including many of Barnet's best-known titles – "Redskin Rhumba", "Cherokee" and more.

Drop Me Off In Harlem (1942–6; MCA/GRP). Another excellent selection, picking up where the previous one leaves off; features "Skyliner", Dodo Marmarosa's "The Moose" and Roy Eldridge's marvellous "Drop Me Off In Harlem".

The Capitol Big Band Sessions (1948–50; Capitol). Excellent scholarly collation of Barnet's Capitol sides including such well-remembered titles as "Bebop Spoken Here", "Redskin Rhumba" and "Claude Reigns", plus four with strings. Sleevenotes by Loren Schoenberg.

Cherokee (1939–44;ASV). Excellent representative collection of Barnet's best-known titles, including "Pompton Turnpike", "Charleston Alley", "Skyliner" and others.

Joey Baron

Drums, composer.

b. Richmond, Virginia, 26 June 1955.

Although celebrated chiefly for his longtime association with guitarist Bill Frisell, Joey Baron is a versatile and intensely musical drummer whose collaborators range from Jim Hall and Belgian harmonica virtuoso Toots Thielemans to the customary open-eared New York downtown stalwarts such as saxophonists Tim Berne and John Zorn (in the bands Naked City and Masada). As well as appearing on a wide range of recordings as a sideman – in the 1990s he appeared on albums by French multi-instrumentalist Michel Portal and accordionist Richard Galliano, in addition to contributing to albums by bassist Marc Johnson, and pianists Steve Kuhn and Misha Mengelberg – Baron has co-led a trio with Berne and cellist Hank Roberts. He has also led his own band, Barondown, featuring trombonist Steve Swell and tenor saxophonist Ellery Eskelin, an uncategorizable trio playing everything – in true downtown style – from punk-jazz to more considered material in a highly sophisticated, occasionally arch, manner. [CP]

Joey Baron

⊙ **R A Isedpleasuredot** (1993; New World). Highly intelligent, utterly distinctive, varied music from odd instrumentation of trio Barondown.

⊙ **Crackshot** (1995; Avant). Characteristically garrulous, swinging fun with trombonist Steve Swell and tenor player Ellery Eskelin.

Bill Frisell

⊙ **Go West** (1994; Elektra Nonesuch). Music composed to accompany Buster Keaton film of same name, part of a series of such projects undertaken by the US guitarist.

➤➤ **John Zorn** *(Spy Vs Spy).*

Dan Barrett

Trombone/cornet.

b. Pasadena, California, 14 Dec 1955.

Barrett took up trumpet, then trombone, in high school and worked early on with the South Frisco Jazz Band before making the decision to adopt music full-time following a trip to the Breda jazz festival in 1977 with the West Coast-based Sunset Music Company. Playing around local jazz societies improved Barrett's technique, and after meeting guitarist Howard Alden he made the move to New York in February 1983, while working with the Widespread (Depression) Jazz Orchestra, and began sitting in at Eddie Condon's. After striking up musical and personal associations with Scott Hamilton and Warren Vaché, like them Barrett became a regular at jazz parties and in 1985 joined Benny Goodman and later Buck Clayton's orchestra. Regularly with Concord Records from the mid-80s, Barrett continued to collaborate with Howard Alden in a delicate acoustic-level quintet which featured music from the John Kirby library. Into the 1990s, he has become recognized as the trombonist/leader of the new-generation American swing revivalists and began prolific recording for the Arbors label. A skilled and good-humoured musician, Barrett's impeccable trombone (frequently recalling Teagarden, Dickenson and all the great classicists) is almost matched by his skills as a cornettist, and he is also a first-class arranger. His close partnership with singer Rebecca Kilgore, as well as a new school of committed Swing players (all to be found on Arbors), has produced consistently delightful and often profound music which clearly places him as a central force in the new Swing revival. [DF]

⊙ **Get Ready For Bed** (2002; Blue Swing). Barrett combines with Kilgore and guitarist/banjoist/singer Eddie Erickson (plus bassist Dave Stone) combining wit, humour and charm; likeably light-hearted selections only serve to emphasize the premier skills of these irresistible performers.

Alden-Barrett Quintet

⊙ **Swing Street** (1988; Concord). A small classic of an album, featuring the Alden-Barrett Quintet completed by Chuck Wilson (reeds), Frank Tate (bass) and Jackie Williams (drums): exquisite small-band swing.

⊙ **Moon Song** (1995; Arbors). Barrett has recorded prolifically for Arbors and this set – humorous, expert and superbly arranged – features Barrett on (excellent) cornet and trombone plus Scott Robinson, Rebecca Kilgore and friends on selections including "Moon Song", "With A Smile And A Song", and more.

⊙ **Being a Bear** (1999; Arbors). A charmer of a record designed for a jazz cartoon (which is yet to appear). Barrett is teamed with Kilgore, trumpeter-singer Spanky Davis and friends in a set radiating fun, humour and good music, including several musically and lyrically fine originals.

Ray Barretto

Conga, percussion.

b. New York, 29 April 1929.

Born of Puerto Rican parents, Barretto grew up playing Afro-Latin music and became involved in jazz in the late 1940s while with the US army in Germany. After jamming in Harlem, in 1954 he turned professional with Tito Puente and others. He succeeded Candido as the first-choice player for jazz albums requiring a single conguero (for example by Lou Donaldson, Gene Ammons, Red Garland and Joe Zawinul), and augmented other percussionists with Herbie Mann in 1960–1. A Latin-pop crossover hit, "El Watusi" (1963), sealed the success of his own groups, which he has continued to lead ever since, helping to incorporate bebop influences into salsa styles. [BP]

⊙ **Tomorrow** (1976; Messidor). After helping to establish the Fania label, Barretto signed with Atlantic, and this first album, recorded live at the Beacon Theater, took the salsa crossover a stage further. Guitarist Barry Finnerty was perhaps overdubbed, but there is a guest vocal by Ruben Blades and, in a closing "Que Viva La Musica", a *timbales* contest with Tito Puente.

Kenny Barron

Piano, composer, educator.
b. Philadelphia, 9 June 1943.

Having studied piano since the age of twelve, Barron's first job, in 1957, was with Mel Melvin's orchestra, a jazz-oriented R&B outfit, of which Barron's saxophonist older brother Bill was a member. He worked briefly with Philly Joe Jones in 1959, and the following year played for one week with Yusef Lateef in Detroit. After moving to New York in 1961 he worked with many leading musicians including James Moody, Lee Morgan, Roy Haynes and Lou Donaldson. Moody recommended him to Dizzy Gillespie, and Barron replaced Lalo Schifrin in the trumpeter's quintet, staying for four years from 1962–6. Tours and LPs with Gillespie brought him to international notice. He spent four years with Freddie Hubbard, from 1966–70, and five with Yusef Lateef from 1970–75. The following year he joined the Ron Carter quartet, staying until it broke up in 1980. Since 1973 he has been a full-time instructor at Rutgers University, teaching theory, keyboard harmony and piano. He has also worked with many others including Milt Jackson, Jimmy Heath, Stan Getz, Buddy Rich and Esther Marrow. In the 1980s he co-led with Charlie Rouse the group Sphere, which included Buster Williams and drummer Ben Riley. An inventive, consistent and very versatile performer in the mainstream-bebop mould, Barron has been much in demand as a sideman and has made well over fifty albums with other leaders, but has also led and recorded with numerous groups of his own. Barron is a very fine composer of small-group themes.

In 1995, Barron's trio with bassist Ray Drummond and drummer Ben Riley appeared at the (Welsh) Brecon Festival and their concert was recorded for BBC Radio 3. Barron's playing seemed to have reached an even higher level of passionate expression, and when asked he said: "I'm just taking more chances that's all." His trio played a mixture of Barron originals, Monk tunes and standards, but one of the high spots was a scalding solo piano version of Monk's "Shuffle Boil". In the later 1990s, he reformed the group Sphere (Monk's middle name) which disbanded after Charlie Rouse died in 1988. The troupe regrouped with the original Sphere bassist and drummer, Buster Williams and Riley; Barron recruited Gary Bartz on alto and soprano saxophones to complete the line-up. In 1998 they recorded an album, *Sphere*, and as The Sphere Quartet (they were forced to adjust their name for legal reasons) they still appear live. **[IC]**

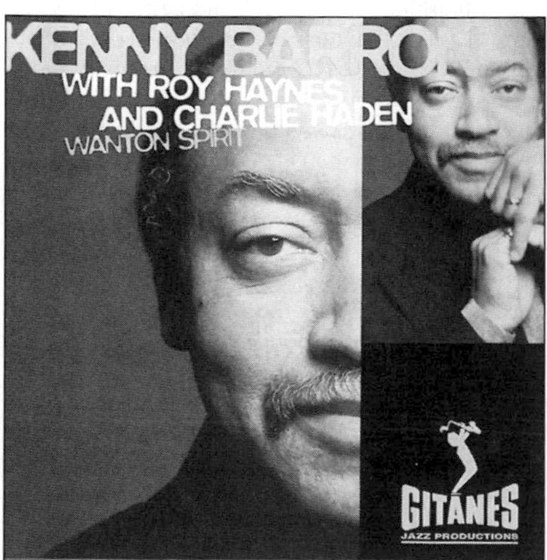

⊙ **What If** (1986; Enja). There are four quintet tracks with Wallace Roney, John Stubblefield, Cecil McBee and Victor Lewis on this album, and the other three tracks involve a trio (McBee's ballad "Close To You Alone"), a piano/drums duo (Parker's "Dexterity") and solo piano (Monk's "Trinkle Tinkle"). Barron is excellent throughout and particularly fine on his opening composition, the lightly rocking "Phantoms".

⊙ **Other Places** (1993; Verve). A very fine album with six superb compositions by Barron and concentrated playing all round. Ralph Moore is on saxophones, Bobby Hutcherson in great form on vibraphone, Rufus Reid on bass and Lewis again on drums. On some tracks the percussionist Mino Cinelu is added. There are a couple of marvellous duo tracks – vibes and piano on the standard "For Heaven's Sake", and piano and bass on "I Should Care". Barron scintillates, the sonorities shimmer, the musicians are at one – an exceptionally benign album.

⊙ **Wanton Spirit** (1994; Verve). An exquisite trio album with Charlie Haden and Roy Haynes, it covers a wide spectrum from bebop and ballad to semi-abstract, and from waltz to loose rock. Haden's warm counterlines and long "singing" notes, and Haynes's freedom and accuracy, create a wonderful feeling of space, a looseness, and the music ebbs and flows, sizzling with warmth.

⊙ **Swamp Sally** (1995; Verve). Barron performs solo and in duo with percussionist Mino Cinelu who also plays guitar, banjo, mandolin and synthesizer. The duos are subtly coherent and Barron, secure in his collaborator, "takes his chances" magnificently.

⊙ **Sphere** (1998; Verve). The quartet play a couple of Monk pieces – "We See" and "Hornin' In" – but healthily tend to play more of their own compositions. They also feature some standards including "Surrey With The Fringe On Top", and seem to be in a state of transition from a Monk repertory group to a more independent status. That is as it should be, and the next album should clarify Sphere's current direction.

➤➤ **Gary Bartz** *(There Goes The Neighborhood).*

Gary Bartz

Alto and soprano saxophones, clarinet, flute.
b. Baltimore, Maryland, 26 Sept 1940.

Bartz's father ran a local jazz club, and Gary got an alto sax at eleven years of age. He studied the instrument at the Juilliard School, and continued in Baltimore at the Peabody Conservatory. His first professional work was with Max Roach-Abbey Lincoln in 1964, followed by a stint with Art Blakey in 1965–6. He played with Roach again, and also with McCoy Tyner and Blue Mitchell in 1968–9. In 1970–71 he worked with Miles Davis, and was strongly featured, making a big impact with his excellent solo work. He then formed and led his own group, Nu Troop, which achieved international popularity and appeared at major festivals, including Montreux in 1973 and Berkeley in 1974. He has also composed music for TV. With Nu Troop he stated that he was not playing jazz but American music. In the later 1970s he had a recording contract with Capitol and made records which were definitely not jazz but essays in disco-funk, spiced with the occasional improvised solo. However, in the 1980s he returned to his Parker/Coltrane roots and the hard-boppish mainstream tradition.

In the later 1990s, Bartz took a stand against record companies, in an effort to retain artistic and financial control over his own music, and in 1998 he began producing and recording his albums – retaining ownership of the master tapes. In addition to playing at this time, he also began an acting career and appeared in *The Connection with Morgan Freeman*, a play about musicians and junkies that was first performed in 1959. The production was a success and Bartz performed in another play, *Bebop: The Hip Musical* with Walter Davis Jnr., Bob Cunningham and Charli Persip. He also acted in and wrote the score for a film, *Jazz Story*, with Turkish director Mevlut Akkaya. Bartz has also been very active as a player, performing with many musicians of different persuasions including trombonist Craig Harris and trumpeter Roy Hargrove's group Crisol, with which he recorded; he is also part of the re-formed Sphere (now Sphere Quartet), with Kenny Barron, Buster Williams and Ben Riley. [IC]

⊙ **West 42nd Street** (1990; Candid). This is an inspired quintet session with trumpeter Claudio Roditi and a superlative rhythm-section – John Hicks, Ray Drummond and Al Foster.

⊙ **There Goes The Neighborhood** (1990; Candid). This quartet session, recorded live at Birdland, has an often tumultuous intensity. Blues, ballads, originals are given absolutely compelling performances. Bartz is on scintillating form, and the rhythm-section (Kenny Barron, Drummond and Ben Riley) are outstanding.

⊙ **Alto Memories** (1993; Verve). Bartz with fellow ex-Miles Davis sideman, Sonny Fortune (alto sax), and the exceptional rhythm-section of Barron, Buster Williams and Jack DeJohnette make the sparks fly on standards and jazz originals.

⊙ **The Red And Orange Poems** (1996; Atlantic). Bartz is here in septet format with ever-improving trumpeter Eddie Henderson, John Clark on French horn, pianist Mulgrew Miller, bassist Dave Holland and Greg Bundy and Steve Kroon respectively on drums and percussion. The sonorities glow, and the whole thing is user-friendly without setting the world on fire.

➤➤ **Miles Davis** *(Live-Evil).*

Basia

Vocals.

b. Jaworzno, Poland.

A professional singer from eighteen, Basia Trzetrzelewska first joined a Russian all-female group called Ali Babki and toured Russia with them. Later she went to the USA and then to Britain to join the group Matt Bianco, which also featured her present MD, pianist Danny White, as well as (on record) the British baritone saxophonist Ronnie Ross. After leaving Matt Bianco to follow a solo career in 1987, she released her first album, containing the US Top Twenty hit "Prime Time TV". A natural contralto who can also sing from bass to altissimo Annie Ross range, Basia has continued to build her solo career, notably in Japan and the USA, although a convincing British breakthrough is still awaited. Basia and White are a formidable and ever-improving partnership, and with a team of highly gifted British-based players around them – including trumpeter Kevin Robinson, guitarist Peter White, and a sensational trio of female singers – their music receives the high-level performance it deserves, both on and off record. [DF]

⊙ **Time And Tide** (1987; Epic). Her debut solo album, containing "Prime Time TV", "Astrud", and "Miles Away"; sidemen include Guy Barker and Ronnie Ross.

⊙ **The Sweetest Illusion** (1994; Sony). Her best yet, featuring the irresistible "Third Time Lucky", plus the roaring samba "An Olive Tree" (co-authored by Robinson) and the murmuring "Perfect Mother".

Count Basie

Piano, organ.

b. Red Bank, New Jersey, 21 Aug 1904; d. 26 April 1984.

Bill Basie became a professional musician in the early 1920s, playing in Asbury Park, New Jersey, and in New York clubs. He toured as a vaudeville accompanist, including two years with Gonzelle White (1925–7). Settling in Kansas City and working in local theatres, he then joined Walter Page's Blue Devils on tour in Dallas (1928–9). He moved to the Elmer Payne band, along with Eddie Durham, both of them going on to Bennie Moten from 1929–34, a period during which other Blue Devils such as bassist Page, trumpeter Hot Lips Page, Jimmy Rushing, Buster Smith and Lester Young also joined Moten. These musicians formed the nucleus of Basie's own Kansas City groups (first in 1934 and again, after Moten's death, in 1935–6), in which they were augmented by baritonist Jack Washington, Jo Jones, Buck Clayton and Herschel Evans. Signed to a national band agency and record contract, the band moved to New York in late 1936, quickly enlarging to a twelve-piece with the addition of rhythm guitarist Freddie Green and lead saxophonist Earl Warren. Work at the Roseland Ballroom in 1937 and the Famous Door nightclub in 1938 established Basie's reputation, and the band's character was maintained by the arrival of Harry Edison and Dicky Wells in 1938 and the replacement of Evans and Young by Buddy Tate (1939) and Don Byas (1940).

World War II caused more rapid personnel turnover, but many of Basie's recruits in the 1940s

Count Basie

were unique soloists, especially Vic Dickenson and saxophonists Lucky Thompson, Illinois Jacquet and Paul Gonsalves. For economic reasons, the big band was folded and Basie led an octet (1950–1) before starting a new sixteen-piece line-up in 1952; significant new members during the 1950s included Ernie Wilkins, Frank Foster, Thad Jones (these three also arranging), Joe Newman, Eddie Davis and Joe Williams. The first of many European tours in 1954 and a couple of extremely successful records gave the impetus for the band to remain in business for a further three decades, although economic considerations in the mid- and late 1960s dictated the recording of several albums backing middle-of-the-road singers. In the 1970s, Basie played in many all-star sessions without the band, but his only absences from its public appearances were occasioned by illness, which in his last years obliged him to perform from a wheelchair.

Always underrated as a pianist, Basie received informal guidance as a teenager from Fats Waller (exactly three months older), and his early records with Moten and a few of his own show him playing excellent "stride piano". But the style forever associated with him is slimmed down by comparison, and it was impossible to achieve except with a cohesive and balanced rhythm-section. The amazing mobility and drive of the Green-Page-Jones combination, who were together for most of the period 1937–49, enabled Basie also to prod the band in a way which – though heard in the work of other Kansas City players such as Mary Lou Williams and Pete Johnson, and even Earl Hines – was brought to perfection by the Count.

The crucial role of the rhythm-section in his first famous big band was magnified because the ensemble functioned with the freedom of a traditional sextet. Soloists were continually supported by spontaneous "riffs", a feature particularly prevalent in Kansas City jazz, and some of these were then memorized as "head arrangements" which later became famous. ("One O'Clock Jump", the band's theme tune, was partly created in this way by Buster Smith and first organized on paper by Buck Clayton, though copyrighted by Basie.) By the late 1930s, however, as it became desirable for the popular instrumental numbers and the arrangements for vocalists to assume a fixed form, scores were commissioned first from Eddie Durham and Buster Smith, then from outside writers such as Andy Gibson and Buster Harding, who were also working for many others including white bands. Basie was saved from anonymity by his unique rhythm-section, and gradually the new 1950s unit pared down the prolix arrangements of the late swing era so that its best performances made predictability a virtue, just like the predictability of the twelve-bar blues which still inspired much of its repertoire.

If imitation is the sincerest form of flattery, Basie's achievement has been the most fawned-over, whether by rehearsal bands, youth bands, semi-professional bands or studio-produced bands all round the world. And it has inspired by far the most convincing of official "ghost bands", in the ensemble led first by Thad Jones (1984–6), then by Frank Foster (1986–96) and Grover Mitchell, who have maintained authenticity, while perpetuating the vitality of the original. [BP]

⊙ **The Original American Decca Recordings** (1937–9; MCA). This three-CD edition of the band's first two years on record brims with classics featuring the early stars – Clayton, Edison, Evans and Young – in uniquely loose-fitting garb. Anyone preferring a single CD should go to the competing albums on CDS, Hep (*Listen... You Shall Hear*) or Classics (*Count Basie 1936–38*), noting that the latter also begins with the four quintet tracks that introduced Lester Young.

⊙ **Verve Jazz Masters: Count Basie** (1954–65; Verve). A successful compilation with some of the 1950s band's hits such as "Paradise Squat" (with Basie on organ), "Shiny Stockings" and "April in Paris", along with four remakes of 1930s material, including a long, live "One O'Clock Jump".

BASIE
The Complete Atomic Basie
E=MC² – COUNT BASIE ORCHESTRA + NEAL HEFTI ARRANGEMENTS

The Complete Atomic Basie (1957; Roulette). The Count's best-known single album, including "Whirlybird" and "Li'l Darlin' ". Tenor soloist, and later band manager, Lockjaw Davis enlivens several of the tracks, all written by prolific Basie contributor Neal Hefti.

For The First Time (1974; Pablo/OJC). The opening shot in a late campaign to force the Count to be less modest about his piano work, this trio matches him with Ray Brown and Louie Bellson.

Ian Bateman

Trombone.

b. Catford, London, 29 March 1959.

A tough-toned hard-swinging stylist with a natural leaning towards Swing and Dixieland, Ian Bateman joined the National Youth Jazz Orchestra (NYJO) in 1976 and was with them for four years. He has subsequently played with various bands including the Pete Allen Jazz Band (1980–87), Rod Mason (1993–4), Terry Lightfoot (from 1995), Kenny Ball (as deputy for John Bennett in 1998), Digby Fairweather (2001–2), and the Back to Basie Big Band (2001). Bateman is a highly versatile player, capable of working equally successfully with modern figures such as Barbara Thompson, Don Weller and Art Themen. He also works on a semi-regular basis with Mason, Fairweather, the Pasadena Roof Orchestra and Andy Cooper and is one of the few graduates of NYJO to embrace traditional styles of jazz as the core of his own musical activities. [DF]

Moonlight Serenade (2003; own label). A fine, and comparatively rare, example of a trombonist holding the attention of the listener for an entire CD playing only with a pianist; in this case, Bateman's longtime colleague Craig Milverton. An excellent and wide-ranging choice of tunes combined with Bateman's powerful athletic approach make this album an important addition to British trombone discography.

Collin Bates

Piano.

b. Sydney, Australia, 1931; d. Aug 17 1991.

Bates played boogie piano to win a Sydney talent contest while at public school and later took a day job, playing in local jam sessions by night. After an exploratory visit to London in 1954 he returned there to live four years later, and soon joined Bruce Turner's Jump Band (1960–4); thereafter he worked at Flanagan's Restaurant as a music-hall entertainer, as well as playing every Sunday at New Merlins Cave, Clerkenwell, London (where George Melly was a frequent visitor) with John Chilton's Feetwarmers. From 1974 he joined Chilton with Melly on the road full-time, then freelanced for six years before rejoining Melly in 1983 for seven more years of touring, including the Far East and Australasia. In March 1990, after a series of dates with Melly, he remained behind in Australia to settle in his home town. Bates was a universally liked and respected musician whose springily vivacious piano playing took in influences from classics to modern; he is well-represented on CD reissues with Bruce Turner and Melly. [DF]

Django Bates

Piano, keyboards, tenor horn, composer.

b. Beckenham, UK, 2 Oct 1960.

Because his father collected jazz, Romanian folk and African music, Bates grew up with diverse influences. He heard jazz records at home when very young and played piano by ear. From 1971–7 he studied trumpet, piano and violin at the Centre for Young Musicians in London, then took the young musicians' course at Morley College in 1977–8. He went to the Royal College of Music to study composition, but left, disenchanted, after two weeks. He joined Tim Whitehead's quartet, Borderline, in 1981, staying for three and a half years, but in 1983 his dream came true when he was recruited into Dudu Pukwana's group, Zila.

The same year, he became a founder member of Loose Tubes, a 21-piece ensemble for which he did much of the composing. He was also a member of First House, a quartet led by saxophonist Ken Stubbs, which, in 1984, won the third European Jazz Competition at Leverkusen. Bates was also a founder member of Bill Bruford's Earthworks in the mid-1980s, but left at the beginning of 1994 to concentrate on his own groups.

Among them was Human Chain, a small group that he had started in 1979, the permanent members of which eventually became Iain Ballamy, Michael Mondesir and Martin France. When Loose Tubes disbanded Bates made Human Chain the core of a large orchestra, Delightful Precipice, which he formed in 1991. The orchestra's first performances were with one of Europe's leading new circus companies, Snapdragon, for which Bates wrote a series of works inspired by the late Angela Carter's book, *Nights At The Circus*. Since then,

Jak Kilby

Django Bates

cross-media collaborations have become an important part of his work.

Bates has worked with international composers and bandleaders George Russell, George Gruntz and Michael Gibbs. He also collaborates as a duo with concert pianist Joanna MacGregor. Since 1986 he has performed in twenty-five countries in Europe, Asia, and North and South America. He has had many composing commissions including, in 1995, one to compose a film soundtrack and one to write a piano concerto for Joanna MacGregor.

In the later 1990s, Bates's touring schedule and composing commitments were unabated. With Delightful Precipice he played festivals in Norway, Holland, Denmark, Portugal and Italy. In 1997 he received the Danish Jazzpar Prize, and a version of Delightful Precipice was involved in the recording of his *Jazzpar music – Like Life* (1998; Storyville). Bates also performs worldwide and collaborates with a diverse range of artists from the classical, jazz, Indian and pop worlds. He composed "My Dream Kitchen" for percussionist Evelyn Glennie, and in 1998 wrote "A Fine Frenzy" for the Shobana Jeyasingh Dance Company. Bates has also composed music for his own circus project, Circus Umbilicus, and a keyboard concerto, "They Think It's All Over". During his Jazzpar activities, he met the young Swedish vocalist Josefine Cronholm, who began singing with Human Chain, with Django's arrangments becoming more romantic, mellow and understated. For saxophonist Tim Berne's new independent label, Screwgun, they recorded *Quiet Nights* in 1998, and toured the following year.

Bates is one of the most prodigiously talented musicians Britain has produced, and his work refers to the entire jazz spectrum – from early jazz through bebop and free jazz to jazz-rock fusion. He also uses a mixture of acoustic and electronic instruments. As well as his protean musical abilities, he has a surreal sense of humour, an acute visual sense, and an interest in language and literature – an often explosive melange. Bates is consistently brilliant and adventurous, both as instrumentalist and as composer. [IC]

⊙ **Autumn Fires (And Green Shoots)** (1994; JMT). This is a superb solo piano album – at times densely complex, but often spacious and deeply considered. "Autumn Leaves" is given a Tatumesque but abstract and oblique exploration. Bates's own composition, "Ralf's Trip", is funky and bluesy, while Ellington's "Solitude" is wonderfully sparse and brooding.

⊙ **Winter Truce (And Homes Blaze)** (1995; JMT). This is primarily a Delightful Precipice album, with much bravura contrapuntal writing and Django's vision more focused than ever. Bates's unflagging invention, whether composing or improvising, is astonishing.

⊙ **Like Life** (1997; Storyville). This is a record of the musical results of Bates's Jazzpar Award, featuring the Danish Radio Orchestra and Human Chain, including Iain Ballamy, bassist Michael Mondesir and drummer Martin France. The imagination, flair and emotional power of this music is remarkable.

⊙ **Quiet Nights** (1998; Screwgun). This features Human Chain and Josefine Cronholm, who can sing with ineffable sweetness, and on the title track even sounds a little like Astrud Gilberto. The standards, which include "Speak Low", "Over The Rainbow", and Ellington's "Solitude", are full of surprises, while Bates's own work ranges from the jokey "Like Someone In Love" to the eerily hypnotic "Is There Anyone Up There?"

➤➤ **Loose Tubes** *(Open Letter).*

Alvin Batiste

Clarinet, saxophone, piano, composer.

b. New Orleans, c. 1937.

A hugely gifted clarinettist and a working musician in New Orleans from around 1950, Alvin Batiste is unfortunately under-recorded. His work, rather like Tony Coe's in Britain, is brilliantly eclectic, based on a cross-culture of classic and modern jazz and including synthetic music and contemporary classical devices. Batiste lives and teaches in Baton Rouge. His extended works include three *New Orleans Suites* written for the New Orleans Philharmonic, and his regular musical colleagues include Billy Cobham (with whom he has recorded) and Ornette Coleman. [DF]

Milton Batiste

Trumpet.

b. New Orleans, 5 Sept 1934; d. 29 March 2001.

One of the stars of Harold Dejan's Olympia Brass Band of the 1960s and 70s, Batiste was taught trumpet at Joseph S. Clarke's High School and led his own boy's band the House Wreckers before joining Professor Longhair at the Hi-Hat Club, a residency which continued into the 1960s. He also toured with Champion Jack Dupree and Big Joe Turner, and joined the Olympia in 1964 alongside Kid Shiek Cola and Andy Anderson (trumpets). Amid a reduced format, Batiste continued to lead the Olympia after Dejan became ill and also led the Young Olympians, a finishing-school for young brass band players, until failing health restricted his activities. [DF]

⊙ **With The Rue Conti Jazz Band** (1995; Ghb). A showcase for Milton Batiste's powerful and energetic trumpet playing, on which he also sings and plays flugelhorn.

Ray Bauduc

Drums, composer.

b. New Orleans, 18 June 1906; d. 15 Jan 1988.

Bauduc worked around his home town with leaders such as Johnny Bayersdorffer (as well as guitarist Nappy Lamare, a lifelong friend) before going to New York in 1926 with the Scranton Sirens. After time with bandleader Fred Rich as drummer and featured dancer, in 1928 he took over the drum chair from his new leader Ben Pollack (while Pollack conducted) and stayed until 1934 when he and most of the rest of the band left to join

Bob Crosby. With Crosby, Bauduc found a perfect frame for his sensational New Orleans style, a collage of clicking woodblocks, press rolls, rimshots, splash and Chinese cymbals; swaying gracefully behind his kit, he was nicknamed "The Seal" by his colleagues. He became a central figure in Crosby's band, often directing the musical traffic, offering ideas and laying down guidelines. After Crosby's band broke up in 1942, Bauduc served in the army, then worked with a big band, with his own swing quartet (he was tired of the Dixieland tag), with Crosby again, with Jimmy Dorsey (1948), and with Jack Teagarden (1952–5). Then came a spell co-leading with Lamare, a highly successful band which lasted until 1960, when Bauduc moved out to California, where he played clubs. By 1970 he was living in Texas and semi-retired. **[DF]**

➤➤ **Bob Crosby** *(Bob Crosby 1936–38 [Halcyon]).*

Billy Bauer

Guitar.

b. New York, 14 Nov 1915.

Bauer played with a number of big bands from 1939, including Woody Herman (1944–6), the Chubby Jackson group (1947) and occasionally Benny Goodman, but his main jazz association was with the Lennie Tristano trio/sextet from 1946–9. One of the few original guitarists to emerge in the 1940s, Bauer avoided the elastic phrasing of the Charlie Christian school. Obtaining a rather ugly metallic sound which was the equivalent of Tristano's glassy piano tone, he aspired to a mirror-image of the pianist, but without achieving a similar idiosyncratic strength. Apart from recording with J.J. Johnson-Kai Winding (1954), Bobby Hackett-Jack Teagarden (1957) and Cootie Williams-Rex Stewart (1957), and reunions with Tristano and Lee Konitz, he was largely occupied with session work and teaching. Many of the original compositions of Konitz, Tristano, etc are registered with William H. Bauer Publishing Co. **[BP]**

➤➤ **Lennie Tristano** *(Live At Birdland 1952).*

Johannes Bauer

Trombone.

b. Halle, Germany, 22 July 1954.

One of the key figures in the "second wave" of East German improvisers, Bauer studied trombone in Berlin from 1971–7. He has two sibling improvisers, a younger brother Matthias, who plays bass, and his older brother Konrad (formerly Conrad), who is also a trombonist, but who exerted very little musical influence on his younger relative (as is evident in their different approaches). Starting in 1979, Bauer began working as a freelance improviser in quite a wide range of contexts, including important East German ensembles led by Manfred Schulze, Ulrich Gumpert, Hannes Zerbe, Hans Rempel, and his older brother, and West European groups including Peter Brötzmann's Alarm Orchestra and März Combo (with which he recorded for FMP in 1981 and 1993 respectively), Cecil Taylor European Orchestra, Tony Oxley Celebration Orchestra, Barry Guy New Orchestra and the Fred van Hove T'Nonet.

A notably loud, punchy player even by the trombone's pugilistic standards, Bauer works well in aggressive settings like the rock driven Slawterhaus, but he is an organic improviser and adapts equally well to quieter, even delicate assemblages like the trio he played in with pianist Van Hove and singer Annick Nozati until her untimely death in 2000. With them he recorded Organo Pleno in 1992 for FMP. He has also recorded duets with Konrad – *Bauer Bauer* (1995; Intakt) – and the two of them are part of the unique line-up of twin trombones and guitars in DoppelMoppel, which released *Aventure Québécoise* (1999; Victo), as well as the earlier *Reflections* (1996; FMP), originally recorded in 1986. With Alan Silva and Roger Turner he is part of the Tradition Trio, formed in 1992. Their music is more about extending tradition than preserving it, and they celebrated their 10 year anniversary with Tone, a dynamic, abrasive album recorded live at the Free Music Festival in Antwerp. **[JC]**

Konrad Bauer

Trombone.

b. Halle, East Germany, 1943.

Konrad Bauer (earlier spelling, "Conrad") studied at the Musikhochscule in Dresden. In the late 60s he played with the important East German jazz ensemble Manfred-Ludwig Sextett, alongside saxophonist Ernst-Ludwig Petrowsky, as well as playing in various rock bands. Into the 1970s, Bauer was one of the most influential figures in free-jazz and improvised music in East Germany, founding the quartet FEZ and diverse small groups, and playing with the Hans Rempel Octet. Through concerts and recordings organized by the West Berlin organization, Free Music Production, Bauer was one of the first musicians from the East to work regularly on the other side of the wall, and he made a small batch of excellent records including *Was Ist Denn Nun?* (1980; FMP). A veritable East German all-star band, Zentralquartett, was established in the early 80s, with Bauer, Petrowsky, pianist Ulrich Gumpert and percussionist Günter "Baby" Sommer, and this ensemble has continued to play and record, making two relatively straightahead records, *Plie* (1984; Intakt) and *Careless Love* (1997; Intakt). He is also a member of the quartet DoppelMoppel, with guitarists Joe Sachse and Uwe Kropinski and his younger brother (also a trombonist) Johannes. He has played with top-flight avant-gardists such as Han Bennink, Anthony Braxton and Peter Brotzmann and Aki Takase.

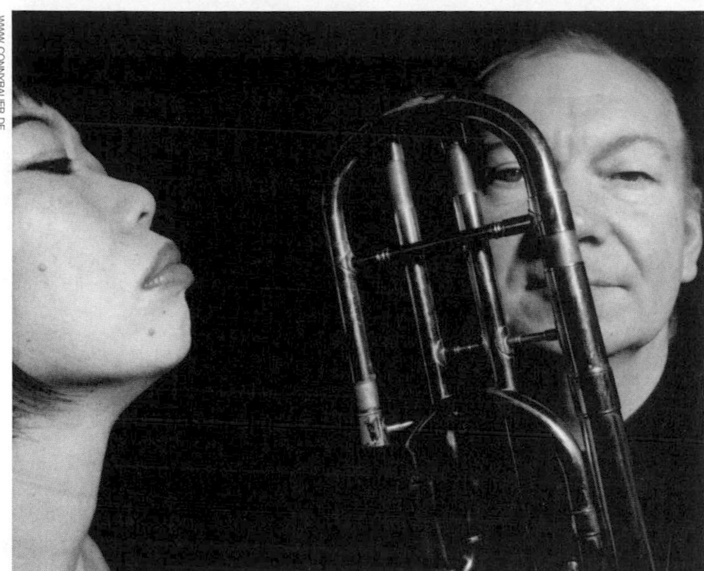
WWW.CONNYBAUER.DE

Konrad Bauer with Aki Takase

Bauer is a tremendous technician who is perfectly comfortable circular-breathing (not common among trombonists) and deploying a range of extended techniques, some of which he has personally innovated. His special vocabulary is most evident on his solo records, including *Toronto Töne* (1992; Victo), which features electronic manipulations, and his approach is very different – rather softer and less punchy – from that of Johannes, as is clear from their duo disc, *Bauer Bauer* (1995; Intakt). [JC]

Three Wheels – Four Directions (1993; Victo). Absolutely stellar trio interplay from the Konrad Bauer Trio, with Eastern drummer Günter Sommer and West German bass legend Peter Kowald. Muscular, angular, full of drive and wit and play, this is both a showcase for Bauer and a breathtaking document of free improvisation.

News from Berlin (1998; Victo). Conny teams up with Aki Takase. His fat but spritely trombone tone provides a wry ballast for Takase's fleet scampering: a romp that sounds like a suite of Thelonious Monk tunes being effortlessly played five times too fast.

Mario Bauzá

Trumpet, alto saxophone, arranger, composer.
b. Havana, 28 April 1911; d. New York, 11 July 1993.

Bauzá played clarinet, bass-clarinet and oboe with the Havana Philharmonic but moved to New York in 1930, working two years later with Noble Sissle, with whom he switched to trumpet. He played with Chick Webb, for whom he became musical director, from 1933–8, with Don Redman in 1938–9 and with Cab Calloway from 1939–41. From then until 1975 he was musical director of the band led by his brother-in-law Machito. Only after Machito's death did Bauzá begin fronting his own ensembles, cutting three albums in the last two years of his life. Bauzá was a mentor of Dizzy Gillespie, whom he met sitting in at Harlem's Savoy Ballroom, and brought him into the Calloway band, later introducing him to percussionist Chano Pozo. By that period, Bauzá's work with Machito had led to a significant increase in the influence of jazz on Afro-Latin music, a development in which he was the main catalyst; specifically, his piece "Tanga" is honoured as the first to include a *montuno* with jazz improvisation. [BP]

➤➤ **Machito** *(The Original Mambo Kings).*

Ted Beament

Piano, composer.
b. Basingstoke, Hants, 10 February 1941.

Growing up in Willesden, North London, Beament began the piano at the age of thirteen and played his first gig just two years later. He turned professional in 1969 performing on cruise-ships, as well as accompanying visiting Americans including Sonny Stitt, Joe Newman, Harry Edison, Allan Eager and Jon Eardley. Beament worked freelance with most of Britain's best-known contemporary players before joining Humphrey Lyttelton in 1995. Thereafter he toured and recorded countrywide forming a highly effective trio, entitled Trio Time, with two members of Lyttelton's rhythm section – bassist Paul Bridge and drummer Adrian Macintosh. A powerful and skilled stylist with a formidable technique, Beament is well grounded in all areas of jazz music. [DF]

How Beautiful Is Night (1999; Calligraph). Witty trio album on which the opening track, "The Kerry Dancers", reveals Beament's originality, fleet touch, creative freshness and – when required – technical power. Very highly recommended.

Jim Beard

Keyboards, percussion.
b. Chester, Pennsylvania, 26 Aug 1960.

Having studied classical piano from the age of six, with Mary Ann Rietz and (1979–83) John Ogden, and jazz with George Shearing (1974–8), Jim Beard graduated from Indiana University music school in 1984, and moved to New York the following year. He had also studied clarinet, tenor saxophone and bass in his teens and quickly earned a reputation, especially in jazz fusion circles, for his versatility and musicality. Leaders using these qualities in the late 1980s and 90s form a virtual who's who of the genre: John McLaughlin, the Breckers, saxophonist Bill Evans, Wayne Shorter, Mike Stern, Victor Bailey, Bob Berg, Wayne Krantz, Dennis Chambers, Pat Metheny and Michael "Patches" Stewart have all featured Beard on various recordings, often playing some of his compositions. His albums as leader include *Song Of The Sun* (1991; CTI) and *Lost At The Carnival* (1995; Lipstick), an album held together by a "fairground organ" concept. When executive producer Joachim Becker left Lipstick to form ESC Records, Beard went with him to record *Truly...* (1997) and *Advocate* (1999). Though Dennis Chambers's *Outbreak* (2002; ESC) carried the drummer's name as leader, Beard was responsible for the arrangements and production as well as the keyboards. All are more adventurous than many so-called fusion recordings and revolve around Beard's subtly varied keyboard sounds and textures, for which he remains in great demand by the more original contemporary exponents of the form. [CP/CI]

⊙ **Truly... (1997; Escapade).** Light, jazzy funk, intelligently arranged to feature Beard's keyboards in the company of fusion studio stalwarts, plus vocalists Mark Ledford and David Blamires.

Heinie Beau

Clarinet, saxophones, composer, arranger.

b. Calvary, Wisconsin, 8 March 1911; d. 19 April 1987.

One of the best yet most neglected Dixieland-to-swing clarinettists, Heinie Beau came from a big-band background (with Tommy Dorsey, 1940–43) and later settled in Hollywood, where he worked as a freelance arranger and musician in radio, TV and recording. He rapidly gravitated to the jazz-based areas regularly occupied by arranger Paul Weston, and recorded with great singers such as Peggy Lee and Frank Sinatra, as well as with a variety of bands and musicians, most notably Red Nichols. "Red and his music were my first introduction to jazz and my biggest influence", Beau wrote later (his first arrangement ever was a copy of Nichols's "Washboard Blues" for a family band). His long friendship with the cornettist resulted in some classic recordings from the late 1950s, in which Beau not only rearranged many of Nichols's greatest hits but also wrote new compositions which lovingly retained Nichols's favourite devices: timpani, mellophone, bass saxophone lead and so on; these important jazz recordings are long overdue for reissue on CD. After Nichols's death, Beau continued his studio commitments and in the 1970s visited Europe, including England, where he sat in at top London jazz clubs. [DF]

Sidney Bechet

Soprano saxophone, clarinet.

b. New Orleans, 14 May 1897; d. Paris, 14 May 1959.

As a boy Sidney Bechet heard powerful trumpeters such as Freddie Keppard in New Orleans. Lessons followed with Lorenzo Tio, Louis Nelson and George Baquet, and soon he was playing with every leading light in his home town, as well as teaching – Larry Shields and Jimmie Noone were two pupils. By 1917 he was in Chicago and there joined Will Marion Cook's orchestra, with whom he travelled in 1919 to New York and then to Europe. In London that year the young clarinettist found a straight soprano saxophone in a junkshop, liked it, and began to feature it onstage in a stately version of "Song Of Songs". He made headlines. The young Ernest Ansermet was enthralled with Bechet's sound, so was the Prince of Wales, and the young man even played for the king at Buckingham Palace. "It was funny to look at your money and see someone you knew", he mused later. But after deportation for minor assault, the love affair with England was over: "On the boat", he wrote, "I took all the English money I had and dropped it overboard." Back in New York, Bechet worked with revues, with James P. Johnson, with Duke Ellington (who would have liked to have him in the band) and taught Johnny Hodges. In 1925 came his first trip to Paris to play for the famous Revue Nègre, then four years of globetrotting in Russia, Germany and France as musical director for the Revue and as a bandsman. Then in 1929, in Paris, he was jailed for eleven months for a shooting offence. He emerged a bitter man.

He worked with Noble Sissle regularly over the next ten years and during the period struck up a firm friendship with trumpeter Tommy Ladnier, a fellow traveller, wit and survivor. With Ladnier in New York he co-led bands in clubs, put together the Bechet-Ladnier Feetwarmers for a spell at the Savoy Ballroom, and opened a tailor's shop. He also got back together with his old teacher Lorenzo Tio, who had come to New York to work at the Nest. By the end of the decade, Bechet was working along 52nd Street with Ladnier and other friends including Joe Marsala, Bobby Hackett and Eddie Condon. In 1940 he made some historic sides with Louis Armstrong, and the two stars saw no need to bend the knee to one another. "A man like Louis", said Bechet later, with just a trace of guile, "he's not just a musicianer any more. He's got himself a name and he's got to live up to that name. I don't even blame him!" Most of the other players on titles such as "Coal Cart Blues" and "Down In Honky-Tonk Town" knew what was happening and seldom talked about the results: jazz temperament was showing its claws. In the early 1940s Bechet did well enough, playing clubs, dances, parties and in a band with Vic Dickenson,

WILLIAM GOTTLIEB

Sidney Bechet

as well as appearing regularly for Eddie Condon's Town Hall concerts during the war, and briefly in 1945 at the Savoy Club, Boston, with the often-drunk Bunk Johnson.

By that time Bechet had settled in Brooklyn, where he began teaching to help his pocket. He taught aspiring saxophonists like Richard Hadlock and Bob Wilber – the latter, his most famous pupil, took a daily lesson and actually moved into a spare room in Bechet's house. But the old master was far from busy, although in 1946 he took part in a jazz-based Broadway play, *Hear That Trumpet*, and worked Jimmy Ryan's and clubs up and down 52nd Street, as well as back in Chicago. The year 1949 was his turning point. That year he was welcomed like a son at the Salle Pleyel jazz festival in Paris, and after one more trip back to New York his mind was set. In November 1949 Bechet went back to Paris (stopping off in London to play with Humphrey Lyttelton on an illegal London stage) and soon began working with André Reweliotty. The approval was ecstatic. In 1951 Bechet married his second wife (a German woman) in Antibes, quickly acquired a manager (Claude Wolff, who later married Petula Clark), and became a French hero of Chevalier-like proportions. In 1955 his music for the ballet *La Nuit Est Une Sorcière* was performed – "an extended piece", says Bob Wilber, "which he worked on, so far as I can see, all his life". He travelled back to America to star with Bob Scobey and others at festivals, and by the late 1950s police had to be called in whenever he played in Paris. When he died in 1959, of cancer, a square was named for him in Antibes and a statue erected in a local park.

Around Bechet's life there hangs an aura of otherworldliness, chiefly the result of his rambling, poetic autobiography *Treat It Gentle*, in which he portrayed himself as a kind of jazz nature boy, wandering a strange land of his own creation. The truth was harder. "Some people say Sidney was the most temperamental son-of-a-bitch in music", says Barney Bigard, "others say he was the nicest man you ever met." Whatever aspect of his personality Bechet chose to display, he was above all a man of personal and musical authority, and very few trumpeters, apart from Louis Armstrong – who brooked no opposition – were ever able to blow him down. His jazz contribution is gigantic. His compositions were melodically stronger than those of any other classic jazz musician, his creation of a vocabulary for his instrument was as great an achievement as Coleman Hawkins's for tenor, and his records are majestic. [DF]

⊙ **The Chronological Sidney Bechet** (1923–41; Classics). This five-CD series (each volume available separately) offers Bechet-led recordings in chronology from his earliest recording years.

⊙ **The Bluebird Sessions 1932–43** (RCA Bluebird). A four-CD set featuring nineteen bands on 84 tracks and including classic titles by the Feetwarmers (with Ladnier) plus alternate takes.

⊙ **Really The Blues** (ASV; 1932–41) Definitive collage of vintage Bechet with twenty-five indispensable tracks including "Really the Blues" as well as titles with Armstrong, the Bechet/Spanier Big Four and Bechet's "one man band".

⊙ **Sidney Bechet 1932–51** (Giants of Jazz). Well-selected three-CD collection of Bechet tracks, including those with Tommy Ladnier's orchestra, Louis Armstrong (1940), the Mezzrow-Bechet quintet and various editions of Bechet's Feetwarmers (1932–50).

⊙ **Sidney Bechet In New York 1937–40** (JSP). An intriguing collection including collaborations with Noble Sissle, Grant and Wilson, Trixie Smith and Louis Armstrong. Superb sound remastering by John R.T. Davies.

⊙ **Jazz Classics Vols. 1/2** (1939–51; Blue Note). Comprehensive collection of Bechet from a definitive period of his recorded history, partnered by Sidney de Paris, Teddy Bunn, Bunk Johnson and other greats.

⊙ **Masters Of Jazz Vol. 4: Sidney Bechet** (1945–7; Storyville). Essential material by the Mezzrow-Bechet partnership, featuring quintet and septet titles.

⊙ **Spreadin' Joy** (1940–50; Naxos). Interesting selection of later Bechet (including tracks with Humphrey Lyttelton's band); excellent sound quality and a good portrait of later Bechet.

Gordon Beck

Piano, electric piano, synthesizers, composer.
b. London, 16 Sept 1938.

Beck studied the piano at school but was largely self-taught. He became a professional musician after nine years as a design draughtsman in aero-engineering in London and Canada, where he was inspired by the playing and popularity of George Shearing and Dave Brubeck. Back in London he began at the top, working with groups led by Tony Kinsey, Vic Ash, Bobby Wellins and Tony Crombie. In 1962 he joined the Tubby Hayes quintet and with it made his first tours abroad, including to the San Remo festival.

In 1965 he formed his own trio, which worked regularly as the house rhythm-section at Ronnie Scott's. He made his own first albums – jazz versions of the film scores *Doctor Doolittle* and *Half A Sixpence* – in 1967, and began working extensively as a studio musician. In 1969 he replaced George Gruntz in Phil Woods's European Rhythm Machine and began an international career playing festivals, concerts, radio, TV and clubs throughout Europe, and by 1971 the USA as well. In 1972, after three albums, the group disbanded. Beck then formed Gyroscope, re-formed his mid-60s trio and eased off the purely commercial studio work.

In the years since 1974 Beck has worked, recorded and composed for many people including Lena Horne, Phil Woods, Gary Burton, Cleo Laine, Mel Tormé, Mike Gibbs, Clark Terry, Charles Tolliver, Sonny Rollins, Joe Henderson, Milt Jackson, Annie Ross, Alan Holdsworth, Don Sebesky and Didier Lockwood. In the early 1970s he was a member of Piano Conclave, the six-keyboard group led by George Gruntz. Since 1978 he has been recording for the French labels JMS and OWL, both in Paris. In 1985 he began working in duo with Helen Merrill, toured California and Japan with Alan Holdsworth, and recorded an album in New York with Didier Lockwood, Cecil McBee and Billy Hart, after which the group toured Europe extensively. The quartet with Lockwood disbanded after two years and two albums.

Beck has been active in jazz education for some time and from 1974–87 he was a tutor at the Barry Jazz Summer School in Wales. He has had composing commissions in England including his "May Song Variations", based on a Fenland folk song, for the 1985 Cambridge festival. In 1988 he began working with computers and MIDI technology and in 1990, working with sequencers and synthesizers as well as piano, he toured the UK in trio with Jeff Clyne and John Marshall. He has continued to work with Helen Merrill and with Alan Holdsworth, and during the 1990s has played solo concerts in Europe, Israel and the USA. There have also been collaborations with Steve Lacy, Lee Konitz and Tom Harrell.

Beck was one of the first of a growing number of British jazz musicians to acquire a really solid international reputation. In the 1970s the French took him to their hearts and he has since become a virtual superstar in France.

In the later 1990s, Beck was able to pick and choose his concerts. In 1996 his duo concert with alto saxophonist Phil Woods, at London's Wigmore Hall, was recorded and released on a double CD. In 1997 the Gordon Beck trio played in Kalisz, Poland. The following year, he played solo, duo and trio concerts in England, Ireland, France, Spain and Poland, and was a member of the very distinguished jury for the second Martial Solal International Jazz Piano competition. In 1999, he continued to tour and in 2003 released a solo album, *Reflections*.

He has the eccentricity of genius (eg, his 1994 project to "explore the harmonic, rhythmic, and visual potential of powered machinery in the context of structured musical performance") and it is astonishing that he and his work are so little known and appreciated in his native country. Like his many influences – among them Herbie Hancock, Bill Evans, Keith Jarrett and Horace Silver – Beck is technically brilliant with an apparently inexhaustible flow of ideas, great lyricism and tremendous rhythmic drive. [IC]

⊙ **Dreams** (1989; JMS). A mark of Beck's quality as an artist is the way he has developed over the decades, continuing to search for new modes of expression in both playing and composing. This album is an adventure in solo playing and using electronics and synthesizers to build up the picture – the only other live ingredient being Rowanne Mark's voice. It's a long way from Beck's dynamic spontaneity, but the music is often very attractive.

⊙ **For Evans Sake** (1991; JMS). Beck leads an all-star quartet with Didier Lockwood, Dave Holland and Jack DeJohnette in this heartfelt tribute to pianist Bill Evans. The result is a masterpiece – very fine compositions and superlative playing by a group that is even greater than the sum of its illustrious parts.

⊙ **The Complete Concert** (1996; JMS). Beck and Phil Woods, both virtuosi, have played together off and on for years, and their rapport is magical. On this two-CD live set they play a mixture of originals written by each of them, and standards, in an utterly compelling concert. Stand-out pieces are the opener, "Quill", composed by Woods in memory of his recently deceased friend Gene Quill, who was one of the best lead alto saxists, and the duo's tremendous version of Miles Davis's "Solar".

⊙ **November Song** (1998; JMS). This features Beck's quartet with Stan Sulzmann, bassist Steve Watts and drummer Gene Calderazzo, in an album of Gordon Beck compositions. The title track is one of his finest pieces, and it had been performed when he played on Didier Lockwood's 1985 album, but Beck had felt ever since that it had been taken too fast on that occasion. Now he makes it the title piece at the right tempo, and the month of November becomes the theme of this masterful CD.

➤➤ **Alan Holdsworth** *(With A Heart In My Song).*

Uli Beckerhoff

Trumpet, piano, composer.
b. Münster, Westphalia, Germany, 6 Dec 1947.

Beckerhoff had piano lessons when he was young and began on trumpet at the age of fifteen with five years of private lessons from an American classical player. After one semester studying law he changed to music, with three years of classical studies at the Münster Conservatory and two years in Cologne. He played first with local groups and won the Best Musician Award in 1966 and 67 at the International Jazz Jamboree in Osnabrück. In 1971 he won the Best Musician Award at the Loosdrecht jazz festival in Holland. He formed his own group, Jazztrack, which played extensively across Europe and appeared at numerous jazz festivals in the early 1970s. In 1974 Beckerhoff formed a quintet with Jasper van't Hof, Palle Danielsson, Edward Vesala and Wolfgang Enstfeld for concerts and radio broadcasts in Germany. He appeared at the 1975 Berlin jazz festival with Jazztrack and with the Michael Gibbs orchestra, following on with more radio and television broadcasts and workshops, this time with Joachim Kuhn, Wolfgang Dauner, Zbigniew Seifert, Charlie Mariano and John Scofield, among others. His group, Riot, also worked throughout Europe. In 1979, as a member of Volker Kriegel's Mild Maniac orchestra, Beckerhoff darted around Africa played concerts on a Goethe Institute tour. Aside from numerous commissions for radio big bands and symphony orchestras, The Uli Beckerhoff trio of 1986–8 (featuring Jasper van't Hof and John Marshall) consumed much of Uli's energy during the mid 1980s. More recently he turned up playing alongside dance outfit Boom Boom on their *Resurrection Lounge* album, with stunning and eclectic results.

Beckerhoff is a virtuoso trumpeter with an excellent range and sound. His favourites include Miles Davis, Kenny Wheeler, Terumaso Hino and Freddie Hubbard. Other inspirations are Joe Zawinul, Keith Jarrett, Wayne Shorter, Herbie Hancock, Claude Debussy, Maurice Ravel and John Coltrane. He has made over twenty albums either under his own name or with other leaders. [IC]

⊙ **Secret Obsession** (1990; Nabel). Beckerhoff leads a magnificent quartet with John Abercrombie, Arild Andersen and John Marshall for this live recording. The music covers a wide spectrum, from rock to jazz, from ballad to uptempo. High spots are Beckerhoff's lovely ballad "Follow Her Heart", with Andersen's ravishing bass sound and fine solo; the leader's four-minute-long unaccompanied trumpet solo, a brilliant *tour de force*; and Andersen's composition, "If You Look Far Enough", which has Beckerhoff using harmon mute and sounding eerily like Miles Davis as he calls plaintively over arco bass drones.

Harry Beckett

Trumpet, flugelhorn, piano.
b. Barbados, 30 May 1935.

Beckett came to the UK in 1954 from Barbados and played in nightclubs. In 1961 he worked with Charles Mingus in London, making the film *All Night Long*. He joined Graham Collier in the early 1960s, playing in his various groups for several years. Since then he has played with many leading UK musicians including John Surman, the New Jazz Orchestra, Mike Westbrook, Nucleus, Stan Tracey, Chris MacGregor's Brotherhood of Breath, Mike Gibbs, Elton Dean, Dudu Pukwana's Zila, Ronnie Scott and John Dankworth. Beckett also leads groups of his own, varying in size from trio to sextet or more. He has played at festivals and toured all over western and eastern Europe as well as Scandinavia, the Middle East and India. He has received Arts Council bursaries to compose, perform and record his own works. He has also been active in jazz education, taking workshops and giving lectures and recitals in schools and colleges. He worked for some years with the Jazz Warriors as a player/composer/arranger, and spent five years (1986–91) working and recording every year with the Ellington-inspired Danish band, The New Jungle Orchestra. At the beginning of the 1990s, the German record company ITM signed him and have recorded him (and all his compositions) in the company of a variety of leading contemporary musicians. In the later 1990s, Beckett continued with his trio of bassist Fred T. Baker and drummer Tony Marsh, and also worked with trombonist Annie Whitehead's band Rude. Between 1997 and 2000 he was a member of the Orchestre National de France. While in the orchestra's ranks he met saxophonist Chris Biscoe, who joined Beckett's trio, making it a quartet and, augmented by pianist Alastair Gavin, the Harry Beckett Quintet recorded the album, *A Tribute To Charles Mingus*. Gavin was replaced by Liam Noble and the Quintet morphed into The Harry Beckett Band; a live album, *Before and After,* hit the streets in 2001.

Jak Kilby

Harry Beckett

Beckett's playing is all quicksilver and lyricism with an often sardonic edge. He is an original, with his own way of phrasing and his own rhythms and timbres, and can run the gamut from wild aggression to great delicacy. His concept encompasses most areas from bebop and chord changes to modal and free playing. **[IC]**

⊙ **Live: Vol. 2 (1987; West Wind).** Beckett in sparkling form with Chris McGregor, Fred Thelonious Baker, Clifford Jarvis and the young lion of the 1980s, Courtney Pine.

⊙ **Passion And Possession (1991; ITM).** Beckett composed nine ballads for this session, and performs them in duo with three pianists – Django Bates, Joachim Kuhn and Keith Tippett – who each play three of them. The interplay of these very different personalities with Beckett's mercurial temperament results in fascinating and varied music.

⊙ **Images Of Clarity (1992; Evidence).** Beckett in trio formation with bassist Didier Levallet and drummer Tony Marsh. The title is apt – in this elemental setting the outlines are stark, there is nowhere to hide, and the music is wonderfully concentrated.

⊙ **A Tribute To Charles Mingus (1999; Basic).** This is one of Beckett's finest albums. Biscoe is a dynamic frontline partner, and the rhythm-section is excellent. They perform six Mingus pieces, including "Pussycat Dues", "Goodbye Porkpie Hat" and "Jellyroll" from *Mingus Ah Um*, and "Slop", a 6/4 descendant from "Better Git It In Your Soul" (also on *Ah Um*). Two of Beckett's pieces are performed, including one of his very best compositions, "Intimate Feelings", the performance of which is one of the high spots of this highly focused album.

Bix Beiderbecke

Cornet, piano, composer.

b. Davenport, Iowa, 10 March 1903; d. 7 Aug 1931.

Bix went to the High School in Davenport, then to Lake Forest Academy near Chicago for a year. He came from a prosperous middle-class family and his mother was an accomplished pianist. He was a "natural" musician, largely self-taught on piano from early childhood and on cornet which he began playing at fifteen. He was inspired by recordings of the Original Dixieland Jazz Band and their trumpet player Nick La Rocca, and heard music on the riverboats that came up the Mississippi from Memphis, St Louis and New Orleans. He certainly heard Louis Armstrong on one of these riverboats and also a white trumpet player called Emmett Hardy whom Bix later acknowledged as an influence but who never recorded. In 1923 Beiderbecke was the star soloist with the Wolverines, with whom he made his first records, and went to New York to play at Roseland. In 1925 he was with Charlie Straight's commercial orchestra in Chicago and spent much time listening to, and sitting in with, the pioneer black musicians there – King Oliver, Louis Armstrong, Jimmie Noone and others. He worked with Frankie Trumbauer's orchestra in 1926 at the Arcadia Ballroom, St Louis. After working with Jean Goldkette in Detroit, he joined Paul Whiteman's band as a featured soloist from 1928–30, but with many absences due to ill health caused by the alcoholism which ultimately

MAX JONES FILES REDFERNS

Bix Beiderbecke

killed him. The last year of his life was spent in Davenport and New York, gigging with Glen Gray's Casa Loma Orchestra and others. He died of pneumonia and was buried in Davenport.

Bix was appreciated by only a handful of musicians and fans during his brief lifetime. Some years after his death, Dorothy Baker's novel *Young Man with a Horn*, which was inspired by but not based on his life story, began the whole process which was to make him into a legendary figure. Musically he was already an immortal – a seminal influence and an inspiration to many other musicians. He was jazz's first great lyricist; the hallmarks of his style and music are delicacy of phrase and nuance, wonderfully poised rhythmic sophistication and rich sonority. For the first time in the history of that noble and martial instrument, the cornet projected a delicate sensitivity and a new, inward-looking thoughtfulness. Bix's emotional and technical palette was smaller than that of Louis Armstrong, whose epic imagination was pushing his trumpet technique to the extreme limits. But Bix had a burnished, bell-like sound, a sure attack, a natural sense of swing, and although he always played well within his technical abilities, his sound and the sweet logic of his thought made him one of the major jazz soloists. This line of playing, begun by Bix and his saxophonist friend Frankie Trumbauer, has been carried on by Bobby Hackett, Lester Young, Charlie Parker, Miles Davis and others right down to the present day. Bix was probably the first white musician ever to be admired and imitated by black jazzmen: Rex Stewart and others learned to play his most famous solo (the Trumbauer record of "Singing the Blues") note for note. As a pianist and composer Bix was one of the first jazzmen to be influenced by Debussy's harmonic ideas; the irony was that because his ear was so good, because he was such a "natural", he never learned to read music very well, and even his own compositions for piano had to be written down for him. Bill Challis, Jean Goldkette's arranger, transcribed the only Beiderbecke compositions we have, a mere five – and Bix nearly drove him to distraction because he never played one of them the same way twice. His most famous composition is "In a Mist". Although the piano pieces have great charm, it is by his cornet solos that Bix Beiderbecke must be judged: his major contribution on cornet keeps the piano pieces alive.

Possibly because of the influence of his family Bix seemed to aspire to the state of classical music while always feeling inferior to it. Had he been more disciplined, he might have continued to develop as a player and composer. He was a man of enormous talent but meagre character or self-discipline, and his creative despair, induced by technical inadequacy and lack of vision, made him take refuge in alcohol. All of his work is still available on record. [IC]

⊙ **The Complete Bix Beiderbecke In Chronological Order** (1924–30; IRD). This nine-CD set contains the entire Beiderbecke opus – his recorded work with the Wolverines, Bix And His Gang, Frankie Trumbauer and the orchestras of Jean Goldkette and Paul Whiteman. A musical legacy of extraordinary lyricism and humanity.

⊙ **Bix Beiderbecke And The Wolverines** (1924; Timeless). Bix's first year in the recording studios and this CD has almost everything he did. The music is fascinating historically, and Bix's young genius already immortal.

⊙ **Bix Lives** (1927–30; Bluebird). This has 23 tracks of Bix with the Jean Goldkette and Paul Whiteman orchestras, and also his last recording under his own name.

⊙ **Bix Beiderbecke Vol. 1: Singin' The Blues** (1927; Columbia); **Bix Beiderbecke Vol. 2: At The Jazz Band Ball** (1927–28; Columbia). These two CDs have all the classic tracks from Bix's most fruitful period in the recording studios, February 1927 to April 1928, some by Bix And His Gang, and others under Frankie Trumbauer's leadership. Essential and delightful.

Richie Beirach

Piano, electric keyboards, composer.

b. Brooklyn, New York, 23 May 1947.

Beirach had classical piano lessons from the age of six, but when he heard Red Garland, Miles Davis and John Coltrane he became interested in jazz. He studied at Berklee, Boston, then took a degree in theory and composition at the Manhattan School of Music, New York, followed by a one-year post-graduate fellowship which enabled him to study with Stan Getz, Dave Holland and Jack DeJohnette. In April 1974 he became a member of Dave Liebman's Lookout Farm, and began playing electric piano. Lookout Farm was one of the most creative jazz-rock groups and toured widely in Europe, playing major festivals. Beirach has also worked with Stan Getz, Freddie Hubbard, Lee Konitz and Chet Baker. During the 90s his work with saxophonist Henrik Frisk was particularly note-worthy. Beirach's jazz influences include Art Tatum, Bud Powell, Paul Bley and Herbie Hancock, though the denticulated romanticism of his playing often draws much from classical inspirations such as Schoenberg, Berg, Scriabin, Debussy and Ravel. [IC]

⊙ **Richie Beirach-Masahiko Togashi-Terumasa Hino** (1976 & 78; Konnex). Here Beirach plays a series of duos with drummer Togashi and with the superb trumpeter Hino.

⊙ **Some Other Time** (1989; Triloka). Beirach with an all-star sextet – Randy and Mike Brecker, John Scofield, George Mraz and Adam Nussbaum – in an album tribute to Chet Baker.

⊙ **Convergence** (1990; Triloka). A very creative duo session with George Coleman.

⊙ **Trust** (1993; Evidence). Beirach with the dynamic partnership of Dave Holland and Jack DeJohnette is propelled to his best form in an album of largely his own compositions plus a Holland original and Wayne Shorter's "Nefertiti".

Bob Belden

Soprano and tenor saxophones, piano, keyboards, arranger, producer.

b. Evanston, Illinois, 31 Oct 1956.

Raised in South Carolina (on a former plantation converted into a country club), with a mother who sang and a sister and brother who both played piano, Belden started on piano at age three. By the age of twelve he was gigging with his brother's band, eventually moving on to study at North Texas State University from 1973–8. He followed Joe Lovano into Woody Herman's band (1979–80), then played for the next few years with Donald Byrd. In 1989 he began a series of recordings with his own large Ensemble and became a busy freelance arranger and producer, working with artists as varied as Sting, Cassandra Wilson, McCoy Tyner and Herbie Hancock (the *New Standard* album). He has also produced reissues on several labels and earned three Grammy awards for the Miles Davis/Gil Evans set and the Davis Quintet 1965–8 set. Many of his own albums feature all-star casts reinterpreting the music of Sting, Prince, Carole King, The Beatles and Puccini (in the case of *Turandot*, which was subsequently banned for copyright reasons). His favourite artists are "too many to name, but at the top of the list would be Woody Herman". [BP]

⊙ **When Doves Cry** (1993; Metro Blue). Produced for the Japanese market, like all Belden's recent albums, these rearrangements of ten Prince songs feature a huge revolving personnel, seven of them with vocalists such as Holly Cole and Phil Perry. The standout title track features Cassandra Wilson plus soprano commentary by Greg Osby.

Graeme Bell

Piano, bandleader.

b. Melbourne, Australia, 7 Sept 1914.

The founding father of the Australian jazz revival, Bell took over the band led by his brother Roger and soon after formed the Uptown Club (an early centre for Australian revivalism) as well as helping to inaugurate the still flourishing Australian Jazz Convention. In 1947–8 he toured Europe including England, where his originality, energy and "jazz for dancing" policy blew a refreshing breeze through the dustier corners of British revivalism. Bell's second visit to England (1950–51) produced great recorded collaborations with Humphrey Lyttelton and players of similar energy and ability (including multi-instrumentalist Lazy Ade Monsbourgh and the young John Sangster) – "Apples Be Ripe" and "Take A Note From The South" are classics of their kind. Having founded the Swaggie record label in 1949, Bell continued playing and travelling internationally until 1957, when he settled in Sydney. From then on he continued to lead his own bands and to record; in 1977 he was awarded the Queen's Medal, followed in 1978 by the MBE. In 1992 he produced an autobiography, and in 1993 appeared at the Edinburgh jazz festival in a reunion with Humphrey Lyttelton; in 1998 he visited Britain again to take part in a BBC celebration of fifty years of Lyttelton's band. **[DF]**

Louie Bellson

Drums, composer.

b. Rock Falls, Illinois, 6 July 1924.

Louie Bellson (Luigi Paolino Balassoni) received copious big-band experience with Benny Goodman (1943, 1946), Tommy Dorsey (1947–9) and Harry James (1950–1), and co-led a sextet with former Dorsey colleague Charlie Shavers in 1950. He joined the Ellington band following the final departure of Sonny Greer from 1951–3. Having married singer Pearl Bailey in London in 1952, he spent much of the next few years acting as her musical director with his own band. He also made tours with Jazz at the Philharmonic in 1955, 1967, and in Europe in 1972, rejoined Dorsey (1955–6) and the posthumous Dorsey band (1964), Ellington (1965–6) and James (1966). Since the 1960s, he has been involved in much educational and demonstration work, and has led his own big bands in the USA and abroad, for which he arranges most of the material himself.

Bellson first became noted as a composer through his features with the early 1950s Ellington band – "The Hawk Talks" and "Skin Deep" – in which the dovetailing of the writing with his dynamic drumming was particularly impressive. His later small-group recordings sometimes result in merely ticking off the up-beats, instead of providing real propulsive power, which is a far cry from Bellson's more creative drumming in a big-band context. **[BP]**

⊙ **Black, Brown And Beige** (1992; Musicmasters). Though this may seem an unrepresentative choice, Bellson's band plays a convincing version of the Ellington masterwork (misleadingly advertised under Ellington's name), preceded by remakes of "The Hawk Talks" and "Skin Deep" and followed by Bellson's interesting "Ellington-Strayhorn Suite". Clark Terry is a guest soloist throughout.

➤➤ **Art Tatum** *(Tatum Group Masterpieces Vol. 1).*

Tex Beneke

Tenor saxophone, vocals.

b. Fort Worth, Texas, 12 Feb 1914; d. Santa Ana, 30 May 2000.

Tex Beneke came to fame after joining Glenn Miller's newly re-formed orchestra of 1938 as featured vocalist, doubling tenor. Beneke's Southern-sunny voice became the voice of Miller's orchestra on immortal hits like "Chattanooga Choo Choo", "I Gotta Gal In Kalamazoo" and "Don't Sit Under The Apple Tree" (despite his self-confessed inability to remember words), and his booting blues-flavoured tenor was always heavily featured by Miller, sometimes to the chagrin of section mate Al Klink. A humorous and relaxed character, he was popular with all the band (including the leader) and despite featured roles in films such as *Sun Valley Serenade* (1941) and *Orchestra Wives* (1942) – after which he topped polls in *Down Beat* and *Metronome* – he never became big-headed. "Tex's big ambition", says drummer Maurice Purtill, "was to get back to Texas, eat some chili, and play some blues." After serving in the US Navy during World War II (he never played in Miller's AAF orchestra), he was requested by the Miller estate to take the Glenn Miller orchestra back on the road; with this sometimes bop-flavoured band, and later on with his own, Beneke's career carried on successfully until the 1980s; in a 1990s video, *Glenn Miller: America's Musical Hero* (BMG), he was as enthusiastic as ever about his lifelong central role in Miller's story. **[DF]**

➤➤ **Glenn Miller** *(Glenn Miller In Hollywood).*

Tommy Benford

Drums.

b. West Virginia, 19 April 1905; d. 24 March 1994.

One of the founding names of jazz drumming, Benford is remembered principally as drummer on several sides with Jelly Roll Morton (1926–30), but his career began as a member of the celebrated Jenkins Orphanage Band of South Carolina in the 1910s. After that Benford worked with minstrel shows and during the 1920s with many eminent New York leaders, including Morton, Elmer Snowden and Edgar Hayes. In the following decade he worked in Europe with Eddie South, Freddie Taylor and Willie Lewis, then in the 1940s with Noble Sissle, Snub Moseley, Bob Wilber and others. The following twenty years saw him drumming with Jimmy Archey, Muggsy Spanier, Rex Stewart, Joe Thomas, Edmund Hall, Danny Barker, and the Saints and Sinners; at the close of the 1960s Benford reverted to part-time playing, but continued to appear with Franz Jackson, Clyde Bernhardt's Harlem Blues and Jazz Band and others. **[DF]**

➤➤ **Jelly Roll Morton** *(Jelly Roll Morton 1926–28).*

Cuban Bennett

Trumpet.

b. 1902; d. 28 Nov 1965.

"You could call him the first of the moderns": Roy Eldridge said about Benny Carter's cousin, Cuban (Theodore) Bennett, a trumpeter of phenomenal harmonic knowledge and endurance who predated Dizzy Gillespie by ten years. "He played changes like I've never heard", said Dickie Wells, and Benny Carter agreed: "Cuban was the greatest", he told Stanley Dance. "You wouldn't believe that anyone could play that way in the Twenties, yet it's hard to talk about him if you've nothing to substantiate it with. He was so advanced. They're doing today what he did then!" Bennett never recorded, never seems to have worked steadily with a band (apart possibly, from an obscure spell with Bingie Madison in a New York taxi dance hall), and he drank a lot. He was a jazz nomad who enjoyed the free and easy life in clubs, experimenting and working underground. "He just liked to hang around and blow in the joints", says Dickie Wells, "and the joints finally gave out. Later I understand he was on a farm his people left him." [DF]

Tony Bennett

Vocals.

b. New York, 13 Aug 1926.

The phrase "jazz singer" might defy precise definition (so, after all, does jazz), but there is no doubt that Tony Bennett (Anthony Dominick Benedetto) is a deeply jazz-influenced singer. He was discovered on the Arthur Godfrey Talent Scout show, after work as a singing waiter, and his hits began in 1951 with "Because Of You", followed by "Cold Cold Heart", "Rags To Riches", "Stranger In Paradise" and twenty more up to 1964. But the histrionic quality of some of these songs temporarily de-focused the image of a singer who was deeply influenced by Louis Armstrong and Billie Holiday amongst others. An early example of his jazz-related work was the album *Cloud Seven* (Columbia), which teamed him in jazz settings with guitarist Chuck Wayne and trumpeter Charles Panely, and over the ensuing decades Bennett regularly continued to seek out jazz company on and off the record. First and foremost is his longtime MD, the British jazz pianist Ralph Sharon, but the full roll call would include Count Basie and his orchestra, Bill Evans, Joe Marsala, Herbie Mann, Nat Adderley, Gene Krupa, Stan Getz, Chico Hamilton, Al Cohn and two incomparable cornet players – Ruby Braff and Bobby Hackett (who travelled regularly with Bennett and made two exquisite records with him, "The Very Thought Of You" and "Sleepy Time Gal"). For an artist who has never had difficulty landing a major-label contract, Bennett has also been generous in his associations with small-scale projects undertaken by jazz players, including Marian and Jimmy McPartland, for whom he recorded the delightful *Make Beautiful Music* collection. Bennett's extraordinary resurgence of popularity in the 1990s was largely due to undimmed talent cannily represented by his son Danny; the album *Unplugged* (with guests Elvis Costello and k.d. laing) helped reintroduce Bennett to a completely new generation of fans, and since then he has become classic American popular music's most powerful ambassador to the generations raised on rock. [DF]

⊙ **Bennett/Berlin** (1987; Columbia). Bennett, Gordon, Gillespie and Benson combine in a carefree salute to America's greatest popular composer.

⊙ **Perfectly Frank** (1992; Columbia). A weathered collection of Sinatra's torch and saloon songs, presented with a jazzman's panache.

⊙ **Unplugged** (1995; Columbia). Bennett doing what comes naturally in front of an audience of new youthful fans; a landmark in his career, this collection won a l995 Grammy award.

Han Bennink

Percussion, other instruments.

b. Zaandam, Netherlands, 17 April 1942.

Bennink started working with local groups in 1960, and from 1962–9 backed a range of visiting American musicians including Ben Webster, Don Byas, Johnny Griffin, Lee Konitz, Sonny Rollins, Dexter Gordon and Eric Dolphy, with whom he was recorded on the saxophonist's last visit to Europe. However, Bennink has mostly been identified with the free-improvisation scene in Europe, having contributed to some of the key performances in the evolution of that music, appearing on Peter Brötzmann's *Machine Gun* in 1968, and in the first performances of Derek Bailey's Company in the mid-1970s. He was part of the Dutch Instant Composers Pool with Misha Mengelberg and Willem Breuker, musicians with whom he shares an absurdist humour and with whom he has continued to collaborate; he worked in Breuker's parodic big band, and in the 1980s, in a rather more serious vein, produced a series of records with Mengelberg (and Steve Lacy and others) exploring the compositions of Monk and Herbie Nichols. He has done much small-group work and duos, often freely improvised, with players such as Brötzmann, Bailey, John Tchicai, Cecil Taylor, Don Cherry, Gary Peacock, Paul Bley and Evan Parker, and was the drummer for Andy Sheppard's Carla Bley-inspired *Soft On The Inside* big-band record. He can also be found in the Cluesone Trio, alongside the woodwinds of Michael Moore and Ernst Reijseger's cello.

Bennink, as the range of his work indicates, is a versatile percussionist; he has been influenced by African music, and traces of early jazz drum styles are evident in his playing, but his versatility does not stop at his drumming; he has been known to perform on banjo, clarinet (which he studied as a teenager), viola

JAK KILBY

Han Bennink

and other similarly disparate instruments, and has given solo performances without a drum kit in sight. The absence of a kit is not necessarily an impediment to Bennink the percussionist, however, as he stamps and bangs on anything that comes to hand or foot. His humour is best appreciated in performance, assuming due precaution is taken to avoid flying fragments of drum stick. [IC & RP]

Serpentine (1996; Songlines). Bennink the joker and debunker is here in duo with trumpeter Dave Douglas, one of the most original and consummate brass talents on the international jazz scene. Douglas also has an occasionally impish sense of humour, but the wellsprings of both men's music run deep and jokes are rationed in this meeting. Of the thirteen pieces, some were freely improvised, and there are anarchic performances of two standards, "Cherokee" and "Too Close For Comfort". A couple of the pieces, including the title track, were written by Douglas.

➤➤ **Derek Bailey** *(Han); Peter Brötzmann (Machine Gun; The Berlin Concert); Andy Sheppard (Soft On The Inside).*

David Benoit

Piano, keyboards.

b. Bakersfield, California, 18 Aug 1953.

Benoit became active in studio work in the 1970s, recording with, among others, drummer Alphonse Mouzon and touring with various singers. After five albums on small West Coast labels, the GRP company gave Benoit the chance to record in a variety of contexts, and become a popular exponent of contemporary MOR-fusion featuring acoustic piano rather than electronic instruments. His 1990 album *Waiting For Spring* enjoyed great success, and he has displayed considerable versatility in showcasing his "smooth-jazz" style. [BP]

Letter To Evan (1992; GRP). An untypical album which shows Benoit flexing his jazz muscles, with the title track and one other written by Bill Evans. Accompanists include guitarist Larry Carlton, also taking a break from fusion formulas.

George Benson

Guitar, vocals.

b. Pittsburgh, 22 March 1943.

After singing and playing ukulele as a child, Benson cut his first vocal records at eleven for an R&B label. Studying guitar from then on, Benson at nineteen was already touring with Jack McDuff's group, staying from 1962–5. In 1965 he formed his own quartet including Lonnie Smith on organ, going on to record under his own name and take part in the Spirituals to Swing Anniversary Concert in 1967. He then began a series of increasingly successful, basically instrumental middle-of-the-road albums, such as the record-breaking *Breezin'* of 1976. After that he concentrated increasingly on singing in a style closely modelled on Stevie Wonder and Donny Hathaway, but still looks back from time to time, and in 1990 recorded with the Count Basie band. Like Nat "King" Cole, an illustrious predecessor with a similar career pattern, many of his more commercial efforts include fine jazz solos, usually in unison with his scatting. And, especially in extended improvisation, the influence of Wes Montgomery and Tal Farlow still fires some remarkably fluent and inspired playing. [BP]

The New Boss Guitar (1964; Prestige/OJC). Unless the 1973 Casa Caribe live set shows up again, you have to go back to his early Jack McDuff period to get the full flavour of Benson's straightahead jazz playing.

Ivy Benson

Bandleader, saxophone, keyboards.

b. Leeds, Yorkshire, UK, 11 Nov 1913; d. 6 May 1993.

Remembered as the leader of a legendary all-woman orchestra, Benson began her career with Edna Croudson's Rhythm Girls in 1928; later she worked with Teddy Joyce and The Girl Friends, and Hylda Baker's "Meet The Girls" show. She formed her first band for Mecca Ballroom appearances in 1940 and led a resident band at the BBC three years later, also touring and playing concerts for the armed forces. Benson continued radio and TV work, and leading bands, into the 1980s, and in her last years appeared regularly as a soloist, playing piano and keyboards at Clacton-on-Sea, where she died. [GC]

Ivy Benson And Her All Girls Band 1943-48 (2000; Harlequin). A 23-track sampler of Benson's sweet swing in its wartime and post-war heyday.

Phillip Bent

Flute, alto flute, piccolo, keyboards.

b. London, 16 Sept 1964.

Bent started on flute at the age of twelve and had private flute lessons at seventeen. He also attended the jazz courses at the Weekend Arts College (WAC) at Interchange, North London, from 1982–6. He then studied for two years at the Guildhall School of Music. Bent rapidly developed into an extraordinary flute virtuoso and, at eighteen, began intermittent session work in the recording studios with groups such as Womack & Womack and guitarist Ronnie Jordan. He soon established himself as one of the leading members of the group of young black musicians who became prominent in the 1980s. He worked with the Jazz Warriors from 1986–9 and formed his own five-piece band in 1987, touring and playing at the Camden jazz festival. Also in 1987 he and two other members of the Jazz Warriors, saxophonists Steve Williamson and Courtney Pine, worked in London with Art Blakey's Jazz Messengers.

He managed to get his own recording facilities and sent finished demonstration tapes to GRP Records, who signed him up in 1992. Unfortunately, his already recorded tracks were overproduced, which dismayed him. After an argument over the concept of a follow-up album, the record company dropped him, a common setback which his remarkable talents should soon overcome. [IC]

The Pressure (1993; GRP). Hints of Bent's brilliance shine through the superimposed urban smog of fashionable but unhip hip-hop.

Bob Berg

Tenor and soprano saxophone.

b. Brooklyn, New York, 7 April 1951; d. 5 Dec 2002.

Berg played in a school band and began listening to jazz at the age of thirteen. He dropped out of the High School of Performing Arts, but then went to the Juilliard School for a year on a special non-academic music programme. Influenced by the later Coltrane, he became deeply involved in free jazz from 1966 to the end of the decade when, he told Mark Gilbert, "I got totally sick of free jazz and went back and really studied the classics like 1950s Miles and Coltrane, and the Bird things." To this end he worked with organist Jack McDuff in 1969 playing the Gene Ammons type of funkier tenor. Throughout the 1970s he wanted to play only acoustic bebop, and was deeply opposed to the jazz-rock music of the time. From 1974–6 he was with Horace Silver, and from 1976–81 in Cedar Walton's quartet, touring and playing festivals internationally. Berg lived and played in Europe from 1981–3, then returned to the USA in early 1984 to join Miles Davis. With Davis he toured worldwide, staying with the band until 1986. Talking of joining Davis's electric fusion group, Berg said, "I needed a change, and I always felt I had the ability to do it and not just play straightahead jazz. Playing with Miles is different from being in a fusion band because you don't have to play funk licks." After a stint with Chick Corea the 90s found Berg producing some of his most accomplished work: both *Riddles* (1994) and *Another Standard* (1996) were a delight.

Tragically, Berg was killed in a car accident at the end of 2002; his absence is sure to be felt in the jazz world. Bob Berg was one of the most gifted of the post-Coltrane generation of saxophonists, with a flawless technique, great harmonic awareness, a beautifully poised sense of time and a massive, emotive sound. [IC]

Short Stories (1987; Denon). The eight musicians involved in this album include Don Grolnick, Peter Erskine and Mike Stern, with David Sanborn having a cameo role on one track, "Kalimba". This is a production job (by Don Grolnick) with superb rhythms, intercomplementing electric instruments and longish written themes. It is brilliantly executed, Berg plays with great fire and contributes four attractive compositions, and the time-playing and dynamics are exquisite.

Riddles (1994; Stretch). This continues Berg's well-produced (this time by Jim Beard) and brilliantly realized fusion music. The personnel includes Beard on key boards, Gil Goldstein on accordion, guitarist John Herington, Steve Gadd, and percussionist/vocalist Arto Tuncboyaciyan. There's a subtle ethnic and country flavour to the music and some excellent compositions by James Taylor, Chick Corea and Pat Metheny among others. Berg plays consistently well, and the overall performance is impeccable.

Another Standard (1996; Stretch). This is primarily a quartet album with Berg leading pianist David Kikoski, bassist Ed Howard and drummer Gary Novak, but Randy Brecker is added on two tracks, "My Man's Gone Now" and "I Could Write A Book", and guitarist Mike Stern also on "No Trouble". Berg is in superb form as both leader and player throughout this inspired album.

Karl Berger

Piano, vibraphone, composer, percussion, educator.

b. Heidelberg, Germany, 30 March 1935.

Berger started on piano, taking up the vibes in 1960. He studied at Heidelberg Conservatory in 1948–54, then did a postgraduate course in musicology and sociology at the University of Heidelberg, obtaining his PhD in 1963. He was inspired to take up vibes by French vibist Michel Hausser, with whom he played in Germany and Paris. Berger was steeped in the work of Ornette Coleman, and he moved to Paris in March 1965, met Don Cherry and played with him for eighteen months. In the autumn of 1966 he played with Steve Lacy, then followed Cherry to New York working with him, Roswell Rudd, Marion Brown, David Izenzon, Sam Rivers and others. With drummer Horace Arnold, he played school and college concerts with a group funded by Young Audiences Inc from 1967–71, and also taught for two years at the New School for Social Research, conducting improvisation classes.

In 1971, with Coleman, Berger formed the Creative Music Foundation, moving in 1973 to Woodstock, where he set up the Creative Music Studio to give full-time classes in all aspects of music, including its relation to dance. More than thirty leading musicians have instructed there on a temporary basis, among them Sam Rivers, George Russell, Roscoe Mitchell, John Cage, Richard Teitelbaum, Lee Konitz and Steve Lacy, and they have usually created large orchestral works with the students.

Berger is a virtuoso player who has always been associated with the more abstract side of improvisation. He has led his own groups from time to time since 1966, has won several US jazz polls, and has toured extensively in Europe and Canada, playing many festivals. He has also recorded with Lee Konitz and John Surman. [IC]

⊙ **We Are You** (1971; Enja). A quartet album with Peter Kowald, drummer Allan Blairman and singer Ingrid Sertso.

⊙ **Transit** (1986; Black Saint). Berger in trio format with Dave Holland and Ed Blackwell, and such fast jazz company concentrates his mind wonderfully.

⊙ **Conversations** (1994; In + Out). Berger is here in a series of dialogues with individual musicians – trombonist Ray Anderson, saxophonist Carlos Ward, violinist Mark Feldman, guitarist James "Blood" Ulmer, bassist Dave Holland and vocalist Ingrid Sertso. The variety of both instrumental sound and the personalities of the guest "conversationalists" makes this an intriguing effort.

⊙ **No Man Is An Island** (1995; Douglas Music). The title is the well-known quote from John Donne's *Meditation XVII*, and this loose suite in nine parts was a radio commission for the annual music festival in the little South German town of Donaueschingen which, in 1954, was the first classical music festival in the world to include jazz in its programme. Berger's ensemble includes trumpeter Enrico Rava, Ingrid Sertso, plus French horn, saxophone, accordion, cello, bass, drums and a string trio. The sixth part of the suite is also a tribute to the memory of Don Cherry, who had died in October that year.

➤➤ **Don Cherry** *(Live At Montmartre Vols. 1 & 2).*

Jerry Bergonzi

Tenor saxophone; also piano, drums.

b. Boston, Massachusetts, 21 Oct 1947.

Bergonzi studied clarinet and alto from the age of eight, then took up the tenor at twelve, studying with instructors from Berklee College while in high school. He moved to New York in 1972 and began working with Tom Harrell, Harvie Swartz and others. In 1973 he joined the Two Generations Of Brubeck group, and later became a member of the Dave Brubeck quartet from 1979–81. Returning to Boston in 1981 to teach and play, he formed a quartet called Con Brio and the trio Gonz. He also started his own record label, overdubbing all the piano and drum parts for one album, and appeared on albums by Bennie Wallace and pianist Joey Calderazzo. Bergonzi, whose favourites include Coltrane, Rollins, Wayne Shorter and Joe Henderson, has a tough, uncompromising sound which effectively communicates his trenchant ideas. [BP]

⊙ **Lost In The Shuffle** (1998; Double-Time). The Gonz's second album with the duo of Adam Nussbaum and organist Dan Wall (who also work with John Abercrombie) finds him blowing creatively on some varied originals and "Have You Met Miss Jones?", adapted slightly to bring it closer to the "Giant Steps" chords that fascinate so many players.

Bunny Berigan

Trumpet, vocals.

b. Hilbert, Wisconsin, 2 Nov 1908; d. 2 June 1942.

At the start of his short career Bunny (Rowland Bernart) Berigan worked with college bands, and in 1928 was heard by bandleader Hal Kemp. Kemp's pianist John Scott Trotter (later Bing Crosby's MD) reports that "Kemp didn't hire Bunny, because he had the tinniest, most ear-splitting tone you ever heard", but two years later Berigan had acquired one of the hugest, most generous sounds any jazz trumpeter ever had and Kemp hired him for a trip to Europe and hotel work in New York.

In 1931 he joined Fred Rich's CBS studio band and continued working busily in studios before joining Paul Whiteman's highly successful, and by now very commercial, orchestra as a late replacement for Bix Beiderbecke. The arrangement was not a success: Berigan felt fettered by the limited solo space he was offered, disliked Whiteman's musical policy, and in any case was seldom happy working for others. So he left again and returned to studio work. By June 1935 he was playing for Benny Goodman (and drinking heavily) and he was in on that great night when Goodman, after ten months of touring, first sent the crowds wild at the Palomar Ballroom in Los Angeles. "When Bunny stood up and blew 'Sometimes I'm Happy' and 'King Porter Stomp' ", recalled Goodman, "the place exploded."

But Berigan had leadership ideas of his own. Trumpeter Pee Wee Erwin joined Goodman in Berigan's place, and in 1936, after a spell back in the studios and work in the evening for Red McKenzie, Berigan floated a big band: it sank at the rehearsal stage. Yet that year he topped the *Metronome* poll with five times as many votes as his nearest competitor (at a period when Louis Armstrong was at his peak) – a first recording of "I Can't Get Started", with a small group, had caught the public's attention. In June he began a set of appearances on the networked *Saturday Night Swing Club* for CBS. From 1937 Berigan's big band got on the road at last, and with it he was to record a second, definitive "I Can't Get Started", on 7 August 1937. It was to remain his

Max Jones Files Redferns

Bunny Berigan

classic. His live appearances too were often of unbeatable brilliance. "Bunny's band stole the show from us at the Savoy", recalls Haywood Henry, who was with Erskine Hawkins at the period. "There were only three bands that could do that: Duke, Lionel and Bunny. We didn't prepare for Bunny 'cos we thought we had him! But Buddy Rich and Georgie Auld were with him, and the house came down. As for Bunny I've no doubt he was the best white trumpeter."

At the end of 1940, however, Berigan was bankrupt, was drinking heavily, and (in the opinion of trumpet authority Charles Colin) may have been suffering spells of temporary mental imbalance. He rejoined Tommy Dorsey's band for six months, but on 20 August left abruptly after an NBC broadcast: "I couldn't bring him round," said hard-man Dorsey with an unfamiliar note of real regret, "so I had to let him go. I hated to do it." Berigan was Dorsey's most vital cornerman (his solos three years before on Dorsey sides like "Marie" had helped to seal his leader's future), but the role didn't suit his temperament. "There wasn't enough chance to play", he said irritably. "Most of the time I was just sitting there waiting for choruses." In 1941 George T. Simon reported on Berigan's newest band, and observed that Berigan had "lost at least thirty pounds" and put in a deputy for the first half of the show; Henry "Red" Allen observed that Berigan was now playing sitting down. On 1 June 1942 Berigan was scheduled to play at New York's Manhattan Center: the band turned up but Bunny never did. Seriously ill with cirrhosis and internal haemorrhaging (he had been drinking rotgut liquor in his last, poorer days), he was rushed to Polyclinic Hospital and died there. Tommy Dorsey paid the funeral expenses.

Louis Armstrong and Bunny Berigan may have been trumpet talents of a similar mettle but there the resemblance stopped. Armstrong was black; Berigan was white. Armstrong, underneath his easy-going bonhomie, had a streak of steel; Berigan had none. Armstrong saw his career as a "hustle", a means of survival to be jealously guarded; Berigan, for whom most things from trumpet playing to women came easily, looked at life more casually. Armstrong's solos were polished setpieces; Berigan's were audacious creations which either equalled Armstrong's for technique and inspiration or developed so fast that they aborted. Berigan remains, with Bix Beiderbecke, the trumpet tragedy of the 1930s: a super-talent which, like Beiderbecke's, blew itself away too soon, leaving Armstrong at the top of the heap. Armstrong's tribute offers a rare criticism of his rival: "Bunny was great, but he had no business dying *that* young." [DF]

⦿ **Portrait** (1932–7; ASV Living Era). Bunny in a variety of settings, including with Connee Boswell, Gene Gifford, Benny Goodman and Bud Freeman; contains the indispensable big-band "I Can't Get Started".

⦿ **Bunny And Red** (1935–6; Archives of Jazz). Fine collection of McKenzie-Berigan collaborations with Carmen Mastren, Forrest Crawford and others.

⦿ **Bunny Berigan 1935–6/1936–37/1937/1937–38/1938/1938–42** (Classics). Six CDs following Berigan's recorded career as a bandleader from start to finish, and quite the best chronology so far, with all his greatest sides from "I Can't Get Started" to the rarely heard big-band Beiderbecke settings.

⦿ **Bunny Berigan And The Rhythm Makers: Vol. 1** (1936 & 1938; Jass). In company with the likes of Artie Shaw and Georgie Auld, Berigan is outstanding on these recordings from NBC transcriptions.

Sonny Berman

Trumpet.

b. New Haven, Connecticut, 21 April 1924; d. 16 Jan 1947.

Named Saul by his parents, the young Berman played as a teenager with big bands led by such as Tommy Dorsey and Benny Goodman. He was working with the Woody Herman band at the time of his death following a drug overdose. One of the promising young soloists of the "Second Herd", Sonny makes his fiery, Gillespie-inspired presence felt on a small number of Herman band and small-group tracks, and on one informal session (see below). [BP]

⦿ **Woodchopper's Holiday** (1946; Cool And Blue). The only competing disc is a Dial studio session that's usually reissued under Serge Chaloff's name, which gives a lesser account of Berman's potential than this private apartment jam, also with Chaloff and Ralph Burns. The CD adds ten tracks with Herman's small group and big band.

Tim Berne

Alto and baritone saxophones.

b. Syracuse, New York, 16 Oct 1954.

Berne started playing saxophone in high school. Inspired initially by a run of concerts he attended by Sun Ra's Arkestra, he pursued jazz, moving to New York in 1974 by way of California. There, he studied briefly with Anthony Braxton and at greater length with the late Julius Hemphill, whose blues-saturated playing and compositional approach deeply influenced him. Berne released his first records on his own label, Empire; subsequent work on Soul Note involved groups with a variety of players including drummers Paul Motian and Joey Baron, trumpeter Herb Robertson, trombonist Ray Anderson, and cellist Hank Roberts. These colourful ensembles enabled Berne to explore a wide range of compositional and improvisational strategies, including long-form, multi-sectional suites. In 1987, Berne released the critically lauded *Sanctified Dreams* as part of a short deal with the major label Columbia Records. He teamed up with Joey Baron and Hank Roberts – a trio named Miniature – in 1988, and was also a member of John Zorn's hardcore Ornette Coleman project, *Spy Vs. Spy*. Berne started a new label named Screwgun in 1996, releasing records by his groups Paraphrase and Bloodcount, as well as outings by Marc Ducret, Michael Formanek, Django Bates, and reissuing Blue Boyé by his original mentor Hemphill. Many of his projects overlap co-collaborators past and present: his albums *Science Friction* and *The Sevens* (2002) both used the charismatic sound (and occasional co-composition) of producer David Torn, and both were bolstered by virtuosi of the Screwgun stable. [JC]

⊙ **The Shell Game** (2001; Thirsty Ear). Dense, muscular corkscrews of fusion reminiscent of Ornette Coleman's Tone Dialling (or Steve Coleman's M-Base) are juxtaposed with ambient electronics evocative of Tibetan temple music: a funky, medicinal experience.

Bloodcount

⊙ **Unwound** (1996; Screwgun). Ambitious live three-disc set of Berne's working group with reedsman Chris Speed, Formanek on bass and hyper-intense Jim Black on drums. Long, winding, circuitous pieces with lots of open improvising and involved unison sections. Packaged, like all Screwgun products, in pleasingly grungy brown cardboard cover.

Clyde Bernhardt

Trombone, vocals.

b. Goldhill, North Carolina, 11 July 1905; d. 20 May l986.

A fine swing trombonist and veteran of touring shows in the early 1920s, Bernhardt moved to New York in 1928, joined King Oliver in 1931, worked with Marion Hardy's Alabamians, then spent three years with Vernon Andrade (1934–7). Thereafter he worked regularly for Edgar Hayes, Cecil Scott, Luis Russell, Claude Hopkins and Dud Bascomb, among others, and by the 1950s was leading his own R&B-slanted groups around clubs. In the late 1960s he attracted more attention with his Harlem Blues and Jazz Band, featuring Viola Wells (professionally known as "Miss Rhapsody"), who until then had turned up only on a few obscure recordings for Savoy in the 1940s. The outfit, containing seasoned veterans like Franc Williams (trumpet, ex-Duke Ellington), Charlie Holmes (alto) and Tommy Benford (drums), recorded, toured and achieved huge publicity, due in part to a British champion, critic Derrick Stewart-Baxter. In the 1980s Bernhardt was touring with the Legends Of Jazz, and his ex-band was successful still, touring with Al Casey and pianist Gene Rodgers and sometimes with British honorary members like Roy Williams, Danny Moss, Stan Greig and Jim Shepherd. [DF]

Bill Berry

Trumpet, cornet, flugelhorn, composer, leader; also vibes.

b. Benton Harbor, Michigan, 14 Sept 1930; ; d. 13 Nov 2002.

A young veteran of Duke Ellington's orchestra, which he joined in 1962, Berry worked in studios for much of the 1960s (including Merv Griffin's TV show, for which Bobby Rosengarden was MD), then in 1971 formed the LA Big Band, a highly successful aggregation. In the 1970s and 80s he developed a solo career, made small-group recordings and undertook European tours, on which his schooled approach (absorbing mainstream influences from Armstrong to Joe Newman), creative flair and reliability won him a big reputation. In 1985 he was in Britain to work London venues, and thereafter he made regular appearances around the international festival circuit, as well as directing the Monterey jazz festival All Stars. In 1991 he led his LA Big Band at the annual Duke Ellington conference in Los Angeles. [DF]

⊙ **Hello Rev** (1976; Concord). Perhaps the best-known Berry album, leading his LA Big Band in a highly enjoyable and mainly Ellington programme.

Chu Berry

Tenor saxophone.

b. Wheeling, West Virginia, 13 Sept 1910; d. 30 Oct 1941.

Leon Berry arrived in New York in 1930, carrying his tenor in a red velvet bootbag and wearing a goatee beard which earned him the nickname "Chu" after Billy Stewart remarked that Berry looked like Chu Chin Chow. After spells with several bands (including immortal recordings with Spike Hughes's pick-up bands for Decca) he majored with Benny Carter and Teddy Hill at the Savoy, and in November 1935, against offers from Duke Ellington, he joined Fletcher Henderson. By then he had become close friends with the young Roy Eldridge ("When Fletcher wanted Chu he had to take Roy too", recalls Walter C. Allen) and the two would terrorize New York jam sessions after hours, cutting down opposition with deadly skill. Berry's style – "based on riff patterns and speed", according to Milt Hinton – was spotted by Hinton's new boss Cab Calloway, who hired him in 1937. Berry became vital to Calloway's entourage, and not just for his well-nigh unbeatable tenor skills. "Chu was very frank and Cab liked him", says Hinton. "He was a swapper, a real saving-man, and he used to swap arrangements with Chick Webb which he thought would fit Cab's band. He was very much responsible for us having good music in the band. Chu had the kind of confidence that made Cab listen."

Fortunately, Berry recorded prolifically, with Eldridge, with Lionel Hampton and with Calloway on at least one classic outing, "I Don't Stand A Ghost Of A Chance With You". When he died four days after suffering severe head injuries in a car crash with Andy Brown, another Calloway saxophonist, it was for Calloway "like losing a brother, someone I had joked with and hollered at. There was a quiet around the band for weeks and we left his chair empty."

Chu Berry is still underrated. He was the only jazz tenor saxophonist who presented a real challenge to the omnipotent Coleman Hawkins on Hawkins's full-blown, fast-fingered terms, although Berry's sound was in some ways different from his rival's: blowzier, fuller, with a more emotive vibrato and a strange crying sound in his frequently used upper register. But he died young without being different enough from Hawkins to be regarded as an alternative, and he missed the late 1940s' onset of jazz intellectualism by a few years. Also, he worked, by and large, in second-rank bands. But he was – the ultimate accolade – a musician's musician. "Chu was about the best," said Coleman Hawkins. **[DF]**

⊙ **Blowing Up A Breeze** (1933–41;Topaz). Excellent and comprehensive collection, spanning Berry's entire career, and including his classic "Ghost Of A Chance" with Cab Calloway.

⊙ **Chu Berry Story 1936–39** (Jazz Archives). Excellent Berry portrait, with Gene Krupa, Wingy Manone, Lionel Hampton and others.

⊙ **Chu Berry 1937–41** (Classics). Classics have started on Berry now and there are important performances here with Roty Eldridge, Buster Bailey, Benny Payne, Sid Catlett and including Berry's challenging version of "Body And Soul".

⊙ **Giants Of The Tenor Sax** (1938 & '41; Commodore). This CD features sides recorded with Roy Eldridge, Hot Lips Page and others just before Berry's death, including "Body And Soul" and "On The Sunny Side Of The Street".

➤➤ **Cab Calloway** *(Cab Calloway And His Orchestra).*

Emmett Berry

Trumpet.

b. Macon, Georgia, 23 July 1915.

Berry's fiery, full-toned and flawless playing was enough to guarantee him the soloist's chair with Fletcher Henderson (1936–9), replacing Roy Eldridge – a formidable challenge. From short stints with Horace Henderson and Earl Hines he moved to Teddy Wilson's Café Society sextet for two years of radio, records and live dates, and then to Raymond Scott's much publicized CBS band – the first integrated band of its kind. From 1945–50 Berry worked with Count Basie, then with Buck Clayton in the legendary small band that Jimmy Rushing led at the Savoy. He toured from 1951–4 with Johnny Hodges' fine small band, then in 1955 with Sammy Price's Bluesicians in Europe (*A Real Jam Session*, a rare album by Price, is a copybook sample of Berry at his best); all through the decade he took part in countless jazz and session recordings in New York and Los Angeles with everyone from Count Basie to Gil Evans (admirers may have spotted him backing Miles Davis in Evans's orchestra on a New York TV show). In the 1960s Berry was busily freelancing still, but in 1970 he retired to Cleveland, and jazz has been the poorer for his absence. Like Bobby Hackett, Dick Ruedebusch and Joe Wilder, he deserves to be more than a trumpet-specialist's delight. **[DF]**

Sammy Price

⊙ **Sam Price And His Bluesicians** (1955; Vogue). Berry at unfailingly high level amid the Bluesicians – fat-toned, rhythmically immaculate and flexibly creative.

⊙ **The Price Is Right!** (1956; Jazztone). Berry was a regular colleague of Sammy Price, and he's in typically good form on this live session with Herbie Hall, George Stevenson and Pops Foster.

Steve Berry

Bass, bass guitar, cello.

b. Gosport, Hampshire, UK, 24 Aug 1957.

Although he first came to public attention as a founder member of the Loose Tubes big band, Steve Berry began as a singer/guitarist in Shropshire. Extremely active in jazz education in the north of England, and a prolific composer, he is a virtuosic but utterly dependable bassist, active in musical fields ranging from big bands to cross-arts projects involving dancers, poets and dramatists. Berry was at the heart of Loose Tubes, as both a composer and bassist, and formed the Steve Berry Trio in 1988 with fellow band member and saxophonist Mark Lockheart and drummer Peter Fairclough. He has also played and recorded with maverick guitarist Billy Jenkins, appearing on four of his Voice Of God Collective albums; with trumpeter Ian Carr; with Django Bates's Powder Room Collapse Orchestra; with numerous singers, including Dagmar Krause and June Tabor; and he is a member of Mike Westbrook's Big Band, and trumpeter Steve Plews's Ascension (with whom he recorded 1995's *Live in Manchester*). In 1996, he toured with Westbrook's "Bar Utopia" project, and the following year recorded *Berlin Cabaret Songs* with Ute Lemper and the Matrix Ensemble, and toured with US pianist

Jessica Williams. Based in the north of England, he is locally and nationally active in the promotion of what he likes to call "Practical and Creative Musicianship" (as opposed to "Improvisation", which he judges too intimidating) and runs Jam Factory, a community-based creative jazz orchestra involving twenty-three members, including his entire family (four children and his partner Cats, who plays tenor). They recently released a double CD of Berry's compositions, *Fruits of 2002* (2002; rfm), featuring guest contributions from Iain Dixon and Chris Batchelor. [CP/CI]

Trio (1988; Loose Tubes). Berry wrote all but one of the pieces for this trio, and his bass also anchors the album, which covers ground between funk and hard bop.

Snap (1998; Room for Music). Self-produced album by Berry's band Foolish Hearts (pianist Nikki Iles, vibraphone player Anthony Kerr, percussionist Paul Clarvis, alongside Berry on bass). Multi-textured, thoughtful but wholly enjoyable music mostly written by Berry himself.

➤➤ **Loose Tubes** *(Open Letter).*

Vic Berton

Drums, percussion, vibes.

b. Chicago, 6 May 1896; d. 26 Dec 1951.

Vic Berton (Victor Cohen) had played percussion in the Alhambra Theater, Milwaukee, by the time he was eight, and during World War I he played for Sousa's navy band – so by 1924, when he took over the drum stool of the Wolverines from Vic Moore (as well as the management, briefly), he was already a senior figure in the jazz firmament. Berton's recorded work with Red Nichols and others made him the best-remembered white jazz drummer of the 1920s and helped to pave the way for later "personality drummers" such as Gene Krupa. From 1930, after work with Roger Wolfe Kahn, Paul Whiteman and others, he moved into studio work at Paramount and later Twentieth Century Fox. Berton was a powerful personality, a cocksure businessman with a fast-talking line in hard sell. His larger-than-life reputation grew after 1931, when he was arrested for smoking marijuana with Louis Armstrong, and Frank Driggs records that Berton regularly dabbled in occultism and "often greeted his students in flowing black robes". [DF]

Red Nichols and his Five Pennies

Rhythm Of The Day (1925–38; ASV/LivingEra). Berton at his percussionistic peak with Nichols's Five Pennies and orchestra and Miff Mole's Molers; Berton's skills well to the fore on "Boneyard Shuffle" plus other classics including "Feelin' No Pain".

Denzil Best

Drums, composer.

b. New York, 27 April 1917; d. 24 May 1965.

Denzil DaCosta Best took up drums only in 1943, after playing piano, trumpet and bass. He worked with Ben Webster in 1943–4, Coleman Hawkins in 1944–5, Illinois Jacquet in 1946 and Chubby Jackson in 1947, and also recorded with musicians such as Lee Konitz. After a record date with George Shearing in 1948, he became a founder member of Shearing's quintet (1949–52), a phase terminated by a car accident. He then played with the Artie Shaw group in 1954 and Erroll Garner's trio from 1955–7, and did further gigs with Nina Simone and Tyree Glenn. Best was gradually crippled by calcium deposits in his wrists, and died after falling down steps in the New York subway. In his heyday a driving but discreet drummer, he specialized in playing with brushes rather than sticks. He was also the composer of such bebop anthems as "Move", "Wee" (aka "Allen's Alley") and "Dee Dee's Dance"; his tune "45 Degree Angle" was recorded by Herbie Nichols and Mary Lou Williams, and he co-wrote "Bemsha Swing" with Thelonious Monk, his colleague in the 1944 Hawkins group. [BP]

➤➤ **Erroll Garner** *(Concert By The Sea).*

Johnny Best

Trumpet.

b. Shelby, North Carolina, 20 Oct 1913; d. 19 Sept 2003.

Johnny Best started his career with a young Les Brown in 1934, going on to work during the war with a string of top-ranking swing bands, including Artie Shaw, Charlie Barnet, Glenn Miller and the US Navy band. Like Billy Butterfield, for whom he subbed later in the World's Greatest Jazz Band, Best combined the strength of a lead trumpeter with high-powered solo ability (a valuable and by no means commonplace double talent), and with all the above bands his intense rather Butterfield-like solo work was featured heavily. After the war, Best worked with Benny Goodman, joined NBC for studio work, played regularly for leaders such as Jerry Gray, Billy May (an old friend) and Bob Crosby (with whom he toured Japan in 1964), and worked in nightclubs such as the Honeybucket in San Diego. A regular associate of the World's Greatest Jazz Band in the 1970s, Best was still playing regularly in the 1980s despite a serious fall in 1982, which confined him to a wheelchair; in 1992 he visited Britain to play with a Glenn Miller Alumni Reunion for BBC Radio 2. "A sort of cross between Bunny Berigan and Bobby Hackett", said George Chisholm of one of the best and most underrated swing trumpeters. [DF]

Ed Bickert

Guitar.

b. Hochfeld, nr Winnipeg, Manitoba, 29 Nov 1932.

Ed Bickert worked regularly in Toronto from the 1950s with clarinettist Phil Nimmons and reedman Moe Koffman, then with trombonist Rob McConnell and Paul Desmond in the 1970s. Yet in the mid-1970s Leonard Feather was still able to say that his reputation was "mainly local, but he is highly regarded by the Americans who have played with him". In the mid-1970s Bickert formed his own trio and toured the USA with Paul Desmond, then in 1983 a Concord album with Rosemary Clooney (*Sings Harold Arlen*) unobtrusively introduced his talents to a wider audience. His quiet assurance and flowing lines (recalling Kenny Burrell and Jim Hall as much as Charlie Christian) showed up on equal terms with better-recognized players such as Dave McKenna and Jake Hanna, and quickly turned him into a new international star at over fifty. From then on Bickert appeared regularly on Concord, with Scott Hamilton and Warren Vaché, and frequently as a leader and soloist in his own right. In the 1990s Bickert has continued to record for Concord and to appear internationally as well as in and around Toronto. [DF]

⊙ **Mutual Street** (1982–4; Jazz Alliance). A duet album with valve trombonist Rob McConnell; superbly musical and technically flawless.

⊙ **I Wished On The Moon** (1986; Concord). A fine example of Bickert's talents as leader and soloist.

⊙ **This Is New** (1990; Concord). An excellent collaboration between old-master Bickert and new-arrival guitarist Lorne Lofsky, frequent duettists on the Toronto club-scene.

Barney Bigard

Clarinet, tenor saxophone.

b. New Orleans, 3 March 1906; d. 27 June 1980.

Barney (Albany Leon) Bigard was taught clarinet by Lorenzo Tio Jnr, the finest teacher in New Orleans, but early in his career bought a new "novelty instrument", a tenor saxophone, and featured himself in a slap-tonguing duo with bandleader/clarinettist Albert Nicholas at Tom Anderson's Café in New Orleans. Soon after, late in 1924, the two of them were invited to join King Oliver in Chicago's Plantation Club; Oliver bought Bigard a brand new Albert-system clarinet and hired him as a clarinettist. When Oliver found himself short of work in 1927, Bigard freelanced, then joined Duke Ellington in New York for his first Cotton Club season. "Barney had that woody tone that Pop always adored", said Mercer Ellington, and he had something else besides: a creative imagination for inventions which later became a part of Ellington compositions. Theme two of "Mood Indigo", the athletic opening of "East St Louis Toodle-oo" (a routine for comedian "Pigmeat" Markham) and "C-Jam Blues" were all derived from Bigard contributions to the creative free-for-all that was the early Ellington band. "Ellington's got Barney Bigard, a good New Orleans boy sitting right by him telling him what to do", said Jelly Roll Morton, a mischievous overstatement which had a germ of truth in it.

Bigard left Ellington in 1942, having helped create classics like "Barney Goin' Easy!", "Across The Track Blues" and "Clarinet Lament" (his favourites). After relaunching and recording with Kid Ory, and playing a part in the film *New Orleans* (1947), he joined Louis Armstrong and his All Stars for five happy years. During that time his translucent tone, snaky mobility and celebrated "waterfalls" were integral to Armstrong's show, but by the time he departed Bigard was exhausted by travel and drink. After a rest and spells with Ben Pollack and Cozy Cole he was back with Louis again in 1960 (and, for Trummy Young, "sounding a whole lot better than before"), but left again in autumn 1961. Freelancing followed, and though he gave up full-time music in 1965 he still came back regularly for tours, guest appearances and radio and TV work, until his death in 1980. He was perhaps the greatest Tio pupil of all; moreover, in the words of Jo Jones – "Barney made the clarinet famous. This was *before* Benny Goodman." [DF]

➤➤ **Louis Armstrong** *(Louis Armstrong Plays W.C. Handy)*; **Duke Ellington** *(The Duke's Men: Small Groups Vols. 1 & 2)*.

Acker Bilk

Clarinet, vocals, bandleader.

b. Pensford, Somerset, UK, 28 Jan 1929.

Acker (Bernard Stanley) Bilk began his career in the mid-1950s working with Ken Colyer, and soon after formed his own band. "Summer Set", co-written by Bilk and pianist Dave Collett, climbed to number eight in the British hit parade, and Bilk's band shot to success, aided by publicist Peter Leslie, who clothed them in Edwardian outfits and bowler hats. (He was later to work for the Beatles.) Bilk was the biggest star of Britain's trad boom, producing a string of shuffle-beat hits (recalling one of his favourites, Louis Prima) and, most significant of all, "Stranger On The Shore", a track which Bilk wrote for his daughter Jenny and was later used in a children's TV serial – he calls it "my old-age pension". His band played in films and on TV and radio until the advent of the Beatles, when Bilk moved into cabaret, played jazz clubs on spare nights, and built up a strong following in Europe. His band of the late 1960s (featuring Bruce Turner and trumpeter-MD Colin Smith, as well as pianist-arranger Barney Bates) was one of the best-ever British mainstream bands. In the 1970s Bilk was still leading his jazz band, and recording with them and with large string orchestras – he easily surpasses Bobby Hackett as the jazzman to have recorded most with strings. Another hit, "Aria", came in 1976. After Rod Mason left the band, Bilk hired a much underrated British trumpeter, Mike Cotton, and trombonist/singer Campbell Burnap replaced longtime sideman Johnny Mortimer; following their departure early in the 1990s Mick Cooke (trombone) and longtime co-leader Colin Smith became his frontline partners; Bilk has now marginally cut his schedules in order to concentrate on a second love, painting (like Tony

Bennett he is a gifted artist), but still tours regularly with longtime sidemen Cooke, pianist Colin Wood and drummer Ritchie Bryant, joined by newcomers Malcolm Creese (double bass) and Enrico Tomasso (trumpet).

Critical tendencies to underrate Bilk's playing simply because of his popularity are misplaced, but regrettably widespread. One of the best-known and best-loved of British jazzmen, Bilk is a jazz clarinettist of world class, blessed (as Humphrey Lyttelton has described it) with "that 'here's me' quality of originality in his soloing". [DF]

At Sundown (1992; Calligraph). Bilk and Humphrey Lyttelton on the latter's own label, in an overdue collaboration by two of the great voices of British traditional jazz; with Dave Cliff, Dave Green and Bobby Worth.

Chalumeau – That's My Home (1993; Apricot Music). Fine, high-powered example of a Bilk band recorded live.

David Binney

Alto saxophone.

b. Miami, Florida, Aug 2 1961.

Raised in Ventura, California, Binney moved to New York in 1981, where he has worked with a cross-section of electric and acoustic jazz ensembles. He studied with Phil Woods, Dave Liebman and George Coleman. A member of Windham Hill group Lost Tribe, which has recorded a self-titled record (1993) and *Soulfish* (1994), Binney has also recorded with the popular funky soul-jazz trio Medeski Martin & Wood on *It's A Jungle In Here* (1994; Gramavision), and as a sideman on bassist Lonnie Plaxico's *Short Takes* (1993; Muse) and *Dreamtime* (1993; Fibre Records). He's been a member of the Marvin "Smitty" Smith Electric Band, Global Theory, Maria Schneider's critically acclaimed orchestra, Drew Gress's Jagged Sky, and has played in the Gil Evans Orchestra under the direction of Miles Evans. Binney has contributed to recent recordings by Chris Potter (*Traveling Mercies*, 2002) and John Zorn (*Voices In The Wilderness*, 2003) and under his own leadership he has released *Point Game* (1991; Owl), *The Luxury Of Guessing* (1995; Audioquest) and *Free To Dream* (1998; Mythology), the latter on his own label. Signing to German label ACT in the early 2000s, Binney produced *South* (see below) and *Balance* (2002). [JC]

South (2001; ACT). Original, adept and free-thinking music, unencumbered by stylistic conformity and full of imagination. A stellar supporting cast includes saxist Chris Potter, pianist Uru Caine and drummer Brian Blade.

Chris Biscoe

Alto, soprano and baritone saxophones, alto clarinet, piccolo, flute, tenor sax.

b. East Barnet, Herts, UK, 5 Feb 1947.

Biscoe started on alto in 1963 and is entirely self-taught. After studying English and education at Sussex University from 1965–8, he moved to London. He played with the National Youth Jazz Orchestra from 1970–73, and then began working professionally with various London groups. In 1969 he began composing and writing music for his own occasional groups. Since 1979 he has worked with Mike Westbrook's various bands, touring throughout Europe, playing international festivals in Australia, Singapore, Hong Kong, Canada and the USA, and making a major contribution to many of Westbrook's recordings. He formed his own quartet in 1979 with Peter Jacobsen on piano, and added Italian trombonist Danilo Terenzi in 1986 for a tour, recording and broadcast. The quartet Full Monte, formed in 1988 by Biscoe, guitarist Brian Godding, bassist Marcio Mattos and drummer Tony Marsh, toured the UK in 1993 and released an album the following year. In 1992 Biscoe had also formed a quintet which included Marsh and trumpeter/cellist Paul Jayasinha.

From 1983–93 Biscoe also toured nationally and internationally with the Brotherhood Of Breath. He has worked and recorded with George Russell's Anglo-American Living Time Orchestra, in 1994 toured the UK with Hermeto Pascoal's big band, and has also played regularly in France and elsewhere with Didier Levallet. In the later 1990s, Biscoe was very active, working with the Ben Davis Quartet (1994–9), and the band Mingus Moves, which included pianist Veryan Weston and trumpeter Henry Lowther. He worked with the French Orchestre National de Jazz (1997–9), and in 1998 Biscoe and his group Full Monte collaborated with The Blowpipes, a trombone trio, performing concerts together, with music co-written by Biscoe and Blowpipes trombonist Mark Bassey. In 1999, Biscoe joined trumpeter Harry Beckett's band making it a quintet, and they recorded an album, *A Tribute to Charles Mingus* (1999; Basic), which was followed by *Before And After* in 2001. With the Orchestre National de Jazz, Biscoe recorded the album *ONJ Express* (1997; Evidence), and with the Ben Davis quartet, *Double Dares Are Sometimes Different* (1996; FMR).

Biscoe is a saxophone virtuoso of great lyricism, passion, stamina and considerable versatility. He is steeped in the jazz tradition and his conception embraces everything from blues and gospel roots to free improvisation and jazz-rock. [IC]

Chris Biscoe Sextet

Chris Biscoe Sextet (1986; Walking Wig). Five of the six pieces on this set were composed by Biscoe, and the music is freeish but organized and coherent.The rhythm-section is excellent and high spots are the bravura opening piece, "Granada", which features the whole sextet; "South Ghost", which is a gloriously lyrical alto and piano duo performance; and "I Porcellini" (young pigs), which features a wonderfully gruff and grunting duet by Biscoe (on baritone sax) and Terenzi.

Full Monte

Spark In The Dark (1994; Slam). All seven compositions are attributed collectively to the four members of the group and, for once, this kind of aesthetic democracy seems to work well. The collective rapport is excellent, tension is created and released satisfactorily, and each man sounds inspired. Biscoe is in tremendous form, and Brian Godding's dynamic guitar contributions are unfailingly apt.

➤➤ **Chris McGregor** *(Country Cooking)*; **George Russell** *(The London Concert)*; **Mike Westbrook** *(London Bridge Is Broken Down)*; **Harry Beckett** *(A Tribute to Charles Mingus)*; **George Russell Living Time Orchestra** *(It's About Time)*.

Walter Bishop Jnr

Piano.

b. New York, 4 Oct 1927; d. 24 Jan 1998.

The son of the Jamaican-born songwriter of the same name (composer of "Swing, Brother, Swing"), Walter Bishop was an early disciple of Bud Powell, becoming the pianist most frequently employed by Charlie Parker during the first half of the 1950s, when he also recorded with Miles Davis. After teaching at the University of Hartford in the 1980s under Jackie McLean, he was still active in the 1990s as both soloist and sideman, bringing an authentic bebop feel to any situation. Stylistically important for his incorporation of Erroll Garner's right-hand chording into the bop piano style, he influenced Red Garland and those who followed him, but his work has been unjustly neglected. [BP]

⊙ **What's New** (1990; DIW). After not recording in his own right for a decade, Bishop suddenly emerged with this excellent trio session featuring Kenny Washington and bassist Peter Washington, taking standards and classic jazz originals such as "Una Mas" and showing how creative he could be within a well-worn formula.

➤➤ **Charlie Parker** *(South Of The Border)*; **Ken McIntyre** *(Looking Ahead)*.

Raoul Bjorkenheim

Guitar, composer.

b. Los Angeles, 11 Feb 1956.

Having travelled extensively with his parents (his mother was an internationally acclaimed actress and singer) Bjorkenheim eventually settled in Finland in his teens. Inspired by Jimi Hendrix, he took up the guitar and enrolled at the Helsinki Conservatory. In 1976 he founded the group Arbuusi, but then decided to make a trip to the USA, where he took private guitar lessons in New York, and studied composition at the Berklee School of Music in Boston. He graduated from Berklee in 1981 and returned to Finland to continue working with Arbuusi and other musicians. After a year or two, Bjorkenheim began working and recording with legendary Finnish composer/drummer, Edward Vesala, playing on three of his albums, *Bad Luck Good Luck* (1983), *Kullervo* (1985) and *Lumi* (1987). He also became a touring member of Vesala's group, Sound & Fury, for two years. In 1985, he founded Krakatau, the group for which he is best known, and which has been described as "a satellite group to Edward Vesala's Sound & Fury", the initial band having featured Vesala on drums. Bjorkenheim led various editions of Krakatau, with many of Finland's finest young musicians passing through the line-up, together with international stars, including Ronald Shannon Jackson, Anthony Braxton and Muhal Richard Abrams. Bjorkenheim has also composed music for dance, and premiered a major work for the Finnish big band, UMO. But Krakatau has remained the principal focus of his activities. In 1990 they performed at the Helsinki Sea jazz festival and also played their first festivals abroad, in Le Mans, France, and Moers, Germany.

Bjorkenheim's work with Krakatau has produced a dynamic amalgam of rock, jazz, free jazz and ethnic elements, as characterized by the group's first album, *Ritual*. For their second album, *Alive* (1990), the group was pared down to a trio, which recorded a high-energy live concert. Then in 1992, they began recording for ECM. More recently Bjorkenheim has toured with the Swedish jazz group Surge and has contributed to Paul Schutze's Phantom City project; the latter collaboration has since led Bjorkenheim to work with legendary producer Bill Laswell. [IC]

⊙ **Volition** (1992; ECM). The other three members of this edition of Krakatau – Jone Takamaki (tenor sax and ethnic instruments), Uffe Krokfors (bass) and Alf Forsman (drums) – had also worked with Edward Vesala. Much of this album, including the title track, is in the often dour, uncompromising free-jazz tradition, but the opening piece, "Brujo", concludes with a slow, hypnotic dance rhythm and some lyrical guitar. "Nai" and "Dalens Ande" are coherent free ballads, and "Changgo" has some powerfully plangent slow single-string guitar.

⊙ **Matinale** (1993; ECM). Percussionist Ippe Katka replaces Forsman, but the personnel is otherwise as above. This album is much more musical and varied in approach. There is more light and shade, a greater emphasis on different textures, and a stronger melodic content. The title track features affecting sax and guitar melodies over rolling bass and drums, "Jai Ping" has a clear swinging and rocking rhythm, "For Bernard Moore" combines attractive melodic motifs with unambiguous rhythms and strong improvising, and "Sarajevo" is a deeply felt, ominous anti-war tone poem.

Black Artists Group

The Black Artists Group (BAG) was a short-lived vanguard jazz union formed in St Louis, Missouri, in 1968. Founding members included drummers Phillip Wilson, Charles "Bobo" Shaw, and Abdullah Yakub, saxophonists Oliver Lake and Julius Hemphill, trumpeter Floyd LeFlore, and poet, actor, and director Ajule Rutlin; other members included trombonist Joseph Bowie, reedmen Hamiet Bluiett, Marty Ehrlich, Luther Thomas and J.D. Parran, and trumpeter Baikida Carroll. Modelled in part on Chicago's pioneering Association for the Advancement of Creative Musicians (AACM), BAG made an effort to be more interdisciplinary, incorporating dance, poetry, theatre and performance, and visual art. The organization, per se, disbanded in the early 70s when funding dried up and most of the principal members moved to New York. [JC]

Black Benny

Drums.

Place of birth and dates unknown.

A legendary bass drummer around 1915 with the New Orleans Brass Band, Black Benny (Benny Williams) supposedly played louder and stronger than any other in the city. One of Louis Armstrong's early minders (he appears in Satchmo's autobiography), Benny was a lowlife who spent regular time in jail and was sometimes released by the police for important parades. But he carried a gun and on one occasion at least shot a bystander during a Canal Street march-past. "Benny got killed", recalls Pops Foster. "He hit this woman and then turned his back on her and she cut him down." [DF]

Jim Black

Drums.

b. Seattle, 1967.

Raised in Seattle, Jim Black grew up playing in a wide range of stylistic arenas, especially rock and jazz. He moved to Boston in 1985 and began studies at Berklee College of Music, and while there he studied privately with Jeff "Tain" Watts, Joe Hunt and Jeff Hamilton. Black subsequently settled in New York, where he has quickly become one of the most in-demand drummers both on the downtown creative music scene and on the more adventurous side of the straightahead jazz scene. He has worked steadily with saxophonist Tim Berne in different combinations, most notably in the group Bloodcount (which has recorded six CDs), and is co-leader of the ensembles Human Feel and Pachora; he composes for both these groups. He is also a regular member of trumpeter Dave Douglas's highly regarded Tiny Bell Trio. A consistent musical companion has been saxophonist Chris Speed in Human Feel – CDs include *Scatter* (1992; GM), *Welcome To Malpesta* (1994; New World/ CounterCurrents) and *Speak To It* (1996; Songlines) – and in Pachora, who have released three albums on Knitting Factory, *Pachora* (1997), *Unn* (1999) and *Ast* (2000), and one on Winter & Winter, *Astereotypical* (2003). Winter & Winter is also the home of Black's rockier project, Alasnoaxis – also featuring Speed – with which he has released two albums; *Alasnoaxis* (2000) and *Splay* (2002).

His playing is very busy, active, sometimes hectic, with boundless energy and an emphasis on constant motion and broad coloration. His work since the mid 1990s in the ensemble fronted by tenor saxophonist Ellery Eskelin is consistently some of his finest. [JC]

Ellery Eskelin with Andrea Parkins and Jim Black

⊙ **Arcanum Moderne** (2003; hatOLOGY). One of the most highly regarded groups in their field, tenorist Eskelin, accordionist/keyboardist Parkins and Black continue to collide with brio and sensitivity on a set of Eskelin's adventurous, cogent originals.

Cindy Blackman

Drums, composer.

b. Yellow Springs, Ohio, 18 Nov 1959.

A fast-rising star operating chiefly in the hard-bop field, Cindy Blackman has a blisteringly energetic drumming style controlled by a faultless technique somewhat reminiscent of one of her chief influences (along with Art Blakey), Tony Williams. She came to public attention freelancing with the likes of Joe Henderson, Don Pullen and Jackie McLean, but made her Muse debut as a leader with Arcane in 1987, featuring Henderson alongside alto player Kenny Garrett and trumpeter Wallace Roney. She consolidated her reputation with the Rudy Van Gelder-engineered *Code Red* (1992; Muse), dedicated to Art Blakey and featuring Steve Coleman in the front line with Roney, but became celebrated in rock circles as well as jazz courtesy of her work with singer/songwriter Lenny Kravitz. A 1995 album, *The Oracle*, featured a distinguished cast of mature masters (pianist Kenny Barron, bassist Ron Carter, saxophonist Gary Bartz), but – like Art Blakey and Betty Carter – she also provided up-and-coming players such as pianist Jacky Terrasson and saxophonist Ravi Coltrane with valuable live and recording experience. On the other hand, her recent albums, *Works On Canvas* (1999; High Note) and *Someday* (2001; High Note), both featured her regular acoustic quartet (J.D. Allen on tenor, Carlton Holmes piano and George Mitchell bass) and benefit from a discernible group synergy. Her most recent touring group featured the electric-based power trio line-up of David Gilmour on guitar and Matt Garrison on bass. [CP/CI]

⊙ **Trio + Two** (1990; Free Lance). A *tour de force* of tightly controlled exuberance featuring a core trio of Blackman, guitarist Dave Fiuczynski and bassist Santi Debriano augmented by Greg Osby on three tracks.

⊙ **Telepathy** (1992; Muse). Fierce, tight but surprisingly subtle music from Blackman aided by Antoine Roney on saxophones, Jacky Terrasson on piano and Clarence Seay on bass.

⊙ **In The Now** (1998; HighNote). Typically punchy but intelligent Blackman originals, centring on a lengthy tribute to the late Tony Williams, "A King Among Men", but also featuring Wayne Shorter, Ornette Coleman and Lenny Kravitz compositions played by Jacky Terrasson, Ravi Coltrane and Ron Carter.

Ed Blackwell

Drums.

b. New Orleans, 10 Oct 1929; d. 8 Oct 1992.

Blackwell began gigging in the late 1940s with Plas Johnson, singer Roy Brown and Ellis Marsalis in

New Orleans, where he first met Ornette Coleman. In 1951 he moved to Los Angeles, rehearsing regularly with Coleman but returning home before Coleman's first records and first New York appearances. In the late 1950s he toured with Ray Charles and did freelance gigging and R&B session work in New Orleans with musicians such as Earl King and Huey "Piano" Smith. He then joined the Coleman quartet in New York from 1960–2, recorded with John Coltrane-Don Cherry and Eric Dolphy-Booker Little, and worked with Cherry's quartet in 1965–6 and Randy Weston from 1965–7, including African tours, before rejoining Coleman (1967–8, 1970–73) and playing briefly with Thelonious Monk and Alice Coltrane. He taught from 1972 at Wesleyan University. His playing activity was restricted through kidney disease, which required regular use of a dialysis machine for many years. He was a member of Old and New Dreams with Cherry, Dewey Redman and Charlie Haden, playing material associated with Coleman (1976–9), and in the 1980s worked with Anthony Braxton, Archie Shepp, David Murray and Cherry's Mu. He regularly led his own groups in the 1980s, and younger musicians with whom he recorded include Jane Ira Bloom and Joe Lovano.

Blackwell's most important work was with Coleman, whose early music thrived on the drummer's alertness. However, the same control and clarity that made him so suitable in that context appears in all Blackwell's playing. Tonally, he obtained a very alive sound from the drums, which may derive from his interest in early New Orleans players such as Paul Barbarin, Baby Dodds and Zutty Singleton. [BP]

Ed Blackwell And Don Cherry

⦿ **Mu (The Complete Session)** (1969; Affinity). The best way to appreciate Blackwell's contribution is either on early albums with Ornette Coleman, or in this now hard-to-find free-form duo which shows the responsiveness which the drummer brought to every situation.

➤➤ **Ornette Coleman** *(This Is Our Music; Free Jazz).*

Brian Blade

Drums.

b. Shreveport, Louisiana, 25 July 1970.

Blade's first profound musical experiences were in the Baptist church where his father was a minister and where he played drums from the age of twelve. While at college in New Orleans, he met fellow students Myron Walden, pianists Peter Martin and Jon Cowherd and bassist Chris Thomas, and also worked with Ellis Marsalis. Commuting for a while between New Orleans and New York, he joined Kenny Garrett and later toured with Joshua Redman, as well as performing and recording with such as Marcus Roberts, Marcus Printup and Brad Mehldau. From 1996, he began playing live and in the studio with singer-songwriter Joni Mitchell, whose sensibilities appear to have influenced Blade's own budding talents as a composer (and closet guitarist). His other favourite musicians include Neil Young and drummers Elvin Jones, Levon Helm, Art Blakey, Max Roach and Paul Motian. Blade's contribution is tremendously assured, whether as a bandleader or a creative supporting player, for instance in his work with Wayne Shorter since 2001.

⦿ **Fellowship** (1997; Blue Note). Featuring a septet with saxophonists Myron Walden and Melvin Butler, Blade's debut album is filled with original compositions of a lyrical, folky bent effortlessly incorporating hints of world music. The rhythm section throughout includes not only the "jazz guitar" of Jeff Parker but the gentle pedal-steel of Dave Easley and, on two tracks, producer Daniel Lanois's mando-guitar.

➤➤ **Joshua Redman** *(Mood Swing)*, **Wayne Shorter** *(Footprints Live).*

Eubie Blake

Piano, composer.

b. Baltimore, Maryland, 7 Feb 1883; d. 12 Feb 1983.

Ragtime's centenarian began on a home harmonium playing hymns, but the rhythms of a revolutionary music were all around him. On the local streets he heard brass bands "raggin' the hell out of the music"; in saloons and dance halls he later heard the virtuoso ragtime piano professors who ceremoniously spread out their coats, velvet lining upwards, dusted off the keys with a new silk handkerchief, and sat down to produce magic. Early masters like "One Leg Willie" Joseph pointed the way for Blake: a trained classical pianist, Joseph had stopped trying to follow up his degree in music in a white man's world, and after three years at Boston Conservatory had taken to ragtime and drink. His showstopper was "The Stars And Stripes Forever" (an ironic choice) played in march time, ragtime and boogie, and as far as Blake was concerned he was only equalled by Johnny Guarnieri.

David Redfern

Eubie Blake

Blake learned his craft in sporting houses (including three years at Aggie Shelton's) and wrote his first rag, "The Charleston Rag", around 1899. By the 1900s, young, ambitious and talented, he was touring with medicine shows, accompanying singers such as Madison Reed, and playing for Baltimore hotels. His piano show by then encompassed classical themes in ragtime, popular tunes, flash ragtime specialities, a classical waltz and perhaps a Bert Williams recitation. Early songs he wrote included "Poor Jimmy Green" (1908) and two very successful rags, "Chevy Chase" and "Fizz Water Rag".

In 1915, Eubie teamed with an ambitious young entrepreneur, Noble Sissle, for vaudeville appearances. Earl Hines remembers Blake at the time: "He used to wear a raccoon coat and a derby and he always carried a cane. He was the first one I ever saw playing piano with one hand and conducting with the other. He used to lift his hands high off the keyboard, which was my first lesson in the value of showmanship. He and Sissle were all the rage when they came to town." By 1921, Blake and Sissle were on Broadway with a colossal success, *Shuffle Along*, the first all-black musical, starring Florence Mills and featuring comedy duo Miller and Lyles. Auditions for *Shuffle Along* stretched three times round the theatre, and its success was to pave the way for more black extravaganzas, among them *Revue Nègre* (in which Sidney Bechet appeared), *Plantation Review*, *Rhapsody In Black* and *Bamville Review*. While Sissle continued his solo treks around Europe, Blake stayed in New York to write prolifically for such hit shows as the *Blackbirds Review*, producing hits like "Memories Of You" (with Andy Razaf, 1930) and "You're Lucky To Me". He was to work with Sissle again, up to World War II, assembling more shows, but then he retired to study the Schillinger system beloved of Glenn Miller at New York University, where he won his degree.

In 1969 John Hammond recorded a vital double album for Columbia, *Eighty-Six Years Of Eubie Blake*. The LP, featuring Eubie's songs, solo piano, reminiscences and a reunion with Sissle, paved the way for a Blake revival in the ragtime-conscious early 1970s, and so did a successful appearance at the 1970 New Orleans jazz festival. That year Blake was awarded the annual James P. Johnson Award. Two years later he won the Duke Ellington Medal, and was writing new rags and travelling internationally to appear at jazz festivals and on TV and radio. In 1976 he collaborated with Terry Waldo on an authoritative book, *This Is Ragtime*, started his own record label and replaced Rudolf Friml as ASCAP's oldest living member. Perhaps his greatest triumph was reserved for 1978, when a full-scale Broadway review, *Eubie* (which came to London and was televised worldwide), strung his songs together in a vivid "song by song" presentation. In 1981, Blake received the Presidential Medal of Honour. He died just five days after his one-hundredth birthday. [DF]

Blues And Rags Vol. 1 (1917–21; Biograph). One of two LPs of Blake's piano rolls, leading off with his first recording ("Charleston Rag") and including several standards-to-be such as Perry Bradford's "Crazy Blues".

Wizard Of The Ragtime Piano Vol. 1 (1958; 20th Century Fox). Blake's second comeback (his first was in the late 1940s) produced this session with a couple of vocals by Noble Sissle, and solos by Blake on material by himself, Scott Joplin and Jess Pickett's "The Dream" from 1890.

Ran Blake

Piano, keyboards, composer, educator.
b. Springfield, Massachusetts, 20 April 1935.

Blake's early influences were classical music (particularly from the twentieth century) and the black gospel music of the Church of God in Christ at Hartford, Connecticut. He graduated from Bard College, where he was the first student to major in jazz. He also spent several of his college summers at the Lenox School of Jazz, which had been opened by John Lewis and Gunther Schuller. In 1957, he began a long association with singer Jeanne Lee, and they were among the first to attempt total voice and piano improvisation. They toured Europe in 1963 and achieved some recognition, but success eluded them in the USA. Since the late 1960s, he has been a member of the staff of the New England Conservatory of Music of which Schuller is president. At first he taught improvisation and acted as co-director of the conservatory's community service projects, then in 1973 he was made chairperson of the Third Stream Department. He has defined Third Stream as "an improvised synthesis of ethnic cabaret or Afro-American music with what has been called for the last few years European avant-garde".

Blake collaborated with tenor saxophonist Ricky Ford off and on in the 1970s, and has worked with singer Eleni Odoni, but he generally prefers to perform solo. That said, 2001 saw the release of a 2CD set, *Sonic Temples*, largely comprising jazz standards and recorded by the trio of Blake and Schuller's two sons, Ed and George. His favourites include George Russell, Thelonious Monk, Ray Charles and Max Roach, though the darker elements of his work betray a fascination with composers such as Messiaen and Bartok. [IC]

⊙ **Short Life Of Barbara Monk** (1986; Soul Note). Blake is a man of passionate enthusiasms and, though an intrepid musical adventurer, he is in thrall to the whole jazz tradition. Here he leads a quartet with Ricky Ford and a young bassist and drummer; the title track is in memory of Thelonious Monk's daughter, Barbara, who died in 1984, and the rest of the album deals with other manifestations of death, but also aspects of the jazz tradition which are not so moribund. Blake's composing and playing are, perhaps ironically, bristling with life.

⊙ **Epistrophy** (1991; Soul Note). This is a solo piano album with Blake paying homage to Monk the father. Blake's solo performances are always intriguing because he has an unpredictable cast of mind, an elephantine memory, and is apparently bilingual in classical and ethnic music.

⊙ **Unmarked Van** (1994; Soul Note). Blake's solo piano (plus drummer Tiziano Tononi), in extended homage to Sarah Vaughan – all her qualities, her phrasing, range and mannerisms in pianistic metaphor ... a virtuosic appreciation.

Art Blakey

Drums.

b. Pittsburgh, Pennsylvania, 11 Oct 1919; d. 16 Oct 1990.

Starting out as a self-taught pianist, Blakey was already leading a big band at fifteen; suddenly displaced in his own group by Erroll Garner, he migrated to drums. After working with several local bands, he joined Mary Lou Williams's first New York group in 1942. Big-band experience followed, with Fletcher Henderson in 1943–4 and the adventurous young outfit of Billy Eckstine – a founder member in 1944, Blakey stayed until the band's demise in 1947. He led an occasional big band, the Seventeen Messengers, and recorded an eight-piece Art Blakey's Messengers, also in 1947. Much freelance gigging and recording with such as Tadd Dameron-Fats Navarro, Thelonious Monk, Charlie Parker, Miles Davis and Horace Silver alternated with longer stints with Lucky Millinder in 1949 and Buddy DeFranco in 1952–3. Occasionally leading his own groups in New York and on out-of-town gigs, he fronted a famous live recording with Clifford Brown and Horace Silver in 1954. A convert to Islam, he was given the name Abdullah Ibn Buhaina, hence his later nickname, "Bu".

A 1954 Horace Silver studio date caused the formation of the Jazz Messengers as a cooperative with Blakey, Silver, Kenny Dorham (later Donald Byrd), Hank Mobley and Doug Watkins, until the other four left (mid-1956) and the Messengers became the trade name for all Blakey's subsequent groups. Although there was a fairly steady turnover of personnel, the proportion of major soloists is high: even a selective list must include Jackie McLean, Johnny Griffin, Wayne Shorter, John Gilmore, Billy Harper, Bobby Watson, Lee Morgan, Freddie Hubbard, Woody Shaw, Wynton Marsalis, Curtis Fuller, Slide Hampton, Cedar Walton, Keith Jarrett, Chick Corea and Joanne Brackeen. Blakey has occasionally appeared with special reunions of former Messengers (at the Kool Jazz festival 1981, in Japan 1983, and at the Blue Note relaunch in 1985) and for one tour the group became a ten-piece band in 1980. But the basic quintet or (since 1961) sextet sound of the Messengers became the virtual definition of the style known as "hard bop".

Although he continued to freelance on records, notably with Sonny Rollins, Milt Jackson, Cannonball Adderley and Hank Mobley, Blakey was rarely heard in public away from the Jazz Messengers after 1955; the major exception was with the Giants of Jazz (1971–2). His brilliant playing remained largely unchanged for three decades and his solo work, in its concentration on the snare drum, is a reminder that his style was formed during the swing era. Yet his accompaniment relies on the rhythmic complexity of bebop. For, in addition to the driving beat of his right hand and left foot (and even the left hand on the snare, at medium tempos such as "Moanin'"), Blakey introduces all manner of cross-rhythms behind a soloist. If the soloist's inspiration begins to flag, Blakey lifts him onto another plane – as Johnny Griffin put it, "He'd make one of those rolls and say, 'No, you can't stop yourself *now*!'"

These effects used to be considered an unwelcome distraction by listeners and critics not attuned to polyrhythms. Indeed, certain youthful band members who were not quite ready for their task may have been swamped by such a tidal wave of percussion. But those who were adequately prepared clearly relished the challenge, and emerged even stronger from the ordeal. Most important of all, perhaps, is that in his long career Blakey always exuded excitement but channelled it to enhance the ensemble, just as the swing-era drummers did. As a result the ensembles he led – no matter what the personnel at any particular moment – became cornerstones of the jazz tradition. [BP]

⦿ **A Night At Birdland Vols. 1 & 2** (1954; Blue Note). This Blakey quintet preceded the famous Messengers by a few months, and features Lou Donaldson and the brilliant Clifford Brown playing recent Horace Silver material and reviving bop tunes from ten years earlier, such as "Confirmation" and "A Night In Tunisia".

⦿ **The Jazz Messengers** (1956; Columbia). The Messengers who first caught the public's imagination were the group that included Donald Byrd, Hank Mobley, Doug Watkins and musical director Horace Silver (before they split to join Silver's own quintet). The latter's compositions, "Ecaroh" and "Nica's Dream", are perhaps the highlights but the standard "It's You Or No One" is a classic definition of hard bop.

⦿ **Orgy In Rhythm** (1957; Blue Note). Blakey's third attempt in three months to capture a multi-percussion, Afro-jazz celebration, this has Herbie Mann's flute, piano, bass and an all-star gathering of drummers: Jo Jones, Art Taylor, Sabu Martinez, Patato Valdes and several others working together.

⦿ **Moanin'** (1958; Blue Note). The most striking solo work here is by Lee Morgan, while Benny Golson and Bobby Timmons try a bit too hard to sound trendy. But, between them, they contributed the first versions of two more Blakey anthems, "Blues March" and "Moanin' ".

⦿ **Free For All** (1964; Blue Note). Here Morgan, Golson and Timmons were replaced by Freddie Hubbard, Wayne Shorter and Cedar Walton (and Curtis Fuller was added to provide a bigger frontline sound), and the new material reflected the influence of Coltrane as well as Shorter's growing maturity.

⦿ **Straight Ahead** (1981; Concord). The next such heavyweight team to grace the Messengers had Bobby Watson and James Williams (both soon to leave) joined by the nineteen-year-old Wynton Marsalis, for a mainly standard programme plus Watson's "E.T.A."

➤➤ **Thelonious Monk** *(Genius Of Modern Music Vols.1 & 2);* **Sonny Rollins** *(Movin' Out);* **Horace Silver** *(Horace Silver And The Jazz Messengers);* **Jimmy Smith** *(The Sermon).*

Terence Blanchard

Trumpet, composer.

b. New Orleans, 13 March 1962.

Blanchard studied piano from age five and composition from fifteen. Inspired by hearing Alvin Alcorn, he took up trumpet in 1976 at the New Orleans Center for Creative Arts, run by Ellis Marsalis, then in 1980 won a Pee Wee Russell Scholarship to Rutgers University in New Jersey. Recommended by Paul Jeffrey, he played with Lionel Hampton from 1980–82 while still a student. He joined Art Blakey as trumpeter and musical director, replacing Wynton Marsalis from 1982–86, then left to form his own quintet with Blakey sideman Donald Harrison with whom he had made three albums. After playing in Spike Lee's films *Do The Right Thing* and *Mo' Better Blues*, also coaching actor Denzil Washington for the latter, he became the musical director for many subsequent films by Lee (including *Malcolm X*) and other directors. In the early 2000s he became artistic director for the Thelonious Monk Institute of Jazz Performance in Los Angeles.

Initially, Blanchard's arrival on the national scene was overshadowed by his precocious predecessor from New Orleans; but, all comparisons with Marsalis left aside, it was soon evident that Blanchard was uncommonly talented for one so young. He showed an early absorption of Clifford Brown and the 1950s Miles Davis along with more fashionable neo-bop archetypes such as Freddie Hubbard and Woody Shaw; although the latter pair predominate in his more mature work, he combines their excitement with an intriguing edge of reserve in his tone-quality. His writing for the Jazz Messengers and for his quintet albums again reveals a strong neo-bop influence with some individual touches, while his film writing has absorbed the influence of European classical music. [BP]

Terence Blanchard and Donald Harrison

⦿ **Eric Dolphy & Booker Little Remembered Vols. 1/2** (1986; Paddle Wheel). Nailing their colours to the mast of post-bop with avant-garde touches, the two principals remade five pieces recorded 25 years earlier by Dolphy and Little with the same rhythm-section of Mal Waldron, Richard Davis and Ed Blackwell.

Terence Blanchard

⦿ **The Billie Holiday Songbook** (1993; Columbia). With his experience of working with strings for his film music, Blanchard took up the challenge of Wynton Marsalis's *Hot House Flowers,* and his commanding performance is not diminished by three vocals by Jeanie Bryson.

Jimmie Blanton

Bass.

b. Chattanooga, Tennessee, 5 Oct 1918 (or 1919); d. 30 July 1942.

Blanton studied violin as a child, then switched to bass while in college and played with the Tennessee State Collegians in 1936–7, also working during summer vacations with Fate Marable. He left college to play full-time in St Louis with the Jeter-Pillars band, with whom he made his recording debut (1937–9). He joined Duke Ellington in October 1939, but after only two years was admitted to hospital with ultimately fatal tuberculosis.

Blanton was the crucial figure in giving the bass greater prominence. Previously John Kirby and the two bassists from Chicago, Milt Hinton and Israel Crosby, had been moving towards more melodic "walking lines", while the great Basie band of the late 1930s had shown the advantage of allowing Walter Page to be heard as the foundation of the rhythm-section. Blanton, however, combined the melodic tendencies of the first group with the marvellously alive pulse of Page, and a beautiful rounded tone which enhanced his brief solo passages. His facility in all these fields could not have had such a speedy impact if Ellington had not known immediately how to exploit it, and taken the trouble to have him exceptionally well captured by the recording engineers of the period – and by the public address systems on live performances. The right man in the right place at the right time, Blanton set new standards of technique and fluency, and set the ball in motion for the development of contemporary bass playing. [BP]

➤➤ **Duke Ellington** *(The Indispensable Vols. 5/6).*

Carla Bley

Composer, piano, organ, synthesizers.
b. Oakland, California, 11 May 1938.

Carla Bley's father was a piano teacher and church organist, and he gave her piano lessons as soon as she could walk. After the age of five she had no formal lessons, but played hymns in churches and sang in church choirs. She became interested in jazz at seventeen: "I liked Miles Davis and Thelonious Monk, people who had only a few notes and chose them well." She went to New York, working as a waitress, and in 1957 married pianist Paul Bley, who encouraged her to start composing, which she did in 1959. She began to devote all her time and energy to music in 1964, after being inspired by Ornette Coleman and Don Cherry, and she worked with Charles Moffett and Pharoah Sanders at a New York club in January of that year. Other musicians began to play and record her compositions, among them George Russell, Jimmy Giuffre and Art Farmer.

With trumpeter/composer Michael Mantler (who was to become her second husband), she was co-leader of the Jazz Composers' Orchestra (JCO) from December 1964, and wrote her first orchestral piece, "Roast", for it. The JCO was an attempt to give the free (abstract) music of the day an orchestral setting, and at this point in her career Carla Bley was deeply involved with the free-jazz scene. In January 1965 she went to Holland to record and do radio and TV work. Back in the USA the JCO played a series of concerts in New York and appeared at the Newport jazz festival. Late in 1965 she returned to Europe, playing in Germany and Italy and forming a quintet with Mantler and Steve Lacy. In 1966, while touring Europe with Peter Brötzmann and Peter Kovald playing high-energy free jazz, she suddenly became disenchanted with total abstraction. She went back to the USA and began working on her composition *A Genuine Tong Funeral*. Later she said: "That's when my life started. I stopped being part of the stream I was in and struck out as a protest to that stream." *A Genuine Tong Funeral* (subtitled *Dark Opera Without Words*) was recorded for RCA in 1967 by the Gary Burton quartet augmented by Gato Barbieri, Jimmy Knepper, Steve Lacy, Howard Johnson, Mantler and Bley.

From this point on, she was more of a composer than an instrumentalist. That same year she began working on her massive composition *Escalator Over The Hill*. In 1969 she arranged all the music on Charlie Haden's *Liberation Music Orchestra* album, and also composed some of it. She spent three years composing and recording *Escalator Over The Hill*, completing it in June 1971, and it was released as a triple-album set on the record label that she and Mantler created: JCOA Records. *Escalator* was inspired by the lyrics of Paul Haines, and is a kind of jazz opera, which J.E. Berendt has called "the largest complete work that has so far emerged from within jazz". It was also a kind of summary of her musical ideas to date, using jazz and rock musicians and covering the gamut from abstraction to set structures and harmonies, rock rhythms and elements from Indian music. In 1973 it was awarded the French Oscar du Disque de Jazz.

Jak Kilby

Carla Bley

Also in 1973, with Don Cherry, she played on the film score of Jodorowski's *Holy Mountain*, and with Mantler set up Watt Records to handle their own compositions separately from their JCOA label, which was used thereafter to release the music of other people. She was commissioned to write a piece for classical musicians, and produced "3/4", which was performed at the Alice Tully Hall in 1974 with Keith Jarrett playing the solo part. Later that year she had a short stint playing with the Jack Bruce band.

From 1976 she led her own bands, which usually included French horn and tuba as well as trumpet and reeds, touring and playing major festivals internationally. In 1985 she completed an opera based on Malcolm Lowry's novel *Under The Volcano*, which was given its premiere in Los Angeles. In the 1990s she began to feature herself as a player much more, performing in duo with Steve Swallow and in trio with Swallow and Andy Sheppard.

She also began to be commissioned to compose for other organizations and ensembles. In the autumn of 1994 she had three major commissions: a classical piece ("Tigers In Training") for the Hamburg L'Art Pour L'Art festival, one for the Carnegie Hall Women In Jazz series, and a piece for Les Percussions de Strasbourg, premiered in the spring of 1995.

In 1995, her album *Big Band Theory* was nominated for a Grammy in the Best Big Band Album category, and the release of *Songs With Legs* was followed by the Bley/Swallow/Sheppard trio's European promotional tour. That year, she and Swallow also played duo concerts in Brazil and worked in Norway rehearsing and performing her music with Norwegian musicians. In 1996, Bley was commissioned to compose *Les Trois Lagons* based on three cut-outs from Henri Matisse's book *Jazz*, for the BSS trio to perform at the French Grenoble jazz festival in the spring, and in the summer her big band completed a week of workshops and master classes at the Paris Conservatory and a final concert at the Paris jazz festival.

Carla Bley's masterwork, *Escalator Over The Hill*, had never been performed live, but in 1997 she received an invitation to stage the work in Cologne, Germany. To do so she needed to scale down the orchestration to manageable size, and find a new and readily available cast. She used four singers – Syd Straw, Phil Minton, Davis Moss and Linda Sharrock – and an ensemble which included key members of her big band. With Bley conducting and Paul Haines, the original librettist, as narrator, the opera was revived to ecstatic reviews. In 1998, it toured with the same cast in France, Germany, Austria and Italy, and to coincide with the tour, ECM/Watt issued a double CD of the original classic album. In 2002 she returned to the big-band for the release of *Looking For America*, which featured many old friends.

From the moment she began composing in the early 1960s, Bley was an original with an extraordinary melodic flair. Two classics of that decade, "Sing Me Softly Of The Blues" and "Ad Infinitum", show her genius for creating evocative and memorable tunes, and "Ida Lupino" and "Wrong Key Donkey" have the same qualities. She developed slowly into one of the most important bandleaders and composing-arranging talents on the entire jazz scene. Her early influences were hymns and church music and later Erik Satie's *Parade* (1917), of which she said, "For a long time it was almost the only music I listened to." But she has stated that her greatest influence was *Sergeant Pepper*-era Beatles. All this gave her earlier orchestral music more of a European than an African-American flavour. The theatricality and parody in her work are European in origin, as are the discontinuous rhythms of some of her earlier work. During the 1970s there was a gradual strengthening of the African-American rhythms, and her music gained enormously in pith and impact, becoming brilliantly concentrated after the diffuseness of *Tropic Appetites* (1973–4). Beginning with *Dinner Music* in 1976, she has released a series of magnificent albums which continued into the 1990s. Since the late 1980s, Lew Soloff has been virtually the only trumpet soloist in her band, and Andy Sheppard has been the main saxophone soloist. Talking of her writing, Sheppard said: "The thing with Carla is you get given a note which you might have to hold for three bars or something, but that note is a fantastic note and you really feel that it's got value in the chord. That's a really gratifying experience." Although her medium-sized bands have an instrumentation similar to the Gil Evans bands, and although her writing for lower instruments such as trombone and tuba is, like Evans's, superb and crucial to her music, her orchestral sound is all her own and instantly recognizable. **[IC]**

⊙ **Escalator Over The Hill** (1971; JCOA). It takes a double CD to accommodate this mighty if diffuse landmark, which summarizes and synthesizes her musical experiences to date and points to future developments. The parts may be more absorbing than the whole, but *Escalator* is a unique testimony to the optimism and adventure of that era.

⊙ **Tropic Appetites** (1974; Watt). This was the album that launched the Carla Bley/Michael Mantler Watt label. Her eight-piece band includes singer Julie Tippetts, tenor saxophonist Gato Barbieri, Howard Johnson on tuba and a multitude of other instruments, Dave Holland, Mantler, Paul Motian and violinist Toni Marcus. The music is powerfully rhythmic, often with multiple percussion, and the resonances are global – African, Latin, Oriental and European/Germanic oompah rhythms, violin and vocals.

⊙ **Musique Mécanique** (1978; Watt). This shows the other side of Carla Bley – theatricality and quirkiness taking precedence over the business of swinging – her European heritage expressing itself in satirical pastiche. Some people are irritated by the at times almost grotesque whimsy, but she and her musicians are having a lot of fun.

⊙ **Social Studies** (1980; Watt). The balance between Europe and America is finely drawn on this excellent album. The writing is deft and full of dry wit, and the performance highly focused. The sardonic element appears fitfully, but never dominates.

⊙ **Fleur Carnivore** (1988; Watt). This is a concert performance by Bley's fourteen-piece band which features some Europeans including Andy Sheppard and the German tenor saxophonist Christof Lauer, as well as American stalwarts such as Gary Valente, Bob Stewart and Steve Swallow. Lew Soloff is also at the beginning of his long and fruitful association with Bley. Both writing and performance are superb.

The Very Big Carla Bley Band (1990; Watt). This time it's a seventeen-piece band with four main soloists – Soloff, Valente, Sheppard and the alto saxophonist/flautist Wolfgang Pushnig. The orchestral textures vary subtly and the music is alive with incident – written and improvised.

Go Together (1992; Watt). Bley plays acoustic piano in duo with Steve Swallow, and their rapport projects extraordinary warmth on this delightful album. Several of her famous pieces, including "Sing Me Softly Of The Blues" and "Ad Infinitum", are featured, and Swallow, who's also a fine composer, contributes a thirteen-minute suite and another shorter piece. Bley, as a player, distils like Miles Davis and has something of Monk's eccentricity.

Big Band Theory (1993; Watt). Bley led an eighteen-piece Anglo-American band on this occasion, with violinist Alex Balanescu added for her twenty-minute suite "Birds Of Paradise". This has some of her most subtle scoring to date, and the whole album bristles with ideas and powerful feeling. The context produces some exceptionally fine solo playing. Soloff has never sounded so good – his tone fat and full, his range phenomenal. Gary Valente's idiosyncrasy blazes out of the ensemble, and Balanescu acquits himself well.

Songs With Legs (1995; Watt). Bley the pianist has been working in trio formation with Steve Swallow and Andy Sheppard for some time now, and the rapport among them all is very fine. There are five compositions by Bley including her brilliant theme, "Wrong Key Donkey", and her lovely arrangement of Monk's "Misterioso". Bley's piano accompaniments are always pithy and full of little surprises, while Sheppard seems to create out of the essential jazz tradition. The resonances of this trio – emotional and musical – are wondrous.

Fancy Chamber Music (1997; Watt). Carla Bley had been asked at various times to compose pieces for classical musicians and decided to record them. This features Bley on piano and Steve Swallow on bass guitar, with six members of the chamber ensemble Opus 20 playing flute, clarinet doubling glockenspiel, violin, viola, cello and percussion. The music is not jazz, but has considerable charm.

>> **Charlie Haden** *(Liberation Music Orchestra).*

Paul Bley

Piano, synthesizer, composer.
b. Montreal, 10 Nov 1932.

From 1950–52 Bley studied composition and conducting at the Juilliard School in New York. Established musicians quickly recognized his extraordinary musical gifts, and by 1951 he had recorded an album with the great bass player Oscar Pettiford – though it was not released at that time. At twenty, Bley played with Charlie Parker and was also leading his own trio in New York. Charles Mingus championed his cause and got him his first album release – *Introducing Paul Bley* (1953) – an impressive trio debut with Mingus and Art Blakey as his rhythm-section. In the later 1950s he was associated with the burgeoning avant-garde movement, playing with Mingus, Ornette Coleman, Don Cherry, Jimmy Giuffre, Don Ellis, Sonny Rollins and Gary Peacock. He also encouraged his wife, Carla Bley, to begin composing. In 1959 he disbanded his own group, which included Bobby Hutcherson and Scott La Faro, in Los Angeles and returned to New York. In January 1960 Bley and Bill Evans were the two featured soloists and duettists with the fifteen-piece orchestra which recorded George Russell's massive composition *Jazz In The Space Age*. With Steve Swallow, Bley was also a member of Jimmy Giuffre's ground-breaking trio of 1960–62. The following year, with his own trio which included Steve Swallow and Pete LaRoca, he recorded the classic and highly influential album *Footloose*. He was a member of the Jazz Composers' Guild in 1964–5, the aim of which was to further the jazz avant-garde. He toured Japan with Rollins in 1963 and Europe with his own quintet in 1965.

In the 1970s he pioneered the use of electronics in jazz, incorporating Arp Odyssey synthesizers and electric keyboards into his solo shows; at around this time he was also closely associated with Annette Peacock, who sang with him. The duo appeared at festivals in the USA and Europe. He continued to appear solo on the European circuit throughout the 70s.

Paul Bley has always been a musical adventurer of the highest order, with an unerring ear for vitally creative collaborators. Although he first came to prominence with the 1960s' avant-garde, Bley's music is steeped in jazz history and he is thoroughly at home with all approaches from the abstract and non-tonal to the diatonic and harmonic. In 1975 he formed his own production company, Improvising Artists Inc, to release records of his own and of other artists, including Ran Blake, Sam Rivers and Sun Ra. In 1999 he published an enthralling autobiography entitled *Stopping Time*; he continues to perform live. [IC]

Introducing Paul Bley (1953; Debut/OJC). Bley's amazingly assured trio debut at the age of twenty-one, with Mingus and Blakey.

The Fabulous Paul Bley Quintet (1958; Musidisc). The adventurer in at the deep end having briefly annexed the Ornette Coleman quartet, with Don Cherry, Charlie Haden and Billy Higgins.

Footloose (1963; Savoy). This trio album with Swallow and LaRoca comes after Bley's stint with Giuffre's chamber jazz. The quiet, focused intensity persists throughout this fine album, which influenced many, including Keith Jarrett, who said it was "a record I've listened to thousands of times".

Barrage (1964; ESP). Bley leads a quintet for this with trumpeter Dewey Johnson and alto saxophonist Marshall Allen (both of whom were to join Sun Ra), Milford Graves, one of the leading avant-garde drummers, and bassist Eddie Gomez. Bley draws this disparate personnel into a coherent unit. The music bucks and kicks but is always under control ... just.

Open, To Love (1972; ECM). After his love affair with electronics, Bley slowly returned to acoustic music in the 1970s. The stark resonance of this solo piano album pointed the way.

Solo (1987; Justin Time); **Changing Hands** (1991; Justin Time). These two solo piano albums, recorded in his native Montreal, follow the starkly brooding trail but throw in a few references to the roots of jazz.

BeBopBeBopBeBopBeBop (1989; Steeplechase). With Bob Cranshaw and Keith Copeland, Bley brings his radical imagination to bear on bebop with dynamic results.

Memoirs (1990; Soul Note). With the superb rhythm-section of Charlie Haden and Paul Motian, Bley conjures up things past on his journey into the future.

Paul Plays Carla (1991; Steeplechase). Bley leads another trio with bassist Marc Johnson and drummer Jeff Williams, in this warm tribute to his ex-wife.

Time Will Tell (1994; ECM). Bley, with Barre Phillips and Evan Parker, creates a resolutely abstract album which yet has eloquent sonorities and is awash with human feeling.

Reality Check (1994; Steeplechase). Paul Bley, with the superlative bassist Jay Anderson and excellent drummer Victor Lewis, seems to be reconsidering his identity here, and checking out his relationship with the jazz tradition. The abstraction is still there in the title track, but Bley is the pianist who, when asked in the 1950s about his main influences, replied "Louis Armstrong". This personal quest with his trio has a remarkably dynamic beauty.

Kenny Wheeler and Paul Bley

Touché (1996; Justin Time). This was the first time the two men had recorded together, and Bley suggested that nothing was to be predetermined, there was to be no discussion before each piece, or after each recording, he and Wheeler were to have a thirty-minute period of relaxation before they re-entered the studio to play again. In this way, six duo performances were recorded in one day, plus three solo trumpet or flugelhorn performances by Wheeler and four solo piano improvisations by Bley. The results are magical – two great masters at play with open hearts and minds.

➤➤ **Jimmy Giuffre** *(1961)*; **John Surman** *(Adventure Playground)*.

Jane Ira Bloom

Soprano saxophone.

b. Newton, Massachusetts, 12 Jan 1954.

Picking up the soprano at age twelve, Bloom studied at Boston's Berklee School of Music until going to college at Yale in 1972. There she met pianist Anthony Davis, trombonist George Lewis, trumpeter Leo Smith, and percussionist Gerry Hemingway. In the late 70s, she settled in New York where she studied with saxophonist George Coleman. Bloom's first two records were issued on her own Outline label; subsequent recordings from the 80s include a duo with pianist Fred Hersch, *As One* (JMT), and a fine quartet with Hersch, bassist Charlie Haden and drummer Edward Blackwell, *Mighty Lights* (Enja).

A strong composer as well as an undramatic, thoughtful voice on the soprano, Bloom gained wide exposure and critical acclaim with her two records on Columbia, *Modern Drama* and *Slalom*, both of which utilized electronics; however it is her consistent output on Arabesque since the early 1990s which represents her mature body of work. *Art And Aviation* (see below) was followed by *Nearness* (1995), in the estimable company of trumpeter Kenny Wheeler, trombonist Julian Priester, Hersch, bassist Mark Dresser and drummer Bobby Previte, the latter three of which were also on hand for *Red Quartets* (1999) and the excellent musical portrait of Jackson Pollock's art, *Chasing Paint* (2003). [JC]

Art And Aviation (1992; Arabesque). Bloom's first record after a long hiatus, this project was adapted from compositions she was commissioned to write for NASA, and offers the best examples of her unorthodox mixture of electronics and (relatively) straight jazz.

Johnny Blowers

Drums, percussion.

b. Spartanburg, South Carolina, 21 April 1911.

Blowers went to New York to join Lou McGarity in 1937, and the following year worked for Bobby Hackett, Bunny Berigan's orchestra and others. One of the very best Dixieland drummers (in the school of Leeman, Fatool et al), he was a busy studio man from 1940, and turned up regularly on fine Dixieland recording dates for Eddie Condon, Louis Armstrong, Billie Holiday and others. From the mid-1960s he could be heard regularly in clubs such as Condon's, and in 1981 came to Europe and made the rounds of the London jazz scene. A biography of Johnny Blowers written by Warren W. Vaché, *Back Beats And Rim Shots: The Johnny Blowers Story*, was published by Scarecrow Press in 1997. [DF]

Warren Vaché Snr

Jazz: It's A Wonderful Sound (1977; Starfire). Uncomplicated, highly professional Dixieland; Blowers is perfect in this setting, under the leadership of Warren Vaché on cornet.

Johnny Blowers And his Giants Of Jazz (1991; JGB). Cohesive date for Blowers's all-star band including John Bunch, Randy Sandke, Harry Allen and singer Lynn Roberts; a welcome reminder of this under-rated but highly qualified swing drummer.

Hamiet Bluiett

Baritone saxophone, alto clarinet.

b. Lovejoy, Illinois, 16 Sep 1940.

Raised near East St Louis, Illinois, Bluiett studied flute and clarinet before taking up the big baritone. While on leave from the navy, he recorded a session with local group Leo's Five, released as *Spider Burks Presents Leo's Five*; after the navy he moved to St Louis, Missouri, where he joined the Black Artists Group (BAG), though he finally settled in New York in 1969. There he worked with the Thad Jones/Mel Lewis Big Band and Charles Mingus, played and recorded as a leader and solo. In 1974, he played a four-saxophone composition by Anthony Braxton, with Braxton and fellow BAG members Julius Hemphill and Oliver Lake. That ensemble, with David Murray replacing Braxton, established itself in the mid-70s as the World Saxophone Quartet, with whom Bluiett continues to work. His beefy sound and rock-solid sense of time has anchored the WSQ since it began, and with his own groups he's consistently drawn on blues and gospel, as well as free jazz and creative composition. Bluiett has been quite active in the

90s and beyond, releasing live and studio recordings on Soul Note, Mapleshade and a string of latterday albums on Justin Time with the WSQ as well as under his own name and that of his four-baritone group Bluiett Baritone Nation. These included *Libation For The Baritone Saxophone Nation* (1998) and the curious if typically diverse *The Calling* (2001) featuring organist D.D. Jackson and drummer/vocalist Kahil El'Zabar. [JC]

Resolution (1977; Black Saint). Super record by Bluiett's mid 70s quintet, still his very best, with bassist Fred Hopkins, pianist (and cohort in the Mingus band) Don Pullen, and twin drummers Billy Hart and Famoudou Don Moyé.

Arthur Blythe

Alto and soprano saxophones, composer.
b. Los Angeles, 5 July 1940.

Blythe first squeezed a note from the alto saxophone at the age of nine; he then studied with local saxophonists and played with R&B bands until, in his teens, he discovered jazz. Moving back to Los Angeles, he worked with Horace Tapscott from 1963–73 and with Stanley Crouch and the Black Music Infinity from 1967–73. He also began leading his own groups in 1970. In 1974 he moved to New York working with Leon Thomas, Julius Hemphill and Chico Hamilton, with whom he visited California in the summer of 1975. He was with the Gil Evans orchestra from 1976–80, recording several albums with him and touring. From 1978–80 he played occasionally with groups led by Lester Bowie and Jack DeJohnette. He was also leading his own groups and recorded for Columbia from 1979 until the later 1980s.

Jak Kilby

Arthur Blythe

Blythe is one of the most gifted alto saxophonists to have emerged in the 1970s. His playing has all the emotional power of the blues and gospel music and great harmonic awareness allied to the linear freedom of abstract improvisation, a combination of qualities which has made him much in demand. He is also a fine composer. Three of his Columbia albums, *Lenox Avenue Breakdown*, *Illusions* and *Elaborations*, use unusual instrumentations, including tuba and cello, and must rank with the most creative small-group music of their time. But after his relationship with Columbia ended, he seemed to lose his impetus, which diminished him as a force on the jazz scene. His influences include Coltrane, Charlie Parker, Miles Davis, Monk, Ellington and Eric Dolphy. [IC]

In Concert (1977; India Navigation). This is pre-Columbia Blythe with a sextet which includes some of his later associates including Bob Stewart (tuba) and Abdul Wadud (cello). The rest of the instrumentation comprises trumpet, drums and percussion. The music is a dynamic preliminary to the Columbia masterpieces, which are unfortunately currently deleted.

Hipmotism (1991; Enja). This is post-Columbia Blythe leading a septet which includes Stewart again, plus guitar vibraphone/marimba, drums and percussion and guest artist baritone saxophonist Hamiet Bluiett. There is much of interest here, but the performance lacks a certain spark.

Today's Blues (1997; CIMP). Blythe on alto sax with David Eyges on amplified cello achieve a rich and resonant duo album, with the former setting the pace and the latter in supportive role.

>> **Lester Bowie** *(The Fifth Power)*; **Jack DeJohnette** *(Special Edition)*.

Jimmy Blythe

Piano, composer.
b. Keene, Kentucky, c. 20 May 1901; d. 21 June 1931.

Jimmy Blythe was a house pianist in the 1920s for companies such as Paramount and Champion and recorded an enormous number of sides as a soloist, accompanist (to singers such as Trixie Smith) and bandleader: his studio groups include the State Street Ramblers, Washboard Band and Washboard Ragamuffins. Besides his regular percussionist Jimmy Bertrand, the groups corralled star names including Natty Dominique, Stump Evans and the Dodds brothers. These names give a clue to his subsequent obscurity; like Lovie Austin and Clarence Williams, Jimmy Blythe has become a victim of musical fashion. [DF]

State Street Ramblers 1927–8 (RST). An excellent set containing all of Blythe's piano solos plus sides with Jimmy Bertrand and piano duos with Charlie Clark.

Willie Bobo

Percussion, drums; also vocals.
b. New York, 28 Feb 1934; d. 15 Sept 1983.

The son of a Puerto Rican who played folk guitar, William Correa was self-taught on bongos from the age of fourteen and worked with bands including Marcelino Guerra and Perez Prado in his teens. The nickname "Bobo", given him by Mary Lou Williams, became his professional name as he moved from Tito Puente (1954–7) to Cal Tjader (1957–61), playing alongside his mentor Mongo Santamaria in both groups. After working for Herbie Mann (1961–4), making his first album in 1963 and freelancing (for instance, with Miles Davis, Chico Hamilton, Wes Montgomery and on Tjader's *Soul Sauce*), he formed his own band in 1966 in Los Angeles. Albums of the late 1960s successfully covered current pop and soul songs with an Afro-Latin groove, but were rather superficial compared to his live performances. Bobo also performed as a guest with Santana (in the 1971 film *Soul To Soul*) and appeared regularly on television with Bill Cosby. [BP]

⊙ **Talkin' Verve: Willie Bobo** (1965–8; Verve). A reasonable compilation of Bobo's most influential music, including "Spanish Grease" and "Evil Ways" (later a hit for Santana), covers of pops ("The Look Of Love") and of instrumentals such as "Mercy, Mercy, Mercy" and Herbie Hancock's "Blind Man, Blind Man".

➤➤ **Mongo Santamaria** *(Afro-Roots)*; **Cal Tjader** *(The Monterey Concerts)*.

Francy Boland

Piano, arranger.
b. Namur, Belgium, 6 Nov 1929.

Boland played at the 1949 Paris jazz fair and contributed arrangements to record dates by Bobby Jaspar and others in the mid-1950s. He then worked with Chet Baker in Europe in 1955–6, following the death of Richard Twardzik, and began writing charts for radio studio bands such as Kurt Edelhagen. This led to a series of albums and transcription recordings featuring Kenny Clarke (from 1961), gradually leading to live appearances with the all-star Clarke-Boland big band, which revealed Boland as a retiring but effective ensemble pianist. However, his reputation rests on his arranging ability: as well as maintaining an excellent balance between the band sound and his renowned soloists, he was especially noted for his improvisatory writing for the saxophone section. Although there was a comparative lack of invention in his original compositions, Boland's qualities show through strongly in his fresh arrangements of standards that in other people's hands were already hackneyed. [BP]

➤➤ **Kenny Clarke** *(Two Originals)*.

Buddy Bolden

Cornet.
b. New Orleans, 6 Sept 1877; d. 4 Nov 1931.

According to the legend of Buddy (Charles Joseph) Bolden, the first-ever jazz trumpeter – young, handsome and with his shirt "busted open to the waist for all the girls to see that red flannel undervest" (Jelly Roll Morton) – used to parade the streets of New Orleans, four or five women on his arm, playing with a trumpet sound that could be heard fourteen miles away on a clear night. In his spare time he ran a barber shop and a scandal sheet, and went spectacularly insane on a street parade.

All this is standard Bolden folklore, and it seems a pity that most of it is untrue. A piece of clear-eyed research by Don Marquis finally revealed the truth: Bolden never ran a barber shop, although his first bandleader Charlie Galloway did, and Bolden was often in there. Rather than being a scandal-sheet editor, Bolden was a part-time plasterer and labourer, and no trumpet, even on a clear night, could possibly penetrate for more than a quarter of a mile.

The facts unearthed by Marquis reveal that Bolden was raised at 2309 1st Street in New Orleans and left school in 1890. All around him were brass bands, street hawkers' cries, church revival meetings and the ragtime of leaders such as John Robichaux. He was taught cornet by Manuel Hall, a friend of his mother, and played early in his career with Charlie Galloway's band, a small dance group that included Albert Gleny, later a Bolden sideman on string bass. Bolden by degrees took over leadership of the band, retaining Galloway (guitar), Frank Lewis (violin) and in 1897 Willie Cornish (valve trombone). A cylinder recording, which Cornish swore was made before 1898, has never been traced.

Buddy Bolden (back row, second left)

At this time Bolden was developing his cornet playing. What he sounded like is conjecture, but his improvisation, if any, would have been primitive, harmonically elementary (probably confined to melody embellishment) and with a rhythmic approach reflecting the current ragtime vogue. But Bolden was a riveting performer of personal charisma and crowd-pleasing musical power. Marquis proves that by 1900 he was playing all over New Orleans in saloons and dance halls, parks and cabarets, for every stratum of black New Orleans. A gregarious man, he was known as "King" Bolden by 1904 and for two years after was taking more and more work, in the uncomfortable knowledge that young innovators like Freddie Keppard and King Oliver were coming up fast.

Bolden began to drink more, to behave eccentrically, and in 1906, during a Labor Day parade, was put under arrest for dementia. He was soon released and lived at home for another year, but there was no more playing. Bolden moved himself and his family into a rougher area of New Orleans and began drinking heavily: a report in the local paper of an attack on his mother and mother-in-law by the cornettist preceded a phone call to the police by Mrs Bolden on 13 March 1907. That day Buddy Bolden was taken first to jail, then to Jackson Mental Institute in New Orleans; he remained there for 24 years. [DF]

Claude Bolling

Piano, composer.
b. Cannes, France, 10 April 1930.

A child prodigy, Bolling won a jazz contest in 1944 and formed his own small group. He played at the 1948 Nice jazz festival and recorded with Rex Stewart in 1948, Roy Eldridge in 1951 and Lionel Hampton in 1953 and 56. He then formed a big band, which has been regularly reconvened, and was musical director for record sessions (including vocals by Brigitte Bardot) and for films. His later jazz-influenced classical compositions for Jean-Pierre Rampal, Maurice André, Elena Duran and Yo-Yo Ma vastly increased his reputation worldwide. As a jazz pianist, his early ragtime approach broadened into a style reflecting Earl Hines, bebop and Ellington, who also influenced his big-band writing. [BP]

Roy Eldridge

⊙ **French Cooking** (1950-1; Vogue). Bolling's one session with Eldridge is remarkable for the 20-year-old pianist's part in "Fireworks" and "Wild Man Blues", in which he plays Earl Hines to Eldridge's Louis Armstrong.

Claude Bolling

⊙ **Live At The Meridien** (1984; CBS). The majority of Bolling's original big-band albums (as opposed to the classical-crossover works) are gradually being reissued on CD, and this live set with stalwarts such as saxophonist Claude Tissendier is full of delightful Ellingtonian touches.

Sharkey Bonano

Trumpet, vocals, bandleader.
b. Milneburg, Louisiana, 9 April 1904; d. 27 March 1972.

Sharkey (Joseph) Bonano was active in his home town by 1920 (and briefly that year in New York with Eddie Edwards) and all through the 1920s played with fine local bands like the New Orleans Harmony Kings and the Prima-Sharkey orchestra (with Louis Prima's brother Leon); he also auditioned unsuccessfully as a replacement for Bix Beiderbecke in the Wolverines in 1924. Bonano made regular forays into the "big time" early on, including a spell with Jean Goldkette in 1927, and by 1936 was leading his own band in New York. Isolated references seem to indicate that he may have talked a greater game than he played. Nevertheless, Bonano was a fine hot trumpeter, and after the dawn of the New Orleans revival he turned into a highly successful solo act and bandleader, travelling back to New York and Chicago for prestige engagements while still basing himself at home. All through the 1950s he produced a string of albums and singles which became near best sellers, and often featured blues singer Lizzie Miles and "Bugle" Sam deKemel, a well-known local attraction. He played the New Orleans jazz festival in 1969, three years before he died. [DF]

⊙ **Sharkey Bonano 1928–1937** (Timeless). Compiled by John R.T. Davies and Chris Ellis, this is a fine portrait of one of the most colourful New Orleans trumpeters in vintage playing years, with Irving Fazola, Eddie Condon, Georg Brunis and others.

Graham Bond

Alto saxophone, piano, Hammond organ, vocals.
b. Romford, Essex, UK, 28 Oct 1937; d. 8 May 1974.

Adopted by Edwin and Edith Bond from a Dr Barnardo's Home, Graham had lessons on piano, cello and oboe and played in his school orchestra, but was largely self-taught on saxophone. A member of the London scene of the early 60s, between 1961–2 he was a member of the Don Rendell quintet; he then joined Alexis Korner's Blues Incorporated, which included Jack Bruce (bass) and Ginger Baker (drums), but left in 1963 taking Bruce and Baker with him, to start his own group, the Graham Bond Organization (GBO). At first guitarist John McLaughlin was with the group, but after a few months he was replaced by saxophonist Dick Heckstall-Smith. GBO II was formed in 1966 with Jon Hiseman on drums. From 1967–9 Bond led various pick-up groups and visited the USA, jamming with Hendrix, Jefferson Airplane, Dr John and Buddy Miles among others. He was with Ginger Baker's Air Force in 1970–1, and in the following two years formed various short-lived groups.

Bond's two greatest influences were Charlie Parker and Ray Charles, and his music was shot through with elements from the blues and hot gospel, as well as with passionate improvisatory aspects coming out of Parker but veering towards the contemporary avant-garde. He was something of a charismatic figure, one of the pioneers of improvisation on the popular music scene and, with Korner and John Mayall, one of the founding fathers of British R&B. His later years were clouded by a growing obsession with the occult, mystical learning and magic which was most probably a direct or indirect cause of his death: in mysterious circumstances he fell under a London underground train. His seminal albums *The Sound Of '65* and *There's A Bond Between Us* were in 1999 issued as a single disc by Beat Goes On, and are well worth checking out. [IC]

Sterling Bose

Trumpet.

b. Florence, Alabama, 23 Feb 1906; d. June 1958.

Certainly Sterling "Bozo" Bose's credentials are top notch: he worked early on for Jean Goldkette, for Ben Pollack in 1930 and with Joe Haymes's highly disciplined band until Tommy Dorsey took it over in 1935. For the rest of the decade he seems to have moved quickly in and out of most of the best bands: a few months with Benny Goodman, Glenn Miller, Bobby Hackett, Bob Zurke and Bud Freeman. In the early 1940s he was back in New York with small groups led by Miff Mole, Art Hodes and others at Nick's Club. For the last thirteen years of his life, Bose freelanced between Chicago, New York and Mobile, led his own band in Florida and worked clubs, but his reputation seemed to have vanished with the war years and his post-war activities, largely unrecorded and undocumented, are a sad echo. The only anecdotes we have of the pre-war Bose seem to be drunken ones – he was once dragged out of the sea near death from trying to play his trumpet to the fishes, and as a 1930s Decca house musician he was part of an alcoholic quintet known as the Falling-Down Five. Yet appearances on other people's record dates provide a tantalizing glimpse of what he had to offer. [DF]

Earl Bostic

Alto saxophone, arranger.

b. Tulsa, Oklahoma, 25 April 1913, d. 28 Oct 1965.

Bostic played alto in high school and, while at Xavier University, New Orleans, added trumpet and guitar. He worked in several territory bands including those of Bennie Moten and Fate Marable, before joining the bands of Don Redman and Edgar Hayes in New York in 1938, and made his record debut with a Lionel Hampton group including Charlie Christian in 1939. He then led his own

groups, and played and arranged for Hot Lips Page in 1941. After a year with Hampton's band (1943–4), he became busy with freelance recording and arranging, including work for Artie Shaw, Paul Whiteman and Louis Prima. In 1945 he formed a regular group, making the first records under his own name, with an enlarged all-star band; the next year, he began cutting discs with his septet, so successfully that he stayed with the same label for the remainder of his career. The band members usually had to take a back seat to Bostic on records, but among those who gained worthwhile experience with him were Jaki Byard, Jimmy Cobb, Johnny Coles, John Coltrane, Benny Golson, Blue Mitchell and Stanley Turrentine.

Admired by fellow saxophonists for his mastery of the instrument, Bostic also had a considerable influence on R&B styles. His early 1940s' hit "Let Me Off Uptown" was typical of the Louis Jordan era, but his own playing took the vibrant tone and the special effects of southwestern tenor players and turned them into a way of life. His 1945 solo on "The Man I Love" shows him beginning to apply this method to standard songs, a policy which, with the addition of a heavy upbeat, paid off handsomely in "Temptation" (1948) and "Flamingo" (1951). In an era when 99 percent of hit records were vocal, Bostic kept a distinct jazz influence alive in popular music. [BP]

That's Earl, Brother (1943–5; Spotlite). An interesting collection of early work, concluding with his own first session and "The Man I Love", but incorporating a session led by Rex Stewart and airshots of Lionel Hampton with Dinah Washington.

Flamingo (1943–51; Proper). A 2-CD set that overlaps with the above, but includes all the development leading up to the first big international hit "Flamingo" and its follow-up "Sleep".

Boswell Sisters

The Boswell Sisters grew up comfortably in white New Orleans, learning black music from their black staff. Martha (1908–58) played piano, Helvetia (1909–88) played banjo, guitar and violin, and Connee (1907–76), who was confined to a wheelchair by polio, played saxophone, cello, trombone and piano. Connee's finest instrument, though, was her voice; very early on she recorded "Crying Blues" with Martha, and not long after all three sisters were in Los Angeles for a five-nights-a-week radio series. With other broadcasting commitments for CBS the girls were constantly on air, and they discovered their close-blended timbre one night when Connee, suffering from a cold, lost her high notes: singing at half-volume close to a microphone produced their unique sound. In 1931 at the Paramount Theater, New York, the trio created a sensation: they were signed by Brunswick Records and appeared on the first-ever American TV transmission. Their work over the next five years was to be the model for dozens of "sister acts", from Andrews to Beverley, which flourished for the next twenty years.

Most of the Boswell Sisters' 75 or so classic Brunswick records were recorded between midnight and dawn after live radio or theatre shows with stars such as Bunny Berigan, the Dorseys, Mannie Klein and the underrated Larry Binyon. Connee wrote their arrangements, which were neat and complex but with plenty of room for hot solos, and at one point imposed a liquor ban on sessions (it was broken by Artie Bernstein, who kept a bottle of scotch in a trap door at the back of his bass). Now at the peak of their popularity, the sisters made films, including *The Big Broadcast Of 1932, Moulin Rouge* (1934) and *Transatlantic Merry Go Round* (1934); they appeared twice in Britain and in Holland (where they recorded, respectively, with Ambrose and the Ramblers).

By the mid-1930s all three were married, Connee to Harold Leedy, their manager. Thereafter Connee embarked on a highly successful solo career, including radio, TV, films (*Artists And Models*, 1937; *Syncopation*, 1942), cabaret and records (with Bing Crosby, Bob Crosby, Victor Young and Ben Pollack). Her jazz treatment of light classical items such as "Martha", "My Little Gypsy Sweetheart" and "Ah! Sweet Mystery of Life" were early examples of their kind and caused controversy as well as consternation to Decca's prim A & R man Jack Kapp. In the 1950s Connee took a leading role in a successful TV series, *Pete Kelly's Blues* (as Savannah Brown, opposite Jack Webb), and worked tirelessly for charity until her husband's death; she then retired, and died eighteen months later. Perhaps her greatest disciple was Ella Fitzgerald, who said "Who influenced me? There was only one – Connee Boswell. She was doing things that no one else was doing at the time." Those vital things included singing correctly, rather than belting as the older acoustic-bound blues singers had to do. Connee Boswell was the first of the microphone-based singers and she exerted a crucial influence over the new 1930s generation of popular song-stylists. [DF]

⊙ **It's The Girls** (1925–31; ASV). Excellent representative selection of Boswell tracks including "Roll On Mississippi Roll On", "Heebie Jeebies" and "When I Take My Sugar To Tea". Discographic information is slim (unlike volume 2 below) but the music is marvellous.

⊙ **Shout Sister Shout** (1931–36; ASV). Continuing their championship, ASV presents 26 tracks of later Boswells and despite a small amount of duplication, this worthwhile collection includes marvellous tracks here with the Dorsey Brothers, Victor Young and others and a host of star sidemen including Bunny Berigan. Standout tracks include the full band version of "Heebie Jeebies", "An Evening In Caroline" (with great Berigan) and "Rock And Roll" (first use of the phrase!) from the film *Transatlantic Merry-Go-Round*.

Allan Botschinsky

Trumpet, flugelhorn.

b. Copenhagen, 23 Sept 1940.

The son of a professional bassoonist, Botschinsky studied at Copenhagen's Royal Conservatory and joined Ib Glindemann's big band at sixteen. From 1961 he was a member of Danish Radio's Jazz Group and then Big Band, which he later conducted, and he played in small groups with visiting musicians such as Kenny Dorham, Dexter Gordon, Lee Konitz and George Russell. In the 1970s he worked all over Europe with Jan Garbarek and Terje Rypdal, the Nordic Big Band, Swedish pianist Nils Lindberg, Peter Herbolzheimer, Jasper Van't Hof and the European Jazz Ensemble. Awarded the Ben Webster Prize in 1983, he settled in Hamburg in 1985, founded the label MA Music with Marion Kaempfert (daughter of MOR maestro Bert) and taught at Holland's Hilversum Conservatory. Teaching and playing visits have taken him to London (where he has lived in recent years), New York, Brazil and New Zealand, and he remains an astute improviser with an individual approach. [BP]

⊙ **The Bench** (1995; Storyville). Recorded in concert as a winner of one of the Danish Jazzpar awards, Botschinsky leads a quintet including Alex Riel, Jesper Lundgaard and Stan Sulzmann. As well as his exemplary playing, he features five attractive original pieces including two based on standards, "Ray's Delight" and the title track.

Lillian Boutte

Vocals.

b. New Orleans, 6 Aug 1949.

Boutte studied music and sang in a church choir before playing a leading role in the jazz-based musical *One Mo' Time*, after which she teamed with her husband-to-be, the German saxophonist Thomas L'Etienne, to form the group known first as their Music Friends and later as the Boutte-L'Etienne Jazz Ensemble. During the 1980s Boutte became a regular on the British and European festival circuit (she is Official Jazz Ambassador for the City of New Orleans) and in 1987, after their appearance together at the 1987 Edinburgh international jazz festival, began a musical association lasting several years with

Humphrey Lyttelton. A fine and stylistically flexible singer, Boutte continues to tour and make the festival rounds today. [DF]

The Dazzling Lillian Boutte (1988; Calligraph). This excellent album on Lyttelton's Calligraph label illustrates Boutte's combination of delicacy, vaudevillian strength and all-round versatility.

Lester Bowie

Trumpet, flugelhorn, vocals, percussion, composer.
b. Frederick, Maryland, 11 Oct 1941; d. 9 Nov 1999.

Bowie was brought up in Little Rock, Arkansas, and St Louis, Missouri, and began playing at the age of five. At sixteen he led a youth group in St Louis and he used to practise his trumpet by an open window in the hope that Louis Armstrong might pass by and discover him. After military service he worked with R&B bands and also with his wife, singer Fontella Bass. He played on R&B sessions for Chess Records and also helped to form BAG (Black Artists Group) and the Great Black Music Orchestra in St Louis. In 1966 he moved to Chicago, got involved with AACM, and joined the band of saxophonist Roscoe Mitchell. In the later 1960s he and Mitchell were founder members of the Art Ensemble Of Chicago, one of the key groups of the 1970s and 80s. In 1969 Bowie recorded with Archie Shepp, Sunny Murray, Jimmy Lyons and Cecil Taylor, among others. He was also involved in intermittent solo projects and recordings over the years. He composed, conducted and recorded "Gettin' To Know Y'All" with the fifty-piece Baden-Baden Free Jazz Orchestra in 1969, performing it again at the 1970 Frankfurt jazz festival. In 1974 he toured Senegal, performing with African drummers, and in 1979 played a New York concert with his 59-piece Sho Nuff Orchestra. He also recorded with Jack DeJohnette and Fela Kuti.

Bowie was a flamboyant performer with a flair for comedy and musical parody, and became a major contributor to the theatrical side of the Art Ensemble's concerts. He was also a fine trumpet player with a beautifully rounded tone and a technique and imagination which encompassed the whole trumpet tradition from Bubber Miley's growls to modern musings and the whole improvising field from blues and popular songs to the most severe abstraction. In the mid-1980s Bowie began leading his Brass Fantasy, a ten-piece (or more) ensemble which harked back to the brass-heavy marching bands of early New Orleans music. The danger of Bowie's theatricality and parody was that they could simply be attempts (conscious or otherwise) to conceal an emptiness of real musical purpose. This was sometimes the case with Brass Fantasy, and the growls, slurs and other mannerisms of his trumpet playing could be tedious when not expressing genuine feeling or creative imagination. [IC]

Jak Kilby

Lester Bowie

The Fifth Power (1978; Black Saint). Bowie leads a powerful quintet with altoist Arthur Blythe in fine form. Blues and hot gospel feelings galvanize the whole album.

Works (1981–6; ECM). This is a useful compilation of tracks from Bowie's four ECM albums. Also included is one track from the Art Ensemble's 1980 Full Force album – Bowie's own moody composition "Charlie M", which inspires some highly focused trumpet playing.

My Way (1990; DIW). This is one of the more purposeful performances by Brass Fantasy. The solos are meatier and even the more jokey performances (cf. the title track) have redeeming features.

The Fire This Time (1992; In + Out). This has excellent arrangements full of incident, and much fine ensemble work and soloing. Bowie himself seems curiously offhand in his solos, but ready and voluble with the verbals. On "Night Life", for example, the pith and purpose of E.J. Allen's trumpet solo rather puts his leader in the shade.

>> **Jack DeJohnette** *(New Directions)*; **David Murray** *(Live At The Lower Manhattan Ocean Club)*.

Dave Bowman

Piano.
b. Buffalo, New York, 8 Sept 1914; d. 28 Dec 1964.

A great jazz pianist who worked in the musical area of Bushkin, Schroeder et al, Dave Bowman studied at Hamilton Conservatory, Ontario, and the Pittsburgh Music Institute, and also toured Britain with Jack Hylton's band before moving into Nick's Club, New York, in 1936. There he worked with Bobby Hackett and with the Summa Cum Laude Orchestra until 1940, when he joined Jack Teagarden's band. Months with Joe Marsala and

Muggsy Spanier followed in 1941, after which Bowman became a staffman for ABC and NBC, often working as accompanist to singer Perry Como. From 1954 he worked with Bud Freeman's trio, then moved to Florida to freelance; in 1964 he was working for Phil Napoleon and in a Miami hotel band when, three days after Christmas, his car plunged into a drainage canal near Miami and he drowned. [DF]

➤➤ **Bud Freeman** *(It's Got To Be The Eel).*

Gary Boyle

Guitar, composer.

b. Patna, India, 24 Nov 1941.

Boyle is an extraudinary jazz-rock guitarist with few equals. His family moved to London when he was eight and he started on guitar at fifteen. He worked for twelve months with Brian Auger and Julie Driscoll in 1966, then studied from 1967–9 at Leeds College of Music, after which he spent another year with Auger. From 1970–73 he played with Mike Westbrook and Mike Gibbs and recorded with Stomu Yamashta. He led his own jazz-rock group Isotope from 1973–5, which toured in Europe; he then moved to Manchester and freelanced. In 1978, Boyle's solo album *The Dancer* received the Montreux Jazz/Pop Award.

He often works in duo and other formations with John Etheridge, and in 1992 he toured the UK in duo with Eberhard Weber. His trio played the Brecon festival in 1993 and the Glasgow festival the following year. In 2003 Boyle released a new trio album, *Games*, with Riaan Vosloo (bass) and Patrick Illingworth (drums); the set also featured Zoe Rahman's piano. Boyle's influences are many, but his favourite guitarists are John McLaughlin, Robben Ford and Mike Stern. [IC]

⦿ **Triple Echo** (1994; The Jazz Label). This features Boyle with bass and drums playing acoustic and electric guitars and synthesizers, with a strong world music emphasis.

Charles Brackeen

Tenor and soprano saxophones.

b. White's Chapel, Oklahoma, 13 May 1940.

Brackeen studied violin and piano in his youth. In his teens, he moved back and forth between New York and California (where he met his wife, pianist Joanne Brackeen, and worked with members of Ornette Coleman's band); he settled in New York in the early 60s. Clearly influenced by Coleman, with a loose, bluesy, roughly harmolodic approach, Brackeen worked extensively with Edward Blackwell over the years. In 1973 he recorded *Rhythm-X* as leader for Strata-East, with Blackwell, cornettist Don Cherry, and bassist Charlie Haden (ie Ornette's classic quartet). He also played with percussionist Paul Motian, recording with him for ECM. After a long, reportedly reclusive hiatus, Brackeen was convinced by trumpeter Dennis Gonzalez to begin recording again in 1986; for the Silkheart label he made three excellent records (*Bannar*, *Attainment* and *Worshippers Come Nigh* – see below) and appeared on Dallas-based Gonzalez's Debenge Debenge. Like various other members of his generation – Sonny Simmons, Fred Anderson, Olu Dara – Brackeen has never quite broken as the major figure his music indicates he could be. From the 90s, sadly, he slipped again from public earshot. [JC]

⦿ **Worshippers Come Nigh** (1987; Silkheart). The last of Brackeen's troika for Silkheart, recorded at the same session as *Attainment* with cornet great Dara, bassist Fred Hopkins and drummer Andrew Cyrille, this is a lesser-known gem of free jazz, featuring ebullient soloing and five excellent original Brackeen tunes.

Joanne Brackeen

Piano, composer.

b. Ventura, California, 26 July 1938.

As an adolescent, Joanne Brackeen (née Grogan) learned piano by copying Frankie Carle records and making her own "inner music". She had a few private lessons, but left Los Angeles Conservatory of Music after only three days. By 1958 she was playing West Coast clubs with Dexter Gordon, Harold Land and others. In 1959 she played with Teddy Edwards and Charles Lloyd, then, after marrying saxophonist Charles Brackeen, she gave up performing to devote time to their four children. In 1966 she moved to New York and began to play in public again. She worked with Woody Shaw and Dave Liebman in 1969 and then spent two years from 1969–71 with Art Blakey's Jazz Messengers. After three years with Joe Henderson, in 1975 she joined Stan Getz, who brought her to the attention of a wider public, particularly in Europe where she was much appreciated. By 1977 she had established herself as a major solo voice, receiving much critical recognition. Leonard Feather has commented that she was as important to the 1980s as Bill Evans and Herbie Hancock were to the 1960s and McCoy Tyner and Keith Jarrett to the 1970s. Since the 1980s she has led her own small groups, frequently playing tours and festivals in Europe.

Brackeen seems to have digested the whole jazz tradition including abstraction and jazz-rock, as well as various ethnic elements, and her compositions emerge from this brew eloquently, with sometimes asymmetrical rhythms and often idiosyncratic melodies. She has said: "I prefer using my own material to standards. Different songs are like babies, and I feel better playing one that I created and nurtured than one I adopted, no matter how good it is." [IC]

⦿ **Special Identity** (1981; Antilles). Brackeen leads a dream rhythm-section with Eddie Gomez and Jack DeJohnette.

Havin' Fun (1985; Concord). Another definitive trio with Cecil McBee and Al Foster.

Live At Maybeck Recital Hall Vol 1 (1989; Concord). Brackeen playing dynamic solo piano with a mixture of standards and originals.

Where Legends Dwell (1991; Ken). Again the virtuoso trio with Gomez and DeJohnette playing a series of Brackeen compositions including the richly asymmetrical "Picasso".

Power Talk (1994; Turnipseed Music). Brackeen easily holds her own in a man's world, and this superb trio album, with bassist Ira Coleman and drummer Tony Reedus, shows why and how. She reinvents that old chestnut, "There Is No Greater Love", and generally has the vision and technique to take risks and live on the edge of time in these performances of standards and one or two of her originals.

Don Braden

Tenor and soprano saxophones, flute.

b. Cincinnati, Ohio, 20 Nov 1963.

Raised in Louisville, Kentucky, Don Braden began playing saxophone at the age of thirteen. After moving to New York in 1984, Braden played with the Harper Brothers, organist Lonnie Smith and the doyenne of talent scouts and nurturers of youthful jazz talent, Betty Carter, making his recording debut on the singer's Grammy-winning album *Look What I've Got* (1988; Verve). Having toured with Wynton Marsalis (1986–8), Braden also played with drummers Roy Haynes and Tony Williams, trumpeter Freddie Hubbard and trombonist J.J. Johnson before becoming a leader in his own right and working as musical supervisor on *The Cosby Show*. In addition to sideman recordings with singers Jeanie Bryson and Freddy Cole, trumpeters Tom Harrell, Valery Ponomarev and Scott Wendholt, organist Melvin Rhyne and fellow Carter alumnus, pianist Stephen Scott, Braden has made a series of hard-swinging but tasteful albums as a leader, landing a major deal with RCA that resulted in his most celebrated album, *The Voice Of The Saxophone*. Live, Braden reveals a warmly elegant, cultured tenor tone, but he is a surprisingly gutsy improviser on material ranging from hard-bop staples by the likes of Hank Mobley, through Coltrane pieces, to his own vigorous compositions. [CP]

The Voice Of The Saxophone (1997; RCA). Octet versions of saxophone classics ranging from Wayne Shorter's "Speak No Evil" and Jimmy Heath's title track, through lesser-known gems like Sam Rivers's "Point Of Many Returns", to Coltrane's "After The Rain". An all-star band (Vincent Herring, Randy Brecker, Hamiet Bluiett, Frank Lacy, plus pianist Darrell Grant, bassist Dwayne Burno and drummer Cecil Brooks III) interprets Braden's arrangements (he also produces) faultlessly.

Bobby Bradford

Trumpet.

b. Cleveland, Mississippi, 19 July 1934.

Brought up in Dallas from age twelve, Bobby Bradford played in high school and college with Cedar Walton and David Newman, and gigged with Buster Smith and others. In 1953, he moved to Los Angeles, began collaborating with Ornette Coleman, and appeared with Wardell Gray, Gerald Wilson and Eric Dolphy. After military service and further studies, he replaced Don Cherry with the Coleman quartet in New York from 1961–3. Back on the West Coast, he co-led a group with John Carter from 1965–71, then made visits to Europe in 1971, 1972–4 and 1986, recording each time with John Stevens. More recently, he has been teaching in Los Angeles and leading his own groups. None of Bradford's early 1960s work with Coleman was recorded, although he was on Ornette's 1971 *Science Fiction* and *Broken Shadows* sessions, but his dates under his own name reveal a thoughtful and melodic player who benefited from the "free jazz" experience to define his individual style. [BP]

John Carter & Bobby Bradford

Seeking (1969; hat Art). The original quartet, with bassist Tom Williamson and drummer Bruz Freeman (brother of Von), pursue their extension of Coleman's methods on this reissued album. The same label also has a live 1988 reunion of Carter and Bradford with an all-star rhythm trio.

Perry "Mule" Bradford

Piano, composer.

b. Montgomery, Alabama, 14 Feb 1893; d. 20 April 1970.

Described by Pops Foster as "one of those old honky-tonk pianists that played with one finger", Perry "Mule" Bradford travelled between the South and New York in the 1910s playing for shows, rent parties, saloons and singers. He went to New York to stay around 1920, while managing vaudeville singer Mamie Smith, and it was her recording of "Crazy Blues" (written by Bradford as part of the score for his show *The Maid Of Harlem*) which single-handedly launched the 1920s blues craze, "race recordings", Smith's career and Bradford's. From then on he toured with Mamie Smith and worked busily as a black talent scout, song-plugger, publisher (in 1923 he was jailed for infringement of copyright laws) and composer. His famous compositions include "That Thing Called Love", "Evil Blues" and "You Can't Keep A Good Man Down". Bradford recorded as a bandleader in the 1920s under the title Perry Bradford's Jazz Phools: the "phools" included Louis Armstrong, Don Redman, Charlie Green and James P. Johnson. [DF]

Will Bradley

Trombone, composer.

b. Newton, New Jersey, 12 July 1912.

After work with CBS as a staffman from 1931, Will Bradley (Wilbur Schwichtenberg) joined Ray Noble's new American orchestra in 1935, where his section mate was Glenn Miller. "He can do more things better than any trombone player I've ever heard", said Miller then, and Bradley stayed in demand in studios until 1939, when with drummer Ray McKinley he formed a band which quickly created a successful style of its own, playing big-band boogie. But Bradley enjoyed playing ballads as well as up-tempo tunes and had a questing mind which was later to take him into the world of contemporary classical composition. From 1942 he returned to studio work and played the Tonight show, while also studying composition and pursuing a spare-time interest in gemstones. In the words of a fan letter to *Metronome* magazine in 1946: "He is as fluent as the early Teagarden, as graceful as Dorsey even in the fastest of passages and as imaginative as McGarity at his Goodman best." [DF]

⊙ **Will Bradley 1940** (Tax). Good collection of two radio broadcasts (excellent sound) by the Bradley-McKinley orchestra.

Tiny Bradshaw

Piano, vocals, drums, bandleader.
b. Youngstown, Ohio, 23 Sept 1905; d. 26 Nov 1958.

Tiny (Myron) Bradshaw is remembered as a pioneer R&B bandleader (he had several hits during the early 50s, including "Well, Oh Well") but his professional career began twenty years before that when, after graduating from Wilberforce University (where he sang with Horace Henderson's Collegians), he went on to work with the Alabamians, Mills Blue Rhythm Band and Luis Russell. In 1934 he formed his own band and began recording regularly, switching to a permanent R&B policy in the mid-1940s and continuing to play regularly until he was incapacitated by strokes. [DF]

Ruby Braff

Cornet, trumpet.
b. Boston, Massachusetts, 16 March 1927; d 9 Feb 2003.

Ruby (Reuben) Braff was working around Boston in the late 1940s, but it was some classic records by Vic Dickenson's septet in 1953–4 that brought him into the spotlight. However, the 1950s were less than kind to Braff in working terms: the critical acclaim that surrounded his prolific recordings was seldom reflected in his datesheet. He arrived at a time when all players of his age were expected to sound like Dizzy Gillespie or Clifford Brown: his swing-based alternative was ignored by jazz fashion. For the next few years he worked on and off at jazz festivals, in clubs and on radio and TV (as well as playing an acting role in *Pipe Dreams* on Broadway in 1955–6), but by 1960 was able to report to Leonard Feather that he had been "almost continuously out of work for five years". If so, it showed no effect on his recorded output, which was the most revolutionary

Jak Kilby

Ruby Braff

of any trumpeter/cornettist operating in his jazz area at the time: albums such as *Holiday In Braff* (a re-creation of Billie Holiday splendours with Bob Wilber's saxophone section), *Easy Now!* (on which he teamed with Roy Eldridge without being bested or cowed) and *Ruby Braff – Featuring Dave McKenna* (which shows him at his hard-blowing 1950s best) all prove it.

By the 1960s Braff was working more regularly: with George Wein's Newport All Stars (he formed a love-hate relationship with Wein's piano playing) and often in Europe as a soloist, where one of his happiest partnerships was with Alex Welsh's fine British band. In the 1970s, now established as a star solo cornettist who often appeared with pianist Dick Hyman and the New York Jazz Repertory Company, he formed one of his few regular groups, with guitarist George Barnes. In its short, sometimes stormy career (both leaders were quick-tempered artists), the Braff-Barnes quartet created small-group jazz to set alongside Louis Armstrong's Hot Five and the groups of Benny Goodman and Teddy Wilson: music that was delicate but never precious, strong but never strident, tasteful but never effete. After quarrels parted the leaders, Braff returned to solo performance, making a conscious decision to work only with those whose musical viewpoint matched his own. Crucial collaborations included classics such as *America The Beautiful* with Dick Hyman, a Crosby set with strings titled *Swingin' On A Star*, which Armstrong could scarcely have bettered, and duets with pianist Gene de Novi. Other partners on and off the record included guitarist Ed Bickert and more regularly guitarist Howard Alden, who with bassist Frank Tate formed the perfect delicate backing for Braff's controlled creativity. Another regular partner in later years was Scott Hamilton, with whom Braff worked effortlessly; their *New England Songhounds* albums are high art. Despite a severe illness in 1993, he was performing in 1994 with undiminished excellence in a new two-guitar quartet featuring Gray Sergeant and continued to work and record despite a recurring asthmatic condition and developing emphysema until a few weeks before his death. During a last tour of Britain in 2002, his mastery and creative flair were audibly undimmed.

Braff remains the most artistic trumpeter/cornettist to emerge since Louis Armstrong, who represented everything that Braff respects in music: honesty, lyricism, strength, sound, and the kind of polished-jewel creations that Braff has called "the adoration of the melody". Unlike most late impressionists, Braff not only absorbed Armstrong's philosophies but constructively added to them. First, he developed a mobile facility which revolutionized the technique of many trumpeters in the 1950s but never toppled over into the "fast fingering" that Armstrong justly dismissed. Second, he introduced a sound in the low cornet register that is as arresting as Armstrong's yet different: a cello-round tone-cavern that no trumpeter had achieved before. Third, he evolved, like Bobby Hackett, an individual and challenging harmonic route through chords which avoided the stock devices of bebop. In later years his style refined and modified itself, but never lost the grace and beauty which made Braff's work inimitable. In 2003 the jazz world, in the words of Eddie Cook, is "just coming to terms with his death". The life that preceded it irrevocably established Ruby Braff as one of the greatest classic jazz musicians of any period. [DF]

⦿ **With An Extra Bit Of Luck** (1989; Concord); **Younger Than Swingtime** (1990; Concord). Braff and Hyman play music from the score of *My Fair Lady* and *South Pacific* respectively; both superb throughout.

⦿ **Bravura Eloquence** (1990; Concord). Featuring his regular young guitarist partner Howard Alden with Jack Lesberg on bass; superbly musical chamber jazz.

⦿ **Calling Berlin Vols. 1 & 2** (1994; Arbors). Two old masters (and lifelong collaborators) at work on the music of Irving Berlin. Braff is as toweringly lyrical as ever; Ellis Larkins's shaded originality at the piano supports him as understandingly as it did in the 1950s.

⦿ **Braff Plays Wimbledon: The First Set/The Second Set** (1996; Zephyr). Recorded in Britain for John Bune this set has Ruby with Warren Vaché and Howard Alden plus Roy Williams, Brian Lemon, Dave Green and Allan Ganley. All is excellence, but on Vol. 1 the trio selections (with Lemon and Ganley) are miniature masterpieces.

⦿ **America The Beautiful** (2002; Arbors). A simply exquisite set with Dick Hyman (possibly Braff's most sympathetic and co-creative partner) playing pipe organ. Originally issued as *A Pipe Organ Recital Plus One* but with seven new tracks, this is definitive Braff.

⦿ **Variety Is The Spice Of Braff** (2002; Arbors). Something close to a swansong for Braff, this great collection presents him playing as well as always in settings from quintet to big band.

Dollar Brand

➤➤ *see entry for* **Abdullah Ibrahim**

Wellman Braud

String bass.

b. St James Parish, Louisiana, 25 Jan 1891; d. 29 Oct 1966.

First on violin, then on bass, Wellman Braud (originally Breaux) played in Tom Anderson's New Orleans saloon, moved to Chicago in 1917 to work with Sugar Johnnie and Charlie Elgar's band, and by 1923 was on tour with James P. Johnson's *Plantation Days* review. After three more years with Will Vodery, vaudevillian Wilbur Sweatman, Jelly Roll Morton and others, he joined Duke Ellington in 1927 and became a stylish focus of attention as well as a musical pacesetter. "The way he was slapping the bass!" recalls Mercer Ellington. "When they recorded he always made sure he was close to the mike and it's amazing how his sound still comes through on those old records." After leaving Ellington in 1935 he managed the Spirits Of Rhythm, ran his own restaurant, got involved in other Harlem business ventures and led his own trio. Although officially retired from 1944 he remained active in jazz, touring with Kid Ory in 1956 and returning to regular gigs after a heart attack in 1961.

Like Pops Foster, Braud had a colossal impact on younger contemporaries like Milt Hinton and Tiny Winters, and he set a style for most pre-Blanton bassists. "I just worshipped him – he was my mentor", said Hinton. "He had such dignity and power – a real New Orleans gentleman." [DF]

Duke Ellington

⦿ **Jungle Nights In Harlem** (1927–32; RCA Bluebird). Produced by Orrin Keepnews, this is a superior collection of Duke Ellington and his Cotton Club Orchestra, with Braud soloing on "Freeze And Melt" and "Creole Love Call".

⦿ **Swing 1930–38** (BBC Records). Braud's bass shows up clearly here, including in solo on "Blue Harlem".

Anthony Braxton

Saxophones, clarinets, flute, composer; also vocals, electronics, percussion, accordion, harmonica, musette.

b. Chicago, 4 June 1945.

Braxton had lessons from 1959–64 with Jack Gell of the Chicago School of Music, and studied harmony and composition at Chicago Musical College and philosophy at Roosevelt University. He met

Roscoe Mitchell and Jack DeJohnette while at Wilson Junior College. His early influences were Paul Desmond, Coltrane and Schoenberg, and later Miles Davis, Eric Dolphy, Lee Konitz and Jackie McLean.

He was in the army from 1964–6 where he played in bands and began leading small groups. Back in Chicago, he joined the AACM and has said of that experience: "There was a degree of unification among musicians in Chicago that wasn't attainable in New York ... There was so much communication and interchange, and careful study and research ... It wasn't as competitive." In 1968 he created a milestone in jazz history when he recorded a double LP of solo alto saxophone, *For Alto*, not released until 1971. He went to Paris in 1969 with the Creative Construction Company, which included Leroy Jenkins (violin), Leo Smith (trumpet) and Steve McCall (drums), but the group had little success there. Braxton said, "Our music was perceived as being cold, and that has stuck with me."

Back in the USA he went to New York at Ornette Coleman's invitation, staying with him for a while. Then for a year Braxton gave up music and worked as a chess hustler in Washington Square Park, New York. In 1970 he began an informal association with Chick Corea, playing with him and studying scores by Stockhausen, Boulez, Xenakis and Schoenberg. He joined Corea's newly formed group Circle, which included Dave Holland and Barry Altschul. Circle lasted two years (1970–2) and played in the USA and France, where the group recorded a live double album.

The release of *For Alto* in 1971 brought high praise and several accolades. It encouraged the fashion for solo instrumental performances and by 1972 was one of Delmark Records' best-selling albums. That year Braxton made his concert debut as a leader, playing at the Town Hall, New York, in duo, trio and quintet formations; he also played solo at Carnegie Hall.

Since then he has continued to lead his own groups, touring and playing festivals in the USA, Canada and Europe. In the early 1970s he also worked with the Italian group Musica Elettronica Viva, playing contemporary classical and improvised music. In the mid-1970s he led a trio with Holland and Altschul, sometimes augmented by Kenny Wheeler (trumpet). Braxton signed a recording contract with Arista Records in 1974 and moved to Woodstock. In 1975, with the quartet, he toured Europe and played festivals including Graz and Hamburg, and in September his trio played at the concert of Arista jazz artists in New York and were the only acoustic group in a programme otherwise entirely made up of heavily electronic jazz-rock-fusion bands. The trio seemed like an oasis of sanity in a desert of decibels; their severe music was warmly received. In 1976 Wheeler left the quartet and his place was taken by trombonist George Lewis. In the

1980s Braxton continued touring in Europe and elsewhere; in 1985 he toured Britain with a quartet for the Arts Council Contemporary Music Network, and Leo Records recorded a double CD-worth of material at each of three of the concerts. He has continued to lead this quartet – Marilyn Crispell (piano), Mark Dresser (bass) and Gerry Hemingway (drums) – intermittently since.

Braxton is as much a composer as an improviser, and he has used mathematical relationships, diagrams and formulae as a basis for both composing and playing. He is one of the first black musicians working in abstraction to acknowledge a debt to contemporary European art music, and his music often seems to have a kind of wilful intellectualism. He has been accused of being swingless; as Gary Giddins put it: "His heavy involvement with the fashions of the European avant-garde seemed to stifle the exuberant vitality of his best work." Whether he swings or not, his restless creativity is constantly seeking new outlets. The range of his ambition is vast: at one end of the spectrum there are the solo saxophone performances and duo performances with musicians such as Derek Bailey and Evan Parker; at the other extreme are the totally composed works for huge ensembles such as his *For Four Orchestras*, which has been described as "a colossal work, longer than any of Gustav Mahler's symphonies and larger in instrumentation than most of Richard Wagner's operas". However, whether Braxton's large orchestral works are as listenable as those of Mahler or Wagner is a moot point. [IC]

⊙ **Three Compositions Of New Jazz** (1968; Delmark). This is Braxton's recording debut as leader with some of the Chicago AACM heavies – trumpeter Leo Smith, violinist Leroy Jenkins and pianist Muhal Richard Abrams – in his quartet.

⊙ **Composition No. 96** (1981; Leo). Braxton has composed for a 37-piece orchestra which he conducts here. The music breathes in its own way with pauses and dynamics, but the relentless abstraction and angularity ultimately seem cliché-ridden and become wearisome. The ludicrously voluminous liner notes read like a parody of depraved academicism.

Quartet (London) 1985; Quartet (Birmingham) 1985; Quartet (Coventry) 1985 (all Leo). Braxton always seems most convincing in small-group formats – anything from solo to quartet or quintet. These double-CD sets were made during a British tour with one of his finest groups comprising pianist Marilyn Crispell, bassist Mark Dresser and drummer Gerry Hemingway. The music has great clarity and variety, and the group played a different programme for each concert. The Coventry recording has the added bonus of two interviews with Braxton.

Seven Compositions (Trio) 1989 (hat Art). This trio with bassist Adelhard Roidinger and drummer Tony Oxley is a superb unit. The resulting music is powerful, packed with incident and most accessible; the trio's hurtling reading of "All The Things You Are" makes nonsense of claims that Braxton can't play jazz.

Duo (London) 1993 (Leo). This is an inspired performance by Braxton and Evan Parker at the Bloomsbury Theatre during the first London jazz festival. The listening and thinking are almost palpable, the feeling often tender, the phrases sculpted, sometimes delicately, sometimes marmoreally. Occasionally the calm is ruffled by some brilliant saxophone squabbling.

Trio (London) 1993 (Leo). Braxton and Parker a day later, playing at the same place, this time augmented by trombonist Paul Rutherford who brings a swashbuckling insouciance to the proceedings. It may not be as exquisite as the duo, but the trio performance makes up for it in drama and incident.

Lenny Breau

Guitar.
b. Auburn, Maine, 5 Aug 1941; d. 12 Aug 1984.

Breau's parents were Canadian country-music singers and he began playing this music professionally in Canada. His jazz work absorbed the ideas of Tal Farlow, Barney Kessel and Johnny Smith, but also introduced some of the techniques of country exponent Chet Atkins into his jazz style. Atkins later offered Breau his first recording contract with RCA in 1968. Breau adopted a pianistic approach to the guitar, using a classical fingerstyle technique to provide beautifully voiced accompanying chords to his own improvised lines. He also adapted aspects of Bill Evans and McCoy Tyner's styles for the guitar, and his musical curiosity extended further afield to flamenco. These elements all contributed to a unique and fertile style, but Breau's career was fractured by his dependency on drugs and by long periods without public performances. He contributed technical articles to *Guitar Player* magazine and collaborated with John Knowles on an instruction book, *Lenny Breau Fingerstyle Jazz*. [CA]

The Velvet Touch Of Lenny Breau (1969; One Way). One of the best of a dozen Breau albums, and the sole CD reissue, this live collection of standards and originals includes five solo tracks.

Michael Brecker

Tenor and soprano saxophone, EWI, flute; also piano.
b. Philadelphia, 29 March 1949.

Brecker studied with Vince Trombetta from 1965–9 and then Joe Allard. At first he was interested in rock – Cream and Hendrix – and later in King Curtis, Junior Walker and Coltrane. One of his initial inspirations was an Alan Skidmore tenor saxophone solo on a John Mayall album. In 1970 he went to New York where his brother, trumpeter Randy Brecker, had been based for four years. Michael's first professional job was with an R&B band led by Edwin Birdsong, and in 1970 he also played with Billy Cobham. He was a member of a jazz-rock group called Dreams, which functioned for two years or so and also recorded, but had no success. In 1973 he worked with James Taylor, then in 1973–4 he was with Horace Silver. From 1974–5 he was again with Billy Cobham and also played with Yoko Ono in Japan. With Randy he formed the Brecker Brothers, which became one of the most successful jazz-rock groups of the mid-70s.

DAVID REDFERN

Mike (left) and Randy Brecker

At the end of the decade, he was a member of the all-star group Steps, which eventually changed its name to Steps Ahead. Originally formed for a Japanese tour, they became one of the most successful bands of the early 1980s, touring and playing festivals all over the world. Their first albums were recorded in Japan and imported into the USA, but they eventually signed with a US company. Brecker eventually left the group, which carried on under Mike Mainieri's leadership. In the 1980s Brecker became the leading exponent of the EWI (Electronic Wind Instrument), which is blown like a saxophone but has a range of over nine octaves – from basso profundo to bat squeak – and toured internationally with his own small groups. He also toured as soloist with

Paul Simon, and in the 1990s Michael and Randy re-formed the Brecker Brothers.More recently he has been worked on his own solo albums, but with the help of such greats as Charlie Haden, Herbie Hancock and Pat Metheney.

Brecker developed into perhaps the most comprehensive saxophone talent of the 1970s and 80s, with a burnished, incisive sound and a fluency and drive which are unsurpassed. He can set his stamp on virtually any kind of context – big band, small group, electronic jazz-rock – which is why he has been one of the busiest studio musicians and certainly the most recorded saxophonist since 1975. [IC]

Brecker Brothers

⊙ **The Brecker Brothers Collection Vols. 1 & 2** (1975–81; RCA). This is a selection of some of the Brothers' classic fusion tracks. Occasionally guilty of overkill, there is nevertheless much subtlety and exhilarating virtuosity in the performances. It's a fascinating document of those heady, hearty times.

Michael Brecker

⊙ **Michael Brecker** (1987; Impulse). Brecker's first album under his own name has a dream line-up – a rhythm-section of Charlie Haden and Jack DeJohnette plus Pat Metheny and Kenny Kirkland. It bristles with intention and has much excellent playing, particularly from the leader. As a session man, Brecker learned to "say something" in short solos and this density and completeness of ideas persists even when he's stretching out.

⊙ **Now You See It (Now You Don't)** (1990; GRP). This is an intelligent fusion album with various personnel, and again Brecker's playing is awesome.

⊙ **Tales From The Hudson** (1997; GRP). An all-star band, again featuring DeJohnette, produce one of Becker's finest recordings.

Brecker Brothers

⊙ **Return Of The Brecker Brothers** (1992; GRP). Michael and Randy share the composing on this brilliant album. The music often has ethnic undertones, and it ebbs and flows with great subtlety. The EWI is used to good effect, and the blend of acoustic and electric instruments is imaginatively done. The playing is superlative, but the real triumph is the warm and expansive atmosphere which pervades the album.

➤➤ **Pat Metheny** *(80/81).*

Randy Brecker

Trumpet; also piano, drums.

b. Philadelphia, 27 Nov 1945.

Randy Brecker played gigs with R&B bands while still at school. While at the University of Indiana from 1963–5 he played in the big band and small groups, and had private lessons with David Baker. The Indiana big band won a competition at Notre Dame festival and did a US State Department tour of Europe and the Middle East, after which Brecker stayed on in Europe for three months working free-lance. Back in the USA he moved to New York, working with Blood Sweat and Tears in 1966. He worked with Horace Silver in 1967, 1969 and 1973. He also played with Janis Joplin, Duke Pearson, Clark Terry's big band, Stevie Wonder and Art Blakey. In 1970, with his saxophonist brother Mike, he joined the jazz-rock group Dreams, staying with it until 1972. In the early 1970s he was also with Larry Coryell's Eleventh House and Billy Cobham's group, and he worked with Deodato and Johnny and Edgar Winter. He was also very active as a studio musician playing in brass sections on the albums of many artists, including James Brown and Gladys Knight. In 1974, with Michael Brecker, he formed the hugely successful jazz-rock group the Brecker Brothers.

In the later 1970s the Brecker brothers opened a successful club in New York. As well as continuing to do studio work, they have also worked together as sidemen in acoustic bands playing neo-bop; in 1978, in this capacity, they recorded a magnificent live album (*Speak With A Single Voice*) with a group led by Hal Galper.

In the 1980s Randy continued to tour internationally with his own groups. He was also in the huge orchestra which recorded and toured performing Charles Mingus's monumental composition *Epitaph.*

After a long silence, the Brecker Brothers reformed in the early-90s and in 2003 Randy was on the road again, touring a new CD, *34th N Lex*, with his own quintet.

Randy Brecker's style comes out of the Clifford Brown-Freddie Hubbard school, and he is a virtuoso performer who has many fine acoustic and electric (amplified trumpet) solos on record. [IC]

⊙ **In The Idiom** (1986; Denon). With a sublime rhythm-section, Ron Carter and Al Foster, the gifted young pianist David Kikoski and the magical Joe Henderson, Brecker revisits his acoustic jazz roots. The benign spirit of the past is clearly evident – shades of Horace Silver, Blakey, Clifford Brown – but rhythmically, harmonically and melodically, these deft performances of Brecker's eight compositions are also very much music of the 1980s.

⊙ **Live At Sweet Basil** (1988; Sonet). Another tribute album, this time with Bob Berg, bassist Dieter Ilg, the excellent Joey Baron on drums and Kikoski again. This is a light-hearted live session, with six neat Brecker compositions and some excellent all-round playing.

➤➤ **Larry Coryell** *(Introducing The Eleventh House).*

John Wolf Brennan

Piano, prepared piano, pipe organ, melodica, conductor.

b. Dublin, 13 Feb 1954.

Brennan has a strong classical music background. His mother was a leading classical singer in Ireland, while his father was an accomplished pianist. Brennan's brother, Peter Wolf, was a founder member of the successful art-rock group Flame Dream (early 1970s–1986), and in 1974 Brennan was also briefly a member of that band.

In 1961, Brennan's family moved permanently to Switzerland, where he went to school in Lucerne.

John Wolf Brennan

He began piano lessons in 1965 and continued through his teens. His discovery of The Beatles, Pink Floyd, Cream, Miles Davis and Hendrix inspired him in 1970 to take up bass guitar and join Crossbreed, a blues-rock band. By 1974, he was playing electric keyboards, and after his short stint with Flame Dream he turned to jazz-rock, then went back to acoustic piano to play music that included African, Indian and Irish elements.

In 1977 he formed his first free-improvisation jazz group, Freemprovisations, with trumpeter Peter Scharli; the troupe ranged from a duo to a quartet. From 1979, he began leading other groups, beginning with the quintet Impetus, which had the unusual line-up of violin, recorder, saxophone, marimba, guitar, bass guitar, drums, piano and electric piano, and which recorded his first LP, *Opening Seed*. In the 1980s he led groups ranging from duos to big bands. 1988, though, was a crucial year, during which Brennan lived for six months in New York, recorded two duo CDs, and married Beatrice Schmidlin, a Swiss classical pianist.

In 1989 he formed a more permanent quartet, Pago Libre, with Steve Goodman (violin), Lars Lindvall (trumpet and flugelhorn) and Daniele Patumi (double bass), which toured Germany, Austria and Hungary. The following year Pago Libre was augmented with leading Europeans, making it a thirteen-piece band. In 1990, Brennan also made a solo piano concert tour of the Ukraine.

During the 1990s there were more tours, festivals, different groupings of musicians, and more compositions. In 1995, he performed solo piano recitals in Moscow and St Petersburg, and a year later toured Russia with Pago Libre. In 1997 a fellowship from the Swiss Art Foundation enabled him to live for six months in London's East End, which resulted in his solo piano album *The Well-Prepared Clavier*, and *Hextet...Through The Ear Of A Raindrop*. Brennan also performed and/or recorded with other British musicians while in London, including Eddie Prevost, Simon Picard and Elton Dean. Although his favourite pianists include Bill Evans, John Taylor, Gordon Beck, Keith Jarrett and Carla Bley, he was probably more influenced by non-pianists such as guitarists John McLaughlin and Fred Frith. Brennan now resides back in Switzerland, but continues to compose for a wide range of conceptual settings and installation environments.

Brennan is a virtuoso pianist and improviser, and an excellent composer, whose work combines elements from jazz, rock, ethnic and classical music. His recorded output is large and ever-growing. [IC]

Christy Doran/John Wolf Brennan

⊙ **Henceforward** (1988; Leo Lab). Doran is a fine guitarist and also a gifted composer. His rapport with Brennan is excellent and the duo's twelve performances of original compositions cover the emotional and musical spectrum, from the romantic melody and resonant harmony of "Cascades" to the ebullient free improvisation of "Collages".

John Wolf Brennan

⊙ **Moskau-Petuschki**; **Felix-Szenen** (1997; Leo Lab). Of his forty theatrical works, these are the only two which have been issued on disc, and Brennan regards them as his best. Using two violins, a French horn doubling hand-horn, plus Lars Lindvall (trumpet and flugelhorn) and Daniele Patumi (bass), and voices, Brennan creates 35 allusive and atmospheric pieces which, even without knowledge of the texts for which they were written, are compelling and profoundly focused.

⊙ **Hextet ... Through The Ear Of A Raindrop** (1998; Leo Records). Brennan here works with some of the strongest musical personalities on the international scene – soprano and tenor saxophonist Evan Parker, singer Julie Tippett, trombonist Paul Rutherford, bass-clarinettist Peter Whyman and drummer Chris Cutler. Brennan plays piano and prepared piano in this project, which mixes Brennan compositions based on various poems (from Seamus Heaney to Shakespeare) with improvised commentary on the text. Brennan's piano, prepared or not, is often a focal point in the proceedings, and the response of the improvisers is superb.

⊙ **The Well-Prepared Clavier** (1998; Creative Works Records). Brennan plays piano or prepared piano on 24 short pieces that are like a kind of musical diary, in which the poetic and the abstract create a bracing tension.

Willem Breuker

Reeds.

b. Amsterdam, 4 Nov 1944.

Dutch saxophonist, clarinettist, and composer Willem Breuker formed his first band (23 pieces) in 1966, and the same year he recorded with a large ensemble led by German pianist Alexander von Schlippenbach on Globe Unity (MPS). A year later, he was a co-founder – with pianist Misha Mengelberg and percussionist Han Bennink – of the Instant Composers' Pool, a collective and record company that he eventually left in 1973. In the mid-70s, he formed the Willem Breuker Kollektief, the pioneering eclectic jazz ensemble that has been his primary vehicle since that time. Combining elements of free jazz, Nino Rota soundtracks, late romantic and vanguard classical, marching band, European folk musics, and anything else it could find, the Kollektief presaged later cut-up artists like John Zorn, though in so doing they looked back to vaudeville and earlier New Orleans traditions. Breuker has continued to work on other projects sporadically with Bennink (as the New Acoustic Swing Duo) and to run his own BVHAAST record label (on which he has released nearly thirty of his own albums), scoring films (like *De Illusionist/Kkkomediant*, with filmmaker Freek de Jonge, and *Music For His Films* 1967/1994, with Johan van der Keuken, both released on BVHAAST), and augmenting the Kollektief with strings, orchestra, singers, and barrel organ (on Psalm 122, also BVHAAST). [JC]

⊙ **To Remain** (1983–9; BVHAAST). The two finest Kollektief records – *Live In Berlin* (1975; FMP) and *In Holland* (1981; BVHAAST double LP) – still haven't made their way onto CD. Still, this disc, which comes packaged as if it were a vinyl LP, is a good indication of the band in full-force shtick; loads of fun, but also masterfully executed (makes most straight big bands sound under-rehearsed) and brilliantly blueprinted by architectural (and comic) master Breuker.

Dee Dee Bridgewater

Vocals.

b. Memphis, 27 May 1950.

Dee Dee (Denise) Garrett married trumpeter Cecil Bridgewater in 1970, sang with the Thad Jones-Mel Lewis Jazz Orchestra in the early 1970s and appeared in the stage version of *The Wiz* in 1975. By 1980 she had broadened her scope to include pop music (including a hit record with Ray Charles, "Precious Thing"), but then in Europe re-established her jazz activities with the show Lady Day. From then on she has continued to appear at European jazz festivals and in concert, singing regularly with her own trio and even teaming with opera singer Julia Migenes for live shows. Influenced by Nancy Wilson, Nina Simone and Tina Turner, she is a gifted all-round performer whose style – despite regular forays into pop music territory during the 1970s and after – is rooted in jazz: "Jazz is my soul, my roots – it's me", she told Don Waterhouse in 1993. She is frequently hailed as a successor to Ella Fitzgerald. [DF]

⊙ **Live at Montreux** (1990; Verve). Bridgewater tackles "hard" jazz material on this set (including "A Night In Tunisia" and the challenging "Strange Fruit") amid the surroundings of a standard jazz trio led by pianist Bert Van Den Brink.

⊙ **Live at Yoshi's** (2000; Verve). Again with a trio (this time led by organist Thierry Eliez), Bridgewater furnishes a convincing display of her jazz talents, including scat and an effective version of "What A Little Moonlight Can Do".

Arthur Briggs

Trumpet.

b. Charleston, South Carolina, 9 April 1899; d. 15 July 1991.

One of the legendary trumpet-founders of jazz, Briggs trained at Jenkins' Orphanage under the private tuition of Eugene Mikell and later worked in army-based bands before joining Will Marion Cook's Southern Syncopated Orchestra (starring Sidney Bechet) from 1919–1921. Throughout the 1920s Briggs travelled widely in Europe, playing with Noble Sissle (1928) and leading his own orchestras; after work with Freddy Johnson and Barretto's Cuban Orchestra he once again led for himself (in Paris and Egypt), recording with Coleman Hawkins in 1935. After internment during World War II, Briggs continued a successful career in France, and subsequently taught both brass and saxophones before retiring c. 1970. [DF]

Alan Broadbent

Piano, arranger, composer.

b. Auckland, New Zealand, 23 April 1947.

A luminously delicate but rhythmically robust pianist, Alan Broadbent composes for classical ensembles as well as arranging for jazz ensembles ranging from big bands to singers. After studying at Auckland's Royal Trinity College of Music, he attended Berklee (1966–9) and was given private tuition by Lennie Tristano. At 22, he became Woody Herman's pianist and arranger; six years later, an ambitious work involving chamber groups and the Houston Symphony Orchestra alongside the Herman big band was premiered as "Variations On A Scene". Jazz ensemble work with Bud Shank, a quintet featuring both Warne Marsh and Gary Foster, and with Charlie Haden's Quartet West followed, but Broadbent continues to involve himself both in solo work and in composing chamber music. He is much in demand as an arranger for both strings and horns, having worked in this capacity for both singer Karin Allyson and pianist Marian McPartland, and he frequently collaborates with fellow Concord artists, appearing on Scott Hamilton's *With Strings* album (1992) and arranging the same tenorman's *Christmas – Love Song* (1997).

Although his great influences are Bud Powell, Lennie Tristano and Bill Evans, Broadbent is instantly recognizable for his mellifluous, bright sound and his intense musicality. Broadbent himself claims he owes "everything" to Charlie Parker, whom he terms his "abiding inspiration". [CP]

Charlie Haden

⊙ **Quartet West** (1987; Verve). Theme album (all musicians – Ernie Watts and Billy Higgins, along with Haden and Broadbent – reside in LA, where the album was recorded) of great depth and beauty, its repertoire ranging from Charlie Parker and Ornette Coleman material to Haden originals.

Alan Broadbent

⊙ **Live At The Maybeck Recital Hall Vol. 14** (1991; Concord). Definitive solo Broadbent in supremely sympathetic surroundings, playing sparkling but superbly sensitive versions of everything from Tristano's "Lennie's Pennies" to Powell's "Parisian Thoroughfare".

⊙ **Personal Standards** (1997; Concord). Exquisitely played by a supremely sensitive trio – bassist Putter Smith and drummer Joe LaBarbera alongside Broadbent – these are the pianist's own favourite compositions, plus one from Smith.

Alan Broadbent-Gary Foster

⊙ **Live At The Maybeck Recital Hall** (1993; Concord). As above, but with Stan Getz-like Foster on alto and tenor.

Sheila Jordan

⊙ **Heart Strings** (1994; Muse). Best example of Broadbent's arranging and accompanying skills since his mid-1970s album with Irene Kral.

Bob Brookmeyer

Valve-trombone, arranger; also piano.

b. Kansas City, Missouri, 19 Dec 1929.

After working as pianist with several big bands, Brookmeyer joined the Stan Getz quintet in 1953. Work with the Gerry Mulligan quartet/sextet (1954, 1955–7) was followed by a spell with the Jimmy Giuffre trio in 1957–8, after which he freelanced in New York as player and arranger and toured with Mulligan's big band, for which he also wrote. Co-leader with Clark Terry of an occasional quintet from 1961–6, he was also a founder member of the Thad Jones-Mel Lewis band (1965–7), while becoming more active as a freelance writer and studio musician, first in New York and then in Los Angeles. His jazz profile revived in New York in the late 1970s, playing with his own quartet and writing new arrangements for the Mel Lewis band. As well as continuing to compose more complex works, he has taught arranging and composition in New York and Holland and performed in duo with Jim Hall. In 1995 he toured Britain with Tony Coe, and was appointed composer/conductor of the Danish Radio Big Band from 1996–7, since when he has retained a base in Europe while also teaching at the New England Conservatory.

Brookmeyer's valve-trombone sound initially seems rather unemotional but is capable of considerable variation – from the deliberately deadpan tone which he uses for unaccented and apparently aimless Tristano-esque doodling, to the warm yet fuzzy quality shown when injecting some swing-era phrasing. His best solos result from a mixture of these approaches, combined with the occasional full-throated shout. This approach blended especially well with Clark Terry during their partnership, and it shows also in his big-band arranging, which marries the influences of early Gil Evans and Gerry Mulligan in a way that makes them appear almost over-serious by comparison. Of Brookmeyer's own tunes, "Open Country" (recorded with both Mulligan and Getz) and "Jive Hoot" have been popular with other players. [BP]

⊙ **Traditionalism Revisited** (1957; Pacific Jazz). Brookmeyer has always displayed a liking for the uncomplicated humour which pervades some early jazz, particularly the work of its trombonists. Here, with partners Jimmy Giuffre and Jim Hall, he also indulges his taste for material such as "Louisiana" and "Ja-Da", and the CD contains two extra tracks previously only on compilations.

⊙ **Dreams** (1988; Dragon). Recorded with a Swedish big band, this involved and occasionally dour writing typifies Brookmeyer's composition in his post-Mel Lewis period.

➤➤ **Stan Getz** *(At The Shrine)*; **Gary McFarland** *(How To Succeed In Business)*; **Clark Terry** *(Gingerbread)*.

Tina Brooks

Tenor saxophone.

b. Fayetteville, North Carolina, 7 June 1932; d. 13 Aug 1974.

Harold Floyd Brooks was the younger brother of tenorman David (Bubba) Brooks Jnr, who played with Sonny Thompson (1950s) and Bill Doggett (1970s–80s). "Tina", as he was known from childhood, moved with the family to New York in 1944 and went on to tour with the R&B bands of

Sonny Thompson in 1950–51, Charles Brown, Joe Morris, Amos Milburn and Lionel Hampton (1955). Then, associating with Benny Harris and Elmo Hope, he worked in various Bronx and Harlem clubs in 1956–7 and recorded with Jimmy Smith ("The Sermon" etc, in 1958) and Kenny Burrell. After a brief recording career lasting until 1961, he slid into obscurity and drug problems. The conviction and fluency of his playing, reminiscent of Hank Mobley, were until recently undervalued (only one album under his own name was released during his lifetime). But reissues, followed by first-time issues of sessions previously withheld, have led to a renewed interest in his work. [BP]

Back To The Tracks (1960; Blue Note). This initially unreleased album (with Blue Mitchell and Art Taylor) attained legendary status before finally appearing in the 1980s, and is recommended for Brooks' quiet, logical invention.

➤➤ **Jimmy Smith** *(The Sermon).*

Brotherhood Of Breath

A band formed in London in 1970 by South African pianist Chris McGregor from a nucleus of fellow expatriates (the Blue Notes) and a number of British free-jazz musicians, Brotherhood of Breath produced a rumbustious mix of exuberant riff-based music, bebop, African polyrhythms and freely improvised jazz. They were active chiefly in the early 1970s, until McGregor moved to France, but he continued to cherish the dream of keeping the band on the road full-time as Ellington used to do, "not as an institution, but as a community", and it continued to play together – even touring Mozambique in the 1980s – until McGregor's premature death in May 1990. The band's original core members were the South Africans Dudu Pukwana (alto), Mongesi Feza (trumpet), Johnny Dyani (bass) and Louis Moholo (drums), augmented by a stellar selection of 1970s UK-based jazz musicians, including trumpeters Harry Beckett and Marc Charig and saxophonists Evan Parker, Mike Osborne and John Surman. The 1980s version of the Brotherhood featured, along with Beckett, a new generation of UK-based players, among them trumpeter Claude Deppa, trombonist Annie Whitehead and saxophonists Steve Williamson, Julian Argüelles and Chris Biscoe.

In 1992, the Spirits Rejoice Trust was formed, to assist burgeoning musical talent in South Africa, and the Dedication Orchestra, assembled from a nucleus of the old Brotherhood (Louis Moholo the only survivor of the original Blue Notes, but joined by Keith Tippett, Evan Parker, Claude Deppa, Chris Biscoe etc), played to launch the fund. The orchestra produced two albums, 1992's *Spirits Rejoice* (studio and live recordings), and, two years later, *Ixeska* (Time), both on Ogun. In 1993 the same label brought out another album in the Brotherhood spirit: *Freedom Tour Live In South Afrika*, by Moholo's Viva La Black. Keeping the Blue Notes/Brotherhood flame burning, the Dedication Orchestra regrouped (with Steve Beresford conducting) for a special concert broadcast by the BBC in 2003. [CP]

Travelling Somewhere (2001; Cuneiform). A powerfully energetic live date (recorded a week before *Live at Willisau*, but not unearthed until decades later) on which the band sound inspired and the audience thrilled.

Live At Willisau (1974; Ogun). Pretty representative sample of the band's live sound, including the straightforwardly tuneful "Tungis Song".

Country Cooking (1988; Venture). Buoyant, invigoratingly eclectic music from new-generation Brotherhood.

Peter Brötzmann

Saxophones, clarinets.
b. Remscheid, Germany, 6 March 1941.

Brötzmann studied painting at art school in Wuppertal and was self-taught as a musician. He began playing traditional jazz and swing at eighteen, but graduated rapidly to the free jazz of the 1960s, and since then has stayed with abstraction. In 1966 he worked with Carla Bley, Michael Mantler and Steve Lacy, touring Europe with the group Jazz Realities. Subsequently he played with Don Cherry and most leading European free improvisers. From 1968, he led his own trio with Fred van Hove (piano) and Han Bennink (drums). Brötzmann has also worked and recorded with Globe Unity Orchestra and Albert Mangelsdorff. Since the late 1960s he has been a member of Free Music Production (FMP), a musicians' collective concerned with promoting abstract music nationally and internationally, and which produces records and organizes concerts and festivals. Brötzmann is one of the most important pioneers of free jazz, though he has often been overlooked by historians with a Stateside focus; his technique is dynamic and unrelenting, and the sound he makes can truly take your breath away. [IC]

JAK KILBY

Peter Brötzmann and bass clarinet, with Peter Kowald

Machine Gun (1968; FMP). Brötzmann leads several key free-jazz players including Evan Parker, Willem Breuker, Peter Kowald and Han Bennink in this effort to turn the recording studio into a combustion chamber with a mighty free-for-all. It's astonishing that everyone had enough energy after this freak-out to end all freak-outs to do two alternative takes – which are included on the CD, making it another fascinating document of those heady times.

The Berlin Concert (1971; FMP). This has Brötzmann's trio with pianist Fred van Hove and Han Bennink augmented by trombonist Albert Mangelsdorff, performing at the Berlin Free Music Market.

No Nothing (FMP; 1990). Brötzmann's third solo saxophone album, and perhaps his most coherent.

Nipples (2000; Atavistic). Brötzmann's 1969 sextet at their most explosive and powerful; a classic session.

Anthony Brown

Drums, percussion, leader.
b. San Francisco,17 Mar 1953.

Born to Japanese and African-Native American parents, Brown was raised in California, Japan and Germany. He gained BSc degrees in music and psychology at the University of Oregon (1975) while playing locally, then spent four years in the US army, during which he played in Europe and hooked up with the James Newton-John Carter quartet in 1978. Further academic achievements followed, including a PhD in ethnomusicology from the University of California at Berkeley, while teaching percussion and lecturing on music history. Brown played with Anthony Davis in the 1980s and with the San Francisco-based group United Front, which mixed jazz and non-Western instruments, as he did again with Jon Jang's Pan-Asian Arkestra in the early 1990s. Since then, he has performed with Sir Roland Hanna, David Murray, Cecil Taylor and Zakir Hussain among others, and in 1998 he formed his own Asian American Jazz Orchestra, recording an album inspired by the World War II imprisonment of Asian Americans in the US, and an adaptation of the Ellington-Strayhorn Far East Suite. He is the author of a book of modern jazz drumming, *Give The Drummer Some* (2003). [BP]

Monk's Moods (2000; Water Baby). The comparison of bebop with "Chinese music" is brought to triumphant life in Brown's adaptation of several famous Monk tunes for his Asian American Orchestra. In particular, the Chinese dulcimer played by Yang Qin Zhao sounds closely akin to Monk's piano.

Boyce Brown

Alto saxophone.
b. Chicago, 16 April 1910; d. 30 Jan 1959.

Boyce Brown was a jazz eccentric with an angular playing style who for most of his life stayed in Chicago. He worked through the 1930s and 40s in good company, including Wingy Manone, Paul Mares and Danny Alvin, as well as leading his own bands, but recorded only a few sides (with Wild Bill Davison amongst others) before entering a Servite monastery in 1953. In 1956, as "Brother Matthew", he emerged to make his only album and appear on TV with Eddie Condon, who remembered him later: "a slow reader, blind in one eye with about one tenth vision in the other! But he was an intellectual who listened to Delius and wrote poetry." Some of that poetry, reprinted in Condon's scrapbook, suggests that Brown was no stranger to earthly pleasures. [DF]

Cleo Brown

Piano, vocals.
b. Meridian, Mississippi, 8 Dec 1909 (or 1907); d. 15 April 1995.

When her Baptist minister father moved to Chicago in 1919, Cleo Brown played piano in church and learned boogie from her pianist brother. She worked for a touring show, and from the late 1920s had Chicago club and radio residencies. In 1935 she replaced Fats Waller on his New York radio series and, as a result, began recording. Working in New York, Chicago, Los Angeles, San Francisco and Las Vegas regularly until 1953, she gained international popularity. She then took up full-time nursing, but after retirement to Denver in 1973 she played and sang religious "inspirational music" under the name C. Patra Brown.

Her version of "Pinetop's Boogie-Woogie" influenced many subsequent players, male and female; it is all the more surprising that she only ever made thirty tracks during the 78rpm era (eighteen in one year, 1935–6). Her singing is cute rather than profound (providing an unmistakable cue for Rose Murphy and Nellie Lutcher), but the driving piano work is what really counts. [BP]

The Legendary Cleo Brown (1935–6; President). This collection of seventeen Decca sides includes her solo track "Pelican Stomp" and her "Boogie Woogie" hit, but emphasizes her coyly rhythmic vocals and Waller-influenced stride piano.

Living In The Afterglow (1987; Audiophile). A brief rediscovery after 35 years of obscurity led to an appearance on radio with Marian McPartland, who guests on four duets. The other tracks have Brown singing and playing solo on a mixture of traditional gospel items and original compositions.

Clifford Brown

Trumpet, composer.

b. Wilmington, Delaware, 30 Oct 1930; d. 26 June 1956.

Brown's father, an amateur musician, gave him a trumpet when he was fifteen. He studied trumpet privately in Wilmington, also taking lessons in jazz harmony, theory, piano, vibes and bass. By 1948 he was playing gigs in Philadelphia with people such as Miles Davis, Kenny Dorham, Max Roach, J.J. Johnson and Fats Navarro. The latter encouraged and influenced him. In 1949 he entered Maryland State University to study music, and did some arranging for the college band. From June 1950 to May 1951 he was in hospital after a car crash which almost killed him, but resumed playing with the encouragement of Dizzy Gillespie and others. From 1952–3 he played trumpet and piano with an R&B group, Chris Powell and his Blue Flames, and briefly worked and recorded with Tadd Dameron. From August to December 1953 he worked with Lionel Hampton's band, touring Europe and recording as leader with a French rhythm-section. Early in 1954 he was briefly with the Art Blakey quintet, recording two magnificent live albums with them. In mid-1954 he joined Max Roach in a group that became known as the Clifford Brown-Max Roach quintet, spending the rest of his life with it. He won the New Star award in the *Down Beat* critics' poll in the same year, but was killed in a road accident at the age of 25.

Clifford Brown had genius as both a trumpet soloist and a composer/bandleader. He absorbed his main influences (Gillespie and Navarro) very rapidly, and by the age of 22 was already an original stylist. His was one of the fullest and most beautiful trumpet sounds in jazz, and it was this which brought him nearer to Navarro than Gillespie. The latter had always sacrificed fullness of tone in order to achieve almost supernatural speed, flexibility and range. Navarro and Brown sought for tonal beauty, with Brown having just the edge in terms of breadth and resonance: a crackling, brassy sound with plenty of vibrato. He had an excellent range, great stamina, superb execution and an apparently inexhaustible capacity for melodic invention which expressed itself fluently at any tempo, whether breakneck, medium or slow. But above all his music exuded warmth and joy, and it is these qualities which gave his brilliance such human eloquence.

The quintet he co-led with Max Roach, one of the finest groups of the 1950s, included pianist Richie Powell (Bud Powell's brother), bassist George Morrow and, at various times, saxophonists Sonny Stitt, Harold Land and Sonny Rollins. During the quintet's two-year existence, Brown's sound gained in fullness and beauty and his technique in sureness, and his ideas became more daring. Some of the live recordings of the group rank with the very greatest in jazz. Brown was an excellent composer for small groups, and several of his themes, such as "Joy Spring", "Daahoud" and "Sandu", have become part of the standard jazz repertoire. As a trumpet stylist, his influence lives on in the work of Lee Morgan, Freddie Hubbard and Wynton Marsalis, and every subsequent jazz trumpeter has been influenced by him either directly or indirectly. His music reflected his personality and character: he was clean-living, disciplined, and had a warm gentle disposition which made him much loved by his associates. [IC]

HERMAN LEONARD

Clifford Brown

Clifford Brown Memorial (1953; OJC); **The Complete Paris Sessions Vols. 1, 2 & 3** (1953; Vogue). In 1953, Brown was already a magnificent player but hadn't quite reached the full heights of his genius. The warmth and lyricism are already apparent, but the supremely incisive imagination and technique have not yet quite coalesced. Nevertheless, these historic recordings have the optimism and expectancy of a major talent on the verge of realization.

Jazz Immortal (1954; Pacific Jazz). By February 1954, when, with Art Blakey's quintet, Brown recorded *A Night At Birdland*, his incandescent genius was fully in evidence. Later that year he did the *Jazz Immortal* sessions on the West Coast with a septet including Shelly Manne and Zoot Sims. The music is not as fiery as the earlier Blakey recording, but in this genial and relaxed company Brownie sounds like a supreme master.

Brownie (1954–6; Emarcy). This ten-CD boxed set covers Brown's most productive period and includes nine previously unreleased takes. All the superlative Brown-Roach quintet tracks are here plus a wealth of other material including the *Clifford Brown With Strings* album, and albums on which he accompanies Sarah Vaughan and Helen Merrill.

Alone Together (1954–6; Verve). This is a double CD, but only the first one features Clifford Brown. However, it has some of the finest Brown-Roach performances and an assortment of other tracks from the period. The second CD is devoted to Max Roach with other musicians.

➤➤ **Art Blakey** *(A Night At Birdland Vols. 1 & 2).*

Damon Brown

Trumpet, Piano.

b. London, 24 Dec 1965.

There was always a piano in the young Damon Brown's house, but it was his art teacher at secondary school who really got him started. Study at Leeds College of Music was followed by the Guildhall School in London and weekend jazz workshops at Interchange. While still a student, Brown began to play with groups on the UK pop and reggae scenes with artists such as Paul Weller, Prince Buster, The Pasadenas and Roco Rodriguez. He also performed with the group Push alongside Rubin Wilson, Weldone Irvine and Big Jon Patten.

In 1996 Brown began to focus entirely on leading and composing for his own jazz group, developing into a superb musician with a unique style on both trumpet and flugelhorn. His first album, *Rhythmic Indicative* (1998), received very favourable reviews and helped to establish him on the British jazz scene. It was followed by *Blues On The Run* (2001) on Ronnie Scott's Jazz House label, *Good Cop Bad Cop* with pianist Jonathan Gee, and his finest album to date, *A Bigger Picture* (2002). [IC]

A Bigger Picture (2002; 33 Records). Eleven of the twelve pieces were composed by Brown, and the variety and originality of both the writing and playing is striking. Excellent support from the rhythm section of Ben Hazleton (db), Sebastian Rochford (d) and pianist Leon Greening.

Donald Brown

Piano, composer.

b. Hernando, Mississippi, 28 March 1954.

Brown grew up in Memphis, having moved with his family at the age of two. His five sisters all played piano but he started out on drums, baritone horn and trumpet, which won him several awards. Taking up a music scholarship to Memphis State University (1972–5), he specialized in piano and was encouraged to concentrate on jazz by fellow student James Williams. After doing R&B session work and gigging in Memphis, he replaced Williams with Art Blakey in 1981–2, finally being forced to leave by rheumatoid arthritis in his hands. While teaching at Berklee (1983–5) and the University of Tennessee (from 1988), he took occasional gigs with such as Freddie Hubbard and Lockjaw Davis, and continues to make his own albums. Already a prolific writer while with Blakey, his new tunes have since been recorded by Williams, Art Farmer, Donald Byrd, Jon Faddis, Wynton Marsalis, Kenny Garrett and Wallace Roney. [BP]

Cause And Effect (1991; Muse). As well as straightahead tracks featuring vibraphonist Stéve Nelson, James Spaulding and guest Joe Henderson (a remake of his "Black Narcissus"), Brown's compositions briefly incorporate voices on several socially conscious titles reminiscent of the late 1960s.

Lawrence Brown

Trombone.

b. Lawrence, Kansas, 3 Aug 1907; d. 5 Sept 1988.

The serious-minded son of a minister (he never smoked, gambled or drank), Lawrence (Olin) Brown studied to be a doctor, then began his musical career in bands led by Charlie Echols and Paul Howard. He became a kingpin of Duke Ellington's mighty trombone section in 1932 (he was christened "Deacon" for his mournful demeanour), and was given a new feature every year – they included "Ducky Wucky", "Slippery Horn", "Sheikh Of Araby", "Yearning For Love", and his own composition "Golden Cress". Brown especially loved the cello, an instrument whose sound and approach he applied to the trombone – Brown's style was revolutionary in its speed, creamy tone, neurotic vibrato and range. He later reluctantly took over "Tricky Sam" Nanton's role as plunger specialist. "I don't like using the plunger", he said, "but I imitate the tops: Tricky Sam. That buzzing breaks your lip down and you have to wait a little while to get back to normal." Brown left Ellington in 1951 ("I was tired of the sameness of the big band", he said), and joined Johnny Hodges's breakaway small group until 1955, when he took "the best job in the business" – a staff position replacing Warren Covington at CBS. But in 1960 he was back with Ellington for another ten years, then left again with the pronouncement:

"We have to realize that being popular is nowadays more important than producing anything of value." After 1970 he was active in business consultancy, took part in the Nixon re-election campaign and later took up the post of recording agent for Hollywood's branch of AFM.

Brown made splendid solo recordings with Hodges, Joe Turner and Jackie Gleason, to name just three, and his smooth yet highly personal creations were an incalculable influence on trombonists from Tommy Dorsey to Bill Harris. [DF]

➤➤ **Johnny Hodges** *(Everybody Knows Johnny Hodges).*

Les Brown

Bandleader/saxophone

b. Reinerton, Pennsylvania, 14 Mar 1912; d. 4 Jan 2001.

After learning the clarinet with his bandmaster father, Brown studied harmony, arranging and composition at Ithaca Conservatory, New York, before completing his musical training at Duke University, North Carolina. While at university he joined – and soon led – the campus dance band The Blue Devils before forming a new band, Les Brown's Orchestra, with arranger Glenn Osser. In 1940 Brown recruited Doris Day as the band's singer but she stayed for less than a year befor being replaced by Betty Bonney with whom the band had their first big hit "Joltin; Joe DiMaggio". In 1942 the band appeared in the comedy-musical film *Seven Days' Leave* alongside Lucille Ball, and it was around this time that Brown settled on the name Band of Renown for his orchestra. Day's return in 1943 provided Brown with his biggest hit, "Sentimental Journey", which was followed by the instrumental "I've Got My Love To Keep Me Warm". In March 1947, following a successful Hollywood Bowl concert, he teamed up with Bob Hope for an association that included radio and TV, and which lasted into the 1980s. At its peak in the 1950s Brown's fine ensemble included a number of significant jazz cornermen; amongst whom were saxophonist Dave Pell, trumpeters Jimmy Zito, Al Porcino and Don Fagerquist, and drummer Mel Lewis. Though the band's recordings are rather milder than hard-line big band jazz they still make for enjoyable listening. [DF]

Les Brown and his Band Of Renown

⊙ **Best Of The Capitol Years** (2002; Capitol). Brilliantly re-mastered 1940s material when Brown and the band really knew how to swing. Includes "I've Got My Love To Keep Me Warm".

Marion Brown

Alto saxophone, composer, ethnomusicologist.

b. Atlanta, Georgia, 8 Sept 1935.

Brown studied saxophone, clarinet and oboe at school and college. After playing in an army band and, in 1957, with Johnny Hodges in Atlanta, he went to New York. There he became involved with the free improvisation of the day and recorded with Archie Shepp (*Fire Music*) and John Coltrane (*Ascension*). He led his own group in the mid-1960s, having been introduced to Impulse records by Shepp; he later acknowledged Shepp's part in his success when he recorded the album *Three For Shepp*. Brown then spent some years in Europe, playing and recording with, among others, Sun Ra and Gunter Hampel. While there, he became deeply interested in African music. In 1970 he returned to the USA where he has taught and studied oral tradition, linguistics and compositional disciplines in African music. He also explored the possibilities of African instruments, and invented his own instruments, while his solid, earthy alto sound remains distinct. [IC]

⊙ **Why Not** (1966; ESP). Brown's work is leavened with memories of ethnic music, and it is hardly ever declamatory. Here in the company of pianist Stanley Cowell, bassist Sirone and drummer Rashied Ali, his meditative and lyrical cast of mind prevails.

⊙ **Gemini (1983; Birth).** Brown in duo with Gunther Hampel playing vibraphone and bass-clarinet. The context and sonorities suit Brown's gentle temperament.

Marshall Brown

Leader, composer, arranger, educator, valve-trombone.

b. Framingham, Massachusetts, 21 Dec 1920; d. 13 Dec 1983.

In the 1950s Marshall Richard Brown was a musical educationalist and an innovator in the youth jazz movement as bandmaster for high school bands – one of which, Farmingdale, played the 1957 Newport jazz festival. In the 1960s he worked in eclectic adult company, including Ruby Braff, Eddie Condon, Roy Eldridge and, in particular, with a Gerry Mulligan-type pianoless quartet which showcased a new-style Pee Wee Russell and featured Brown's own compositions. In the 1970s he worked just as easily with Lee Konitz's quintet, for whom again he wrote the book. His compositional talents produced several quite successful pop songs, and he was a shining-toned, technically able soloist who, like Bob Wilber, Dick Cary and Rusty Dedrick, was often to be found at the inspirational centre of intelligent jazz projects. [DF]

⊙ **New Groove** (1962; Columbia). Now very hard to find, but this old vinyl album shows off Brown's cultivated technique in the uncluttered surroundings of a piano-less quartet, Mulligan-style, with Pee Wee Russell.

Pete Brown

Alto and tenor saxophones; also trumpet, violin, piano.

b. Baltimore, Maryland, 9 Nov 1906; d. 20 Sept 1963.

Some swing musicians survived the onslaught of bebop more comfortably than others. Charlie Parker, its central figure, presented a challenge to the older generation which it was necessary either to ignore (as Johnny Hodges calmly did) or to come to terms with. Of the swingmen who plumped for the second option, Pete Brown is perhaps the most uncomfortable example.

He played piano first, and went to New York in 1927 with Bernie Robinson's band, by which time he was doubling trumpet and saxophone. For the next ten years he worked for lesser-known leaders such as Charlie Skeets and Fred Moore and struck up a strong friendship with trumpeter Frankie Newton which found its way onto record from the mid-1930s. Together they joined John Kirby's first band in 1937 but it was a brief stay: a year later Brown was once again leading his own groups up and down 52nd Street and by 1940 was co-leading with Newton at Kelly's Stables. Over the next ten years he stayed busy enough: he commuted between Boston, Chicago and New York with and without Newton, briefly fronted Louis Jordan's band in 1943, and continued club work into the 1950s.

Up to this time his style was a grit-toned, happy statement of all the best qualities of swing, and he single-handedly invented the "jump style" of alto. But then his style seemed to change for the worse: his sound coarsened and elements of Parker's innovations appeared, then disappeared, from his solo work, like an unwelcome spectre at a feast. On a 1954 recording date for Bethlehem, Brown's selection of repertoire, as much as his style, hovers uncertainly between contemporary vehicles ("There Will Never Be Another You") and familiar stand-bys ("The World Is Waiting For The Sunrise"), and his solo contributions are dwarfed by trumpeter Joe Wilder. Brown was to make only one more record, for Verve in 1959, before he died. In later years he was ill, too, from diabetes and weight problems, and he spent a lot of time teaching as well as playing club residencies. But on Joe Turner's *Boss Of The Blues* album, from the very period when, according to received opinion, Brown was no longer a force to be reckoned with, he sounds just as good as he ever did, surrounded by such compatible friends as Walter Page, Lawrence Brown and Pete Johnson. [DF]

>> **Joe Turner** *(The Boss Of The Blues).*

Pud Brown

Trumpet, reeds.

b. Wilmington, Delaware, 22 Jan 1917; d. 27 May 1996.

One of a highly musical family who toured America as The Brown Family Band, Pud (Albert J.) Brown was billed (at five years old) as "The World's Youngest Saxophone Virtuoso". After the family act broke up in 1933 Brown worked around Chicago with Bud Freeman, Jimmy McPartland and later Phil Lavant and Lou Breeze, as well as Jimmy Dorsey and Lawrence Welk, before opening a motor-cycle shop in Shreveport (1945–50). From 1948 he relocated to Los Angeles, working with Nappy Lamare, Pete Daily (with whom he recorded a best-selling version of "Johnson Rag" for Capitol), Rosy McHargue, Jack Teagarden, Teddy Buckner and Kid Ory, amongst others. From the 1960s he began doubling on trumpet and cornet, and from 1973, when he returned to Shreveport, appeared regularly in New Orleans, working with British musicians Les Muscutt and Trevor Richards, and playing for the review *One Mo' Time.* [DF]

⊙ **Tenor For Two** (1977; New Orleans Jazz). A fine illustration of Brown's later work in great company including Dick Cary, Monty Budwig, Shelley Manne and tenorist-partner the great Eddie Miller.

Ray Brown

Bass; also cello.

b. Pittsburgh, Pennsylvania, 13 Oct 1926; d. 2 July 2002.

After gigging with local bands, Brown was just nineteen when he began working with Dizzy Gillespie (1945–7). He formed his own trio (1947–51) to tour with Ella Fitzgerald, to whom he was married from 1948–52. From 1951–66 he worked with the Oscar Peterson trio, while recording prolifically with others. He then settled in Los Angeles and became involved in the personal management of, among others, Quincy Jones, Milt Jackson and the re-formed Modern Jazz Quartet, as well as continuing to record and perform. A founder member of the LA 4 in 1974, he also led his own trio with Monty Alexander, later with Gene Harris, Benny Green and more recently still with Geoff

HERMAN LEONARD

Ray Brown

Keezer. He has also acted as producer of albums by Jackson and others.

One of the immediate successors of Jimmy Blanton, Brown stepped onto the New York small-group scene as Oscar Pettiford left it in order to join Ellington. Ray's conception did not add significantly to the Blanton style except for a more bluesy inflexion in his solos, although this became rather overblown in some of his later recordings. But what he did triumphantly was to take the full-toned rhythm playing and build it to a peak that few have equalled. [BP]

Ray Brown and Jimmy Rowles

As Good As It Gets (1977; Concord). Amid a stream of trio albums (with occasional guests) for the same label, this duo session stands out for the consummate but unhurried work of the two giants on tunes such as "Sophisticated Lady" and "Morning Of The Carnival".

>> **Monty Alexander** *(Facets)*; **Dizzy Gillespie** *(Roy And Diz)*; **Oscar Peterson** *(The Jazz Soul of Oscar Peterson)*; **Sonny Rollins** *(Way Out West)*.

Sandy Brown

Clarinet, bass-clarinet, vocals, composer, leader.
b. Izatnagar, India, 25 Feb 1929; d. London, 15 March 1975.

Sandy Brown grew up in Edinburgh and came south to London in 1954 with pianist Stan Greig and trumpeter Al Fairweather to form the Fairweather-Brown All Stars. A musician of questing harmonic sense and total authority, and a world-class blues player, he was quick to move from a revivalist paraphrase of Louis Armstrong's Hot Five to a more sophisticated "mainstream" area: his compositions of the late 1950s (and albums such as *McJazz* and *Dr McJazz*) were highly original. By the 1960s Brown's band, featuring front-rank British players such as Tony Milliner (trombone), Brian Lemon (piano), Tony Coe (tenor) and Fairweather, had reached a peak, captured on the album *The Incredible McJazz*. By then Brown was pursuing his second career as an acoustic architect (Sandy Brown Associates designed hundreds of recording studios for the BBC and worldwide), but his frequent return to clubs and festivals and to the recording studio – including his last LP, a seminal quartet recording with Brian Lemon's trio – showed that his genius never dimmed. His health, however, did. By the mid-1970s Brown had become seriously ill, and he died one Saturday afternoon in March 1975, watching Scotland lose to England in the Calcutta Cup. His collection of writings, *The McJazz Manuscripts*, helps to illuminate the mind of this brilliant and complex jazzman. [DF]

Historic Usher Hall Concert 1952 (Lake). From Brown's formative years, this has his longtime partner Al Fairweather, Stan Greig and other Edinburgh stalwarts in an echoing concert full of revivalist flaming youth; Brown's likeable announcements are retained.

McJazz And Friends (1956–8; Lake). An important collection, containing the complete (classic) *McJazz* album from 1957 ("Go Ghana", "Onoliya" etc) plus collaborations with Al Fairweather and Dick Heckstall-Smith.

McJazz Lives On (1959–63; EMI). A retrospective collection of definitive Fairweather-Brown, including "Portrait Of Willie Best", "Wind Of Change" and "Blues March".

Dr McJazz (1961; Columbia). Seventeen ingenious Brown miniatures, with at least one classic blues, "Two Blue" (with guitarist Bill Bramwell).

In The Evening (1971; Hep). Brown in a quartet setting with Brian Lemon on his last great album; possibly the greatest single portrait of his world-class talent.

Work Song (1962–8; Lake). Very good eighteen-track collection, featuring three by the Fairweather-Brown All Stars (1962), four more from 1963 with the welcome addition of Tony Coe, and Brown's complete album of the music from *Hair* with George Chisholm, Kenny Wheeler, John McLaughlin et al.

Tom Brown

Trombone, bass.
b. New Orleans, 3 June 1888; d. 25 March 1958.

In the first years of the century Tom Brown was very active in New Orleans, playing for parades and brass bands. However, he is remembered particularly for being the first New Orleans bandleader to present his band in Chicago: "A fine group", Ed Garland remembers, "and Brown played good trombone; he tried to copy Ory." Brown's Chicago band featured Larry Shields. who later swapped jobs with Alcide "Yellow" Nuñez to join the Original Dixieland Jazz Band. When Brown received an offer to visit Reisenweber's cabaret in New York his band had broken up, and he recommended the ODJB, who went on to fame and fortune; Brown continued an active career in New Orleans, with Ray Miller, Harry A. Yerkes, and later regularly with Johnny Wiggs. His later records for GHB, Southland and Oriole are worth hearing. [DF]

Vernon Brown

Trombone.
b. Venice, Illinois, 6 Jan 1907; d. 18 May 1979.

The most stylish trombonist of Benny Goodman's late 1930s band had already been playing in classy company before he joined Goodman: with Frank Trumbauer and Bix Beiderbecke at the Arcadia Ballroom, St Louis, in 1926, then with Jean Goldkette in 1928. Vernon Brown never made the logical career move made by his friends – into Paul Whiteman's orchestra – but instead freelanced for ten years before signing with Goodman in 1937 for a two-year stay in which his warm-toned, sophisticated style (midway between Cutty Cutshall and Jack Teagarden) was well featured on record. After Goodman he worked with Artie Shaw (1940), Muggsy Spanier (1941–2) and soon after began a career in radio and TV, with regular returns for Goodman reunions. He was still active in the early 1970s. [DF]

>> **Benny Goodman** *(At Carnegie Hall 1938: Complete)*.

Tom Browne

Trumpet.

b. Queens, New York, 30 Oct 1954.

Known as "Mr Jamaica Funk", Tom Browne appeared regularly in the jazz and R&B charts in the 1980s with his highly danceable, accessible, groove-based music. Browne entered the jazz scene under the wing of such trumpeters as Roy Eldridge and Jimmy Nottingham, but it was with leader Sonny Fortune that he first came to real public attention, contributing his trademark warm trumpet to 1976's *Infinity Is* album. Signed to GRP Records in 1979, he regularly earned Gold Albums in the 1980s for both GRP and, later, Arista. After a brief musical retirement (when he worked as a charter pilot), Browne signed with independent label Hip Bop Records. Touching all bases from Miles Davis and Lee Morgan through to A Tribe Called Quest, the range of Browne's trumpet playing has been sympathetically showcased by his new label.

In addition to recording with both the Essence All Stars (Essence of Funk, 1995) and Polish violinist Michal Urbaniak's Urbanator project, Browne has also recorded, as a self-conscious corrective to his reputation as a funk player, an album appropriately entitled *Another Shade Of Browne* (see below), and an album featuring singer Dianne Reeves, produced by Bob Belden, *R & Browne* (1999). [CP]

⊙ **Mo' Jamaica Funk** (1994; Hip Bop). Featuring Browne reunited with the likes of Marcus Miller and Bernard Wright; another high-energy, populist album.

⊙ **Another Shade Of Browne** (1996; Hip Bop). In relatively straightahead company (saxophonist Javon Jackson, pianist Larry Goldings, bassist Ron Carter and drummer Idris Muhammad), Browne explores the legacy of trumpeters Freddie Hubbard, Kenny Dorham, Lee Morgan and Booker Little, as well as performing Ellington's "In A Sentimental Mood".

Dave Brubeck

Piano, composer.

b. Concord, California, 6 Dec 1920.

A group leader of unparalleled popularity in the 1950s and 60s, Brubeck did much to promote jazz with the white middle-class audience. As a composition student with Darius Milhaud, he led experimental and strongly European-influenced jazz groups in San Francisco in the late 1940s, before his quartet (featuring Paul Desmond from 1951) established him as an international attraction. After Desmond left in 1967, first Gerry Mulligan became a member of the group and then Brubeck's sons – keyboardist Darius, bassist/trombonist Chris and drummer Danny. (Cellist Matthew Brubeck also worked with Dave in the early 1990s.) In succession from the late 1970s, reedmen Jerry Bergonzi, former San Francisco colleague Bill Smith and Bobby Militello have toured with Brubeck, who has devoted more of his time to large-scale composition. He appeared with the London Symphony Orchestra in 1990, 1995 and 2000, and in 1996 was given a Lifetime Achievement Grammy award.

Although a prolific writer, and forever associated with his hit record of Desmond's "Take Five", Brubeck's only originals to have become standards were the two covered by Miles Davis, "In Your Own Sweet Way" and "The Duke". Similarly the popularization of "odd" time-signatures (five, seven or nine beats per bar) and of two instruments improvising simultaneously (in his case, saxophone and piano) were not achieved by Brubeck alone. As for his piano work, Brubeck in his early days often lacked the technique to carry out his ideas, except when indulging in heavy chording; in later years, a greater sense of relaxation imparted more ease, and swing, to his execution. [BP]

⊙ **Jazz At Oberlin** (1953; Fantasy/OJC). The first breakthrough album, taped by Brubeck himself on one of his self-promoted college concerts, has the leader building a harmonic fantasia on "These Foolish Things" and tripping over his fingers on "Perdido", contrasting with the Getz-like invention of Desmond.

⊙ **Time Out** (1959; Columbia). The mega-breakthrough was the album containing pieces in 3/4, 9/4 and "Take Five", a track which (perhaps inspired by Max Roach's pioneering) turned over what would have been Brubeck's solo to drummer Joe Morello.

Jack Bruce

Bass, vocals, composer, keyboards, synthesizer, harmonica.

b. Glasgow, 14 May 1943.

Bruce went to the Royal Scottish Academy of Music at seventeen, studying cello and composition. In 1962 he worked with Alexis Korner's Blues Incorporated and was with the Graham Bond Organization from 1963–5. He worked briefly with John Mayall and Manfred Mann, before forming Cream with Ginger Baker and Eric Clapton. Cream became one of the international supergroups on the

1960s' rock scene. After Cream broke up, Bruce was an original member of Tony Williams's Lifetime, which included John McLaughlin and Larry Young. When that first Lifetime disbanded, Bruce pursued a solo career using various combinations of friends including John Marshall, Chris Spedding, Larry Coryell and Jon Hiseman. He also performed on Carla Bley's album *Escalator Over The Hill*. From the mid-1970s he started a series of short-lived bands. Bruce is an immensely talented musician who only occasionally realizes his full potential. He is an excellent singer, a masterful songwriter, a very good composer/arranger for small groups and big bands, and with Cream he brought bass guitar playing to a new level of brilliance. [IC]

➤➤ **Carla Bley** *(Escalator Over The Hill)*; **Michael Mantler** *(Live)*.

Bill Bruford

Drums, composer.

b. Sevenoaks, Kent, UK, 17 May 1949.

Beginning as a rock drummer with Yes, King Crimson, Gong and Genesis, Bill Bruford moved into jazz-rock in 1978 by leading a band called Bruford, featuring electric guitarist Allan Holdsworth, bassist Jeff Berlin and keyboard player Dave Stewart, which split up in 1980, having recorded three albums. After collaborating with keyboard player Patrick Moraz and guitarist David Torn and some studio work with Kazumi Watanabe and bassist Jamaaladeen Tacuma in the early 1980s, Bruford formed Earthworks, a quartet comprising the leader behind Loose Tubes, Django Bates and Iain Ballamy on keyboards and saxophones respectively, and bassist Mick Hutton, later replaced by Tim Harries. Basically a fusion outfit propelled by Bruford's muscly drumming, Earthworks covered a lot of musical ground in typical 1980s fashion: cool funk, house music, jazz-rock. In 1994, King Crimson re-formed in their double-trio manifestation and gave 120 concerts worldwide with Pat Masteletto drumming alongside Bruford. During this period he also worked with David Torn, the Buddy Rich Orchestra, a re-formed Yes and Al Di Meola, among others. In 1997, Earthworks released a "best of" compilation, including some new material, and Bruford relaunched the group featuring a new line-up, focusing less on electronica than acoustic interaction – the recent culmination of which was a sizzling live album and DVD, recorded in NYC, *Footloose And Fancy Free* (2002; Discipline). [CP/CI]

Earthworks

⦿ **Earthworks** (1986; Editions EG). Bright, glossy, punchy music with just enough collective improvisation to locate it in jazz.

⊙ **All Heaven Broke Loose** (1991; Editions EG). Earthworks' third album of polished fusion, laced with musical humour, featuring Bates, Ballamy and Harries.

⊙ **If Summer Had Its Ghosts** (1997; Discipline). Bruford's tenth album as leader sees him in stellar acoustic company with guitarist Ralph Towner and bassist Eddie Gomez. Including everything from Bruford's trademark subtle electronic percussion to a reworking of his boyhood idol Joe Morello's solo on "Far More Drums". A light, pleasantly airy album.

⊙ **A Part, And Yet Apart** (1998; Discipline Global Mobile). An entire change of personnel for Bruford's Earthworks band: the late-1990s crop of UK jazz talent (gutsy saxophonist Patrick Clahar, sparkling pianist Steve Hamilton, eloquent bassist Mark Hodgson) has replaced the Loose Tubes generation, resulting in a sparkier, more straightforwardly gutsy, more immediately accessible sound driven by the leader's punchy, brisk drumming.

Rainer Brüninghaus

Piano, synthesizers.

b. Bad Pyrmont, Germany, 21 Nov 1949.

Brüninghaus studied classical piano at Cologne Conservatory, then from 1973–6 was with Volker Kriegel's Spectrum. He was a member of Eberhard Weber's Colours from 1975–80 and played in Manfred Schoof's quintet from 1978–81. Since 1981 Brüninghaus has been leading his own trio, which includes Markus Stockhausen (trumpet) and Fredy Studer (drums). Since the later 1980s Brüninghaus has been a member of Jan Garbarek's various groups. He also composes and arranges for radio big bands and for symphony orchestras, and does some teaching at a music college in Cologne. He has worked with many other leading jazz musicians including Archie Shepp, George Adams, Kenny Wheeler, Charlie Mariano, Carla Bley, Toots Thielemans, Albert Mangelsdorff and Bobby McFerrin. [IC]

⦿ **Freigeweht** (1980; ECM). This is basically a trio album with Brüninghaus playing acoustic piano and synthesizers, Kenny Wheeler on flugelhorn, Jon Christensen on drums, and occasionally the added sound of Brynjar Hoff's oboe or English horn. The music is atmospheric, hypnotic, drenched in romantic melancholy at times, and very European with lots of airy keyboard patterns. Only the redoubtable Christensen occasionally creates a pulse which mercifully stirs things up a bit and Wheeler responds with some passionate lyricism.

⦿ **Continuum** (1983; ECM). This features Brüninghaus's regular trio with Markus Stockhausen and Fredy Studer. The keyboard ostinati persist, though occasionally we get flashes of the leader's consummate acoustic piano work. Stockhausen varies the sonorities and textures by using piccolo trumpet and flugelhorn as well as the usual B-flat trumpet. Studer initiates some unashamed grooves, but there is no bass and the rhythm is never ecstatic. The playing is impeccable but the colours so pastel that one begins to yearn for some blood and sweat.

➤➤ **Jan Garbarek** *(Legend Of The Seven Dreams)*; **Eberhard Weber** *(Yellow Fields)*.

Georg Brunis

Trombone, vocals.

b. New Orleans, 6 Feb 1902; d. 19 Nov 1974.

The best-known of five musical New Orleans brothers, Georg Brunis (George Clarence

Brunies) played at eight with Papa Jack Laine's "Junior Band". Eleven years on, he was part of the Friars Society Orchestra with Paul Mares, Mel Stitzel and drummer Ben Pollack, a band that turned into the New Orleans Rhythm Kings. Then came the first long stint with clarinettist Ted Lewis (1924–34), whose much-maligned act was nonetheless a headliner and for Brunis a lesson in presentation. In 1934 he was at the Famous Door with another master showman, Louis Prima, and from 1936 began a long residency at Nick's. By now his playing – "on the nose, never mixed up with a lot of phony tricks", as Amy Lee said – was complemented by cut-up routines: playing trombone with his foot, bullfrog-voiced songs, unscheduled parades into the ladies room and invitations to (lighter) customers to stand on his stomach. But he always played "like it was his last night on earth", said Matty Walsh, and he forged two classic partnerships at the period: with Muggsy Spanier's Ragtimers for five and a half months (and sixteen great records) and with Wild Bill Davison in 1944 for definitive recordings on Commodore. By 1943 Brunis was with Lewis again, then he was at Eddie Condon's (1947–9), and for nine years after that at Club Eleven Eleven in Chicago (1951–9). For the last fifteen years of his life, despite illness in the late 1960s, he stayed busy, continuing to define the role of a trombone in Dixieland ensemble ("George's taste in jazz ranges from New Orleans to New Orleans", said Bud Freeman) and perfectly embodying the sophisticated end of tailgate trombone. [DF]

⊙ **Tin Roof Blues** (1923/46; ASV). Excellent and overdue survey of an important Dixieland artist with perfect company – Muggsy Spanier's Ragtimers, Wild Bill Davison's Commodores and his own band. Twenty-five tracks also illustrate Brunis with Ted Lewis, the New Orleans Rhythm Kings and Louis Prima.

Bill Brunskill

Trumpet, leader.

b. London, 2 Feb 1920; d. 17 Nov 2002.

Bill Brunskill personified the proud amateur traditions of British revivalism. A local government officer until his retirement in 1985, he played New Orleans jazz to generations of London jazz fans since the 1940s, working most of the major venues. Early on in his career Brunskill worked with Cy Laurie, Lonnie Donegan and Bob Dawbarn before forming his own band in 1955. His group played long London residencies at the Fighting Cocks in Kingston, Surrey, and later at the Lord Napier in Thornton Heath, where in 1984 he was the central figure in a TV documentary, written by George Melly and researched by John Chilton, *Whatever Happened To Bill Brunskill?*, tracing the story of British revivalist jazz. [DF]

⊙ **Thirty Years On** (1980; VJM). A good representative collection by a long-serving British revivalist.

Ray Bryant

Piano.

b. Philadelphia, 24 Dec 1931.

Ray Bryant became known to colleagues as house pianist at Philadelphia's Blue Note club, where he worked with elder brother Tom on bass. (His sister, who sang gospel music, is the mother of Kevin and Robin Eubanks.) This position led to recordings with Miles Davis, Sonny Rollins, Carmen McRae, Coleman Hawkins and Jo Jones in the late 1950s, and to a continuing career as trio leader and soloist. One of the few pianists of his generation to show an affinity for unaccompanied playing, Bryant has a wide-ranging left hand and a straightforward harmonic vocabulary which suggests predecessors such as Teddy Wilson. More rhythmically outgoing than the latter, he was able to incorporate aspects of gospel keyboard work into a mainstream jazz style, without sounding merely derivative. [BP]

⊙ **Trio** (1957; Prestige/OJC). This session with Carmen McRae's rhythm-section provides several examples of Bryant's happy-sounding approach on such tunes as Clifford Brown's "Daahoud".

Willie Bryant

Vocals, leader, compere.

b. New Orleans, 30 Aug 1908; d. 9 Feb 1964.

Willie Bryant began his career as a dancer and first fronted his own big band at the famous Howard Theater, Washington. From 1933 he was in New York, first as a dancer and revue artist, and from 1934 as leader of a big band which worked clubs including the Savoy Ballroom. The band had arrangements by Teddy Wilson and starred musicians such as Wilson, Cozy Cole, Benny Carter, Ben Webster, Edgar Battle and Taft Jordan. Bryant himself was no musician, but his likeable personality and good looks won him jobs as an actor, disc jockey and MC at the Apollo after the band broke up in late 1938. His band, including Panama Francis on drums, re-formed in 1946–8, after which Bryant resumed his freelance career. [DF]

Owen Bryce

Trumpet, bandleader.

b. London, 8 Aug 1920.

The guiding light who encouraged George Webb's full-scale adoption of jazz revivalism, Owen Bryce partnered Reg Rigden and briefly Humphrey Lyttelton in the first George Webb Dixielanders (re-formed in 1949 as the Original Dixielanders), and in 1956 formed his own band from the High Society Jazz Band. In later years he also published instructional books, wrote widely for the jazz press and set up residential jazz courses on his barge-home and elsewhere. In the 1980s he played regularly, including

George Webb reunions, and in the 1990s was still playing and writing as enthusiastically as ever. [DF]

>> **George Webb** *(Dixielanders).*

Beryl Bryden

Washboard, vocals.

b. Norwich, Norfolk, UK, 11 May 1920; d. 14 July 1998.

Britain's "Queen of the Blues" was one of the most colourful figures in European jazz. Her big, friendly voice, professional presentation and wide-ranging repertoire (which ran from Bessie Smith to 1930s standard tunes such as "Miss Brown To You") took her a long way from the post-war London days when she first sang with George Webb's Dixielanders and Humphrey Lyttelton. Her career was based as much in continental Europe as in Britain: in Paris 1953–4 she sang for Lionel Hampton and around the clubs, and later she worked with such bands as Fatty George's and the Tremble Kids in Holland and Germany. During the 1960s she played the Antibes festival and toured the Far East and Africa, then paid her first visit to New York in 1970. Then came a busy decade in which, weathering the changes in musical tastes as successfully as ever, she continued her European travels, recorded prolifically for Ted Easton's Riff label in Holland (where she was crowned "Queen of Jazz" in 1978) and others, appeared regularly at South Bank concerts in London (often with her close friend Alex Welsh and his band), and won the BBC Jazz Society's Musician of the Year award. In the 1980s, appearing at festivals, clubs and with Pete Allen's band in a new theatre production, *Jazzin' Around*, Beryl Bryden showed no sign of slowing up. In 1994 she toured with her centenary tribute to Bessie Smith, *I've Got What It Takes*, and from 1995 was featured in a revised version of *Salute To Satchmo* with the Alex Welsh Reunion Band. Her last recording session with old friend Nat Gonella took place in Holland in March 1997, by which time health problems had begun to recur, stemming from the cancer she had first suffered in 1992. She died of lymphoma; a joyous memorial service was held at St Mary's, Paddington Green, on 2 September 1998. [DF]

⊙ **Two Moods Of Beryl Bryden** (1975–84; Audiophile). Excellent, finely contrasted showcase of Bryden's later work, combining a classy session with Lennie Felix and Bud Freeman (under the leadership of Ted Easton) and a Dixieland set with the Sweetwood Dixie Stompers.

⊙ **I've Got What It Takes (1995; Lake).** Fine tribute to Bessie Smith with Beryl in good voice amid good company: Keith Nichols, Denis Field, Roy Williams and the late Cy Laurie. Well worth hearing.

Milt Buckner

Piano, organ, arranger.

b. St Louis, Missouri, 10 July 1915; d. 27 July 1977.

Raised in Detroit from age nine, Milt Buckner was the younger brother of altoist Ted Buckner, who played with the Jimmie Lunceford band (not to be confused with the unrelated Teddy Buckner featured below). He played piano and arranged for many Detroit-based bands from 1930, including McKinney's Cotton Pickers, but came to fame with the Lionel Hampton band (1941–8, 1950–52). In between he led his own seventeen-piece band, later reducing to a ten-piece (1949–50). From 1952 he led an organ trio: his 1955 edition included Sam Woodyard, who promptly joined Ellington, and saxophonist Danny Turner, who was later in the Basie band. He continued with this format for the rest of his life, teaming up with Illinois Jacquet from 1971. Extremely popular in Europe from the late 1960s, Buckner was one of the pioneers of the electric organ in jazz and its use in replacing a big-band brass section, and his early arranging experience clearly influenced this conception. [BP]

⊙ **Green Onions** (1975; Black & Blue). Instead of backing a big-toned tenor player, as on many of his best later sessions (all recorded in Europe), Buckner here convenes blues guitarist Roy Gaines to make explicit links with other popular formats, such as the Booker T & the MGs title track.

Teddy Buckner

Trumpet, flugelhorn, vocals.

b. Sherman, Texas, 16 July 1909; d. 22 Sept 1994.

Like most of his generation, Buckner grew up in the shadow of Louis Armstrong, but unlike some of his contemporaries (Henry "Red" Allen or Rex Stewart, for example) he never felt the need to develop an alternative route to his idol's. On the contrary, Buckner declared his allegiance to Armstrong very early on (by 1936 he was working as Louis's stand-in on the film *Pennies From Heaven*), and all through his career he regularly sang and played the praises of his inspiration: in Lionel Hampton's bebop band of 1948 (where he played an Armstrong-style feature), with Kid Ory's band 1949–54 (where his trumpet is very difficult to distinguish from Armstrong's), in Armstrong-style tributes at Gene Norman's Dixieland festivals, in Floyd Levin's 1970 TV production of *Hello Louis* (in which he played Armstrong in his Hot Five role) and, as late as 1975, in a tribute film for ABC, *Louis Armstrong – Chicago Style!*

As well as work in and around Los Angeles with Speed Webb, Sonny Clay, Edythe Turnham, Lorenzo Flennoy and Les Hite, Buckner went to Shanghai with Buck Clayton's band in 1934, and a year later took over Lionel Hampton's at the Paradise Club, Los Angeles. In the 1940s he was regularly to be found with R&B shows as well as with big bands led by Benny Carter, Gerald Wilson and others. He led his own New Orleans-style bands through the 1950s (recording with Sidney Bechet in 1958) and early 1960s; after 1965 he was regularly at Disneyland for sixteen years. From the 1930s to the 70s he appeared in numerous films as well.

Buckner's espousal of traditional jazz was never dictated by limited technique: a huge-toned, sometimes flashy performer with a fondness (unlike Armstrong) for muted effects, he was capable of playing more or less anything. [DF]

Teddy Buckner and Sidney Bechet

Parisian Encounter (1958; Vogue). A studio-recorded selection in which Buckner shows up in fine form, uncowed by the dominance of the great Bechet.

Hiram Bullock

Guitar.

b. Osaka, Japan, 11 Sept 1955.

One of the world's top guitarists, in great demand both as a leader and as a studio musician, Hiram Bullock rose to prominence in the 24th Street Band, which recorded three albums for Columbia Japan and toured extensively in that country. In the USA, he became popular for his work on *The David Letterman Show* and, with David Sanborn and Marcus Miller, on *Night Music*. In the 1980s, in addition to working with Carla Bley, Miles Davis and Gil Evans, he fronted his own band, recording his Atlantic debut album, *From All Sides*, in 1986, and following it up with *Give It What You Got* in 1987. Always noted for his restrained power and passion, Bullock has worked with a number of rock and pop figures, Sting, Paul Simon and Billy Joel among them, as well as with a great many of jazz's finest musicians, including Jaco Pastorius and singer Al Jarreau. In the mid-1990s, he toured and recorded with a stellar fusion line-up led by Miles Davis producer and multi-instrumentalist Marcus Miller. He has latterly appeared on the records of top fusioneers Bob James and Bill Evans, among many others, and in one of his occasional dips into left-field, the contemporary progressive album *Karen Mantler's Pet Project*, led by the daughter of Carla Bley and Michael Mantler. [CP/CI]

Carla Bley

Heavy Heart (1984; Watt). Bullock brings welcome tautness and grit to this airily appealing album, which also features Kenny Kirkland on piano and Steve Slagle on reeds.

Jaco Pastorius

PDB (1986; DIW). Surprisingly tasteful album from stellar trio; Bullock shines on a selection ranging from "Dolphin Dance" to "Ode to Billy Joe", although drummer Kenwood Dennard is a mite too assertive for comfort.

Hiram Bullock

World Of Collision (1994; Big World). Debut album for this label, but basically same formula as his Atlantic albums: rock-influenced, but with a jazz sensibility.

Marcus Miller

Live & More (1996; Dreyfus). Alongside such luminaries as alto player Kenny Garrett and trumpeter Michael Stewart, Bullock brings his customary jazz-rock sensibility to material such as Miller's "Panther" and "Tutu".

John Bunch

Piano.

b. Tipton, Indiana, 1 Dec 1921.

Bunch took up the piano at the age of eleven but began playing professionally only in his mid-30s, working early on with Georgie Auld in Los Angeles and then in the mid- to late 1950s with Woody Herman, Benny Goodman and Maynard Ferguson, as well as in small groups led by Buddy Rich, Al Cohn, Zoot Sims and Gene Krupa. From 1966–72 he worked as MD for Tony Bennett, as well as with Buddy Rich's band (1966), and regularly with Benny Goodman throughout the 1960s and 70s. It was at this point that Bunch's unobtrusive excellence began to be more widely recognized; from 1975–7 he recorded five albums as leader (including three for Harry Lim's Famous Door label) and from then on recorded regularly, often in the company of the new-generation mainstream stars like Warren Vaché Jnr (whose trio he joined in 1979) and Scott Hamilton (whose quintet he joined in 1982). From the 1990s Bunch was semi-resident in Britain and played regularly at jazz clubs and festivals (including Blackpool 2003), always in the best company and regularly leading his own trio and playing solo. A musician of immense taste, skill and versatility, he deserves the widest recognition. [DF]

Solo (1996; Arbors). The Arbors label has done much to remind people of Bunch's underrated talent, and this relaxed and lyrical recital meets all the highest criteria of mid-period jazz piano.

A Special Alliance (2002; Arbors). With a British rhythm section (Dave Green and Steve Brown), Bunch presents a seasoned selection – Monk to Matt Dennis – with the grace and wit that once saw him dubbed "The Fred Astaire of the piano".

➤➤ **Warren Vaché Jnr** *(Midtown Jazz).*

Teddy Bunn

Guitar, vocals.

b. Freeport, Long Island, 1909; d. 20 July 1978.

The most important black guitarist of the 1930s before Charlie Christian, Teddy Bunn is still often neglected, perhaps because Eddie Lang had created such a gigantic impression just before him and the revolutions of Christian were soon to make the older man appear just a little out of fashion. But Bunn's music is fondly remembered by musicians and critics everywhere. "He was a true guitar-master", says Max Jones. "The urge he gave to a band, his rhythmic support, whether heard in a washboard band, swing combo, blues or big-band context, was nearly as impressive as his beautiful soloing." Bunn's solo talents in the 1930s were featured with the Spirits Of Rhythm (his cutting-toned single-string creations were their strongest solo voice) and he made strong contributions to record sessions by the Mezzrow-Ladnier quintet of the same period. By August 1940, when he recorded with Lionel Hampton, Bunn had changed permanently to electric guitar. For the next ten years he played in various re-formations of the Spirits and with his own small groups, and by the mid-1950s was following the new road for guitar into R&B and rock'n'roll, working with Jack McVea, Edgar Hayes and others, and with touring rock'n'roll shows. By the late 1960s Bunn worked less often; he suffered a mild stroke in 1970, and it was followed by three heart attacks which rendered him partly blind and paralyzed. He died after ten years' illness, almost forgotten, except, says Max Jones, a faithful fan, "among musicians and collectors who remember his top-flight solos and accompaniments". [DF]

➤➤ **Spirits Of Rhythm** *(The Spirits of Rhythm 1933–4, Featuring Teddy Bunn).*

Jane Bunnett

Flute, soprano sax.

b. Toronto, 22 Oct 1955.

Having played clarinet and flute in high school, Bunnett studied classical piano until the age of 19 when she was hampered by tendonitis. After hearing Charles Mingus in San Francisco she devoted herself to jazz, taking up the soprano at 22 and eventually commuting by bus to New York for lessons with Barry Harris. While working with a Greek function band, she and her subsequent husband (trumpeter Larry Cramer) set up her first group for a radio recording, which led to numerous festival gigs and a debut album (*In Dew Time*, with Dewey Redman and Don Pullen as guests). Mainly heard thereafter as a bandleader, she also recorded under the leadership of Paul Bley and Cuban pianist Hilario Durán. She and Cramer have regularly visited Cuba since 1982, finding its music more inspiring than neo-bop. While making several albums there, including *Cuban Odyssey* which in 2003 gained an award from the Jazz Journalists' Association, she emphasized the continuity between Cuban roots and those of jazz. Favourite instrumentalists are Steve Lacy, Coltrane, Shorter and Roland Kirk, while other inspirations are Charlie Parker, Clifford Jordan, Redman, Pullen, Mingus and Ellington. [BP]

⊙ **The Water Is Wide** (1993; Evidence). One of Bunnett's straigtahead but not straightforward jazz albums, this includes a Roland Kirk, an Ellington and two Monks, plus appearances by the unique vocalists Sheila Jordan and Jeanne Lee.

⊙ **Cuban Odyssey** (2002; Blue Note). A large-scale effort with indigenous material and performers, including Hilario Durán and veteran Guillermo Rubalcaba on piano. Also available as a package with the Spirits Of Havana (1991).

Albert Burbank

Clarinet.

b. New Orleans, 25 March 1902; d. 15 Aug 1976.

Burbank was a pupil of Lorenzo Tio in 1916, then played in New Orleans and nearby resorts through the 1920s. During the Depression he worked with drummer Kid Milton's band and after the war (during which he served in the US Navy) was regularly with trumpeter Herb Morand. During the 1950s he worked with internationally famous names including Paul Barbarin and Kid Ory, but thereafter moved back home to play for local leaders such as Octave Crosby and Bill Matthews and brass bands like the Eureka and Young Tuxedo, as well as doing a long stint with Papa French's jazz band. Regularly with the Preservation Hall band in the early 1970s (when he toured Australia with them), Burbank played right up until 1975 when he suffered a stroke, but he kept on playing until he died. [DF]

⊙ **Albert Burbank With Kid Ory And His Creole Jazzband** (1954; Storyville). Taken from concerts at the Hangover Club, San Francisco, these are good represen tative examples of an under-recorded clarinettist in compatible company; an eleven-minute "Blues For Jimmy" is outstanding.

Campbell Burnap

Trombone, vocals.

b. Derby, UK, 10 Sept 1939.

Burnap played around New Zealand and Australia before returning to Britain, via New Orleans, in the 1960s to work for a variety of leaders including Terry Lightfoot, Monty Sunshine and Alan Elsdon, as well as leading his own quintet with saxophonist Geoff Simkins and freelancing with leaders such as Alex Welsh. He played whenever possible with the trombone quintet Five-a-Slide and from 1980 played with Acker Bilk. After leaving the band in 1987, he developed his talents as a broadcaster and jazz researcher, presenting shows on Jazz FM and BBC Radio 2. One of Britain's most stylish trombonists, Burnap plays a burry combination of Jack Teagarden and Bill Harris and sings with a lazy, charming delivery akin to Teagarden's own; in 1994 he appeared in a concert honouring Teagarden at London's Queen Elizabeth Hall. In 2003 he continues to lead his own band, to play guest spots and present radio shows. [DF]

⊙ **Night Workers** (1997; Mainstem). A relaxed blowing session with Burnap in convivial company, including clarinet/tenorist Ron Drake and featuring guests Bob and Tony Barnard.

Ralph Burns

Piano, arranger, composer.

b. Newton, Massachusetts, 29 June 1922; d. 21 Nov 2001.

After studies at New England Conservatory, Burns moved to New York, joining Charlie Barnet in 1942–3, Red Norvo in 1943 and Woody Herman in 1944–5. Contributing important compositions to both Barnet ("The Moose") and

Herman ("Apple Honey", "Bijou"), he then became non-playing arranger for Herman until the 1950s. Active as a freelance musical director, he wrote orchestral backings for Ben Webster, Harry Carney, Ray Charles and for the Broadway stage. In the 1970s he was busy composing for Hollywood films (including *Lenny* and *New York, New York*) and he still writes occasional vocal arrangements. His early work for the mid-1940s Herman band was significant in focusing the spirit of the band, while his more thoughtful compositions "Lady McGowan's Dream" and "Summer Sequence" rivalled Ellington in the field of extended writing; the latter also contained the theme of the subsequent song "Early Autumn". [BP]

➤➤ **Woody Herman** *(The Thundering Herds).*

Ronnie Burrage

Drums, keyboards, percussion, vocals.
b. St Louis, Missouri, 19 Oct 1959.

At the age of nine Burrage performed with Duke Ellington and, until he died, Ellington wrote to encourage Burrage's interest in music. He sang in the St Louis Cathedral boys' choir and worked with funk and R&B groups. From 1980–83 he worked with the St Louis Metropolitan Jazz Quintet, accompanying many visiting soloists including Arthur Blythe, Jackie McLean, Andrew Hill, Jaco Pastorius and McCoy Tyner. In 1983 he worked for a month with Chico Freeman and, from 1983–5, with Woody Shaw's quintet. By the early 1980s Burrage already had a tremendous reputation among US musicians and by 1985 had worked with most contemporary stars, from Pat Metheny to Lester Bowie and members of the World Saxophone Quartet. He has led several groups of his own too: in 1984 he opened the Kool Jazz festival in Philadelphia with the Burrage Ensemble and in 1986 he toured with his own Third Kind Of Blue, which included John Purcell (reeds) and Anthony Cox (bass). His composition "Endless Flight" was written for McCoy Tyner and was recorded on the Young Lions' double album. He has been heard latterly on the recordings of Sonny Fortune and Luther Thomas while Burrage's own album *Just Natural* (WestWind) – an updated take on the classic sax-organ-drums lineup, featuring saxist Eric Person and organist Terence Conley – appeared in 2001. Burrage's influences range from Jack DeJohnette, Art Blakey, Max Roach, Elvin Jones to Bobby Hutcherson, Herbie Hancock, Egberto Gismonti, Milton Nascimento and Toots Thielemans. [IC]

⊙ **Shuttle** (1993; Sound Hills). For this adventurous debut album Burrage leads a septet which includes Hamiet Bluiett, trombonist/flugelhornist Frank Lacy and saxophonist Joe Ford.

➤➤ **Chico Freeman** *(Destiny Dance).*

Dave Burrell

Piano.
b. Middletown, Ohio, 10 Sept 1944.

Pianist Dave Burrell (born Herman Davis Burrell) grew up in Hawaii, where he went to college before studying music at Berklee in Boston. In the mid-60s he moved first to Cleveland, then settled in New York, where he played with many of the leading lights of free jazz, including Marion Brown, Pharoah Sanders, Giuseppi Logan, Sunny Murray and Archie Shepp. He recorded frequently as a sideman, including several releases for the BYG label and his own self-titled debut on Douglas. Together with trombonist Grachan Moncur III and drummer Beaver Harris, he initiated the 360 Degree Music Experience in 1968. In the last few decades, Burrell has worked frequently with reedman David Murray, making numerous duo records (most recently *Windward Passages* on Black Saint) and participating in Murray's larger groups. Burrell's style is comparable, in certain respects, to that of Don Pullen; given to lyricism and an accomplished comper, he sometimes explodes into extremely energetic playing, usually returning to the theme with a strong sense of resolved tension. [JC]

⊙ **The Jelly Roll Joys** (1991; Gazell). Though the solid *Murray duet In Concert* [1991; Victo] may be a more representative slice of the pianist's output, this wonderfully strange record represents at least part of what Burrell gets up to when left to his own devices, playing Jelly Roll Morton tunes as well as stride takes of bop tunes like "Giant Steps", "Billy's Bounce", and "Moment's Notice".

Kenny Burrell

Guitar, vocals.
b. Detroit, Michigan, 31 July 1931.

Part of the 1950s exodus from Detroit, Burrell made his first recording there with a visiting Dizzy Gillespie (1951). He continued working locally, then in 1955 toured with the Oscar Peterson trio during Herb Ellis's illness, and moved to New York, where he freelanced and recorded prolifically. After playing for Benny Goodman in 1957, he worked under his own name with a trio/quartet and formed several associations on record, especially with Jimmy Smith. His records have occasionally included either big-band backing (by such as Gil Evans or Don Sebesky) or all-star small groups. He has toured Europe and Japan, and since 1973 has done studio work and taught at the University of California. There have been reunions with Smith in 1985 and 1993–4, and frequent appearances at Duke Ellington conferences.

Burrell has never achieved the wide popular appeal of a Wes Montgomery or a George Benson, despite his vocal work in the early 1960s. Yet he is utterly reliable in an accompanying role, and he gives the same impression of infallibility when soloing.

Managing to be both boppy and bluesy without being boring, he has furthered the Charlie Christian style better than almost anyone else. [BP]

Kenny Burrell And John Coltrane (1958; New Jazz/OJC). This stands out from Burrell's early albums (which were typically just Prestige "blowing sessions"), for its duet track by the principals and for its rhythm-section of Tommy Flanagan, Paul Chambers and Jimmy Cobb.

Ellington Is Forever Vol. 1 (1975; Fantasy). A long-time student of Duke's music, Burrell here convened a mix-and-match jam session, whose contents are every bit as good as the personnel. Includes Thad Jones, Jon Faddis and Snooky Young on brass, Joe Henderson and Jimmy Smith.

➤➤ **Gary McFarland** *(How To Succeed In Business).*

Gary Burton

Vibraphone, educator, composer.
b. Anderson, Indiana, 23 Jan 1943.

Burton began teaching himself the piano at the age of six and studied composition and piano at high school, but was self-taught on vibes. He attended the Berklee School, Boston, at the beginning of the 1960s, where he met composer/arranger Mike Gibbs, beginning a long and fruitful association. In 1963 he toured the USA and Japan with George Shearing and the following year Shearing recorded an LP (*Out Of The Woods*) of Burton's compositions. From 1964–6 he was with the Stan Getz quartet, which involved appearances at the White House and in two films, *The Hanged Man* and *Get Yourself A College Girl*. In 1967 he formed his own quartet with Larry Coryell (guitar), Steve Swallow (bass) and Bob Moses (drums), and the fully mature Burton sound and style were clearly evident for the first time. The quartet's music had all the jazz virtues – harmonic sophistication, swing, good dynamics – but it also fused elements from rock and country music, creating a fresh, attractive, totally contemporary sound and anticipating the jazz-rock movement of the 1970s.

Jak Kilby

Gary Burton

Burton himself was generally recognized as being the new voice on vibes. He asserted that he was not influenced by other vibists and that his main inspiration had been pianist Bill Evans. In fact, his whole approach to the vibes was pianistic, with brilliantly fleet linear runs and rich four-mallet chording that was without precedent in jazz. Later he explained the genesis of this: "I played a lot at home by myself when I was first learning. I naturally started filling things in and accompanying myself because it sounded too empty as a single line instrument."

Also in 1967 he asked Carla Bley to arrange her *A Genuine Tong Funeral* for his quartet augmented by Gato Barbieri, Jimmy Knepper, Steve Lacy, Howard Johnson, Michael Mantler and Bley herself. It was recorded in November and was Carla Bley's first major exposure on an LP; it was also the beginning of a long association with Burton, who would go on playing and recording her compositions over the years.

Since 1970, Burton has also played solo concerts, and has worked in duo with Keith Jarrett and frequently with Chick Corea. From 1974–6 he recorded and toured with his quartet, featuring bassist Eberhard Weber as a soloist and melodist and fifth member of the group. In 1974, with his longtime friend and associate Steve Swallow, he recorded a superb duo album of which he said: "*Hotel Hello* ... strikes me as the best representation of my playing that I've ever gotten on record." In fact the early 1970s were something of a rebirth for him; he began recording for Manfred Eicher and ECM, and for the first time the actual sound of his vibes was captured on record.

During the 1960s and early 70s he was also active as an educator, conducting workshops and presenting lecture/concert programmes with his quartet at universities all over the USA. In 1971, he became a permanent staff member at Berklee, and in 1985 he was made Dean of Curriculum there. In the late 1970s and the 1980s, he toured in duo with Chick Corea, visiting Europe and Japan as well as playing many cities in the USA. In 1982 he was featured soloist on Corea's "Lyric Suite" for piano, vibes and string quartet. He has also visited Russia, playing solo concerts at the US embassy for invited Russian musicians and critics. In the mid-1980s his quartet included Steve Swallow, Adam Nussbaum (drums) and the young Japanese pianist Makoto Ozone. Though soon to retire from Berklee, Burton continues to tour with the likes of Corea and Ozone, and is always looking for new projects to involve himself in – he is soon to make a film about contemporary tango music.

Burton is not only a great player and fine bandleader, but an inspirational figure, a discoverer of new talent and a catalyst through whom people can focus and find themselves. Many leading musicians have emerged from his groups and his projects, including Bob Moses, Larry Coryell, Pat Metheny, Mike Gibbs, Carla Bley, Tiger Okoshi and Danny Gottlieb. He is a major stylist on vibes, and he was one of the initiators of the trend of playing without a rhythm-section. [IC]

⊙ **Artist's Choice** (1963–8; Bluebird). This a selection of tracks from Burton's deleted but brilliantly creative early albums. There are pieces from Carla Bley's masterpiece *A Genuine Tong Funeral*, and other seminal tracks including the cliffhanging slow blues "Country Roads", composed jointly by Burton and Steve Swallow and played by many other musicians.

⊙ **Works** (1972–80; ECM). A useful selection of tracks of Burton's various groups during the 1970s.

⊙ **The New Quartet** (1973; ECM). I973 saw the high water-mark of the jazz-rock movement, and this album was one of the most accomplished of the time. Burton leads guitarist Michael Goodrick, bassist Abraham Laboriel and drummer Harry Blazer in a performance of eight excellent compositions – two each by Mike Gibbs and Gordon Beck and one each by Carla Bley, Chick Corea, Keith Jarrett and Burton himself. The performance has terrific panache and bites deep rhythmically and emotionally.

⊙ **Hotel Hello** (1974; ECM). This duo album is a masterpiece. The vibraphone sound is wonderfully recorded and has great presence, and Burton also plays some organ and marimba on occasion. Steve Swallow plays bass guitar and piano, and the rapport between the two men is magical. Swallow is also one of the best composers around, and five of the eight pieces are his, including the title track. The whole thing exudes life and warmth.

⊙ **Passengers** (1976; ECM). This is the Burton quartet with Metheny, Swallow and drummer Dan Gottlieb which toured featuring Eberhard Weber as bass melodist and soloist. Weber's plangent sonorities meld well with vibes and guitar, though one can have too much of this mellifluous brew.

⊙ **Reunion** (1989; GRP). Metheny left the Burton quartet in the mid-1970s and eventually became a superstar. He makes the fifth member of the group for this recording, which includes pianist Mitch Forman, bassist Will Lee and the fine drummer Peter Erskine. The compositions – two by Forman, two by Metheny and a few others by friends and associates – are consistently good, and the playing superb. This is a very musical, exceptionally listenable album, except that towards the end one yearns for a hint of struggle, a wrong note, an unfinished phrase.

⊙ **Chick Corea/Gary Burton Native Sense** (1997; Stretch Records). Corea and Burton had been touring and recording as a duo at intervals since 1972, and this album is something of a masterpiece. Eight of the eleven pieces were composed by Corea, and the remaining three are two of Béla Bartók's "Bagatelles", and Thelonious Monk's tricky "sheets of sound" composition "Four In One" which they handle with playful nonchalance. Corea and Burton are virtuosi whose playing speaks directly to the human heart because it is very lyrical and also rhythmically superb – it sings and emphatically swings.

Joe Bushkin

Piano, composer, trumpet, flugelhorn.
b. New York, 7 Nov 1916.

Joe Bushkin was first spotted by Artie Shaw around 1935 as "a very young, bright-eyed, intense kid who hung out with the Chicago crowd". Bushkin was on 52nd Street with Bunny Berigan, Eddie Condon, Muggsy Spanier and Joe Marsala until 1940, when he was hired by Tommy Dorsey, whose frequent raids on Marsala's bands were a standing joke. In Dorsey's band Bushkin recorded over one hundred sides, wrote "Oh Look At Me Now" for Frank Sinatra and, according to Sinatra, "introduced the band to Pernod. Suddenly all the Coca Cola turned green!" During the war he directed a GI show, *Winged Victory*, which toured the Pacific and Japan, and co-wrote "Hot Time In The Town Of Berlin" with John de Vries (a small hit for Crosby and Sinatra). In 1946 he joined Benny Goodman, taught the young Burt Bacharach to play jazz in spare moments, and acted in a jazzman's Broadway play, *Rat Race*, with Georgie Auld and others. From 1950 he was regularly at the Embers (with Jo Jones, Charles Mingus et al), a small club into which Jonah Jones recalls, "nobody else but Joe would take a trumpet". The "muted jazz" which resulted set a lucrative trend for Jones straight after and a pattern for trumpet-led quartets for ten years more. Bushkin's solo albums of the period, often with strings (such as *Midnite Rhapsody* and *Listen To The Quiet*), were commercial hits and ensured the continuance of his solo career through the 1960s at the Embers, in New York and in Las Vegas. By 1970, partly retired, he was in Hawaii breeding horses, but he returned triumphantly to back Bing Crosby in London, New York and Norway, and for radio and TV spectaculars. A classic album (see below) recalls this period. Throughout the 1980s and on into the 90s Bushkin was as busy as ever, playing concerts, clubs, festivals and jazz parties. [DF]

⊙ **The Road To Oslo/Play It Again Joe** (1977; DRG). This excellent compilation has a remastered reissue of the LP *Celebrates 100 Years Of Recorded Sound*, on which Bushkin talks, sings, and plays piano and flugelhorn in the company of Johnny Smith, Milt Hinton, Jake Hanna and Jack Parnell's orchestra (and Bing Crosby sings on one track). Added to it are nine tracks featuring Warren Vaché, Dan Barrett and Howard Alden, among others.

Richard Busiakiewicz

Piano
b. 14 January I963.

Busiakiewicz took classical piano lessons at six and was drawn to jazz after hearing Oscar Peterson recordings at fourteen. By his late teens he was playing in London hotels, restaurants and jazz clubs and turned professional in February 1987. After working with Tommy Chase's band he formed his own outfit with trumpeter Gerard Presencer working regularly at the Bulls' Head, Barnes. From 1994 he has been pianist with Ray Gelato, touring Europe and North America as well as playing two seasons at Ronnie Scott's, London. He also works regularly with Karen Sharp, Dunstan Coulber and the group Tough Tenors, and has accompanied Scott

Hamilton, Teddy Edwards, Art Farmer, Charles McPherson, Ken Peplowski, Herb Geller and Warren Vaché et.al. An eclectic and versatile artist, Busiakiewicz is also a fine solo pianist with a wide-ranging and tasteful repertoire. [DF]

John Butcher

Soprano and tenor saxophones.

b. Brighton, UK, 25 Oct 1954.

As a college student, John Butcher began playing saxophone; he initially worked in jazz ensembles, with dance and theatre groups, and was introduced to improvised music playing Stockhausen. After completing a doctorate in physics at the beginning of the 80s, Butcher devoted himself to improvising – though he still teaches to support himself – and, less frequently, to contemporary classical music. A key member of the third generation of British improvisers, he has quickly taken a place as one of the most important new voices in European free music. His longterm groups have included various ensembles of varying size with pianist Chris Burn (a frequent collaborator since his university years), wind player Jim Denley, and bassist/cellist Marcio Mattos; and his trio with guitarist John Russell and violinist Phil Durrant. He has also regularly played with trombonist Radu Malfatti, percussionist Paul Lovens, pianists Georg Gräwe and Steve Beresford, bassist Hans Schneider, and drummers such as Martin Blume and Steve Noble. Butcher is an accomplished solo performer: he has released striking solo CDs such as *Thirteen Friendly Numbers* (1992) on his own Acta label (making use of overdubs), as well as a lone venture on Rastascan, London and *Cologne Saxophone Solos* (1997) and the *Fixations* (14) compilation on Emanem, upon which 14 different concert ambiences from across the world are subjected to his poignantly frosty sax tone. He was a member of the last incarnation of drummer John Stevens's Spontaneous Music Ensemble, documented on *A New Distance* (1995; Acta), and has made a stunning record with a quartet of drummer Roger Turner, pianist Veryan Weston and singer Phil Minton, based on texts from James Joyce's Finnegan's Wake, *Mouthfull of Ecstasy* (1996; Victo), as well as a trio with Minton and guitarist Erhard Hirt, *Two Concerts* (1997; FMP). He replaced Malfatti in the otherwise Austrian group Polwechsel, and appears on *Polwechsel 2* (1999; hatNOW). Like that of Derek Bailey, Butcher's music often sounds severe, focused and unswerving: paradoxically, the more inflexible and rigorous it forces itself to be, the more limitlessly plastic and imaginative it becomes. [JC]

⊙ **Concert Moves** (1995; Random Acoustics). Butcher's trio with Russell and Durrant is a model of the type of close listening interplay that British improvisers have explored so deeply. Careful, but not overly-cautious, intimate and engrossing, but also spiky and abrasive, Concert Moves catches the group after a decade working together. While he's advanced the saxophone vocabulary and developed a range of unique extended techniques, Butcher's predilection is to avoid anything showy or demonstrative, and he's said he's happy when a listener comes away not remembering there was a saxophone present.

Butterbeans and Susie

A legendary vaudeville team (they married on stage in 1916), Butterbeans (Jody Edwards; b. 19 July 1895, d. 28 Oct 1967) and Susie (Susie Hawthorne; b. 1896, d. 5 Dec 1963) worked early on with comedian Budd "Stringbeans" LeMay until his death in 1917 and then branched out with their own act in St Louis. They began recording in 1924 for OKeh and between then and 1930 they recorded more than sixty sides for the label, as well as touring to play theatres, music halls and cabarets, with their accompanist Eddie Heywood Senior. They continued working regularly for three decades (including regularly at the Apollo) and in 1960 recorded again, this time with Eddie Heywood Jnr playing piano in the band. [DF]

⊙ **Elevator Papa, Switchboard Mama** (1927–30; JSP). Scholarly selection of their early work, featuring pianist Eddie Heywood Senior and including "I Ain't Scared Of You", 'Get Yourself A Monkey Man" and "Radio Papa".

Billy Butterfield

Trumpet, flugelhorn, leader.

b. Middleton, Ohio, 14 Jan 1917; d. 18 March 1988.

Billy Butterfield took up music at thirteen and played in campus bands while he studied medicine. During a stint with Austin Wylie, an eccentric bandleader who also featured Claude Thornhill and Artie Shaw early in their careers, he was spotted by Bob Crosby's band and joined them in autumn 1937 in Cleveland. Crosby featured Butterfield's wide-range, huge-toned trumpet until 1940, when Artie Shaw made an offer. Butterfield, who had already recorded the soundtrack for a Shaw film, *Second Chorus*, with Bobby Hackett, moved over, stayed for six months and recorded more classics including "Stardust". By 1941 he was with Benny Goodman until petrol rationing and the draft reduced the workload.

Joe Glaser, Louis Armstrong's powerful manager, then helped him back into studio work, but Butterfield had his eye on a band of his own and after the war formed one with clarinettist Bill Stegmeyer. "But the whole thing came to a shuddering stop", he later recalled. "It was very much a one-man concern and I had to do everything: set the band up, take it down, drive the bus – even take vocals!" With relief, but in debt, he moved back to studio work (often with Hackett at ABC, a much-loved team), doubling up with small bands at Nick's and Condon's, and playing with a six-piece band featuring saxophonist Nick Caiazza for dates in colleges around Norfolk.

The 1950s were perhaps Butterfield's greatest recorded decade: with Condon, Jackie Gleason and

Ray Conniff he produced work of matchless invention, which echoed Louis Armstrong but had ideas of its own. In 1968 he was invited to join the World's Greatest Jazz Band, "at its best one of the finest groups I ever worked with", he said, and here his playing, especially early on, took on new fire: flaring, daring, high-register bursts which complemented Yank Lawson's hectoring co-lead to perfection. In the 1970s came regular partnerships with Flip Phillips (a favourite), solo tours and prolific recording in Europe, and a maturity which, once in a while, attractively fluffed up the edges of his tone. Butterfield's gifts were a natural extension of Armstrong's strengths: warm, buttered tone, and a magician's ability to pull melodic creations of arresting originality from battered jazz hats. Butterfield continued working until cancer finally immobilized him; with Bobby Hackett, he remains the most artistic swing trumpeter of post-war America, and is still criminally under-represented on CD. [DF]

Billy Butterfield and Ray Conniff

Conniff Meets Butterfield (1958–9; Columbia). An example of Butterfield's immense versatility and technical skill in an unusual partnership with Ray Conniff.

Billy Butterfield

Billy Plays Bix (1959; Epic). One great brassman salutes another: Butterfield at peak form with Tommy Gwaltney (clarinet) and a fine band of underrated players. Worth searching for.

Billy Butterfield: The Issued Recordings 1944–7 (1999; Jazz Band). Butterfield with his big band proving that, if not quite Harry James, he still had all of the technique and inspiration to stand out in front and strike fire.

Billy Butterfield And His Modern Dixie Stompers "Soft Strut" (2001; Fresh Sound). Recorded in 1956, this is a small group date including Lou McGarity, Hal McCusick and Boomie Richman that spotlights determinedly "contemporary" arrangements. Nice, although more Billy would (as ever) be welcome.

World's Greatest Jazz Band

Extra (1968; Project). Latter-day Butterfield with Yank Lawson at peak form in a band that (within its style) deserved its name; Billy's "Alfie" is a masterpiece.

Billy Butterfield and Dick Wellstood

Rapport (1975; 77 Records). The rather flat recording quality of this set does little to diminish the commanding work of its master duettists.

Jaki Byard

Piano, saxophones, arranger.

b. Worcester, Massachusetts, 15 June 1922; d. 11 Feb 1999.

Jaki (John) Byard was an enormously versatile musician who was working professionally from fifteen, before army service in World War II. He toured on piano with Earl Bostic in the late 1940s and played tenor saxophone throughout the 1950s in Boston's Herb Pomeroy band, for which he wrote "Aluminum Baby", a second cousin to "Satin Doll". After replacing Joe Zawinul with the Maynard Ferguson band in 1959, Byard began recording albums under his own name and, although finding a sympathetic forum for pianistic virtuosity during two stints with Charles Mingus (1962–5 and 1970), he was heard to best advantage as a soloist. He also led an occasional big band, the Apollo Stompers, and taught at New England Conservatory. Byard's familiarity with the whole gamut of jazz pianists from Tatum and Waller to contemporary players matched his knowledge of European music, a range reflected in Byard's kaleidoscopic performances. [BP]

Blues For Smoke (1960; Candid). Originally unreleased due to the demise of the record label, Byard's first album was unaccompanied and illustrates the range of his concerns, as well as including items he would return to, such as "Aluminum Baby" and "Tribute To The Ticklers".

➤➤ Don Ellis *(How Time Passes).*

Don Byas

Tenor saxophone.

b. Muskogee, Oklahoma, 21 Oct 1912 (or 1913); d. Amsterdam, 24 Aug 1972.

Carlos Wesley Byas gained early experience with Bennie Moten, Walter Page and his own band before switching from alto to tenor in 1933. He settled in California and worked in succession with Lionel Hampton (1935), Eddie Barefield and Buck Clayton (1936). In 1937 he moved to New York, playing with numerous name bands such as Don Redman, Lucky Millinder, Andy Kirk and Benny Carter. He made a considerable impact by replacing Lester Young in Count Basie's band from 1941–3, and during these three years became heavily involved in New York's "underground" scene at Minton's and elsewhere. In 1944 he played in Dizzy Gillespie's first small group on 52nd Street and the next year replaced Gillespie in a quintet with Charlie Parker and led his own quartet/quintet, recording prolifi-

cally under his own name and others'. He was widely regarded as the prime tenor player of the period, superior to the current work of either Coleman Hawkins or Lester Young. In 1946, while visiting Europe with Redman's small group, he decided to settle in Paris and became the first American jazz superstar there since Hawkins. He played the 1949 Paris jazz fair with Hot Lips Page, and toured Europe with the Ellington band in 1950 and with JATP in 1960, also performing regularly as a soloist. He later settled in Amsterdam, and returned only once to the USA, featuring at the 1970 Newport festival and with Art Blakey (with whom he toured Japan in 1971).

Although derived ultimately from Hawkins, Byas's style was more involved harmonically, a fact attributable to the direct influence of Art Tatum. Johnny Griffin has commented: "I used to say Don was the Tatum of the saxophone. ... He was using his harmonic solutions." In this respect he could justifiably claim to have had a decisive effect on Parker; and, while his on-the-beat accentuation was shunned by Parker, it came back with a vengeance in the work of the Coltrane school. His huge tone could sometimes sound unwieldy at fast tempos, but it was particularly sumptuous on the ballads which were the source of his post-war popularity, first in the USA and then in Europe. [BP]

⊙ **Savoy Jam Party** (1944–6; Savoy). This material is a forceful reminder of the imperious sound of Byas at the top of his game. With short solos and swing-to-bop rhythm-sections, it shows the tenorist's synthesis of Hawkins and Tatum carrying all before it.

⊙ **Lover Man** (1953–5; Vogue). Also recorded with 78rpm singles in mind, these tracks with either Martial Solal or Maurice Vander (piano) reflect the French equivalent of the Gene Ammons school of "sexophone". But it's not all ballads and current pops, and the mixture includes up-tempos such as the Byas speciality "Just One Of Those Things".

⊙ **A Night In Tunisia** (1963; Black Lion). An opportunity to hear Byas stretch out on this live recording with a sharp European rhythm-section. As well as bebop blowing vehicles such as the title track, Byas gives an oblique treatment to the ballads "Loverman" and "Yesterdays".

Charlie Byrd

Guitar.

b. Suffolk, Virginia, 16 Sept 1925; d. 30 Nov 1999.

Byrd played guitar from age ten, and later toured with name groups including that of Joe Marsala from 1947–9. He then studied European guitar music (including with Andrés Segovia) and settled in Washington, DC, working there in clubs and recording for a locally based label. He was with the Woody Herman sextet (1958–9), including a UK tour with Anglo-American Herd and the Monterey festival (both in 1959). He returned to Washington, and did a South American tour for the US State Department; contact with Brazilian popular music enabled him to appear on the first Stan Getz bossa-nova album in 1962, whose enormous success caused a lawsuit over royalties. He continued leading his own trio and recording for major labels, often with augmented backing. Compared with either his jazz contemporaries or expert bossa-nova guitarists such as João Gilberto or Luiz Bonfa, Byrd sounds very stiff, but his chief attraction lies in the use of the unamplified finger-style sound in a semi-jazz context, which influenced Earl Klugh and others. [BP]

⊙ **Bossa Nova Pelos Passoros** (1962; Riverside/OJC). According to the album title this is strictly for the birds but, coming from the same year as the Getz collaboration and with the same regular Byrd rhythm-section, it summarized a superficial perception of the bossa.

Donald Byrd

Trumpet, flugelhorn, educator, composer.

b. Detroit, Michigan, 9 Dec 1932.

Educated at Wayne University and the Manhattan School of Music, Byrd came to national and international prominence with Art Blakey's Jazz Messengers in the mid-1950s. He also worked with many leading modernists including Max Roach, John Coltrane, Red Garland, Pepper Adams, Sonny Rollins and Thelonious Monk. By 1958 he was also leading his own quintet and played festivals in Europe. He continued to lead his own groups and tour internationally during the 1960s, and also did a great deal of teaching at jazz clinics and at the Music and Art High School, New York. In 1963, he studied with Nadia Boulanger in Paris and in the USA acquired two educational degrees. He received his PhD in college teaching and administration in 1971 from Columbia University School of Education, then took up the post of chairman of the Black Music Department at Howard University, Washington, DC.

His 1973 jazz-soul album entitled *Black Byrd*, made for Blue Note, became the best-selling LP in the company's entire history, rocketing him to superstardom. He made a few more albums in the same vein and toured in the USA and internationally, but success did not unsettle him and he continued steadily with his educational and self-educational work, studying law and lecturing at various campuses on education, black music and law as it applies to music and musicians, and also conducting workshops. He left Howard in the autumn of 1975, but has continued to teach at university level. More recently he popped up on Guru's hip-hop fusion project *Jazzmatazz*.

Byrd's main influences are Dizzy Gillespie, Miles Davis and Clifford Brown, and his work in the 1950s and 1960s revealed immense assurance and lyricism. [IC]

⊙ **First Flight** (1955; Delmark). Twenty-two-year-old Byrd's first album as leader was recorded at a concert with a sextet which includes the great saxophonist Yusef Lateef, pianist Barry Harris, and euphonium, bass and drums. In this fast company, Byrd sounds slick and assured.

Early Byrd (1960–72; Blue Note). This is a composite album of fine tracks from various Byrd albums over a twelve-year period.

Free Form (1961; Blue Note). Byrd's quintet for this album comprised Wayne Shorter, Herbie Hancock, bassist Butch Warren and Billy Higgins, and the performances have the dynamism and optimism of newly arriving talents. This was two years before Hancock joined Miles Davis and it was Byrd who was to introduce Miles to the young pianist.

The Best Of Donald Byrd (1969–76; Blue Note). Another composite, including some of Byrd's (pretty feeble) jazz fusion.

Don Byron

Clarinet, composer.

b. New York, 8 Nov 1958.

A virtuosic performer equally at home in klezmer (Jewish street music from eastern Europe), classical and jazz-based musics, Don Byron was eased into musical appreciation by his father, a bassist in a calypso band, and his pianist mother, who took him to both jazz clubs and the New York Philharmonic. After studying classical clarinet, Byron became interested in salsa bands, subsequently turning to jazz at the New England Conservatory of Music in Boston. His music still reflects this broad-based outlook. He rose to prominence with his klezmer project, *Don Byron Plays The Music Of Mickey Katz*, enshrined on an Elektra Nonesuch album of the same name, and quickly established himself as a sell-out attraction in the genre. Since the mid-1980s, Byron has also become a stalwart of the New York contemporary jazz scene, playing with the likes of Craig Harris, David Murray, Marc Ribot, Bill Frisell, Bobby Previte and Ralph Peterson, in the process helping to re-establish the clarinet as a front-rank jazz instrument. In the late 1990s, Byron formed a band, Existential Dred, an "attempt to present a more literary view of African American poetry than rap in a contemporary context". To this end, the band included poet/rapper Sadiq Bey alongside pianist Uri Gaine, bassist Reggie Washington and drummer Ben Wittman. Byron is an imaginative but deliberate musician, open-minded and adventurous; he characterizes himself thus: "I tend to gravitate to whoever is playing the trickiest, outest stuff." [DF]

Bobby Previte

Weather Clear, Track Fast (1992; Enja). Bustling, almost Mingusian music composed by drummer/leader Previte, to which Byron brings astringent inventiveness.

Don Byron

Tuskegee Experiments (1992; Elektra Nonesuch). Debut as leader, containing originals, an Ellington arrangement and a transcription of a Schumann song, played by Byron with band including guitarist Bill Frisell and drummer Ralph Peterson.

Music For Six Musicians (1995; Elektra Nonesuch). Intriguing mix of Latin rhythms and tricky time-signatures, racial politics and virtuosic soloing from cream of New York's contemporary musicians: Graham Haynes (cornet); Edsel Gomez (piano); Kenny Davis (bass); Jerry Gonzalez (congas); Ben Wittman (drums), in addition to the ever-inventive Byron.

Nu Blaxploitation (1998; Blue Note). Many-hued album, touching on funk, rap and Jimi Hendrix, with power, politics and race pungently debated.

C

George Cables

Piano.
b. New York, 14 Nov 1944.

After studying at the High School of Performing Arts and Mannes College, Cables worked in the mid-1960s with both Art Blakey and Max Roach (recording with both in the early 1970s). He played regularly with Sonny Rollins in 1969, Joe Henderson from 1969–71 and Freddie Hubbard from 1971–6 and in 1980; Cables also backed Dexter Gordon for two years after his return to the USA in 1977, and Art Pepper, first in New York (1977) and then for the last three years of his career (1979–82), when they recorded two duo albums. Other important associations in the last two decades have included work with Bobby Hutcherson, Frank Morgan, Chico Freeman and the group Bebop And Beyond. As well as being a prolific composer for others, Cables occasionally appears under his own name and is an invaluable sideman; his backing is always intensely rhythmic and supportive, and his solo work is sure-footed and stimulating. [BP]

Night And Day (1991; DIW). A relatively conventional programme – apart from Jaco Pastorius's "Three Views Of A Secret" and Cables's own "Ebony Moonbeams" (partly in 5/4) – finds him in sparkling form with the beautifully loose rhythm-section of Cecil McBee and Billy Hart.

Ernie Caceres

Baritone and alto saxophones, clarinet.
b. Rockport, Texas, 22 Nov 1911; d. 10 Jan 1971.

Ernie (Ernesto) Caceres worked with his brothers, Emilio (violin) and Pinero (trumpet and piano), in the early 1930s around Detroit and later New York. There, in 1938, he joined Bobby Hackett's band for the start of a musical relationship which lasted, on and off, for thirty years. A booming-toned, agile and versatile musician, Caceres was, with Harry Carney, the first baritone stylist to achieve a solo reputation, but his sound - less lush and more edgy than Carney's - was heard in a wider variety of contexts than his black contemporary's: with, among others, Jack Teagarden (1939), Bob Zurke, Glenn Miller (1940–2) and later Benny Goodman, Tommy Dorsey and Woody Herman. By 1948 Caceres was winner of a Metronome poll and the following year won again, against strong opposition from the burgeoning bebop movement. Although he was capable of standing his ground in such company, as he shows on a 1949 Metronome All Stars recording date ("Overtime" and "Victory Ball"), his style gravitated more naturally to swing and Dixieland, and from 1946, when he moved into Nick's Club in New York,he was more and more associated with Eddie Condon's circle of "timeless" jazzmen. He recorded regularly with them, led his own quartet at the Hickory Log in 1949, and from 1950 was a staffman and featured artist on Garry Moore's TV show for six years. In 1956–7 he played for Bobby Hackett's Henry Hudson band (his brother Pinero also appeared with them) and kept working all through the 1960s with Billy Butterfield and later with Jim Cullum's Happy Jazz Band. [DF]

Eddie Condon

Town Hall Concerts Vol. 7 (1944; Jazzology). This double CD set has Caceres not only on his baritone saxophone but on a rarer clarinet feature ("Cherry"), demonstrating that he was one of the greatest clarinettists ever to play Dixieland music.

Jackie Cain

>> *see entry for* **Jackie And Roy**.

Michael Cain

Piano.
b. Los Angeles, 2 Apr 1966.

Raised in Las Vegas, Cain started playing at the age of four, initially studying classical music. He pursued both classical and jazz studies at North Texas State University, and in California at the University of Southern California and Cal Arts. On the West Coast in the late 80s, he gigged with Gerald Wilson, flautist James Newton and drummer Billy Higgins. Settling in New York in 1990, and hooking up with members of the M-Base collective, Cain's career began to flourish, bolstered by his joining drummer Jack DeJohnette's new ensemble (for which he was pianist of choice for a number of years) which was recording for ECM. He has also played and recorded with Dave Holland, John Scofield, Marty Ehrlich and Ray Anderson, and he was reportedly commissioned to write music for President Clinton's inaugural gala. Cain can be impressionistic, but also has the melodic power and drive to keep the flowers from wilting. As a leader, Cain has recorded twice for Candid (*Strange Omen*, 1990; *What Means*

This, 1991) and, with trumpeter Ralph Alessi and saxist Peter Epstein, once each for ECM (*Circa*, 1996) and the M.A. label (*Phfew*, 2000). A solo album *Evidence Of Things Unseen*, recorded in Japan in 1994, appeared on M.A. in 1999. Cain teamed up with drummer and composer Pheeroan akLaff for *Brooklyn Waters*, a duo project for Telepathy Records. [JC]

⊙ **Circa** (1996; ECM). Unusual, evocative writing inspired by the Nevadan landscape, and outstandingly nuanced playing from Cain within the singular grouping of trumpeter Alessi and saxist Epstein.

Uri Caine

Piano, keyboards.
b. Philadelphia, 8 June 1956.

Caine began piano lessons at the age of eight, and while still a high-school student he played in pick-up bands led by trumpeter Johnny Coles, saxophonists Odean Pope and Hank Mobley, and drummers Mickey Roker and Philly Joe Jones. He moved from Philadelphia to New York, where he has instituted himself as an important player straddling the downtown and straightahead scenes, successfully playing with such diverse figures as Donald Byrd, Bobby Watson and Freddie Hubbard, on one hand, and Rashied Ali, Don Byron and Sam Rivers on the other. As a sideman, he has recorded with a variety of players, including Byron, trumpeters Clark Terry and Dave Douglas, bassist Cornell Rochester, and vibes player Gust William Tsilis. Sometimes on synthesizers, more often on acoustic piano, Caine is a very versatile musician, a melodically inclined individual with wide tastes reflected in his eclectic, playful, but never superficial playing and composing. He was a member of the JMT stable of artists before that label went defunct, recording a couple of promising CDs, *Sphere Music* (1994) and *Toys* (1995), for them. He has since recorded a string of nearly a dozen albums for ex-JMT label boss Stefan Winter's new company Winter & Winter, an astonishing body of work ranging from ingenious interpretations of Wagner (*Wagner in Venice*, 1996 and *I Went Out This Morning Over The Countryside*, 1998), early Tin Pan Alley (*The Sidewalks Of New York*, 1999), Schumann (*Love Fugue*, 1999) and hip-hop (*Bedrock*, 2001), and that marks Caine as one of the most intrepid, prolific musicians on the scene. [JC]

⊙ **Solitaire** (2002; Winter & Winter). After the percussion and synths have been packed away and the DJs have gone home (this was recorded the same year as his Latin album *Rio* and the cut-up funk of *Bedrock*), here Uri is alone at the piano making music perhaps as compelling as anything he has done.

Joey Calderazzo

Piano, composer.
b. New Rochelle, New York, 27 Feb 1965.

After taking up classical piano at seven under the tutelage of Juilliard's Bella Schumlatcher, Joey Calderazzo discovered jazz in his mid-teens, playing in a band with his drummer-brother Gene. He became known to a wider jazz public once he joined saxophonist Michael Brecker's band in 1987, recording two albums, *Don't Try This At Home* (Impulse; 1988) and *Now You See It... (Now You Don't)* (GRP; 1990), with him before signing to Blue Note. A sparky but circumspect improviser with a penchant for dramatic, slow-building climaxes, Calderazzo has contributed his pungent but fleet piano to albums by saxophonist label-mates Jerry Bergonzi and Rick Margitza, guitarist Dave Stryker and UK tenor/soprano player Dave O'Higgins. He can also be heard on Bob Belden's Blue Note album of Sting compositions, *Straight To My Heart*, and on Bob Mintzer's tribute to bassist Jaco Pastorius, *I Remember Jaco*. Although heavily indebted to Herbie Hancock, and a strong admirer of Wynton Kelly, Calderazzo has audibly matured into a more individual player with each successive album as a leader, and in 1995 he left Blue Note and began to leaven what his producer Bob Belden refers to as his "scorched earth policy" with a more thoughtful approach, concentrating on texture, timbre and mood as much as on straightforward momentum, as heard on his well-received debut for Columbia (see below). A regular member of Branford Marsalis's groups since the mid 1990s, talk of a signing to the saxophonist's label Marsalis Music is in the air. [CP]

⊙ **In The Door** (1990; Blue Note). In stellar company – Branford Marsalis, Michael Brecker, Peter Erskine and Adam Nussbaum are all featured, among others – Calderazzo produces a highly enjoyable, if somewhat glib set.

⊙ **To Know One** (1992; Blue Note). Improved by having the same rhythm-section – Jack DeJohnette (drums) and Dave Holland (bass) – throughout, with guest appearances again from Branford Marsalis and Jerry Bergonzi, a lively set of originals leavened with one Holland and one Richie Beirach composition.

⊙ **The Traveler** (1993; Blue Note). Maturing music, featuring two trios on post-bop staples such as "Blue In Green", Wayne Shorter's "Black Nile" etc, plus three Calderazzo originals.

⊙ **Secrets** (1995; AudioQuest). With orchestrations by Bob Belden interspersed with trio tracks with bassist James Genus and drummer Clarence Penn, this is a move into more considered music for Calderazzo.

⊙ **Joey Calderazzo** (2000; Columbia). In the brilliant company of John Pattitucci on bass and his drumming colleague in the Marsalis group, Jeff "Tain" Watts, Calderazzo fashions a complete culmination and fruition of his earlier promise with his most measured music yet. It features his intriguingly spiralling original composition "Haiku", already sounding like a modern classic.

Happy Caldwell

Tenor saxophone, clarinet.
b. Chicago, 25 July 1903; d. 29 Dec 1978.

"A great and unheralded influence on tenor saxophone", said cornettist Rex Stewart of Happy (Albert) Caldwell, one of the most gifted players in the formative years of his instrument. "He was playing like mad", affirms Coleman Hawkins, and all through the 1920s and 1930s Caldwell stayed busy, touring with Bernie Young's band, then with Mamie Smith and later with a succession of fine American big bands, including Fletcher Henderson's, Vernon Andrade's, Charlie Johnson's and Tiny Bradshaw's. In the 1920s Caldwell was all over New York playing clubs and dance schools; Rex Stewart describes the two of them commuting from band to band: "It was Happy and Rex against the world! [But] Happy knew his way around. We spent part of each day finding a sheltered place to sleep and the rest of the time hustling hot dog money." Caldwell also appeared on such classic records as Louis Armstrong's 1929 "Knockin' A Jug" sides with Jack Bland's Rhythmakers (featuring Henry "Red" Allen) and even Jelly Roll Morton's 1939 remake of "Winin' Boy Blues".

Recorded examples of early Caldwell sound much like Hawkins, but there is little evidence that he kept up his former admirer's relentless progression. By 1939, according to Kenny Clarke, Caldwell was leading "a little band in the back room of Minton's ... a rather drab place frequented by old men". Caldwell at 36 was hardly old, but his style (rather like Prince Robinson's) never quite kept up with Hawkins, and no records exist to chart his reactions to bebop. But around New York his name stayed well known for years longer: he regularly led a band at Smalls' Paradise (1950–53) and was a familiar face at New York functions until his death. [DF]

➤➤ **Billy Banks** *(Billy Banks And His Rhythmakers).*

California Ramblers

The California Ramblers were managed by Ed Kirkeby, who later became manager to Fats Waller. At its height the band contained a rich selection of white stars, including Red Nichols, the Dorseys, Adrian Rollini (who took up bass saxophone at Kirkeby's request) and drummer Stan King; from 1921 they played at the Pelham Bay Park, Westchester County, which Kirkeby renamed the California Ramblers Inn. Throughout the ensuing decade the California Ramblers – with a huge variety of players – recorded hundreds of sides for a plethora of different labels (sometimes under the pseudonym "The Golden Gate Orchestra") and much of their music stands the test of time. In the 1970s and 1980s cornettist Dick Sudhalter re-formed the Ramblers for US concerts and club dates, using some of their most attractive material. [DF]

⊙ **California Ramblers With Adrian Rollini** (1923–7; Village). A useful compendium which collects many of the Ramblers' better sides.

Red Callender

Bass, tuba.

b. Haynesville, Virginia, 6 March 1916; d. 8 March 1992.

George Sylvester Callender went to school in New Jersey, then took a touring band job at seventeen. He settled on the West Coast, working with, among others, Buck Clayton in 1936, Louis Armstrong in 1937–8, Lester Young (1941–3), his own trio (1944–6), Erroll Garner (1946–7), Johnny Otis (1947) and Cee Pee Johnson (1947). After that he led his own band in Hawaii (1947–8, 1949–50) and in San Francisco (1948), and did production work for small record companies. His prolific recording included sessions with Charlie Parker (1947) and the last albums of Art Tatum (1955–6). Everything mentioned so far was on string bass but, becoming heavily involved in session work from the 1950s, he also used tuba with everyone from Frank Sinatra and Stan Kenton to Stevie Wonder; live appearances on tuba, such as with Mingus and Monk (Monterey festival, 1964) and James Newton (from 1980, including a 1981 European tour), maintained his strong jazz connection.

Following the premature death of the slightly younger Jimmie Blanton, Callender first drew favourable attention through his 1942 trio recording with Lester Young and Nat "King" Cole. His style combines a Blantonesque approach to melody and timing with a penetrating pizzicato tone which strongly influenced his friend and pupil Charles Mingus. [BP]

➤➤ **Charlie Parker** *(The Dial Masters).*

Cab Calloway

Vocals, leader.

b. Rochester, New York, 25 Dec 1907; d. 18 Nov 1994.

Cab (Cabell) Calloway began his long and distinguished jazz career as a hustler and part-time singer in Baltimore's clubland. In 1927 he joined an all-male quartet in the famous black revue *Plantation Days*, and when they arrived in Chicago he stayed on to work solo as singer, drummer and MC in the Dreamland and Sunset cafés. In 1929, while introducing the Sunset shows, he took over leadership of the Alabamians, an eleven-piece band from Chicago. It was a happy period, but once in New York the Alabamians fared badly against tough opposition. They parted company with Calloway, who at Louis Armstrong's recommendation joined the company of Connie's Hot Chocolates at Connie's Inn, then, in the spring of 1930, went into the Savoy as contracted frontman for the Missourians, another touring band that was to form the base for Calloway's great orchestra.

At the Savoy he developed a spectacular new line in showmanship, got noticed by the Mafia men who ran it, and found himself forcibly transferred to the Cotton Club as relief band to Duke Ellington's. As work at the Cotton Club regularized, Calloway took over leadership of the Missourians (previously they had worked as a co-operative) and filled them out with spectacular cornermen: showman trumpeter Reuben Reeves, trombonist Ed Swayzee (from Sam Wooding's glo-

Cab Calloway

betrotting orchestra), trumpeter Doc Cheatham and pianist Benny Payne, a longtime partner. From 1931 the band began recording and broadcasting for network radio and became a smash hit: their theme song "Minnie The Moocher", a creation by Calloway and Irving Mills, was to become Calloway's lifelong *pièce de résistance*.

For the next decade and a half Calloway's noisily extroverted band, fronted by its wild-haired, white-suited conductor, made headlines at the Cotton Club, in theatres countrywide, in films and on radio, with Calloway's singalong specialities and histrionic high tenor voice generating hysterical approval. Conditions on the road were often appalling (especially for black bands) but morale stayed high. And Calloway – personally if not always musically – was loved and respected by his musicians. Says Benny Payne: "You could get drunk with him and bring him home on your back – but next day when he raised his hand for the downbeat he didn't want to know what had happened the night before!" The band spent as much as fifty weeks a year on the road and produced a string of hit records, "The Lady With The Fan", "Za-Zuh-Zaz" and others, many of them containing explicit references to drugs.

Perhaps the best Calloway bands came after 1940, producing classic sides, often with solo contributions from the likes of Milt Hinton, Hilton Jefferson, Chu Berry and Jonah Jones. But by 1947 Calloway's regular bandleading days were coming to an end. The following year he reduced to a septet, then a trio, and one brief big-band revival was a flop. His solo career, though, hardly faltered. From 1952–4 he played Sportin' Life in a Porgy and Bess revival opposite Leontyne Price, toured with the show regularly thereafter and in 1965 was warm-up man for the Harlem Globetrotters before spending three years playing Horace Vandergelder opposite Pearl Bailey in an all-black production of *Hello Dolly!*. In the 1970s he appeared on Broadway in Bubbling Brown Sugar, cameoed in the Belushi/Aykroyd movie *The Blues Brothers*, and continued appearing in musicals and one-off shows for the rest of his life – finding the time to act as a consultant for Francis Ford Coppola's film *The Cotton Club* in 1985.

Calloway was a grand survivor whose contribution to jazz history deserves a second look. Like Earl Hines and Wilbur de Paris he was a vocational bandleader, but he treated his men to wages higher than did any other bandleader of the swing years, and his name remains universally popular among musicians who knew him. [DF]

⊙ **Cab Calloway And The Missourians** (1929–30; JSP). Interesting collection covering early titles by the Missourians and Calloway's first recordings as their new leader.

⊙ **Kickin' The Gong Around** (1930–1; ASV Living Era). Excellent compilation of early Cab including "Minnie", "Trickeration" and the title track. Produced by the late Kevin Daly, an informed swing authority.

⊙ **The Chronological Cab Calloway** (1931–45; Classics). This ten-CD set (available in separate volumes) is the definitive Calloway memorial.

⊙ **The King Of Hi-De-Ho** (1934–47; Giants of Jazz). Excellent budget collection of Calloway classics, including "Minnie The Moocher", "The Jumpin' Jive" and later greats like the hilarious "Everybody Eats When They Come To My House".

Michel Camilo

Piano.

b. Santo Domingo, Dominican Republic, 4 April 1954.

Camilo played accordion at family gatherings (his nine uncles were all musicians), and then switched at the age of sixteen to piano, which he studied at conservatory level while playing percussion and piano in the National Symphony Orchestra. Moving to New York in 1979, he studied at Mannes

College and the Juilliard School, while gigging frequently. As a member of the group French Toast he recorded his tune "Why Not?", which was also done by Manhattan Transfer and Paquito D'Rivera, while his "Caribe" was performed by Dizzy Gillespie. After playing at Carnegie Hall with his own trio opposite Tania Maria in 1985, he recorded several popular albums, as well as conducting classical European music and composing works such as his "Rhapsody" for piano duettists Katia and Marielle Labèque (1992). Camilo's own piano style is full of technical bravura and the verve of Afro-Latin rhythms, a fusion of which he is one of the most impressive performers. [BP]

⊙ **One More Once** (1994; Columbia). The high energy of Camilo's piano is balanced here by his excitable writing for a big band, including soloists such as Paquito D'Rivera and Chris Hunter; the repertoire includes remakes of "Why Not?" and "Caribe".

Candido

Bongo, conga drums.

b. Havana, 22 April 1921.

Candido Camero went to the USA in the 1950s, playing with Dizzy Gillespie, Stan Kenton and Billy Taylor. One of the most accomplished Latin percussionists, over the years he has worked under bandleaders including Sonny Rollins, Elvin Jones and Duke Ellington, and has led his own bands across a varied musical terrain of latin, soul-jazz and jazz-funk. [IC]

➤➤ **Dizzy Gillespie** *(Gillespania/Carnegie Hall)*; **Billy Taylor** *(The Billy Taylor Trio With Candido).*

Mutt Carey

Trumpet.

b. Hahnville, Louisiana, 1891; d. 3 Sept 1948.

Mutt (Thomas) Carey's brother Jack ran the Crescent Brass Band in New Orleans, but Mutt took up trumpet late, at 22. He worked first with Frankie Dusen, Joe Oliver, Jimmy Brown and Bebe Ridgeley in clubs and on parades. In 1914 he joined Kid Ory to begin a partnership of more than thirty (sometimes fiery) years. With his mellow-toned mid-range playing, Carey was one of the most popular New Orleans trumpetmen, with a special gift for playing softly, emulating the muted techniques of his friend King Oliver. The self-named "Blues King of New Orleans" moved to California in 1919 to join Kid Ory, and when Oliver himself came to California in 1921 to cover jobs for Ory, audiences dismissed him as a Carey imitator: Oliver quickly left for Chicago and greater things. From 1925 Carey took over Ory's small group, renamed it the Jeffersonians and expanded it to big-band size for work in the silent film studios. During a quiet spell in the 1930s he combined music with work as a Pullman porter and mailman, then returned to Ory's band for the Standard Oil broadcasts (narrated by Orson Welles) which accelerated the revivalism of the mid-1940s. He remained a much-loved star until he died. [DF]

⊙ **Giants Of Traditional Jazz** (1944–52; Savoy). Includes the recordings made by Mutt Carey's New Yorkers (with Ed Hall), just after he left Ory in 1947; marvellous illustrations of a great jazz trumpeter.

➤➤ **Kid Ory** *(Creole Jazz Band).*

Johnny Carisi

Arranger, composer, trumpet.

b. Hasbrouck Heights, New Jersey, 23 Feb 1922; d. 8 Oct 1992.

After playing in several big bands, including the Glenn Miller service band (1943–6) and Claude Thornhill's, Carisi began formal study of composition in 1948, while writing for record dates by Brew Moore and Miles Davis ("Israel" was his contribution to *Birth Of The Cool*). His later jazz associations include playing and writing for an Urbie Green big-band album (1956, one tune from which was used on *Miles Ahead*) and three pieces for a Gil Evans date (*Into The Hot*, 1960); he also wrote a more conventional album for trumpeter Marvin Stamm in 1968. Carisi was involved in all aspects of music from pop to ballet, and his compositions include a saxophone quartet and a tuba concerto. His jazz output was minuscule but, thanks to his association with Davis and Evans, his thought-provoking work with medium-sized ensembles has received due attention. [BP]

Gil Evans, Johnny Carisi and Cecil Taylor

⊙ **Into The Hot** (1961; Impulse). Although featuring solo contributions from Phil Woods and guitarist Barry Galbraith, the three scores Carisi wrote for this album are most notable for reanimating the ideas and textures associated with 1950s experimental arranging.

Hoagy Carmichael

Composer, vocals, piano.

b. Bloomington, Indiana, 11 Nov 1899; d. 28 Dec 1981.

In his early years as an aspiring lawyer, Hoagy (Hoagland Howard) Carmichael worshipped the young Bix Beiderbecke – who, with the Wolverines, recorded Carmichael's first composition, "Free Wheeling", later titled "Riverboat Shuffle". Soon after, the young composer – abandoning law and moving into the young jazz circles – wrote a classic duet, "Rockin' Chair", which he recorded with Louis Armstrong. From the very start his compositions were marked by references to the jazz he loved: "Stardust", the 1929 masterpiece that sealed his songwriting future, quotes directly from a Louis Armstrong solo (bar 4 is bar 26 of Armstrong's "Potato Head Blues" solo); "Skylark", played in strict straight quavers, turns into a Bix Beiderbecke pas-

tiche. The lyrics, too, sometimes included jazz references: "Riverboat Shuffle" celebrates Coleman Hawkins and Louis Jordan, while "The Monkey Song" cites Beiderbecke and Charlie Parker ("Bird") in quick succession. (Carmichael's muse is often quirky: as well as monkeys, his songs contain mice, spiders, whales, and a whole menagerie in his 1951 award-winning fantasy, "In The Cool Cool Cool Of The Evening", co-composed with Johnny Mercer.)

A huge list of compositions through the 1930s established Carmichael in Hollywood as well as in Tin Pan Alley, and by the 1940s he was also playing effective cameo roles in enduring films such as Howard Hawks's *To Have And Have Not* (1945) as well as in more forgettable ones like Michael Curtiz's *Young Man With A Horn* (1950), ostensibly based on the life of Bix Beiderbecke. In the 1940s his Decca sides were regularly staffed by stars such as Dick Cathcart and Eddie Miller, and at least one 1950s album teamed him with modern jazzmen including Art Pepper, Jimmy Rowles and Don Fagerquist. Regular radio shows and television and solo appearances in the USA and Europe kept him busy all through the 1950s and it was only with the coming of the Beatles that Carmichael at last sat back on his royalties. His songs have continued to be steady favourites with jazz instrumentalists and singers. [DF]

⊙ **Hoagy Carmichael Vols 1 & 2** (1924–32; JSP). The best overall survey of Carmichael's early years, this set has his own first recordings plus significant recordings of his work by others, crowned by a definitive annotation from Carmichael biographer Richard M. Sudhalter.

⊙ **Stardust And Much More** (RCA Bluebird). Covering 1927–34, plus two late and skilfully edited pieces from 1960, this is another set of classic tracks, also with fine notes by Richard M. Sudhalter.

⊙ **Hoagy Carmichael 1927–39** (Timeless). Produced by Chris Ellis, this set has Hoagy with Paul Whiteman, Irving Mills, Louis Armstrong and his own orchestra; interesting choice of material includes "Rockin' Chair", "Washboard Blues", "Lazybones" and "Moon Country", and a few rarities.

⊙ **Classics: The Collection** (1930–45; Collection). A very interesting set for its inclusion of rare V-disc material and some esoteric titles, including "No More Toujours L'Amour" and "Ginger And Spice".

⊙ **Stardust** (1942–54; AAD). Possibly the best collection of mid-period Carmichael including "My Resistance Is Low", "A Tune For Humming", "Casanova Cricket" and twenty-one more. Entertaining, humorous and regularly moving with superb musicianship all around.

Harry Carney

Baritone, bass and alto saxophones, clarinet.

b. Boston, Massachusetts, 1 April 1910; d. 8 Oct 1974.

Harry Howell Carney began playing the clarinet in youth bands in Boston; a few doors away lived Johnny Hodges and Charlie Holmes, and all three made exploratory New York trips in 1927 to visit the Rhythm Club. Carney played other venues too – the Savoy, in a relief band, and the Bamboo Inn, where Duke Ellington heard him and invited the young saxophonist to join his band for a trip back to Boston. Once there Ellington persuaded Carney's parents to let their son join him on the road: a first contract involved Ellington in guardian duties. He used his protégé to play alto first, alongside Rudy Jackson, then third alto (after Otto Hardwicke had joined the band yet again), but Carney had his eye on the big baritone saxophone. "I wanted to impress everyone with the idea that the baritone was *necessary*," he said. Ellington quickly fell for Carney's huge sound (modelled in the top register on Coleman Hawkins, in the bottom on Adrian Rollini), and apart from a clarinet solo on "Rockin' In Rhythm", Carney played little else but baritone for his leader for the next 45 years.

A cultured, knowledgeable and good-natured man, Carney had "the look of a man who has lived in nothing but comfort", remarked Rex Stewart in the 1960s. Jimmy Staples added: "He has a characteristic not always evident in some famous musicians – humility." In later years Carney became Ellington's closest associate, because he drove Ellington everywhere. On drives of up to six hundred miles Ellington would sit alongside to compose, think or sleep, and the only time his driver got agitated was when his employer was late for the pick-up. "He's a great fellow," said Carney, "and it's not only been an education being with him but also a great pleasure. At times I've been ashamed to take the money!" After Ellington died in 1974, Carney told Don George: "This is the worst day of my life. Without Duke I have nothing to live for." His own death followed just four months later – "Carney died of bereavement", said Whitney Balliett. Carney's contribution to Ellington's oeuvre was immeasurable: his huge sound, which shouldered and sometimes led Ellington's saxophones, was – with that of Johnny Hodges – the most irreplaceable of his leader's woodwind voices. [DF]

➤➤ **Duke Ellington** *(Such Sweet Thunder; Far East Suite).*

Ian Carr

Trumpet, flugelhorn, keyboards, composer, writer, educator.

b. Dumfries, Scotland, 21 April 1933.

Older brother of pianist and composer Mike Carr, Ian started teaching himself the trumpet at the age of 17. From 1960–62 he played with the EmCee Five, based in Newcastle, and then moved to London, joining Don Rendell. He became co-leader of the Rendell-Carr quintet in 1963, staying with it until July 1969, making five albums and performing at international festivals. Between 1970–72 he also played and recorded with the New Jazz Orchestra, Michael Garrick, Neil Ardley, Guy Warren of Ghana (Ghanaba), John Stevens and Trevor Watts, and worked with Joe Harriott, John McLaughlin, Mike Westbrook and Don Byas.

In September 1969 Carr formed Nucleus, which pioneered jazz-rock fusion and electronics in jazz. In 1970 the group recorded their first album, *Elastic Rock*, won first prize at the Montreux festival, and performed at the Newport festival and the Village Gate in New York. Throughout the 1970s Nucleus toured throughout Europe, playing major festivals and appearing on radio and TV; in 1974 an augmented Nucleus toured the UK for the Arts Council Contemporary Music Network, performing Carr's long composition, *Labyrinth*. In 1984 Nucleus undertook a seven-week British Council tour of Latin America; the following year Nucleus played for one week at the Rome spring festival, and recorded a live album at the Stuttgart festival.

CAROLINE IRWIN

Ian Carr

Since 1975 Carr has also been a member of the United Jazz and Rock Ensemble, and alongside various incarnations of Nucleus, he has played with the NDR Big Band, Hamburg, under the direction of Michael Gibbs, toured with George Russell's Anglo-American Living Time Orchestra. Carr has had many composing commissions, writing for all sizes of ensembles from small groups to full orchestra with strings; in 1986 he wrote "Northumberland Sketches" for string ensemble and soloists, which was performed at the Bracknell classical and jazz festivals and later became part of his longer work *Old Heartland*.

Carr's books on Miles Davis and Keith Jarrett are classics of jazz biography (In August 1982 he received the Calabria award for "outstanding contribution in the field of jazz") and he is a regular jazz columnist for the BBC Music Magazine.

Nucleus re-formed in 1998 to play a concert in a "Music Of The 1970s" series, which concluded with a performance of Neil Ardley's *Kaleidoscope Of Rainbows*; in 1999 the concert was performed again, and recorded. In January 1999 Carr spent ten days in Germany with the United Jazz and Rock Ensemble, recording an album and playing concerts. In May 2001, Carr reunited with Don Rendell at the Royal Festival Hall as part of the South Bank's 50th Anniversary celebrations. [CA]

⊙ **Elastic Rock/We'll Talk About It Later** (1994; BGO). A two-CD reissue – with new sleevenotes – of the first two Nucleus albums, recorded in 1970. (BGO have also reissued the 1971/72 albums *Solar Plexus/Bella Donna*, the 1973 albums *Labyrinth/Roots* and the 1974/75 albums *Under The Sun/Snakehips Etc* – all good value twofers.)

⊙ **Out Of The Long Dark/Old Heartland** (1998; BGO). The combination of jazz and strings is rarely successful but *Old Heartland* is a shining exception. Carr's writing for the Kreisler String Orchestra is skilful and exciting, and his four "Northumbrian Sketches" provide outstanding settings for soloists, evoking both the industrial energy of Newcastle and the rural peace of its hinterland.

➤➤ **Neil Ardley** *(Virtual Realities)*.

Mike Carr

Organ, piano, vibes.

b. South Shields, Durham, UK, 7 Dec 1937.

Self-taught on piano, Carr organized the Newcastle-based group EmCee Five (1960–62) which included Malcolm Cecil (who later worked with Jim Hall and Stevie Wonder) and his elder brother Ian Carr. He then played in London with R&B singer Herbie Goins in 1966 and his own trio, including John McLaughlin in 1967, and accompanied Coleman Hawkins (1967) and Don Byas (1968). His duo with Tony Crombie in 1969–70 became the Ronnie Scott trio from 1971–5, which played a Carnegie Hall concert in 1974. He toured the UK with the Kenny Clarke trio in 1978 and has gigged and/or recorded with Buddy Tate, Illinois Jacquet, Eddie Davis, Johnny Griffin, Arnett Cobb, Sonny Payne, Art Taylor and Jimmy Witherspoon. His own groups have included Jim Mullen, Dick Morrissey, Peter King, Tony Coe and Phil Lee, and a successful jazz-funk recording group Cargo.

A dynamic performer whose pedal work emulates Jimmy Smith, Carr produces right-hand lines that are more bebop-oriented than most organists'. His subsequent incorporation of electric piano caused no less a figure than Oscar Peterson to comment, "I have never heard an organist in the States who has all that swinging, the organ, the electric piano, and the bass pedals." In 2001 he formed a new hard-bop quintet featuring the brothers Steve and Matt Fishwick. [BP]

Bebop From The East Coast (1960–7; Birdland). The EmCee Five, with a frontline of brother Ian and neglected tenorist Gary Cox, in its only surviving recordings (including a session originally released by EMI). Carr plays bustling piano, for the most part, although the lone track from 1967 features his organ trio with young John McLaughlin.

Good Times And The Blues (1993; Cargogold). The excellent rhythm-section (Carr and drummer Mark Taylor) plays host to both Jim Mullen and Dick Morrissey on a varied programme of Carr originals, including "The One That Got Away", a minor classic first recorded by the EmCee Five (see above).

Terri Lyne Carrington

Drums.

b. Medford, Massachusetts, 4 Aug 1965.

Carrington came from a musical family – her mother studied piano, her father was a saxophonist, her paternal grandmother played "saloon-style piano" and her paternal grandfather was a drummer. Discovering her grandfather's drum kit, she began playing at seven, was performing professionally at ten, and at eleven gained a full scholarship to Berklee College, where she later studied full-time for a while. Receiving early encouragement from Clark Terry, she has performed and recorded with a huge variety of musicians, from swing to M-Base to fusion. Important collaborators whom she lists (apart from Terry) are Nat Adderley, Kenny Barron, Lester Bowie, George Coleman, Stan Getz, Herbie Hancock, Joe Henderson, Al Jarreau, Joe Sample, Dave Sanborn, Pharoah Sanders and Wayne Shorter. Her 1989 solo album, *Real Life Story*, was nominated for a Grammy, as was Dianne Reeves's 1998 *That Day* which Carrington produced. In the late 1990s she has worked as house drummer on several TV series, and since 1999 she has toured internationally with Herbie Hancock, as well as taking part in a tribute to Jimi Hendrix with guitarist Nguyên Lê. [BP]

Jazz Is A Spirit (2001; ACT). Demonstrating Carrington's effortless versatility and musicality, this set features recent employer Herbie Hancock plus Terence Blanchard, Wallace Roney and Gary Thomas. A couple of brief spoken-word tracks relate to the album title, and the drum solo "Mr. Jo Jones" features his voice.

≫ **Greg Osby** *(Greg Osby And Sound Theatre)*; **Danilo Perez** *(PanaMonk)*; **Nguyên Lê** *(Purple: Celebrating Jimi Hendrix)*

Benny Carter

Alto saxophone, trumpet, arranger, composer; also tenor saxophone, clarinet, trombone, piano.

b. New York, 8 Aug 1907; d.12 July 2003.

Benny Carter began with lessons from Harold Procter and a couple of other teachers, it seems on a semi-casual basis. His inspirations for trumpet (which he played first) included Bubber Miley and his own cousin Cuban Bennett, who in very early jam sessions showed him what could be done with harmony; for saxophone, the young Benny adored Frank Trumbauer, an elegant, technically flawless and tasteful player. After tentative beginnings (at John O'Connor's club he was dismissed from the stand to pass out handbills), Carter developed fast as both musician and arranger and by 1928 was working with and arranging for bands like Fletcher Henderson's and Duke Ellington's. "I started off by writing saxophone choruses along the chords", he said later; the device was to remain a favourite all his life.

By 1928 he also had his own band, working at New York's Arcadia Ballroom, and re-formed it regularly over the next eight years for specific projects. His groups became a guarantee of musical excellence. "If you made Benny Carter's band in those days the stamp was on you", says Danny Barker. "Then you could go with Chick Webb or Fletcher or any of the other bands. It was like major and minor league baseball." Quiet-mannered, easygoing, soft-spoken and affable, but confidently aware of his own abilities, Carter moved in and out of great bands, including Charlie Johnson's, Chick Webb's and Fletcher Henderson's, until 1935, when he sailed for Paris to join Willie Lewis's orchestra at Chez Florence. A year later he took up the job of staff arranger for Henry Hall's BBC Dance Orchestra to which, from March 1936, he contributed as many as six new arrangements per week: recordings of the period, such as the revolutionary "Waltzing The Blues", are still much reissued. Then came two years in Holland, Belgium, Scandinavia and France before a return to the USA in 1938 (with violinist Eddie South, on board the *Ile de France*), after which he formed a big band.

Carter's project (just like South's big band earlier in the decade) was an elegant musical success but not a commercial one – perhaps it was just too refined for the "killer-diller" years. "And he probably came home too late", says Dave Dexter. "There were so many swing bands being booked by 1939 that his great organization never seemed to get the right bookings nor the network radio time to make it a favourite." And it was led by a black.

In 1941 he cut down to a sextet, and by 1943 was leading a band at Billy Berg's club on the West Coast. When he was offered work writing for Twentieth Century Fox films (including *Stormy Weather* in 1943) he eagerly accepted and in 1945 moved to Hollywood permanently to write in the day and play club residencies at night. Over the next forty years he was to write scores for films such as *The Snows Of Kilimanjaro* (1952), *The Five Pennies* (1959), *Flower Drum Song* (1961), *Buck And The Preacher* (1971), and television music for series such as *Bob Hope Presents*, *M-Squad*, *Ironside*, *Banyon* and numerous "specials". But he was not lost to the jazz world, for he continued to lead his own bands, work solo, and to be involved in essential recordings – for example, *Further Definitions* (which teamed him with Coleman Hawkins to re-create Carter classics from 1937, including "Honeysuckle Rose"), and *Kansas City Suite*, which he wrote in 1961 for Count Basie to five-star reviews. In the 1970s he toured Europe and Japan, signed recording contracts with Norman Granz (for Pablo) and in 1985 was back in England to play and record. Since then Carter has continued to garner honours and awards, and to perform at his invariably immaculate level.

A superb trumpeter and a classic alto-saxophonist, Benny Carter made one of the most artistic contributions to swing saxophone. Throughout his career he presented an elegant alternative to his two contemporaries, Willie Smith and Johnny Hodges: where Smith devoured solos with a surging urgency and Hodges catwalked a sequence with sinewy grace, Carter negotiated lines with urbane panache, his improvisation a graceful exercise in perfection. Says Rex Stewart – "His gentility seems to be out of a forgotten age. He moves with the grace and poise of those accustomed to walking with kings. Perhaps that's why those who know him best call him 'King'." [DF]

⊙ **Symphony In Riffs** (1930-7; ASV Living Era). Selection of Carter's work from the 30s, with Hawkins, Higginbotham, George Chisholm, Teddy Wilson and others.

⊙ **The Complete Recordings:1930–40 – Vol. 1** (Affinity). Three-CD set representing Carter's career from dates with the Chocolate Dandies (1930) to the Ramblers (1937). Covers his European sojourn, including British recordings with Tommy McQuater and Elizabeth Welch.

⊙ **All Of Me** (1934–59; RCA Bluebird). An outstanding collection covering all facets of Carter's work from bandleading to TV composition, with some alternate takes and seldom-heard tracks.

⊙ **The Complete Benny Carter On Keynote** (1946; Mercury). Carter weathering the bebop revolution with accustomed elegance, with Arnold Ross and his own quartet.

⊙ **The Verve Small Group Sessions** (1950s; Verve). Tracks with Benny in trio, quartet and quintet settings. Teddy Wilson, Don Abney and Oscar Peterson co-feature.

⊙ **Jazz Giant** (1957–8; Contemporary/OJC). One of Benny Carter's best solo dates, in the company of Ben Webster and the great Jimmy Rowles.

⊙ **The King** (1976; Pablo/OJC). With Milt Jackson on towering form as Carter's partner, this is one of the best Pablo sessions – and that's saying a lot.

⊙ **Live And Well In Japan** (1977; Fantasy). A superbly arranged concert with an all-star band including Cat Anderson, Joe Newman, Budd Johnson and Cecil Payne. Essential mainstream jazz.

Betty Carter

Vocals.

b. Flint, Michigan, 16 May 1929; d. 26 Sept 1998.

Born Lillie Mae Jones, Betty Carter studied piano and began working as a singer in Detroit clubs in 1946, sitting in with Dizzy Gillespie's big band and Charlie Parker's quintet. As Lorraine Carter she toured with Lionel Hampton (1948–51), making her record debut and writing occasional arrangements. Work in nightclubs and theatres was followed by touring and recording with Ray Charles in 1961, and appearances in Japan (1963) and Europe (1964). She retired from performance to raise her children, then returned to performing in 1969, with ever-increasing success. She formed her own label, Bet-Car Records, and started to work exclusively with hand-picked trios, including such pianists as Norman Simmons, John Hicks, Mulgrew Miller, Benny Green, Stephen Scott, Marc Cary and Cyrus Chestnut, and a long list of equally promising bassists and drummers.

Considered until the 1970s to be too far-out for even the jazz public, Carter saw the taste-makers catch up with her. Initially inspired by Billie Holiday and especially Sarah Vaughan, she sang in a way which was more instrumentally conceived than any other vocalist using largely standard material; this was not true merely of her scatting (which prompted Hampton to rename her "Betty Bebop") but, even more so, of her fragmentation of a given tune and lyrics. Miraculously, the lyrics survived and were sometimes enhanced by the process, although this perception depended (like melodic decoration) on the original being familiar to listeners. But Carter's improvisations, combined with her husky, saxophone-like voice quality, often created marvellous effects and influenced a whole generation of younger singers including Cassandra Wilson. [BP]

Jak Kilby

Betty Carter

I Can't Help It (1958–60; Impulse). These relatively early recordings, mostly with tidy backing arranged by Melba Liston, display a typical mixture of standards and obscure material, with Carter going boldly beyond Sarah Vaughan.

Feel The Fire (1993; Verve). This London concert has Geri Allen, Dave Holland and Jack DeJohnette contributing to a masterly performance which sums up all Carter's originality and flair.

➤➤ **Bobby Bradford** *(Seeking)*.

James Carter

Soprano, alto, tenor and baritone saxophones, bass-clarinet.

b. Detroit, Michigan, 3 Jan 1969.

Carter sprang on the scene in the early 90s, confounding mainstreamers and outcats alike with a multidimensional outlook that blurred facile distinctions. An extremely prodigious saxophonist, equally at home in extended technique territory (circular breathing, slap-tonguing), playing restructuralist works by Braxton or blowing hard through changes, Carter is perhaps only hindered by a lack of discretion – he's often quote-happy (tasteless TV theme quotes included), show-offy, sometimes too handy with expressive devices. But he's also a quite astounding technician and a young artist with plenty of room to develop. Carter's been documented on record with fellow Detroiters Jaribu Shahid on bass and Tani Tabbal on drums – both members of Griot Galaxy – and Craig Taborn on piano. His two records on the Japanese DIW label – *JC On The Set*, (1993) and *Jurassic Classics* (1994) – during a short-lived spell when the label was affiliated with Columbia in the USA, gained him widespread exposure, and he subsequently signed to Atlantic and produced *Real Quiet Storm* (1994) and *Conversin' With The Elders* (1996) and *In Carterian Fashion* (1998) while 2000 saw him release simultaneously a funk album *Layin' In the Cut* and a tribute to Django Reinhardt, *Chasin' The Gypsy*, the latter of which was generally better received. Bowing out from the duties of recorded leader, at least for the time being, Carter has been heard latterly on albums by Hamiet Bluiett, Cyrus Chestnut and 85-year-old Flip Phillips, and in the live line-ups of Bluiett and organist Lonnie Smith. The jazz world eagerly awaits the next development from this modern virtuoso. [JC]

Conversin' With The Elders (1996; Warner) In which Carter meets the sort of players who have inspired him, like Lester Bowie, Harry "Sweets" Edison, Buddy Tate and Hamiet Bluiett, a good idea in which the results – covering bases from Pres to Braxton – are ultra-Carterian. The old guys are good too.

John Carter

Clarinet, alto saxophone.

b. Fort Worth, Texas, 24 Sept 1929; d. 31 March 1991.

John Carter played with Ornette Coleman and Charles Moffett in Fort Worth in the late 1940s, and taught Julius Hemphill. Holding a BA in music from Lincoln University, Missouri, and an MA in music education from the University of Colorado, he also studied at North Texas State and California State universities. Based on the West Coast since 1961, he formed a quartet with Bobby Bradford in 1965, then led his own groups from 1973. A member of James Newton's woodwind quintet from 1980, he formed the group Clarinet Summit, including Alvin Batiste, Jimmy Hamilton and David Murray, in 1981. After teaching music in the public school system, he also founded the Wind College in Los Angeles, and during the 1980s he wrote five suites collectively titled *Roots And Folklore: Episodes In The Development Of American Folk Music*. Red Callender, who once described working alongside Carter and Newton as his most enjoyable experience since playing with Art Tatum, has said of Carter, "I had never heard anybody with such control on the clarinet. ... His complete mastery of the instrument is astounding." [BP]

Clarinet Summit

Southern Bells (1987; Black Saint). The best-realized of the few recordings by this quartet covers the ground from standards to freer material, and shows Carter playing excellently while keeping a loose hand on the reins.

John Carter

Shadows On A Wall (1989; Gramavision). The final part of *Roots And Folklore* deals with twentieth-century urban black music, transmuted through Carter's writing and the playing of Bobby Bradford, Andrew Cyrille, Marty Ehrlich and others. The earlier albums of the series (*Dauhwe, Castles Of Ghana, Dance Of The Love Ghosts* and *Fields*) are also recommended.

Regina Carter

Violin.

b. Detroit, Michigan, 6 Aug 1966.

Having begun learning violin in grade school by the Suzuki method, Regina Carter swiftly established herself on Detroit's musical scene by playing not only with the city's Civic Symphony Orchestra and the all-female group Straight Ahead, but also with the pop/funk band Brainstorm and jazz musicians including trumpeter Marcus Belgrave and organist Lymon Woodard. After graduating from the New England Conservatory and Oakland University, she moved to New York in the early 1990s, playing with Oliver Lake, bassist Mark Helias (*Loopin' The Cool*, 1995; Enja) and Tom Harrell (*The Art of Rhythm*, 1997; RCA Victor). In 1992, she replaced Charles Burnham (himself a replacement for founder member Billy Bang) in the String Trio Of New York and made three albums for the group, two in the first year, and *With Anthony Davis* (Music & Arts) in 1997. Two years previously, Carter made her eponymous debut album as a leader for Atlantic and in 1997 released a second album, dedicated to her mother and entitled *Something For Grace*. The same year, she was placed first in the violin category of the *Down Beat* critics' poll. She has performed with Wynton Marsalis in his Pulitzer-winning *Blood On The Fields*, with Cassandra Wilson in her *Travelin' Miles* performances, and with trombonist/shell player Steve Turré, alongside cellist Akua Dixon, in the former's sextet, best captured on *Lotus Flower* (1998; Verve). In the same year, she signed to Verve herself, and produced *Rhythms Of The Heart* (see below). Her sophomore album of 2000, *Motor City Moments*, paid homage to her home town of Detroit, via her highly personal interpretations of material by the city's favourite musical sons and daughter's.[CP]

⊙ **Rhythms Of The Heart** (1998; Verve). In various-sized groups formed round a core of guitarist Rodney Jones, bassist Peter Washington and drummer Lewis Nash, Carter explores a wide range of styles, from standards to Afro-Cuban and West African music, from Tadd Dameron to the Strong/Whitfield classic "Papa Was A Rolling Stone", sung by Cassandra Wilson.

Jak Kilby

Regina Carter

Ron Carter

Bass, cello, bass guitar, composer; also violin, clarinet, trombone, tuba.

b. Ferndale, Michigan, 4 May 1937.

Carter began on cello at the age of ten, and was soon playing chamber concerts; he changed to double bass in high school. His first professional jazz engagement was with Chico Hamilton in 1959; he then freelanced until 1962 with Eric Dolphy (with whom he recorded several times on cello), Cannonball Adderley, Jaki Byard, Randy Weston, Bobby Timmons and Mal Waldron among others. Musicians quickly recognized Carter's outstanding qualities – his perfectly poised sense of time, brilliant technique, and a sound so resonant that in ballads it seemed as if the notes were being artificially sustained – but it was not until he joined Miles Davis in 1963 that he came to prominence in the USA and internationally.

He stayed with Davis's quintet until 1968 and, with Tony Williams on drums and Herbie Hancock on piano, made perhaps the greatest jazz time-playing rhythm-section ever. By the mid-1960s each of the three men was *the* dominant influence on his instrument, and as a unit they had transformed rhythm-section playing – they swung as never before, and they took outrageous liberties with the pulse without ever losing the beat, playing with a freedom bordering on, but never disintegrating into, total abstraction. It was a way of playing which required immense virtuosity and it spawned disciples and would-be imitators through successive decades.

Carter gained a great deal by association with Davis, but he also found time to freelance, and in 1965 played in Europe with Friedrich Gulda. He continued to be active in education and was on the faculty of several summer clinics.

In the early 1970s Carter worked with the New York Bass Choir, Lena Horne (for her New York appearances), Michel Legrand, and the New York Jazz Quartet, and he freelanced with Stanley Turrentine, Hubert Laws, George Benson and others. He recorded for CTI Records and toured with some of their artists in Europe and Japan. Throughout the jazz-rock boom, the acoustic bass always remained his first love and first choice, but he did double occasionally on electric bass, practising it only one hour a week "just to stay in tune".

In 1976 he formed his first quartet with Kenny Barron (piano), Buster Williams (bass) and Ben Riley (drums). Carter was the main soloist and melodist, playing piccolo bass, which he tuned higher than a standard acoustic bass and which therefore projects more clearly over a rhythm-section. In 1977, he was reunited with Herbie Hancock and Tony Williams in the all-star group VSOP, which also included Wayne Shorter and Freddie Hubbard. This toured worldwide and recorded a studio and a live album. In 1978 he also toured with an all-star quartet led by Sonny Rollins, which included McCoy Tyner and Al Foster. Since the later 1970s he has usually done an all-star tour every summer.

In 1981 he was again reunited with Hancock and Williams, when the Hancock quartet, featuring Wynton Marsalis on trumpet, toured the USA, Europe and Japan, where they recorded a double album. Carter also played on Marsalis's 1984 album *Hot House Flowers* and assisted Robert Freedman with the arrangements for a large string ensemble plus French horn, tuba and woodwind. Carter has been perennially in demand as a session bassist and has played on well over five hundred albums. He has remained active in education, and the 1990s saw him tackling quasi-classical projects (he has an abiding preoccupation with Bach). He has since recorded Brazilian-tinged repertoire with Bill Frisell, and played with artists such as Joey Baron, Kenny Barron and Herb Ellis on various studio albums for his long-term patrons Blue Note. [IC]

⊙ **Where?** (1961; New Jazz/OJC). Carter's unruffled calm and Eric Dolphy's adventurous huffing make this a remarkable album. The rest of the group is pianist Mal Waldron and drummer Charlie Persip, and when Carter plays cello on a couple of tracks, George Duvivier takes over on bass. The rhythm-section is excellent and the music grips and delights.

⊙ **Peg Leg** (1977; Milestone/OJC). Carter augments his first quartet with three reeds and Jay Berliner's guitar for this lively session.

⊙ **Third Plane** (1978; Milestone/OJC). Carter leads the great rhythm-section with Tony Williams, and Herbie Hancock plays acoustic piano on a trio album of standards and originals. A superlative session.

⊙ **Études** (1982; Discovery). A pianoless quintet formation with other Miles Davis alumni - drummer Tony Williams and saxophonist Bill Evans along with flugelhornist Art Farmer: an exquisite album.

⊙ **Telephone** (1984; Concord). Carter performing standards in duo with Jim Hall.

➤➤ **Miles Davis** *(The Complete Concert; ESP; Miles Smiles).*

Deirdre Cartwright

Guitar.

b. London, 27 July 1956.

Cartwright, a self-taught guitarist, played with various London small groups and big bands from 1973–81, before she joined the Guest Stars, an all-female fusion band (somehow finding the time to be guitar presenter for two series of the now cult status 1980s BBC TV programme *Rockschool).* Their first album was highly acclaimed in the UK, and the Guest Stars toured in seventeen countries and recorded two more albums before they split up. Since then Cartwright played with leading British musicians including Ian Shaw, Carol Grimes, Peter King and Annie Whitehead, forming her own quintet, featuring fellow Guest Star Alison Rayner on bass, in 1992. They have received several commissions, and regularly tour the UK and Europe. Cartwright's influences include Jimi Hendrix, Pat Metheny, Charlie Christian, Alan Holdsworth, Mingus and Pastorius. [IC]

⊙ **Debut** (1994; BTF Records). Cartwright's guitar leads an unpretentious quartet of drums, bass and tenor/flute, across an interesting, albeit polite, range of original compositions - from palatable funk to pleasant bop via languid bossa nova.

Wayman Carver

Flute, saxophones, clarinet.

b. Portsmouth, Virginia, 25 Dec 1905; d. 6 May 1967.

Although it's true that there was a flute and piccolo specialist called "Flutes" Morton playing regularly at the Sunset Café, Chicago, in the mid-1920s, Wayman Carver was one of the first jazz flautists of note, and the first to be featured on record. He took up the instrument at fourteen, and after a stay with Elmer Snowden (1931–2) joined Benny Carter for two years, featuring on Spike Hughes's 1933 session in New York that produced "Sweet Sue, Just You". From 1934–40 Carver worked for Chick Webb and Ella Fitzgerald, contributing arrangements such as "My Heart Belongs To Daddy" and "Down Home Rag". After quitting full-time bandwork he turned to teaching, later becoming professor of music at Clark College, Georgia, where he taught until he died. George Adams and Marion Brown were two of his most prominent pupils. [DF]

Chick Webb

Chick Webb 1935–8 (Classics). This set has three tracks by Webb's Little Chicks, teaming Chauncey Haughton's clarinet with Carver's skilful flute in gorgeous swing-era miniatures.

Dick Cary

Piano, alto horn, trumpet, arranger.

b. Hartford, Connecticut, 10 July 1916; d. 6 April 1994.

Cary began his professional jazz life as a pianist with Wild Bill Davison in 1941 at Nick's Club, New York. After work with Benny Goodman, Joe Marsala, Brad Gowans and the Casa Loma Orchestra he joined the army, and it was in the army band that he acquired his second instrument, an alto horn. His main instrument, though, was still the piano and in 1947 he joined Louis Armstrong for Ernie Anderson's first All Stars concert at New York's Town Hall. He stayed for a few months before swapping the highly paid piano chair with Earl Hines and going on to study twelve-tone theory with Stefan Wolpe. Regular work with Jimmy Dorsey, Tony Parenti, Muggsy Spanier and Eddie Condon followed (Cary's alto horn is a central sound on important Condon sessions of the mid-1950s, including "The Roaring 20s" and "Bixieland"), and then a partnership which gave Cary all the artistic headroom he needed – with Bobby Hackett, resident at the Henry Hudson Hotel, New York.

After this milestone, Cary moved to Los Angeles in 1959 to pursue freelance arranging and rehearsing, as well as work with Eddie Condon. The 1970s brought a resurgence: he worked jazz festivals, toured Europe as a soloist and recorded for the Riff label (on, among other instruments, the intriguing F trumpet he found in a pawnshop). By the mid-1980s he was working with Bob Ringwald's Great Pacific Jazz Band and rehearsing his own Tuesday Night Band, which played over 1500 Cary arrangements and appeared at the LA Classic jazz festival. Cary himself appeared throughout the 1980s at the LACJF and at Sacramento, where in 1987 he was honoured as the "Emperor of Jazz". [DF]

Eddie Condon

Classic Columbia Condon Mob Sessions (1940–59; Mosaic). This 8-CD boxed set has lots of Cary, both with his "Dixieland Doodlers" and also with Jimmy McPartland (whose "Music Man" set, arranged by Cary, is a masterpiece).

Complete CBS Recordings Of Eddie Condon and his All Stars (1953–62; Mosaic). Contains the Condon sessions cited above.

Dick Cary

Dick Cary's Tuesday Night Friends: Got Swing? (2001; Arbors). Nineteen of Cary's originals and arrangements beautifully re-created by founder members of his Tuesday Night band, led by Dick Hamilton.

Casa Loma Orchestra

Masterminded by saxophonist Glen "Spike" Gray, the Casa Loma Orchestra was a cooperative which laid the groundwork for later successful swing kings such as Benny Goodman. Named for a never-to-be-opened hotel, the Casa Loma was formed by Gray from the Orange Blossoms, an orchestra contracted to Jean Goldkette, and in 1929 were booked into New York's Roseland Ballroom by the Tommy Rockwell-Cork O'Keefe office. There they were heard by Bob Stevens, an OKeh talent scout who offered them a contract: between then and 1931 (with a book written by guitarist Gene Gifford) the Casa Lomans built their sound up, adding cornermen such as clarinettist Clarence Hutchenrider, trombonist-singer Pee Wee Hunt, spectacular high-note trumpeter Sonny Dunham and singer Kenny Sargent.

The great years for Casa Loma were 1931–5: they produced strings of records for Victor, Brunswick and Decca, broadcast on the Camel Cigarette programme and played summers at the Glen Island Casino. Here the Casa Lomans' impeccably drilled music – murmuring sentimental items mixed in with swing specialities such as "White Jazz" (later covered by Lew Stone) – became the anthems of a generation, easily surviving Benny Goodman's high-powered onslaught of a year or two later. By 1935 the Casa Loma Orchestra was resident at the Rainbow Room on top of New York's Radio City; soon after, Glen Gray took over fronting the band from violinist Mel Jenssen. In 1939 the band had a hit with "Sun Valley Serenade", two months ahead of Glenn Miller.

In the 1940s key men like Dunham went out on their own, the draft took more, but Gray replaced them with fine young talent such as pianist Lou Carter, guitarist Herb Ellis and singer Eugenie Baird, as well as tried-and-trusted players like cornettists Red Nichols and Bobby Hackett. Gray retired from touring in 1950 but continued to record regularly with his orchestra until he died in 1963; later Capitol albums featuring Jonah Jones, Conrad Gozzo, Si Zentner, Nick Fatool and other stars are worth finding. [DF]

Casa Loma Stomp (1929–31; Hep); **Maniac's Ball** (1931–37; Hep). As usual from the admirable Hep label, a first-class presentation. Here are the formative Casa Loma years, featuring (on Volume 2) their most well-remembered sides including "Black Jazz", "White Jazz" and others.

Al Casey

Guitar.

b. Louisville, Kentucky, 15 Sept 1915.

Two uncles and two aunts of Al Casey sang in a gospel quartet for a nightly show on Radio WLW, Cincinnati; on the show they befriended Fats Waller, who was in search of a guitarist, and they recommended their nephew. Until graduation in 1933 he played on Waller's records in school holidays, and from 1934–42 (with a year away in 1939) Casey's playful chorded acoustic guitar solos were the most graceful feature of Fats Waller's Rhythm. His nine years with Waller included films, sellout concert tours and countless records ("Buck Jumpin'", a clever feature based on guitar harmonics, was a small hit). When Waller died in 1943 Casey laid off work, but came back with Clarence Profit's trio (which he later took over, replacing Profit with Sammy Clanton), and found himself playing alongside young bebop stars such as Fats Navarro. The same year he won the Esquire guitarists' poll and featured in a famous All-American Award Winners' concert, sponsored by Leonard Feather at the New York Metropolitan Opera House.

After the war and the fall of 52nd Street it was "back to all kinds of jobs, weekend gigs and so on" followed by four years playing R&B with King Curtis (1957–61), and more of the same with drummer Curley Hamner's sextet, including a long New York residency. In the early 1970s Casey worked part-time, then gave up completely for two years, but in 1980 – despite a leg injury sustained in a fall – he resumed a busy round of solo work in England. By 1986 he was playing annually to packed British clubs and back home with the highly successful Harlem Blues and Jazz Band. He continued solo appearances unflaggingly into the mid-1990s, recording a tribute album to his mentor and muse Fats Waller in 1994. [DF]

⊙ **Jumpin' With Al** (1983; Black and Blue). A good later-day Casey set with Arnett Cobb among others, plus quartet sides with Jay McShann; Casey plays acoustic guitar most of the time.

Geoff Castle

Piano, electric piano, synthesizers, composer.

b. London, 8 June 1949.

After eight years of classical piano, Castle spent two years studying jazz with Tubby Hayes, Don Rendell and Graham Collier. He was a member of the National Youth Jazz Orchestra from 1967–70, and then was with Graham Collier's band from 1970–74. He worked with Nucleus from 1974–82, touring western and eastern Europe and India, and also gigged with other UK musicians. In 1977 he formed his own group, Strange Fruit, and, in 1981, his *Impressions Of New York suite* was performed at the Camden Jazz Festival. He worked with Brian Smith's quartet in New Zealand in 1983–4, and in the later 1980s and the 1990s he continued to lead his own groups, freelance as a sideman and compose music for TV, setting up his own record label, Turret Records, in 1994. Steeped in the whole jazz tradition and in rock and world music too, he is a superbly versatile performer on acoustic piano and electric keyboards. [IC]

⊙ **Expanded** (1994; Turret). Castle leads an excellent ten-piece group of young British stars, including saxophonist Tim Garland. The composing is pithy and assured – Castle never overwrites – and the ten tracks run the gamut from funk, reggae, blues and rock to ballads and straight jazz, as in his piece "Moving On". The rhythm-section of Rufus Philpots and Steve Taylor is exemplary, and there are sparkling solos by the young lions and by the leader himself.

Lee Castle

Trumpet.

b. New York, 28 Feb 1915; d. 16 Nov 1990.

One of five musical brothers, Castle played in the 1940s with Artie Shaw, Red Norvo, Tommy Dorsey, Glenn Miller, Jack Teagarden, Will Bradley, Benny Goodman and others, as well as regularly leading his own bands. In 1950 he worked with Shaw again and from 1953 with the Dorsey Brothers Orchestra; after its leader died he fronted Jimmy Dorsey's Orchestra, and continued to do so until the 1980s. A talented swing musician whose principal influence was Louis Armstrong, Castle is difficult to find on disc; but the deleted LP listed below is well worth tracking down. [DF]

⊙ **Dixieland Heaven** (1954 & 57; Davis). A compilation of three dates with Dick Cary, Lou McGarity, Peanuts Hucko and others, clearly illustrating Castle's graceful style and mastery of the Dixieland idiom.

Mario Castronari

Bass, composer.

b. Berlin, 31 May 1954.

A bassist equally adept in wholly improvised and composed music, Mario Castronari began his career in Europe, playing with trombonist Albert Mangelsdorff and saxophonist Heinz Sauer before establishing himself permanently in the UK. He has contributed his big, booming sound to the Duncan Lamont Big Band and to the improvisation of his Feathers trio – alongside pianist Howard Riley and drummer Tony Marsh – but it was for his work, as both leader and composer, with the classy fusion outfit, Roadside Picnic, that he was most celebrated in the late 1980s and early 1990s. In its first manifestation as a quartet featuring saxophonist Dave O'Higgins, the band made two highly acclaimed, brightly accessible albums for BMG; in its subsequent quintet form, propelled by drummer Winston Clifford, cemented by keyboard player Graham Harvey, and with a frontline featuring saxophonist Matt Wates and guitarist Ivor Goldberg, it made *La Famille* in 1995 (see below). In the late 1990s, Castronari continued his association with Howard Riley, appearing with Riley and Art Themen on *Classics (Live)* (Slam; 1996), and with Riley and Elton Dean on *Descending Circles* (Blueprint; 1996). Castronari has also recorded with Gail Thompson's Jazz Africa, and with New Zealand pianist John Taberner (*More Jazz From The Café*, JT; 1998). In 1999, he began working with a string quartet led by cellist David Hughes and has been heard on twenty-first century albums by singer Lee Gibson and pianist Mark Latimer. [CP]

Riley, Castronari, Marsh

Feathers (1988; Spotlite). Improvised trio music of the highest order, plus witty and cogent version of standard "Yesterdays".

Roadside Picnic

Roadside Picnic (1988; Novus). Strident, anthemic music from Castronari, O'Higgins, plus keyboard player John G. Smith and drummer Mike Bradley.

For Madmen Only (1990; Novus). "Concept" album inspired by Hesse's Steppenwolf, all written by Castronari, and featuring band as above.

La Famille (1995; B&W). New line-up Roadside Picnic (see above), augmented by guests, saxophonist Mornington Lockett and trumpeter Steve Waterman, in wholly Castronari-composed session indebted to 1970s UK jazz-rock and progressive rock as well as more jazz-based influences.

Pete Cater

Drums.

b. Lichfield, Staffs, 8 February 1963.

Encouraged by his drummer father (also called Peter), Cater took up drums at a very early age, and whilst a teenager played drums with the Midland Youth Jazz Orchestra. During the 1980s he worked around the Birmingham area in various capacities before relocating to London in 1992. He formed his innovative big band in 1995 (which has been running ever since) which was voted "Best Big Band" in the British Jazz Awards in 2000, and "Critics' Choice" in the same awards in 2002. Away from his big band Cater is a versatile and gifted drummer at home in all contexts; he toured with the jazz revue shows *Let's Do It* and *Thank You Mr Gershwin* (starring Elaine Delmar) during the 1990s, and was a regular member of Spike Robinson's Quartet. He appeared with Robinson's Tribute to Stan Getz tour (which also included Johnny Williams and Bill Crow) and on his last recording "Young Lions Old Tigers". In addition he has played with many outstanding American artists including Benny Carter, Harry Edison, Tony Scott, Terry Gibbs and Buddy de Franco. From 2001 he has played with The Best of British Jazz touring package show. [DF]

Pete Cater Big Band

Upswing (2000; Vocalion). Recorded at Abbey Road studios, this collection spotlights Cater's excellent big band in a programme of standards, jazz classics and originals excitingly arranged in a contemporary, and decidedly "un-nostalgic" style.

Dick Cathcart

Trumpet, vocals.

b. Michigan City, Indiana, 6 Nov 1924; d. 8 Nov 1993.

Dick Cathcart began his career with the USAAF band, Alvino Rey and Ray McKinley, and was lead trumpeter with Bob Crosby's post-war big band, a Basie-style ensemble which owed nothing to Crosby's pre-war Dixieland approach. From 1946–9 Cathcart worked for the MGM film studios, then with Ben Pollack, Ray Noble and Frank de Vol. His versatility and creativity came to the fore in 1952 when he was invited to direct the music and ghost the trumpet for a radio series, *Pete Kelly's Blues*, which brought his perfectly smooth, graceful and glass-clear playing to wider public attention. Thereafter, apart from a spell on the road with the Modernaires (he was a fine singer), Cathcart was the offstage trumpet for a Pete Kelly decade that included a radio series, a feature film (1955) and – from 1959 – a TV series starring William Reynolds as cornettist Kelly and Connee Boswell as blues singer Savannah Brown. A string of albums for RCA, Capitol and Warner Bros, including music from these productions and later music by Pete Kelly's Big Seven (as Cathcart's band became known), featured stars such as Eddie Miller, Matty Matlock, Moe Schneider, Ray Sherman, Nick Fatool and George Van Eps. They worked together regularly in a variety of contexts, including sessions for Paul Weston and Harry James. The music that resulted was sublimely good: so was another album by Cathcart with Warren Barker's orchestra, *Bix MCMLIX*. Later in the 1960s Cathcart was regrettably absent from recording (although he kept on singing) but in 1985 was back to full form with Dick Cary's rehearsal band at the Sacramento jazz festival, and with a re-formed Pete Kelly's Big Seven, as well as blowing around the festival circuit, frequently with pianist Ray Sherman. He remained busy, playing as beautifully as ever, until cancer finally robbed the swing world of one of its most elegant brassmen. [DF]

Bix MCMLIX (1958; Warner Bros). This Beiderbecke tribute, with the luxurious strings of Warren Barker's orchestra on some tracks and premier-quality soloing from Cathcart, is very rare but essential listening.

Pete Kelly's Blues (1999; Collectors Choice). Top-grade Dixieland, this movie soundtrack from 1955 is also available in a version featuring vocals from Ella Fitzgerald and Peggy Lee.

Classic Columbia Condon Mob Sessions (1940–59; Mosaic). This multi-disc set has Cathcart with Matty Matlock's All Stars; eight titles worth the price of the whole thing alone.

Philip Catherine

Acoustic and electric guitars, guitar synthesizer.

b. London, 27 Oct 1942.

Philip Catherine's mother was English, his father Belgian and he grew up in Brussels after World War II. Inspired at first by Django Reinhardt and Rene Thomas, he turned professional at seventeen and toured with organist Lou Bennett, playing during the 1960s with various Belgian musicians including Jack Sels and Fats Sadi. Then, inspired by John McLaughlin and Larry Coryell, he began playing jazz-rock, working with Jean-Luc Ponty from 1970–72. After studying for a year at the Berklee School in Boston, he went back to Europe in 1973 and founded, with Charlie Mariano and Jasper van't Hof, the group Pork Pie, which was a great success on the European festival circuit. He also played with the Mike Gibbs band and Klaus Doldinger's Jubilee. In 1975 he made his first album as leader, with van't Hof, Mariano, John Lee (bass) and Gerry Brown (drums), and recorded another with the same personnel in 1976. That year he and Larry Coryell played a spontaneous duet at the Berlin festival, the start of a fruitful musical partnership, and they have since recorded and toured together extensively. But Catherine has always divided his energies between fusion and more trad styles - he played on Mingus' late *Three or Four Shades of Blue* and from 1980-85 he regularly accompanied Chet Baker - a hallmark of his work with the regular trio and quartet he leads. [IC]

Sleep My Love (1979; CMP). This is one of the most beautiful albums of the 1970s, made by a trio of equals: Catherine, Mariano and van't Hof. Using acoustic and electric instruments they create perpetually shifting soundscapes; the mood is romantic with a muscular edge. The rapport between the three men is so fine that all seven performances seem to have the unity and coherence of a suite.

September Sky (1988; September). Catherine leads a trio with bassist Hein Van De Geyn and drummer Aldo Romano in a very sure-footed performance, mostly of standards.

I Remember You (1990; Criss Cross). This trio recording with bassist De Geyn and the trumpeter Tom Harrell on flugelhorn is a tribute to Chet Baker, who had died two years previously, but also harks back to the drummerless jazz of Django Reinhardt and the Hot Club of France. The mood is exquisitely elegiac, yet at the same time achieves something of Django's rhythmic dynamism.

➤➤ **Larry Coryell** *(Twin House)*; **Niels-Henning Ørsted-Pedersen** *(Double Bass)*.

Big Sid Catlett

Drums.

b. Evansville, Indiana, 17 Jan 1910; d. 25 March 1951.

An easy-going, soft-hearted giant, often dressed in green chalk-striped suits and brightly flowered necktie, Sid Catlett came to New York in 1930 to join Elmer Snowden's band. "He was a musician's drummer", says Rex Stewart. "He would ask you, 'What kind of rhythm shall I play for you?' That was as soon as you came in the band and after you'd told him you'd get the same thing every night." Catlett combined music with a strong line in showmanship (verbal asides, cavernous rimshots to accompany "business", and a giant powder puff for his armpits), a combination that ensured work with the elite 1930s bands from Fletcher Henderson to Benny Goodman, in all of which he became a centre of attention. "Though he was such a powerful fellow he could play very lightly and delicately without sounding weak," says Max Kaminsky, "and his generosity matched his size. He'd give you the shirt off his back if you needed it."

The 1940s bebop revolution clearly pinpointed Catlett's versatility. Where the conflicts of jazz fashion helped to kill Dave Tough, the easy-going Catlett simply crossed 52nd Street and sat in, as a matter of course, with Charlie Parker and Dizzy Gillespie. "Sid was the first guy I was aware of who was the complete drummer", says Billy Taylor. "He could play any style. I remember when Buddy Rich was with Tommy Dorsey he used to cut all the drummers, but not Sid. It used to annoy Buddy so much. He'd play all over his head and then Sid would gently play his simple melodic lines on drums – and make his point!" Catlett played non-stop through the 1940s (he seldom bothered to go to bed), including two years (1947–9) with Louis Armstrong's All Stars, where he got on well with his leader despite a chronic inability to be onstage for curtain-up. By the late 1940s Catlett was visibly ill; he took time away from the All Stars after a heart attack and was replaced by Cozy Cole. In 1950, shortly after his ritual Christmas trip back to visit his mother, he collapsed in the wings of the Chicago Opera House at a Hot Lips Page benefit, and died aged 41. [DF]

Sid Catlett 1944–6 (Classics). Tracks with Barney Bigard, Ben Webster, Roy Eldridge and others; a valuable set illustrating Catlett's immense adaptability and incomparable senses of swing and taste.

➤➤ **Louis Armstrong** *(Louis Armstrong And The All Stars At Symphony Hall)*.

Papa Celestin

Trumpet, vocals.

b. La Fourche, Louisiana, 1 Jan 1884; d. 15 Dec 1954.

A legend of New Orleans jazz who was quickly famous for his off-centre embouchure, Papa (Oscar) Celestin was with the Algiers Brass Band by the early 1900s, with Henry Allen senior's Olympia band soon after, and led the band at Tuxedo Hall from 1910–13. Not long afterwards his Tuxedo Brass Band became one of the city's most popular bands, and in 1917 the Original Tuxedo Orchestra – which he co-led with trombonist William "Bebe" Ridgely – began playing dances for white society, featuring star names like Zutty Singleton, Kid Shots Madison, Manuel Manetta and Paul Barnes.

Celestin recorded a lot in the 1920s for OKeh and Columbia, toured widely and remained a big New Orleans attraction, but in the Depression years he retired from full-time music, then worked in shipyards during the war. With the post-war onset of revivalism he reorganized his band for a late burst of success. He recorded again for De Luxe in 1947, and by 1949 was starring on Bourbon Street at the Paddock Lounge, recording regularly and doing TV and radio work. Celestin played for President Eisenhower in 1953; a bust of him, bought by the New Orleans Jazz Foundation, stands today in the Delgado Museum, New Orleans. [DF]

Papa Celestin

New Orleans Classics (1925–8; Azure). This CD collates all the titles (including one additional take) recorded by Celestin's Original Tuxedo Orchestra for Columbia.

Bill Challis

Arranger, piano, saxophone, clarinet.

b. Wilkes Barre, Pennsylvania, 8 July 1904; d. 4 Oct 1994.

A self-taught pianist, Challis played a central role (with Tom Satterfield, Lennie Hayton and Matty Malneck) in creating a style for Jean Goldkette's orchestra (1926) and Paul Whiteman's great orchestra of 1927–30. His highly modernistic arrangements were always charming as well as ingenious, and often much more than that. Scores such as "Changes", "Oh Miss Hannah" and "San" (with its celebrated trumpet trio for the Dorseys and Bix Beiderbecke) were notable for their brilliant exploitation of tone colours, unconventional voicing and revolutionary harmonies (in jazz terms). In Dick Sudhalter's words, "Challis was easily on a par with Don Redman and other outstanding black orchestrators"; indeed, it could be argued that most of Challis's work is much more complex and daring than the contemporary output of Redman or even Duke Ellington, neither of whom had to write for orchestras as huge as Whiteman's. Even the more contrived moments in Challis's 1920s work are hard to dislike, and his settings for Beiderbecke, Trumbauer and their brilliant contemporaries are often ravishing.

After leaving Whiteman in 1930 he began working as a full-time arranger, writing for a variety of top-line bands including Fletcher Henderson, the Dorseys and Glen Gray's Casa Loma Orchestra. Challis's later work for such artists as Bobby Hackett, stripped of its obligation to break new ground, is a mature delight. By the mid-1980s he was no longer arranging because of failing sight but was still fit and active, and continued to show up at jazz events as an honoured guest for the rest of his life. [DF]

Vince Giordano

The Goldkette Project (1986; Circle Records). Challis's arrangements for Jean Goldkette re-created by longtime colleague and his Nighthawks. Cornettist Tom Pletcher is featured in the Beiderbecke role.

➤➤ **Bix Beiderbecke** *(The Complete Bix Beiderbecke In Chronological Order).*

Serge Chaloff

Baritone saxophone.

b. Boston, Massachusetts, 24 Nov 1923; d. 16 July 1957.

Son of a symphonic musician and a noted piano teacher, Chaloff played with several big bands as a teenager, then Boyd Raeburn (1944–5), Georgie Auld (1945–6) and Jimmy Dorsey (1946–7). He made small-group recordings both before and during his stay with Woody Herman (1947–9), and also with Count Basie (1950). In the early 1950s he returned to Boston and, though less active, did some teaching and made further albums under his own name; by the time of his final date, a February 1957 reunion of the Herman band's Four Brothers, he was crippled by spinal paralysis. Herman's popularity had helped Chaloff become the first baritonist to make a reputation during the bebop era. Unlike some who followed, he avoided the mistake of forcing endless streams of notes through the horn at a pace which neutralized its characteristic sound. Instead, he built on the baritone's tonal richness and, especially in his later work, attained a profundity matched by few players of any instrument during this period. [BP]

The Fable Of Mabel (1954; Black Lion). Since his late and classic quartet set, Blue Serge, is only to be found in a four-CD boxed set, these Boston recordings are recommended for their clear impression of how forthright Chaloff was, even compared to such individualistic colleagues as Charlie Mariano and Dick Twardzik.

Dennis Chambers

Drums.

b. Baltimore, Maryland, 9 May 1959.

After coming to prominence with George Clinton in a straightforward funk context, Dennis Chambers swiftly established himself – courtesy of his virtuosic, powerhouse work with John Scofield's influential 1980s fusion band – as the first-call drummer for guitarists, like Scofield, on the cusp of jazz and rock. "I like it when a drummer has so much to say that you have to fight to stay afloat", was Scofield's tribute to Chambers, and fellow guitarists such as Mike Stern, Steve Khan, Wayne Krantz and Mitch Watkins all used Chambers's vigorously emphatic yet surprisingly subtle drumming on late 1980s and 1990s recordings. Saxophonists Bob Berg, Gary Thomas, Gato Barbieri and Bill Evans also employed him, but it was his appearances and recordings as part of John McLaughlin's power trio, Free Spirits, with organist/trumpeter Joey DeFrancesco, captured on *Tokyo Live* (1994; Verve), that brought him as much jazz-world attention as had his work with Scofield. Chambers also appears on McLaughlin's 1997 Verve album *The Heart Of Things*, alongside Jimmy Garrison's son Matthew on bass, Gary Thomas and keyboard player Jim Beard, who also arranged and served as MD for Chambers's debut recording as a leader, *Getting Even* and his similarly muscular 2002 follow-up *Outbreak* on the German fusion label ESC. [CP]

⊙ **Getting Even** (1991; 101 South). Involving three of the Chambers associates listed above (Scofield, Berg, Beard), plus Scofield rhythm-section mate Gary Grainger on bass, this is not a ground-breaking album, but one that packs a solid punch and showcases Chambers's brisk, supple drumming to perfection.

Henderson Chambers

Trombone.

b. Alexandria, Louisiana, 1 May 1908; d. 19 Oct 1967.

Chambers began his career in the 1930s in territory bands such as Speed Webb's and Zack Whyte's, and in Al Sears's group in Kentucky (1935–6). In 1941 he joined Louis Armstrong's big band for two years, and from then on worked in a starry selection of orchestras and small bands including those of Don Redman (1943), Ed Hall (1944–8), Lucky Millinder, Cab Calloway, Duke Ellington (1957), Mercer Ellington (1959), Ray Charles (1961–3) and Count Basie (1964–6). Perhaps because his soloing was never as highly individual as, say, Dickie Wells's or Vic Dickenson's, Chambers never quite achieved their high reputation; he is nevertheless a neglected name. [DF]

➤➤ **Buck Clayton** *(Complete CBS Jam Sessions); Jimmy Rushing (His Complete Vanguard Recordings).*

Joe Chambers

Drums, piano.

b. Stoneacre, Virginia, 25 June 1942.

Chambers studied in Philadelphia and Washington, DC, where he did regular gigging from 1960–63, before moving to New York to play with the likes of Eric Dolphy, Freddie Hubbard, Lou Donaldson, Jimmy Giuffre and Andrew Hill. Work with Bobby Hutcherson from 1965–70 included a European tour and eight albums; he also recorded with many others such as Archie Shepp, Wayne Shorter and Joe Henderson. A member of Max Roach's percussion group M'Boom, to which he contributes compositions, he has appeared at Carnegie Hall (playing his own suite, *The Almoravid*, 1974) and at the Moers festival (1982). He has made one album playing keyboards and percussion, and one of solo piano, while continuing to work and record with younger musicians including David Murray, Gary Thomas and Rickey Woodard. Chambers's qualities as a sensitive but dynamic drummer were compared by Archie Shepp to the work of Roy Haynes, which was high praise indeed. [BP]

⊙ **Mirrors** (1998; Blue Note). With his few earlier albums hard to find, this recent programme may already have joined them, but is worth seeking out. A satisfying feature for Chambers the composer, leading a quintet with Eddie Henderson, Vincent Herring, Mulgrew Miller and bassist Ira Coleman.

➤➤ **Bobby Hutcherson** *(Dialogue);* **Wayne Shorter** *(Adam's Apple).*

Paul Chambers

Bass.

b. Pittsburgh, Pennsylvania, 22 April 1935; d. 4 Jan 1969.

Chambers grew up in Detroit, where he studied tuba, then between 1954–5 toured with Paul Quinichette, Bennie Green, J.J. Johnson-Kai Winding and George Wallington. In the latter year he joined the Miles Davis quintet and remained seven and a half years, a period during which he enjoyed an enormously prolific recording career, despite the problems of being a heroin user. He then worked regularly with the Wynton Kelly trio (1963–6), and continued freelance gigging in New York, with Tony Scott, Barry Harris and others, until shortly before his premature death.

"Mr P.C.", as he was called in Coltrane's tune-title, was one of the most influential rhythm-section players ever. In addition to his springy articulation and propulsive time-feeling, his oblique walking lines made interesting detours around the more obvious notes that other bassists used. At slow tempos, the fill-in phrases which Jimmie Blanton had introduced on bass were converted by Chambers into upper-register countermelodies, and even his up-tempo lines were often strong enough to be described in the same way. In featured solos (and he was one of the first bassists to be accorded these on a regular basis) he added new and exceptionally horn-like bebop phrasing to the bass repertoire. Although his bowed tone and phrasing left something to be desired, he certainly helped popularize the greater use of the bow, and his pizzicato playing set new standards for rhythm-sections all over the world. [BP]

➤➤ **John Coltrane** *(Blue Train; Giant Steps);* **Miles Davis** *(Cookin' And Relaxin'; Milestones; Kind Of Blue).*

Thomas Chapin

Saxophones, flutes.

b. 9 March 1957, Manchester, Connecticut; d. 13 Feb 1998.

Chapin studied with Jackie McLean at the University of Hartford and with pianist Kenny Barron at Rutgers University, where he graduated in the mid-80s. He was music director of the Lionel Hampton Orchestra for six years (1981–7), after which he joined drummer Chico Hamilton's quintet. In 1989, Chapin began a fruitful period leading, recording and writing for his own groups. As a stalwart member of the downtown Manhattan new jazz scene, he was the first artist signed to the Knitting Factory's record label, and he recorded a number of times for them, both with his longstanding trio, including bassist Mario Pavone and drummer Michael Sarin (hear 1995's *Menagerie Dreams*, with two cameos by John Zorn), and with that group augmented by strings (hear 1996's *Haywire*). He recorded for other labels as well, including two slightly more straightahead outings for Arabesque, who issued *I've Got Your Number* (quartet from 1993, with pianist Ronnie Matthews) and *You Don't Know Me* (quintet from 1995, featuring trumpeter Tom Harrell). Chapin was an extremely exuberant player, capable of being extremely slick and facile at one moment, pulling out commercial licks from a deep trick bag, then turning rough and outré the next, delving into a range of unexpected techniques. Though he initially concentrated on alto saxophone, Chapin's arsenal expanded later to include most of the saxophone family; he was devoted to the jazz flute, and he wrote quite beautifully for the unloved instrument. Long before his time, this important member of the New York creative music community died after a year-long struggle with leukemia. [JC]

⊙ **Insomnia** (1992; Knitting Factory Works). Chapin's flexible trio, spotlighting the leader's ranging saxophone and flute and Mario Pavone's undersung, woody bass playing, here supplemented by a five-piece brass ensemble. Rich compositions and arrangements, considered improvising all around.

Bill Charlap

Piano.

b. New York, 15 Oct 1966.

Bill Charlap's father, Moose Charlap, was a songwriter and his mother, Sandy Stewart, was a professional singer. He had his first piano lessons at the age of three, subsequently studying classical music at the New York Performing Arts High School, as well as taking private lessons with Kenny Barron and Richie Beirach. With Gerry Mulligan's quartet from 1988–90, he began working for singers such as Helen Merrill, Sheila Jordan and Barbara Lea, later joining Phil Woods' quintet in 1995. He appeared in duo with several bassists such as Michael Moore and Sean Smith and, more unusually, with fellow pianists including Derek Smith, Dick Hyman – a distant cousin – and Sir Roland Hanna. He has backed Scott Hamilton and Harry Allen and toured in the European Jazz Piano Trio with whom he has recorded. A sensitive accompanist of horn players and singers (Tony Bennett and Shirley Horn both make guest appearances on one of his albums), he is equally impressive in duo and trio formats. [BP]

⊙ **Written In The Stars** (2000; Blue Note). Hints of Ahmad Jamal, Bill Evans and Tommy Flanagan inform Charlap's trio versions of standards (with Kenny Washington and bassist Peter Washington), and his command of touch, harmony, feel and tempo make him a worthy successor.

Dennis Charles

Drums, percussion.

b. St Croix, Virgin Islands, 4 Dec 1933; d. New York, 26 Mar 1998.

When he moved to New York in 1945, Charles was already playing congas, but he didn't begin teaching himself on the drumkit until 1954. Between 1955–60 he gigged with African-Latin and African-Caribbean groups in Harlem and worked with Cecil Taylor's group, where his straightahead but admirably loose style was a useful foil. He recorded albums with Gil Evans in 1959 and Sonny Rollins in 1962; live work included the Steve Lacy quartet (1963–4), Archie Shepp and Don Cherry. From the mid-1960s he was out of music for a long period before returning in the 1980s with, among others, the Jazz Doctors (including saxophonist Frank Lowe and Billy Bang). [BP]

Wilber Morris

⊙ **Wilber Force** (DIW; 1983). This live date with another frequent colleague, bassist Morris, features a trio completed by the ubiquitous David Murray, and displays a wide variety of approaches including a compelling "West Indian Folk Song".

Ray Charles

Vocals, piano, arranger; also alto saxophone.

b. Albany, Georgia, 23 Sept 1932.

Ray Charles – born Ray Charles Robinson – was blind from childhood and self-taught on piano. Brought up in Florida, he became a freelance entertainer at fifteen. Travelling to the West Coast, he formed his McSon trio in Seattle in 1949, and made his first recordings. He also recorded using the frontline of Lowell Fulson's band (with which he toured in 1950–51), and backed Guitar Slim on record (1953). In 1954 he formed his seven-piece band, backing Ruth Brown, then played for dances, R&B package shows and festivals, as well as recording with top jazz soloists. Increasing success with white audiences led in 1961 to the creation of his big band, which toured internationally with backing vocalists and featured singers such as Betty Carter (1961) and Billy Preston (1966–8). He still

Jak Kilby

Ray Charles

maintains links with jazz in occasional recordings and festival appearances.

Most of Charles's records from around 1960 have extremely middle-of-the-road accompaniment, but his way with material from "You Are My Sunshine" to "Georgia On My Mind" demonstrates the universality of jazz singing in the tradition of Louis Armstrong and Billie Holiday. Moreover, the same kind of far-reaching fusion created by his vocal style (gospel + blues + jazz = soul) occurred equally effortlessly in his keyboard playing. Although this never made the same impact as his singing, Charles's 1950s instrumental albums provided a considerable boost to the recognition of gospel's influence on hard bop, and indeed on the swing and R&B bands that inspired the hard boppers in the first place. [BP]

Ray Charles and Milt Jackson

⊙ **Soul Brothers/Soul Meeting** (1957–8; Atlantic). Making a good case for a renewed interest in Charles's piano work (as Nat "King" Cole's has gained), this combination of two LPs has much enjoyable and stylistically well-matched playing from the two principals.

Teddy Charles

Vibes, composer.

b. Chicopee Falls, Massachusetts, 13 April 1928.

Teddy Charles (Theodore Charles Cohen) worked on vibes, piano or drums with various big bands from 1948–51, including Benny Goodman, Chubby Jackson, Artie Shaw and Buddy DeFranco. From 1951 he played in small groups with Oscar Pettiford, Roy Eldridge and Slim Gaillard, while studying composition. He led his own quartet from 1953, and was a member of the Jazz Composers' Workshop from 1953–5 with Teo Macero and Charles Mingus, appearing with this group at the Newport festival in 1955 and 1956, and writing arrangements for a Miles Davis album produced by Mingus in 1955. Having produced his own albums in 1953, he specialized in production from 1956: often featuring Charles's own writing, these sets used not just conventional line-ups such as Pepper Adams-Donald Byrd and Booker Little-Booker Ervin, but also unusual groups, such as three trumpets and rhythm, or John Coltrane and two baritones. His vibes playing made a brief return in the late 1980s, including an appearance at the Verona festival. [BP]

Teddy Charles and Shorty Rogers

⊙ **Collaboration: West** (1953; Prestige/OJC). This is the music that Charles is most associated with: a genuinely thoughtful project, aided greatly by the unhackneyed contributions of Rogers and Shelly Manne.

Dick Charlesworth

Clarinet, tenor saxophone.

b. Sheffield, Yorkshire, UK, 8 Jan 1932.

Charlesworth moved to London in 1952 and played in dance and jazz bands, including Jim Weller's in 1956, before forming his own, Dick Charlesworth's Jazzmen, in the same year. Twelve months later they won the South London Jazz Band Championship, turned professional in 1959 and then signed a recording contract with EMI. Remarketed as Dick Charlesworth's City Gents, with bowler hat and pinstripe uniform, the band played interesting, often out-of-the-way repertoire and became comfortably successful (although it never reached the trad boom heights of Barber, Bilk and Ball), featuring excellent sidemen such as trombonist Dave Keir and mellifluous trumpeter Robert Masters (later a highly successful agent). When the arrival of the Beatles laid the jazz world temporarily to waste, Charlesworth worked on P & O liners (1964–9), then ran a music bar in Spain which became a regular stopping-off point for jazzmen in transit. In 1976 he returned to the UK, and since then has played all over London's club and pub scene, amongst others with John Petters's "Legends of British Trad" package show. [DF]

Tommy Chase

Drums.

b. Manchester, UK, 22 March 1947.

Initially inspired by the Clifford Brown-Max Roach track "Clifford's Axe", Chase became a largely self-taught drummer, turning professional at seventeen to play in summer shows, cabaret and on cruise liners. Based in London from the early 1970s, he gigged regularly with guitarist Dave Cliff, Ray Warleigh, Art Themen and Harry Beckett, and formed his own sextet including these four in 1975. He worked with visiting Americans Joe Albany, Al Haig and Jon Eardley, also touring Germany and recording with the last-named. His mid-1980s quartets, featuring

Alan Barnes and many other younger musicians, gained considerable success, and he has remained a tireless campaigner for bebop and 1960s-style soul-jazz. [BP]

⊙ **Rebel Fire** (1990; Moles). More into the Blue Note organ sound than Chase's earlier sets, this nevertheless does a presentable job of showcasing the leader's driving percussion, with acceptable solos from altoist Ben Waghorn and organist Gary Baldwin.

Doc Cheatham

Trumpet.

b. Nashville, Tennessee, 13 June 1905; d. 2 June 1997.

Doc (Adolphus Anthony) Cheatham worked first in vaudeville theatres backing visiting blues singers (including Clara and Bessie Smith) and playing for burlesque shows. By 1926 he was in Chicago, playing saxophone until the influence of Louis Armstrong and Freddie Keppard took over; soon after he was recording on trumpet with Ma Rainey. After short stays with Bobby Lee and Wilbur de Paris he travelled to Europe with Sam Wooding (his friend Tommy Ladnier shared the trumpet solos), then went back to New York to work with Marion Hardy. A slim, trim, almost frail man, Cheatham played lead for the next ten years with McKinney's Cotton Pickers and with Cab Calloway (1933–9), but then had a breakdown. After recuperation he joined Teddy Wilson and then Eddie Heywood, both of whom used Cheatham's delicate style to great advantage.

JAK KILBY

Doc Cheatham

In 1945, out of sympathy with bebop, he took a job with the post office, opened a New York teaching studio, and took stock. But he was soon back, perhaps surprisingly playing jazz solos with a variety of Latin American bands, including Ricardo Rey's, Marcelino Guerra's, Machito's and Perez Prado's. By the 1950s he was once again to be heard in more traditional jazz contexts, working for Wilbur de Paris (playing second to Sidney), Sammy Price and Herbie Mann, then led his own band for five years at Broadway's International Hotel. After a spell with Benny Goodman (1966–7), Cheatham came back to work with Red Balaban at Your Father's Moustache, and in the 1970s began to build an international soloist's reputation on record and on tour. Over the ensuing twenty years, Cheatham's worldwide appearances in jazz clubs, at concerts and at festivals established him as a father figure of jazz's golden era. [DF]

⊙ **Doc Cheatham And Jim Galloway At Berne Jazz Festival** (1983; Sackville). Superior live session, also featuring trombonist Roy Williams.

⊙ **The Eighty-Seven Years Of Doc Cheatham** (1992; Columbia). A fine illustration of Cheatham's talents with his New York quartet, including pianist Chuck Folds; his trumpet playing is as secure as ever.

⊙ **Duets And Solos** (1976–9; Sackville). With Sammy Price as his partner, Cheatham's duets here – rags, stomps and blues – are in a format allowing him maximum creative flexibility.

Don Cherry

Trumpet, piano, organ, wooden flutes, doussn'gouni, melodica, vocals.

b. Oklahoma City, Oklahoma, 18 Nov 1936; d. 19 Oct 1995.

Cherry started on trumpet in junior high school. As a teenager he played the piano in an R&B band with drummer Billy Higgins, and in 1956 they began playing with Ornette Coleman. In 1959 Cherry and Coleman spent the summer at the Lenox School of Music, and in the autumn made their New York debut in a quartet with Higgins and Charlie Haden. Cherry worked with Coleman, recording a series of groundbreaking albums with him, until the end of 1961. He also played briefly with John Coltrane, Steve Lacy and Sonny Rollins. In 1963 he founded the New York Contemporary Five, which included Archie Shepp and John Tchicai and which toured and recorded in Europe before disbanding in early 1964. Cherry returned to Europe with Albert Ayler, then formed a group with Gato Barbieri which lasted until autumn 1966, recording in Europe and New York. He recorded with George Russell at a concert in Stuttgart in 1965 and worked with Giorgio Gaslini in Milan the following year. For the rest of the decade he wandered the world, playing and soaking up its music, though still finding the time to record the explosive duet album *Mu* (Actuel) with Ed Blackwell in 1969 – a meeting of two voraciously inquisitive musical minds that's a fascinating com-

JAK KILBY

Don Cherry

panion to Coltrane and Ali's *Interstellar Space*. Cherry and his wife Moki eventually settled in Sweden in the early 1970s, living in a schoolhouse, working an organic farm, making music programmes for children on radio and TV and taking music workshops on the road to schools.

From the mid-1960s Cherry had become more and more deeply involved in different ethnic musics, studying the techniques and instruments of Tibet, China, Africa and India. In Sweden he acquired a doussn'gouni, a hunter's guitar from Mali, with a calabash soundbox, six strings and a rattle, and began to play it regularly. In 1973 he and his wife (voice and percussion) and children gave a concert of "Organic Music Theater" in Central Park, New York, as part of the Newport jazz festival. They covered the stage with multicoloured banners, whilst percussion, vocals and Cherry's trumpet were utilized in an unclassifiable melange.

From the early 1970s he and his wife and their associates rarely played clubs, but divided their time between working with children (introducing them to the music of different lands), teaching and playing festivals. Cherry explained that he and Moki were "trying to work on all the senses, with incense for smells, and tapestries you can touch and see ... tapestries with the songs on them so that people can learn to sing them."

He still kept in touch with the US, and in 1975 played a two-week engagement at the Five Spot in New York with a quartet which included Billy Higgins, Hakim Jami (bass) and Frank Lowe (reeds), and Cherry also played some electric piano as well as trumpet. In 1976, he began working and recording with a group of his (and Ornette Coleman's) old associates: Dewey Redman (reeds), Charlie Haden (bass) and Ed Blackwell (drums). Their first album for ECM was entitled *Old And New Dreams*, and this became the name of the band which toured, played some festivals and recorded a live album, *Playing*, in 1980. The music of this group featured many of the old Ornette Coleman compositions, but also pieces written by Cherry, Coleman and Haden.

In the later 1970s he began a fruitful association with Collin Walcott, who shared his interest in the ethnic musics of the world, and who played sitar, tabla and percussion. In 1977 Cherry played on Walcott's album *Grazing Dreams*, one of the best-realized fusions of elements from ethnic music with the harmonies and structural sense of jazz. On this small masterpiece, Cherry's playing on trumpet, wood flute and doussn'gouni is given superb coherence and pith by clearly defined musical structures. In 1978 he and Walcott formed a trio with Brazilian percussionist Nana Vasconcelos, calling it Codona. They played concerts and eventually recorded three albums on ECM.

Cherry received a National Endowment grant in 1982 to work in Watts, where he was brought up, visiting schools and introducing black children to the music of Thelonious Monk, Charlie Parker and Ornette Coleman. He continued to tour and play international festivals during the 1980s (and guested memorably with daughter Neneh's "improv-punk" group Rip Rig and Panic) and into the 1990s. In 1993 he did a reunion tour with Ornette Coleman and an acoustic group. However, in latter years he seems to have had embouchure problems which tended to curtail his solos. He died of liver failure while on tour in Spain in 1995.

Don Cherry was a natural and an original in both his music and his life. Everything he did seemed to come directly from the heart, with the same immediate response as birdsong, and in this sense he was a man at one with himself; his art seemed to be an attempt to become at one with the world outside himself. Like all the main innovators in jazz, he was also a fairly prolific composer. From the moment he appeared on the scene with Coleman at the end of the 1950s he showed a virtually fully-formed original trumpet style, and his playing was always full of lyricism and freshly honed phrases. He always swung, and if he was sometimes rather diffuse it was a by-product of his generous, "street music" philosophy of the social and "disarming" function of music. He said, "I'm a world musician", and has called his music "Primal Music". As a trumpet stylist he had a huge influence; as part of the questing movement in jazz to know and absorb vital elements of ethnic music, he was a pioneer. [IC]

⊙ **Live At The Montmartre: Vols. 1 & 2** (1965 or '66; Magnetic). The Montmartre club in Copenhagen was an open house for avant-garde jazz groups in the mid-1960s, and these historic sessions show just how international free jazz had already become. Cherry's group comprises an Argentinian saxophonist (Gato Barbieri), a German vibraphonist (Karl Berger), a Danish bassist (Bo Stief) and an Italian drummer (Aldo Romano). Jazz and improvisation were in the crucible and these albums document one particular meltdown.

⊙ **Brown Rice** (1976; A&M). This is one of Cherry's more successful fusions of jazz and ethnic music. Charlie Haden is on three of the four tracks and his relationship with Cherry always produces some fine results. The tenor saxophonist Frank Lowe also makes a vital contribution, and Billy Higgins is on drums. There are chanting, rocky world music rhythms and a hypnotic atmosphere. Cherry is in good lip, and on "Malkauns", aided and abetted by Haden, he plays a ten-minute trumpet solo with a lovely sound and plenty of power and control.

⊙ **El Corazon** (1982; ECM). This duo album with drummer Ed Blackwell brings out a more tuneful and diatonic side of Cherry. His sound is full and forthright and he also plays Monk's "Bemsha Swing" on piano briefly. In addition there seems to be a little pre-recording of piano and then overdubbing of trumpet, but for the most part this warm and engaging album happens spontaneously in the studio.

⊙ **Multi Kulti** (1988–90; A&M). Quintessential world music by Cherry with a large cast of players – brass, reed, percussion, electronic and vocal.

➤➤ **Charlie Haden** *(Liberation Music Orchestra); Collin Walcott (Grazing Dreams).*

Laurie Chescoe

Drums, bandleader.

b. London, 18 April 1933.

Laurie Chescoe worked professionally from the late 1950s in a wide variety of classic-style jazz bands from Monty Sunshine's (1960–4) and Bruce Turner's (1965) to Bob Wallis's (1966–70) and George Webb's Dixielanders in their 1970s re-formation. By the middle of the 1970s he was a regular colleague of pianist Keith Nichols (with Nichols's Midnite Follies Orchestra and on the pianist's touring shows), was playing regularly for Alan Elsdon's band and long-standing groups such as the Black Bottom Stompers, as well as organizing his own groups, featuring Alan Elsdon (trumpet) and Dave Jones (clarinet). By the mid-1980s Chescoe was featured with Nichols's re-creation of King Oliver's Dixie Syncopators, with the Midnite Follies Orchestra on their occasional appearances, and with the Alex Welsh Memorial Band (he had worked with Welsh for the last two years of the trumpeter's career, 1981–2). Into the 1990s, his self-led Good Time Jazz group was establishing a solid reputation around the international club and festival circuit; after disbanding in 2002, Chescoe joined cornettist Phil Mason's band in 2003. A Cliff Leeman-style player who delights in the drum philosophies of such seminal figures as Baby Dodds and plays with all their attention to shades of sound and dynamics, Chescoe upholds traditions of Dixieland jazz drumming that could easily disappear. [DF]

⊙ **London Pride** (1994; Jazzology). The Chescoe band at full power, in characteristically well-chosen repertoire, with Alan Littlejohn's Butterfield-esque trumpet and Dave Jones's world-class clarinet to the fore throughout.

Cyrus Chestnut

Piano, composer.

b. Baltimore, Maryland, 17 Jan 1963.

Musically inspired by his father who played hymns on the piano, Cyrus Chestnut made his first public appearance as a musician at Baltimore's Calvary Star Baptist church at the age of seven. After attending the Peabody Preparatory Institute and the Berklee College of Music – from which he graduated in 1985 with a degree in jazz composition and arranging – he began his professional life working with singer Jon Hendricks (1986–8), Terence Blanchard and Donald Harrison (1988–90), and Wynton Marsalis (1991). Chestnut then joined Betty Carter's trio, making his recording debut as a leader with *Nut* (1992; Evidence), with bassist Christian McBride and drummer Carl Allen, and following it with a second Evidence album, *Another Direction*, with the same trio the following year. His major-label debut, *Revelations* (1993; Atlantic), with Carter's rhythm-section (bassist Christopher J. Thomas, drummer Clarence Penn), attracted considerable critical acclaim and topped US jazz charts, and its follow-up, *Dark Before The Dawn* (1994; Atlantic), upon which Steve Kirby replaced Thomas on bass, exploited Chestnut's penchant for gospel music, a musical seam mined even more thoroughly by another Atlantic album, *Blessed Quietness* (1996), a solo recording featuring hymns, carols and spirituals. A further Atlantic album the same year, *Earth Stories*, also won widespread praise. Chestnut has also appeared on albums by drummers Carl Allen, Ronnie Burrage and Jae Sinnett, bassists Christian McBride, Rodney Whitaker and George Mraz, vocalists Jeri Brown, Freddy Cole, Kathleen Battle and Kevin Mahogany, as well as on recordings by trumpeter Roy Hargrove and saxophonists Vincent Herring, Bud Shank, James Carter and Steve Wilson, but it was his 1998 album *Cyrus Chestnut* (see below) that cemented his reputation as one of the music's most versatile and virtuosic young pianists, while *Soul Food* (see below) and *You Are My Sunshine* (2003; Warner) continued to enhance it.

In addition to his regular trio appearances, Chestnut also performs solo and with symphony orchestras, playing his arrangements of spirituals, standards and classical pieces. A determinedly eclectic performer, he refuses to set stylistic limits for himself: "If I say to myself, 'Oh, I can't do that', then I'm robbing myself. I hope one day to headline at Carnegie Hall or even Madison Square Garden." [CP]

⊙ **Cyrus Chestnut** (1998; Atlantic). Featuring singer Anita Baker and a stellar jazz cast – Joe Lovano, James Carter, Ron Carter, Billy Higgins and Lewis Wash are all involved – Chestnut swings mightily yet tastefully through a mix of standards and originals ranging from trio blues to hymn-like solo meditations.

⊙ **Soul Food** (2001; Atlantic) Another top-class, all-star outing for Chestnut's expert, rich hard bop, this time featuring Marcus Printup on trumpet, Christian McBride on bass, Stephan Harris on vibes and Wycliffe Gordon on trombone.

John Chilton

Trumpet, flugelhorn, leader, arranger, composer, writer.
b. London, 16 July 1932.

Chilton came to prominence with Bruce Turner's Jump Band (1958–63); with Turner he recorded classics such as *Jumping At The NFT*, made a film (*Living Jazz*), and toured consistently. Later in the 1960s he worked with big bands led by Alex Welsh and Mike Daniels, led his own band – the Swing Kings (1966–8), which toured with Americans such as Charlie Shavers – and opened his own jazz book shop. In 1971, with Max Jones, he produced his first big book, *Louis*, a detailed biography/critique of Louis Armstrong; a year later came his *Who's Who of Jazz: Storyville to Swing Street*, an encyclopedia of jazzmen born before 1920 which quickly became a standard source. Then, in quick succession, came a wealth of studies including *Billie's Blues* (1975), *McKinney's Music* (1978), *Teach Yourself Jazz* (1979), *A Jazz Nursery: The Story Of The Jenkins Orphanage Bands* (1980), *Stomp Off Let's Go!: The Story Of Bob Crosby's Bobcats* (1983), *Sidney Bechet: The Wizard Of Jazz* (1987), *The Song Of The Hawk: The Life And Recordings Of Coleman Hawkins* (1990) and *Let The Good Times Roll: The Story Of Louis Jordan And His Music* (1992), *Who's Who of British Jazz* (1997) and *Ride Red, Ride* (2000). A full-time author would be proud of such an output, but all through this prolific period Chilton also worked as songwriter, partner and musical director for George Melly, a collaboration which began informally at a London pub, New Merlins Cave, and in 1974 became a very successful act after a best-selling LP, *Nuts!*. Chilton continued to tour nationally and internationally with Melly until December 2002, when he retired to concentrate on writing and musical freelancing. Chilton's trumpet playing – a crackling-to-fractured mix of Cootie Williams, Rex Stewart and Armstrong – has been constantly featured on TV, radio, records, and at all the major jazz venues and festivals in America, Australia and the Far East. He remains a gifted polymath: a jazz historian to set alongside Leonard Feather and Stanley Dance, as well as a highly original and creative musician. [DF]

➤➤ **George Melly** *(Puttin' On The Ritz).*

James Chirillo

Guitar, banjo.
b. Waltham, Massachusetts, 2 May 1953.

Chirillo majored in music composition at North Texas State University, then worked with singer Marilyn Maye (1977–9), the United States Military Academy Band West Point (1979–82), and moved to New York in 1982 where he studied and played with guitarist Tiny Grimes, and sat in with artists including Eddie Barefield, Joe Newman and Earle Warren. Thereafter, Chirillo worked with the Benny Goodman Orchestra (1985–6), Buck Clayton Orchestra (1987–91), Ed Polcer (1987 onwards), Ruby Braff (1988), Dick Sudhalter (1988 onwards), Claude Williams (1989 onwards), Jack Wilson, Loren Schoenberg, Kenny Davern, Peanuts Hucko, and was a charter member of the Smithsonian Jazz Masterworks Orchestra co-directed by Gunther Schuller and David Baker (1991 onwards). Having studied composition and arranging with John Carisi, he premiered Carisi's "Counterpoint 2" for electric guitar and trumpet (1991), and in 1995 completed the "Homage Concerto For Clarinet And Jazz Orchestra", composed for Ken Peplowski with Loren Schoenberg's Jazz Orchestra. A master of jazz guitar in all the classic styles, Chirillo is also a highly gifted writer and has continued his studies most recently with veteran Bill Finegan. [DF]

➤➤ **Ken Peplowski** *(A Good Reed);* **Bob Wilber** *(A Perfect Match).*

George Chisholm

Trombone.
b. Glasgow, Scotland, 29 March 1915; d. 6 Dec 1997.

George Chisholm came from Scotland to join Teddy Joyce in London in 1936, then Ambrose in 1938, and was soon leading his own groups for recording sessions. By then it was clear that, in Leonard Feather's words, Chisholm was "a superlative musician with an ageless style". It showed up to advantage on sides the young trombonist made with Fats Waller in London in 1938, and by 1941 he was leading the trombone section and arranging for the Squadronaires, Britain's RAF-based dance orchestra (his duets with Eric Breeze became a central feature of the show).

After the war Chisholm freelanced, then in 1952 joined the BBC Show Band where – on the BBC's *Goon Show* – he was able to indulge his gift for comedy, often taking speaking roles (he remained a close friend and occasional partner of Spike Milligan). In 1956 he played the Hungarian Relief Fund concert alongside Louis Armstrong at London's Royal Festival Hall, and soon after began a long TV residency doing comedy routines on the hugely popular *Black And White Minstrel Show*, a decision that caused a certain amount of controversy among jazz critics. Throughout the 1960s and 70s Chisholm recorded and played clubs and concerts, and by the later decade was touring in tributes to Louis Armstrong, as well as leading his own Gentlemen Of Jazz and guesting at US jazz festivals such as Colorado. After heart surgery in 1982 he was back to full strength, touring with Keith Smith in mid-decade, and in 1985 was awarded the OBE. He continued to appear until the end of the decade, but slowed down after the death of his wife; by 1995 he was no longer playing.

Chisholm's majestic tone, biting style and use of what became known as "Chisholm intervals" (based on the emphasis of lower neighbour tones in his lines) were an irreplaceable feature of British jazz. He is one of the few international-standard jazz figures to emerge from Britain, yet there is a dearth of Chisholm on CD; the discs listed below are worth searching out. [DF]

⊙ **Early Days 1935–44** (Timeless). A vital collection of early Chisholm, this set has him with Danny Polo, Gerry Moore and Lew Stone as well as leading groups of his own; a fascinating oddity is "Pardon Me Pretty Baby" recorded privately with Benny Winestone and Leonard Feather on the day Chisholm arrived in London from Scotland.

⊙ **In A Mellow Tone** (1972–3; Lake). Perhaps Chisholm's greatest late recording with Kenny Baker, Tommy Whittle, Tony Coe (on alto) et.al. The music is as good as the production and two live quartet tracks are added as a bonus.

Herman Chittison

Piano.

b. Flemingsburg, Kentucky, 15 Oct 1908; d. 8 March 1967.

Early in his career Chittison worked with Zack Whyte's territory band (which also contained, at various times, stars such as Sy Oliver and Quentin Jackson) and stayed for three years until 1931. Working as accompanist to singers Ethel Waters and Adelaide Hall, as well as comedian Stepin Fetchit, he attracted great attention, and by 1934 was starring with bandleader Willie Lewis in Paris as well as touring with Louis Armstrong. (Agent N.J. Canetti said Chittison's crowd-pleasing contribution to Armstrong's show may have been the cause of the trumpeter's premature return to New York, an uncharitable thought which nevertheless gives some idea of the pianist's solo powers.) After he left Lewis in 1938, Chittison took ex-members of Lewis's band, including Bill Coleman, to Egypt for a two-year stay, returning home in 1941; for the last 25 years of his life he led his own trio around New York, helped by a weekly appearance on a popular series, *Casey – Crime Photographer*, which ran for seven years on CBS radio. He recorded regularly too, often in a "pop" format recalling Eddie Heywood: his last album to be issued officially was in 1964, three years before his death. [DF]

⊙ **PS With Love** (1964–7; IAJRC). Previously unissued piano solos which, despite only fair recording quality, do much to illustrate the full breadth of Chittison's powerful style.

Jon Christensen

Drums.

b. Oslo, 20 March 1943.

In 1960 Christensen won the Norwegian Jazz Amateur Competition, and from 1961–5 he played at clubs and festivals in Norway with local and international musicians, including Bud Powell, Dexter Gordon, Sonny Stitt, Don Ellis, Don Byas, Jan Garbarek, Karin Krog and Kenny Dorham. From 1966–8 he played in Sweden with Monica Zetterlund, the Steve Kuhn trio and George Russell's sextet and big band (appearing on Russell's *Electronic Sonata for Souls loved by Nature*). He was with the Jan Garbarek quartet from 1970–73, and has had a long and prolific recording career on ECM in addition to touring with Garbarek, Terje Rypdal, Eberhard Weber, Ralph Towner, Enrico Rava, Keith Jarrett, Miroslav Vitous and John Surman. In the later 1990s, Christensen continued to work with pianist Bobo Stenson's trio with Anders Jormin on bass, and with Polish trumpeter Tomasz Stanko's sextet, which recorded the film music of the late Polish composer Krystof Komeda. In 1997, with the Bobo Stenson trio, he recorded the album *War Orphans*, and in 1998, he recorded an ECM album with Stanko, John Surman, Dino Saluzzi and Jormin, for release in 1999. He also plays with the Lars Danielsson/Dave Liebman Quartet and is a regular collaborator of John Scofield's.

Christensen has every virtue as a drummer, including great rhythmic power and extreme sensitivity. He can handle any area, rock, jazz or free, with immense musicality, and always projects without ever obtruding. Having been a member of three of the most important and influential groups in 1970s jazz - Keith Jarrett's European quartet, Eberhard Weber's Colours and Jan Garbarek's quartet - he has played a key role on some classic albums. In particular, the studio albums with Jarrett, Garbarek and Palle Danielsson, *Belonging* and *My Song*, rank with the finest quartet records in jazz and have been a huge inspiration to musicians everywhere. [IC]

➤➤ **Keith Jarrett** *(Belonging; My Song)*; **Tomasz Stanko** *(Litania: Music of Krystof Komeda)*; **Bobo Stenson Trio** *(War Orphans)*.

Charlie Christian

Guitar.

b. Dallas, Texas, 29 July 1916; d. 2 March 1942.

The seminal influence on modern jazz guitarists until the 1960s, Christian was a professional in the Oklahoma City area by 1934, then toured with Anna Mae Winburn's band, Alphonso Trent (on bass), Lloyd Hunter and Nat Towles. By 1937 he was specializing on electric guitar, often with Lesley Sheffield's band, meanwhile jamming in Benny Hooper's basement on Walton Street with another legend, tenorist Dick Wilson. John Hammond introduced him to Benny Goodman on a recording date to little avail, but the same night Hammond and bassist Artie Bernstein smuggled Christian on stage at the Victor Hugo Hotel, Beverley Hills, for a ninety-minute version of "Rose Room"; Goodman hired Christian on the spot as the newest star in his sextet.

In 1939, Christian was brought by pianist Mel Powell to Minton's Playhouse, the shrine of bebop, and became a fixture. Every Monday, when the Goodman band took a night off from their residency at Pennsylvania Hotel in Meadowbrook, NY, the young guitarist would play at Minton's, creating music that has been regularly reissued since. Most other nights he was there after work and he frequently played all day too, just for good measure. "Later when I was in New York", says Mary Lou Williams, "I'd look Charlie up and we'd go to a basement room in the Dewey Square hotel, usually around ten in the morning, and sometimes we'd jam, just the two of us, until eleven at night. It smelled down there and the rats ran over our feet and only ten keys on the piano played – but we just didn't pay any attention."

In October 1940 Goodman's doctors found TB on one lung, but touring continued until Christian was taken ill in the Midwest and admitted first to New York's Bellevue Hospital, then to the Seaview Sanatorium on Staten Island. Visiting wellwishers brought him marijuana, drink and even women, and in early 1942 they managed to sneak Christian out to a party: he contracted pneumonia and died. "He was a sweet loving man with few defences against the world", remembers Hammond. "His only resource was music and when he was unable to play he was unable to live." Christian's funeral was in Harlem: he was buried in the cheapest coffin available.

His influence on guitarists was huge. He was the first to establish a mature vocabulary for electric guitar, which younger players such as Jim Hall and Barney Kessel had cause to be grateful for, and it was only with the emergence of a rock-based vocabulary in the 1960s that Christian's approach fell into historic perspective. Dizzy Gillespie makes a perceptive point: "Charlie was *bad!* He knew the blues and he knew how to do the swing. He had a great sense of harmony and he lifted up the guitar to a solo voice in jazz ... but he never showed me a total knowledge of the harmonic possibilities of the instrument." However, Christian's flowing lines, pawky sound and rhythmic grace (very like his friend and influence Lester Young) carried him to jazz immortality. [DF]

⊙ **Genius Of The Electric Guitar** (1939–41; CBS). This disc has essential titles with Goodman's small groups ("Wholly Cats", "Till Tom Special") as well as Christian's big-band feature with Benny on "Solo Flight" and the informally recorded "Blues In B" with Georgie Auld and Johnny Guarnieri.

⊙ **Live Session At Minton's Playhouse** (1941; Jazz Anthology). Historic live titles which bring you the birth of bop on record, with Christian's central contribution to the process.

Keith Christie

Trombone.

b. Blackpool, UK, 6 Jan 1931; d. 16 Dec 1980.

Christie began his high-pressure career as a revivalist with Humphrey Lyttelton's band, with whom he played fondly-remembered features such as "The Dormouse", written by Lyttelton. He then moved on to form the Christie Brothers' Stompers (with brother Ian on clarinet), but was soon rapidly broadening his approach. In 1953 he joined John Dankworth's highly modern big band, then went over to Tommy Whittle and began freelancing around London's club scene, and by 1957 was partnering Don Lusher in Ted Heath's trombone section. After leaving Heath, Christie worked in studios and played regularly with Tubby Hayes's big band. From 1970–2 he toured Europe with Benny Goodman, also continuing a wide-based variety of activities which veered from work with Kenny Wheeler's big band to re-creating Jelly Roll Morton's Red Hot Peppers (under pianist Max Harris) for American choreographer Twyla

Tharp. By the late 1970s he was working in the London production of the jazz-based show *Bubbling Brown Sugar*: there he suffered an accident one night when he fell off the raised theatre set. After recovering he returned to work, including concerts with the *Best Of British Jazz* package, but alcoholism had claimed him and he died in 1980. His brother Ian (b. 24 June 1927) became a Fleet Street television critic after early years with Humphrey Lyttelton, Mick Mulligan and the Christie Brothers' Stompers, among others, and in the 1980s returned to regular performing with Graham Tayar's Crouch End All Stars, as well as recording with Wally Fawkes. [DF]

Christie Brothers

A Tribute To Humph (1949–50; Dormouse). The very valuable Dormouse catalogue of British jazz has yet to reappear on CD; in the meantime, this LP gives a fine example of the Christies' inspired traditional style.

Christie Brothers' Stompers (1951–3; Cadillac). This splendid collection has the Christies co-leading a project that's well remembered in British jazz circles; all their commercial recordings are here, plus unissued acetates.

Tubby Hayes

100% Proof! (1966; Fontana). The perfect example of Christie's towering solo powers, with one of the greatest modern British big bands ever assembled on record.

June Christy

Vocals.

b. Springfield, Illinois, 20 Nov 1925; d. 21 June 1990.

The cool-voiced June Christy was one of the leaders of a hip vocal school founded by Anita O'Day, whom she replaced with Stan Kenton's band in 1945. Christy had hit records with Kenton (including "Tampico", "Shoo Fly Pie", "Across The Alley From The Alamo" and "Ain't No Misery In me"), then recorded her first solo single in 1947, one year before Kenton's band broke up; by that time she had married tenor soloist Bob Cooper. From the late 1940s Christy was a regular poll-winner and remained one of the stars of the Capitol label, producing best-selling albums such as *Something Cool*, with its art-song of a title track, composed by her friend Billy Barnes and superbly arranged by colleague Pete Rugolo. Some of Christy's output during the 1950s was more commercial (including "My Heart Belongs To You", which charted), but that work is less remembered now than her nine magnificent LP collaborations with Rugolo, including *Something Cool* and *The Misty Miss Christy*. [DF]

Something Cool (1953–5; Capitol). "Something Cool" is a great vocal performance by any standards, and a most under-rated composition. Rugolo's arranging is state-of-the-art and still surprises.

The Misty Miss Christy (1955–6; Capitol). Accompanied by the cream of West Coast sessionmen (including Maynard Ferguson, Pete Candoli, Milt Bernhardt, George Roberts, Bud Shank and Shelly Manne), Christy presents a selection of classic standards brilliantly arranged by Rugolo.

Mino Cinélu

Percussion; also keyboards, guitar, flute etc.

b. St. Cloud, France, 10 Mar 1957.

Born into a musical family from Martinique, Dominique Cinélu grew up in Paris and played as a teenager, both with his brothers in the group Chute Libre and with leading French jazzmen. Moving to New York in 1979, he recorded with Dizzy Gillespie and Gato Barbieri, and then toured with Miles Davis from mid-1981 to late 1983 and again in 1987. He also worked with Weather Report, Gil Evans (both 1984), Sadao Watanabe, Sting, Headhunters Two, Pat Metheny and Nguyên Lê, as well as leading his own groups. Possessing an equal talent for working in acoustic contexts, he has collaborated with Michel Portal and pianists Kenny Barron (mid-1990s) and Geri Allen (2001). As a "world musician" with an affinity for playing alongside jazz and fusion musicians, Cinélu is emblematic of the wide-ranging interests of his generation. [BP]

World Trio (1995; VeraBra). Joined by guitarist Kevin Eubanks and bassist Dave Holland, Cinélu shows his great powers of invention in open-ended situations of superb musicality.

>> **Kenny Barron** *(Swamp Sally); Miles Davis (We Want Miles).*

Johnny Claes

Trumpet.

b. Belgium 1916; d. 3 Feb 1956.

A protégé of Nat Gonella, Claes was leading bands in Britain by the mid-1930s and in 1937 recorded with Valaida Snow. By 1941 he was resident at the Nuthouse in Regent Street, leading a band featuring singer Benny Lee; he went on to build a band library written for trumpet and saxophone section, to record ten titles for Columbia (including two with Gonella) and to play regularly at nightclubs in London's West End, as well as leading a band at Boston's Gliderdrome (including Britain's bop guru, pianist/trumpeter Denis Rose). A personable and good-looking bandleader, Claes was a capable if not outstanding player; his band can be heard and seen in the 1946 George Formby film *George In Civvy Street* (trumpeter Terry Brown and saxophonist Ronnie Scott are in the ranks). In the late 1940s Claes abandoned jazz for a career in motor racing. [DF]

Kenny Clare

Drums.

b. London, 8 June 1929; d. 11 Jan 1985.

Clare was a consummate big-band drummer. He worked with the Oscar Rabin band from 1949–54, with Jack Parnell in 1954–5, the Johnny Dankworth orchestra from 1955–60, the Ted Heath band in 1962–6, the Clarke-Boland band in 1967–72 and with a big band led by the German trombonist/composer Peter Herbolzheimer in 1973–4. Clare also worked with the Bobby Lamb-Ray Premru orchestra. He played on a superb LP with Ella Fitzgerald, *Can't Buy Me Love*, and he became the permanent UK drummer for Henry Mancini, involved in all the *Pink Panther* film scores, though he later spent three years in the US working with Basie, Herman and Ellington while backing singer Tom Jones. Clare also played on film soundtracks scored by Michel Legrand and spent the 1980s working with John Dankworth and Cleo Laine. [IC]

➤➤ **Kenny Clarke** *(Two Originals).*

Clark Sisters

The Clark Sisters were one of the most esteemed, influential and musical of the many "sisters" acts which sprang up from the 1920s. The four sisters – Anne, Jean, Mary and Lillian – began as the Sentimentalists with Tommy Dorsey's orchestra and, coached by arranger Sy Oliver, rapidly made their mark. Featured on Dorsey's classics "I'm Getting Sentimental Over You" and "On The Sunny Side Of The Street" (as well as "Chicago", also featuring Oliver), their close harmonies were to influence later groups like the Four Freshmen. They broke up their group in 1948 but re-formed in 1958 for a classic LP *Sing Sing Sing* – vocal re-creations of swing-era big-band arrangements with Bud Dant's orchestra. A further LP, *Swing With The Clark Sisters*, is of comparable quality, but neither set has yet been re-issued on CD. [DF]

Garnet Clark

Piano.

b. Washington, DC, c. 1914; d. 1938.

A child prodigy, Clark was playing piano and arranging for Tommy Myles's band in Washington, DC, at the age of sixteen. He went to New York in 1933, worked at Pod's and Jerry's Club that year and caused a sensation, but in 1935 he emigrated to Europe. With Benny Carter in Paris he briefly joined Willie Lewis's Entertainers, and with Bill Coleman and Django Reinhardt made his only record session – apart, says Dan Morgenstern, from an "obscure Alex Hill big-band session" the previous year. He was the first to put on disc the chord sequence for "I Got Rhythm" invented by Art Tatum, later used by Don Byas, Thelonious Monk and, occasionally, Charlie Parker. After solo work and time as accompanist for Adelaide Hall in Switzerland, Clark was committed to an asylum and died at 24. [DF]

⦿ **Piano & Swing** (1935–8; Pathe). This collection also features Teddy Weatherford and Garland Wilson, and has the only two known solos by Clark. One is the above-mentioned "I Got Rhythm" from his Reinhardt session, and "Improvisation" was actually recorded in the mental hospital.

Sonny Clark

Piano.

b. Herminie, Pennsylvania, 21 July 1931; d. 13 Jan 1963.

Clark made his record debut on the West Coast with Wardell Gray in 1953, and was the regular pianist with Buddy DeFranco, replacing Kenny Drew. Settling in New York in 1957, he participated in numerous album sessions, notably for Blue Note, and was much admired by other pianists – Bill Evans's "NYC's No Lark" was titled in memory of Clark, whose premature death was hastened by alcohol abuse, an attempt to counteract his dependence on heroin. Both his right-hand lines and driving accompaniments contain hints of Horace Silver and Hampton Hawes, although arrived at independently, and his rhythmic ebullience and melodic sense are more than a match for either of them. [BP]

⦿ **Leapin' And Lopin'** (1961; Blue Note). Clark's piano playing is here set in a typical Blue Note quintet album with Charlie Rouse and trumpeter Tommy Turrentine; the ballad "Deep In A Dream" has a beautiful solo by production assistant Ike Quebec.

Kenny Clarke

Drums, composer; also vibes.

b. Pittsburgh, Pennsylvania, 9 Jan 1914; d. 26 Jan 1985.

After gigging locally, Clarke worked briefly with Roy Eldridge in 1935 and then with the Jeter-Pillars band. In New York he joined Edgar Hayes (1937–8), with whom he toured Europe, and then, after making records under his own name in Stockholm, he played with the Claude Hopkins (1939) and Teddy Hill (1940–41) bands. In 1941 he led the house group at Minton's, using Thelonious Monk and encouraging advanced sitters-in such as Dizzy Gillespie, Charlie Christian and Charlie Parker. He was briefly with Louis Armstrong and the Ella Fitzgerald band (both in 1941), then with Benny Carter's sextet in 1941–2, working in both the latter alongside Gillespie. In 1943 he played with Henry "Red" Allen's group in Chicago, and with Coleman Hawkins and under his own name in New York. Then, after army service in Europe, he was with Gillespie's big band, touring Europe in 1948, and remained in Paris several months before working with Tadd Dameron there and in New York. He spent more time in France, where he married, then played in the USA from 1951 with Billy Eckstine, and in Milt Jackson's quartet which included John Lewis and which also backed Parker in 1951–2. Recordings by Jackson led to the formation of the Modern Jazz Quartet, which Clarke left in 1955 for freelance gigging and recording: in the jazz record boom of the mid-1950s he cut well over one hundred albums in the space of a year.

In 1956 he settled in France, doing a lot of studio work and live appearances with visiting Americans including Miles Davis (1957) and the Jazz From Carnegie Hall group (1958). He played regularly with Bud Powell and Oscar Pettiford, known unofficially as the Three Bosses (1959–60), then worked with his own organ/guitar/drums trio, an instrumentation he maintained for several years. Clarke also ran a famous but intermittent big band co-led by Francy Boland from 1961–72, whose surprisingly stable all-star line-up included, over the years, Johnny Griffin, Tony Coe, Ronnie Scott, Benny Bailey, Art Farmer, Ake Persson, Jimmy Woode and second drummer Kenny Clare. Clarke continued to freelance, recording for instance with Dexter Gordon (1963, 1973) and Gillespie (1974), and operated his own teaching studio in Paris. He made brief return visits to the USA in 1972, for the dedication of commemorative plaques on 52nd Street in 1979 and for the 1984 Kool festival. He was living in semi-retirement near Paris at the time of his death.

Although originally prized as the founder of bebop drumming in the early 1940s, Kenny rapidly became the embodiment of straightahead playing. Even his sometimes insistent snare-drum commentary was essentially supportive, just as his bass drum helped to underline rather than dictate; his nickname "Klook" was abbreviated from "Klookmop", which describes a rimshot on the snare followed by the bass drum, sounds which he used as punctuation of others' phrases rather than a statement in themselves. The fact that Clarke was initially inspired by Jo Jones (even down to the very idea of punctuating improvisations) doubtless explains why he was such a superb big-band drummer, never flashy or even noisy but always appropriate. But perhaps the greatest joy of his playing, most clearly audible on small-group recordings, was the pulse of his cymbal work, so marvellously alive yet effortless that fellow musicians called it his "heartbeat".

Clarke wrote a number of tunes that were recorded by others, but is especially noted as co-composer of two key early bop items, "Epistrophy" (aka "Fly Right") with Thelonious Monk, and "Salt Peanuts" with Dizzy Gillespie. Both pieces are built around the cross-rhythm of 3 against 4, which was the source of so much of the freedom of bebop. [BP]

⊙ **Special Kenny Clarke** (1938–59; JazzTime). Recorded for various EMI labels in Europe, this set includes Clarke's first session in Stockholm and various post-war Paris dates, most notably the 1957 quartet featuring Lucky Thompson, Martial Solal and Pierre Michelot.

⊙ **Meets The Detroit Jazzmen** (1956; Savoy). This typically straightahead "blowing session" from the period of Clarke's maximum studio involvement finds him backing youngsters Pepper Adams, Kenny Burrell and Tommy Flanagan, and making them sound even better than they are.

Kenny Clarke-Francy Boland Big Band

⊙ **Two Originals** (1967–8; MPS). The series title for two-LPs-on-one-CD (namely *Sax No End* and *All Blues*) might as well refer to the co-leaders. Francy Boland's original material brings out the best in soloists as different as Griffin and Scott, Bailey and Persson and, on the earlier set, guest Eddie "Lockjaw" Davis.

➤➤ **Miles Davis** *(Walkin'; Bags' Groove);* **Dizzy Gillespie** *(Groovin' High);* **Milt Jackson** *(Milt Jackson Quartet; Opus de Jazz).*

Stanley Clarke

Bass, bass guitar, piccolo bass guitar, keyboards.
b. Philadelphia, 30 June 1951.

Clarke studied bass while at school and at a local music academy and spent the late 1960s playing with rock groups before, in 1970, he landed six months with Horace Silver, then a year with Joe Henderson, followed by periods with Pharoah Sanders and Stan Getz. Clarke came to real international prominence with Chick Corea's Return To Forever, of which he was an original member. A master of both acoustic and electric basses, he was the new star in the early 1970s, winning polls in both categories. He soon had his own contract with CBS, and recorded a series of highly polished albums using some of the leading jazz, rock and Latin instrumentalists of the time, teaming up with George Duke on some collaborative albums in the later 1970s into the

Jak Kilby

Stanley Clarke

80s. Clarke is one of the most technically brilliant bass guitarists, and a virtuoso soloist on the instrument - on piccolo bass guitar his speed approaches the fleetness of John McLaughlin - but he is also capable of spare and moody playing. He had considerable influence on bass guitarists in the earlier 1970s, many of whom copied his fast rhythmic slapping of the strings. Clarke continues to play and tour with peers such as Jean-Luc Ponty and Chick Corea, whilst his funky, cult cachet has assured him the respect of the elders of the hip-hop generation. [IC]

Stanley Clarke (1974; CBS). This first album under his own name was recorded at the height of the jazz-rock movement. It has a surprising variety of music and reveals the extraordinary instrumental versatility of Clarke. His basic group here comprises Tony Williams, Jan Hammer and Bill Connors, and as well as some really dynamic jazz-rock performances there are also more spacey, meditative pieces. On "Spanish Phases For Strings And Bass", composed and arranged by Michael Gibbs, Clarke is featured on double bass and acquits himself well. Clarke composed all the rest of the music, but his final four-part suite "Life Suite" is orchestrated for strings and brass by Gibbs.

School Days (1976; CBS). This is probably Clarke's most popular album. The personnel varies and includes Steve Gadd, Billy Cobham and on one track John McLaughlin. Clarke sings on a couple of tracks, plays an array of instruments and produces a brilliant piccolo bass guitar solo on "The Dancer".

>> **Chick Corea** *(Return To Forever).*

Jazz Photos

Paul Clarvis

Paul Clarvis

Drums, percussion.
b. London, 9 April 1963.

At the age of twelve, Clarvis began playing in his school's Dixieland band. He also played with rock groups and on percussion with the National Youth Orchestra. A scholarship to the Royal College of Music followed, but he left after only two years to gig professionally, playing jazz regularly after hours with guitarist Phil Lee and bassist Simon Woolf.

Clarvis became interested in folk music and ethnic percussion and had lessons with Dave Hassel, Jim Blackley and Dawson Miller. Then, in 1991, he formed Orquesta Mahatma with Stuart Hall. In 1992, he began a long association with pianist Nick Weldon's trio. Clarvis also has a trio jointly with saxophonist Stan Sulzman and pianist Tony Hymas, and is a member of trumpeter Henry Lowther's band Stillwaters. In 1998, with violinist Sonia Slany, he formed his own independent record label Village Life Records. Clarvis is a prodigiously gifted drummer and percussionist: he is equally at home with jazz, world or classical music (his playing with the BBC Symphony Orchestra on Harrison Birtwistle's *Panic* (1995) is savage and thrilling), big bands or small groups. His time sense is beautifully poised and his playing is always intensely musical. He is much in demand and when Markus Stenz, the conductor of the London Sinfonietta, decided it needed jazz musicians for London's historic first performance of the Miles Davis and Gil Evans orchestral music in 1996, Clarvis was his first choice on drums and percussion.

His favourites include Baby Dodds, Big Sid Catlett, Mel Lewis, Tony Oxley and Elvin Jones, and other inspirations are John Surman, Stuart Hall and Ahmad Jamal. [IC]

Orquestra Mahatma: A Young Person's Guide (1996; Babel). This features Stuart Hall on violin and guitar, Thad Kelly on double bass, and Clarvis on assorted percussion from around the world, including tabla. The results are delightful – airy and imaginative world music on the wing, including performances of Joe Sullivan's "Little Rock Getaway", and Ellington's "I Got It Bad And That Ain't Good", with several compositions by the three performers.

Clarvis/Sulzmann/Hymas

For All The Saints (1996; Village Life). With Sulzmann on sax and flute, and Hymas on piano and synths, disparate idioms from Latvia, Scotland and the Middle East sound as convincing on the trio's own compositions as on the traditional folk pieces they attempt. The music is often exquisitely haunting and occasionally riotous with synthesizer textures and percussive sounds.

Buck Clayton

Trumpet, arranger, composer.

b. Parsons, Kansas, 12 Nov 1911; d. 8 Dec 1991.

One of the greatest classic trumpeters, Buck (Wilbur Dorsey) Clayton came from a musical family and was taught the trumpet by Bob Russell (from George E. Lee's band). In early years he worked for bands led by Duke Ellighew, Lavern Floyd, Charlie Echols (a famous territory band) and promoter Earl Dancer, and then at 21 went to China for two years, leading his own band. Back in California he did the same at Frank Sebastian's Cotton Club, before joining Count Basie at the Reno Club, Kansas City, in 1936 as a replacement for Hot Lips Page. By 1937 Basie's band was successful in New York, and Clayton stayed with them until 1943, when he was called up. He spent his army years in bands led by pianist Dave Martin and Sy Oliver.

On discharge he joined Norman Granz's newly formed *Jazz At The Philharmonic* show, playing the trumpet spectaculars Granz expected and, as he once joked, "keeping Lester Young and Coleman Hawkins apart". From 1947 he was back in New York and in 1948 played at the Savoy Ballroom with Jimmy Rushing's band, which a decade later was to form the basis of a band with which he toured Europe. In the 1950s Clayton partnered Joe Bushkin in the first of the pianist's influential Embers quartets and worked at Lou Terrassi's with Tony Parenti ("he taught me Dixieland") and with two highly contrasted clarinettists, Benny Goodman and Mezz Mezzrow. He is best remembered at this period for a set of irreplaceable recordings in which he and kindred spirits from the swing era played chorus after chorus on standard tunes: the resulting *Buck Clayton Jam Sessions* (often one tune per album side) cemented the mainstream jazz boom and illustrated the value of extended performances in jazz recording.

In 1959 Clayton toured with a memorable team (including Emmett Berry, Dickie Wells and Buddy Tate) which visited England and recorded classic albums such as *Songs For Swingers*. In the 1960s he worked and recorded with Eddie Condon, toured Europe as a soloist (including Britain with old friend Humphrey Lyttelton) and played jazz festivals. The first signs of lip trouble surfaced in 1969, and in the 1970s this became a recurring condition: one operation required 39 stitches in his top lip. The problem reached its height in 1979 when, after a month in Denmark, Clayton applied himself more to teaching, arranging (including Lyttelton commissions), lecturing and directing recording sessions. During the 1980s he taught at Hunter College, toured Europe with The Countsmen (1983) and from 1987 led his own big band, featuring his compositions and arrangements. [DF]

Buck Clayton 1945–7 (Classics). A good set for Clayton completists, including titles with Freddie Green, J.C. Heard and others.

Complete CBS Jam Sessions (1953–6; Mosaic). The definitive collection of Clayton's best-remembered contributions to jazz history.

Songs For Swingers (1958; Philips). A great mid-period Clayton unit which featured co-stars Emmett Berry, Dickie Wells, Earl Warren and Buddy Tate, and which achieved great prominence via widespread touring.

Buck Clayton Meets Joe Turner (1965; Black Lion). Clayton is at a career peak in this recording with Turner and the Zagreb Jazz Quartet, featuring vibraphonist Bosko Petrovic.

A Swingin' Dream (1988; Stash). Recorded live in New Jersey, this album by Buck Clayton and his Swing Band illustrates Clayton's skills as a writer and leader long after he had retired from trumpet playing.

➤➤ **Count Basie** *(The Original American Decca Recordings).*

Rod Cless

Clarinet, saxophones.

b. Lennox, Iowa, 20 May 1907; d. 8 Dec 1944.

Rod Cless began his short and often brilliant musical life learning violin then cornet, saxophone and clarinet, playing the last in the high school orchestra. At school and university in Iowa he was a star pupil: good at maths, captain of the baseball team, a promising swimmer and diver. After university he moved to Des Moines, where in 1925 the Wolverines played a six-week residency at Riverview Park Ballroom. Cless went there every night, befriended Frank Teschemacher, and two years later took the plunge in Chicago, rooming with Tesch and working with him in Charles Pierce's orchestra and others. There were a few records ("Jazz Me Blues" with Teschemacher, Krupa and Mezzrow is one), and Cless survived the Depression none too happily with teaching and playing for dance band bounces. By the debut of Muggsy Spanier's brilliant band at the Sherman (Cless's work on their sixteen Bluebird recordings is legendary) he had suffered a broken marriage (to Bud Freeman's sister) and was cultivating a drinking problem. For the next four years, however, Cless continued to work on the jazz circuit, with Art Hodes, Bobby Hackett, Wild Bill Davison and Max Kaminsky, among others. One night in December 1944, Kaminsky noticed that the clarinettist was very drunk and offered to walk him home. Cless refused, Kaminsky reluctantly let him go, and Cless fell badly on the way to his apartment. He died four days later at the age of 37. [DF]

➤➤ **Muggsy Spanier** *(Muggsy Spanier 1931 and 1939).*

Jimmy Cleveland

Trombone.

b. Wartrace, Tennessee, 3 May 1926.

A member of the Lionel Hampton band from 1949–53, Cleveland afterwards became an in-demand freelance soloist on the New York recording scene. This provided entry into the general session world and, apart from a few months with the Quincy Jones band in Europe in 1959–60 and a European tour with Thelonious Monk in 1967, this continued to be his main employment. He moved to Los Angeles at the end of the 1960s, and occasionally emerges in all-star West Coast big bands. Cleveland is probably the most dazzling disciple of J.J. Johnson and, especially at slower tempos, shows a real flair for solo work. [BP]

➤➤ **Lucky Thompson** *(Tricotism).*

Andrew Cleyndert

Double bass.

b. Warwickshire, UK, 8 Jan 1963.

Nicholas Andrew de Jong Cleyndert took up the double bass at school and turned professional on leaving. His first job was at the George Chisholm Jazz Club in Manchester where he backed visiting American soloists including Art Farmer and Joe Newman. After moving to London in 1982 his excellent playing brought him early recognition from musicians, and he worked with bands led by saxophonists Bobby Wellins, Don Weller and Bobby Watson, and trumpeters Ted Curson and Red Rodney, also accompanying visiting American legends like Bud Shank, George Coleman, Ray Bryant, John Hicks and Lee Konitz, as well as playing with the cream of London musicians and broadcasting with Kenny Wheeler's big band. In the later 1980s, he took two years off to get his degree in maths and psychology, after which he returned to the jazz scene, and became a member of Ronnie Scott's sextet and quartet. In the later 1990s he joined Stan Tracey's bands, and worked regularly with singer Annie Ross, and with Nick Weldon's trio. He also toured Britain and Europe with the Gene Harris Quartet. Nominated for the British Jazz Awards for three years running (1996–8), he has released two albums as co-leader, *Sing The Line* on Red Dot Records and *My Ideal* on Trio Records (his own label), though playing in the Stan Tracey Trio appears to be his steadiest current gig. [IC]

The New Stan Tracey Quartet

⊙ **For Heaven's Sake** (1995; Cadillac). With the Traceys Stan and son Clark, and young trumpeter Gerard Presencer, Cleyndert plays flawlessly through a wide range of material.

➤➤ **Nick Weldon Trio** *(Lavender's Blue).*

Dave Cliff

Guitar.

b. Northumberland, UK, 25 June, 1944.

Cliff began his career in local rock bands before attending Leeds College of Music in 1967, where a principal tutor was Peter Ind. He then moved to London in 1971 where he became established on the jazz scene working with Ind and others. He toured Holland, Italy and Denmark with Lee Konitz/Warne Marsh in 1976, and toured with Soprano Summit and Charlie Ventura in Sicily in 1977. During the 1980s his reputation continued to grow with appearances at major festivals (Northsea in 1986 and Nice the following year) and in 1987 he recorded his first self-led album *The Right Time,* co-featuring a long-time collaborator, altoist Geoff Simkins.

Cliff has accompanied many visiting Americans over the years, including Slide Hampton, Nina Simone, Warren Vaché, Benny Waters, Herb Geller, Scott Hamilton, Harry Allen, Eddie "Lockjaw" Davis and others, and more recently he has worked with Georgie Fame, Irene Reid and Mike Carr. He has toured in Britain with Ruby Braff's quartet and in Spain with Kenny Davern. In 1994 he also appeared with André Previn's trio for Kiri Te Kanawa's 50th birthday concert televised at the Albert Hall, London. Festival appearances for Cliff during the 1990s include Cork (1992/3 with Mike Carr/Summit Reunion), Brecon (1994 with Warren Vaché/Kenny Davern), Berne (1996, with Bob Wilber) and Jersey (1996, with Ken Peplowski), and between such engagements he has also maintained a busy teaching schedule including Wavendon, Barry, Jamie Aebersold's London Summer School and elsewhere. The gifted alto saxophonist Geoff Simkins is a regular duet partner of his.

A schooled, eclectic but always melodic guitarist, Cliff now belongs amongst the elite of mainstream British jazz, traversing international barriers with reliable regularity. [DF]

⊙ **Sipping at Bells** (1994; Spotlite). A fine overall group performance, with special mention for the duo tracks co-featuring Cliff's old partner Geoff Simkins.

⊙ **Dave Cliff And Friends – When Lights Are Low** (1997; Zephyr). A charming and relaxed guitar date, co-featuring Cliff in a variety of combinations (quartet/duo/solo) with American Howard Alden and two more world-class talents: Dave Green (bass) and Allan Ganley (drums).

Winston Clifford

Drums.

b. London, 19 Sept 1965.

A vigorously assertive but subtle drummer, Winston Clifford made his name by playing with a fairly representative sample of London's 1980s generation of jazz musicians – Courtney Pine, Steve Williamson, Julian Joseph – and with a number of US visitors – Monty Alexander, Eddie Harris, Art Farmer – as well as with established UK residents such as Ronnie Scott and Slim Gaillard. In the 1990s, Clifford became a close associate of pianist Jonathan Gee, playing with him in all his various-sized bands and alongside him in tenor/soprano player Ed Jones's quartet and quintet. He also joined Mario Castronari's cultured fusion band Roadside Picnic and Dylan Fowler's eclectic Frevo, and played regularly in the second half of the decade with saxophonist Tim Garland, guitarist Ciyo Brown and – as a singer – with Jan Ponsford's Vocal Chords. He also remains one of the UK's first-call drummers for US visitors like singer Carmen Lundy (with whom he has recorded, and toured Europe and India), Stanley Turrentine, Gary Bartz and Freddie Hubbard. [CP]

➤➤ **Mario Castronari** *(La Famille)*; **Orphy Robinson** *(When Tomorrow Comes; The Vibes Describes)*.

Rosemary Clooney

Vocals.

b. Maysville, Kentucky, 23 May 1928; d. 29 June 2002.

Rosemary Clooney began her career singing with her sister Betty on local radio and with Tony Pastor's band, before embarking on a solo career with a contract with Columbia. From the early 1950s she produced a string of pop hits and, by 1954, she had broken into films. On the jazz side, Clooney recorded with Benny Goodman, Duke Ellington, Woody Herman and the Hi-Los, and after a period of retirement returned to co-star with Bing Crosby on stage and resume a full-time performing career. In the late 1970s she became Concord Records' most prestigious signing, and she has continued to record with new depth and musical maturity in a variety of contexts, frequently in the company of Warren Vaché and/or Scott Hamilton until her death from cancer in 2002. Clooney's always musical and occasionally gently ironic approach marked her out as one of the great individual voices of twentieth-century popular music. [CP]

⊙ **Tribute To Billie Holiday** (1979; Concord). One of Clooney's first appearances on Concord, with the young Vaché and Hamilton on fine form; the rueful quality of her later work suits the subject to perfection.

⊙ **Sings Rodgers, Hart And Hammerstein** (1990; Concord). In addition to the luxurious LA choir (arranged by John Oddo), this album has the bonus of Chauncey Welsch on trombone and Jack Sheldon on trumpet (and hilarious vocally on "People Will Say We're In Love").

⊙ **Do You Miss New York** (1993; Concord). Excellent collection of songs with New York connections, featuring the touching title track by Dave Frishberg.

Jeff Clyne

Double bass, bass guitar.

b. London, 29 Jan 1937.

Clyne was self-taught, though spent some short periods studying with orchestral players. In 1955 he became a military bandsman during his National Service and played in London with Tony Crombie's Rockets and with Stan Tracey. He joined the Jazz Couriers, a group co-led by Tubby Hayes and Ronnie Scott in 1958, and continued to work with Hayes for about ten years. Clyne branched out into the avant-garde in the early 1960s playing with John Stevens and Trevor Wattst in the Spontaneous Music Ensemble and Amalgam. In 1965 he joined Stan Tracey's quartet, which recorded the classic album *Under Milk Wood,* before spending the later 1960s working with musicians from right across the jazz spectrum: Gordon Beck, Tony Kinsey, John McLaughlin and Tony Oxley. Then he took up bass guitar, and joined Nucleus at its beginning in 1969, staying until 1971. The 1970s saw him playing with Keith Tippett and Gary Boyle's Isotope among others, though he formed Turning Point in 1976 with singer Pepi Lemer, a fusion band for which he composed much of the music and which recorded two acclaimed albums, *Creatures Of The Night* and *Silent Promise*. He has accompanied singers Blossom Dearie, Marion Montgomery, Annie Ross and Norma Winstone, and worked with many US musicians, including Lucky Thompson, Zoot Sims, Phil Woods, Jim Hall, Lockjaw Davis and Tal Farlow. Though he plays regularly, he has been active in education for several years and is currently co-director of the Wavendon Summer Jazz Course and also on the faculty of both the Guildhall School of Music and the Royal Academy of Music jazz courses. [IC]

⊙ **Twice Upon A Time** (1987; Cadillac). This duo album by two quiet masters – Clyne on double bass and Phil Lee on guitar – has great finesse and warmth. They play a few lesser-known standards, a couple of Steve Swallow's pieces and one of Keith Jarrett's. "P.S. For Scott" is Clyne's solo bass tribute to the late Scott LaFaro, complete with pin-point harmonics and bravura passages. Both men are highly melodic improvisers and this, coupled with the delicate blend of the two instruments, creates a supremely intimate atmosphere.

➤➤ **Stan Tracey** *(Under Milk Wood)*.

Arnett Cobb

Tenor saxophone.

b. Houston, Texas, 10 Aug 1918; d. 24 March 1989.

Born Arnette Cleophus Cobbs, Arnett Cobb worked first with the Texas-based bands of Chester Boone (1934–6) and Milt Larkin (1936–42, including a West Coast period fronted by Floyd Ray). Cobb succeeded his former Larkin colleague Illinois Jacquet with Lionel Hampton (1942–7), then formed his own seven-piece band, which was interrupted by serious illness in 1950. He re-formed it successfully, only to be disabled by a car crash in 1956. Despite frequent hospitalization and permanent reliance on crutches, Cobb continued to work in the 1970s and 1980s as a soloist, making tours of Europe and taking part in all-star reunions with Hampton.

One of many stylistically related tenor saxophonists from Texas, Cobb, along with the younger Jacquet, virtually defined which aspects of the style were to be incorporated in the standard R&B approach, and the efforts of his own group – including the hit "Smooth Sailing" – were largely aimed at the R&B audience. His later work demonstrated convincingly that, without abandoning the virtues of R&B, he was more than capable of creating extended jazz solos. [BP]

⊙ **Blue And Sentimental** (1960; Prestige). Two days with the Red Garland trio produced a ballad set fit to put alongside Gene Ammons's *Gentle Jug*; the soulful title track pays tribute to the first "Texas tenor" of them all, Herschel Evans.

⊙ **The Wild Man From Texas** (1974–6; Black & Blue). One of a number of albums done in Europe, this has a five-piece frontline (with Earl Warren and fellow tenorist Eddie Chamblee) reproducing the atmosphere of Cobb's touring band of the post-war years.

Jimmy Cobb

Drums.

b. Washington, DC, 20 Jan 1929.

After working with leading local musicians, Cobb toured with Earl Bostic in 1951 and with his then wife Dinah Washington, for whom he acted as musical director until 1955. After freelancing in New York and joining Cannonball Adderley (1957–8), he played briefly with Stan Getz and Dizzy Gillespie, then followed Cannonball into the Miles Davis group (1958–63). Next he played regularly with Wynton Kelly until the latter's death in 1971. He accompanied Sarah Vaughan in the 1970s, while copious freelance work and a long relationship with Nat Adderley's groups continued into the 1990s. In recent years he has led his own groups and continued to be active as a sideman.

Cobb's strength lies in his time-playing, which is very much out of the Kenny Clarke school – though he's less of a living metronome than Clarke, and even sounds compelling while slowing down (especially when partnered by Paul Chambers in the Davis and Kelly groups). Although perfectly capable of well-constructed improvisations based largely on the snare drum, Cobb is rarely in the solo spotlight, but the way he uses accents to steady or to spur other soloists is a delight. [BP]

➤➤ **Miles Davis** *(Kind Of Blue)*; **Wes Montgomery** *(Full House)*.

Billy Cobham

Drums, percussion, electronics, composer.

b. Panama, 16 May 1944.

Cobham's family moved to New York when he was three. He began on percussion when still a toddler and at eight was adept enough to play publicly with his pianist father. In 1959 he got his first complete drum set when he went to the High School of Music and Art. School friends included future jazz stars George Cables (piano), Jimmy Owens (trumpet) and Eddie Gomez (bass). After high school he went into the army, playing with a military band until his demobilization in 1968, when he joined the Horace Silver quintet. He stayed with Silver for eight

Jak Kilby

Billy Cobham

months, working in the USA and touring Europe, and Cobham's brilliant playing began to attract attention. After leaving Silver he became active as a session musician, playing on film and TV soundtracks and advertising jingles. With Randy and Mike Brecker he formed and worked with a jazz-rock group called Dreams in 1969–70, and in the same period also played on some key Miles Davis albums including *Bitches Brew*, *Live-Evil* and *Jack Johnson*. In 1971 he was a founder member of John McLaughlin's Mahavishnu Orchestra, which many consider to have been the greatest jazz-rock fusion group of all. Cobham made a vital contribution to the group's music, which was innovative and enormously influential.

When the first Mahavishnu Orchestra disbanded in 1973, Cobham began leading his own bands and recording under his own name; his first album, *Spectrum*, is one of the classics of the jazz-rock genre. He toured the USA and Europe in 1974–5 with his own groups, playing concerts and major festivals. In September 1975 he formed a new group, named after his debut album, which included George Duke (keyboards) and John Scofield (guitar), but in the later 1970s he stopped leading groups and freelanced, oversaw drum clinics and did some teaching. In the early 1980s he was lived in Switzerland and freelanced in Europe. From 1984–5 he played with German trumpeter Johannes Faber's group Consortium, recording one album with them, but he left Consortium to lead his own group again, and recorded a highly successful album called *Warning*.

Cobham was the dominant drummer of the first half of the 1970s, spawning disciples and imitators all over the world. His playing combines great power and rhythmic clarity with a most musical sensitivity and subtlety. With the Mahavishnu Orchestra, his magnificent handling of asymmetry (in both rhythms and structures) set new standards of excellence for everyone. But after his spectacular start with *Spectrum*, when he (and Jan Hammer) were still under the visionary spell of the Mahavishnu Orchestra, he seemed to rather lose his way. Subsequent albums faltered and rarely ever reached the same heights of creative intensity. [IC]

⊙ **Spectrum** (1973; Atlantic). This classic jazz-rock album bristles with new rhythms, new ideas, vitality and optimism. It is also notable for its light and shade, ebb and flow. Jimmy Owens plays some excellent trumpet and the late Joe Farrell is his usual impeccable self. But the real star is the rhythm-section plus Jan Hammer and guitarists Tommy Bolin and John Tropea.

⊙ **Billy's Best Hits** (1985/87; GRP).This compilation of tracks from *Warning* (1985), featuring Cobham with a guitar and keyboard quintet, and *Picture This* (1987), on which he leads a group of stars including Ron Carter, Randy Brecker, Grover Washington and Tom Scott, has some of his better performances from the later 1980s.

➤➤ **Larry Coryell** *(Live From Bahia).*

Tony Coe

Tenor and soprano saxophones, clarinet, bass-clarinet, composer.

b. Canterbury, Kent, UK, 29 Nov 1934.

Coe had private lessons on clarinet (though is self-taught on saxophone) and studied composition with Donald Leggatt, Alfred Nieman, Richard Rodney Bennett and Vinko Globokar. He worked with Humphrey Lyttelton's band from 1957–62, touring the USA, UK and Europe, but led his own group from 1962–4. Count Basie offered him a place in the Basie band saxophone section in 1965, and only red tape stopped Coe from taking up the offer. He was with the John Dankworth orchestra from 1966–9 and the Kenny Clarke-Francy Boland band from 1967–73. During the 1970s he began working with Derek Bailey's shifting free-improvisation group Company, and with Stan Tracey, as well as leading a series of groups of his own including (with Kenny Wheeler) Coe, Wheeler & Co, Three (with Bob Cornford), Coe Oxley & Co and Axel. In 1978 he toured in Europe with the United Jazz and Rock Ensemble and in 1983 toured the UK with the Mike Gibbs band. He went to the USA in 1984 to be one of the featured soloists on Bob Moses's album *Visit With The Great Spirit* and he has also worked intermittently with Matrix, a small ensemble formed in 1971 by clarinettist Alan Hacker, which is not exactly a jazz group but has a wide-ranging repertoire of early, classical and contemporary music. With Matrix, Coe has performed at the Edinburgh festival, done broadcasts for the BBC and ORTF (Paris), and played the music for films such as Ken Russell's *The Devils* (1970) and *The Boy Friend* (1971). Coe's playing has also been heard by millions in the unlikely context of Henry Mancini's music for the *Pink Panther* films, for which he is the featured tenor saxophone soloist.

Coe's film score work took him across the Channel for *Mer de Chine* (1986), *Camomille* (1987), and in 1995, for the 1928 silent film *Peau de Pêche*, directed by Marie Epstein, for which he composed two hours of music for chamber orchestra. (When Coe was working on the score, Marie Epstein (b. 1899) sent a spy to make sure there wasn't any jazz content, and was reassured to find there wasn't).

Coe is a player of astonishing versatility and brilliance. As a mainstreamer with Lyttelton and others, he was influenced by Barney Bigard and Johnny Hodges, but he rapidly assimilated the innovations and stylistic developments of Charlie Parker and Paul Gonsalves. His playing reveals the disparate influences of Alan Hacker, Debussy, Berg, Boulez and Louis Armstrong, yet he is one of the finest exponents of free improvisation. He has remained catholic in his tastes and protean in his abilities: he can function with perfect ease in a mainstream group playing a standard; with a post-Coltrane small group or a jazz-rock band; with a freely improvising ensemble; or with a European art music chamber group.

He is an immensely gifted composer, his works performed by Matrix, the Danish Radio Big Band and the Metropole Orchestra and Skymasters in Holland. *Zeitgeist* (1975) is an extended work deftly fusing jazz and rock elements with techniques from European art music, which deploys a very large orchestra including woodwind and cellos. First performed and recorded in 1976, it moved the composer Richard Rodney Bennett to write (prompted by the work's dedication to Alban Berg): "Berg's music grew from a brilliantly fertile imagination controlled by a beautifully planned and articulated structure. *Zeitgeist* possesses precisely these admirable qualities."

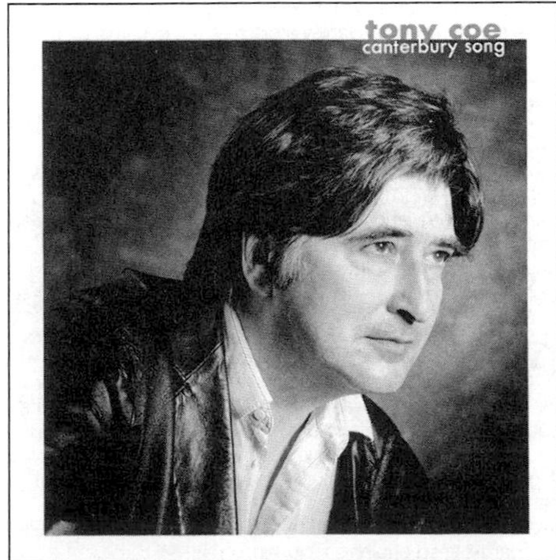

By the mid-1980s Coe was generally considered to be the finest and most original living clarinettist in jazz, and one of the most individual stylists on tenor saxophone. He is a sophisticate who, behind a smokescreen of vagueness, hides an incisive chess-player's mind, always improvising "compositionally", with an overall view of the music and of his place in it. [IC]

Tony Coe

Tournée Du Chat (1981–2; Nato). Centrepiece of this set is Coe's seventeen-minute-long composition "The Jolly Corner", here performed live. He and Alan Hacker play clarinets, with the late Bob Cornford on piano, bassist Chris Laurence and percussionist Nic Williams. Wonderfully economically written passages and bravura improvisation create a mysterious drama. The other pieces are all improvised by Coe either solo or with bassist John Lindberg – uncompromisingly abstract yet eloquent constructions.

Tony Coe, Chris Laurence and Tony Oxley

Nutty On Willisau (hat Art; 1983). Coe in trio format with Chris Laurence, doyen of jazz and classical bass playing, and Tony Oxley, doyen of both conventional jazz and free improv. This is a virtuoso set by three musicians at home with any idiom, and it includes some standards.

Tony Coe

Canterbury Song (Hot House; 1988). Coe leads some fine Americans – trumpeter Benny Bailey, pianist Horace Parlan, bassist Jimmy Woode and drummer Idris Muhammad. Coe the jazzman extraordinary is in evidence here, in a performance of standards and a couple of his excellent compositions – the title track and "Lagos". The rhythm-section "cooks", and Bailey, as usual, plays superbly.

Captain Coe's Famous Racearound (1995; Storyville). This recording was part of Coe's Danish Jazzpar Prize, and it features him with the Danish Radio Orchestra and with the 1995 Jazzpar combo. The orchestra was conducted by valve-trombonist and composer Bob Brookmeyer, who also played in the small group. Coe composed and arranged the title track, and arranged the opening orchestral performance of "Prelude/How Long Has This Been Going On?/Postlude". But his role was primarily as the star soloist of the whole occasion, which produced some magnificent music.

Blue Jersey (1995; ABCD). This is a live recording by Coe's quintet at the Jersey festival. Coe led pianist John Horler, drummer Allan Ganley, Horler's brother Dave on valve-trombone, and bassist Malcolm Creese. They played a mixture of standards and originals – the title track by Coe and three by John Horler. Ganley's discreet but dynamic drumming is exactly what Coe requires, and the session is a gem.

In Concert (1997; ABCD). Coe, John Horler and Creese are the virtuoso (drumless) trio on this superlative live recording – this is chamber jazz at its most adventurous. The fare includes a couple of excellent Horler originals, Duke Ellington's "Blue Rose", Bill Evans's "Re: Person I Knew", and three standards including "You Stepped Out Of A Dream" which was also featured on *Blue Jersey*, but every time Coe plays a piece it's freshly minted. The highly empathetic listening of the trio and their interplay are thrilling.

Ruby (1998; Zah Zah). In 1999 Coe won the Best Clarinettist award at the annual BT British Jazz Awards, for the fourth time. It was at the 1997 BT Awards that he first had pianist Brian Dee and bassist Matt Miles in his quartet and on this album they are joined in his group by Steve Argüelles, a drummer who has the discreet dynamism that has made him a frequent associate of Coe's. Once again, this is a ravishing album of standards with a couple of Coe's standard-based originals included.

➤➤ **Kenny Clarke** *(Two Originals)*; **Humphrey Lyttelton** *(Back To The Sixties)*; **Bob Moses** *(Visit With The Great Spirit)*; **Norma Winstone** *(Somewhere Called Home)*.

Alan Cohen

Composer, arranger, soprano and tenor saxophones.

b. London, 25 Nov 1934.

A graduate of the Royal Academy of Music, Cohen formed a band to appear at Ronnie Scott's Club in 1967 and quickly became known as one of the most important British arrangers, supplying scores for Humphrey Lyttelton, the New Jazz Orchestra and American visitors such as Bing Crosby. In 1972 Cohen's recorded re-creation of Ellington's "Black, Brown And Beige" suite won high praise, and he continued writing on a semi-freelance basis until 1978, when he formed the Midnite Follies Orchestra with Keith Nichols. The MFO, featuring Alan Elsdon, John Barnes, Pete Strange and others, recorded and toured for six years, after which Cohen arranged for Charlie Watts's big band in 1985 and in the following year formed his own quintet, playing soprano saxophone. [DF]

Duke Ellington's Black Brown And Beige (1972; Argo). A great reconstruction of Ellington's complete suite, featuring British-based jazzmen like Olaf Vas and Harry Beckett; a British jazz milestone and long overdue for re-issue on CD.

➤➤ **Midnite Follies Orchestra** *(Hotter Than Hades)*.

Avishai Cohen

Bass, composer.

b. Naharia, Israel, 20 April 1970.

Having begun playing piano at the age of nine – marking the keys with seashells so that he could remember the melodies he'd made up – Avishai Cohen began formal musical studies at eleven. In 1984, his family moved from Israel to St Louis. On switching to electric bass, his playing was revolutionized by exposure to the music of Jaco Pastorius, leading him to fusion, and on to Chick Corea, and Stanley Clarke. At sixteen, Cohen moved back to Israel and enrolled in the Music and Arts High School in Jerusalem, but dropped out after a year to pursue his musical interests. After a spell in the Israeli army, during which he played rock bass, he took up the acoustic instrument and moved to New York in 1992. There, he performed with Paquito D'Rivera, Roy Hargrove, Joshua Redman and Leon Parker before being hired by Panamanian pianist Danilo Perez, and forming his own band with drummer Jeff Ballard, saxophonists Ravi Coltrane and Steve Wilson, and pianist Jason Lindner. After recording Panamonk (1996; Impulse!) with Perez, Cohen was signed by Chick Corea's Stretch label and recorded *Adama* (see below), *Devotion* (1999) and *Colors* (2000). He also joined the pianist's Origin band, an acoustic sextet that can be heard on a six-CD Stretch set, *The Complete 1998 Live At The Blue Note Recordings*. Cohen formed and led the International Vamp Band in 2000: their album *Unity* (2001) was a successful fusion of Latin rhythms, Sephardic melodies and Middle Eastern modes with a jazz idiom. [CP]

⊙ **Adama** (1998; Stretch). All Cohen originals (except a trio version of "Bésame Mucho" featuring pianist Brad Mehldau and drummer Jordy Rossi) that make up a fine debut, showcasing Cohen's regular band (as above, but with trombonist Steve Davis instead of Coltrane) playing music that is unmistakably jazz-based but frequently anchored in the sound of the oud, played by guitarist Amos Hoffman.

Al Cohn

Tenor saxophone, arranger.

b. Brooklyn, New York, 24 Nov 1925; d. 15 Feb 1988.

Al Cohn began as a sideman with several big bands, including Georgie Auld (1944–6), Buddy Rich (1947), Woody Herman (1948–9) and Artie Shaw (1949–50). He was then mainly busy as an arranger, making many jazz recordings in the 1950s and doing mostly non-jazz work thereafter. He also appeared frequently as a tenor soloist, co-featuring from the late 1950s with fellow Herman and Shaw colleague Zoot Sims, and in the 1980s with his son, guitarist Joe Cohn.

Cohn created such notable big band pieces as "The Goof And I", used by both Rich and Herman, and the small-group numbers written for his own recordings include the standard "The Underdog" (aka "Ah Moore"), with words by Dave Frishberg. His work on tenor was sometimes compared unfavourably with that of Sims, but any apparent lack of fluency was amply compensated by the melodic intelligence of his Young-derived style. During his 1980s return to more regular playing, this quality was emphasized by a more meaty tone, reminiscent of such players as Buddy Tate. [BP]

Al Cohn – Zoot Sims

⊙ **You 'N' Me** (1960; Verve). Cohn and Sims did much to set the fashionable approach to tenor-playing in the 1950s, with Sims joyous and fluent and Cohn thoughtful and driving. This set, with Mose Allison on piano, includes effortless playing on an equal number of old standards and swinging originals.

⊙ **Nonpareil** (1981; Concord). The mature Cohn here chooses interesting material – tunes by Gary McFarland and Dave Frishberg, and the almost forgotten Kurt Weill song "This Is New" – and also appears as a totally commanding tenor soloist.

➤➤ **Zoot Sims** *(Zoot Case)*.

Cozy Cole

Drums.

b. East Orange, New Jersey, 17 Oct 1909; d. 29 Jan 1981.

Cozy (William Randolph) Cole was first inspired by Sonny Greer's playing with Duke Ellington's band, and moved to New York in 1926 to work as a barber and shipping clerk, while building his musical career and taking lessons with Charlie Brooks, the pit drummer at Lincoln Theater. (Cole never missed an opportunity to study – later he went to the Juilliard and in 1964 opened a New York drum tuition school with Gene Krupa.) By the early 1930s he was building a big reputation with bands led by Blanche Calloway, Benny Carter and Willie Bryant, and from 1936 was playing with Stuff Smith and Jonah Jones at the Onyx (their version of "I'se A Muggin'" was a big hit). Cole worked from 1938 with Cab Calloway, from 1942 with Raymond Scott's "integrated" band at CBS, and by 1944 was busy with film and pitwork, playing for the *Carmen Jones Show*, in Billy Rose's Ziegfeld Theater (with Don Byas) and briefly in 1946 with Benny Goodman, doing the eight-a-day at New York's Paramount Theater.

By 1949 he had replaced Sid Catlett with Louis Armstrong's All Stars for a three-year stay, and all through the 1950s he played in studios and taught drums. In 1957 he toured Europe with Earl Hines and Jack Teagarden and in 1958 had a surprise hit record of his own, "Topsy", arranged by Dick Hyman and financed by Alan Hartwell, a fan from the Metropole where Cole regularly appeared. Thereafter he toured with his own band (featuring tenorist George Kelly), went to Africa in 1962 and by 1969 had rejoined Jonah Jones at the Embers. In the 1970s Cole stayed active: he played for a 1973 Calloway reunion at Newport jazz festival, and in 1976 for a *Night In New Orleans* package starring Benny Carter, which toured the UK. One of the greatest classic drummers, he belongs in the class of Catlett and Singleton. [DF]

➤➤ **Louis Armstrong** *(The California Concerts)*.

Nat "King" Cole

Piano, vocals.

b. Montgomery, Alabama, 17 March 1917; d. 15 Feb 1965.

Like several musicians whose solo work moved beyond the realm of jazz – both Jimmy and Tommy Dorsey, for example – Nathaniel Adams Cole created a brilliant playing style that set new standards for followers of his instrument. Other musicians admired his playing unreservedly, though some were distracted by the popularity of his vocals, which were also widely influential but fairly insignificant in the development of jazz singing. His youngest brother, Freddy Cole (b. 15 Oct 1931) still maintains the family tradition as a singer-pianist.

The inspiration of Earl Hines can clearly be heard in Nat's one early recording as a sideman, for his elder brother Eddie, but by the time he began leading his trio in 1939, Nat – in common with Billy Kyle – was taking a key role in turning the idea of "trumpet-style" right-hand lines into a conception more akin to the saxophone or clarinet. Simultaneously, the left-

HERMAN LEONARD

Nat "King" Cole

hand punctuations became more streamlined and predictable than those of Hines, but the smoothness of the whole approach consolidated the piano's vocabulary in a way that was crucial for its adaptation to bebop.

Cole's popularity is evidenced by the fact that his line-up of piano, guitar (initially Oscar Moore) and bass dictated the trio format for countless performers from Art Tatum to Oscar Peterson. But far more significant is Cole's direct influence on the pianists of a whole generation, including those influential in their own right – namely Peterson, Powell, Horace Silver and Bill Evans. [BP]

Lester Young

Lester Young Trio (1943–6; Verve). Also including four very early Dexter Gordon-Nat Cole tracks as makeweights, this programme has the pianist displaying his great rhythmic expertise and completely disguising the lack of a bass on the Young session.

Nat "King" Cole

Best Of The Nat "King" Cole Trio (1943–9; Capitol). A canny selection of instrumental-only tracks by the group which first established Cole's reputation. Using Oscar Moore as a brilliant foil, Cole plays originals and jazz standards with superb flair.

>> **Jazz At The Philharmonic** *(The First Concert).*

Richie Cole

Alto, tenor and baritone saxophones.

b. Trenton, New Jersey, 29 Feb 1948.

Cole studied alto as a teenager with Phil Woods, with whom he did some gigging in the mid-1970s, after working with Buddy Rich and Lionel Hampton bands. He began recording under his own name in 1976 and led the regular backing group for Eddie Jefferson from 1976–9; after that he formed his own group Alto Madness, based in San Francisco since 1981 but touring internationally. Though he's an impressive technician, Cole's heated playing is often a vulgarization of the work of Woods and others closer to the bebop source. [BP]

New York Afternoon (1976; Muse). The title track and one other item benefit from the guest appearance of Cole's employer Eddie Jefferson, and the comparatively unambitious programme actually works in the altoist's favour on this well-known (but currently hard-to-find) album.

Bill Coleman

Trumpet, flugelhorn, vocals.

b. Paris, Kentucky, 4 Aug 1904; d. Toulouse, France, 24 Aug 1981.

Bill Coleman first played the clarinet (a fact perhaps reflected in his later mobile approach to trumpet), but like Doc Cheatham became a permanent brass convert after he heard Louis Armstrong. "My first inspiration", he remembered later, "and 'Money Blues' with Fletcher Henderson was my first impression of him." In 1927, Coleman went to New York with brothers Cecil and Lloyd Scott in a great band that included another fine trumpeter, Frankie Newton. For the next five years his quicksilver creations graced such fine New York bands as Lucky Millinder's, Benny Carter's and Charlie Johnson's, and his sides with Fats Waller at this period dwarf the efforts of Waller's lesser trumpeters.

In 1935 he moved to Paris, his base for the next five years, to work with Freddie Taylor and the great Willie Lewis orchestra. There he found none of the travails of black musicians in New York – "it was a mellow, cultural city where you were accepted for what you were". He recorded solos with Garnet Clark, Dickie Wells and Lewis's orchestra, recorded with the Hot Club of France quintet, and became a celebrity. After a year in Egypt he went back to New York in 1940 to work with such stellar names as Teddy Wilson, Ellis Larkins, Andy Kirk, Benny Carter, Teddy Wilson, Coleman Hawkins, Lester Young, Mary Lou Williams and Sy Oliver.

Perhaps the rise of bebop and young turks such as Dizzy Gillespie (who surpassed Coleman in technique if not elegance) made life less comfortable in the USA than it had been in Paris, and in 1948, in response to a telegram from Charles Delaunay, he returned to play for the opening of a Paris nightclub. He stayed on to live in France, commuting regularly to other European countries, including trips to Britain in the 1960s with Bruce Turner's Jump Band. In the year he died his adopted home town, Limeray, pronounced him an honorary free citizen. [DF]

Hangin' Around (1929–43;Topaz). An attractive collection of Coleman, spanning 1929 (with Luis Russell) through to Joe Marsala and Coleman Hawkins in the 1940s. Midway are some of his greatest Parisian titles including "I Got Rhythm" and "Hangin' around Boudon" with Dickie Wells and "I'm In The Mood For Love" with Herman Chittison.

⦿ **Bill Coleman 1936–38** (Classics). A worthwhile set, overlapping with the above but adding extra titles including five with clarinet/tenorist Eddie Brunner.

⦿ **Bill Coleman In Paris** (2003; EMI France). Some of Coleman's most delightful work from his earlier years is on his Paris sessions; there are also appearances here from Stephane Grappelli, Django Reinhardt and Frank "Big Boy" Goodie.

⦿ **Town Hall Concert** (1945; Commodore). An occasionally uncomfortable-sounding New York concert with pianist Billy Taylor, but Bill Coleman's contributions stand out with unflurried panache.

⦿ **Meets Guy Lafitte** (1973; Black Lion). Lafitte matches Coleman's elegant sophistication to perfection in this classy musical pairing.

George Coleman

Tenor and alto saxophones.

b. Memphis, 8 March 1935.

After early experience in blues bands, including touring with B.B. King (1952 and 1955–6), Coleman moved to Chicago with Booker Little, then recorded in New York with Lee Morgan and Jimmy Smith. Spells followed with the Max Roach quintet in 1958–9, the Slide Hampton octet from 1959–61 and Wild Bill Davis in 1962. In 1963–4 he was a member of the Miles Davis quintet, then a sideman with Lionel Hampton (1964), and, during the next ten years, with Lee Morgan, Elvin Jones, Shirley Scott and Cedar Walton. Since then he has led his own quintet, quartet and octet, and worked as visiting soloist with local rhythm-sections. An extremely fluent post-bop stylist with a beautifully even tone, he has an ability to run the changes at lightning speed, which has made him an uncompromising figurehead of pre-free jazz. He is also capable of considerable sensitivity at slower tempos, and of occasional recourse to his blues roots. His son, George Jnr, is active on the New York scene as a drummer. [BP]

Jak Kilby

George Coleman

⦿ **At Yoshi's** (1987; Evidence). This half-live, half-studio album features his high-school buddy Harold Mabern on piano and mixes shorter tracks with long workouts on tracks such as "Up Jumped Spring" and "Soul Eyes".

➤➤ **Miles Davis** *(The Complete Concert).*

Ornette Coleman

Alto saxophone, composer, tenor saxophone, trumpet, violin.

b. Fort Worth, Texas, 19 March 1930.

Coleman began on alto at fourteen and was largely self-taught. He played in his school marching band with fellow students and future jazz musicians Dewey Redman, Charles Moffett and Prince Lasha. In 1946, he took up the tenor saxophone, inspired by the best local tenor player, Thomas "Red" Connors, who taught him the elements of bebop and introduced him to the work of Charlie Parker. He worked in Connors's band for a while, playing mostly blues, and also worked with R&B groups, eventually forming his own, and backing up singers such as Big Joe Turner. In 1949 he toured on tenor with a minstrel show and was left stranded in New Orleans. He eventually got a job with Pee Wee Crayton's R&B band, leaving it in Los Angeles where, apart from one brief period back in Fort Worth, he made his home until 1959. There he did a variety of non-musical jobs while studying theory and harmony textbooks and working on his own music. Coleman's concept was so unorthodox that most musicians dismissed and derided him, and it was not until the mid-1950s that he found his regular playing associates. He played with trumpeter Bobby Bradford and drummer Ed Blackwell in 1953–4, then, after working briefly with Paul Bley, he began regular private sessions with Don Cherry (trumpet), Billy Higgins (drums) and Charlie Haden (bass), who ultimately became the Ornette Coleman quartet.

In 1958 bassist Red Mitchell helped Coleman to get his first recording contract with the Los Angeles company Contemporary Records, and the two albums on that label, *Something Else!* and *Tomorrow Is The Question*, served notice on the jazz world that a radical new talent had arrived. Coleman was championed by Nat Hentoff, one of the most eminent jazz critics of the 1950s, and he was befriended and helped by John Lewis and Gunther Schuller. He signed with Atlantic Records, who sponsored his attendance (with Don Cherry) at the Lenox School of Jazz in 1959. In the autumn of that year, Coleman took his quartet into the Five Spot in New York and, in an explosion of publicity and controversy, "free jazz" became an established fact. Coleman recorded seven albums for Atlantic between 1959–62, and played with his quartet in the New York area and at the Newport and Monterey jazz festivals. Then he retired from performing for two years.

Coleman had arrived on the New York scene at 29 years old with his musical concept fully formed. No one except his immediate associates had witnessed his gradual development, and most critics and musicians were unprepared for such a radical new sound. His quartet had no chordal instrument – no piano or guitar – and his music was non-harmonic and not based on chord changes. His highly original compositions embodied other new factors: rhythmic accents were displaced in unexpected ways, melodic phrases often had unusual, asymmetrical lengths, and bass and drums sometimes took a much more melodic role than previously, either phrasing with the horns or in counterpoint to them. To cap it all, Coleman and Cherry played with fluency, maturity, and a kind of freedom which showed that this was their natural mode of expression: the compositions, solos and whole performances were all of a piece.

The traditional features and familiar roots of Coleman's music were at first overlooked. It was not entirely abstract: although there were no harmonies, it was often tonal, the improvisation taking place in a basic key and often in common time with the superbly swinging rhythm-section of Haden and either Higgins or Blackwell. Coleman and Cherry always swung mightily too, and their phrases were shot through with the human cry of the blues. The influence of Charlie Parker and Thelonious Monk was evident in the music, and nearly all Coleman's compositions were either based on the blues or were variations on the AABA format of popular songs. Furthermore, the Coleman quartet's performances always "breathed" beautifully, creating and releasing tension with great artistry.

Coleman's early music was enormously influential, affecting and inspiring musicians on all instruments and stimulating the whole free-jazz movement in the USA and Europe. John Coltrane visited the Five Spot regularly to hear Coleman, became friendly with him, and the two of them played together a great deal. His approach did not negate more conventionally structured music, but could simply create another dimension to it, which is why his influence was also potent among non-free players of all persuasions.

Between 1963–4 he took up trumpet and violin, and after studying them for two years emerged from retirement in 1965, appearing at the Village Vanguard, New York, with a trio featuring David Izenzon (bass) and Charles Moffett (drums). He took the trio to Europe, visiting several countries and recording a live double album at the Golden Circle in Stockholm, Sweden. At the Fairfield Halls in Croydon, England, a chamber group played a scored Coleman composition, which consisted (in accor-

dance with his "harmolodic theory") of a series of interweaving melodic lines with no underlying harmonic structure.

In the later 1960s he led a quartet with Dewey Redman (tenor), Charlie Haden and either Ed Blackwell or Coleman's son Denardo on drums. In 1967 he played at the Village Theater with his quartet and the Philadelphia Woodwind Quintet, and in 1969 there was a brief reunion with Don Cherry for a New York University concert. In 1971 he opened his own Artist House in the Soho section of Manhattan as a centre for exhibitions and concerts. He seemed to find more fulfilment in composing than in performing at this time, and spent much time at home writing and doing most of his playing there. In 1972 his quartet performed with a symphony orchestra at the Newport festival, playing his *Skies Of America*, composed in accordance with his harmolodic theory. From 1975, using electric bass and guitars, he began to work with rock rhythms, in what became known as his Prime Time band. But the results of Coleman's rock experiments are extremely patchy, the old compositional skill is little in evidence, and interacting lines which might sound attractive in an acoustic band often seem cluttered and monotonous in an electric rock group.

In 1985 Prime Time opened a week-long festival in Coleman's honour at Hartford, Connecticut. He was presented with the key to the city, and a documentary film, *Ornette: Made In America*, directed by Shirley Clarke, was shown. The core of the Hartford festival was a performance of three of Coleman's chamber pieces: a 1962 string quartet, *Dedication To Poets And Writers: The Sacred Mind Of Johnny Dolphin*; a 1983 work, *Time Design*, for string quartet and percussion, written in memory of Buckminster Fuller; and a 1984 work for strings, two trumpets and percussion. In 1987 he made a double album, *In All Languages*, using Prime Time for one disc and his "original" acoustic quartet for the other. In the mid-1990s he was touring with acoustic groups including, at different times, his son Denardo, Cherry, pianist Geri Allen and Charnett Moffet (the son of drummer

Charles) on bass. He was also featured on the soundtrack of the film *The Naked Lunch* (1991).

Ornette Coleman's debut was so stunning that the rest of his career, going in fits and starts as it has, with long reclusive periods, seems something of an anticlimax. His most intensely creative work was done in the 1950s and on the nine seminal albums recorded from 1958–61. His profoundly original music seemed to flow out of him effortlessly and naturally. It split the music world into those who thought he was the new Messiah (John Lewis, Leonard Bernstein and others), and those who thought he was, if not the Devil incarnate, then at least a charlatan who could not really play. The resulting publicity rocketed Coleman to international stardom before he had left American shores. Nothing else he would ever do would place him so firmly in the centre of the stage again. There has been little development in his subsequent acoustic music, and his use of trumpet and violin as well as alto sounds sometimes like a desperate search for new colours and textures. His supporters make all kinds of claims for the idiosyncratically "creative" way he uses the new instruments, but his alto playing is vastly superior.

He admires European classical music, and has aspired to compose in that tradition since the early 1960s. In fact, Coleman is first and foremost a composer, but his compositions are born from his playing and improvising. Harmolody offers an inevitably limited approach to music-making, and his compositions in this vein have not received recognition from the classical music establishment. There is no doubt, however, about the quality of his best compositions for small group; they rank among the finest pieces in jazz and several of them have entered the general repertoire – "Tears Inside", "Ramblin'" and "Una Muy Bonita", for example (though most of them were written before he developed his theory of music-making).

Musicians not only listen to Coleman's music and learn from it; they seek him out to study with him and discuss their musical ideas. As with his friends John Coltrane and Albert Ayler, his commitment is total, and he has made his music, to adapt Val Wilmer's expression, "as serious as his life". [IC]

⊙ **Something Else** (1958; Contemporary/OJC); **Tomorrow Is The Question** (1959; Contemporary/OJC). On these first two albums, Coleman is still searching for his ideal personnel. Don Cherry is on both, but the first has pianist Walter Norris, bassist Don Payne and drummer Billy Higgins, and the second has either Percy Heath or Red Mitchell on bass and the great West Coast drummer Shelly Manne. The 1958 sessions have a raw, unfinished quality, but the "shock of the new" shines through. Coleman's music becomes more focused on the 1959 recording which includes his sublime ballad "Tears Inside".

⊙ **The Shape Of Jazz To Come** (1959–60; Atlantic); **Change Of The Century** (1959; Atlantic). The classic Coleman quartet – Cherry, Haden and Higgins – made these two marvellous albums which are clearly focused expressions of his music and enshrine some of his finest compositions – "Lonely Woman" and "Congeniality" on the first and "Ramblin'", "Bird Food" and "Una Muy Bonita" on the second.

⊙ **This Is Our Music** (1960; Atlantic); **Free Jazz** (1960; Atlantic). These are the third and fourth epoch-making albums Coleman recorded for Atlantic in this astonishing fourteen-month period. The great quartet included Ed Blackwell on both occasions, and on *Free Jazz* Coleman's group is joined by Freddie Hubbard, Eric Dolphy, Scott LaFaro and Billy Higgins. The pairings offer rich contrasts in personality and timbre which, with the innate musicality of the participants, give this essay in abstract expressionism an exhilarating coherence.

⊙ **At The Golden Circle, Stockholm: Vols. 1 & 2** (1965; Blue Note). These are live sessions by Coleman's touring trio with bassist Izenzon and drummer Charles Moffett. There are violin and trumpet extravaganzas but, for the most part, Coleman is in his most commanding form on alto and Izenzon is an ideal foil and inspiration.

⊙ **Colors** (1996; Verve/Harmolodic). This vital duo album with Joachim Kuhn the virtuoso, genre-bending German pianist, was recorded live at the Leipzig Opera. Coleman was relaxed and intensely focused on this genial occasion, and the two men simply opened their hearts and minds, threw caution to the winds, and lived in the heat of each moment. The resulting music is full of delightful surprises.

➤➤ **Paul Bley** *(The Fabulous Paul Bley Quintet)*; **Pat Metheny** *(Song X)*.

Steve Coleman

Alto saxophone, composer.

b. Chicago, 20 Sept 1956.

Growing up on Chicago's South Side, exposed to blues through soul to jazz, and with a Charlie Parker fan for a father, Steve Coleman's taking up the alto in his teens was entirely natural (although he was more into Maceo Parker than Charlie). By his early twenties, however, his jazz taste had broadened and Coleman moved to New York in 1978 to land jobs with the Thad Jones-Mel Lewis big band and with those led by Cecil Taylor and Sam Rivers. Recording dates with David Murray, Dave Holland and Branford Marsalis followed, but it was with his own band, Five Elements (the name comes from a kung-fu movie), that Coleman began to carve out his own style: M-Base (Macro-Basic Array of Structured Extemporization), based on what he terms "a certain balance of structure and improvisation which will express our lives and time". Three JMT albums and one on Pangaea featuring like-minded spirits such as Graham Haynes, Geri Allen and Robin Eubanks came out in the mid-to-late 1980s, but Coleman came to a wider jazz public's notice with his signing to RCA Novus in 1990. After producing half a dozen albums showcasing his slippery, virtuosic alto against a heady mix of street-smart rhythms from hip-hop to funk, jazz and soul, Coleman branched out in the mid-1990s, running three bands at once: the Afro-Cuban-influenced Mystic Rhythm Society, the fusion-based Metrics and the regular Five Elements. His live concerts continued to be heady, almost hypnotic affairs, featuring street beats, rappers and the occasional dancer. His work has become increasingly ambitious, and albums such as *The Sonic Language of Myth* (see below) are epic in both concept and execution. Coleman remains one of the music's most vital improvisers and catalysts, [CP]

Black Science (1990; Novus). Archetypal M-Base recording, all eel-like alto soloing over snappy, funky beats. Guitarist David Gilmore is a welcome addition to the crew, and regulars Marvin "Smitty" Smith (drums) and Cassandra Wilson (vocals) both perform with their customary aplomb.

The Tao Of Mad Phat/Fringe Zones (1993; Novus). Most adventurous album thus far from Coleman: a species of suite cleverly balancing solo and ensemble playing from the likes of Roy Hargrove (trumpet), Andy Milne (piano) and the ever-present Gilmore.

The Sign And The Seal (1996; RCA). A Mystic Rhythm Society album recorded in Havana with a slightly murky overall sound produced by a plethora of guests including Ravi Coltrane and a Cuban contingent of vocalists and percussionists.

The Sonic Language of Myth (1999; RCA). A slithery, restless collection, its syncretic attitude to composition and improvisation recalls the work of Sun Ra, Anthony Braxton and Prince (often at the same time).

Johnny Coles

Trumpet, flugelhorn.

b. Trenton, New Jersey, 3 July 1926; d. 21 Dec 1997.

Resident in Philadelphia in the 1940s, Coles toured with leading R&B bands such as those of Eddie Vinson (1948–51), Bull Moose Jackson (1952) and Earl Bostic (1955–6). His time with James Moody from 1956–8 led to important solo contributions to Gil Evans's albums and band from 1958–60. He was with Charles Mingus briefly in 1964, George Coleman in 1966, and Herbie Hancock's sextet in 1968–9. Other famous affiliations include Ray Charles (1969–70 and mid-1970s), Duke Ellington (1970–74), Art Blakey (1976) and the Count Basie band (1985–6), and in the early 1980s he appeared with both Dameronia and Mingus Dynasty. An underrated and extremely effective improviser, influenced by Miles Davis and probably Kenny Dorham, he had a tonal variety that was capable of expressing a lot in a few notes, but could summon a fluent technique when required. [BP]

New Morning (1982; Criss Cross). Recorded in Europe, this is a sparkling quartet session with European resident Horace Parlan, and confirms the enormous talent of someone normally seen as the perennial sideman.

Buddy Collette

Tenor saxophone, clarinet, flute.

b. Los Angeles, 6 Aug 1921.

Buddy (William Marcel) Collette worked with several LA groups before becoming leader of a navy band during World War II. A member of a short-lived cooperative group with Britt Woodman and Charles Mingus in 1946, he then did extensive freelancing and session work, becoming the first black musician to hold a permanent position in a West Coast studio band (1951–5). A founder member of the popular Chico Hamilton quintet in 1955–6, he soon returned to freelance playing, teaching and composing. He also assembled big bands for Monterey festivals, led by Mingus, Monk (both in 1964), Dizzy Gillespie (1965) and Gil Evans (1966). A discreet, swinging saxophonist of the Lester Young school, Collette is also a brilliant clarinettist and flautist who has made a better case than many post-swing players for the use of these instruments in jazz. [BP]

A Nice Day (1956–7; Contemporary/OJC). Done while he was riding high with the Chico Hamilton group, this is a convincing sampler of Collette's work.

Scott Colley

Bass.

b. Pasadena, California, 24 Nov 1963.

His older brother was a drummer, and Colley took up the bass aged 11, winning a scholarship to California Institute of the Arts in 1984. He also studied privately with Charlie Haden, and from 1986-90 worked with Carmen McRae, subsequently gigging with Dizzy Gillespie, Roy Hargrove, Art Farmer, Joe Lovano and Pat Martino. In the early and mid-1990s he was a member of groups led by Fred Hersch, T.S. Monk and Jim Hall (the latter a partnership that continued into the new century) and during the same period he formed separate trios with Chris Potter, David Binney and Ravi Coltrane. Towards the end of the 1990s he began an association with Andrew Hill, and in 2003 he was in the touring band of Herbie Hancock. In all these contexts, Colley's supple sound mirrors his supportive stance towards fellow performers. [BP]

Subliminal (1997; Criss Cross). Well titled for a bass-led album, this has some intriguing originals by Colley and drummer Bill Stewart, with solo realizations by Chris Potter and on some tracks pianist Bill Carrothers.

➤➤ **Jim Hall** *(Dialogues)*; **Andrew Hill** *(Dusk)*; **Chris Potter** *(Vertigo)*.

Max Collie

Trombone, vocals, leader.

b. Melbourne, Australia, 21 Feb 1931.

Max Collie's most remarkable achievement (like Pete Allen's a decade later) was to build a national reputation for his New Orleans-style band at a time when demand for new names working in that jazz area was practically nil. A rudimentary trombonist with a degree in marketing, Collie arrived in Britain in 1962, and after forming his own band in 1966 set out to persuade the jazz public that they needed him. By dint of a long residency at Chelsea's Trafalgar pub, a string of LPs (first for Black Lion), then a self-financed tour of the USA with a hard-swinging, chummily presented show,

Collie soon amassed a huge following for his hard-working band. By the 1980s Collie was highly successful and well paid and was looking for fresh achievements. In 1983 he opened the Dixie Strand Café with American tycoon Sam Johnson: it was one of his few unsuccessful ventures. Soon he was back on the road in full swing playing the kind of rough-edged revivalist music which had all too often polished itself out of its convictions in Britain. In 1985 Collie completed more than a hundred performances of his new presentation, *New Orleans Mardi Gras*, in collaboration with two other committed New Orleans figureheads, Ken Colyer and Cy Laurie; throughout the 1990s he was still working regularly and tirelessly. [DF]

Sensation (1988; Timeless Traditional); **The High Society Show** (1992; Reality). Both these are good examples of Collie's rough-hewn traditional jazz message.

Graham Collier

Composer, director, keyboards, bass.

b. Tynemouth, Northumberland, UK, 21 Feb 1937.

Collier's father, a drummer for silent movies and a semi-pro for the rest of his life, encouraged him to play trumpet in local orchestras. After playing in army bands, he won a *Down Beat* scholarship to the Berklee School of Music, USA, in 1961 where he studied with Herb Pomeroy, becoming the school's first British graduate in 1963. He returned to the UK and since 1964 has led his own bands, known as Graham Collier Music and varying in size from sextets to very large ensembles. His personnel has included most leading British musicians such as John Surman, John Marshall, Mike Gibbs and Kenny Wheeler, and sometimes players from Europe and the USA including Ted Curson, Palle Mikkelborg and Manfred Schoof. In 1967 he was the first jazz composer to win an Arts Council bursary, and wrote *Workpoints* for a twelve-piece band. In 1976 he formed his own record company, Mosaic Records, which produced not only Collier's music but also the work of some of his contemporaries and associates: Howard Riley, Stan Sulzmann, Roger Dean and Alan Wakeman. He was instrumental in establishing the crucible of UK talent Loose Tubes in the 1980s. As a composer he has had commissions from many major festivals as well as European radio stations and he has scored documentary films and stage plays. His latest projects include The *Jazz* Ensemble, a cross-Atlantic, cross-generational "ad-hoc big band", showcased on the albums *Charles River Fragments* (Jazzprint; 2003) and *The Third Colour* (Jazzprint; 2003). [IC]

Jazz at the Royal Academy of Music

Spirits Rising (1993–4; RAM Records). "One By One The Cow Goes By", Collier's first generally available composition for some time, occupies the second half of this album and demonstrates his ever-evolving writing as well as the fine ensemble of the Academy's big-band soloists.

Cal Collins

Guitar.

b. Medora, Indiana, 5 May 1933.

Cal Collins grew up listening to country and western music, but soon became aware of jazz and was playing the electric guitar for fun by the age of thirteen. In the 1950s he worked commercially with a quartet, playing jazz wherever possible, and after two years in the army settled in Cincinnati for club work, studio dates and session work for local radio and TV. International fame came with a three-year spell with Benny Goodman (on Jack Sheldon's recommendation) where he found himself in the company of Scott Hamilton, Warren Vaché, John Bunch, Keter Betts and Spike Moore. Here Carl Jefferson heard him for the first time and signed him to Concord for a set of jazz-filled dates with his new colleagues. Regular appearances with Vaché and Hamilton plus others at jazz festivals and concerts in the USA, Europe and Japan further consolidated Collins's reputation, and he continued to lead groups in the Cincinnati area, including a quartet with flugelhornist Jerry Van Blair. [DF]

Ohio Style (1990; Concord). An excellent recording by Collins's Cincinnati-based quartet, with Jerry Van Blair, Lou Lausche (bass) and Tony Sweet (drums).

Lee Collins

Trumpet, vocals.

b. New Orleans, 17 Oct 1901; d. 3 July 1960.

Although he was never quite as good as Armstrong or "Red" Allen, Lee Collins was a highly rated player in New Orleans from the early 1920s, and in 1924 he went to Chicago, where he replaced Louis Armstrong with King Oliver's band and recorded with Jelly Roll Morton. Back in New Orleans by the decade's end, he had built a big reputation, working with an A-team of local heroes: Dave Jones, Earl Humphrey and Theodore Purnell. In 1930, in New York, he briefly replaced Henry "Red" Allen in Luis Russell's orchestra, but throughout the decade he was in Chicago, working with the Dodds brothers, Zutty Singleton and Dave Peyton, and leading his own bands. Shortly after the war he was resident at Chicago's Victory Club. In later years he had a variety of prestigious jobs with top names, including Kid Ory (1948) and Mezz Mezzrow (all round Europe in 1951). Despite failing health – he was suffering from the emphysema which was to finish first his career and then his life – he played on through the 1950s at Club Hangover, San Francisco, then back in Chicago. A fine trumpeter, much influenced by Bunk Johnson, Collins wrote an autobiography which throws much light on a dedicated professional jazzman. [DF]

Mutt Carey And Lee Collins (1923–9; American Music). Collins's titles here include tracks with Bertha Hill and Lovie Austin.

Shad Collins

Trumpet.

b. New Jersey, 27 June 1910; d. May 1978.

The son of a minister, Shad (Lester Rallington) Collins played early on in Charlie Dixon's band and all through the 1930s with a front-rank collection of big bands, including those of Chick Webb, Benny Carter, Teddy Hill, Don Redman and Count Basie. In the 1940s he was regularly with Cab Calloway, then in the 1950s appeared with R&B leaders such as Sam "The Man" Taylor. In the 1960s he left full-time music to work as a cab driver.

Collins was one of the most respected trumpeters of the swing era, although he never wished to move with the times – Dizzy Gillespie made some cutting remarks about Collins's reaction to his experiments when they worked together with Teddy Hill. Unfortunately his recorded dates often seemed to be with more famous trumpeters, who in one way or another overshadowed him. A 1937 Paris session with Dickie Wells ("Devil and the Deep Blue Sea", etc) shows Bill Coleman in a form so devastating that it leaves little room for anyone else, and a 1953 date with Vic Dickenson fanfared the emergence of Ruby Braff, whose legato runs and fat, full tone make Collins's swing-style phrasing and punchy delivery sound almost pedestrian. Nevertheless, Collins is a significant figure in jazz history whose work deserves attention. [DF]

Shad Collins with Paul Quinichette

Basie Reunions (1957–8; Prestige). A fine sample of Collins's fat-toned, strong performance, in company with Paul Quinichette, Buck Clayton and Nat Pierce's Basie-based rhythm-section.

Alice Coltrane

Piano, organ, harp.

b. Detroit, Michigan, 27 Aug 1937.

Alice McLeod first worked in Detroit with her trio and with female vibes-player Terry Pollard, and was touring with the Terry Gibbs quartet (1962–3) at the start of her association with John Coltrane – they were married in 1966 after his divorce (and hers, from singer Kenny Hapgood). After playing piano in his group from 1965 until his death, she formed her own groups, gradually turning the music of her husband's final years into something more suitable as a background for prayer or meditation. By the early 1970s she had issued an album of John Coltrane overdubbed with her own arrangements for strings, and in *Lord Of Lords* she reorchestrated a piece by Stravinsky under "divine instruction", following a visitation from the late composer. In the late 1980s she briefly led a group containing her son, saxophonist Ravi Coltrane, and made a guest appearance at his 1998 New York Town Hall concert. [BP]

Journey In Satchidananda (1970; Impulse). Featuring Pharoah Sanders and Rashied Ali, this is probably the strongest of her ten albums (along with *Ptah, The El Daoud* from the same year).

John Coltrane

Tenor, soprano and alto saxophones, composer.

b. Hamlet, North Carolina, 23 Sept 1926; d. 17 July 1967.

Moving to Philadelphia after graduating from high school, Coltrane began formal saxophone study and gigging on alto. He spent part of his military service in a navy band, then toured with King Kolax in 1946–7 and Eddie Vinson in 1947–8. Back in Philadelphia, he rehearsed with the Jimmy Heath big band in 1948, then joined Dizzy Gillespie's big band (alongside Heath and other Philadelphians). He remained when Gillespie cut down to a sextet in 1950–51 and switched permanently to tenor, which he had previously used while with Vinson. Further touring with Gay Crosse (1952), Earl Bostic (1952) and Johnny Hodges (1953–4) alternated with stays in Philadelphia and work with local musicians, including briefly with Jimmy Smith in 1955. He became a member of the new Miles Davis quintet from 1955–7, and began to record prolifically with Davis, Paul Chambers and others, when he earned the nickname "Trane".

In 1957, during what turned out to be his final stay at home, Coltrane managed to break his long-standing addiction to alcohol and hard drugs, and experienced a spiritual awakening which had immediate musical consequences. He now recorded the first of many albums under his own name, and also performed with Thelonious Monk on records and live, prior to rejoining Miles Davis from 1958–60. At the end of this association the John Coltrane quartet was formed, the classic line-up consisting of pianist McCoy Tyner (who joined in summer 1960), drummer Elvin Jones (autumn 1960) and bassist Jimmy Garrison (end of 1961). Despite the financial and artistic success of this group, which made four tours of Europe, Trane was continually seeking to expand his horizons. Eric Dolphy became an additional member for a while in 1961–2, and Coltrane regularly invited younger, more free-thinking players to join in his performances until, in the latter half of 1965, he radically changed his personnel, introducing first Pharoah Sanders on tenor, then Rashied Ali on drums and his second wife, Alice Coltrane, on piano. But only a year later, after touring Japan, he began to decline engagements on the grounds of fatigue and, shortly afterwards, died of liver cancer.

Though the stylistic detail of Coltrane's playing varied considerably over the years, the one common thread was its intensity. On the evidence of eyewitnesses and his lamentably few pre-Miles recordings, this was as true of his first struggles as it was during the experimentation of his last years. Some of the earliest Trane, even while with Davis, sounds comparatively unformed, as if adapting the honking

REDFERNS

John Coltrane

approach derived via Dexter Gordon from Lester Young in order to incorporate flowing Charlie-Parker-out-of-Don-Byas lines. This conflict between a relatively rigid rhythmic feel and an advanced harmonic conception was only resolved when, around 1957, Coltrane developed sufficient fluency to overcome the apparent obstacles. In fact the speed and accuracy of his execution became the envy of saxophonists of many persuasions, and it was only achieved through obsessive devotion to technical mastery. Lee Konitz said that Trane must have been "an eight- or ten-hour-a-day practiser to play the way he did".

It is sometimes forgotten that Trane could also display an admirable restraint in his interpretation of standard popular ballads, and yet do so without losing intensity. Some of his original ballads, notably "Naima" (1959), exemplify this ability, so different from the relentless harmonic exploration of *Giant Steps* (composed 1957). The sound which most typifies his mature work, however, is of restless, sometimes anguished floods of notes (usually with an explicit or implied fast-tempo feel) which, although harmonically correct, are not melodically appealing or even rhythmically interesting in any obvious way. Rather, there is a full frontal assault on all these technical categories and on the listener's senses; the well-known description "sheets of sound" is significant for, although the individual notes are precise, the approach heralds the desire to go beyond fixed pitch to pure emotion.

How far Coltrane was ever a member of the mid-1960s avant-garde is likely to remain a controversial question, but he certainly facilitated its arrival, and he was indisputably the leading exponent of the "modal" school of improvisation. "Impressions" (1961), an original tune widely used by others, is really just an excuse for extensive examination of one scale (or mode) and, as with its companion piece, the themeless blues "Chasin' The Trane", the recorded version broke all conventions about the length of continuous improvisation which an audience could be expected to take. Undoubtedly this prolixity was attributable in part to Trane's interest in Eastern music; although he modestly disclaimed precedence in this area, it was he who popularized the use of the soprano saxophone played with a distinctly oriental tone and also legitimized the idea of jazzmen gaining inspiration from such musicians as the sitarist Ravi Shankar. And, just as Indian improvisers need their rapport with a good tabla player, Coltrane found his ideal percussionist in Elvin Jones, without whom his most exhaustive and self-exhausting work would have been inconceivable.

Both in length of performance and in expanding the horizons of jazz in the direction of "world music", Coltrane has had an enormous influence, for good and bad, on younger players of all instruments. While he also spawned a huge number of outright imitators (as did Armstrong and Parker before him), his encouragement of lesser-known musicians more "modern" than himself set a new and exemplary standard of selflessness and diversity. Perhaps this is why no single performer has come along to dominate the succeeding decades as Coltrane dominated the 1960s. [BP]

⊙ **Traneing In** (1957; Prestige/OJC). A comparatively straightahead quartet featuring Red Garland, redolent of Coltrane's first stint with Miles Davis, especially in the long medium-tempo blues of the title track.

⊙ **Blue Train** (1957; Blue Note). The would-be hard-bop sextet used on this session, with Lee Morgan and Curtis Fuller, introduces Trane's new harmonic interests in "A Moment's Notice" and "Lazy Bird", balanced by a ballad and by the blues of the title track and "Locomotion".

⊙ **Giant Steps** (1959–60; Atlantic). The first album to consist of original material, including "Naima" and others developed a couple of years earlier such as the title track. The CD edition also contains the takes of these tunes rejected by Coltrane in favour of the famous LP versions with Tommy Flanagan.

⊙ **My Favorite Things** (1960; Atlantic). The debut album of the quartet with McCoy Tyner and Elvin Jones introduced Trane's soprano and crystallized his modal approach

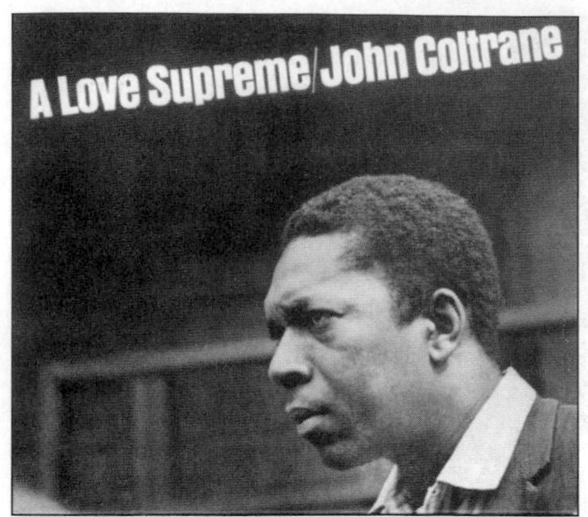

to standards such as the title waltz and an affecting "Ev'ry Time We Say Goodbye".

Complete Africa/Brass Sessions (1961; Impulse). A solitary experiment with an almost conventional big band has them doubling up for Tyner's piano on "Greensleeves" but sounding more jungleistic on "Africa"; this, like earlier Gillespie, added weight to the jazz/Afro-Latin crossover than just copying the rhythms.

Live At The Village Vanguard – The Master Takes (1961; Impulse). The tracks originally selected by Coltrane from four nights of recording (available complete in a box set) include "Chasin' The Trane" and "Impressions", which each have Coltrane soloing for fifteen straight minutes. Eric Dolphy is added to the quartet on another long live track, "India".

The Gentle Side Of John Coltrane (1961–3; Impulse). Like the compilation *In A Soulful Mood*, this is a record company's repackaging of one of Trane's strongest suits. As well as the quartet, there are guest appearances by Duke Ellington and singer Johnny Hartman.

A Love Supreme (1964; Impulse). The apotheosis of the Tyner-Garrison-Jones quartet, as well as Coltrane's religious beliefs.

Ascension (1965; Impulse). A recommended reissue combining two versions of the benchmark piece, which saw new players such as Archie Shepp and Pharoah Sanders in an eleven-piece line-up that incorporated dense collective improvisations.

➤➤ **Miles Davis** *(Cookin' And Relaxin');* **Duke Ellington** *(Duke Ellington And John Coltrane);* **Johnny Hartman** *(John Coltrane And Johnny Hartman);* **Thelonious Monk** *(Monk With John Coltrane).*

Ravi Coltrane

Tenor and soprano saxophones.

b. Huntington, New York, 6 Aug 1965.

The third child of pianist Alice Coltrane and saxophonist John Coltrane, Ravi Coltrane lost his father when he was two, and he moved with his mother and siblings to Woodland Hills, California, when he was six. He played clarinet in public school but didn't become seriously involved with jazz or the saxophone until 1986, when he began four years at the California Institute for the Arts under the tutelage of Paul Melrose and Charlie Haden. In 1991, referred by Wallace Roney, he was recruited by Elvin Jones, his father's former drummer, into Jones's Jazz Machine, and he followed the leader to New York. Parting ways with Jones in 1993, Coltrane became a favoured sideman for several progressive peers, including Roney, Geri Allen and Steve Coleman, as well as Joanne Brackeen, with whom he recorded. He also made several albums as co-leader (with fellow tenor Antoine Roney) of the group Grand Central, and finally recorded and toured under his own name with various quartets in the late 1990s and in special projects with his mother, Alice. He evolved an understated, personalized approach to his instruments, influenced by Joe Henderson and Sonny Stitt, manifest on his first two albums, *Moving Pictures* and *From the Round Box* (2000; RCA), although his music since has become more concentrated, focused and compelling on all fronts. [JK]

Moving Pictures (1998; BMG). Coltrane showcases an airy compositional style more concerned with spirit than groove, although the percussion unit, augmenting a fine rhythm-section, connects the young saxophonist with West African roots. Altoist Steve Coleman and trumpeter Ralph Alessi help spur Coltrane to some fine improvisation, while the leader's reading of standards by Joe Henderson, Wayne Shorter, Horace Silver and his father's former pianist McCoy Tyner displays an introspection and tenderness somewhat evocative of his departed dad.

Mad 6 (2002; BMG). Coltrane's third album begins with a restless take on his father's "24-7" and contains a dispensable version of "Round Midnight", but it really lifts off on "Avignon", and its wilder successor "The Mad 6" – both are beautifully single-minded exercises in group polyrhythm, the band following an *idée fixe* towards irresistible conclusions. Throughout, Jeff Hass' drums are hard and powerful, lending a muscular "drum'n'bass" feel to the album's rhythm-section.

Randolph Colville

Clarinet, saxophones, arranger.

b. Glasgow, Scotland, 23 May 1942; d. 15 Jan 2004.

Randolph (Randy) Colville graduated from the Northern School of Music in Manchester and later taught clarinet at his alma mater. Around Manchester he played anything from solo recitals to circuses, and was a later member of two famous local units, the Jazz Aces and the Saints Jazz Band. After his move south in the late 1970s Colville's warm tone, elegant improvisation and Matty Matlock-inspired approach produced a string of offers, and by the 1980s he was working regularly with Keith Nichols's Ragtime Orchestra, the Midnite Follies Orchestra (co-led by Nichols and Alan Cohen), and Alan Elsdon's band; from 1984 he was also an occasional substitute for Bruce Turner in Humphrey Lyttelton's band. More recently Colville continued to collaborate with Keith Nichols, starred in South Bank concerts (performing tributes to Benny Goodman and Artie Shaw, as well as the Mozart *Clarinet Quintet*), and led his own band, The Colville Collection. Apart from his clarinet skills, he was a painstaking arranger whose work has been featured by the Midnite Follies Orchestra, Elsdon, the all-trombone band Five-a-Slide and his own sextet. [DF]

Ken Colyer

Trumpet, guitar, vocals, leader.

b. Great Yarmouth, Norfolk, UK, 18 April 1928; d. 8 March 1988.

The spiritual and musical leader of British New Orleans jazz, Ken Colyer very early made it clear where his allegiances lay. "Ken played traditional not revivalist jazz", says George Melly. "His wavery vibrato and basic melodic approach was based on Bunk Johnson." Colyer's love was for the pure music of New Orleans, and after a controversial period of bandleading ("to ears attuned to Morton's Red Hot Peppers", says Melly, "Ken's band was a horrible noise") he rejoined the Merchant Navy, deserted in Mobile, Alabama, and took a Greyhound bus to New Orleans. There he sat in with such old masters as George Lewis and recorded with Emile Barnes and others. "The logical thing was to get there while the old men were still playing", said Colyer later. He was deported from the USA, went back to London, and after a brief collaboration with Chris Barber (whose ideals were different from his) formed his own band and began touring, playing clubs and recording.

For the next three decades this was, broadly speaking, to be Colyer's career pattern. In the 1950s he toured Britain with George Lewis (a close friend), led London's best jazz brass band, and recorded all through the decade. The collapse of the trad boom in 1962 made very little difference to Colyer's progress, as his aims had nothing to do with commercial appeal. Through the 1960s he continued touring Britain and Europe and recorded for a variety of independent labels, as well as regularly going back to his spiritual home, New Orleans. After a bout of stomach cancer he was forced to retire temporarily, but by the end of the 1970s he was back to full power, and in the 1980s was assuming legendary status in Britain. By 1987, however, after recurrent illness, he was living in a caravan in France and no longer playing. An autobiography published at that time, *When Dreams Are In The Dust*, testified to his occasional feelings of dismay at the state of jazz, but his life's work has been honoured since: by the Ken Colyer Trust, by a blue plaque mounted in his memory at the 100 Club in London, and by a steady stream of reissues. [DF]

⊙ **In The Beginning: The Decca Years Vol. 6** (1953–4; Lake). This important set contains Colyer's great "New Orleans To London" collection with Barber and Sunshine, plus the first tracks to feature his re-formed band with Ed O'Donnell and the young Acker Bilk.

⊙ **Marching Back To New Orleans: The Decca Years** (1955 & '57; Lake). The first sessions by Colyer's front-line with Mac Duncan and Ian Wheeler, plus Britain's first-ever parade-band recordings, led by Colyer.

⊙ **Serenading Auntie** (1955–60; Upbeat). BBC recordings by Colyer's Jazzmen; a high level of excitement throughout, and well recorded too, of course.

⊙ **Studio 51 Revisited** (1958; Lake). Live recordings from the Colyer club near Leicester Square, his spiritual home during the 1950s.

⊙ **Colyer's Pleasure** (1962–3; Lake). One of the great Colyer recordings with Sammy Rimington and Geoff Cole, augmented by five previously unissued tracks.

Eddie Condon

Guitar, banjo, composer, leader.

b. Goodland, Indiana, 16 Nov 1905; d. 4 Aug 1973.

The figurehead of Chicago jazz, Eddie Condon was a professional jazz banjoist at seventeen (with Hollis Peavey's Jazz Bandits) and by the 1920s had built a circle of gifted young friends, including Frank Teschemacher, Jimmy McPartland and Bud Freeman. On 10 December 1927 he co-led (with Red McKenzie) the first Chicago-style jazz records – "although", he qualified later, "we were just a bunch of musicians who happened to be in Chicago at the time!"

By 1928 he was in New York, working briefly and unhappily with Red Nichols, then more contentedly with Red McKenzie's Mound City Blue Blowers. With McKenzie, a kindred fighting spirit, Condon helped to set up great multiracial recording dates, with black musicians such as Louis Armstrong, Leonard Davis and Happy Caldwell alongside white ones including Jack Teagarden, Joe Sullivan and Gene Krupa: classics like "Knockin' A Jug" and "Mahogany Hall Stomp" were the result. In the early to mid-1930s he was busy sorting out his musical life up and down 52nd Street and by 1938 had formed two significant relationships: one with record producer Milt Gabler, who amended his Commodore re-issue policy to record Condon for the first time, and the other with club owner Nick Rongetti, at whose influential club he opened that year with Bobby Hackett. Nick's – or "Sizzlin's" as Condon called it – was a noisy, cheerful club and the guitarist made it his base of operations for the next eight years, combining work there with hotel concerts at the Park Lane and Belmont, co-promoted by Paul Smith and Ernie Anderson. In 1939 came the most polished of Condon's bands to date, the Summa Cum Laude, formed after a Princeton fraternity dance and made up of some of Condon's most compatible partners, including Max Kaminsky, Bud Freeman and Pee Wee Russell. The band recorded, toured and played onstage for an attractive but unsuccessful musical, *Swingin' The Dream*, starring Maxine Sullivan and Louis Armstrong, which, said Condon, "was open on Broadway for about three minutes".

By 1942 he had cemented a third professional relationship, with manager and publicist Ernie Anderson, and together they presented a Fats Waller concert at Carnegie Hall (a modest success), and soon after a set of Town Hall concerts, the last of which was televised for CBS. "A few weeks later", Condon recalled, "jazz was the hit of television." The concerts, developed and extended all through the war

years, were broadcast and issued on disc, making a valuable contribution to morale as well as presenting Condon's determined policy of desegregated, free-spirit jazz.

THE CHRONOGICAL
EDDIE CONDON
1944 - 1946
WITH JAMES P. JOHNSON, LEE WILEY, JACK TEAGARDEN, PEE WEE RUSSELL, BUD FREEMAN, BOBBY HACKETT, LOU McGARITY...
CLASSICS

In 1945 he opened his own club on West 3rd Street, round the corner from his Washington Square home, and it became the late spot for a crowd of stars: Robert Mitchum, John Steinbeck, Yul Brynner, Bing Crosby and Johnny Mercer were habitués. Looking sharp in his formal suit and bow tie, Condon would circulate, chatting in his bewilderingly fast staccato, laying groundwork for new plans (he called it "parish business"), filling his pockets with tiny indecipherable memos, and on occasion playing guitar. The band, on a stand at one end of the room, played long, loud and beautifully. House cornettist Wild Bill Davison recalls: "I've gone in there and felt like death but three minutes in and I forgot my illness. It went on till 4 every morning, never stopped swinging, people screaming and whiskey flying. It was New Year's Eve every day."

From the late 1940s Condon's name became international. Thanks to Anderson and personal manager John O'Connor, he had his own TV programme, the *Eddie Condon Floorshow*, a best-selling autobiography and a column in the *New York Journal-American*, "Pro and Condon". In the 1950s he began a long, fruitful recording relationship with George Avakian of Columbia: it produced albums which defined Condon's music and were in their time revolutionary with their inclusion of Condon's spoken comments at the ends of tracks. From that time he devoted himself to his club, to touring and to occasional writing: in 1957 *Eddie Condon's Treasury Of Jazz*, a classic compilation, was published. Condon toured Britain with his group in 1957, presenting music which critics tended to underplay while they sensationalized Condon's legendary drinking abilities. Back home, Condon grew tired of New York and began commuting to work three days and nights a week from a rambling house on the Jersey shore, where he lived lazily and enjoyed a steady stream of callers, from Muggsy Spanier to Bing Crosby (the period is enchantingly captured in Condon's last *Scrapbook Of Jazz*). But he continued to pursue a busy schedule – touring Australia, New Zealand and Japan in 1964 (in Japan he was once introduced as "the king of bop and the mayor of Greenwich Village"). That year he was taken into hospital, severely ill. A lightning recovery allowed him to appear at his own Carnegie Hall benefit concert but the following year he was ill again, and gently slowed down until his final trip to hospital in 1973.

It would be hard to overestimate Condon's contribution to jazz. He created an image for Chicago jazz and, more importantly, a collection of faultless recorded music. He was fiercely loyal to the musicians he loved, created a professional frame for them to shine in, and was a fine judge of humanity who liked the good things about people: genuineness, creativity, humility. "And", says Sidney Bechet, whose cause Condon championed, "he was a real fine musicianer." Says Bobby Hackett, "Eddie was the greatest rhythm guitarist you ever heard", and no one who knows the records will forget that sweet and plangent chime. [DF]

⊙ **Chronological Eddie Condon 1927–38, 1938–40 & 1942–3** (Classics). Part one of this chronology contains all Condon's titles under his own name from the McKenzie-Condon Chicagoans via his Hot Shots to the Commodore sessions of April 1938 ("Embraceable You", "Meet Me Tonight In Dreamland"). The second volume shows Condon's career maturing, with Teagarden and Hackett at peak form, plus classic Kaminsky sides ("Strut Miss Lizzie", "It's Right Here For You", etc) and the extended jam session at Commodore, "A Good Man Is Hard To Find – parts 1–4". Part three contains twelve favourite Condon titles, with fine contributions from Brad Gowans and Pee Wee Russell, plus Kaminsky on all tracks except the two with Yank Lawson ("Squeeze Me" and "That's A Plenty").

⊙ **Eddie Condon 1928–31** (Timeless). Likeably concentrating on Condon rather than his ever-stellar roster of sidemen, this issue has him with Miff Mole, the Mound City Blue Blowers and groups of his own; transfers by John R.T. Davies are superb as ever, and there are two alternate takes.

⊙ **Eddie Condon Dixieland All Stars: The Original Decca Recordings** (1939–46; MCA/GRP). This has many of Condon's best studio recordings of the period, with alternate takes; gold standard jazz, beautifully arranged and flawlessly performed.

⊙ **The Town Hall Concert Volumes 1–10** (1944; Jazzology). Ten double CDs (plus one triple) furnish complete transcriptions of Condon's weekly radio shows for the NBC Blue Network. In addition to appearances from Condon's seminal associates, there's talk by Condon, stylish announcements from Fred Robbins, bit-parts by Condon cronies from James P. Johnson to John Steinbeck – even war news flashes have been retained. Social history in the making – and great music too.

⊙ **Definitive Eddie Condon And His Jazz Concert All Stars** (1944; Stash). Tracks recorded for a radio transcription service with a roster of stars: Hackett, Hot Lips Page, Caceres, Butterfield, Pee Wee Russell and more. Includes breakdowns, false starts and other intriguing trivia.

⊙ **From Eddie Condon's, 47 West 3rd Street** (1951–2; Storyville). Lively Condon broadcasts with Cutty Cutshall, Ed Hall and Gene Schroeder, but most noticeable for the presence of the under-recorded and hugely talented trumpeter Johnny Windhurst.

Ringside At Condon's (1951–2; Savoy). Long unavailable, this is the definitive portrait of Condon music as it was heard night by night at his club (despite one or two inexplicable jumps in the CD repressing): Cutshall, Hall and Wild Bill Davison all caught at peak form.

Complete CBS Recordings Of Eddie Condon And His All Stars (1953–62; Mosaic). Absolutely essential Condon collation during his later period; included are "Jammin' At Condon's", "Bixieland", "Treasury Of Jazz", "Roaring Twenties", "Midnight In Moscow", "Dixieland Jam", the Condon portions of *Jam Session Coast To Coast* and *Armstrong/Condon Live At Newport* plus more. All Condon's greatest sidemen – Davison, Butterfield, Cutshall, Schroeder, Hucko, Cary and their peers – on peak form; this is possibly the greatest Dixieland ever.

Dixieland Jam (1957–8; CBS). First-class Condon in the form of unissued stereo sessions plus alternate takes; stars in attendance include Butterfield, Dickenson, Davison, Bob Wilber, Schroeder and an A-team rhythm-section.

Harry Connick Jnr

Piano, vocals.

b. New Orleans, 11 Sept 1967.

A former student at the New Orleans Center for Creative Arts (where he was taught by Ellis Marsalis), Connick played piano and sang in Bourbon Street saloons before recording two widely praised albums. But it was his contribution to the soundtrack of the Meg Ryan/Billy Crystal film *When Harry Met Sally* which focused widespread attention on Connick's chunkily individualistic piano playing (which incorporates elements of Garner, Hines and Monk), and on his singing, which is often compared to the young Frank Sinatra but has a grittier edge. He won a Grammy for the score, and from there has quickly achieved international success with concerts (fronting a high-powered big band since 1990), television, a string of best-selling albums and a further contribution to the movies – the soundtrack of *Sleepless In Seattle* (also starring Ryan, this time with Tom Hanks).

Although greeted with suspicion by the hard-core jazz community because of his matinee-idol looks and the hype which surrounded his apparently fully formed appearance on the musical scene when barely out of his teens, Connick rendered their opinions increasingly irrelevant in the mid-1990s by broadening his approach with the pop-funk of *She* (1994) and *Star Turtle* (1996), then with the romantic balladry of *To See You* (1998). He remains, however, a compelling performer with a serious interest in the history and development of New Orleans music, which, of course, embraces everything from traditional jazz to the greasiest funk. By 2003 Connick could be seen as father-figure to later emergents including Jamie Cullum. [DF/CP]

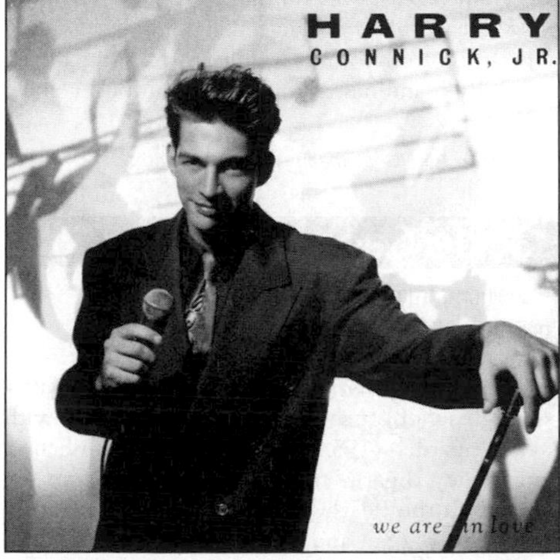

20 (1989; CBS). A detailed exposition of Connick's solo piano talent and lazily charming singing, encompassing tunes from "Avalon" (played as a piano solo) and "Do You Know What It Means To Miss New Orleans" (with Dr John) to Arlen's "If I Only Had A Brain" from *The Wizard of Oz* and "Please Don't Talk About Me When I'm Gone" (with the late Carmen McRae).

We Are In Love (1990; Columbia). Attractive, if derivative selection of standards and originals sung to strings and Connick's own trio fleshed out by saxophonist Branford Marsalis and guitarist Russell Malone.

Lofty's Roach Soufflé (1990; Columbia). Fair representation of Connick's pianistic talents with regular trio.

25 (1992; Columbia). Guests Ellis Marsalis, Johnny Adams, Ray Brown and Ned Goold join Connick on this jazz-weighted collection ranging from Coltrane's "Moment's Notice" to Ory's "Muskrat Ramble", plus ballads like "This Time The Dream's On Me" and "Music Maestro Please".

Ray Conniff

Trombone, arranger.

b. Attleboro, Massachusetts, 6 Nov 1916; d. 12 Oct 2002.

Conniff began his career with Dan Murphy (1936), then joined Bunny Berigan's band in 1937 before moving on to join Bob Crosby (1939–40). A brief period with Artie Shaw followed (a notable Conniff solo is the striking tight-muted outburst on Shaw's "Beyond The Blue Horizon"), then Conniff led his own octet in 1941 before working with Harry James, Dave Matthews and Shaw again before moving into studio work including for ABC (1954). A year later Conniff gave up trombone to concentrate on developing "the Conniff sound", an orchestral device comprising male and female groups of session singers, singing currently popular songs in a wordless swing-style paraphrase, block harmony or unison, along with a trumpet, trombone or saxophone section. Conniff's highly successful formula won him a Grammy in 1966 (for "Somewhere My Love", also known as "Lara's Theme"), and his orchestra and singers also toured with Johnny Mathis as well as appearing in concert. The highly successful formula had little to offer jazz followers, but on at least two recorded occasions Conniff teamed up again with his old Bob Crosby colleague Billy Butterfield, producing two worthwhile albums, *Just Kiddin' Around* and *Mr Conniff Meets Mr Butterfield*. [DF]

➤➤ **Billy Butterfield** *(Mr Conniff Meets Mr Butterfield).*

Chris Connor

Vocals.

b. Kansas City, Missouri, 8 Nov 1927.

A one-time clarinettist, Chris Connor achieved international fame after she was hired by Stan Kenton in 1952 on the recommendation of June Christy. (By that time she had already sung with Claude Thornhill's vocal group The Snowflakes, then as featured soloist with Thornhill.) After Kenton she turned solo in 1953, signing to Bethlehem for a series of albums including *The Rich Sound Of Chris Connor, Lullabies Of Birdland* and *This Is Chris*, followed by a period with Atlantic, producing more well-rated albums such as *Chris Craft* (1958) and *Ballads Of The Sad Café* (1959). Connor's career stayed steady in the 1960s, but with the revival of interest in jazz in the 1970s she staged a comeback, recording for Progressive, Stash and Contemporary, and in the 1990s was still touring internationally. [DF]

⊙ **Sings The George Gershwin Almanac Of Song** (1985; Atlantic). This double CD set is a connoisseur's collection of Gershwin classics and should-be classics.

Junior Cook

Tenor saxophone.

b. Pensacola, Florida, 22 July 1934; d. 4 Feb 1992.

After a brief stay with Dizzy Gillespie in 1958 Cook worked for ten years with basically one group, first as the Horace Silver quintet (1958–64), then as the Blue Mitchell quintet (1964–9). He then taught at Berklee School, and gigged with Freddie Hubbard, Elvin Jones and George Coleman before co-leading quintets with Louis Hayes in 1975–6 and Bill Hardman from 1979–81, and recording with Eddie Jefferson. From 1988–91 he made several albums, and also performed and recorded with the McCoy Tyner big band. He was an extremely competent player who sometimes ran the risk of sounding somewhat anonymous through his complete mastery of post-bop tenor styles. [BP]

⊙ **On A Misty Night** (1989; Steeplechase). Cook is completely in command here with a quartet including pianist Mickey Tucker, playing material such as the Tadd Dameron title track and the Arthur Schwartz song "By Myself".

Willie Cook

Trumpet.

b. Tangipahoa, Louisiana, 11 Nov 1923; d. 22 Sept 2000.

Willie Cook's first band after leaving school was King Perry's Fletcher Henderson-style orchestra, after which he moved to Jay McShann in early 1943 and then to Earl Hines for four years. "My first real influence on trumpet was Harry James", he told Stanley Dance later, "then Louis Armstrong and a little later on Charlie Spivak. I always did like melodic playing and I guess I intended to be a first horn man from the beginning." After Hines he worked with Jimmie Lunceford's orchestra for six months, then with Dizzy Gillespie (1948–50), Gerald Wilson and Billie Holiday (as her MD for a year), before joining Duke Ellington in 1951. From then until Ellington's death he was regularly coming and going. "Willie Cook has always been potentially the best first trumpeter in the business. ... his taste as a soloist is quickly proved to anyone who listens to his records", said Ellington, though the presence in the orchestra of outstanding soloists such as Clark Terry sometimes masked Cook's solo strength. In the decade after Ellington's death he toured Europe, recorded prolifically in Sweden and elsewhere, and became far better known as a soloist, working in Britain at clubs such as Pizza Express in 1985 and, also that year, attending the annual Duke Ellington Convention with fellow guests Bob Wilber and Jimmy Hamilton (as he did again in 1994). [DF]

Count Basie

⊙ **Kansas City Six** (1981; Pablo/OJC). Not to be compared with the early sessions of the same name, this sextet has Basie leading "Cleanhead" Vinson on alto and vocals, plus the forthright Cook as the other frontline man.

Micky Cooke

Trombone.

b. Hyde, Cheshire, UK, 6 Aug 1945.

Cooke worked with Terry Lightfoot's band in the 1960s, where his shouting Abe Lincoln-influenced style attracted much attention. Later, after freelance work for leaders including Dave Shepherd, Lennie Hastings, Pete Allen and Alan Elsdon, he joined Keith Smith's Hefty Jazz, with whom he worked regularly, taking part in all of Smith's highly successful ventures and touring the USA with him in 1985. He is one of the hottest and most technically able British trombonists. In July 1987 Cooke joined Acker Bilk, and has remained with him ever since. [DF]

➤➤ **Acker Bilk** *(Chalumeau – That's My Home).*

Jackie Coon

Flugelhorn, trumpet.

b. Beatrice, Nebraska, date unknown.

Coon took up cornet at eleven years old and after high school turned professional working with Jack Teagarden (1954), Bob Crosby, Red Nichols and Barney Bigard, amongst others. He spent ten years with the Pearly Band at Disneyland, before moving to Big Sur and concentrating on the flugelhorn. A regular at festivals, jazz parties and cruises in later years, Coon's career lacks the high profile of stylistic contemporaries such as Yank Lawson or Billie Butterfield, and until recently he was notably under-recorded. But he is a lyrical player of great value whose work is now gaining international attention via solo recording for the Arbors label. [DF]

⊙ **Jack Teagarden: The Club Hangover Broadcasts 1954** (1995; Arbors). A double CD of Teagarden live takes from "Doc" Dougherty's famous San Francisco venue. Coon had just replaced trumpeter Charlie Teagarden in Jack's band, and his work – if marginally less commanding – has much of the same elegance, fire and technique.

⊙ **Softly** (1998; Arbors). Later Coon in compatible company, including Johnny Varro, Bob Haggart, Ed Metz and guests. His flugelhorn here – audacious, fluffy-toned and friendly – occasionally recalls later Billy Butterfield, and he sings appealingly too on "Look For The Silver Lining".

Coon-Sanders Nighthawks

The Coon-Sanders Nighthawks were a highly successful jazz-based dance orchestra, co-led by drummer Carlton Coon and pianist Joe Sanders, originally formed in Kansas City after World War I. Resident at the Muehlebach Hotel, the band also broadcast for station WDAF from 1921, and their polished, sometimes hot music was soon in such demand that they secured a long residency at Chicago's Blackhawk Restaurant from 1926. From here they broadcast regularly and gained a following among jazz lovers: many of their arrangements, "Brainstorm" for one, were published as "stocks" (ie standard arrangements for purchase by amateur, and sometimes professional, orchestras in search of repertoire). Coon died on 5 May 1932, after an operation on a septic tooth, but Sanders took over leadership, billed the orchestra as the Original Nighthawks and remained active in the Midwest until 1950 (with regular trips back to the Blackhawk). He died in Kansas in May 1965, but ex-members of the orchestra (eg Leonard Schwartz) were still active in the late 1980s. [DF]

⊙ **The Best Of Coon-Sanders Original Nighthawk Orchestra 1924–32** (Retrieval). Overdue reissue and as good as you'd expect. Compiled by Chris Ellis and remastered by John R.T. Davies, important titles including "Brainstorm", "Too Busy" and "Flamin' Mamie".

Alan Cooper

E flat, B flat and bass-clarinet.

b. Leeds, UK, 15 Feb 1931.

Cooper is a veteran of the Yorkshire Jazz Band, Anglo-American Alliance and Temperance Seven (which suited his naturally zany sense of humour). His intriguing gas-pipe lower register and stifled bronchial sound in the upper were the perfect expression for his piquant, very melodic and defiantly original ideas. A naturally eccentric but highly talented player, Cooper is – after Sandy Brown – the most original clarinettist on Britain's classic jazz scene. [DF]

Bob Cooper

Tenor saxophone, oboe.

b. Pittsburgh, Pennsylvania, 6 Dec 1925; d. 6 Aug 1993.

Cooper first came to prominence playing tenor with Stan Kenton from 1945–51, during which period he married June Christy. He then settled on the West Coast to become a freelance, and added the oboe to his arsenal. A regular member of the Lighthouse All Stars from 1952–62, he recorded with Shorty Rogers, Pete Rugolo and Christy, with whom he also toured. He made his living as a studio musician from the late 1960s, and also appeared regularly from the late 1970s with the occasional big bands of Frank Capp-Nat Pierce and Bob Florence. In the late 1980s and early 1990s he worked again with Rogers and the re-formed Lighthouse All Stars. As well as being the first person to record convincing jazz on the oboe, Cooper was a highly respected tenor soloist in the 1950s post-Lester Young style. [BP]

⊙ **Coop!** (1957; Contemporary/OJC). An effective, if somewhat low-key, showcase for Cooper's tenor, featuring mostly a sextet with Victor Feldman on vibes and the great Frank Rosolino on trombone.

➤➤ **Digby Fairweather** *(Songs For Sandy).*

Lindsay Cooper

Bassoon, piano, sopranino and alto saxophones, oboe, composer.

b. London, 3 March 1951.

Cooper had a brief career as a freelance classical bassoonist, followed by work with various pop, theatre and improvised-music groups from 1970–73. She played with the post-Frank Zappa rock group Henry Cow from 1974–8; the Feminist Improvising Group from 1977–82; and the Mike Westbrook orchestra from 1979–83. From 1982–5 she also worked with David Thomas and the Pedestrians. Since 1984 she has led her own group, the Lindsay Cooper Film Music Orchestra, but has found time to play with most of the big guns of the European and US free improv scene: Derek Bailey's group Company, Maggie Nicols, Irene Schweizer, Joelle Leandre, George Lewis, John Zorn, Lol Coxhill, Georgie Born and Lauren Newton, among others. She has written many scores for films and TV, including *The Gold Diggers* (1983), directed by Sally Potter, and also several compositions for dance and theatre including *Face On* (1983), a dance show by Maedee Dupres.Her song-cycle *Oh Moscow* was recorded live at the 1989 Victoriaville festival in Canada, and in 1991 an album of her contemporary dance pieces, *Schrödinger's Cat*, was released.

In 1992 she premiered her *Concerto for Sopranino Saxophone And Strings* in London, and her *Songs For Bassoon And Orchestra* was performed in Bologna. Cooper has developed into a virtuoso of the sopranino saxophone and an extraordinarily versatile composer. *A View From the Bridge* (1999), spanning two CDs, compiled a long-overdue retrospective of her work. [IC]

Oh Moscow (1989; Victo). Inspired by Sally Potter's texts about twentieth-century history and German nationalism, Cooper's music is scored for a septet comprising tenor saxophone and piano, Sally Potter's and Phil Minton's voices, bassist Hugh Hopper and percussionist Marilyn Mazur. The writing is taut and full of incident and the band responds with great panache.

>> **Mike Westbrook** *(Westbrook-Rossini).*

Marc Copland

Piano, alto saxophone.
b. Philadelphia, 27 May 1948.

Copland played in his hometown before going to New York to study music at Columbia University. Under his family name of Cohen, he worked as a saxophonist with Chico Hamilton and others in the early 1970s, before leaving New York for the next decade in order to develop his piano playing. When he returned to the jazz scene he specialized as a pianist and, from 1985, spent three years with James Moody before leading his own groups with such musicians as Bill Stewart, Billy Hart, John Abercrombie and Gary Peacock. Recordings and tours in the 1990s featured these collaborators and others including both Brecker brothers, Bob Berg, Joe Lovano, Greg Osby and Kenny Wheeler, while a spate of records since 2000 has included duo sets with Osby and Dave Liebman. On visits to Europe he has also performed and recorded with Stan Sulzmann. While his playing behind saxophonists is beneficially informed by his own background, his lyrical and sensitive interpretations reveal an innate understanding of the piano. [BP]

Marc Copland And... (2002; Hat Hut). Copland's current trio, with bassist Drew Gress and drummer Jochen Rueckert, plays host to John Abercrombie on five numbers and Michael Brecker on two long tracks, "Canteloupe Island" and "See You Again".

>> **Stan Sulzmann** *(Never At All).*

Chick Corea

Piano, composer, keyboards; also drums.
b. Chelsea, Massachusetts, 12 June 1941.

Corea began on piano at the age of six and drums at eight. From 1962–6 he worked with Mongo Santamaria, Willie Bobo, Blue Mitchell and Herbie Mann, going on to record with Stan Getz in 1967 and also started leading his own groups. From 1968–70 he worked with Miles Davis, touring internationally, appearing at most major festivals, and playing on some of the trumpeter's most important and influential albums, including *Filles De Kilimanjaro, In A Silent Way*, *Bitches Brew* and *Live-Evil*. Until he joined Davis, Corea had been known on the New York scene as a brilliant acoustic pianist notable for his composing, his familiarity with Latin idioms, and for an eclectic style compounded of his main influences: Tatum, Hancock, Tyner, Monk, Bud Powell and Bill Evans. His 1968 trio album, *Now He Sings, Now He Sobs*, shows his consummate ability at that time and also hints at his growing interest in the freer and more European aspects of the contemporary avant-garde.

The exposure with Davis made him an international jazz star, establishing him as one of the leading performers on electric keyboards, and the group's non-harmonic, often polytonal jazz-rock music gave Corea the freedom to explore abstraction as much as he wished. In 1970 he and bassist Dave Holland left the Davis band to form Circle, with Anthony Braxton (reeds) and Barry Altschul (drums), which, for the most part, went even more deeply into the European vein of abstraction. It created an acoustic music which often bore no relation to African-American forms such as the blues or gospel, no coherent physical rhythmic grooves, but which featured much scurrying and chittering non-tonal improvisation. Circle toured in the USA and Europe, recording a live double album in Paris and two studio LPs for Blue Note, but, at the end of 1971, Corea left the group suddenly. Years later, recalling this period, he said to John Toner, "When I see an artist using his energies and technique to create a music way beyond the ability of people to connect with it, I see his abilities being wasted."

He played briefly with the Stan Getz quartet, then at the beginning of 1972, with Stanley Clarke, Airto Moreira, Airto's wife Flora Purim, and Joe Farrell, he formed Return To Forever (RTF), an electric, jazz-rock group with a strong Latin flavour, and one of the most delightful and original fusion groups of the 1970s. Its music combined elements from rock, jazz, Latin and classical music, and it became one of the most successful groups of the decade. RTF went through several line-ups and included Bill Connors, Steve Gadd, Al DiMeola, Lenny White and Gayle Moran among its members. The final version broke up in 1980, but there was a reunion tour in 1983.

In the later 1970s and early 1980s Corea began concentrating again on acoustic piano and toured worldwide in duo with Herbie Hancock and with Gary Burton. He also collaborated from 1980–85 with Mike Brecker, Steve Gadd, Eddie Gomez, Roy Haynes, Miroslav Vitous, Keith Jarrett, Friedrich Gulda and various classical musicians. In 1984 he recorded Mozart's concerto for two pianos, and in 1985 he composed his own piano concerto which had its premiere in the USA in February 1986 and was performed later that year in Japan. That year he also returned to electric keyboards, launching his new Elektric Band with bassist John Patitucci and drummer Dave Weckl. Later there was an Akoustic Band, and in the 1990s he toured playing solo piano (although, like RTF, the Elektric Band reunited for a tour in 2003).

Raffaella Cavalieri

Chick Corea

In 1992, Corea set up his own successful record label, Stretch Records, to release his own recordings and that of kindred spirits. He also put together an all-star group of Roy Haynes, Kenny Garrett, Christian McBride, Joshua Redman and Wallace Roney to record a tribute to the memory of pianist Bud Powell, a dynamic attempt to re-examine his bebop roots. In 1998, Corea toured with a band of young virtuosi – Bob Sheppard and Steve Wilson on saxophones, trombonist Steve Davis, bassist Avishai Cohen and drummer Adam Cruz – because he had begun to feel a need for a steady band for which he could compose and arrange regularly. He also kept in touch with his classical roots by collaborating with Singer Bobby McFerrin in *The Mozart Sessions* (Sony Classical) with the Saint Paul Chamber Orchestra, and in 1999 he came to London and recorded his piano concerto and an arrangement of his composition "Spain" with the London Philharmonic Orchestra conducted by Steven Mercurio, also for Sony Classical. In a move reminiscent of his Elektric/Akoustic Band dichotomy, he recorded two complementary solo piano albums in 2000: one of his own compositions; one addressing standards.

Chick Corea ranks alongside Herbie Hancock and Keith Jarrett as one of the leading pianists and bandleaders since the late 1960s. He is one of the most original and gifted composers in jazz, and many of his pieces, including "Spain", "La Fiesta", "What Games Shall We Play Today", "Spanish Song", "Tones For Joan's Bones" and "Return To Forever", have entered the standard jazz repertoire. He told John Toner in 1974, "What I am striving for is incorporating the discipline and beauty of the symphony orchestra and classical composers – the subtlety and beauty of harmony, melody and form – with the looseness and rhythmic dancing quality of jazz and more folky musics." [IC]

Chick Corea

⊙ **Now He Sings, Now He Sobs** (1968; Blue Note). This, Corea's first recording under his own name, is one of the great albums of the 1960s. His trio with Miroslav Vitous and Roy Haynes is a superlative unit, and Corea himself is simply bursting with fresh ideas. Apart from one standard, "My One And Only Love" and Monk's "Pannonica", all the other eleven compositions are by Corea and they range from structured to semi-free and totally abstract. Haynes and Vitous handle this great diversity of approach with breathtaking panache.

⊙ **The Song Of Singing** (1970; Blue Note). Another trio album, this time with Dave Holland and Barry Altschul. The approach is freer and a couple of totally improvised ballads are included. Corea and Holland had been with Miles Davis since 1968 and had developed a considerable rapport, and Altschul had worked with Paul Bley, that early pioneer of free improvisation, all of which forged the effortless three-way communication on this occasion.

Circle

⊙ **Paris Concert** (1971; ECM). To the above trio was now added avant-garde saxophonist Anthony Braxton. Abstraction is the name of the game, but the group also play a long workout on Wayne Shorter's "Nefertiti", albeit taken pretty far out, and give a more conventional, though violent, performance of the standard "No Greater Love". In his gushing sleevenote, Corea asserts that "the moment's forever" but the following year he was to drop abstraction and Circle like a hot potato and "return to forever" another way.

Chick Corea

Piano Improvisations Vols. 1 & 2 (1971; ECM). This collection of short improvisations with some assistance from Ida Kavafian's violin and Fred Sherry's cello was recorded just two months after the Circle double album. At this point in time, Corea's life and musical conceptions were in the melting pot and his mind was wonderfully concentrated – with the result that these pieces are brief and distilled to the essence.

Return To Forever

Return To Forever (1972; ECM). The clarity, lightness and tunefulness of the music come as a pleasant surprise: electric piano, Joe Farrell confined to flute and soprano saxophone, Flora Purim's sweet treble and the masterstroke – the light touch of Latin genius Airto Moreira on drums. Corea's composing, whether minimal or full-blooded, always has a touch of magic: the long title track moves through a series of rhythmic and textural changes, and "Crystal Silence", a duo performance by electric piano and soprano saxophone, is played with unfixed tempo throughout – shades of Miles Davis's *In A Silent Way*.

Light As A Feather (1972; Polydor). This is the second and last album by the first RTF band, and it is even more brilliant than the debut, with some of Corea's best compositions – "Captain Marvel", "500 Miles High" and "Spain" all performed by a great band in the full flush of its joyous creative dynamism.

Chick Corea

Crystal Silence (1979; ECM). An inspired duo album with vibist Gary Burton.

Three Quartets (1981; Stretch). Corea's group here comprises Michael Brecker, Eddie Gomez and Steve Gadd. In composing these quite tightly structured quartets Corea tried to synthesize his jazz and classical experience, with surprisingly satisfying results. The musicians take the structures in their stride, and Brecker is in great form. The second quartet is in two parts – the first dedicated to Duke Ellington and the second to John Coltrane. The band also lets its hair down with a few looser pieces, including a wild duo performance of "Confirmation" by Brecker and Gadd.

Expressions (1993; GRP). A superb solo piano album consisting of three Corea originals and twelve standards. The whole thing is dedicated to Art Tatum, whose benign spirit infuses several of the performances.

Remembering Bud Powell (1996; Stretch). Corea arranged nine of Powell's pieces and also composed his own "Bud Powell" for this loving act of homage. Both the young(ish) lions and the elder statesmen (Corea and Haynes) rise to the occasion.

Native Sense (1997; Stretch). The duo of Corea and Gary Burton play eleven of the former's compositions plus two of Bartok's "Bagatelles" and Monk's "Four In One", with tremendous muscularity, swing, panache and feeling.

Bob Cornford

Piano, keyboards, composer, arranger.

b. Brazil, 15 May 1940; d. London, 18 July 1983.

Cornford studied at the Royal College of Music, London, and became interested in jazz after hearing Bill Evans. He worked as the pianist/arranger for John Dankworth in the early 1960s and wrote many arrangements for the BBC, featuring singers including Mark Murphy, Sandra King, Norma Winstone, Elaine Delmar and soloists including Tony Coe, Bobby Wellins and Kenny Wheeler. In 1969 three performances of his own music and a public concert with the Danish State Radio Orchestra were broadcast. The North German Radio Orchestra (NDR) performed Cornford's thirty-minute composition *Coalescence* in memory of Ben Webster, and in 1982 they performed his *In Memoriam*, a tribute to Bill Evans. From 1977 Cornford was a member of Tony Coe's small group Axel, and he also played in groups with Wellins, Wheeler, Alan Skidmore, Phil Lee and others. In June 1983 he played with Lee Konitz at the Canteen in London. One month later Cornford died of a heart attack at the age of only 43. He had a consuming interest in all types of music, his favourite pianists being Bill Evans and Herbie Hancock, and other particular inspirations were Gil Evans and Ben Webster, but he was also fascinated by the post-Romantic soundworlds of Webern, Debussy and Ravel. A superb composer and arranger and a sensitive pianist, if he had a fault (if such a thing can be called a fault) it is that he lacked the essential ego flaunted by many jazz artists, which is why so little of his work is available on record. [IC]

>> **Tony Coe** *(Tournée Du Chat).*

Larry Coryell

Guitar, composer.

b. Galveston, Texas, 2 April 1943.

As a teenager, Coryell played rock'n'roll guitar in a group run by seventeen-year-old Mike Mandel. He then studied journalism at the University of Washington in Seattle, though continued playing in rock and jazz groups. But he left university before his final year and moved to New York in 1965, joining Chico Hamilton. In 1966, with Bob Moses and Jim Pepper, he formed Free Spirits, possibly the first electric jazz-rock group. Then he and Moses joined Gary Burton's quartet, touring internationally with it in 1967–8. Coryell played briefly with Herbie Mann, recording *Memphis Underground*, one of the seminal albums of the period, before forming his own group Foreplay with saxophonist Steve Marcus and Mike Mandel on keyboards.

In 1970 he recorded the album *Spaces* with the dizzying line-up of John McLaughlin, Chick Corea, Miroslav Vitous and Billy Cobham, and in 1973 formed another jazz-rock group, The Eleventh House, which included Mandel, Randy Brecker and Alphonse Mouzon. The group was a great success, touring extensively, in Europe and Japan.

When it broke up, Coryell concentrated on acoustic guitar for some years. He toured in Europe in 1975 playing solo acoustic guitar, and began playing duos with Philip Catherine in 1976, touring Europe twice with him and playing major festivals including Montreux and Newport. Coryell also toured in an acoustic trio with McLaughlin and Paco De Lucia. In the late 1970s he played on two of

Mingus's albums, and in 1979 recorded with guitarist John Scofield. Extending his range in the 1980s, he recorded some classical pieces for Nippon Phonogram – his versions of Rimsky-Korsakov's *Scheherazade* and Stravinsky's *Firebird, Petrushka* and *The Rite Of Spring*. By the mid-1980s Coryell was touring again, returning to electric guitar with a trio consisting of Mouzon and French bass guitarist Bunny Brunel.

Coryell's career has been dogged by crises of both confidence and identity, because he has rarely been able to unify the opposing facets of his enormous talent. He has been, at one time or another, a brash, loud, electrified rock'n'roller, an urbane jazz soloist, a sensitive acoustic guitarist, and a classical performer. In a sense, his dilemma is the dilemma of jazz today. But throughout all his anguish and soul-searching since he appeared on the scene in the mid-1960s, he has been one of the most consistently interesting performers – a brilliant and compelling soloist with a superb technique and the ability to surprise delightfully. [IC]

Spaces (1970; Start). The band is an all-star affair with John McLaughlin, Miroslav Vitous, Billy Cobham and Chick Corea added for one track, and the music is a mixture of straight jazz and jazz-rock – all executed with great strength and sensitivity. "Rene's Theme" is an acoustic guitar duet which harks back to Django Reinhardt in its rhythmic bite and brilliance.

The Eleventh House (1973; Vanguard). One of the more creative albums of the jazz-rock era. With Randy Brecker, Alphonse Mouzon, keyboardist Mike Mandel and bassist Danny Trifan, Coryell ran the gamut from extreme virtuosity to spacey, atmospheric minimalism. The bulk of the composing was done by the leader, Mandel and Mouzon, but there is a spirited performance of Wolfgang Dauner's wayward but wonderful "Yin".

Twin House (1976–7; Act). A series of guitar duets with Philip Catherine (although pianist Joachim Kuhn makes an apearance on one track), it nods to the past, but the two guitarists mainly come up with new themes and ideas.

Tributaries (1978–9; Novus). This acoustic guitar album has five solo tracks by Coryell; a duo with Joe Beck and one with John Scofield; and five more performances by this guitar trio. At this point in his career, Coryell seems to be feeling his way back to straight jazz playing.

A Quiet Day In Spring (1983; Steeplechase). The chemistry works well on this trio outing with violinist Michael Urbaniak and bassist Jesper Lundgaard. The music is airy and evocative, resonant with feeling.

Together (1985; Concord). Coryell is in duo here with guitarist Emily Remler, who died very prematurely of a heart attack in 1990. She and Coryell toured internationally as a duo and were also romantically linked, and their intimacy informs and illuminates the entire album.

Equipoise (1985; Muse); **Toku Du** (1987; Muse); **Shining Hour** (1990; Muse). The small groups on these three albums all have conventional jazz trio rhythm-sections, and Coryell gets down to some highly focused playing with them. The personnel varies, but bassist Buster Williams is on all three discs and Pamela Sklar's flute is added to *Equipoise*.

Live From Bahia (1992; CTI). Here, Coryell collaborates with the legendary Brazilian singer, songwriter and guitarist Dori Caymmi, aided by Billy Cobham, saxophonist Donald Harrison and nine Brazilian musicians including the superb trumpeter Marcio Montarroyas. The result is world music full of rich sonorities and mellow feeling, often enhanced by Caymmi's gentle voice. On Coryell's "Bloco Loco" and Montarroyas's "Bahian Night Walk" the band digs deep rhythmically, breaking the mould, and there are blazing solos from Coryell's guitar and Marcio's trumpet.

Spaces Revisited (1997; Shanachie). The main thing in common with his 1970s *Spaces* album is the instrumentation of two guitars, bass and drums. Billy Cobham is back, but in place of John McLaughlin is guitarist Birelli Lagrene, and the African bassist Richard Bona replaces Miroslav Vitous. The sound is different from the original, but long experience has sharpened the pith and moment of Coryell and Cobham without blunting their passion, and the quartet's performances are inspired.

➤➤ **Herbie Mann** *(Memphis Underground)*; **Jack Walrath** *(Out Of The Tradition).*

Eddie Costa

Piano, vibes.

b. Atlas, Pennsylvania, 14 Aug 1930; d. 28 July 1962.

Costa played with Joe Venuti in New York in 1949, then after army service did freelance work with Kai Winding and others. He worked and recorded on piano with Tal Farlow's trio from 1956–8 and, doubling on vibes, with Woody Herman's sextet in 1958–9 and his own trio. He was increasingly in demand for studio work on vibes by the time of his death in a car accident. Costa's piano style, long underrated, was characterized by a combination of percussiveness and mobility; the sound particularly identified with him was the use of the lower half of the keyboard for fast-running bebop lines (sometimes in octave unison), but his attacking accompaniments were also noteworthy. [BP]

Guys And Dolls Like Vibes (1958; Verve). The only one of his few feature albums to be reissued, this places Costa's inventive vibraphone alongside a rhythm section featuring Bill Evans and Paul Motian.

➤➤ **Tal Farlow** *(The Swinging Guitar).*

Mike Cotton

Trumpet, flugelhorn, harmonica, vocals, leader.

b. Hackney, London, 12 Aug 1939.

From early years as a Dixieland bandleader, Mike Cotton cannily moved with the times, changing to a format embracing rock'n'roll, R&B and soul music, and in 1964 re-forming his band as the Mike Cotton Sound. From then until 1971 his group was highly successful and backed a succession of American soul visitors including Doris Troy, Solomon Burke and Sugar Pie DeSanto. After Cotton broke up his band he freelanced briefly, then joined the Kinks, a British rock legend whose leader Ray Davies had a weakness for jazz. After two more successful years Cotton came back to jazz, took over Bill Nile's band briefly and then joined Acker Bilk in 1973. After leaving in 1991 Cotton played with the Harry Strutters Hot Rhythm Orchestra, in a quintet with John Barnes, and with Bob Hunt's Ellington tribute group. In 1994 he joined The Great British Jazz Band (on lead trumpet) and in addition to freelancing on land cruised regularly, leading jazz bands for comedian Jim Bowen and others. From 2002 he also joined clarinettist Andy Cooper's Euro Top Eight.

A strong, powerful soloist with an enviable range and occasional interest in electronic experiments (at one point he used a set-up similar to trumpeter Don Ellis's), Cotton works naturally in the mainstream area occupied in America by players such as Bill Berry, and is a consistently impressive if underrated musician. [DF]

➤➤ **Dave Shepherd** *(The Great British Jazz Band).*

Stanley Cowell

Piano, keyboards.

b. Toledo, Ohio, 5 May 1941.

Taught first by his sisters, Cowell studied the piano from the age of four. In New York from 1966, he played with Marion Brown in 1966–7, Max Roach from 1967–70, Stan Getz in 1969 and the Bobby Hutcherson-Harold Land quintet from 1968–71. In the early 1970s he formed the quartet Music Inc, the record label Strata-East and the organization Collective Black Artists Inc, all with Charles Tolliver, his colleague in the Roach group. A member of the Heath Brothers band from 1974–83, he also organized the Piano Choir, recorded solo piano works by Jimmy Heath and received a National Endowment for the Arts grant for his own writing. Since 1981 he has been an associate professor at the City University of New York, and in 1991 he wrote a piano concerto in honour of Art Tatum, whom he first heard at the age of six. He made few records until recent years, but his total command of jazz piano, especially in solo performances, is impressive. [BP]

⊙ **Back To The Beautiful** (1989; Concord). Mostly by a trio including Joe Chambers, this set of standards and four originals features a guest appearance by Steve Coleman, and ends with an unaccompanied version of "A Nightingale Sang In Berkeley Square".

Anthony Cox

Double bass, electric bass, acoustic bass guitar.

b. Ardmore, Oklahoma, 24 Oct 1954.

Cox writes, "My career seems to be one of many styles and an ever evolving network of players", and it is certainly true that he is so consummate a bassist, with such a broad concept of music, that he has been, and still is, much in demand across styles and genres. He has played with saxophonists Charles Lloyd, Sam Rivers, Stan Getz, Henry Threadgill, Joe Lovano and Gary Thomas; guitarists Jon Scofield, Kenny Burrell and Marc Ducret; brass players Craig Harris and Jon Faddis; drummers Elvin Jones, Ronnie Burrage, Ed Blackwell and Gene Jackson; and pianist Geri Allen. Cox has also co-led groups including Rios, with frequent collaborator David Friedman and Dino Saluzzi, Third Kind've Blue, with Burrage and John Purcell, Other Worlds with Jean Louis Matinier and Friedman, and his own Anthony Cox Group, a quartet with Michael Cain, Billy Higgins and Dewey Redman. Cox has recorded many albums with other musicians, and one each with his co-led groups Rios and Other Worlds. He has also recorded two albums with the leading German saxophonist Christof Lauer, *Evidence*, and most recently, *Fragile Network* (1998; ACT) which features an all-star quintet comprising Lauer, Marc Ducret, Michel Godard, Cox and Gene Jackson – all on the cutting edge of the music. 2003 saw an elegant pair of albums released on the French label Sketch that complement each other beautifully: on *Work* Cox joined Steve Lacy and Daniel Humaire for a typically Lacyan session of Monk-ish abstraction; and on *This That*, a solo acoustic bass album Cox recorded directly afterward, his deep, generous grooves are intriguingly informed by the spirit of the Lacy set. [IC]

Anthony Cox

➤➤ **Christof Lauer** *(Fragile Network).*

Ida Cox

Vocals.

b. Toccoa, Georgia, 25 Feb 1896; d. 10 Nov 1967.

Ida Cox began her career with minstrel shows, then made the transition to vaudeville and by the early 1920s was a star of the Theater Owners' Booking Association (TOBA) circuit. Bill-topping in the 1920s, her show was built on a formula, "three letters each name, three jokes between songs, three songs!", and many of those songs were hits, like "Monkey Man Blues", popular in the Midwest in 1924. Others were "Death Letter Blues", "Black Crepe Blues", "Coffin Blues" and "Graveyard Bound Blues" – a macabre formula and an intriguing link between the Victorian way of death and later hit-making "death discs" such as "Gloomy Sunday" or "Ebony Eyes". Ida Cox recorded regularly for Paramount from 1923–9 (accompanists included Lovie Austin and Fletcher Henderson's group) and toured successfully with her own tent show through the 1930s. John Hammond brought her to New York in 1939 to play Café Society, make broadcasts, cut records with Hot Lips Page and others (including the marvellous "Four Day Creep") and appear in the epoch-making *Spirituals To Swing* concert on Christmas Eve at Carnegie Hall. From 1941 she toured successfully with her *Raising Cain!* and *Darktown Scandals* shows until she suffered a stroke in 1944. She came out of retirement in 1961 for a last recording for Riverside with Coleman Hawkins, Roy Eldridge and Sammy Price (substituting for her longtime accompanist, husband Jesse Crump). [DF]

I Can't Quit My Man (1939–40; Affinity). Titles including Cox specialities like "Death Letter Blues" and "Four Day Creep" with Hot Lips Page, J.C. Higginbotham, Ed Hall and Charlie Christian on guitar on eleven tracks.

With The Coleman Hawkins Quintet (1961; Riverside/OJC). Cox was still in fine voice for this, her final recording session.

JAK KILBY

Lol Coxhill

Lol Coxhill

Soprano and other saxophones, vocals.
b. Portsmouth, UK, 19 Sept 1932.

By rights, Lol Coxhill ought to have the international stature of an Ornette Coleman or an Archie Shepp by now (in terms of respect from those in the know, he arguably already does): both his sax tone and his selfless enthusiasm for collaboration and practise have been consistently distinctive for decades. From 1962–9 he performed solo saxophone sets whilst also playing with several R&B groups including Otis Spann and Alexis Korner. He continued his solo performances and played duos with David Bedford and others in 1970–73, during which time he spent a year as musical director for Welfare State Theatre and did some acting with various companies. In 1974–5 he worked with Chris McGregor's Brotherhood of Breath and played occasional gigs with rock groups including Henry Cow and Hatfield and the North, touring with punk group The Damned at the height of the punk era's notoriety. He also worked with Trevor Watts's Moire Music and played with stalwarts of the UK's free-improvisation scene such as Evan Parker, Tony Coe (he was a member of the Melody Four with Coe and Steve Beresford) and Derek Bailey; he has also played with renowned figures such as Dave Holland and Misha Mengelberg. Recognition of his tireless commitment to music came via an Arts Council of Great Britain documentary film, *Frog Dance*, in 1983. Under his own name he has recorded albums for the French label Nato, including *The Dunois Solos* (1982) and *Coucou* (1983), but none is currently available. Coxhill is an amiable oddball, at home with free-form, conventional jazz or folk music. His favourite sopranos are Sidney Bechet, Lucky Thompson, Evan Parker and Steve Lacy. Other inspirations are Pee Wee Russell, Edgard Varèse and Ornette Coleman. [IC]

Boundless (1998; Emanem). Coxhill, on soprano saxophone, duets with pianist and frequent sparring partner Veryan Weston (other meetings of theirs are collected on Emanem's excellent *Worms Organising Archdukes* CD, released in 2002). Both players' calls and responses find each other with a superlative rapport.

Spectral Soprano (2002; Emanem). "Spectral" seems an unlikely epithet to apply to Coxhill in terms of both his sax tone and his solid presence in British music. This 2-CD set spans the years1959–99 and covers a startling range of musical ground: from honking R&B to free jazz fire to collaborations with poets and artists.

Ray Crane

Trumpet, piano.

b. Skegness, Lincolnshire, UK, 31 Oct 1930; d 29 June 1994.

A fine Nottinghamshire-based trumpeter, Ray Crane moved south in 1963 to join Bruce Turner's Jump Band. After Turner broke up the band, Crane stayed in London, working regularly with pick-up groups including Brian Lemon's, and in the 1970s was a mainstay of Stan Greig's London Jazz Big Band, by which time his hot, Roy Eldridge-influenced style had broadened to encompass Rex Stewart (a favourite) as easily as Harry James. During this decade he also ran his own rehearsal band (including Guy Barker and Martin Taylor) and after that worked with Trevor Swale's Dixie Syncopators, Dick Laurie's Elastic Band and saxophonist Trevor Whiting. His last appearance with Turner was at Aberystwyth (July 1993), by which time cancer had struck; his last gig (with Pete Strange) was New Year's Eve 1993. One of the best British swing trumpeters, with a broad eclectic interest in most areas of jazz, Crane was recorded less often than he deserved, but his debut with Turner (see below) clearly demonstrates his talents. [DF]

Bruce Turner

⊙ **Jumping For Joy** (1962–3; Lake). On sixteen track-miniatures from Turner's fine *Going Places* collection, recorded in l963, Crane's trumpet shines out in a close-to-stunning record debut.

Digby Fairweather

⊙ **Songs For Sandy** (1970–82; Hep). In the CD reissue of this album is hidden a second – Brian Lemon's *Our Kind Of Music* (for 77 Records, 1970) which features Crane to good effect, along with Tony Coe, Bruce Turner, John Picard et al.

Bob Cranshaw

Bass.

b. Evanston, Illinois, 10 Dec 1932.

After starting on piano and drums, Cranshaw played bass around Chicago with musicians such as Eddie Harris, and co-led the Modern Jazz Two plus Three (MJT+3) with drummer Walter Perkins (1957–60). He then moved to New York, played with Carmen McRae, Sonny Rollins and the Junior Mance trio, and did a lot of freelance recording, which led to full-time involvement in the studio scene from the mid-1960s. Further spells with Rollins (1972–4 and from the mid-1980s to the present) have run in parallel with continued studio, club and Broadway stage work.

Cranshaw is an intensely rhythmic performer whose lines, though never deliberately attention-seeking, are admirably straightahead. A couple of key albums which include established figures coming to terms with "free jazz" have Cranshaw as their most conservative element, namely Rollins's *Our Man In Jazz* (1962) and Grachan Moncur's *Evolution* (1963). But the solid virtues of his playing are perhaps best appreciated in slightly more conventional albums such as that shown below. [BP]

Sonny Rollins

⊙ **Alternatives** (1964; Bluebird). This compilation, including some material originally on the *Now's The Time* album, has Cranshaw on some tracks and Ron Carter on others, an instructive comparison which shows them both on top form.

➤➤ **Lee Morgan** *(The Sidewinder).*

Hank Crawford

Alto and baritone saxophones; also piano.

b. Memphis, 21 Dec 1934.

Crawford played in Memphis with B.B. King, Bobby Bland and Ike Turner, then studied music at Tennessee State College in Nashville. He joined Ray Charles (1958–63) and, after Charles left Atlantic, began recording his own albums for the label (1960–70). His jazz reputation was widened by a series of crossover albums produced by Creed Taylor (1971–8), whereas his recordings of the 1980s were closer to the R&B music of his background; they also led to a recording and touring partnership with Jimmy McGriff. Crawford's simple but telling phraseology has always been linked to an emotive tone, derived ultimately from Louis Jordan, and is an acknowledged influence on David Sanborn. [BP]

⊙ **Groove Master** (1990; Milestone). One of several albums which feature Dr John on keyboard instead of Jimmy McGriff, this has Crawford strutting in front of an octet and creating a convincing soul-jazz version of "Saving All My Love For You".

Jimmy Crawford

Drums.

b. Memphis, 14 Jan 1910; d. 28 Jan 1980.

Jimmy Crawford began his career in Jimmie Lunceford's band of promising pupils at Manassas County High School and worked the hard road upwards with Lunceford until their first great successes at the Lafayette Theater, New York, in 1933 and the Cotton Club in 1934. He stayed with Lunceford until the break-up in 1943 then, with Shelly Manne's help, made the difficult transition back to small-group work – "my greatest achievement", he told Stanley Dance later. After demobilization in 1945 he worked with Edmond Hall, Harry James and for Fletcher Henderson's sextet and from then on in a succession of Broadway shows, including *Pal Joey*, *Gypsy*, *Jamaica* and *Delilah*, combining this with regular recording and small-group work wherever possible. Crawford's jazz contribution is comparable to Milt Hinton's: a master whose presence was always a guarantee of professionalism and inspiration. [DF]

➤➤ **Jimmie Lunceford** *(The Chronological Jimmy Lunceford).*

Ray Crawford

Guitar; also tenor saxophone.

b. Pittsburgh, Pennsylvania, 7 Feb 1924; d. 30 Dec 1997.

During 1941–3 Crawford played tenor with the Fletcher Henderson band. Forced by ill-health to give up saxophone, he switched to guitar and worked with Ahmad Jamal in the Four Strings (1949–50) and the Jamal trio (1951–5). He then settled in New York, playing with Jimmy Smith, Tony Scott and Gil Evans, with whom he recorded two key sessions in 1959–60 (*Old Wine, New Bottles* and *Out Of The Cool*). In the early 1960s he moved to Los Angeles, teaching and playing yet remaining in obscurity until the late 1970s, when the Japanese release of his previously unissued album from 1961 led to two new records. His playing is unhurried and unhackneyed, and he is reputed to have originated the "bongos" sound of tapping deadened strings, which was later used by Tal Farlow and others. On leaving Jamal, he was replaced not by another guitar but by a drummer, and he remains the only guitarist to have added a distinctive voice to Gil Evans's music. [BP]

⊙ **Smooth Groove** (1961; Candid). Though less sensational than the Evans albums, this set (formerly known as *I Know Pres*) is enlivened by contributions from Johnny Coles, Cecil Payne and Junior Mance.

➤➤ **Gil Evans** *(Out Of The Cool).*

Wilton Crawley

Clarinet.

b. Smithfield, Virginia, 18 July 1900; d. sometime after 1948.

One of the more bizarre figures in jazz history, Crawley was essentially a variety artist who toured with great success through the 1920s and 1930s; he recorded with Jelly Roll Morton and also made solo sides with, among others, Eddie Lang. Crawley's clarinet playing (rather like Ted Lewis's or Wilbur Sweatman's) was determinedly comedic, making great use of slap-tonguing, exaggerated glissandi and other popular 1920s effects, and his music-hall act was based on these and his abilities as a contortionist. Legend has it (and it may be true) that Crawley was unable to separate his contortionist's tricks from his clarinet playing and so proved extremely difficult to record in studio conditions: however, he managed it and a collection of his solo sides is planned. [DF]

Malcolm Creese

Double bass.

b. Bristol, UK, 24 Aug 1959.

Creese's mother was a classical pianist and music teacher and his father a professional violinist, and it was not until the age of sixteen that Creese first discovered jazz. He attended the Choir School at St

David Sinclair

Malcolm Creese

John's College, Cambridge (1967–72), and gained the top music scholarship to Radley College (1972–5). Then he spent a year studying cello at London's Guildhall School of Music, after which he worked as a classical cellist playing with chamber ensembles and orchestras. Jazz grew on him and at 25 he bought a double bass, taught himself to play it and was soon gigging and working with some of the finest London jazz musicians and singers. In 1990, he was asked to join Stan Tracey (he continued to tour the world with Tracey's various bands until 1996) and in 1991 Creese was recruited by John Dankworth and Cleo Laine, with whom played for a decade. Creese also began working in a drumless trio with Tony Coe and pianist John Horler to great acclaim. He has accompanied many visiting American musicians including Johnny Griffin, Scott Hamilton, Clark Terry, Art Farmer and Mel Tormé.

Creese runs his own independent label, ABCDs (Audio B limited), to record bands with which he plays, and he acts occasionally as an independent producer for other labels. Acoustic Triangle, his trio with Tim Garland and John Horler, is his primary ongoing concern, its musical focus paralleling that of the ECM label in tackling compositions by Ravel, Ralph Towner and Kenny Wheeler. Still active as a classical bassist, Creese works occasionally with the London Symphony Orchestra among others. His favourite bassists include Dave Holland, Paul Chambers and Charles Mingus, but he also admires Duke Ellington, Messiaen and J.S. Bach. [IC]

Tony Coe, John Horler & Malcolm Creese

In Concert (1997; ABCDs). A superlataive showcase for Creese's solid, big-toned bass, this live recording was in the *Independent* newspaper's Top 10 Jazz Records of 1997, and has been hailed by some as one of the greatest British jazz albums of all time.

Roy Crimmins

Trombone.

b. Perth, Scotland, 2 Aug 1929.

Early in the 1950s Roy Crimmins worked with Mick Mulligan and Freddy Randall before joining Alex Welsh to play a concert at the Royal Festival Hall. Crimmins was a guiding light in the early years of Welsh's band, and he partnered Welsh for eleven years until April 1965, when he took his own band to Germany for a season in Lübeck: the season turned into a thirteen-year stay. Later in the period Crimmins gave up playing for three years but was tempted back to playing by trumpeter Oscar Klein, re-formed his own band (the Roy King Dixielanders) and then moved into studio work until 1978 when he went back to England to freelance. Almost immediately he was invited by Alex Welsh to rejoin the band, and he stayed with his old friend until their last job together in Nottingham, shortly before Welsh's death in 1982. Crimmins then freelanced, working regularly with Harry Gold, with the trombone quintet Five-a-Slide, and with his own five-piece. In 1987 he moved permanently to Tel Aviv. [DF]

Marilyn Crispell

Piano, composer.

b. Philadelphia, 30 March 1947.

Starting piano lessons at age seven, Marilyn Crispell grew up in Baltimore, Maryland, and studied piano and composition at the New England Conservatory, Boston. After a six-year hiatus from music, she moved to Cape Cod and began playing free jazz after the epiphany of hearing Coltrane's *A Love Supreme* and the piano playing of Cecil Taylor. After more studies in Boston, she participated in vibraphonist Karl Berger's Creative Music Studio in Woodstock, New York, where she eventually relocated. In 1978, she toured extensively with Anthony Braxton, whose brilliant quartet she joined in the early-80s. Near-telepathic, the quartet recorded astonishingly incendiary yet focused music, compacting the sound-worlds, melodies and rhythms of Boulez, Ligeti, Thelonious Monk and Cecil Taylor into a joyous synthesis. Crispell's own first record, *Spirit Music*, was released on Cadence in 1983, and since then she has been a very prolific recording artist, releasing music on Leo, FMP, Black Saint, Victo, Music & Arts, Knitting Factory, Okka Disk and ECM. As a leader, she has had several ongoing groups, including trios with percussionist Gerry Hemingway and bassist Reggie Workman or bassist Mark Dresser, as well as the gorgeous string quartet that made *Santuerio* (Leo, 1993), and her forceful solo work has also been amply documented. Though she has inevitably drawn comparisons with Taylor, Crispell is very much her own artist. There has been an increasingly lyrical lushness complementing her abrasive dynamism. Her two late-1990s trio albums on ECM – with Paul Motian and Gary Peacock – share a more crepuscular, contemplative mood, with the odd pianistic gesture towards the impressionism of Bill Evans. [JC]

Nothing Ever Was, Anyway (1997; ECM). Tremendous trio disc with Gary Peacock on bass and Paul Motian on drums, playing the quirky, fascinating music of Annette Peacock. While it is in line with a rising use of pastels and Keith Jarrett-like lyricism, it's free of any self-absorption or cloying pedal pushing; really one of the most beautiful piano recordings of the 90s and an excellent portal into the sound-world of Marilyn Crispell.

Sonny Criss

Alto and soprano saxophones.

b. Memphis, 23 Oct 1927; d. 19 Nov 1977.

In the late 1940s Sonny Criss worked on the West Coast with Johnny Otis, Howard McGhee and Billy Eckstine. After that he led his own groups intermittently, toured with the Buddy Rich quintet (1955), performed in Europe in the mid-1960s, then resumed playing in the USA, where he also did rehabilitation work with young offenders. A further tour of Europe came in 1974, and three years later he appeared with Dizzy Gillespie at Monterey. He was about to make his first tour of Japan when he died from a self-inflicted gunshot. One of the first generation of altoists to be deeply marked by Parker, Criss came up initially with an awkward compromise between the rhythmic approaches of Parker and Willie Smith (the direct comparison between Criss and his idol on Parker's *Inglewood Jam* is revealing). His later work achieved a more homogeneous style while retaining great intensity. [BP]

Portrait Of Sonny Criss (1967; Prestige/OJC). Playing with a quartet featuring Walter Davis, Criss here sounds like a bebop version of Hank Crawford on "God Bless The Child" and "On A Clear Day".

John Critchinson

Piano.

b. East London, 24 Dec 1934.

Raised in the West Country, John Critchinson began his musical career by working in

Chippenham's Icebox Club (while a teenage apprentice electrician) in the 1950s, backing visitors such as Tubby Hayes, Jimmy Deuchar and his eventual employer, Ronnie Scott. He led his own trios and payed his dues working local gigs throughout the 60s and into the 70s before moving to London in 1978. There, he played with saxophonist Kathy Stobart and, in the early 1980s, with the Morrissey-Mullen band, but it was his work with Ronnie Scott, from 1979 onwards, that brought him to national attention. In addition to playing with Scott in his various bands, and with the Martin Drew quartet, Critchinson has, like fellow pianist Stan Tracey, backed a great number of US stars at Ronnie Scott's – Chet Baker, James Moody, Joe Henderson and George Coleman prominent among them. After Scott's death in December 1996, Critchinson toured in the UK for several years in The Ronnie Scott Legacy band, a tribute to his erstwhile employer, with saxophonist Pat Crumly, bassist Leon Clayton and drummer Martin Drew. The RSL played its final gig in 2002, by which time the quartet featured Crumly, Tim Wells (bass) and Mark Fletcher (drums). [CP/CI]

First Moves (1996; Jazz House). Featuring saxophonist Art Themen, bassist Dave Green and drummer Dave Barry on a brisk selection of material by Sonny Rollins, Cedar Walton, Jobim and Mal Waldron, along with a couple of originals.

Excuse Me, Do I Know You? (1997; Jazz House). Vigorously interactive quartet music paying tribute to Ronnie Scott, with Mark Fletcher and Martin Drew sharing the drumming and Pat Crumly on saxophones. Scott favourites are here ("This Heart Of Mine", "Seven Steps To Heaven"), while pithy originals and vocal guest appearances by Flora Purim and Georgie Fame make a worthy musical memorial to one of the UK's most respected musicians.

➤➤ **Ronnie Scott** *(Never Pat A Burning Dog).*

A.J. Croce

Piano, vocals, composer.
b. Philadelphia, 28 Sept 1971.

The son of singer Jim Croce, who was killed in an air crash when A.J. (Adrian James) was a week short of his second birthday, A.J. Croce took up piano at six, performed his first professional engagement at thirteen, and enrolled at his home town San Diego's School of Creative and Performing Arts at fifteen, dropping out in his final year. Inspired initially by the stride pianists and blues shouters he had heard in his father's record collection, Croce quickly assimilated a number of other jazz-based styles, from the jumping, humorous jive of Louis Jordan to the richly emotional soul of Ray Charles, into a highly marketable but sincerely held and personal approach. Citing everyone from Dylan Thomas through Mark Twain and e e cummings to Chilean Nobel Prize-winning poet Pablo Neruda as influences on his sparky lyric-writing style, Croce gained critical plaudits for his eponymous debut album (see below) and for 1995's *That's Me In The Bar* (Private Music). In the late 1990s, Croce signed for the German label, Ruff (distributed by the House of Blues), and though talk of his emulating Harry Connick as the next big thing in youthful vocal jazz began to subside somewhat, the albums *Fit To Serve* (1998; Ruf) and the left-turn into sophisticated pop *Transit* (2000; Higher Octave) were characterful enough to suggest that this cult artist is in for the long haul. [CP]

A.J. Croce (1993; Private Music). Witty songs from all parts of the US tradition, leavened with the odd original, all played with great panache by the rollicking Croce piano, backed by a hard-swinging stellar band.

Tony Crombie

Drums, composer; also piano.
b. London, 27 Aug 1925; d. 18 Oct 1999.

Crombie's mother was a silent-movie pianist, and he was self-taught. He toured with Lena Horne, Carmen McRae, Annie Ross and others and led his own bands in the mid-1950s – including, in 1959, Jazz Inc., which included Bobby Wellins and Stan Tracey. He also wrote original scores for TV films and feature films. In 1963 he led his own band in Israel with Jeff Clyne and Pete Lemer. He has done many European tours with jazz and pop artists including Tony Bennett and Jack Jones. He also worked with Coleman Hawkins, Ben Webster, Jimmy Witherspoon and others at Ronnie Scott's club. Since the 1970s he has worked with Georgie Fame's Blue Flames. His compositions include "So Near So Far", recorded by Miles Davis in 1963 and Joe Henderson in 1993; "Debs Delight", recorded by Paul Gonsalves; "Child's Fancy", recorded by Ray Nance; "That Tune" and "Restless Girl", recorded by Stephane Grappelli. Miles Davis was very complimentary about "So Near So Far" and said, "I like the tunes drummers write because they have a good sense of space." He was about to record a ballad which Crombie had recently composed for him but Davis's death put a stop to that. Leonard Feather has described Crombie as an "outstandingly imaginative drummer; talented leader, writer and pianist". Crombie's protean abilities have always been rather overlooked in his own country. [IC]

Bing Crosby

Vocals.
b. Tacoma, Washington, 2 May 1903; d. Madrid, 14 Oct 1977.

Bing (Harry Lillis) Crosby played drums in his local high school band before exploring singing. While studying law at Jesuit-run Gonzaga University he met Al Rinker, with whom he formed a double act in Los Angeles. Paul Whiteman heard them, teamed the duo with Harry Barris, and the Rhythm Boys were on their way. They had a highly successful period performing and recording with Whiteman, but after a dispute with Abe Frank, the boss of the Coconut

Grove, where the trio was appearing, Crosby found himself suspended. At the same time, Everett Crosby interested William Paley (director of CBS) in his brother's voice, and the result was that Paley signed Bing for a series of fifteen-minute CBS radio programmes. Jack Kapp then heard the shows and signed Crosby to Brunswick Records in 1931.

Crosby's work at this period is full of heights, typified by the soaring, unlimitable vocal resources of his Hollywood recordings with Whiteman, Lennie Hayton and others ("Black Moonlight" is a melodramatic masterpiece) and, best of all, the jazz sides with Bix, the Rhythm Boys ("Changes", "Ain't No Sweet Man", "From Monday On") and Whiteman-based small groups. "Listening to Bing on the 1932 recording of 'Some Of These Days' with Trumbauer and Lang behind him", says Sid Colin, "you can hear him express all his jazz aspirations." With the Kapp signing – and the death of Eddie Lang, whose jazz guitar he loved and regularly employed – Crosby honed his pyrotechnic approach. From the young man who sang with all the ardour of Jolson but with much more taste and technique, he gradually recultivated himself as the casual, pipe-smoking Bing that was his public personality in later life. Perhaps this was a reaction to Kapp's contractual demands: "He had me doing things that I thought insane", said Bing later, "Herbert, Friml, and Viennese waltzes." No doubt it was also that Crosby was becoming the property of America (rather like Elvis Presley, 25 years on): his defences against the commercial machine may have been in part to "sing down" as a way of conserving energy, as well as, on occasion, to parade a justifiable detachment.

He made his first feature film, *The Big Broadcast*, in 1932 (more than sixty were to follow), and from then on most of Crosby's commercial output consisted of top-of-the-heap songs which people could hum. Crosby's work was unfailingly professional, but Whitney Balliett noted that some of his work has an "absent-minded" quality. His most reactive performances sometimes came in collaborations with other competitive stars, while his most relaxed and humorous work (on radio, records and TV) seemed to come with the jazz musicians he loved: notably in films such as *Rhythm On The River* (1940, with Wingy Manone), *The Birth Of The Blues* (1941, based, just, on the Original Dixieland Jazz Band and starring Jack Teagarden), *Holiday Inn* (1942, with Bob Crosby's orchestra, but not Bob) and *High Society* (1956, with Louis Armstrong, among others). On record and in radio shows with the likes of Red Nichols and Connee Boswell, there were countless confirmations of his claim: "When all's done, my favourite music is Dixieland." Even jazz fans who find most later Crosby too bland will notice the warmth in his voice on sessions with Bob Scobey, Eddie Condon, Matty Matlock, Louis Jordan and Wingy Manone. Best of all are his duets with Louis Armstrong, which reveal in four bars a side of Bing that never went away.

By the 1970s Crosby ran a baseball club and golf tournaments, and he slowed down before a dramatic return to performance just before his death. Ruby Braff heard him at the London Palladium and pronounced him "the greatest popular singer ever". [DF]

⊙ **Bing Crosby** (1926–32; Timeless). Many of Crosby's early jazz collaborations are on this set, including "Mary" and "Changes" (with Whiteman), "Mississippi Mud" (with the Rhythm Boys) and the magnificent "St Louis Blues" with Duke Ellington. Produced by Chris Ellis with John R.T. Davies' audio restoration, an unbeatable team.

⊙ **Bing Crosby: His Greatest Hits Of The 30s** (1931–39; ASV). Twenty-five definitive titles, including "Love In Bloom", "June In January" and jazzier outings including "Bob White" (with Connee Boswell) and "You Must Have Been A Beautiful Baby" with Bob Crosby.

⊙ **The Jazzin' Bing Crosby 1927–40** (Affinity). This fine double-CD represents excellent value, with "Mr Gallagher And Mr Sheen" (co-starring Johnny Mercer) and "Rhythm On The River" (with Wingy Manone) among 48 well-chosen titles.

⊙ **Bing Crosby And Some Jazz Friends** (1934–51; MCA/GRP). Bing with Louis Jordan, Connee Boswell, Joe Sullivan, Louis Armstrong, Jack Teagarden, Eddie Condon, Lee Wiley, Woody Herman, Bob Crosby and Lionel Hampton. What more could you want?

⊙ **Bing Crosby And Friends** (1949–50; Magic). This has Louis Armstrong on two tracks plus other wonderful collaborations with Bob Hope, Judy Garland, the Andrews Sisters and others.

⊙ **Bing Crosby (With Louis Armstrong): Havin' Fun Havin' More Fun!** (1949–51; Jazz Unlimited). Crosby's most chemical work was frequently with Armstrong, and these two CDs are taken from live airshots of Bing's radio shows of the period. Co-stars include Peggy Lee, Jack Teagarden, Dinah Shore and Joe Venuti.

Bob Crosby

Vocals, leader.

b. Spokane, Washington, 25 Aug 1913; d. 9 March 1993.

Bob Crosby already had experience as a singer with Anson Weeks and the Dorsey brothers (including the intractable Tommy) when in 1935 he was invited to act as frontman for a group of musicians – led by Gil Rodin and including Yank Lawson, Matty Matlock and Dean Kincaide – who had left Ben Pollack after a dispute. They were to form Bob Crosby's Band and a breakaway small group, the Bobcats. The chance to front a group of groundbreaking jazzmen, to sing regularly and create his own identity was an attractive option, and for the next seven years, despite inexperience which gave him trouble even counting off the band, Bob Crosby learned his profession. A charming presenter and a likeable, plum-toned singer with a natural jazz feeling (although he lacked his brother Bing's technique), Crosby recorded prolifically and very soon forged a career that was a success on its own terms (no doubt Bing envied his brother all that jazz). The band broke up in 1942, and after the war Bob worked solo on radio and TV, led his own big bands (including an up-to-the-minute aggregation owing little to Dixieland) and regularly got the Bobcats together for reunions. Late in life he was touring festivals and appearing at the Reagan White House (1985). His name will always be synonymous with the best of organized Dixieland. [DF]

⊙ **Bob Crosby 1936–38** (Jazz Classics). Good selection of tracks by orchestra and Bobcats, with notes by Crosby authority John Chilton.

⊙ **Stomp Off, Let's Go** (1936–40; ASV). Excellent introduction to Crosby's Orchestra and Bobcats, featuring many of their best sides – including "South Rampart Street Parade" and "March of the Bobcats".

⊙ **Bob Crosby 1936–38** (Halcyon). Issued in separate volumes, this sixteen-volume set is a complete chronology of Crosby's orchestra and Bobcats titles.

⊙ **South Rampart Street Parade** (1936–42; MCA/GRP). Good representative selection of classics by Crosby's orchestra, including "SRSP", "My Inspiration", "I'm Prayin' Humble" and "Little Rock Getaway".

⊙ **Bob Crosby And His Bobcats** (1937–40; Swaggie). Four CDs which gather all the Bobcats sides, with orchestra tracks as a filler on vol. 2 (1939); this treasury is amongst the best of Dixieland.

⊙ **Bob Crosby And His Orchestra** (1938; Circle). Sides recorded for World Broadcasting Systems, including what are thought to be vocalist Kay Weber's last recordings with the Crosby organization.

Gary Crosby

Bass.

b. London, 26 Jan 1955.

Although he started his musical life as a trumpet player in 1968, Gary Crosby was tutored on the bass by Peter Ind in 1974 and was one of the founder members of the big band the Jazz Warriors in the early 1980s. He has since established himself as one of the UK's leading bassists, having performed all over Europe with the likes of UK saxophonists Courtney Pine and Steve Williamson and vibes player Orphy Robinson, and with touring Americans such as Art Farmer, Larry Coryell, Gary Bartz, Joey Calderazzo, Stanley Turrentine, Jimmy Witherspoon, Sonny Fortune and Johnny Griffin. As a leader, he has taken his band Jazz Jamaica to festivals worldwide, but he is also extremely active in jazz education, his Tomorrow's Warriors project – established in 1991 – providing apprenticeships for young, upcoming jazz musicians, and spawning two award-winning acoustic ensembles, the sextet Nu Troop and the quintet J-Life. In 1995, Crosby organized the recording of a Bob Marley tribute album, *One Love* (Mercury; 1996), involving ten UK jazz artists (Cleveland Watkiss, Steve Williamson, Orphy Robinson, Tony Rémy et al), and in 1997 formed Dune Records to showcase both his own ensemble and the work of Tomorrow's Warriors graduates. The quality of music produced quickly established Dune as a premier UK jazz label and introduced to the world the extraordinary young talents of Denys Baptiste, Robert Mitchell and Soweto Kinch. Crosby remains a committed player, educator and bandleader and continues to generate awards both for himself (notably, in 2002, for Consistent Contribution to Music In Jamaica) and for his groups, particularly the Jazz Jamaica All-Stars, which deservedly won the BBC Radio Jazz award for Best Band in 2002. [CP]

Jazz Jamaica

⊙ **Skaravan** (1994; Skazz). A heady mix of traditional Jamaican music and jazz and R&B, but includes versions of Juan Tizol's "Caravan" and Charlie Parker's "Barbados".

⊙ **Blue Note Beat Vol. 1** (1994; Toshiba-EMI). Blue Note classics given the Jazz Jamaica treatment.

⊙ **Double Barrel** (1998; Rykodisc). Danceable, cogent, intelligent jazz/reggae versions of everything from "Monkey Man" to "Walk On By" and "I Heard It Through the Grapevine".

⊙ **Massive** (2001; Dune). More infectious, intelligent fun, in which Shorter and Hancock material exists happily next to "My Boy Lollipop". On many lists for best album of the year 2001.

Nu Troop

⊙ **Migrations** (1997; Dune). Mostly original material from a versatile, whip-smart, vigorous band: saxophonists Tony Kofi and Denys Baptiste, trumpeter Neil Yates, pianist Alex Wilson and drummer Robert Fordjour, alongside Crosby.

Israel Crosby

Bass.

b. Chicago, 19 Jan 1919; d. 11 Aug 1962.

Israel Crosby took up the bass at fifteen and a year later was noticed by John Hammond as "the phenomenal ... bass player" who worked with Albert Ammons at Club de Lisa, Chicago. Hammond promptly booked him on a record date with Gene Krupa, which was to produce a small jazz classic, "Blues Of Israel", and Crosby attracted widespread attention as a result. "He plays with a rare speed and accuracy and unusual precision", noted Hugues Panassie, "and he improvises very rich counter-melodies behind the soloists." From Fletcher

Henderson (1936–8) Crosby moved to the Three Sharps and a Flat, then Horace Henderson's orchestra (1940), Teddy Wilson's group (1940–42) and Raymond Scott's multiracial studio group at CBS. For most of the 1940s he was to work regularly in studios, but in 1951 began a great partnership with pianist Ahmad Jamal which lasted on and off until 1962. That year Crosby joined George Shearing and recorded with him (as well as with progressive arranger Bill Russo), but died of a heart attack two months later. A neglected bass virtuoso (whose work is regularly under-rated as well as rediscovered), Crosby's achievements stand comparison with Jimmy Blanton's. [DF]

➤➤ **Ahmad Jamal** *(At The Pershing).*

Stanley Crouch

Drums, writer.

b. Los Angeles, 14 Dec 1945.

Crouch began playing drums at twenty while working as an actor with Jayne Cortez, former wife of Ornette Coleman. Gigging with various musicians led in 1967 to the formation of a co-operative band, the Quartet, with Arthur Blythe and Bobby Bradford. When teaching drama at Claremont College, he led Black Music Infinity (1969–75), including James Newton and David Murray, then in 1975 he moved to New York with Murray's trio and almost immediately began writing about jazz for *Village Voice*. Long inactive as a player, his reputation rests on his general political and social commentary; in the jazz field, he initially espoused players such as Murray, then those of the Wynton Marsalis persuasion, as well as tackling key historical figures like Ellington and Parker. A man of wide knowledge and interests (gospel singer Andrae Crouch is his cousin), he is the first musician, established initially as a performer, to have become more influential as a critic. [BP]

David Murray

⊙ **Flowers For Albert** (1977; West Wind). Not Murray's original recording of the previous year (which had Phillip Wilson on drums), this European live date is by a quintet with Butch Morris and Don Pullen, and shows how promising Crouch was as a musician.

Pat Crumly

Saxophones, flute.

b. Oxford, UK, 9 Feb 1942.

Having learnt his trade by jamming on the university jazz scene, Pat Crumly made his reputation in the jazz world by touring and gigging with singers Jack Jones and Cleo Laine, and with tenor player Ronnie Scott. Equally adept in the rock, blues and R&B fields, Crumly has lent his gutsy tenor and strident alto sound to the bands of musical figures as diverse as Alan Price, Eric Burdon, Chris Farlowe, the Drifters, Lulu and Helen Reddy, but his forte is producing blues-inflected post-bop jazz in the manner of his chief influences, Phil Woods and Cannonball Adderley. A stalwart of the UK jazz world, Crumly also teaches at Wavendon, and in addition to a Chiltern Sound recording with a band called Edge, *Uneasy Peace*, made in 1978, he has made three albums for the Spotlite label, 1984's *Third World Sketches* and the two 1990s CDs listed below. He was a member of the John Critchinson quartet formed to pay tribute to the late Ronnie Scott, touring extensively and recording a memorial album, *Excuse Me, Do I Know You?* (1997; Jazz House) before the group disbanded in 2002. He has toured with rock/blues band The Shortlist, featuring ex-Family singer Roger Chapman, and currently leads a quartet featuring Nick Weldon on piano and ex-RSL colleagues Tim Wells on bass and Mark Fletcher on drums. [CP]

⊙ **Behind The Mask** (1992; Spotlite). Switching easily between alto, soprano, tenor and flute, Crumly – leading his regular band of John Pearce (piano), Simon Woolf (bass), Simon Morton (drums) – produces lively and accessible versions of everything from Ornette Coleman's "Tears Inside" through Kenny Barron's "Voyage" to McCoy Tyner's "Contemplation", laced with cogent originals.

⊙ **Flamingo** (1994; Spotlite). Same band as above, occasionally augmented by Guy Barker (trumpet), Richard Edwards (trombone), in eclectic, vibrant mix of Mancini, Rodgers and Hart, etc standards with Crumly originals. The album's title track is a reworking of the famous Mingus *Tijuana Moods* arrangement.

➤➤ **John Critchinson** *(Excuse Me, Do I Know You?).*

Adam Cruz

Drums, percussion.

b. New York, 13 Feb 1970.

Although his chief musical impetus came from his drummer father Ray, who worked with Mongo Santamaria and Richie Ray, and who runs his own Latin band, Cruz Control, Adam Cruz's maternal grandfather was the trumpeter Ricky Trent. After spending two years studying at Rutgers under Kenny Barron and Keith Copeland, Cruz attended the New School for Social Research (1990–93), an institution with a thriving jazz department. Early experience with trumpeter Charlie Sepulveda, singer Willie Colón, Panamanian pianist Danilo Perez, Puerto Rican pianist Hilton Ruiz and Cuban saxophonist Paquito D'Rivera gave Cruz a thorough grounding in both Latin and jazz music, but he opted to follow the latter route, resisting the commercial pressures of the former to play with the likes of pianist/composer Edward Simon, Chick Corea (in his Origin band, documented on the six-disc Stretch set *The Complete 1998 Live At The Blue Note Recordings*), percussionist Leon Parker, trumpeter Tom Harrell, Puerto Rican saxophonist David Sanchez (appearing on his 1994 Columbia album *Sketches Of Dreams* and on *Obsession* on the same label in 1998) and the Mingus Big Band. Naming Roy Haynes as his biggest influence "for his connection to the history of the music, but also for the integrity of his individual voice", Cruz is a supple but crisp drummer particularly adept at propelling music on the cusp between Latin and jazz. [CP]

Ronnie Cuber

Baritone saxophone; also soprano, flute, bass-clarinet.
b. Brooklyn, New York, 25 Dec 1941.

Cuber's mother was a pianist and his father played accordion. Starting on clarinet at the age of nine, he took up tenor in high school and joined the Newport Youth Band on baritone in 1958–9. He toured with Maynard Ferguson from 1963–5 and with George Benson's first group in 1966–7. Subsequently working with Lionel Hampton and Woody Herman, he joined the occasional big band White Elephant in 1970 and then toured with King Curtis and Aretha Franklin. In the 1970s he began playing with Afro-Latin leaders such as Eddie Palmieri, an interest he maintains to the present, having unveiled his own Latin quartet in the early 2000s. As well as considerable studio work, he has been in demand for small-group jazz recordings (eg with Steve Gadd, Lee Konitz and Horace Silver) and frequently appears with the McCoy Tyner big band and the Mingus Big Band. A forthright soloist who lights up any session he takes part in, Cuber plays the baritone with commendable fluency and edge. [BP]

The Scene Is Clean (1993; Milestone). As the only horn player on most tracks, Cuber fronts both a straightahead line-up, for instance on the Tadd Dameron title piece, and a Latin-fusion group including Geoff Keezer on material such as his own "Mezambo".

Laurent Cugny

Arranger, composer, keyboards, writer.
b. La Garenne-Colombes, France, 14 April 1955.

Cugny studied piano from age ten and began gigging in 1975. Self-taught as a composer, he formed his Big Band Lumière in 1979. He received his first commission, from France's Ministry of Culture, in 1986 and the following year completed a tour and two albums with Gil Evans directing his band, which was commemorated in the video *Jazz à Paris*. John Scofield was their guest soloist in 1990, and Cugny wrote arrangements for recordings by Abbey Lincoln and bluesman Lucky Peterson, with whom he toured in 1995. In the meantime, he became leader of the Orchestre National de Jazz from 1994–97, writing the music for four of their albums. The holder of a Master's degree in economics and a degree in cinematography, Cugny has written numerous articles on jazz and film since 1978, and authored two prize-winning books, *Las Vegas Tango* on Gil Evans (published 1989) and *Electrique, Miles Davis 1968–75* (1993). [BP]

Laurent Cugny

Personal Landscape (2001; Emarcy France). A light but pleasingly detailed orchestral jazz album featuring cloudy expositions on themes by Sting ("Fields Of Gold"), McCartney ("Blackbird") and Joni Mitchell ("Man From Mars") among Cogny's originals.

Orchestre National De Jazz

Merci, Merci, Merci (1996; Verve). Apart from two tracks by other composers, Cugny produced and arranged the whole album. The inclusion of Miles's "Frelon Brun" and a piece by Willie Tee gives an idea where Cugny is coming from, and his rock-influenced originals inspire an excellent performance from the ONJ and soloists such as Stefano di Battista and Flavio Boltro.

>> **Gil Evans** *(Rhythm-A-Ning).*

Jamie Cullum

Piano, vocals, guitar.
b. Rochford, Essex, 20 August 1979.

Jamie Cullum's Burmese mother and English father were self-taught part-time club and function singers who also worked together in bands. Cullum had piano lessons at school until he was 11 or 12, but after that, he was largely self-taught on both piano and guitar. As a teenager, he played in all types of bands – pop, rock and hip-hop – but swiftly developed an interest in songs and songwriting from Stevie Wonder to Cole Porter. After taking a year out to study Film and English Literature at Reading University, he met bassist Geoff Gascoyne, who asked him to appear on his CD *Songs of the Summer*. Then Cullum formed a trio with Gascoyne and drummer Sebastian DeKrom and began recording

UMUSIC

Jamie Cullum

Pointless Nostalgic, which was picked up by Candid Records. Cullum's obvious star quality meant that Candid was able to get him bookings in significant London clubs, where he made a powerful impression on audiences. Talkshow host Michael Parkinson heard him and was so impressed that he recommended Cullum to Universal Records, who signed him to a six-figure contract in April 2003. Cullum's approach is always accessible and can be rather middle-of-the-road, but he is already developing as an artist and should go from strength to strength. [IC]

⊙ **Pointless Nostalgic** (2003; Candid). A mature and deftly achieved album which features Cullum backed by some of the finest musicians on the London scene. There are two of his own compositions on offer – the title track and "I Want To Be A Popstar". The rest consists of Monk's "Well You Needn't" and ten standards – all performed with great panache.

Jim Cullum

Cornet, leader.

b. San Antonio, Texas, 20 Sept 1941.

Jim Cullum is the second-generation leader of a famous San Antonio-based jazz band, Jim Cullum's Happy Jazz, originally formed by his clarinettist father, who began playing in his college band (immortalized by Johnny Mercer in his song "Jamboree Jones" after he heard them at a 1934 New York football game) and afterwards played for Jack Teagarden, but gave up music to run his grocery business. He later formed a family band with Jim Jnr playing cornet, and in 1969 he founded a record company to record his band and other musical events (including a musical meeting for brothers Emilio and Ernie Caceres). Jim Cullum Jnr has carried on the traditions of his father and co-owns (with other band members, including clarinettist Allan Vaché) a hugely successful jazz room open seven nights a week in the Landing Hotel on San Antonio's plush River Walk. By the mid-90s Cullum's band had become a central focus in jazz revivalism, with a series of fine recordings to their credit; in 2003 – just as busy – it may also be seen as a university for fine young players including Allan Vaché, Randy Reinhardt and John Sheridan. [DF]

⊙ **Fireworks: Red Hot And Blues!** (1989–95; Pacific Vista). Cullum's high-powered joyful band with a spectacular roster of guests recorded from live radio, among them Clark Terry, Dick Hyman, Ken Peplowski and Joe Williams. Beautifully recorded and entertaining all the way.

⊙ **New Year's Jam Live From New York** (1993; Pacific Vista). An excellent and typical live session, with guests Bob Haggart, Marty Grosz and Carol Woods.

Ted Curson

Trumpet, piccolo trumpet, pocket trumpet, flugelhorn.

b. Philadelphia, 3 June 1935.

Curson went to Granoff Musical Conservatory and also studied privately with Jimmy Heath. In the 1950s he went to New York, working with Mal Waldron, Red Garland, Philly Joe Jones and Cecil Taylor. From 1959–60, he played in Charles Mingus's quartet, which included Eric Dolphy, making the music he will probably always be best known for: Curson made his first recordings with Mingus in 1960, playing on some classic tracks such as "Folk Forms No. 1". He went on to co-lead a band with Bill Barron from 1960–65, and also played with Max Roach and led his own groups. In the late 1960s and throughout the 1970s he was a regular on the concert and festival scene in Europe (with Chris Woods, Andrew Hill, Lee Konitz and Kenny Barron, among others) becoming an in-house member of the Schauspielhaus theatre orchestra in Zurich for a year in 1973. He has always been concerned with promoting interest in jazz and encouraging young musicians, and in that cause he has played and lectured at campuses of the University of California, Vallekilde Music School, Denmark, and the University of Vermont. With Gato Barbieri and Aldo Romano he appeared in the film, *Notes For A Film On Jazz*. Curson is at home with all kinds of playing approaches because he has always lived adventurously, experimenting and pushing musical frontiers to their limits without losing touch with the roots of jazz. [IC]

⊙ **Plays Fire Down Below** (1962; New Jazz/OJC). This features Curson with a rhythm-section plus an added percussionist. George Tucker and Roy Haynes make a great bass and drums team, and the pianist is Gildo Mahones. Curson's fiery, all-round trumpet abilities are very much in evidence.

⊙ **Tears For Dolphy** (1964; Black Lion). Curson led a piano-less quartet for this session, with Bill Barron on tenor and clarinet, and Herb Bushler and Dick Berk on bass and drums. Eric Dolphy had died only a few weeks before, and Curson's grief pervades the lovely title track. Barron is as adventurous a player as Curson, and also contributes some meaty compositions including "7/4 Funny Time" – a time-signature that was virtually unknown in jazz in those days. The rhythm-section handles it, and everything else, with panache.

➤➤ **Charles Mingus** *(Charles Mingus Presents Charles Mingus).*

King Curtis

Tenor and soprano saxophones.

b. Fort Worth, Texas, 7 Feb 1934; d. 14 Aug 1971.

King Curtis (born Curtis Ousley) played in the same high school band as Ornette Coleman, then led his own group and toured with Lionel Hampton (1953) before settling in New York and leading a trio containing Horace Silver. He became involved in session work with the Coasters vocal group and many more (predominantly as featured soloist), and replaced Red Prysock in the Alan Freed radio show band. Live appearances regularly at Smalls' Paradise club (late 1950s) and at Apollo Theater, Harlem (early 1960s), led to his becoming the musical director for Aretha Franklin and studio producer for her and others. He was at a peak of fame when he was stabbed to death outside his New York house. Curtis earned his reputation for the superb appropriateness of his brief solos on R&B and pop records – though, as many of these were overdubbed, appropriate did not necessarily mean spontaneous. His background knowledge of the "Texas tenor" tradition, however, emerges strongly on his occasional jazz albums such as the one below. [BP]

⊙ **The New Scene Of King Curtis** (1960; New Jazz/OJC). A dynamic rhythm-section of Wynton Kelly, Paul Chambers and Oliver Jackson, and the frontline contributions of "Little Brother" (Nat Adderley), set the scene for Curtis's brief move into straightahead jazz.

Cutty Cutshall

Trombone.

b. Huntington County, Pennsylvania, 29 Dec 1911; d. 16 Aug 1968.

A busy professional by his mid-20s, Cutty (Robert Dewees) Cutshall came to fame when he joined Benny Goodman in 1940. Replacing Red Gingler, he joined Lou McGarity to form Goodman's finest trombone team and stayed for two years until call-up. After discharge he rejoined Goodman briefly, then freelanced with Billy Butterfield and Jimmy Dorsey's Dixielanders, among others. In 1949 he joined Eddie Condon, and the almost continuous twenty-year spell that followed is the one for which he is best remembered, producing records to spare. In the 1960s he was again freelance, but at his death he was working with Condon once more at the Colonial Tavern, Toronto. Cutshall is one of three swing trombonists – Lou McGarity and Abe Lincoln were the others – whose best work was aesthetically, technically and harmonically comparable to Jack Teagarden's, without quite possessing that smooth and elusive genius-stroke. A courteous, humorous professional, his creativity and melodic ingenuity was an influence on fine players such as George Chisholm. [DF]

Eddie Condon

⊙ **The Complete CBS Recordings Of Eddie Condon And His All Stars** (1953–62; Mosaic). Cutshall was a fixture in Condon's band during these years and makes stirling contributions to classic albums including "Bixieland', "Roaring Twenties", "Midnight In Moscow" and more.

➤➤ **Eddie Condon** *(Ringside at Condon's; Dixieland Jam).*

Andrew Cyrille

Drums, composer.

b. Brooklyn, New York, 10 Nov 1939.

Cyrille studied privately from 1952–7 and with Philly Joe Jones in 1958. He worked with Nellie Lutcher, Roland Hanna, Illinois Jacquet, Walt Dickerson, Bill Barron and Rahsaan Roland Kirk from 1959–63 but it was with Cecil Taylor that he came to prominence in 1965, playing by his side for ten years (though he also played with Stanley Turrentine, Gary Bartz and Junior Mance in the 1960s). In 1971 he formed Dialogue Of The Drums,

Jak Kilby

Andrew Cyrille

a percussion trio with Milford Graves and Rashied Ali. After leaving Taylor in 1975 Cyrille formed his own group, Maono, which had a broader musical base and usually comprised trumpeter Ted Daniel, saxophonist David S. Ware and bassist Nick DiGeronimo. Since then he has worked with many musicians including Leroy Jenkins, Muhal Richard Abrams, Reggie Workman, Marilyn Crispell, Billy Bang and Anthony Braxton. In 1990 he toured Britain with a trio featuring the free-improviser bassist Paul Rogers and guitarist Mark Hewins. He currently plays with two trios: Trio 3, with Oliver Lake and Reggie Workman; and the CDE Trio, with Marty Ehrlich and Mark Dresser. Cyrille's is an inclusive, all-embracing conception of music – abstraction, conventional jazz, African and ethnic elements and other types of vernacular music are all grist to his mill. He is a consummate percussionist who always thinks and plays compositionally, with an overall view of the performance. [IC]

⊙ **Metamusicians' Stomp** (1978; Black Saint). Featuring Cyrille's quartet, Maono, its very title reflects his life and aims – the neologism "metamusician" suggesting changes of state, and one of the oldest words in jazz, "stomp", implying dance and invoking the music's early roots. This is a strong, highly committed set with much improvisation, excellent group rapport, and one ballad – Kurt Weill's "My Ship".

⊙ **Nuba** (1979; Black Saint). Nuba is the name of an African tribe living in southern Sudan and of their language, and this album featuring Cyrille with alto saxophonist Jimmy Lyons and vocalist Jeanne Lee is a dynamic exploration of the African/African-American relationship.

⊙ **Galaxies** (1990; Music & Arts). Cyrille plays a duo here with the Russian percussionist Vladimir Tarasov, formerly with the Ganelin trio. There are three compositions by Tarasov, one by Cyrille and "One Up One Down" by John Coltrane. The uncompromising commitment of the music renders it more exciting in small doses.

⊙ **My Friend Louis** (1991; DIW). The heart of this album is the wonderful rhythm-section of Cyrille and Workman. The rest of the quintet comprise trumpeter Hannibal, saxophonist Oliver Lake and pianist Adegoke Steve Colson. Everyone contributes a composition and there's also a performance of Dolphy's "The Prophet". Lake is in tremendous form, and the other soloists aren't far behind him.

➤➤ **Horace Tapscott** *(The Dark Tree Vols. 1 & 2).*

Renato D'Aiello

Tenor saxophone.

b.21 March 1959, Naples, Italy.

After studying with virtuoso saxophonist Antonio Andolfi, D'Aiello started performing in 1979. In 1984 he was first alto with the Bologna Big Band but left to take up the same role with the Big Band of the Capolinea Jazz Club in Milan. In 1987 he received a full tuition scholarship from Berklee College in Boston, met Sal Nistico – who became something of a mentor – and began leading his own quartet. Although he began as an alto sax player, he gradually switched to tenor – an instrument more suited to his warm and expansive temperament. In the 1990s he worked with the great trumpeter, Art Farmer, and for the past four years he's moved between Paris and the UK, moving to the latter in 2000 – the year of his first album, *Like Someone In Love*. His next album, *Introducing Renato D'Aiello*, was a scintillating selection of twelve standards with D'Aiello leading an all-star sextet. A tenor player for all seasons with a broad and beautiful sound, D'Aiello possesses both strength and sensitivity and can boot it with the best or play the ardent lover in a breathy ballad. [IC]

⊙ **Introducing Renato D'Aiello** (2001; Spotlite). A very pleasing album of twelve standards, some familiar and some less well known. D'Aiello shines throughout and the whole thing swings like the clappers.

Pete Daily

Cornet, valve-trombone.

b. Portland, Indiana, 5 May 1911; d. 23 Aug 1986.

Pete (Thaman Pierce) Daily started on baritone horn, later played tuba and bass saxophone, and borrowed his first cornet from a girl in his high school band. A talent to watch by 1930, he formed a close musical relationship with pianist Frank Melrose, and by the end of the decade had spent time with Bud Freeman, Boyce Brown and Art Van Damme as well as leading his own bands. After the war he organized his own West Coast group, which quickly achieved commercial success and recorded regularly through the first half of the 1950s for small labels, then Capitol, featuring such fine Chicago-style players as Warren Smith, Nappy Lamare, Joe Darensbourg and Jerry Fuller. In the early 1960s Daily switched to valve-trombone and moved to Indiana, continuing regular work with Smoky Stover's band. He appeared in the mid-1970s at Sacramento's jazz festival, but could no longer play after a stroke in 1979. [DF]

Dave Dallwitz

Piano, composer, leader.

b. Adelaide, Australia, 25 Oct 1914.

Australia's ragtime conservative to set beside the headily progressive John Sangster, Dallwitz runs a scholarly ragtime orchestra which plays classic rags and his own compositions. He also writes material in the contemporary mainstream area, and always uses the very best of his Australian colleagues to play it on record, including Sangster, Bob and Len Barnard and their peers. There are many excellent recordings by Dallwitz on Swaggie and other labels, but few have yet been transferred to CD. [DF]

Tadd Dameron

Composer, arranger, piano.

b. Cleveland, Ohio, 21 Feb 1917; d. 8 March 1965.

Tadley Ewing Peake Dameron began gigging locally as pianist with the legendary Freddie Webster (mid-1930s), then touring with the Zack Whyte and Blanche Calloway bands and writing arrangements. In 1939 he worked in New York with Vido Musso's band and was arranger for the Kansas City-based Harlan Leonard band (1939–41). He was soon contributing to other famous bands such as those of Jimmie Lunceford, Georgie Auld, Billy Eckstine, Count Basie (including one of Dameron's best-known originals, "Good Bait"). Occasional sitting-in on piano with Dizzy Gillespie and Charlie Parker led to their recording his "Hot House" (1945), and arrangements for Gillespie's big band (1945–7) and for Sarah Vaughan. In 1947 he was gigging with Babs Gonzales's Three Bips and a Bop (Dameron on piano and backing vocals) and recording with a quintet/sextet under his own name and Fats Navarro's. He was resident at the Royal Roost with a sextet in the summer and autumn of 1948, augmented to a ten-piece (early 1949) with Miles Davis replacing Navarro.

He co-led a quintet with Davis at the Paris Jazz Fair, 1949 and, encouraged by Kenny Clarke, stayed in Europe several months and wrote briefly for the Ted Heath band. Back in New York (late 1949) he wrote for Artie Shaw, singer Pearl Bailey and others, then doubled on piano and arranging for the Bull Moose Jackson R&B group (1951–2). In 1953, he led his own nine-piece band featuring Clifford Brown and Philly Joe Jones in Atlantic City, but became less active because of drug problems; he wrote for Max Roach-Clifford Brown and for Carmen McRae (1956) and recorded two albums, but was then imprisoned for three years. Released in 1960, he arranged albums by Sonny Stitt, Blue Mitchell, Milt Jackson and his own last recording (1962), but worked infrequently in the last couple of years preceding his death from cancer.

Undervalued during his lifetime, except by fellow musicians, Dameron was a unique contributor at the crossroads between swing and bebop. The lasting qualities of "Good Bait" and "Hot House", though claimed as being written before the crystallization of bop, did reflect its harmonic language (like a number of his lesser-known lines), but rhythmically they are close to the swing era. Many of Dameron's most representative items such as "Tadd's Delight" (aka "Sid's Delight") and "Lady Bird", though beautifully melodic, are built almost entirely of notes derived from his typically lush chords; similarly, his piano style gained its interest from the use of harmony rather than independent lines. In this respect, Dameron was a strong influence on the compositions of Horace Silver and many of the "hard bop" writers, as well as on Benny Golson, Gigi Gryce, Paul Jeffrey and others who emulated him more directly. Many of his nine-piece orchestrations were re-created note for note by arrangers Don Sickler and John Oddo for the 1980s group Dameronia led by Philly Joe Jones. [BP]

⊙ **Fontainebleau** (1956; Prestige/OJC). A continuation of the medium-sized groups Dameron led in 1949 and '53, this studio reunion with Kenny Dorham and Cecil Payne is distinguished by a superior blowing vehicle, "The Scene Is Clean", and the fully notated title track tone-poem.

⊙ **The Magic Touch** (1962; Riverside/OJC). Returning to the big-band format of his early work, with Johnny Griffin and Bill Evans, Dameron reprised "Fontainebleau" and several earlier items such as his vocal ballad "If You Could See Me Now".

➤➤ **Fats Navarro** *(The Complete Blue Note and Capitol Recordings of Fats Navarro and Tadd Dameron; Featured With The Tadd Dameron Band).*

Hank D'Amico

Clarinet.

b. Rochester, New York, 21 March 1915; d. 3 Dec 1965.

A highly able clarinettist who played broadly in Benny Goodman's style, D'Amico worked with Red Norvo on and off until 1939. He then joined Bob Crosby (1940–41) before leading his own band (1941–2) and playing with Les Brown, Benny Goodman, Red Norvo, Raymond Scott's multiracial studio group at CBS, Tommy Dorsey and Miff Mole. From 1944 he worked for ten years as a staffman for ABC, then played with Jack Teagarden as well as doing TV, club and radio sessions, and freelancing. In 1964 he worked at the New York World's Fair with Morey Feld's trio. [DF]

Franco D'Andrea

Piano, keyboards, composer.

b. Merano, Italy, 8 March 1941.

D'Andrea is self-taught and began playing piano at seventeen after having tried the trumpet, clarinet, bass and saxophone. From 1964–5 he played with Gato Barbieri and co-led the Modern Art Trio, an avant-garde group, from 1968–72 before spending five years (1972–7), with Perigeo, a jazz-rock group. In the late 1970s he led a own trio whilst beginning to perform solo concerts and teaching intensively before forming his own quartet in 1981 with Tino Tracanna (saxophones), Attilio Zanchi (bass) and Gianni Cazzola (drums), touring with it extensively in Italy and Europe and playing several international festivals. He also played with Lee Konitz, Johnny Griffin, Steve Lacy, Enrico Rava, Pepper Adams, Conte Candoli, Frank Rosolino, Max Roach, Jean-Luc Ponty and Toots Thielemans among others. In 1982 and 1984 he was voted Best Italian Jazz Musician in the magazine *Musica Jazz*, and his albums *Es* and *No Idea of Time* won the Italian critics' award. D'Andrea is a prolific composer, and in 1984 was commissioned by the Teatro Lirico di Cagliari to collaborate with contemporary composer Luca Francesconi and African percussionist Fode Youla, to create a piece based on the interaction of different musical languages.

Despite (or perhaps because of) his late start, D'Andrea developed into a virtuoso performer with a quicksilver technique sometimes reminiscent of Art Tatum. Relentless in his output (he released eight albums of solo piano in 2002, each one focussing on a different aspect of jazz practice), he displays an effortless familiarity with all styles and eras of jazz – from stride piano to bebop, jazz-rock and total abstraction. [IC]

⊙ **No Idea Of Time** (1983; Red). On this quirky and audacious album D'Andrea leads an Italian-American quartet including the excellent Tino Tracanna on saxophones and a rhythm-section of bassist Mark Helias and drummer Barry Altschul. There are only three long pieces, including two very different takes of the title track. Group virtuosity, subtlety and rampant imagination make this music most joyous.

⊙ **Airegin** (1991; Red). A superb trio of D'Andrea, bassist Giovanni Tommaso and drummer Robert Gatto shed new light on canonical jazz standards with loving reinterpretations of Monk's "Epistrophy", Miles's and Bill Evans's "Blue In Green" and Rollins's classic pieces, "Doxy" and "Airegin". There are also some fine compositions by the leader and Tommaso.

Putney Dandridge

Piano, vocals.

b. Richmond, Virginia, 13 Jan 1902; d. 15 Feb 1946.

A vaudeville artist in the 1920s, Putney (Louis) Dandridge worked as accompanist to tap-dancer Bill Robinson in the early 1930s, led his own band, and from 1935 had solo residencies up and down 52nd Street, at the Hickory House and elsewhere. His records, modelled on Fats Waller and his Rhythm, are less well known than they should be, for they feature superior repertoire, Dandridge's engaging singing and a string of star accompanists (see review below), as well as specially recruited pianists including Teddy Wilson, Ram Ramirez and Clyde Hart. A neglected artist of the swing era. [DF]

Putney Dandridge: A Chronological Study In Three Volumes (1935–6; Rarities). A valuable set which should be re-issued on CD: Dandridge's stellar sidemen include Roy Eldridge, Dick Clark, Bobby Stark, Henry "Red" Allen, Chu Berry, Ben Webster, Joe Marsala, Dave Barbour and Cozy Cole.

Eddie Daniels

Tenor saxophone, clarinet, flute.

b. New York, 19 Oct 1941.

A supremely technically gifted clarinettist and a dependable saxophonist, Eddie Daniels is one of the few practitioners on the former reed to have made fusion recordings. After attending New York's High School of the Performing Arts and graduating from Brooklyn College in 1963, he obtained an MA from the Juilliard in 1966. The same year, he joined the prestigious and influential Thad Jones-Mel Lewis orchestra, retaining his chair there until 1972, and made his recording debut as a leader. In the late 1960s and early 1970s, he recorded with a great many stellar names, including Freddie Hubbard, Joe Henderson, Richard Davis, Bucky Pizzarelli and Airto Moreira. In 1984, he premiered Jorge Calandrelli's *Concerto for Jazz Clarinet and Orchestra*, subsequently recording it, along with other pieces for clarinet and orchestra, on his album *Breakthrough*. In the late 1980s, he was also featured in the Mercer Ellington-led orchestra which produced the highly regarded album *Digital Duke*. Recording highlights in the 1990s included some sparkling live interplay with UK pianist Julian Joseph, caught on *In Concert at the Wigmore Hall* (East West; 1994), and participation in an all-star reworking of classic bop and hard bop numbers under the leadership of Cuban trumpeter Arturo Sandoval, *Swingin'* (GRP; 1996). Daniels's own recording career, however, saw him leave GRP for Shanachie, where he produced a somewhat saccharine album, *Beautiful Love* (1996), including arrangements of Bach, Satie and Rachmaninov – before a majestic big band album, *Swing Low Sweet Clarinet* (2000). Despite his output being characterized by a certain aesthetic unevenness, Daniels is – like Don Byron, in more avant-garde jazz circles – widely credited with helping to bring the clarinet out of undeserved jazz obscurity. [CP]

Nepenthe (1989; GRP). Jaunty fusion session featuring Chick Corea's rhythm-section, John Patitucci (bass) and Dave Weckl (drums), among other fusion stalwarts such as guitarist Chuck Loeb.

Benny Rides Again (1992; GRP). Lively Benny Goodman tribute, with Gary Burton unusually assertive on vibes, backed by excellent rhythm-section: Mulgrew Miller (piano), Marc Johnson (bass) and Peter Erskine (drums).

Under The Influence (1992; GRP). Quartet record, concentrating largely on tenor, featuring keyboard player Alan Pasqua, bassist Michael Formanek and drummer Peter Erskine.

Two Of A Kind (2002; Sittel). Daniels in a head-to-head swing session with Swedish clarinet king Putte Wickman. A high-scoring draw.

Joe Daniels

Drums, bandleader.

b. Zeerust, South Africa, 9 March 1908; d. 2 July 1993.

Daniels took up drums at eleven and in the same year played Frascati's Restaurant, London, before work on Cunard liners with bands led by Al Kaplan, and dates in London clubs, restaurants and ballrooms. In 1926 he teamed with trumpeter Max Goldberg in a small group and soon after played with Fred Elizalde, Al Tabor and Billy Mason before joining Harry Roy (1931–7). Roy's famous Hotshots, featuring Daniels's spectacular "drumnastics", were formed during this period for EMI studio recordings, and continued throughout the war when he served in the RAF and ran a quintet. After the war Daniels formed his Dixieland Group (featuring at various times Dave Shepherd and Alan Wickham) and recorded for the Parlophone "Rhythm Style" series until 1957. In later years he ran a band at Butlin's holiday camps and in 1984 briefly appeared with Denny Wright and Tiny Winters in the wacky comedy film *Top Secret*. [DF]

Swing Is The Thing (1937; Empress). Good representative collection of Daniels's "drumnastics" from 1937 et seq, featuring Max Goldberg, Nat Temple, Harry Lewis and others.

Maxine Daniels

Vocals.

b. London, 2 Nov 1930; d 20 October 2003.

Maxine Daniels's career began after she won a local talent competition in Stepney, followed by a long residency with bandleader Denny Boyce at the Orchid Room in Purley. In 1953 she won a TV talent show and was signed by Bernard Delfont for cabaret and appearances at all of London's principal theatres, including the London Palladium. She also appeared on TV shows for Humphrey Lyttelton, among others. During this busy period Daniels toured with Tony Crombie and also appeared with leading entertainers including Tony Hancock, Alma Cogan and Frankie Vaughan, as well as Americans Billy Eckstine, Sarah Vaughan and Les Brown. Following illness she took a long rest, but made a return in the later 1970s, subsequently presenting two shows compered by longtime admirer Benny Green

(*Evergreens* and *Songs Of Irving Berlin*) and singing nationally with bands including Lyttelton's, Harry Gold's, and the Dutch Swing College Band. She continued to appear regularly at jazz clubs and festivals into the 1990s - often with Benny Green or with bandleaders including John Petters and Terry Lightfoot – but later chose to retire from performance again. A warm-toned singer who always respected the melody, Maxine Daniels' vocal timbre sometimes recalled Rosemary Clooney, but her approach was distinctly personal and despite a discontinuous career in later years her recordings bear testimony to a singer of international standard. [DF]

A Memory Of Tonight (1996; Calligraph). Though recorded late in her career (for Humphrey Lyttelton's label), this collection of standards highlights the clarity and directness of Daniels' vocal style; with able support from Ted Beament (piano), Dominic Green (guitar) and John Rees-Jones (bass).

Mike Daniels

Trumpet, leader.

b. Stanmore, Middlesex, UK, 13 April 1928.

Daniels led a superior British revivalist jazz band of the 1950s and early 1960s which (like Bruce Turner's Jump Band) was renowned for its convincing re-creation of the Morton/Oliver/Armstrong repertoire. Featuring fine players such as John Barnes (clarinet/reeds) and Gordon Blundy (trombone) as well as Daniels's own Oliver-style lead, the Delta Jazzmen won a strong following among aficionados; so did Daniels's big band, which featured later stars such as John Chilton and Keith Nichols and played regularly in the London area. Daniels went abroad in the mid-1960s (the band continued to thrive under the direction of saxophonist Trevor Swayle), but in 1985 he made a trip back to Britain, worked a string of provincial dates and, with his band reassembled, found queues stretching round the building for his appearances at London's Pizza Express. Soon after he moved back to Britain full-time and, with a band regularly including Daniels veterans Des Bacon (piano) and Arthur Fryatt (drums), was once again making the rounds of clubs, festivals and recording studios in the 1990s and on into the twenty-first century. [DF]

Mike Daniels Delta Jazzmen (1957–9; Harlequin). A good selection of jazz standards in spirited and skilful re-creations.

Palle Danielsson

Double bass.

b. Stockholm, 15 Oct 1946.

Danielsson began violin lessons when he was eight, studying for about five years. He became interested in jazz, Stravinsky and Bartok, and took up the double bass, starting his professional career at fifteen as a bass player doubling on harmonica, which he managed to juggle with studying for five years (1962–6) at the Stockholm Royal Academy of Music. He began playing with leading Scandinavian musicians including the trombonist Eje Thelin, pianist Bobo Stenson and saxophonist Jan Garbarek, and he accompanied American musicians such as Bill Evans, George Russell, Ben Webster and Charlie Shavers. Danielsson also recorded an album *Watch What Happens* with the Steve Kuhn trio in 1968. He co-led the Swedish group Rena Rama from 1972–86, which included Stenson and saxophonist Lennart Aberg but Danielsson really entered the realms of music history when he became a member of Keith Jarrett's European quartet throughout its short but immensely influential life (1974–9). This was a defiantly acoustic group in the age of electronics, and it brought a fresh dynamism to jazz. Danielsson is a tower of strength on the two magnificent, seminal studio albums, *Belonging* (1974) and *My Song* (1977), and also on the two 1979 live albums, *Nude Ants* and *Personal Mountains*. His sound has been integral to ECM records for decades, fundamental to many albums by Charles Lloyd, Kenny Wheeler and Peter Erskine. In the 1990s, he toured with Erskine and the pianist John Taylor. His own band is currently Contra Post, a quintet with piano and guitar, which recorded an eponymous album in 1994. [IC]

Contra Post (1994; CAP). Danielsson's greatest recorded work is with other leaders, and this is his debut album as a leader at the ripe age of 48, a classy quintet recording with saxophonist Joakim Milder, pianist Rita Marcotulli, drummer Anders Kjellberg and guitarist Goran Klinghagen. There are some fine moments, particularly his duo track with the latter.

>> **Keith Jarrett** *(Belonging; My Song).*

Danish Radio Big Band

Formed in 1964 as the New Radio Dance Orchestra, it became the first permanent, state-financed jazz big-band and its excellence is the epitome of house bands employed by European broadcasting organizations. From 1967 it was known as the Radio Big Band, then from 1997-2002 as the DR Jazz Orchestra and now in 2003 as the DR Big Band. Its first regular conductor was Ib Glindemann and, as well as drawing on a gradually permutating list of top Danish musicians, it sometimes had visiting Americans among its personnel and especially its contributing arrangers. Full-time directors have included Palle Mikkelborg, Thad Jones, pianist Ole Kock Hansen, Bob Brookmeyer and Jim McNeely, and it has appeared on albums with Jones, Stan Getz, Georgie Fame, Ernie Wilkins, Mike Mantler and Miles Davis (*Aura*). Unlike most of its counterparts in other countries, the orchestra undertakes regular appearances in the UK and elsewhere. [BP]

This Train (1991; Dacapo). One of the only albums featuring the band without a guest, this consists of instrumentals (and three songs) written and arranged by US keyboardist-saxophonist Ray Pitts who, while resident in

Denmark from 1962-75, was one of the band's first musical directors.

➤➤ **Tony Coe** *(Captain Coe's Famous Racearound)*; **Ben Webster** *(No Fool, No Fun)*.

Harold Danko

Piano.

b. Sharon, Pennsylvania, 13 June 1947.

Danko's parents both sang and his father played button accordion, while two brothers became professional saxophonists. Harold was already accompanying his brother's pupils by the age of twelve and, after receiving his Bachelor of Music Education from Youngstown State University in 1969, he briefly attended the Juilliard and studied with Jaki Byard and Chick Corea. He played for Woody Herman in 1972, Chet Baker (1973–6), Lee Konitz (1974–5), Thad Jones-Mel Lewis (1976–8) and Gerry Mulligan (1980). In addition to accompanying various vocalists from Anita O'Day to Liza Minnelli, he has recorded prolifically as sideman and, since 1975, with his own groups. He formed his current quartet, featuring saxophonist Richie Perry, in 1990, and taught at college level in New York, Hartford and New Haven before becoming an associate professor at the Eastman School of Music in 1998. He is influenced by Armstrong, Parker and Coltrane as well as the musicians he worked with, while favourite pianists are Hines, Powell and Artur Rubinstein. [BP]

⊙ **New Autumn** (1995; Steeplechase). One of four albums by the quartet with Rich Perry, bassist Scott Colley and drummer Jeff Hirshfield, this collection of Danko originals includes what he considers some of his "most personal and adventurous playing and writing".

➤➤ **Mel Lewis** *(Thad Jones-Mel Lewis Quartet)*.

Alec Dankworth

Bass, composer.

b. London, 14 May 1960.

After studying at Boston's Berklee School of Music in 1978, Alec Dankworth joined his father, John Dankworth, and his mother, Cleo Laine, in their quintet, touring the USA, Australia and Europe between 1980–83. Work with drummer Tommy Chase, the BBC Radio Big Band and Clark Tracey's quintet followed in the mid-1980s, and he recorded two albums, *Stiperstones* and *We've Been Expecting You*, with the last of these before their break-up in the early 1990s. In 1988 Dankworth worked with the classical violinist Nigel Kennedy, recording Duke Ellington's *Black, Brown and Beige* and performing Vivaldi's *Four Seasons* with him, and he also played with ex-Jazz Messenger Jean Toussaint and pianist Michael Garrick. By the late 1980s he had established himself as something of a stalwart of the UK jazz scene, appearing with the Tommy Smith quartet, the Julian Joseph quartet, Birmingham-based tenorman Andy Hamilton's band, and his own quartet, featuring Robin Aspland on piano, Andy Panayi on saxophones and Mark Taylor on drums.

In 1993 Dankworth toured Europe and South Africa with Abdullah Ibrahim. He also frequently backs visiting Americans such as Mose Allison, Clark Terry, Mel Tormé and Anita O'Day, and in the late 1990s was invited by Dave Brubeck to join his band, where he stayed for three years until 2001. As well as recording with a who's who of the UK scene – saxophonists Alan Barnes, Peter King, Dave O'Higgins, Bobby Wellins, Jean Toussaint, Tommy Smith, David-Jean Baptiste, pianist David Newton, guitarist Martin Taylor – Dankworth continues his association with his father in their fourteen-piece Generation Band, recording two albums with them, *Nebuchadnezzar* (Jazz House; 1993) and the live recording below. In 2002 he formed his own acoustic trio, performing an eclectic mixture of originals and standards by composers ranging from Dave Brubeck to Abdullah Ibrahim and featuring Phil Robson on guitar and Julian Argüelles on saxes. The trio's debut album *If You're Passing By* appeared on Candid in 2003. [CP]

Clark Tracey Quintet

⊙ **We've Been Expecting You** (1992; 33 Records). Pithy hard-bop-based music from drummer/leader's band, opening with Dankworth's composition "Descendant".

Generation Band

⊙ **Rhythm Changes** (1995; Jazz House). A stellar band, including saxophonists Tim Garland and Andy Panayi, trumpeters Guy Barker and Gerard Presencer, bring great collective and solo skills to mainly in-house originals.

➤➤ **Guy Barker** *(Into The Blue)*; **Dave O'Higgins** *(All Good Things)*.

John Dankworth

Alto and soprano saxophones, clarinet, arranger.

b. London, 20 Sept 1927.

Dankworth played clarinet in trad bands (mid-1940s), then studied at the Royal Academy of Music. Interested in bebop, he worked on transatlantic liners to hear music in New York. Playing in the Tito Burns sextet alongside Ronnie Scott, he also did some arranging for Ted Heath. A founder member of the Club 11 (1948–50), he then formed the Johnny Dankworth Seven (1950–3). His big band toured from 1953–64, featuring singer Cleo Laine (they married in 1958) and re-formed for annual engagements till 1971. He began writing film scores from 1959, and became increasingly busy from the mid-1960s to mid-1970s. From 1971, he also acted as musical director for Laine's tours of the USA, Australia, etc and undertook engagements conducting symphony orchestras, recording in this capacity with Dizzy Gillespie (1989). He formed a new occasional big band (1990) and from 1993 co-led the Dankworth Generation Band with his son

Alec. He was awarded the CBE in 1974 and published his autobiography in 1998.

John's own alto work, reflecting the influence of Charlie Parker and perhaps Lee Konitz, retains a light, nonchalant tone and a considerable inventive edge. Though sometimes too fussy, his early writing for septet and big band at its best encouraged relaxed and idiomatic performances from such notable contributors as Don Rendell, Kenny Clare and Kenny Wheeler. In its heyday, the big band also developed inventive head arrangements of classic Ellington and Basie warhorses, which were performed during its brief US visit for the Newport festival in 1959. [BP]

The Best Of John Dankworth (1956–72; Redial). A somewhat middle-of-the-road compilation, covering John's two hits "African Waltz" and the witty "Experiments With Mice"; several Dankworth movie and TV themes; excerpts from his Dickens and Zodiac suites; and the Mike Gibbs arrangement of Jarrett's "Grow Your Own".

Moon Valley (1998; ABCDs). Dankworth's first small-group recording for nearly two decades finds him leading his regular rhythm-section (John Horler, Malcolm Creese, Allan Ganley), and the programme of originals and three standards reveals a fine maturity in his playing.

Olu Dara

Cornet, guitar, harmonica, vocals.

b. Louisville, Mississippi, 12 Jan 1941.

At the age of seven, Olu Dara (born Charles Jones III) began playing trumpet solos for the Women's Auxiliary Clubs in Natchez, Mississippi, where he was raised. There he learned many modes of entertainment, including singing and dancing. He attempted to play music in college, but left in 1959 and joined the Navy, where he played in a variety of musical settings from small groups to big bands. He served out the last year of his duty in New York in 1963, then remained in the Big Apple, continuing to listen but shelving his musical aspirations for eight years. In the early 70s, he joined Art Blakey's Jazz Messengers, alongside saxophonist Carter Jefferson, and as the decade pushed on he became a fixture on the city's so-called loft scene, working with the movement's main figures including Sam Rivers, David Murray, Henry Threadgill and Julius Hemphill. He played on some of the era's classic LPs, such as Murray's *Flowers For Albert* (1976; India Navigation), *Ming* (1980; Black Saint) and *Home* (1981; Black Saint), Threadgill's *When Was That?* (1982; About Time) and *Just The Facts And Pass The Bucket* (1983; About Time), and Hemphill's *Flat-Out Jump Suite* (1980; Black Saint). Later he continued to work with Threadgill and led his own sadly undocumented groups, but more or less vanished, making a surprise cameo on some Silkheart records, on Cassandra Wilson's breakaway *New Moon Daughter* (1995; Blue Note), and on records by his rap-star son, Nas. More surprising, though, was Dara's comeback (and technically first record as a leader), *In The World: From Natchez To New York* (1998; Atlantic), on which he returned to his early training as singer and entertainer, putting the more strictly jazz-oriented material in the context of blues, R&B and Afro-Caribbean music. On his follow-up, *Neighbourhoods* (2001; Atlantic), he surprised by concentrating on a kind of contemporary country blues, often forsaking his cornet for voice and guitar. He remains a unique-sounding horn player whose distinctive cornet can cut through any blowing with a subtle curve or whispered nuance. A great member of the loft generation, one hopes Dara will continue to make more concentrated creative music for years to come. [JC]

Joe Darensbourg

Clarinet, saxophones.

b. Baton Rouge, Louisiana, 9 July 1906; d. 24 May 1985.

By the 1920s Darensbourg was active in New Orleans, working with such as Buddy Petit, Fate Marable, Charlie Creath and Jelly Roll Morton, as well as for medicine shows and, from around 1925, with Mutt Carey's Jeffersonians in Los Angeles. In the 1930s he played all the saxophones instead of clarinet, leading bands around Seattle, Vancouver and the West Coast, working on cruise liners and teaching a star pupil, saxophonist Dick Wilson, who was later to work with Andy Kirk. Darensbourg's move back to traditional jazz came in the wake of America's jazz revival: he worked with pianist Johnny Wittwer around Seattle and joined Kid Ory in 1944 for the first of several stints spread over ten years; doubled up with pianist Joe Liggins, comedian Redd Foxx and Wingy Manone; and, after more freelancing, started his own band, the Dixie Flyers, in 1956. Thereafter he became a familiar figure at Disneyland, on a mock-up riverboat, playing with the Young Men Of New Orleans. After three years with Louis Armstrong (he was on the record of *Hello Dolly!*), Darensbourg worked at Disneyland again in the 1970s and with Barry Martyn's Jazz Legends, as well as at festivals before heart trouble slowed him down.

On clarinet, Darensbourg is remembered for his featuring of the "slap-tongue" technique: a reed player's show stopper in the 1920s which very few of its practitioners (they included Albert Nicholas and Barney Bigard) bothered to carry over to later decades. Darensbourg continued to feature it, however, and a highly successful single by Darensbourg's Dixie Flyers, "Yellow Dog Blues", repopularized the sound in 1958. [DF]

The New Orleans Statesmen (1995; GHB). Good example of Darensbourg in later years, with Clive Wilson on trumpet and veteran guitarist Danny Barker.

David Darling

Cello, electric cello, percussion, composer.

b. Elkhart, Indiana, 4 March 1941.

Darling is a classically-trained cellist who began his career teaching, from 1966–9, in US public schools. From 1969–70 he was the faculty cellist and community orchestra conductor at Western Kentucky University, before he joined the Paul Winter Consort (1970–78), touring extensively throughout the USA and recording four albums. After leaving Winter, he began to compose more, and several of his pieces for large orchestra were played by the Indianapolis and Cincinnati symphony orchestras. Part of the pool of musicians based around the ECM record label, he played on Ralph Towner's album *Old Friends, New Friends* with Kenny Wheeler, Eddie Gomez and Michael Di Pasqua in 1979, and co-founded the group Gallery in 1980 with Di Pasqua (drums), Dave Samuels (vibraharp) and Paul McCandless (reeds), recording for ECM in 1981 and touring the USA and Europe in 1982.

Darling plays both the traditional cello and an eight-string solid-bodied cello of his own design which is amplified and filtered through various electronic attachments such as echoplex, ring modulator and fuzz box. This practice enables him to combine elements from the classical tradition with jazz, rock and other musics, and lends his solo cello music an extraordinarily wide palette of sounds. [IC]

Cello (1992; ECM). This solo cello outing is Darling's third and most focused album. It features his normal acoustic cello and his eight-string electric cello, often overdubbed. This combination of the two instruments affords him a very broad spectrum of timbres and he produces some ravishing sonorities. The mood is profoundly meditative, the compositions evocative, and Darling's playing faultless.

>> **Terje Rypdal** *(Eos);* **Ralph Towner** *(Old Friends, New Friends).*

Julian Dash

Tenor saxophone.

b. Charleston, South Carolina, 9 April 1916; d. 25 Feb 1974.

The greater part of Dash's career was spent in Erskine Hawkins's orchestra, which he joined in 1938, emerging occasionally to record as a soloist. Later – after Hawkins reduced to a small group – he led his own band and recorded with his own quintet in 1970, but afterwards retired from music. His principal influence, Chu Berry, is clearly audible in his style, which shows up to advantage on Buck Clayton's 1953 "Hucklebuck" jam session. [DF]

>> **Buck Clayton** *(Complete Buck Clayton Jam Sessions).*

Wolfgang Dauner

Piano, keyboards, composer.

b. Stuttgart, Germany, 30 Dec 1935.

Dauner was brought up by his aunt, a piano teacher who gave him lessons from the age of five. He first worked as a mechanic, but took up music professionally in 1957. Bill Evans was his main early influence, but Dauner's curiosity and theatrical side led his music in more chaotic directions and the trio he formed in 1963, with Eberhard Weber and Fred Braceful, caused a sensation at German festivals with its unconventional performances. He played sideman to visiting jazz stars and began composing, whilst gaining a notoriety for his live performances in the latter half of the 1960s – he set fire to a piano on stage on one occasion, and on another he covered the heads of one of Germany's most renowned choirs in nylon stockings so that they could only emit garbled noises. Around this time he recorded *Free Action*, a septet featuring Jean-Luc Ponty, and ambitious pieces for choir and jazz group at German festivals. In 1970 he formed the group Et Cetera, a loud, psychedelic, jazz-rock outfit prone to extended synthesizer freak-outs. He branched out in 1974 with his own music TV show for children, *Glotzmusik*.

In 1975 he founded the United Jazz and Rock Ensemble, a project for TV that became so popular that it began regular tours, and Dauner set up Mood Records (with Volker Kriegel, Albert Mangelsdorff and Ack van Rooyen) to record it. The late 1970s saw him collaborating on film scores and, into the 1980s, he recorded duo albums with Mangelsdorff and wrote works for symphony orchestra (his arrangements used prepared tapes and idiosyncratic combinations of musicians).

In 1986 he began working with the singer/songwriter Konstantin Wecker for concert tours and recordings; the mid-eighties also saw a blossoming musical partnership with Charlie Mariano. The pair played together on several ponderous but beautiful albums, ably complemented by Dino Saluzzi (see below). In the later 1990s, Dauner played a number of solo concerts, continued to play with trombonist Albert Mangelsdorff, and co-led the Mangelsdorff-Dauner quintet, which recorded the album *Hut Ab* (1998; Mood). Dauner joined an all-star band of German jazz veterans, Old Friends, including Mangelsdorff, Weber and Doldinger, which toured the USA in 1999.

Dauner's is a massive talent embracing (as both player and composer) every facet of contemporary music-making. His favourite pianist is Glenn Gould, and other inspirations include Coltrane, Webern, Debussy and Ravel. [IC]

Two Is Company (1982; Mood). Dauner and Albert Mangelsdorff have an almost preternatural rapport. Here they perform in duo four longish pieces, each of which moves through several phases and moods. The spiky theme of the title track inspires powerful piano vamps and vaulting melodic lines. "Wheat Song" begins with muted trombone and spacey, rubato piano, but develops a hot gospel-like exultation.

Meditation On A Landscape – Tagore (1988; Mood). Dauner's other close associate since the early 1980s is Charlie Mariano. They're joined by percussionist Ernst Stroer for this music for a film on the life of Bengali poet Rabindranath Tagore. This is, fundamentally, high-class mood music, but Mariano and Dauner nevertheless always have absorbing things to say.

One Night In '88 (1988; Mood); **Pas De Trois** (1989; Mood). For these two albums Stroer is replaced by the great bandoneon (a type of accordion) virtuoso Dino Saluzzi, whose musical antennae match the sensitivities of Dauner and Mariano. The interplay and sonorities sing out with brilliant consonance. Both albums are excellent with *Pas De Trois* having just the edge in terms of focus and pith.

Solo Piano 2 (1994; Mood). A rich and lovely album, Dauner plays acoustic piano throughout three of his own pieces, three Gershwin preludes and finally all five parts of Ravel's *Le Tombeau de Couperin*. This whole album is lyrical and performed with a lightness of touch and delightful clarity.

Cow-Cow Davenport

Piano, vocals, composer.

b. Anniston, Alabama, 26 April 1895; d. 2 Dec 1956.

The career of Cow-Cow (Charles) Davenport, which began in vaudeville, was dogged by bad health, bad luck and a spell in jail, but by the 1940s, at the height of the boogie boom, he was a regular broadcaster and club attraction. He part-composed "I'll Be Glad When You're Dead, You Rascal You" and "Mama Don't Allow", and recorded the seminal piano solo "Cow-Cow Blues", which has links with Jelly Roll Morton's "New Orleans Joys" and Ray Charles's "Mess Around". He was honoured in a song called "Cow-Cow Boogie", written by Benny Carter and others, which was a big hit for Ella Mae Morse and Ella Fitzgerald in the 1940s. [DF]

Complete Recorded Works In Chronological Order Vol.1 (1925–9; Document). The famous "Cow-Cow Blues", heard in three takes, and Davenport's other piano features (with occasional vocals) demonstrate a wide variety of voicings and rhythm patterns.

Kenny Davern

Clarinet, saxophones.

b. Huntingdon, Long Island, 7 Jan 1935.

Davern fell under the spell of Benny Goodman when young, then of Pee Wee Russell, whom he heard on a Ted Husing programme. His first professional job was with Jack Teagarden (who always encouraged good young players), and thereafter he played on the New York club circuit, including Nick's, Eddie Condon's and Central Plaza with stars including Billy Butterfield, Wild Bill Davison, Pee Wee Erwin, Condon and Dick Wellstood. Davern first achieved worldwide recognition in the supergroup Soprano Summit, which he co-led with Bob Wilber. The end of the group (after three years and nine albums) signalled his disenchantment with saxophone and the beginning of a solo career playing clarinet only. In later years he has toured internationally with the Blue Three (Dick Wellstood and Bobby Rosengarden), with Bob Wilber for "Summit Reunion" dates, and as a soloist – and his 1984 album *The Very Thought Of You* was an award-winner. Tempting as it is to bracket Davern and Wilber together, there's a world of difference between them. Whereas Wilber ploughs the rich soils of Armstrong and Bechet, Davern walks the wilder byways of such eccentrics as Pee Wee Russell and Rex Stewart. His playing and stage demeanour (slim fingers lifted high off the keys, mobile shoulders) recall Russell, too, but Davern is his own man. Witty, sometimes acerbic, always eclectic, he is a classicist who has also explored avant-garde jazz to great effect, while maintaining a strong campaign against certain contemporary jazz trends, such as amplification in every form. [DF]

Soprano Summit In Concert (1976; Concord); **Soprano Summit Live At Concord** (1977; Concord). Two classy sessions recorded live at the Concord summer festival, the former with Marty Grosz, Ray Brown and Jake Hanna, the latter with Grosz and Hanna joined by Monty Budwig on bass.

Stretchin' Out (1983; Jazzology). Davern at his very best, accompanied by the still underrated Dick Wellstood.

My Inspiration (1991; Limelight). Davern with a large string orchestra directed by Bob Haggart, who wrote the arrangements: one of the very best sessions of its genre.

A Night With Eddie Condon (2001; Arbors). Concert recording from 1971 at Westwood High School, Syracuse. Davern, on fine form, is teamed with Bernie Privin, Lou McGarity and a rhythm-section led by Condon, and perhaps most notably, trumpeter Bernie Privin, who plays marvellously in a rare illustration of his superb Dixieland powers.

The Jazz Kennection (2001; Arbors). Peplowski is a brilliant talent on clarinet, and his fluent creativity matches Davern's in an exemplary set accompanied by John Bunch and a quartet including Howard Allden.

John R.T. "Ristic" Davies

Trumpet, trombone, saxophones, piano, banjo.

b. Wivelsfield, Sussex, UK, 20 March 1927.

Davies worked with Mick Mulligan's band before, in 1949, joining the revolutionary Crane River Jazz Band, which set out to replay New Orleans jazz properly (and was still doing so, with line-up unaltered, in 1985). The same year he formed Ristic, the first of his two excellent record companies, then spent time in bands led by Steve Lane and Cy Laurie, and in 1955 joined Sandy Brown's band for what he later said were "the sixteen most valuable months in my career". In 1959 Davies joined the Temperance Seven for nine years as arranger/multi-instrumentalist and from 1968 worked regularly with cornettist Dick Sudhalter, in the Anglo-American Alliance (his favourite), the New Paul Whiteman Orchestra (playing the role of Frank Trumbauer) and elsewhere. Then in 1972 he became co-director of Retrieval Records, which over twenty years reissued a priceless catalogue of vintage jazz – often from old masters restored to mint quality by Davies's expert processes. Although his playing appearances became a little rarer after this, "Ristic" played on reunions with the Crane River Jazz Band (1972), recorded with the likes of Jimmie Noone Jnr and Dick Sudhalter, and still runs his own band, John R.T.'s Gentle Jazz (other regular members include trombonist Jim Shepherd and another senior master, guitarist Nevil Skrimshire). In 2003, following major surgery, he was working his way back to uninterrupted activity again. Davies is a jewel of British jazz: a musician of unimpeachable taste and creativity and a record producer whose work has set standards for all to follow. [DF]

➤➤ **Dick Sudhalter** *(After Awhile)*; **Dick Sudhalter And The Anglo-American Alliance** *(The Tuesday Band)*.

Anthony Davis

Piano, keyboards, composer.

b. Paterson, New Jersey, 20 Feb 1951.

Davis's father was a university professor, and he was brought up in the campus towns of Princeton and State College, Pennsylvania. His father knew Art Tatum, and pianist Billy Taylor was a neighbour. Davis studied classical piano as a child and graduated in music at Yale in the early 1970s, meeting and playing with trombonist George Lewis and others while he was there. From 1974–7 he played with trumpeter Leo Smith's band New Delta Ahkri, recording two albums. In 1975, he led his own quartet with Ed Blackwell (drums), Mark Helias (bass) and Jay Hoggard (vibes) before moving to New York in 1977, performing with Oliver Lake, Anthony Braxton, Barry Altschul, Chico Freeman and George Lewis. He also joined Leroy Jenkins's trio, staying with it until 1979. In the late 1970s he recorded his first album as leader, *Song For The Old World* and, into the 1980s, he ran a duo, led a quartet with flute player James Newton, and played solo piano concerts. In 1981 he formed his octet Episteme to play his own music and that of composers such as Earle Howard and Alvin Singleton. Davis has said: "...we're now getting to a period in music where the harmonic dimensions are coming back ... Most of my own music is composed – written. I think that improvisation is one compositional tool within the framework of a given piece." Certainly composition now seems to be his main interest – he has written the successsful operas *X*, based on the life of Malcolm X, and *Amistad*, and he continues to juggle composing classical pieces and music for Broadway theatre with his teaching post at Yale. [IC]

⊙ **I've Known Rivers** (1982; Gramavision). Davis is something of an intellectual with an academic bent, which tends to what Sidney Bechet called "kind of freezing" the music. But in trio format, here with flautist James Newton and cellist Abdul Wadud, Davis thaws out somewhat.

⊙ **Hemispheres** (1983; Gramavision). Davis leads a nine-piece ensemble featuring the contemporary "heavies" trumpeter Wadada Leo Smith and trombonist George Lewis, with instrumentation that includes saxophones, woodwind, vibes, marimba, and cello, so the textures and colours are greatly varied. There's also a bracing dynamic creative tension between the written and improvised passages.

⊙ **Middle Passage** (1984; Gramavision). Davis plays solo piano in a musical response to the history of slavery in America – ground he would later return to in his opera *Amistad*.

>> **George Lewis** *(Homage To Charles Parker)*; **David Murray** *(Ming)*.

Art Davis

Bass.

b. Harrisburg, Pennsylvania, 5 Dec 1934.

After studying at the Juilliard and Manhattan schools of music, Art Davis toured with Max Roach (1958–9) and Dizzy Gillespie (1959–61). In succeeding years he worked with several folk singers and with Lena Horne, becoming a radio studio musician and playing in symphony orchestras. Having been the first black string player to be a full staff member of the New York studio scene, he then became inactive as a player ("for reasons connected with racial politics") from 1970 to the end of the decade, while earning several degrees in music and psychology. From the 1980s he worked as a psychologist and resumed occasional playing.

A splendidly rhythmic performer, Davis amply justified John Coltrane's choice of him as occasional second bassist (1961, 1964–5), and he deserves to be far better known for his jazz work. [BP]

>> **Abbey Lincoln** *(Straight Ahead)*.

Eddie "Lockjaw" Davis

Tenor saxophone.

b. New York, 2 March 1921; d. 3 Nov 1986.

After stays with Cootie Williams (1942–4) and Andy Kirk (1945–6), Eddie "Lockjaw" Davis began leading his own group and recording under his own name in 1946. He was with the Count Basie band in 1952–3, and returned on several occasions, later doubling as saxophonist and road manager for four distinct spells – 1957, 1964–5, 1966 and

JAK KILBY

Eddie "Lockjaw" Davis

1967–73. While his own leader again, he had one of the first permanent tenor-and-organ trios (1955–60, though he had already recorded in this format in 1949). He co-led a two-tenor quintet with Johnny Griffin (1960–62), then gave up playing to work as a booking agent (1963–4). Resuming appearances as a guest soloist between stints with Basie, he sometimes teamed up with Roy Eldridge (1974) and Harry Edison (1975–82).

Lockjaw was a tough and trenchant stylist who seemed to have learned early on to emulate the style of "Texas tenors" such as Illinois Jacquet and Arnett Cobb, whom he resembled in his mid-1940s work especially. But he rapidly developed an individual and inimitable tone quality, by turns mellow and exasperated, which enhanced his jerky and somewhat repetitive phrasing. At ballad tempo Lockjaw showed familiarity with the achievements of Hawkins and more particularly Webster, as the tone becomes the chief vehicle for interpretation. [BP]

Eddie "Lockjaw" Davis

Jaws Strikes Again (1976; Black & Blue). A French-recorded quartet in which Wild Bill Davis fills the organ spot and Lockjaw takes on old warhorses like "Stompin' At The Savoy" and "Jumpin' With Symphony Sid".

Eddie Davis & Johnny Griffin

Live At Minton's (1961; Prestige). Minton's Playhouse was not the experimental hub of twenty years ago, but committed music was still being played for the locals. This fine document of the tough tenors' regular quintet (including Junior Mance) includes a choice of excellent Monk tunes.

➤➤ **Harry Edison** *(Jawbreakers).*

Jesse Davis

Alto saxophone, composer.
b. New Orleans, 11 Sept 1965.

Encouraged to take up the alto (after breaking his collarbone in sixth grade) by his tuba-playing brother Roger, Jesse Davis was initially interested in Grover Washington's music, but soon began to tread a more strictly jazz-oriented path courtesy of his introduction by mentor Ellis Marsalis to the music of Charlie Parker and Sonny Stitt. From Marsalis, Davis "learned that jazz is about your life, expressing who you are through your instrument and the music you make", and he continued to study jazz at Northeastern Illinois University, the William Paterson College in New Jersey and the New School in New York. Sideman work with the likes of Illinois Jacquet, Clark Terry, Benny Carter, the Lincoln Center Jazz Orchestra and trumpeter Nicholas Payton was followed by an offer – initially rejected – of a Concord contract, and Davis has now made several albums for the label. His debut, *Horn Of Passion* (1991), was hailed by Gary Giddins in the *Village Voice* magazine as "one of the most impressive debuts in years" and helped win Davis a nomination for a NAIRD Indie award. Four more albums – 1992's *As We Speak* with pianist Jacky Terrasson, *Young At Art* (1993) with Brad Mehldau at the keyboard, *High Standards* (1994) with trombonist Robert Trowers and Payton sharing frontline duties, and *From Within* (1996) with Payton, Hank Jones, Ron Carter and Lewis Nash – cemented his reputation as one of the brightest young stars in the jazz firmament, and his appearance in Robert Altman's *Kansas City* raised his profile, but he really shows his class as both improviser and composer on *First Insight* (see below) and his seventh Concord release, and swansong with the company, *Second Nature* (2000). A new deal on Alltribe Records started reliably enough with *The Setup* (2003) but by now some commentators have ventured to interpret Davis's everyday consistency as a lack of musical ambition. [CP]

First Insight (1998; Concord). With regular guitarist Peter Bernstein, pianist Mulgrew Miller, bassist Ron Carter and drummer Kenny Washington on board, Davis swings hard but intelligently through a richly varied set of originals, some inspired by his return in 1996 to live in the city of his birth.

Lem Davis

Alto saxophone.
b. Tampa, Florida, 22 June 1914; d. 16 Jan 1970.

Lem Davis's career began in the 1940s (with pianist Nat Jaffe) at a time when bebop was making some swing-based musicians sound listless and dull. Players such as Roy Eldridge, Bill Coleman and particularly Pete Brown suffered crises of identity at that period, and some of Davis's later work (very like Brown's) sounds as if he was trying to come to terms with modernity without quite believing in it.

A star of Coleman Hawkins's septet in 1943, and later with Eddie Heywood's small group (which became hugely successful), he was constantly working in the best jazz company all through the 1940s and made a late extended appearance on Buck Clayton's 1953 "Hucklebuck" recording, though by this time his lines sound incomplete and his tone suggests his emotional reservations about what he was playing. "Davis is one of the great swing altos gone modern", wrote annotator/producer George Avakian, "and his occasional bop phrases kept us all on our toes."

As he deserved, Davis stayed busy around New York through the 1950s, but little more was heard from him thereafter. [DF]

Miles Davis

Trumpet, flugelhorn, keyboards, composer.
b. Alton, Illinois, 26 May 1926; d. 28 Sept 1991.

Miles Dewey Davis moved to East St Louis in 1927. He had a wealthy middle-class background – his grandfather was a landowner in Arkansas and his father was a successful dentist who also owned a ranch; his mother played violin and his sister played piano. Davis got his first trumpet at the age of nine or ten, took private lessons from Elwood Buchanan and played in his high school band. He also played with a St Louis R&B band, Eddie Randall's Blue Devils, while still at school. Clark Terry befriended him, influencing his sound and style, and Davis also met Dizzy Gillespie and Charlie Parker when the Billy Eckstine band played in St Louis.

In September 1944 his father sent him to New York to study at the Juilliard, but he left to play in the small clubs on 52nd Street with Coleman Hawkins and others, though mainly with Parker. In November 1945, aged only nineteen, he joined the Parker quintet which recorded the first true bebop tracks, including the classic blues performance "Now's The Time", which established Davis immediately as a master of understatement and an alternative trumpet stylist to Gillespie. From 1946–8 he worked mostly with Parker, playing on the saxophonist's best sextet and quintet recordings. He left Parker's group in late 1948 and began leading his own groups in New York, including a nine-piece band which created a revolutionary new sound.

The nonet grew out of extensive discussions between Davis and a small coterie of the most vital young talents of the day, who met informally at Gil Evans's apartment. Some, including Evans, Gerry Mulligan and Lee Konitz, were from the Claude Thornhill band which used French horns and tuba, and their aim was to achieve a full orchestral palette from a minimum number of instruments. The result was an instrumentation new to jazz: French horn, trumpet, trombone, tuba, alto and baritone saxophones, piano, bass and drums. The nonet's urbane sound, the subtle, innovatory scoring and the calm, unhurried solos seemed to be a reaction against the frenetic flurries of bebop and ushered in what came to be called the "cool school" of jazz. This was perhaps the first example of key musicians of the time focusing and finding themselves through Miles Davis. The band was a failure as a working unit, its only public appearances being a two-week engagement at the Royal Roost in September 1948 and one week a year later at the Clique Club. However, several tracks were recorded for Capitol and released on 78s, spawning a host of imitators and admirers. Years later they were issued on an LP under the title *Birth Of The Cool*, which has since become recognized as a classic album and sold steadily throughout successive decades. The nonet established Davis as a leader and a talent quite independent of Charlie Parker.

He continued to work with various small groups on a casual basis in New York, and in 1949 played at the Paris jazz festival, which gave him his first international exposure. But then his brilliantly promising career suddenly lost all impetus and direction, and for four years (1949–53) he hardly worked at all. 1954 saw the beginning of his fully mature style and from that year until the end of the decade there was a succession of recorded masterpieces which astonished and delighted musicians and non-musicians alike, opened up several new avenues of musical development, influencing subsequent generations of artists all over the world, and brought Davis a huge audience, many of whom knew little about jazz in general.

The first great Miles Davis quintet (1955–6), with John Coltrane, Red Garland, Paul Chambers and Philly Joe Jones, was a group so brimful with new ideas that they recorded six influential albums in a twelve-month period. In 1957 he played and recorded the soundtrack for Louis Malle's film *Lift To The Scaffold*, and in collaboration with Gil Evans recorded their first orchestral masterpiece, *Miles Ahead*, which was followed by two others – *Porgy And Bess* and *Sketches Of Spain*. In the last two years of the decade there were also two albums by the great Miles Davis sextet (with Coltrane and Cannonball Adderley), *Milestones* and *Kind Of Blue*, both seminal but the latter probably the most influential LP in jazz history. During the latter half of the 1950s Davis became the dominant figure in jazz: his rhythm-sections were regarded as the key units of the time, and his quintet and sextet were generally recognized as the leading groups of the period. The orchestral works with Gil Evans were not only innovative – creating new sounds, textures and techniques – but they also brought the integration of soloist and ensemble to a new and sustained peak. With *Kind Of Blue*, Davis had fully established the relevance and beauty of modal improvisation, and it soon became part of the current jazz language. He had also introduced (for the first time in 1954) a totally new instrumental sound – that of the trumpet with a metal harmon mute (without its stem) played close to the microphone, and had established the flugelhorn, which he played on *Miles Ahead*, as an important expressive instrument; by the early 1960s harmon mutes and flugelhorns were employed ubiquitously in jazz.

Between 1963–4 Davis gradually formed a new quintet, yet again drawing together some of the most gifted young musicians of the time: Herbie Hancock (piano), Ron Carter (bass), Tony Williams (drums) and Wayne Shorter (saxophones). This particular rhythm-section is generally considered to be perhaps the greatest time-playing unit in jazz, and its brilliant fluidity can be heard on a series of live albums of 1963–4, on which Davis and the group explore conventional structures – standard tunes, ballads, modal pieces and blues – so radically that they are sometimes taken to the verge of disintegration. The best of these, and one of the finest live recordings in jazz history, is *The Complete Concert*. From 1965 Davis and his group began perfecting a new way of playing which came to be called "time-no changes". This was a form of abstraction in that the improvisation occurred in regular time, but without prearranged harmonies; in other words, there were composed themes, the group played in 4/4 or 3/4 at various tempos, but after the theme statement, the soloist and the pianist and bassist were free to choose what notes or chords they wanted. This approach added yet another dimension to the current jazz language and soon had practitioners everywhere. Its genesis and development are documented on four studio albums Davis recorded between 1965–7. Leonard Feather commented in the later 1960s that Davis had taken small-group improvisation to such a pitch of brilliance that he had "nowhere to look except down".

Up to this point virtually all Davis's small-group music had been based on themes which related clearly to popular song structures, but in 1968 he began to think more in terms of longer pieces, often without written themes. He also began to change the instrumentation of his group, using electric keyboards, electric guitars, multiple percussion and sometimes Indian musicians and instruments (sitar, tabla and others). The harmonic and linear abstraction remained, but he employed rock rhythms which created a coherent pulse, giving his music a human face. Yet again, some of the most gifted of that generation of players were drawn to his band: John McLaughlin, Chick Corea, Keith Jarrett, Dave Holland, Jack DeJohnette, Billy Cobham, Dave Liebman and Joe Zawinul. In two years of furious creative activity, 1969–70, Davis recorded more than twenty LP sides, focusing and launching the jazz-rock-fusion movement. The key albums which had a global influence were *In A Silent Way*, *Bitches Brew* and, to a lesser extent, *Live-Evil* and *Jack Johnson*. Davis continued exploring this vein until 1975, when illness and physical and creative exhaustion incapacitated him. He was inactive until 1980, when he began to perform again.

In the 1980s he felt his way slowly into a new phase which was like a summary of his whole career. He steadily regained all his trumpet magnificence – the huge singing sound, the stamina, the use of the entire range from the lowest notes to the extreme upper register, and his characteristic gift for epigrammatic melodic phrases. Once more he drew to his band some key people from the current generation: Bill Evans and Bob Berg (saxophones), Mike Stern and John Scofield (guitars), Marcus Miller and Daryl "The Munch" Jones (bass guitar). He returned to using structures related to popular songs, and on his recordings he functioned more as a producer/composer/arranger than ever before. His studio albums, such as *Decoy* and *You're Under Arrest*, are tightly organized, with an immense attention to detail and considerable complexity, yet they seem like blueprints for the looser live performances where the magic and the music really happen. After his return Davis toured once or twice a year in the USA, Europe and Japan, playing to huge and ecstatic crowds everywhere. Although he still employed electronics and rock rhythms, the whole of his past glowed in the music, and yet he was neither coasting nor purveying nostalgia. Some of his most eloquent and moving playing was done during these tours, and he was still pushing himself to the limit. In 1984 he went to Denmark to receive the Sonning Award, presented for a lifetime achievement in music. Davis

ROBERT SERRA

Miles Davis

was the first non-classical musician to receive it. Three months later he was back in Denmark to play on the recording of an hour-long suite, *Aura,* which Danish trumpeter Palle Mikkelborg had composed in his honour. For his London appearances in 1985 he was on stage for over five hours, playing for long stretches and actively directing his band. But after 1985 his strength began almost imperceptibly to leave him over the years up to his death.

In these final years, Davis changed record companies for the first time in thirty years. Disgusted at Columbia's reluctance to release *Aura*, he signed with Warner Bros. and recorded for them two magnificent albums, *Tutu* in 1986, which Mike Zwerin called " the soundtrack to the decade", and *Amandla* in the autumn and winter of 1988 and 1989. He continued to play and tour right up to the end. On 10 July 1991, at the Montreux festival, just two months before his death, he astonished the jazz world by performing again some of his great orchestral music from the 1950s, even though his frailness was apparent. Two days later, in Paris, he received a decoration from the Minister of Culture, then played another revisitation concert with several ex-members of his various bands including Herbie Hancock, John McLaughlin, Jackie McLean, Wayne Shorter, Dave

Holland and Joe Zawinul. He played at the Royal Festival Hall, London, on 19 July and the Hollywood Bowl five weeks later. Then he went into hospital and died a few weeks later of pneumonia, respiratory failure and a stroke.

Miles Davis is a unique figure in jazz because his creativity and his influence as both player and conceptualist were sustained for more than four decades, an example which introduced the idea of permanent conceptual development into the jazz life. That is why he has been an inspirational figure for successive generations of musicians since the 1940s. With Louis Armstrong and Dizzy Gillespie, he is one of the three most influential trumpet players, but whereas the first two each introduced basically one stylistic approach Davis has evolved at least three interrelated trumpet styles: the lyrical minimalist approach of *Bags' Groove* or of his work on *Kind Of Blue* in the 1950s, the voluble brilliance and dramatic use of space of the live albums of 1961–4, and the abstraction, chromaticism and the electric trumpet of the late 1960s and early 1970s. Few, if any, players, can match his emotional scope, which ranges from the extreme violence of "What I Say" (*Live-Evil*) to the melancholy introspection of ballad performances such as "Blue In Green" (*Kind Of Blue*), the ominous disquiet of "The Buzzard Song" (*Porgy And Bess*), or the sheer joy of "Straight No Chaser" (*Milestones*).

His development is minutely documented by his huge body of recorded work, and every phase has its masterpieces which have defined areas and set standards for other musicians. Herbert Marcuse said that "the truth of art lies in its power to break the monopoly of established reality to define what is real", and Davis's work has broken this monopoly decade after decade, forcing people to ask "Is it jazz?" and making them revise and expand their ideas of the music's identity and possibilities.

Posthumously, Davis has become more famous than ever – an irony that he would have appreciated. The acute sense of loss among musicians can be measured by the unceasing flow of tribute albums that began immediately after he died – Mark Isham's impassioned *Miles Remembered: The Silent Way Project* (Columbia; 1999) being particularly poignant. There's an entire industry geared to reissuing and repackaging the Davis oeuvre for completists, with different Miles periods gathered into handy multi-CD box-sets: the most satifying and fascinating being the magnificent *Complete Bitches Brew Sessions 1969–70*; *Panthalassa* (the Miles of 1969–74 remixed by Bill Laswell); and the recent *Complete Jack Johnson*. [IC]

⊙ **The Complete Birth Of The Cool** (1948–50; Capitol). These tracks changed the course of jazz, introducing the urbane cool school of playing and establishing Davis as an important leader in his own right. He was still only 24 years old, and Mulligan and Konitz were both a year younger. The ensemble playing and soloing of all three is astonishingly original and assured.

⊙ **Walkin'** (1954; Prestige/OJC). 1954 was a miraculous year for Miles, in which his vision became sharper and his playing even pithier. The two masterpieces on this compilation are the title track and "Blue 'n' Boogie". With a superlative sextet – Lucky Thompson, J.J. Johnson, Horace Silver, Percy Heath and Kenny Clarke – Davis created two of the greatest instrumental blues performances of all time and helped to initiate the hard bop movement.

⊙ **Bags' Groove** (1954; Prestige/OJC). This is another compilation with tracks from two very significant sessions in June and December 1954. The June session was with the same Silver-Heath-Clarke rhythm-section plus Sonny Rollins, three of whose new compositions for this date, "Airegin", "Oleo" and "Doxy", were to become jazz standards. Miles used the harmon mute for the first time on record, thus introducing a new sound to jazz. It also affected the way he phrased, and his solo on "Oleo" is not only utterly non-boppish, but unlike any previous jazz. For the Christmas Eve session, Silver was replaced by Milt Jackson and Thelonious Monk. This compilation includes only the two takes of "Bags' Groove" from that session, and these are exquisite performances where Miles plays, as Barry Ulanov put it, "like a man walking on eggshells".

⊙ **Cookin' And Relaxin'** (1956; Ace/Prestige). Davis had formed his great quintet with John Coltrane, Red Garland, Paul Chambers and Philly Joe Jones towards the end of 1955, and in order to fulfil his contract with Prestige (so that he could sign up with Columbia) he recorded four LPs' worth of material in two marathon sessions in May and October 1956, two of which are coupled on this single CD. One of the supreme groups in jazz (and one of the best loved) is documented here in the white heat of creation. The ecstatic joy of the rhythm-section and the depth of feeling projected by Miles and Coltrane gave this band a unique human resonance.

⊙ **Miles Ahead** (1957; Columbia). This collaboration with Gil Evans has Davis as the only soloist with an orchestra of twelve brass, alto saxophone, three woodwinds, bass and drums. By now, each new Davis release brought with it the "shock of the new", and this was perhaps the biggest shock to date. The lyricism of Miles' flugelhorn plus Evans's inspired arrangements give the nine separate pieces (all composed by different people) the unity of a suite. Each side of the LP ran continuously, with bridge passages edited in between the pieces – another startling innovation. This remains a masterpiece and one of the glories of twentieth-century orchestral music.

⊙ **Milestones** (1958; Columbia). Alto saxophonist Cannonball Adderley was now in the Davis band, making it a sextet. Again, it is a working band playing on a knife-edge of creativity in the studio with spectacular results. Old material is brilliantly reinterpreted – there are three blues in F including an ecstatic version of Monk's "Straight No Chaser". The title track is the one new composition and it's a radically different-sounding modal piece by Miles himself.

⊙ **Porgy And Bess** (1958; Columbia). If *Miles Ahead* is the most perfect of the three orchestral albums, *Porgy* has greater majesty and profundity. The harmon mute's new sonorities and attack give a sharp edge to the ensembles and Evans's scoring has the mark of genius – textures are wonderfully varied, tension created and released in many subtle ways.

⊙ **Kind Of Blue** (1959; Columbia). This is one of the most famous, influential and most loved albums in jazz history. It is a perfect expression of Davis's contemplative self, the tempos leisurely, his themes spare and sonorous. The sextet now had Jimmy Cobb on drums and Bill Evans on piano for everything except the blues "Freddie Freeloader", on which Wynton Kelly played. This was also the first modal jazz album and its grave elegance and mysteriously profound feeling spoke directly to the hearts of musicians and non-musicians alike. The "singing" resonance of Evans's chords were matched by the sculptural eloquence of the soloists. Miles's solo on "So What" was so beautifully constructed that it has since been orchestrated and played by many musicians.

⊙ **Miles In Antibes** (1963; Columbia). After Coltrane left the band in 1960, Miles slowly assembled a new group. By 1963, he already had his new rhythm-section in Herbie Hancock, Ron Carter and the seventeen-year-old Tony Williams. The saxophonist at Antibes was the excellent George Coleman. Here, once again, is a brand-new group bristling with adventure and new ideas. This is a tumultuous concert, and again Davis is reinventing himself with freshly minted phrases and group interplay so audacious that it flirts with disaster.

⊙ **The Complete Concert** (1964; Columbia). The same group played this concert at New York's Philharmonic Hall in February 1964. The concert was originally released on two separate LPs – *My Funny Valentine* and *Four And More*, which are brought together on this double CD. The *Valentine* material contains all the medium and slow pieces, and Davis's playing is unearthly in its starkness of phrase and feeling, while the rhythm-section's fluidity and freedom border on the superhuman. Coleman is superb, and his more conventional solos provide a useful counterweight to the proceedings. *Four And More* isn't quite so good though, as the fast tempi employed give a sense of scramble and strain.

⊙ **ESP** (1965; Columbia). After a spate of live albums offering the old repertoire, it became necessary to explore some fresh musical territory. All of the band, except Tony Williams, had a hand in one or other of the seven superb compositions, and the playing is at an exceptionally high level. The album seems to indicate two different musical directions. On the title track Miles plays powerfully and very chromatically at times, as if he is moving halfway towards abstraction. But on his joint composition with Ron Carter, "Eighty-One", he is reworking the blues with a rock rhythm, and his majestic trumpet solo is one of the high spots of the whole album. This seesawing between abstraction and the blues (and their eventual synthesis) would be a recurring theme in his work.

⊙ **Miles Smiles** (1966; Columbia). This is also a powerful album full of new ideas. Miles had said he didn't want to play chord sequences after the themes had been stated, and Hancock said in that case he wouldn't know what chords to play. Davis replied, "Then don't play." The two most abstract pieces on *Smiles* are "Orbits", which opens the album, and "Dolores", both by Shorter. Hancock plays no chords during the themes of both, nothing behind the solos of Miles and Shorter, and both of his own piano solos are played with the right hand only. However, there is a magnificent reworking of the blues in Wayne Shorter's composition in 6/4, "Footprints".

⊙ **In A Silent Way** (1969; Columbia). This is another sublime expression of Miles's meditative self, but the context and the method have changed radically once more. Miles had been gradually moving away from popular song structures and was now beginning to abandon them altogether. The astonishing touch was the use of three electric keyboards – Chick Corea, Herbie Hancock and Zawinul – and John McLaughlin's electric guitar. Their improvised, ever-changing figures produced textures and an ensemble sound which were new to jazz. Tony Williams's crystal-clear rock rhythms, which give the music a wonderful coherence, make this radical album attractively familiar to contemporary ears.

⊙ **Bitches Brew** (1969; Columbia). This turbulent, massive album was recorded just six months after *Silent Way*. The big ensemble bucks and heaves like a live animal under Miles's direction. The mood is often dark and brooding, and an atmosphere of barely suppressed passion suffuses the proceedings. There are longueurs, of course, and on "Spanish Key" Davis can actually be heard shouting instructions to John McLaughlin and others. The process of music creation is more important on *Bitches Brew* than the end product. However, even with its failings, this is an heroic, extraordinarily thrilling document.

⊙ **Jack Johnson** (1970; Columbia). The band is a sextet, the palette smaller, and the music buoyant and brilliant ("Right Off"), and dramatically spacious and meditative ("Yesternow").

⊙ **We Want Miles** (1981; Columbia). This is Miles's first live recording after his return to music. The young band is superb, and Miles came back with some new and dynamic rhythms – particularly the feel on his folky "Jean-Pierre", and his imaginative updating of the Gershwin tune from *Porgy And Bess*, "My Man's Gone Now".

⊙ **Amandla** (1989; Warner). Miles's last really beautiful album – the sculpted phrases still sing and linger in the memory. His open trumpet tribute to Pastorius is highly emotional and ends, as if as an afterthought, with little upward flurries of unaccompanied trumpet.

⊙ **Panthalassa** (1998; Columbia). Bill Laswell remixed and re-edited passages from *In A Silent Way*, *On The Corner*, *Agharta* and *Get Up With It*, putting them together in a coherent and very attractive suite. Miles Davis would certainly have approved of this intelligent and sensitive recycling, re-editing and reissuing of aspects of his more discursive music.

➤➤ **Charlie Parker** *(The Charlie Parker Story; The Dial Masters; Charlie Parker Memorial Vol.1; Complete Live Performances On Savoy).*

Nathan Davis

Tenor saxophone, soprano saxophone, flute, bass-clarinet.

b. Kansas City, Kansas, 15 Feb 1937.

Davis's mother sang gospel and his father played drums. Nathan began on trombone, then played saxophone in school and briefly with Jay McShann (c.1955). At the University of Kansas he led a group including Carmell Jones and, after moving to Chicago (c.1959), army service took him to Berlin (1960–63), where he played weekends with Benny Bailey. Later he worked in Paris with Kenny Clarke (1963–9), also touring Europe with Art Blakey and Ray Charles, and studied composition and ethnomusicology. He returned to the USA to become professor of jazz at the University of Pittsburgh (from 1969) and more recently at Moorhead State University. He continued playing in Pittsburgh, running the record label Segue (one of whose tracks had a belated dance-floor success in Europe), and has toured internationally, fronting the Paris Reunion Band (1985–9) and the band Roots (from 1991). Davis's style is a persuasive blend of his early grounding in Coleman Hawkins and Don Byas with influences from John Coltrane onwards. [BP]

London By Night (1987; DIW). Mainly performed by a quintet with Dusko Goykovich, plus one three-saxophone track prefiguring the Roots group, this shows Davis at the top of his post-bop form.

Richard Davis

Bass.

b. Chicago, 15 April 1930.

Part of the generation of Chicago musicians that included Johnny Griffin, John Gilmore and Clifford Jordan, Davis played in local symphony orchestras as well as with local pianists Ahmad Jamal (1953–4) and Don Shirley (1954–6). He toured and recorded with Charlie Ventura (1956), Sarah Vaughan (1957–60, including a tour of Europe) and Kenny Burrell (1959). Freelancing in New York from 1960, his brief engagement with Eric Dolphy (1961) led to important 1963–4 albums together. He also formed a recording association with Jaki Byard and Alan Dawson, backing Booker Ervin, Roland Kirk, etc (1963–6). He became heavily involved in session work for artists as varied as Igor Stravinsky and Van Morrison, while gigging with the Thad Jones-Mel Lewis band (1966–72). Teaching in university from the mid-1970s, Davis returned to Chicago until the mid-1980s; he then recorded live sets with Donald Harrison-Terence Blanchard, Bobby Bradford-John Carter and Archie Shepp (late 1980s). A couple of live albums under his own name and a studio series by the "New York Unit" led by drummer Tatsuya Nakamura (1990–92) brought him to the fore again, but he is still underrecognized.

Possessed of an enormous sound and a springy beat, he was the most dominant bassist to appear since Charles Mingus, and required a flexible yet driving drummer such as Dawson or Elvin Jones in order to be heard at his best. In these favourable circumstances, Davis was fond of breaking up the beat in a manner probably inspired by fellow Chicagoan Wilbur Ware, and his accompaniments as well as solos usually mixed high-register notes (including double-stops) with the low sounds of the open strings. At times, when surrounded by less suitable collaborators, Davis's work could sound too mannered, but his great contribution and influence should not be overlooked. [BP]

>> **Eric Dolphy** *(Iron Man)*; **Booker Ervin** *(The Blues Book)*; **Thad Jones** *(Central Park North)*.

Walter Davis Jnr

Piano.

b. Richmond, Virginia, 2 Sept 1932; d. 2 June 1990.

No relation to the prolific blues pianist and singer Walter Davis (b. 1 March 1912; d. 22 Oct 1963), the bebop-based pianist Walter Davis Jnr was brought up in New Jersey, where his mother played gospel music. Moving to New York after a gig with Charlie Parker, he was befriended by Bud Powell and Thelonious Monk, and worked with Max Roach (1953) and Dizzy Gillespie (1956 and mid-1980s). A European tour with Donald Byrd's quintet (1958) led to recording his own album with Byrd and Jackie McLean, and to work with Art Blakey (1959, 1975–7) and Philly Joe Jones (1960, 1982–3). Other important associations were with Betty Carter and Sonny Rollins (1973), and he was one of the pianists on the soundtrack of the film *Bird* (1987). As with his tunes for Blakey which have become widely known, such as "Gypsy Folk Tales", his mature playing showed an ability to blend the demands of modal jazz with the fire of Powell-style bebop. [BP]

>> **Jackie McLean** *(New Soil)*.

Wild Bill Davis

Piano, organ, arranger.

b. Glasgow, Missouri, 24 Nov 1918; d. 17 Aug 1995.

Wild Bill Davis studied music at Tuskegee Institute and Wiley College, Texas (late 1930s), while playing guitar and arranging for the Milt Larkin band before their departure to the West Coast. Davis moved to Chicago, doing some arrangements for the Earl Hines band (early 1940s). He joined Louis Jordan's group as pianist/arranger (1945–8), then returned to Chicago and began playing electric organ; he recorded on organ, guesting with Jordan (1950), and had piano backing from Duke Ellington on one of his own first records (1951). He formed a successful organ/guitar/drums trio (1951), working at Birdland and in Atlantic City, etc. He did occasional arrangements for Ellington, Count Basie and others and, from 1961, did a series of albums with Johnny Hodges. In 1969–70 he joined the Ellington band for several months, playing featured organ solos, then resumed his own trio. He worked with Lionel Hampton's ten-piece band (1979), was teamed in tenor/organ/drums trios with Illinois Jacquet, Eddie Davis, Guy Lafitte, etc and continued to appear as a soloist until his death. Davis's dynamic arranging is best known via his organ version of "April In Paris" as transcribed for the Basie band, but the same forthright qualities permeate all his playing. In addition, he deserves to be honoured as a pioneer, for, of the pianists of the late swing/early R&B era, he switched on to the organ earlier than either Milt Buckner or Bill Doggett. [BP]

Impulsions (1972; Black & Blue). Davis's trio (with guitarist Floyd Smith and drummer Chris Columbus) reproduces the ensemble style of the big bands. Here he reprises "Night Train" and "Ooh! Ah! De-De-De" from his live Birdland album of eighteen years earlier.

Wild Bill Davison

Cornet.

b. Defiance, Ohio, 5 Jan 1906; d. 14 Nov 1989.

From the early 1920s Wild Bill (William Edward) Davison was building a career with, among

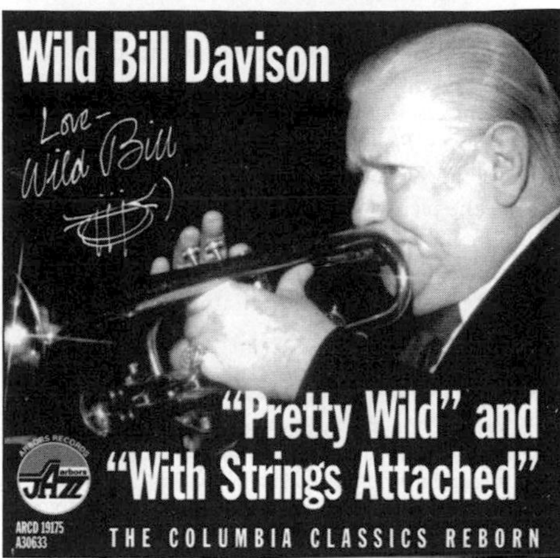

others, the Ohio Lucky Seven, the Chubb-Steinberg Orchestra (for which Davison recorded at eighteen for OKeh), the Seattle Harmony Kings and Benny Meroff's Chicago-based orchestra, where he first met Eddie Condon. For most of the 1930s he was in Milwaukee, billed as "Trumpet-King" Davison, then arrived on the New York scene in 1941, despite a lip injury sustained when he was hit in the mouth by a flying beer mug (appropriately for Milwaukee). Work at Nick's saloon and with an Original Dixieland Jazz Band re-creation for the Katherine Dunham show culminated in twelve sides recorded with Georg Brunis a week before his 38th birthday – brilliant recordings which showed that Davison had found a new style of his own.

A two-year spell in the army followed, and after discharge he joined Eddie Condon's house band in 1945. A commanding front man, and a tough, reliable and original lead cornettist, Davison was perfect for the long nights and hard pace of Condon's club. His physico-musical style – growls, rips, flares, long tones brusquely cut with a peremptory shake, giving way to heart-on-sleeve Irish sentimentality on ballads – personified Condon's Chicago jazz image and was quickly singled out for star treatment. TV presenter Garry Moore first recorded Davison with strings (for the compendium album *My Kind Of Music* with, among others, Percy Faith) and this session lit the way for two more incandescent dates, *With Strings Attached* and *Pretty Wild*, an enchanting jazz classic. As well as making Condon recordings and playing quartet dates of his own, Davison by 1960 was a soloist, with his wife Anne as manager. Reunions with Condon now punctuated a pattern of bandleading and touring: between 1965–75 Davison appeared with more than a hundred bands and recorded over twenty albums. A thorough professional for all his hard drinking, Davison was honoured in 1980 with Carnegie Hall concerts, and continued globetrotting, despite illness in mid-decade, until very shortly before his death.

Because Wild Bill Davison made his name in a jazz age dominated by the omnipotent Louis Armstrong, his work has occasionally been downgraded as a less effective paraphrase of the Armstrong prototype. In fact Davison's style remains a brilliant alternative which, though it was once based on admiration – "just to make one note sound like Louis is enough to accomplish in one lifetime", he once said with typically rash generosity – soon outgrew its creative inspiration to become a self-sufficient entity. [DF]

Wild Bill Davison and Georg Brunis

◉ **The Davison-Brunis Sessions Vols. 1–3** (1943–5; Commodore). The classic recordings which established Davison internationally as a force to reckon with.

Wild Bill Davison

⊙ **The Commodore Master Takes** (1943–6; Commodore). All the sides by Wild Bill with his Commodores; Brunis again, but also Lou McGarity, Edmund Hall, Vernon Brown and others plus Eddie Condon in the rhythm-section throughout.

⊙ **Memories** (1966; Jazzology). With the Alex Welsh band at the Manchester Sports Guild, Davison is in good and compatible 1960s company; he and Welsh make a perfect cornet partnership and Davison high spots include his specialities "Blue Again" and "Blue And Brokenhearted". An "informal" live recording, the quality and balance are acceptable nevertheless.

⊙ **Lady Of The Evening** (1971; Jazzology). A marvellous small-group session featuring Davison with four-piece rhythm-section; his emotive version of Irving Berlin's title track is outstanding.

⊙ **"Pretty Wild" And "With Strings Attached": The Columbia Classics Reborn** (2000; Arbors). One of the late Anne Davison's last missions accomplished: the reissue of Davison's two with-strings masterpieces. *Pretty Wild* sees him with Percy Faith's orchestra, while on *With Strings Attached* he teams with Deane Kincaide's Orchestra and a Dixieland band including Cutty Cutshall, Bob Wilber and Gene Schroeder. Unmissable for Davison lovers.

➤➤ **Eddie Condon** *(Dixieland Jam).*

Alan Dawson

Drums; also vibes.

b. Marietta, Pennsylvania, 14 July 1929; d. 23 Feb 1996.

Dawson studied at the Charles Alden Drum Studio in Boston in 1947 and also studied vibes there in 1949. He spent three years, 1949–52, playing with local and army dance bands, then in 1953 he played with Lionel Hampton for three months, making his first trips to Africa and Europe and his first recording – with Clifford Brown and Gigi Gryce. From late 1953 to 1956 he worked with Sabby Lewis, then taught at the Berklee School of Music in Boston until 1975, cramming in recordings and gigs with Earl Hines, Booker Ervin, Teddy Wilson, Jaki Byard, Phil Woods, Sonny Stitt, Frank Foster and others during the 1960s. At the 1965 Berlin jazz festival he played with Sonny Rollins and Bill Evans. From 1968–74 he was a member of the Dave Brubeck quartet, touring worldwide and playing major festivals. His drums can be heard on innumerable recordings with leading musicians including Quincy Jones, Sonny Stitt, Lee Konitz and Terry Gibbs.

Dawson had all the virtues of a born drummer – beautiful time, taste and great stamina – but perhaps his true genius was for teaching, as his first student was one Tony Williams, and Harvey Mason, Joe La Barbera and Vinnie Colaiuta also took lessons from him. [IC]

➤➤ **Booker Ervin** *(The Blues Book).*

Sebastiaan De Krom

Drums.

b. Dordrecht, Netherlands, 6 February 1971.

De Krom got his basic skills from his father – a talented amateur drummer – but thereafter taught himself by listening to records. In 1991 he formed a sextet that came third in the European Jazz contest in Hoeilaart, Belgium, and in the same year won a scholarship to Berklee College of Music in Boston USA where he won the Buddy Rich award. He later took a master's degree in Jazz Studies at the New England Conservatory where he came under the influence of Ron Carter and Charlie Persip. In 2000 De Krom moved to England and joined the Guy Barker Quintet and Tommy Smith Quartet, and also performed on the sound track of the film *The Talented Mr Ripley*. Of his own recordings, the one he rates most highly is *The Horizon* which was recorded with alto saxophonist (and fellow Berklee graduate) Phil Stockli in 1998. More recently he has provided dynamic support for Jamie Cullum along with bass-player Geoff Gascoyne. [IC]

➤➤ **Jamie Cullum** *(Pointless Nostalgic).*

Maria Pia De Vito

Voice, piano.

b.Naples, Italy, 17 August 1960.

Maria Pia De Vito is a brilliant and astonishingly versatile singer who combines the widest of ranges – from basso semi-profundo to bat squeak – with an ability to improvise and scat. She began as a classical musician, with a degree in music and ten years of operatic training. In 1976 she started to sing with groups specializing in traditional music from the Mediterranean and the Balkans, but by 1980 was singing jazz. Four years later she was performing at the Rome Festival with her own quartet. In1987 she joined trumpeter Paolu Fresu's quintet, and made her first jazz recording with the TinoTracanna Sextet on "Mr Frankenstein Blues". Throughout the 1990s she performed with several other major musicians – American as well as Italian – including Joe Zawinul, Bobby Previte, Kenny Wheeler and Gianluigi Trovesi.

In 1994 De Vito formed the group Nauplia, with pianist Rita Marcotulli, a project which fused Neapolitan and improvisational music. Two years later she began a long term collaboration with the English composer Colin Towns, and recorded with his Mask Orchestra the CD *Nowhere and Heaven*. Her continuing fascination with world music can be heard on her album *Phoné* (1998), an eclectic blend of influences including Macedonian and Italian folk. John Taylor, the pianist for *Phoné*, was another regular collaborator, as was the guitarist Ralph Towner. Since 1998 the three have performed regularly together and in 2000 produced the highly impressive *Verso* for Provocateur Records. [IC]

De Vito/Taylor/Towner

⊙ **Verso** (2000; Provocateur Records). A trio of real virtuosi, with all the material composed by the artists themselves. The title track, written by all three, has De Vito scatting away as Taylor and Towner bang ecstatic rhythms on the wood of their instruments. Other highlights include Taylor's bravura "Afterthought", and De Vito and Towner's haunting lament "L'Ombra E La Grazia".

Elton Dean

Alto saxophone, saxello.

b. Nottingham, UK, 28 Oct 1945.

A self-taught musician, Dean worked in 1967 with Long John Baldry's Bluesology, and his long association with Keith Tippett began in 1968. Dean was with the prog-rock band Soft Machine from 1969–72, after which he began leading his own group Just Us. In 1972 he joined the London Jazz Composers' Orchestra and, in 1974, led his own quartet which comprised Louis Moholo, Harry Miller and Tippett. The following year he formed his nine-piece band Ninesense, which included Mongezi Feza, Alan Skidmore and Marc Charig, and in 1976 co-led a group (El Skid) with Alan Skidmore. He toured internationally and recorded with the Carla Bley band in 1977. Dean formed Soft Heap in 1978, the first in a series of bands built around former Soft Machine players (such as Soft Head, SoftWare, SoftWorks et al). He joined the band In Cahoots with veteran "Canterbury band" stalwart Phil Miller, with whom he still plays. Keeping busy, Dean spent the 1990s leading a quartet drawing heavily on ex-Mujicians (Keith Tippett's band). Latterly Dean has begun to release his own music on his tape-only label – ED Tapes. Dean is a passionate improviser, with wide terms of reference. His favourite saxophonists are Coltrane and Joe Henderson, and other inspirations have been Miles Davis and Bill Evans. An excellent free jazz player, he's also at home with more conventional jazz.[IC]

⊙ **Unlimited Saxophone Company** (1989; Ogun). Dean leads Trevor Watts, altoist Simon Picard, Paul Rogers and Tony Levin on drums in a cooperative cutting session.

⊙ **The Vortex Tapes** (1990; Slam). This was recorded at London's Vortex club during a season of improvisations led by Dean. The *Unlimited* players take part as well as Keith Tippett, Howard Riley, Louis Moholo, Marcio Mattos and two or three musicians from the rising generation.

Twos And Threes (c.1994; Voiceprint). Dean plays first a series of duos in turn with Howard Riley, Keith Tippett, Mark Hewins (guitar), Marcio Mattos and Paul Rogers, then adds John Etheridge and Fred Thelonious Baker to the proceedings and plays a series of trios with the same musicians.

Newsense (1997; Slam). Dean is here on excellent form with a nine-piece band that harks back to his Ninesense band in the later 1970s. This has the ever-improving trumpeter Jim Dvorak, with three trombones – the legendary American Roswell Rudd, Paul Rutherford and Annie Whitehead – plus pianist Alex Maguire, Marcio Mattos on cello, bassist Roberto Bellatalla and drummer Mark Sanders.

➤➤ **Dennis Gonzalez** *(Catechism).*

Roger Dean

Piano, synthesizer, double bass, vibraphone.

b. Manchester, UK, 6 Sept 1948.

Roger Dean was a classically-trained double bass prodigy at an early age and began performing jazz whilst studying biology at Cambridge in the late 1960s. From 1973 until 1988 he played keyboards with Graham Collier Music and formed his own group, Lysis, in 1974. He also played with the London Jazz Composers' Orchestra, Barry Guy, Tony Oxley, Derek Bailey, Harry Beckett, Terje Rypdal, Arild Andersen, Ted Curson, Tony Scott, Tony Coe and others. A critic and writer on improvisation, his performances and compositions have firmly established his reputation in contemporary music practice – he has worked with Stockhausen, Penderecki and Kagel. Australia became his home in 1989, where he put together a new group, australYSIS. These days his musical interests appear to focus upon computer-related composition and the interface between music and new media. [IC]

The Next Room (1992; Tall Poppies). Dean's group australYSIS plays two hour-long free improvisations, the second including some electronic sounds.

Blossom Dearie

Vocals, piano.

b. East Durham, New York, 28 April 1928.

Dearie's career began in New York in vocal groups for Woody Herman and Alvino Rey in the mid-1940s. Early in the 1950s she moved to Paris to form her eight-piece vocal group, The Blue Stars, which subsequently evolved into the Swingle Singers. Following a signing to Norman Granz's Verve label, Dearie moved back to the USA and commenced a solo career, which by the 1960s had achieved international attention through hits such as her versions of two Dave Frishberg songs, "Peel Me A Grape" and "I'm Hip", and two self-penned dedications to pop stars – "Sweet Georgie Fame" and "Hey John" (for John Lennon). Dearie's unique high-pitched voice, quirky lyrics and muscular piano playing marked her out as a true original, but major companies showed so little interest that in 1974 she formed Daffodil Records to record for herself. In 1985 she won the Mabel Mercer Foundation Award, and, like Mercer, Dearie sits at the centre of a devoted salon which appreciates her commitment to musical and lyrical excellence and her refusal to compromise. [DF]

At Ronnie Scott's (1998; Polygram). A classic collection – Dearie as she's best known, in cabaret at Ronnie's, with Jeff Clyne (bass) and Johnny Butts (drums) in an inimitable programme including "I'm Hip". "When In Rome", and "Once Upon A Summertime".

John D'Earth

Trumpet.

b. Holliston, Massachusetts, 30 March 1950.

Having studied and worked initially with alto/baritone saxophonist Boots Mussulli, John D'Earth subsequently attended Harvard, where he read English literature, before leaving for New York and establishing himself as a jazz musician. Work with the likes of Buddy Rich, the Thad Jones-Mel Lewis big band, a number of Latin bands and Lionel Hampton led to his recording with drummer/leader Bob Moses, bassist Harvie Swartz, vibes player/composer Gunter Hämpel and the late guitarist Emily Remler, with whom he formed a particularly fruitful musical relationship, his flaring but tasteful playing beautifully complementing her flowing lines.

D'Earth began the 1990s in stellar company, contributing to the Montreux concert honouring Miles Davis shortly before the great trumpeter's death, and continued contributing his surefooted sound to recordings by trombonist Ray Anderson (*Big Band Record*, Gramavision; 1994), composer Klaus Konig's satirical *Reviews* (a 1995 Enja release dedicated to the spirit of Frank Zappa and featuring quotes from critics' reviews of previous Konig work), and a hard-bop session, *Listen* (Heart Music 20; 1996), led by drummer Jae Sinnett, in which D'Earth shares solo duties with alto player Jesse Davis and tenorman Billy Pierce. [CP]

Emily Remler

Transitions (1984; Concord). D'Earth's Latin experience proves extremely useful on this wide-ranging album which also features bassist Eddie Gomez and drummer Moses.

John D'Earth

One Bright Glance (1989; Enja). Repeats attractive guitar/trumpet frontline, this time with John Abercrombie; the rhythm-section is Marc Johnson (bass) and Howard Curtis (drums).

Rusty Dedrick

Trumpet, composer.

b. Delevan, New York, 7 Dec 1918.

Rusty (Lyle F.) Dedrick trained with big bands led by Dick Stabile, Red Norvo, Claude Thornhill and Ray McKinley among others, then after the war worked for NBC TV. From 1950 he produced a small number of fine records (including duets with Don Elliott and a solo review of *The Trumpet Greats*), and it was not until after 1970 – when he began appearing at jazz festivals again – that the public saw more of him again. By then Dedrick had formed a partnership with Bill Borden of Monmouth Evergreen, and some later albums for Borden show off his broad-based trumpet style to perfection. Like Bob Wilber and Dick Cary, Dedrick is often found at the centre of educational jazz enterprises, and from 1971 he taught jazz studies at the Manhattan College of Music before becoming its director. [DF]

Salute To Bunny (1957; Counterpoint). Perhaps Dedrick's most frequently seen album, this is a worthy tribute to Berigan, with Dedrick sounding full-toned and full of confidence.

Twelve Isham Jones Evergreens (1964; Monmouth Evergreen). Arranged for septet and big band, this classy collection features a lot of Dedrick's authoritative swing soloing.

Barrett Deems

Drums.

b. Springfield, Illinois, 1 March 1914; d. 15 Sept 1998.

Often billed as "the world's fastest drummer", Deems tends to be thought of as a post-war star who came to fame with Louis Armstrong's All Stars. In fact he was working professionally by the late 1920s (with Paul Ash) and led his own bands around Chicago in the 1930s before joining Joe Venuti for seven years in 1937. Then came work with a variety of top leaders including Jimmy Dorsey (1945), Red Norvo (1948) and Muggsy Spanier (1951). After his four-year spell with Armstrong – during which he contributed to such great records as *Satch Plays Fats* and *Louis Armstrong Plays W.C. Handy*, as well as appearing in the 1956 film *High Society* – Deems led his own band again (at Chicago's Brass Rail club), worked with Jack Teagarden (1960–64), and from 1964 formed a partnership with the Dukes of Dixieland. In the 1970s and 1980s he worked around Chicago with a variety of groups (including Joe Kelly's Gaslight Band), played and recorded with Art Hodes, and toured in tribute packages such as Keith Smith's *Wonderful World Of Louis Armstrong*. In the mid-1990s he was still as active as ever and continued playing around Chicago until shortly before he died. [DF]

➤➤ **Louis Armstrong** *(Louis Armstrong Plays W.C. Handy).*

Joey DeFrancesco

Organ, trumpet.

b. Springfield, Philadelphia, 4 Oct 1971.

Brought up in the centre of the Northeast Corridor by a Hammond B3-playing father, "Papa" John DeFrancesco, surrounded by the most fertile club scene in the world for organ-centred jazz, Joey DeFrancesco is a musician steeped in the tradition surrounding his particular instrument. A useful extra string to his bow, however, is his trumpet playing, particularly handy on live dates for varying the texture of his music, but also featured on many of the recordings listed below. DeFrancesco can be heard on Miles Davis's *Amandla*, but it was his work – particularly his live performances, worldwide – with John McLaughlin in the guitarist's Free Spirits trio in the mid-1990s (initially with Dennis Chambers, subsequently with Elvin Jones on drums) that really brought him to prominence in the jazz world. Like many organists, DeFrancesco has particularly close musical relationships with guitarists; he has recorded with Paul Bollenback, Jimmy Bruno and Dave Stryker, most memorably on *Double Gemini* (Challenge; 1997) in a classic trio with Bollenback and drummer Jeff "Tain" Watts. DeFrancesco has also beefed up albums by saxophonists Ronnie Cuber and Ron Holloway. An attempt to muscle Joey beyond the jazz charts as a rough and ready crooner with *Singin' And Swingin'* (2001; Concord) didn't quite come off, though *Falling In Love Again* (2003; Concord) gets closer, with the vocals handled by Joe Doggs. However, it is probably his instrumental recordings – generally no-nonsense, rousing, totally unpretentious affairs – which underline his importance as one of the most unfussily virtuosic torch-bearers of contemporary organ jazz. [CP/CI]

Live At The Five Spot (1993; Columbia). With a central trio – DeFrancesco, Bollenback and drummer Byron "Wookie" Landham – augmented by regular trumpeter Jim Henry and a host of exciting guests (Grover Washington, Jack McDuff, Illinois Jacquet, Houston Person, Robert Landham), this is an irresistibly good-time album packed with great solos over familiar themes ("Embraceable You", "Song", "Impressions", "All of Me", etc).

All in the Family (1998; HighNote). More familiar material ("My Buddy", "Tuxedo Junction", "Bags' Groove" – even "The Saints") given the DeFrancesco treatment, but this time featuring father and son with saxophonists Bootsie Barnes and Houston Person, guitarist Melvin Sparks and drummer Byron Landham.

Buddy DeFranco

Clarinet; also alto saxophone, bass-clarinet.

b. Camden, New Jersey, 17 Feb 1923.

Buddy (Boniface Ferdinand Leonardo) DeFranco played with several name bands on alto including Gene Krupa (c.1942–3), Charlie Barnet (1943–4) and Tommy Dorsey (three stints in 1944–8, during which he was featured on clarinet). In between, he did prolific small-group work in California, New York and Chicago. He was a member of the Count Basie octet (1950–51), playing in a film short but not allowed to be seen with the otherwise all-black group (he was replaced on screen by Marshall Royal). He formed his own big band (1951), then a quartet

(1952–5) including Art Blakey and Kenny Drew, later Sonny Clark. He settled on the West Coast, led a new quartet (1961–4), and then became leader of the Glenn Miller "ghost band" (1966–74). Involved in education in the late 1970s and occasional work as a soloist, he made several tours of Europe in the 1980s and (from 1981) began an ongoing partnership with Terry Gibbs. A consummate technician who invariably provokes the envy of struggling performers, DeFranco incurs the same criticism of technique without taste which can be levelled against Oscar Peterson and Buddy Rich. In addition, wind instruments in jazz have benefited from non-standard tone-quality employed to enhance the player's structures and to express his emotional depths, whereas the mechanical perfection of DeFranco appeals mainly to listeners with different priorities. [BP]

Mr. Clarinet (1953; Verve). A version of DeFranco's early quartet, with Blakey and Drew joined by Milt Hinton for the record date, has him demonstrating his virtuosity in the most straight-ahead, driving context.

Buddy DeFranco and Terry Gibbs

Holiday For Swing (1988; Contemporary). DeFranco and Gibbs are real contemporaries, and revisit both late swing repertoire ("Seven Come Eleven", "Serenade In Blue") and early bebop ("Yardbird Suite" and Bud Powell's "Parisian Thoroughfare").

David DeFries

Trumpet, flugelhorn, tenor horn, percussion.

b. London, 24 May 1952.

Defries attended various jazz courses and spent two terms as a student at Leeds College of Music. In the 1970s he worked with various groups in London, including Julian Bahula's Jabula, Don Weller's Major Surgery and Dudu Pukwana's Zila. In 1981, with guitarist Mark Wood, he founded the group Sunwind, which the following year won first prize in the Greater London Arts Association jazz competition. In the early 1980s he joined Chris McGregor's Brotherhood of Breath, and also played with Rip Rig & Panic, the Breakfast Band and Loose Tubes. At the beginning of the 1990s he went to live in France. He recorded with the Brotherhood of Breath, with Sunwind (*The Sun Below*; 1983), and, under his own name, *The Secret City* in 1985. His favourites range from Louis Armstrong to Miles Davis, Clark Terry to Mongezi Feza, and he cites Chris McGregor, Hermeto Pascoal and Collin Walcott as inspirational figures. [IC]

Harold "Duke" Dejan

Alto saxophone.

b. New Orleans, Louisiana, 4 February 1909; d. 5 July 2002.

Dejan was known principally as the leader of the internationally acclaimed Olympia Brass Band which he formed in 1962 in New Orleans. Having studied clarinet with Lorenzo Tio and Albert Nicholas, Dejan began working with some of the leading figures of the New Orleans jazz world including Tink Baptiste, Oscar Celestin, his brother Leo's Moonlight Serenaders (later the Black Diamonds), Sax Jefferson, Bebe Ridgeley and Clarence Desdune. From 1930 he began a series of riverboat jobs on the SS Dixie and worked with Manuel Perez, Arnold Depass's Olympia Band, and Henry "Kid" Rena. Following wartime service in the US navy, he replaced John Handy in Frank Moliere's Trio and played around New Orleans with a variety of luminaries including Alec Bigard's Mighty Four. After the group disbanded Dejan worked with trumpeter Willie Pajeaud in the Eureka Brass Band; thereafter forming his own Eureka Number Two band and later changing its name to the Olympia. In 1986 Dejan and Milton Baptiste started the Junior Olympia Brass Band as a way of replenishing the tradition. A much loved figure at New Orleans' Preservation Hall, Dejan continued playing there until a stroke sadly curtailed his activities in 1990. [DF]

Olympia Brass Band

Best Of New Orleans Jazz (1987; Mardi Gras Records). The raw and authentic sound of one of the greatest New Orleans brass bands. Direct and emotional playing of some great standards, including "When The Saints Go Marching In" and "Just A Closer Walk With Me".

Jack DeJohnette

Drums, piano, keyboards, composer, melodica, vocals.

b. Chicago, 9 Aug 1942.

DeJohnette had classical piano lessons for ten years and graduated from the American Conservatory of Music, Chicago. He began playing drums with his high school concert band after being inspired by Max Roach. During his early years in Chicago, he paid his musical dues playing everything from R&B to free jazz, and he was practising four hours on piano and four hours on drums every day. In 1966 he moved to New York, playing drums with organist John Patton and later gigging with Jackie McLean and singers Betty Carter and Abbey Lincoln. From early 1966 to 1969 he was with the Charles Lloyd quartet, which included Keith Jarrett and Ron McClure, establishing his international reputation. The Lloyd quartet was the first jazz group to play in US rock concert halls, and was the first band of modern jazz musicians to play in Russia. DeJohnette also gigged around New York with Coltrane, Monk, Freddie Hubbard, Bill Evans, Jarrett, Chick Corea and Stan Getz.

In August 1969 he played on Miles Davis's seminal album *Bitches Brew*, and in April 1970 joined the Davis band, staying on until the summer of 1971. During this period he began leading his own groups and, as well as playing drums, performed on melodica, piano, clavinet and organ. After leaving

RAFFAELLA CAVALIERI

Jack DeJohnette

Davis, he led his own band Compost, touring in the USA and internationally. During the 1970s he recorded two albums for Prestige and appeared as sideman on ECM recordings with many people including Kenny Wheeler, John Abercrombie and Jan Garbarek. He also began recording for ECM as leader, and the first album by his quartet New Directions, with Abercrombie, Lester Bowie and Eddie Gomez, received the Prix du Jazz Contemporain de l'Académie Charles Cros in 1979. In 1980 he formed a group with varying personnel, calling it Jack DeJohnette's Special Edition, which has recorded a series of magnificent albums.

He has been a member of Keith Jarrett's standards trio since it first recorded in January 1983, during which time he has virtually reinvented the role of drummer, with an astonishing variety of new approaches. In the 1990s he also played in Voicestra, a trio with Bobby McFerrin and keyboardist Lyle Mays in which all three vocalize. As a result of his interest in "world music" DeJohnette began to practise hand percussion and singing. He is also a gifted composer, writing for his own groups and also occasionally for other people. In 1992 he completed *Concerto For A Better World*, a commission from the ROVA Saxophone Quartet. In 1994 he did an international tour, including festivals, playing solo piano.

DeJohnette is one of the most gifted and complete musicians in jazz. As a drummer, he has everything – a perfectly poised sense of time, an unerring instinct for knowing when to sustain a rhythm and when to disturb the pulse, and he always plays orchestrally with immense attention to detail. As well as Roach, his early favourites were Philly Joe Jones and Elvin Jones, and he embodies all their virtues and has added his own dimension, becoming a master of every style and genre from R&B to rock, ethnic, reggae, bebop and free improvisation. An example of his sheer power is the track "What I Say" from the Miles Davis album *Live-Evil*, on which DeJohnette sustains a ferocious rock pulse for fifteen minutes and then plays a long drum solo. Not surprisingly most contemporary drummers cite him as one of their favourites. He is also an excellent pianist and a considerably talented composer, who with his Special Edition recordings created some of the most interesting jazz of the 1980s. [IC]

⊙ **New Directions** (1978; ECM). DeJohnette leads a quartet with Lester Bowie, John Abercrombie and Eddie Gomez. The funky and atmospheric "Bayou Fever" opens up this genial album. The leader plays piano throughout his fine ballad, "Silver Hollow", with Bowie using harmon mute.

⊙ **Special Edition** (1979; ECM). This is another quartet with David Murray, Arthur Blythe and bassist/cellist Peter Warren. The complex theme and dynamic rhythms of DeJohnette's Dolphy tribute "One For Eric" are matched by Murray's bass-clarinet, while "Zoot Suit" has the group sounding initially like a 1940s jump band – until they take off. A deft album with much variety of idiom and style.

⊙ **Tin Can Alley** (1980; ECM). A quartet with Freeman, Purcell and Warren recorded this, one of DeJohnette's most focused albums. Four of his compositions are evocative and muscular. His other piece is a solo effort with overdubbed congas, drums, organ and timpani. Freeman and Purcell seem in their element with this music.

⊙ **Inflation Blues** (1982; ECM). There's a considerable range of sonorities on this quintet album, with John Purcell's flutes, clarinets and saxophones, Chico Freeman's saxophones and bass-clarinet, and Baikida Carroll's trumpet. All five pieces are by DeJohnette and he sings the blues convincingly and engagingly on the title track.

⊙ **Album Album** (1984; ECM). A series of terrific compositions by DeJohnette and a resonant arrangement of "Monk's Mood" from a group featuring Purcell and Murray again, with Howard Johnson on tuba and baritone saxophone and Rufus Reid on acoustic and electric bass.

⊙ **Earth Walk** (1991; Blue Note). This is also a beautifully realized album. This special edition has two of the hottest younger saxophonists in Gary Thomas and Greg Osby plus pianist Michael Cain, guitarist Mick Goodrick and bassist Lonnie Plaxico. The leader concentrates on the drums and is on superlative form, and his nine compositions have great variety and human resonances.

⊙ **Dancing With Nature Spirits** (1995; ECM). DeJohnette is here in trio formation with Michael Cain on piano and keyboards and Steve Gorn on bansuri flute, soprano saxophone and clarinet. The music has a strong ethnic feel and seems to follow on from Dejohnette's *Music For The Fifth World*, in which he began examining his Native American roots. The title track and "Healing Song For Mother Earth" are both totally improvised and each is over twenty minutes long. Three more composed pieces – Gorn's "Anatolia", Cain's "Emanations", and the glorious "Time Warps" by Cain and DeJohnette, with its wonderful groove and lyrical soprano, all provide a welcome relief from the two epic improvised performances.

⊙ **Oneness** (1997; ECM). DeJohnette and Michael Cain are joined by guitarist Jerome Harris in this trio, and percussionist Don Alias guests in duo with DeJohnette in the opening track "Welcome Blessing". Again there are two long collectively improvised performances – "Free Above Sea" and "From The Heart" – and two pieces are DeJohnette compositions – "C.M.A." and a reinterpretation of his "Jack In". Again, a highly focused and dynamic album.

➤➤ **Pat Metheny** *(80/81)*; **Kenny Wheeler** *(Gnu High).*

Barbara Dennerlein

Hammond organ, composer.

b. Munich, Germany, 25 Sept 1964.

In a field dominated by the towering figure of Jimmy Smith and his many acolytes, Barbara Dennerlein has managed to bring genuine innovation to her chosen instrument by adapting it electronically so that it can produce string-bass sounds through its foot pedals, which she operates with astonishing facility. She began playing at eleven, but by fifteen was gigging in Munich clubs and quickly established herself as a big draw on the European festival circuit. Her playing is totally different from Smith's, more broad-based, taking in aspects of blues, bebop and free music, but she has his massive swing, despite being a more adventurous improviser than the Hammond legend. Since her main label debut as a leader in 1988, she has carved out a niche for herself as a supremely entertaining, hard-driving player capable of considerable subtlety. In 1995, her major-label debut *Take Off!* (Verve) won her the Preis der deutschen Schallplattenkritik (German Critics' Award) for the third time, and was that country's best-selling album of the year. Her follow-up, *Junkanoo* (Verve; 1996), drew on Bahamian festival ritual and, like *Take Off!*, involved a star-studded cast (Randy Brecker, David Murray, Frank Lacy, etc). Her 1999 swansong for Verve, *Outhipped*, was probably the most accomplished and eclectic of her major label offerings but the sheer brio of her playing is perhaps best represented by the albums below. [CP/CI]

Straight Ahead (1988; Enja). Excellent debut as leader of stellar band comprising trombonist Ray Anderson, guitarist Mitch Watkins and drummer Ronnie Burrage. Exuberant mix of Anderson's blues and free-music offerings with Watkins's rock guitar and Burrage's superbly propulsive drumming.

Hot Stuff (1990; Enja). Consolidates progress of first album, but features UK's Andy Sheppard and Mark Mondesir along with Watkins in swirling, exhilarating music.

That's Me (1992; Enja). Same personnel as debut, only with Dennis Chambers instead of Burrage and Bob Berg on tenor. Excellent, punchy, innovative music, all but one tune composed by Dennerlein.

Love Letters (2001; Bebab). Back on her own label with no guest stars – a good place to hear lots of latter-day Dennerlein playing in the sole company of Daniel Messina on drums.

Matt Dennis

Songwriter, singer, piano.

b. Seattle, 11 Feb 1914; d. 21 June 2002.

Dennis was born into a vaudeville family, studied piano from an early age and began his professional career with Horace Heidt in 1933. For much of the 1930s, he sang and played in nightclubs and worked as vocal coach and/or accompanist for singers including Martha Tilton and vocal groups including the Merry Macs, Six Hits And A Miss, and the Pied Pipers, with whom he joined Tommy Dorsey (1940–42). He worked as staff-arranger/composer/vocal coach for Dorsey, writing a succession of hits for Frank Sinatra including "Will You Still Be Mine", "Let's Get Away From It All", "Everything Happens To Me" and "Violets For Your Furs", all of which – like other Dennis tunes including "Angel Eyes" – instantly achieved standard-status. As a songwriter Dennis was well ahead of his time and his principal collaborator early on was lyricist Tom Adair. After leaving Dorsey for Military Service, he worked briefly for Glenn Miller's AAF orchestra, continuing to broadcast, and after discharge carried on playing club dates and to arrange for radio (1946–8). Thereafter, settled in LA, he worked for many years as a supper-club single, and later teamed with his wife, singer Ginny Maxey, with whom he recorded in 1991 before his career began to slow up in the mid-1990s. A hugely underrated singer-pianist and stylistically unmistakable composer, Dennis recorded sparingly (CD reissues are still thin on the ground), but the albums listed below are worth the search. [DF]

Play Melancholy Baby (1956; RCA). Dennis with trumpeter Don Fagerquist – a frequent recording partner – in superb form.

Matt Dennis Plays And Sings (1957; Kapp). Live at the Tally Ho club in Hollywood, this fine performance includes lesser-known beauties such as "Compared To You" and "Junior And Julie".

Willie Dennis

Trombone.

b. Philadelphia, 10 Jan 1926; d. 8 July 1965.

Willie Dennis (William DeBerardinis) played with Elliot Lawrence, Claude Thornhill and Sam Donahue (late 1940s). He first performed with Charles Mingus in 1953 and returned several times, while working largely with big bands such as Woody Herman (1958) and Benny Goodman (1958, 1962). He was a member of the Buddy Rich quintet (1959–60) and the Gerry Mulligan band (1960–61), while becoming involved in studio work. Married to singer Morgana King, he was much admired by other trombonists for, in the words of David Baker, his "style of articulation or lack of it [and his] marvellous facility and ease with the horn". [BP]

➤➤ **Charles Mingus** *(Blues And Roots).*

Sidney De Paris

Trumpet, tuba, vocals.

b. Crawfordsville, Indiana, 30 May 1905; d. 13 Sept 1967.

Sidney De Paris was in New York from 1925, then over the next few years worked with Charlie Johnson (the longtime bandleader at Smalls' Paradise), Fletcher Henderson (replacing Louis Armstrong's replacement Rex Stewart in late 1931), and Don Redman's band, with whom he recorded classics such as "Cherry", "Four Or Five Times" and "Shimme Sha Wabble"). In the ten years from 1936 his career diversified, as he worked for bandleaders as different as Mezz Mezzrow and Charlie Barnet, led his own groups, and played in theatre orchestras. All this thoroughly equipped him for the demands of his brother Wilbur's "New" New Orleans Jazz Band, which formed in 1947 and for the next sixteen years was a success playing everything from blues to light classics. De Paris's range, fluent creativity, unique rhythmic sense, and attractive New Orleans vibrato are all over his brother's successful albums. He remains a neglected talent. [DF]

Wilbur De Paris

Trombone, leader, drums.

b. Crawfordsville, Indiana, 11 Jan 1900; d. 3 Jan 1973.

Wilbur De Paris began his career around 1912 in carnival bands and tent shows, and heard a feast of music on his travels. Canny, observant and with a strong sense of what was commercial, he soon had "eyes to be a bandleader" (in Dickie Wells's words) and by 1925 had his own short-lived band, Wilbur De Paris's Cotton Pickers, at the Cinderella Ballroom in New York. For the next eighteen years, however, he worked as a sideman for other leaders, including three years in Luis Russell's orchestra (alongside his future sideman, banjoist Lee Blair), backing master showman Louis Armstrong.

In 1943 he formed a band briefly with brother Sidney, then left it for two years to join Duke Ellington (playing "Tricky Sam" Nanton's role) before finally, in 1947, putting together his "New" New Orleans Band. The outfit aimed to make discoveries within old traditions: "We try to play as the early New Orleans masters would if they were alive today", he explained. The De Paris band sounded like no one else: often using unorthodox instruments (Wilbert Kirk's harmonica, the leader's valve-trombone, his brother's tuba) and unusual repertoire (originals, classic pastiches, pop tunes), they produced, in Brian Rust's words, "forthright mellow music – an object lesson to most of our revivalists". Many UK revivalists – Chris Barber for one – learned much from the De Paris formula, which laid the foundations for the style and approach of Britain's trad-boom bands of the early 1960s. In New York the band broke records with a famous eleven-year residency at Jimmy Ryan's (1951–62), and in 1952 De Paris signed a lucrative contract with Atlantic which gave him free rein to produce a string of small classics. When Jimmy Ryan's finally made a change, De Paris continued bandleading in other New York clubs until shortly before his death. [DF]

⊙ **"New" New Orleans Jazz** (1955; Atlantic). Perhaps De Paris's best album, including the cleverly constructed "Madagascar".

⊙ **Wilbur De Paris At Symphony Hall** (1956; Atlantic). Excellent live programme featuring the outstanding Omer Simeon ("Juba Dance") and Wilbert Kirk's harmonica on "Sister Kate".

Claude Deppa

Trumpet.

b. Cape Town, South Africa, 10 May 1958.

Although he is best known as a fiery trumpeter in both free and structured big- and small-group jazz, Claude Deppa also operates as a first-call freelance for a number of visiting bands whose music ranges from calypso through juju to swing and improvised music. He arrived in the UK at seventeen, and has since toured worldwide not only with British Council-sponsored units but with a variety of other projects, including the "Havana Greets Ronnie Scott" jazz festival. In addition to his work with smaller bands such as Andy Sheppard's quintet In Co-Motion and Brian Abrahams's District Six, Deppa has also contributed his unpredictable, tart sound to bigger aggregations such as the Jazz Warriors, the Brotherhood of Breath, Carla Bley's Very Big Band and Andy Sheppard's Big Co-Motion. In the 1990s, Deppa participated in two African-influenced projects: in 1993, he joined drummer Louis Moholo for a celebratory series of concerts and workshops in the recently liberated South Africa, caught on *Freedom Tour* (Ogun; 1993), and in 1995, after Gail Thompson's tour of thirteen African countries, from Morocco to Kenya, he played on her Jazz Africa suite (Enja), recorded by a thirteen-piece band in Duisburg, Germany. He has led several bands including Frontline, the Spontaneous Urban Ensemble, Horns Unlimited and most recently African Jazz Explosion, carrying on the proud tradition of the original Blue Notes by injecting South African musical values into UK jazz. [CP/CI]

Harry Beckett's Flugelhorn 4+3

⊙ **All Four One** (1992; Spotlite). Delightful, unusual album featuring frontline of four flugelhorns (Beckett, Deppa, Jon Corbett, Chris Batchelor) performing Beckett material and Mingus's "Better Get It in Your Soul".

➤➤ **Carla Bley** *(Big Band Theory)*; **Andy Sheppard** *(Rhythm Method).*

Lorraine Desmarais

Piano, keyboards.

b. Montreal, 15 Aug 1956.

Desmarais is one of Canada's leading jazz musicians. She had extensive classical training, receiving her Master's degree in classical piano in 1979. She also studied jazz-combo at McGill University, Montreal (1978–9), and arranging at the University of Montreal in 1981. From 1983–4 she studied jazz piano in New York with Kenny Barron, then from 1992–3 she studied jazz improvisation with Charlie Banacos in Boston. Throughout her studies, she was also playing concerts and touring.

In 1984, she won first prize in the Montreal international jazz festival's Yamaha contest, and in 1986 made her first appearance in the USA, winning first prize in the Great American Jazz Piano Competition at the Jacksonville jazz festival, Florida – the first non-American and the first woman ever to win this event. In 1988 she played at festivals throughout Canada, worked in collaboration with trumpeter Tiger Okoshi and, as a last-minute substitute for Paquito D'Rivera's pianist at the Rimouski (Quebec) festival,

Lorraine Desmarais

acquitted herself superbly. Since then, Desmarais has toured Asia, given concerts in Moscow, played in duo with pianists Marian McPartland and Joanne Brackeen, and in 1993 toured Canadian jazz festivals with her quartet, featuring Tiger Okoshi on trumpet. She has also played with trumpeter Kenny Wheeler and recorded with percussionist Don Alias. Desmarais has a formidable piano technique and her passionate improvising swings mightily. She is also an excellent composer and has recorded six CDs. [IC]

Lorraine Desmarais (1995; Scherzo). With her superb rhythm-section of bassist Michel Donato and drummer Magella Cormier, plus Tiger Okoshi on trumpet and flugelhorn, Desmarais performs eight of her compositions and two standards – "Body and Soul" which she and Okoshi dissect and reconstitute incandescently, and "My One And Only Love", which she performs solo. Her originals include bravura experiments with structure ("One For Chick") and beautifully paced elegaic pieces ("Olivier").

Paul Desmond

Alto saxophone.

b. San Francisco, 25 Nov 1924; d. 30 May 1977.

Originally Paul Emil Breitenfeld, Desmond studied clarinet at high school and college, and in 1948–50 he rehearsed and recorded with the Dave Brubeck octet. He worked with bands locally, and was then added to Brubeck's regular trio from 1951. He left after sixteen years in order to freelance, rejoining Brubeck for specific tours (1972, 1973, 1975). He also appeared in concert with the Modern Jazz Quartet (1971) and worked occasionally under his own name in New York and Toronto before his death from cancer.

It was only too easy to think of Desmond as merely the best thing in a not very interesting group, and certainly his effortless superiority when matched against Brubeck was the most easily noticeable aspect of his work; the extreme popularity of his tune "Take Five" (now an anthem of street musicians) did nothing to lessen his identification with the pianist's group. But despite a certain over-cleverness in his musical humour he was a much more intuitive soloist, capable of great invention and swing much akin to Zoot Sims. One of a whole generation of saxophonists initially inspired by Lester Young, he was also marked by Lee Konitz but used a purer, more forthright tone. He was the only altoist in the early 1950s (apart from Earl Bostic) employing the upper harmonics of the instrument, and it was probably the questing nature of his improvisation that attracted Anthony Braxton, an early admirer. Away from Brubeck, for instance in his recording partnerships with Gerry Mulligan and Jim Hall, there was an added relaxation and gentleness to his playing which was well exploited in a series of middle-of-the-road albums made during his last decade. [BP]

Easy Living (1963–5; RCA). One of a long series of studio albums featuring Jim Hall and Connie Kay, this has splendid versions of the title track and other standards such as "Polka Dots And Moonbeams".

Like Someone In Love (1975; Telarc). From the same live Toronto sessions as two previous releases, this catches Desmond in sublimely relaxed mode with another guitar-based trio (Ed Bickert does him proud).

Jimmy Deuchar

Flugelhorn, mellophonium, composer, arranger.

b. Dundee, Scotland, 26 June 1930; d. 9 Sept 1993.

Deuchar began by playing out around the Dundee area. He moved to London in 1950, playing with the Johnny Dankworth Seven, and from

1952–5 he played bebop with Jack Parnell, Ronnie Scott and Tony Crombie. In 1956 he toured with Lionel Hampton and in 1957 he toured the USA with Scott, before joining Kurt Edelhagen's radio big band in Cologne. From 1960–62 he again worked with Scott, and then with Tubby Hayes from 1962–6. During the mid-1960s Deuchar played with the Benny Golson orchestra on TV in the UK. From 1966 he worked as a soloist and staff arranger with the Edelhagen orchestra and played with the occasional big band led by Kenny Clarke and Francy Boland. He returned to the UK in 1971, moving back to Scotland during the 1970s. In the 1980s he was again active in London. He recorded with Tubby Hayes, Victor Feldman, Edelhagen and Ronnie Scott. Deuchar was an excellent arranger and a fine soloist in the bop and post-bop tradition. [IC]

Laurent de Wilde

Piano, composer, writer.
b. Washington, D.C., 19 Dec 1960.

Raised in France from the age of three, de Wilde earned a degree in philosophy and literature from the École Normale Supérieure. Influenced in his early teens by Peterson, Evans, Hancock and Corea, he then won a music scholarship to Long Island University, where he studied from 1983–6. He worked with Reggie Workman, Greg Osby, Ralph Moore and Eddie Henderson, the two last-named playing on de Wilde's first album in 1987. He made four albums in New York for the French label IDA (all including Ira Coleman on bass) and in 1990 moved back to Paris. There he played with Johnny Griffin, Ernest Ranglin, Aldo Romano and Dee Dee Bridgewater among others, and in 1995 began recording for Sony which released his records internationally; during 1997–8 his trio toured Europe, USA, the Middle and Far East. His book on Monk was published in 1996 and, like his albums, received several awards. [BP]

⊙ **Spoon-A-Rhythm** (1996; Columbia). Omitting the horns present on some of his recordings, this is a trio recording (with added percussion on half the tracks) featuring Ira Coleman and Caribbean drummer Dion Parson. One of three standards is "Round Midnight", while among the rhythmically tricky originals are "Tune For T." and "Edward K.", dedicated to Monk and Ellington respectively.

Julie Dexter

Vocals.
b. Birmingham, UK, 2 Sept 1971.

In the 1970s, Julie Dexter's father sang in an R&B band called The Robusters, and she grew up studying violin, clarinet, piano and djembe. At the age of twenty, she went to Radford University, Virginia, USA, where she had been planning to major in classical clarinet, but decided to take up singing, and completed her degree majoring in jazz vocals.

In 1992, Dexter began attending jam sessions at London's Jazz Café, with Gary Crosby's Nu Troop, and a year later was performing with pianist Nikki Yeoh and saxophonist Jean Toussaint. In 1994, she recorded "You'd Be So Nice To Come Home To", with Gary Crosby's Jazz Jamaica, and a year later spent three months in South Africa with the a cappella group Shades, rounding off 1995 with a gig at London's Rhythmic Club with saxophonist Steve Williamson.

Dexter sang with Courtney Pine's band (1996–7), touring the UK, Europe and Japan, and playing at Switzerland's Montreux jazz festival. She was a member of the workshop group Tomorrow's Warriors, out of which came the group J-Life, led by saxophonist Jason Yarde. In 1996, the CD *Tomorrow's Warriors Presents J-Life* was recorded with Dexter's vocals strongly featured, and in October J-Life won first prize as Best European Jazz Band at Germany's Leverkusen festival. The following year, Dexter won Best Vocalist at the Perrier Awards, and J-Life won Best Ensemble; they subsequently joined forces to tour Mexico, Colombia and Ecuador, and also performed at the Glastonbury and Edinburgh festivals. She later moved back to the US and released the album *Dexterity* on her own label, Ketch A Vibe, in 2002; it was an appealing, earnest pursuit of the musical middle-ground between classic soul, dub and jazz. Like many of the British post-Acid Jazz acts, Julie Dexter's principal genre has become mellow soul marked by a jazz background, but her quiet and compelling singing has something of Billie Holiday's heartfelt intimacy and bitter-sweetness. Her favourites include Holiday, Nancy Wilson, Cassandra Wilson, Ella Fitzgerald, Sarah Vaughan and Stevie Wonder. [IC]

Tomorrow's Warriors

⊙ **Tomorrow's Warriors Presents J-Life** (1996; Dune). J-Life is a quintet with soprano and alto saxophonist Jason Yarde as musical director, Robert Mitchell on piano, Darren Taylor on double bass, Daniel Crosby on drums, and Julie Dexter on vocals. She composed the song "To Be Poor

Is A Crime", in a beautifully rocking 7/4 rhythm, and had a hand in two or three of the other compositions.

➤➤ *see entry for* **Jason Yarde**.

Stefano Di Battista

Saxophones.

b. Rome, 14 Feb, 1969.

As a teenager, Di Battista played in a "banda", the uniquely Italian, horn-heavy popular ensemble that performs light versions of opera and other instrumental songs. In the same period, he fell under the influence of legendary Italian alto saxophonist Massimo Urbani, with whom he studied, and began listening fervently to the records of Art Pepper. Although classically trained, he played in various pop settings for money after graduating from conservatory. He was invited by Jean-Pierre Como to play in Paris in 1992, which initiated a period of commuting between Rome and the French capital, but soon afterwards he began playing regularly with drummer Aldo Romano and as a member of the National Jazz Orchestra and has since, for all intents and purposes, become a full-fledged member of the Parisian jazz scene. Di Battista has recorded as a sideman with Romano, Enrico Rava, Michel Petrucciani (*Both Worlds*; 1998) and Jacky Terrasson (*A Paris*, 2001). His debut as leader, *Volare* (1997; Label Bleu), was followed by his signing to Blue Note and the albums *A Prima Vista* (see below), *Stefano Di Battista* (2000) – both of which featured his long term musical partner, fellow ex-pat trumpeter Flavio Boltro – and a lush orchestral homage to his birthplace, *Round About Roma* (2003). [JC]

⊙ **A Prima Vista** (1999; Blue Note). Exuberant post bop, full of fun and skill. Mainly skittish Di Battista originals, but also with a look at "Lush Life", featuring a Euro scene lineup of Flavio Boltro (trumpet), Eric Legnini (piano), Rosario Bonnacorso (bass) and Benjamin Henocq (drums).

➤➤ **Laurent Cugny** *(Merci, Merci, Merci)*; **Rita Marcotulli** *(The Woman Next Door)*.

Vic Dickenson

Trombone, vocals.

b. Xenia, Ohio, 6 Aug 1906; d. 16 Nov 1984.

One of the first jazz trombonists (like Dickie Wells) to use the humour of the slide trombone to full artistic effect, Vic Dickenson heard Mamie Smith's Jazz Hounds while still at school but felt, he said, "the trombone part was too limited. So I learned what everybody played on the records – the sax and clarinets too." A natural "ear" player with little formal training, he worked in territory bands (including Speed Webb's and Zack Whyte's) before, in the 1930s, playing with big bands like those of Bennie Moten, Blanche Calloway (Cab's most successful sister) and Claude Hopkins. In the next decade he was with Eddie Heywood, then after a spell of illness in 1947 he became "house-trombonist" at the Savoy, Boston (1949). After that he worked in and around the area with such as Buster Bailey, Bobby Hackett and the McPartlands before returning to New York for work at the Metropole (replacing J.C. Higginbotham) and eight years with the very successful Saints and Sinners. More stints with Bobby Hackett followed, as well as spells with Eddie Condon, the World's Greatest Jazz Band, and (from 1975), Red Balaban and Cats at Condon's.

Like his frequent colleague Bobby Hackett, Dickenson was one of the most respected of jazz musicians. Famous for an encyclopedic knowledge of songs, he played with fluent assurance, burry tone and a great repertoire of droll inventions. Benny Morton, who described him as "The Will Rogers of the trombone", said: "Vic has more to say on the trombone than anybody I know. He gets musicians laughing when he plays, yet he can say the most serious things with a touch of humour." Dickenson's humour, kindness and humility also made him one of the best-loved figures on the scene. "One night Vic was late back on the stand", recalls Warren Vaché, a lifelong fan and regular colleague, "and the club owner bawled him out, quite rudely. Vic just smiled and tiptoed back onto the stand. And you know what he played? 'I Apologize'!" Dickenson's favourite phrase was "Music am a bitch"; so in the nicest way was he. [DF]

⊙ **Breaks Blues And Boogie** (1941–6; Topaz). An excellent Topaz compilation; Dickenson in telling form as always amid varied surroundings: James P. Johnson's Blue Note Jazzmen, Coleman Hawkins, Edmond Hall and four tracks with Louis Armstrong.

⊙ **Vic Dickenson Septet** (1953–4; Vanguard). A double CD containing the classic recordings which established Dickenson and his young trumpet partner Ruby Braff, and created the "mainstream" genre of jazz. This is indispensable music in jazz history, and along with his leader Braff is on incomparable form.

⊙ **Gentleman Of The Trombone** (1975; Storyville). A five-star quartet date for Dickenson, with the added bonus of Johnny Guarnieri at his most fantastical on piano.

➤➤ **Bobby Hackett** *(Melody Is A Must)*.

Carroll Dickerson

Violin, leader.

b. 1895; d. Oct 1957.

Resident bandleader at Chicago's Sunset Café from 1922–4, Dickerson took his orchestra on the road for a 48-week tour of the Pantages Theater circuit, and when he arrived back in Chicago was the centre of attention. At the Sunset Café once again, and now featuring Louis Armstrong, he was in charge of a high-powered show until Joe Glaser sacked him and made Armstrong leader instead. Dickerson took over at the Savoy Dance Hall, Armstrong rejoined him, and in early 1929 Armstrong, Dickerson and the band travelled to New York to join the Great Day company. After a season at Connie's Inn they disbanded, but Dickerson stayed in New York to try his luck, briefly led the Mills Blue Rhythm Band, then toured with King Oliver. By 1935 he was back in Chicago and stayed there until he died, leading bands in clubs and dance halls.

A strict disciplinarian who demanded the best, Dickerson cut an impressive onstage figure in his rhinestone-studded velvet smock and tam-o'-shanter, but his violin playing was less impressive than his wardrobe. As Earl Hines remembers, when Dickerson got drunk, which he frequently did, "he sometimes didn't know if he was using the front of the bow or the back". [DF]

Neville Dickie

Piano.

b. Durham, UK, 1 Jan 1937.

One of Britain's most powerful and gifted traditional jazz pianists, Dickie took piano lessons from the age of seven, and by 1953 was playing in working men's clubs in his home town. After National Service he moved to London in 1958 to work for ten years with a trio in London pubs. He first recorded in 1966, joined Brian Green's Jazzmen in 1968 and Spencer's Washboard Kings in 1969, then played regularly on Radio 2's *Jimmy Young Show*. Also in 1969 he recorded "The Robin's Return", which reached the UK pop chart and sealed a recording contract with Major Minor records. In 1975 Dickie re-signed to the Stomp Off label and has since produced four albums for them. In 1985 he formed his Rhythmakers (based on Billy Banks's recording band of 1932) and has continued to work in Britain, the USA and Canada with his own band, a Fats Waller tribute show (1992–3) and with Alan Elsdon. He also leads his own groups in the London area and beyond. [DF]

⊙ **Don't Forget To Mess Around** (1998–9; Stomp Off). A re-creation of Louis Armstrong's 1920s repertoire spotlighting Dickie's forceful swinging style, flanked by the delicate guitar of Martin Wheatley and veteran clarinettist Alex Revell.

Bill Dillard

Trumpet, vocals.

b. Pennsylvania, 20 July 1911; d. 1995.

A New York performer by 1929, Dillard worked early on with Jelly Roll Morton and all through the 1930s with a selection of fine big bands, including Luis Russell's (1931–2), Benny Carter's (1933) and Teddy Hill's (1934–8). While he was with Hill, Dillard became friends with Dizzy Gillespie, who said of him: "he'd show me how to hold notes out, how to sing on the trumpet. He helped me change the little things I did that weren't professional." After three more years working with other star names, including Coleman Hawkins and Louis Armstrong, Dillard embarked on an acting career which took him into Broadway shows such as *Carmen Jones* (1943) and Kurt Weill's *Lost In The Stars* (1950) and radio series such as *Love Of Life*, besides regular commitments with his own big band and freelancing. During the 1980s he continued his stage work in the show *One Mo' Time*, toured Europe and Australia, and recorded with British guitarist Denny Wright and others. [DF]

Al Di Meola

Guitar.

b. Bergenfield, New Jersey, 22 July 1954.

Di Meola started on drums and, inspired by the Beatles, took up guitar at the age of nine. At fifteen he was playing country music on pedal steel guitar, but heard the Miles Davis band with Chick Corea and knew immediately that "that was the new sound I wanted to get into". He went to the Berklee College of Music and while there in 1973 played with Barry Miles and Joe Kaye's Neophonic Orchestra. In 1974 he joined Corea's Return To Forever and in the later 1970s he led his own groups, releasing his virtuosic debut album *Land of the Midnight Sun* in 1976 and toured in an acoustic trio with John McLaughlin and Paco DeLucia, playing major international concert halls. In the mid-1980s he led his own group, the Al Di Meola Project, with Airto Moreira (percussion), Danny Gottlieb (drums), Phil Markowitz (keyboards) and Ron McClure (bass). Di Meola is strongly influenced by classical guitarists, Julian Bream in particular, but also by the jazz-rock fusion of Larry Coryell, who helped and encouraged him in his early years. Recently, Di Meola's playing has been increasingly informed by Argentinian tango styles, audible in performances of his large acoustic ensemble, World Sinfonia, which, ably assisted by the warm bandoneon of Dino Saluzzi, has interpreted Astor Piazzola's pieces. [IC]

Gene DiNovi

Piano, arranger.

b. Brooklyn, New York, 26 May 1928.

Interested in jazz from the age of twelve, DiNovi became a professional musician in 1943, playing with several name big bands. After sitting in with Gillespie and Parker at sixteen, he performed in small groups on 52nd Street and recorded with Lester Young, Brew Moore and Benny Goodman. In the 1950s he accompanied singers such as Peggy Lee, Tony Bennett and Lena Horne, and published several songs written with Lee and Johnny Mercer. He studied with composers such as Mario Castelnuovo-Tedesco as well as playing again with Goodman in 1959. Settling in Los Angeles in the 1960s, he wrote for films and TV series. By the 1980s he was resident in Toronto and had his own radio slot. In more recent years, he has toured internationally and recorded again under his own name. [BP]

Live At The Montreal Bistro (1993; Candid). With local bassist and drummer Dave Young and Terry Clarke, the Toronto venue hosts DiNovi in an interesting selection of originals and unfashionable standards, plus two tunes by legendary drummer Tiny Kahn.

Michael Di Pasqua

Drums, percussion.

b. Orlando, Florida, 4 May 1953.

Between 1969–75 Michael Di Pasqua played with the Zoot Sims/Al Cohn quintet, and with Don Elliott, Gerry Mulligan and Chet Baker, Jackie Cain and Roy Kral, to name a few. From 1976–80 he co-led a group with Dave Friedman, Dave Samuels and Harvie Swartz, recording the albums *Dawn* and *Double Image*; he played on Ralph Towner's 1979 album *Old Friends, New Friends*; and then in 1981 co-led the group Gallery with Dave Samuels and Paul McCandless. He joined Eberhard Weber's Later That Evening band in 1982, playing on its eponymous recording, and in the same year he joined Jan Garbarek's group, playing on the albums *Wayfarer* and *It's Okay to listen to the Gray Voice* (alongside David Torn). His favourites are Jack DeJohnette, Nana Vasconcelos, Trilok Gurtu, Tony Williams and Philly Joe Jones; his other inspirations are Miles Davis, Keith Jarrett and Bill Evans. [IC]

Dirty Dozen Brass Band

Brass band music is an integral part of the New Orleans jazz tradition, but the group that most convincingly redefined the genre for popular purposes is the Dirty Dozen Brass Band, who overlay the "European traditional" concept of the genre with more contemporary approaches, including funk and R&B. Formed in the late 1970s, the DDBB attracted widespread attention with their 1984 album *My Feet Can't Fail Me Now*, and a string of similar successes for major labels followed. They continue to play in New Orleans and to tour internationally, and are recognized as the leaders in their field, with a "second line" of copyists following in their tradition. [DF]

Watcha Gonna Do For The Rest Of Your Life (1991; Columbia). An album composed principally of original compositions by DDBB members, including the spritely "Use Your Brain" by baritonist Roger Lewis, and trumpeter Gregory Davis's menacing "Darker Shadows".

Jelly (1993; Columbia). An album dedicated to Jelly Roll Morton and his music, including "Georgia Swing", "Deep Creek" and others, and linked by guitarist Danny Barker's brief reminiscences of Jelly Roll.

Diz Disley

Guitar, bandleader.

b. Winnipeg, Manitoba, 27 May 1931.

Canadian-born Diz (William Charles) Disley spent his youth in Wales and Yorkshire. A graduate of Leeds College of Art and a gifted cartoonist (his work later featured in the *Radio Times*, *Spectator*, *Melody Maker* and *Jazz Journal*), he played early on with the Yorkshire Jazz Band, then as freelance soloist and occasional sideman with all the best British bands of the 1950s (Welsh, Brown, Ball, Bob Cort and Nancy Whiskey), as well as leading his own Hot Club-style string quintets. In the 1960s he became a popular figure in folk clubs, an occasional radio presenter (he also introduced the Beatles on their first London concert), and was the first to reintroduce Stephane Grappelli to the British music scene when in June 1973 he organized a tour of folk clubs for the violinist backed by Disley's own trio. Thereafter he worked regularly as guitarist partner to Grappelli, led occasional bands of his own and in 1985 was consultant for a projected full-length film about Reinhardt. There could be no better consultant: one of the great eccentrics of British acoustic music, Disley is one of Django's spiritual sons. In the 1990s he was freelancing as busily as ever, and in 1994 was reportedly drawing for the Walt Disney studios, before returning to London to live later in the decade. Among other recording activities at this time, he took part in Nat Gonella's final recording session in February 1998. [DF]

➤➤ **Stephane Grappelli** *(I Got Rhythm).*

Bill Dixon

Trumpet, flugelhorn, composer.

b. Nantucket, Massachusetts, 5 Oct 1925.

The Dixon family moved to New York in 1933. Bill's mother was a writer and blues singer, an artistic background that clearly left its mark on him, as he studied painting at Boston University, deciding to play trumpet aged 20 and studying music from 1946–51. He freelanced around New York as a trumpeter and arranger, led his own groups and befriended Cecil Taylor, with whom he subsequently worked, in 1958. In the early 1960s he co-led the Archie Shepp-Bill Dixon quartet before forming the New York Contemporary Five, which toured Europe in 1963, with Shepp, John Tchicai and Don Cherry. In 1964 he organized the Jazz Composers' Guild, and the October Revolution in Jazz, which aimed to promote the "new thing", free jazz, and to improve the working conditions of the avant-garde musicians who created it. In 1966 Dixon premiered his composition "Pomegranate" at the Newport jazz festival with dancer Judith Dunn, and this performance led to a contract with RCA and his orchestral recording *Intents And Purposes*, which was highly acclaimed. The same year he also played on Cecil Taylor's *Conquistador* album, Dixon's understated lyrical style making a welcome contrast to the pianist's prolixity.

In 1968 he took up a teaching post at Bennington College, Vermont, and there he established a Black Music department during the 1970s, going on to create the post of musician in residence, which has since been filled by Jimmy Lyons, Jimmy Garrison, Alan Shorter and Alan Silva. Education has been his primary concern ever since, although in 1976 Dixon – with Stephen Horenstein (tenor saxophone) and Alan Silva (bass) – performed his *Autumn Sequence, From A Paris Diary* at the Paris autumn festival, an ambitious piece attempting to show musical development as contemporary history, presented in five sections over five nights. This trio was augmented to a septet at the Verona jazz festival in 1980, resulting in two albums released on the Soul Note label. Dixon has also exhibited his paintings in the USA and Europe, and in 1986 he published *L'Opera*, a collection of letters, writings, musical scores and drawings. The 1990s saw Dixon playing regularly – or as regularly as Dixon ever has – with veteran virtuosi such as Tony Oxley, William Parker and Barry Guy (all of whom have circled Cecil Taylor's orbit at some point). *Odyssey*, a towering 6-CD retrospective of Dixon solo works – though he does overdub and layer, occasionally using minimal backing – since 1970, was released in 2001 on his own label. It's an intimidatingly gestalt artwork, complementing his restlessly exploratory music with reproductions of his angular, modernist paintings; an epic that should more than placate those frustrated by his infrequent recorded appearances.[IC]

⊙ **Bill Dixon In Italy** (1980; Soul Note). This studio recording has Dixon with two other trumpeters, Stephen Horenstein on saxophones, bassist Alan Silva and drummer Freddie Waits. Part of the music is dedicated to Cecil Taylor and his spirit pervades the whole album – the rhythm-section boils and the horns wail.

⊙ **Son Of Sisyphus** (1988; Soul Note). One of Dixon's most fully realized albums, this features a quartet including John Buckingham (tuba), Mario Pavone (bass) and Laurence Cook Dixon's penchant for dark low sounds is much in evidence – particularly on the title track. His own playing has a pithy lyricism with a sorrowful edge which is disarming and attractive. He also plays some piano on this expansive and moving album.

Iain Dixon

Tenor sax, clarinet, bass clarinet.

b.Clitheroe, Lancashire, UK, 6 Aug 1966.

Dixon started learning the tenor sax at school when he was eleven, and took up the clarinet some three years later. From 1984–88 he studied with Tommy Cudley at the Royal Northern College of Music, and while still a student worked and recorded with the rock group Simply Red. An outstanding multi-instrumentalist, from1996–98 Dixon was a member of the BBC Radio Big Band. Since 1998 he has played with the Dave Green Trio, alongside bassist Green and drummer Gene Calderazzo. With no piano or guitar this is a very exacting and exposing context, but Dixon seems to revel in it. Dixon is admired both in Britain and internationally and is much in demand. In 2001 he played as a session musician on Joni Mitchell's album *Both Sides Now*, and in 2002 he toured the UK with Michael Brecker and featured on bass clarinet on Brecker's album *Wide Angles*. [IC]

➤➤ **Dave Green Trio** *(Time Will Tell)*.

Baby Dodds

Drums.

b. New Orleans, 24 Dec 1898; d. 14 Feb 1959.

The younger brother of Johnny Dodds, and always a bad young brother, Baby (Warren) Dodds began drinking young, bought his first drums at the age of sixteen and played in Willie Hightower's band that year for ice creams. He was soon playing all over New Orleans in a showy style that used every one of his drums, then in Fate Marable's highly able Streckfus orchestra and by 1922 with King Oliver's great Creole Jazz Band (Oliver's records clearly show Dodds's groundbreaking talent). After the financial quarrel that broke up Oliver's band, Baby Dodds was around Chicago for twenty years (often with his disciplinarian elder brother: "very hard for me", he said ruefully), and supplementing his income working with a taxi firm. In 1945, in New York to work with Bunk Johnson, his style was still controversial: "the way he played drums behind the band was a solo in itself", says George Wettling. The approach was disturbing to Johnson (and to other musicians, including Lester Young, who also preferred a discreet tick) but it had an affinity with the liberated role of African drums in modern and avant-garde jazz. In 1947 on a Rudi Blesh show, Dodds listened with interest to Max Roach, and his stated ambition, "to work out a drum symphony for five or six drummers", found an echo in Roach's own M'Boom percussion ensemble. From 1949 Dodds suffered a series of strokes that curtailed his playing; "physically he's about 95", said Jo Jones. "He did more living than three men." [DF]

⊙ **Baby Dodds** (1944–5; American Music). An excellent portrait of Dodds, featuring his famous "talking records" along with musical examples featuring Bunk Johnson, Jim Robinson, George Lewis and others.

Johnny Dodds

Clarinet, alto saxophone.

b. Waverly, Louisiana, 12 April 1892; d. 8 Aug 1940.

Johnny Dodds sang "real high tenor" in the family quartet, then graduated to penny whistle and clarinet, which – despite early lessons from Lorenzo Tio – he always played by ear. After ten years in and around New Orleans (from 1910 with, among others, Frank Dusen, Kid Ory and Billy Mael's vaudeville troupe) he joined King Oliver's Creole Jazz Band in Chicago and stayed for three years, during which his fervent clarinet was recorded on

MAX JONES FILES/REDFERNS

Johnny Dodds

more than forty sides. When he left in 1924, after a pay disagreement, it was to begin a successful solo career at Burt Kelly's Stables, a Mafia-controlled club on Chicago's Rush Street. Dodds combined his residency at Kelly's, and occasionally other small South Side clubs, with regular studio work, recording with his own band, with Jelly Roll Morton, Lovie Austin, and Louis Armstrong (for whom he recorded all the Hot Five and Seven classics).

He took music very seriously, insisted on regular rehearsals for his own band and refused to tolerate drunkenness or slack behaviour from his younger brother Baby, whom he kept on a tight rein. "I'd say they did regard themselves as artists in the sense we use the term today", says Garvin Bushell. "They knew they were doing something new that nobody else could do." This was less true by 1930, although by that time the canny Dodds had invested his money wisely in property, including an apartment block. Nevertheless, work and money were getting harder to come by and Dodds began a round of tireless hustling, playing for saloons, clubs, rent parties and jam sessions. One regular fan in Chicago was Benny Goodman, but by 1935, with Goodman's rise to fame, the craze for sophisticated big-band swing, and a new clarinet star, Jimmie Noone, making headlines in the city, Dodds's currency was waning. In 1938 he recorded in New York with Charlie Shavers, then the year after he made more records in Chicago and had a residency with old friends Lonnie Johnson and Natty Dominique at the Hayes Hotel, but soon after Dodds suffered a stroke. He died the following year, missing the jazz revival by a whisker; his style of playing lives on in the work of aficionados such as Kenny Davern and in particular Cy Laurie. [DF]

⊙ **Johnny Dodds 1926–28** (JSP). Definitive Dodds sessions with the New Orleans Wanderers, Bootblacks, Black Bottom Stompers and Chicago Footwarmers. Remastered by John R. T. Davies.

⊙ **The Myth Of New Orleans** (1926–9; Giants of Jazz). Strange title but a typically good and well-priced Giants of Jazz selection, containing many of the best-known recordings of the groups mentioned above.

⊙ **Wild Man Blues** (1923–40; ASV). Excellent all-round survey of Dodds's work, moving from King Oliver to his last recordings and featuring numerous indispensables along the way including his Trio, Black Bottom Stompers, New Orleans Wanderers and Bootblacks.

⊙ **The Chronological Johnny Dodds** (1926–40; Classics). Four separately available CDs containing all of Dodds's recordings under his own name, including those with the New Orleans Wanderers and Bootblacks and moving up to the intriguing 1938 collaborations in which Dodds's intense New Orleans style is pitted against a group of swing sophisticates including Charlie Shavers.

⊙ **Johnny Dodds 1926–40: Part I** (Affinity). All of Dodds's solo recordings, beginning with modest collaborations with singers Teddy Peters and Edonia Henderson and finishing (so far) with Jimmy Blythe's Owls in 1927.

➤➤ **Louis Armstrong** *(Louis Armstrong Volume 1, 1925–7).*

Bill Doggett

Piano, organ, arranger.

b. Philadelphia, 16 Feb 1916; d. 13 Nov 1996.

After playing with local groups, Doggett led his own locally based big band (1938), which then toured for a year under Lucky Millinder before breaking up. He was with the Jimmy Mundy big band (1939), then with a new Millinder band (1940–42). He arranged for the Ink Spots vocal group (1942–4) and as a freelance for Louis Armstrong, Lionel Hampton and Count Basie, also scoring the debut recording of "Round Midnight" for Cootie Williams. He recorded on Johnny Otis's first big-band session (1945) during a West Coast stay, and four times with early Illinois Jacquet groups (1945–7). He replaced Wild Bill Davis in the Louis Jordan band (1948–51) and, inspired by Davis, took up the organ and recorded with Eddie Davis and Ella Fitzgerald (1951). He led his own quintet (octet from 1958) with great success in the R&B field, his 1956 record "Honky Tonk" being of classic simplicity. Not much of Doggett's early big-band writing (even for Millinder) has been positively identified as his, but there can be no doubt that this talent carried over directly into his own small group. [BP]

⊙ **Every Day I Have The Blues** (1971; Black & Blue). Probably the best Doggett combo album currently available, with a handful of undistinguished vocal tracks failing to disguise the leader's relaxed groove. Of interest are Doggett's two takes on the Booker T number "Green Onions".

Klaus Doldinger

Tenor and soprano saxophones, composer; also clarinet and keyboards.
b. Berlin, 12 May 1936.

Doldinger studied piano from 1947 and clarinet from 1952 at the Robert Schumann Conservatory, Düsseldorf. In the 1960s he did jazz workshops with visiting Americans such as Kenny Clarke, Max Roach and Donald Byrd. He toured in Europe, North Africa, the Middle East and South America with his own quintet. In 1970 he formed a jazz-rock group, which from 1971 was known as Passport, and played festivals and made TV appearances in Europe and the Far East. Beloved by aficionados of the fusion era – their 1970s albums have all the pomp, mystical song titles, and virtuosity a fan could ask for – Passport have continued to be Doldinger's vehicle ever since, releasing a prolific amount of albums. Doldinger has also written music for major feature films and TV series such as *Das Boot*. His influences include Sidney Bechet, Charlie Parker, John Coltrane, Ornette Coleman, Gil Evans and Miles Davis. [IC]

Doldinger's Best (1963–77; ACT). This compiles highlights of Doldinger's music over some fifteen years of his career, and a cast as varied as Donald Byrd, Johnny Griffin, Herbie Mann, Idrees Sulieman, Albert Mangelsdorff and Etta James conveys some idea of the versatility of Doldinger's talent.

Eric Dolphy

Alto saxophone, bass-clarinet, flute, clarinet.
b. Los Angeles, 20 June 1928; d. Berlin, 29 June 1964.

Dolphy began playing clarinet in junior high school, and studied with noted ex-Les Hite bandsman Lloyd Reese. He gained playing experience with various West Coast groups including the bebop-influenced Roy Porter big band (1948–9), and with army bands (1950–52). Gigging with Gerald Wilson, Buddy Collette and his own groups led to joining the popular Chico Hamilton quintet in early 1958. Late in 1959 he settled in New York, then worked with Charles Mingus small groups (and big band on record) and became busy recording under his own name and for others. Freelance work from late 1960 included albums with Max Roach and George Russell, and he led his own quintet and did a solo tour of Germany and Scandinavia. After contributing to Coltrane's 1961 recordings, he became a full member of his group until spring 1962. A further period of freelance gigging (though little recording) included playing European straight music and working with John Lewis's Orchestra USA. He rejoined Mingus in early 1964 in time for his tour of Europe, after which Dolphy undertook his own engagements in the remaining weeks before his sudden death, as a result of uraemia and/or undiagnosed diabetes.

Despite a mere six years on the US national scene, Dolphy had as much long term influence as other prematurely deceased artists such as Beiderbecke, Blanton, Christian, Navarro. This is partly because of the manner in which he defined a role for such hitherto peripheral instruments as the flute and bass-clarinet, that is, the role they would fill in the new jazz of the last three decades. It is also not unconnected with the mere fact of being a convincing multi-instrumentalist. Virtually all previous such musicians were identified with one main instrument to which their others were clearly secondary: Dolphy was a force to be reckoned with on each of his three main horns, and the tendency of players since his time (reedmen especially) to make a virtue of versatility stems mostly from him.

His work on alto is the most easily distinguishable from his predecessors. He had great admiration for Charlie Parker but only occasionally referred directly to his style; instead of Parker's precise and taut rhythmic mechanism, Dolphy came on like a conveyor belt running too fast (like Ornette Coleman or John Coltrane, his timing was more often in "even 8ths" than "dotted 8ths"). Unlike Ornette or Trane, however, he relished playing on strict chord sequences while appearing not to follow them strictly. In a famous interview he once said, "I play notes that would not ordinarily be said to be in a given key, but I hear them as proper. I don't think I 'leave the changes' as the expression goes; every note I play has some reference to the chords of the piece."

The huge, guffawing tone he used also carried over to his bass-clarinet playing, and in the middle register of both instruments it was evident that the combination of tone and phrasing closely resembled human speech patterns, whether of weighty philosophizing or garrulous chatter. The second is more typical of the flute work because of its pitch range, which has perhaps made this aspect of Dolphy harder to hear for those listeners unconvinced of the importance of the instrument itself. But the significance of his contribution in the eyes of fellow flautists can hardly be overestimated.

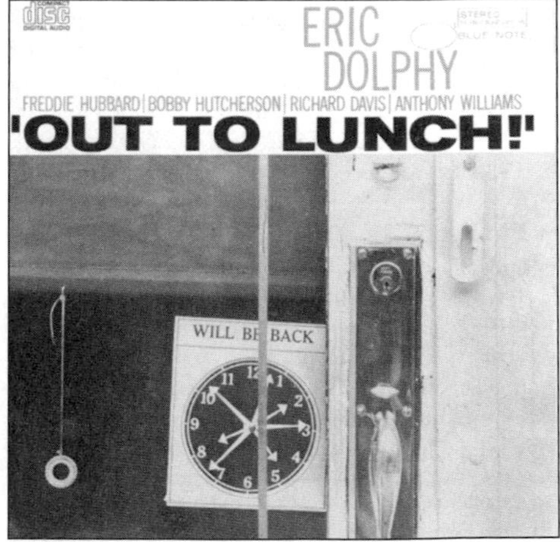

Like most jazz players since about 1960, he wrote a large number of original compositions which were only ever performed by his own groups. But the younger generation of "free" players, many of whom have reverted to the use of chord changes but in a loosely defined manner, has reflected the influence of Eric Dolphy more and more. [BP]

Outward Bound (1960; New Jazz/OJC). Dolphy's first recording under his own name still has a unique angle on post-bop, with Freddie Hubbard, Jaki Byard and Roy Haynes combining to take nearly normal material and play it with energetic hints of polytonality.

Out There (1960; New Jazz/OJC). A more subdued quartet album has Ron Carter (Dolphy's former colleague in the Chico Hamilton group) playing as the second frontline instrument, and no keyboard instrument.

At The Five Spot Vol. 1 (1961; New Jazz/OJC). The energy level rises again on this famous live session (which produced several further albums) with the Mal Waldron-Richard Davis-Ed Blackwell rhythm-section backing Dolphy and Booker Little, another advanced harmonic thinker.

Iron Man (1963; West Wind). Dolphy in a variety of contexts, including Woody Shaw and Bobby Hutcherson and two fine duets with Richard Davis, from which the sympathetic interplay between bass and bass-clarinet on "Come Sunday" stands out.

Out To Lunch (1964; Blue Note). The last great studio album has Hubbard and Davis returning plus new Blue Note stars Bobby Hutcherson and Tony Williams, and some of Dolphy's greatest work on bass-clarinet ("Hat And Beard") and flute ("Gazzelloni").

>> **Andrew Hill** *(Point Of Departure);* **Charles Mingus** *(Presents Charles Mingus);* **George Russell** *(Ezz-thetics).*

Natty Dominique

Trumpet.

b. New Orleans, 2 Aug 1896, d. 30 Aug 1982.

An able, versatile trumpeter who studied with Manuel Perez (New Orleans' best teacher), Natty (Anatie) Dominique moved to Chicago in 1913 and all through the 1920s was an in-demand talent. He was good enough to tour with Carroll Dickerson's orchestra, and later, for Dickerson again, played second trumpet to Louis Armstrong at Sunset Café. He also worked with the two leading Chicago-based clarinettists, Jimmie Noone and Johnny Dodds, forming a partnership with Dodds that lasted until the clarinettist's death. (There are lots of his records at this time with Noone, Dodds, Jelly Roll Morton, Jimmy Bertrand, Jimmy Blythe, Jasper Taylor, Sippie Wallace and others.) In the 1940s Dominique retired to work as a porter at Chicago airport, but by 1950 he was playing again – notably in his self-led Creole Dance Band with Baby Dodds, Volly de Faut, Preston Jackson and Jasper Taylor, which in 1953 was still playing around the city. Dominique was last active at jazz concerts in the mid-1960s. [DF]

Natty Dominique's Creole Dance Band (1953; American Music). Recorded at a hotel with Preston Jackson, Darnell Howard and Baby Dodds, an intriguing (and unexpected) late illustration of Dominique's pioneering work.

Arne Domnérus

Alto saxophone, clarinet.

b. Stockholm, 20 Dec 1924.

Domnérus has been one of Sweden's top jazz musicians almost since the start of his career in the 1940s with leaders Simon Brehm and Thore Ehrling. He played at the Paris Jazz Fair (1949) and his group, including Lars Gullin and pianist Jan Johansson (1950s), recorded in Sweden with James Moody, Clifford Brown-Art Farmer and others. From 1956–78 he worked with the Swedish Radio Big Band and Jazz Group and wrote for films and TV, and (from late 1970s) he recorded several duos with Bengt Hallberg, including music with explicitly religious themes. Initially influenced by Parker, his playing was then marked (like many Europeans') by Lee Konitz, while later still he acknowledged his debt to Johnny Hodges. Now he is a commanding, if laid-back, soloist who plays pure melody without reference to stylistic models. [BP]

Portrait (1946–93; Phontastic). Covering Domnérus's recording career to date, this includes two collaborations with Hallberg, bringing in the Hodges connection with "Blood Count", and sessions with Clark Terry in New York and Clifford Brown-Art Farmer in Sweden.

>> **Clifford Brown** *(Memorial Album).*

Sam Donahue

Tenor saxophone, trumpet, arranger.

b. Detroit, Michigan, 18 March 1918; d. 22 March 1974.

Sam Donahue began with Gene Krupa (1938–40) and worked with Harry James and Benny Goodman before joining the navy in 1942. He led the US Navy Dance Band, which toured Europe throughout the war years and achieved a great reputation – most ranked it above Glenn Miller's AAF band for jazz feeling, swing and adventurousness. Donahue led the band until 1946, when he re-formed his own, and all through the 1950s he worked for top leaders like Tommy Dorsey and Billy May. In 1961–5, after a spell with Stan Kenton, he fronted the Tommy Dorsey Memorial Band (featuring Frank Sinatra Jnr and Charlie Shavers) and thereafter carried on bandleading, as well as working for the Playboy chain of clubs, until he died. Donahue's long career was a success, but his saxophone playing was seldom quoted as a major jazz influence: like Tony Pastor and Tex Beneke he worked most happily in a swing style which by the end of the war had been superseded by the new giants of bebop. But Donahue was canny enough, and a good enough musician and leader, to weather the fickleness of jazz fashion: a considerable achievement on its own. [DF]

Lou Donaldson

Alto saxophone.

b. Badin, North Carolina, 1 Nov 1926.

Donaldson moved to New York in the early 1950s, recording sessions for Milt Jackson, Thelonious Monk and, continuously from 1952, under his own name. He also worked briefly with Art Blakey (1954) and Charles Mingus (1956), and led his own group with little interruption from the mid-1950s onwards. He made his first tours of Europe in the 1980s. Initially strongly influenced by Charlie Parker, Donaldson had a more strident tone which suited ideally his simplification of Parker's lines. Concentrating on blues phrasing hitherto associated more with R&B tenor saxophonists, he helped to create an alto approach to "soul jazz"; throughout the 1960s his backing group usually contained an organist (and more often than not an extra percussionist). From the late 1970s, for the duration of the neo-bop revival, he used a pianist once more, but during the 1990s reverted to employing an organist, usually Dr Lonnie Smith. Historically, Donaldson can be seen to have paved the way for such altoists as Cannonball Adderley, Gary Bartz and even David Sanborn. [BP]

⊙ **Blues Walk** (1958; Blue Note). The first time that Donaldson's quartet added a conga accompaniment (by Ray Barretto) produced a classic of simplicity which has proved hard to beat.

➤➤ **Art Blakey** *(A Night At Birdland Vols. 1 & 2).*

Dorothy Donegan

Piano.

b. Chicago, 26 April 1922; d. 19 May 1998.

Donegan started piano at six and by the age of eleven was hired for parties and church functions. She studied at Chicago's famous DuSable High School, and at seventeen began regular night-club work. In 1942 her first recordings included jazz versions of the classical warhorses, "Prelude In C Sharp Minor" and "Minuet In G", and at twenty she became the first black performer to play a concert at her home town's Orchestra Hall, which led to informal tuition from Art Tatum. A flamboyant populist, she appeared on film and on Broadway in the mid-1940s, and developed her boogie-woogie specialities. Success in 1950s supper-clubs and at 1970s and 80s festivals led to her adding occasional vocals and impersonations of famous singers, but verbal and visual humour were often the keynote of her appeal (she even performed opposite former Chicago buddy, Sun Ra, in 1979). Pianist-journalist Dempsey Travis claimed that Tatum was the only player with a better technique than Donegan. [BP]

⊙ **Live In Copenhagen** (1980; Storyville). Abetted by bassist Mads Vinding and local resident Ed Thigpen, Donegan carries all before her in a typical onslaught on such items as "Take The A Train", and even the sceptical listener is eventually won over by her relentless entertainment.

Pierre Dørge

Guitar, composer.

b. Copenhagen, 28 Feb 1946.

While in his mid-teens Dørge's group, the Copenhagen Jazz Quintet, won first prize in Radio Denmark jazz competitions (1961–3). By the late 1960s he was active in experimental musical circles and as guitarist with John Tchicai's group, Cadentia Nova Danica. Influences as varied as Ellington and free jazz, African music and contemporary European composition found expression in his quartet Thermaenius (1978), including Marilyn Mazur and his wife, keyboardist Irene Becker. His New Jungle Orchestra (1980) was originally an eighteen-piece; its size and instrumention varied over the years, as Dørge constantly widened its sources of material and influences to include Arabic, African and Balinese music alongside reworkings of classics by Monk and Ellington and a reinterpretation of Grieg's *Peer Gynt* suite. Dørge and the New Jungle Orchestra were selected as the Danish State Ensemble for the period 1993–6. In recognition of his prolific creativity, Denmark awarded Dørge a life-long composer's grant in 1998 and with the NJO making regular appearances worldwide, his international reputation continues to grow. [CA/CI]

⊙ **Different Places – Different Bananas** (1988; Olufsen). This set is typically diverse in its sources: tributes to Fats Waller and Sun Ra feature together with compositions inspired by *gamelan* and *kora*, while Harry Beckett's trumpet solos generate the heat.

⊙ **Zig Zag Zimfoni** (2001; Stunt). Vibrant, eccentric and exotic enough to satisfy lovers of the left field, but also full enough of the jazz tradition for some to hail Dørge as the globalized alternative to Marsalis's US-centric classicism.

⊙ **Live At Birdland** (2003; Stunt). In this recording from their triumphant 2002 trip to the US, the New Jungle Orchestra in full flight.

Kenny Dorham

Trumpet, composer.

b. Fairfield, Texas, 30 Aug 1924; d. 5 Dec 1972.

Dorham started the piano at age seven and took up the trumpet in high school. From 1945–8 he played with Dizzy Gillespie, Billy Eckstine, Lionel Hampton and Mercer Ellington. He replaced Miles Davis in the Charlie Parker quintet from 1948–50, playing with Parker at the Paris jazz festival in 1949. After freelancing in New York during the early 1950s, he became was a founder member of Art Blakey's Jazz Messengers in 1954. That year Dorham was a star soloist on the great album which was the blueprint for the Messengers, *Horace Silver And The Jazz Messengers.* From 1956–8 he replaced Clifford Brown in the Max Roach quintet, and played superbly on another classic

Herman Leonard

Kenny Dorham

bass/drums/brass trio is elemental, and Dorham's pauses, rhythmic attack and serpentine phrases speak out with great eloquence.

⊙ **Quiet Kenny** (1959; New Jazz/OJC). This trumpet quartet album, with Tommy Flanagan, Paul Chambers and Art Taylor, is a quite exquisite affair of fluid lyricism and subtle rhythmic poise.

⊙ **Jazz Contemporary** (1960; Time). Dorham is in ebullient mood for this quintet album with Charles Davis on baritone, pianist Steve Kuhn, plus bass and drums. Dorham's technique was always excellent but he seems to be pushing it to the limits with even more passionate urgency. Another departure is his composition "Tonica", which is a wholly composed piece without solos.

➤➤ **Charlie Parker** *(Complete Live Performances On Savoy);* **Sonny Rollins** *(Moving Out);* **Horace Silver** *(Horace Silver And The Jazz Messengers).*

album of the 1950s, *Max Roach 4 Plays Charlie Parker*. During the late 1950s and the 1960s he led various groups of his own, composed and played music for some films, worked with Joe Henderson and Hank Mobley, toured internationally and played major festivals. Dorham successfully straddled the bop and hard-bop eras of jazz, and contributed to the louche sound of Blue Note's more "out" records of the 1960s. His trumpet sat naturally alongside Parker, Coltrane, Monk, Oliver Nelson, Tadd Dameron, J.J. Johnson and Sonny Rollins; some of his finest playing was done on other people's albums before his early death from kidney failure.

One of the first bebop trumpeters, he had something of the fleetness of Gillespie and the sonority of Miles Davis. By the beginning of the 1950s he had absorbed his influences and found his own individual voice on trumpet. A brilliant player, he was never glib, and could project great lyricism even at fast tempos, producing astonishingly long lines of fluid triplets. Yet he was also a magnificent blues player, because his fluidity of execution was accompanied by all the tonal inflexions of the vocal blues tradition. Dorham influenced and inspired countless trumpeters all over the world, but never himself broke through to a wider audience or got all the recognition he was due, because he was overshadowed by Davis and Fats Navarro in the 1940s and Clifford Brown and others in the 1950s and 1960s. A fine composer, one of his best pieces, "Blue Bossa", has become part of the jazz canon. [IC]

⊙ **Kenny Dorham Quintet** (1953; Debut/OJC). Dorham's first album under his own name was produced at the age of 29, with Jimmy Heath, Walter Bishop, Percy Heath and Kenny Clarke. Dorham's blues-drenched urgency and wit are thrilling.

⊙ **Two Horns/Two Rhythm** (1957; Riverside/OJC). From around the same time as the *Max Roach 4 Plays Charlie Parker* album, the same instrumentation is used, only here it's Ernie Henry on alto, the great Wilbur Ware on bass and Granville T. Hogan on drums. Without a piano, the

Bob Dorough

Vocals, piano, composer.

b. Cherry Hill, Arkansas, 12 Dec 1923.

A cult singer favoured by hip musicians and by younger connoisseurs, Dorough was raised in Texas and studied music at school and at North Texas State College. His performing career included two years working for boxer Sugar Ray Robinson in the 1950s, when he also appeared with his own trio in Paris, New York, Chicago and Los Angeles. His first album, recorded in 1956, included his original "Devil May Care", later covered by Miles Davis (with whom Dorough recorded two more of his songs in 1962). He also recorded an album of jazz-and-poetry in 1958 and a jazz version of the musical *Oliver*, and collaborated on the songs "Comin' Home Baby" (with bassist Ben Tucker) and "I'm Hip" (with Dave Frishberg). He composed for advertising and for TV series such as *Schoolhouse Rock*, of which he was musical director for twenty-five years. His sporadic (and mostly rare) later recordings were often completed live with bassist Bill Takas, with whom he toured Europe again in the 1990s. In the early 2000s he was performing weekly at New York's Iridium nightclub.[BP]

⊙ **Right On My Way Home** (1997; Blue Note). His first studio album in decades features Dorough's mock-ironic vocalizing and quirky piano on a programme of obscurities topped and tailed by "Moon River" and "Spring Can Really Hang You Up", partly accompanied by Bill Takas and partly by guests Joe Lovano and Christian McBride.

Jimmy Dorsey

Clarinet, alto saxophone, trumpet.

b. Shenandoah, Pennsylvania, 29 Feb 1904; d. 12 June 1957.

In his early years Jimmy Dorsey worked with his brother Tommy in Dorsey's Novelty Six, the

Scranton Sirens (a jazz-based group which often featured sitters-in such as Joe Venuti and Eddie Lang), the California Ramblers (a prototype big band, managed by Ed Kirkeby) and from 1925 in studios and big bands led by Jean Goldkette, Paul Whiteman and others. From 1934 he co-led the Dorsey Brothers orchestra with Tommy, then after a quarrel over the tempo for the popular song "I'll Never Say 'Never Again' Again" he took over leadership, replacing his brother with trombonist Bobby Byrne. In 1935 they became resident band on the Kraft Music Hall programme starring Bing Crosby, and from then on Jimmy Dorsey – a milder man than his brother – led a succession of highly successful bands, had a number of hits (eg "Amapola", "So Rare", and "Green Eyes") and in 1937 supplied the soundtrack music for the Fred Astaire-Ginger Rogers box-office success *Shall We Dance?*

A good part of Dorsey's success was attributable to his singers – initially Bob Eberly and Helen O'Connell, later replaced by fine singers such as Kitty Kallen, Bob Hughes and Bob Carroll. As a clarinettist he never seriously competed with masters like Goodman and Shaw, and later recordings (with his marvellous Dorseyland Band) reveal an occasionally stilted turn of phrase. But his band featured a succession of fine if lesser-known jazzmen, including tenor saxophonist Herbie Haymer, trumpeter Shorty Sherock, drummer Ray McKinley and lead trumpeter Ralph Muzillo. By 1943 Dorsey's Band had reached its peak, yet it remained highly successful after the war, when bright young stars such as Herb Ellis and Lou Carter joined the ranks. As late as 1948 Dorsey was still organizing new bands (his brass section featured Maynard Ferguson and Charlie Teagarden together), but was featuring more regularly a small Dixieland unit, the Dorseyland Band, which that year played a season at Tommy Dorsey's own Casino Garden ballroom in Santa Monica. From 1953, no longer a bandleader, Jimmy Dorsey was once again featured in a soloist's set with his brother's orchestra, and after his brother's death he again took over leadership briefly. [DF]

⊙ **Amapola** (1936–43; ASV). Excellent collection of most of Jimmy Dorsey's greatest hits, including "Green Eyes", "Besame Mucho" and the title track.

⊙ **Classic Columbia Condon Mob Sessions** (1940–59; Mosaic). This set contains twenty-one tracks by Jimmy's Dorseyland jazz band, an enormously skilled ensemble featuring the flyaway trumpet of Charlie Teagarden alongside Dorsey's biting clarinet. These sides (regularly issued as single albums too) are top-notch Dixieland.

Tommy Dorsey

Trombone, trumpet.

b. Shenandoah, Pennsylvania, 19 Nov 1905; d. 26 Nov 1956.

With his elder brother Jimmy, Tommy Dorsey spent his early years around Scranton, then worked with famous bands led by Paul Whiteman and Jean Goldkette, and in 1934 formed the Dorsey Brothers orchestra, a project dissolved after a quarrel during a Glenn Island Casino residency. (Arranger Billy May believed this group to be the brothers' greatest achievement.) From there Dorsey took over Joe Haymes's orchestra – "a very disciplined band", says Charlie Barnet – and began his ambitious climb. First he brought in arranger Axel Stordahl, trumpeter Joe Bauer, arranger/guitarist Carmen Mastren and singer Jack Leonard, and continued building all through the 1930s. By offering blank cheques to talent he wanted to poach from other orchestras, he brought in such star instrumentalists as Bud Freeman, Max Kaminsky, Yank Lawson, Ziggy Elman and Pee Wee Erwin, as well as a succession of great singers, including Frank Sinatra, Dick Haymes, Jo Stafford and the Pied Pipers, plus arranger Sy Oliver. The result was a highly versatile, sternly drilled jazz orchestra: "of all the hundreds of bands Tommy's could do more things better than anyone else", says George T. Simon.

Max Jones Files/Redferns

Tommy Dorsey

Dorsey devised a host of promotional tactics, which at various times included a nationwide "Amateur Swing Contest", programmes dedicated to specific songwriters and subjects on his long Raleigh-Kool radio series, and in 1939 a dual band show with Jimmy, with whom he had been reconciled in 1937. The result was a string of hits, notably "I'm Getting Sentimental Over You" (his theme song), "Song Of India", "Marie" and "Sunny Side Of The Street", featuring The Sentimentalists (later the Clark Sisters).

By 1941, Dorsey had taken over his bookings and opened his own Santa Monica ballroom; a year later he had added a string section to his orchestra, and by 1945 he had brought Charlie Shavers – a much valued cornerman – into his show. He stayed successful enough for the rest of the decade: in 1947 a Hollywood fantasy, *The Fabulous Dorseys*, starred both brothers and in the same year they introduced pseudo-classical works like "Dorsey Concerto" (Leo Shuken) and "The Quest" (Roy Harris) in concerts. From May 1953 the Dorsey brothers worked together again – under Tommy's banner, "featuring" Jimmy – until 1956, when Tommy Dorsey choked to death in his sleep at 51. The Tommy Dorsey Memorial Band, under leaders Warren Covington and Sam Donahue, remained successful until the mid-1960s.

Dorsey was billed as "The Sentimental Gentleman of Swing" after his famous theme song, but he was neither sentimental nor altogether a gentleman: "a totally cold person", says Bob Crosby, who sang with the Dorsey Brothers orchestra. Few accounts of Dorsey fail to mention his ruthless drive for perfection, his unshakeable ambition and his occasional enjoyment of others' discomfiture (he once sent songwriter Johnny Mercer a mock birthday cake filled with old leadsheets of Mercer's less successful songs). On the other hand Dorsey could show a more supportive side; one sideman described him as "horrible when sober and delightful when drunk – the exact opposite to Jimmy". As a trombonist Dorsey was technically unfaultable: he invented a smooth-as-silk upper register which was revolutionary for its time and was framed in such classics as his signature tune and "Song Of India". But his jazz ideas were limited, based on an affection for fine 1920s players such as Miff Mole, whose talents had been in part at least eclipsed by Jack Teagarden, a musician with whom Dorsey never (for once) tried to compete. The now-legendary Tommy Dorsey was perhaps most noticeable for doing everything well rather than any one thing outstandingly. [DF]

⊙ **The Complete Tommy Dorsey And His Orchestra 1928–35** (Le Jazz). Covers Dorsey's solo recordings from trumpet solos with Eddie Lang and Arthur Schutt up to "Don't Give Up The Ship", but omitting sides by the Dorsey Brothers orchestra.

⊙ **The Fabulous Dorsey Brothers And Their Orchestra** (1928–35; ASV). Worthwhile survey of the Dorseys' early days with endless star sidemen including Bunny Berigan, Glenn Miller, Dick McDonough and many others; titles include "By Heck", "Weary Blues", "Lullaby Of Broadway" and twenty-one more.

⊙ **The Music Goes 'Round And Around** (1935–50; ASV). Dorsey's Clambake Seven with a host of stars:Yank Lawson, Pee Wee Erwin, Bud Freeman, Johnny Mince, Bobby Hackett, Peanuts Hucko, Billy Butterfield et al; plus singer Edythe Wright. Interesting if occasionally slightly formalized Dixieland-to-swing but with those players plenty of surprises still.

⊙ **Stop Look and Listen** (1935–42; ASV). Excellent cross-selection of Dorsey sides with his orchestra and Clambake Seven, including such indispensables as "Marie", "Liebestraum", "Easy Does It" and "Song Of India".

⊙ **Yes Indeed** (1939–45; RCA Bluebird). Taken from his peak years, this has Dorsey at his jazziest, including Sy Oliver's "Swanee River", "Opus One" and "Looselid Special".

⊙ **Well Git It!** (1943–6; Jass). An excellent collection with Charlie Shavers and Buddy DeFranco amongst the soloists plus a guest spot from Gene Krupa on the title track.

⊙ **At The Fat Man's 1946–48** (Hep). Later Dorsey caught on air checks with DeFranco, Shavers, Ziggy Elman and vocalist Lucy Ann Polk, a neglected and talented singer.

⊙ **The Dorsey Brothers Live In The Big Apple** (1954–5; Submarine). The brothers together for their last partnership in a combination of live broadcasts from the Café Rouge and excerpts from stage shows. With Dick Haymes and Kitty Kallen.

Dave Douglas

Trumpet, composer.

b. New Jersey, 24 March 1963.

Dave Douglas is one of the busiest composers and performers of jazz and new music, and one of the most critically acclaimed musicians of the last decade. He began playing improvised music during a high school year abroad in Barcelona, after which he studied composition and performance at the Berklee College of Music and the New England Conservatory in Boston. He moved to New York in 1984, completing his BA degree at New York University's Gallatin Division while also performing in the streets of the city with other young musicians. His education continued when he joined Horace Silver's band and toured internationally with it in 1987. Since then, Douglas has released eleven CDs under his own name and four as a co-leader, including over one hundred of his own compositions. He was voted Best Trumpeter of 1998 by the Jazz Journalists' Association, and the 1998 *Down Beat* critics' poll voted him Jazz Artist of the Year and Best Trumpeter in its Talent Deserving Wider Recognition category.

Douglas is not only a magnificent trumpet player, but also something of a visionary. He has a beautifully warm and expressive sound with a whole armoury of tonal effects, a fluent technique and excellent range, plus the knack of investing every note and phrase with pith and moment. His compositions are extraordinarily varied and develop organically as they move from one musical area to another. He writes mainly for his own numerous ensembles: the Tiny Bell trio, the Dave Douglas string group, his jazz quartet, quintet (featuring Uri Caine) and sextet, and the electric octet Sanctuary. Other projects of his explore the relationship of improvisation with Indian music, *musique concrète*, and even literature – his *Word* project of autumn 2003 set poems by Beckett, Kerouac and Basho to music.

Douglas is also much in demand by other musicians and groups. He is a member of John Zorn's

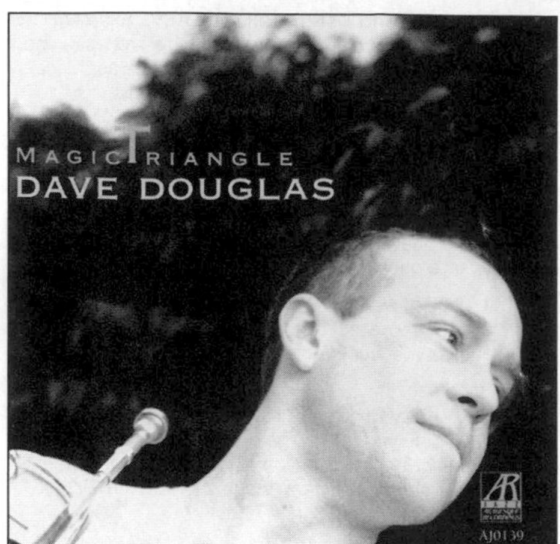

Masada, Myra Melford's The Same River Twice, and has recorded with Don Byron, Fred Hersch, Anthony Braxton, Han Bennink, Tim Berne, Uri Caine and Vincent Herring among (many) others. [IC]

⊙ **Tiny Bell Trio Live In Europe** (1996; Arabesque). Douglas, with guitarist Brad Schoeppach and drummer/percussionist Jim Black, creates an astonishing variety of music, from the ribald humour of "Around The Bend", to the sustained seriousness of the 11.41-minute "Zeno".

⊙ **Stargazer** (1996; Arabesque). Douglas here leads a sextet with Chris Speed (tenor saxophone and clarinet), Joshua Roseman (trombone), Uri Caine (piano), James Genus (bass) and Joey Baron (drums). The album is a tribute to Wayne Shorter, and Douglas composed six of the nine pieces. The rhythm-section is excellent, and Uri Caine makes several intensely lyrical contributions.

⊙ **Magic Triangle** (1997; Arabesque). Douglas's all-star quartet comprises Chris Potter (tenor saxophone), James Genus (bass) and Ben Perowsky (drums). Douglas composed all nine items on this superb album, and his writing deploys the group so skilfully that we hardly notice the absence of a chordal instrument.

Jim Douglas

Guitar, banjo.

b. Gifford, East Lothian, Scotland, 13 May 1942.

Douglas worked early on with the Clyde Valley Stompers and in 1964 joined Alex Welsh, with whom he remained until the trumpeter's death in 1982. One of Britain's most elegant and experienced jazz guitarists, he played in Welsh's band with a string of American visitors from Earl Hines to Ruby Braff, all of whom praised his softly supportive rhythm guitar and solo abilities which ran the gamut from swift single-string lines to lightly floating chorded creations recalling Kress and Van Eps. Douglas has worked with Keith Smith on package shows, leads the Alex Welsh Legacy Band, and freelances; in 1993 he toured with Ed Polcer's *Salute To Eddie Condon*, and from 1994 began recording and touring regularly in Germany with American musicians such as Warren Vaché. He also worked with The Great British Jazz Band from 1995 and regularly plays a leading role in reissue programmes on CD for Welsh. [DF]

➤➤ **Ed Polcer** *(Salute To Eddie Condon);* **Alex Welsh** *(Classic Concert; Doggin' Around).*

Tommy Douglas

Clarinet, reeds, leader.

b. Eskridge, Kansas, 9 Nov 1911; d. Sioux Falls, South Dakota, 9 Mar 1965.

Of all the territory bandleaders the one who achieved the highest reputation as a soloist was Tommy Douglas, who formed his first band in Kansas City in 1930. A spectacular technician – he was a graduate of Boston Conservatory where star names Johnny Hodges, Harry Carney and others had been contemporaries – Douglas played early on as a sideman for Jelly Roll Morton and later Bennie Moten, but worked as a leader from 1930–42. Young sidemen who gained experience in his bands included Jo Jones, Paul Webster and Charlie Parker, and, according to biographer Ross Russell, Parker learned much from Douglas. "Tommy was the kind of man who could play anything. He could play all of the saxophones. He knew his harmony inside out. Charlie took his place … watching the leader's fingers … asking questions … calling him 'Mr Douglas'." Douglas briefly disbanded his orchestra in 1937, but soon reformed and, apart from a late 1930s stint as MD for George E. Lee, and a short stay with Duke Ellington (1951), continued leading his big band – and, later on, small groups – for the rest of his working life. Why this magnificent musician has never progressed to the starry end of jazz history has regularly been conjectured: perhaps his preference for Kansas rather than the fast pace of New York was one reason. [DF]

Bob Downes

Concert, alto and bass flute, Chinese, Japanese and South American bamboo flute, tenor, alto and soprano saxophones.

b. Plymouth, UK, 22 July 1937.

Downes's first inspiration was his mother's "lovely singing voice", and he was basically self-taught. At nineteen he took up the saxophone, but in 1968 he began to devote most of his energy to the flute. From 1969–70 he played with the Mike Westbrook band and also formed his own Open Music Trio. Since 1974 he has performed mainly on unaccompanied flutes in Germany, where he took up residence in the late 1970s. He formed his Alternative Medicine Quintet in 1978, and in 1984 formed the Flute Orchestra in Germany. Downes is something of a maverick, and, although he admits to being inspired by saxophone players such as Sonny Rollins, "Fathead" Newman and Roland Kirk, he admires no flautists. His other influences are Horace Silver, Stan Kenton, and Miles Davis's late 1950s music, but Downes's music also owes much to rock, vocal blues and ethnic music of various kinds, and his emotional range can veer from lyricism to the more abrasive aspects of free jazz. He has composed many scores for contemporary dance companies including the Rambert. [IC]

Kenny Drew

Piano.

b. New York, 28 Aug 1928; d. Copenhagen, 4 Aug 1993.

Drew attended the High School of Music and Art, and was the accompanist of Lester Young, Sonny Rollins, Buddy DeFranco and others in the early 1950s. He then worked on the West Coast for a couple of years before playing for Dinah Washington and returning to New York. During this period he appeared on important albums by John Coltrane and Dexter Gordon, among others, and he continued to record prolifically after moving to Florida (c.1959) and Paris (1961) and from 1964 when he made his home in Copenhagen and where he married the daughter of 1940s Danish bandleader Leo Mathisen. He was co-owner of the Copenhagen-based Matrix record label and formed a long-standing duo with Niels-Henning Ørsted Pedersen. A dynamic and sought-after accompanist, Drew was also an exciting soloist somewhat influenced by Bud Powell and Hampton Hawes, with a special fondness for long right-hand lines full of rhythmic verve. His son Kenny Drew Jnr is also a fine pianist (see below). [BP]

⊙ **Recollections** (1989; Timeless). From the many recordings made with Ørsted Pedersen, this is a trio date including drummer Alvin Queen and combining standards such as "The Gentle Rain" and originals by both pianist and bassist.

>> **John Coltrane** *(Blue Train);* **Dexter Gordon** *(Both Sides Of Midnight).*

Kenny Drew Jnr

Piano.

b. New York, 14 June 1958.

Drew's father (see above) and uncle played piano, as did his aunt and grandmother who were responsible for his upbringing. Taught European classical music by his aunt from the age of four, he was later inspired by awareness of the expatriate Drew Snr and began taking an interest in jazz. In his teens he played in rock and funk bands, and in the 1980s he worked with singer Smokey Robinson, Stanley Turrentine, Out Of The Blue and Slide Hampton. He made his first three albums in the late 80s, and in 1990 won the Great American Jazz Piano Competition. Since then, he has appeared at major venues and international festivals with his own groups, as well as performing and recording with such as Charnett Moffett, Ronnie Cuber and the Mingus Big Band. Kenny has also continued to play classical music at a high level, with concerts in the USA, Europe and Australia, and this is frequently discernible in his jazz work. [BP]

⊙ **Follow The Spirit** (1997; Sirocco Jazz). Part trio and part quartet with saxophonist Steve Wilson, this collection of standards, jazz standards, two originals and one by his father does justice to the talents of the pianist, who closes with a rhapsodic solo ballad by Astor Piazzolla.

>> **Charles Mingus** *(Live In Time).*

Martin Drew

Drums.

b. Northampton, UK, 11 Feb 1944.

Drew first became interested in drums when he was five or six years old and took lessons at eleven, playing his first professional gig at thirteen. Over the years he has played countless engagements at Ronnie Scott's club in London, accompanying leading artists of the day. He was part of Ronnie Scott's quintet from 1975–1995, and (since 1974) has also played with the Oscar Peterson trio, the guitarist Joe Pass' band, and his own band, which included John Critchinson, Ron Mathewson, Dick Morrissey and Jim Mullen. He has worked with innumerable musicians of all styles and persuasions, from singers such as Ella Fitzgerald and Nina Simone to mainstreamers such as Harry Edison and Buddy Tate, and more contemporary stylists such as the Brecker brothers, Freddie Hubbard and Gil Evans. He has recorded with Ray Brown, Peterson, Buddy DeFranco, Hubbard and Arturo Sandoval. [IC]

>> **Oscar Peterson** *(If You Could See Me Now);* **Ronnie Scott** *(Never Pat A Burning Dog).*

Paquito D'Rivera

Alto saxophone, clarinet, soprano saxophone, flute.

b. Havana, 4 June 1948.

Taught by his father Tito, Paquito D'Rivera played with him in public at six and was advertising Selmer saxophones at seven; he was a featured soloist with the Havana Municipal Band and played a clarinet concerto with the National Symphony Orchestra in his teens. He had met Chucho Valdés while a student at the conservatory, and with him and Arturo Sandoval (1967) formed the group which became Irakere. After appearing with them in Europe and the USA (1978–9), he defected from Cuba and settled in New York (1980). There he worked with David Amram, McCoy Tyner and Dizzy Gillespie, in both a small-group setting and the United Nation Orchestra, which D'Rivera directed following Gillespie's death. In his own groups and solo guest appearances, Paquito has furthered the combination of post-bebop with Cuban rhythms and demonstrated great instrumental skill and passion. [BP]

Tico Tico (1989; Chesky). An absorbing programme, with Danilo Perez on piano, covers the ground from relatively conventional Afro-Latin dance music with bop solos to deliberately old-style renditions of the title track (with virtuoso clarinet) and three Venezuelan waltzes.

Buzzy Drootin

Drums.

b. Russia, 22 April 1920.

Buzzy (Benjamin) Drootin came along ten years after the first generation of great Dixieland drummers which included Dave Tough and Cliff Leeman, but he belongs in their class. He was first noticed nationally during a four-year term at Eddie Condon's (1947–51), and all through the 1950s his swing-to-Dixieland style backed the classiest of his contemporaries: Billy Butterfield, old friend Ruby Braff and Bobby Hackett among others. They all liked Drootin's loose, athletic time-sense, sensitive attention to dynamics and history-conscious style, at a time when younger players were dropping bebop bombs. He appeared on such classic records as Hackett's *Jazz Ultimate* with Jack Teagarden, held down a residency at George Wein's Boston Jazz Club (1953–5), and worked all over New York between times with kindred spirits Ralph Sutton, Pee Wee Erwin and Wild Bill Davison. In the 1960s Drootin joined the Newport All Stars (under Wein, with Braff) and formed his own Jazz Family with Herman Autrey and Benny Morton (1967–9), and in the 1970s was back in Boston running his Drootin Brothers orchestra with relations Al and Sonny. He also appeared at festivals including the Los Angeles Classic (1984) and continued to work into the 1990s, despite the onset of partial deafness. [DF]

Ray Drummond

Bass, composer.

b. Brookline, Massachusetts, 23 Nov 1946.

After working with Michael White and Bobby Hutcherson in San Francisco in the early 1970s, Ray Drummond attended Stanford Business School between 1974–7 and was inactive in music. Subsequently, he has played as first-choice sideman with a large number of musicians, most notably David Murray and Pharoah Sanders, but he has also contributed his solid, propulsive sound to the music of the New York Jazz Quartet, guitarist Joshua Breakstone, the Mingus Dynasty, Slide Hampton and many others. As adept a contributor to adventurously modern music as to mainstream singer-led sessions, Drummond is an entirely dependable, rock-solid presence both on the stand and in the studio, and in the 1990s has produced a series of intriguing albums as leader. *Excursion* (Arabesque; 1992) is a loose, rumbustious session of originals featuring the contrasting saxophones of Joe Lovano and Craig Handy; *Vignette* (Arabesque; 1995) centres on the superb rhythm-section work of pianist Renee Rosnes and drummer Billy Hart. *When You Wish Upon A Star* (2000; 32 Jazz) sees Rosnes join with husband drummer Billy Drummond (no relation to Ray), and the bassist in an excellent straightahead trio called, reasonably enough, The Drummonds. The pick of the bunch, though, is *Continuum* (see below). [CP/CI]

David Murray

Fast Life (1991; DIW). Definitive Murray outing featuring pianist John Hicks and drummer Idris Muhammad alongside Murray and Drummond, with Branford Marsalis guesting on two tracks.

Ray Drummond

Excursion (1992; Arabesque). Loose, rumbustious session of Drummond compositions featuring contrasting saxophone playing from Craig Handy and Joe Lovano over the percussive rhythm-section of pianist Danilo Perez, and drummers Marvin "Smitty" Smith and Mor Thiam.

Continuum (1994; Arabesque). Blues-based album with unusual group sounds and textures produced by combination of Thomas Chapin's flute and Steve Nelson's vibes. With guitarist John Scofield, pianist Kenny Barron and trumpeter Randy Brecker also on hand, and Marvin "Smitty" Smith and percussionist Mor Thiam driving the rhythm-section, this is a heady brew of post-bop jazz.

John Donaldson

Meeting In Brooklyn (1993; Babel). Intensely tuneful session featuring UK pianist Donaldson and saxophonist Iain Ballamy with US rhythm-section of Drummond and Victor Lewis.

Marc Ducret

Guitar.

b. Paris, France, 19 Aug 1957.

A self-taught guitarist, Ducret began playing in various live and studio settings in 1975. He was a member of France's first National Jazz Orchestra (1986), played with many luminaries, both American and European, and led his own trio. In the early 90s, he achieved higher visibility by joining Louis Sclavis and Dominique Pifarely's group, which recorded *Acoustic Quartet* (1993; ECM), and different ensembles associated with saxophonist Tim Berne, including Caos Totale and Bloodcount (both of whom recorded more than one record for the now-defunct JMT label). Ducret also recorded for JMT, as a leader, *News From The Front* (1991), more recently for Berne's Screwgun label leading a trio, *L'Ombra di Verdi* (1999), and with Francois Jeanneau, Larry Schneider, Klaus König, Bobby Previte, Peter Herborn, and a collective trio with Berne and drummer Tom Rainey called Big Satan – *I Think They Liked It, Honey* (1997; Winter & Winter). He continues to be heard in Tim Berne's various outfits as well as Belgian experimentalists AKA Moon and drummer Daniel Humair's group.

An outstanding technician, Ducret has some of the brilliance and pastel orientation of Ralph Towner on acoustic, but he's also possessed of an evil streak – grimy textures, feedback, power improvising – on electric, nicely illustrated on his solo outing *Un Certain Malaise* (1998; Screwgun). [JC]

Gerd Dudek

Tenor and soprano saxophones; also clarinet, flute, shehnai.

b. Gross Döbern, Germany, 28 Sept 1938.

Dudek had private clarinet lessons at 15 and in 1954 went to music school in Siegen. From 1960–64 he played with the Berlin Jazz Quintet. In the later 1960s he worked with Kurt Edelhagen, touring Russia with him, and also played with the Manfred Schoof quintet, Globe Unity Orchestra, Wolfgang Dauner, Albert Mangelsdorff, Don Cherry and George Russell, as well as leading his own groups. From 1977–81 he was with Alan Skidmore in the European Jazz Consensus and the European Jazz Quintet. In 1985 he toured with the Tony Oxley quintet which included Enrico Rava, Joachim Kuhn and Ali Haurand. Dudek is one of the most accomplished of European saxophonists, a veteran of sessions with such formidable firebrands as Peter Brötzmann, Misha Mengelberg and Tony Oxley. Yet his own material shows marked, perhaps surprising, influences of classic jazz and his tone often nods to early Coltrane. [IC]

⊙ **After All** (1991; Konnex). Dudek, in trio with the fine bassist Ali Haurand and pianist Rob Van Den Broeck, is consistently interesting and inspired, prompting surprise that he hasn't a higher profile.

⊙ **Smatter** (1991; Psi). His first album under his own, sole name is very much in the jazz – rather than Euro free improv – tradition and is utterly beautiful, with unimpeachable takes on tunes by Kenny Wheeler and George Coleman, among others.

Urszula Dudziak

Vocals, percussion, synthesizer, composer.

b. Straconka, Poland, 22 Oct 1943.

Dudziak studied piano at a music school in Zielona Góra and had private singing lessons for two years. She was inspired by Ella Fitzgerald, whom she heard on Willis Conover's Voice of America *Jazz Hour* and, later, Miles Davis was a big influence. She married the violinist and saxophonist Michal Urbaniak and played with his group, travelling throughout Europe from 1965, playing jazz festivals in Warsaw, Molde and various others in France and Italy. She and Urbaniak went to live in the USA in the autumn of 1973.

Dudziak has an exceptional five-octave range and mostly uses her voice "instrumentally". Her wordless singing made an immediate impact in America, and was once described, by Herb Nolan in *Down Beat*, as a "four-octave vocal soundscape with [a] lyricless myriad of scats, squawks, groans, screeches, mellow harmonies, subtle counterpoint and wild improvisations". Much of her music has been in a jazz-rock vein, both on the string of albums she recorded under her own name through the '70s and on various sideperson gigs, and she also uses electronics extensively to extend the possibilities of her voice. A superb musician, she has frequently worked with musicians of the calibre of Archie Shepp and Lester Bowie, and was also a member of the a cappella group Vocal Summit which included Jay Clayton, Bobby McFerrin, Jeanne Lee and Lauren Newton, with whom she recorded *Sorrow Is Not Forever ... But Love Is* in 1983. At the end of the 1980s she toured with Norma Winstone and other singers and it has been said, understandably, that Winstone and Dudziak are the only next-generation singers to approach Betty Carter and Sheila Jordan in terms of originality and innovation. She was a beautifully apposite guest on a track on DJ Vadim's *USSR: The Art of Listening* (Ninja Tune; 2002) as her ingeniously lithe vocals danced colourfully and acrobatically around twenty-first century beatboxing – turning the wheel of jazz fusion full circle. [IC]

➤➤ **Michal Urbaniak** *(Polish Jazz Vol. 9).*

George Duke

Keyboards, synthesizer, composer, vocals.

b. San Rafael, California, 12 Jan 1946.

After studying the piano at school, where he ran a Les McCann-inspired band, Duke obtained his Bachelor of Music in composition from San Francisco Conservatory in 1967. He then worked with his trio in San Francisco accompanying stars such as Dizzy Gillespie, Bobby Hutcherson and Kenny Dorham. From 1967–70 his trio also travelled with a vocal group, the Third Wave, for which he wrote most of the arrangements. In 1969 Duke played with Jean-Luc Ponty, using electric piano to accompany Ponty's amplified violin, and played on *King Kong*, the album Frank Zappa composed for Ponty. After spending eight months with the Don Ellis band, Duke began recording with Frank Zappa and joined his group the Mothers Of Invention from 1970–75, with one year away (1971–2) to tour with Cannonball Adderley. With Zappa he played on the 1975 album *Roxy & Elsewhere* which, in true Zappa style, combined jazz with rock, shock and avant-garde elements. It was Zappa who loosened up Duke as an entertainer, encouraging him not to shy away from singing and joking around. During this period he began working with his own groups, and in 1975 he co-led a group with Billy Cobham, and also began a long association with bassist Stanley Clarke which led to a series of joint albums in the 1980s. But he had already become an international star with his own electronic jazz/rock/funk/soul group, touring and playing festivals in Europe and elsewhere in the late 70s, managing to somehow squeeze in time to work with the Brecker Brothers.

Duke is a highly accomplished player and composer, in whose playing you can hear the gloriously mishmashed influences of Ravel, Stravinsky, Stockhausen, Herbie Hancock, Miles Davis and Zappa, among others. However, his later albums, particularly the collaborations with Clarke, moved more towards easy-listening disco music; it is pop music sometimes flavoured with jazz improvisation with no questions asked and no doubts disturbing the glossy surface. In 1986 Duke did a fine arrangement of "Backyard Ritual" on the Miles Davis album *Tutu* and also assisted with keyboards on one track of Davis's lovely 1989 album *Amandla,* and it may be that Duke's finest jazz playing has been with other leaders. [IC]

➤➤ **Jean-Luc Ponty** *(King Kong).*

Dukes Of Dixieland

A commercially and musically successful group formed in New Orleans in 1948 by teenage brothers Frank and Fred Assunto, the Dukes Of Dixieland won a Horace Heidt talent contest and toured with Heidt before settling in New Orleans (under the management of their father and second trombonist, "Papa Jac" Assunto) to turn professional. Their biggest break came with a signing to the Audio Fidelity label which provided them with huge publicity. The Dukes' Audio Fidelity-inspired logo "You Have To Hear It To Believe It" got short shrift from the jazz press, but their music was never less than enjoyable, and – in its early days – was reminiscent of the Yerba Buena Jazz Band. Besides the considerable talent of trumpeter/singer Frank Assunto, the band later featured proven names such as Jerry Fuller (clarinet), Herb Ellis and Jim Hall (guitars) and Gene Schroeder (piano). Sadly, Fred Assunto died young in 1966; his brother Frank died in 1974; and Papa Jac then retired from the group in order to teach, which he did until his death in 1985. A team of reconstituted Dukes, led by trumpeter Mike Vax and featuring New Orleans clarinettist Otis Bazoon, still played successfully at the Dukes' Place club in the late 1970s. In 1985 they were re-formed as an inter-racial group for Hollywood appearances, including Frank Trapani (trumpet), Frank Hooks (trombone) and Phamons Lambert (piano/vocals). [DF]

⊙ **Radio Broadcasts 1961–2** (Hindsight). This valuable retrospective from the Dukes' golden years, with the Assuntos, Gene Schroeder, Jim Hall, is the only CD in the catalogue, but their classic albums from the 1950s and 60s – particularly *Breakin' It Up On Broadway* – are well worth searching for on vinyl, as are their earlier rumbustious collaborations with Louis Armstrong.

Candy Dulfer

Alto and other saxophones, vocals.
b. Amsterdam, 19 Sept 1969.

After taking up the saxophone at five, Candy Dulfer was playing professionally by her early teens, encouraged by her tenor-saxophonist father Hans. At fifteen, she formed her own band, Funky Stuff, and by her early twenties she had appeared on pop recordings by Prince and Dave Stewart – the latter spawning a hit single, "Lily Was Here" – and had supported Madonna on the latter's Dutch tour. Sessions with Van Morrison and Aretha Franklin followed, but Dulfer's own recording debut as a leader, *Saxuality*, was not released until 1991. A follow-up, *Sax-a-go-go*, like its predecessor produced by Funky Stuff's keyboard player, Ulco Bed, was released in 1993. She has been promoted more as a sex symbol than as a saxophonist; her playing ability seems to have been obscured by careful career moves. [BP & CP]

⊙ **Sax-a-go-go** (1993; BMG). Soft-centred fusion with slightly harder edge than its 1991 predecessor, *Saxuality*, but usual mix of funk beat with little surges of jazz improvisation.

Ted Dunbar

Guitar, composer.
b. Port Arthur, Texas, 17 Jan 1937; d. 29 May 1998.

Dunbar was self-taught as a musician, but played trumpet and guitar in jazz groups at Texas Southern University where he obtained a degree in pharmacy. In 1963 he studied George Russell's "Lydian concept" of music theory with David Baker in Indianapolis and played with Baker, Red Garland, Billy Harper among others. In 1966 he moved to New York, working in theatre orchestras, in music education, and in small groups and big bands with leading players including Jimmy Heath and McCoy Tyner. He was with the Gil Evans orchestra from 1970–73, and with Tony Williams's Lifetime in 1971–2, though his gigging and recording took second place to his academic position for the rest of his life. When not playing in a jazz-rock context and left to his own devices, Dunbar was an even-keeled, almost subfusc performer, but there was subtlety and meat in his musings and idiosyncratic turns of thought that ensured his playing – though indebted to Wes Montgomery and also steeped in the blues – was always distinctive. [IC]

⊙ **Jazz Guitarist** (1982; Xanadu). A beautifully realized solo album, featuring some surprising choices of compositions by pianists popularized as band numbers and rarely heard as solo guitar performances, such as Horace Silver's "Nica's Dream", Monk's "Epistrophy" and Randy Weston's "Hi-Fly".

⊙ **Gentle Time Along** (1991; Steeplechase). With pianist Mickey Tucker, bassist Ray Drummond and drummer David Jones, Dunbar plays a subtle and rhythmically buoyant set.

Hank Duncan

Piano.
b. Bowling Green, Kentucky, 26 Oct 1894; d. 7 June 1968.

One of the creators of stride piano, Duncan ran his own band in Louisville and after going to

New York in the mid-1920s worked for bandleader "Fess" Williams for five years. After that he was with King Oliver, Charles "Fat Man" Turner and the Bechet-Ladnier Feetwarmers at the Savoy, and was second pianist on tour with Fats Waller's big band. For much of the rest of his long life he turned up in small groups (for example, Zutty Singleton's trio in 1939) or as a soloist in New York clubs including Nick's (1947–55 and again 1956–63) and the Metropole (in between). After leaving Nick's he continued to work solo until a long terminal illness. [DF]

➤➤ **Sidney Bechet** *(The Legendary Sidney Bechet).*

Paul Dunmall

Saxophones, clarinets, bagpipes, other wind instruments.

b. Barnehurst, Kent, UK, 6 May 1953.

Known chiefly as a volcanic improviser in all forms of freely improvised music, Paul Dunmall is also a highly skilled and disciplined soloist in more straightahead jazz contexts ranging from the original Spirit Level to bassist Danny Thompson's folk/jazz group Whatever. Although self-taught on the saxophone, he studied clarinet for five years at the Blackheath Conservatoire of Music before joining the group Marsupilami and touring Europe with them. In 1973, he went to America and played with Alice Coltrane and toured with Johnny "Guitar" Watson. On his return to the UK, he played with folk musicians Kevin Dempsey, Martin Jenkins and Polly Bolton before becoming a founder member of the band Spirit Level in 1979. In the 1980s, he collaborated with fellow tenorman Alan Skidmore in the band Tenor Tonic and joined Barry Guy's improvising big band, the London Jazz Composers' Orchestra, in 1987, the same year he first played with Whatever. It is with Keith Tippett, Paul Rogers and Tony Levin in the improvising quartet Mujician, however, that Dunmall's talents are given fullest expression, his burly, sinewy inventiveness the perfect foil for Tippett's cascading freedom. Bassist Rogers is also the saxophonist's partner in a duo folk project which toured the UK to great acclaim in 1994. In 1995, Dunmall formed trios with tuba player Oren Marshall and drummer Steve Noble, and with guitarist John Adams and drummer Mark Sanders, which occasionally operated as a quintet. The following year he toured with the British Saxophone Quartet (Elton Dean, Simon Picard and George Haslam), Mujician (including a visit to South Africa) and with pianist John Law's Extremely Quartet. In 1998, Dunmall worked on projects involving live electronics with Joe Hyde and Alistair McDonald, and with Irish composer Brian Irvine's fourteen-piece band. Leading his own well-regarded Octet since 1997, Dunmall also founded his own CD label Duns Limited Editions in 2000 on which to release his prolific output. [CP/CI]

Mujician

⊙ **The Journey** (1990; Cuneiform). Seamless, nearly hour-long improvisation recorded at the 1990 Bath festival, and playing off Dunmall's high-energy Coltrane-influenced saxophone against wonderfully inventive rhythm-section work from Levin and Rogers and Tippett's free romanticism.

Paul Dunmall

⊙ **Babu** (1994; Slam). Double CD featuring Dunmall's protean talent in various contexts: a quartet with Rogers, Levin and Simon Picard; a sextet and a trio with Rogers and Levin. The best showcase for Dunmall's extraordinary playing.

⊙ **Bebop Starburst** (1999; Cuneiform). Octet recording featuring, as a nucleus, Mujician, with tenor player Simon Picard, trombonists Annie Whitehead and Chris Bridges and trumpeter Gethin Liddington on a powerful mix of bebop-derived themes and fierce improvisation.

⊙ **Solo Bagpipes II** (2001; Duns). Released on his own label, a typically forthright recording featuring Dunmall on a selection of pipes.

➤➤ **Tim Richards** *(Killer Bunnies).*

Johnny Dunn

Trumpet.

b. Memphis, 19 Feb 1897; d. Paris, 20 Aug 1937.

A jazz trumpet pioneer, Dunn worked with W.C. Handy (c.1916–20) and subsequently joined Mamie Smith's Jazz Hounds before working with a second pack of Hounds (under his leadership) for singer Edith Wilson. Work with Perry Bradford and Will Vodery followed, and it was with Vodery that Dunn made his first important visit to Europe. He returned there with the *Blackbirds* of 1926 review and two years later worked in Paris with Noble Sissle, rejoined the cast of *Blackbirds* of 1928 and by the end of the decade had formed his New Yorkers band for regular work in Holland, Denmark and Belgium. Dunn died in the American hospital in Paris, aged just forty. [DF]

Eddie Durham

Guitar, trombone, arranger.

b. San Marcos, Texas, 19 Aug 1908; d. 6 March 1987.

As a teenager Eddie Durham played guitar and then trombone with six siblings in the Durham Brothers band. He toured from the mid-1920s with circus bands and top territory groups including Walter Page's Blue Devils, moving (along with Count Basie) to the Elmer Payne band and then Bennie Moten (1929–33). Briefly with Cab Calloway, Andy Kirk and Willie Bryant, he spent two years with Jimmie Lunceford (1935–7) and a year with Basie (1937–8); in all these bands, he contributed arrangements and trombone section-work plus occasional guitar solos. Then he became a freelance writer for Artie Shaw, Glenn Miller, etc and in the 1940s leader of various bands including the International Sweethearts of Rhythm and later his own all-women group. After further freelancing, he led his own groups from 1957, and joined the Buddy Tate band (1970s) and the Harlem Jazz and Blues Band (1980s), including touring and recording in Europe.

An important but neglected figure in the development of jazz guitar, he devised a non-electric method of amplification, so that his contributions to the 1929 Moten records leap out with a verve worthy of Charlie Christian – and in a bluesy style which must surely have influenced him. But Durham was better known to his colleagues as an arranger, responsible for the classic "Moten Swing" and such Basie numbers as "Sent For You Yesterday" and "Topsy". Although not his own composition, he also scored possibly the most famous swing-era arrangement, the Glenn Miller version of "In the Mood". [BP]

>> **Count Basie** *(Original American Decca Recordings)*; **Bennie Moten** *(Basie Beginnings)*.

Dutch Swing College Band

Europe's longest-playing jazz band was formed on 5 May 1945 under the leadership of Peter Schilperoort (clarinet/saxophones). Early members of the Dutch Swing College band included guitarist Wout Steenhuis, trumpeter Kees van Dorser, clarinettist Dim Kesber and the brilliant Jan Morks, who combined outstanding solo clarinet talent with a career in law (he died in 1984). From 1952, Schilperoort formed a long partnership with guitarist/banjoist Arie Ligthart, and by the late 1950s the DSC was well established as a commercially successful and highly rated unit. By 1959 more key men were in the ranks, including the fiery Armstrong-inspired trumpeter Oscar Klein and fluent trombonist Dick Kaart (who died in 1985), whose brother Ray (a brilliant lyric trumpeter whose life was complicated by a severe road accident and alcohol problems) was to join in 1963, replacing Klein. In the 1960s the eclectic repertoire of the DSC broadened further to include popular and rock repertoire, and in 1968 Ray Kaart was replaced by Bert de Koort, later a successful touring soloist, whose understanding of Bobby Hackett's vocabulary is close to uncanny.

In the 1970s the DSC reached its peak. Schilperoort formed his own record company, DSC Productions, to produce a string of impressive albums, some with Americans including Billy Butterfield, Joe Venuti and Teddy Wilson, others exploring unusual areas such as country and western, and one with full military band. The European touring continued, and Peter Schilperoort was knighted by Queen Juliana of the Netherlands for his contributions to jazz. In the 1980s the DSC wagon continued to roll smoothly along. Featuring British cornettist Rod Mason until 1985, when cornettist Sytze von Duin and trombonist Bert Boeren joined, the band presented a polished, highly arranged repertoire with all the skill of its American inspirers. After the death of Schilperoort on 17 November 1990 the DSC regrouped and continued touring, just as Count Basie's band survived as a performing unit after the death of its leader, thanks to its strong identity. [DF]

⊙ **Forty Years At Its Best 1945–85** (Timeless Traditional); **Best Of The Dutch Swing College Band** (PMF). Two good retrospectives of the DSC's output, the latter spreading over two CDs.

Honoré Dutrey

Trombone.

b. New Orleans, 1894; d. 21 July 1935.

Dutrey's early work in New Orleans brass bands and small groups was followed by a spell in the US Navy in 1917, involving him in a powder-room accident which severely damaged his lungs. From then on Dutrey used an inhaler, but was fit enough to join King Oliver's great band in Chicago in 1920. He played on all the classic records of Oliver's Creole Jazz Band and, after the split with Oliver in 1924, led his own band at Lincoln Gardens, before spending time with other Chicago-based stars, including Johnny Dodds, Louis Armstrong and Carroll Dickerson's big band. He gave up music in 1930 and died before he was forty from the consequences of his disability. [DF]

>> **King Oliver** *(King Oliver Vol. 1 1923–29)*.

George Duvivier

Bass, arranger.

b. New York, 17 Aug 1920; d. 11 July 1985.

Duvivier studied violin and composition as a teenager, also playing bass with the Royal Baron Orchestra (c.1937). Turning professional, he worked with the Coleman Hawkins band (1941) and Lucky Millinder (1941–2). He wrote arrangements for Jimmie Lunceford (and played on one recording) while in the army (1943–5), then became a full-time writer for Lunceford (1945–7). Employed full-time on bass from 1950 with singers Nellie Lutcher, Pearl Bailey, Billy Eckstine and Lena Horne, he also made jazz appearances and recordings with Terry Gibbs (1952), Bud Powell (1953–6, including assisting with arrangements) and with Eric Dolphy and Oliver Nelson (1960). Primarily involved from the 1950s in non-jazz studio work, he also appeared at several jazz festivals in the USA and Europe. Duvivier's excellence was proven by the breadth of his associations over a long career. As well as having the ability to be simultaneously interesting and unflamboyant, he made the creation of a driving pulse appear effortless. [BP]

>> **Eric Dolphy** *(Outward Bound)*; *Bud Powell (The Amazing Bud Powell Vol. 2)*.

Mbizo Johnny Dyani

Bass, vocals, composer.

b. East London, South Africa, 30 Nov 1945; d. Berlin, 25 Oct 1986.

Dyani joined Chris McGregor's Blue Notes in 1962 and left South Africa with them in 1965, going to Europe and playing in France and Switzerland before settling in Britain. He spent five years based in London, working mostly with the avant-garde of the time, playing freely improvised abstract music in small-group settings. Dyani toured South America with Steve Lacy, Enrico Rava and Louis Moholo; the quartet recorded an album in 1968. Dyani also played with the Spontaneous Music Ensemble in 1969 and the Musicians' Co-op in 1971.

He continued with the Blue Notes, but was beginning to feel that they were coming too much under the influence of the American free-players and losing touch with their African roots. So in the early 1970s he moved to Denmark, working with John Tchicai and Don Cherry, and also with Abdullah Ibrahim (aka Dollar Brand), of whom Dyani said, "Only Abdullah Ibrahim and Makhaya Ntoshko are being true to themselves. They are the ones working for Africa. With them there is a real exchange – as with Don [Cherry] – we don't seem to need to talk, we just communicate." He also worked with David Murray and Joseph Jarman and in the trio Detail with John Stevens and the saxophonist Frøde Gjerstad, which became Detail Plus when Bobby Bradford and others guested with them.

Dyani also led various groups of his own. Something of a visionary, his music has a flavour and feeling that is unique. It fuses elements from contemporary jazz with a spaciousness and rhythmic coherence which were rarely evident in the "free" jazz of the 1960s. It is music of the heart, the expression of an exile's angers, sorrows and joys. After his death several albums were dedicated to his memory including *Blue Notes For Johnny* by McGregor, Pukwana and Moholo, and Tchicai's *Put Up The Fight*. [IC]

JAK KILBY

Mbizo Johnny Dyani

⊙ **Witchdoctor's Son** (1978; Steeplechase); **Song For Biko** (1978; Steeplechase). Both of these are from Dyani's most creative period. The first features a sextet which includes John Tchicai and Dudu Pukwana, and *Biko* is a quintet album with Pukwana, Don Cherry and drummer Makhaya Ntoshko.

⊙ **Angolian Cry** (1985; Steeplechase). This features a superb quartet with Harry Beckett's quicksilver trumpet and flugelhorn, Tchicai, and the great American drummer Billy Hart. Vitality pervades this album – whether in lamentation or celebration.

➤➤ **Abdullah Ibrahim** *(Echoes From Africa);* **Steve Lacy** *(The Forest And The Zoo).*

Allen Eager

Tenor and alto saxophones.
b. New York, 27 Jan 1927; d. 13 April 2003.

After experience with name bands such as Tommy Dorsey while still a teenager, Eager played on 52nd Street (1945) and began to make records under his own name (1946), then worked with Buddy Rich (1947, 1952) and Tadd Dameron (1948). Intermittent playing in New York (1953–5, 1957), Paris (mid-1950s), Los Angeles (mid-1960s, appearing on Frank Zappa's first album) and Miami (1970s) was interspersed with activities such as skiing, riding and car racing. He made a brief, nostalgic jazz comeback in the early 1980s, including a European tour in 1982. A disciple of Lester Young, Eager will be remembered for having made a distinctive and memorable contribution to the jazz world in the late 1940s. [BP]

➤➤ **Fats Navarro** *(Featured With The Tadd Dameron Band).*

Jon Eardley

Trumpet.
b. Altoona, Pennsylvania, 30 Sept 1928; d. Cologne, 2 April 1991.

Eardley's father was a trumpet player, and Jon began playing at eleven. After being in an air-force band and in his own local group (1950–53), he worked in New York with Phil Woods (1954). He joined Gerry Mulligan's quartet and sextet, first replacing Bob Brookmeyer and then playing alongside him (1954–5, 1956–7). After working again in his home area he moved to Europe, playing in Belgium (from 1963) and in a Cologne radio band (from 1969). He made several recordings in Europe, including two albums in London (1977), and continued playing into the early 1990s. His early solos with Mulligan showed a bright tone and a melodic feel which survived in the best of his later work. [BP]

Gerry Mulligan

⊙ **California Concerts Vol.1** (1954; Pacific Jazz). The inevitable comparison with Chet Baker shows the more light-hearted Eardley to advantage, in a set whose previously unreleased material includes "Ontet" (Mulligan's shout-chorus from the Miles Davis version of "Godchild") and "Darn That Dream", where Mulligan re-creates his Davis arrangement at the piano.

Charles Earland

Organ, keyboards; also saxophones.
b. Philadelphia, 24 May 1941; d. 11 Dec 1999.

Earland learned the saxophone at the high school where Bobby Timmons had studied and Lew Tabackin was a contemporary. From age seventeen he played tenor with Jimmy McGriff and formed his first group two years later. After working with Pat Martino, he took up the organ and, from 1968–9, played in Lou Donaldson's touring band. Leading his own group from January 1970 (which soon contained Grover Washington), he had considerable success and later added his own contributions on soprano and synthesizer, the latter programmed by Patrick Gleeson who earlier assisted Herbie Hancock in a similar role. His performing and recording career was very consistent, despite emphasizing different dance beats in the late 1970s and 80s and, particularly since the late 80s, he has reverted to a more traditional view of the organ combo with added horns. [BP]

⊙ **Black Talk** (1969; Prestige/OJC). The first big success for Earland featured guitarist Melvin Sparks and Idris Muhammad from Lou Donaldson's group, plus the horns of Houston Person and trumpeter Virgil Jones. The funky title-track theme is distantly derived from "Eleanor Rigby" and there's also a fast modal version of "Aquarius".

Peter Ecklund

Cornet, trumpet, guitar.
b. Woodbridge, Connecticut, 27 Sept 1945.

Ecklund is a highly versatile and accomplished musician, as capable of playing authoritative lead trumpet as furnishing original thought to a small traditional jazz ensemble. Classically trained, he began playing jazz while still working as a high-school teacher in Boston. He turned professional with David Bromberg in the early 1970s, specializing in pop and roots music, including the Bromberg album *Americana*. By 1990 his track record included lead trumpet with Vince Giordano's Nighthawks, as well as work with the New Haven Symphony Orchestra, Leon Redbone, Woody Allen, the Black Eagle Jazz Band and Dick Hyman. His studio work ranged from films (*The Civil War*) to shows, including leading the trumpet section for a 1990 recording of Gershwin's *Girl Crazy*. His most regular exposure in recorded jazz circles during the 1990s has been with groups organized by Marty Grosz and Keith Ingham for specialist projects rich in scholarship but never devoid of humour. Ecklund is also the author of two books *Louis Armstrong: Great Trumpet Solos* and *Bix Beiderbecke: Great Cornet Solos* (published by Charles Colin). [DF]

The Orphan Newsboys: Laughing At Life (1990; Stomp Off). One early definitive date for Grosz's collection of classicists; Ecklund's cornet sounds commanding on "Lonesome Road" and lyrical on Carmichael's "Judy"; he also whistles prettily (and plays) on "Beyond The Blue Horizon".

With Strings Attached (1996; Arbors). A comparatively rare solo date for Ecklund, with colleagues Greg Cohen, Chris Flory, Grosz and others. Eclectic in inspiration but artistically unified, this album demonstrates Ecklund's sense of fun as well as his effortless story-telling cornet.

Billy Eckstine

Vocals, trumpet, valve-trombone, guitar.

b. Pittsburgh, Pennsylvania, 8 July 1914; d. 8 March 1993.

Not to be confused with the 1920s ragtime pianist Willie Eckstein (which is how Billy's family name was originally spelled), Billy Eckstine worked in Washington (early 1930s), Buffalo, Detroit (1937) and then Chicago (1938). He found fame with the Earl Hines band (1939–43), singing ballads but scoring particularly with a smooth and sexy blues "Jelly, Jelly". Leaving Hines, he soon formed his own big band (1944–7) with first Dizzy Gillespie and then Budd Johnson as musical director; a short list of the most important musicians who played with him includes Charlie Parker, Dexter Gordon, Gene Ammons, Sonny Stitt, Fats Navarro, Miles Davis and Art Blakey. The septet he fronted next had Wardell Gray on tenor (1947), and thereafter he toured internationally as a soloist with jazz-based accompanists such as pianist Bobby Tucker (1950s–1960s) and drummer Charli Persip (late 1960s–early 1970s). Very successful with both black and white audiences throughout the 1940s, when he was easily the most imitated of singers, Eckstine's more middle-of-the-road backing on later records made him an enormous superstar. It is to his credit, therefore, that his later performances still made regular reference to his instrumental work. [BP]

Mr. B. And The Bebop Band (1944–5; President). Together with the overlapping two-CD compilation of mid-1940s work, *The Legendary Big Band* (Savoy), this covers the all-star band mentioned above and, as well as superior vocals (two by Sarah Vaughan), includes several exciting instrumentals such as "Love Me Or Leave Me" featuring Ammons and Navarro.

HERMAN LEONARD

Billy Eckstine

Harry "Sweets" Edison

Trumpet.

b. Columbus, Ohio, 10 Oct 1915; d. 27 July 1999.

The half Native American Harry "Sweets" Edison fell under the spell of Louis Armstrong after hearing him on Bessie Smith records and live with Bennie Moten at Valley Dale dance hall, Ohio. Early on he worked in the best territory bands (among them Jeter-Pillars, Earl Hood and Morrison's Grenadiers), then moved to New York where, after six months with Lucky Millinder, he joined Count Basie in June 1938. He remained until 1950, when Basie disbanded to form a small group and Edison found himself without a band or a father figure, but with a wife and family to support. He took work with Norman Granz's Jazz at the Philharmonic and with Josephine Baker (as her MD), and from 1952 began regular studio work and a permanent association with Frank Sinatra, as well as playing for any number of other singers. (With Bobby Hackett, Edison was one of the few master trumpet-accompanists, often – as with Sinatra – playing into his trademark harmon-mute.) In the 1960s he continued his heavy studio commitments as well as regular appearances at festivals (solo and with his own quartet), with JATP, with Count Basie as guest soloist, and on TV's Hollywood Palace show. In the 1970s he also made numerous tours with "Lockjaw" Davis and Benny Carter and taught at Yale for the Duke Ellington Fellowship. In the mid-1990s he was still appearing in concerts and festivals (notably with Lionel Hampton) and playing beautifully if more sparely.

A natural player, rather like Louis Armstrong, Edison was one of the most distinctive voices in jazz, single-handedly developing a vocabulary for the harmon mute, and evolving from a blustery-wild young style to a mature controlled perfection (like Armstrong again) with a rare gift for "stretching out" in extended solos without losing creative steam. [DF]

The Inventive Mr Edison (1953; Pacific Jazz). One of the classic Edison dates from the Lighthouse Club, with "Sweets" stretching out on standards in a set that quickly assumed near-classic status.

Harry "Sweets" Edison (1956–59; Giants of Jazz). A budget collection of great Edison recording; nothing cheap about the company which includes Ben Webster, Oscar Peterson and four tracks from the Johnny Hodges classic *Back to Back*. Essential listening.

Jawbreakers (1962; Prestige/OJC). This set teams "Sweets" with his regular partner "Lockjaw" Davis in an inspired quintet; an excellent version of "A Gal In Calico" is a highlight.

Swing Summit (1990; Candid). A fine live session recorded at Birdland with Buddy Tate and Frank Wess (tenors) alongside the old master, here playing with apparently undiminished strength at 75.

➤➤ **Frank Sinatra** *(Songs For Swingin' Lovers).*

Teddy Edwards

Tenor saxophone, arranger.

b. Jackson, Mississippi, 26 April 1924; d. 20 April 2003.

Edwards worked with many territory bands before moving to Los Angeles (1944). Switching from alto to join Howard McGhee (1945–7), he recorded with him and on a two-tenor session with Dexter Gordon (1947). He played in groups led by Red Callender (1948), Benny Carter, Gerald Wilson and Max Roach-Clifford Brown (1954). His own quartet was active in Los Angeles (1958–61) and he continued to be in demand for recording and live work with a wide variety of artists including Carter, Wilson, Benny Goodman (1964), Milt Jackson (1969–76), Jimmy Smith (1972), Sarah Vaughan (1974) and Tom Waits (1982). He made several solo tours of Europe in the 1980s, and began recording again under his own name in the 1990s.

As well as being a dependable back-up artist, Edwards was a forthright soloist who has been consistently undervalued. His typical Southwestern sound reveals an affinity for the blues and the tone quality that goes with it, but this is only the background to an extremely fluent use of post-bop vocabulary. [BP]

Teddy's Ready (1959; Contemporary/OJC). From the opening "Blues In G", this quartet session with Billy Higgins and the little-known pianist Joe Castro shows Edwards at the height of his form.

Mark Egan

Bass; trumpet.

b. Brockton, Massachusetts, 14 Jan 1951.

Egan started on trumpet at ten and took up the bass at sixteen, playing in local R&B bands. He had private music lessons, then studied with Jerry Coker at the University of Miami, taking a Bachelor's degree in applied music. Bass became his main instrument and for two years he played with Ira Sullivan's group. In 1976 he moved to New York, touring and recording with the Pointer Sisters and David Sanborn. The following year he joined Pat Metheny's group and toured with it extensively for three and a half years. He left the group in 1980 to pursue a solo and freelance career. Since then he has worked with many leading musicians, including Stan Getz, Flora and Airto Moreira, Jim Hall, the Gil Evans orchestra (from 1983–5), Randy Brecker, saxophonist Bill Evans and John McLaughlin. In 1982, with drummer Danny Gottlieb, Egan formed and co-led a group called Elements. With the Gil Evans band he toured Japan in 1983 and 1984. Egan has spent much time studying ethnic music (from Bali, South India, Africa and Brazil) and with Gottlieb has spent long periods in Kauai, Hawaii, "playing music in nature – in valleys, during very extreme weather conditions (wind, rain, etc)". [IC]

Beyond Words (1990–1; Bluemoon). The gloriously singing tones Egan coaxes from his fretless four- and eight-string basses are a dominant colour on this world music album. With jazz associates including Danny Gottlieb and saxophonist Bill Evans, plus percussionists, keyboards and guitars, Egan has created subtly varied textures – often by using synthesizers to create the sound of panpipes, marimba or the sea.

➤➤ **Pat Metheny** *(American Garage);* **Lew Soloff** *(Little Wing).*

Marty Ehrlich

Reeds, flute.

b. St Louis, Missouri, 31 May 1955.

As a sixteen-year-old high school student, Marty Ehrlich made his first recording in 1972 with the Human Arts Ensemble in St Louis. In the mid-70s he majored in African-American music at Boston's New England Conservatory of Music, studying with pianists Jaki Byard and Ran Blake and composers George Russell and Gunther Schuller. In 1978 Ehrlich moved to New York, where he has played with many key musicians, including Muhal Richard Abrams, Anthony Braxton and Julius Hemphill. In the mid-80s, he began releasing records as a leader, and has maintained a productive relationship with the German Enja label, recording his own compositions with his quartet on *Pliant Plaint* (1988), *The Traveller's Tale* (1990) and *Side By Side* (1992). He featured his saxophone (soprano, alto and tenor) and flute in duet with bassist Anthony Cox on *Falling Man* (1991; Muse), while his elegant clarinet playing marks *Light At The Crossroads* (1996; Song Lines), co-led with Ben Goldberg, as well as *Emergency Peace* (1991; New World), *Just Before The Dawn* (1995; New World) and *Live Wood* (1995; Music & Arts), all of which feature his string-intensive Dark Woods Ensemble. Ehrlich's compositions are expansive and architectural, terrifically coloured, and reminiscent at times of Hemphill or John Carter. [JC]

Can You Hear A Motion? (1994; Enja). The Ehrlich quartet, with longterm reed partner Stan Strickland on tenor and flute, Michael Formanek on bass, and Bobby Previte on drums. Each of this group's records is better than the last; this one has two pieces dedicated to Carter, as well as the classic Ehrlich tune "The Welcome", which he recorded on his first record as a leader.

>> **Don Grolnick** *(Nighttown)*; **Andrew Hill** *(Dusk)*.

Either/Orchestra

A Boston-based, horn-dominated ensemble founded in 1985 by saxophonist Russ Gershon, Either/Orchestra revels in the colourful and adventurous eclecticism that might typify an ideal post-Mingus, Sun Ra-influenced large band. Featuring some standout members – clarinetist Andrew D'Angelo, baritone saxophonist Charlie Kohlhase, drummer Matt Turner, trombonist Curtis Hasslebring – emphasis is nevertheless on the group and arrangement. Various members have written for the ensemble and the group has also covered stylistically wide-ranging material from King Crimson, Ellington, John Tchicai, Richie Beirach and Mal Waldron through to Bob Dylan. In 1987, Gershon founded Accurate Records and Either/Orchestra has made eight albums, bearing such decadently romantic titles as *More Beautiful than Death* and *Half-life of Desire*. 1993's *The Brunt* is arguably the best of the batch, while *Across The Omniverse* (1995), a two-disc compilation of unreleased material spanning the group's first decade, provides an excellent overview. [JC]

Joe Eldridge

Alto saxophone; also violin.

b. Pittsburgh, Pennsylvania, 1908; d. 5 March 1952.

Eldridge worked in a variety of territory bands around Pittsburgh and paid a visit to New York in 1927 with Henry Saparo's group, before forming the Eldridge Brothers Rhythm Team with his younger brother Roy in Pittsburgh in 1933. Soon afterwards they joined McKinney's Cotton Pickers, then in 1936 Joe joined Roy's band in Chicago and moved to New York with it (1938–40). From then on he worked with Zutty Singleton in New York, with Roy again and with Hot Lips Page, lived for a while in Canada in the late 1940s, and finally moved back to New York shortly before he died. "I never did know the real cause", said Roy later. "He had got real overweight, drinking wine and stuff – it could have been his heart. I'd go to play something and I'd remember the things he had taught me like running the changes. [He was] *down* you know!" [DF]

>> **Roy Eldridge** *(Heckler's Hop)*.

Roy Eldridge

Trumpet, flugelhorn, vocals, drums, piano.

b. Pittsburgh, Pennsylvania, 30 Jan 1911; d. 26 Feb 1989.

In jazz lore, Roy Eldridge forms the link between Louis Armstrong and Dizzy Gillespie, but in fact the young Roy Eldridge, who "began tearing up Chicago in the 1920s" (said Doc Cheatham), preferred Red Nichols, Rex Stewart, Coleman Hawkins and Benny Carter to Armstrong. He started on trumpet and drums in carnival, circus and dance bands, one of which – the Nighthawk Syncopators – played a lightning trumpet transcription of Coleman Hawkins's "Stampede". From the first, Eldridge was impressed by speed and range: he liked Jabbo Smith and later remembered being worn out by the older man in a cutting contest. "Little Jazz", as he was soon to be dubbed by bandleader Elmer Snowden, worked his way up through the territory bands of Zack Whyte, Lawrence "Speed" Webb and the rest, and by 1931 had arrived in New York to work with Snowden, McKinney's Cotton Pickers and Teddy Hill. In Hill's band he became close friends with Chu Berry, and the two would go out on the town to cut down opposition; it was a vocation that Eldridge would continue to pursue all his playing life.

With Berry he joined Fletcher Henderson's band in 1935 and one year later opened with his own band at the Three Deuces in Chicago, with broadcasts seven nights a week. By this time his formidable stamina, range and waspish attack were the talk of New York, and in 1939 he reopened at the Arcadia Ballroom with an augmented band, broadcasting most days and dominating jam sessions in spare moments. By 1941, back in Chicago, he had joined Gene Krupa's orchestra for a successful but traumatic spell: Krupa hired him after an ignominious trouncing in battle with Jimmie Lunceford's band, and from then on used Eldridge as a cornerman, featuring his stratospheric trumpet and show drumming, and teaming him in a centre-stage double act with young hip singer Anita O'Day. This on occasion produced temperament problems, but it was more than these that drove Eldridge from the band. The appalling conditions to which black musicians were subjected on tour caused the volatile trumpeter to suffer a nervous breakdown and after one more brief stint with Artie Shaw's band in 1944 he promised: "As long as I'm in America I'll never in my life work with a white band again."

The period was an unhappy one overall. Soon afterwards his own big band folded ("they couldn't hold their whiskey", he said later); worse still, he was starting (like Dave Tough) to question his musical validity in the fast-moving bebop revolution. One night at Minton's Dizzy Gillespie cut him in public; soon after, on a 1949 Jazz at the Philharmonic tour, bebop trumpeter Howard McGhee began taunting Eldridge and didn't let up. For a sensitive and vulnerable competitor like "Little Jazz" it was a crisis point. "I felt I was out of step. I was torn whether I should do that sort of thing, or go for myself. It stopped being fun anymore." So, as Bill Coleman was to do, he took a long sabbatical in France. It worked, and from 1951 Eldridge was regularly with JATP again, his phenomenal range and endurance

HERMAN LEONARD

Roy Eldridge with Benny Carter and Coleman Hawkins

making him the greatest ever trumpeter of Norman Granz's show. He worked regularly with old colleague Coleman Hawkins and in 1956 at Café Bohemia was keenly disappointed that Miles Davis wasn't appearing opposite him. "If it were possible", recalled Nat Hentoff, "he'd have tried for a cutting contest with Buddy Bolden!"

From 1960–65 he had his own quintet, backed Ella Fitzgerald, joined Count Basie briefly, and from 1966 led a quintet again with Richie Kamuca. After this period it was occasionally possible to hear that for "Little Jazz" the trumpet sometimes felt heavier, but in 1970 came the start of a long residency at Jimmy Ryan's, and he was still taking on all comers until a stroke in 1980 curtailed his playing. A definitive biography by John Chilton, *Roy Eldridge: Little Jazz Giant*, was published by Continuum in 2002. [DF]

ROY ELDRIDGE

⦿ **Little Jazz** (1935–40; CBS). A fascinating collection of Eldridge's formative work, including sides with Fletcher Henderson, Teddy Wilson, Mildred Bailey and solo *tours de force* including "Heckler's Hop" and "Wabash Stomp".

⦿ **Heckler's Hop** (1936–9; Hep). Classic early Eldridge set, containing sides with Gene Krupa, Chu Berry and his "Little Jazz" Ensemble, plus Eldridge solo titles.

⦿ **After You've Gone: The Original American Decca Recordings** (1936–46; MCA/GRP). Fine selection, mostly from the 40s, including Little Jazz standards like "The Gasser", "Fish Market", "Yard Dog" and "Hi Ho Trailus Boot Whip" as well as his version of "After You've Gone".

⦿ **Little Jazz: The Best Of The Verve Years** (1951–60; Verve). An excellent selection; Eldridge at his peak years in the company, variously, of Benny Carter, Sonny Stitt and Oscar Peterson, George Williams's orchestra and others. Recommended.

⦿ **Swingin' On The Town!** (1960; Verve). Recorded as a high-powered echo of the successful Jonah Jones "muted jazz" formula popular during the period, this has a fluent Eldridge with a neat quartet headed by pianist Ronnie Ball.

ROY ELDRIDGE AND COLEMAN HAWKINS

⦿ **With Coleman Hawkins Live In 1959** (Stash). Hawkins was in many respects Eldridge's most compatible partner-in-swing; here they are captured in maturity, with Don Wilson, Bob Decker and Buddy Dean.

➤➤ **Dizzy Gillespie** *(Roy And Diz);* **Gene Krupa** *(Uptown; Drummer Man).*

Eliane Elias

Piano; also vocals.

b. São Paulo, Brazil, 19 March 1960.

Work with the big band of guitarist Sebastião Tapajos and bassist Eddie Gomez brought Eliane Elias to prominence; she moved to New York in 1981, joined Steps Ahead, and married trumpeter Randy Brecker in 1983, the same year she appeared on Polish violinist Michal Urbaniak's *Sorrow Is Not Forever But Love Is*. She made her debut recording as a leader, *Illusions*, for Denon in 1986, and followed it with another Denon album featuring Gomez,

Crosscurrents. Since signing for Blue Note in 1989, she has carved a niche for herself in an attractive Brazilian/jazz fusion corner of the music, most overtly on her debut for the label, *Plays Jobim*, but more subtly and effectively since with a string of light but infectiously likeable albums with stellar company. In 1995, still with Blue Note, Elias recorded an album of solo piano, plus six duets with Herbie Hancock (*Solos And Duets*), and in 1997 she revisited Jobim in both vocal and instrumental capacities (*Sings Jobim*). Partly pursuing – despite the complaints of some jazz critics – the idea of the glamorous, modest-voiced Brazilian singer/pianist through *Everything I Love* (2000; Blue Note) and *Kissed By Nature* (2002; BMG), perhaps her finest recorded work can be found on *The Three Americas* (see below), material from which she interpreted on tour with drummer Satoshi Takeishi and bassist Marc Johnson, with whom she has forged a musical relationship as rewarding as her earlier one with Eddie Gomez. [CP/CI]

Plays Jobim (1990; Blue Note). Airy, intelligent versions of Jobim tunes, including "Desafinado" and "One Note Samba", featuring Gomez, Jack DeJohnette and Nana Vasconcelos (percussion).

Paulistina (1992; Blue Note). Chiefly interesting for unusual version of "Black Orpheus" and for Elias's sparing use of her vocal talents and of synthesizer to vary the music's texture.

The Three Americas (1997; Blue Note). "To capture the musical essence of each America [North, Central and South] and combine their various rhythms and sounds to beat as one heart" is Elias's intention here, and she succeeds perfectly, with the help of flautist Dave Valentin, guitarist Oscar Castro-Neves and others, including the rhythm-section mentioned above.

Fred Elizalde

Piano, composer, leader.

b. Manila, Philippines, 12 Dec 1907; d. 16 Jan 1979.

Elizalde formed his all-British Quinquaginta Ramblers, an undergraduate jazz band, for a Cambridge ball in 1927. The novelty of a fully fledged British jazz band (featuring, incidentally, star cricketer Maurice Allom on saxophone) created a sensation, and Elizalde became a headliner: before the year's end he had written pieces for *Melody Maker*, composed a suite called *The Heart Of A Nigger* for Ambrose's orchestra (which had a good press, was recorded but then withdrawn after one public performance) and made records with an Ambrose contingent (including Nichols-style trumpeter and future DJ Jack Jackson). Then Elizalde took a band into the Savoy with a nucleus of US musicians, including Chelsea Quealey, Bobby Davis and – direct from a failed bandleading stint back home – Adrian Rollini. Elizalde's impressive band, led by the youthful pianist in the reflection from a glass-fronted piano, influenced young British musicians such as Harry Gold, who sneaked backstage to listen to Rollini and to learn. But it was too hot for the Savoy's dignified music policy, and in 1929 Elizalde was politely asked to leave. After a final concert at Shepherd's Bush Empire he moved to Spain, studied under Manuel de Falla and, as Federico Elizalde, became a classical composer and conductor. [DF]

Jazz At The Savoy: The 20s (1927–8; Decca). Classic Elizalde, greatly in need of CD reissue, with his solo piano on four tracks and contributions from US visitors Chelsea Quealey, Bobby Davis and Adrian Rollini.

Kurt Elling

Vocals.

b. Chicago, 2 Nov 1967.

Elling began listening to jazz rather late, as a college student, but his rise to the top ranks of male vocalists – a short list in the 1990s – was mercurial. After Blue Note signed him, based on a demo cassette, Elling recorded a couple of extremely successful records, *Close Your Eyes* (1995), his acclaimed debut, and *Messenger* (1997). Inspired in no small part by Mark Murphy, the Chicagoan has consciously drawn connections with beat-culture heroes like Allen Ginsberg and Jack Kerouac, and he's elaborated on Eddie Jefferson's vocalese tradition of putting original lyrics to beloved horn solos, as he does on Dexter Gordon's 1965 solo on "Tanya Jean". Subsequent albums on Blue Note – *This Time It's Love* (1998), *Live In Chicago* (2000), *Flirting With Twilight* (2002) and *Man In The Air* (see below) – have not only maintained scrupulous standards, they have established Elling as nothing less than the consummate vocal jazz artist of his generation, with the heart and chops to pull off anything that occurs to him. His ongoing collaboration with amazingly resourceful pianist/arranger Lawrence Hobgood is showing all the signs of being one of the music's great partnerships. [JC]

Man In The Air (2003; Blue Note). Elling lyricises Zawinul ("Time To Say Goodbye"), Hancock ("A Secret I") and Metheny ("Minuano"), among others, to superb effect. Joined by Stefon Harris and the reliably inspired Lawrence Hobgood Trio on perhaps the highpoint of a recording career that has been, in any case, mostly highpoints.

Duke Ellington

Composer, arranger, piano.

b. Washington, DC, 29 April 1899; d. 24 May 1974.

After studying piano as a child, Ellington became interested in local ragtimers such as Lester Dishman, for whom he deputized at fifteen. Working as a freelance sign-painter from 1917, he began assembling groups to play for dances, and in 1919 met drummer Sonny Greer from New Jersey who encouraged Duke's ambition to become a professional musician. They played together (with early home-town associates Otto Hardwicke and Arthur Whetsol) in Wisconsin and Atlantic City before settling in New York in 1923, working first as a sextet under Elmer Snowden (also from Washington), then as the embryonic Duke Ellington and his Washingtonians (1924). Successful nightclub residencies culminated in a long stay at the Cotton Club with an enlarged, ten-piece band (from the end of 1927), with regular broadcasts establishing his reputation nationally. There were lengthy absences from New York in order to tour the West Coast and make his first film appearance (in 1930, when he was replaced at the Cotton Club by Cab Calloway) and for tours of Europe and Southern USA (both in 1933, when the replacement was Jimmie Lunceford). During the second half of the 1930s, band numbers had increased to fifteen with two basses, and US tours playing at theatres, hotels and dances (virtually constant from 1934) were only broken by further work at the Cotton Club (1937, 1938 – the latter season there was the first to which Duke contributed songs as well as backing music for dancers) and by a second tour of Europe in 1939. Ellington played for and wrote the score of the revue *Jump For Joy* (1941) and a musical comedy, *Beggars' Holiday* (1947).

A series of annual concerts at Carnegie Hall (from early 1943 to late 1948) and one at Metropolitan Opera House (1951) was another breakthrough, and each occasion saw the premiere of an extended composition. The temporary inactivity of the big band (1948) enabled Ellington to tour the UK with Ray Nance, singer Kay Davis and a local trio; the reconvened band was his largest ever (eighteen pieces, dropping to sixteen by the next European tour in 1950, and usually fifteen thereafter) but marked by the departure of Sonny Greer (1951) and the simultaneous temporary withdrawal of longterm members Johnny Hodges and Lawrence Brown, all of them playing in Hodges's own group. The declining popularity of Duke's band in the USA was arrested by a newsworthy Newport festival appearance (1956). He became the first black composer commissioned to write major film soundtracks (notably *Anatomy Of A Murder*, 1959) and TV series theme music. (Benny Carter had preceded him but as an uncredited "ghostwriter".) Further foreign tours multiplied: Europe (1958, 1962–71 annually and 1973); Middle East and India (1963); Japan (1964, 1970); West Africa (1966); South America (1968); Australia (1970); Soviet Union (1971). Ellington continued to produce quantities of new pieces and suites, including "sacred concerts" in various cathedrals, and to appear in public until a couple of months before his death from cancer. In 1999 the annual Pulitzer Prize for music – which he was recommended for but which was denied him back in 1965 – was awarded to him posthumously.

First recorded soon after the start of his bandleading career, Duke seems to have been initially inspired by the successful white dance bands of the 1920s and their rather maudlin (and middle-class) view of what jazz was all about. However, the arrival of Sidney Bechet (briefly in 1925), Joe Nanton (1926–46) and especially the continued presence of Bubber Miley from the Elmer Snowden days (1924–9) introduced him, virtually for the first time in his life, to the passion and poetry of black jazz. Early masterpieces such as "Black And Tan Fantasy" (co-written with Miley) are compounds of both approaches, and ever afterwards Ellington performed not one but several stylistic balancing acts. Additional soloists in the next few years – Harry Carney (1927–74), Barney Bigard (1927–42), Johnny Hodges (1928–51, 1955–70), Cootie Williams (1929–40, 1962–74), Lawrence Brown (1932–51, 1960–70) and Rex Stewart (1934–45) – were all sophisticated technically but, all being influenced by Louis Armstrong, were also in touch with the earthy roots of his music. Ellington responded with (or, rather, used their talents to help him come up with) such widely differing successes as "Mood Indigo", "It Don't Mean A Thing", "Sophisticated Lady" and countless instrumental-only conceptions.

A significant new wave of contributors who signed up within a few months of one another included Ben Webster (1940–43, 1948–9), Jimmy Blanton (1939–41) and Duke's writing collaborator Billy Strayhorn (1939–67). They brought him up to date with the jazz of the late 1930s and, particularly in the case of Blanton and Strayhorn, foreshadowed many of the rhythmic and harmonic developments of the 1940s. Ellington's compositional penchant for cannibalizing what they had to offer and in turn stretching their abilities – in virtuoso vehicles such as "Cotton Tail", "In A Mellotone" and "Perdido" (a tune by Juan Tizol arranged by Duke) – surfaced again a decade later with the induction of established "modernists" such as Clark Terry (1951–9) and Paul Gonsalves (1950–74). Fewer Ellington "standards" may have emerged thereafter (and those that did were less innovative, eg "Satin Doll"), but items from *Such Sweet Thunder* and *Suite Thursday* were dramatic demonstrations of his facility for keeping up with the times and yet sounding always like himself. As late as 1966–7, the *Far East Suite* and "La Plus Belle Africaine" showed him convincingly coming to terms with modal jazz, and also with the increasing popularity of the Latin-jazz crossover which he and Tizol had started off with "Caravan" back in 1936.

Combining all these innovations within the ongoing history of one band is only half the story, despite the fact that no other figure managed to be creatively involved in so many different stages of jazz development. If it was merely a matter of anthologizing typical phrases of various jazz styles, then numerous other arrangers have achieved this – indeed, that is what arrangers are for. But Ellington set his sights much higher, absorbing the utterances of his hired soloists into his own compositional expression so that the two frequently became indistinguishable. And this was possible because his sensitivity to notes (therefore, to harmony and rhythm) was matched by his sensitivity to textures. In this way, saying that Duke "always sounded like himself" is tantamount to saying that he sounded like

HERMAN LEONARD

Duke Ellington

Harry Carney and Johnny Hodges and Cootie Williams. But it is at least arguable that they would have sounded less like themselves, had it not been for Duke continually showing them in the best light and thus encouraging them to play at their best.

This is an area in which very few writers have ever tried to emulate Ellington; other aspects of his work have proved more influential, if not always beneficially so. The concept of a specially written series (or suite) of shortish pieces, interlinked either musically or merely by circumstance, has inspired many of those looking for a way of lending spurious dignity to their normal output. Similarly, the idea of featuring just one soloist per piece, which Duke inaugurated with four "concertos" in 1936 (and came to rely on increasingly thereafter), found immediate favour with several other big bands in the swing era. Less far-reaching was the effect of his longer compositions, starting as far back as the two quite different versions of "Creole Rhapsody" in 1931; Ellington's own successful follow-ups included "Reminiscing In Tempo" (1935), "Diminuendo And Crescendo In Blue" (1937), "Black, Brown And Beige" (1943) and "Tone Parallel To Harlem" (1951). The retention of a jazz feel despite a minimum of improvisation in these larger structures seems to have eluded other writers.

The crucial factor in Ellington's evolution was his enormous receptivity to everything he ever heard (and saw and felt, hence his choice of evocative titles); as a result, while there was a consistent, and no doubt fairly egotistical, emotional core, his sources of inspiration were constantly expanding. Just as an improviser has to learn to think while on his feet, so Duke learned how to write his kind of jazz while doing it. Indeed, perhaps the writing process is more easily understood by comparing it with his own solo work on piano, and by contrasting the brief and rather bland pseudo-ragtime contributions on his earliest recordings with the dynamic and totally original playing on two albums thrown together in a few hours with Charles Mingus-Max Roach and with John Coltrane-Elvin Jones. It may well be that the small school of pianists who have learned from Duke's use of the instrument – Thelonious Monk, Randy Weston, Abdullah Ibrahim, Stan Tracey, Cecil Taylor and a few others – have perpetuated the spirit of Ellington more meaningfully than those who try to copy his composition and orchestration.

One of the problems in considering Ellington's achievement is that it exists on an astonishing variety of levels. Not only do the writing and playing offer a convenient contrast – for each extended work there are several straightahead ballads, simple in conception but immensely sophisticated in their execution. And the number of different uses Duke found for the twelve-bar blues is bewildering to behold. Then there is his success as a songwriter (which subsidized the continued existence of the Ellington band in its last 25 years or so): some of the few titles mentioned above had lyrics added and became twice as popular, as did numerous other standards; the quality and quantity of his song output places Duke in the Gershwin and Porter category. However, his uniqueness lies not only in the breadth and universality of the music which reached the greatest number of listeners, but in those irreplaceable and inimitable icons such as "Harlem Air Shaft", "Concerto For Cootie" and "Ko-Ko", all recorded within a few months in 1940, which have been an inspiration to several generations of jazz musicians. [BP]

DUKE ELLINGTON

⊙ **Early Ellington** (1926–31; MCA). A three-CD completist approach to Duke's early Brunswick and Vocalion records shows the band with Miley, Greer and Nanton being joined along the way by Carney, Bigard, Hodges, Williams and Brown, and producing such gems as "Black And Tan Fantasy", "The Mooche", "Mood Indigo", "Rockin' In Rhythm" and "Creole Rhapsody".

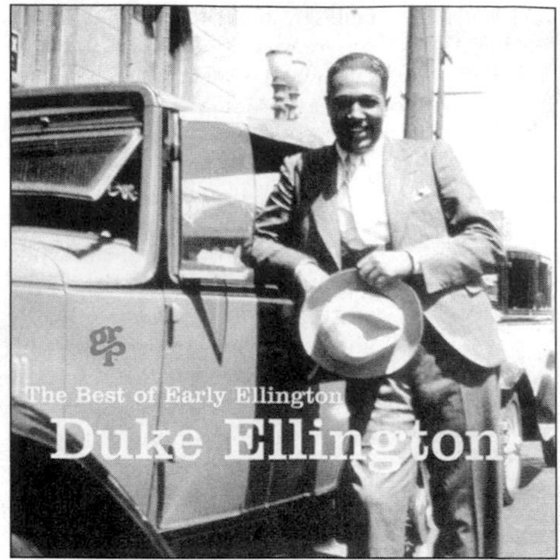

⊙ **Early Ellington** (1927–34; Bluebird). This is probably the best single-CD approach to its era, containing alternative versions of all the above but with the inclusion of "Creole Love Call", "Daybreak Express", "Solitude" and the more interesting version of "Creole Rhapsody".

⊙ **Playing The Blues** (1927–39; Black & Blue). As a quick glance at the pre-1940 period, there is much to be said for this cross-section of music linked by Ellington's varied approaches to the blues form, including "Black And Tan Fantasy" and the stunning 1937 "Diminuendo And Crescendo In Blue".

⊙ **Duke Ellington 1935–36** (Classics). This volume of the huge chronology put together by Classics has two significant aspects, one being "Reminiscing In Tempo" (Duke's longest piece so far and, in the eyes of many, least successful). There is no such controversy about the first of his solo concertos, "Echoes Of Harlem" for Williams and the under-appreciated "Clarinet Lament" for Bigard.

⊙ **The Duke's Men: Small Groups Vols. 1 & 2** (1936–8; Columbia). Practical necessity frequently stimulated Duke's creative juices, as here when his record producer required jukebox singles built around Ellington soloists Williams, Stewart, Bigard and Hodges. These septets include the original "Caravan". Vol. 2 has comparatively more Hodges, including "Jeep's Blues".

⊙ **The Indispensable, Vols. 5/6** (1940; RCA). This is the album which has the output of the peak line-up with Webster, containing "Harlem Air Shaft", "Concerto For Cootie" and "Ko-Ko", plus nineteen others almost as famous and eight duets of Duke's piano and Blanton's bass.

⊙ **The Indispensable, Vols. 7/8** (1941; RCA). This album, almost as good as Vols. 5/6, contains the best of Mercer Ellington's compositions.

⊙ **Sophisticated Lady** (1941–6; Bluebird). The other side of the coin is shown in this collection of hits, some in their original versions such as "Take The A Train" and "Just Squeeze Me" (both with Nance), and others like the title track in Billy Strayhorn-arranged remakes from 1945. Many later albums revisit the song hits and (unless in concert medleys) nearly always cast new light on them.

⊙ **Carnegie Hall Concert January 1943** (Prestige). Most of the 1940 band were still present for Duke's Carnegie Hall debut, which included current repertoire and introduced his 48-minute "symphonic" masterpiece "Black, Brown And Beige".

⊙ **At Newport** (1956; Columbia). This became Ellington's best-selling album because of the (studio-sweetened?) crowd noise but the music is compelling, contrasting remakes of "Jeep's Blues" (featuring Hodges) and "Diminuendo And Crescendo" (Gonsalves) with new material; reissued in 1999 on 2-CDs with the revived original gig.

⊙ **Such Sweet Thunder** (1956–7; Columbia). One of the most durable of Duke's album-sized suites of disparate numbers, at least one of which existed before the commission for a Shakespeare tribute. Key contributors are Clark Terry, Gonsalves and the perennial Hodges.

Duke Ellington-Johnny Hodges

⊙ **Back To Back** (1959; Verve). Renewed attention was focused on Duke's piano work in this casual sextet session, with Harry Edison and Jo Jones, which completely avoided Ellington material in favour of jazz standards such as "St Louis Blues" and "Basin Street Blues".

Ellington, Mingus and Roach

⊙ **Money Jungle** (1962; Blue Note). The pianist goes out on a limb with two respectful but demanding accompanists, and material mostly improvised with minimal preparation ("Fleurette Africaine"). A couple of Ellington hits, especially "Caravan", are forcefully updated.

Ellington and Coltrane

⊙ **Duke Ellington And John Coltrane** (1962; Impulse). Midway in intent between the last two items above, Duke puts Trane in the spotlight on simple new material and earlier hits such as "In A Sentimental Mood", while his knowledge of piano textures rivals his sensitivity to horn players.

Duke Ellington

⊙ **The Far East Suite (Special Mix)** (1966; RCA Victor). The band meanwhile was anything but a spent force, and this music (compiled during the preceding three years) is a late masterpiece, updating Ellington's use of modal materials and Afro-Latin rhythms.

Mercer Ellington

Trumpet, composer, arranger.

b. Washington, DC, 11 March 1919; d. Copenhagen, 8 Feb 1996.

Mercer Ellington studied informally with his father Duke, and "Pigeons And Peppers", written at the age of eighteen, became his first piece to be recorded by Duke (with a Cootie Williams group, 1937). He spent several periods leading his own bands (1939, 1946–9, 1959), often hiring musicians later employed by Duke such as Clark Terry, Harold Ashby, Wendell Marshall, Joe Benjamin and singer Al Hibbler, plus non-Ducal notables Dizzy Gillespie, Kenny Dorham, Idrees Sulieman, Chico Hamilton, Charles Mingus and Carmen McRae. He also worked as road manager for the Cootie Williams band (1941–3, 1954), as musical director for singer Della Reese (1960–62) and as a DJ with a daily show in New York (1962–5). Periods of working for his father included, in 1940–41, contributing original compositions; in 1950, playing E-flat horn; in 1955–9, acting as general assistant and copyist; and from 1965–74, as trumpeter and road manager.

On Duke's death, Mercer took over his band on a regular basis, making European tours (1975, 1977). He also published a memoir of his father and in the early 1980s he was the original conductor of the house band for a Broadway musical of Duke tunes, *Sophisticated Ladies*. From the late 1980s he was based in Denmark, undertaking only occasional engagements, but it is important to remember the masterly pieces written by him in his early twenties, such as "Things Ain't What They Used To Be", "Jumpin' Punkins", "Moon Mist" and especially "Blue Serge". His daughter Mercedes is a choreographer, while son Edward played in his band in the late 1970s. His youngest son, Paul (b. 1978), now directs the latest descendant of the Ellington orchestra. [BP]

Music Is My Mistress (c.1981–9; Musicmasters). Several editions of Duke's posthumous band are heard, mainly with Roland Hanna on piano, playing some vintage scores retranscribed and new music by Mercer such as the 25-minute title suite.

➤➤ **Duke Ellington** *(The Indispensable, Vols. 7/8).*

Ray Ellington

Drums, vocals.

b. London, 17 March 1916; d. 27 Feb 1985.

Born to a Russian-Jewish mother and a black American comedian from St. Louis, he was christened Henry Pitts Brown but changed his name after seeing the Duke Ellington band in London in 1933. From 1937 to 1947 (with a break for war service) Ray Ellington worked with top bands such as that of Harry Roy and Tito Burns's sextet. In the late 1940s Ellington added his drums and rhythmic vocals to the Caribbean Trio (Coleridge Goode on bass, pianist Dick Katz and guitarist Lauderic Caton). Formed in 1950, the resulting Ray Ellington Quartet became the most popular black British group of the era, aided by its weekly radio appearances on the *Goon Show*, in which Ray also had occasional acting parts. Ellington pioneered local acceptance of rhythm-and-blues with bop overtones, and was equally happy covering Louis Jordan, Duke Ellington or the latest hit-parade rock and-roll tunes. [BP]

The Three Bears (1948–49; Avid). The early quartet repertoire featuring their hip adaptations of "Old King Cole" and "Little Bo(p) Peep" plus several instrumentals, including four tracks with a visiting American trumpeter Ray Nance.

Chris Ellis

Vocals.

b. Shrewsbury, UK, 25 Dec 1928.

Ellis's rather too infrequent singing appearances in Britain have included spells with Alan Elsdon, the Anglo-American Alliance (leader Dick Sudhalter) and the New Paul Whiteman Orchestra (ditto), as well as periods in pubs and clubs with like-minded musicians such as Keith Nichols and Alan Leat, the Midnite Follies Orchestra and Tiny Winters's Kettners Five and Orchestra. A man with encyclopedic knowledge of everything from songs to the backwaters of jazz discography, Ellis worked on and off as a record producer for EMI during the 1960s and 1970s, fighting hard for worthwhile talent to be recorded: musicians to benefit from his unobtrusive but dedicated championship included Keith Ingham, Susannah McCorkle and Keith Nichols. Ellis's compilations of classic recordings (including most of Louis Armstrong's 1920s output, and most of Bix Beiderbecke's) set new standards, as did his later – highly skilful – records for visiting Americans such as Ginger Rogers, Elaine Stritch and Sammy Cahn. In the early 1990s he moved to Amsterdam, where he has continued to sing and to produce fine jazz recordings, notably for Timeless and for his own labels, Challenge and A Records. [DF]

Vocal With Hot Accompaniment (1988; Dormouse). This long-overdue solo album is an elegant song recital with Martin Litton (piano), Paul Sealey (acoustic guitar), Tiny Winters (bass) and Digby Fairweather (cornet).

Dick Sudhalter

The Tuesday Band (1997; Jazzology). CD reissue of Ellis's "Sweet And Hot" session for Sudhalter and the Anglo-American Alliance in 1968, originally on EMI and featuring his light-voiced, tasteful singing in ideal surroundings. Six bonus tracks included.

➤➤ **Dick Sudhalter** *(After Awhile).*

Don Ellis

Trumpet, drums, composer.

b. Los Angeles, 25 July 1934; d. 17 Dec 1978.

Ellis played trumpet in high school dance bands and in 1956 graduated with a Bachelor of Music in composition from Boston University. From 1956–60 he played in various big bands, including Maynard Ferguson's, and then, in New York, he worked with George Russell from 1961–2, establishing himself as an interesting new voice on trumpet and playing on one of the seminal albums of the 1960s, *Ezz-thetics*, with Russell's sextet. His early influences were Gillespie, Navarro and Clark Terry, and Ellis displayed a brilliant conventional technique as well as an interest in tonal and structural experimentation. He began leading his own small groups in the early 1960s, and in 1964 went back to Los Angeles, beginning postgraduate studies at UCLA and studying Indian music with Hari Har Rao, forming the Hindustani Jazz Sextet, one of the first groups to fuse elements from Indian music and jazz.

From 1965 he began leading a series of big bands which introduced a series of new devices and new approaches into big-band music. With rock rhythms, multiple percussion, electronic instruments like the Fender-Rhodes piano, clavinet, ring modulator, phaser and other devices, and the use of odd, asymmetrical time-signatures, he anticipated most of the elements of the jazz-rock movement of the 1970s. He used an amplified string quartet on occasion, and deployed a vocal quartet as an instrumental section; he introduced sitar and elements from Indian music to big-band music; from time to time, he would have the entire trumpet section playing quarter-tones on the four-valve trumpets he played from 1966 onwards; and he took asymmetry to extraordinary lengths. On one of his best albums, *Electric Bath*, not one piece is in common time, yet the music seems effortless and natural, and its range is broad – from a very funky eastern-sounding blues in 7/4 ("Turkish Bath") and a fast funky piece in 5/4 ("Indian Lady"), to spacey, out-of-time sections and the more floating asymmetry of "New Horizons" and "Open Beauty".

Ellis was immensely articulate: he wrote about music in magazines such as *Down Beat* and spoke on campuses, and from the early 1960s appeared many times on TV, with and without his bands. Remaining active in education, he taught theory, composition, arranging and trumpet in New York and Los Angeles. His piece *Contrasts For Two Orchestras And Trumpet* was played by the Los Angeles Philharmonic (conducted by Zubin Mehta) and he scored the soundtracks for several films including *The French Connection* (1972).

In February 1978 he appeared with a small group at the first Jazz Yatra in Bombay, once more using his four-valve trumpet. He played with all his old brilliance and fire, giving a sparkling performance. He died later that year, having never entirely recovered from a serious heart attack in 1975.

Without doubt Ellis was a virtuoso trumpet player, but in some ways his sound lacked warmth, and his big-band music, for all its tremendous brilliance and spirit, seems more the product of mind and will than of the mysteriously sensuous feeling which imbues the work of Duke Ellington, or Miles and Gil. But he was a man of great energy and intelligence, and an inspiring bandleader who reinvigorated jazz, broadening its rythmic and sonic possibilities. [IC]

⊙ **... How Time Passes ...** (1960; Candid). Ellis was immersed in the jazz avant-garde at the beginning of the 1960s and brought to it his knowledge of the classical world. Half the album is a suite for which the soloists have to improvise on a Schoenbergian twelve-tone row. The title track uses accelerations and decelerations of tempo that were almost unheard of in jazz. Ellis has lots of new things to say on trumpet and Jaki Byard's piano is a dynamic support and foil: Byard's composition, "Waste", is one of the high spots.

⊙ **Out Of Nowhere** (1961; Candid). Paul Bley and Steve Swallow were in Ellis's working band at this time, and their rapport with the leader is excellent on this more conventional album, featuring a few standards. Ellis is on brilliant form and Bley, as usual, plays masterfully.

⊙ **New Ideas** (1961; OJC). The Byard, Carter, Perkins rhythm-section, augmented by vibraphonist Al Francis, make up Ellis's quintet for this session, which runs the gamut from the blues to atonality, and offers compositions and solos of considerable originality.

⊙ **Electric Bath** (1968; Columbia). This is one of the most exciting and creatively successful big-band albums of the jazz-rock period, and it sounds just as fresh over 30 years after the recording.

➤➤ **George Russell** *(Ezz-thetics).*

Herb Ellis

Guitar.

b. McKinley, Texas, 4 August 1921.

Ellis studied at North Texas State College alongside Jimmy Giuffre and arranger Gene Roland. He played with the Casa Loma Orchestra and the Jimmy Dorsey band (mid-1940s) and then with the Soft Winds trio, co-composers of "Detour Ahead", recorded by Billie Holiday. He joined Oscar Peterson on the departure of Barney Kessel (1953–8), then backed singers Ella Fitzgerald and Julie London. He was involved in studio work on the West Coast from the 1960s, making occasional small-group appearances with The Great Guitars and with Ray Brown from the early 1970s onwards. Ellis has made several European tours, and is highly regarded as a gutsy guitarist whose unforced blues inflexions made him a natural Charlie Christian disciple. [BP]

⊙ **Nothing But The Blues** (1957; Verve). An excellent piano-less quintet session (supplemented by extra tracks with Peterson) features Ellis's guitar as the lead instrument with Roy Eldridge and a surprisingly down-home Stan Getz.

Seger Ellis

Piano.

b. Houston, Texas, 4 July 1906; d. 29 Sept 1995.

A versatile and flexible musician, by 1921 Ellis was broadcasting piano solos on early radio (KPRC), and in 1925 had big hits with records including "Prairie Blues" and "Sentimental Blues". After this he became an exclusive OKeh artist whose highly successful records as pianist and vocalist frequently featured top names including Manny Klein, the Dorsey Brothers, Muggsy Spanier, Eddie Lang and Louis Armstrong. While on tour in Cincinnati, Ellis discovered the Mills Brothers (1931) and became involved in their management; he also continued a successful solo career with, among others, Paul Whiteman, and appeared in the 1934 film *One Rainy Afternoon*. He led a variety of orchestras in the 1930s, plus his unique Choir of Brass (eight brass, one reed) in 1936 and 37. After being called up (1942–3), Ellis settled in Texas and returned to songwriting, arranging and – his first love – the piano. [DF]

⊙ **Choirs Of Brass 1937** (Alamac). Ellis's interesting and progressive orchestra (including Nate Kazebier, King Jackson and Irving Fazola) in a programme of Dixieland standards seen from a new angle.

Ziggy Elman

Trumpet, multi-instrumentalist.

b. Philadelphia, 26 May 1914; d. 26 June 1968.

Ziggy Elman (Harry Finkelman) began his career playing trombone with Alex Bartha's house band at Atlantic City's Steel Pier ballroom. In 1936 he moved to Benny Goodman, replacing lead trumpeter Pee Wee Erwin, and stayed with Goodman for four years, forming the trumpet triumvirate (Elman/James/Griffin) that topped Goodman's greatest band. In 1938, as featured soloist, Elman recorded sixteen highly successful sides for Bluebird (an RCA subsidiary): two of these, "Fralich In Swing" and "Bublitchki", were to be incorporated into Goodman's repertoire as the thrilling "And The Angels Sing" (words by Johnny Mercer) and "Who'll Buy My Bublitchki?" (Elman also played clarinet for Goodman on occasion: reputedly he learned the instrument in one day for a live performance of "Bach Goes To Town".) From 1940–47 he was regularly with Tommy Dorsey, usually leading the trumpet section, and after that he based himself in Los Angeles. He had two unsuccessful tries at running his own big band (at a time when big bands were winding down anyway), and was badly affected by the second American Federation of Musicians recording ban (1948), so worked instead for film studios, radio and TV; one late album, *Tribute To Benny Goodman* by Jess Stacy and the Famous Sidemen, shows his creative flame burning bright as ever. He appeared in *The Benny Goodman Story* (1955), although his playing was dubbed by Manny Klein, and in later years he kept active until succumbing to a nervous breakdown and drinking problems. Elman, a trumpeter to compare with Harry James, personifies the Jewish "fralich" trumpet style. [DF]

⊙ **Ziggy Elman 1938–9** (Classics). Elman's massive talent – and tone – on display in company with his format of trumpet plus saxophone section and rhythm. Great performances here including "Fralich In Swing" (later "And The Angels Sing") and "Bublitchki".

⊙ **Ziggy Elman And His Orchestra** (1947; Circle). Powerful trumpet playing in music from the end of Elman's short career as bandleader.

Alan Elsdon

Trumpet, flugelhorn, leader, vocals.

b. Chiswick, London, 15 Oct 1934.

Elsdon worked in the 1950s with Cy Laurie, Graham Stewart and Terry Lightfoot before forming his own band in 1961, shortly before the British trad boom ended. For that reason his band never quite achieved the popular status of earlier arrivals such as Barber, Bilk and Ball, but established a high musical reputation which gave Elsdon the option to work in cabaret with a variety of singers including Cilla Black, the Isley Brothers and Dionne Warwick. Later in the 1960s, as well as busily working the jazz circuits, Elsdon's band became a temporary backing group for George Melly. He continued to play for clubs and concerts with and without his band, and in 1978 joined the Midnite Follies Orchestra, a move which focused attention on the strength, versatility and flair of his re-creation of jazz roles from Louis Armstrong to Cootie Williams. In the 1980s he became a regular working partner to leader Keith Nichols; in the later 1980s and into the 1990s he has maintained his career as one of Britain's best traditional trumpeters, working with Nichols and blues singer Beryl Bryden amongst others, while continuing to lead his band and to work solo. [DF]

⊙ **Featuring Alan Elsdon...** (2001; Lake). Excellent and overdue studio compilation of Elsdon's fine trumpet-playing in the company of various British contemporaries.

Sidsel Endresen

Vocals.

b.Trondheim, Norway, 19 June 1952.

A potent and dramatic jazz artist, Sidsel Endresen is a largely self taught vocalist, though she has studied privately with Radka To Neff and Meredith Monk. She began collaborating with guitarist Jon Eberson in the late 1970s and together they recorded

Sidsel Endresen

five pop CDs winning Norwegian Grammies for two – *Jive Talk* (1980) and *City Visions* (1981). After this early success, Endresen sought a more subtle and minimalist approach and aimed to get rid of the showy aspects of her performance. In 1990 this more poetic approach was revealed in her debut album on ECM, *So I Write*. During the 1990s her profile continued to grow internationally with the release of *Exile* (1994) and *Duplex Ride* (1998). More recently Endresen worked in duo with Bugge Wesseltoft, and in 2001 they recorded the haunting *Undertow* for Jazzland. That same year, Endresen received Norway's prestigious Buddy Award in recognition of her vocal achievements. Like Sarah Vaughan, Endresen is both a contralto and a soprano, and like Joni Mitchell she has an occasional conversational style of delivery. [IC]

⊙ **Undertow** (2001; Jazzland). Bugge Wesseltoft plus four other musicians supply intriguing electronic backgrounds for Endresen's vocals. After the opener, "Western Wind", with its mournful, droning bass and austere wind blasts, the whole soundscape starts to lighten up.

Peter Epstein

Saxophones.

b. Eugene, Oregon, Jan 18, 1967.

Raised in Portland, Oregon, Peter Epstein was taught clarinet from the age of ten by his father, Ed Epstein, a saxophonist. At a young age, he played with Portland-based bassist Glen Moore of the group Oregon. He attended Cal Arts in LA, where he studied with bassist Charlie Haden, flautist James Newton and clarinettist John Carter, as well as pursuing ethnomusicological studies on various cultures. Since relocating to New York in 1992, he has been active recording with various figures, joining drummer Bobby Previte's Weather Clear, Track Fast group, guitarist Brad Shepik's international-minded group the Commuters, drummer Jerry Granelli's Badlands, and Ralph Alessi's Modular Theatre. He leads a quartet with drummer Jim Black, bassist Chris Dahlgren and keyboardist Jamie Saft, heard on *The Invisible* (1999; M.A.), and has recorded with pianist Michael Cain, notably on *Circa* (1996; ECM). He produced a series of albums for M.A. Records including an unaccompanied record, *Solus* (1998; MA Recordings), on soprano and alto saxes, featuring transcribed violin music of Bach, a theme of Verdi's and some original pieces. His appearance with drummer Peter Erskine and bassist Scott Colley on the well-received, quirky-but-accessible trio recording *Old School* (2001; M.A.) further raised his profile. [JC]

Rolf Ericson

Trumpet.

b. Stockholm, 29 Aug 1922; d. 16 June 1997.

Ericson took up trumpet at the age of nine, heard Louis Armstrong in Stockholm in 1933 and turned professional in 1943. He moved to the USA (1947–50, 1953–66), where he was a sideman with many big bands including Benny Carter, Charlie Barnet (1949), Charlie Ventura (1950), Woody Herman (1950), Harry James, Stan Kenton (1959), Maynard Ferguson (1960–1). His small-group work included the Lighthouse All Stars (1953, replacing Shorty Rogers), Dexter Gordon, Curtis Counce-Harold Land (1958), and the ten-piece Charles Mingus band (1962–3). He toured Sweden with Charlie Parker (1950) and with Duke Jordan, Cecil Payne and others in 1956. A regular member of Duke Ellington's band (1963–4), he also rehearsed and recorded with the Rod Levitt octet (1963–5). He then led his own Swedish big band (late 1960s), followed by radio studio work in Berlin into the 1980s and further playing visits to the USA. Already a bright, boppish soloist in his twenties, Ericson's contact with the very best American musicians helped him to form a markedly individual style. [BP]

➤➤ **Harold Land** *(Harold In The Land Of Jazz)*; **Rod Levitt** *(Dynamic Sound Patterns).*

Peter Erskine

Drums, composer.

b. Somers Point, New Jersey, 5 June 1954.

At the age of six Erskine attended the Stan Kenton National Stage Band camps, and continued doing so each summer for several years. In 1972 he joined the Stan Kenton orchestra, touring the USA, Europe and Japan and teaching at Kenton clinics. Erskine was with Weather Report from 1978–82, in one of its most vital and creative phases, and with Jaco Pastorius formed one of the finest rhythm-sections of the 1970s and early 1980s; his exposure with the group brought him to worldwide attention. In 1979 he began playing with Steps (with Mike Brecker, Mike Mainieri and Eddie Gomez), later renamed Steps Ahead, and he toured Japan, the USA and Europe with the group in the 1980s. Later in the decade he led his own group, which included Brecker (whom he still often plays with) and John Abercrombie. He also worked with Kenny Wheeler's quintet and big band, recording with both. Erskine divides his time between his current group (a classic piano-bass-drums trio with Alan Pasqua and Dave Carpenter) and freelance music with such diverse figures as Joni Mitchell, Elvis Costello, Sadao Watanabe and Mark Anthony Turnage. He is one of the most brilliantly accomplished and versatile drummers on the jazz scene, and can handle everything from the most complex jazz-rock charts, to the most delicate and subtle acoustic jazz, as well as being a gifted composer. [IC]

⊙ **Transition** (1986; Denon). This is notable for the pristine clarity of Erskine's acoustic and electronic drum sound and the terrific variety of the music. The eight musicians include Abercrombie, Joe Lovano and Bob Mintzer, all of whom solo wonderfully. Stand-out tracks are the loosest ones – the title track is in the Coltrane/Tyner mould, and the most moving piece of all is a straightforward trio feature with

KAREN MILLER

Peter Erskine

Abercrombie, Marc Johnson (bass) and Erskine playing a glorious version of "My Foolish Heart".

⊙ **Sweet Soul** (1991; RCA Novus). The group is virtually the same here as above, except that Randy Brecker replaces Peter Gordon (French horn) and John Scofield replaces Abercrombie. Again the excellent compositions are by Erskine, pianist Kenny Werner and producer Vince Mendoza, and again the album soars, exhilarating and stirring.

⊙ **Time Being** (1993; ECM). The trio heard here – Erskine with bassist Palle Danielsson and pianist John Taylor – sounds ravishing. The mood is mostly meditative, the pulses expansive and loose. Erskine writes and plays beautifully in this contemplative vein, but there's a wonderful moment when his piece "Bulgaria" takes a fierce rhythmic grip and everybody has to dig in.

⊙ **As It Is** (1995; ECM). The same trio, the same label, and the same exceptional rapport. Taylor's romanticism has immensely appealing resonances: "Glebe Ascending" harks back in impulse to Vaughan Williams's "Lark Ascending" and is impressionistic with a feathery lyricism. Danielsson has a gloriously singing tone, and Erskine's drumming is exacting and prescient.

➤➤ **Don Grolnick** *(Weaver Of Dreams);* **Kenny Wheeler** *(Music For Large And Small Ensembles);* **Joe Zawinul** *(Night Passage).*

Booker Ervin

Tenor saxophone, composer.

b. Denison, Texas, 31 Oct 1930; d. 31 July 1970.

After playing trombone and then taking up tenor during service in the air force (1949–53), Ervin studied at Berklee (1954) and toured with Ernie Fields (1955). Then he worked in Dallas, Denver and Pittsburgh until moving to New York in 1958. He was immediately recommended to Charles Mingus, who employed him for several periods between 1958–64. He also played with pianists Roland Hanna (1959) and Randy Weston (1960, 1964, 1966). Work under his own name from 1960 included live gigs and recording in Europe (1964–6, 1968) and he was performing again in the USA at the time of his death from kidney disease.

Although his father Booker Ervin Snr played alongside the great Buddy Tate, Booker Jnr's style is far removed from the bluesy mainstream playing identified with other "Texas tenors". Though his tone is subject to similar inflexions, it is not merely hot but scalding, and his line and time feeling owe something to both Dexter Gordon and John Coltrane. His original compositions and solos on others' material reflect a sophisticated sense of harmony and polytonality as well as the explicit emotionalism he projects. [BP]

⊙ **The Blues Book** (1964; Prestige/OJC). Now that several of Ervin's sessions are reissued, one is spoilt for choice, but this has four long blues hovering between polytonality and modal jazz played by a quintet including Carmell Jones and the redoubtable rhythm-section of Richard Davis and Alan Dawson.

➤➤ **Charles Mingus** *(Blues And Roots; Mingus Ah Um).*

Pee Wee Erwin

Trumpet.

b. Falls City, Nebraska, 30 May 1913; d. 20 June 1981.

Pee Wee (George) Erwin was learning the trumpet from his father by the age of four and at eight was featured on Kansas City radio with the Coon-Sanders Nighthawks. At eighteen he made the New York trip to join Joe Haymes's band, then worked with Isham Jones and Freddy Martin, and by 1935 was with Benny Goodman, playing lead and solos for the famous "Let's Dance" programmes. In 1936 he had a second stint with Ray Noble's orchestra, for which Glenn Miller was fixer and staff arranger. Miller, at Erwin's request, wrote his trumpet high and voiced with the saxophones; when Erwin's successor couldn't play the parts, they were given to the clarinettist, and Miller's sound – which he credited to Erwin – came to be.

For the remainder of the 1930s Erwin was first trumpeter for Goodman, Ray Noble and Tommy Dorsey (replacing Bunny Berigan, an indicator of his ability), then from 1940 he took over Berigan's band for two years. From 1942–9 he was in the studios as an almost permanent deputy for Manny Klein, and then led the band at Nick's Saloon for ten years from 1949 – a period that produced many fine Erwin recordings, including his definitive Jelly Roll Morton tribute with Kenny Davern. In the 1960s he continued busy studio work (including replacing Bobby Hackett on Jackie Gleason's later recordings), ran a trumpet school with Chris Griffin in New Jersey (his most famous pupil is Warren Vaché Jnr) and played festivals. From the early 1970s he worked with the NYJRC, on fourth trumpet, and in his last years was with Warren Vaché Snr's band around New Jersey. [DF]

⊙ **Dr Jazz Volume 14: Pee Wee Erwin** (2000; Storyville). On this "marvellous" (Cook/Morton) set, Erwin is at his most uninhibited, producing solos that combine his acknowledged technique with a truly fluent imagination. It seems amazing that, at the time, at least one prominent British critic dismissed him as just "a competent run of the mill professional who finds it profitable to play Dixieland jazz".

Ellery Eskelin

Tenor saxophone.

b. Wichita, Kansas, 16 Aug 1959.

Eskelin was raised in Baltimore where his mother was a bandleader and professional Hammond B-3 organist (stage name Bobbie Lee) who immersed him in jazz at a very young age. His father, whom he barely knew, was also a musician and composer, Rodd Keith, whose unusual work in the 60s and 70s writing and recording music for a "send-us-your-lyrics" venture was explored by his son in a compilation *I Died Today* (1996; Tzadik). He also utilized snips of Keith's strange songs on the disc *Green Bermudas* (1996; Eremite).

In 1983 Eskelin moved to New York to pursue jazz professionally, though he eventually found the neo-conservative climate of the straightahead scene less interesting, and by 1987 was active in various creative improvising ensembles including the collective Joint Venture (with trumpeter Paul Smoker and frequent early partners bassist Drew Gress and drummer Phil Haynes); with this group he recorded *Joint Venture* (1987; Enja), *Ways* (1990; Enja) and *Mirrors* (1993; Enja). Eskelin's first record as a leader was a group of reworked standards, *Setting The Standard* (1988; Cadence), in a trio context – his preferred ensemble size – and other trios have included *Forms* (1991; Open Minds), with Gress and Haynes (as was his debut), *Figure Of Speech* (1993; Soul Note), with Joe Daley on tuba and Arto Tuncboyaciyan on percussion, and *The Sun Died* (1996; Soul Note), a programme of Gene Ammons tunes with guitarist Marc Ribot and drummer Kenny Wollesen. Across this work, Eskelin has established a unique approach to the tenor – he often shifts colour and texture rapidly, in the space of a single line, and his breathy, sometimes swaggering phrasing has drawn comparison with Ben Webster and Archie Shepp. His solo outing, *Premonition* (1993; Prime Source), gives a sense of his developing style.

In 1994, Eskelin formed a group with Andrea Parkins on accordion, sampler and keyboards and Jim Black on drums, and this amalgam has been his prime vehicle since then, exploring a highly personal, wide-perspective take on contemporary composition and improvisation. This group has released seven records thus far, including *Jazz Trash* (1995; Songlines), *Kulak 29* and *30* (1998; hatOLOGY), *12 (+1) Imaginary Views* (2001; hatOLOGY) and *Arcanum Moderne* (2003; hatOLOGY), and continues to be one of the most interesting, challenging ensembles in today's jazz. [JC]

⊙ **One Great Day ...** (1997; hatOLOGY). A super live recording from Germany, the best yet by this extremely creative line-up. Eskelin's at-once-fluttery, at-once-razor-sharp lines, Black's hyperpropulsive drumming, and oddly cold accordion and samples from wildcard Parkins are all spun together in the leader's unique charts; there's also a totally reconceived version of Roland Kirk's "The Inflated Tear".

John Etheridge

Guitars.

b. London, 12 Jan 1948.

Etheridge taught himself guitar when at school and went on to obtain a history of art degree at Essex University. From 1971–4 he played with jazz-rock groups in London, then spent three years with Soft Machine from 1975–8. He joined Stephane Grappelli's touring band from 1977–81, then teamed up with violinist Ric Saunders (formerly of Fairport Convention), forming a well-received group called Surrounding Science. They recorded the album *Second Vision* in 1982 – a fusion album with rock, folk and neo-classical touches. Throughout the 80s and 90s he toured and recorded in a number of different musical contexts: solo concerts across the globe; trios and quartets (often in a "Hot Club" style); as part of a re-formed Soft Machine; in duo with Gary Boyle; with Danny Thompson's Whatever from 1989–93; with violinist Nigel Kennedy in both his jazz and rock projects (still an ongoing musical relationship); and with fellow guitarists such as Andy Summers

(formerly of the rock group The Police), Jim Mullen and Herb Ellis.

Pat Metheny, with whom Etheridge has duetted on TV and radio, once described him as "one of the best guitarists in the world". Though it's a generalisation, his interests are in a sense polarized by his two main influences: Django Reinhardt and John McLaughlin. On the one hand, he's a keeper of the Reinhardt/Grapelli flame, recording a handsome tribute to his late bandleader, *Sweet Chorus* (Dyad Records) with violinist Christian Garrick in 1998. On the other, he's happy firing off blistering solos with the Zappatistas, his tribute band cum homage to Frank Zappa. [IC]

ANDY SUMMERS/JOHN ETHERIDGE

⊙ **Invisible Threads** (1994; Inak). A warm and friendly duo album of seven Summers compositions, three joint compositions and two jazz classics – Django Reinhardt's "Nuages" and Monk's haunting reverie "Monk's Mood". Both men play acoustic and twelve-string guitars and acoustic bass.

JOHN ETHERIDGE

⊙ **Ash** (1994; Voiceprint). Etheridge, in a quartet, straddles a number of idioms here, from solo acoustic (almost classical) guitar to jazz-rock fusion. Two of the high points are a lovely version of Brubeck's "In Your Own Sweet Way" and a dynamic reading of Cedar Walton's "Ugetsu".

⊙ **Sweet Chorus** (1998; Dyad). A wonderfully spirited tribute to Grappelli, and of course to Django, whose "Nuages" is one of the five pieces the pair wrote. The other eight tunes are all standards, including Lennon and McCartney's "Here There and Everywhere". The group swings effortlessly, Etheridge shines throughout, and violinist Christian Garrick, in the Grapelli hot seat, drives the whole thing with a jaunty finesse.

➤➤ **Danny Thompson** *(Elemental)*.

Ethnic Heritage Ensemble

Chicago percussionist Kahil El Zabar established the Ethnic Heritage Ensemble in the mid-70s as a sextet. In 1976, reed player Edward Wilkerson Jnr, a new member of the Association for the Advancement of Creative Musicians (AACM), joined the group, which soon pared down to a trio. The group's music mixes deep African influences (El Zabar had visited Ghana in 1973) with open improvisation, folkish modal harmonies and explorative soloing. Various third reedmen rounded out the Ensemble, including Kalaparusha, Maurice McIntyre and the late "Light" Henry Huff. These groups toured Europe and made several records for small European labels, including *Welcome* (1982; Leo/Finland) and *Three Gentlemen From Chikago* (1981; Moers). In 1986, trombonist Joseph Bowie (brother of trumpeter Lester Bowie and leader of avant-funk band Defunkt) became the permanent third member, and this group has recorded on the Silkheart, Open Minds, and Chameleon labels). Wilkerson left the band in the late 90s, replaced by Chicago saxophonist Ernest Dawkins; this line-up has recorded for CIMP and Delmark and did a 25th Anniversary tour of the USA in 2002. [JC]

⊙ **Dance With The Ancestors** (1993; Chameleon). This was the Ethnic Heritage Ensemble's big-label break on the unfortunately short-lived Chameleon subdivision of Elektra. It provides a picture-perfect snapshot of the band: well recorded, with plenty of hand drums and percussion augmenting El Zabar's fine kitwork, the gorgeous alto and clarinet playing of Wilkerson, and Bowie's tough, punchy 'bone.

Kevin Eubanks

Guitar.

b. Philadelphia, 15 Nov 1957.

Eubanks studied music at Berklee and with Ted Dunbar. Up to around 1970 his biggest influence was John McLaughlin and the Mahavishnu Orchestra, but then he began to check out Wes Montgomery – a major influence on his clean playing. From 1980–81 he was with Art Blakey's Jazz Messengers and played briefly with Roy Haynes and Slide Hampton. In 1982 he toured with Sam Rivers, whose free-improvising concept radically altered Eubanks's ideas about music. He has played with numerous other musicians including Gary Thomas and Dave Holland, and has been leading his own group since 1983.

Eubanks has shown himself to be an interesting composer, though during the later 1980s he made a series of fusion albums for GRP, which brought him a wider public but tended not to extend his remarkable abilities. However, he remains one of the more interesting figures swimming in the jazz mainstream. [IC]

⊙ **Face To Face** (1986; GRP). This is one of his better efforts, and the personnel includes Dave Grusin, Ron Carter and Marcus Miller. Eubanks and Carter play a couple of dynamic duos which liven things up.

⊙ **Promise Of Tomorrow** (1989; GRP). After some indifferent albums, overloaded with personnel and production, Eubanks here reduces to quartet and does some serious playing in this leaner context.

Turning Point (1991; Blue Note). Eubanks's group here includes Dave Holland, Kent Jordan (alto flute), Charnett Moffett, and two of the most dynamic younger drummers – the British Mark Mondesir and the American Marvin "Smitty" Smith. Eubanks is really playing again and the band kicks hard.

Robin Eubanks

Trombone, bass trombone, keyboards.
b. Philadelphia, 25 Oct 1955.

Dedicated to countering the view of the trombone as "this little bastard instrument over in the corner", Robin Eubanks has made himself into one of the horn's most versatile virtuosi since arriving in New York in 1980 under the wing of his mentor, Slide Hampton. Equally adept in styles ranging from straightahead jazz through free playing to the street-smart, funky eclecticism favoured by M-Base, Eubanks traces his open-mindedness back to a childhood spent listening not only to jazz but to Led Zeppelin and Frank Zappa in a highly musical family. After serving his musical apprenticeship in the bands of Slide Hampton and Sun Ra, he spent three years on Broadway, then toured with Stevie Wonder before becoming Art Blakey's musical director. He also involved himself with Steve Coleman et al in the M-Base movement, but continues to play in a wide variety of musical contexts, chief among them big bands, for a large number of which he is a first-call trombonist. Bobby Watson, Joe Henderson, J.J. Johnson, arranger/conductor Peter Herborn, as well as the Philip Morris Superband and the Mingus Big Band, have all used him, and he is also a frequent collaborator with New York-based small-group leaders such as saxophonists Antonio Hart and Greg Osby, and drummer Bobby Previte. In 1997, he was invited to inaugurate a new UK label, Sirocco Jazz, with an album, *Wake Up Call*, also involving Hart. Heard recently in the critically applauded, award-winning Dave Holland Quintet (see below), he also leads his own eclectic group, Mental Images, performs a solo live show incorporating trombone and electronica, and is Professor of Jazz Trombone at the Oberlin Conservatory. [CP/CI]

Different Perspectives (1988; JMT). Varied personnel (participants include Hampton and Coleman, brother Kevin on guitar, and Jeff Watts on drums) play a rich selection of tightly arranged pieces.

Dedication (1989; JMT). Credited to fellow trombonist Steve Turre as co-leader with Eubanks, a sparky but wonderfully lively and immediately accessible album, touching a number of contemporary musical bases.

Karma (1990; JMT). Contains some superb trio work with Dave Holland and Marvin "Smitty" Smith, and some heavy workouts with M-Base stalwart Greg Osby, trumpeter Earl Gardener and Branford Marsalis on tenor.

Mental Images (1994; JMT). Eubanks plays electric as well as ordinary trombone on this gutsy album, which embraces M-Base and other styles, and features brother Kevin on guitar, pianist Michael Cain and saxophonist Antonio Hart.

Get 2 It (2001; Robin Eubanks Music). A diverting continuance (still with brother Kevin and pianist Cain) of Eubanks's exploration of the possibilities of the electric 'bone.

Dave Holland

Prime Directive (2000; ECM). Eubanks on top sideman form – alongside Chris Potter, Steve Nelson and Billy Kilson – in one of the most celebrated acoustic groups of recent times.

Jim Europe

Bandleader, entrepreneur, songwriter.
b. Mobile, Alabama, 22 Feb 1881; d. 10 May 1919.

A pioneer of ragtime and jazz, Jim Europe (James Reese) took part in a public concert of syncopation for singer Ernest Hogan in 1905, and the same year formed an association with legendary dance team Vernon and Irene Castle. During World War I he toured with an internationally renowned US army band which incorporated jazz and ragtime, and played a wildly successful concert in Paris in 1918. The following year Europe embarked on a similarly spectacular US tour, but was stabbed to death by a fellow musician in Boston. His contribution to jazz development in its formative years is plain in recorded examples of his work ("Too Much Mustard" and "Down Home Rag" from 1913; "Darktown Strutters' Ball", "That Moanin' Trombone", "Memphis Blues" and others from 1919), but none has yet been issued on CD. [DF]

Bill Evans

Piano, composer.
b. Plainfield, New Jersey, 16 Aug 1929; d. 15 Sept 1980.

An enormously influential figure, Bill (William John) Evans seemingly sprang upon the jazz scene fully formed. He made his first solo album in 1956 shortly after joining Tony Scott, whom he rejoined briefly in 1959 following a crucial eight months with Miles Davis. He also made important contributions to projects by such as Charles Mingus (*East Coasting*) and George Russell (*All About Rosie*, *Jazz In The Space Age*, etc). From 1959 he led his own trio, but his career was marked by brief drug-related absences, and readdiction preceded Evans's death at the peak of his career.

Evans's recordings with Davis had a decisive effect on the trumpeter, as well as vice versa, despite comprising less than two whole albums (the *Jazz Track* session and *Kind Of Blue*). His harmonic approach, especially, was significant in softening the edges of conventional sequences and pointing the way for pianists to cope with modal jazz; it also dictated the emotional content of his work, which became almost too rarefied at times and can be seen as foreshadowing the restrained gestures of much European jazz of the 1970s and 1980s. Archie Shepp articulated a widely held view when saying, "I think Bill's best work was done with the Miles Davis quintet. A good deal of that energy seems to me to have gone by the way. ... I like him on ballad material ... but Debussy and Satie have already done those things."

An extraordinarily prophetic example of Evans's affinity with these composers is "Peace Piece" (from *Everybody Digs Bill Evans*), where the improvised melody unfolds over a completely open-ended non-harmonic background. His up-tempo playing betrays the early inspiration of Bud Powell, Horace Silver, even of Nat "King" Cole, but the shape and length of his lines shows his admiration for Lennie Tristano. But Evans is far more expressive than Tristano, displaying a wide range of touch and accentuation; the singing tone of his right-hand work and his left-hand voicings were utterly distinctive although universally imitated. Similarly, the interplay within his trio (initially with bassist Scott LaFaro and Paul Motian, later with Eddie Gomez and a variety of drummers) added a new sound to the vocabulary of rhythm-section work.

Although he was a prolific composer, Evans's creations are closely bound to his style of improvisation and not many have become standard material. "Blue In Green", written for *Kind Of Blue*, is an exception, as is "Waltz For Debby" (to which lyrics were added by Gene Lees), while others such as "Turn Out The Stars" have gained wider currency in recent years. At the same time the more easily assimilated aspects of his work, as with Teddy Wilson before him, have been swallowed whole by so many lesser players that they are usually heard in heavily diluted form. But the combination of strength and sensitivity in his playing is ultimately what will be remembered about Evans and, since a whole generation of individualistic keyboard artists from Herbie Hancock to Keith Jarrett also absorbed aspects of his style, it is necessary to listen to his early recordings in order to appreciate his unique contribution. [BP]

⊙ **Everybody Digs Bill Evans** (1958; Riverside/OJC). Early, energetic, bop-derived playing with Philly Joe Jones on drums.

⊙ **Portrait In Jazz** (1959; Riverside/OJC). The debut of the LaFaro-Motian group, with brilliant interplay on "Autumn Leaves" and others. Evans's own trio's take on "Blue In Green" compares favourably with the *Kind Of Blue* version, recorded earlier the same year with Miles Davis.

⊙ **Waltz For Debby** (1961; Riverside/OJC). The eighteen months since *Portrait* produced a much greater looseness in the trio conception, halted by LaFaro's death ten days after this live set.

⊙ **Conversations With Myself** (1963; Verve). Evans's first and best overdubbing experiment, including "Round Midnight" and "Stella by Starlight".

⊙ **You Must Believe In Spring** (1977; Warner). As well as the Michel Legrand title song, this last recording with Eddie Gomez includes Evans's own "B Minor Waltz" (unusual for its structure and harmonic scheme) and his Legrand-influenced "We Will Meet Again".

➤➤ **Miles Davis** *(Kind Of Blue);* **Jim Hall** *(Undercurrent).*

Bill Evans

Tenor and soprano saxophones, flute, keyboards, composer.

b. Clarendon Hills, Illinois, 9 Feb 1958.

Evans began on piano at the age of five, later taking up the clarinet and tenor saxophone. He played classical piano concerts at sixteen and after one year of studying music at North Texas State University he transferred to William Paterson College in New Jersey, while also studying sax with Dave Liebman, who recommended Evans to Miles Davis. After graduating, Evans joined Davis in 1980 and stayed with him until 1984. With Davis he did several major tours, taking in the USA, Europe and Japan, appearing at all the leading festivals in almost every country in which the band played. From 1984 he worked with John McLaughlin's re-formed Mahavishnu Orchestra, and also led his own groups and recorded albums under his own name. In the early 1990s he led a fusion band, Petite Blonde, notably featuring Dennis Chambers on drums, which toured internationally. Davis said of Evans, "He's one of the greatest musicians I've ever come upon", and he is certainly one of the most gifted players to have emerged in the 1980s, with a pure singing sound on soprano, a crisp, dry tone on tenor, and tremendous rhythmic flow. [IC]

⊙ **Moods Unlimited** (1982; Paddle Wheel). This superb album came rather out of the blue. Here's Evans in an acoustic situation playing with two seasoned masters, Hank Jones and Red Mitchell, and sounding to the manner born. They lovingly explore five standards and the whole session has the magic of a chance encounter at a perfect moment.

⊙ **Petite Blonde** (1992; Lipstick). The tracks here were taken from a couple of concerts recorded in Germany and this is fusion at its best, with Evans passionate, deft, and absolutely compelling. The whole band has a remarkable fluidity with subtle changes of mood and shifting textural and spatial effects which make the music breathe in a very satisfying way.

⊙ **Push** (1993; Lipstick). A studio-recorded dance album, with a heavy backbeat often in evidence and the rapper K.C. Flight active on three of the twelve tracks. So far so bad, but Evans plays virtually throughout the entire album, most of the time on soprano, and the consistency of his brilliance borders on genius.

Doc Evans

Cornet, leader.

b. Spring Valley, Minnesota, 20 June 1907; d.10 Jan 1977.

Doc (Paul Wesley) Evans specialized on cornet in the late 1920s, and in the late 1930s worked with Red Dougherty's band before leading his own bands throughout the 1940s in Chicago and occasionally New York. A lyrical, technically accomplished and highly respected player, Evans worked with many better-known jazz stars such as Miff Mole, Tony Parenti and Joe Sullivan, and from 1947 recorded with his own band, including an extensive series with Audiophile in the 1950s (often co-featuring pianist John "Knocky" Parker) which established him as a major-league figure in the jazz revival. Evans continued bandleading throughout the 1960s and also directed the Mendota Symphony Orchestra; his last recordings were made at the 1975 Manassas jazz festival, with Bill Allred, Tommy Gwaltney and others. [DF]

Gil Evans

Composer, arranger, piano.

b. Toronto, 13 May 1912; d. 20 March 1988.

After hearing some Louis Armstrong records Gil Evans became interested in jazz at fourteen, and taught himself composing and arranging. From 1933–8 he led his own band in Stockton, California, and when it was taken over by Skinnay Ennis stayed on as arranger until 1941. He then worked as arranger with the Claude Thornhill orchestra until 1948, except for three years of army service from 1943–6. As well as the usual big-band line-up of brass, reeds and rhythm, the Thornhill orchestra employed French horns and tuba, and Evans soon became noticed by musicians for the variety and originality of the tonal textures of his arrangements.

In 1947 Evans was the central figure in a series of discussions with some of the leading young players of the day, including Gerry Mulligan, John Lewis and Miles Davis. They wanted to use the smallest number of instruments possible to get a fully orchestral sound, and this resulted in a nine-piece band under Davis's leadership which made a series of classic recordings and launched the "cool" school of jazz at the beginning of the 1950s. Evans arranged two of the pieces in its repertoire, "Moondreams" and "Boplicity"; French critic Andre Hodeir was moved to laud Evans as "one of jazz's greatest composer/arrangers".

In the USA, however, Evans still worked in obscurity as a freelance arranger. No critics noticed him or wrote about him, so he spent the first half of the 1950s filling in the gaps in his musical education – listening to recorded music, reading musical history, biographies and criticism. Then between 1957–60, again in collaboration with Miles Davis and using a nineteen-piece orchestra, he recorded three albums which rank with the finest orchestral music of the twentieth century: *Miles Ahead*, *Porgy And Bess* and *Sketches Of Spain*. All three were like concertos for trumpet (or flugelhorn) with Davis the only soloist, and his contribution was brilliantly integrated with the orchestral setting. British critic Max Harrison pointed out that Evans could handle the orchestra with "a freedom and plasticity that have been surpassed only in a very few works such as Stockhausen's *Gruppen für drei Orchester*". In the USA, too, critics were lavish with their praise, and Evans, then in his late 40s, at last became well enough known to lead his own bands on recording sessions and for concerts.

In 1961 his orchestra performed with Miles Davis at the latter's Carnegie Hall concert, which was recorded for a live album. He collaborated with Davis on another studio album, *Quiet Nights*, which neither of them felt happy about, recorded some albums of his own, and wrote arrangements for other artists including Kenny Burrell and Astrud Gilberto. In 1968 he played a concert in New York and was reunited with Davis for a concert at UCLA. These, however, were rare performances; during the late 1960s he spent most of his time writing.

In 1970 he began staging weekly performances at the Village Vanguard, usually with larger ensembles composed of some of New York's leading contemporary players. These sessions became somewhat of an institution and went on into the 1980s whenever Evans was at home. This music often used rock rhythms extensively, with massed percussion and electric bass and piano. From 1971 onwards he went even more deeply into electronics, using synthesizers and blending them with acoustic instruments.

By 1973 Evans's authority as a jazz composer had become sufficiently assured for the New York Jazz Repertory Company to put on three Evans concerts featuring different themes: "Jazz In The Rock Age", "Gil Evans Retrospective" and "The Music of Jimi Hendrix" over three years. The Evans orchestra had been due to record with Hendrix in 1970, when the guitarist died, and an album of Hendrix tunes was ultimately made in 1974, featuring two arrangements by Evans and six by other members of his orchestra.

Almost every aspect of Gil Evans's extraordinary career reversed the normal pattern. Although a competent pianist, he was not a virtuoso, and he only began playing professionally in 1952, when he was forty. He did not lead bands of his own until he was almost fifty; his most intense period of public performance began ten years later and showed no sign of diminishing in his seventies, until illness intervened.

He once said that "all form originated from spirit" – everything Evans did comes from this "spirit", which is why his music always sounds so fresh and so alive. Although primarily a composer, he loved fluidity and improvisation because, like Duke Ellington, he wanted music to always be in a state of becoming. [IC]

Gil Evans

⊙ **Great Jazz Standards** (1959; Pacific Jazz). Evans's love of the whole jazz tradition shines out from this brilliant album. The band, including trumpeter Johnny Coles and saxophonists Steve Lacy and Budd Johnson, and all the arrangements newly mint Beiderbecke's "Davenport Blues", Don Redman's "Chant Of The Weed", and pieces by Monk, John Lewis and Clifford Brown. Evans's "La Nevada" has Budd Johnson and the great Elvin Jones in full cry.

⊙ **Out Of The Cool** (1960; Impulse). Perhaps Evans's most perfectly realized album under his own name. Johnny Coles had a strong enough musical personality to take over the Miles Davis role in Evans's bands and makes his presence felt. Gil has such rapport with the soloists that his written arrangements have the immediacy of improvisation.

⊙ **The Individualism Of Gil Evans** (1963-64; Verve). The format is rangier and looser on this lovely album, with longer solos and more open written contexts. High spots are Kurt Weill's "Barbara Song", hauntingly dressed in French horns, woodwinds and lower brass (no trumpets), plus Wayne Shorter's lyrical tenor solo, and the swaggering 12/8 blues/gospel feel of "Hotel Me", with brass, reeds and woodwind backings trilled in harmony.

⊙ **Plays The Music Of Jimi Hendrix** (1974–5; Bluebird). Only three of the nine arrangements are by Evans, but nevertheless this is a stunning fusion of rock and jazz, and "Little Wing" and "Up From The Skies" remained part of the Evans band repertoire for years afterwards.

⊙ **Priestess** (1977; Antilles). This is the minimalist side of Evans at its most sublime. His orchestra worked only once in 1977 (on his 65th birthday) and the music comes from that joyous concert. Although the arrangements are merely sketches from the old master's pen, the music is highly concentrated and totally coherent. Highlights are Lew Soloff and Arthur Blythe on the title track, David Sanborn's glorious alto on "Short Visit", George Adams on "Orange Was The Colour Of Her Dress", and "Lunar Eclipse", featuring the whole ensemble in improvised and written passages.

⊙ **Farewell** (1986; Electric Bird). As Evans became older his art became younger and more spontaneous: the improvisations longer, the orchestral sections more skeletal. *Farewell* features Johnny Coles, Lew Soloff, Dave Bargeron, Chris Hunter and Hamiet Bluiett among others, all on cracking form.

➤➤ **Miles Davis** *(Miles Ahead; Porgy And Bess; Sketches Of Spain)*; **Claude Thornhill** *(Transcription Performances)*.

Herschel Evans

Tenor saxophone, alto saxophone, clarinet.
b. Denton, Texas, 1909; d. 9 Feb 1939.

Early on Herschel Evans played with territory bands in Texas, sometimes on tenor, sometimes on an alto that, according to Buddy Tate, had "about a hundred rubber bands around it". By the mid-1930s he was working with name bands such as Bennie Moten, Dave Peyton, Charlie Echols, Buck Clayton and Lionel Hampton. In 1936 he joined Count Basie to form a team with Lester Young. They were very different characters: Evans, direct, blustery, a "man's man", would tear up a band part if he couldn't read it; Young, a superior reader, looked at the world through amused, half-closed eyes, and lived by his philosophy of "to each his own". Their music, which echoed their personal contrasts to the note, instituted Basie's lifelong tradition of battling tenor saxophones, and was to pass into general jazz lore. But, says Jo Jones, "There was no real friction: Lester and Herschel were brothers in rivalry." Evans's hit record "Blue And Sentimental" showed his heart-on-sleeve tenor to perfection, but he was not with Basie long. Late in 1938 he became ill with dropsy and, said Dickie Wells, "swelled up so he couldn't get his hat on. It could have been cured if he'd gone to the doctor earlier." Buddy Tate dreamed that Evans had died and that a telegram came from Basie offering him the tenor chair; the telegram arrived in 1939. [DF]

➤➤ **Count Basie** *(The Original American Decca Recordings)*.

Stump Evans

Saxophones.
b. Lawrence, Kansas, 18 Oct 1904; d. 29 Aug 1928.

Paul Anderson Evans, called Stump because of his tiny build, played in Kansas City's Lawrence

High School band, then moved to Chicago. A potentially brilliant soloist and a good reader, he was soon a featured player with Erskine Tate's Vendome Orchestra (alongside Louis Armstrong and show trumpeter Reuben Reeves), King Oliver, Jimmy Wade, and Carroll Dickerson's orchestra at Sunset Café, featuring Earl Hines and Louis Armstrong again. "Stumpy Evans played beautiful tenor", remembered Hines. "Everyone was trying to get him then." Evans recorded too, with Oliver, Dickerson, Jelly Roll Morton and Jimmy Blythe, and for a time was MD at the Moulin Rouge Club. But he contracted TB while working with Tate and moved back to Kansas, where he died at only 23. His highest accolade came from Coleman Hawkins, who acknowledged Evans as an influence. [DF]

➤➤ **Jelly Roll Morton** *(Jelly Roll Morton Vol. 1: 1926–7).*

Sue Evans

Drums, percussion.

b. New York, 7 July 1951.

Sue Evans's father was a music teacher, and she had piano lessons as a child, before taking up drums at eleven. She then studied with Warren Smith at the Third Street Drum School and also with Morris Lang and others. From 1969–73 she played drums in Judy Collins's backing group, then was the percussionist with the Steve Kuhn quartet from 1972–4. She also worked with the Jazz Composers' Orchestra, and recorded with James Brown, Roswell Rudd, Billy Cobham, Blood Sweat and Tears and others. From the late 1960s until 1978 she played percussion and sometimes drums with the Gil Evans orchestra, and she recorded at least five albums with him – she is the only drummer on Evans's wonderful *Priestess*. During the 1980s and early 1990s she recorded on percussion with Sadao Watanabe, Hubert Laws and Terence Blanchard. [IC]

➤➤ **Gil Evans** *(Priestess).*

Don Ewell

Piano.

b. Baltimore, Maryland, 14 Nov 1916; d. 9 Aug 1983.

Tempting as it is to bracket Ewell with Ralph Sutton as the premier latter-day jazz piano revivalists, Ewell was active around Baltimore by the mid-1930s, ten years or so before Sutton's career got under way, and his inspirations were different. Sutton reworked the disciplines of Waller and Beiderbecke; Ewell delighted in the New Orleans-based music of Jelly Roll Morton and his peers. He began his post-war career alongside Bunk Johnson and George Lewis, and worked regularly thereafter with New Orleans-based musicians such as Bechet and Kid Ory, as well as hard-blowing leaders like Doc Evans, Georg Brunis and Muggsy Spanier. Ewell's piano style – delicate and academically perfect – was showcased in Jack Teagarden's marvellous band, in which, despite occasional ideological brushes with trumpeter Don Goldie, he stayed from 1956–62. After Teagarden's death Ewell moved back to New Orleans and played there in hotels and for bands, also making regular European tours: one of his last was undertaken to pay for costly cancer treatments for his daughter. She died, and Ewell carried on working in a daze until his own death, after several strokes. [DF]

⦿ **Music To Listen To Don Ewell By** (1956; Good Time Jazz). A well-rated LP at the time of its issue, this session is equally welcome on CD, featuring Ewell's crafted piano in company with Darnell Howard (clarinet) and Minor Hall (drums).

F

Johannes Faber

Trumpet, flugelhorn, piano, violin, composer.
b. Munich, Germany, 7 Nov 1952.

Faber's father was a composer, and he began on trumpet at the age of ten. He studied at the Richard Strauss Conservatory in Munich, at the University for the Performing Arts and Music in Graz, and at Berklee. He began his first fully professional job at eighteen, playing in the orchestra for various musicals and also working with Wolfgang Dauner, Sal Nistico, Dusko Goykovich and Mal Waldron, among others. In 1980 he joined the Stuttgart Radio Orchestra and in 1985 formed his own group, Johannes Faber's Consortium, featuring Billy Cobham on drums. The group made one eponymous album for Mood records in 1985. Faber toured with the United Jazz and Rock Ensemble in 1983 and 1984. At the end of the 1980s he became a member of the Hamburg Radio Orchestra. Faber is a virtuoso trumpeter and improviser with a full, rich sound and an excellent range. His favourites range from Louis Armstrong and Maurice André to Miles Davis, Don Cherry, Clifford Brown and Freddie Hubbard. [IC]

Jon Faddis

Trumpet, flugelhorn.
b. Oakland, California, 24 July 1953.

Faddis studied trumpet from the age of eight, and played with R&B groups and rehearsal big bands from the age of thirteen. He toured with Lionel Hampton in 1971–2, and then settled in New York. He worked with Gil Evans and Charles Mingus (including a European tour) in 1972 and the Thad Jones-Mel Lewis band, for whom he played lead trumpet, from 1972–5. In 1974 he began guesting with Dizzy Gillespie, recording with him and Oscar Peterson. He was already involved in studio work, and specialized in this field until the early 1980s, before emerging on the jazz scene again. He has since undertaken numerous festival and club appearances in his own right, and was appointed musical director of the Carnegie Hall Jazz Orchestra in 1993. Initially he was markedly influenced by Gillespie, even before he played with him, but Faddis possesses all the ensemble qualities of big-band players as well as a dazzling upper-register technique. His resurgent jazz work exhibits his brilliant combination of exuberance and discipline. [BP]

Legacy (1985; Concord). Preferable to his unavailable and over-populist Epic albums, this quintet session with Harold Land and Kenny Barron includes tributes to Gillespie, Thad Jones ("A Child Is Born") and Louis Armstrong ("West End Blues").

Al Fairweather

Trumpet, arranger, composer, leader.
b. Edinburgh, Scotland, 12 June 1927; d. 21 June 1993.

Al Fairweather is most famous for his long partnership with Scottish clarinettist Sandy Brown, which began in Edinburgh, then moved to London to produce Britain's most creative mainstream jazz in the years 1956–64. A forthright, powerful trumpeter who played in the Armstrong mode, Fairweather took over leadership of the band as Brown's preoccupation with acoustic architecture grew; he also produced many of the neat arrangements which encapsulated Brown's often startling ideas: LPs such as *Dr McJazz* show the partnership at its working peak. After he left Brown, Fairweather worked for Acker Bilk in the mid-1960s, then reverted to full-time teaching, playing in his spare time. In the 1970s he was featured soloist and a highly effective arranger for Stan Greig's London Jazz Big Band, took part in Sandy Brown reunions, and freelanced around London's clubs and pubs. A heart attack in 1983 slowed him down for a couple of years, then later in the decade he moved back to Edinburgh, where he worked with Groove Juice Special, led by pianist/critic Ralph Laing, with whom he collaborated on a variety of other projects including a tribute to Sandy Brown and a proposed musical based on Kingsley Amis's *Lucky Jim*. He also appeared regularly at the Edinburgh jazz festival until the year of his death. [DF]

Fairweather Friends; Made To Measure (1957–61; Lake). Outstanding Fairweather solo album from 1957 with kindreds Red Price, Tony Coe, Tony Milliner, Stan Greig et al, along with a reissue of a very rare John R.T. Davies session, also featuring Kenny Ball, John Picard, Bruce Turner, Dick Heckstall-Smith and others.

➤➤ **Sandy Brown** *(Historic Usher Hall Concert 1952; McJazz And Friends; McJazz Lives On).*

Digby Fairweather

Cornet, trumpet.

b. Rochford, Essex, UK, 25 April 1946.

Before turning professional on 1 January 1977, Digby Fairweather worked for seven years in various Essex-based bands from New Orleans-style to avant-garde jazz – with his own band (Dig's Half Dozen), then latterly with Eggy Ley, Hugh Rainey, Eric Silk, Gene Allen, Ron Russell, Lennie Hastings, Dave Shepherd and Alex Welsh, with whom he recorded his first album in 1975 (as deputy trumpeter with Welsh's band). As a professional, he was a founder member of Keith Nichols's Midnite Follies Orchestra, joined the cooperative quartet Velvet, and recorded solo albums. In 1979 he was voted the BBC Jazz Society's Musician of the Year and for two years after was placed in polls in *Jazz Journal International*. From that year he became involved in jazz education (as co-director, with pianist Stan Barker, of a non-profit-making educational trust, Jazz College) and at the same period joined the Pizza All Stars for three years. After leaving, he led his own quartet, re-formed the Kettners Five with veteran bassist Tiny Winters, toured and appeared on TV with a Nat Gonella tribute (starring Nat), taught more and worked for Brian Priestley's septet (featuring Don Rendell). By 1985 he had written a successful trumpet tutor (*How To Play Trumpet*), was broadcasting busily (including deps for Humphrey Lyttelton on BBC's *Best Of Jazz* and a World Service series) and had produced three new albums, one of which (*Let's Duet* with Stan Barker) was shortlisted as record of the year by *Cadence* magazine. He has contributed short pieces to a variety of recent books.

In 1987 Fairweather founded the Association of British Jazz Musicians and the National Jazz Foundation Archive, and in 1990 played a leading role in establishing the jazz section of Britain's Musicians' Union. In the early 1990s he presented a live weekly radio show on London's Jazz FM, then BBC Radio 2's *Jazz Parade* and *Jazznotes*. He has won British Jazz Awards twice, received the Freedom of the City of London (1992), Freedom of (his hometown) Southend (2000) and at the 1993 Cork jazz festival won the Benno Haussman Award for services to jazz. From 1987 he led the Jazz Superkings (with Dave Shepherd, Roy Williams and Brian Lemon), and from 1994 co-led (and still does) the Great British Jazz Band (GBJB) with trombonist Pete Strange, as well as maintaining solo appearances. Then in 1998 he retired from the BBC after six years to concentrate on full-time playing, including his own Half Dozen and, from 2000, appearances as Kenny Baker's replacement with Don Lusher's Best Of British Jazz. His autobiography *Notes From A Jazz Life* appeared in 2002, published by Northway. [JLS]

⊙ **Portrait** (1979–84; Black Lion). Duo, quartet and quintet recordings featuring Velvet (with Denny Wright, Ike Isaacs and Len Skeat), pianist Stan Barker, and titles from Fairweather's award-winning "Goin' Out Steppin' " with Brian Lemon, Wright, Chris Ellis and friends.

⊙ **Something To Remember Us By** (1984; Jazzology). The complete studio and live duets of Fairweather with his longtime playing partner Stan Barker; a double CD and concentrated listening but worth hearing.

⊙ **Squeezin' The Blues Away** (1994; FMR). Duo date with accordionist Tony Compton, plus singer Liza Lincoln featured on two tracks. "One of Fairweather's major performances on record", to quote *Jazz Journal International*.

⊙ **Recorded Delivery** (1997; Loose Tie). Fairweather with an all-star band (Shepherd, Gay, Williams, Lemon, Douglas, Skeat, Ganley) in an album sponsored by the Post Office; mainly the repertoire of his Jazz Superkings group formed in 1987.

⊙ **Special Delivery** (1998; Loose Tie). Fairweather's second "Post Office" album; wide-ranging in style, specifically "postal" in theme, and with a number of originals including Fairweather's "Unsweet Letter From You", "Letter Fellow Get Some Sleep" and the title track.

⊙ **Twelve Feet Off the Ground** (1998; Flat Five). This all-new group, featuring Julian Marc Stringle (clarinet), Malcolm Smith (trombone), Craig Milverton (keyboards) and others, fulfils Fairweather's wish for a stylistically broad-based group, with strong vocal element. Originals include Fairweather's close harmony "Babe" and "Twelve Feet Off The Ground" and Smith's "Morning Song". "There cannot be another band with quite this range – relaxed, witty, amazingly accomplished." (Dave Gelly, *Observer*, 1998).

➤➤ **Pete Strange** *(Great British Jazz Band)*; **Val Wiseman** *(Lady Sings The Blues).*

TIM HALL

Digby Fairweather

Jack Fallon

Bass.

b. London, Ontario, 13 Oct 1915.

Fallon arrived in Britain with the Canadian Air Force in 1946 and joined Ted Heath's orchestra for six months. His highly modern bass playing attracted huge attention, and after leaving Heath he worked with the cream of British jazz talent, as well as playing with visiting talent such as Duke Ellington, Django Reinhardt, Lena Horne, Sarah Vaughan, Maxine Sullivan and Mary Lou Williams, and working as staff bassist for the Lansdowne series, for which he recorded with Josh White, Jack Elliott, Kenny Baker, Bruce Turner and Humphrey Lyttelton amongst others.

From 1952 he ran his highly successful Cana Agency, which later represented stars like Kenny Ball (as well as the Beatles and the Rolling Stones for occasional work in their early days), and also pursued a third career as a country and western violinist (he can be heard on the Beatles' *White Album*). Despite concentrating on his agency from the early 1960s, he was often persuaded out of retirement by Lennie Felix and in the 1980s by pianist Stan Greig, Digby Fairweather and others. In the 1990s Fallon was still running his agency and freelancing, but by 2003, following a minor stroke, had stopped playing. [DF]

➤➤ **Dick Sudhalter** *(After Awhile).*

Georgie Fame

Vocals, piano, organ.

b. Leigh, Lancashire, UK, 26 June 1943.

Born Clive Powell, Georgie Fame was given his stage name by impresario Larry Parnes prior to forming his Blue Flames to back pop singer Billy Fury, although Fame had travelled to London at sixteen with Rory and the Blackjacks. Post-Fury, the Blue Flames established themselves at Soho's Flamingo Club, producing Fame's debut album, *Rhythm And Blues At The Flamingo*, in 1963. Pop hits "Yeh Yeh", "Getaway" and "The Ballad Of Bonnie And Clyde" followed, but Fame's heart has always been in jazz and R&B, and he toured Europe in 1967–8 with Count Basie. He spent the early 1970s working with Alan Price, but then returned to the Blue Flames, recording *Georgie Fame*, an R&B album, with them in 1974. An accomplished arranger – he has worked with Van Morrison in this capacity – Fame continues to commute between pop, R&B and jazz (he works frequently with Scandinavian big bands), and his club gigs for which he is now able to call on a who's who of UK jazz talent – among them Guy Barker, Anthony Kerr, Alan Skidmore, Peter King and Geoff Gascoyne, along with Fame's sons Tristan and James Powell – are both erudite (name-checking a plethora of jazz legends in flights of vocalese) and wholly enjoyable. In the early 1990s he signed with Ben Sidran's Go Jazz label, which resulted in a series of fine albums (see below) culminating in 2000's *Poet In New York*, which won the French Académie du Jazz's Best Jazz Vocal Album award. Continuing to release albums on his own Three Line Whip label, in 2003 he celebrated forty-five years in the business, and was able to look back on over thirty albums and fourteen hit singles. [CP/CI]

Rhythm And Blues At The Flamingo (1963; RSO). Definitive 1960s live R&B album featuring "Parchman Farm", "Let The Good Times Roll", "Baby Please Don't Go" and other favourites.

The First Thirty Years (1989; Connoisseur). Pop hits plus R&B, jazz ("Moody's Mood For Love") in thirty-year retrospective.

Cool Cat Blues (1991; Go Jazz). Slick, tight album featuring fusion's finest, including Robben Ford, Steve Gadd and Richard Tee, on material ranging from Van Morrison's "Moondance" to Hoagy Carmichael's "Rockin' Chair" as well as R&B classics.

Walking Wounded (1998; Go Jazz). Although named for the flu bug which was afflicting his band (see above) for this Ronnie Scott's gig, the Fame magic is still apparent in every track, whether they're touching Fran Landesman songs, visits to familiar hits or Fame's trademark vocalese.

Farley and Riley

When the Onyx Club on 52nd Street reopened after a fire in 1935 the resident group assembled by Red McKenzie contained Eddie Condon, Eddie Farley (trumpet/vocals; b. Newark, New Jersey, 16 July 1904) and Mike Riley (trombone; b. Fall River, Massachusetts, 5 Jan 1904; d. 2 Sept 1984). While rehearsing for the reopening, singer Ruth Lee introduced the band to a novelty song, "The Music Goes Round And Round", written (it later transpired) by Chicago trumpeter Red Hodgson. After trying out the tune and adding their own chords, the group appropriated the song for themselves. Condon, appalled by Riley and Farley's antics ("they poured water over each other, scuffled, mugged and did everything but play music"), left the band soon after, but the duo recorded their novelty item. It sold over 100,000 copies, became the biggest jazz hit of the 1930s, and focused attention on "The Street". During 1935–6 the "House Full" signs were constantly up at the Onyx, clubs were opening in droves, and the smart set were turning right for 52nd Street instead of left into Harlem. Paramount made a film of the song in 1936, and two years later the Casa Lomans were still featuring it sung by Pee Wee Hunt, with special material by Sammy Cahn. Both Riley and Farley formed bands of their own; Mike Farley was active in Chicago until the 1950s. [DF]

➤➤ **Red McKenzie** *(Red McKenzie 1935–7).*

Tal Farlow

Guitar.

b. Greensboro, North Carolina, 7 June 1921; d. 25 July 1998.

Talmage Farlow only took up the guitar at the age of 21. He worked with pianist/singer Dardanelle Breckenbridge in 1947, and then with the Margie Hyams trio in 1948 and the Buddy DeFranco sextet in 1949. He played in the innovative Red Norvo trio from 1950–53, and with Norvo's quintet from 1954–5; in between he was with Artie Shaw's last Gramercy Five. During this period, he made the first records under his own name. He formed a trio, including pianist Eddie Costa, which worked in 1956 and 1958 with a break for Farlow's retirement. This became virtually complete for a decade, as he became a freelance signpainter (possibly the only jazzman with this alternative career since Duke Ellington). Occasional local gigs, and a recording in 1967, led to Newport festival appearances and to touring with the George Wein group in 1969. Although still only performing part-time and teaching, he recorded more regularly after 1976 and undertook European tours, both with Norvo in 1982 and, into the 1990s, alone. An extremely fluent improviser who grasped the essential rhythmic variety of bebop, Tal fell into the trap (especially with his own 1950s group) of using too many notes with a minimum of inflexion, for all the world like those transitional mid-1940s guitarists who recorded with Dizzy Gillespie and/or Charlie Parker. Latterly, while retaining all his facility, Farlow allowed far more lyricism into his playing, and the result was correspondingly more captivating. [BP]

The Swinging Guitar Of Tal Farlow (1956; Verve). Farlow's buoyant lines are matched by the driving piano work of Eddie Costa in the drummer-less trio completed by bassist Vinnie Burke.

A Sign Of The Times (1977; Concord). A more reflective Farlow, again in his favourite drummer-less trio format but this time with Hank Jones and Ray Brown.

Addison Farmer

Bass.

b. Council Bluffs, Iowa, 21 Aug 1928; d. 20 Feb 1963.

The twin brother of Art Farmer, Addison Farmer freelanced in New York in the 1950s, playing with Charlie Parker, Miles Davis, Benny Carter, Howard McGhee and many others. He was with the Art Farmer-Benny Golson Jazztet from 1959–60. From 1960–62 he worked with Mose Allison and others. Farmer played bass under his brother's leadership on one of the finest albums of the 1950s – *Modern Art*. He also recorded with Allison, Gene Ammons, Teo Macero, Mal Waldron and Stan Getz. [IC]

➤➤ **Art Farmer** *(Portrait Of Art Farmer).*

Art Farmer

Flugelhorn, trumpet.

b. Council Bluffs, Iowa, 21 Aug 1928; d. 4 Oct 1999.

Farmer was brought up in Phoenix, Arizona, and moved to Los Angeles in 1945 with his twin brother Addison. Art's late-1940s playing experience included the bands of Johnny Otis, Jay McShann, Roy Porter, Gerald Wilson and Benny Carter. In 1951–2 he was gigging and recording with Wardell Gray. In 1952–3 he toured with Lionel Hampton, cutting discs with Clifford Brown and under his own name with other Hampton sidemen including Gigi Gryce. He settled in New York and worked in succession with Gryce from 1954–6, Horace Silver from 1956–8 and Gerry Mulligan from 1958–9. He appeared on albums with writers as different as George Russell and Quincy Jones and became co-leader, with Benny Golson, of the Jazztet which lasted from 1959–62, then led a quartet with Jim Hall, and later Steve Kuhn, from 1962–5. He made his first solo tours of Europe in 1965 and 1966, and worked in the USA with a quintet including Jimmy Heath. He became a member of the Austrian Radio Orchestra in 1968, also appearing solo and with the Kenny Clarke-Francy Boland and Peter Herbolzheimer bands, and making brief returns to the USA. Since the 1980s he has spent more time in the USA, reuniting with Benny Golson and appearing under his own name, often using Clifford Jordan or Jerome Richardson on tenor.

The gentle surface of Farmer's playing has been mistaken for blandness by some, and his 1953 recording with Clifford Brown finds him seemingly at a disadvantage. Even at this stage, however, he was markedly individual and, though inspired by the "modal" implications of early Miles Davis, he also foreshadowed the wistfulness of later Kenny Dorham, with phrasing behind the beat and achingly wide melodic leaps. As his work matured in the late 1950s, there was an apparent lack of attack in his articulation which, perversely, enhanced the unusual shapes of Farmer's lines. The final touch was added when, in the early 1960s, he began to solo exclusively on flugelhorn (though he still used trumpet for big-band section work), so that what had sounded merely forlorn was given a further profundity. Late in his career he adopted a hybrid instrument called a "flumpet". Partly as a result, Farmer managed to broaden his emotional range with growing strength and even glimpses of something approaching gaiety, without jettisoning his unique style. [BP]

Portrait Of Art Farmer (1958; Contemporary). A seemingly casual quartet session (with brother Addison, Hank Jones and Roy Haynes) highlights the best of pre-flugelhorn Farmer.

Sing Me Softly Of The Blues (1965; Atlantic). Though other Farmer Atlantics have appeared on CD, this is the one to look for, with its fresh-sounding work from Steve Kuhn, Steve Swallow and Pete LaRoca, and a stunning debut recording of Carla Bley's title track.

Jak Kilby

Art Farmer

Blame It On My Youth (1988; Contemporary). One of three albums with Clifford Jordan and James Williams, representing a more varied programme than the previous year's excellent all-Strayhorn album *Something To Live For*.

>> **Clifford Brown** *(Clifford Brown Memorial)*; **Quincy Jones** *(This Is How I Feel About Jazz)*.

Joe Farrell

Tenor and soprano saxophones, flute.

b. Chicago Heights, Illinois, 16 Dec 1937; d. 10 Jan 1986.

Farrell played with Ira Sullivan and others in Chicago before moving to New York in 1960. There he joined the Maynard Ferguson band in 1960–61. He then worked with the Slide Hampton octet in 1962, the Charles Mingus and George Russell sextets in 1964 and the Jaki Byard quartet in 1965. He was a founder member of the Thad Jones-Mel Lewis band in 1966, and he also toured with the Elvin Jones trio between 1967–71. He worked with Chick Corea (on whose first album he played in 1966) in the first Return To Forever of 1972–3 and in the enlarged edition of 1977–8. He was making his own albums regularly after 1970, but moved to California in the late 1970s and became heavily involved in studio work. After a period of reassessment, he reverted to more frequent jazz playing and co-led European tours with Louis Hayes in 1983 and Woody Shaw in 1985. Farrell was a driving force on his main instrument, the tenor, and his improvisations reflected an intelligent appreciation of both Coltrane and Rollins. [BP]

Joe Farrell-Louis Hayes

Vim 'n' Vigor (1983; Timeless). The teaming of the co-leaders with two Dutch musicians is less exciting than the Elvin Jones below, but offers a fair representation of Farrell's latter-day work.

>> **Elvin Jones** *(Puttin' It Together)*.

Nick Fatool

Drums.

b. Milbury, Massachusetts, 2 Jan 1915; d, 26 Sept 2000.

Fatool learnt his craft with big bands led by Benny Goodman (1939–40), Artie Shaw (1940–1), Les Brown, Alvino Rey, Eddie Miller and others, and later worked in studios – as a staffman on Bing Crosby shows, for example, and for Dick Cathcart in the *Pete Kelly's Blues* radio, TV and film hit of the 1950s. From the 1960s he was a regular associate of Bob Crosby as well as working with Pete Fountain and other kindred Dixieland spirits, and he was still active in the 1990s. Recalling Baby Dodds in his controlled use of percussion colours, Fatool had the ability to propel a band unrelentingly at the kind of level over which an acoustic guitar could still be comfortably heard. [DF]

Malachi Favors

Bass, banjo, zither, bells, gongs, log drum, whistles, vocals.

b. Chicago, 22 Aug 1927; d. 30 Jan 2004.

Favors began playing double bass after high school, at the age of fifteen, inspired by Wilbur Ware. From 1958–60 he worked with pianist Andrew Hill. He met Roscoe Mitchell and Muhal Richard Abrams in 1961 and worked with Abrams's big Experimental Band which evolved into the AACM. He played with Roscoe Mitchell and Lester Bowie, joining with them and Joseph Jarman in 1969 to form the Art Ensemble Of Chicago, one of the most important groups of the 1970s and 1980s. He also played on Mitchell's and Bowie's individual albums as well as on other AACM members' albums. An album of duos with Abrams was released in the mid-1970s. [IC]

>> **The Art Ensemble Of Chicago** *(Urban Bushmen)*.

Pierre Favre

Drums, percussion.

b. Le Locle, Switzerland, 2 June 1937.

Favre began on drums at fifteen, turning professional two years later. He worked with various European bands and at nineteen was percussionist in the Basle Radio Orchestra. In 1960 he freelanced in Paris and in 1961 he played in Rome with the American Jazz Ensemble. In 1962 he joined the Max Greger band, also playing and recording with George Gruntz, Chet Baker, Bud Powell, Lou Bennett and many others. From 1966–70 he worked with Irene Schweizer, Peter Kowald and Evan Parker, and played at international festivals. He also did lecture tours in Europe, the USA and Japan and headed the Paiste Drummer Service. From 1970–75 he performed with Michel Portal and John Tchicai and was a member of the Zurich Radio Orchestra. He also composed music for theatrical productions, played solo concerts, worked with Interchange (with Joachim Kuhn and Peter Warren) and collaborated with contemporary composers U. Lehmann, R. Boesch and U. Schneider. In 1976 he did some work with dancers, and performed frequently with Albert Mangelsdorff. Since then he has worked in duo with various partners and played solo concerts in North and South America, Asia and Europe. He also conducts rhythm workshops and has worked with the groups Drum Orchestra, Music By and Madrugada. [IC]

Singing Drums (1984; ECM). Favre with fellow percussionists Paul Motian, Freddy Studer and Nana Vasconcelos, on an album which seems to be largely intended for other percussionists.

>> **Irene Schweizer** *(Irene Schweizer & Pierre Favre)*; **John Surman** *(Such Winters Of Memory)*.

Wally Fawkes

Clarinet, soprano saxophone.

b. Vancouver, 21 June 1924.

Wally Fawkes was first heard in the George Webb band and subsequently joined Humphrey Lyttelton, with whom his throbbing broad-toned clarinet found a perfect showcase: his records with Lyttelton, from 1947–55, are British jazz classics. He then decided to give up full-time music to pursue his other love, cartoon drawing; for nearly forty.years he drew *Flook* for the *Daily Mail* and was also behind the Trog cartoons in the *Observer*. Yet he still found time for the clarinet: in the late 1950s his Troglodytes and collaborations with Bruce Turner produced jazz of special quality, and in the 1960s he played regularly at New Merlins Cave, a Clerkenwell jazz centre, and for Humphrey Lyttelton reunions. In the early 1970s he was a founder member of John Chilton's Feetwarmers, appearing in tandem with an old partner, George Melly, before Chilton's group cut down to a quartet format, and in the following decade was still regularly to be heard playing in pubs and clubs around London, and for reunions with Lyttelton. Into the 1990s Fawkes continued to work with kindred piano spirits including Doug Murray and Stan Greig, and is most often to be heard in London jazz pubs, though one distinguished occasion in the 1990s found him playing clarinet duets with Bob Wilber at Pizza on the Park. In 2003, he was regularly teaming with trumpeter John Chilton, again in London pubs. [DF]

⊙ **Flook Digs Jazz** (1957–9; Lake). Valuable reissue of all Fawkes' records (EPs plus one ten-inch LP) with his Troglodytes, featuring the underrated trumpeter Spike Mackintosh (father of showbusiness tycoon Cameron). Fine liner notes by Ralph Laing.

⊙ **Jazz Jurassics** (2002; Macjazz). A new date for Fawkes – his soaring clarinet teamed with pianist Stan Greig and long-time partner, trumpeter Colin Smith (a most welcome guest), in a session of vintage quality.

⊙ **Juicy And Full-toned** (1954–6; Lake). All the tracks recorded by the Fawkes-Turner Sextet (with Bruce Turner,1954) and the Fawkes-Brown Quintet (with Sandy Brown, 1956). This is British jazz which deserves to be termed "classic" for its craftsmanship and musical substance.

➤➤ **Humphrey Lyttelton And His Band** *(The Parlophones Vols. 1–4).*

Rick Fay

Clarinet, soprano saxophone, tenor saxophone.

b. Evanston, Illinois, 25 December 1926; d. 22 March I999.

Fay began on clarinet after hearing Barney Bigard's solo on Duke Ellington's "I Don't Know What Kind Of Blues I've Got", and turned professional in 1945 at the age of nineteen. Not much is known of his early activities in and around Los Angeles but he worked with drummer Nick Pelico at the Gaslight Club in 1966 and thereafter at Disneyland California for ten years before transferring to Orlando Florida until 1997. Fay's career is all the more shadowy because he did not record until 1989 when Arbors' owner Mat Domber renewed his acquaintance with the saxophonist after a gap of twenty-three years. Fay's late recordings for the label suggest a musician intent on stamping his name on jazz history via a variety of means; his albums include singing and spoken poetry as well as his warm tenor sax and Bechet-influenced soprano. His final album *With A Song In My Heart* bears all the marks of a last testament from a much-under-rated musician. [DF]

⊙ **With A Song In My Heart** (1998; Arbors). Recorded in the twilight of Fay's career, this album mixes ballads with brighter tunes in a setting that most musicians of his generation only dreamed of; a full string section cocooning his breathy and occasionally flawed tenor. A moving memorial nevertheless.

Irving Fazola

Clarinet, saxophones.

b. New Orleans, 10 Dec 1912; d. 20 March 1949.

Irving Fazola was born Irving Henry Prestopnik – the *nom de plume* was a Louis Prima massacre of "fah-so-lah", a reference to Prestopnik's classical training. He began in New Orleans in the 1920s (playing with Prima, Armand Hug, Julian Lane and Sharkey Bonano, among others), went to Ben Pollack's training band in 1935, moved in 1937 to Glenn Miller (a frequent sparring partner), then after several returns to New Orleans went to Bob Crosby's band in 1938, where he stayed all of two years until a spectacular fight with Ray Conniff. In 1941 he spent a year with another New Orleans man, Claude Thornhill, then returned to his Dixieland roots with Muggsy Spanier and Georg Brunis, among others. He went back to New Orleans in 1943 and for the last five years of his life played all the best jobs in the city. With a sound like honey and a virtuoso's technique, Irving Fazola was arguably the finest clarinettist to emerge in the swing era, but he was unmarketable and unapproachable. Fat, taciturn, quick-tempered, violent when it suited him, he had few ambitions beyond food, drink, sex and Dixieland jazz, and in all of them (in John Chilton's marvellous phrase) "he thought in double portions". High blood pressure and cirrhosis of the liver ended his music at the age of 36. [DF]

⊙ **Faz** (1936–45; ASV). Excellent and intelligent Fazola compilation, including famous titles with Bob Crosby ("My Inspiration", "Hindustan") plus sides with Ben Pollack, The Musical Maniacs, Glenn Miller, Jess Stacy, Muggsy Spanier and his own band.

➤➤ **Bob Crosby** *(Bob Crosby And His Bobcats: Vols. 1 & 2).*

Leonard Feather

Piano, composer, producer, journalist.

b. London, 13 Sept 1914; d. Sherman Oaks, California, 22 Sept 1994.

After studying the piano informally, Feather became involved in writing about jazz (and film) in his late teens, and paid his first visits to the USA in 1935–6 and 1938. After producing record sessions in the UK and USA, he took up permanent residence in New York where he stayed from 1939–60, when he moved to Los Angeles. Large numbers of his compositions have been recorded, mainly on the many sessions supervised by him, the most famous being the songs "Evil Man Blues" and "How Blue Can You Get". Feather was for a long time the most widely read and most influential writer on jazz. Nevertheless, he was on several occasions an effective organizer and composer for musicians he admired, and his sympathies (except for the avant-garde) were extremely wide. [BP]

Leonard Feather 1937–45 (Classics). Although Feather plays piano on some of these tracks, it's his arrangements (some of them being English folk songs!) that are the best excuse for the all-star small groups. Brief glimpses of London-based Caribbean musicians like Dave Wilkins and Bertie King give way to New York line-ups including Bobby Hackett, Benny Carter, Coleman Hawkins and Leo Watson.

Buddy Featherstonhaugh

Clarinet, tenor and baritone saxophones.

b. Paris, 4 Oct 1909; d. London, 12 July 1976.

Buddy (Rupert Edward Lee) Featherstonhaugh came to prominence as a tenor saxophonist with Spike Hughes's British orchestra (1930–32), toured with Louis Armstrong in Britain (1932) and in 1935 recorded for Decca with his own band, the Cosmopolitans (also featuring Harry Hayes and Alan Ferguson). Featherstonhaugh also recorded for Benny Carter in Britain (1936–7) and remained busy until he joined the RAF, leading a group which included trombonist Don McCaffer, and subsequently took over from Harry Parry on the BBC's *Radio Rhythm Club* half-hour show. This group recorded extensively for HMV but after the war Featherstonhaugh slipped from public attention. He re-emerged in 1956 (on baritone) for eight bop recordings (also featuring the young Kenny Wheeler and Bobby Wellins) but had retired from jazz by the 1960s. [DF]

Morey Feld

Drums.

b. Cleveland, Ohio, 15 Aug 1915; d. 28 March 1971.

Morey Feld belongs with Cliff Leeman, Nick Fatool and Buzzy Drootin in the echelons of great Dixieland drummers. From a grounding in 1936 with Ben Pollack – the university of so many later great names – he worked on and up with Joe Haymes, the Summa Cum Laude band (1940), Benny Goodman (1943–5), Eddie Condon (1946 and after), Billy Butterfield, Peanuts Hucko, Bobby Hackett, and as a staffman for ABC (1955–60). In the 1960s he returned to Goodman, to Condon's, led his own bands and opened a drum school before moving in 1968 to Denver, where he joined Peanuts Hucko's quintet and was founder drummer with the World's Greatest Jazz Band. He died in a fire at his home. [DF]

Mark Feldman

Violin.

b. Chicago, 17 July 1955.

Feldman began playing violin at the age of nine, studied music with George Swigart, Adia Ghertovici, pianist Irwin Helfer and saxophonist Joe Daley. Rather than go to college at eighteen, he began to work the northside Chicago bar scene. He moved to Nashville in 1980, where he became immersed in the studio scene, appearing on more than two hundred records of country and western and contemporary Christian music (including Jimmy Swaggart); he played extensively with Loretta Lynn, Ray Price and George Strait. Feldman studied informally with guitarist Jimmy Raney in the early 1980s and twice attended Abersold jazz clinics in Louisville (1982–3), and a clinic in Banff (1985).

The following year, he relocated to New York, where he has made over one hundred records as a sideman in a variety of contexts, and become part of the downtown scene. He made a vital contribution to the string ensembles of John Zorn's sprawling *Masada* catalogue, and has also recorded with Tim Berne, Lee Konitz, Ray Anderson, Anthony Davis, Ned Rothenberg and Dave Douglas. Indeed, Feldman was spotlit particularly well as a member of Douglas's string-oriented group on their three records, *Parallel Worlds* (1993; Soul Note), *Five* (1996) and *Convergence* (1998). His clean, Webern-like notes on *Music For Violin And Piano* (1999) – duets with pianist Sylvie Courvoisier, both improvised and composed – are lucent and alert. [JC]

Music For Violin Alone (1995; Tzadik). Feldman claims this solo record as his "debut recording as a leader". It is a perfect powerhouse showcase for his dazzling playing – swooping, darting, double-stopping like nobody's business, mixing adrenaline-primed improvising adventure, impeccable wood tone and a classical sureness of pitch.

Victor Feldman

Vibraharp, drums, percussion.

b. London, 7 April 1934; d. Los Angeles, 12 May 1987.

One of quite a long list of British keyboard players who made their home in the USA, Feldman emigrated in order to join Woody Herman in 1955. Previously the child prodigy of a highly musical family (playing professionally from the age of seven), he had been a significant contributor to the UK scene, working with Ted Heath and Ronnie Scott in 1954–5. Feldman settled in Los Angeles in 1957 and, with a few breaks such as six months with Cannonball Adderley in 1960–61, he specialized in session work as a miscellaneous percussionist. His tune "Seven Steps To Heaven" (recorded by Miles Davis) has become a standard. [BP]

Merry Olde Soul (1960–61; Riverside/OJC). With four tracks featuring vibes (backed by Hank Jones) and the balance with Feldman's piano, a session dating from his period of maximum visibility and maximum finesse.

Lennie Felix

Piano.

b. London, 16 Aug 1920; d. 20 Dec 1980.

Lennie Felix made his debut playing in pre-war nightclubs and after 1945 quickly established a reputation as a piano entertainer. He was a devotee of Fats Waller (he looked like him and in later years cultivated his mannerisms, if not his girth), but his albums of the 1950s showed that his influences also included great soloists such as Art Tatum, Earl Hines and Teddy Wilson. He preferred playing in trios, and was less commonly to be found in bands: one exception was Nat Gonella's 1960 Armstrong-style group, in which Felix played the Hines role with great gusto and fine technique. In the 1960s and 1970s he continued to work solo, playing London clubs as well as travelling abroad for long periods to work in Denmark, Germany and elsewhere; he also toured England with Ruby Braff, one occasion on which Felix's accompanying style was swiftly at odds with his guest. He died from injuries sustained when he was knocked down by a speeding car outside the 606 Club in Fulham, London. [DF]

Maynard Ferguson

Trumpet, flugelhorn, baritone horn, valve-trombone, bandleader.

b. Montreal, 4 May 1928.

Ferguson studied at the French Conservatory of Music in Montreal, then came to international notice with the Stan Kenton band, which featured him prominently, from 1950–53. Ferguson had brilliant technical abilities and specialized in screaming high notes which he seemed to be able to produce and sustain at will; his prowess in the upper register was unequalled at that time. From 1953–6 he freelanced in Los Angeles and in 1957 began leading big bands, continuing to do so until 1965 when economics forced him to work with a sextet. In the later 1960s he moved to the UK, working with an Anglo-American big band which toured the USA in 1971, and also played in continental Europe. He moved back to the USA in the early 1970s, again leading big bands and featuring a programme of current jazz-rock and pop hits as well as some updated material from his past. Ferguson's music often has more to do with athletics than aesthetics, and his bands play brash, brassy, high-energy music. But it is astonishing that he has managed to sustain his youthful ebullience and the supreme strength needed for such high-register work into middle (and even older) age. There are signs now that he is beginning to take things more easily, but he continues to lead his young Big Bop Nouveau Band. Ferguson has been intermittently active in education, conducting instrumental clinics and group workshops. In sympathetic company, he is also capable of fine and sensitive solo work. [IC]

The Birdland Dreamband (1956; Bluebird). Ferguson was in the heyday of his youth and reputation when this was recorded, and his Dreamband was awash with talent, including Hank Jones, Milt Hinton, Budd Johnson and Herb Geller. The arrangements, by some of the most gifted writers of the time – Johnny Mandel, Bob Brookmeyer and Jimmy Giuffre among others – are superb.

Two's Company (1961; Fresh Sound). Ferguson plays with considerable sensitivity and invention here, with a band including Joe Farrell and Jaki Byard, and the very fine singer Chris Connor.

Maynard Ferguson '93 Footpath Café (1992; Hot Shot). This is a live recording of Ferguson's Big Bop Nouveau Band, a young outfit that supplies the volcanic energy Ferguson seems to need, though he often turns to the less demanding and more poetic flugelhorn.

Mongezi Feza

Trumpet, flute.

b. Queenstown, South Africa, 1945; d. London, 14 Dec 1975.

Feza got his first trumpet at the age of eight, and at sixteen was already playing with groups. In 1962 he joined Chris McGregor's Blue Notes, which in 1963 won the Best Group Award at South Africa's national jazz festival. In 1965 they left for Europe and played in France and Switzerland before settling in Britain. Feza continued working with McGregor's sextet and his larger group, the

JAK KILBY

Mongezi Feza with Harry Miller on bass

Brotherhood of Breath, and also with Dudu Pukwana's groups Spear and Assagai and Keith Tippett's Centipede. In 1972 he worked in Denmark with bassist Johnny Dyani and Turkish percussionist Okay Temiz. With McGregor and others he toured and played festivals throughout the UK and Europe. He recorded with the Blue Notes, the Brotherhood of Breath, Robert Wyatt and Dudu Pukwana. Mongezi was a dynamic soloist, and his style fused elements from kwela, bebop and free jazz into a highly individual synthesis. His premature death deprived the European scene of one of its most adventurous and benign musicians. [IC]

➤➤ **Brotherhood of Breath** *(Live At Willisau).*

Kansas Fields

Drums.

b. Chapman, Kansas, 5 Dec 1915; d. May 1995.

One of the best and most versatile jazz drummers, Fields worked early on with Eddie Mullins, Horace Henderson and others, before joining Roy Eldridge at the Capitol Lounge (1940–41), and then Ella Fitzgerald – who had taken over Chick Webb's orchestra. He also worked with Benny Carter, Edgar Hayes and Charlie Barnet before a spell in the US Merchant Marine, during which time he doubled concerts with Eddie Condon and club work at Minton's, bridging the stylistic gap between Dixieland and Bop as easily as Dave Tough or Sid Catlett. After the war, Fields continued his all-purpose career with artists as diverse as Dizzy Gillespie and Mezz Mezzrow, and in 1953 (following a French tour with Mezzrow) settled in Paris working and recording with Sidney Bechet, Buck Clayton, Teddy Buckner, Benny Waters and others. From 1965 he moved back to Chicago to work and record, notably with Gillespie, and to play for studio sessions. In his later years the work began to dry up, and at the time of his death he was employed as doorman in an apartment building. [DF]

➤➤ **Sidney Bechet And Teddy Buckner** *(Parisian Encounter).*

Firehouse Five Plus Two

A Los Angeles-based revivalist band which enjoyed great popularity from the late 1940s through to the 1960s, the Firehouse Five Plus Two consisted of a team of cartoon animators from the Disney Film studios, led by trombonist Ward Kimball, a situation maintained throughout their twenty-year career on records. Decked out in firefighters' uniforms and surrounded by sirens, bells and a firetruck, the band combined hard-driving two-beat Dixieland with regular infusions of vaudeville-style comedy. A residency at the Mocambo Club on Sunset Strip in 1949, plus network radio on Bing Crosby's *Chesterfield Programme* (1950) and TV exposure, helped establish the group, and their first recordings for Good Time Jazz in May 1949 were followed by a string of successful LPs. Throughout their semi-professional career, the Firehouse Five Plus Two played dances, parades, parties, concerts and clubs, and their music is now regularly re-created by teams of younger US firefighters. [DF]

⦿ **Goes South** (1954–6; Good Time Jazz). One of the original FF+2 albums and a definitive portrait of this lighthearted but influential troupe of West Coast revivalists.

⦿ **Sixteen Dixieland Favourites** (1959–69; Good Time Jazz). Exactly what the title suggests, full of what Louis Armstrong would have called "very good spirit".

⦿ **At Disneyland Live** (1962; Good Time Jazz). The FF+2 sounded even more unbuttoned live than they did on record; here they are on home territory, knocking 'em dead.

Clare Fischer

Piano, organ, arranger.

b. Durand, Michigan, 22 Oct 1928.

Fischer studied music at Michigan State University. He moved to Los Angeles in 1957, wrote arrangements and was accompanist for the Hi-Los vocal group in the late 1950s. He was also the arranger/conductor for albums by Donald Byrd in 1957 (though the former was not released until 1980) and Dizzy Gillespie in 1960. He led his own occasional big band in the 1960s but, as well as freelance arranging for everybody from Earl Klugh to Prince, he is better known as a keyboard player specializing in trio and solo work. Fischer has taken a particularly close interest in Brazilian music, living there and studying Portuguese, and one of his bossa nova originals, "Pensativa", has become something of a standard. His playing is a thoughtful but unstilted extension of methods associated with Lennie Tristano and Bill Evans. [BP]

⦿ **Just Me** (1995; Concord). Fischer's first solo piano recording in a long time, and the only one easily available, doesn't disappoint. There are free-ranging investigations of standards and three delighfully rhythmic originals, including a thoughtful return visit to "Pensativa".

Ella Fitzgerald

Vocals.

b. Newport News, Virginia, 25 April 1917; d. 15 June 1996.

In 1934, as a dare, Ella Fitzgerald sang "Judy" on an amateur night at Harlem's Apollo Theater; her ingenuous charm, crystal-clear diction and translucent voice (Connee Boswell was her primary influence) won her $25, and a job with Tiny Bradshaw's band immediately followed, after an audition at Harlem's Opera House. Soon after, Benny Carter and comedian Bardu Ali, who fronted Chick Webb's band, brought her to the attention of Webb, who let her sing on a one-nighter at Yale University, then for a week at the Savoy Ballroom, and finally

Ella Fitzgerald

hired her permanently to sing with his orchestra (he also became her guardian after her mother died). In 1938, while Webb was in hospital, Ella and arranger Van Alexander dressed up a nursery-rhyme routine, "A-tisket, A-tasket", which then became Webb's biggest hit. As a result he built his show around her, and when Webb died in 1939 she took over his band for two years before going solo. For the next 45 years she was to establish a queenly reputation as America's finest female interpreter of popular song.

From 1948, as a part of Norman Granz's organization, she became almost as well known for her improvisatory powers (on high-speed scat extravaganzas such as "Lady Be Good" and "Flying Home") as for her interpretations of great songs, which were always guaranteed to win the approval of their composers. Through the 1950s, she recorded for a variety of labels and teamed regularly with Louis Armstrong and others for great duets, but her greatest triumphs were reserved for Granz; she often toured with him, and from the late 1950s he financed her seminal "songbook" albums, dedicated to the works of George Gershwin, Harold Arlen, Johnny Mercer, Jerome Kern, Cole Porter, Irving Berlin and Duke Ellington. As Benny Green said later, Ella's "perfect intonation, natural ear for harmony, vast vocal range and purity of tone helped to make Ella's versions of these beautifully witty, gay, sad, lovingly wrought songs the definitive versions".

In the 1960s Ella continued to tour festivals, jazz rooms and concert halls internationally, her voice broadening with the years and her act evolving into a finely honed cabaret formula featuring longterm accompanists such as Tommy Flanagan, Keter Betts and Joe Pass. By the 1980s her voice had acquired a rough edge which, though it indicated the inevitable passage of time, lent a new profundity to much of what she did – with the younger, insouciant Fitzgerald, there was sometimes the feeling that all was just a little too right with the world. In autumn 1986 she was admitted to intensive care for heart trouble, but soon returned to performing (in 1990 she starred in a London concert with the Count Basie orchestra); however, by the mid-1990s she was confined to a wheelchair. [DF]

⊙ **The Complete Recordings 1935–39** (Affinity). A three-CD set of Ella's recordings from her first with Chick Webb, through sessions with Teddy Wilson, Benny Goodman, Webb again, the Mills Brothers and her own Savoy Eight featuring trumpeter Taft Jordan. A perfect microcosm of the swing era.

⊙ **The Complete Songbooks** (1956–64; Verve). Probably Fitzgerald's finest work of all, the Granz "songbooks" featuring all the greatest American composers are required listening. Also available separately (fortunately!) the sets within this mighty box represent dual microcosms: of Fitzgerald and American popular music. Whether they appeal to jazz ears is incidental, but they should.

⊙ **For The Love Of Ella** (1956–88; Polygram). A tasty two-CD compilation, including titles with JATP, Marty Paich, Louis Armstrong, Duke Ellington's orchestra, Nelson Riddle and Count Basie. One disc is up-tempo tunes; the second ballads.

⊙ **At The Opera House** (1957; Verve). Ella at her peak, in a quartet session with Oscar Peterson and two scat *tours de force* with the full JATP team – "Oh Lady Be Good" and "Stompin' At The Savoy", which Norman Granz calls "the most incredible brilliant jazz vocal performance ever put to wax".

⊙ **Ella And Basie** (1963; Verve). Another summit conference, with arrangements by Quincy Jones. Ella shines on "Shiny Stockings" (her lyrics), and there are two excellent small-group titles with Joe Newman, Urbie Green and Frank Foster – "Them There Eyes" and "Dream A Little Dream Of Me".

⊙ **These Are The Blues** (1963; Verve). Ten superb blues tracks, featuring a great rhythm-section (Wild Bill Davis, Herb Ellis, Ray Brown and Gus Johnson) plus Roy Eldridge at his best on trumpet.

⊙ **Take Love Easy** (1973; Pablo). Later Ella, occasionally rusty, but still in first-class form, duetting with Joe Pass.

David Fiuczynski

Guitar.

b. Newark, New Jersey, 5 March 1964.

David grew up in Germany before returning to the US to attend the New England Conservatory, where he was taught by guitarist Mick Goodrick and composer-pianist George Russell. He toured with the latter's band in 1989 and then worked with several other established leaders such as Muhal Richard Abrams and Ronald Shannon Jackson. His debut album was a collaboration with avant-garde keyboard player John Medeski entitled *Lunar Crush* (1994). Fiuczynski's long-running and charmingly named band, Screaming Headless Torsos, have made several albums and in 1998 he formed his own label, FuzeLicious Morsels. As well as playing on the first two albums of Me'Shell NdegéOcello, he has performed with a host of acoustic and electric musicians, from Branford Marsalis and John Zorn to Victor Bailey and Vernon Reid. Based in Massachusetts, Fiuczynski is a professor at Berklee College and has taught privately since the early 1990s. [BP]

Screaming Headless Torsos

⊙ **Screaming Headless Torsos** (1995; FuzeLicious Morsels). Originally issued by Warner and now re-released on Fiuczynski's own label, the debut of his best-known group placed the leader's abundant technical ability in a heavy rock context.

David Fiuczynski

⊙ **Kif** (2002; FuzeLicious Morsels). With a line-up including cellist Rufus Cappadocia and saxist Matt Darriau, this "Arabo-funk-jazz group" blends Eastern textures with Western grooves.

➤➤ **Ronald Shannon Jackson** *(Raven Roc).*

Tommy Flanagan

Piano.

b. Detroit, Michigan, 16 March 1930; d. 16 Nov 2001.

Flanagan played clarinet from the age of six, switching to the piano at eleven, and his work as a teenager in Detroit – alongside such players as Kenny Burrell and Thad Jones – quickly established his reputation as a sensitive and stimulating accompanist. His move to New York in 1956, simultaneously with Burrell, led to recordings and live appearances with Jones, J.J. Johnson, Miles Davis (*Collectors' Items*), Sonny Rollins, John Coltrane and Coleman Hawkins. For a long time Flanagan's skill in backing soloists involved total immersion in servicing singers, notably Ella Fitzgerald from 1963–5 and 1968–78 and Tony Bennett. From the mid-1970s, however, he began a new career as an independent trio leader and soloist, producing many fine albums and notable partnerships with George Mraz and, in the 1990s, with drummer Lewis Nash. His achievements were recognized by the award of Denmark's Jazzpar Prize in 1993. Flanagan's surprisingly delicate touch combined with his ever-present rhythmic resilience to create a uniquely refined approach to bebop piano. [BP]

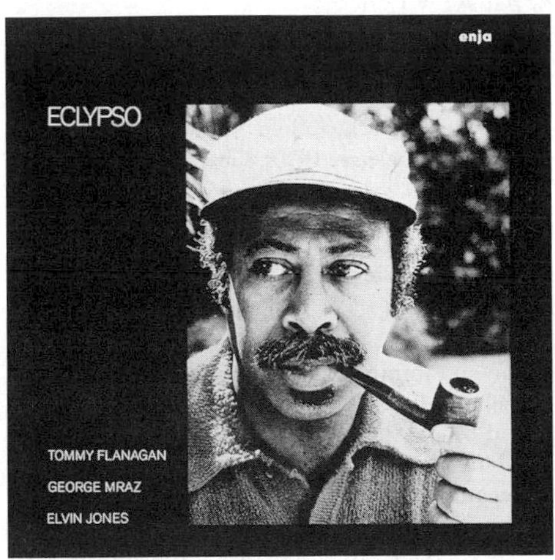

enja
ECLYPSO
TOMMY FLANAGAN
GEORGE MRAZ
ELVIN JONES

⊙ **Eclypso** (1977; Enja). Backed by George Mraz and former Detroit companion Elvin Jones, a mix of obscure bebop tunes (by Dameron and Denzil Best) and extremely well-known ones (by Parker and Rollins) is capped by Flanagan's own title track.

➤➤ **John Coltrane** *(Giant Steps);* **Sonny Rollins** *(Saxophone Colossus).*

Phil Flanigan

Bass, cello.

b. Geneva, New York, 28 June 1956.

Flanigan began on piano, trombone and guitar before switching to bass to study at the Eastman School of Music from 1972–4, and joined Scott Hamilton in 1976 as a founder member of the tenorist's quintet in Providence, Rhode Island. He also worked with Bob Wilber (1977–81) and Benny Goodman (1977–83), including a Carnegie Hall concert in 1982 with Lionel Hampton and Teddy Wilson. During the 1980s and in the early 1990s

Flanigan worked with Warren Vaché, John Bunch, Louis Bellson and Ira Sullivan. In a varied career, he has also worked and recorded with Roy Eldridge, Ruby Braff, Rosemary Clooney, Helen Humes and Maxine Sullivan, with whom he recorded five albums. A exponent of the classic role of bass in jazz, Flanigan's influences include Oscar Pettiford, Ray Brown and Scott LaFaro, and he is at home in all the established contexts of jazz from traditional to bebop and beyond. [DF]

Scott Hamilton and Warren Vaché

With Scott's Band In New York (1978; Concord). An early classic of the New York swing revival of the I970s, this collection includes Flanigan, whose warm-toned, perfectly accurate bass is heard on nine tracks including a typically relaxed solo on "You're Getting To Be A Habit With Me".

Bela Fleck

Banjo.

b. New York, 7 July 1958.

Inspired by the film *Deliverance*, with its famous "Duelling Banjos" sequence, to take up the instrument, Bela Fleck joined the bluegrass group Spectrum in the early 1970s, subsequently moving to Nashville in 1981 and becoming a first-call session musician there. He spent eight years with New Grass Revival, producing an album, *Deviation*, in 1984, before forming the Flecktones, with harmonica player Howard Levy, bassist Victor Wooten and Roy Wooten on drumitar (a guitar wired to an electric drum) and immediately hitting pay dirt with their first album, *Bela Fleck And The Flecktones*, swiftly followed by 1992's *Flight Of The Cosmic Hippo* and *UFO TOFU* the following year. Fleck has appeared on recordings by everyone from Bruce Hornsby and the Range, through Nanci Griffith and the Nashville Bluegrass Band, to V.M. Bhatt, the mohan vina player whose Tabula Rasa, featuring Fleck, was Grammy-nominated in 1996. A player as at home in jazz settings as in bluegrass, he guested on Ginger Baker's 1996 Atlantic album *Falling Off The Roof*, contributing characteristically cogent banjo to an unusual version of "Au Privave", though the majority of his output resides in the progressive country field. [CP/CI]

Carl Fontana

Trombone.

b. Monroe, Louisiana, 18 July 1928; d. 9 Oct 2003.

One of the great jazz trombonists, Fontana came to prominence in Woody Herman's band (1952–3) and after work with Lionel Hampton and Hal MacIntyre joined Stan Kenton, where his solo on "Intermission Riff" caused a sensation. In 1956 he joined Kai Winding's four-trombone band, then for much of the 1960s worked out of Las Vegas in house bands and studios. By the end of the decade Fontana was playing for Dick Gibson's Jazz Parties in Denver, and after the death of Cutty Cutshall he joined Gibson's project, The World's Greatest Jazz Band, in which his faultless technique and challenging creativity found perfect expression. In the mid-70s a bandleading project with drummer Jake Hanna further enhanced his reputation, and in the 1990s – like Urbie Green – he joined the echelon of senior trombonists who just kept on performing superbly. [DF]

Hanna-Fontana Band Live At Concord (1975; Concord). Something of a mainstream classic, this album has Fontana at peak form along with Bill Berry and Plas Johnson in the frontline, and a rhythm-section with Dave McKenna and Herb Ellis. Grandmasters of swing at full power.

Ricky Ford

Tenor saxophone.

b. Boston, Massachusetts, 4 March 1954.

Ford studied locally at the New England Conservatory, making his recording debut with Gunther Schuller in 1974 and subsequently recording for his tutors Jaki Byard and Ran Blake. His first touring job was with Mercer Ellington from 1974–6. He was a member of the Charles Mingus quintet in 1976–7, until the leader's illness, and then worked with the Dannie Richmond quintet from 1978–81. He also played with, and wrote arrangements for, the Lionel Hampton big band in 1981 and with Mingus Dynasty in 1982, including two European tours. He has made several albums and done gigs with his own groups, and made European appearances under his own name in 1982 and 1985, and with Abdullah Ibrahim's group Ekaya in 1986. Ford's playing, already highly competent by the time of his Ellington stint, was considerably stretched while with Mingus. Now he has an all-embracing style which mixes modal jazz and bebop but also enabled him to stand alongside Illinois Jacquet and Arnett Cobb in the 1981 Hampton band. Described by Ran Blake as "a marvellous player", Ford's increasing maturity has not yet brought him the fame that he deserves. [BP]

Ebony Rhapsody (1990; Candid). A live quartet date (with veterans Jaki Byard and Milt Hinton) extends Ford in several directions, including the updating of the title track and the equally venerable "Broadway".

Reginald Foresythe

Composer, arranger, piano.

b. London, 28 May 1907; d. 28 Dec 1958.

Son of a British father and West Indian mother, Foresythe played piano in American nightclubs until 1930, when he met Earl Hines in Chicago. Hines took Foresythe under his wing and into his home, wrote "Deep Forest" with him and introduced him to Paul Whiteman, who signed him to play extended classical pieces (*Rhapsody In Blue* included) as well as his own quirkily titled creations, such as "Dodging A Divorcee" and "Serenade To A Wealthy Widow". Foresythe carried a cane and an Eton accent with equal aplomb, and Charlie Carpenter (Hines's manager) remembers his outburst when ordered to dine in the kitchens of Chicago's College Inn: "How dare you have the audacity to call me a negro! Must I show you my passport? I'm an Englishman, and I'll go straight to the embassy and cause this place more trouble than you can stand!" By 1933 Foresythe was regularly in London as well as New York (he returned to Whiteman for a second spell in 1934) and a year later was a British fixture, bandleading at the 400 Club and making appearances in British films until the war, when he joined the RAF as an intelligence officer. After the war he worked in British nightclubs, his life complicated by alcoholism and the prevailing attitudes towards homosexuality. [DF]

Michael Formanek

Double bass.

b. San Francisco, 7 May 1958.

Formanek studied bass privately in San Francisco and New York. His first professional engagement, in 1974, was in San Francisco with saxophonist Norman Williams. He then worked with Eddie Henderson, Joe Henderson, Tony Williams and Dave Liebman. In 1978 he moved to New York, working with Tom Harrell, Herbie Mann, Chet Baker, Bob Moses and Bill Connors. From February 1980 to January 1981 he recorded and performed as soloist and accompanist with the Media Band at West German Radio in Cologne. In 1982 he joined Gallery, which included Paul McCandless, David Darling, David Samuels and Michael DiPasqua. In the past fifteen years, Formanek has performed his music with a wide range of ensembles. His band Wide Open Spaces played at the Leverkusener Jazztage in Germany, the Espoo Festival in Finland, Lincoln Center Out-Of-Doors in New York, and many clubs and concert halls in the USA and Europe. He also works with Tim Berne's Bloodcount, and a new cooperative trio Relativity, with Peter Erskine and Marty Ehrlich, plus the Tim Berne/Michael Formanek duo. Most recently he popped up on Elvis Costello's 2003 album, *North*. [IC]

⦿ **Extended Animation** (1991; Enja). Formanek has developed into an extraordinarily resourceful composer, and all eight pieces here are by him. The broken rhythms, angularity and often wide interval leaps of the compositions relate to avant-garde classical music, and that is reflected in the solos. The quintet comprises Tim Berne (alto and baritone saxophones), Mark Feldman (violin), Wayne Krantz (guitar) and drummer Jeff Hirshfield – Formanek and Hirshfield work superbly together.

⦿ **Loose Cannon** (1992; Soul Note). Krantz and Feldman are omitted here and the partnership of Formanek and Hirshfield comes into sharp relief, with saxophonist Berne really getting into his stride. Berne also composed five of the eight pieces.

⦿ **Nature Of The Beast** (1996; Enja). One of Formanek's finest albums with a line-up of trumpeter Dave Douglas, trombonist Steve Swell, alto saxophonist Tim Berne, tenor saxophonist Tony Malaby, clarinettist Chris Speed and drummer Jim Black. The reeds play on just four of the eight tracks, but this is contemporary 1990s jazz at its most focused and intense. Dave Douglas's playing illuminates and at times dazzles, and Formanek's writing grows and deepens constantly.

⦿ **Am I Bothering You?** (1997; Screwgun). Formanek's first-ever solo bass album reveals a virtuoso in essentially playful mood. We hear the slapping of strings, the intakes of breath, and the lavish bass tone both pizzicato and arco. He also sometimes plays high fast scratchy rhythms below the bridge. The eighth piece is all bowed and comically speech-like with high shrieks and bowed chords so vocal that they recall Mingus's bass conversations with Eric Dolphy's alto.

➤➤ **Jane Ira Bloom** *(Art And Aviation).*

Helen Forrest

Vocals.

b. Atlantic City, New Jersey, 12 April 1918; d. 11 July 1999.

Perhaps the most stylish of the white swing-era singers, Helen Forrest began her high-profile career with Artie Shaw in 1938, replacing Billie Holiday. From 1939–41 she was with Benny Goodman, then partnered Harry James, with whom she created major hits like "I've Heard That Song Before" and "I Had The Craziest Dream". After leaving James in 1943 she teamed with her co-singer in James's organization, Dick Haymes, for radio and a series of hit recordings. From the 1950s Forrest appeared less often, but returned to tour with the re-formed Tommy Dorsey Orchestra (1961–2) and as recently as 1983 released an album (*Now And Forever*), which featured Hank Jones, Frank Wess and young trumpeter Glenn Zottola. Her autobiography, *I Had The Craziest Dream* (1982), though now out of print, is well worth searching for. [DF]

Jimmy Forrest

Tenor saxophone.

b. St Louis, Missouri, 24 Jan 1920; d. 26 Aug 1980.

Forrest worked with several St Louis bands, such as that of Fate Marable, as a teenager, and then played with Jay McShann in 1941–2, including a visit to New York. He played in the Andy Kirk band from 1943–7, and with Duke Ellington in 1949–50. In the 1950s he led his own group in St Louis, and then worked with the Harry Edison quintet. After returning to St Louis for several years, he joined Count Basie, staying from 1973–8, and then appeared as a soloist (sometimes with Al Grey) until his death. Forrest was the first person to record the R&B standard "Night Train", which combines two Ellington tunes "That's The Blues Old Man" and "Happy-Go-Lucky Local". The style that made the number a hit used his typical "Southwestern tenor" tone to project lines full of blues and bop, which proved very adaptable to a number of different settings. [BP]

Most Much (1961; Prestige/OJC). What appears on the surface to be a straight tenor-and-rhythm date (with the then ubiquitous Ray Barretto) is salvaged by the meaty sound and melodic conviction of the leader.

Sonny Fortune

Alto and soprano saxophones, flute.
b. Philadelphia, 19 May 1939.

Having studied at Wurlitzer's and Granoff School of Music, Fortune began working locally in R&B groups. In 1967 he moved to New York where he spent ten weeks working with Elvin Jones. He then joined Mongo Santamaria in 1968, staying for two years. In 1970 he worked with singer Leon Thomas, then spent two years (1971–3) with McCoy Tyner. After a few months with Roy Brooks, he led his own group briefly, then played with Buddy Rich for five months in 1974. In August that year he joined Miles Davis, staying with him until midsummer 1975, when illness incapacitated Davis and he disbanded. He played on the Davis albums *Agharta* and *Pangaea*. Fortune has also played with George Benson, Roy Ayers, Oliver Nelson and Pharoah Sanders.

Fortune is a powerful soloist with a superb technique and plenty of creative stamina, but after recording a promising solo album, *Awakening*, for A&M in 1975, he seemed to half disappear from the scene, keeping a very low profile for some years. In general he seems to play better as a sideman than as leader, and in the later 1980s he began to appear again on other people's albums, and toured with Elvin Jones and Nat Adderley.

Coltrane has always been of key importance to Sonny Fortune, and in 2000 he released a mesmerizing album to make the point: *In The Spirit Of John Coltrane*. [IC]

Laying It Down (1989; Konnex). With the fine rhythm-section of Cecil McBee and Billy Hart, and pianist Kenny Barron, Fortune plays a quite conventional jazz set, though with slight ethnic/African overtones in his playing.

Monk's Mood (1993; Konnex). This is another quartet album with bassist David Williams, Joe Chambers on drums and pianist Kirk Lightsey. The results are generally excellent.

➤➤ **Elvin Jones** *(When I Was At Aso-Mountain)*; **McCoy Tyner** *(Sahara)*.

Dudley Fosdick

Mellophone.
b. Liberty, Indiana, 1902; d. 27 June 1957.

Although the mellophone has made isolated appearances in jazz history – Don Elliott featured one, bands as different as Lew Stone's and Stan Kenton's used sections of them, and later Dixieland players such as Jack Coon doubled on one – Dudley Fosdick was the true "father of mellophone". He was a fine musician who worked in the 1920s with Red Nichols, Don Voorhees and Roger Wolfe Kahn, and recorded prolifically as a soloist with Nichols and others. From the early 1930s he combined studio work with a ten-year stay with Guy Lombardo's Royal Canadians, and by the mid-1950s was teaching full-time at Roerich Academy of Arts. [DF]

➤➤ **Red Nichols** *(Rhythm Of The Day)*.

Al Foster

Drums, tenor saxophone, piano, bass.
b. Richmond, Virginia, 18 Jan 1944.

Foster's family moved to New York when he was five. He had no formal lessons, but he learned from watching his uncle, drummer Ron Jefferson (his father also played drums). His first professional work was with Hugh Masekela in 1960, then with Ted Curson. He was with Illinois Jacquet from 1962–4, and Blue Mitchell and (briefly) Erskine Hawkins in 1964–5. In 1966 he played with Lou Donaldson, then with Kai Winding at the Playboy Club in New York, after which he spent five years with the Earl May quartet in a club called the Cellar. During that time he turned down offers to join Cannonball Adderley and Horace Silver because he did not wish to leave his family in order to tour. In 1972 Miles Davis heard the band in the Cellar, and that was the beginning of a long association. After playing on *On The Corner*, Foster stayed with the band, touring in the USA, Europe and Japan, until it broke up because of Davis's ill-health in 1975. From then until 1980, Foster led his own groups at the Cellar and worked with other people. When Davis resurfaced in 1980, Foster was soon back in the band, staying with it until early 1985. He was a pillar of strength during Davis's comeback and played on *We Want Miles*, *Star People* and *Decoy*. He understood the later music of Miles Davis perfectly and made an immense contribution to it. His rapport with Davis was such that the transitions from one piece to another in live performance always seemed to happen like magic.

Foster is a magnificent all-round drummer, capable of handling anything from bebop to free-form and jazz-rock. Since his time with Davis he has been in great demand as a sideman, touring and/or recording with several leading musicians including McCoy Tyner, Freddie Hubbard, Sonny Rollins and Michel Petrucciani. He also works with his own Al Foster Quartet. [IC]

➤➤ **Miles Davis** *(We Want Miles)*.

Frank Foster

Tenor and soprano saxophones, arranger.
b. Cincinnati, Ohio, 23 Sept 1928.

After studying at Wilberforce University, Foster played in Detroit with Wardell Gray, Elvin Jones and others in 1949. He followed army service by joining Count Basie, with whom he played and arranged from 1953–64. He then became a successful freelance writer, contributing to albums by Sarah Vaughan and Frank Sinatra, and has been involved in educational work in New York and elsewhere. As well as playing with Elvin Jones from 1970–72 and on later albums, and with the Thad Jones-Mel Lewis band in 1972 and 1975, he has led his own small groups and the Living Color and The Loud Minority big bands, visiting Europe and Japan several times. One of his own albums was recorded in Japan fronting the Jones-Lewis band. He also co-led a quintet with Frank Wess from 1983 and appeared in Europe as a member of the Jimmy Smith quintet in 1985. In mid-1986 he took over from Thad Jones as the leader of the Basie band for the next ten years. Since then he has revived The Loud Minority and led several small groups, including with Marlena Shaw in 1998.

As a writer, Foster has created a large body of work, and it is perhaps a pity (except financially) that he is always identified with one enormously popular standard, "Shiny Stockings". His solo work has been consistently excellent since his early days with Basie and an important 1954 session with Thelonious Monk (which featured "Locomotive", etc). At that period his tone and phrasing suggested a slightly harder-edged Wardell Gray, but from the early 1960s he has managed to incorporate the phraseology (and the facility) of John Coltrane without being dominated by it, which cannot be said of many players. [BP]

⊙ **Here Comes Frank Foster** (1954; Blue Note). Foster's 1954 rash of small-group recordings followed his discovery by Basie, and this quintet album under his own name (with Kenny Clarke and Basie trombonist Bennie Powell) is paired with the following week's session by George Wallington featuring Foster, Jimmy Cleveland and charts by Quincy Jones.

⊙ **Shiny Stockings** (1977–8; Denon). The part-time big band run by Foster before his decade running the ex-Basie band does two Basie remakes (including Foster's famous title track) and his arrangement of the traditional "Hills Of The North Rejoice", with Charli Persip on drums.

➤➤ **Julius Watkins** *(Monk).*

Pops Foster

Bass, tuba.

b. McCall, Louisiana, 18 May 1892; d. 30 Oct 1969.

Pops (George Murphy) Foster was born on a sugar plantation 68 miles north of New Orleans and played cello in a family trio, with brother Willy on guitar and sister Elizabeth on mandolin. By 1905 he was specializing on double bass and from 1908 worked regularly with the Magnolia Band, King Oliver, Kid Ory, Jack Carey and Armand J. Piron as well as on riverboats. By 1918 he was regularly with Fate Marable's Streckfus showband and soon was working upriver in St Louis with Charlie Creath and Ed Allen's Whispering Gold Band (with Allen he played tuba to combat the fashionable three-saxophone frontline). Foster was busy all through the 1920s with Kid Ory and others, moved to New York to join King Oliver in 1928 and one year later joined Luis Russell's New Orleans-based orchestra for eleven years (backing Louis Armstrong from 1935). In the 1940s he was reduced to subway portering, but with the jazz revival he moved back into the spotlight to work with Sidney Bechet and Art Hodes, for Rudi Blesh's influential *This Is Jazz* programme, and then (after a visit to Nice with Mezz Mezzrow) for Bob Wilber. Thereafter Foster played in New York and at the Hangover in San Francisco (1956–61), where Earl Hines showed him some new approaches to bass. For his last few years, however, Foster (like Wellman Braud) was the emblem of good old New Orleans slap bass, travelling from his California home to tour America and Europe. [DF]

➤➤ **Luis Russell** *(Savoy Shout).*

Pete Fountain

Clarinet, saxophones.

b. New Orleans, 3 July 1930.

Fountain began in his home town in the mid-1940s with Monk Hazel's band, the Junior Dixieland Band, Phil Zito and others, before working with the Basin Street Six. His international success began in 1957 when he teamed up with Lawrence Welk for live appearances, records and a networked TV series for ABC which featured him in a Dixieland group drawn from Welk's band. The contract with Welk landed him a prestigious recording deal with Coral which lasted through the 1960s; his club, Pete's Place at 231 Bourbon Street, opened at the same period. Throughout the 1960s Fountain was a familiar figure on American TV and radio, a clarinet counterpart to New Orleans's newest trumpet king Al Hirt, with whom he worked frequently. In the 1970s he was headlining at his own club (alternating with two months a year at Las Vegas), appearing on TV specials with such superstars as Bing Crosby, Bob Hope and Johnny Carson, and living in New Orleans's plush Garden district. Because some jazz critics regard commercial success as unforgivable, Fountain is often ignored. But he was a peach-toned clarinettist, the musical heir of such artists as Irving Fazola and Matty Matlock. "Never mind what people say about him", said Wild Bill Davison, "he's a fine clarinettist, fine tone, lovely ideas – and he can really play the blues when the mood takes him." *A Closer Walk: The Pete Fountain Story*, by Pete Fountain and Bill Neely, was published in 1972. [DF]

⊙ **Do You Know What It Means To Miss New Orleans** (1959–65; GRP). A valuable representation of Fountain's Fazola-esque gifts in a variety of settings from quartet to big band. He is outstanding amid superb support, which includes welcome stars such as Charlie Teagarden, Eddie Miller and his longtime colleague, vibraharpist Godfrey Hirsch.

Four Freshmen

The founder members of the Four Freshmen were Don Barbour (guitar/vocals) and younger brother Ross (vocals/trumpet) who in 1947, while they were freshmen at the Arthur Jordan Conservatory in Indianapolis, teamed with Hal Kratsch and Marvin Pruitt to form Hal's Harmonizers, a barbershop quartet which ran parallel with their more jazz-influenced project, The Toppers. Soon after, lead singer Pruitt was replaced by the Barbours' cousin Bob Flanigan (trombone/bass/vocals), whose phenomenal vocal range would later be the Freshmen's trademark. Informal work with Woody Herman followed, then in 1950 the Freshmen were spotted by Stan Kenton in Dayton, Ohio, and a contract with Capitol Records was arranged. Their subsequent sides, featuring low sensuous unisons flowering into glorious jazz-based four-part harmony and topped by Flanigan's inimitable lead, earned them widening recognition and a film appearance in *Rich, Young And Pretty* opposite Jane Powell. In 1952 their contract with Capitol was dropped, then renewed after their hit "It's A Blue World"; the next year Hal Kratsch was replaced by Ken Errair, who gave way to Ken Albers in 1955, just after their second album, *Four Freshmen And Five Trombones*.

By this time the Freshmen were winning polls, appearing on TV and riding high internationally, and they continued to perform throughout the 1960s and 1970s with their longtime MD Dick Reynolds. The indomitable Flanigan led the Freshmen through various personnel changes until after a British tour in 1992, when he finally retired to be replaced by another phenomenal lead singer, Greg Stegeman. For many the Freshmen's combination of lush harmony, hard swing and high comedy make them the greatest vocal group of their era. [DF]

⊙ **The Four Freshmen** (1952–63; Capitol). A perceptively selected sampler of Freshmen tracks from their Capitol period, including major hits ("It's A Blue World", "We'll Be Together Again"), tracks from the *Five Trombones* album arranged by longtime colleague Pete Rugolo, and later beauties like Bobby Troup's "Their Hearts Were Full Of Spring".

⊙ **Five Trombones And Five Trumpets** (1956-7; EMI Capitol). The *Five Trombones* album (arranged by Pete Rugolo) is the Freshmen's best-remembered and set a pattern for three follow-ups including the excellent *Five Trumpets* (arranged by Dick Reynolds) which came next.

⊙ **Five Saxes And Five Guitars** (1957–9; EMI Capitol). *Five Saxes* is a brilliant development of the theme with arrangements by Rugolo/Reynolds again; tracks such as "Liza" and the extraordinary "Very Thought Of You" are outstanding. *Five Guitars* (arranged by Reynolds and Jack Marshall) is less dynamically varied but still of top quality.

⊙ **Voices In Love/Love Lost** (1958–9; EMI Capitol). Two more vintage Freshmen albums on one CD; *Voices In Love* is Ross Barbour's personal favourite and contains a yearning "Time Was", a poignant and immensely skilled "I'm Always Chasing Rainbows" and much more.

⊙ **Live At Butler University With Stan Kenton** (1972; Creative World Records). A perfect example of the Freshmen live: hip announcements from Ross Barbour, Bob Flanigan's amazing "lead-trumpet" of a voice, and fine collaborations with Kenton, including "After You" and Willie Maiden's glorious "Hymn To Her".

⊙ **Fresh** (1986; Ranwood). A later team of Freshmen, still headed by Flanigan, and this time dignifying pop material (including "Sailing" by Christopher Cross and "Do I Do" by Stevie Wonder) with treatments that often surpass the originals.

⊙ **Voices In Standards** (1993; Hindsight). An all-new team of Freshmen headed by Greg Stegeman with Lew Anderson's orchestra. Some of the humour is gone but the technical level is higher than ever and so is the selection of songs, which are all pre-rock.

⊙ **Golden Anniversary Celebration**. (Collectors' Choice Music). Spanning l951–69, this fascinating compilation includes the Freshmen's first single, "Then I'll Be Happy", multi-track adventures including "Tuxedo Junction", live tracks and later songs from their Liberty contract years.

Charlie Fowlkes

Baritone saxophone.

b. New York, 16 Feb 1916; d. 9 Feb 1980.

Fowlkes was best known as the baritone saxophonist with Count Basie's orchestra, which he joined in 1953 and stayed with until he died, except for the years 1969–75. Before then he had worked long stints with Tiny Bradshaw (1938–44), Lionel Hampton (1944–8) and Arnett Cobb (1948–51), and a rare chance to hear his pleasant soloing turns up on Buck Clayton's "Hucklebuck" and "Robbins' Nest". [DF]

➤➤ **Buck Clayton** *(Complete CBS Jam Sessions).*

Martin France

Drums.

b. Rainham, Kent, UK, 29 Feb 1964.

After learning the basics of drumming in Manchester, Martin France became a professional musician on leaving school at sixteen, and by the mid-1980s he had established himself on the London jazz scene. Work with Loose Tubes followed and led to subsequent work with the band's composer/keyboard player Django Bates in his groups Delightful Precipice and Human Chain. Tours and records with Scandinavian singer Sidsel Endresen and the Kenny Wheeler quartet (a stellar band also featuring pianist John Taylor and bassist Dave Holland alongside the Canadian trumpeter) are interspersed with France's regular work with bands such as Perfect Houseplants, guitarist Billy Jenkins's various aggregations and saxophonist Iain Ballamy's quartet. A drummer more given to subtle embellishment than to gutsy propulsion, France is an important part of the UK jazz scene, and has, with Django Bates, contributed to many cross-cultural projects, including film soundtracks, jazz theatre and recordings with classical orchestras. In the 1990s, France collaborated fruitfully with Julian Argüelles in the saxophonist's quartet and octet, and extended his playing with a move into midi, electronic and sequenced drums and percussion, heard to great effect on Django Bates's *Quiet Nights* (see below), and recently with his own group Spin Marvel, featuring Bates, Ballamy, guitarist John Parricelli and bassist Tim Harries. [CP/CI]

Django Bates

Music For The Third Policeman (1990; Ah Um). Eastern Jazz commission inspired by Flann O'Brien's novel and featuring many Loose Tubes alumni along with France.

Quiet Nights (1998; Screwgun). Eccentric, adventurous arrangements of everything from Kurt Weill's "Speak Low" to "Over The Rainbow", with France particularly impressive alongside bassist Michael Mondesir in a sensitive rhythm team.

Perfect Houseplants

Perfect Houseplants (1993; Ah Um). Wistful, gentle music from band spearheaded by Mark Lockheart's breathy saxophones and also featuring pianist/accordion player Huw Warren and bassist Dudley Phillips in the rhythm-section with France. Other albums from this excellent group include *Clec* (1995; EFZ) and *Modern Folk Songs* (1999; Linn), while their delicate collaboration with early music vocal ensemble the Orlando Consort now runs to two beautiful volumes: *Extempore* (1998; Linn) and *Extempore II* (2003; Harmonia Mundi).

➤➤ **Iain Ballamy** *(Balloon Man).*

Nic France

Drums, percussion, piano, steel pan.

b. Standon, Herts, UK, 30 March 1956.

A cathedral chorister from 1964–9, France took a degree in music at Cambridge College of Arts and Technology. From 1978–80 he worked with various groups in the Cambridge area, including the Trevor Kaye quartet, which won first prize at the San Sebastian jazz competition. He worked with Nucleus from 1980–82, touring in the UK and Europe and playing on the album *Awakening*. He took part in a television drum workshop with Billy Cobham. During the 1980s he also worked with Chucho Merchan's Macondo, which won the Greater London Arts Association Young Jazz Musicians' Award in 1981, and with Sunwind, which won the same award in 1983. Macondo also won the 1984 European Young Jazz Group competition, and played Detroit Kool jazz festival. In 1983 he played on the Sunwind album *The Sun Below*; in 1984 he was on the first eponymous Loose Tubes album; and in 1988 he played on saxophonist Tim Whitehead's album, *Decision*. He is an excellent teacher and has conducted many workshops. [IC]

Panama Francis

Drums.

b. Miami, Florida, 21 Dec 1918; d. 11 Nov 2001.

Panama (David Albert) Francis played for church revival meetings before joining saxophonist George Kelly's band the Cavaliers in Florida. Francis moved to New York in 1938 and a year later joined Roy Eldridge's band at the Arcadia Ballroom, and recorded with them; it was Eldridge who gave him his lifelong nickname, derived from his customary headgear. During the war he worked with Lucky Millinder's riff-proud band at the Savoy: "It was mostly the Savoy Sultans opposite us: only eight pieces but from the time they hit to the time they finished they were swinging!" Francis loved the Sultans (with their famous riveted Chinese cymbal) and after he left he formed his own version of the group, but had little success, and six years with Cab Calloway followed. From 1953, with the help of percussionist Fred Albright, he began a studio career (often gravitating to R&B – "until people forgot I ever played jazz"), doubled as house drummer at Central Plaza, and widened his connections to record with Sy Oliver, Perez Prado and Ray Charles, as well as working on TV for Ed Sullivan, Jackie Gleason and Dinah Shore, with whom he toured (1963–7). By 1972, back in New York, he worked with Sy Oliver and the NYJRC, and in 1974 reformed his own Savoy Sultans (including George Kelly), this time with huge success: they played for eight years at New York's Rainbow Room, headlined at festivals, topped polls, and made best-selling records. In later years Francis returned to Florida, led a New York quintet, took jobs at Disneyland and toured with the Statesmen of Jazz before his career slowed following diabetes complications in 1996. [DF]

Gettin' In The Groove! (1979; Black and Blue). A CD reissue of an essential Francis album, with arrangements by his fine tenorist George Kelly; well recorded, with fine playing and solos from all involved.

Parke Frankenfield

Multi-instrumentalist, vocals, arranger, bandleader.

b. Allentown, Pennsylvania, 6 July 1929.

Frankenfield led bands around Pennsylvania from 1950, including the Dixieland All Stars (featuring Ben Ventura on trumpet and Bob Levine on reeds) and a thirteen-piece big band which re-created the swing music of the 1930s and 1940s. As well as regularly appearing at major US jazz festivals and on riverboat cruises, Frankenfield promotes concerts and festivals, runs his own label and writes all his own arrangements. In 1985 his band affiliated with Bob Crosby to form the New Bob Cats, who appeared that year at Ronald Reagan's presidential inauguration; at the same period Frankenfield moved his base to Florida where he has played with Billy Butterfield, John Mince, Chubby Jackson and others. [DF]

Aretha Franklin

Vocals, piano.

b. Memphis, 25 March 1942.

Aretha Franklin's father, C.L. Franklin, was pastor of the New Bethel Baptist Church and a revered figure in gospel music. From early childhood she sang in choirs, and from fourteen was a featured soloist with her father's touring gospel troupe. At eighteen she changed to secular music, working at the Apollo Theater in Harlem on a show with Count Basie, Lambert, Hendricks & Ross, and Joe Williams, and recording her first album for Columbia in 1960. She received immediate acclaim in jazz circles and was frequently compared to Ray Charles and Dinah Washington. In the early 1960s she played mostly in clubs, but after signing with Atlantic Records in 1966 she had a hit single and album (*I Never Loved A Man The Way I Love You*) in 1967, which made her a superstar overnight. She toured major concert halls all over the USA and Europe, with tumultuous receptions everywhere. By the mid-1970s she had six gold LPs (each having sold a million) and has had fourteen hit singles. That same year, the Reverend Martin Luther King presented her with a special Southern Christian Leadership Council Award.

Her singing is a unique combination of the raw, direct and intensely personal style of the country blues, and the more polished, professional, outgoing style of the urban blues, and it is shot through with the exultation of her gospel roots. Her voice is a marvellously expressive instrument which can move instantly from a sweet murmur to jubilant shouts which dominate an ensemble. She projects extreme emotion, but it is always finely controlled, and she is a brilliant exponent of the gospel "call and response" technique, playing "preacher" to her vocal backing group's "congregation".

Talking of her versatility, Jon Hendricks has said: "Born and raised in the church and singing all her life in the church, when she sings what we call jazz, there's no difference ... she can do anything, she can sing anywhere, she can sing with anybody ... without anybody!" [IC]

⊙ **Columbia Jazz 1960-1965** (2003; Columbia). A fine CD that documents Franklin's first record deal; the set beautifully defines the moment when her name was made in the jazz community.

Jack Free

Trombone.

b. London, 28 March 1932.

One of Britain's best Dixieland trombonists, Free learnt trombone in the Boys' Brigade and started playing jazz at Leyton Youth Club (his contemporaries included clarinettist Dave Jones and cornettist Johnny Rowden). His first band was Harry Walton's Jazzmen (1954–60), after which he joined Freddy Randall (1962–5) and Dave Shepherd's Jazz Band (1965–70). Since then he has freelanced, working with various bands, with visiting Americans (including Billy Butterfield) and recording with Wild Bill Davison, Art Hodes and Yank Lawson. Free plays in the mould of Georg Brunis and fellow Condon alumni such as Cutty Cutshall, Lou McGarity and Jack Teagarden. [DF]

Bud Freeman

Tenor saxophone, clarinet, composer.

b. Chicago, 13 April 1906; d. 15 March 1991.

Bud (Lawrence) Freeman took up C melody saxophone in 1923 but by 1925 had changed to tenor. Somewhere in between Eddie Condon heard him playing "a saxophone green with corrosion [which] sounded the way it looked", but a year later Freeman's sound and technique had improved dramatically. For the next nine years he was working with a formidable list of leaders including Red Nichols, Meyer Davis, Roger Wolfe Kahn, Ben Pollack, Zez Confrey, Joe Venuti and Gene Kardos, and was regularly recording: focal points charting his progress are the 1927 "Sugar/Nobody's Sweetheart" by the McKenzie-Condon Chicagoans (their first recording), and a hit from 1933, "The Eel", based on a deceptive *trompe l'oreille* which he afterwards used frequently.

From Joe Haymes's influential band (also featuring young trumpet turk Pee Wee Erwin), Freeman joined Ray Noble at New York's Rainbow Room in July 1935, then moved on to Tommy Dorsey's great band in 1936, then to Benny Goodman for nine months in 1938. But he quickly tired of nine shows a night and left to front the immortal Summa Cum Laude orchestra for hotel work and a spot in *Swingin' The Dream*, a short-lived Broadway musical (also starring Louis Armstrong and Maxine Sullivan) based on Shakespeare's *A Midsummer Night's Dream*.

From 1940 came more freelancing, then two years in the army (he led service bands) and regular appearances at Eddie Condon's from 1945. Despite his frequent association with Condon on record, Freeman carefully forged a solo career of his own, recording prolifically under his own name, taking solo work in Peru and Chile and leading his own bands around New York and Chicago. (He even found time to study under Lennie Tristano.) By the early 1960s he was a globetrotter, travelling light as a soloist and creating best-selling albums. In 1968 he was a founder member of The World's Greatest Jazz Band and stayed for three years before solo work prevailed. In the 1970s he lived in London for a while before going back to Chicago to settle, and continued to play into his eighties, until failing health forced him to retire. He died in 1991, a matter of days after his old friend and founder Austin High colleague Jimmy McPartland.

Along with Coleman Hawkins, Bud Freeman was the most recognizable creator of a tenor-saxophone style back in the 1920s. Most remarkably, he presented an alternative to the monolith created by Hawkins, as Bix Beiderbecke did to Louis Armstrong, and he created the vocabulary for a generation of white pre-bop tenors. The music of Eddie Miller, Boomie Richman, Nick Caiazza and Tony Pastor bears testimony to an influence that is still being felt today. [DF]

Jazz Classics 1927–28 (Jazz Classics). Early Freeman titles, well rebalanced by Robert Parker, giving a fascinating insight into the evolution of Freeman's style from its primitive beginnings.

Bud Freeman 1928–38/1939–40 (Classics 781/811). The Classics series have got around to Freeman now, and his sidemen include an encyclopedic spectrum of swing stars from Bunny Berigan and Bobby Hackett to Gene Krupa and Dave Tough with everyone in between.

Swingin' With The Eel (1927–45; ASV). As usual, a near-definitive collection from ASV. Beginning with the McKenzie-Condon Chicagoans, Freeman's career is charted through central sides with his Windy City Seven and Trio, Tommy Dorsey, Condon, Spanier and the Summa Cum Laude Orchestra.

It's Got To Be The Eel: A Tribute To Bud Freeman (1939–40; Affinity). Classic titles by Freeman's Summa Cum Laude band, the greatest Chicago-style ensemble of its day, along with Muggsy Spanier's Ragtimers and Bob Crosby's Bobcats. Kaminsky, Gowans, Russell and Freeman are all at their peak here, and four band sides with singer Teddy Grace are included.

Chicago/Austin High School Jazz In Hi Fi (1958; RCA). Perfect re-creation of Freeman's Summa Cum Laude orchestra, featuring Teagarden and Butterfield in one of the few such projects that doesn't suffer in comparison to the original.

Something To Remember You By (1962; Black Lion). A typically urbane Freeman quartet set with the impressive rhythm-section of Dave Frishberg, Bob Haggart and Don Lamond.

Chico Freeman

Tenor and soprano saxophones, bass-clarinet, flute.

b. Chicago, 17 July 1949.

The son of saxophonist Von Freeman, Chico (Earl) Freeman began on trumpet, switching to tenor while at Northwestern University. He studied with Muhal Richard Abrams and Joe Daley in the early 1970s, and holds a Master's degree in composition from Governors State University. In 1976 he appeared successfully with a university group at the Notre Dame festival and in Brazil. He settled in New York, working, from 1976, with bassist Cecil McBee, Elvin Jones, Sam Rivers, Don Pullen and Sun Ra. He toured Europe with Jones, with an AACM big band in 1979 and with his own quartet in 1979 and 1980. Freeman recorded and toured with his father and with various editions of The Leaders in the 1980s. Since 1989 he has fronted a more amplified band with additional percussion, called Brainstorm, and in 1999 he toured Europe with an all-star Latin Jazz Explosion group. Like almost every other young tenor player, Freeman initially mirrored the work of John Coltrane but is both more individual and more versatile than most of his contemporaries. With a tone that, though not reminiscent of his father's, is recognizably of the Chicago school, Chico is able to incorporate mainstream virtues without imitating specific earlier players. As well as being probably the first jazzman of his generation to record an album of standards (see the first album below), he seems engaged on a longterm consolidation which has yet to reach fruition. [BP]

Spirit Sensitive (1978; India Navigation). Possibly inspired by his father and by a general move among his generation, Freeman tackled such material as "Autumn In New York" and "Don't Get Around Much Anymore" with Cecil McBee and John Hicks.

Destiny's Dance (1981; Contemporary/OJC). The contributions of Bobby Hutcherson and, on three tracks, Wynton Marsalis make this superior to the once-prized and now unavailable *Kings Of Mali*.

Russ Freeman

Piano.

b. Chicago, 28 May 1926; d. 27 June 2002.

Not to be confused with the fusion guitarist who leads the Rippington, Russ Freeman became involved in bebop after studying piano on the West Coast, initially working with Howard McGhee, trumpeter Al Killian and Dexter Gordon, and playing on informal recordings by Charlie Parker (all in 1947). In the early 1950s he performed with Shorty Rogers, the Lighthouse All Stars and Art Pepper, with whom he recorded in 1952, 1956 and 1978. His most important associations were with Chet Baker in 1953–4 and 1956, and Shelly Manne from 1955–66. He also supervised some recordings, including some by his successor with Baker, Dick Twardzik, and assisted film writers Johnny Mandel and André Previn in the late 1950s. Thereafter he became a musical director in clubs and for television. Freeman's piano style on his most notable work was influenced by Horace Silver and had a pleasing angularity. His ballad "The Wind", originally recorded by Baker and June Christy, was published through his own company and, when covered by Mariah Carey, afforded him a comfortable retirement. [BP]

Russ Freeman and Dick Twardzik

Trio (1953–7; Pacific Jazz). Freeman's twelve tracks, balanced by Twardzik's more idiosyncratic eight contributions, show that not only black Los Angeles pianists could get into the muscular areas thrown up by the combination of bebop and cool jazz.

➤➤ **Chet Baker** *(Chet Baker Sings).*

Von Freeman

Tenor saxophone.

b. Chicago, 3 Oct 1922.

Von (Earl Lavon) Freeman worked with the Horace Henderson group in the late 1940s and Sun Ra's band in the early 1950s. During the same period he played with his brothers, drummer Bruz (Eldridge) Freeman and guitarist George Freeman; the group's pianists were successively Ahmad Jamal, Andrew Hill and Muhal Richard Abrams. In the early 1960s he toured with vocalist Milt Trenier of the Trenier Brothers. Since the 1970s he has been making brief appearances in New York and Europe, but remains based in Chicago. Freeman is an unsung progenitor of the "Chicago tenor" style along with Gene Ammons, who was a couple of years his junior. His very personal, rather querulous tone is sometimes echoed by Johnny Griffin, and he has a tremendous fluency which must have impressed his son Chico. [BP]

Lester Leaps In (1992; Steeplechase). Freeman's programme of hoary anthems (the title track, "Scrapple From The Apple", and a few ancient pop songs) gives little indication of the idiosyncratic playing by the leader and his Chicago rhythm-section.

Paolo Fresu

Trumpet, flugelhorn, composer, arranger.
b. Berchidda, Sardinia, Italy, 10 Feb 1961.

Fresu began trumpet at the age of eleven in the town band, with which he played for eight years. Also involved in pop music, he finally discovered jazz in 1980 and began his professional career in 1982, while studying at Cagliari Conservatory. He made his own first album in 1984 and, as well as leading his own groups, has collaborated with leading Italian and international musicians such as Kenny Wheeler, Dave Liebman, Daniel Humair, Albert Mangelsdorff, Gerry Mulligan, Phil Woods, John Zorn, Trilok Gurtu, Gunther Schuller, etc. He has played contemporary orchestral music with Michael Nyman and Giancarlo Schiaffini, and composes for theatre and film. Active in music education since 1985, he has taught all over Italy and in Boston, Atlanta, Melbourne and Beijing. In recent years he has been based in Paris, and in 1996 won two French awards after signing with BMG France. Inspired initially by Armstrong, Davis and Chet Baker, and more recently by Tom Harrell, he has recorded two albums with fellow trumpeter Enrico Rava; he also lists Billie Holiday and John Coltrane among his numerous influences. [BP]

Kind Of Porgy And Bess (2002; RCA Victor). Despite the challenging album title, Fresu treads the tightrope of homage and personal lyricism, featuring a quartet with guitarist Nguyên Lê and vocalist (and oud player) Dhafer Youssef.

Bill Frisell

Guitar, electric guitar, banjo, guitar synthesizer, effects, composer.
b. Baltimore, Maryland, 18 March 1951.

Frisell, whose father played tuba and string bass, grew up in Denver, Colorado. Beginning on clarinet and saxophone before taking up guitar, he majored in music at the University of North Colorado from 1969–71, and then took a diploma in arranging and composition at Berklee College in 1977, receiving the Harris Stanton guitar award the same year. He had private guitar lessons with Jim Hall, Johnny Smith and Dale Bruning. Frisell is one of the most accomplished and sought-after of the younger American guitarists. Since the late 1970s he has performed in the USA and throughout Europe with leading contemporary players such as Paul Motian, Jan Garbarek, Eberhard Weber, Bob Moses, Charlie Haden's Liberation Music Orchestra, Michael Mantler, Carla Bley, Mike Gibbs's orchestra, Julius Hemphill's Jah band, Gunter Hampel's Galaxie Dream Band, Lyle Mays, John Scofield and Peter Erskine.

Frisell is in demand because he invests his playing with such strong intention – he really means what he plays and communicates that compellingly.

He makes much use of electronics and sound distortion, including feedback, and often uses long sustained notes and legato lines with a sometimes violent vibrato. His choice of notes (and sounds) is always interesting, and while he can grace any context – abstract or tightly structured – he can also boogie happily with the best; he is also an excellent composer.

In the 1990s he toured Britain and Europe with his own groups. His favourite guitarists are Wes Montgomery, Jim Hall and Jimi Hendrix. In 1996, Frisell's long-standing trio with bassist Kermit Driscoll and drummer Joey Baron disbanded, and he formed a quartet with new voice on trumpet Ron Miles, violinist/tuba player Eyvind Kang and trombonist Curtis Fowlkes. This seems to have given him a new lease of musical life, and the album they recorded that year, *Quartet*, had a wonderful freshness and dynamism. That same year he also played a crucial role on Kenny Wheeler's exquisite quartet album, *Angel Song*, which included Lee Konitz and Dave Holland. He has also recorded with Ginger Baker, Gary Peacock, Paul Motian and Elvis Costello.

He is currently exploring global music themes with a new band that incorporates styles from Brazil, Greece and Mali, among others. They released an album, *The Intercontinentals*, in 2003. [IC]

Before We Were Born (1988; Elektra Musician); **Is That You?** (1989; Elektra Musician). Frisell examines his American roots in these albums, both of which have the excellent Joey Baron on drums. The former features a ten-piece ensemble with three saxophones, cello and percussion, and there's great vitality in Frisell's composing and arranging, as well as in the playing. The later album is a quartet effort with Frisell playing guitars, bass, banjo, ukulele and clarinet: a highly focused session, it covers the spectrum from rock to rag to free to funky.

Have A Little Faith (1991; Elektra Musician). Frisell breaks new ground in this album, which has his version of Aaron Copland's *Billy The Kid* plus pieces by Charles Ives, John Phillip Sousa, Bob Dylan and Madonna. There's also a superbly funky version of "I Can't Be Satisfied", with far-out clarinet from Don Byron.

This Land (1992; Elektra Musician). With Byron, Driscoll and Baron, augmented by trombonist Curtis Fowlkes, Frisell plays a robust session with wonderful rhythmic grooves, much lyrical impressionist writing, and eloquent solos all round.

RICK MALKIN

Bill Frisell

Quartet (1996; Nonesuch). This is Frisell's new quartet album, and there is a visual inspiration behind much of the music. Frisell draws on music he wrote for the Buster Keaton short silent film *Convict 13*, for the Italian film *La Scuola*, and also for Gary Larson's *Tales From The Far Side*, shown on TV in 1994. The personalities of the quartet and their huge range of sounds and sonorities – guitar, tuba, violin, trumpet and piccolo trumpet and trombone, made this an exceptional album.

Gone, Just Like A Train (1997; Nonesuch). Another trio with two musicians Frisell had long admired – drummer Jim Keltner and bassist Viktor Krauss. All fifteen titles were composed by Frisell, and seem profoundly rooted in his American roots – musical, social and domestic.

Dave Frishberg

Piano, composer, lyricist, vocals.
b. St Paul, Minnesota, 23 March 1933.

After giving up his job in journalism for full-time music, Dave Frishberg played intermission piano at Eddie Condon's for a year, then played with Bud Freeman's quartet and with Gene Krupa, and worked regularly at the Metropole, besides taking his first steps in songwriting. An early success, the drily witty "Peel Me A Grape", cemented his professional credibility and good relations with like-minded song people such as Blossom Dearie (for whom it was a hit) and Bob Dorough. In the 1960s he worked for Ben Webster, and with Al Cohn and Zoot Sims for a long famous stay at New York's Half-Note. In 1971 he left New York to write for a weekly TV show, and then (a testimony to Frishberg's broad mind) he joined Herb Alpert. "When I heard the personnel I jumped at the chance. I loved it – it was the most fun I'd had. I got a solo spot and played some of my Jelly Roll Morton stuff." A solo career was becoming more important to him: two 1970s albums, *Getting Some Fun Out Of Life* and *You're A Lucky Guy*, focused attention on his connoisseur's taste in songs and his avuncular singing. They were followed by three valuable albums of original songs, sung by himself: *Oklahoma Toad* and the *Dave Frishberg Song Book* volumes one and two. Frishberg's re-emergence as a pianist/singer in the Carmichael mould has continued into the 1990s on the American and European club circuits. [DF]

Getting Some Fun Out Of Life (1977; Concord). The album that brought Frishberg to international attention. With Bob Findley on trumpet and Marshall Royal on alto, he presents a moody "Lotus Blossom", a rollicking "Old Man Harlem" and his own quite beautiful "Dear Bix".

Classics (1982–3; Concord). A compendium of most of Frishberg's best songs, including "I'm Hip", "Van Lingle Mungo", "Do You Miss New York" and "My Attorney Bernie".

Let's Eat Home (1989; Concord). A concept similar to Frishberg's *Getting Some Fun Out Of Life* collection, mixing witty songs like "Brenda Starr" and the title track with instrumentals like "The Mooche" and an Al Cohn medley. Snooky Young (trumpet) and Rob McConnell (valve-trombone) join Frishberg's rhythm-section.

Double Play (1993; Arbors Jazz). An enjoyable album of piano-cornet duets featuring the gifted Jim Goodwin and some superb selections, including "Easy Come Easy Go", "Blue River" and "Winin' Boy Blues".

By Himself (1997; Arbors). Frishberg has found an ideal home in the shade of Arbors, and this album features substantial amounts of his solo piano as well as several (as usual) funny and hip songs including "I Want To Be A Sideman" and "Can't Take You Nowhere".

Do You Miss New York (2003; Arbors). Very welcome new live concert in which Frishberg lays down his quilt of musico/lyric concepts, from funny ("Jaws", "Quality Time") via nostalgic ("Eastwood Lane") to wryly observant "The Difficult Season") and touchingly gentle ("Heart's Desire").

➤➤ **Jimmy Rushing** *(The You And Me That Used To Be).*

Curtis Fuller

Trombone.

b. Detroit, Michigan, 14 Dec 1934.

Fuller played with Kenny Burrell and with Yusef Lateef's Detroit quintet in 1955–6. He moved to New York in 1957, and within a year had worked for Miles Davis, Dizzy Gillespie, Sonny Rollins and, in 1958, Lester Young. He immediately began recording prolifically, including sessions with Bud Powell and John Coltrane. He was a founder member of the Jazztet with Art Farmer and Benny Golson in 1959–60, and then worked with Art Blakey's Jazz Messengers from 1961–5. He has been less active on the jazz scene since, but made more recordings under his own name in the 1970s. He toured with Count Basie in the late 1970s and early 1980s, with Lionel Hampton in 1979, with Kai Winding in 1980 and with the revived Jazztet in 1982, as well as freelancing in New York. Fuller has a style which exploits the technical discoveries of J.J. Johnson but in a more subdued manner. His phrasing is sometimes clipped and repetitive at up-tempo, but with slower vehicles his melodic approach is very distinctive. [BP]

⊙ **Blues-ette** (1959; Savoy). Probably the pick of his early albums, this has Fuller leading a quintet with Benny Golson and Tommy Flanagan, and includes Golson's "Five Spot After Dark" and "Minor Vamp".

➤➤ **Art Blakey** *(Free For All)*; **John Coltrane** *(Blue Train)*.

Steve Gadd

Drums.

b. Rochester, New York, 1945.

Gadd was encouraged by his uncle, a drummer in the army. He took drum lessons from the age of seven and sat in with Dizzy Gillespie at eleven. He studied music at Eastman College, Rochester, playing in a wind ensemble and concert band, and at night in a club with Chick Corea, Chuck Mangione, Joe Romano and Frank Polero. After college he was drafted into the army and spent three years in a military band. After the army, he gigged and worked with a big band in Rochester, and in 1972 he formed a trio with Tony Levin and Mike Holmes, going to New York with it. The trio fizzled out but Gadd began to work extensively as a studio musician and also played with Corea's first Return To Forever. In the 1970s and 1980s he toured internationally and recorded with Paul Simon and Al Di Meola's Electric Rendezvous Band. By the end of the 1970s Gadd was the most in-demand and probably the most imitated drummer in the world. In Japan transcriptions of his solos were on sale, and all the leading Japanese drummers were sounding like him. In the 1980s Gadd was working with the all-star Manhattan Jazz Quintet, and formed, with Eddie Gomez and Ronnie Cuber, the Gadd Gang. He has also recorded with Carla Bley (*Dinner Music*) and George Benson (*In Concert*), as well as a hoste of rock and pop acts. Chick Corea commented: "Every drummer wants to play like Gadd because he plays perfect ... He has brought orchestral and compositional thinking to the drumkit while at the same time having a great imagination and a great ability to swing." Gadd's favourites are Elvin Jones, Tony Williams, Jack DeJohnette, Buddy Rich and Louie Bellson, among others. [IC]

➤➤ **Chick Corea** *(Three Quartets).*

Slim (Bulee) Gaillard

Vocals, piano, guitar vibes, tenor saxophone, composer.

b. Detroit, Michigan, 4 Jan 1911; d. London, 26 Feb 1991.

In the mid-1930s Slim Gaillard worked as a comic variety act, playing guitar and tap-dancing simultaneously, then formed the "Slim and Slam" double act with bassist Slam Stewart (1937–43), which caused a sensation with its hit "Flat Foot Floogie" and landed a long series on Radio WNEW. Gaillard presented his routines in "vout" (an invented jive talk which finished off every other word with "oreenee"), veering off into manic machine-gun Spanish patter, while his highly original songs were often about food ("Avocado Seed Soup Symphony", "Matzoh Balls" and "Yip Roc Heresy", which he composed from an Armenian menu), or about machinery ("Cement Mixer", "Poppity-Pop!"), or were just marvellous nonsense ("Ya Ha Ha", "Laughing In Rhythm", "Flat Foot Floogie"). After army service (1943–4) he was again a big attraction in Los Angeles clubs, including the Regency – where Hollywood stars dropped in nightly – and he had already appeared in films himself, notably *Star Spangled Rhythm* and *Hellzapoppin!* (both 1942).

Recording and radio followed, but by the 1950s Gaillard's career was slowing temporarily; in 1963 he managed a motel in San Diego, after which, in the 1970s, he bought an orange farm near Seattle. Then came a revival: he moved to London to live, and record producer Alastair Robertson both reissued old Gaillard sides and recorded new ones for his Hep label. Gaillard turned back into a celebrity, touring, appearing at jazz festivals and featuring on TV. His act – playing guitar, piano (with the backs of his hands) and singing his old hits – was once again big news and his striking looks, dark-brown voice and gently surreal comedy caused as big a hit as they had forty years earlier. By 1985 he was commuting from country to country, playing jazz festivals, concerts

and clubs, and he continued to do so until cancer quickly laid him low in 1991. Now seen as one of the forefathers of rap, his last recorded appearance was on a single by the Dream Warriors. [DF]

Slim And Slam: Complete Recordings (1938–42; Affinity). Definitive three-CD set including many classics, such as "Flat Foot Floogie", "Tutti Frutti" and "Buck Dance Rhythm".

Legendary McVouty (1945–6; Hep). Hilarious recordings from the mid-40s, with guest appearance by Harry "The Hipster" Gibson.

Laughin' In Rhythm: The Best Of The Verve Years (1946–54; Verve). Perhaps the best-known of the Gaillard collections, featuring his "Opera In Vout", "Yip Roc Heresy" and "Chicken Rhythm".

The Legendary McVouty (1982; Hep). Recorded with an Anglo-American group, including Buddy Tate, Jay McShann, Allan Ganley, Peter Ind and Digby Fairweather, this set has a remake of "Slim's Jam" plus Gaillard's wonderfully eccentric "OK In The UK".

Charlie Galbraith

Trombone, leader.

b. London, 13 Aug 1920; d. 16 Jan 1997.

A longtime member of Britain's Dixieland fraternity who played in a charming Teagarden-influenced style, Galbraith took up trombone while in the RAF (1940–46) and played with John Haim, Mike Daniels, Joe Daniels and Cy Laurie before forming his first band in 1950 after a visit to Paris to play with Sidney Bechet. After seven years Galbraith formed a second band with Kenny Ball (trumpet); he worked for Ball and Bobby Mickleburgh (from 1958) and from 1960–62 led the Charlie Galbraith All Stars, recording one hit with singer Clinton Ford ("Too Many Beautiful Girls And Not Enough Time)" and touring widely in Turkey, France, Belgium and Holland. Galbraith's last band, formed in 1969, frequently featured trumpeter Alan Wickham, and he remained a familiar figure in London and also in Northampton where, at Pollacks Hill, he ran a longtime residency, often in the company of fellow trombonist George Chisholm. His last residency was in a London wine bar with pianist Angus McLarty. [DF]

On Tour (1962; 77 label). Galbraith's All Stars featuring Bryan Jones (trumpet), Martin Downer (soprano) and Pat Mason (piano) recorded at the very end of Britain's "Trad boom".

Eric Gale

Guitar.

b. New York, 20 Sept 1938; d. 25 May 1994.

Gale's parents arrived in New York from Barbados shortly before his birth, and his early musical inspiration was derived from the music of Charlie Parker, Sonny Rollins, Lester Young, John Coltrane and Thelonious Monk. He described himself, however, as an "R&B musician" and abandoned an embryonic career as a chemist to spend the early 1960s on the road playing guitar with the Drifters, the Flamingos, Jackie Wilson and other popular acts. By the mid-60s Gale had created an identifiable style that blended elements of R&B, jazz and the funk rhythms of the period with the clear, soft tone of his large-bodied Gibson L-5 and Super 400 guitars. While house guitarist for Creed Taylor's CTI label, he recorded several solo albums from 1973 onwards, and teamed up with keyboardist Bob James and others to form the succcessful recording and touring band Stuff. [CA]

Blue Horizon (1982; Pinnacle). With perhaps more of his R&B than his jazz roots on display, Gale's expressive style is featured on a variety of styles and grooves from samba to reggae, with trumpeter Hugh Masakela guesting on the title track.

Richard Galliano

Accordion, bandoneon, composer.

b. Cannes, France, 12 Dec 1950.

The son of an accordion teacher, Richard Galliano was playing the instrument at four, and by the age of twelve was seen as an infant prodigy. He studied harmony, counterpoint and trombone at the Nice Conservatoire, then moved to Paris in 1973. For seven years, he was *chanson* singer Claude Nougaro's musical director, but he also collaborated and recorded with jazz musicians, among them Chet Baker (appearing on an album of Brazilian pieces), Jimmy Gourley, Eddy Louiss, Steve Potts and – a longtime associate – Michel Portal. Galliano played in a trio with pianist Daniel Goyone and percussionist Trilok Gurtu, in duos with US bassist Ron Carter and cellist Jean-Charles Gapon, and also, in the 1980s, with Louis Sclavis and Marc Ducret. In the 1990s, just as his great inspiration Astor Piazzolla had done with "nuevo tango" in Argentina, Galliano spearheaded "new musette", and recorded as a leader with Belgian guitarist Philip Catherine, Pierre Michelot and Aldo Romano, receiving the Prix Django Reinhardt de l'Académie du Jazz in 1991. In 1994, he made what many consider his finest album, *Laurita* (Dreyfus), with Portal playing bass-clarinet, Didier Lockwood (violin), Toots Thielemans (harmonica), Palle Danielsson (bass) and Joey Baron (drums). The following year, he played accordion on the folk song "The Shepherd of Breton" as part of Mike Gibbs's Europeana project (ACT), while also continuing with duo work, most notably with Michel Portal, memorably captured on *Blow Up* (see below). The most recent release of his rich tenure at Dreyfus is a passionate, virtuosic septet tribute to his abiding inspiration, *Piazzolla Forever* (2003; Dreyfus). [CP]

Blow Up (1997; Dreyfus). One of the most elegantly virtuosic pairings in recent Jazz – Galliano playing both accordion and piano, Portal playing bass-clarinet, bandoneon, soprano saxophone and jazzophone publicly, recorded in Paris, and mixing graceful originals with material by Piazzolla ("Libertango", "Oblivion") and characteristically eccentric pieces by Hermeto Pascoal.

Jim Galloway

Saxophones, clarinet.

b. Kilwinning, Scotland, 28 July 1936.

A committed jazzman who includes among his principal influences Armstrong, Teagarden, Coleman Hawkins, Lester Young, Ellington, Basie and Lunceford, Jim Galloway (James Brodie) took up the clarinet in his teens in Glasgow (Forrie Cairns was an occasional clarinet colleague) and later doubled on alto saxophone, playing with local bands such as the Jazzmakers. In 1964 he moved to Canada, where he added soprano and baritone saxophone to his collection and set about broadening his experience, working with the Metro Stompers, which he led from 1968. In 1976 he was asked to take a band to the Montreux festival (including Buddy Tate and Jay McShann), which was followed by a trip to Nice and a long European tour with Tate again. Since then he has become a regular at jazz festivals worldwide, as well as touring Europe as a soloist and leading his own quartet, sextet and "Wee Big Band" (Toronto, 1979 onwards). In 1985 a Galloway commission, *Hot And Suite*, featuring himself, two jazz bands and a symphony orchestra, stole the show at Edinburgh's jazz festival. From 1987 he was artistic director for Toronto's Du Maurier Downtown Jazz Festival and remains busy (including UK tours with Randy Sandke in 2001). [DF]

⊙ **Thou Swell** (1981; Sackville). Galloway stretching out in a quartet setting with his regular colleague Jay McShann.

Hal Galper

Piano, keyboards, composer.

b. Salem, Massachusetts, 18 April 1938.

Hal (Harold) Galper studied classical piano from 1945–8, was at the Berklee School of Music from 1955–8 and had private tuition with Jaki Byard, Herb Pomeroy and others. He played with the Pomeroy big band and small group in Boston, and with the Sam Rivers quartet, Tony Williams and Chet Baker. With Bobby Hutcherson, Joe Henderson, Stan Getz, Randy Brecker and Attila Zoller he has played European festivals, and has also accompanied many singers including Joe Williams, Anita O'Day and Chris Connor. From 1972–5 he worked with the Cannonball Adderley quintet, in which he replaced George Duke. He also played with Lee Konitz, John Scofield and Billy Hart. During the 80s he was a member of the Phil Woods quintet. He left in 1990 to concentrate, throughout the 90s, on his own trio, featuring Steve Ellington (drums) and Jeff Johnson (bass). Galper is a highly accomplished player, at home with any idiom from jazz to rock. Today, his schedule is augmented by teaching and writing. [IC]

⊙ **Reach Out** (1976; Steeplechase). Features the Brecker brothers and presents Galper's playing and writing at their best.

⊙ **Now Hear This** (1977; Enja). Galper is here in quartet format with the excellent trumpeter Terumasa Hino, and a brilliant rhythm-section of Cecil McBee and Tony Williams.

⊙ **Ivory Forest** (1979; Enja). A quartet this time with John Scofield in marvellous form, with bassist Wayne Dockery and the superb drummer Adam Nussbaum.

⊙ **Portrait** (1989; Concord). Galper leads bassist Ray Drummond and Billy Hart in a fine trio outing which shows his excellent technique and artistry in fine equilibrium.

Frank Gambale

Guitar.

b. Canberra, Australia, 22 Dec 1958.

A guitarist from the age of seven, Gambale started his own blues band at thirteen. The music of John McLaughlin and the Mahavishnu Orchestra kindled his interest in jazz and jazz fusion, and in his early twenties he enrolled at the Guitar Institute of Technology (GIT), Hollywood. While still a student, he wrote his first instructional book, *Speed Picking*, later followed by *The Frank Gambale Technique – Vols. 1 and 2*. From 1983 for three years he was a member of GIT's teaching faculty. As a performer Gambale has attracted widespread attention for his virtuosic work with Jean-Luc Ponty, Jeff Berlin and, in particular, the Chick Corea Elektric Band (1986–93). Gambale has also recorded and toured with drummer Steve Smith's Vital Information and with former Santana keyboardist Tom Coster, and released a series of solo albums.

His "sweep-picking" technique (a combination of single direction picking, pull-offs and hammer-ons) enables him to play ultra-fast runs throughout the range of the guitar and this, together with his fluency over complex chord progressions, is a hallmark of his style. To some critics his exceptional facility governs his choice of notes, and he is often accused of having a jazz musician's musical knowledge and a rock musician's aesthetic sense. In spite of this continuing controversy, Frank Gambale is undoubtedly one of the foremost fusion guitarists to emerge in the 1980s.

Appointed Head of Guitar Department LAMA (Los Angeles Music Academy) in 1996, he continues to do good business, not least with his instructional videos, the latest of which was suitably entitled *Chop Builder*. In 2002 he rejoined Corea's reformed Elektric Band for touring and recording projects. [CA/CI]

⊙ **Passages** (1994; JVC). With its production values and its guitar sound rooted firmly in contemporary rock, this album nevertheless includes some excellent, adventurous soloing from Gambale.

Ganelin Trio

Vyacheslav Ganelin (b. Kraskov, USSR, 17 Dec 1944) began on piano at the age of four and has played jazz since 1961 (he also plays synthesizer, basset, electric guitar and percussion). He graduated from the Vilnius Conservatory, and was a member of the USSR Composers' Union. He has written a number of operas and film scores.

Vladimir Chekasin (b. Sverdlovsk, USSR, 24 Feb 1944) began on violin at the age of six, started the clarinet at eleven and alto saxophone at eighteen. He graduated from Sverdlovsk Conservatory, and has played jazz since 1967. In 1970 he won first prize at the international competition organized by the Czechoslovak Society of Composers. He teaches at a conservatory and directs an orchestra.

The third member of the trio, percussionist Vladimir Tarasov (b. Archangelsk, USSR, 29 June 1947), is self-taught. He plays drums with the Lithuanian Radio Symphony Orchestra and the Lithuanian State Symphony Orchestra.

These three virtuosi, assembled in 1971 in the USSR by Ganelin, created a kind of abstract music which grew out of the European free jazz movement of the 1960s but had its own, very different, identity. Composition seemed to play a more important role in Ganelin's music, and every piece, every album, was different, offering a tremendous variety of textures, timbres, instrumental combinations and approaches. They were capable of good time-playing and occasionally set up some nice sustained rhythms. Their performances could range from grotesque parody and burlesque to the wide-eyed simplicity of children's nursery songs or the romantic melancholy of European – and particularly Slavonic – folk music and classical music. Although their music was sometimes totally abstract and often semi-abstract, there was always a sense of form and an intelligent use of space.

In 1976 they performed at the Warsaw Jazz Jamboree and their first album, *Con Anima*, was released in the USSR. By the 1980s they were playing concerts both in the Soviet Union and abroad. In 1980 they performed at the West Berlin jazz festival, to an ecstatic audience; J.E. Berendt wrote: "With three musicians playing approximately fifteen instruments with a breathtaking intensity, building their set to a euphoric climax, it was the wildest and yet the best organized and most professional free jazz I've heard in years."

Because the official Soviet record label Melodiya was reluctant to release their albums in the USSR a London company, Leo Records, undertook the release and distribution of their recordings, and those of other Russian jazz musicians, in Britain and the West. The trio broke up in 1987 when Ganelin left the Soviet Union and settled in Israel – they had spent their intensely creative performing lives in opposition to political repression, and when *glasnost* and *perestroika* removed the cork from the bottle, the genie evaporated. Duo albums appeared in the late 1980s and early 1990s, when Ganelin also formed a new trio and released a solo album, *Onstage … Backstage*. [IC]

⊙ **Poco A Poco** (1978; Leo); **Catalogue: Live in East Germany** (1979; Leo). The tapes of these live recordings were smuggled out of the Soviet Union and the sound quality is only fair. However, the trio were in their heyday of creativity, and these are fascinating and important documents of a brilliant group living their historical moment to the hilt.

⊙ **Encores** (1978, 80 & 81; Leo). This is an anthology of pieces and encores for concerts in Moscow, West Berlin and Leningrad. The vitality and variety of the music are astonishing, ranging as it does from ethnic drones and folk tunes to echoes from classical music, total abstraction and versions of "Mack The Knife" and "Summertime".

⊙ **Non Troppo** (1982; hat Art). This includes both parts of "Ancora Da Capo", and "Non Troppo", which is one of the group's finest suites.

⊙ **San Francisco Holidays** (1986; Leo). This double CD is another historical document – the trio's first visit to the United States. The American ROVA saxophone quartet were the supporting group, opening the concert with a 45-minute performance, and they also joined the trio for the final fifteen minutes of the concert. There are some excellent moments and hilarious happenings, but the proceedings generally have an end-of-term slackness.

⊙ **Opuses** (1989; Leo). After moving to Israel, Slava Ganelin (as he now calls himself) formed a new trio with Victor Fonarev (cello, double bass and gamelan) and Mika Markovich (drums, percussion and gamelan). The anarchic humour and wit have gone, but the new sobriety yields some spacious and resonant music with Ganelin adding flute and synthesizer to his armoury. The bass is a fountainhead of stimulating sounds, and Ganelin's piano, whether violent or elegaic, is ever eloquent.

⊙ **Onstage … Backstage** (1992; Leo). Ganelin's solo album, with some piano romanticism reminiscent of Keith Jarrett, and edifices of sound created by synthesizer.

Allan Ganley

Drums, composer, arranger.

b. Tolworth, Surrey, UK, 11 March 1931.

Ganley is mainly self-taught, but in 1970 he did one semester at Berklee College. He worked with Jack Parnell's band and the Ambrose orchestra in the early 1950s and then joined the first John Dankworth orchestra, staying with it for two years. Then he formed a quintet called the Jazzmakers, which lasted two years and did a major US tour. In the early 1960s he was with the new Tubby Hayes quintet, and was also busy as a studio musician and had begun composing and arranging. Ganley's impeccable technique and taste make him much in demand and he has worked with many leading musicians, including Stan Getz, Freddie Hubbard, Roland Kirk, Al Cohn, Clark Terry, Dizzy Gillespie and Jim Hall, and has recorded with many others including Albert Mangelsdorff, Al Haig and Art Farmer. Ganley is still very active as a player, having frequently worked in the early 1990s with the Scottish pianist Dave Newton, with whom he recorded the album *Eyewitness*. His band, The Allan Ganley Quartet, can still be found on the road, though his main interest is arranging/composing and he has written regularly for the BBC Radio Big Band. [IC]

Jan Garbarek

Soprano, tenor and bass saxophones, flutes.

b. Mysen, Norway, 4 March 1947.

Garbarek, who was born to a Norwegian mother and a Polish father, is self-taught and wanted to play saxophone after hearing John Coltrane on the radio in 1961. In 1962 he won a competition for amateur jazz players, which led to his first professional work. He enrolled at Oslo University, but soon dropped out because he was getting too much work as a musician. Since the early 1960s he has led groups of his own, but he worked with George Russell, who was resident in Scandinavia for four years in the later 1960s, and studied Russell's book *The Lydian Chromatic Concept Of Tonal Organisation*. He also played with singer Karin Krog. In 1970 Garbarek was given a government grant to go to the USA and listen to jazz, and began recording for ECM; he has been with the label ever since. He has also played with Chick Corea and Don Cherry, and in the mid-1970s, with Keith Jarrett, Palle Danielsson (bass) and Jon Christensen, he played on two classic albums: *Belonging* and *My Song*. Garbarek's work on these sets established him as one of the major saxophone voices of the post-Coltrane period. This quartet, known as the Belonging Band, toured in Europe, Japan and the USA towards the end of the decade, recording a live double album of new material at the Village Vanguard, New York.

ECM Records

Jan Garbarek

In the 1980s Garbarek led a very distinguished quartet with Eberhard Weber on bass, Christensen (who was succeeded by Michael Di Pasqua and later Nana Vasconcelos) on drums and percussion, and a series of guitarists including Bill Frisell, Moss Trout and David Torn; towards the end of the 1980s, the guitarists were replaced by German keyboardist Rainer Brüninghaus. In the later 1980s and the 1990s Garbarek explored a number of contexts for his saxophone playing; he has recorded with a variety of Nordic singers, with Eastern musicians, and with the Hilliard Ensemble he performed and recorded a set of medieval and Renaissance liturgical music. His critical reputation has grown steadily as has his international audience and, in artistic as well as financial terms, he is one of the most successful European jazz musicians. His favourite saxophonists are Johnny Hodges, John Coltrane, Albert Ayler, Pharoah Sanders, Archie Shepp and Gene Ammons, and other inspirations are Miles Davis, Ornette Coleman and Jarrett.

In the middle and later 1990s Garbarek and the Hilliard Ensemble toured worldwide with *Officium*, and because of its musical success and the enormous popular appeal of the album and the concerts, in 1997 Garbarek was the first-ever jazz musician to be BBC Radio 3's "Artist of the Week". In the 90s, he continued touring with his own superlative regular group – pianist/keyboardist Rainer Brüninghaus, bassist Eberhard Weber and percussonist Marilyn Mazur. They recorded and released the double CD *Rites* in 1998, and toured with it in the latter half of the year, and their London concert in the Royal Festival Hall at the beginning of December was packed to capacity. In 1998, *Jan Garbarek: Deep Song* by Michael Tucker was published by EastNote – a very scholarly critical study of his music in the context of his Scandinavian background and the world jazz scene.

Manfred Eicher, Garbarek's ECM producer, has described him as "a very ascetic person, with an ascetic appearance, and an ascetic sound". The asceticism, however, is in the spareness of his phrasing, not in the feeling that underlies it. Garbarek does not play

"licks" (preconceived or habitual patterns), but his improvisations sound like distilled thought, ideas conceived, edited and expressed on the spur of each moment. Underneath this icy clarity he burns with a feeling which is the more potent for being so tightly controlled. Every note, every phrase is meant: there is no rhetoric, only poetry. The intense feeling is conveyed in the extraordinary tonal quality of his work; he employs a great variety of subtle inflexions, timbres and ways of articulating notes which are emotionally eloquent. He is a fine small-group composer, his music full of resonances from the past – echoes of Nordic folk song and old church music. [IC]

⊙ **Afric Pepperbird** (1970; ECM). This was a double debut – Garbarek's and ECM's first album. It was an auspicious beginning – the album points towards the haunting impressionistic concept of Garbarek's later years, but also shows his visceral, declamatory approach which owed so much to Coltrane and Ayler. The title track also relates to Miles Davis's then current work.

⊙ **Places** (1977; ECM); **Paths Prints** (1981; ECM). Garbarek's passionate, keening romanticism and sonorous composing get full rein on these two quartet albums – the first with guitarist Bill Connors, John Taylor and Jack DeJohnette, and the second with Bill Frisell, Eberhard Weber and Jon Christensen.

⊙ **Legend Of The Seven Dreams** (1988; ECM). With Rainer Brüninghaus, Eberhard Weber and Nana Vasconcelos now in the group, Garbarek began to go much more deeply into Nordic folk music. The naked emotion on this album haunts and hypnotizes.

⊙ **Ragas And Sagas** (1990; ECM); **Madar** (1992; ECM). Garbarek is completely at home with the Indian musicians on these two albums. His sparse phrases are marmoreally sculpted and perfectly suit the stark context.

⊙ **Twelve Moons** (1993; ECM). Garbarek, Brüninghaus and Weber are joined by rock drummer Manu Katche, percussionist Marilyn Mazur and two women vocalists. Garbarek's passionate soprano swoops and soars, and the rhythm-section bites deep: an exquisite album of beautiful dynamics, sonorities and great lyricism.

⊙ **Officium** (1993; ECM). Garbarek here improvises to complement the Hilliard Ensemble, a British vocal quartet which specializes in early music. The gloriously sonorous liturgical atmosphere is leavened by Garbarek's soprano and tenor saxophones. The album must have touched a nerve with the international public because within a few weeks of its release it had sold 350,000 copies.

⊙ **Rites** (1998; ECM). This double CD is a masterwork, drawing together all the disparate strands of his experience into diverse and compelling new syntheses. He's a jazz musician through and through, yet has said: "I'm really fascinated by the connection between Norwegian music and that of India via the Balkans and Asia Minor", and that connection is really the subject of the album. Garbarek's poetic playing, the amazing variety of superb rhythms and the terrific emotional resonances make this one of his greatest albums.

Jan Garbarek/The Hilliard Ensemble

⊙ **Mnemosyne** (1998; ECM). This double CD is a follow-up to the single CD *Officium*, and has the same hauntingly ecstatic atmosphere. It, too, was recorded in the monastery of St Gerold. On this occasion, however, not all the pieces are conventionally notated, and several are improvisations, by the singers and Garbarek, based on fragments of unearthed old music.

➤➤ **Keith Jarrett** *(Belonging; My Song);* **L. Shankar** *(Song For Everyone);* **Ralph Towner** *(Solstice);* **Kenny Wheeler** *(Deer Wan).*

Freddy Gardner

All saxophones, clarinet.

b. Kilburn, London, 23 December 1910; d. 26 July 1950.

Along with Tubby Hayes, Freddy Gardner was one of Britain's greatest saxophonists. His career began when he won an award in a *Melody Maker* contest in 1929, and by 1933 he was working with Sidney Lipton and playing and recording with Ray Noble. During the remainder of the 1930s Gardner operated mainly as an in-demand freelancer who was quickly recognized as a superb talent. One of Gardner's best-remembered partnerships on record is with George Scott Wood's influential Six Swingers (with whom he toured England and Scotland in 1937), but he also led bands himself, broadcast and played for film soundtracks. From 1940 to 1945 Gardner served in the navy and after demobilization worked with Ted Heath (1945) and Billy Munn (1945–6). However he remained principally a soloist whose natural jazz feeling and great technique was as much at home with Mark White's BBC Jazz Club as it was with Peter Yorke's Concert Orchestra. [DF]

⊙ **Freddy Gardner And His Golden Tone Saxophone** (1935–50; ASV). Gardner's opening track "Smoke Gets In Your Eyes" reveals the poise and tone of a classical saxophonist, though he could get hot at the drop of a reed as tracks like "China Boy" prove. Gardiner charges into his alto solo with glorious abandon switching effortlessly to baritone during Albert Harris's guitar break, before moving to clarinet and back to alto!

Lou Gare

Tenor saxophone.

b. Rugby, Warwickshire, UK, 16 June 1939.

Although a prime mover in freely improvised music in the UK, Lou Gare has never achieved the prominence enjoyed by a number of his contemporaries in the field. After meeting and teaming up with drummer Eddie Prévost in 1963, Gare played briefly with Mike Westbrook, where he formed a close musical relationship with guitarist Keith Rowe and bassist Lawrence Sheaff, both of whom later joined Gare and Prévost in the improvising ensemble AMM. Remaining with – indeed for periods solely constituting (with Prévost) – the process-dominated group for nearly a decade, Gare eventually moved to Exeter, formed a free-jazz trio and supported himself with solo gigs and the odd film soundtrack, although he still performs with Prévost from time to time. [CP]

AMM

To Hear And Back Again (1973–5; Matchless). Duo with Prévost featuring music from three separate sessions.

The Nameless Uncarved Block (1990; Matchless). Live recording from AMM in quartet format – John Tilbury (piano), Keith Rowe (guitar, electronics), Eddie Prévost (drums), plus Gare on tenor – showcasing their subtle dynamic variation and the understated self-communing of Gare himself. From the massive "Igneous" to the noise drones of "Sedimentary", this is a consistently absorbing and wholly original album.

>> **Eddie Prévost** *(AMM Music 1966; The Crypt – 12 June 1968).*

Ed "Montudi" Garland

Bass.

b. New Orleans, 9 Jan 1885; d. 22 Jan 1980.

The father of jazz double bass, Garland first played on "a stick attached to a hole in a milk can with a string run to the top". At fifteen he was playing bass drum in Frank Duson's Eagle Band (Black Benny was in it too), but soon specialized on double bass and worked with Buddy Bolden at Hank's Saloon, Funky Butt Hall and all over Storyville. He played with Buddy Petit and Manuel Babes before pioneering around the South with Mabel Lee Lane's vaudeville troupe, and by 1917 was raising a riot in Chicago with Sugar Johnny's Creole Band: "Montudi, Tubby Hall and I beat out a rhythm that put the Bechuana tribes of Africa to shame", Lil Hardin Armstrong recalled later. Garland went to California with King Oliver in 1921 to help out Kid Ory with a double booking, liked the climate as well as the music, and stayed.

From 1922, when with Ory he recorded the first-ever black New Orleans jazz for the Spikes Brothers' Sunshine label ("Ory's Creole Trombone" and "Society Blues"), Montudi lived on America's West Coast, working with Ory and others, leading his own One-Eleven Club band, and playing mood music for Hollywood silent films. In the 1930s came a spell of Hollywood parties and a quieter period until he reteamed with Kid Ory for the Standard Oil Broadcasts, compered by Orson Welles, which helped to establish the American jazz revival. From then on Garland worked constantly, with stars including Ory, Earl Hines, Turk Murphy, Joe Darensbourg and Andrew Blakeney. In 1974 he was still touring Europe and America (with Barry Martyn), nearly blind but still immaculate (he was nicknamed after a legendary New Orleans dandy). In September that year he was honoured by President Gerald Ford as "the oldest living sideman". [DF]

Kid Ory

Kid Ory's Creole Jazz Band 1954 (Good Time Jazz). A regular colleague of Ory, Garland's slap-happy playing shows up to advantage here with Mutt Carey, Omer Simeon and the leader.

Joe Garland

Tenor, baritone and bass saxophones, arranger.

b. Norfolk, Virginia, 15 Aug 1903; d. 21 April 1977.

Joe Garland's career resembles Eddie Barefield's in more ways than one: both men were outstanding soloists, experienced musical directors, and more than competent arrangers, as well as versatile multi-reedmen. Garland's New York career began in 1925 at the Bamville Club with Elmer Snowden's band, after which he played under a variety of leaders and with Mills Blue Rhythm Band under Lucky Millinder (1932–6). Then came year-long stays with Edgar Hayes (1937) and Don Redman (1938), before in 1939 he joined Louis Armstrong's big band for an association which was to last until 1947. After Luis Russell's connection with Armstrong was severed in late 1940, Garland took over musical direction of Armstrong's orchestra as well. Said Louis, "he couldn't stand hearing wrong notes! He'd make a funny noise in his throat – and that cat didn't need telling again!" After Armstrong gave up his big band, Garland – by now well known as the composer of Glenn Miller's hit "In The Mood" – worked for Claude Hopkins and as musical director for Earl Hines. But from the early 1950s he left full-time music and put together bands for fun as well as cultivating an intense interest in photography. A highly competent professional, Joe Garland deserves re-assessment; after all, Louis Armstrong called him "one of the greatest musicians I ever worked with". [DF]

>> **Louis Armstrong** *(Louis Armstrong 1939–40 [Classics]).*

Red Garland

Piano.

b. Dallas, Texas, 13 May 1923; d. 23 April 1984.

Red (William) Garland was a rather idiosyncratic stylist, whose wide influence stemmed from his work in the Miles Davis group between 1955–8. Previously he had accompanied several name soloists in Philadelphia and Boston, and toured with Eddie Vinson in the late 1940s alongside John Coltrane. By the time of his first recordings with Davis, Garland was strongly indebted to Ahmad Jamal (and perhaps also to Parker's pianist Walter Bishop) and his use of boppish but tinkly solo lines was actively encouraged by Miles; so too was his right-hand chording which, however, had a distinctive sound due to the frequent inclusion of "wrong" notes. After a period of success as a trio leader in the early 1960s Garland returned first to Philadelphia and then to Dallas, and despite being "rediscovered" he seldom recaptured the jaunty confidence of his 1950s recordings. [BP]

⊙ **All Mornin' Long** (1957; Prestige/OJC). As well as featuring typical Garland solos and backings, this is one of three albums from marathon sessions featuring Donald Byrd and John Coltrane, just before he and Garland rejoined Miles for the *Milestones* period.

>> **John Coltrane** *(Traneing In).*

Tim Garland

Tenor and soprano saxophones, woodflute, synthesizer.

b. Ilford, Essex, UK, 19 Oct 1966.

Garland studied composition at the London Guildhall School of Music. He was commissioned to write a suite for his college quintet and composed "Points On The Curve" in 1988. He had been playing saxophone for only three years when the music was recorded on an eponymous album. In 1990 he spent six months with Ronnie Scott's band, playing in the UK and northern Europe. He also won the BBC soloist award in 1989. He met guitarist Don Paterson and started writing very folk-oriented material; they formed Lammas, which was originally a trio with a tabla player. The final line-up recorded an album in 1991 and went on to win the British Jazz Award for Best Ensemble in 1993. Since 1994 Garland has also led a quintet which included the brilliant young trumpeter Gerard Presencer. He plays regularly with Jim Mullen, John Dankworth, Anthony Kerr and the London Jazz Orchestra (LJO). Garland has also composed and arranged several excellent pieces for the LJO. He is now Composer-in-residence at Newcastle University. [IC]

⊙ **Points On The Curve** (1988; FMR). Garland's debut album is astonishingly brilliant. Nine of the ten compositions are his, and his playing is mature with a sinuous flow of invention. His quintet is a wonderfully flexible and sure unit, with trumpeter Paul Dias-Jayasinha, pianist Robin Aspland, bassist Howard Britz and drummer Mark Fletcher.

⊙ **Enter The Fire** (1997; Linn Records). Featuring Garland's quartet of young lions – pianist Jason Rebello, bassist Mick Hutton and drummer Jeremy Stacey, with trumpeter Gerard Presencer added on five of the ten tracks. Garland wrote all of the pieces except "Only Child" (Bill Evans's lovely ballad), Gershwin's "I Loves You Porgy", and Ornette Coleman's "Rejoicing". His band is terrific and he is very much his own man.

Lammas

⊙ **This Morning** (1993; EFZ). Garland with Fletcher again and acoustic guitarist Don Paterson, Steafan Hannigan on Uillean pipes, bodhran and percussion, and Christine Tobin on vocals make up Lammas, which fuses folk and jazz in a fascinating synthesis.

Erroll Garner

Piano.

b. Pittsburgh, Pennsylvania, 15 June 1921; d. 2 Jan 1977.

Garner, who was recognized in early childhood as a gifted musician, had an elder brother, Linton Garner, who also became a professional pianist (b. 25 March 1915; d. 6 Mar 2003). Erroll appeared from the age of ten with the Kan-D-Kids entertainers on KQV Radio, and at sixteen he joined local saxophonist Leroy Brown. After work with singers and piano duettists, he moved to New York in 1944 and achieved immediate nightclub success. Apart from a year with Slam Stewart in 1944–5, and the occasional all-star jam session, he worked only as a soloist or as the leader of his own trio and, thanks to strong management, graduated in the 1950s from nightclubs to top-class hotels and international concert tours.

Garner may have been inspired by the example of Earl Hines, a fellow Pittsburgh resident but eighteen years his senior, and there were resemblances in their elastic approach to timing and the use of right-hand octaves. Erroll's style, however, was unique and had neither obvious forerunners nor competent imitators (although at an amateur level more players attempted to imitate him than any other pianist in jazz history). A key factor in his sound was the independence of his springy but rock-steady left hand from the seemingly wayward melodies of the right. Whether in ultra-slow ballads or rampant up-tempo improvisation, this never failed to convey a humorous and titillating attitude to both the material at hand and the audience.

Although his tune "Misty" rapidly became a standard with singers, it was never a favourite with fellow instrumentalists. Erroll, however, was a jazz musician

Herman Leonard

Erroll Garner

through and through, his popular appeal arising directly from his playing. It was achieved without the aid of jocular vocals or ingratiating announcements, in the manner of Armstrong or Waller (the only comparable figures in terms of earning universal affection), and it seems equally unlikely that he tailored his music to the demands of success. He merely found the way to people's hearts and never lost it. [BP]

⊙ **Body And Soul** (1951–2; Columbia). Recorded for 78rpm singles, these twenty trios (with John Simmons and Shadow Wilson) hardly suffer from the time restriction, with brief ballads balanced by effervescent effusions on "The Way You Look Tonight" and a great "Honeysuckle Rose".

⊙ **Contrasts** (1954; Verve). Garner's best-known original, "Misty", heard during a marathon Chicago studio session, before the strings got to it.

⊙ **Concert By The Sea** (1955; Columbia). A famously casual date originally recorded for local radio, with Erroll stretching "Autumn Leaves" to the limit and blowing the blues on "Red Top".

Carlos Garnett

Tenor, alto and soprano saxophones; also piano, drums, ukulele, congas, flute.

b. Red Tank, Panama, 1 Dec 1938.

Although his grandfather was a guitarist-organist and his mother played organ, Garnett taught himself saxophone as a teenager. He worked with several groups in Panama from 1957, then moved to New York in 1962, initially playing rock and soul and then co-leading BAJI (Brooklyn Afro Jazz Inc). He worked with Freddie Hubbard, Andrew Hill, Woody Shaw, Art Blakey, Charles Mingus and Miles Davis (appearing on *On The Corner* and other sessions in 1972). He recorded with Pharoah Sanders, Mtume and on five dates by drummer Norman Connors, and formed "Universal Black Force" to combine jazz influences with Afro-Caribbean music and soul, making albums such as *Black Love*. Largely inactive in the 1980s, Garnett formed a new quartet in the 1990s and made three albums. Blakey, Davis, Hubbard and McCoy Tyner have all been a source of inspiration, as well as his favourite saxophonists Coltrane, Shorter, Johnny Griffin, Harold Land (for his "mellow and almost-spiritual tone"), Hank Mobley, Branford Marsalis, Joshua Redman and Courtney Pine. [BP]

⊙ **Under Nubian Skies** (1997; HighNote). Augmenting his quartet with young trumpeter Russell Gunn, Garnett now plays in a lighter, straightahead, neo-bop style but, alongside the Mellin-Wood standard "My One And Only Love", he creates melodically captivating originals with solo work to match.

Kenny Garrett

Alto and soprano saxophones, flute.

b. Detroit, Michigan, 9 Oct 1960.

Although initially famous chiefly for his spell with Miles Davis – he is featured on the albums *Amandla* and *Dingo* – Kenny Garrett swiftly established himself as a substantial presence on the 1990s jazz scene, both as a scorching frontline soloist on others' projects, and as a leader of his own sharp band, which purveyed passionate straightahead jazz with a street-smart edge. He has contributed his virtuosic, sinewy alto to the music of many leaders, from the funky jazz of Headhunters drummer Mike Clark, to the post-bop subtleties of pianists Geri Allen, Stephen Scott, Chick Corea and Mulgrew Miller, as well as sharing solo duties with the likes of trombonist Clifton Anderson, trumpeter Terence Blanchard and saxophonist David Sanchez. He began by playing with local musicians Bill Wiggins and Marcus Belgrave and gained valuable experience in Mercer Ellington's orchestra before moving to New York in 1980 and making his debut album as leader, *Introducing Kenny Garrett*, in 1984. A stint with neo-bop band Out Of The Blue followed, but his considerable reputation now rests on his mid-1990s offerings. *Pursuance* (Warner Bros; 1996), featuring Pat Metheny, was one of the finest Coltrane tributes of the many 30th-anniversary offerings; *Songbook* (Warner Bros; 1997), with the late Kenny Kirkland leading the rhythm-section, offered pithy originals throughout. His most representative album of the period, however, may be *Trilogy* (see below). Continuing to be in demand by the likes of Herbie Hancock (*Gershwin's World*) and John Scofield (*Works For Me*), his prolific output as leader on Warners remains of the highest quality. [CP/CI]

⊙ **Introducing Kenny Garrett** (1984; Criss Cross). Promising debut leading stellar band including trumpeter Woody Shaw (who plays beautifully throughout), Mulgrew Miller (piano), Nat Reeves (bass) and drummer Tony Reedus.

⊙ **Garrett 5** (1988; Paddle Wheel). Similar band as above, but with Wallace Roney taking on trumpet duties and Charnett Moffett on bass. Mulgrew Miller is outstanding, his sparkling but delicate runs complementing Garrett's bluesiness perfectly.

⊙ **Trilogy** (1995; Warner Bros). Featuring Garrett's then working trio – bassist Kiyoshi Kitagawa, drummer Brian Blade – plus a couple with Charnett Moffett, this no-nonsense set of originals, warhorses ("Giant Steps") and standards puts a whip-smart band through its hugely enjoyable paces in a conscious emulation of previous masters of the saxophone-trio genre, Sonny Rollins and Joe Henderson.

⊙ **Standard Of Language** (2003; Warner). Following on from albums – *Simply Said* (1999; Warner) and *Happy People* (2002; Warner) – in which Garrett's technique, imagination and passionate swing are in full flow, this eighth Warners release features a set of intense originals (plus a searing romp through "What Is This Thing Called Love") in the estimable company of regulars – pianist Vernell Brown Jnr, bassist Charnett Moffett and drummer Chris "Daddy" Dave.

➤➤ **Miles Davis** *(Amandla)*; **Mulgrew Miller** *(Hand In Hand)*; **Roy Haynes** *(Birds Of A Feather)*.

Michael Garrick

Piano, pipe organ, keyboards, composer.

b. Enfield, Middlesex, UK, 30 May 1933.

Garrick took a BA in English Literature at London University, but as a musician he was self-taught, except for some classes at the Ivor Mairants School of Dance Music. In the 1970s he attended Berklee College, Boston, as a mature student. He began leading small groups back in the late 1950s and was one of the pioneers of Poetry and Jazz concerts, working with various British poets and leading a quintet which included Joe Harriott and Shake Keane. From 1965–9 he was pianist with the Rendell-Carr quintet, and from 1966 was regularly leading his own sextet.

He is a prolific composer and several of his compositions were an important part of the Rendell-Carr repertoire. In 1967 he composed *Jazz Praises*, a cycle of religious pieces for his sextet and a large choir, which was performed and recorded in St Paul's Cathedral, London, the following year. As well as being deeply versed in jazz and church music, Garrick has studied Indian music, and several of his compositions are inspired by Indian scales and techniques. He is very active in jazz education, teaching at schools, on short courses and at London's Royal Academy of Music. Among his favourite pianists are Bill Evans, John Taylor, Duke Ellington and Herbie Hancock, and he also cites John Lewis and Kenny Wheeler as inspirational figures. Poetry is an abiding interest for him, and for years he has been studying Rudolf Steiner's Anthroposophy. Some of Garrick's best, and best-known, compositions are *Dusk Fire*, *Black Marigolds* and *Cold Mountain*, all small-group pieces, and bigger works such as *Jazz Praises*, *Mr Smith's Apocalypse*, *Zodiac Of Angels*, *The Royal Box* (a big-band work inspired by the marital turmoils of the British royal family) and *Bovingdon Poppies*, a composition for choirs, string orchestra and Garrick's quintet. [IC]

⊙ **Meteors Close At Hand** (1994; Jazz Academy). Garrick's first big-band album, this double CD features excellent and varied writing for the leader.

⊙ **Down On Your Knees** (1998; Jazz Academy). This is a rich and delightful big-band album featuring the fine singer Anita Wardell on four of the thirteen tracks. Garrick has cunningly rearranged some of his earlier music and given it fresh life. But his new compositions, including the title track with its pointed lyrics beautifully sung by Wardell, are excellent and the band is strong in soloists.

Jimmy Garrison

Bass.

b. Miami, Florida, 3 March 1934; d. 7 April 1976.

Garrison was raised in Philadelphia where he played with local groups until 1958, when Philly Joe Jones brought him to New York. There he gigged with various people including Lennie Tristano, Benny Golson, Bill Evans and Kenny Dorham, but only began to be noticed when he joined Ornette Coleman's group at the Five Spot. Coltrane sat in with Coleman's group and liked Garrison so much that he offered him the job with his own quartet. From 1961–6 he was a fundamental force in Coltrane's group, and as Elvin Jones commented, "He was the turning point ... his aggressiveness, his attitude toward the instrument gave us all a lift." Garrison left in the summer of 1966, and co-led a group with Hampton Hawes for six months. Then, with Archie Shepp's group, he toured and played festivals in the USA and Europe during 1967–8. He was with the Elvin Jones trio in 1968–9 and then taught for a year (1970–1) at both Bennington College and Wesleyan University, performing as a soloist at the Bennington graduation ceremony. In 1972 he was with Alice Coltrane and he rejoined Jones in 1973. Then ill-health beset him; he had trouble with a hand in late 1974 and a lung operation in 1975. He died of lung cancer in 1976.

Garrison played the bass as a bass – as the rock-solid fundament of a band. He was not interested in the Scott LaFaro style which "liberated" the instrument from the "tyranny" of roots, giving it a front-line role. Talking of Garrison's role in the Coltrane quartet, McCoy Tyner said, "He was like the pivot in the group. He had excellent time, good supportive work, knew the function of the bass." Yet Garrison was also a powerful soloist both pizzicato and with a bow, and he was a master of double and multiple stopping, strumming the instrument with his thumb like a guitar. [IC]

➤➤ **John Coltrane** *(A Love Supreme)*; **Elvin Jones** *(Puttin' It Together)*.

Leonard Gaskin

Bass.

b. Brooklyn, New York, 25 Aug 1920.

A bassist remarkable for his versatility, and latterly a teacher of note, Gaskin took up bass in high school and worked first among the emergent bebop generation of the early 1940s, including Duke Jordan, Dizzy Gillespie and Charlie Parker. He remained busy for another ten years, recording with Miles Davis and others, and in 1956 joined Eddie Condon, with whom he toured in 1957 as well as staying busy with studio work. In the 1960s and after he remained a central figure in New York's bass fraternity and by the late 1970s was touring Europe, with the Oliver Jackson trio, Panama Francis, Sy Oliver, and the educational ensemble International Art of Jazz. [DF]

➤➤ **Eddie Condon** *(Dixieland Jam)*.

Giorgio Gaslini

Piano, composer, synthesizer.

b. Milan, 22 Oct 1929.

Gaslini had piano lessons as a child and studied composition at Milan Conservatory of Music. He appeared at the Florence jazz festival in 1947 with his own trio. From 1957–60 he was active as a player and composer and as a conductor of symphony orchestras, and he composed and played the music for Antonioni's film *La Notte* (1960). From 1963 he led his own quartet. In 1965 he wrote and performed the music for another film, Vermuccio's *Un Amore*. During the 1960s Gaslini took his music to the people, playing with his quartet in factories, hospitals, universities, cinemas and concert halls, in an attempt to make jazz part of the fabric of Italian life, but he has also played many festivals in Italy and elsewhere in Europe. He has worked with Gato Barbieri, Max Roach, Don Cherry and others, and has been active in music education. In 1970 his jazz opera, *Colloquio con Malcolm X*, was performed in Genoa and recorded. He was friendly with Eric Dolphy, and after the saxophonist's death he composed "I Remember Dolphy".

Gaslini is a consummate pianist and composer, and his concept in both capacities is pluralistic; he is at home with any area or context – classical, neo-bop, total or partial abstraction. He has remained active though was at the height of his powers in the 1980s and 1990s, having recorded some of the most outstanding piano albums of both decades. [IC]

⊙ **Gaslini Plays Monk** (1981; Soul Note). Gaslini playing solo piano pays profound homage by finding his own space and meaning inside Monk's idiosyncratic compositions.

⊙ **Schumann Reflections** (1984; Soul Note). Gaslini, with bassist Piero Leveratto and drummer Paolo Pellegati, plays the thirteen pieces which comprise Schumann's *Kinderszenen* and at intervals inserts one of the four movements of his own *Reflections*, which is a kind of commentary on the Schumann.

⊙ **Ayler's Wings** (1990; Soul Note). This is a bold and brilliant solo piano exploration of some of Albert Ayler's most famous pieces.

⊙ **Lampi** (1994; Soul Note). This quartet album with bass, drums and Daniele Di Gregorio on vibes, marimba and percussion is another *tour de force* – packed with incident and drama.

⊙ **Jelly's Back In Town** (1996; DDQ). This Gaslini tribute album is to Jelly Roll Morton, and he deploys the Ensemble Mobile, a 19-piece orchestra with brass, reeds, woodwinds, rhythm-section with percussion, and a vocalist. There are three guest soloists, trumpeter Paolo Fresu, tenor and soprano saxophonist Tino Tracanna and Gianluigi Trovesi on alto saxophone and bass-clarinet. Gaslini explores the New Orleans music which Morton drew on to make his own seminal contribution to jazz, with fascinating results.

Al Gay

Clarinet, tenor, alto and soprano saxophones.
b. London, 25 Feb 1928.

An original member of the Jive Bombers, who won the *Melody Maker* All-British championship of 1946, Gay went on to work with Freddy Randall (1953–7), then Bobby Mickleburgh, Laurie Gold, Joe Daniels and Harry Gold. In 1961 he joined Bob Wallis's younger Storyville Jazzmen, for whom he provided an elegant dash of sophistication, and by 1963 had joined Alex Welsh's new band. With Welsh he recorded prolifically, broadcast on radio and TV, and toured alongside great American visitors such as Earl Hines and Ruby Braff. In the 1970s and 80s he freelanced with Stan Greig, Randall again and with Ron Russell's band before rejoining Welsh in 1977, replacing John Barnes. He also led his own quartet for BBC work and club dates and in 1978 toured with The World's Greatest Jazz Band. More recently Gay has worked regularly with trumpeter Keith Smith in a variety of package shows, as well as with the Val Wiseman package *Lady Sings The Blues* and Digby Fairweather's Jazz Superkings and First Class Sounds. From 1999 he joined Laurie Chescoe's Good Time Jazz. With Danny Moss, Gay is one of Britain's most distinguished mainstream tenormen, but where Moss paints in the deep oils of Ben Webster, or Arnett Cobb, Gay's lines are watercolour – somewhere between Zoot Sims and Eddie Miller. [DF]

➤➤ **Val Wiseman** *(Lady Sings The Blues).*

Charles Gayle

Tenor saxophone, bass-clarinet, piano.
b. Buffalo, New York, 28 Feb 1939.

Not a great deal is known about Charles Gayle's relationship to the 60s New York free-jazz scene, to which he reputedly contributed: he remained out of the spotlight until the late 80s, when constant concerts at the Knitting Factory and numerous records helped catapult him into the limited stardom open to a furious free-jazzer. Gayle's saxophone sound is clearly indebted to Albert Ayler, with whom he shares rough, at times jagged, tone and boundless energy; Gayle's bass-clarinet playing suggests the extremes that instrument can achieve, making David Murray's altissimo reach seem stifled.

He moved into the public ear starting with appearances at the mid-80s Sound Unity festival, New York, where he met bassist Peter Kowald. Enamoured of his playing, Kowald helped take Gayle on a tour of Europe, during which he played in trios with bassist Torsten Müller and drummer Sven Ake-Johansson. Gayle's reclusive street existence – squatting and at times homeless – and the born-again Christian, anti-gay, anti-abortion preaching with which he sometimes peppered his performances (which he has thankfully stopped), all threatened to overshadow his identity as a player, but records like *Spirits Before* (1988; Silkheart), *Consecration* (1993; Black Saint) and *Repent* (1992; Knitting Factory) have cemented him as one of the major "fire music" players of the decade. He has recorded an album of solos, *Unto I Am* (1995; Victo), and highlighted his piano playing – piano was his first instrument – on *Kingdom Come* (1994; Knitting Factory) with bassist William Parker and drum legend Sunny Murray. On *Daily Bread* (1998; Black Saint) he even played viola. After an overabundance of recordings, many of them sub-par, his output slowed considerably at the end of the 90s, although a more overt melody of sorts began to infuse his playing on albums such as the uplifting, gospel-influenced *Delivered* (1997; Thirsty Ear) and *Jazz Solo Piano* (2001; Knitting Factory). [JC]

⊙ **Touchin' On Trane** (1993; FMP). This is Gayle at his best, with bassist Parker and another free-drumming legend, Rashied Ali. They don't play any Coltrane, but the feel is more relaxed, less constantly aggressive than Gayle can be. Where he has too often recorded with musicians of far lower calibre than he, Gayle is in good company with this rhythm team.

Jonathan Gee

Piano, composer.

b. Jaffa, Israel, 6 March 1959.

Since winning *Wire* magazine's "Most Promising Newcomer" award in 1991, Jonathan Gee has established himself as a central figure on the UK jazz scene, both with his own trio of bassist Steve Rose and drummer Winston Clifford, and as a regular collaborator with visiting Americans. He began with classical training at the age of five, but abandoned it for rock music as a teenager, performing on the guitar and singing. He played jazz piano while at university in Sheffield, and on graduating enrolled at London's Guildhall School of Music, but left after a week to immerse himself in the UK jazz scene, playing with Bobby Wellins, Iain Ballamy, Eddie Parker, Dylan Fowler's Frevo and Dick Heckstall-Smith. In 1988, he released a trio album, *Blah, Blah, Blah, Etc, Etc*, on cassette, featuring bassist Thad Kelly and drummer Peter Fairclough, but it was not until 1997 that his first CD as leader, *Closer To* (ASC), with Rose and Clifford, was released. In the 1990s, Gee played at many festivals worldwide, in places ranging from Zagreb to Yaoundé, and Cork to Thessaloniki; he also became a regular pianist for saxophonist Ed Jones in his various projects, and played with a large number of well-established jazz names, including Benny Golson and Joe Lovano (in week-long residencies at Ronnie Scott's), Teddy Edwards, Art Farmer, Sonny Fortune, Andy Sheppard, Courtney Pine and David Murray. A gutsy but thoughtful pianist equally adept at scintillating runs and chunkily propulsive comping, Gee is also one of the UK's hardest-working jazz musicians, constantly touring – including visits to New York, Israel and Spain in the spring of 2002 with his international Quartet, featuring trumpeter Damon Brown and Israeli musicians Yorai Oron on bass and Yaaki Levy at the drums – and appearing on albums by artists ranging from singers Claire Martin and Alison Bentley to vibes player Orphy Robinson and Blue Note hit-makers US3. Having latterly developed his own singing voice, Gee has recently been performing a set of sophisticated standards in the company of another pianist/vocalist, Dominic Aldiss. [CP/CI]

⊙ **Your Shining Heart** (1998; ASC). Featuring Gee's regular trio on ten in-house originals, mostly by Gee himself, a fair representation of a fiercely interactive band, with Gee's sparkling but vigorous piano propelled by Rose and Clifford, one of the UK's tightest young rhythm-sections.

Herb Geller

Alto and soprano saxophones, flute.

b. Los Angeles, 2 Nov 1928.

After working with Joe Venuti in 1946, Geller moved to New York and played with Claude Thornhill and Billy May among others. In 1951 he returned to Los Angeles and worked with several small groups; he also led an occasional quartet with his pianist wife Lorraine. He then went on tour with Benny Goodman, and played for Louie Bellson in 1959 and 1961. This was followed by a move to Europe in 1962. After doing some studio work in Berlin, he has worked since 1965 in studio bands of the NDR (Hamburg) under various leaders including Peter Herbolzheimer. In the 1950s Geller was more Parker-influenced than many altoists based on the West Coast and, though not overexposed as a soloist recently, he has updated his style considerably. [BP]

⊙ **That Geller Feller** (1957; Fresh Sound). A rare LP sometimes known as *Fire In The West*, this reissue teams Geller with players such as Harold Land and Kenny Dorham for a demonstration that 1950s hard bop was not restricted to the East Coast.

Stan Getz

Tenor saxophone.

b. Philadelphia, 2 Feb 1927; d. 6 June 1991.

Getz's big-band experience began when he was fifteen, and included work with Jack Teagarden in 1943, Stan Kenton in 1944–5, Jimmy Dorsey in 1945 and Benny Goodman in 1945–6. He made the first recordings under his own name at nineteen. From 1947–9 he played with the Woody Herman band, and then began leading his own quartet/quintet. He also worked as a soloist in Scandinavia in 1951, as a guest with Kenton in the winter of 1953–4 and with Jazz At The Philharmonic in 1957–8, including a trip to Europe. He was out of circulation during 1954 owing to drug offences, and he remained in Europe for three years from 1958–61, settling in Copenhagen. He returned to the USA to lead his own quartet and, between 1962–4, made popular albums with Charlie Byrd, Luiz Bonfa and João and Astrud Gilberto. Members of his regular groups over the years have included vibes player Gary Burton, keyboard players Chick Corea, Stanley Cowell, Joanne Brackeen and Kenny Barron; bassists Steve Swallow, Miroslav Vitous and Stanley Clarke; and drummers Roy Haynes, Jack DeJohnette, Tony Williams, Billy Hart and Victor Lewis. In 1972 Getz started producing and leasing his own albums and thereafter his successes of the 1960s enabled him to live in semi-retirement and re-form his group for specific engagements. He was artist in residence at Stanford University in 1986, but he continued to make occasional tours, even in early 1991, while under the shadow of his terminal cancer.

HERMAN LEONARD

Stan Getz

Getz is one of the most renowned of jazzmen, and one of comparatively few who have achieved widespread acclaim while retaining the admiration of their fellow musicians. The reasons lie, on both sides, in his appealing sense of melody and his often exquisite tone. Neither was attained overnight, and many of his early records are closely based on the vocabulary of Lester Young but with a less expressive sound. But as early as the 1948 "Early Autumn" with Herman and his 1951 recordings in Sweden, the distinctive featherweight tone matches the floating quality of his lines. In the second half of the 1950s a more metallic ring underlines his acquisition of some overt blues influence, and both aspects are blended into a new melodic refinement in his mature 1960s style.

Despite the enormous popularity of his bossa nova albums of this period, such material always formed a small proportion of his repertoire. The paramount importance of melody in the pop outings and the much greater rhythmic development in his other work, especially live, created an artistic tension which gave his later playing its all-encompassing strength. Certainly his sound-quality displayed an extraordinary combination of emotive colour and cutting edge. [BP]

STAN GETZ

⊙ **The Complete Roost Recordings** (1950–4; Roost). A cross-section of early work, with the translucent studio ballads (and interesting but polite versions of Horace Silver and Gigi Gryce compositions) contrasted with unbuttoned live work from the Storyville club, which was once also available on a separate CD.

⊙ **At The Shrine** (1954; Verve). This famous live set with Bob Brookmeyer on trombone has much jaunty interplay between the two, presaging the one-off *At The Opera House* set with J.J. Johnson.

STAN GETZ AND EDDIE SAUTER

⊙ **Focus** (1961; Verve). A uniquely successful setting for Getz among a small string ensemble, playing original material by Sauter and with Roy Haynes on one track.

STAN GETZ

⊙ **Getz/Gilberto** (1964; Verve). So named for the bossa nova guitar and vocals of João Gilberto, although it was the waif-like Astrud who made the album a hit. With Jobim at the piano, Getz is more appropriately supported than on *Jazz Samba* with Charlie Byrd.

⊙ **Sweet Rain** (1967; Verve). A return to straight quartet playing with a version of "Con Alma" and Mike Gibbs's excellent title track. Acoustic work by Chick Corea contrasts with the 1972 *Captain Marvel* to which he contributed some Return To Forever material.

⊙ **The Dolphin** (1981; Concord). Typical of Getz's late work after a flirtation with electronics in the 1970s, this is distinguished by his take on "The Night Has A Thousand Eyes" with Lou Levy.

➤➤ **J.J. Johnson** *(At The Opera House).*

Ghanaba

Drums, African percussion, composer.

b. Accra, Ghana, 4 May 1923.

Born Guy Warren, Ghanaba went to the Government Elementary Boys' School, Accra, from 1928–39, and was leader of the school band in his last two years. In 1940 he drummed for the Accra Rhythmic Orchestra, and in 1941 he won a teacher-training scholarship to Achimota College, Accra, but dropped out in 1943. He visited the USA that year while working for the US army. During the years 1943–52 he was back in Africa, where he worked as a reporter, newspaper editor, radio disc jockey and musician – playing with one of the most famous African jazz groups, the Tempos. In 1950 he spent some time in London, playing with Kenny Graham's Afro-Cubists. In 1953 he took his own band, the Afro-Cubists, to play at the inauguration of President W. Tubman of Liberia, and stayed on there in the capital, Monrovia, working as a DJ. In 1955 he went to Chicago, joining the Gene Esposito band as co-leader, percussionist and arranger. With this band he recorded his album *Africa Speaks, America Answers*, in 1956, which sold over a million copies and includes his composition "That Happy Feeling". In 1957 he moved to New York, leading his own trio at the African Room and recording his classic album *Themes For African Drums*. While working in the USA he was associated with many of the leading musicians of the time including Max Roach, Dizzy Gillespie, Lester Young and Billie Holiday. Since the early 1960s Ghanaba has lived on the outskirts of Accra, returning to the UK and USA only occasionally to record or play concerts.

Ghanaba, also known as "Kofi" and "The Divine Drummer", has created a music all his own; it is profoundly African, but it is leavened with the linear improvisation of jazz and with some European harmonic elements. His music also has a surprisingly wide emotional and tonal scope, ranging from the violent energy and passion of "Burning Bush" (percussion, brass, saxophone) to gentle tone poems such as "I Love The Silence" (voice, African xylophone and guitar) and the joyous lilt of "That Happy Feeling". Historically, he is one of the founders of black pride and was the main African influence on jazz in the USA and Europe in the 1950s. Max Roach wrote in 1974: "I met Ghanaba in Chicago in 1956 ... Ghanaba was so far ahead of what we were all doing, that none of us understood what he was saying – that in order for Afro-American music to be stronger, it must cross-fertilize with its African origins ... We ignored him. Seventeen years later, Black Music in America has turned to Africa for inspiration and rejuvenation, and the African sound of Ghanaba is now being imitated all over the United States..." Ghanaba recorded the albums *Afro-Jazz* (1968) and *That Happy Feeling* (1978) in London with Ghanaian and British musicians. **[IC]**

Mike Gibbs

Trombone, piano, composer, arranger.
b. Harare, Zimbabwe, 25 Sept 1937.

Gibbs took piano lessons for ten years from the age of seven, and studied the trombone from seventeen. From 1959–62 he was at Berklee, and in 1961 he won a full scholarship to the Lenox School of Jazz, where he studied with Gunther Schuller, George Russell and J.J. Johnson. In 1962 he graduated from Berklee with a diploma in arranging and composition, and recorded his first album as an arranger for Gary Burton, with Phil Woods, Tommy Flanagan and Joe Morello. In 1963 he gained a BMus from Boston Conservatory and a scholarship to Tanglewood Summer School studying with Aaron Copland, Iannis Xenakis, Schuller and Lukas Foss. He briefly went back to Rhodesia, then moved to the UK in 1965, playing trombone and arranging with Graham Collier, John Dankworth, Cleo Laine, Tubby Hayes and working as a studio musician. From 1968–74 he played concerts and clubs and did radio broadcasts in the UK and Europe with his own bands, and performed his music with the radio big bands of Denmark, Sweden and Hamburg, and with the Hanover Radio Symphony Orchestra. In the early 1970s he won several *Melody Maker* awards, and his LP *In The Public Interest* was voted best album of 1974.

By the late 1960s Gibbs was generally recognized as being one of the leading younger composer/arrangers in jazz. He had already absorbed his main influences (Gil Evans and Olivier Messiaen – particularly the *Turangalîla* symphony) and found his own sound and style. His buoyant rock rhythms and his use of asymmetry anticipated the jazz-rock movement of the 1970s, and compositions such as "Family Joy, Oh Boy!" and "Tanglewood '63" showed an extraordinary melodic gift as well as great orchestral sonority. In particular, his writing for the lower instruments was often powerfully dramatic, and his work already showed considerable emotional resonance, ranging from the ominous brooding of "On The Third Day" to the irrepressible high spirits of "Family Joy", one of the most joyous compositions in jazz or any other music. In 1974 he moved to the USA to take up the post of composer in residence at Berklee, but continued to do occasional tours and concerts with his own bands. From 1975–8 he played the Berlin festival and twice toured the UK. In 1978–81 he performed his music with the radio orchestras of Sweden, Finland and Cologne. In 1982 he produced guitarist Kevin Eubanks's first solo album, and acted as musical director for the Young Lions at the Kool jazz festival concert at Carnegie Hall, producing a live double album for them.

In 1983 he resigned from his Berklee post to freelance in New York as a composer/arranger/producer, and co-produced saxophonist Bill Evans's first album. His composition *Interviews*, commissioned by the Foundation of New American Music, was performed by the Orchestra (Los Angeles). By 1984, Gibbs had become a globetrotting orchestrator and producer, commuting between the USA and Europe. He orchestrated a ballet for John Dankworth and also Michael Mantler's composition for orchestra and soloists, *Twenty Five*; Gibbs conducted the first performance of this with the Cologne Radio Symphony Orchestra featuring Carla Bley, Steve Swallow, Nick Mason, Bill Frisell and Mantler. In 1985, he orchestrated Pat Metheny's film score for *Twice In A Lifetime*, and also John McLaughlin's *Concerto For Guitar* for the Los Angeles Philharmonic. He also moved back to London that year.

Mike Gibbs has composed and arranged music for several feature films, and for two ballets for the Ballet Rambert, London. His compositions have also been recorded by Gary Burton, Stan Getz, Cleo Laine, John Dankworth, Stanley Clarke and others. His most recent project is a collaboration with pianist Joachim Kuhn, who is the principal soloist on an album called *Europeana Jazzphony No. 1*, for which Gibbs arranged thirteen European folk songs using the Hanover Radio Philharmonic Orchestra and featuring some other leading European jazz soloists as well as Kuhn. He has worked as an arranger on albums for many people including Joni Mitchell, Lenny White, Michael Walden, Peter Gabriel, Jaco Pastorius, Sister Sledge, Mantler and McLaughlin. He also currently leads his own Mike Gibbs Big Band. [IC]

⊙ **The Only Chrome Waterfall Orchestra** (1975; Ah Um). This is one of Gibbs's finest albums. Using a large orchestra in differing units and combinations he runs the gamut of emotion and musical architecture, from the airy textures of "Nairam" to the seething interlocking rhythms of "Blackgang" or the sonorous dialogues of "To Lady Mac: In Retrospect". Bob Moses and Steve Swallow mastermind the rhythm and the main soloists are Charlie Mariano, Philip Catherine and Tony Coe.

⊙ **Big Music** (1988; Virgin). This features another all-star big-band ensemble recorded in America with additional solos recorded in London. Again the music ranges from the overtly African "Kosasa" with its bustle and complex bass riff, to "Mopsus" (dedicated to Gil Evans) with its humorous reggae rhythm and easy pace. The main soloists are Bill Frisell, Chris Hunter, Lew Soloff, John Scofield and Dave Bargeron.

⊙ **By The Way ...** (1993; Ah Um). This is basically a British big band, but with Steve Swallow and Bob Moses or John Marshall on drums; the music is compelling, with fine solos from Kenny Wheeler, Evan Parker and Mariano.

⊙ **Europeana Jazzphony No. 1** (1994; ACT). This giant work, featuring Joachim Kuhn, also features soloists Django Bates, Albert Mangelsdorff, Markus Stockhausen, Klaus Doldinger, Christof Lauer and accordionist Richard Galliano. Gibbs handles with his usual aplomb the giant task of melding folk music, symphony orchestra and Kuhn's jazz trio into a rich fusion.

Terry Gibbs

Vibes; also drums.

b. Brooklyn, New Jersey, 13 Oct 1924.

Terry Gibbs (who changed his name from Julius Gubenko) came from a musical family. He won a radio amateur contest at twelve and played drums professionally before army service in World War II. He did small-group work, playing vibes, on 52nd Street in 1945–6, followed by touring jobs with Tommy Dorsey, Chubby Jackson, Buddy Rich in 1948 and the Woody Herman band in 1948–9. He led his own groups, and also worked with the Charlie Shavers-Louie Bellson band and Benny Goodman in 1951–2. He then led his own quintet or quartet and, after settling in Los Angeles in 1957, a part-time big band composed of jazz-inclined studio musicians. In 1964 he started working in television, becoming musical director of various shows. In the 1980s he was more active in live appearances, sometimes with Buddy DeFranco, and in the meantime his son Gerry Gibbs developed into an impressive drummer. An early enthusiast of bebop, Gibbs was nevertheless closer rhythmically to Lionel Hampton than Milt Jackson, but he was frequently an inventive soloist. His big band, which often included Mel Lewis on drums, was a precursor of the similar organization run by Lewis and Thad Jones, and was excellent of its kind. [BP]

⊙ **Main Stem** (1961; Contemporary). Part of a series of rediscovered live sessions by the West Coast big band, this has soloists such as Frank Rosolino and drumming by Mel Lewis to complement the updated swing-era feel of the exciting ensemble.

➤➤ **Buddy DeFranco** *(Holiday For Swing).*

Harry "The Hipster" Gibson

Piano, vocals.

b. New York, 1914; d. May 1991.

Harry Gibson (Harry Raab) began at the Yacht Club in New York as intermission pianist for Fats Waller, and later teamed with singer Ruth Gibson in a double act before working solo on 52nd Street in clubs such as the Hickory House, Onyx and Three Deuces. Gibson's hilarious and highly expert act included self-penned compositions such as "Handsome Harry The Hipster" and "Who Put The Benzedrine In Mrs Murphy's Ovaltine?", witty creations delivered in a voice that should have belonged to a black rather than a white hipster. By the mid-1940s Gibson was headlining in New York and on the West Coast (in 1947 he was on the cover of *Down Beat*), but his movements during the later 1940s and after are ill-documented. He is said to have become the conductor of the choir in the female prisoners' wing during imprisonment for drugs; to have written a hymn accepted by the Vatican for the Marian Year; and to have become involved in a car crash on an Indian reservation, after which he married the chief's daughter, a compulsive shoplifter. During the 1970s Gibson led a family band featuring his sons, but was apparently inactive from then until his death. In 1991 Arlena Gibson and Flavyn Feller produced an invaluable documentary on Gibson, including interview material, entitled *Boogie In Blue* (K Jazz KJ109). [DF]

⊙ **Boogie Woogie In Blue** (1944–6; Musicraft). This definitive Gibson collection has "Who Put The Benzedrine In Mrs Murphy's Ovaltine?", "Who's Goin' Steady With Who?", "What's His Story?" and other hipster essentials.

Gilberto Gil

Guitar, accordion, composer, singer.

b. Salvador, Brazil, 29 June 1942.

Although he began his musical life playing accordion, Gilberto Gil switched to guitar on hearing the bossa nova of João Gilberto. Other influences include everyone from legendary South American singer Yma Sumac to Miles Davis. Gil became a full-time musician after studying business administration at Salvador's Federal University, and quickly established himself as a protest singer extremely popular with Brazilians involved in the Tropicália movement, which opened up Brazilian music to all kinds of influences. Gil was not, however, popular with the Brazilian authorities, who arrested him in 1969, prompting him to emigrate on his release, and he did not return until 1972. Ever open to the music of others, he has collaborated with a variety of musical figures, including Stevie Wonder, Fela Kuti and the Wailers, with whom he recorded in 1978. A desire to "re-Africanize" Bahia led to his involvement in politics in the 1980s, and his music has always betrayed this interest. In 1997, however, Gil revealed himself as something of a Renaissance man with *Quanta*, a rich, thought-provoking confection touching on everything from particle physics to the commercialization of medicine, and from simple love songs to the workings of divine grace. As a sellout world tour the same year proved, he is a star of almost Bob Marley-esque proportions. [CP]

⊙ **Parabolic** (1991; WEA). Attractively lilting music produced by bassist Liminha; one of Gil's most instantly accessible albums.

⊙ **Amoroso/Brasil** (1993; WEA). Reissue of early 1980s music and featuring Gil alongside one of his great influences, João Gilberto.

⊙ **Quanta Gente Veio Ver** (1997; WEA). Live from the Teatro João Caetano in Rio, Gil leads a supple, vital septet through a selection of his most intriguing songs.

Astrud Gilberto

Vocals.

b. Bahia, Brazil, 1940.

Gilberto's family moved to Rio when she was two. Her professional debut as a singer occurred in 1963, at the beginning of the bossa nova impact on jazz, when she was asked to sing the English lyrics to "The Girl From Ipanema" on an album Stan Getz was making with her then husband João Gilberto, *Getz/Gilberto*. In 1964 she also sang on the album *Getz Au Go Go*, which was recorded live by a band which included Gary Burton and Kenny Burrell. Her deadpan delivery and girlish voice were an instant hit, and she subsequently toured several times with Getz.

She continues to tour and play international festivals, and was inducted into the 'International Latin Music Hall of Fame' in April 2002. [IC]

⊙ **Look To The Rainbow** (1966–7; Verve). Most of this disc has Gilberto with an orchestra conducted by Gil Evans, which doesn't prove to be the happiest of pairings – her voice is too unresponsive to Evans's characteristic textures. Six tracks added to this reissue with the organ trio of Walter Wanderley work rather better. Nothing, however, is quite the equal of Astrud's (brief) interjections on the Getz disc below.

➤➤ **Stan Getz** *(Getz/Gilberto)*.

João Gilberto

Vocals, guitar.

b. Juaseiro, Bahia, Brazil, June 1931.

Gilberto first played drums in a local band, then taught himself guitar, developing into a solo performer. The bossa nova style was invented by Antonio Carlos Jobim, who wrote "The Girl From Ipanema", but it was Gilberto who, in July 1957, made the first bossa nova record, a Jobim piece entitled "Desafinado" (Out Of Tune). It was an instant hit in Brazil, launching the whole bossa nova (new wave) movement which made an impact in the USA during the early 1960s. Gilberto went to the USA in 1963 and recorded an influential album with Stan Getz (*Getz/Gilberto*), which remained a best seller for several years. [IC]

➤➤ **Stan Getz** *(Getz/Gilberto)*.

Dizzy Gillespie

Trumpet, composer, vocals, conga, piano.

b. Cheraw, South Carolina, 21 Oct 1917; d. 6 Jan 1993.

Dizzy (John Birks) Gillespie's father was an amateur musician who played bass, mandolin, drums and piano, and through him Dizzy gained a working knowledge of several instruments. However, he died when Dizzy was ten, and the boy was mostly self-taught as a musician. He started on trombone at twelve and on trumpet about a year later. At sixteen he won a scholarship (for sports and music) to Laurinburg Institute in North Carolina, and spent two years there playing music but not studying it. From 1935 he lived in Philadelphia, playing in small groups and a big band led by Frank Fairfax. He developed precociously and was soon a virtuoso soloist in the style of his idol Roy Eldridge, whose role in the Teddy Hill band he inherited early in 1937. He stayed with Hill for two years, visiting Europe and recording his first solos with the band. From 1939–41 he was one of the three instrumental stars in Cab Calloway's band and his style was beginning to develop some of the elements of bebop. During this period he also began writing big-band arrangements, became friends with Charlie Parker and was already sitting in at Minton's Playhouse, where he, Thelonious Monk, Kenny Clarke and others were working out their revolutionary new ideas. From 1941–3 he was with various big bands including those of Benny Carter, Charlie Barnet, Lucky Millinder and Earl Hines. During 1944 he worked with small groups on 52nd Street, joining Billy Eckstine's band in June, and by the end of that year Gillespie's fame had spread among musicians and fans, and bebop had gained cult status.

He left Eckstine in early 1945 and led a small group at the Three Deuces, then he formed and toured with his first big band. In May, with his All Star Quintet which included Charlie Parker, Al Haig (piano), Curley Russell (bass) and Sid Catlett (drums), he recorded the first full-blooded bebop tracks including "Shaw 'Nuff", "Salt Peanuts" and "Hot House", which shook up the jazz world with their brilliant and alien virtuosity. In December 1945 Gillespie took his sextet to California for eight weeks, with Parker, Milt Jackson (vibes), Ray Brown (bass), Haig and Stan Levey (drums), but the new music was so foreign to audiences that it had a very mixed reception. In 1946 he re-formed a big band, touring and recording with it, and playing two months in Scandinavia at the beginning of 1948; it disbanded early in 1950.

ROBERTO SERRA

Dizzy Gillespie

The 1940s were for Gillespie a period of sustained and almost superhuman creative energy during which he changed the face of jazz in three ways: first, he created a totally original trumpet style which took virtuosity to undreamed-of limits, redefining the technical possibilities of the instrument; second, with Parker and others he established bebop as the valid contemporary style for both small groups and big bands; third, he changed the way jazz musicians behaved towards one another: whereas previous generations of musicians had been reluctant to share their knowledge with up-and-coming players, Gillespie proselytized, taught and encouraged musicians on all instruments, drawing them into the music and recommending them for various jobs. His generosity and his confidence in his own abilities were such that he assisted and nurtured the talents of potential rivals including Fats Navarro, Kenny Dorham, Miles Davis, Clifford Brown, and later Lee Morgan and Jon Faddis. If Bird was the intuitive genius of bebop, Dizzy was the organizing genius, the passionate, rational force.

Virtually all his important compositions were written in that creative heyday – "Night In Tunisia", "Groovin' High", "Woody 'N' You", "Salt Peanuts", "Blue 'N' Boogie", and others, most of which have become standard themes in the subsequent jazz repertoire. His solo style had reached its fully mature glory by the mid-1940s; the trumpet had never before been played with such speed, such flexibility, dynamism and drama. The whole essence of a Gillespie solo was cliff-hanging suspense: the phrases and the angle of approach were perpetually varied, breakneck runs were followed by pauses, by huge interval leaps, by long, immensely high notes, by slurs and smears and bluesy phrases; he was always taking listeners by surprise, always shocking them with a new thought. His lightning reflexes and superb ear meant that his instrumental execution matched his thought in its power and speed. And he was concerned at all times with swing – even when he was taking the most daring liberties with the pulse or beat, his phrases never failed to swing. Gillespie's magnificent sense of time and the emotional intensity of his playing grew from childhood roots. His parents were Methodists, but as a boy he used to sneak off every Sunday to the uninhibited services in the Sanctified Church. He said later, "The Sanctified Church had a deep significance for me musically. I first learned the meaning of rhythm there and all about how music could transport people spiritually."

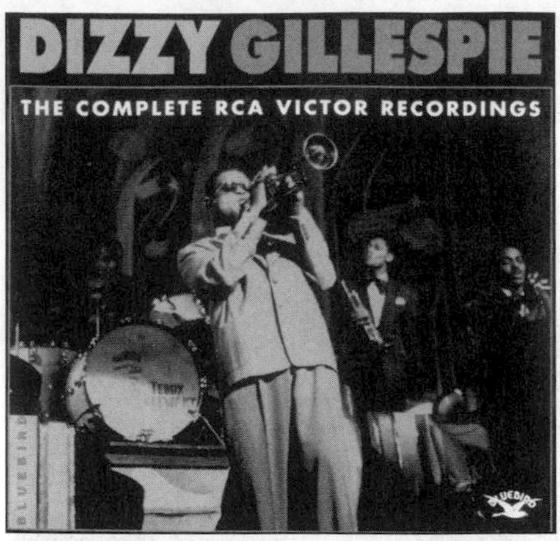

DIZZY GILLESPIE
THE COMPLETE RCA VICTOR RECORDINGS
BLUEBIRD

After 1950 he mostly led small groups, worked as a soloist with Norman Granz's Jazz At The Philharmonic, but occasionally led big bands and played one-off special projects at festivals and concerts. In 1956 he formed a big band and did two long tours for the US State Department, the first from March to May in Pakistan, Lebanon, Syria, Iran, Turkey, Yugoslavia and Greece, the second that autumn in Latin America. This was the first time that the US government had used a jazz ensemble as its cultural representative, and as the tours were immensely successful they continued to use jazz in this capacity, a significant change in the music's status in America.

Gillespie kept the big band going until January 1958, when he resumed leading a quintet. During the early 1960s his pianist was the Argentinian Lalo Schifrin, a composer who wrote several pieces for Gillespie including "Gillespiana" which was performed at the Monterey jazz festival in 1961, "Tunisian Fantasy", an orchestral version of Dizzy's early composition "Night In Tunisia", and in 1962 "The New Continent", which featured Gillespie as soloist with a large orchestra conducted by Benny Carter. The same year, Dizzy improvised a solo trumpet soundtrack for a short film showing the Dutch painter Karel Appel at work, which won first prize at the Berlin film festival. During the 1960s he also did projects with Gil Fuller, who had been the chief arranger of Gillespie's 1940s band, and took part in educational television shows.

During the 1970s he continued to tour worldwide and to appear at major festivals everywhere, both as a soloist and with his own groups. In 1975 Gillespie was given the equivalent of a painter's retrospective exhibition: this was a "Tribute To Dizzy Gillespie" concert in September at the Avery Fisher Hall, New York, and consisted of big-band and small-group performances featuring him with friends and associates from different stages in his career including Percy and Jimmy Heath, James Moody, John Lewis, Max Roach, Stan Getz and Lalo Schifrin. The same year the award of Musician of the Year from the Institute of High Fidelity was presented to him by Miles Davis in San Francisco. He had also received an honorary Doctorate from Rutgers University in 1970, and the Handel Medallion from New York in 1972.

Dizzy Gillespie was one of the most important figures in the entire history of jazz and, like Louis Armstrong and Miles Davis, he influenced players on all instruments. There are other parallels with Louis; in fact, Gillespie's whole career was like a magnification and extension of Armstrong's. Louis created a whole trumpet style and a complete musical language in his small-group recordings of 1925–8, and then spent the next decade refining and polishing it, after which there were no significant changes or developments. During the 1940s Dizzy created a new trumpet style and, with Parker and others, a new language for small groups and big bands; during the 1950s he continued refining his art, after which there were few significant changes. Dizzy was always much more the conscious artist than Louis, and so there were interesting new compositions after the 1940s ("Con Alma", "Kush", "Brother King") and some ambitious musical projects, but his playing and his conception remained, in essence, the same. Both he and Louis were accused by solemn jazz purists of demeaning themselves by clowning and humour in an attempt to "commercialize" their music. Such accusations betray a dismal lack of understanding. To both men humour and clowning were the natural outcome of their high spirits and the way they viewed the world, and humour is a way of distancing and dealing with an often unsympathetic and sometimes openly hostile environment. The dizziness of Dizzy helped him to survive, and he did so without ever really breaking through to a wider audience: his was always the cult following of the jazz world. Great artists are always of their time, never ahead of it, and the general public always lags behind. By the time of his death bebop was history, a known quantity fixed and safe – and therefore more popular – and its surviving creator, Dizzy Gillespie, at last began to get his due recognition from a wider public. Gillespie remained active as a musician until about eleven months before his death. In the late 1980s he toured internationally with a big band which included his protégé John Faddis, whose trumpet playing was featured quite prominently. But Dizzy himself was on good form. At that time he was very much the benign elder statesman of jazz, and friends and fans and the media openly showed their admiration and affection for him. In preparation for his 75th birthday in October 1992, he was booked for the first two months of that year at the Blue Note in Greenwich Village to perform with different trumpeters and groups of his choice for the eight weeks. This was a very happy time for him; he was surrounded by musicians who loved him and visited by fans from America and abroad. Although not as strong as he used to be he could still play beautifully, and on one occasion Jon Hendricks sat in with him and the two of them scatted a rip-roaring version of "Ool Ya Koo", swapping choruses and fours and pushing each other to the limit. After that eight-week series, however, Dizzy was soon in hospital and cancer of the pancreas was discovered. He had ten months or so to live and during that time was honoured and feted on many occasions. [IC]

Dizzy Gillespie

Groovin' High (1945–6; Savoy). Here are some of the key bebop small-group and big-band recordings. Gillespie's playing in the 1940s, like Armstrong's in the 1920s, can never be surpassed because he was defining territory that everybody on all instruments would inhabit. He used intervals far more extreme than Parker's and created a huge vocabulary of new kinds of phrase.

Pleyel '48 (1948; Vogue). Dizzy took his big band to Europe on a shoestring in 1948 and they got stranded in Holland. The Frenchman Charles Delaunay fixed them up with a month's work in Paris. Here was a hungry (literally) band with a dynamic new music, bursting with enthusiasm. The excitement is palpable – history in the making. The reissue also includes Max Roach's 1949 Paris recordings with Kenny Dorham and James Moody.

The Champ (1951–2; Savoy). Gillespie's fortunes went up and down and he had to resort to clowning and showmanship to get work in the early 1950s. *The Champ* has more substance than some of his other work of the period, with solid versions of the title track, and Dizzy's classics – "Tin Tin Deo" and "Birk's Works".

Roy Eldridge and Dizzy Gillespie

Roy And Diz (1954; Verve). Accompanied by Oscar Peterson, Herb Ellis, Ray Brown and Louie Bellson, Eldridge and Gillespie play brilliantly competitively – two old pals egging each other on. Gillespie is wonderful – magnificent time and swing and a flow of perfectly formed ideas.

Dizzy Gillespie

Groovin' High (1956; Bandstand). This album is drawn from two live concerts by Gillespie's State Department-sponsored big band. Dizzy, in buoyant mood, is on great form and the star-filled band does him justice.

Gillespiana/Carnegie Hall Concert (1960–61 Verve). Lalo Schifrin wrote the *Gillespiana* suite for Dizzy, who responds to it brilliantly, and this studio recording is coupled on a double-CD set with a live concert at Carnegie Hall a few months later.

Dizzy Gillespie And The Double Six Of Paris (1963; Philips). Dizzy in succinct but brilliantly fruitful collaboration with the French vocal group.

Max Roach and Dizzy Gillespie

Max And Dizzy, Paris 1989 (A&M). Two elder statesmen – the definitive bop drummer and definitive bop trumpeter – in flowing dialogue.

Dizzy Gillespie

To Diz With Love (1992; Telarc). This is an anthology drawn from Dizzy's last sessions, and it presents him in the company of eight other trumpeters including Wynton Marsalis, Red Rodney, Wallace Roney, Jon Faddis, Doc Cheatham and Lew Soloff. It's a very touching record of homage to a great musician.

>> **Charlie Parker** *(Jazz At Massey Hall).*

John Gilmore

Tenor saxophone, drums.

b. Summit, Mississippi, 28 Sept 1931; d. 20 Aug 1995.

Gilmore was raised from the age of two in Chicago. He played saxophone in school and clarinet in the army from 1948–52. He worked with the Earl Hines group in 1952, and in 1953 he joined Sun Ra in a quartet, beginning an association which lasted almost continuously until the bandleader's death. He was a regular member of the Art Blakey group in 1964–5, including a European tour. He also recorded with Freddie Hubbard, Andrew Hill, Pete LaRoca (on an album reissued as being by Chick Corea) and under his own name.

Apart from his role as an auxiliary drummer with Sun Ra, Gilmore is known for two rather different styles of tenor playing. On performances of a straight-ahead post-bop character (which include many of those with Sun Ra), he runs the changes with a fluency and tone halfway between Johnny Griffin and Wardell Gray, and with a rhythmic and motivic approach which he claims influenced Coltrane. On more abstract material, he is capable of long passages based exclusively on high-register squeals. Especially when heard live, Gilmore was one of the few musicians who carried sufficient conviction to encompass both approaches. [BP]

John Gilmore and Clifford Jordan

Blowing In From Chicago (1957; Blue Note). This quintet debut with his exact contemporary (and a Horace Silver-Art Blakey rhythm-section) shows Gilmore's hard-bop roots in contrast to his work on dozens of Sun Ra albums.

>> **Sun Ra** *(Jazz In Silhouette; Space Is The Place).*

Adèle Girard

Harp.

b. 1913; d. 7 Sept 1993.

Girard – who along with Casper Reardon was the most well-known harpist of the swing era – worked with Harry Sosnick, joined Joe Marsala in 1937 and married him the same year. From then on they continued to work successfully together (most regularly at the Hickory House) until Marsala retired from full-time jazz in the late 1940s. In later years Girard worked in clubs as a soloist, and also played piano and sang; her last recording was with clarinettist Bobby Gordon (a protégé of Marsala's) in 1992. [DF]

Egberto Gismonti

Guitar, piano; also Indian organ, vocals, percussion, composer.

b. Rio de Janeiro, 5 Dec 1947.

Gismonti had piano lessons from the age of six and studied classical music for fifteen years, including two years in Paris with Nadia Boulanger (orchestration and analysis) and one with composer Jean Barlaque. Back in Brazil he worked as an arranger and concert artist.

Gismonti was attracted by Ravel's ideas of orchestration and chord voicings, but at the same time was drawn to his Brazilian musical heritage, in particular to *choro* – the orignial Carnaval music. In 1967 he took up the classical guitar in order to play *choro*, and in 1973 switched to an eight-stringed instrument with a range of five octaves, enabling him to play all kinds of moving bass lines, drones and inversions of chords. Between 1973 and 1975 he experimented with different tunings and searched for new sounds, using flutes, *kalimbas* (thumb pianos), voice and bells. He also listened to Django Reinhardt, Jimi Hendrix, Wes Montgomery and John McLaughlin.

Gismonti has recorded and performed extensively in Brazil and has worked with Airto Moreira, Flora Purim and Paul Horn. In 1976 he spent four weeks with the Xingu Indians in the Amazon jungle before recording his first album for ECM, *Danca Das Cabecas*, and said, "They influenced me a lot in ways of approaching my instruments..." *Danca Das Cabecas* was nominated Album of the Year by *Stereo Review* and also received the Grosser Deutscher Schallplattenpreis. In 1979, with Charlie Haden and Jan Garbarek, he recorded two albums and toured Europe, returning in 1981. He has also composed and played background music for eleven films; he continues to record for ECM.

Gismonti is a virtuoso performer with a very pianistic guitar style, and his music is a delicate fusion of all the influences he has absorbed – folk music, classical, jazz, blues, African, Brazilian and various other ethnic musics. [IC]

⊙ **Musica de Sobrevivencia** (1993; ECM). This brooding, ravishing music combines elements mostly from classical music, with some ethnic undertones. The quartet includes Nando Carneiro on synthesizers, guitar and caxixi, Jaques Morelenbaum on cello and bottle, Zeca Assumpcão on bass and rainwood (*pau de chuva*). The sounds are sumptuous and the percussion very sparse and light, all the rhythmic vitality coming from the stringed instruments and the piano.

Jimmy Giuffre

Clarinet, saxophones, composer, flutes.
b. Dallas, Texas, 26 April 1921.

Giuffre studied music at the North Texas College and played with name bands such as those of Jimmy Dorsey in 1947, Buddy Rich in 1948 and Woody Herman in 1949. He settled on the West Coast and worked with the Lighthouse All Stars in 1951–2, Shorty Rogers from 1953–5, and recorded under his own name. He led a regular trio with Jim Hall and either Bob Brookmeyer or various bassists from 1956–9; later trios featured Paul Bley and Steve Swallow from 1960–62 (they reunited early in 1989), Don Friedman and Barre Phillips in 1964–5 and Kiyoshi Tokunaga and Randy Kaye in the 1970s. Giuffre has been active since the 1960s as a composer and academic, teaching at the New England Conservatory in the late 1970s and early 1980s.

Giuffre's career has covered many different phases, and it is perhaps understandable that not all have been

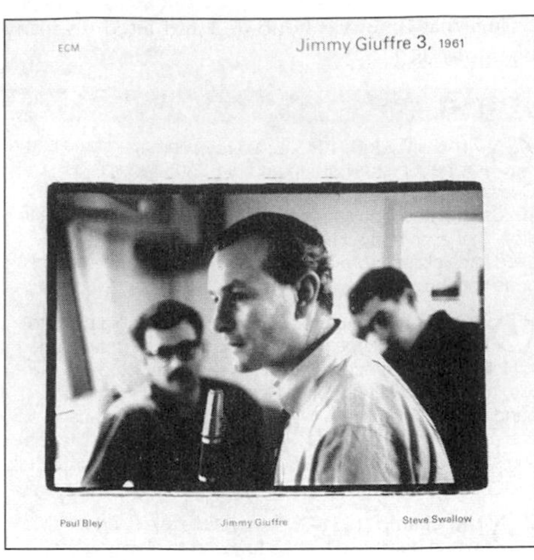

equally noteworthy. His excellence as a straightforward big-band writer is exemplified by his classic original for Herman, "Four Brothers", and its less well-known follow-up, "Four Others". In the early 1950s and the 1960s Giuffre was an avowed experimentalist and, whether with the West Coast thinkers or the New York avant-garde, he sounded less than convincing. Similarly, his composed works for large ensemble ("Pharaoh", "Suspensions" and "Hex") seem somewhat barren. But the subdued clarinettist and saxophonist, who discovered a folksy element in the work of Lester Young, mined one narrow vein that was not without its charm, as the continuing popularity of "The Train And The River" demonstrates. [BP]

⊙ **The Jimmy Giuffre 3** (1956; Atlantic). Unlike the famous *Jazz On A Summer's Day* version of "The Train And The River", this debut of Giuffre's trio features him with Jim Hall and guitarist Ralph Peña and, alongside other folksy material, there are versions of standards such as "Crazy He Calls Me".

⊙ **1961** (ECM). A reissue of the Giuffre-Bley-Swallow trio, now rehabilitated as a precursor of subdued European free improvisation. Old live recordings and new sessions by the group have also been made available.

Adam Glasser

Piano, keyboards, chromatic harmonica, percussion.
b. Cambridge, UK, 20 Sept 1955.

The son of Stanley Glasser, a South African composer and former head of music at London's Goldsmith's College, Adam Glasser only had occasional piano lessons as a child and was primarily self taught. He began playing jazz while at university in the late 1970s and in 1981 spent one semester at Berklee College, Boston, USA. In 1983 he turned professional and the following year he formed the Adam Glasser Trio playing London jazz venues. He was with Dudu Pukwana's Zila for a year, and his first composition, "August One", was recorded on Dudu's album *Zila* (1986). Glasser also played piano with the South African township vocal group The Manhattan Brothers, and has worked with the Dominic Alldis Quartet and with the Ana Maria Velez Quintet, playing mainly harmonica and keyboards. Despite being such an excellent musician, Glasser's reticence has kept him out of the limelight and he is yet to be captured on record as leader. He did, however, win a Peter Whittingham Award in 1996, which allowed him to continue exploring the crossover between jazz and South African township music. [IC]

Jackie Gleason

Musical director.

b. Brooklyn, New York, 26 Feb 1916.

A survivor of burlesque shows who became a highly rated TV and film actor (his best-known film is *The Hustler*), Gleason established his jazz credentials in the 1950s when Capitol produced a series of Gleason albums to tie in with a long-running TV series called *Music For The Love Hours*, for which he conducted a big string orchestra. Featuring a similarly lush orchestra, and in the early days cornettist Bobby Hackett, the albums became best sellers, but have been persistently downgraded since: "the results belong more to the category of mood music than jazz music", says critic Jorgen Jepsen, a widely accepted view. But early Gleason albums such as *Rendezvous*, *Music To Make You Misty* and *Music For The Love Hours* contain irreplaceable examples of an irresistible combination: Bobby Hackett and the great American ballad. After financial disagreements ended the partnership, Gleason – a longtime jazz buff, 52nd Street habitué and smart operator – used other soloists including Pee Wee Erwin (who took over from Hackett), Don Goldie, Lawrence Brown, Toots Mondello, Charlie Ventura, Hank Jones and Jimmy Cleveland. His recordings continued into the late 1960s, when Gleason decided to concentrate on his acting career. [DF]

⊙ **Music To Make You Misty/Night Winds** (1954; Capitol). *Music To Make You Misty* has luxurious solos by Bobby Hackett and altoist Toots Mondello amid Gleason's strings.

Tyree Glenn

Trombone, vibes, vocals.

b. Corsicana, Texas, 23 Nov 1912; d. 18 May 1974.

In his early years Glenn worked with Tommy Myles, Charlie Echols, pianist Booker Coleman's Bellhops, Eddie Barefield's big band, Eddie Mallory and two top names: Benny Carter, at the Harlem Savoy in 1939, and Lionel Hampton at the Paradise Nightclub, Los Angeles, with trumpeter Teddy Buckner. From 1939–46 he worked with Cab Calloway's best big band, leading a trombone section of Quentin Jackson, Keg Johnson and Claude Jones, and playing the trombone he features in Calloway's small group the Cab Jivers. After the war he toured Europe in Don Redman's band (along with Don Byas) and then in 1947 joined Duke Ellington. He played the "Tricky Sam" Nanton role to perfection for four years, then left Ellington in Chicago in 1951. From 1952 he was active in studio work (including Jack Sperling's CBS radio show, playing vibes), led his own quartet at the Embers and a New York quintet with Shorty Baker, and, like Joe Bushkin and Georgie Auld, took up acting part-time. In 1965 he joined Louis Armstrong, playing vibes and trombone and subjugating his solo career to do for Louis what Trummy Young had done before him. After Armstrong's death Glenn led his own small group until February 1974. He died six days before Duke Ellington and was laid to rest in the same funeral home as Ellington and Paul Gonsalves. His sons, Roger Glenn (flute/vibes) and Tyree Glenn Jnr (tenor saxophone), have kept their father's memory alive. [DF]

Globe Unity Orchestra

The Globe Unity Orchestra was a large ensemble concerned with the freer end of the jazz spectrum, founded by German pianist Alexander von Schlippenbach in 1966 to perform his composition "Globe Unity" at the Berlin festival. It developed into an international ensemble with leading musicians from Germany, the UK, the USA and Italy, including Albert Mangelsdorff, Kenny Wheeler, Evan Parker, Manfred Schoof and Paul Rutherford. It performed at the World Exhibition in Osaka, Japan, 1970, but until 1974 worked mostly in Germany. In 1975 it played the Rheims festival with guest artists Enrico Rava and Anthony Braxton, and in 1977 undertook a ten-day tour of the UK. Since then the orchestra has played several concerts in Paris and festivals in Grenoble, Rome, Bologna, Berlin, Moers and Lisbon, has toured the Far East for the Goethe Institute, and performed at Jazz Yatra in Bombay, India. In 2002 they released a new album, *Globe Unity 2002*, recorded that year and featuring Peter Brötzmann, Manfred Schoof, Evan Parker, E. L. Petrowsky, Hannes Bauer, Paul Rutherford, Paul Lytton and Paul Lovens, among others. [IC]

⊙ **Rumbling** (1975; FMP). *Rumbling* is an eleven-piece version of what was often a large big band, with solo, duo and other small combinations of instruments juxtaposed with collective written or improvised passages.

Michel Godard

Tuba, serpent.

b. Héricourt, France, 3 Oct 1960.

Godard's parents were amateur musicians; his mother played accordion and his father trumpet.

Michel Godard

Godard studied at the conservatory in Besançon and the Paris Academy of Music, and also had private lessons with Roger Bobo and Mel Culberson. He very soon became an extraordinary tuba virtuoso, and also mastered the serpent – a medieval bass horn. Godard developed an exceptionally broad conception of music, so that from 1979 onwards he has divided his career between jazz, free improvisation, and classical music. He has played with several classical orchestras including the Radio France Philharmonic Orchestra, and is currently a member of an ensemble called La Fenice.

Godard also conducts many master classes in France and abroad. In the jazz and improvized music worlds, he was a member of the French National Jazz Orchestra, 1989–91, and has worked with many leading jazz musicians including Michel Portal, Martial Solal, Barry Altschul, Kenny Wheeler and Ray Anderson.

In 1989, he formed his own band, Le Chant du Serpent, in which he featured both tuba and serpent, with guitarist Philippe Deschepper, trumpeter Jean-François Canape, drummer Jacques Mahieux, and vocalist Linda Bsiri. In 1995, he formed an international quartet with Sylvie Courvoisier (piano), Tony Overwater (double bass) and Mark Nauseef (drums), and in 1997 a trio with saxophonist Wolfgang Puschnig and Linda Sharrock.

Godard has given the tuba the speed and flexibility of a saxophone, and made it a highly melodic instrument. He has also increased its upper range dramatically, and developed a rich vocabulary of tonal effects. In 1998, he performed and recorded with a French/Italian band which included Pino Minafra, Jean Luigi Troversi and Pierre Favre, and the same year he was featured on German saxophonist Christof Lauer's album, *Fragile Network*, with Americans Anthony Cox (bass) and Gene Jackson (drums), plus Godard's fellow countryman, guitarist Marc Ducret. He has also made several albums under his own name. [IC]

>> **Christof Lauer** *(Fragile Network).*

Brian Godding

Electric and acoustic guitars, guitar synthesizer.
b. Wales, 19 Aug 1945.

Godding, who is self-taught, started in a rock band in the 1960s. At the beginning of the 1970s he played in Keith Tippett's Centipede and joined Mike Westbrook's Solid Gold Cadillac. He has continued working with Westbrook's various bands since then. Godding has also worked with many other UK musicians, and in 1990 formed Full Monte with fellow Westbrook collaborator Chris Biscoe, and Tony Marsh and Marcio Mattos. He has also co-written numerous songs with Kevin Coyne. His taste in guitarists runs from McLaughlin and Allan Holdsworth to Jeff Beck and Jimi Hendrix. [IC]

➤➤ **Chris Biscoe** *(Spark In The Dark)*; **Mike Westbrook** *(Citadel/Room 315; The Cortege; On Duke's Birthday)*.

Harry Gold

Bass, tenor saxophone, clarinet, reeds, leader, arranger, composer.

b. Dublin, Ireland, 26 Feb 1907.

Harry Gold played early on with the Metronomes dance band at the London Astoria, and later with Roy Fox, Bert Firman, Freddy Gardner and Geraldo, as well as working as staff arranger for the BBC. His Pieces Of Eight, formed in 1940 as a band-within-a-band for Oscar Rabin, featured such well-known names as Geoff Love (trombone), Norrie Paramor (piano and arranging) and Bert Weedon (guitar), as well as trumpeters including, at various times, Freddie Tomasso, Bruts Gonella and Joe Macintyre. They achieved solid commercial success but post-war sometimes fell between the two stools of jazz revivalism (for which they were too polished) and the developing trend of bebop, to which their Bobcats style of Dixieland did not belong. A busy worker in the music industry and an in-demand arranger, Gold handed over his band to his brother Laurie in the 1960s and slipped from view until Dick Sudhalter (a champion of pre-war British musicians) featured him in the New Paul Whiteman Orchestra, 1975. Soon afterwards Gold re-formed his Pieces Of Eight, with trumpeter Al Wynette and other old colleagues Bob Lazell and Don Lowes, and a successful round of albums, festival appearances and broadcasts soon re-established the group as Britain's most polished Dixieland outfit. In the 1990s his band continued to work semi-regularly, and Gold starred as a soloist at jazz festivals in Britain and America, but by 2003 he was retired. [DF]

⊙ **Octagonal Gold** (1980; Black Lion). There is as yet no Harry Gold on CD, but several LPs, notably this one, illustrate his finely polished output.

Stu Goldberg

Keyboards, composer.

b. Massachusetts, 1954.

Goldberg was raised in Seattle where he began learning music on piano and trombone at the age of ten. At twelve he took up the organ, influenced by Jimmy Smith and Jimmy McGriff, but continued to study classical music. At sixteen he was featured at the Monterey jazz festival in a quartet with Ray Brown, Louie Bellson and Mundell Lowe. He studied jazz for two and a half years at the University of Utah, graduating *magna cum laude*. In 1974 he moved to Los Angeles and joined John McLaughlin's Mahavishnu Orchestra, touring the USA and Europe with it in 1975, eventually leaving to freelance. Since then he has toured the USA with Miroslav Vitous, Europe with Alphonse Mouzon, and worked with Al Di Meola. In 1978 he joined Freddie Hubbard, played a successful series of solo concerts in Europe and recorded his first album as leader, *Stu Goldberg: Solos, Duos And Trio*, with Larry Coryell and L. Subramaniam. He has recorded with Charlie Mariano, Mahavishnu (*Inner Worlds*), and with McLaughlin, and scores a considerable amount of music for films and TV. His influences include Herbie Hancock and Joe Zawinul. [IC]

Don Goldie

Trumpet.

b. Newark, New Jersey, 5 Feb 1930; d. 19 Nov 1995.

Don Goldie was the son of Harry "Goldie" Goldfield, Paul Whiteman's assistant conductor, entertainer and trumpeter. After playing in a wide variety of groups, from country blues to the bands of Lester Lanin and Buddy Rich (a regular colleague), Don joined Jack Teagarden in 1959, fulfilling the leader's need for a sure-lipped and imaginative trumpet player with showman experience. With Teagarden he recorded brilliantly (his solos on set pieces such as "Blue Dawn", "High Society" and "Riverboat Shuffle" are startling), often playing his solos into a muffler mute of his own invention, which gave him a distinctive shaded sound. After Teagarden's death more fine recordings followed for Argo and for Jackie Gleason. In the 1970s and beyond Goldie was trumpet king of Miami, playing at top venues (Houston Astrodome, Fontainebleau Hotel Miami Beach) and recording a score of albums for the Jazz Forum label (solo and with his Lords Of Dixieland) as well as for Jazzology with his Jazz Express (1983). Goldie continued to play for hotels, clubs and festivals (including Sacramento), as well as running his successful music agency and subbing for Al Hirt until his suicide.

Don Goldie was perhaps the last great original of Dixieland trumpet. A Goldie solo is a model of melodic ingenuity spiced with perky-tongued triplets, audacious vibrato and rhythmic awareness – indeed, in the early days with Teagarden his approach was simply too exuberant for some critics, but time has placed his work in perspective. [DF]

➤➤ **Jack Teagarden** *(Jack Teagarden Sextet Live In Chicago 1960–61; Think Well Of Me)*.

Jean Goldkette

Leader, piano.

b. Valenciennes, France, 18 March 1899; d. Santa Barbara, California, 24 March 1962.

A classically trained pianist, Goldkette spent his childhood in Greece and Russia, arrived in America in 1911 and a few years later, leading a dance band in Chicago, caught the eye and ear of entrepreneur Edgar Benson, who led the mightily successful Benson Orchestra of Chicago. Full of charm and quick with business acumen, Goldkette became Benson's MD, moved to Detroit to run a second Benson orchestra there, and after a successful run at the Book-Cadillac Hotel acquired the lease of an unfinished Chinese restaurant. This he converted into the Graystone Ballroom, which quickly became the premier Detroit venue for visiting bands and was staffed with Goldkette's legendary Victor Recording Orchestra – a fantastic collection of stars including, at various times, Bix Beiderbecke, Frank Trumbauer, Danny Polo, Joe Venuti, Eddie Lang, Tommy and Jimmy Dorsey, Don Murray, Bill Rank and arranger Bill Challis. (On one famous occasion they "cut" Fletcher Henderson's band on Henderson's home ground at New York's Roseland.) Goldkette widened his operations quickly and dramatically: according to Rex Stewart, "he created several orchestras, built many ballrooms and operated through the Midwest on such a large scale that he became the most important impresario in the area bounded by Buffalo, Chicago, Toronto and New York". By the 1930s Goldkette had stopped creating bands (most of the Victor Orchestra was with Whiteman by 1928) and confined himself to agency work and classical piano performance. [DF]

BIX BEIDERBECKE

⊙ **Bix Beiderbecke Vol. 2** (1927; Masters of Jazz). This CD set has a fair selection of Beiderbecke-Goldkette tracks.

➤➤ **Bill Challis** *(The Goldkette Project).*

Gil Goldstein

Piano, accordion.

b. Washington, DC, 6 Nov 1950.

Goldstein's mother, Lili Goldstein, owned a jazz club in Washington from 1947–9 and knew all the players of that time. Goldstein's father played harmonica and encouraged his children to jam with him: Gil playing the accordion and his brother Miles the piano. Goldstein had started on accordion aged four, initially playing by ear, but had private lessons from the age of five. He played cello in public school orchestras, then switched to piano when he was ten. He stopped playing accordion at sixteen, but rediscovered it when he was thirty-three. In his later teens, he studied with jazz pianist John Phillips in Washington, DC, and from 1968–70 studied music at the American University before going to Berklee College of Music 1970–71. He completed his BA degree at the University of Maryland, 1971–3, followed by a postgraduate jazz-based programme of study at the University of Miami from 1973–4. While in Miami, he met Pat Metheny, Jaco Pastorius, Danny Gottlieb and Mark Egan. Goldstein's meeting with Metheny and Pastorius seems to have been his most inspirational early experience, and it was through Pastorius that he began working with guitarist Pat Martino in 1975. While working with Billy Cobham in Switzerland in 1982, Goldstein met Gil Evans, and became a regular member of his band, remaining so to this day.

Goldstein is a prolific composer and arranger, as well as a virtuoso keyboardist, and is permanently in demand as a sideman, composer/arranger of film music, conductor, or album producer. He received a 1998 Grammy for producing Randy Brecker's album *Into The Sun*, and he has arranged music for artists such as Milton Nascimento, David Sanborn, James Moody and Wallace Roney. Goldstein has also performed as pianist and accordionist on over two hundred and fifty albums and CDs.

As so much of Goldstein's work has been behind the scenes, he has a rather low profile as a musician, and albums under his own name are not always available. His own favourites are a duet album with Pat Martino, *We'll be Together Again* (1976; Muse Records), and as a sideman with guitarist Jim Hall, *All Across The City* (1989; Concord Records). [IC]

➤➤ **Tiger Okoshi** *(Echoes Of A Note).*

Benny Golson

Tenor saxophone, composer, arranger.

b. Philadelphia, 25 Jan 1929.

Golson first toured with the R&B band of singer Bull Moose Jackson when it contained Tadd Dameron in 1952. He did a summer season with Dameron in 1953, then worked with the Lionel Hampton band in 1953–4. He briefly replaced his friend John Coltrane with Johnny Hodges in 1954, and replaced Stanley Turrentine with Earl Bostic from 1954–6. He played and arranged for the Dizzy Gillespie big band from 1956 to early 1958, and was also writing for record sessions by Donald Byrd, Oscar Pettiford, Art Farmer and others during this period. Following twelve months with Art Blakey in 1958–9, his own quintet with Curtis Fuller became the Jazztet through the addition of Art Farmer, a band which lasted from 1959–62. He gradually gave up playing to concentrate on writing, first for jazz-related big-band and vocal albums, then for television commercials and serials. He returned to playing in the late 1970s, making records and touring, including visits to Europe in 1982 with the reunited Jazztet, and a solo tour in 1985. In 1993 he premiered a bass concerto featuring Rufus Reid, and in 1996 toured Europe with the all-star group Roots, while continuing to appear as a guest soloist.

Golson's tenor work originally followed the lines of Lucky Thompson, and then adopted some of the Byas-derived developments of Coltrane. But it took second place to his writing even in the 1950s, when he created many well-received originals reminiscent of the harmonic approach of Dameron (although he also admired the work of Quincy Jones, Gigi Gryce and Ernie Wilkins). His tunes were frequently recorded by others in this period and then fell into disuse, but they have achieved more staying power than those of his colleague Gryce. "I Remember Clifford", inspired by Clifford Brown, is the most long-lived, although the modal "Killer Joe" has been more successful with non-jazz listeners. [BP]

Benny Golson

⊙ **Benny Golson's New York Scene** (1957; Contemporary/OJC). With its eighth track restored on CD, Golson's debut album includes three *Birth Of The Cool*-type charts (including "Whisper Not") and healthy-sounding quintet tracks with Art Farmer and Wynton Kelly.

Benny Golson and the Art Farmer Jazztet

⊙ **Real Time** (1986; Contemporary). Work by the turn-of-the-60s Jazztet remains unavailable, and this live set is the best of their reunions with Curtis Fuller, featuring Golson's "Whisper Not", "Are You Real?" and "Along Came Betty".

➤➤ **Art Blakey** *(Moanin').*

Eddie Gomez

Bass.
b. Santurce, Puerto Rico, 4 Oct 1944.

Gomez was brought up in New York and joined the Newport Festival Youth Band in 1959 at the age of fourteen, staying until 1961. He studied at the Juilliard School in 1963, and in the same year gigged with the Rufus Jones sextet. He worked with the Marian McPartland trio in 1964 and the Gary McFarland sextet in 1965, but was also active on the "free jazz" scene with Paul Bley in 1964–5, recording with him and with Giuseppe Logan (both featuring drummer Milford Graves). He then joined the Bill Evans trio and remained for over a decade, from 1966–77. He continued to make albums with performers such as the Jazz Composers' Orchestra, Jeremy Steig, Bennie Wallace, and with others. Charles Mingus chose Gomez to deputize for him in 1978, shortly before Mingus's death. He was increasingly busy with studio work from the late 1970s onwards, and was a founder member of the group Steps (later Steps Ahead) which made several tours of Japan and Europe from 1979–84.

His early work followed the example of Scott LaFaro in exploiting the upper range of the bass and playing it with the melodic fluency expected of any other instrument. It was fitting, therefore, that he inherited LaFaro's position with Bill Evans, for he seemed (perhaps because of superior amplification) to further this approach with even greater aptitude and authority. Moving gradually into the fusion area, he demonstrated that in the right hands the amplified acoustic bass loses nothing in comparison with the electric axes of Jaco Pastorius or Eberhard Weber. He now seems less flamboyant than either of these players, though his technique remains as staggering as ever. [BP]

➤➤ **Bill Evans** *(You Must Believe In Spring);* **Mike Mainieri** *(Modern Times).*

Nat Gonella

Trumpet, mellophone, leader, vocals.
b. London, 7 March 1908; d. 6 Aug 1998.

Nat Gonella was born in a rough area of East London, brought up in a Board of Guardians school and played first in a junior review band, Archie Pitt's Busby Boys. He became intrigued by jazz (and in particular Louis Armstrong, whom he resembled physically, even at fifteen) after hearing "Wild Man Blues" in a Nottingham record shop while on tour. After Pitt broke up the band in 1928, Gonella joined Bob Dryden's band at the Dreamland in Margate, left to join Archie Alexander's band at Brighton, and was signed by Billy Cotton (with whom he first recorded) for a season at the Streatham Locarno. After two more career jumps – with Roy Fox and headlining success with Lew Stone's band – Gonella formed his Georgians, first as a band-within-a-band for Lew Stone, later as an independent unit featuring Pat Smuts (tenor) and Harold "Babe" Hood (piano). The Georgians packed theatres, broadcast frequently and appeared in films up to the war; Gonella's trumpet – a highly original variant of the Armstrong prototype – would later inspire the likes of Humphrey Lyttelton and Kenny Ball.

After the war, Gonella's New Georgians Big Band operated successfully enough, but then he formed a bebop band, a brief and unhappy flirtation with jazz fashion. After that came a spell on the halls with comedians Max Miller and Leon Cortes until in 1959 his jazz career was relaunched by agent Lyn Dutton with the six-piece Armstrong-style New Georgians, an appearance on TV's *This Is Your Life* and a record contract with EMI (including an Armstrong-style *Autobiography* album). Gonella's new-found success was curtailed by the arrival of the Beatles and the collapse of the trad boom. For the next fifteen years he lived in Lancashire, recorded infrequently and played northern clubs. In 1984 a tour by Digby Fairweather's New Georgians celebrated his music; the next year a biography, a discography by Ron Brown plus a set of reissues continued the trend. By then resident in Hampshire, Gonella was regularly to be seen at the Gosport Jazz Club, singing with visiting bands; in 1994 his eighty-sixth birthday party at the club attracted four hundred guests. The same year a square in Gosport was named in his honour. In February 1998 Gonella recorded for the last time (with Teddy Layton, Kenny Baker, Fairweather et al) and just before his ninetieth birthday appeared to full houses at Pizza on the Park (with Digby Fairweather's Half Dozen). His sudden death five months later was an unexpected end to Britain's longest and most eminent jazz career. [DF]

⊙ **A Jazz Legend Through The Years 1930–1998** (Avid). Produced by Dave Bennett, a remarkable set, spanning Gonella's career from first sides with Billy Cotton and Roy Fox, through solo recordings to the Georgians, his Georgia Jazz Band (1960) and on to Gonella's last recordings just before his ninetieth birthday at the Concorde Club, Southampton.

Georgia On My Mind (1931–41/ASV). Excellent Gonella portrait, including early sides with Brian Lawrence, Roy Fox et al. Following are seventeen titles by the classic Georgians plus two from Gonella's American session (1939) and a 1941 "Georgia On My Mind" with his New Georgians big band.

The Dance Band Years (1940–6; Pulse). Deceptive title for a valuable double CD including fifty titles by Gonella's New Georgians Big Band; a neglected area of his career.

Paul Gonsalves

Tenor saxophone; also guitar.

b. Boston, Massachusetts, 12 July 1920; d. London, 14 May 1974.

Gonsalves played in Boston's Sabby Lewis band both before and after World War II service. He then joined Count Basie from 1946–9, followed by several months with Dizzy Gillespie in 1949–50 and 24 years with Duke Ellington. Most of his few brief absences during this long period were associated with drug and alcohol addiction but, thanks to Ellington's tolerance and encouragement, he was musically more in control than many others in his situation.

Although Gonsalves initially guaranteed himself a place in Duke's band through his knowledge of Ben Webster's work, it was the harmonically involved experimentation of Don Byas which most strongly influenced him. His development of this approach, however, was more extreme than that of anyone else of a similar persuasion. Every note could be justified logically, but the angularity of Gonsalves's style was such that he was flirting with atonality long before either Coltrane or Dolphy. As a result, he has received belated recognition from much younger players such as David Murray.

One of the roles taken by Gonsalves in the Ellington band was that of the combative and inexhaustable rabble-rouser featured, from the early 1950s onwards, in extended versions of "Take The A Train" and "Diminuendo And Crescendo In Blue", the latter becoming especially popular. While these medium up-tempos were very suitable for highlighting his serpentine phrasing, it was on ballads especially that his vocalized but fragile tone was most affecting. In addition, they allowed free rein to his polyrhythmic skill, so that the slow "Happy Reunion" or "Chelsea Bridge" became saxophone showpieces in the grand tradition, but sounded like no one else before or since. [BP]

Paul Gonsalves

Gettin' Together (1960; Jazzland/OJC). With a splendid Wynton Kelly-led rhythm section and Nat Adderley on several tracks, Gonsalves underlines the distance between hard bop and his angular mainstream extensions.

Paul Gonsalves and Ray Nance

Just A-Sittin' And A-Rockin' (1970; Black Lion). Ellington partner-in-crime Nance and a less boppish backing put Gonsalves in his element, with a programme half-composed of Ellington tunes.

➤➤ **Duke Ellington** *(The Far East Suite).*

Babs Gonzales

Vocals.

b. Newark, New Jersey, 27 Oct 1919; d. 23 Jan 1980.

After singing in various clubs on both the East and West coasts, Babs Gonzales (Lee Brown) organized his own group, Three Bips and a Bop, from 1946–8. The group, which included Tadd Dameron and Rudy Williams, first recorded "Oop-Pop-A-Da", which was later covered by Dizzy Gillespie. He was the vocalist and road manager with the James Moody band from 1951–3, and also participated in record sessions by Jimmy Smith, Bennie Green and Johnny Griffin. He worked as a soloist thereafter, including frequent visits to Europe; he was, in 1962, one of the first US performers at Ronnie Scott's. He published his own albums on a variety of labels, as well as two books of autobiography which he also distributed. A tireless promoter and pusher of jazz into unlikely outlets, his efforts in that direction were probably more important that his actual performances. He was involved in several other activities on the fringe of show business, including work as chauffeur to Errol Flynn. [BP]

Bennie Green

Soul Stirrin' (1958; Blue Note). Like several Blue Notes of the period, this is something of a Gonzales party, with his singing on a couple of tracks perhaps less essential than his general vibrations.

Dennis Gonzalez

Trumpet, pocket trumpet, flugelhorn.

b. Abilene, Texas, 1954.

A second-generation Mexican-American, Dennis Gonzalez grew up in a musical family; his mother was pianist at their Southern Baptist church, and his father was a big-band enthusiast. As a child he had unsuccessful piano lessons, but picked up trumpet in sixth grade. In high school, his band director introduced him to Sam Rivers's Contours, which impressed him deeply. Self-taught on many instruments including alto saxophone and bass, he moved to Dallas in 1977, where, inspired by pianist Errol Parker, he started his own record label, Daagnim (originally an acronym for Dallas Association for Avant-Garde and Neo-Impressionist Music). Along with his self-produced records, Gonzalez made a flurry of excellent records at the end of the 1980s, all for the Silkheart label. He coaxed missing-in-action saxophonist Charles Brackeen to play on *Debenge Debenge* (1988) and utilized mixed ensembles including underdocumented musicians from New Orleans (Kidd Jordan, Alvin Fiedler) and

Chicago (Douglas Ewart). In 1991 he released a surprising record with an electric group, *The Earth And The Heart* (Konnex; reissued in 1996 on Music & Arts), anchored by drummer Andrew Cyrille, and was heard latterly on *Home* (2001; Daagnim) by a group called Yells At Eels comprising his sons Aaron on bass and Stefon on drums. [JC]

⊙ **Catechism (The Names We Are Known By)** (1987; Daagnim). While Gonzalez's Silkheart records with his New Dallasorleanssippi group are all in the pocket, this outing with his Dallas-London Sextet is particularly nice, with elements of South African jive, New Orleans looseness (out-takes are integrated into the programme with interesting results), and lovely horn charts. Pianist Keith Tippett, reed player Elton Dean, bassist Marcio Mattos and drummer Louis Moholo constitute the British component, while Gonzalez is joined by fine trumpeter Rob Blakeslee.

Jerry Gonzalez

Trumpet, percussion.

b. New York, 5 June 1949.

A key figure in the resurgence of Latin jazz in the 1980s and 1990s, Gonzalez began playing in Afro-Latin bands as a teenager alongside his brother, bassist Andy Gonzalez, who formed the salsa band Conjunto Libre and the Grupo Folklorico y Experimental Nuevayorquino in the 1970s. He studied at New York College Of Music and New York University, and played with, among others, Dizzy Gillespie in 1970, Tony Williams, Eddie Palmieri, George Benson and, in the 1980s, with Tito Puente and McCoy Tyner. In 1980 Gonzalez, who teaches percussion at the New School, formed the influential Fort Apache Band which he described as being "about young blacks and Latinos who grew up in New York listening to *all* this music and can deal equally with the complexities of Afro-Cuban rhythms and bebop". [BP]

⊙ **Crossroads** (1994; Milestone). Slimming down to a tight sextet in the 1990s, Gonzalez features John Stubblefield and soprano/alto man Joe Ford with his regular rhythm-section of Larry Willis, bassist Andy Gonzalez (his brother) and drummer Steve Berrios. The leader's trumpet is adequate but less exciting than the band as a whole on pieces such as "Rumba Columbia" and Willis's "Malandro".

Coleridge Goode

Bass; also violin.

b. Jamaica, 29 Nov 1914.

Coleridge (George Emerson) Goode's first instrument was the violin. From 1934–40 he studied electrical engineering at Glasgow University, at the end of which he studied bass privately. In 1945–6 he played and broadcast with the Stephane Grappelli quartet and recorded with Django Reinhardt and the Quintet of the Hot Club of France. In 1958 he began his long association with Joe Harriott's quintet, which pioneered abstract, free-form jazz and then, in the mid-1960s, blazed another new trail with Indo-Jazz Fusions, playing festivals all over Europe. Goode also worked and recorded with Michael Garrick in the 1960s. He pioneered double-bass amplification, first using it on a broadcast in 1946. He can still be found playing a weekend lunchtime slot at The King's Head, Crouch End, North London.

His favourite bassists include Jimmy Blanton, Slam Stewart and Ray Brown, and like Stewart, Goode usually plays bowed solos singing in octave unison with his bass. [IC]

➤➤ **Joe Harriott** *(Abstract)*.

Benny Goodman

Clarinet, alto saxophone, leader.

b. Chicago, 30 May 1909; d. 20 June 1986.

Goodman took up the clarinet at eleven, studied under the great teacher Franz Schoepp (who also taught Buster Bailey and Jimmie Noone), and by thirteen was working professionally. Apart from Frank Teschemacher – who in any case lacked Goodman's steely nerves – there was no clarinettist in Chicago to challenge his potential, and by 1925 he was working for Ben Pollack, who quickly latched on to Goodman as a central feature of his show. Ambitious, self-assured and with a healthy disregard for authority, Goodman treated his leader with ill-concealed disregard, took recording dates using Pollack's men but never Pollack, and in 1929 resigned along with Jimmy McPartland after his aggrieved leader had complained that his protégés had appeared on stage in dirty shoes.

Goodman went on to work with Red Nichols, then in the studios for five years, using the money he earned to support his mother and eleven siblings after his father had been killed in a taxi accident. In 1934 – at 25 – he was leading his own band for Billy Rose's Music Hall, broadcasting weekly for NBC and attracting attention with a closing hour of hot arrangements. One night, despairing after a nondescript tour, he threw in one of his hottest numbers at

a dance at the Palomar Ballroom, Los Angeles, and caused a riot in the student audience. Over the next five years, first in Chicago, then in New York, he achieved an international reputation, playing (to riots again) at the Paramount Theater, New York, and in 1938 at a legendary (recorded) Carnegie Hall concert, at a time when jazz was still largely foreign to concert-hall settings. By now, with the aid of rich young talent scout John Hammond, Goodman had strengthened his team to include trumpeter Harry James, showman-drummer Gene Krupa (one of his nearest friends in the period) and, in a much publicized and important step, black musicians such as Teddy Wilson and Lionel Hampton. The Benny Goodman small groups, featuring Wilson, Hampton, Krupa and – a dramatic later addition – electric guitarist Charlie Christian, created a second revolutionary sound of the period.

By now Goodman was also beginning to acquire a reputation among musicians for being "difficult". Singer Helen Forrest left, so she said, "to avoid a nervous breakdown"; Harry James left in 1938 claiming that he'd "never really understood Benny"; and pianist Jess Stacy was later to remember "Benny was a terrific leader – but if I'd had any spunk I'd probably have thrown the piano at him!" Goodman, a reticent, often aloof man, was a skilled perfectionist who expected the best, and may have seen his own early struggles as a justification for not being soft with others; he also insisted (not unreasonably) on being the centre of attention in any orchestra he formed.

By 1940 he had rebuilt his orchestra, and although the replacement names never created the impact of his first-generation stars, newer additions – including Cootie Williams, Billy Butterfield, Lou McGarity, Jimmy Maxwell, Charlie Queener, Aaron Sachs, Red Norvo, John Best, Peanuts Hucko, Frank Beach and singer Peggy Lee (who fronted the 1942 hit "Why Don't You Do Right?) – continued to set unfaultable standards. By the end of the decade Goodman was effectively incorporating bebop into his programmes, featuring musicians such as Doug Mettome, Milt Bernhardt and Wardell Gray, and was simultaneously moving into the world of classical music, an area in which he could fully explore his first love – clarinet playing – away from the pressures of bandleading.

Decades of successful international touring followed, including a 1962 tour of Russia for the US State Department; there were also appearances in films (including *A Song Is Born*, 1947), and in 1955 Hollywood filmed *The Benny Goodman Story*. He continued to tour Europe through the 1970s – a 1978 Carnegie Hall concert, forty years on from the great original, was amiably chaotic – and in the 1980s was still mounting occasional concerts and shining in a small group featuring Scott Hamilton and Warren Vaché. Although late Goodman conveys little of the hot urgency that informs his early work (his later playing sometimes levels into a mildly interested urbanity), he remained the master of the jazz clarinet, a virtuoso who, according to Warren Vaché, could play rings around the opposition right up to his death. [DF]

⊙ **Benny Goodman 1928–31/1931–3/1934–5/1935/1935–6/1936 Vols. 1 and 2/1936–7/1937/1938 Vols. 1 & 2** (Classics). The admirable Classics series are marching ahead with their chronology of Goodman studio recordings, and as they're available separately collectors can build by degrees. Not everything is wonderful here, but of course the Goodman classics are numerous and irreplaceable, and small-group recordings are included too.

⊙ **BG And Big Tea In NYC** (1929–34; MCA/GRP). Young Goodman and Teagarden in classic sides with Red Nichols, Irving Mills, Joe Venuti, Eddie Lang and Adrian Rollini.

⊙ **The Birth Of Swing** (1935–6; RCA Bluebird). Produced by Orrin Keepnews and with impressive notes by former Goodman associate Loren Schoenberg, this three-disc collection chronologizes Benny from his first Victor sessions in April 1935 through to "Did You Mean It" (with Ella Fitzgerald) in November 1936. The formative Goodman years, with Bunny Berigan, Ziggy Elman, Jack Teagarden, Vido Musso, Jess Stacy and Gene Krupa co-starring.

⊙ **After You've Gone** (1935–7; RCA Bluebird); **Avalon** (1937–9; RCA Bluebird). Produced by the indefatigable Keepnews and Schoenberg, these CDs contain timeless performances by the Goodman trio, quartet and quintet.

⊙ **The Small Groups** (1935–42; ASV). Excellent selection of twenty-five tracks by Goodman's trio, quartet, quintet and sextet, including many classics – "Gone With What Wind", "Good Enough To Keep", "Wholly Cats" and his 1941 "Sunny Side Of The Street" with Peggy Lee and Lou McGarity.

⊙ **The Harry James Years Vol. 1** (1937–8; RCA Bluebird). Again produced by Keepnews with notes by Schoenberg, this set picks up Goodman's story from the arrival of Harry James and his first recorded solo with the band ("I Want To Be Happy") up to "One O' Clock Jump" in February 1938. Magnificent swing, with all the heat of youth.

⊙ **Benny Goodman On The Air** (1937–8; Columbia). Superb airshots of the Goodman band at its peak, recorded from the radio by Bill Savory and originally issued by Columbia. On this set, produced by Michael Brooks with notes by Dick Sudhalter, there are twelve bonus tracks by Benny's trio, quartet and orchestra – all are swing summits.

⊙ **Carnegie Hall Concert** (1938; Avid); **Second Carnegie Hall Concert** (1939; Giants Of Jazz). Goodman's finest in-concert hours are captured in full on these issues; the 1938 concert is the great event of Goodman's career, featuring such masterpieces as "Sing Sing Sing" (with Jess Stacy's immortal piano tailpiece), the "Honeysuckle Rose" jam session (with Ellington and Basie alumni on board), and Goodman's quartet titles with Lionel Hampton. The AVID set includes the full original recorded edition of the concert (which some longtime record collectors may prefer to the expanded Schaap edition below) and completes its three CDs with small group recordings (l944–7) and further big band tracks. An excellent collection with fine sound restoration by Dave Bennett.

⊙ **The Famous 1938 Carnegie Hall Concert** (1999; Sony). Produced by Phil Schaap, this expanded edition of Goodman's concert presents the entire show in real time with announcements, extra tracks and an unedited "Honeysuckle Rose" jam session. Ideal for historians and completists.

⊙ **Goodman – The Different Version Vols. 1–5** (1939–47; Phontastic). A highly impressive ten-CD set featuring alternate Goodman takes; many of exceptional quality and all very well-recorded.

Benny Goodman: His Orchestra And His Combos 1941–55 (Giants Of Jazz). Another well-selected budget-price collection, with Goodman latterday classics including "Clarinet À La King" and "I Got Rhythm", plus tracks from the splendid *Benny Goodman In Hi Fi* sessions of November 1954, with Ruby Braff on trumpet.

Complete Capitol Recordings Of Benny Goodman 1944–55 (Mosaic). Four-CD boxed set. Goodman may have passed his flaming youth by now but Capitol regularly presented him in inspiring surroundings. Here are the sides with accordionist Ernie Felice and other inspired (and regularly high-powered) sidemen include Red Norvo, Charlie Shavers, Doug Mettome, Wardell Gray, Mel Powell and Ruby Braff.

Benny Goodman Sextet (1950–52; CBS). In 1950 Goodman formed a full-time sextet initially for the *Star Time* TV series. These recordings, co-featuring Terry Gibbs on vibraphone, are a neglected part of his history and well worth hearing.

Benny Goodman And Friends (1984; Decca). An informal session in which Goodman teamed with a group of sidemen including Scott Hamilton and Warren Vaché. Goodman in his later, more disconnected years, but still able to outswing the opposition when he could be bothered.

Mick Goodrick

Guitar.

b. Sharon, Pennsylvania, 9 June 1945.

After graduating from the Berklee School in 1967, Goodrick taught there for four years before joining Gary Burton's group in 1973, where he played alongside fellow guitarist Pat Metheny. After Metheny's departure, Goodrick stayed with Burton until 1976, recording five albums with the vibraphonist. For almost a decade he maintained a low profile, studying, teaching (privately and at the New England Conservatory) and performing locally in the Boston area, occasionally interrupting this pattern for recording, for example *In Pas(s)ing* (1978) as leader with John Surman, Eddie Gomez and Jack DeJohnette, and for a tour with Charlie Haden's Liberation Orchestra in 1985. Goodrick is highly regarded as a music educator and has influenced the development of several leading guitarists, among them John Scofield, Mike Stern and Emily Remler. His instructional book *The Advancing Guitarist* (Third Earth/Hal Leonard), setting out his technical and artistic concepts, was published in 1987. In the same year he resumed his international performing career with Jack DeJohnette's Special Edition. Heard latterly on a fine pair of edgily inventive releases by Steve Swallow (*Deconstructed* [1996; ECM] and *Always Pack Your Uniform On Top* [2000; ECM]), Goodrick's latest self-published advanced guitar tutor *Mr Goodchord's Almanac Of Guitar Voice-Leading For The Year 2001 and Beyond* was acclaimed by educators and guitarists as a major work. [CA/CI]

Claudio Fasoli

Cities (1993; RAM). On this album, recorded in Italy with Claudio Fasoli (tenor/soprano), bassist Paolino Dalla Porta and drummer Bill Elgart, Goodrick displays his mastery both as soloist and accompanist on Fasoli's cityscape compositions.

Bill Goodwin

Drums.

b. Los Angeles, California, 8 Jan 1942.

The son of an actor, Bill Goodwin studied piano from the age of five, took up saxophone under the tutelage of Frank Chase and then drums under Stan Levey. Charles Lloyd was his first serious employer, but Goodwin also played with keyboard player Mike Melvoin (1961–5), and with a number of West Coast jazz luminaries – Bud Shank, Frank Rosolino, Howard Rumsey, Art Pepper and Paul Horn – before moving to New York in 1970. Work with Toshiko Akiyoshi, Stan Getz, Gerry Mulligan, Al Cohn and Zoot Sims took up the early 1970s, but it was his association with alto player Phil Woods as both drummer and producer – particularly in his classic quintet, also featuring trumpeter Tom Harrell, pianist Hal Galper and bassist Steve Gilmore – that substantially raised his profile in the jazz world during the later 1970s and 80s. The ongoing Goodwin/Woods relationship was heard as recently as 2002 on *You And The Night And The Music* (Venus).

Goodwin is a regular on Concord recordings, having made albums for the company with guitarist Howard Alden, singer Dave Frishberg and the owner of the Maybeck Recital Hall, pianist Dick Whittington, but he has also contributed his briskly propulsive, cultured drumming – one of his chief influences is Pete LaRoca – to sessions by everyone from Chet Baker and David Liebman to saxophonist Anthony Ortega and his Woods-band colleagues, Galper and Harrell. As well as his continuing appearances as producer and/or drummer on albums by the likes of pianist Mike Melvoin and singer Stephanie Nakasian, Goodwin recently oversaw and played on Lee Konitz's album *Parallels* (2001; Chesky). [CP/CI]

Phil Woods

Integrity (1984; Red). The classic Woods quintet (see above) caught at their peak, live in Bologna, playing material by Neal Hefti ("Repetition"), Duke Ellington ("Azure"), Charlie Mariano, Wayne Shorter et al in their customary classy but peppy style.

Bobby Gordon

Clarinet.

b. Hartford, Connecticut, 29 June 1941.

A student of Joe Marsala who called him "my most gifted student and protégé", Gordon worked with Eddie Condon, Wild Bill Davison, Bobby Hackett and Muggsy Spanier and was house clarinettist at Eddie Condon's (1977–80). He also had a long association with Jim Cullum and blues singer Leon Redbone, recording with both of them. Gordon's recent activities include work with Redbone (*The Johnny Carson Show*), regular appearances at jazz festivals (Atlanta, Los Angeles, JVC), and tours with Marty Grosz's Orphan Newsboys in Japan (1995–6), and at the Lincoln Center (1996). He records regularly for the Arbors label. Gordon now lives in San Diego, California, where he heads his own quartet at Milligan's in La Jolla. [DF]

⊙ **Don't Let It End** (1992; Arbors). The sensitive teaming of Gordon with harpist Adèle Girard, his former teacher's wife, for a connoisseur's selection of tunes. The group is completed by Gene Estes, Morty Corb and the great pianist Ray Sherman.

Dexter Gordon

Tenor and soprano saxophones.

b. Los Angeles, 27 Feb 1923; d. 25 April 1990.

Gordon joined the new Lionel Hampton band at the age of seventeen, staying from 1940–43. He then worked briefly with the Lee Young sextet in 1943 and toured with the bands of Fletcher Henderson in 1943–4, Louis Armstrong in 1944 and Billy Eckstine in 1944–5. He moved to New York as a freelance soloist, working with Charlie Parker and others in 1945 and making regular recordings under his own name. He returned to Los Angeles in 1946, and travelled to Hawaii with drummer/singer Cee Pee Johnson in 1947. He started an informal partnership with Wardell Gray, which lasted on and off until 1952, when Gordon began the first of two sentences (from 1952–4 and from 1956–60) for drug offences. Both comebacks led to recordings, those of 1960–62 being particularly well received. His first trip to Europe, in the autumn of 1962, found Gordon settling in Copenhagen for a total of fourteen years with only brief returns to the USA in 1965, 1969, 1970 and 1972. Huge acclaim for his visit of 1976–7 encouraged him to move back and, after several years of successful playing, he was virtually in retirement until taking the lead role of a US musician in the Bertrand Tavernier film *Round Midnight* (1986). There was one further brief film role and very little playing in Gordon's last years as ill-health finally caught up with him.

Dexter's style in the mid-1940s was probably the most popular approach to the tenor, influencing many players whose primary allegiance was to Lester Young (such as Sonny Stitt, early Stan Getz and, especially, John Coltrane). His combination of bop-inspired lines with an essentially pre-bop time feeling produced an inherent tension which was excruciatingly enjoyable. His tone-quality, always vibrantly hot even when playing ballads, remained virtually unchanged for forty years, despite adopting a few mannerisms from Coltrane in the 1960s and occasionally taking up the soprano. His authoritative delivery, however, only increased with the passing years. [BP]

⊙ **Dexter Rides Again** (1945–7; Savoy). A clutch of singles recorded when Dexter was the new young tenor in New York, with sidemen such as Bud Powell and Max Roach.

⊙ **Go!** (1962; Blue Note). The best of the resurgent Gordon, with Sonny Clark and Billy Higgins, and including the up-tempo "Love For Sale" and two ballads, "Where Are You?" and "I Guess I'll Hang My Tears Out To Dry".

⊙ **Our Man In Paris** (1963; Blue Note). A reunion with Bud Powell and Kenny Clarke from early on in Gordon's European sojourn finds him in magisterial form on "Scrapple From The Apple" and "Night In Tunisia".

⊙ **Both Sides Of Midnight** (1967; Black Lion). The first of several albums from a single night at the Montmartre in Copenhagen with Kenny Drew on piano, this has extended versions of two Rollins tunes, "Doxy" and "Sonnymoon For Two".

Herman Leonard

Dexter Gordon

Joe Gordon

Trumpet.

b. Boston, Massachusetts, 15 May 1928; d. 4 Nov 1963.

Gordon studied trumpet at the New England Conservatory, and played in Boston with the Sabby Lewis band, Georgie Auld, Lionel Hampton, Charlie Mariano and Charlie Parker. He was briefly with Art Blakey in 1954, Don Redman in 1955 and Dizzy Gillespie's big band in 1956; even more briefly, he replaced Donald Byrd with Horace Silver in 1956. He worked with Herb Pomeroy in Boston in 1957–8, and then moved to Los Angeles, recording with Barney Kessel, Benny Carter, Harold Land, Thelonious Monk and Shelly Manne, with whom he played from 1958–60. While freelancing, he was badly burned in a fire and died thereafter. Though never earning more than an underground reputation, Gordon's approach to bebop trumpet deserves to be far better known. [BP]

Shelly Manne

⊙ **At The Blackhawk Vol. 1** (1959; Contemporary/OJC). Part of a series of five CDs recorded on three consecutive nights, this has Gordon and the rest of Manne's quintet eating up three standards and two takes of Frank Rosolino's "Blue Daniel".

Jon Gordon

Alto and soprano saxophones; also flute, clarinet.

b. Staten Island, New York, 23 Dec 1966.

Gordon's mother was a singer who kept the name of her first husband, baritonist Bob Gordon (who died in 1955). Jon studied at the Performing Arts High School (winning several classical competitions in his teens), then at the Manhattan School of Music and privately with Bob Mintzer, Phil Woods, Charles McPherson, Joe Lovano and others. While still a student, he played professionally with Roy Eldridge, Al Grey, Barney Kessel, Doc Cheatham and Mel Lewis, and in 1988 joined the Red Rodney quintet. The following year he recorded in Norway with Red Holloway and formed his own quartet, whose first two albums featured Woods and Benny Carter as guests. Subsequent affiliations include Maria Schneider, Clark Terry, pianist Bill Mays and T.S. Monk, while in 1996 Gordon won the Thelonious Monk Competition. Among his favourite altoists are Hodges, Parker, Adderley and Woods, as well as Paul Desmond, Lee Konitz, Kenny Garrett and Steve Wilson. Other inspirations are Lovano, Schneider and tenorist Mark Turner, plus Coltrane and Joe Henderson. [BP]

⊙ **Currents** (1998; Double-Time). Gordon leads a quintet including Ben Monder (guitar), Ed Simon (piano) and drummer Bill Stewart and the material, all original apart from "Comecar De Novo (The Island)", covers a wide variety of approaches. The leader's playing is full of verve when necessary but is also thoughtful and thought-provoking.

Wycliffe Gordon

Trombone, tuba, didgeridoo, voice.

b. 29 May 1967, Waynesboro, Georgia.

Starting on trombone at the age of twelve, Wycliffe Gordon became truly immersed in jazz after hearing Louis Armstrong's "Keyhole Blues" a year later. While at high school in Augusta, he played with the All-State Concert and Jazz Band and with the McDonald's All-American High School Marching Band and Jazz Band. While studying at Florida A&M University in Tallahassee he met Wynton Marsalis, which led to the trombonist's swapping his gig playing bass at the local Pizza Hut for the trombone chair in the trumpeter's band, which he has held since 1989. Nicknamed "Pine Cone" because, in Marsalis's words, he is "country by choice", Gordon also plays trumpet, bass, piano, drums and tuba as well as his main instrument, and he has lent his distinctive sound to the Lincoln Center Jazz Orchestra and to *Musicale* by pianist Eric Reed (Impulse!; 1996) as well as to Marsalis's many projects in the 1990s. Since 1996, he has been an authoritative and spirited leader on eight albums, including three on the Criss Cross label and four on Nagel Heyer. Gordon also founded and teaches at the Augusta Music and Dance Company in his native Georgia. [CP/CI]

⊙ **The Joyride** (2003; Nagel Heyer). Generally considered to be the high-point of Gordon's work as leader, this all-original set showcases his vocal and piano skills along with his virtuosic trombone, in the playfully inventive company of another of Marsalis's alumni, reedman Victor Goines.

Wynton Marsalis

⊙ **Citi Movement** (Griot New York) (1993; Columbia). Cultured, elegant yet hard-swinging suite with roots in Ellington and Mingus, but imbued with Marsalis's sweet precision. Gordon's contribution is crucial to the band's texture.

Danny Gottlieb

Drums.

b. New York, 18 April 1953.

Gottlieb was raised in Union, New Jersey. He began on drums at fourteen, playing in a high school band during his last years at school. He studied with Joe Morello and Mel Lewis and from 1971–5 studied music at the University of Miami. While there, he played with Paul Bley, Jaco Pastorius, Ira Sullivan and Pat Metheny, and also gained much experience playing shows on Miami Beach. On graduating he moved to New York, working with Joe Farrell, Clark Terry, Pat Martino and others. In 1976 he joined the Gary Burton quartet and in 1978 he toured Europe with Eberhard Weber's Colours. With Pat Metheny, he broke away from Burton's group in order to form the Pat Metheny Group, with Lyle Mays and Mark Egan. The group toured extensively in the USA, Europe and Japan and played most major festivals, becoming one of the most successful jazz groups of the 1970s and early 1980s. He left Metheny and in 1984 became a member of John McLaughlin's reconstituted Mahavishnu Orchestra. He continues to be an in-demand drummer. [IC]

>> **Gary Burton** *(Passengers)*; **Pat Metheny** *(American Garage)*.

Frank "Big Boy" Goudie

Tenor saxophone, clarinet, trumpet.

b. Royville, Louisiana, 13 Sept 1899; d. 9 Jan 1964.

"Big Boy" Goudie was taught trumpet by Bunk Johnson, was working in Papa Celestin's Tuxedo Band by 1910, played in New Orleans for ten years and by 1921 was touring with minstrel shows. In 1925 he moved to Paris and from there played in Europe with a variety of famous leaders (including Noble Sissle, Sam Wooding and Willie Lewis) until the outbreak of war, when he took refuge in Brazil and Argentina. In 1946 he was back in France working for Arthur Briggs, Glyn Paque and Bill Coleman, among others, then from 1951–6 led his own band in Berlin. After that he went back to San Francisco to play with more than twenty different bands and run a furniture upholstery business from home. [DF]

Brad Gowans

Valve-trombone, clarinet, cornet, saxophones.

b. Billerica, Massachusetts, 3 Dec 1903; d. 8 Sept 1954.

Gowans was jazz's first valve-trombonist of historic significance. A dandy who sported a small gaucho moustache and was mad on sports cars, he played all his instruments in bands led by the likes of Tommy de Rosa, Jimmy Durante, Mal Hallett and Joe Venuti in the 1920s. He retired for a time before coming back to join Bobby Hackett in Boston's first great jazz band, at the Theatrical Club in 1936: from then on, valve-trombone was his first choice. In New York in 1938 he was again working for Hackett as well as for Wingy Manone and Eddie Condon, and the year after was founder member of one of the greatest of all jazz bands, the Summa Cum Laude, led by Bud Freeman. From then on he was regularly at the heart of 52nd Street life, playing on Jimmy Ryan's first jam session (with Shavers, Higginbotham, Hackett and others), working very successfully as staff arranger for Ray McKinley, and playing for Condon for much of the rest of the 1940s (including Condon's first jazz concerts, and the opening of his new club). Spells with Jimmy Dorsey (in 1948) and Nappy Lamare (from 1949) followed, by which time Gowans was living in Los Angeles. His last date was with Ed Skrivanek's band in 1954; he died of cancer after a long illness. [DF]

⊙ **Brad Gowans And His New York Nine** (1946; Victor). Extremely rare and never reissued but a ringing classic, with Billy Butterfield (his "Carolina In The Morning" is sensational), Arthur Rollini, Joe Dixon, Paul Ricci (bass saxophone) and Dave Tough on his last recording date – plus Gowans, whose arranging and playing created a classic of swing here. Pay whatever they want for it!

>> **Eddie Condon** *(Eddie Condon 1942–3)*; **Bud Freeman** *(It's Got To Be The Eel)*.

Chris Gower

Trombone, bass trombone.

b. Hammersmith, London, 19 December 1948.

Chris Gower started playing the trombone after moving with his family to Shanklin on the Isle of Wight in 1959. Though his father taught oboe and woodwind and conducted the Shanklin military band, Gower was mainly self taught. In 1963 he joined the Unity Stompers combining a love of traditional jazz (fostered during Britain's "Trad Boom") with interests in modern jazz, rock and soul. Gower turned professional in 1967 and after playing holiday camps for two years moved to London to join a British band backing US soul artists like Ben E. King, Jimmy Ruffin and the Fantastics. Thereafter Gower worked with Iguana, Jess Roden and Graham Parker And The Rumour. In the 1980s Gower worked with a variety of rock and pop musicians including Randy Crawford, "Shakin' " Stevens, Desmond Decker, Kirsty McColl, Cliff Richard, Amazulu, Musical Youth, the O-Jays and Odyssey as well as the Andy Ross Orchestra. In the 1990s Gower's jazz abilities were heard more widely with the Glenn Miller Orchestra UK, the BBC Big Band, the Pizza Express All Stars and Syd Lawrence's Orchestra. A big-toned, accurate and hard-hitting trombone stylist who can hold his own in most musical situations, he is currently a member of Digby Fairweather's Half Dozen. [DF]

Dusko Goykovich

Trumpet, composer.

b. Jajce, Yugoslavia, 14 Oct 1931.

Goykovich was active in Europe during the 1950s, then from 1961–3 studied at the Berklee School. He played with Maynard Ferguson in 1963–4 and with Woody Herman from 1964–6. He played in Europe for eight months with Sal Nistico in the International Jazz Quintet in 1966. Returning to live in Europe in 1967 he led his own groups, and did some composing, arranging and teaching, and also played with the Clarke-Boland band until it disbanded in 1973. He also worked with Mal Waldron, Jimmy Woode, Philly Joe Jones and others. He co-led a Euro-American twelve-piece band with Slide Hampton in 1974–5. He is still an active musician and in 2000 released *In My Dreams*, a quartet album with pianist Bob Degen, Isla Eckinger (bass) and drummer Jarrod Cagwin.

His influences are Roy Eldridge, Dizzy Gillespie, Kenny Dorham, Clifford Brown and Miles Davis.

Goykovich is a fine all-round player, at home with big bands and small groups. With his own groups he has combined elements from Slavonic folk music, both rhythmic and melodic, to produce a highly individual synthesis. [IC]

⊙ **Swinging Macedonia** (1966; Enja). Goykovich's sextet is a mixture of American and European musicians including Mal Waldron and Nathan Davis from the States and German bassist Peter Trunk and Dutch drummer Cees See. The music has all the jazz virtues, but is strongly flavoured with eastern European rhythms and scales.

⊙ **Celebration** (1987; DIW). Goykovich in quartet formation with an excellent rhythm-section of Kenny Drew, Jimmy Woode and drummer Al Levitt. This is less Slavonic and includes versions of "Blues In The Closet" and Ray Noble's "The Touch Of Your Lips". Goykovich doesn't play safe and sounds really good.

⊙ **Bebop City** (1995; Enja). Goykovich assembled a superlative sextet for this fine recording – the great rhythm-section of pianist Kenny Barron, bassist Ray Drummond and drummer Alvin Queen, plus two of the most gifted younger saxophonists, Abraham Burton (alto) and Ralph Moore (tenor).

➤➤ **Woody Herman** *(Woody's Winners).*

Teddy Grace

Vocals.

b. Arcadia, Louisiana, 26 June 1905; d. 4 Jan 1992.

One of the best singers of her swing generation, Teddy Grace turned professional in 1931 when she appeared on local Montgomery radio, then toured with Al Katz (1933), sang with Tommy Christian (1934) and with Mal Hallett (1934–5, 1937), and recorded regularly under her own name for Decca. Sadly she stopped singing after military service, but her 1930s' recordings with Hallett, Bob Crosby and Bud Freeman's Summa Cum Laude Orchestra attest to her remarkable talent. [DF]

⊙ **Teddy Grace** (1937–40; Timeless). Stylish performances by Grace, with sidemen including Bobby Hackett, Jack Teagarden and Charlie Shavers, plus her four sides with Freeman's Summa Cum Laude Orchestra.

Kenny Graham

Tenor saxophone, keyboards, composer, arranger.

b. London, 19 July 1924; d. 17 Feb 1997.

Kenny Graham (Kenneth Thomas Skingle) learned banjo from the age of six and later took up the C-melody sax, before switching to alto. Adopting music as a profession in 1940, he worked after 1945 with Jiver Hutchinson, Nat Gonella and Jack Parnell before forming his influential band, the Afro Cubists, in which he played tenor saxophone alongside trumpeter Jo Hunter. Graham's drum-based and world-music-influenced work of this period – including the *Moondog* and *Suncat* suites – anticipated jazz trends which only fully materialized thirty or more years later. Graham became ill in 1958 and thereafter gave up performing but continued to write – notably for Humphrey Lyttelton, who has remained a champion of Graham's work. From the mid-1980s Graham was playing electronic keyboards and alto again, but his public activities were confined to occasional informal duo dates with Paul Sealey and a few others. [DF]

Stephane Grappelli

Violin.

b. Paris, 26 Jan 1908; d. 1 Dec 1997.

Grappelli played harmonium at ten, acquired his first violin at twelve and soon after was studying at the Paris Conservatoire. At sixteen he was working summer seasons, playing in silent cinemas and in Paris courtyards for centimes, until Stephane Mougin, a young fellow musician, introduced him into the Gregorians, a big band modelled on Jack Hylton's and led by a flamboyant French dancer-entrepreneur, Gregor. Grappelli first played piano, then violin. Soon after, he met Django Reinhardt at the Croix du Sud club, and one night at the Hotel Claridge their acquaintance turned into a musical partnership. "We were all in the dressing room waiting to go on", Grappelli remembered later, "and Django was as usual plucking at his guitar. I just started improvising on the chords, and Louis Vola thought it would be fun to add his bass fiddle to our duo: he joined in and so did Django's brother. Thus was born a new jazz!" The little group (with the addition of a third guitarist, first Roger Chaput, then a variety of others) was adopted by the newly formed Hot Club of France, which presented it at a Salle Pleyel concert with Coleman Hawkins. The Quintette du Hot Club de France, as it became known, became a sensational success at chic clubs such as Bricktop's and Chez Florence, playing its quiet but spectacularly creative music.

The partnership between Grappelli and Reinhardt often threatened to founder: Grappelli – conscientious, hard-working, never really "one of the boys" – played to lengths that suggested a rivalry with Reinhardt, and he worried constantly about his partner's gypsy tendencies. But they worked together, recording prolifically and achieving international fame until 1939 when, caught on the hop by the war, Grappelli stayed in London. "I don't think he did very much to begin with", says Denny Wright, his guitarist partner of the 1940s and 1970s, "but later he played the club at 96 Piccadilly and then moved into Hatchett's with George Shearing and a quartet (including me for a year) and worked all through the Blitz. After that he took the show on tour of the Moss Empires."

After the war, Grappelli and Reinhardt were reunited for concerts in Britain and at home, but the guitarist seemed to have lost his urgent motivation. Grappelli enjoyed fishing and painting as much as working and, despite regular recording and club work, their partnership operated on a more casual basis until Reinhardt's death, just before a projected American trip. After that, said Grappelli in 1964, he passed his time "between Paris, Italy and England, working steadily: nightclubs, concerts, radio and TV". It seemed as if his career had reached a comfortable plateau, but in 1972 British-based guitarist Diz Disley, a lifelong Reinhardt follower, brought Grappelli to Britain to play the rounds of local folk clubs (jazz clubs expressed little interest in the idea) with a Reinhardt-style quartet featuring, in addition to himself, Denny Wright (guitar) and John Hawkesworth (bass). After the unexpected success of that tour – "it was the first time he'd gone back to the Hot Club format", explains Wright – Grappelli rapidly turned into a superstar.

He played Carnegie Hall in 1974 and toured America and Europe with his quartet – Disley, Wright (later Ike Isaacs) and Len Skeat (bass). Grappelli albums soon to follow included collaborations with talents as different as Bill Coleman, Gary Burton and Teresa Brewer; prestige sets with Yehudi Menuhin also sold hotly. As the 1980s progressed, Grappelli's soaring improvisational talent – backed by Martin Taylor as well as Disley – seemed to mature like vintage wine: his colossal technique, sculptured lines and elegant repertoire remained one of jazz's most gracefully creative sounds. Into the 1990s he continued to play at full strength with a variety of partners, as his formidable sixty-year discography re-emerged on CD. [DF]

Feeling Plus Finesse Equals Jazz (1962; Atlantic). One of Grappelli's most famous albums prior to his rise to super-stardom in the 1970s, and as good as anything he's ever recorded.

Live In London (1970; Black Lion). Exciting performance from the years when Grappelli was re-establishing himself as a major solo force in Britain and Europe, with the British trio that helped in the process – Diz Disley, Denny Wright and Len Skeat.

Stardust (1973; Black Lion). Duets with the late great British pianist Alan Clare, full of elegant creativity. The CD contains unreleased alternate takes and titles not featured on the LP release.

I Got Rhythm (1973; Black Lion). A hugely exciting concert recorded at the Queen Elizabeth Hall, with the Disley-Grappelli partnership complemented by Denny Wright and Len Skeat.

Meets Earl Hines (1974; Black Lion). Duets with the spectacular Earl Hines, containing two previously unreleased takes.

Reunion With Martin Taylor (1993; Linn). One of Grappelli's most sympathetic guitarist partners is Martin Taylor; all their collaborations are musically immaculate and this is one of their best.

➤➤ **Django Reinhardt** *(Swing In Paris).*

Frank Gratkowski

Soprano and alto saxophones, clarinet, bass-clarinet, flute.

b. 1963, Hamburg, Germany.

Gratkowski began playing saxophone at sixteen, then studied at the Hamburg Musikhochschule and Cologne Conservatory of Music (1985–90). He has studied with Steve Lacy, Sal Nistico and Charlie Mariano, and he participated in a workshop ensemble led by Muhal Richard Abrams in 1988. Gratkowski began performing solo in 1990 and has released *Artikulationen* (1991; 2nd Floor), an impressive lone saxophone disc. In 1992, he began collaborating with pianist Georg Gräwe; the two released a duo, *Vicissetudes* (1993; Random Acoustics), which features Gratkowski on Braxtonesque alto, and he is also a member of the Georg Gräwe quartet, which waxed *Melodie Und Rhythmus* (1997; Okka Disk). A versatile player with a particularly nice, large sound on clarinet, prone to highly expressive outbursts, Gratkowski has been a favoured member of various large ensembles, including the Klaus König Orchestra, Tony Oxley's Celebration Orchestra, the WDR Big Band, and Gräwe's GrubenKlangOrchester. The Frank Gratkowski trio, with drummer Gerry Hemingway and bassist Dieter Mandersheid, has released two strong CDs, *Gestalten* (1996; JazzHausMusik) and *The Flume Factor* (1998; Random Acoustics) while Hemingway remained in the various Gratkowski-led ensembles on *Kollapse* (2001: Red Toucan) and *Spectral Reflections* (2003: Leo). [JC]

Milford Graves

Drums, percussion.

b. New York, 20 Aug 1941.

Graves is self-taught, initially playing congas and subsequently studying Indian tabla, as well as the drumkit. He worked on dance gigs and with Hugh Masekela and Miriam Makeba in the early 1960s. He then became involved in the avant-garde scene with the New York Art Quartet and Paul Bley, making albums with them and with reedman Giuseppe Logan (the last-mentioned being the first jazz recording of Graves, Eddie Gomez and Don Pullen). He was also with the original 1964 edition of the Jazz Composers' Orchestra Association. He performed in duo with Don Pullen in 1966, in a duo with Andrew Cyrille and a trio with Cyrille and Rashied Ali. He was with Albert Ayler in 1967–8, and did regular duo work with reed player Hugh Glover. He taught at the Black Arts Repertory Theater in the late 1960s, and at Bennington College, Vermont, alongside Bill Dixon in the 1970s. He made tours of Europe in 1973 and 1974 and of Japan in 1977. From 1983–6 he played with the all-percussion quartet Pieces Of Time featuring Andrew Cyrille, Don Moye and Kenny Clarke (later Philly Joe Jones).

Probably the most influential of the early "free jazz" drummers, Graves has a highly mobile style which is not perceived in any schematic manner. Technically complex and demanding, his playing nevertheless interacts constantly with the musical activity around him and thus stimulates further activity, without being overbearing. As a soloist he has been a pioneer of extended percussion-only performances from the time of his first album. [BP]

Milford Graves and Sunny Morgan

⊙ **Percussion Ensemble** (1965; ESP). Alongside his striking work of the same period with such as the New York Art Quartet and Paul Bley, this duo with fellow percussionist Morgan opened listeners' ears to the possibilities of non-metric but dynamic drumming.

Georg Gräwe

Piano.

b. 1956, Bochum, Germany.

Raised in the industrial Ruhr region of Germany, near Cologne, Gräwe played in rock bands starting in 1971 and formed an outward-oriented jazz quintet in 1974. In 1976, at the suggestion of pianist Alexander von Schlippenbach, the FMP label released the twenty-year-old sensation's first record, *New Movements*, followed the next year by *Pink Pong*. An agile, tremendously gifted improviser, Gräwe has one of the most advanced harmonic sensibilities in contemporary improvising; he's a serious student of Schœnberg and imports a chamber sensibility into much of his work, but also has some of the wavelike linearity of Lennie Tristano, filtered through the more energetic intensity of 60s free music. Gräwe founded a larger group, the GrubenKlangOrchester (1982–93), which recorded several times, including a set of Hanns Eisler pieces (1984; AufRuhr) and *Songs And Variations* (1989; hat Art). Other larger works include *Chamber Works 1990–92* (1993), released on Gräwe's own Random Acoustics label, which he founded in 1993.

In 1989, he began playing in a trio with cellist Ernst Reijseger and drummer Gerry Hemingway, a group that has worked sporadically since and has released a number of outstanding records, including *Zwei Nacht In Berlin* (1994; Sound Aspects), *The View From Points West* (1994; Music & Arts), *Flex 27* (1994; Random Acoustics), *Saturn Cycle* (1996; Music & Arts) and *Counterfactuals* (2001; Nuscope). Other working groups include a duo with fine Italian trombonist Sebi Tramontana and a new group called Torque with reed player Peter van Bergen and tuba expert Melvyn Poore. Gräwe has also recorded with van Bergen along with bassist Barre Phillips on *Other Songs* (2001; Nuscope). Gräwe's 1991 encounter with Anthony Braxton was released as duo *Amsterdam 1991* (1997; Okka Disk), as was a later duet with Evan Parker, *Unity Variations* (1999; Okka Disk).

He frequently performs solo piano recitals, and his *Gedächtnisspuren* (1995; Music & Arts) gives a clear, unaccompanied picture of his strengths in this setting. [JC]

⊙ **Melodie Und Rhythmus** (1997; Okka Disk). A startling free quartet, one of Gräwe's main vehicles now, with longterm Cologne cohort Frank Gratkowski on clarinet and alto saxophone and an exceptional Chicago team of Kent Kessler on bass and Hamid Drake on drums. Drake, in particular, draws more direct rhythmic interaction from the often oblique pianist, and Gräwe rises unfalteringly to the challenge. Non-stop improvising excitement from a signal player of the current free-music generation.

Wardell Gray

Tenor saxophone.

b. Oklahoma City, 13 Feb 1921; d. 25 May 1955.

Gray was raised in Detroit and, after working locally, toured with the Earl Hines band from 1943–5. He settled on the West Coast and made the first records under his own name in 1946, though they were initially only released in Europe. He spent time freelancing, including with Benny Carter in the mid-1940s and 1955 and the Billy Eckstine septet in 1947, and had regular jam sessions and recording dates from 1947–52 with Dexter Gordon. He worked briefly with Benny Goodman, Count Basie and Tadd Dameron, all in 1948, then had longer stays with Goodman in 1949 and the Basie octet in 1950–51. He did further gigs on the West Coast during his last years. The cause of his death was rumoured to be a drug overdose while working in Las Vegas in company with the dancer (and heroin addict) Teddy Hale (not to be confused with bandleader Teddy Hill).

Though not as immediately influential as his partner Gordon, Wardell converted their common interest in Lester Young into a more mobile style than most of his contemporaries. His great fluency, combined with a mellow yet compact tone, enabled him to fit easily into a bebop context, and to bring its flavour into the swing-oriented groups with which he usually worked. His tune "Twisted", now a standard thanks to singers Annie Ross, Joni Mitchell and Crystal Waters, is an excellent example of Gray at his best. [BP]

⊙ **Memorial, Vols. 1/2** (1949–53; Prestige/OJC). Available separately, these two CDs encapsulate the best of Gray. "Twisted" and two lovely ballads with Al Haig are on Vol. 1, while Vol. 2 has the "Farmer's Market" session with Art Farmer and two live tracks with Basie colleague Clark Terry (and Dexter Gordon joining in on one).

Buddy Greco

Singer, pianist, composer, arranger.

b. Philadelphia, 14 Aug 1926.

Like Nat Cole, Buddy Greco's talents as a jazz pianist are sometimes overlooked because of his international success as a singer in his later years. Greco first led a trio (1944–8) with whom he made a million-selling hit for Musicraft "Ooh Look-A-There Ain't She Pretty". He then joined Benny Goodman, travelling with him to Britain in 1949, before re-forming his trio and scoring a Top 30 hit with "I Ran All The Way Home". Greco's duo album, *At Mr. Kelly's* (1955), was also highly successful and from the mid-50s he was recording regularly as a solo singer with a number of highly rated albums for Epic (including *Songs For Swinging Losers, Buddy And Soul, I Like It Swinging*), plus a hit single reworking of "The Lady Is A Tramp" (1960) which again sold over a million copies in Europe. Greco's final US hit was "Mr Lonely" (1962) but he continued a successful career into the 70s and 80s keeping up with repertoire changes. His regular appearances in Britain included performing at the Talk Of The Town and at the Royal Variety Performance, as well as recording an album with the London Symphony Orchestra. By the 1990s he was recording more regularly in jazz surroundings, touring with his own small group and appearing at clubs, jazz festivals and in concert, notably at the Tavern on the Green and New York's Algonquin. [DF]

⊙ **'Round Midnight** (1992; Bay City). With a team of kindred spirits – Jack Sheldon, Terry Gibbs, Buddy DeFranco and Grover Washington – Greco performs a typically wide-ranging programme spanning "Nobody Knows You When You're Down and Out" to the title track.

⊙ **Talkin' Verve** (1955–8; Verve). Interesting selection of Greco's small-group sides of the period with Billy Bauer, Mundell Lowe, Johnny Frigo and others.

Bennie Green

Trombone.

b. Chicago, 16 April 1923; d. 23 March 1977.

Green joined the Chicago-based Earl Hines band in 1942–3 when he was nineteen (other sidemen at the time included Gillespie and Parker), and rejoined several times later, including from 1946–8 and 1951–3. He worked with Charlie Ventura (replacing Kai Winding) in 1948–9, with Gene Ammons-Sonny Stitt in 1950, and then led his own quintets from the mid-1950s to the early 1960s. After a period of inactivity, he reappeared with his own group in 1968 and played with Duke Ellington in 1969, before working in Las Vegas hotel bands. Green was probably the first trombonist to consort with beboppers, and the first whose ear enabled him to adopt aspects of their harmonic approach. Nevertheless he retained a swing-era phraseology and a warm singing tone, which adapted well to the R&B-influenced repertoire of his later groups. [BP]

⊙ **Glidin' Along** (1961; Jazzland/OJC). A romping session with Johnny Griffin, Junior Mance and (for part of the time) Paul Chambers finds Green on good form, and slowing the pace briefly for "Stardust" which he previously recorded with a Mingus-led trombone workshop.

➤➤ **Charlie Ventura** *(Gene Norman Presents).*

Benny Green

Piano.

b. New York, 4 April 1963.

Growing up in Berkeley, California and studying piano privately, Benny Green gigged as a teenager with Joe Henderson, Woody Shaw and Peter Apfelbaum's Hieroglyphics Ensemble. Moving back to New York in 1983, he studied further with Walter Bishop and Walter Davis, and joined Betty Carter from 1983–7. He then worked with Art Blakey from 1987–9 and Freddie Hubbard from 1989–92; during this period he was also much in demand for freelance recording. From 1992–7, he joined Ray Brown's trio and has worked steadily with his own trio, which includes Christian McBride and drummer Carl Allen, who both played with him in Hubbard's group. From an original appreciation of Bud Powell and Thelonious Monk, Green has moved to absorb some of the slickness associated with Oscar Peterson, whose protégé he was officially named when Peterson won Canada's Glenn Gould prize in 1993. In 1996, he took part in both a New York Town Hall tribute concert to Peterson and a two-piano recording with his mentor. [BP]

⊙ **Lineage** (1990; Blue Note). The album which preceded the tightly organized Green-McBride-Allen sets (four so far), this employs a highly meaningful approach to a collection of jazz standards and a couple of Green's own, including the attractive "Phoebe's Samba".

Charlie "Big" Green

Trombone.

b. Omaha, Nebraska, c. 1900; d. Feb 1936.

Green had a thorough training in tent and carnival shows around Omaha and by the time he joined Fletcher Henderson in 1924 was one of the finest blues players. One of the A-team of Henderson's soloists (along with Coleman Hawkins, Buster Bailey, Joe Smith and Louis Armstrong), he was humorously unflappable, with a vast appetite for life, food and drink, and the ability to make a joke of practically anything. Green's blues can be heard to perfection on a number of sides made with Bessie Smith (their most famous recorded feature was "Trombone Cholly") and with all the other blues singers for whom Henderson was staff pianist at Black Swan. But more than that he was a fine all-round musician who could play almost anything in any key, read a score at sight and play a straight waltz just as well as he could play jazz. Green relished solo playing and tended to make short work of opposition: he kept a feud going with tuba player Ralph Escudero (who, says Louis Armstrong, sometimes doubled Green's trombone parts on his tuba) and later sparred with Jimmy Harrison. After he left Henderson for the last time in 1930, "Big" Green worked with heavyweight bands led by Don Redman, Chick Webb, Benny Carter and others, and was working with Kaiser Marshall's band when in 1936 he passed out on his doorstep one snowy night and froze to death. [DF]

➤➤ **Fletcher Henderson** *(The Chronological Fletcher Henderson 1924–30).*

Dave Green

Double bass.

b. London, 5 March 1942.

Green had no formal lessons, started playing at sixteen and turned professional four years later. He has had several long associations in his career: from 1963–9 he was with the Rendell-Carr quintet, from 1965–83 with Humphrey Lyttelton, from 1967–78 with Stan Tracey, and from 1964 onwards with Michael Garrick. He formed his own band, Fingers, in 1979, and recorded an album, *Fingers Remember Mingus*, the same year. Fingers also did a British Council tour of Yugoslavia in 1984. The same year he played at the Nice jazz festival, and in 1985 played with the Jim Galloway-Carl Fontana group at the Berne jazz festival. That summer he toured Europe with Didier Lockwood and Gordon Beck. Green has also worked with many Americans, from mainstreamers such as Benny Goodman, Coleman Hawkins, Ben Webster, Pee Wee Russell and Scott Hamilton to modernists such as Roland Kirk, Sonny Rollins, George Coleman and Milt Jackson.

From 1994–7, Green played regularly in Europe with New Orleans blues and Gospel singer Lillian Boutte, and in July 1996 he toured the USA with the Charlie Watts quintet which included Peter King, Gerard Presencer and Brian Lemon. In 1998, he played in Berne, Switzerland, with the John Lewis trio and the Warren Vaché/George Wein quartet. The same year, Green formed his own trio with saxophonist Iain Dixon and drummer Gene Calderazzo. In 1999, he appeared at several major jazz festivals in Britain, and also in Jersey and Switzerland. Green has won the Best Bass category at the annual BT British Jazz Awards six times. [IC]

⊙ **Time Will Tell** (2001; Jazz House Records). This rich and dynamic album opens with the trio in swaggering form on "I Hear A Rhapsody". Iain Dixon contributes three excellent compositions, including the funky and emotive "Ellie's Wellies", and there's a hilarious improvised freak-out over mobile phones entitled "Mo-bile".

➤➤ **Scott Hamilton** *(East Of The Sun)*; **Stan Tracey** *(Portraits Plus).*

Freddie Green

Acoustic guitar.

b. Charleston, South Carolina, 31 March 1911; d. 1 March 1987.

Freddie Green went to New York in his teens, working by day as an upholsterer and by night in jazz clubs, including the Yeah Man Exclusive Club and Black Cat in Greenwich Village. At the latter he was heard by impresario John Hammond, who recommended him to Basie as a replacement for Claude Williams. Basie reluctantly auditioned him in a Roseland dressing room – and the next day Green was on the band bus, bound for Pittsburgh. He stayed for thirteen years, cementing the smooth pulse of Basie's all-American rhythm-section. "They had a kind of throb going", says Nat Pierce, "no one instrument louder than the other, so it was a real section!" Harry Edison emphasizes: "Freddie, Walter and Jo would follow Basie until he hit the right tempo, and when he started they *kept* it." In future years, when less reliable timekeepers joined Basie, Green's metronomic guitar was his leader's rock. Comfortable in the Basie band – he played softball in the band team, went swimming with friend Harry Edison, crabbing with Preston Love and had an affair with Billie Holiday – it was a shock to Green when Basie's small group of 1950 excluded him: he climbed back on the stand one night, uninvited, and never allowed himself to be left out again. For the next 35 years the sight of "Old Freddie Green sitting there like a sheep dog looking round to see that nothing is going wrong" (Don Byas) was as familiar as the confident ring of chords produced by his agile left hand on the guitar strings. He stayed until Basie died, and in 1985 was still recording – he played on Manhattan Transfer's tribute to Basie, "Rambo". [DF]

➤➤ **Count Basie** *(The Original American Decca Recordings).*

Grant Green

Guitar.

b. St Louis, Missouri, 6 June 1931; d. 31 January 1979.

Green worked with Jimmy Forrest in his home town in the 1950s, making his record debut when Forrest cut a Chicago session with Elvin Jones in 1959. He played in the organ groups of Sam Lazar in 1960 and Jack McDuff in 1961, recording with them and with Lou Donaldson, Stanley Turrentine and drummer Dave Bailey. He began making albums under his own name, using musicians such as Yusef Lateef, Joe Henderson, Hank Mobley, Herbie Hancock, McCoy Tyner, Elvin Jones, and organists John Patton and Larry Young. His career was interrupted by drug problems in the late 1960s, but he enjoyed his greatest popularity in the 1970s, until he was hospitalized in 1978. Some later recordings have really tedious pseudo-funk backings, and Green graces them with the performances they deserve; but he was capable of moving in very fast company musically, and some albums, unreleased at the time, which have appeared posthumously make this even more evident. [BP]

Matador (1964; Blue Note). Including Green's alternative version of "My Favourite Things", this has McCoy Tyner and Elvin Jones acting as backup and sounding less profound but no less rhythmic than in their work with Coltrane.

>> **Stanley Turrentine** *(Up At Minton's).*

Urbie Green

Trombone, bandleader.

b. Mobile, Alabama, 8 Aug 1926.

A trombone student by the age of twelve, Urbie Green progressed with amazing speed: after four years with Gene Krupa (1946–50), he joined Woody Herman, taking over Bill Harris's featured chair. At not much over 24 he had developed the approach of Jack Teagarden without sounding like an imitator or an exhibitionist. As with Teagarden, everything Green played sounded like the only musical way to play it, and he added some new gifts of his own to Teagarden's master-method: an ability to play high up in the trombone super-register without effort (and never for effect), an ear-boggling speed of execution, and a joyfully developed use of the slide – more pronounced than Teagarden's – which was specially welcome in an era when most of Green's contemporaries were trying to sound like valve-trombonists. All this was quickly spotted by musicians and critics: Green won the *Down Beat* New Star poll for 1954 and soon after was a regular colleague of Benny Goodman – he appeared in *The Benny Goodman Story* (1955) and led Goodman's orchestra for a three-month tour in 1957. By then Green was a star in his own right, appearing on record with musicians twenty years his senior (including Buck Clayton and Jimmy Rushing) and producing a string of albums of his own which have since turned into trombonists' textbooks. By the 1960s he was bandleading still, fronting Tommy Dorsey's orchestra, and in 1969 was with a rock-based small group at New York's Riverboat, experimenting with electronic octave-dividers. From the 1970s Green – who by now had taken up farming too – was most often to be seen and heard teaching at clinics, leading his own small groups, appearing at prestigious one-offs (including Duke Ellington's 70th birthday celebrations at the White House), and playing jazz festivals. By the mid-1990s his appearances on record were becoming more sparse, but he has continued to play regularly, including a visit to London to perform with a large trombone ensemble. [DF]

>> **Bobby Hackett** *(What A Wonderful World).*

Sonny Greer

Drums.

b. Long Branch, New Jersey, 13 Dec 1895; d. 23 March 1982.

Duke Ellington's first drummer, and for many his greatest, Sonny (William Alexander) Greer was four years older than Ellington and arrived in New York with Elmer Snowden's band well before the young pianist – and so was well qualified to become a senior member of Ellington's "family". A fast-talking hipster who hustled in pool halls to get his drums out of hock, and drank with the best, Greer worked with Ellington's five-piece Washingtonians, and then moved, with a few reservations, into the Cotton Club with the augmented orchestra, for which he built up a $3000 edifice of drums supplied by Indiana's Leedy Drum Company (for whom Greer was a designer), plus chimes, vibes, timpani and gong. Greer, a powerful drummer and an inspiration to later drummer-showmen like Gene Krupa, was fundamental to all Ellington's greatest work until 1950. But that year, conscious of Greer's heavy drinking and occasional fallibility in performance, as well as of changing fashion, Ellington took a second drummer, Butch Ballard, on a Scandinavian tour. The quarrel that followed was much worse than their regular "cussings-out", and it ended the partnership. For the next twenty years Greer freelanced with Johnny Hodges's small band, "Red" Allen, Tyree Glenn and others, and appeared in films (including *The Night They Raided Minsky's*). In 1974 he joined Ellington scholar Brooks Kerr for a tribute to his old boss which was hugely successful all over the USA. "I never heard a better drummer for the Ellington band than Sonny Greer", says Don Byas. "It's funny, for alone or with another band he was nothing exceptional. But he fitted with the Duke as has no one else!" [DF]

Duke Ellington

Swing 1930–1938 (Jazz Classics). In Robert Parker's re-mastering the big-band aspect of Greer's contribution to Ellington's early peak years is clearly – and beautifully – audible.

>> **Duke Ellington** *(The Duke's Men: Small Groups Vols. 1 & 2).*

Stan Greig

Piano, drums, bandleader.

b. Edinburgh, Scotland, 12 Aug 1930.

Greig grew up in Edinburgh, joined Sandy Brown's band at the Royal High School in 1945 and came to London to join Ken Colyer (on drums) in 1954. From then on he worked with Humphrey Lyttelton (1955–6), the Fairweather-Brown All Stars (1956–60) and Acker Bilk (1960–68), then from 1969 had his own trio and quintet (featuring Colin Smith and Al Gay), playing mainstream jazz and specializing in boogie-woogie. In 1975 Greig formed the London Jazz Big Band, a top-rate fifteen-piece orchestra which, despite the presence of such musicians as Picard, Milliner, Fairweather, Gay and Smith, never achieved the recognition it deserved and was never recorded. In the mid-1980s, after a spell with George Melly, Greig was once again with Humphrey Lyttelton, taking time off to appear with his own boogie band, the Harlem Blues and Jazz Band, and solo in pubs and clubs. He left Lyttelton early in 1995 to concentrate on solo activities. [DF]

⊙ **Boogie Woogie** (1971/1997; Lake). A welcome CD reissue of a rare Greig trio album recorded in 1971 for Rediffusion. A bonus is three new solo tracks spread through the collection.

➤➤ **Humphrey Lyttelton** *(Beano Boogie)*; **Wally Fawkes** *(Jazz Jurassics)*.

Al Grey

Trombone.

b. Aldie, Virginia, 6 June 1925.

Grey's early years, during World War II, were spent in a navy band and after demobilization he joined Benny Carter. Subsequently he worked with Jimmie Lunceford, Lucky Millinder and Lionel Hampton, then, after a spell with Dizzy Gillespie (1956–7), he joined Count Basie, a vital career association which lasted, on and off, for twenty more years. His pungent plungermute contributions to Basie masterpieces such as "Blues In Hoss' Flat" made Grey – along with Lockjaw Davis – the most striking band soloist of Basie's "atomic" recording period. By the 1960s he had established an international reputation and recorded – as leader – albums such as *Thinking Man's Trombone*. Later he worked in studios, toured for Jazz At The Philharmonic, played occasionally with George Wein's Newport All Stars and continued to build his soloist's reputation. By the mid-1970s he was touring regularly with Jimmy Forrest in duo and in the 1980s, after Forrest's death, he teamed with Buddy Tate for more tandem appearances. A regular star of the festival and club circuit, Grey continued to commute from country to country – in the mid-80s he appeared at the Edinburgh jazz festival, led a quintet with Al Cohn in New York, and performed regularly with Lionel Hampton. In the 1990s he led a quintet and recorded for the last time in 1996 (*Matzoh and Grits* on Arbors). An ebullient extrovert, often billed as "the last of the great plungers", Grey worked in the area previously occupied by such great names as "Tricky Sam" Nanton, and always produced a high-octane performance. [DF]

⊙ **The New Al Grey Quintet** (1988; Chiaroscuro). A two-trombone date featuring Mike Grey – Al's son – with Al Cohn's son Joe playing guitar and J.J. Wiggins (son of Gerald) on bass. Good playing all round.

⊙ **Fab** (1992; Capri). The king of the plunger in typically powerful form, with Clark Terry and others.

Chris Griffin

Trumpet.

b. Binghampton, New York, 31 Oct 1915.

A new trumpet talent on the 1930s New York scene, Griffin was playing with Charlie Barnet's big band in his late teens, and from 1936 formed Benny Goodman's legendary trumpet section with Harry James and Ziggy Elman. Although programme items such as "Blue Skies" and "Blue Room" included solos for him, Griffin was featured sparingly with Goodman – but it would have been difficult for any trumpeter not to be overshadowed by the bravura presence of James and Elman, as reviewers of the time occasionally remarked. After he left Goodman in 1939 Griffin concentrated on studio work, following up an earlier connection with CBS; he stayed with the company for thirty years and co-ran a trumpet school with Pee Wee Erwin in the 1960s and 1970s. After Erwin's death in 1981, Griffin replaced his partner in Warren Vaché senior's small group, based in New Jersey. [DF]

➤➤ **Benny Goodman** *(Carnegie Hall Concert; Second Carnegie Hall Concert)*.

Johnny Griffin

Tenor saxophone.

b. Chicago, 24 April 1928.

Griffin was on the road at seventeen with Lionel Hampton, with whom he worked from 1945–7, before joining the breakaway Hampton group of trumpeter Joe Morris from 1947–50, which enjoyed great success in the R&B field. After stays with Jo Jones in 1950 and Arnett Cobb in 1951, he was stationed in Hawaii from 1952–4. He returned to Chicago leading his own group and also worked there in 1955 with Thelonious Monk. In 1957 he toured with Art Blakey, and then with the Monk quartet in 1958. He worked as a soloist in Chicago and elsewhere, until the formation of the Eddie Davis-Johnny Griffin quintet which operated from 1960–62. In autumn 1963 he followed in the footsteps of Dexter Gordon by touring Europe and staying on, based in Holland and then France. He was a regular member of the Kenny Clarke-Francy Boland band between 1967–72, and of other occasional all-star groups. He also worked as a guest soloist with various European rhythm-sections, sometimes reunited with Eddie Davis, as in 1977 and 1984, and Arnett Cobb as in 1984. From 1978 onwards he began to spend part of each year touring in the USA with his own quartet.

Although he is fully conversant with the tenor tradition of Hawkins, Byas, Webster and Young, it has often been remarked how close in spirit Griffin's playing is to that of Charlie Parker. The headlong rush of ideas, and the rhythmic variety and freedom that go with them, all point in this direction. In addition his tone combines a vocalized sound with a slightly hysterical edge that, at his best, can evoke almost uncontrollable exhilaration – except perhaps for other tenor players, since Griffin is one of the fastest and most accurate ever on his instrument. [BP]

⊙ **A Blowing Session** (1957; Blue Note). How to make your mark on Blue Note, with a frontline combining the talents of Griffin, Hank Mobley and John Coltrane. Griffin is the most at ease with the standard changes and the relentless tempos of his then employer Art Blakey.

The Man I Love (1967; Black Lion). Griffin is effortlessly in charge of this live date with Kenny Drew. Favourite vehicles include "Sophisticated Lady" and the title track.

The Cat (1990; Antilles). Now conserving his energy but no less sure-footed, Griffin presents an all-original programme including the impressive ballad "Woe Is Me".

➤➤ **Kenny Clarke** *(Two Originals)*; **Eddie "Lockjaw" Davis** *(Live At Minton's)*.

Henry Grimes

Bass.

b. Philadelphia, 3 Nov 1935.

Grimes studied at the Juilliard School in 1953, and gigged with Arnett Cobb and Willis Jackson. He played with the Gerry Mulligan quartet in 1957, Charles Mingus (with Mingus on piano) also in 1957, Tony Scott in 1958 and the Sonny Rollins trio in 1958–9. With Rollins he played at the 1958 Newport festival, where he also backed Thelonious Monk. He worked with Cecil Taylor in 1961–2, then in 1962–3 (including a European tour) rejoined Rollins, whose group then included Don Cherry. He gigged with the Steve Lacy quartet in 1963 and did further work with Taylor. During 1965 he recorded with, among others, Albert Ayler, Archie Shepp, Frank Wright, Mose Allison, Perry Robinson and Cherry (the first of three albums). Turning his back on music from 1967 onwards, he was involved in poetry and painting, until being discovered by a social worker in 2002. Given a new bass by William Parker, he began playing in public again in 2003 – a cause for great rejoicing, since the strength gained from his wide experience was always evident in whatever context he performed. [BP]

Sonny Rollins

In Stockholm 1959 (Dragon). As on a couple of other live recordings from the same European tour, Grimes is the only harmony instrument in Rollins's trio and performs admirably in a way which fuelled his later "free" work.

Tiny Grimes

Guitar, vocals.

b. Newport News, Virginia, 7 July 1916; d. 4 March 1989.

Tiny (Lloyd) Grimes started playing four-string guitar in 1937 ("I always tell people I can't afford the other two strings"), after several years as a drummer, and was entirely self-taught. Eight months later he joined a string group, The Cats And A Fiddle, but soon after teamed with Slam Stewart (after Stewart's former partner Slim Gaillard had gone into the army) and the two of them then joined Art Tatum to form a legendary trio – their fantastic interplay and Tatum's occasional stylish singing were, in Frank Driggs's words, "the talk of the jazz world". After Tatum, Grimes's bluesy guitar was all over 52nd Street until clubs began closing; when work slowed he went to Cleveland and Atlantic City, where he formed an embryonic rock'n'roll show, The Rocking Highlanders (who played in kilts). Grimes continued touring and playing small-group residencies until a serious illness in 1964, but he recovered in two years to return to New York clubland. From 1970 he was back in the swing of jazz festivals and club dates with Earl Hines and others. [DF]

Callin' The Blues (1958; Prestige/OJC). A later Grimes date which also marked the return to the studio of trombonist J.C. Higginbotham. Earthy, occasionally laboured, but a significant addition to Grimes's discography.

Tiny In Swingville (1959; Swingville/OJC). A fine studio date featuring Jerome Richardson and Grimes displaying his immense jazz talents to full effect, despite some novelty "Highland" material.

One Is Never Too Old To Swing (1977; Sonet). Superb swing session with Roy Eldridge in attendance and on keen form.

➤➤ **Art Tatum** *(I Got Rhythm)*.

Don Grolnick

Piano, composer.

b. Brooklyn, New York, 23 Sept 1947; d. 1 June 1996.

Fascinated by jazz after being taken by his guitar-playing father to a Count Basie concert when he was eight, and after seeing Erroll Garner at Carnegie Hall shortly afterwards, Don Grolnick played accordion (like Stan Tracey) before switching to piano. He played in a rock'n'roll band in his teenage years, but listened almost exclusively to Miles Davis, Cannonball Adderley and early John Coltrane. After reading philosophy at Tufts University, Grolnick joined Dreams, a band featuring John Abercrombie and the Brecker brothers. In the 1970s, he became a highly sought-after session player, appearing on albums by Bette Midler, Roberta Flack, Carly Simon, Steely Dan and James Taylor, with whom he has had a twenty-year association as player, musical director and producer. In the 1980s, in addition to continuing his work with the likes of Randy and Mike Brecker, Joe Farrell and George Benson, Grolnick played with drummer Peter Erskine, the Bob Mintzer big band, David Sanborn, and guitarists John Scofield and Mike Stern. In 1986, however, he realized his ambition to record his own music with *Hearts And Numbers*, following it up with two Blue Note releases (see below). A slyly inventive, rather than a sparklingly virtuosic pianist, Grolnick will be sorely missed, not only as a superb arranger and MD for the classier pop and rock acts, but most importantly as a composer of deceptively simple themes that reveal more depths on every playing, and as a linchpin of the New York jazz scene, able to draw magnificent performances from, typically, four-horn frontlines, of music deeply but unpretentiously informed by his encyclopedic knowledge of post-war jazz. [CP]

Hearts And Numbers (1986; VeraBra). Mike Brecker (trumpets), Hiram Bullock (guitar), Marcus Miller (bass) and Peter Erskine (drums) all help lift this album out of the ordinary fusion mould.

Weaver Of Dreams (1989; Blue Note). Erskine and both Breckers, trombonist Barry Rogers, Bob Mintzer (bass-clarinet) and Dave Holland (bass) are beautifully handled by Grolnick's haunting but accessible music – top-class fusion.

Nighttown (1992; Blue Note). Superb, classy, elegant music featuring Randy Brecker (trumpet), Steve Turre (tuba), Joe Lovano (tenor saxophone), Marty Ehrlich (bass-clarinet), Dave Holland (bass) and Bill Stewart (drums). Grolnick's own "Heart Of Darkness" and his arrangement of "What is This Thing Called Love" are particular highlights.

Steve Grossman

Saxophones.

b. Brooklyn, New York, 18 Jan 1951.

Grossman started on alto in 1959, studying with his brother Hal, who later taught at Berklee. He took up soprano saxophone at fifteen and tenor a year later. In November 1969 he made his first recording with Miles Davis. From March to September 1970 he was a member of Davis's group, playing on some key albums. In 1971 he was with Lonnie Liston Smith, from 1971–3 with Elvin Jones and in 1975 he formed Stone Alliance with Gene Perla and Don Alias. Grossman spent the 80s and early 90s leading his own groups.

Though Grossman was much maligned by critics during his stint with Miles Davis, the then nineteen year old made a very positive contribution to the music, playing with great emotional intensity and creating some excellent melodic lines. With other ex-Davis alumni Grossman was united with Miles for a concert in Paris a few months before the master's death. [IC]

In New York (1991; Dreyfus). This is a dynamic live session with McCoy Tyner, bassist Avery Sharpe and Art Taylor. The fast company keeps Grossman on his toes, and, despite his curiously dry, unresonant sound, he gives as good as he gets.

A Small Hotel (1993; Dreyfus). Another trio, more expansive and less hard-hitting, with Cedar Walton, David Williams and Billy Higgins, but again Grossman is at his very best, which is very good indeed.

>> **Miles Davis** *(Jack Johnson).*

Marty Grosz

Guitar, banjo, vocals, composer.

b. Berlin, 28 Feb 1930.

A fine rhythm guitarist and constantly surprising soloist, Marty Grosz worked for years in Chicago in comparative obscurity. Although early albums such as *Hooray For Bix* clearly showed where he was bound, it was after Grosz joined Soprano Summit at the invitation of Bob Wilber that he started to get talked about. He took a major part in Wilber's project, writing a number of fine arrangements, but after three years and eight more albums went back to freelancing around New York, often with Dick Sudhalter, Kenny Davern or his own groups. A notable musical project with Sudhalter, a kindred spirit, was the Classic Jazz Quartet (or Bourgeois Scum), featuring clarinettist Joe Muranyi and pianist Dick Wellstood – quality music with a sense of humour. Since the CJQ parted company (after the death of Wellstood) Grosz has consolidated his solo status as guitarist and singer with a developing roster of appearances at jazz rooms and festivals in America and Europe. He has also built up an impressive discography in which respect for classic jazz's heritage is mingled with a likeable reluctance to present his devotion overseriously. Like Wellstood and Sudhalter, Grosz is also an outstanding jazz journalist. [DF]

Marty Grosz and Keith Ingham

Unsaturated Fats (1990; Stomp Off). Wittily titled examination of Fats Waller's less well-known compositions, and all excellent.

Donaldson Redux (1991; Stomp Off). Ingham, Grosz and their Hot Cosmopolites present a scholarly but never pompous exploration of the tunes of Walter Donaldson.

Marty Grosz

Thanks (1993; J and M). One of Grosz's own favourites, this CD has him on peak form with Ecklund, clarinettist Bobby Gordon, Hal Smith and Ingham again; one outstanding track is the peppy "Alarm Clock Stomp", with its Waller-ish top and tail.

Just Imagine: The Music Of DeSylva, Brown And Henderson (1994; Stomp Off). More finely-researched levity in a collection which, as usual, digs deep into the compositional files of its subjects. Titles like "This Is The Missus", "Southwind" and "Let's Call It A Day" are brightly re-established by the Hot Cosmopolites, co-led by Grosz and Keith Ingham, whose research, performance and sleevenotes are all impeccable.

Going Hollywood (1997; Stomp Off). As usual, scholarly, witty and full of connoisseurs' references, a retrospective study of tunes from the early "Talkies" as they might have been played at the time of release. Keith Ingham and Grosz steer their Hot Cosmopolites including Ecklund, Robinson and violinist Andy Stein on six tracks.

George Gruntz

Piano, organ, harpsichord, Rhodes piano, synthesizer, composer.

b. Basle, Switzerland, 24 June 1932.

Gruntz studied music at Basle and Zurich conservatories. He won several prizes at Zurich jazz festivals during the 1950s, but did not become a fully professional musician until 1963. He was a member of the European all-star group called the Newport International Band, performing at the Newport festival and in New York. Since then he has appeared at most major jazz festivals throughout the world. In 1968–9 he was a member of Phil Woods's original European Rhythm Machine. He has also played with Don Cherry, Roland Kirk, Mel Lewis and others. Since 1970 he has been Musical Director of the

Zurich Schauspielhaus, and from 1972–94 he was the artistic director/producer of the Berlin jazz festival. In 1972 Gruntz, together with Swiss musicians Flavio and Franco Ambrosetti and Daniel Humair, formed an all-star big band called The Band which toured Europe that year and in 1976; in 1978 he took over the band, calling it the George Gruntz Concert Jazz Band. In 1973 he created the Piano Conclave: from a pool of ten leading European pianists, he drew six for the Conclave performances, and they used twenty keyboard instruments from harpsichord to synthesizer, working with a rhythm-section. The Conclave played major festivals all over Europe.

Gruntz is a prolific composer and arranger, writing for all kinds of ensembles from small groups and big bands to symphony orchestras. In 1974 he was given an Arts Council of Great Britain composition award and wrote *The Rape Of Lucrece*, which was performed in London in 1975 at the Shakespeare birthday celebrations concert at Southwark Cathedral. In 1977 he was commissioned to write a long piece for a percussion orchestra, and the premiere of *Percussion Profiles* was given at the Monterey festival. In 1987 he led a big band on a tour of the USA. He has also written a jazz opera and a ballet, collaborated with various composers including Hans Werner Henze, and composed for art-film soundtracks and for contemporary theatrical productions. He has won polls in the USA and Europe for composing, arranging, his keyboard work and his big band.

During the 1990s he has continued to tour and record with his various Concert Jazz Bands (CJB). Gruntz and the CJB were augmented by members of the Gil Evans Orchestra at the 1991 Montreux festival, and under Quincy Jones's direction the huge ensemble performed the famous Evans orchestral arrangements with Miles Davis. In November 1992 his CJB made the first official tour of China, playing seven concerts in Beijing, Shanghai and Guangzhou, and in April 1994 they had a week's residency at Ronnie Scott's club in London. They have toured extensively since and in 2000 released their *Global Excellence* album to critical acclaim. [IC]

⊙ **Beyond Another Wall: Live In China** (1992; TCB). Gruntz is a very adventurous composer/arranger, but he also plays pieces by members of the band. The quality of the live recording in China is not good, but the bristling vitality of the written and improvised sections is clearly apparent. There are powerful solos by Lew Soloff, Chris Hunter and Ray Anderson. Gruntz's concept embraces the whole spectrum from structured pieces to free improvisation, and the results are usually exhilarating.

Dave Grusin

Piano, composer.

b. Denver, Colorado, 26 June 1934.

After studying at the University of Colorado, where he played with Terry Gibbs and Johnny Smith, Dave Grusin was singer Andy Williams's musical director for seven years, commencing 1959, and also established himself as a composer of film and TV music. A versatile and thoroughly professional pianist, Grusin has collaborated with jazz figures as wide-ranging as Benny Goodman, Gerry Mulligan and Lee Ritenour in everything from swing through hard bop to fusion music, but he is perhaps mainly celebrated as a prolific writer of film soundtracks – *The Fabulous Baker Boys* and *Havana* (see below) are prominent examples – and as the "G" of the GRP (Grusin-Rosen Productions) label, formed with drummer Larry Rosen. GRP produced a great deal of popular "jazz-lite" in the 1980s and 1990s, undemanding but impeccably played fusion music epitomized by the albums recorded by the label's cream session men, collectively known as the GRP All Stars, and drawing players from a pool including the likes of Lee Ritenour, Steve Gadd, Tom Browne and Eric Gale. [CP/CI]

Gerry Mulligan

⊙ **Little Big Horn** (1988; GRP). Interesting session, mimicking big-band sound with electronics and featuring tenorman Michael Brecker as well as Grusin on electric piano and synthesizer.

Dave Grusin

⊙ **Havana** (1990; GRP). Bustling, suitably atmospheric soundtrack packed with subdued virtuosity and textural variety.

⊙ **West Side Story** (1997; N2K). Inventive all-star presentation of Grusin's reworking of Bernstein's score, featuring Michael Brecker, Arturo Sandoval and Bill Evans as outstanding soloists.

➤➤ **Kevin Eubanks** *(Face To Face).*

Gigi Gryce

Alto saxophone, flute, composer.

b. Pensacola, Florida, 28 Nov 1927; d. 17 March 1983.

After extensive studies, including some months in Paris, Gryce (aka Basheer Qusim) secured his reputation by stays with Tadd Dameron and Lionel Hampton in 1953, the latter also giving rise to many small-group recordings by band members, arranged by Gryce and Quincy Jones. He wrote and played for the Oscar Pettiford band from 1955–7, and during the same period co-led the Jazz Lab quintet with Donald Byrd, sometimes expanding it to a nine-piece line-up for records. From 1959–61 he led a quintet, but then became less active as a performer and, from 1963 until his death, dedicated himself to schoolteaching.

Gryce's alto work, although passionate and articulate in a Parkerian vein, was largely overshadowed by his writing, which appeared on albums by Clifford Brown, Art Farmer, J.J. Johnson and others. In particular a couple of tunes, "Social Call" and "Nica's Tempo", enjoyed a considerable vogue in the mid-1950s and were recorded by several groups. Alongside Horace Silver – whose work his own resembles – Gryce was one of the first black musicians to retain the publishing rights to his pieces. [BP]

⊙ **The Rat Race Blues** (1960; New Jazz/OJC). Gryce's next-to-last album before he ceased recording in 1961 finds him with a programme of originals that deserve to be better known, and an excellent line-up including Richard Williams and pianist Richard Wyands.

Frank Guarente

Trumpet.

b. Montemilletto, Italy, 5 Oct 1893; d. 21 July 1942.

According to John Chilton, Frank (Francesco Saverio) Guarente went to the USA in 1910 and while living in New Orleans in 1914 took advice from King Oliver. After a lot of freelance work he joined violinist Paul Specht's highly successful orchestra in 1921, and became the centrepiece of Specht's hot band-within-a-band, the Georgians. Including trombonist Russ Morgan and pianist Arthur Schutt, the Georgians recorded for Columbia, played a long residency at the Alamec Hotel on Broadway and visited London for a 1923 summer season. From 1924–7, Guarente led the New Georgians in America and Europe, including a 1926 summer in Scheveningen, a Dutch jazz stronghold that later played host to jazzmen such as Ray Noble and Nat Gonella. After that he came to London to join the original Savoy Orpheans, alongside trumpeter Max Goldberg. After a trip to Prague the group broke up on return to London and Guarente took his Oliver-flavoured trumpet into the Savoy and other major London venues before returning to the USA in 1928. For the next twelve years he was active in studio work with Victor Young and the Dorseys, among others, until ill health caused his retirement. [DF]

Johnny Guarnieri

Piano, composer.

b. New York, 23 March 1917; d. 7 Jan 1985.

Johnny Guarnieri heard Fats Waller when he was fifteen and turned professional two years later; his early work was with George Hall, Farley and Riley ("a comedy band and not really for me"), Benny Goodman (1939) and Artie Shaw (1940). Versatility and a vivid imagination assured him work, and after a non-stop period seeing in "the dark hours to dawn" along 52nd Street, doubling with Raymond Scott's CBS orchestra (he slept in a CBS lounge to make the calls) and recording all over, Guarnieri moved into studio work as a staffman for NBC. His jazz interests never flagged, however, and through the 1950s occasional albums illustrated his bravura abilities: "in performance he might offer a lighter-than-air 'My Funny Valentine' with the left hand only, a 5/4 treatment of 'Maple Leaf Rag' and then perhaps 'I'm Just Wild About Harry' with a dozen key changes", observed critic Floyd Levin. A warm-hearted and enthusiastic communicator, Guarnieri taught selflessly in later years; his pupils responded by financing a label, TazJazz, to record him. By 1970 the pianist had recorded an album of originals and composed a piano concerto, and by the early 1970s was enchanting visitors at the Tail of the Cock club in Studio City, California, where he worked regularly until 1982. He collapsed and died suddenly on a date with Dick Sudhalter in New York. [DF]

⊙ **Guarnieri Stealin' Apples** (1978; TazJazz). The brilliant Guarnieri with eleven examples of his piano showcases, recorded live at Pasadena City College.

Lars Gullin

Baritone saxophone, composer, piano.

b. Visby, Sweden, 4 May 1928; d. 17 May 1976.

Gullin began on clarinet and played alto regularly until taking up the baritone at the age of 21. He played with the Arne Domnérus sextet, which included Rolf Ericson, from 1951–3, and then formed his own quintet in 1953. Thereafter he worked principally as a guest soloist with local rhythm-sections, and also made frequent recordings, including with visiting Americans such as Clifford Brown. He toured in Italy with Chet Baker in 1959, and subsequently made a considerable impression as a composer. Much of Gullin's career was shadowed by narcotics (the fictional saxophonist of the Swedish film *Sven Klang's Combo* is based on Gullin), and some periods in which he was inactive as a player were only survived with the aid of artists' grants from the Swedish government.

As the first European musician after Django Reinhardt to have an impact in the USA without relocating there, Gullin has never been duplicated or surpassed. His facility and relaxation, especially in the 1950s, were able to make the baritone feel like a delicately handled tenor. But his tone (thanks to the Tristano influence detectable in many Swedish and German musicians of this period) was so light and pure that it recalled not so much a tenor as altoist Lee Konitz. Konitz in turn was an admirer of Gullin and participated in a posthumous album of Gullin tunes, under the title of one of them, *Dedicated To Lee* (1983; Dragon). Local commentators detect the inspiration not only of folk music but of nineteenth-century Swedish composers in Gullin's distinctive writing. His son Peter Gullin (b. Milan, 12 April 1959) is highly regarded as a promising alto and baritone saxophonist. [BP]

⊙ **Lars Gullin Vol. 2 1953** (Dragon). This contains the original two versions of "Dedicated To Lee" recorded with Konitz and others from the touring Stan Kenton band, plus mainly quartet performances of standards.

⊙ **Lars Gullin Vol. 1 1955–56** (Dragon). The slender fruits of Gullin's internationally available recordings conclude with this selection, which includes more Gullin originals and a set with the 1955 Chet Baker quartet.

➤➤ **Clifford Brown** *(Memorial Album).*

Trilok Gurtu

Percussion, tabla, drums, conga.

b. Bombay, India, 30 Oct 1951.

Gurtu studied tabla with Ahmed Jan Thirakwa, but in jazz, percussion and conga, he was self-taught.

He studied tabla from the age of six, regularly accompanying his mother and other musicians at his home. In 1965, with his brother, he led a percussion group in Bombay and, influenced by Miles Davis and John Coltrane (particularly *Coltrane Plays The Blues*), he began playing jazz. In 1973 he went to Europe with an Indian jazz-rock group, staying in Italy until 1975. He went to the USA in 1976, playing with various jazz groups in New York and beginning his long association with Charlie Mariano. He also worked with Don Cherry and Barre Phillips. Gurtu was active as a teacher in New York and played Woodstock every year until 1982. In the 1980s he played the New York Kool jazz festival with Lee Konitz, worked with Karl Berger, with Mariano and Philip Catherine, and with Archie Shepp. He has also toured Europe with Nana Vasconcelos in duo with break dancers, with a quartet including Shankar, Garbarek and Vasconcelos, and with Mariano and Jasper van't Hof. In the mid-1980s, Gurtu was working with Rainer Brüninghaus (keyboards) and John Abercrombie (guitar), and was also a member of the group Oregon, in which he replaced the late Collin Walcott. In the late 1980s and early 1990s he toured and recorded with John McLaughlin, and in the 1990s he toured internationally with his own groups. Gurtu's favourites are Thirakwa, Roy Haynes and Elvin Jones; other inspirations are Chopin, Ellington, Shobha Gurtu (his mother), Miles Davis, Booker Little, Ahmad Jamal and the music of Africa. His compositions include "Paschlove", dedicated to Collin Walcott, and a commission for the West German Radio with Airto Moreira and Flora Purim. [IC]

⊙ **Crazy Saints** (1993; CMP). Gurtu displays his effortless mastery of Eastern and Western percussion. This is not a drum-dominated session, however, as he fuses Indian scales and structures with Western instrumentation; the clarinet of Louis Sclavis and cello of Ernst Reijsiger are used particularly effectively. Two tracks performed with and written by Joe Zawinul, though interesting in themselves, disturb the unity of the disc somewhat.

⊙ **The Trilok Gurtu Collection** (1997; CMP). This is a fascinating selection of tracks from six of Gurtu's albums covering the period 1987–96. The roll call of sidemen's names is impressive – Don Cherry, saxophonist Bill Evans, Jan Garbarek, Pat Metheny, Ralph Towner and Joe Zawinul are only a few of the people featured in this collection, which shows Gurtu's immense talent as both composer and arranger, as well as his extraordinary skills as a percussionist.

➤➤ **John McLaughlin** *(Live At The Royal Festival Hall; Que Allegria)*; **Barre Phillips** *(Three Day Moon)*; **L. Shankar** *(Song For Everyone)*; **Ralph Towner** *(Always Never And Forever)*.

Barry Guy

Double bass, chamber bass, violone, composer.
b. London, 22 April 1947.

Guy became interested in jazz at school, then studied double bass and composition at the Guildhall School of Music and Drama. In the mid-1960s he began playing with John Stevens and Trevor Watts in the Spontaneous Music Ensemble, which was totally dedicated to free improvisation. Since then, he has pursued a dual career on the European art music circuit and on the free-improvisation circuit. He has also worked with the Howard Riley trio, Bob Downes's Open Music, Trevor Watts's Amalgam, Iskra 1903, and various groups with Tony Oxley, Evan Parker and Peter Kowald.

By the end of the 1960s it was becoming apparent that there was not much of an audience for improvised abstract music and, faced with an unsympathetic world, the players drew together for mutual support in an organization called the Musicians' Co-operative. Guy was a founder member and, to celebrate the event, he composed "Ode" for a 21-piece ensemble of free improvisers which he called the London Jazz Composers' Orchestra (LJCO), following a precedent created in the USA by Michael Mantler in 1964, when he too formed an ensemble called the Jazz Composers' Orchestra. The aim of both orchestras was to try to explore the relationship of individual improvisers to organized ensemble sound and to translate abstraction from a small-group setting to an orchestral one. The situation was complicated in the British ensemble by the fact that several of its members were ideologically opposed to any kind of formal composition at all. The LJCO has undergone various transformations over the years, and has appeared at festivals in the UK and Europe.

Guy has composed many pieces for "classical" ensembles of all sizes, and has written several works for the LJCO, including *Polyhymnia* and *Four Pieces For Orchestra*. He is a virtuoso player, often giving solo concerts. Among his influences he names Charles Mingus, Scott LaFaro, Gary Peacock, Albert Ayler, Eric Dolphy, Ornette Coleman, John Coltrane, Bill Evans and all his UK improvising associates. [IC]

London Jazz Composers' Orchestra

⊙ **Harmos** (1989; Intakt). The problems of orchestral coherence and its relation to each individual musician's freedom is solved in many ingenious ways here. Trevor Watts, another pioneer who has also matured over the years, is strongly featured.

Barry Guy

Arcus (1990; Maya). Guy is here in felicitous duo with Barre Phillips. Both were pioneers of free improvisation in the 1960s and, like most of their contemporaries who have persevered in this vein, they have matured and mellowed.

You Forget To Answer (1995; Maya) This is a playful and highly focused trio album with Swedish saxophonist and fluteophonist (a flute with a saxophone mouthpiece on one end) and drummer/percussionist Raymond Strid. The quality of listening is formidable and the free/abstract improvising has impressive coherence.

➤➤ **Evan Parker** *(Atlanta)*; **Eddie Prévost** *(Supersession).*

Fred Guy

Guitar, banjo.

b. Burkesville, Georgia, 23 May 1897; d. 22 Nov 1971.

At the start of his career Fred Guy worked with Joseph Smith's band in New York, then led his own before joining Duke Ellington in 1925. A close friend of Ellington, Guy provided a stabilizing influence: "He was one of the more mature, level-headed people in the band", says Mercer Ellington. Guy switched to guitar in the mid-1930s after Eddie Lang's influence had been widely acknowledged, and played it regularly thereafter until he left Ellington in 1949 to work for twenty years as a dance hall manager. His suicide was a severe shock to his former leader in his declining years. [DF]

Joe Guy

Trumpet.

b. Birmingham, Alabama, 20 Sept 1920; d. 1962.

Guy worked in the late 1930s with Teddy Hill and Coleman Hawkins and from 1941 led the house band at Minton's, which included Thelonious Monk and Kenny Clarke. The following year he joined Cootie Williams's orchestra, and in 1944 took part in Norman Granz's first-ever JATP concert. For a couple of years after that Guy was Billie Holiday's partner: he led her orchestra on tour, recorded a number of classic titles with her, and from 1946 fronted a quintet for her long residency at the Downbeat Club on 52nd Street. By the end of the 1940s he had become inactive, possibly owing to drug abuse. [DF]

➤➤ **Billie Holiday** *(The Complete American Original Decca Recordings).*

Tommy Gwaltney

Alto and tenor saxophones, clarinet, vibes, xylophone.

b. Norfolk, Virginia, 28 Feb 1921.

From 1945 Gwaltney was an active performer in and around Washington, DC, with bands led by Benny Goodman, Billy Butterfield and Bobby Hackett (including Hackett's legendary Henry Hudson band, in which he regularly replaced Bob Wilber). Around 1960 he based himself in Norfolk, Virginia, to lead jazz and dance bands; this period produced one classic album, *Goin' To Kansas City*, which showed Gwaltney as a performer and researcher with the potential to rival Wilber. In the ensuing years less was heard from him than should have been, but in 1965 he began a long residency at Washington's Blues Alley and used the club as a platform to help relaunch singer Maxine Sullivan – an intelligent move, reflecting his strong sense of musical history. He was also active at the Manassas jazz festivals into the 1970s. [DF]

Goin' To Kansas City (1960; Riverside). With an amazing line-up, mixing established KC men such as Buck Clayton and Dickie Wells with younger men including John Bunch and Charlie Byrd, this old album is the best example of Gwaltney as arranger and player.

Bobby Hackett

Cornet, trumpet, guitar; also ukulele, banjo.
b. Providence, Rhode Island, 31 Jan 1915; d. 7 June 1976.

In the early years of his career Bobby Hackett was almost as well known for his guitar playing as for his brass work. He first specialized on cornet while working in a trio with Pee Wee Russell in Boston, 1933, and by the mid-1930s his small translucent sound, subtle harmonic twists and elegant lines seemed to make him the natural successor to Bix Beiderbecke (though his primary influence was always Louis Armstrong). For the rest of the decade he worked with bandleaders such as Horace Heidt, briefly led his own orchestra and made the rounds of New York's club circuit.

From 1941–2 he played acoustic guitar, then cornet, for Glenn Miller, a close friend. By 1944, when he joined Glen Gray's Casa Loma Orchestra, Hackett had a severe drink problem, which helped induce the diabetes that would eventually kill him, but he controlled his habit and by 1946 was a staffman for ABC with Billy Butterfield, and was working regularly at Eddie Condon's and other clubs. In 1947 he was MD for Louis Armstrong's revolutionary Town Hall concert as well as second cornettist. Hackett's gift for playing second made him a regular companion and recording colleague to Armstrong, who supplied the best one-line reason for having him there: "Bobby's got more ingredients!"

From 1951 some of Hackett's greatest recordings were made for Jackie Gleason's best-selling "mood music" albums such as *Music For Lovers Only*. He later perpetuated the sound on records with pipe-organ played by Glenn Osser, and he recorded with strings until the end of his career – but not for Gleason, who paid Hackett only just above union scale, causing a deep rift between them. Combining studio and clubwork, Hackett produced more masterpieces with Jack Teagarden (*Coast To Coast* might be the greatest Dixieland record ever) and by 1956 was leading a band at the Henry Hudson Hotel, featuring clarinettist Tommy Gwaltney (later replaced by Bob Wilber) and staff arranger Dick Cary. Formed at the peak in his career, Hackett's Henry Hudson band is remembered nearly as well as Muggsy Spanier's Ragtimers, but it broke up after only a year. Hackett returned to studio work, a spell with Benny Goodman (1962–3), another for Ray McKinley, and in 1965 became "official accompanist" for Tony Bennett. In the late 1960s Hackett ran a quintet with Vic Dickenson, guested with The World's Greatest Jazz Band, and played with Dave McKenna; in 1974 a European tour teamed him with fellow cornettist Dick Sudhalter. Eighteen months later he was dead.

Hackett was universally loved by the jazz community for his graceful, unobtrusive music and for his inability to say anything bad about anyone – asked about Hitler, he said, after a pause, "Well, he was the best in his field." Moreover, he was the perfect accompanist, adored by singers from Teresa Brewer to Lee Wiley. [DF]

⊙ **That Da Da Strain** (1938–40; Portrait). Early Hackett small groups including his *tour-de-force* "Jada", plus six titles by his big band.

⊙ **A String Of Pearls** (1938–44; Topaz). Twenty-three tracks from Hackett's formative years; his shining cornet is heard with (amongst others) Eddie Condon, Adrian Rollini, Maxine Sullivan, Teddy Wilson, Miff Mole and his own groups. Selection (as regularly with Topaz) is outstanding and includes Miller's "String Of Pearls" with Hackett's classic chord-tone solo.

⊙ **Coast Concert/Jazz Ultimate** (1955 & 57; EMI/Capitol). Capitol is now regularly issuing Hackett twofers from the 1950s and l960s and all are worth buying, but this is perhaps the greatest of them all (both are with Teagarden on board). *Coast Concert* is rightly revered for its glorious artistic unity and a luxurious version of "I Guess I'll Have To Change My Plan". *Jazz Ultimate* might lack such intense high spots, but is high art nevertheless, and a first call for Hackett study.

⊙ **Gotham Jazz Scene** (1957; Dormouse). A beauty from one of Hackett's best post-Armstrong periods; he had strong chops on this one, and the date is graced by Dick Cary's fine arrangements.

⊙ **Plays the great music of Henry Mancini/Bert Kaempfert** (1963; Sony). Superior productions and superb lounge music; the Kaempfert sides have the bonus of immensely skilled arrangements by the great Dick Hyman including the charming "A Powdered Wig".

⊙ **Melody Is A Must/Live At The Roosevelt Grill Vols. 1 & 2** (1969; Phontastic). The close partnership between Hackett and Vic Dickenson is on ravishing display here, in a relaxed quintet which defines the elusive quality of "jazz taste". Dickenson's humorous approach slouches around Hackett's elegance like a shaggy friendly dog.

⊙ **What A Wonderful World** (1973; Signature). Latter-day Hackett with small group (including Vic Dickenson) and big band in a selection of beautifully recorded standards. Teresa Brewer sings on two tracks.

➤➤ **Jackie Gleason** *(Music To Make You Misty/Night Winds).*

Charlie Haden

Bass.

b. Shenandoah, Iowa, 6 Aug 1937.

Born into a musical family, Charlie Haden played on a daily radio show as a child. He moved to Los Angeles, and worked with Art Pepper in 1957 and Elmo Hope and Hampton Hawes in 1958–9. He had regular gigs with the Paul Bley group from 1957–9, which briefly included Ornette Coleman and Don Cherry. He was with the classic Coleman quartet from 1958–60 and rejoined him on several occasions after 1966, including a European tour Coleman made with the two basses of Haden and David Izenzon in 1968. After curing his drug addiction at the Synanon Foundation in the early 1960s, Charlie undertook counselling of addicts while resuming regular playing with Denny Zeitlin from 1964–6. He worked with the Jazz Composers' Orchestra Association in the late 1960s, and in 1969 assembled a group of its members to record the Liberation Music Orchestra album; similar line-ups have since convened for recording and touring. He made frequent appearances and recordings with Alice Coltrane from 1968–72 and the Keith Jarrett quartet from 1967–75. He recorded a series of duo sessions with Coleman, Jarrett, Hawes and others in 1975–6, and the first album of the Old and New Dreams quartet (Cherry, Haden, Dewey Redman and Ed Blackwell) in 1976 led to touring from 1979 onwards. He also recorded and toured in 1982–3 with a trio including Jan Garbarek and guitarist Egberto Gismonti. A "straightahead" project, Haden's Quartet West (formed in 1986), featured Alan Broadbent and Ernie Watts.

RAFFAELLA CAVALIERI

Charlie Haden

A powerful yet extremely adaptable player, Haden was probably the first to apply the freedoms of the "avant-garde" to the role of bassist. Accepting the traditional task of being supportive but stimulating, he went one step further and, by his intuitive choice of phrases, suggested new directions for the other participants in collective improvisation. Although he expressed admiration for Wilbur Ware there was little of Ware's work to model himself upon when Haden began to make an impact, and all of it was in a bebop context. Haden's group playing was at first paramount, though Coleman quartet pieces such as "Lonely Woman" and "Ramblin'" hinted at the bassist's virtuoso capabilities. While his ability in group playing is undiminished, he has since developed into a riveting soloist and, despite concentrating more than most of his contemporaries on the lower and middle range of the instrument, displays a ravishingly beautiful tone. [BP]

Charlie Haden

⊙ **Liberation Music Orchestra** (1969; Impulse). The flavour of the politics is conveyed by Haden's "Song For Che", the Spanish Civil War melodies and the amazing "Circus '68 '69", which depicts musically the punch-up of the previous year's Democrat Party convention. Featuring such as Don Cherry, Gato Barbieri and Dewey Redman, this is also a tribute to Haden's and arranger Carla Bley's organizational powers.

⊙ **The Golden Number** (1976; A&M/Horizon). The duos with Don Cherry, Ornette Coleman, Archie Shepp and Hampton Hawes (a whole album is available with the latter) give an excellent indication of Haden's positive contribution.

Old and New Dreams

⊙ **Old And New Dreams** (1979; ECM). This second album of the reunited Coleman quartet (but with Ornette replaced by family member Dewey Redman) includes a new version of "Lonely Woman".

Quartet West

⊙ **Haunted Heart** (1990; Verve). Treating Glenn Miller's "Moonlight Serenade" reverentially, Haden plays nostalgia for all it's worth, with Ernie Watts's tenor almost as evocative as the records (not sampled but included complete) by Jo Stafford, Jeri Southern and Billie Holiday.

➤➤ **Geri Allen** *(Etudes)*.

Shafi Hadi

Tenor and alto saxophones.

b. Philadelphia, 21 Sept 1929.

Hadi, otherwise known as Curtis Porter (he was listed as such on a couple of albums), began touring with leading R&B bands such as Paul Williams (c. 1951) and the Griffin Brothers. He settled in New York and joined Charles Mingus from late 1956–8, and again in 1959. He is thought to have been collaborating with Mary Lou Williams in the mid-1970s, but otherwise inactive in music since the early 1960s. Apart from recordings with Mingus and Hank Mobley, and his solo saxophone work for the film *Shadows* (1959), little is known of Hadi. But his distinctive mixture of bop and blues, combined with a very individual tone, is likely to remain in the memory of anyone who has ever heard him. [BP]

➤➤ **Charles Mingus** *(New Tijuana Moods).*

Wolfgang Haffner

Drums.

b. Wunsiedel, Germany, 7 Dec 1965.

Having begun playing drums at seven, Wolfgang Haffner studied privately in Nuremberg for four years before turning professional and establishing himself as one of Germany's most in-demand drummers. He is most celebrated for his work with big bands, notably the radio orchestras based in Cologne (the WDR) and Hamburg (NDR), and Peter Herbolzheimer's Rhythm Combination And Brass, but he has also been a member of the Albert Mangelsdorff/Wolfgang Dauner quintet since 1986, and plays regularly with the jazz-rock band Klaus Doldinger's Passport. He was also a member of the Chaka Khan Band in the mid-1990s. Haffner has played with a who's who of visiting jazz luminaries – Michael Brecker, Jan Garbarek, Johnny Griffin, Cassandra Wilson, Roy Ayers, Tom Harrell, John Abercrombie and many others – and appeared on over one hundred albums by artists ranging from Eddie Daniels and Nelson Rangell to Joe Pass and Chuck Loeb. Since 1994 he has played and toured with Metro, featuring bassist Victor Bailey (replacing founder member Anthony Jackson), guitarist Chuck Loeb and keyboardist Mitch Forman. [CP/CI]

Al Cohn

⊙ **Al Cohn Meets Al Porcino** (1987; Red Baron). Among the US saxophonist's last dates, with a mainly German big band – one of Haffner's most consistently available albums, and one that finds him doing what he does best: sparking a large ensemble, yet playing with grace and elegance behind a featured soloist.

Paul Heller

⊙ **Paul Heller** (1994; Mons). Good example of Haffner's small-group work, driving along a tenor-led date with bassist Ingmar Heller.

Metro

⊙ **Metrocafé** (2000; Hip Bop). Second album by the all-star progressive fusioneers Haffner, Bailey, Loeb and Forman, and fairly representative.

Tim Hagans

Trumpet, flugelhorn.

b. Dayton, Ohio, 19 Aug 1954.

After studying music at Bowling Green State University, 1972–4, Tim Hagans played with Stan Kenton's orchestra before leaving for Sweden in 1977, where he played with numerous Scandinavian outfits and contributed his elegant sound to Thad Jones's Eclipse big band, appearing on their eponymous Storyville album in 1979. Back in his home country, he played with the Blue Wisp Big Band, the Groove Organizers and the Steve Schmidt trio, as well as with George Schuller's repertoire-based big band, Orange Then Blue, but his neat, cultured tone is heard to best advantage on small-group sessions with the likes of tenor player Joe Lovano, bassist Ron McClure and saxophonist Steve Slagle.

In the 1990s, Hagans signed with Blue Note, sharing frontline duties with Joe Lovano and John Abercrombie on *No Words* (1993), and with fellow trumpeter Marcus Printup on a tribute to Freddie Hubbard, *Hubsongs* (1997). A latter-day exploration of the territory mapped out by late-period Miles Davis resulted in *Animation-Imagination* (1999; Blue Note), though perhaps his best recording is 1994's *Audible Architecture* (see below). Hagans is a thoroughly dependable, accomplished trumpeter, and among those demanding his services as a sideman are saxophonists Bob Belden, Seamus Blake, Jon Gordon, Greg Osby and Don Braden. He has also contributed to big-band projects by ex-Woody Herman trombonist John Fedchock and reedsman/arranger Bob Mintzer. [CP/CI]

Rick Margitza

⊙ **This Is New** (1991; Blue Note). Hagans is featured only on one of the album's longest tracks, "Beware of the Dog", but his is an excellent performance.

Joe Lovano

⊙ **Universal Language** (1993; Blue Note). Lovano's cultured sound provides a near-perfect setting for Hagans, and he takes full advantage on an album also featuring bassists Steve Swallow and Charlie Haden.

Tim Hagans

⊙ **Audible Architecture** (1994; Blue Note). Basically a trumpet trio recording (although Bob Belden is featured on four tracks) with Hagans's unhurried eloquence on both post-bop and funkier themes propelled by bassist Larry Grenadier and drummer Billy Kilson.

➤➤ **Joe Lovano** *(Worlds)*; **Maria Schneider** *(Evanescence).*

Bob Haggart

Bass, composer, arranger.

b. New York, 13 March 1914; d. 2 Dec 1998.

Bob Haggart began as a guitar player (his teacher was George Van Eps) and then taught himself bass in high school. At school he heard the finest jazz on record (including Louis Armstrong's Hot Five, which made a lifelong impression) and soon after was making his way in professional music, working all kinds of gigs, becoming well known as a bright new bass talent and turning down offers from Benny

Goodman and Tommy Dorsey – "I felt I wasn't ready", he later told John Chilton. In 1935 he became a founder member of Bob Crosby's band, which introduced Dixieland to the swing-happy 1930s. He recorded the classic hit "Big Noise From Winnetka" (which, with its whistling and drumsticks on bass strings, was to become a showpiece for Dixieland bands) and composed or arranged much of Crosby's most distinguished repertoire, such as "South Rampart Street Parade" (a creation with Ray Bauduc, scribbled on a hotel tablecloth), "Dogtown Blues" and "Diga Diga Doo".

In 1942, when Crosby's band broke up, Haggart became a busy studio musician, working with giants such as Bing Crosby, Duke Ellington and Louis Armstrong, then from 1950 was with Yank Lawson for recordings with the Lawson-Haggart Jazz Band, which Dixieland aficionados rate as the best ever of its kind. In the 1960s he was a familiar bass at Crosby reunions (including a famous one at New York's Rainbow Grill in 1966), and played at every Dick Gibson jazz party in Colorado from their inception in 1963. In 1968 the Gibson house band turned into The World's Greatest Jazz Band, which Haggart co-led with enormous success (and occasional personal reservations) for ten years. In the 1980s he was happy to be back in a re-formed Lawson-Haggart Jazz Band, producing a touching, reminiscent LP for George Buck, *Sentimental Journey*, and into the 1990s he continued to record and tour – including an Eddie Condon tribute led by Ed Polcer in 1993. In early 1994 he was honoured in the USA with a starry eightieth birthday celebration, co-featuring his old partner Yank Lawson. Haggart also enjoyed painting and held several exhibitions in later years; he continued playing until just before his death. [DF]

The Legendary Lawson-Haggart Jazz Band (1952–3; MCA). Double-album collection of many of the best tracks by the LHJB, with Billy Butterfield, Peanuts Hucko, Cutty Cutshall, Lou McGarity, George Barnes and Lou Stein; Haggart's arrangements frame nonpareil soloists.

Hag Leaps In (1995; Arbors). As part of a classy trio (completed by John Bunch and Bucky Pizzarelli) Haggart plays through a sophisticated set with undiminished power and accuracy; he also brings back "Big Noise From Winnetka" for a late run.

>> **Bob Crosby; World's Greatest Jazz Band.**

Al Haig

Piano.

b. Newark, New Jersey, 22 July 1924; d. 16 Nov 1982.

One of the first pianists to develop an idiomatic bop style, Haig was active with Dizzy Gillespie and Charlie Parker by late 1944. After service under the leadership of Gillespie from 1944–6, Parker from 1948–50 (including his first trip to Europe) and Stan Getz from 1949–51, much of his time was spent playing solo background music or in non-jazz organizations. Only in the last decade of his life did he experience a personal renaissance, which led to many foreign tours and frequent recording. The contradictions of his career were evident quite early on, for some of his work as a featured performer in his own right seems to err on the side of caution, especially when using standard songs. However, when backing superior soloists as on the Parker and Getz discs listed below, or dealing with specifically jazz-based material, he displayed a special combination of commanding calm and dynamic drive. [BP]

Al Haig Quartet (1954; Fresh Sound). A typical programme of standards finds Haig getting under the skin of such as "The Man I Love" and "Woody'n'You".

>> **Stan Getz** *(Complete Roost Recordings);* **Charlie Parker** *(Complete Live Performances On Savoy).*

John Haim

Cornet, leader.

b. London, 1929; d. Jan 1949.

John Haim formed his first band in 1945 and was one of the brightest talents of post-war London revivalism. Haim's band, including his brother Gerry (tuba) and Eric Silk (banjo), was creating a stir around London's clubs when the *Melody Maker* inexplicably reported his death in a headline. Haim had never told his sidemen that he was in fact suffering from a lung disorder; days later he died from a heart attack brought on by his condition. He was nineteen. A memorial album entitled *Blues For Johnny* was issued, but, said Rex Harris, "it gives no indication of the lusty sound which the band made in the flesh". That Haim's replacement for the tribute was Freddy Randall, however, gives a hint of the high level of Haim's performance. [DF]

Sadik Hakim

Piano.

b. Duluth, Minnesota, 15 July 1922; d. 20 June 1983.

Hakim was active on New York's 52nd Street scene in the mid-1940s, under his original name of Argonne Thornton. He participated in significant recording sessions by Charlie Parker and Lester Young, and also did regular work and recording with Ben Webster and "Lockjaw" Davis. Later he worked with the James Moody band from 1951–4 and the Buddy Tate band from 1955–60. He lived in Canada from the late 1960s, except for a visit to Europe in 1972, until returning to New York during the late 1970s. A prolific writer in his later years, Hakim also wrote the tune "Eronel" recorded by and credited to Thelonious Monk. His 1940s style, though indicative of the problems of adapting to bebop, was strongly individual and possibly more interesting than his later work. [BP]

>> **Charlie Parker** *(The Charlie Parker Story).*

Pat Halcox

Trumpet, flugelhorn, cornet, arranger, leader.
b. London, 17 March 1930.

Halcox joined Chris Barber in 1954 from the Albemarle Jazz Band and has stayed with him ever since. A New Orleans-based player to begin with, Halcox rapidly broadened his approach with Barber's, until by the 1960s he was as skilled at playing in a rock setting as he was at leading a collective ensemble. Thanks to Barber's catholic tastes, Halcox has had every opportunity to parade his broad-based abilities, and he remains one of Britain's best loved and respected trumpeters. A bout of illness in the early 1990s forced him into brief retirement from the Barber ranks, but by 1994 he was back in harness and blowing at full strength for his leader's fortieth anniversary concert tour. By 2003 he had been joined by trumpeter Mike Henry in Barber's expanded line-up, also featuring trombonist Bob Hunt. [DF]

⊙ **Pat Halcox All Stars** (1978–9; Lake). Really Chris Barber's band, regularly led by Halcox during the leader's summer recess, this group features Campbell Burnap in place of Barber in a good-humoured, regularly sensitive session co-featuring the excellent Johnny Parker on piano and John Crocker on reeds.

⊙ **There's Yes Yes In Your Eyes** (1989; Jazzology). A rare solo outing for Halcox, spotlighting his always tasteful lead and solo powers amid a group also featuring Bruce Turner playing clarinet.

➤➤ **Chris Barber** *(40 Year Jubilee).*

Simon Hale

Piano, keyboards, synthesizers, composer.
b. Birmingham, UK, 23 April 1964.

Hale had classical lessons on piano and violin, then took a music degree at Goldsmiths' College from 1982–5. In the summer of 1984 he was in the USA, where he completed a course on the mechanics of film scoring. The following year he was commissioned to compose *East Fourteen* for piano and strings and performed it at Valley College, Los Angeles. From 1984–94 he worked as a session musician for various rock and pop stars, and was also a member of the superb jazz-rock group System X. During that time he also composed his four-part suite, *East Fifteen*, featuring young British jazz lions Dave O'Higgins, Tim Garland, Noel Langley and Ralph Salmins, with the Guildhall string ensemble. His favourite pianists include Dave Grusin, Richard Tee and Russell Ferrante, and other inspirations are the composer John Williams, David Sanborn, Stevie Wonder and Quincy Jones. [IC]

⊙ **East Fifteen** (1992; EFZ). This includes the eponymous suite in four movements and four additional tracks. The harmonic and melodic language of the suite smacks of nineteenth-century romanticism leavened sometimes by some heavy Stravinskian punctuations. But the whole thing is very well done, and there are good and sometimes ecstatic moments from Langley, O'Higgins and Garland. Salmins, as usual, handles the written percussion parts superbly.

Adelaide Hall

Vocals.
b. Brooklyn, New York, 20 Oct 1901; d. London, 7 Nov 1992.

Hall was taught to sing by her father, and made her show business debut in a variety of black musical shows in New York, including *Shuffle Along*, *Chocolate Kiddies*, *Desires Of 1927* and *Blackbirds Of 1928*, the last of which introduced several songs closely associated with Hall, including "I Can't Give You Anything But Love" and "Diga Diga Doo". It was with this show that Hall first went to Paris, around the time she married a British seaman named Bert Hicks, who opened La Grosse Pomme club for her. Throughout the 1930s she stayed busy in America and Europe, recording with Art Tatum, Duke Ellington and Fats Waller amongst others (her most famous recording is the 1927 "Creole Love Call" with Duke Ellington, on which she sang wordless responses to Ellington's theme), as well as with European bands led by Kai Ewans and John Ellsworth. During World War II, the Florida Club, which she had opened in London with Hicks, was destroyed in a bombing raid, but Hall's career continued unabated. She toured for ENSA, sang in theatres, clubs and on radio, and in 1951 appeared in

Adelaide Hall

the London edition of *Kiss Me Kate*, continuing a theatrical career which had begun with her 1938 appearance in *The Sun Never Sets* at Drury Lane. In 1957 she went back to Broadway to co-star in *Jamaica* with Lena Horne, but during the 1960s, after the death of her husband, she worked less intensively. However, during 1969–70 she returned to the recording studios for two jazz albums with Humphrey Lyttelton and an all-star British band, and soon after began touring theatres again. In 1974 Adelaide sang at the memorial service for Duke Ellington at St Martin-in-the-Fields, London, and thereafter made regular concert appearances, including a one-woman show at Carnegie Hall in 1988. She continued singing until shortly before her death. [DF]

⊙ **A Centenary Collection** (1927–45; Avid). Superb CD celebration of Hall – 52 tracks with Ellington, Tatum, Waller and fascinating later tracks wih Jay Wilbur, Phil Green, broadcasts by ENSA and more. Highly recommended.

Edmond Hall

Clarinet, baritone saxophone.

b. New Orleans, 15 May 1901; d. 11 Feb 1967.

Edmond Hall was one of four clarinet-playing sons of Edward Hall, a member of the great Onward Brass Band which played in New York in 1891 as well as New Orleans. From 1919, young Ed Hall – playing an Albert system like many of his New Orleans colleagues – worked in a variety of bands (including Jack Carey, Lee Collins, Buddy Petit, Chris Kelly and Kid Thomas) and finally went to New York with Alonzo Ross in 1928. From here he jobbed around, and by 1930 was working with Claude Hopkins. Despite the often appalling touring conditions suffered by black musicians in the 1930s, Hall stayed with Hopkins until 1935, when Chauncey Haughton replaced him. Much of his work for the next ten years or so was New York-based: after playing with Lucky Millinder, Zutty Singleton and Joe Sullivan, in 1940 he joined Henry "Red" Allen's brand-new band, then in 1941 moved to Teddy Wilson's classy sextet, which broadcast and recorded regularly. From 1944–6 Hall led his own group (including Jimmy Crawford) for a famous New York residency at Café Society, then after four years in Boston he joined Eddie Condon (1950–5), moving on to Louis Armstrong's All Stars for three years after that (replacing Barney Bigard). The Armstrong schedule encouraged Hall to think about retirement in 1958, but in the 1960s he was still busy working with Condon, with his own quartet around New York, and touring abroad until his sudden death – he suffered a heart attack after shovelling snow from his driveway. Much loved by all who met him, Hall was a calm and placid man (he practised yoga and "inner cleanliness" – one practice involved swallowing a roll of bandage inch by inch then pulling it back up again), whose grittily fierce clarinet playing always came as a surprise. [DF]

Ed Hall

⊙ **Profoundly Blue** (1937–44; ASV). A reliable portrait, homing in on excellent sides with Red Allen, Zutty Singleton, Billie Holiday, Lionel Hampton and a variety of Hall's own groups including his Celeste Quartet (1941) with Meade Lux Lewis and Blue Note Jazzmen (1943).

⊙ **Edmond Hall 1936–44/1944–5** (Classics). Chronological survey of a great clarinettist, and well worth the thought. Titles include *(1936–44)* sessions for Blue Note involving the marvellous Emmett Berry, Teddy Wilson, Meade "Lux" Lewis, James P. Johnson and Vic Dickenson; the all superb *(1944–5)* has sides with Benny Morton, Harry Carney and eight quartet sides with elegant Teddy Wilson.

⊙ **In Copenhagen** (1966; Storyville). A solo version of "It Ain't Necessarily So" is one of the many high spots in this collection, recorded with Papa Bue's rhythm-section (plus band on a couple of tracks) only a few weeks before Hall's death.

Louis Armstrong

⊙ **Louis Armstrong All Star Dates 1947–50; With Edmond Hall's All Stars 1947** (Forlane). An early collaboration between Hall and Louis in concert at Carnegie Hall. The recording quality is mediocre but Hall's power cuts through as always.

Herbie Hall

Clarinet.

b. Reserve, Louisiana, 28 March 1907; d. 5 March 1996.

The younger brother of Edmond Hall, Herbie began his professional career playing banjo and guitar with the Niles Jazz Band. He then switched to clarinet and alto saxophone, playing with Augustin Victor in Baton Rouge (1926) and Sidney Desvigne in New Orleans (1927), before joining trumpeter Don Alberts for a successful eleven-year stay (1929–40). After the war, Hall worked with trumpeter Herman Autrey, with Harvey Davis and Doc Cheatham in 1955, as well as Sammy Price, Wilbur De Paris, "Red" Allen, Eddie Condon (replacing Bob Wilber), Max Kaminsky and Roy Eldridge. From 1967, following his brother Edmond's death, Herbie worked regularly in Toronto, first with Don Ewell, then with Wild Bill Davison and others. In 1973 Hall joined Bob Greene's World of Jelly Roll Morton, and from 1977 returned to Texas, working with Jim Cullum, amongst others. A highly skilled and individual stylist, Hall was a superb alto and baritone saxophonist but concentrated on clarinet from the 1950s, producing an unobtrusive body of recorded work which is sometimes unreasonably minimized against the achievements of his older brother. [DF]

Jim Hall

Guitar.

b. Buffalo, New York, 4 Dec 1930.

After playing in local bands, Hall moved to Los Angeles in 1955. He first became prominent with the Chico Hamilton quintet in 1955–6, and was then a member of the Jimmy Giuffre trio from 1956–9. He was part of the Ella Fitzgerald rhythm-section in 1960–61, also working in New York in a duo with Lee Konitz. In 1961–2 he spent half a year with the new Sonny Rollins group and then co-led a quartet with Art Farmer from 1962–4. He made recordings with all the aforementioned, and with Gerry Mulligan, Bill Evans and others. He settled into New York studio work, and, since 1965, has led his own trio on frequent gigs, including numerous tours abroad. Since 1972 he has made duo appearances and records with Ron Carter, and has done much unaccompanied playing. During the 1990s Hall's albums have emphasized his arranging and composition, which is after all what he studied as a youth, and in 1998 his all-round ability was recognized by the award of the Jazzpar prize.

Hall is definitely not one of those after-Christian, after-bebop, afternoon-nap guitarists. In fact, far from blinding the listener with science and technique, he is often so subtle in the use of both as to bypass some listeners altogether. His extremely mellow sound often disguises his rhythmic and harmonic finesse and, like the very best players of conventional frameworks, he manages to sound totally free within them. Backing other soloists, too, his choice of textures is usually unexpected but sounds absolutely right; both this ability and his fine contrapuntal sense are best revealed alongside musicians who share the same qualities such as Sonny Rollins or Bill Evans or indeed Ron Carter. [BP]

Bill Evans and Jim Hall

⊙ **Undercurrent** (1962; Blue Note). A classic for both participants, and Hall's contributions on his own dead-slow "Romain" and two fast versions of "My Funny Valentine" are the equal of Evans in sensitivity and resourcefulness.

Jim Hall

⊙ **All Across The City** (1989; Concord). Conveying something of the range of Hall's music, this quartet with Gil Goldstein includes some free improvisation as well as "Bemsha Swing" and straightahead but challenging originals.

⊙ **Dialogues** (1995; Telarc). Hall's choice of guest soloists, heard one at a time, reveals much about his still-questing spirit: Joe Lovano, Tom Harrell, Gil Goldstein on accordion, Mike Stern and Bill Frisell all have material specially written for them by Hall, and all make the most of it.

➤➤ **Sonny Rollins** *(The Bridge)*.

Bengt Hallberg

Piano, organ, accordion.

b. Gothenburg, Sweden, 13 Sept 1932.

Hallberg was already active on the Swedish jazz scene as a teenager, but he gained attention abroad through his recordings with Stan Getz (*Tenor Contrasts*, 1951) and Clifford Brown. In the 1950s he worked and recorded regularly with Lars Gullin and Arne Domnérus, while, since then, he has made his living largely as a composer and session musician. Despite this, his enthusiasm for jazz remains undiminished, and the freshness of his early work has matured into a style of considerable originality. Whereas the harmonically updated Teddy Wilson approach of the 1950s was already very distinctive, Hallberg's later playing (especially unaccompanied) is a totally individual amalgam of many elements from stride to post-modal jazz. [BP]

⊙ **Hallberg's Happiness** (1977; Phontastic). One of a series of solo piano records which find Hallberg exploring his quirky approach to standards and, as here in "Herdesang", the occasional traditional Swedish melody.

➤➤ **Clifford Brown** *(Memorial Album)*.

Andy Hamilton

Tenor saxophone, composer.

b. Port Maria, Jamaica, 26 March 1918.

Having learnt to play on a bamboo saxophone, and influenced not only by American radio transmissions of Duke Ellington and Count Basie but also by the Kingston bands of Redver Cook and Roy Coburn, Andy Hamilton formed his first band, Silvershine, at eighteen. After leaving Jamaica for the USA, where he worked as a cook and farm labourer, he played brief residencies in Buffalo and Syracuse before returning to Jamaica and becoming musical arranger on Errol Flynn's yacht, the *Zaka*. In 1949, Hamilton moved to the UK, settling in Birmingham, where he worked in a factory by day and played jazz by night, frequently with visiting Americans like Art Farmer and David Murray. Hamilton's regular band, the Blue Notes, comprises longtime associates such as pianist Sam Brown (with him for forty years) and drummer Johnny Hoo (twenty years); he also plays with his sons Graeme (trumpet) and Mark (alto, tenor). In 1991, at 73, Hamilton made his debut album as a leader, involving not only a host of young UK jazz players – Andy Sheppard, Steve Williamson, Orphy Robinson, Mark Mondesir – but also US guest David Murray and pop singer Mick Hucknall. His follow-up album, *Jamaica By Night*, was inspired by Hamilton's revisiting the Caribbean and features his smooth, mature, unhurried saxophone in a mixture of calypsos, spirituals and jazz. In his ninth decade, Hamilton shows few signs of slowing down: he still plays regularly at the Bear and Ty's in Birmingham, guests on the odd World Circuit album, and a recent recording project, involving both his sons, saxophonist Luke Shingler, plus longtime associates Hoo and Brown, was an album of self-penned ska and bluebeat pieces. In 1998, the Birmingham City Council awarded him Freedom of the City, and in 1999 he was presented with a Millennium Fellowship for his work in community education. [CP/CI]

⊙ **Silvershine** (1991; World Circuit). The Blue Notes (plus Ralf DeCambre, guitar, and Ray "Pablo" Brown, bass), augmented by a host of guests, ease their way through a soulful mix of standards ("I Can't Get Started", "Body And Soul", etc) and Hamilton originals.

Jamaica By Night (1994; World Circuit). Jean Toussaint-produced album featuring Guy Barker's pianist Bernardo Sassetti, Graeme Hamilton (trumpet) and many more UK players in attractive, laid-back music. Hamilton: "Play sweet and you can baptize anybody, wild animals included. Play rough and you don't baptize no one."

Chico Hamilton

Drums.

b. Los Angeles, 21 Sept 1921.

Chico (Foreststorn) Hamilton played regularly in high school with a band including fellow students Dexter Gordon, Ernie Royal, Buddy Collette and Charles Mingus and later Illinois Jacquet. He then spent time freelancing with Floyd Ray, Lionel Hampton, Slim Gaillard and others, until his army service which ran from 1942–6. In 1946 he worked with the Jimmy Mundy band, briefly with Count Basie, and with Lester Young. He toured with the singer Lena Horne from 1948–55, and, based in Los Angeles between tours, did studio work and played with Charlie Barnet and the original Gerry Mulligan quartet in 1952–3. He formed his own quintet in 1955, which became popular internationally through the use of a flute or clarinet and cello; in 1962 he replaced the cello with a trombone to achieve a harder sound. Hamilton toured regularly until the mid-1960s when he wrote the music for Polanski's *Repulsion*, and again, usually with two reeds, in the early 1970s. Since then he has been active in writing advertising jingles and film music, and, in the late 1980s, he began playing with a new quartet which has toured Europe several times.

Bob Willoughby/Redferns

Chico Hamilton with his quintet

Hamilton's original reputation as an excellent Jo Jones-tutored drummer has been largely forgotten. His quintet veered constantly between being the unacceptable face of capitulation to European influence and an acceptable forum for aspiring improvisers. In the latter field, Chico deserves credit for offering their first touring opportunities to such interesting musicians as Buddy Collette, Jim Hall, Paul Horn, Eric Dolphy, Ron Carter, Charles Lloyd, Gabor Szabö, John Abercrombie, Arthur Blythe and Tom Chapin. [BP]

Gongs East (1958; Discovery). The best available album of the early quintet has Eric Dolphy on a tight leash, threatening to unbalance the mix with his reading of Strayhorn's "Passion Flower" and other briefer interventions.

Jimmy Hamilton

Clarinet, tenor saxophone, arranger.

b. Dillon, South Carolina, 25 May 1917; d. Virgin Islands, 20 Sept 1994.

Hamilton was brought up in Philadelphia, where he studied piano and brass instruments, playing the latter with local bands in the mid-1930s. He switched to saxophone and clarinet, then worked for both Lucky Millinder and Jimmy Mundy in 1939 and concurrently with Bill Doggett. He was a member of the Teddy Wilson sextet from 1940–42, and then worked with the Eddie Heywood and Yank Porter groups. He joined Duke Ellington in 1943, filling the post vacated eight months earlier by Barney Bigard, and remaining till 1968. He then did freelance arranging and playing, and followed that by teaching music in public schools in the Virgin Islands in the 1970s and 80s. He returned to the USA for appearances with John Carter's group Clarinet Summit from 1981 onwards, and was a special guest at the Ellington Conference in Manchester, England, in 1985. After retiring from teaching he played further New York gigs with his own groups in 1989–90.

In performance Hamilton often exhibited something of a split personality. His comparatively rare tenor solos sounded like the better R&B players; on clarinet, however, he had an academically correct tone and admirable fluency, and the possible jazz deficiencies of this approach were cleverly minimized by Duke Ellington during his long tenure. Some of his features within the band were initially composed by Hamilton himself, such as "Air Conditioned Jungle", "Monologue" and "Ad Lib On Nippon". [BP]

➤➤ **John Carter** *(Southern Bells)*; **Duke Ellington** *(The Far East Suite)*.

John “Bugs” Hamilton

Trumpet.

b. St Louis, Missouri, 8 March 1911; d. 15 Aug 1947.

Hamilton's short career, spanning only fifteen years, included New York spells with Billy Kato, Chick Webb and Kaiser Marshall in the early 1930s, before the period for which he is best remembered: four years with Fats Waller, 1938–42, replacing Herman Autrey. Hamilton's style – on record anyway – was close to Autrey's, although a few degrees more elegant and musical on occasion. Very little more was heard from him after Waller's death, apart from a brief spell with Eddie South's fine small group: he died of tuberculosis at 36. [DF]

➤➤ **Fats Waller** *(The Last Years 1940–43).*

Scott Hamilton

Tenor saxophone.

b. Providence, Rhode Island, 12 Sept 1954.

Scott Hamilton played first around New England, then moved to New York to follow up connections with Roy Eldridge, Tiny Grimes, Carol Sloane and John Bunch. Bunch recommended him to Benny Goodman, whom Hamilton then joined, having already met his frequent partner, cornettist Warren Vaché, in a New York club. While with Goodman, Hamilton signed a contract with Concord Records, and the huge publicity that followed for him and Vaché guaranteed these mainstream messiahs a heady round of clubs, festivals and recordings in America and Europe. Though born into the post-Beatles generation, Hamilton had emerged as a mature tenor-saxophonist whose natural vocabulary was that of Ben Webster, Lester Young, Don Byas and Zoot Sims, and the demands placed on Hamilton were heavy. By the early 1980s he was working with the Concord Super Band and with his own quintet of young mainstreamers, as well as recording solo and with Bob Wilber, Buddy Tate, Rosemary Clooney and regularly with Warren Vaché. By 1985 he was with the Newport Jazz Festival All Stars (George Wein at the piano), busily recording, touring and making the festival rounds. As the 1990s progressed he became recognized as the leader of his field, with several followers such as tenorist Harry Allen acknowledging Hamilton as a primary influence. In 2003 he was working as busily as ever. [DF]

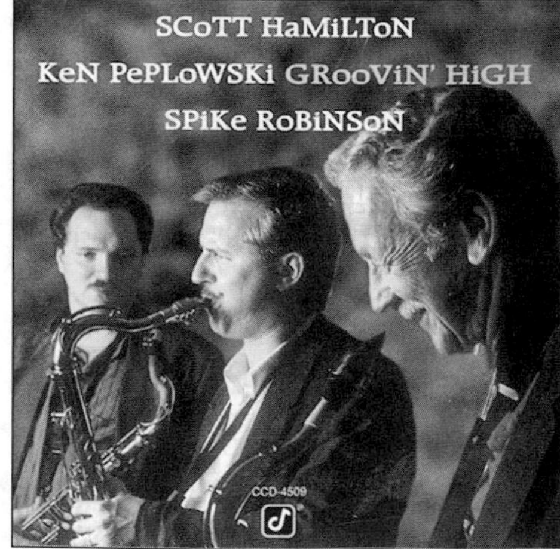

Scott Hamilton and Warren Vaché

With Scott's Band In New York City (1978; Concord). Hamilton emerged onto the international jazz scene with cornettist Vaché. Their longtime partnership is well represented on this LP, with Vaché's highly melodic and feisty playing a fine foil for Scott's urbanity.

Scott Hamilton

Ballads (1989; Concord). One of Hamilton's best albums; relaxed and assured jazz tenor at its classic best.

Groovin' High (1991; Concord). Hamilton's Concord contract has given him the chance to record in a wide variety of settings, and on this date he shares the studio with two kindred tenor spirits: young Ken Peplowski and veteran Spike Robinson.

With Strings (1993; Concord). A longterm ambition of Hamilton's is realized on this set, where a twenty-piece string orchestra surrounds his luxuriously creative lines. Arranged by Alan Broadbent.

East Of The Sun (1993; Concord). The first of Hamilton's recorded collaborations with his regular British rhythm-section: Brian Lemon, Dave Green and Allan Ganley. The results were so good that a second album has been issued.

Organic Duke (1994; Concord). Tenors mate naturally with Hammond organs, and this set has Mike LeDonne (Widespread Depression Orchestra, Milt Jackson et al) playing a real Hammond B-3 and soloing impressively on favourite territory: the music of Duke Ellington.

Jan Hammer

Piano, electric keyboards, synthesizer, drums, composer.

b. Prague, Czechoslovakia, 17 April 1948.

Hammer began on piano at the age of four and also took up the drums. As a teenager he was influenced by the Beatles, Jimi Hendrix and James Brown, then by Coltrane and Elvin Jones. While in high school he played in a trio with Miroslav and Alan Vitous and then studied classical composition and piano at Prague Conservatory, won an international music competition in Vienna in 1966, and a scholarship to the Berklee School of Music.

In 1967 he played at the Warsaw Jazz Jamboree with Stuff Smith. When the Russians invaded Czechoslovakia in 1968, he left for the USA, working around Boston and attending some classes at Berklee. In 1970–71 he was with Sarah Vaughan, touring the USA, Canada and Japan. He then based himself in New York, working with Jeremy Steig, Elvin Jones, and others. From May 1971 to December 1973 he was with the Mahavishnu Orchestra, then with Billy Cobham's Spectrum until the autumn of 1975, before leading his own groups. In the early 1980s the commercial success of his theme to *Miami Vice* reduced his interest in playing jazz.

Hammer is a virtuoso performer: equally at home with acoustic and electric music, he can handle all areas of improvisation from abstraction to conventional forms, and he is a master of the complex asymmetry of jazz-rock. He made an important contribution to some of the classic albums of the 1970s with the Mahavishnu Orchestra and with Cobham. [IC]

➤➤ **Billy Cobham** *(Spectrum);* **John McLaughlin** *(The Inner Mounting Flame; Birds Of Fire).*

Gunter Hampel

Vibraphone, clarinet and bass-clarinet, saxophones, flutes, piano, composer.

b. Göttingen, Germany, 31 Aug 1937.

Hampel started leading his own band in 1958, touring Germany and Europe. In the 1960s he became deeply committed to free jazz, his group improvising collective abstract music, and guitarist John McLaughlin worked with him for six months in the middle of the decade. Hampel toured extensively for the Goethe Institute in Africa, Asia and South America. At the end of the 1960s he formed Birth Records to put out his own music, and in the early 1970s he started his Galaxie Dream Band, with which his wife, singer Jeanne Lee, has also worked. Apart from work with the group, Hampel has played unaccompanied concerts, including an appearance at the 1972 Munich Olympic Games. He has composed music for films, and appeared at most major international festivals. Hampel lives in New York for half of each year and in Germany for the other half. Most recently he has been spotted on tour with both the Gunter Hampel Jazz Quintet and Next Generation. [IC]

Gunter Hampel, Anthony Braxton, Willem Breuker and Jeanne Lee

⊙ **The 8th of July 1969** (Birth). The date may be the birthday of Birth Records. It was also the day when American free improvisation (Braxton) met European free in the form of Hampel, Lee and Breuker. A significant date.

Gunter Hampel

⊙ **Fresh Heat – Live At Sweet Basil** (1985; Birth). Hampel is another pioneer from the 1960s who shows signs of maturing. On this disc, recorded in New York with a partly American band, a certain amount of control is evident and the music recalls Mingus's spirit and method.

Lionel Hampton

Vibes, drums, piano, vocals.

b. Louisville, Kentucky, 20 April 1908; d. 31 Aug 2003.

Hampton was raised in the Catholic Church and was sent to school at the Holy Rosary Academy in Kenosha, Wisconsin, where he was taught snare-drum rudiments by a Dominican nun. Back in Chicago he joined the Chicago Defender Newsboys' Band and learned timpani and marimba under Major N. Clark Smith. Spare evenings were spent watching percussionist Jimmy Bertrand, his idol and occasional teacher, at the nearby Vendome Theater. Hampton's uncle, Richard Morgan (who later shared Bessie Smith's turbulent life), bought Hampton "everything: silk shirts, the finest clothes, my first marimba and my first set of drums – it had a light in it!" (like Bertrand's). Soon after, Hampton was working with bands led by Detroit Shannon, Curtis Mosby, Vernon Elkins, Paul Howard and Reb Spikes before joining Les Hite to back Louis Armstrong at the Los Angeles Cotton Club. There he met dancer Gladys Riddle, who was to become his wife and business manager: she bought a "little set of vibes", encouraged him to practise them and then sent him to the University of Southern California to study theory.

Thereafter Hampton formed his own band, finding that was the only way to feature himself as he wished on vibes. In 1936 he was offered a residency at the Paradise Café in Los Angeles, and one night Benny Goodman came in: "The next thing I knew Benny was on stage playing clarinet, Gene Krupa was at the drums and Teddy Wilson was at the piano." They recorded together and six weeks later Hampton was featured artist with Benny Goodman's quartet on the Camel Cigarette programme. A year later RCA offered their new star carte blanche to record with whomever he pleased whenever he was in New York: the ninety resulting sides (along with Teddy Wilson's, Billie Holiday's and Mildred Bailey's) are the best records of the swing era at its zenith, and feature practically every star of the period. He was with Benny Goodman until 1940, creating the kind of excitement that jazz had seldom experienced, and then – with Goodman's blessing – left to start his own highly successful big band, which in 1986 was the longest-established orchestra in jazz history.

Over the years, Hampton's band became a university for young talent, including Charles Mingus, Art Farmer, Joe Newman, Illinois Jacquet, Dexter Gordon, Lee Young, Ernie Royal, Clark Terry, Joe Williams and Dinah Washington. "They all got a living and a chance", said Hampton later, "and I didn't hold 'em back, but I was strict and I disciplined 'em!" – vital in the wild years of the 1940s, when hard drugs and hard living were taking their toll on the post-war jazz generation. By and large, Hampton led a happy band, though there were occasional rumours of the leader being too hard on his sidemen: Clifford Brown once fled down a fire escape after his leader posted a lookout in the lobby of their Paris hotel to prevent his sidemen from sneaking out to recording studios.

A 1942 hit, "Flying Home", clearly established the Hampton formula: high energy, screaming brass, and rhythms which could drive an audience to the kind of near-hysterical excitement that he had first

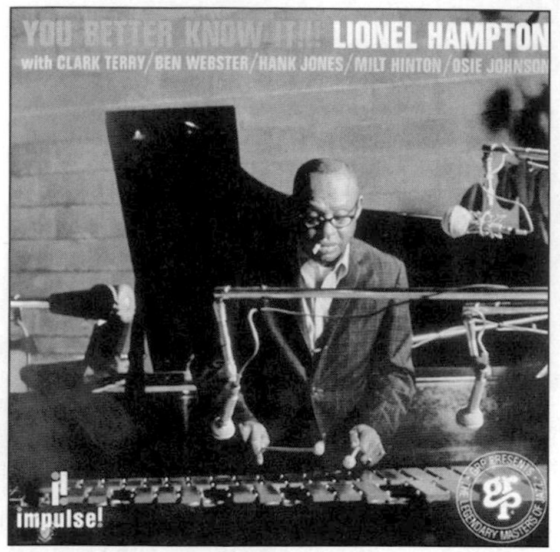

created with Goodman's quartet. Hampton's big band – fronted by its energetic dynamo of a leader, who did everything from jump on his drums to just fail to hammer his vibraphone into the stage – was, in a sense, a rock'n'roll band conforming to jazz conventions, and all through the 1950s and after it remained hugely successful, appearing at all the best festivals (including Newport, 1967 and 1972). Hampton also led a successful small group, Lionel Hampton's Inner Circle, played regularly at Benny Goodman reunions, recorded often with all-star small groups (*You Better Know It*, starring Hank Jones, Clark Terry and Ben Webster, is a late classic), and was often to be seen in Europe. By the mid-1970s his services to music were reaping tangible rewards: he ran his own publishing companies, his own record label (Who's Who In Jazz), and had founded the Lionel Hampton Development Corporation, which erected two multimillion-dollar apartment complexes in Harlem and by 1980 was planning a full-scale university. By the mid-1980s, Dr Lionel Hampton (the Doctorate came from Pepperdine College, California) was moving in the senior circles of New York politics as well as leading his big band around the jazz circuits of the world. In 1988 The Lionel Hampton Center for the Performing Arts was opened in Idaho, one of many public dedications to Hampton's life in music; he also received a masters fellowship from the National Endowment for the Arts (1988) and the Kennedy Center Lifetime Achievement Award (1992). In 1997 a fire at his home destroyed much of his music, but that year he was also awarded the National Medal of Arts by President Clinton. Despite a stroke in 1995 he continued to tour with his big band, and small bands, and with his Golden Men Of Jazz (with Clark Terry, Harry Edison and others), capping a career that was one of the monumental achievements of jazz. Following a series of further strokes Hampton died of heart failure at Mount Sinai Medical Centre, NY, in 2003; one of the last founding-fathers of jazz to pass away. [DF]

⊙ **Early Hamp** (1929–38; Affinity). An admirable collation of Hampton's early foundation work: as drummer/pianist/vocalist with Paul Howard's Quality Serenaders; on drums with Louis Armstrong and Eddie Condon; and on vibraphone with Teddy Wilson's orchestra.

⊙ **Lionel Hampton All Star Sessions Vols. 1 & 2** (1937–41; Avid). In fine re-mastered sound (by Dave Bennett) all of Hampton's RCA Victor recordings in New York, Chicago and Hollywood plus alternate takes and broadcasts to produce one hundred indispensable (and underrated) swing sides.

⊙ **Flying Home** (1930–49; ASV). Typically thorough two-CD survey of Hampton's formative years, opening with "Flying Home" and jumping back to his brief vibraphone debut with Armstrong ("Memories of you", 1930). It also covers definitive 1930s sides with Goodman and his own groups, plus early big band extravaganzas ("Airmail Special", "Hamp's Boogie Woogie" et al) and an admittedly incomplete concluding excerpt from his l947 Pasadena-recorded "Stardust".

⊙ **Lionel Hampton 1937–8/1938–9/1939–40/ 1940–41/ 1942–4/1945–6/1946** (Classics). For completists; everything recorded by Hampton from his formative swing years to his rocking big band. Not everything is indispensable here, but those who want the full story will invest accordingly, and volumes as usual are available singly.

⊙ **Lionel Hampton And His Orchestra** (1942–9; Giants Of Jazz). A well-selected collection of Hampton's storming big-band hits of the 40s, including "Flying Home" (nos. 1 and 2), "Hamp's Boogie Woogie" (nos. 1 and 2) and "Airmail Special".

⊙ **Stardust** (1947; MCA). This legendary concert features Hampton's *tour-de-force* "Stardust" (one of his greatest on-record performances) plus tracks with fellow masters like Charlie Shavers, Willie Smith and Corky Corcoran.

⊙ **European Tour** (1953; Royal Jazz). Hampton's big band of 1953, containing the famed trumpet section of Clifford Brown, Art Farmer, Quincy Jones and Walter Williams, in live performances which fully capture Hampton's unsurpassable on-stage excitement.

⊙ **Hamp's Big Band** (1959; RCA). A very well-remembered and superb session, featuring trumpeter Cat Anderson along with Donald Byrd and others.

⊙ **You Better Know It !!!** (1964; Impulse!). This session – starring Ben Webster, Clark Terry, Hank Jones, Milt Hinton and Osie Johnson – presents the relaxed side of Hampton: mostly mid-tempos, mellow vocals here and there, and masterful solos.

⊙ **Made In Japan** (1982; Timeless). A fine latterday Hampton big band featuring two gifted newcomers – John Colianni (piano) and Ricky Ford (tenor) – in a programme of Hampton standards and new works, all played with conviction.

⊙ **For The Love Of Music** (1995; Motown). Extraordinary that this man introduced the vibraphone with Louis Armstrong in 1930; here he is in 1995 with Chaka Khan, Stevie Wonder and others playing his music on their terms. It works well too – Khan's "Gossamer Wings" is especially delightful.

➤➤ **Benny Goodman** *(After You've Gone; Avalon).*

Slide Hampton

Trombone, tuba, arranger.

b. Jeannette, Pennsylvania, 21 April 1932.

Slide (Locksley) Hampton played with Buddy Johnson in 1955–6 and with the Lionel Hampton band in 1956–7. He played and arranged for Maynard Ferguson from 1957–9, then formed his own octet which he led from 1959–62. After working as the musical director for singer Lloyd Price and doing freelance arranging, he joined Woody Herman in 1968 and toured Europe with him. Hampton settled there, doing much arranging for radio studio bands and playing in all-star contexts. He returned to New York in 1977 and began leading his own World of Trombones, a twelve-piece group, and was also involved in jazz education. One of the few prominent left-handed trombonists, Hampton has an amazingly fluent technique but, unlike some of the busier players on his instrument, he is also blessed with a fine melodic sense. [BP]

Roots (1985; Criss Cross). A useful quintet session with Clifford Jordan and the Cedar Walton trio, this has Hampton effortlessly carving mere trombone technicians with his meaningful solos.

Herbie Hancock

Keyboards, electronics, composer.
b. Chicago, 12 April 1940.

Hancock had piano lessons from seven, making rapid progress; at eleven he played Mozart's D major piano concerto with the Chicago Symphony Orchestra, and in his teens performed in Bach's Brandenburg Concerto no. 2.

In January 1961 he went to New York with trumpeter Donald Byrd and made an immediate impact. He worked with Phil Woods and Oliver Nelson, and recorded his first album as leader, *Takin' Off*, which has been described as "one of the most accomplished and stunning debuts in the annals of jazz". One of the tracks, "Watermelon Man", became a hit single and versions have since been recorded by more than two hundred artists. He worked briefly, in 1962–3, with Eric Dolphy, then in May 1963 joined the Miles Davis quintet. He stayed with Davis for five and a half years, leaving in 1968, but continuing to play on some later record sessions. His time with Davis established him internationally as one of the most important pianists of the time, and also as a fine composer of small-group material.

Throughout the 1960s he continued to record under his own name, and several of his compositions became part of the jazz repertoire: "The Sorcerer", "Riot", "Canteloupe Island", "Dolphin Dance", "Maiden Voyage" and "Speak Like A Child".

When he left the Miles Davis group, Hancock led a sextet which included Eddie Henderson (trumpet, flugelhorn), Benny Maupin (reeds and flutes), Julian Priester (trombone), Billy Hart (drums) and Buster Williams (bass), touring and playing festivals in the

Columbia Records

Herbie Hancock

USA and Europe. With this group he began to feature electronics more and more as a source of colour and atmosphere, but although the music was excellent, alternating spacey free sections with some marvellously rhythmic passages, there were not enough bookings to make the sextet viable economically. The jazz scene was in such a parlous state at the time that even though his albums sold reasonably well, and he was still recognized internationally as one of the leading forces in the music, he lacked the status, financial or otherwise, to keep the sextet together. He disbanded it in June 1973, forming a quartet with Maupin on reeds and featuring funky rhythms and electronic sounds.

It was not just money that made Hancock change tack; he had done much soul-searching and analysed his own situation ruthlessly. He was upset that friends had his albums on their shelves, but never played them. He said: "I realized that I could never be a genius in the class of Miles, Charlie Parker or Coltrane so I might just as well forget about becoming a legend and just be satisfied to create some music to make people happy. I no longer wanted to write the Great American Masterpiece."

Ironically, he immediately created a small American masterpiece with his new group's first recording, *Headhunters*, which became the best-selling jazz album in history. The first track, "Chameleon", also became a hit single – both album and single were instrumental. The music was heavily electronic, with electric bass, keyboards and synthesizers; it featured the kind of hypnotically repeating interlocking rhythms which Hancock admired so much in the music of Sly Stone. *Headhunters* had a new sound and it radically transformed Hancock's fortunes, turning him into a superstar with a huge international following. He and his group toured as the main attraction in major concert halls throughout the USA, Europe and Japan and made some more best-selling instrumental albums.

In the later 1970s Hancock began to make albums with vocals, his music became much more pop-oriented and, indeed, his popularity was huge. But at the same time he began to play and record acoustically again and work with old associates. In 1977 he initiated and toured worldwide with VSOP – the old Miles Davis band with Freddie Hubbard standing in for Davis. Later he toured with Chick Corea, performing acoustic piano duets; in 1982 he toured Europe and Japan with a quartet made up of himself, Tony Williams, Ron Carter and Wynton Marsalis. He won an Oscar in 1987 for his soundtrack to the film *Round Midnight*. He has also made more heavily electronic funky hit records and continued to break new ground in that area. Collaborating with the rock group Material, he co-wrote a tune, "Rockit", which inspired an award-winning video and helped to make the album *Future Shock* a best seller.

Hancock's restless creativity seems to find its main satisfaction in pioneering new electronic music – though he also works fitfully as a producer of other people's albums and tours playing acoustic piano or in groups such as the 1990s quartet with Jack DeJohnette, Dave Holland and Pat Metheny, and in 2001 a trio with Michael Brecker and Roy Hargrove. [IC]

Herbie Hancock

⊙ **Maiden Voyage** (1964; Blue Note); **Empyrean Isles** (1964; Blue Note). These are two classic albums from the 1960s. The rhythm-section on both is from the Miles Davis group – Ron Carter and Tony Williams – and Freddy Hubbard is the trumpeter. On *Maiden Voyage* saxophonist George Coleman was added to the quartet. All the pieces were composed by Hancock and at least three have since become jazz standards – "Maiden Voyage" and "Dolphin Dance" from the first album and "Canteloupe Island" from the second. The playing is faultless on both and Hubbard is at his best.

⊙ **Headhunters** (1973; CBS). Hancock created this gem with Benny Maupin on reeds and flute, Paul Jackson on bass and Harvey Mason and Bill Summers on drums and percussion respectively. The sound is composed and orchestrated with immense care, and improvised solos are beautifully integrated into performances which embody all Hancock's virtues: superb time and flawlessly executed rhythms, graceful melodies, brilliantly creative and catchy riffs, and an atmosphere of urbane contemplation laced with joy.

⊙ **Gershwin's World** (1998; Verve). Hancock exonerates himself to a great degree with this dynamic homage to George Gershwin in his centenary year. His strikingly imaginative tribute is full of rare feeling and creative surprises. Even the opening piece, "Overture (Fascinating Rhythm)", delightfully wrong-foots the listener, because Gershwin's tune never appears and instead we get five fascinating African percussionists playing rhythm for 53 seconds. Pure Hancock, and he finds new angles on several of Gershwin's pieces and on music that influenced Gershwin.

VSOP

⊙ **The Quintet** (1977; CBS). This was an attempt to resurrect the great 1960s Miles Davis quintet with Freddie Hubbard taking Miles's role. The whole thing was done very well, but it is impossible to re-create the "shock of the new" which, of course, was the essential ingredient that had given the original band its dynamism.

Herbie Hancock and Chick Corea

⊙ **An Evening With Chick Corea And Herbie Hancock** (1978; Columbia). Corea seems to have emerged from the mid-1970s immersion in electronics rather better than Hancock, and, although there are marvellous passages, Hancock sounds less at home on acoustic piano than does his partner.

Herbie Hancock, Wynton Marsalis, Ron Carter and Tony Williams

Quartet (1982; CBS). This album perhaps represents the genesis of neo-bop. The great 1960s rhythm-section takes under its wing Marsalis, the embryonic icon of the next generation. The playing is excellent, and Ron Carter's funky, minimalist "A Quick Sketch" is a delight, with Marsalis on fiery form.

>> **Miles Davis** *(The Complete Concert; ESP; Miles Smiles).*

"Captain" John Handy

Alto saxophone, clarinet.

b. Pass Christian, Missouri, 24 June 1900; d. 12 Jan 1971.

John Handy first specialized on alto saxophone in the late 1920s (having also played clarinet in a variety of bands) and during the 1930s played his new speciality with his own group, the Louisiana Shakers, on tour and in residence at La Vida Dance Hall, New Orleans. By the 1960s he was regularly to be heard with trumpeter Kid Sheik Cola's band, as well as at Preservation Hall. He achieved international popularity after touring Europe as a soloist in the mid-1960s, playing with a variety of New Orleans-style bands: his gutty, hard-swinging approach (which sometimes recalled Pete Brown, as well as Johnny Hodges and Sidney Bechet) was an eloquent demonstration that saxophones – the bane of hard-line jazz revivalists in the 1950s – had never really been out of place in a New Orleans ensemble. He played with the Preservation Hall Jazz Band at the 1970 Newport jazz festival, where his stomping style created a sensation. [DF]

Captain John Handy And His New Orleans Stompers Vols 1 & 2 (1965; GHB). Excellent illustration of Handy's strong, vibrant style in the good company of Kid Thomas Valentine, Jim Robinson and the ever-rewarding Sammy Rimington.

Craig Handy

Tenor, soprano and alto saxophones.

b. Oakland, California, 25 Sept 1962.

As a teenager, Handy played in the Hieroglyphics Ensemble with Peter Apfelbaum and others, then won a Charlie Parker Scholarship to study at North Texas State University from 1981–4. Invited to New York by Roy Haynes, he made his recording debut with the Mingus Dynasty in 1987 and played with Abdullah Ibrahim, Art Blakey, Wynton Marsalis, Haynes and, in the early 90s, with Betty Carter. In 1991 he made his own first album (his third awaits issue as the time of writing), and an ongoing relationship with the Mingus Big Band has bracketed work for Steve Coleman and the movie *Kansas City*, where he took part in the "tenor battle" sequence with Joshua Redman. A member of the recording groups Essence All Stars and Chartbusters, he toured internationally with Herbie Hancock during 1998–9. In the words of Betty Carter: "He has one of those wonderful, good tenor sax sounds that's been missing. He's a lyricist, he can play pretty, but he can also fire it up." [BP]

Split Second Timing (1991; Arabesque). This quartet session with Ralph Peterson (augmented on three tracks by Robin Eubanks) features Handy's brief Dexter Gordon imitation, plus a confidently lyrical alto ballad and much convincing up-tempo improvisation.

>> **Roy Haynes** *(When It's Haynes It Roars).*

John Handy

Reeds, composer, educator; also flute, piano, vocals, percussion.

b. Dallas, Texas, 3 Feb 1933.

Handy (no relation to "Captain" John Handy) was self-taught on clarinet from thirteen, began on alto saxophone in 1949, and studied theory at college. He moved to New York in 1958, working with Mingus in 1958–9 and playing a crucial role on the classic album *Mingus Ah Um*. He formed his own group in 1959 which played around New York and, in 1961, did a US government tour of Europe; Handy later worked in Sweden and Denmark as a soloist. In 1963 he was soloist with the Santa Clara Symphony Orchestra and San Francisco State College Symphonic Band. In 1964 he played with Mingus at the Monterey jazz festival, where he returned the following year with his own quintet (with Michael White on violin) and made a great impression. In 1966–7 he toured with the Monterey All Stars in the USA and played in Gunther Schuller's opera *The Visitation*, and in 1968 he formed a new band with Mike Nock, White and Ron McClure, all of whom broke away two years later to form one of the first jazz-rock groups, Fourth Way. In 1970 Handy finished writing his *Concerto For Jazz Soloist And Orchestra*, playing with the San Francisco Symphony Orchestra for its premiere. His career since 1971 has been diverse; he has collaborated with Indian musician Ali Akbar Khan in a group called Rainbow, had a pop hit with "Hard Work" in 1976, and was also a member of Mingus Dynasty, a band composed of associates of the bassist, formed after his death.

Since 1968 Handy has been active as an educator in California, teaching courses in jazz history, black music and improvisation at various universities and conservatories. He was a judge at the Monterey High School jazz festival in 1973–4, and has acted in the same capacity at various other secondary school jazz gatherings. He has also played major festivals with his various groups and collaborators all over the USA and Europe.

Handy was initially schooled in bebop, but with Mingus he rapidly developed a more flexible and adventurous approach. With an alto sound somewhere between those of Parker and Eric Dolphy, he is an impassioned soloist with a highly individual style and a concept which can embrace anything from bebop to abstraction, Indian music or contemporary classical. [IC]

Where Go The Boats (1988; Inak). Handy leads thirteen musicians here, including guitarist Lee Ritenour, in a programme that comes out of jazz-rock fusion with Indian tinges. It has its moments and the title track has some charm, but in general it lacks dynamism.

Musical Dreamland (c. late 1980s; Boulevard). Handy was a vital force in the 1960s, but his once-strong vision seems to have evaporated. Here he leads a quartet of musicians in a half-baked curryfication of music.

➤➤ **Charles Mingus** *(Mingus Ah Um).*

W.C. Handy

Composer, bandleader, cornet.

b. Florence, Alabama, 16 Nov 1873; d. 28 March 1958.

Known as "the Father of the Blues", W.C. (William Christopher) Handy was the composer – or at least the copyrighter – of a huge number of classic blues themes, beginning with "Memphis Blues" (his first success, originally an electioneering song known as "Mr Crump"), "St Louis Blues", "Beale Street Blues" and "Old Miss Rag", and many others. The inspiration for many of Handy's songs came from folk tunes, rural blues and others that he heard from street performers and other wandering musicians, but he brought discipline and structure to what he heard. At a century's distance it may never be established which passages among these compositions actually were Handy's own creations: "Handy is not the inventor of the genre", says Isaac Goldberg, "[but] he was the first to set down jazz on paper – to fix the quality of the various breaks, as these wildly filled-in pauses were named."

Max Jones Files/Redferns

W.C. Handy

After the success of "Memphis Blues" in 1912 and his masterpiece, "St Louis Blues", in 1914, Handy, a highly trained bandmaster and cornettist, opened a publishing firm in Memphis with Harry Pace. In 1918 the operation moved to New York, where it flourished on Broadway as Handy Brothers Music Company Incorporated. From the 1920s Handy suffered periods of blindness, but carried on with his publishing concerns and played concerts and tours all through the 1930s; he also recorded in 1939 with J.C. Higginbotham and others. After a subway accident in 1943 he became a more elusive figure, turning up at special concerts to hear his inventions played by musicians such as Eddie Condon. Handy's engrossing autobiography, *Father Of The Blues* (a truly remarkable portrait of its times), was published in 1941; in 1958, the year of his death, Paramount filmed *St Louis Blues*, an approximation of Handy's story starring Nat "King" Cole and Eartha Kitt. In 1960 a statue of Handy was unveiled in Memphis, but perhaps his best memorial is Louis Armstrong's *Plays W.C. Handy* collection from 1954. [DF]

Father Of The Blues: A Musical Autobiography (1952–3; DRG). Contains fascinating personal reminiscences by this gentle "father of the blues", plus examples of his work played by pianists Katherine Handy, Charles Cooke and Adele Brown Whitney, with Handy himself on vocals, guitar and trumpet.

Jake Hanna

Drums.

b. Roxbury, Massachusetts, 4 April 1931.

A Boston-based musician until the late 1950s, Hanna worked with Marian McPartland and Woody Herman before starting a ten-year stint on American TV's *Merv Griffin Show* in 1964. During that period he worked in an impressively eclectic variety of settings, from the Clark Terry-Bob Brookmeyer quintet to the Oscar Peterson trio in 1974 and played for Bing Crosby in Joe Bushkin's quartet in mid-decade. Later in the decade he was working with younger swingmen including Warren Vaché, Scott Hamilton and the Concord Super Band. Through the 1980s and into the 1990s Hanna stayed busy on the West Coast, and regularly made the rounds of festivals, concerts and club dates at home and abroad (including Britain's Swinging Jazz Parties, Blackpool, 2002–3). As dynamic a personality as he is performer. Hanna's understanding of every area of jazz drums – from Baby Dodds to Ed Thigpen and beyond – makes him a riveting sight and sound, and like Louie Bellson he functions equally happily in a big band or small group. Although he emerged too late to achieve quite the reputation of Buddy Rich, his talents are comparable. [DF]

Live At Concord (1975; Concord). A rare opportunity to hear Hanna as leader with regular partners Carl Fontana, Bill Berry and Plas Johnson in a swing set of finest quality.

The Joint Is Jumpin' (1997; Arbors). An informal date; not much in the way of charts, but delights include Jack Sheldon singing and playing, the phenomenal John Allred (trombone) and Hanna's crisp full drumming.

Sir Roland Hanna

Piano, composer.

b. Detroit, Michigan, 10 Feb 1932; d. 13 Nov 2002.

Hanna played regularly in Detroit and elsewhere before studying at music college in the mid-1950s. He worked with Benny Goodman in 1958 and Charles Mingus in 1959 (also recording with him in 1971). He led his own trios and duos regularly from 1959, but also worked with the Thad Jones-Mel Lewis band from 1967–74. He toured as a soloist in Europe and Africa in 1968–9, and in 1974 founded the New York Jazz Quartet with Frank Wess, Ron Carter and drummer Ben Riley. Hanna is an excellent ensemble player. He took part in the re-creation of Mingus's *Epitaph* in 1989, and in several concerts by the Lincoln Center Jazz Orchestra in the 1990s, and he was a professor at the Aaron Copland School of Music, Queens College, The City University of New York. In addition to several albums under his own name, Hanna was notable for backing work in ensemble contexts which is always exciting and to the point. As a soloist, he displayed an improvisatory flair in various European "classical" styles besides his brilliant jazz work. His knighthood was bestowed by the President of Liberia. [BP]

Perugia (1974; Freedom). A live solo set that begins with "Take The A Train" (also a feature for him with the LCJO) finds Hanna's own material equally absorbing.

Wilbur Harden

Trumpet, flugelhorn, composer.

b. Birmingham, Alabama, 31 Dec 1924; d. June 1969.

Harden's first professional touring jobs were with R&B stars such as Roy Brown (in 1950) and Ivory Joe Hunter. After playing in the navy, he moved to Detroit and played and recorded with Yusef Lateef's quintet in 1957. The following year he recorded with Coltrane, and made four albums under his own name; three have been reissued as by Coltrane, the fourth as by Tommy Flanagan. In 1960 he again recorded with Curtis Fuller but gave up regular playing as a result of ill health. His mellow flugel work deserves to be more widely remembered, and the original compositions on his sextet records were some of the earliest to be titled in honour of African subjects. [BP]

Wilbur Harden and John Coltrane

Tanganyika Strut (1958; Savoy). Although these sessions may not quite live up to the promise of their personnel (Coltrane, Fuller, Flanagan), the conception of their original leader and his solo work stand up extremely well.

Buster Harding

Arranger, piano.

b. Ontario, Canada, 19 March 1917; d. 14 Nov 1965.

Buster (Lavere) Harding was brought up in Cleveland, where he started his own band as a teenager. After working in Buffalo and Boston, he arranged for the Teddy Wilson big band in 1939–40. He also wrote for the Coleman Hawkins band and for Cab Calloway in 1941–2. Turning freelance, he contributed arrangements to Roy Eldridge, Artie Shaw, Count Basie, Calloway, Dizzy Gillespie and others. He was the musical director for record sessions by Billie Holiday in 1949 and played the piano for her in 1951, and worked for Gillespie in 1954. Apart from playing briefly with Jonah Jones in the early 1960s, his performing was restricted by illness, although he continued to write. Harding's block-chord voicing for brass focused the Calloway band during one of its best periods and helped to set the style of the post-war Basie band; his 1947 "Mr Roberts' Roost" for Basie was adapted in the later jukebox hit "Paradise Squat". [BP]

➤➤ **Cab Calloway** *(The Chronological Cab Calloway 1940–1941).*

Bill Hardman

Trumpet.

b. Cleveland, Ohio, 6 April 1933; d. Paris, 5 Dec 1990.

Hardman was frequently associated with Charles Mingus, playing with him in 1956, 1969–70 and with Mingus's big band of 1972, and with Art Blakey with whom he worked from 1956–8, 1966–9, 1970 and in 1975–6. He also worked briefly with Horace Silver, singer Lloyd Price's big band, and spent several years with Lou Donaldson from 1959–66. He ran his own group, the Brass Company, and played in the USA and Europe with Junior Cook from 1979–81. An admirer of Clifford Brown, Hardman in his early work had a limited phraseology and a peculiarly acrid tone which were very identifiable. He built on this foundation to become a wide-ranging stylist who deserves to be more widely known. [BP]

What's Up (1989; Steeplechase). A reunion with Junior Cook, plus the trombone of young Robin Eubanks, has Hardman at the top of his game on both up-tempo material and ballads.

Otto Hardwicke

Alto, bass and baritone saxophones.

b. Washington, DC, 31 May 1904; d. 5 Aug 1970.

A childhood friend of Duke Ellington, Otto James "Toby" Hardwicke began as a bass player in Carroll's Columbia Orchestra and was persuaded to take up C-melody saxophone by Ellington around 1920. "Toby was a great saxophone player so far as tone and execution were concerned", says Mercer Ellington, "and he was also valuable from the standpoint of thought and ideas." But for a variety of reasons (wanderlust, girlfriends, drink) Hardwicke had a habit of disappearing at inconvenient moments in Ellington's early career-building campaign. In 1928 he went to Europe to work with Noble Sissle and Nekka Shaw, and by 1930 was leading his own band, featuring an innovative five-man saxophone section, in Harlem. (His band once bested Ellington's in a famous battle, and may have helped Ellington towards his idea for an enlarged saxophone section.) When he rejoined Ellington in 1932, Hardwicke found Johnny Hodges leading the section and the band more of an autocracy than the freewheeling club it had been ten years before. But he stayed with Ellington, on the whole happily, until 1946, when the demands of travel, his increased drinking and personal differences finally caused a rift with his leader. In later life Hardwicke worked in hotel management and ran his own farm. [DF]

Emmett Hardy

Cornet.

b. Gretna, Louisiana, 12 June 1903; d. 16 June 1925.

The best-remembered "fact" about the legendary Emmett Hardy is that he influenced the young Bix Beiderbecke, but because no records of his work exist there will always be some contentiousness about the subject. Because Hardy was a graduate of Papa Jack Laine's "Children", a New Orleans university for jazzmen (another student was Nick La Rocca, who unquestionably influenced Bix), and later regularly worked on the steamship *Capitol*, which he joined in Beiderbecke's home town of Davenport, Iowa, it seems certain that Bix at least heard him play. After a brief visit to Chicago, where an attempt to join the New Orleans Rhythm Kings was foiled by the American Federation of Musicians, Hardy returned to New Orleans and died soon after of tuberculosis, aged just 22. [DF]

Roy Hargrove

Trumpet, composer.

b. Dallas, Texas, 16 Oct 1969.

Greeted with considerable acclaim for the purity and brilliance of his tone when he burst onto the scene in the late 1980s, Roy Hargrove established himself in the following decade as one of the most in-demand trumpeters in the music, appearing on small-group sessions with everyone from Jackie McLean and T.S. Monk, through budding pianists like Stephen Scott and Marc Cary, to young lions like Christian McBride and Nicholas Payton. A neo-classicist who eschews fusion in favour of a bright, hard-swinging post-bop style, Hargrove made five well-received albums in quick succession for Novus between 1989–93, involving the likes of pianists Geoff Keezer, Stephen Scott and Marc Cary, bassists Christian McBride and Rodney Whitaker, and sharing frontline duties with a college colleague, alto player Antonio Hart. He has also played with the Jazz Masters, a big band specializing in large-scale arrangements of jazz composers' work. Although he is a fine, fiery player on up-tempo material, his forte is the slow-burning ballad, so his work behind singers (he plays a Miles role on Shirley Horn's 1997 album *I Remember Miles*, and a Clifford Brown role on Helen Merrill's 1994 recording *Brownie*) is particularly memorable, though this aspect of his craft hit a peak with the orchestrated album *Moment To Moment* (1999; Verve). Latter-day moves into street-beat adorned crossover jazz mark a new direction for this gifted trumpeter. [CP/CI]

⊙ **Diamond In The Rough** (1990; Novus). Auspicious debut featuring pianist Geoff Keezer, who provides the most memorable of the album's original tunes, although Denzil Best's "Wee" and Monk's "Ruby My Dear" are also included.

⊙ **Public Eye** (1991; Novus). Similar to above, only featuring Billy Higgins on drums. The Warren/Dubin classic "September In The Rain" is a standout, also included on *Approaching Standards*.

⊙ **With The Tenors Of Our Time** (1994; Verve). Frontline sparring partners include Johnny Griffin, Joe Henderson and Branford Marsalis, but Hargrove holds his own well, and surpasses himself on "Never Let Me Go".

⊙ **Parker's Mood** (1995; Verve). The pick of Hargrove's 1990s Verve output, an irrepressibly sparky visit to sixteen Charlie Parker themes by three utterly compatible players: Hargrove, again showing his class on ballad material, vigorous pianist Stephen Scott and young bass maestro Christian McBride.

⊙ **Hard Groove** (2003; Verve). With rap, funk and guest vocals from the likes of Erykah Badu, for some this was a hipper Hargrove, for others disappointingly modish. Either way, it's a virtual reinvention.

John Harle

Soprano and alto saxophones, composer.

b. Newcastle upon Tyne, UK, 20 Sept 1956.

Like a number of his near-contemporaries – Nigel Kennedy and Joanna MacGregor are other obvious examples – John Harle commutes without a hint of contrivance or condescension between jazz, classical and rock music, playing Berio and Ellington, Weill and Woods (Phil) with equal ease and commitment. He studied at London's Royal College of Music (1978–81), and subsequently at the Paris Conservatoire, and won the Amcon Award in 1984, giving a recital shortly afterwards in Carnegie Hall. He has performed various concerti in New York, London, Germany and Japan, and in 1988 appeared in the highly acclaimed TV feature, *One Man And His Sax*. The same year, his score for the film *Prick Up Your Ears* won an award at Cannes. In 1995, Harle's performance of Sir Harrison Birtwistle's *Panic*, a saxophone concerto, at the Last Night of the Proms brought him to an international audience, and he has written *Terror and Magnificence* (1996), settings of medieval texts involving pop singer Elvis Costello, soprano Sarah Leonard and saxophonist Andy Sheppard, and an opera, *Angel Magick*, heard at the Proms in 1998. Sheppard also collaborated with Harle in a project highlighting the contrasting sounds and musical contexts of their instrument, "Twentieth Century Saxophones", which toured the UK in 1995. In addition to participating in numerous projects with the likes of Sir Paul McCartney, Michael Nyman and Ute Lemper, Harle continues to write film and TV music, perform and compose in a variety of musical contexts and genres (including, latterly, trip-hop), teach at London's Guildhall School and receive plaudits of the following sort from the *Daily Telegraph*: "no one," it writes, "is certainly doing more to extend the saxophone's musically restricted repertoire." [CP/CI]

Habanera (1987; Hannibal). Elegies for Coltrane and Piaf rub shoulders with Satie, Richard Rodney Bennett and Poulenc, all played with exquisite delicacy and faultless technique by Harle and Lenehan.

John Harle's Saxophone (1987; Hyperion). Highlight is Phil Woods's sonata, but Michael Berkeley, Edison Denisov, Richard Rodney Bennett and Dave Heath all have music featured by Harle and Lenehan.

The Shadow Of The Duke (1992; EMI). "Caravan", "The Mooche", "Isfahan" and many more (including a Harle original, "The Shadow of the Duke", sung by Sarah Leonard) receive creamy-toned treatment from Harle and his band.

Terror and Magnificence (1996; Argo). Settings of medieval texts sung by pop composer Elvis Costello and soprano Sarah Leonard, and also featuring Andy Sheppard and countertenor William Purefoy.

Billy Harper

Tenor saxophone, flute, vocals, composer.
b. Houston, Texas, 17 Jan 1943.

Harper began learning the saxophone at twelve and had lessons at school, playing in the school marching and jazz bands. He was at North Texas State University from 1961–5 where he did special jazz studies, graduating in saxophone and theory. He also played with R&B bands and in 1966 moved to New York. From 1967 until the mid-1970s he worked with Gil Evans, touring Japan with him in 1972 and playing on several Evans albums including that classic melange of acoustic and electric instruments, *Svengali*. From 1968–70 he also worked with Art Blakey and toured Japan with him. In 1971 he joined the Thad Jones-Mel Lewis big band, touring Europe with them in 1973. He led groups of his own in the early 1970s and worked with Max Roach, Lee Morgan, Elvin Jones and others. In 1975 he took his quintet to Europe, performing throughout Scandinavia, and also in Holland, France and Italy.

He has been active in music education since the mid-1960s teaching improvisation, saxophone and flute, privately and in schools and colleges. With his own and various other groups he has played major festivals in the USA, Europe and North Africa. Harper is a fine composer, and Gil Evans arranged and recorded some of his pieces including the blues/gospel masterpiece "Thoroughbred" (on the *Svengali* album), one of the definitive performances of 1970s fusion music. Harper's influences include Rollins, Coltrane and Gil Evans. [IC]

Capra Black (1973; Strata East). This features a septet plus four vocalists, and reveals the strength and variety of Harper's composing which is infused with his blues and gospel roots.

Live On Tour In The Far East, Vol. 2 (1991; Steeplechase). Harper leads another marvellous quintet which includes the great trumpeter Eddie Henderson. There's an excellent version of "Priestess" and some fine Henderson on "My Funny Valentine".

>> **Gil Evans** *(Svengali)*; **Thad Jones** *(Complete Solid State Recordings Of The Thad Jones-Mel Lewis Orchestra)*.

The Harper Brothers

Although there are signs of late that their artistic scope is widening somewhat, Phil Harper (trumpet; b. Baltimore, 10 May 1965) and his brother Winard (drums; b. Baltimore, 4 June 1962) are basically hard-bop musicians who rose to prominence on the wave of reawakened interest in that branch of the music in the late 1980s. Both had top-class teachers: Phil occupied the trumpet chair in Art Blakey's Jazz Messengers between Terence Blanchard and Brian Lynch, in a band also including tenor player Javon Jackson, trombonist Robin Eubanks and pianist Benny Green; Winard drummed for Betty Carter – also alongside Green – in a rhythm team with bassist Michael Bowie. After his Messengers stint, Phil recorded with two other drummer/leaders, Cecil Brooks III and Joe Chambers, with Algerian-born drummer/pianist Errol Parker, singer Etta Jones, saxophonist Houston Person and the Mingus Big Band, as well as fellow trumpeter Terence Blanchard. Winard has recorded with pianist Ray Bryant, and saxophonists Dan Braden and James Clay as well as with Carter. With the group splitting in 1993, Phil recorded two albums for Muse as leader (before returning to the Mingus Big Band, with whom he still appears), while Winard led several releases, mostly on Savant, in a generally classic neo-hard bop style – sharp, lively and accessible in the Messengers mould. [CP/CI]

⊙ **The Harper Brothers** (1988; Verve). Featuring Betty Carter alumni pianist Stephen Scott and bassist Michael Bowie, plus alto player Justin Robinson alongside the brothers, an enjoyable, straightforwardly unpretentious hard-bop session.

⊙ **Remembrance** (1989; Verve). Bassist Kiyoshi Kitagawa replaces Bowie for this sparky live set from the Village Vanguard, respectful of the tradition but always uplifting and with enough new slants on the hard-bop form to reward repeated listenings.

⊙ **You Can Hide Inside the Music** (1990; Verve). Much more diffuse, ambitious recording, touching on bluesy modern mainstream as well as strict hard bop, with guest appearances from Harry "Sweets" Edison and Jimmy McGriff.

Winard Harper

⊙ **Trap Dancer** (1997; Savant). The drummer's finest album as leader, showcasing his considerable composing and bandleading talents as he drives a vigorous band, including pianist George Cables, through an intelligent selection of standards and originals.

⊙ **Time For The Soul** (2003; Savant). Ten years after the Harper Brothers went their own ways to pursue "new directions", Winard's fifth album as leader finds him ploughing the same hard bop furrow with considerable flair.

Tom Harrell

Trumpet, flugelhorn, composer.

b. Urbana, Illinois, 16 June 1946.

Harrell moved to the San Francisco area with his family at the age of five. He joined Woody Herman in 1970–71 and Horace Silver from 1973–7. He also worked with Carlos Santana, Azteca, Arnie Lawrence's Treasure Island, the National Jazz Ensemble, and did studio work. The Phil Woods quartet was expanded to a quintet by the addition of Harrell from 1983–9. He continued to maintain his career throughout this period despite a diagnosis of schizophrenia, and has gradually risen to the top echelon of trumpeters. Freelancing throughout the 1990s, he has performed and recorded with a stylistically wide variety of players such as Charlie Haden, Art Farmer, Tom Chapin, Charles McPherson, Jim Hall and Joe Lovano, and has led his own groups. After making albums for various labels, in 1996 he signed with RCA Victor who to date have released two widely acclaimed recordings. His style was described by Horace Silver: "He's got his own thing, but you can hear Dizzy, Miles, Hubbard, Kenny Dorham, Blue [Mitchell] and Clifford [Brown]." Very fluent technically, Harrell's playing nevertheless gives the impression of understatement and restrained lyricism. [BP]

⊙ **The Art Of Rhythm** (1997; RCA Victor). More than its comparatively robust predecessor *Labyrinth*, this programme of original material amplifies the subtlety of Harrell's own playing in varied settings, including at different times guitarists Mike Stern and Romero Lubambo and saxophonists Greg Tardy, David Sanchez and Dewey Redman.

Joe Harriott

Alto saxophone, composer; also baritone saxophone, piano.

b. Jamaica, 15 July 1928; d. 2 Jan 1973.

Harriott studied clarinet at school, then played saxophone in dance bands. He emigrated to the UK in 1951, freelancing in London. In 1954 he played at the Paris festival with Tony Kinsey, and later in the decade worked with Ronnie Scott, the Modern Jazz Quartet and others. He began leading his own groups in 1958 and performed with his quintet at the 1959 San Remo jazz festival, after which he contracted tuberculosis and spent six months in hospital. He had begun as a Parker-inspired altoist, and by the end of the 1950s was a very fine player in the conventional post-bebop mould, with everything played in common time (4/4 or 3/4), themes played at the beginning and end of pieces, and improvisations based closely on harmonic sequences. In hospital he conceived the idea of a music (written and improvised) without set rhythmic and harmonic patterns – abstract music – and immediately began composing "freeform" pieces. Once out of hospital in late 1959 he began rehearsing the pieces with his quintet, which comprised Shake Keane (trumpet and flugelhorn), Pat Smythe (piano), Coleridge Goode (bass) and Phil Seamen (drums), all of whom grasped the new concept immediately.

David Redfern

Joe Harriott

They recorded the album *Free Form* in 1960, and their 1962 album *Abstract* received great critical acclaim in the USA.

Harriott's abstract music was nothing like the free-form jazz created by Ornette Coleman around the same time. Coleman's was shot through with the blues and the African-American tradition and, although harmonically abstract, it usually featured a swinging rhythm-section, thus occurring in clearly defined time. Harriott's abstraction often had no regular rhythm, sometimes featured total silences as an integral part of the music, fused African-Caribbean elements with the jagged lines and dissonances of western European avant-garde music, and occasionally included totally unaccompanied improvisation by any one of the five players. Abstraction simply added a new dimension to the Harriott quintet's music, and the group often juxtaposed conventionally structured pieces with free-form ones. In the early 1960s they performed the new music at several festivals in Europe.

During the mid-1960s Harriott pioneered another trend-setting innovation, collaborating with the Indian violinist and composer John Mayer to create Indo-Jazz Fusions. Using a sextet of jazz musicians and a quartet of Indian musicians, they compounded elements from jazz and Indian music into a rich new synthesis. Three albums were recorded and, again, the ten-piece fusion group performed at many European festivals.

Joe Harriott was a compelling and original soloist with a searing, passionate sound, an inexhaustible fund of rhythmic and melodic ideas and great technical mastery. He was perfectly at home in any context – big band, small group or fusion orchestra – and the master of any idiom, whether conventional, abstract or mixed genre. He was also an important innovator, the creator of European free jazz as opposed to the American kind, and one of the first jazz musicians to revitalize his music by integrating it with elements from ethnic music. Unfortunately, his achievements went virtually unrecognized in the UK, and he neither worked enough nor made enough money to survive comfortably. It became impossible for him to lead a regular group, and he was forced to travel around as a soloist playing with local rhythm-sections in provincial towns, sleeping on people's couches or their floors, or wherever he could. In this sense, his last years were horribly similar to those of Charlie Parker, and perhaps even more tragically lonely. He died of cancer at the age of 44. [IC]

Joe Harriott

Abstract (1961–2; Redial). This was the Joe Harriott quintet album given a four-star review by *Down Beat* magazine. The great trumpeter, Shake Keane (who was also a fine poet), and Harriott have an uncanny rapport, pianist Pat Smythe complements them subtly, bassist Coleridge Goode is the intelligent pivot of the band, and legendary drummer Phil Seamen plays on the four tracks recorded in 1961, while the other great drummer, Bobby Orr, plays on the four 1962 tracks. Seven of the eight pieces are composed by Harriott, and the ninth performance is of Sonny Rollins's "Oleo", which is given a very abstract interpretation. This is a glowing memorial to a benign and formative moment in jazz history.

Movement (1963; EMI). This is an excellent introduction to many aspects of Harriott's work. The nine tracks alternate between blues and gospel-inspired compositions such as "Count Twelve" and "Revival", and completely abstract performances like the title track or "Beams" and "Spaces". The group was Harriott's classic quintet, but with the great drummer Bobby Orr replacing Phil Seamen.

Joe Harriott-John Mayer Double Quintet

Indo-Jazz Fusions; Indo-Jazz Fusions II (1967–8; Redial). These records, like the one above, may need some searching out. The themes are nearly all by Mayer, but the jazz sensibilities of Harriott and Keane (replaced by Kenny Wheeler on the second LP) are hardly diluted, and Harriott's beautiful tone and phrasing are shown to advantage. Some compromises are noticeable – the complex Indian metre is replaced by a 3/4 rhythm for the jazz soloists on "Purvi Variations", for example, but the collaboration not only broke new ground but remains more satisfying than many similar experiments.

Barry Harris

Piano.

b. Detroit, Michigan, 15 Dec 1929.

Like his contemporary and fellow Detroiter Tommy Flanagan, Harris is an important second-generation bop stylist. After brief tours with Max Roach in 1956 and Cannonball Adderley in 1960, he moved to New York and has remained there teaching and playing, mostly under his own name. He became the favourite accompanist of Coleman Hawkins in the mid-1960s, and deputized for Thelonious Monk in rehearsals for the New York Jazz Repertory Company tribute in 1974. Over the years, Harris has shown an increasing affinity to the music of Monk, in addition to his close involvement in the styles of Powell and Parker. While less intense than any of these players, Harris has a beautifully crisp and lithe approach which readily explains his influence on a number of young players. For most of the 1980s, he ran the Jazz Cultural Center, a combined nightclub and school in New York, and was given an award from the National Endowment for the Arts in 1989. Now travelling internationally in the cause of jazz education, Harris is one of the surviving paragons of the bebop style. [BP]

Live At The Maybeck Recital Hall Vol. 12 (1990; Concord). Harris's solo set contains moving ballads by Powell ("I'll Keep Loving You") and Parker ("Parker's Mood"), as well as homages to Monk and Tatum and the theme music of "The Flintstones" and "I Love Lucy".

Beaver Harris

Drums.

b. Pittsburgh, Pennsylvania, 20 April 1936; d. 22 Dec 1991.

Beaver (William) Harris played clarinet and alto saxophone as a teenager. He became involved in baseball, playing in all the major black leagues, but didn't drum until he joined the army. After his discharge in 1963 he moved to New York, working with Sonny Rollins, Thelonious Monk, Joe Henderson, Freddie Hubbard and others. He joined Archie Shepp in 1966, touring Europe with him, where he working with Albert Ayler. He also worked with Sonny Stitt, Dexter Gordon and Clark Terry.

At the end of the 1960s he formed a cooperative group with Grachan Moncur III, the 360 Degree Experience. In 1970 he played with Shepp for LeRoi Jones's play *Slave Ship*, and in 1973 for Aishah Rahman's *Lady Day: A Musical Tragedy*. 1973 also found him playing on the Newport jazz festival tour of Japan with Shepp, Konitz, Gato Barbieri and others. Harris also recorded with Steve Lacy, the Jazz Composers' Orchestra and Larry Coryell. His influences included Kenny Clarke, Max Roach, Roy Haynes and Sonny Rollins. [IC]

➤➤ **Archie Shepp** *(Montreux One).*

Benny Harris

Trumpet, composer.

b. New York, 23 April 1919; d. 11 Feb 1975.

Harris worked with Tiny Bradshaw in 1939 and Earl Hines in 1941 and 1942–3, as well as doing small-group work on 52nd Street with Coleman Hawkins, Don Byas and others. He took part in an important early bebop record session by the Clyde Hart All Stars in December 1944. Later he was only intermittently active as a player, for example with the Dizzy Gillespie band in 1949 and with Charlie Parker in 1951–2. Harris contributed to the bop repertoire by combining the chords of "How High The Moon" with Parker's solo on "Jumpin' Blues" to create "Ornithology". Other compositions include "Little Benny" (aka "Bud's Bubble" or "Crazeology"), "Reets and I" and "Wahoo". [BP]

➤➤ **Don Byas** *(Savoy Jam Party).*

Bill Harris

Trombone.

b. Philadelphia, 28 Oct 1916; d. 19 Sept 1973.

Harris came to prominence as one of the leading soloists of the Woody Herman band, which he rejoined several times during his career in 1944–6, 1948–50, 1956–8 and 1959. He co-led groups with Charlie Ventura in 1947, and bassist Chubby Jackson in 1953, and made annual tours with Jazz At The Philharmonic from 1950–54. In the 1960s he was occupied playing in backing bands at various Las Vegas nightspots, and then retired to Florida.

Harris's style was especially distinctive during the period of his greatest popularity, the late 1940s and early 1950s. Though not unaware of bebop, he based himself firmly on swing-era greats such as J.C. Higginbotham. His forthright delivery, complete with a variety of articulation and slurring, conveyed his frequently outrageous sense of humour, reminiscent of a vulgarized Vic Dickenson. Nowadays overlooked except by Herman fans, Harris's always enjoyable solo work deserves wider recognition. [BP]

⊙ **Bill Harris And Friends** (1957; Fantasy/OJC). Partnered in a quintet with Jimmy Rowles and Ben Webster, this is virtually Harris's only extended studio session in his own right. As well as forthright playing, it contains a priceless moment of musical and verbal comedy too.

Craig Harris

Trombone.

b. Hempstead, New York, 10 Sept 1954.

After studying composition at the State University of New York, Craig Harris played with Sun Ra 1976–8, Abdullah Ibrahim 1979–81, and in the pit band for Lena Horne's *The Lady And Her Music*. He was subsequently in bands led by figures as diverse as Henry Threadgill and Jay McShann, David Murray and Olu Dara, but his highly personal, vocalized style is best showcased in his own projects, the bands Tailgater's Tales and the later, funkier, Cold Sweat, an outfit featuring bassist Melvin Gibbs, reedsman Sam Furnace and trumpeter Eddie Allen. Harris's trombone playing, like that of Robin Eubanks, revived interest in his instrument by combining the traditional style of early innovators like Kid Ory with elements of later jazz-related styles like funk and free-form, and he joined three like-minded souls, fellow trombonists Ray Anderson, George Lewis and Gary Valente, on Anderson's engaging hatArt album *Slideride* (1994). In addition to collaborating with the likes of Muhal Richard Abrams and Don Byron, Harris continues to work in David Murray's various aggregations and has collaborated with the likes of Muhal Richard Abrams, Don Byron, singer Carla Cook and hip-hop group The Roots. [CP/CI]

Craig Harris

⊙ **Black Bone** (1983; Soul Note). Appealing, intelligent mix of old and new jazz featuring tenorman George Adams and bassist Fred Hopkins.

Tailgater's Tales

⊙ **Shelter** (1986; JMT). Lively session particularly noteworthy for the musical drumming of Pheeroan akLaff. Also features virtuoso clarinettist Don Byron.

Cold Sweat

⊙ **4 Play** (1990; JMT). Rich, funky music, a fitting setting for both Harris and the stridently assertive tenor of George Adams.

Craig Harris

⊙ **F-Stops** (1993; Soul Note). An intriguing contrast with Harris's funkier work, this album involves saxophonists John Stubblefield and Hamiet Bluiett in a suite that sees the leader play didjeridu as well as trombone.

DAVID MURRAY

Now Is Another Time (2003; Justin Time). A Latin jazz tour-de-force from saxophonist Murray, who imports trusted sidemen like Harris and baritonist Hamiet Bluiett into a large Cuban ensemble.

Eddie Harris

Tenor saxophone, electric piano, organ, reed trumpet, vocals, composer.

b. Chicago, 20 Oct 1936; d. 5 Nov 1996.

Harris's professional debut was as a pianist with Gene Ammons. In the 1950s he toured all over France and Germany with the 7th Army Symphony Orchestra. Back in Chicago as a civilian, he recorded a single in 1960 of the movie theme "Exodus", and it became a national hit, selling a million copies. This commercial success badly damaged his reputation in the jazz community, and after that Harris was always something of a loner, following his own path and starting trends rather than following them.

During the 1960s he further alienated himself by using rock rhythms and experimenting with electronics – which were anathema to the reactionary purism of the jazz scene. At the Newport jazz festival in 1970 he also astonished the crowd with another of his technical innovations: a trumpet and flugelhorn each played with a reed instead of the usual mouthpiece. Although he patented this idea, and one or two people did use the hybrid instruments, the reed trumpet never really caught on, perhaps largely because its sound and attack lacked the true characteristics of the trumpet. As a result of the prejudice against Harris he rarely, if ever, received any serious critical attention, only the dismissive variety. He was an excellent player, a master of electronics and a prolific composer with a large body of work on record. His influence was more extensive than some people might imagine – the innovative trombonist, George Lewis, for example, cites as one of the major factors in his musical growth the fact that he practised exercises out of Eddie Harris saxophone books. Harris's magnificent composition "Freedom Jazz Dance" was recorded by Miles Davis in the mid-1960s, and has since become part of the repertoire and consciousness of subsequent generations of musicians.

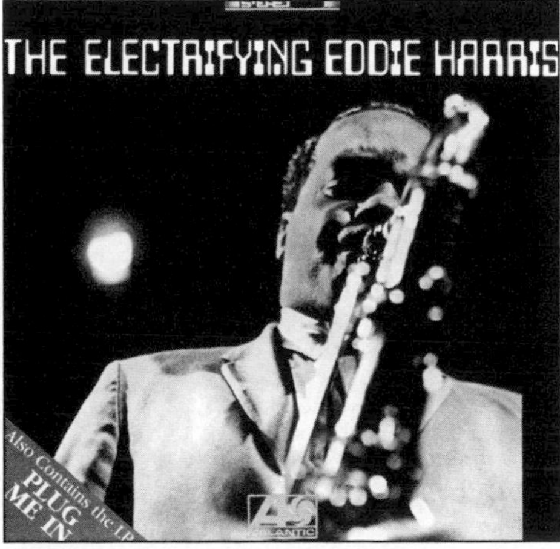

In March 1996, Harris, though suffering from cancer, played a two-week residency in a club in London, UK, accompanied by the young trio of pianist Nikki Yeoh, with bassist Michael Mondesir and drummer Keith Leblanc, and he revelled in their company. That month was his last time in Europe. [IC]

The Electrifying Eddie Harris/Plug Me In (1967/8; Rhino/Atlantic). This double CD set gives some idea of Harris's musical versatility – the first disc showing the clarity and drive of his funky rhythms, and the second pitting him against brass-section backgrounds.

Artist's Choice: The Eddie Harris Anthology (Atlantic). This two-CD anthology offers an even richer fare, with some marvellous tracks from sixteen albums. "Freedom Jazz Dance" is here, and an irreverent version of "Giant Steps" on electric saxophone. And in general Harris boogies along with great bite and panache.

Freedom Jazz Dance (1994; MusicMasters). Harris in the fine jazz company of pianist Jacky Terrasson, bassist George Mraz and drummer Billy Hart. Harris was always underrated as a player by critics, though not by musicians. He was profoundly steeped in the whole jazz tradition and a consummate, highly versatile soloist who loved to play. The quartet here is a joy, and Harris plays his heart out.

➤➤ **Les McCann** *(Swiss Movement).*

Gene Harris

Piano, keyboards.

b. Benton Harbor, Michigan, 1 Sept 1933; d. 16 Jan 2000.

Harris started as a self-taught boogie-woogie specialist; he later played in an army band from 1951–4. He then formed a local group with bassist Andy Simpkins and drummer Bill Dowdy, which became known in New York as the Three Sounds, recording prolifically for Blue Note and others between 1956–74. After personnel and stylistic changes leaning towards jazz-funk, Harris moved in 1977 to Boise, Idaho, gradually re-emerging to play with the Ray Brown trio in the mid-1980s. Thereafter he recorded under his own name and led the Philip Morris Super Band, touring Europe and Japan between 1989–91, and he formed his own quartet in 1991. Drawing on the piano trio and blues traditions, Harris was an eclectic and effervescent performer. [BP]

Gene Harris Trio Plus One (1985; Concord). The renewal of a recording partnership with Stanley Turrentine begun 25 years earlier finds Harris's trio, with Ray Brown and Mickey Roker, rocking New York's Blue Note club.

Donald Harrison

Alto and soprano saxophones, bass-clarinet, composer.

b. New Orleans, 23 June 1960.

Harrison studied under Ellis Marsalis and Alvin Batiste in New Orleans while still at school, and at Berklee College from 1979–82. He worked with Roy Haynes in 1980–81, Jack McDuff in 1981, and then joined Art Blakey, with whom he stayed from 1982–6. As well as recording with the Jazz Messengers, he co-led albums with fellow Messenger Terence Blanchard, with whom he also played in a quintet. Like many American jazzmen of his generation, Harrison has a strong sense of the tradition, for example arranging "When The Saints" for the Blanchard-Harrison album *Discernment* and featuring himself on weighty standards such as "Body And Soul" and "I Can't Get Started". In more recent years, Harrison has shown increasing interest in his New Orleans musical heritage, and has also played regularly in the Afro-Latin band of Eddie Palmieri. But stylistically, he is firmly of the post-Dolphy generation, with a heated tone to his improvisations and an impressive command of high harmonics. [BP]

⦿ **Indian Blues** (1991; Candid). Harrison's bold combination of post-bop saxophone with the music of the New Orleans Indians includes an adaptation of "Cherokee" and four tracks featuring the piano of Dr John (Mac Rebennack). Successfully unclassifiable.

⦿ **Free To Be** (1998; Impulse). A relatively conventional album showing Harrison's mature solo style, mostly in a quartet setting but with guest appearances by guitarist Rodney Jones, trumpeter Brian Lynch and pianists Eddie Palmieri (on one track) and Mulgrew Miller (on four).

➤➤ **Terence Blanchard** *(Eric Dolphy And Booker Little Remembered)*; **Eddie Palmieri** *(Palmas)*.

Jimmy Harrison

Trombone, vocals.

b. Louisville, Kentucky, 17 Oct 1900; d. 23 July 1931.

Jimmy Harrison had varied early experience, including carnival bands (for which he developed a Bert Williams stand-up routine) and occasional trio and duo work which helped to develop his revolutionary trombone technique, often played high up near the trumpet register, fast and melodic and very much in the style of Louis Armstrong. After arriving in New York in 1923 (with Fess Williams's band) he played Ed Small's Sugarcane Club with his best friend June Clark (young "Bill" Basie played the piano), with Duke Ellington briefly, and with a variety of other bands including Elmer Snowden's. In 1927 Harrison joined Fletcher Henderson, was fired for his slow reading, then later re-hired: he became Henderson's star trombone soloist, a funny and likeable cornerman, and close buddy of Coleman Hawkins, who arranged "Singin' In The Rain" and several other songs to spotlight his Bert Williams-style routines. Jack Teagarden and Harrison became inseparable friends: the trombone titans of their generation, they must have been an attractive pair, immaculately suited, easy-going, always laughing and partying. They played together in clubs and rent parties (where Teagarden loved the soul food), often with Coleman Hawkins pumping a piano accompaniment. In 1930, however, Harrison became ill and a year later he died of stomach cancer. He remained a primary influence on black trombonists for ten more years. [DF]

➤➤ **Fletcher Henderson** *(A Study in Frustration)*.

Antonio Hart

Alto saxophone, composer.

b. Baltimore, Maryland, 30 Sept 1968.

Hart began playing the saxophone in elementary school, and continued his musical education at the Baltimore School for the Arts and Berklee College of Music (where he met longtime associate Roy Hargrove), and at Queens College, where he studied under Jimmy Heath. He began his musical career with Latin and jazz gigs in the Boston area, then moved to New York in 1991. Work with Memphis pianist James Williams and with Out Of The Blue followed, but Hart's chief employment was with Hargrove, with whom he not only toured Europe and Japan, but made four Novus albums between 1989–91. He then formed his own quintet, making his recording debut with *For The First Time* for Novus, alongside Hargrove, in 1991. Three more Novus albums followed, including a tribute to Cannonball Adderley and Woody Shaw, featuring associates of the two jazzmen, which appeared in 1992. His last Novus album, *It's All Good* (1995) included more contemporary material, but his finest hour came with *Here I Stand* (titled for Paul Robeson's autobiography), his debut album for the revivified Impulse! label in 1996 (see below). Hart has also recorded with pianists Monty Alexander, Laurent De Wilde, Benny Green and McCoy Tyner, vocalists Freddy Cole and Claire Martin, trombonist Robin Eubanks and drummer Winard Harper. An inventive, thoughtful player, Hart has clear ideas about his artistic goals: "I'm really trying to get to the point where the music reflects what I'm living, where I'm at as an artist. They have a lot of us young musicians making records with nothing but standards and tunes that aren't very personal to us. It's great for study purposes, but it's time for us – this generation – to step out there." His return to recording after four years' self-imposed absence from the scene was a further personal "step out there" (see below). Also heard with the award-winning Dave Holland Big Band in 2002, Hart was appointed full-time professor at Queens College, City University of New York, in 2003, teaching advanced improvisation. [CP/CI]

⦿ **Here I Stand** (1996; Impulse!). It all comes together for Hart on this disc, which is propelled by Freddie Waits's drummer son Nasheet, but also features Shirley Scott on both piano and organ, plus core band-members James Hurt (piano) and John Benitez (bass). The material is taken from all phases of Hart's career, but is bound together by his newfound confidence as a player.

Ama Tu Sonrisa (2001; Enja). An eclectic recording demonstrating world music influences and following on from a period of reflection, re-evaluation and travel, it features pianist Kevin Hays and vocalist Lenora Zenzalai Helm and is shot through, as ever, by Hart's impeccable musicality.

Billy Hart

Drums.

b. Washington, DC, 29 Nov 1940.

Hart's early professional work was with local saxophonist Buck Hill (to whom he returned the favour twenty years later by setting up Hill's album debut), and with singer Shirley Horn. He worked briefly with the Montgomery Brothers in 1961, then with Jimmy Smith from 1964–6, including a European tour, and with Wes Montgomery from 1966–8. He spent time gigging with Eddie Harris, Pharoah Sanders and Marian McPartland, and joined the Herbie Hancock sextet from 1969–73. Known during this period by the name "Jabali", he worked with McCoy Tyner in 1973–4, and with Stan Getz from 1974–7, but also made freelance appearances and recordings with a wide variety of musicians, including visits to Europe. Hart is equally capable of straight-ahead time playing with a creative flair, and of the more impressionistic approach. His wide sensibilities are well illustrated by the album issued under his own name reviewed below. [BP]

Amethyst (1992; Arabesque). As with his earlier and unavailable *Enhance*, Hart has chosen an eclectic personnel to reflect the range of music he can contribute to, with a front-line balancing saxophonist John Stubblefield and violinist Mark Feldman.

Clyde Hart

Piano, arranger.

b. Baltimore, Maryland, 1910; d. 19 March 1945.

Hart played with big bands, including Blanche Calloway's, from 1931–5. He was based in New York after 1936, and recorded with such important soloists as Henry "Red" Allen, Billie Holiday, Stuff Smith, Lionel Hampton, Chu Berry, Roy Eldridge and Lester Young. He replaced Billy Kyle with the John Kirby sextet in 1942, and was working with Tiny Grimes's group when Charlie Parker was added for the latter's first small-band recording in 1944. During the last couple of months before his death from tuberculosis, Hart cut the only discs under his own name, including the first studio appearance of Parker and Gillespie together. An unhackneyed player, he demonstrated the continuity between 1930s jazz and bebop. [BP]

Charlie Parker

Complete Savoy Studio Sessions, Vol. 1 (1944–5; Savoy). Should the CD reissue of Parker's tracks with Tiny Grimes ever be remastered to include three missing piano solos, it will provide the memorial to Hart which so far has to be sought on this LP.

Johnny Hartman

Vocals.

b. Chicago, 13 July 1923; d. 15 Sept 1983.

Studying piano and voice from the age of eight, Hartman gained a vocal scholarship to Chicago Musical College in 1939. Active professionally before army service in World War II, his career was later resumed with the bands of Earl Hines in 1947 and Dizzy Gillespie from 1948–9. He worked thereafter as a single, recording a session backed by Erroll Garner in 1949, followed by several more in the 1950s (some with non-jazz backings) and a 1960s series initiated by the famous album with John Coltrane. The rarity of his late albums reflects his cult status, but his 1980 Grammy-nominated recording *Once In Every Life*, with Joe Wilder, Frank Wess and Billy Taylor, was used on the hypnotic soundtrack of Clint Eastwood's film *The Bridges Of Madison County*, giving him a posthumous best seller. [BP]

John Coltrane And Johnny Hartman (1963; Impulse!). The unbeatable combination of rich-toned ballad singing with the backing of Coltrane at his gentlest remains the high spot of Hartman's recording career. "My One And Only Love", "You Are Too Beautiful" and "Lush Life", with additional obbligatos dubbed in by the saxophonist, are classics of their kind.

Eddie Harvey

Trombone, piano, composer, arranger, educator.

b. Blackpool, UK, 15 Nov 1925.

Harvey, whose mother played the piano and sang, began in traditional jazz, and was a founder member of George Webb's Dixielanders from 1943–6. After National Service he played with Freddy Randall from 1949–50, then graduated to modern jazz, playing with Vic Lewis. He was a founder member of the Johnny Dankworth Seven in 1950, and worked with Dankworth's big band until the mid-1950s. During the later 1950s and the 1960s, he worked with many leading jazz musicians including Don Rendell and Tubby Hayes, and toured with Woody Herman's Anglo-American Herd and the Maynard Ferguson big band. He has written arrangements for many people including Humphrey Lyttelton (in whose band he played piano for a time) and the Jack Parnell Orchestra at Associated Television. Harvey is very active in education, running regular courses and annual summer schools, he has given regular lectures on jazz at the City Literary Institute, London, and from the early 1970s until 1985 he was Assistant Music Master at Haileybury College, Hertfordshire. [IC]

Michael Hashim

Soprano, alto and baritone saxophones.
b. Geneva, New York, 9 April 1956.

Hashim took up saxophone at school, heard Johnny Hodges early on, and teamed up with bassist Phil Flanigan and then guitarist Chris Flory while all three were still in their teens. In 1975 he moved to Providence, Rhode Island, to work with Flory, and thereafter joined the Widespread Depression Orchestra, of which he subsequently assumed leadership. Later the orchestra moved to New York, where Hashim began playing with Benny Carter, Roy Eldridge, Brooks Kerr, Sonny Greer, Eddie Barefield and Jo Jones; he also studied informally with Jimmy Rowles, and formally with Albert Regni. In the 1990s he continued to work busily in the studio and live: as well as playing festivals from Cork to Nice, he toured Britain regularly as a soloist, and in 1992 became the first jazz musician to tour the People's Republic of China. [DF]

⊙ **Lotus Blossom** (1990; Stash). With pianist Mike LeDonne leading the accompanying trio, Hashim here celebrates Billy Strayhorn's compositions with aptitude, passion and creative flare.

Stan Hasselgard

Clarinet.
b. Sundsvall, Sweden, 4 Oct 1922; d. Illinois, 23 Nov 1948.

Åke Stan Hasselgard's early days in Sweden involved work with Gosta Torner, Arthur Osterwall and Simon Brehm amongst others, then in 1947 – having taken his music degree at Uppsala University – he moved to New York. There he sat in with Jack Teagarden, Bud Freeman and others on 52nd Street, and also with modernists such as Charlie Parker, Dizzy Gillespie and Miles Davis. In November 1947 he was invited to appear with Count Basie's rhythm-section at a Gene Norman *Just Jazz* concert and a month later, with the help of Barney Kessel and other friends, recorded four now-legendary sides for Capitol, including "Swedish Pastry". During early 1948 Hasselgard played two concerts with Benny Goodman on the West Coast, after which the two clarinettists formed a septet featuring tenorist Wardell Gray, plus Teddy Wilson, Billy Bauer, Arnold Fishkind, Mel Zelnick and singer Patti Page. By October 1948 Hasselgard was fronting a quintet with Max Roach on drums and planning a further group of his own, but he was then killed in a car crash outside Decatur. He remains a legend, as one of jazz's most elegant clarinettists. [DF]

Stan Hasselgard and Benny Goodman

⊙ **At Click 1948** (Dragon). Air checks of the short-lived Hasselgard-Goodman septet, which never recorded commercially as a result of an AFN ban. Goodman and his protégé are both on peak form, and recording quality is excellent.

Stan Hasselgard

⊙ **The Permanent Hasselgard** (1945–8; Phontastic). Excellent collection of Hasselgard, including early recordings for Dragon and four fine quintet recordings. "A generously filled and respectful memorial to a fine player" (Cook/Morton).

Lennie Hastings

Drums, piano, bandleader.
b. London, 5 Jan 1927; d. 14 July 1978.

Hastings worked around the British post-war modern jazz scene before joining Freddy Randall's band during their Cooks Ferry Inn tenure. A devotee of the style of Cliff Leeman, he moved to Alex Welsh's band in 1954 and stayed with him for nearly twenty years, apart from isolated bandleading spells and stints with Nat Gonella and Johnny Duncan's Blue Grass Boys in the early 1960s. From 1973, when ill health led to his departure from the Welsh outfit, Hastings led his own band, toured with American visitors (including Wild Bill Davison, Ruby Braff and Soprano Summit), broadcast regularly, worked with Fred Hunt's trio and was often to be found at Pizza Express. He collapsed from a stroke in 1978 and died six weeks later. [DF]

➤➤ **Alex Welsh** *(Classic Concert).*

Martin Hathaway

Saxophones, clarinet, flute, piano, vocals, composer, arranger.
b. Chelmsford, Essex, UK, 6 Aug 1969.

Hathaway studied privately and at music school from 1979–87. He was at the London Guildhall School of Music from 1987–91, obtaining a first-class honours degree and a diploma in jazz studies. He played in the Essex Youth Jazz Orchestra from 1984–90, and was lead alto in the Guildhall Jazz Orchestra from 1987–91. He worked with various Michael Garrick groups from 1988 onwards, became a regular member of the London Jazz Orchestra and a regular deputy in the Mike Westbrook orchestra.

Hathaway has led his own quartet since 1989 and his own big band since 1992. An exceptionally promising soloist and an extremely gifted composer/arranger, Hathaway is very active in jazz education – as a professor at the Guildhall School and Goldsmiths College and director of the Essex Youth Jazz Orchestra (since 1991). He also runs his own jazz club in East London. [IC]

Ali Haurand

Bass, composer.
b. Viersen, Germany, 15 Nov 1943.

From 1965–71 Haurand studied music in Essen, and in 1969 started his own trio, playing concerts in Germany, San Sebastian, Belgium and France. He formed the group, Third Eye, in 1970 and, with different personnel (including Kenny Wheeler, Alan Skidmore, Tony Levin and Gerd Dudek), it continued into the mid-1980s. Since 1977 Haurand has been a member of the European Jazz Quintet, and since 1978 of SOH, a trio consisting of Skidmore, Tony Oxley and himself, from time to time augmented to a quartet with either Wheeler or John Surman.

In 1985 Haurand founded the Quintet with Joachim Kuhn and Enrico Rava. He has also worked with many other leading European and American musicians. With his trio he won prizes at the 1969 festivals in San Sebastian and Bilzen (Belgium). In the 1990s he was working as musical consultant for a German television company. He cites bassists Charles Mingus and Jimmy Garrison as his main initial inspiration but is also influenced by John Coltrane and his quartet, Bill Evans and Gil Evans. [IC]

➤➤ **Gerd Dudek** *(After All)*.

Bob Havens

Trombone, vibes.

b. Quincy, Illinois, 3 May 1930.

Havens's early work around Chicago in the mid-1950s was followed by a spell with Ralph Flanagan's orchestra, during which he found himself in New Orleans for a month's residency. He fell in love with the city, moved there in 1956 and joined George Girard's band. When Girard became ill the following year, Havens moved over to join Al Hirt's spectacular group, which had also featured young clarinettist Pete Fountain, by then a featured star with the enormously popular Lawrence Welk orchestra. In 1959, after success with Hirt's much-recorded group, Havens joined Welk too (one of his specialities was a high-speed "Tiger Rag") and stayed for over twenty years, appearing on TV regularly and doubling up with studio work in spare moments. In the 1980s he became first call for the kind of classic Dixieland that Bob Crosby patented (in 1985 he worked with Crosby, Dick Cathcart and Don Goldie) and he still leads his own band, as well as teaching and working as a soloist with high school and college bands. A gifted all-round trombonist, Havens is influenced above all by Jack Teagarden and Lou McGarity. [DF]

➤➤ **Ed Polcer** *(A Salute To Eddie Condon)*.

Dick Hawdon

Trumpet, flugelhorn, bass, mellophone.

b. Leeds, UK, 27 Aug 1927.

Hawdon's brilliant career began post-war in the Yorkshire Jazz Band and Chris Barber's two-trumpet group (his partner was Ben Cohen), and by 1951 he was living in London and developing his style to encompass the modern jazz players he loved: Clifford Brown, Fats Navarro and a Scottish mentor, Jimmy Deuchar. By the middle of the decade he was playing traditional music with the Christie Brothers' Stompers, as well as working with Don Rendell's band and Tubby Hayes's octet, and recording advanced contemporary material with Hayes. After work with Ivor and Basil Kirchin (1956–7), he was featured soloist and then lead trumpet for Johnny Dankworth (1957–63). After this astonishing stylistic development, controversy was created by Hawdon's decision in 1962 to join the traditionalist Terry Lightfoot's Jazzmen, but he ignored the critics and carried on playing as he pleased. In the late 1960s, after another stint with Dankworth and several years playing lead at the Talk of the Town, he became a senior lecturer back home at Leeds College of Music. He also took up double bass, and thereafter made regular appearances at Midlands jazz clubs backing Americans such as Art Farmer. In the mid-1980s he was continuing to double on trumpet and bass, and amongst numerous freelance gigs took part in a TV documentary on the Yorkshire Jazz Band. After retiring from Leeds College early in the 1990s Hawdon concentrated once again on the trumpet, and he remains one of the best and most eclectic trumpeters in British jazz history, though largely inactive in 2003. [DF]

Hampton Hawes

Piano.

b. Los Angeles, 13 Nov 1928; d. 22 May 1977.

Hawes was one of the few influential black musicians to have remained resident on the West Coast of the USA. He began gigging as a teenager with R&B saxophonist Big Jay McNeely, and worked briefly with Charlie Parker in 1947. In the early 1950s Hawes was successfully employed by the figureheads of the budding "West Coast movement", Shorty Rogers and Howard Rumsey's Lighthouse All Stars. After army service in Japan, he formed his own trio, with Red Mitchell on bass, which made a series of impressive albums. Incarcerated in the late 1950s for drug offences and released in 1963 through the executive clemency of President Kennedy, Hawes began recording again for Contemporary but found the jazz scene changed and less welcoming. A privately arranged round-the-world tour in 1967–8 led to Hawes cutting half a dozen albums in Europe and Japan, but on his return to the USA he remained in unwarranted obscurity. He visited Europe again in 1971, and the Montreux festival in 1973, with other Prestige artists (Dexter Gordon and Gene Ammons). The ups and downs of his career were detailed in his short but moving autobiography.

In his debut recording, made in 1947 with Dexter Gordon and Wardell Gray, the germ of Hawes's mature style is quite discernible. His most renowned work in the 1950s found him combining the glittering precision of Bud Powell and Charlie Parker with some of the blues tinge later associated with "funky" pianists. This development ran parallel to the work of Horace Silver at the same period, and indeed Hawes's sense of timing was then very similar to that of Silver, but the Hawes right hand was usually more florid and boppish, influencing Oscar Peterson. On his comeback during the 1960s Hawes adopted some of the then popular mannerisms derived from Bill Evans which, as with his espousal of the electric keyboard in the 1970s, did not mix well with his earlier, eminently percussive approach. He can hardly be overestimated, however, as an important figure in jazz piano history. [BP]

The Trio Vol. 2 (1955–6; Contemporary/OJC). Hawes's regular line-up of the period with Red Mitchell and drummer Chuck Thompson, in casual but intense sessions including "Stella By Starlight", "Round Midnight" and two brilliant blues.

For Real! (1958; Contemporary/OJC). A quartet set with Harold Land and the young Scott LaFaro on material such as Bennie Harris's "Crazeology", plus standards and a couple of Hawes originals. Compare also his three albums with Jim Hall (*All Night Session Vols. 1–3*).

Coleman Hawkins

Tenor saxophone.

b. St Joseph, Missouri, 21 Nov 1901; d. 19 May 1969.

"He's the person who played the tenor saxophone, who woke you up and let you know there was a tenor saxophone", says Lester Young, Hawkins's principal rival for the first thirty years of jazz history. Hawkins created what was, to begin with, an omnipotent vocabulary for the tenor, and for 45 years he maintained and consolidated his seniority.

He was playing to school audiences by the age of twelve, and in his early teens was regularly to be heard in Kansas and travelling at weekends over to Chicago, where he heard pacesetters such as Stomp Evans, Buster Bailey (renowned for his speed), Happy Caldwell, and headlining acts such as Sophie Tucker and Ted Lewis, a Hawkins favourite. In 1921 he joined Mamie Smith's Jazz Hounds, a hit-making touring group; in later years Hawkins claimed that at this period he was so young that he needed a guardian, though in fact he was twenty and, by his own admission, "as big as I am now" – an example of Hawkins's sly habit of lopping years off his age. In 1924 he joined Fletcher Henderson for ten years, and instantly became a star: with his roller-coaster speed he was one of the team of omnipotent Henderson "killers" that included his old idol Buster Bailey and trombonist Jimmy Harrison, who became a close friend. Hawkins dressed in the most expensive clothes, drove the fastest car on Henderson's tours and quickly established himself as the Attila of jazz saxophone, ruthlessly cutting down anyone rash enough to challenge him. His contribution to the unbridled stomping power of Henderson's orchestra was mighty, as demonstrated by an early classic "Stampede". In spare moments the killer also arranged for Henderson's band, including a Bert Williams pastiche of "Singin' In The Rain" for Jimmy Harrison, which, he admitted, "sounded a little different!"

By 1934 he was becoming disillusioned with Henderson, sent a telegram to "Jack Hylton, London, England" (on the advice of June Clark, Henderson's bass player) and on 29 March stepped off the *Ile de France* to begin a five-year tour of Europe in the UK. He played the London Palladium with Hylton's band and for the next five years was to work not only in England but in Holland, France, Denmark (his favourite), Switzerland, Sweden and elsewhere. Away from the American downgrading of his race, Hawkins could cut the dash he felt he deserved, but in 1939 he made his leisurely way back to Chicago. "Fletcher was playing. He knew I was out in the audience and sent a waiter with a note saying, 'Don't you think it's about time the leave of absence is over?' And signed his name at the bottom!" While he was re-establishing his saxophone supremacy at Kelly's Stables on 52nd Street in 1939, Hawkins recorded the side forever to be most associated with his name. "Body And Soul", which he used as a ten-chorus feature at Kelly's, was recorded in a two-chorus abbreviation for RCA Victor, and the record – a prototype of jazz saxophone, with subtly amended changes, graceful swooping improvisations

WILLIAM GOTTLIEB/REDFERNS

Coleman Hawkins

and faultless execution – became a jazz classic to place alongside Armstrong's "West End Blues".

Hawkins's involvement with bebop in the years that followed was confident, swift and all-embracing. Where other musicians, such as Dave Tough or Roy Eldridge, felt inadequate and bruised by the revolution, modern jazz supplied Hawkins with the new harmonic challenges he needed. By 1943 he led a sextet with Don Byas, Thelonious Monk and trumpeter Benny Harris, and he took an active interest in the careers of young musicians such as Fats Navarro, Oscar Pettiford, Max Roach and Dizzy Gillespie. He was also regularly with Norman Granz's Jazz At The Philharmonic from 1946 (with Lester Young), led a quintet with frequent colleague Roy Eldridge and continued to forge a solo career which never suffered real decline. Even in the fashion-conscious 1950s, when Hawkins's heavy-toned, gruff saxophone occasionally seemed to take second place to young Turks such as Stan Getz or Zoot Sims, there was never any serious doubt that he was still the finest exponent of his instrument. In the 1960s, as undeposed king of New York, he was playing hotels and still recording prolifically with much younger men, including Thad Jones and even Sonny Rollins, and beating them at their own game. Even the revolution of rock'n'roll did nothing to shake his aplomb: "rock doesn't sound too bad", he said at the time, "but I don't think the right people are playing it yet". Later in his career, suitably bearded like a prophet, Hawkins continued handing down his huge-toned jazz commandments until in 1969, taciturn and worn thin from a permanent diet of lentil soup and brandy, he died. [DF]

⊙ **Coleman Hawkins 1929–34/1934–7/1937–9/1939–40/1943–4/1944/1944–5/1945** (Classics). Jazz's first great tenorist in an eight-volume chronology (so far) from early beginnings with the Mound City Blue Blowers et al through to his admirable associations with youthful bebop constituents including Monk and Howard McGhee. Almost all the music in between is indispensable.

⊙ **The Complete Recordings 1929–41** (Charly). This six-CD boxed set chronicles Hawkins from his dates with the Mound City Blues Blowers through his years in Europe (with the Ramblers, Michel Warlop, Jack Hylton and many more) via "Body And Soul" up to titles with Metronome All Stars and Count Basie in spring 1941. A full panorama of Hawkins's stylistic development from its headlong earlier years to glorious maturity.

⊙ **Picasso** (1929–49; Giants Of Jazz). A handy budget-price set containing some of the best material included in the above, but moving forward to well-selected titles by Hawkins with Thelonious Monk, Miles Davis and Fats Navarro, plus his classic unaccompanied "Picasso".

⊙ **Body And Soul** (1939–56; RCA Bluebird). A very good collection, including his session with Navarro and J.J. Johnson, the sublime title track, and later five-star examples of the Hawk in flight.

⊙ **Coleman Hawkins: The Bebop Years** (1939–49; Properbox). Comprehensive survey of Hawkins' American recordings after his European sojourn. It begins with "Body And Soul" and moves on to sides (88 in all) with Basie, Feather, JATP, and of course his junior bop partners, including Howard McGhee, Miles Davis, Oscar Pettiford.

⊙ **Hollywood Stampede** (1945; Capitol). This set shows the master in transition, amid a new generation of bop men including Howard McGhee, Oscar Pettiford and Denzil Best.

⊙ **The Bean** (1951–7; Giants Of Jazz). The companion to *Picasso*, this similarly well-selected budget set includes the solo "Foolin' Around", "The Bean Stalks Again" (with Billy Byers's orchestra), four 1957 titles with Oscar Peterson's quartet and more.

⊙ **Coleman Hawkins Encounters Ben Webster** (1957; Verve). A classic on-record meeting between two entirely individual tenor giants, backed by the Oscar Peterson quartet; simply indispensable.

⊙ **Bean And The Boys** (1958 & 64; Le Jazz). Live recordings from two French concerts, with Roy Eldridge, Harry Edison, Vic Dickenson and veteran Hubert Rostaing in the ranks. Good-quality sound.

⊙ **Hawkins! Eldridge! Hodges! Alive At The Village Gate** (1962; Verve). A well-remembered date for Hawkins in fitting company, including his longtime partner Roy Eldridge. Four quartet tracks are included.

➤➤ **Henry "Red" Allen** *(World On A String).*

Erskine Hawkins

Trumpet, bandleader.

b. Birmingham, Alabama, 26 July 1914; d. 12 Nov 1993.

In 1930s America a generation of young trumpeters grew up whose speciality was impersonating Louis Armstrong. One of the best was Erskine Ramsay Hawkins, who had taken up trumpet at thirteen and was soon able to deliver a high-powered parody of Armstrong's showier *tours de force* such as "Shine", with its one hundred top Cs rounded off with a super-F. "That's what Erskine was doing all through the South", remembers Dud Bascomb, who was himself to become featured soloist with Hawkins's big band, which formed from a group based at Alabama State Teachers' College. The "Bama State Collegians", as they were first known, opened at Harlem's Opera House, a vaudeville theatre, on 11 August 1934, worked a variety of clubs thereafter and began recording for Vocalion. After the death of Chick Webb, their manager Moe Gale booked them into the Savoy Ballroom, where they were to take over Webb's old position as unofficial house band. More success followed, including a contract for the prestigious Bluebird label, and throughout the 1940s Hawkins's rocking band, dispensing the same kind of gutbucket swing that Fletcher Henderson had featured at Roseland ten years before, regularly drew record crowds and easily dwarfed more famous names like Count Basie.

A string of successful records – including "Tuxedo Junction" (1939), "After Hours" (1940), "Someone's Rockin' My Dreamboat" (1941) and "Tippin' In" (1945) – bolstered Hawkins's popularity, and his band, featuring Dud Bascomb (trumpet), Haywood Henry (bar) and Avery Parrish (piano), easily survived the big-band decline until 1955, when reduction to a small-group format at last became essential. From 1960 Hawkins led a quartet at the Embers and continued recording, re-forming his big band and working hotels with his small group; in the 1970s he was still playing strong and guested at the 1979 Nice jazz festival. A spectacular technician who, said trumpeter Sammy Lowe, "had the potential to become a legend", Hawkins continued to work sporadically into the 1980s. [DF]

⊙ **Erskine Hawkins 1938–9/39–40/40–41/41–5/46–7/47–9** (Classics). For Hawkins specialists, the ultimate collection though some may prefer to sample the music of this highly able big band fronted by "the twentieth century Gabriel".

Clancy Hayes

Banjo, drums, vocals, composer.

b. Caney, Kansas, 14 Nov 1908; d. 13 March 1972.

The banjo-playing seventh son of a seventh son, Hayes began his career in vaudeville in the early 1920s and from 1928 (as "Bob Sheridan") was presenter for shows such as *Mother's Cakes And Cookies* and *Tune Termites* for NBC Radio, San Francisco. Ten years on he was frontman for Lu Watters's big band, and he remained with Watters for twelve years, all the way through the era of the Yerba Buena Jazz Band. Then, after Bob Scobey broke away from Watters to form his hugely successful Frisco Jazz Band, Hayes's lazy vocalizing and humorous "point material" became central to Scobey's show. With Scobey he recorded more than two hundred titles including, on occasion, his own compositions: two fine examples are "Ten To One It's Tennessee", recorded by no less than Hoagy Carmichael, and the surreal "Huggin' And A-Chalkin'", recorded by both Carmichael and Johnny Mercer. Sadly, Hayes never had a hit record himself, but he continued working for Scobey until 1959 when he finally took up a solo career based in San Francisco and continued regular recording. After ten well-recorded solo years he died of cancer: his last record, *Mr Hayes Goes To Washington* with Tommy Gwaltney, was almost as good as anything from his earlier catalogue. [DF]

➤➤ **Bob Scobey** *(Frisco Band Featuring Vocals By Clancy Hayes).*

Harry Hayes

Alto saxophone.

b. London 23 March 1909; d. 17 March 2002.

Harry Hayes, widely regarded as one of Britain's greatest saxophonists, began on soprano saxophone at eleven, and by sixteen he was playing professionally. In December 1927 he joined Fred Elizalde's historic Anglo-American band at the Savoy Hotel, London, alongside Adrian Rollini, Fud Livingstone and Chelsea Quealey. Rapidly achieving widespread recognition as a young virtuoso, Hayes worked for Sidney Kyte, Billy Mason, Spike Hughes, Sydney Lipton, "Hutch", and toured with Louis Armstrong in 1932 in Billy Mason's band.

Throughout the 1930s he also played as lead alto with Maurice Winnick, Harry Roy, Sydney Lipton and Geraldo. In 1944, after completing his military service, Hayes began recording for EMI with small groups whose members included Kenny Baker, George Shearing, George Chisholm, Tommy Whittle and Norman Stenfalt. Later he opened a music shop on Shaftesbury Avenue in London's West End. Hayes also taught extensively, published and sold his own "hot choruses" for students including British clarinettist/saxophonist Roy Willox. From 1952 he played lead for Kenny Baker's Dozen and also led his own groups for London nightclub and theatre work, including a lengthy residency from 1957 to 1965 at Winston's Club, Mayfair, before retiring to run instrument and record shops in Fulham.

Hayes occasionally reappeared to play during the 1990s and enterprisingly reissued all his EMI recordings (1944–47) on CD in this period. [DF]

⊙ **Harry Hayes And His Band, Vols. 1 and 2** (1995; Harry Hayes Records). These two CDs include all of Hayes' EMI output of the l940s. This is dashing and enterprising British jazz of the highest order, and some of trumpeter Kenny Baker's best recorded work.

Louis Hayes

Drums.

b. Detroit, Michigan, 31 May 1937.

Hayes worked with the Detroit-based Yusef Lateef quintet at eighteen in 1955–6, and then toured with Horace Silver from 1956–9. There was also freelance recording during this period, including with John Coltrane and Cecil Taylor. He was a member of the Cannonball Adderley quintet from 1959–65, until joining the Oscar Peterson trio from 1965–7, returning for a second spell in 1971–2. He co-led the Jazz Communicators group with Freddie Hubbard and Joe Henderson in 1967–8, and later worked with the Hubbard quintet in 1970–71. Then he co-led a quintet in 1975–6 with Junior Cook, who was succeeded by Woody Shaw in 1976–7, and he later co-led a quartet with Joe Farrell in 1983–4. As well as continued freelance work, he toured with the McCoy Tyner trio in 1985 and with Freddie Hubbard in 1994. An alert and driving accompanist since his earliest professional days, Hayes rapidly matured into a versatile and dependable group player whose work is consistently exciting. [BP]

⊙ **Ichi-Ban** (1976; Timeless). A strong quintet session, with added percussion, this features Junior Cook and Woody Shaw on Shaw's "The Moontrane" and Monk's "Pannonica".

➤➤ **Horace Silver** *(Blowin' The Blues Away).*

Tubby Hayes

Tenor saxophone, flute, vibraphone, composer.

b. London, 30 Jan 1935; d. 8 June 1973.

Tubby (Edward) Hayes started playing the violin at the age of eight, changed to tenor at twelve and

JAK KILBY

Tubby Hayes

turned professional at fifteen. In 1951 he joined Kenny Baker and later played with the big bands of Ambrose, Vic Lewis and Jack Parnell. He led his own octet from April 1955 to October 1956, touring the UK with it. Encouraged by Victor Feldman, he began playing vibes in December 1956. With Ronnie Scott he co-led the Jazz Couriers from 1957–9, and he toured Germany with Kurt Edelhagen in 1959. His international reputation grew rapidly, and he was the first British contemporary soloist to appear at regular intervals in the USA: he played at the Half Note, New York, in 1961, 1962 and 1964, and also played at the Boston Jazz Workshop in 1964 and Shelly Manne's Manne-Hole, Los Angeles, in 1965.

In London he led his own big band, for which he did most of the writing, and had his own TV series in 1961–2 and 1963. He deputized for Paul Gonsalves with the Ellington orchestra at the Royal Festival Hall in February 1964. With Mingus, Brubeck and others, he appeared in the film *All Night Long* (1961) and with his own quintet in *The Beauty Jungle* (1964) and Dr Terror's *House Of Horrors* (1965). He played at many major festivals in Europe including Antibes in 1962, Lugano in 1963, Vienna (with Friedrich Gulda) in 1964 and 1965, and Berlin in 1964. In the later 1960s he underwent open-heart surgery, and then was out of action from 1969–71, when he began working again. He died while undergoing a second heart operation.

Tubby was a virtuoso performer on tenor and flute, an excellent vibist, and a composer/arranger of rare talent. He could play with great sensitivity, and his technique and knowledge were such that he could compete on equal terms with most US musicians: he twice recorded as leader of all-American groups which included Clark Terry, Roland Kirk and James Moody. He also had the energy and courage to assert himself and his music in a basically unsympathetic environment – which the UK certainly was as far as "modern" jazz was concerned. He was a charismatic big-band leader, and he also led some distinguished small groups including two particularly fine quartets: one in the late 1950s which included Terry Shannon (piano), Jeff Clyne (bass) and Phil Seamen or Bill Eyden (drums), and one in the later 1960s with Mick Pyne (piano), Ron Mathewson (bass) and Tony Levin (drums). His early influences were Charlie Parker, Sonny Rollins and Stan Getz. [IC]

⊙ **For Members Only** (1967; Mastermix). This features the great quartet Hayes led when he returned to playing after open-heart surgery, with pianist Mick Pyne, bassist Ron Mathewson and that doyen of the drums, Tony Levin. The music is taken from three radio broadcasts with Hayes on flute as well as tenor saxophone, and the programme includes a couple of his own compositions. Tubby was living on borrowed time and the rhythm-section seemed to feel that and give their all – either in quiet intensity or gargantuan swing.

⊙ **Live 1969** (Harlequin). Levin is replaced on drums by Spike Wells, and the tracks are drawn from a couple of live gigs. Hayes lacked the Dionysian energy of his pre-operation days, and spread the solo space much more democratically among his group.

Dick Haymes

Vocals.

b. Buenos Aires, 13 Sept 1916; d. 28 March 1980.

After replacing Frank Sinatra in Harry James's band in 1941, Haymes swept to solo stardom with a string of hits in conjunction with starring appearances in successful movie musicals such as *State Fair* (1945) and the less memorable *Do You Love Me?* (1946 with Harry James). Like Sinatra, his voice was a perfect instrument, full of tonal quality and an appealing vulnerability, but Haymes never quite equalled Sinatra's charisma, and in the 1950s his career failed to maintain the impetus of his predecessor's, although he recorded for Decca and Capitol with reasonable commercial (and complete musical) success.

Into the 1970s he still appeared regularly on the US cabaret circuit (including a recorded date at the Coconut Grove with Les Brown's band), and made excellent albums with pianist Loonis McGlohon, but he remained a connoisseur's figure rather than turning into an icon as Sinatra did.

Graham Haynes

Cornet.

b. Hollis, Queens, New York 16 Sept 1960.

Graham Haynes is the son of bebop legend, drummer Roy Haynes. He began playing cornet at the age of thirteen, having been surrounded by jazz musicians throughout his entire childhood. He studied with trumpeter Dave Burns (a Gillespie-alumnus and fine, underrated player), studying classical music at Queens College and playing in church. In the early 80s, Haynes formed Five Elements with alto saxophonist Steve Coleman, and he worked in various M-Base groups. Haynes moved to Paris in the early 90s, when he began recording as a leader; early work includes *What Time It Be!* (1990; Muse) and *Nocturne Parisian* (1992; Muse). At this time, he also made some wonderful recordings with the Ed Blackwell Project, *What It Is?* (1993; Enja) and *What It Be Like?* (1994; Enja), partnered with great saxophonist Carlos Ward; these are perhaps the best straight jazz setting in which to hear him. Haynes's trajectory shifted as the decade moved along, and he has of late embraced various musics from around the world – hear the Indian classical music on *The Griot's Footsteps* (1994; Antilles), check out the uneven avant-pop of *Transition* (1995; Antilles) and *Tones For The 21st Century* (1996; Verve) and the space-age Wagner of *BPM* (Knitting Factory). A regular contributor to bassist/producer Bill Laswell's projects, Haynes has latterly brought his horn and electronics to recordings by Pharoah Sanders and Lucky Peterson. [JC]

Roy Haynes

Drums.

b. Roxbury, Massachusetts, 13 March 1925.

Haynes's parents were originally from Barbados, and he was taught by Herbert Wright, former drummer with Jim Europe. He worked in Boston with the Sabby Lewis band, and with Frankie Newton and Pete Brown in the early 1940s. He toured with Luis Russell from 1945–7 and the Lester Young sextet from 1947–9. In New York he gigged with Kai Winding in 1949, and recorded with him, Bud Powell and others. He joined the Charlie Parker quintet in 1949–50, whose rhythm-section also worked with Wardell Gray and Stan Getz. After a hiatus, he became the regular drummer for Sarah Vaughan from 1953–8, and then spent 1958 free-lancing with Miles Davis, Lee Konitz and Thelonious Monk. In the next few years he led his own trio and quartet, and also appeared with George Shearing, Lennie Tristano, Kenny Burrell and Getz in 1961, and with Coltrane in 1961 and 1963. He toured regularly with Getz from 1965–7 and with the Gary Burton quartet in 1967 and 1968. He then led his own Hip Ensemble for many years, including such players as George Adams and Hannibal Peterson in 1972, Ralph Moore in the mid-1980s, and Craig Handy from 1989. He also recorded and toured internationally with Chick Corea in 1981 and 1984 and Pat Metheny in 1989–90. He was awarded the Danish Jazzpar prize in 1994, and again recorded and toured with Corea in 1996 in a tribute to Bud Powell. Since then, he has continued leading his own groups into the twenty-first century. [BP]

⊙ **We Three** (1958; New Jazz/OJC). A regular partnership with Phineas Newborn sparks this trio, with the addition of Paul Chambers, who take in the blues classic "After Hours" as well as Newborn's "Sugar Ray".

⊙ **When It's Haynes It Roars** (1992; Dreyfus). Haynes's quartet with Craig Handy and Dave Kikoski in splendid form on a programme of jazz and song standards, which opens with the calypso "Brown Skin Gal" and ends with a jazz version of Jolson's "Anniversary Waltz".

J.C. Heard

Drums.

b. Dayton, Ohio, 8 Oct 1917; d. 27 Sept 1988.

J.C. (James Charles) Heard's topline career began in 1939 with Teddy Wilson's band, after which he worked with Benny Carter (1942), Cab Calloway (1942–5) and his own sextet (1946–7). From 1946–53 he was regularly with Norman Granz's Jazz At The Philharmonic and then moved to Japan to lead his own band, which included for a while the Japanese pianist Toshiko. In 1957 he returned to New York, where he worked, played with Coleman Hawkins's quintet (co-led by Roy Eldridge) and renewed acquaintance with JATP, as well as gigging with society leader Lester Lanin. From 1961 he worked with Teddy Wilson again for a year, then, after a spell with pianist Dorothy Donegan, led bands in Las Vegas and Detroit. In the 1970s and 1980s Heard continued to lead an all-star band and to tour. While never achieving the international name of a Jo Jones or Gene Krupa, Heard – rather like Gus Johnson – was a graceful drummer who knew every inch of his art, and after the death of Jo Jones he was the keeper of a musical flame that at one time threatened to expire. [DF]

➤➤ **Ben Webster** *(King Of The Tenors)*; **Lester Young** *(The President Plays)*.

Albert "Tootie" Heath

Drums.

b. Philadelphia, 31 May 1935.

The younger brother of Jimmy and Percy Heath, Albert moved to New York in 1957, making his record debut with fellow Philadelphian John Coltrane. From 1958–60 he toured with J.J. Johnson, and then had trio gigs with Cedar Walton and Bobby Timmons in 1961. He emigrated to Europe in 1965, working with George Russell and pianist Friedrich Gulda, and had a residency with Kenny Drew in Copenhagen in 1967–8. Returning to the USA, he became the original drummer of the Herbie Hancock sextet in 1968–9, then joined the Yusef Lateef quartet from 1970–4. He recorded in Copenhagen with Kenny Drew and Anthony Braxton in 1974, remaining in Europe for a year before joining the Heath Brothers group in 1975. He left the group in

1978 for further freelance work, rejoining them from time to time, and he played some dates with the Modern Jazz Quartet in the mid-90s following the death of Connie Kay. Also a composer in his own right, Heath is a dynamic and driving drummer who has developed the Kenny Clarke style of discreet directness. Never unduly attracting attention to himself, he is extremely versatile and supportive in whatever musical situation he encompasses. [BP]

➤➤ **Dexter Gordon** *(Both Sides Of Midnight).*

Jimmy Heath

Tenor and soprano saxophones, flute, composer, arranger.

b. Philadelphia, 25 Oct 1926.

Heath played on alto with Nat Towles in the mid-1940s and with the Howard McGhee sextet in 1947–8. He wrote for and led his own big band in Philadelphia in 1948–9, though it was also briefly fronted by Howard McGhee in New York, and then joined Dizzy Gillespie in 1949–50. Heath took up freelance writing and recording, now on tenor, including work for Miles Davis in 1953. During an absence from playing he did further writing for Chet Baker in 1956 and Art Blakey in 1957. On his return he worked for Davis, Kenny Dorham and Gil Evans, all in 1959, and began making albums under his own name as well as writing for others. He had recording and gigging partnerships with Milt Jackson and Art Farmer from the mid-1960s, and did much educational work in college and for the Jazzmobile project. He was a member of the Heath Brothers group for several years from 1975, and continued composing and arranging, for example for his new big band, in the 1990s. From 1987–1998 he taught at New York's Queens College.

Jimmy's excellence as a player was first noticed on alto in the late 1940s, when he was known in Philadelphia as "Little Bird". While extremely competent on soprano and flute, he is most effective on tenor, and his tough post-bop style is a match for many better-known players. His playing, however, has frequently been overshadowed by arranging which, whether for big band or quintet, is always able to draw the best from the resources available. Among the many Heath tunes recorded by other musicians, "C.T.A." and "Gingerbread Boy" were both used by Miles Davis and have since become standards. Jimmy's son, percussionist Mtume, also worked with Miles Davis in the 1970s and is now a successful producer of soul and funk records. [BP]

⊙ **Really Big!** (1960; Riverside/OJC). A small big band premieres Jimmy's "Big P" (dedicated to brother Percy, who is in attendance) and features the Adderley brothers on such tunes as "Green Dolphin Street" and "Dat Dere".

⊙ **You've Changed** (1991; Steeplechase). Heath leads a quartet with Albert Heath and former Heath Brothers guitarist Tony Purrone, beginning with "Soul Eyes" and working back to Kenny Dorham's 1940s classic "Prince Albert".

Percy Heath

Bass, cello.

b. Wilmington, North Carolina, 30 April 1923.

Percy Heath only began serious study of music in 1946 after air force service. He worked alongside his younger brother Jimmy in the Howard McGhee sextet and big band in 1947–8, then freelanced in New York with Miles Davis, Fats Navarro and J.J. Johnson. He joined the Dizzy Gillespie sextet from 1950–52, and followed that by freelance gigging and recording with Milt Jackson, Miles Davis, Clifford Brown, Thelonious Monk, Charlie Parker and many others. He was a founder member of the Modern Jazz Quartet (MJQ) in 1952, staying until 1974, but during this period he also recorded and did occasional gigs with Jimmy Heath. Then he worked with Sarah Vaughan in 1975 and the Heath Brothers band from 1975–82. He rejoined the MJQ in 1981, and in the 1990s revived the Heath Brothers.

Although the pattern of his career has caused him to be unfairly pigeonholed, "Big P" (the name of Jimmy Heath's tune dedicated to him) was and is a superb bass player. All the basic jazz virtues of relaxation and buoyancy come across in his straightahead playing which, whether with the MJQ or others, reveals considerable admiration for Ray Brown. In addition, the demands made by the more ambitious aspects of MJQ's repertoire not only brought the bass into greater prominence, without straining its traditional vocabulary, but drew particularly fine performances from Percy. [BP]

➤➤ **Miles Davis** *(Walkin'; Bags' Groove);* **John Lewis** *(Django).*

Ted Heath

Trombone, bandleader.

b. London, 30 March 1900; d. 18 Nov 1969.

Britain's most celebrated bandleader, Heath took up the trombone at fourteen and in his early years worked with Bert Firman, Jack Hylton (1925–7), Ambrose (1927–35), Sid Lipton and Geraldo. He first assembled an orchestra for BBC broadcasts in 1944, but began serious bandleading in 1945; a year later his orchestra played for the British film musical London Town directed by Tutti Camarata which helped to finance the organization. Premier British musicians such as Kenny Baker and Jack Parnell headed the band in its first years; later replaced by two further generations of star sidemen: Bobby Pratt, Tommy Whittle, Henry Mackenzie, Ronnie Chamberlain, Don Lusher, Roy Willox, Ronnie Verrell. Along with later newcomers such as trumpeter Tony Fisher, they were all with Heath's orchestra during its fifteen years of maximum success (which only lapsed with the emergence of rock'n'roll, and the Beatles in particular).

His series of Sunday night concerts at the London Palladium (which began in 1945) became legendary in British jazz circles – the one hundredth was recorded by Decca in February 1954. Regular BBC broadcasting and hit records such as "Hot Toddy" and "Swingin' Shepherd Blues" helped maintain the band's reputation (and enhance its finances), and so did Heath's forward-thinking policies – at various times, for example, he recorded Fats Waller's *London Suite* in orchestral form, employed Tadd Dameron as staff arranger, and produced an album of the ingenious compositions of Raymond Scott.

The adventurousness of Heath and his superb team of staff arrangers (including at various times Reg Owen, Johnny Keating and Alan Bristow) ensured that the band's output stayed fresh and challenging. After the relaxation of the Musicians' Union restrictions on Anglo-American exchanges in 1956 the Heath band visited America regularly from that year. Heath insisted on perfectionism in his musicians, demanding that "improvised" solos be repeated note for note, night by night, and refusing to tolerate sloppiness in performance or appearance. This naturally placed pressure on his sidemen, but those who thrived on the team spirit within the organization contributed to a band that is now generally recognized as the best of its kind ever to play in Britain.

Heath ceased bandleading following a stroke in 1964, but his orchestra continued performing (amongst others with singer Tom Jones) under the leadership of Ralph Dollimore and others until 1979 when trombonist Don Lusher (a longtime Heath protégé) took over until the orchestra's final concert in December 2000. [DF]

⊙ **Listen To My Music** (1944–6; Hep). Interesting and valuable 25-track survey of Heath's formative years, studded with the solos of cornermen Kenny Baker, Jack Parnell and Norman Stenfalt. Tracks from *London Town* are here plus ten more rarities, originally issued as Baker's orchestra and the Brass Hats.

⊙ **Listen To My Music** (1944–50; ASV). Some duplication with the above on early tracks, but valuable nonetheless for Heath's adaptation of Waller's "London Suite" (in five movements) and two of Tadd Dameron's arrangements, "Lyonia" and "Euphoria". It's worth noting that a great deal of Heath's later output is currently being re-released on the Vocalion label.

Dick Heckstall-Smith

Tenor and soprano saxophones.

b. Ludlow, Shropshire, UK, 26 Sept 1934.

A pioneer in his 1960s commuting between jazz and blues and in his 1980s interest in so-called world musics, Dick Heckstall-Smith is a crucially important, if relatively unsung, figure in UK jazz-related music. After studying at Cambridge University, becoming co-leader of the university jazz band in 1954, and touring Switzerland with it in 1956, he immersed himself in the London jazz scene, joining clarinettist Sandy Brown's band in 1958 and collaborating with a great many of the capital's musicians, including trumpeter Bert Courtley and drummer Ginger Baker. After an eighteen-week engagement with the Ronnie Smith quintet at Butlin's in Filey in 1958, Heckstall-Smith freelanced until 1962, when he joined Alexis Korner's Blues Incorporated. The following year, he formed the Graham Bond Organization with Bond, Ginger Baker and Jack Bruce, and in 1967 he joined John Mayall's Bluesbreakers. From August 1968 until November 1971, he was a member of Jon Hiseman's jazz-rock band Colosseum, embarking on a solo career thereafter. In 1972, he formed Manchild, but left music to study for a social sciences degree in 1973–6. In the late 1970s, he formed Big Chief, Tough Tenors and made occasional appearances with the Famous Blues Blasters, a group which became Mainsqueeze in 1981, and toured Europe with Bo Diddley in 1983. From the mid-1980s onwards, Heckstall-Smith became a galvanizing force in UK jazz, employing many young musicians such as tenor player Ed Jones in his sextet DHSS, and playing with Julian Bahula in Electric Dream. In the late 1990s, Colosseum re-formed and toured Germany and the UK with their original line-up (guitarist Clem Clempson, singer Chris Farlowe and bassist Mark Clarke alongside Heckstall-Smith and Hiseman), and produced an album, *Bread And Circuses* (Cloud Nine; 1998). Heckstall-Smith also played with the Hamburg Blues Band, a quintet that utilized his baritone and electric-saxophone playing skills, and recorded an album, *Rollin'* (Newmusic; 1999). Another blues project, *Blues And Beyond* (2001; Eagle), featured such star cohorts as Jack Bruce, Peter Green and John Mayall, and an incarnation of DHSS featuring ex-luminaries was heard at the London Jazz Festival as recently as 2003. [CP/CI]

⊙ **Woza Nasu** (1990; Aura). Features Heckstall-Smith alongside a galaxy of young UK talent, including Ed Jones, Ike Leo, Frank Tontoh, etc, in a bluesy, eclectic mix of styles liberally embellished with percussion. Recently reissued on Voiceprint.

⊙ **Live 1990** (1990; L+R). Collaboration with longtime partner John Etheridge (guitar), bassist Rainer Glas and the late Joe Nay (drums) recorded in Erlangen.

⊙ **Obsession Fees** (1992; R&M). Same as above, but with Evert Fraterman on drums and Chris Beier on piano.

⊙ **Celtic Steppes** (1995; 33 Records). A 20-piece band, representing all styles (and generations) of UK jazz, negotiate an exhilarating suite that draws on Celtic traditional music as well as on contemporary jazz and blues.

Neal Hefti

Composer, arranger; also trumpet.

b. Hastings, Nebraska, 29 Oct 1922.

Hefti's teenage arrangements were bought by black bandleader Nat Towles in the late 1930s. He wrote for Earl Hines in the early 1940s, and then both played and wrote for several bands including, briefly, Charlie Barnet in 1942 and Woody Herman from 1944–6. He then wrote for the short-lived Charlie Ventura big band in 1946, Harry James in 1948–9 and for Count Basie from 1950–62. In 1951 he also started recording under his own name and leading a band for live appearances, featuring his vocalist wife Frances Wayne. By the late 1950s he had become involved full-time in writing for television and films. Before this, however, his work for the Basie band (especially pieces such as "Whirlybird" and "Li'l Darlin'") made him one of the best-known non-playing arrangers and the model for many lesser writers such as Sammy Nestico. He also wrote the rather banal "Repetition" (1947), which went into the repertoire of the Charlie Parker with strings group. [BP]

➤➤ **Count Basie** *(The Complete Atomic Mr. Basie)*; **Woody Herman** *(The Thundering Herds)*.

Mark Helias

Bass, electric bass.

b. Brunswick, New Jersey, 1 Oct 1950.

Bassist Mark Helias began studying bass relatively late, at the age of twenty. He studied music at Yale University in New Haven, Connecticut, where he was an important member of the mid-70s scene, playing with trumpeter Leo Smith, pianist Anthony Davis and percussionist Gerry Hemingway, among others. Possessed of a deep, woody sound and rock-solid time, Helias established himself as one of the best bassists of his generation, turning in stellar recordings with Anderson and drummer Barry Altschul and with Anderson and Hemingway as BassDrumBone. He's also doubled on electric bass in the funky group Slikophonics. An active session musician, playing in various groups led by Anthony Braxton, Muhal Richard Abrams and many others, Helias began a string of excellent records featuring his own writing on the Enja label in the mid-80s; these include *Split Image* (1984), *The Current Set* (1987) and *Desert Blue* (1989), *Loopin' The Cool* (see below) and *New School* (2001) featuring a new trio Open Loose comprising saxist Tony Malaby and drummer Tom Rainey. A recent highlight however was *Fictionary* (1998; GMR), documenting a European festival appearance of a Helias-led quartet featuring Ellery Eskalin. He has also written for symphony orchestra and worked with performers, dancers, and film- and video-makers. His long relationship with drummer Edward Blackwell produced some fine music, including two quartet dates on Enja, and he has played periodically with Cecil Taylor. [JC]

⊙ **Loopin' The Cool** (1994; Enja). A glorious quintet date with tenor saxophonist Ellery Eskelin, violinist Regina Carter and twin percussion entourage of Epizio Bangoura on djembe and Tom Rainey on traps. As well as spotlighting his great timing and improvisational finesse, these ten tunes give a good sense of Helias's talents as a composer and arranger.

Gerry Hemingway

Drums, percussion.

b. New Haven, Connecticut, 1955.

Gerry Hemingway

Gerry Hemingway studied at Wesleyan College and Yale, though his approach to multiple percussion is largely self-taught. In New Haven during the mid-70s he began collaborating with trombonist George Lewis, pianist Anthony Davis and trumpeter Leo Smith, and in 1978 he established his record label Auricle, on which he released several LPs including Oahspe, with trombonist Ray Anderson and bassist Mark Helias; this trio became known as BassDrumBone and recorded for the Italian Soul Note label. On Auricle, Hemingway also made his first solo percussion LP *Soloworks*, which documented his developing ideas about time and extended technique. While he often utilizes "unpulsed" percussion and explores textures, Hemingway also cites Art Blakey as a key influence, and in his confident time-playing the connection is evident. Hemingway is a frequent collaborator with pianist Marilyn Crispell, with whom he played in Anthony Braxton's breathtaking early-1980s quartet, and he plays with a trio featuring pianist Georg Gräwe and cellist Ernst Reijseger. The Gerry Hemingway quintet (which included Reijseger, trombonist Wolter Wierbos, reedsman Michael Moore and bassist Mark Dresser), active through the late 80s and 90s, was arguably Hemingway's ideal outfit, incorporating his strong, multi-sectional compositions with his highly detailed percussion work. Dresser, another Braxton veteran and a long-term sparring partner of Hemingway, is part of his current quartet, with tenor saxophonist Ellery Eskelin and usually either Ray Anderson or Robin Eubanks on trombone, and together they have recorded a string of acclaimed albums. Hemingway's music now moves in many directions. He has confidently branched out with solo performances that augment his percussion with sampled birdsong and similarly exotic colours. In 2002 he even turned his hand to songwriting, recording an album of songs with an unlikely line-up that included John Butcher and Thomas Lehn. [JC]

⊙ **Acoustic Solo Works; Electro-Acoustic Solo Works** (1996; Random Acoustics). Two separate discs focusing on Hemingway's work for unaccompanied percussion since the mid-80s; detailed notes on various, varied compositions and concepts exploring electronics and traditional drumset.

Julius Hemphill

Alto saxophone, composer.

b. Fort Worth, Texas, 24 Jan 1938; d. 2 April 1995.

Hemphill studied clarinet in the early 1950s and began his professional life with various Texan bands, and with Ike Turner. In 1968 he moved to St Louis, becoming a member of BAG (Black Artists Group) with Lester Bowie and Oliver Lake. In the early 1970s he played with Anthony Braxton in Chicago, and worked in Paris and Sweden. Hemphill was also something of a lyricist and poet, and in 1972 he presented his *Kawaida*, a collage of instrumental music, voices, dance and drama, at Washington University, St Louis. In 1977 he was a co-founder of the World Saxophone Quartet, with Hamiet Bluiett, Oliver Lake and David Murray. This group built up a substantial international following in the 1980s, appearing at major festivals all over the world. Hemphill left in 1990, but continued playing and recording until his death. [IC]

⊙ **Flat Out Jump Suite** (1980; Black Saint). Hemphill, with trumpeter Olu Dara, cellist Abdul Wadud and percussionist Warren Smith, creates some intensely quiet acoustic music of great subtlety and warmth.

⊙ **Julius Hemphill Big Band** (1988: Elektra Musician). Hemphill did the composing and arranging for this sixteen-piece band, which includes several players on the cutting edge of the music – John Purcell, John Stubblefield, Bill Frisell and Ronnie Burrage.

⊙ **Fat Man And The Hard Blues** (1991; Black Saint). Hemphill composes here for a saxophone sextet, with conspicuous success.

➤➤ **World Saxophone Quartet** *(Point of No Return).*

Bobby Henderson

Piano, trumpet.

b. New York, 16 April 1910; d. 9 Dec 1969.

A brilliant and very underrated pianist, Henderson began playing piano at parties and at Pod's and Jerry's Club in New York, before meeting Billie Holiday, with whom he struck up a close musical and personal relationship (for a short time they were engaged, but it was called off in December 1934). Thereafter Henderson remained in semi-obscurity until John Hammond recorded him in 1956, after which he appeared at the 1957 Newport jazz festival and recorded for Chiaroscuro. [DF]

Eddie Henderson

Trumpet, flugelhorn, composer.

b. New York, 26 Oct 1940.

Henderson studied trumpet at school from 1950–54 and then theory and trumpet at San Francisco Conservatory from 1954–7. From 1958–61 he served in the air force. Henderson was encouraged by Miles Davis to take an interest in jazz, but from 1961–4 he studied at the University of California, Berkeley, graduating with a BSc in zoology; from 1964–8 he was at Howard University, Washington, DC, graduating in medicine. During the summer vacations, however, he played with John Handy. In 1968 he played with Handy and Philly Joe Jones, and from 1970–73 with Herbie Hancock's sextet, recording, touring internationally and playing major festivals. He also worked with Pharoah Sanders, Joe Henderson and others. In 1973 he played for six months with Art Blakey's Jazz Messengers. Since 1974 he has led his own groups, and he recorded a series of albums as leader for Capitol Records. He has continued to work in his medical capacity both as a general practitioner and as a psychiatrist. In 1991 he toured with Billy Harper, and in 1992 he made a great contribution to Mulgrew Miller's album *Hand In Hand*. [IC]

⊙ **Dark Shadows** (1995; Milestone). Henderson's daughter, whom he'd not seen for fifteen years, turned up at the studio, giving the session an extraordinary emotional charge. Henderson's trumpet work, particularly with the harmon mute, is intensely affecting, and his sextet – vibes, piano, bass, drums and percussion –were also wonderfully concentrated on ten tracks of varied material.

➤➤ **Billy Harper** *(Live On Tour In The Far East, Vol. 2);* **Mulgrew Miller** *(Hand In Hand).*

Fletcher Henderson

Piano, arranger, composer.

b. Cuthbert, Georgia, 18 Dec 1897; d. 28 Dec 1952.

Fletcher Henderson went to New York in 1920 with hopes of a career in chemistry, but in 1921 took a job as recording manager for Black Swan, a black record label owned by Harry Pace. By 1923 he was well known for the organized, no-nonsense fashion in which he made sense of the material handed to him by a succession of blues singers (from Bessie Smith on) who recorded for the label. More than just an administrator, he was a highly skilled musician with a shrewd eye for talent and a gift for leadership, and he had his eye on a big band.

In 1924 he auditioned for the Club Alabam, assumed leadership of the band there and then took up residency at New York's Roseland with a band which, by the year's end, contained an A-team of soloists including Coleman Hawkins, Buster Bailey, Charlie "Big" Green and Louis Armstrong. Though just up from Chicago, Armstrong survived with the super-confident city-slicker Hendersonians on talent and a sense of humour, but you had to be very good to play with Fletcher Henderson, as Pee Wee Russell found out one night when he sat in for Coleman Hawkins. "My God, those scores. They were written in six flats, eight flats – I never saw anything like it! Buster Bailey was next to me and after a couple of numbers I told him, 'Man, I came up here to have a good time, not to work. Where's Hawkins?' " Yet the Fletcher Henderson band never sounded academic. It was a powerhouse rhythm machine which delivered a beat that could drive dancers to exhaustion.

As time went on the band played and recorded in a more disciplined fashion (though for Hawkins it lost too much of its stomp) and also broadened its approach with more sophisticated arrangements by Henderson himself, Benny Carter and others, and new material swapped with bands such as Jean Goldkette's and the Casa Lomans. But Henderson had problems to contend with, notably personnel changes and, more seriously, a car accident in 1928 in which he was badly injured. Prior to the crash he and wife Leora had run the band independently of agents, hustling the night away; afterwards he seemed to slow up. By the mid-1930s Henderson was working in a variety of provincial venues but was better known as a staff arranger for Benny Goodman, whom he joined briefly on piano in 1939. Through the 1940s he still ran bands around New York and Chicago, arranged for lots of newer outfits, and by 1950 had a sextet at New York's Café Society. That year he suffered a stroke; Benny Goodman kept his name before the public with benefits and appeals, but Henderson died a couple of years later, at 55. [DF]

⊙ **A Study In Frustration** (1923–38; CBS). This three-CD boxed set chronicles the best of Henderson's career from beginning to end, and has long been looked upon as a classic.

⊙ **Louis With Fletcher Henderson** (1924–5; Forte). Armstrong's arrival with the Henderson orchestra is often perhaps simplistically seen as marking its transformation to greatness. On this triple-CD set all Armstrong's titles (superbly remastered by John R.T. Davies) are presented in chronology, with alternate takes.

Max Jones Files/Redferns

Fletcher Henderson

⊙ **The Chronological Fletcher Henderson** (1924–38; Classics). Available in fifteen separate volumes, this set covers all of Henderson's major recordings and is therefore an essential chronicle of big-band jazz in its formative years. Beginners should start with the later Twenties, by which time central stars like Coleman Hawkins, Buster Bailey, Rex Stewart, Charlie Green and Jimmy Harrison were soloing at full power.

Horace Henderson

Piano, arranger, composer.

b. Cuthbert, Georgia, 22 Nov 1904; d. 29 Aug 1988.

Horace Henderson formed his first band at Wilberforce University in the 1920s and was established in New York bandleading by the turn of the decade (later Don Redman took over leadership). He then worked for Redman and for his brother Fletcher Henderson, as well as regularly organizing bands of his own. After military service he was accompanist for Lena Horne, then re-formed his orchestras until the failing big-band scene reduced him to a small group. Though he recorded seldom and rarely appeared in New York, Henderson toured throughout the 1950s and 1960s with groups of various sizes, and in the late 1960s was active in and around Denver. He earned a fine reputation as an arranger whose work was often used by great bandleaders such as his brother, Benny Goodman, Charlie Barnet, Tommy Dorsey, Earl Hines and Jimmie Lunceford. [DF]

⊙ **Horace Henderson 1940 (Classics).** Sixteen titles illustrating the underrated excellence of Henderson's brother-organization with soloists including Ray Nance and the great Emmett Berry.

Joe Henderson

Tenor saxophone, composer, soprano saxophone, flute.
b. Lima, Ohio, 24 April 1937; d. 30 June 2001.

Henderson, whose brother is also a saxophonist, first came to prominence co-leading a group with Kenny Dorham in 1962–3. He was with Horace Silver from 1964–6 and co-led the Jazz Communicators with Freddie Hubbard in 1967–8. He joined the Herbie Hancock sextet during 1969–70 and in 1971 he spent four months with Blood Sweat And Tears. After 1970 he led his own groups. In the mid-1970s he moved to California and became active in music education. In 1985 he played with Herbie Hancock, Ron Carter and Tony Williams at the televised concert *One Night With Blue Note*, to celebrate the relaunching of the Blue Note label, with which he was once closely associated. Henderson was prolific in the years that followed, and was frequently called upon to add authority to the work of younger musicians.

Henderson was one of the most gifted of the post-Coltrane saxophonists. He rapidly absorbed his main influences – Sonny Rollins, John Coltrane and Ornette Coleman – finding his own voice and approach on tenor saxophone. He was exposed to a great variety of music as a child and adolescent, and told Ray Townley: "I heard a lot of country and western music on the radio ... A lot of rhythm and blues, a lot of Chuck Berry, Bo Diddley, and all those real deep blues players ... When I went to college, I got just a bit more esoteric – Indian music, Balinese music."

His playing transcended categories, incorporating elements from bebop, R&B, abstraction, rock and ethnic music. He had an extraordinary melodic gift, and his work never sounded like exercises or "licks" because he was a master of thematic development. Over the years he steadily grew in stature and, apart from the odd relapse, his vision and playing sharpened and deepened. He died of heart failure in 2001. [IC]

⊙ **The Blue Note Years** (1963–90; Blue Note). Either as leader or sideman, Henderson appeared on 34 Blue Note albums, and this four-disc compilation includes many of his classic tracks, plus some lesser-known gems. The collective personnel reads like a who's who of jazz greats.

⊙ **Inner Urge** (1964; Blue Note). This is a powerful quartet session with McCoy Tyner, Bob Cranshaw (bass) and Elvin Jones. Henderson is at his most incisive, and McCoy and the rhythm-section bristle with energy.

⊙ **Mirror Mirror** (1980; MPS). Henderson is as consistently creative as ever, and this fruitful collaboration with Chick Corea produces some sinewy romanticism.

⊙ **The State Of The Tenor Vols. 1 & 2** (1985; Blue Note). Henderson is a long-distance improviser, and in this two-CD set, in trio format with Ron Carter and Al Foster, he has the chance to stretch out luxuriously. Carter's own lyricism and rhythmic invention are also well featured, and the trio functions as an integrated creative unit. A superb effort all round.

⊙ **Lush Life** (1991; Verve). Henderson plays Billy Strayhorn compositions on this lovely album. Using a basic group of pianist Stephen Scott, basist Christian McBride and drummer Gregory Hutchinson, Henderson plays a solo version of the title track, then does a duo with each member of the rhythm-section, a quartet performance of "Blood Count", and three pieces with Wynton Marsalis making the group a quintet.

⊙ **So Near, So Far (Musings For Miles)** (1992; Verve). This is an exquisitely moving tribute to Miles Davis by a quartet which includes three of his ex-musicians – John Scofield, Dave Holland and Al Foster. Henderson plays Davis compositions and tunes associated with the trumpeter, and the quartet breathes fresh life into everything. The music glows.

➤➤ **Andrew Hill** *(Point Of Departure);* **Lee Morgan** *(The Sidewinder);* **Bheki Mseleku** *(Timelessness);* **Horace Silver** *(Song For My Father).*

Jon Hendricks

Vocals, lyricist.
b. Newark, Ohio, 16 Sept 1921.

Hendricks was brought up from the age of eleven in Toledo, where he sang on local radio. After high school and frequent performing, then army service from 1942–6, he took up law studies. He was dissuaded from a legal career by praise from Charlie Parker. As a self-taught drummer he led groups in Rochester and Toledo. From 1952 he was based in New York as a part-time songwriter; his "I Want You To Be My Baby" (lyrics added to the earlier jazz tune "Rag Mop") was recorded by Louis Jordan. He gave up his day job in 1957 after recording his own lyricized versions of "Four Brothers" and Sam "The Man" Taylor's tenor solo on the R&B disc *Cloudburst* (by Claude Cloud and his Thunderclaps); his backing group for the occasion, the Dave Lambert Singers, then narrowed down to Lambert, Hendricks and Ross, first on records and then, from 1958, as a working unit, with Hendricks adding words to classics by Count Basie, Horace Silver, Miles Davis and Art Blakey. After Dave Lambert's departure in 1964, Hendricks was active as a soloist, though he briefly teamed up with Annie Ross and Georgie Fame in 1968 while living in Europe from 1967–73. Before his return to the USA, he had involved his wife and daughter in a new singing group, which in the late 1970s also included non-family members such as Bobby McFerrin. Since 1979 he has also written for and guested with Manhattan Transfer. Of his hundreds of lyrics added to jazz solos (sometimes termed vocalese), many brilliantly mirror the rhythmic contours of the original instrumentals, and their success on this level excuses the lack of verbal profundity. [BP]

Freddie Freeloader (1990; Denon). Over-the-top title track has Hendricks, George Benson, Al Jarreau and Bobby McFerrin singing the solos. Other guests on this extravaganza include Stanley Turrentine, Wynton Marsalis, Manhattan Transfer and the posthumous Basie band.

➤➤ **Lambert, Hendricks And Ross** *(Sing A Song Of Basie).*

Ernie Henry

Alto saxophone.

b. Brooklyn, New York, 3 Sept 1926; d. 29 Dec 1957.

Henry was a worthy associate of several important composer/bandleaders. He worked with Tadd Dameron in 1947, Dizzy Gillespie in 1948–9 and 1956–7, and Charles Mingus and Thelonious Monk, both in 1956. Despite the brevity of his career, and a gap in the middle of it following work with Illinois Jacquet in the early 1950s, Henry stands out as an intelligent adapter of the style of Charlie Parker. As such, he pointed to some of the developments effected in the 1950s by Sonny Rollins (their one recording together, Monk's *Brilliant Corners*, is thought-provoking in this respect) and to the emotional intensity of Jackie McLean. [BP]

➤➤ **Thelonious Monk** *(Brilliant Corners).*

Peter Herbolzheimer

Trombone, composer, arranger.

b. Bucharest, Romania, 31 Dec 1935.

Dubbed "probably the best large-scale arranger of blues themes working outside the United States", Peter Herbolzheimer started his musical career by playing guitar in Detroit, before returning to Germany in 1957 to attend the Konservatorium in Nuremberg, where he remained in the 1960s, playing trombone in the city's radio dance orchestra. In 1969 he formed his big band, the Rhythm Combination And Brass, featuring, among many others, US figures such as Herb Geller and Art Farmer, but also a host of European players including the UK's Derek Watkins and Ray Warleigh. In 1972, he was commissioned to provide the music for the Olympic Games in Munich and won the International Jazz Composers Competition. His many recordings on his own Koala label document his band's skill in the fields of bebop, dance-band material and straightforward swing, and the consistency of its personnel through the years has resulted in its being almost unrivalled for professionalism and sheer cohesiveness. [CP]

Jazz Gala Concert (1979; Rare Bid). Stellar cast including Herb Geller, Tony Coe and Don Menza (saxophones); Art Farmer and Palle Mikkelborg (trumpets); Niels-Henning Ørsted Pedersen (bass) and Grady Tate (drums). Contains excellent versions of "Giant Steps" and "Bluesette".

Bigband Bebop (1983; Koala). Music as per album's title, featuring trumpeter Allan Botschinsky and trombonist Jiggs Whigham, and including a particularly fine version of Charlie Parker's "Au Privave".

Latin Groove (1986; Koala). Outstanding Latin big-band album also featuring Botschinsky and Whigham alongside percussionists Freddie Santiago and Dom Um Romao.

Friends And Silhouettes (1991; Koala). Another high-class big-band album, but with alto player Charlie Mariano and vibes player David Friedman aboard, a slight but welcome change from the series of genre-specific albums that preceded it.

Woody Herman

Clarinet, alto and soprano saxophone, vocals.

b. Milwaukee, Wisconsin, 16 May 1913; d. 29 Oct 1987.

Herman was a child singer in vaudeville, and started learning saxophone at eleven. From the age of fifteen he played in numerous touring bands, ending up with Isham Jones from 1934 until Jones retired from leading in 1936. The members of the band who wished to continue elected Herman as leader. Despite changes in personnel, he worked steadily until 1946, when economic difficulties forced him to follow up his success as a singer. He formed a new band, active from 1947–9, followed by a small group. He made further records as a singer accompanied by studio groups, and then formed a new regular band, now called the Third Herd, which worked from 1950–58, recording for his own Mars label from 1952–4. This was followed by a sextet which was augmented for records and for a European tour in 1959. The Fourth Herd, formed in 1961, continued until the 1980s although, during the 1970s, it became customary to take annual breaks and then reconvene; hence the non-numerical designation of the Swinging Herd and finally the Thundering Herd. The latter was featured with many former sidemen in a fortieth anniversary concert at Carnegie Hall in 1976, and a fiftieth anniversary celebration at the Hollywood Bowl in 1986.

Herman managed the difficult feat of maintaining a feeling of continuity among his different bands, while allowing a gradual stylistic evolution to take place over the decades. This reflects in part his openness to the desires of his soloists, but also his ability as a talent-spotter of section players, which paid off early on in performances such as "At The Woodchoppers' Ball". Although his publicity catchphrase, "The Band that Plays the Blues", might have justifiably been claimed by Basie, Herman's first band and his down-to-earth clarinet work (as opposed to that of Goodman and Shaw) did much to live up to it. It was

DAVID REDFERN

Woody Herman

not until the mid-1940s that the band acquired other strong soloists such as Bill Harris and Flip Phillips, along with a bunch of slightly younger men (and two women, Margie Hyams and trumpeter Billie Rogers) who leavened the late swing era with a new excitement on pieces such as "The Good Earth" and "Caldonia" – the latter a slightly boppish approach to a Louis Jordan hit which was also still the blues.

The band of the late 1940s, identified in retrospect as the Four Brothers era, was the first large unit anywhere to reflect the then increasing influence of Lester Young by featuring such promising players as Stan Getz, Zoot Sims and Serge Chaloff. Furthermore, in the mid-1950s Herman and musical director Nat Pierce acknowledged the ascendancy of East Coast "hard bop" with the first of several Horace Silver tunes, "Opus De Funk" (ie the blues yet again). The traditional aspect of the big-band sound was always adhered to as were, still more so, the drive and dynamism of a rhythm-section style which was modernized almost imperceptibly, like the repertoire. The early 1960s found Herman adopting pieces by Monk ("Blue Monk"), Mingus ("Better Get It In Your Soul") and Herbie Hancock ("Watermelon Man"), and by the 1970s the young generation working for him introduced Coltrane pieces including "Giant Steps", while Woody himself took up the soprano saxophone, playing it with the same hint of Johnny Hodges which always informed his alto work. Throughout this entire development he answered nightly requests for "Woodchoppers' Ball", and continually made it and his current musicians sound just as lively as in the 1930s – a considerable achievement, unequalled by any other white bandleader. [BP]

Blues On Parade (1937–42; MCA). What might have initially sounded unadventurous, compared to other clarinettist/leaders such as Goodman and Shaw, was perhaps closer to the real thing and paid off with hits such as "Woodchoppers' Ball".

The Thundering Herds 1945–47 (Columbia). The band which would ensure Herman's reputation if the others hadn't existed, with Harris and Phillips plus arrangers Neal Hefti and Ralph Burns playing as well as writing. Add a rhythm-section of Chubby Jackson and Dave Tough, and a brass team to match them for excitement, plus, at the end of the album, the arrival of the "Four Brothers".

Keeper Of The Flame (1948–9; Capitol). A reconvened Second Herd with some of the same people and all the same qualities, featuring early Getz on "Early Autumn" and Serge Chaloff in a couple of great solos.

Woody's Winners (1965; Columbia). The 1960s Herd had played itself in for a few years before this live set, which includes "Opus De Funk" featuring Nat Pierce, excellent new material in "23 Red" and "Greasy Sack Blues", and a remake of the First Herd's "Northwest Passage".

Vincent Herring

Alto, soprano and tenor saxophones.
b. Kentucky, 19 Nov 1964.

Herring moved to New York from California in 1982, earning money as a street musician. This led to gigging with Lionel Hampton, and then with David Murray, Abdullah Ibrahim, Art Blakey, Horace Silver, Cedar Walton and Larry Coryell. He joined the Nat Adderley quintet from 1987–93, and began recording under his own name in 1986 while studying music at Long Island University. Herring's full sound and love of boppish blues articulation had him rapidly tagged as the reincarnation of Cannonball Adderley. This is the highest praise in Herring's own scale of values, though he also admires Parker, Coltrane, Ornette Coleman and Wynton Kelly. [BP]

Change The World (1997; Musicmasters). Joined on one track by Roy Hargrove, Herring is otherwise out front with just a rhythm-section led by Joey Calderazzo. The all-original programme finds him sounding less derivative than at times but still joyously authoritative.

➤➤ **Nat Adderley** *(The Old Country).*

Fred Hersch

Piano, composer.
b. Cincinnati, Ohio, 21 Oct 1955.

Hersch's musical career began in 1973 when he began playing with guitarist Cal Collins and others in his home town. In 1975 he moved on to Boston to study at the New England Conservatory (where he is now a part-time faculty member). From 1977, he worked steadily in New York with Art Farmer's quartet, recording and touring also with Sam Jones, Jane Ira Bloom, Billy Harper, Joe Henderson and Stan Getz. During the 1980s he played with the Mel Lewis orchestra, Eddie Daniels and Toots Thielemans, and started his own trio in 1986. In more recent years, he became noted for his unaccompanied playing, both live and in a series of albums, and he has also worked with singers such as Chris Connor, Janis Siegel (of Manhattan Transfer) and soprano Dawn Upshaw. In addition, he has gained a reputation as a producer, particularly of vocal albums, and an organizer; a notable success in this area is his work on behalf of AIDS research, including production of the fund-raising album *Last Night When We Were Young*. Hersch is also a composer of ballet and other music, and his sensitive piano work goes from strength to strength. [BP]

⊙ **Thelonious** (1997; Nonesuch). The dedicatee is obvious, but this solo recital is anything but. Initially an unlikely-seeming project, given Hersch's Bill Evans leanings, it soon convinces the listener that there's more meat in Monk's repertoire than overt imitators usually locate.

Conrad Herwig

Trombone.

b. Fort Sill, Oklahoma, 1 Nov 1959.

Herwig's grandmother played the organ in church and two aunts earned BMus degrees, while an uncle played Dixieland trumpet and another uncle donated his modern-jazz record collection to Herwig when he was twelve. By then he had played for four years in school bands and studied with military musicians (his father was an army colonel). From 1977 he was at North Texas State University, moving in 1981 to New York and working with Clark Terry and Buddy Rich. In 1983 he began playing with Toshiko Akiyoshi and Mario Bauza (remaining with both into the 90s), and soon with several other name bands including Slide Hampton, Paquito D'Rivera and Eddie Palmieri (the latter two continuing until the present). In the 90s he played regularly with Frank Sinatra, the Mingus Big Band and Joe Henderson, and since 1987 has made nine albums as a leader. He lists as favourites Trummy Young, Carl Fontana, Frank Rosolino, J.J. Johnson, Slide Hampton and Albert Mangelsdorff, while being inspired by Coltrane, Shorter, Woody Shaw and composers Berg, Takemitsu and Mompou. [BP]

⊙ **The Latin Side Of John Coltrane** (1997; Astor Place). Herwig's wide experience and knowledge of Afro-Latin music help to make this project unexpectedly successful. The trombonist is only one of several forthright soloists and Trane's tunes are given an authentic feel by rhythm-sections including Eddie Palmieri and Danilo Perez.

➤➤ **Charles Mingus** *(Live In Time)*; **Eddie Palmieri** *(Palmas)*.

Eddie Heywood

Piano, composer, arranger.

b. Atlanta, Georgia, 4 Dec 1915; d. 2 Jan 1989.

Eddie Heywood's father played piano, trumpet and saxophone, recorded prolifically in the 1920s with his own Atlanta-based band and was MD for vaudeville team Butterbeans and Susie. Eddie junior played piano in his father's 81 Theater orchestra when his father was away on tour and five years later joined Clarence Love's orchestra, with whom he went to New York in 1937. Thereafter he worked with Benny Carter's short-lived big band and for Zutty Singleton and Georgie Auld at the Three Deuces, and by 1941 had his own group at Village Vanguard. This sextet – including Doc Cheatham, Lem Davis and Vic Dickenson – achieved great success at New York's Café Society Downtown, and from 1943 they recorded classic sides with Billie Holiday, Ella Fitzgerald, Bing Crosby and the Andrews Sisters, as well as a version of "Begin The Beguine" which turned them into bill-toppers in their own right. From 1947 Heywood was afflicted with arthritic paralysis of the hands; when the trouble cleared he found a comeback difficult and began to develop a gift for composition, with the encouragement of Cole Porter. Several big hits, including "Canadian Sunset", "Land Of Dreams" and "Soft Summer Breeze", all featuring the Heywood trademark of repeated bass and a simple right-hand theme, re-established him, and a string of expensively produced US albums for Mercury, Sunset and RCA Victor followed. In the 1960s Heywood found himself out of step with popular trends (although one more big hit, Mary Wells's "My Guy", drew largely from Heywood's "Canadian Sunset") and once more had health problems, but he re-emerged in the 1970s for New York club work and an appearance at the 1974 Newport jazz festival. [DF]

⊙ **Eddie Heywood 1944/44–6/46–7** (Classics). Useful survey of Heywood's output; this set is calm in the main, but regularly and usefully featuring soloists including Doc Cheatham and the great Vic Dickenson.

Al Hibbler

Vocals.

b. Tyro, Mississippi, 16 August 1915; d. Chicago, Illinois, 24 April 2001.

Vocalist Hibbler was born blind and attended the Little Rock Conservatory for the Blind where he sang treble in the school choir. Later, as a plummy baritone, he sang in clubs and bars and led a band in Texas before joining Jay McShann in 1942 and then Duke Ellington in late 1943. With Ellington his lush, suave sound became part of many classic recordings; among them "Do Nothin' 'Til You Hear From Me", "Don't Get Around Much Anymore", "Don't You Know I Care", "I'm Just A Lucky So And So" and the atmospheric "Pretty Woman".

By the 1950s Hibbler was singing solo and later recorded with Count Basie and Johnny Hodges as well as soloing for Aladdin, Mercury and Decca. He scored a major hit in 1955 with his version of "Unchained Melody", and a further hit a year later "When The Lights Go Down Low". From then on Hibbler recorded sporadically notably in 1964, 1972 (with Roland Kirk) and 1982. Hibbler continued to appear in public at festivals and concerts throughout the 1980s but the passage of pop fashion wreaked its inevitable revenge on his onetime popularity. He remains however, in Donald Clarke's words, "an unforgettable voice". [DF]

Starring Al Hibbler/Here's Hibbler (1996;Jasmine). Useful "twofer" reissue containing twenty-four tracks of Hibbler's idiosyncratic, yet likeable, solo recordings including his hit "After The Lights Go Down Low", as well as "Shanghai Lil" and "Just A Kid Named Joe".

Rahsaan Roland Kirk and Al Hibbler

Meeting Of The Times (1999; Collectables). Originally issued on Atlantic in 1972, this contains such Hibbler classics as "Don't Get Around Much Anymore" and "Do Nothin' 'Til You Hear From Me". Seven songs in total, all backed with great panache by Kirk. The CD also includes an Ornette Coleman album from 1961.

John Hicks

Piano.

b. Atlanta, Georgia, 21 Dec 1941.

Hicks started learning the piano at the age of six, and majored in music at Lincoln University, where the student band included Lester Bowie, Julius Hemphill, Ronald Shannon Jackson and Oliver Lake. He also attended the Berklee School and worked around Boston, before moving to New York in 1963. He was the regular pianist for Art Blakey in 1964–5 and 1973, Betty Carter from 1966–8 and 1975–80, and Woody Herman from 1968–70. Other important partnerships, live and on record, include those with Bowie, Lake, Arthur Blythe, Chico Freeman, Pharoah Sanders and David Murray, his work with the last four being mainly associated with their more straightahead playing. Hicks is a versatile post-Tyner pianist, yet readily identifiable; in the words of Betty Carter, "You hear his way of phrasing, his way of attacking the piano ... He's got things he's gonna do to let you know 'This is John Hicks here'." [BP]

Is That So? (1990; Timeless). The emphasis on standards here, apart from the title track by fellow Atlantan Duke Pearson, focuses the listener on Hicks's qualities, as does the backing of Idris Muhammad and bassist Ray Drummond.

>> **Gary Bartz** *(West 42nd Street).*

J.C. Higginbotham

Trombone.

b. Social Circle, near Atlanta, Georgia, 11 May 1906; d. 26 May 1973.

J.C. (Jack) Higginbotham began his career in 1921 with Neal Montgomery's orchestra in Georgia, and he had worked with various vaudeville troupes, tent shows and jazz bands by the time he got to New York in 1928. There he joined Henry "Red" Allen (a lifelong friend) in Luis Russell's orchestra at Club Saratoga and stayed until 1931 – classic sides including "I Can't Give You Anything But Love", "Bessie Couldn't Help It" and "St Louis Blues", all with Louis Armstrong, are rich dividends from the period. For six years after that Higgy's huge sound, confident range and pawky tone were to be heard in Fletcher Henderson's orchestra, with Benny Carter (he was sacked for sending a love note by mistake to the club-owner's wife) and Lucky Millinder. Then in 1937, in response to a request from Louis Armstrong, Higginbotham rejoined Luis Russell's orchestra (by this time it was backing Armstrong full-time) and stayed until the whole band was dismissed by Armstrong's manager Joe Glaser in 1940.

Then came seven years working with "Red" Allen in a high-octane small band, at Café Society, Kelly's Stables, the Garrick Lounge, Chicago, and Jimmy Ryan's. George Hoefer points up the fascinating duality of Higginbotham at this period: "While he could arrive in New York in 1947 for an Esquire concert with two cases – one holding his trombone, the other containing nine bottles of whiskey – and wind up playing seated on the floor, he could write at the same time in a national magazine an article entitled 'Some of my best friends are enemies!' illustrating a sensitive and keen judgement of the racial situation as applying to Negro musicians." By the mid-1950s Higginbotham, though working with "Red" Allen again at the Metropole jazz bar in New York, was suffering a period of obscurity: an album of that period, *Callin' The Blues*, with Tiny Grimes, sounds unhappy and forced. During the 1960s, however, he was active at clubs and festivals, and it took illness in 1971 to stop his fifty-year career. [DF]

>> **Henry "Red" Allen** *(The Chronological Henry "Red" Allen And His Orchestra 1935–6; World On A String).*

Billy Higgins

Drums.

b. Los Angeles, 11 October 1936; d. 3 May 2001.

After playing with R&B bands and singers Brook Benton and Sister Rosetta Tharpe, Higgins joined the Red Mitchell quartet in 1957. He replaced the departing Ed Blackwell with Ornette Coleman, performed on Coleman's early West Coast-recorded studio albums in 1958–9 and appeared with him during a New York nightclub residency in 1959–60. He left Coleman to work with the Thelonious Monk quartet and the John Coltrane quartet in 1960. He worked with Sonny Rollins & Co in 1962–3, including a European tour. Many freelance gigs and albums followed in the 1960s with such musicians as Dexter Gordon, Hank Mobley, Donald Byrd, Herbie Hancock and Lee Morgan (including the original recordings of both "Watermelon Man" and "The Sidewinder"). A regular association with Cedar Walton, usually with bassist Sam Jones, or, later, Dave Williams, which began in 1966, continued into the 1990s despite Higgins undergoing a liver transplant in 1996. In 2000 he did a reunion gig with Ornette and played

Billy Higgins

with Charles Lloyd, who organized fund-raising during Higgins's final illness. Noted for his copious freelance recording, with and without these favourite associates, he also taught regularly at his studio in South Central LA.

As long ago as 1957, Red Mitchell said, "Billy Higgins, I think, is really destined to be recognized as one of the great drummers in the country ... He has great imagination and is a wonderful group player as well as being able to solo." The apparent flexibility required to work for the many leading stylists who have employed Higgins is very real; but, more than that, it is a reflection of the responsiveness present in his playing at any given moment. The dancing pulse of his cymbals is sufficiently mesmeric to make soloists of whatever persuasion totally relaxed in his company, and any group of which he is a member functions at its optimum level. [BP]

⊙ **Mr Billy Higgins** (1984; Evidence). An interesting programme highlighted by "John Coltrane", composed by bassist Bill Lee (Spike's father), finds Higgins being supportive of Los Angeles players Bill Henderson (piano), Tony Dumas (bass) and Gary Bias (reeds).

➤➤ **Dexter Gordon** *(Go!)*; **Lee Morgan** *(The Sidewinder)*.

Andrew Hill

Piano, composer.

b. Chicago, 30 June 1937.

Andrew Hill (or Hille) worked with the Paul Williams R&B blues band in 1953, and played alongside such Chicago musicians as Gene Ammons, Von Freeman, Johnny Griffin and Malachi Favors during the 1950s. He toured with Dinah Washington in 1961, and accompanied singers Al Hibbler and Johnny Hartman in New York. In Los Angeles in 1962–3, he worked with Roland Kirk, saxophonist Jimmy Woods and others. Returning to New York in 1963 he played with Joe Henderson and began recording under his own name. He was active in California again in the late 1960s, and then became composer in residence at Colgate University in 1970–1 and lectured at other colleges. He was involved with the New York State Council for the Arts in 1972–3 and the Smithsonian Institution the following year. He made visits to the Montreux festival in 1975, Japan in 1976, Italy in 1980 and England in 1991. A renaissance of Hill's US career in the late 1990s led to new recordings, further international touring and the award of the Jazzpar Prize in 2003.

Hill is one of a strong line of pianist/composers who, like Thelonious Monk or Cecil Taylor, are impossible to categorize except as individualists. Although he produces recognizable, even catchy tunes, these are very much part of his improvisational playing style, and vice versa. Whether he is implying Caribbean rhythms or using a more abstract approach, he always seems totally controlled and totally spontaneous. He commented in an interview: "I can't see limiting myself to one harmonic or rhythmic conception. ... As far as I'm concerned, my thing is to create a situation to play in, as interesting a situation as possible." His success is demonstrated by the manner in which he stimulates different players in his various groups, and equally the manner in which he uses different aspects of the piano. [BP]

⊙ **Point Of Departure** (1964; Blue Note). One of Hill's excellent mid-1960s series, this combines post-boppers Kenny Dorham and Joe Henderson with Eric Dolphy in challenging material that brings the best out of them.

⊙ **Shades** (1986; Soul Note). Made on the same Italian trip as one of his solo albums (*Verona Rag*), Hill's original material is reminiscent of Monk but also of Mal Waldron's obsessiveness. The group consists of Rufus Reid and drummer Ben Riley plus, on most tracks, Clifford Jordan.

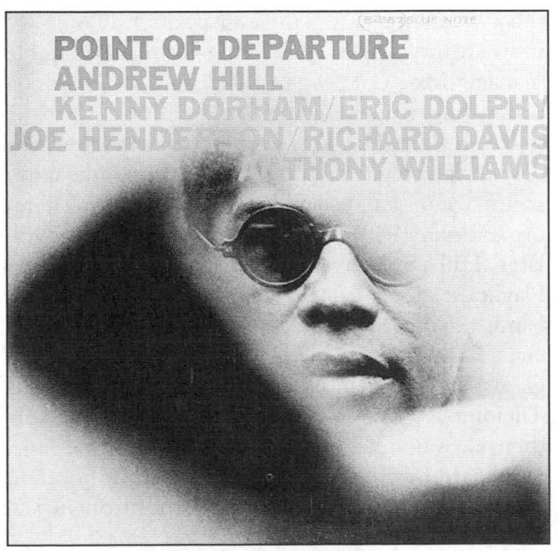

POINT OF DEPARTURE
ANDREW HILL
KENNY DORHAM/ERIC DOLPHY
JOE HENDERSON/RICHARD DAVIS
ANTHONY WILLIAMS

Chippie Hill

Vocals.

b. Charleston, South Carolina, 15 March 1905; d. 7 May 1950.

One of sixteen children, Chippie (Bertha) Hill was working at Leroy's club in Harlem by 1916. Later she was on the road with Ma Rainey's show, moved to Chicago around 1925 and recorded important titles with Louis Armstrong and Richard M. Jones, including "Lonesome All Alone", "Trouble In Mind", "Georgia Man" and "Pratt City Blues". Other work in Chicago at this period included spells with King Oliver, one-night stands opposite Ma Rainey, and club and theatre work. She retired to marry in the late 1920s, and worked spasmodically thereafter until she was rediscovered by Rudi Blesh in 1946. Chippie sang on Blesh's *This Is Jazz* radio series, recorded for his Circle label (including "Blues Around The Clock", a thematic predecessor to "Rock Around The Clock") and scored huge successes at the Village Vanguard in 1947 and the Paris jazz festival of the following year. Back in New York she was the victim of a hit-and-run driver and died in Harlem Hospital. [DF]

Teddy Hill

Saxophones, bandleader.

b. Birmingham, Alabama, 7 Dec 1909; d. 19 May 1978.

Teddy Hill was a competent saxophonist in New York by 1927, worked with Luis Russell over the next two years, and in 1932 formed his own band which played the Savoy regularly as well as clubs such as the Ubangi. They visited Florida in 1936, recorded for Bluebird in 1937, and in that year toured Europe as well as acquiring a young Eldridge-inspired trumpeter, Dizzy Gillespie. By now Hill was fronting the band rather than playing in it, attracting attention with his charm and good looks. The band was full of stars such as Chu Berry, Bill Coleman, Roy Eldridge, Frank Newton and Cecil Scott throughout most of the 1930s, but it lacked the combination of luck and individuality necessary for long-term survival. His manager Moe Gale, when faced with the option of promoting either Hill or the second band in his stable, Erskine Hawkins's, opted for the latter, and despite fairly regular returns to the Savoy some of the steam went out of Teddy Hill's orchestra. They broke up in 1940 after the World's Fair, and a year later Hill took over management of Minton's Playhouse, dispensed with Happy Caldwell's resident band, and turned the room over to the young musicians with whose aims he sympathized. Youthful giants such as Dizzy Gillespie, Kenny Clarke, Thelonious Monk and Charlie Christian worked out their ideas under Hill's eye and, though little more was heard from him, Minton's was an honourable epitaph, for it occupies a central position in jazz development. [DF]

⊙ **Uptown Rhapsody** (1935–7; Hep). Fine collection of Hill sides, including "King Porter Stomp", "Study In Brown" and "Twilight In Turkey".

The Hi-Los

The Hi-Los – Clark Burroughs, lead singer Bob Morse (a phenomenal counter-tenor), Gene Puerling and Robert Strasen (replaced by Dan Shelton in 1958) – were, along with the Four Freshmen, the most prominent vocal quartet of their generation. Formed in 1953 and discovered by Jerry Fielding (who arranged their first recording for Trend Records), the Hi-Los quickly established themselves as technically unsurpassable all-rounders, capable of tackling a range from carefree swinging standards like "Life Is Just A Bowl Of Cherries" (one of their bigger hits) to *a cappella* renditions of dramatic songs like "Black Is The Colour Of My True Love's Hair". Beginning with a Las Vegas hotel season, followed by a tour supporting Judy Garland and a season on Red Skelton's TV show, the quartet went on to record with Marty Paich and Rosemary Clooney, and a string of healthily selling albums followed, along with concerts, cabaret, radio and TV, until the group disbanded in 1964. Two years later Puerling and Shelton went on to form Singers Unlimited, and a Hi-Los reunion album, *Back Again*, was recorded in 1978 with Rob McConnell's orchestra. [DF]

⊙ **Best Of The Hi-Los** (1954–6; VSD). The formative years of the Hi-Los prior to their signing with Columbia but "if I told you they were done last week you'd probably believe it" (Tim Hauser). Remarkable, with headlong comedy ("Chinatown") alongside vocal tenderness ("Shadow Waltz").

⊙ **The Hi-Los: The Columbia Years** (1956–60; Columbia). After signing to Columbia in 1956, the Hi-Los kept doing what they already did superbly, producing hip humoresques like "Life Is Just A Bowl Of Cherries" alongside magnificent *a cappella* creations like "Brahms's Lullaby". In the rock generation they were simply too good.

Earl "Fatha" Hines

Piano, vocals, composer.

b. Duquesne, Pennsylvania, 28 Dec 1903; d. 22 April 1983.

Earl "Fatha" Hines grew up in Pittsburgh, where he was inspired by Sissle and Blake revues, and by the age of 21 was leading a band at a club in Chicago: his precocious talent was to make him, with Louis Armstrong, the city's most spectacular star in the 1920s. For several years, on and off, Hines was Armstrong's close associate (he even invented a style of jazz piano known as "trumpet style"), but from the very start their relationship was often marked by professional rivalry: their early duets, such as "Weather Bird Rag" (1928), with its squally multi-directional rhythmic challenges, plainly show two masters fighting their way to a draw, while "My Monday Date", a Hines composition from the same year, was composed to commemorate Armstrong's inability to remember appointments. Right at the end of 1928, after working as MD for Louis Armstrong's Stompers at Sunset Café and with Jimmie Noone's hit-making band, Hines took his own outfit into Chicago's Grand Terrace Ballroom, fulfilling his ambition to be a bandleader.

For the next twelve years the Mafia-controlled Grand Terrace was Hines's home. "So far as I know", says Jo Jones, "Earl had to play with a knife at his throat and a gun at his back the whole time he was in Chicago." If this was the case, Hines made the best of it. He formed a regular association with Reginald Foresythe (who co-wrote Hines's ingenious theme song "Deep Forest"), expanded to big-band size, MC'd, broadcast regularly all through his tenure, ran shows with Valaida Snow and earned a lot of money. Later, after he left the Grand Terrace, Hines contemplated a double act with Billy Eckstine but instead (like Eckstine) went on to lead another big band full of young jazzmen including Dizzy Gillespie, Charlie Parker, Wardell Gray and singer Johnny Hartman. He disbanded in 1947 to run a club in Chicago, and that same year Joe Glaser approached Hines to ask him to rejoin Armstrong. Hines agreed, but both leaders had come too far to give as much as was necessary. "More than once", says Humphrey Lyttelton, recalling the All Stars at Nice, "Earl Hines's exuberance was curbed by Louis with a sharp 'Cut it, boy!'" Resenting the discipline of Armstrong and the Glaser organization, Hines left in 1951. "I didn't think the new contract they offered me was like it should have been", he explained later. "They wanted to list me merely as a sideman!" He formed a group in Los Angeles before moving into the Hangover Club to front a back-to-the-roots Dixieland band for the next five years: his group included Darnell Howard (clarinet), Jimmy Archey (trombone), Pops Foster (bass) and a variety of trumpeters including Muggsy Spanier and Eddie Smith.

Hines toured for the rest of the 1950s (including Europe, 1957) but it was a grey period: his Oakland nightclub, the Music Crossroads, folded ("when they began to realize I was a Negro owner"), and he thought of taking a store. Then in 1964 Stanley Dance engineered the engagement that saved Hines's career: three concerts at New York's Little Theater, solo and with a quartet featuring Budd Johnson. The concerts sold out, and the master's resurrection was confirmed by a long piece in the *New Yorker* by Whitney Balliett, a season at Birdland and a set of recordings for Dance. His albums attained five-star ratings in *Down Beat* and by the end of the decade he was a jetsetter. Before the 1970s were out he had toured Britain, Russia, Italy, Japan and Australia, had met the pope, and played at the White House for President Ford. By the 1980s Hines was owning up to feeling tired, but he entertained determinedly until the weekend he died, aged 79. By that time his reputation as the greatest pianist after Art Tatum in the annals of classic jazz was far too secure to die with him. [DF]

William Gottlieb/Redferns

Earl "Fatha" Hines

Earl Hines 1928–32/1932–4/1934–7/1937–9/1939–40/1941/1942–5 (Classics). In seven volumes, Hines's earlier career from ravishing solo piano on Vol. 1 through to the last days of his big-band and small-group dates with Charlie Shavers and others. Variable quality but essential for completists.

Fine And Dandy (1949; Vogue). With Barney Bigard and Buck Clayton in attendance, this set has Hines at top form in a period of his career that's less well represented on record than it should be.

Live At The Village Vanguard (1965; CBS). Recorded within a year of Hines's resurgence into jazz consciousness, this set captures him with longtime partner Budd Johnson in high form.

Plays Duke Ellington (1971–5; New World). Produced by Stanley Dance over a four-year period, this well-considered and deeply satisfying set re-examines lesser-known Ellington pieces (eg "Black Butterfly" and "The Shepherd") as well as standards.

Tour De Force (1972; Black Lion); **Tour De Force Encore** (1972; Black Lion); **Live At The New School** (1973; Chiaroscuro). Hines was one of jazz's great solo piano talents, and these three sessions are late illustrations of the fact, and of his incomparable skills as a showman.

>> **Louis Armstrong** *(Louis Armstrong And His Orchestra 1928–29 [Classics]; The California Concerts).*

Motohiko Hino

Drums.

b. Tokyo, 3 Jan 1946; d. 13 May 1999.

The brother of trumpeter Terumasa Hino, Motohiko began on drums at ten and turned professional at seventeen. He worked with various bands, including K. Saijo's quartet, then played in his brother's group until it disbanded in 1975. He then led his own trio, playing extensively in jazz clubs until he moved to the USA in 1978, where he worked with Joe Henderson, Chuck Rainey, Hal Galper, Ronnie Mathews and others. In 1979 he joined Hugh Masekela's band and after 1980 was a regular member of Joanne Brackeen's trio. He has recorded with Henderson, Lew Tabackin, Mal Waldron, Roland Hanna, Terumasa Hino and others. He cites as his influences Terumasa Hino, Tony Williams and Elvin Jones. [IC]

⊙ **Sailing Stone** (1991; Pinnacle). This very pleasant album is full of surprises. Hino has assembled some stars for the occasion – Mike Stern, Dave Liebman, Steve Swallow, and his brother Terumasa (on one track). They perform four Rolling Stones tunes including "Lady Jane" – a ballad feature for Terumasa – and "Satisfaction", on which Mike Stern is given his head. Hino also contributes four of his own deftly rocking compositions.

Terumasa Hino

Trumpet, flugelhorn, composer.
b. Tokyo, 25 Oct 1942.

Hino's father, a tap-dancer and trumpet player, taught him to tap-dance at the age of four; he began on trumpet at nine. His greatest loves became Miles Davis and Louis Armstrong, but he also studied the work of Clifford Brown, Lee Morgan, John Coltrane and Freddie Hubbard, transcribing their solos for himself. He told Sally Placksin in 1985, "It took a long time to transcribe the solos. But that was a great help. . . . Little by little, one note by one note, you're copying. His [Coltrane's] information came through my heart, then I never forget that."

He played with various bands and groups during the later 1950s and early 1960s, then joined the Hideo Shiraki quintet, the top Japanese jazz group. In 1965, with Shiraki, he played the Berlin jazz festival and recorded for the German label MPS. In 1964–5 he also led his own group and recorded *Hinology*, which won two awards including a Golden Disc. In the later 1960s he left Shiraki in order to concentrate on his own group, which started with a residency in a small jazz coffee shop in Tokyo. He established himself rapidly as Japan's top trumpeter, working with his own group and with American musicians, doing TV shows and playing on film soundtracks.

In 1975 he moved to the USA, working with Gil Evans, Jackie McLean, and others. During the late 1970s he was a member of Dave Liebman's group, touring internationally with it and playing major festivals. In 1979 they did a two-month tour in Europe, culminating in a performance at the Ljubljana festival, Yugoslavia. During the 1980s Hino was spending half his time in the USA and half in Japan, where he was still extremely popular.

Among Hino's influences are bassist Reggie Workman, and his style is a synthesis of elements from Miles Davis, Coltrane and Freddie Hubbard. He has a magnificent technique, a full singing sound, and a concept that can embrace any kind of improvisation from neo-bop to abstraction, ballads and fusion. He said to Sally Placksin: "I want to be as simple as possible. Still now, there are so many notes I'm playing, so many notes I don't need. But it's very hard to throw away ... and always for me very important is space, quiet ... Miles does the same thing, Stravinsky, whoever, great people. Painters know how to make space. That's the whole idea of art, I think. Space and simplicity. That's why I love Duke Ellington and Satchmo, because of the space." [IC]

⊙ **Live At The Warsaw Jazz Festival** (1991; Jazzmen). Hino leads a sextet which includes bassist Jay Anderson and guitarist John Hart. The material ranges from a Hino original, "Kimiko", to "Over The Rainbow" and some bravura uptempo pieces. Hino is exhilarating and Hart captivates. A fine set.

➤➤ **Dave Liebman** *(Doin' It Again)*.

Milt Hinton

Bass.
b. Vicksburg, Mississippi, 23 June 1910; d. 19 Dec 2000.

Hinton took up the bass in high school, studied music at Northwest University and worked early on with bands led by Boyd Atkins and Tiny Parham. From 1931 he was bassist for the "dark angel of the violin", Eddie South, then for three great trumpeters – Jabbo Smith, Guy Kelly and an ailing Freddie Keppard. After a spell with Zutty Singleton's trio at Chicago's Three Deuces, Hinton joined Cab Calloway in 1936 and stayed – albeit with mixed feelings – for fifteen years. Calloway's band, the highest-paid in swingdom, played its nightly show competently and Hinton was featured in Calloway's small band, the Cab Jivers (another member, briefly, was Dizzy Gillespie). In 1951, when the whole band was fired, he moved into the New York club scene (with Joe Bushkin at the Embers), then worked briefly with Count Basie and did two short tours with Louis Armstrong's All Stars. In 1954, tired of touring, he took a staff job at CBS, recording thousands of sides, including both Billie Holiday's last sessions (with Ray Ellis) and Bobby Darin's most famous hits from "Mack The Knife" on. He also worked with Sam Jones, Ron Carter and Richard Davis in the New York Bass Violin Choir. Throughout the 1970s and into the 1980s Hinton appeared regularly at Dick Gibson's jazz parties, and at international festivals and clubs, and in 1990 his eightieth birthday was celebrated at New York's Town Hall. Into the 1990s Hinton continued to appear as a senior jazz ambassador worldwide and as a regular commentator in jazz books and TV documentaries. [DF]

⊙ **Old Man Time** (1989; Chiaroscuro). Hinton reminisces and plays bass features in an overdue showcase, with a well-matched band of stars including Dizzy Gillespie, Lionel Hampton, Clark Terry and Ralph Sutton, plus a couple of "talking tracks" with Cab Calloway.

Chris Hinze

Flute, composer.

b. Hilversum, Holland, 30 June 1938.

Hinze's father was a child-prodigy violinist who later became a conductor, and Chris studied flute at the Royal Conservatory in The Hague and afterwards studied arranging at Berklee. At the Montreux jazz festival in 1970 he won the Press Prize as Best Soloist, and the following year launched his jazz-rock-fusion group Chris Hinze Combination at the Lake Geneva Casino. In 1972, for the Holland festival, he was commissioned to compose a suite, *Live Music Now*, for 42 musicians and string orchestra, and for this composition he received the Beethoven Award of the City of Bonn.

During the 1970s Hinze also composed and recorded other symphonic works, including *Parcival*, *New York* and *Silhouettes*, the last of which was recorded with the London Philharmonic Orchestra and arranged by Michael Gibbs; he also made three LPs in Japan, three in India and several in the USA, after which he went to live in New York in 1976. In the later 1970s he made several tours of the Benelux countries with a group called Chris Hinze And Friends and a programme entitled *Music From The Past Till Now*. In 1980 he collaborated with Peter Tosh in recording a reggae album, and also formed a duo with German guitarist Sigi Schwab; in 1983 the guitarist joined the Combination for a tour of Holland and Germany. In 1985 Hinze included Indian and African musicians in his Combination, touring widely in Europe with a programme called *African-Indian and World Fusion* and recording a double album, *Saliah*. Hinze also works as record producer for other musicians.

His favourite jazz flautist is James Moody, with whom he has recorded, and other inspirations are Miles Davis, Duke Ellington, Gil Evans, Gunther Schuller and J.S. Bach. [IC]

Al Hirt

Trumpet.

b. New Orleans, 7 Nov 1922; d. 27 April 1999.

Al Hirt took up the trumpet at eight and, after sitting enthralled through Benny Goodman's 1938 Carnegie Hall concert, went on to train at the Cincinnati Conservatory. Over the next couple of decades came work with the New Orleans Symphony Orchestra, tours with Horace Heidt (whose talent contests he won weeks in succession), club residencies all over New Orleans, and stints with Tommy Dorsey, Jimmy Dorsey and Ray McKinley (with whom he toured Europe for a year). In 1958 came a vital contract with Audio Fidelity, who also signed the Dukes Of Dixieland. This contract ensured Hirt and the Dukes a period of blanket publicity in hi-fi magazines and turned him into a star. By 1960 he was settled in New Orleans with his family, running his own club, and signed to RCA Victor for a set of albums and singles which made him the most talked-about trumpet man of the 1960s. He had hits with singles such as "Java", and LPs with figures such as Ann-Margret and Chet Atkins followed, but Hirt's jazz roots were always audible – especially on *Horn-A-Plenty*, which was arranged by Billy May and pitted Hirt against a trumpet team of Manny Klein, Conrad Gozzo, Frank Beach and Uan Rasey. In the late 1960s Hirt's progress was temporarily slowed by a lip injury sustained in a street parade, but a few years later he was back in stratospheric form at his club on Bourbon Street. Hirt is often dismissed by jazz critics for his supposed "vulgarity" and his undoubted commercial success, but his jazz recordings are usually fun at least, and often much more. [DF]

⊙ **Pete Fountain Presents The Best Of Dixieland: Al Hirt** (1956; Verve). Originally issued as *Al Hirt's Jazz Band Ball*, this CD presents Hirt along with Fountain and super-trombonist Bob Havens, three superstars of post-impressionist Dixieland. Though sometimes showy – the three frontline members occasionally clash amid the demonstrations of technical brilliance – this music is enormously skilful.

⊙ **Horn A-Plenty** (1961; RCA). One of the best Hirt albums, in which he blows with colossal power over Billy May's orchestra; some showcases (including the galloping "Holiday For Trumpet") but regular lyrical outings too, including an enchanting "I'll Take Romance". May's arrangements are full of skill and gusty humour.

⊙ **Brassman's Holiday** (1963; Hindsight). A valuable collection of previously unreleased Hirt leading his six-piece Dixieland band with Bob Havens (trombone), Pee Wee Spitelera (clarinet) et al. Hirt's trumpet-playing gloriously disregards the disciplines of Dixieland trumpet-lead but that's just what you'd expect from a virtuoso, and it's spectacular fun.

Jon Hiseman

Drums.

b. London, 21 June 1944.

Hiseman studied violin and piano until he was thirteen, but is self-taught on drums. He played in amateur jazz, blues and dance bands from 1958–65, and was a founder member of the New Jazz Orchestra (NJO), which operated between 1964–9. From 1966–7 he was with the Graham Bond Organization, and was then with Georgie Fame And The Blue Flames from 1967–8.

From the early 1960s Hiseman was associated with Mike Taylor (pianist and composer), playing in his quartet and recording with him. Their quartet album *Pendulum* was the first real statement on record by the new generation of British musicians, and it remains a little-known icon of the 1960s. He was also involved in trio projects with Jack Bruce and John Surman. After six months playing with John Mayall's Bluesbreakers in 1968, he started his own group, Colosseum, which continued until 1971. He spent a year doing studio session work and then started another group of his own, Tempest, at the beginning of 1973, disbanding at the end of 1974. In 1975 he joined the United Jazz and

Rock Ensemble (UJRE) at its inception and from 1975–8 led Colosseum II. He first met Barbara Thompson in the NJO in 1964, and they later married. In 1979 he joined her group Paraphernalia, and has continued with it and with the UJRE. Since 1977 both he and Thompson have worked intermittently for Andrew Lloyd Webber on various projects including *Variations* and the musical *Cats*.

Since 1983 Hiseman has been deeply involved in engineering and producing in the studio, but has continued to tour and record with Thompson and with the UJRE. In 1994 he re-formed Colosseum with the original personnel and, using the original repertoire (now played rather better than originally), the group performed a few concerts in Germany. The response was so overwhelming that Hiseman released a video of one of the concerts, and in early 1995 Colosseum did a 25-concert tour to packed houses.

In the later 1990s, Colosseum seemed more popular than ever. Hiseman eventually recorded and co-produced two albums and a live video of the band, *Colosseum Lives – The Reunion Concerts*, and the band released a new studio album, *Bread And Circuses*, in 1997. Hiseman is famous for his drum solos, and *About Time Too!*, his 1986 album of drum solos played during concerts with Paraphernalia and the UJRE, was reissued on CD in 1999 by Intuition. Hiseman continues to work with and record Paraphernalia, to play with the UJRE and to tour with Colosseum, and when not on the road he is perpetually busy in his studio or producing film and TV scores.

Hiseman is a drummer of tremendous power and stamina, and has what musicians call "great chops". He is equally at home in jazz or rock contexts, though his early influences were mostly jazz drummers such as Joe Morello, Roy Haynes and Elvin Jones, and he was steeped in Coltrane's music. Later influences were Joni Mitchell, Stevie Wonder, Lenny White and Ellington. Hiseman's great energy is mental as well as physical, and extends to the business and organizational side of the music. He has his own record company (TM Records), his own recording studio, a music publishing company, a PA hire company, and he provides management and agency for Thompson. [IC]

Colosseum & Colosseum II

⊙ **Live** (1971; Sequel); **Electric Savage** (1976; Pinnacle). Colosseum was one of the pioneering jazz-rock groups, using powerful amplification, electronics, and generating Dionysian energy. It was immensely successful, and these sets show why.

➤➤ **Barbara Thompson** *(Breathless; Everlasting Flame).*

Art Hodes

Piano.

b. Nikoliev, Russia, 14 Nov 1904; d. Park Forest, Illinois, 4 March 1993.

"The South Side of Chicago became my alma mater", Art Hodes once declared with typical romanticism, remembering his early career, when soaking up the music of bar-room piano professors in gangster-controlled South Side clubs was as important to him as his work with Wingy Manone and Dick Voynow's Wolverines and any number of lesser bands. By 1938 he had arrived in New York to work up and down 52nd Street, but was soon widening his activities to work as a jazz DJ and to edit (with Dale Curran and Harold Hersey) a vital magazine, *The Jazz Record*. In spare moments Hodes found time to become a pioneering jazz lecturer in schools and colleges, and he stayed in New York until 1950 when he decided to move back to the Chicago area. From 1959 he was resident at Bob Scobey's Chicago nightclub, and during the 1960s he was playing solo, bandleading all over, writing for *Down Beat* magazine, hosting an educational TV series (one programme, *Plain Ol' Blues*, won an Emmy) and teaching piano. Throughout the 1970s and 1980s he continued to play and record internationally, and he kept going right up to the year of his death. [DF]

⊙ **Sessions At Blue Note** (1944; Dormouse International). Hodes in ideal company, including the straight-leading Max Kaminsky who suits the pianist's direct-to-blues approach perfectly. Their trio sessions are outstanding.

⊙ **Parkwood Creative Concept Sessions Vol. 1** (1987–9; Parkwood). Combining Christmas tunes with Hodes originals, this set is an unlikely mixture which, however, shows off Hodes at his solo best.

Johnny Hodges

Alto and soprano saxophones, composer.

b. Cambridge, Massachusetts, 25 July 1907; d. 11 May 1970.

Johnny "Rabbit" Hodges (Cornelius Hodge) lived on Hammond Street, Boston, in what later turned out to be a saxophonists' ghetto: Howard Johnson, Toots Mondello, Charlie Holmes and Harry Carney were all near neighbours. Very early in his career Hodges met Sidney Bechet (who was working in Boston for burlesque entrepreneur Jimmy Cooper), asked for lessons, and soon after worked at his Club Bechet in New York, filling in until the older man arrived, and playing duets such as "I Found A New Baby" or "Everybody Loves My Baby" after he turned up. Hodges at this time was still living in Boston, where Duke Ellington first heard the precociously poised and gloriously talented young saxophonist and signed him on 18 May 1928 to replace Otto Hardwicke. Seated impassively at the centre of Ellington's saxophone section, Hodges (nicknamed "Rabbit" because of his taste for lettuce and tomato sandwiches) directed his section through all of Ellington's creations for the next 22 years. A set of small-group recordings (part of a trend for bands-within-bands) issued in 1938 and 1939 portrays his sensual art perfectly on classic Hodges titles such as "Jeep's Blues", "Empty Ballroom Blues", "Hodge Podge" and "Krum Elbow Blues"; they offer a last chance to hear him playing his first instrument, soprano saxophone, which he gave up in 1940 when Ellington began featuring his alto saxophone so heavily that another instrument turned into a burden.

HERMAN LEONARD

Johnny Hodges

In 1948, while Ellington was touring Britain with a variety show following a serious operation, Hodges was offered a residency at the Apollo Bar on 125th Street, New York, with a small band into which he invited Lawrence Brown, Sonny Greer and other old friends. The "House Full" signs were up most nights, and soon after – in the wake of rows with Ellington's band and in a lean period for big bands generally – Hodges decided to take a band out on his own. It lasted from 1951 for four successful years but, said Hodges, "It was a whole lot of work – and a whole lot of headaches too!" In August 1955 he rejoined Ellington, his stately, blues-inflected creations scoring a huge hit at the 1956 Newport jazz festival and apparently giving a new thrust to his leader's writing: recordings such as *Such Sweet Thunder* (1957), *Jazz Party* (1959) and *Nutcracker Suite* (1960) might have been possible without Hodges but would never have been so great. In the mid-1960s, however, his health began to deteriorate: three hospital stays and numerous doctors' warnings went unheeded as Hodges continued to follow Ellington's punishing schedule. He died while visiting the dentist. "Because of this great loss", Ellington mourned, "our band will never sound the same." [DF]

⊙ **Jeep's Blues** (1928–41; ASV). A similarly good selection to the above with gratifyingly little duplication. Sides with Lionel Hampton, Mildred Bailey, Ivie Anderson, Billie Holiday, and his own orchestra – plus Hodges's "Blue Reverie" from Goodman's 1938 Carnegie Hall concert.

⊙ **Classic Solos 1928–42** (Topaz). Finely chosen selection of Hodges's early work including Ellington (1928–40) and moving through regularly-ravishing titles with Mildred Bailey, Teddy Wilson (with Billie Holiday) and his own groups.

⊙ **The Complete Johnny Hodges And His Orchestra** (1937–8; Le Jazz). All the Hodges-led small-group sessions for Vocalion and Variety; some indifferent singing here, but great jazz too, including classics like "The Jeep Is Jumpin' ".

⊙ **Passion Flower** (1950–60; Giants of Jazz). Another in this regularly outstanding budget-label series; later Hodges lollipops including sides with his orchestra, Ellington, and four selections from the *Back To Back/Side By Side* sessions.

⊙ **Used To Be Duke** (1954; Verve). With Harold "Shorty" Baker, Lawrence Brown, Jimmy Hamilton, Harry Carney and – more surprisingly – the young John Coltrane, this is a premier example of Hodges's occasional attempts at small-group leading.

⊙ **Side By Side** (1958; Verve). An essential set teaming Hodges at his greatest with fellow masters Harry Edison, Roy Eldridge, Lawrence Brown, Ben Webster, Duke Ellington and Billy Strayhorn in a session that deserves reissue with the great contemporaneous set, *Back To Back.*

⊙ **Compact Jazz: Johnny Hodges And Wild Bill Davis** (1961–6; Verve). Like many great jazz players, Hodges enjoyed the comfortable sustains of a Hammond organ as a backdrop, and Davis's rich voicings suited his mix of sensuality and blues to perfection.

⊙ **Everybody Knows Johnny Hodges** (1964–5; Impulse!). A combination of two late and classic Hodges dates – the title session and *Inspired Abandon*, issued originally under the name of The Lawrence Brown All Stars with Johnny Hodges. Essential.

➤➤ **Duke Ellington** *(The Duke's Men: Small Groups Vols. 1 & 2).*

Colin Hodgkinson

Bass guitar, vocals, composer.

b. Peterborough, UK, 14 Oct 1945.

Hodgkinson's first professional job was in 1966 with a jazz trio. In 1969 he began working with Alexis Korner in various formations ranging from their brilliant and popular duo to quartets and larger groups. This relationship continued until Korner's terminal illness in 1983. Hodgkinson was a founder member of the group Back Door, which worked from 1972–7, with Ron Aspery (reeds) and Tony Hicks (drums). They played the Montreux festival and did numerous tours of the USA and Europe. In 1978 Hodgkinson began working with Jan Hammer, and continued with him into the 1980s. From 1985 he also worked with Brian Auger's Blues Reunion.

Hodgkinson is an extraordinary virtuoso of the bass guitar, with an engaging vocal style – everything he does is shot through with blues feeling and the sheer joy of music-making. His favourites are Mingus and Eddie Gomez, and particular inspirations are Hammer and Miles Davis. [IC]

Jay Hoggard

Vibraphone, xylophone, balaphon.

b. Washington, DC, 24 Sept 1954.

After playing piano and saxophone as a child, Hoggard turned to vibraphone in the 1960s. In the early 70s he studied ethnomusicology at Wesleyan University, and simultaneously began working with various members of the New Haven scene, including pianist Anthony Davis and trumpeter Leo Smith. In 1977, he moved to New York, where he recorded with Davis, Chico Freeman, James Newton and Anthony Braxton, among others. He worked frequently both as a sideman and as a leader, incorporating African and Asian musics into his creative jazz outlook. His records include *Rain Forest* (1980; Contemporary), *Riverside Dance* (1985; India Navigation), and the strong *The Little Tiger* (1990; Muse). Among more straightahead efforts, Hoggard appeared on one of Kenny Burrell's best latterday albums, *Guiding Spirit* (1989; Contemporary), and continued issuing as a leader on Muse: *In The Spirit* (1992), *Love Is The Answer* (1994) and *Night In Greenwich Village* (1996). Currently he is a Professor Of Music at the Connecticut Wesleyan University, where he himself studied. [JC]

Allan Holdsworth

Guitar, SyntheAxe, violin, composer.

b. Leeds, UK, 6 Aug 1946.

Holdsworth started on saxophone and clarinet and took up the guitar at seventeen. He wanted the guitar to sound like a saxophone, more as if he were blowing it than plucking it, and so from the beginning he experimented with electronics. He played around the Leeds area, then came to London at the end of the 1960s, where he was one of the pioneers of jazz-rock-fusion in the early 1970s. In 1972 he worked briefly with Nucleus, playing on the album *Belladonna*, then left to join Jon Hiseman's Colosseum. He left in November 1973 to join Soft Machine, leaving that group in March 1975 to join Tony Williams's Lifetime in the USA.

From 1976 he played with Bill Bruford's various bands, and worked and recorded with Jean-Luc Ponty. At the end of the 1970s he was again with Tony Williams, and then settled in the USA and led his own bands. In 1985 his group, with Gordon Beck on keyboards, toured California and then Japan. In the 1980s and 1990s his brilliance became more widely recognized.

He is a highly individual stylist, with a gloriously fluid technique and an endless flow of linear ideas. He has said: "I tend to hear flurries of notes as a whole, from beginning to end, rather than hearing one note after the other." [IC]

⊙ **I.O.U.** (1985; Cream). The composing and playing here are tremendously restless, with guitar speed bordering on the superhuman, and drummer Gary Husband playing so much during the ensembles that his solo on "Checking Out" seems redundant. The few moments of calmness and space are a wonderful relief – the beautiful and eery unaccompanied guitar on "Shallow Sea", and Husband's piano solo on "Temporary Fault".

⊙ **With A Heart In My Song** (1988; JMS). Holdsworth and Gordon Beck in duo making music of the heart and soul. There is space, expansive feeling, and a considerable rapport between the two, who have been friends and collaborators for many years now.

⊙ **Wardenclyffe Tower** (1992; Cream). The music is very electronic and seesaws between pieces which recall 1970s fusion and others which seem to have a different story to tell. On seven of the eight tracks, Holdsworth is accompanied by drums, bass guitar and keyboards, but on the final and most beautiful piece, "Oneiric Moor", he plays solo guitar accompanied only by sounds of the wind whistling.

Billie Holiday

Vocals, composer.

b. Baltimore, Maryland, 7 April 1915; d. 17 July 1959.

Billie Holiday's early life is obscure, but was apparently hard: she was confined to an institution as a victim of childhood rape and became a prostitute in her early teens. By November 1933, when she made her first sides with Benny Goodman ("Your Mother's Son-In-Law" and "Riffin' The Scotch"), she had discovered that although she was "scared to death" of recording, singing could save her from drudgery or whoring. In July 1935, when she made her first great records with friends like Buck Clayton, Lester Young (a platonic soul-brother) and canny Teddy Wilson, the thought of release from such a life still rang joyously in her performances.

She signed with Joe Glaser, Louis Armstrong's manager, in 1935 and toured with Count Basie in 1937 and with Artie Shaw (briefly her lover) in 1938. But she bitterly resented the second-class treatment that Shaw, as an ambitious leader, was prepared to tolerate, and from 1939 turned herself into a solo act at Barney Josephson's multiracial Café Society club. Despite a hit with "Strange Fruit", an anti-lynching song which struck like a hammer on ears attuned to Ella Fitzgerald's satchel-swinging "A-Tisket, A-Tasket", Billie was ill-equipped for a solo career: her progress through a series of nightclubs – Famous Door, Kelly's Stables, Billy Berg's Downbeat, Spotlite and a clutch of others – was accompanied by a heroin habit, drinking problems and a desperate search for a husband/father figure. With a strong sexual appetite and plenty of money to spare, the still childlike Billie was easy prey for a succession of men who came, used her and went; Jimmy Monroe, trumpeter Joe Guy, practised lowlife John Levy, finally Louis McKay, a mafioso heavy – she was helplessly dependent on each in turn. As early as the mid-1940s it was easy to hear that her spontaneous talent was being remorselessly eaten away: "Billie is not singing her best, nor does she sing often enough", scolded *Down Beat* magazine in 1944, by which time she was visibly addicted to heroin. In 1947, after being arrested for drug use, she took a cure in Alderson Reformatory, West Virginia. The resulting notoriety terrified her: by the time she played a packed Carnegie Hall concert in 1948 (to a thunderous ovation) she was beginning to believe that audiences came to see the scars on her arms (which she hid under long gloves) rather than to hear her voice.

Billie desperately wanted to work in films and in 1947 had played a maid in *New Orleans*: servant roles

HERMAN LEONARD

Billie Holiday

were of course standard for black performers, but Billie must have felt the indignity of the role and resented the white people who made her feel guilty for accepting it. She responded with the film's only worthwhile performance, taking out her resentment on-set but off-camera. By 1952, after taking a second cure at Belmont Sanitarium, she was working clubs again and had signed with Norman Granz, who was to record her regularly for five years. But she was out of sympathy with the intellectualism of modern jazz, and lacked the musical knowledge to discuss the problems created by rhythm-sections who professed ignorance of her tunes: no wonder that her voice sometimes sounded like a sad caricature. Granz summed up the stance that her admirers gladly adopted: "It was obvious to me that she was less of a singer physically – but you have to use a different set of values. A singer's range might become more narrow – but their understanding might become more profound."

In 1953 Billie's *Comeback Story* was networked on TV; in 1954 she toured Europe including Britain; by 1956, when her bitter-flavoured autobiography *Lady Sings The Blues* was published, she was working harder than ever. In 1957 a TV jazz show reunited her with Lester Young, and the momentary vision is still terribly moving, as the disarmingly youthful-looking singer nods approval at Young's languid lines. By 1958 she was living alone near Central Park, New York, with her chihuahua (she had recently been refused permission to adopt a child and sometimes fed her dog from a baby's bottle). On 31 May 1959 she collapsed and was taken to hospital where, on her deathbed, she was arrested for possession of narcotics.

At her peak, in the swing-happy 1930s, Billie Holiday was unquestionably the greatest jazz singer of all, an avant-garde artist who polished unremarkable popular songs into iridescent gems. She ecstatically re-created their melodies in a small, worldly voice that, in Barney Josephson's words, "rang like a bell and went a mile"; she conveyed a vulnerability which, as kind Johnny Mercer once said, "made you feel she needed help"; and she projected an intoxicating sensuality when she sang lines like "If you wanna make love, OK" in "Too Hot For Words". Outwardly she was strong, proud and independent (only the young Lena Horne shares that defiant tilt of the head), but unlike Horne – and other contemporaries who, like Ethel Waters, fought the system on its own doubtful terms – Billie's insecurities led her to drink, drugs and a succession of men, making her an easy target for a witch-hunting white society. Naïve as it normally is to equate singers with their songs, Billie's numbers bear out her own assertion that "anything I do sing, it's part of my life". Songs like "Lover Man (Oh Where Can You Be?)" (a longtime stayer in her act), "Don't Explain" (her hymn to forgiveness for male infidelity) and "T'Ain't Nobody's Business If I Do" all speak directly of the problems that quickly devastated her. [DF]

⊙ **The Voice Of Jazz: The Complete Recordings 1933–40** (Affinity). With very few omissions (to be issued on CD shortly) this eight-CD set comprehensively covers Billie's recordings from what is generally thought to be her golden age. These sessions teamed her with the greatest swing musicians of the 1930s, notably Buck Clayton, Lester Young and pianist Teddy Wilson, and there are contributions from Louis Armstrong, Charlie Parker, Dizzy Gillespie, Miles Davis and John Coltrane. The collective results are required listening. These recordings are also available separately and in chronology on two parallel sets: *The Quintessential Billie Holiday* (Columbia) and in the *Chronological Classics* series, though the sound is variable on the latter.

⊙ **The Complete Original American Decca Recordings** (1944–50; GRP). Produced by Milt Gabler, Billie's recordings for Decca presented her as a popular singer rather than as a jazz artist, but the results are almost as ravishing. Great songs like "Lover Man" (her first for Decca with strings), "That Old Devil Called Love", "No Good Man" and "Crazy He Calls Me" receive definitive treatment on these two CDs.

⊙ **The Complete Billie Holiday On Verve** (1945–59; Verve). This magnificent award-winning ten-disc set (produced by Phil Schaap), spanning the fourteen years of Billie Holiday's association with Verve, has all her concert and studio recordings (including alternate takes) plus on-record rehearsals and conversations. Complete with luxuriously produced and informative booklet, this commemorative masterpiece contains much indispensable material, although Buck Clayton's unselfish claim that the Verve records are better than Billie's pre-war output will always be a subject for debate. Many of Billie's best later sessions for Verve are available as single CDs, as listed below.

⊙ **Lady In Autumn** (1946–59; Verve). A fine double CD including live JATP tracks, plus some of Billie's best studio performances.

⊙ **The Great American Songbook** (1952–9; Verve). Newly assembled two-CD collation of Billie recordings for Verve, covering the same composers as Ella Fitzgerald's "Songbooks". Billie slowed down in the 1950s but intelligent programming helps this collection to keep moving, and there are bright solo spots from Edison, Webster and Shavers.

⊙ **Compact Jazz: Billie Holiday** (1955–6; Verve). A fine compilation from the Verve years, including Harry Edison, Webster Rowles and Benny Carter.

⊙ **Songs For Distingué Lovers** (1957; Verve). Weathered Billie with Edison, Webster and Rowles; fine solos from all concerned.

Dave Holland

Bass, cello, composer; and piano, guitar, bass guitar.
b. Wolverhampton, UK, 1 Oct 1946.

Holland studied at the Guildhall School of Music and Drama in the late-1960s, where he was the principal bassist in the college orchestra. He became active on the London jazz scene, working with John Surman, Kenny Wheeler, Evan Parker, Ronnie Scott, Tubby Hayes and others. He already had all the virtues – beautiful tone, perfect time, harmonic knowledge and a brilliant technique – when Miles Davis heard him in London in the summer of 1968 and invited him to New York to join his quintet.

He worked with Davis from September 1968 to the autumn of 1970, playing on some of the trumpeter's key albums, then left with Chick Corea to form Circle with Barry Altschul and Anthony Braxton. Circle toured in the USA and Europe, but broke up when Corea left in 1972. Holland and the other members, with the addition of Sam Rivers, recorded Holland's album *Conference Of The Birds*, a classic of acoustic, semi-abstract music.

During the 1970s Holland worked with the Sam Rivers trio, touring worldwide and playing major festivals. During the 1980s he began leading his own group, which initially featured Kenny Wheeler, Julian Priester and saxophonist Steve Coleman. The association with Coleman (who was retained when he reduced his group to a quartet) brought him into contact with the younger M-Base group of American musicians, and he recorded with both Coleman and saxophonist Gary Thomas. In 1985 Holland worked with a Euro-American group led by Franco Ambrosetti, which performed at the Berlin festival. Since the early 1980s Holland has been a tutor at the Banff summer school in Canada, and his groups have formed the core of the tutorial staff there. He also teaches privately. Holland has steadily grown in stature over the years, and has become more and more in demand for recordings and tours, often by jazz supergroups such as the Holland-DeJohnette-Hancock-Metheny unit which toured internationally in the 1990s. He was among the other ex-Miles Davis musicians who joined the trumpeter for one of his last concerts on 10 July 1991 in Paris, and he was a member of the Miles Davis Tribute Band, with Tony Williams, Herbie Hancock, Wayne Shorter and Wallace Roney, which toured internationally in the autumn of 1992.

In the later 1990s, Holland worked much more often with Herbie Hancock, and went to Brazil with him in 1996. He also continued to work and record with Kenny Wheeler, and was a member of the latter's drumless quartet which made the beautiful album *Angel Song* in 1996. In the summer of 1997, Holland toured extensively with a new quintet which included two of his old associates, vibraphonist Steve Nelson and trombonist Robin Eubanks, but brought in saxophonist Steve Wilson and drummer Billy Kilson. They recorded the album *Points Of View* in September 1997. In December 1998, having recorded the album *Prime Directive*, Steve Wilson was replaced by the new voice on tenor saxophone, Chris Potter, but the rest of the personnel remained the same. In May 1999, the quintet had a dynamic week's residency at London's Ronnie Scott's Club,

Laurance Labat/ECM Records

Dave Holland

Jumpin' In (1983; ECM). This was a blueprint for Holland's groups for the next several years. He, Steve Coleman and Kenny Wheeler are joined on this occasion by drummer Steve Ellington and trombonist Julian Priester. The music runs the gamut from bustling, uptempo pieces, to elegaic and moody performances, and on "The Dragon And The Samurai" (composed by Coleman) there's a rocky groove and some collective improvisation. The other six compositions are all by Holland, and again we have the "shock of the new" plus all the basic jazz virtues superlatively displayed.

Seeds Of Time (1984; ECM); **The Razor's Edge** (1987; ECM). The variety and quality are maintained on both of these fine albums. Only the personnel changes slightly. On *Seeds*, Marvin "Smitty" Smith replaces Ellington, and on *The Razor's Edge*, Robin Eubanks replaces Priester.

Points Of View (1997; ECM). This music has immense warmth and clarity. Five of the pieces were composed by Holland, and three are by other members of the band. Wilson has a very pure sound on soprano and alto saxophones, and Eubanks blends easily with him. Vibist, Steve Nelson, creates excellent colours and textures and is a fine soloist. There's plenty of solo strength here, not least from the leader.

Prime Directive (1998; ECM). The band has now benefited from the impassioned tenor saxophone of Chris Potter who is so immersed in the music that he dances while he plays. Billy Kilson is a tremendous drummer, and he and Holland have developed a euphoric rapport.

and in the years since his reputation has been cemented by numerous awards and an honorary Doctorate from the Berklee School of Music.

Holland's favourites range from Mingus and Scott LaFaro to Ray Brown and Paul Chambers; other influences are Davis, Coltrane, Monk, Ellington and Dolphy. [IC]

Conference Of The Birds (1972; ECM). Holland's first album under his own name is a masterpiece of its genre and still sounds utterly contemporary. His compositions have great linear and rhythmic vitality, the band swings and everyone plays as if there were no tomorrow.

Life Cycle (1982; ECM). Holland has occasionally featured cello solos during live performances, and this is a solo cello album. The strength of this recording, as of all his work, is that it is rooted in his humanity – melodies, textures and rhythms, with their marvellous invention, are so listenable because they are so emotionally eloquent.

➤➤ **Chick Corea** *(Paris Concert);* **Miles Davis** *(In A Silent Way; Bitches Brew);* **Joe Henderson** *(So Near So Far);* **Sam Rivers** *(Waves);* **Collin Walcott** *(Cloud Dance);* **Kenny Wheeler** *(Deer Wan).*

Peanuts Holland

Trumpet, vocals, composer.

b. Norfolk, Virginia, 9 Feb 1910; d. Stockholm, 7 Feb 1979.

A veteran of Alphonso Trent's territory band, which he joined in 1928 and stayed with for five years, Peanuts (Herbert Lee) Holland led his own very successful showband in 1938, and then lent his talent to a variety of top bandleaders such as Jimmie

Lunceford, Willie Bryant, Coleman Hawkins and Fletcher Henderson, as well as Charlie Barnet – a close friend and regular employer – for five years from 1941. In 1946 he travelled to Europe as lead trumpeter for Don Redman and settled there, commuting between Paris and Scandinavia with his own small group and regularly recording with names as diverse as Mezz Mezzrow, Don Byas, Billy Taylor and Claude Bolling. [DF]

Major Holley

Double bass, violin, tuba.
b. Detroit, Michigan, 10 July 1924; d. 26 Oct 1990.

Major "Mule" Holley played violin first, then tuba in a navy band before studying bass at Groth School of Music. Early work included stints with Dexter Gordon and Wardell Gray, Charlie Parker, Ella Fitzgerald and Oscar Peterson (1950), and from 1952 he worked in the studios of BBC TV in Britain where he became a familiar and well-loved figure. After returning to the USA Holley worked for Woody Herman, the Zoot Sims-Al Cohn quintet and Duke Ellington (1964) before freelancing for three years and teaching for three more at Berklee College, Boston. From the early 1970s Holley was house bassist at Jimmy Ryan's and stayed busy playing festivals, concerts and jazz parties, recording (as leader and with Rose Murphy amongst others), and touring with Helen Humes and the Kings Of Jazz. A remarkable later recorded appearance was on Bob James's *Sign Of The Times* album (1981), where on the enchanting title track Holley adopts his longtime trademark of bowing the bass while singing in unison with the line he is playing (similar to Slam Stewart singing an octave above). [DF]

KENNY BURRELL

⊙ **Midnight Blue** (1963; Blue Note). On this popular blues-mood album Burrell and Stanley Turrentine are joined by the no-nonsense rhythm-section of Holley, drummer Bill English and Ray Barretto.

Red Holloway

Alto, tenor and baritone saxophones.
b. Helena, Arkansas, 31 May 1927.

The blues-influenced saxophone of Red (James) Holloway first became prominent in post-war Chicago, where he played with Roosevelt Sykes, Willie Dixon, Lloyd Price, Muddy Waters, Chuck Berry, B.B. King and many other seminal blues artists. However, his career has regularly involved high-level jazz activities too, with amongst others Lionel Hampton and Brother Jack McDuff in the 1960s, as well as the big band Juggernaut. But it was his partnership with Sonny Stitt – from 1977 – which drew full international attention to Holloway's gifts as a lyrical and technically assured jazz player. [DF]

⊙ **Locksmith Blues** (1989; Concord). A superb double date with Clark Terry, including a magnificent workout on the title track plus satisfying dips into Ellington repertoire.

Bill Holman

Tenor saxophone, arranger.
b. Olive, California, 21 May 1927.

After studying music at Westlake College, Holman was a sideman in the bands of Charlie Barnet in 1950–51 and Stan Kenton from 1952–5, for which he also wrote. Settling again on the West Coast, he worked with Shorty Rogers and others, while writing further arrangements for Kenton, Woody Herman, Maynard Ferguson, Herb Pomeroy and Gerry Mulligan. From the 1960s he arranged occasionally for Count Basie, Buddy Rich and trumpeter Doc Severinsen's band, but concentrated on studio work for pop records, TV and films. He formed an occasional big band to play his own music in 1975 while continuing with his commissioned work, which included the new scores for Natalie Cole's *Unforgettable* album of 1991. Despite mentioning Mingus and Charles Ives as inspirations for his more recent writing, he is chiefly associated with the Mulliganesque work that Kenton and others recorded in the 1950s. [BP]

⊙ **A View From The Side** (1995; JVC). Even more than his Monk album *Brilliant Corners*, this represents Holman's current writing, some of it commissioned by college big bands or European state-radio orchestras. Along with three standards, originals like "Make My Day" and "Petaluma Lu" are involved but logical, and so are soloists such as saxophonists Pete Christlieb and Bill Perkins.

➤➤ **Stan Kenton** *(Complete Bill Holman And Bill Russo Arrangements).*

Charlie Holmes

Alto and soprano saxophones, clarinet, oboe, flute.
b. Boston, Massachusetts, 27 Jan 1910; d. Sept 1985.

In the 1920s Holmes lived on Boston's Tremont Street, around the corner from Johnny Hodges, and first played the oboe in local orchestras. He then took up an easier option, the fashionable alto saxophone, and began visiting New York with another near neighbour, Harry Carney. There he worked with bands led by Billy Fowler, George Howe, Luis Russell, Lew Henry (at the Savoy) and guitarist Henri Saparo, before joining Russell's band again at Casper Holstein's Saratoga Club. The Russell band – a romping, stomping New Orleans family – felt like home to Holmes and he stayed, with one short break in 1932, until 1940 (backing Louis Armstrong for the last five years), when Joe Glaser dismissed the band *en bloc*. After a quiet period back in Boston, Holmes worked with Cootie Williams and briefly with John Kirby in 1947, playing an old tattered book, the remnant of former glories. His last record for a long time was made in 1952 with Al Sears ("a lot of people thought it was Johnny Hodges", he later said wistfully); Holmes retired soon after to work on Wall Street. "I never cared about making records", he told Stanley Dance later. "... I liked to play where people were dancing and not paying attention to you." In the 1970s he was persuaded to perform and record with Clyde Bernhardt's Harlem Jazz and Blues Band. [DF]

➤➤ **Luis Russell** *(Savoy Shout).*

Richard "Groove" Holmes

Organ; also piano.

b. Camden, New Jersey, 2 May 1931; d. 29 June 1991.

After teaching himself to play organ, Holmes was discovered by Les McCann in Pittsburgh, and his first two albums, both made in 1961, featured McCann, Ben Webster and Gene Ammons. As well as guesting with Gerald Wilson and recording with big-band backings, he worked steadily through the 1960s, 1970s and 1980s with his organ-guitar-drums trio. He occasionally added a pianist to his group in the mid-1970s, and his albums from 1977 onwards were usually augmented by horns, especially the saxophone of Houston Person. His swinging style and fleet footwork undoubtedly aided the return to wider popularity of the organ in the 1990s, which sadly he did not live to see. [BP]

⊙ **Misty** (1965–6; Prestige/OJC). Bouncy trio performances of perennials like "Summertime" and "The Shadow Of Your Smile" are augmented by Holmes's hit version of the title track from an earlier session.

Elmo Hope

Piano, composer.

b. New York, 27 June 1923; d. 19 May 1967.

St Elmo Sylvester Hope was a boyhood friend of Bud Powell; he also studied European music. He first toured with the Joe Morris R&B band that included Johnny Griffin and Philly Joe Jones in 1948–9, and with Etta Jones. During the 1950s he did freelance gigging and recording with Sonny Rollins, Clifford Brown and under his own name. He lived in Los Angeles from 1957–60, working with Harold Land, Lionel Hampton and others. Returning to New York, he recorded with an all-star group and in duo with his wife, pianist Bertha Hope, but was also imprisoned for drug offences. Remaining intermittently active until his death, Hope was strongly marked by the influence of Powell and especially Thelonious Monk; but he had a personal sound at the piano and was an interesting, and greatly underrated, composer. In the 1990s Bertha Hope (b. 1936) has enjoyed a career renaissance, which has led to her recording several albums, including some of Elmo's music. [BP]

⊙ **Homecoming** (1961; Riverside/OJC). Divided between trio tracks with Percy Heath and Philly Joe Jones, and a sextet adding Blue Mitchell, Frank Foster and Jimmy Heath, this has absorbing Hope originals such as the unusually structured "La Berthe" and the lyrical "A Kiss For My Love".

Claude Hopkins

Piano, bandleader, arranger, composer.

b. Alexandria, Virginia, 24 Aug 1903; d. 19 Feb 1984.

A childhood friend of Rex Stewart in Washington, Claude Hopkins was bandleading by 1924 and in 1925 travelled round Europe with Sidney Bechet in the Revue Nègre. He returned to the USA to work in dancing schools and clubs in New York and Washington, and tour for the Theater Owners' Booking Association (TOBA) with the Ginger Snaps revue. By 1927, in Atlantic City, he had set his band's style – "I always stressed cup mutes and soft rhythm" – and the formula brought success, at New York's Savoy Ballroom, then at Roseland for three years from 1931. Here the band reached a peak, appearing in films and employing Bill Challis, Paul Whiteman's premier arranger, to swell their book. After Roseland they took over from Cab Calloway at the Cotton Club, bringing in Russell "Pops" Smith (the old reliable lead trumpeter from Fletcher Henderson's orchestra) and popular falsetto singer Orlando Smith. From 1937 the Hopkins band took to the road, playing to packed houses: Hopkins himself – a tough streetwise leader who once achieved the near-impossible double of punching both Cab Calloway and Joe Glaser – doubled as a staff arranger for CBS. He continued bandleading until the boom was over, then in 1947 reverted to small-band work, touring with revues, and backing familiar faces such as Sol Yaged, Herman Autrey and Henry "Red" Allen. (A delightful record from the period, issued by Gala as *The Golden Era Of Dixieland Jazz*, with Pee Wee Erwin and Buster Bailey, allows an extended view of Hopkins's fleet piano, moving from Waller to Basie and back with easy grace.) In the 1960s and 1970s this work pattern prevailed, but a tour of Europe in 1982 with Earle Warren and Dicky Wells revealed a sad and disillusioned Hopkins, his wife dead, his motivation gone. [DF]

⊙ **Claude Hopkins** (1932–40; Classics). During the 1930s Hopkins's orchestra – though never an international headliner – featured star players including Edmond Hall, Hilton Jefferson, Jabbo Smith and Snub Mosley (as well as the arranging skills of Jimmy Mundy) and this three-volume chronology regularly demonstrates how underrated the Hopkins heritage remains.

John Horler

Piano, composer.

b. Lymington, UK, 26 Feb 1947.

Horler's father Ron played trumpet in the Eric Delaney band, while elder brother Dave is a trombonist-arranger with the WDR band in Cologne. John studied piano and clarinet at the

Royal Academy of Music and, since 1967, has been continuously active with such leaders as Peter King, Ronnie Ross, Tommy Whittle and Tony Coe; since 1984 he has been the pianist for John Dankworth and Cleo Laine. He performed at Ronnie Scott's with many visiting musicians including Zoot Sims, Chet Baker and Victor Feldman and, among other studio work, recorded with Kenny Wheeler, Harry Allen and Elaine Delmar. In the late 1990s and early 2000s, he played in a trio with Coe and Malcolm Creese and in its successor, Acoustic Triangle. As well as the initial inspiration of Bill Evans, he admires Feldman, Chick Corea and Richie Beirach, and other favourites include Miles, Brookmeyer, Jim Hall, Clifford Brown, J.J. Johnson, Stan Getz, Gil Evans and Gary McFarland. An excellent accompanist and fluent soloist, Horler is also a stimulating and unconventional composer. [BP]

⊙ **Gentle Piece** (1992; Spotlite). One of two Horler albums under his own name, this has music for quartet, trio and duo (the Bill Evans/Jim Hall-inspired "My Funny Valentine" performed with Phil Lee) and the meat is the original material, with a title track by Kenny Wheeler. Interestingly, the Japanese issue of this session includes three more recent standards, such as "Candle In The Wind".

➤➤ **Tony Coe** *(In Concert)*; **John Dankworth** *(Moon Valley)*; **Kenny Wheeler** *(Kayak)*.

Paul Horn

Flute, alto saxophone, clarinet.

b. New York, 17 March 1930.

After studies at music college and work with the Sauter-Finegan orchestra, Paul Horn replaced Buddy Collette in the Chico Hamilton quintet from 1956–8 and worked briefly with Cal Tjader in 1959. He did studio work in Los Angeles, and made appearances and recordings with his own groups from 1957 onwards. In 1964 he became one of the first musicians after Mary Lou Williams to be featured in church performances of jazz music, and in 1968 he was also one of the first jazzmen after Tony Scott to play in the Far East. He has performed in China and Russia, and runs his own Golden Flute record label. Horn has a notably pretty sound, which is his chief means of communication with his large and broadly based following. [BP]

⊙ **China** (1983; Kuckuck). One of a series of reissues from Horn's own label, recorded in various parts of the globe, this double CD is a duo performance with Chinese multi-instrumentalist David Mingyue Lung.

Shirley Horn

Vocals, piano.

b. Washington, DC, 1 May 1934.

Starting on piano at the age of four, Horn later studied music at Howard University. After forming her own trio in 1954, she was encouraged by Miles Davis and Quincy Jones, with whose backing she recorded two albums in 1963. Continuing to work mainly around the Washington area, her underground reputation finally led to further recordings, made from 1978, and a first tour of Europe in 1981. This in turn led to renewed appreciation in the USA, and a major label contract which has brought her far wider recognition. Many of Horn's most distinctive recordings are live sets, while her studio albums are also based on her own accompaniments, even when larger ensembles are overdubbed. She shares with the very different Blossom Dearie the ability to incorporate delicate piano shadings behind her equally subtle vocal delivery. [BP]

⊙ **You Won't Forget Me** (1990; Verve). Horn's intimate voice and piano work subdues various guests, including a reflective Miles Davis on the title track, and her husky delivery and use of space is a perfect vocal equivalent of the Miles ballad style.

Lena Horne

Vocals.

b. Brooklyn, New York, 30 June 1917.

Lena Horne's career began in 1934 at the Cotton Club, after which she sang with Noble Sissle (1935–6), toured with Charlie Barnet (1940–41), and recorded with Artie Shaw, plus strings and a pep section of Henry "Red" Allen, J.C. Higginbotham, Benny Carter and Sonny White. Tracks like "Love Me A Little, Little" and "Don't Take Your Love From Me", both cut in 1941, demonstrate her ease in jazz surroundings. From the early 1940s Horne's talent and striking looks took her into a string of films (including *Cabin In The Sky* with Ethel Waters, Eddie Anderson, Duke Ellington and Louis Armstrong, *Two Girls And A Sailor*, with Harry James, and *Ziegfeld Follies*) – appearances which were sometimes "clipped out" for showings in the Southern states, but which struck an early blow for black equality. In 1947 Horne married MD Lennie Hayton and by that period she was an international star, capable of topping the bill at London's Palladium, as well as at all the best concert halls and clubs in America. In the 1950s hits such as "Love Me Or Leave Me", "Honeysuckle Rose" and the risqué "New Fangled Tango" kept her on top, and in 1957 she starred on Broadway in *Jamaica* (with Adelaide Hall also in the cast); a quarter of a century later her one-woman show, *The Lady And Her Music*, ran on Broadway for over a year. Since then Horne has continued to appear regularly, and to receive awards for her achievements as entertainer. Like Pearl Bailey, much of her recorded work is jazz-friendly rather than jazz as such, but the unique caustic quality of her singing makes hers a true jazz voice. [DF]

⊙ **Stormy Weather** (1941–58; Blackbird). With a variety of backings, including two tracks each with Charlie Barnet and Artie Shaw, Horne's individualistic style is displayed on great standards (the title track to "It's All Right With Me") and on obscurities.

Ron Horton

Trumpet, flugelhorn.

b. Bethesda, Maryland, 12 Feb 1960.

Horton's parents and older sister were all amateur musicians and his father started him on the trumpet at age five. After studying arranging with famous locals such as Bill Potts, he went to Berklee College, Boston from 1978–80. Moving to New York in 1982, he played with Jane Ira Bloom for the next 12 years and with the East Down Septet. Horton was a founder member of the Jazz Composers Collective in 1992 and of the Herbie Nichols Project in 1994. He joined the Andrew Hill Sextet in 1998 and became the co-arranger and director of Hill's big band in 2000. Horton also leads his own quartet, and cites artists such as Kenny Wheeler, Henry Threadgill, Maria Schneider and Django Bates as key inspirations. [BP]

⊙ **Genius Envy** (1999; OmniTone). Horton's basic quartet is joined by guests including Jane Ira Bloom in a varied and descriptive set that hardly justifies the Freudian wordplay.

➤➤ **Jane Ira Bloom** *(Art And Aviation)*; **Tom Varner/East Down Septet** *(Out Of Gridlock)*.

Wayne Horvitz

Piano, synthesiser, organ.

b. New York, 1 Sep 1955.

With a father who played piano and clarinet and a guitarist/composer for a brother, Horvitz took up the piano at twelve. Raised in California, he went to university in Santa Cruz and studied privately with pianist Art Lande. After moving to New York, he worked with Eugene Chadbourne and formed a trio with bassist William Parker and cornet player Butch Morris. In the early 1980s Horvitz began a long association with John Zorn, appearing with many of his groups such as Naked City and the Sonny Clark Memorial Quartet. His own many bands include the New York Composers Orchestra, The President, Pigpen (named after the Grateful Dead keyboardist), Zony Mash and the Four Plus One Ensemble. In the 1990s he relocated to Seattle, where he has also worked as an album producer for Bill Frisell, Peter Apfelbaum and Fontella Bass.

A prodigious composer, Horvitz has a finger in many pies, taking commissions from the Kronos Quartet and collaborating with a variety of choreographers and movie directors. He also records and regularly performs with his wife, the singer, Robin Holcomb. [BP]

⊙ **This New Generation** (1985; Nonesuch). Originally released as *Dinner At Eight*, Horvitz's first album (after the Parker/Morris trio) includes notable "downtown" musicians such as Bobby Previte and guitarists Elliott Sharp and Bill Frisell in a kaleidoscopic variety of settings and instrumentation.

⊙ **Four Plus One Ensemble** (1998; Intuition). The unusual quartet of piano, second keyboardist, violin (Eyvind Kang), trombone (the great Julian Priester) plus programmer includes a sample of Ellington's piano and, from there on, gets more abstract and more groovy.

Darnell Howard

Clarinet, violin, saxophones.

b. Chicago, 25 July 1895; d. 2 Sept 1966.

As well known among musicians for his violin playing as for his huge-toned clarinet (which in

WAYNEHORVITZ.COM

Wayne Horvitz (second from left) with his Four Plus One Ensemble.

approach and vibrato sometimes echoed the violin sound), Howard was good enough to play for W.C. Handy's famous orchestra on Handy's first New York recordings in 1917. For the next six years he was playing and touring with, among others, his former teacher Charlie Elgar, who led a band at Chicago's Dreamland Ballroom in 1921; after that he was with James P. Johnson's touring revue *Plantation Days* in 1923, and by the mid-1920s was working with top leaders including King Oliver, Carroll Dickerson and Erskine Tate. In 1931 he joined Earl Hines's brilliant big band, and there he stayed until 1937, playing alto saxophone, featuring his violin, and taking a small group from Hines's orchestra on tour each summer, when the Grand Terrace was closed. After a lull in the early 1940s, when Howard became a shopkeeper, he worked with Kid Ory, Muggsy Spanier and Bob Scobey, concentrating on clarinet. From 1955–62 he was back with Hines at the Hangover Club in San Francisco, and worked regularly after then (including a tour of Europe with the New Orleans All Stars) until his death from a brain tumour. [DF]

Kid Howard

Trumpet.

b. New Orleans, 22 April 1908; d. 28 March 1966.

Kid (Avery) Howard began as a drummer in bands led by Andrew Morgan and trumpeter Chris Kelly. He was so impressed by Kelly that he switched instruments and later became a regular with the Young Tuxedo Brass Band, Allen's Brass Band and others, as well as playing in small groups and a brass band of his own. In the 1930s he played in clubs and theatres, then in 1943 recorded with George Lewis, with whom he worked regularly from 1952. A familiar figure at Preservation Hall in the early 1960s, Howard was held in high regard for his hot, driving style. His funeral, attended by the Eureka, Olympia and Onward brass bands, was one of the biggest processions ever held in his home town. [DF]

⊙ **Kid Howard's La Vida Band** (1961; American Music). A good representative selection of Howard's later work with Israel Gorman (clarinet), Eddie Sommers (trombone) and others; Howard's tribute to Chris Kelly is outstanding.

Freddie Hubbard

Trumpet, flugelhorn, composer, piano.

b. Indianapolis, Indiana, 7 April 1938.

Hubbard's first professional engagements were with Wes and Monk Montgomery in Indianapolis, and he also used to go to Chicago every Sunday to blow at a club where Bunky Green, Frank Strozier and trumpeter Booker Little worked. He moved to New York at the end of the 1950s, sharing rooms with Eric Dolphy for eighteen months. He was with Sonny Rollins for four months in 1959, then played with Slide Hampton, J.J. Johnson and Quincy Jones. In 1961 he joined Art Blakey's Jazz Messengers, staying with them for a few years and rapidly establishing a national and international reputation; in 1961 he won the *Down Beat* New Star Award for trumpet. Although Hubbard's prime influences were Clifford Brown and Little, he also learned much from Dolphy, and has said: "He opened me up with the register playing, intervallic playing. I was making two-octave jumps, because he was doing that on the clarinet and bass-clarinet. He had me practising from books ... and he had me interested in Ravi Shankar, which helped me play modally."

Hubbard's debut in jazz was even more remarkable than the bald facts indicate. He not only worked with some of the leading and most influential players (Wes Montgomery, Rollins and Blakey), but at only 22 he walked straight into the history books: in December 1960, with Dolphy, he participated in the Ornette Coleman double quartet album *Free Jazz*, one of the seminal albums of the early 1960s avant-garde, and only two months later, again with Dolphy, Hubbard played an equally important part in another classic and influential recording – Oliver Nelson's *Blues And The Abstract Truth*. Even at that early stage Hubbard's style was fully formed. He had absorbed his influences and created his own sound: a crisp, full-blooded, brassy tone, a highly personal way of rhythmic inflexion, a brilliantly fleet technique, and a vocabulary of tonal resources and effects which were new to the trumpet. He was also perfectly at home with chords and set structures and with semi- or total abstraction.

After leaving Blakey he led his own groups for a while, then joined Max Roach; he rejoined Blakey to tour Europe and Japan, and in 1965 worked in Austria with Friedrich Gulda. With Quincy Jones he also played on the soundtrack of the film *The Pawnbroker* (1965). In the mid-1960s Hubbard played on yet more classic and seminal albums: with Dolphy, *Out To Lunch*, with Coltrane, *Ascension*, and with Herbie Hancock, *Maiden Voyage* and *Empyrean Isles*. Between 1966–70 he recorded a series of his own albums for Atlantic, on which his music began to show rock influences.

During the 1970s he toured internationally with his own groups, playing major festivals, and also made more recordings for CTI and later Columbia. In 1972 he moved to California, and the same year his album *First Light* won a Grammy award as the best jazz performance of the year by a small group. By the later 1970s he was leading a group of young unknown musicians who functioned more as a backing band for a "star" than as collaborators in the act of making music, and his music was heavily electronic and rock-based. Several of his associates from the 1960s had become huge international stars – Herbie Hancock, Wayne Shorter (with Weather Report) and others with the jazz-rock-fusion movement of the 1970s which they had helped to create, and Hubbard was looking for that kind of stardom and a hit record. He was doomed to disappointment, and in the 1980s was performing once more with an acoustic group, playing the contemporary neo-bop at which he excels.

In 1977 he was reunited with old friends Herbie Hancock, Wayne Shorter, Ron Carter and Tony Williams, in an acoustic band called VSOP which toured worldwide and recorded. In 1985 there was a similar reunion for a concert to celebrate the relaunching of the old Blue Note record catalogue. The concert was filmed for television and shown internationally.

As a trumpet player, Freddie Hubbard is an important stylist, and several subsequent players, including Charles Tolliver, Randy Brecker, Woody Shaw and Wynton Marsalis, are indebted to him. Virtuosity and versatility are the hallmarks of his highly individual style and, because of this, he has seemed at times to be all circumference and no centre, which is one of his weaknesses as a bandleader: no central, driving vision or profound commitment to a particular musical direction. He told Howard Mandel: "My problem has been switching my music, but that's also what keeps me going, being able to play a little bit of everything. I want to play a little bit of rock, I want to play a lot of jazz, I want to play a little bit of soul. That way I get to meet so many different types of people." As a result, much of his jazz-rock-fusion output sounds like easy-listening mood music: it is impeccably performed, but it has no demons and lacks emotional tension. All his most important recordings – which include several of the crucially influential albums of the 1960s – are with other leaders.

Hubbard's trumpet-playing was severely impaired in 1993 when he ruined his embouchure by forcing himself to play with a damaged lip. He recorded an album, *M.M.T.C. (Monk, Miles, Trane, Cannon)* (Musicmasters) in 1994, which did not help his recovery; it is still doubtful if he will ever be able to play again at his previous best. [IC]

⊙ **Hub-Tones** (1962; Blue Note). Hubbard, at the time of this recording, was just 24 years old and his playing was wonderfully cocky and optimistic. He's in partnership with the excellent but undersung James Spaulding (alto saxophone and flute), and a superb rhythm-section of Herbie Hancock, Reggie Workman and Clifford Jarvis. The title piece and "Prophet Jennings" are two fine Hubbard compositions, and the playing is full of pith and moment. It's an early 1960s classic.

⊙ **Backlash** (1966; Blue Note). Hubbard and Spaulding are together again, with pianist Albert Dailey, bassist Bob Cunningham, drummer Otis Ray Appleton and percussionist Ray Barretto added on three tracks. The rocky influence begins to appear particularly on the title track, but Hubbard and Spaulding are on great form, and the music has considerable variety, including some warm lyricism on Hubbard's waltz "Up Jumped Spring", which he plays on flugelhorn with sublime echoes of Clifford Brown.

⊙ **First Light** (1972; CTI). Hubbard is featured here with woodwinds, French horns, strings and a jazz ensemble which includes George Benson, Ron Carter, Jack DeJohnette and Airto Moreira. Hubbard's fine sound and instincts elevate the proceedings.The original LP has been remastered for CD and includes some previously unreleased tracks.

➤➤ **Art Blakey** *(Free For All);* **Ornette Coleman** *(Free Jazz);* **Eric Dolphy** *(Out To Lunch);* **Herbie Hancock** *(Maiden Voyage);* **Oliver Nelson** *(Blues And The Abstract Truth).*

Eddie Hubble

Trombone.

b. Santa Barbara, California, 6 April 1928.

Hubble was an early associate of Bob Wilber: they met at Scarsdale High School and worked together briefly in the school jazz band, where Dick Wellstood was the pianist. The start of Hubble's career proper came in 1947 when he worked for nine months with singer Red McKenzie at Jimmy Ryan's: the band included a brilliant young trumpeter, Johnny Windhurst, who became Hubble's close friend. For the next few years the trombonist worked around, with Alvino Rey and Buddy Rich among others, but more often alongside Windhurst at the Storyville Club, Boston, or in Windhurst's Riverboat Five, commuting between Ohio and New York. He also worked with Billy Maxted's band, with Phil Napoleon's fine band in the late 1950s at Napoleon's Retreat in Miami, and led his own small group round Fort Lauderdale. By 1966 Hubble was playing with the Dukes of Dixieland, after the death of trombonist Fred Assunto. He stayed a year, then settled in New Jersey with George Morrow's band, and in 1968 became a founder member of The World's Greatest Jazz Band. In 1973–4 he worked in Florida with Flip Phillips and toured Europe with the Kings Of Jazz, then continued work as a freelance until a serious car crash temporarily immobilized him in 1979. After moving to Texas, Hubble joined Jim Cullum's band (1986–7) and then resumed freelancing, but his fine Teagarden-style playing is heard too seldom. [DF]

Peanuts Hucko

Clarinet, tenor saxophone.

b. Syracuse, New York, 7 April 1918; d. 19 June 2003.

Michael Andrew Hucko (nicknamed "Peanuts" for his schoolboy love of them) began his career playing smooth tenor saxophone (his early influences were Bud Freeman and Eddie Miller) with trombonist Jack Jenney, and later with Will Bradley, Joe Marsala, Charlie Spivak and Bob Chester. In 1941 he joined the air force, where he concentrated more on clarinet ("because we did a lot of marching in sand which was awkward with the tenor") and soon after was featuring his new speciality in a breakneck "Stealin' Apples" with Glenn Miller's Uptown Hall Gang. He reverted to tenor for spells with Benny Goodman (his section mate was Stan Getz) and Ray McKinley before joining Eddie Condon (on clarinet), filling in for Pee Wee Russell from 1947–50.

After Condon came five years as a studio man for CBS and ABC, where Hucko met Louis Armstrong; in 1958 he joined Armstrong's All Stars for two years. From 1960 Hucko divided his time between Condon and studio work, and from 1966 was regularly at Dick Gibson's Colorado jazz parties playing with the Ten Greats Of Jazz, later The World's Greatest Jazz Band.

In the 1970s he led the Glenn Miller Orchestra at home and abroad, played clarinet solos for Lawrence Welk, worked the studios, and opened his own nightclub, Peanuts Hucko's Navarre, featuring Ralph Sutton and his singer-wife Louise Tobin. The 1980s brought renewed success: European tours (solo and with his award-winning Pied Piper quintet), work with Syd Lawrence's Miller-style orchestra, and best-selling recordings. Later in the decade Hucko toured and recorded regularly with his own Dixieland groups (often including trumpeter Randy Sandke) and into the 1990s was still busy, maintaining a distinguished link between Benny Goodman and post-war virtuosi such as Bob Wilber. [DF]

⊙ **Tribute To Louis Armstrong** (1983; Timeless); **Tribute To Benny Goodman** (1983; Timeless). The first of these sessions includes Hucko's longtime partner Billy Butterfield and trombonist Trummy Young, while the second (only slightly less successful) features a high-powered front-line completed by young Randy Sandke along with trombonist Al Grey.

⊙ **Swing That Music** (1993; Starline). With a super-group of American and European colleagues including Danny Moss (tenor) and Roy Williams (trombone) alongside Sandke, Hucko leads a live concert that's not only note-perfect but blessed with the energy of a bunch of teenagers.

Spike Hughes

Composer, bass.

b. London, 19 Oct 1908; d. 2 Feb 1987.

A self-taught double-bassist (he played a German string bass made of tin), Spike (Patrick C.) Hughes arranged for British dance bands before auditioning for Philip Lewis at Decca. Some fine jazz records followed, by Spike Hughes's orchestra, Three Blind Mice and Decca-Dents, featuring amongst others trumpeters Max Goldberg and Sylvester Ahola, and the outstanding Philip Buchel (who played alto, tap-danced and later, with his wife Betty, choreographed British musical films). From the late 1920s Hughes was very busy: touring Holland with his band, writing and orchestrating music for C.B. Cochran and Noël Coward, and (in a more specifically jazz vein) devising items such as *A Harlem Symphony* (composed on William Walton's piano) and the hit ballet *High Yellow*, which juxtaposed jazz and classically trained players in the same piece. From 1931 Hughes played bass regularly for Jack Hylton's band, then in 1933 he went to New York. There he stayed with John Hammond, wrote songs with Ned Washington (including "Let's Drink To Love") and, most importantly, recorded fourteen masterpieces of Ellingtonian stature with Benny Carter's band, which included such stars as Dicky Wells, Coleman Hawkins, Chu Berry and Henry "Red" Allen. By 1934 he had packed it in for the world of classical music – "I left jazz behind at the moment I was enjoying it most: the moment when all love affairs should end", wrote Hughes fifteen years later. Spike seems to have been too bright, and too much a trained musician, to take the early excesses of jazz (and the limitations of his own bass playing) easily in his stride. His autobiography, larded with classical references, eyebrow-raising chauvinism and determinedly "modern" attitudes, is a wonderfully entertaining book that ends with a detailed critique of Toscanini: a penance, presumably, for his bohemian dealings with jazz. [DF]

⊙ **Spike Hughes: His Orchestra, Three Blind Mice And Decca-Dents** (1930s; King's Cross Music). Featuring British stars Goldberg, Buchel, Jack Jackson, Buddy Featherstonhaugh and many more, this is an excellent two-disc chronology, remastered by John R.T. Davies.

⊙ **Spike Hughes: All His Jazz Compositions** (1930–33; Largo). This fascinating collection, spotlighting Hughes as composer, has twenty outstanding tracks from his British and American orchestras, and brings together all that exists of his music for the ballet *High Yellow*.

⊙ **Spike Hughes And Benny Carter 1933** (Retrieval). All of Hughes's indispensable American recordings with Benny Carter's orchestra; required first-stop listening for Hughes-fanciers.

Daniel Humair

Drums, composer.

b. Geneva, 23 May 1938.

Humair played clarinet and drums from the age of seven, and committed himself to jazz after winning a competition for young amateurs. By 1958 he was regularly accompanying Americans in Paris clubs, including a long spell at the Chat Qui Pêche with Lucky Thompson. By 1962 he had become France's number one drummer in both talent and popularity. He played with the Swingle Singers in the early 1960s, appearing at numerous European festivals. In the late 1960s and early 1970s he was a regular member of Phil Woods's European Rhythm Machine. He also worked with Herbie Mann, Lee Konitz, Anthony Braxton, Roy Eldridge, Stephane Grappelli, Joachim Kuhn and his own group. He has played on the soundtracks of several films, including Bertolucci's *Last Tango in Paris* (1972). Humair has recorded as a sideman with many people including Martial Solal, Chet Baker, Jean-Luc Ponty and Jim Hall, and he has made many albums under his own name. Since the mid-1960s he has also had a second career as a successful painter. His main influences are Elvin Jones, Roy Haynes and Philly Joe Jones. [IC]

⊙ **Surrounded** (1964–87; Blue Flame). A kind of greatest hits, which covers many areas, and the list of his sidemen reads like a who's who of leading American and European jazzmen, including Eric Dolphy, Johnny Griffin, Joachim Kuhn and Martial Solal.

Derek Humble

Alto saxophone, clarinet.

b. Livingston, Durham, UK, 1931; d. 22 Feb 1971.

Humble turned professional at the age of sixteen, and toured with the bands of Teddy Foster, Vic Lewis and Kathy Stobart in 1951. He was a member of the Ronnie Scott band from 1953–6, also recording with Vic Feldman and others. From 1957–67 he worked with the Kurt Edelhagen radio band, and he recorded regularly with the Kenny Clarke-Francy Boland band from 1961 onwards; he began touring with the latter group and freelancing in 1967. He died from the after-effects of street violence, despite a temporary recovery and work in the UK with the Phil Seamen quartet in 1970–71. Ronnie Scott described Humble after his death as "the complete lead alto saxophonist and a great soloist". [BP]

➤➤ **Kenny Clarke** *(Two Originals).*

Helen Humes

Vocals, piano.

b. Louisville, Kentucky, 23 June 1913; d. 9 Sept 1981.

Helen Humes fell under the spell of Ethel Waters early in her career, and recorded four sides for OKeh in Chicago when she was just fourteen. In the early 1930s she worked with Stuff Smith and Jonah Jones, with Vernon Andrade, and with tenorist Al Sears's band in Cincinnati, where Count Basie hired her in 1938 to replace Billie Holiday. With Basie, Humes worked New York theatres, clubs and the Famous Door until 1941, then left to work with Teddy Wilson, Art Tatum and others. By 1944 she was touring with package shows, featuring the high-powered blues singing that was her trademark, but her jazz approach – clear-toned, rhythmic, note-perfect – also won regular work with Red Norvo in the 1950s and 1960s. In 1964 she settled in Australia (having toured there with Norvo in 1956), but returned to the USA after her mother became ill in 1967 and was soon singing again: in 1973 she scored a huge success at the Newport festival in a *Tribute To Count Basie*. The dividends that followed included new recordings, headline appearances at New York's Cookery and the Nice jazz festival, and European tours, including a visit to Ronnie Scott's in 1978. [DF]

⊙ **Blue Prelude** (1927–47;Topaz). Excellent survey of twenty years of Humes's remarkable career demonstrating her range of recorded settings from country blues ("Cross Eyed Blues", 1927) to Harry James's orchestra and beyond.

⊙ **T'Aint Nobody's Business If I Do** (1959; OJC). With André Previn on piano plus Teddy Edwards, Frank Rosolino and Benny Carter in the frontline, this set was rightly acclaimed as one of Humes's finest efforts at the time of its original release.

⊙ **Songs I Like To Sing** (1960; OJC). Probably Humes's best album, with arrangements by Marty Paich and four tracks featuring Ben Webster.

⊙ **Swingin' With Helen** (1961; OJC). Twelve tracks of premier quality from Humes's golden period, with the under-recorded Joe Gordon on trumpet.

Percy Humphrey

Trumpet.

b. New Orleans, 13 Jan 1905; d. 22 July 1995.

The son of clarinettist Willie Eli Humphrey, and grandson of Professor James Humphrey (one of New Orleans's greatest music teachers), Percy Humphrey began on drums before switching to trumpet, playing for much of his life in his home town while pursuing a second career as an insurance salesman. During the 1920s he worked with Willie Cornish and Kid Howard, amongst others, and later led bands of his own, as well as playing and recording with George Lewis's band (1951–3). A technically well-qualified player, Humphrey played for and then led the Eureka Brass Band from the 1950s until the early 1970s (when it disbanded), and, from 1972, the New Orleans Joymakers. Humphrey was also semi-resident at Preservation Hall, working there with his own Preservation Hall Jazz Band which, from 1964, regularly played at festivals and at Disneyland. He also appeared with "Sweet Emma" Barrett, and Billie Pierce (replacing DeeDee Pierce) from 1973. His last appearance was at the New Orleans Fair Grounds as part of that city's 1995 jazz festival. [DF]

⊙ **Percy Humphrey Featuring Sweet Emma** (1974; Smokey Mary). A spirited and well-recorded set, including two tracks by "Sweet Emma" Barrett, and with a band including Jim Robinson and Percy's brother Willie. Humphrey, confining himself to lead for much of the session, plays nevertheless with clear tone, invention and great facility.

Willie Humphrey

Clarinet, saxophones.

b. New Orleans, 29 Dec 1900; d. 1994.

One of the central figures of New Orleans clarinet, Humphrey took up the instrument at fourteen and worked with local bands before moving to Chicago in 1919 to play with such musicians as Manuel Perez, Freddy Keppard and Joe Oliver (for the "Black Sox" World series). After returning to New Orleans (1920) Humphrey freelanced until 1925, when he moved to St Louis and worked for leaders including Fate Marable and Dewey Jackson, for another seven years. During the mid-1930s he worked for Lucky Millinder and recorded with Henry "Red" Allen, but after wartime naval service he returned to New Orleans to work with the Young Tuxedo and Eureka Brass Bands, with his brother Percy and Paul Barbarin, and at Preservation Hall. A mainstay of the Preservation Hall Band from the later 1960s, Humphrey toured regularly with the group as well as appearing and recording solo. [DF]

⊙ **New Orleans Clarinet** (1974; Smokey Mary). A fine solo outing for Humphrey, showcasing his big-toned clarinet and spirited vocals against a hard-swinging rhythm-section.

Fred Hunt

Piano, bandleader.

b. London, 21 Sept 1923; d. 25 April 1986.

Hunt worked with clarinettist Cy Laurie's quartet before joining Alex Welsh's Dixieland band in 1954. For the next twenty years or so his fine jazz piano – a mix of Hines, Hodes, Bushkin and his own recipes – was a central feature of Welsh's band. Several early recordings, including the classic *Music For Night People* featuring Welsh and Archie Semple, show off Hunt's Hines-ish flourishes, grumbling blues interludes and chiming declamations. From the mid-1960s, American visitors toured constantly with Welsh's second great band (featuring John Barnes and Roy Williams), and all of them – from Peanuts Hucko to Ruby Braff – were unanimous in their praise of Hunt's sympathetic and highly creative performance. His filigree-to-muscular solos were for long a cherished centrepoint of Welsh's concerts (as were their trumpet-piano duets, such as "Sleepy Time Gal"), but in the later 1970s he left to build a solo career and began a busy round of performances at home and abroad, returning occasionally for Welsh reunions. From 1983 terminal cancer made Hunt's appearances rarer. [DF]

➤➤ **Alex Welsh** *(The Great Concert).*

Alberta Hunter

Vocals.

b. Memphis, 1 April 1895; d. 18 Oct 1984.

The phenomenal career of Alberta Hunter (also known as May Alix, Helen Roberts or Josephine Beatty) began in vaudeville in Chicago, where she sang with many great jazz musicians including King Oliver, Tony Jackson and Sidney Bechet. All through the 1920s she worked constantly, recording with the likes of Fletcher Henderson, Louis Armstrong, Perry Bradford and Fats Waller, and replacing Bessie Smith in the show *How Come* in New York in 1923. Later in the decade Hunter commuted between America and Europe, starring in *Showboat* with Paul Robeson (1928–9) at the London Palladium before spending time in Paris, then returning to New York for more shows. During the mid-1930s she replaced Josephine Baker at the Casino de Paris, and sang with Louis Armstrong; during the war years she worked for USO, then in peacetime toured the UK with Snub Mosley. In 1956, shortly after understudying for Eartha Kitt in *Mrs Patterson*, Hunter left show business to become a nurse, although she recorded again in 1961, and in 1977, aged 82, made a starring comeback at Barney Josephson's Cookery in Greenwich Village and recorded the soundtrack of Alan Rudolph's 1978 film, *Remember My Name*. Alberta Hunter's career – rather like Adelaide Hall's – suffered only from a comparative lack of recordings, but her work well deserves re-examination. [DF]

⊙ **Young Alberta Hunter** (1920–40; Jass). Good overview of Hunter's earlier work with Eddie Heywood, Charlie Shavers, Louis Armstrong and more.

Charlie Hunter

Eight-string guitar.

b. Rhode Island, 23 May 1968.

Hunter grew up surrounded by guitars (his mother repaired them for a living), and bought his first instrument when he was twelve for $7. His first lessons were with Joe Satriani in Berkeley, California, and he attended the same high school as Joshua Redman and Benny Green. Blues, rockabilly, soul and funk initially attracted him, but he discovered jazz at eighteen by listening to the recordings of Charlie Parker, Charlie Christian and John Coltrane. Organ jazz – an important ingredient of his mature sound – also made an impact via the work of Jimmy Smith, Big John Patton and Larry Young. In the late 1980s, he busked in Paris and Zurich and, on returning to the USA, he met up with poet/rapper Michael Franti and joined the Disposable Heroes Of Hiphoprisy. In 1993, Hunter formed his own trio with saxophonist Dave Ellis and drummer Jay Lane and recorded an eponymous debut album for Prawn Song Records the following year. Signing to Blue Note, the trio produced *Bing, Bing, Bing!* in 1995 before Hunter recorded *Ready... Set... Shango!* (see below) with dummer Scott Amendola and Canadian alto player Calder Spanier. Both albums dispense a highly infectious, accessible brand of "improvisational-oriented pop" (in Hunter's words) but, until 1997, Hunter also ran a James Brown/Thelonious Monk/Roland Kirk-oriented quartet, TJ Kirk (originally James T. Kirk until Paramount Pictures – *Star Trek*'s company – complained), signed to Warner Bros.

Hunter has since recorded prolifically and variously: a Bob Marley "cover" album, *Natty Dread* (1997; Blue Note); quartet and quintet albums featuring Amendola, vibes player Stefon Harris and percussionist John Santos; a set of duets with percussionist Leon Parker; a solo guitar album in 2000; collaborations with rapper Mos Def and singer Norah Jones on *Songs From The Analog Playground* (2001); and the Brazilian-influenced *Right Now Move* (2003; Ropeadope). Hunter's self-proclaimed mission is to "turn a generation of people on to a much more spiritually and soulfully executed music than what gets played on MTV". [CP]

⊙ **Ready ... Set ... Shango!** (1996; Blue Note). More jazzy than his previous Blue Note outing, Hunter describes this lively mix – of throaty tenor (Ellis), grainy alto (Spanier) and his own multi-textured guitar ranging from organ sounds to spangly solo runs, all with his trademark bass-playing built in, courtesy of the bottom three strings of his eight-string instrument – as "a pre-funk funk record with no backbeat".

Chris Hunter

Alto, tenor and soprano sax, flute.

b. London, 21 Feb 1957.

Hunter got his first saxophone at twelve and at sixteen began two years of private lessons with

Les Evans. He then began taking part in jazz workshops and studying improvisation with Don Rendell. At nineteen he joined the National Youth Jazz Orchestra, touring Europe and the USSR. During 1978–9 he was with the Mike Westbrook Brass Band touring Europe, and in the early 1980s began doing studio work, mostly as a soloist, including work in 1982 with the Metropole Orchestra, Holland. In 1983 he played with the Gil Evans British Orchestra, and was then in New York for one week with the Westbrook Brass Band. The same year he toured Japan with Gil Evans, and in October 1983 he moved to New York. In 1984 he again toured Japan with the Gil Evans orchestra featuring Jaco Pastorius; Hunter remained with Evans right up to the latter's terminal illness. In 1984 he also joined the Michel Camilo sextet which featured Lew Soloff, and began his association with Mike Gibbs; that year he was soloist with the Cologne Radio Orchestra for a Gibbs project, and after that played in the Gibbs orchestra at the 1987 UK Bracknell festival and featured on Gibbs's 1989 album *Big Music*.

Hunter's progress was meteoric: in seven years (1976–83) he moved from being a closet saxophonist to a world platform, and by the end of the 1980s he had shown that he has what it takes to survive in fast company. His favourite saxophonists are Cannonball Adderley, Mike Brecker, Jan Garbarek, Charlie Parker, Dave Sanborn and Tom Scott. [IC]

⊙ **This Is Chris** (1988; Paddle Wheel); **Scarborough Fair** (1989; Paddle Wheel). Hunter is in fast company on both of these albums and comes out of the experience very creditably. The first one is a quartet with keyboardist Gil Goldstein, bassist Ratzo Harris and drummer Terri Lyne Carrington, with Emily Remler being added on one track. The second album has an eleven-piece band which includes Goldstein, Howard Johnson, John Clark and Adam Nussbaum.

➤➤ **Mike Westbrook** *(The Cortege)*.

Ian Hunter-Randall

Trumpet.

b. London, 3 Jan 1938; d. 13 Feb 1999.

Ian Hunter-Randall was one of the most schooled and inspired trumpet talents in British Dixieland: a talent whose phenomenal range, crackling tone and fresh creativity deserved wider recognition. Early on in his career he worked with Ken Barton, Monty Sunshine, Alexander's Jazzmen (and briefly with Acker Bilk) but came to national attention after joining Terry Lightfoot early in the 1970s for a stay of around twenty years. During this time Hunter-Randall's power, range and reliability stood Lightfoot in good stead; after leaving, he joined Pete Allen's band, and after years freelancing replaced Alan Littlejohn in Laurie Chescoe's Goodtime Jazz (from 1996). He died unexpectedly of a heart attack. [DF]

➤➤ **Terry Lightfoot** *(Stardust)*.

Clyde Hurley

Trumpet.

b. Fort Worth, Texas, 3 Sept 1916; d. Sept 1963.

Inspired by Louis Armstrong, Clyde L. Hurley played in local bands around his home town before joining Ben Pollack in 1937 to replace Harry James. Glenn Miller signed him in 1939 for what was to be a none-too-happy stay, and Hurley moved to Tommy Dorsey's band for a year from 1940, then to Artie Shaw's in 1941, and a year after that moved back to Hollywood to take studio work. For the next thirteen years he was a Hollywood staffman and a freelance for NBC-TV, but he still found time to work the jazz circuit, notably with Ralph Sutton at Club Hangover in 1954, with Matty Matlock's marvellous studio band, the Rampart Street Paraders, and as a guest with Bob Scobey's Frisco band for other recording assignments. Hurley may also be heard on Hollywood soundtracks such as *Drum Crazy: The Gene Krupa Story* (1959) and *The Five Pennies* (1959), starring Danny Kaye and Louis Armstrong. [DF]

The Rampart Street Paraders

⊙ **Dixieland, My Dixieland** (1954; Columbia). Hurley's strong lead and muscular soloing shows off well in this A-team of West Coast Dixielanders.

Robert Hurst

Bass.

b. Detroit, Michigan, 4 Oct 1964.

Although he is chiefly celebrated as the Marsalis brothers' "house bassist", Robert Hurst has also lent his thickly propulsive sound to the work of a great many hard-bop and post-bop leaders. He has played with pianists Geri Allen, Bruce Barth and ex-Jazz Messengers Donald Brown and Mulgrew Miller; Harry Connick (on his breakthrough recording *20*) and the New Orleans singer's guitarist Russell Malone; saxophonists Ricky Ford and Rick Margitza; and drummers Marvin "Smitty" Smith and Tony Williams. Hurst also appeared on singer Carmen Bradford's 1993 Evidence album, *With Respect*, but his own album from the same year, *One forNamesake* (Columbia/DIW), despite the presence of Elvin Jones and the late Kenny Kirkland, was thought to miss the presence of horns. However, it was his almost telepathic understanding with drummer Jeff "Tain" Watts that perhaps produced Hurst's best and most distinctive work; their presence on any recording is a sure-fire guarantee of quality. [CP/CI]

⊙ **Robert Hurst Presents Robert Hurst** (1992; DIW). Finely wrought music featuring trumpeter Marcus Belgrave and bass-clarinettist Ralph Miles Jones III along with the regular Branford Marsalis quartet under Hurst's leadership.

⊙ **Unrehurst Vol. 1** (2002; Bebob). Hard-edged contemporary jazz in the customary Hurst style, again in a trio format but this time featuring pianist Robert Glasper and drummer Damion Reid.

➤➤ **Geri Allen** *(The Nurturer);* **Branford Marsalis** *(Crazy People Music);* **Wynton Marsalis** *(Live At Blues Alley).*

Gary Husband

Drums, piano.

b. Leeds, UK, 14 June 1960.

Husband started learning the piano at seven and the drums at ten, and studied theory with his father, a flute player and composer. Since the late 1970s he has worked with many leading UK musicians in London, including Gordon Peck, Jim Mullen and Barbara Thompson. Throughout the 80s and 90s he regularly worked with Allan Holdsworth's group, touring the USA and making a significant contribution to the albums *I.O.U.* (1985) and *Wardenclyffe Tower* (1992). Husband's influences and inspirations range widely, and include jazz greats like Bill Evans and John Coltrane, as well as Eastern and Western classical music, and much pop. In 1987 he joined the jazz/funk outfit Level 42 with whom he enjoyed great success until its demise in 1994. Four years later he formed The New Gary Husband Trio, with Mick Hutton on bass and Gene Caldarazzo on drums, as a showcase for his all-round talents – in particular allowing his brilliant piano playing to take centre stage. The double album, *From The Heart*, appeared the following year on the Jazzizit label. Combining sharply arranged standards with Husband's own compositions, the album had guest appearances from, among others, Georgie Fame, Steve Topping and Jack Bruce. The Trio's second album for Jazzizit, *Aspire*, appeared in 2004. [IC]

⊙ **Aspire** (2004; Jazzizit). An exciting and eclectic selection that reveals both Husband's ambition and his flair. Guest spots include Mark King singing Jobim's Dindi and Christin Tobin giving her all in "Willow Weep For Me", but the highpoint is Husband's own powerfully emotive "New York City – Suite in Four Parts".

➤➤ **Allan Holdsworth** *(I.O.U.)*

Zakir Hussain

Tabla, percussion.

b. Bombay, India, 9 March 1951.

Hussain was introduced to tabla by his father, Ustad Allarakha, a revered master of the instrument. Substituting for Rakha in the ensemble of sitarist Ravi Shankar, Hussain toured the USA in 1969 and joined the ethnomusicological faculty at the University of Washington. His ensuing teaching position with the Ali Akbar Khan College of Music in northern California allowed him to mature in the classical Indian tradition and broadened his experience with such Californian fusion pioneers of the 1970s as John Handy in jazz and Mickey Hart in rock, leading to the formation of such groups as Diga and The Rhythm Experience.

On tour with Khan in 1973, Hussain encountered guitarist John McLaughlin, with whom he created Shakti, the first of their continuing collaborations. Performing and recording with eclectic percussionists such as Tito Puente, Airto Moreira and Olatunji, as well as with Joe Henderson, Yusef Lateef, Pharoah Sanders and other hornsmen expanded Hussain's percussion kit. In 1992 he founded Moment Records, headquartered near his home in San Anselmo, California, which maintains a catalogue of new and reissued albums of fusion and classical Indian material. Hussain has since composed on commission for jazz festivals, ballet and film, and was awarded a National Heritage Fellowship by the United States in 1999. McLaughlin and Hussain regrouped for an international tour that summer – a "Shakti" missing L. Shankar's violin, but with the addition of electric mandolin – and this new incarnation, Remember Shakti, has been caught on several incendiary live albums since. [JK]

⊙ **Making Music** (1987; ECM). The almost humanly articulate sound of the tabla is deployed both in rapid, rhythmically intricate improvised solos and in delicious support of McLaughlin's guitar, the flutes of Hariprasad Chaurasia, and the tenor and soprano saxophones of Jan Garbarek. The compositions by Hussain and McLaughlin helped establish the label's world music consciousness.

Clarence Hutchenrider

Clarinet.

b. Waco, Texas, 13 June 1908; d. 18 Aug 1991.

Clarence Behrens Hutchenrider played with local bands including Austin Wylie (replacing Artie Shaw in 1931) and thereafter the Casa Loma Orchestra (1931–43). From there he embarked on a career in studio work, later combining that with club residencies including Gaslight and Bill's Gay Nineties. Later in his career he worked, amongst others, with Vince Giordano and David Ostwald. Hutchenrider was a fine clarinettist, whose principal influences included Larry Shields and Jimmy Lytell, and whose later recordings reveal a very underrated player. [DF]

➤➤ **Bobby Hackett** *(What A Wonderful World).*

Bobby Hutcherson

Vibes, marimba.

b. Los Angeles, 27 Jan 1941.

Hutcherson only became interested in jazz after hearing a Milt Jackson record. He started playing vibes while at school, getting some tips from Dave Pike and some help with harmony from a local pianist. He worked locally with saxophonists Curtis Amy and Charles Lloyd, then played in San Francisco with the Al Grey-Billy Mitchell group, going with them to New York in 1961 and playing at Birdland. In 1964 he played on Eric Dolphy's seminal album *Out To Lunch*, then freelanced in New York for another year, playing with Archie Shepp, Hank Mobley, Charles Tolliver and Jackie McLean, among others. Back on the West Coast, he worked with small groups and played in Gil Fuller's big band at the Monterey jazz festival in 1965. He won US polls as new star and best vibist in the mid-1960s, and in the later 1960s began to record regularly under his own name for Blue Note. From 1968–71 he co-led a quintet with Harold Land and, when the group split up, Hutcherson stayed in San Francisco leading small groups.

He is a fleet, technically excellent player, who has always performed to a consistently high standard, but towards the end of the 1960s he faded into the backwaters of the jazz scene. However, he re-emerged in the 1980s with renewed confidence and vigour. In the early 1990s he began a very fruitful association with pianist McCoy Tyner, playing and touring internationally with the latter's trio in 1993, and in 1995, recording and touring in duo with Tyner. At this stage in his career, Hutcherson had become an extraordinary virtuoso capable of breathtaking imaginative flights or heart-stopping performances of ballads such as "I Loves You Porgy". They played two concerts at the 1995 Brecon jazz festival, Wales, with a programme of originals, standards and blues. [IC]

⊙ **Dialogue** (1965; Blue Note). This is a classic album of the decade. Each member of the sextet was on the cutting edge of the music – the leader plus Freddie Hubbard, Sam Rivers, Andrew Hill, Richard Davis and Joe Chambers.

⊙ **Happenings** (1966; Blue Note). A marvellous quartet album with Hutcherson and Herbie Hancock in the heyday of their youthful exuberance and a rhythm-section of Albert Stinson and Chambers.

⊙ **Total Eclipse** (1967; Blue Note). A very happy pairing of Hutcherson and Harold Land on tenor and flute, with new star Chick Corea on piano, Reggie Johnson and the redoubtable Chambers.

⊙ **In The Vanguard** (1986; Landmark). This is an exceptional quartet album by any standards. Recorded live at the Village Vanguard in New York, it has Hutcherson in brilliantly compatible company with pianist Kenny Barron and the dream rhythm-section of Buster Williams and Al Foster. The interaction of vibes and piano has a dynamism which recalls the 1970 Gary Burton and Keith Jarrett exchanges on record.

McCoy Tyner/Bobby Hutcherson

⊙ **Manhattan Moods** (1994; Blue Note). The music from this album was performed at the Brecon festival. The two virtuosi, at the height of their powers, were in buoyant mood and their genial and sometimes boisterous playfulness was generated on a basis of equality. They had a lot of shared experiences from the 1960s and they had played duets in previous years, but their rapport was now supreme.

➤➤ **Kenny Barron** *(Other Places)*; **Eric Dolphy** *(Out To Lunch)*.

Margie Hyams

Vibes.
b. New York, 1923.

Hyams's early career is not well documented, but she was playing with a group in Atlantic City when she was "discovered" by Woody Herman. She played for one year with the Herman band in 1944–5, and was replaced by Red Norvo when she formed her own trio, which operated from 1945–8, and included, for a while, Tal Farlow. She took part in the all-women groups led by Mary Lou Williams, on record and at Carnegie Hall in 1947. She was a member of the George Shearing quintet, staying for eighteen months in 1949–50. Since women-only big bands were so common in the late 1930s and during World War II, it is hardly surprising that many of their members were capable of joining previously all-male bands – in practice, however, this happened even more rarely than black musicians joining white bands, though there was clearly less resistance from the public. Hyams's vibes solos were a distinct aural asset to both Herman and Shearing (her trio apparently made no records), but she married trumpeter Rolf Ericson and promptly retired from active playing to concentrate on teaching. [BP]

➤➤ **George Shearing** *(Verve Jazz Masters)*.

Ken Hyder

Drums, percussion, vocals.
b. Dundee, Scotland, 29 June 1946.

Equally at home with jazz standards, free jazz and folk-based music, Ken Hyder began playing at fourteen, influenced by Elvin Jones and Paul Motian, but soon immersed himself in folk music, setting up Talisker at the end of the 1960s to play a mixture of Celtic music and jazz. After recording several albums and touring Europe with the band, Hyder began to interest himself in indigenous musics of all kinds, including the shamanic music of the Inuit native Canadians and throat singing from Tuva, on Siberia's Mongolian border. He has collaborated with an extraordinary variety of singers and musicians, including the UK's Elton Dean and Phil Minton, Japanese shakuhachi player Shiku Yano, and Altai throat singer Anatoly Kokov, and he has recorded with folk singer Frankie Armstrong, uilleann pipes player Tomas Lynch and Tuvan singer Sainkho Namchylak, whose home base, Siberia, is currently the source of Hyder's strongest musical influence. In the mid-1990s, Hyder joined up with two other enthusiasts for "spirit music", bassist Marcio Mattos and trumpeter Jim Dvorak, in the Bardo State Orchestra, and produced two albums, *The Ultimate Gift* (Impetus; 1994), full of lengthy but absorbing collective improvisations, and *Wheels Within Wheels* (see below). Two of his recent projects included the acclaimed trio K-Space (see below) and Hoots And Roots, a duo with fellow avant-garde Scot Maggie Nichols. [CP]

Big Team

⊙ **Under The Influence** (1984; Konnex). Suite touching on many areas of Hyder's musical and extra-musical influences, from the jute mills of Dundee through Lord Buckley to free jazz. A heady, highly emotional album featuring saxophonists Elton Dean and Chris Biscoe and bassist Paul Rogers.

Talisker

Humanity (1985; Impetus). Folk-based jazz featuring violinist Sylvia Hallett and poet/guitarist Don Paterson in his pre-Lammas days.

Vladimir Rezitsky

Hot Sounds From The Arctic (1994; Leo). Compilation of the work of seminal alto player Rezitsky; Hyder is featured on voice and drums on two tracks – one, "Planet Rezitsky", recorded at Jazz Days Arkhangelsk 1992.

Bardo State Orchestra

Wheels Within Wheels (1995; Impetus). The BSO are joined by monks from a Nepalese Buddhist monastery for this extraordinary album, and their doubled-reeded instruments etc bring great textural variety to the overall group sound.

K-Space

Bear Bones (2002; Slam). Featuring ex-Henry Cow saxist and guitarist Tim Hodgkinson and the shamanic throat-singing of Gendos Chamzyryn, further striking exploration of Hyder's preoccupation with the freeform and the ritualistic.

Dick Hyman

Piano, composer, organ, clarinet.
b. New York, 8 March 1927.

A pupil of Teddy Wilson, Hyman played with Red Norvo in 1949 and Benny Goodman in 1950, but he first came to notice in the 1950s as a staffman for WMCA, MGM and NBC (sometimes linked to jazz, sometimes not), though even here his output gave little indication of either his world-class ability or his eclectic jazz interests: an early pointer to his real stature was the series of *History Of Jazz* concerts, for which he collaborated with critic/commentator Leonard Feather. Throughout the 1960s Hyman was again involved in a wide spread of musical areas, including free jazz, jazz-rock, symphonic composition (he wrote a piano concerto) and early experimentation with synthesizers (as recorded on the album *The Electric Eclectics Of Dick Hyman*).

In the 1970s he began to re-examine the classic areas of jazz with the New York Jazz Repertory Company, playing concerts and recording albums which re-created the music of Louis Armstrong, James P. Johnson, Jelly Roll Morton and Scott Joplin. By the late 1970s Hyman's work had placed him alongside Bob Wilber as the most dedicated and scholarly of jazz researchers, and his Perfect Jazz Quintet had become a delightful addition to America's classic small groups. In the 1980s he shone as a virtuoso performer, often playing in the company of Ruby Braff, with whom he created duet music as profound as that created by Hines and Armstrong. Since then Hyman has continued to work internationally, most regularly with musicians of classic persuasions. His unobtrusive skills as archivist, arranger and musical director are matched by his Tatum-esque mastery of the piano – a level of talent still to be fully acknowledged by the critical fraternity. [DF]

Dick Hyman

The Music Of Jelly Roll Morton (1973; Columbia). Surrounded by musical equals – including violinist Joe Venuti – Hyman re-creates much of the best of Morton in a way that the inventor would have liked.

Satchmo Remembered: The Music Of Louis Armstrong At Carnegie Hall (1975; Atlantic). Hyman's New York Jazz Repertory Company created some of the best jazz homages, and this tribute to Armstrong is one of their finest, with harmonized re-creations of Armstrong solos by trumpeters Mel Davis, Pee Wee Erwin, Joe Newman and Ray Nance. Ruby Braff is also in attendance.

Charleston (1975; Columbia). A wonderful re-creation of James P. Johnson's compositions, featuring Hyman solo and in duos with Braff, plus his seven-piece jazz band (with Bob Wilber and Vic Dickenson) and full-scale Theater Orchestra.

Dick Hyman and Ruby Braff

A Pipe Organ Recital Plus One (1982; Concord). One of Hyman's principal later achievements was to tame the mighty Wurlitzer organ for duets with the great Braff; his skills produce the perfect colourful backdrop for Braff's creations.

Dick Hyman

Music Of 1937 (1990; Concord). All Hyman's strengths show up here, chiefly intelligent and detailed programming, and solo piano work of faultless quality.

Cheek To Cheek (1995; Arbors). A masterly trio date with Bob Haggart and Howard Alden encompassing Monk and Flip Phillips through to popular standards, all treated with understanding and inspiration.

>> **Ruby Braff** *(With An Extra Bit Of Luck; Younger Than Swingtime).*

I

Susie Ibarra

Drums, percussion, gongs.
b. Anaheim, California, 15 Nov 1970.

Brought up in Texas, Ibarra played classical piano and organ before beginning on drums at sixteen. She studied art in New York but, after hearing Sun Ra live, switched to Mannes College of Music. She has also studied privately with legendary drummer, Vernel Fournier, and drummer and musical therapist, Milford Graves. In addition to mastering the techniques of classical and free jazz drumming, Ibarra has studied and become adept at the percussion music of Bali, Java and her ancestral home, the Philippines. Throughout the 1990s Ibarra's unique style of playing has been in high demand and she has worked with a host of key figures including John Zorn, Derek Bailey and Dave Douglas. Regular collaborations with bassist William Parker and pianist Mathew Shipp resulted in the album *Go See The World* (1998), on which the three were joined by David S. Ware as leader on tenor sax. In addition to leading her own groups, Ibarra has given many solo performances and created an interactive sound installation for the Pope John Paul II Cultural Center, Washington DC. In either group or solo context, whether free or more groove-oriented, Ibarra is sensitive, superbly dynamic and less overbearing than many contemporary drummers. [BP]

⊙ **Flower After Flower** (1999; Tzadik). Working with several regular collaborators including violinist Charles Burnham, Ibarra features the horns of Chris Speed, Assif Tsahar (her ex-husband) and Wadada Leo Smith in four long pieces, with brief percussion links between tracks.

➤➤ **Matthew Shipp** (*Multiplication Table*).

Abdullah Ibrahim (aka Dollar Brand)

Piano, composer, Indian-African flute, soprano saxophone, cello, vocals.
b. Cape Town, South Africa, 9 Oct 1934.

Ibrahim was born Adolph Johannes Brand and adopted Dollar Brand as a stage name; he later

CLAUDIO CASANOVA

Susie Ibarra

Jak Kilby

Abdullah Ibrahim

changed his name to Abdullah Ibrahim when he converted to Islam. His grandmother played piano in church and he had private piano lessons from the age of seven. He grew up with the hymns, gospel songs and spirituals of the American-influenced African Methodist Episcopal Church, but also heard Louis Jordan and the Tympany Five popular hits blaring from the township ice-cream vans. Duke Ellington's music was so familiar that he was "not regarded as a foreign musician, but rather as something like a wise old man of our community *in abstentia*".

His first professional job was with a vocal group, The Streamline Brothers, singing traditional songs, American popular songs, doo-wop and spirituals; then he played piano with the Tuxedo Slickers, followed by a period with the Willie Max dance band in 1959. In 1960–61, he led his own band, the Jazz Epistles, which included Hugh Masekela (trumpet) and Kippie Moeketsi (alto saxophone) and was the first black group in South Africa to record an LP.

He moved to Europe in 1962, playing for two years at the Café Africana in Zurich. In February 1963 his wife-to-be Bea Benjamin persuaded Duke Ellington to hear him play, and Duke was so impressed that he fixed up a recording session for him. As a result of Ellington's sponsorship, Ibrahim played at the Antibes, Juan-les-Pins and Palermo festivals in 1963. In 1964–5, he played at the Montmartre in Copenhagen. At Ellington's urging he went to the USA in 1965, played at the Newport festival and stayed on in New York for three years, where he got deeply involved with the free jazz scene, working with John Coltrane, Don Cherry, Ornette Coleman and Sunny Murray, and playing with the Elvin Jones quartet in 1966. From then until the mid-1970s he divided his time between Africa, Europe and the USA.

His early influences included Monk as well as Ellington, and also Moeketsi and his own African heritage, but all of these tended to become obscured during his involvement in free jazz. After his return to Africa in 1968 and his conversion to Islam, he rejected total abstraction and returned to his African roots, changing in the process from a very good musician into a great one. In his music of the 1970s and 1980s composition and structure were as important as improvisation, a great variety of rhythms were explored, and there was a tremendous harmonic, melodic and emotional resonance. Having rediscovered his own identity, his art gained immense power and projection, incorporating African chants, carnival music, rural laments, and the sonorities of church hymns – the inner-voicing of chords and moving (and emotive) bass lines.

From 1970–76 he toured and played major festivals in Europe, the USA, Scandinavia, Japan, Australia and Canada. Most of his appearances were as a solo pianist, but in 1974 he toured with a ten-piece band. In 1976 Ibrahim organized a South African jazz festival which flouted all the rules of apartheid, and a few days afterwards he left the country. In 1977 he moved to the USA, basing himself in New York, and since then has toured as solo performer, in duo, trio and quartet formations and with larger groups, his wife Sathima (Bea Benjamin) often appearing with him.

In 1982 he and Sathima spent two weeks on a cultural mission to Mozambique; the same year, Ibrahim's *Kalahari Liberation Opera*, a multimedia collage of drama, music and dance, was first performed, and was hailed as "one of the most important artistic productions of the South African resistance". In the mid-1980s he began leading a seven-piece ensemble called Ekaya ("home"), dedicating its work to the people of his home country still under the tyranny of apartheid. The group, which lasted several years, featured Carlos Ward (alto saxophone and flute), Ricky Ford (tenor), Charles Davis (baritone), Dick Griffin (trombone), Ben Riley (drums) and Essiet Okon Essiet (bass). Of this group Thomas Rome commented, "The creative challenges ... are fuelling an intense but measured compositional outpouring on Ibrahim's part. As the members of the ensemble grow more and more intimate with Ibrahim's compositions, the harmonic brilliance of Ekaya's sound seems to be reaching audiences ever more profoundly."

In the later 80s Ibrahim wrote and performed the music for two French films, *Chocolat* (the soundtrack was released under the title *Mindif*) and *No Fear No Die*. The changing political situation in South Africa encouraged him to renew musical association with players who had stayed there, notably the saxophonist Basil Coetzee, and by 1993 Ibrahim was once more spending much of his time in the country of his birth. [IC]

Abdullah Ibrahim

⊙ **African Piano** (1969; Japo). The reborn Ibrahim re-examines his African roots, but the European and jazz traditions also leaven his playing. He can make the piano sing with his resonant chord voicings and bass notes, and the jubilant and ecstatic sometimes turn to an exile's melancholy. This is a rich and moving album.

⊙ **African Sketchbook** (1973; Enja). This begins with an unaccompanied flute solo which is simple and haunting, but the piano playing lacks the homogeneity of the earlier album. There are good moments, but the improvisations are at times wild and even scrappy. However, it concludes with Ibrahim's great hymn "Salaam – Peace – Hamba Khale", which always delights and reassures.

⊙ **African Space Programme** (1973; Enja). The eleven-piece band is full of stars including Cecil Bridgewater, Enrico Rava, Hamiet Bluiett, Sonny Fortune, Carlos Ward and bassist Cecil McBee. It's a bit of a bash with some dour and heavy chords in the totally written opening and a hot gospel piece in 6/4 which starts promisingly but becomes a series of solos with loud backing riffs.

Abdullah Ibrahim and Johnny Dyani

⊙ **Good News From Africa** (1973; Enja); **Echoes From Africa** (1979; Enja). The rapport between these two exiles is wondrous to witness. Singing and playing (and Ibrahim plays some flute on the earlier album), they celebrate and yearn for their homeland. *Echoes* opens with a seventeen-minute hypnotic groove on one chord with the voices in unison and harmony punctuated by passionate piano interludes and occasional shouts. Other pieces are sonorously elegaic or have a poignant atmosphere of exultation and sorrow.

Abdullah Ibrahim

⊙ **At Montreux** (1980; Enja). For this live session, Ibrahim led a quintet which included Carlos Ward and trombonist Craig Harris, with electric bass and drums. Several of Ibrahim's most beautiful compositions are on this programme, including "The Wedding" and "The Perfumed Forest Wet With Rain". The rhythm-section pushes things along, and Ward and Harris dig deep. A fine album with lots of colour and space.

⊙ **Zimbabwe** (1983; Enja). Carlos Ward was magnified by his association with Ibrahim, and the latter's music was served brilliantly by Ward. Here they are in quartet format with Essiet Okun Essiet on bass and Don Mumford on drums. There are four strong compositions by Ibrahim and three standards including "Don't Blame Me" and "It Never Entered My Mind". The balance of African and jazz elements is well nigh perfect and the group plays superbly.

Ekaya

⊙ **Water From An Ancient Well** (1985; Tiptoe). This features Ibrahim's band Ekaya, with Ward, Ricky Ford, plus baritone saxophone, trombone and rhythm-section. The emphasis is on Ibrahim's writing, which is much more deft and eloquent than on *African Space Programme*. "Daughter Of Capetown" pays moving homage to his wife, Sathima (Bea Benjamin), and again there is a good balance between Africa and America in these performances.

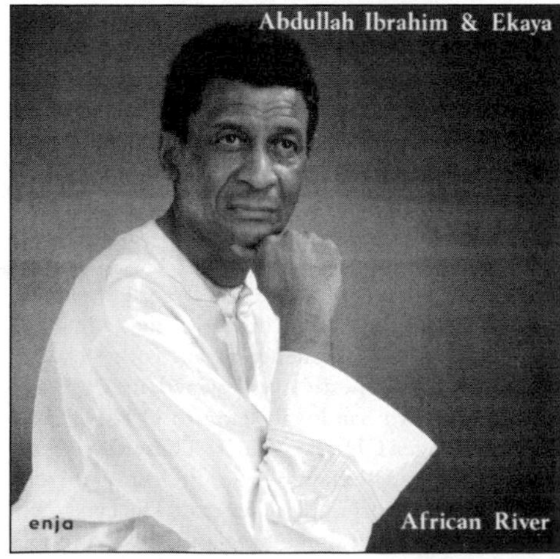

⊙ **African River** (1989; Enja). This beautiful and deeply considered album has some glorious composing and arranging by Ibrahim and superb solos from Robin Eubanks (trombone), John Stubblefield and Horace Alexander Young on reeds and flute/piccolo, and the multi-instrumentalist Howard Johnson. The rhythm-section with Buster Williams (bass) and the South African Brian Abrahams (wrongly listed as Adams) on drums is also excellent. One of Ibrahim's most brilliant and humane albums.

Abdullah Ibrahim

⊙ **Cape Town Flowers** (1997; Tiptoe). With his trio, bassist Marcus McLaurine and drummer George Gray, Ibrahim, the charismatic storyteller in music (as are all the greatest jazz musicians) plays eleven "tales" for us. The war is over, the old soldier has returned home and his music exudes the warmth of this consummative afterglow. Delightful.

⊙ **African Suite For Trio and String Orchestra** (1997; Tiptoe). All eleven compositions are by Ibrahim, but the arrangements for string orchestra were written by Daniel Schnyder. The recording was done at L'Abbatiale de Payerne, Switzerland, thus following the trend set by Garbarek's *Officium* of using church acoustics. Some of Ibrahim's most beautiful pieces are here, such as "The Wedding". His attractive melodies and often sumptuous harmonies are enhanced by the strings, and by the fact that he plays minimal piano throughout – except in the piece "Aspen" which is a charming romantic solo piano effort. His brief, very rhythmic piece "Blanton" is played by the strings alone. At times, it all seems perilously near easy-listening music, but Ibrahim's charisma and quality prevail.

Nikki Iles

Piano, accordion.

b. Dunstable, Bedfordshire, UK, 16 May 1963.

Iles was a junior exhibitioner at London's Royal Academy of Music, 1974–81, studying clarinet and piano. She then went on to study piano and alto saxophone at the Leeds College of Music (1981–84). Iles had started out in youth orchestras and youth big bands in Bedfordshire, before moving to Leeds to study and settle there. She eventually moved back to London in September 1998.

The first platform for her own composing was the group Emanon, led by Richard Iles (whom she married), which also included guitarist Mike Walker and Iain Dixon. The meeting of these kindred spirits was significant for all of their developments. They were all founder members of the Creative Jazz Orchestra, working with Vince Mendoza, Anthony Braxton, Mike Gibbs, Kenny Wheeler and Bobby Previte. Iles also began working with other groups including Julian Argüelles, Mick Hutton's Straight Face, Stan Sulzmann's quartet, the Tina May quartet, Norma Winstone, Kenny Wheeler and other lions young or mature of the UK scene. She also played with Americans Art Farmer and Scott Hamilton.

In 1996, Iles won John Dankworth's Special Award at the BT Jazz Awards and that same year she recorded a duo CD, *Treasure Trove* (ASC Records), with Stan Sulzmann, which was the beginning of an ongoing musical relationship. A year later, she recorded a duo CD with Tina May, *Change Of Sky* (33 Records), and a CD with Martin Speake, *The*

Tan Tien (FMR). Composition remains a major part of her musical life, and she has had commissions from the Creative Jazz Orchestra for "The Printmakers Suite" (1994), from John Willians's *New Perspectives* (1998–9) celebrating the role of women in jazz, and others from the Berkshire Youth Jazz Orchestra, January 1999, and the London Sinfonietta Ellington Celebrations, April 1999. In 2003 her quintet released a new album, *Veils*, which was followed by an outstanding tribute album, *Everything I Love* (2004; Basho), by the Nikki Iles Trio. [IC]

Stan Sulzmann/Nikki Iles

⊙ **Treasure Trove** (1996; ASC Records). This is a quiet, exquisite duo album. Three of the compositions are by Iles, and reveal her great melodic gifts and the singing subtlety of her harmonies. These qualities also inform her piano-playing – her fine touch, the sonorities and her flow. Five of the compositions are by Sulzmann, who plays saxophones, clarinet and flutes, and as player and composer he has similar poetic qualities to Iles, which is why the music they make together is so ecstatic.

Peter Ind

Bass.

b. Uxbridge, Middlesex, UK, 20 July 1928.

Ind studied piano and harmony at Trinity College, Cambridge, and took up the bass in 1947. He moved to the USA in 1951 and studied with Lennie Tristano, playing with Lee Konitz, Coleman Hawkins, Buddy Rich, Paul Bley, Roy Eldridge and others. From 1963–6 he lived in Big Sur, California, and then returned to the UK, living in London, freelancing and teaching. He has recorded as a sideman with many leading musicians including Tubby Hayes (*Jazz Tête a Tête*), Lee Konitz (*Lee Konitz*) and Lennie Tristano. He started his own record company, Wave Records, and during the 1970s opened a recording studio and, in the 1980s, his own club, the Bass Clef, which presented jazz and related music (often with Ind backing visiting musicians) until it closed in 1994. Since then his focus has been the release of fine recordings on Wave. [IC]

➤➤ **Lennie Tristano** *(Lennie Tristano/The New Tristano).*

Keith Ingham

Piano.

b. London, 5 Feb 1942.

A strong all-rounder whose tastes run from Bunk Johnson to John Coltrane and beyond, Ingham began in the mid-1960s working with most of the best British mainstream musicians, including Sandy Brown, Bruce Turner, Dick Sudhalter, Lennie Hastings and Ron Russell. In the following decade he also formed a professional relationship with singer Susannah McCorkle and built a reputation amongst musicians and perceptive critics as a pianist of encyclopoedic repertoire, formidable technique and extraordinary power matched by delicacy according to context. As a soloist with the help of producer/singer Chris Ellis he recorded excellent albums for EMI at the period. A natural choice for visiting Americans such as "Red" Allen, Pee Wee Russell, Charlie Shavers and Ben Webster, Ingham made an exploratory trip to New York, accompanying McCorkle at the Riverboat Room in 1975, and three years later moved there permanently. He worked with Ed Polcer and others at Eddie Condon's, with Benny Goodman and with The World's Greatest Jazz Band, as well as accompanying McCorkle (with whom he recorded several albums), and also worked the rounds of hotels, piano bars and jazz festivals as a soloist. In the mid-1980s he toured Britain with the Eddie Condon Memorial band (led by Polcer), and collaborated with singer Maxine Sullivan – their album *Songs From The Cotton Club* was nominated for a Grammy. Since then he has continued to perform solo and in the best company in the USA (with occasional visits back home), often with guitarist Marty Grosz and tenorist Harry Allen, two strong kindred spirits. [DF]

Keith Ingham

⊙ **Out Of The Past** (1990; Sackville). Enormously skilful piano-solo recital, moving with comfortable ease from "Jazzin' Babies Blues" by Richard M. Jones to "Sphere" by Barry Harris.

⊙ **Music From The Mauve Decades** (1993; Sackville). Ingham's powerful left hand effortlessly replaces the bass in this trio with clarinettist Bobby Gordon and drummer Hal Smith, playing music from the dawn of jazz.

Keith Ingham and Harry Allen

⊙ **My Little Brown Book/The Intimacy Of The Blues: A Celebration Of Billy Strayhorn's Music Vols. 1 & 2** (1993; Progressive). This two-disc set is a major undertaking, in which Ingham and Allen examine in detail the special beauties of the music of Billy Strayhorn, whose work is all too often aurally confused with Ellington's. Music of prime quality.

⊙ **New York Nine** (Vols. 1 & 2) (1994; Jump). An ambitious and finely conceived project: to re-create the freshness of groups like Brad Gowan's original New York Nine (1946) with the sophistication of West Coast Dixieland of the period, as featured on the original Jump label! Much joyful music here, starring Ingham, Dan Barrett, Phil Bodner, Scott Robinson et al.

⊙ **A Mellow Bit Of Rhythm** (1997; Sackville). A typically thorough example of Ingham research; the music of black woman composers including Irene Wilson, Bessie Smith, Lil Armstrong, Una Mae Carlisle and more. With Bob Barnard (cornet) – excellent.

➤➤ **Marty Grosz** *(Unsaturated Fats; Donaldson Redux).*

Irakere

The Cuban band Irakere has its origins in the Orquesta Cubana de Música Moderna, a name chosen to signal the influence of jazz without specifying it. This orchestra was formed in 1967 and included Arturo Sandoval, Paquito D'Rivera and pianist-arranger Chucho Valdés. These three were the key players who then went on to form Irakere in 1973, with Valdés as musical director. The band's aim was to further the fusion of jazz and rock with both contemporary and traditional Cuban styles, developed independently of New York salsa. Their work was highly praised in 1977 by such as Dizzy Gillespie and Stan Getz, among the first official US visitors to Cuba for nearly two decades, and in 1978 the band appeared in Europe and New York. Despite the departure of Sandoval to form his own group, D'Rivera's defection from Cuba, and the virtual non-existence of further US appearances in the 80s and 90s, Irakere (currently led by Chucho's son, Luís Valdés) has maintained its international reputation and popularity. [BP]

La Colección Cubana (1977–95; MCI/Nascente). Although Sandoval is hardly heard, there are voluble saxophone and guitar solos in this wide survey of the band's locally made albums. But the most arresting contributor is Valdés with his Tyner-influenced keyboard work and Latin-bop compositions such as "Estela Va A Estallar" (based on "Stella By Starlight") and the "Confirmation"-inspired "Las Margeritas".

Charlie Irvis

Trombone.

b. New York, c. 1899; d. c. 1939.

By the early 1920s Irvis was playing clubs with Willie "The Lion" Smith, among others. He also worked regularly with Bubber Miley, a boyhood friend, with whom in 1923 he introduced a revolutionary "new sound" at the Bucket of Blood Club, on 135th Street. Using a whole set of mutes, including half a yo-yo, Irvis produced growling music that set a pattern for future specialists such as "Tricky Sam" Nanton, and attracted the attention of famous leaders including Paul Whiteman. Young Duke Ellington hauled Irvis and Miley into Elmer Snowden's Washingtonians (soon to become Duke Ellington's), and began to write material for them. Ellington said later: "There was a kind of mute they built at the time to go into a trombone and make it sound like a saxophone but he dropped his one night and the darned thing broke – so he picked up the part that was left and started using it. That was his device and it was greater than the original thing. He got a great big fat sound at the bottom end of the trombone – melodic, masculine, full of tremendous authority." Some of that sound can be heard on records Irvis made with Clarence Williams, Fats Waller ("Minor Drag", "Harlem Fuss") and Jelly Roll Morton ("Tank Town Bump", "Burning The Iceberg"). He went on working with Charlie Johnson and Miley into the 1930s but was inactive by 1939. [DF]

Dennis Irwin

Bass.

b. Birmingham, Alabama, 28 Nov 1951.

A clarinettist from the age of nine, Irwin studied music at North Texas State University from 1969–74, switching to bass while there and playing in Dallas with Red Garland. He then moved to New York, gigging widely and working with Betty Carter in 1976 and Art Blakey from 1977–80. Other important associations were with the Mel Lewis band from 1981–90, Johnny Griffin from 1988–91 and John Scofield from 1992–4. A great believer in the use of gut instead of metal strings, he has said, "Young players don't realize until they try, that that's why Wilbur Ware and Paul Chambers sound the way they do." [BP]

JOHN SCOFIELD

Hand Jive (1993; Blue Note). Irwin's strong bass work is heard more prominently in this set than many, especially in the repeated riffs on several numbers which recall the acoustic jazz-funk trends of the 1960s.

Ike Isaacs

Guitar.

b. Rangoon, Burma, 1 Dec 1919; d. Sydney, Australia, 10 Jan 1996.

Isaacs came to Britain in 1946 and worked many years with Ted Heath and with the BBC Showband, as well as leading his quartet for the BBC's weekly Guitar Club in the 1950s. Later he worked as a prolific studio man and in the 1970s toured with Stephane Grappelli's quartet, the co-operative quartet Velvet (with Denny Wright, Len Skeat and Digby Fairweather) and played regularly in duo with Martin Taylor. A master technician who for many years wrote about guitar technique in professional journals, Isaacs moved to Australia to take up a professorship at Sydney Guitar School in the early 1980s. After that he continued to teach, play and record, visiting Britain for solo dates and all-star guitar shows, until illness immobilized him in 1995. [DF]

Intimate Interpretations (1992; Ike Isaacs Music). A very welcome late solo CD, beautifully recorded, showing off his guitar mastery in an unhurried recital.

Mark Isham

Trumpet, flugelhorn and flumpet.

b. New York, 7 Sept 1951.

From an early age Isham studied classical piano, violin and trumpet, and after the family moved to California, he played trumpet in the Oakland and San Francisco Symphony Orchestras and the San Francisco Opera Orchestra. Isham also began playing in jazz and rock bands and, in his early twenties, became interested in electronic music, earning a reputation as a synthesizer programmer. But the trumpet remained his first love, and he was soon much in demand in the recording studio as a solo instrumentalist or rock accompanist. During the 1970s, he recorded and/or toured with The Beach Boys, Ester

Phillips, Charles Lloyd, Pharoah Sanders and Van Morrison. He was also a member of pianist Art Lande's Rubisa Patrol and produced two of Lande's solo albums. During the 1980s and 90s, Isham's trumpet-playing was featured on albums by several rock stars, including David Sylvian, Tanita Tikaram and The Rolling Stones.

The early 90s saw him form the Mark Isham Jazz Band, playing acoustic jazz. Around that same time, he began to explore his classical background, and composed *Five Short Stories For Trumpet And Orchestra*, his first commissioned work for the St Louis Symphony Orchestra. It was premiered in 1992, with Isham playing the solo trumpet part. He is also much in demand as a film composer in Hollywood, and has scored more than thirty movies since 1986. Today, Mark is still heavily involved in film, but has also found time to radically remix a few classics, from the likes of Ella Fitzgerald and Cole Porter, for an advertising campaign.

Isham is an excellent trumpet player, a fine musician and a talented composer. Although he loves Miles Davis, when playing jazz on open trumpet, Isham sometimes sounds detached, as if barely involved. Some of his most incisive playing is achieved using the harmon mute, which is in a Milesian mode, and seems to release Isham's passion to communicate. [IC]

⊙ **Blue Sun** (1995; Sony Music). Isham composed seven of the nine pieces on this brooding and mostly elegaic album, which is performed by a quintet with David Goldblatt (keyboards), Steve Tavaglione (tenor saxophone), Doug Lunn (electric bass) and Kurt Wurtman (drums). Isham is highly focused on trumpet and flugelhorn, and he's an inventive composer. There's some excellent harmon mute work on the fast rock piece "Trapeze", and moody harmon on the title track.

⊙ **Afterglow** (1998; Sony Music). Isham composed all ten pieces for the eponymous film starring Julie Christie and Nick Nolte, and recruited some leading jazz musicians – tenor saxophonist Charles Lloyd, Gary Burton (vibes), Geri Allen (piano), Billy Higgins (drums), Jeff Littleton (bass). The mood again is generally romantic and melancholy, with Lloyd's passionate improvising emphasizing Isham's detachment on open trumpet.

Chuck Israels

Bass, composer.
b. New York, 10 Oct 1936.

Israels studied music in the USA and Paris, becoming interested in jazz at eighteen. He recorded with the Cecil Taylor studio group in 1958 (the music was reissued as by John Coltrane) and with Eric Dolphy in 1961. He formed regular working associations with the George Russell sextet in 1960 and Bill Evans from 1961–6. In 1966 he formed a rehearsal band and had his compositions played by European radio orchestras. He also founded the National Jazz Ensemble repertory group, which operated from 1973–8, and for which he conducted and (with others) arranged. Resident in the San Francisco area, he appeared on record with the Kronos string quartet in 1984 and with his own trio in Moscow and Germany. Israels's contribution to the Evans trio was far less flamboyant than other incumbents, but he has said recently, "My growth has come late. I think I'm a much better musician now than I was when I was with Bill." [BP]

Bill Evans

⊙ **At Shelly's Manne-Hole** (1963; Riverside/OJC). A live set that amply demonstrates Israels's fluency and responsiveness, despite his apparently back-seat role compared to Scott LaFaro.

Chuck Israels

⊙ **On Common Ground** (1991; Anima). Israels leads an international trio of Azerbaijani pianist David Gazarov and Yugoslav drummer Lala Kovacev on material such as the leader's "New Sarabande" and several pieces by Gazarov.

Italian Instabile Orchestra

This "unstable" orchestra was formed in 1990, and after a few teething problems has proved to be a very stable unit, with few personnel changes. By 1998, it had released three CDs and given over forty international performances. The orchestra was created to challenge the predictability of much post-modernist jazz in the 1980s – the neo-bop, the bland fusionists, the lax acceptance of existing forms. It took live wire trumpeter, Pino Minafra, from Puglia in southern Italy, and a dynamic organizer, Riccardo Bergerone, from Turin in the north, to make the whole thing happen. Jazz musicians have been notoriously purist about their personal ideological musical stances, but Minafra managed to recruit around twenty leading Italian musicians, from at least three generations of musicians, who learned to respect one another's disparate musical aims. Minafra was the prime mover, but the orchestra has no leader and is a democratic unit with its own committee, which includes Bergerone, and which determines who will write for the band, and monitors the allocation of solo space. So far, fifteen of the twenty-four musicians have contributed pieces to the book.

The orchestra's musical scope is very broad, encompassing elements from jazz, free improvisation, popular song, folk, ethnic and classical music. Its essential Italian identity encourages an emphasis on melody, a preference for the narrative, and a geniality in its music-making, and it succeeds in balancing composition with improvisation, and tonality with harmonic abstraction. The orchestra's first and eponymous CD featured recordings from June 1991 and January 1992. [IC]

Skies Of Europe (1994; ECM). The Italian Instabile Orchestra's second album is a *tour de force*. It consists of two long suites, "Il Maestro Muratore" (The Master Mason) by the bassist, Bruno Tomaso, and "Skies of Europe" by the pianist Giorgio Gaslini. The inspirations for both suites are leading figures in the visual arts. For Tomaso – the sculptor Constantino Nivola and the architect Le Corbusier; and for Gaslini – Duchamp, Kandinsky, Marlene Dietrich, Antonioni and Fellini. Both suites celebrate things European, and encompass a huge variety of music, with marvellous lyrical passages by Gaslini, wonderful strings – Paolo Damiani (cello), Renato Geremia (violin) – and huge orchestral edifices, both written and improvised. Much sublety in the quieter moments, and powerful solo work.

Ethan Iverson

Piano.

b. Menomonie, Minnesota, 11 Feb 1973.

Iverson had the benefit of classical piano tuition when young, but soon developed an ear for jazz. A long-standing partnership with Minneapolis native and bassist, Reid Anderson, began with a performance of Monk's "Bemsha Swing" in 1989, when Iverson was a high-school senior and Anderson a college freshman. After moving to New York in the early 1990s, he continued his studies with Sophia Rosoff and Fred Hersch, and became the musical director of the Mark Morris Dance Group for five years. This position allowed Iverson to explore a wide range of musical genres, from collaborations with tabla great, Zakir Hussain, to reworkings of popular songs from the 1930s. Iverson maintained his jazz credentials through recordings with guitarist Kurt Rosenwinkel and saxophonist Mark Turner, as well as making several trio albums with Anderson released on Spain's Fresh Sound label. The last of these records, made in 2000, and incorporating fellow Minnesotan drummer David King, was titled *The Bad Plus*, which henceforth became the group's name and led to them signing a contract with Columbia Records. With The Bad Plus one sees the intensity of Iverson's approach well balanced by the more mischievous and populist instincts of the other trio members. [BP]

The Bad Plus

These Are The Vistas (2002; Columbia). An impressive onslaught of post-modernist techniques are brought to bear on both original material by all three group members, along with deconstructions of popular songs by Nirvana, Aphex Twin and Blondie.

David Izenzon

Bass, composer.

b. Pittsburgh, Pennsylvania, 17 May 1932; d. 8 Oct 1979.

Izenzon took up the bass in 1956, playing locally until 1961 when he moved to New York. He became deeply involved with the avant-garde, working with Paul Bley, Archie Shepp, Bill Dixon and Ornette Coleman, but also gigged with less abstract players such as Sonny Rollins and Mose Allison. He came to international prominence with the Ornette Coleman trio in the mid-1960s, touring and recording in Europe. In the later 1960s, he led his own quintet in the New York area, and also worked with Perry Robinson, Jaki Byard and others. From 1968–71 he taught music history at Bronx Community College. From 1972 he curtailed his playing in order to devote time to his son Solomon, who was born with severe brain damage. In 1973 he received a PhD in psychotherapy from Northwestern University, and started a private practice in New York. In 1975, he composed and performed a jazz opera, *How Music Can Save The World*, dedicated to all those who helped care for his son. He also performed in the late 70s alongside Paul Motian. [IC]

➤➤ **Ornette Coleman** *(Live At The Golden Circle Vols. 1 & 2).*

Jackie and Roy

The best-known vocal duo in jazz history, Jackie and Roy (Jackie Cain, b. Milwaukee, 22 May 1928; Roy Joseph Kral, b. Chicago, 10 Oct 1921; d. 2 Aug 2002) sprang to prominence with Charlie Ventura's high-powered Bop For The People combo. Their vocal routines on jazz hits like "I'm Forever Blowing Bubbles", "Euphoria" and "East Of Suez" created a stir for Ventura, notably at a 1949 Pasadena concert hosted by Gene Norman and recorded by the group. The album became an international hit, but after marrying a matter of weeks after the concert they left Ventura and formed their own group, including guitarist Joe Romano and bassist Kenny O'Brien. After six years in Chicago the duo went to New York to continue work as a duo, worked Las Vegas (1967–73) and over the following decades produced a formidable discography of ever-brilliant vocal albums. They also composed and sang TV commercials as well as appearing at festivals and clubs and producing TV specials, not least their PBS *Alltime American Songbook*. Jackie and Roy continued performing until a matter of weeks before Kral's death; the story of their career is a triumph of good music over prevailing fashion and an inspirational example to musicians everywhere. [DF]

Charlie Ventura

⊙ **Bop For The People** (1945–9; Properbox). Back where the story started; disc 4 of this set is the complete Pasadena concert which established Jackie and Roy as international stars. Much of their other work is confined to vinyl but time will put that right.

Jackie and Roy

⊙ **High Standards** (1982; Concord). Recorded with a quartet – Kral (piano), Paul Johnson (vibes), Dean Johnson (bass) and Jeff Brillinger (drums) – the ten tunes show off every aspect of their high art.

Chubby Jackson

Bass.

b. New York, 25 Oct 1918; d. 1 Oct 2003.

Jackson played the clarinet at sixteen, then switched to bass, working professionally from 1937 onwards. He worked with Charlie Barnet from 1941–3 and with Woody Herman from 1943–6 and in 1948. He was also with the Charlie Ventura septet in 1947, had his own small group in 1947–8 and a short-lived big band in 1948–9. Freelance and studio work followed in the 1950s, and he also became a TV personality and songwriter. He worked briefly with Harold Baker in 1963, and led occasional groups in New York, Florida, Los Angeles and Las Vegas. He reappeared on the jazz scene with the Lionel Hampton all-star band of 1978–9. His son Duffy Jackson (b. 3 July 1953) played drums in both the Hampton and Count Basie bands in the early 1980s. Chubby's own sprightly bass work is still associated most strongly with the Herman band, to which he gave a tremendous rhythmic lift. He was also known, several years before Charles Mingus, for shouting out his encouragement of the band's soloists. [BP]

➤➤ **Woody Herman** *(The Thundering Herds).*

Cliff Jackson

Piano.

b. Culpeper, Virginia, 19 July 1902; d. 24 May 1970.

"He can beat sense into any box!" said Maxine Sullivan, talking about her husband and regular accompanist, one of the greatest classic stride pianists. He went to New York from Washington, DC, in 1923 and after work with a variety of bands (including Elmer Snowden's) formed his own Krazy Kats in 1927. From then on – rather like Willie "The Lion" Smith – Jackson made his name as a soloist (on occasion he would make short work of younger opposition like Duke Ellington), led his own bands, accompanied singers and made the rounds of clubs from the Radium to Café Society Downtown, where he was house pianist from 1944–51. Through the 1950s and early 1960s he worked in New York with such old friends as Garvin Bushell, J.C. Higginbotham and Joe Thomas, and by 1963 was resident at Jimmy Ryan's with clarinettist Tony Parenti. In 1965 he was prominent in Maxine Sullivan's return to live performance, and he recorded solo in 1969, the year before he died of heart failure during a residency at the RX Room, Manhattan. [DF]

⊙ **Carolina Shout** (1962; Black Lion). One of Jackson's rare solo albums, this features him in classic repertory such as "Honeysuckle Rose" and James P. Johnson's "Carolina Shout", and reveals a stomping, dynamic approach.

D. D. Jackson

Piano, organ, keyboards.

b. Ottawa, Canada, 25 Jan 1967.

Born into a multi-ethnic, musical family Robert Cleath Kai-Nien Jackson ("D.D." is a nickname meaning "Little Brother" in Chinese) started playing piano at six. He studied classical piano at Indiana University as an undergraduate and took a masters degree in jazz at the Manhattan School of Music. There he studied with multi-talented Jaki Byard and the ailing pianist and composer, Don Pullen, whom he assisted in the completion of his final jazz composition, "Earth Eagle First Circle".

In the early 1990s Jackson played with composer-pianist David Murray in big band, octet and duo formats, and worked with violinist Billy Bang and saxophonist Jane Bunnett. In the second half of the decade he backed musicians such as James Carter, Chico Freeman and Dewey Redman, and formed a trio with saxophonist Hamiet Bluiett and Senegalese djembe player Mor Thiam, with whom he recorded "Same Space" (1998). As well as a series of varied albums under his own name, he recorded Gershwin's "Rhapsody In Blue" with the Pro Musica Chamber Orchestra, and wrote an opera, *Québécité*, for the 2003 Guelph Jazz Festival. He also writes a regular column for Downbeat magazine. [BP]

⊙ **Paired Down, Vol.1** (1996; Justin Time). Jackson's diverse approach to the piano is showcased in a series of duets, with David Murray, Hamiet Bluiett, James Carter and Billy Bang.

⊙ **Suite For New York** (2002; Justin Time). A fascinating suite, inspired by the city and haunted by the September 11th attacks, sees Jackson leading regular companions Christian Howes (violin), Ugonna Okegwo (bass) and Dafnis Prieto (drums) and guests such as flautist James Spaulding.

Gene Jackson

Drums.

b. Philadelphia, 16 Oct 1961.

After studying at Berklee College of Music, Gene Jackson established himself on the New York scene, first with brothers Kevin and Robin Eubanks – both of whom he went on to record with throughout the 1990s – and then with Dave Holland's Dream Of The Elders band. He has also played with Branford Marsalis and Dianne Reeves, touring Europe in summer 1995 with Dave Holland on bass. His most high-profile (but alas, unrecorded) job, however, is with Herbie Hancock's working trios and quartets with whom he toured through the 1990s, latterly accompanied by saxophonist Craig Handy and bassist Kenny Davis. Jackson's fiercely percussive sound has propelled albums by several important artists, including *Mental Images* (1994) by trombonist Robin Eubanks; *Harvest* (1993), *Spirit* (1993) and *Somethin' Else* (1994) by pianist Michele Rosewoman; *MusiCollage* (1995) by saxophonist Jorge Sylvester; and *Moment To Moment* (1994) and *Sound Tracks* (1996) by vibraphone player Joe Locke. Jackson is also part of the large pool of musi-

Justin-Time Records

D. D. Jackson

cians upon which the Mingus Big Band regularly draws, appearing both on Dreyfus's 1997 album, *Que Viva Mingus!*, and on *Alto Blue* (1997; Steeplechase) and touring with them as recently as 2001. He has also been seen recently with pianists Antonio Farao and Jason Lindner as well as saxist Sam Newsome. The main influences on his supple but assertive drumming include Elvin Jones, Philly Joe Jones, Roy Haynes and Billy Higgins. [CP]

Javon Jackson

Tenor saxophone, composer.

b. Carthage, Missouri, 16 June 1965.

Having completed his studies at the Berklee College of Music in the late 1980s, Javon Jackson became the tenorman in the last manifestation of Art Blakey's Jazz Messengers, alongside trumpeter Bryan Lynch and trombonist Steve Davis, then worked with another legendary drummer, Elvin Jones, in his Jazz Machine. Jackson's studio sideman work began with fellow Messengers and band alumni – he appears on late-1950s albums by Lynch and pianist Benny Green, and several under the leadership of Freddie Hubbard 1988–94 – but he also established himself with albums led by trumpeters Rebecca Coupe Franks, Tim Hagans and Tom Williams, pianists Roberta Piket and Mickey Tucker, singer Freddy Cole and drummer Louis Hayes. Jackson's recording career as a leader began with Gerry Teekens's perspicacious Criss Cross label: he made two albums for them, *Me And Mr Jones* and *Burnin'*, in 1991. Betty Carter produced his first major-label album, for Blue Note, *When The Time Is Right* (1994), and he has subsequently risen to considerable prominence in the jazz world with a string of solid, thoughtful but vigorous albums for the company: *For One Who Knows* (1995), *A Look Within And Good People* (1996) and *Pleasant Valley* (1999; see below). A new deal with Palmetto began with a funky soul-jazz date, *Easy Does It* (2003), featuring Dr Lonnie Smith on Hammond. Jackson's musical philosophy was inpired by Hubbard, who advised him "to find a way to get the soul back into the music". Consequently, Jackson says, "While I study jazz of the 1950s and 1960s, I don't live there. I'm searching to find myseif through different types of vehicles as opposed to always taking a straightahead approach. I'm a risk-taker." [CP]

⊙ **Pleasant Valley** (1999; Blue Note). Continuing his association with producer Craig Street, Jackson retains drummer Billy Drummond from previous albums, but brings in organist Larry Goldings and guitarist Dave Stryker (who learned his trade with Jimmy Smith and Jack McDuff). Material ranges from Ellington's "Sun Swept Sunday" to Stevie Wonder's "Don't You Worry 'bout A Thing" and Al Green's "Love And Happiness", plus Goldings's "Jim Jam" and four Jackson originals.

Milt Jackson

Vibes, piano.

b. Detroit, Michigan, 1 Jan 1923; d. 9 Oct 1999.

Milt "Bags" Jackson played in local groups alongside such players as Lucky Thompson, and studied music at Michigan State University. He moved to New York for work with the Dizzy Gillespie sextet, in time for a West Coast visit, in 1945–6. Then he was a founder member of the Gillespie big band of 1946–7, followed by freelance work with Howard McGhee, Thelonious Monk (with both of whom he recorded) and Tadd Dameron. The first sessions recorded under his own name came in 1948, during a return visit to Detroit. Several months with Woody Herman in 1949–50 were followed by work with the new Gillespie sextet from 1950–52. He recorded with his own quartet in 1951 for Gillespie's Dee Gee Records, and then undertook live appearances, including backing Charlie Parker and Ben Webster. He made further quartet records (and records with guest soloists Lou Donaldson, Sonny Rollins and Horace Silver) until the Milt Jackson Modern Jazz Quartet's title was abbreviated to the last three words, and a regular group under the musical direction of John Lewis was established in 1954.

Throughout the next twenty years Jackson continued to work with the Modern Jazz Quartet (MJQ) and to make albums under his own name, collaborating with Frank Wess, Lucky Thompson, Coleman Hawkins, John Coltrane and Wes Montgomery, and guesting on records by Kenny Clarke, Miles Davis, Quincy Jones and others. Starting in the mid-1960s he also appeared in public with his own quintets including James Moody, Jimmy Heath, Cedar Walton, Monty Alexander and former Gillespie colleague Ray Brown. He departed from the MJQ, bringing about its break-up, in 1974, partly because he thought the members were being financially exploited. From 1975 he appeared as a guest artist or with his own groups, for example in Montreux in 1975 and 1977, Japan in 1976 and London in 1975 and 1982. Then he returned to the re-formed MJQ, but continued to tour and record with his own groups.

Jackson's attempts to overcome the limitations of his chosen instrument were remarkably successful; at the start of his career the current model's mechanical problems were considerably greater than more recently manufactured models. Lionel Hampton and his followers had capitalized on its ringing tones and, at faster tempos, treated the vibes percussively like a recalcitrant piano, but Milt managed against the odds to make it sound more like a trumpet or saxophone. To that end he employed a great variety of attack in articulating his phrases, and allowed the vibrato mechanism to emphasize the occasional longer note. This is especially true of the way in which he caressed a ballad or a slow blues, on which all of his melodic lyricism emerges in a seemingly unstoppable flow. Despite using a considerable quantity of notes, there was always an essential simplicity about Jackson's playing. It is no coincidence that his eponymous twelve-bar blues "Bags' Groove", and to a lesser extent "Bluesology", are known the world over as easy but effective standards for jamming. [BP]

⊙ **Wizard Of The Vibes** (1948-52; Blue Note). Strictly speaking, the earliest material was recorded under the leadership of Thelonious Monk, with whom Milt enjoyed a percussive partnership, making a telling contrast with John Lewis on the quintet session (Lou Donaldson added) that includes the debut version of "Bags' Groove".

⊙ **Milt Jackson Quartet** (1954; Prestige/OJC). The last early Jackson album not to have John Lewis readying the MJQ. Soul-mates Horace Silver and Kenny Clarke bring out Milt's bluesy side, even on Artie Shaw's song "Moon Ray".

⊙ **Opus De Jazz** (1955; Savoy). Hank Jones takes over on piano, with Frank Wess's flute making it a quintet, on a unique version of Silver's "Opus De Funk", which has the principals taking repeated solos that gradually increase in urgency as they diminish in length.

⊙ **Plenty, Plenty Soul** (1957; Atlantic). The apotheosis of Jackson's collaboration with Quincy Jones, in two groups which have Lucky Thompson, Joe Newman and Silver in common, while the larger band adds Art Blakey and Cannonball Adderley.

⊙ **Soul Fusion** (1977; OJC). One of Jackson's recordings with Monty Alexander, a most suitable colleague on the title track (much prized by the 1980s dance-floor crowd) and a splendid version of "Isn't She Lovely".

➤➤ **Miles Davis** *(Bags' Groove)*; **John Lewis** *(Django)*.

Oliver Jackson Jnr

Drums.

b. Detroit, Michigan, 28 April 1933; d. 29 May 1995.

Jackson played first in the Detroit area with R&B bands (one, led by Gay Crosse, featured a young John Coltrane) and signed his first union card in 1949. Thereafter he worked in trios – with Tommy Flanagan, Barry Harris and Dorothy Donegan – and in 1953 formed a successful tap-dancing duo, Bop and Locke, with drummer Eddie Locke. They danced at the Apollo and around the theatre circuit until Jackson signed with Tony Parenti's trio in 1954, working afternoons at the Metropole and then evenings at the same venue with Henry "Red" Allen, succeeding Cozy Cole. He stayed with Allen until 1961 when he joined Charlie Shavers, a constant working companion for the next ten years, in a Jonah Jones-patterned quartet which recorded widely. Jackson also worked variously with Benny Goodman, Lionel Hampton, Buck Clayton, Earl Hines, Erroll Garner, Oscar Peterson (for a year) and in 1967 toured with a package show, *Jazz From A Swinging Era*, which teamed him with Roy Eldridge, Clayton and Hines. In 1969 he became a founder member of the JPJ Quartet, a group featuring Budd Johnson, Bill Pemberton and Dill Jones, which played all over the USA in concerts for the John Manville Corporation. From 1975 he worked with Sy Oliver's fine new band at New York's Rainbow Room and led his own trio in New York and for European tours. In the 1980s Jackson played regularly with George Wein's Newport Jazz Festival All Stars, featuring Scott Hamilton and Warren Vaché, and in 1985 toured the UK with Eddie Condon's Memorial group. Until his death in 1995 he was still with the Newport Festival All Stars, and freelancing with various swing-based players, including tenorist Harry Allen and the all-star Yamaha International Band. [DF]

⊙ **Billie's Bounce** (1984; Black And Blue). A good straightforward swing session, featuring altoist Norris Turney on fine form along with Oliver's brother Ali on bass.

➤➤ **Randy Sandke** *(Happy Birthday Jazz Welle Plus)*.

Preston Jackson

Trombone.

b. New Orleans, 3 Jan 1902; d. 12 Nov 1983.

Preston Jackson (James Preston McDonald) moved to Chicago at fifteen, having soaked up the music of his home town, and was immediately enthralled by the city's elite of ex-New Orleans jazz men. "I didn't play anything then", he later told Shapiro and Hentoff, "but I was thinking of taking the clarinet. We used to hang around Joe [King] Oliver's band [and] I used to sit behind Dutrey every night. He was wonderful about showing me fine points on the horn. I learned lots from him." Jackson also took lessons from Roy Palmer. After ten years working in territory bands, he came back to Chicago for ten more, playing and recording with Louis Armstrong (1931–2), Carroll Dickerson, Jimmie Noone and Zilmer Randolph's big band. In the 1940s he took up a full-time union post but continued bandleading for fun, and reunited with Lil Hardin Armstrong on record in 1959. At the end of his life he moved back to New Orleans, where he joined the Preservation Hall Band; he died while touring with them.

Jackson was not only one of the most technically able and creative of the New Orleans trombonists but also an observant commentator on jazz history – Shapiro and Hentoff's *Hear Me Talkin' To Ya* contains a number of his reminiscences, and he wrote a regular column for *Jazz Hot* and *Hot News* magazines. He was also a capable administrator who from 1934–1957 served on the board of Chicago's Associated Federation of Musicians. [DF]

➤➤ **Louis Armstrong** *(Louis Armstrong 1930–31 & 1931–3)*.

Quentin Jackson

Trombone; also vocals, bass.

b. Springfield, Ohio, 13 Jan 1909; d. 2 Oct 1976.

Jackson first played violin and organ for hometown church services and in his school orchestra before taking up the trombone at eighteen. He progressed fast and was soon working with territory bands led by Gerald Hobson, Lloyd Byrd, Zack Whyte and Wesley Helvey, whose Troubadours sported an eminent succession of trombonists including J.C. Higginbotham and Vic Dickenson. In December 1930 he joined McKinney's Cotton Pickers primarily to sing as replacement for George "Fathead" Thomas, who had been killed in a car crash. Don Redman was staff arranger for McKinney at the time and when he left to form his own band Jackson (whom Redman named "Butter" because he was "kind of chubby") went with him, staying until the end of 1939 to play in a revolutionary three-trombone section that Duke Ellington quickly copied. Then came eight years in Cab Calloway's band and eleven with Duke Ellington, replacing Claude Jones. From the late 1950s his career diversified, with pit work under Quincy Jones's baton for *Free And Easy*, a European tour with Jones's band, a year with Count Basie, time with Charles Mingus (who had worked with Ellington for ten days while Jackson was there), and in the 1970s big-band work with Sammy Davis, Louie Bellson, Gerald Wilson and others. **[DF]**

>> Duke Ellington *(Such Sweet Thunder)*; **Charles Mingus** *(Black Saint And The Sinner Lady).*

Ronald Shannon Jackson

Drums, flute, miscellaneous instruments.

b. Fort Worth, Texas, 12 Jan 1940.

As a teenager Jackson played regular sessions in Dallas with Ray Charles sidemen James Clay and Leroy Cooper. He studied history and sociology in Texas, Missouri and Connecticut, and obtained a music scholarship in New York in the mid-1960s. He recorded there with saxophonist Charles Tyler in 1966, and worked as a drummer with Albert Ayler, Betty Carter, Charles Mingus and Stanley Turrentine. Less involved in music in the early 1970s, Jackson returned to the forefront with Ornette Coleman in 1975–6 and with Cecil Taylor in the late 1970s. He then worked with the James "Blood" Ulmer group before forming his own Decoding Society in 1981. In 1985–6 he recorded and toured in Last Exit with Peter Brötzmann, Sonny Sharrock and bassist Bill Laswell, and in the early 1990s in Power Tools with bassist Melvin Gibbs and Bill Frisell, subsequently leading new editions of the Decoding Society. Jackson's style, initially focused by the influence of Milford Graves and Sunny Murray, proved adaptable to the further developments of Ornette's group approach. But, as with Coleman himself, Jackson seems to have simplified his music in the quest for greater popularity. **[BP]**

⊙ **Taboo (c. 1988; Virgin).** With key collaborators Melvin Gibbs, guitarist Vernon Reid (founder of the Black Rock Coalition) and saxophonist Zane Massey (son of Cal), Jackson covers a lot of ground in trying to combine what used to be avant-garde improvisation with the textures of heavy rock.

⊙ **Raven Roc (1992; DIW).** A sort of Power Tools in all but name, with the frontline consisting of two guitarists, Jef Lee Johnson and Dave Fiucynski, and the drumming to the fore especially on "Sexual Drum Dance".

Tony Jackson

Piano, vocals.

b. New Orleans, 5 June 1876; d. 20 April 1921.

Tony Jackson worked in bands well before the turn of the century (including Adam Olivier's) and spent some years in New Orleans entertaining at bagnios such as Gypsy Schaeffer's and Antonia Gonzales's. He was an epileptic and an alcoholic, with severe tooth decay, and regular outbreaks of unsightly sores which he hid under his hat; he was also an enchanting singer/entertainer. "He was the outstanding favourite of New Orleans", said Jelly Roll Morton. "We all copied Tony", said Clarence Williams. "He was so original, and a great instrumentalist ... certainly the greatest piano player and singer in New Orleans." Jackson moved to Chicago in 1912, where he worked at cafés such as the DeLuxe and Pekin until the year of his death (probably due to syphilis). As well as being an unbeatable one-man show he composed fine tunes, including "Some Sweet Day", "The Naked Dance" (re-created by Jelly Roll Morton) and his most famous, "Pretty Baby", dedicated, said Alberta Hunter, "to a tall, skinny fellow". Jackson never recorded. **[DF]**

Pete Jacobsen

Piano.

b. Newcastle upon Tyne, UK, 16 May 1950; d. 29 April 2002.

Having taught himself the rudiments of harmony as a child, Pete Jacobsen later studied classical piano, attending London's Royal Academy of Music for three years after moving to the capital in 1969. Work in the fusion band Morrissey-Mullen, and with leading UK saxophonists Don Weller, Bobby Wellins and Barbara Thompson, plus the odd visiting American such as trombonist Jimmy Knepper, followed. In the 1980s and 1990s, Jacobsen was featured in the bands of saxophonists Chris Biscoe and Tim Whitehead; Biscoe commented: "His ability to play melodic lines which extend the writing and counterpoint other musicians' solos is remarkable." He also played folk-based music in a band, Carmina, with fellow jazz musicians Rigel Thomas (bass), saxophonist Julian Nicholas and drummer Nic France, as well as working in a trio, with France and bassist Simon Woolf, that concentrated on Jacobsen's own compositions. Like many of his generation of UK musicians, Jacobsen never received quite the degree of critical acclaim his sensitive yet vigorous playing deserved, despite being equally adept in the fields of straightahead jazz, funk and wholly improvised music. His early passing left the UK music scene a poorer place. **[CP]**

Ever Onward (1994; FMR). Engaging solo-piano album featuring a mix of originals, favourite standards and free improvisations.

>> **Chris Biscoe** *(Chris Biscoe Sextet);* **Bobby Wellins** *(Birds Of Brazil);* **Tim Whitehead** *(Authentic; Silence Between Waves).*

Illinois Jacquet

Tenor saxophone and bassoon.

b. Broussard, Louisiana, 31 Oct 1922.

Jean-Baptiste Jacquet was brought up in Houston, Texas, where he was tap-dancing in a stage act with his older brothers at the age of three. He learned the soprano saxophone in high school and worked with the Milt Larkin band in 1939–40, including a move to the West Coast. He was briefly with Floyd Ray in late 1940, and became a key member of the new Lionel Hampton band in 1941–2. Then he worked with Cab Calloway in 1943–4 and Count Basie in 1945–6, also appearing at early Jazz At The Philharmonic concerts in 1944, and on subsequent national tours in 1947 and 1955. He had his own seven-piece bands in 1945 and from 1947 onwards. Later he alternated between work as a guest soloist and his own groups, including trios with Milt Buckner from 1966–74 and Wild Bill Davis in 1972 and 1977. He took part in all-star reunion bands with Hampton in 1967, 1972 and 1980 and made frequent solo tours of Europe. He also organized his own Jazz Legends big band from 1984 into the 90s.

Jacquet may be the essential encapsulation of the "Texas tenor", for he managed to combine the mobility of the best blues players with the pungent yet fruity tone of more mainstream men such as Arnett Cobb and Buddy Tate. Despite a popular reputation for upper-register harmonics, Jacquet has had a considerable and usually unacknowledged influence on several generations of tenorists from Eddie Davis to King Curtis to Scott Hamilton. And, although not known for putting pen to paper as a composer, his 64-bar solo on the original Lionel Hampton record of "Flying Home" (complete with quotation from Herschel Evans) is the longest example in existence of an improvisation which was then habitually incorporated wholesale into later written arrangements. [BP]

Flying Home (1951–8; Verve). A compilation by the above contributor, tracing the ground from covers of Ben Webster ("Cotton Tail") and himself (the title track), to a duet with Ben and hot sessions with either Harry Edison or Roy Eldridge.

The Comeback (1971; Black Lion). A typical live date with longtime collaborator Milt Buckner, supplemented by Tony Crombie, blowing the daylights out of chestnuts such as "C Jam Blues", "Take The A Train" and his Basie hit, "The King".

>> **Jazz At The Philharmonic** *(The First Concert).*

Ahmad Jamal

Piano.

b. Pittsburgh, Pennsylvania, 2 July 1930.

Like jazz-based vocalists, the jazz pianist who attains commercial success moves closer to the show-business world than most horn players ever have the opportunity to do. For instance, Jamal (christened Fritz Jones, a name he repudiated after Idrees Sulieman interested him in Islam) is seen by outsiders as a star, yet his influence on jazz has been considerable. After touring with the St Louis-based George Hudson band, he formed his first group c.1949 featuring Ray Crawford on guitar, and gained an early hit record with his arrangement of the folk song "Billy Boy". Around 1956, the guitar was replaced by drums and, with bassist Israel Crosby playing a prominent role, Jamal developed his distinctive sound on several best-selling albums. He continues to work, usually with just bass, drums and percussion but sometimes with additional musicians.

Jamal's popularity was enhanced by the advocacy of Miles Davis and by the example of Miles's pianist of the mid-1950s, Red Garland. The bouncy left-hand voicings and tinkly, tantalizing right – contrasted from time to time with mobile block chords – were a streamlined version of fellow Pittsburgher Erroll Garner. But Miles went so far as to cover much of Jamal's repertoire (his composition "New Rhumba" and numerous standards such as "Autumn Leaves" and "But Not For Me") and also to adopt the two-beat rhythm-section style and four-bar tags associated with the pianist. Given Davis's great influence on other musicians, the knock-on effect has been incalculable; not only later pianists with Miles (Wynton Kelly and Herbie Hancock particularly) but also everyone who has imitated them reflect the work of Jamal to some degree. [BP]

At The Pershing (1958; Chess). Jamal's popular breakthrough album, with Israel Crosby and drummer Vernell Fournier, finds him in live versions of early hit arrangements such as "But Not For Me" and "Surrey With The Fringe On Top" (which had inspired Miles Davis to record them) and his new Latin-jazz hit "Poinciana".

Leon Morris/Redferns

Ahmad Jamal

Chicago Revisited (1992; Telarc). Titled in honour of his success at the above Chicago venue, the trio (bassist John Heard and the much younger drummer Yoron Israel) is still just a backdrop to the leader, who is in great form on tunes such as Clifford Brown's "Daahoud".

Bob James

Piano, composer, organ synthesizer.

b. Marshall, Michigan, 25 Dec 1939.

James received his Master's degree in composition from the University of Michigan in 1962. He worked for Maynard Ferguson for three months in 1963, then became pianist and arranger for Sarah Vaughan until 1968. James is a highly professional composer/arranger who has done much studio work, and arranged and performed with Quincy Jones, Dionne Warwick and Roberta Flack. In 1973 he was signed as exclusive arranger for CTI Records, and wrote albums for Eric Gale, Grover Washington, Hank Crawford and Stanley Turrentine as well as making his own albums for the label. Later in the 1970s he was signed to CBS, making a series of highly produced albums with a disco flavour, often with strings and an orchestra which included several leading jazz musicians, all combining to create a glossy attractive surface. Typical examples are the 1979 *One On One*, in collaboration with Earl Klugh, and the 1980 *H*.[IC]

Explosion (1965; ESP). This trio album, with bassist Barre Phillips and drummer Bob Pozar, was recorded before fame and fortune overtook James. He plays piano and uses some pre-recorded electronic tapes, and the results are surprisingly adventurous; Phillips is a tower of strength.

Harry James

Trumpet.

b. Albany, Georgia, 15 March 1916; d. 5 July 1983.

Harry Hagg James began playing professionally at nine, in a circus orchestra led by his father Everett James, who was also a trumpet player. Harry learned technique from him (the two men later co-wrote a trumpet tutor); he learned how to make a show from the circus. After a bout of lip trouble during a stint with Herman Waldman's band he was soon working all over Texas, with the enthusiastic backing of his proud father. By 1935 the skinny, voracious-looking teenager had joined Ben Pollack, and even by then was a trumpet master, blessed with strength, steely control, concentration and a pugnacious creativity (his records of the period suggest that he might be trying to blow the trumpet out straight). He was quickly accepted in New York's studio world, and almost as quickly by his jam session colleagues, black and white. "James was pretty hostile at first as I remember him", says Billie Holiday. "He came from Texas where negroes are looked on like they're dirt. It showed. We had to break him out of that – and also of the idea that he was the world's greatest trumpet player. But it only took a few earfuls of Buck Clayton's playing and Harry wasn't so uppity. He'd had his lesson and after that he came up to jam and loved it!" James's records of the period, with Teddy Wilson, Buster Bailey, Johnny Hodges and others, make it clear that his confidence remained unshaken, and with good reason.

In 1937 he left a chagrined Ben Pollack to join Pollack's younger rival Benny Goodman, and in two brief years his reputation was made. Not only was he Goodman's most brilliant trumpet soloist ever ("he ripped hungrily at the solos", wrote Irving Townsend, "as if he hadn't had one in weeks"), but he led the trumpet section with a fire that would stay with him for life. He worked for Goodman for two years almost to the day, and a month later formed his own band, which made its debut at the Benjamin Franklin Hotel, Philadelphia: from then on James would be a leader.

After a short consolidation period, during which Frank Sinatra joined him at Roseland in July 1939, James began parading his limitless trumpet technique in virtuosic pieces such as "Concerto For Trumpet" (November 1939), "Carnival Of Venice" (March 1940), the "Flight Of The Bumble-Bee" (May 1940) and "Trumpet Rhapsody" (March 1941 – by which time he had lost Sinatra to Tommy Dorsey and acquired Dick Haymes). It was a trumpet feature from May 1941 which established James as the most commercially successful jazzman of the 1940s. "You Made Me Love You", which Judy Garland had sung in *The Broadway Melody* of 1938, introduced his new "sweet style", a strong, sensuously vibratoed "adoration of the melody" with generous embellishments and a sound like hot gold. He became a pop-music idol: at one stage Columbia, amid wartime shortages, was unable to press enough of his records to meet demand. James married Betty Grable (after a torrid affair with his singer Helen Forrest and a previous marriage to Louise Tobin), added strings to his orchestra, toured and broadcast constantly, and made a number of films, including the marvellous *Springtime In The Rockies* (1942). By 1944 his band featured longterm members such as Willie Smith, "Corky" Corcoran, Juan Tizol and singer Helen Forrest.

The swift changes in post-war jazz fashion briefly dented James's success story: he was neither modern enough for bebop nor rough-hewn enough for the revival, and his swing orchestra epitomized "commerciality". He formed a small group (the Music Makers, featuring cornermen Smith, Tizol and Buddy Rich), and took time off to recoup energy and inspiration, but by 1957 was touring Europe with a re-formed big band which chose to use the work of more contemporary arrangers including Neil Hefti, Ernie Wilkins and Thad Jones. From then on James was seldom out of the spotlight.

James's orchestra was often unjustifiably regarded as a pale copy of Count Basie's, for two chief reasons: Basie employed young arrangers such as Neal Hefti and Ernie Wilkins whom James had used earlier but publicized less; and sometimes James "covered" Basie records such as "M-Squad Theme". In fact Harry James's show was quite different from Basie's: it featured a succession of familiar swing stars (such as Corcoran and Smith) rather than Basie's new-generation men; it was characterized by James's "sweet style" and a Dixieland frontline which gave his band the sound of a supercharged Bob Crosby; and it had a more catholic repertoire, which returned happily to Armstrong as well as creating new material. All this was all-fashioned, but James was fiercely impatient with jazz fashion. "What do you mean, 'commercial'?" he demanded. "I don't believe we've ever played or recorded one tune that I didn't love to play." During the 1970s grandmaster James – a powerful hard-living man – continued touring, but he was ill in the 1980s and succumbed to cancer at 67. British trumpeter Kenny Baker, a comparable talent, was asked to take over his role, but declined. [DF]

⊙ **Yes Indeed** (1936–42; ASV). A wide-ranging collection, moving from early recordings with Ben Pollack (Harry sings on one title too) through sides with Goodman to the earlier years of James's commercial success with Sinatra and Helen Forrest. Also included are James's Boogie Woogie Trio sides and the magnificent "Just A Mood" with Teddy Wilson.

⊙ **Harry James: His Orchestra And The Boogie Woogie Trio** (1937–9; Affinity). First-class selection of James from his hungry years, when he recorded with studio groups, culled here from the Count Basie, Benny Goodman and Duke Ellington stables. Sides with Pete Johnson and Albert Ammons (1939) are a bonus, and James plays thrillingly throughout.

⊙ **I've Heard That Song Before** (1938–47; Jasmine). Excellent comprehensive double CD assembling 49 tracks of James's showstoppers. Just about everything is here and the sound quality is uniformly good. Fine notes by Brian Belton of the Harry James Appreciation Society.

⊙ **Bandstand Memories 1938–48** (Hindsight). A three-CD boxed set of James airshots from the private collection of James's band-manager and friend PeeWee Monte. Excellent presentation and music, with vocalists including Frank Sinatra, Dick Haymes et al.

⊙ **Harry James 1954–66** (Giants Of Jazz). Another excellent budget set including latterday James stand-bys like "The Jazz Connoisseur" and a ravishing "Lush Life", plus three Dixieland beauties.

⊙ **One Night Stand/Soft Lights, Sweet Trumpet** (1951–2; Sony). Sony have now begun reissuing James's important vinyl albums as 'two-fers' and this combines an outstanding live concert from the Aragon, Ballroom, Chicago (James in impressive form), with a studio session featuring the sweeter side of his horn.

⊙ **Compact Jazz: Harry James** (1959–62; Verve). James's later bands were often underrated because of his enjoyment of repertoire that embraced TV themes as well as Dixieland and contemporary big-band writing. This set reflects his catholicity, and open-minded listeners should enjoy it all.

Jon Jang

Piano.

b. Los Angeles, 11 March 1954.

Jang began piano lessons at the age of nineteen, and he studied at Oberlin Conservatory of Music. His initial exposure to a broader audience came at the end of the 1980s as a member of Fred Ho's Afro-Asian Music Ensemble. A driving force in the Asian-American jazz movement, Jang was, with producer Francis Wong, a co-founder of Asian Improv Records in 1987, and he has used his Chinese-American ancestry as a platform for the musical and meta-musical directions he's taken over the last decade, mixing Occidental and Asian genres and instrumental techniques and dealing with politically charged themes. Musically, Jang has tended to emphasize composition and arrangement over soloistic showmanship, citing Mingus and Ellington as influences, and he has a sweeping use of colour and orchestration in the works he's written for his larger ensemble, the Pan Asian Arkestra, and various smaller groups. His compositions have been consistently documented, thanks in part to an ongoing relationship with the Italian Soul Note label, which has released *Self-Defence!* (1992) and *Tiananmen!* (1993) by the Arkestra; *Two Flowers On A Stem* (1995) by his sextet and *Island: The Immigrant Suite No. 1* (1997) by his octet. Latterly his own Asian Improv label has released *Beijing Trio* (1998) featuring Jiebing Chen on *ehru* (a traditional Japanese violin) along with veteran drummer Max Roach, a meditative solo piano recording *Self Portrait* (1999) and *River Of Life* (2000), a duet album with David Murray. [JC]

Joseph Jarman

Sopranino, soprano, alto, tenor and bass saxophones, bassoon, oboe, flute, clarinets, piccolo, composer, vocals, percussion.

b. Pine Bluff, Arkansas, 14 Sept 1937.

Having studied drums in high school, and saxophone and clarinet in the army, Jarman attended the Chicago Conservatory of Music, and in 1965 began performing with the AACM. He had earlier played bebop with saxophonist Roscoe Mitchell at college, and freely improvised music with him in Abrams's Experimental Band. By the later 1960s he was leading a group which explored poetry and elaborate programme music with a strong theatrical slant. In 1965 he played his composition *Imperfections In A Given Space* with John Cage. 1966 saw him record his first album, *Song For*, and premiere the theatre pieces *Tribute To The Hard Core*.

In 1969, when two of his musicians, pianist Christopher Gaddy and bassist Charles Clark, died suddenly (the former from heart disease and the latter from a stroke), Jarman disbanded his group and joined the Art Ensemble Of Chicago. He left the group in 1993, and has since been involved in numerous musical projects and teaches martial arts. [IC]

⊙ **Song For** (1966; Delmark). Jarman's first album includes both Gaddy and Clark and is an example of the general AACM approach to music-making. Jarman fancied himself as a poet and treats us to some declamatory verbals; the music is loose and largely improvised.

Keith Jarrett

Piano, composer, soprano saxophone.

b. Allentown, Pennsylvania, 8 May 1945.

The eldest of five brothers, all of whom were musically inclined, Jarrett was a child prodigy, studying piano from the age of three and presenting a full-length solo recital when he was seven. He toured extensively as a child, performing solo recitals of classical music and his own compositions. He also took up the drums, vibraphone and soprano saxophone. Although he had piano lessons throughout his childhood and adolescence, he received no training in orchestration or composition.

At seventeen he played a two-hour solo concert of his own compositions, and turned down the offer of a scholarship to study privately in Paris with Nadia Boulanger. After a year at the Berklee School on a scholarship he left to lead his own trio in the Boston area. Then he moved to New York, playing with Tony Scott and others until he joined Art Blakey's Jazz Messengers in December 1965. In February 1966 he left Blakey to join the Charles Lloyd quartet, which included Jack DeJohnette and bassist Cecil McBee, later replaced by Ron McClure. This was an important, trail-blazing group, and Jarrett stayed with it until 1969. With Lloyd, he toured Europe six times, the Far East once, and the USSR – the first time that a group of modern jazz musicians had played there. They also played the international jazz festival in Prague, where the Moscow Radio and TV Orchestra performed an arrangement of Jarrett's composition *Sorcery*.

The seeds of Jarrett's mature style can be seen in his work with the Lloyd quartet, which recorded several albums: his intensely rhythmic left hand, the brilliant right-hand linear runs, the emotional heat redolent of the blues and gospel music are all in evidence. His exposure with the group laid the foundations for his national and international reputation. He left Lloyd in 1969 to lead his own trio with Charlie Haden and Paul Motian. In 1970–71 he played electric keyboards with Miles Davis, which further enhanced his reputation. He had recorded for various labels with his trio, but in 1971, while with Davis, he was signed by CBS, and recorded a superb double LP, *Expectations*, only to have his contract terminated abruptly two weeks later. However, that year he began his vital association with Manfred Eicher and the German ECM label, starting with the solo piano album *Facing You*, which made a big impact in Europe. As a result Jarrett performed eighteen solo concerts on a tour of Europe in 1973, and a triple album was released of his Bremen and Lausanne concerts. It caused a sensation and was voted 1974 Record of the Year in four influential US publications: *Down Beat*, *Stereo Review*, *Time* and *New York Times*. His increasing recognition and burgeoning record sales resulted in a unique recording arrangement: he was signed by the American label Impulse! to record with his US quartet (saxophonist Dewey Redman added to the trio), while he remained with ECM for solo LPs and special projects. He also began recording for ECM with a European quartet (Jan Garbarek, Jon Christensen and Palle Danielsson), which many prefer to the US group.

As well as his solo and small-group projects, he has written totally composed music. In the early 1970s he was awarded a Guggenheim Fellowship in composition, and the result was the double album, *In The Light*, which has the string section of the Stuttgart Philharmonic, the American Brass Quintet, the

PATRICK HINLEY/ECM RECORDS

Keith Jarrett

Sonnleitner String Quartet and guitarist Ralph Towner, all performing with Jarrett. In 1980 he recorded *The Celestial Hawk*, a forty-minute work featuring himself on piano with a symphony orchestra. During the rest of the 1970s and in the early 1980s there were more solo and quartet tours, and he then began to give performances of classical music.

Keith Jarrett is one of the very few people to begin as a child prodigy and slowly mature into a prodigious adult talent. His early influences were Art Tatum, Bud Powell, Bill Evans and McCoy Tyner, but he quickly absorbed them, becoming in the mid-1980s the most influential living jazz pianist. After his stint on electric keyboards with Miles Davis he turned his back on electronics and played acoustic piano; this was when his fully mature work began. The solo concerts of that time were unique and totally improvised: there were no preconceived themes or structures, and Jarrett attempted to begin them with a blank mind, so that audiences were witnessing the very act of creation. He seemed to be able to sustain his creative ecstasy throughout every concert, often egging himself on with little cries (a mannerism which irritated some critics). These marathons showed Jarrett to be one of the greatest improvisers in jazz, with an apparently inexhaustible flow of rhythmic and melodic ideas, one of the most brilliant pianistic techniques, and the ability to project complex and profound feeling. They also showed that, though he is steeped in jazz lore and tradition, he is just as deeply versed in European classical music. It was only after his relationship with ECM began that his European strain was given free rein, and his persona became complete.

The new maturity also resulted in two masterpieces with his European quartet, *Belonging* and *My Song*, on both of which all the compositions are by Jarrett. In May 1981 he recorded another superb solo piano concert in Bregenz, Austria, which was different yet again from the previous ones in terms of its passionate intensity and often exhilarating abstraction. In January 1983 he recorded for the first time with what was to become his Standards trio, with Gary Peacock and Jack DeJohnette, and during the rest of the year he played fifty solo piano concerts. Then he spent 1984 playing exclusively orchestral classical concerts and composing some classical pieces himself. That year he played no jazz at all and said later that being deprived of the opportunity to improvise was like being prevented from praying. In 1985 he began touring with his Standards trio, but was still deeply involved in classical performances.

That summer the tension between the demands of the classical world and his needs as a maker of music reached such a crisis point that he withdrew from the spotlight, recording about thirty pieces of improvised "ethnic" music at home on primitive cassette recorders. Twenty-six of the pieces were later released on a double LP, *Spirits*, by ECM. This experience was so revelatory for Jarrett that he subsequently saw his whole life in terms of "before or after" *Spirits*. Immediately after, he and the Standards trio toured in Europe. A Paris concert was recorded and released under the title *Standards Live*.

Each year from 1985 on, Jarrett has usually worked in three areas – solo piano concerts, touring with the Standards trio, and classical concerts. There have been several magnificent recordings in all three categories. Jarrett's solo piano concert on 13 July 1991, *Vienna Concert*, was so special for him that he and Manfred Eicher held a special international press conference in the autumn, at which the journalists first listened to the recording and then questioned Jarrett. His trio has, over the years, produced a host of extraordinarily brilliant reinterpretations of standard tunes, and Jarrett's classical playing is at last getting some recognition from the classical world. He has received many prizes and awards, including two Grammy nominations in 1988 for his recording of Bach's *Well-Tempered Clavier Book I*, and three awards in 1992 for *Shostakovich Preludes* and *Fugues*. Keith Jarrett is one of a handful of musicians who are admired by their peers and honoured by national and international institutions, and who also have a substantial popular following all over the world.

The years 1994–6 saw some of Jarrett's most extraordinary achievements. In 1994, three nights with his trio at the Blue Note Club in New York were recorded, and the results issued the following year in a six-CD box-set, which revealed an almost superhuman level of creativity by Jarrett, Peacock and DeJohnette. Then in February 1995, Jarrett played perhaps his greatest ever concert of totally improvised solo piano, at Milan's La Scala opera house, which was the first non-classical event to be presented there. In March 1996 his trio performed one of their finest concerts in Tokyo, and in May – with the Stuttgart Chamber Orchestra in Stuttgart's Mozart Saal, and his longtime associate and friend Dennis Russell Davies conducting – Jarrett recorded superlative performances of three Mozart piano concertos, "No. 9 in E flat" K271, "No. 17 in G major" K453 and "No. 20 in D minor" K 466.

Jarrett was at the supreme height of his powers, but then in the autumn of 1996, he was tragically stricken with what became diagnosed as Chronic Fatigue Immune Dysfunction Syndrome, which forced him to cancel all his concert dates. There were tentative attempts at public performance in 1998, but he was forced to withdraw from an October concert in Chicago. By 2003, however, Jarrett's schedule was as full as ever, with many concerts scheduled for the near future. [IC]

Keith Jarrett

⊙ **Expectations** (1971; Columbia). This was recorded a month before *Facing You*. Using his trio and quartet, plus guitarist Sam Brown, Airto Moreira, a brass section and strings, Jarrett pulled together all the disparate strands of his musical influences into a brilliantly diverse album which has the unity of a suite, and with his hallmark on every note.

⊙ **Facing You** (1971; ECM); **The Köln Concert** (1975; ECM). These albums reinstated the acoustic piano as a solo instrument in jazz at the height of the electronic jazz-rock movement. *Facing You* was a studio album, mostly of short pieces, and its brilliance, glowing sonorities and emotional resonances stunned the public. Jarrett had had little sleep the night before *The Köln Concert*, and the piano was an inferior one. He wanted to cancel the recording, but in a mood of somnolent and good-humoured resignation went ahead with it. The result was a benign masterpiece.

⊙ **Spheres** (1976; ECM). Originally released as a double LP, *Hymns/Spheres*, this series of solos on organ at a Benedictine abbey reinvented the instrument. Jarrett used all its conventional resources, but vastly enriched its expressive potential by radically experimenting with the stops – having some half open with others completely open or closed. A daring and enthralling session.

⊙ **Concerts** (1981; ECM). In 1976 Jarrett went back to serious piano practice, and the results show in these 1981 concerts at Bregenz and Munich. Everything is heightened – the technical brilliance and the audacious risks. There are sustained minimalist sections, and the Munich concert culminates in a long, tumultuous abstract workout.

⊙ **Spirits** (1985; ECM). The process of creating this home-recorded "ethnic" music helped Jarrett to weather his crisis and get back to full music-making. The music on this two-disc set has its own direct depth and beauty – the glorious rhythm and Pakistani flute on "Spirits 21" for example, or the liturgical vocal drones and haunting soprano saxophone on "Spirits 17" – but it also stands as a record of a unique revelatory experience.

⊙ **Vienna Concert** (1991; ECM). Jarrett was usually never wholly satisfied with his solo concerts but, for the first time, he expressed complete satisfaction with his *Vienna Concert*, so much so, in fact, that he said later he wouldn't mind if he never did another solo concert.

⊙ **Keith Jarrett At The Blue Note I–VI, The Complete Recordings** (1994; ECM). Over six hours of recorded music are enshrined here and 39 separate performances of standards with one or two Jarrett originals. The opening track on CD III, an ecstatic, mind-blowing version of the old chestnut "Autumn Leaves", encapsulates the magical transforming power of Jarrett and the trio.

⊙ **La Scala** (1995; ECM). This totally improvised solo piano concert is in two parts. *La Scala Part I* is over 44 minutes long and begins prayerfully with sonorous chords, slowly evolving through a long, Eastern-flavoured episode, to a jubilant gospel finale and a quiet, hymn-like conclusion. Jarrett's courage to wait and let the music find its own length is remarkable. *La Scala II* is, by contrast, a riotous *tour de force*. Jarrett plays with amazing speed and brilliant clarity of thought and execution.

⊙ **Tokyo 96** (1996; ECM). This was the last great trio album before Jarrett fell ill. It's all standards except for Parker's "Billie's Bounce", Bud Powell's "John's Abbey" and Jarrett's "Song". Here there's yet another totally different version of "Autumn Leaves" and the music throughout is freshly minted and covers the gamut of the emotions.

Jarrett, Jan Garbarek, Palle Danielsson and Jon Christensen

⊙ **Belonging** (1974; ECM). This is an inspirationally dynamic and beautiful acoustic quartet album. "The Windup" is one of the most joyous pieces to be heard, while the long ballad "Solstice" has a most exquisitely beatific finale. Garbarek, Danielsson and Christensen perform superbly and are perfect associates.

⊙ **My Song** (1977; ECM). This studio recording contains some of Jarrett's most beautiful pieces, and the mood is more lyrical and romantic than *Belonging*. Garbarek and Jarrett have tremendous rapport, the saxophonist matching Jarrett's intensity, and the melodies and solos are truly exquisite. Only one piece, "Mandala", approaches the unbuttoned intensity of the groovier *Belonging* performances and, being more abstract, seems out of place in this context.

Jarrett, Jan Garbarek, Charlie Haden and String Ensemble

⊙ **Arbour Zena** (1975; ECM). This suite in three movements, with three improvising soloists, fuses classical, ethnic, folk and jazz elements in a highly original synthesis. Garbarek is at his most eloquent and Haden injects rhythmic muscle. The mood is elegaic, but there is more movement in the string writing and Jarrett's piano is prominently featured, reinforcing the strings and playing solo.

Jarrett, Dewey Redman, Charlie Haden and Paul Motian

⊙ **The Survivor's Suite** (1976; ECM). Jarrett's American quartet was much more experimental than his European quartet. With Garbarek and Co the process of making music and the end product were of equal importance, but with the American group the process itself seems to have been the *raison d'être* – Jarrett was able to try things out, playing soprano and other instruments. The results were often patchy, but with *Survivor's* process and product became one in a triumphantly successful album. There are strong references to folk and ethnic music and the whole suite is shot through with the most intensely focused emotion.

Jarrett, Peacock and DeJohnette

⊙ **Standards Live** (1985; ECM). The crucial factors about Jarrett's trio are the magical empathy among the three men and the fact that Jarrett was virtually reborn after *Spirits*, which seems to have communicated itself to DeJohnette and Peacock. The whole concert is exceptional, and "Too Young To Go Steady" is one of the most perfect and exultant trio performances in the whole of jazz. DeJohnette's loping, unstoppable rhythmic feel, right out of the Big Sid Catlett tradition, fires and sustains the whole performance, Peacock sticks to the half feel, thus adding to the depth of the pulse, and Jarrett plays a superlatively swinging and ecstatically emotional solo.

Clifford Jarvis

Drums, congas.

b. Boston, Massachusetts, 26 Aug 1941; d. 26 Nov 1999.

Jarvis began playing professionally in Boston in the late 1950s with Jaki Byard and Sam Rivers, and went to New York at the end of the decade. There, during the 60s, he played with Randy Weston, Coleman Hawkins, Eddie "Lockjaw" Davis, Johnny Griffin, Sonny Stitt, Charles Mingus and John Coltrane. He joined Sun Ra in 1961, working with him throughout the 1960s.

In 1973 he left the USA, touring internationally with Sun Ra and with Pharoah Sanders. From 1976–81 he was with Archie Shepp's group, after which he spent fourteen weeks in Norway appearing as a guest artist. In 1983 he rejoined Sun Ra for an international tour with an all-star band which included Don Cherry, Lester Bowie and Shepp. He moved to England in the 1980s, leading a group called the Prophets of Jazz.

He recorded with Yusef Lateef, Sun Ra, Archie Shepp, Randy Weston and Barry Harris, and made an important contribution to Freddie Hubbard's 1962 album, *Hub-Tones*. Prior to his death, he also worked in education, appearing as guest instructor at the University of Massachusetts and other New England colleges. [IC]

➤➤ **Freddie Hubbard** *(Hub-Tones).*

Bobby Jaspar

Tenor saxophone, flute.

b. Liège, Belgium, 20 Feb 1926; d. 28 Feb 1963.

After gigging at US army bases in Germany, Jaspar moved to Paris in 1950 and quickly established his reputation. He worked and recorded with many US musicians such as Jimmy Raney and Chet Baker, then moved to New York with his wife, singer Blossom Dearie. He toured with the J.J. Johnson quintet in 1956–7 and worked briefly with Miles Davis in 1957. He was a member of the Donald Byrd quintet on an extended tour of Europe in 1958, then worked in New York as a guest soloist with Bill Evans in 1959 and with singer Chris Connor in 1960. He made a further tour of Europe with Belgian guitarist René Thomas in 1962. His death, following heart surgery, was hastened by drug abuse. He was a superior flute player who was highly valued during his American stay. His tenor work perhaps borrowed more than was the norm in the USA from Lester Young, especially tonally, but his somewhat Rollins-tinged lines were notably individual. [BP]

Hank Jones-Bobby Jaspar

⊙ **Hank Jones Trio Plus Bobby Jaspar** (1956; Savoy). Savoy's house rhythm-section (with Kenny Clarke on one of his very last appearances) plays host to Jaspar, confined to his sprightly flute-playing on such as "Relaxin' At Camarillo".

Bobby Jaspar

⊙ **The Bobby Jaspar Quartet at Ronnie Scott's 1962** (Mole). With Jaspar mainly on tenor, this was a regular quartet featuring René Thomas and stretching out on live versions of Rollins tunes and standard material such as "Like Someone In Love" and "Darn That Dream".

Jazz At The Philharmonic

Jazz At The Philharmonic was originally the billing for a 1944 benefit concert organized by Norman Granz for victims of anti-Chicano rioting in Los Angeles; recordings of the concert were leased for an album of 78s, of which "Blues Part 2", featuring Illinois Jacquet, became a jukebox hit. Demand for more concerts and records was so great that, beginning in 1946, Granz was able to set up lengthy national (later international) package tours of star soloists such as Lester Young, Coleman Hawkins, Roy Eldridge, etc. Early editions traded for their success on R&B-inspired rabble-rousing and were responsible for formulating the idea of "cutting contests" between two or more players of the same instrument; while much of this was released on record, much of a less obvious nature is apparently still in the can. The last of the annual US tours was in 1957 (with a follow-up in 1967), but the name continued to be used for Granz packages in Europe and Japan. [BP]

Jazz At The Philharmonic: The First Concert (1944; Verve). The landmark event which begat "Blues Part 2" finds Illinois Jacquet and the young J.J. Johnson whipping up the excitement, complemented by the wit of Nat "King" Cole and the jazz side of Les Paul.

Jazz Composers' Orchestra

>> *see entry on* **Michael Mantler**.

Jazz Crusaders

>> *see entry on* **Joe Sample**.

Jazz Group Arkhangelsk

In 1967–8 Vladimir Rezitsky – founder and leader of Jazz Group Arkhangelsk – travelled from the far-north USSR port-city that gave the ensemble its name to Vilnius, to study with drummer Vladimir Tarasov and keyboardist Vyacheslav Ganelin (later two-thirds of the Ganelin Trio). With keyboardist Vladimir Turov (at that time a singer), Rezitsky started a trio in 1972, and this group grew into Arkhangelsk in 1975. Theatrical, noisy, with elements of European free improvised music and free jazz, as well as pop and traditional musics, Arkhangelsk played Soviet festivals throughout the 80s. Comparisons with Sun Ra's Arkestra go far deeper than mere name – Arkhangelsk used a similar sense of pageantry and fanfare in their surreal soundscapes. In 1987, the band gained official status, which slightly improved its working conditions, and they continue to function into the post-Cold War period. Although they released 30-odd albums in their lifetime, two the few CD releases featuring JGA music are *Portrait* (1991; Leo) and *Hot Sounds From The Arctic* (1995; Leo) released under Rezitsky's name. Vladimir Rezitsky died in May 2002 of a heart attack at the age of fifty-six, a Russian jazz hero. [JC]

Jazz Warriors

Formed in the mid-1980s as both an incubator and a platform for the UK's young black musicians, the Jazz Warriors was the brainchild of Abibi ("Africa" in Ghana's Twi language) Jazz Arts, an organization based in London and dedicated to the promotion of black music and culture.

A guiding light and founder member was the saxophonist Courtney Pine, and the band attracted a large number of musicians frustrated at the lack of musical opportunities for them outside funk and reggae. Their first gig took place at the Fridge in Brixton in January 1986, and set a pattern for their subsequent performances by striking an informal, egalitarian but fundamentally musicianly note. The band's peak was reached in 1987, when they not only won *The Wire*'s Best Band award, but also saw their singer Cleveland Watkiss win the award for Best Vocalist and their main soloist, Courtney Pine, win the Best Instrumentalist poll. Although they received both critical and popular acclaim, particularly for a countrywide tour honouring Jamaica-born saxophonist Joe Harriott, the difficulties involved in keeping a big band together led to its demise in the early 1990s. Prominent members, however – among them Pine himself, fellow saxophonists Steve Williamson and Gail Thompson, tuba player Andy Grappy, flautist Rowland Sutherland, bassists Ike Leo and Gary Crosby, vibes player Orphy Robinson and singer Watkiss – went on to establish themselves firmly in the UK jazz world.

In 1991, Gary Crosby kept the Warriors' name alive by establishing Tomorrow's Warriors as an outlet for up-and-coming UK jazz talent. Spin-off bands include the bassist's own Nu Troop, who won the Best Ensemble award at the Festival Jazz à Vienne Concours International d'Orchestres in 1998, and J-Life, who, in addition to being voted European Jazz Artists 1997, won the Best Ensemble award and (via singer Julie Dexter) Best Young Vocalist award in 1998's Perrier Young Jazz competition. Crosby's contribution won him an award for services to the industry from the magazine *Straight No Chaser* the same year. [CP]

Out Of Many, One People (1987; Antilles). Somewhat diffuse but energetic and compelling music featuring cream of UK's young black talent in concert at London's Shaw Theatre, 14–15 March 1987.

Eddie Jefferson

Vocals.

b. Pittsburgh, Pennsylvania, 3 Aug 1918; d. 9 May 1979.

Jefferson alternated between work as a dancer and as a singer from an early age, appearing on radio with the same children's group as Erroll Garner. He sang with Coleman Hawkins (c. 1940), but was discouraged from improvisation (scatting) by the excellent Leo Watson; instead, he started creating lyrics to fit recorded instrumental solos by Hawkins, Lester Young, Charlie Parker, James Moody and others. The first opportunity to record such material came in Pittsburgh in 1952, a few months after his then more popular imitator King Pleasure. Jefferson replaced Babs Gonzales as vocalist and road manager of the James Moody band from 1953–7. He seemingly fell into obscurity during the ascendancy of Lambert, Hendricks and Ross, but he reappeared as a dancer in 1967, and then rejoined Moody when the latter left Dizzy Gillespie, working with him from 1968–73. He co-led the Artistic Truth group with drummer Roy Brooks in 1974–5, and then worked regularly with Richie Cole until his death. He was shot to death in front of a Detroit club after performing.

The quality of Jefferson's lyrics was always appropriate to the melodies he found in recorded improvisations, and these covered a wide stylistic range: from his famous versions of "Parker's Mood" and "Moody's Mood For Love" (he used different titles from those associated with King Pleasure, because of copyright conflicts) to solos by Miles Davis ("So What") and Horace Silver ("Psychedelic Sally"). Manhattan Transfer recorded a posthumous tribute to Jefferson in their version of "Body And Soul". [BP]

⊙ **Body And Soul** (1968; Prestige/OJC). Backed by James Moody, who begat vocalese's biggest hit (here recorded as "There I Go, There I Go Again"), Jefferson also includes "Psychedelic Sally", "Mercy, Mercy, Mercy" and his version of Coleman Hawkins's title track.

Hilton Jefferson

Alto saxophone.

b. Danbury, Connecticut, 30 July 1903; d. 14 Nov 1968.

Jefferson began his career in 1926 with Claude Hopkins's soft and smooth ensemble, and for the next 25 years was with most of the greatest big bands, including Chick Webb (1929–30), McKinney's Cotton Pickers (1931) and Fletcher Henderson (1932–4). His longest stay in one band was with Cab Calloway (1940–49), for whom he led the saxophone section and recorded one now-classic feature, "Willow Weep For Me". From 1949–51 he worked at Billy Rose's legendary Diamond Horseshoe in New York, where Kelly was staff choreographer – a Fox musical was made about the club, starring Betty Grable and Dick Haymes. After this highly paid period Jefferson joined Duke Ellington for eight months in 1952–3, but soon after was working as a bank guard in New York to supplement irregular work with Rex Stewart's reassembled Fletcher Henderson orchestra and with his own small group. He continued to work sporadically until the year he died.

Jefferson's translucent sound, harmonic ingenuity (he could run a chord progression into any other key) and graceful technique were objects of awe to musicians better known than he. Said Ben Webster: "I've seen fellers ... made to cry by Jeff – people I didn't think had a tear in them." [DF]

➤➤ **Cab Calloway** *(The Chronological Cab Calloway 1940–41).*

Paul Jeffrey

Tenor saxophone, arranger.

b. New York, 8 April 1933.

Jeffrey worked in many different areas of the USA between 1956–60 with R&B singers Wynonie Harris, Big Maybelle and B.B. King. He also worked with Illinois Jacquet in 1958 and, after his return to New York in the 1960s, with Sadik Hakim, Howard McGhee, Dizzy Gillespie and Count Basie. He played with the Thelonious Monk quartet from 1970–72 and conducted a concert of Monk music at the Newport festival in 1974. He also arranged and conducted Mingus's music on his last albums in 1977–8, and at Newport in 1978. In the early 1980s he was head of Jazz Studies at Rutgers University. Jeffrey has also led his own octet and, though his ensemble writing is functional rather than inspiring, his infrequently heard tenor work was seemingly influenced by Sonny Rollins and promised greater individuality. [BP]

⊙ **Electrifying Sounds** (1968; Savoy). Not yet the subject of a reissue, any more than his two mainstream albums, this features Jeffrey with Jimmy Owens and George Cables, putting the Varitone (an early electric saxophone) through its paces.

Billy Jenkins

Guitarist, composer.

b. Bromley, Kent, UK, 5 July 1956.

Billy Jenkins is routinely described as a maverick, and he did indeed consistently provide the perfect antidote to the retrogressive winebar-friendly jazz in vogue in mid-1980s Britain. The description, while basically accurate, is a little misleading, since Jenkins's anarchic demeanour conceals both a skilful musician and a shrewd thinker on all matters musical. He released a plethora of thought-provoking but amusing albums in the latter half of the 1980s on his own label (including his most famous work, Scratches of Spain), operating in all fields from oddly askew rock through jazz to free music and documenting a series of encounters with many of the UK's top improvising musicians on tapes under the overall title "Big Fights". In the early 1990s, he continued his individual, quirky journey, collaborating with the Fun Horns of Berlin and leading his own band, the Voice Of God Collective, in repeated assaults on various icons of contemporary musical culture.

As the decade progressed, two further strands emerged in Jenkins's work: the Blues Collective and the True Love Collection. The former, immortalized on the album *S.A.D.* (Babel; 1996), usually involved Whispering Gerry Tighe on harmonica, bassist Thad Kelly, keyboard player Dave Ramm and drummer Mike Pickering in a band that – in typical Jenkins fashion – actually produced a great deal of fine blues playing, particularly from Jenkins himself, while satirizing the excesses of the genre. The latter took a similarly wry look at popular love songs such as "How Deep Is Your Love", but featured a searing version of "Dancing In The Street" from vocalist Christine Tobin (Babel; 1998). The Blues Collective, often with Dylan Bates sparring on violin, has earned a reputation for ferocious live shows, and the albums *Life* (2001; Babel) and *Blues Two Zero* (2002; Babel) draw on collaborators past and present who are more than a match for Jenkins's ever acerbic wit. [CP]

⊙ **Scratches Of Spain** (1987; Babel). Humorous, rumbustious music involving a large number of Loose Tubes members alongside Jenkins's fractured guitar.

Jak Kilby

Billy Jenkins

First Aural Art Exhibition (1992; VOTP). A sort of "Best of" the previous decade's Jenkins music featuring various Collective members including Iain Ballamy on saxophone, Steve Watts on bass and Roy Dodds on drums.

The Shakedown Club (1994; Babel). Jenkins showcases his improvising side, playing guitar, keyboards and *Scalextric* cars alongside drummer Steve Noble and bassist Roberto Bellatalla.

Leroy Jenkins

Violin, viola, composer, educator.

b. Chicago, 11 March 1932.

Jenkins began on violin at eight, playing regularly in church; he learned basic musicianship with Walter Dyett at Du Sable High. He also took up alto saxophone in high school, playing bebop under the influence of Charlie Parker. He graduated with a B. Mus (violin) from Florida's A & M University, having by then abandoned the alto. From 1961–5 he taught string instruments in schools in Mobile, Alabama. He taught music in the Chicago school system from 1965–9, also working during that period with the AACM. Jenkins developed into one of the most important musicians to emerge from the AACM. J.E. Berendt has written: "His cluster-like, 'pounded' violin sounds have a kind of manic drive. Jenkins uses the violin as percussion instrument or noise producer – without scrupling about the traditional rules of violin and harmony." Jenkins also fuses elements from the romanticism of the European classical tradition with his blues roots.

In 1969 there was an exodus of AACM musicians from Chicago, and Jenkins left for Europe with Anthony Braxton and trumpeter Leo Smith. In Paris, with drummer Steve McCall they formed the Creative Construction Company. He also played with Ornette Coleman while there. He returned to Chicago, and then, in February 1970, moved to New York with Braxton, staying at Coleman's house and studying with him for three months. He played with Cecil Taylor in 1970 and with Braxton from 1969–72. During this period he also worked with Albert Ayler, Cal Massey, Alice Coltrane, Archie Shepp and Rahsaan Roland Kirk.

In 1971 he formed the Revolutionary Ensemble with Sirone (Norris Jones) on bass and trombone and Jerome Cooper (drums and piano), recording an eponymous album for ESP in 1972. Gary Giddins wrote of the group: "It could be pastoral and urban, derivative and distinctive, bluesy and classical, baroque and austere." After it broke up in 1977 Jenkins led a trio with Andrew Cyrille and Anthony Davis, which toured the USA and Europe in the late 1970s. He continued to lead groups throughout the 80s, including his blues-based band Sting, and in 1987 he played and recorded with Cecil Taylor. He is still an active musician and is today recognized as an innovator of his instrument. [IC]

Leroy Jenkins and Muhal Richard Abrams

Lifelong Ambitions (1977; Black Saint). An eventful duo album by two men who are rooted in the whole jazz tradition and yet remain on the cutting edge of the music. Jenkins wrote all the pieces, and despite the rather staid atmosphere the music flows.

Jenkins, George Lewis, Anthony Davis, Andrew Cyrille

Space Minds, New Worlds, Survival America (1978; Tomato). Virtuosity, academicism, earthiness and lyricism combine in this quartet summit meeting.

Leroy Jenkins

Live (1992; Black Saint). Jenkins's band comprises guitarist Brandon Ross, Eric Johnson on synthesizer, bassist Hill Greene and drummer Reggie Nicholson. This visceral live session at a New York school has the headlong excitement of black street music on the move.

➤➤ **Carla Bley** *(Escalator Over The Hill)*; **Anthony Braxton** *(Three Compositions Of New Jazz)*.

Jean-François Jenny-Clark

Bass; also cello.

b. Toulouse, France, 12 July 1944; d. 6 Oct 1998.

Jean-François studied classical music, including at the Paris Conservatoire. Already involved in jazz in his teens, he played with Jackie McLean (appearing in Paris with The Connection) in 1961. He specialized in free jazz in the mid-1960s and performed with visitors Don Cherry, Gato Barbieri and Steve Lacy. He then played fusion music with Jean-Luc Ponty until the latter's emigration, and worked with Barbieri in New York, with Chet Baker and Paul Motian. In the 1980s he partnered European musicians such as Martial Solal, Michel Portal, Albert Mangelsdorff and Michel Petrucciani, and played regularly in trio with Joachim Kuhn and Daniel Humair from 1984 until his death from cancer. He appeared on albums by all the above and by Joe Henderson, Enrico Rava, George Russell and Kenny Wheeler, among many others. Steve Lacy wrote of him that: "Apart from his impeccable musicianship, which included the bow, reading, chord changes or free, swinging time or rubato, what I thought made JF so remarkable was his soloing, which was never predictable." [BP]

➤➤ **Joachim Kuhn** *(From Time To Time Free)*; **Albert Mangelsdorff** *(Three Originals)*; **Aldo Romano** *(Il Piacere)*.

Ingrid Jensen

Trumpet, flugelhorn.

b. Vancouver, Canada, 12 Jan 1966.

Jensen's mother, a classical and stride pianist, directed the school choir Ingrid sang with, while younger sister Christine is a professional saxophonist, pianist and composer. She began trumpet at thirteen with the school band, played with a rehearsal big band at sixteen, then studied at college in Nanaimo, B.C. (1985–7), and at Berklee from 1987–9. She toured with the Vienna Art Orchestra in 1991 and became professor of trumpet and big band at the Bruckner Conservatory; while there, she toured with Lionel Hampton. Based in New York since the mid-1990s, she has led her own group and worked with the Mingus Big Band, Maria Schneider, the all-woman big band Diva and vocalist Ethel Ennis. Inspirational figures for her include Schneider, Wayne Shorter and Woody Shaw, while other favourite trumpeters are Miles, Brownie, Clark Terry, Lee Morgan, Freddie Hubbard, Booker Little, Kenny Wheeler, Tom Harrell and Tim Hagans. Maria Schneider has said of listening to Jensen: "I find myself mesmerized by sensuous lines and spellbound by the warmth and richness of her tone ... She is quite simply one of the most compelling improvisers I know." [BP]

Higher Grounds (1998; Enja). With a heavy quintet featuring Gary Thomas, David Kikoski, bassist Ed Howard and Victor Lewis, Jensen's most complete album yet finds her mobile, meaningful trumpet deployed on a variety of contemporary material plus 1960s jazz standards by Freddie Hubbard and Chick Corea.

Papa Bue Jensen

Trombone, bandleader.

b. Copenhagen, 8 May 1930.

Papa Bue (Arne) Jensen formed his Danish Jazz Band in 1956 (renamed the Viking Jazz Band in 1958), and achieved international recognition during the trad boom of the early 1960s. Featuring longtime sidemen such as Jorgen Svarre (clarinet) and Bjarne "Liller" Petersen (banjo), as well as later additions like Keith Smith and Finn Otto Hansen (trumpet), Papa Bue's jazz was New Orleans-based, but with a lilting swing and sophisticated soloists. During the 1960s and 1970s his band worked alongside a series of American visitors including Wingy Manone, Wild Bill Davison, Ed Hall, George Lewis, Albert Nicholas and Art Hodes. Into the 1980s he continued to record prolifically at home and abroad, as well as playing the best Copenhagen venues and international jazz festivals. [DF]

On Stage (1982; Timeless). Excellent in-concert recording by the Bue band.

Jerry Jerome

Tenor saxophone, clarinet, flute, arranger.

b. New York, 19 June 1912; d. 17 Nov 2001.

Jerome began with Harry Reser's Cliquot Club Eskimos, then turned full-time professional with Glenn Miller (1937–8), before going on to work with Red Norvo (1938), Benny Goodman (1938–40) and Artie Shaw (1940–41). After this starry beginning, he turned to full-time studio work at NBC (as conductor/director 1942–6 and 1948), later working in television and the record industry, and running his own successful jingles company. One famous recording from this period (featuring Jerome appropriately in top-class company) is Capitol's *Session At Riverside* (1956). For the next forty years his solo recording activities as a jazzman ceased altogether although, after his retirement to Florida, Jerome reappeared at jazz concerts, festivals, and on record – thanks to the ever-vigilant Arbors label. He also toured Germany in 1996 and played for the Arbors March of Jazz Festival 2001. Jerome's style resembled a well-stirred mixture of Hawkins and

Lester Young, and his reappearance on the international jazz scene was highly welcomed. [DF]

Something Old, Something New (1996; Arbors). A fascinating audio-biography of Jerome on a two-CD set. Vol. I brings together significant and fascinating pre-war recordings (many unissued) with contemporaries from Charlie Christian to Johnny Guarnieri. Vol. 2, recorded in 1996, with Randy Sandke, George Masso and Dick Hyman, demonstrates that his talent is virtually unmarked by time.

Something Borrowed, Something Blue (1939–64/2001; Arbors). A matching scrapbook to the above. Volume one has Jerome with old colleagues including Charlie Shavers, Teddy Wilson and others; volume two presents him in a contemporary group with Lou Colombo, John Allred and Dick Hyman.

Jeter-Pillars Orchestra

After the break-up of Alphonso Trent's hugely successful territory band in Columbus, Ohio, in 1934, two of Trent's sidemen, Mexican saxophonists James Jeter and Hayes Pillars, decided to form a band for themselves. "They were very good musicians", remembers Harry Edison, "and they stressed quality in their band, which was more of a sweet band – there wasn't much room for playing solos!" The Jeter-Pillars orchestra was nevertheless an important training ground for young musicians such as Edison, Walter Page, Jimmy Blanton (now believed to have made his first records with the orchestra), Sid Catlett, Charlie Christian and Jo Jones (who left to join Count Basie). To begin with they worked around Cleveland, Ohio, then the co-leaders moved their operation further south to St Louis for three more years before disbanding. [DF]

Antonio Carlos Jobim

Composer, guitar, piano.

b. Rio de Janeiro, 25 Jan 1927; d. New York, 8 Dec 1994.

Antonio Carlos Jobim and his friend João Gilberto were the founders of the bossa nova movement which spread to the USA in 1962. Jobim was the composer of excellent songs, much favoured by jazz musicians as vehicles for improvisation. Some of his best-known pieces are "Chega de Saudade" (English title, "No More Blues"), "Desafinado", "One Note Samba", "The Girl From Ipanema", "Quiet Nights", "Wave", "Triste" and "Jazz Samba". His tunes have been played and recorded by Stan Getz, Dizzy Gillespie, Miles Davis, Gil Evans, and many others. [IC]

➤➤ **Stan Getz** *(Getz/Gilberto).*

Jan Johansson

Piano.

b. Söderhamn, Sweden, 16 Sept 1931; d. 9 Nov 1968.

Originally an engineering student and maths whiz, Johansson worked avocationally in various jazz ensembles and other musical endeavours in the early 1950s – including the unusual "spex" burlesque shows produced at Swedish universities, eventually turning professional in 1955. He worked with Swedish groups, including Kenneth Fagerlund, Gunnar Johnson (1956–9), and Arne Domnérus (starting in 1961), but in 1959 he joined the Stan Getz quartet, touring Europe, recording with them and with bassist Oscar Pettiford. In the mid-60s, Johansson recorded some very influential albums, making jazz arrangements of folk material from Scandinavia and eastern Europe; these included *Jazz Pa Svenska* and *Adventures In Jazz And Folklore*. An original composer and a very dexterous, nimble pianist (invocations of Bill Evans are not unusual), Johansson was a bright light on the Swedish scene. As well as valuable mainstream records with his own trio and variously sized assemblages, he made some very adventurous, freely oriented music toward the end of his life, including the as yet unreissued *M*, which has rightly been compared to Sun Ra's *Arkestra*. Many of his LPs have been made available on disc, however, on the Heptagon label, and Erik Kjellberg's monograph *Jan Johansson: A Visionary Swedish Musician* (1998; Svensk Musik) chronicles his life. Johansson died tragically in a car accident in 1968. His compositions were performed by the Swedish Radio Jazz Group on *Longing* (1993; Phono Suecia) and in 1998, Erik Kjellberg's biography *Jan Johansson: A Visionary Swedish Musician* was published. [JC]

Steve Johns

Drums.

b. Boston, Massachusetts, 25 Nov 1960.

Stephen Samuel Johns's mother, Goldie Johns, composed music and was a member of ASCAP (American Society of Composers, Authors and Publishers). Johns studied with the famous drummer and teacher, Alan Dawson, in 1977, and then attended the New England Conservatory of Music (1979–82). While at the Conservatory, Johns won the "Outstanding Drummer" Award at the Notre Dame jazz festival and played in Boston with many visiting jazz stars including Bob Berg, Mick Goodrick, Tom Harrell, Dave Liebman and Mike Stern. He moved to New York in 1982, and was immediately in demand, playing with John Hicks, Larry Coryell, Bobby Watson, Gary Bartz and Diane Schuur. Johns has toured the USA with the Count Basie Orchestra directed by Frank Foster, and Europe with the Gil Evans Orchestra, the George Russell Living Time Orchestra (several times), and the Mingus Epitaph Orchestra conducted by Gunther Schuller. He is proud to have also played with that legendary jazz survivor, alto saxophonist Benny Carter.

When not on the road, or at the Kennedy Centre as a member of pianist Billy Taylor's trio, Johns can frequently be found at the Time Café in New York with the Mingus Big Band, a group with which he performed as part of National Public Radio's Jazzset, hosted by Branford Marsalis. He was also filmed and recorded for American WGBH-TV's documentary *An Evening with Stanley Turrentine*.

An exceptionally gifted and versatile drummer, combining great subtlety with great power and stamina, Johns made a major contribution to George Russell's magnificently demanding music, during his five years (1988–93) with the Living Time Orchestra. He has recorded with Russell, Billy Taylor and others. His favourites are many, including Elvin Jones, Jack DeJohnette, Max Roach, Roy Haynes and Louie Bellson. Other inspirations are Miles Davis, John Coltrane, Duke Ellington, Herbie Hancock, Chick Corea and Gil Evans. Johns teaches each summer in the University of Massachusetts Jazz in July programme.

Some of his most interesting work of recent years has been with saxophonist Peter Brainin, their CD *Ceremony* (1998) being a fine addition to Johns' body of work. **[IC]**

Peter Brainin/Steve Johns

⊙ **Ceremony** (1997; Cats Paw Records). A beautifully performed album and an impressive debut. The other members of the quartet – guitarist Ben Monder and bassist Sean Smith – were also in their thirties when this album was recorded, and all were working in New York, but underrated and, except for Johns, unknown outside of the USA. All four men are excellent players, and the composing, mostly by Johns and Brainin, is also excellent.

Bill Johnson

Bass, guitar, banjo.

b. Talladega, Alabama, 10 Aug 1872; d. 3 Dec 1972.

At 28 years old Bill Johnson switched from guitar to double bass and began working around the saloons of New Orleans and in parade bands (for which he doubled on tuba). In his late thirties he moved to California, and in 1914 teamed with Freddie Keppard to form the Original Creole Orchestra, a band which achieved headlining success on the Orpheum theatre circuit and – with Keppard's brilliant, versatile and high-powered trumpet – was an influence on young musicians everywhere. Johnson may have originated a now standard convention of jazz bass. "I think Bill, who travelled with Keppard, plucked the bass first", says Ed Garland, himself often credited with the innovation, "after a drunk broke his bow one night." Later Johnson organized more bands and played with King Oliver (1918–23, the greatest period), and remained a senior figure on Chicago's music scene for another thirty years, a strong influence on young players such as Milt Hinton. His name is less familiar than that of Ed Garland or Pops Foster only because he took a less active role in the post-war New Orleans revival. **[DF]**

Budd Johnson

Tenor, soprano and alto saxophones, clarinet, arranger.

b. Dallas, Texas, 14 Dec 1910; d. 20 Oct 1984.

Much of Budd's early career paralleled that of his elder brother, trombonist Keg Johnson (b. 19 Nov 1908; d. 8 Nov 1967), including work around Texas with Terrence Holder's Twelve Clouds Of Joy, whose personnel were taken over by Jesse Stone and then, from 1929–31, by George E. Lee. Both brothers moved to Chicago in 1932 and played with the Louis Armstrong band in 1933, then Budd began eight years' nearly continuous membership of the Earl Hines band from 1935–42. He started arranging for other bands during this period, and he concentrated increasingly on it in the 1940s, but he also played for Dizzy Gillespie in 1944 and 1948, Billy Eckstine in 1944–5, Sy Oliver in 1947, and Machito in 1949. In the 1950s he arranged and produced many early rock-'n'roll records, thanks to Jesse Stone, and he partnered Al Sears in publishing such material and organizing the house band for the Alan Freed shows. He played with Benny Goodman in 1956–7, Gil Evans in 1959, Quincy Jones from 1959–61 and Count Basie in 1961–2. There was further freelance playing and frequent quartet reunions with Hines from 1964–9, including a Russian tour with a septet in 1966. He then took the Hines rhythm-section and replaced Hines with Dill Jones to form his own JPJ quartet from 1969–75. In the mid-1970s he worked arranging and playing for the Smithsonian Institution repertory project and the New York Jazz Repertory Company, including a further Russian trip in 1975; he worked on Kool festival tribute concerts from 1979. He also had regular work as a guest soloist, making many tours of Europe and visits to the Nice festivals and the Colorado Jazz Party.

Johnson's arranging work was especially important during the 1940s, when he was musical director for Hines and then for the Billy Eckstine band. As in his freelance writing, for Gillespie and other bands, he was adept at combining a bebop influence with solid swing-era sounds. Budd's significance as a player only became evident to most listeners from 1959 onwards, when he was given more space by his bandleaders. The warmth of his mainstream approach was matched by a very contemporary-sounding fluency, and tonally he leaned towards the Lester Young side of the typical Southwestern sound, but with a restrained edge that was nevertheless very penetrating. **[BP]**

⊙ **Budd Johnson & The Four Brass Giants** (1960; Riverside/OJC). With a rhythm-section and the brass of Harry Edison, Nat Adderley, Clark Terry and Ray Nance, Johnson proves himself a strong personality, and his original material includes a fine two-part "Memories Of Lester Young".

⊙ **Let's Swing** (1960; Swingville/OJC). Recorded, like the above, when Johnson was in the solo spotlight almost for the first time, this is a quintet blowing date with brother Keg and Tommy Flanagan, but Budd's own playing and writing make it a standout.

Bunk Johnson

Trumpet.

b. New Orleans, 27 Dec 1889; d. 7 July 1949.

Bunk (Geary) Johnson began playing in and around New Orleans with bands led by Adam Olivier,

Bob Russell and Buddy Bolden, generally taking second trumpet player – in New Orleans, where jobs could last for six hours in a row, a second trumpeter was a vital backup. "Bunk played funeral marches that made me cry!" said Louis Armstrong; Mutt Carey supplied details: "Bunk always stayed behind the beat – he wasn't quite the drive man that Joe Oliver and Freddie Keppard were." Like Buddy Petit, Johnson also established a reputation for unreliability, taking jobs for Red Duson's band agency, disappearing with the advance and forgetting to play the job.

He left New Orleans around 1915 and played all around the South in bands, theatres and clubs alongside entertainers as diverse as Louis Fritz (with whom he first met George Lewis), Ma Rainey and Julia Lee. Then, one night in 1931, bandleader Evan Thomas was stabbed to death as he played alongside Johnson on the stand. The tragedy seems to have marked a slowing of Johnson's career: already suffering from dental problems, he soon after settled in New Iberia, where he worked at various trades, including caretaking and truck driving as well as, possibly, labouring in the rice fields.

In 1939 Frederick Ramsey and William Russell, researching their book *Jazzmen*, picked up references to Johnson by Clarence Williams and Louis Armstrong. The young writers located him and began to correspond. By 1942 Russell had supplied his discovery with a new trumpet and new teeth (Sidney Bechet's brother Leonard made the plate), and recorded him with the aid of producer David Stuart in a room above Grunewald's Music Shop in New Orleans. Between 1944–5 Johnson recorded nearly one hundred sides: they created enormous interest and were hailed as a triumph for pure jazz over the commercial excesses of swing.

Johnson was crucial to the jazz revival, but he was still working daytime jobs and playing only irregularly – a week at the Gary Theater in San Francisco (May 1943), concert lectures with Rudi Blesh, recording and concerts with the Yerba Buena Jazz Band, nights with Sidney Bechet at the Savoy Café, Boston. The chief problem was that Johnson had firmly entrenched and sometimes anti-social approaches to music and life. He drank as heavily as he once had in New Orleans: "Bunk really got bad on my hands, full of liquor all the time", said Bechet of the Boston residency. "There was just no music to be gotten out of him." (Johnny Windhurst finally completed the season.) More pointedly, Johnson had fixed ideas about the musical company he wanted to keep. When he reopened at Stuyvesant Casino in April 1946 with a band including George Lewis, Jim Robinson and Baby Dodds, Johnson hated the sound of his sidemen and found it hard to make himself heard against Dodds's ferocious drums. He drank through his frustration, swore at his men onstage and, once at least, locked them out of their living quarters. (Contradictorily Johnson was often the soul of charm: "He was intelligent, gracious and sensitive", said Nesuhi Ertegun of the "other" Johnson.)

The group with Lewis disbanded and Johnson began working as a soloist in New York, Louisiana, Chicago and elsewhere, then returned to New York in 1947, the year after he appeared in a Hollywood fantasy, *New Orleans*, starring Louis Armstrong and Billie Holiday (all but one of Johnson's scenes were later cut). Now an ex-GI named Harold Drob moved into the picture. He helped Johnson to assemble a band of latterday swing-based players, including Ed Cuffee (trombone), Garvin Bushell (clarinet), Don Kirkpatrick (piano) and Alphonse Steele, a more discreet drummer than Dodds. The new band played at Stuyvesant Casino again, recorded successfully in late 1947, and at last provided Johnson with the musical surroundings he had been hearing all along. Soon after, he went home to New Iberia where, in 1949, he died after a succession of strokes. History has made him – with George Lewis – the figurehead of revivalism and an inspiration to younger New Orleans jazz musicians ever since. [DF]

⊙ **A Trumpet Stylist** (1942-45; MM). Very good introduction to Johnson featuring nineteen tracks by Bunk with his own band, the Yerba Buena Jazz Band (1944), Bunk's Brass Band, Sidney Bechet and more.

⊙ **Bunk Johnson And His Superior Band** (1942; Good Time Jazz). The product of one three-hour session, these spirituals, marches and blues were Bunk's first recordings with George Lewis and Jim Robinson and are therefore of central historic and musical interest. The set also includes the fascinating "Bunk Johnson talking records", recorded one day later and giving Johnson's view of jazz history.

⊙ **In San Francisco** (1943–7; American Music). Bunk playing with an intriguing mix of sidemen, including Kid Ory, Jim Robinson plus latterday revivalists; the CD also features a live *This Is Jazz* broadcast and six beautiful duets with pianist Bertha Gonsoulin.

⊙ **Bunk And Lu** (1944; Good Time Jazz). Fascinating and highly satisfactory meld of Watters's two-beat with Johnson's New Orleans roots; Bunk called Watters's outfit "the best band I had during my comeback".

⊙ **King Of The Blues** (1944; American Music). This disc contains thirteen wonderful tracks by Bunk's Blues Band, including unissued takes and notes by William Russell, who recorded the music originally.

Second Masters (1944; American Music). Continuing American Music's coverage of Bunk's career (many volumes to go), this set combines New Orleans specialities with standards played by the legendary team of Johnson, Robinson, Lewis, Marrero, "Slow Drag" Pavageau, Sidney Brown and Baby Dodds.

Bunk's Brass Band And Dance Band (1945; American Music). Bunk in a parade-band setting, plus tracks by his regular colleagues of the period (Lewis, Robinson, etc), recorded at George Lewis's home; especially valuable in that it shows two sides of the great man.

Bunk Johnson And Mutt Carey In New York (1947; American Music). Bunk at the Caravan Ballroom with a new team of revivalists, including Dick Wellstood.

Last Testament (1947; Delmark). Johnson's last band with a team of sophisticated swingmen. Ragtime specialities ("Kinklets", "The Entertainer") seem to contradict Johnson's purpose but he plays pop tunes too, including an atmospheric (if approximate) "Out Of Nowhere".

Charlie Johnson

Piano, bandleader.

b. Philadelphia, 21 Nov 1891; d. 13 Dec 1959.

Charlie "Fess" Johnson (the nickname probably comes from "professor") is mainly remembered as the leader of a fine band which for more than ten years was resident at Ed Smalls's Paradise in Harlem. By the early 1930s Johnson's orchestra included Sidney De Paris, Leonard Davis, Benny Carter (who wrote arrangements), Billy Taylor (bass) and trombonist Dicky Wells, who draws a hilarious picture of the band in his autobiography *Night People*. "Charlie loved to leave the piano and come out front to start his band so much that if only one cat had arrived he would still come out front and start him off, smiling as if the whole band were there! And he was a swell guy. Paynight there'd be a line around the booth and Charlie would sometimes be high and pay you twice!" Johnson's band recorded a few sides in the 1920s, but never achieved the reputation it deserved. "With any sort of management it might really have been something", said Eddie Condon later, "a rival to Duke Ellington or anyone else." After his orchestra broke up in 1938, Johnson continued playing around New York, but became ill in the 1950s and died in Harlem Hospital after a long illness. [DF]

Gus Johnson

Drums.

b. Tyler, Texas, 15 Nov 1913; d. 6 Feb 2000.

Gus Johnson played the bass drum for hometown parades and cinema bands before going to college in Kansas City, where he met and learned much from Jo Jones. After working in a variety of bands from 1935, he joined Jay McShann in 1938 and stayed until army service intervened in 1943. After his demobilization he played in New York with Jesse Miller's showband and with big bands led by Eddie Vinson, Earl Hines and Cootie Williams before joining Count Basie in 1948. The stay was short (Johnson was replaced by Butch Ballard) but in 1950 he rejoined Basie's small group at the Brass Rail in Chicago and later moved into the big band for another stay. Basie replaced him with Sonny Payne while Johnson was in hospital for an appendectomy. After his operation Johnson planned to concentrate on studio work, but soon after joined Ella Fitzgerald for a nine-year spell which he combined with more session work, a period with Woody Herman's band (1959) and club appearances accompanying everyone from Ralph Sutton to Stan Getz. A regular attender at Dick Gibson's Colorado Jazz Parties, Johnson was a member of The World's Greatest Jazz Band from 1969, was a star of Peanuts Hucko's Pied Piper quintet at the end of the next decade, and over a long and distinguished career has recorded with Herman, Basie, Gerry Mulligan, Johnny Hodges, Ralph Sutton and countless others. [DF]

➤➤ **Johnny Hodges** (*Everybody Knows Johnny Hodges*).

Howard Johnson

Baritone saxophone, tuba, composer, arranger, flugelhorn, clarinets, bass saxophone.

b. Montgomery, Alabama, 7 Aug 1941.

Johnson, who is self-taught, started on baritone saxophone in 1954, and took up the tuba in 1955. Between 1964–6 he played with Mingus, Hank Crawford and Archie Shepp. From 1966 he played various instruments with Gil Evans orchestras. In 1967 he was in Los Angeles working with Gerald Wilson, Big Black and Oliver Nelson. He has toured and played festivals in the USA and internationally with Shepp, Evans and others. His influences are Clifford Brown, Mingus, Evans, Ellington and Herb Bushler. Johnson is at home with all styles and types of music, and is a strong soloist on several instruments. He has written arrangements for Taj Mahal, Gil Evans and B.B. King. [IC]

Gravity!!! (1996; Verve). Gravity is the name of Johnson's working group of tuba virtuosi, and on this album he has nine tuba players including Dave Bargeron and Bob Stewart, with various rhythm-sections. The material includes a couple of Johnson's excellent pieces and his imaginative arrangement of some jazz originals including "Round Midnight" and "Stolen Moments", plus a standard "Yesterdays", and a marvellous version of the gospel/soul piece "Way 'Cross Georgia", with Johnson playing the melody on penny whistle and Bargeron's lovely euphonium solo ranging from bass to bat-squeak.

Right Now! (1997; Verve). This time there is a regular rhythm-section for the session – pianist Ray Chew, bassist James Cammack and drummer Kenwood Dennard – and Johnson's old associate Taj Mahal sings on a couple of the tracks, including the funky soul piece "It's Getting Harder To Survive". The performances and arrangements are also more adventurous, with brief passages of wilder collective improvising in the hard-hitting title track. The penny whistle features again, and in general the variety of sound and texture, aided and abetted by the skill of the fine rhythm-section, is absorbing. Again, Johnson's booklet notes are excellent.

➤➤ **Jack DeJohnette** *(Album Album)*; **Gil Evans** *(Plays The Music Of Jimi Hendrix)*; **Bob Moses** *(Visit With The Great Spirit)*.

J.J. Johnson

Trombone, arranger, composer.

b. Indianapolis, Indiana, 22 Jan 1924; d. 4 Feb 2001.

After working with territory bands, Johnson joined the Benny Carter band at the age of eighteen, staying from 1942–5 and moving on to Count Basie in 1945–6. In 1946 he did some small-group gigging in New York, and recorded under his own name and with the Esquire All Stars. This was followed by a period in the Illinois Jacquet group from 1947–9 and brief stints with Dizzy Gillespie in 1949 and 1951, and Oscar Pettiford in 1951. He was working out of music in 1952, except for recordings with Miles Davis and others. Then he co-led a quintet with fellow trombonist Kai Winding from 1954–6, which reunited for a European tour in 1958 and for recording in 1960 and 1968. He worked with his own quintet or sextet from 1956–60, and toured with Miles Davis in 1961–2, and with Sonny Stitt in Japan and Europe in 1964. Gaining a reputation as a writer in the late 1950s and 1960s, he moved to Los Angeles in 1970 to score film and TV background music, making only occasional records as player from then on, although he appeared in public from time to time during the 1980s and later.

Johnson adapted bebop to the trombone rather than the other way around, and achieved a quantum leap in what could be done with the unwieldy mechanism of the instrument. His immediate stylistic predecessors were people such as Trummy Young and Dicky Wells (whom he played alongside in the Basie band); their rhythmic concepts were firmly rooted in the swing era, but they easily overcame any limitations on their mobility or melodic thinking. The little-known and prematurely deceased Fred Beckett, trombonist with the Harlan Leonard and Lionel Hampton bands, was said by Johnson to have inspired his fast articulation, which for the 1940s was exceptionally clean and precise. While his contemporaries Kai Winding and Bill Harris both occasionally doubled on valve-trombone, J.J. never did but was often suspected of doing so.

Perhaps because of a certain blandness of tone, Johnson's early playing seems in retrospect a trifle academic, his choice of notes and especially of rhythms sounding somewhat stilted compared to leading modernists on other instruments. This approach also tends to carry over to his writing, which is at its best in relatively complex compositions such as "Poem For Brass" and "El Camino Real"; in more improvisatory contexts, even including the famous duo with Winding, his arrangements can be too fussy. However, Johnson's mature trombone work of the mid-1950s onwards, relieved of the need to prove itself alongside the beboppers, makes the instrument a more convincing vehicle for extended soloing than in the hands of almost anyone else. [BP]

Raffaella Cavalieri

J.J. Johmson

J.J. Johnson-Kai Winding

⊙ **Jay And Kai** (1947–54; Savoy). Placed first chronologically because of a single 1947 track by Johnson, which is balanced by some solo Winding material, the album's meat is the eight 1954 tracks which marked their first studio collaboration and led to their popular touring quintet.

J.J. Johnson

⊙ **The Eminent Jay Jay Johnson: Vol. 1** (1953; Blue Note). The album which encapsulates the best of J.J.'s early playing, done (ironically, while he was working in a day job) with an all-star group including the young Clifford Brown, Kenny Clarke and John Lewis.

J.J. Johnson-Stan Getz

⊙ **At The Opera House** (1957; Verve). Two casual Jazz At The Phil sessions which find both principals at the top of their game, goosed by the Oscar Peterson trio and Connie Kay.

J.J. Johnson

⊙ **The Trombone Master** (1957–60; Columbia). An excellent compilation of mainly quartet tracks, featuring Victor Feldman-Sam Jones-Louis Hayes or Tommy Flanagan-Paul Chambers-Max Roach.

⊙ **The Brass Orchestra** (1996; Verve). An impressive review of J.J.'s large-ensemble writing over forty years, with part of the 1956 "Poem For Brass", part of his *Perceptions* album for Dizzy Gillespie (recently reissued in its original version) and material from his mostly unreissued *J.J.!* The line-up of top New York brassmen is even more impressive, and soloists include Eddie Henderson, Robin Eubanks, Jon Faddis, Joe Wilder and of course Johnson.

James P. Johnson

Piano, arranger, composer.

b. New Brunswick, New Jersey, 1 Feb 1894; d. 17 Nov 1955.

By 1912 James P. (Price) Johnson was playing regularly in New York and the following year was established in the "Jungle", a tough area between 60th and 63rd streets, playing in clubs such as Jim Allan's, Barron's and Drake's Dance Hall. A big, horse-faced man with a modest manner, Johnson found his popularity and reputation growing quickly, and in 1916 he began to cut piano rolls for the Aeolian Company, then for QRS, which had a bigger circulation. In the following year he made his first record.

All through the 1920s he recorded constantly with stars, from Jabbo Smith to Bessie Smith (he directed music for her short film, *St Louis Blues*), appeared at clubs and rent parties, toured in England and elsewhere with *Plantation Revue* and worked as an MD. In 1923 he composed the score for a Broadway show, *Running Wild*, and by 1928 had written an extended work, *Yamecraw*, which was premiered at Carnegie Hall but met the fate of most serious music by black composers of the time. In the 1930s Johnson wrote stage works (including a collaboration with the poet Langston Hughes) and composed a symphony, as well as occasionally assembling bands; from 1939 he was playing regularly in bands once more. In spite of progressive illness he stayed reasonably active all through the 1940s, recording, playing at Jimmy Ryan's and with bands such as Wild Bill Davison's and Eddie Condon's; he also appeared to spectacular effect at Condon's Town Hall concerts for Blue Network Radio. By 1946 he was intermission pianist at clubs such as Condon's and the Pied Piper in Greenwich Village, where he met the young Dick Hyman. In 1951 a severe stroke disabled him for the rest of his life.

James P. Johnson is often called the "father of stride piano", merely because he was the teacher of Fats Waller, but there is evidence that he was in some respects a superior musician. "His basslines", says Dick Wellstood, "are better constructed, his right hand is freer and less repetitive, his rhythm is more accurate and his playing not so relentlessly two-beat." Famous for his later extended works and compositions such as "If I Could Be With You One Hour Tonight", "Old-Fashioned Love" and "Running Wild", Johnson was a highly trained musician who based his music on a wide range of influences – church music, dances, ragtime, blues and reels (rags like "Carolina Shout", featured by Fats Waller, are derived from square dances). Twenty years after his death his pupil Dick Hyman retranscribed and recorded a celebration of Johnson's ageless music. [DF]

James P. Johnson 1921–8/1928–38/1938–42/1943–4/1944 (Classics). Johnson is served by the chronological Classics series and these five volumes document his on-record career from early solos and sides with Jimmy Johnson's Jazz Boys through to the dusk of the swing era.

Hot Piano (1921–45; Topaz). Excellent selection of definitive Johnson, with piano solos spanning 1921–43, duets with Clarence Williams, his own orchestra (1939) and group tracks with Pee Wee Russell, Frank Newton and Omer Simeon.

Snowy Morning Blues (1930–44; GRP). The very best from Johnson, including four titles recorded for Brunswick in 1930 (Johnson at his peak) plus an eight-track Waller tribute and eight of Johnson's own specialities, including "Carolina Shout" and "Keep Off The Grass".

Lonnie Johnson

Guitar, vocals.

b. New Orleans, 8 Feb 1899; d. 16 June 1970.

Lonnie (Alonzo) Johnson studied violin and guitar in New Orleans, and visited London for the first time in 1917 to work in revue. Returning home, he found that most of his family had died in the great flu epidemic, and he left New Orleans for St Louis and Chicago. In 1925 he won a talent contest for the OKeh company, and became staff musician for the label, making records with emerging stars such as Duke Ellington, Louis Armstrong, Eddie Lang, Victoria Spivey and Spencer Williams. From 1932–7 he worked around Cleveland, playing for radio and working a day job; for three years after that he teamed regularly with Johnny Dodds in Chicago and led for himself. For the next four years he was commuting between Chicago, Detroit and Kansas City, and by the mid-1940s was featuring amplified guitar and a contemporary ballad style which earned him a best seller, "Tomorrow Night", in 1948. But when Johnson came to London in 1952, "he seemed out of practice on his guitar", *Jazz Journal* reported, "and insisted on featuring too many of his own ballad compositions". Johnson moved to Cincinnati, then to Philadelphia (1958–62), where he worked as a chef, before touring in 1963 in a blues package with Otis Spann and others. From the mid-1960s he lived and performed in Toronto and was a popular figure with local fans. [DF]

Playing With The Strings (1927–40; JSP). A fine selection of Johnson's work in jazz company – Armstrong, Ellington, Williams, Dodds, Ory and others.

Marc Johnson

Bass.

b. Omaha, Nebraska, 21 Oct 1953.

After attending Texas North State University, Marc Johnson played with a number of superb leaders in both small and large groups: Woody Herman (1977), Bill Evans (1978–80), Stan Getz (1981–2) and John Abercrombie (1983). He also collaborated, during this period, with Joanne Brackeen, Lee Konitz, John Lewis and Bob Brookmeyer. His most famous recording, however, *Bass Desires*, was made in 1985, and featured a two-guitar frontline of Bill Frisell and John Scofield along with drummer Peter Erskine; a follow-up with the same line-up two years later attracted fewer plaudits. In 1991, Johnson formed another band, Right Brain Patrol, which made two albums for JMT, an eponymous recording featuring guitarist Ben Monder and singing percussionist Arto Tunçboyaciyan, and a follow-up, *Magic Labyrinth* (1994), upon which Bonder was replaced by fellow guitarist Wolfgang Muthspiel. Work continued with pianists Eliane Elias, Lyle Mays and Enrico Pieranunzi, and in 1999 Johnson collaborated with Canadian cellist Eric Longsworth on an intriguing duo album, *If Trees Could Fly* (Intuition). An in-demand sideman and the anchor of well over 100 recordings in the last 25 years, he has latterly been heard with Charles Lloyd (*Lift Every Voice*; ECM 2002) and singers Patricia Barber (*Nightclub*; Blue Note, 2000) and Kurt Elling (*Flirting With Twilight*, Blue Note, 2001), but the bassist's clear predilection for guitars found its ultimate expression in his 1998 date as leader, *The Sound Of Summer Running* (see below). [CP]

⊙ **Bass Desires** (1985; ECM). Highly influential album, still sounding fresh thanks to Frisell's and Scofield's pleasingly contrasting styles, and featuring the leader on electric bass. A highlight is a ringingly positive version of Coltrane's "Resolution", from *A Love Supreme*.

⊙ **2 X 4** (1989; Emarcy). Series of duos with Gary Burton (Bill Evans's "Time Remembered" and "Monk's Dream"), Toots Thielemans ("Goodbye Pork Pie Hat") and others.

⊙ **Right Brain Patrol** (1991; JMT). Trio album featuring guitarist Ben Monder and ace percussionist Arto Tunçboyaciyan.

⊙ **The Sound Of Summer Running** (1998; Verve). Bill Frisell and Pat Metheny's guitars mesh beautifully on this "American heartland" album, which features six Johnson compositions, tastefully propelled by drummer Joey Baron.

Margaret Johnson

Piano.

b. Kansas City, 1919; d. 1939.

One of the pioneer woman jazz performers, and known as "Countess" or "Queenie", Johnson worked in her teens with Harlan Leonard's territory bands, was leading her own band at fifteen, and at seventeen replaced Count Basie as pianist with his band while Basie visited Chicago. She also briefly replaced Mary Lou Williams in the Andy Kirk band. A powerful player whose style recalled both Basie and Earl Hines, she became close friends with Lester Young during Basie's Kansas City years, and her authoritative style may be heard on four titles recorded by Billie Holiday's orchestra with Lester Young in New York, September 1938. She died the following year of tuberculosis. [DF]

Pete Johnson

Piano.

b. Kansas City, 24 March 1904; d. 23 March 1967.

A highly versatile pianist (Duke Ellington loved his work), Pete Johnson was mainly active as a soloist in 1930s clubs, but also accompanied Joe Turner and occasionally worked in bands during that decade. He was featured in the 1938 Carnegie Hall "Spirituals to Swing" concert, featuring Albert Ammons and Meade "Lux" Lewis, and rode the boogie boom with Ammons at Café Society, New York (they also formed a highly successful trio with Lewis). He later worked again as a soloist; and in the 1950s, despite a day job, he was still appearing occasionally at festivals and for Jazz At The Philharmonic, as well as accompanying Jimmy Rushing and getting together with Joe Turner for reunions. [DF]

Pete Johnson

⊙ **Pete Johnson 1938–9 & 1939–41** (Classics). These two volumes contain everything recorded by Johnson during the years in question: part one has titles with Joe Turner, Harry James, his Boogie Woogie Boys and Blues Trio; part two has more from his Blues Trio, plus sessions by his band (with Hot Lips Page and Don Byas) and Joe Turner's Fly Cats, and duos with Albert Ammons.

⊙ **Roll 'em Pete** (1938–47; Topaz). Johnson was a delicate and sophisticated musical mind whose blues always sounded as refined as they were barrelhouse; tracks here include his marvellous "Death Ray Boogie", "Sixth Avenue Express" (with Albert Ammons) and the high-spirited "Mr Drum Meets Mr Piano" (with J.C. Heard).

Joe Turner

⊙ **Big Joe Turner: The Blues Boss** (1946–58; Blues Encore). This excellent budget selection has eight of the eleven selections Turner recorded with Johnson in their classic 1956 "Boss of the Blues" collaboration, including "Roll 'em Pete", "Morning Glories", "Cherry Red" et al.

Plas Johnson

Tenor and other saxophones, flute.

b. Donaldsville, Louisiana, 21 July 1931.

Johnson learned the soprano from his father, and then graduated to tenor in the New Orleans-based Johnson Brothers Combo with pianist Ray in the early 1950s. Moving to the West Coast, he worked with Johnny Otis and pianist/singer Charles Brown, and became heavily involved in R&B session work. He was the tenor soloist in the first *Pink Panther* movie (1963) and in *Lady Sings The Blues* (1972), and was heard on countless MOR albums by everyone from Linda Ronstadt to Ella Fitzgerald. From the 1970s onwards he also performed more frequently in jazz contexts, including touring Europe as a soloist and with the Gene Harris SuperBand in 1990. In such situations, his love of Illinois Jacquet, Gene Ammons, Don Byas and Johnny Hodges comes through strongly. [BP]

The Blues (1975; Concord). This simply titled album points to the common thread in all of Johnson's work, from ballads such as "Georgia" and "Please Send Me Someone To Love" to the swinging "Parking Lot Blues" by Ray Brown, who underpins the quintet with Jake Hanna.

Sy Johnson

Arranger, piano.

b. New Haven, Connecticut, 15 April 1930.

Johnson studied music and played jazz in high school and in the air force. He moved to Los Angeles and began freelance arranging, but was also involved with Ornette Coleman and Paul Bley. Hoping to hear Bley in New York in 1960, he played in place of him for two weeks with Charles Mingus. In the 1960s he worked in New York with his own trio, the Rod Levitt octet, and the singer Yolande Bavan. He arranged for the Mingus big band and small group from 1971–8, as well as for the Thad Jones-Mel Lewis band and Quincy Jones. He wrote and occasionally played piano for the Lee Konitz nine-piece band from 1975–9. He was involved in the musical re-creations for the film *The Cotton Club* (1984). Like most professional arrangers, Johnson does a considerable amount of non-jazz work, but the above associations demonstrate his versatility and wide knowledge of the jazz field. He is also an entertaining journalist and perceptive photographer of jazz subjects. [BP]

Charles Mingus

Let My Children Hear Music (1971; Columbia). One of Mingus's few big-band albums and excellent in its own right, with much of the adaptation of Mingus's compositions entrusted to Johnson, and a wide variety of soloists from Mingus faithfuls to James Moody and Julius Watkins.

Carmell Jones

Trumpet.

b. Kansas City, 19 July 1936; d. 7 Nov 1996.

After making his mark in student band contests in Kansas, Jones moved to Los Angeles in 1961, gigging and recording with Harold Land, Bud Shank and under his own name. In 1964 he moved on to New York for more recording and touring with Horace Silver. He transplanted to Berlin in 1965 for radio studio work, combined with solo appearances throughout Europe. In the 1980s he returned to Kansas City. An interesting bop-oriented trumpeter who, through accidents of timing and geography, has been consistently underrated. [BP]

Carmell Jones (1961–3; Mosaic Select). This 3-CD set collects Jones's three albums from his West Coast stay, plus one led by Harold Land and an unissued date with pianist Frank Strazzeri.

>> **Booker Ervin** *(The Blues Book)*; **Horace Silver** *(Song For My Father)*.

Claude Jones

Trombone, vocals.

b. Boley, Oklahoma, 11 Feb 1901; d. 17 Jan 1962.

One of the trombone pioneers who helped free the trombone from its traditional tailgate role, Jones was a star of McKinney's Cotton Pickers (where his melodic improvisation and mobility reminded Quentin Jackson of Miff Mole), then worked with Fletcher Henderson from 1929 and Don Redman from 1931. His career went on to include years with Chick Webb, Cab Calloway and Duke Ellington (from 1944); he left music in the early 1950 to go to sea and died while Chief Steward on the *SS United States*. [DF]

>> **Bill McKinney** *(McKinney's Cotton Pickers 1928–9)*.

Dave Jones

Clarinet, baritone saxophone.

b. Ilminster, Somerset, UK, 22 Feb 1932; d. 1998.

Dave Jones worked around the East London area in the 1950s with bands such as Charlie Galbraith's before joining Kenny Ball's newly formed band in 1959. There his fruity, substantial tone, superior technique, powerful sound and driving approach became one of the strongest points of Ball's strong frontline and helped to establish a new high standard for British Dixieland. Jones's clarinet was heard on all the Kenny Ball hits from "I Love You Samantha" onward, and he became a star with an international reputation. After he left Ball in 1965 he became a freelance, worked with the Kinks (on baritone saxophone), and played locally on the Dixieland scene with friends including Galbraith, Mike Cotton, Pat Mason and Bill Nile; he also subbed for Acker Bilk. In the 1970s he was often heard with bassist Ron Russell's small group (featuring Keith Ingham, Pete Strange and Digby Fairweather) and from the later 1980s played regularly for drummer Laurie Chescoe's band, his superlative technique and creativity undiminished thirty years after the trad boom. [DF].

>> **Kenny Ball** *(Strictly Jazz)*.

Davey Jones

Trumpet, mellophone, horn, drums, saxophone.

b. Lutcher, Louisiana, c. 1888; d. c. 1953.

A multi-instrumentalist, Davey Jones worked in a Lutcher brass band from 1910, then in 1918 joined Fate Marable to work on the *SS Capitol*. During his time on board he played a part in Louis Armstrong's musical education, helping him to learn to read music and possibly more than that. "Jones was a phenomenal musician", recalls Danny Barker. "He played trumpet, but his instrument really was the mellophone and French horn! Now I can appreciate what he was doing – I didn't then. He was running all kinds of strange changes and I think he was some help to Louis – 'cos Louis could see what could be done with that horn. Nobody had taken liberties, other than clarinet players – here was Davey Jones doing it on the mellophone." Barker's remark about "strange changes" suggests that Jones was a harmonically advanced player, and Armstrong's own harmonic sophistication by the time he joined King Oliver in 1922 may have owed something to Jones's early lessons. Furthermore, Oliver was "a punch man", in George James's words, who could hardly have been the inspiration for flexible masterpieces such as "Cornet Chop Suey" or "West End Blues", which Armstrong was effortlessly producing five years on.

Jones himself worked with Oliver in 1921 for a year, and by mid-decade was leading his own band at the Pelican Dance Hall, New Orleans. In 1929 he cut four historic sides on saxophone with the Jones-Collins Astoria Hot Eight and later in the 1930s ran a student band (at one stage Joe Newman was a member). As with Cuban Bennett, the full depth of his influence and originality is one of the casualties of jazz history. [DF]

⊙ **New Orleans 1923–9** (Collectors Classics). This set includes the classic Jones-Collins Astoria Hot Eight sides.

Dill Jones

Piano.

b. Newcastle Emlyn, Wales, 19 Aug 1923; d. New York, 22 June 1984.

Jones played jazz while in the navy from 1942–6, then studied at music college in London in the late 1940s. He was associated with a wide variety of players including Joe Harriott, Don Rendell, Ronnie Scott, Jimmy Skidmore, Bruce Turner and Tommy Whittle during the 1950s; he also introduced a BBC radio jazz series. He moved to New York in 1961, working regularly with Yank Lawson, Max Kaminsky, Roy Eldridge, Bob Wilber, Jimmy McPartland and the Gene Krupa quartet in the 1960s. He then worked with former members of the Earl Hines quartet as the JPJ quartet, led by Budd Johnson from 1969–74. He resumed freelance activity and made frequent solo appearances (including a return trip to the UK in 1983). The breadth of Jones's knowledge, from stride piano to "modern jazz", was already evident during the 1950s when he was a "mainstreamer" before the term was invented; by the time of his death from throat cancer, he had become a highly respected member of the New York jazz community. [BP]

⊙ **The Music Of Bix Beiderbecke** (1972; Chiaroscuro). Beiderbecke's few piano pieces plus a fine "Davenport Blues" are combined with other material associated with him, all played in an eclectic manner that has a nostalgic feel but doesn't ape the style of the era.

Ed Jones

Saxophones, bass-clarinet, flute, composer.

b. Amersham, Bucks, UK, 8 July 1961.

Musically encouraged by a violinist father and a mother who had sung in school choirs, Ed Jones took up saxophone at fifteen, and was playing in the school jazz band two weeks later. He began playing with local rock, jazz and funk bands in 1977, and in 1978 he joined the Bedfordshire Youth Jazz Orchestra. The following year, he played with Quasar, a jazz-rock band, but played his first London gig in 1981 with Julian Bahula and Simon Picard. After graduating in art (with a music major) from Middlesex Polytechnic in 1984, a spell of street musicianship followed, but by 1986, Jones was performing with Bahula's Jazz Africa, and in 1987 he joined bassist Rob Statham's Kew Street, forming his own quartet – with Statham, pianist Geoff Williams and drummer Winston Clifford – a year later. He also joined Dick Heckstall-Smith's DHSS. In 1989, Jones's quartet undertook their first UK tour, and brought out a debut album, *The Homecoming*, on Acid Jazz. Jones also joined drummer John Stevens's trio with bassist Paul Rogers. The following year, Jones again toured the UK with his band – now a quintet with the addition of Bosco De Oliveira on percussion – and with the John Stevens quintet and DHSS. Jones formed a new quartet – Jonathan Gee (piano), Wayne Batchelor (bass) and Brian Abrahams (drums) – in 1991, and recorded *Piper's Tales* with it (released on ASC in 1995). Tours of Europe followed in 1990–94, with both the quartet and with US3, and in 1994 Jones recorded for Blue Note both with a new quintet (Gee, bassist Arnie Somogyi, Clifford and trumpeter Byron Wallen – which remained unreleased) and with organist Lonnie Smith. In 1995, Jones joined Incognito, recording and touring with them, and the next year formed a sextet with actor/vibes player Max Beasley, bassist Geoff Gascoyne, Gee, Wallen and Clifford, which can be heard on *Out Here* (see below). In 1997, Jones began playing with Finnish trumpeter Mika Myllari, and toured and recorded (see below) with him in Finland. Jones has written scores for TV and theatre, brass arrangements for Incognito, US3 and Herbie Hancock's Headhunters, and added his gutsy but cultured saxophone sound to the music of everyone from the Brand New Heavies and Boy George to Queen Latifa and George Benson.

Though he regards his current quintet as his main solo platform (releasing *Seven Moments* on ASC in 2002), his other projects often reflect his interest in modern trends. These include Ed/Ge, a jazz/beats/electronica fusion in collaboration with Us3 drummer programmer Geoff Wilkinson and Nu Quartet, an exploration of the classic and contemporary possibilities of the pianoless quartet, featuring Wallen, bassist Ben Hazleton and drummer Sebastian Rochford. [CP]

Out Here (1997; ASC). All-original album (except for "Chelsea Bridge") showcasing Jones's blustery, vigorous tenor spearheading one of the UK's most fiercely interactive bands in top gear throughout.

Blue Reflections (1999; ASC). Recorded in the middle of Jones's Finnish tour with Mika Myllari. All tracks are originals, featuring some of Jones's most effective soprano-playing and more superbly cohesive work from his tastefully rumbustious band.

Elvin Jones

Drums, composer.

b. Pontiac, Michigan, 9 Sept 1927.

Elvin is the younger brother of Hank and Thad Jones, but is unrelated to the other famous drummers Jo and Philly Joe Jones. After army service from 1946–9, he began playing locally in the Detroit area in a group led by Billy Mitchell, making his record debut with them on two early 1950s sessions. He moved to New York in 1955 and worked with Teddy Charles-Charles Mingus and the Bud Powell trio and recorded with Miles Davis and Sonny Rollins. He joined the new J.J. Johnson quintet in 1956–7, Pepper Adams-Donald Byrd in 1958, Tyree Glenn in 1958–9, and the Harry Edison quintet in 1959–60. He then became a member of the classic John Coltrane quartet, staying until early 1966, when he started leading his own trio, quartet or quintet. Among musicians working regularly for him have been saxophonists Joe Farrell, Frank Foster, George Coleman, Dave Liebman, Pat La Barbera and Sonny Fortune; they have frequently chosen the group's repertoire, but some original material has been contributed by Elvin's Japanese wife Keiko Jones.

The dynamic drummer is an asset to any group and has done a certain amount of performing and recording in mainstream and all-star contexts, but he is particularly associated with Coltrane (and the post-Coltrane soloists of his own group). The driving, and psychologically driven, quality of his work was especially appropriate to the emotional climate of the new jazz in the 1960s, and it is difficult to imagine the eviscerating explorations of mature Coltrane without Elvin's percussive outpourings playing a simultaneous, indeed equal role. But, along with his all-enveloping energy and high volume level (that is, for someone playing unamplified pre-rock drums), there is an essential clarity to Jones's drumming, both tonally and rhythmically. The sounds he obtains from the standard kit are instantly recognizable and easy to follow, which is important since his rhythmic feel is very personal; the cross-rhythms, often complicated by omitting or underemphasizing the downbeat, may seem almost impossible to count aloud. Their ebb and flow, however, is so constant that they always come out sounding absolutely right in the end.

These stylistic innovations were a vital step beyond the polyrhythms of Max Roach and Art Blakey. Although he was not personally identified with either

Jak Kilby

Elvin Jones

free jazz or jazz-rock, Elvin's contribution was crucial both for the multidirectional drumming of the former school and for the complex percussion of some fusion music. Throughout the varying fortunes of jazz itself in the last two decades he has maintained his own individuality, which is a considerable achievement in itself. And, in a more specific manner, his rhythmic independence (just like the sheer speed of Buddy Rich) is seen as an ultimate standard by which all other drummers are measured, and which affords them continual and limitless inspiration. [BP]

Puttin' It Together (1968; Blue Note). This was Elvin's first working trio after his Coltrane period, with Jimmy Garrison on bass and saxophonist Joe Farrell holding his own against the percussion on "Ginger Bread Boy" and the one-time bossa nova "Reza".

When I Was At Aso-Mountain (1990; Enja). Altoist-flautist Sonny Fortune was the main horn in Elvin's 1980s groups, sometimes joined by Pat La Barbera (and briefly by Alan Skidmore or Courtney Pine), and Fortune carries the day here with strong contributions from Cecil McBee.

Going Home (1992; Enja). Indicative of Elvin's frequent featuring of younger musicians, this group features trumpeter Nicholas Pyton, flautist Kent Jordan and saxophonists Javon Jackson and Ravi Coltrane.

➤➤ **John Coltrane** *(My Favourite Things; Complete Africa/Brass Sessions; Live At The Village Vanguard; A Love Supreme)*; **Gil Evans** *(The Individualism of Gil Evans)*; **Sonny Rollins** *(A Night At The Village Vanguard Vols.1 & 2)*.

Etta Jones

Vocals.

b. Aiken, South Carolina, 25 Nov 1928; d. 16 Oct 2001.

Etta Jones has an R&B background, from touring with Buddy Johnson's band at the age of sixteen. She also recorded with Barney Bigard and Pete Johnson and toured with the Earl Hines sextet in the early 1950s. Established as a solo star, she had a hit single and album, *Don't Go To Strangers*, in 1960, and has since made numerous albums. She toured Japan alongside Art Blakey in 1970 and, since the mid-1970s, she also performed regularly with her partner, Houston Person. Possessed of a clear, round voice, she combines the influence of Billie Holiday and the blues in a way which is both middle-of-the-road and thoroughly jazz-based. [BP]

Don't Go To Strangers (1960; Prestige/OJC). Her second jazz album, which included the successful title track, finds her confidently fronting a quartet with Frank Wess on tenor and flute.

Hank Jones

Piano.

b. Vicksburg, Mississippi, 31 July 1918.

The elder brother of Thad and Elvin Jones, Hank was also the founder of the Detroit "school" of pianists (which includes players such as Tommy Flanagan, Barry Harris and Roland Hanna). He moved to New York in 1944 and worked with Hot Lips Page, Andy Kirk and Coleman Hawkins from 1946–7. He backed Ella Fitzgerald from 1947–53, which included touring with Jazz At The Philharmonic. Subsequently he took part in innumerable recording sessions with virtually every pre-"free jazz" soloist of any consequence (and in many non-jazz situations as well). A musician for all seasons, Jones has a distinctive but seemingly subdued style, which has made him a superbly responsive accompanist. The strength and resilience of his contributions are often best savoured in recordings designed to feature others, but his solo playing, on which he has concentrated from the mid-1970s, is worthy of close attention. [BP]

The Oracle (1989; Emarcy). At the age of seventy, Jones was just as on top of things as 35 years earlier and this programme, with Dave Holland and Billy Higgins, has him proclaiming his eminence in typical understated manner.

➤➤ **Abbey Lincoln** *(When There Is Love).*

Isham Jones

Saxophones, bass.

b. Coalton, Iowa, 31 Jan 1894; d. 19 Oct 1956.

Isham Jones led a famous band which worked Chicago's hotel circuit in the early 1920s, played at one stage for Streckfus Line steamers (along with Fate Marable and Ralph Williams) and recorded prolifically with fine players such as Louis Panico (trumpet), Leo Murphy (violin) and Roy Bargy (piano). By 1935 there were new stars in Jones's band including Pee Wee Erwin, Jack Jenney (trombone), singer Eddie Stone and staff arranger Gordon Jenkins, who later called it "the greatest sweet ensemble of that time – or any other time". A sad-faced leader, Jones played his farewell engagement in 1936 opposite Benny Goodman and retired to concentrate on composition. His orchestra was taken over by sideman Woody Herman, who, with the help of flugelhornist/arranger Joe Bishop, created his own first big band from it.

Isham Jones is remembered as the composer of fine songs including "The One I Love Belongs To Somebody Else", "Swingin' Down The Lane", "On The Alamo", "There Is No Greater Love", "Spain" and "I'll Never Have To Dream Again". His music has been re-created by Rusty Dedrick, among others. [DF]

Jimmy Jones

Piano.

b. Memphis, 30 Dec 1918; d. 29 April 1982.

Jones's early career included work with Stuff Smith (1943–5) and J.C. Heard (1946–7), and as accompanist to Sarah Vaughan, first from 1947–52, and then again after a two-year illness from 1954–8. During this time Jones recorded prolifically, including a celebrated return to the studios for the Buck Clayton Jam Session. During the 1960s Jones worked as arranger and MD (notably for Duke Ellington's *My People* in 1963), accompanied Ella Fitzgerald (1966–8) and wrote for TV and films (he moved to LA in 1969) – *Shaft's Big Score* was an early film credit. In the 1970s he also worked with guitarists Kenny Burrell and John Collins.

Jones was a gently original jazz pianist, producing work distinguished by a veiled piano sound (not unlike Ellis Larkins's), audacious single-note lines, and particularly by the habit of letting right-handed block chords, interrogatively voiced, move polyrhythmically over the rhythm-section's steady pulse. [DF]

The Piano Collection Vol. 2 (1953–4; Vogue). Reissued with trio sessions by Al Haig and George Wallington, Jones leads what was Sarah Vaughan's rhythm-section (Roy Haynes and bassist Joe Benjamin) in a set of six standards, all given imaginative and harmonically distinctive treatments.

➤➤ **Buck Clayton** *(Complete CBS Jam Sessions).*

Jo Jones

Drums.

b. Illinois, 7 Oct 1911; d. 4 Sept 1985.

"Jo Jones reminds me of the wind", said Don Lamond in a familiar quotation. "He has more class than any drummer I've ever heard: with Jo there's none of that dam' raucous tom-tom beating or riveting-machine stuff. Jo makes sense." Jo (Jonathan) Jones made sense in a lot of ways. Musically he was the finest, fastest drummer of the swing era, the pulse that powered Count Basie's unmatchable "All-American Rhythm Section". Personally he was the most pertinent (and sometimes painful) commentator on the jazz life. "As of today I don't know nobody I can talk to but Roy Eldridge, because there's nobody playing in the music business that's had the kind of experience he and I had", said Jones not long before he died.

His earliest musical memories were often of fairgrounds – "I remember my aunt taking me to a circus when I was a kid, and I can still feel that bass drum!" – and on the way up he worked successively in carnival bands (two important teachers were bandleaders Henri Woode and Samuel Brothers, both from Omaha), territory bands and for such well-known leaders as Bennie Moten and Tommy Douglas. From 1934, with one or two false starts, he was working for Count Basie ("I joined for two weeks and stayed for fourteen years") and defining what modern jazz drummers were to do ten years later. "He was playing that modern stuff and it sounded good", says Eddie Durham of that period. "I don't know where he got it from", Gus Johnson agrees: "The way Jo played was something else, it was smooth as you'd want to hear anybody play and right easy!" Like any great craftsman, the ever-smiling Jones made difficult things look easy and the result was classic jazz's finest rhythm-section. "We worked at it to build a rhythm-section every day and night", Jones recalled. "Basie's rhythm-section had a kind of throb going – no one instrument louder than the other", explains Nat Pierce.

Jones was with Basie until 1944, when he was called up, then again from 1946–8, when he was replaced by Gus Johnson. By now established as a star in his own right, he turned freelance, working with Illinois Jacquet and Lester Young, with Joe Bushkin's trio at the Embers, with old friends such as Teddy Wilson, Coleman Hawkins and Roy Eldridge, and with Jazz At The Philharmonic, as well as leading his own groups in clubs and for recordings arranged by John Hammond. "I think Jo can do more things superlatively well than any drummer I ever heard", said Hammond, "he's always been my favourite." The result of Hammond's enthusiasm was classic albums such as *Jo Jones Special* and *Jo Jones + 2* for Vanguard. By the mid-1960s, however, the "wide smile" that Jones had worn for so long was starting to be replaced by the quizzical look of a man out of place: "I'm a loner – a street boy – fifty years without a home!" In later years Jones brought a keenly observant eye to the fallibilities of the jazz life, and tended to speak the truth with no compromise. He was a consummate professional, who dismissed the non-comprehension of followers: "We haven't got time to explain our references." In the 1980s Jones became ill; benefits were organized by musical heirs such as Jack DeJohnette, and the master happily recovered, but only for a while. [DF]

HERMAN LEONARD

Jo Jones

⊙ **Jo Jones Trio** (1959; Fresh Sounds). With Ray and Tommy Bryant on piano and bass, this is an enjoyable trio session from years when Jones was still at the heart of the swing generation.

⊙ **Jo Jones Sextet** (1960; Fresh Sounds). With an A-team of sidemen including Harry Edison, Jimmy Forrest and trombonist Benny Green, this is one of Jones's best albums as a leader.

➤➤ **Count Basie** *(The Original American Decca Recordings).*

Jonah Jones

Trumpet, vocals.

b. Louisville, Kentucky, 31 Dec 1908.

Jonah Jones started his playing career with an alto horn in Louisville's Community Center Band, and after an apprenticeship in local groups he worked with Horace Henderson and Jimmie Lunceford (among others) before beginning a partnership with Stuff Smith (1932–4), latterly at the Lafayette Theater. A year later Lil Hardin Armstrong took over the band and billed Jones remorselessly as "King Louis II". He rejoined Smith soon after and, when bandleader Dick Stabile offered the duo a residency at the Onyx on 52nd Street, their brand of knocked-out showmanship, combined with catchy hit songs such as "I'se A Muggin'" and the reefer-happy "If You'se A Viper", made them a hot property. A sixteen-month stay at the Onyx, and four more successful years together, followed.

In 1941 Jones began an eleven-year stay with Cab Calloway, who celebrated his arrival with a record, "When Jonah Joined The Cab", a cheeky reference to Raymond Scott's "When Cootie Left The Duke". After 1952 Jones worked the Embers for a while with Joe Bushkin; his second stay there, from 1955, proved his biggest career step. A recording session, *Jonah Jones At The Embers*, produced a throwaway end-of-session side: a shufflebeat paraphrase of "On The Street Where You Live" from *My Fair Lady*, which had opened that year on Broadway. The album featuring the track sold more than a million copies and was followed by a string of others, all featuring Jones's singing and unmistakable trumpet, full of veiled glissandi, attacking climbs and fuzzy vibrato. Setting a style for trumpet quartets for the next decade, Jones was the star of the Embers for seven years and an international star for years after that, playing for LBJ, Prince Rainier on Sunset Strip and network American TV with stars including Fred

Astaire. In the 1970s he played festivals and continued touring, then in the 1980s was relaunched in a loosely swinging new format. By the 1990s he was semi-retired but still practising daily. [DF]

⊙ **Jonah Jones 1935–6** (Classics). Jones's totally original 1950s style was still developing at this point, but he was a powerful and impressive player from day one, and it shows on this initial chronology featuring tracks with Dick Porter and titles under his own name.

⊙ **Jonah Jones At The Embers** (1956; RCA). Jones's record-breaking run at the Embers helped establish his inimitable quartet sound, well illustrated on this collection.

⊙ **Jumpin' With Jonah** (1958; Capitol). In full swing at this point, a good example of Jones's internationally successful quartet formula which spawned a section of trumpet-copyists. Hank Jones is on piano and there are four bonus tracks for luck from related collections.

⊙ **Confessin': The definitive Black and Blue sessions** (1978; Black and Blue). With the great Andre Persiany on piano, Jones plays marvellously on seven beautifully recorded tracks sounding more like 25 years old than 70. Anyone foolish enough to berate him for commercial success will have all their "strict-jazz" demands fulfilled here – Jones was a technically superb and stylistically individual player, a fact faithfully re-illustrated on this set.

Leroy Jones

Trumpet.

b. New Orleans, 20 Feb 1958.

One of the most interesting and creative of new-wave black traditionalists, Jones took up cornet in 1971 and trained with Danny Barker in the Fairview Baptist Church Christian Marching Band. By the time he was sixteen Jones was co-leading the Hurricane Brass Band with fellow trumpeter Gregory Davis (of the Dirty Dozen Brass Band) and working in numerous brass bands. In 1974 he won a scholarship to Loyola Music Conservatory, New Orleans, but stayed only half a semester; he went on to work with singer Leroy Bates, then with clarinettist Hollis Carmouche (1978) and a variety of other bands before joining Harry Connick's big band in 1990. Since then Jones has achieved international recognition and recorded as a soloist. [DF]

⊙ **Mo' Cream From The Crop** (1994; Columbia). Jones's debut album as a soloist, in the company of Thaddeus Richard (piano) and Lucien Barban (trombone), with repertoire including "How Come You Do Me?'" and "Mood Indigo".

Oliver Jones

Piano.

b. Montreal, 11 Sept 1934.

The son of Barbadian immigrants, Oliver Jones began musical life in Montreal by studying classical piano with Madame Bonner at the age of seven. At nine, he was studying with Oscar Peterson's sister, Daisy, and by high-school age he was playing gigs in local clubs. In 1962 Jones formed an international showband, doing occasional gigs in Las Vegas, but

mostly playing in Puerto Rico, where Jones settled. In 1980 he moved back to Montreal and joined bassist Charlie Biddle in his jazz trio at his own club, Biddle's Jazz and Ribs. He made his debut album for CBC in 1983, but has since made a number of recordings for Justin Time, establishing himself as an internationally famous musician with a gospelly sound liberally laced with the subtle felicities of his chief inspirations, Art Tatum, Erroll Garner and Oscar Peterson. In 1995, Jones decided to go into semi-retirement, but this didn't prevent him from producing one of the finest recordings of his career in 1997, *Have Fingers, Will Travel*, with a top-flight rhythm-section (see below) and a good live album *Just In Time* (Justin Time; 1998). Despite the appearance of *Then And Now* in 2002 (a mixture of 1986 and 2001 sessions), Jones's current efforts at retirement seem successful. [CP]

⊙ **Cookin' At Sweet Basil** (1987; Justin Time). Rumbustious but surprisingly delicate when need be, Jones leads bassist Dave Young and drummer Terry Clarke in a highly enjoyable set at New York's famous jazz club.

⊙ **Just Friends** (1989; Justin Time). Chiefly notable for the enlivening presence of trumpeter Clark Terry, another accessible, sparky Jones recording.

⊙ **A Class Act** (1991; Justin Time). Jones's classiest recording to date, featuring bassist Steve Wallace and drummer Ed Thigpen in thoughtful but lively renditions of a mix of Jones originals and tunes such as Kenny Wheeler's "Everybody's Song But My Own" and Bill Evans's "Very Early".

⊙ **Have Fingers, Will Travel** (1997; Justin Time.) Six originals plus old chestnuts like "If I Were A Bell" and "Without A Song", performed with all Jones's customary elegance and verve, with bassist Ray Brown and drummer Jeff Hamilton, thus underlining the Oscar Peterson conection.

Philly Joe Jones

Drums; also piano and other instruments.

b. Philadelphia, 15 July 1923; d. 30 Aug 1985.

Jones worked extensively in his home town (hence the nickname, bestowed to distinguish him from the other drumming Jo Jones) before touring with trumpeter Joe Morris, whose R&B group included Johnny Griffin and Elmo Hope. He played with Ben Webster in 1949, then moved to New York, freelancing with Zoot Sims, Lee Konitz, Tony Scott and Tadd Dameron in 1953. From 1952–5 he worked in partnership with Miles Davis, who often used Philly Joe to bolster locally based rhythm-sections when gigging outside New York. Jones then played with the regular Davis quintet/sextet from 1955–7, and again in 1958 and 1962. He did many record dates during this period and in the early 1960s, and worked with the Gil Evans band in 1959, and led a quintet from 1959–62. He was a member of the Bill Evans trio in 1967 and 1976. He moved to England in 1967, and then lived in France from 1969–72, gigging and teaching all over Europe. He returned to Philadelphia for the rest of the 1970s, leading his own groups. From 1981–5 he led the nine-piece band Dameronia, dedicated to performing works of Tadd Dameron, and also briefly replaced the deceased Kenny Clarke in Pieces Of Time in 1985, shortly before his own death.

Jones is indelibly associated with the first classic Miles Davis quintet; he not only masterminded its rhythm-section, but created one of its most distinctive (and most imitated) sounds, the once-per-bar rim-shot played with the heel of the drumstick, as in the title track of *Milestones*. Equally adept with the wire brushes, he was nevertheless at his best when using sticks to play an interactive commentary behind a suitably strong soloist such as John Coltrane. His style could be said to combine the intelligence of Max Roach with the power of Art Blakey, although in detail it was unique. Dismissing obliquely the criticisms of Joe's musical idiosyncrasy and drug-related unreliability, Miles once said, "I wouldn't care if he came up on the bandstand in his BVDs [underwear] and with one arm, just so long as he was there. He's got the fire I want." [BP]

⊙ **Drums Around The World** (1959; Riverside/OJC). Good work from a nine-piece band with Cannonball Adderley and either Lee Morgan or Blue Mitchell includes Tadd Dameron's drum feature "Philly J.J." and is capped by a solo track "Tribal Message".

➤➤ **John Coltrane** *(Blue Train)*; **Miles Davis** *(Cookin' And Relaxin'; Milestones)*; **Bill Evans** *(Everybody Digs Bill Evans)*.

Quincy Jones

Composer, arranger; also trumpet, piano.

b. Chicago, 14 March 1933.

Jones moved to Seattle when he was ten and played with locally based teenager Ray Charles, who interested him in arranging. His early efforts were recorded by Lionel Hampton, with whom he played for two and a half years from 1951–3, including a European tour. He then became a freelance arranger, including work on many small-group record sessions. He was the musical director for the Dizzy Gillespie big band in 1956, before returning to freelance work. In 1957–8 he spent eighteen months in France and Scandinavia, studying composition and working for Barclay Records. He formed his own all-star big band for the European opening of the show *Free and Easy* in 1959 and then, first in Europe and later in the USA, he toured regularly for two years. He also wrote albums for Count Basie and recorded backings for Sarah Vaughan, Dinah Washington, Billy Eckstine and other singers. He held an executive post at Mercury Records, where he continued to produce his own albums, although they were increasingly aimed at the popular market. Since the mid-1960s he has written music for about fifty films, and since the mid-1970s he has run Qwest Productions, arranging and producing hugely successful albums by Brothers Johnston, Michael Jackson and Frank Sinatra. From 1991 he became co-producer of the famous Montreux festivals.

Although now at a professional peak previously undreamed of for black musicians, Jones was also something of an innovator in the early and mid-1950s, using the concept of chords built in fourths long before McCoy Tyner (or even Richie Powell) discovered them as a piano device. In this way he obtained a sound as rich as that of Tadd Dameron or the arrangers for the Miles Davis band (and often with smaller forces at his disposal), and added a bluesy pungency that eluded other writers. To that extent, Quincy's work for musicians such as Clifford Brown (during the Hampton European tour) predicted the strengths which pervaded his collaborations with artists remote from jazz, and which have made him capable of the far-reaching fusions he has helped to create. [BP]

⊙ **This Is How I Feel About Jazz** (1956–7; Impulse!). The 1956 sessions constitute Jones's masterpiece, with (inevitably all-star) nine- and fifteen-piece bands playing his light-fingered but dynamic arrangements of such as "Walkin'" and "Sermonette". Art Farmer and Lucky Thompson are the key soloists among many.

⊙ **Walking In Space** (1969; A&M). An echo-laden attempt to tread similar ground but with more pop-jazz material. Freddie Hubbard and Hubert Laws are featured on Benny Golson's "Killer Joe", which ends with a female backing-vocal group.

➤➤ **Dizzy Gillespie** *(Groovin' High)*; **Dinah Washington** *(The Swingin' Miss "D")*.

Richard M. Jones

Piano, composer.

b. Donaldsville, Louisiana, 13 June 1889; d. 8 Dec 1945.

Richard M. ("Myknee") Jones worked around New Orleans in clubs and cabarets in his teens and in 1919 joined Clarence Williams's publishing company. By 1925 he was A&R man for OKeh (producing the "race" records which were popular with both black and white audiences in the 1920s), from whom he later moved to Decca. A longtime friend of King Oliver, for whom he engineered recording contracts with OKeh, Columbia and other companies, Jones was also a fine pianist who recorded prolifically himself from 1923. From 1925 he made records with his Jazz Wizards, which included such famous names as Albert Nicholas, Shirley Clay (cornet), Darnell Howard (clarinet) and Preston Jackson (trombone). He also composed famous tunes such as "Trouble In Mind" and "Riverside Blues". From the 1940s he was most active as an arranger and talent scout for Mercury. [DF]

Richard M. Jones 1923-7/1927-44 (Classics) Admirable if patchy selection of Jones's work featuring good trio sides with Albert Nicholas, the (very rarely heard) Hightower's Nighthawks featuring cornettist Willie Hightower.

Rodney Jones

Guitar, bass, drums.

b. New Haven, Connecticut, 30 Aug 1956.

Jones went to City College of New York for two years, studying improvisation with John Lewis and playing in Lewis's ensemble. From 1966–73 Jones led his own small groups around the New York area. In 1974 he worked at the Five Spot with the Music Complex Orchestra led by Jaki Byard, and with other groups in New York, doing many disco and Latin recordings. In 1975 he was recommended to Chico Hamilton by a friend of Arthur Blythe and played with Hamilton for almost a year. In 1976 he joined Dizzy Gillespie's quartet, staying for almost three years, and from 1978–80 worked in the USA with Chico Hamilton, Maxine Brown and numerous others, and formed his own group with Kenny Kirkland (piano), Ronnie Burrage (drums) and Ben Brown (bass).

From 1980–83 he worked with his group in the New York area, did a world tour with the Subtle Sounds jazz group, and played with Darwin Gross in the USA and Europe. In 1983 he started working as guitarist for Lena Horne, writing and arranging her "London Opener", and was with her until 1985. In the late 1980s he recorded with Hilton Ruiz (*Strut*) and Maceo Parker (*Roots Revisited*). In 2001 he released *Soul Manifesto*, an explosive set that embraced funk over and above the more traditional material that he had produced in the years previous. The album featured heavyweights Maceo Parker, Arthur Blythe and Lonnie Smith.

Jones' favourite guitarists are Wes Montgomery, Barney Kessel, Grant Green and Bruce Johnson. He has said, "I try to bring out the subtle aspects of music when I play, and to make each note have a meaning." [IC]

Salena Jones

Vocals.

b. Virginia, 29 Jan 1944.

Jones (born Joan Shaw) began singing in church and school and began club work at the age of fifteen. After winning a talent contest at New York's Apollo, she began making demonstration records (for Peggy Lee and Lena Horne), acquired her own contract and appeared in New York before touring in Spain (1965) and Britain (1966), where she appeared for an extended season at Ronnie Scott's. Since then she has appeared at most leading concert halls and clubs in Europe, Africa, Australasia, South America and Asia, and appeared regularly on radio and TV, with her own series in the UK. Since visiting Japan for the first time (1978) she has appeared there annually, memorably in the Unesco *Save The Children Telethon* (1988), and on a concert tour with the Royal Philharmonic Orchestra (1992). Jones's contained dry-sherry contralto fits effortlessly into any musical situation, and her recent return to recording in Britain is good news; she also briefly opened a club of her own in London's Shepherd's Bush in 2001. [DF]

Sings Jobim With The Jobims (1994; Vinegate Music). A major artistic statement; Jones, recorded in Rio, with the Jobim family (son Paulo, grandson Daniel) and including two duos with Antonio Carlos 'Tom' Jobim himself. A beautiful recording and one of her best.

It Amazes Me (1995; Vinegate). A considered selection of sixteen fine songs (including "Canadian Sunset" and "Imagine My Frustration") with Jones surrounded by generously featured British soloists, including Guy Barker, Richard Edwards, Iain Dixon and pianist/arranger Paul Sawtell.

Salena Jones Meets Kenny Burrell And Richie Cole (undated; Vinegate). An exhilarating trio of talents: Richie Cole's chemical alto joins Jones in a straightahead small group, while Burrell is her musical partner in a larger orchestral setting. The usual classy songs.

Sam Jones

Bass, cello.

b. Jacksonville, Florida, 12 Nov 1924; d. 15 Dec 1981.

After moving to New York, Jones worked with Tiny Bradshaw, Illinois Jacquet and Kenny Dorham in 1955–6. He was a member of the first Cannonball Adderley quintet in 1956–7, then worked with Dizzy Gillespie and the Thelonious Monk quartet. As well as recording with these artists he had frequent album dates with players such as Clark Terry, Bill Evans, Johnny Hodges and Duke Ellington. When Adderley re-formed his band, Jones was with him from 1959–66, until he replaced Ray Brown in the Oscar Peterson trio from 1966–9. Thereafter he worked as a freelance in New York, and, after 1971, did regular work with the Cedar Walton trio plus various tenor players. During the last years of his life Jones led a part-time twelve-piece band. Despite occasional doubling on cello, in the manner of his forebears Brown and Pettiford, Jones made relatively little impression as a soloist. However, in his partnerships with drummers Louis Hayes (in both the Adderley and Peterson groups) and Billy Higgins (via the Cedar Walton connection), he revealed himself as a rhythm-section player par excellence. Two of his tunes used by Adderley,

"Unit 7" and "Del Sasser", have gradually become standard material. [BP]

Cannonball Adderley

At The Lighthouse (1960; Riverside/OJC). One of Adderley's most popular live albums, this has Jones being superbly unobtrusive in his rhythm-section role with Louis Hayes, and soloing on "Sack O'Woe".

Sam Jones

The Soul Society (1960; Riverside/OJC). Jones is featured on cello for four tracks, including the standards "Just Friends" and "There Is No Greater Love", in a sextet including Bobby Timmons and Nat Adderley or Blue Mitchell.

Thad Jones

Trumpet, cornet, valve-trombone, arranger, composer.
b. Pontiac, Michigan, 28 March 1923;
d. Copenhagen, 21 Aug 1986.

After working locally and in Oklahoma City, Jones joined Count Basie from 1954–63, and though he was not generously featured as a soloist he wrote many arrangements of original compositions. He left to become a freelance arranger and studio player, and in the meantime he started, with Mel Lewis, a once-a-week rehearsal band of leading studio band jazz musicians. The Thad Jones-Mel Lewis orchestra ran from 1965–78 (continuing thereafter under Lewis alone), gained an international reputation and made several foreign tours. Jones migrated to Denmark from 1978–84, writing for the radio orchestra and running his own jazz big band, Eclipse. During this period, he also took up valve-trombone and studied composition formally. In late 1984 he was contracted to work in the USA with the Basie band following the death of its leader, but he gave up touring and returned to Denmark a couple of months before his own death.

Jones's playing was unfortunately overshadowed by his arranging and bandleading ability, but the printed comment of Charles Mingus made in 1954 – "the greatest trumpeter that I've heard in this life" – gives an idea of his stylistic freshness at the time. While with Basie, he appeared on several records (under his own name and with Mingus, Coleman Hawkins and Thelonious Monk), combining Gillespie's rhythmic alertness with an advanced approach to thematic improvisation. His big-band arrangements, especially post-Basie, employed similar rhythmic lines with astringent block-chord voicings demanding great virtuosity from the performers. They also incorporated some of the more recent freedoms of small-group work, especially when Jones directed his own music, and set new standards now aimed at by semi-professional and college bands. A few of his tunes have become extremely well-known (especially "A Child Is Born") but more attention should be devoted to absorbing the lessons of his recorded trumpet solos. [BP]

David Redfern

Thad Jones

Thad Jones

The Fabulous Thad Jones (1954; Debut/OJC). Jones's first two sessions under his own name were produced, and accompanied, by Mingus in quartet/quintet settings which underline his surprising but coherent improvisation.

Thad Jones-Mel Lewis Orchestra

Central Park North (1969; Blue Note). This Continental reissue is the only available representation of Jones's writing for the all-star band of studio musicians, in which the looseness of the rhythm-section (Lewis and Richard Davis) infects the sections and soloists.

➤➤ **Count Basie** *(Verve Jazz Masters; The Complete Atomic Mr. Basie)*; **Mel Lewis** *(Thad Jones-Mel Lewis Quartet).*

Herbert Joos

Flugelhorn, trumpet, alphorn, composer, arranger.
b. Karlsruhe, Germany, 21 March 1940.

Joos studied music at Karlsruhe University, and during the 1960s was a member of the Karlsruhe Modern Jazz Quintet, which developed from hard bop to free jazz. In 1974 he took part in the Baden-Baden Free Jazz Meeting, organized an NDR (Hamburg) jazz workshop, started flugelhorn workshops for SDR (Stuttgart) with Kenny Wheeler, Ack Van Rooyen, Ian Carr, Harry Beckett, and was an occasional leader of his own ten-piece band.

In 1975 he was a member of the Mike Gibbs orchestra at the Berlin festival, and played with the Hans Koller-Wolfgang Dauner Free Sound and

Super Brass. In 1976 he toured Africa with the New Jazz Ensemble for the Goethe Institute and that December recorded with Hans Koller and the classical Blaser Quintet for German TV. In 1979 he joined the Vienna Art Orchestra, an association that has continued, and in 1984 was awarded the South West German TV jazz prize. Joos also does drawings and paintings of jazz musicians. His main inspirations are Miles Davis, Gil Evans and Mahler. [IC]

Daybreak (1976; Japo). Joos is a fine musician who can handle virtually any musical genre, and he sounds very much at home with the strings of the Stuttgart Radio Symphony Orchestra. There was a precedent – two and a half years previously, Jan Garbarek had been featured with the same string section playing Keith Jarrett's *Luminessence*. The passionate lyricism of Joos has a cutting edge – incisive but user-friendly.

Scott Joplin

Piano, composer.

b. Texarkana, Texas, 24 Nov 1868; d. 1 April 1917.

The "King of Ragtime", Scott Joplin taught himself piano first, then at eleven years old began studying with a German piano teacher. In his teens he left home and from 1885–93 lived in St Louis, a centre for fine pianists, playing in local cabarets and saloons such as the Silver Dollar. In 1894 Joplin's band of strolling players performed on the outskirts of the World's Fair in Chicago, and in the same year he settled in Sedalia, touring with his Texas Medley Quartet, which introduced many of his most famous compositions. In 1896 he enrolled at George Smith College, a black academy, which enabled him to write down the ragtime music he heard: "Joplin was the one and only ragtimer who had the nerve to put it down on paper", said Eubie Blake, years after.

Joplin's rags became hits in Sedalia's red-light district, and in his local Maple Leaf club (a rendezvous for local piano professors) – in 1899 his "Maple Leaf Rag" was published by John Stark and sold 75,000 copies in the first year. It was soon followed by "Swipsey Cake-Walk", the success of which encouraged Stark to move to St Louis and expand his publishing activities. Joplin followed but not before he had staged an extended ballet, *The Ragtime Dance*, at the Woods Opera House in Sedalia. The presentation was well received but the music, published soon after, made little impact; Joplin's ragtime opera of three years later, *The Guest Of Honor*, may have been performed but was never published. By that time Joplin was producing a string of successful rags – "Easy Winners", "Elite Syncopations" and "The Entertainer" – but the failure of his extended works was a preoccupying worry, complicated by a marriage breakdown and the death of his baby daughter.

In 1907, after a visit to Chicago and a second term in St Louis, he arrived in New York, where he met and married the loving and supportive Lottie Stokes. He had already contracted syphilis and was becoming ill. By 1910, talking with difficulty and almost unable to play, Joplin cut a sad figure amid the stylish society of young piano professors around New York. The year before he had split up with his old friend and publisher Stark over a royalty disagreement and he was to produce only three more rags before he died, along with the controlling obsession of his last years, a ragtime opera called *Treemonisha*. In 1915 Joplin financed a makeshift production of the work but it met with indifference, and this final blow to his aspirations was too much for him: syphilis took hold, and in 1916 he was admitted to Ward's Island Hospital in Manhattan, where he died the following year.

Recordings Joplin made in his declining years sound sad and inept; scores of unpublished works disappeared after the death of his wife. However, in the 1970s a ragtime revival was boosted by *The Sting* (1973), a Redford and Newman vehicle which used "The Entertainer" as a theme tune and featured other Joplin rags. Soon after, his works were recorded in scholarly sets by Joshua Rifkin and others. [DF]

King Of Ragtime (c.1898–1913; Giants Of Jazz). Classic Joplin compositions, including "The Entertainer" and "Maple Leaf Rag", recorded as piano rolls by the composer; generally good recording quality and vivacious performances.

Clifford Jordan

Tenor saxophone.

b. Chicago, 2 Sept 1931; d. 27 March 1993.

Clifford Jordan went to school with Johnny Griffin and Richard Davis; he played in Chicago with R&B bands and gigged with Sonny Stitt. He briefly replaced Sonny Rollins with Max Roach in 1957, then worked with Horace Silver in 1957–8. He was a regular member of the J.J. Johnson sextet in 1959–60, the Kenny Dorham quintet in 1961–2, and the Max Roach quartet from 1962–4 and in 1965. In 1964 he spent four months with Charles Mingus, including a European tour, and he did further work in Europe as a soloist and arranger in 1966, 1969–70 and 1974. He was in a quartet with Cedar Walton in 1974–5, and did much educational work in public schools in New York. In the doldrums of the late 1960s, Jordan produced several albums independently and, in the late 1980s, he was active in an advisory capacity with Mapleshade Records.

Jordan's tenor style shows considerable individuality, particularly in terms of tone-quality, although there are similarities to other Chicago tenors such as Griffin and Von Freeman. As the majority of his own records were in a quartet format, his composing and arranging talents have been underplayed; the first album below emphasizes these aspects as well as his excellent instrumental work. [BP]

These Are My Roots (1965; Koch). With contributions by Cedar Walton and Richard Davis (plus a couple of vocals and even a bit of banjo), Jordan's arrangements of material by Leadbelly(!) work musically and stand as an early example of black pride in an earlier tradition.

The Highest Mountain (1975–8; Camden). A two-CD compilation of Muse sessions, this has Jordan fronting Cedar Walton, Tommy Flanagan, Dizzy Reece and others, and its new title track (debuted in shorter form on the Koch above) is only one of the attractions.

>> **Art Farmer** *(Something To Live For).*

Duke Jordan

Piano, composer.

b. Brooklyn, New York, 1 April 1922.

Duke (Irving Stanley) Jordan worked with Coleman Hawkins and the original Savoy Sultans during the early and mid-1940s; he spent a year with Charlie Parker in 1947–8, and nine months with Stan Getz in 1952. His periods of absence from the jazz scene have made for a rather erratic career, but Jordan was not only active, but also appeared on records regularly in the mid-1950s, early 1960s and the mid-1970s. The increased interest in jazz during the latter period led to well-received tours of Europe and Japan and the recording of his complete output of compositions for the Steeplechase label in Denmark, where he still lives.

Several of Jordan's tunes have been taken up by other musicians; "Jor-du" became a standard, while two of his originals (published by the copyright owners under the name of a fictitious composer) were popularized in the Roger Vadim film *Les Liaisons Dangereuses* (1959). They reflect an inherently melodic style which, in improvisation, is enlivened by a delightfully crisp touch and unexpected turns of phrase. [BP]

Two Loves (1973; Steeplechase). Jordan has recorded his compositions prolifically while in Europe, and his catchy "Jor-du" is included, but his ability with the standards here highlights his springy rhythmic and melodic approach.

Kent Jordan

Flute.

b. New Orleans, 28 Oct 1958.

Although often regarded as a fusion musician, Kent Jordan is an assertive, cogent player of modern jazz as well, particularly on alto flute. He has contributed his powerful, large-toned flute sound to recordings by Elvin Jones (for whose medium-sized band he also plays piccolo), Bheki Mseleku and Wynton Marsalis as well as to albums by his younger brother, trumpeter Marlon, and guitarist Kevin Eubanks. He also plays occasionally with Wynton Marsalis's Lincoln Center Jazz Orchestra, and can be heard (on piccolo) on the trumpeter's "Express Crossing", featured on the orchestra's *They Came To Swing* (Columbia 1994). He was heard also as featured soloist on drummer Warren Smith's *Cats Are Stealing My Shit* (Mapleshade 1998). [CP]

Marlon Jordan

For You Only (1988; Columbia). Not overawed by stellar company (Branford Marsalis is his frontline partner), Kent Jordan contributes surprisingly muscular flute to this promising session by his brother.

>> **Kevin Eubanks** *(Turning Point);* **Elvin Jones** *(Going Home);* **Bheki Mseleku** *(Timelessness).*

Louis Jordan

Vocals, alto saxophone, bandleader.

b. Brinkley, Arkansas, 8 July 1908; d. 4 Feb 1975.

Jordan came to prominence in New York, where he worked with Chick Webb on alto saxophone and as occasional vocalist from 1936–8. He formed his own group, the Tympany Five, a proto-R&B outfit with a strong jazz slant, in 1938, working at Elks' Rendezvous in Harlem and R&B venues. During the 1940s, he broke through to national and international stardom with a series of hit 78rpm records, including "Choo Choo Ch'Boogie" which sold a million, "Saturday Night Fish Fry", "I'm Gonna Move To The Outskirts Of Town", and "Ain't Nobody Here But Us Chickens". His version of "Caldonia" was also a hit and was later covered by Woody Herman's mid-1940s band.

Jordan recorded duets with Bing Crosby, Ella Fitzgerald and Louis Armstrong, and he and the Tympany Five were featured in one or two films. He was a great showman with an irrepressible personality and his singing was notable for its timing, its marvellous rhythms and its humour. His music always swung, was always well played and featured improvised solos, and it brought many people,

William Gottlieb/Redferns

Louis Jordan

including musicians, to jazz. His influence in this sense was considerable in the 1940s and 1950s. He was active in the 1960s, touring the UK in 1962 with Chris Barber, playing in the USA, and, after a long gap, resuming his recording career. In the 1970s he worked intermittently, leading a new version of his Tympany Five and appearing at the Newport jazz festival in 1974. His music is generally considered to have been a seminal influence on rock'n'roll. [IC]

Louis Jordan 1934–40/1940–41/1941–3/ 1943–5/ 1945–6 (Classics); **Best Of Louis Jordan** (1942–5; MCA). The period 1934–45 was Jordan's creative heyday, and these five albums cover his hilarious and salty rise. He always seemed intensely alive and his marvellously deft singing and alto-playing are as eloquent and entertaining today as they ever were. The Classics are full of good things, but the MCA has most of his hit singles.

Ronny Jordan

Guitar.

b. London, 29 Nov 1962.

Emerging from London's "acid jazz" scene in 1992, Jordan's debut album *The Antidote* (with its post-Candy Dulfer cover of "So What") was commercially successful around the world. Jordan combines elements of Wes Montgomery's style (and warmth of sound) with tough hip-hop dance rhythms and rap, while his breezy Benson-lite gestures – as on his 2003 album *At Last* – sit perfectly within the lucrative smooth jazz movement. [CA/CI]

The Quiet Revolution (1993; Island). Jordan performs Wes's "Mister Walker" with many of his mentor's hallmark phrases and devices such as octaves, but any comparison stops there. The attractively undemanding guitar lines have neither the emotional depth of Montgomery nor his improvisational strength.

Sheila Jordan

Vocals.

b. Detroit, Michigan, 18 Nov 1928.

Sheila Jordan, née Dawson, was raised until the age of fourteen in Pennsylvania, where she sang in school and on amateur shows on the radio. She became interested in jazz in her Detroit high school, which was also attended by Kenny Burrell, Tommy Flanagan and Barry Harris. Encouraged by Charlie Parker, she moved to New York in 1950, and studied with Lennie Tristano in 1951–2. In 1952 she married pianist Duke Jordan, though they later divorced. She began singing regularly in small New York clubs in 1959, continuing until 1965, and in 1962 she recorded with George Russell and made her own first album. In the late 1960s she performed in churches and concerts with Don Heckman. She was involved in collaborations with Jazz Composers' Orchestra Association members such as Carla Bley (on *Escalator Over The Hill*), and Roswell Rudd, on big-band and small-group records made in 1973–4.

Jak Kilby

Sheila Jordan with Steve Kuhn

Visits to Europe as a soloist, including to London in 1966 and Norway in 1970 and 1977, led to an increased reputation in the USA. She toured with the Steve Kuhn trio in the late 1970s, and co-led the group on records. In 1981 she performed on an album of music written by Steve Swallow. She has continued working as a soloist or in duo with bassist Harvie Swartz, expanding her reputation and influence into the 1990s, and she is noted for her stimulating vocal workshops.

Jordan, who is entirely self-taught, resembles other prominent jazz singers only in the fact that she sounds like no one else. Her voice can sound alternately – or even simultaneously – bitter and sweet, soft and strained, pure and distorted, and all without any electronic treatment. Aptly described by Dick Sudhalter as "a difficult singer who demands much but is never less than absorbing", she relies on spontaneity to such an extent that a single performance can be full of ups and downs. Like her Detroit contemporary Betty Carter, she is equally capable of using scat, standard songs or little-known original material and making it all sound unique to her. [BP]

Portrait Of Sheila (1962; Blue Note). Her debut album, with minimal accompaniment including Steve Swallow and guitarist Barry Galbraith, still sounds marvellous and includes a version of "Dat Dere" which must have been heard by Rickie Lee Jones.

Lost And Found (1990; Muse). With a "conventional" trio led by Kenny Barron (and including Harvie Swartz), Jordan enhanced her status still further in a variety of material from Kurt Weill's "Lost In The Stars" to "Good Morning Heartache".

Stanley Jordan

Guitar.

b. Chicago, 31 July 1959.

Jordan was brought up in California, where he started studying the piano at the age of six; he took up the guitar at eleven. He studied for a music degree at Princeton University from 1977–81, followed by two years of practising and playing in small clubs or on the street. After living in the Chicago area, he moved to New York only months before an invitation to play at the Kool and Montreux festivals in 1984. He was signed by Blue Note, and his album *The Magic Touch* (released in 1985) sold extremely well. He has since toured with his own trio and appeared with Michal Urbaniak, Richie Cole and Quincy Jones.

Jordan's thoroughgoing use of the "hammering-on" technique (instead of plucking his notes) may have opened up new avenues for the guitar, but his concept of what to play seems limited to the clichés of jazz piano. Finding his creativity somewhat paralysed by his technical demands, in the 90s Jordan forsook his playing career to study music therapy. Now an active promoter of musical healing and spokesperson for the American Music Therapy Association, he can also be seen regularly on the US concert circuit, and reports he can "play better" when he doesn't "take it all so seriously". [BP]

Stolen Moments (1991; Blue Note). While all of Jordan's recorded output is a mix of pearls and gravel, this album, recorded live with Charnett Moffett and drummer Kenwood Dennard, contains a majority of excellent tracks such as "Impressions" and "Autumn Leaves".

Steve Jordan

Guitar.

b. New York, 15 Jan 1919; d. 13 Sept 1993.

A pupil of Allan Reuss (a gifted swing guitarist who studied with George Van Eps and worked for Benny Goodman), Jordan played with several big bands from the late 1930s, including Will Bradley's and Artie Shaw's, and after the war worked with Glen Gray, Stan Kenton, Boyd Raeburn and others. Jordan is best remembered as a rock-steady guitarist who lent his sound to the "All-American"-style rhythm-sections that followed in Count Basie's footsteps during the 1950s, often on John Hammond's recording sessions. As well as studio work he completed three years with Benny Goodman (1954–7), but then was more regularly employed as a tailor until 1965, when he came back to regular work with Tommy Gwaltney's group at Chicago's Blues Alley. He also appeared regularly at the Manassas jazz festival into the 1970s, and was regularly featured thereafter with Jack Maheu's Salt City Six and Brooks Tegler's Hot Jazz. [DF]

>> **Vic Dickenson** *(Vic Dickenson Septet).*

Taft Jordan

Trumpet, vocals.

b. Florence, South Carolina, 15 Feb 1915; d.1 Dec 1981.

As a boy James Taft Jordan was entranced by Louis Armstrong's revolutionary reworking of "When You're Smiling", took up the trumpet seriously and, after a time with a variety of Philadelphia-based bands, moved to New York. In 1933 drummer Chick Webb heard him at a musicians' hang-out, the Radium Club, and took him on to play with his band at the Savoy. Most bands of the day had their own Armstrong soundalike, and Jordan became Webb's, as well as playing lead, all the high notes, and most of the rest of the trumpet solos. Jordan's centre-stage role with Webb was later taken over by Ella Fitzgerald (from "A-Tisket A-Tasket" onwards), but he stayed with the band until 1941, two years after Webb's death, and then, after a bandleading period at New York's Savoy, joined Duke Ellington in 1943 for four years. In the 1950s he was busy with studio work, and with bands led by Lucille Dixon, Don Redman and Benny Goodman. In the 1960s he played on Broadway for such shows as *Hello Dolly!*, led his own quartet and quintet, and worked in studios again; in his last ten years he played for the New York Jazz Repertory Company, as well as in a marvellous salute to Ella Fitzgerald at the 1973 Newport jazz festival. [DF]

Duke Ellington

Duke Ellington 1941–50 (Giants Of Jazz). Jordan is well featured on Ellington classics "It Don't Mean A Thing" and "Trumpet No End".

Julian Joseph

Piano, composer.

b. Hammersmith, London, 11 May 1966.

Joseph's father was a singer with a blue beat group; Julian studied the piano at school, where he formed his first trio. He attended the jazz classes at the Weekend Arts College in northwest London from 1983–5 and was a member of the first London Fusion Orchestra which was formed there. He also formed a rehearsal group at that time, which comprised Courtney Pine, Philip Bent, Mark Mondesir and Paul Hunt. In 1985 he won a scholarship to Berklee, studying composition, and in 1986 joined the Branford Marsalis quartet, making a video with Marsalis directed by Spike Lee. Joseph also sat in with Wynton Marsalis and vocalist Bobby McFerrin.

Back in London in 1990, Joseph formed his own quartet, which performed his compositions almost exclusively. He was signed by East West Records and his debut album, *The Language Of Truth,* with Jean Toussaint, Alec Dankworth, Mark Mondesir and vocalist Sharon Musgrave, was released in 1991. Around the same time he also signed with Warner

James Joseph Music Management

Julian Joseph

Classics as a composer and pianist and subsequently became a Steinway Piano Artist. After that he made regular appearances at Ronnie Scott's club and the Jazz Café in London, performing with artists such as Johnny Griffin and George Coleman, and toured Europe for three weeks with Chico and Von Freeman and Gary Bartz. He has toured Britain and Europe with his own quartet and played festivals at Montreux and Nancy. In August 1992 he also completed writing and recording a film score for *A Tale Of A Vampire*, starring Julian Sands. His second album, *Reality*, was released in 1993, and in 1994 he toured America and Australia, and in Britain did an Arts Council Network tour.

Inspired by the examples of Wynton Marsalis and Keith Jarrett, Joseph intends to pursue a classical career parallel with his jazz work, and in 1993 he played Gershwin's *Piano Concerto* as well as one of his own compositions with the BBC Scottish Symphony Orchestra, and wrote a vibraphone solo for Evelyn Glennie. Joseph has said that despite his international commitments he remains committed to the British jazz scene: "No other place in the world has such a vibrant and varied jazz potential where so many great young players are coming through. ... The developments in jazz in the 90s will include musicians from London: that's where it's going to be and I will make sure I'm there when it happens." Joseph favourites on piano are legion, ranging from Duke Ellington and Fats Waller to Monk and Keith Jarrett, and other inspirations include Prokofiev, Bartók, Stravinsky, Weather Report, Miles Davis and Gil Evans. In 1995, Joseph was the first British-born black jazz musician to be given his own late-night Prom concert at London's Royal Albert Hall. He performed there with his trio – drummer Mark Mondesir and bassist Jeremy Brown – then conducted and played piano with his All-Star Big Band, for which he had written all the arrangements. In the later 1990s he has continued performing nationally and internationally. [IC]

⊙ **The Language Of Truth** (1991; East West). A very impressive debut record, the writing is very fine – such as the impishly tricky theme on "Don't Chisel The Shisel" – and Joseph, playing with great brio, is full of surprises. Jean Toussaint plays with great feeling and focus and the rhythm-section is excellent. Sharon Musgrave's couple of vocals are all right, but one wonders what they are doing on this album.

⊙ **Reality** (1993; East West). Joseph really shows his piano "chops" on this; the second track is a lovely version of "Body And Soul" with an exquisite piano solo in the spirit of Herbie Hancock. Jean Toussaint handles the saxophone role on most of the pieces, with the impeccable Mark Mondesir on drums, Charnett Moffett or Wayne Bachelor on bass, and a guest appearance by Peter King on alto saxophone. Some of Joseph's writing is excellent (in particular, "The Empty Dream" and "The Whispering Dome") but, again, one wonders why he sings a couple of songs.

⊙ **In Concert At Wigmore Hall** (1994; East West). These recordings came from a series of duets Joseph played with established stars saxophonist Johnny Griffin and clarinettist Eddie Daniels, and with his contemporary, pianist Jason Rebello. Alec Dankworth's bass underpinned all the duets except the Joseph/Rebello meeting which was a performance of Herbie Hancock's "Maiden Voyage" on two pianos only. Joseph acquitted himself well with the established stars.

K

Alfie Kahn

Saxophones, clarinet, flute, piano, harmonica.

b. (place unknown), 18 Feb 1914; d. 16 Feb 1996.

To British jazz history Kahn is best remembered for legendary sides with Fats Waller in London (August 1938), but his long career began with Lou Preager in 1935. Thereafter, jazz connections included Gerry Moore (1937), Harry Roy (1937–8), George Shearing (1939), while, after the war, he worked on ocean liners and with bandleaders like Geoff Love, Harry Gold and George Fierstone from 1954. In his later career he was a regular on the harmonica, playing it for films and TV before retiring in the mid-1980s. [DF]

Fats Waller

⊙ **Fats Waller 1938** (1997; Classics). Probably the most comprehensive collection of Kahn's contributions to Waller's London sessions available.

Roger Wolfe Kahn

Leader, multi-instrumentalist.

b. Morristown, New Jersey, 19 Oct 1907; d. 12 July 1962.

The millionaire son of a millionaire banker-cum-art dealer, Kahn led a highly successful dance band from 1924–33. Much of its music was purely commercial (Kahn worked a circuit of high-society hotels before finishing up in his own, the Perroquet de Paris on West 57th Street), but his orchestras, especially those assembled for recording sessions, often bristled with jazz talent: a shortlist could include Leo McConville, Mannie Klein, Miff Mole, Joe Venuti, Arthur Schutt, Eddie Lang, Vic Berton and Jack Teagarden. Kahn featured his guest stars sparingly on record (one famous exception is Jack Teagarden's outing on "She's A Great Great Girl" from 1928), but his orchestra was an influence on young men such as Benny Goodman, and his string writing in particular intrigued Glenn Miller, who went to see Kahn every night for two weeks in 1927, garnering ideas which he later used in Ben Pollack's orchestra (and perhaps his own). Kahn last played in 1933 at the Hotel Pennsylvania and his own Perroquet de Paris; that year he left the music business to become a test pilot. [DF]

➤➤ **Jack Teagarden** *(That's A Serious Thing).*

Max Kaminsky

Trumpet.

b. Brockton, Massachusetts, 7 Sept 1908; d. 6 Sept 1994.

Max Kaminsky played his early gigs in the Boston area and studied (like Manny Klein) with a great local trumpet teacher, Max Schlossberg. Soon he was commuting between his home town, New York and Chicago, working with George Wettling, "Red" Nichols, Leo Reisman and others, and learning from friends such as Bud Freeman, Frank Teschemacher and Wingy Manone.

A quiet three years was followed by work with Joe Venuti and others, and in 1936 a spell with Tommy Dorsey. Kaminsky's reputation as a powerful and accurate lead/trumpeter, as well as a proficient small-band soloist, was spreading, and, after turning down offers from Benny Goodman and Glenn Miller, he joined Artie Shaw in 1938. A quarrel over leadership ended the partnership: Kaminsky joined Dorsey again, then Bud Freeman's now legendary Summa Cum Laude band (1939–40) and Tony Pastor (1940–41), before reuniting with Shaw in his 1942 navy band, which included Conrad Gozzo, Frank Beach, John Best, Dave Tough and Claude Thornhill.

After discharge from the armed services, Kaminsky led his own band in Greenwich Village, worked for Art Hodes at the Village Vanguard and, after a brief attempt at club-owning in Boston, returned to New York to play Eddie Condon's for a year. It was an unsettling period: the two trends of bebop and New Orleans jazz meant that there was less work for a classic stylist, and clubs were closing all over the place. But he found work at the Village Vanguard, and even played with Charlie Parker for the opening night of Birdland. Through the 1950s Kaminsky carried on in big bands and small groups at Jimmy Ryan's and Eddie Condon's, as well as travelling to Europe with Jack Teagarden and Earl Hines. After 1960 he was often to be found playing in New York clubs, including a long residency at Jimmy Ryan's, and kept recording steadily into the following decade.

A skilled, versatile and forthright jazz trumpeter (as happy in a big band as a small group) and master of the plunger-mute, Kaminsky also wrote one of the most intelligent and informative of jazz autobiographies, *Jazz Band: My Life In Jazz.* While never as creatively innovatory as Billie Butterfield or later

Wild Bill Davison he remains a hero of the music whose work with Condon in the early 1940s provided the workhorse Dixieland lead trumpet (an elusive Dixieland art) required in Condon's formative years. [DF]

Max Goes East (1963; United Artists). An example of Kaminsky's later work with fellow masters Peanuts Hucko, Bob Wilber and Urbie Green on a "concept set" of tunes with Eastern connections. Entertaining, inspired and very musical.

>> **Eddie Condon** *(Town Hall Concerts; Chronological Eddie Condon 1942–3)*; **Bud Freeman** *(It's Got To Be The Eel)*.

Richie Kamuca

Tenor saxophone.
b. Philadelphia, 23 July 1930; d. 23 July 1977.

Kamuca worked with the big bands of Stan Kenton, from 1952–3, and Woody Herman from 1954–6. This was followed by small-group work on the West Coast with Chet Baker and Maynard Ferguson, both in 1957, the Lighthouse All Stars in 1957–8, Shorty Rogers in 1959 and Shelly Manne from 1959–61. Kamuca was based in New York from 1962 with the Gerry Mulligan band, Gary McFarland group and the Roy Eldridge quintet with which he worked from 1966–71, including occasions backing Jimmy Rushing. He also made an occasional third tenor with Zoot Sims and Al Cohn. From 1972 onwards he did TV studio work in Los Angeles, but remained active in small-group jazz until shortly before his death from cancer. Kamuca was a firm adherent of the Lester Young approach, and his always sensitive playing was flexible enough to fit well in a number of different contexts. [BP]

Drop Me Off In Harlem (1977; Concord). Overdue for reissue, this is one of a clutch of albums from just before Kamuca's passing, and features him with either Herb Ellis and Ray Brown or just Frishberg. As well as his affecting saxophone, he also sings on Frishberg's "Dear Bix".

Dill Katz

Bass guitar, double bass, acoustic guitar.
b. London, 12 Jan 1946.

Dill (David) Katz's became a professional musician in 1962, playing with Irish showbands and doing general session work. In the mid-1970s he was with Dave MacRae's Pacific Eardrum. From 1978–9 he was a member of Nucleus and from 1979–82 could be found in Barbara Thompson's Paraphernalia. He left to form a trio with Nic France and pianist Colin Dudman called 20th Century Blues.

He has since worked with two London-based African groups: Julian Bahula's Jazz Afrika and Brian Abrahams's District Six. He rejoined Nucleus in 1984, staying with it until its demise in 1988. Katz is very active in jazz education, and is Electric Bass Consultant at the Guildhall School of Music, London. In 1985, with pianist Colin Dudman, he opened a rehearsal studio, The Premises, in East London, and has since built a recording studio in it. Katz acts as producer/engineer in his own studio with conspicuous success. However, he is still active as a player. His favourites are Jaco Pastorius and Scott LaFaro. [IC]

>> **Brian Abrahams** *(Imgoma Yabantwana)*; **Ian Carr** *(Old Heartland)*.

Connie Kay

Drums.
b. Tuckahoe, New York, 27 April 1927; d. 30 Nov 1994.

Connie Kay (Conrad Kirnon, also known professionally as Connie Henry) played with Sir Charles Thompson and Miles Davis in the mid-1940s, and with the Cat Anderson Band (c. 1949). In the early 1950s he played at Birdland with musicians such as Stan Getz and Miles Davis (both in 1952), but he also did much R&B studio work (including the hit records "Mama, He Treats Your Daughter Mean" by Ruth Brown and Joe Turner's "Shake, Rattle And Roll"). He toured with Lester Young from 1953–5, then spent the next nineteen years with the Modern Jazz Quartet (MJQ) until their break-up in 1974, rejoining them in 1981. During the late 1970s he played in many semi-Dixieland contexts and with Benny Goodman, including an appearance at Carnegie Hall in 1978. Kay is most strongly identified with the carefully detailed playing he contributed to the MJQ. He not only managed to provide a light and bouncy swing suitable to the group's low volume level, but even – occasionally – to hint at his knowledge of R&B and Dixieland in this most demanding context. [BP]

>> **John Lewis** *(Concorde)*.

Cab Kaye

Vocals, piano, guitar.
b. London 3 Sept 1921; d. 13 March 2000.

A much loved singer whose style unashamedly recalled Billie Holiday's and a capable pianist, Cab Kaye (born (Augustus Kwamlah Quaye) began his show business career in London nightclubs at the age of fourteen. Throughout the 1930s he worked for the prominent band leaders: Billy Cotton, later star of early BBC Sunday television, Ivor Kirchin, and Ken "Snakehips" Johnson. After a period of service in the merchant navy during World War II, Kaye worked with Welsh saxophonist Harry Parry's band, Princes of Rhythm. Kaye formed his own band in 1943 before touring India with trumpeter Leslie "Jiver" Hutchinson, and thereafter worked with Tito Burns and Paul Fenoulhet, director of the Skyrockets, before spending time playing in Europe from 1950–56. After returning to Britain, he worked with leader of the revivalist movement Humphrey

Lyttelton, with whom he recorded a very likeable (and now collectable) LP, *Humph Meets Cab* (1960). He then took up the post of Government Entertainments Director in Ghana and worked there for most of the 1960s before moving back to Britain in 1970. Kaye was regularly to be heard at his own Amsterdam Piano Bar in the late 1970s and 1980s. [DF]

Shake Keane

Trumpet, flugelhorn.

b. St Vincent, West Indies, 30 May 1927; d. 10 Nov 1997.

Shake (Ellsworth) Keane was taught music by his father from the age of five. He also began writing verse at an early age, developing into an excellent poet (his nickname is short for Shakespeare).

In 1952 he came to the UK, playing with Mike McKenzie's Harlem Allstars which included Joe Harriott, and working with many other groups while spending two years studying English literature at London University. From 1959–65 he played with Joe Harriott, pioneering free improvisation and recording some classic and seminal albums with him, including *Free Form*, *Abstract*, *Movement* and *Indo-Jazz Fusions*. He toured Europe and played major festivals with the Harriott quintet. In 1965 he joined the Kurt Edelhagen Orchestra in Cologne, Germany, as featured soloist. In the 1970s he went back to St Vincent where he was Minister of Culture for a while, but was temperamentally unsuited for it. The same thing happened when he was made Principal of Bishop's College in Georgetown. He had stopped playing music, but wrote more poetry. In 1989, he began playing seriously again and visited England, whereupon Michael Garrick, with whose band Keane had played in the 1960s, re-formed the remaining members of the Harriott quintet for a British tour. However, that was Keane's swan-song, and he spent his last years in Brooklyn, New York. His health declined and the genial multi-talented giant (he was well over six feet tall) died of cancer.

Keane's main influences were Dizzy Gillespie and Miles Davis, but he had forged his own powerful and distinct identity by the beginning of the 1960s. His excellent technique and good range were at the service of a brilliant and unpredictable imagination, and he could handle anything from bebop to contemporary classical ensemble playing to austere and total abstraction. [IC]

➤➤ **Joe Harriott** *(Abstract; ; Movement; Indo-Jazz Fusions).*

Geoff Keezer

Piano.

b. Eau Claire, Wisconsin, 21 Nov 1970.

Both Keezer's parents were piano teachers, and he began studying as a child. He was only seventeen when he became the last pianist in Art Blakey's band, which he worked with from 1988–90. Since then he has played and recorded several albums with Art Farmer, and guested on sets by Jim Hall, Ray Brown and others. In 1997 he became a member of Brown's regular trio, and also toured with his own trio, making considerable use of keyboards as well as acoustic piano. Keezer has made half a dozen albums of his own since 1988, demonstrating considerable potential. He also has the ability to create arresting tunes such as "Proclamation", written for Roy Hargrove. [BP]

⊙ **Zero One** (1999; Dreyfus). Demonstrating what Keezer is capable of, this unaccompanied set features mostly acoustic piano, with a little overdubbing and sampling from his own playing. A considerable breadth of material and an expansive technique makes for absorbing listening.

➤➤ **Ulf Wakenius** *(Summertime).*

Roger Kellaway

Piano, composer.

b. Waban, Massachusetts, 1 Nov 1939.

Kellaway began classical piano lessons at the age of seven and later studied composition and piano at the New England Conservatory from 1957–9. His first professional jobs were on bass. He moved to New York, working as a pianist with Kai Winding in 1962, with Clark Murphy in 1963, and also worked with Al Cohn-Zoot Sims. From 1964–6 he led his own trio and also worked with Clark Terry and Bob Brookmeyer. He moved to Los Angeles in 1966, spending nine months with the Don Ellis band. He was music director for singer Bobby Darin from 1967–9 and worked regularly with Tom Scott for several years, at first in a quartet with Chuck Domanico (bass) and John Guerin (drums), which was later augmented by Howard Roberts (guitar).

From the later 1960s he began writing film music and composing for classical ensembles and for TV. In 1973 he recorded with Gerry Mulligan, Tom Scott and others, and his classical composition *Esque*, for trombone and double bass, was recorded. In 1974 he toured with Joni Mitchell and Tom Scott's LA Express in the USA, Canada and the UK. Since the mid-1970s he has been active as an arranger, and also as a producer and conductor. Kellaway is a technically brilliant and often exceptionally adventurous pianist as well as an excellent composer. [IC]

⊙ **A Portrait Of Roger Kellaway** (1963; Fresh Sound). Kellaway has the whole jazz heritage at his fingertips and much of it is displayed on this wonderful album. Bassist Ben Tucker and drummer Dave Bailey provide support on four tracks, and on the other tracks Jim Hall, Steve Swallow (then regular members of Art Farmer's quartet) and drummer Tony Inzalaco create more active and interactive responses to Kellaway's piano. The result is an album of terrific variety and vitality.

⊙ **Live At Maybeck Recital Hall Vol. 11** (1991; Concord). All those years of writing for films and TV have not dimmed Kellaway's quicksilver pianistic genius. Like Earl Hines, he's a Houdini of the piano who can tie himself in knots and extricate himself brilliantly. There is space as well as brilliance, however, on this beautifully contemplative set.

Peck Kelley

Piano.

b. Houston, Texas, 1898; d. 26 Dec 1980.

Peck (John Dickson) Kelley led a famous band, Peck's Bad Boys, around Texas in the early 1920s, featuring soon-to-be stars such as Jack Teagarden, Pee Wee Russell and trumpeter Leon Prima. Kelley was a shy, kind man who took care of his musicians; he was also a virtuoso pianist, and his band played a famous residency at Sylva Beach on Galveston Bay in 1924: soon after he was persuaded to join Russell, Bix Beiderbecke and Frank Trumbauer at the Arcadia Ballroom, St Louis. But union problems prevented him getting a work permit and, says Russell, "Peck went home more convinced than ever that it was a mistake to leave home!" From then on Kelley turned down offers from (among others) Paul Whiteman, the Dorseys, Rudy Vallee and Bob and Bing Crosby, and refused to record. He was seldom forgotten for long: a pop tune, "Beat Me Daddy, Eight To The Bar", was said to have been written about him during the boogie boom, and in 1940 *Collier's Magazine* ran a feature. Kelley stubbornly stayed home, nonetheless, and worked locally: one of his last groups was a Shearing-style quintet, and after a final season at Houston's Dixie Bar in 1949 he retired. Much later *Down Beat* reporter Richard Hadlock interviewed him, tall, grey and nearly blind, in a dim, dusty house with no piano in working order. "I guess people think it's strange I didn't go with the big names in the 1930s", Kelley told Hadlock. "Maybe the real reason was I never felt the need to entertain people – I like to play for myself!" The old pianist went blind, contracted Parkinson's disease and died at 82. [DF]

Peck Kelley Jam Vols. 1 & 2 (1957; Commodore). These two albums with Dick Shannon's quartet show Kelley as a fine but blunted talent; a necessary set for historians, however.

Brian Kellock

Piano.

b. Edinburgh, 28 Dec 1962.

Born on the very same day as fellow jazz pianists Rachel Z and Michel Petrucciani, Brian studied music at Edinburgh University from 1982–6. During this period he formed a trio with drummer John Rae and bassist Brian Shiels, and played with saxophonist Bobby Wishart and R&B singer Tam White. In 1988 he joined the John Rae Collective, and the drummer's rhythm-section with Kenny Ellis on bass became Kellock's new trio. This group has backed many visiting artists including Sheila Jordan, Charlie Rouse, Scott Hamilton and Herb Geller, and recorded with saxophonists Spike Robinson and Joe Temperley and trumpeter James Morrison, with whom he has toured Europe since the mid 1990s. In 1996 he made the first of two trio albums, the second of which (see below) was voted album of the year in the 2002 BBC Radio Jazz Awards. [BP]

Live At Henry's (2000; Caber). An ebullient pianist who would always rather be spontaneous than over-prepared, Kellock is well captured at his Edinburgh club base, in a programme that runs from bebop through Tristano to Jimmy Rowles and Kenny Wheeler.

>> **Tommy Smith** *(Bezique).*

Jon-Erik Kellso

Trumpet, cornet, Puje trumpet-cornet.

b. Dearborn, Michigan, 8 May 1964.

Kellso grew up in Dearborn, Michigan, began big-band work at eleven, and by thirteen had joined the International Youth Symphony Orchestra; he also featured regularly in the Montreux-Detroit jazz festival and played with J.C. Heard's big band. Since 1988 he has played with James Dapogny's Chicago Jazz Band and moved to New York to join Vince Giordano's Nighthawks (1989–93); during and after that period he began playing and recording with (amongst others) Howard Alden, Dan Barrett, Marty Grosz, Milt Hinton, Bob Haggart and Kenny Davern. Kellso is also a regular at American jazz parties and festivals, and has toured Brazil, Spain, Germany, Switzerland and the UK, as well as Japan with The World's Greatest Jazz Band. Currently he works with Dapogny, Giordano, Dan Levinson and DanBarrett's 'Blue Swing'. His work is well documented by the Arbors label, including two albums with his principal influence Ruby Braff, two as leader, and around a dozen more as featured sideman. A technically assured player, firmly based in the lyric-to-hot school of Braff, Kellso is the newest to join Vaché, Sandke and their trumpet-swing contemporaries. [DF]

The Plot Thickens (1995; Arbors). A thoroughly enjoyable collection – bright arrangements, good tunes and replete with "swing authenticity" – it surprisingly, but effectively, co-features Kellso's longtime colleague Mike Karoub on cello, plus a compatible team including Harry Allen and Scott Robinson.

Chris Kelly

Trumpet.

b. Deer Range Plantation, Louisiana, 18 Oct 1885 (or 1890); d. 19 Aug 1929.

One of the early trumpet kings of New Orleans, Chris Kelly never recorded and no photograph of him has ever been traced. He arrived in New Orleans somewhere between 1913–15 and once other musicians had got over his eccentric dress – he was a raggedy man who went to work in whatever clothes he could find – they were struck by the power and originality of his playing. Soon Kelly was working every night, mostly in low-class joints where the poorest paid strata of black New Orleans society gathered to dance and fight. At one of these – Perseverance Hall – he worked regularly in the 1920s with clarinettist George Lewis. Kelly's famous feature was "Careless Love" which (says researcher Len Page) he played into a plunger-mute at a time when the technique was new: the effect of the rendition (it was claimed) made men weep and women tear their clothes off. To at least one New Orleans citizen, Kelly's wife Edna, the song was really titled "Kelly's Love", and so it became to his admirers, who knew his whispered, deep-muted variations note for note. Kelly became a musical hero, was constantly surrounded by fans and frequently took his band to venues in Biloxi and Mobile where – just possibly – Cootie Williams might have heard him. By the late 1920s Kelly was using relief trumpeters and in 1929 he died in the Algiers Naval Base Hospital: the consensus was that drink had ended his life by a heart attack. [DF]

George Kelly

Tenor saxophone, vocals, arranger.

b. Miami, Florida, 31 July 1915; d. 24 May 1998.

Kelly played piano from the age of nine, but added saxophone to his armoury from the age of fifteen, and was soon leading high-school groups of his own including the Cavaliers (which also featured Panama Francis (drums)). After the group disbanded Kelly later joined Zack Whyte's Chocolate Beau Brummels (including Tadd Dameron), then worked with Hartley Tootes and from 1941 joined Al Cooper's Savoy Sultans at the Savoy Ballroom, New York. After conscription (1944) Kelly played with Rex Stewart (1946), Lucille Dixon, Babs Gonzales, Tiny Grimes and his Rocking Highlanders, Cozy Cole (after the hit parade success of Cole's "Topsy") and regularly subbed for Buddy Tate in Tate's Celebrity Club Orchestra. From 1970–77 Kelly played piano for the Ink Spots vocal group, but thereafter joined the re-formed Savoy Sultans under Panama Francis until disputes over billing led him to resume a solo career. This included trips to Britain (1982 and 1983), solo recording, and appearances with the Harlem Blues and Jazz Band. Kelly's stylish singing and playing was a grace to jazz and, although his work never achieved universal recognition, it's worth seeking out on record. [DF]

⊙ **Fine And Dandy** (1982; Barron). Recorded in England by Dave Bennett with guitarist Paul Sealey's expert trio, this is "probably the definitive guide to Kelly's solo skills" (Peter Vacher).

Guy Kelly

Trumpet.

b. Scotlandville, Louisiana, 22 Nov 1906; d. 24 Feb 1940.

An important trumpeter in the early era of jazz, Kelly settled in New Orleans in the mid-1920s, to work with Papa Celestin and Kid Howard before moving up to Chicago for work with many of the city's headlining bands including Erskine Tate, Dave Peyton, Carroll Dickerson, Jimmie Noone and Albert Ammons, with whom his short career concluded in 1939. Kelly is affectionately remembered for his contribution to a Jimmie Noone classic, "The Blues Jumped A Rabbit" (1936), which reveals his dry-toned style rather like Tommy Ladnier's. [DF]

➤➤ **Jimmie Noone** *(Jimmie Noone 1934–40).*

Wynton Kelly

Piano.

b. Brooklyn, New York, 2 Dec 1931; d. 12 April 1971.

An important stylist, but largely unrecognized except by fellow pianists, Kelly was raised in Brooklyn from the age of four. He began working in the R&B field with Ray Abrams in 1946, and recorded with "Cleanhead" Vinson, Hal Singer and "Lockjaw" Davis. He cut his own first album for Blue Note at the age of nineteen, and in 1951–2 he worked with Dinah Washington, Dizzy Gillespie and Lester Young. After army service he rejoined Washington in 1955 and Gillespie's big band in 1957, worked briefly with Charles Mingus in 1956–7, and then led his own trio. Four years with Miles Davis, from January 1959 to March 1963, led to the setting-up of Miles's whole rhythm-section (completed by Paul Chambers and Jimmy Cobb) as the new Wynton Kelly trio. Frequently backing Wes Montgomery and other major soloists, the trio remained a regular unit for several years, although Kelly undertook other freelance accompaniment work until his death following an epileptic fit.

The pianist's mature style was hinted at in his earliest recordings and was similar in origin to that of Horace Silver. He combined boppish lines and bluesy interpolations, but with a taut sense of timing quite unlike anyone else except his many imitators. The same quality made his equally individual block

chording into a particularly dynamic and driving accompanying style that was savoured by the many soloists he backed on record, such as Cannonball Adderley and Hank Mobley. [BP]

Kelly Blue (1959; Riverside/OJC). Kelly's masterpiece, done in a couple of weeks either side of his first date with Miles (when they recorded "Freddie Freeloader"), has a sextet including Benny Golson and Nat Adderley on a couple of tracks and the famous trio with Chambers and Cobb carrying the day on the rest.

➤➤ **Cannonball Adderley** *(Quintet In Chicago);* **Hank Mobley** *(Soul Station);* **Wes Montgomery** *(Full House).*

Rodney Kendrick

Piano.

b. Philadelphia, 30 April 1960.

Kendrick grew up in a musical household. His father was a pianist who worked with Illinois Jacquet for seven years and gigged with Sonny Stitt, Lou Donaldson and Sam Rivers. By the time he was eighteen, Kendrick had already turned professional, touring and playing keyboards with R&B and funk acts including Harold Melvin & The Blue Notes, James Brown and George Clinton. At twenty-one, he delved more deeply into jazz, moving to New York where he worked steadily, supporting Freddie Hubbard, Terence Blanchard, Stanley Turrentine and others, and studying with pianist Barry Harris. In 1993, Kendrick secured a deal with Verve, who issued his debut, *The Secrets Of Rodney Kendrick*, and a year later the follow-up, *Dance World Dance*; these both feature a range of musicians, from the smooth soul jazz saxophonist Houston Person to post-bop cornettist Graham Haynes and alto saxophonist Arthur Blythe. His most recent record as a leader is *Last Chance For Common Sense* (1996; Verve) and *We Don't Die We Multiply* (1998; Verve). He also appears on some Verve outings by vocalist Abbey Lincoln, *Bop* (1996; Telarc), with veteran alto man Frank Morgan, and Cassandra Wilson's *Traveling Miles* (1999; Blue Note). Kendrick cites Randy Weston and Sun Ra as influences; his playing has some of the African patterning of the former and a vein of the adventurousness of the latter, but his records have never quite risen above uneven mix-and-match hodgepodges. [JC]

Stacey Kent

Vocals.

b. New York, 27 March 1968.

Kent grew up in New York and studied piano from childhood, before moving to London where she studied at the Guildhall School of Music, and joined the Ritz Hotel's resident big band, Vile Bodies, as well as appearing in the film of *Richard III* starring Ian McKellen. Her first album, *Close Your Eyes* (1997), was well received, but her second, *The Tender Trap* (1998), achieved more success with a launch at New York's Birdland. In 1998 Kent toured in the USA and was profiled for US television on *CBS Sunday Morning*. She also toured Scandinavia and appeared on the Big Band Legends concert at London's Queen Elizabeth Hall, with Les Brown, Billy May and Ray Anthony. Recently she has achieved new levels of recognition, including American seasons at New York's Algonquin Hotel and elsewhere and formed an affectionate (and musically profitable) partnership with Humphrey Lyttelton; their travelling show 'Between Friends' tours countrywide.

Kent is a relaxed swing singer whose preoccupation with great standards has found enormous favour with critics and public alike. Her roots reach back to inspirations including Mildred Bailey and Lee Wiley and in an era when such styles are less than fashionable she has refocused public attention on them, as well as on her own assured recorded interpretations which always respect the composer's intentions. She is married to saxophonist Jim Tomlinson. [DF]

Love Is – The Tender Trap (1998; Candid). Kent amid regular associates – David Newton (piano) and husband Jim Tomlinson (tenor) – in a well-judged selection of standards, neatly arranged to showcase her swing-based approach.

Between Friends (2000/Calligraph). Recorded illustration of the Lyttelton-Kent collaboration with his nine-piece band (including Tomlinson on clarinet plus alto tenor and baritone saxophones) and Stacey featured on fine standards including "Everything But You", "Sugar" and "I'm Just A Lucky So-and-so".

Stan Kenton

Piano, arranger, composer.

b. Wichita, Kansas, 15 Dec 1911; d. 25 Aug 1979.

Kenton was raised from the age of five in California, where he played piano as a teenager with a high school group. He began touring at eighteen, worked in Las Vegas and Arizona, and then, in 1938–9, in San Francisco and Los Angeles with locally based bands including those of Gus Arnheim and Vido Musso. He formed his own first band in California, becoming extremely successful through broadcasts and then touring nationally from 1941–8. In this period the band played for dancing as well as having a brash air of mild experimentation exemplified by such pieces as "Eager Beaver" and "Intermission Riff". With the arrival of Shelly Manne in 1946 and Art Pepper in 1947, the music was described by Kenton himself as "progressive jazz". When he tried to earn his reputation as an experimentalist with the forty-piece Innovations In Modern Music Orchestra from 1950–2, which had sixteen string players, he included some totally composed avant-garde works such as Bob Graettinger's "City Of Glass", and even the presence of improvisers such as Maynard Ferguson and Bud Shank hardly refuted accusations of Kenton's rampant pretentiousness.

Having alienated many of his fans, he thereafter decided that discretion was the better part of valour, reverting to updated swing and acquiring a particularly strong contingent of soloists (Frank Rosolino, Lee Konitz and briefly Zoot Sims) between 1952–4. He continued for the rest of his career in the same vein, except for such occasional ventures as the Neophonic Orchestra of 1965–6 and a *Kenton Plays Wagner* album in 1964, and retained the standard trumpets/ trombones/saxophones/rhythm configuration augmented only by a quartet of mellophoniums from 1960–63 and a Latin percussionist from 1968 onwards. Despite carefully contriving an impression of single-mindedness, Kenton was musically quite versatile in a rather heavy-handed way; he even recorded a couple of comedy numbers including "Blues In Burlesque" and, though not noted for a sense of humour, was once heard to say in a live album, "We've tried everything from playing music backwards; we've played three tunes at a time simultaneously, getting all kinds of polytonal effects, we've gotten so progressive that we went off the end and had to go back around and jump on again!" [BP]

The Best Of Stan Kenton (1943–61; Capitol). A useful single-CD compilation containing the original 1940s instrumental hits "Artistry In Rhythm", "Peanut Vendor", etc (less punchy remakes are on the 1956 *Kenton In Hi-Fi*) and overlapping the era of the next recommendation.

Complete Bill Holman And Bill Russo Arrangements (1952–61; Mosaic). Now hard to obtain, this boxed set is what many observers would call the best of Kenton, for the two arrangers (both of whom started as playing members of the early 1950s band) knew how to satisfy Kenton's pretensions and link up with the jazz potential of his personnel.

HERMAN LEONARD

Stan Kenton

New Concepts Of Artistry In Rhythm (1952; Capitol). Despite the original album title, these were not remakes but excellent new material for the Rosolino-Konitz band, written by Holman and Russo and, on two tracks, Gerry Mulligan. (Also included is Kenton's ludicrous meet-the-band monologue "Prologue", added to the LP but originally a pair of 78rpm singles!)

Cuban Fire (1956–60; Capitol). Kenton's interest in Latin music went back to the 1940s (hear the above-mentioned "Peanut Vendor") and the 1956 pieces commissioned from composer Johnny Richards, with Mel Lewis powering the band, are his most satisfying venture in this field.

Freddie Keppard

Cornet.

b. New Orleans, 27 Feb 1890; d. 15 July 1933.

Keppard was playing with John Brown's band from Spanish Fort by the time he was twelve, and by 1906 was leading his own Olympia Orchestra (featuring Alphonse Picou). Soon after that he was New Orleans's newest trumpet king: he blew with huge power, could play for hours on end without faltering, and covered his hands with a handkerchief to keep his fingerings secret. Late in 1914 he left New Orleans and began working with Bill Johnson, George Baquet and Eddie Vinson in the Original Creole Orchestra, which toured the prestigious Orpheum circuit of theatres. Mezz Mezzrow heard them: "That band really upset Chicago, and paved the way for the rest of the New Orleans jazzmen ... Before harmon mutes were ever thought of he was getting his glissandos and tones with a water glass and a beer bottle too. Freddie's cornet was powerful and to the point: the way he led the ensemble breaking at the right breaks and carrying the lead there was never a letdown." In 1918 Keppard settled in Chicago, first as a featured star with orchestras and bands led by Doc Cooke, Erskine Tate and Jimmie Noone, a regular drinking buddy: perhaps it was the sight and sound of younger men such as Louis Armstrong surpassing him that drove the older cornettist to drink more and more. By the mid-1920s, says Milt Hinton, "he was blowing loud but not very good!" Keppard, his water bottle full of whisky under his arm, became a notorious figure and later a mere sideman in lesser bands. He died of tuberculosis after a long illness in Cook County Hospital, Chicago.

Freddie Keppard is probably the closest recorded link with Buddy Bolden, but he was a more developed and sophisticated player than his forerunner: says Sidney Bechet, "He played practically the same way as Buddy Bolden but he really played!" [DF]

REDFERNS

Freddie Keppard

The Legend (1923–7; Topaz). Keppard's complete recorded output admirably collected by Topaz; big-band sides with Doc Cooke and Erskine Tate as well as titles with Jimmy Blythe, Jasper Taylor and Keppard's own Jazz Cardinals. He may have been past his prime but there's much of interest here.

Anthony Kerr

Vibraphone, marimba.

b. Belfast, Northern Ireland, 16 Oct 1965.

After studying percussion at the City of Belfast School of Music (1981–4), Anthony Kerr went to New York to study vibes and marimba with David Friedman, and composition and improvisation with Kenny Werner, winning a scholarship to the New School of Jazz and Contemporary Music in the city in 1987. After experience as a percussionist with the RTE Symphony Orchestra and employment in a freelance capacity at the UK's National Theatre, Kerr gradually established himself on the jazz scene, finding work with pianist John Taylor, Irish guitarist Louis Stewart, alto player Peter King, singer Norma Winstone and composer/bandleader Mike Westbrook, with whose big band he has toured extensively in Europe. In addition to occasional work with popular-music figures like Charlie Watts and Georgie Fame, Kerr has also led his own groups and conducted jazz improvisation workshops in Belfast, Southampton and London, in addition to tutoring the percussion section of the Irish Youth Jazz Orchestra. Latterly, as well as giving solo recitals, fulfilling his duties as featured soloist and percussionist with the BBC Big Band and collaborating with singer Ian Shaw and saxophonist Dale Barlow, Kerr leads various groups including his own quartet (recently comprising bassist Orlando le Flemming, pianist Tom Cawley and drummer Steve Brown) and The Mallet Band featuring Justin Woodward (xylosynth and vibes), Steve Brown (drums) and Geoff Gascoyne (bass and xylosynth). [CP]

First Cry (1994; EFZ). Kerr composed, arranged and performs the vast bulk of the music on this unusual album with vocalist Jacqui Dankworth. A gently lyrical, intimate recording, it also features the percussion of Bosco De Oliveira and Paul Clarvis and the flute of Stan Sulzmann.

Now Hear This (1997; Jazz House). Elegant but gutsy quartet (pianist Albert Bover, bassist Matt Miles and drummer Stephen Keogh) giving renditions of standards (some transcribed from Milt Jackson and Bobby Hutcherson recordings), pieces by modern jazz masters like Jimmy Rowles, and the odd original.

Brooks Kerr

Piano.

b. New Haven, Connecticut, 26 Dec 1951.

Kerr graduated from the Manhattan and Juilliard schools of music and in the early 1970s became a close friend of Duke Ellington (like Ellington he studied with Willie "The Lion" Smith), subbing for him regularly and assisting him on teaching projects. Kerr is known as the leader of a small group featuring Russell Procope and Sonny Greer, which after Ellington's death in 1974 worked all round New York in hotels and Greenwich Village clubs, playing a tribute programme and often starring Ellington alumni such as Ray Nance and Francis Williams. Kerr's eclectic piano talent (he could play "Soda Fountain Rag" or "Satin Doll" to order) made a strong and favourable impact. "His style is steeped in Ellington", wrote critic Lee Jeske in *Jazz Journal*, "and he comes out with names, dates and places at a rate to make even Stanley Dance quiver! Duke couldn't ask for a finer quartet to keep his sound alive." [DF]

Trudy Kerr

Vocals.

b. Brisbane, Australia, 3 Jan 1963.

A self-taught natural singer, Trudy Kerr began working professionally in Brisbane at seventeen. She performed in clubs and at festivals throughout the East Coast of Australia and the Far East, then came to England in 1990, settling and performing in London. She attended the London Guildhall School of Music's postgraduate jazz course 1994–5, then formed her own band with some of the young lions of the London jazz scene. Since then, she has performed throughout the UK, worked at London's main jazz venues (including the Ronnie Scott club and Pizza On The Park), and in 1998 performed for a week at the Pizza Express, Istanbul, Turkey. She has also appeared at London's Soho and Greenwich jazz festivals and Holland's Jazz in Duketown.

Kerr's first CD, *Sweet Surprise*, recorded in 1997, received excellent reviews and featured her regular rhythm-section – pianist Phil Peskett, bassist Andy Hamilton and drummer Mark Fletcher – with the excellent saxophonist Dave O'Higgins guesting on a couple of tracks, and virtuoso Australian guitarist Mark Johns added for the blues, rock or soul tracks. Kerr is superbly versatile and can handle any kind of song with total conviction, even at the two extremes of jazz singing – the subtle, tender self-communing of Billie Holiday, or the earthy declamatory style of soul or gospel singers such as Aretha Franklin.

Kerr's own favourites are Carmen McRae, Nancy Wilson and Norma Winstone, and other inspirations are Antonio Carlos Jobim and Miles Davis. Trudy Kerr also teaches a BA course in singing at Colchester Institute, Essex. [IC]

⊙ **Sweet Surprise** (1997; FMR). This is a fine debut with twelve dynamic performances of extremely varied material. A couple of well-known standards, Vernon Duke's "Taking A Chance On Love", and Cole Porter's "All Of You", are included, but the rest of the pieces are refreshingly unfamiliar. Kerr delivers the title track, an unusual love song by Blossom Dearie, with sweet intimacy and urgency, breathing life into the tricky lyrics. Then she's raunchy and passionate for the witty soul song "I've Got To Be Me". Her diction is cleverly varied to suit her material, and her trio are superb accompanists.

⊙ **Trudy** (1998; Jazzizit). This is an even more confident and adventurous album. Nick Weldon has replaced Phil Peskett on piano, and the guest stars are saxophonist Mornington Lockett, and on one track only, Acker Bilk, who shares the spirited vocal with Kerr in "I Can't Believe That You're In Love With Me" and plays a husky, moody clarinet solo. There are thirteen tracks in all and not one dull moment.

Barney Kessel

Guitar.

b. Muskogee, Oklahoma, 17 Oct 1923.

Kessel's first name job was with a big band fronted by Chico Marx. He settled in Los Angeles, and worked with the bands of Charlie Barnet in 1944 and 1945, and Artie Shaw, also in 1945. He made the first records under own his name with Shaw sidemen Dodo Marmarosa and Herbie Steward the same year. For the next twenty years he was busy with studio work, first in radio and then in TV and films, but he still frequently appeared on jazz records, for example with Charlie Parker. He joined the Oscar Peterson trio for one year in 1952–3, including Jazz At The Philharmonic tours of the USA and Europe, and appeared on the many recordings that arose from them. From 1953 onwards he made regular albums under his own name and played jazz gigs as a sideline to his studio work; from 1957 he made albums with the Poll-Winners trio, including Ray Brown and Shelly Manne. He toured Europe with the Newport fes-

TIM BURKITT

Trudy Kerr

tival package in 1967, and returned the following year to make records and perform in various European countries. Back in the USA he resumed public appearances and became involved in teaching, with annual trips to Europe to give seminars. He also toured with an occasional group including Herb Ellis and Charlie Byrd, under the name Great Guitars. He has not played since suffering a stroke in 1992.

Frequently viewed as the most complete of the immediate inheritors of Charlie Christian (who was brought up in the same state, Oklahoma), Kessel's best work displays a lithe, boppish style with distinct blues overtones. These have sometimes been allowed to predominate, to the detriment of his overall playing, and the adaptability required in the studios has often caused him to sound too bland. However, given the right setting and stimulating colleagues, Kessel can be a brilliant jazz player. [BP]

⊙ **Easy Like** (1953–6; Contemporary/OJC). Sounding superficially like superior mood-music with Bud Shank on flute (replaced by Buddy Collette on the 56 session), Kessel's first album contains some excellent jazz playing.

⊙ **Straight Ahead** (1975; Contemporary/OJC). Billed as by the Poll Winners, this is a follow-up to three late 1950s albums with Shelly Manne and Ray Brown illustrating, rather better than Kessel's albums with European musicians, how he could still blow up a storm.

Steve Khan

Guitar.

b. Los Angeles, 28 April 1947.

The son of lyricist Sammy Cahn, Steve Khan played drums and piano before taking up guitar in the mid-1960s. After graduating from UCLA, he moved to New York in 1970 and found work as a session musician, playing with Steely Dan, James Brown, Hubert Laws, Maynard Ferguson, Blood Sweat And Tears, Billy Joel, Billy Cobham and many others. His work with the Brecker Brothers and Joe Zawinul's Weather Update heightened his profile, and he toured Japan with the CBS Jazz All Stars in 1977. His increasing interest in jazz led him to form the band Eyewitness in 1981 with singing percussionist Manolo Badrena, bassist Anthony Jackson and drummer Steve Jordan. In the early 1990s, Khan began recording straightforward jazz albums as a leader for Polydor, beginning with *Let's Call This* (1991), featuring Ron Carter and Al Foster, and visiting Monk, Shorter and standard material. Two more albums followed, with Dennis Chambers on drums and the second, *Crossings* (Verve Forecast; 1993), also featuring Michael Brecker, but Khan's best album is generally thought to be *Got My Mental* (see below). Latterly involved in the Caribbean Jazz Project with ex-Spyra Gyra marimba player Dave Samuels with whom he recorded the well-received *Paraiso* (Concord, 2001), Khan continues to be in demand as a jazz educator; his latest improvisation tutor is entitled *Pentatonic Khancepts*. [CP]

⊙ **Local Color** (1987; Denon). A series of duets with keyboard player Rob Mounsey, worthy but lacking true improvisational vitality.

⊙ **Public Access** (1989; GRP). Eyewitness as above, but with Dave Weckl instead of Jordan. Virtuosic but rather formulaic, Sammy Cahn's gentle "Dedicated To You" aside.

⊙ **Got My Mental** (1996; Evidence). A superb core band – Khan, bassist John Patitucci, drummer Jack DeJohnette – augmented by percussionists Cafe, Don Alias et al, perform an intriguingly varied set, including Ornette Coleman's "R.P.D.D.", with delicacy and verve.

Sibongile Khumalo

Vocals, violin.

b. Johannesburg, 24 Sept 1957.

Khumalo's father, a professor of music and a music historian, took her musical education in hand from an early age, and she studied violin, singing, drama and dance. In 1978, she graduated with a music degree from the University of Zululand, followed by an honours degree from the University of the Witwatersrand. While studying, she took a job organizing the music department at The Federated Union of Black Arts (FUBA), and also worked on her singing. In 1993, she turned professional after winning the Standard Bank Young Artist Award.

Throughout her extensive classical music education as a mezzo-soprano, Khumalo was also absorbing her South African musical heritage, and was very much aware of jazz singers such as Sarah Vaughan, Ella Fitzgerald, Carmen McRae, Al Jarreau and Bobby McFerrin, among others. But she was equally inspired by three South African singers, commenting: "I always wanted to emulate Letta Mbulu's sound," stating that Sophie Mgcina was and continues to be her mentor, and that Tandi Klaasen taught her that a good sense of humour enhances the enjoyment of a performance.

As early as 1992, she performed in Johannesburg, a concert entitled *The Three Faces of Sibongile Khumalo*, and these three aspects would seem to refer to her equally natural expertise in classical music, South

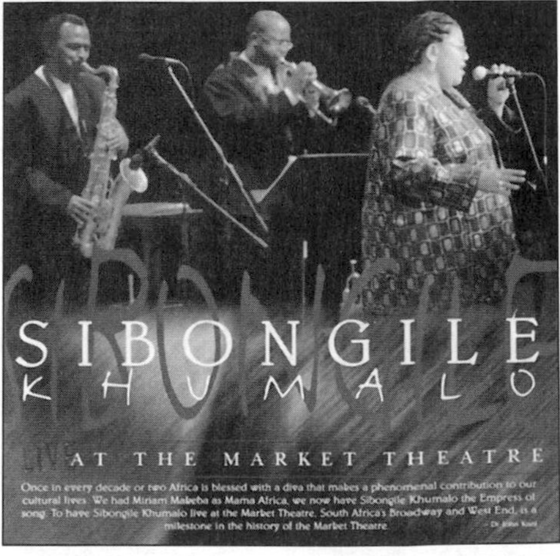

African music and jazz. During the 1990s, she had major successes performing in all three disciplines. In 1996, she made her operatic debut as Carmen in Durban, and also signed a contract with Sony Music Entertainment South Africa, releasing her first album, *Ancient Evenings*. That same year, she performed the *Two Nations* concert in London to honour Nelson Mandela. In 1997, she and her excellent South African band were recorded live at the Market Theatre, Johannesburg, and the superlative album *Live At The Market Theatre* was released in 1998. Khumalo has also performed classical concerts in France and Egypt, and in September 1998, with her South African band, she performed for a week at London's Ronnie Scott jazz club.

Khumalo is an extraordinary phenomenon – an artist who is world-class in three different musical disciplines. She is regarded as a mezzo-soprano, but seems to have the range of both a contralto and a soprano. When she is singing with her band there is no trace of the classical background in her sound or her phrasing, except that, when needed, she has all the power of a classically trained singer at her disposal. She can scat sing – rhythmically without words, and she can also sing wordlessly with great feeling and lyricism. She's a diva with a real difference. [IC]

⊙ **Live At The Market Theatre** (1997; Sony Jazz). The opening track, "Tsakwe/Royal Blue", has Khumalo singing wordlessly, and her every note and phrase is organic and charged with feeling. Her rhythm-section is a fine unit, her pianist and musical director, Themba Mkhize, is very accomplished and so are her main soloists, trumpeter Prince Lengoasa and tenor saxophonist Khaya Mahlangu.

Dave Kikoski

Piano, composer.

b. Milltown, New Jersey, 29 Sept 1961.

Taught by his father to play Basie and Ellington material at the piano as well as Chopin and Beethoven, Dave Kikoski attended New Brunswick High School, where he played in both rock and jazz bands, later cementing the latter interest by studying at Berklee. On graduating in piano performance in 1984, Kikoski remained in Boston, holding down a regular gig at Ryle's and thus meeting a number of future musical collaborators, including Pat Metheny and Roy Haynes. On moving to New York, Kikoski was introduced into Roy Haynes's band by saxophonist Ralph Moore and he also became involved with a number of other New York-based musicians, appearing on Randy Brecker's *In The Idiom*, gigging with bassist Santi Debriano and saxophonist Bob Berg, and becoming a regular member of Puerto Rican saxophonist David Sanchez's band. A firm believer in "knowing the tradition and using your own original voice to add to it", Kikoski made two albums as a leader, a debut for the French Freelance label, a second (produced by Steely Dan's Walter Becker), *Persistent Dreams*, for Triloka, before attracting major-label attention for his third, *Dave Kikoski*. His sparkily ebullient, yet intelligent playing, makes Kikoski an ideal sideman, and he has been used in this capacity through the 1990s and beyond by figures as diverse as drummer Billy Hart, trumpeter Eddie Henderson, vibes player Joe Locke, Spanish alto player Perico Sambeat, Japanese singer Monday Michiru (daughter of Toshiko Akiyoshi) and French violinist Didier Lockwood.

But perhaps one of his most typically telling contributions to a recording project can be heard on the Mingus Big Band's *Que Viva Mingus!* (Dreyfus; 1997), on which his rhythmic adventurousness and subtlety make him the ideal interpreter of the great bassist's Latin compositions. A firm believer in "knowing the tradition and using your own original voice to add to it", Kikoski made two albums as a leader, a debut for the French Freelance label (see below), a second (produced by Steely Dan's Walter Becker), *Persistent Dreams*, for Triloka, before attracting major-label attention for his third, *Dave Kikoski*. Thereafter followed a quartet of albums for Criss Cross, two decent Beatlejazz albums for Zebra and a pair for Japanese label DIW, the cumulative sum of which is building into an impressive body of contemporary jazz piano work. [CP]

Dave Kikoski

⊙ **Presage** (1989; Freelance). Particularly good at reinterpreting standards – "In The Still Of The Night" and "A Nightingale Sang in Berkeley Square" - Kikoski receives firm and sensitive support from bassist Eddie Gomez and drummer Al Foster.

⊙ **Dave Kikoski** (1994; Epicure). Consistently fresh, inventive trio music, again with Al Foster, but with bassist Essiet Essiet, balancing the experimental ("E" and "Chant") with Kikoski's trademark reworking of the familiar ("Giant Steps").

⊙ **Surf's Up** (2001; Criss Cross). The fourth Kikosky-led album for the label, and probably the best, with the pianist taking in Zappa, Monk and delivering a 14-minute exposition on the Brian Wilson-composed title track in the blue chip company of bassist James Genus and drummer Jeff 'Tain' Watts.

Roy Haynes

⊙ **Te-Vou!** (1994; Dreyfus). Classy music from a stellar band – Donald Harrison (alto saxophone), Pat Metheny (guitar) and Christian McBride (bass) along with Haynes and Kikoski. The material is a mix of Metheny and Harrison originals with the odd Monk and Ornette Coleman tune thrown in. Kikoski is in sparkling form throughout.

Masabumi Kikuchi

Piano, composer.

b. Tokyo, 19 Oct 1939.

Kikuchi led his own trio and toured with Lionel Hampton in 1962 and Sonny Rollins in 1968. He went to Berklee on a *Down Beat* scholarship in September 1968, returning to Japan in 1969, where he led his own groups again, and also worked (from 1969–71) with Woody Herman, Mal Waldron and

Joe Henderson. Since 1970 he has commuted between Japan and the USA, working with Elvin Jones until January 1974, and with others during the same period including McCoy Tyner. In 1972 he played under Gil Evans's direction in a band of Japanese musicians with Billy Harper and Hannibal Peterson, which gave concerts in Tokyo and recorded an album. From 1974 he worked with Sonny Rollins. He was also closely associated with Terumasa Hino in the mid-1970s and played and recorded with Evans again in 1980.

Since then Kikuchi has remained active, playing with established figures such as Paul Motian and Charlie Haden, as well as exploring new areas of experimentation with young DJs and also drummer Tatsuya Yoshida, a well-respected alternative/avant-garde rock musician. **[IC]**

➤➤ **Sadao Watanabe** *(Bossa Nova Concert).*

Rebecca Kilgore

Vocals, guitar.

b. Waltham, Massachusetts, 24 Sept 1949.

Kilgore is arguably the most sophisticated and naturally gifted swing singer in America today. Coming from a musical family, she moved to Portland, Oregon, in 1979 and joined the swing group Wholly Cats playing rhythm guitar (1981), before branching out with Ranch Dressing (Western swing), Woody Hite's big band, and her own country sextet Beck-a-Roo. From 1991 she appeared at the Heathman Hotel, Portland, singing twice a week with pianist Dave Frishberg; her schedule at that period included work with her trio (Kilgore, Randy Porter (keyboards), Neil Masson (drums)), as well as with Art Abrams' Swing Machine, Tall Jazz, Casey MacGill's Spirits Of Rhythm, Hite and the Western swing group Cactus Setup, co-led by violinist James Mason. Kilgore's most exquisite partnerships since then (regularly documented on the Arbors label) include numerous collaborations with Dan Barrett and pianist John Sheridan and off the record she appears widely at jazz parties and festivals with Barrett, Sheridan Dave McKenna, Cal Collins, Ken Peplowski, Scott Hamilton and Keith Ingham, amongst others. Kilgore has also taught singing and guitar in Washington, DC. A model jazz singer, the effortless musicality of her style regularly recalls but never imitates Maxine Sullivan; her light touch, perfect intonation and diction combine with a near-infallible ear for repertoire to produce a major new performer in her genre. **[DF]**

⊙ **I Saw Stars (1994; Arbors).** With outstanding Kirby-esque arrangements by Dan Barrett for his Celestial Six (hear "No Love No Nothing" for a referential miniature of crafted conceptual perfection), Kilgore's singing is an unqualified delight. The CD includes a graceful PS, "Princess" (based on Brubeck's "The Duke").

⊙ **Not A Care In The World (1996; Arbors).** The fruits of a long partnership with Dave Frishberg, this collection is genuinely investigative. "In The Land Of Oo-Blah-Dee", "South American Way", "Samba Da Minha Terra" and the (irresistible) title track are all very different songs bound together only by excellence. Seventeen superb tracks with Dan Faehnle guesting regularly and effectively on guitar.

⊙ **The Starlit Hour (1997; Arbors).** Recorded on the final night of their long-standing residency at the Heathman Hotel, Portland, Oregon, a predictably five-star set including beauties such as "I Go For That", "You Smell So Good" and "Thief In The Night", with Frishberg's vintage piano a worthy match for Kilgore's effortless artistry.

⊙ **Moments Like This (2001; Heavywood).** Kilgore with her own trio in an immaculate programme of should-be standards including "Oh! You Crazy Moon'' "You Say You Care" and the title track.

Billy Kilson

Drums.

b. Washington, DC, 2 Aug 1962.

One of the most versatile drummers to appear in a long while, Kilson had no musical antecedents in his family. He studied at Berklee College, graduating in 1985, and also privately with Alan Dawson. Working in the late 80s with Walter Davis Jnr, Donald Byrd and Ahmad Jamal, in 1989 he started six years with Dianne Reeves. 1991 saw him working with musicians as diverse as Marcus Roberts, Marvin Hamlisch, Greg Osby and George Duke, and in subsequent years he appeared or recorded with Bob Belden, Steps Ahead, Mike Stern, Tim Hagans and saxophonist Bill Evans. In 1995 an ongoing relationship with Bob James-Kirk Whalum-Larry Carlton began, and in 1997 he joined Dave Holland, recording Grammy-nominated albums with both groups. Particular inspirations were Ahmad Jamal, Walter Davis and Alan Dawson, while twelve other favourite drummers run from Jo Jones to Lenny White (via Shadow Wilson and Frankie Dunlop). Dave Holland summarized Kilson's qualities as follows: "His groove is impeccable and he's always coming up with different rhythmic settings. He can enter into dialogue without overshadowing the band, he's got a great sense of dynamics." **[BP]**

➤➤ **Bob Belden** *(When Doves Cry);* **Dave Holland** *(Points Of View);* **Greg Osby** *(Man Talk For Moderns);* **Dianne Reeves** *(Quiet After The Storm).*

Frank Kimbrough

Piano, composer.

b. Roxburgh, North Carolina, 2 Nov 1956.

Kimbrough's mother and grandmother were both piano teachers, and his father was also a keen amateur musician. He began playing piano by ear as a child and then studied formally for fourteen years. After three years of composition studies at university, he left to play jazz and moved to Washington DC in 1980, where he was mentored by pianist and singer Shirley Horn. Settling in New York in 1981, Kimbrough regularly performed solo gigs and won the Great American Jazz Piano Competition in 1985.

A member of the quartet of hard-bop saxophonist Ted Nash from 1989, he helped found the musician-run, non-profit Jazz Composers Collective in 1992 with bassist Ben Allison and, two years later, set up the Herbie Nichols Project to play the pianist's compositions. He joined the Maria Schneider band in 1993 and has worked more recently with vibes man Joe Locke, as well as his own group Noumena which comprises saxophonist Scott Robinson, guitarist Ben Monder and drummer Tony Moreno. Kimbrough cites both Paul Bley and Andrew Hill as key inspirations. [BP]

Quickening (1998; OmniTone). This belatedly released, live JCC concert effectively captures the fluid, free-tempo interaction between Kimbrough, Ben Allison and drummer Jeff Ballard. It's an absorbing programme of the pianist's originals, which includes "Svengali", a continuation of Gil Evans's "Las Vegas Tango".

Frank Kimbrough and Joe Locke

The Willow (2002; OmniTone). Kimbrough describes his second album with the vibist as possessing a "peaceful feeling" and "an empathy that can't be rehearsed". Five of the ten tracks feature the duo while on the other five they are joined by reedman Tim Reis and percussionist Jeff Ballard.

>> **Herbie Nichols Project** *(Strange City)*.

Soweto Kinch

Alto saxophone, rap vocals.
b. London, England, 10 Jan 1978.

Coming from a West Indian theatrical family, Soweto Kinch began playing music in church in his teens. He studied history at Hertford College, Oxford University, and, in 1999, joined Tomorrow's Warriors, the non-profit making jazz organization founded by bassist Gary Crosby, aimed at fostering young musicians attempting a career in jazz. Through Tomorrow's Warriors Kinch joined the internationally acclaimed Jazz Jamaica All Stars, a twenty-one piece big band, who blend jazz with reggae, ska and other Caribbean rhythms. The resulting album, *Massive* (2001) gave Kinch the opportunity to show his abilities as both soloist and arranger. The album's release catapulted Kinch to further successes in 2002, a year in which he received the prestigious BBC Radio Jazz Award for Rising Star and won the inaugural White Foundation International Saxophone Competition at the Montreux Jazz Festival. These wins led to shows for his own band at the 2003 Montreux Jazz Festival, the IAJE Annual Festival in Toronto, at the famed Ronnie Scott Club in London and Highlights of Jazz in New York. Kinch, frequently in demand for guest appearances with the likes of Wynton Marsalis and Julian Joseph, has also dedicated a considerable part of his career to working in theatre, writing scores for plays and musicals, including a 2002 production of *It's Just A Name* written by his father, Don. Soweto Kinch is an intelligent, multi-talented, new voice on the saxophone whose recent performances have confirmed his authority and originality on both sax and vocals. [IC]

Conversations With The Unseen (2003; Dune Records). This brilliant, overpowering debut begins with some dynamic rapping, before revealing Kinch's real virtuosity on the second track, "Doxology". All twelve pieces were written and arranged by Kinch, and the performances are always stunning – not least on the beautifully compassionate title track.

King Pleasure And The Biscuit Boys

Generally recognized as Britain's leading jump-jive band, King Pleasure And The Biscuit Boys were formed in Walsall in 1986 as Some Like It Hot (later The Satellites) around saxophonist-singer King Pleasure (Mark Skirving, b. 13 March 1966); fellow founder members included "P. Popps" Martin (saxophone) and "Bullmoose" K. Shirley (guitar). After re-forming in late 1987 under their current name, and signing up to Jim Simpson's Big Bear label, the group (now a seven-piece) recorded in 1988, 1990 and 1991 and, championed by manager Simpson, steadily built a local, then a national, reputation. Changes and additions to the line-up strengthened the group's musical resources further, and Al Nicholls (tenor) completed a three-man saxophone section in 1993, staying for one year. By the mid 1990s the group had worked and recorded with R&B legend Charles Brown, Howard McCrary and Gene "Mighty Flea" Connors, as well as toured the USA and Europe. Combining humour with solid musical ability, the Kaypees are busier than ever today; their current line-up (1999) includes Pleasure, Shirley and Martin, fellow founder members "Slap Happy" (bass) and "Bam Bam" Beresford (drums), along with "Ivory Dan" McCormack (piano), John Battrum (tenor) and "Big Mally" Baxter (trumpet). [DF]

Smack Dab In The Middle (1998; Big Bear). Right down to the splendidly non-pc cover, this is a definitive illustration of what the Kaypees do; high-standard musicality, inexhaustible energy and strong solo ability, all fronted by hoarse-voiced King Pleasure and his driving tenor.

Peter King

Alto, tenor and soprano saxophones, clarinet.
b. Kingston-upon-Thames, Surrey, UK, 11 Aug 1940.

King, who is entirely self-taught, began playing clarinet at fifteen, soon changing to alto saxophone. In 1959 he got his first important engagement when Ronnie Scott booked him to appear at the opening of the first Ronnie Scott's club in London. In 1960–61 he worked with the Johnny Dankworth orchestra. Since then he has worked with the big bands of Maynard Ferguson, Tubby Hayes, Harry South and Stan Tracey, and played in small groups with Philly Joe Jones, Zoot Sims, Al Cohn, Red Rodney, Hampton Hawes, Nat Adderley, Al Haig, Bill Watrous and others. He has also done a European tour with the Ray Charles band, and has worked with singers such as Jimmy Witherspoon, Joe Williams, Jon Hendricks and Anita O'Day.

In recent years he has continued to lead his own small groups, and regularly appears with Stan Tracey. King has always been a brilliant soloist in the bebop tradition, but he has developed over the years into very much more than that. His great technical virtuosity and powerful swing have gradually been leavened by a very advanced harmonic element and a penchant for pan-tonality. During the 1990s he has been a star soloist with the Colin Towns Mask Orchestra, which has extremely adventurous charts written by the leader. The Peter King Quintet released a new CD, *Speed Trap*, in 2003. [IC]

⊙ **Tamburello** (1994; Miles Music). King has an unusual line-up for this session – two keyboardists, Steve Melling and James Hellawell, bassist Alec Dankworth and drummer Stephen Keogh. It's an adventurous effort, with some fine playing, but the results are uneven.

➤➤ **Stan Tracey** *(Portraits Plus).*

Tony Kinsey

Percussion, piano, composer, arranger.
b. Sutton Coldfield, Warwickshire, UK, 11 Oct 1927.

Kinsey studied percussion with Tommy Webster in Birmingham and Bill West in the USA, and also studied composition and orchestration with Bill Russo. He went to London in 1948 and worked with various small groups. He was a founder member of the Johnny Dankworth Seven, staying with them from 1950–52. He then led his own small groups featuring many of the finest British musicians. He has also accompanied Oscar Peterson, Ben Webster, Clark Terry, Billie Holiday, Ella Fitzgerald, Lena Horne, Sarah Vaughan and played on eight tracks of Mary Lou Williams's *The London Sessions* (1954). His favourite drummers include Kenny Clarke, Buddy Rich, Tony Williams, Phil Seamen and Max Roach, and he has gained inspiration from Duke Ellington, Miles Davis, Thelonious Monk and several European composers from Beethoven to Bartók. He writes music for TV shows, commercials, documentaries and films. Two of his best compositions are *Pictures*, an orchestral suite, and *The Colour Quadrant Suite*, pieces for string quartet and alto saxophone. He remains active as a drummer in London. [IC]

John Kirby

Bass, tuba, arranger.
b. Baltimore, Maryland, 31 Dec 1908; d. 14 June 1952.

Kirby was originally the tuba player for Bill Brown's Brownies in New York, but changed over to bass after joining Fletcher Henderson's orchestra in 1930. From 1934 he was in and out of orchestras led by Chick Webb, Lucky Millinder and Charlie Barnet, until in 1937 he moved into the Onyx Club on 52nd Street with a six-piece band containing the old team of Frankie Newton and Pete Brown, soon to be replaced by Charlie Shavers and Russell Procope. Daily rehearsals, during which Kirby was officially appointed leader of the group, combined with Shavers's brilliant little arrangements (often of classical material such as Grieg's "Anitra's Dance"), quickly made John Kirby's sextet the talk of the Onyx, then of 52nd Street. Dressed in immaculate white suits, "the biggest little swing band in the world" played all the best hotels (including the Waldorf Astoria), worked up and down Swing Street and landed a three-a-week NBC radio series, *Flow Gently, Sweet Rhythm*, featuring Kirby's wife Maxine Sullivan. Their success lasted until the early 1940s, when Billy Kyle was drafted, drummer O'Neill Spencer was forced to leave for serious health reasons (Cliff Leeman replaced him), and Shavers left to work in the studios. Charlie Holmes joined briefly in 1947, by which time the band was in decline. Never much of a businessman or a disciplinarian, Kirby saw his band slip out of fashion, and a Carnegie Hall reunion concert attracted few customers. He went to California to plan a new band but died of diabetes with complications at 43. [DF]

⊙ **The John Kirby Sextet 1939–41** (Columbia). Kirby's sides in chronological order on a two-CD set, including titles with Maxine Sullivan – the apotheosis of small-band swing. Excellent remastering.

⊙ **John Kirby 1938-9/1939-41/1941–3/1945–6.** The full Kirby saga; this small precise ensemble was supercharged with solo talent and only the later sides after Kirby's A-team had all dispersed (1945-6) show signs of fatigue.

Bill Kirchner

Soprano saxophone, clarinet, arranger, composer, writer.
b. Youngstown, Ohio, 31 Aug 1953.

Kirchner began clarinet at the age of seven and saxophone at twelve, and wrote arrangements for his school's stage band. Taking an English degree in New York, he studied with Lee Konitz and Harold

Danko, then moved to Washington, DC, from 1975–80, playing locally, writing reviews and working on oral-history projects. Back in New York he led his own nonet and played in the Mel Lewis and Mario Bauza bands, among others. He wrote arrangements for Konitz, Dizzy Gillespie and singer Patti Austin and, since 1991, has taught at the New School. In 1993, surgery to remove a tumour on the spinal chord restricted his playing to a modified soprano saxophone, but he then became more active as a journalist, record annotator and reissue producer. He has also edited two books, *A Miles Davis Reader* (1997) and *Jazz: A Reader's Companion* (2000). [BP]

⊙ **Trance Dance** (1990; A-Records). This 2-CD live concert features Kirchner's nonet, with trumpeter Brian Lynch and tenorist Ralph Lalama. Arrangements of a standard each by Ivan Lins, Peter Nero, Burt Bacharach and Wayne Shorter sit alongside originals by band members and others such as Jane Ira Bloom.

⊙ **Some Enchanted Evening** (1996; A-Records). A series of duets with three different pianists, Mike Abene, Marc Copland and Harold Danko. The disc features Kirchner's quirky and melancholic dissections of "Autumn Leaves" and several less frequently used standards.

Andy Kirk

Bass and baritone saxophones, tuba.
b. Newport, Kentucky, 28 May 1898; d. 11 Dec 1992.

Kirk had been a postman and part-time musician for more than ten years when in 1929 he took over leadership of Terrence Holder's Dark Clouds Of Joy from Dallas. The band that year included young Buddy Tate and over the next ten years other keymen such as drummer Ben Thigpen, singer Pha (pronounced Fay) Terrell, electric guitarist Floyd Smith and saxophonists Dick Wilson and John Williams were to join; in 1931 Williams's wife, pianist Mary Lou Williams, became Kirk's staff arranger. "I used to write with the flashlight on in the car when we did one-nighters", she later told Stan Britt, "and sometimes we didn't eat for four, five or maybe even six days, because we were afraid to stop at a particular city. After all they were lynching blacks. It was very difficult." By 1936, when Kirk's band had a hit record featuring Terrell, "Until The Real Thing Comes Along", it was playing more in New York than down South, often at big venues such as the Savoy, and in 1939 the band took over the residency at the Cotton Club from Cab Calloway. It was a brief stay: the club closed because of tax problems. All through the 1940s Kirk continued to lead successful bands: later keymen included Ken Kersey, Don Byas (who replaced Dick Wilson), Shorty Baker and Howard McGhee (who recorded "McGhee Special" with Kirk in 1942). In 1948 the Clouds Of Joy blew away forever and Kirk settled into a string of careers: hotel management, real estate and in the 1980s as a Musicians' Union official in New York. [DF]

⊙ **The Chronological Andy Kirk: 1936–8** (Classics). A comprehensive three-volume set which reveals the very high output level of the Kirk band, featuring Mary Lou Williams's piano and spritely, sometimes testing arrangements, as well as legendary tenorist Dick Wilson. The 1936–7 volume has classics like "Walkin' And Swingin'", "Moten Swing" and "Froggy Bottom".

Rahsaan Roland Kirk

Tenor saxophone, flute, manzello, stritch, clarinet, composer, whistles.
b. Columbus, Ohio, 7 Aug 1936; d. 5 Dec 1977.

Kirk was blinded soon after his birth, and was educated at Ohio State School for the Blind. He played saxophone and clarinet with a school band from the age of twelve, and by 1951 was leading his own group for dances and playing with other bands around Ohio. At sixteen he dreamed he was playing three instruments at once, and the next day went to a music shop and tried out all the reed instruments. He was taken to the basement to be shown "the scraps", and found two archaic saxophones which had been used in turn-of-the-century Spanish military bands, the stritch and the manzello; the first is a kind of straight alto saxophone, and the second looks a little like an alto, but sounds more like a soprano. Kirk took these and worked out a way of playing them simultaneously with the tenor saxophone, producing three-part harmony by trick fingering. As there were often slight tuning discrepancies between the three instruments, the resulting sound could be harsh, almost with the characteristic of certain ethnic instruments, and this gave Kirk's music an added robustness. He also used sirens, whistles and other sounds to heighten the drama of his performances.

He made his first album in 1956, but it went virtually unnoticed. Then in 1960, through the help of Ramsey Lewis, he recorded for the Cadet label, and immediately caused controversy. People accused him of gimmickry, and Kirk defended himself, saying that he did everything for a reason, and he heard sirens and things in his head when he played. He was, in fact, rooted very deeply in the whole jazz tradition, and knew all the early music, including the work of Jelly Roll Morton (and Fats Waller) in which sirens, whistles, car horns and human voices had figured to brilliant effect. For Kirk, jazz was "black classical music", and he was steeped in its wild, untamed spirit.

In 1961 he worked with Charles Mingus, playing on the album *Oh Yeah* and touring with him in California. His international reputation was burgeoning, and after his stint with Mingus he made his first trip to Europe, performing as soloist at the Essen jazz festival in Germany. From 1963 he began a series of regular tours abroad with his own quartet, and played the first of several residencies at Ronnie Scott's club. For the rest of the 1960s and into the 1970s he led his group the Vibration Society in clubs, concerts and major festivals throughout the USA, Canada, Europe, Australia and New Zealand.

Rahsaan Roland Kirk

past forms. Even today his music does not sound dated – it sounds ever-present, beyond time. Playing one instrument – either tenor saxophone or the manzello – Kirk showed clearly that he was one of the great improvisers. He was an enthusiast who was always listening and learning, and he was generous in his encouragement of aspiring young musicians. He was a composer of memorable tunes: some of the better-known ones are "From Bechet, Byas And Fats", "No Tonic Pres", "Bright Moments", "Let Me Shake Your Tree" and "The Inflated Tear".

J.E. Berendt said that Kirk had "all the wild untutored quality of a street musician coupled with the subtlety of a modern jazz musician", and Michael Ullman wrote: "Hearing him, one can almost feel that music, like the Lord in 'Shine On Me', can 'heal the sick and raise the dead'." [IC]

⊙ **Does Your House Have Lions** (1961–76; Rhino). This two-disc compilation of seventeen tracks from twelve albums is an excellent introduction to Kirk's work from his 25th year to the year before his death, and it has comprehensive liner notes by Stanley Crouch.

⊙ **Kirks Work** (1961; OJC). Kirk is in effervescent form here, with organist Jack McDuff, bassist Joe Benjamin and Art Taylor. The organ sound suits him; the band is exuberant and Kirk drives them on with three saxophones foghorning, and incredible virtuosity on flute and individual reeds.

In 1975, Kirk had a stroke which partially paralysed one side of his body. With tremendous courage he began performing again with one arm – an almost impossible handicap for a saxophonist – and he managed to tour internationally, play some festivals and appear on TV. In 1977 a second stroke caused his death.

Kirk was much loved, not only by his audiences but also by other musicians. He was unclassifiable: a completely original performer whose style carried in it the whole of jazz history from early New Orleans roots, through swing and bebop, to the abstraction of the 1960s and 1970s avant-garde. Throughout his career he recorded tributes to people he particularly loved, and they included Fats Waller, Billie Holiday, Duke Ellington, Lester Young, Thelonious Monk, Sidney Bechet, Don Byas, Roy Haynes, Charles Mingus, Clifford Brown, Barney Bigard and John Coltrane. Yet he could be classified neither as a traditionalist nor as an avant-gardist; his music was always of the present, but contained the essence of

⊙ **Rip Rig And Panic/Now Please Don't You Cry, Beautiful Edith** (1965; Emarcy). *Edith* is one of Kirk's less well-known albums, but it covers a wide spectrum from jazz to ironic kitsch to rock'n'roll. *Panic* is one of his very finest albums, with Jaki Byard, Richard Davis, Elvin Jones, some of Kirk's most inspired tribute compositions including "From Bechet, Byas And Fats", and powerful playing from all four men.

⊙ **The Inflated Tear** (1967; Atlantic). This is another of Kirk's superlative albums, yet he was the only star in this quartet, which was his working group of the time. It's one of his most personal statements because the title refers to his blindness and the suffering he endured as a child. Spurred by his example, the group gives a dynamic, compassionate and totally enthralling performance.

⊙ **Volunteered Slavery** (1968; Rhino). With five strong studio tracks and an exhilarating live set from the 1968 Newport festival, Kirk is on great form here.

⊙ **Blacknuss** (1971; Rhino). Kirk was playing quite a lot of pop music at this point, and on the title track he talks, sings and shouts. Whitney Houston's mother, Cissy, assists him with the vocals on this and other tracks.

Kenny Kirkland

Piano, composer.

b. Brooklyn, New York, 28 Sept 1955; d. 12 Nov 1998.

Kirkland started piano lessons at the age of six, and later attended Manhattan School of Music, studying classical piano performance for eighteen months, then classical theory and composition, graduating as a teacher. He joined Michal Urbaniak's group on keyboards and synthesizer, touring Europe and Scandinavia in 1977. Back in the USA, he played with Angela Bofill, Don Alias and others from 1979–81, and then joined Terumasa Hino and toured in Japan where he met Wynton Marsalis. From 1982 he worked with Marsalis, touring and recording several albums with him. Two years later he toured Japan with Jim Hall, Eddie Gomez and Grady Tate. In 1985–6, with Branford Marsalis, Omar Hakim and Darryl Jones, Kirkland accompanied the pop/rock musician Sting, recording *Dream Of The Blue Turtles* with him and doing a massive international tour. The main influences which brought him to jazz were Larry Willis – who played electric piano with Blood Sweat And Tears – Kenny Barron and Herbie Hancock. Kirkland has recorded with many people, including Urbaniak, Miroslav Vitous, Bofill, John Scofield, Chico Hamilton, Chico Freeman, David Liebman, Dewey Redman and Carla Bley. **[IC]**

➤➤ **Branford Marsalis** *(Requiem)*; **Wynton Marsalis** *(Wynton Marsalis)*; **Charnett Moffett** *(Nettwork)*.

Don Kirkpatrick

Piano, arranger.

b. Charlotte, North Carolina, 17 June 1905; d. 13 May 1956.

A veteran of Chick Webb's and later Don Redman's bands in the first half of the 1930s, Don Kirkpatrick was as highly rated for his arranging talents as he was for his piano-playing. As well as writing for Webb and Redman (another great arranger), he was one of the first to contribute scores to Count Basie's band at a time when it had relied largely on head arrangements: according to Dicky Wells, Kirkpatrick's work was complicated enough to defeat Herschel Evans (who would tear up the music accordingly). Surprisingly, Kirkpatrick's playing companions often included more hard-line traditionalists such as Mezz Mezzrow, and he had a solo spot at Nick's from 1944. Perhaps his most dramatic change of stylistic course was a spell with Bunk Johnson in 1947, where he provided (for concerts and records) the kind of light, swing-based piano that Johnson by that time preferred. During the period 1952–5 he worked with Wilbur de Paris's New New Orleans Jazz which – with its mix of old and new traditions – should have provided a perfect setting for Kirkpatrick's trained versatility (some of these dates are currently in the process of reissue on CD). He died soon after of pneumonia. **[DF]**

Manny Klein

Trumpet.

b. New York, 4 Feb 1908; d. 31 May 1994.

A pupil of trumpet guru Max Schlossberg (like Max Kaminsky), Manny Klein was later in boys' bands and New York's Junior Police Band. He was so good so young that from 1928 he was in constant demand as a freelance, working on record and live with practically every important white band, from Roger Wolfe Kahn to Benny Goodman and Red Nichols. With very occasional breaks for isolated bandleading ventures (he co-led a technically superb band with Frank Trumbauer in 1938), Klein remained a studio musician for the rest of his life. He moved to Los Angeles in 1937, where he played powerful lead, immaculate hot choruses or classical concertos to perfect order: it would be difficult to find a top-class studio trumpet section of the 1940s and 1950s that did not include him and his longtime playing colleague Conrad Gozzo. Klein appeared in the 1939 Bing Crosby film *This Side Of Heaven*, and his trumpet featured on countless film soundtracks, including *From Here To Eternity*, for which he ghosted trumpet solos for Montgomery Clift, and *The Benny Goodman Story*, in which he doubled for a sick Ziggy Elman. In the 1970s he suffered the first of a series of strokes which rendered him dyslexic and unable to read music, but he could still play perfectly. Retired by the 1990s, Klein was honoured with the nickname "GOMOTS" (Grand Old Man Of The Trumpet Section), a fair description, for despite his superlative talents Klein's solo jazz recordings could be counted on the valves of half a dozen trumpets. **[DF]**

Manny Klein And His Sextet (1959; Imperial). Manny in a small-group setting of his own, with Ronnie Lang on reeds; unfortunately the programme concentrates on selections from *The Sound Of Music*, but the value of the set lies in its rarity.

John Klemmer

Saxophones, flute.

b. Chicago, 3 July 1946.

After learning guitar initially, John Klemmer took up saxophone at eleven, studying with Joe Daley and leading the school band. He toured, at sixteen, with Ted Weems's dance band, but continued to learn his craft at a number of Stan Kenton's summer workshops. His recording career began with Cadet, for whom he produced a number of psychedelic jazz fusion albums in the late 1960s, but he came to the jazz public's attention through his work with Don Ellis's band (1968–70). Settled on the West Coast, he worked with Oliver Nelson and Alice Coltrane, as well as the Crusaders, before leading his own groups in the 1970s and making a number of light fusion albums, employing electronic effects, for MCA. He studied orchestration in Los Angeles (1970–74) and received acclaim for two more adventurous albums, *Cry* (notable for the electronic effects it applied to solo saxophone) and *Nexus For Duo And Trio*. He has also collaborated with fellow experimenter saxophonist Eddie Harris. Although celebrated for his electronic experimentation, Klemmer is a gifted technician on all his horns despite his rather patchy recorded output and his mid-1980s retirement from the public eye. 1997 saw him performing again and promoting himself as a Godfather of Smooth Jazz, stating on the release of *Making Love Volume 1* (Touch, 1998) his intent to "try to make the most beautiful music on the planet". [CP]

⊙ **Waterfalls** (1972; MCA). Although a little bland, and with its electronics sounding more than a little dated, this gives a fair idea of Klemmer's 1970s concerns.

⊙ **Barefoot Ballet** (1976; MCA). Perhaps Klemmer's most popular recording, featuring West Coast fusion stalwarts Dave Grusin (piano), Larry Carlton (guitar) and John Guerin (drums).

⊙ **Nexus for Duo and Trio** (1978; Arista). A break from the fusion mould, featuring bassist Bob Magnusson and drummer Carl Burnett.

⊙ **Simpatico** (1998; JVC). Made twenty years before release, a celebration, in Klemmer's words, of "melodicism, tenderness and romance": duo performances with Brazilian guitarist Oscar Castro Neves from the late 1970s, recorded with ocean sounds "acting as the third party to create a trio".

Al Klink

Saxophones.

b. Danbury, Connecticut, 28 Dec 1915; d. 7 March 1991.

One of the most stylish white swing saxophonists, Al Klink played with Glenn Miller from 1939–42 (he shares the tenor solo on "In The Mood" with Tex Beneke but was underfeatured in general) and then moved on to a succession of fine bands including Benny Goodman's and Tommy Dorsey's. Later in the 1940s he concentrated on studio work for WNEW and NBC, and appeared regularly on jazz albums too (including Ruby Braff's Billie Holiday tribute, *Holiday In Braff*). A busy freelance for much of the 1970s, he was with The World's Greatest Jazz Band from 1974–82, and continued to play freelance at festivals and in studios and to record with George Masso, Glenn Zottola and others. [DF]

Earl Klugh

Guitar.

b. Detroit, Michigan, 16 Sept 1954.

Influenced by Chet Atkins, Earl Klugh took up and taught himself guitar as a child, playing on Yusef Lateef's album, *Suite 16*, at fifteen. In 1973, he joined George Benson's band, having contributed to the guitarist's *White Rabbit* album two years earlier. In 1974, he joined Return To Forever, playing electric guitar alongside his customary acoustic model with nylon strings. In the mid-1970s he established himself as a leader and made a large number of light, accessible but always intensely musical albums in a fusion mould. In 1979, his album *One On One* won him a Grammy. In addition to his highly successful fusion albums, Klugh has also made a niche for himself in film music: *How To Beat The High Cost Of Living* (1980, with flautist Hubert Laws) is his most prominent example. In the 1990s, Klugh's radio-friendly recordings remained popular: Warner Bros issued seven albums, all save one (*Cool*, from 1992, co-produced with Bob James) produced by Klugh himself. They included *Sounds And Visions* (1993), which contained "Jo Ann's Song", featured in the film *Tequila Sunrise*, and 1997's *The Journey*, featuring vocalist Eddie "Key" Bullard. His archetypical 1999 album, *Peculiar Situation*, marked his debut for Windham Hill but has not as yet led to a similarly prolific output. [CP]

⊙ **Two Of A Kind** (1982; EMI Manhattan). Like *One On One*, this album features pianist/composer Bob James along with a tasty fusion band including ace percussionist Sammy Figueroa.

⊙ **Best Of Earl Klugh** (1991–3; Blue Note). Perhaps the easiest way into Klugh's light but tasteful musicianly world, featuring the highlights from his EMI albums.

⊙ **Ballads** (1994; EMI Manhattan). Highly palatable, easy on the ear, but laced with subtleties, featuring Dave Grusin and Paulinho Da Costa alongside Klugh.

⊙ **The Best Of Earl Klugh** (1998; Warner Bros). Culled from the guitarist's fifteen-year association with the company, showcasing his undemanding but impeccably performed music in a variety of settings.

Jimmy Knepper

Trombone, arranger.

b. Los Angeles, 22 Nov 1927; d. 14 June 2003.

Knepper gained his early experience with a band led by Chuck Cascales (brother of the arranger Johnny Richards) and with saxophonist Dean Benedetti in the mid-1940s. He toured with pianist Freddie Slack in 1947, altoist Johnny Bothwell in 1948, as well as with other name bands, and rehearsed and recorded in the Roy Porter band in 1948–9 alongside Eric Dolphy, a fellow student at LA City College. Further big-band work, including time with Claude Thornhill in 1956, took him to New York, where he immediately replaced trombonist Willie Dennis in Charles Mingus's Jazz Workshop. He played with Mingus in 1957–8, rejoining him briefly in 1959, in 1961 twice, in 1976 and 1977. He also spent a few months each with Stan Kenton and Tony Scott, both in 1958, Gil Evans in 1960 and Benny Goodman in 1962. Then, following injury to his mouth and jaw inflicted by Mingus in 1962, he worked steadily in Broadway pit bands and did session work, becoming a member of the Thad Jones-Mel Lewis band from 1967–73 and of the Lee

Konitz nonet from 1975–9. He was one of the regulars, and sometimes musical director, of Mingus Dynasty from 1979 onwards, and has also done numerous tours abroad as soloist.

Knepper's solo work is most frequently associated with Mingus, but it is remarkably consistent whatever the context. While taking account of the harmonic and melodic advances of bebop, he steered clear of the staccato attack of J.J. Johnson. ("He plays the trombone fast like a fast trombonist rather than a machine-gunner; false slide positions are the secret", according to Mike Zwerin.) His extremely nimble technique enabled him to articulate more in the manner of a saxophonist, and at the same time to incorporate aspects of earlier trombonists, such as the slurs and tonal variations of Vic Dickenson. Following his re-emergence as a soloist in the mid-1970s, Knepper became widely acknowledged as one of the leading performers on his instrument. [BP]

⊙ **Cunningbird** (1976; Steeplechase). Knepper's first solo album in nearly twenty years displayed his marvellously idiosyncratic playing style (and intelligent compositions) in company with Al Cohn and Roland Hanna.

⊙ **I Dream Too Much** (1984; Soul Note). The title track shows Knepper's impeccable taste in obscure Hollywood tunes, and his arrangements for the whole album (with French-hornist John Clark, trumpeter John Eckert and Knepper's drummer of choice, Billy Hart) enhance his own playing beautifully.

➤➤ **Charles Mingus** *(Mingus Ah Um; New Tijuana Moods).*

Franz Koglmann

Trumpet, flugelhorn, composer.

b. Mödling, Austria, 22 May 1947.

Austrian hornman and composer Franz Koglmann studied music in high school, then jazz at the State Conservatory of Vienna between 1969–72; he travelled to New York and Philadelphia in the early 70s as well. Throughout that decade he had a group called the Masters Of Unorthodox Jazz. In 1973 he founded Pipe Records, on which he released music with guests saxophonist Steve Lacy and trumpeter Bill Dixon, as well as his own *Schlaf Schlemmer, Schlaf Magritte*. Indeed, Dixon and Koglmann have comparable sounds, accenting fuzziness and warmth over brassiness or pitch. In the 80s, Koglmann played with a variety of groups, including East German pianist Ulrich Gumpert's Workshop Band, guitarist Eugene Chadbourne, and pianist Georg Gräwe's GrubenKlangOrchester. In 1983 he established his own group, the Pipetet; later in the decade he started other ensembles including KoKoKo and the Pipe Trio. His partnership with hat Art records, which started in 1986, has produced a series of highly successful releases; these utilize elements of cool jazz, free improvisation, European chamber music, atonality, and pastiche. More recent collaborations have included *Annette* (1992; hat Art), with pianist Paul Bley and bassist Gary Peacock, and *We Thought About Duke* (1995; hat Art), with guest alto saxophonist Lee Konitz. Koglmann and Ingrid Karl started the Wiener Music Gallerie, where they present an annual festival. Koglmann has increasingly featured his writing and arrangements to very good advantage on two releases based on the writings of Ezra Pound, *Cantos I-IV* (1993; hat Art) and *O Moon My Pin-Up* (1998; hat Art/Wespennest), the latter of which comes packaged with an elaborate 130-page book of images and essays. A letter spell with Frankfurt label Between The Lines Records produced *Make Believe* (1999) - inspired by Jean Cocteau - and *An Affair With Strauss* (2000), both releases featuring Tony Coe, followed by *Venus In Transit* (see below) and *Don't Play Just Be* (2001). [JC]

⊙ **L'Heure Bleue** (1991; hat Art). This record barely nudges out the Pipetet disc *The Use Of Memory* (1990; hat Art) and the quintet with soprano master Lacy, *About Yesterday's Ezzthetics* (1988; hat Art), both of which are fabulous for their own reasons. *L'Heure Bleue* features the Monoblue Quartet, with clarinettist and tenor saxophonist Tony Coe, guitarist Burkhard Stangl and bassist Klaus Koch, and a batch of nutty duets with Dutch pianist Misha Mengelberg.

⊙ **Venus In Transit** (2001; Between The Lines). Inspired variously by Marilyn Monroe and beautiful architecture and weighted toward composition over improvisation in Koglmann's latter style, his music here is deep, fluid and effortlessly attractive. Featuring reedsman Chris Speed, guitarist David Fiuczynski and violinist Mat Maneri.

Eero Koivistoinen

Saxophones, composer.

b. Finland, 13 Jan 1946.

Koivistoinen is one of the all-time greats of Finnish jazz. He studied classical violin at first, but became interested in jazz and, in the mid-1960s, enrolled at the Sibelius Academy to begin his saxophone and composition studies. He soon formed an improvising trio which included drummer Edward Vesala and bassist Pekka Sarmanto. In 1967, the newly founded Finnish Jazz Federation recognized his remarkable talents by presenting him with their first-ever Georgie Award. In 1969, Koivistoinen's group won first prize at the Montreux international jazz festival's band competition: this was the first international recognition of Finnish jazz. In the 1970s, he pursued further studies in composition with one term at the Sibelius Academy and three terms at the Berklee College of Music in Boston. Since then he has taught at the Sibelius Academy and the pop and jazz Conservatory. He has been a member of the Finnish UMO orchestra since its inception in 1975, starting in the saxophone section, then also composing for the orchestra, and finally becoming its conductor. He also made appearances as a conductor in Germany, Norway and Denmark. In 1996 Koivistoinen was appointed artistic director of the UMO which, by then, had an international reputation.

Finnish literature has inspired several of his compositions, and his extensive list of works includes a ballet, *aita maa* (Mother Earth), and a suite inspired by Charles Baudelaire's "Les Fleurs du Mal". He has recorded several albums, and in 1982 recruited a group of international jazz stars to record *Picture In Three Colours*. The band included Jack DeJohnette and John Scofield and re-formed in 1992 to record the critically lauded *Altered Things*. In 1997, Koivistoinen was one of the arrangers of a special UMO/Tim Hagans (trumpet) project – "The UMO Plays Electric Miles". [IC]

➤➤ **UMO Jazz Orchestra** *(UMO Jazz Orchestra).*

Hans Koller

Tenor and soprano saxophones, clarinet, sopranino, alto and baritone saxophones.

b. Vienna, 12 Feb 1921; d. 22 Dec 2003.

Koller studied clarinet at Vienna Music Academy from 1935–9. He entered the German army in 1940, and was one of very few jazz musicians who played during Nazi dominance. He became one of the leaders of post-war jazz in Germany, forming the first important modern combo, which included Albert Mangelsdorff. He toured with Gillespie, Lee Konitz, Stan Kenton and others during the 1950s. He made a short film, *Jazz Yesterday And Today*, for J.E. Berendt, and continued to lead his own groups during the 1960s and 1970s. His early influences were Lennie Tristano and Lee Konitz, and he later became inspired by John Coltrane. He appeared at many European festivals and won polls on tenor and soprano and for his group. Since 1957 he has been active as an abstract painter with international exhibitions. [IC]

➤➤ **Oscar Pettiford** *(Vienna Blues).*

Hans Koller

Piano, composer, arranger.

b. Landshut, Germany, 10 Nov 1970.

Hans Koller was born into a musical family: his father was a jazz-loving Lutheran pastor, his mother was a classically trained music teacher and his four sisters all played instruments. Growing up in rural Bavaria, Koller first came into contact with jazz musicians in his teens while attending jazz summer schools run by Brian Abraham's District Six in Ingolstadt. In 1991 he came to England to study music, first at Middlesex University, where he majored in composition, then at the School of Oriental and African Studies where he obtained a masters degree in Ethnomusicology.

Koller started playing in bands with saxophonist Stan Sulzman and trumpeter Chris Batchelor and went on to form his own group, Neverland, with bass player Dave Whitford, saxophonist Rob Townsend and drummer Stuart Lawrence. This group was augmented into a nine-piece outfit for Koller's debut album *Magic Mountain* (1997), which established him as one of the leading new jazz composers in the UK. Three years later he won the JOEY Award for composers organised by Eastern Arts, and subsequently was awarded major commissions by Birmingham Jazz and by the Freden International Music Festival. In 2001 he released *Lovers And Strangers*, an album featuring his trio alongside the harpist Helen Tunstall, the singer Christine Tobin, and the percussionist Corrina Silvester. His next album, *New Memories* (2002), was hailed as "the most expansive, expressive and exciting new jazz orchestral sound to have emerged in this country since the late-lamented Loose Tubes" by John Fordham in the *Guardian*. As well as playing the piano in Mike Gibbs's new big band, Koller is currently composing/arranging for a new collaboration with saxophonist Steve Lacy. An exuberant and remarkable talent, Koller's music is full of surprises. [IC]

⊙ **New Memories** (2002; 33 Records). For his big band album Koller composed and arranged nine of the ten pieces and radically rearranged the tenth, "My One and Only Love" (Wood/Mellin). While the music sometimes sounds upside down or inside out, it inevitably resolves into a coherent statement, with Koller's humanity always in evidence.

Krzysztof Komeda

Composer, piano.

b. Poznań, Poland, 27 April 1931; d. 23 April 1969.

Born Krzysztof Trzcinski, Komeda studied music as a child but was apparently a self-taught composer. Although trained as a medic, he became an active amateur musician and from the 1950s appeared at Polish jazz festivals, as well as performing in Russia and Scandinavia. During the following decade, he moved from conventional "modern jazz" to the beginnings of a Polish free-jazz movement, working with Tomasz Stanko, Zbigniew Namysłowski and Michal Urbaniak. At the same time, Komeda was involved in jazz-and-poetry, song-writing and particularly theatre and film music, for directors such as

Skolimowski and Polanski. For the latter, he created the soundtrack music of *Knife In The Water* (featuring Swedish saxophonist Bernt Røsengren), *Cul-De-Sac* and, having followed Polanski to Hollywood, *Rosemary's Baby*. Fatally injured in January 1969, he had brain surgery and was flown home but died without regaining consciousness. Although not a virtuoso player, Komeda was extremely versatile as a writer and exerted an important influence on Polish jazz. [BP]

Astigmatic (1965; Power Bros). A remarkably mature statement for its time, this classic album finds Komeda leading Stanko and Namyslowski in three long pieces. "Kattorna" (Kittens) began life as film music but this is a jazz performance, while the title track has a chromatic motif treated freely. The closing "Svantetic", apparently based on a Polish boy-scout song, is spacious but builds to an appropriate climax.

Toshinori Kondo

Trumpet, electronics.
b. Japan, 1948.

Kondo recorded in 1976, with Yosuke Yamashita's Jam Rice Sextet, *Jam Rice Relaxin'* (Frasco), and a year later with American percussion innovator Milford Graves, *Meditation Among Us* (Kitty). His connections with various European and American players have made him perhaps the most international of the Japanese free improvisers. Kondo was very active in the late 70s and in 1979 alone he issued records with guitarist Henry Kaiser and saxophonist John Oswald, *Moose And Salmon* (Music Gallery Editions), with British drummer Roger Turner and guitarist John Russell, *Artless Sky* (Caw), large group recordings in New York, *2000 Statues And The English Channel* (Parachute), duets with guitarist Eugene Chadbourne, *Possibilties Of The Color Plastic*, and a solo record, *Fuigo From A Different Dimension* (the latter two of these released on Kondo's own short-lived Bellows label). In the 80s, he collaborated frequently with cellist Tristan Honsinger, recording in quartet with Japanese drummer Sabu Toyazumi and German bass colossus Peter Kowald, *What Are You Talking About?* (1983; IMA), in a sextet, *Picnic* (1985; Data), and co-leading the group This, That And The Other, which made an eponymous LP for ITM in 1987. In the late 80s, he shifted his attention primarily to his funky, extremely Miles Davis-oriented group IMA, which gained high visibility and popularity in Japan. The pop world bottomed out for him in 1993, however, and he briefly left music altogether, moving to Amsterdam for half the year and finally returning to play again in both free-music settings, like saxophonist Peter Brötzmann's superb *Die Like A Dog Quartet* (with which he has recorded several times for FMP), in a more hip-hop-oriented setting with DJ Krush and on a pair of solo albums for Japan's DIW label, *Nerve Tripper* (2002) and *Death Is Our Eternal Friend* (2003). [JC]

The Last Supper (1980; Po Torch). Still available on Paul Lovens's exquisite vinyl-only Po Torch label, this captures Kondo at the height of his non-electric, non-Miles powers, playing intense little sounds with speed, listening acuity and tremendous creativity. It helps, too, that he's abetted by Lovens – arguably the finest improvising percussionist in the world. Top-shelf free duets.

Lee Konitz

Alto, soprano and tenor saxophones.
b. Chicago, 13 Oct 1927.

After meeting Lennie Tristano on commercial gigs in Chicago in the mid-1940s and studying under him, Konitz became deeply involved in jazz and toured with Claude Thornhill's band in 1947–8. He settled in New York, working with Miles Davis in 1948 and making recordings with him during 1949–51. He recorded for Tristano and under his own name from 1949 onwards, and was also a member of the Stan Kenton orchestra in 1952–3. Since that time, apart from occasional reunions with Tristano and/or fellow student Warne Marsh, Konitz has been a freelance soloist and private teacher. He has made regular trips to Europe since 1951, and led his own trio and (in the late 1970s) nonet. He has recorded prolifically, especially in Europe, and was awarded the Jazzpar Prize in 1992.

The influence of Tristano was predominant in the early work of Konitz, so that in the late 1940s he was one of the few altoists of his generation not to be overwhelmed by the example of Charlie Parker. His

Jak Kilby

Lee Konitz

playing instead was characterized by extremely long lines, with irregular but not strong accents and a thin, deliberately uninflected tone. Submitting to the demands of the Kenton band during his stay, he strengthened the tone and, in subsequent decades, allowed a much greater variety of emotion to be expressed by the sound-quality alone. A similar development showed in the rhythmic accentuation and fragmentation of his lines, which gradually took on more vitality and complexity, demonstrating a thorough understanding of greats such as Armstrong, Young and of course Parker. A unique and immediately identifiable performer. [BP]

⊙ **Subconscious-Lee** (1949–50; Prestige/OJC). From Konitz's Tristano period, and including four tracks issued (without his agreement) under Tristano's name, this contains fascinating improvisations on standard sequences but with abstract bop lines on top (eg "Marshmallow" and the title track).

⊙ **Live At The Half Note** (1959; Verve). A live date with the Konitz-Warne Marsh frontline and with the Bill Evans-Jimmy Garrison-Paul Motian rhythm-section which became the first working Evans trio. He is fairly subdued here, but Konitz and Marsh's soloing and duetting is some of their best ever.

⊙ **Yes Yes Nonet** (1979; Steeplechase). One of a handful of recordings of the *Birth Of The Cool-ish* nine-piece band Konitz led for a few years, including Jimmy Knepper, pianist Harold Danko, Billy Hart and, on this outing, Tom Harrell.

⊙ **Alone Together** (1996; Blue Note). This live album, jointly credited to Konitz, Charlie Haden and Brad Mehldau, is a superior example of the altoist's more recent work and features extended dialogues on standards such as "What Is This Thing Called Love?", "Cherokee" and the title-track.

➤➤ **Paul Motian** *(On Broadway Vol. 1)*; **Gerry Mulligan** *(Mullenium)*.

Jan Kopinski

Tenor, alto and soprano saxophones, composer.
b. Lincoln, UK, 10 March 1948.

The son of a Polish bomber pilot and a mother interested in Egyptian mythology and opera, Jan Kopinski became interested in music through listening to the work of figures as diverse as Yma Sumac (a Peruvian singer with a four-octave range), Jimi Hendrix and John Coltrane, and to blues and soul. Having glimpsed what he terms "the possibility of Hendrix in the setting of Coltrane or Coltrane in the setting of a power back-beat", he was confirmed in his path by hearing Prime Time, and his band Pinski Zoo purveys a heady mix of harmolodics, heavy funk and Albert Ayler-style saxophone stridency. A quartet comprising bassist Karl Wesley Bingham (b. Nottingham, UK, 1966), keyboard player Steve Iliffe (b. Leicestershire, UK, 1951) and drummer Steve Harris (b. Mansfield, UK, 1948) alongside Kopinski, Pinski Zoo rose to prominence in 1980s UK jazz through regular gigging both in Nottingham and at London's original Jazz Café, for whose label the band made their debut and follow-up CDs, showcasing their anthemic sound but never quite capturing the visceral impact achieved in live performance.

Away from Pinski Zoo in the later 1990s, Kopinski collaborated with film-maker Frank Abbott in a project utilizing film shot in Poland, *Drive Me Crazy*, featuring Steve Iliffe on keyboards and samples, and Melanie Pappenheim on vocals. He also formed the band PZ Basscorp with Iliffe, Bingham and son Stefan on bass and programs. In 1997, he released *Ghost Music* (see below), strongly influenced by visual media, particularly Tarkovsky films. Live performances featured three Kopinskis (Jan, Stefan and viola-playing daughter Janina), plus Iliffe and drummer Patrick Illingworth. Kopinski père has also performed in duo with Iliffe, in collaboration with Polish composer and pianist Wojciech Konikiewicz and, occasionally, solo; Pinski Zoo re-formed for a tour (and a rumoured live album) in 2003. He teaches part-time at the universities of Salford and Derby on improvisation, and became artist in residence at Leeds University in 2003. [CP]

⊙ **Rare Breeds** (1989; Jazz Café Records). Raw, energetic, electric jazz-funk-harmolodics with drum duties shared between Tim Bullock, Frank Tontoh and Steve Harris.

⊙ **East Rail East** (1990; Jazz Café Records). The musical mix as before, but with Harris established on drums – a rousing, relentlessly powerful album with composing credits shared pretty equally among band members.

⊙ **De-Icer** (1993; Slam). Live recordings from Austria, New York and the UK of the band in spirited, slightly extended renditions of such staples as the title track and "Slab", also featured on *East Rail East*.

⊙ **Ghost Music** (1997; ASC). Atmospheric, swirling music, full of absorbing textures, featuring Kopinski's keening saxophones against a highly original soundscape formed from programming, keyboards and Janina Kopinska's viola.

Alexis Korner

Guitar, piano, vocals.
b. Paris, 19 April 1928; d. London, I Jan 1984.

Korner was the son of a Greek mother and an Austrian cavalry officer father, and when Germany invaded France, the Korner family fled from Paris via Switzerland and North Africa to the UK, where they settled. Alexis had classical piano lessons from the age of five, but in 1940 he discovered a record by blues and boogie-woogie pianist Jimmy Yancey, and from then on was totally and passionately committed to playing blues and jazz.

By the late 1940s Korner's blues quartet was part of trombonist Chris Barber's band, playing for thirty minutes in the middle of each of Barber's jazz concerts. Although Korner failed to fit into the fanatically purist traditional jazz scene (he also loved Charlie Parker and bebop because of the "great blues feeling in it"), he again worked with Barber's band in 1952, and in 1953 played in the skiffle group within Ken Colyer's band alongside Colyer and guitarist Lonnie Donegan.

Skiffle broke the American domination of the pop charts, and was the initial inspiration of many of the

British rock groups of the 1960s, including the Beatles. It was also the source of the whole British blues movement, spearheaded by Korner; in the mid-1950s Barber began to bring American blues artists such as Big Bill Broonzy and Muddy Waters to the UK, and for the third time he gave Korner a spot in his band, playing electric blues with Cyril Davis on harmonica. The heavily amplified music deeply offended traditional jazz purists, and Korner left to form his own band, Blues Incorporated, which rapidly became an inspiration and focal point of blues enthusiasts all over the UK. It provided a direct experience of the blues for young musicians who came to listen, to sit in and sometimes to join the band, including Mick Jagger, Charlie Watts, John Mayall, Eric Burdon, Long John Baldry, Paul Jones, Robert Plant and many others. Improvisation was so germane to Alexis's concept that many of the most talented young jazz musicians of the 1960s worked with Blues Incorporated, including Jack Bruce, Ginger Baker, Graham Bond, John Marshall, Phil Seamen, John Surman, Kenny Wheeler, Ian Carr, Ray Warleigh, Dave Holland, Alan Skidmore, Art Themen and Dick Heckstall-Smith.

In 1968 Korner disbanded the group and went solo, touring with Continental groups. In 1969 he began a long and fruitful association with the Danish blues singer Peter Thorup, forming first a band called New Church, which included virtuoso bass guitarist (and singer) Colin Hodgkinson, and then the very successful bigger band CCS. Throughout the 1970s and into the 1980s Korner and Hodgkinson worked together a great deal as a duo. From the late 1970s until his death, he had a BBC radio show, on which he played and talked about records he liked, mostly vernacular music, covering everything from blues and rock to gospel music, folk and all eras and types of jazz; the programme's benign catholicity attracted a wide cross-section of listeners. He also wrote and recorded some excellent songs including "Robert Johnson", "Tap Turns On The Water" and "Lend Me Some Time".

Alexis Korner's influence is incalculable. He was a passionate enthusiast who wanted to share his knowledge and experience with everyone. He was always generous with his help and advice, always quick to recognize quality in other artists and to preach their virtues. He brought direct experience of R&B to a whole generation of British rock and jazz musicians and during the 1960s various of his disciples, such as the Rolling Stones, helped to make Americans aware of their own blues artists. [IC]

Bootleg Him (1957–69; RAK). This double LP, now hard to find, features a huge number of different line-ups with soloists from Cyril Davies to John Surman and Dave Holland, and the material is equally wide-ranging.

Teddy Kotick

Bass.

b. Haverhill, Massachusetts, 4 June 1928; d. 17 April 1986.

Kotick moved to New York in 1948, working with, among others, Buddy Rich, Buddy DeFranco and the Artie Shaw band. He played fairly regularly for Charlie Parker in 1951–2 and with Stan Getz from 1951–3. He recorded with Herbie Nichols and Tony Scott in 1956, and in the same year was on the first album of Scott's pianist, Bill Evans. He toured with the Horace Silver quintet in 1957–8, and then began freelancing in the New York area. From the early 1970s he was again based in Massachusetts, one of his only recordings thereafter being with Allen Eager in 1982. A light-fingered and light-toned bassist, Kotick in the early 1950s paralleled the development of Red Mitchell and predicted some of the innovations of Paul Chambers and even Scott LaFaro. Both his walking and his occasional solos managed to avoid the obvious and nevertheless sound absolutely right. [BP]

Bill Evans

New Jazz Conceptions (1956; Riverside/OJC). Usually studied for Evans's developing style (and one of his brief unaccompanied tracks is an early "Waltz For Debby"), this is an excellent representation of Kotick's mobile sound in combination with Paul Motian.

Peter Kowald

Bass, tuba, alphorn.

b. Masserberg, Germany, 21 April 1944.

Captivated as a teenager by Louis Armstrong, Peter Kowald began playing free jazz in Wuppertal, Germany with saxophonist Peter Brötzmann in the early 1960s. Under the prevailing influence of Albert Ayler and others on the American ESP and Impulse! labels, Kowald, Brötzmann and percussionist Sven-Ake Johansson performed as a trio, recording For Adolphe Sax in 1967; with the Brötzmann Octet he recorded the seminal *Machine Gun* a year later. In 1972 he released *Peter Kowald Quintet*, with trombonists Günter Christmann and Paul Rutherford, drummer Paul Lovens, and alto saxist Peter van de Locht. Kowald was a member of pianist Alexander von Schlippenbach's large ensemble Globe Unity Orchestra starting in 1966, and again when it was revived in 1973. In 1969, he helped found Free Music Productions (FMP), the important record and concert producers based in Berlin, and he has continued to work with FMP ever since. He has worked with most of the major players in European free improvised music, as well as African-American free-jazz figures like Bill Dixon, Charles Gayle, Andrew Cyrille, David S. Ware, Leo Smith, Fred Anderson and fellow bassist William Parker.

With trumpeter Smith and East German percussionist Günter Sommer, he had a trio that made two beautiful records for FMP, *Touch The Earth* and *Break The Shells*. He recorded the stellar *Three Wheels – Four Directions* (1992; Victo) with Sommer and trombonist Konrad Bauer, and the live trio date *Fred Anderson Trio* (1999; Okka Disk) with Chicago tenor legend Anderson and drummer Hamid Drake. An international, intermedia artist at heart, Kowald pursued multi-cultural ensemble improvising under the banner "Global Village" (playing with Sainkho Namtchylak, Zeena Parkins and Xiao Min Fen among others) and in 1998 released a lavish book/CD/video work documenting a year-long multidisciplinary project he undertook using his apartment in Wuppertal. Kowald was a powerhouse bassist, with a heavy, thick sound and massive arco style; his solo concerts were astoundingly rich and bountiful sonically (hear his outstanding lone venture *Was Da Ist* from 1995 on FMP) and he would often accompany himself on charmingly deep, multiphonic singing. [JC]

⊙ **Duos Europa/America/Japan** (1984–9; FMP). Released simultaneously with a three-LP set of additional material, this chronicles Kowald's ongoing encounters with players from many lands, from Greek clarinettist Floros Floridis to Japanese biwa expert Junko Handa to American vocalist Diamanda Galas (who sings without effects).

Diana Krall

Piano, vocals.

b. Nanaimo, Canada, 16 Nov 1964.

One of the most high-profile of new jazz arrivals, Krall came from a musical family and studied piano at school before winning a scholarship to Berklee College in Boston, and later playing in Canada again, where associates included Ray Brown, Jeff Hamilton and (following temporary relocation to Los Angeles) Jimmy Rowles. At this point in her career Krall developed her singing talents, at first tentatively, but following work in Toronto (with regular returns to the USA) she began to attract wider attention and by the mid-1990s was achieving a premier reputation as both singer-pianist and leader of her own trio (completed at this point by Russell Malone (guitar) and Paul Keller (bass)). A regular association with producer Tommy LiPuma produced fruitful results on record including the 1997 album *Love Scenes*, which attests to Krall's continued artistic development. An accessible performer whose easy, regularly sexy contralto and rooted piano style confirm a sound base in jazz traditions, her work at one stage was strongly inspired by the trio concept of Nat Cole, but it has continued to develop – amid high-powered and glamorous marketing – to unqualified approval from the international jazz scene. [DF]

⊙ **Love Scenes** (1997; Impulse!). With Russell Malone and Christian McBride (bass), an effortless exposition of standards and niceties including "Garden In The Rain", "Gentle Rain" and eleven more.

Carl Kress

Guitar.

b. Newark, New Jersey, 20 Oct 1907; d. 10 June 1965.

A brilliant guitarist whose name is synonymous with the art of chorded guitar solos, Kress was discovered when, at the instigation of Bill Challis, he subbed at short notice for Eddie Lang on a Paul Whiteman recording date. From then on he was a New York studio habitué, and recorded with Beiderbecke and Trumbauer on a Chicago Loopers session (with most of the best of the rest of the white studio fraternity, from Red Nichols to the Dorseys). By the 1930s he was rich enough to go into partnership with Joe Helbock as co-owner of the Onyx Club on 52nd Street at the height of its success (the partnership was later dissolved after a quarrel). Kress's guitar duets, recorded with such kindred spirits as Eddie Lang and Dick McDonough during the 1930s, are classics, and he remained a busy studio man until the 1960s, working for radio and TV (including the Garry Moore programme), and duetting with a later partner, George Barnes, until his death.

Like many of his guitarist contemporaries (including his pupil George Van Eps), Kress played banjo first, and he continued to retain banjo tuning on the guitar's top four strings. He played banjo with Clarence Hutchenrider's trio in 1960, recording albums which were later to fetch collectors' prices. His wife was singer Helen Carroll, whom he backed regularly (with the Merry Macs). [DF]

⊙ **Pioneers Of Jazz Guitar 1927-39** (Retrieval) An invaluable release (Ellis/Davies) which documents important titles by Kress including two duets with Eddie Lang, four with Dick McDonough and six solos including his fascinating three-part "Afterthoughts".

Volker Kriegel

Guitar, composer.

b. Darmstadt, Germany, 24 Dec 1943; d. 14 June 2003.

Kriegel, who was self-taught, began on guitar at fifteen. At eighteen he formed his own trio, which in 1963 was voted Best Band at the German Amateur jazz festival, Kriegel getting the Best Soloist award. While at Frankfurt University he became involved with the scene centred on the Frankfurt Jazzkeller, which included Albert and Emil Mangelsdorff and bassist Peter Trunk.

In 1968 Kriegel joined the US vibraphonist Dave Pike in the Dave Pike Set, with drummer Peter Baumeister and Austrian bassist Hans Rettenbacher; the immediate success of the group led Kriegel to abandon his studies for music. The group played concerts and festivals throughout Europe and twice toured extensively in South and Central America (1971 and 1973) for the Goethe Institute, with Eberhard Weber on bass for the second tour. Pike then returned to the USA, and in late 1973 Kriegel formed his own band, Spectrum, with Weber, Rainer Brüninghaus (keyboards), and Joe Nay (drums). In 1976 Weber left to concentrate on his own band, Colours, taking Brüninghaus with him. Kriegel formed an entirely fresh band called the Mild Maniac Orchestra, with very young and virtually unknown musicians including Hans Peter Stroer (bass guitar) and Thomas Bettermann (keyboards). The group began as a quartet but eventually became a sextet with the addition of percussion and saxophone, and as such it continued into the mid-1980s.

In 1975 Kriegel was a founder member of the United Jazz and Rock Ensemble, and in 1977, with Wolfgang Dauner, Mangelsdorff, Ack Van Rooyen and Werner Schretzmeier, he co-founded Mood Records. With Spectrum he toured North Africa in 1974 and did his third tour of Brazil in 1975, spending one month teaching at the Goethe Institute in Salvador, Bahia. With the Mild Maniac Orchestra he has toured widely in Germany, played at Montreux in 1977, and in 1979, augmenting the group with Uli Beckerhoff (trumpet) and Wolfgang Engstfeld (tenor saxophone), he did a two-month tour in Africa for the Goethe Institute. He has also worked as a sideman for other leaders including Klaus Doldinger and Peter Herbolzheimer. With the United Jazz and Rock Ensemble he has played festivals all over Europe.

Kriegel was also an established cartoonist with work published regularly in German papers and magazines, the author of two books (*Der Rock "n" Roll König* and *Hallo*, both published in 1982) and a regular radio broadcaster presenting analytical programmes on music. In 1980 he completed an animated cartoon film (*Der Falschspieler*) which was shown in many countries and won a prize at a Los Angeles film festival, and he has also directed two long TV documentary films about music. In the late 1980s he wrote and recorded the music for a series of historical programmes on German television H.R.

Kriegel's work was permeated with influences from rock, pop and ethnic music, as well as jazz. His groups played jazz-rock with a rare lightness of touch, and his music combined an often very subtle harmonic sense with great rhythmic deftness and invention. In his ballads there was a brooding romantic strain, while his uptempo pieces could express unbridled joy. He was a prolific composer and has also written much music for TV programmes and animated films.

He continued to play live until 2002, and died of a heart attack the following year. Gaines wrote of him: "Wit, consummate grace, humanity, these are the hallmarks of Kriegel's style in all his multifarious activities." [IC]

⊙ **Schöne Aussichten** (1983; Mood); **Palazzo Blue** (1987; Mood). These are perfect examples of two sides of Kriegel's work. The earlier has eight short tracks – all between about four and six minutes – with composition and improvisation in fine balance. The later album has four long tracks which move through several stages and have longer solos. The music is poetic and evocative jazz-rock with rich harmonies and sonorities, subtle rhythms and a kaleidoscope of human moods.

Karin Krog

Vocals.

b. Oslo, Norway, 15 May 1937.

Krog had private lessons with Anne Brown (Bess in the first *Porgy And Bess*). She began to appear in Oslo and Stockholm in the early 1960s with Jon Christensen, Jan Garbarek and Arild Andersen, and in 1964 she performed at the Antibes jazz festival. She played and recorded with the Don Ellis orchestra and the Clare Fischer trio in the USA in 1967 and toured Japan in 1970 with a group of European poll-winners which included Albert Mangelsdorff, John Surman and Jean-Luc Ponty. She has often toured in the USA. She did a world tour in 1975, and performed at the first Indian Jazz Yatra in 1978. She has also appeared throughout Europe at festivals and on radio and TV. In 1974 she took a course in TV production and has since produced a number of jazz programmes for Norwegian TV. Between 1965–83, she won several prizes and awards in the USA and Norway. Her recordings with Dexter Gordon (*Some Other Spring*, 1971) and with Archie Shepp were both voted jazz vocal record of their respective year in Japan.

STUART NICHOLSON

Karin Krog

Karin Krog has developed into one of Europe's most accomplished and original singers. Since 1978 she has often concentrated on duo work with Bengt Hallberg, Red Mitchell and John Surman. In 1985, she and Surman toured Australia, and they have continued subsequently to tour internationally. In 2003 she released a new album with the Steve Kuhn trio, *Where You At?*, and has also collaborated with young electronic jazzer Mathew Herbert. [IC]

Karin Krog

⊙ **Gershwin With Karin Krog** (1974–89; Meantime). Krog sings Gershwin superbly – both the torch songs and the swingers.

Karin Krog with Archie Shepp

⊙ **Hi-Fly** (1976; Meantime). Krog is impressive with Shepp, surviving a sometimes overbearing context and making an exquisite job of Carla Bley's "Sing Me Softly Of The Blues", for which Krog wrote her own lyrics.

Karin Krog with John Surman

⊙ **Freestyle** (1985–6; Odin). Krog is at her most adventurous with her longtime companion John Surman, who's playing saxophone, synthesizer and percussion here, aided and abetted by oboist Brynjar Hoff. The electronics and overdubbing create some strikingly unusual soundscapes, and they perform some pretty offbeat compositions by Scandinavian composers.

Krog, Drew, Ørsted Pedersen and Riel

⊙ **Something Borrowed ...Something New** (1989; Meantime). *Something Borrowed* is a delight. The trio – Kenny Drew, Niels-Henning Ørsted Pedersen and Alex Riel – is a marvellous working unit with which Krog seems relaxed but fired up as if working in a club. The thirteen pieces are all fairly short and mingle standards with ballads in an exquisite bout of straight jazz singing.

Gene Krupa

Drums.

b. Chicago, 15 Jan 1909; d. 16 Oct 1973.

Gene Krupa's first record, made in 1927 with the McKenzie-Condon Chicagoans, was a groundbreaker: "I'm afraid Krupa's bass-drum and those tom-toms will knock the needle off the wax", said producer Tommy Rockwell. In December 1934 Krupa joined Benny Goodman and became a riveting central figure, whose innovatory drumnastics were dangerously likely to steal the limelight from his leader. "Gene was as magnetic as a movie-star", says Anita O'Day, "filled with wild exuberance as his raven-coloured hair, flashing brown eyes and black suit contrasted with the snow-white marine pearl drums around him." His image caused concern among middle-class Americans. "He's much more normal at home!" promised a caption to his picture in Timme Rosenkrantz's 1939 Swing Album.

In 1938 an onstage fracas between Goodman and Krupa temporarily ended their partnership, and Krupa formed his own band for an April debut at Atlantic City's Steel Pier. Soon after, following a drubbing from Jimmie Lunceford's orchestra, he augmented with Anita O'Day and trumpeter Roy Eldridge, who became two vital features of his show. Fascinated by African percussion, Krupa tried featuring every band member playing tom-toms in sectionally arranged cross-rhythms: the memory of these experiments was to endear Krupa to modern drummers such as Max Roach. In 1943, an international star on record and in films, Krupa was arrested, ostensibly for employing an underage bandboy, and briefly jailed (society's correction, perhaps, for his larger-than-life image), but he was back with Goodman for an emotional reunion in September 1943, on which he played like a king, got a standing ovation, and cried. After Goodman he worked briefly with Tommy Dorsey's band, then re-formed his own for a second successful run from 1944, using new arrangers, including Eddie Finckel, Gerry Mulligan and George Williams, and young bop soloists such as Don Fagerquist, Lennie Hambro and Frank Rehak.

drummer
man
GENE KRUPA BIG BAND
featuring Anita O'Day • Roy Eldridge
Verve

Gradually, however, the modern jazz revolution began to make Krupa's style sound inflexible and four-square, a problem that recurred when, after 1951, he formed a trio with pianist Dave McKenna and saxophonist Charlie Ventura: their attempts to re-create the excitement of Benny Goodman's quartet of fifteen years before sounded contrived and ran at odds with the "cool school". From 1954 Krupa ran a drum school with Cozy Cole in New York and in 1959 the Hollywood film *Drum Crazy: The Gene Krupa Story* appeared. In 1960 he had his first heart attack, but he continued leading his own quartet and playing reunions with Benny Goodman until 1967, when he decided to take life more easily. Their last reunion was in 1973, the year of Krupa's death. Sadly, a fire destroyed his houseful of memorabilia shortly before he died.

In three ways at least Krupa was lucky in his career: he was born at the right time; he was a natural performer (unlike, say, Dave Tough, a contemporary of equal talents); and he was white – black showman contemporaries such as Sid Catlett were never allowed the career opportunities that Krupa had. Musically his influence was colossal: "I succeeded in doing two things", he summed up later. "I made the drummer a high-priced guy, and I was able to project enough so that people were drawn to jazz." [DF]

⊙ **Gene Krupa 1935–8/1938/1939/1939–40/1940 Vols. 1, 2 & 3** (Classics). Krupa's formative years including small-group sides made while he was with Goodman, but not – of course – those with Goodman himself. From 1938 Krupa led his own big band, regularly producing substantial music (*Symphony In Riffs* (1939)), but his greatest years were later with Eldridge and Anita O'Day.

⊙ **The Gene Krupa Story** (1936–47; Proper Records). Impressive and reasonably priced four-CD set spanning 1936–47, containing almost all of Krupa's major self-led recordings from small group to big band, spanning the eras from swing to bop, and gloriously starring cornerpersons Anita O'Day and Roy Eldridge amid other delights. Vol. 4 has valuable live performances and transcriptions. Produced by Joop Visser.

⊙ **Drummin' Man** (1938–47; Charly). Worthy reissue of an old vinyl set on 2 CDs containing most (though not quite all) of the Krupa big band classics.

⊙ **Uptown** (1941–9; CBS). Now deleted but well worth searching for; his definitive set has all the Krupa/Roy Eldridge/Anita O'Day triumphs ("Let Me Off Uptown", "Walls Keep Talkin'", etc) plus one unissued side ("Barrelhouse Bessie From Basin Street") and later tracks with underrated O'Day successor Delores Hawkins including "Bebop Boogie".

Compact Jazz: Gene Krupa (1953–8; Verve). A useful selection concentrating, for all but four tracks, on Krupa's many fine small-group sides from the 1950s; Charlie Shavers, Willie Smith, Bill Harris and JATP alumni are all represented, as is Krupa's regular partnership with reedman Eddie Shu.

Drummer Man (1956; Verve). One of the few "remake" sessions where the results were comparable (and arguably better) than the originals; Eldridge and O'Day back together again for their hits, with Roy in particularly sparkling form throughout.

➤➤ **Benny Goodman** *(The Carnegie Hall Concert).*

Gunther Kuermayr

Piano, composer.

b. Linz, Austria, 8 June 1967.

Although he studied classical piano from the age of seven, Gunther Kuermayr was strongly influenced by Keith Jarrett, Bill Evans, Chick Corea and Herbie Hancock while studying at Graz's Hochschule für Musik und darstellende Kunst. After a spell as jazz piano tutor at the Prayner Konservatorium in Vienna, Kuermayr attended the Berklee College of Music – where he studied under Laszlo Gardony, Ray Santisi and Herb Pomeroy – graduating in 1996 with a diploma in professional music. The following year, he moved to London, where he has worked with many of the capital's musicians and singers, including Holly Penfield, Sheena Davies, Andy Hamill, Caroline Taylor, Francesca Payne and Iain Dixon. Kuermayr has performed, solo and with both small groups and big bands, all over Europe and America, and also in Egypt and Kyrgyzstan. His wife, Chinara Sharshenova – a violinist and komuz player with whom Kuermayr frequently plays as a duo – hails from this last country, and composes all the music the duo play, a mix of Kyrgyz folk and classical music. Kuermayr also leads his own quartet, which features tenor/soprano player Ian Ritchie and concentrates on Kuermayr originals and standards. His compositions include a nuptial mass for piano trio and numerous works for solo piano and groups of various sizes, and he has recorded with Sharshenova, Penfield and tenor player Jerry Bergonzi (*What I'm Doing Now ... Must Be Done!*, 1994, X-Records; *The Window* – see below). [CP]

The Window (1998; A-Records). Packed with neat, airy themes written by Kuermayr, impeccably played by the mellifluous, lucid leader plus Jerry Bergonzi on tenor and soprano, Johan Sievert (electric basses) and drummer Marc Gratama, a fine introduction to Kuermayr, both as soloist and composer.

Joachim Kuhn

Piano, composer, alto saxophone.

b. Leipzig, Germany, 15 March 1944.

Joachim, the brother of clarinettist Rolf Kuhn, studied classical piano and composition privately from 1949–61, playing classical concerts throughout that period, then became a professional jazz pianist. From 1962–6 he led his own trio and from 1966–9 co-led a quartet with his brother in Hamburg. He spent the years 1969–71 with his own group in Paris. In the early-70s he was with the Jean-Luc Ponty Experience, then co-led a group with Eje Thelin. With Association PC, he went on to tour Asia, North Africa, Portugal and Spain.

In the 1980s he was also a member of the Tony Oxley quintet, with Enrico Rava, Gerd Dudek and Ali Haurand. In 1994–5 Kuhn collaborated with Mike Gibbs in a huge project with the Hanover Radio Philharmonic Orchestra, the results of which came out on an album called *Europeana Jazzphony No. 1*. With Kuhn as the main soloist, Gibbs chose and orchestrated thirteen European folk songs for symphony orchestra and Kuhn's jazz trio. Kuhn said: "I liked the idea from the start, even though it was a departure from the musical area in which I normally work. But the discipline involved in following the orchestral arrangements was, in fact, a creative element ... It was also a great advantage to be able to work with Jean-François Jenny-Clark. He has been my bass player for 29 years, but he still does things which surprise me!" [IC]

Joachim Kuhn, Jean-François Jenny-Clark and Daniel Humair

From Time To Time Free (1988; CMP). Joachim Kuhn's superb trio with Jenny-Clark and Humair was the backbone of his performing life for almost thirty years, and provided the ideal setting for his improvising style.

Joachim Kuhn and Walter Quintus

Get Up Early (1991; Ambiance). *Get Up Early* is a strangely interesting "duo" album in that Kuhn plays while Quintus, using an electronic soundboard, transforms the sound of the piano.

➤➤ **Mike Gibbs** *(Europeana Jazzphony No. 1).*

Steve Kuhn

Keyboards, composer.

b. Brooklyn, New York, 24 March 1938.

Kuhn began piano lessons at the age of five. From 1959–63 he played with Kenny Dorham, John Coltrane and Stan Getz, and from 1964–6 was with the Art Farmer quartet and led his own occasional trio. From 1967–71 he lived in Stockholm, working with his own trio throughout Europe, and after 1971 he worked with his own quartet back in New York. He played many festivals with Getz and Farmer, including Newport and Monterey, and, with his own group, festivals in Europe. Kuhn is steeped in the whole jazz piano tradition and is a vastly accomplished player and a prolific composer. His favourites range from Fats Waller and Art Tatum to Bud Powell and Bill Evans, and other inspirations are Charlie Parker, John Coltrane and Miles Davis. [IC]

Oceans In The Sky (1989; Owl). One of a series of fine, tradition-oriented albums Kuhn made around the turn of the decade, this has Miroslav Vitous and Aldo Romano playing material by Kenny Dorham, Jobim, Ivan Lins (a non-bossa nova version of "The Island") and Brubeck.

➤➤ **Kenny Dorham** *(Jazz Contemporary).*

Sergey Kuryokhin

Piano, multi-instrumentalist, composer.

b. Murmansk, Russia, 16 June 1954; d. 9 July 1996.

Kuryokhin moved to Leningrad in 1971, where he showed a startling independence and non-conformism from an early age, being thrown out of both the Leningrad Conservatory and the Institute of Culture for failing to attend classes. He played in rock groups at school but changed course after hearing McCoy Tyner with John Coltrane on Voice Of America radio programmes. Despite this his music seems pianistically more in thrall to the classical tradition than to jazz. He also stated that his main inspirations were saxophonists including Anthony Braxton, Evan Parker and Russian associates Vladimir Chekasin and Anatoly Vapirov. He came to prominence playing with Vapirov in 1977, then worked with Chekasin and co-led the rock group Aquarium with Boris Grebenshikov. He also formed his own performing group, Crazy Music Orchestra, which, like all jazz in the USSR at that time, was subversive and anti-establishment. Kuryokhin used words and theatrical happenings as well as music to cock a snook at the authorities, and soon had a large, enthusiastic, clandestine audience. Tapes of his first record, a solo effort, *The Ways Of Freedom*, were smuggled out of Russia and released by Leo Records in 1981.

From 1984 on, he called all his ensembles Pop Mechanics, and his performances became increasingly anarchic, while he himself became an underground superstar. His albums, *Introduction In Pop Mechanics* and *Pop Mechanics No. 17,* may still be found on Leo. In 1989 he had one Dada-esque performance in Liverpool, UK, then toured America playing with different US musicians including John Zorn and Boz Scaggs. He was the first individual international star to emerge from the Russian jazz scene, and, as a composer, had collaborated with Alfred Schnittke and the Kronos string quartet.

Kuryokhin was a brilliant, flamboyant pianist, composer and musical stuntman, but he had lamented the advent of *glasnost* and *perestroika* which brought the end of official suppression of improvised music in the USSR. Under Communism his wild, theatrical opposition to the regime had enormous vitality, but the question was, could he live as intensely when not oppressed? Apparently not; he died at the age of 42 from cancer of the heart muscle, a very rare condition. [IC]

Some Combination Of Fingers And Passion (1991; Leo). This is a recording of Kuryokhin's solo piano concert in London. He is of course technically brilliant, but the title track, which is almost thirty minutes long, seems little more than a clever ragbag of classical echoes with a snippet of unfunky boogie-woogie thrown in towards the end. His tribute to Dave Brubeck, a series of variations on "Blue Rondo À La Turk" called "Blue Rondo À La Russ", is much more focused, but for all his pianism and subtle use of the pedals, Kuryokhin can't compensate for his lack of jazz feeling.

Sergey Kuryokhin (1999; Leo Records). This invaluable four-CD box-set has almost five hours of his music and extensive notes on the man, his music, his Russian background, and his hectic, but brief, life outside the USSR. It is also lavishly illustrated, and is a fascinating document of our times.

Billy Kyle

Piano, arranger.

b. Philadelphia, 14 July 1914; d. 23 Feb 1966.

Kyle studied piano from the age of eight and was a professional at eighteen, playing with bands such as Tiny Bradshaw's as well as (briefly) his own and Lucky Millinder's. He joined John Kirby's band in 1938, and when he left in 1942 after call-up the loss was a severe blow to the band. After demobilization he rejoined briefly, then worked in pit bands for Broadway shows (including *Guys And Dolls*), led his own small group and worked for Sy Oliver. In autumn 1953 Kyle joined Louis Armstrong's All Stars (replacing Earl Hines) and for the rest of his life was to remain the perfect band pianist. With the All Stars Kyle recorded classics such as *Plays W.C. Handy* and *Plays Fats*, appeared in the film *High Society* (1956) and weathered the touring until he died quite suddenly in Youngstown, Ohio, while on tour.

Although Billy Kyle never achieved the reputation of pianists such as Earl Hines and Teddy Wilson (whose approaches he somehow melded into one style), he was a brilliantly able pianist. "In my opinion", says Barney Bigard, "Billy was the best piano player Louis ever had." [DF]

Billy Kyle 1937-8/1939-46 (Classics). It's good that Classics have taken account of Kyle's pearl-scattering piano and these sets have outstanding sides including trio sides for Decca and four fine titles with Nat Gonella on holiday in America in l939.

➤➤ **Louis Armstrong** *(Louis Armstrong Plays W.C. Handy; Satch Plays Fats; California Concerts; Complete Decca Studio Recordings Of Louis Armstrong And The All Stars).*

Pat La Barbera

Tenor, soprano and alto saxophones, clarinet, flute.
b. Mt Morris, New York, 7 April 1944.

La Barbera first became known for being featured tenor sax soloist with the Buddy Rich band between 1967–73, doing TV shows and playing many international festivals, which he joined more or less straight from Berklee. But he also led his own groups at the same time, and worked with Louie Bellson and Woody Herman. After moving to Canada he joined Elvin Jones' band in 1975 and in 1979 toured Europe with him, appearing at the Messina (Sicily) festival. He recorded the album *From The Heart* in 2001 with his brother and long-term collaborator Joe, with George Cables on piano. John Coltrane's ballad playing has had a significant and oft-cited influence on La Barbera, both in his tone and in his choice of material. [IC]

⊙ **JMOG** (1987; Sackville). JMOG is an acronym for Jazz Men On The Go. La Barbera plays a swinging, highly competent set with quartet which includes brother Joe on drums. There's not a standard in sight, and the seven originals are all by La Barbera, bassist Neil Swainson or pianist Don Thompson.

➤➤ **Buddy Rich** *(Swingin' New Big Band/Keep the Customer Satisfied).*

Steve Lacy

Soprano saxophone, composer.
b. New York, 23 July 1934.

Lacy's whole career is a rare example of sustained artistic development, which has taken him from total immersion in traditional jazz in the early 1950s, through bebop to the free improvisation of the 1960s and the pluralism of the 1970s and 1980s. In 1958–9 he worked with Gil Evans, Mal Waldron and Jimmy Giuffre, and began studying Thelonious Monk's music, which would become a lifelong obsession of his. He played with Monk's quintet in 1960, then led his own quartet with Roswell Rudd (trombone), Dennis Charles (drums) and various bassists, mostly playing Monk tunes. In 1965 he played at Cafe Montmartre in Copenhagen with Kenny Drew, and at the Bologna festival in Italy, where he formed a quartet with Enrico Rava, and toured in South America for eight months. He then returned to New York, working for a year with a quintet which comprised Rava, Karl Berger, Kent Carter and Paul Motian, before moving to Europe in 1967 with his Swiss wife.

He spent three years in Rome working in various contexts, including Musica Elettronica Viva, which combined improvised contemporary music with electronics, and experimented with sound and language in music. (His various interests in composition date from this time, and he has since written settings for the works of poets such as Robert Creeley and Anna Akhmatova; works to accompany modern dance companies; and a commission in 1989 for the French Ministry of Culture to mark the bicentenary of the French Revolution.) In 1970 he moved to Paris, and in 1972 began playing solo soprano saxophone concerts, though alongside his small groups and occasional bigger ensembles. The later 1970s and 80s saw him playing intermittently with Derek Bailey and Evan Parker. At that time Lacy called his music "poly-free" because it was a mixed approach containing elements from the previous two decades – including abstract improvisation and more structured passages. At the beginning of the 1980s he started to assemble the group of musicians with whom he is still associated, including Bobby Few (piano), Steve Potts (saxophones), Jean-Jacques Avenel (bass) and Lacy's wife Irene Aebi (vocals, violin, cello). He has, however, continued to tour and to record solo sets, and to perform in duos, particularly with the pianist Mal Waldron.

His soprano sound is more rounded than Sidney Bechet's, with less vibrato, and less reedy than Coltrane's, but Lacy has explored the tonal resources of the instrument far more than the other two and his fresh, fleet lines have a stark beauty.Lee Jeske wrote: "His work is interspersed with growls and short stop-time phrases which sound like dialogue in a Beckett play ... Once in a while Lacy will hold a high, shrill squeak until it dissipates in the air. ... Sometimes his playing takes on a vaudevillian tone ... occasionally he uses his corduroyed leg as a mute to produce a cow-like mooing." Lacy's soprano-playing, in the late 1950s, inspired Coltrane to take up the instrument, and his quiet but steely integrity has made him a contemporary force throughout his career. [IC]

⊙ **Reflections** (1958; OJC). Lacy became obsessed early in his career with the work of Thelonious Monk, and this is his first recording devoted entirely to Monk compositions. The quartet includes the Monkishly wise pianist Mal Waldron, bassist Buell Neidlinger and Elvin Jones. Lacy is very exposed in this context and rises impressively to the occasion.

⊙ **Schooldays** (1963; hat Art). Another Monkish outing, this time with Roswell Rudd, bassist Henry Grimes and

ROBERT SERRA

Steve Lacy

drummer Dennis Charles. They play variations on Monk tunes, but only after faithfully stating the original themes. Trombonist Rudd, who has been disgracefully overlooked in latter years, produces some eloquent sonorities and linear comments on the proceedings.

⊙ **The Forest And The Zoo** (1966; ESP). 1966 was the heyday of free (abstract) jazz, and this consists of two freely improvised long tracks, but the music is greatly enriched by the cultural diversity of the quartet – Italian trumpeter Enrico Rava, and the great South African musicians Johnny Dyani and Louis Moholo on bass and drums.

⊙ **More Monk** (1989; Soul Note). This is a solo saxophone outing on several of Monk's most famous pieces, including the dazzling "Trinkle Tinkle", "Crepuscule With Nellie" and "Epistrophy". Lacy is at his most focused and incisive when paying homage to this master.

⊙ **Anthem** (1989; Novus). Lacy's nine-piece ensemble here includes trombone and two singers (one his wife Irene Aebi) in a series of orchestral performances both celebratory and elegiac.

⊙ **Five Facings** (1996; FMP). Lacy's soprano duets with five very different pianists: Marilyn Crispell, Ulrich Gumpert, Misha Mengelberg, Vladimir Miller and Fred Van Hove. The performances include four Lacy compositions and three of Monk's, proving that Lacy's is a steely talent which becomes more tempered and durable with time.

➤➤ **Gil Evans** *(Gil Evans And Ten).*

Tommy Ladnier

Trumpet.

b. Florenceville, Louisiana, 28 May 1900; d. 4 June 1939.

A childhood pupil of Bunk Johnson (with whom he played in several bands), Tommy Ladnier went to Chicago sometime before 1917, then worked briefly in trumpeter Charlie Creath's fine St Louis band (with Gene Sedric, a frequent colleague), but soon after was back in Chicago again. For the next four years he worked with Chicago stars such as Jimmie Noone and King Oliver (as replacement for Lee Collins who in turn had replaced Louis Armstrong), and in 1925 joined Sam Wooding's globetrotting orchestra. A year later he joined Fletcher Henderson in New York but in 1928 was back in Europe with Wooding, rooming with Doc Cheatham, and by this time drinking heavily.

Back in the USA in the Depression years, he opened a tailor's shop with Sidney Bechet and formed a great band with him, the New Orleans Feetwarmers, which played in 1932 to a half-empty Savoy Ballroom but recorded classic sides for Victor. This low period, combined with a broken marriage, sent Ladnier to heavier drinking but in 1938, thanks to the determined promotion of Hugues Panassié, he recorded again after years in retirement: classics such as "Really The Blues", "Jada" and "Comin' On With The Come On!" were the result. The plain and simple trumpet-playing of these sides is priceless, but it was Ladnier at reduced power, and he died soon after from a heart attack, while rooming with Mezz Mezzrow. Mezzrow made a collection for the funeral and on 9 June Ladnier was buried in Frederick Douglass Memorial Cemetery, Staten Island. "There's a guy who had a natural swing," said Buster Bailey. "Listen to the way he plays – the way he takes a melody and swings it. That's what I mean by swing!" [DF]

⊙ **Goose Pimples** (1926–39;Topaz). The best on-record collection of Ladnier, this set represents his early work with Fletcher Henderson and covers all his most important sides with the New Orleans Feetwarmers, plus Ladnier classics including "Really The Blues" and "If You See Me Comin'" with Mezzrow, Bechet et al. (If this issue is hard to find, ASV have a similar one with considerable duplication; it's *Steppin' on the Blues* and was released in 2000.)

➤➤ **Sidney Bechet** *(The Bluebird Sessions 1932–43).*

Scott LaFaro

Bass.

b. Newark, New Jersey, 3 April 1936; d. 6 July 1961.

Scott (Rocco) LaFaro took up the bass in 1953, when he began gigging in R&B groups. He toured with Buddy Morrow in 1955, and then worked in California with Chet Baker, Barney Kessel and Cal Tjader. After moving to New York, he played with Benny Goodman in 1959 and led his own group. He joined the Bill Evans trio, with which his name is still indelibly associated, from 1959–61, but he also recorded with Vic Feldman, Hampton Hawes, and made two albums with Ornette Coleman (replacing his close friend Charlie Haden). At the 1961 Newport festival he played with Stan Getz, shortly before his untimely death in a car accident.

LaFaro has been, for both better and worse, one of the most influential bassists since Jimmy Blanton. During his brief period of prominence he took for granted the new mobility that Mingus had demonstrated and, inspired in part by the style of Red Mitchell, constructed his solos entirely from the sort of boppish lines used by pianists and especially guitarists of the late 1950s. In his solo work with Evans he achieved a kind of parity with the pianist, audibly expanding the role of the bass in piano-led trios far beyond the then norm. To achieve this required a low action (ie with the strings lying close to the fingerboard, producing correspondingly lower volume and necessitating extra-close miking), which was contrary to standard practice at the time. But the facility gained in the upper range ensured that everyone would eventually follow the same path and that better amplification would become essential.

Less frequently noted is LaFaro's rhythm-playing in the same group which, in partnership with Paul Motian, used a number of different gradations between straightahead and almost-out-of-tempo. This approach, quite distinct from either Ornette Coleman's rhythm-section with Charlie Haden or John Coltrane's, made a considerable impact on Miles Davis's 1963 group and, through them, on nearly everyone else. [BP]

➤➤ **Bill Evans** *(Portrait In Jazz; Waltz For Debby);* **Hampton Hawes** *(For Real!).*

Guy Lafitte

Tenor saxophone.

b. St Gaudens, France, 12 Jan 1927; d. 10 July 1998.

Lafitte first became active in the Toulouse area, and then toured nationally with Big Bill Broonzy in 1951, Mezz Mezzrow in 1951–2, and Bill Coleman-Dicky Wells, also in 1952. He was based in Paris from 1954, leading his own groups regularly, and appeared with American musicians such as Emmett Berry and Lionel Hampton in the 1950s, Bill Coleman in 1973 and Wild Bill Davis in 1985. Lafitte was a notably forthright soloist, whose early allegiance to Coleman Hawkins was particularly noticeable in terms of his tone-quality. But his individuality matured with the passing years and his playing, sometimes spiced with the inflexions of R&B, seemed totally effortless. [BP]

⊙ **The Things We Did Last Summer** (1990; Black & Blue). Lafitte continues along the classic tenor trail of playing American standards such as the title track and "God Bless The Child", with Jacky Terrason on piano.

Bireli Lagrene

Guitar, electric bass.

b. Saverne, France, 4 Sept 1966.

A child prodigy on guitar, Lagrene has become known as an "infant Django" to a generation of jazz fans. Lagrene's background – he was born a Sinti gypsy – uncannily resembles Reinhardt's, and so does his prodigious talent: he took up guitar at four and, encouraged by his father Fiso Lagrene (a well-known guitarist of the 1930s), was playing jazz by the time he was seven. In his teens he began touring Europe with musicians such as Diz Disley and Denny Wright, and after his first album, *Routes To Django* (1980), he became a regular at festivals, worked with Benny Carter, Benny Goodman and Stephane Grappelli, and toured with Jaco Pastorius (1986). On record and in live performance he has continued to develop his faultless and spectacular style, which takes in contemporary musical trends as much as it harks back to Reinhardt. [DF]

⊙ **Routes To Django** (1980; Jazzpoint). Lagrene's first album – a spectacular debut in concert.

⊙ **Stuttgart Aria** (1986; Jazzpoint). Lagrene's on-record meeting with Jaco Pastorius, an artist from an era quite different from Django's. This album of jazz fusion demonstrates perfectly that Lagrene had evolved into a gifted multistylist by the tender age of twenty.

⊙ **Standards** (1992; Blue Note). This set with bassist Niels Henning Ørsted Pedersen might be a return to old territory, but it shows off Lagrene's awesome technique and exuberant imagination.

Cleo Laine

Vocals.

b. Southall, Middlesex, UK, 27 Oct 1927.

After singing semi-professionally, Cleo Laine (Clementina Campbell) worked with the Johnny Dankworth Seven and big band from 1951–7. After marriage to Dankworth she continued to make guest appearances with the band, but was mainly involved in various stage shows, such as *The Seven Deadly Sins* by Kurt Weill, *Show Boat* and *Colette* (co-written by Dankworth), as well as taking straight acting roles. Since 1972 she has undertaken many successful tours of the USA, including regular appearances at Carnegie Hall and New York's Blue Note. Laine's performances since then have aimed for the middle-of-the-road audience, although a 1995 release featured her with the posthumous Duke Ellington band. Her extraordinarily wide vocal range is easily admired, but, especially in her more intimate recordings, the sensitivity and phraseology still derive directly from her love of jazz. One of the first jazz-related personalities to be so honoured, Laine was awarded the OBE in 1979 and was made a Dame in 1997. Her autobiography was published in 1994. [BP]

Jazz (1991; RCA). Abetted by Dankworth, her musical director on all her album projects, Laine addresses a suitable repertoire of standards, with guest appearances by such old friends as Clark Terry, Gerry Mulligan and Jane Ira Bloom.

Papa Jack Laine

Drums, alto horn, leader.

b. New Orleans, 21 Sept 1873; d. 1 June 1966.

Born at the dawn of jazz, George Vital Laine – called "Papa Jack" because he was a father figure to dozens of young white New Orleans jazzmen – formed his own ragtime band in 1888 and soon after was leading his Reliance Brass Bands. Most of the great names of early white jazz (Nick La Rocca and Tom Brown are two famous examples) worked with one of Laine's bands, as did some of the best "Creoles of colour", such as clarinettist Achille Baquet. The demand for Laine's services was intense, and for a long time he exercised a monopoly in supplying music to white upper-class New Orleans society and all over the neighbouring Gulf Coast states. Playing ragtime by ear, Laine's bands continued their successful spell until 1917 when he retired from music, but during the revival of the 1940s and 1950s he was again a familiar and revered figure. Records of Papa Laine's Children were reissued on various labels in the 1950s. [DF]

Rick Laird

Double bass, bass guitar.

b. Dublin, Ireland, 5 Feb 1941.

Laird's family moved from Ireland to Auckland, New Zealand, where he began playing bass in 1959. He moved to Australia, and played with Mike Nock and others, then came to London in the early 1960s, studying at the Guildhall School of Music and working with John Dankworth, Tubby Hayes, Ronnie Scott and others. In 1966 he emigrated to the USA, studying at Berklee and playing with Charlie Mariano, Phil Woods and Zoot Sims, and touring with Buddy Rich for eighteen months. From 1971–3 he was with John McLaughlin's first Mahavishnu Orchestra. In the later 1970s he freelanced in New York with John Abercrombie, Nock and many others, and in the 1980s worked with Chuck Wayne and a group called Timepiece,whilst teaching in New York. Although the double bass was his first love – his main influences are Ray Brown, Paul Chambers and Scott LaFaro – it was on bass guitar that he made the first three trailblazing albums with the Mahavishnu Orchestra. He has written one book: *Improvising Jazz Bass* (Amsco; 1980). [IC]

➤➤ **John McLaughlin** *(The Inner Mounting Flame; Birds Of Fire).*

Laka Daisical

Piano, vocals.

b. Oxford, UK, 8 Jan 1953.

Laka Daisical (the stage name of Dorota Koc), began piano lessons aged three, and studied the cello for four years; she also played timpani in her school orchestra. From 1972–84 she played with various pop groups, funk bands, small groups and big bands; in 1982 she joined the Guest Stars, an all-women fusion group (she also organized the first British Women's jazz festival that year) ; and from 1983–5 she worked with the Annie Whitehead band. In 1984 the Guest Stars' first album was released to high acclaim in the UK; in September they toured the US East Coast, and in December did a short UK tour. Koe remains a regular collaborator (both live and on record) with Annie Whitehead and Kate Westbrook. [IC]

Oliver Lake

Alto saxophone, composer, flute.

b. Marianna, Arkansas, 14 Sept 1942.

Lake was raised in St Louis, and he first learned percussion, before starting to play alto saxophone in 1960. In the later 60s he was involved with BAG (Black Artists Group), the St Louis equivalent of Chicago's AACM. He played in Paris in the early 1970s and in 1974 he moved to New York. In 1977 he was a co-founder of the World Saxophone Quartet, with whom he has remained, though he has continued to record as leader. Lake is steeped in the blues and the black American music tradition, and he's equally at home with funk or free jazz. An admirer of Eric Dolphy, he has something of the late great reedman's plasticity and subtlety, an influence acknowledged on the quintet recording *Dedicated to Dolphy* (Black Saint; 1996). [IC]

Zaki (1979; hat Art). The Lake trio with guitar and drums at the 1979 Willisau jazz festival. Freedom reigns supreme.

Prophet (1980; Black Saint). Lake with conventional jazz quintet – trumpet, saxophone, piano, bass and drums – playing unconventional music, including a couple of Dolphy's best compositions, "Hat and Beard" and "Something Sweet, Something Tender".

Compilation (1982–8; Gramavision). This is a useful anthology drawn from *Gallery* (with the *Prophet* quintet plus a second trumpet and pianist Geri Allen) and two now unavailable albums, *Impala* and *Otherside*.

➤➤ **World Saxophone Quartet** *(WSQ; Dances And Ballads).*

Nappy Lamare

Guitar, banjo, vocals.

b. New Orleans, 14 June 1907; d. 9 May 1988.

Nappy (Hilton Napoleon) Lamare began in New Orleans, where he played banjo in bands led by

Sharkey Bonano, Monk Hazel and Johnny Wiggs, among others, and toured with Johnny Bayersdorffer and Billy Lustig before joining Ben Pollack's band – a clearing-house for talent – in 1930. Five years later, Nappy (the nickname supposedly came from a childhood habit of oversleeping – though having the middle-name Napoleon just might have something to do with it!) joined Bob Crosby's band of "Pollack rebels" and for eight great years was an irreplaceable part of his rhythm-section. Then came a spell with Eddie Miller's reconstituted band, studio work, bands of his own, a year with Jimmy Dorsey (1948), and from 1947 part-ownership of a Los Angeles club, the 47, which lasted until 1951. In 1950, Lamare and his Straw Hat Strutters began a weekly TV show for KTLA; five years of successful touring followed, then Lamare co-led the Riverboat Dandies with Ray Bauduc, performing and recording high-entertainment Dixieland. From the early 1960s, following a bad car crash, he worked more sparingly but regularly, with Bauduc, clarinettist Joe Darensbourg, and for Crosby reunions. [DF]

➤➤ **Bob Crosby** *(Bob Crosby 1936–38).*

Donald Lambert

Piano.

b. Princeton, New Jersey, 1904; d. 8 May 1962.

One of the most underrated masters of stride piano, Donald "The Lamb" Lambert was taught by his mother and by the late 1920s had become a pillar of Harlem clubs and rent parties. For many years in the 1930s he worked at the Town House, Montclair, before another long residency at Wallace's Bar in East Orange, New Jersey. He made his first recordings in 1941 (for Bluebird), then sporadically to the end of his life; he preferred working in home-town venues, but appeared at the 1961 Newport jazz festival. [DF]

⊙ **1959–61** (1959–61; Storyville). A collection of live recordings, mostly from Wallace's, New Jersey, of Lambert playing solo late in life, but still demonstrating his Tatum-esque talents. Grieg's *Anitra's Dance* is played straight and melancholy, then in a vengefully swinging uptempo stride style – a moment of hilarious but beautiful bathos that was a favourite party trick of Lambert's.

Lambert, Hendricks and Ross

The greatest group practitioners of vocalese (the art of adding words to existing jazz solos), Lambert, Hendricks and Ross began after singer Dave Lambert (b. Boston, 19 June 1917; d. 3 Oct 1966) and Jon Hendricks assembled a group of singers to rehearse vocalese arrangements of Count Basie standards. The experiment was not working, so Annie Ross (already an established singer) was called in as vocal coach. Subsequently it was decided, by the artists and producer Creed Taylor, to multitrack the arrangements using a basic rhythm-section plus Lambert, Hendricks and Ross overdubbing (a comparatively early example of the technique), and *Sing A Song Of Basie* was recorded in New York over a four-month period in 1957. The album caused a sensation and launched Lambert, Hendricks and Ross as a top-line act that regularly broke audience records at clubs in New York, Chicago and on the West Coast, as well as producing a string of albums including *Sing Along With Basie* (1958), *The Swingers*, *The Hottest New Group In Jazz* (both 1959) and *Lambert, Hendricks And Ross Sing Ellington* (1960). In 1962 Annie Ross retired from the group and was replaced by Yolande Bavan, but after Bavan left in 1964 the group soon broke up. They are remembered as the leaders in their field: Annie Ross's lead-trumpet of a voice, combined with Lambert's sour-edged sound and Hendricks's warmer timbre and skills as a lyricist, made them unbeatable. [DF]

⊙ **Sing A Song Of Basie** (1957; Impulse!). The great sessions that inaugurated LHR, accompanied by the rhythm-section of Nat Pierce, Freddy Green, Eddie Jones and Sonny Payne; masterpieces here include Hendricks's high-speed "Lil' Pony", Ross's languorous "Fiesta In Blue" and two medium-tempo beauties – "Down For The Count" and "Blues Backstage".

⊙ **Sing Along With Basie** (1958; EMI Roulette). This time, LHR are with the Basie band itself plus Joe Williams; highlights include "Shorty George", "Rusty Dusty Blues" and "Goin' To Chicago" with its definitive opening choruses by Hendricks.

⊙ **The Hottest New Group In Jazz** (1959–62; Columbia). Very good value, three LPs on two CDs under one title. Included are the title album (definitive with "Charleston Alley", "Bijou" and more) plus *LHR Sing Ellington* (later but important) and a lesser-known collection *High Flying* – all with the Ike Isaacs trio.

⊙ **Swinging Till The Girls Come Home** (1962–3; RCA Bluebird). With Yolande Bavan's attractively deadpan voice in place of Ross, this set has the very funny "Doodlin'" and fourteen more tracks; guest spots by Clark Terry, Coleman Hawkins, Pony Poindexter and others.

Niels Lan Doky

Piano, composer.

b. Copenhagen, 3 Oct 1963.

The son of a Vietnamese doctor who played classical guitar, and a Danish mother who as a teenager had several hit records singing with Arne Lambert's orchestra, Niels Lan Doky was an award-winning guitarist between the ages of seven and eleven, but switched to piano, having caught the ragtime bug after watching the movie *The Sting*. His jazz interests soon blossomed, and he played his first paid gig in 1976 and began working in Denmark with Thad Jones at 15. Two years later, encouraged by Jones, Lan Doky left for the USA to attend Berklee, graduating in 1984 having received the Oscar Peterson Jazz Masters Award in 1983 and the Boston Jazz Society Achievement Award a year later. Settling in New York, he played with Ray Barretto and Thad Jones, among others, before making his recorded debut as a leader, *Here Or There* (Storyville; 1986), with a trio comprising his most famous jazz compatriot, Niels-Henning Ørsted Pedersen, and drummer Alvin Queen. Half a dozen Storyville albums followed in swift succession, plus a session with John Scofield, Randy Brecker, Bob Berg, brother Christian on bass and Adam Nussbaum on drums (*Dreams*, 1989; Milestone), followed by a second album for the label with an enlarged personnel, *Friendship*, in 1990. The Lan Doky Brothers were signed to Blue Note in the mid-1990s, and produced a couple of albums with stellar casts blending jazz and pop with variable results. In 1998, Niels Lan Doky made a poppy, eponymous album for Verve (see below), but by dividing his time between homes in New York and Paris – not to mention drawing on his native city's scene – he has kept his live sound fresh, collaborating with musicians from widely varying musical traditions, such as the violinist Didier Lockwood, including a number from his father's country. [CP]

⊙ **Niels Lan Doky** (1998; Verve). Glossy production and pop material (Eric Clapton's "Tears In Heaven", Peter Gabriel's "Sledgehammer", Prince's "Kiss", etc) almost overwhelm the torrential virtuosity of Lan Doky's jazz piano, which is probably better appreciated in the more jazz-oriented material available on Storyville.

Harold Land

Tenor saxophone, flute.

b. Houston, Texas, 18 Feb 1928; ; d. 27 July 2001.

Land was brought up from the age of five in San Diego, California. He worked there with trumpeter Froebel Bingham, whose group he used on his own first recording in 1949. After moving to Los Angeles in 1954, he toured nationally with the Max Roach/Clifford Brown quintet. He was a regular member of the Curtis Counce quintet from 1956–8, the Gerald Wilson band from 1955 onwards, and Shorty Rogers's Giants in 1961. From 1961–2 he co-led his own quintet with Red Mitchell, doing some studio work and live backing of vocalists in the 1960s, as well as composing and arranging. He co-led a quintet with Bobby Hutcherson from 1969–71, recording several albums with changing rhythm sections. One of the group's pianists was Harold Land Jnr (b. 25 April 1950) who continued to work with his father thereafter. Land also toured Europe with the Timeless All-Stars and with Cedar Walton.

The tenor-playing Land first came to attention holding his own in the fast company of Roach and Brown, thanks to a thoughtful combination of interesting ideas and an insinuating tone. This somewhat undemonstrative approach was overtaken in the 1960s by a strong Coltrane influence, until he gradually began to achieve a satisfying balance between the two approaches. [BP]

⊙ **Harold In The Land Of Jazz** (1958; Contemporary/OJC). A minor classic with fine playing by all concerned: Rolf Ericson, Leroy Vinnegar and drummer Frank Butler, plus Carl Perkins, whose "Grooveyard" gave its name to one of the earlier issues of this music.

Steve Lane

Cornet, leader.

b. London, 7 Nov 1921.

Steve Lane's revivalist band, the Southern Stompers, have played around Britain's jazz clubs (and further afield) for more than thirty years, always presenting scholarly repertoire with a rare dedication to authenticity. His partnership in the VJM label, with John Wadley and Trevor Benwell, has produced classic reissues of historic jazz as well as regular new albums documenting the progress of his own band, renamed in 1985 the Red Hot Peppers. Into the twenty-first century Lane continues to produce revivalist jazz of delicate quality and stylistic precision. [DF]

Eddie Lang

Guitar.

b. Philadelphia, 25 Oct 1902; d. 26 March 1933.

Eddie Lang (Salvatore Massaro) began his career on violin at seven years old, then studied banjo and guitar, played his first duets with Joe Venuti in school, and in 1923 joined Venuti in pianist Bert Estlow's Atlantic City band. The following year he was with the Scranton Sirens (a hot band that featured the young Dorsey brothers, and trombonist Russ Morgan), then joined the Mound City Blue Blowers, with whom he toured the USA and played a season at London's Piccadilly Hotel. By 1925, back in the USA, he was in constant demand for session work: he had become the first of the guitar heroes (previously the guitar had been a rhythm instrument), and Lang's chiming rococo solo lines were super-fast and machine-accurate. Never a great reader, whenever he was faced with a complicated big-band arrangement Lang would listen once, then add his own part the second time round; he was also a skilful guitar duettist, recording classics with Carl Kress and (as "Blind Willie Dunn") with Lonnie Johnson.

In 1926 Lang worked with Joe Venuti's band and Roger Wolfe Kahn's society orchestra (two regular connections all his life); in the following year he toured with Jean Goldkette's band and, when it broke up in New York, joined Adrian Rollini's legendary (and short-lived) Club New Yorker band. In 1929 Lang and Venuti were teamed again in Paul Whiteman's orchestra, and from 1932, when Bing Crosby developed his solo career, Eddie Lang was his staff accompanist. (In spare hours Lang visited the pool halls – "he made more at pool than he did accompanying me," said Crosby.) In 1933 he recorded classic sides with Venuti as the Blue Five, including "Raggin' The Scale"; the same year, troubled with chronic throat problems, he underwent surgery to have his tonsils removed, and died of an embolism under the anaesthetic.

Inventor of the solo vocabulary for the guitar, Eddie Lang was, said Bing Crosby, "in the opinion of all the guitar players of his day, and many since, the greatest one of the craft that ever lived". Lang's partnership with violinist Joe Venuti set the standard for chamber jazz (indeed, Django Reinhardt and Stephane Grappelli were often dismissed as a country-style parody of Venuti-Lang), and Lang's plangent guitar – though temporarily superseded by the rise of electric guitar, and Charlie Christian, ten years on – is still regarded as being of central importance in jazz history. [DF]

⊙ **Joe Venuti And Eddie Lang Vols. 1 & 2** (1926–31; JSP). This excellent collection covers five years of Lang in duo, trio, quartet and quintet format, complete with alternate takes, recorded for three major companies. Remastering by John R.T. Davies (superb); notes by Nevil Skrimshire (likewise).

⊙ **The Quintessential Eddie Lang 1925–32** (Timeless). Undoubtedly the best (and beautifully mastered) Lang reissue currently available, with the Mound City Blue Blowers, Jean Goldkette, Ukelele Ike, Paul Whiteman, Lonnie Johnson, Louis Armstrong et. al.

Don Lanphere

Tenor and soprano saxophones.

b. Wenatchee, Washington, 26 June 1928; d. 9 Oct 2003.

Lanphere studied music at Northwestern University, Illinois, from 1945–7. He moved to New York at the age of nineteen, and made the first of two recordings with Fats Navarro in 1948, before playing with Woody Herman in 1949, Artie Shaw from 1949–50, and with Claude Thornhill, Charlie Barnet, Billy May and Sonny Dunham. He was arrested as a heroin user in 1951, and returned home to run the family music store. Apart from three years, including a period playing with Herb Pomeroy and with Herman again from 1959–61, which was followed by a further arrest, he remained there until the 1980s. His comeback albums, beginning in 1982, resulted in playing visits to New York and Kansas City (both in 1983) and to Europe in 1985.

Lanphere was impressed early on by Lester Young and Charlie Parker, his private recordings of whom have been issued on various labels. The great facility and interesting ideas of his own early work have grown considerably in recent performances, which display markedly unpredictable phrasing and a delightfully individual tone. [BP]

Don Lanphere and Larry Coryell

⊙ **Don Lanphere/Larry Coryell** (1990; Hep). One of a series of fine albums from his comeback years in which Lanphere performs with Seattle-based musicians, this has the advantage of an on-form guest appearance by Coryell.

Ellis Larkins

Piano.

b. Baltimore, Maryland, 15 May 1923; d. 29 Sept 2002.

Larkins's mother was a pianist, his father a violinist, and he was taught privately to a high standard. He made his debut with the Baltimore City Colored Orchestra at eleven, and was hailed as a prodigy. Graduation from the Peabody Conservatory and Juilliard School followed (a considerable achievement for a black musician at that time), and then Larkins began work as a jazz pianist with Billy Moore, Ed Hall and his own trio around New York, settling into a regular shuttle between the Village Vanguard and the Blue Angel that lasted twenty years. During this period he recorded classic duo albums with Ella Fitzgerald and Ruby Braff, and worked as accompanist for Fitzgerald and Helen Humes. During the 1960s he accompanied Joe Williams, Anita Ellis, Jane Harvey, Eartha Kitt, Georgia Gibbs and Harry Belafonte. In the 1970s he recorded for Chiaroscuro both solo and with Braff, and began regular club work at venues such as Gregory's, Michael's Pub, the Cookery and the Carnegie Hall Tavern. He returned to his old haunt, the Carnegie Tavern, in 1985, and was still working regularly into the 1990s. [DF]

⊙ **Concert In Argentina** (1974; Jazz Alliance). Recorded during a tour of South America, this concert by four solo pianists (Marian McPartland, Teddy Wilson and Earl Hines are the others) has four solo items clearly illustrating Larkins's unique sound and approach – pastel-brown, with interrogative lines and harmonies.

⊙ **Live At Maybeck Recital Hall Vol. 22** (1992; Concord). The best latterday illustration of Larkins the soloist; an extended concert in the extensive Maybeck series of piano recitals, this is a welcome portrait of a pianist whose work has remained (at least in Europe) one of the elusive pleasures of jazz.

Pete LaRoca

Drums.

b. New York, 7 April 1938.

LaRoca was born on the same day as Freddie Hubbard, and was equally precocious. He was recommended to Sonny Rollins when he was nineteen by Max Roach, and played with him until Rollins retired in 1959. He then played with Jackie McLean (from 1959–1961), the Tony Scott quartet in 1959 and the Slide Hampton octet from 1959–60 before becoming the first drummer of the John Coltrane quartet in 1960. He led his own group from 1961–2, and worked with the Art Farmer quartet in 1964–5, the Freddie Hubbard quintet in 1965, Mose Allison also in 1965 and the Charles Lloyd quartet in 1966. Finding gigs too sparse in the late 1960s, he began working as a lawyer under his "Anglo" name, Peter Sims. He then reappeared in the 1990s playing as well as ever, recording an album for Blue Note, and leading a sextet which in 1998 included Jimmy Owens, Don Braden and Steve Kuhn. His early work showed enormous promise and he was the first person to record a totally free-tempo drum solo (in May 1959, on the Jackie McLean album *New Soil*). His remarkably fluid backing of a very varied list of soloists is extremely impressive, and his return to music very encouraging. [BP]

⊙ **Basra** (1965; Blue Note). One of LaRoca's two 1960s albums as a leader (the other, *Turkish Women at the Bath*, with John Gilmore, has sometimes been issued as a Chick Corea album), this has Steve Kuhn and Steve Swallow, as on the Art Farmer album below, with Joe Henderson as the solitary horn on a lovely "Lazy Afternoon".

➤➤ **Art Farmer** *(Sing Me Softly Of The Blues)*.

Bill Laswell

Bass.

b. Salem, Illinois, 12 Feb 1955.

A prime exponent of the cut'n'paste aesthetic, with credits as bassist and/or producer on more than two hundred albums across an awesome variety of genres, Bill Laswell first came to prominence as the bassist in the avant-rock-jazz-punk-disco fusion band, Material. With Michael Beinhorn (keyboards), Fred Maher (drums), and Fred Frith (guitar), Material was the house band for New York's multicultural, hybridizing avant-garde. Their first LP, *Temporary Music* (1981), was a startling mixture of funk and punk whilst *Memory Serves* (1982), with guests Sonny Sharrock, Henry Threadgill and Billy Bang created the unholiest meeting of jazz and rock since Miles met McLaughlin. *One Down* (1983) was Material's finest moment. Combining the best of the jazz underground (Archie Shepp, Oliver Lake, Ronnie Drayton) with the best of New York's disco scene (Chic's Nile Rodgers and Tony Thompson, Bernard Fowler, Yogi Horton, Nona Hendryx, and Whitney Houston), it was a perfect evocation of the strange glamour of the Big Apple.

Laswell produced Herbie Hancock's brilliant *Future Shock* in 1983, which spawned the electro hit, "Rockit"; at the same time, as a member of Last Exit (with guitarist Sonny Sharrock, saxophonist Peter Brötzmann, and drummer Ronald Shannon Jackson) he churned out some of the most explosive music ever made – free jazz as nihilistic punk rock.

His appreciation of hip-hop and new technology, his willingness to jump across generic boundaries, and his identifiable sound made him a producer much in demand during the mid-80s. His best outside production was Sly And Robbie's *Rhythm Killers* (1987). By uniting the Jamaican rhythm-section with hip-hoppers Rammelzee and Grandmixer DST, percussionists Deng and Daniel Ponce, avantists Threadgill and Nicky Skopelitis, and funkateers Mudbone Cooper and Bootsy Collins, Laswell made an album that flattered his fusion/fission concept. Unfortunately, this became something of a Laswell blueprint, and on albums like Material's *The Third Power* (1991), the Axiom Funk all-star project *Funkcronomicon* (1995) and the Bahia Black project's *Ritual Beating System* (1992) Laswell's melting-pot groove failed to become more than the sum of its parts.

But Laswell didn't stop there. His interest in William Burroughs and poet Brion Gysin led him to Morocco's mystical trance music. His recordings of the musicians of Jajouka are both definitive documents of these musical styles, while *The Trance Of Seven Colors* (1994) is an intriguing pairing of saxophonist Pharoah Sanders and trance musician Maleem Mahmoud Gania. On his Axiom label Laswell has produced and released albums by co-conspirators past and present such as Jackson, Sharrock and Threadgill. His Subharmonic label is the home of his most out-there recordings – the best of these being *Execution Ground* (1994), the third album by Painkiller, his noise trio with saxophonist John Zorn and ex-Napalm Death and Scorn drummer Mick Harris, on which din-scapes were processed into an insect-ridden nightmare of treated sounds and backwards loops by co-conspirator Robert Musso.

Laswell leavens his prolific slew of ambient, dub and "world music" collaborations with occasional returns to unadulterated improv bass playing: in 1998 he recorded a duet album with Peter Brötzmann, and a kind of evolved, mature revision of the Painkiller blueprint (a quartet with Zorn, Fred Frith and thrash metal drummer Dave Lombardo) toured a powerful, thrilling, occasionally ponderous set in 2001.

Bill Laswell treats music as pure sound to be manipulated any which way, and funk is the key to his approach. When it fails, it's because his music becomes rhythm about rhythm, or funk that isn't funky. When it works it's because his ideas and his rhythms truly gel with each other. [JK]

⊙ **Deconstruction: The Celluloid Recordings** (1993; Restless). A collection of Laswell's 80s recordings with the wide-reaching Celluloid label. Moving from Afro-fusion to art-punk to conceptual hip-hop to bruising jazz massacres, this album provides a neat overview of Laswell's cut'n'paste artistry.

⊙ **Sacred System, Nagual Site** (1998; BMG/Wicklow). In this fascinating showcase of Laswell's influences and talents, he produces a meeting of jazzmen Dave Liebman and Graham Haynes with vocalists Gulam Mohamed Khan and Sussan Deyhim from the Sufi Qawwali tradition. Khan, Haynes and Laswell also composed some of the material, and Laswell plays eclectic bass, keyboards and percussion.

Yusef Lateef

Tenor saxophone, flutes, oboe; also percussion and other instruments.

b. Chattanooga, Tennessee, 9 Oct 1920.

Lateef, under his earlier name William Evans, went to school in Detroit, and moved to New York in 1946, where he worked with Lucky Millinder, Hot Lips Page and Roy Eldridge. He embraced Islam in the late 1940s and, after nearly a year with the Dizzy Gillespie band in 1949, he went to study at Wayne University, and led his own Detroit-based group from 1955–9, which made several albums for New York record labels. Returning to New York, he played with his own group; briefly with Charles Mingus in 1960 and 1961; and with percussionist Michael Olatunji from 1961–2. He then joined the Cannonball Adderley sextet, with which he worked from 1962–4. After 1964 he alternated between leading his own group and academic studies; he holds an MA and Doctorate in education and an associate professorship, and has published books of philosophy and short stories. In the 1980s he spent several years teaching in Nigeria, before returning to the USA to teach at the University of Massachusetts and Amherst College. Since retiring from academia, he has started his own record label and performed internationally in a duo with percussionist Adam Rudolph.

Lateef's use in the 1950s of first the flute, then the oboe and various "miscellaneous" instruments (including a 7-Up bottle) marks him as one of the earliest diversified talents. Though ultimately less dedicated to multi-instrumental excellence than Eric Dolphy or the generation that followed him, Yusef is certainly a brilliant flautist. The exotic aspects of his early work were a musical and ideological influence on many people, such as John Coltrane, who acknowledged him in 1960: "Yusef Lateef has been using [Eastern music] in his playing for some time." Interestingly, his tenor work has always retained the sound of straightahead blues-and-bebop, and indeed some of his late 1960s and 1970s albums emphasized this to the point of banality. But when his compositional flair comes into play, and binds together the various strands of his music, the results are extremely impressive. [BP]

Jazz Moods (1957; Savoy). Lateef's Detroit group with Curtis Fuller and Louis Hayes, in a programme of original material that involves pseudo-Oriental percussion, with the leader playing not only tenor and flute but the *arghul,* an Arabian double-reed clarinet.

Eastern Sounds (1961; Prestige/OJC). Not quite the album its title suggests, but an impressive quartet date which, as well as the Chinese clay flute and European oboe, features straightahead tenor on such tracks as "Don't Blame Me".

Live At Pep's (1964; Impulse!). Lateef's post-Adderley quintet, with trumpeter Richard Williams and New Orleans drummer James Black, has soulful oboe on a slow "See See Rider", funky flute on "Slippin' And Slidin'" and the Indian shenai on a boogaloo-style "Sister Mamie".

The African-American Epic Suite (1993; ACT). Sharing the same subject matter as Ellington's *Black, Brown And Beige*, this is also a moving work of substantial proportions, in which Lateef's 1990s quintet is heard with the WDR strings.

Jak Kilby

Yusuf Lateef

Christof Lauer

Tenor and soprano saxophones.

b. Melsungen, Germany, 25 May 1953.

Lauer started playing piano as a child, then studied violin at Dr Hoch's Conservatory in Frankfurt. In 1971 he started playing saxophone, studying at the Music High School in Graz, Austria, from 1972–4. He played with various jazz groups in Austria, then, back in Frankfurt in 1978, he became a member of the jazz ensemble of Frankfurt Radio. In 1982 he began teaching in the jazz department of Dr Hoch's Conservatory, and at the same time began playing with various bands including the Uli Beckerhoff group, Toto Blanke's Electric Circus, Joachim Kuhn quartet, United Jazz and Rock Ensemble (UJRE), Carla Bley band, Jasper van t'Hof-Alphonse Mouzon quartet, Volker Kriegel band and the Michel Portal quintet. He has also led his own bands, including a trio with Palle Danielsson and Billy Hart, and a quartet with Wolfgang Puschnig (reeds), Bob Stewart and drummer Thomas Alkier. In the mid-1990s, Lauer was playing with vocalist Maria Joao and his own trio with bassist Anthony Cox and Daniel Humair, and in 1994 became a regular member of the UJRE when Charlie Mariano left the band. He is also one of the main soloists with the Hamburg NDR Radio Orchestra.

Lauer is one of the most impressive European saxophonists to have emerged during the 80s. His technique, ear and harmonic sense are formidable, and he can handle virtually any tempo or mood. [IC]

Christof Lauer (1989; CMP); **Bluebells** (1992; CMP). The eponymous album with contemporary heavies Joachim Kuhn, Palle Danielsson and Peter Erskine demonstrates all Lauer's qualities and has four of his excellent and very diverse compositions. *Bluebells,* however, is a complete departure in that the line-up is two saxophones, tuba and drums (with Puschnig, Stewart and Alkier) and composition duties are shared, with one piece improvised by the quartet.

Fragile Network (1998; ACT). Lauer assembled a band and a half for this one – bassist Anthony Cox, drummer Gene Jackson, tuba and serpent virtuoso Michel Godard and wild-card guitarist Marc Ducret. On Lauer's "Flying Carpets" saxophone and tuba play the tricky theme in unison, as they also do in Godard's own piece "Vernasio", where he solos with great agility.

Chris Laurence

Double bass.

b. London, 6 Jan 1949.

Chris Laurence studied at the Royal Junior College of Music and the Guildhall School. He began playing in the later 1960s with many London-based musicians, including Frank Ricotti. In the 1970s he worked with the Mike Westbrook orchestra, John Taylor sextet and the Mike Pyne sextet, as well as with Kenny Wheeler's occasional big band and small groups. In the 1980s he also worked in trio format with Tony Oxley and Alan Skidmore, and with Oxley and Tony Coe.

Laurence is equally at home with European classical music and jazz and has always been active in both fields. During the 1980s he played second bass with the Academy of St Martin-in-the-Fields chamber orchestra, and from 1984 was a member of the London Bach Orchestra. He has been a member of John Surman's British quartet, with John Taylor and John Marshall, for several years now, touring internationally and playing festivals. Their album *Stranger than Fiction* is one of the most beautiful quartet recordings of the 1990s; in quality of execution and depth of feeling it approaches the work of Keith Jarrett's European quartet.

Laurence has recorded with many people, including Ricotti, Norma Winstone, John Taylor and Alan Skidmore (he played bass on *El Skid*, a fun, convivial Skidmore/ Elton Dean album of 2001). He is a virtuoso player who is massively dependable. [IC]

➤➤ **Tony Coe** *(Nutty On Willisau);* **John Surman** *(The Brass Project; Stranger Than Fiction).*

Cy Laurie

Clarinet, vocals, leader.

b. London, 20 April 1926; d. 18 April 2002..

Originally a Johnny Dodds disciple, Cy Laurie worked around the London jazz clubs with his quartet (featuring Les Jowett on trumpet and Fred Hunt on piano) and later his band, which in the 1950s enjoyed great success at their Windmill Street premises. The "Cy Laurie all-night raves" are still well remembered by greying British jazz aficionados, and the band's first-class publicity agent Les Perrin (who later worked for the Beatles) helped their records achieve best-selling status in jazz terms. "Cy's band attracted and held all of Humph's disappointed revivalist fans," points out George Melly, "and won the adherence of the self-styled beatniks too." Chris Barber's inexorable rise to fame eclipsed Laurie, however, and in 1960 he left music to study meditation in India. At the end of the decade he was back: he played regularly around the London scene, briefly joined the Blackbottom Stompers, formed a band to work in the Essex area and for a time led a quintet with saxophonist Eggy Ley. By the 1980s he had based himself in the Southend area, working with musicians such as Terry Pitts (trombone), Hugh Rainey (banjo) and Dennis Field (cornet). He continued bandleading and soloing on the British revivalist scene until his death in 2002. [DF]

Cy Laurie blows Blue Hot (1954-5; Lake). Possibly Laurie's best-remembered album, with one of his greatest bands including Al Fairweather (trumpet) and John Picard (trombone): definitive British revivalist jazz with Laurie's studious liner notes included.

Charlie LaVere

Piano, leader, vocals.

b. Salina, Kansas, 18 July 1910; d. 28 April 1983.

Charlie LaVere (Charles LaVere Johnson) is principally remembered for a set of irresistible recordings made with his Chicago Loopers, a studio group featuring Jack Teagarden, Billy May, Matty Matlock, George Van Eps, Floyd O'Brien and little-known cornettist Rico Vallese. The man behind these sessions was at the time one of Hollywood's busiest musicians, a studio regular who accompanied Bing Crosby (1939–47) and played on sessions for Frank Sinatra, having already worked with Teagarden, Wingy Manone and Paul Whiteman. A capable singer and fine composer, LaVere later played at Disneyland (1955–9) and with Bob Crosby, but his Chicago Loopers remain his seminal contribution to jazz history. [DF]

LaVere's Chicago Loopers (1944–50; Jump). Recorded in four sessions, these titles have become the definition of Dixieland perfection. The superbly arranged "Carolina In The Morning" and LaVere's own lovely "It's All In Your Mind" are highlights, but all sixteen tracks are essential listening.

Hubert Laws

Flute, composer, saxophone, guitar, piano.

b. Houston, Texas, 10 Nov 1939.

Hubert is the brother of saxophonist Ronnie Laws. His first professional job was at fifteen with the Jazz Crusaders, with whom he stayed until 1960, but he also played symphonic music during his teens. In the 1960s he played with Mongo Santamaria, Gunther Schuller's Orchestra USA,

Sergio Mendes, Lena Horne, Benny Golson, Jim Hall, James Moody, Clark Terry and many others. During the early 1970s he established an international reputation leading his own groups and touring worldwide. Laws was a member of the Metropolitan Opera Orchestra from 1968–73, and worked with the New York Philharmonic from 1971–4. He is a virtuoso player, equally at home with jazz and classical music. Laws has attempted to create jazz adaptations of some classical music compositions by Bach, Mozart, Debussy, Stravinsky, Ravel, Satie and others, and has also made many jazz-rock and fusion records. These days he frequently plays with like-minded musicians who share his interest in sophisticated arrangement and the hinterland between jazz improvisation and classical composition. [IC]

⊙ **The Laws of Jazz/Flute By Laws** (1964/6; Rhino/Atlantic). This CD combines two albums, the first featuring Laws with a rhythm-section, and the second with the backing of a big band. Both show what an excellent improviser he is and how versatile he is in handling different tempos and moods.

Ronnie Laws

Tenor saxophone.

b. Houston, Texas, 3 Oct 1950.

The younger brother of Hubert, Ronnie began on saxophone at twelve and then took up flute, studying at Texas Southern University. Inspired by David "Fathead" Newman, he moved to Los Angeles in 1971, working with Quincy Jones, Hugh Masekela, Kenny Burrell and Walter Bishop Jnr. He recorded with his brother and with Ramsey Lewis, and toured with Earth, Wind And Fire. Recording under his own name from 1975, he was first associated with disco-style funk, playing in a debased version of the "Texas tenor" style and enjoying success with his tune "Always There". However, since the 1990s he has turned his attention to a more anodyne music known on US radio as "smooth jazz". [BP]

⊙ **The Best Of Ronnie Laws** (1975–80; Blue Note). A compilation from five albums, the first three produced by the Crusaders' Wayne Henderson, and leading off with the inevitable "Always There".

Yank Lawson

Trumpet.

b. Trenton, Missouri, 3 May 1911; d. 18 Feb 1995.

Yank (John Rhea) Lawson took up the trumpet in his teens, played with college bands and worked his way round the South with Wingy Manone before joining the Ben Pollack band in 1933, replacing Sterling Bose. Two years later – following a disagreement over Pollack's determination to feature his girlfriend as singer – Lawson freelanced in New York and then joined Bob Crosby's orchestra, frequently leading their band-within-a-band, the Bobcats, for classic recordings. He left in 1938 after a financial dispute with Gil Rodin, Crosby's business manager, and moved to Tommy Dorsey, who often let his new sideman write his own cheque. This stay lasted a year, after which Lawson freelanced, worked briefly with Crosby again (1941), then with Benny Goodman. Thereafter he combined jazz with studio work in premier contexts including radio (from 1942) and as NBC staffman 1950-68. From 1950 Lawson's jazz trademarks – harmon-to-open muted technique, hectoring phrasing, a frank vibrato and a feeling for the blues that recalled King Oliver – were paraded on marvellous records by the Lawson-Haggart Jazz Band, at Crosby reunions, in jazz clubs (including Eddie Condon's 1963-6) and on tour. In 1968 Lawson joined The World's Greatest Jazz Band, where his driving creations sat perfectly back to back with the shifting lyricism of Billy Butterfield. In the 1980s he co-led the Lawson-Haggart band again, toured Europe as a soloist and played jazz festivals; up to his death he regularly led reunions of The World's Greatest Jazz Band (sometimes with Warren Vaché as co-lead trumpeter), as well as continuing with guest and touring commitments. Like Manny Klein and Pee Wee Erwin, Lawson was a player of enormous strength, versatility and trained orthodox technique; his trumpet typified the sound of Bob Crosby's Bobcats, and his contribution to a vast number of fine recordings marks him out as one of the great Dixieland trumpeters. [DF]

⊙ **Something Old, Something New, Something Borrowed, Something Blue** (1988; Audiophile). Yank as powerful as ever amid a Dixieland team of old friends – George Masso, Johnny Mince, Lou Stein, Bucky Pizzarelli, Bob Haggart and Nick Fatool.

⊙ **Singin' The Blues** (1990; Jazzology). A selection of blues and blues-related tunes with the old master in fine fettle, notably on "Singin' The Blues" and "Tin Roof Blues".

➤➤ **Bob Crosby** *(South Rampart Street Parade).*

Barbara Lea

Vocals.

b. Detroit, Michigan, 10 Apr 1929.

One of jazz's most underrated singers, Lea sang first with Detroit dance bands while still at school, before studying at Wellesley College, Harvard, where she sang with the college jazz band, the Crimson Stompers, as well as working as jazz DJ for WBS and critic for the *Wellesley News*. From there she worked Boston cocktail lounges and New Jersey clubs, before being "discovered" on Art Ford's talent show, *One Week Stand*. Immediately booked into Childs Paramount Restaurant in Times Square, she began radio and TV work, and produced two fine albums in the mid-1950s for Riverside and Prestige. Yet despite Eddie Condon's prediction that "she has nowhere to go but up", Lea's career was curtailed by the pop era, during which she did voice-overs, acted in stage productions and taught at the American Academy of Dramatic Arts. She began singing again in the 1970s (including PBS broadcasts) and thereafter was heard more regularly, singing with Loren Schoenberg's orchestra and recording with Dick Sudhalter and Ed Polcer, among others. She also began recording for Challenge Records, with pianist Keith Ingham, including admirable collections celebrating women songwriters and Noël Coward. Her devotion to the "Great American Songbook" continues to wow audiences internationally. [DF]

⊙ **Barbara Lea With The Johnny Windhurst Quintets** (1956; Fantasy/Prestige). Lea's first major recordings from 1955–6 with the near incomparable trumpet of Windhurst – essential listening on both counts.

⊙ **Lea/In Love** (1957; Fantasy/Prestige). Music of comparable value to the above with similarly exquisite selections ("Am I In Love", "Will I Find My Love Today"). Arrangements and solo contributions are by Dick Cary (alto horn), with more from the underrated Windhurst.

➤➤ **Ed Polcer** *(At The Atlanta Jazz Party);* **Dick Sudhalter** *(Getting Some Fun Out Of Life).*

Brian Leake

Piano, alto saxophone.

b. South Wales, 9 Nov 1934; d. 10 Nov 1992.

One of Britain's most gifted swing pianists, Leake took up clarinet to work with Mike Harris's jazz band while training as an architect. National Service followed and then Leake moved to London, where he worked as a door-to-door salesman before leading his own band during the later days of Britain's trad boom. In the early 1960s he worked with Dick Charlesworth on P&O liners, and at the end of the decade joined Alan Elsdon's band, with which he played for the rest of his life. In addition, Leake led a fine mainstream sextet, Sweet and Sour, and the Al Fresco Marching Band (playing alto saxophone); he was also a genuinely original composer. [DF]

⊙ **Benign Jazz** (1993; Inxent). This valuable album, taken from broadcasts, features Leake's fine Sweet and Sour aggregation and highlights not just his vivacious piano but also his talent as a composer.

Dave Lee

Piano, arranger, composer, vocals, leader.

b. London, 12 Aug 1930.

An eclectic pianist whose work runs from Bud Powell to Earl Hines with equal ease, Dave Lee won the *Melody Maker* contest for jazz pianists when he was sixteen, and joined the John Dankworth Big Band in 1955, with which he toured the USA and recorded prolifically. In the 1960s he ran his own trio, issued a number of best-selling albums (including *New Big Band from Britain*, which was in the *Cashbox* Top Ten for six weeks) and worked as musical director for Judy Garland and for a number of British TV shows, including *That Was The Week That Was.* Lee's compositions also became well known: he wrote the scores for the musical *Our Man Crichton* (1965) and the film *The Solid Gold Cadillac* (1956), and a best-selling hit for Peter Sellers and Sophia Loren, "Goodness Gracious Me" (from *The Millionairess*, 1960). In the 1980s he was still involved in writing for revues and TV, and re-emerged as a solo act at London venues. A longtime campaigner for jazz radio, Lee was responsible for the establishment of Britain's first jazz radio station, Jazz FM, and served on its board before resuming freelance activities. [DF]

Julia Lee

Piano, vocals, composer.

b. Boonesville, Missouri, 31 Oct 1902; d. 8 Dec 1958.

Julia Lee was the sister of George E. Lee, who led a novelty band which in the early 1930s worked in competition with McKinney's Cotton Pickers. Julia sang regularly with her brother's band until it broke up in 1934 (she also worked solo on some occasions), and then spent fourteen years working clubs on Kansas City's 12th Street. In 1944 she was discovered by Capitol talent scout Dave Dexter, who recorded her regularly, first with Jay McShann's and Tommy Douglas's bands, later under the banner of Julia Lee's Boyfriends. The "boyfriends" included such great men as Benny Carter, Ernie Royal, Vic Dickenson, Red Norvo, Red Nichols, Nappy Lamare and Douglas, and the salty songs they recorded (usually Lee compositions, such as "King Size Papa" and "I Didn't Like It The First Time") often became hits. Julia Lee continued to work in Kansas City for most of her life, with a year in LA (1949–50). With artists such as Nellie Lutcher and Louis Jordan, her work represents one early transition from jazz towards rock'n'roll. [DF]

Peggy Lee

Vocals.

b. Jamestown, Ohio, 26 May 1920; d. 22 Jan 2002.

Born Norma Dolores Egstrom, Peggy Lee was a world-class popular singer whose talents led her regularly into jazz surroundings. Her early years with Benny Goodman (1941–3) established her as a blues singer of outstanding talent, with recordings like "Blues In The Night" and "Why Don't You Do Right". At that point Lee married Dave Barbour and temporarily retired, but she came back in 1944 for recordings with the Capitol Jazzmen ("Ain't Goin' No Place", "That Old Feeling"). Over the next fifteen years she became a much-loved radio star, singer and comedienne (with Bing Crosby and others) and recorded numerous hits for Capitol and Decca, including the once-controversial "Lover", "Mr Wonderful", "Fever" (1958) and the Grammy-award winning "Is That All There Is" (1969). Compositions

Bob Willoughby/Redferns

Peggy Lee

of hers (co-written with Barber) such as "It's A Good Day" (1947), "Mañana" and "I Don't Know Enough About You" constitute a catalogue that renders her one of the great twentieth-century popular composers. Most notably perhaps, in cinematic terms, she wrote the score for Walt Disney's *Lady and the Tramp* (1955) in collaboration with Sonny Burke and provided the on-screen voice for Disney's Siamese cat characters.

Amid her later, more commercial output, there are regular returns to strict jazz formats (and the blues), notably for her classic album *Black Coffee* (1953), which featured the magnificent twelve-bar title track. Two years later her portrayal of an alcoholic singer in *Pete Kelly's Blues* (still one of the best jazz films) won her an Academy award nomination for best supporting actress and, musically, placed her in the company of Dixieland masters such as Dick Cathcart and Matty Matlock. The albums *Beauty And The Beat* (with George Shearing's Quintet) and *Mink Jazz* attained classic status at the start of the next decade, and Peggy Lee showed little intention of slowing down in later years despite illness in the later 1980s, and a complicated court case with Disney's studios over royalties over the re-release of *Lady and the Tramp* on video (Lee received a two million-dollar settlement). By 2000 her performing days were over and she died two years later from a heart attack; in retrospect an unecessarily sad end for one of the twentieth century's most widely-gifted and sunny popular talents. [DF]

⊙ **It's A Good Day** (1941–1952; ASV). Valuable collection of early Lee with Goodman, the Capitol Jazzmen, Dave Barbour, Frank de Vol and Billy May including "It's A Good Day", "You Was Right Baby" and "I Don't Know Enough About You".

⊙ **Black Coffee/Sea Shells** (1953–6; MCA). Two important Lee albums on one CD. The first is a classic, with Jimmy Rowles and Pete Candoli on top trumpet form. *Sea Shells* is more abstruse; Lee recites poetry as well as sings but the album repays concentrated attention, and there is one Lee standard, "I Don't Want To Play In Your Yard".

⊙ **Beauty And The Beat** (1959; Capitol). A central item in Lee's long discography, this concert was recorded at a DJs' convention in Miami, with George Shearing's quintet. A sultry version of "You Came A Long Way From St Louis" is one highlight.

Phil Lee

Guitar.

b. London, 8 April 1943.

Lee played with various London-based groups in the 1960s, including the Graham Collier sextet and one with Dudu Pukwana, and since the 1970s has played with Henry Lowther's groups. In the mid-1970s he was co-leader, with Tony Coe, of Axel and also played

with Michael Garrick and Jeff Clyne in progressive rock bands, Alan Gowen's Gilgamesh being the most successful and longest-lived. In 1979 he toured with the Michel Legrand quartet, and in 1983 with Gordon Beck's nonet. He regularly records and gigs as a duo with saxophonist Martin Speake. [IC]

➤➤ **Jeff Clyne** *(Twice Upon A Time)*; **John Horler** *(Gentle Piece)*.

Cliff Leeman

Drums.

b. Portland, Maine, 10 Sept 1913; d. 29 April 1986.

After work as a teenage percussionist with the Portland Symphony Orchestra, Leeman joined Artie Shaw at the State Ballroom, New York (he played on all Shaw's hit records), then worked for a succession of great bandleaders – Glenn Miller, Tommy Dorsey, Charlie Barnet and Woody Herman. In 1944, at Charlie Shavers' instigation, he joined John Kirby's band (replacing O'Neill Spencer) and doubled with Raymond Scott's famous and short-lived "integrated" studio band for CBS, which included Johnny Guarnieri, Ben Webster, Trummy Young and Shavers. From 1945 Leeman worked with, among others, Jimmy Dorsey, Glen Gray's Casa Lomans, Jean Goldkette and Barnet again (though uncomfortable with Barnet's reluctant bebop policy). In the 1950s he was active in the studios, his work for Eddie Condon, Pee Wee Erwin, Billy Butterfield, Wild Bill Davison and the Dukes of Dixieland setting a standard for younger drummers such as Lennie Hastings and Tony Allen. In the 1970s Leeman played with Bobby Hackett, Joe Venuti, The World's Greatest Jazz Band and the European group the Kings of Jazz (featuring Pee Wee Erwin, Bernie Privin, Kenny Davern and Dick Hyman), and he stayed active into the 1980s, despite occasional hearing problems.

Cliff Leeman, whose formative years were spent in the shadow of Gene Krupa, had neither Krupa's flash nor the troubled intellect that endeared Dave Tough to his followers. In every other way, though, he was their equal, and his recordings are included in the Smithsonian Institution's archive of classic jazz. [DF]

KENNY DAVERN

⊙ **Kings of Jazz** (2003/Arbors). A polished group led by trumpeter Pee Wee Erwin, recalling The World's Greatest Jazz Band, and recorded live at the Atlantic Club, Stockholm, in 1974, featuring Leeman's kicking drums in familiar territory.

➤➤ **Bobby Hackett** *(Live At The Roosevelt Grill)*.

Michel Legrand

Arranger, composer, piano, vocals.

b. Paris, 24 Feb 1932.

Michel is the son of a bandleader and brother of session singer Christiane Legrand (heard, for instance, with the Blue Stars, the Double Six and the Swingle Singers, and on the soundtrack of *Les Parapluies De Cherbourg*). He studied at the Paris Conservatoire, and became a commercial arranger at nineteen. He became extremely prolific as a writer of film music (beginning with *La Porte Des Lilas*, released in 1957 and the source of his first standard, "Once Upon A Summertime"), first in Paris and then in Hollywood. Before that, he recorded an all-star jazz album with Miles Davis and Ben Webster (1958) and later wrote albums for Stan Getz (1971), Sarah Vaughan (1972), Phil Woods (1975), Stephane Grappelli (1992) and Arturo Sandoval (1993). A kind of French Quincy Jones, Legrand is universally admired by musicians fond of good arranging, whether jazz-oriented or not, and the number of tunes he has contributed to the standard repertoire for improvisers is considerable. [BP]

⊙ **Legrand "Live" Jazz** (1973–5; Novus). Unlike the activity described above, this is drawn from two of the few occasions when Legrand played piano with his own small group (including Randy Brecker, Ron Carter, drummer Grady Tate and Phil Woods, featured on a definitive "You Must Believe In Spring").

Pepi Lemer

Vocals.

b. Ilfracombe, Devon, UK, 25 May 1944.

Lemer had singing lessons with classical teachers from the age of five, before going on to stage school where she studied singing and dancing. This led to theatrical work and cabaret in the UK and abroad. She has played with John Stevens' Spontaneous Music Ensemble, her then husband Pete Lemer's E, Keith Tippett's Centipede, Mike Gibbs, and Barbara Thompson's Paraphernalia. During the 1970s she co-led Turning Point with Jeff Clyne, who did an Arts Council tour of the UK with guests Alan Holdsworth and Neil Ardley in 1981 and recorded three albums. Pepi Lemer has a very wide range, and is able to handle anything from a popular song to the most difficult abstract lines and free improvisation. She has latterly become best known for her vocal tuition to the stars – strange to think that a singer influenced by Urszula Dudziak, Ella Fitzgerald and Miles Davis has buffed and toned the larynxes of Boyzone, the Spice Girls and Liberty X. [IC]

Pete Lemer

Piano, electric piano, synthesizer.

b. London, 14 June 1942.

Lemer had private classical piano lessons when young, and then went to the Royal Academy of Music in London. He later took lessons from Paul Bley and Jaki Byard. It was during his first professional engagement, in Haifa in 1963 with Tony Crombie and Jeff Clyne, that the latter introduced him to the music of Ornette Coleman and Scott

LaFaro. When he returned to London he started leading his own groups – a trio, quartet, quintet and a group he called E. Since the mid-1960s he has played with many leading British musicians and groups, including Barbara Thompson's Paraphernalia and Jubiaba, Harry Beckett, Don Rendell, the Spontaneous Music Ensemble, Amalgam, Baker-Gurvitz Army, Mike Oldfield, Annette Peacock, Neil Ardley and Mike Westbrook. (He garnered a certain cult cachet amongst prog-rock obsessives via his involvement in the "Canterbury scene" with Gilgamesh, Pierre Moerlin's Gong, Mike Oldfield and, latterly, with Phil Miller's band In Cahoots.)

He remains a tower of strength in Barbara Thompson's various groups, and regularly tours with Paraphernalia. His favourite pianists range from Ellington, Zawinul and Twardzik to Sun Ra, Stevie Wonder and Meade "Lux" Lewis, and other influences are Coltrane and Ornette Coleman. Lemer's own concept covers a similarly broad spectrum and he is perfectly at home with free jazz, conventional jazz, or rock. [IC]

⊙ **Local Color** (1965; ESP). This is an iconic album of the young lions of the 1960s – Lemer with John Surman, bassist Tony Reeves and drummer Jon Hiseman, plus saxophonist Nisar Ahmad Khan. Lemer's compositions are full of dynamism and the playing is exemplary.

➤➤ **Barbara Thompson** *(A Cry from the Heart; Everlasting Flame).*

Brian Lemon

Piano, arranger.

b. Nottingham, UK, 11 Feb 1937.

Lemon came south from Nottingham in the mid-1950s to join Freddy Randall's band, then moved to saxophonist Betty Smith's quintet. He quickly became the centre of attention among British mainstreamers, and after a spell with the Fairweather-Brown All Stars he began working all over, in Danny Moss's quartet, Dave Shepherd's quintet and small groups led by George Chisholm, as well as subbing for Dudley Moore at the Establishment and accompanying American visitors such as Milt Jackson, Charlie Shavers, Ben Webster, Harry Edison, "Lockjaw" Davis and Buddy Tate – "Professor" Lemon works as easily with post-bebop players as he does with Dixieland (for which he admits a special fondness). During the 1970s and 1980s he played for Benny Goodman, shared TV programmes with Ray Brown, organized his own small groups and large string ensembles for BBC sessions, and worked with Alex Welsh and Peter Boizot's Pizza All Stars.

Into the 1990s he was still first-call for many visiting Americans, in particular Warren Vaché and Scott Hamilton (with whom he tours Britain bi-annually). Lemon is also a member of the Charlie Watts quintet and appeared with Kenny Baker's Best of British Jazz package, which toured the USA in 1994. A regular British Jazz Award winner, Lemon has recently concentrated on developing his talents as a solo performer. From 1995 Lemon's talents were recognized by producer John Bune in a comprehensively excellent series of self-led recordings which rightly restored him to a central position in British recorded jazz history. [DF]

⊙ **But Beautiful** (1995; Zephyr). Lemon in the first of his many albums as a leader for John Bune, and a beauty. Dave Cliff, Dave Green and Allan Ganley are his hand-picked support and the leader shines from the poised title track to the end.

⊙ **An Affair To Remember** (1995; Zephyr). Lemon is joined by a favourite partner, Warren Vaché, for a frequently exquisite exploration of Harry Warren's music. A two-handed pianist, he shines in duo and these performances (regularly concise) belong in the top rank of an exclusive genre.

⊙ **Over The Rainbow** (1995; Zephyr). Lemon's relationship with Bune involves promotion of worthy causes, and Derek Watkins – better known as a lead trumpeter of legendary status – is one, here playing through a straight-jazz programme flawlessly – and usually in middle register.

➤➤ **Scott Hamilton** *(East Of The Sun);* **Charlie Watts** *(From One Charlie; With Strings – A Tribute To Charlie Parker).*

Bill Le Sage

Piano, accordion, vibraphone, percussion.

b. London, 20 Jan 1927; d. 31 Oct 2001.

Le Sage taught himself to play piano by working out chords he'd learned to play on the ukulele given to him as a child (though he did, in the late 1940s, snatch eight lessons with Lennie Tristano when the cruise ship he was working on was in port Stateside). In 1945 he formed his own sextet, then from 1945–8 he played in army bands. He was then snapped up by Johnny Dankworth, playing with his "Seven" in the early 1950s and with his big band from 1953–4. From 1954–61 he played with the Tony Kinsey trio, and began scoring British B-movies and TV films, working at such a pace that he was soon astounded to find he could write music faster than he could read it.

He played with Ronnie Ross from 1961–5 and afterwards led trios and quintets of his own. Over his long career he worked with many UK musicians and with leading US jazzmen such as Dizzy Gillespie, Benny Goodman and Red Rodney, returning regularly to sage old cohorts Dankworth and Laine whilst juggling commissions for radio and music education that broadened his musical horizons, honed his orchestrating skills and developed in him an informed, respectful influence from Brazilian music. [IC]

Jack Lesberg

Bass.

b. Boston, Massachusetts, 14 Feb 1920.

From 1945 Lesberg doubled a bass chair in the New York Symphony Orchestra (under Leonard

Bernstein) with a five-year residency at Eddie Condon's. From 1950, when he began freelancing, Lesberg's all-round talent took him at various times to Louis Armstrong's All Stars; on tour in Britain with Earl Hines and Jack Teagarden's band in 1957; and in and out of studios as a busy sessionman (for Wild Bill Davison, Sarah Vaughan, Benny Goodman, Coleman Hawkins and Sidney Bechet, to name a few). His appearances on record are countless and, although he eventually moved to Australia, he managed to tour with the Eddie Condon Reunion Band, featuring Tom Artin, Ed Polcer, Kenny Davern, Keith Ingham and Oliver Jackson, in the mid-1980s and continued to gig and record from time to time. [DF]

➤➤ **Ruby Braff** *(Bravura Eloquence).*

Johnny Letman

Trumpet.

b. McCormick, South Carolina, 6 Sept 1917; d. 17 July 1992.

A fine, strong-blowing trumpeter and more than capable soloist who regularly led his own small groups, Letman worked with Nat Cole in 1933 and through the 1940s with a succession of big bands, including those of Horace Henderson (1941), Lucky Millinder, Claude Hopkins, John Kirby, Phil Moore, Cab Calloway (1947-9) and Count Basie. In the 1950s he worked around with Eddie Condon, Wilbur de Paris (1956) and others, and led his own bands; he also toured in the 1960s with Tiny Grimes and Milt Buckner and during the 1970s and 80s worked with Sammy Price, the New Orleans Blues Serenaders (1985-6) and the Harlem Blues and Jazz Band (1990). During these later years he also freelanced, recording with Lionel Hampton, Earl Hines and Cozy Cole. Letman was underrecorded but his solo talents are comparable to those of another neglected tower of strength, Emmett Berry. [DF]

Didier Levallet

Double bass, composer, leader.

b. Arcy-sur-Cure, France, 19 July 1944.

Levallet studied journalism in Lille from 1963–6, and studied bass briefly at the Lille Conservatory, but is otherwise self-taught. His professional debut was in Paris in 1969, working in clubs with Ted Curson, Chris Woods, George Arvanitas, Siegfried Kessler, Hank Mobley, Mal Waldron and others. He also toured France with Johnny Griffin, Kenny Clarke and Slide Hampton. From 1970–77 he worked with a free-jazz quartet, Perception, touring in France, Belgium, Germany and Norway. In 1976 he founded and led ADMI (Association pour le Développement de la Musique Improvisée) and also played in the USA with saxophonist Byard Lancaster. Since the later 1970s he has formed and composed for several groups with unusual instrumentation (often using strings) including Didier Lockwood, Steve Lacy, Tony Coe, Marc Charig, Radu Malfatti and Tony Oxley. Levallet also played during the early 1980s with Archie Shepp, Frank Lowe and Chris McGregor's Brotherhood of Breath, though he increasingly preferred composition and arrangement to improvisation. The Levallet-Marais-Pifarely string trio joined Mike Westbrook's "A Little Westbrook Music" unit for concerts and festivals in France and the UK in 1985–6. With reed player Louis Sclavis he was half of the Tony Oxley-Didier Levallet double quartet project, which appeared in France and the UK from 1984–6. Levallet has also long been active in education, teaching at L'Ecole Nationale de Musique. His favourites are Charlie Haden and Gary Peacock; other inspirations are Mingus, Ellington and Gil Evans. [IC]

➤➤ **Harry Beckett** *(Images Of Clarity).*

Stan Levey

Drums.

b. Philadelphia, 5 April 1926.

Levey started learning drums at the age of seven, and was playing with Dizzy Gillespie in Philadelphia in 1942. Moving to New York in 1944, he worked with Oscar Pettiford, Coleman Hawkins, Ben Webster and the Dizzy Gillespie quintet with Charlie Parker (1945–6). He also toured with Woody Herman (1945), Charlie Ventura, Georgie Auld and Stan Kenton (1952–4), before settling on the West Coast as a member of the Lighthouse All Stars from 1954–60. In the 1960s he toured with Peggy Lee, Ella Fitzgerald and Pat Boone, and did prolific studio work with the orchestras of Nelson Riddle and Henry Mancini, playing mallet instruments. He also composed music for short films before retiring in 1973 to run a photography and video business. Initially inspired by Chick Webb, Sid Catlett and Dave Tough, he was hailed as one of the first white drummers with a feel for bebop, saying "Bird and Max [Roach] were responsible for the way I thought about music. I came to realize that being 'musical' on drums was the most important thing." [BP]

Dizzy Gillespie, Sonny Stitt and Stan Getz

⊙ **For Musicians Only** (1956; Verve). At one level just another Jazz At The Phil studio jam session, three of these four tracks are taken at the fast bebop tempos that Levey could handle easily while remaining creative.

Milcho Leviev

Piano, keyboards, arranger.

b. Plovdiv, Bulgaria, 19 Dec 1937.

Leviev obtained a Master's degree in composition in 1960, becoming successively music director for the state drama theatre and the radio/TV big band.

He led the quartet Jazz Focus '65 from 1965–9, which won a prize at the first Montreux festival in 1967, and recorded in West Germany, where Leviev defected in 1970. He then moved to Los Angeles in 1971, becoming a US citizen in 1977 and playing with Don Ellis (1971–6), Billy Cobham, Airto Moreira, Roy Haynes, Art Pepper (1979–80) and Manhattan Transfer (for whom he arranged Parker's "Confirmation"). He led a classical/fusion quartet Free Flight from 1980–3, and worked in duo with both Charlie Haden and Dave Holland, recording in Japan with Holland and with Ray Brown, as well as doing solo European tours (1990–95). In 1995 he received an honorary Doctorate and an award from the Paris Académie Internationale des Arts. His favourites include players from Fats Waller to Joe Zawinul. Also inspired by Ellington, Gil Evans and Don Ellis, his writing and playing ably mix the odd-metered music of his Balkan background with an excellent post-bop technique. [BP]

⊙ **Blues For The Fisherman** (1980; Mole Jazz). Recorded live in London, this was in reality a classic Art Pepper quartet session with Leviev named as leader for contractual reasons, but it is nonetheless a powerful document of his dynamic and inventive playing.

Tony Levin

Drums.

b. Much Wenlock, Shropshire, UK, 30 Jan 1940.

One of the UK's top drummers, Tony Levin is equally adept in both wholly improvised and straightahead jazz, having played with a veritable who's who of UK musicians since joining the Tubby Hayes quartet in 1965, with which he recorded the classic *Mexican Green* two years later. In 1969, he joined the Alan Skidmore quintet and worked with the Humphrey Lyttelton band, and a year later drummed for pianist John Taylor in both his trio and his sextet. In the 1970s he toured Italy with Ian Carr's band Nucleus, played with the Stan Sulzmann quartet and Gordon Beck's Gyroscope, and joined John Surman for a duet recording of a Moers festival concert (1975). In 1979 Levin joined the German band Third Eye and the following year collaborated with Dutch pianist Rob Van Den Broeck in his trio, which recorded for Timeless. Levin's long-standing musical relationship with saxophonist Paul Dunmall began in 1980 when they formed the Tony Levin trio with bassist Tony Moore, and throughout the 1980s, 1990s and beyond they have continued to play together in various formations, most famously in the band Mujician (with Keith Tippett and Paul Rogers), but also as a duo.

Yet Levin also squeezed in the time to play with a number of other musicians, including Alan Skidmore again (in Tenor Tonic); the European Jazz Ensemble; the Philip Catherine quintet; Germany's Trumpet Summit; and Sophia Domancich (with whom Levin toured France and the Middle East in 1994 and recorded three albums). He maintained his musical relationships with the other members of Mujician, in the 1990s, making a string of albums including *Spacetime* (Cuneiform; 2002), playing with Paul Rogers's quartet and recording *Time Of Brightness* with the band in 1997. Duo work with Paul Dunmall also continued, and recordings with various combinations of UK free musicians appeared on Levin's label, Rare Music. Levin also played with Charlie Mariano in the European Jazz Ensemble Octet, in a trio with US saxophonist John Roucco and Belgian bassist Philippe Aerts and with German saxophonist Gerd Dudek with whom he made an evocative album, *Smatter* (Psi; 2002). [CP]

Mujician

⊙ **The Journey** (1990; Cuneiform). Continuous near hour-long collective improvisation recorded at the Bath festival, featuring four peerless free players in almost telepathic communication.

Tony Levin and Paul Dunmall

⊙ **Spiritual Empathy** (1994; Rare Music). Series of gripping – often volcanic – duets perfectly illustrating the extraordinary rapport between Levin and Dunmall.

➤➤ **Tubby Hayes** *(For Members Only).*

Bobby "Lips" Levine

Clarinet, bass-clarinet, saxophones.

b. Easton, Pennsylvania, 9 April 1923.

Levine was a regular at Capitol Records for most of their great post-war years and played with a classy selection of big bands, including Billy Butterfield, Sam Donahue's re-created Tommy Dorsey Orchestra, Warren Covington (with whom he toured England), Vaughn Monroe, Sammy Kaye, Tex Beneke and Art Mooney. He also worked with some fine small groups led by Chris Griffin, trumpeter Ben Ventura, Parke Frankenfield and latterly Bob Crosby. In 1974 he appeared with Sy Oliver in a Tommy Dorsey tribute at Carnegie Hall; in 1985 he won the All Star Award (for reeds) with Frankenfield's band at Sacramento's jazz festival; and he was still busy in the 1990s. [DF]

Henry "Hot Lips" Levine

Trumpet.

b. London, 26 Nov 1907; d. May 1989.

Henry "Hot Lips" Levine lived in New York from the age of six months, learned the bugle in a Boy Scout troop, was taught by Max Schlossberg, graduated to trumpet soloist in Brooklyn Boys' High School, and thereafter worked with bands all over New York (a close friend was trumpeter Phil Napoleon). In 1926 he replaced Nick La Rocca in the Original Dixieland Jazz Band, then played with Vincent Lopez, and in 1927 joined Ambrose's band in London. Back in New York he worked for theatre orchestras and bandleaders, and from 1940 directed the Chamber Music Society of Lower Basin Street, an NBC in-house Dixieland band which had its own programme (*Strictly Dixie*) and recorded with Dinah Shore, Jelly Roll Morton, Sidney Bechet and others. In later years Levine became MD for Radio NBK and NBC TV in Cleveland, and continued bandleading in Miami and Las Vegas. [DF]

⊙ **NBC's Chamber Music Society Of Lower Basin Street** (1940–41; Harlequin). Invaluable document of Levine's work. Powerful, accurate lead and soloing amid sophisticated New York Dixieland surroundings.

Rod Levitt

Trombone, composer, arranger.

b. Portland, Oregon, 16 Sept 1929.

A member of the Dizzy Gillespie big band from 1956–7 and the Gil Evans band in 1959, Levitt has mostly made his living through studio work. Early in the 1960s he formed his own octet with other studio-based players, such as pianist Sy Johnson and trumpeters Rolf Ericson or Bill Berry, which made several concert appearances and four delightful albums. Now hard to find, the records feature a wide range of material, all written or arranged by Levitt himself and showing an intelligent blend of musicality and humour with influences as varied as Evans, Mingus and 1920s jazz. [BP]

Various Artists

⊙ **Dynamic Sound Patterns** (1963; Riverside/OJC). From the opening "Holler", humorously recalling early Ellington, to the tongue-in-cheek exoticism of "Ah! Spain" and "El General", Levitt's writing for the five horns is unlike anyone else's of the period. Ericson on trumpet is the only big name among the performers, whose solo contributions belie their reputations as studio musicians.

Lou Levy

Piano.

b.Chicago, Illinois, 5 March l928; d. 23 Jan 2001.

Though Levy is one of the great jazz pianists of the twentieth century, he is mentioned far less often than he deserves. A superb musician (comparable to Hank Jones) who could turn his hand to any jazz style, Levy worked with Georgie Auld (1947), Chubby Jackson (1947–8), Woody Herman (1948–9) and Tommy Dorsey (1950), before temporarily retiring for three years. He returned to solo performance in 1954, and thereafter recorded with West Coast heroes, including trumpeter Conte Candoli, and regularly accompanied Peggy Lee and Ella Fitzgerald. His reputation as a sensitive accompanist led him to work with such luminaries as Anita O'Day, Tony Bennett, Nancy Wilson and Frank Sinatra, and he also played with Benny Goodman, Stan Getz and Terry Gibbs. From 1973 he joined Supersax and also taught at the Dick Grove School of Music. Levy underwent brain surgery in 1999 but carried on performing until his death from a heart attack. [DF]

Conte Candoli & Lou Levy

⊙ **West Coast Wailers** (1955; Atlantic). Levy's light Bud-Powell influenced piano is well displayed on this classy small group date, featuring Candoli and his Quintet with Bill Homan on tenor sax.

George Lewis

Clarinet, alto saxophone.

b. New Orleans, 13 July 1900; d. 31 Dec 1968.

George Lewis (George Louis Francis Zeno) heard his first jazz as it blew in from neighbouring dance halls (Hope's was across the street) and bought his first clarinet around 1917. By 1919 he was working in brass bands and small groups with such musicians as trumpeter Buddy Petit, whom he idolized. Like Petit – and many other fine New Orleans players – Lewis did not make the trip north to Chicago. All through the 1920s he led bands in New Orleans with Henry "Red" Allen, Chris Kelly, Arnold Dupas, Sam Morgan and Evan Thomas – another Lewis favourite, who was murdered onstage, alongside him, in 1932. In the 1930s came work with Kid Howard, Billie Holiday and Dee Dee Pierce, but Lewis, as a convinced clarinettist, found himself out of fashion – "everyone was saxophone crazy then", he remembered later. By the end of the decade he was still playing regularly at night – but working as a stevedore by day.

In 1941 researcher William Russell came to New Orleans, in search of Bunk Johnson and the real jazz; at the suggestion of trombonist Jim Robinson, Lewis played clarinet on a 1942 recording session with Johnson, and a brief but memorable partnership was forged. For the next five years, with and without his new partner, Lewis recorded for Russell – classics include the 1944 American Music series with Johnson, Lewis-led masterpieces such as "Burgundy Street Blues" (recorded in his bedroom after an accident), and titles with Kid Howard. In 1945 he took a band starring Bunk Johnson to New York to play a season at Stuyvesant Casino, a new jazz venue opened by Russell and Gene Williams. The band became a central point for a new breed of jazz followers, who saw it as a vital restatement of the music's best and most honest qualities. The triumph lasted only a year: Johnson wanted to play with swing-style musicians, and Lewis wanted to go home. Lewis took his band back to New Orleans in 1946, and the following year began a residency at Manny's Tavern.

In 1950 *Look* magazine ran a feature on Lewis ("The best New Orleans band in New Orleans"), his band moved up to Bourbon Street (New Orleans's commercial music centre), and from then on he was to remain the frail figurehead for hardline jazz revivalism. By 1952 he had again left New Orleans with his band, beginning an unrelenting round of major venues such as the Beverly Cavern in Los Angeles and San Francisco's Hangover Club (at $1000 a week), and acquiring a full-time manager, Dorothy Tait (she wrote his biography, *Call Him George*, under the pseudonym Jay Alison Stuart). From the mid-1950s he toured Europe and Japan as a soloist or in ensemble; in 1957 and 1959 he came to Britain, first with Ken Colyer, then with his own venerable group.

For lovers of New Orleans jazz Lewis's music possessed a simple beauty that was otherworldly in its lack of artifice. Yet even some of his admirers commented on his technical fallibilities – an occasional tendency to play out of tune, for example, was blamed on lack of judgement, rather than his willingness to record with pianos that went a semitone flat in the hot New Orleans climate. Lewis was a natural talent rather than a highly sophisticated one, with a musical philosophy that was different from that of Dixieland, rather than just a simplification of it. "It's a conversation," he told Tom Bethell, " ... and it's rough music! You don't want nothin' smooth in it. When I play music I like those people around me, especially people dancing. Then you don't think too much!" [DF]

⊙ **George Lewis With Kid Shots** (1944; American Music); **Trios And Bands** (1945; American Music). Classic Lewis with Louis "Kid Shots" Madison, a worthy partner from the formative days of America's great jazz revival. The second CD is from the same sessions, and includes titles with banjo and bass alone – a formula that frequently produced Lewis's most moving work.

⊙ **The George Lewis Ragtime Band of New Orleans: The Oxford Series Vols. 1–17** (1952–3; American Music). This indispensable series, recorded by the American Folklore Group at Miami University, mixes studio and concert recordings (including a party on Vol. 10), and remains the most comprehensive documentation of this great New Orleans clarinettist. Primary listening.

⊙ **Jazz At Vespers** (1954; OJC). A superlative Lewis session with Kid Howard, Jim Robinson and others, recorded at a Sunday service in Ohio.

⊙ **George Lewis And The Barry Martyn Band** (1965; GHB). Lewis on tour with a gifted band of British New Orleans men, sounding fully at home and as inspired as usual.

➤➤ **Bunk Johnson** *(Second Masters; Bunk's Brass Band And Dance Band).*

George Lewis

Trombone, sousaphone, tuba, electronics, composer.

b. Chicago, 14 July 1952.

Lewis took up the trombone aged nine, and played in school bands with fellow pupil Ray Anderson, who was to become the other leading trombonist to emerge in the 1970s. Three years later, Lewis was copying tenor saxophone solos from a Lester Young-Oscar Peterson trio album. He took a BA in philosophy at Yale, playing with the Anthony Davis sextet while he was there, before hooking up with the AACM School (see Art Ensemble of Chicago) in 1971 and was taught theory by Muhal Richard Abrams, an experience that led him, in 1973, to commit himself totally to music. He rapidly became a virtuoso on the trombone, with terms of reference that covered everything from the tailgate style of classic jazz to the fleet lines of bebop, to abstraction and the multiphonics (playing more than one note simultaneously) pioneered by Albert Mangelsdorff. Lewis has stated that the major influences on his playing are saxophonists Coltrane, Young and Parker, and in the 1970s he was also practising exercises out of Eddie Harris's saxophone books. Early in 1976 he spent two months with the Count Basie band, which put the finishing touches to his education. In the winter of 1976 he began his long and fruitful association with Anthony Braxton, recording duo, quartet and orchestral pieces with him, including *Elements Of Surprise* and *Creative Orchestra Music*, both in 1976. He has also played and recorded with Euro improvisers such as Evan Parker, Derek Bailey and Dave Holland. Yet the company he keeps isn't exclusively free-improv and avant garde: he toured Europe and Japan with Gil Evans and has also played with Randy Weston. In 1987, with John Zorn and Bill Frisell, he recorded *News For Lulu*, an album of hard bop pieces which straddled the bebop/free divide brilliantly.

Lewis' is a very comprehensive talent embracing early roots to bebop and free playing, as well as inventing some new areas of exploration for himself – since the 1980s he has performed improvised duets with programmed computers. [IC]

⊙ **Shadowgraph 5** (1977; Black Saint). A powerful freely improvised session by some of the genre's key musicians – Roscoe Mitchell, multi-wind instrumentalist Douglas Ewart, Muhal Richard Abrams, Leroy Jenkins and Abdul Wadud, all under Lewis's direction.

⊙ **Homage To Charles Parker** (1979; Black Saint). The same group, plus Anthony Davis and Richard Teitelbaum (synthesizer), combine improvisation with predetermined structures in a superbly adventurous exploration of the Parker legacy.

➤➤ **John Zorn** *(News For Lulu).*

John Lewis

Composer, arranger, piano.

b. La Grange, Illinois, 3 May 1920; d. 29 Mar 2001.

Lewis' mother was a trained singer and he learned the piano from the age of seven. He studied music and anthropology at the University of New Mexico and had his first arrangements accepted by the Teddy Wilson sextet. After army service between 1942–5, Lewis replaced Thelonious Monk in the Dizzy Gillespie band from 1946–8, at the suggestion of Kenny Clarke. Following the band's European tour, he and Clarke remained for a few months in Paris. He also sat in and recorded with Charlie Parker in 1947 and 1948, and arranged for and performed with Miles Davis's nine-piece band in 1948. He toured with the Illinois Jacquet group in 1948–9, and with the Lester Young quartet in 1950–51. He also made many freelance recordings with players such as J.J. Johnson,

Zoot Sims, Parker, Davis and singer King Pleasure. The first recordings of the Milt Jackson quartet, made in 1951–2 with Lewis, Clarke and Ray Brown, the original rhythm-section of the Gillespie band, led to public appearances. These in turn (in 1954) led to the full-time Modern Jazz Quartet, with the replacement of Brown by Percy Heath and, from 1955, of Kenny Clarke by Connie Kay. Lewis became musical director, composing or arranging all their material.

He also wrote soundtrack music for *No Sun In Venice* (1957) and *Odds Against Tomorrow* (1959), and for ballets, stage plays and TV documentaries. He was involved in forming the Jazz and Classical Music Society in the mid-1950s, and Orchestra USA from 1962–6, both ensembles comprising players fluent in jazz and European music, and both committed to using newly written "third stream" compositions. Late in the 1950s he organized jazz summer schools at the Music Inn, and was musical adviser to the Monterey festival from 1958–82. The Modern Jazz Quartet disbanded in 1974, and in 1977 Lewis became professor of music at City College, New York. He received honorary doctorates from the University of New Mexico, Columbia College in Chicago and the New England Conservatory. A reunion concert of the MJQ (in Japan in 1981) led to regular concert tours from the summer of 1982 onwards, until the death of Jackson. Lewis made occasional appearances in his own right (visiting Stockholm in 1994 and London in 1997), and recorded two new albums in 1999.

Lewis's reputation is identified almost totally with the Quartet, and his promising early compositions, "Two Bass Hit" for Gillespie and "Rouge" for Davis, were both rewritten for the group – as "La Ronde" and "The Queen's Fancy" respectively. His choice of instrumentation, and the watercolour textures it produces, seem entirely appropriate to the dispassionate counterpoint of his pseudo-baroque writing. The key element in the Quartet is not, in fact, Milt Jackson, but Lewis's own piano-playing, delicate and even tentative, as if picking at a dish of food. Even at his most convincing, he doesn't scintillate so much as insinuate. The fact that he has popularized a whole area of Bach-goes-to-town superficiality was acknowledged when the MJQ recorded an album with the Swingle Singers, and more recently Lewis (without the Quartet) emulated his own imitator, Jacques Loussier, by tackling Bach's "48". Among fellow musicians his very distinctive work seems to have aroused neither great enthusiasm nor even very much hostility, although the tune "Django" (in memory of Django Reinhardt) rapidly became a standard. Jazz listeners, on the other hand, tend to be strongly divided about Lewis. [BP]

⊙ **Grand Encounter** (1956; Blue Note). Lewis and the MJQ's Percy Heath, plus Chico Hamilton, Jim Hall and Bill Perkins, make for a surprisingly successful session, with a minimum of organization, which includes a laid-back "Skylark" and the slow blues "Two Degrees East, Three Degrees West".

⊙ **Afternoon In Paris** (1979; Dreyfus). Not to be confused with the reissued 1956 quintet session featuring Barney Wilen and the jazz guitar of Sacha Distel, this solo recital sounds initially rather uninvolved, yet "unemphatic" is a better word for these new versions of "Django", "Two Degrees East" and Lewis's oft-covered title track.

The Modern Jazz Quartet

⊙ **Django** (1953–5; Prestige/OJC). The early edition of the quartet, with Kenny Clarke on drums, in a classic early album plus the even earlier "The Queen's Fancy" baroque pastiche. Highlights are the title track, the four-part "La Ronde Suite" and the ballad "Milano" (based on a piece Lewis wrote for Miles Davis).

⊙ **Concorde** (1955; Prestige/OJC). The first album in which Connie Kay replaced Clarke is notable for the fugue-like title track, a relaxed "Softly As In A Morning Sunrise" (with Bach co-opted to write the intro and coda) and Milt Jackson's "Ralph's New Blues".

Meade "Lux" Lewis

Piano, composer.

b. Louisville, Kentucky, 4 Sept 1905, d. 7 June 1964.

The most famous of the boogie performers, Meade "Lux" Lewis played around Chicago in the 1920s and worked with Albert Ammons in a taxi firm, where they sorted out their ideas on the owner's piano. In 1928 Lewis recorded "Honky Tonk Train Blues", which was little noticed until recording executive John Hammond heard it, whereupon he traced Lewis through Ammons – by that time he was washing cars for a living. Hammond teamed Lewis and Ammons with Pete Johnson in the 1938 Carnegie Hall concert *Spirituals to Swing*, which initiated an international boogie craze. From then on Lewis remained a celebrity, living in California, working up and down the West Coast and for radio and TV. [DF]

Max Jones Files/Redferns

Meade "Lux" Lewis

Meade Lux Lewis 1927–39; 1939–41; 1941–44 (Classics). Three volumes of Lewis presenting all his work in chronology; "Honky Tonk Train Blues" shows up regularly in various forms but much other good music too, including solos on harpsichord, celeste and his remarkable five-part investigation of *The Blues* (1939).

Boogies And Blues (1936–41;Topaz). Excellent cross-section of Lewis's work, including generous illustration of his Blue Note output. "'Honky Tonk Train" is here once again (1940 version), plus sides with Edmond Hall and the Port of Harlem Seven.

Mel Lewis

Drums.

b. Buffalo, New York, 10 May 1929; d. 2 Feb 1990.

Mel Lewis (Melvin Sokoloff) had a professional drummer for a father and began working full-time at fifteen. He worked with several big bands, including Boyd Raeburn's in 1948 and Stan Kenton's from 1954–6. He also did small-group work with Frank Rosolino and Hampton Hawes in 1955, and led his own quintet with tenorist Bill Holman in 1958. He was involved in studio sessions in Los Angeles after leaving Kenton, but also toured with the Gerry Mulligan band from 1960–63, Benny Goodman in 1962, and deputized with the Dizzy Gillespie quintet for a European tour in 1961. He moved back to New York in 1963, continuing studio work and forming a band of top studio players co-led by Thad Jones from 1965–78. Originally this was a once-a-week venture, but the band toured Europe in 1969, 1973, 1976 and 1978, and, as it undertook more US work in the 1970s, employed younger, less well-known musicians. When Jones left in 1978, Lewis continued to lead the Jazz Orchestra, with further arrangements contributed by Bob Brookmeyer and others. Though he was often heard with small groups on record, he appeared with them less frequently in public, and Lewis is thought of as pre-eminently a big-band drummer. His ability to underline and drive forward a complicated ensemble was valued by many different leaders and was the equal of some more renowned players. [BP]

Thad Jones-Mel Lewis Quartet (1977; A & M/Horizon). A rare small-group album, recorded live by the co-leaders with the rhythm-section of their big band featuring Harold Danko and Rufus Reid. Extended versions of four standards reveal new depths to the playing of all concerned.

Naturally! (1979; Telarc). Lewis's first recording with the orchestra after the departure of Jones finds him still using several Thad arrangements, but somehow Jones's absence underlines the great contribution of the drummer to the band's sound.

➤➤ **Thad Jones** *(Central Park North).*

Ramsey Lewis

Piano, electric keyboards, synthesizer, composer.

b. Chicago, 27 May 1935.

Lewis had private piano lessons from the age of six, and later studied at Chicago Music College and De Paul University. In 1956 he formed his own trio with bassist Eldee Young and drummer Red Holt, recording his first album for Argo Records (later renamed Cadet Records). Lewis also recorded with Sonny Stitt, Clark Terry, Max Roach and others in the late 1950s. His trio album made a strong impact and in 1959 he played Randall's Island jazz festival, New York, followed by a residency at Birdland. In 1965 he had a big hit with the title track of his LP *The In Crowd*, and both the single and the album gained gold discs for selling over a million copies. Lewis said, "In June of 1965 we were earning something like $1500 to $2000 a week. By September we were earning something like $15,000 to $25,000 a week ... After that we started finding problems with each other, dissension set in and then that trio broke up." He formed a new trio, continued with Chess through the 1960s, then signed with Columbia in 1971. Lewis's original influences were John Lewis, Oscar Peterson, Bud Powell and Art Tatum, but since the early 1970s he has produced MOR, easy-listening disco music. [IC]

Sky Islands (1993; GRP). Lewis's lite-funk quintet is augmented by altoist Art Porter and various vocalists on remakes of early hits, including the inevitable "In Crowd".

Ted Lewis

Clarinet, vocals.

b. Circleville, Ohio, 6 June 1892; d. 25 Aug 1971.

Known as the "top-hatted tragedian of jazz", Ted Lewis was the clarinet-playing leader of a vaudeville-based band show that was enormously successful over 30 years from 1917, and survived for 20 more after that. Lewis exploited to the full the comedic possibilities of jazz clarinet (as did many other 1920s reedmen, for example Barney Bigard and Wilton Crawley), but his playing had plenty of technique and kitsch style. "I'd never miss seeing Lewis when he came into town. He was fine!" said Coleman Hawkins. "Lewis made the clarinet talk," said Eddie Condon (who loathed show-offs), "and it usually said, 'Put me back in the case'." Like him or not, Lewis was so popular that Benny Goodman's Boys could score a commercial success with "Shirt Tail Stomp", an irreverent imitation of his style. By the late 1920s Lewis – who "talked" his songs and usually signed off all but his hottest records with a lugubrious "Is everybody happy?" – was a radio and film star, and earning $10,000 a week. His bands, often staffed by such great jazzmen as Muggsy Spanier (who worked with Lewis for a dozen years off and on), Georg Brunis and Fats Waller, were influential on later (sometimes inferior) comedy-based bands such as Harry Roy and Spike Jones. [DF]

Ted Lewis And His Band: Classic Sessions 1928–29 (JSP). A mixed bag of Lewis titles: there's some standard dance-band fare here, but the band takes off on "A Jazz Holiday", "Shimme Sha Wabble", "Clarinet Marmalade" and two takes of "Lewisada Blues".

Is Everybody Happy? 1925-38 (ASV). Excellent collection of twenty-five of Lewis's hottest sides in the regular company of Muggsy Spanier, Georg Brunis, Benny Goodman et al. and including the immortal "Some of these days" with Sophie Tucker.

Vic Lewis

Guitar, leader; also trombone.

b. London, 29 July 1919; d. Nov 1999.

A remarkable survivor with a career that spans almost sixty years, Lewis began on four-string guitar in London clubs and in 1938 travelled to New York to play at Nick's with established figures like Jack Teagarden and Louis Armstrong, as well as newly emerging stars, including Eddie Condon and Bobby Hackett. While serving in the RAF during the war, Lewis worked with saxophonist Buddy Featherstonhaugh's group (which recorded extensively), and a year later teamed up with Featherstonhaugh's drummer, Jack Parnell, in a well-remembered British group, the Lewis-Parnell Jazzmen. After 1945 he formed a close association with Stan Kenton, and a formed a big band to play Kenton-style music; several of its recordings (including "Come Back To Sorrento") are now British jazz classics. Lewis continued leading orchestras regularly until the 1960s and then became involved in management – Dudley Moore, Elton John, Count Basie, Judy Garland, Nina Simone and Johnny Mathis were all on his roster. However, he retained his jazz connections with old West Coast friends, including Bill Holman, Bud Shank and Shorty Rogers, and resumed recording regularly in the 1990s in conjunction with a longterm champion, Alan Bates of Candid Records. [DF]

Vic Lewis And His American Jazzmen 1938/British Jazzmen 1945–47 (Baldwin). The American recordings feature Americans Bobby Hackett, Dave Bowman, Pee Wee Russell and other habitués of Nick's; the British sides come from unissued Parlophone masters featuring Reg Arnold, Jimmy Skidmore, Ronnie Chamberlain and others.

Vic Lewis West Coast All Stars Play The Music Of Bill Holman (1989; Mole Jazz). From another end of Lewis's spectrum of interests, new Holman arrangements played by an all-star West Coast group featuring Sheldon, Shank, Cooper, Bill Perkins and (on one track) Dudley Moore.

A celebration of West Coast Jazz (1994; Candid). Tied in with the indefatigable Lewis's 75th birthday, this date continues to celebrate his championship of an older order. Supremely polished playing and regularly creative soloing shows that time changes little where good music is concerned; trombonist Andy Martin stands out.

Victor Lewis

Drums, composer.

b. Omaha, Nebraska, 20 May 1950.

The son of a piano-playing mother and a saxophonist father, Victor Lewis studied cello and piano between the ages of seven and eleven before studying drumming with Luigi Watts, who led him to the work of Art Blakey, Elvin Jones, Max Roach and Baby Dodds. In 1968, Lewis studied classical percussion at the University of Nebraska and was subsequently helped to turn professional by fellow drummer Billy Hart. In the 1970s, he launched himself into one of the most successful and prolific drumming careers in contemporary jazz, initially playing with fusion-oriented bands led by the likes of Earl Klugh and David Sanborn, but subsequently with a who's who of the music: trumpeters Art Farmer, Chet Baker, Eddie Henderson; pianists Kenny Barron, Paul Bley, George Cables, Cedar Walton – plus the younger generation of Benny Green, Geoff Keezer and Stephen Scott; and saxophonists Gary Bartz, Oliver Lake, David Murray, Dexter Gordon and Bobby Watson. A host of other leaders, including trombonists Steve Turre and J.J. Johnson, and bassists Steve Swallow and Mark Helias, have all recorded with Lewis, as have singers Carmen Lundy, Andy Bey and Janis Siegel, not to mention big-band leaders such as Carla Bley and George Russell. But it is for his long-standing musical association with Stan Getz in the saxophonist's most cultured quartet of the 1980s that he is most celebrated as a sideman.

His own albums showcase not only his sharp, musical drumming but also his considerable compositional gift: they include *Family Portrait* (1992; Audioquest), with John Stubblefield, Cecil McBee and others, and *Know It Today, Know It Tomorrow* (1992; Red), with Eddie Henderson, Seamus Blake, Eduardo Simon and Christian McBride, in addition to the Enja recording below. [CP]

Eeeyyess! (1997; Enja). Featuring Seamus Blake (soprano and tenor saxophones), Terell Stafford (trumpet, flugelhorn), Stephen Scott (piano), Ed Howard (bass) and percussionist Don Alias, a band whose togetherness was honed in New York and Italy before recording this rich and varied album, mainly composed of Lewis's own pieces and featuring the leader on vocals as well as drums.

Willie Lewis

Saxophones, clarinet, vocals.

b. Cleburne, Texas, 10 June 1905; d. 13 Jan 1971.

Willie Lewis was a graduate of European swing bands such as Will Marion Cook's and Sam Wooding's (1924–31), the latter being the best of its kind. After Wooding's disbanded, Lewis formed his own orchestra, named Willie Lewis and his Entertainers, and by 1934 had moved into a Paris nightclub, Chez Florence. A year later he was recording for Pathé, working with such strong soloists as Herman Chittison and Benny Carter, who were joined in 1936 by trumpeter Bill Coleman. Along with other cornermen, including Frank "Big Boy" Goudie and legendary trumpeter Arthur Briggs, Lewis's band continued touring and recording until 1941, when he sailed for home. Apart from an appearance in a Broadway play called *Angel in the Pawnshop* (1951), he did little more in show business and ended up working as a waiter and bartender. [DF]

Classics 1932–1936 (2000; Classics). Entertaining versions of "Nagasaki" and "I Can't Dance" sit alongside more serious selections, all superbly played; solos from Benny Carter, Bill Coleman and "Big Boy" Goudie.

Eggy Ley

Soprano and alto saxophones, vocals, leader.

b. London, 4 Nov 1928; d. Dec 20 1995.

Eggy (Derek) Ley took up soprano saxophone in 1949, and led a top-rated Dixieland band in Germany from 1955–61. After returning to London he joined Radio Luxembourg and played resident at the Tatty Bogle Club (1961–9), then freelanced, produced for BFBS (1969–83), and co-led Jazz Legend with Hugh Rainey. From 1983 he fronted his Hot Shots, ran a jazz magazine called *Jazzin' Around*, and successfully toured abroad and recorded. One of the pioneers of classic soprano saxophone in Britain, Eggy Ley moved to Canada in the late 1980s but soon after was immobilized by a stroke. [DF]

Dave Liebman

Tenor and soprano saxophones, flute, composer, piano, drums.

b. Brooklyn, New York, 4 Sept 1946.

Liebman had piano lessons as a child, later turning to the clarinet and eventually the saxophone. He began gigging at fourteen, inspired and helped by Bob Moses, with whom he played from the age of sixteen. Liebman also studied privately with Joe Allard, Charles Lloyd and Lennie Tristano. He graduated from New York University in the late 1960s with a degree in American history and a teaching diploma. His first professional engagement was in 1970 with the rock group 10 Wheel Drive. From 1971–3 he was with Elvin Jones, and from 1973–4 with Miles Davis. In April 1974 he formed his own group, Lookout Farm, with Richie Beirach (keyboards), Frank Tusa (bass), Jeff Williams (drums) and Badal Roy (percussion), which toured and played festivals in the USA and Europe. In the mid-1970s he was also playing in Open Sky, a group he and Bob Moses had first started at the end of the 1960s. Talking of Lookout Farm's music to Chuck Berg, Liebman said: "I hear New York and I hear the Caribbean. Then, of course, I hear some Middle East stuff. . . . And the East Indian with Badal. Then there's the African influence. . . . There's the European thing with the acoustic piano, the chords and the way we associate with each other harmonically. In a way it's a world music with all the elements that we have."

In the late 1970s and the early 80s Liebman led a very distinguished quintet with Terumasa Hino (trumpet), John Scofield (guitar), Ron McClure (bass) and Adam Nussbaum (drums). By the mid-1980s Liebman was touring as a soloist, whilst appearing at European festivals with Albert Mangelsdorff, the Swiss trumpeter Franco Ambrosetti and others. He is also active in jazz education, giving personal tuition and conducting workshops (often internationally with the Jamey Aebersold organization), and was instrumental in founding the International Association of Schools of Jazz in 1989. Liebman's art remains a various one: in addition to his ongoing regular band he has recorded *Colors* (2000; ECM), a solo, improvised concept album synaesthetic in its designs; and revisited past compositions in new, big band arrangements on *Beyond the Line* (2003; Omnitone).

Steeped in the work of John Coltrane, other influences of his include Sonny Rollins, McCoy Tyner, Elvin Jones, Miles Davis and Wayne Shorter. He is one of the most gifted of the post-Coltrane saxophonists, and his work is always shot through with human feeling; his groups have created some of the most vital music of the last thirty years. [IC]

Doin' It Again (1980; Timeless). Featuring Liebman's marvellous band of the late 1970s, with Terumasa Hino, John Scofield, Ron McClure and Adam Nussbaum, this has everything – imagination, swing, energy, the sound of surprise.

Trio + One (1988; Owl). Liebman leads Dave Holland, Jack DeJohnette and oboist Caris Visentin (Liebman's wife) in a powerful set largely consisting of his own excellent originals.

Classic Ballads (1990–91; Candid); **Setting the Standard** (1992; Red). Liebman is a fine interpreter of ballads and is here in trio with guitarist Vic Juris and bassist Steve Gilmore. *Standard* is a straightforward, hard-swinging jazz quartet session with stalwarts Mulgrew Miller, Rufus Reid and Victor Lewis.

Miles Away (1994; Owl). A heartfelt tribute to his late boss and good friend, Liebman leads his working band on this session, just as Miles had usually done. Guitarist Vic Juris, pianist Phil Markowitz, bassist Tony Marino, drummer Jamey Haddad and percussionist Scott Cutshall are supplemented by English horn player Caris Visentin who plays a star part on Gil Evans's "Pan Piper". All the pieces have some association with Miles in various parts of his long career.

Double Edge (1985; Double Edge). Liebman and pianist Richard Beirach had worked together for years, and their empathy glows in this meaty duet re-examination of standards such as "Lover Man", "On Green Dolphin Street" and "Naima".

Spirit Renewed (1982; Owl). This live trio session with Eddie Gomez and Bob Moses is a summit meeting between three virtuosi – all listening, responding and initiating with great dynamism. Sheer class.

➤➤ **Steve Swallow** *(Home)*.

Terry Lightfoot

Clarinet, alto saxophone, vocals, leader.

b. Potters Bar, Middlesex, UK, 21 May 1935.

Terry Lightfoot formed his first band in 1955 and by 1959 had established a strong reputation: that year he toured with Kid Ory and played for the BBC's Festival of Jazz at the Royal Albert Hall, making a strong impression with his clean-cut, well-rehearsed act. A headliner through Britain's trad boom years (he appeared in Dick Lester's 1962 fantasy *It's Trad Dad*), Lightfoot was strong competition for Bilk, Barber and Ball, with sidemen including Colin Smith, Alan Elsdon and Dick Hawdon (trumpets), John Bennett, Roy Williams, Phil Rhodes (trombones) and Colin Bates (piano). After the boom he carried on very successfully through the 1960s, touring clubs and theatres, appearing on radio and TV, and joining Kenny Ball for a year in 1967. His band of the 1970s featured another strong brass team, Ian Hunter-Randall (trumpet) and Mike Cooke (trombone), and stayed busy in clubs and theatres. Lightfoot ran a pub from 1978–83 but never turned his back on performing, and in 1983 went fully professional again. In the 1990s he continued to play in clubs, festivals and special theatre presentations, including a salute to Louis Armstrong, featuring a new team of sidemen including Ian Bateman (trombone) and Paul Lacey (trumpet). Following heart surgery in 2002 Lightfoot was quickly back to full performing-strength in 2003. [DF]

⊙ **Stardust** (1990; Timeless). Studio set by Lightfoot's well-drilled band, with the leader and trumpeter Ian Hunter-Randall outstanding.

⊙ **Down On Bourbon Street** (1993; Timeless). This is a fine live set, again with longtime sidemen Ian Hunter-Randall and Phil Rhodes.

Kirk Lightsey

Piano.

b. Detroit, Michigan15 Feb 1937.

After taking up piano at five, Kirk Lightsey became a full-time jazz musician in his late teens and by the early 1960s was accompanying artists such as Melba Liston, Ernestine Anderson, O.C. Smith and Damita Jo. In the mid-1960s he became a sideman for both Chet Baker and Sonny Stitt, but it was his work with Dexter Gordon (1979–83) that brought him to the attention of a wider jazz public. Other leaders with whom Lightsey has recorded include: trumpeters Brian Lynch and Woody Shaw; saxophonists James Clay, David Murray, Clifford Jordan, James Moody and Harold Land; vibes player Steve Nelson; and guitarists Peter Leitch and Jimmy Raney. But he was also a vital member of two contrasting bands: the Leaders and the Satchmo Legacy. The former beautifully exploited Lightsey's classy, post-bop sensibility in state-of-the-art 1980s jazz; the latter, a band dedicated to presenting Armstrong's legacy in contemporary settings, relied heavily on Lightsey's versatility and wit. A highly polished, virtuosic but always architecturally minded player, Lightsey continued to be in great demand for sideman duties through the 1990s and beyond. Among those calling on his services were singer Jeri Brown (*"Unfolding" The Peacocks*, Justin Time; 1992) and drummer Lotus Hayes (*The Super Quartet*, Timeless, 1994) and tenorist Bobby Wellins, with whom he was heard live in the UK in 2003, but perhaps his unique talents shine best on two Monk tributes by saxophonist Sonny Fortune, *Monk's Zood* (Konnex; 1993) and *Four In One* (Blue Note; 1994). Lightsey also recorded a large number of albums under his own name in the 1980s and 1990s, mostly for Sunnyside and Criss Cross. [CP]

⊙ **Lightsey Live** (1985; Sunnyside). Unshowy, but surprisingly subtle solo album taking in Monk ("Trinkle Tinkle"), Tony Williams and Rodgers and Hart, along with a showstopper, "Fee Fi Fo Fum".

⊙ **From Kirk To Nat** (1990; Criss Cross Criss). A tribute to Nat "King" Cole, but a highly individual one, featuring Lightsey's gravelly singing and guitarist Kevin Eubanks taking the Oscar Moore role, plus the supple, propulsive bassist Rufus Reid.

The Leaders Trio

⊙ **Heaven Dance** (1988; Sunnyside). Lightsey in sparkling form, especially on the album's title track, but Cecil McBee (bass) and Famoudou Don Moye (drums) also shine.

Lincoln Center Jazz Orchestra

A key element of the Jazz At Lincoln Center project, this standard-size big band was founded in 1988, and was initially directed by arranger-transcriber David Berger before Wynton Marsalis took over in 1993. It usually tours the USA and elsewhere for at least half the year, featuring the sound of live big band performance and a mixture of repertory and new material. Among the many alumni of the orchestra are Marcus Roberts, Nicholas Payton and Wycliffe Gordon while, especially in the early years, several veteran players provided the backbone for the repertory performances. [BP]

⊙ **They Came To Swing** (1992-4; Columbia). Recorded live, all but three tracks are by the full LCJO, covering mainly Ellington and Strayhorn plus material by Monk, Gillespie and the Billy Eckstine band, and an excerpt from the premiere of Marsalis's piece *Blood On The Fields*.

Abbey Lincoln

Vocals, composer.

b. Chicago, 6 Aug 1930.

One of twelve children, Lincoln was brought up on a farm in Michigan, and then at the age of fourteen she moved with her mother to Kalamazoo, where she started performing in high school. She began singing with a local band there and, after moving to California, worked professionally both there and in Honolulu, under the name Anna Marie. After other name changes she became Abbey Lincoln and made her first album, backed by Benny Carter. Meeting Max Roach (who was her husband from 1962–70), she started singing with small jazz groups, and recorded on her own and Roach's albums. She began writing some of her own material, often full of social and political comment, and has also worked as an actress in films by Spike Lee; she was given the new name Aminata Moseka, which she has used professionally, by African politicians. In the 1980s she employed younger musicians such as Steve Coleman, and in the 1990s her recording and performing career moved into a higher gear altogether as the world woke up to what a poignantly charismatic and startling talent she has always been. Her distinctive style, an influence on Cassandra Wilson among others, is marked by the example of Billie Holiday, but the subject matter of her writing aspires to the wisdom and simplicity of a folk singer. [BP]

Straight Ahead (1961; Candid). Performing with most of Max Roach's current band plus Eric Dolphy, this is Lincoln's socially conscious statement, with fine singing and playing to back it up. "Retribution" is a warning, while the nineteenth-century poem "When Malindy Sings" is "innocent" praise of the former slave race.

Abbey Lincoln and Hank Jones

When There Is Love (1992; Verve). This unlikely duet treads a fine line between Lincoln's current devotion to her own material and her early adherence to standards, with perhaps the most unobtrusively perfect accompaniment she ever received.

Abe Lincoln

Trombone.

b. Lancaster, Pennsylvania, 29 March 1907; d. 8 June 2000.

Lincoln came from a musical family (three of his five brothers played, and his father was a cornet virtuoso) and he began playing trombone at the age of five. From 1921 he played with brother Bud Lincoln's band, recorded in 1924 (with Ace Brigode) and played with the California Ramblers (replacing Tommy Dorsey) from 1926. Thereafter he led his own band in Pennsylvania in 1933 and worked with a string of famous leaders, including Paul Whiteman, Leo Reisman, Roger Wolfe Kahn and Ozzie Nelson, before moving into studio work in Los Angeles working for radio shows including Bing Crosby, Al Jolson, Fibber McGee and Molly, Fred Astaire and others as lead trombonist; a career that would span 25 years. In the 1940s and 1950s, amid the jazz revival, he worked with Wingy Manone, Wild Bill Davison, Matty Matlock, Red Nichols and others; his explosive contributions to Matlock recording dates for groups such as the Rampart Street Paraders (1953-60) – wide-intervalled, like a souped-up Miff Mole with a stratospheric top range thrown in for good measure – are a reliable high spot. In the 1960s and 1970s he was still a busy freelancer, working with, among many others, Pete Fountain and Wild Bill Davison and he continued playing on the festival circuit (notably Sacramento) into the 90s.

Like Cutty Cutshall and Lou McGarity, Lincoln played for most of his life in the shadow of Jack Teagarden, but his roistering style and unique sense of humour marked him out, and on one famous date for Bobby Hackett (see below) there's evidence of Lincoln playing Teagarden at his own game and hitting a home run. "I just got out of the way when it was Abe's turn" recalled Teagarden at the time. [DF]

➤➤ **Bobby Hackett** *(Coast Concert/Jazz Ultimate).*

John Lindberg

Bass.

b. Royal Oaks, Michigan, 16 March 1959.

John Lindberg played percussion in school bands from the age of ten, and left school at sixteen to pursue music professionally. He moved to New York in 1977, where he introduced himself to drummer Charles "Bobo" Shaw, with whom he subsequently worked. Still very young, he recorded with Shaw, saxophonist Frank Lowe, and in Shaw's group the Human Arts Ensemble. He formed the New York String Trio with violinist Billy Bang and guitarist James Emery, whom he had met in the mid-70s at the Creative Music Studio in Woodstock. The NYST has continued to work and record since, with a succession of violinists including Charles Burnham, Regina Carter and Rob Thomas. Lindberg played in the Anthony Braxton quartet from 1979–85, also recording duos with Braxton. Among his dates as a leader are *Trilogy Of Works For Eleven Instrumentalists* (1985; Black Saint) and the unbeatable trio with trombonist George Lewis and percussionist Barry Altschul, *Give And Take* (1983; Black Saint). In 1981 he moved to Paris, then returned to the USA two years later, settling in upstate New York. In the 90s Lindberg played with swingful drummer Ed Thigpen (aka Mr Taste), pianist Eric Watson and German trombone innovator Albert Mangelsdorff, recording *Dodging Bullets* (1992, sans Thigpen), *Quartet Afternoon* (1994) and *Resurrection Of A Dormant Soul* (1996) for Black Saint. In 1997 he recorded *Bounce* with an unusual ensemble mixing Thigpen, trumpet star Dave Douglas and ROVA Saxophone Quartet member Larry Ochs. His solo disc, *Luminosity* (1996; Music & Arts), dedicated to David Izenzon (an oft-cited influence of his), is an excellent place to study Lindberg's limber, rather light-fingered and glassy-textured approach. A latter association with Frankfurt label Between The Lines has produced *A Tree Frog Tonality* (2000) with Ochs, trumpeter Leo Smith and drummer Andrew Cyrille, *Two By Five* (2001) for string ensemble and *Ruminations Upon Ives And Gottschalk*, all evidence that Lindberg is developing into a substantial modern composer. [JC]

Ruminations Upon Ives And Gottschalk (2002; Between The Lines). Trumpeter Bakida Carrol, drummer Susie Ibarra and Steve Korn on bansuri flute among other wind instruments contribute to an intriguing, mature set characterized by intertwining musical lines and a faintly Asian atmosphere. A highlight is Lindberg's post 9/11 sombre tribute to Gottschalk's "Holy Spirit, Light Divine": "Spirit Great, Golden Shrine".

Jimmy Lyons/Sunny Murray Trio

Jump Up – What To Do About (1980; hat Art). Though the billing doesn't even list Lindberg, this fantastic trio session may be his best playing ever. Most of his early records as a leader are well worth having, especially for their extraordinary group feel, but on this sympathetic threesome Lindberg plays some quite astounding arco (a strong Paul Chambers feel) and assured unpulsed interplay.

Jason Lindner

Piano, composer.

b. Brooklyn, New York, 1 Feb 1973.

Lindner played by ear at the age of three and had piano lessons for five years from the age of seven. He attended the High School of Music and Art from 1989–91 and spent a year at Mannes College before learning with Barry Harris and Chris Anderson. Playing in art galleries and other small venues from 1989, he worked with Junior Cook, Dennis Charles and many others. A regular performer at Smalls in Greenwich Village from its opening in 1994, he has led a big band there weekly since 1995 – according to Lindner, "It's the only big band today dedicated to new, original music, and it's bringing jazz into new areas previously untouched." His debut album *Premonition* (2000; Stretch) was a little too complacent and polite, despite its Brazilian influences and Ellingtonian flourishes. Yet it at least displayed the hallmark cosmopolitanism of America's younger jazzers – like the music of Avishai Cohen or Claudia Acuna, Lindney's curiosity is fired by time signatures and melodies sourced from different musics from all over the globe. [BP]

Various Artists

Jazz Underground: Live At Smalls (1997; Impulse!). One of the five top-selling new jazz albums of 1998, this has Lindner's more conventional playing on two tracks with saxophonist Charles Owens. Two other tracks feature his regular big band including Owens and Myron Walden, with solos by trumpeter Diego Urcola and trombonist Ari Lebovich and a collective spirit reminiscent of the early Mike Westbrook band.

>> **Avishai Cohen** *(Adama).*

Ray Linn

Trumpet.

b. Chicago, 20 Oct 1920; d. 1996.

One of the West Coast's greatest jazz all-rounders, Linn was a powerful lead-trumpeter with Tommy Dorsey (1939–41), Woody Herman (1942 and 1945), Artie Shaw (1944) and Boyd Raeburn (1946), amongst others. From 1945 he settled in Los Angeles, playing for TV, films and radio, and took part in countless sessions, initially developing a bop style (including four 1945 small-group titles under his own name) but later reverting to Dixieland. From the 1950s he regularly led and played for bands in the company of such fellow West Coast masters as Matty Matlock, Abe Lincoln, Ray Sherman, Eddie Miller, but recorded sparely as a leader – only two self-led albums appear in the discographies. A dedicated musician of high standards, Linn's work is always of the highest order and worth seeking out on record. [DF]

Empty Suit Blues (1981; Trend). Immaculate Dixieland arranged by Linn, supported by Eddie Miller, Bob Havens, Dave Frishberg, and with vocals by the great Mary Ann McCall.

Melba Liston

Trombone, arranger.

b. Kansas City, Missouri, 13 Jan 1926; d. 23 April 1999.

Melba Liston's family moved to Los Angeles in 1937, where she studied trombone in high school. She played in a theatre pit band led by Bardu Ali, a former frontman for Chick Webb, from 1942–4, and her first arrangements were written for this group. She was a member of the Gerald Wilson big band from 1944–7, and later worked alongside Wilson in the Count Basie band from 1948–9. She joined Dizzy Gillespie in the last year of one big band, 1950, but stayed for the whole lifespan of another, from 1956–7. She worked in New York and Bermuda with her own all-female quintet in 1958, and began freelance arranging. She was one of two women members of Quincy Jones's touring band from 1959–61 (the other being pianist Patti Bown). Thereafter, she was occasionally active as a player but always busy as a writer, arranging on jazz albums for Randy Weston, Johnny Griffin and Milt Jackson; whilst also for popular singers such as Tony Bennett and Diana Ross and for TV commercials. She spent time teaching in Harlem and Brooklyn in the late 1960s, Watts in the early 1970s and in Jamaica from 1974–9. Following the second annual Kansas City Women's jazz festival in 1979, she returned to full-time playing, based in New York, and in the early 1980s she led a seven-piece mixed group, Melba Liston and Company. Following a serious stroke in 1985, her activity was severely restricted but she continued her arranging via computer software, resuming a writing relationship with Randy Weston.

Liston's 1947 recording with Dexter Gordon ("Mischievous Lady") gives a favourable indication of her potential as a jazz trombonist, but in her big-band playing she was rarely featured except on ballads. However, her arranging, though not always credited, made a big impression, from the 1950 Gillespie band onwards. As Liston recalled, Gillespie asked her to bring an arrangement to her first rehearsal with the band, "And of course they got about two measures and fell out, and got all confused and stuff. And Dizzy said, 'Now who's the bitch?'" [BP]

>> **Randy Weston** *(The Spirits Of Our Ancestors).*

Booker Little

Trumpet.

b. Memphis, 2 April 1938; d. 5 Oct 1961.

Little was part of the 1950s Memphis jazz underground, which included George Coleman, Charles Lloyd and pianists Harold Mabern and Phineas Newborn. He moved to Chicago in 1957, and then joined Max Roach in 1958, remaining associated with him for most of his brief career, which was prematurely terminated by uremia. He also recorded and gigged with Mal Waldron, John Coltrane and Eric Dolphy, with whom he played and recorded in 1960–61.

Little had tremendous fluency and a bright, clear sound which, although descended from Clifford Brown, was more emotionally ambiguous. His harmonic approach was similarly adventurous, stretching the bonds of tonality without straining the logic of his lines. [BP]

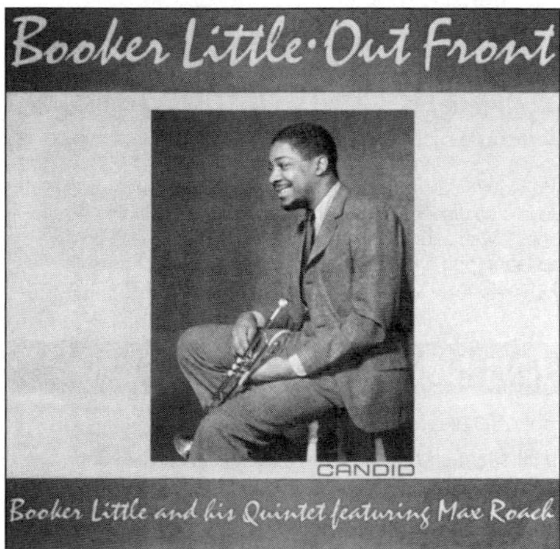

Out Front (1961; Candid). The last of Little's recordings, apart from the Dolphy set below and a further sextet *Victory And Sorrow*, this has an impressive line-up (Dolphy, Ron Carter, Max Roach, etc) and even more impressive playing and writing from the leader.

➤➤ **Eric Dolphy** *(At The Five Spot Vol. 1).*

Alan Littlejohn

Trumpet, flugelhorn, leader.

b. London, 4 Jan 1929; d. 12 Nov 1995.

A veteran of of the Cy Laurie (1952) and Eric Silk bands (1953), Littlejohn worked around the British jazz scene for over thirty years, leading a variety of bands including the Littlejohn-Milliner sextet, featuring Lew Hooper (tenor), which played an ambitiously eclectic repertoire: in the 1960s they backed a series of visiting Americans such as Earl Hines, Ben Webster and Bill Coleman. Later in the 1970s Littlejohn's Jazzers, a seven-piece Dixieland group, was resident at London's 100 Club. In between he often worked with co-trumpeter Al Fairweather, in bands such as the Sonny Dee (Stan Daly) band and as a touring duo, and all around the London club and pub circuit as a soloist and sideman. From August 1990 he was the trumpet-leader of Laurie Chescoe's Goodtime Jazz, his straight lead (and occasional singing) providing a reliable centre for this fine new Dixieland group. A thorough student of classic jazz, Littlejohn was a close friend of Billy Butterfield, an association reflected in his performance: his flugelhorn in particular carried the same flurries of lyricism that mark Butterfield's best latterday work. [DF]

Martin Litton

Piano.

b. Grays, Essex, UK, 14 May 1957.

After obtaining a BA in music at Colchester Institute, Litton worked with Steve Lane (1978–80), Harry Gold (1980–83) and, after a freelance period with George Melly, Ken Colyer and others, joined Kenny Ball (1983–5), with whom he toured the Middle East and Russia. In 1985 he began freelancing, regularly accompanying Kenny Davern on British visits, recording with Kenny Baker and George Chisholm, and subbing with Humphrey Lyttelton's band on records and live dates. From 1983 he also appeared on London's South Bank with shows including *Tribute To Benny Goodman*, *Tribute To Fats Waller*, *From Dixieland To Swing*, *Creole Clarinets* and *Giants Of Jazz Piano*. A strong, sophisticated soloist with an eclectic repertoire and an eye to presentation, he now works regularly with Harry Strutter's Hot Rhythm Orchestra and Randy Colville's Collection, as well as deputizing with Ray Wordsworth, Bob Hunt, Humphrey Lyttelton and others, and often performs solo at festivals. Litton plays in the areas of Jelly Roll Morton through to Teddy Wilson, and is Britain's most gifted latterday swing pianist. [DF]

Martin Litton Jazz Piano (1992; Solo Art). Litton's first solo album, full of delicacy and strength, playing sophisticated piano repertoire with Peter Morgan (bass) and Allan Ganley (drums).

Charles Lloyd

Tenor and soprano saxophones, flutes, composer.

b. Memphis, 15 March 1938.

As a teenager Lloyd played alto with R&B bands, including those of B. B. King and Bobby Bland. From 1956 he studied composition at the University of Southern California. After graduating he taught music until 1961, when he joined Chico Hamilton, switching to tenor saxophone and playing more flute. In 1964–5 he worked with the Cannonball Adderley sextet, touring and recording with the group, which

RAFFAELLA CAVALIERI

Charles Lloyd

brought him to international attention. In 1966 he formed his own quartet with Keith Jarrett, Jack DeJohnette and first Cecil McBee, later Ron McClure on bass, which rapidly established itself as one of the most dynamic and successful groups of the late 1960s.

Lloyd's early influences were Coleman Hawkins, Ben Webster and Lester Young, and he also became steeped in the work of Sonny Stitt, Sonny Rollins and John Coltrane. But by the mid-1960s he was a virtuoso performer whose passionate style incorporated elements from the whole tenor saxophone tradition, yet was unmistakably contemporary. His rhythm-section of brilliant young virtuosi had a similarly broad concept and the quartet's music covered everything from churchy gospel pieces to blues, modal music, abstraction and rock. Lloyd and Jarrett did virtually all the composing, but the repertoire would often extend to the occasional Lennon and McCartney tune. The quartet had a huge success at the Newport and Monterey jazz festivals in 1966, and in 1967 was the first jazz group to perform at one of the new cathedrals of rock music – the Fillmore Auditorium in San Francisco.

During the early 1970s he toured and played festivals in the USA, and he began undertaking more teaching and academic work (and not just music – he also became a transcendental meditation instructor). He kept a low profile at the decade's end, but he did perform with Michel Petrucciani at the Montreux festival in 1982, and on the *One Night With Blue Note* album and documentary. He returned to recording, with ECM, in the late 80s with mixed results.

Lloyd and his first quartet (1966–9) made an immense contribution to jazz at a very difficult time: when the entire scene was dominated by rock music he showed that it was possible to make music that could communicate to young audiences without having to cheapen itself in the process. [IC]

⊙ **Forest Flower/Soundtrack** (1968; Atlantic). A reissue coupling two of Lloyd's finest mid-60s records. *Forest Flower* has the original quartet (bassist Cecil McBee was replaced by Ron McClure for *Soundtrack*) and is the pick of the two. Partly recorded at the Monterey festival, it features originals by band members and "East Of The Sun", and, contrary to some critics' complaints, the result is a pure joy.

⊙ **Voice In The Night** (1998; ECM). Since his return to playing in the late 1980s, Lloyd has grown constantly. Yet on ECM albums prior to this one (of which *Notes From Big Sur* is the most consistent), his compositions were often nondescript and his playing occasionally showed signs of torpor – despite featuring beautiful playing from the likes of Stenson, Danielsson, Jormin and Hart. Here in the company of guitarist John Abercrombie, bassist Dave Holland and legendary drummer Billy Higgins, Lloyd plays with ecstatic lyricism. His title track is a glorious ballad and he gets the most subtle support from Abercrombie. They play an excellent version of an Elvis Costello tune, "God Give Me Strength", and Lloyd's "Dorotea's Studio" is a romantic Latin piece. But Lloyd also glances back at his earlier music including "Island Blues", with a funky, bluesy bass and guitar groove and wailing tenor, and a fifteen-minute performance of "Forest Flower: Sunrise/Sunset".

Jon Lloyd

Soprano and alto saxophones.

b. Stratford-upon-Avon, Warwickshire, UK, 20 Oct 1958.

Always a player who operates at the freer end of the jazz spectrum, despite his quartet's music occasionally beginning with written heads, Jon Lloyd first became involved in improvised music in 1985, when he formed the Lloyd-Fowler-Garside trio, featuring Dave Fowler on drums and Gus Garside on bass and percussion. This trio later constituted the musical core of the Air Ensemble, an improvised dance and music project involving dancers Claire Carnell and Thomas Kampe. Lloyd, in addition to his involvement with a number of short-lived or one-off projects – the nine-piece improvising group Anacrusis, featuring Evan Parker, Jon Corbett, Marcio Mattos, Sylvia Hallett and others; the Extempore Saxophone Quartet featuring John Butcher, Pete McPhail and Tony Bevan; a duo with violinist/viola player Phil Wachsmann – formed his own quartet in 1989 with pianist John Law, bassist Paul Rogers (replaced when he moved to France by US-born bassist Tim Hells) and drummer Mark Sanders. This band made the highly regarded *By Confusion* (hat Art; 1997). The same year, Lloyd was commissioned by the Arts Council to write music for an international sextet including US-born cellist Stanley Adler, and the resulting album, recorded live in Colchester, was released by FMR in 1998 as *Praxis*. The music reflects one of Lloyd's chief artistic concerns: "to create structures which encourage creative improvisation ... to lay down harmonic and rhythmic ideas around which a soundscape can develop". Adler is also involved in Lloyd's group Four, featuring percussionist Paul Clarvis and bassist Marcio Mattos, made *Four And Five* (see below) while in 2000–01, Lloyd toured and recorded as part of John Law's group Abacus. [CP]

⊙ **Syzygy** (1990; Leo). Lively but cultured free-ish jazz, its impact heightened by the pleasing contrast between the freedom of Rogers and the more structured approach of Law.

⊙ **Head!** (1993; Leo). Same personnel as above, but recorded at three locations on the band's Arts Council tour. Extended improvisations give four of the UK's top free players space to really stretch out.

⊙ **Four And Five** (1999; hatOLOGY). Thoughtful, provocative and evocative in equal measure, this may be the highlight of Lloyd's output to date.

Joe Locke

Vibes.

b. Palo Alto, California, 18 March 1959.

Although he took private lessons in percussion and studied theory at the Eastman School of Music, Locke is self-taught as a jazz vibes player. He became active on the New York jazz scene in the early 1980s, making his own first album co-led with pianist Phil Markowitz in 1983. He has enjoyed a long-standing musical partnership with Eddie Henderson, touring Europe with him in 1989 and appearing on several of his albums, but has recorded with numerous other artists, including George Cables, Ronnie Cuber, Barbara Dennerlein, Dave O'Higgins and the Mingus Big Band. He has led his own quartets, with either Mark Soskin or Billy Childs on piano, and in 1999 he briefly joined Cecil Taylor's quartet. In the new century he led a new group including Bob Berg, and played alongside Tim Garland in a trio with Geoff Keezer called Storms/Nocturnes (with whom he recorded the highly praised album *Rising Tide*). Locke's favourite vibists are Bobby Hutcherson, Milt Jackson, Gary Burton, Mike Mainieri and Dave Pike, while other inspirations run from Coltrane to Joni Mitchell to composers Sibelius and Takemitsu. [BP]

⊙ **Inner Space** (1995; Steeplechase). A programme of standards such as "Fly Me To The Moon", jazz standards like "Django" and "Quiet Now" and originals showcases Locke's thoughtful and stimulating approach with his quartet (including Mark Soskin and bassist Harvie Swartz).

⊙ **Four Walls Of Freedom** (2002; Sirocco). Two lengthy compositions by Locke, the title-suite and "Suite De Morfeo", form the meat of this stimulating programme played by a quintet including Gerard Presencer and, on one of his last recordings, Bob Berg.

Mark Lockheart

Tenor and soprano saxophones.

b. Lymington, Hampshire, UK, 31 March 1961.

Mark Lockheart was introduced to the music of jazz musicians like Miles Davis and Frank Sinatra by his father, an amateur alto saxophonist. Lockheart studied classical saxophone and clarinet at London's Trinity College of Music from 1979–83. After graduating, he began working with London-based musicians including Django Bates, bassist Steve Berry and Roger Dean's Lysis. In 1984, Lockheart was a founder member of the idiosyncratic big band, Loose Tubes, which gathered together some of the most gifted musicians of that generation. The ensemble disbanded at the beginning of the 1990s, and in 1991 Lockheart formed the quartet Perfect Houseplants, with pianist Huw Warren, bassist Dudley Phillips and drummer Martin France – who released their debut eponymous album in 1993. In 1995, Lockheart toured with Django Bates's large orchestra, Delightful Precipice, appearing all over Europe including the Berlin jazz festival, Le Mans, Copenhagen and the Norwegian Molde jazz festival. He also toured with the maverick guitarist Billy Jenkins, and released a duo album, *Matheran*, with guitarist John Parricelli, and the second Perfect Houseplants album, *Clec*. The same year, Perfect Houseplants began collaborating with the early music vocal quartet, The Orlando Consort,

Mark Lockheart

and they recorded two successful albums together, *Extempore* and *Extempore 2*. In 1998 Lockheart was given the Peter Whittingham Award to finance his composing for an eleven-piece band and to record an album. Using Perfect Houseplants as the nucleus, he added brass, reeds, woodwind and guitar to make up The Scratch Band. The album, *Through Rose-Coloured Glasses*, under Lockheart's name, was released that year, and the successful experiment later produced a wistful and nostalgic follow-up, *Imaginary Dances*.

Lockheart is a consummate saxophonist and a versatile composer. His eclectic tastes and pursuits have brought him work with experimental pop groups such as Stereolab and Radiohead, yet he regularly plays with John Paricelli's quartet and with Seb Rochford's chunky, drum'n'bass influenced group Polar Bear. His favourites include Wayne Shorter, Jan Garbarek and Dewey Redman, and other inspirations include Egberto Gismonti, Django Bates and Pat Metheny. [IC]

⊙ **Extempore** (1997; Linn). Houseplants meet the Orlando Consort, the two groups interacting freely to produce a wide variety of music without losing the haunting resonances of plainchant or other medieval church music. Subtlety and sonority are the hallmarks of the eleven actual collaborations of the two quartets.

⊙ **Through Rose-Coloured Glasses** (1998; Subtone). Lockheart's first album under his own name is a genial *tour de force*. He composed and arranged all eight pieces for a line-up which includes French horn, bass trombone, tuba, flute and alto flute, and his changes of texture are often exquisite and dramatic. All the pieces have their own way of breathing, and the solos are integrated into the ensemble.

Didier Lockwood

Violin.

b. Calais, France, 11 Feb 1956.

Lockwood's father was a violin teacher, and Didier began on violin at six, going on to study at the Paris Conservatoire. Whilst there he heard Jimi Hendrix, Johnny Winter and John Mayall, and began playing rock and blues; Jean-Luc Ponty's album with Zappa, *King Kong*, first got Lockwood interested in jazz. In 1972, at sixteen, he stopped his formal training, and soon after joined the French rock group Magma, recording a live double album with them. He began playing gigs in Paris with Daniel Humair, Aldo Romano and others. At the North Sea festival he met Zbigniew Seifert and Stephane Grappelli, and was soon playing standards and doing tours with the latter violin master aged just 21. Lockwood was deeply immersed in the music of Coltrane when he formed a group called Surya (from the Sanskrit meaning "sun"), which fused jazz and rock with classical overtones, following the work of Jerry Goodman, Michal Urbaniak and Jean-Luc Ponty. (Though unlike them Lockwood wasn't playing electric violin but a 160-year-old acoustic instrument with a pick-up). He diversified even further in the late 70s, playing with five or six bands of jazz and rock persuasions, touring with Grappelli and recording with Tony Williams.

He now has a solid international reputation and tours regularly in the USA and Europe. His assertion that "musicians have to be itinerant" is substantiated by his appearances on over 30 albums with diverse musicians such as Paco de Lucia, Yehudi Menuhin, Astor Piazzola and John Petrucciani. In 2000 he recorded the ineluctable homage to his mentor, *A Tribute to Stephane Grappelli*; whilst the 2003 double *Globe-Trotter* saw him taking stock of various musics and collaborations past and present. [IC]

➤➤ **Gordon Beck** *(For Evans Sake).*

Steve Lodder

Piano, synthesizers, organ, harmonium.

b. St Helier, Jersey, UK, 10 April 1951.

Stephen John Lodder's paternal grandmother was an organist and violinist, and his maternal grandfather was a choral singer. Lodder was a classical organ scholar and graduated with a BA Hons in music from Cambridge University. After teaching at post-graduate level in Nottingham, he gained his Associateship of the Royal College of Organists. In the late 1970s, he began playing jazz-rock-fusion, and soon began working with many of London's leading musicians including Paul Nieman's Elephant, John Etheridge, Harry Beckett, Brian Abraham's District Six and Annie Whitehead. In 1987, Lodder became a member of George Russell's Living Time Orchestra, remaining with it throughout the 1990s. He also began a long and artistically fruitful association with saxophonist and bandleader Andy Sheppard, working with Sheppard's Commotion, 1991–5, his Big Commotion, 1993–5, and his Small Commotion, 1993–7. Lodder is also a member of the trio Inclassificable, with Sheppard and Brazilian percussionist Nana Vasconcelos and his collaborations with Sheppard has involved composing music for television.

Lodder is one of the growing number of musicians who are bilingual in classical music and jazz, and he has toured with classical saxophonist, John Harle. He is a virtuoso on his acoustic and electronic instruments, and his great versatility keeps him much in demand. [IC]

⊙ **Inclassificable** (1994; Label Bleu). This pithy and delightful fusion of many musical strands uses acoustic and electronic instruments, with Vasconcelos's subtle percussion and his breathy voice often humanizing the soundscape. The music is very imaginative and deftly played and might be classified as a kind of idiosyncratic world music.

Mark Ramsden/Steve Lodder

⊙ **Above The Clouds** (1995; Breathe). This haunting duo album was recorded live and unedited in St Thomas's Church, London, with Lodder playing the church organ and Ramsden producing ravishing sonorities on the soprano saxophone. The two performers arranged some anonymous, early music pieces, and music by Albinoni, Fiocco and Stanley alongside their own. The lyrical, brooding, timeless atmosphere is sustained throughout.

Julie London

Singer.

b. Santa Rosa, Cal., 26 Sept 1926; d. 18 Oct 2000.

Born Julie Peck, Julie London was one of the best-loved torch singers of her generation with a sultry and intimate voice that was enormously appealing. She began as a film actress appearing in Nabonga (1944), *On Stage Everybody* (1945) and the thriller *The Red House* (1947) with Edward G. Robinson. But her second husband, Bobby Troup, was a jazz musician and the composer of "Route 66", "Their Hearts Were Full Of Spring" and "Julie Is Her Name"; it was Troup who persuaded London to begin a singing career and her 1956 recording of "Cry Me A River" became a million-seller. By the late 1950s she was recording prolifically and working extensively on TV, radio and in nightclubs, as well as taking the occasional film role, until 1961. Her last album was made in 1969, after which she returned to TV acting. Her greatest hit "Cry Me A River" however found new fame amid the nouveau jazz revival of the 1990s, and she is remembered for both her clear delivery and a spectacular appearance that is celebrated on numerous LP covers. [DF]

⊙ **Julie Is Her Name Vol.1 & 2** (1992; Liberty). London's work is now widely reissued on CD, but this "twofer" is a good place to start: two of her classic recordings, including the original l955 session (with Barney Kessel and Ray Leatherwood) which produced "Cry Me A River" and twelve more coolly-seductive titles including "No Moon At All" and "Easy Street".

Loose Tubes

A 21-piece band of young London-based musicians, Loose Tubes was one of the most original large ensembles of the 1980s. Its orthodox big-band line-up was augmented by tuba, bass-clarinet, flute and percussion, and was totally unlike the conventional jazz/dance orchestra. No bandleader fronted it and it functioned democratically. It set up in either a "V" formation, or played in the round, affording the eye-contact that enabled cues to be given by anyone in the

Jak Kilby

Loose Tubes

band who was free to do so at that moment. The brilliantly assured writing was done largely by Django Bates (keyboards) and Steve Berry (bass), and occasionally by other members, and it showed an understanding not only of the whole jazz tradition but of rock, African and other ethnic music. Rich melodies, ebullient solos, sonorous harmonies and beautifully executed rhythms were played with great fire. The band's first public performance was in London in June 1984, and thereafter it played clubs, theatres and festivals in the London area, including several spells at Ronnie Scott's and an appearance at the BBC Promenade concerts in 1987. The group disbanded in the early 1990s, but most of the musicians involved still collaborate on a variety of projects. [IC]

⊙ **Open Letter** (1988; Editions EG). This, the third Loose Tubes album, was produced by Teo Macero and he caught the band at its very best. The eight tracks, all written by members, cover a wide area of music and are a superb blend of vernacular roots with highly literate harmony and orchestration.

Joe Lovano

Saxophones.

b. Cleveland, Ohio, 29 Dec 1952.

Although he began playing with his father's bands in his teens, Joe Lovano came to true prominence only in his late twenties when his vital contribution to the various recordings of Paul Motian began to be recognized. Prior to this, Lovano's smoky tenor had graced the bands of Lonnie Liston Smith (1974–6) and Woody Herman (1976–9), but his classy yet impassioned interpretations of Motian originals, Monk tunes and even Broadway show favourites on such albums as *Misterioso* (1986), *On Broadway* (three volumes, 1988–91) and *One Time Out* (1987) brought him great critical acclaim. Particularly effective when forming a frontline with a guitarist (Bill Frisell in the Paul Motian trio and John Scofield in his band), Lovano is also a considerable leader in his own right, as evidenced by his Wind Ensemble's *Worlds* and his extraordinarily consistent run of albums for Blue Note in the 1990s. These ranged, in the second half of the 1990s, from *Celebrating Sinatra* (1996), more than a cut above the usual tributes, through a duo recording with Cuban label-mate, pianist Gonzalo Rubalcaba, *Flying Colours* (1998), to the ultimate test of the tenor player aspiring to true greatness, a trio album (see *Trio Fascination* below). Into the new millennium, Lovano's output remained prodigious with, among other albums, *Flights Of Fancy: Trio Fascination Vol 2* (2001), in part featuring performances by different line-ups edited together, and *Viva Caruso* (2002), a tribute to the Italian tenor whose third stream-esque approach recalled 1995's *Rush Hour*. Deservedly one of the busiest saxophonists, courtesy of his supremely cultured tone and an intelligent but swinging approach encompassing influences ranging from swing players through to

John Coltrane and even Ornette Coleman, Lovano is one of the most mature talents currently operating in the music. [CP]

⊙ **Worlds** (1989; Label Bleu). An excellent live album documenting Lovano's innovative and multitextured music, featuring Bill Frisell and Paul Motian as well as Tim Hagans and trombonist Gary Valente.

⊙ **Landmarks** (1990; Blue Note). Lovano's Blue Note debut, its sophistication and polish setting the standard for the saxophonist's later 1990s recordings for the company.

⊙ **From The Soul** (1991; Blue Note). A masterful album, perfectly cast (Michel Petrucciani, piano; Dave Holland, bass; Ed Blackwell, drums) and beautifully executed – "Body And Soul" receives yet another definitive rendering and Lovano's own compositions are pithy and cogent, yet swinging.

⊙ **Rush Hour** (1995; Blue Note). Lovano's most ambitious project to date, involving various Gunther Schuller ensembles and a repertoire touching most bases in modern and not-so-modern jazz.

⊙ **Trio Fascination** (1998; Blue Note). Cultured yet vigorously inventive playing from Lovano (occasionally playing straight alto) in first-class company. Dave Holland is characteristically elegantly propulsive on bass, Elvin Jones his inimitable self on drums.

⊙ **On This Day ... At The Vanguard** (2003; Blue Note). An expansive live nonet album ranging from a swing chart based on "Stomping At The Savoy" to a 15-minute improv inspired by the death of Billy Higgins.

» **Paul Motian** *(Misterioso; On Broadway Vol. 1).*

Paul Lovens

Drums and cymbals, musical saw.

b. Aachen, Germany, 6 June 1949.

Certainly the most dapper player on the European free-improv scene, Lovens is said to sport his trademark black suit and tie no matter what the occasion or outside temperature. He played drums as a child, and from the age of fourteen worked with pop groups and jazz groups of different styles. Totally self-taught, from 1969 onwards he worked almost exclusively as a free improviser and built his own customized drumset, heavily infleunced by Han Bennink. Since then, he has played with almost all the leading musicians of the international free-jazz and free-improvisation scene, and has done concert tours in more than forty countries. He is a founder member of a musicians' cooperative, and in 1976, in collaboration with Paul Lytton, he created his own record label, Po Torch Records. Alexander von Schlippenbach and Evan Parker have been regular collaborators of his, a trio that continues to tour, and he has also played with Schlippenbach in the Globe Unity Orchestra. He has also performed with Sven Ake Johansson, Gunter Christmann, Evan Parker, and regularly plays with rigorous European improvisers such as Barry Guy, John Edwards, Thomas Lehn and Martin Theurer. [IC]

>> **Globe Unity Orchestra** *(Rumbling);* **Alexander von Schlippenbach** *(Elf Bagatellen; Physics).*

Mundell Lowe

Guitar.

b. Laurel, Massachusetts, 21 April 1922.

One of the senior guitar-masters of jazz, Lowe has been a part of almost every major area of the American jazz scene. A highly schooled player, he began his career with Jan Savitt in 1942 and after military service joined Ray McKinley, working thereafter with Ellis Larkins, Red Norvo, Fats Navarro and Benny Goodman, as well as recording with Charlie Parker, Billie Holiday, Lester Young and others. In the 1950s Lowe worked for NBC New York and produced a series of solo albums for RCA Victor and Riverside, featuring anything from trios to ten-piece bands; he also recorded a well-regarded *Porgy And Bess* set for Camden in 1958, featuring Art Farmer, Tony Scott and Ben Webster. From the mid-1960s Lowe wrote for TV on the West Coast, but also found time to perform live with Richie Kamuca, Benny Carter and his wife Betty Bennett among others, as well as with his small group Transit West, which debuted at the 1983 Monterey festival. He toured, both solo and with groups, throughout the 1980s and 90s, and regularly plays with the André Previn trio. [DF]

⊙ **Mundell Lowe Quartet** (1955; Riverside/OJC). A very enjoyable quartet record (featuring Dick Hyman), which reveals Lowe's all-round musicianship and perfectly tasteful style.

⊙ **Souvenirs** (1992; Jazz Alliance). This set has Lowe with Mike Wofford (another fine but underrecorded musician) in a tribute to Lowe's former drummer Nick Ceroli.

Henry Lowther

Trumpet, flugelhorn, cornet.

b. Leicester, UK, 11 July 1941.

Lowther was orginally taught cornet by his father and he played with the local Salvation Army band. He learned the violin in his teens and studied at the Royal Academy of Music, but returned to the trumpet after getting into jazz, having heard Sonny Rollins. During the 1960s he led various groups of his own, and also worked with Mike Westbrook, the New Jazz Orchestra and rock and blues bands such as John Mayall's and Keef Hartley's. In the 1970s he played with many leading musicians in London, including Mike Gibbs, Kenny Wheeler, Tony Coe, Norma Winstone, Michael Garrick and John Dankworth. He was again leading his own bands in the 1980s, and played with John Surman, Gordon Beck, John Taylor, Gil Evans and the London Brass Virtuosi. In the mid-1990s he began working with George Russell's Living Time Orchestra. Lowther is a superb all-round trumpeter, capable of playing lead in a big band, and is also a fine soloist. [IC]

>> **Barry Guy** *(Harmos);* **John Surman** *(The Brass Project);* **Kenny Wheeler** *(Music For Large And Small Ensembles).*

Jimmie Lunceford

Multi-instrumentalist, leader, arranger.

b. Fulton, Mississippi, 6 June 1902; d. 12 July 1947.

After school in Denver (where he studied music with Paul Whiteman's father, Wilberforce) and a music degree at Fisk, Lunceford worked with New York bands led by Elmer Snowden, Wilbur Sweatman and others, before taking up teaching at Manassa High School. At Manassa he formed a school dance band – Jimmy Crawford (drums), Moses Allen (bass) and Henry Clay (trumpet) were founder members – and after augmenting it with some old colleagues from Fisk, including Willie Smith (alto), Ed Wilcox (piano) and Henry Bowles

William Gottlieb

Jimmie Lunceford

(trombone), Lunceford took his well-drilled band of teenagers on the road. Four hard years followed, living on morale and peanuts, until in 1933 the band was booked into New York's Lafayette Theater and then invited to play the Cotton Club. More touring from 1934 quickly turned Lunceford's young band into the hottest property on the road. "Willie Smith would put his bonnet on and sing a sort of nursery rhyme," remembered Eddie Durham. "Eddie Tompkins hit the high notes and did a Louis Armstrong deal. Then they had a Guy Lombardo and a Paul Whiteman bit. Then the lights would go down and they'd all lay down their horns and come out and sing as a glee club." The trumpeters threw their horns at the ceiling and caught them in regimented unison, or came down front for a dance routine, topping the show with a repertoire of rehearsed bows, Lunceford calling a number for each.

Detractors called Lunceford's band "the trained seals", but the band was musically perfect as well as being showy. Individual section rehearsals were standard practice, and Willie Smith's saxophone team, inspired by its masterful boss, rehearsed the fine points of each bar. Powerful cornermen such as Smith, tenorist Joe Thomas and trombonist Trummy Young (who joined in 1937) were soloists of premier quality, their talents powerfully featured by two arrangers: Sy Oliver (whose name is synonymous with Lunceford's) and Ed Wilcox, whose work for saxophones was especially outstanding and who after Oliver's arrival concentrated mainly on ballads and blues. The band was unbeatable, but it maintained a crippling schedule of profitable one-nighters and by 1942 Lunceford's men felt overworked and underpaid. "We knew Jimmie was making a lot of money," says Willie Smith, "because he was forever buying planes, wrecking them and buying new ones." An angry meeting at the YMCA, New York, at which Smith spoke up for the band, produced no pay rise, and a succession of cornermen – including Young and old-timers like Smith and Moses Allen – decided to move on. The band never returned to full power, though Lunceford treated his later sidemen more fairly, and claimed that his band manager had misled him over wages. A few years later, he collapsed and died while signing autographs at a music shop in Seaside, Oregon. [DF]

⊙ **Jimmy Lunceford 1930–41** (Classics). The Classics series provides the whole Lunceford story in eight volumes, available separately. Beginners should examine first the 1939–40 period, which features classics such as "White Heat", "Uptown Blues", "Lunceford Special" and "Ain't She Sweet".

⊙ **For Dancers Only** (1935–7; MCA). A fine selection, including "My Blue Heaven", "For Dancers Only", "Charmaine" and the hilarious "Merry Go Round Broke Down". Wonderful sound reproduction and faultless presentation.

⊙ **Lunceford Special: 1939–1940** (Columbia). These were the peak years of Lunceford's organization and it shows on titles including "White Heat", "What's Your Story, Morning Glory" and "T'aint What You Do".

Jesper Lundgaard

Bass.

b. Hillerød, Denmark, 12 June 1954.

Lundgaard started on Spanish guitar before taking up the bass at age sixteen. Studying music at Aarhus University, he worked with local bands and, from 1976, accompanied among others Dexter Gordon, Johnny Griffin and Pepper Adams. After playing with Thad Jones-Mel Lewis during much of their 1978 European tour, he moved to Copenhagen and worked with Jones's Eclipse big band and for two years with the Radio Jazz Group. Winner of the Ben Webster Prize in 1982 and the JASA Prize in 1991, he freelanced with resident Americans including Horace Parlan, Duke Jordan, Doug Raney and Ernie Wilkins, and toured with such as Warne Marsh, Chet Baker, Tommy Flanagan, Paul Bley and Benny Carter. In the 1990s he has played in Svend Asmussen's quartet, and was leader/producer/engineer of the Repertory Quartet. Appearing on some four hundred albums, Lundgaard always displays his superb time-playing and beautifully melodic solo-work. [BP]

The Repertory Quartet

⊙ **Hear Us Talking To You** (1995; Music Mecca). This tribute album to Armstrong (others involved music by Thad Jones and Fats Waller) finds Lundgaard leading drummer Alex Riel, guitarist Jacob Fischer and saxophonist Bob Rockwell in straight-ahead but imaginative versions of 1920s repertoire. His stunning bass solos are consistent highlights.

➤➤ **Allan Botschinsky** *(The Bench)*; **Larry Coryell** *(A Quiet Day In Spring)*; **Horace Parlan** *(Glad I Found You)*.

Carmen Lundy

Vocals.

b. Miami, 1 Nov 1954.

Carmen Lundy studied theory at Miami University and sang with the college band. Moving to New York in 1978, she first worked with Ray Barretto and then started her own trio in 1980, her pianists including John Hicks and Onaje Allan Gumbs. She made her own debut album in 1985 (*Good Morning Kiss*) and has recorded with such diverse leaders as saxophonist Charles Austin, trombonist Fred Wesley and composer Kip Hanrahan. Inspired by Sarah Vaughan and Betty Carter, she has a more bland tone than either and has a somewhat soul-influenced style which has proved very popular. Her brother Curtis (b. 1 Oct 1955) is a bassist who has worked with Betty Carter, Bobby Watson and Johnny Griffin. [BP]

⊙ **Moment To Moment** (1991; Arabesque). Her most musically successful album so far has Gumbs on keyboards, with guest appearances by Chico Freeman and Kevin Eubanks, and includes a pleasing fusion arrangement of "Invitation" as well as "Samba De La Playa" and the title track.

Jak Kilby

Carmen Lundy

Don Lusher

Trombone.

b. Peterborough, UK, 6 Nov 1923.

A virtuoso performer – his showstoppers include Leroy Anderson's "The Typewriter" played with machine-gun accuracy – Don Lusher has been the master technician of British trombone since the 1950s. Salvation-Army trained, he first worked with Joe Daniels (1947), Lou Preager and Maurice Winnick (1948), and then as replacement for Eric Breeze partnering George Chisholm in the Squadronaires (1948–51) before spells with Jack Parnell, Eric Delaney and Geraldo. His best-remembered partnership is as lead-trombonist with Ted Heath (1952-61) during which time Lusher toured internationally (including America on four occasions) and achieved a premier reputation. After leaving Heath he worked with Jack Parnell's ATV Orchestra; played on innumerable live and studio sessions; worked with Americans in London including Henry Mancini and Nelson Riddle; was lead trombonist for Frank Sinatra in London, Europe and the Middle East; and led his own big band from 1974. Later, at the invitation of Kenny Baker, he toured with The Best of British Jazz package show (with Betty Smith plus Tony Lee's Trio; later Roy Willox, Brian Lemon, Lennie Bush and Parnell), conducted master classes for the International Trombone Association, and continued his round of guest spots as a trombone celebrity. From 1975 he led the re-formed Ted Heath Orchestra until its final concert at London's Festival Hall in 2000. Lusher received the OBE in 2003. [DF]

⊙ **Don Lusher Pays Tribute To The Great Big Bands** (Horatio Nelson). A four-volume set in which Lusher and his all-star big band pay tribute to a whole range of big bands from Geraldo to Stan Kenton. Played with technical flawlessness, fire and many original touches, Lusher's re-creations are not mere cover-jobs.

Jimmy Lyons

Alto and baritone saxophones, flute, composer.

b. Jersey City, New Jersey, 1 Dec 1932; d. 19 May 1986.

In 1941 Lyons moved to New York, living with his grandfather in Harlem. He began playing alto at fifteen, and was mainly self-taught. From 1960 onwards he was associated with Cecil Taylor, becoming identified with the free jazz movement. In 1969 he played concerts with Taylor at the Maeght Foundation in France, and made his first record as leader for Byg records in Paris. In 1970–71 he taught music for Narcotic Addiction Control, and from 1971–3, with Taylor, he was artist in residence at Antioch College, Ohio. He said of this period: "I continued writing and trying to develop a more compositional sense. At Antioch College I got a chance to hear the things that people like Fletcher Henderson, Coleman Hawkins, Ben Webster had done ... I went back and listened to that music and really got turned on." In 1975 he was composer-instrumentalist and director of the Black Music Ensemble at Bennington College, Vermont. During the early 1970s he toured Japan twice with Taylor, and throughout the decade appeared with Taylor's groups at major festivals in Europe and the USA.

Lyons also worked with David Murray and with Mary Lou Williams, and in the 1980s collaborated in quartet formation with Andrew Cyrille, Joseph Jarman and Don Moye. After his untimely death from lung cancer, a concert tribute was organized in New York by his longtime associate Andrew Cyrille, and the performers included Archie Shepp, Sun Ra, Lester Bowie, Anthony Davis and Rashied Ali. [IC]

Jump Up (1980; hat Art). This is a live session at the 1980 Willisau festival, with Lyons, bassist John Lindberg and drummer Sunny Murray creating quintessential free improvisation.

Give It Up (1985; Black Saint). Lyons keeps a fairly low profile in this quintet of trumpet (Enrico Rava), bassoon (Karen Borca), bass and drums.

Jimmy Lyons and Andrew Cyrille

Something In Return (1981; Black Saint). Lyons and Cyrille always seemed to bring out the best in each other – out of their strength (and subtlety) comes forth sweetness.

➤➤ **Cecil Taylor** *(Student Studies).*

Jimmy Lytell

Clarinet.

b. New York, 1 Dec 1904; d. 26 Nov 1972.

A very classy but very neglected clarinettist, with a sound and technique recalling Irving Fazola, Lytell replaced Larry Shields in the Original Dixieland Band for two years, then joined the Original Memphis Five (1922–5), which he left to join the Capitol Theatre Orchestra in New York, under Eugene Ormandy. In 1930 he joined the staff of NBC but re-formed the OMF in 1949 and again in the mid-1950s, continuing to work on Long Island until a long illness curtailed his activities. [DF]

Original Memphis Five

Columbias 1923-1931 (2001; Retrieval). The OMF in its original incarnation and in a 1931 reunion in which Lytell can be compared to clarinet up-and-comer Jimmy Dorsey.

Johnny Lytle

Vibraphone.

b. Springfield, Ohio, 13 Oct 1932; d. 15 Dec 1995.

Given a vibraphone stick as a child by Lionel Hampton (as was Roy Ayers), Lytle began his career as a drummer with Ray Charles (1950) and Gene Ammons (1953). He then played vibes with a group led by Boots Johnson (1955–7), after which he led his own bands, which often included organ. On records, he was joined by such as Johnny Griffin and Houston Person, and his albums have sold steadily to the urban black audience. As with Roy Ayers, in the mid-1980s he finally reached young white listeners of the acid-jazz generation, and toured England as a result (1989). Less fusion-oriented than Ayers, his records often have a heavy R&B background with deliberately flashy vibes, regularly incorporating a single note repeated quickly enough to sound like a continuous tone. [BP]

The Loop/New And Groovy (1966; BGP). These twenty organ-based tracks are very danceable and very short. They display the qualities mentioned above, but several such as the modal "Selim" are musically enlivened by the improvisation of an unnamed musician who could only be Wynton Kelly.

Humphrey Lyttelton

Trumpet, clarinet, tenor horn.

b. Berkshire, UK, 23 May 1921.

Humphrey Lyttelton emerged as a bright young trumpeter right after World War II, playing with George Webb's Dixielanders at Britain's revivalist shrine, the Red Barn at Barnehurst. By 1948 he had formed his own band from the remnant of Webb's and recorded his first sides for London Jazz; over the next six years he was quickly established as Britain's premier revivalist, recording with Australian Graeme Bell and others, and in 1954 producing the first of several volumes of autobiography, *I Play As I Please*. In the same year, with a band including saxophonist Bruce Turner, Lyttelton's musical policies broadened to encompass mainstream: by the end of the decade he had assembled a classic saxophone section including Tony Coe (alto), Jimmy Skidmore (tenor) and Joe Temperley (baritone). In the 1960s his career expanded with writing, broadcasting and TV work, and his band continued to grow, with a variety of new and familiar names – Dave Castle, Danny Moss, Tony Roberts and Eddie Harvey – all adding new chapters to his band's history.

From 1970 a stabilized line-up (featuring Bruce Turner, Kathy Stobart and Mick Pyne) and a long, productive contract with Black Lion Records refocused attention on Lyttelton's band. The momentum was maintained through personnel changes into the 1980s, and Lyttelton's group made fine records in a stimulating variety of creative contexts (as he still does) on his own label, Calligraph. By the late 1980s he had acquired Alan Barnes in a chemical partnership that produced much fine on-record music. Barnes's departure in 1993 signalled the arrival of Jimmy Hastings, and two years later Stan Greig left, to be replaced by Ted Beament. Lyttelton's musical output (steered by staff arranger Pete Strange) achieved new heights in the mid-1990s. With the dawn of the new century Lyttelton showed no signs of either looking back or slowing down and in 2003 was touring busily with his band and (regularly) singer Stacey Kent and tenorist Jim Tomlinson as

DAVID REDFERN

Humphrey Lyttelton

well as headlining on Jack Higgins' "Giants of Jazz" package tour.

In addition to his obvious talent as a trumpeter, which made him for Louis Armstrong "the top trumpet man in England", "Humph" has made vital contributions to jazz as a communicator. His successive volumes of autobiography were the first really intelligent writings from a jazz musician (apart from Eddie Condon's) and helped incalculably to establish jazz as a literate and intelligent art form. He is now Britain's senior jazz ambassador and has constantly demonstrated an admirably open ear for new developments in the music. As bandleader he has constantly kept an eye out for new young talent, latterly offering musicians (from Alan Barnes to Stacey Kent) a prestigious platform from which to display their developing talents. [DF]

⊙ **The Parlophones 1949–59** (Calligraph). In four volumes, this invaluable chronology carries you through Lyttelton's first 100 recordings (on 78rpm singles); ten peak years, from his first band (with Fawkes and the Christie Brothers), progressing to mainstream with Bruce Turner and Picard and finally to the first great sides by his "three saxophone" band with Tony Coe, Jimmy Skidmore and Joe Temperley.

⊙ **Jazz At The Royal Festival Hall/Jazz At The Conway Hall** (1954 & 51; Dormouse). Two concerts on one CD – the RFH date features Lyttelton's second great band (with Turner), while the Conway is a rare treat, featuring Lyttelton and Wally Fawkes at white heat.

⊙ **Back To The Sixties** (1960–63; Philips). A five-star selection of Lyttelton titles, with his great three-saxophone band (Coe, Skidmore and Temperley), Buck Clayton, Cab Kaye and more.

⊙ **Beano Boogie** (1989; Calligraph). The first Lyttelton CD to include Alan Barnes, this set has the atmospheric "The Strange Mr Peter Charles" (a feature for Pete Strange) plus Kenny Graham's "Ficklefanny Strikes Again" and the riotous Stan Greig title track.

⊙ **Humph 'n' Helen: I Can't Get Started** (1990; Calligraph). Lyttelton's regular collaboration with Helen Shapiro has produced a lot of good music; tracks here include the multivocal "Elmer's Tune" and a rip-roaring "Choo Choo Ch'Boogie".

⊙ **Hear Me Talkin' To Ya** (1993; Calligaph). Jimmy Hastings joins the band on this CD, with a spectacular circular-breathing feature on "I Got Rhythm". Other high spots include the title track and Pete Strange's reworking of Carla Bley's feature for Gary Valente, "The Lord Is Listening To Ya – Hallelujah!"

⊙ **Sing, Swing Together … Again!** (1997; Calligraph). Lyttelton's admirably prolific Calligraph output has yet to be properly recognized; this delightful set (arranged by Lyttelton's staffman Pete Strange) has Helen Shapiro flawless as ever, a catchy Inkspots medley (with Lyttelton and Strange vocalizing) and at least two outstanding Humph compositions – the lyrically clever "That Old Familiar Trouble" and the exquisite "Moving Into Spring".

➤➤ **Buddy Tate** *(Long Tall Tenor).*

Paul Lytton

Percussion.

b. London, March 1947.

Since the mid-60s, Lytton has been active in the London free-music scene and was co-founder of the London Musicians Cooperative. He made his first recorded appearance on the electronics collage project and cult classic of David Vorhaus, *White Noise* (1969; Island). One of the key European improvisers, he settled in Belgium in 1975, making frequent excursions over the border to nearby Aachen, Germany, where he co-founded the Aachen Musicians Collective with Paul Lovens, a frequent collaborator. Together they recorded *Moinho Da Asneira, A Cerca Da Bela Vista A Graca* (1979; Po Torch) and *The Fetch* (1984; Po Torch), and Lytton made the solo *The Inclined Stick* (1983) for the same label. During this period, his massive percussion set-up included live, ramshackle but fluent electronics, and a largely reinvented drumkit.

Lytton has maintained several long-standing musical partnerships (though he has also supported himself working as a dentist), most importantly with saxophonist Evan Parker, with whom he had a significant, influential duo. Their early years are well documented on the Emanem label, whilst the Evan Parker trio, augmented by bassist Barry Guy, is one of the premier improvising ensembles and has recorded a number of stellar records. Lytton also played on three of Parker's Electro-Acoustic Ensemble records on ECM, group music ideally suited to his "extended kit" playing, and the same ethos later informed an even more concentrated album of beautiful duets with violinist Phil Wachsmann for the same label. Lytton also drummed with Guy's London Jazz Composers Orchestra (appearing on their Intakt records) and with Wolfgang Fuchs's large but intimate free ensemble King Ubu Orchestru. He is a highly textural percussionist, using colour and dynamic shifts masterfully, and is brilliantly interactive in demanding, abstract terrain. [JC]

➤➤ **Philip Wachsmann** *(Some Other Season)*.

Harold Mabern

Piano.

b. Memphis, 20 March 1936.

Self-taught as a teenager, Mabern admired Memphis pianists Charles Thomas and Phineas Newborn. He moved to Chicago in 1954, studying with Ahmad Jamal and replacing Richard Abrams in the group MJT+3. Settling in New York, he played with Lionel Hampton, Art Farmer-Benny Golson (1961–2), Donald Byrd, Miles Davis (1963, briefly), J.J. Johnson (1963–5) and Wes Montgomery (touring Europe with him in 1965). He worked with Joe Williams, Sarah Vaughan and Arthur Prysock, and toured Japan with Billy Harper (1977) and Europe with the George Coleman octet (1981). He has also been a member of Piano Choir, organized by Stanley Cowell (1970s), and James Williams's Contemporary Piano Ensemble (1993–4). A dynamic soloist and accompanist (who also teaches at William Paterson University, New Jersey), Mabern has kept alive some of the techniques introduced by Newborn and written some compelling tunes, a couple of which have found favour with dance-music fans. [BP]

⊙ **The Leading Man** (1992–3; Columbia/DIW). A good representation of Mabern's forceful playing in a trio setting occasionally augmented by guests such as Kevin Eubanks, and an illustration of his fund of melodic compositions in the title track and "B&B" (dedicated to Booker Little and Clifford Brown).

Laura MacDonald

Alto and soprano saxophones.

b. Glasgow, Scotland, 17 July 1974.

Inspired by her father, who was a singer, Laura MacDonald began playing the saxophone at the age of 16 and was fronting her own quartet within two years. From 1992–4 she studied at the Royal Scottish Academy of Music and Drama, and in 1995 won a full scholarship to Berklee College of Music, Boston, where she went on to win the Frederick Cameron Weber award for saxophone performance. Returning to Scotland at the end of 1997 she joined up with the great Scottish saxophonist Tommy Smith – the pair were married for several years – playing with his sextet on tours of Sweden, Kazakstan, France, England and Scotland. MacDonald also plays and composes for the Scottish National Jazz Orchestra and has performed with her own quartet throughout England and Scotland, supporting both George Benson and Michel Camillo at the 2000 Glasgow Jazz Festival. Her debut album, *Laura*, was the first disc to be recorded for Tommy Smith's own Spartacus label. The sessions took place in the USA, with an all-star American trio: drummer Jeff "Tain" Watts, bassist James Genus and pianist David Budway. Released in August 2001, the album deservedly won much critical acclaim. [IC]

⊙ **Laura** (2001; Spartacus). MacDonald clearly thrived in such fast company producing a brilliant debut album on which she plays four of her own compositions and four by others, including a beautiful solo version of Pat Metheny's "Always And Forever". There's an amazing rapport between the players – a measure of just how mature and confident an artist MacDonald has become.

Teo Macero

Composer, saxophone, producer.

b. Glens Falls, New York, 30 Oct 1925.

Teo (Attilio Joseph) Macero attended the Navy School of Music in Washington, DC, from 1943–4. He spent 1947 in Glens Falls, teaching and playing before he moved to New York in 1948, studying at the Juilliard and getting Bachelor's and Master's degrees in 1953. He began composing jazz-influenced atonal classical works: they received more than one hundred performances between 1955–60; and he received two Guggenheim awards for composition, in 1957 and 1958. Macero also played and recorded with Mingus in the early and mid-1950s. Then, in 1957, he joined the staff of Columbia Records, initially as a music editor, and he was to stay with the company until the end of the 1970s becoming in-house producer for some of the best music in recorded history. It was there, in the same year, that he began his long and fruitful association with Miles Davis, which continued into the 1980s. Macero was the perfect producer for Davis, and his musical understanding, wisdom and vision helped the trumpeter in his quest for new forms and new standards of excellence. [IC]

➤➤ **Charles Mingus** *(Jazz Composers' Workshop).*

Machito

Vocals, percussion, leader.

b. Havana, 3 Dec 1907; d. London, 15 April 1984.

Machito (born Raúl "Frank" Grillo) was brought up in Cuba and moved to New York in the 1930s where he sang with various Afro-Latin ensembles. He formed his own band in 1941, Machito and his Afro-Cubans, which he organized with his brother-in-law Mario Bauza, and he continued to lead this ensemble for 40 years; beginning in 1975, he began to tour with a smaller ensemble in Europe and further afield. Although engaged full-time in Latin music, Machito was important in the Latin/jazz crossover of the mid- and late 1940s. The mambo style he helped to found (especially the brass-section work) represented the first major influence of jazz on Latin music and, in return, he inspired the Latin ventures of Stan Kenton and Dizzy Gillespie and backed Charlie Parker on records. As well as employing several jazz players, such as Doc Cheatham, on a longterm basis, he remained open to later stylistic trends such as salsa and, at the time of his death while working in London, had found a new, younger audience. [BP]

Various Artists

⊙ **The Original Mambo Kings** (1948–54; Verve). With Machito's band involved in the majority of the tracks, this compilation represents the jazz-Latin crossover aspect of his work, with the addition on most items of soloists such as Charlie Parker ("Mango Mangue"), Flip Phillips (the legendary "Tanga") and Howard McGhee-Brew Moore. The remaining material includes the Chico O'Farrill-arranged "Manteca Suite", featuring Gillespie.

Adrian Macintosh

Drums.

b. Tadcaster, Yorkshire, UK, 7 March 1942.

Macintosh moved to London in 1966 and played with pianist John Taylor's trio before joining Alan Elsdon's band in late 1969. For the next 14 years

William Gottlieb/Redferns

Machito

he freelanced with a variety of leaders including Lennie Felix, Ted Beament and Brian Leake (with whose band, Sweet and Sour, he worked throughout its existence), as well as backing American visitors such as Sonny Stitt, Red Holloway, Teddy Edwards, Cecil Payne, Jimmy Witherspoon, Doc Cheatham, Al Casey and Earle Warren. In May 1982 he joined Humphrey Lyttelton, and he has remained with him ever since, as well as freelancing and leading his own sextet. He has also played regularly with Ted Beament in a trio formed from the rhythm section of Lyttelton's band. In addition to his musical pursuits Macintosh is active within the British Musicians' Union and is a founder member of the Association of British Jazz Musicians. [DF]

➤➤ **Brian Leake** *(Benign Jazz)*; **Humphrey Lyttelton** *(Beano Boogie)*.

Billy Mackel

Guitar.

b. Baltimore, Maryland, 28 Dec 1912; d. 5 May 1986.

Mackel played guitar, banjo and ukulele around Baltimore at the start of his career and was leading a band in Club Orleans, Philadelphia, when in 1944 he was heard by Roy McCoy from Lionel Hampton's band. Hampton invited Mackel to play a concert, and from then on Mackel was Hampton's guitarist, contributing to the nightly excitement of jazz's most exciting big band. He cites Charlie Christian and Wes Montgomery as his prime influences, and his funky, bluesy lines can be heard as a harbinger of rock'n'roll. [DF]

Lionel Hampton

⊙ **Paris All Stars** (1953; Vogue). Mackel as support for Hampton in a wonderfully catholic jam session with Jimmy Cleveland and Mezz Mezzrow; his comping – like Freddy Green's with Basie – was an audible trademark, and he was a good soloist too.

Fraser Macpherson

Flute, clarinet, tenor saxophone.

b. Winnipeg, Manitoba, 10 April 1928; d. 28 Sept 1993.

Macpherson's career was spent largely in studio work from the late 1940s, but in the 1980s he made a late emergence into the jazz world, winning a Juno Award in 1983 for his album *I Didn't Know About You*, recorded for Sackville with guitarist Oliver Gannon. Later he recorded an album for Concord that similarly displayed a mellow mid-period style somewhere between Zoot Sims and Al Cohn. He visited the USSR several times and was made a Member of the Order of Canada in 1988. [DF]

⊙ **In The Tradition** (1991; Concord). With Ian McDougall partnering Macpherson in the frontline, this album is an outstanding one-off demonstrating Macpherson's tenor talent.

Dave MacRae

Piano, electric piano, synthesizers.

b. Auckland, New Zealand, 2 April 1940.

Apart from some study at Sydney Conservatory, Australia, MacRae is self-taught as a musician. From 1960–68 he worked in Australia as a record producer and arranger before moving to the USA in 1969 where he joined the Buddy Rich band. In 1971 he came to the UK, working with many Americans at Ronnie Scott's, notably Clark Terry, Chet Baker, Jon Hendricks and Gil Evans. He is best known for his association with the jazz-rock and prog scene: from 1971–3 he was with Ian Carr's Nucleus, played with Robert Wyatt's Matching Mole, Mike Gibbs, Mike Westbrook, Back Door and several other UK groups. From 1978–82 with his wife, singer Joy Yates, he co-led Pacific Eardrum. In 1984 he returned to Australia with Yates and has remained fairly quiet ever since, bar a residency at Ronnie Scott's club in London in January 1998 in duo with Joy. MacRae's influences range from Art Tatum, Wynton Kelly and Bill Evans to Ellington, Monk and Zawinul, and his playing encompasses a similarly broad spectrum. [IC]

➤➤ **Mike Westbrook** *(Citadel/Room 315; Love/Dream And Variations)*.

Magic Malik

Flute and voice.

b. Abidjan, Ivory Coast, 29 July 1969.

Born Malik Mezzadri to a French mother and an African father, Magic Malik and his family moved from the Ivory Coast to Guadeloupe soon after he was born. After early recorder lessons, he took up the flute at 15, studying in Pointe-à-Pitre (the Guadeloupe capital) with Marc Rovelas. In 1986 he moved to France for further studies at the Marseilles Music Conservatory and at CIM in Paris. Three years later he joined the eclectic, multi-cultural Human Spirit – one of the most exciting bands of the period – working with them for ten years. A meeting with saxophonist and bandleader Julien Lourau in 1997 led to Malik joining Lourau's equally eclectic jazz fusion group Groove Gang and appearing on the album *Gambit*. He has also played with the Malian singer Rokia Traore and the Buena Vista Social Club bassist Cachaito Lopez. Malik leads his own groups, including the thirteen-piece HWI Project and the seven-piece Magic Malik Orchestra, and has produced two innovative albums with the latter, the cryptically titled *69 96* (2001) and *00-237/XP-1* (2003) for Label Bleu. A highly receptive musician, his flute playing possesses all the immediacy and flexibility of the human voice, and, indeed, is often accompanied by his own strange vocalizing. [IC]

⊙ **00-237/XP-1** (2003; Label Bleu). An experimental double album that is both challenging and accessible,

Malik's compositions employ a fluid improvisatory language partly inspired by the M-Base style of saxophonist Steve Coleman who appears on some tracks. More reflective than its predecessor, this is a rich and often poetic album of varied moods on which the inspiration never flags.

Alex Maguire

Piano, composer.

b. London, 6 Jan 1959.

Although primarily viewed as an improvising pianist, Alex Maguire usually works, in his own words, "in the area where improvisation and composition meet", and in his music he attempts a corollary to the techniques of contemporary dance, theatre and cinema that inspire him – cutaway, close-up, montage, flashback and so on. A similar openness is reflected in the wide variety of music on which he draws, ranging from South African kwelas through jazz standards to pointillism. After studying at London University and attending the Barry Jazz Summer School in 1978, he founded the Ping Pong club in London with drummer Steve Noble, and began long-standing musical relationships with not only Noble but also other UK improvisers such as Evan Parker, Phil Minton and Paul Rutherford, as well as dancers Katie Duck and Julian Hamilton. In addition to working with his own large band, Cat O' Nine Tails, which has toured all over the UK and Europe, he has also played with saxophonists Paul Dunmall and Alan Wilkinson, guitarist Derek Bailey and drummer Tony Oxley in his Celebration Orchestra. He has acted as MD for a number of theatre companies as well as for the Italian dance company Group O, and since 1984 he has held regular workshops in the UK and Holland. In the late 1990s, work with Elton Dean's Newsense led Maguire to form a regular band from its rhythm-section, bassist Roberto Bellatalla (celebrated for his work with the improvising sextet Dreamtime) and drummer Mark Sanders. Maguire, a composer whose pieces have been performed by Tristan Honsinger, Sean Bergin's M.O.B. and the Michael Moore quartet, among others, provided all the trio's material. He continues to contribute to Elton Dean's projects and has recently appeared in the groups of bassist/composer Simon H. Fell and Dutch saxophonist Sean Bergin. [CP]

Alex Maguire and Steve Noble

Live At Oscar's (1987; Incus). Serious but always entertaining duo improvisation, recorded live; despite sound-quality problems, this is a fair representation of their *modus operandi*.

Michael Moore

Négligé (1992; Ramboy). Maguire's compositions "Sparky" and "Epigram" are two of the fifteen tracks featuring US expat reedsman Moore with cellist Ernst Reijseger and percussionist Michael Vatcher, and his mix of structure and complete freedom sits well with this group's approach.

Kevin Mahogany

Singer.

b. Kansas City, Missouri, 30 July 1958.

Having put his childhood musical studies to use by playing baritone saxophone in Eddie Baker's New Breed Jazz Orchestra and singing in his high school choir, Kevin Mahogany formed a jazz choir at Baker University, and began his professional career by singing in the Midwest with a trio. Signed to Enja in the early 1990s, he made three albums for the company. *Double Rainbow* (1993), with saxophonist Ralph Moore, pianist Kenny Barron, bassist Ray Drummond and drummer Lewis Wash, includes material by Charlie Parker and Charles Mingus, plus a James Baldwin recitation; *Songs And Moments* (1994) is a more ambitious affair with a larger band and backing singers, but contains intriguing versions of "Take The A-Train" and "My Foolish Heart". Enja's *You Got What It Takes* (1995) was followed by a move to Warners in 1996, where his eponymous debut for the company contained material by Stevie Wonder, James Carr ("The Dark End Of The Street") and Fats Domino, but it was *Another Time, Another Place* (see below) that really won over both fans and critics. In addition to his own albums, Mahogany has also lent his rich, dark baritone (which Ray Brown predicted would "fill the gap between Billy Eckstine and Joe Williams") to albums by Brown himself, drummers Carl Allen, Elvin Jones and T.S. Monk, and to 1991's *Dangerous Precedent* (Sea Breeze) by arranger/keyboard player Frank Mantooth. [CP]

Another Time, Another Place (1997; Warner Bros). With Joe Lovano guesting on three tracks and a stellar team including pianist Cyrus Chestnut and drummer Clarence Penn backing him, Mahogany brings class, sophistication and great sureness of touch to such material as "In The Wee Small Hours Of The Morning" and "Nature Boy".

Pride And Joy (2002; Telarc). The culmination to date of Mahogany's affinity with quality pop, this is a mostly Mahogany-arranged, imaginative and persuasive set of Motown classics like "Reach Out (I'll Be There)" and "Signed Sealed Delivered", with Jon Faddis guesting.

Mike Mainieri

Vibes, keyboards, percussion, composer.

b. Bronx, New York, 24 July 1938.

Mainieri began on vibes at the age of twelve. He played with the Buddy Rich band until 1962, touring South America and Asia, then led his own groups from 1963, recording the quartet album *Insight* in 1968 and the large ensemble album *Journey Thru An Electric Tube* in 1970. He was a busy studio musician from the late 60s onwards, writing and arranged music for feature films and TV programmes, and playing for Tim Hardin, Jack McDuff and Billy Cobham among others. A dab hand with a soldering iron, he invented an instrument called a "synthivibe", which enables him to treat the vibes sound electronically, and he set up his own recording studio in a converted barn at his home in Woodstock, New York. In 1975 he formed a new quartet, and in 1979 became a founder member of the all-star fusion group Steps – formed to tour Japan, the original personnel included Steve Gadd, Eddie Gomez and Mike Brecker. Later known as Steps Ahead, it became one of the most successful jazz acts of the 1980s, touring and playing festivals all over the world, and still reconvenes in various forms. Mainieri's energies of late seem to be concentrated in producing records for his label NYC. [IC]

STEPS AHEAD

Modern Times (1984; Elektra). The classic line-up with Brecker, Peter Erskine, Warren Bernhardt on keyboards and Gomez playing amplified acoustic bass in a manner whose subtlety eludes all other fusion groups.

Ivor Mairants

Guitar.

b. Rypin, Poland, 18 July 1908; d. 20 Feb 1998.

Mairants came to the UK in 1913, took up the banjo at fifteen and turned professional at twenty. By the 1930s he was well established as a premier player and spent years in leading bands including Ambrose, Roy Fox, Lew Stone, Geraldo and Ted Heath, before moving into the world of sessions after the war. Frequently heard on BBC's *Guitar Club* in the 1950s, he was also featured with Mantovani's orchestra, 'Manuel and his Music of the Mountains', and many other session and recording ensembles. In the 1950s he also established his Central School of Dance Music in London, and in 1958 opened Ivor Mairants' Musicentre in the West End, which became a legendary guitar shop. Mairants also wrote regularly about jazz music and guitars, and in 1980 published his autobiography *My Fifty Fretting Years*. In 1995 he also produced *The Great Jazz Guitarists*, a plush and scholarly collection of guitar solo transcriptions. During these later years he was a regular at London's Coda Club and continued to play occasionally with the Coda Club All Stars. A central figure in Britain's guitar history, Mairants's solo recordings are scattered, but his duets with a second guitar master from the swing years, Albert Harris (sadly last issued on cassette tape only), are worth seeking out. [DF]

Adam Makowicz

Piano, keyboards, composer, bass guitar.

b. Czechoslovakia, 18 Aug 1940.

Makowicz's mother, a piano teacher, gave him his first lessons. He attended the Chopin Secondary School of Music in Cracow, where in 1962 he played his first jazz gig with Polish trumpeter Tomasz Stanko. Moving to Warsaw in 1965, he led his own trio, then toured throughout Europe, and in Cuba, India, Australia and New Zealand with Zbigniew Namyslowski and the Novi singers. He began composing, arranging, and writing music criticism in 1970 and joined Michal Urbaniak's group in 1971. He also recorded a duo album with Urbaniak's wife, Urszula Dudziak, in 1974. He then played with the Tomasz Stanko trio, and in 1975 formed the Tomasz Stanko and Adam Makowicz Unit.

Since the late 1970s he has frequently worked unaccompanied. He did take part in solidarity concerts protesting against martial law in Poland in the early 1980s (which earned him *persona non grata* status until 1989), and he recorded albums with like-minded musicians Dave Holland, Charlie Haden, Palle Danielsson and John Christensen in the late 80s. But it is his solo piano interpretations of the likes of Tatum, Gershwin and Irving Berlin – not forgetting his soloist chair on orchestral recordings – that seem to be his chief preoccupation. [IC]

The Solo Album: Adam Live In Stockholm (1986; Verve); **Live At The Maybeck Recital Hall** (1992; Concord). Makowicz is well versed in classical piano music and also in the jazz tradition. Both areas nourish these two piano recitals, mostly of standards with one or two of his original compositions.

➤➤ **Michal Urbaniak** *(Polish Jazz Vol. 9)*.

Russell Malone

Guitar, composer.

b. Albany, Georgia, 8 Nov 1963.

Having received a green plastic four-string guitar at four, Russell Malone was confirmed in his desire to play the real thing by seeing B.B. King perform "How Blue Can You Get" on television. Exposure to blues, the jazz of George Benson and Wes Montgomery and the country music of Chet Atkins and Johnny Cash all influenced Malone's playing, as did the spirituals which he had heard in his childhood. After breaking into live performance with Jimmy Smith in 1988, Malone joined Harry Connick Jnr and played with the singer's orchestra from 1990–94. Recordings with saxophonists Don Braden and Branford Marsalis, pianist Benny Green, trumpeters Terrell Stafford and Roy Hargrove followed, and Malone also appears on Mose Allison's 1998 Blue Note album *Gimcracks And Gewgaws*. In the mid-1990s, he joined singer/pianist Diana Krall's band, appearing on her Impulse! albums *All For You* (1995) and *Love Scenes* (1997), and on the worldwide tours that established her, by the end of the 1990s, as one of the biggest-selling artists in the music. Malone's albums as leader include an eponymous debut for Columbia featuring Connick on piano (1992), a follow-up for the same company (*Black Butterfly*, 1993). His signing in the late 1990s to Universal produced the well-received *Sweet Georgia Peach*, the mature straightahead jazz of *Look Who's Here* (2001) and *Heartstrings* (2001), a strings-laden ballad album, though his most exciting recorded playing may be on the 2003 meeting with pianist Benny Green on *Jazz At The Bistro*. A soulful, engaging player whose music is always accessible without ever lapsing into cliché, Malone (who played the cigar-smoking guitarist in Robert Altman's *Kansas City*) is as likely to lend his elegant sound to the music of Clarence Carter, Little Anthony or Eddie "Cleanhead" Vinson as to that of Bucky Pizzarelli, Jack McDuff or Regina Carter. [CP]

⊙ **Sweet Georgia Peach** (1998; Impulse!). With an all-star band (pianist Kenny Barron, bassist Ron Carter, drummer Lewis Wash, plus percussionist Steve Kroon), Malone not only showcases his facility on uptempo tunes and luxurious ballads, but also closes with a solo version of "Swing Low, Sweet Chariot" that emphasizes his church roots.

⊙ **Jazz At The Bistro** (2003; Telarc). An alternately sensitive and incendiary live date from Malone and pianist Benny Green, two of the hottest straightahead players on the scene.

Junior Mance

Piano.

b. Chicago, 10 Oct 1928.

Julian Mance was active on the Chicago jazz scene with Gene Ammons in 1947–8. After moving to New York he became the pianist in Lester Young's bop-oriented group of 1949, and then worked with the Gene Ammons-Sonny Stitt touring band in 1950–51. After army service he accompanied Dinah Washington from 1954–5. He made tours and regular recordings with Cannonball Adderley's early quintet in 1956–7, Dizzy Gillespie from 1958–60 and the "Lockjaw" Davis/Johnny Griffin group of 1960–61. He formed his own trio, which also accompanied singer Joe Williams and, apart from a period of illness, has continued to work steadily (but record less prolifically) for the past forty years. He teaches regularly at New York's New School University, and his students included Brad Mehldau.

A strong accompanist, heard on record with performers as varied as Aretha Franklin and bluesman Buddy Guy, his trio and duo routines are sometimes predictable, but very effective with a live audience. Known principally for a highly rhythmic, bluesy approach somewhat similar to that of Ray Bryant, Mance is capable in the right company of a much wider range of expression. [BP]

⊙ **Junior's Blues** (1963; Riverside/OJC). Mance's regular trio with Bob Cranshaw on bass covers different facets of the blues, from originals to Monk, Ellington and Parker to more folky material such as "Yancey Special" and Leroy Carr's "In The Evening".

➤➤ **Eddie "Lockjaw" Davis** *(Live At Minton's).*

Joe Maneri

Alto and tenor saxophones, clarinet, piano.

b. Brooklyn, New York, 1927.

One of the most remarkable Cinderella stories in creative music, Maneri played clarinet from the age of eleven (initially studying with cobbler Pietro Bruno, furniture maker Joseph Nalbone and drummer Giuseppe DeLuca) but was not recognized as the consummate tonal and improvisational genius he is until Paul Bley championed him at the Montreal Jazz Festival in 1992.

In 1947, he began a ten-year set of composition and theory studies with Alban Berg follower Josef Schmid, leading to various classical works including a commission from the Boston Symphony Orchestra (a piano concerto that was debuted in 1960). At that time he played various ethnic musics (Armenian, Syrian, Greek, Irish) as well as jazz, to support himself. Musically apperceptive, in the mid-50s he manipulated (via varying tape speed and mixing) several completely free improvisations he had recorded for a film score. In 1965, he performed with Gunther Schuller's Twentieth Century Innovations Ensemble at Carnegie Hall; Schuller was very impressed by Maneri and tried unsuccessfully to convince Atlantic Records to issue an LP of his original music. (The demo material produced in the attempt was eventually issued on *Paniots Nine* (1998; Avant), a fascinating collection of early Maneri work which also features his traditional Greek and Klezmer music, as well as some surprising, innovative jazz from the 60s). In 1970, Schuller hired Maneri at the New England Conservatory in Boston, where he continues to teach.

Maneri did issue a record in 1989, *Kalavinka* (Cochlea), but it was not until 1995 and the release of his first CD, *Get Ready To Receive Yourself* (Leo) that Maneri, by then nearly 70, gained international notice. Since then, he has recorded a steady stream of exciting dates, including *Let The Horse Go* (1996; Leo), *In Full Cry* (1997; ECM), *Coming Down The Mountain* (1997; hatOLOGY), and *Tenderly* (1999; hatOLOGY) with his quartet (which includes his son Mat on violin). He has an extended family, as it were, of regular collaborators – Mat, Randy Peterson, Ed Schuller and the Boston guitarist Joe Morris (*Three Men Walking*, a 1996 trio album with Morris and Maneri junior, is terrifically intense) – an empathetic axis who all seem to play on each other's albums.

Maneri's concept draws on decades of work with microtonal music, both in Mediterranean and in post-serial spheres; he is a tremendously original reed player, a very fine pianist and as open-eared a septuagenarian as they come. [JC]

⊙ **Dahabenzapple** (1996; hat Art). Twenty-minute tracks let Maneri stretch more than elsewhere, and that's a plus on this quartet outing with son Mat on lightly amplified fiddle, Cecil McBee on bass and the outstanding Randy Peterson on drums. It may take a minute to adjust to the Maneri microtonal free interplay, which can sound out of tune to a new ear, but once you've adjusted it's a splendid new sound world they've invented.

Albert Mangelsdorff

Trombone, composer.

b. Frankfurt am Main, Germany, 5 Sept 1928.

Mangelsdorff comes from a musical family and his brother Emil is a noted saxophonist in

Germany. Jazz was banned by the Nazis, but Albert and his brother attended secret meetings at the Hot Club in Frankfurt, and in 1940, at twelve, he decided that jazz was the kind of music he wanted to play. He did not take up the trombone until he was twenty, but began playing modern jazz (bebop) immediately, since after the war American Forces Radio in Europe would broadcast Charlie Parker records. By the early 1950s he was listening to Lee Konitz and Lennie Tristano – in particular the latter's 1949 performance of "Intuition", the first recording of free (abstract) jazz improvisation.

A second epiphany that shaped his practice came later, at the beginning of 1964, when his group did a three-month tour of Asia. "We heard Indian music and played with Indian musicians," he said. "All of a sudden you could do without all this playing on chord structures and themes. So, my playing started to get freer all by itself." He incorporated some of the Indian *ragas* into his own music and recorded a work by Ravi Shankar. These ethnic influences, and the development of free improvisation, brought Mangelsdorff to his mature musical identity.

He continued to tour worldwide, playing Newport in 1965, 1967 and 1969. From the late 1960s he was a regular member of the Globe Unity Orchestra, a large ensemble devoted almost exclusively to free music. He also began to develop a radical new approach to trombone-playing, a technique that produced multiphonics (more than one note played simultaneously) on the trombone. "You play a note and you sing another, usually a higher note" Mangelsdorff explained. "In the interval between ... overtones are created which become so audible that you end up with real chords – sometimes up to four notes ... all that has to do with how far you can control your voice." After this discovery he began playing unaccompanied trombone concerts (often for as long as two hours!) and tours, appearing at festivals including Monterey in 1975. Solo playing led him to re-examine his jazz roots and to reject certain aspects of free jazz. "Jazz is rhythm," he reflected, " ... there were too many people who forgot that for a while".

Mangelsdorff played with French saxophonist Michel Portal in his quartet and quintet from 1976–82. During the 80s and 90s he played around Europe with a multitude of musicians in various contexts: with French bassist Jean-Francois Jenny-Clark, co-leading the French/German Jazz Ensemble; with the Pierre Courbois quintet; in a trio with Anders Jormin (bass) and Rune Carlsson (drums); assisting Wolfgang Dauner's ambitious ensemble and orchestral projects; his own trio with Pierre Favre (drums) and Leon Francioli (bass); occasional reconventions of the United Jazz and Rock Ensemble; and duet tours with John Surman.

As with Miles Davis, his career shows an extraordinary capacity for artistic growth allied to rigorous standards of self-discipline and self-criticism, minutely documented in his huge body of recorded work. As a musician he is an innovator and an influential stylist with enormous physical and creative stamina. As a composer, he harnesses drama and surprise – brilliant angular lines are juxtaposed with dense dissonant chords, displaced accents, sudden silences and percussive eruptions. [IC]

Albert Mangelsdorff

⊙ **Animal Dance** (1962; Atlantic); **New Jazz Ramwong** (1964; L+R). Mangelsdorff is superbly lyrical and inventive on *Animal Dance*, on which he leads a quartet with bass, drums and the great John Lewis on piano. The later album is by his piano-less working group, with bassist Gunther Lenz, drummer Ralph Hubner and two reeds. The relationship of precomposed passages with the more freely improvised solos is a powerful dynamic.

⊙ **Room1220** (1970; Konnex). Mangelsdorff's quintet for this set includes John Surman, Eddy Louiss, Niels-Henning Ørsted Pedersen and Daniel Humair. Surman is somewhat diffident but Mangelsdorff is in wonderful form and the rhythm-section is excellent.

⊙ **Three Originals** (1975, 76 & 80; MPS). This is a really superb two-CD package of one studio and two live trio albums: *The Widepoint* with Palle Danielsson and Elvin Jones; *Trilogue* with Jaco Pastorius and Alphonse Mouzon; and *Albert Live in Montreux* with Jean-Francois Jenny-Clark and Ronald Shannon Jackson. The three sessions are surprisingly different but all are fascinating, with *Montreux* just having the edge. Mangelsdorff's originality, his range from gruff basso profundo to bat-squeak, his technical ability and vaulting imagination, and his multiphonics (which seem to get richer and richer through this series) astonish and delight.

⊙ **Purity** (1990; Mood). 14 pieces on this unaccompanied set have a distinct identity and sound by subtle use of mutes, growls, voice, attack, extremely varied multiphonics and composed structures. A masterpiece.

➤➤ **Wolfgang Dauner** *(Two Is Company)*; **Globe Unity Orchestra** *(Rumbling)*.

Chuck Mangione

Trumpet, flugelhorn, keyboards, composer.
b. Rochester, New York, 29 Nov 1940.

Chuck Mangione studied at the Eastman School of Music in his home town. From 1960–64, with his brother Gap (a pianist and composer), he co-led the Jazz Brothers before moving to New York in 1965 and playing with Woody Herman, Kai Winding and Maynard Ferguson. From 1965–7 he worked with Art Blakey's Jazz Messengers, and some of his very finest playing is on Blakey's 1966 live album *Buttercorn Lady*, which also features Keith Jarrett. He formed his own quartet in 1968, and in 1970, with the Rochester Philharmonic Orchestra, recorded a live album, *Friends And Love*, which blended jazz, rock, folk and classical elements; it received good critical notices and also sold well. The first track, a Mangione composition called "Hill Where The Lord Hides", was released as a single and became a hit. In 1973 he toured with his quartet, making appearances with various US and Canadian symphony orchestras, and recording *Land Of Make Believe* with the Hamilton Philharmonic, Ontario. During the early 1970s he also toured extensively in the USA and Europe, playing at major festivals, and appearing at Ronnie Scott's club in London.

In 1974 Mangione formed his own recording company in order to release records by his friends. He also published arrangements of his compositions designed for high school choirs. His compositions have been recorded by jazz and pop artists such as Cannonball Adderley, Herb Alpert, Ray Bryant, Mark Murphy and Percy Faith.

Mangione produces a lovely lyrical sound and, although he has a superb technique, he plays with great economy. As a composer and a player, he makes benign fusion music, often with a delicate Latin tinge. He also plays very "tasty" piano. [IC]

⊙ **Recuerdo** (1962; OJC). Quintet session with Joe Romano on tenor, and the classy rhythm-section of Wynton Kelly, Sam Jones and Louis Hayes. The music is a user-friendly but unspectacular venture into the mainstream hard bop of the time, but nowhere does Mangione reach the sustained brilliance of his 1966 performances on Blakey's *Buttercorn Lady*.

⊙ **Land Of Make Believe** (1973; Polygram). This is a rocky extravaganza with Mangione's quartet plus symphony orchestra, choir and guest performers. It's a bit of an overblown effort, not helped by the poor recording quality.

Manhattan Jazz Quintet

Brought into the world by the editor of Japan's *Swing Journal*, Yasuki Nakayama, the Manhattan Jazz Quintet's *raison d'être* was providing pianist and veteran studio sessionman David Mathews with an outlet for both his own compositions and his unfussy arrangements of Blue Note-type jazz of the 1950s and 1960s. The presence of some of Manhattan's finest 1980s musicians – Lew Soloff (trumpet), George Young (tenor), Charnett Moffett (bass) and Steve Gadd (drums) or, after 1988, John Patitucci (bass) and Dave Weckl (drums), along with Mathews – ensured that the band's nine albums (ten if you count the inevitable "reunion" album featuring John Scofield, issued in 1990) were no mere re-creations but up-to-the-minute interpretations of material such as "Jordu", "Airegin", "Cheese Cake", "Moanin'"and so on. Soloff remained with Mathews as the quintet expanded to become the Manhattan Jazz Orchestra on the Milestone-released albums *Bach 2000* (2001) and *Hey Duke* (2002). Mathews's arrangements are never less than cogent, but there is perhaps, on occasion, rather too much polish on the band's music and too little danger for it to generate true excitement. [CP]

⊙ **Manhattan Jazz Quintet** (1984; Paddle Wheel). The highlight here is a highly unusual Mathews arrangement of "Summertime", which brings the best out of Soloff in particular – an auspicious debut album from the stellar quintet.

⊙ **Autumn Leaves** (1985; Paddle Wheel). Same formula as before, but with an unusually tricksy "Jordu" the highlight.

⊙ **Plays Blue Note** (1988; Paddle Wheel). Tribute to the label which put out the quintet's core repertoire, with Weckl and Patitucci. Sonny Clark's "Cool Struttin'" and Woody Shaw's "Sweet Love of Mine" are the highlights.

Manhattan Transfer

Formed in 1969 under the leadership of Tim Hauser, Manhattan Transfer had taken definitive shape by October 1972, with the line-up of Hauser, Alan Paul, Janis Siegel and Laurel Masse. In the early years they combined pop, doo-wop music, pastiche 1930s jive and great standards, a hybrid repertoire reflected in the albums that followed their 1974 signing to Atlantic. Their 1976 set, *Coming Out*, contains a lavish version of "Poinciana", as well as their hit "Chanson D'Amour", and by 1978 their parameters had been extended to include vocalese (check out "Four Brothers" on their *Pastiche* album). *Extensions*, one year later (by which time Laurel Masse had been replaced by the phenomenal high-note lead singer Cheryl Bentine), showed further evidence of their maturing talent, containing now-classic vocalese adaptations of Joe Zawinul's "Birdland", "The Shaker Song" (featuring joyful soloing from altoist Ritchie Cole) and a close-harmony expansion of Coleman Hawkins's "Body and Soul", dedicated to Eddie Jefferson. After three more fine albums, 1985 saw the release of ManTran's sensational *Vocalese*, which earned two Grammy awards. The subsequent *Vocalese Live* album added weight to their reputation, which was futher enhanced by *Brasil*, featuring Brazilian artists such as Djavan and Milton Nascimento, plus old bossa nova friends like Stan Getz, in a collection that looked back to the moods of Jobim and Gilberto while also reflecting the state of Brazilian music in the 1980s. On later albums including *Swing* (1997), the pop celebration *Tonin'* (1994), and the Louis Armstrong tribute *Spirit of St. Louis* (2000), and throughout the solo projects of its members, Manhattan Transfer continue to thrive. [DF]

⊙ **Down In Birdland** (1975–88; Atlantic). Fine anthology from the vinyl years: early ManTran hokum like "That Cat Is High", through to late masterpieces like the exquisite "Capim" (from *Brasil*), "Sing Joy Spring" (from *Vocalese*), plus seventeen other tracks including the sensational "Spice Of Life", previously a B-side.

⊙ **Vocalese** (1985; Atlantic). Studded with star guests – McCoy Tyner, Dizzy Gillespie, James Moody, Ray Brown, The Four Freshmen, Count Basie's orchestra, lyricist Jon Hendricks – this album showcases the group at the height of its powers.

⊙ **The Offbeat Of Avenues** (1991; Columbia). This set features the cocktail-smooth and very raunchy "Ten Minutes Till The Savages Come", plus tributes to Sarah Vaughan and Miles Davis (an exquisite "Blues For Pablo") and some fine new songs.

Herbie Mann

Flute, tenor saxophone, composer.
b. Brooklyn, New York, 16 April 1930; d. 1 July 2003.

Mann began on clarinet at the age of nine. He was stationed in Europe with the US army and played with a band in Trieste for three years. From 1954–7 he was active on the West Coast of the USA, playing and writing, and directing music for TV dramas. Henceforth specializing on flute, in 1959 he formed his Afro-Jazz Sextet, which he took on a US State Department tour of 15 African countries in 1960. In 1961 he played in Brazil, discovered the bossa nova style and began playing in this idiom. He had a best-selling album (*Herbie Mann At The Village Gate*) and a hit single ("Comin' Home Baby") in 1962. By now established as the most popular flautist in jazz, as well as African, Latin and Brazilian influences, he also incorporated elements from Arabian, Jewish and Turkish music into his performances. In the late 60s he introduced elements from rock, recording the seminally hip *Memphis Underground* – his most convincing music – with a group that included Larry Coryell, Miroslav Vitous and Sonny Sharrock.

He continued his exploration of the jazz-rock-funk galaxy in the 1970s, calling his band the Family of Mann. A pallid reggae album with Tommy McCook and novelty disco hits in 1975 were low points, though on his own record label, Embryo, he produced albums by Ron Carter, Vitous, Attila Zoller and others. Mann's music was always closely related to the dance rhythms of the day, which could be both an asset and a weakness in his music. Yet, towards the end of his life, cut short by a long battle against prostrate cancer, he returned to his Eastern European, Jewish heritage, making music he described as a kind of "gypsy jazz". [IC]

⊙ **Herbie Mann At The Village Gate** (1962; Atlantic). Mann has had much critical stick over the years, but is essentially a benign force with an ear for good musicians. His band here, with vibes, bass, drums and two percussionists, is a fine, cohesive, swinging unit and he plays with considerable force.

⊙ **Memphis Underground** (1968; Atlantic). This deservedly was one of the hit albums of that decade. The title track has a fetching innocence about it – it's merely a hypnotic groove on one chord, but it breathes and it works. The ensemble is rather innovatory, with three guitarists (including Larry Coryell and Sonny Sharrock), organ and electric piano, Roy Ayers on vibes and two bass players with a third (Miroslav Vitous) added for one track. There's plenty of substance and high spirits in the proceedings.

➤➤ **Art Blakey** *(Orgy In Rhythm)*.

Shelly Manne

Drums, composer.

b. New York, 11 June 1920; d. 26 Sept 1984.

Manne played on boats to Europe in the late 1930s, and then worked with several leading big bands between 1939–42. He was also with the Joe Marsala group on 52nd Street in 1940–41. While in the navy from 1942–5, he played on and helped to organize sessions for Signature records with Coleman Hawkins, Barney Bigard and others. He was the drummer for Stan Kenton in 1946–7, 1947–8 and 1950–51, and for Woody Herman in 1949. He also did small-group work with Charlie Ventura in 1947 and Bill Harris in 1948. After leaving Kenton for the last time, he settled in Los Angeles and became

HERMAN LEONARD

Shelly Manne

heavily involved in studio work, eventually not only as a player but also as a composer of film and TV music. At the same time he continued making small-group records and live appearances, billed as Shelly Manne and his Men. He ran a successful nightclub, Shelly's Manne-Hole, from 1960–74, and was a founder member of the L.A.4, with whom he played from 1974–7.

An example of true versatility, Manne was widely respected in all the spheres he moved in. The West Coast experimentalists of the early 1950s and the more vital jazz stylists he worked with before and after – not to mention those who wielded power in the demanding world of the studios – all valued his musical contributions and his personal reliability. His jazz drumming was marked by the kind of responsiveness that makes the life of other group members so much easier, and some of the unusual effects he came up with may have paved the way for the freer approach to drumming that surfaced in the mid-1960s. [BP]

⊙ **The Three And The Two** (1954; Contemporary/OJC). Manne plays melody rather than time in this brief flirtation with the West Coast intellectuals, led by Jimmy Giuffre and Shorty Rogers; they are the other two-thirds of the "Three", while the duo is with Russ Freeman.

⊙ **My Fair Lady** (1956; Contemporary/OJC). A much more typical session is this famous album featuring the jazz playing of André Previn (with Leroy Vinnegar completing the trio), with Manne again bringing considerable creativity to his role.

Bill Evans-Shelly Manne

⊙ **Empathy** (1962–6; Verve). The reissue combines the original album of this title with the return match four years later, Monte Budwig being replaced by Eddie Gomez on the second date. Here it sounds as if Manne's invention had found a worthy home.

➤➤ **Lennie Niehaus** *(Vol.1: The Quintets)*; **Sonny Rollins** *(Way Out West)*.

Wingy Manone

Trumpet, vocals.

b. New Orleans, 13 Feb 1900; d. 9 July 1982.

Wingy (Joseph Matthews) Manone worked round the Southern states with leaders such as Peck Kelley and Doc Ross, before going to New York in 1927 and then settling in Chicago. Fast-talking, amiable and ambitious, during the late 1920s and early 1930s he toured in shows, recorded with Benny Goodman and Red Nichols and even appeared in a revue in which he was billed as "the one-armed Indian" (he had lost his right arm in a streetcar accident), but by 1934 he was leading his own band in New York, and recording prolifically. One Manone title of the period, "Isle Of Capri", full of nonsense delivered in his appealing Italianate style, was a big hit, and the formula made him a headliner on 52nd Street as well as in Chicago, New Orleans and Los Angeles. "I'd like to be up at RKO myself", Manone sang in another anarchic rewrite (of Dorothy Fields's "A Fine Romance"), and by 1940 he was, for *Rhythm on the River*, starring Bing Crosby (who befriended Manone and kept him around as a "court jester"), and four other, less successful low-budget movies. Now living in Hollywood, Manone was the star he wanted to be and in 1948 he wrote a high-spirited autobiography, *Trumpet on the Wing*, one of the funniest of all jazz books. For most of the 1950s, living in Las Vegas, he was still warding off jazz fashion, bandleading and working with Crosby on radio shows. But by the 1960s cracks were starting to show – nursing an ambition to write a suite based on his New Orleans memories, worried that his son might be drafted into Vietnam, and touring Britain to audiences who seemed slightly out-of-touch with Manone's irrepressible humour, he grew disillusioned. "You can't make it playing honest nowadays," he told a *Down Beat* reporter in 1970, a sad comment from the trumpeter who had billed his shows with the byline "Come in and hear the truth!" Since then Manone's fine records of the 1930s have been reissued: a much happier epitaph. [DF]

⊙ **Swingin' at the Hickory House** (1924-45/ASV). Very good all round illustration of Manone from early titles by the Arcadian Serenaders (1924) via many favourites ("Tar Paper Stomp", "Isle of Capri") through to "Where Can I Find A Cherry?" with his Cats in 1945.

⊙ **Wingy Manone Collection Vols. 1/2/3/4** (1927–36; Collectors' Classics). Four volumes, demonstrating the chronological development of Manone's workmanlike trumpet and wonderfully hip singing on record. His biggest hit "Isle Of Capri" is on Vol. 3, but much of the music is comparably enjoyable, with class-A sidemen. Fine production, remastering by John R.T. Davies and alternate takes.

⊙ **Wingy Manone 1936/1936–7/1937–8** (Classics). Classics take up the story of Manone's later 1930s work; equally enjoyable with famous sidemen including Joe Marsala, Matty Matlock, Babe Russin and more.

Michael Mantler

Composer, trumpet.

b. Vienna, 10 Aug 1943.

Mantler studied trumpet and musicology at Vienna Academy of Music and University, then in 1962 moved to the USA, studying at the Berklee School of Music. In 1964 he moved to New York and played trumpet with Cecil Taylor's group, probably the closest he has ever got to being a gigging jazzman – his interests always seem to have lain more in composition and orchestral arrangement. He was involved in the formation of the Jazz Composers' Guild with Taylor, Bill Dixon, Roswell Rudd, Archie Shepp and others, struggling for better working conditions and opportunities to present their new (abstract) music without compromise. Together with Carla Bley, whom he later married, he formed a large orchestra to perform new compositions by members of the Guild; and, after touring Europe with Bley and Steve Lacy in the Jazz Realities quintet, he formed the Jazz Composers' Orchestra Association (JCOA), a non-profit-making foundation to perform new compositions for jazz orchestras.

In the late 60s his trumpet contributed to some idiosyncratic classics of the jazz album canon – Carla Bley's *A Genuine Tong Funeral* (by Gary Burton's augmented group) and Charlie Haden's *Liberation Music Orchestra* project. Mantler's own music during the 1960s was uncompromisingly abstract and perhaps a little severe – there has often been a dour, angst-ridden strain in Mantler's music. Nevertheless, *Communications* (JCOA; 1968), an award-winning double album recorded with the JCOA, was a landmark of the decade, setting a precedent for organized abstraction by large improvising ensembles. It featured stellar soloists such as Taylor, Rudd, Don Cherry and Pharoah Sanders.

His thriving creative partnership with Carla Bley continued, and he helped to manage (and played on) the logistical nightmare but ambitious success that was *Escalator Over The Hill*. Mantler has never looked back. With the aid of a grant he was able to record his ambitious *13* for two orchestras and piano. and later works "revelled" in judicious use of characterful musicians and distinctive vocalists from any and all genres, deployed (or juxtaposed) almost as if they were orchestral parts in a score. He did, however, carry on gigging and recording with the Carla Bley Band until 1985, recording and touring Europe with Charlie Haden's reconvened Liberation Music Orchestra in 1982.

He wrote a series of orchestral suites, including 1984's *Twenty Five* (premiered in Cologne under the direction of Mike Gibbs) in the 1980s, often with literature as inspiration, and several quasi-operas and grand schemes. *Many Have No Speech* (1988; ECM) was a sombre project with snatches of beauty: Mantler's settings of poems by Samuel Beckett, Ernst Meister and Philippe Soupault, powered by Rick Fenn's rock guitar and his own trumpet, with full orchestral backing and vocals from Robert Wyatt, Marianne Faithful and Jack Bruce. He has been resident in Copenhagen since the early 1990s. **[IC]**

⊙ **The Hapless Child** (1976; Watt). Mantler's involvement in Carla Bley's *Escalator Over The Hill* seems to have been a turning point for him, and he too became interested in the rock, folk and ethnic music traditions. *Hapless Child* is much less abstract than his 1960s work, with a small jazz group (Carla Bley, Steve Swallow, Jack DeJohnette, Terje Rypdal) and four vocalists, including Nick Mason from Pink Floyd and Robert Wyatt.

⊙ **Folly Seeing All This** (1992; Watt). This is a lament for the lost ideals, cruelties and corruption of our century. Using the Balanescu string quartet (with added viola and cello), vocals by Jack Bruce, plus Wolfgang Puschnig on alto flute, Rick Fenn on guitar, Karen Mantler on pianos and vocals and Dave Adams on vibraphone, Mantler has created a suite of often singular beauty. It has more to do with European art music than jazz and sounds as if it is entirely written, but there may be improvised passages by the individual soloists.

➤➤ **Carla Bley** *(Escalator Over The Hill; Social Studies; Live!)*; **Charlie Haden** *(Ballad Of The Fallen)*.

Davide Mantovani

Bass, bass guitar, composer.
b. Ferrara, Italy, 23 May 1965.

As a child, Mantovani had three years of piano and a year of guitar lessons, but his bass playing, which he began at the age of 17 (and for which he is best known) was self taught. The peak of his Italian career was touring with the Italian singer/songwriter, Francesco Guccini, in 1991. In the same year he moved to London where he soon became a sought-after bassist, playing with Antonio Forcione, Carol Grimes, Juan Martin, Roberto Pla, Jim Mullen,Tim Richard's nine-piece Great Spirit and on Monica Vasconcelos' album *Nóis* (1999). He formed the Davide Mantovani Quintet in 1999 and his first album, *Square One*, appeared the following year. On this very impressive debut, Mantovani's regular team of Gerry Hunt (guitar and sax), Roger Beaujolais (vibes), Steve Lodder (keyboards) and Davide Giovanni (drums) were supplemented on some tracks by Kim Burton's accordion and Wade Austin's steel pan.

Mantovani does not consider himself exclusively a jazz musician. He also loves to play salsa, Brazilian music and fusion, and is stimulated by the creative freedom of being able to move easily between different genres. The eclecticism of his own compositions is testament to his disregard for musical boundaries. **[IC]**

⊙ **Square One** (2000; Stay Tuned). There's never a dull moment in this varied collection of Mantovani compositions. The opening "Promenade" evokes the poetic spirit of Eberhard Weber's music, with its soprano sax lead and deft changes of pace, while "Brotherly" has an easy loping Latin rock feel and a catchy melody, with a big percussion outing and fine vibraphone and guitar solos.

Fate Marable

Piano, calliope, bandleader.
b. Paducah, Kentucky, 2 Dec 1890; d. 16 Jan 1947.

One of the three bandleaders who led bands for the Streckfus riverboat line, Fate Marable played on boats for most of his life – indeed, he worked so long for Streckfus that he became known as "Streckfus's son". A bandleader by 1917, he was a highly talented piano and calliope player and a sternly disciplined leader, who reputedly kept his wild bunch of young musicians – many of them straight from rough-house New Orleans – in strict order. All of them had to be able to read music and tackle a varied repertoire of popular tunes, classical selections and singalongs (to please the predominantly white clientele that rode the steamers), as well as play jazz, which more often came into its own on specially advertised "coloured nights", when admirers stood six feet deep around the band. New music was rehearsed daily, band members were encouraged to listen to the orchestras on neighbouring boats, and visits were organized for the purpose. The greats-in-the-making who worked for Marable included Louis Armstrong, Henry "Red" Allen, Pops Foster, Jimmy Blanton, Gene Sedric, Zutty Singleton, the Dodds Brothers and mellophonist Dave Jones, who is said to have helped Louis Armstrong with technique and ideas; the music they produced had a colossal effect on still younger talents, two examples among hundreds being Bix Beiderbecke and pianist Jess Stacy, who heard riverboat bands often at Cape Girardeau. Marable left only disappointing recordings made with a second-line band, Fate Marable's Society Syncopators, in New Orleans in 1924, but his bands were a vital training ground. "Fate knew that just by being around musicians who read music I would automatically learn myself", said Louis Armstrong; whether reading or improvising, Marable provided a free university to people who otherwise could never have even seen one. [DF]

Rita Marcotulli

Piano, composer.

b. Rome, 10 March 1959.

Marcotulli's father was a sound engineer who recorded classical musicians and film composers such as Nino Rota and Ennio Morricone. Rita began piano at the age of five and later studied at the Santa Cecilia Conservatory. Since the early 1980s she has performed and recorded with many local and visiting players including Enrico Rava, Aldo Romano, Sal Nistico, Palle Danielsson, Michel Portal, Dewey Redman and Billy Cobham, with whom she toured in Europe and the USA in 1988. She recorded her first album in 1984 and worked more recently in a trio with Danielsson and Bob Moses, and also with vocalist Maria Pia De Vito. She duetted in 1996 with Pat Metheny, and in a piano trio with Paul Bley and John Taylor. Marcotulli's influences extend beyond jazz to artists such as the Brazilian singer Elis Regina, and to Indian and African music. "The most important aim," she says "is trying to find a personal sound which is more than virtuosity and mere technique." [BP]

⊙ **The Woman Next Door** (1997; Label Bleu). Inspired by the work of François Truffaut, this wide-ranging suite incorporates the film director's voice in a landscape populated with accordion, Celtic harp and Indian rhythmic patterns, as well as jazz solos from Enrico Rava, Stefano Di Battista and the leader herself.

Sam Margolis

Clarinet, tenor saxophone.

b. Boston, Massachusetts, 1 Nov 1923; d. 20 March 1996.

Like Ruby Braff, Margolis grew up in Boston and was a stylistic throwback, preferring to concentrate on the swing styles of Lester Young and Bud Freeman rather than the vocabulary of bebop. As such he made the ideal musical partner for Braff early on, and after time playing round Boston with Bobby Hackett, Vic Dickenson and others, the two of them worked regularly and recorded together in New York, as well as appearing at the 1957 Newport festival. Margolis retrned to Boston in 1958, but recorded again with Braff in 1973 and continued to play at festivals, clubs and jazz parties. [DF]

Tania Maria

Vocals, piano.

b. São Luiz, Maranhão, Brazil, 9 May 1948.

Tania Maria Correa Reis, to give her her full name, studied classical music as a child and became involved in jazz as a teenager in Rio de Janeiro. She settled in Paris in 1974, becoming famous for her residency at the Via Brazil restaurant, and toured Europe, visiting England in 1980. Moving to New York in 1981, she worked with Eddie Gomez and increased her reputation with many popular records. Her rhythmic piano-playing tends to be dominated on records by her vocals, often scatting in unison with her instrument à la George Benson (or, earlier, singer-pianist Nellie Lutcher). Singing lyrics, she has a typical musician's untrained voice, which is nevertheless strangely attractive. [BP]

⊙ **Bela Vista** (1990; World Pacific). With backing musicians including Gomez, Steve Gadd and Lew Soloff (who has one tiny solo), Maria lets loose on "I Can't Give You Anything But Love", the Rolling Stones' "Satisfaction", and one of her catchy originals, "Ca C'est Bon".

Charlie Mariano

Alto and soprano saxophones, flutes, nadaswaram.

b. Boston, Massachusetts, 12 Nov 1923.

Mariano's whole career is an object lesson in gradual artistic growth. Like Miles Davis, he has at every stage played contemporary music, always remaining open to new ideas and never allowing his creative arteries to harden. While studying at Berklee School of Music he played around Boston with an astonishing amount of jazz masters, such as Jaki Byard, Nat Pierce, Sam Rivers and Quincy Jones (to name but a few). He first made an international impression, in the early 1950s, as an impassioned alto soloist, coming out of Parker but already showing originality. From 1953–5 he worked with Stan Kenton's band, then spent two and a half years in Los Angeles playing with Frank Rosolino, Shelly Manne and others. In 1959 he married Japanese pianist Toshiko Akiyoshi and formed a quartet with her in 1960, playing in the USA and Japan. By 1963, when he worked and recorded with Mingus (on the classic album *The Black Saint And The Sinner Lady*), he was even more individual, and was described by critic John S. Wilson as "a brilliant combination of authority, virtuosity and inspiration". There then followed six years teaching at Berklee (during which time he also played with Astrud Gilberto) which made him examine the whole basis of his music.

He was introduced to the *nadaswaram* (a South Indian wind instrument with a double reed, like an oboe) whilst in Malaysia on a five-month US government sponsored trip to coach the Radio Malaysia orchestra, and he would later make several prolonged trips to India to study and play. From 1971–84 he lived in Europe, working with artists and groups such as Ambush (Stu Martin, Barre Phillips and Peter Warren), Eberhard Weber's Colours, Jasper van't Hof and Pork Pie, the United Jazz and Rock Ensemble (UJRE), Philip Catherine, and various other bands under his own name. The European environment was conducive to his art – he found that musical athleticism played very little part in Europe, whereas the creation of atmosphere and mood were of crucial importance.

Charlie Mariano

Since the late 1980s Mariano has been a featured soloist with the singer/songwriter Konstantin Wecker. whilst leading his own groups. In the later 1990s, Mariano formed a quartet, Nassim, which fused Eastern and Western musical elements, in which alto sax met African vocals, oud, darabouka, percussion, bass and baritone guitar. The group toured Germany and in 1997 recorded a live album, *Charlie Mariano's Nassim*, at the Leverkusen and Westerstede jazz festivals, for which their cross-cultural pollination became even broader, augmented by Indian drums and percussion.

Mariano's profound interest in other musical cultures has broadened and deepened his vision, and his greatest work has been done since he reached fifty. In his later compositions, his solos are often quite extraordinary – marmoreally sculpted, every note telling and every note meant, his soprano and alto sound projecting a powerful, almost anguished, lyricism, as if the music were being wrung out of him. There are few parallels in jazz to the voluptuous austerity of Mariano's later work. [IC]

⊙ **Jyothi** (1983; ECM). Mariano is one of the few Western musicians who can play Indian music on an equal footing with Indian musicians, and the enthralling performances on *Jyothi* include singer Ramamani's composition *Raga Yagapryia* in 7/4 time, which Mariano later adapted for the UJRE.

⊙ **Mariano** (1987; Intuition). Mariano with guitarist Paul Shigihara and pianist/keyboardist Michael Hertin, in a series of moody performances, including a version of Ravel's *Pavane Pour Une Infante Défunte*.

⊙ **Adagio** (1991; Lipstick). A beautifully contemplative album from the same trio, reinterpreting a series of classical pieces and excerpts (some associated with Miles Davis) including Delibes's "Filles De Cadiz" and "En Aranjuez Con Tu Amor".

⊙ **Charlie Mariano's Nassim** (1997; Off The Wall Records). Mariano is well versed in Indian music, and the non-Western musicians on the album are also well versed in harmony, with the result that the unforced and natural cooperation creates marvellous music that has the best of both worlds. The seething rhythms are wonderfully varied throughout, and the solos blaze with feeling. The music breathes beautifully – light and shade, tension and release.

➤➤ **Philip Catherine** *(Sleep My Love)*; **Charles Mingus** *(The Black Saint And Tho Sinnor Lady)*; **Eberhard Weber** *(Yellow Fields)*.

Dodo Marmarosa

Piano.

b. Pittsburgh, Pennsylvania, 12 Dec 1925; d. 17 Sep 2002.

Michael "Dodo" Marmarosa worked in his late teens with the big bands of Gene Krupa, Tommy Dorsey and Charlie Barnet (whose recorded "The Moose" was his piano feature). After more than a year with Artie Shaw from 1944–5, he settled on the West Coast, as did fellow Shaw sideman Barney Kessel, with whom Marmarosa had already recorded. Prolific freelance work, including record dates with Lester Young and Charlie Parker, followed. In the 1950s he was living in Pittsburgh and inactive through illness, but he resurfaced in the early 1960s to cut three albums (one with Gene Ammons), before returning to total obscurity. The brilliant sound and highly original bop-influenced lines of his 1940s playing made most of his contemporaries, and even his own later work, feel like an anticlimax. [BP]

⊙ **On Dial** (1946–7; Spotlite). Combining one track with Charlie Parker and a sextet session led by Howard McGhee with some of the few early recordings under his own name, this amply illustrates Dodo's inventive flair, original tone and fresh style during his heyday.

➤➤ **Charlie Parker** *(The Dial Masters)*.

Lawrence Marrero

Banjo, guitar.

b. New Orleans, 24 Oct 1900; d. 5 June 1959.

Marrero was taught banjo by his brother John and from about 1919 played with leaders such as Wooden Joe Nicholas, Chris Kelly, Frank Dusen and John Robichaux; by the late 1930s he was working regularly with George Lewis in clubs and cabarets in New Orleans. In 1942, alongside Lewis, he made the recordings for Gene Williams that were to help launch the jazz revival – and Bunk Johnson – and he stayed on in New York until 1946, when Lewis went home to work at Manny's Tavern, New Orleans. Marrero went with him and became inseparable from his leader (he called Lewis his "brother-in-law"). A simple, content-to-accompany banjoist, Marrero was the ideal support for Lewis, and saw himself rise to unexpected stardom in the 1950s, despite the onset of his worrying high blood pressure. Lewis replaced him in 1955 before a heavy spell of touring, and for the rest of his life Marrero led his own bands in New Orleans. [DF]

Joe Marsala

Clarinet, saxophones, composer.

b. Chicago, 4 Jan 1907; d. 4 March 1978.

Joe Marsala was born into a musical family living in a black neighbourhood of Chicago. By 1937 he had held down a wide range of non-musical jobs, as well as working ten years in clubs, circuses and touring bands in and out of New York and Chicago. That year he moved into 52nd Street's Hickory House, a steak joint owned by John Popkin, with a band that included Eddie Condon, Joe Bushkin and Ray Biondi (violin); soon after Marsala brought in black trumpeter Henry "Red" Allen to complete the group – "In the 1930s," says Leonard Feather, "Joe was responsible in his quiet, unpublicized way for more attempts to break down segregation in jazz than Benny Goodman." (Allen was later replaced by another black player, Otis Johnson.) After illness in 1938, Marsala moved back into the Hickory House (this time featuring harpist Adèle Girard, whom he later married), where he was based for most of the next decade. Apart from Girard, Marsala's group featured bright up-and-comers such as Carmen Mastren, Buddy Rich, Shelly Manne and Dave Tough, many of whom later joined Tommy Dorsey (Marsala once sent Dorsey a half-joking telegram: "How about giving me a job in your band so I can play with mine?"); singer Frankie Laine was another early protégé. In 1944 Marsala wrote the first of several hit tunes, "Don't Cry Joe" (performed by Gordon Jenkins's orchestra); later ones included "Little Sir Echo" and "And So To Sleep Again". But the winds of change were sweeping through jazz and Marsala (despite being open-eared enough to feature trumpeters Neal Hefti and Dizzy Gillespie in future projects) retired from full-time performing in 1948. He went into music publishing and in 1962 was vice-president of Seeburg's jukebox-based recording company. Bandleading occasionally in the 1960s, he made some intriguing late records with Bobby Hackett and Tony Bennett, still playing the low-register clarinet that had made him famous. [DF]

⊙ **Joe Marsala 1936–42/1944–6** (Classics). Two chronological surveys of Marsala: *(1936–42)* has him with Pee Wee Erwin, the Delta Four, brother Marty, Adèle Girard and his Chosen Seven; *(1944–6)* has fine Joe Thomas and an intriguing appearance by Dizzy Gillespie exploding into "My Melancholy Baby", plus one other track.

Marty Marsala

Trumpet.

b. Chicago, 2 April 1909; d. 27 April 1975.

Marty Marsala began in Chicago, where the New Orleans Rhythm Kings were an early inspiration, and worked locally before moving to New York in 1936 to join his brother Joe's band. The two of them worked together regularly until 1946, with periods in between during which Marsala led his own band, toured with Chico Marx, and worked with leaders including Miff Mole and Tony Parenti. By the late 1940s he was commuting ever more regularly between Chicago and San Francisco, where his powerhouse trumpeting, sense of humour and onstage presence made him a much loved part of the West Coast scene; he appeared at Victor's and Roxie's, the Downbeat (where he backed Sidney Bechet), and at Doc Dougherty's Hangover Club with his own band and Earl Hines's. Marsala soon settled in San Francisco, making occasional visits back to Chicago, but he became ill in the 1960s and gradually gave up music. While never a great individualist, his sound evoked a well-stirred mix of Muggsy Spanier, Wild Bill Davison and more technical latterday players such as Don Goldie. [DF]

Earl Hines

⊙ **At Club Hangover 1955** (2001; Storyville). Marsala's excellent strong lead and multifaceted style show up well on this fine date with Earl Hines.

Branford Marsalis

Soprano and tenor saxophones.

b. Breaux Bridge, Louisiana, 26 Aug 1960.

The son of Ellis Marsalis and brother of Wynton, Branford began on alto, replacing Bobby Watson in Art Blakey's band in 1981. He then switched to tenor and soprano, joining his brother's band in 1982, and released *Scenes in the City* (Columbia), an accomplished but non-committal debut album of mainstream jazz, the following year. He has led his own trios and quartets since the mid-1980s, playing forceful neo-bop, though he, notably, played on Miles Davis's album *Decoy* and, alongside Kenny Kirkland, Darryl Jones and Omar Hakim, he accompanied Sting on the album *The Dream Of The Blue Turtles*, touring internationally with him. The exposure got him deserved recognition as a leading jazz and fusion saxophonist, and in 1986 he toured Europe with the Herbie Hancock quartet.

During the early 1990s he led the house band on *The Tonight Show*, a top American TV talk show, and in 1993, Marsalis won a Grammy Award for his album *I Heard You Twice The First Time*. His 1994 album with a new band, *Buckshot LeFonque*, was a daring attempt to fuse jazz with hip-hop (he had previously co-written hip-hop act Gang Starr's "Jazz

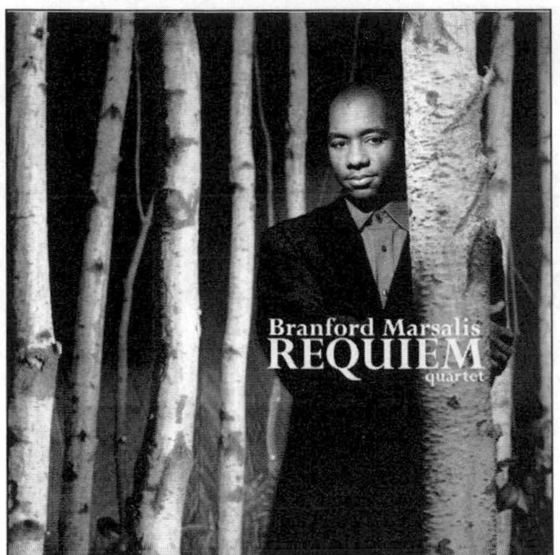

Thing" for the Spike Lee movie *Mo' Better Blues* in 1990). In latter years, Marsalis has joined the faculty of Michigan State University in East Lansing, where he teaches in the Jazz Studies department. He has also worked as an A&R man and producer with Columbia Records, and is a relaxed and interesting TV broadcaster and writer. Branford Marsalis is also something of a polymath, with wide intellectual interests and a great love for the work of William Shakespeare. Black history profoundly and self-consciously informs his music – *Romare Bearden Revealed* (2003; Marsalis Music) honours the Harlem Renaissance artist of its title with Branford's takes of the jazz classics that inspired Bearden and compositions inspired by him. [IC]

⊙ **Crazy People Music** (1990; Columbia); **The Beautyful Ones Are Not Yet Born** (1991; Columbia). *Crazy* has Branford with Kenny Kirkland, bassist Robert Hurst and Watts, and is very much more focused and pithy than his earlier work. On the latter album, Marsalis plays with great invention in trio format with Hurst and Watts, with brother Wynton added on one track.

⊙ **I Heard You Twice The First Time** (1992; Columbia). During the 1980s both Marsalis brothers began to rediscover Louis Armstrong and the whole blues tradition, and this multi-personnel affair is Branford's commendable tribute to that legacy, with guest appearances from John Lee Hooker, B.B. King and Linda Hopkins.

⊙ **Branford Marsalis Quartet: Requiem** (1998; Columbia). This was the last ever recording by pianist Kenny Kirkland, who died tragically in his early forties before the last piece, "Elysium", was recorded. Marsalis, bassist Eric Revis and drummer Jeff "Tain" Watts recorded it later as a trio and the album is a fitting memorial to the much admired and loved pianist. It's Marsalis's most adventurous album to date. Kirkland plays superbly throughout, not least on "Trieste", which was composed by Paul Motian.

Ellis Marsalis

Piano, composer.

b. New Orleans, 14 Nov 1934.

After learning clarinet at elementary school and playing it in his high-school marching band, Ellis Marsalis gained a Bachelor of Arts degree in music education from Dillard University in 1955. In addition to playing the saxophone, Marsalis took up piano, influenced chiefly by Oscar Peterson and Nat "King" Cole, and established himself in the New Orleans music scene as both an educator and a player. In the latter capacity, he has played and recorded with trumpeters Nat Adderley and the Rebirth Brass Band's Kermit Ruffins, with saxophonists David "Fathead" Newman and the UK's Courtney Pine, as well as participating in local New Orleans-based projects such as the American Jazz Quintet and the Heritage Hall Jazz Band. In his capacity as an educator, he has worked, since 1983, for the National Endowment for the Arts, since 1989 as the Director of Jazz Studies at the University of New Orleans, and since 1990 as the Vice President of the International Association of Jazz Educators, not retiring from teaching until 2003. As well as gracing the local and, less frequently, the international jazz scene with his cultured, elegant but robust piano-playing, Marsalis has also been highly influential in encouraging the development of many younger players, among them Harry Connick Jnr, in addition to his own sons Branford, Wynton, Delfeayo and – the latest member of the clan to make an impact on the jazz scene – drummer Jason (though they weren't all heard playing together until 2003). In 1995, Ellis and Branford made a duo album, *Loved Ones* (Columbia), with Ellis's solo piano tracks a highlight, and in 1999 the expansive solo piano *Duke in Blue* (Columbia) was a standout tribute in Ellington's centenary year. [CP]

⊙ **Ellis Marsalis Trio** (1990; Blue Note). The classic Marsalis rhythm-section of Bob Hurst (bass) and Jeff Watts (drums) propels Marsalis père through an educational yet swinging range of tunes embracing waltzes, standards and originals, but the highlight is an unaccompanied "I Thought About You".

⊙ **Whistle Stop** (1993; Columbia). To some extent a rerun of *The Classic Ellis Marsalis* (1963; Boplicity), containing five tunes from that date, this features sons Branford and Jason with Hurst and Watts in careful virtuosic playing.

⊙ **Joe Cool's Blues** (1995; Columbia). An album shared with son Wynton and dedicated to Peanuts-cartoon music. Ellis Marsalis's trio (bassist Reginald Veal and drummer Martin Butler) interprets Vince Guaraldi's music, while Wynton plays his own incidental music.

⊙ **Marsalis Family: A Jazz Celebration** (2003; Rounder). A joyous live recording of the first time the entire musical dynasty had ever performed together and a fine tribute to the patriarch on the occasion of his retirement from teaching.

Wynton Marsalis

Trumpet.

b. New Orleans, 18 Oct 1961.

The son of Ellis Marsalis and another of the four musical Marsalis brothers, Wynton was given his first trumpet when he was six. In his mid-teens he had extensive experience in marching bands, jazz

Wynton Marsalis

bands, funk bands and orchestras playing European classical repertoire. At 17 he met Gunther Schuller and impressed him with his precocious knowledge of jazz. At 18 he went to the Juilliard School in New York, and a few months later joined Art Blakey's Jazz Messengers.

Tours with the Herbie Hancock quartet in the US and Japan, and playing at the Newport jazz festival, established his international reputation. The quartet recorded a double album and Marsalis recorded his own first LP as a leader. By the spring of 1982 he was leading his own quintet and touring extensively in the USA, participating in the all-star tribute *Musicians for Monk*, and the Young Lions of Jazz concert in the summer. In December he recorded his first classical album, of Haydn, Hummel and Leopold Mozart trumpet concertos, in London, where the famous classical trumpeter Maurice André pronounced him "potentially the greatest [classical] trumpeter of all time". He would later become the first instrumentalist to win two simultaneous Grammy awards in the categories of Jazz (Best Soloist) and Classical Music (Best Soloist with Orchestra).

By now, he was getting extensive media coverage in the USA, and a documentary film was made about him for British TV. At the age of 22 he was a jazz superstar. Five astonishingly accomplished albums charted his initial progress, beginning with *Wynton Marsalis* (1982), which marked his weaning off the VSOP rhythm-section and Art Blakey, and culminating in *J Mood*, recorded in December 1986, the year in which his first quintet broke up. Marsalis had shown the world his technical genius: a beautiful sound, good range, superb articulation, brilliant control and an apparently intuitive grasp of whatever music he played. As a jazz player, however, he had not done anything new either stylistically or conceptually in his first five records.

At this point, realizing that if you don't know where you've come from, you can't know where you're going, Marsalis wisely went back to acquaint himself with the earliest roots of the music – the whole blues tradition, gospels, worksongs, and particularly the early work of Louis Armstrong and the music of Duke Ellington. This was his Pentecost, and by the 1990s it had brought to his playing a new passion and depth, and to his composing and arranging a greater richness of rhythms, timbres and emotional resonances. A series of recordings dealt with his discovery of the music's great past and its influence and, to accommodate his compositional and tonal ideas, he added to the classic quintet line-up trombone and alto saxophone, making his working band a septet.

Marsalis is also a highly literate and tireless proselytizer for jazz and has spent a considerable amount of time and energy speaking in American schools and conducting master classes nationally and internationally. This resulted in a brilliant series of four TV films, *Marsalis On Music*, explaining and demonstrating the resemblances and the differences between jazz and

European classical music. In 1994, his book *Sweet Swing Blues On The Road* was published, which showed that he is also a capable writer – lucid, genial and humane. The only off-note he sounds is his bizarre idea that there is one singular thing called "real jazz". Like all great arts, jazz is, and ought to be, incorrigibly plural. But Marsalis is probably the only major jazz musician whose early thinking was formed by critics – Albert Murray and Stanley Crouch were early mentors, and Crouch has continued in the role of personal guru and sleevenote writer for the Marsalis albums. However, the expressive and emotional scope of Marsalis's trumpet-playing and composing continues to grow impressively, and the future years promise new riches. [IC]

⊙ **Wynton Marsalis** (1982; Columbia); **J Mood** (1986; Columbia). During the period that produced these albums Marsalis was concerned with the 1960s bands of Ornette Coleman, Miles Davis and Coltrane. Together they comprise a graphic record of Marsalis's brilliance and habit of controlling the overall shape of each piece, and while the first has the excitement of new discovery (and, on some tracks, Miles's 1960s rhythm-section), *J Mood,* with a group of his peers, is a summation of his work to that point.

⊙ **Marsalis Standard Time: Vol. 1** (1986; Columbia); **Live At Blues Alley** (1986; Columbia); **The Majesty Of The Blues** (1988; Columbia). In 1986 Marsalis began recording performances of standards. The first has the dynamism of the new and Marsalis sparkles all the way, in the company of Marcus Roberts, bassist Leslie Hurst and Jeff Watts. On the *Blues Alley* live session he reviews pieces from his own earlier albums with stunning virtuosity and daredevil risks. *Majesty* is half superb and half noble failure. The title track and "Hickory Dickory Dock" are small masterpieces, his young sextet playing contemporary music that contains essences and elements of the blues, but the grafting of old New Orleans players onto the young group is an oil-and-water mix.

⊙ **Blue Interlude** (1992; Columbia). This marked the official debut of Marsalis's septet, which rapidly developed into one of the finest working bands on the scene. Marsalis's 37-minute title piece suite sets up a kaleidoscope of moods and motifs.

⊙ **Citi Movement (Griot New York)** (1992; Columbia). Marsalis wrote this septet music for a collaboration with the New York Ballet – "six and a half syncopated movements for jazz band and dancers". The result is a highly evocative musical portrait of America, and is probably Marsalis's first full masterpiece.

⊙ **Marsalis Plays Monk–Standard Time Vol. 4** (1994; Columbia). Marsalis leads an octet for this dynamic exploration of Monk's music. Monk's unique compositions arose out of the jazz tradition, and Marsalis's great plan was to draw on the same tradition, adapting the ideas of Armstrong (and Jelly Roll Morton) in their 1920s music – strange introductions and codas, breaks, very long solos, very short ones, surprises, drama all the way – to get inside Monk's music, and he has succeeded brilliantly.

➤➤ **Art Blakey** *(Straight Ahead).*

Warne Marsh

Tenor saxophone; also clarinet, flute.

b. Los Angeles, 26 Oct 1927; d. 18 Dec 1987.

Marsh played with Hoagy Carmichael's group in 1944–5 before army service. He then toured with Buddy Rich in 1948 and settled in New York, working with the Lennie Tristano sextet from 1949–52. Otherwise he worked outside music except for recordings with Lee Konitz and under his own name in the mid-1950s. There were reunions with Tristano in 1959 and 1964–5. He returned to California in 1966, teaching music and working at other jobs, as well as playing occasionally. In 1972 he became an early member of the Supersax ensemble. He made two tours of Europe with Konitz, using local rhythm-sections, in 1975 and 1976, and revisited the continent alone in 1982 and 1983.

Marsh was an extremely fluent but not facile thinker, full of unusual turns of phrase, despite a flow of notes that in most other players would hinder rather than encourage invention. He was, for instance, far more in command of high-speed technique than his frequent collaborator Konitz. Changing less over the years than Konitz, his later playing was more obviously marked by his work with Tristano; in fact, the shifting accents and veiled tonality often make him sound like a saxophone transcription of Tristano's piano solos. The overall impression, though, is more vital, thanks to Marsh's unique tone – an acquired taste, which has tempted few other saxophonists apart from Teo Macero, Wayne Shorter (more obliquely) and Mark Turner, but its glacial edge accords well with the otherworldliness of Marsh's lines. [BP]

⊙ **Ne Plus Ultra** (1969; hat Art). This reissued material from the small Revelation label finds Marsh perpetuating his ascetic approach without a piano (important because most pianists sound too conventional for him) but with a younger disciple, altoist Gary Foster.

➤➤ **Lee Konitz** *(Live At The Half Note);* **Lennie Tristano** *(Live At Birdland 1952).*

Eddie Marshall

Drums, recorder.

b. Springfield, Massachusetts, 13 April 1938.

After gigging with his father's swing band and student R&B groups in high school in Springfield, Edwin Marshall Jnr went on to study with a variety of New York drummers in 1956, developing a crisp groove under the influence of Max Roach and Art Blakey. Two years later he was recruited by Charlie Mariano into a quartet with the saxophonist's then wife, Toshiko Akiyoshi, and he returned to Akiyoshi (without Mariano) in 1965 after two years in the army, sustaining a musical relationship that continues on-call. He spent a year with Stan Getz while anchoring the house band at The Dom in New York, alongside pianist Mike Nock; played with Nock on tour with pop singer Dionne Warwick; and in 1967 was convinced to join the pianist in a groundbreaking San Francisco fusion band, The Fourth Way, which also included John Handy, Michael White and Ron McClure. From his Bay Area base, Marshall toured and recorded for Capitol until The Fourth Way's break-up in the early 70s, and then teamed up with vibraphonist Bobby Hutcherson. A heart operation in 1984 encouraged him to make jazz use of the recorder, a less stressful instrument, though rare to jazz. Marshall went on to a heavier groove in electrified hip-hop with a couple of his sons, and has gigged of late with Jon Jang and with Bobby McFerrin's Bang! Zoom, Marian McPartland, Charles Lloyd, Bobby Hutcherson and Cedar Walton. Active in San Francisco's jazz education scene, he releases recordings by his group Holy Mischief (comprising pianist Paul Nagel, bassist Jeff Chambers, and sax player Kenny Brooks) on his own Ruddy Duck label. [JK]

⊙ **Dance Of The Sun** (1977; Timeless). Marshall's fellow members of the legendary Keystone Korner's house rhythm-section (George Cables on piano and James Leary on bass) are joined by Hutcherson on vibes and Manny Boyd on saxophones for a spirited session that showcases both Marshall's rapid-fire propulsion (on Dizzy's "Salt Peanuts") and his tasteful swing through several of his own breezy compositions.

John Marshall

Drums.

b. London, 28 Aug 1941.

One of the few European drummers with a solid international reputation, Marshall began playing at school and became seriously involved with music at Reading University, where he took a degree in psychology. He had private lessons with several teachers, including Philly Joe Jones. In the 60s he played with Alexis Korner's Blues Incorporated, the Graham Collier sextet and with John Surman, John McLaughlin, Dave Holland, Mike Westbrook, Joe Harriott, Keith Tippett and others. In 1969 he was a founder member, along with Ian Carr, of Nucleus, which he juggled with regular membership of the Mike Gibbs orchestra.

The 1970s saw him playing with Jack Bruce and Soft Machine, becoming a permanent band member for most of the decade. He also played with many leading US and European musicians, including Larry Coryell, Gary Burton, Mary Lou Williams, Ronnie Scott, Ben Webster, Roy Eldridge, Milt Jackson, John Taylor, Norma Winstone and Volker Kriegel. In 1973, at the Baden-Baden Free Jazz Meeting, he met and began playing with Charlie Mariano, Jasper van't Hof and Philip Catherine. In 1977 he joined Eberhard Weber's Colours, one of the most important and influential groups of its time, staying with it until it disbanded at the end of 1981. Since then he has rejoined Nucleus and played with John Surman, Kenny Wheeler, the Gil Evans orchestra, van't Hof, Coryell, Anthony Braxton, Albert Mangelsdorff and many others. He played with John Surman in the early 90s, and can be heard on the *Brass Project* album in 1992 and on Surman's English Quartet album, *Stranger Than Fiction*, in 1993 – one of the saxophonist's most beautiful recordings. Marshall has tended to play more and more free jazz, but regularly returns to playing with long-term friends and collaborators Surman, John Etheridge, and other stalwarts of the European chamber jazz and fusion scenes. [IC]

⊙ **Marshall/Travis/Wood** (1998; 33 Jazz). Marshall, saxophonist Theo Travis and guitarist Mark Wood are three virtuosi who have such an intensely compositional approach to improvisation that, though none of the music on this album was premeditated, the majority of the performances are achieved with such artistry that they sound almost pre-composed. The concentrated intelligence of the trio results in several exquisitely elegaic or romantic pieces and much dynamic music.

➤➤ **Ian Carr** *(Old Heartland)*; **Mike Gibbs** *(By the Way…)*; **Nucleus** *(Elastic Rock)*; **John Surman** *(The Brass Project; Stranger Than Fiction)*; **Eberhard Weber's Colours** *(Silent Feet)*.

Kaiser Marshall

Drums.

b. Savannah, Georgia, 11 June 1899; d. 3 Jan 1948.

Marshall's first important connection was with Fletcher Henderson, with whom he played from 1924–30. Thereafter he led his own bands, subbed for other leaders including Duke Ellington, Cab Calloway, Bill McKinney and Chick Webb, and during the 1940s worked with, among others, Wild Bill Davison, Art Hodes, Sidney Bechet, Garvin Bushell and Bunk Johnson at the Stuyvesant Casino. His drumming is vividly captured on Louis Armstrong's immortal "Knockin' A Jug". [DF]

➤➤ **Louis Armstrong** *(Louis Armstrong And His Orchestra 1928–9 [Classics])*.

Wendell Marshall

Bass.

b. St Louis, Missouri, 24 Oct 1920; d. 6 Feb 2002.

While in college Marshall played briefly with the Lionel Hampton band in 1942. He spent three years in the army, then worked with the Stuff Smith trio in 1946–7 and led his own group back in St Louis. He joined the Mercer Ellington band in 1948, followed by a successful transfer to Duke Ellington that lasted from 1948–55. He was recorded on many sessions from the mid-1950s with such players as Art Blakey, Donald Byrd, Gigi Gryce, Milt Jackson, Hank Jones and Kenny Clarke, before specializing in Broadway pit-orchestra work. The bassist who replaced Oscar Pettiford in Duke's band, he took occasional solo features in a typical Blanton/Pettiford style, while his later jazz work concentrated almost exclusively on excellent rhythm-playing. Interestingly, he was a first cousin of Blanton, inheriting one of Blanton's instruments, but sadly he was soon lost to the jazz scene as he specialized more and more in Broadway stage work. [BP]

➤➤ **Bobby Jaspar** *(Hank Jones Trio With Bobby Jaspar)*.

Claire Martin

Vocals.

b. London, 6 Sept 1967.

A professional singer since the age of seventeen, Claire Martin travelled the world after leaving stage school, singing in piano bars and occasionally on the *QE2*. Back in London, she established herself on the jazz scene there with a gruelling series of gigs in clubs, hotel lounge bars and arts centres, singing with Ray Gelato's Giants and delivering her debut album, *The Waiting Game*, in 1992. As at home with the popular music of the 1970s as with the work of the conventional jazz-standards writers, her virtuosic but relaxed and engaging live performances generally featured a lively mix of the more recherché songs of Rodgers and Hart, Irving Berlin or Noël Coward, with the odd Joni Mitchell, Tom Waits or Dave Frishberg song thrown in. She performed in duos with fellow singer Ian Shaw and guitarist Jim Mullen, with Martin Taylor's Spirit Of Django band, and – in 1995 – on a "Rising Stars" tour of Europe that also featured Diana Krall, Cyrus Chestnut and David Sanchez. Martin's Shirley Horn influence was underlined in 1997, by her use of the latter's producer, Joel E. Siegel, for her fifth Linn album, *Make This City Ours*, a characteristically eclectic recording made in New York with some of the city's finest – bassist Peter Washington, drummer Gregory Hutchinson, saxophonist Antonio Hart – and one that raised her profile considerably in the USA. In 1999, Martin released her most wide-ranging album to date, *Take My Heart* (Linn), including an affecting version of Nick Drake's "Riverman" and an emotive visit to Elvis Costello's "Baby Plays Around". *Perfect Alibi* (Linn, 2000) continued her mid-career dalliance with contemporary pop but, by now established as the fortnightly presenter of BBC Radio 3's *Jazz Line Up*, she returned to jazz in 2002 with *Too Darn Hot!* and remains one the UK's most engaging performers. [CP]

⊙ **The Waiting Game** (1992; Linn). Martin backed by regular band – Jim Mullen (guitar), Jonathan Gee (piano), Arnie Somogyi (bass) and Clark Tracey (drums) – in an appealing mix of the tastefully salacious (Leiber & Stoller's "Some Cats"), the melancholic (Rupert Holmes's "The People That You Never Get To Love") and less well-known standards, plus Joni Mitchell's "Be Cool".

⊙ **Devil May Care** (1993; Linn). Same band, plus Nigel Hitchcock (alto), Iain Ballamy (soprano and tenor) and Rick Taylor (trombone, percussion), covering similar ground: intelligent pop, unusual minor standards, plus the odd original by Rick Taylor or Martin herself.

⊙ **Old Boyfriends** (1994; Linn). Martin's finest album to date, a carefully selected crop of unusual songs from a wide variety of sources, beautifully sung in her trademark controlled, smokily intimate manner.

⊙ **Too Darn Hot!** (2002; Linn). A return to the Great American Songbook plus some specialist material (including a song written for her by guest Geoff Keezer) with some sparkling arrangements and exciting playing, notably from Martin's regular, still undervalued pianist Gareth Williams.

Pat Martino

Guitar.

b. Philadelphia, 25 Aug 1944.

Martino took up the guitar at the age of eleven, encouraged by his father, a singer and guitarist who had taken lessons with Eddie Lang. By fifteen he was a professional, playing initially with R&B bands before graduating to the organ-led combos of Don Patterson, Jimmy Smith, Jimmy McGriff, Jack McDuff and Richard "Groove" Holmes – a great training ground for many jazz guitarists – and to groups led by Sonny Stitt and John Handy. Martino plays with a thick plectrum on heavy-gauge strings – contributing to his robust, round sound. The influence of guitarist Johnny Smith is evident in his precise technique and excellent articulation, and in his ability to improvise long, involved lines at any tempo and with unerring drive and swing. Wes Montgomery, with whom he often jammed, also left a mark on his style. From 1967 he recorded a series of critically acclaimed albums as a leader, marking a progression from hard bop through a period of interest in Indian music and on to a form of fusion. Martino's career was interrupted in 1980 when he suffered an aneurysm on the brain.

His life was saved by a successful operation but he was unable to perform again for several years. Recent recordings show that his musical powers are fully recovered. In 1996 he recorded *All Side Now* for Blue Note, a collections of collaborations with guitarists from varying musical backgrounds including Les Paul, Michael Hedges, Joe Satriani, Kevin Eubanks, Charlie Hunter, Mike Stern and Tuck Andress. Warner Bros Music have published a collection of his transcribed recorded solos entitled *Pat Martino: The Early Years*, and in 1993 Martino recorded a pair of instructional video/book/CD packages for REH/Manhattan Music. One of the most remarkable comebacks in jazz continued with a latter-day deal with Blue Note, which saw him address his roots with a rousing 2001 update of the organ trio on *Live At Yoshi's* (featuring Joey DeFrancesco and Billy Hart), for which he received two Grammy nominations. [CA]

⊙ **El Hombre** (1967; Prestige/OJC). On his first album as a leader, Pat Martino elected to stay with the organ-combo format in which he had served his apprenticeship. Weaving his lyrical, flowing lines throughout this judicious mix of funky blues, ballad, bossa, jazz waltz and standards ("Just Friends"), the guitarist creates full and satisfying musical statements.

Hugh Masekela

Trumpet, flugelhorn.

b. Witbank, South Africa, 4 April 1939.

Helped by the priest Trevor Huddleston, Masekela got his first trumpet from the Johannesburg Native Municipal Band, and his first lessons from its leader, Old Man Sowsa. Later he had lessons from saxophonist Kippie Moeketsi and met trombonist Jonas Gwanga and Dollar Brand (Abdullah Ibrahim). Their musical experience consisted of their African roots – *kwela* and the music of the black townships – church music, and imported American records: they were listening to Ellington, Louis Jordan, Basie, Dizzy and Bird. Together with Brand and Gwanga, Masekela formed the Jazz Epistles, the first black band to record a jazz LP in South Africa. The Jazz Epistles played "township bebop", but had only a brief existence because of the worsening political situation. All gatherings of more than ten people were banned, which effectively prohibited public musical performances. John Dankworth and Harry Belafonte procured a passport for Masekela, enabling him to leave South Africa. He studied for a few months at the Guildhall in London, then went to the Manhattan School of Music, New York. He began to record, and went to live in California, forming his own record label, Chisa Records. But living in US society and playing "American" jazz made him lose his sense of identity to some extent and it became essential to re-establish contact with his African roots. He went to London with Makhaya Ntshoko (drums), Larry Willis (piano) and Eddie Gomez (bass), and with fellow South African emigré Dudu Pukwana on alto saxophone they recorded a dynamic album, *Home Is Where The Music Is* (1972). Helped by Fela Ransome Kuti, Masekela began to tour in Africa with an African group called Hedzoleh Soundz, then took it to California for some years, during which time they recorded six albums. Again the US episode was not a success. In 1980 he returned to Africa, living first in Zimbabwe, then moving to Botswana in 1982. His "Going Home" concert, with his wife, singer Miriam Makeba, was attended by 35,000 people. Masekela contains to tour internationally; his music continually develops and has come to include some township *marabi* and *mbaqanga* plus African-American funk and soul. [IC]

⊙ **Hope** (1994; Triloka). A live recording of Masekela's greatest hits with a newly formed band.

Harvey Mason Jnr

Drums, percussion, piano, composer.
b. Atlantic City, New Jersey, 22 Feb 1947.

Mason began on drums at the age of four, studied at Berklee, and gained a BEd from the New England Conservatory. Early on he worked with Jan Hammer, George Mraz, Erroll Garner and George Shearing. He moved to Los Angeles in 1971, becoming very active as a studio musician and working with jazz and rock groups and symphony orchestras. He played with many leading musicians, including Ellington, Quincy Jones, Freddie Hubbard and Gunther Schuller. Mason made an important contribution to Herbie Hancock's classic jazz-rock-funk album *Head Hunters* (1973); as well as playing drums, he was co-writer of the brilliant piece "Chameleon", and did a rearrangement of Hancock's old hit tune "Watermelon Man" that was so imaginative that it amounted to virtual recomposition. [IC]

➤➤ **Herbie Hancock** *(Head Hunters)*.

Phil Mason

Cornet.
b. London, 10 April 1940.

A prominent British New Orleans-style cornettist, Mason studied at Trinity College Dublin, where he began playing jazz, and thereafter returned to London to work with Eric Silk's Southern Jazz Band (1966–9) and Max Collie's Rhythm Aces (from 1970). He carved himself out a career as a freelance, and in 1992 formed his New Orleans All Stars, featuring several of Europe's top traditional musicians. Resident in the Isle of Bute, Scotland, Mason has recorded some fifty LPs, including several solo albums, and is also director of the Isle of Bute jazz festival. [DF]

⊙ **You do something to me!** (1993; Lake). Good example of Mason's forthright revivalism with an A-team of players including Colin Bowden and longtime sidemen Jim McIntosh (banjo), Martin Bennett (trombone) and Trevor Williams (bass).

Rod Mason

Trumpet, cornet, leader.
b. Plymouth, UK, 28 Sept 1940.

Mason worked first with Cy Laurie in 1959 and by 1962 was working for Monty Sunshine, with whom he stayed for four years. During this period he temporarily contracted Bell's palsy, a disease attacking the nerves of the lip, but the necessary embouchure switch coincidentally improved Mason's range, and by 1970, when he joined Acker Bilk's band, he had turned into a world-class trumpeter with a phenomenal range, limitless endurance and an uncanny ability to sound like Louis Armstrong around 1927. Later in the 1970s Mason led his own band and became well known in Europe, recording prolifically for the Riff label with musicians from Brian Lemon to Dick Wellstood and Bob Wilber. By the 1980s he had joined the prestigious Dutch Swing College Band, but he left in 1985 to bandlead again in Europe, which he continued to do into the 1990s with his Hot Five. Mason's natural modesty and light-hearted approach to jazz have unfairly tended to obscure his considerable talents. [DF]

⊙ **Struttin' With Some Barbecue** (1977; Black Lion). Combination of two LPs recorded with Mason's quintet (featuring clarinettist Pete Allen); his blistering technique, audacious creativity, rip-roaring sense of fun and likeable singing are all on show here.

⊙ **Rod Mason's Hot Five** (1990; Timeless). A live date in Düsseldorf, featuring Mason's delicate Hot Five with guest blues singer Angela Brown.

Cal Massey

Composer, trumpet.

b. Philadelphia, 11 Jan 1928; d. 25 Oct 1972.

Massey was brought up in Pittsburgh, and toured briefly with Jay McShann in the mid-1940s before returning to Philadelphia. He toured with Billie Holiday, Eddie Vinson, B.B. King and (in 1959) with the George Shearing big band. He contributed compositions to record dates by Charlie Parker ("Fiesta", 1951), John Coltrane ("Bakai", 1957; "Nakatini Serenade", 1958; "The Damned Don't Cry", 1961) and many others. He also led his own group in Philadelphia from the mid-1950s, which included McCoy Tyner. Massey then moved to New York, and co-led the ROMAS big band in 1970–72. He played trumpet with Archie Shepp in Europe in 1969, and collaborated with him on albums and on the musical play *Lady Day* (1972). An under-recognized figure, Massey's work was a considerable influence on certain free-jazz players. His son Zane Massey played the saxophone in the early 1980s with Ronald Shannon Jackson's group. [BP]

⊙ **Blues To Coltrane** (1961; Candid). A slightly disappointing set for Massey's only recording under his own name. It includes a version of "Bakai" and, as well as Massey's own probing playing, is valuable for a rare extended outing by Julius Watkins.

George Masso

Trombone, composer, leader; also piano, vibes.

b. Cranston, Rhode Island, 17 Nov 1926.

The son of Tommy Masso, a well-known Rhode Island trumpet player, George Masso was inspired to take up trombone in his teens by Lou McGarity's record of "Yours"; Jack Teagarden and Trummy Young were also major influences. At 22 Masso found himself working with Jimmy Dorsey's band for two years on lead trombone, but gave up professional music for teaching in order to support his wife and family. In 1973, with the encouragement of friends such as Bobby Hackett, he returned to professional music, working full-time with Hackett, with Benny Goodman for a year and a half, with Bobby Rosengarden's band at the Rainbow Room, and at Eddie Condon's. Thereafter Masso continued to play at clubs, concerts and festivals, and regularly toured Europe as a soloist. His numerous records in recent years – with his own quintet, Buck Clayton and The World's Greatest Jazz Band among others – reveal an elegant and highly gifted trombonist. [DF]

⊙ **Just For A Thrill** (1990; Sackville). In a quintet setting with Dave McKenna and Bucky Pizzarelli, this is Masso at his free-blowing best.

George Masso and Dan Barrett

⊙ **Let's Be Buddies** (1994; Arbors). It would be difficult to find a better-matched pair of trombonists than Masso and Barrett, and together they demonstrate exactly how swing trombone was meant to sound.

Carmen Mastren

Guitar, banjo.

b. Cohoes, New York, 6 Oct 1913; d. 31 March 1981.

Carmen Mastren (Carmine Niccolo Mastandrea) began as a banjo player, like George Van Eps, Dick McDonough, Nappy Lamare and Carl Kress – the last of whom, along with Mastren, perfected the art of chorded melodic solos and so helped liberate the acoustic guitar from its rhythmic function. Mastren's tight, fleet four-to-the-bar and agile solos were first heard with Wingy Manone in New York in 1935, and the following year he replaced Mac Cheikes in Tommy Dorsey's orchestra for a five-year stay; by 1939 his work with Dorsey had put him at number one in *Down Beat's* guitar poll. A capable reader and versatile creative soloist, Mastren was a natural for studio work, and from 1941 he worked regularly for NBC along with Raymond Scott and Bob Chester, before joining Glenn Miller's AEF band to form part of the unbeatable rhythm-section that included Mel Powell, Trigger Alpert and Ray McKinley. After the war he returned to the studios and in 1953 rejoined NBC, where until 1970 he played for the *Today* and *Tonight* shows. Then, at 57 years old, he went freelance, writing jingles, playing with the New York Jazz Repertory Company and recording with them on guitar and banjo. (Like Herb Ellis, Mastren is now well known for his banjo playing, and his later LPs, such as *Banjo* for Mercury, now fetch collectors' prices.) By the late 1970s he was taking things easy and working round New York with singer Betty Comora, among others. [DF]

➤➤ **Sidney Bechet** *(Chronological Sidney Bechet: 1940).*

Ron Mathewson

Double bass, bass guitar.

b. Lerwick, Shetland Isles, Scotland, 19 Feb 1944.

Mathewson took up the bass at fifteen and had six months' tuition to learn proper fingering and how to play arco (with a bow). His first professional job was with a Scottish Dixieland band in Germany in 1962. Then he played with various London-based traditional and R&B bands from 1963–6. He joined Tubby Hayes in October 1966, playing with him in all his active phases until his final illness and death in 1973. From the mid-1960s Mathewson also played with groups led by Stan Getz, Charles Tolliver, Carmell Jones, Leo Wright, Budd Johnson, Joe Henderson, Ben Webster, Frank Rosolino, Roy Eldridge, Oscar Peterson, the Brecker Brothers, Philly Joe Jones and Bill Evans among others, as well as with several UK bands, including the Kenny Wheeler big band, Stan Sulzmann quartet, Gordon Beck and John Taylor. He has also occasionally led his own groups, including the Ron

Mathewson Six Piece with Sulzmann and Alan Skidmore (saxophones), Dick Pearce (trumpet), Beck or Taylor (piano) and Spike Wells (drums). He was a regular member of Ronnie Scott's quartets and quintets from 1975 until the early 1990s, when he left to freelance. His live appearances have become less frequent than he deserves, for his is a prodigious natural talent: he is blessed with good time, a good ear and great speed of thought and execution. [IC]

>> **Tubby Hayes** *(For Members Only; Live 1969)*; **Daniel Humair** *(Surrounded)*; **Ronnie Scott** *(Never Pat A Burning Dog)*.

Matty Matlock

Clarinet, saxophones, arranger.

b. Paducah, Kentucky, 27 April 1907; d. 14 June 1978.

Matty (Julian Clifton) Matlock joined Ben Pollack in 1929, replacing Benny Goodman as clarinettist and arranger, and developed his arranging style from such gifted contemporaries as Fud Livingston. He stayed with Pollack until 1934, when a band delegation for which he was spokesman complained to their leader over his favouring of singer-girlfriend Doris Robbins. After a "freelance period" with the "Pollack Orphans" in New York, Matlock joined Bob Crosby in 1935 as clarinettist, though he was often seconded to write full-time for the orchestra and the Bobcats. When Crosby's outfit broke up in 1942, Matlock became a busy studio musician, sideman and freelance arranger, writing whenever perfect Dixieland scoring was required: for Eddie Miller's reconstituted Crosby band in 1943; for Bing Crosby's radio shows; and all through the 1950s for skilled men such as Paul Weston (a constant associate), Billy May and Harry James. Classic Matlock creations of this period include the series *Pete Kelly's Blues*, which started on radio, went to TV and in 1955 became a feature film (all the music arranged by Matlock featured trumpeter Dick Cathcart), albums by his Rampart Street Paraders (with Clyde Hurley) and his Paducah Patrol (a Crosbyesque mid-size band), and one-offs such as *Coast Concert* for Bobby Hackett. In the 1960s Matlock took part in Crosby reunions, freelanced, played for Dick Gibson's jazz parties and sometimes led bands of his own.

Matty Matlock was, with Irving Fazola, the most inspired and spontaneous clarinettist in the Dixieland style, and as a truly original arranger he perfected the sound of "arranged white Dixieland" as we know it today. [DF]

Dixieland Story Vols. 1 & 2 (1958; Warner Bros). With an all-star team including Johnny Best, Shorty Sherock, Eddie Miller, Moe Schneider and Abe Lincoln, these brilliantly conceived Dixieland arrangements transform old standards into monuments to the style.

Marcio Mattos

Double bass, cello, acoustic guitar, electronics.

b. Rio de Janeiro, 20 March 1946.

Marcio Mattos started on classical guitar, later studying double bass and composition at the Villa Lobos Institute, Rio de Janeiro. After coming to the UK, he attended workshops in improvisation and jazz at the Barry Summer School, Wales, and at London's Morley College, as well as studying electronic music and composition at West Square, in London. He has recorded and broadcast in Britain and abroad with many leading musicians including

Dennis Austin

Marcio Mattos

John Surman, Evan Parker, John Stevens, Roswell Rudd, Dewey Redman and Marilyn Crispell. Mattos has also worked with dance companies such as Ballet Rambert and The Extemporary Dance Theatre Company Ensemble, and in electro-acoustic music groups such as the West Square Electronic Music Ensemble. He has been a long-standing member of the Eddie Prévost quartet and various groups led by Elton Dean. Other projects he is involved with include Wooden Taps with Maggie Nichols, and Embers and Full Monte with Chris Biscoe. International projects in Europe have included the Bardo State Orchestra, which involves Mattos with trumpeter Jim Dvorak and percussionist Ken Hyder making music with Tibetan monks. Mattos is also involved with several other groups, such as Tony Oxley's Celebration Orchestra, and has regularly duetted with shakuhachi player Shiku Yano. A virtuoso bassist and cellist with a gloriously singing sound on both instruments, Mattos is interested primarily in free improvisation and the more experimental areas of music, inspired by bassists like Mingus, LaFaro and Charlie Haden, and the music and ideas of Coltrane, Monk and John Cage. [IC]

Bennie Maupin

Tenor saxophone, bass-clarinet, flute, soprano saxophone, saxello.

b. Detroit, Michigan, 29 Aug 1946.

Maupin undertook extensive instrumental studies from 1954–62, both privately and at the Detroit Institute of Musical Art. From 1966–8 he was with Roy Haynes, and from 1968–70 with Horace Silver. In 1971 he joined Herbie Hancock, working with him for several years. He also played with Lee Morgan, McCoy Tyner, Miles Davis, Freddie Hubbard and Miles Davis. It is perhaps his relationship to the latter for which he is best known: his bass-clarinet improvisations are an important ingredient on the Miles album *Bitches Brew*. Maupin wrote himself into a second chapter in jazz history when he played on Hancock's seminal album *Head Hunters*. One of the most accomplished players of the post-Coltrane period, he can handle any area from jazz to rock and abstraction. [IC]

➤➤ **Miles Davis** *(Bitches Brew)*; **Herbie Hancock** *(Head Hunters)*.

Jimmy Maxwell

Trumpet.

b. Stockton, California, 9 Jan 1917; d. 20 July 2002.

From a long family line of brass players, Jimmy Maxwell took up trumpet at the age of four and studied with a string of legendary American brass teachers, including Herbert Clarke, over a ten-year period. Maxwell in turn became a trumpet teacher of guru-like knowledge, whose advice has been sought by countless well-known players. Besides being a world authority on trumpet-playing, Maxwell was a premier leadman and gifted soloist. He worked first with the young Gil Evans (1933–4), then with Jimmy Dorsey, Maxine Sullivan, Skinnay Ennis and Benny Goodman (1939-42) before joining the CBS staff orchestra for TV shows, including Perry Como's and the *Tonight* show. Throughout the 1960s he stayed busy – with Gerry Mulligan, Quincy Jones, Oliver Nelson and others – and in the 1970s-80s was heard on and off record with the New York Jazz Repertory Company (with whom he toured Europe), Dick Sudhalter's New California Ramblers, the Louis Armstrong Tribute Band and the new Duke Ellington Orchestra, led by son Mercer.

In 1982 Maxwell published his trumpet manual, *First Trumpeter*. Though his on-record solos are comparatively rare, Maxwell was a versatile musician who during his career recorded with everyone from Duke Ellington to Charlie Parker, and he can be heard on Peggy Lee's hit "Why Don't You Do Right" with Goodman. [DF]

Tina May

Vocals.

b. Gloucester, UK, 30 March 1961.

A trained actress, Tina May was a founder member of the Back Door Theatre Company before concentrating on singing. A pure-toned soprano, she listened widely to jazz in her teens (especially Fats Waller and Duke Ellington), took singing lessons from sixteen onwards, and has given recitals of music ranging from baroque music to Fauré. She has also had considerable experience in cabaret/club singing, but her forte is jazz, her smooth delivery particularly well suited to the slow-burning ballad. After rising to some prominence in a trio with bassist Thad Kelly and guitarist Dylan Fowler (with whom she also collaborated in the nonet Frevo, an adventurous band specializing in an intelligent mix of world music and jazz), she consolidated her reputation with a series of albums for 33 Records. These showcase her flawless pitch and control, and her dramatic but relaxed delivery, and all feature bands including her husband, drummer Clark Tracey. In 1998, however, May broke new ground in her recording career with a French-language album, *Jazz Piquant*, which set her impeccable French accent (acquired while studying and performing in Paris in the early 1980s) against the cultured reeds of Tony Coe and a tasteful band featuring pianist Brian Dee. May recorded a pair of albums, *Change of Sky* and *One Fine Day*, with pianist and frequent accompanist Nikki Iles that perfectly showcased the intense rapport between them, honed in performances across Europe; their partnership continues, often supplemented by Tony Coe. In 2003 May moved to Linn records for *I'll Take Romance* which opted for a more mainstream approach with no discernible compromise in quality. The same year

Tina May

she cemented her jazz diva reputation by recording classics of the American songbook with pianist Ray Bryant (veteran accompanist of Ella, Billie and Betty Carter, who knows a good voice when he hears one). [DF]

⊙ **Never Let Me Go** (1991; 33 Jazz). May's first album, featuring the rhythm-section as above plus tenorist Don Weller. Outstanding tracks include "Lush Life", a sensuous "Lazy Afternoon" and May's own jaunty "Ol' Blue Eyes", co-written with Newton.

⊙ **It Ain't Necessarily So** (1994; 33 Jazz). There are substantial originals on this set (including "Writer's Block", written with Clark Tracey), of which the outstanding track is a luxurious "Chelsea Bridge" with the Britten string quartet, arranged by Colin Towns.

⊙ **I'll Take Romance** (2003; Linn). New label, higher profile, Scott Hamilton produced and guested on this engaging set of straightahead standards featuring Nikki Iles and Robin Aspland sharing piano duties.

John Mayall

Vocals, harmonica, guitar, piano.
b. Macclesfield, Cheshire, UK, 29 Nov 1933.

Mayall taught himself music from the age of thirteen. He began as a commercial artist, playing blues in his spare time. Inspired and assisted by Alexis Korner, he moved to London in the early 1960s and, after forming his Bluesbreakers, turned fully professional. He and his various groups sang and played the blues with conviction and authority, with influences such as Sonny Boy Williamson, Otis Rush and Django Reinhardt, and helped to create the 1960s blues boom. By the end of the decade, Mayall had become immensely successful internationally and went to live on the West Coast of the USA, doing one or two big tours a year, rounding off the 60s with a blistering set at the Newport festival. His UK bands included Eric Clapton, Jack Bruce and Jon Hiseman, among others, while his US groups often included leading jazz musicians such as Blue Mitchell, Victor Gaskin, Ernie Watts and Don Harris. [IC]

Lyle Mays

Keyboards.
b. Wausaukee, Wisconsin, 27 Nov 1953.

Mays grew up playing piano and improvising from an exclusively bebop point of view. In 1975 he attended North Texas State University in Denton, joining the University Lab band for which he composed and orchestrated an album, the first by a college band to be nominated for a Grammy award. That same year he met guitarist Pat Metheny at the Wichita jazz festival and this was the beginning of their immensely fruitful association.

Mays made his first recording with Metheny's group in 1977 (*Watercolors*), and since then has co-written many of the compositions in their repertoire. They have also co-written film scores and background music for TV documentaries. Although Mays plays most of his solos on acoustic piano, he has developed a brilliant mastery of electronic sound, which he deploys in Metheny's group to create different textures, moods and spatial densities. He was co-billed with Metheny on the Grammy-nominated album *As Falls Wichita, So Falls Wichita Falls* (1981), and something of Mays's electronic artistry can be heard on the twenty-minute title track. In the 1990s Mays, with Jack DeJohnette, made up the Bobby McFerrin Voicestra, whose performances were wholly improvised, with Mays and DeJohnette singing as well as playing their instruments. [IC]

⊙ **Street Dreams** (1988; Geffen). The second and best of Mays's solo albums, this covers everything from unaccompanied music, through a duet and quartet with Bill Frisell, to the ambitious title suite, with brass, woodwind and strings.

➤➤ **Pat Metheny** *(As Falls Wichita, So Falls Wichita Falls; Travels).*

Marilyn Mazur

Percussion, vocals, composer, piano.
b. New York, 18 Jan 1955.

Born of Danish and American parents, Mazur was brought up in Denmark from the age of six. She worked as a pianist and dancer with several dance groups in the early 1970s, then played drums and sang with bands that included the Feminist Improvising Group with Irene Schweizer and Lindsay Cooper in the late 1970s. She led her own all-women music-theatre group Primi Band (1982–4), and collaborated with John Tchicai and Pierre Dørge. After recording with Miles Davis (*Aura*, 1985), she toured with his group for nine months, before playing with Gil Evans in 1986 and touring with Wayne Shorter in 1987. She returned to Denmark in 1989 to lead her own groups Future Song and then Pulse Unit, with which her husband Klavs Hovman plays bass. She has also worked with Mathias Rüegg, Charlie Mariano and Jan Garbarek, and was awarded the international Jazzpar Prize in 2001. Possessing a wide variety of exotic instruments as well as playing excellent kit drums, she says "Obviously the music contains ... jazz, rock and ethnic elements, but it is none of them – and does not try to be." [BP]

Circular Chant (1994; Storyville). A wide variety of approaches, from world music and free jazz, are brought to life by Mazur's discreet percussion, and the contributions of Norwegians Nils Petter Molvaer's trumpet and Per Jørgensen's ethnic vocalizing.

Cecil McBee

Bass.

b. Tulsa, Oklahoma, 19 May 1935.

After studying clarinet, McBee began on bass at the age of seventeen. He gained a music degree from Ohio Central State University, and was a band director in the army. He played with the Paul Winter sextet from 1963–4, and then with leading New York players such as Jackie McLean in 1964, and Wayne Shorter from 1965–6, on gigs and records. His main affiliations were with the Charles Lloyd quartet in 1966, Yusef Lateef from 1967–9, and Alice Coltrane from 1969–72. But in 1975 he started leading his own group, often featuring Chico Freeman, and he also played under Freeman's leadership. From the late 1970s he was much in demand for work with musicians as varied as Archie Shepp, Art Pepper, Abdullah Ibrahim, Joanne Brackeen and Harry Edison-Buddy Tate. In the late 1980s he was a founder member of the group The Leaders, and worked throughout the 1990s with Yosuke Yamashita. As well as having established a reputation for creative versatility in both "free" and "time" contexts, McBee has a rounded, expressive tone and an enviably strong pulse. [BP]

Unspoken (1996; Palmetto). McBee has not cut very many albums under his own name – this one features a quintet with younger players such as trumpeter James Zollar and drummer Matt Wilson. As usual McBee not only holds everyone together but pushes them forward selflessly.

>> **Elvin Jones** *(When I Was At Aso-Mountain)*; **Kirk Lightsey** *(Heaven Dance)*; **Charles Lloyd** *(Forest Flower)*; **Yosuke Yamashita** *(Kurdish Dance)*.

Christian McBride

Bass.

b. Philadelphia, 21 May 1972.

McBride's father was an R&B session-player on bass guitar, while his great-uncle, Howard Cooper, worked on upright bass with Sunny Murray and was a bebop fan. Christian started on electric bass at eight and played classical music in high school, while studying privately and taking R&B gigs. Encouraged by schoolfriend Joey DeFrancesco and by the visiting Wynton Marsalis, McBride was already into jazz before studying at New York's Juilliard School (from 1989). He started playing with the bands of Bobby Watson, Benny Golson, Roy Hargrove and Freddie Hubbard, also joining the trio of Hubbard bandmate Benny Green. Inspired by Ron Carter, Paul Chambers, Ray Brown and Jaco Pastorius, McBride gained immediate acceptance as the best new bebop bassist for a generation, Brown saying of him, "This guy has really got a handle on it, and he's going to be magnificent." His albums for Verve have been varied in style: 1998's *A Family Affair* saw him arrange the Afro-American soul songbook for jazz ensemble; *Sci-Fi* (2000) was a successful consolidation of his music's various strands and featured Herbie Hancock; whilst *The Philadelphia Experiment* was a intriguing dip into hip-hop and funk with Pat Martino, Uri Caine and former schoolmates from The Roots. [BP]

Gettin' To It (1994; Verve). McBride demonstrates his excellent rhythmic feel, mellow tone and great melodic sense in trio-to-sextet setting with artists such as Hargrove and Joshua Redman, while one odd track features him with just the 150-year-old team of Brown and Milt Hinton.

Steve McCall

Drums.

b. Chicago, 30 Sept 1933; d. May 1989.

Steve McCall played in different contexts – blues, mainstream jazz – before establishing contact with pianist, composer and organizer Muhal Richard Abrams in 1961. In 1964, playing an early form of post-bop, McCall worked in Detroit as part of a trio led by saxophonist Fred Anderson. Along with Abrams, saxophonists Joseph Jarman and Anderson, and others, he co-founded Chicago's Association for the Advancement of Creative Musicians (AACM) in 1964. McCall was a key drummer in the AACM, playing with Jarman on *Song For* (1966; Delmark), the Association's first record. Like many of the post-free jazz generation, McCall moved to Paris in 1967, where he was based until 1970. While in Europe, he worked extensively with Gunter Hampel, as well as in groups with Anthony Braxton, Marion Brown and Roscoe Mitchell. In the early 70s, McCall began a long association with saxophonist/flautist Henry Threadgill and bassist Fred Hopkins; as a trio, they began performing as Air in 1975, after McCall moved to New York. This highly important ensemble was the perfect vehicle for McCall, who played cymbals and mallets with extreme sensitivity and was able to interact with precisely the directness or obliqueness that the occasion called for. In the early 80s McCall left the group, which was never the same without him. He recorded *Vintage Duets Chicago 1-11-80* (Okka Disk) with Anderson, and with the David

Murray octet on *Ming* (1980; Black Saint) and *Home* (1982; Black Saint). In the mid-1980s, he was a member of the Cecil Taylor Unit, alongside old AACM percussion partner Thurman Barker, and he played regularly in the Roscoe Mitchell quartet until his death from a stroke in 1989. [JC]

>> **David Murray** *(Ming; Home)*; **Henry Threadgill** *(Air Lore)*.

Paul McCandless

Oboe, English horn, bass-clarinet, composer.

b. Indiana, Pennsylvania, 24 March 1947.

Both McCandless's parents were public school music teachers; his father taught him clarinet, his mother taught him the piano. At thirteen he was playing and writing for a Dixieland band. He was educated at Duquesne University, where he played both with the Pittsburgh Symphony and in jazz clubs. In 1967 he went to the Manhattan School of Music to concentrate solely on oboe. From 1968–73 he was with Paul Winter's Winter Consort which, from 1970, included Ralph Towner, Glen Moore and Collin Walcott. With these three McCandless left the Winter Consort in the early 1970s and formed Oregon, one of the key groups of the 1970s. In 1980 McCandless also joined Gallery with Michael Di Pasqua, David Samuels and David Darling. With Winter Consort, he toured and played festivals all over the USA, and with Oregon he continues to play extensively on the international circuit. He has recorded as a sideman with many artists, including Billy Hart, John Scofield, Jerry Goodman, Zbigniew Seifert, Eddie Gomez and Bob Moses and, since 1988, has recorded solo albums for the Windham Hill label. [IC]

>> **Ralph Towner** *(Distant Hills)*; **Eberhard Weber** *(Later That Evening)*.

Les McCann

Piano, vocals.

b. Lexington, Kentucky, 23 Sept 1935.

After studies and naval service, McCann accompanied singer Gene McDaniels in 1959, and formed his own trio just in time to profit from the popularity of soul-jazz. When, in the 1960s, he began featuring his own singing with the trio, he scored two sizeable hits ("Compared To What", written by McDaniels, and the standard "With These Hands"). While eminently capable of setting up a compelling groove, his piano does little except pile cliché upon cliché and, like his dull singing voice, has few redeeming qualities other than confidence in its ability to entertain. [BP]

Les McCann-Eddie Harris

⊙ **Swiss Movement** (1969; Atlantic). The ultimate fun-funk record, which did almost as much for the Montreux festival as it did for the careers of the two principals. It includes guest trumpeter Benny Bailey, and the famous "Compared To What", before it was ruined by Candy Dulfer.

Ron McClure

Bass, piano, composer.

b. New Haven, Connecticut, 22 Nov 1941.

McClure began on accordion at the age of five, and played piano in his school band. He then studied bass, graduating from the Julius Hartt Conservatory, Hartford, Connecticut, in 1962. He played with Buddy Rich, Maynard Ferguson, Herbie Mann, Don Friedman, Marian McPartland, and replaced Paul Chambers in the Wynton Kelly trio during 1965–6. He was a member of the Charles Lloyd quartet from 1967–9, which became one of the most successful jazz groups of the later 1960s and pioneered jazz-rock. With Lloyd he recorded the albums *Love In* and *Charles Lloyd In The Soviet Union*, both in 1967. In 1969 he was a founder member of Fourth Way, which featured more sophisticated jazz-rock, recording *Sun and Moon* (1969) before leaving in 1970, playing with Joe Henderson, Dionne Warwick, Gary Burton and Mose Allison. From 1971–4 he also freelanced with many people, including Thelonious Monk, Keith Jarrett, the Pointer Sisters, Freddie Hubbard and Airto Moreira. In 1974 he joined Blood Sweat and Tears, and in the later 1970s and early 1980s freelanced in New York. He joined the Al Di Meola Project in 1985, which included Danny Gottlieb and Moreira, recording and touring in the USA and Europe. He churned out albums prolifically throughout the 1990s and continues to record under his own name in a variety of line-ups and contexts, registering an ever-refining rapport with regular collaborators Marc Copland and Billy Hart. [IC]

⊙ **Descendants** (1980; Ken). McClure wrote some fine compositions for this date with a quintet that includes Tom Harrell and John Scofield. The playing is first-class, and there's also some humour in the ironical free-form outing "Life Isn't Everything".

⊙ **Yesterday's Tomorrow** (1989; EPC). This trio with John Abercrombie and Aldo Romano has some of McClure's most eloquent writing, with a looser, freer approach.

>> **David Liebman** *(Doin' It Again; Quest/Natural Selection)*.

Rob McConnell

Valve-trombone, composer, arranger, leader.

b. London, Ontario, Canada, 14 Feb 1935.

McConnell is principally known as an arranger and bandleader who, with his Toronto-based big band the Boss Brass (formed in 1968), set new standards for jazz writing, including the use of complex unaccompanied passages played in close harmony section by section. His group, which originally omitted a sax section, acquired one in 1971 and later in the 1970s began recording, making their American debut at the Monterey Jazz Festival and Concerts by the Sea 1981. The band's 1983 album *All In Good Time* won a Grammy soon after; a 1986 album with Mel Tormé received rapturous reviews but – after six Grammy nominations and other awards – McConnell began teaching at the Dick Grove Music School in California (1988-90). He returned to bandleading in 1990 with a residency at Toronto's "Bermuda Onion" club and the beginnings of a long and rewarding association with the Concord label beginning with a now famous collection, *The Brass is Back!*. A small-group album of the same period (with his Jive Five) was a welcome opportunity to hear his smooth solo talents at length. All McConnell's recordings are distinguished by his brilliant arranging and by the superb technical abilities of his players. [DF]

⊙ **The Brass Is Back!** (1991; Concord). With a band studded with Canadian stars, including guitarist Ed Bickert and phenomenal lead trumpeters Arnie Chycoski and Steve McDade, this is an example of McConnell at his best.

⊙ **Riffs I Have Known** (1997; Snapper). Excellent compilation of McConnell's best work with the Boss Brass; inspiration harnessed to innovative writing and incomparable technical ability.

Susannah McCorkle

Vocals.

b. Berkeley, California, 1 Jan 1946; d. 19 May 2001.

A onetime languages student, as well as interpreter and translator, Susannah McCorkle first got into jazz after hearing Billie Holiday records in Paris around 1971, and she moved to England soon after where she played with Bruce Turner, Keith Nichols, Dick Sudhalter and pianist Keith Ingham (for several years her accompanist and musical director). Around the same time she played major concerts with visiting Americans such as Ben Webster, Dexter Gordon and Bobby Hackett (who called her "the best singer since Billie Holiday"), and in 1975 played a season at the Riverboat jazz room, Manhattan, to plaudits from Alec Wilder and his circle. After another year in England (during which she played Ronnie Scott's and recorded two solo albums), she returned to America with Keith Ingham. Albums that followed included a Yip Harburg tribute and a Grammy-nominated collection, *The People That You Never Get To Love*, and in the later 1980s she signed to Carl Jefferson's Concord label. McCorkle's clear-sounding, natural voice combines Billie Holiday inflexions with a surprising occasional hint of Marilyn Monroe, and her discography since signing for Concord has revealed an impressive "all music" approach, trawling songs from a repertoire of classic standards, blues, Brazilian music and the best of current pop. An ambitious and intelligent performer, she also wrote for the New Yorker and published a number of short stories. Reportedly a long-term sufferer from clinical depression, she committed suicide by jumping from her Manhattan apartment. [DF]

⊙ **Sabia** (1990; Concord). McCorkle had been singing bossa nova in Portuguese since the 1970s and she does so here with Lee Musiker (piano and MD), Emily Remler (on her last studio date) and Scott Hamilton (tenor).

⊙ **I'll Take Romance** (1991; Concord). Selected with an expert's ear, this is McCorkle in standard territory; great songs including "My Foolish Heart", "It Never Entered My Mind" and "Where Do You Start".

⊙ **From Bessie To Brazil** (1993; Concord). A typically eclectic McCorkle collection, spanning Smith to Paul Simon. Alan Farnham's backing is outstanding with trumpeter Randy Sandke well to the fore.

Bob McCracken

Clarinet, saxophones.

b. Dallas, Texas, 23 Nov 1904; d. 4 July 1972.

A player with an elegant "timeless" style, McCracken worked in Jack Teagarden's company in Doc Ross's band in 1924, and later based himself in Chicago, where he worked from 1939 with musicians such as Jimmy McPartland and Wingy Manone. He is best remembered for a brief spell with Louis Armstrong's All Stars in the early 1950s and for his time with Kid Ory later in the decade. Later in his career he combined business interests with music, but kept up his playing, rejoining Teagarden in 1962 and working with Wild Bill Davison in 1967. [DF]

Dick McDonough

Guitar, banjo.

b. 1904; d. 25 May 1938.

A pioneer of single-string solo guitar as well as the ringing "chorded-solo" style that was such a joyous aspect of 1930s jazz, Dick McDonough began as a banjoist, playing regularly with Red Nichols. From the late 1920s until his death he was a constantly busy studio man, recording on guitar with musicians as varied as Nichols, Red McKenzie, the Boswell Sisters, the Dorseys, Benny Goodman, Joe Venuti, Mildred Bailey, Adrian Rollini and Glenn Miller (he was guitarist for Miller's orchestral debut on record in 1937). A sociable youngster who numbered Johnny Mercer among his many friends, in the 1930s McDonough was often to be found at the Onyx club on 52nd Street, discovering new music, playing, and drinking the night away. One regular colleague was guitarist Carl Kress, with whom McDonough recorded duets and played "New York's First Swing Concert" at the Imperial Theater on 24 May 1936. Two years later McDonough collapsed at the NBC studios. "Dick's dead for much the same reason as Bix and Bunny," lamented Artie Shaw later. [DF]

Pioneers Of Jazz Guitar 1927-39 (1999; Retrieval). Sadly under-recorded as a soloist, McDonough nevertheless has four fine duos with Carl Kress on this set.

Brother Jack McDuff

Organ, piano; also bass.

b. Champaign, Illinois, 17 Sept 1926; d. 23 Jan 2001.

McDuff was self-taught on piano, and then moved to the organ. He worked with Chicago-based groups in the mid-1950s, and then toured with Willis Jackson until 1959. Forming a trio, he recorded under his own name, and with Roland Kirk in 1961, usually in the soul-jazz idiom. He employed Grant Green as guitarist in his group in 1961, and replaced him with George Benson from 1962–5. He continued leading a regular unit into the 1990s, featuring himself on electric piano as well as organ, and moving for a while towards vocal-based soul music; he later returned to instrumental soul, renaming his group The Heating System. Initially, like all the organists of his generation, McDuff was heavily indebted to Jimmy Smith. Unlike some of the more excitable players of this group, however, Jack had a less grating tone and a sober, coherent approach to improvisation. [BP]

That's The Way I Feel It (1996; Concord). You know there's an organ revival going on when you see the veteran leader surrounded by the all-young all-white sidemen of his Heating System. Augmented by Chris Potter on flute for this session, they do well by "The Age Of Aquarius" and "Theme From Mission Impossible" and four oldies including "Saturday Night Fish Fry", on which McDuff sings.

➤➤ **Rahsaan Roland Kirk** *(Kirk's Work).*

Murray McEachern

Trombone, alto saxophone, trumpet.

b. Toronto, Canada, 16 Aug 1915; d. 28 April 1982.

McEachern was a child prodigy concert violinist and by his late teens had mastered clarinet, alto and tenor saxophones, trumpet, trombone, tuba and bass. He was featuring his array of instruments in Chicago floor shows by the mid-1930s and in 1936 joined Benny Goodman on trombone for just over a year. From 1938–41 he was with the Casa Loma Orchestra, then, after a year as assistant MD for Paul Whiteman, moved to the West Coast, where he became an in-demand studio man. A regular concert artist (with David Rose), McEachern often turned up as a soloist for TV specials as well as on record, and his work on any instrument suggested that he might have made a lifelong study of that one alone – his trombone solos, for example, rival Tommy Dorsey's for fluency, range and control, while his saxophone would do credit to such seasoned performers as Toots Mondello. In the 1970s he joined Duke Ellington for a short spell and led the re-formed Tommy Dorsey orchestra. [DF]

Gary McFarland

Composer, arranger, vibes.

b. Los Angeles, 23 Oct 1933; d. 3 Nov 1971.

McFarland's interest in jazz only began at university in Oregon, and he briefly took up trumpet, trombone, piano and finally vibes while in the army. He studied music at San Jose City College from 1957–8 and at Berklee in 1959. Encouraged by John Lewis and Bob Brookmeyer, he moved to New York and in 1961–4 had his compositions recorded by Lewis, the MJQ, Gerry Mulligan, Johnny Hodges and J.J. Johnson. During the same period he arranged whole albums for Anita O'Day and Stan Getz, and made several discs of his own, the second featuring the piano of Bill Evans. Forming a quintet in 1965 led by his vibes and synchronized singing (later emulated by Roy Ayers), he recorded such lightweight fare as *Soft Samba* and *Tijuana Jazz*. He was a co-founder of the short-lived Skye record label, but fell prey to alcoholism and died of a heart attack. [BP]

How To Succeed In Business Without Really Trying (1961; Verve). A single CD reissue also containing his mentor Bob Brookmeyer's album *Gloomy Sunday And Other Bright Moments*, this is one of the best jazz transformations of a Broadway musical. Featuring Clark Terry, Phil Woods and Kenny Burrell, McFarland's vivid writing with its touches of Ellington and especially Gil Evans is hugely enjoyable.

Bobby McFerrin

Vocals.

b. New York, 11 March 1950.

McFerrin's father was an opera singer, his mother a classical soprano. He began as a pianist, taking lessons from the age of six, and worked as a singer/pianist whilst in college but soon abandoned the piano. He was discovered by Jon Hendricks with whom he sang some duets before making a big impact at New York's Kool jazz festival, going on to tour with George Benson and an all-star band. Since then he has toured internationally with Chico Freeman, Grover Washington Jnr and Herbie Hancock's VSOP, among others. As a pianist, McFerrin was inspired by Keith Jarrett, and it was the latter's solo piano performances that made McFerrin think of singing unaccompanied, which he began doing in 1983. He is best known for his chart hit of 1988, "Don't Worry, Be Happy", a pop reggae song on which he overdubbed all the parts himself, but it belies his seriousness: he has studied the music of Bach and was invited to perform at classical music festivals, both to sing pieces as they were written and to improvise variations on them. In the 1990s he formed a trio with Lyle Mays and Jack DeJohnette, calling it Bobby McFerrin and the Voicestra. Their performances are wholly improvised and Mays and DeJohnette, as well as playing their instruments, also sing.

Raffaella Cavalieri

Bobby McFerrin

McFerrin has an extraordinarily flexible voice, which he often uses to imitate musical instruments. In order to avoid breaking the flow of the music, he produces notes even when he breathes in, and can produce cross rhythms by "drumming" with his voice and keeping a pulse with his hand on his chest. [IC]

The Voice (1984; Elektra). A solo concert recording with material ranging from bebop to pseudo-Baroque by way of the Beatles. McFerrin's ability to maintain (and improvise on) more than one melodic line at once is astonishing, but his light touch makes this disc more than a simple display of virtuosity.

Lou McGarity

Trombone, vocals.

b. Athens, Georgia, 22 July 1917; d. 28 Aug 1971.

Lou McGarity began on violin at seven, took up the trombone in his teens, moved to New York with Nye Mayhew's band, and then joined Ben Bernie's excellent and often jazz-influenced dance band towards the end of "old maestro" Bernie's career (he died two years later, at 46). McGarity's accurate lead and creative solos prompted an offer from Benny Goodman, whom he joined on 25 October 1940, to work with Cutty Cutshall in a superb trombone team. For McGarity it was a good period: he recorded influential and popular features with Goodman ("Yours" much influenced younger players such as George Masso), sang with Goodman's sextet, and appeared in a 1942 film, *The Powers Girl*. In 1942 he left Goodman to work with Raymond Scott at CBS, then served in the navy for four years before rejoining Goodman. By 1947 he was back in New York, working the studios and doubling with Eddie Condon; the 1950s were to produce big-band sessions, small-group sides with Muggsy Spanier, Cootie Williams, Neal Hefti and Wild Bill Davison, and above all a string of studio-based Dixieland recordings with the Lawson-Haggart Jazz Band. A Condon regular until illness slowed him down in 1957, McGarity was visible in the 1960s both in the studio orchestra for Arthur Godfrey's popular TV show, and in Bob Crosby's band. He was also a founder member of The World's Greatest Jazz Band (1968–70), and continued working right up to his death. [DF]

Lawson-Haggart Jazz Band

The Best Of Dixieland (MCA Coral). McGarity in his element, with master Dixielanders including Yank, Bob and Billy Butterfield; this album is in urgent need of CD reissue but worth the search on vinyl.

Howard McGhee

Trumpet.

b. Tulsa, Oklahoma, 6 March 1918; d. 17 July 1987.

McGhee's main early big-band affiliations were with Charlie Barnet in 1942–3, and Andy Kirk in 1941–2 and 1943–4; with the latter he wrote his own feature number "McGhee Special". He played in Coleman Hawkins's small group in 1944–5, and then with his own groups in Los Angeles from

1945–7, which sometimes included Charlie Parker. Back in New York, he organized a sextet in 1947, visiting the Paris Jazz Fair the following year, and he briefly used Jimmy Heath's big band as his own in 1948. He was only occasionally active in the 1950s, owing to drug problems. Work after his comeback included a George Wein tour of Europe and Japan, a short spell with Ellington in 1965, and his own small groups and big band, with both of which he made recordings. A significant stylist of the 1940s, McGhee was a great admirer of Roy Eldridge but was also impressed by Fats Navarro and Dizzy Gillespie. More than capable of holding his own technically, he developed a compromise between the rhythmic approach of the swing-era players and the long lines of bebop, which is not only musically successful but highly individual. [BP]

⊙ **Maggie's Back in Town!** (1961; Contemporary/OJC). McGhee's only quartet album finds him in excellent form (he also recorded a good quintet set with Teddy Edwards during this period), and with Phineas Newborn on piano he shines on "Softly As In A Morning Sunrise" and "Brownie Speaks".

Chris McGregor

Piano, composer.

b. Somerset West, South Africa, 24 Dec 1936; d. France, 26 May 1990.

McGregor's father taught in a Church of Scotland mission school in the Transkei province; among McGregor's earliest experiences were the hymns of the mission church and the music of the Xhosa people. He spent four years at Cape Town College of Music, studying western European classical music by day, and at night playing jam sessions in local jazz clubs with both white and black musicians. In 1962 he formed the Blue Notes with Dudu Pukwana (alto saxophone), Mongezi Feza (trumpet), Nick Moyake (tenor saxophone), Johnny Dyani (bass) and Louis Moholo (drums). It became virtually impossible for racially mixed groups to function in South Africa, and when they were invited to play at the French Antibes festival in 1964 they left their country for good. Their compatriot Dollar Brand (later Abdullah Ibrahim) had preceded them to Europe and helped them find work there. They spent almost a year in Switzerland, playing at the Blue Note, Geneva, and the Afrikaner Café in Zurich, then came to the UK in 1965, playing at Ronnie Scott's club and settling in London. In 1966 McGregor and the band played a four-week engagement at the Montmartre club in Copenhagen, which was then presenting most of the leading avant-garde players of the time, including Albert Ayler, Archie Shepp and Cecil Taylor. From this point on, the music of McGregor and the Blue Notes was to fuse their African roots with elements from free jazz, creating a highly distinctive sound.

In 1970 McGregor augmented his band, calling the larger ensemble the Brotherhood of Breath. It toured the UK and Europe, playing many major festivals and gaining a solid international reputation. The Brotherhood also recorded the soundtrack for the film of Wole Soyinka's *Kongi's Harvest*. In the mid-1970s McGregor went to live in the southwest of France, commuting to engagements in the UK. In the early 1970s he toured Africa with the Blue Notes; the Brotherhood of Breath continued to function internationally, and McGregor also played solo piano concerts. In 1983 he did an Arts Council Network tour of the UK with a very big band, for which he had done all the composing and arranging. He was a consummate pianist with a style that often employed immense percussiveness. [IC]

➤➤ **Harry Beckett** *(Live Vol. 2)*; **Brotherhood of Breath** *(Live At Willisau; Procession)*; **Mike Osborne** *(Outback)*.

Jimmy McGriff

Organ.

b. Philadelphia, 3 April 1936.

A decade younger than the generation of Jimmy Smith and Jack McDuff, McGriff comes from the same town as Smith and Shirley Scott. Both his parents were pianists, and he learned to play bass, saxophones, vibes and drums, gigging on bass with Archie Shepp, Charles Earland (then also a saxophonist) and R&B singer Big Maybelle. After working as a policeman for two years, he studied organ in Philadelphia and at the Juilliard School, also taking tuition from Jimmy Smith, Groove Holmes and Milt Buckner. Forming his own trio in the early 1960s, he had hit singles with Ray Charles's "I Got A Woman" and "All About My Girl", using a bright trumpet tone which he alternated with flute-like chording on slower numbers. He toured and recorded with the great Buddy Rich for two years in the mid 70s. Later adding synthesizers to his arsenal, he returned to more blues-oriented playing in the late 1980s, teaming up for records and touring with Hank Crawford. His bluesy, feel-good sound has enlivened some 100 albums, and he has performed in concert with greats such as Count Basie, Wynton Marsalis, Dizzy Gillespie, James Moody, Lou Donaldson and the Thad Jones-Mel Lewis Big Band. [BP]

⊙ **The Starting Five** (1986; Milestone). Joined here by Crawford's ex-Ray Charles colleague David Newman and drummer Bernard Purdie, McGriff leads a straightahead date with a couple of ballads ("Georgia") and blues such as "BGO", dedicated to the New Jersey jazz radio station.

James Eugene "Rosy" McHargue

Clarinet, saxophones, vocals.

b. Danville, Illinois, 6 April 1902; d. 7 June 1999.

One of the best-loved veterans of classic jazz, McHargue's career spanned over eighty years. He started off playing C-Melody saxophone before concentrating on the clarinet, and began his professional career with the Novelty Syncopators in 1917. During the 1920s he played with Roy Schoenbeck's Orchestra, the Wolverines, the Seattle Harmony Kings, before a sustained spell with bandleader Ted Weems from 1934 to 1942. In 1943, after moving to Los Angeles, he had brief stints with Eddie Miller and Benny Goodman, thereafter he was with Kay Kyser from 1943 to 1946, and Red Nichols from 1947 to 1951. In 1948 McHargue featured as the lively clarinet soloist on bandleader Pee Wee Hunt's mammoth hit "Twelth Street Rag". From the early 1950s he also led his own bands (Rosy McHargue's Ragtimers and Rosy McHargue and His Dixieland Band) around the west coast. In the twilight of his career he became something of a historian of early jazz, performing – as a singer – many old and forgotten numbers. On his ninety-seventh birthday he was still performing at the monthly Jazz Forum session at Elk's Hall, Santa Monica. [DF]

Rosy McHargue's Ragtimers: The Complete Recordings 1952–1956 (2003; Jump). Lovingly comprehensive compilation of one period of McHargue's unique music, featuring (among others) trombonist Moe Schneider and Earle Sturgis on piano. As well as jazz standards, the titles include McHargue specialities like "They Gotta Quit Kickin' My Dawg Aroun'", "Rosy's Hangover Rag" and "Don't Bring Me Posies".

Kalaparusha Maurice McIntyre

Tenor saxophone, clarinet, bass-clarinet, percussion, flute.

b. Clarksville, Arizona, 24 March 1936.

Maurice Benford McIntyre started playing drums at the age of seven, switching to reeds after a couple of years. He attended Chicago Musical College and played with many of the city's most open-minded musicians, including John Gilmore, Nicky Hill and Roscoe Mitchell, before joining the nascent Association for the Advancement of Creative Musicians (AACM) in 1965. He played on several of the AACM's earliest records, including Mitchell's *Sound* (1966) and his own *Humility In The Light Of The Creator* (1969), and he was a member of Muhal Richard Abrams's Experimental Big Band. He continued to play with blues musicians like J.B. Hutto and Little Milton while pursuing creative music with the AACM. In 1969, the year he took his Muslim name, he moved to New York, where he participated in the so-called "loft scene". Throughout the 70s, he played with Jerome Cooper, with whom he recorded the double LP *Positions 369* (1977; Karma), and he led recording dates for Black Saint, Trio and Cadence. In the early 80s he was a member of Kahil El Zabar's Ethnic Heritage Ensemble, recording *Welcome* (1982; Leo/Finland), though in the subsequent decade he reportedly went into semi-retirement. In 1998, McIntyre returned playing tenor saxophone as a member of the AACM group Bright Moments, alongside Joseph Jarman (also returning from retirement), Malachi Favors, Steve Colson and Kahil El Zabar, to record *Return Of The Lost Tribe* (Delmark). He also released the sax-bass-drums trio album *Dream Of...* (1998; CIMP), his first as leader for 16 years, and followed that with *South Eastern* (2002; CIMP) featuring the unusual trio of McIntire's reeds, tuba by Jesse Dulman and drums by Ravish Moman. [JC]

Forces And Feelings (1970; Delmark). Kalaparusha has so far been ill-served in CD reissues. (His 1979 Black Saint LP *Peace And Blessing* is well worth tracking down.) This record, his second as a leader, is perhaps most remarkable as a vehicle for bassist Fred Hopkins, who makes a startling debut here. Along with McIntyre's multi-instrumentalism – *de rigueur* for AACM musicians at the time – and forceful, gritty tenor (audible in a different context on a single memorable track on guitarist George Freeman's contemporaneous *Birth Sign*, also on Delmark), *Forces And Feelings* features Rita Warford's cosmic vocals and Sonny Sharrock-like guitar from Sarnie Garnett.

>> **Muhal Richard Abrams** *(Levels And Degrees Of Light)*.

Ken McIntyre

Alto saxophone, composer, educator, flute, oboe, bass-clarinet, bassoon, piano.

b. Boston, Massachusetts, 7 Sept 1931; d. 13 June 2001.

McIntyre had classical piano lessons from 1940–45 and later studied saxophone with Gigi Gryce, Charlie Mariano and others. He gained degrees in composition from Boston Conservatory and taught in New York schools in the later 1950s, leading his own group in clubs. In 1960 he met and recorded with Eric Dolphy and became an active member of the avant-garde, playing clubs and festivals. From 1961 he became deeply involved in education, teaching in the New York school system until 1967, at Central State University in Wilberforce, Ohio, from 1967–9, and from 1969–71 at Wesleyan. He received a Doctorate in education from the University of Massachusetts and since 1971 has been director of the African-American Music and Dance concentration at the State University of New York, as well as professor of humanities. He changed his name to Makanda Ken McIntyre in the early 90s – "Makanda" means "many skins" in the Ndebele language and "many heads" in Shona.

The series of albums he recorded on Steeplechase in the 1970s show his originality as a composer and player. His compositions are full of surprises and odd twists; they often feature asymmetrical numbers of bars, and sometimes asymmetrical time-signatures. It has been said that Ornette Coleman and Dolphy were influences on McIntyre, but he always protested – he is about the same age and was already mature when he met them – and claimed his main inspiration was initially Charlie Parker. [IC]

Looking Ahead (1960; OJC). McIntyre in fast company – Eric Dolphy, Walter Bishop Jnr, Sam Jones, Arthur Taylor – with good, but unspectacular, results.

Tribute (1990; Serene). Another quintet with Thierry Bruneau (reeds) – also a Dolphy fan – vibist Severi Pyysalo, Richard Davis and drummer Jean-Yves Colson, and this time McIntyre's playing is more focused, the spirit of Dolphy is conjured up and the results are fine.

Dave McKenna

Piano.

b. Woonsocket, Rhode Island, 30 May 1930.

McKenna was playing piano by seven, and taught himself to play jazz through radio and records. He joined Charlie Ventura in 1949, worked with Woody Herman from 1950–51, and then found himself in Korea until 1953. He spent the rest of the decade commuting between Gene Krupa, Stan Getz, Zoot Sims and Ventura, and most of the 1960s working with Eddie Condon or Bobby Hackett (fine records with Hackett's quartet include the classic *Blues With A Kick* on Capitol). In 1967 McKenna and his family moved out to Cape Cod, near to Hackett (who called him "the best piano player alive"), and there began club work with seven years at the Columns. By the late 1970s he was back on the international circuit, touring and recording with Bob Wilber and Pug Horton. In 1979 McKenna signed with Concord Records, a deal which brought his talents to international attention – by the early 1980s he was making the rounds of the festival circuit with Concord's Superband, including kindred spirits such as Warren Vaché and Scott Hamilton. Since then he has continued to produce CDs that illustrate his piano talents in full. "McKenna is his own rhythm section," Ira Gitler observes; he's also, as George Shearing adds, "the hardest-swinging of them all". [DF]

No Bass Hit (1979; Concord). Trio set with Scott Hamilton and Jake Hanna, proving that McKenna's playing could approach Tatum level.

Live At Maybeck Recital Hall Vols. 1 & 2 (1990; Concord). Solo recital in which McKenna plays great tunes like "Detour Ahead" and one of his famous thematic medleys – this one, "Knowledge", blends together "I Didn't Know About You", "I Wish I Knew" and "I Never Knew". Sleevenote writer Cyra McFadden calls this set a "bliss bomb".

Shadows And Dreams (1990; Concord). More concept-linked material, played by a pianist who sounds as if he has forty-nine fingers.

An intimate evening with Dave McKenna (1999; Arbors). Now safely re-located amid the Arbors bower, McKenna plays a solo recital of concept-related tunes (a favourite device); his medleys here cover wide territory from stride and Dixieland to wonderful obscurities like "Don't forget 127th Street" and "Thinking of you".

Red McKenzie

Vocals, kazoo.

b. St Louis, Missouri, 14 Oct 1899; d. 7 Feb 1948.

Red (William) McKenzie was a jockey before he broke both arms in a fall, then worked as a bellhop at the Claridge Hotel, St Louis, where he met guitarists Dick Slevin and Jack Bland. With them he formed a "jug band", the Mound City Blue Blowers, which became a success working opposite Gene Rodemich's band in Chicago. Isham Jones engineered a recording date, and their first single, "Arkansas Blues", featuring McKenzie's red-hot comb and paper and his plummy, punctilious singing, sold over a million copies. For the next eight years fast-talking, straight-speaking McKenzie led the Blowers for concerts, society parties and recordings such as "Hello Lola" and "One Hour" which, with guests including Coleman Hawkins and Glenn Miller, became classics. Two famous guitarists with the Blowers were Eddie Lang and Eddie Condon, who loved McKenzie's kindred cockfighting spirit; McKenzie helped Condon further by setting up his first record date, the McKenzie-Condon Chicagoans. From 1932 McKenzie was with Paul Whiteman for a year, then worked 52nd Street with success; but after his wife died he moved back to St Louis to look after his son and work as a beer salesman. He came back to record twice with Condon in 1944, and by 1947 was leading a band again at Jimmy Ryan's, shortly before he died of cirrhosis. Ed Hubble remembers: "His death was the end of the band. It was a stomping band and Red was singing beautifully, but his personal life was very lonely – he was taking it out on the bandstand and drinking entirely too much." [DF]

Mound City Blue Blowers (1935–6; Timeless Historical). Concentrating on the later days of the Blowers, with only McKenzie's comb as an echo of their "spasm-band" (the trad American sound akin to skiffle) roots, this has Red singing wonderfully, with Bunny Berigan as chief alumnus.

Red McKenzie 1935–7 (Timeless Traditional). Another good collection of McKenzie-led titles with a variety of studio groups, including Farley and Riley, and Bobby Hackett.

Al McKibbon

Bass.

b. Chicago, 1 Jan 1919.

McKibbon was raised in Detroit, and played in local bands, before touring with the Lucky Millinder band in 1943–4 and the Tab Smith small group in 1944–5. He did further small-band work with J.C. Heard in 1946 and Coleman Hawkins from 1946–7. In 1947 he replaced Ray Brown with the Dizzy Gillespie band, in time for the Carnegie Hall concert and European tour. He worked briefly with Count Basie in 1950, and was then with George Shearing from 1951–8 and with vibist Cal Tjader in 1958–9. He also recorded with Thelonious Monk in 1951, though he claimed to have heard his music as early as 1939, and Herbie Nichols in 1955. He toured with Monk in the Giants of Jazz from 1971–2. In the 1960s he settled in Los Angeles, and was busy with studio work and live appearances with singers, including Sammy Davis, with whom he worked in 1975. A veteran whose tone recalls the pre-amplification days of the 1940s, his lines similarly stick to the basics of the bop era without being too predictable.

He proved extremely adaptable to the material of Monk and Nichols and, when playing Latin jazz with Shearing and Tjader, submitted readily to the collective style of this type of rhythm-section. [BP]

➤➤ **Thelonious Monk** *(The London Collection Vol. 3)*; **Mongo Santamaria** *(Afro-Roots)*; **Cal Tjader** *(Monterey Concerts)*.

Ray McKinley

Drums, vocals, leader.

b. Fort Worth, Texas, 18 June 1910; d. 7 May 1995.

"Ray McKinley always was an amazing drummer," says critic George T. Simon. "He propelled a swinging beat, very often with a two-beat Dixieland basis, that inspired musicians to play better. [And] he spent more time on getting just the right sound out of his drums than any other". McKinley was in the class of contemporaries such as Cliff Leeman and Dave Tough, but more than either he was a vocational leader and all-round entertainer. He played early in his career in local "territory-style" bands such as Duncan Marion's, Savage Cummings's and Milt Shaw's, later with Smith Ballew, the Dorsey Brothers and Jimmy Dorsey, with whom he stayed until 1939. That year he teamed up with Will Bradley, a very underrated trombonist, to form a big band which cornered the market for big-band arrangements of boogie-woogie – the craze of the period. McKinley played drums, sang, co-led with Bradley and even composed special material: his biggest hit was "Beat Me Daddy, Eight To The Bar" and it was followed by others like "Scrub Me Mama With A Boogie Beat", "Bounce Me Brother With A Solid Four" and "Fry Me Cookie With A Can Of Lard". After three years the co-leaders disagreed over material (Bradley, a smooth stylist, enjoyed ballads more than McKinley did) and the drummer formed his own band, then moved to Glenn Miller's AEF band, taking over leadership of the organization after Miller's death. It was a role he was to play for another ten years from 1956, after a decade leading his own band again (featuring go-ahead arrangements by Eddie Sauter and cornermen such as Peanuts Hucko and guitarist Mundell Lowe) and working as a solo singer and DJ. From 1965 McKinley was semi-retired but continued to work through the 1970s, taking over from Tex Beneke to lead a Miller tribute band (1973–8), and in 1985 came to Britain for TV work with old colleagues Hucko and Zeke Zarchy. In the mid-1990s he was still active and contributed extensively to the video tribute *Glenn Miller: America's Musical Hero*. [DF]

Bill McKinney

Drums, leader.

b. Cynthiana, Kentucky, 17 Sept 1895; d. 14 Oct 1969.

Bill McKinney took over the leadership of Milton Senior's Synco Septet (later the Synco Jazz Band) in Springfield, Ohio, where they were succeeding as a novelty band. ("We played typical dance music of the early 1920s," remembered pianist Todd Rhodes, "complete with paper hats and whistles.") In Detroit the band was heard by Jean Goldkette, who spotted their potential, booked them into his newly acquired Graystone Ballroom and changed their name to McKinney's Cotton Pickers. He also hired Don Redman from Fletcher Henderson, at $300 a week, to build their repertoire, and a year later, in 1928, the band began recording for Victor (after Goldkette threw a party for Victor's boss at Edgewater Park Ballroom, Detroit): classic sides from that year, featuring John Nesbitt (trumpet) and Prince Robinson (tenor/clarinet), include "Cherry", "Shimme Sha Wabble" and "Four Or Five Times". The Pickers drew such crowds for their dances at Graystone (they also appeared regularly on local radio) that Goldkette refused them permission to take up an offer to record in New York, only relenting when keymen including Claude Jones, Dave Wilborn, Joe Smith and Don Redman went anyway (they recorded marvellous sides featuring Coleman Hawkins and Fats Waller in November 1929); the band then began touring and recording where they pleased. By 1931 the Cotton Pickers had left Detroit (and Goldkette) to work at Frank Sebastian's Cotton Club in Culver City, and Quentin Jackson had joined as singer, replacing George Thomas. The same year several McKinney cornermen left with Don Redman to join his new band; new members Rex Stewart and Benny Carter joined McKinney, and Carter took over musical direction. He stayed only a year, however, and after more touring the Cotton Pickers broke up in 1934. McKinney continued to lead bands and run an agency until the mid-1940s. [DF]

⊙ **The Band Don Redman Built** (1991; RCA Bluebird). An excellent representative set of McKinney titles from their hottest period.

⊙ **McKinney's Cotton Pickers 1928–9 & 1929–30** (1996; Classics). All the Cotton Pickers titles from the period on two CDs; some stronger than others but necessary for completists.

⊙ **McKinney's Cotton Pickers 1930–31/Don Redman 1939–40** (Classics). Later Cotton Pickers titles including the marvellous "Never Swat A Fly", plus eight Redman titles from the end of the decade, showing how his writing style had moved on with the swing era.

Hal McKusick

Alto saxophone.

b. Medford, Massachusetts, 1 June 1924.

McKusick worked with several big bands, his longest affiliations being with Boyd Raeburn in 1944–5, Claude Thornhill in 1948–9 and Elliot Lawrence from 1952–7. He played in small groups led by Terry Gibbs (1950–51), Don Elliott and others, and led his own septet (1958–9). Having recorded prolifically, he became a studio staff musician in 1958 and gradually decreased his involvement in jazz. A fluent player in the Lester Young-influenced style favoured by Art Pepper and Bud Shank in the 1950s, he is mainly remembered for having fronted several interesting and mildly experimental record projects. [BP]

Triple Exposure (1957; Prestige/OJC). Though not the most complex or absorbing McKusick session (see the compilation described under Rod Levitt), this quintet date with trombonist Billy Byers and Eddie Costa is the best representation of his excellent alto work.

John McLaughlin

Acoustic and electric guitars, piano, synthesizer, composer.

b. Kirk Sandall, Yorkshire, UK, 4 Jan 1942.

McLaughlin started off playing blues guitar and listening to Muddy Waters, Big Bill Broonzy and Leadbelly, then later to Django Reinhardt with Stephane Grappelli, and Tal Farlow. He moved to London in the early 1960s, playing in R&B groups with Alexis Korner, Graham Bond, Eric Clapton, Ginger Baker and others. Through Bond's influence, he joined the Theosophical Society, becoming interested in Eastern philosophy and religion and, after hearing Ravi Shankar, in Indian music. In the later 1960s he worked with Gunter Hampel in Germany for six months, playing free jazz. His first album as leader, *Extrapolation*, made in 1969 with John Surman (reeds), Tony Oxley (drums) and Brian Odges (bass), was one of the classic albums of the decade: a virtual summary of small-group playing techniques of the time, a catalyst of the jazz-rock movement of the 1970s and one that proved McLaughlin to be both a fine composer and a sublimely original guitar stylist. That busy year he went to New York to join Tony Williams's Lifetime, and recorded with Miles Davis, making a vital contribution to two of the latter's most influential albums, *In A Silent Way* and *Bitches Brew*. Lifetime included Jack Bruce (bass/vocals) and Larry Young (keyboards) and was one of the first jazz-rock bands, but it was dogged by bad luck and McLaughlin left in 1970. His 1970 album, *My Goal's Beyond*, featured him on one side playing standards on solo guitar, and it seems likely that this triggered off the spate of solo guitar records that followed.

After more recording sessions and concerts with Davis, he started his own group, the Mahavishnu Orchestra, in 1971, with Jerry Goodman (violin), Billy Cobham (drums), Jan Hammer (keyboards) and Rick Laird (bass guitar). McLaughlin had become a disciple of the guru Sri Chinmoy, who suggested the name Mahavishnu ("divine compassion, power and justice"). The band had a strong philosophical and spiritual basis and was revolutionary both musically and as a phenomenon; it was immensely successful, touring worldwide, playing major festivals everywhere, selling thousands of albums, and will probably never be usurped as the greatest jazz-rock band.

Musically the group deployed the resources of electronic sound superbly, and integrated drums with highly rhythmic melodies in a novel way. It used asymmetrical rhythms in a manner totally new to jazz, and juxtaposed immensely detailed and complex written passages with long sections of improvisation. It also combined extreme virtuosity with an Indo-European romantic lyricism and tenderness. Their first two albums, *The Inner Mounting Flame* and *Birds of Fire*, are masterpieces of the genre they virtually created.

Concurrently, McLaughlin had been taking vocal lessons in Indian music, and lessons from Ravi Shankar and other master instrumentalists. In 1973 he began playing with the violinist L. Shankar, Zakir Hussein (tabla) and Raghavan (*mridangam*). Through the strains of massive success and internal conflicts, Mahavishnu broke up at the end of 1973, and in 1974 McLaughlin unveiled a new line-up with Jean-Luc Ponty (violin) and Gayle Moran (vocals/keyboards). This toured internationally and made two albums before it too disbanded in 1975. Thereafter McLaughlin concentrated on playing acoustic music with his Indian musician friends, calling the group Shakti ("creative intelligence, beauty and power"). Shakti made a big impact internationally and recorded three albums before breaking up in 1978. McLaughlin went back to electric guitar, making an album called *Johnny McLaughlin, Electric Guitarist*, which was a reunion with the Mahavishnu players. For a while he led another electric group, the One Truth Band, but then reverted to acoustic guitar, touring in the late 1970s and early 1980s in trio with either Paco De Lucia and Larry Coryell, or De Lucia

RAFFAELLA CAVALIERI

John McLaughlin

and Al Di Meola, and in duo with French guitarist Christian Escoudé.

In 1975 he moved back to Europe, living in France, because he felt that in Europe and Japan jazz was understood and respected as an art, whereas the American music business regarded it as a commodity. McLaughlin played on some tracks of Davis's heavily electric album *You're Under Arrest* in 1984. He also played guitar on the 1985 recording of *Aura*, the orchestral tribute to Miles Davis, composed and conducted by Palle Mikkelborg, on which Miles himself played. He was commissioned to compose a guitar concerto featuring himself with the Los Angeles Philharmonic, and Mike Gibbs orchestrated it for the premiere in November 1985. It is a densely composed, long (about 30 minutes) and complex piece, which includes passages of guitar improvisation. In the mid-1980s, McLaughlin resurrected the name "Mahavishnu", forming another group that included saxophonist Bill Evans, bassist Jonas Hellborg and others. This toured internationally and played festivals, but by the later 80s McLaughlin was on the road with a trio comprising bassist Kai Eckhardt and the superlative percussionist Trilok Gurtu. By 1993 McLaughlin was touring and recording with another trio (Joey DeFrancesco on organ and trumpet and Dennis Chambers on drums), playing a mixture of standards and jazz originals. Remember Shakti was a more successful, durable and flexible reunion, touring to rapturous crowds and recording several albums with a slightly altered line-up, but one that still featured virtuosos of carnatic music.

McLaughlin is as equally dedicated to acoustic and electric guitar and continues to be influential on both. He is a visionary and a true artist, constantly searching and growing, who describes himself as "a musician for people who are not musicians". Like Miles Davis, Keith Jarrett and Weather Report, he has gained both a huge public following and the admiration of his peers. A prolific composer, his music always communicates the warmest emotions, and very often beatific joy. [IC]

⊙ **Extrapolation** (1969; Polydor). Everything about this album is exceptional. The music is full of emotional resonances, and "Binky's Beam", in 19/8 time, is one of the most thrilling reworkings of the blues in the entire history of jazz.

Mahavishnu Orchestra

⊙ **The Inner Mounting Flame** (1971; Columbia); **Birds Of Fire** (1972; Columbia). The key album of this pair is the first one, which sounds as fresh today as it did on the day of its release. The originality and beauty of McLaughlin's compositions, his virtuosity and that of the whole group, and the sheer clarity of even the bravura passages, all combined to produce a totally new sound that was stunningly attractive. *Birds Of Fire* is excellent but not quite so magical.

Shakti

⊙ **Shakti** (1975; Columbia). McLaughlin was now exploring the Indian heritage, with quietly spectacular results. Again, new trails of energy, interplay and virtuosity are blazed, but this time the intensity is at low volume, though none the less dynamic.

John McLaughlin

⊙ **Johnny McLaughlin, Electric Guitarist** (1978; Columbia). McLaughlin here re-establishes his electric credentials with several stars from the fusion movement, and also holds out an olive branch to Cobham and Goodman from the original Mahavishnu Orchestra.

⊙ **Que Alegria** (1991; Verve). The same trio with bassist Dominique De Piazza added on a couple of tracks – "Reincarnation" and "1 Nite Stand". McLaughlin's genius as a leader and player are well in evidence here, and the band responds powerfully.

⊙ **Tokyo Live** (1993; Verve). This trio with the superb organist (and nifty Miles impersonator on trumpet) Joey DeFrancesco, and the great drummer Dennis Chambers, is a wonderful working band. McLaughlin is enjoying himself, playing superbly, giving at times strong direction to the proceedings, and the repertoire covers a wide spectrum of standards and originals.

➤➤ **Carla Bley** *(Escalator Over The Hill);* **Miles Davis** *(In A Silent Way; Bitches Brew);* **Tony Williams** *(Emergency!).*

Jackie McLean

Alto saxophone, composer.
b. New York, 17 May 1931.

After studying with his neighbour Bud Powell and gigging with Thelonious Monk in the late 1940s, McLean was recommended by Powell to Miles Davis, with whom he worked in 1951–2. A year's formal music education at the North Carolina A & T College (where Lou Donaldson and Dannie Richmond were also to become students) was followed by gigs with Paul Bley in 1954 and the George Wallington quintet in 1955. He also played with Charles Mingus in 1956 and Art Blakey in 1956–7. He acted and played in the long-running stage play *The Connection* from 1959–61, including performances in London and Paris. He toured Japan in 1964 and Scandinavia in 1966, and then began part-time teaching and counselling users of narcotics, which had earlier interrupted his own career. In 1968 he began teaching at the University of Hartford, Connecticut, and in 1972 became full-time head of department; some of his protégés have included saxophonists Antoine Roney and Abraham Burton, and Winard and Philip Harper. Even before becoming an educator, Jackie had made a practice of encouraging young musicians such as Tony Williams, Grachan Moncur III, Charles Tolliver, Woody Shaw and Cecil McBee. After a period in which he performed mainly during summer vacations, often with a group led by his saxophonist son Rene (b. 16 Dec 1946), McLean increased his playing activity in the late 1980s and has since enjoyed a career renaissance.

Although they never recorded together, Jackie was a close friend of Charlie Parker and his style is an individual and oblique reflection of Parker's, in which intensity replaces fluency and linear invention is more important than harmonic interest. McLean himself points to the stylistic example of Dexter Gordon and, in the 1960s, he was capable of absorbing creatively the influence of both Ornette Coleman (who recorded with him on the album *New And Old Gospel*) and John Coltrane. Several of McLean's compositions have become standards, for instance "Dig" (aka "Donna"), "Dr Jackle" (or "Dr Jekyll") and "Little Melonae", all of which were recorded by Miles, and "Hip Strut". His uniquely tart sound and his forceful lines have also rubbed off on a whole generation of altoists such as Gary Bartz and Sonny Fortune. [BP]

⊙ **4, 5 and 6** (1956; Prestige/OJC). A superior example from the many sessions McLean turned out for Prestige during a rather untogether period, this has a basic rhythm-section led by Mal Waldron, joined on two tracks by Hank Mobley and/or Donald Byrd.

⊙ **New Soil** (1959; Blue Note). A resurgent McLean led a dynamite quintet with Byrd and Walter Davis Jnr through material by the pianist and McLean's own "Minor Apprehension" (entitled "Minor March" when it was recorded by Miles) and the gripping "Hip Strut".

⊙ **The Jackie Mac Attack: Live** (1991; Birdology). A quartet date with his regular rhythm-section of the period, including drummer Carl Allen and pianist Hotep Idris Galeta (aka Cecil Barnard), finds McLean aiming to prove he's thirty years younger, and actually succeeding.

John McLevy

Trumpet, flugelhorn.

b. Dundee, Scotland, 2 Jan 1927; d. Nov 2003.

McLevy became prominent on the British jazz scene in the 1960s, after formative years in London hotel bands and at the BBC working for Cyril Stapleton. His humorous, hard-swinging style attracted attention when in 1970 he featured in Benny Goodman's British big band and toured Europe (on Bobby Hackett's recommendation) in Goodman's small group with Hank Jones, Slam Stewart, Bucky Pizzarelli and George Masso. In the 1970s McLevy worked in studios (he played the Harry Edison role on 21 LPs with singer Max Bygraves), formed a highly successful quartet with accordionist Jack Emblow, and worked the British club circuit (often with Kenny Baker and later Tommy McQuater). Throughout the 1980s he continued to work regularly in clubs, pubs and with Bob Wilber's big band, although in the 1990s he was heard less often than he deserved before Alzheimer's disease put an end to his playing. A middle-range trumpeter and flugelhornist who never wasted a note, McLevy used short, attacking phrases and had a highly original approach – for example, he adapted the in-and-out harmon-muted effect of Clark Terry with striking ingenuity. [DF]

➤➤ **Roy Williams** *(Royal Trombone).*

Jim McNeely

Piano, arranger, composer.

b. Chicago, 18 May 1949.

Jim studied piano, clarinet and saxophone privately from 1958–67, played French horn and snare drum in his high-school band, then earned a BMus at the University of Illinois in 1975. Moving to New York, he worked consecutively with Ted Curson, Chet Baker, Thad Jones and Mel Lewis from 1978–84, Stan Getz (1981–5) and Phil Woods (1990–95). He has written for the Stockholm Jazz Band, WDR Big Band and the Carnegie Hall Jazz Orchestra, and in 1996 returned to the (ex-Jones-Lewis) Vanguard Jazz Orchestra as composer-in-residence. Since 1998, he has been chief conductor of the Danish Radio Jazz Orchestra. His favourites on piano are Monk, Wynton Kelly, McCoy Tyner and Earl Hines, while inspirational composers are Thad Jones, Bob Brookmeyer and Coltrane. He values his father's advice: "You could play football and have fun for a few years, or play music and have fun for the rest of your life." [BP]

Jim McNeely

⊙ **The Plot Thickens** (1979; Muse). Possibly hard to obtain, this is McNeely's most intriguing small-group album. The all-original material is played by a trio containing Billy Hart plus, on the title track and a couple of others, John Scofield.

Vanguard Jazz Orchestra

⊙ **Lickety Split** (1997; New World). The programme, entirely written by McNeely, contains one track each dedicated to the band's founders, Thad and Mel, the latter evoked by drummer John Riley. Among the many other soloists are altoists Billy Drewes and Dick Oatts.

Jimmy McPartland

Trumpet.

b. Chicago, 15 March 1907; d. 13 March 1991.

Jimmy McPartland took up jazz seriously at Austin High School where, with fellow students and outside friends known collectively as the "Austin High School Gang", he learned New Orleans Rhythm Kings records note for note. In 1923 he heard Bix Beiderbecke for the first time and in 1925 replaced him in the Wolverines in New York (Beiderbecke gave him a cornet and worked the first five nights with him). McPartland then played with Ben Pollack and with Eddie Condon on seminal recording sessions with the McKenzie-Condon Chicagoans. In the 1930s he toured, then settled in Chicago in 1937 and shuttled between there and New York until he was called up in 1942. Three years later he met his British wife Marian (see below) in Belgium while playing *Bandwagon* (an ENSA service show), then worked back in Chicago and New York after demobilization. Club work, touring, festival appearances and a busy recording schedule kept him busy through to the 1970s, and he was regularly to be heard with Marian in the late 1970s (although divorced, they remained great friends, and remarried a matter of weeks before Jimmy's death). He continued playing until shortly before he died, which came just two days before that of Bud Freeman, his old colleague from the Austin High School Gang.

With Wild Bill Davison, Jimmy McPartland was the last classic ambassador of jazz cornet. He was always associated with Bix Beiderbecke, whom he revered; while McPartland never quite possessed the same elusive genius, he shared Beiderbecke's attractive tonal and melodic approaches, and could drive down a band with a force and excitement that sometimes recalled Muggsy Spanier as much as Bix. [DF]

Chicago Rompers (1956; Jazztone). With an all-style group featuring Dickenson, Stegmeyer, Freeman, Hinton, Morello and Marian McPartland, this album – later reissued as *The Middle Road* – is Dixieland at its near-best.

That Happy Dixieland Jazz (1959; RCA). Another superb Dixieland session with Dick Cary arrangements; Cutshall, Wilber and Wettling play to the strong trumpet/cornet lead of McPartland and Charlie Shavers.

>> **Dick Cary** *(The Music Man Goes Dixieland).*

Marian McPartland

Piano, songwriter.

b. Slough, Berkshire, UK, 20 March 1918.

Marian Turner studied music at the Guildhall before working in music hall with pianist Billy Mayerl's Claviers. In 1945 she met and married Jimmy McPartland, and returned to the USA with him. She worked in the 1950s as a solo pianist at Condon's, the Embers, the London House and the Hickory House, where she led a great trio for a while with Bill Crow and Joe Morello. The 1960s, an unsettling period for many jazz musicians, were unhappy for McPartland: her marriage failed and a spell with Benny Goodman ended unhappily. Yet by the end of the decade she was on an upswing: she had a new record label, Halcyon, and was soon busily performing in clubs, concert halls and workshops. From 1978 she began recording for Concord (an important outlet) and has carried on busily playing and recording, including classical repertoire such as Grieg's piano concerto.

Besides being an important jazz pianist, Marian McPartland is a diversifier: her early work with black students in Washington predated most jazz educational work by five years, and continues today. She has served on a number of jazz boards, writes beautifully about her music (a collection of her writings, *All In Good Time*, was published in 1987), and broadcasts regularly: her Peabody-award-winning *Piano Jazz* programmes for NBC, New York, are frequently rebroadcast (some of the best are now issued on Jazz Alliance CDs). Marian is also a gifted composer, whose creations include "In The Days Of Our Love", "With You In Mind" and "Ambience". [DF]

Plays The Music Of Alec Wilder (1973; Jazz Alliance). McPartland is a lifelong champion of the music of her good friend Alec Wilder, and this is one of a very few comprehensive celebrations of his work.

Marian McPartland's Piano Jazz With Guest Eubie Blake (1979; Jazz Alliance). Conversation and music with veteran Blake, as heard on National Public Radio; an invaluable piece of aural history.

Max Jones Files/Redferns

Marian McPartland

Plays The Music Of Billy Strayhorn (1987; Concord). McPartland was one of the first to separate Strayhorn's output from Duke's on record, and she and altoist Jerry Dodgion make magnificent work of the project.

Live At Maybeck Recital Hall Vol. 9 (1991; Concord). An eclectic demonstration of McPartland's mastery as a soloist: Ellington to Ornette Coleman.

The Silent Pool (1995; Concord). McPartland's "Silent Pool" (dedicated to a calm water-hole near Abinger Hammer, Surrey) is one of her many finely wrought originals and it is luxuriously presented – together with eleven more – amid Alan Broadbent's strings. Superb.

>> **Ellis Larkins** *(Concert In Argentina).*

Joe McPhee

Saxophones, trumpet, flugelhorn, valve-trombone.

b. Miami, Florida, 3 Nov 1939.

Joe McPhee's father played trumpet and gave him lessons at the age of eight. In Poughkeepsie, New York, where he still lives and works, McPhee played in his high school band, and while in the infantry in 1963 he played in the military band in Germany. His first recording was with Clifford Thornton, on *Freedom And Unity* (1967; Third World). In the late 60s he began playing reeds and releasing his own ferocious free jazz records on Craig Johnson's CjR label, including *Underground Railroad* (1969), *Nation Time* (1970), *Trinity* (1971) and *Pieces Of Light* (1974), the latter with John Snyder on ARP synthesizer. In 1975, hat Hut Records was formed by Swiss producer Werner X. Uehlinger, specifically to release music by McPhee. Records on hat Hut have seen McPhee grow more ambitious in his compositions and arrangements, while *Tenor* (1976) – one of several superb solo outings – remains among the very best lone saxophone records ever made. McPhee lived in Europe in the mid-70s, when he began playing with Marseilles-based guitarist Raymond Boni and reedman André Jaume; with others, these players appear on McPhee's excellent *Old Eyes & Mysteries* (1979) and *Topology* (1981). Among various other hat Hut and hat Art commitments, McPhee recorded *Impressions Of Jimmy Giuffre* (1991; CELP) with Boni and Jaume. In the second half of the 90s, McPhee has grown more active, recording an exciting new solo program, *As Serious As Your Life* (1998; hatOLOGY) – which includes a multitracked take on George Gershwin's "The Man I Love" for tenor and synthesizer – several sessions with tenor player Frank Lowe for the CIMP label, a duet with Canadian violinist David Prentice titled *Inside Out* (1996; CIMP), tenor duets with Evan Parker, and a trio with reed player Ken Vandermark and bassist Kent Kessler called *A Meeting In Chicago* (1996; Okka Disk). His willingness to play with young, unknown musicians, his prolific gigging and recording, and his tirelessly uncompromising blowing have made him a hero to a whole new generation of avant-improvisers. [JC]

⊙ **Oleo & A Future Retrospective** (1982; hat Art). This CD presents McPhee's fantastic quartet date *Oleo* with a live concert recorded the same day (without bassist François Mechali). McPhee plays pocket cornet and tenor throughout, while Boni and Jaume draw from a big timbral palette with effects and clarinets. With the leader's melancholic balladry and nifty sense of space, Benny Golson's "I Remember Clifford" and Sonny Rollins's revamped title cut, this disc is gorgeous at all levels.

Charles McPherson

Alto, saxophone.

b. Joplin, Missouri, 24 July 1939.

McPherson grew up in Detroit, and played as a teenager with Barry Harris. Moving to New York in 1959, he joined Charles Mingus in 1960 with his Detroit partner, trumpeter Lonnie Hillyer. Apart from a period co-leading a quintet with Hillyer in 1966, McPherson mainly performed with Mingus until 1972. He then became a soloist playing with local groups, including a spell in San Diego, where he moved in 1978. He was employed to rerecord the ensemble playing on Charlie Parker records used for the soundtrack of *Bird!* (1988), and this increased his international reputation. Highly regarded for his faithfulness to the language of Parker, his work with Mingus showed his ability to extend this idiom meaningfully. [BP]

⊙ **First Flight Out** (1994; Arabesque). With a quintet including Tom Harrell and drummer Victor Lewis, McPherson plays a programme of largely original material (plus Mingus and Monk and a couple of standards) and infuses everything with his tremendous commitment.

Tommy McQuater

Trumpet, flugelhorn.

b. Maybole, Ayrshire, Scotland, 4 Sept 1914.

Tommy McQuater was playing with Lew Stone by 1935, then went on to create a sensation as the brightest young British trumpet soloist of his era, working with Ambrose (where he partnered George Chisholm), recording with Benny Carter and Chisholm, and playing in the short-lived but legendary Heralds of Swing in 1939. From the outbreak of war McQuater played lead trumpet with the Squadronaires, and after 1945 worked as a freelance and with the BBC Showband. Although his post-war reputation was occasionally eclipsed by the younger Kenny Baker, he remained a connoisseur's delight, playing and recording regularly with Chisholm (they also made a formidable comedy team), and for Jack Parnell's band, in addition to working at Elstree film studios and at the London Palladium. During the 1970s and 1980s McQuater was still to be heard at Bill McGuffie's Niner Club, often with John McLevy, as well as in studios, and, though he played less often in the 1990s following a lip injury, he was still occasionally to be heard with big bands and in 2003 made the latest of his annual guest appearances at the Ealing Jazz Festival at the age of 89 ('Still annoying the neighbours!' he joked). McQuater – as well as a great lead-trumpeter - is also a great teacher: his former pupils include Ian Carr, Alan Elsdon and Digby Fairweather. [DF]

Carmen McRae

Vocals.

b. New York, 8 April 1920; d. 10 Nov 1994.

A keen student of the piano and of singers, Carmen McRae wrote the song "Dream Of Life", which was recorded by Billie Holiday when Carmen was eighteen. She worked with the Benny Carter band in 1944, and briefly with Count Basie. She married and divorced the drummer Kenny Clarke in the 1940s, and sang under the name Carmen Clarke with the Mercer Ellington band in 1946–7. Later she worked as an intermission pianist/singer at various New York clubs. She began making records under her own name, initially for small labels, in 1953, and went on to record successful albums for major companies. From the late 1950s on she was accompanied by her own trio, featuring such pianists as Ray Bryant, Norman Simmons and Duke Pearson. She made many international tours, doing both nightclub and concert work, and did occasional acting work in films (*Hotel*, 1967) and television (*Roots*, 1976). She retired from performing in public in 1991, and suffered a long period of illness terminated by a stroke.

Although her admiration for Billie Holiday dated from the start of her career, there was never any hint

of stylistic dependency and, in any case, Carmen's personal, rather acid tone-quality did much to disguise what little similarity there was. The chief legacy of Holiday, in fact, lay in her rhythmic expertise and in the depth of feeling that Carmen managed to extract from her interpretation of lyrics, an art which the majority of would-be jazz singers seem determined to ignore. [BP]

Here To Stay (1955–9; MCA). Though sounding less idiosyncratic than some of her later work, this has all the characteristics of Carmen at her best, in both a small-group session (including a rare appearance by Billy Strayhorn) and a big-band set.

Carmen Sings Monk (1988; Novus). With impressive support from Clifford Jordan, McRae interprets the various words added to Monk tunes, including both sets for "Round Midnight". One gem of the lyricist's art is the line supplied for "Straight No Chaser": "He [Monk] knew you can't pack up the moment and take it with you on the road".

Jay McShann

Piano, vocals.

b. Muskogee, Oklahoma, 12 Jan 1916.

Jay McShann, also known as Hootie, played the piano from the age of twelve. He moved to Kansas City in the mid-1930s, and worked both with local groups and under his own name; his 1938 group included Charlie Parker. When Kansas City nightlife slowed down he played briefly in Chicago in 1939, but then went back to leading his own Kansas City group, enlarging it to a twelve-piece band from 1940–43 and appearing with success in New York and elsewhere. After army service he re-formed his band in 1945, and from 1946–50 led an eight-piece group mainly active on the West Coast. Boomeranging back to Kansas City in 1951, he led a band (later a trio) with which he sang numbers associated with his former band vocalists Walter Brown and Jimmy Witherspoon. Trips to France in 1969 and Canada in 1971 led to gradually lengthier touring schedules, including several further European visits. Still working occasionally in North America, he made an album with ex-Chuck Berry pianist Johnnie Johnston in 2001, and in 2003 visited New York to receive an award from the New School University.

As well as his latter-day blues singing, McShann is noted for his compelling solo playing, an indefinable blend of blues, boogie, Basie and a bit of Earl Hines. On occasion during the 1970s he was again able to call on the services of Gene Ramey and Gus Johnson, who not only worked briefly together for Basie (in 1952–3) but were also the foundation of McShann's 1938–43 band – and what a foundation! Their work then combined brilliantly with the leader's choice of blues-based section-players and forward-looking soloists such as Parker and trumpeter Buddy Anderson (who, though reported dead in 1944, was playing locally in the 1980s). It is this band which, despite its small recorded output, is likely to prove McShann's most enduring claim to fame. [BP]

Blues From Kansas City (1941–3; MCA). The total recorded output of McShann's loosely swinging band, with Parker making history on seven tracks, and a great feel to the ensemble throughout, even on a couple of scores more adventurous than the blues that were their meal-ticket.

Kansas City Memories (1970–73; Black & Blue). Two different European sessions featuring a variety of blues-oriented players, from Arnett Cobb to guitarist Gatemouth Brown, with McShann and his post-Gus Johnson drummer Paul Gunther providing a groovy foundation.

Jack McVea

Tenor and baritone saxophones.

b. Los Angeles, 5 Nov 1914; d. 27 Dec 2000.

The son of banjoist-entertainer "Satchel" McVea, Jack McVea worked with his father until 1932 before joining trumpeter Dootsie Williams' Harlem Dukes. During the 1930s he played with Charlie Echols, Lorenzo Flennoy, Claude Kennedy, Cee Pee Johnson and Eddie Barefield. In 1940 he joined Lionel Hampton's crowd-pleasing big band for three years playing baritone saxophone and scoring a big hit with "Flying Home". Thereafter he worked regularly for Norman Granz's JATP concerts, broadcast with Count Basie, and made a famous appearance with Charlie Parker and Dizzy Gillespie on Slim Gaillard's immortal "Slim's Jam". In 1946 he scored his biggest success with the internationally famous R&B hit "Open The Door, Richard". In the 1950s and early 60s, as well as leading his own R&B band and playing with Benny Carter, he also ran a scrap-iron business. Then in 1966 he joined a Disneyland-based trio, the Royal Street Bachelors, an association that lasted for twenty-five years. McVea's only self-led album *Nothin' But Jazz!* is well overdue for CD re-issue. [DF]

McVoutie's Central Avenue Blues (2002; Delmark). A fully-comprehensive CD survey of McVea has yet to emerge, but this bluesy collection finds him – along with Wynonie Harris, Rabon Tarrant and others – playing his tough but finely-honed tenor on titles including "Don't Blame Me" and "Okay For Baby!".

John Medeski

Piano, Hammond organ.

b. Louisville, Kentucky, 28 June 1965.

Anthony John Medeski grew up in Florida, and began piano lessons at the age of five. In his teens he worked with local and national musicians including Jaco Pastorius and Mark Murphy, and in 1983 began studying at Boston's New England Conservatory with Ran Blake, Leonard Shure and Bob Moses. While there, he also gained invaluable experience as a sideman in the Boston area with jazz stars such as Dewey Redman, Billy Higgins, Bob Mintzer and Alan Dawson, and legendary New England blues man, Mr Jellybelly, who initiated Medeski's enthusiasm for the B-3 organ. Concurrently, Medeski was keyboardist for various jazz groups, including the Either/Orchestra, Mandala Octet and Chris Hollyday quartet.

In 1991, Medeski moved to New York, where he played with many musicians and groups, including Reggie Workman, John Lurie's Lounge Lizards and John Zorn's Masada. He formed the trio Medeski, Martin & Wood (MMW) with drummer/percussionist Billy Martin and bassist Chris Wood. Medeski's album, *Lunar Crush* (1994; Gramavision), was an "avant-rock-jazz-hop" collaboration with ex-George Russell virtuoso guitarist David "Fuze" Fiuczynski. Medeski also played on David Byrne's 1994 eponymous album, and in the same year, he and his musical partners Martin and Wood performed on arranger Ken Schaphorst's album, *When The Moon Jumps* (Accurate Records). MMW took a leaf out of Pat Metheny's book: travelling on a shoestring, they took their music to the people by touring in a camper and playing rock clubs and coffee houses, achieving (as Metheny had done) a cult status that is rare in instrumental music. Although Medeski seems to be the driving force, it is a trio of equals, and most of their compositions are attributed to all three men. They are all virtuosi with a vision that combines rock, funk, ethnic and jazz rhythms with electronics, tonalities, harmonies non-tonal sounds and outright free improvisation. [IC]

⊙ **Friday Afternoon In The Universe** (1994; Gramavision). The opening piece, "The Lover", sustains a wonderfully funky rhythm all the way, while "House Mop" shuffles along with tongue in cheek. There's much humour and sardonic wit here, and an astonishing variety of sounds.

⊙ **Shack – Man** (1996; Gramavision). The opening track, a warm loping MMW arrangement of the traditional gospel piece "Is There Anybody Here That Love My Jesus", sets the tone for the whole album, which is rich in ecstatically sustained rhythms. "Jellybelly" is a tribute to Medeski's inspirational blues man, with gutbucket shuffle and chuntering synth rhythms. "Bubblehouse" slowly accelerates from medium funk to racing funk, then slowly decelerates to its original medium tempo. Again, MMW demonstrate their restless invention and absorbing music.

➤➤ **John Scofield** *(A Go Go).*

Brad Mehldau

Piano.

b. Jacksonville, Florida, 23 Aug 1970.

Mehldau began investigating the piano when he was four and, growing up in Hartford, Connecticut, took classical lessons between the ages of six and fourteen. After becoming interested in jazz, he studied at New York's New School with Junior Mance, Kenny Werner and Fred Hersch. He worked with Jackie McLean and, from 1991, recorded albums with altoist Christopher Hollyday, guitarist Peter Bernstein and Jesse Davis, as well as completing three albums in Spain with Perico Sambeat and drummer Jorge Rossy, who subsequently became part of Mehldau's long-lived trio with Larry Grenadier. One of the band's aims, he has said, is to "keep the trio interesting for each of us ... It's real improvisation on a group level." In 1994 they worked together on saxophonist Mark Turner's debut session, and the pianist's first record with Joshua Redman led to international tours and his own contract. The trio have recorded a series of consistent albums, and Mehldau has more recently recorded a couple of solo albums, garnering a reputation for ingenious cover versions (a penchant for Radiohead and *White Album* era Beatles). [BP]

⊙ **Art Of The Trio Vol.4** (1999; Warner). With the fiercely interactive ensemble (Jorge Rossy and bassist Larry Grenadier) pushing him every step of the way, Mehldau shines throughout a wide-ranging selection, from hard-driving standards to the odd contemporary pop song (Radiohead's "Exit Music").

⊙ **Elegiac Cycle** (1999; Warner). Whereas his trio recordings sometimes sound like Jarrett out-takes, this unaccompanied set is more individual and darker in tone. The influence of nineteenth-century European composers is unmistakable but the improvising clearly draws on the jazz tradition and is wholly compelling.

➤➤ **Lee Konitz** *(Alone Together);* **Joshua Redman** *(Mood Swing; Timeless Tales).*

Myra Melford

Piano.

b. Glencoe, Illinois, 5 Jan 1957.

Melford's first classical piano studies were with Erwin Helfer, a renowned boogie-woogie specialist, and she subsequently studied with Art Lande in Washington State and later with Henry Threadgill. She is perhaps best known for the trio she formed with bassist Lindsay Horner and drummer Reggie Nicholson in New York in 1990. This group recorded *Jump* (1990; Enemy), *Now & Now* (1991; Enemy) and the classic *Alive In The House Of Saints* (1993; hat Art), all of which spotlit Melford's method of composition – including some unusual major-scale, sometimes poppy or pastel elements (as heard on her multi-part dedication to the architect who designed the house in Chicago in which she lived

Myra Melford

from three to eighteen, "Frank Lloyd Wright Goes West To Rest") – and her passionate playing. In 1994 she recorded duets with Dutch drummer Han Bennink, *Eleven Ghosts* (1997; hatOLOGY), and has since played and recorded with like-minded musicians such as Josph Jarman, Leroy Jenkins and Henry Threadgill (all of whom, significantly, are free jazz players who nonetheless owe much to the blues tradition). Melford has expanded her trio to a quintet, first adding Dave Douglas on trumpet and Marty Ehrlich on reeds on *Even The Sounds Shine* (1994; hat Art), then switching Chris Speed for Ehrlich, Erik Friedlander's cello for Horner, and Michael Sarin for Nicholson. She continues to write long, sectional pieces that allow ample space for improvisation. Expanding her pianistic horizons, she has learned the harmonium, studying North Indian music in Calcutta in 2000–01, and has played it in Dave Douglas' group Satya. [JC]

⊙ **The Same River Twice** (1996; Gramavision). Elegant lines shared by Douglas, Friedlander, Speed and Melford, whose debt to Don Pullen is evident in the way she bursts into energy playing (she's seriously studied martial arts), then slips gracefully back into overtly lyrical melodicism. Melford evidently learned a great deal about transitions from Threadgill, and she deftly negotiates this very twisty highway.

Steve Melling

Piano.

b. Accrington, Lancashire, UK, 12 July 1959.

Steve Melling was brought up in Preston and continued his music studies at Goldsmiths' College in London before joining the National Youth Jazz Orchestra. In the late 1970s he began playing professionally when he toured with Harry Beckett and Elton Dean. In 1986 Melling received the first Pat Smythe Memorial Trust Award, a financial prize for the most exceptionally promising pianist. He played with Barbara Thompson's Paraphernalia (1986–7), and in 1987 and 1989 toured the Far East with the Clark Tracey quintet, as well as playing on three of the group's albums. He worked with Tim Whitehead's band (1988–9), and recorded the album *Decision* (EG) with him, an experience he described as "a lesson in using the studio to develop musical ideas rather than just to record predetermined ones". Melling also recorded *East To West* with Alan Skidmore, and played on the title track of Skidmore's exquisite ballad album *After The Rain* (both on Miles Music).

Having worked and recorded with Claire Martin and with Peter King's quartet and quintet, in 1996 Melling recorded his own album *Trio Duo Solo*. From 1996–8, he was Professor of Jazz Piano at London's Royal College of Music. Melling is one of the most comprehensively gifted of pianists, with a great technique and an abundance of ideas. [IC]

⊙ **Trio Duo Solo** (1996; Ronnie Scott's Jazz House). Melling handles very varied material with terrific authority: standards by Cole Porter, Ellington and Leonard Bernstein, originals by Monk, Coltrane and Bud Powell, and a couple of his own excellent pieces, "In A Monochrome", with its restless, hard-hitting rhythms in the Tyner style, and "Leona", a delightful romantic waltz.

Steve Melling

George Melly

Vocals.

b. Liverpool, UK, 17 Aug 1926.

Melly's first career, roistering around Britain in the 1950s with Mick Mulligan's band, is wickedly replayed in his first, still scandalous volume of autobiography, *Owning Up*, probably the funniest book ever written by a jazzman. In the early 1960s he was a freelance journalist, occasional TV and radio presenter and art critic, while his sporadic pub performances were praised by critics such as Chris Welch in *Melody Maker* for their showmanship and sauciness (songs like Eva Taylor's "Hot Nuts" helped the publicity, as did Melly's avowed bisexuality). By the time Melly published his book of rock and roll criticism, *Revolt into Style* (he is the only traditional jazzman flexible enough to write well about rock), his career had been relaunched in 1960s terms by Beatles publicist Derek Taylor, with the occasionally chaotic live album *Nuts*. Melly's restoration to fame was helped by Jack Higgins, holding the managerial reins, and by John Chilton, Melly's right-hand man and resident jazz authority. In the 1970s and 1980s Melly's show, featuring Chilton, Steve Fagg (bass), Chuck Smith (drums) and talented pianists such as Collin Bates, became Britain's most successful of its kind, combining Melly's deeply loved classic repertoire (from Bessie Smith on) with new material by Chilton. Melly, able to talk wittily about most subjects, became a TV personality, his larger-than-life image bolstered by later autobiographical volumes, and he is now a familiar and well-loved media figure, still working and touring tirelessly. [DF]

⊙ **Meet Mick Mulligan and George Melly** (1959; Lake). Mostly from old Pye recordings but with some valuable extras (four tracks from the old Saga label), this is a good portrait of the rumbustious hard-blowing jazz of Mulligan, his capable friends and stylish singer.

⊙ **Puttin' On The Ritz** (1990; Legacy). Melly has recorded very widely but this fine selection of classic jazz material (plus one or two originals) is as good a representation of his show as any; crackling trumpet by John Chilton.

Vince Mendoza

Trumpet, piano, guitar, composer, arranger.

b.Norwalk, Connecticut, USA, Nov 1961.

Mendoza had guitar lessons with his uncle, Frank Falcone, from the age of five, and later learned the trumpet with Raymond Crisara and Carmine Caruso in New York. He went on to study composition at Ohio State University, and obtained a Masters degree from the University of Southern California. Today he is widely regarded as one of the most versatile and multi-talented musicians around, highly sought after as a composer, arranger, producer and conductor. Artists such as Gary Burton, Pat Metheny, Michael Brecker, Charlie Haden, Andy Narell, Kurt Elling and John Abercrombie have all featured his compositions and arrangements on their albums, and he won acclaim for his orchestral arrangements for two Joni Mitchell Albums, *Travelogue* (2002) and *Both Sides Now* (2000). Mendoza's arrangements can also be heard in Lars van Trier's film *Dancer in the Dark* (2000), while his work with the Dutch Metropole Orchestra and the WDR Big Band means that he is as well known in Europe as he is in the US. In 1992 he collaborated with Arif Mardin on a Jazz-Flamenco album, *Jazzpaña* (1993), recorded by the WDR Big Band, which was twice nominated for a Grammy award. His own compositional projects – on the albums *Start Here* (1989), *Instructions Inside* (1991), *Sketches* (1993) and *Epiphany* (1997) – reveal a wide range of influences from classical masters Stravinsky and Ravel, to jazz giants Gil Evans and Miles Davis.

⊙ **Epiphany** (1999; Zebra Acoustic). Mendoza's latest foray into the problematic arena of symphony orchestra plus jazz soloists is largely successful, if somewhat subdued. The musicianship is always superb, with outstanding contributions from Kenny Wheeler, Michael Brecker, John Abercrombie and Joe Lovano.

The Merry Macs

Vocal group.

The Merry Macs were a close-harmony vocal trio formed in the mid-1920s by Ted McMichael (baritone) and his brothers Joe and Judd (both tenors) while at school in Minneapolis. Following a 1926 appearance (as The Mystery Trio) on Eddie Dunstedter's WCCO Radio show, the group toured with bandleader Joe Haymes who renamed them The Personality Boys. In 1930 lead singer Cheri McKay joined and the group became the Merry Macs – on account of their similar surnames. Broadcasting from 1930 for NBC Chicago, they made their first record, "The Little White Church On The Hill", for Victor in 1932. Radio work continued throughout the 1930s and 40s, as well as tours with Glenn Miller, Jack Hylton and other big bands. In 1936 Cheri McKay left and was replaced by Helen Carroll, then Mary Lou Cook (1939), before Marjory Garland took over in 1941, remaining until the group disbanded in 1964. After signing for Decca in 1938, The Merry Macs had a succession of hits including "The Hut-Hut Song" (1941), "Jingle Jangle Jingle" (1942), "Sentimental Journey" (1943) and – biggest of all – "Mairzy Doats" which remained at number 1 for five weeks in 1944. The group also appeared in several films, notably *Love Thy Neighbor* (1938), with Jack Benny and Fred Allen, *Ride 'Em Cowboy* (1942), with Abbott and Costello (on which they sang "A Tisket, A Tasket"), and *Mr. Music* (1950) with Bing Crosby. [DF]

⊙ **Mairzy Doats** (2001; ASV). A well-judged selection illustrating The Merry Macs' wonderful close-harmony talents on material ranging from novelty hits like "Pop Goes The Weasel" and "Ta Ha Wa Nu Wa" to more touching songs like "I Get The Blues When It Rains". There can be few more skilled examples of group singing than the Merry Macs' rendition of Burke and Van Heusen's delightful "Isn't That Just Like Love".

Misha Mengelberg

Piano, composer.

b. Kiev, Ukraine, 5 June 1935.

From a musical family – both his father Karel and great-uncle Willem were conductors – Misha Mengelberg studied piano and composition first in Darmstadt in 1958, and thereafter at the Royal Conservatory in The Hague (1958–64). After involvement with the experimental theatre/music group Fluxus (1961–3), and a high-profile appearance on Eric Dolphy's last recording (1964), Mengelberg (with alto player Piet Noordijk) led a quartet at 1966's Newport jazz festival and won the Dutch National Jazz Prize the same year. The following year, he founded the avant-garde self-help organization the Instant Composers Pool, and in 1968 formed a duo with the like-minded, theatrical improviser, drummer Han Bennink. Always interested in finding new directions for free piano-playing, Mengelberg studied Moroccan music in the early 1970s, and has involved himself not only with large-scale European oufits such as the Berlin Contemporary Jazz Orchestra and the ICP Orchestra, but also with sympathetic US players such as Lee Konitz and Roswell Rudd. In the mid-1990s, he worked with drummer Joey Baron, who appeared on both 1994's Avant album, *Who's Bridge* – an uncharacteristically conventional piano trio album also featuring bassist Brad Jones – and *No Idea* (DIW; 1996), where bass duties were performed by Greg Cohen. Mengelberg's most intriguing 1990s album, though, is the series of live duets below. His quartet album of 2002, *Four in One* (Songlines), was well-received, and doffed a cap to a significant influence of his, Thelonious Monk. Mengelberg continues to compose for, and improvise with, the ICP on a regular basis. [CP]

⊙ **Change of Season** (1984; Soul Note). Featuring trombonist George Lewis and the soprano of Steve Lacy alongside bassist Arjen Gorter, Mengelberg and Bennink, an album showcasing the pianist's experiments with freedom and structure.

⊙ **Impromptus** (1988; FMP). Thirteen ostensibly unlinked pieces for Mengelberg's solo piano.

⊙ **The Root Of The Problem** (1996; hatOLOGY). Recorded in Cologne, a thoroughly absorbing set of duets and trios with various combinations of French serpent/tuba player Michel Godard, German trumpeter Thomas Heberer, saxophonist Steve Potts and German drummer Achim Kremer.

Berlin Contemporary Jazz Orchestra

⊙ **Berlin Contemporary Jazz Orchestra** (1989; ECM). Excellent album of music for improvising orchestra. Mengelberg provides two highlights: "Salz" and "Reef Und Kneebus", which characteristically draw on classical structures to produce thoughtful jazz.

Johnny Mercer

Vocals, songwriter.

b. Savannah, Georgia, 18 Nov 1909; d. 25 June 1976.

A dripping-with-charm white Southerner, Johnny Mercer began singing with Paul Whiteman and writing material for him in 1932: hits that emerged included "Pardon My Southern Accent" and "Here Come The British, Bang Bang!" (a jazzy epitaph for the Empire), as well as two duets with Jack Teagarden, "Fare Thee Well To Harlem" and its follow-up "Christmas Night In Harlem". (In this period a black social club from the South voted Mercer "our favourite colored singer on radio".) In the 1930s he recorded regularly with young stars such as Wingy Manone, Benny Goodman, Teagarden and Eddie Condon, and after leaving Whiteman he became a radio personality, introducing Benny Goodman's band and Bob Crosby's orchestra on the 1939 Camel Caravan programmes (and singing his own material with them). From 1943 he introduced his own series, *Johnny Mercer's Music Shop*, which lasted two years.

In 1941 (the year he wrote "Blues In The Night" with Harold Arlen, the greatest blues lyric after "St Louis Blues") Mercer founded Capitol Records, employing young talent such as Paul Weston, Matty Matlock and Eddie Miller as staffers, signing young jazzmen such as Nat Cole and Stan Kenton to long contracts, and recording duets with the likes of Wingy Manone, Bing Crosby and Cole. Later he gave up Capitol to concentrate on writing lyrics (and sometimes music), plus "special material" for albums such as *Bing And Louis*, on which he wrote all the lyrics and the sleevenotes. In 1961, with Henry Mancini, Mercer wrote probably his most famous song of all, "Moon River", for *Breakfast at Tiffany's*. His 1960s solo albums (some recorded in London with Pete Moore) are reflective pieces, bringing to the fore a strange yearning quality that was always implicit in his singing. He remains one of the most loved personalities in twentieth-century popular music, and one of its greatest lyricists. [DF]

⊙ **Pardon My Southern Accent** (1932–40; Conifer). The perfect complement to the CD below, this set has treasures to spare, including duets with Jack Teagarden, Wingy Manone and Ginger Rogers, plus four classics with Bing Crosby, including the irresistible "Mr Meadowlark".

⊙ **Johnny Mercer** (1942–9; Capitol Collectors). Beginning with "Strip Polka", Mercer's first for Capitol, this has classics like "I Lost My Sugar In Salt Lake City", "GI Jive" and "Glow Worm", plus rarer specialities like "Save The Bones For Henry Jones" (with Nat Cole). The best all-round Mercer collection so far, along with the set listed below.

⊙ **Personality; Johnny Mercer sings** (1933–50; ASV). While there's some duplication with the above, this ASV collection has a number of delicious rarities including his 1933 "Lazybones", "Hooray For Love" (1947) and "She's Shimmyin' On The Beach Again!" with Ben Pollack and the Skylarks (1950) amid 26 fine tracks.

⊙ **An Evening With Johnny Mercer** (1971; DRG). Mercer reminiscing and singing in concert as part of Maurice Levine's "Lyrics And Lyricists" series. Although the show is edited, his reminiscences are delightful and the songs (with Margaret Whiting and Robert Sands) as great as they come.

Chucho Merchan

Bass, electric bass, guitars.

b. Bogotá, Colombia, 25 Dec 1953.

From 1968 Merchan was playing in Colombia with salsa, Latin and rock bands. In 1970 he went to the USA to play and study, then in 1972–3 toured in South America from his base in Colombia. From 1974–9 he was in Britain studying music and taking a degree at Cambridge College of Arts and Technology. Then he came to London and, from 1980–82, was with Nucleus, playing on the 1980 album *Awakening* and touring internationally. He formed his own band, Macondo, in 1980; in 1983 it won the GLAA Young Jazz Artists of the Year and the European Young Jazz Artists of the Year. Merchan also played with the award-winning group Sunwind and has worked as a session musician with various rock and pop stars, as well as jazz musicians such as Mose Allison, Gordon Beck, John Taylor and Hank Crawford, and with Working Week. [IC]

Helen Merrill

Vocals.

b. New York, 21 July 1930.

After early work as a singer with seminal members of the bop generation (including Charlie Parker), Merrill married clarinettist Aaron Sachs and sang with the Earl Hines sextet (1952). From 1954–8 she recorded extensively for Emarcy, including a classic album with Clifford Brown, before moving first to Italy, then back to the USA, and then to Japan, where she lived and recorded from 1969–72. After coming back to Chicago, Merrill continued recording regularly, with, among others, pianist John Lewis (1976), Pepper Adams (1979), Bucky Pizzarelli (1980), Urbie Green and Stephane Grappelli (1986). She is a deeply committed jazz singer who, like Barbara Lea, has refused to allow changing music fashions to compromise her musical beliefs. [DF]

⊙ **Helen Merrill** (1954–7; Verve). A good sampler of Merrill's early work with Hal Mooney, Quincy Jones and Gil Evans.

Merseysippi Jazz Band

Based in Liverpool, the Merseysippi Jazz Band has been one of Britain's best revivalist jazz ensembles for nearly fifty years. Semi-professional since its formation in 1948, the band has achieved a remarkable consistency of personnel, with founder members John Lawrence (cornet), Ken Baldwin (guitar/banjo), Frank Robinson (piano) and Don Lydiatt (clarinet) still in attendance in 1999. During the 1950s the band created a national impact with club and concert appearances in Liverpool, London and elsewhere (in 1957 they opened Liverpool's Cavern Club as resident band and stayed for two years), and recorded regularly for Esquire. From the 1960s they continued playing and recording, and appeared regularly at Liverpool's Mardi Gras and Sportsman clubs before beginning a residency at Hartley's Wine Bar in 1984 which continues in 1999. They have also been regular visitors to Sacramento's jazz festival and in February 1999 celebrated their 50th anniversary in Liverpool. Their regular use of a two-trumpet line-up allows the Merseysippi Jazz Band to specialize in the two-beat West Coast style of Lu Watters, but they play across the complete range of classic jazz with enviable originality of repertoire and stylistic nicety. [DF]

⊙ **Mersey Tunnel Jazz** (1956–7; Lake). Two vintage albums – *Mersey Tunnel Jazz* and *West Coast Shout* – both recorded for Esquire, and both featuring the efficient two-trumpet team of Pete Daniels and John Lawrence. The band's repertorial adventure was apparent even then; "Duff Campbell's Revenge", "Hop Frog" and "Tres Moutard" are far from trad standards.

⊙ **The Quality Of Mersea** (1996; MJB). On their own label, a well-recorded programme with niceties including Dick Cary's "Henry Hudson", "Smokey Mokes" and Clarence Williams's splendidly titled "I'm Going Back To Bottomland".

Louis Metcalf

Trumpet, vocals.

b. St Louis, Missouri, 28 Feb 1905; d. 27 Oct 1981.

During the 1920s Metcalf recorded with most of the best of the period, including Charlie Johnson, Sidney Bechet, Sam Wooding, Willie "The Lion" Smith, Jelly Roll Morton, Duke Ellington, Luis Russell and King Oliver. By the early 1930s he was working regularly in Canada, then came back to New York to run his own Heatwave Club during the late 1930s and early 1940s, as well as bandleading and playing riverboats. From 1947–50 he was back in Canada again with his own club and band, then led at various New York clubs, including the Embers. Recorded examples of Metcalf in later years are regrettably scarce, although he made titles for Franwell Records in 1954–5, as well as a session for Stereocraft in 1958. [DF]

➤➤ **Duke Ellington** *(Early Ellington [MCA])*.

Pat Metheny

Guitars.

b. Lee's Summit, Missouri, 12 Aug 1954.

Metheny played French horn throughout his time at high school and took up the guitar when he was thirteen. At first he was totally under the influence of Wes Montgomery, but soon began to find his own personal style, inspired by the example of two local Kansas City musicians, a trumpet player called Gary Sivils and a drummer called Tommy

Ruskin. He developed with amazing precocity and while still in his teens was teaching at both the University of Miami and Boston's Berklee School of Music. At 19 he joined Gary Burton's band, staying with it for three years (1974–7) and playing on three of Burton's ECM albums. After leaving he formed his own group with Lyle Mays on keyboards, and before the end of the decade had become a superstar, pulling in huge crowds wherever he played, his albums selling hundreds of thousands of copies. Like Weather Report, he achieved this without in any way diluting his art or "playing down" to the public.

Since the mid-1970s he has played or recorded with many of the most vital musicians in contemporary jazz, including Paul Bley, Sonny Rollins, Steve Swallow, Dave Liebman, Eberhard Weber, Julius Hemphill, Jack DeJohnette, Mike Brecker, Charlie Haden and Billy Higgins. Metheny has also blossomed into a fine small-group composer, as well as completing three film scores, including one for John Schlesinger's *The Falcon and the Snowman* (1985). By then he had recorded twelve records in nine years, three of them receiving Grammy awards. That busy year he also recorded *Song X* with one of his idols, Ornette Coleman.

In the later 1980s Metheny recorded, co-produced and contributed compositions to Jack DeJohnette's *Parallel Realities* album; Herbie Hancock, who was featured on the recording, joined Metheny, DeJohnette and Dave Holland for a world tour in 1990. In June that year Metheny released a trio recording with Holland and Roy Haynes, touring with them in the USA and Europe that autumn. Metheny's "Change of Heart", from that album, won a Grammy as the best instrumental composition of 1990.

In the 1990s, Metheny continued to tour with his group, but also worked and recorded with other stars including John Scofield, Herbie Hancock, Michael Brecker, Dave Holland and Jack DeJohnette. In 1996, he spent some time with free-improvising guitarist Derek Bailey and then recorded a three-CD album with him live at The Knitting Factory, New York. Near the end of the decade, Metheny left his record company Geffen, signed with Warner Bros, and in 1997 recorded the album *Imaginary Day* for them. During tours in 1998 he would frequently open each concert by playing his latest invented instrument, the forty-two-string Pikasso guitar which is so large that it has to be played while on a stand that has been specially made for it. The long-term group recorded almost an album a year throughout the 80s and 90s. Metheny's other established, regular unit is a trio with Christian McBride and Antonio Sanchez.

Pat Metheny's music, whatever the context, has its roots in jazz, rock and country music and it is characterized by intensely melodic compositions, clear rhythms perfectly executed, and an inexhaustible flow of melodic improvisation. Metheny has an extraordinary understanding of, and insight into, the making of improvised music. [IC]

⊙ **As Falls Wichita, So Falls Wichita Falls** (1981; ECM); **Travels** (1983; ECM). *Wichita* features a trio with Mays and Nana Vasconcelos, creating atmospheric and gloriously romantic music. Bassist Steve Rodby and Danny Gottlieb are added on *Travels* (originally released as a double LP), a live session full of dynamism and incident.

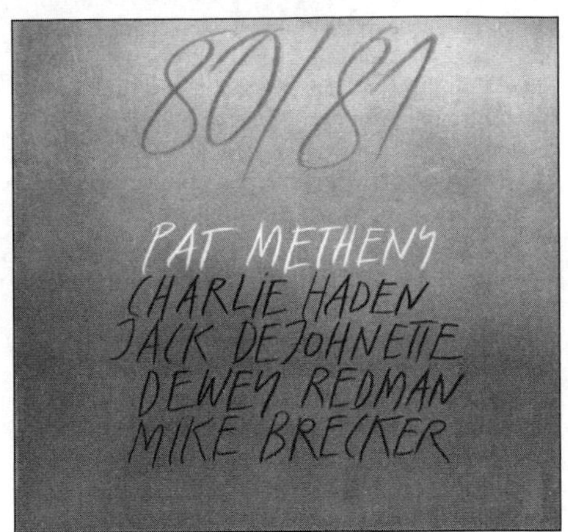

Pat Metheny and Ornette Coleman

⊙ **Song X** (1985; Geffen). Metheny and his hero get together at last, with Haden, DeJohnette and Ornette's drumming son, Denardo. Metheny shines incandescently in this company, and produces music of a furious intensity that contrasts sharply with his usual output.

Pat Metheny

⊙ **Question And Answer** (1989; Geffen). Metheny with Dave Holland and Roy Haynes, playing a mixture of standards and pieces by himself and Coleman. Metheny is at his most eloquent in pared-down ensembles where his guitar speaks directly to listeners, and Haynes and Holland are ideal support.

⊙ **The Sign Of 4** (1996; Knitting Factory). Metheny and Derek Bailey with percussionists Gregg Bendian and Paul Wertico, creating music that is surprisingly more user-friendly than Metheny's *Zero Tolerance For Silence*. Metheny said: "I feel he's [Bailey's] somebody who has distilled a particular way of thinking about music to such a point, that the whole idea of idiom is completely obliterated ... In my case it's kind of the opposite – I feel like I embrace almost everything to the point where there is no idiom."

⊙ **Imaginary Day** (1997; Warner Bros). This is Metheny's most orchestral album, though the musical architecture that so fascinates him is created electronically. But he also has two acoustic multi-instrumentalists in the group, Mark Ledford and David Blamires, both of whom are also vocalists. Seven of the nine compositions are jointly by Metheny/Lyle Mays. Only the gorgeous ballad, "Too Soon Tomorrow", is by Metheny alone, whose featured guitar solo is superb, and "Into The Dream", which is his solo Pikasso guitar feature. There is a huge variety of music on the album, and, as always, the rhythmic grooves are excellent.

Mezz Mezzrow

Clarinet, saxophones.

b. Chicago, 9 Nov 1899; d. Paris, 5 Aug 1972.

Eddie Condon, in his book *We Called It Music*, slandered Mezz Mezzrow (real name Milton Mesirow) so wickedly that he turned into a cartoon figure; Mezzrow's own *Really the Blues*, full of Spillane-speak, Chicago wind and drumbeating, sealed the image of a character much larger, and funnier, than life. The young Mezzrow possessed limited musical ability and compounded the problem by spending a lot of time among the young white musicians of Eddie Condon's circle, where his constant preoccupation with black players (Condon called him "Southmouth") and his determination to identify with them was a source of embarrassment all round. "When a man is trying so hard to be something he isn't," said Sidney Bechet cruelly, "then some of that will show in the music. The idea of it will be wrong."

As his career progressed, Mezzrow's projects increasingly included black players: during the 1930s he put together big bands containing Benny Carter, Pops Foster and Teddy Wilson, but they seldom lasted long because of Mezzrow's waywardness, fondness for drugs and role as a marijuana supplier. "Mezz got a big band together," Condon recalled, "to audition for some Bond Bread commercials. We all assembled and the bakers were sitting there waiting for him to give the downbeat. Just before he did Mezz turned round to the prospective sponsors and said, 'Man, am I high!' We didn't get the job." However, many of Mezzrow's records – his 1933 big band, his sessions with Frankie Newton, the faultless sets with Tommy Ladnier and Bechet for Hugues Panassié in 1938, the post-war Mezzrow-Bechet masterpieces on his King Jazz label – are marvellous creations, revealing his deep feeling for the blues, well-thought-out lines, agility and appealing acid tone. Following his appearance at the 1948 Nice jazz festival, Mezzrow became a big star in Europe, touring regularly with bands including Buck Clayton, Gene Sedric and Jimmy Archey, recording in Paris with Lionel Hampton, and working part-time as tour "gofer" and marijuana supplier for Louis Armstrong. [DF]

⊙ **Mezz Mezzrow 1928-36; 1936–9; 1944** (Classics). Classics have at last got around to Mezz, and much of this work, though eccentric, is appealing. Volume three has sides by the Mezzrow-Bechet partnership which remains a central influence on postwar Revivalism and great music in itself.

⊙ **The Quintessential Milton Mezz Mezzrow** (1928–53; King Jazz). Eccentric but useful collection which includes several of Mezz's incidental wanderings into jazz history (playing drums on the Chocolate Dandies' "Krazy Kapers" for one), as well as important titles with Ladnier, Bechet and Clayton.

⊙ **In Paris 1955** (Jazz Time). Mezzrow's last major sessions, originally titled *A La Scola Cantorum* and consisting of two extended 12-bar improvisations. Mezz plays wonderfully on his home territory – the blues – and there are some fine bonus titles from a couple of months later too.

➤➤ **Sidney Bechet** *(Masters Of Jazz: Sidney Bechet).*

Pierre Michelot

Bass, arranger.

b. Saint Denis, France, 3 March 1928.

After taking up the bass at sixteen, Michelot soon began working with US musicians in Paris and making records, for example with Coleman Hawkins in 1949. He worked regularly, gigging and recording with Kenny Clarke, Miles Davis in 1956 and 1957, and Bud Powell from 1960–62. He became more involved in studio work and arranging for the next two decades, and took part in the filming of *Round Midnight* (1985). Michelot is a beautifully propulsive and melodic player, easily the best bebop bassist that Europe has produced; while the opportunity to play with leading Americans clearly refined it further, his style was already perfectly balanced by the time he came to the fore. [BP]

➤➤ **Dexter Gordon** *(Our Man In Paris).*

Velma Middleton

Vocals.

b. St Louis, Missouri, 1 Sept 1917; d. 10 Feb 1961.

After working as a chorus girl, Velma Middleton joined Louis Armstrong's big band in 1942 and remained with him throughout the great days of the All Stars. A good-humoured performer whom one critic described as looking like "a sequinned football" on stage, she was always the female singer that Louis liked working with best. Middleton's voice was not her strongest point – "Actually," says Barney Bigard, "she was a mediocre singer but one hell of an entertainer!" – yet her amiable singing fitted admirably with the broad style of Armstrong's group, frequently turning up in hilarious duos like "Baby It's Cold Outside" and "That's My Desire". Her end was sudden and tragic: she had a stroke on tour with Louis in Africa, was too ill to be moved far and died in Sierra Leone three weeks later. [DF]

➤➤ **Louis Armstrong** *(Plays W. C. Handy; Satch Plays Fats).*

Midnite Follies Orchestra

Formed in 1978 by ragtime pianist Keith Nichols and arranger Alan Cohen, the Midnite Follies Orchestra was Britain's best jazz repertory orchestra, performing re-creations of important items by Ellington, Calloway, Wooding, Henderson and others, as well as imaginative originals composed by the leaders. Musicians featured within the MFO included, at various times, Alan Elsdon, Nick Stevenson, Dave Saville, Digby Fairweather (trumpets), Gordon Blundy, Pete Strange (trombones), John Barnes, Will Hastie, Olaf Vas, Mac White, Alan Cohen, Randolph Colville (reeds), as well as Keith Nichols (piano/soprano/trombone/vocals), Richard Warner, Keith Greville (guitars), Bob Taylor (bass) and Laurie Chescoe (drums). The MFO was swiftly contracted to EMI after a first night at London's 100 Club, then appeared regularly on radio and TV, produced two well-reviewed albums, and played the club circuit and festivals in Britain and Europe, as well as starring regularly in London concert halls. By the 1990s it had become inactive. [DF]

⊙ **Hotter Than Hades** (1978; EMI). The Follies' first album, featuring singer Johnny M, arrangements by Nichols and Cohen, and hot solos from Barnes, Elsdon and Hastie.

Palle Mikkelborg

Trumpet, composer, conductor.

b. Copenhagen, 6 March 1941.

Mikkelborg is self-taught as a trumpet player, but studied conducting at the Royal Music Conservatory, Copenhagen. He began to play the trumpet in 1956 and earned his stripes playing at the Vingaarden and Montmartre clubs in Copenhagen in the early 60s. Long-term, stable commitments of his were the Danish Radio Jazz Group and its Big Band, for which he played for the decade's latter half and into the 1970s, eventually conducting his own compositions and interpreting the work of other composers. But he also led his own bands from 1965 and formed a quintet with drummer Alex Riel in 1966, which in 1968 played at the Newport jazz festival and won first prize at the Montreux festival. Since then he has continued to lead his own groups: V8 in the early 1970s, again with Alex Riel; and from the late 1970s to the mid-1980s the group Entrance. He was also a regular member of the Peter Herbolzheimer big band in the early 1970s. Mikkelborg has also played, for varying periods, with George Russell, Dexter Gordon, Jan Garbarek, Abdullah Ibrahim, Charlie Mariano, Maynard Ferguson, Don Cherry and Gil Evans.

His main influence, both conceptually and as a trumpet player, is Miles Davis. But he has absorbed his influences and created a way of making music that is all his own. He is a magnificent acoustic trumpet player with a lyrical sound and huge range, and he is also perhaps the very finest exponent of electric trumpet, deploying the new sounds and timbres with great artistry. A prolific composer, he has written long pieces for big ensembles. Some key works are: *Journey To ...* (1978), for symphony orchestra and soloists; *Dis* (1981), for flute and percussion; *A Simple Prayer* (1981), for choir, gamelan ensemble and soloists; *Pictures* (1983), for bass, piano, soloists and symphony orchestra; and *Aura* (1984), a tribute to Miles Davis, for big band and soloists, featuring Davis himself. His interests appear to increasingly favour composition over performance, and his music has found a spiritual home of sorts at ECM records. [IC]

⊙ **Heart To Heart** (1986; Storyville). Mikkelborg in a poetic trio with keyboardist Kenneth Knudsen and bassist Niels-Henning Ørsted Pedersen.

➤➤ **Shankar** *(Vision).*

Joakim Milder

Tenor and soprano saxophones, composer.

b. Stockholm, Sweden, 24 Sept 1965.

Having taken up the saxophone in his mid-teens, Joakim Milder studied improvisation at the Conservatory in his native Stockholm, an institution at which he currently teaches himself. His first professional job was with Fredrik Norén, Sweden's equivalent of Art Blakey (both for the hard-bop orientation of his band – which Milder attempted to broaden with his more contemporary compositions – and for his talent-spotting prowess), but Milder has also contributed his adventurous, highly original sound to both the Stockholm Jazz Orchestra and the Stockholm Big Band, with which, in 1986, he recorded an album of material arranged by pianist Nils Linberg and sung by Lena Jansson. In addition to recording with reedsmen Cennet Jonsson (in his ten-piece) and Jonas Knutsson, bassist Palle Danielsson and (a free/standards duo) pianist Soren Norbo, Milder began recording as a leader in the late 1980s, producing a series of highly distinctive albums. *Still In Motion* (Dragon; 1989) was all originals, *Consensus* (Opus 3; 1992) took a sideways look at twelve standards including "My Funny Valentine" and "Someday My Prince Will Come", and *Ways* (Dragon; 1992) was chamber music involving French horn, euphonium and strings, and these three strands continue to manifest themselves in Milder's music. He can also be heard on the highly rated 1997 album of Krzysztof Komeda music by Tomasz Stanko, *Litania*, where he is effectively contrasted with the hotter saxophone playing of Bernt Rosengren. He has latterly also made his mark as a string arranger for hire, featuring on recordings by electronic specialists Covenant and pop albums by ex-Boyzone Stephen Gately and mature Nordic popsters A-ha. [CP]

⊙ **Sister Majs Blouse** (1993; Mirrors). Dedicated to the music of the late Swedish saxophonist Borje Fredriksson, and involving his rhythm-section – pianist Bobo Stenson, bassist Palle Danielsson, drummer Fredrik Norén – this is a fine, vigorously interactive quartet recording.

Butch Miles

Drums.

b. Ironton, Ohio, 4 July 1944.

A drummer who follows in the grand tradition of old masters like Jo Jones and Gus Johnson, Miles is as capable of working brilliantly in a big-band context (Count Basie 1975–9) as in a Dixieland band (he has worked with everyone from Wild Bill Davison to Gerry Mulligan), and has also spent time accompanying singers as prestigious (and demanding) as Mel Tormé (1972–4) and Tony Bennett (1980). A musician who brings energy and visible enjoyment to every bar of music he plays, Miles is the embodiment of the grand values of classic jazz drumming; in recent years he has also recorded as a singer. [DF]

Lizzie Miles

Vocals.

b. New Orleans, 31 March 1895; d. 17 March 1963.

After early work in medicine shows, tent shows and the vaudeville circuit, Lizzie Miles (Elizabeth Mary Landreaux) became prominent in the 1920s, working first in Chicago and later in New

York, where from 1922 she recorded with stars such as Jelly Roll Morton, Clarence Williams, Louis Armstrong and Kid Ory. In 1924 she travelled to Europe with Alexander Shargenski's troupe, scoring a hit in Paris, where she became known as "La Rose Noire". In 1925, back in the USA, she had a big hit with a version of "I'm Confessin'". Throughout the rest of the 1920s and 1930s she stayed busy (she worked with Fats Waller briefly) but, as happened to many of her contemporaries, her blues singing went out of fashion in the early 1940s. A New Orleans DJ, Joe Mares (brother of the trumpeter Paul Mares), rediscovered her around 1950, recorded her with a trio and began playing her records. Then she started singing again at the Mardi Gras Lounge on Bourbon Street, with Paul Barbarin's band, and by 1955 was featured with Bob Scobey's hugely successful Dixieland band. She went on to sing with bands such as Joe Darensbourg's, but retired in the late 1950s to study religion. [DF]

Ron Miles

Trumpet.

b. Indianapolis, Indiana, 9 May 1963.

Ronald Glen Miles began playing trumpet at the age of eleven, during a summer school in Indiana. After the family moved to Colorado, he studied for his Bachelor of Music at the University of Denver, where he met Fred Hess and the Boulder Creative Music Ensemble, which introduced him to structural improvisation and free music. He attended the postgraduate course at the Manhattan School of Music (1985–6), then returned to Colorado University to study for his Master of Music (1986–99), during which period he recorded an album, *Distance For Safety*, for the small Prolific label. He began teaching at the Metropolitan State College in 1988.

In 1992, when Miles was in the band which toured Europe performing *Sophisticated Ladies* (the musical based on Duke Ellington tunes), he met Mercer Ellington, and for a year after that Miles was in the Ellington orchestra. In 1995 he began playing with Bill Frisell and met Ginger Baker, with whom he also began playing a year later. (Throughout these periods he had been fronting groups of his own). He played on Bill Frisell's magnificent album, *Quartet*, in 1996, and the same year recorded his own second album, *My Cruel Heart*, which established him not only as a new voice on trumpet, but also as a very able and adventurous composer. In 1997 he recorded *Woman's Day*, which further consolidated his reputation, and also that year, worked on Ginger Baker's album *Coward Of The County* – as co-producer, trumpet player and writer of six of the eight tracks.

Miles's playing can veer between ice and fire. He has a reserve and economy which are illuminated by a beautifully rounded sound, but he is also capable of abstract conflagrations in the free jazz vein. His inspirations include Miles Davis, Jelly Roll Morton, Prince and Bill Frisell. [IC]

⊙ **My Cruel Heart** (1996; Gramavision). Drawing from a pool of 14 musicians, Miles's pieces range from big rocky grooves and fusion outings, to the elemental sound of his trumpet plus bass (Artie Moore) and drums (Rudy Royston) – a trio with a stark eloquence. Miles's wife, Kari, plays flute on the title track, a lyrical, ever-changing soundscape, with a rocking finale.

⊙ **Woman's Day** (1997; Gramavision). Miles leads a quartet with Frisell, Moore and Royston for this album of twelve of his compositions, but adds another bass, guitar, bass-clarinet and/or piano on some tracks. The writing is more assured here, and Frisell is a major asset with his range of moody electronic colours. The opening "Dew" is a short and beautifully simple tune, but with "Born Liar" Miles shows he can also write long, totally absorbing pieces.

Bubber Miley

Trumpet, composer.

b. Aiken, South Carolina, 3 April 1903; d. 20 May 1932.

Bubber (James Wesley) Miley began in clubs and cabarets around New York, and toured with blues singer Mamie Smith. (While on tour with her in Chicago he heard King Oliver, and went back every night for two weeks to listen and learn.) In 1923 Duke Ellington heard him in the basement of the Bucket of Blood club on 135th Street, New York, with trombonist Charlie Irvis. Miley then joined Ellington in Elmer Snowden's Washingtonians at the Kentucky club and caused a sensation: spies including Paul Whiteman and his featured trumpeter Henry Busse came to listen to his revolutionary, growling style, and to steal. A handsome good-time youngster who loved to make music and who enjoyed battling with his competitors, Miley next formed a strong team with "Tricky Sam" Nanton in Ellington's new band: "They were always blowing for each other and getting ideas for what they wanted to play," recalled Ellington. Miley helped Ellington to develop many of his compositions and occupied a central role in the band, but by 1929 he was drinking heavily and becoming unreliable (when he did appear, he was often unable to play). Cootie Williams took his place with Ellington and he left to freelance in Europe, working in France with Noble Sissle and at home with Zutty Singleton and Leo Reisman: Miley's records of the period show a disintegrating talent. By 1931 he was playing for revues, including Roger Pryor Dodge's *Sweet And Low* and Billy Rose's *Third Little Show*, and later that year had a show of his own, *Harlem Scandals*, built around his band by Ellington's manager Irving Mills. But tuberculosis set in while he was on the road with the show and he died at 29.

Bubber Miley was a central figure in Duke Ellington's first band and to all Ellington's subsequent music. "Our band changed character when Bubber came in," said Ellington. "That's when we forgot all about the sweet music." [DF]

➤➤ **Duke Ellington** *(Early Ellington).*

Eddie Miller

Tenor saxophone, clarinet, vocals.
b. New Orleans, 23 June 1911; d. April 1991.

A second-generation New Orleans musician, Eddie Miller (Edward Raymond Muller) played the clarinet in home-town groups such as the New Orleans Owls, before driving to New York in 1928 in a Model T Ford to work with bandleaders including Red McKenzie, the Dorseys and Ben Pollack. After Pollack's band broke up, Miller stayed with the re-formed unit under Bob Crosby until 1942, a strong cornerman with his blues singing, showmanship, gift for composition (a 1938 Miller tune, "Slow Mood", with words added by Johnny Mercer, became a 1944 hit for them both), and urbane "white tenor". (Miller also played the legendary clarinet solo on Crosby's hit "South Rampart Street Parade".) After Crosby's band split up, Miller led his own in 1943, then began a round of studio work, including nine years with Twentieth Century Fox, staff work for Capitol and other labels, and a lengthy association with clarinettist Matty Matlock for recordings, radio and the hugely successful *Pete Kelly's Blues* series on radio, TV and film. During this period Miller's saxophone became one of the most familiar sounds on radio and record, even though his work was frequently uncredited (rather like Harry Edison's trumpet). Bob Crosby reunions, a tour of the UK with Alex Welsh (1967) and nine years with Pete Fountain's band back in New Orleans took Miller into the 1970s; in the 1980s he was with Crosby and travelling Europe as a soloist until the onset of senility slowed then stopped his career. His frank, svelte saxophone remains the smoothest graduate of Bud Freeman's school. [DF]

➤➤ **Bob Crosby** *(South Rampart Street Parade).*

Glenn Miller

Trombone, arranger, composer, leader.
b. Clarinda, Iowa, 1 March 1904; reported missing 15 Dec 1944.

Miller flunked music at Colorado University, but gained early trombone experience with territory bands, and in 1926 joined Ben Pollack as trombonist-arranger, arranging mainly the sweet side of Pollack's book. The young trombonist's dual talent quickly became apparent (his writing for strings was influenced by Roger Wolfe Kahn's orchestra), but when Gil Rodin introduced Jack Teagarden's fluent gifts to the band, Miller – who hated being second best – tactfully moved on. By 1930 he was working for Red Nichols and others in pit orchestras (for shows including *Strike Up The Band* and *Girl Crazy*), arranging for radio, and freelancing. In 1932, as MD for film star Smith Ballew's dance band, Miller polished his bandleading style ("He was a hard taskmaster," said Ballew, "often resented by musicians in the band"), and by 1934 was touring with the Dorsey brothers, singing "Annie's Cousin Fanny", and studying in spare moments with Dr Joseph Schillinger. In 1935 he collaborated with Ray Noble to assemble an all-star band to play the Rainbow Room on top of the RCA Building in Radio City, New York, a job for which Noble paid him the high salary of $175 a week. In this band Miller found his elusive "sound", when trumpeter Pee Wee Erwin, famed for his range and endurance, asked to play lead alto parts transposed specially for his instrument (later players, less able than Erwin, declined the pleasure and the music was handed to a clarinettist instead). Noble and Miller – two strong characters – parted company the next year, and Miller began to make serious bandleading plans of his own. Early keymen such as Hal McIntyre and Rolly Bundock joined him; in 1937 the first, slow-moving records were made; and after a year of touring, playing hotels and running at a loss of $19 a week, Miller disbanded.

In 1938 he re-formed with keymen including Willie Schwartz, Tex Beneke and singer Ray Eberle, made his first records for RCA Victor and took an arranger, Bill Finegan. Finegan, whose new boss stringently edited his work, liked Miller, but was bemused by his blunt reluctance to communicate: "Glenn seemed to have the feeling that if he complimented a guy he would ask for a raise," he remembered. By 1939 Miller's fame was growing: a spring season at Glen Island Casino (a teenage centre installed with broadcasting lines) broke records, and so did the one-nighters that followed. A string of singles for RCA helped, as did a radio series for Chesterfield Cigarettes, and by 1940 Miller had taken on more keymen: trumpeters Billy May and Ray Anthony, bassist Trigger Alpert, cornettist Bobby Hackett, the Modernaires vocal group, and arranger Jerry Gray, whose creations such as "Elmer's Tune", "Chattanooga Choo-Choo" and "I've Got A Gal In Kalamazoo" sealed Miller's success. By 1941 he was grossing more than any other bandleader (apart, strangely enough, from Kay Kyser), and that year the hugely successful film *Sun Valley Serenade* (starring John Payne and Sonja Henie) endeared him to audiences worldwide; it was followed by *Orchestra Wives* in 1942.

By then Miller – a staunch patriot – had registered for the draft; later that year he was accepted as a captain in the army. His band split up and Harry James took over the Chesterfield broadcasts, but Miller was soon appointed Director of Bands for the Army Air Force Technical Training Command (AAFTTC); Alpert, Gray and Zeke Zarchy rejoined him, along with new stars including Mel Powell, Bernie Privin and Carmen Mastren, and in 1944 the Glenn Miller AEF (American Expeditionary Forces) Orchestra sailed for England on the *Queen Elizabeth.* They arrived in London in the middle of the Blitz and Miller insisted that his band be rebilleted out of

London in Bedfordshire; their London quarters in Sloane Court were bombed to the ground the same night. Working for the BBC, Miller caused a stir with his attitude, at one stage insisting on tripling the number of microphones for a broadcast – the BBC responded with a battery of additional equipment, none of it connected. He caused a musical sensation too. His *Strings With Wings* feature, broadcast every Saturday morning, was as much admired by the jazz fraternity as it was by Adrian Boult; his Uptown Hall Gang, featuring Privin, Hucko and Powell, was a small-group delight; and his full orchestra was simply better than anything heard in Britain before. In December 1944 Miller went ahead of his orchestra, which had been posted to Paris, to spy out the musical land. His plane disappeared, and a year later he was pronounced officially dead and received a posthumous Bronze Star. "He left before we did – as he usually did!" says Peanuts Hucko. "He didn't leave it to anybody; he didn't send a scout."

Glenn Miller himself was only an average trombonist ("pedestrian, and he knew it," said Benny Goodman), but he led the most commercially successful big band of all, and at its best it ranked with Artie Shaw's as the hardest-swinging white orchestra of its time. The Miller band introduced at least one totally original scoring device (clarinet lead above a section of saxophones); and it featured stronger, more inventive material than any of its rivals. His music has been kept alive in later years by American reassemblies (led by Hucko, among others) and by British bandleaders including the late Syd Lawrence, as well as the Herb Miller organization. [DF]

⊙ **The Complete Glenn Miller And His Orchestra 1938–42** (RCA Bluebird). This 13-disc set is the definitive survey of Miller's greatest years, with superb notes by Mort Goode and complete discographic information.

⊙ **Moonlight Serenade: His 50 finest recordings 1939–43** (Living Era). Two hours and 38 minutes of vintage Miller in superb sound. All the hits are here, but it's still possible to be surprised by the power and swing of Miller's organization on sides like "Caribbean Clipper" – which could easily give Woody Herman's First or Second Herds a gallop for their money!

⊙ **Big Band Bash** (1938–42; Giants of Jazz). Good selection of Miller hits and near-hits from this reliable budget label; excellent sound.

⊙ **Glenn Miller In Hollywood** (1941–2; Mercury). Excellent CD filling in a gap in all the above by collating Miller's music for *Sun Valley Serenade* and *Orchestra Wives*; several hits including the uncut "Chattanooga Choo-Choo" and enchanting "It Happened In Sun Valley", plus "I've Got A Gal In Kalamazoo" with Beneke, Marian Hutton and the Modernaires.

Harry Miller

Bass, cello.

b. South Africa, 21 April 1941; d. 16 Dec 1983.

Miller had music lessons in South Africa and began playing with R&B groups there. He came to the UK in 1961, playing with various people, and then joined Geraldo's Navy for eighteen months on the New York run, which enabled him to experience jazz in New York. Back in London he played with many leading musicians, including John Surman, Mike Osborne, Mike Westbrook's small and big bands, and he joined Chris McGregor's Brotherhood of Breath. In the late 1960s and the 1970s he led his own group, Isipingo, and played with Stan Tracey, Keith Tippett, Elton Dean's Ninesense and Louis Moholo's Culture Shock. He helped to form Lambeth New Music Society, which ran a regular jazz club (Grass Roots), and he was involved in the creation of the Ogun Record Company, for which he and many of his associates recorded. Miller was also a member of the Alan Skidmore quintet when it won the Press Prize at the Montreux festival in 1969. He died following a car crash. [IC]

➤➤ **Mike Osborne** *(Outback)*; **Dudu Pukwana** *(In The Townships)*.

Marcus Miller

Bass guitar, multi-instrumentalist, composer/arranger.

b. Brooklyn, New York, 14 June 1959.

Marcus Miller's family moved, when he was a child, to Rochdale Village in the Jamaica section of Queens, New York, and he grew up there. He took up clarinet at the age of ten, studying it at the New York High School of Music and Art, and then at Queens College. He started playing bass after hearing Larry Graham's slap technique, and other bass influences include Stanley Clarke, Anthony Jackson and Jaco Pastorius. But he also played several other instruments – bass-clarinet, soprano saxophone, keyboards, guitar, drums.

Miller played his first professional gigs with Harlem River Drive and Lonnie Liston Smith, and made his first recording with the flute player Bobbi Humphrey. He has played with many jazz artists and is a slick studio producer but probably his most important work so far has been with Miles Davis in

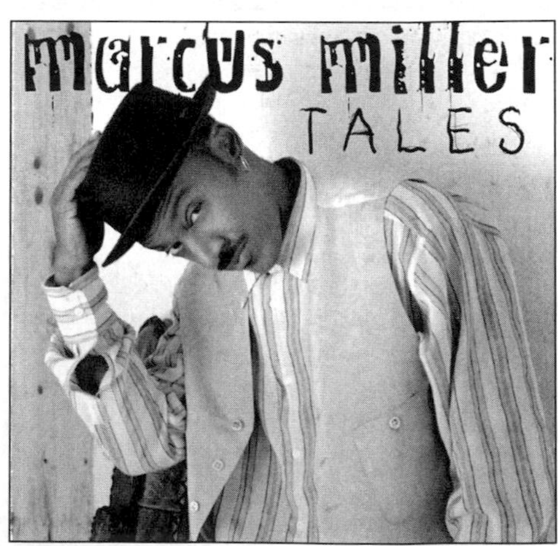

Marcus Miller

the 1980s. He played bass in Davis's band (1981–2), and made an important contribution to the trumpeter's comeback, touring with him and recording the albums *We Want Miles* and *Star People*. Later in the decade, Miller, working in close collaboration with Davis, composed, arranged and often played instruments on the superb albums *Tutu*, *Siesta* and *Amandla*. In the same period, he produced many of David Sanborn's albums, as well as albums by Dizzy Gillespie, George Benson, the Brecker Brothers, Dave Liebman and Kenny Garrett, to name but a few, and played as a session musician for prestigious rock, pop and soul artists (including Frank Sinatra, Aretha Franklin and Luther Vandross).

Marcus Miller is a brilliantly gifted musician and composer/arranger, but his role seems to consist largely in helping others to realize their visions – and in that capacity, his work with Miles Davis had touches of genius. His own albums don't manifest a coherent personal vision, yet there is plenty of time for that to emerge. [IC]

⊙ **The Sun Don't Lie** (1992; Dreyfus). Shades of Miles, Tutu and Pastorius stalk the tracks, but there are some ecstatic rhythms here, and some fine bass playing and soloing by Miller and a few famous guests. The final piece, "The King Is Gone", a tribute to Davis, is extremely moving, with Miller on bass-clarinet and bass guitar, Wayne Shorter on tenor saxophone, and Tony Williams on drums.

⊙ **Tales** (1995; Dreyfus). The spirit of Miles looms even stronger on this. Trumpeter Michael "Patches" Stewart takes the Davis role on horn while Kenny Garrett on the title track duets with him, echoing the trumpet phrases as he often did with Miles – whose voice is even sampled on "True Geminis".

Mulgrew Miller

Piano.

b. Greenwood, Mississippi, 13 Aug 1955.

Miller studied music privately, as well as at school and Memphis State University, at the same time playing in gospel and R&B groups. He toured with the Mercer Ellington band in the late 1970s, including a European visit in 1977. He worked regularly with Betty Carter in 1980, and then was a member of the Woody Shaw quintet from 1981–3, as well as doing prolific freelance work. He joined Art Blakey and the Jazz Messengers from 1983–6, and was subsequently a member of Tony Williams's quintet. In addition he has led his own trio and, as well as making several albums under his own name, has been much in demand for others' recording sessions, including vocalists such as Dianne Reeves and Cassandra Wilson. Miller is a brilliant technician who has absorbed all the influences of 1960s and 1970s jazz piano, and has been one of the key figures in consolidating the piano tradition. [BP]

⊙ **Hand In Hand** (1992; Novus). As hinted by his curriculum vitae, Miller is often at his best with more than just a piano trio, and this session with Kenny Garrett, vibist Steve Nelson and Hendersons Joe and Eddie brings the best out of him, from both the playing and writing points of view.

➤➤ **Tony Williams** *(Foreign Intrigue).*

Punch Miller

Trumpet, vocals.

b. Raceland, Louisiana, 14 June 1894; d. 2 Dec 1971.

Punch Miller (Ernest Burden) was a Louisiana trumpeter who, like many of his fellows (Guy Kelly, Joe Suttler), felt that he had been unjustifiably overshadowed by Louis Armstrong. While Miller's talent could never seriously be compared to Armstrong's, their early years at least show a striking similarity: a publicity shot of the time shows Miller handsome, young, in a brilliant white suit, looking uncannily like Louis. He was a powerful trumpeter who knew how to make a show and was proud of his fly-fast fingering: "Some of the men from that school had a few things that they did even better than Louis," says Milt Hinton. (In fact, "fast-fingering" is a spectacular but easy device which Armstrong consciously abandoned early on for something greater, on King Oliver's advice.) Miller's career showed signs of following Louis's, too: he played with Kid Ory's band in New Orleans, with Erskine Tate, Freddie Keppard and Earl Hines (for one night) in Chicago, and by the mid-1930s was in New York with second-line bands such as Leonard Reed's. By the 1940s Miller was back in Chicago for club work, then tours with carnivals and circuses. Apart from work with George Lewis (1964–5), this was the pattern for the rest of his life, except for one fine final fling: *Till The Butcher Cuts Him Down* (1971), one of the most moving jazz films, shows Miller, on leave from a terminal hospital, defiantly playing his show-stopping routine to an enthralled audience at Newport, with such great trumpeters as Dizzy Gillespie and Bobby Hackett in respectful attendance. [DF]

⊙ **Prelude To The Revival Vol. 1** (1941; American Music). The fast-fingered Punch is at his powerful best here, with just piano and drums to accompany him.

⊙ **New Orleans 1957** (504 Records). Later Miller, but he kept his technique in good fettle and his playing here is as impressive as ever.

Lucky Millinder

Leader.

b. Anniston, Alabama, 8 Aug 1900; d. 28 Sept 1966.

Lucky (Lucius) Millinder was a natural choice to take over Irving Mills's third band, the Mills Blue Rhythm Band, when it moved into the Cotton Club in 1934, replacing Cab Calloway. Like Calloway, Millinder was a high-powered frontman with a gift for showmanship and a canny eye for commercial appeal. He also had such a retentive ear for music that reputedly he could conduct the hardest score after one hearing, including the difficult and revolutionary arrangements devised by Chappie Willett – though in fact Millinder worked hard on the scores, stayed up all night to study them, and took advice from his deputy, Bill Doggett. Besides being "the best conductor I've ever seen" (Dizzy Gillespie), Millinder was a popular and personable employer and ran a successful band: one great line-up from 1943 included Gillespie, Doggett, Freddie Webster and Tab Smith. In 1952 he retired to become a liquor salesman and later a successful DJ. [DF]

⊙ **Mills Blue Rhythm Band** (1931–6; Classics). The saga of the Mills Blue Rhythm Band in four volumes; variable output but at its best magnificent with solos from "Red" Allen, Buster Bailey, J. C. Higginbotham and Tab Smith.

⊙ **Lucky Millinder 1941–2** (Classics). A fascinating collection of later Millinder after the final demise of the Mills Blue Rhythm Band, with contributions from Bill Doggett, Rosetta Tharpe, Tab Smith and Dizzy Gillespie.

Mills Brothers

One of the twentieth century's most successful brother acts, the Mills Brothers consisted of John (1899–1935), Herbert (b.1912), Harry (1913–82) and Donald (b.1915). Beginning at an early age on the radio in Cincinnati, they graduated to New York in 1930 and started their own coast-to-coast radio show a year later. Their trademark was imitating instruments as well as singing, and this device earned them international fame, several hit records, and regular appearances in films (*Big Broadcast Of 1932*, *Rhythm Parade* (1943), and *When You're Smiling* (1950), to name just three). Apart from their solo success the Brothers regularly teamed up on record and radio with fellow stars like Louis Armstrong, Ella Fitzgerald and Bing Crosby. After the death of elder brother John, the brothers' father, John Senior, took over the role of bass singer, continuing until 1956 when he retired. After this the Brothers toured as a trio, continuing to score success at home and internationally. Their biggest hits included "Paper Doll" (1943), "Lazy River", "Glow Worm" (1952) and, their last hit for Decca, "Queen Of The Senior Prom" (1957). After switching from Decca to Dot Records, the Brothers also made their presence felt in the rock years with two US Top 30 hits, "Get A Job" and "Cab Driver". A well-remembered album *Board of Directors* teamed them up with Count Basie in 1967. After Harry's death in 1982, Donald and Herbert continued touring, and in 1989 Donald was joined by his son John singing old and new material. [DF]

⊙ **The 1930s Recordings** (2000; JSP). Covers the Mills Brothers' formative recordings in a beautifully re-mastered 5-CD set.

Irving Mills

Impresario, publisher, composer, lyricist, leader.
b. New York, 16 Jan 1884; d. 21 April 1985.

While Mills's contribution to jazz was as an organizer rather than a musician, his achievements are central to jazz history. After founding a publishing company, Mills Music, in 1919, he became Duke Ellington's manager (1926–39) and by his skilled promotion helped turn Ellington into the star he deserved to be; other acts that Mills helped along the way included Cab Calloway, Benny Carter and Fletcher Henderson. He was also active in organizing record sessions, notably for the Whoopee Makers, the Irving Mills Hotsy Totsy Gang (featuring Bix Beiderbecke, Benny Goodman, Jack Teagarden and Hoagy Carmichael) and the Mills Blue Rhythm Band. In 1936 Mills founded the Master and Variety record labels, and after his partnership with Ellington had ceased he remained active in a variety of entrepreneurial roles, as well as reaping the rewards of his publishing activities with Ellington and others. [DF]

Craig Milverton

Piano, keyboards, vocals.
b. Bexley, Kent, 20 Aug 1967.

Milverton began on the piano at the age of 7 and first performed in public when he was 10. Moving to Devon in 1985, he toured with R&B band Junkyard Angels from 1987 to 1991. He had a brief stint playing in Zurich with trombonist Roger Mark's Quintet in 1989, before sustained spells with the Pete Allen Jazz Band (1992-5) and Terry Lightfoot's Band (1995-8). From 1995 to the present he has been a regular member of Digby Fairweather's Half Dozen, and has also worked with trumpeter Paul Lacey's Quintet, and the seven-piece Orjazzmic led by trombonist Ian Bateman. More recently he has toured with George Melly and Digby Fairweather in their *Singing And Swinging The Blues* show. A busy leader and soloist, he also runs two trios; one without drums (in tribute to Nat Cole), and another, with drummer Steve Brown and bassist Orlando Le Fleming, that covers standards, originals and more contemporary jazz styles. Milverton's main influences are Oscar Peterson, Nat Cole and Bill Evans, but he is a multi-faceted soloist just as happy to play boogie-woogie as jazz fusion. [DF]

⊙ **A Time To Move** (1998; Loose Tie Records). This brilliant collection illustrates Milverton's polymath approach to jazz piano ranging from the jazz-funk of the title track to standards including "Sophisticated Lady" and "Corcovado". Guests include reedmen Ian Ellis and Julian Stringle, and trombonist Ian Bateman.

Pino Minafra

Trumpet, flugelhorn, bugle, dijeridoo, ocarina, percussion, voice, megaphone.
b. Ruvo di Puglia, Italy, 1951.

Minafra played in banda ensembles (brass groups performing Verdi, Puccini and arrangements of other opera works) as a child, then studied under Nino Rota at the Bari Conservatory. He led his own Dirty Half Dozen on a Splasc(h) LP, made a disc with the

December Thirty Jazz Trio, and has recorded on different occasions with Dutch musicians Misha Mengelberg, Willem Breuker, Ernst Reijseger and Han Bennink. Minafra has a propensity for madcap antics – playing horn through megaphone, wildly quoting or jumping around on stage – and for genre jumping, but he is also possessed of a lovely tone, not un-Miles-y, when he turns romantic. Minafra established the Italian Instabile Orchestra in 1990 – a large ensemble containing many of the leading lights of Italian improvised music and creative jazz, and the group has now made four records: *Skies Of Europe* (1995; ECM), *Live In Noci And Rive de Gier* (1992; Leo), *European Concerts '94–'97* (1997; NelJazz), and the two-disc *Italian Instabile Festival* (1998; Leo). His ongoing group is the Sud Ensemble, which released the fine studio date *Sudori* (1995; Victo), but has a long-standing, regular association with Giovanni Trovesi's Octet and Keith Tippett's band Tapestry. An important organizer, Minafra is the artistic director of the Europe jazz festival in Noci and also directs the Talos festival in Ruvo di Puglia. [JC]

Johnny Mince

Clarinet, saxophones.

b. Chicago, 8 July 1912; d. 23 Dec 1994.

After an early spell with Joe Haymes' well-schooled band, Johnny Mince (John H. Muenzenberger) worked for Ray Noble from 1935–7, and with Bob Crosby and Tommy Dorsey from 1937–41. With all these bands he provided the technically able jazz clarinet that every swing band after Goodman and Shaw was expected to supply, with an attractive and recognizable grit-edged tone that he was to keep for life. He also is credited with creating Glenn Miller's "sound" during a rehearsal with Ray Noble by playing a trumpet part intended for an absent Pee Wee Erwin on clarinet. During the war Mince played for shows (including Irving Berlin's *This Is The Army*), moving into studio work at CBS and television (including twenty years on the Arthur Godfrey show) after demobilization. His reappearances on the jazz scene were regular from the 1960s: he led his own bands, played at festivals, toured with the Kings of Jazz (a 1974 package featuring Pee Wee Erwin, Bernie Privin and Dick Hyman) among others, and collaborated regularly with Yank Lawson and Bob Haggart. He also made recordings with the likes of Bobby Hackett and Urbie Green in the 1970s, and in the 1980s he was a featured star in Keith Smith's 100 Years Of American Dixieland package. [DF]

Charles Mingus

Bass, composer; also piano.

b. Nogales, Arizona, 22 April 1922; d. Cuernavaca, Mexico, 5 Jan 1979.

Mingus was brought up in Watts, Los Angeles, and started on trombone and cello as a child,

REDFERNS

Charles Mingus

switching to the bass at sixteen. He played with high school colleagues in the Buddy Collette group, the Al Adams band and the rehearsal band of Lloyd Reese, with whom he studied piano and theory. He worked with the Barney Bigard group in Los Angeles in 1942, before touring briefly with the Louis Armstrong band. He replaced his bass teacher Red Callender in the Lee Young sextet in 1943, then formed his own Strings and Keys trio in 1944, making the first recordings under his own name in 1945. Then he spent some time freelancing and had stints with the co-operative Stars of Swing and with bandleaders Floyd Ray and Cee Pee Johnson. He toured and played with Lionel Hampton, the Red Callender sextet and the Red Norvo trio until 1951, when he settled in New York, gigging with Miles Davis, Billy Taylor, Charlie Parker, Stan Getz, Lennie Tristano, Duke Ellington, Bud Powell and Art Tatum. He formed his own company, Debut Records, in 1952, in which he was later joined by Max Roach, and co-founded the Jazz Composers' Workshop with Teo Macero, John LaPorta and Teddy Charles (1953–5).

Mingus began leading his own quintet or sextet in 1955, known for many years as the Charles Mingus Jazz Workshop, with frequently changing personnel albeit for the virtual permanence of Dannie Richmond after 1956. Mingus deployed the front-line partnerships of Jimmy Knepper-Shafi Hadi in

1957–8, Booker Ervin-John Handy in 1958–9, and Eric Dolphy-Ted Curson in 1959–60. In the summer of 1960 he was the musical director, with Max Roach, of an "alternative festival" at Newport; he was also a founder member of the short-lived Jazz Artists' Guild. After augmenting his group for record sessions, he assembled a big band for the magnificent Town Hall concert in 1962, and led eleven-piece groups for club and record work from 1962–4 and an eight-piece group in 1965–6. He made another attempt at running his own record label, and then spent the year 1967–8 out of music. A new quintet/sextet formed in 1969 – including from 1973–5 Don Pullen and George Adams – and the publication of his "autobiography" *Beneath the Underdog* (1971) both increased Mingus's popularity. Big-band work and records (1971–2 and 1977–8) were aimed successfully at a wider audience but Mingus's regular quintet activity was halted late in 1977 by the onset of sclerosis. Within months of his death the Mingus Dynasty group was formed, led at first by Dannie Richmond, then by Jimmy Knepper and later Jack Walrath, and in 1989 his previously unperformed double-big-band extravaganza *Epitaph* was realized by Gunther Schuller. Since 1991 the Mingus Big Band has performed weekly in New York and tours Europe annually. One of his sons (Eric Mingus, b. 8 July 1964) is a vocalist and bassist, who has recorded his own album, as well as with the Dynasty and with Karen Mantler.

Mingus was unlike any previous jazz composer, although his combination of egocentricity and generosity towards (some of) his sidemen resembled that of his idol Duke Ellington. Since he and his collaborators grew up during or after the bebop era, the structures Mingus evolved from the mid-1950s onwards were looser and lengthier than the majority of Ellington's work. Perhaps as a result, Mingus became one of the forces favouring the development of both "modal jazz" (by introducing passages without chord movement) and "free jazz"; he later deplored what he considered the excesses of the latter, despite revelling in the concept of collective improvisation and encouraging the use of vocalized instrumental tone and similar colouristic devices. A couple of his ballads, such as "Duke Ellington's Sound Of Love", have been widely used by others, and two of his twelve-bar blues have become standards: "Goodbye Pork Pie Hat" and "Wednesday Night Prayer Meeting" (or the related "Better Git It In Your Soul"); it should be emphasized, however, that no one else's versions, nor even his own remakes, sound anything like the enlarged small groups on the 1959 originals.

Like Ellington too, Mingus was aware of the whole history of jazz and this fact, as well as his own innovations, has provided a strong example to others in recent decades. He was frequently not only adding to it but quoting from it, and his output contains somewhat sardonic tributes to musicians such as Jelly Roll Morton and Fats Waller, as well as Duke. Some listeners consider this a disadvantage, finding his

major work, *Black Saint And The Sinner Lady*, too overtly Ellington-influenced. The only thing it lacks, however, is Mingus's magnificent solo bass-playing, which became influential in its own right since he was the first bassist of his generation to ignore the harmonic fundamentals when soloing and to imitate saxophone and piano lines. His larger-than-life personality, underscored by his book, occasionally overshadowed his music but, as his presence recedes further into the past, it becomes clear that his was a unique contribution to jazz. [BP]

⊙ **Charles 'Baron' Mingus** (1945-49; Uptown). There's everything here from attempts at early R&B, Billy Eckstine clones, intelligent small-band modern jazz and adventurous big-band writing. The solos are fairly anonymous (the few bars credited to Eric Dolphy are actually by Art Pepper) but, for anyone remotely into Mingus, this rare material is intriguing.

⊙ **Jazz Composers' Workshop** (1954; Savoy). Fascinating for its hints of what was to come in terms of collective improvisation and occasional suspension of the chord sequence, this is rendered untypical of Mingus because of the sometimes stiff playing of saxophonists John LaPorta and Teo Macero.

⊙ **Pithecanthropus Erectus** (1956; Atlantic). Exactly fifteen months later – it seems like years – the use of sound-effects and the deployment of saxophonists J.R. Monterose and Jackie McLean (against their own instincts, apparently) in R&B techniques of vocalization, along with the "modal" sections of the title track and "Love Chant", cracked open the door to free jazz.

⊙ **New Tijuana Moods** (1957; RCA Victor). The finest hour of the Hadi-Knepper frontline, with the addition of trumpeter Clarence Shaw, is this Mexican extravaganza in which Mingus's moods become those of the whole group.

⊙ **Blues And Roots** (1959; Atlantic). Conceived by its producer as a way of making Mingus more accessible, this nine-piece band has the appearance of a jam session but structured by exhortations from the composer. It includes the original "Wednesday Night Prayer Meeting" and "My Jelly Roll Soul".

⊙ **Mingus Ah Um** (1959; Columbia). Three months later, the above pieces had turned into "Better Git It In Your Soul" and "Jelly Roll Soul", with different melodies but the same feel, and, as well as much other new material, "Goodbye Pork Pie Hat" surfaced for the first time in tribute to the recently deceased Lester Young.

Charles Mingus Presents Charles Mingus (1960; Candid). Mingus's most stripped-down regular group, this quartet is filled out by the dynamic virtuosity of Eric Dolphy, Ted Curson and Dannie Richmond (who is on all these recommended records except the first two). "Folk Forms No. 1" covers the ground from the avant-garde to the backwoods.

The Black Saint And The Sinner Lady (1963; Impulse!). This eleven-piece band was virtually a working group and, with outstanding contributions from the seemingly disparate soloists Quentin Jackson and Charlie Mariano, it is in fact a marvellous conglomeration of everything from nineteenth-century piano to flamenco guitar.

Changes One (1974; Rhino). A late-flowering Mingus group including George Adams, Don Pullen and Jack Walrath breathes life into the composer's obituary tributes to Ellington ("Sound Of Love") and Harry Carney, as well as the extraordinary "Sue's Changes".

Mingus Big Band

Live In Time (1996; Dreyfus). Caught at their regular gig, the posthumous band defies all the odds, because the mainly younger players who populate it really want to put their own energies into this music.

>> **Charlie Parker** *(Jazz At Massey Hall).*

Phil Minton

Vocals, trumpet.

b. Torquay, Devon, UK, 2 Nov 1940.

Minton's father and mother were both singers. He sang as a choirboy, had trumpet lessons from a local teacher and then worked with local bands around south Devon in the late 1950s. In 1962 he moved to London and joined Mike Westbrook, leaving in 1964 to play with rock and blues bands in Europe. He rejoined Westbrook in 1972, and was involved in many of Westbrook's projects through the 1970s and 1980s, including the Blake songs, *Mama Chicago* and *The Cortege*. But from the late 60s Minton has steered from singing to free vocal music – a one-man sound library of larynx-derived musique concrète.

He also played with Maggie Nicols and Julie Tippett in the vocal group Voice, and performed in theatre and improvised duos with other singers. He has been a member of Lindsay Cooper's Film Music and Trevor Watts's Moire Music, and is an institution of the European free improv scene, startling and delighting audiences whether solo or with the likes of John Butcher, Lol Coxhill and Veryan Weston. Minton has matured into a uniquely versatile singer, with a range that stretches from baritone to tenor, from pathos to grand guignol, and from the muscularly operatic to near supersonic bat-squeak. [IC]

Phil Minton, Veryan Weston and Voices From Somewhere

Songs From A Prison Diary (1991; Leo). *Prison Diary* features the extraordinary choir Voices From Somewhere, alternating with Minton and pianist Veryan Weston. Minton is in full, rich, conventional voice here and sings texts by Ho Chi Minh superbly and movingly.

Phil Minton and Roger Turner

Dada Da (1993; Leo). With percussionist Turner, Minton is – as the title suggests – at his most dada-esque, indulging in grotesque abstract noises and freakish vocal timbres – extraordinary and unique.

>> **Lindsay Cooper** *(Oh Moscow);* **Mike Westbrook** *(The Cortege).*

Bob Mintzer

Saxophones, clarinets, flutes.

b. New Rochelle, New York, 27 Jan 1953.

From 1969–70 Mintzer attended Interlochen Arts Academy, and from 1970–74 Hartt College of Music and Manhattan School of Music. He began playing saxophones, flutes and clarinets and writing professionally in 1974, working with Deodato and Tito Puente. In 1975 he worked with Buddy Rich and Hubert Laws, then in 1977 he was with the Thad Jones/Mel Lewis band, Sam Jones and Eddie Palmieri. From 1978–80 he played with Ray Mantilla, Mel Lewis and his own (Bob Mintzer) band. From 1980–82 he played with Jaco Pastorius, Mike Mainieri, Louie Bellson and Joe Chambers; from 1982–4 with Bob Moses, the New York Philharmonic, Brooklyn Philharmonic, American Ballet Theater, the Bob Mintzer big band and quintet, Liza Minnelli and the American Saxophone Quartet. Between 1982–4 he also appeared with the radio bands of Rome, Helsinki and Hamburg as a soloist and composer. In 1991 he became a regular member of the Yellowjackets, a popular fusion group. He has written music for Buddy Rich, Mel Lewis, Art Blakey and Jaco Pastorius, as well as for more commercial ventures. But his forte has always been, and continues to be, meticulously honed and executed big-band jazz. [IC]

Incredible Journey (1985; DMP); **Camouflage** (1986; DMP); **Spectrum** (1988; DMP). Mintzer is a virtuoso saxophonist and a highly competent big-band composer/arranger, as shown by these big-band albums with all-star personnel. The writing is deft and there are some excellent solos by the leader and sidemen.

>> **Peter Erskine** *(Transition);* **Bob Moses** *(Visit With The Great Spirit).*

Billy Mitchell

Tenor and other reeds.

b. Kansas City, Missouri, 3 Nov 1926; d. 18 April 2001.

Mitchell studied in Detroit, and then toured briefly with Nat Towles, Lucky Millinder in 1948 and Woody Herman in 1949, replacing Gene Ammons. He made his recording debut with the Milt Buckner band in 1949. Early in the 1950s he led his own group in Detroit, backing visiting soloists. In 1956–7 he was a member of the Dizzy Gillespie big band, and then replaced "Lockjaw" Davis with Count Basie from 1957–61 and 1966–7. He co-led a six-piece group from 1961–4 with Al Grey and sidemen such as Bobby Hutcherson. In the mid-1960s he was musical director for Stevie Wonder, and in the 1970s was busy with educational seminars and workshops. He also worked as a freelance soloist, and toured the UK in 1984. Mitchell was consistently impressive with his edgy but full-blooded tone and his fluent, linear approach. [BP]

⊙ **This Is Billy Mitchell** (1962; Verve). One of a small number of albums under Mitchell's own leadership, these tracks feature either a quintet (with Bobby Hutcherson) or sextet (trumpeter Dave Burns added) and spotlight his muscular sound on originals by a variety of writers plus a couple of standards.

Blue Mitchell

Trumpet.

b. Miami, Florida, 13 March 1930; d. 21 May 1979.

Richard "Blue" Mitchell began working in R&B bands such as those of Paul Williams in 1951, Earl Bostic from 1952–5 and Red Prysock in 1955. He later settled in New York and became firmly established during the six years he spent with the Horace Silver quintet from 1958–64. When Silver re-formed, it became the Blue Mitchell quintet (initially with Chick Corea on piano) from 1964–9. He then toured with Ray Charles from 1969–71, and with John Mayall from 1971–3, as well as doing prolific freelance work in Los Angeles until his death from cancer. A forthright soloist, he was capable of making a personal contribution in a variety of situations. [BP]

⊙ **The Cup Bearers** (1963; Riverside/OJC). This was the current Horace Silver group with Cedar Walton in place of the leader, with material by trombonist Tom McIntosh as well as a couple of standards. The follow-up album *The Thing To Do*, with Chick Corea at the piano, is worth looking for.

George Mitchell

Cornet, trumpet.

b. Louisville, Kentucky, 8 March 1899; d. 27 May 1972.

George Mitchell's dependable trumpet (he played trumpet-cornet after 1924) first showed up in Southern minstrel shows, where he was taught by Bobby Williams from Kansas City ("one of the outstanding brass bandleaders and very successful at that time", says Dicky Wells), and by 1920 he was working in Chicago with Tony Jackson. Mitchell is remembered mainly for his handful of classic recordings with Jelly Roll Morton, but these formed only a fraction of his career. Throughout the 1920s he was an in-demand sideman, touring out of town and working in Chicago with Carroll Dickerson, Doc Cooke, Lil Hardin Armstrong, Dave Peyton, Earl Hines (he was in Hines's first Grand Terrace band) and Jimmie Noone, among others. "Every so often George would come back home to Louisville from Chicago to help teach the kids in the Booker T. Washington youth band," remembers Jonah Jones, himself a former member. Mitchell retired from music in 1931 to become a bank messenger; later he played with Elgar's Federal Concert Orchestra, but never (contrary to legend) with the Chicago Symphony Orchestra. [DF]

➤➤ **Jelly Roll Morton** *(Jelly Roll Morton Vol. 1: 1926–7).*

Red Mitchell

Bass, piano, vocals.

b. New York, 20 Sept 1927; d. 8 Nov 1992.

Keith Moore Mitchell played piano while becoming established as a bassist, and continued to use it occasionally. He played the piano in the Chubby Jackson band in 1949, but bass with Charlie Ventura in the summer of 1949 and with Woody Herman from 1949–51. He had small-group exposure with the Red Norvo trio of 1952–3 and the Gerry Mulligan quartet in 1954–5. Settling in Los Angeles, he worked regularly with the Hampton Hawes trio from 1955–7, his own quartet in 1957, and Shelly Manne and André Previn from 1957–61, while becoming involved in copious studio work. He co-led a quintet with Harold Land in 1961–2 and resumed his partnership with Hawes in 1965–6. Turning his back on commercial studio recording, he moved to Scandinavia and gigged with the similarly inclined Phil Woods in 1968. He lived in Stockholm until shortly before the end of his life, freelancing successfully, leading his own groups, and returning only occasionally to the USA; he received the Swedish official honour, the Illis Quorum.

Mitchell's early small-group work was strikingly unclichéd, in both accompanying and solo roles. His solos, in particular, sounded different from the then norm because of his varied articulation, often leaving notes to be heard simply through the change of left-hand fingering, without the right hand plucking the string at all. The result of this, and the choice of phraseology to go with it, was a distinctly horn-like approach that can be said to have foreshadowed the style of Scott LaFaro. Perhaps in order to counteract his generally light sound, Mitchell in the 1960s retuned his strings exactly an octave lower than those of the cello, thus giving himself a bottom C as the lowest note on the bass, some years before Ron Carter and others acquired one.

Red's brother, Whitey (Gordon B.) Mitchell (b. 22 Feb 1932), also played bass, working in the rhythm-section of the band led by Oscar Pettiford in 1956 among others, but moved out of the jazz field in the 1960s. [BP]

Red Mitchell

⊙ **Presenting Red Mitchell** (1957; Contemporary/OJC). A quartet featuring elusive tenorman James Clay, pianist Lorraine Geller and a young Billy Higgins is highlighted by the driving work of Mitchell, whether in the rhythm-section or in his superbly phrased solos.

Red Mitchell and Clark Terry

⊙ **To Duke And Basie** (1986; Enja). This first of two duo albums by this pair is great fun: Mitchell sings (for instance, on the miscredited "Thank You For Everything", which is Edmund Anderson's lyric to Strayhorn's "Lotus Blossom"), and his work as a sole accompaniment instrument is exemplary.

Robert Mitchell

Piano, keyboards, composer.

b. Ilford, UK, 28 May 1971.

Son of the singer Norman Mitchell, Robert Mitchell studied piano and classical music privately, before taking a music degree at the City University in London, which included piano study at the Guildhall School. Mitchell began improvising and composing in 1988. From 1991–6 he worked with Quite Sane, a rap/jazz/experimental octet which performed in the UK and abroad. He was also with The Jazz Warriors (1992–5), a band formed by Courtney Pine and Gary Crosby, and rejoined them for a tour of Nepal in 1997. Mitchell has also played with cutting-edge Americans, touring Europe with saxophonist Greg Osby in 1992, and with saxophonist Steve Coleman in 1998. He was a key member of the award-winning crossover band J-Life, and a regular member of Steve Williamson's quartet. In 2000 he assembled the electro-acoustic sextet, Panacea, and recorded an eponymous album for Dune records: talents as formidable as Williamson, Barak Schmool and Michael Mondesir lending their energies to its infectious pan-cultural grooves. Mitchell's piano technique is as quicksilver and comprehensive as is his imagination, and he is an extremely promising composer. [IC]

Roscoe Mitchell

Soprano, alto, tenor and bass saxophones, flute, piccolo, oboe, clarinet, percussion, vocals.

b. Chicago, 3 Aug 1940.

Mitchell played baritone saxophone in his high school band and alto in his senior year. He played both instruments in an army band during military service in Germany, and after demobilization in 1961 played with Henry Threadgill in an Art Blakey-style group. He then joined Richard Abrams's Experimental Band and met Joseph Jarman, Anthony Braxton and others in an association that evolved into the AACM. He led his own sextet in the middle and late 1960s, eschewing the uproarious abstraction of the current avant-garde, and, with his *Sound* and *Congliptious* albums, reintroduced space and silence into a music that breathed freely. In 1969, with Jarman, Lester Bowie and Malachi Favors, he formed the Art Ensemble of Chicago, which became one of the most important groups of the 1970s and 1980s. Mitchell continued to perform and record solo projects, and still regularly teams up with AACM and Art Ensemble veterans. [IC]

⊙ **Roscoe Mitchell** (1978; Chief). Experimental music with some great moments: Mitchell plus trumpeter Leo Smith and trombonist George Mitchell play a long trio for brass and woodwind; eight percussionists, of whom only two are drummers, play a long piece; and Mitchell provides a quiet seventeen-minute saxophone solo.

⊙ **After Fallen Leaves** (1989; Silkheart). Mitchell plus the Swedish Brus trio (piano, bass, drums) play with focus and force.

Hank Mobley

Tenor saxophone.

b. Eastman, Georgia, 7 July 1930; d. 30 May 1986.

Mobley was raised in Newark, New Jersey, and played there with the Paul Gayten R&B band from 1950–51, until discovered by Max Roach, with whom he worked from 1951–3. He also played with Tadd Dameron, Dizzy Gillespie in 1954, and with the Horace Silver quartet, which merged into the Jazz Messengers, from 1954–6. He began a prolific recording career under his own name, while working with Silver, Max Roach and Art Blakey in the later 1950s. He was a member of the Miles Davis quintet in 1961–2, between two absences from the scene due to drug convictions. He continued from 1965 to work and record with Lee Morgan, Kenny Dorham and Elvin Jones. He toured in Europe as a soloist in 1967, 1968 and 1970, and co-led a quintet with Cedar Walton from 1970–72. He moved from New York to Philadelphia in 1975, where ill health later forced him to abandon music. He made a non-playing appearance at the Blue Note relaunch concert in 1985, and played briefly with Duke Jordan in 1986, shortly before his death from double pneumonia.

Donald Byrd said in the mid-1960s, "Hank is to me just as much a personality as Sonny Rollins. I mean, he has so definitely established his own sound and style." Though far less flamboyant than Rollins,

and therefore less widely appreciated, Mobley shared with him an extremely flexible rhythmic approach. This enlivened a choice of notes that would otherwise have come close to being banal but, with a suitably no-nonsense accompaniment, created an exciting air of brinkmanship. His somewhat introverted tone often makes his lines seem a little too laid-back, but the logic of their construction amply repays the dedicated listener. [BP]

Soul Station (1960; Blue Note). The classic Mobley quartet album, with Wynton Kelly, Paul Chambers and Art Blakey, led to several follow-ups, but *Soul Station* is the one that contains "This I Dig Of You", "Dig Dis" and of course the "Doxy"-esque title track.

No Room For Squares (1963; Blue Note). In quintet with Lee Morgan (and on four tracks Andrew Hill), Mobley gets into more challenging modal material. The dance-floor crowd prefer the slightly later *Dippin'*, also with Morgan, for Mobley's rhythmic approach to "Recado Bossa Nova".

➤➤ **Horace Silver** *(Horace Silver And The Jazz Messengers).*

Modern Jazz Quartet (MJQ)

➤➤ *see entry for* **John Lewis**.

Modernaires

The Modernaires were founded as a vocal trio in Buffalo by Hal Dickinson in the early 1930s, and later expanded to a quartet working with Fred Waring and recording with Charlie Barnet (1936). Popular in clubs, theatre and on radio, the Modernaires (Chuck Goldstein, Bill Conway, Ralph Brewster and Dickinson) worked with Paul Whiteman (1938–40) where their extraordinary innovations – high male-vocal lead, close harmony and adventurous voice-leading (all arranged by Bill Conway) – set new artistic precedents for vocal groups and were described by Mel Tormé as "bordering on genius". From 1940 the group sang with the Glenn Miller Orchestra and were later joined by Dickinson's wife, Paula Kelly. The group also appeared in Miller's films *Sun Valley Serenade* and *Orchestra Wives*. Their inimitable close harmony lent much of the character to Miller's most enduring hits, including "Chattanooga Choo-Choo", "I've Got A Gal In Kalamazoo", and "Don't Sit Under The Apple Tree". After Miller disbanded the orchestra they toured theatres, clubs and broadcast as a single act, Paula Kelly joining permanently from the mid-1940s. Later they toured with Bob Crosby (1951), starred on the *Club 15* radio show (1952), *The Bob Crosby TV Show* (mid-1950s) and in 1953 appeared in the film *The Glenn Miller Story*. Hal Dickinson died in 1970 but the group remained active with Tex Beneke and Ray Eberle in Miller revival projects. Their work was an influential forerunner to groups such as the Pastels, Four Freshmen and Hi-Los, and from the 1930s dramatically advanced the art of vocal close harmony. [DF]

Paul Whiteman 1938 – Featuring Jack Teagarden And The Modernaires (Solid Sender). At this period the Modernaires were at their most innovative, and their finely crafted collaborations with Teagarden are extraordinary for the time; listen to "Small Fry" for an example of vocal voicings at least a decade in advance of their time.

Singin' and Swingin' (1951–7; Varese Sarabande). Valuable collection of later Modernaires including knockout versions of "April In Paris" and "The Milkman's Matinee", amongst others. Tex Beneke, Ray Eberle and Marian Hutton all join the regulars on various tracks.

Reunion In Hi Fi (1959; Jasmine). With the surprising addition of trumpeter Dick Cathcart (he sang with them regularly in the 1950s), the Modernaires present a nostalgic re-creation of old hits in the company of fellow Miller singers Marion Hutton, Ray Eberle and Tex Beneke.

Charles Moffett

Drums, trumpet.

b. Fort Worth, Texas, 6 Sept 1929; d. 14 Feb 1997.

Moffett played as a teenager with Ornette Coleman, Dewey Redman and Leo Wright. After navy service in the late 1940s, he taught high-school music in Texas, as well as playing with Little Richard. He moved to New York in 1961, and joined the Ornette Coleman trio, which was intermittently active from 1962–7, including a European tour. During this period he also worked with Archie Shepp and led his own group which included Pharoah Sanders, Alan Shorter and Carla Bley. In the 1970s he moved to San Francisco, teaching music again and gigging with the Moffett Family, including his several children (such as drummer Cody and bassist Charnett). In the 1980s he moved back to New York to teach mentally retarded children.

Moffett was very much a swing-oriented drummer but open to free styles of improvisation; as such, he certainly brought out the more traditional aspects of those "avant-garde" soloists with whom he performed. [BP]

➤➤ **Ornette Coleman** *(At the Golden Circle, Vols. 1 & 2).*

Charnett Moffett

Bass.

b. 10 June 1967.

Charnett Moffett was named after his father, Charles, and Ornette Coleman, who had been best man at his father's wedding. As a teenager he was involved in the family band, and in the early 1980s he acquired a reputation in his own right, working with Wynton Marsalis (c.1983–5) and then with Branford Marsalis (1986). In demand for freelance work, he has played with a wide variety of performers, recording with artists such as David Benoit, Kevin and Robin Eubanks, Kenny Garrett, Mulgrew Miller, Courtney Pine, Wallace Roney, Arturo Sandoval and Sonny Sharrock, and touring with

Ornette in the mid-1990s and both Kenny Garrett and McCoy Tyner in the early 2000s. Since the late 1980s he has also recorded and occasionally appeared under his own name. Charnett is an excellent section player, but his own albums have been disappointingly bland. [BP]

Nettwork (c.1990; Manhattan). Marginally preferable to *Beauty Within*, this edges close to a kind of new-age funk in which the chief elements are the lush synthesizers of co-producer Kenny Kirkland and the warm post-Ron Carter sound of Moffett's melodically simplistic lead lines.

Louis Moholo

Drums, vocals, cello, percussion.

b. Cape Town, South Africa, 10 March 1940.

In 1956 Louis, who is self-taught, co-founded a big band, The Cordettes. At the 1962 Johannesburg jazz festival he received the Best Drummer award, before he joined the Blue Notes, a band of local stars assembled by the white South African pianist Chris McGregor. Under apartheid, racially mixed bands were illegal, and, as the reputation of the Blue Notes began to grow, it became almost impossible for the band to play together. They secured passports through an organization called Union Artists, and left for Europe in 1964. They played at the Antibes festival, appeared at some of the most important jazz centres in Europe and arrived in the UK in 1965, making their home in London. In 1966 Moholo toured South America with Steve Lacy, recording with him and staying abroad for about a year, during which time he also played with Roswell Rudd, John Tchicai and Archie Shepp, among others. He returned to the UK in 1967, playing then and subsequently with former Blue Notes in McGregor's Brotherhood of Breath, the Mike Osborne trio, Isipingo, the Irene Schweizer trio, the Peter Brötzmann trio and big band and with Keith Tippett, both as a duo and in the pianist's very large ensemble, the Ark. He has also led various groups of his own, including Moholo's Unit, Spirits Rejoice, Culture Shock, African Drum Ensemble and Viva La Black.

Moholo, like his compatriot Dudu Pukwana, has made a great contribution to the British jazz scene, bringing to it the whole ethos of African drumming and music-making: energy, passion, superb time and flexibility. He seems equally at home with jazz 4/4 time, free (abstract) improvisation and rock rhythms, which is why his presence has been felt in such a wide range of musical contexts. With the Brotherhood and other groups he has toured and played festivals all over Europe. With Peter Brötzmann and Harry Miller he toured the USA in 1979, and with Chris McGregor and the Blue Notes toured Africa during the 1970s. Despite serious ill health in the late 1980s, he has continued to work in a variety of contexts. His favourite percussionists are Michael Olatunji (Nigeria) and Bra Punk (Port Elizabeth, South Africa), and other inspirations are Eubie Blake, Harry Miller and three African composer/arranger/lyricists: Mnyataza, Tyhamzashe and Jolobe. He remains a tireless, elegant player who still plays regularly on the European free improv scene. [IC]

The Blue Notes (from left): bassist Johnny Dyani, pianist Chris McGregor, trumpeter Mongezi Feza, drummer Louis Moholo and altoist Dudu Pukwana

Exile (1990; Ogun). A powerful quartet session with Sean Bergin and Steve Williamson on saxophone and bassist Paul Rogers.

➤➤ **Derek Bailey** *(Village Life);* **Steve Lacy** *(Forest And The Zoo);* **Mike Osborne** *(Outback);* **Dudu Pukwana** *(In The Townships).*

Miff Mole

Trombone.

b. Roosevelt, Long Island, 11 March 1898; d. 29 April 1961.

Miff (Irving Milfred) Mole began his career in bands led by Gus Sharp and pianist Jimmy Durante, but by 1923 was working with Phil Napoleon's Original Memphis Five: they produced dozens of highly polished chamber jazz classics, and in turn influenced young Red Nichols, who heard Mole with Napoleon in Atlantic City that year. From 1925 Nichols and Mole were virtually inseparable for five years, producing on-record classics (eg "That's No Bargain", "Feeling No Pain" and "Boneyard Shuffle") under their own and a variety of other names – The Arkansas Travellers, The Redheads, Miff and Red's Stompers and so on. Mole also worked independently with large society orchestras such as Roger Wolfe Kahn's, and by 1927, rather than join the young band of Condon-led Chicago hopefuls taking their first uncertain steps, he had moved into studio work, first at WOR, then at NBC (he played for Toscanini *and* Bessie Smith). In the

1940s he worked with Benny Goodman and led a band at Nick's on and off for four years, but a period out of the limelight and the new omnipotence of Jack Teagarden (whose playing somehow seemed more charming than Mole's) presented major problems, exacerbated by illness. Like Joe Sullivan (in some ways a kindred spirit), Mole worked less and less, and by the 1950s his health was worsening. By 1960 he had had six hip operations and was walking with a stick; that year a Newport concert featuring him and Henry "Red" Allen was unceremoniously cancelled, and Mole was sent home unrecognized. That winter he was seen selling pretzels in a New York subway: benefits organized by Jack Crystal at New York's Central Plaza came too late and Mole died the following April.

"The J. J. Johnson of the 1920s," in Dicky Wells's words, and "one of the first fine technical trombones I heard", Mole was a revolutionary trombonist whose clean, quick technique, like Frankie Trumbauer's technically unsurpassable playing, made a deep impression on black and white players alike in the formative jazz years. [DF]

⊙ **Slipping around 1927–30** (Frog). Sessions by Miff's Molers, Red and Miff's Stompers, and Red Nichols illustrating Mole's central position in 1920s jazz which (with Nichols) achieved international impact long before either Jack Teagarden or Louis Armstrong.

⊙ **Slipping around ...again 1927-37** (Frog). Six more titles by Red and Miff's Stompers plus fifteen by the Molers and bonus tracks helping to complete the musical picture of one of jazz's most unobserved and undeserved tragedies.

Nils Petter Molvaer

Trumpet.
b.Sula, Norway,18 Sept 1960.

Trumpeter Nils Petter Molvaer is a leading light of the burgeoning, and highly original, Scandinavian jazz scene. A gifted performer with a very individual sound and style who, in his two albums for ECM, creates richly ambient soundscapes in which acoustic and electric elements form the backdrop for his own haunting solos. Much in demand as an instrumentalist, he has played on about 120 albums as a session musician, working with Marilyn Mazur, Django Bates, several rock groups and Sidsel Endresen (his wonderfully spare and poetic solo on the last track of Endresen's 2001 album *Undertow* is a must-hear).

Molvaer was introduced to jazz at an early age by his musician father, and got his first trumpet at the age of six. After playing in school bands and local clubs, he left Sula in 1979 to study for two years at the Trondheim Conservatory. From the start he seems to have been interested in electric and acoustic music, as well as certain aspects of the pop, rock and funk scenes. From 1982–92 he played with Masqualero, which was co-led by Jon Christensen and Arild Andersen and, through Masqualero's association with ECM records, Molvaer recorded his first album, *Khmer*, for the label in 1997. It received extraordinary public and media response, winning the German Record Critics Award and a Norwegian Grammy. Unusually for a jazz artist, Molvaer made remixes of *Khmer*, alongside dance programmers Herbaliser, Rockers Hi Fi and Mental Overdrive. The next album, *Solid Ether* (2000), continued along this trajectory; the vulnerable sound of Molvaer's trumpet hovering over electronically programmed drum beats with breaks from DJ Strangefruit. [IC]

⊙ **Khmer** (1997; ECM). A ground-breaking album that at the same time gives the nod to Miles Davis's *Bitches Brew* period. Highly atmospheric, in a bleakly North European way, Molvaer's superb trumpet playing gets excellent support from, among others, Eivind Aarset on guitar and electronics, and Per Lindvall and Rune Arnesen on drums.

➤➤ **Sidsel Endressen** *(Undertow)*.

Grachan Moncur III

Trombone, composer.
b. New York, 3 June 1937.

Grachan Moncur III's father, Grachan II (b. 2 Sept 1915; d. 3 Nov 1996), was the bassist with the original Savoy Sultans and played on records with Billie Holiday and Mildred Bailey. Grachan III studied music at the Manhattan School of Music and Juilliard School and toured with the Ray Charles band from 1961–3, and with Art Farmer-Benny Golson in 1962. He then settled in New York, working and recording with Jackie McLean, Sonny Rollins and under his own name. He's probably best known for being part of Blue Note's more experimental strain in the early/mid-sixties, contributing an arch waywardness to the label's albums much as Eric Dolphy and the young Anthony Williams did. From 1967–9 he played with Archie Shepp, including a European tour in 1967 and a trip to Algiers in 1969. He also played with drummer Beaver Harris in the 360 Degree Music Experience. In 1974 he wrote *Echoes Of Prayer* for the Jazz Composers' Orchestra Association in 1974. He returned to Newark, where he was raised, to do educational work, and played there with organist John Patton, with whom he recorded again in 1983. He also recorded with saxophonist Frank Lowe and with Cassandra Wilson, and toured Europe with the second edition of the Paris Reunion Band in 1986. Unlike the expressionist exclamations of most trombonists involved in the 1960s avant-garde, Moncur's style was based on the approach of J. J. Johnson, which he successfully adapted and made work in a free setting. [BP]

⊙ **Evolution** (1963; Blue Note). The all-star band at Moncur's disposal for this minor classic (Lee Morgan, Jackie McLean and the young Bobby Hutcherson and Tony Williams) is given challenging material by the leader-for-a-day, including his memorable "Monk In Wonderland".

Jane Monheit

Vocals.

b. New York, USA, 3 Nov 1977.

Jane Monheit is one of the most gifted young vocalists around, with a warm and seductive vocal style that reveals the influence of her great heroine Ella Fitzgerald. Born into a highly musical family – both her aunt and grandmother were professional singers – Monheit started singing at a very young age. Formal vocal training came from Peter Eldridge at the Manhattan School of Music where she gained her Bachelor of Music degree and met her future husband, drummer Rick Montalbano. Although she started singing professionally at the age of 16, her career really took off after she came second in the 1998 Thelonious Monk Institute's vocal competition, and was signed to the N-Coded Music label. Her first, highly-acclaimed album, *Never Never Land*, appeared in 2000, on which she was supported by, among others, jazz veterans Kenny Barron on piano, bassist Ron Carter and saxophonists David "Fathead" Newman and Hank Crawford. Concerts at the prestigious Village Vanguard and the Algonquin in Manhattan cemented her reputation, and she has recorded two further albums, *Come Dream With Me* (2001) and *In The Sun* (2002). She has also performed on albums of several other artists including Ivan Lins (with whom she toured Brazil), Terence Blanchard, Freddy Cole and Mark O'Connor. [IC]

⊙ **In The Sun** (2002; N-Coded Music). Monheit's third album didn't please everyone, but it is much more expansive, both musically and emotionally, than the preceding two. With a string section accompanying her on four tracks, and the services of two great arrangers – Alan Broadbent and Vince Mendoza – she performs an extremely varied selection of songs from jazz standards to rock, including lively versions of "Tea For Two", "Cheek To Cheek" and an outstanding rendition of Bernstein's "Some Other Time".

Mark Mondesir

Drums.

b. London, 12 Dec 1964.

Mondesir had private lessons on drums with Trevor Tomkins, studied music at school and from 1984–6 attended the jazz workshops at the weekend arts course at Interchange in North London. He joined Courtney Pine's band in 1985, and that year played a drum duet with Art Blakey on British television. He became a freelance after 1989, playing with Joanne Brackeen, Art Farmer, John Scofield, Larry Coryell, Hermeto Pascoal, Julian Joseph, Andy Sheppard and many others. He has also sat in with Wynton and Branford Marsalis, Mike Stern and other leading Americans. Mondesir played on the 1991 Kevin Eubanks album *Turning Point*, alongside Dave Holland. Mondesir is a brilliantly gifted drummer with great musicality, strength and subtlety. [IC]

➤➤ **Barbara Dennerlein** *(Hot Stuff)*; **Courtney Pine** *(Journey To The Urge Within)*; **Jean Toussaint** *(What Goes Around)*.

Michael Mondesir

Electric bass guitar, composer.

b. London, 6 Feb 1966.

Brother of Mark Mondesir, Michael began playing bass guitar at 16, after four years of playing drums. Listening regularly to radio programmes, he discovered Billy Cobham, the Mahavishnu Orchestra, Weather Report and other musicians and groups., latching on to the rhythmic, melodic and harmonic ideas of Jan Hammer, Zakir Hussain, Shankar, Subramaniam and Frank Zappa (he had no formal training). In 1983 he formed a trio, EMJIEM, with brother Mark and guitarist Hawi Gondwe. From 1984–6 he attended the jazz workshops at Interchange in North London, where he met Julian Joseph, Courtney Pine and Phillip Bent, and from the late 1980s Mondesir played with Pine, Steve Williamson, Jason Rebello, Annette Peacock, Django Bates and Billy Cobham. He regularly plays with like-minded alumni of various strands of the 1980s Brit scene, such as Django Bates and Iain Ballamy. Mondesir is a superb bassist with phenomenal concentration and excellent time. [IC]

Thelonious Monk

Piano, composer.

b. Rocky Mount, North Carolina, 10 Oct 1917; d. 17 Feb 1982.

Thelonious Sphere Monk was brought up in New York from the age of five, and took piano lessons at eleven or twelve. Two years later he began playing at Harlem rent parties and accompanying his mother's singing in church. He led a trio in a neighbourhood bar (c.1934) and then spent two years touring in a quartet with an evangelist. He studied briefly at the Juilliard School and freelanced with all kinds of groups. He played regularly with the Keg Purnell quartet in 1939, and with Kenny Clarke at Minton's and at Kelly's Stables from 1940–42. He also worked with the Lucky Millinder band in 1942, and was back at Minton's under Kermit Scott in 1943. He was the regular pianist with Coleman Hawkins's sextet from 1943 to early 1945, and made his recording debut with him. In 1943 he rehearsed with Dizzy Gillespie's first quintet, and briefly worked with the Cootie Williams band in 1944. He gigged with the Skippy Williams band in 1945, and then with Gillespie's big band in 1946. He began recording with his own groups in 1947 and appearing with them at Minton's, the Royal Roost and the Village Vanguard. Among his sidemen in this period were Art Blakey, Milt Jackson, Sahib Shihab and Sonny Rollins. He was falsely imprisoned for possession of drugs in 1951, and was deprived of New

Herman Leonard

Thelonious Sphere Monk

since his death. Some of them, however, were standard material as early as the mid-1940s: "Round Midnight" was put on record by Dizzy Gillespie and Cootie Williams (who used Monk's "Epistrophy" as his radio theme song), "52nd St Theme" was recorded by Gillespie and Bud Powell, while Charlie Parker used both on broadcasts. In the 1950s Miles Davis's versions of "Well You Needn't" and "Straight, No Chaser", and Monk's own *Jazz On A Summer's Day*, the filmed performance of "Blue Monk", succeeded in placing them in the same evergreen category. In fact, these and the rest of his output always sound at their best when played by him and are best understood by reference to his piano style, and vice versa. Starting from an admiration for Teddy Wilson and the stride players, Monk achieved a much more economical and much more percussive manner; the way in which he would analyse and develop the phrases of his own pieces in improvisation illustrated how they had been put together in the first place.

Although he contributed harmonically to bebop, he criticized the boppers for being more interested in straightahead blowing than in exploring the ins and outs of his material. Monk was equally frustrated by later generations of soloists, although Rollins, Coltrane and Griffin each approached his ideal from different directions. Steve Lacy, after working with him briefly in 1960, spent several years using only Monk tunes, and the motivic improvisation Monk favoured was quite prevalent in the 1960s avant-garde movement and has enjoyed renewed interest in the 1980s and 1990s. In terms of pianistic influence, while the great majority of keyboardists always want to play the maximum number of notes, the select few who have followed Monk are more thoughtful and thought-provoking. But his influence on other instrumentalists and writers has been enormous, and it is appropriate that the Thelonious Monk Institute's annual competitions, begun in 1987, are open to practitioners of a different instrument each year. [BP]

York employment for six years after his release. However, he continued recording with some regularity and occasionally gigging elsewhere, making an appearance at the Paris Jazz Fair in 1954.

In the summer of 1957 he assembled a quartet with John Coltrane, Shadow Wilson (originally Philly Joe Jones) and Wilbur Ware for the first of several long residencies at the 5 Spot Café. His later collaborators included Johnny Griffin and Roy Haynes in 1958, and Charlie Rouse, who worked with him from 1959–70. Monk was presented in big-band concerts at the Town Hall in 1959, Lincoln Center in 1963 and the Monterey festival in 1964. His reputation blossomed in the USA, and then internationally, with his first tours of Europe in 1961 and Japan in 1964. He toured Europe with an octet in 1967, but the quartet continued to be his usual format, featuring saxophonists Pat Patrick in 1970 and Paul Jeffrey in 1970–72, and, on drums, Thelonious Monk Jnr (now known as "T.S. Monk"). He accepted fewer engagements in the late 1960s and early 1970s, but toured widely with the Giants of Jazz in 1971–2. Thereafter a combination of illness and voluntary inactivity kept Monk from public performance, one of his last appearances being at the 1974 Newport festival concert of orchestrated arrangements of his compositions.

No longer inevitably associated with his piano-playing, Monk's tunes have enjoyed renewed interest

⊙ **Genius Of Modern Music Vol. 1/2** (1947–52; Blue Note). Monk's initial breakthrough sessions (for the label too, this was an impressive step) include his first recordings of "Round Midnight", "Ruby My Dear" and "I Mean You", already several years old at the time. Art Blakey is an almost constant presence, but, unlike the previous CD edition, the quartet session with Milt Jackson is now on his own Blue Note reissue.

⊙ **Thelonious Monk/Sonny Rollins** (1953–4; Prestige/OJC). Along with a couple of trio tracks ("Work" and "Nutty" with Blakey), this celebrates the two principals in excerpts from two sessions. Rollins leads on standard material with Monk prodding him forward, while Monk draws out his minimal "Friday The 13th" to extraordinary lengths.

Solo 1954 (Vogue). Monk's first European recording was unaccompanied, partly because local accompanists couldn't stay with him, but the versions of "Reflections", "Hackensack" and the standard "Smoke Gets In Your Eyes" sound very complete in themselves.

Brilliant Corners (1956; Riverside/OJC). An exceptional band performance of challenging new material, played by the returning Rollins and Max Roach, plus Monk's regular saxophonist of the day, Ernie Henry, who sounds convincing and undaunted by the fast company.

Thelonious Monk with John Coltrane (1957; Jazzland/OJC). Rather than the indifferently recorded live album of their work at the 5 Spot, Monk's short-lived quartet with Coltrane is at its most probing on three quartet tracks, including the "impossible" "Tinkle Tinkle". Trane is also heard in two items with the septet which recorded *Monk's Music*.

At Town Hall (1959; Riverside/OJC). A famous apotheosis in concert with a ten-piece band (à la *Birth Of The Cool* without the cool) includes the ensemble re-creation of Monk's solo on "Little Rootie Tootie" and good work by Phil Woods and Charlie Rouse, before his playing with Monk became unbearably routine.

The London Collection: Vol. 3 (1971; Black Lion). Superficially a collection of out-takes, this has solo versions of "The Man I Love" and a spontaneous "Something In Blue", and five trio tracks with Al McKibbon and Blakey. The fascinating "Chordially", not even an out-take but a warm-up, is included.

➤➤ **Miles Davis** *(Bags' Groove).*

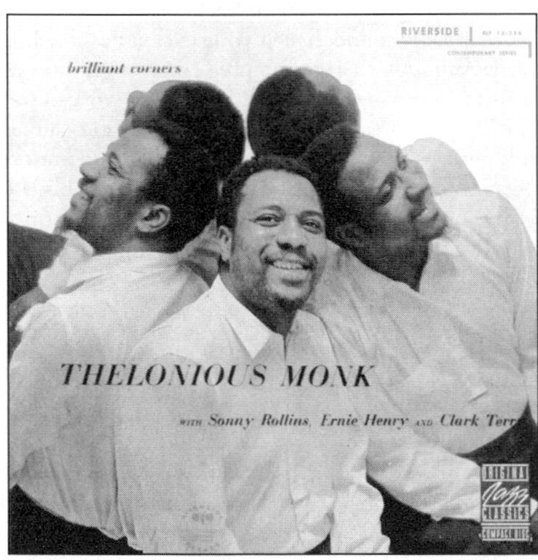

T.S. Monk

Drums, percussion.
b. New York, 27 Dec 1949.

Nicknamed by his father "Little Rootie Tootie" (soon shortened to "Toot"), Thelonious Sphere Monk III grew up surrounded by music but with no parental compulsion to play. He had no formal music education but tried the trumpet and piano before taking up drums at fifteen and studying with Max Roach. Playing with pop groups initially, he only became interested in jazz at nineteen and then worked in his father's group from 1970–72 and with saxophonist Paul Jeffrey, recording with him in 1972 and with Louis Hayes (on conga) in 1974. He studied African and Brazilian percussion and formed his own soul-oriented band, whose *House Of Music* (Mirage/Atlantic) reached the R&B Top 5 in 1980. In the late 1980s, he set up the Thelonious Monk International Competition and an educational foundation, the Thelonious Monk Institute of Jazz. In the early 1990s he started his own jazz sextet, which toured internationally in 1992, expanding to a ten-piece in 1997–8. His favourite drummers are Roach, Blakey, Jo Jones, Elvin Jones, Tony Williams and Buddy Miles, while Hancock, Shorter, Ellington and Jimi Hendrix are particular inspirations. A committed spokesman for jazz, he is a dynamic drummer and an engaging bandleader. [BP]

Monk On Monk (1997; N2K Encoded Music). Arranged and co-produced by Don Sickler, an all-star cast of 27 instrumentalists including Herbie Hancock, Wayne Shorter, Grover Washington, plus singers Kevin Mahogany, Dianne Reeves and Nnenna Frelon, contribute to one or more tracks of T.S.'s only album devoted solely to the music of his father.

"Lazy Ade" Monsbourgh

Alto saxophone, clarinet, trombone, trumpet, recorder.
b. Melbourne, Australia, 14 Aug 1926.

One of the most trenchant originals of Australian classic Jazz, Monsbourgh (born Adrian Herbert) began playing with Graeme Bell while in his early teens and soon became immersed in the Melbourne jazz scene, working with Bell's bands, and with other central figures including Roger Bell, Don Roberts, Dave Dallwitz and their contemporaries. From 1944 until the 1970s he continued to lead bands of his own (regularly under the generic title Lazy Ade's Late Hour Boys), and after the war regularly played throughout Australia and further afield including eastern Europe (1947) and Britain (1950–51). It was while in Britain (as part of Graeme Bell's band) that he formed an integral element in the Anglo-Australian alliance with Humphrey Lyttelton, producing classic recordings such as "Don't Monkey With It!" and "Hoppin' Mad" (1951). After his return to Australia, less was heard of Monsbourgh internationally, but his playing and recording continued unabated, losing none of its in-built creative focus and dedication. Despite professed retirement in the 1970s, he was still visible (and audible) thereafter, playing for jazz clubs, conventions and making recordings, notably for the Brighton Jazz Parade sessions in 1984. [DF]

Wild Life (1971; Swaggie). Recorded by Monsbourgh's Late Hour Boys in 1956/70 – "an object lesson in the performance of a small-group back-room musicians' type of jazz" (Roger Bell) – with the leader on alto saxophone and clarinet. His strong compositions include "More Than Good Lookin'", "All Steamed Up", and the title track.

Marian Montgomery

Vocals.

b. Natchez, Mississippi, 17 Nov 1934; d. 22 July 2002..

Marian Montgomery (Maud Runnels) grew up working nightclubs and jazz clubs in the USA and by the mid-1960s had graduated to the best venues in New York and Las Vegas. She moved to Britain in 1965 after marriage to British pianist/MD Laurie Holloway, and then worked on TV as well as presenting one-woman shows and performing in cabaret. Montgomery had a deep feeling for the blues and a cool and smoky delivery that relied for much of its effect on understatement; she also possessed an actress's grasp of stagecraft, which made her performances visually riveting as well as musically rewarding. Her death from cancer was a sad and premature loss. [DF]

⊙ **I Gotta Right To Sing** (1987; Jazz House). With a superb rhythm-section (including Laurie Holloway, Mitch Dalton, Lennie Bush and Allan Ganley), Montgomery is here on peak form in a live set from Ronnie Scott's.

⊙ **Makin' Whoopee** (1993; Bowstone). A rare chance to hear Marian singing Dixieland (which she does beautifully) along with a peppy ensemble – clarinettist Mart Rodger and his Manchester Jazz.

Wes Montgomery

Guitar.

b. Indianapolis, Indiana, 6 March 1925; d. 15 June 1968.

Montgomery taught himself the guitar during his teenage years, and soon started gigging on the local scene. He toured with the Lionel Hampton band from 1948–50, appearing briefly in a film short and performing his first recorded solo on "Moonglow", released in the late 1970s. He returned to Indianapolis, working through most of the 1950s at a day job and playing every night at local bars such as the Flame and the Missile Room. He made recordings in Chicago in 1957 and Los Angeles in 1958 with bassist Monk (William) Montgomery (b. 10 Oct 1921; d. 20 May 1982) and vibraharpist Buddy (Charles) Montgomery (b. 30 Jan 1930), who formed the Mastersounds group from 1957–62, but were known as the Montgomery Brothers after 1960.

Returning home again, Wes worked with his own organ trio in 1958–9, until he started cutting albums in New York under his own name in 1959. He lived in San Francisco with his brothers in 1960–61, and during this period he briefly worked with the John Coltrane sextet in San Francisco and at the Monterey festival. He then toured with his own trio or quartet, along with club and TV work with Stan Tracey during his only British visit in 1965. He also recorded with the Wynton Kelly trio in 1962, and later played regularly in public with them. In 1964 he began making a series of albums with big-band backing, enjoying unprecedented success even for middle-of-the-road instrumentals. In 1967 he made a TV

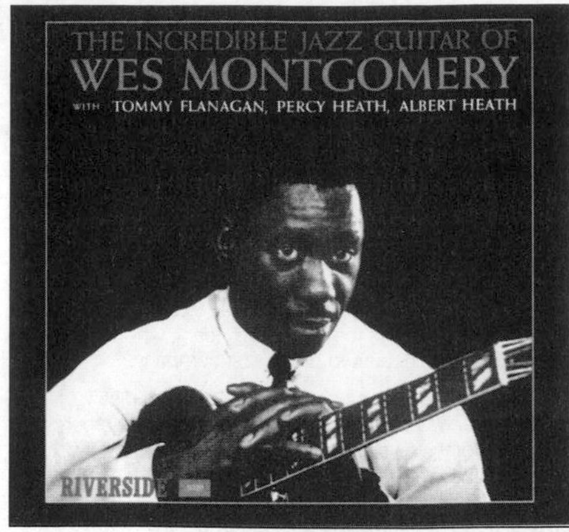

appearance with Herb Alpert, to whose record company he was contracted in the last year before his death from a heart attack.

Easily the most accomplished guitarist since the emergence of Charlie Christian, Montgomery had all the rhythmic verve associated with his original idol, and covered a wider range on the instrument. To this he added the four-note parallel chording that Barney Kessel had essayed and the unison octaves perfected by Django Reinhardt. Throughout his career he used his thumb to pick the strings (as opposed to the folky finger-style or the plectrum favoured by previous jazz stylists), which gave him a more mellow sound than anyone except possibly Jim Hall. Although there was a predictable aspect to the way he constructed many of his solos, his work of the late 1950s and early 1960s still feels brilliantly alive. It is perhaps a pity that the mellow sound and unison octaves were marketed so mercilessly during his last years, but the positive influence of his work on a whole generation of players is still strong. [BP]

⊙ **Incredible Jazz Guitar** (1960; Riverside/OJC). Montgomery's first quartet album (including Tommy Flanagan and Percy Heath) remains a definitive statement, with the original version of "West Coast Blues" and other riffs such as "Mister Walker", later covered by Ronny Jordan, plus dynamic improvisation on standards.

⊙ **Full House** (1962; Riverside/OJC). A live set with the Wynton Kelly trio (then still working for Miles Davis) plus Johnny Griffin, who offers Wes a real challenge in terms of speed and invention. The CD reissue contains three additional takes from the same date.

⊙ **Verve Jazz Masters: Wes Montgomery** (1964–6; Verve). A compilation which shows how big-band backing, Creed Taylor production and commercial simplification happened to Wes all at once. The inclusion of two long live tracks co-led by Wynton Kelly shows up how facile the rest is.

Tete Montoliu

Piano.

b. Barcelona, Spain, 28 March 1933; d. 24 Aug 1997.

Born blind, Vincente Montoliu studied the piano and became interested in jazz as a child. He played with Don Byas on his visits to Barcelona, and began recording with US musicians such as Lionel Hampton in 1956, Roland Kirk in 1963 and Anthony Braxton in 1974. From the early 1960s he worked regularly in Denmark and Germany, and visited the USA in 1967 and 1979. Through his own albums, including duos with George Coleman and Chick Corea, Montoliu gradually acquired an international reputation; possessing an excellent technique, his unaccompanied performances were less vacuous than those of other technical heavyweights, and he was also impressive in a group context. [BP]

⊙ **Yellow Dolphin Street/Catalonian Folk Songs** (1977; Timeless). An excellent way to explore the depth of Montoliu's work, these two sets on one CD feature his approach to the contrasting material of standards on the one hand and the folk music that is one of his inspirations on the other.

James Moody

Tenor and alto saxophones, flute, vocals.

b. Savannah, Georgia, 26 March 1925.

Moody's father was a trumpeter with Tiny Bradshaw. James took up the alto in 1941, and tenor the following year. He played regularly in the air force from 1943–6, joining Dizzy Gillespie's band on tenor when he left. He was based in Paris from late 1948 to 1951, working with Miles Davis-Tadd Dameron, recording with Max Roach (both in 1949), and touring throughout western Europe. He returned to the USA, and led his own septet from 1951–62, adding flute to his performances from the mid-1950s. He was briefly with a three-tenor group with Gene Ammons and Sonny Stitt in 1962, and then featured in the Gillespie quintet of 1963–8, and the Gillespie big band in Europe in 1968. He then toured as a soloist, followed by a spell in Las Vegas backing bands from 1974–80. Since re-emerging on the jazz scene, he has been in demand for recording and has often toured Europe.

Moody was one of the earliest tenor players to be at home playing bop in the mid-1940s, when he sounded a little like Dexter Gordon with a softer tone. He created a jukebox hit with his first-ever alto recording, the 1949 Swedish version of "I'm In The Mood For Love", which demonstrated a fine command of ballads. He is also extremely fluent on flute, although the tenor seems to be his most impressive instrument. A commitment to communicating with audiences comes across in his engaging stage presentation, even including the occasional vocal chorus. [BP]

⊙ **Moody's Mood for Blues** (1954–5; Prestige/OJC). Moody's travelling group (including Sadik Hakim) has bustling band work, two guest vocals by band manager Eddie Jefferson, and a handful of the leader's alto ballads, all with crisp arrangements by Quincy Jones.

⊙ **Young At Heart** (1996; Warners). One of several Sinatra tributes that preceded his demise, this is a relaxed demonstration of the 71-year-old Moody's continued command of his saxophones and flutes (plus the odd vocal), cutting across the horn-and-sometimes-strings arrangements of Gil Goldstein.

Brew Moore

Tenor saxophone.

b. Indianola, Mississippi, 26 March 1924;
d. Copenhagen, 19 Aug 1973.

Moore was active in New York in the late 1940s with Claude Thornhill, Gerry Mulligan and Kai Winding, as well as recording under his own name. He took part in live sessions with trumpeter Tony Fruscella in 1953, then lived in San Francisco from 1955–60. He was based in Europe from 1961–7, New York from 1967–70, and in the Canary Islands in 1970, before returning to Europe. Addiction to alcohol contributed to his fatal fall down a flight of stairs. Moore was the originator of the phrase, "Anyone who doesn't play like Lester [Young] is wrong", and certainly his playing backed up the assertion. He never attained the fluency and unpredictability of the master, but he was definitely one of his most faithful followers. [BP]

⊙ **Svinget 14** (1962; Black Lion). Named after his address in Copenhagen, this finds Moore near the top of his form with a rhythm-section including Niels-Henning Ørsted Pedersen, and joined on two tracks by the equally vagabond Lars Gullin, who arranged a Swedish folk song for the occasion.

Michael Moore

Bass, piano.

b. Glen Este, near Cincinatti, 16 May 1945.

Not to be confused with the saxophonist listed below, Moore began on bass at 15 and played locally with guitarist Cal Collins and pianist-arranger Dave Matthews. After touring and recording with Woody Herman in 1966, he moved to New York and briefly took up bass guitar for economic reasons. Specializing on double bass in the 1970s, he worked with musicians such as Marian McPartland, Benny Goodman and the Ruby Braff/George Barnes quartet. The following decades have found him performing with a wide variety of mainstream musicians, including pianists Jimmy Rowles, Kenny Barron, Roger Kellaway and Bill Charlap, and guitarists such as Howard Alden, Charlie Byrd and Jim Mullen. The latter association dates from Moore's period of living in London (1989-92) but, since returning to New York, he has been one of the most in-demand bassists for melodic yet solid accompaniments. In addition he has written well-received bass tutor books, and in 2002-3 his schedule included touring in the Dave Brubeck quartet. [BP]

⊙ **Dedications: The History Of Jazz Vol. 2** (2001; Arbors). Moore's trio, with Ken Peplowski and drummer Tom Melito, features the leader on piano as well as bass, and includes six originals inspired by such heroes as Bill Evans, Jimmy Rowles and Herbie Nichols.

Michael Moore

Alto saxophone, clarinets.
b. Eureka, California, 4 Dec 1954.

Michael Moore's father was a musician and teacher, and when Moore was ten he moved to Rochester, New York, while his father attended the Eastman School of Music for two years. While there, an earlier interest in clarinet was rekindled, and when he returned to California he played clarinet until high school, at which point he began playing alto saxophone. He studied with Jaki Byard at the New England Conservatory, and while in Boston he played with Ran Blake and Joe Allard. He subsequently spent a short stint in New York, but in the summer of 1978, Moore joined his brother, trombonist and electric bassist Gregg Moore, in Amsterdam. For a period, he moved back and forth between New York and Holland, settling in Amsterdam in about 1984.

Moore has been a key figure in the Dutch new jazz scene ever since, playing in and recording with Misha Mengelberg's ICP Orchestra and in prestigious groups led by bassist Maarten Altena and pianist Guus Janssen. He was also one third of the Clusone 3, with cellist Ernst Reijseger and drummer Han Bennink, which released several playful, very enjoyable records before breaking up in 1998, none better than their last, *Rara Avis* (1999; hatOLOGY), an all-ornithological thematic set of tunes. Moore runs his own label, Ramboy, which has issued a number of his projects. He is quite active as a leader, playing with and composing for a variety of groups; he has released quartet, *Négligé* (1992; Ramboy), and quintet, *Home Game* (1990; Ramboy), outings, as well as several trio CDs, two of which – *Monitor* (1999) and *Air Street* (2002) – featured Cor Fuhler on keyboard and keyolin ("a two-stringed violin on a frame suspended above small keyboard") and Tristan Honsinger on cello.

His musical interests are wildly eclectic, from the Beach Boys to Ellington, to traditional music from Madagascar – a facet well reflected in the arrangements and compositions he has made for the group Available Jelly. They're nicely documented on several records in various line-ups over the years, including *In Full Flail* (1989; Ear-Rational) and *Happy Camp* (1996; Ramboy). Soft-toned, West-Coast imbued, with a gorgeous clarinet sound and terrific velocity and ideas on alto, Moore is as versatile as he is his own man, and his talents are well utilized by various sectors of the bustling Dutch scene. [JC]

⊙ **Bering** (1997; Ramboy). With his American trio of pianist Fred Hersch and bassist Mark Helias, Moore's recorded *Chiacoutimi* (1993; Ramboy) and this understated wonder, both nodding in the direction of Jimmy Giuffre's clarinet, piano and bass trios. It's a showcase for Moore's outstanding clarinet work (he leaves the alto at home) and is simply glowing music, including versions of standards, some Greek and Brazilian music, and some of his own clever tunes.

Oscar Moore

Guitar.
b. Austin, Texas, 25 Dec 1912; d. 8 Oct 1981.

Oscar Moore made a striking contribution to Nat "King" Cole's trio in the 1940s, when his use of electric guitar and his cool hip lines (recalling Charlie Christian) made him an innovator. Moore first met Cole after the pianist had been asked to assemble a quartet for a 1937 residency at the Swanee Inn, Santa Monica, and soon after that they began touring and club work with bassist Wesley Prince (later replaced by Johnny Miller). A 1942 contract for Capitol led to a string of hits ("Straighten Up And Fly Right", "Sweet Lorraine", "Route 66" and "It's Only A Paper Moon") that did much to popularize the electric guitar. The partnership lasted until 1947, when Moore left to pursue the possibilities of a band co-led with his guitarist brother John (Johnny Moore's Three Blazers, with Charles Brown on piano and vocals). From then on very little was heard from Oscar Moore, although he remained a busy freelance and returned to professional work in the 1960s after working as a bricklayer. [DF]

➤➤ **Nat "King" Cole** *(Best Of The Nat "King" Cole Trio).*

Ralph Moore

Tenor and soprano saxophones.
b. London, 24 Dec 1956.

A US resident since 1970, Ralph Moore studied at Berklee (1975–7), then stayed in Boston as a freelance musician, playing with such figures as guitarist Kevin Eubanks and drummer Marvin "Smitty" Smith, before moving to New York in 1980, where he joined Horace Silver's band and became a sideman for Roy Haynes, Dizzy Gillespie, Freddie Hubbard and J.J. Johnson, among others. A thoroughly reliable but gutsy, cogent player in the modern-mainstream style, Moore has made half a dozen albums under his own name since the mid-1980s and is much valued for his consistency and professionalism, epitomized both by his stint with the all-star Phillip Morris Superband and by his winning the 1990 emerging-talent polls in *Down Beat* and *Jazz Times*. In the 1990s, Moore participated in many high-profile recordings as a sideman: with Kenny Barron, Ray Brown and Dusko Goykovich, and – alongside old associate, trumpeter Roy Hargrove – on both *Oscar Peterson Meets Roy Hargrove and Ralph Moore* (Telarc; 1996), and Cedar Walton's *The Composer* (Astor Place; 1996), the last a classy outing well suited to Moore's controlled, sophisticated approach. A regular member of NBC's *Tonight Show* orchestra since 1995, his recorded jazz career as leader seems to have gone on hold, though notable cameos have been heard on recordings by singer Ruth Cameron (*Roadhouse*, 2000) and organist Joey DeFrancesco (*Falling In Love Again*, 2003). [CP]

Rejuvenate! (1988; Criss Cross Criss). Technically proficient, highly enjoyable post-bop with Steve Turre (trombone), Mulgrew Miller (piano), Peter Washington (bass) and Marvin "Smitty" Smith (drums). A highlight is Moore's own "Song For Soweto".

Furthermore (1990; Landmark). An attractive mix of Moore originals and Monk ("Monk's Dream"), Hefti ("Girl Talk") and pianist Benny Green's tunes, this album also features trumpeter Roy Hargrove on four tracks.

Who It Is You Are (1993; Savoy Jazz). Regular collaborators Green and Washington are augmented by Billy Higgins on the usual mix of modern standards and Green and Moore originals.

"Big Chief" Russell Moore

Trombone, vocals.

b. near Sacaton, Arizona, 13 Aug 1912; d. 15 Dec 1983.

Russell Moore was taught the trombone by his uncle, lived in the Chicago area during the 1920s and played locally before working with Lionel Hampton's Los Angeles band in 1935. After that he was with Eddie Barefield, and then was active around New Orleans with men such as Oscar Celestin, Paul Barbarin, Noble Sissle and Harlan Leonard. From 1944–7 he worked with Louis Armstrong's big band (which also featured young Dexter Gordon), and by the 1950s was working with such names as Eddie Condon, Wild Bill Davison, Tony Parenti, Sammy Price, Buck Clayton, Don Byas, Hot Lips Page and Henry "Red" Allen. Perhaps his most prestigious career step was to join Louis Armstrong for a year in 1964 (replacing Trummy Young); thereafter he led his own band again, gigged with Lester Lanin and was busy until 1981, when a tour of Europe with Keith Smith revealed, at last, an old tired Chief. [DF]

>> **Louis Armstrong** *(Hello Dolly!).*

Jason Moran

Piano.

b. Houston, Texas, 21 Jan 1975.

Moran began studying piano in the first grade but it was only after hearing his father's collection of Monk records that he determined to become a jazz musician. He studied at Houston's High School for Performing and Visual Arts (leading its jazz quartet), and at the Manhattan School of Music (1993-7), where he was taught by Jaki Byard, with additional private tuition from Muhal Richard Abrams and Andrew Hill. After working with David Murray, Steve Coleman, Cassandra Wilson and others, he joined saxophonist Greg Osby's Quartet in 1997 and made four albums with the group. Osby also produced and played on Moran's first albums for Blue Note, *Soundtrack To Human Motion* (1998), alongside vibist Stefon Harris, drummer Eric Harland and bassist Lonnie Plaxico. For Moran's third album, *Black Stars* (2001), he was joined by veteran saxophonist Sam Rivers plus regular colleagues Nasheet Waits and bassist Tarus Mateen – what Jazz Times called "the most exciting rhythm section in jazz". Since then, Moran's challenging playing, with its huge range of stylistic references from Bartok to James Johnson, has become increasingly prominent and promises great things for the future. [BP]

The Bandwagon (2002; Blue Note). Recorded live, Moran's trio with Waits and Mateen put on a dazzling display of mutually challenging supportiveness. Moran's repertoire reinterprets everything from Brahms to Jaki Byard via some pop-music, and he also creates some fascinating lines suggested by speech samples.

>> **Greg Osby** *(Zero; Banned In New York).*

Herb Morand

Trumpet, vocals.

b. New Orleans, 1905; d. 23 Feb 1952.

Lizzie Miles's half-brother, Herb Morand was broadcasting from New Orleans by the early 1920s and in 1925 moved to New York to work with Cliff Jackson's band. For most of his career from the late 1920s he was Chicago-based, working with Joe Lindsey at Tony's Taverns (1934–5), recording with Frank Melrose and the Dodds Brothers, and running the Harlem Hamfats, a mellow, entertaining group for which Morand was trumpeter-manager. (Hamfats, in Harlemese, were country boys who used ham fat to grease their valves: the Hamfats' great records have just a trace of country style in them.) Morand was a latecomer to Chicago at a time when giants like Louis Armstrong were tearing up the town, and by the 1940s he was back in New Orleans, leading resort bands and working with artists such as Joe Watkins and George Lewis. From 1950 he was plagued by illness (complicated by obesity) and he died during an engagement with Lewis at the El Morocco club, New Orleans. [DF]

Chauncey Morehouse

Drums, percussion.

b. Niagara Falls, 11 March 1902; d. 31 Oct 1980.

Morehouse began work playing in silent-movie houses around Pennsylvania with his pianist father. Then came the Gettysburg College dance band and from 1922 the coveted drummer's chair with Paul Specht's Society Serenaders, who quickly came east from Detroit to New York. He recorded classic sides with the Georgians, Specht's band-within-a-band (led by Frank Guarente), but left three years on to work with Howard Lanin and Ted Weems, before joining Jean Goldkette at Detroit's Graystone Ballroom: Morehouse's records with Beiderbecke and Trumbauer from this period are classics. After Goldkette's band broke up in New York he joined Adrian Rollini briefly, then Don Voorhees for pitwork in a Broadway show,

Rain Or Shine. From then on (with a break for bandleading in 1938, for which he invented a set of chromatic tuneable drums), theatre and studio work were to be Morehouse's life: he played for commercial radio and TV, wrote and recorded jingles, and later became house drummer for Decca. After retiring in the late 1960s, he re-emerged in the 1970s to play for the New York Jazz Repertory Company, Bix Beiderbecke tributes, for a Goldkette reunion at Carnegie Hall and elsewhere. [DF]

Airto Moreira

Percussion, drums, vocals, composer.

b. Itaiopolis, Brazil, 5 Aug 1941.

Moreira studied acoustic guitar and piano from 1948–50, and at twelve was performing with groups. From the age of 19 he spent three years playing in nightclubs all over Brazil. He formed his own group, which included Hermeto Pascoal, and later the two of them formed the Quarteto Novo. During these early years travelling through the various areas of Brazil – the Amazon jungle, the dry northeast and the Mato Grosso prairies – he collected and studied about 120 different instruments.

In 1968 he and his wife, singer Flora Purim, moved to the USA, and came to international notice with Miles Davis in 1970, playing on records and in live concerts. He worked with Lee Morgan early in 1971, and later that year played percussion in the first Weather Report with Joe Zawinul, Wayne Shorter, Miroslav Vitous and Alphonse Mouzon. In 1972, with Flora Purim, he was a member of Chick Corea's first Return to Forever. He became one of the most sought-after percussionists in the USA, working with many people in all sorts of contexts, including Stan Getz, Cannonball Adderley, Gato Barbieri, Don Friedman and Reggie Workman. He formed his own group in 1973, moving to Berkeley, California, with Flora Purim, playing on her albums and also recording under his own name. In the mid-1980s he was a member of the Al Di Meola Project, recording with them and touring in the USA and Europe. Moreira was the first of the contemporary Latin percussionists to work on the US scene and has made the biggest reputation, having been in so many key groups at an extraordinarily dynamic time in jazz history. [IC]

⊙ **The Colours Of Life** (1987; In & Out). This marvellously buoyant Latin album is attributed to Moreira and Flora Purim. It includes the fine saxophonist Gary Meek and various added musicians – usually Brazilian. Sunblessed music.

⊙ **Killer Bees** (1989; B & W Music). A gloriously different album: nine totally improvised performances by trios or quartets drawn from a pool of friends – Hiram Bullock, Stanley Clarke, Chick Corea, Mark Egan, Herbie Hancock and Gary Meek, with Flora Purim singing on one track.

➤➤ **Chick Corea** *(Return To Forever)*; **Flora Purim** *(The Flight; Speed Of Light)*; **Joe Zawinul** *(Weather Report)*.

Joe Morello

Drums.

b. Springfield, Massachusetts, 17 July 1928.

A near-contemporary of Phil Woods, who was born in the same town, Morello was partly blind from childhood. After playing locally, he toured with the Glen Gray band in 1950, then worked in New York with guitarist Johnny Smith in 1952 and with the Stan Kenton band. He was a regular member of the Marian McPartland trio from 1953–6, and of the best-known edition of the Dave Brubeck quartet from 1956–67. Since then, his fairly infrequent appearances have been to promote drum manufacturers or of an educational nature. His work with Brubeck might be seen in the same light, since he was the first drummer to make the group sound like a jazz band, and, unlike its leader when he joined, Morello was an extremely precise player who nevertheless managed to be relaxed and swinging. As a result, he set standards of excellence for many young listeners who were just becoming interested in jazz, and prepared them to appreciate players such as Max Roach and Art Blakey. [BP]

➤➤ **Dave Brubeck** *(Time Out)*.

Frank Morgan

Alto saxophone.

b. Minneapolis, Minnesota, 23 Dec 1933.

Frank Morgan's father, Stanley, played guitar with the Ink Spots vocal group, and Frank started on clarinet at the age of seven and on alto at ten. After the family moved from Milwaukee to Los Angeles in 1947, he made his record debut at fifteen in a talent contest run by bandleader Freddie Martin. Becoming involved in bebop, he recorded with Teddy Charles in 1953 and Kenny Clarke in 1954, and the next year was given his own album. In 1955 he was sentenced for narcotics abuse and, for the next twenty years, was in and out of jail. After performing locally from around 1977, he finally received national recognition in 1985, and went on to record twelve albums in the next eight years. Acclaimed as the new Art Pepper, he remained adept at rekindling the flame of bebop. [BP]

⊙ **Easy Living** (1985; Contemporary/OJC). The first of Frank's comeback records to be granted mid-price reissue has him backed by Cedar Walton and Billy Higgins, heralding an outburst of uncontained energy on material by Parker, Shorter, Gershwin and Morgan himself.

⊙ **Bebop Lives!** (1986; Contemporary). Recorded live at the Village Vanguard (where Art Pepper finally established his readiness for a comeback), Morgan is flanked by the Cedar Walton trio and Johnny Coles on a programme of Ellington, Monk, Parker and McLean, plus two bop-era standards.

Lee Morgan

Trumpet, composer.

b. Philadelphia, 10 July 1938; d. 19 Feb 1972.

Morgan died after being shot in a New York club where his quintet was performing, after a quarrel with a woman. His career had also begun with a bang, when at 18 he joined the Dizzy Gillespie big band, staying with it for two years (1956–8). He then joined Art Blakey's Jazz Messengers in one of the group's best phases (1958–61). Benny Golson was writing much of the material, and Morgan made a big impact internationally with brilliantly funky open-horn solos on Golson's "Blues March" and fine harmon-mute work on "Whisper Not". He was a little overshadowed when Freddie Hubbard burst on the scene in the early 1960s, and spent some years playing in the Philadelphia area with Jimmy Heath and others. From 1964–6 he again toured internationally with Blakey, and was also recording regularly for Blue Note with his own groups. In 1964 one of his compositions, a blues called "The Sidewinder", was a hit, and the eponymous album became a best seller: this commercial success and popularity did not please the jazz critics. Morgan's instantly recognizable sound and style grew out of his main influences – Clifford Brown, Dizzy Gillespie and Fats Navarro. He had a fat, crisp tone, a good range, and he played with immense expressiveness and urgency – a style rooted in the inflexions of the blues, with slurred and bent notes, funky phrases and great rhythmic momentum. [IC]

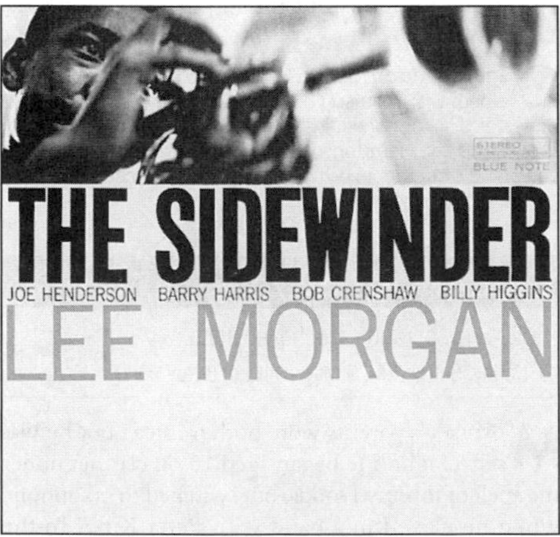

⊙ **Introducing Lee Morgan** (1956; Savoy). The 18-year-old Lee was cocky and irrepressible, and this album – in seasoned company – is a triumphant debut.

⊙ **The Sidewinder** (1964; Blue Note). *An* excellent album, full of good compositions and great playing. The title track is a small masterpiece, which swings and breathes beautifully.

⊙ **At The Lighthouse** (1970; Blue Note). *The Lighthouse* is a live quintet session, with Morgan playing as if there were no tomorrow.

➤➤ **Art Blakey** *(Moanin');* **John Coltrane** *(Blue Train).*

Sam Morgan

Trumpet.

b. Bertrandville, Louisiana, 1895; d. 25 Feb 1936.

An important New Orleans trumpeter with a big local following, Morgan (the brother of bassist Al Morgan) played in and around the city for ten years, at venues such as the Savoy on Rampart Street, where George Lewis was an early sitter-in. In 1925 he suffered a severe stroke but one year on had re-formed his band with keymen such as Jim Robinson (trombone), Rene Hall (banjo) and Isaiah Morgan (lead trumpet). In 1927 the band made some now famous records for Columbia at Werlein's Music Shop on Canal Street in New Orleans, and they played on until 1932 (running a profitable sideline – a treasure-hunting service complete with tents and divining rods), when Morgan had a second stroke. His band broke up a year later. [DF]

⊙ **Papa Celestin And Sam Morgan** (1927; Azure). An essential purchase: Morgan's eight titles, including "Steppin' On The Gas", "Sing On" and "Mobile Stomp", are true classics of New Orleans jazz.

Butch Morris

Cornet, composer.

b. Long Beach, California, 10 Feb 1947.

Born Lawrence Douglas Morris, the brother of bassist Wilber Morris, Butch Morris is chiefly celebrated for his participation in David Murray's most outré music, but he first gained experience with Horace Tapscott, Arthur Blythe and Bobby Bradford in the early 1970s, and subsequently with tenor player Frank Lowe, touring Europe with him in 1976 and living in Paris for a year. While in Europe, he played with Steve Lacy, Alan Silva and Frank Wright, but on returning to the USA he began his extremely fruitful musical relationship with Murray, although he was also a frequent participant in New York "loft" sessions, forming improvising groups with the likes of trombonist/electronics exponent J.A. Deane, guitarist Bill Frisell, keyboard player Wayne Horvitz and drummer Bobby Previte. A prolific and highly original composer of everything from works for solo piano and harpsichord to complex orchestral pieces, Morris has also devised a system – known as "conduction" – for organizing improvised music with gestures of the conductor's baton, and his chief ambition is "to further the whole idea of ensemble music". His dedication to conduction led to his playing less since the 1990s although he did release a trio album, featuring J.A. Deane on trombone and electronics and percussionist Le Quan Ninh, which was recorded at a Total Music Meeting in Berlin (FMP; 1993). His major work from this period, however, was collected on a ten-CD set documenting his conduction activities with (usually) large ensembles in America, Europe, Turkey and Japan (see below). [CP]

Current Trends In Racism In Modern America (1985; sound aspects). Utilizing the talents of old associate Frank Lowe and a host of New York's most open-eared musicians (John Zorn, Zeena Parkins, Christian Marclay and Thurman Barker, among others), a rowdy, polemical piece of organized improvisation.

Homeing (1987; sound aspects). Typically adventurous line-up (electronics, French horn, oboe, vibes, violin, etc) producing innovative, consistently challenging music.

Testament: A Conduction Collection (1995; New World/Countercurrents). Meticulously annotated collection of seven years' activity worldwide, featuring pieces ranging from a few minutes to an hour in length, and involving a veritable who's who of contemporay improvised music.

➤➤ **David Murray** *(Ming).*

Joe Morris

Electric and acoustic guitar, banjo ukelele, mandolin.

b. New Haven, Connecticut, 1955.

A self-taught musician, Morris began playing in the late 60s, and into the early 70s he was inspired and influenced by the exciting creative music scene in New Haven. In 1975, he moved to Boston and began playing with important, all-but-undocumented, multi-instrumentalist Lowell Davidson. Through the 80s, he was a key mover and shaker on the Boston underground scene, setting up innumerable concerts and preventing the city from becoming completely absorbed in a conservatory mentality. A clean-toned guitarist, Morris eschews electronic effects in favour of linear directness; he's a fluid player with a highly personal, spidery melodic sense and a variety of patented picking techniques that draw on African string traditions. Though he's most often found on solid-body electric, Morris is equally accomplished on the acoustic guitar, mandolin and banjo ukelele. He began releasing records on his own Riti label in 1982, including his debut *Wraparound, Sweatshop* (1988), *Flip And Spike* (1992) and a collective trio with alto saxophonist Rob Brown and drummer Whit Dickey, *Youniverse* (1992). Though he has spent a great deal of time in New York, playing with New Yorkers like Brown, pianist Matthew Shipp – with whom he recorded the duo *Thesis* (1997; hatOLOGY) – and William Parker, Morris stayed in Boston. There he has had a fruitful collaboration with Joe and Mat Maneri (their impressive, serpentine *Three Men Walking* (1996) album casts a restlessly despondent shadow over the ECM catalogue). In 1993, fed up with lack of opportunities and frustrated by the scene in general, Morris almost quit music altogether; ironically, this was precisely the moment when his proverbial star was rising, and he has in the following years made a staggering number of very worthwhile records for various labels, including Aum Fidelity, Incus, No More, Homestead, Leo, Soul Note, Okka Disk and Knitting Factory. [JC]

Antennae (1997; Aum Fidelity). Morris shines in trio contexts, and this one with drummer Jerome Deupree and stellar young bassist Nate McBride – dedicated in its entirety to Lowell Davidson – is among his very best. Intriguing tunes and expansive improvising, all featuring a guitarist with an original vision. For his solo work, the uncompromising *No Vertigo* (1995; Leo) is also highly recommended.

James Morrison

Trumpet, trombone, saxophone, piano, miscellaneous instruments.

b. Australia, 11 Nov 1962.

Known with some justification as the "Wizard Of Oz", Morrison took up cornet at seven, but had soon mastered most other instruments while at school. In 1975 he studied at the New South Wales Conservatorium while working with Don Burrows's quartet and also debuted at America's Monterey jazz festival at the age of seventeen. Quickly recognized as a national celebrity (he is also a champion racing driver, bungey-jumper and more), Morrison also co-led a big band with his brother John, appeared in duo with veteran trumpeter Red Rodney, and struck up a relationship on and off record with bassist Ray Brown, with whom he recorded the hit single "Snappy Doo". By the end of the 1980s Morrison was working with the Philip Morris Super Band (on trombone), and in the 1990s expanded his horizons by performing equally effortlessly in classical surroundings, including the Queensland Symphony Orchestra, and at London's Covent Garden Royal Opera House. In 1996 he travelled to Davenport, Iowa, to perform Lalo Schifrin's *A Rhapsody for Bix*, and has since continued his phenomenal roster of solo activities. A player who can justifiably be termed a prodigy, Morrison's talents are seemingly unlimited and have yet to receive the international recognition that are their due; perhaps he simply makes it all look and sound too easy, but the music is there to hear! [DF]

Snappy Doo (1989; WEA). A world-class big-band album with Morrison playing four trumpets, four trombones, five saxophones and piano, with Herb Ellis, Ray Brown and Jeff Hamilton in support. He even played different-brand instruments within each section to ensure a "human" mix of sound!

Dick Morrissey

Tenor and soprano saxophones, flute.

b. Horley, Surrey, UK, 9 May 1940; d. 8 Nov 2000.

Morrissey's parents were both musical, but he was self-taught. He began aged 16 on clarinet under the spell of Johnny Dodds, but switched to saxophone when he played in a band with Peter King. In the early 1960s he was leading a quartet with pianist Harry South, bassist Phil Bates and Phil Seamen on drums. At the beginning of the 1970s he formed and co-led the jazz-rock band If with Terry Smith. He met Jim Mullen in 1976 and formed Morrissey-Mullen in order to record in New York with the Average White Band, then stayed on in New York, playing with his own band and with Herbie Mann. Back in the UK his association with Mullen continued until 1985, since when he was a familiar face on the UK scene, working regularly at Ronnie Scott's. [IC]

Life On The Wire (1982; Beggars Banquet); **Happy Hour** (1988; Coda). Morrissey-Mullen were one of the most popular jazz groups in London. They swung beautifully, projected great warmth and handled the whole jazz spectrum from ballads to booting uptempo numbers.

➤➤ **Mike Carr** *(Good Times And The Blues).*

Benny Morton

Trombone.

b. New York, 31 Jan 1907; d. 28 Dec 1985.

A graduate of the Jenkins Orphanage Band (he was taught by Professor Rohmie Jones), Morton was influenced by church music as well as by Mamie Smith's star trombonist Dope Andrews. By 1923 he was working with Clarence Holiday's orchestra, gaining experience that stood him in good stead when he joined Fletcher Henderson's in 1926. "For a young person it was like a school," Morton said, "because the youngest man close to my age was five years older and it went up to the first trumpet who was twenty years older." Two stays with Henderson were followed by six years with Don Redman and three more with Count Basie (1937–40); there are wonderful records of Morton with Billie Holiday at this time, including "My First Impression Of You" (1938). After Basie, he worked in the 1940s with Teddy Wilson and Ed Hall, and led his own band, before playing in the pit for Broadway shows including *Guys And Dolls* and for Radio City Music Hall (1959). Throughout the 1960s and 1970s, and into the 1980s, he was back among high jazz society, including Wild Bill Davison, Bobby Hackett, the Saints and Sinners (replacing his friend Vic Dickenson) and The World's Greatest Jazz Band.

Morton was a gentle and self-effacing man, who never had the spectacular technique of a Trummy Young or the humour of a Wells or Dickenson ("that's why Vic has been recorded two thousand times and I and others twenty times," he admitted), yet he was one of the most sophisticated trombonists of the swing era. [DF]

Jelly Roll Morton

Piano, composer, arranger, vocals.

b. New Orleans, 20 Oct 1890; d. 10 July 1941.

Until recently the career of Jelly Roll Morton (Ferdinand Lemott) was veiled with grandiose claims and doubtful facts, many of them conjured up by "The Originator of Jazz Stomps and Blues", as Morton styled himself. Researchers such as Lawrence Gushee, John Chilton and Laurie Wright have now cleared the mists, but Morton's career – full of pizazz and tireless self-promotion – remains one of the most colourful in jazz.

By 1906 he was playing piano in the Storyville brothels, hustling, playing pool and learning how to survive. These hard-won lessons were to involve him in vaudeville (he worked in a double act as "Morton and Morton" with a partner called "Rose"), music publishing with the Spikes brothers, running a tailor's shop, boxing promotion, pimping, black-face minstrel shows, work in cabarets, dance halls and gambling houses (as manager as well as pianist), and running a club-hotel with his canny wife Anita, the sister of bassist Bill Johnson. By 1923 he was in Chicago and at the dawn of his greatest creative period: a good relationship with the Melrose brothers (who published his tunes) and a string of successful piano solos recorded for Gennett (including "King Porter Stomp", "Kansas City Stomp" and "The Pearls") drew early attention to his style. When not recording, Morton was touring with his own groups – and occasionally for other leaders such as Fate Marable and W.C. Handy, which he usually strenuously denied.

In 1926, at the behest of Frank Melrose, he recorded the classic Red Hot Peppers sessions, acknowledged as his greatest. Baby Dodds supplies memories: "There was a fine spirit in that group at rehearsal. Jelly used to work on each and every number until it satisfied him! You did what Jelly Roll wanted you to do, no more no less." Morton would supply every last routine of the performance, always hired reliable men (preferably Creoles from New Orleans), paid generously for rehearsals ($5) and recording ($15), and maintained an easy but disciplined atmosphere: the results were such closely worked masterpieces as "Dead Man Blues" and "Sidewalk Blues", which established the Peppers as Victor's number-one hot band.

In 1928 Morton followed his success to New York, but there – for the first time – he began to lose ground. The new big-band era could not accommodate his preference for small-band jazz and his fondness for New Orleans, and his attempts over the next two years to hold together a big band were half-hearted and unhappy. By 1930 he was finding it hard to book the musicians and find the amount of work he had been used to; his contract with Victor then expired and was not renewed, and within two years he was working in theatre pits for musical revues and hanging out at the Rhythm Club over at Lafayette Theater. Four years on, in 1936, he was living in Washington and, in George Hoefer's memorable phrase, "suing the world for recognition" as he played in a tiny second-floor club to a clique of dedicated admirers, including Roy Carew. Later Alan Lomax, the curator of the Library of Congress folklore archives, joined them, and in 1938 recorded Morton reminiscing at length in a small room in the library's music section, recordings which are a crazy quilt of memory, romance and invention. In the same period, infuriated by a Robert Ripley radio programme which introduced W.C. Handy as "the originator of jazz and the blues," Morton fired off a letter to *Down Beat* magazine: "I myself," he said, "happened to be the creator of jazz in the year of 1902." The controversy reminded people that

MAX JONES FILE/REDFERNS

Jelly Roll Morton and his Red Hot Peppers

Morton was still alive, but he was not well. In 1939, living in New York again ("that cruel city", he called it), he made more recordings, as he did in 1940. And that year, plagued with asthma and a heart condition, he drove to California in search of warm weather and perhaps success; the following year he died insensate in hospital. Ten years on the Jelly Roll Morton Society, at the instigation of Floyd Levin, finally marked his grave at Calvary Cemetery, Los Angeles.

Morton took classic small-band jazz to its artistic limits: "Jelly Roll was to the small band what Ellington was to the large," says Art Hodes. His music has been perpetuated in clubs, concert halls, theatres and on record by artists as varied as Dick Hyman, Pee Wee Erwin, Kenny Ball, Max Harris and choreographer Twyla Tharp. [DF]

⦿ **Jelly Roll Morton 1923–24/1924–26/1926–28/ 1928–29/ 1929–30/1930–39/1939–40** (Classics). The comprehensive chronology of Morton's work, including titles omitted from the two sets below. Quality is variable and some of the core Morton work is better presented on the other sets, but only here will you find his very last recordings, with "Red" Allen, Albert Nicholas and others.

⦿ **Jelly Roll Morton Vols. 1–5** (1926–30; JSP). Available as five separate volumes, and only excluding Morton's 1939 sessions, this set is a magnificent chronology, superbly mastered by John R.T. Davies; alternate takes are included.

⊙ **The Original Mr. Jelly Lord 1923–41** (Avid). Very good fifty-track 2-CD selection of Morton's work with most of his greatest sides (plus some oddities including "Hyena Stomp"); fine sound restoration by Dave Bennett and excellent documentation by Clarrie Henley, Martin Litton and Brian Rust. A well-informed collection for non-completists.

⦿ **The Library Of Congress Recordings** (1938; Affinity). A three-CD set collating the best of Morton's playing with some of his reminiscences. Essential for Morton aficionados.

⦿ **Last Sessions: The Complete General Recordings** (1939–40; Commodore). Morton's final sessions are often criticized but with the presence of musicians like Henry "Red" Allen and charming tunes like "My Home Is In A Southern Town" it's hard to see why. Fine sound and booklet make this set an attractive choice.

Bob Moses

Drums, piano, vibes, bass-clarinet, flutes, kalimba, electric bass, synthesizer, vocals, composer.
b. New York, 28 Jan 1948.

Bob (Rahboat) Moses's father, Richard, was press agent for musicians including Charles Mingus, Max Roach and Rahsaan Roland Kirk, all of whom were close family friends and powerful influences on young him. When he was about twelve he used to sit in with Mingus on Sunday afternoon sessions (mostly playing drums, his first instrument), but his first professional gigs were as a teenage vibraphonist on New York's Latin music scene. In 1964–5 he spent six months with Kirk and drummed on two of the saxophonist's albums. In 1966 he helped to form Free Spirits with saxophonist Jim Pepper and Larry Coryell, which was perhaps the first electric jazz-rock group. In 1968 he played briefly in Open Sky with Dave Liebman, then joined the Gary Burton quartet, which then included Coryell and bassist Steve Swallow. Although he left after 14 months in 1969, he would return to Burton's groups throughout the 70s.

Moses formed another jazz-rock band, Compost, in 1973, with Jack DeJohnette and tenor saxman Harold Vick. He toured the UK with the Mike Gibbs orchestra in 1974, before playing and recording with the Pat Metheny trio along with Jaco Pastorius, and Hal Galper's group with the Brecker brothers. In 1980 he formed an all-star quintet with Dave Liebman, Terumasa Hino, Steve Kuhn and Steve Swallow. He spent 1981–3 with the Steve Kuhn-Sheila Jordan band, and 1984 with the George Gruntz big band. In 1984–5 he formed his own quintet.

In the mid-1970s he began composing for big ensembles, and created his own record label, Mozown Records, to release *Bittersuite In The Ozone*, for a line-up which included Randy Brecker, Eddie Gomez, Howard Johnson, Dave Liebman, Jeanne Lee, Billy Hart and Stanley Free. This was followed by two superb albums, *When Elephants Dream of Music* (1982) and *Visit With The Great Spirit* (1983), which showed Moses to be a highly accomplished and most original composer and orchestrator. He had always been an incipient visionary, and with these albums the seer came out in all his glory: he was now writing and reciting poetry and painting, and the album covers bore his texts and brightly coloured semi-abstract pictures. The music, too, had many resonances, from other periods of jazz, other cultures; it was dense and deft but also full of wit and humour. The albums received universal critical acclaim, and Nat Hentoff wrote: "No orchestral composer of this scope, mellow wit and freshly distinctive range of colours has come along since Gil Evans." As a drummer and as an orchestrator, Moses shows wide terms of reference, from Evans, Mike Gibbs, Mingus, Monk, Ellington and Miles Davis to African and Latin American music. The music he makes always swings; he once said, "Several years ago, I got tired of playing subdued, non-physical, abstract music for a small audience of elite aficionados who sit there and politely applaud; I want to play some loud, powerful people's music ... Everything I do I want to swing. I think music needs to swing, no matter how abstract it gets. In fact, the more abstract, the more intellectual it gets, the more it *needs* to swing, because that's the balancing factor." [IC]

⊙ **Visit With The Great Spirit** (1983; Gramavision); **Wheels Of Coloured Light** (no date; Open Minds). *Spirit* has a huge star-studded personnel and is full of colour and drama. *Wheels* has Moses in quartet with Terumasa Hino, Dave Liebman and vocalist Jeanne Lee – a microcosm, airier and freer.

➤➤ **Mike Gibbs** *(By The Way...)*; **Steve Swallow** *(Home)*.

Snub Mosley

Trombone, slide saxophone, vocals.

b. Little Rock, Arkansas, 29 Dec 1905; d. 21 July 1981.

While Snub (Lawrence Leo) Mosley was never in the front rank of early trombone soloists such as Jimmy Harrison or even Claude Jones, he was a talent to watch right from the start. From 1926–33 he was featured soloist with Alphonso Trent's hugely successful territory band, where his stabbing, staccato attack and high-register work attracted attention, and for the rest of the 1930s he worked in some of the best big bands, including Claude Hopkins's, Luis Russell's, Fats Waller's and Fletcher Henderson's. From 1938 he led his own six-piece band at hotels, clubs and on tour, and produced at least one hit record, "The Man With The Funny Little Horn!", featuring a remarkable "slide saxophone" – his own invention, it looked like a big metal Swanee whistle and produced a spectral sound. For forty years, Mosley fronted his sometimes R&B-flavoured bands, mainly in the New York area; he recorded in 1959 for Stanley Dance and twenty years on was touring Europe, fronting Fred Hunt's trio. [DF]

Danny Moss

Tenor saxophone, reeds.

b. Sussex, UK, 16 Aug 1927.

Moss built his reputation in the best 1940s and 1950s British big bands, including Tommy Sampson's, Ted Heath's and John Dankworth's, in all of which he was a featured soloist. Although chronologically a member of the post-war bebop generation (and a master of it), Moss found himself by 1960 identifying more strongly with jazz's classic era and began returning to the vocabulary of Ben Webster and Coleman Hawkins, regularly sitting in with Dixielanders such as Alex Welsh and mainstreamer Sandy Brown. In the 1960s, with pianist Brian Lemon, he formed his quartet and worked with Humphrey Lyttelton; in the 1970s he was regularly with Freddy Randall's Bobcats-style band (co-led by Dave Shepherd), and was featured soloist with Stan Reynolds's swing band, working in studios only when necessary. In the 1980s he played as easily for Tony Bennett (as featured accompanist, succeeding Bobby Hackett and Ruby Braff) and for Bobby Rosengarden's New York band as he did for Peter Boizot's Pizza All Stars in Britain. In the 1990s Moss moved to Australia, but he tours for part of the year as a soloist and with Peanuts Hucko, and records regularly with Americans such as Randy Sandke for the Nagel-Heyer company in Germany. Still underrated, he did in Britain what Scott Hamilton was to do later in America, but to fewer fanfares. [DF]

⊙ **Keeper of the flame** (1998; Nagel-Heyer). Moss in a fine representative quartet setting accompanied by three peers; John Pearce (piano), Len Skeat (bass) and Charlie Antolini (drums). One of the best of his many Nagel-Heyer recordings; playing what comes naturally.

➤➤ **Randy Sandke** *(Happy Birthday Welle Plus)*.

Michael Mossman

Trumpet, flugelhorn, piano.

b. Philadelphia, 12 Oct 1959.

Mossman gained a BA in sociology and anthropology, and a BMus in trumpet, both from Oberlin College in 1982; he also did postgraduate trumpet studies at Rutgers University. Though his chosen medium is hard-bop, he first came to international notice touring Europe in the late 70s with more left-field players: the Anthony Braxton orchestra, and Roscoe Mitchell. But he went on to play with Lionel Hampton's orchestra in 1984, and, for one month, with Art Blakey's Jazz Messengers. In 1985 he was lead trumpet with Machito, for a Spanish tour, and was featured soloist with the Gerry Mulligan orchestra, as well as with two classical orchestras. He was also co-leader of Blue Note Records' young artist group, Out of the Blue. [IC]

Out of the Blue

⊙ **Live At Mt Fuji** (1986; Blue Note). Mossman co-leads this young neo-bop sextet, recorded at the Japanese 1986 Blue Note festival. The band includes alto player Kenny Garrett, later of Miles Davis fame, but the group in general tends to overplay. Mossman's funky composition "OTB" is one of the best performances.

Mossman-Schnyder Quintet

⊙ **Granulat** (1990; Red). Mossman co-leads this quintet in music that is crisp, clear, but tricky and demanding. All compositions except one are by Schnyder – the exception is Mossman's "Cage Of Ice". Mossman handles the written parts and solos with great panache.

Bennie Moten

Piano, leader, composer.

b. Kansas City, Missouri, 13 Nov 1894; d. 2 April 1935.

One of the three best-known Kansas big-band leaders of the 1920s (the other two were his arch-rival George E. Lee and Walter Page), Moten "started out with just three pieces" (said Jimmy Rushing), playing ragtime and New Orleans-style jazz, and by 1923 had recorded for OKeh. His band policy, geared to public demand and designed for dancing, made Moten very popular around Kansas (for a long time he held down a residency at the El Torreon Ballroom) and by 1925 his band had augmented to six pieces. Three years on, when Moten came to New York for the first time, more big changes occurred. "When Walter Page had trouble with bookings," remembers Rushing, "Bennie began to take guys from his Blue Devils. Basie went first, then Lips Page and I. Later Walter Page broke up his group and joined Bennie too." (So did guitarist Eddie Durham and accordionist Bus Moten, Bennie's young nephew.) The improvement was audible to all apart from the die-hard fans who resented his change in style, and gradually Moten's original men were replaced by new stars: Ben Webster and Eddie Barefield joined in 1932, Herschel Evans and Lester Young the year after. By 1935, Moten's "first band" (he ran several others at the period) had reached a peak and travelled to Chicago for a booking at Rainbow Gardens and an audition for the Grand Terrace Ballroom. Moten stayed behind to have his tonsils out and died on the operating table; his band was taken over (after a struggle with Walter Page) by Count Basie – the start of something big. [DF]

⊙ **Bennie Moten 1923–32** (Classics). The complete Moten saga in four volumes, from the early OKeh recordings, through the arrival of Count Basie and Eddie Durham, to the glory days of 1932, when the band produced a string of classic-status recordings, such as "Moten Swing". Jimmy Rushing, Hot Lips Page and Basie shine in solos as well as ensemble.

Paul Motian

Drums.

b. Providence, Rhode Island, 25 March 1931.

Motian began gigging in New York in the mid-1950s with George Wallington and Russell Jacquet. He then got regular work with the Tony Scott quartet of 1956–7, where he began his association with pianist Bill Evans. He also worked with Oscar Pettiford, Zoot Sims, Lennie Tristano and Al Cohn-Zoot Sims in the late 1950s. He was with the Bill Evans trio from 1959–64, and worked with the Paul Bley trio from 1963–4. In the mid-1960s he worked with singers such as Mose Allison, Morgana King and Arlo Guthrie, but was also with Charles Lloyd. He formed a lasting partnership with Charlie Haden in Keith Jarrett's trio and quartet from 1967–76, recording and touring with Haden's Liberation Music Orchestra in 1969, 1982, 1985 and 1990. In the 1970s he recorded and played in concerts with the Jazz Composers' Orchestra Association under different leaders, such as Carla Bley and Don Cherry. Since 1977 he has led his own groups, notably a quintet with Bill Frisell and Joe Lovano (later reducing to a trio) since the early 1980s, and in the 1990s he formed his Electric Bebop Band with two guitarists and Joshua Redman (later Chris Potter).

Motian's ground-breaking work in the Bill Evans trio originally followed the example of Philly Joe Jones, but went much further in fragmenting the beat and interacting with the other members of the group. This ability lent itself extremely well to situations involving more avant-garde soloists, and Motian developed to the point of playing authoritatively in all manner of contexts. His playing is still, however, underrated by many listeners, despite his increasing profile in the last ten years. [BP]

⊙ **Misterioso** (1986; Soul Note). Two tracks of this quintet album, with Lovano, Frisell, bassist Ed Schuller and saxophonist Jim Pepper, pay tribute to Monk (later the subject of a whole album) but the meat of the entire performance lies in the often subtle interaction of Motian and his colleagues.

⊙ **Paul Motian On Broadway: Vol. 1** (1988; JMT). Like Charlie Haden – his Jarrett-era colleague here added to the basic trio – Motian began reinvestigating show tunes at this period. Hoary standards like "Someone To Watch Over Me" and "Over The Rainbow" (plus a couple of more interesting choices) emerge with surprising freshness.

➤➤ **Bill Evans** *(Portrait In Jazz; Waltz For Debby).*

Alphonse Mouzon

Drums, keyboards, composer, arranger, vocals.
b. Charleston, South Carolina, 21 Nov 1948.

Mouzon left for New York at seventeen, working as an orderly in a hospital and studying at night school to be a medical technician. He also studied drama for two and a half years, and at weekends played with Ross Carnegie's Society Band. During his second year in the Big Apple, 1969, he made his first record date – with the Gil Evans orchestra – and in 1970–71 he played with Roy Ayers. But it was the the jazz-rock-fusion movement that really brought Mouzon to prominence. In 1971–2 he was a member of the first line-up of Weather Report (with Zawinul, Shorter, Vitous and Moreira). In 1972–3 he played with McCoy Tyner, and from 1973–5 he was with Larry Coryell's Eleventh House. Mouzon then freelanced, playing festivals and occasionally touring with groups. In 1976 he played the Berlin festival with the Albert Mangelsdorff trio (Jaco Pastorius on bass). In 1984 he was once more with Coryell, in a trio with French bass guitarist Bunny Brunel, which did a long European tour.

Mouzon is a flamboyant character and a drummer of great power. Although he has brought "jazz polyrhythms to a rock pulse", to use his own words, his whole identity as a musician is rooted more in commercial rock than in jazz. [IC]

➤➤ **Albert Mangelsdorff** *(Three Originals)*; **McCoy Tyner** *(Sahara; Enlightenment)*; **Joe Zawinul** *(Weather Report)*.

Famadou Don Moye

Drums, congas, bongos, bass marimba, miscellaneous percussion, whistles, horns, vocals.
b. Rochester, New York, 23 May 1946.

Moye took percussion classes at Wayne State University, Detroit, from 1965–6 before playing with Detroit Free Jazz, going with it to Europe in 1968. He played with Steve Lacy in Rome, North Africa and Paris, where he also worked with the Gospel Messenger Singers, Sonny Sharrock, Dave Burrell, Gato Barbieri, Pharoah Sanders and Alan Shorter. In 1969 he joined the Art Ensemble of Chicago in Paris and has been with it ever since, an integral part of its joyous, pan-cultural folking-up of the jazz avant-garde. Much of his work has been with his Art Ensemble colleagues, notably with Lester Bowie in both The Leaders (since 1984) and Brass Fantasy, and also with musicians who have gravitated about the Chicago and AACM scene – such as Don Pullen, Cecil McBee, Hamiet Bluiet and Julius Hemphill. He regularly convenes righteous meetings of the Sun Percussion Summit, a group dedicated to exploring and extending the traditions of African American percussion music. [IC]

➤➤ **The Art Ensemble of Chicago** *(Urban Bushmen)*; **Lester Bowie** *(The Fire This Time)*.

George Mraz

Bass.
b. Písek, Czechoslovakia, 9 Sept 1944.

George (Jiří) Mraz began studying violin aged seven and played alto saxophone in high school, before specializing on double bass at Prague Conservatory at age sixteen. He graduated and then left Prague at around the same time as Miroslav Vitous, both having played there with Jan Hammer. Mraz moved first to Munich where he stayed from 1966–7, and won a scholarship to study composition and arranging at Berklee. While based in Boston, he worked with Dizzy Gillespie, the Oscar Peterson trio and Ella Fitzgerald, the latter two both in 1972. He settled in New York, and became the replacement for Richard Davis in the Thad Jones-Mel Lewis band from 1972–6. He toured with Stan Getz in 1974, and then freelanced and did studio work. He has also had duo partnerships with pianists such as Jimmy Rowles, Tommy Flanagan and Barry Harris. Extremely reliable in the rhythm-section, Mraz's excellent harmonic sense also translates into marvellously melodic improvised solos. [BP]

⊙ **Jazz** (1995; Milestone). The first-ever US album under his own name features for the most part a trio with Billy Hart and Richie Beirach, with tenorman Rich Perry on two tracks. Mraz shines in a low-key but affecting set of tunes by Shorter, Abercrombie, Bill Evans, Jimmy Rowles (multitrack bass on "The Peacocks") and a couple of standards including the theme from "Cinema Paradiso".

➤➤ **Tommy Flanagan** *(Eclypso)*.

Bheki Mseleku

Piano, alto and tenor saxophones, vocals.
b. Durban, South Africa, 1955.

Mseleku's father died prematurely of diabetes, and his family were so poor that they had to chop up the piano for firewood – Mseleku said he had to "go where there was a piano and hassle my way in". He played with various local bands, then joined one called Malumbo which, sponsored by Atlantic Records, went to play at the Newport jazz festival in the USA. Malumbo went on to New York, playing with Dave Brubeck's sons before going on to the Montreal jazz festival. Back in South Africa, a friend bought Mseleku a plane ticket to Sweden in 1980 and he spent three years there working with bassist Johnny Dyani and trumpeter Don Cherry; elsewhere in Europe he worked with Abdullah Ibrahim and Chris McGregor. He came to England in 1987, where he gigged with Steve Williamson and Courtney Pine, played on Cleveland Watkiss's album *Green Chimneys*, and collaborated with Jonas Gwanga on the film score *Cry Freedom* and Channel Four's *Land Of Dreams*. Then, disillusioned by the musical rat race and the few work opportunities, he gave up music and retired to a Buddhist temple for two years.

JAK KILBY

Bheki Mseleku

Back in London, in November 1991 Mseleku made an impact with some Jazz Café gigs with American bassist Michael Bowie and drummer Marvin "Smitty" Smith, and London musicians Steve Williamson, Jean Toussaint and Eddie Parker. Adding Courtney Pine and South African percussionists, the band recorded Mseleku's first album, *Celebration*, which was produced by his friend Russell Herman. After this breakthrough came tours, festivals and the 1992 live solo album, *Meditations*, and then in August 1993 a trip to New York to record the album *Timelessness*, which was again produced by Herman and again featured Bowie and Smith, as well as special guests singer Abbey Lincoln, flautist Kent Jordan, Pharoah Sanders, Joe Henderson and, on one track, Elvin Jones. It seemed that Mseleku had arrived at last. *Star Seedings* (1995) and *Beauty Of Sunrise* (1997) with Polygram were highly acclaimed and won him a wider audience. His 2003 album *Home At Last* saw him re-evaluate his South African roots, drawing on the talents of fellow countrymen Feya Faku on trumpet and Winston Mankunku Ngozi on sax. It was something of a concept album – and one that actually worked – in that in addressing the paradox of "home" and "roots" for a displaced musician such as Mseleku, he made rich, moving and uplifting music: music that exists in two worlds simultaneously. [IC]

⊙ **Celebration** (1991; World Circuit). Mseleku is an excellent small-group composer. His ten pieces on this album are in recognizable jazz and African traditions, and his piano-playing – rangy, full-chorded and fleet – echoes those traditions too. A very satisfying set with a fine rhythm-section and strong solos all round.

⊙ **Meditations** (1992; MCPS/Verve); *Meditations* consists of just two pieces: the title track, which is just over 32 minutes long, and *Meera-Ma* (Divine Mother), which is nearly 15 minutes. The set has great charm and much feeling, and some piano passages are superb, but it's sometimes a little over-extended.

⊙ **Timelessness** (1993; Verve). The compositions here are brilliant, and the playing likewise. The title track is a small masterpiece, and the standard is consistently good throughout, with a great variety of music.

Eska Mtungwazi

Vocals, keyboards.

b. Bulawayo, Zimbabwe, 22 Aug 1971.

Eska Gillian Mtungwazi studied classical violin, cello and piano through her teens. Having come to live in London, in 1994 she became the vocalist with Anthony Tidd's M-Base Project, and began singing with Quite Sane, a rap/jazz experimental octet. In 1996 she played keyboards and sang backing vocals for gospel artist Judy Bailey, and in 1998 she became the vocalist with Tomorrow's Warriors. She also worked with various hip-hop artists and performed with vocalist Julie Dexter, pianist Nikki Yeoh, Courtney Pine (with whom she also recorded), and former J-Lifers pianist Robert Mitchell and saxophonist Barak Schmool. In 1999, she went to Tennessee to record a gospel album with Judy Bailey, for whom Mtungwazi did all the vocal arrangements and the backing vocals. She is a sweet and powerful gospel singer, and during the 1990s she broadened her techniques to include standard songs and other vocal areas as well as jazz. In 2000, she sang with Panacea, Robert Mitchell's electroacoustic band, on the album *Voyager* (Dune). She sang on New Sector Movement's chic and of its time *Download This* album – 2001's soundtrack of choice for plush West London wine bars due to its slightly louche updating of early-70s Roy Ayers. And her "eerie vocal blend of the majestic and the childlike" (John Fordham) spooked up "Good Nyooz" on Soweto Kinch's *Conversations with the Unseen* (2003; Dune). [IC]

Idris Muhammad

Drums.

b. New Orleans, 13 Nov 1939.

Idris was born Leo Morris to a father from Pakistan and a mother from Paris. At sixteen Idris recorded with Fats Domino. He toured with singers Larry Williams, Lloyd Price and Jerry Butler, before joining the house band at Harlem's Apollo Theatre. He later toured with Lou Donaldson (1966–70), changing to his present name, and then played for the Broadway musical *Hair!* in the early 1970s, during which time he sessioned, and recorded a series of albums under his own name. After touring with singer Roberta Flack from 1974–8, he visited India and Pakistan for six months and then played successively with Johnny Griffin, Pharoah Sanders and George Coleman. In 1986 and 1988, Muhammad toured with the Paris Reunion Band and took up residence in Europe, living for a time in the UK and working with Tommy Smith and many visiting US musicians. His name is a byword for creative versatility: he is capable of covering the thrusting bebop required by his 1980s associations, the subtle swing needed for Hank Jones and Tommy Flanagan, and that zestful New Orleans funk which made his name(s). [BP]

Kabsha (1980; Evidence). Although his 1970s soul and funk albums are collectable items among dance-floor fans, this post-bop date features Ray Drummond, no keyboard or guitar, and both George Coleman and Pharoah Sanders (who have solo features and combine on two takes of the blues).

➤➤ **Tony Coe** *(Canterbury Song)*; **Charles Earland** *(Black Talk)*; **Ernest Ranglin** *(Below The Bassline)*.

Jim Mullen

Guitar.

b. Glasgow, Scotland, 2 Nov 1945.

Mullen started on guitar at the age of ten, switched to bass at fourteen, and started gigging locally. In 1963 he reverted to guitar, running his own bands in Glasgow before moving to London in 1969, playing with Pete Brown until 1971. He played with Brian Auger's Oblivion Express from 1971–3, and with blues band Vinegar Joe and others from 1973–5. From 1975–7 he played in the USA with acts such as the Average White Band and Herbie Mann.

He is probably best known to European audiences for his long-term partnership with Dick Morrissey, a duo that lasted from the mid-70s until 1985. The pair continued to work together in more straightforward jazz contexts until Morrissey's death. Among his favourites are Django Reinhardt, Charlie Christian, Barney Kessel, Kenny Burrell and John McLaughlin. [IC]

Soundbites (1993; EFZ). Mullen leads a quartet with tenor sax star Dave O'Higgins, bassist Laurence Cottle and drummer Ian Thomas. Mullen's playing has deepened and sharpened over the years so that he always seems to mean every note – to be permanently inspired – and O'Higgins never puts a foot wrong.

➤➤ **Mike Carr** *(The Good Times And The Blues)*; **Dick Morrissey** *(Happy Hour; Life On The Wire)*.

Gerry Mulligan

Baritone and soprano saxophones, arranger, composer.

b. New York, 6 April 1927; d. 20 Jan 1996.

Mulligan was raised in Philadelphia and, after selling arrangements to a local radio band, he specialized as a writer. His first recorded works were for Gene Krupa in 1947 and Claude Thornhill in 1948; in both bands he also briefly played alto. Through Thornhill he made contact with Gil Evans, and this led to him writing and playing baritone for the Miles Davis nonet of 1948; Mulligan later recorded with his own similar-sized groups in 1951, 1953 and 1972, and rerecorded the Davis repertoire in 1992. He wrote for Stan Kenton's band in 1953, and meanwhile increased his performing reputation by organizing his popular quartet on the West Coast, in which he shared the frontline with Chet Baker from 1952–3, Jon Eardley from 1954–5, Bob Brookmeyer from 1956–7 and Art Farmer from 1958–9. He also led a sextet in 1955–6 with Eardley, Brookmeyer and Zoot Sims, and other small ensembles in the mid-1960s and mid-1970s. He had his own twelve-piece big band from 1960–63, and intermittently revived it from 1978–96. He appeared with the Dave Brubeck group from 1968–72 and, resident in Italy from 1974, he did annual tours with a quartet.

Most of Mulligan's most popular tunes, such as "Walkin' Shoes" or "Line For Lyons", date from his 1950s quartets, which were the first regularly organized groups without a chord instrument such as a piano or guitar. His writing for larger bands, much of it original material but also including intelligent treatments of standards, is more absorbing. Whether using fully voiced chords or unison lines, there is always a light-hearted and light-textured feel about Mulligan's work. Typically, he operated at medium volume, always preferring two or three trumpets to everyone else's four, and the boring big-band blast-off is not his bag at all.

Sadly, this arranging style has not been as influential as his playing, which represents one of the few peaks of the baritone's history. By comparison with Serge Chaloff or later entrants, Mulligan always sounded like a product of the swing era; indeed, in phraseology and timing, not much separated him from the bass-saxophone work of Adrian Rollini. Even the advanced harmonic knowledge in some of his arranging was usually banished from his own solos, whose rhythmic and melodic verve made him "the Zoot Sims of the baritone". Given the ponderous nature of the instrument, there can be no higher praise. [BP]

Mullenium (1946–57; Columbia). An excellent expanded reissue of a 1977 LP that included then new material by a 1957 studio-only big band, featuring Zoot Sims, Lee Konitz, Bob Brookmeyer and Charlie Rouse. Mulligan's light-toned, swinging scores are usefully contrasted with early work for the bands of Gene Krupa (when he was nineteen) and Elliot Lawrence.

The Best Of The Gerry Mulligan Quartet With Chet Baker (1952–7; Pacific Jazz). A justifiable title for a compilation which (apart from the closing 1957 track) concentrates on the *annus mirabilis* of Mulligan's first quartet. All the hits are here, plus other highly melodic and virtually forgotten originals that would have made anyone else's reputation.

Gerry Mulligan Meets Ben Webster (1959; Verve). The straightforward blowing side of Mulligan's persona came out in a series of quintets with one other veteran saxophonist. Both Gerry and Ben contribute new tunes, singably simple riffs designed just to get everyone off the ground.

The Age Of Steam (1971; A&M). Given the apparent unavailability of both earlier and later big-band albums, this classic takes on new importance. Here was a get-together of studio veterans (from Harry Edison to Tom Scott) giving their all to realize some splendidly judged, and surprisingly funky, Mulligan originals.

Mick Mulligan

Trumpet, leader.

b. Harrow, Middlesex, UK, 24 Jan 1928.

The Mulligan band was so wickedly documented in George Melly's book *Owning Up* that its music is now lost under a tidal wave of largely well-founded legend. A man of boundless charm and bawdy humour, Mulligan was a sturdy Armstrong-style trumpeter whose music was later overshadowed by Alex Welsh's longer-lived organization. Occasionally chaotic in public performance, his band was marvellous on record: it featured two fine players in Ian Christie (clarinet) and Frank Parr (trombone), as well as regular guests such as Betty Smith and Denny Wright, and often dug into obscure repertoire, which it played in an enjoyable, "timeless" style. The band had a highly successful fifteen-year career until 1962, when Mulligan decided to concentrate on his business concerns, very occasionally playing for fun. [DF]

Jimmy Mundy

Tenor saxophone, arranger, composer.

b. Cincinnati, 28 June 1907; d. 24 April 1983.

Originally a tenor saxophonist, Mundy learnt the craft of arranging in Washington in the mid-20s, working for Erskine Tate, Tommy Miles and Carroll Dickerson before moving on to Earl Hines (1932–6), for whom he played tenor and supplied arrangements (Hines especially enjoyed "Everything Depends On You"). In 1935, however, Mundy sold Goodman an arrangement of "Madhouse" and the following year became his staff arranger, producing many successful scores including "Swingtime In The Rockies", "Jumpin' At The Woodside", "Air Mail Special", "Bugle Call Rag", "Sunny Disposish", "Clarinet Marmalade", "Moonlight On The Highway" and "Solo Flight". Mundy also wrote extensively for Count Basie (c.1940–47), as well as Paul Whiteman, Gene Krupa, Charlie Spivak and others, and briefly led his own band in 1939. After military service he returned to arranging for Basie, Harry James and others, and then in 1959 moved to Paris as musical director for Barclay Records. Back in the USA from the 1960s, he remained reasonably active as a writer, consolidating his central contribution to jazz arranging. [DF]

Jimmy Mundy 1937-47 (Classics). A very worthwhile collection from Classics, combining V-Disc material from 1947 with sides by his small groups and big band (1939) plus vocal group the Ginger Snaps.

➤➤ **Benny Goodman** *(Benny Goodman On The Air).*

Joe Muranyi

Clarinet, soprano saxophone, vocals.

b. Ohio, 14 Jan 1928.

Of Hungarian descent, Joe Muranyi did his first playing with a balalaika orchestra, and later attracted attention as one of the American post-war revivalists who flew in the face of fashion by re-examining the music of Armstrong and Morton (two regular playing associates then, and more recently, were Marty Grosz and Dick Wellstood). In the 1950s, still only in his mid-twenties, he played with bands led by Danny Barker, as well as the Red Onion Jazz Band, and also worked successfully as a producer and sleevenote writer for major labels such as Atlantic, Bethlehem and RCA. Recording, club and festival work with senior partners such as Max Kaminsky and Jimmy McPartland helped further Muranyi's reputation, and from 1967–71 he hit a career peak as clarinettist with Louis Armstrong's All Stars, providing the supportive role that Armstrong required and becoming a close friend in the process. The partnership was terminated only by the trumpeter's death, after which Muranyi moved into Jimmy Ryan's to work alongside another old master, Roy Eldridge, then deputized with The World's Greatest Jazz Band in 1975. In 1983 he became one quarter of the Classic Jazz Quartet, a highly successful (and in its own way groundbreaking) quartet with cornettist Dick Sudhalter and old friends Grosz and Wellstood, which played at acoustic level, explored rare and original repertoire, and – best of all – never took itself too seriously. Since the CJQ disbanded, Muranyi has continued to freelance and to tour as a soloist and with trumpeter Keith Smith, and has appeared in two TV documentaries about Louis Armstrong; the Gully Low Jazz Band, featuring Joe, marked the opening of Louis Armstong's Queens, New York, house as a museum in swinging style in autumn 2003. A witty commentator and beguiling composer, Muranyi is a multifaceted jazzman whose swooping soprano and dry-toned clarinet evoke the memory of Sidney Bechet and Jimmie Noone. [DF]

The Classic Jazz Quartet; the complete recordings (1986; Jazzology). Muranyi's solo powers on both clarinet and soprano saxophone show up well in the scholarly and instrumentally economical setting of this gentlemen's musical club, and he has a fine original too; "Medusa".

➤➤ **Dick Sudhalter** *(Classic Jazz Quartet; Classic Jazz Quartet MCMLXXXVI).*

Mark Murphy

Vocals.

b. Syracuse, New York, 14 March 1932.

Murphy gained early experience with a band led by his elder brother. He began working in New York jazz clubs and appearing on TV in the late 1950s, making albums under his own name backed by arrangers such as Ernie Wilkins and Al Cohn. He toured the UK and Europe as a soloist in 1964, and then settled in Europe for the next ten years. He returned to the USA in 1975, and started recording regularly again, as well as working in Europe on tour. Murphy's popular success with two different generations of young listeners, in the early 1960s and since the 1980s, speaks well for his dedication. Stylistically very consistent, he frequently uses jazz-associated material for his own melodic improvisation and scat singing that sounds infallibly "hip". [BP]

What A Way To Go (1990; Muse). Despite the title, Murphy is still highly active, reinterpreting standards such as "I Fall In Love Too Easily" and the less well-known "All My Tomorrows", while expanding the repertoire with his own words to, for instance, Lee Morgan's "Ceora".

Rose Murphy

Piano, vocals.

b. Xenia, Ohio, 1913; d. 16 Nov 1989.

Murphy made her name as a club performer in the 1940s and became known as the "chee-chee" girl after a piece of scat she introduced in her inimitable high-pitched voice on "Busy Line" and other big-selling records of the period. A disciple of Fats Waller, she played the London Palladium in 1950, and continued for the next three decades to appear at clubs (including the Cookery, New York, during the 1960s), concerts and festivals; in 1980 she recorded at the Nice jazz festival with Major Holley. [DF]

Turk Murphy

Trombone, composer.

b. Palermo, California, 16 Dec 1915; d. 30 May 1987.

After an apprenticeship with Mal Hallett, Will Osborne and cabaret bands, Turk (Melvin) Murphy spent ten very successful years with Lu Watters's Yerba Buena Jazz Band, the figurehead of San Francisco's classic jazz revival. From 1940–50 Murphy's racketing tailgate trombone was central to the rolling two-beat music of the Yerba Buenas: his natural gift for ensemble playing and forthright solos were showcased in features such as his own "Trombone Rag". After the band broke up, Murphy formed his own, retaining ex-Yerbas such as Bob Helm and Wally Rose and digging – with a scholar's judgement – into the classic jazz repertoire. He also became a spokesman for revivalist jazz, writing regularly and intelligently about his jazz in books and on sleevenotes, and was wellknown enough to be portrayed by Eddie Condon in his *Treasury of Jazz* ("a husky guy with a stir trim, somewhat like Fred MacMurray, who looks capable of staying a round or two!"). Murphy's music – in contrast to his quick wit and verbal gifts – stayed close to the roots and was sometimes criticized: "The music that I have been making for the past fifteen years," he wrote in 1956, "has been the subject of a concerted critical animosity almost unanimous in the music trade press." Murphy's music was actually great fun, and he weathered the criticism to play in New York at Child's Restaurant in the 1950s, as well as in New Orleans and San Francisco, where in 1960 he opened his own club, Earthquake McGoon's. Murphy continued to play at his (later relocated) club when not appearing at Disneyland, at festivals (including the St Louis Ragtime festival, 1977) or on the road. [DF]

Jazz Band Favourites (1949–51; Good Time Jazz). Vintage Murphy from the morning of America's jazz revival; his music has spawned a school of West Coast imitators, and the roots of its inspiration are here.

San Francisco Jazz Band In Concert Vols. 1 & 2 (1972; GHB). Live recordings by Murphy's band from later in his career but full of the roaring revivalist spirit that turned him into a legend.

David Murray

Tenor and soprano saxophones, bass-clarinet, flute, composer.

b. Berkeley, California, 19 Feb 1955.

Murray's mother, who was a pianist in the Pentecostal Church, taught him elementary music harmony. He played tenor from the age of nine, and at twelve he got into R&B, playing in groups as a teenager. After studying at Pomona College, Los Angeles, with Stanley Crouch and Margaret Kohn (piano) he left for New York in 1975. Murray began his professional career as a free player sitting in with Cecil Taylor, Don Cherry and Anthony Braxton, and working with Sunny Murray. By the late 1970s he was working with James "Blood" Ulmer's harmolodic free-funk Music Revelation Ensemble, Jack DeJohnette's Special Edition and the World Saxophone Quartet. However, his music gradually moved back into the area of coherent swing and clear structures, and he quickly began leading his own groups, touring Europe regularly and making records. In the early 1980s he led his own octet and quartet and recorded for the Italian Black Saint label.

Since 1984 he has led a big band, when finances allow, which appeared at the Kool festival, and through the later 1980s and into the 1990s Murray has recorded prolifically with a variety of musicians and in 1991 he was awarded the Danish Jazzpar

DAVID REDFERN

David Murray

prize. His main influence is perhaps Paul Gonsalves, whom he much admires and considers underrated. He is a player of outstanding passion and plasticity, and his music has all the fervour of hot gospel and the blues. He is also a gifted composer and arranger. [IC]

⊙ **Live At The Lower Manhattan Ocean Club** (1977; India Navigation). The live session is by a piano-less quartet with bassist Fred Hopkins, drummer Phillip Wilson and Lester Bowie, partnering Murray in a re-examination of the jazz tradition.

⊙ **Ming** (1980; Black Saint); **Home** (1981; Black Saint). Several aristocrats of the avant-garde feature in Murray's octet on both of these albums, including George Lewis, Henry Threadgill, Anthony Davis and drummer Steve McCall; the results are superbly focused fusions of tradition and innovation, and Murray's dynamic originality astonishes.

⊙ **The Hill** (1986; Black Saint). Murray's trio with Richard Davis and Joe Chambers in a powerful and affecting interpretation of jazz standards and original compositions. Incisive playing all round plus some superb bass-clarinet.

⊙ **Ballads** (1988; DIW); **Spirituals** (1988; DIW); **Special Quartet** (1990; DIW). *Ballads* and *Spirituals* are deservedly two of Murray's most popular quartet albums – with pianist Dave Burrell, Hopkins and drummer Ralph Peterson, playing fine original compositions by members of the group. *Special Quartet* is indeed that, with McCoy Tyner, Hopkins and Elvin Jones, exploring a tradition that two of them had helped to create.

⊙ **Body And Soul** (1993; Black Saint). Murray is a masterful interpreter of ballads, and he continues to explore the Hawkins legacy here with a quartet and vocalist Taana Running.

➤➤ **Jack DeJohnette** *(Album Album)*; **World Saxophone Quartet** *(WSQ; Dances And Ballads).*

Don Murray

Clarinet, saxophones: also violin.
b. Joliet, Illinois, 7 June 1904; d. 2 June 1929.

A clarinettist who often played tenor saxophone, Don Murray is principally remembered as a colleague and early champion of Bix Beiderbecke, whom he joined after early work with a reconstituted New Orleans Rhythm Kings, with Jean Goldkette's orchestra, Adrian Rollini's short-lived New Yorker band and bandleader Don Voorhees. His records with Beiderbecke under the banner of Bix and his Gang, as well as with related small groups from 1927–8, are some of the greatest ever made, and his premature death, after hitting his head in a fall while filming with Ted Lewis in Hollywood, was a tragic loss. [DF]

➤➤ **Bix Beiderbecke** *(Vol 2: At The Jazz Band Ball).*

Sunny Murray

Drums.
b. Idabel, Oklahoma, 21 Sept 1937.

James Murray moved to New York in 1956, where he started his career working with players such as Henry "Red" Allen, Willie "The Lion" Smith, Jackie McLean and Ted Curson. He began playing with Cecil Taylor in 1959 and stayed with him five years, including a European tour in 1962. Meeting Albert Ayler in Scandinavia, he formed a trio with him and Gary Peacock which was active in 1964–5, and which also toured Europe. He also did gigs with Don Cherry, John Coltrane, Ornette Coleman, Roswell Rudd and John Tchicai in the mid-1960s. He was based in France from 1968–71, performing and recording with local musicians; made unaccompanied appearances in London and other cities in 1968; and worked with visiting Americans such as Archie Shepp and Grachan Moncur, including performances at the Pan-African festival in Algiers in 1969. In the 1970s he moved to Philadelphia, co-leading, with vibist Khan Jamal, the Untouchable Factor, and working with Philly Joe Jones, whom he had met in Paris.

Murray's pioneering work with Taylor found him building a bridge between a recognizable pulse and the totally abstract style typical of his period with Ayler. Though full of vitality, he was less domineering than many of the so-called "energy" players, and devoted considerable attention to the cymbals, from which he drew a great variety of tonal contrast. Although this was often submerged by the contexts in which he chose to perform, it is equally true that his example was not lost on European drummers of the "free" persuasion. [BP]

➤➤ **Albert Ayler** *(Spiritual Unity; Witches And Devils).*

Vido Musso

Tenor saxophone, clarinet.
b. Carrini, Sicily, 17 Jan 1913; d. 9 Jan 1982.

To the white tenor-saxophone vocabulary patented by Bud Freeman and continued by such men as Tony Pastor and Eddie Miller, Vido William Musso brought a new Italianate fervour, a tone as big as a mountain and the rasping throat-growl that was to be adopted by rock'n'roll saxophonists a generation later. His career proper began with Benny Goodman in 1936 and he quickly became a crowd-pleasing favourite, who over an eleven-year period worked with most of swingdom's famous leaders: Gene Krupa (1938), Harry James (1940–41), Goodman again, Woody Herman (1942–3), Tommy Dorsey (1945) and Stan Kenton (1946–7). Musso's contribution to Kenton classics such as "Painted Rhythm" and "Artistry In Rhythm" are fondly remembered by jazz people, and had a powerful influence on younger modern jazzmen, including Ronnie Scott. But by the time he joined Kenton it was a sad fact that Musso sounded uncomfortable set against the harmonic advances of bop, the tight-lipped cool fashions of modern jazz and Kenton's austere innovations; in a word, he sounded dated, and – perhaps because he was a "natural" player who never learned to read music, nor studied a lot – he found himself unable to do much about it. From 1947 Musso carried on bandleading on the West Coast but, despite fairly regular recording, he failed to maintain the reputation of his younger years. Perhaps he was simply born too early: the jazz climate of the 1980s would have suited him better. **[DF]**

Stan Kenton

Retrospective (1943–68; Capitol). Disc 1 of this four-disc boxed set has many of Kenton's formative hits featuring Musso's huge-toned generous tenor, probably Kenton's principal solo voice in his earliest years.

Wolfgang Muthspiel

Guitar, violin, composer.
b. 2 March 1965, Judenburg, Austria

Raised in a musical family – his father was an amateur choirmaster, his brother Christian is a trombonist – Wolfgang Muthspiel began playing the violin at six and switched to guitar at fifteen, studying both the classical and jazz instrument at the Hochschule für Musik und Darstellende Kunst in Graz. In addition to various national classical competitions, Muthspiel also won the International Guitar Competition in Mettmann, Germany, but – a passion for Bach (which saw him, inspired by Glenn Gould, transcribe and record Bach's *Goldberg Variations* for two guitars) aside – became frustrated at the relative lack of classical repertoire for guitar. Following his penchant for improvisation, he formed a duo with his brother Christian in 1982, and they, as *Duo Due*, performed extensively in Europe, the USA and North Africa, and made two albums for Amadeo. In 1986, Muthspiel emigrated to the USA to study at the New England Conservatory under Mick Goodrick and David Leisner, later attending Berklee and graduating in 1989. Joining the Gary Burton quintet, he toured the world, appearing in nearly two hundred concerts and recording for the GRP label. Muthspiel has also recorded with bassist Marc Johnson, drummers Paul Motian and Brian Blade, and the Vienna Art Orchestra, but his own albums provide the best showcase for his wide-ranging, protean talent, which draws as easily on Bach and The Beatles as on jazz. His Amadeo/Polygram albums include *Timezones* (1989, with Bob Berg), *The Promise* (1990, with Berg and Richie Beirach), *Black And Blue* (1993, with Tom Harrell and George Garzone), *In and Out* (1994, with Harrell and Chris Cheek), *Loaded, Like New* (see below) and *Perspective* (1996, with Paul Motian and Marc Johnson). A trio of albums on his own label Material Records in 2001 saw Muthspiel take a turn into left-field electronica and progressive dance music. **[CP]**

Loaded, Like New (1995; Amadeo/Polygram). A horn-less band – bassist Tony Scherr, drummer Kenny Wolleson, percussionist Don Alias – interacts perfectly with Muthspiel's wholly distinctive guitar and guitar-synth sound on an intriguing selection of originals, leavened with The Beatles' "With a Little Help from My Friends".

Amina Claudine Myers

Piano, organ, vocals.
b. Blackwell, Arkansas, 21 March 1942.

Myers studied the piano as a child and sang in a gospel choir; she described hearing Mozart's Requiem at school being a musical epiphany. Moving to Chicago, she became involved with the AACM in the mid-1960s and played with Lester Bowie, Kalaparusha Maurice McIntyre and Muhal Richard Abrams. In the 1970s she also worked with drummer Ajaramu (aka Gerald Donovan), Sonny Stitt-Gene Ammons and blues singer Little Milton, before moving to New York and forming her own group. She has freelanced widely, often with former Chicago colleagues, and in 1985 toured with Charlie Haden's Liberation Music Orchestra. In the late 1980s she signed a recording contract with RCA/Novus that resulted in several fusion-inspired albums. Her more typical playing shows a deep respect for blues and gospel roots, while being highly versed in open-ended improvisation. **[BP]**

Salutes Bessie Smith (1980; Leo). A trio recording with Cecil McBee, which rejoices in Myers's sonorous gospel-influenced vocals on several tracks but is ultimately more impressive for her dynamic piano work.

Zbigniew Namyslowski

Alto saxophone, composer, flute, cello, trombone, piano.
b. Warsaw, Poland, 9 Sept 1939.

Namyslowski began on the piano at four, started music lessons at six and was playing the cello at twelve. He studied theory at the High School of Music in Warsaw, played trombone with a trad band and cello with a modern group before taking up alto saxophone in 1960. With Andrzej Trzaskowski's Jazz Wreckers he toured the USA and Europe, then left to form his own quartet in 1963. He toured in Europe, including the UK, in India, Australia, New Zealand and the USSR. In London in 1964, he and his quartet were the first Polish jazz musicians to record an album in the West – *Lola*, which was released on Decca. In 1965 he played on Krzysztof Komeda's seminal album *Astigmatic*. He has also played on film soundtracks and worked with C. Niemen, the Novi singers and Georges Arvanitas. Since 1971 he has led quintets and quartets. Namyslowski performed with his group at the first Indian jazz festival, Jazz Yatra in Bombay, in 1978. He has composed and arranged for radio, TV and films; he is also a member of the Polish Radio Jazz Studio Band. Namyslowski's favourites include Charlie Parker, John Coltrane and Sonny Rollins. J.E. Berendt calls him a "timeless improviser, in line with the great saxophone tradition in jazz". But Namyslowski is more than that: he has created a music all his own, an impassioned Polish jazz compounded of his American influences and the rich heritage of Polish folk music. [IC]

⊙ **Polish Jazz: Vol. 4 – Zbigniew Namyslowski** (1966–87; Polskie Nagrania); **The Last Concert** (1991; Polonia). This compilation and the *Last Concert* (which concluded the 1991 Warsaw Jazz Jamboree) give a graphic picture of the passionate Polish character of Namyslowski's rich and original music.

➤➤ **Krzysztof Komeda** *(Astigmatic)*.

Ray Nance

Trumpet, violin, vocals, dancer.
b. Chicago, 10 Dec 1913, d. 28 Jan 1976.

For most of the 1930s Nance worked in clubs around Chicago and for bandleaders such as Horace Henderson and Earl Hines. With them, and with his own little band, he gained a reputation as a hard-swinging violinist, mellow cornettist and especially as an entertainer who could sing, dance, do comedy routines and front a show. After he joined Ellington (who nicknamed him "Floorshow"), replacing Cootie Williams in 1940, Nance's talents were featured to the full: his cornet was teamed with "Tricky Sam" Nanton for the growling role that Williams had in turn inherited from Bubber Miley, his violin featured on tone poems such as "Moon Mist", and his jivey infectious vocals were heard on swing tunes such as "A Slip Of The Lip". It was Nance, too, who on Ellington's 1941 record of "Take The A-Train" contributed passages of inspired solo work that soon became an integral part of the composition. In 1948 he came to Britain, as the natural choice for Duke Ellington's partner to tour variety theatres. Jack Fallon, who played bass, remembers: "He was the king of stage presentation. When Duke would be playing he'd do a kind of jig, peckin' round the stage, and every time he'd shoot his cuffs he made his coat tail go up. Then he'd pull his coat down – and up went his cuffs! ... He used to carry a pile of 78s around of all his old friends, and I would say he was insecure, timid though not aggressive." Nance stayed with Ellington until 1963, then led a solo career for a dozen years, toured Britain again in 1966 (a not so happy time) and carried on leading his own quartet, featuring his heavy-toned cornet and witty violin, up to the time of his death. [DF]

➤➤ **Duke Ellington** *(The Indispensable, Vols. 7/8)*.

Joe Nanton

Trombone.
b. New York, 1 Feb 1904; d. 20 July 1946.

Duke Ellington always loved his trombone section best of all, and of all his trombonists it was plunger-mute master "Tricky Sam" Nanton (Joseph N. Irish) who was the most revolutionary. Along with Bubber Miley, with whom he formed a keen team early on, Nanton played Ellington's growling jungle music best. "Tricky had a perfect feeling for it and he could play the proper things to fit the plunger," says Mercer Ellington. "That man could say as much as a human voice on his horn," agreed Dicky Wells. "The wail of a newborn baby, the raucous hoot of an owl, the bloodcurdling scream of an enraged tiger, or the eerie cooing of a mournful dove!" remembered Rex Stewart.

Before he found Ellington in 1926, Nanton – a mild-mannered, cultured Anglophile, who often set up a talking-table near the bar to discuss anything from handmade English clothes to black American politics – had worked in cabaret bands such as Cliff Jackson's, Earl Frazier's and Elmer Snowden's. Subsequently, he worked only for Ellington, refusing to appear or even record with lesser lights, and played on until he suffered a stroke in 1945. Within a few months he came back to tour California and was found dead one morning in his hotel bedroom: heavy drinking may have contributed to his early demise. Afterwards other fine players, including Wilbur de Paris and Tyree Glenn, tried to re-create Nanton's sound: for Ellington it was never quite the same again. [DF]

Duke Ellington

⊙ **Duke Ellington Swing** (1930–38, BBC). In Robert Parker's vivid remix, Nanton's unique sound shines through on "Rockin' In Rhythm", "Saddest Tale", "Truckin'" and more.

➤➤ **Duke Ellington** *(The Duke's Men: Small Groups Vol. 1).*

Marty Napoleon

Piano.

b. Brooklyn, New York, 2 June 1921.

A fine eclectic pianist, Marty Napoleon (Matthew Napoli) received an all-round training in big bands before he joined Gene Krupa's in 1946. Then came time with his uncle Phil Napoleon's Original Memphis Five, and with Charlie Ventura's big bebop band and quintet, beginning an association that lasted on and off for many years. Another longterm connection began in 1952 when Napoleon replaced Earl Hines in Louis Armstrong's All Stars; then came two years duetting with his brother Teddy (1955–6), followed by regular work at the Metropole in New York with Henry "Red" Allen's band. From 1966–71 Napoleon was with Armstrong again, touring, recording and travelling; after that he settled in New York for another brief period with Gene Krupa, as well as making solo appearances and playing festivals. During the 1970s and 1980s he worked with Peanuts Hucko, among others, played a memorial concert for Louis Armstrong (New York, 1986), and appeared in a video documentary celebrating Satchmo (1988). [DF]

Louis Armstrong

⊙ **Mame** (1966; Mercury). Napoleon succeeded Hines and Billy Kyle in Armstrong's All Stars, and he adds much of the same sparkle to their rhythm-section on tracks including "Mame" and "Tin Roof Blues".

Phil Napoleon

Trumpet.

b. Boston, Massachusetts, 2 Sept 1901; d. 30 Sept 1990.

Phil Napoleon (Filippo Napoli) was a formally trained player (like Red Nichols), who by the time he was sixteen had recorded classical cornet pieces. At first undecided on whether to follow straight music or jazz, he chose the latter as a full-time career. "We'd listen to the best records we could get," remembers Napoleon's friend Henry Levine, another underrated trumpeter of the period, "and whenever any good bands came to New York we'd hike across the river from Brooklyn to listen." By 1922 Napoleon had formed the Original Memphis Five, one of the greatest white groups of that decade. Their first two sides ("My Honey's Lovin' Arms" and "Gypsy Blues") were to be followed by hundreds more, most of them best sellers, featuring the revolutionary trombone of Miff Mole as well as other young stars such as the Dorseys, Frank Signorelli and Jimmy Lytell. Napoleon's own clear-toned, clean jazz approach was to influence Red Nichols (who heard him in Kansas City) and Bix Beiderbecke ("I'd take Bix outside and show him what I was doing," Napoleon told Dick Sudhalter): both men were, to some degree, to eclipse their inspiration. Napoleon broke up his band in 1928 and went to work in studios, including NBC, for leaders such as B.A. Rolfe, Sam Lanin and Leo Reisman. Apart from work with big bands (his own in 1938, Jimmy Dorsey's in 1943), he stayed in the studios until 1949, when he re-formed the Original Memphis Five for a seven-year residency at Nick's Club. Soon after that he opened his own club, Napoleon's Retreat, in Miami, ran a band there (including trombonist Ed Hubble), and continued playing the strong, flexible and creative trumpet that jazz has so persistently tended to forget. [DF]

⊙ **The Original Memphis Five/Napoleon's Emperors/The Cotton Pickers 1928-29** (Timeless; 1998). Excellent representation of Napoleon's formative (and prolific) recordings; surrounded by premier sessionmen of the time (Miller, Lang, Signorelli and more).

Teddy Napoleon

Piano.

b. Brooklyn, New York, 23 Jan 1914; d. 5 July 1964.

A fine and very versatile pianist, like his younger brother Marty, Teddy Napoleon (George Napoli) was active with society bands from the 1930s, and is remembered for an association with Gene Krupa that lasted for fourteen years from 1944. After a brief spell with bandleader Tex Beneke, he moved closer to his uncle Phil Napoleon in Florida, and worked there with trios and visiting guests such as Bill Harris and Flip Phillips until his death from cancer. [DF]

Derek Nash

Saxophones, flute, arranger.

b. Manchester, UK, 26 July 1961.

Son of an arranger for the BBC's Northern Dance Orchestra, Derek was a teenage member of

Stockport Schools Stagesound. While studying acoustics at Salford University, he formed the first Saxophone Appeal in 1980 and won a prize in the 1983 National Festival of Music for Youth. The band was re-formed in London in 1984 while Nash was working for BBC-TV and became a busy touring band, visiting festivals in France and Ireland from 1993 and playing for the British Council in Venezuela in 1996. The group's saxophone section also formed part of Barbara Thompson's big band, and Nash has worked with Dick Morrissey and Spike Robinson. He also does pop, soul and blues session work, is a gifted arranger and recording engineer, and in 1999 released his first solo album. His favourites on saxophone include Adderley, Sanborn, Brecker, Turrentine, Peter King, Dave O'Higgins and Tim Garland, while inspirational composer-arrangers are Bob Mintzer, Jaco Pastorius and Ellington. [BP]

Sax Appeal

Let's Go (1993; Jazzizit). The two line-ups on this breakthrough album feature solos by both Dave O'Higgins and Tim Garland, and the material covers funk, swing, fusion, blues and bop. As with subsequent albums, a special guest is US fusion saxophonist Nelson Rangell.

Lewis Nash

Drums, percussion.

b. Phoenix, Arizona, 30 Dec 1958.

Nash's parents and sisters all sang gospel in the church choir, while his mother also listened to blues records. He studied music in school, and privately throughout his school and college career in Arizona. On moving to New York, he began working with Betty Carter in 1985 (alongside Benny Green) and recorded with Green, Branford Marsalis, Renee Rosnes and Clark Terry. After completing his own album, in a single year (1990) he performed sessions with pianists Kenny Barron, Don Pullen, Steve Kuhn and Tete Montoliu and began a continuing relationship with Tommy Flanagan. His subtlety and drive in constant demand at the highest level, Nash has worked with Art Farmer, Dizzy Gillespie, J.J. Johnson, Oscar Peterson, Horace Silver, McCoy Tyner, Joe Henderson and Ron Carter. He lists fifteen favourite drummers including Louis Hayes, Roy Haynes, Alan Dawson, Connie Kay, Billy Higgins, Ben Riley and Jimmy Cobb, while inspirational figures are Gillespie, Parker, Monk, J.J. Johnson, Thad Jones and Oliver Nelson. [BP]

Rhythm Is My Business (1989; Evidence). Nash's only solo album to date features a basic quartet with Mulgrew Miller and Steve Nelson, augmented by a little percussion, one vocal and one guest-spot for Ron Carter, and amply demonstrates the qualities sought by all his various employers.

➤➤ **Tommy Flanagan** *(Let's)*; **Mulgrew Miller** *(Hand In Hand)*.

Ted Nash

Alto and soprano saxophones, clarinet.

b. Los Angeles, 28 Dec 1959.

Nash's extended family was highly musical; both his trombonist father, Dick, and his saxophonist uncle, also called Ted, were busy LA sessionmen – the latter achieving prominence with Les Brown's 1940s big-band. Ted Nash junior studied piano and trombone with his father, before switching to reeds aged 11. As a teenager he worked with an array of jazz stars, including Quincy Jones, Lionel Hampton, Don Ellis, Toshiko Akiyoshi and Louie Bellson who recorded Nash's first composition when he was only sixteen. In 1978 he moved to New York and a couple of years later joined the Mel Lewis/Vanguard Jazz Orchestra for whom he played and wrote arrangements over a period of ten years. During the 1980s Nash also worked with a wide variety of artists, including Gerry Mulligan's Big Band, and formed his own group in 1989. Throughout the 1990s Nash was a member of important repertory organizations such as the American Jazz Orchestra, the Carnegie Hall Big Band and the Lincoln Center Jazz Orchestra. He has also taught improvisation at New York University. A member of the Jazz Composers Collective, he was commissioned in 1994 by the Davos Musik Festival in Switzerland, which led to a well-received CD *Rhyme And Reason* several years later. Nash's latest project involves him leading a fusion, chamber-jazz collective named Odeon. [BP]

Still Evolved (2003; Palmetto). With pianist Frank Kimbrough, bassist Ben Allison and drummer Matt Wilson forming the rhythm-section, this lively quintet is completed by Wynton Marsalis on half the tracks and Marcus Printup on the others. In eight original compositions Nash takes a particularly creative approach to various aspects of the jazz tradition.

➤➤ **Ben Allison/Herbie Nichols Project** *(Strange City)*; **Anthony Wilson** *(Goat Hill Junket)*.

National Youth Jazz Orchestra

While the National Youth Jazz Orchestra (universally known as NYJO) had historic precedents, including the Newport Youth Band directed by Marshall Brown, it remains the finest and most longstanding example of its kind. Formed in 1965 as the London Schools Jazz Orchestra, the NYJO has for thirty years provided an incomparable training ground: a random handful of its dozens of graduates includes Guy Barker, Nigel Hitchcock, Dave O'Higgins, Simon Gardner, Andy Cleyndert, Julian Argüelles, Jamie Talbot, Mike Smith and Gerard Presencer. The success of the NYJO (the only full-time big band operating in Britain today) is due to its founder, Bill Ashton (b. Blackpool, 6 Dec 1936), who has single-mindedly devoted his life to it, producing a string of superb recordings, encouraging (and then publishing) young British composers, and developing the orchestra by touring it on its own (in Britain, Europe and America) and with American players and singers such as Shorty Rogers (1982–3). Ashton's contribution to Britain's jazz heritage is incalculable; he also finds time to write fine songs and publish an excellent magazine, *News from NYJO*. His orchestra has spawned county-based YJOs nationwide. [DF]

⊙ **Portraits** (1990; Hot House). A very valuable NYJO project: fifteen newly commissioned scores from the brilliant British arranger Harry South, who died just after the collection was recorded. Georgie Fame, Ronnie Ross and Dick Morrissey all guest with the orchestra.

⊙ **Remembrance** (1991; NYJO). Containing Paul Hart's moving "Remembrance" suite (dedicated to friends and ex-members of NYJO), as well as new titles by the band.

⊙ **Algarhythms** (1996; NYJO). Recorded at Ronnie's again, and originally scheduled to tie in with an NYJO tour of the Algarve, this album features Latin-based compositions by guitarist Anthony Adams plus others. New impressive soloists include Mick Ball (trumpet), Ross Milligan (guitar) and pianist Simon Carter.

⊙ **Unison** (1996; NYJO). A recorded dedication to NYJO's sponsors (as well as to their late baritonist Mike Page) and mainly straightahead this time, with the gifted Howard McGill (lead alto) regularly featured plus Jon Halton (on baritone saxophone).

⊙ **47 Frith Street** (1997; NYJO). Recorded a matter of weeks after Scott's death, this collection is thematically centred on his club and its associations and features. There's much fine soloing, two great songs by Ashton ("London" and "New London"), as well as the expected superlative playing from the orchestra.

⊙ **The Very Best Of NYJO** (2001; NYJO). 4-CD boxed set including "Portraits And Tributes", "Live Portraits" and "Tributes" (both with Ross, Morrissey and South guesting), "Setting Standards" and "By George It's NYJO!", a Gershwin celebration. Uniformly high standards of ensemble and soloing; an essential high-value set.

Michael Naura

Piano, Indian and Mexican flutes, composer.

b. Memel, Lithuania, 19 Aug 1934.

Naura studied philosophy, sociology and the graphic arts in Berlin, but is self-taught as a musician. He began leading his own groups in the early 1950s, always with Wolfgang Schluter (vibes/percussion). At first they copied George Shearing, then Brubeck, the MJQ and Horace Silver, but evolved their own style in the 1960s which Naura describes as "a collage of blues, bebop and European avant-garde". By the beginning of the 1960s, the two leading German groups were Albert Mangelsdorff's and the Naura quintet. Later in the decade he began working as an editor of music programmes for NDR (North German Radio), Hamburg. Since 1971 he has been head of the NDR jazz department (radio and TV), but continues to play, compose and record occasionally. With Schluter he often accompanies one of Germany's leading lyric poets, Peter Ruhmkorf, in poetry and jazz recitals. Under his own name, Naura recorded for ECM the 1976 album *Kein Apolloprogram für Lyrik* with Schluter, Eberhard Weber and Ruhmkorf, and in duo with Schluter he made the 1977 album *Country Children*.

Under Naura's influence the NDR developed the most dynamic jazz policy of all European radio stations, covering the whole spectrum from traditional jazz to swing, bebop and contemporary, and offering interviews, talks, record recitals and live concerts. Furthermore, it has afforded substantial patronage to leading German and international musicians, with a programme of jazz workshops which Naura inaugurated: these concentrate on contemporary music, and consist of four days of rehearsal in Hamburg and a recorded (sometimes filmed) concert on the fifth day. There have been, on average, just over ten of these workshops a year since the early 1970s, and almost every contemporary US and European musician of note has taken part.

Naura's favourites are Teddy Wilson, Art Tatum, Bill Evans and Keith Jarrett, and particular inspirations are John Lewis, Milt Jackson, Gil Evans, Ben Webster and Stravinsky. [IC]

Fats Navarro

Trumpet.

b. Key West, Florida, 24 Sept 1923; d. 7 July 1950.

Theodore Fats Navarro played in territory bands as a teenager, sometimes doubling on tenor saxophone, and toured with Andy Kirk in 1943–4. He joined the Billy Eckstine band, replacing Dizzy Gillespie, in 1945–6, and then settled in New York. He recorded with Kenny Clarke, Coleman Hawkins, Eddie Davis and Illinois Jacquet in 1946–7, a time when he began his association with Tadd Dameron. In 1948 he toured with Jazz At The Philharmonic and the Lionel Hampton band, and recorded and rehearsed (but never toured) with Benny Goodman. He worked regularly with the Dameron sextet and ten-piece from 1948 to early 1949, and made records with Bud Powell. His last public appearance (which was also recorded) was with Charlie Parker. Like Parker, he was a highly intelligent and articulate person who became a narcotics addict; Navarro contracted tuberculosis which proved fatal.

His premature death did not prevent Navarro from being seen as one of the leading soloists of the bebop era. The clarion quality of his tone is the most immediately recognizable factor distinguishing him from the Eldridge-inspired sounds adopted by Howard McGhee (with whom he played in the Kirk band) and by Gillespie. Navarro aimed for the fullness of tone associated with Charlie Shavers and Freddie Webster, but with a brassy attack that claimed instant attention. His melodic lines gave the impression of being carefully sculpted, and avoided the apparent impetuosity of players such as Parker, Powell or even Gillespie, concentrating on classic and largely non-chromatic phraseology. For this reason, although Navarro's inventive ability was not outclassed even

HERMAND LEONARD

Navarro Fats

by Parker, he was most at home as soloist and lead trumpeter with Tadd Dameron, many of whose pieces were written with him in mind. Similarly, the rhythmic content of his playing was conservative (though not stilted) and, had Navarro's lifestyle permitted more attention to furthering his music, he might have developed in the direction explored a few years later by his disciple Clifford Brown. [BP]

⊙ **The Complete Blue Note and Capitol Recordings of Fats Navarro and Tadd Dameron** (1947-8; Blue Note). A 2-CD set containing the original recordings (and alternate takes) of the famous collaborations of Navarro and composer Dameron, plus a one-off appearance by Navarro with Benny Goodman and tracks led by Dameron, with the young Miles Davis replacing Navarro.

⊙ **Featured With The Tadd Dameron Band** (1948; Milestone). These airshots, featuring Allan Eager and Milt Jackson, as well as Dameron's regular rhythm-section with Kenny Clarke, have Navarro playing at greater length than on most studio sessions and his solos are that much more impressive.

⊙ **Bird And Fats – Live at Birdland** (1950; Cool and Blue). Formerly available as *One Night In Birdland*, this live set would be poignant if Navarro didn't play so brilliantly. So also do Parker, Bud Powell, Art Blakey and Curly Russell. Relatively poor recording means nothing with music as good as this.

Buell Neidlinger

Bass, cello.

b. New York, 2 March 1936.

Buell Neidlinger studied classical cello as a child, and as a teenager he played bass in numerous jazz groups. He led a band while in college at Yale, then in the mid-50s he joined pianist Cecil Taylor, playing in various groups of Taylor's and recording on *Jazz Advance* (1956; Transition) and *Looking Ahead!* (Contemporary), among other seminal free jazz sessions. In this period he also worked closely with fellow Taylorite soprano saxophonist Steve Lacy, playing on several records Lacy made for Prestige, as well as with pianist/composer Herbie Nichols. Always outspoken, in 1963 Neidlinger exchanged heated letters with *Down Beat* magazine on the feeble state of jazz criticism. Neidlinger moved to Los Angeles at the end of the 60s, playing classical music, working as a studio bassist, and recording with Jean-Luc Ponty, and worked busily as a studio bassist through the 1970s, 80s and 90s. A constant genre-jumper, he held first chair on bass in the Los Angeles Chamber Orchestra through the 70s, started a bluegrass band called Buellgrass featuring long-time associate, tenorist Marty Krystall, with whom he also started the label K2B2, and in the 80s made a group of strong jazz records including *Big Day At Ojai* (1981; K2B2) and *Locomotive* (1987; Soul Note). He has also made two albums with his group Thelonious, also featuring Krystall, specializing in harmonically and melodically faithful readings of Monk tunes: *Thelonious* (1988; K2B2) and *Thelonious Atmosphere* (2001; K2B2). [JC]

⊙ **Blue Chopsticks** (1995; K2B2). Another of Neidlinger's figure studies (he's made records updating both Ellington and Monk), *Blue Chopsticks* arranges compositions by Herbie Nichols for a string trio plus horns – in the 50s, Nichols told Neidlinger he'd always wanted to hear his work played on strings. In fact, it works splendidly, with Neidlinger on cello, Richard Greene's violin giving a strong country flavour, and tenor saxophonist Marty Krystall and trumpeter Hugh Shick filling out Nichols's inimitable heads.

Steve Neil

Alto and tenor saxophones, guitar, electric and string bass, drums.

b. Dayton, Ohio, 16 Nov 1953.

Neil's mother played jazz, and as a child he went to see many jazz musicians, including Miles Davis, and was friendly with bassist Jimmy Garrison. At seven he studied saxophone and guitar, then at thirteen he took up the bass. His first professional job was on bass guitar with a band called Chairman of the Board in 1972 in Detroit. He toured the USA and UK with it in 1974, then was with Pharoah Sanders off and on for five years. In 1977 he joined Elvin Jones for a short time and then played with Yusef Lateef's band. He played on the West Coast with Harold Land, then on the East Coast with Mary Lou Williams. In 1977 he was with the Frank Foster big band and in 1979 with Sun Ra. He toured Europe with Hannibal Marvin Peterson in 1976 and 1977, with Lateef in 1978, with Sanders in 1979, with Sam Rivers and Charles Tolliver in 1983 and with Beaver Harris in 1985. He has also worked and recorded with Gil Evans. His main influences are Sun Ra, Monk and Mingus. [IC]

➤➤ **Gil Evans** *(Priestess)*.

Louis "Big Eye" Nelson

Clarinet.

b. New Orleans, 28 Jan 1885; d. 20 Aug 1949.

One of the best Creole clarinettists in New Orleans (he was a Lorenzo Tio pupil), Nelson was a warm-toned, technically able performer. By 1900 he had played bass in Buddy Bolden's band, as well as violin and guitar for other leaders, but by 1904 was concentrating on clarinet (because, according to one version, a clarinet was easier to run with in race-riot-torn New Orleans). For more than ten years after that Nelson was a familiar sound of the city, working in the Ninth Ward band, Golden Rule orchestra, Imperial Band Superior Orchestra and others, and specializing for a long period on C clarinet before moving over to the more familiar B-flat (on which George Lewis, for one, liked him less). As a teacher "He'd show a youngster all he knew – but he knew how to be stern with those of us that were learning," said Baby Dodds (Nelson taught Sidney Bechet, among others). In 1916 Nelson toured with Freddie Keppard's Original Creole Orchestra, but after a year he was home to stay and the rest of his life was spent in New Orleans cabarets, theatres and function rooms. The dawn of the revival brought renewed interest in Nelson's talent: in 1940 he recorded eight sides for Delta with Kid Rena's Jazz Band at the behest of Heywood Broun, and two years after narrowly missed being selected by Bill Russell to record with Bunk Johnson (Russell heard him on a bad night at Luthjen's cabaret). In 1944 Nelson was the subject of a feature article by Robert Goffin in *Jazz Record*. He continued his residency at Luthjen's until 1948 and the following year – just in time – was recorded by Russell. [DF]

Big Eye Louis Nelson Delisle (1949; American Music). Fascinating example of Nelson's latterday work, including home recordings and live performances in a New Orleans dance hall. Nelson is partnered by Wooden Joe Nicholas and others.

Louis Nelson

Trombone.

b. New Orleans, 17 Sept 1902; d. 5 April 1990.

After Jim Robinson, Louis Nelson was perhaps the best-loved New Orleans trombonist. A technically assured, velvet-toned player, he began his musical life playing alto horn, but had taken up trombone by the time he was twenty, and worked regularly with Kid Rena, the Original Tuxedo orchestra, then for fifteen years with Sidney Desvigne's big band in New Orleans. It was probably his big-band training that led to his being equated with such players as Tommy Dorsey by some New Orleans musicians. "Louis Nelson plays a good trombone," said George Lewis, "but he plays nervous trombone, you know, on his out notes. That's because he never came up playing this music. He came up playing big-band music." Nelson worked from 1944 with Kid Thomas's band and – despite the gentle criticism above – with George Lewis regularly in the 1950s. He became, with Jim Robinson, a figurehead for New Orleans trombone, touring Europe as a soloist and with bands such as the Legends of Jazz, and appearing at home at Preservation Hall, maintaining, at more than eighty years of age, his reputation as New Orleans's most sophisticated slideman. [DF]

Louis Nelson Big Four (1963; GHB). Superb small-group set recorded in Tokyo with George Lewis, Joe Robichaux and Emmanuel Sayles.

Louis Nelson And Alton Purnell (1974–5; Jazz Crusade). Nelson features on ten of the CD's tracks with Dave Brennan's excellent New Orleans band and sounds wonderful, playing with combined power and gentility amid dance-hall acoustics.

Live In Japan (1987; GHB). A likeable live session in Tokyo, with Wendell Brunious, Sammy Rimington, Danny Barker and a compatible team around the grand old man.

Oliver Nelson

Alto, tenor and soprano saxophones, arranger, composer.

b. St Louis, Missouri, 4 June 1932; d. 27 Oct 1975.

Starting in 1947, Nelson played in St Louis-based territory bands, and then played second alto and arranged for the Louis Jordan big band in 1951. He followed his navy service with four years studying music at university, and then moved to New York, working with Erskine Hawkins, Wild Bill Davis and, briefly, with the Louie Bellson band on the West Coast in 1959. He played tenor with the Quincy Jones band from 1960–61, including a European tour. Between 1959–61 he recorded his own compositions on six small-group albums, three including Eric Dolphy, and his first big-band album. He arranged the first big-band recordings of Jimmy Smith in 1962, and worked in a similar capacity with Eddie Davis, Billy Taylor, Wes Montgomery and many others from the early 1960s onwards. He also contributed arrangements to the Buddy Rich band and other touring groups. He made occasional live appearances with his own all-star big bands in 1966, at the 1970 Berlin festival, in 1971 at Montreux and in 1975 in New York and Los Angeles. He also led a small group on a tour of West Africa in 1969. He moved to Los Angeles in 1967, spending the greater part of his time writing for television and film soundtracks; he died from a heart attack.

Although he did a certain amount of formal European-style composition, Nelson's jazz writing for both small group and big band was very close in spirit, and often in musical detail, to early Quincy Jones. He displayed many of the same virtues as Jones, though sometimes spread too thinly for comfort, and it is a pity that his original themes were usually too formulaic by comparison with the memorable "Hoe Down" and "Stolen Moments". It is also to be regretted that after the early 1960s he had little time to further his forthright saxophone work. [BP]

⊙ **Blues And The Abstract Truth** (1961; Impulse!). Only slightly more highly rated than Nelson's New Jazz/OJC albums *Straight Ahead* and *Screamin' The Blues*, this, like them, features Eric Dolphy and Roy Haynes, plus in this case Freddie Hubbard and Bill Evans. It also includes the classic versions of "Hoe Down" and "Stolen Moments".

⊙ **Afro/American Sketches** (1961; Prestige/OJC). Nelson's first big-band recording apart from charts for Louis Jordan and "Lockjaw" Davis, this has memorable melodic material and solo work from Nelson himself, both just this side of cliché but showing up his later writing.

Steve Nelson

Vibes; also piano.

b. Pittsburgh, Pennsylvania, 11 Aug 1954.

There were no musicians in Nelson's immediate family, and he had no serious involvement in music until taking up the vibes at sixteen. Moving to New York in the late 1970s, he played with Kenny Barron, Ted Dunbar and James Spaulding, with whom he had made his record debut in 1976. He then became a student on the Rutgers University jazz programme in the early 1980s. Enormously prolific in recordings and live appearances with a wide variety of musicians from Jackie McLean to George Shearing, he has enjoyed continuing relationships with Bobby Watson, Mulgrew Miller and Donald Brown. Since 1995, he has worked regularly with Dave Holland's quartet and quintet. Holland has said of Nelson, "He keeps the harmonic context very open and mobile and spacious. His playing always has the blues in it, it's very profound and thoughtful." His favourites on vibes are Bobby Hutcherson and Milt Jackson, while he has been inspired by Barron, Watson, Miller and "everybody I ever played with". [BP]

⊙ **Communications** (1987–9; Criss Cross). Nelson has recorded little under his own name, and the currently available evidence includes this quartet session with Mulgrew Miller, Ray Drummond and Tony Reedus, where the vibist demonstrates his invention across a selection of standards and five originals.

➤➤ **Donald Brown** *(Cause And Effect)*; **Mulgrew Miller** *(Hand In Hand)*; **George Shearing** *(That Shearing Sound)*.

Phineas Newborn Jnr

Piano.

b. Whiteville, Tennessee, 14 Dec 1931; d. 26 May 1989.

Along with his brother, guitarist Calvin Newborn, Phineas worked in the Memphis R&B bands of Tuff Green and Phineas Snr in the late 1940s. He toured with Jackie Brenston and B.B. King in the early 1950s, and did session work in Memphis, including a piano feature on "Rockin' The Boogie" with Lou Sargent in 1951. He toured briefly with Lionel Hampton and Willis Jackson before army service from 1952–4, after which he formed a quartet and, in 1956, moved to New York, where he started making albums under his own name. He also worked with Charles Mingus in 1958 and with Roy Haynes from 1958–9, and then settled in Los Angeles and recorded with Howard McGhee and Teddy Edwards. After that Newborn's career was extremely intermittent, partly as a result of a nervous breakdown in the 1960s. Like Chet Baker, he suffered from the extravagant praise of his early solo albums, which exhibited a dazzling technique and a rather superficial Petersonesque conception. Subsequent work, including several 1970s recordings and a 1979 Montreux festival appearance, were less overwhelming but, at their best, more considered and more affecting. [BP]

⊙ **A World of Piano!** (1961; Contemporary/OJC). Like the album done for Haynes, this shows Newborn on top of the world, not only technically but inventively, and partnered by the ex-Miles rhythm-section of Chambers and Philly Joe or by Cannonball's current stars Sam Jones and Louis Hayes.

➤➤ **Roy Haynes** *(We Three)*.

New Jazz Orchestra

The New Jazz Orchestra was a British big band, led by composer/arranger Neil Ardley, which served as a crucible for the talents of many of the leading young musicians of the 1960s, including Jon Hiseman, Jack Bruce, Mike Gibbs, Paul Rutherford, Trevor Watts, Barbara Thompson, Ian Carr, Kenny Wheeler, Henry Lowther, Harry Beckett and Michael Garrick. It featured original compositions and arrangements by Ardley, Gibbs, Rutherford, Garrick and other members, and also included in its repertoire occasional pieces by non-members such as Mike Taylor, one of the most gifted and original composers of the 1960s. The NJO played occasional gigs in London, and did a few broadcasts, UK tours and festivals. It made no impact abroad, but several of its members later became known internationally. The band recorded only two albums, the 1965 *Western Reunion* for Decca, and the 1969 *Le Déjeuner Sur L'herbe* for MGM-Verve. [IC]

David "Fathead" Newman

Tenor saxophone.

b. Dallas, Texas, 24 Feb 1933.

After playing, while still a teenager, with alto player Buster Smith (an experience he shares with Charlie Parker), David "Fathead" Newman joined the band led by saxophonist Red Connors (playing alongside Ornette Coleman). A spell in the R&B bands of Lowell Fulson and T-Bone Walker then led to his being hired by Fulson's erstwhile pianist, Ray Charles, with whom he played for a decade, commencing in 1954 on baritone, but later becoming Charles's main tenor saxophone soloist. From the 1950s onwards, Newman also appeared as a driving, tough-toned Texan tenorman on a number of Atlantic albums, alongside everyone from blues man Zuzu Bollinand through Dr John to Aretha Franklin, but he also forged more lasting musical relationships with King Curtis in the mid-1960s and with Herbie Mann (1972–4), in addition to leading his own bands and recording with Blue Mitchell (1970), Roy Ayers (1971) and Junior Mance (1983). Perhaps his best work, however, appears in the relaxed, blues-based sessions undertaken with old sparring partner Hank Crawford and/or fellow tenorman Stanley Turrentine. Rhino have issued two compilations of Newman's recordings in various contexts for Atlantic: *House of David*, an overview of his contributions to albums by everyone from Texas blues man Zuzu Bollinand, through Ray Charles, to Aretha Franklin and Dr John; and *Bigger And Better/ The Many Facets Of David Newman*, a double CD featuring the saxophonist with strings and brass. A latter day spell at High Note records (see below) has produced a handful of albums showing the old master in undiminished form. [CP]

⊙ **House of David** (1952–89; Rhino/Atlantic). A potted history of Newman's Atlantic sideman sessions, all brimming with guts and vitality. Highlights include the classics "Hard Times" and "The Clincher".

⊙ **Still Hard Times** (1982; Muse). Relaxed, big-swinging blues, produced by Michael Cuscuna and featuring Hank Crawford in the trontline alongside Newman and a superb rhythm-section: Larry Willis (piano), Walter Booker (bass) and Jimmy Cobb (drums).

⊙ **Mr Gentle Mr Cool** (1994; Kokopelli). The more soulful side of Newman, applied to a selection of Duke Ellington pieces and featuring Jim Pugh on trombone, Ron Carter (bass) and Lewis Nash (drums).

⊙ **Davey Blue** (2002; High Note). The third of a remarkably consistent autumnal run on High Note from Newman and featuring appropriately measured contributions of Cedar Walton (piano), David Williams (bass), Kenny Washington (drums) and the undervalued vibraphonist Brian Carrott.

➤➤ **Jimmy McGriff** *(The Starting Five).*

Joe Newman

Trumpet.

b. New Orleans, 7 Sept 1922; d. 4 July 1992.

Joe Newman was born into a musical family in New Orleans and first took lessons from multi-instrumentalist David Jones, whose mellophone work with Fate Marable had influenced Louis Armstrong from 1919. While attending Alabama State College, Newman joined the college band, then took it out under his leadership and finally joined Lionel Hampton in 1941 for two years, before Count Basie at the Lincoln Hotel signed him; Newman stayed with Basie (with short breaks) until 1947, when he teamed first with Illinois Jacquet in a touring unit, then with drummer J.C. Heard. From 1952 he was with Basie regularly for nine years, a period which

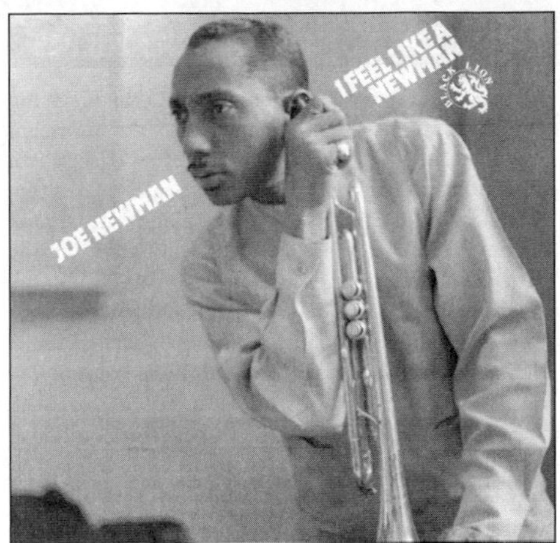

focused international attention on Newman's crackling tone, "neutralist-modern" approach (in Leonard Feather's words) and joyfully creative flair.

It was then that he began a series of solo recordings that were to establish him as the last of Basie's classic trumpeters, an accessible player whose approach acknowledged such masters as Louis Armstrong but was contemporary enough to match fellow "Basie-moderns" such as Frank Foster and Frank Wess. "Louis Armstrong was my first idol and the biggest influence of my whole career," he told Stanley Dance, "but if there's anybody to follow Louis it will be Dizzy Gillespie!"

After he left Basie in 1961, Newman became involved in Jazz Interactions, a non-profit-making trust which (under Newman's presidency from 1967) conducted master classes in schools and colleges, maintained a jazz information service and later formed its own Jazz Interaction Orchestra, for whom Newman wrote extended compositions such as *Suite For Pops*, dedicated to Armstrong. By the 1970s he was touring the international circuit as a soloist, guesting with the New York Jazz Repertory Company and recording solo for Pablo and other major labels. He was to continue this course in the 1980s, featuring a broad-based jazz presentation with homely vocals, eclectic repertoire and all-embracing style, until finally disabled by a stroke in 1991. [DF]

⊙ **I Feel Like A Newman** (1956; Black Lion). Reissue of an important formative session for Newman, teaming him with Billy Byers, Gene Quill and Frank Foster, and on a second grouping with Frank Wess, Sir Charles Thompson and rhythm.

⊙ **The Midgets** (1956/RCA). Another important Newman session from his starring years with Basie; writing by Ernie Wilkins with Joe, Frank Wess fronting an outstanding rhythm section headed by Hank Jones.

⊙ **At Atlantic Restaurant** (1977; Phontastic). Recorded with vibraphonist Lars Estrand and clarinettist Ove Lind, plus a rhythm-section, this is a valuable illustration of Newman stretching out at ease in his mature years.

⊙ **Hangin' Out** (1984; Concord). A later album teaming Newman with the under-recorded Joe Wilder on a weathered two-trumpet workout; two older men pacing themselves and having fun.

New Orleans Rhythm Kings

Organized for a Chicago residency at the Friars Inn by cornettist Paul Mares, the New Orleans Rhythm Kings – Georg Brunis (trombone), Jack Pettis (C-melody saxophone), Arnold Loyacano (bass), Louis Black (banjo), Elmer Schoebel (piano) and Frank Snyder (drums) – were a huge influence on young white Chicagoans such as Jimmy McPartland, Frank Teschemacher and Bud Freeman. The Rhythm Kings, who filled the gap left in Chicago by the Original Dixieland Jazz Band after they had moved on to New York, featured a high-powered programme (arranged by Schoebel, the only band member who could read music) laced with showmanship and clowning, and they soon built a huge reputation: New York promoters such as Sam Lanin from Roseland made enticing financial offers, but no one wanted to leave Friars Inn, with its familiar clientele and informal cabaret atmosphere. (And as Friars Inn was gangster-controlled, it is reasonable to assume that nobody could have left even if they had wanted to.) The New Orleans Rhythm Kings recorded for Gennett in 1922 (before King Oliver), but because they had no business manager, were very young and often rushed into deals, their later career – by which time Mel Stitzel was playing piano, Ben Pollack drums – ended in a whimper in 1925, though there was a brief revival of the band in 1935 for OKeh records, featuring Jess Stacy on piano. By the late 1930s Mares was a restaurateur. He died in 1949, planning a comeback. [DF]

⊙ **New Orleans Rhythm Kings And Jelly Roll Morton** (1922–5; Milestone). All the principal titles by the NORK, with some alternate takes.

Dave Newton

Piano.

b. Glasgow, Scotland, 2 Feb 1958.

Newton studied piano at Leeds College of Music (Alan Barnes was a fellow student) and first led a trio in Bradford in 1978, before returning to Scotland in the early 1980s to develop his talents from an Edinburgh base, working with many visiting Americans. By the mid-80s his reputation was growing: in 1986 he recorded with Buddy DeFranco, and one year later he moved to London, where he worked as pianist/MD for Carol Kidd, and recorded with Alan Barnes and Martin Taylor, among others. Since 1990 he has recorded as a soloist for Linn Records and has now become firmly established as one of Britain's best pianists, teaming with older hands like Dave Green and Allan Ganley, backing American visitors, and working as a member of the poll-winning quintet of Bruce Adams and Alan Barnes. While happiest in modern settings, Newton is a versatile performer capable of covering the jazz spectrum with conviction. [DF]

⊙ **Victim of Circumstance** (1990; Linn). Newton's first self-led trio album, with Alec Dankworth and Clark Tracey; fine playing on Newton originals plus connoisseur's standards like Matt Dennis's "The Night We Called It A Day".

⊙ **Eye Witness** (1991; Linn). Newton on authoritative form, with Green and Ganley in full support in a set of songs with an "eye" theme, such as "Angel Eyes" (by Dennis again), "My Mother's Eyes", and Newton's own "Ol' Blues Eyes" and "Bedroom Eyes".

Frankie Newton

Trumpet.

b. Emory, Virginia, 4 Jan 1906; d. 11 March 1954.

Neat, broad-shouldered and handsome, Frankie Newton was attracting attention with Cecil Scott's Bright Boys by 1929, then quickly graduated to Charlie Johnson's band at Small's Paradise, to Chick Webb and canny Elmer Snowden, and by 1934 had recorded four classics at Bessie Smith's last recording session. From 1935 bouts of ill health were to afflict him, but in 1936 he was with Charlie Barnet's "integrated" band (featuring John Kirby and the very young Modernaires) at Glen Island Casino, as well as with Teddy Hill's band at the Savoy, opposite Chick Webb. In 1937 Newton recorded the hit "Loch Lomond"/"Annie Laurie" with Kirby's wife Maxine Sullivan and worked for the last time with Kirby in the prototype of the soon-to-be-famous John Kirby band: his rapid and unexplained departure from the Kirby project, with altoist Pete Brown, may have been his single most unlucky break. While Kirby's band spun to success, Newton played for Mezz Mezzrow and Lucky Millinder, then led the band at Barney Josephson's new club, Café Society, where he was billed as "trumpet tootin' Frankie Newton", for Billie Holiday (he played on her best recording of "Strange Fruit").

In 1940 he opened Kelly's Stables with Pete Brown again, but for this neglected trumpeter the 1940s were a slow wind-down, with regular commuting from New York to Boston and elsewhere (with Sid Catlett, Ed Hall and James P. Johnson among others), and more time socializing with friends, fishing and playing tennis. In 1948 a fire destroyed his trumpet and other belongings; after a last summer season with his band at Boston's Savoy in 1950, he was more often to be found painting and reminiscing at his Greenwich Village home.

Frankie Newton's handicaps were bad luck, a lack of hit records, occasional ill health and mainly the kind of easy-going unambitious nature that, as Stanley Dance says, "is seldom an asset in the world of jazz". His gifts included a warm, plummy tone, the accuracy and control of a Charlie Shavers (though not quite the range), and an imagination which, as Dicky Wells said, "always believed in giving the people something different". [DF]

⊙ **Frankie's Jump** (1937–9; Affinity). Featuring Newton's tightly planned arrangements and bright vivacious trumpet, in company with Pete Brown, James P. Johnson and Tab Smith, this excellent collection contains some of the best small-group swing on record.

Frankie Newton 1937–39 (Classics). With sidemen including Pete Brown, James P., Slim Gaillard, Mezz Mezzrow and more, Newton's polished, technically effortless style stands out throughout in a variety of spirited settings.

James Newton

Flutes.

b. Los Angeles, 1 May 1953.

Newton's grandmother and aunt sang Baptist hymns and taught him spirituals. In high school he started on electric bass, playing in rock and R&B bands. Then he became proficient on alto saxophone and bass clarinet, and took up the flute just before starting his last year at school. Inspired by Eric Dolphy's flute-playing, he became interested in jazz, listening to Mingus, Ellington, Miles Davis and others. He studied music at California State College, playing in classical ensembles as well as jazz groups. In 1975 he received his degree in music, after which he went to New York, working with David Murray, Anthony Davis and many others. In 1977 he gave up the saxophones and bass clarinet to concentrate entirely on flutes. By the early 1980s his reputation had burgeoned internationally, and he was generally recognized as a major exponent of the instruments.

Newton is a virtuoso with a rich sound, and he has developed the simultaneous use of voice and flute to an unprecedented degree, by using special fingerings. He can sing in unison and harmony with it, which is not so unusual, but he can also improvise on a melody while he is singing it. He has said, "I think very much in a contrapuntal sense, using both voice and flute. I have a piece called 'Choir' that deals in four voices holding a tone, singing a tone and the different tones between the two. This is such a new field that classical flute players in Europe are always ... asking how I get these sounds." Newton has remained active in classical music, both composing and playing it. [IC]

Axum (1981; ECM). A totally absorbing solo album, original, full of variety and innovative techniques, with wonderful flute sonorities and counterpoint to simultaneous vocalizing.

Luella (1983; Gramavision); **Water Mystery** (1985; Gramavision). These albums present Newton in unconventional formations, the first having four string instruments, and the second oboe and bassoon. The flautist runs the gamut of influences from jazz to classical, ethnic, abstract and funk. Always brilliant and often waywardly so.

New York Voices

The most innovative and expert vocal group since Manhattan Transfer, New York Voices were formed, as a six-voice group (including Darmon Meader (director), Peter Eldridge and Kim Nazarian) for a 1986 tour of European jazz festivals by Dave Riley, vocal jazz director of Ithaca College. The group recorded first for GRP in 1989 (*New York Voices*), then again in 1991 (*Hearts of Fire*); Lauren Kinhan joined in 1992 and first appeared on their 1993 release "What's Inside?" Since then the group has continued to grow artistically and win international appreciation; their collaboration with the Count Basie Orchestra (*Live at Manchester Craftsmen's Guild*) won a Grammy award, while their 1998 album *The Songs of Paul Simon* is widely regarded as their best so far. Enormously versatile – they tackle "Cottontail" with as much verve and skill as Simon's "Cecilia" – the group is technically formidable, harmonically innovative as well as great fun. [DF]

The Songs of Paul Simon (1998; BMG). Great pop music was often created despite the technical limitations of its performers, and this collection arguably enriches Simon's originals. The cluster-harmonies of "Overs", the gentle parody of "Punky's Dilemma", and the airy joy of "Me And Julio Down By The Schoolyard" are just three high points of this distinguished album.

Sing Sing Sing (2001/Concord). As the title suggests, a celebration of Swing brought up to date featuring NYV's highly individual close harmonies on titles as diverse as "Ain't Nobody Here But Us Chickens" and "Early Autumn". Occasional pop inflections marginally blur the musical focus here and there, but the band (arranged by Meader who also plays fine tenor and Mike Abene) is outstanding as is the collection.

Nguyên Lê

Guitar.

b. Paris, 14 Jan 1959.

Nguyên Lê acquired his basic knowledge of rock and jazz from the records of Jimi Hendrix and Wes Montgomery and made his first album, *Dé*, in 1989. In the late 1980s he was a member of the Orchestre National de Jazz, and subsequently worked with the singer Claude Nougaro and with saxophonists Michel Portal and Tommy Smith. He has led his own band Ultramarine as well as specially convened all-star recording groups, with such musicians as winds man Paul McCandless, saxophonist Bob Berg and percussionist Trilok Gurtu. Since the late 1990s he has been a regular partner of trumpeter Paolo Fresu, in a line-up sometimes billed as the Angel Quartet, and has also appeared as a soloist with, among others, the WDR Big Band. Inspired by his multi-ethnic Paris milieu, Lê responds to a wide range of cultural influences; from the relationship between black sub-Saharan African styles and North African music to the musical heritage of his Vietnamese family background. [BP]

Bakida (1999; ACT). Interwoven with the many textures provided by the core trio are an astonishing variety of instruments from the Maghreb, Turkey, Vietnam, Europe and the US. With this record Lê vindicates his growing reputation as one of jazz's most inventive contemporary figures.

Purple: Celebrating Jimi Hendrix (2002; High Note). Devoting a whole album to an influence regularly referenced in his other works, Lê involves bassist Me'Shell Ndegé Ocello, keyboardist Bojan Zulfikarpasic and Terri Lyne Carrington on drums and vocals.

➤➤ **Paolo Fresu** *(Kind Of Porgy And Bess).*

Albert Nicholas

Clarinet, saxophones.

b. New Orleans, 27 May 1900; d. Basle, Switzerland, 3 Sept 1973.

One of the mellowest New Orleans clarinettists (he was a pupil of Lorenzo Tio), Nicholas played with all the early stars in his home town, served for three years in the navy (his comrades-in-arms included Zutty Singleton and Charles Bolden) and by 1923 was back in New Orleans and leading his own band, which included Barney Bigard and Luis Russell, at Tom Anderson's cabaret on Basin Street. By early 1925 all three were working with King Oliver's Dixie Syncopators, but after two years Nicholas took work in the Far East (with Jack Carter), returned home the long way (spending a year in Cairo), and finally in 1928 rejoined his old friend Russell, whose New Orleans-based band was happily holding forth in New York, including at Club Saratoga, millionaire Jasper Holstein's personal indulgence. For ten years from 1933, when he left Russell, Nicholas worked at the aristocratic end of New York jazz, playing clarinet for John Kirby's quartet, reading Buster Bailey's difficult book with Kirby's sextet as first deputy, doubling on tenor in Louis Armstrong's sophisticated big band (led by Russell again), and in 1939 working for Jelly Roll Morton at Nick's. In 1941 a flat patch put him out of music, and when he returned it was in the new context of the revival: he worked for Art Hodes and Bunk Johnson (briefly) in 1945, joined Kid Ory a year later, and by 1948 – perhaps with relief – was at Jimmy Ryan's and with Ralph Sutton's trio. In 1953 he settled in France and, like Sidney Bechet, the childhood friend with whom he had run the New Orleans streets, maintained a solo career thereafter. [DF]

Let Me Tell You (1974; Double Up). Produced by Denis Preston, this fascinating album has Nicholas playing (with a group of British sessionmen, including guitarist Dick Abel), singing and reminiscing about his long career. A valuable document, well worth searching for on vinyl.

Herbie Nichols

Piano, composer.

b. New York, 3 Jan 1919; d. 12 April 1963.

Nichols played with the Royal Baron orchestra and other local bands before his army service from 1941–3. After leaving the army he gigged with a wide variety of leaders, including Herman Autrey in 1945, Hal Singer in 1946, Illinois Jacquet, and John Kirby from 1948–9. He appeared on some obscure R&B record dates and, despite recording his own compositions in the mid-1950s, always worked with other leaders, such as Edgar Sampson, Arnett Cobb and Wilbur de Paris. Early in the 1960s he had a club residency backing singers, one of whom was Sheila Jordan, though the others were less interesting. He had just been discovered by a new generation of musicians, including Roswell Rudd and Archie Shepp (with whom he went to Scandinavia in 1962), when he died of leukaemia.

One of the many whose posthumous renown exceeds the reputation he achieved during his lifetime, Nichols's own compositions are completely at odds with the swing, R&B and Dixieland repertoire he played to earn a living. (He could apparently be surprisingly creative in that context too, but the records he made with Rex Stewart and trumpeter Joe Thomas do not provide enough evidence.) As a composer he was impressed by the early work of Thelonious Monk – indeed, he wrote the first article about him ever published – and may be said to have developed the linear, non-Ellingtonian side of Monk's playing. Not that he was uninterested in textures, for the ones he created were recognizably his, but his particular strengths lay in the use of melodic motifs and rhythmic ideas that were unique to him. This explains why, with the exception of "Lady Sings The Blues", written for Billie Holiday, his tunes are not widely known and have been adopted by few others apart from Rudd, Shepp, Misha Mengelberg and Geri Allen. Recent interest from much younger musicians, including the exploration of his unpublished manuscripts, has underlined Nichols's importance, which the albums below (containing most of the 28 originals he recorded) eloquently confirm. [BP]

The Complete Blue Note Recordings (1955–6; Blue Note). With either Art Blakey or Max Roach, these sessions include "Lady Sings The Blues" and the few other Nichols tunes which have been covered by others, but also open up an individual sound-world which no one else has successfully entered.

Love, Gloom, Cash, Love (1957; Rhino). Previously reissued as *The Bethlehem Sessions*, this last trio album benefits from responsive drumming from Dannie Richmond and, along with further intriguing originals, has Denzil Best's "45 Degree Angle" and the then-new songs "Too Close For Comfort" and "All The Way".

Herbie Nichols Project

Strange City (2001; Palmetto). As well as the musicians mentioned above, Matt Wilson and Wycliffe Gordon round out the septet that goes far beyond an average "repertory band" and presents previously undocumented Nichols material lodged at the Library of Congress. Only "Shuffle Montgomery" is an adaptation of a piece officially recorded by Nichols.

>> **Frank Kimbrough** *(Quickening)*.

Keith Nichols

Piano, trombone, reeds, accordion, arranger, leader.
b. Ilford, Essex, UK, 13 Feb 1945.

Keith Nichols was an All-Britain junior accordion champion and child actor, and worked early on with Mike Daniels and a comedy-based group, the Levity Lancers. A ragtime authority with a particular *tendresse* for 1920s jazz, he rapidly gained a reputation in London jazz venues in the early 1970s, when he ran bands such as the New Sedalia and a swing sextet. By mid-decade he was leading his own scholarly Ragtime Orchestra (featuring Paul Nossiter, Mo Morris and Richard Warner), playing in the New Paul Whiteman Orchestra and Dick Sudhalter's smaller bands, recording with the likes of Bing Crosby and as a soloist for EMI, and contributing scores to the New York Jazz Repertory Company, the Pasadena Roof Orchestra and Dick Hyman. From 1978 he co-led the Midnite Follies Orchestra with Alan Cohen, toured shows of his own (including a Fats Waller tribute), and appeared on the South Bank in small-group concerts, full-scale repertory presentations with the MFO (often featuring Ellington and Armstrong re-creations) and occasional one-offs, including a Eubie Blake tribute. In the 1980s he subbed with Harry Gold, led his Paramount Theatre Orchestra and collaborated with reed player Claus Jacobi in re-creating the music of territory bands and early radio dance orchestras; in the 1990s he continued his researches and performs today as busily as ever. Britain's most methodical jazz preservationist, Nichols plays most instruments well, but specializes on piano and trombone. [DF]

Territory Jazz (1986; Stomp Off). One of Nichols's most interesting projects with Claus Jacobi – a re-creation of important music by US territory bands, with sidemen including Colin Smith, Alan Elsdon, John Barnes and John Armatage.

I Like To Do Things For You (1991; Stomp Off). Featuring Nichols's regular partner Guy Barker (trumpet) along with singer Janice Day, this set falls somewhere between jazz and hot dance music; fascinating choice of material and lively soloing.

Syncopated Jamboree (1991; Stomp Off). Another collaboration with Jacobi, plus stars including Bent Persson (trumpet), in a re-creation of 1920s big-band material; well researched and beautifully played.

Harlem's Arabian Nights (1996; Stomp Off). An example of Nichols's jazz repertory at its greatest. Superb re-creations of obscure manuscripts by Ellington, James P. Johnson et al played by an orchestra also featuring researcher/trombonist Bob Hunt. This is music and performance of international standard.

>> **Midnite Follies Orchestra** *(Hotter Than Hades)*.

Red Nichols

Cornet.
b. Ogden, Utah, 8 May 1905; d. 28 June 1965.

Red (Ernest Loring) Nichols was a child performer who played difficult set pieces for his father's brass band at twelve; in his teens (to his father's annoyance) he idolized the Original Dixieland Jazz Band, Bix Beiderbecke and the Wolverines and Phil Napoleon – with whom he first met, in Atlantic City, his long-time partner and musical influence Miff Mole. In 1926, already a busy session and studio man around New York, Nichols began a string of recordings with his Five Pennies. "That was only a number we tied in with my name," he explained later. "We'd generally have eight or nine, depending on who was around for the session and what I was trying to do." The records were often made at the rate of ten to a dozen in a week, under a variety of pseudonyms (The California Redheads, The Charleston Chasers, The Arkansas Travellers and Red and Miff's Stompers), and exerted a huge influence on black and white musicians alike – from Roy Eldridge, who thought Nichols had "something different", to Gil Evans, whose first-ever transcription was of Nichols's "Ida, Sweet As Apple Cider", a close-voiced arrangement led by Adrian Rollini's dark-toned bass saxophone.

By 1930 Nichols was a top bandleader who had worked for Whiteman ("My chair was taken by Bix, and to me that's still the greatest honour I've ever received," he said later, with commendable modesty), regularly directed Broadway shows such as *Girl Crazy* and *Strike Up The Band*, and sometimes taken bands on tour. On one such tour he employed a band of young Chicagoans who drank heavily, read badly, laughed at their leader's taste for commercial success and, through their spokesman Eddie Condon, questioned his decisions. Nichols was a strait-laced disciplinarian (a 1929 Vitaphone short shows his vocal group bowing to their leader before beginning their song), and he sacked Condon for refusing to replay a request: "'Oh no, Red', I said, 'Not "Ida" again.' 'You're sacked!' he said. I was!". So the seeds were sown for the unflattering portrait of Nichols in Condon's book *We Called It Music*.

In the 1930s Nichols was on network radio, leading a fashionable big band and (as "Loring Nichols") conducting radio orchestras for Bob Hope and Ruth Etting. In 1942 he retired briefly and worked in a munitions factory, but he was out of music for less than two years and by 1944 was star soloist again with Glen Gray's Casa Lomans (Nichols's record of "Don't Take Your Love From Me" with Eugenie Baird and Gray's orchestra is an exquisite vignette). In 1945 – after Gray's promise of a "band within a band" failed to materialize and Nichols had moved to the warmer climate of Los Angeles for his polio-stricken daughter's health – he returned to leading small groups again (two years in advance of Louis Armstrong). Throughout the 1940s and 1950s he kept up an unflagging pace, recording, bandleading around California, appearing on radio and TV (with Bing Crosby among others), and generally doing nicely. Following his appearance on *This Is Your Life* (Oct 1956), Paramount began a three-million-dollar life story, *The Five Pennies* (starring Danny Kaye and Louis Armstrong, with Nichols dubbing the music), which supercharged Nichols's career again, leading to a string of Capitol records with such old friends as Joe Rushton, Jack Coon, Manny Klein, and arranger/clarinettist Heinie Beau. These recordings are of exceptional quality and well overdue for CD reissue. At sixty Nichols unexpectedly died in his Las Vegas hotel room; his work, central to jazz history, is still generally under-rated. [DF]

⊙ **On Edison** (1924–7; Jazz Oracle). Scholarly survey of early Nichols as sessionman, including four outstanding titles (with seven alternate takes) by Red and Miff's Stompers. John R.T. Davies remasterings and transfers.

⊙ **Rhythm Of The Day** (1925–32; ASV). This has twenty prime Nichols tracks, including "Feelin' No Pain" and "Boneyard Shuffle", plus titles by Miff Mole and Ross Gorman's band (both featuring Nichols).

⊙ **Red Nichols 1927-8** (Classics). Overdue chronology, welcome from Classics; the Six Hottentots, Five Pennies, Red's Stompers (and Red and Miff's). Essential titles include "Ida", "Cornfed" and the Mole *tour de force* "Slippin' Around".

⊙ **Original 1929 Recordings** (Tax). Remastered by John R.T. Davies, this excellent collection of Nichols's 1929 sides proved to be the welcome harbinger of a complete Nichols chronology.

⊙ **Wail Of The Winds** (1939–40; Hep). Twenty-two invaluable titles by Nichols's mid-period big band plus four by his Five Pennies from an underrated era in his career. Billy Maxted's arrangements are regularly original; Nichols is at his strongest, and there's fun too, on tracks like "Robins and Roses".

⊙ **Red Nichols And His Five Pennies' Vols 2** (1949; Jazzology). Excellent collection of mid-period Nichols illustrating his heat, skills and enterprising repertoire choice.

⊙ **Happy Jazz** (1950; Magic). US Marine Corps broadcasts featuring Nichols's driving cornet and ever-ingenious arranging plus stylish vocals from Dotty O'Brien. Very good illustration of his unflagging creativity amid the jazz Revival, but we're still awaiting those late Capitol dates.

Maggie Nicols

Vocals, piano.

b. Edinburgh, Scotland, 24 Feb 1948.

Nicols's mother, half French, half Berber, was a singer. Nicols herself is self-taught and began as a dancer at London's Windmill Theatre in 1964; her first singing engagement was in 1965. She worked with various musicians in London, including John Stevens and Trevor Watts, from 1968–9, and worked in Keith Tippett's Centipede in 1971. She led her own group, Okuren, in the early 1970s, and later co-founded the vocal quartet Voice with Phil Minton, Julie Tippett and Brian Eley. In 1977 she co-founded the Feminist Improvising Group. She also founded Contradictions, a workshop/performance group which has included many European musicians, for example Uli Lask, Conny Bauer and Irene Schweizer. She also composes, and wrote the music for the Common Stock Youth Theatre's production of Brecht's *The Caucasian Chalk Circle*. Her favourites range from Billie Holiday and Aretha Franklin to Julie Tippett and Phil Minton. Other inspirations are Bill Evans, Coltrane, Dolphy, Schweizer, Stevens and Watts. [IC]

⊙ **Nicols 'N' Nu** (1985; Leo). Nicols's talents range from orthodox jazz singing to wild abstraction and outrageously inventive tonal and rhythmic variations, exemplified here by the duets with pianist Pete Nu.

⊙ **Loverly Play World Wild Music** (undated; ITM). An excellent anthology of Nicols's vocal groups Okuren, Voice and Loverly.

Lennie Niehaus

Alto saxophone, arranger.

b. St Louis, Missouri, 11 June 1929.

Niehaus played with Stan Kenton in 1952 and from 1954–9, but then concentrated on writing for television and educational activities. He has also worked on film music, originally arranging for musical director Jerry Fielding but then working under his own name for Clint Eastwood (including the technically demanding assignment of the film *Bird!*). Niehaus's alto work reflected that of Bud Shank and early Art Pepper, adhering to the West Coast orthodoxy of blending the styles of Charlie Parker and Benny Carter; an interesting comparison is afforded between Parker's "Cherokee", recorded live with Kenton, and Niehaus playing the same Bill Holman arrangement. His own jazz writing revealed a talent for creating interesting original themes, and for finding fresh and sometimes contrapuntal approaches to arranging standard material. [BP]

⊙ **Vol. 1: The Quintets** (1954–6; Contemporary/OJC). The best of several albums from this period featured a mobile three-saxophone quintet (Jack Montrose and Bob Gordon on tenor and baritone) with no chord instrument, while four tracks from 1956 have trumpeter Stu Williamson and Hampton Hawes. Shelly Manne plays drums throughout.

Paul Nieman

Trombone.

b. London, 19 June 1950.

Nieman's father, Alfred, was a composer, pianist and improviser. Nieman studied music under

Brian Richardson at Chiswick Polytechnic, then at the Guildhall School of Music with Denis Wick from 1969–72. From 1969–72 he was also with the National Youth Jazz Orchestra on lead trombone. Since then he has played with Mike Gibbs, George Harrison, the London Jazz Composers' Orchestra, Soft Machine, John Surman, Keith Tippett, Stan Tracey, Mike Westbrook, Gil Evans and Diana Ross, among others. He is also very active in education, teaching on jazz courses, and as professor at the Guildhall, where he initiated the jazz course. He leads his own group, Elephant, for which he does much of the composing. Nieman is the complete trombonist, equally at home with early music and all contemporary styles, equally proficient as a lead player or a soloist, whether working acoustically or with electronics. His influences range from Jimmy Knepper, Jack Teagarden and Bob Brookmeyer to Charles Mingus, the Brecker brothers and Stockhausen. [IC]

Mark Nightingale

Trombone.

b. Evesham, Worcestershire, UK, 29 May 1967.

Mark Nightingale's first teacher was Fred Mercer, and his musical education continued when he became a member of the Midlands Youth Jazz Orchestra (1979–84), and the National Youth Jazz Orchestra (1983–9). He attended London's Trinity College of Music (1985–8) and was tutored by Bobby Lamb. In 1988 he formed and led Bonestructure (five trombones and rhythm section) and produced their album. Nightingale excelled as section player and soloist, and was very much in demand, playing regularly and appearing on albums with the Clark Tracey sextet, the Andy Panayi quartet, the Dankworth Generation Band, and Claire Martin. In 1984, he played on Clark Terry's sextet CD, *Remember The Time*. In 1998 he formed his first regular group, the Mark Nightingale quartet, with pianist Brian Kellock, bassist Mark Hodgson and drummer Steve Brown. Nightingale also composes his own material and is a successful arranger for big bands. He currently plays with the Colin Towns Mask Orchestra, the Laurence Cottle, Stan Tracey and Kenny Wheeler big bands among others, and has had an association with Cleo Laine and John Dankworth, working in their various groups. Nightingale has also worked with Frank Sinatra, Louie Bellson, Claudio Roditi, Lee Konitz and Henry Mancini. In 1994, he recorded his first CD under his own name, *What I Wanted To Say*, with pianist Dado Moroni, bassist Ray Brown and drummer Jeff Hamilton. For his second solo CD, *Destiny*, he recorded as soloist with the RIAS big band in Berlin, and commissioned all the arrangements, including one from the famous West Coast American, Bill Holman. A winner of the Rising Star and Best Trombonist prizes at the British Jazz Awards, Nightingale is a musician who is constantly developing, and has not yet peaked. [IC]

⊙ **What I Wanted To Say** (1994; Mons). This is a virtuoso debut, with five very competent originals by Nightingale and five standards. He's in fast American company, yet never falters or fumbles.

⊙ **Destiny** (1996; Mons). This big-band album, with arrangements by Holman, Duncan Lamont, Allan Ganley, Steve Gray and two by Nightingale of his own compositions, consolidates his reputation as an immensely versatile and brilliant trombonist. He is at ease whatever the tempo or emotional climate, and his arrangements are sonorous and incisive.

➤➤ **Andy Panayi** *(Blown Away).*

Paal Nilssen-Love

Drums, composer.

b. Molde, Norway, 24 Dec 1974.

After playing in his school band from the age of eight and with a local rock band Hekkan, from age fourteen, Paal Nilssen-Love began playing in Pocket Corner, one of Norway's most popular bands, specializing in jazz-rock, in 1990. The following year, he joined Frode Gjerstad's Circulasione Totale Orchestra, in a re-formed manifestation of which – an octet – he still plays. In 1993, he studied for a year in the jazz department of Sund High School and for a further two years at Trøndelag Musikkonservatorium, a period during which he also played with the bands Element, Con Alma, the Øyvind Brandtsæg trio and Vindaloo, with Per "Texas" Johansson and Steinar Raknes. In 1996, he began an association with the SAN International Ensemble, which involved musicians from South Africa and Norway (Zim Ngqawana, Andile Yenana, Ingebrigt Flaten) and formed the Young/Love trio with Jacob Young. In 1997, the [Christian] Wallumrød/[Mats] Eilertsen/Nilssen-Love trio was formed, and Nilssen-Love also plays in trios led by Håkon Kornstad (with Mats Eilertsen), Frode Gjerstad (with Øyvind Storesund) and Svein Finnerud (with Bjørnar Andresen). With Pocket Corner, Nilssen-Love has played all over the world, including New York's Knitting Factory, and in 1996 the SAN International Ensemble toured South Africa on an official visit hosted by Nelson Mandela. He has also toured (and recorded) in Norway with most of the bands mentioned above. He has made four albums, *Slutt* (1995), *Rede For Hugg* (1996), *By-Music* (1997; see below) and *Cosmic Ballet* (1999) with Pocket Corner. Nilssen-Love has also written "Evolution", a composition for percussion, cello and trombone, and "The Storm", incidental music for Shakespeare's *The Tempest*. Among his other recordings is a solo percussion album in 2001 (*Sticks And Stones* on Sofa) and an eponymous album with the Scorch Trio in 2002 (with guitarist Raoul Björkenheim and bassist Ingebrigt Haker Flaten). However, it is perhaps his association with Ken Vandermark's acclaimed School Days band (*Crossing Divisions* and *In Our Times* - see below) that has done most to raise his international profile. [CP]

Pocket Corner

By-Music (1997; Da-Da). Lively, accessible early Miles-style jazz-rock, with trumpeter Didrik Ingvaldsen spearheading a vigorous band including keyboard player Ståle Storløkken and guitarist Stein Ornhaug.

School Days

In Our Times (2002; Okka Disk). Live in Norway, wacky and adept free jazz from Vandermark, Nillsen-Love, trombonist Jeb Bishop, vibraphonist Kjell Nordeson and long-time Nillsen-Love associate, bassist Ingebrigt Flaten.

Sal Nistico

Tenor saxophone.

b. Syracuse, New York, 2 April 1940; d. 3 March 1991.

Nistico played with R&B bands in New York in the 1950s and came to prominence with Chuck and Gap Mangione in 1960–61. He was the featured soloist with Woody Herman for several periods during the 1960s and also played with Count Basie in 1965 and 1967. He worked with Don Ellis and others in Los Angeles in 1970, then played briefly with Herman again in 1971, followed by freelancing with various small groups. He toured Europe with Slide Hampton and, at the end of the 1970s, went to live there, where he freelanced again, touring and playing festivals. Nistico's main influences were Charlie Parker, Gene Ammons and Sonny Rollins, but he developed his own style in the post-bop idiom, a big-toned, fiery approach which swung intensely. [IC]

Live In London (1985; Steam). Touring with Stan Tracey's quartet, including Art Themen, Nistico digs into Monk standards, a Tracey calypso, the ballad "I"ve Grown Accustomed To Your Face") and his own "Backlog" (based on "Stella By Starlight").

Liam Noble

Piano.

b. London, 15 Nov 1968.

Noble was classically trained in piano at school but became intrigued by jazz after hearing the music of Scott Joplin in the film *The Sting*. After gaining his BA in music at Oxford University he went on to study jazz at the London Guildhall School of Music. Rapidly establishing himself as a much sought after pianist on the London jazz scene, he played regularly with the likes of singer Anita Wardell, the late drummer John Stevens, saxophonist Tim Whitehead and legendary trumpeter and composer Kenny Wheeler. In 1994 Noble recorded a solo piano album *Close Your Eyes* for Future Music Records and made his first attempt at composition and free improvisation, discovering that he enjoyed the sense of danger this approach involved. Three years later he joined the Bobby Wellins Quartet with whom he recorded *The Best Is Yet To Come*. He has also appeared with the Christine Tobin Band, the Randy Brecker English Sextet and the Julian Siegel Group.

In 2001, he formed the Liam Noble Group with Stan Sulzmann and Chris Biscoe on sax, bassist Mick Hutton and drummer Paul Clarvis. This all-star quintet recorded the album *In The Meantime* showcasing Noble's abilities as composer to much critical acclaim. Noble's varied influences, which range from techno to Bach, have placed him at the cutting edge of contemporary jazz, which is evident in his recent work for the Tides project: a collaboration between jazz sax player Tim Whitehead and contemporary classical composer Colin Riley. [IC]

Close Your Eyes (1995; FMR). Noble distils his interests and influences in an intimate setting.

In the Meantime (2001; Basho). An outstanding album of mostly Noble's own compositions (plus "Who Will Buy?" from Lionel Bart's *Oliver!*). There's a wide variety of styles on offer from the Monkish "Once Over" to the broad and bluesy "Hello Boys" with its Fats Domino groove. Stan Sulzmann provides brilliant support on tenor sax throughout.

>> **Anita Wardell** *(Why Do You Cry?).*

Ray Noble

Composer, leader.

b. Brighton, Sussex, UK, 17 Nov 1907; d. Santa Barbara, California, 3 April 1977.

One of England's most famous popular composers – he wrote "The Very Thought Of You", "By The Fireside", "The Touch Of Your Lips", "Goodnight Sweetheart" (his signature tune), "Love Locked Out", "Love Is The Sweetest Thing", "Cherokee" (part of his *Red Indian Suite*) and many others – Noble was musical director of HMV from 1929–34, in which capacity he recorded hundreds of brilliant sides featuring British stars such as Nat Gonella, Freddy Gardner, E.O. Pogson and Tiny Winters. In 1934 Noble went to live in the USA (taking drummer/manager Bill Harty and singer Al Bowlly with him) and organized a band to play at the Rainbow Room on top of Radio City in New York. His orchestra – featuring Johnny Mince, Pee Wee Erwin, Will Bradley, Claude Thornhill and George Van Eps, with Glenn Miller as MD – played from 9pm to 3am seven nights a week, and lasted a year until a disagreement arose between Miller and Noble (a strong character beneath a mild British exterior). The orchestra, whose records were seldom as good as those of its British predecessors, broke up after disputes about overtime and other political issues. With his stars gone, Noble moved to Hollywood (with Harty) to work as MD and straight man for the *Burns and Allen Show* (he appeared with them in *A Damsel In Distress*, 1937, starring Fred Astaire), and later worked in the same roles for comedian Edgar Bergen for fourteen years. Noble remained a well-known radio personality and bandleader in America until the 1950s, when he retired with his wife to Jersey in the Channel Islands; he went back to the USA to end his life in Santa Barbara, California. Each month after he died his widow received a romantic legacy – a dozen red roses. [DF]

Mike Nock

Piano, electric keyboards, synthesizer.
b. Christchurch, New Zealand, 27 Sept 1940.

Nock had lessons from his father for six months when he was eleven, after which he was mainly self-taught, although he studied at Berklee, Boston, on a scholarship in 1961. In 1962–3 he was the house pianist in a Boston club, accompanying many jazz stars including Coleman Hawkins. From 1964–7 he toured with Yusef Lateef and worked with Booker Ervin, Stanley Turrentine, John Handy and others. In 1968 he formed Fourth Way, one of the first jazz-rock-fusion groups. The group toured internationally, appearing at many festivals including Montreux in 1970, before it disbanded in 1971, after which Nock became involved in electronic music and freelanced in San Francisco. He moved to Australia in 1985. [IC]

⊙ **Climbing** (1979; Tomato). Nock leads an all-star group for this outing, with a quintet of Tom Harrell, John Abercrombie, Davis Friesen and Al Foster. The solos sparkle and Nock is inspired by the company.

⊙ **Touch** (1993; Birdland). This solo album has Nock at his best with sustained explorations of standards and originals.

➤➤ **Yusef Lateef** *(Live At Pep's).*

Jimmie Noone

Clarinet, soprano and alto saxophones, leader.
b. near New Orleans, 23 April 1895; d. 19 April 1944.

By 1910 Jimmie Noone had made the trip to nearby New Orleans, where he took clarinet lessons from Sidney Bechet. A jolly, roly-poly man who loved to socialize as well as to play, Noone was soon firm friends with Freddie Keppard, his first bandleader, and worked with him regularly as well as with other New Orleans stars such as Buddy Petit and Kid Ory, whose trumpet player at the time was Joe Oliver. Young Noone made his first trip to Chicago in late 1917, to join Keppard, and a year later he was with King Oliver, with whom he worked until 1920. Then came six years with Doc Cooke's Dreamland orchestra. "That was a devil of a band," recalls Barney Bigard, "and Jimmie was the main one for me. While he was with Charlie Cooke he mostly played harmony parts, but after at the Nest he played mostly lead all night because the band was so small." From 1926 the Nest – a famous Chicago nightspot – was renamed the Apex Club, and Noone took up the residency that year with his little band, including Joe Poston (alto) and Earl Hines (piano). He quickly became its star, and records for Vocalion, especially "Sweet Lorraine" and "Four Or Five Times", made him more famous still: soon he was recognized as the newest and most influential clarinet voice in Chicago. Visitors from Benny Goodman to Joe Marsala came in to see Noone "holding the horn over that great belly of his and playing like it was nothing" (in Marsala's words). So did Maurice Ravel: "He showed up one night with the first clarinettist of the Chicago Symphony," recalls Mezz Mezzrow, "and they seesawed back and forth on their unbelief until the joint closed up!"

Noone's pre-eminent position in clarinet history has occasionally been obscured because he never settled for long in New York, the jazz capital, but generally stayed around Chicago, playing a kind of small-group jazz that in the late 1930s – with the dawn of swing – was temporarily out of fashion. But he stayed busy in Chicago, toured in 1938, and formed a big band for broadcasting in 1939. By 1944 he was living on the West Coast and working with Kid Ory's band in the ground-breaking Standard Oil broadcasts. Then, quite suddenly, he died. "He ate himself to death," says Jimmie Noone Jnr (himself a successful clarinettist). "He didn't drink or smoke but he couldn't leave food alone and he had very high blood pressure." Noone was replaced by Barney Bigard, his great admirer: the band played "Blues for Jimmie" in his memory on Ory's show a week after his death. [DF]

⊙ **The Apex Of New Orleans Jazz** (1923-1944/ASV). A very welcome and thorough sampler of Noone's work beginning with titles by Ollie Powers and Cookie's Gingersnaps (1923) and carrying on with thirteen titles from his Apex Club Orchestra plus classics including "Blues Jumped A Rabbit" and sides with the Capitol Jazzmen and Kid Ory.

⊙ **Jimmie Noone 1928-9/1929-30/1930–34 & 1934–40** (Classics). For Noone completists. Without alternate takes but with good general sound quality; the second volume has Noone's well-remembered "Blues Jumped A Rabbit" session from 1936 (with Guy Kelly and Preston Jackson), plus titles with an unstoppable young Charlie Shavers from the year after.

Red Norvo

Vibraharp, xylophone.
b. Beardstown, Illinois, 31 March 1908; d. 5 April 1999.

Red Norvo (Kenneth Norville) began his career as a xylophone specialist (its "novelty" characteristics are reflected in a couple of early recordings). After time with Paul Whiteman in the early 1930s, he formed his own band, active from 1935–44, which had a low-key approach tailored by arranger Eddie Sauter to suit the minimal decibel-count of Norvo's instrument and of the singing of his then wife, Mildred Bailey. Only in the 1940s did Norvo follow the lead of Lionel Hampton and Adrian Rollini in concentrating on vibes, while retaining the rhythmically choppy style and terminal tremolos that made him the Jess Stacy of the mallets.

Keeping abreast of jazz developments without modifying his own playing, Norvo was responsible (during employment with Benny Goodman, from 1944–5) for an all-star record session which introduced many listeners to the work of Dizzy Gillespie and Charlie Parker. After a year with Woody

Herman in 1946, he settled on the West Coast, where the early 1950s found him leading a drummerless trio, initially with Tal Farlow and Charles Mingus. This group not only betrayed the influence of bebop but was the first of the "chamber jazz" outfits that proliferated during that decade. Norvo remained active, frequently in Las Vegas, though he enjoyed a brief semi-retirement in the mid-1970s. Before retiring again (following a stroke in 1986), he toured Europe several times with his colleague Tal Farlow, his playing retaining its essential vitality and underlying humour. [BP]

⊙ **Dance Of The Octopus** (1933–6; Hep). Norvo's best instrumental tracks of the period including the truly avant-garde "Dance Of The Octopus". Excellent notes by Campbell Burnap.

⊙ **Jivin' The Jeep** (1936–7; Hep). Fifteen out of 21 tracks have vocals (all but one by Mildred Bailey) but, unless you're a Bailey fan, attention is liable to focus on Norvo's quaint but absolutely right playing and Eddie Sauter's frequently wonderful arrangements.

⊙ **The Modern Red Norvo** (1945–51; Savoy). Incorporating Norvo's session with Gillespie and Parker, alongside his first trio, which pointed towards the developments of the 1950s. As well as focusing attention on the hitherto obscure Farlow and Mingus, it was a considerable achievement for Norvo not to have sounded in the least outmoded.

Alcide "Yellow" Nuñez

Clarinet.

b. New Orleans, 17 March 1884; d. 2 Sept 1934.

One of the most highly trained New Orleans clarinettists, "Yellow" Nuñez (he was a Creole) worked all around New Orleans in cabarets, saloons and parade bands from 1902, including a stay with Jack Laine's Reliance Band from 1912–16. That year he travelled to Chicago with drummer Johnny Stein and soon after joined the Original Dixieland Jazz Band under leader Nick LaRocca; after an argument with LaRocca, however, he traded places with Larry Shields in Tom Brown's group, which had come back from New York after a none-too-successful comedy season. Nothing happened with Brown in Chicago, so Nuñez went back to leading his own bands, toured with Bert Kelly and played for drummer Anton Lada at the Athenia Café, Chicago, before touring his quartet around the Midwest. By 1927 he was back in New Orleans, where he later played with the New Orleans Police Band. [DF]

Adam Nussbaum

Drums.

b. New York, 29 Nov 1955.

One of the brightest drum stars in America, Nussbaum started on piano, and also played bass and alto saxophone. He studied music at the Davis Center, City College of New York, then from 1978–83 he was with John Scofield, and from 1978–81 with the Dave Liebman quintet. In 1982–3 he was with Stan Getz, from 1983 he worked with the Gil Evans orchestra, and from 1984 with Randy Brecker and Eliane Elias. In 1984 he also worked with the George Gruntz Concert Jazz Band and Gary Burton. He has freelanced with Sonny Rollins, Joe Henderson, Art Pepper, Art Farmer, "Lockjaw" Davis, John Abercrombie, Bob Brookmeyer, Ted Curson, Al Cohn, Sheila Jordan and Hal Galper, and toured with Liebman, Scofield and Steve Swallow, playing major festivals in Europe and the USA. He was in Michael Brecker's touring group with Mike Stern in 1987 and in 1992 performed with Don Grolnick's group at the Red Sea festival.

Nussbaum remains one of the most sought-after drummers on the cutting edge of the music. He has been a member of the John Abercrombie trio from 1991 to the present, the Jerry Bergonzi quartet from 1989, the Sigurd Ulveseth quartet from 1994, and the James Moody quartet and the Kenny Wheeler quartet from 1996. In the later 1990s, he was a member of Steve Swallow's great quintet with Chris Potter, Mick Goodrich and trumpeter Ryan Kisor. Nussbaum has played with many other leading musicians including the Gil Evans orchestra, Randy Brecker, Stan Getz, Bob Brookmeyer, and John Scofield. He is also very active in jazz education, teaching at New York University, Long Island University, Jamey Aebersold's Summer Jazz Band Camps and also holding drum clinics in the USA and internationally. He has also played on well over one hundred albums with other leaders. [IC]

➤➤ **Dave Liebman** *(If They Only Knew)*; **John Scofield** *(Shinola; Out Like A Light)*; **Steve Swallow** *(Deconstructed)*.

O

Floyd O'Brien

Trombone.

b. Chicago, 7 May 1904; d. 26 Nov 1968.

In his early teens Floyd O'Brien was a ringsider at Lincoln Gardens for King Oliver's band, then in 1921 he was discovered by drummer Dave Tough at a fraternity dance. For the next ten years, although he became friends with the Austin High School Gang, he stayed around Chicago, working for leaders such as Charles Pierce and Thelma Terry, and for theatre orchestras. When he finally got to New York, around 1934, he made fine records with Eddie Condon, Fats Waller, Mezz Mezzrow and the Chocolate Dandies, but soon after joined comedian Phil Harris's big band, where he stayed until 1939 (the year he recorded George Wettling's classic *Chicago Jazz* set). Then came work with Gene Krupa, Bob Crosby and Eddie Miller, before opening a shop on the West Coast, playing with Shorty Sherock's band, and finally moving back to Chicago in 1948. From then on O'Brien's career (apart from excellent records with Art Hodes in the late 1950s) was poorly documented, until a *Down Beat* obituary in 1968 told the full story. One of the best Chicago-style trombonists, O'Brien is neglected primarily because he made too few records, and based himself for much of his life outside New York. [DF]

Chicago Jazz (1939–40; MCA Coral). One of the rare examples of O'Brien's fine work, with Condon, McPartland and Wettling; a classic.

Jimmy O'Bryant

Clarinet.

b. Arkansas, c.1896; d. 24 June 1928.

A widely recorded musician in jazz's formative years, O'Bryant worked with the Tennessee Ten (c.1920–21), Jelly Roll Morton and W.C. Handy (1923), and King Oliver (1924). He also recorded with Lovie Austin's Blues Serenaders (1923–6) and his own Washboard Band (1925–6), then – after work with Paul Stuart (1927) – he returned to Chicago, where he died. [DF]

Mystery Man Of Jazz (2002; Frog). Twenty-seven tracks of vintage O'Bryant (1924–6), including "Red Hot Mama".

Helen O'Connell

Vocals.

b. Lima, Ohio, 23 May 1920; d. 9 Sept 1993.

O'Connell joined Jimmy Dorsey in 1939 and from 1940 teamed with Dorsey's male singer Bob Eberly in a series of hit recordings – notably "Green Eyes", which highlighted O'Connell's sexily slurred delivery. In 1940 she topped the *Down Beat* female vocalists poll, but retired three years later after marrying, then returned in 1953 to join Dave Garroway on NBC's *Tonight* show. She later toured with Tex Beneke and others, and was singing at the time of her final illness. [I Cr]

The Sweetest Sounds (1953–63; Hindsight). Fine collection of O'Connell titles, with the hit-making Page Cavanaugh group among others.

Anita O'Day

Vocals.

b. Chicago, 18 Oct 1919.

After singing with local Chicago groups in the late 1930s, O'Day earned a national reputation as a member of the Gene Krupa band from 1941–3 and in 1945. In 1944–5 she also worked with an early Stan Kenton band. She then established herself as a soloist, recording frequently and appearing with local rhythm-sections, though from 1954 she was regularly accompanied by drummer John Poole. In a career marked by personal ups and downs (as documented in her autobiography), her performance has been remarkably consistent, and even well-known highlights such as the Newport festival in 1958 and the Berlin festival in 1970 – captured on film and disc respectively – are only representative of her normal standards.

As well as making one of the first inter-racial vocal duets on record ("Let Me Off Uptown" with Roy Eldridge and the Krupa band), O'Day was the first (only?) feminist big-band singer, appearing in band-jacket and skirt rather than a dress. Musically, she more than earned the right to be treated as a band member rather than a visual exhibit, for her originality was a considerable asset and, after working solo, her style matured marvellously. On ballads there is a distant resemblance to Billie Holiday, while on uptempo numbers, whether scatting or merely stretching the lyrics to breaking point, she has a fine rhythmic sense and an ebullience that is hard to duplicate. Certainly, the many singers who emulated her work, ballads especially, such as June Christy, Chris Connor and Helen Merrill, came nowhere near to swinging as delightfully as O'Day. [BP]

⊙ **Anita Sings The Most** (1957; Verve). O'Day (and John Poole) with the Oscar Peterson trio on a recording which displays her rhythmic invention and accuracy on a set of standards.

⊙ **Tea For Two** (1958–66; Moon). Live sets which include her famous Newport festival repertoire, "Tea For Two" and "Sweet Georgia Brown", plus a European recording backed by Tete Montoliu, which underlines O'Day's free-thinking approach to her material.

⊙ **Rules Of The Road** (1993; Pablo). It seems ungallant to be surprised at such a late success, but here is Anita still singing her mind out in front of a big band directed by sometime singer Jack Sheldon.

Chico O'Farrill

Arranger, trumpet.

b. Havana, Cuba, 28 Oct 1921; d. New York, 27 June 2001.

O'Farrill was raised in Cuba and the USA; he studied music and played in Havana from 1940–48, and then settled in New York. As well as writing for Benny Goodman and Stan Kenton, he did arrangements for Latin jazz albums by Machito (with Charlie Parker and Flip Phillips) in 1950, Dizzy Gillespie in 1954 and 1975, Art Farmer (1959), Cal Tjader (1967), Candido (1973), Gato Barbieri and Larry Harlow (both 1974), Tito Puente and Mario Bauza. From 1965, he arranged other, more conventional, work for Count Basie, Clark Terry and many others, finally recording with his own band again in 1995. Although O'Farrill's big-band scoring is based on fairly banal US styles, he has an enviable knowledge of which Afro-Latin rhythms can blend with them. His son, Arturo O'Farrill Jnr, played with the Carla Bley band and others, and directed his father's group after his death. [BP]

⊙ **Pure Emotion** (1995; Milestone). His first jazz recording for decades, with a big-band including top New York section-men, includes everything from "Perdido" to a Latin version of "Get Me To The Church On Time" along with many O'Farrill originals, both new and old.

➤➤ **Machito** *(The Original Mambo Kings).*

STEVE MARUTA

Chico O'Farrill

Dave O'Higgins

Saxophones, flute, keyboards, drums, composer.

b. Birmingham, UK, 1 Sept 1964.

O'Higgins learned trumpet, drums and piano at school, and played drums with local Derby function bands and the Derbyshire Youth Jazz Orchestra. He started on saxophone at sixteen, and was self-taught. In 1983 he moved to London to study music at the City University, and at the same time joined the National Youth Jazz Orchestra (NYJO) and formed the Dave O'Higgins quintet. Since then O'Higgins has worked regularly with NYJO (1983–6), Mezzoforte (1986–9), Cleo Laine and the John Dankworth quintet, Sax Appeal, Jason Rebello (1990–91), Jim Mullen, Itchy Fingers, Clark Tracey's sextet and Martin Taylor's Spirit of Django. His quartet and quintet have been a continuous feature in his career, but he has also concurrently led other groups, including the Gang of Three (1987–9), the highly regarded fusion band Roadside Picnic (co-leader, 1986–90), and Dave O'Higgins and The Oblivion Brothers (1989–91).

O'Higgins is a stunning player in the neo-bop vein, with an apparently effortless flow of coherent ideas, beautiful time, and a highly developed harmonic sense, and the world has been quick to recognize his outstanding talent. He is also a composer of often memorable themes, and has already appeared on at least ten albums with other leaders, as well as a number of his own. He has toured and played festivals in Europe, Africa, South America, the USA, Japan and Cuba. He has received several awards, including the 1992 John Dankworth Personal Award for Young Soloist, and two of Ronnie Scott's 1994 British Jazz Awards, in the Tenor Sax and Rising Star categories. He is also much in demand as a sideman with artists ranging from Nancy Wilson and Chaka Khan to Evan Parker and Mose Allison. His favourite saxophonists are Charlie Parker, Stanley Turrentine, Bob Mintzer and Michael Brecker. [IC]

All Good Things (1992; EFZ); **Beats Working For A Living** (1994; EFZ). Two genial quartet albums, both mainly of O'Higgins originals with a couple of standards for good measure. The earlier one was recorded in London with a British rhythm-section of Robin Aspland, Alec Dankworth and Jeremy Stacey; the second was recorded in New York with Joe Locke (vibes), pianist Joey Calderazzo, bassist James Genus and Adam Nussbaum. Both albums are excellent saxophone quartet/quintet performances but, if anything, the home product has the greater sense of collective purpose.

Tiger Okoshi

Trumpet, synthesizer, composer.

b. Ashita, Japan, 21 March 1950.

Tiger (Toru) Okoshi has lived in the USA since 1972, playing with Gary Burton, Bob Moses and others, as well as leading his own bands. His music, which he calls "Baku" music after a mythical creature that eats bad dreams, is a jazz-rock fusion, but embraces the whole jazz tradition. In the early 1990s he joined George Russell's Living Time orchestra as featured electric trumpet soloist. Okoshi is a highly accomplished player and composer. He has said of the trumpet, "It is a limited, incomplete, very old-fashioned instrument – but I love it." Miles Davis is a main influence, but more for his jazz-rock experiments on *Bitches Brew* than for his trumpet-playing. Louis Armstrong is also a prime influence, as demonstrated on the recording below. [IC]

Echoes Of A Note (1993; JVC). Leading a sextet of bassist Jay Anderson, drummer Peter Erskine, banjoist Bela Fleck, keyboardist (and accordionist) Gil Goldstein and guitarist Mike Stern, Okoshi recomposes, rearranges and reinvents ten pieces closely associated with Armstrong, including "Hello, Dolly", "Basin Street Blues" and "St James Infirmary", with such imagination that they seem completely contemporary. The playing of the group, especially Okoshi, is utterly brilliant, making this one of the most creative and moving albums of the 1990s.

➤➤ **Bob Moses** *(Visit With The Great Spirit).*

Old And New Dreams

➤➤ *see entry for* **Charlie Haden**

King Oliver

Cornet, composer.

b. Louisiana, 11 May 1885; d. 10 April 1938.

Joe Oliver was a slow developer back in New Orleans. By 1905, although "he had a book thicker than the Good Book with nothing but dates in it" (as Pops Foster remembers it), the future "King" was still a thin-toned, restricted player with a lot of learning to do. Then, around 1914 (Preston Jackson recalls), he began to improve through very hard practice, his own band began to cause a stir, and by 1917 Kid Ory was billing him as "King". On parades, in cabarets and often fronting his own group, Oliver was cutting an impressive figure. "I'll never forget how big and tough he looked," says Ed Souchon, "his brown derby tilted low over one eye, his shirt collar open at the neck and a bright red undershirt peeking out at the V." Oliver was now a more than competent cornettist who played a strong, capable lead with plenty of volume and a battery of muted effects. "Joe did most of his playing with cups, glasses, buckets and mutes", says Mutt Carey, who copied Oliver. "He could make his horn sound like a holy roller meeting!" (He also used the tiny, now obsolete "door-knob" mute beloved of Jabbo Smith.)

Oliver was an ambitious businessman, and by 1919 he knew that jazz was moving upstream to Chicago and that back home in New Orleans a new prodigy – Louis Armstrong – was ready to usurp every other king in the city. So that year he was pleased to join bassist/entrepreneur Bill Johnson (Buddy Petit had turned down the offer), as well as clarinettist Lawrence Duhé, at the Dreamland Ballroom in Chicago. Soon after he took over Duhé's band and in 1921 took his new team (featuring Johnny Dodds, Honoré Dutrey and Lil Hardin) to California. The trip was unsuccessful: Mutt Carey had got there first with Ory, and audiences saw Oliver as an imitator, rather than the originator, of Carey's muted tricks. A year later Oliver returned to Chicago in fighting mood, and opened at the Lincoln Gardens with his band and a new member up from New Orleans: Louis Armstrong. Armstrong – a young, generous boy in search of a father – was far too good-natured to query his second-trumpet post, and it was one of Oliver's cannier moves. "As long as I got him with me", he told pianist Lil Hardin, "he won't be able to get ahead of me. I'll still be King!" The Creole Jazz Band was omnipotent. Nightly the Lincoln Gardens was packed with dancers and musicians listening to what George Wettling called "the hottest band ever to sit on a bandstand", playing 45-minute versions of classics such as "Riverside Blues", "'Working Man Blues" and "Mabel's Dream", and featuring Armstrong and Oliver's staggeringly complex and apparently ad-libbed "hot breaks". Oliver, at the centre of the band, was an imposing leader and a strict one: sidemen could drink only from a bucket of sugar water with a dipper in it, while new boy Armstrong was told to play "more lead" and took the advice. In 1923, at the Gennett Studios in Richmond, Indiana, the first great sides by King Oliver's Creole Jazz Band were recorded. Everyone apart from Lil Hardin was nervous, but the records are still some of the greatest ever made, with Oliver's racketing, joyous lead clearly audible in the pre-electric recording. (However, it may be that his best work never survived studio conditions: "To tell the truth," says Mutt Carey, "I don't believe it is Joe playing on the records sometimes.")

In 1924, Oliver's greatest band broke up, after the Dodds brothers discovered that Oliver was creaming money from his sidemen's salaries; soon only Louis

King Oliver's Creole Jazz Band. Left to right: Johnny Dodds, Baby Dodds, Honoré Dutrey, Louis Armstrong, King Oliver, Lil Hardin and Johnny St Cyr

Armstrong was left, until Lil Hardin, now his wife, secured his departure. Oliver replaced him with Lee Collins, but by the end of 1924 was guesting with Dave Peyton's band. He took it over in February 1925 and formed his Dixie Syncopators, a band featuring the new and revolutionary saxophone team of Barney Bigard and Albert Nicholas. By 1927 Oliver had taken his new package to New York but there – once again – time had beaten him to the punch. "Everybody in New York then," said Louis Armstrong, "was playing King Oliver – even me!" It was hard for the old King to accept. He continued quoting high fees and losing work (including a contract for the Cotton Club, which Duke Ellington won), as well as overeating, which produced weight and dental problems. His last ten years, despite successful recordings and tours in the early 1930s, form a sad picture of a man reduced by jazz fashion, calling shots he could no longer afford to call, seeing such protégés as Armstrong relentlessly overtake him. Plagued by recurrent pyorrhoea, by 1936 he was working as a janitor in a Savannah pool room. "He got stranded down there," remembered Louis Armstrong, "and ended up a very pathetic man." Oliver's course was almost run: a letter to his sister in 1937 sounded like a goodbye: "I know the Good Lord will take care of me. Goodnight dear!" He died in Savannah and was buried in the Bronx: a sad way to get back to New York. [DF]

⊙ **King Oliver 1923/1923–6/1926–8/28–30/30–31** (Classics). The whole Oliver story in five volumes. The first, (*1923*) has the complete oeuvre of the Creole Jazz Band and there's much of interest in later volumes too, including the wonderful "Freakish Light Blues" and "West End Blues".

⊙ **King Oliver's Creole Jazz Band; The Complete Set** (1923-4; Retrieval). Unquestionably the definitive collection of Oliver's greatest years including alternate takes plus titles with Morton and Butterbeans and Susie. Superb sound restoration as ever by John R.T. Davies on this 2CD set.

⊙ **King Oliver Vols. 1 & 2** (1923–9 & 1927–30; BBC). Another desirable collection, collating in separately available volumes 41 of Oliver's best titles with his Creole Jazz Band, Jazz Band and Dixie Syncopators, Blind Willie Dunn's Gin Bottle Four, Clarence Williams, Texas Alexander and others. Robert Parker's restorations are exemplary.

⊙ **Sugar Foot Stomp: The Original Decca Recordings** (1926 & 28; MCA/GRP). With notes by Richard Hadlock and sound restoration by Erick Labson, this set is a fine sampler of Oliver's later years with his Dixie Syncopators, including near-classics like "Snag It", "Sobbin' Blues" and Oliver's own (very capable) "West End Blues".

⊙ **Complete Vocalion And Brunswick Recordings** (1926–31; Affinity). An important two-CD boxed set which brings together all the recordings of Oliver's Dixie Syncopators, plus more with his orchestra and Jazz Band.

⊙ **King Oliver Vols. 1 & 2** (1929–30; JSP). A chronology of Oliver's orchestra sides, including alternate takes; with remasterings by John R.T. Davies (excellent as always) and fine notes by Sally Ann Worsfold.

Sy Oliver

Trumpet, arranger, vocals, composer.

b. Battle Creek, Michigan, 17 Dec 1910; d. 27 May 1988.

Sy (Melvin James) Oliver grew up in a musical household in which he learned to read notes as soon as he learned to read words. A highly intelligent young man, who first wanted to be an attorney and whose nickname was an abbreviation of "Psychology", by his late teens Oliver was working in territory bands led by Cliff Barnett, Zack Whyte and Alphonso Trent, and perfecting his gift for orchestration; in 1933 he joined Jimmie Lunceford as trumpeter and co-staff arranger with pianist Ed Wilcox. Oliver's writing for Lunceford – in arrangements such as "T'ain't What You Do!", "Dinah" and "Ain't She Sweet" – was a dashing parade of innovation that rivalled Ellington's for consistency and originality; when he joined Tommy Dorsey in 1939 (at $5000 a year more than Lunceford gave him) Oliver continued to write "brilliant, full-blooded things", in Frank Sinatra's words, although as he said, "I had to write down for the Dorsey guys because this was before the days when you couldn't tell the difference between a negro and a white musician." ("Sunny Side Of The Street" is one of Oliver's most famous compositions for Dorsey.) From 1946, after a brief band-leading spell, he continued working as a freelance arranger (often for black artists) and produced hugely successful recordings for (among many others) Ella Fitzgerald, Sammy Davis, Frank Sinatra and Louis Armstrong (two of Louis's finest albums, *Louis And The Good Book* and its lesser-known but superior companion *Louis And The Angels*, are Oliver's creations). In the late 1960s he returned to bandleading again, and from 1975–80 was at the Rainbow Room with an all-star band, for which he wrote a book of over 300 arrangements: "At weekends when everybody gets high we play a lot of jazz", recalled Oliver Jackson. One of the most intense, intelligent and educated men of swing, Oliver remained busy as ever in the 1980s. [DF]

➤➤ **Jimmie Lunceford** *(1930–34; 1934–35; 1935–37; 1937–39).*

Oregon

➤➤ *see entry for* **Ralph Towner**.

Original Dixieland Jazz Band

Although nowadays their music sometimes sounds quaintly dated, the ODJB (as they soon became known) played a vital part in a jazz revolution: their 1917 residency at Reisenweber's restaurant in Columbus Circle, New York – which attracted all of New York's bright young society – really launched the jazz age of the 1920s. To musicians left behind in New Orleans, the fast-working white publicity machine that advertised the all-white ODJB as "the creators of jazz" must have seemed unfair, as indeed it was. Its five members – Nick LaRocca (cornet), Larry Shields (clarinet), Eddie Edwards (trombone), Henry Ragas (piano) and Tony Sbarbaro or Spargo (drums) – were young New Orleans men who had played first with such senior New Orleans leaders as Papa Jack Laine, then listened to and learned from older players like King Oliver ("the LaRocca boys used to hang around and got a lot of ideas from his gang", says Preston Jackson).

The band began in 1916, when drummer Johnny Stein led LaRocca, Edwards, Ragas and clarinettist Alcide "Yellow" Nuñez (later replaced by Shields) in work for club-owner Harry James at Chicago's Booster Club. From there, with drummer Sbarbaro replacing Stein, they moved to a rival café, the Del'Arbe, which put in a better offer. Soon after, agent Max Hart gave LaRocca the chance to work at Reisenweber's restaurant, and after a slow start the ODJB were soon packing in crowds with a high-powered jazz-based vaudeville act, featuring Shields's fine playing interlaced with clarinet hokum (he was a prime influence on Ted Lewis), LaRocca and Edwards playing into each other's bell, a battery of tin-can mutes, sock-cymbals and Swanee whistles, and Edwards playing the trombone with his foot. Their records from this time are a mixed bunch: hits such as "Livery Stable Blues", full of trumpet-brays and clarinet cock-crows, and "At The Jazz Band Ball", with its ritualized clarinet routines, remind us how young jazz was then, but other sides, including "I've Lost My Heart In Dixieland" and "Tell Me" from two years after, are great by any standards. Every one of these records, in any case, was a seminal influence on a new generation of jazzmen from Bix Beiderbecke down.

In 1919 the ODJB became the rude invaders of polite London society: they opened in Albert de Courville's *Joy Bells* revue at the Hippodrome, but were hastily removed from the bill at the instigation of George Robey and sent on a tour of variety theatres (including the Palladium). Then on 28 October 1919 they opened at the Hammersmith Palais. LaRocca's press announcements at the time must have sounded as controversial as punk did in the 1970s: "Jazz is the assassination of the melody – the slaying of syncopation. It's a revolution in this kind of music and I confess we're musical anarchists!" A nine-month stay at Hammersmith, however, proved that post-war Britain was ready for all the anarchy it could get, and when the group returned to the USA it was for a spell of busy touring and more recording. But jazz fashion was getting into gear and Paul Whiteman's "Symphonic Jazz" concert at Carnegie

Max Jones Files/Redferns

Original Dixieland Jazz Band

Hall in 1924 in some ways sounded a trump for the ODJB. In 1925, LaRocca – a bundle of high energy, hard sell and ego – collapsed and retired exhausted to New Orleans; his place was briefly taken by Henry Levine, but for ten years the show was suspended. In 1936 the band re-formed for Ed Wynn's network radio programme, toured theatres, made a film and were written up in a perceptive article by J.S. Moynahan in the *Saturday Evening Post*: the ODJB, not Benny Goodman, said Moynahan, were "the real jazz". His article, and the re-formed ODJB, came five years too early for the jazz revival: Shields developed heart trouble and LaRocca retired for ever to New Orleans and the building trade. In the 1940s the memory of the band was preserved by records by Edwards (featuring Bill Davison and Max Kaminsky on trumpets and Brad Gowans on clarinet) and by a tribute in Katherine Dunham's 1944 revue; later a book called *The Story Of The ODJB* set out to substantiate LaRocca's more grandiose claims, but (of course) failed. But the band had left its mark on young players such as Phil Napoleon, Red Nichols and Beiderbecke, and invented a style of presentation that was to live on in some Dixieland music to the present day. [DF]

⊙ **Sensation** (1917–20; ASV). Good representative selection of titles by the very first "Dixieland Five", including their British recordings with pianist Billy Jones.

⊙ **Seventy-Fifth Anniversary** (1917–21; RCA Bluebird). All of the ODJB's Victor sessions up to the end of 1921. Also available on Timeless.

⊙ **Complete ODJB 1917–36** (RCA). Complete recordings for RCA, including the last session from 1936 with the ODJB augmented by a big band.

⊙ **In England** (1919–20; EMI Jazztime). All of the ODJB's British recordings with Jones – an important stage in their recorded career – plus titles by other London-based groups of the period.

Niels-Henning Ørsted Pedersen

Bass.

b. Ørsted, Denmark, 27 May 1946.

Ørsted Pedersen's mother was a church organist. He studied the piano, but was a prodigy on bass, playing with Danish groups at the age of fourteen. At seventeen he was asked to join Count Basie, but was unable to do so. He played with many Americans during the 1960s, including Sonny Rollins, Bill Evans and Roland Kirk, and was the house bassist at Copenhagen's leading jazz venue, Club Montmartre, and a member of the Danish Radio Orchestra. He has won polls in Europe and the USA. In the 1970s he formed a duo with pianist Kenny Drew, and from the mid-1970s until the mid-1980s he was a regular and permanent member of the Oscar Peterson trio. In the early 1980s he hosted a jazz show on TV in the UK. He is a virtuoso double-bass player, equally capable as accompanist or soloist. Only Ray Brown has been more in demand as a sideman than Ørsted Pedersen, who has played bass on more than 150 albums. [IC]

⊙ **Jaywalkin'** (1975; Steeplechase); **Double Bass** (1976; Steeplechase); **Dancing On The Tables** (1979; Steeplechase). Three fine albums under NHØP's leadership. The first is a quartet with Philip Catherine, Billy Higgins and pianist Ole Kock Hansen, who is replaced by a second bassist (Sam Jones) on the the second. The repertoire is basically standards, but *Dancing*, with Dave Liebman, John Scofield and Billy Hart, explores some more adventurous territory.

➤➤ **Chet Baker** *(Daybreak)*; **Dexter Gordon** *(Both Sides Of Midnight)*; **Oscar Peterson** *(If You Could See Me Now)*.

Kid Ory

Trombone, vocals, composer; also bass, cornet, alto saxophone.

b. La Place, Louisiana, 25 Dec 1886; d. Hawaii, 23 Jan 1973.

While he was still playing the banjo in his home town, thirty miles from New Orleans, Kid (Edward) Ory was already setting up musical picnics – and charging admission. When, around 1911, he arrived in New Orleans as a young trombonist, he quickly drummed up more business: "I rented a furniture wagon, and told a fellow to make signs, 'KID ORY', with address and telephone number. After that I began to get lots of calls!" Soon Ory – a very competitive leader who whipped opposition unmercifully and walked off the stage if the musical company failed to suit him – was spellbinding New Orleans with bands featuring strong trumpeters such as Mutt Carey (a lifelong colleague), Joe Oliver and the young Louis Armstrong. In 1917 he received an offer to go to Chicago, but was simply too busy. In 1919 his doctor advised a warmer climate: Ory moved to California, set up his band there, recorded the first-ever titles by an all-black New Orleans-style jazz band ("Ory's Creole Trombone" for the Spike Brothers's Sunshine label), and as early as 1921 was so busy again that he had to delegate a string of double bookings to Oliver's band.

In 1925 he was back in Chicago with King Oliver, and he spent the next seven years playing for leaders such as Dave Peyton, Boyd Atkins and Clarence Black, and recording with (among others) Jelly Roll Morton, Ma Rainey, Tiny Parham, Luis Russell and, of course, Louis Armstrong's Hot Five and Seven. "When we made those records we didn't have any expectation that they would be so successful," said Ory later. "One thing that helped the sales was the fact for a while that the OKeh people gave away a picture of Louis to everyone that bought one."

By 1933 the big bands were taking over, and Ory retired from music to look after his brother's chicken farm. Not much more was heard from him until 1942, when he came back to music with Barney Bigard's band (on trombone), and a year later he was playing concerts with his own group. In 1944 a series of weekly broadcasts hosted by Orson Welles for Standard Oil re-established him as the revival's most resilient star, and for the rest of his life Kid Ory was a prosperous and successful jazzman. He began a long residency at the Jade Palace on Hollywood Boulevard in 1945, took a featured role in the Hollywood film *New Orleans* in 1947, toured nationally in 1948, and the following year moved to the Beverley Cavern back on the West Coast. After Carey left the band in 1948 (the year he died), Ory used a succession of brilliant trumpeters such as Teddy Buckner (who joined him from Lionel Hampton), Marty Marsala and Alvin Alcorn, and all through the 1950s he continued to market his career with skill and vision (his Good Time Jazz albums of the period feature irresistible artwork and New Orleans recipes, as well as notes about the band). A new hit version of his composition "Muskrat Ramble" in 1954 made Ory richer still (in the early years of his career he had failed to collect royalties on the tune until Barney Bigard explained how), and that year he opened his club, On The Levee, in Los Angeles. "Ory has the mentality of a French peasant, with all the charm, shrewdness and stinginess that that implies," said Martin Williams at this time. (British trumpeter Colin Smith remembers Ory's reply to a fan who asked him for tips on trombone playing: "Never do it for nothing!")

Ory's primitive trombone – several observers, including Williams and British trombonist Alan Dean, believe that he was actually a far better player than he let on – was heard in Europe in 1956 and 1959; in the mid-1960s he moved to Hawaii, following the hot weather once more. A very old Ory appeared – but only to sing – at festivals in the early 1970s. He died at 86 and was buried New Orleans-style: "I know they played 'Just A Closer Walk With Thee' over him," remembers Barney Bigard, "and cut down the hill with 'Muskrat Ramble' and 'Ory's Creole Trombone' and that was the end of an era." [DF]

MAX JONES FILES/REDFERNS

Kid Ory

⊙ **Ory's Creole Trombone; Greatest Recordings 1922-44** (ASV). Invaluable for its pre-Revival coverage of Ory as leader and sideman in central settings, this set has his first two sides (with Ory's Sunshine Orchestra) plus essential titles with King Oliver (1926), Armstrong's Hot Five (1926-7), New Orleans Wanderers/Bootblacks (1926), Jelly Roll Morton (1926), plus five with his own band from 1944.

⊙ **Creole Jazz Band** (1944–5; Good Time Jazz). With Carey in the ranks plus clarinettists Darnell Howard and Omer Simeon, this is Ory in the setting he would be known for for two more decades.

⊙ **Kid Ory** (1944–6; American Music). Ory just after his return to the spotlight, with Mutt Carey, Albert Nicholas, Barney Bigard and folk-blues singer Leadbelly all making appearances.

⊙ **This Kid's The Greatest** (1953–6; Good Time Jazz). This album features the brilliant Teddy Buckner, a highly trained musician who provided the Armstrong-esque lead against which the Kid played his old-style tailgate.

⊙ **The Tailgate Trombone** (1956; Giants of Jazz). Good titles with Alvin Alcorn (trumpet) playing alongside the elegant Phil Gomez (clarinet) and a rhythm-section featuring Cedric Haywood.

➤➤ **Louis Armstrong** *(Louis Armstrong Vol. 1 1925–6 & 1926–7)*; **Johnny Dodds** *(The Chronological Johnny Dodds – 1926).*

Mike Osborne

Alto saxophone, clarinet, piano.

b. Hereford, UK, 28 Sept 1941.

Osborne graduated from the Guildhall School of Music, London, and from 1962–72 was a member of Mike Westbrook's band. During the 1960s and 1970s he was also a regular member of Chris McGregor's Brotherhood of Breath and the John Warren big band, and worked with Mike Gibbs, Humphrey Lyttelton and Alan Skidmore. In 1970 he began leading his own trio. He was often associated with Stan Tracey, playing a series of duo concerts with him. He was, in 1973, a founder member of SOS (Surman-Osborne-Skidmore), an innovative three-saxophone group that toured in Italy, Germany and France, and co-wrote and performed music for a ballet, *Sablier Prison*, at the Paris Opera House. With various bands Osborne toured all over Europe. He was voted first on alto saxophone in the *Melody Maker* Jazz Poll every year from 1969–73. His favourite altoists are Jackie McLean and Phil Woods, and Osborne's own playing has an intensity similar to theirs. He has been ill and out of action since 1980. [IC]

⊙ **Outback** (1970; Future Music). Osborne with Harry Beckett, Chris McGregor, Harry Miller and Louis Moholo, and two long tracks, the title piece and "So It Is". The music is passionate, semi-free, rhythmic and with African shadings. Very much of its time.

Greg Osby

Alto and soprano saxophones, flute.

b. St Louis, Missouri, 3 Aug 1960.

After studying jazz at Howard University, Washington, DC (1978–80), Greg Osby took a three-year composing and arranging course at Berklee, after which he moved to New York. Work with Woody Shaw, Jon Faddis, Ron Carter and Dizzy Gillespie followed, and he became a member of Jack DeJohnette's Special Edition in 1985. A meeting with Steve Coleman, and through him introduction into the M-Base scene and its environs, led to Osby not only finding much-needed support in his musical campaign against neo-conservatism, but also to his joining up with like-minded figures such as Marvin "Smitty" Smith and Dave Holland, and to his signing a deal with Blue Note in 1990. His first three albums for the company, *Man Talk for Moderns, Vol. X* (1990), *3-D Lifestyles* (1992) and *Black Book* (1994), contained modish, coolly detached music drawing on street beats, rap and hip-hop in typical M-Base fashion. With 1996's *Art Forum*, however, Osby changed direction somewhat, showcasing his compositional strengths in an acoustic format that drew deeply on his original influences: Herbie Hancock's *Speak Like A Child*, Charles Mingus's *Ah Um*, Duke Ellington's *Indigo* and Miles Davis and Gil Evans's *Miles Ahead*. The following year, Osby released *Further Ado* featuring some fine young players – pianist Jason Moran and tenorman Mark Shim among them – and maintaining his acoustic direction. The two 1998 albums listed below were also acoustic, and Osby commented: "I've discovered how to make grooves and progressions and vertical structures in the acoustic environment ... The challenge is trying to rethink a classic form in a way that makes reference to the people I love so much, like Monk and Andrew Hill, but doesn't patronise their contribution." [CP]

⊙ **Greg Osby And Sound Theatre** (1987; JMT). Featuring Osby in an intriguing partnership with pianist Michele Rosewoman, and with a rhythm-section comprising bassist Lonnie Plaxico and drummers Paul Samuels and Teri Lyne Carrington, this debut album touches many more jazz bases than subsequent Osby recordings.

⊙ **Man Talk For Moderns** (1990; Blue Note). Most of the prominent M-Base crew – Steve Coleman, Gary Thomas, David Gilmour, etc – are featured on this determinedly contemporary album, but jazz struggles to be heard in all the modishness.

⊙ **3-D Lifestyles** (1992; Blue Note). Uneasy mixture of rap, jazz and hip attitude, which falls between several stools despite a stellar line-up including pianist Geri Allen and vocalist Cassandra Wilson.

⊙ **Zero** (1998; Blue Note). Dark, slightly enigmatic but consistently intriguing quintet music from a virtuosic young band with which Osby is trying to attain a "high point of musical independence, expression and interplay" and thereby launch himself into what he refers to as the "Zero Zone", the Buddhist state of "no-mind".

⊙ **Banned In New York** (1998; Blue Note). Got up to resemble a bootleg, a semi-unofficial recording catching Osby's working band steaming through such fare as Sonny Rollins's "Pent Up House" and Charlie Parker's "Big Foot".

Johnny Otis

Drums, vibes, piano.

b. Vallejo, California, 28 Dec 1921.

Born of Greek parents, John Veliotes was brought up in the black community of Berkeley. Starting as a jazz drummer in 1939, he worked with several name bands and, after moving to Los Angeles in 1943, recorded with both Illinois Jacquet in 1945 and Lester Young in 1946. He led his own big band from 1945–7, which included Paul Quinichette and bassist Curtis Counce. He then led a septet, initially with Hampton Hawes and saxophonist Big Jay McNeely, gradually moving from jazz into R&B and featuring such singers as Little Esther Phillips and Willie Mae (Big Mama) Thornton. He also recorded with Dinah Washington, using Ben Webster as guest with his band in 1951. He became a radio DJ and hosted a live R&B revue on a weekly TV series from 1956–61. He was inactive in music in the 1960s and late 1970s, including a period as a preacher in his own church. He successfully spearheaded R&B revivals in the USA from 1969–75 and again in 1984, and helped to relaunch the careers of jazz-based singers Louis Jordan, Slim Gaillard and Eddie Vinson in the early 1970s. In the early 1990s he led an occasional big band, featuring some swing-era veterans and his sons, guitarist Shuggie and drummer Nicky Otis. [BP]

⊙ **Barrelhouse Stomp** (1946–51; Jukebox Lil). An excellent chronological compilation which shows precisely the move from big-band jazz to instrumental R&B. As well as an appearance by Big Jay McNeely, there are early sides arranged by Buck Clayton and Bill Doggett, and a late guest spot for Ben Webster on his favourite "Stardust".

Jimmy Owens

Trumpet, flugelhorn, composer.

b. New York, 9 Dec 1943.

Owens began on trumpet at ten; he attended the High School of Music and Art, and then studied composition with Henry Bryant, and the trumpet with Donald Byrd. During the 1960s he worked with many leading musicians, including Lionel Hampton in 1963–4, Hank Crawford in 1964–5, and Charles Mingus and (separately) Herbie Mann in 1965–6. He also spent briefer periods with Ellington, Gerry Mulligan, Max Roach and Count Basie. He was one of the original members of the Thad Jones-Mel Lewis orchestra. He toured Europe with the Dizzy Gillespie reunion band in 1968, and since then has done many other European tours with different groups and bands. In 1974 he played with radio orchestras in Germany and Holland. Owens's initial influences were Miles Davis, Gillespie and Art Farmer, and he was already a highly polished performer by the mid-1960s, combining something of the sonority of Davis with a superb technique. At the 1970 Newport jazz festival celebration of Louis Armstrong's birthday, Owens was the youngest of a select group of trumpet players chosen to play in tribute to Satchmo; the others included Gillespie, Bobby Hackett and Joe Newman. But Owens was very much of the younger generation, and in 1973 was a featured soloist on one of the classic jazz-rock albums – Billy Cobham's *Spectrum*. Later in the decade Owens made his own fusion albums. He has played on more than eighty albums with other leaders, including Mann, James Moody, Gillespie, Archie Shepp and Booker Ervin.

Owens is also active as a lecturer, lobbyist and educator. From 1972–6 he served on the Jazz-Folk-Ethnic Music Panel of the National Endowment for the Arts; he is one of the founders of Collective Black Artists, Inc., a non-profit-making education and performance organization; he has been on the music panel of the New York State Council on the Arts; and in 1974 was musical director of the New York Jazz Repertory Company. In 1976 he received his Master's degree in education. [IC]

➤➤ **Billy Cobham** *(Spectrum);* **Billy Harper** *(Capra Black).*

Tony Oxley

Drums, percussion, electronics, composer.
b. Sheffield, UK, 15 June 1938.

Oxley taught himself the piano from the age of eight, but he did not get his first drumkit until he was seventeen. From 1957–60, in the Black Watch military band, he studied drums and theory. From 1960–64 he led his own quintet in Sheffield, and from 1963–7 he collaborated with Derek Bailey in exploring freely improvised music. In 1966 he moved to London, becoming the house drummer at Ronnie Scott's club, where he accompanied many visiting Americans including Sonny Rollins, Bill Evans, Stan Getz, Lee Konitz, Charlie Mariano and Joe Henderson. He continued in this capacity until the early 1970s, was in the 1968 Ronnie Scott octet called the Band, and also played with the Gordon Beck trio, Alan Skidmore and the Mike Pyne trio.

By the mid-1960s Oxley had mastered all the arts of conventional jazz drumming, and was already a virtuoso with superb time and a brilliant technique, but he was losing interest in the accepted musical language of the period. He had resumed his association with Bailey, now also living in London, and was becoming deeply committed to abstract music both as a player and as a composer. In 1969 he played on a classic album of the 1960s – John McLaughlin's *Extrapolation* – which was like a summary of small-group playing to date, with pointers to the future. The same year, for CBS, he began recording his own severely abstract music with a quintet that included Bailey, Kenny Wheeler, Evan Parker and Jeff Clyne, producing the 1969 album *The Baptised Traveller.* Paul Rutherford (trombone) was added to make the group a sextet for a second album, *4 Compositions For Sextet,* in 1970. With Bailey and Parker he formed Incus Records, because it was already clear that major labels would not commit themselves to the austere new music. Oxley also became a member of the London Jazz Composers' Orchestra, formed by Barry Guy, and worked with Howard Riley in his trio and other groups. From 1973 he was organizing tutor at the Barry Summer School (Wales) of a course in jazz and improvised music. In 1974 he formed his own group, Angular Apron. He has also worked a great deal in Europe with leading European and American musicians. He has received several composing awards from the Arts Council of Great Britain, and worked with George Gruntz on music for the film *Steppenwolf* (1974).

Although committed to abstraction, Oxley has continued occasionally to play in a more conventional way when accompanying others. However, his own quintet's concert at the Camden festival in 1985 was as abstract as ever. He made further tours of the UK in 1986 with an octet co-led by Didier Levallet, and a quartet with Tony Coe. Through the later 1980s Oxley led his own Celebration Orchestra, and in 1989 toured and recorded with Anthony Braxton. Since the late 80s he has frequently worked with Cecil Taylor.

He has been influenced by contemporary classical composers, and often uses graphic scores. Other influences are Eric Dolphy, Art Blakey, Elvin Jones, John Coltrane and Bill Evans. [IC]

⊙ **The Tony Oxley Quartet** (1992; Incus). Oxley reunited with Bailey and aided and abetted by two younger British improvisers, Pat Thomas (keyboards and electronics) and Matt Wand (drum machine and tape switchboard). The result is intelligent free-playing, informed by acute ears and years of seasoning.

➤➤ **Anthony Braxton** *(Seven Compositions (Trio) 1989);* **Tony Coe** *(Nutty On Willisau);* **John McLaughlin** *(Extrapolation).*

Makoto Ozone

Piano, composer, arranger.
b. Kobe, Japan, 25 March 1961.

Ozone's father, Minoru, is one of Japan's best jazz pianists. Makoto started on organ at the age of four and took up the piano in his teens after hearing Oscar Peterson. In 1980 he went to Berklee, Boston, studying composing and arranging, and there Gary Burton immediately recognized Ozone's extraordinary qualities: he has great virtuosity, is a born improviser, and his playing is already a compendium of the entire jazz piano tradition. In 1983 he opened the Kool jazz festival with a Carnegie Hall recital; in 1984 he recorded his first album as leader with Burton (vibes) and Eddie Gomez (bass). By 1985 he was a regular member of the Burton quartet, and also played in a duo with the French keyboard virtuoso Michel Petrucciani at the Playboy festival at the Hollywood Bowl. His main recent influences are Burton and classical pianist Vladimir Ashkenazy: Ozone is also studying classical piano. [IC]

Gary Burton-Makoto Ozone

⊙ **Face To Face** (1994; GRP). Burton and Ozone in duo tackling a range of material from Latin to blues and impressionistic essays, and even some cod stride piano. Both virtuosi are in fine fettle and good humour.

P

Hot Lips Page

Trumpet, mellophone, vocals.
b. Dallas, Texas, 27 Jan 1908; d. 5 Nov 1954.

"You could take Louis Armstrong and put Lips in there and you couldn't tell 'em apart," said Budd Johnson. "He learned to play every note Louis played on a record, note for note." In fact, Hot Lips (Oran Thaddeus) Page was instantly distinguishable from his idol: his improvisation was wilder and less monumental than Armstrong's, his singing more blues-filled and insidious. But the resemblance was close enough to strike Joe Glaser, who first heard Page while he was appearing with Count Basie at the Reno Club, Kansas City, in 1936, riding over the brass, as Louis did, in the final out-choruses. By that time "The trumpet king of the West", as he was billed, had spent years backing blues singers such as Bessie Smith and Ma Rainey and starring in territory bands, including Walter Page's and Bennie Moten's, and had built a storehouse of confidence, showmanship and technique. Glaser, knowing that Louis Armstrong, his "number one boy", was suffering with a disturbing patch of lip trouble and might be finished, signed Page to a long contract and when Basie left for Chicago with his new band the trumpeter stayed behind to front Bus Moten's group. For the last eighteen years of his career, Lips – a handsome young hepcat, full of charm, talent and a Louis Jordan-esque fondness for rhythm and blues – led bands and appeared solo up and down 52nd Street.

But after Armstrong's lip recovered, Glaser rapidly lost sight of his second-string as a priority and Page had more reason to see himself as an Armstrong alternative. "I went up to Lips at the Plantation," recalls Ahmet Ertegun, "and said 'Would you please play "Satchelmouth Swing"?' He looked at me and laughed and said 'No, but I'll play Hot Lips Page's special message to a young ofay!'" Page's career never achieved the status of Armstrong's: he remained a jam session habitué (something Armstrong never did) and often seemed haunted by bad luck – his hit record of "St James Infirmary" with Artie Shaw came just as Shaw disbanded; a later best seller with Pearl Bailey, "Baby It's Cold Outside", launched Bailey but left Page unremembered. It would be rash to lay all the blame at Glaser's office door: Page was less talented than Armstrong, and – relatively speaking – he was a success, with a string of entertaining and often commercially slanted records to his name. But it is ironic that (as Greg Murphy points out) the first full-scale reissue of Hot Lips Page material on LP came seventeen years after his death – the year that Armstrong died. [DF]

⊙ **Pagin' Mr. Page; His Greatest Recordings 1932-46** (ASV). Page's rough-hewn trumpet and sly sensual singing is well-represented in this sampler which includes a comprehensive portrait of Page in different contexts; with Artie Shaw (the great "St. James Infirmary"), Basie, Eddie Condon ("Uncle Sam Blues" a big hit), Albert Ammons and his Rhythm Kings and Page's own R&B-laced recordings including "They Raided The Joint", "Feelin' High And Happy" and "Just Another Woman".

⊙ **Hot Lips Page 1938–40/1940–44/1946–50** (Classics). The complete Page saga and for completists, the starting point; stars like Earl Bostic, Don Byas and Ben Webster add to the delights along the way, and Page's work is consistently interesting though less refined than many of his contemporaries.

Walter Page

Bass.
b. Gallatin, Missouri, 9 Feb 1900; d. 20 Dec 1957.

Walter Sylvester Page worked with Bennie Moten on and off from 1918, and then went on to lead his own Blue Devils from 1925–31, featuring Basie, Rushing and Hot Lips Page among others. In the latter year Bennie Moten made room in his band for Page's young stars – and subsequently Page himself (1932–4). After Moten died suddenly in 1935, Page came back to work for Basie (who was four years his junior), but he was to form a vital quarter of his new leader's "All American Rhythm-Section". Says Harry Edison: "The whole band would be shouting and then all of a sudden everyone would drop out for the bridge, and there'd be just the rhythm with Page's bass going up and down." "Walter Page you could *hear*," agrees Eddie Durham. "He didn't have the best ear in the world, but he worked hard. Walter Page invented that walkin', walkin'!" Page was a part of Basie's unbeatable section until 1942, when a dispute temporarily hardened him against Basie once more, but by 1946 he was back for three more years. Then he became a freelance with old friends Hot Lips Page (1949–51), Jimmy Rushing (1951–2) and with Eddie Condon from 1952. In December 1957 he collapsed on the way to a TV *Sound Of Jazz* recording, was rushed to hospital and died shortly after.

Jo Jones sets Walter Page in perspective. "The greatest band I ever heard in my life was Walter Page's Blue Devils. Musically Page was the father of Basie, Rushing, Buster Smith – and me too, because without him I wouldn't have known how to play drums. For two years Page told me how to phrase. And aside from that he told me a few of the moral responsibilities that go into making up an artist's life." Walter Page, or "Big One" as he was known to the Kansas City jazz fraternity, was not only the last of the great pre-Blanton bassists, but a figure of authority. [DF]

➤➤ **Count Basie** *(The Original American Decca Recordings).*

Marty Paich

Arranger, piano.

b. Oakland, California, 23 Jan 1925; d. 12 Aug 1995.

Paich started playing and arranging professionally in Oakland at sixteen and, after working with a service band from 1943–6, he studied composition at Los Angeles Conservatory until 1950. He worked as pianist and arranger for Peggy Lee in 1953, and with the Shelly Manne and Shorty Rogers groups in 1953–4. As a freelance writer, he arranged famous 1950s and 60s albums for Mel Tormé, Art Pepper, Ray Charles and many others, before specializing in work for television and films. In the case of the Pepper and Tormé items (and a couple of 1988 reunions with Tormé) he made effective use of the "small big band" sound of his ten-piece Dektette. [BP]

Art Pepper

⊙ **Modern Jazz Classics** (1959; Contemporary/OJC). As well as the size and sound of the group being closely modelled on the *Birth Of The Cool* band, some of Paich's ideas about content are secondhand, viz. the close imitation of Gil Evans's version on "Round Midnight".

➤➤ **Mel Tormé** *(Swings Shubert Alley).*

Roy Palmer

Trombone.

b. New Orleans, 2 April 1892; d. 22 Dec 1963.

Roy Palmer worked all around his home town before making the pioneer jump to Chicago in 1917 to play with Sugar Johnny's headlining band. All through the next decade he remained a busy freelance in the city, playing with Johnny Dodds, Hughie Swift, Jelly Roll Morton, Doc Watson and W.C. Handy, but he left full-time music in the 1930s and by 1940 had opened a laundry. He is said to have influenced the young Georg Brunis, and other early pupils included Albert Wynn and Preston Jackson; he was still teaching trumpet, trombone and music theory in Chicago in the 1950s. [DF]

Eddie Palmieri

Piano, arranger.

b. New York, 15 Dec 1936.

Born to Puerto Rican parents, Palmieri started on piano at eight and studied classical music from the age of thirteen, but also played drums in a traditional Latin band. His elder brother Charlie (1927–88) was a successful pianist and bandleader by the time Eddie began playing with a series of bands, culminating in Tito Rodriguez's in 1958–60. He then formed his influential band La Perfecta, which lasted from 1961–8; its flute and trombone frontline was adopted by Herbie Mann, and Palmieri recorded a 1966 album with Cal Tjader. In the mid-1960s he began formally studying arranging, and his piano work began to echo the styles of Monk and McCoy Tyner. In the 1970s Palmieri temporarily moved closer to a fusion of salsa music with R&B and rock, but his piano solos, including extended introductions as deceptive as Erroll Garner's (though very different in style), ensure that the jazz influence is ever-present. [BP]

⊙ **Palmas** (1993; Elektra Nonesuch). Palmieri's most jazz-oriented album yet features, in place of Latin vocals, the same three horns that take the improvised solos (Donald Harrison, trumpeter Brian Lynch and trombonist Conrad Herwig) playing within a six-piece rhythm-section.

Andy Panayi

Flutes, saxophones, clarinets.

b. London, 18 Jan 1964.

Andreas Lambrov Panayi has Greek Cypriot parents, and his father is a professional bouzouki player. Andy Panayi studied flute, composition and saxophone at London's Trinity College of Music. He began on flute at thirteen, playing in classical groups, wind bands, small band ensembles and big bands; a year later he took up baritone saxophone and, soon afterwards, alto and tenor. At sixteen, he played flute in the London Schools Symphony Orchestra. He joined the Superjazz Big Band and played with them at Ronnie Scott's club, then was with NYJO for a while. Soon he was in great demand as a multi-instrumentalist and played with many other groups and musicians. He won the National Big Band Marty Paich Arranging Award in 1987, the John Dankworth Soloist Award, and the Worshipful Company of Musicians Jazz Medal in 1994. Panayi has worked with Abdullah Ibrahim, Pepper Adams, Jiggs Whigham, Freddie Hubbard, Irene Reid and most leading British jazz musicians, including John Dankworth and Cleo Laine, and Stan Tracey. He has recorded with many musicians and groups, and in 1998 released his own quartet album, *Blown Away*, a live recording of his quartet at the Scott club. His favourites are Harold McNair (flute), Sonny Rollins, Zoot Sims, Cannonball Adderley and Charlie Parker,

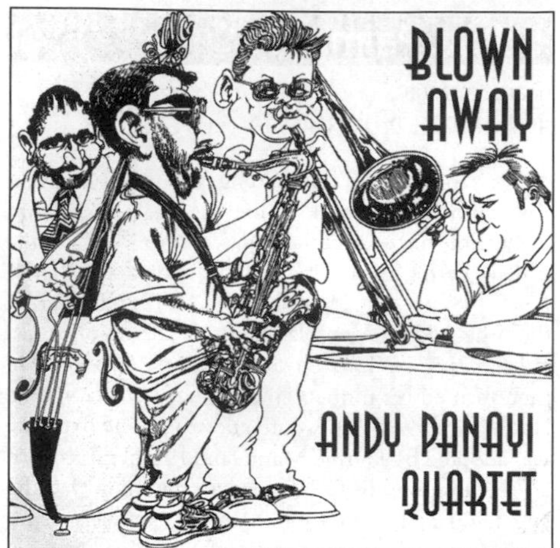

and other inspirations are Bob Brookmeyer, Thad Jones/Mel Lewis, Basie, Ellington and Strayhorn. Panayi still plays classical recitals as well as jazz concerts, and finds inspiration in Debussy, Ravel, Bach and others. [IC]

Blown Away (1998; Jazz House). Panayi leads an all-star quartet in this session, with trombonist Mark Nightingale, bassist Simon Woolf and drummer Mark Taylor. The fare includes some standards, three originals by Woolf and one by Panayi, and some interesting but less well-known originals by leading American jazzmen. This is a dynamic set, working in very familiar jazz territory, but the standard of invention is phenomenal, and the dynamism exhilarating.

Tony Parenti

Clarinet, saxophones.

b. New Orleans, 6 Aug 1900; d. 17 April 1972.

Tony Parenti was a child prodigy who by the age of twelve was playing in ragtime trios and soon after was turning down offers from Paul Whiteman and the Original Dixieland Jazz Band because he was too young to go on the road. But he did work for Papa Jack Laine's band, as well as on board riverboats (including the *Capitol* for Streckfus, where young pianist Jess Stacy was an early partner). By the late 1920s Parenti was busy in New York, "shackin' with my old friend Ray Bauduc" (another New Orleans man), and doing all the best work: playing for Ben Pollack in Benny Goodman's frequent absences, appearing on radio and records with leaders such as Fred Rich, and providing the jazz injection for society bands like Meyer Davis's. "Those jobs accounted for us making a lot of money in those days," he recalled later. "They wanted a man who could play a couple of choruses on the up-tempo things." Parenti, whose abilities in many respects rivalled Irving Fazola's, worked throughout the 1930s as staffman for CBS and for the Radio City Symphony Orchestra, then from 1939 served alongside Muggsy Spanier in Ted Lewis's highly paid show. After 1945 he became better known as a jazzman again, identifying strongly with the New Orleans revival and often recording with a mix of Chicago and New Orleans stars from Wild Bill Davison to Pops Foster. He was also regularly to be seen in New York at Dixieland strongholds such as Jimmy Ryan's, the Metropole and Central Plaza, spent four years in Florida with Preacher Rollo's Five Saints, and subbed briefly for George Lewis in 1959. In the 1960s, following Wilbur de Paris, Parenti led the house band at Ryan's for six years. Parenti's heart was always in New Orleans jazz: "Progressive jazz is really extemporaneous tricks: it lacks feeling and expression, and gives me a cold reaction." [DF]

Tony Parenti And His New Orleanians (1949; Jazzology). Good example of Parenti's virtuosity amid a compatible group – Wild Bill Davison, Jimmy Archey and Art Hodes among them.

Tiny Parham

Piano, organ, arranger, composer.

b. Winnipeg, Manitoba, 25 Feb 1900; d. 4 April 1943.

A quietly talented Chicago-based pianist-arranger, Hartzell Strathdene Parham – called "Tiny" because of his enormous girth – was touring the Pantages theatre circuit by 1925 and later directed music for a variety of clubs and theatres, including the Apollo Theater, Chicago, where he led a high-powered showband featuring high-note trumpeter Reuben Reeves. Parham's recording career was busy, too: he accompanied blues singers and led his own bands, which maintained a constantly high standard – such titles as "Dixieland Doings", "Blue Island Blues" and "Black Cat Moan" reveal an ingenuity comparable to early work from Ellington and Morton. A thoroughly schooled player who arranged for King Oliver, Earl Hines and for club floor shows, Parham led bands all through the 1930s but never graduated to New York, and by the end of the decade was playing the organ in theatres, cinemas and ice-rinks. [DF]

Tiny Parham 1928-30 (Timeless). As usual from Timeless a definitive reissue (including alternate takes) of all of Parham's most important work from his peak period.

Truck Parham

Bass.

b. Chicago, 25 Jan 1911; d. 5 June 2002.

Born Charles Valdez Parham, but commonly known as "Truck", Parham started off playing drums and tuba in a school band led by pianist Albert Ammons. In the 1930s he worked as a singer with Zack Whyte's Chocolate Beau Brummels with whom he later also played bass. Thereafter Parham worked with Art Tatum (1936) and most notably with Roy Eldridge, recording classics including "Heckler's Hop", before joining Earl Hines and Jimmy Lunceford in the early to mid-1940s. In the

1950s he continued to work around Chicago, notably with cornet player Muggsy Spanier and Art Hodes, but also with modernists including Gigi Gryce, Louie Bellson and Herbie Fields. Parham was also active as a sports coach, having played professional American football with the Chicago Negro All Stars in his youth. He continued to work regularly through the 1970s to the 1990s leading his Swing All Stars in Europe and New Orleans until shortly before his death. [DF]

➤➤ **Roy Eldridge** *(Heckler's Hop).*

Jackie Paris

Vocals.

b. Nutley, New Jersey, 20 Sept 1926.

Paris played guitar during the early 1940s and after military service sang regularly on 52nd Street, notably with Charlie Parker, as well as working with Lionel Hampton (1949–50). Voted best new male singer by *Down Beat* magazine in 1953, he recorded regularly through the 1950s, and has continued ever since to record (including with Mingus in 1974) and to appear at clubs, concerts and festivals. [DF]

⊙ **Lucky To Be Me** (1988; Emarcy). Paris's ever-hip talent is unaltered by time in this collection of jazz and popular standards; his splendid trio is made up of Jim McNeely (piano,) Mike Richmond (bass) and Adam Nussbaum (drums).

Charlie Parker

Alto saxophone, composer; also tenor saxophone.

b. Kansas City, 29 Aug 1920; d. 12 March 1955.

Charlie Parker, often known as Bird, or Yardbird, was one of the most striking performers in the entire history of jazz, and one of the most influential. He became aware of the strong local music scene in Kansas City at an early age, even before he took up first the baritone horn and then the alto while in high school. Dropping out of school at fourteen, he concentrated all his efforts on mastering his instrument and watching locally based innovators such as Lester Young and Count Basie. He learned much from employment by altoist/bandleaders Tommy Douglas from 1936–7 and Buster Smith from 1937–8. In between he spent a few months out of town with the band of George E. Lee, and subsequent trips to Chicago and New York contributed to his development, the seal on which was set by his tenure with Jay McShann in 1938, and again in 1940–42.

He played briefly in several more big bands including Earl Hines's from 1942–3 and Billy Eckstine's in 1944, before Dizzy Gillespie, his colleague under both Hines and Eckstine, helped to establish bebop on the small-group scene of New York's 52nd Street. He worked there with Gillespie from 1944–5, with Ben Webster in 1944, and with his own group in 1945. While on the West Coast, Parker was featured with Jazz At The Philharmonic in 1946 and with Howard McGhee from 1946–7, the latter period broken by six months of enforced recuperation from the previous ten years of heroin addiction. His return to New York in 1947 found him at the height of his powers, and leading a highly compatible quintet with Miles Davis, Duke Jordan, Tommy Potter and Max Roach. However, the popularity of his first recordings with strings, issued in 1950, led to public appearances with similar backing, and a corresponding lack of challenge in even the rhythm-sections he employed. Parker spent the remaining years of his life gigging with local pick-up groups in different parts of the USA or touring as guest soloist in the unlikely company of the Woody Herman and Stan Kenton bands, which he did in 1951 and 1954 respectively. His recording projects included a promising series with Latin American accompaniment and an unpromising date with woodwinds and voices, both sabotaged by lack of adequate preparation. Approximately annual reunions with Gillespie and other key associates from the 1940s showed him still capable of superlative playing, but his readdiction to narcotics, plus a huge intake of alcohol, eventually ended his growing musical frustration when he died in the home of jazz benefactor Baroness Pannonica de Koenigswater. Although never excusing or recommending his own habits to others, Parker nonetheless set an example in this sphere as much as in his music, and the number of performers of his generation who lost several productive years, or in some cases their lives, is quite staggeringly high.

What made Parker truly charismatic, however, was his musical genius, the seemingly miraculous way in which he solved problems that were preoccupying his chief colleagues, and then proceeded to set up a whole new series of hurdles which he cleared with one hand tied behind his back, as it were. Parker's impact on saxophonists, from the time of his first records with McShann in 1941 and his second arrival in New York in 1942, may be likened to that of Art Tatum's on pianists. It is hardly coincidental that he was in fact influenced by Tatum, for he managed to give the same impression that executing any musical idea, however difficult, was childishly easy. This facility bestowed the same, perhaps childlike, ability to conceive fantastic ideas that other, more rational beings would have dismissed as technically impossible. The net result of this was to take the fascinating rules of advanced European harmony (already being tapped by saxophonists Coleman Hawkins and Don Byas) and to deploy them at lightning speed, yet with all the linear grace associated with Lester Young. The effectiveness of the conception was made just that bit more authoritative by Parker's tone, which matched the daring of his structures and, once the listener has become accustomed to it, is as irresistible as a knife cutting through butter. His communicative powers surpassed the efforts of Hawkins, Byas and Young, who

William Gottlieb/Redferns

Charlie Parker with Red Rodney

chiefly impressed other saxophonists – Parker impressed and influenced players of every instrument.

The new technical hurdles that he was largely responsible for introducing were above all rhythmic. As in the case of the harmonic extensions inherent in bebop, other leading thinkers such as Gillespie and Thelonious Monk were active in studying and perfecting the new rhythmic variations, but it was Bird who played them as to the manner born, and indeed he had never played any other way, to judge from his earliest recordings. For this reason, his most important collaborators were always drummers, whether the most flexible swing drummers, such as Sid Catlett, or the best Latin percussionists of the day, or his ideal partner, Max Roach. Miles Davis once illustrated Parker's freedom in this area by describing his (literally) off-beat entries: "Every time that would happen, Max Roach used to scream at Duke Jordan not to follow Bird, but to stay where he was. Then, eventually it came round as Bird had planned and we were together again." The full extent of his rhythmic virtuosity became the norm only in the free jazz of the 1960s and the fusion music of the 1970s (or at least in some instances of both): most of the 1970s revival of bebop fell far short in this respect.

One by-product of the bop revival, however, was the rediscovery of Parker's written lines and of their superiority to most other tunes of his era. The mere fact of executing themes such as "Confirmation", "Scrapple From The Apple", "Cheryl" and "Quasimodo" is a constant challenge to try and produce improvisation of equivalent quality to that of their composer. (One way of sidestepping the challenge was demonstrated in the early 1970s by the group Supersax, who transcribed and orchestrated Parker improvisations and played them as compositions, a treatment they are well able to withstand.) In many other ways, Bird is still very much a contemporary figure – either as the supreme example of the art of the soloist and therefore to be emulated, or as a superman whose contribution could only ever be equalled by drawing on the somewhat different strengths of the collective approach. No one individual apart from Louis Armstrong has cast such a long shadow over succeeding generations of jazz musicians. [BP]

⊙ **The Complete Birth Of The Bebop** (1940–46; Stash). Not the best place to start, except for the sake of chronology. Badly balanced and poorly preserved private recordings of Parker, either solo or jamming with records, or playing with his peers. But absolutely fascinating historically, if you've already studied the masterworks and want to know how Parker got where he was.

⊙ **The Complete Savoy And Dial Studio Recordings** (1944-8; Savoy). Not for faint hearts (or empty pockets), this 8-CD set does what it says on the box. It includes absolutely essential Savoy items, like Bird's first session under his own name with the young Miles Davis, Gillespie on piano (and trumpet for the magical "Ko-Ko") and Max Roach;

here too is the 1947–8 working group in iconic tracks such as "Buzzy", "Barbados", "Ah-Leu-Cha" and "Parker's Mood". There is also a three-CD compilation of the Complete Savoy And Dial Master Takes, which duplicates all of the set listed below.

⊙ **The Dial Masters** (1946–7; Spotlite). Covering both the pre-recuperation and the recuperated Parker, this two-CD set includes such items as "Night In Tunisia", "Ornithology" and the infamous "Lover Man", followed by the 1947 quintet with Davis and Roach ("Embraceable You", "Scrapple From The Apple" and more). Classic stuff.

⊙ **Complete Live Performances On Savoy** (1947–50; Savoy). Indifferent airshot sound-quality does not detract from these performances at the Royal Roost. As well as the Roach-Davis quintet, Dorham replaces Davis for a look at "White Christmas" (!) and the four-CD set ends with a Gillespie-Parker 1947 performance at Carnegie Hall.

⊙ **Charlie Parker With Strings: The Master Takes** (1947–52; Verve). Neatly covering all the sessions with the bland backings which actually sold most copies the first time around, this leads off with the highlight of the set, "Just Friends". Elsewhere Bird often tries to play a bit too straight.

⊙ **South Of The Border** (1948–52; Verve). Whether backed by the full Machito band, or just his rhythm-section grafted on to Parker's quintet, this is a fascinating glimpse of a promising collaboration that Bird never took far enough. He sounds perfectly at ease, whether with original material ("Mango Mangue" or his own calypso-style "My Little Suede Shoes") or with Latin standards such as "Tico Tico".

⊙ **The Cole Porter Songbook** (1950–54; Verve). Rather like *The Gentle Side Of John Coltrane*, this compilation repackages performances that had some commercial intent in the first place, and makes Parker's genius for variation accessible to those who need the toehold of a familiar coastline.

⊙ **Now's The Time** (1952–3; Verve). The last great studio sessions also happen to be the last small groups with Max Roach, by no coincidence at all. Including remakes of the title track and the famous "Confirmation", these are quartets with either Hank Jones or Al Haig playing quality piano.

⊙ **Jazz At Massey Hall** (1953; Debut/OJC). The last great live set, under the by-line "The Quintet Of The Year", was an unrehearsed concert with Gillespie, Roach, Mingus and Bud Powell. Reasonably well recorded, all concerned play as if their lives depended on it.

➤➤ **Dizzy Gillespie** *(Groovin' High);* **Jay McShann** *(Blues From Kansas City);* **Fats Navarro** *(Bird And Fats – Live At Birdland).*

Eddie Parker

Flute, composer.

b. Liverpool, UK, 28 May 1959.

From a musical family (his father was a pianist/musical director), Eddie Parker started in music by playing in rock bands influenced by Jethro Tull around Liverpool. Introduced to jazz at York University, Parker joined an early version of Django Bates's Human Chain on moving to London, subsequently playing with John Stevens's Freebop and becoming a member of Loose Tubes. In tandem with his performing activities, Parker also works extensively in jazz education, having run a jazz workshop at London's Morley College and a jazz option for classical students at the Guildhall School. He currently teaches at Middlesex University. In 1991 he began playing with South African pianist Bheki Mseleku, recording and touring with him. He has been a member of Django Bates's Delightful Precipice and also runs the Eddie Parker Group and the bands Mister Vertigo and Twittering Machine using musicians such as Julian Nicholas (saxophones), John Parricelli (guitar), Pete Saberton (piano), Steve Watts (bass) and drummers Roy Dodds, Martin France and Mike Pickering. A fine composer, Parker wrote an orchestral piece, *Tin Tin Goes to Hell*, for Loose Tubes and the Docklands Sinfonietta in 1990 and, among many other projects for large and small ensembles, *Cartoons*, premiered by the Apollo Saxophone Quartet in 1995, and *Autogeddon*, a suite of jazz-influenced pieces for saxophone quintet, vibes, percussion and prepared tape, inspired by the book of the same name by Heathcote Williams. This piece was performed at its London premiere in 1997 by the Saxtet (Andrew Tweed, Karen Street, Chris Gumbley, Richard Exall and Jamie Anderson), vibes player Anthony Kerr and percussionist Paul Clarvis. The previous year, the Eddie Parker Group produced their second album, *Everything You Do To Me* (FMR). [CP]

⊙ **Transformations Of The Lamp** (1994; FMR). Martin France and Jonathan Gee, in addition to the band listed above, in a representative selection of material from the band's eclectic repertoire, all composed by Parker.

➤➤ **Loose Tubes** *(Open Letter);* **Bheki Mseleku** *(Celebration).*

Evan Parker

Soprano and tenor saxophones.

b. Bristol, UK, 5 April 1944.

Parker's mother, an amateur pianist, introduced him to the delights of Fats Waller. He studied saxophone with James Knott from 1958–62, then from 1962–4 he studied botany at Birmingham University, but dropped out to concentrate on music. He rapidly became interested in free (abstract) improvisation, playing occasional gigs with Howard Riley in the Birmingham area. In 1966 he went to London and worked with the Spontaneous Music Ensemble, where he met Derek Bailey, his friend and longtime associate. From 1968–72 Parker and Bailey co-led the Music Improvisation Company, which also included electronics, percussion and voice. In 1969 Parker joined Chris McGregor's sextet, which later (augmented) became the Brotherhood of Breath. From 1969–72 he was also with the Tony Oxley sextet; since 1970 he has played with Alex von Schlippenbach's trio and quartet, and since 1971 with Schlippenbach's Globe Unity Orchestra. In 1979 he took part in Derek Bailey's Company. In 1980 he worked with Kenny Wheeler's quintet, and from 1980 led his own trio and quartet with Barry Guy, Paul Lytton (and trombonist George Lewis). He has a wide international reputation and has toured all over the world, with Globe Unity and other groups, and also as a solo artist.

Parker is a master saxophonist and a radical experimentalist who has pioneered the use of harmonics, unusual note-groupings, and the production of new timbres by tonguing and by splitting up single notes into their component parts. By means of circular breathing he can produce an unbroken column of air for quite long periods of time, and his solo concerts have often consisted of unbroken rhythmic and melodic patterns that undergo gradual and constant variations. The austerity of Parker's music makes it hard to recognize that his original influence was Paul Desmond, while his current favourites are John Coltrane and Steve Lacy. In 1985 he wrote, "I work in a form of free improvisation in which the theme and variations style has been replaced by spontaneous development." Since 1970, Parker and Bailey have owned and run their own record label, Incus Records. [IC]

JAK KILBY

Evan Parker

EVAN PARKER, BARRY GUY AND PAUL LYTTON

⊙ **Atlanta** (1986; Impulse!). A genial meeting of old campaigners from the avant-garde skirmishes of yesteryear.

EVAN PARKER

⊙ **Conic Projections** (1989; Ah Um). These unaccompanied soprano saxophone improvisations perfectly display Parker's astonishing, but never gratuitous, virtuosity. The long pieces, unbroken by pauses for breath, display Parker's method of building his improvisations, overlaid patterns developed with great intensity and range of texture.

EVAN PARKER AND WALTER PRATI

⊙ **Hall Of Mirrors** (1990; MM&T). Parker's tenor and soprano saxophones in relief against Walter Prati's delicate electronic backgrounds.

EVAN PARKER

⊙ **Process And Reality** (1991; FMP). Parker's tenor and soprano multi-tracked in a rich collage of sound.

EVAN PARKER AND JOHN STEVENS

⊙ **Corner To Corner** (1993; Ogun). A final meeting of old friends on record. Stevens's tragically premature death was to occur some eighteen months later.

➤➤ **Anthony Braxton** *(Duo (London) 1993);* **Alexander von Schlippenbach** *(Elf Bagatellen);* **John Stevens** *(Karyobin).*

Johnny Parker

Piano, leader.

b. Beckenham, Kent, UK, 6 Nov 1929.

Johnny Parker worked early on in bands led by Mick Mulligan and Humphrey Lyttelton (he played on Lyttelton's "Bad Penny Blues"), revealing a fine talent for ragtime and boogie-woogie. Later in the 1960s he worked for leaders as diverse as Alexis Korner, Monty Sunshine and Kenny Ball, and led his own small group featuring Wally Fawkes (clarinet) and Chez Chesterman (trumpet). In the 1970s and 1980s he worked solo in clubs and piano bars, backed the vocal group Sweet Substitute in cabaret, organized his own bands, and collaborated regularly with singer Beryl Bryden, as well as recording and broadcasting. From the 1990s Parker was occasionally less active because of illness, but still undertook occasional engagements. He remains one of Britain's most elegant, painstaking and creative classic jazz pianists. [DF]

⊙ **At The 100 Club** (1984; Jazz Crusade). Despite his distinguished career Parker is yet to be fully represented as a soloist-leader on CD. Here his work is as knowledgeable and delicate as always amid a connoisseur's band including Alan Cooper, Graham Stewart and Ken Colyer.

➤➤ **Humphrey Lyttelton** *(Complete Parlophones Vols. 2 & 3).*

Leo Parker

Baritone and alto saxophones.
b. Washington, DC, 18 April 1925; d. 11 Feb 1962.

Parker studied alto at high school, and recorded with Coleman Hawkins's "bebop band" including Dizzy Gillespie and Max Roach at the age of eighteen. Already versed in the new style, he switched to baritone to play in the newly formed Billy Eckstine band in 1944–5 and 1946. He then worked with Gillespie's small group and big band in 1946, in effect replacing Charlie Parker (no relation), and the following year he played on record dates with Fats Navarro, J.J. Johnson and Dexter Gordon. In 1947–8 he joined Illinois Jacquet's septet, recording with him and on spinoff sessions by Russell Jacquet and Jacquet's pianist Sir Charles Thompson, and under his own name. Some of these records attained popularity in the R&B field, but his career was plagued by drug problems. Despite further work for small labels and rejoining Jacquet in 1954, he was largely neglected until recording two albums for Blue Note in 1961, the first of which had just been issued at the time of his death from a heart attack. [BP]

Rollin' With Leo (1961; Blue Note). Leo's beefy sound is heard to advantage on this late session, which shows him bridging the gap between the R&B inflexions he learned from Illinois Jacquet and the bebop he was capable of in the mid-1940s.

Leon Parker

Drums, percussion, composer.
b. New York, 21 Aug 1964.

Raised in White Plains, just north of the Bronx, Leon Parker was one of a number of young New York-based musicians – saxophonist Jesse Davis, guitarist Peter Bernstein were others – who honed their talents at the uptown venue known as Augie's Pub in the late 1980s. Initially, wishing to concentrate on a single sound – as a horn player might – he would arrive at gigs with just a ride cymbal, but was soon persuaded that he would have to play something resembling a kit if he wanted to work regularly, so added a snare and a bass drum. He explains: "As a child, my first drum set had no hi-hat, no cymbal or floor tom. I just had a bass drum, snare and rack tom. My current set-up – unintentionally through experimentation – ended up with one similar to my childhood set." In sideman situations, support, rather than showiness, is his musical priority: "I put my instrument on automatic to listen to the music and let it drive me, instead of trying to control it and play with people at the same time. Having less equipment directs more intensity on the music itself." This "less is more" approach slowly won over leaders, including Jesse Davis and pianist Geoff Keezer, in the early 1990s, and by 1994 Parker had lent his highly effective minimalist drumming and percussion to albums by pianist Bruce Barth and saxophonists David Sanchez, Don Braden and James Carter; trumpeter Tom Harrell has also used him on a couple of recordings. Parker's most high-profile sideman role, however, is with pianist Jacky Terrasson alongside Nigerian/German bassist Ugonna Okegwo. The trio have made three Blue Note albums, all notable for the mutual respect and unselfishness discernible in the music. Parker's own albums, *Above And Below* (1994; Epicure), his 1996 Columbia debut *Belief* (featuring Lisa Parker on flute and Adam Cruz on steel pan, alongside Harrell and saxophonist Steve Wilson), *Awakening* (see below) and *The Simple Life* (see below), are multi-textured explorations of sounds from Africa, the Caribbean, Latin America, etc, all filtered through a jazz-based sensibility. Parker comments: "I'm trying to respect the traditions these sounds and rhythms come from, but I'm not trying to be 'authentic'. I'm trying to let those different acoustic sounds inspire me, trying to do something based on their spirit." [CP]

Awakening (1998; Columbia). Featuring a host of percussionists, Natalie Cushman (gourds, shekere), Adam Cruz on steel pan, bells and his father Ray on timbales, Rita Silva (clavé, wood block) – plus Parker and saxophonists Steve Wilson and Sam Newsome. This is a rich, many-hued album of great depth and subtlety.

The Simple Life (2002; Label M). The most extravagant exploration thus far of his vocal-body rhythmic technique (whereby he utilizes all manner of slaps, thumps and grunts to create elaborate rhythmic patterns), this release further establishes Parker as a great individual artist of range and depth.

➤➤ **Steve Wilson** *(Four For Time)*.

Maceo Parker

Alto, tenor and baritone saxophones.
b. Kinston, North Carolina, 14 Feb 1943.

Parker's father played piano and drums for church services, and both parents sang. He played with two brothers in a teenage band that did intermissions for his uncle's band. At 21 he joined singer/arranger James Brown, on tenor from 1964–5 and 1967–70 (interrupted by army service), and on alto from 1973–6 and 1984–90. In between, he led his own band or, from 1976–80, worked with singer/producer George Clinton and ex-Brown bassist Bootsy Collins, alongside other ex-Brown horn players, saxophonist Alfred "Pee Wee" Ellis and trombonist Fred Wesley. The new band he formed after Brown's imprisonment in 1990, usually featuring Ellis and Wesley, has achieved great success in purveying his brand of jazz-funk, and his own playing has been acknowledged as an influence by a generation of younger musicians who grew up listening to James Brown. [BP]

Southern Exposure (1993; Minor Music/Novus). Parker's most varied album so far features two tracks with New Orleans's Rebirth Brass Band (one a cover of "Mercy, Mercy, Mercy") and several with members of The

Meters. Two tracks with Ellis and Wesley, plus Parker's touring rhythm-section, include a confident version of "The Way You Look Tonight".

William Parker

Bass.

b. Bronx, New York, 10 Jan, 1952.

In junior high school, William Parker played cello, though he says he had no musical interest at that time. By the time he was in high school, he had started listening to the music of John Coltrane, Ornette Coleman and Cecil Taylor. Parker then began playing the bass, which he studied with Jimmy Garrison; he also took some lessons with Milt Hinton. He was active by the mid-70s, and in fact recorded his first LP, *Through Acceptance Of The Mystery Peace* (Centering, recently reissued on Eremite), in phases from 1974–9. In 1974, he first played with Taylor, too, and he was one of the pianist's primary colleagues during the 80s, recording and performing with him regularly. This association is well documented on the trio CD *In Florescence* (1989; A&M). As the energy of New York's "loft scene" of the 70s dissipated, Parker became one of the most important community activists rallying around the music, playing constantly and bolstering the ebbing and flowing free-music scene. In 1984, he was instrumental in organizing the Sound Unity Festival, a focal event of the period that drew European and American improvisers together. The second Sound Unity Fest took place in 1988, and more recently Parker and his wife, dancer Patricia Nicholson, have organized the Vision Festival, arguably the most important new jazz fest (of several) in New York these days.

Parker has become one of the most frequently recorded free jazz musicians since the 80s, as he has appeared on innumerable LPs and CDs with all shapes and sizes of ensemble. In the 90s, the bassist began recording more frequently as a leader, and his work with the group In Order To Survive and with his Little Huey Creative Music Orchestra is well worth seeking out. Parker's own playing, always strong, has grown even more concentrated in recent years, and he is now clearly one of the most imposing figures in the music, as is evident in his work with Peter Brötzmann's Die Like A Dog quartet, particularly on the group's two outstanding volumes of *Little Birds Have Fast Hearts* (1998/99; FMP). Parker works regularly with the lauded David S. Ware quartet and he plays frequently in various ensembles; in duet with pianist Matthew Shipp; in innovative projects for Thirsty Ear, bridging the gap between free jazz and drum'n'bass; and in string trios with Billy Bang. [JC]

⊙ **Testimony** (1998; zero in). Parker alone. Massive sound, woody with high-action palpability and an improvising mind to make use of it. Lengthy tracks allow him to dig in, and he does so with power and sensitivity to spare.

Horace Parlan

Piano.

b. Pittsburgh, Pennsylvania, 19 Jan 1931.

Parlan worked in the R&B field and with Sonny Stitt before moving to New York, where he almost immediately joined Charles Mingus, staying with him from 1957–9. He played in a quartet with Booker Ervin in 1960–61, and recorded frequently as both leader and sideman in the early 1960s. He was the regular pianist with the "Lockjaw" Davis-Johnny Griffin quintet in 1962 and with Roland Kirk from 1963–6. Jazz work became scarce from the late 1960s and in 1973 Parlan took up residence in Copenhagen, where he has performed steadily and made a number of albums, including two duo sets with Archie Shepp.

Parlan's style derives musical strength from his physical disability, arising from polio which partially crippled his right hand in childhood. By combining pungent left-hand chords with stark but highly rhythmic phrases in the right, he creates a very positive contribution to any situation in which he finds himself. Perhaps because of restricted mobility, he avoids blues clichés yet manages to sound more basically blues-influenced than many other pianists of his generation. [BP]

⊙ **Glad I Found You** (1984; Steeplechase). Parlan's quintet for this date has a Danish bass-and-drums team and the oddly well-balanced frontline of Thad Jones (also a Copenhagen resident at the time) and Eddie Harris. The leader's material is melodic as always, and the programme closes with John Lewis's "Afternoon In Paris".

➤➤ **Tony Coe** *(Canterbury Song)*; **Charles Mingus** *(Blues And Roots; Mingus Ah Um)*; **Archie Shepp** *(Trouble In Mind)*; **Stanley Turrentine** *(Up At Minton's)*.

Jack Parnell

Drums, piano, leader.

b. London, 6 Aug 1923.

Nephew of the show-business tycoon Val Parnell, Jack Parnell was quickly marked out as a leader by his natural charm, charisma and talent. Very early on, while in the RAF, he worked with Buddy Featherstonhaugh; then co-led the Vic Lewis-Jack Parnell Jazzmen, featuring Billy Riddick and Ronnie Chamberlain. From 1945, for six years after the war, he became a central feature of Ted Heath's show (as well as a popular music star), driving the orchestra from behind his drumkit and often singing; then, from 1951 he formed his own big band which toured from 1952. Parnell later studied conducting and spent nearly twenty years as a highly successful bandleader, leading the staff orchestra for ATV (from 1956) and providing the music for over 2500 peak-viewing television shows, including *Saturday Night At The London Palladium*. In the late 1970s he returned to jazz work, toured with the "Best Of British Jazz package" (c.1990–2000) (led by his close friend and lifelong colleague Kenny Baker), and played again in clubs and concerts with Danny Moss's quartet, Tommy Whittle, Bob Wilber and others. In the mid-1980s he accompanied his close friend Ruby Braff at London's Pizza Express, and remained a centrepiece in Kenny Baker's Best Of British Jazz (now co-featuring Don Lusher, Roy Willox and Brian Lemon), as well as regularly leading groups of his own. In the 1990s he recorded with his quartet (featuring tenorist Dean Masser) during a season at Ronnie Scott's, directed the BBC's Big Band (1994), and continued working with a wide variety of British and American jazz names including Annie Ross (1995/6). In 2001 he starred on a P and O Jazz Cruise (with Digby Fairweather) and in 2003, at the age of eighty, was still playing, principally around his home county of Norfolk but also working as guest-conductor with Laurie Johnson and Robert Farnon for recording projects. [DF]

⊙ **Best of British Volume 1** (1995:Horatio Nelson). A group which truly lived up to its name with Parnell at its dynamic rhythmic centre; he also sings as appealingly as ever on "The Trouble With Me Is You".

John Parricelli

Guitar.

b. Worcester, UK, 5 April 1959.

Parricelli was born of Italian parents, and his mother is a keen amateur singer. Basically self-taught, he began playing in local rock bands at sixteen, and came to London in 1977 to study social sciences. After completing his degree in 1980, he became interested in a career in music. During the 80s, he played with Tim Whitehead, Annie Whitehead, and was a founder member of Loose Tubes, touring internationally with them and recording three albums. A guitarist for all genres, Parricelli seems to be in permanent demand. He has worked with Kenny Wheeler, Norma Winstone, Lee Konitz, Paul Motian and the German WDR Band (with Peter Erskine and Vince Mendoza). He co-led the group Matheran with Mark Lockheart, recording an eponymous album with them, and currently plays with Iain Ballamy's Acme, Mark Lockheart's quartet, Andy Sheppard, Gerard Presencer, the Colin Towns quintet, the Martin Speake quartet and the Eddie Parker group. Parricelli has also worked and recorded with M People, Judy Tzuke, Mike Oldfield, and he has played in numerous TV and feature films for Mike Figgis, George Fenton, Stephen Warbeck and several others. His favourites are Wes Montgomery, Frisell, Toninho Horta, Joni Mitchell and Pat Metheny, and other inspirations are Jarrett, Miles, Aretha Franklin, Kenny Wheeler, Egberto Gismonti and Antonio Carlos Jobim. [IC]

➤➤ **Iain Ballamy** *(Acme)*; **Loose Tubes** *(Open Letter)*.

Pasadena Roof Orchestra

Formed by bassist/bakery owner John Arthey in the mid-1960s, the Pasadena Roof Orchestra began as an authentic re-creation of a 1920s dance band but later – after enthusiastic publicity in the *Melody Maker* and elsewhere – widened their appeal, bringing in cornermen such as singer John "Pazz" Parry, clarinettist/saxophonist Mac White and trumpeters Clive Baker, Enrico Tomasso and Mike Henry. The PRO gradually built up a European following that made them one of the continent's most commercially successful jazz-based acts of the 1970s. Never really a jazz band in the full sense of the term, the PRO concentrated more on showbizzy re-creations of period material, but their staff arrangers included jazz pianist Keith Nichols, and a great deal of their recorded work is still highly acceptable to ears attuned to 1920s hot dance music. [DF]

⊙ **Breakaway** (1991; Pasadena). Plenty of hot dance and jazz material in this album, including "Temptation Rag", "That's A Plenty" and "Rockin' Chair", with fourteen more titles featuring the orchestra with vocalist Duncan Galloway.

Hermeto Pascoal

Piano, electric piano, flutes, guitar, saxophones, composer.

b. Lagoa da Canoa, Brazil, 22 June 1936.

All Pascoal's family were musical and he started in groups with his father and brother, but had no formal training. He worked with several small groups in Brazil, then, with Airto Moreira, formed the Quarteto Novo, which became very popular. He ventured out of Brazil in the early 1970s, going to New York, where he recorded with Miles Davis, and spending some time in California, but soon returned to his own country. Pascoal is the father-figure and inspiration of a whole generation of Brazilian musicians who, during the 1970s and 1980s, have worked in the USA and Europe, making a considerable contribution to jazz – Moreira, Flora Purim, Milton Nascimento, Hugo Fatteruso, Dom Um Romao and others. Since the later 1970s he has led a sextet of young Brazilian musicians, and although his group rehearses almost every day they still lack the time to perform many of the new pieces he is constantly producing. In 1984–5 he toured Europe extensively with his group, making a big impact. His musicians double on different instruments, so the sextet offers a very broad palette, and Pascoal makes full use of it. The whole group exults in rhythm, performing with passionate energy, handling the most complex passages with consummate ease, and exuding the sheer joy of music-making.

Music flows out of Pascoal unquenchably and without apparent effort. He plays all his instruments with total virtuosity, he composes and arranges for all sizes of ensemble, from very big bands to small groups, and his orchestral writing was much admired by Gil Evans. His music explores elements from jazz and rock, European art music, street music, ethnic and Brazilian folk music. He has recorded with Miles Davis, Antonio Carlos Jobim, Duke Pearson, Airto Moreira and Flora Purim, and under his own name. [IC]

Festa Dos Deuses (1992; Philips). Pascoal's sextet divides its time between energetic Brazilian fusion and more unusual fare: a reharmonized "Round Midnight", synthesized birdcalls, and the melodic transformation of speech recordings, including one of the then Brazilian president.

Joe Pass

Guitar.

b. New Brunswick, New Jersey, 13 Jan 1929; d. 23 May 1994.

After working with name bands, including that of Tony Pastor, before he left high school, Joseph Antony Jacobi Passalaqua toured nationally with Charlie Barnet in c.1947. Navy service was followed by a decade divided between serving time in Las Vegas backing groups and serving time for narcotics offences. He made his first small-group recording with fellow patients at the Synanon Foundation in 1962. On discharge, he began working regularly as a soloist with West Coast-based groups and cutting albums under his own name. He toured with George Shearing in 1967 and with Benny Goodman in 1973, and did frequent studio work. The recommendation of Oscar Peterson led to international touring under Peterson's manager Norman Granz, often with Peterson and/or Ella Fitzgerald. He made albums with both, as well as with Duke Ellington, Count Basie, Dizzy Gillespie and Milt Jackson. His last album, *Songs For Ellen* (1992), followed his marriage to a native of Hamburg, where he had been based since 1989.

A superbly competent guitarist, Pass summarized all of the bop-based practitioners of several decades (only the free-players and the prolific rock-fusion school left him untouched). In addition to his abilities as a stylistic consolidator, he quietly expanded the instrument's flexibility in a jazz context by his frequent work without bass and drums backing; as a result he learned to simulate a bass-line counterpointing his simultaneous chords and melodic lines, and to swing as if he were an entire group. In this respect, and in most others, few guitarists could surpass Joe. [BP]

Virtuoso (1973; Pablo). Pass's first completely unaccompanied album certainly lived up to its title, and the programme of standards (and one blues) is exemplary.

Appassionato (1989; Pablo). Also well titled, this finds Pass with second guitarist John Pisano plus bass and drums, featuring tunes by jazz writers; even the ballads are mostly things like "Gee Baby Ain't I Good To You" and "Lil' Darlin'", while the faster numbers include "Stuffy" and Zoot Sims's "Red Door".

Tony Pastor

Tenor saxophone, vocals.

b. Middletown, Connecticut, 26 Oct 1907; d. 31 Oct 1969.

Tony Pastor (Antonio Pestritto) was raised in New Haven, and played early on – often alongside childhood friend Artie Shaw – in John Cavallaro's band, Irving Aaronson's Commanders and with Austin Wylie. He led his own band from 1931–4, but made his first real impact as the one-and-only tenor saxophonist with Shaw's band from 1936. "Pastor's kidding around and screwy faces help to bring the crowds up to the bandstand," reported George Simon. "He's a vastly underrated hot tenor man with a splendid tone and a simple but pleasantly rhythmic style." By 1940 Pastor was confident enough to start up his own band again and was soon resident at the Hotel Lincoln, where he paid to have radio lines installed: the reward was eighteen broadcasts a week. By 1941 Max Kaminsky was leading Pastor's trumpet section (until he went back to Shaw), guitarist Al Avola was fashioning a stylish book of arrangements, and a succession of singers – including Eugenie Baird, Virginia Maxey (Mrs Matt Dennis), Rosemary Clooney with her singing sister, and Pastor himself – were helping to produce a smooth and enjoyable show. By the mid-1940s Pastor was enlivening his library further with jazz arrangements by Budd Johnson and Gil Fuller, and – with his natural gift for showmanship and near-comedy vocals – he easily survived the demise of big bands until 1959, by which time he had made a string of excellent big-band albums. That year he formed a small group featuring his sons Guy, John and Tony to play Las Vegas, and worked with them until 1968. [DF]

>> **Artie Shaw** *(In The Beginning).*

Jaco Pastorius

Bass guitar, composer.

b. Norristown, Pennsylvania, 1 Dec 1951; d. 22 Sept 1987.

Pastorius's family moved to Fort Lauderdale, Florida, in 1958. His father, a drummer and singer, was Jaco's model, but he had no lessons. At first Pastorius wanted to play drums, but at thirteen he injured his right arm playing football, and it failed to heal properly. He also played piano, saxophone and guitar, and he learned by listening to local Florida musicians, including the legendary saxophone/trumpet player Ira Sullivan. He accompanied visiting stars such as Wayne Cochran and the C.C. Riders, the Temptations, the Supremes and Nancy Wilson, on piano and bass. While still in his teens he began writing arrangements for a local big band and Ira Sullivan's Baker's Dozen. At seventeen he had an operation to put his arm right; a year later it was strong enough to enable him to play the bass properly and from then on this became his main instrument. He got first-hand experience of Caribbean music by working as a show musician on tourist cruise ships off the southern tip of Florida and going for week-long trips to Mexico, Jamaica, Haiti and the Bahamas. In Florida he played country and western music, soul and reggae. There were no local cliques of young jazz musicians, so no peer group pressure to prejudice him against other types of

JAK KILBY

Jaco Pastorius

music, and Pastorius attributes his later musical diversity to this freedom. He liked the Beatles, the Rolling Stones and other rock/pop groups, as well as Max Roach. By the early 1970s he was playing with Ira Sullivan and also with the house band at Fort Lauderdale's Bachelors III Club. He also met and played with some visiting jazz musicians, including Paul Bley and Pat Metheny.

In mid-1975 Blood Sweat And Tears were booked into the Bachelors III Club, and their drummer, Bobby Colomby, immediately arranged for Pastorius to record an album in New York. A few months later, with Colomby as producer and with the aid of Herbie Hancock, Mike Gibbs, Don Alias, Wayne Shorter and Hubert Laws, the album was made. By April 1976, Pastorius was a member of Weather Report, and by May he had also played on Pat Metheny's first album for ECM. Pastorius had arrived and he had done so fully formed, as a mature and original stylist and a composer/arranger with his own individual approach. He always considered himself as much a composer as a bass player, and this was his great strength: he thought, wrote and played orchestrally, which is why his music is so complete.

As Eberhard Weber was doing in Europe, Pastorius redefined the whole conception and role of the electric bass. He gave it the tonal characteristics and articulation of both an amplified acoustic guitar and an amplified double bass, producing an immensely resonant, lyrical sound. He once said, "It sings ... you have to know exactly where to touch the strings, exactly how much pressure to apply. You have to learn to *feel* it. And then it just sings." He used harmonics with brilliant imagination for both rhythmic and melodic colour. Like Weber, he gave the bass a new melodic role, often playing romantic themes or thematic fragments with delicate subtlety and expressiveness. But he also developed the rhythmic and linear aspects of the bass to new levels of complexity and ferocity, playing long rhythmic lines with perfect articulation at astonishing speeds.

He was with Weather Report through one of the group's most creative periods (1976–82) and his qualities contributed greatly to that success. His playing and persona were an inspiration to Joe Zawinul, who wrote some of his finest pieces to feature Pastorius. After leaving Weather Report he pursued a solo career, recording and playing festivals with a big band. In this context, too, his writing shows marked individuality in the way it draws on elements of his musical heritage – jazz, blues, R&B, the classics, reggae riffs, and the Caribbean sound of the steel drum, which seemed to be a staple ingredient of his music. [IC]

Jaco (1974; DIW); **Pastorius-Metheney-Ditmas-Bley** (1974; Improvising Artists). Two quartet sessions with Pat Metheny, Paul Bley and drummer Bruce Ditmas, recorded at the height of the fusion era.

Holiday For Pans (1980–82; Sound Hills). Pastorius in collaboration with Michael Gibbs and an ensemble which includes the great Toots Thielemans, in a joyfully creative orchestral deployment of West Indian steel drums.

Punk Jazz (1986; Big World Music). Pastorius with guitarist Hiram Bullock, drummer Kenwood Dennard, plus trumpet, two saxophones, piano and keyboards. One of Pastorius's major statements of intent, it includes his sensational rendering of Miles Davis's great bebop tune "Donna Lee", and much swashbuckling electric jazz.

>> **Pat Metheny** *(Bright Size Life);* **Joe Zawinul** *(Black Market; Heavy Weather).*

John Patitucci

Bass, composer.

b. Brooklyn, New York, 22 Dec 1959.

Having discovered jazz by accident – his grandfather, who worked for the New York City roads department, brought home an unwanted box of jazz records one day, including albums by Thad Jones, Art Blakey, Wes Montgomery and Ray Charles – John Patitucci was encouraged to take up bass by listening to the work of Ron Carter, but was also influenced (like his guitarist brother) by the phrasing and tone of Montgomery. He was playing rock bass by his early teens, and on his family's moving to California in 1972 he took up acoustic bass in his high school orchestra, although his first gig (in 1978 with Chuck Mangione's pianist brother Gap) was on the electric instrument. A year at California State University, San Francisco, was followed by further study at CSU Long Beach, but by 1982 Patitucci was in Los Angeles, working in the studios with the likes of Stan Getz, David Sanborn, Victor Feldman, Wayne Shorter and Freddie Hubbard. Until he met Chick Corea while playing with Feldman at a Valentine's Day party at Corea's house in 1985, Patitucci's most regular gig was with his brother-in-law, trumpeter Mike Fahn, with whom he played for seven years. A week after meeting Corea, though, he was in the Elektric Band and he stayed with it – and the contemporaneous Akoustic Band – for ten years, making seven albums with both outfits. In 1987, Patitucci made his recording debut as a leader with an eponymous album on GRP, the first of six albums for the company. The following year he toured Japan with the Manhattan Jazz Quartet (replacing Eddie Gomez), but it was not until 1994, after meeting and marrying his second wife Sachi – a cellist – that Patitucci actually returned to the city, leaving both Corea and the West Coast and moving back to New York to raise a family. As well as appearing on albums by, among others, Monty Alexander, Gary Burton, Bob Berg, Mike Stern and Wolfgang Muthspiel, Patitucci continues to make supremely tasteful, virtuosic but accessible albums under his own name, latterly on Concord. The deeply personal *One More Angel* (1997; Concord), featuring Alan Pasqua on piano, drummer Paul Motian and guests including Michael Brecker and Chris Potter, was followed by *Now* (see below), Imprint (2000), *Communion* (2001) and *Songs, Stories And Spirituals* (2003 – see below). Patitucci continues to work with a great many stellar names, including various reformed Chick Corea groups but perhaps most notably with Wayne Shorter's remarkable quartet featuring Patitucci, pianist Danilo Perez and drummer Brian Blade and with whom he was heard on disc and on tour in 2002/03. [CP]

⊙ **Now** (1998; Concord). Brecker and Potter again share solo duties, but guitarist John Scofield taking on the band's chordal role "changes the sonic contours of the band", according to Patitucci, opening space for his booming, yet lithe, sound on eight originals, plus Coltrane's "Giant Steps" and McCoy Tyner's "Search For Peace".

⊙ **Songs, Stories And Spirituals** (2003; Concord). An impressively wide-ranging, semi-original set taking in classical, folk and Brazilian influences, but all focused on conveying what Patitucci calls "my continuing love for the spiritual life." Featuring wife Sachi on cello, singer Luciana Souza and flautist Tim Reis.

➤➤ **Wayne Shorter** *(Footprints Live)*

Big John Patton

Organ and piano.

b. Kansas City, Missouri, 12 July 1935; d. 19 Mar 2002.

Patton played with the Lloyd Price touring band from 1954–9, and then settled in New York. Switching to organ, he worked with Grant Green and others, and made his recording debut with Lou Donaldson in 1962. In 1963 he recorded his first album and started leading his own trio, which included, at different times, Clifford Jarvis and James "Blood" Ulmer. He was also capable of sitting in with Sun Ra's musicians in the 1960s. Patton was initially inspired by Hampton Hawes, Horace Silver and Wynton Kelly, and managed to bring some of their linear invention to the frequently overblown art of jazz organ. Based since the 1970s in East Orange, New Jersey, he started recording again in 1983 and was used as one of the textures in John Zorn's album *Spillane*. [BP]

⊙ **Boogaloo** (1968; Blue Note). Dignified by notes from John Zorn, this session was unreleased for 25 years until the increasing competition to find the rarest of "rare grooves". The pent-up aggression of tenorman Harold Alexander, even on "Barefootin'", sounds more in tune with the genre now than it would have done then.

Emmanuel Paul

Tenor saxophone, banjo, vocals.

b. New Orleans, 2 Feb 1904; d. 23 May 1988.

Emmanuel Paul was trained in an orchestra organized by a New Orleans church foundation and played banjo regularly throughout the 1920s. During the Depression, when saxophones were starting to eclipse the clarinet as a fashionable instrument, he concentrated on tenor and began playing it regularly from 1940 with the Eureka Brass Band. In 1942 he joined Kid Thomas Valentine's band and forty years on was still partnering Valentine regularly at Preservation Hall, playing with huge vigour, unremitting swing and an approach falling somewhere between Benny Waters and Bud Freeman. [DF]

Les Paul

Guitar.

b. Waukesha, Wisconsin, 9 June 1916.

Les Paul (Lester Polfus) did studio work in Chicago from 1932–42, toured with bandleader Fred Waring and first recorded under his own name in 1940. He settled in California and formed his own trio in 1944, also making guest appearances on records by Red Callender, Jazz At The Philharmonic and others, often under the pseudonym "Paul Leslie". In 1948 he began recording best-selling discs as a "one-man band", thanks to primitive overdubbing techniques, with his wife Mary Ford as vocalist. To further this success, he created the first multi-track tape machine and later lent his name to one of the most popular models of guitar. As a result of his pop hits Paul was lost to the jazz world, but he was a very capable Reinhardt-influenced improviser. In 1986 he produced an album by Joe Bushkin, and he still plays weekly in public accompanied by his son, drummer Les Paul Jnr. [BP]

⊙ **Guitar Wizard** (1936–51; Proper). The first half of this two-CD set begins with some anonymous studio work and Paul's attempt at hillbilly singing (as "Rhubarb Red"), before selecting from his mid-1940s trios, some with guest vocalists including Bing Crosby and Helen Forrest. Disc two includes the famous early overdubbed singles, such as "Lover", "Little Rock Getaway" and (with similarly overdubbed Mary Ford) "How High The Moon".

➤➤ **Jazz At The Philharmonic** *(The First Concert).*

Alcide "Slow Drag" Pavageau

Bass.

b. New Orleans, 7 March 1888; d. 19 Jan 1969.

Principally remembered as George Lewis's long-term double-bassist, "Slow Drag" Pavageau (he earned his nickname winning slow-drag competitions in dance halls in his youth) began as a street-corner guitarist and took up the bass when he was forty. "I picked up a barrel on Orleans Street, between Robertson and Villere," he told researcher Tom Bethell, "and I made me a bass, a little bitty three-string bass, and that's how I learned myself to play." He joined Lewis from Herb Morand's band (which played at the Silver Star Café) in 1944 and recorded with him that year, including a classic version of "Burgundy Street Blues". A beautifully dressed French Creole, who smoked a big cigar and spoke in almost incomprehensible patois, Pavageau was one of New Orleans's most relaxed and powerful slap-bassists, and he worked hard for Lewis for 25 years (he was also officially known, on New Orlean's street parades, as Grand Marshal of the Second Line). Afflicted with deafness by his mid-seventies, "Slow Drag" was mugged on his way home from work and died soon after: his spectacular funeral was a tourist attraction. [DF]

➤➤ **George Lewis** *(George Lewis Ragtime Band of New Orleans: The Oxford Series Vol. 1).*

Cecil Payne

Baritone and alto saxophones.

b. Brooklyn, New York, 14 Dec 1922.

After army service, Payne worked in 1946 on alto with J.J. Johnson and on baritone with Roy Eldridge. He then joined Dizzy Gillespie and, in 1949, the Tadd Dameron tentet. He worked with James Moody in 1951 and Illinois Jacquet from 1952–4, and then appeared on many jazz albums while also working at a day job. He was associated with Randy Weston from 1956, and appeared in the play *The Connection* after the original cast went to Europe in 1961. He toured full-time with Machito from 1963–6, Woody Herman from 1966–8, and Count Basie from 1969–71. From the mid-1970s he performed regularly in a duo with his vocalist sister Cavril Payne, and in the 1990s recorded two new albums. Although less of an individualist than Serge Chaloff and largely unknown to the public, Payne was nevertheless one of the pioneers in adapting the instrument to bebop and post-bebop. [BP]

⊙ **Patterns of Jazz** (1956; Savoy). The melodically mobile Payne is partnered by a lucid rhythm-section of Duke Jordan, Tommy Potter and Art Taylor on four tunes, including Randy Weston's "Chessman's Delight", while Kenny Dorham joins in for four more, ending with "Groovin' High".

Sonny Payne

Drums.

b. New York, 4 May 1926; d. 29 Jan 1979.

No relation to Sylvester "Vess" Payne, drummer with the mid-1940s Cootie Williams band, Sonny (Percival) Payne was the son of Wild Bill Davis's drummer Chris Columbus (b. 17 June 1902). Between 1947–9 he worked with Hot Lips Page, Earl Bostic and Tiny Grimes, as well as with Grimes's bassist Lucille Dixon in 1948. He was with the Erskine Hawkins big band from 1950–53, and then had a long stay with Count Basie, from late 1954 to 1964. He rejoined Basie twice, in 1965–6 and 1973–4, and toured with Illinois Jacquet in 1976. The rest of the time he was with the Harry James band, with which he was working at the time of his death. He was a flashy and somewhat overexcitable performer; it was said that Basie's guitarist and timekeeper Freddie Green used to prod Payne with a drumstick when he rushed the tempo. Nevertheless, he possessed all the other qualities of a big-band drummer, and his showmanship was an asset to the Basie band during one of its vintage periods. [BP]

➤➤ **Count Basie** *(The Complete Atomic Basie).*

Gary Peacock

Bass, composer.

b. Barley, Idaho, 12 May 1935.

Peacock studied the piano while at school, and played it in a US army band in Germany during the late 1950s. He stayed on in Germany after demobilization, playing bass and working with Hans Koller, Attila Zoller, and also Tony Scott and Bud Shank. In 1958 he went to California, where he worked with leading musicians including Paul Horn, Terry Gibbs and Shorty Rogers, and in 1962 moved

Roberto Serra

Gary Peacock

to New York, becoming involved in more adventurous music and working with Paul Bley, Jimmy Giuffre, Roland Kirk, George Russell and Bill Evans. He became associated with the avant-garde and worked in Europe with Albert Ayler and Don Cherry in 1964. He also worked with Roswell Rudd, Steve Lacy and Don Ellis. In the later 1960s he was briefly with Miles Davis, then with Bley again, after which he took time off from music to study macrobiotics and Eastern philosophy in Japan. In the mid-1970s, he once more resumed his association with Bley and also did some teaching. He began recording for ECM, leading his own groups, and working with the trio led by Keith Jarrett, a setting in which he still works.

Peacock is a technically brilliant bass player, and a master of both conventional structures and of semi- or total abstraction. His ECM recordings show this mastery and also reproduce his wonderfully resonant sound. [IC]

Gary Peacock, Keith Jarrett and Jack DeJohnette

⊙ **Tales Of Another** (1977; ECM). One of the great records of the decade, and a blueprint for the Keith Jarrett trio, which began six years later. Six excellent compositions by Peacock straddle formal harmonic structures, modal music and more freely improvised areas. The playing by all three is tremendous.

Gary Peacock, Tomasz Stanko, Jan Garbarek and Jack DeJohnette

⊙ **Voice From The Past/Paradigm** (1981; ECM). Half folky and semi-abstract, this is an atmospheric foray into Garbarek territory strained through the Peacock sensibility. Trumpeter Stanko understands the spirit of the music and DeJohnette's drum shadings are unfailingly apt.

Gary Peacock and Paul Bley

⊙ **Partners** (1989; Owl). Despite Peacock's folk and ethnic leanings, he is a jazz musician through and through, as his solos on this album shared with Bley manifest.

➤➤ **Albert Ayler** *(Spiritual Unity).*

Dick Pearce

Trumpet, flugelhorn.

b. London, 19 April 1951.

Pearce's father was a singer, his cousin a pianist and arranger. He had private trumpet lessons at thirteen, but taught himself harmony. From 1968–71 he was in a military band, then in 1971–2 worked with Graham Collier. From 1973–80 he played with the younger generation of London musicians, including Chris Biscoe, Dave Defries and Brian Abrahams. He later worked with Mike Westbrook, Keith Tippett, Dudu Pukwana, Gil Evans and others. In 1981 he joined Ronnie Scott's group. He leads his own occasional band. His favourites are Miles Davis, Art Farmer, Woody Shaw, Kenny Wheeler and Don Cherry. [IC]

➤➤ **Ronnie Scott** *(Never Pat A Burning Dog);* **Mike Westbrook** *(The Cortège).*

Duke Pearson

Piano, composer.

b. Atlanta, Georgia, 17 Aug 1932; d. 4 Aug 1980.

Pearson studied both brass instruments and piano, receiving his nickname because of the latter. He started his career gigging in his home town, both before and after army service, and had his tunes "Tribute To Brownie" and "Jeannine" recorded by the Cannonball Adderley quintet. He moved to New York in 1959 and joined Donald Byrd and, in 1960, the Art Farmer-Benny Golson Jazztet. From 1963–70 he was the assistant producer with the Blue Note label, for which most of his own albums were made. Also in the late 1960s he ran a part-time big band in New York, including musicians such as Randy Brecker and Chick Corea. He was frequently employed as an accompanist to singers, working with Nancy Wilson, Dakota Staton, Carmen McRae and Joe Williams. Pearson modelled himself on the work of Hank Jones and had an appropriately unflamboyant but lyrical solo style. [BP]

⊙ **Sweet Honey Bee** (1966; Blue Note). A typically conservative album for Pearson, blending some of the freedoms of Freddie Hubbard, Joe Henderson and James Spaulding with appealing melodies such as the title track.

Santo Pecora

Trombone.

b. New Orleans, 31 March 1902; d. 29 May 1984.

Early in his career Santo Pecora worked with the New Orleans Rhythm Kings and by the 1930s was enough of an all-rounder to begin working in big bands, including Will Osborne's, Ben Pollack's and Charlie Barnet's, as well as Dixieland groups such as Sharkey Bonano's (1936), and (after a move to the West Coast in 1938) in Hollywood film studios until 1942. For the last forty years of his life he led bands of his own in New Orleans (and occasionally Chicago), often teaming with Bonano at Bourbon Street clubs, including the Famous Door. [DF]

Ken Peplowski

Clarinet, alto and tenor saxophones.

b. Cleveland, Ohio, 23 May 1959.

Peplowski's professional career began with the Tommy Dorsey orchestra (directed by Buddy Morrow) in 1978, and after two and a half years with them he settled in New York. There and on tour, his thorough training allowed him to work in a variety of contexts, from pit and symphony orchestras to jazz bands, including work with Benny Goodman. By the late 1980s "Peps" was a regular visitor to the UK, and at that period signed with Concord Records for a series of albums which revealed his interest in every area of jazz, a likeable sense of humour and, in particular, his delicate pure-toned clarinet-playing. In 1990 he won the *Jazz Times* critics' poll for clarinet and continued to tour, record, and play concerts and festivals, to growing acclaim. By the late 1990s Peplowski had developed into a clarinettist of phenomenal technique and creativity whose every recording appeared to be setting standards for the instrument unheard (in Swing terms) since the days of Goodman and Shaw. [DF]

⊙ **Steppin' With Peps** (1993; Concord). With friends including Howard Alden, Randy Sandke, Joe Wilder and Bucky Pizzarelli, this collection has everything from Louis Armstrong standards to Ornette Coleman tunes.

⊙ **Ken Peplowski And Howard Alden Live At Maybeck Recital Hall** (1993; Concord). High-level duetting on a set ranging from Walter Donaldson's "Changes" to Lennie Tristano's "Two Not One", featuring both participants stretching out in comfortable extended musical conversation.

⊙ **The Other Portrait** (1996; Concord). A milestone for Peps; classical compositions by the jazz-friendly Milhaud and others alongside fine standards including Ellington's "Single Petal Of A Rose". Certainly one of his definitive statements of intent and superbly delivered.

⊙ **A Good Reed** (1997; Concord). Like his colleague Randy Sandke, Peplowski is a multifaceted musician whose settings are increasingly ambitious and fascinating. This set (with Loren Schoenberg's big band on three tracks) includes James Chirillo's seventeen-minute "Homage Concerto For Clarinet" – fleet, witty and enchanting, it deserves classic status.

⊙ **Last Swing of the Century** (1998; Concord). A Goodman tribute in which Peplowski proves himself far more than a faithful imitator. The heat of his creations is apparent on old vehicles like "Stealin' Apples" and the big band benefits from the dual presence of Randy Sandke and Conte Candoli.

Art Pepper

Alto and tenor saxophones, clarinet.

b. Gardena, California, 1 Sept 1925; d. 15 June 1982.

After working at the age of seventeen on Central Avenue (the Los Angeles answer to 52nd Street) with otherwise all-black groups such as the the Lee Young sextet, Pepper briefly joined the Benny Carter and Stan Kenton bands. During his army service, from 1944–6, he was heard jamming in London and then, after freelancing in Los Angeles, rejoined Kenton from 1947–51. He started recording under his own name in 1952, but his career was interrupted by repeated imprisonment for drug offences; he was jailed in 1953–4, 1954–6, 1961–4 and 1965–6. Finally, after further work that included a few months in 1968 with the Buddy Rich band, he was rehabilitated at the Synanon Foundation between 1969–71, and began a slow comeback. He cut his first new album in 1975, played with the Don Ellis band in 1976, appeared at the Newport festival in 1977, and toured Europe and Japan for the first time in 1978, all to great acclaim. During the remainder of his life, he was much recorded and also found wider fame through his brutally honest book and film.

Pepper's playing, during his first popularity in the late 1940s, absorbed the influences of Benny Carter and Charlie Parker into a fluent and individual style. His most affecting performances, especially on his own albums, were often the slow ballads that showed an awareness of the melodic economy of Lester Young, which was also reflected in his 1950s work on tenor and clarinet. A period in the mid-1960s, barely heard on disc, was apparently dominated by Pepper's emulation of John Coltrane. This had been abandoned by the time Pepper was recording regularly again, but he had redoubled the intensity of his earlier work. [BP]

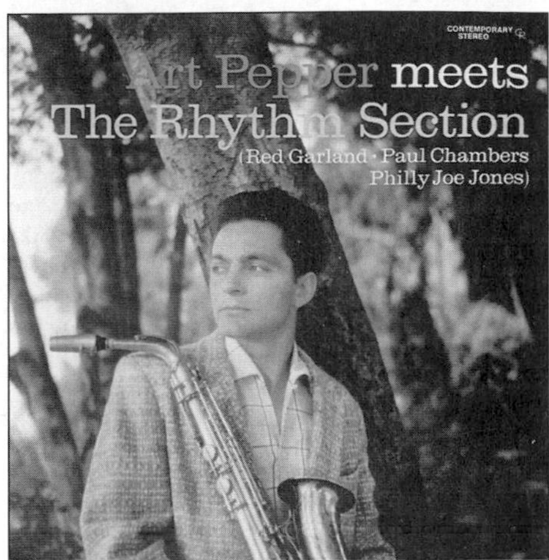

⊙ **Meets The Rhythm Section** (1957; Contemporary/OJC). A great example of how an experienced professional (despite being spectacularly untogether at the time) can not only survive but thrive in fast company, namely Miles Davis's trio of Garland, Chambers and Philly Joe Jones.

⊙ **Smack Up** (1960; Contemporary/OJC). A different kind of intensity imbues this quintet date with Jack Sheldon, in which Pepper covers other writers in the Contemporary catalogue, even including Ornette Coleman's folky blues "Tears Inside".

⊙ **Living Legend** (1975; Contemporary/OJC). Pepper's first new small-group album in fifteen years, this combined him with two fellow survivors, Hampton Hawes and Charlie Haden, plus Shelly Manne. So much is waiting to come out that Art can hardly wait and, as on many records except his final splurge, the original material is exceptional too.

➤➤ **Milcho Leviev** *(Blues For The Fisherman).*

Danilo Pérez

Piano.

b. Panama, 29 Dec 1966.

Pérez began learning music aged three with his father, a bandleader and singer also called Danilo, and studied European classics at Panama National Conservatory from the age of ten. He moved to Boston to attend Berklee College from 1985–8, performing meanwhile with Jon Hendricks, Claudio Roditi and Paquito D'Rivera, appearing on the latter's *Reunion* album in 1990. He was Dizzy Gillespie's pianist from 1989–92, playing with his United

Nation Orchestra and performing on his last four albums. He has led his own groups since 1993, also working with Wynton Marsalis (1995–6) in Poland and the USA, with Gary Burton (1997) and with Wayne Shorter since 2001. He became the first jazz musician to play with the Panamanian Symphony Orchestra in 1995, and has written film music and extended orchestral compositions. Pérez gives workshops in jazz and Afro-Latin rhythms and is a professor of improvisation and jazz studies at the New England Conservatory, while his own playing has become emblematic of the incorporation of Latin techniques in advanced contemporary jazz. [BP]

⊙ **PanaMonk** (1996; Impulse!). Far from being a conventional Monk tribute, this does contain several tunes by him but most of them are given new and often Afro-Latin treatments, while the themes of "Evidence" and "Four In One" are played simultaneously. With percussionists Jeff Watts and Terri Lyne Carrington behind him, Pérez's flair for dynamics and variety is evident throughout.

>> **Paquito D'Rivera** *(Tico Tico)*; **Dizzy Gillespie** *(To Diz With Love)*; **Wayne Shorter** *(Footprints Live)*.

Manuel Perez

Cornet.

b. New Orleans, 28 Dec 1871; d. 1946.

The organizer of the Imperial Brass Band, Perez was a trained player – "a military man who played on a Sousa kick", says Danny Barker – who read music fluently and expected his band to do the same. Very few players of the period in New Orleans had his power, control and exceptionally high register. "He could hit those high notes," says Barker, in probably his only doubtful theory, "because he had eaten two pots of gumbo before he left. Most of them fellows who played the parades were full of whiskey!" Barney Bigard remembers Perez from one of his rare trips out of New Orleans to work with Charlie Elgar's orchestra in Milwaukee: "He taught me a great deal. We would run down studies and reading and then Manuel was showing me how to transpose. He wasn't one of those fly trumpet players that you have nowadays. He was very tasty – a thorough musician." Perez was New Orleans's brass equivalent to clarinettist Lorenzo Tio: one of the last of the town's old-style "legitimate" teachers to work on into jazz's rough-and-ready self-creation. In the 1930s he returned to his second profession of cigar-maker (a popular New Orleans trade); he was incapacitated in the early 1940s by a series of strokes. [DF]

Bill Perkins

Tenor and other saxophones, flutes, clarinets.

b. San Francisco, 22 July 1924; d. 9 Aug 2003.

After serving in World War II, Perkins studied music and engineering at Cal-Tech, at the University of California (Santa Barbara) and at Westlake College. He played in the big bands of Jerry Wald, Woody Herman in 1951–3 and 1954, and Stan Kenton in 1953–4 and 1955–8, touring Europe with both Herman and Kenton. In 1956 he began recording under his own name, including the album with John Lewis (below) on which he was originally billed as co-leader, and has continued to do so into the 1990s. In the 1960s he became a busy studio musician, also doubling as a recording engineer, and from 1970–92 was a member of the *Tonight* show band. Among saxophonists, he admired Young, Parker, Rollins, Coltrane, Joe Henderson, Wayne Shorter and Kenny Garrett, while also being inspired by Miles Davis and arrangers Bill Holman, Rob Pronk, Johnny Mandel and Bob Brookmeyer. Although the Young influence that dominated his style had undergone some modification, Perkins was always a superbly melodic player. [BP]

⊙ **On Stage** (1956; Pacific Jazz). Recorded at exactly the same period as the session with Lewis, Perkins is featured in a swing-influenced octet including Bud Shank and Carl Fontana. Two items from the old Basie band repertoire, "Song Of The Islands" (arranged by Bill Holman) and "Let Me See" (by Perkins), incorporate ensemble versions of Lester Young's recorded solos.

⊙ **I Wished On The Moon** (1989–90; Candid). One of Perkins's own favourites, this has him favouring his tenor on a set of lush charts for strings and big band by Holland's Rob Pronk, played by the Metropole Radio Orchestra.

>> **John Lewis** *(Grand Encounter)*.

Carl Perkins

Piano.

b. Indianapolis, Indiana, 16 Aug 1928; d. 17 March 1958.

Perkins toured with bandleaders Tiny Bradshaw and Big Jay McNeely, and settled on the West Coast in 1949. He was a member of the Oscar Moore trio from 1953–4, and again in 1955, and of the early Max Roach-Clifford Brown quintet in 1954. He played with the hard-bop-inspired quintet led by bassist Curtis Counce from its formation in 1956 and, as well as these affiliations, he was heard on records with Chet Baker, Jim Hall and Art Pepper. His career was not blessed with fame and was beset by drug addiction, but his 24-bar tune "Grooveyard", cut at his last session in 1958 (led by Harold Land), has become a standard. Like Horace Parlan, Perkins was a childhood victim of polio, which restricted his left-hand movement, but he made up for it with playing that resembled a heavier version of Hampton Hawes. Pianist Lionel Grigson wrote of Perkins: "He rarely used double-tempo runs, preferring familiar phrases which he nevertheless inflected in an astonishingly horn- or guitar-like manner by the use of grace-notes, turns, doubling in octaves or fourths." In this respect he resembled the early blues pianists even more than Hawes or Horace Silver did, and was a considerable influence on Les McCann, Bobby Timmons and other soul-jazz pianists. [BP]

>> **Harold Land** *(Harold In The Land Of Jazz)*.

Jukka Perko

Soprano, alto and C-melody saxophones.

b. Finland, 8 Feb 1968.

Perko started on clarinet in 1981, but after a year he switched to alto saxophone, having heard Charlie Parker one night on the radio. Three years later he made a sensational impact when he played in a jam session at the 1985 Pori jazz festival, earning himself the nickname "Little Bird". In 1986, he was chosen to perform with the Dizzy Gillespie 70th Anniversary Big Band, and did so with such success that, in 1988, Gillespie took Perko on the road a second time. After that tour, the 21-year-old saxophonist enrolled at the Sibelius Academy, and six months later he was a full-time member of the UMO Jazz Orchestra. During his years at the Academy, he led the Jukka Perko quartet, and also began composing and playing with other groups. In 1993, with virtuoso vibraphonist Severi Pyysalo, Perko co-founded the astonishingly brilliant Perko-Pyysalo Poppoo group, later called simply The Poppoo. They released the album *Garden Of Time* in 1993, and in 1995 the album *Uuno Kailas*, which presented music based on the poems of Uuno Kailas (1901–33), performed by Perko, Pyysalo and the famous Finnish singer/actor Vesa-Matti Loiri. Perko has received the Finnish Pekka Poyry Award and the Georgie Award, and in 1993 he was chosen as Young Artist of the Year by the Finland Festivals. [IC]

⊙ **Varia** (1998; PoriJazz). Bassist Villo Huolman and drummer Teppo Makynen are perfect musical partners for the two genre-bending leaders. The music runs the gamut from exuberance to melancholy, ranging from the opening witty and ironic "Tango Catastrophique", to unusual standards, excellent originals by Pyysalo (mostly) and Perko, and their haunting arrangements of Finnish folk themes.

Ben Perowsky

Drums, percussion, electronics.

b. New York, 12 May 1966.

His father, Frank Perowsky, played saxophone and clarinet with several of the most famous big bands including those of Woody Herman, Billy Eckstine and Thad Jones/Mel Lewis. Benjamin had drum lessons from age five, studied at the High School of Music and Art in New York, and at Berklee College in Boston. At nineteen, Ben played with James Moody at the Village Vanguard, then toured Europe and Israel with Rickie Lee Jones. He was with Roy Ayres from 1988–9, toured and recorded with Mike Stern from 1990–94, and went on to record with Ronnie Cuber, the Lounge Lizards and Pat Martino. Perowsky began touring and recording with Dave Douglas in 1997, and continues to play with him. He has also played with Michael Brecker, Don Byron and Uri Caine. In 1999 he released his own *Ben Perowsky Trio* CD. A consummate technician and an intensely musical drummer, Perowsky is also co-leader of the co-operative group Lost Tribe, which has released three albums, and he is co-leader of the Ben/Frank Perowsky quartet. His favourites are Tony Williams, Elvin Jones, Jack DeJohnette, John Bonham and Art Blakey, and other inspirations are Monk, Miles, The Beatles, Hendrix, Sly Stone and Messiaen. [IC]

➤➤ **Dave Douglas** *(Magic Triangle).*

Charli Persip

Drums.

b. Morristown, New Jersey, 26 July 1929.

Persip studied drums in Springfield, Massachusetts, and then played R&B and jazz locally in New Jersey. Replacing Philly Joe Jones with Tadd Dameron in 1953, he then joined Dizzy Gillespie's quintet and big band from 1953–8. He recorded prolifically with Gillespie and other leaders, including Quincy Jones, George Russell, Gil Evans, Don Ellis, Roland Kirk, Archie Shepp and Frank Foster's big band, among others. In 1959 he appeared with his own group, the Jazz Statesmen, with Freddie Hubbard and Ron Carter, and later toured as accompanist to Billy Eckstine from 1966–73. In the 1980s he led a part-time big band called Superband, which recorded three albums; changing his name from "Charlie" to "Charli', he has remained in demand as a performer and a teacher at New York's New School. His dynamic but unflamboyant playing is particularly effective in a big-band setting. [BP]

➤➤ **Dizzy Gillespie** *(Groovin' High [1956]).*

Houston Person

Tenor saxophone.

b. Florence, South Carolina, 10 Nov 1934.

After learning piano as a child, Person became involved in jazz and the tenor at the age of seventeen, pursuing his interest at South Carolina State College. He played regularly while on army service in Germany in the 1950s, with Eddie Harris, Cedar Walton and others. He studied music at the University of Hartford, and then toured with the group of organist Johnny Hammond from 1963–6, before forming his own organ-based band. In 1973 he began a touring partnership with Etta Jones that lasted into the 1990s and, as well as recording regularly under his own name, since the mid-1980s he has been a successful producer of other artists. The warmth of Person's tone and the directness of his phrasing owes much to the Gene Ammons school of playing, and experience at the R&B end of the spectrum has done nothing but enhance his jazz work. [BP]

⊙ **Something In Common** (1989; Soul Note). Jointly credited to Person and Ron Carter, this duo performance covers the ground from blues to ballads to bebop, and Person takes them all in his stride.

➤➤ **Charles Earland** *(Black Talk).*

Aake Persson

Trombone.

b. Hässleholm, Sweden, 25 Feb 1932; d. 4 Feb 1975.

Acclaimed at the age of eighteen, Persson toured with bassist Simon Brehm in 1951, and then began freelance gigging and recording, including work with visiting US musicians such as Clifford Brown, Quincy Jones and Stan Getz. He toured with Jones's European-based band from 1959–60, followed by studio work, first in Stockholm and later in Berlin, until his accidental death. He was a founder member of the Clarke-Boland band in 1961, and featured on their records and subsequent live appearances. Persson was a brilliant improviser in a style that may be said to be inspired by J.J. Johnson, but with a melodic grace and fire all his own. [BP]

>> **Kenny Clarke** *(Two Originals)*; **Sahib Shihab** *(And All Those Cats)*.

Bent Persson

Trumpet, cornet, leader.

b. Blekinge, Sweden, 6 Sept 1947.

The star of fine Swedish bands such as Maggie's Blue Five, Kustbandet and Bent's Blue Rhythm Band, Bent Persson came to prominence in Europe as the re-creator of *Louis Armstrong's Fifty Hot Choruses*, a set of Armstrong solos published by Melrose Brothers in 1927, transcribed from long-lost cylinder recordings. After this success Persson formed the Weatherbird Jazzband, collaborated with another fine re-creator, reedman Tomas Ornberg, for a variety of projects, and in the 1980s was recording with Maxine Sullivan as easily as he continued his authentic re-creations of Armstrong, Beiderbecke and others. Since then his fine flexible Armstrong-based playing has been heard in a wide variety of contexts, most regularly with Ornberg. [DF]

⊙ **Louis Armstrong's 50 Hot Choruses For Cornet: Vols1/2, 2/3, 3/4** (Kenneth). Fifty-three solos and 125 breaks by Louis Armstrong lost to record and re-created by Persson. The CD versions are in many cases re-recorded since LP days.

⊙ **Swinging Straight** (1994; Sitel). Good portrait of the straightahead swing of Persson leading a compatible sextet including Ulf Johansson (piano).

"Hannibal" Marvin Peterson

Trumpet, composer.

b. Smithville, Texas, 11 Nov 1948.

Peterson's mother was a pianist and his sister Pat Peterson is a singer. He studied harmony and theory from 1962–5 and played in local bands, then from 1967–9 studied at North Texas State University. He moved to New York in 1970, working with Roy Haynes, Gil Evans, Elvin Jones, Pharoah Sanders, Archie Shepp, Rahsaan Roland Kirk and others. He formed his own Sunrise Orchestra in 1974. Peterson continued leading his own bands and working as a soloist throughout the 1970s and into the 1980s. He also continued his association with Gil Evans up to the mid-1980s, touring many times in Europe, Japan and the USA, and playing on some of Evans's most vital albums. In 1976 Peterson played the Berlin festival with a group that included George Adams in a concert that was recorded by MPS. In 1984 he toured in the UK with the Don Weller-Bryan Spring quartet. A player of great dynamism with an excellent range, Peterson's concept seems to embrace the entire jazz tradition from New Orleans to Coltrane. His influences include Gil Evans, Leadbelly, B.B. King, Coltrane, Ellington, Janáček, Sun Ra and Cecil Taylor. [IC]

⊙ **Kiss On The Bridge** (1990; Ear Rational). Peterson with a classic quintet line-up, demonstrating his fine technique and range and his understanding of the whole jazz trumpet tradition.

>> **Gil Evans** *(Plays The Music Of Jimi Hendrix)*.

Oscar Peterson

Piano.

b. Montreal, 15 Aug 1925.

Like many pianists, Peterson did not first find fame as a sideman and then branch out as a leader: after a brief Canadian apprenticeship he was introduced in 1949 to an unsuspecting US audience in his own right, and it is by his own groups that he is always judged. Despite differences in emphasis at various stages of his career, he has been remarkably consistent; the trios he led until 1959 invariably included a guitarist along with bassist Ray Brown, who remained for several more years when the third member was a drummer (at first Ed Thigpen, then Louis Hayes). From the 1970s onwards Peterson no longer maintained a regular group but appeared variously in trio (often with Niels-Henning Ørsted Pedersen and Martin Drew), duo and unaccompanied formats, while continuing to record more prolifically than almost anyone else in jazz. In 1993 he suffered a severe stroke, but resumed public performance and a new series of recordings the following year.

Inspired initially by the piano work of Nat "King" Cole, he subsequently revealed the influence of Art Tatum (after the latter's death) and sometimes of Hampton Hawes, Phineas Newborn or Bill Evans, while remaining instantly identifiable. The multiplicity of notes Peterson produces in even a relatively subdued context is undeniably exciting, as is the ease with which he works out harmonic variations. But one of the most impressive aspects of his work is an unfailing commitment to swinging which, although often achieved at the cost of repetition in the melodic line, is continually compelling. This is the quality that makes Peterson outstanding as an accompanist, at

Herman Leonard

Oscar Peterson

least to musicians stylistically rooted in the swing era, and the albums below should be compared with his backing work on Jazz At The Philharmonic concerts or on studio sessions with everyone from Louis Armstrong to Lester Young. [BP]

At The Stratford Shakespearean Festival (1956; Verve). Among Peterson's huge output, this stands as the apotheosis of the trio with Ray Brown and Herb Ellis. Despite a less than brilliant recording, the headlong invention of "Swinging On A Star" is balanced by an object lesson in swinging at slow tempo on "Love You Madly".

The Jazz Soul Of Oscar Peterson (1959–62; Verve). Two albums on one CD, with Ed Thigpen replacing Ellis, in which the first set includes classic Peterson arrangements of "Close Your Eyes" and Gillespie's "Con Alma". On the second album Peterson keeps his ears open for new repertoire, such as "Waltz For Debby" and Oliver Nelson's "Six And Four".

Exclusively For My Friends (1963–8; MPS). This four-CD set celebrates the relationship with a small German label, which began quite informally with private recordings in front of a small invited audience, and ended with alternately relaxed and grandiose unaccompanied albums.

If You Could See Me Now (1983; Pablo). A late set with Joe Pass, Niels-Henning Ørsted Pedersen (both of whom have done duos with him) and Martin Drew, which sees Peterson's technique turned onto a couple of unfamiliar vehicles, the Tadd Dameron title track and the bassist's self-composed feature.

Ralph Peterson

Drums, composer.

b. Pleasantville, New Jersey, 20 May 1962.

Born to an oddly specialized musical family – his father, four uncles and a grandfather were all drummers – Ralph Peterson took up the sticks at three. After attending the jazz course at New Jersey's Rutgers University, where he studied trumpet in addition to drums – fellow students included Terence Blanchard and Regina Belle – Peterson immediately became one of the most in-demand musicians on the scene. His most celebrated sideman recordings took place with David Murray – he appears on the Murray series *Lovers*, *Deep River*, *Ballads* and *Spirituals* – but he is also heard on albums by OTB, Donald Harrison-Terence Blanchard, Craig Harris and many more. Off record, he has played with Wynton Marsalis, Jon Faddis, as second drummer with Art Blakey's Messengers, and with a growing number of top-flight US players, among them Michael Brecker, with whose quartet, on a European tour in 1998, Peterson played trumpet (while Brecker took over on drums) for the finale. In addition to the Blue Note albums below, Peterson has also made two for Evidence: 1994's *The Reclamation Project*, upon which he is joined by saxophonist Steve Wilson, vibesman Bryan Carrott and bassist Belden Bullock in an intense study of addiction and recovery; and *The Fo'tet Plays Monk* (1995), in which the same band digs into some of the less obvious corners of the pianist's legacy. Peterson's albums – two on Sirocco, *Back To Stay* (2000) and *Triangular 2* (2000), and three on Criss Cross, *The Art Of War* (2001), *Subliminal Seduction* (2002 – see below) and *Test Of Time* (2003) – are generally intensely thoughtful, virtuosic affairs held together by his sensitive but emphatic playing. His aims remain (as expressed to *Wire* magazine's Philip Watson) "to practise true group improvisation when soloing on a melody or developing a musical idea" and, more generally, to "make my music rich with tradition but moving forward at the same time ... as Roland Kirk used to say: 'You can only go as far forward as you have gone back'". [CP]

Volition (1990; Blue Note). Oddly centreless tunes, but a stellar band – Terence Blanchard (trumpet), Geri Allen (piano), Steve Wilson (soprano and alto saxophones), Phil Bowler (bass), along with the eternally restless Peterson – interprets them with great brio.

Presents the Fo'tet (1991; Blue Note). Fresh band – Don Byron (clarinet, bass clarinet), Bryan Carrott (vibes), Melissa Slocum (bass), plus guests Frank Lacy (trombone, flugelhorn) and David Murray (tenor saxophone, bass clarinet) – contributes compositions as well as skill and commitment to an innovative, constantly inventive session.

Ornettology (1991; Blue Note). Just the core quartet above, but with repertory numbers by Monk, Wayne Shorter and Ornette Coleman added to band originals. As always, Peterson's broodingly energetic drumming binds the session together.

Subliminal Seduction (2002; Criss Cross). Second consecutive release for this group of young turks (pianist Orrin Evans, saxist Jimmy Greene, trumpeter Jeremy Pelt and bassist Eric Revis) and a fine example of Peterson's Blakey-and-beyond approach.

Buddy Petit

Cornet.

b. White Castle, Louisiana, c.1897; d. 4 July 1931.

"A dozen books should have been written about Buddy Petit," says Danny Barker. "The way people rave over Dempsey, Joe Louis or Ben Hogan – *that's* how great Petit was when he played! The kids would come up and say 'Can I shake your hand, Mr Petit?' On parades they'd be ten deep around Buddy as he walked along blowing!" Small, with Indian features and a pronounced stammer, Petit was Armstrong's nearest rival in New Orleans, playing funerals alongside him and setting a fast pace with his superb control and warm mid-register approach. "Outside of Louis," says George Lewis, "Buddy was better liked and better known around New Orleans than any other cornet player: the first one of all the men I've played with."

By 1916 Petit was co-leading a band with Jimmie Noone and he worked constantly up and down the Gulf Coast, playing one-nighters and daytime functions until he could no longer meet the demand; recalls Barney Bigard, "Buddy was so popular that he'd take four or five jobs a night." Petit always took a deposit too, but spoiled his reputation by putting in other bands under his name: finally prospective bookers fought shy, as they could never be sure whether the band that turned up for the date would be his or someone else's. In 1917 Petit answered Jelly Roll Morton's call to work with him on the West Coast but the partnership foundered: Morton ridiculed his new employee's country-boy ways and eating habits (after he once tried to cook up red beans and rice at work) and the trumpeter threatened to kill Morton if their paths crossed again. The following year Petit refused an offer to go to Chicago to join Bill Johnson's band, and King Oliver got the job instead. Petit continued working round the Gulf Coast all through the 1920s and later in the decade was regularly on the riverboats. He died at about 34 from the effects of overeating and drinking at a New Orleans Independence Day picnic: Louis Armstrong was a pallbearer at the funeral. [DF]

Ernst-Ludwig Petrowsky

Reeds, flutes.

b. Güstrow, Germany, 10 Dec 1933.

Ernst-Ludwig Petrowsky studied violin as a child in the north of East Germany. Switching to reeds, he began playing dance music and accompanying theatre before joining jazz groups led by pianist Eberhard Weise in the mid-50s, when government sanctions against jazz eased up. He played for nine years in the Berlin Radio big band. Influenced by composer George Russell and saxophonist Ornette Coleman (whose tunes he discovered in a book), Petrowsky began playing more adventurous jazz, starting an ensemble with fellow reedman Manfred Schulze, the Manfred Ludwig Sextett, which recorded a straight date with singer Dorothy Ellison (1964; Amiga). In the 70s he was very active, playing Colemanesque jazz in various groups, incorporating an eastern European flavour into the music, as well as a strain of free improvisation. Like most creative musicians in eastern Europe during Socialism, Petrowsky was officially required to play as a studio musician in addition to his own work. He recorded for the state label, Amiga Jazz, and in the 70s he was among the first East Germans to play in the West, bolstered by the enthusiastic support of Berlin's Free Music Productions. On FMP he released several excellent records, including *SelbDritt* (1980), a trio that features Coleman's "Enfant", and *Selb Viert* (1979), a quartet that features Coleman's "Blues Connotation". In the mid-70s he was a member of the quartet Synopsis, with pianist Ulrich Gumpert, percussionist Günter "Baby" Sommer and trombonist Conrad Bauer; this group re-formed in 1984 as the Zentral-Quartett, and most recently released the surprisingly conservative *Plie* (1994; Intakt) and *Careless Love* (1997; Intakt). He has continued to work with his wife, experimental pop-jazz singer Uschi Brüning, and as a member of two big bands – the George Gruntz Concert Jazz Band and since 1980 the Globe Unity Orchestra. [JC]

Michel Petrucciani

Piano.

b. Montpellier, France, 28 Dec 1962; d. New York, 6 Jan 1999.

Born with a rare bone disease (osteogenesis imperfecta) that prevents growth to adult size, Petrucciani nevertheless began playing in the family band, with his guitarist father Tony and bassist brother Louis. His professional career started at the age of fifteen by playing for Kenny Clarke and guesting with Clark Terry, following which he moved to Paris and recorded his first album at seventeen. After a visit to New York, he toured France in a duo with Lee Konitz in 1980, and then moved to the USA two years later. He visited Europe as a member of the Charles Lloyd quartet in 1982, made a solo appearance at the Kool festival in 1984, and played a duo/trio set at the Montreux festival of 1986 with Jim Hall and Wayne Shorter. From 1989–92 he led a quartet in which his acoustic keyboard was joined by the synthesizer of Adam Holzman and thereafter, apart from special projects promoting his albums, he made frequent tours as a soloist, often playing uninterrupted sets of ninety minutes or more. After two decades of testing the limits of his physical disability, he died of complications following an attack of pneumonia.

A highly gifted performer, Petrucciani's precocious early work was largely under the sway of Keith Jarrett but he soon exhibited both the delicacy of Bill Evans and the power of McCoy Tyner. His lyrical improvisational style came across clearly in his compositions, matching an abundant technique which presented no obstacles to his imagination. [BP]

⊙ **Power Of Three** (1986; Blue Note). A captivating live set with Hall and Shorter, each of the three occasionally acting as substitute bass and drums. "In A Sentimental Mood" is long but not a moment too long, and Hall's "Bimini" plays fast and loose with its implied calypso rhythm.

⊙ **Conference De Presse** (1994; Dreyfus). Another live, drummer-less collaboration, this time with French organist Eddy Louiss, with spontaneous but enchanting performances of the occasional jazz standard, such as "So What", and simple and stimulating original material.

Oscar Pettiford

Bass, cello.

b. Okmulgee, Oklahoma, 30 Sept 1922; d. Copenhagen, 8 Sept 1960.

Pettiford began on piano, but took up the bass at fourteen, touring with a family band led by his father Harry "Doc" Pettiford. (Of Oscar's many siblings, both trumpeter Ira and trombonist Alonzo worked in 1943 with Jay McShann.) Oscar joined Charlie Barnet for a few months in 1942, and then worked in New York with Roy Eldridge in 1943, as well as recording several key sessions with Coleman Hawkins, Earl Hines and Ben Webster. He co-led a quintet with Dizzy Gillespie in early 1944 and led his own small group. He recorded with Gillespie and with his own big band in early 1945. He went to the West Coast to work with Hawkins later that year, and joined Duke Ellington, with whom he stayed until 1948. After leading his own trio in Los Angeles in 1948, he worked with Woody Herman in 1949. The next year he toured with the Louie Bellson-Charlie Shavers band, followed by a period leading his own small groups, including a residency at the Café Bohemia in 1955, and his occasional big band in 1956–7. He had record dates under his own name, and with Thelonious Monk in 1955–6 and Art Blakey in 1957. He went to Europe with the Jazz From Carnegie Hall package in 1958. He settled in Copenhagen, and worked with Stan Getz in 1959 and Bud Powell in 1960, until his sudden death from a stroke.

Pettiford became, in 1950, the first musician successfully to adapt the pizzicato bass style to the cello, using it frequently on records and in concerts. More strikingly, his exceptionally speedy acceptance by his elders during his first years in New York shows that he was viewed, correctly, as a reincarnation of the recently deceased Jimmy Blanton. His characteristic melodic phrasing is preserved not only in countless recorded solos but in his written lines, such as "Bohemia After Dark", "Trictatism" (apparently the original spelling of what's usually called "Tricotism") and "Laverne Walk", the last two in particular still viewed as test pieces by younger players. One such younger player, Buell Neidlinger, who compared

HERMAN LEONARD

Oscar Pettiford

Pettiford at first hand with all the top bassists of the 1950s, called him "The greatest bass player who ever lived. The man was a monster – he had the most beautiful intonation and time." [BP]

⊙ **Deep Passion** (1956–7; Impulse!). Pettiford's recordings with his own big band are interesting partly for the writing of Gigi Gryce and Benny Golson, and the solos of Lucky Thompson and Art Farmer. But the leader's bass solos (and a couple on cello) are outstanding.

⊙ **Vienna Blues: The Complete Session** (1959; Black Lion). This quartet set with Attila Zoller and Hans Koller on guitar and tenor is an excellent place to concentrate on Pettiford's rhythm playing. His ballad "The Gentle Art Of Love" is reprised from the above album, while his "Blues In The Closet" is an eminently suitable bass feature.

➤➤ **Thelonious Monk** *(Brilliant Corners)*; **Sonny Rollins** *(Freedom Blues)*.

Barre Phillips

Double bass, electronics.

b. San Francisco, 27 Oct 1934.

Phillips began playing in a Dixieland band at Stanford University when he was fifteen, then studied romance languages at Berkeley and afterwards moved to New York. After some belated double bass lessons in 1963, he played with Eric Dolphy at Carnegie Hall as part of Gunther Schuller's Twentieth Century Innovations series. After that he worked with George Russell, visiting Europe with him in 1964, with Jimmy Giuffre, visiting Europe with him in 1965, and played with Archie Shepp at the 1965 Newport festival. He was with guitarist Attila Zoller from 1965–7, and in 1968 he made the first-ever album of solo bass improvisations, which was eventually released under the title *Unaccompanied Barre*. He then began to work more in Europe, playing in a concert with John Lennon and Yoko Ono, working with the Paris-based band Gong and with Mike Westbrook. With John Surman and fellow American Stu Martin (drums), Phillips was a member of The Trio from 1969–71, which was one of the most Dionysian free jazz groups of the time. In 1976 he began recording for ECM with *Mountainscapes*. In 1983 he played and recorded with the classical ensemble Accroche Note, and in 1988 worked with Derek Bailey and Company. A year later he was working with Barry Guy.

Phillips has matured over the years into a player who combines all the basic virtues – lovely tone, superb time, good harmonic knowledge and fine ear – with a perpetual zest for musical adventure. [IC]

⊙ **Mountainscapes** (1976; ECM). There was a reunion of The Trio for this recording, augmented by John Abercrombie and synthesizer player Dieter Feichtener, and the result is a suite of shifting colours.

⊙ **Three Day Moon** (1978; ECM). Phillips with Terje Rypdal, Feichtener and Trilok Gurtu. Rypdal understands this impressionistic mode, and Gurtu's percussive forays enliven the proceedings.

⊙ **Journal Violone II** (1979; ECM). Phillips and Surman are joined by vocalist Aina Kemanis in a moody and meditative session.

⊙ **Camouflage** (1989; Victo). Phillips playing solo bass with grace, sonority and much feeling.

Flip Phillips

Tenor saxophone.
b. Brooklyn, New York, 26 March 1915; d. 17 Aug 2001.

Joseph Flip Phillips worked in Brooklyn on alto and clarinet from 1934–9, then played clarinet with Frankie Newton from 1940–41. He switched to tenor in 1942, working with Benny Goodman that year, Wingy Manone and Red Norvo in 1943, and Woody Herman from 1944–6. He toured with Jazz At The Philharmonic annually for the next ten years, and then moved to Florida and played with Herman and JATP colleague Bill Harris. He made a European tour with Goodman in 1959, followed by fifteen years doing a day job in Florida and leading his own quartet. After occasional playing trips in the early 1970s, he moved to New York in 1975, and worked more regularly, touring Europe in 1982 and recording several new albums in his seventies and eighties.

Phillips came to the fore as a tenor star when all the other contenders idolized Lester Young, and he stood out from the crowd through his interest in Coleman Hawkins and, especially, Ben Webster. Always intensely rhythmic, he took the southwestern-style shouting and honking common to both Webster and Young, and, in the late 1940s, threatened to outdo Illinois Jacquet as a JATP crowd-pleaser. The solid virtues of his playing were more evident, however, in less extrovert surroundings, and his post-1975 comeback in particular was far more convincing than those of many others of his generation. [BP]

⊙ **Flip Wails: The Best Of The Verve Years** (1947–57; Verve). A compilation which eschews the rabble-rousing JATP side of Phillips's best period, and shows what a meaningful improviser he was, even on hackneyed material such as "Singing' In The Rain" or the Bix-associated "Singin' The Blues".

⊙ **A Real Swinger** (1988; Concord). With a rhythm-section led by Dick Hyman (who arranged a later album with strings), Phillips is the only horn on a solid session which goes from "Cotton Tail" to the rather appropriate "September Song".

Sid Phillips

Clarinet, piano, baritone saxophone, arranger, leader.
b. London, 14 June 1902; d. 26 May 1973.

Sid (Simon) Phillips played early on in the Melodians, a band featuring his brothers Harry (trumpet), Ralph (bass) and Woolf (trombone), and later became baritone-saxophonist cornerman of Ambrose's orchestra – to which he contributed scores such as "Cotton Pickers' Congregation" (an intriguing mix of instrumental and choral passages), "Escapada" and "Bwangi", all as good in their way as the writing of Spike Hughes or Ray Noble. Phillips's first band of his own was organized for a Mayfair residency and included Max Goldberg (trumpet), Max Abrams (drums), longtime colleague Bert Barnes (piano) and Ralph Phillips (bass); for the next thirty or more years he was to lead a succession of immaculately arranged, often hot Dixieland bands, which at their best are as good as anything Bob Crosby ever did. Later sidemen who worked for Phillips included two fine trumpeters: the neglected Joe McIntyre (an Irishman whose best work is preserved on Phillips's records; he died early) and Kenny Ball. "Sid's reputation as a hard-driving taskmaster, a perfectionist and to some almost a martinet was well-known," says Ball, "but this supposed hard man was so hard he not only employed and paid me, he sent me for reading lessons every week and paid for them as well." Apart from being a fine arranger, Phillips composed *Symphonie Russe*, a full-length work which was broadcast by the BBC Symphony Orchestra in 1946, conducted by Adrian Boult. His career continued unabated until the 1960s, when his easy-to-like music was heard less often. Phillips's son Simon is a highly rated session drummer; his nephew John Altman is Britain's most prolific writer of TV commercials, a popular music authority and highly gifted reedman. [DF]

⊙ **Hors d'oeuvres** (1936-50/ASV). A very well-chosen introduction to Phillips's work including sides with Ambrose (groundbreakers such as "Cotton Pickers' Congregation") plus titles by his own Trio (with Shearing), Quintet (with Max Goldberg), piano solos and half-a-dozen Dixieland tracks (1949-51). While there is still scope for organised reissue of Phillips's highly influential output of the 1950s, this set makes a good start, and important points too.

John Picard

Trombone, piano.

b. London, 17 May 1934.

John Picard worked with Humphrey Lyttelton's band of the mid-1950s, where his pawky-toned, shouting declamations attracted huge attention and strongly recalled J.C. Higginbotham. But Picard was quick to broaden his approach and by the end of the 1950s (after classic recordings with Lyttelton) was working not only with Bruce Turner's Jump Band but just as notably with Tony Coe's brilliant contemporary-style quintet. Semi-professional in later years (he became a partner in an estate agency), Picard chose his musical surroundings with care, keeping a watchful eye on the progress of modern jazz. Later commitments included a 1970s septet (featuring Colin Smith, Don Weller and Tony Coe) that played Mingus-style jazz as happily as Ellington; lead trombone with Stan Greig's London Jazz Band (for whom he produced stormy avant-garde-tinged scores such as "Meet Mr Rabbit" and "Golden Apples Of The Sun"); and regular work in a hard-swinging rock'n'roll-based band, Rocket 88, featuring Alexis Korner, Don Weller, Colin Smith and sometimes Rolling Stones drummer Charlie Watts. From 1985 Picard was a cornerman in Watts's big band whenever it got together but was working less by the late 1990s. [DF]

➤➤ **Humphrey Lyttelton** *(Jazz At The Royal Festival Hall/Jazz At The Conway Hall).*

Alphonse Picou

Clarinet, composer.

b. New Orleans, 19 Oct 1878; d. 4 Feb 1961.

Alphonse Floristan Picou, the "little big man" of New Orleans clarinet, is most famous for his patenting of a piccolo descant written into a stock military band arrangement of "High Society" – Picou borrowed the theme, played it on his E-flat clarinet, and the solo ever after became a set piece for jazz clarinettists. It was only one discovery in a seventy-year career which began in the 1890s in a bewildering variety of saloon and parade bands. He played for dance halls, functions, funerals, picnics, elections, birthdays, high days, holidays and Mardi Gras (where his speciality was a kazoo stuck down an E-flat clarinet, which he fingered as he sang), as well as in bands led by Buddy Bolden, Dave Peyton, Bunk Johnson, Manuel Perez and Wooden Joe Nicholas, in addition to Papa Celestin's Tuxedo Band and the Olympia band led by Freddie Keppard. He often kept going for three days at a time: "Sometimes my clarinet seemed to weigh a thousand pounds," he remembered later, "but those were happy days! Talk about wild and woolly! There were 2000 registered girls and must have been 10,000 unregistered. And all crazy about clarinet blowers!" Picou kept up the pace until 1932, then returned to his first trade of tinsmith, at which he became prosperous: he acquired property, including several back-of-town bars. By 1940 he was playing again, and took part in Heywood Broun's first-ever record for the American jazz revival, by Kid Rena's band on Delta Records. In 1944 he began a long residency at the Club Pig Pen, then went on to work and recording with Papa Celestin (re-creating his famous solo); in the 1950s he played again for Alexis's Tuxedo band and led his own group at the Paddock Club before confining himself to guest appearances with the Eureka band. He died a rich man, and nearly 2500 people attended his funeral. [DF]

Enrico Pieranunzi

Piano.

b. Rome, 5 Dec 1949.

His father, a guitarist, introduced Pieranunzi to blues and jazz improvisation, and he started piano lessons when he was five years old. He developed his jazz style while studying classical piano, in which he graduated in 1972. In the 1970s and early 80s, he played club and theatre concerts with Johnny Griffin, Kenny Clarke, Sal Nistico, Art Farmer, Kai Winding and Jim Hall. In 1982 and 1985, Pieranunzi toured the USA with Lew Soloff, Michael Moore and Joey Baron, among others. In the 1980s, he also collaborated extensively with Chet Baker and Lee Konitz. He has played at all the major Italian festivals, and has appeared at most of the other European festivals including Berlin, Madrid, Paris and Copenhagen. In 1993, he played a solo piano concert at the Montreal festival. Pieranunzi teaches in both the jazz and classical disciplines, and is currently professor of piano at the Conservatorio di Musica in Frosinone, where he has been teaching since 1978. He has also conducted workshops in Europe and the USA, and has for many years taught at seminars and courses in Siena.

In addition to recording many albums, including trio sets with Marc Johnson and Joey Baron and with Charlie Haden and Billy Higgins, he has written more

than 150 compositions, including "Night Bird", recorded several times by Chet Baker and performed by many others. His regular groups are his American trio with Johnson and Motian and his European trio with Dutch bassist Heyn Van de Geyn and French drummer Andre Ceccarelli. In 1998, Pieranunzi re-formed his Italian trio with bassist Piero Leveratto and the young Mauro Beggio or Francesco Petreni on drums. His album, *Isis*, won the Premio della Critica Discographia in 1982, and the same year he was voted one of the six top jazz musicians in Italy. In 1989, he was voted Musician of the Year in the *Musica Jazz* critics' poll, and in the same poll his Space Jazz Trio was voted best Italian group. Author of a book on the life and art of pianist Bill Evans, Pieranunzi has many of the qualities of Evans, particularly his beautiful touch and the way his virtuoso technique is kept on a tight rein. He can also swing mightily. [IC]

⊙ **The Night Gone By** (1996; Alfa Jazz). This features Pieranunzi's trio with Marc Johnson and Paul Motian, and the collective interplay is superbly done. They dig deep into some standards, transforming the innards of "Body And Soul", and giving an exceptionally dynamic reading of "If I Should Lose You". Several of his excellent originals are featured, and the invention of the trio never flags.

⊙ **The Chant Of Time** (1997; Alfa Jazz). Joey Baron replaces Motian in this trio, and the spirit of Keith Jarrett is a little more prominent on the first two pieces, "Thiaki" and "September Waltz", both composed by Pieranunzi. Fats Waller's "Jitterbug Waltz" swings like the clappers and is treated with impish wit and humour. Lennon/McCartney's "Fool On The Hill" is given a rhapsodic performance on solo piano by Pieranunzi, and his own Monkish piece "The Surprise Answer" is given a wildly ecstatic performance.

Billie Pierce

Piano, vocals.

b. Marianna, Florida, 8 June 1907; d. 29 Sept 1974.

Billie Pierce toured as a pianist/accompanist in the 1920s before settling in New Orleans in 1930. In the 1960s she achieved international fame working in duo with her husband Dee Dee Pierce (Joseph de Lacrois), a prominent local trumpeter (and part-time bricklayer) who worked with the Tuxedo band and others at venues such as Luthjen's. A string of albums all through the 1960s assured the duo a round of work at college and campus jazz festivals, regular appearances at Preservation Hall and even tours of the Far East, until Dee Dee's death in 1973. [DF]

⊙ **New Orleans: The Living Legends** (1961; OBC). So far the only CD of this legendary New Orleans duo, accompanied by Albert Jiles on drums.

Nat Pierce

Piano, arranger.

b. Somerville, Massachusetts, 16 July 1925; d. 10 June 1992.

After studying at the New England Conservatory, Pierce worked with name bands in Boston and on the road. He then ran his own part-time big band in Boston, featuring Charlie Mariano, from 1949–51, while doing freelance writing for Woody Herman and Count Basie. He toured as the pianist/arranger with the Herman band from 1951–5. Based in New York thereafter, he worked with players such as Lester Young, Ruby Braff, Emmett Berry and Pee Wee Russell. He also led an occasional all-star band, including Buck Clayton, Paul Quinichette and Gus Johnson, from 1957–9. Among his arranging credits were the *Sound Of Jazz* TV special in 1957, the Quincy Jones band in 1959, and a Coleman Hawkins-Pee Wee Russell album in 1961. He rejoined Herman from 1961–6, and followed that by freelance work in Los Angeles for Carmen McRae, Louie Bellson and the Bill Berry big band. He co-led the Los Angeles-based big band Juggernaut, with drummer Frankie Capp, on and off during the 1970s and 1980s, and also made a brief playing appearance in the film *New York, New York* (1977). He made European tours as a member of the all-star package The Countsmen in 1980 and 1983, in a Louis Armstrong tribute in 1984 and as a soloist in 1989.

Pierce's writing was predominantly associated with big bands, and managed to retain the simplicity and drive of the best swing-era scores with a minimum of harmonic updating. In his long association with Herman, he was also the chief organizer of the band and even his piano-playing had a functional, cheer-leading aspect. For this reason, he was adept at deputizing for pianist-bandleaders in times of illness, such as Claude Thornhill and Stan Kenton in 1972. The originator of Nat's approach to ensemble playing, Count Basie, chose Nat as his deputy several times from the late 1950s onwards, and used him increasingly during his final years. [BP]

Capp-Pierce Juggernaut

⊙ **Live At The Century Plaza** (1978; Concord). One of the handful of live recordings of this well-oiled monster, with great fun being had by all the studio musicians let out for a day. Someone only has to call a chart "Capp This" and they do, with two closing tracks featuring Joe Williams.

Dave Pike

Vibes, marimba, composer.

b. Detroit, Michigan, 23 March 1938.

Pike began on drums at the age of eight and is self-taught on vibes. He moved to Los Angeles in 1954, playing with Elmo Hope, Carl Perkins, Curtis Counce, James Clay and Paul Bley, and leading his own quartets. In 1960 he moved to New York and played with Herbie Mann from 1961–4, touring Japan with him. Pike performed at the 1968 Berlin jazz festival, and stayed on in West Germany for five years, leading his quartet of German musicians, including guitarist Volker Kriegel and, for one tour, bassist Eberhard Weber. The Dave Pike Set toured throughout Europe and played major festivals. In the early 1970s the group twice made extensive tours in

South America for the Goethe Institute. After the second South American tour, at the end of 1973, Pike returned to the USA and settled in California. [IC]

⊙ **Bluebird** (1988; Timeless). A deft bebop session on which Pike explores three Parker themes with a Dutch rhythm-section, then makes the group a quintet with the addition of altoist Charles McPherson for four more Parker tunes. The whole thing is done with élan, though McPherson tends to steal the show.

Courtney Pine

Tenor and soprano saxophones, bass clarinet, composer.
b. London, 18 March 1964.

Pine began on clarinet, and later took up the tenor saxophone, playing with reggae and funk bands while still at school. Inspired by Sonny Rollins and John Coltrane, he became interested in jazz. In the early 1980s he took part in some of John Stevens's weekly workshops, then graduated to occasional appearances with Stevens's Freebop band. By the mid-1980s Pine was teaching at his own workshops and had formed an organization called Abibi Jazz Arts to encourage black musicians to take more interest in jazz. As an outcome of this project he formed the Jazz Warriors, an all-black big band which included the exceptionally gifted young flautist Phillip Bent, and which developed into a dynamic unit fusing elements from the jazz tradition with elements from West Indian music – calypso, reggae and ska. Pine also formed the World's First Saxophone Posse, a saxophone quartet, and from the mid-1980s he has led his own quartet and quintet, both of which have included the brilliantly promising young pianist Julian Joseph.

In 1986 Pine toured the UK with the George Russell orchestra, played with Art Blakey's Jazz Messengers at the Camden jazz festival and worked for several nights with Elvin Jones at Ronnie Scott's club. In 1988 he appeared before a huge worldwide audience at the Nelson Mandela seventieth birthday concert at Wembley, London. He was also the subject of several television programmes about jazz in the late 1980s, and played on the soundtrack of Alan Parker's film *Angel Heart*.

He has established himself as a focal point and inspiration for young black musicians in London, and he is the first British-born black musician to set his imprint on the UK jazz scene. His influences include Lester Young, Sidney Bechet and Albert Ayler. Pine has established himself as a virtuoso instrumentalist, passionately committed to his music, but there has not as yet been any convincing conceptual innovation. It may be that so many genres are now available, particularly in view of the popularization of world music, that it will take present and future generations of musicians many years to achieve any kind of new synthesis. Pine has made some heroic efforts to explore the jazz terrain and its offshoots, but he still keeps in touch with his reggae roots, which may be a pointer to his future development. [IC]

Jak Kilby

Courtney Pine

⊙ **Journey To The Urge Within** (1986; Island). Pine's debut album drew together some of the most brilliant young black talents in Britain, including Julian Joseph, Mark Mondesir and Cleveland Watkiss, and sold over 100,000 copies – an astonishing figure for a jazz album. Pine plays superbly, and the others acquit themselves well, though as a whole it is something of a hotchpotch.

⊙ **The Vision's Tale** (1989; Island); **Within The Realms Of Our Dreams** (1990; Island). These two records shows Pine's astonishingly comprehensive virtuosity: in fast American company (including Ellis Marsalis and Jeff Watts on the first and Kenny Kirkland, Charnett Moffett and Watts again on the second) he tears through Ornette Coleman and Parker compositions and standards, plus some of his own excellent originals.

⊙ **To The Eyes Of Creation** (1992; Island). This album marks another quest for new syntheses – using a pool of fourteen musicians, Pine draws together elements from jazz, folk, African music, West Indian ska and other sources.

Armand J. Piron

Violin, composer.
b. New Orleans, 16 Aug 1888; d. 17 Feb 1943.

Piron is now remembered primarily as the composer of a huge jazz hit, "I Wish That I Could Shimmy Like My Sister Kate", but he was also a trained violinist who led bands from 1908 and fronted the Olympia Orchestra (1912–14), which included Clarence Williams. A close colleague of Williams from then on (together they formed the Piron and Williams Publishing Company, which published "Shimmy" in 1915), Piron also worked with W.C. Handy and Papa Celestin and in 1918 formed his own orchestra to play at Tranchina's Restaurant at Spanish Fort, Lake Pontchartrain. He made short visits with the orchestra to New York in 1923–4, but after that stayed around New Orleans, working riverboats and nightclubs until his death. [DF]

Piron's New Orleans Orchestra (1923–6; Azure). This fine CD presents the complete recorded output of Piron and of his highly rated pianist Steve Lewis.

Bucky Pizzarelli

Guitar.

b. Paterson, New Jersey, 9 Jan 1926.

A self-taught musician, very early in his career Bucky (John) Pizzarelli tried out new ideas with Joe Mooney's small modern jazz group, then entered the demanding world of studio work in 1954, when he joined NBC. After twelve years (during which he often toured with Vaughn Monroe) he moved to ABC as a staffman for Bobby Rosengarden on the Dick Cavett Show. In the 1970s (rather as with Rosengarden himself) the guitarist's reputation as a jazzman started to blossom: he toured with Benny Goodman, formed a duo with George Barnes, and throughout the decade was to be found at the centre of musical projects, recordings and concerts. Pizzarelli, who like George Van Eps plays a seven-string guitar, has the same all-music approach as his inspiration, and has worked with all the greatest latterday classicists, from Bob Wilber (in the first days of the Soprano Summit quintet) to Bobby Hackett. In the 1980s Pizzarelli formed a duo with his son John (see below), recording several albums including *The Swinging Sevens*. [DF]

The Complete Guitar Duos (1980/4; Stash). Recorded with his son John, these are guitar duos in the grand tradition established by McDonough and Kress.

One Morning In May (2001; Arbors). "There's not a standard or swing tune his seven-string instrument hasn't spun into pure gold" said the New Yorker of Pizzarelli in 2000; here, his dark-toned guitar makes its assured way through a delicious selection of titles including "I Guess I'll Go Back Home This Summer" (Robison), "Serenata" and Strayhorn's "Blood Count".

Legends (2003; Arbors). A very lively date, co-featuring the great Skitch Henderson (piano), son John and a quartet of vioinists including Johnny Frigo in a delightful carefree selection of string-laden standards.. Frigo's solo appearances are especially welcome and veteran Walter Cronkite provides the sleevenotes. Excellent!

John Pizzarelli

Guitar, vocals.

b. Paterson, New Jersey, 6 April 1960.

The son and pupil of Bucky Pizzarelli, John began attracting attention when he sat in with his father and Zoot Sims on a Highlights In Jazz concert in 1980. John continued playing and singing with Bucky in duo thereafter, as well as working in 1986 with Tony Monte's trio, which had a regular slot on Radio WNEW, New York. In 1990 Pizzarelli appeared on his first solo album (for Chesky) and since then has continued to progress as a solo entertainer. By 1995 he was leading a full-time trio (including his brother on bass), and had appeared in a recorded version of Gershwin's *Girl Crazy*. He would seem to be moving into the sort of popular territory occupied by Harry Connick Jnr. [DF]

My Blue Heaven (1990; Chesky). With a compatible team including Bucky, Dave McKenna, Clark Terry and Milt Hinton, Pizzarelli plays and sings with style on wonderful should-be standards like Nat Cole's "I'm An Errand Boy For Rhythm".

New Standards (1994; RCA). Pizzarelli on top form with small groups and orchestra, featuring superior new songs and one or two good old ones, including the jivey "Come On-A My House", previously a hit for Rosemary Clooney.

After hours (1995; Jive). With accompaniments by Randy Sandke and Harry Allen plus the Pizzarelli clan (Bucky plus brother Martin, bass) a charming examination of fine ballads; classy but never over-solemn or pompous.

The Rare Delight Of You (2001; Telarc). A delightful meeting between Pizzarelli and George Shearing including a remake of Shearing's old hit with Nat 'King' Cole, "Lost April".

Lonnie Plaxico

Bass.

b. Chicago, 4 Sept 1960.

Although he came to public attention with the Wynton Marsalis group in 1982, Lonnie Plaxico gained early jazz experience playing with Chet Baker, Sonny Stitt and Junior Cook, and subsequently with Dexter Gordon and Hank Jones. In the mid-1980s he joined Art Blakey's Jazz Messengers and, after the break-up of this band in 1986, continued to play with fellow Blakey alumni Donald Harrison and Terence Blanchard. In the late 1980s and 1990s, Plaxico established himself as a top-flight studio bassist, in demand particularly with M-Base adherents Steve Coleman, Greg Osby and their UK disciple Steve Williamson, but he also played with drummer/leaders Cindy Blackman, Cecil Brooks III, Jack DeJohnette and Marvin "Smitty" Smith, in addition to a host of other well-known musicians, including Bud Shank, David Murray, Robin Eubanks and Don Byron, as well as regularly recording with singer Cassandra Wilson. In the mid-1990s, he appeared on both of German organist Barbara Dennerlein's initial Verve releases, *Take Off!* (1995) and *Junkanoo* (1996), as well as contributing his sinewy, propulsive sound to dozens of recordings, among them albums by Graham Haynes (*Transition*, Verve; 1995) and – particularly memorably – to Greg Osby's Blue Note albums *Art Forumaq* (1996) and *Further Ado* (1997). A leader on eight of his own albums since 1989 (including four on Muse and one – *Mélange*, see below – on Blue Note in 2001), Plaxico also runs his own label, Plax Music. [CP]

Mélange (2001; Blue Note). Signed at Cassandra Wilson's recommendation, Lexico gets tougher than his previous solo efforts, but remains preoccupied by grooves of all sorts. Featuring George Colligan on keyboards, notably Hammond B3, and Tim Ries and Marcus Strickland on tenors.

Steve Coleman

Motherland Pulse (1985; JMT). Vibrant and original album, through which Coleman first made his mark, considerably aided by the commitment and energy demonstrated throughout by Plaxico, trumpeter Graham Haynes, pianist Geri Allen and drummer Marvin "Smitty" Smith.

Michele Rosewoman

Contrast High (1988; Enja). The adventurousness of Rosewoman's playing stretches Plaxico and his rhythm-section partner Cecil Brooks III, but this is a fine album, featuring Greg Osby and Gary Thomas as frontline horns.

Cindy Blackman

Code Red (1990; Muse). High-energy session of the sort Plaxico relishes, especially in such sympathetic company: Wallace Roney (trumpet), Steve Coleman (alto) and Kenny Barron (piano).

King Pleasure

Vocals.

b. Oakdale, Indiana, 24 March 1922; d. 21 March 1981.

The album *King Pleasure Sings* introduced a vast number of listeners to vocalese in the 1950s, though the art of setting words to jazz solos had been invented long before Pleasure (born Clarence Beeks) pursued the idea. But Pleasure did much to popularize the form after he won a talent competition at Harlem's Apollo, singing Eddie Jefferson's version of "Moody's Mood For Love" (subsequently recorded for Prestige, 1952). Over the next two years he continued to record for Prestige, including a second lesser hit, "Parker's Mood" (1953), and thereafter made two further albums that combined new titles with new versions of his previous work. After that Pleasure seems to have retired to California, but his recordings were a central influence on later generations of vocalese-lovers from Georgie Fame to Manhattan Transfer. [DF]

King Pleasure Sings – Annie Ross Sings (1952–4; OJC). The great Pleasure album, combining classics like "Red Top Jumpin' With Symphony Sid" and "Parker's Mood" with four titles by Annie Ross, including "Farmer's Market" and "Twisted".

Stew Pletcher

Trumpet, mellophone.

b. 1907; d. USA, 29 Nov 1978.

Stew Pletcher was a fine swing trumpeter, whose relaxed, Hackett-style playing is heard to advantage on Red Norvo sides such as "Remember". After working with Norvo's band in the 1930s (he also played with Norvo in an interesting drummer-less and piano-less group at the Famous Door, featuring Dave Barbour on guitar), Pletcher worked with Tony Pastor, Billy Bissett, Jack Teagarden (1945), Nappy Lamare (1949) and Teagarden again (1955). He carried on playing into the 1970s, until ill health struck. Stew Pletcher's son, cornettist Tom, is one of the most interesting latterday revivalists, working in the Beiderbecke-celebrating semi-professional Sons of Bix. [DF]

Pekka Pohjola

Bass, composer.

b. Finland, 13 Jan 1952.

Pohjola's formal musical education consisted only of a few years studying violin at the Sibelius Academy, but he started composing early. His basic influences are the Beatles, Weather Report and Frank Zappa, and he is probably more at home with rock rhythms than with straight jazz. He is one of the most Finnish of that country's musicians, and his often densely composed pieces have sometimes massive and disturbing sonorities. He has recorded eleven studio albums and two live ones, and composed one symphony. In his early career he worked mainly as a sideman in other leaders' bands (including Mike Oldfield in 1977–8). In 1992, he formed his regular working group with guitarist Markku Kanerva, pianist Seppo Kantonen and drummer Anssi Nykanen, which has toured in Spain, the USA and Japan. Pohjola also writes, arranges and produces music for singers, groups and theatre companies. His main source of inspiration is the work of painter Akseli Gallen-Kallela (1865–1931), who illustrated the Finnish national epic, the *Kalevala*. [IC]

Pewit (1997; Pohjola Records). All eight pieces were composed by Pohjola, but at the recording he gave the musicians guidelines to a certain mood, then recorded their parts separately without allowing them to listen to the other tracks. The mood ranges from romantic and gentle to heavy rock and dense electro/acoustic soundscapes. The nineteen-minute "Ordinary Music", with violins, violas, cellos and percussion augmenting the ensemble, begins with stately court music before the air-raid sirens and the mayhem erupt.

Ed Polcer

Cornet, vibes.

b. Paterson, New Jersey, 10 Feb 1937.

A mellow mid-period cornettist who works the musical furrows of Hackett, Windhurst and Butterfield without copying any of them, Ed Polcer played early in his career with Stan Rubin's Tigertown Five at Princeton College, while he was studying engineering. After graduation he was active on the jazz scene at Jimmy Ryan's and played at Carnegie Hall, but remained semi-pro, served his time in the US air force from 1960, then in 1963 toured Europe with Mezz Mezzrow. After that he became a familiar sound in New York clubland, subbing for Max Kaminsky at Ryan's and working for a time as house cornettist for Eddie Condon (although Condon was on stage for only about a score of the dates). In 1973, the year that Condon died, Polcer joined Benny Goodman (replacing Bobby Hackett, at Hackett's instigation); when, two years later, Eddie Condon's club reopened at a new location, Polcer became house cornettist, co-owner (with Red Balaban, in whose band he had worked from 1969), and, at last, a full-time musician. From then on his mellifluous, well-stirred trumpet was heard more regularly in New York, and on fine records by Jane Harvey, Peter Dean and the re-formed Eddie Condon house band. In the 1980s he visited Britain twice with his ensemble (featuring Keith Ingham and Kenny Davern), and in the 1990s Polcer still carried the torch for Condon, regularly starring at clubs and festivals. [DF]

⊙ **Barbara Lea And The Ed Polcer All Stars At The Atlanta Jazz Party** (1992; Jazzology). With a similar team to the one above but with Ken Peplowski for Barnes and Marty Grosz guesting on guitar, Polcer provides the perfect musical backup for Lea's classy singing.

⊙ **A Salute To Eddie Condon** (1993; Nagel Heyer). Polcer leads an Anglo-American band including Bob Havens, Bob Haggart, John Barnes and Jim Douglas; he also solos effectively, particularly on a moving "Wherever There's Love".

Ben Pollack

Drums, leader.
b. Chicago, 22 June 1903; d. 7 June 1971.

A fast-talking, kindly, but deeply ambitious man, Ben Pollack had already worked with such commercially successful bands as the New Orleans Rhythm Kings before forming his own in 1926. A musicianly Dixieland drummer ("one of the first to hit all four beats in a measure," said Benny Goodman), he possessed a fine ear for talent and heard much of it in the young, white soon-to-be-stars who lit up the music scene of the late 1920s. In 1928, at the Little Club, New York, Pollack's band was a storehouse of young talent, featuring Benny Goodman, Jimmy McPartland, Glenn Miller and, soon after, Jack Teagarden. Although Pollack was never a tyrant, he soon found he had rebellious young tigers by the tail: his protégés (often with Goodman, six years his junior, as their ringleader) laughed at Pollack's "old-fashioned" plummy singing and commercial eye for presentation, played practical jokes, took record dates without him, and stood up to his views on and off the stand. Animosity finally exploded over an apparently tiny but probably highly significant issue: "Pollack said something to the effect that he didn't want anybody with dirty white shoes playing in his band," recalls Goodman. "Jimmy turned in his notice and I followed."

Pollack survived the crisis and by 1934 was leading another band of young stars, including Yank Lawson, Matty Matlock, Eddie Miller and an old ally, Gil Rodin. This time, however, Pollack made a more serious error of judgement. A new singer, Doris Robbins, who also happened to be Pollack's girlfriend, became his band's favoured artist: "She and Pollack used to sing moist-eyed duets that made the band cringe," Lawson told John Chilton. Pollack was deeply angered and aggrieved by the inevitable walk-out that followed, and he became angrier still at his protégés' rapid success without him under Bob Crosby's nominal leadership. Fuel was added to the blaze as he saw another of his old employees, Benny Goodman, achieve commercial success that Pollack could only dream of. In 1936, Pollack's latest discovery, Harry James, left unceremoniously – to join Goodman. Over the next two years Pollack's fury boiled over. He sued Goodman, Bob Crosby, Paramount Pictures, Victor Records and Camel Cigarettes for $5,000,000 in estimated lost earnings, a desperate move that died in the courts.

For much of the 1940s, after a spell as MD for Chico Marx, Pollack ran a successful agency and record company (perhaps he saw it as a safer commercial option), but by the 1950s was bandleading again, on Sunset Strip in Los Angeles. He also made a tight-lipped appearance as himself in the film *The Benny Goodman Story* (1956). By now most of the old rivalries had been filed away, and Pollack was once again successful in his own right: in 1964 his Pick-A-Rib Boys attracted more than 20,000 people at the Disneyland Dixieland Festival. And yet, in Dick Sudhalter's words, "Pollack never overcame the feeling of bewilderment: never stopped asking what he should have done wrong that he shouldn't have received the rewards due to the Father of Swing." Weighed down by a developing heart condition, Pollack eventually hanged himself in his Palm Springs bathroom. [DF]

⊙ **The Dean Of Swing** (1926-50; ASV). As regularly from ASV, a comprehensive survey of a neglected figure; this Pollack collection has central titles from the 1920s ("Singapore Sorrows", "Futuristic Rhythm") and 1930s, rich in stars including Harry James, Glenn Miller, Jack Teagarden and Benny Goodman. Six tracks from his Pick-A-Rib Boys complete the collection, including two from 1950 with Cathcart/Schneider.

⊙ **Ben Pollack And His Pick-A-Rib Boys** (1950; Jazzology). Pollack always surrounded himself with the cream of Dixieland talent later on, and his compatriots on these World Broadcasting transcriptions include Dick Cathcart, Moe Schneider, Matty Matlock and Ray Sherman.

Marilyn Middleton Pollock

Vocals.
b. Chicago, 25 Oct 1947.

Pollock sang rock'n'roll and folk in the USA before turning to jazz, joining Max Collie's band in 1991. Since then she has appeared regularly at jazz festivals and clubs, presented one-woman shows and recorded regularly for Lake Records. An authority on vaudeville singers, and an enthusiastic collector of songs in the genre, Pollock has a big voice, commanding stage presence and a natural feeling for jazz.

In 1994 she starred in a series of jazz concerts for BBC Radio 2, with Steve Mellor's Chicago Hoods. [DF]

⊙ **With The Lake Records All Star Jazz Band** (1993; Lake). A fine set with accompanists including Paul Munnery (trombone) and Frank Brooker (reeds); Pollock sings standards and rarities like "Washing The Blues From My Soul" and "Big Bad Bill" (also revived by Ry Cooder).

Danny Polo

Clarinet, saxophones.

b. Toluca, Illinois, 22 Dec 1901; d. 11 July 1949.

Son of a clarinettist, Danny Polo worked in a boys' duo with pianist Claude Thornhill, then with Elmer Schoebel and Merritt Brunies at Friars Inn, Chicago, and all over with top American bandleaders such as Ben Bernie, Joe Venuti and Jean Goldkette – he recorded with Bix Beiderbecke and Frankie Trumbauer under Goldkette's baton in 1927. That year Polo sailed to Europe with Dave Tough in George Carhart's New Yorkers, toured the continent, formed a band in Paris for dancer Maurice Loupiau, and ended up in London in 1929. The following year he joined Ambrose (who had just signed a Decca contract with a strong jazz slant to it), and for most of the next nine years was a featured soloist with Britain's best orchestra of the period: records with Ambrose and with Polo's own groups, including the Swing Stars (featuring Tommy McQuater, Eddie Macauley and Dick Ball) and the Embassy Rhythm Eight, show him off to fine advantage. When at last he resettled in the USA, Polo was unforgotten. He recorded with Coleman Hawkins in 1940, doubled on tenor with Joe Sullivan's Café Society Orchestra ("a dry utilitarian style", says Charles Fox) and worked with Jack Teagarden's band: his marvellous playing can be heard on the soundtrack to Bing Crosby's film with Teagarden, *Birth Of The Blues* (1941). For his last seven years Polo rejoined his old friend Claude Thornhill (replacing Irving Fazola), then led bands for himself, but was back with Thornhill in July 1949, when he collapsed and died within two days. [DF]

➤➤ **Claude Thornhill** *(Transcription Performances 1947; 1948 Transcriptions).*

Herb Pomeroy

Composer, trumpet, educator.

b. Gloucester, Massachusetts, 15 April 1930.

Pomeroy studied theory, composition, piano and trumpet at Schillinger House (Boston), which later became the Berklee School of Music. He had extensive experience with jazz groups in the 1950s, working with Charlie Parker, Lionel Hampton, Stan Kenton and Charlie Mariano among others. He joined the staff of the Berklee School in 1955, and continued as an instructor there through succeeding decades into the mid-1980s. He also taught at the Lenox School of Jazz in 1959–60. He took time off from Berklee in 1962 in order to work for the US State Department in Malaysia, directing the Radio Malaya Orchestra. Pomeroy has also continued to lead his own bands, to host a jazz series on TV, and to teach at various summer schools. He has composed for the Boston Ballet Company, the National Jazz Ensemble and other organizations. Keith Jarrett, recalling his time at Berklee, said of Pomeroy: "He was one of the more innovative players – the intervals he would play would be just not what you usually hear on trumpet." [IC]

Valery Ponomarev

Trumpet.

b. Moscow, 20 Jan 1943.

After studying music in his home town, Valery Ponomarev became intrigued by jazz trumpet on hearing a recording of Clifford Brown, and joined a hard-bop band led by pianist Vadim Sakun. In 1973 the trumpeter defected, joining Art Blakey's Jazz Messengers in 1977, where his featured number, appropriately enough, was "I Remember Clifford". In the 1980s, on leaving the Messengers, he formed his own band, Universal Language, and saw a loose adaptation of his life made into a film, *Moscow on the Hudson* (Paul Mazursky, 1984) starring Robin Williams. Throughout the 1980s and 1990s, Ponomarev continued to dispense faultless, vigorous jazz in stellar company: on *Profile* (1991; see below); with Don Braden, John Hicks, Peter Washington and Victor Jones in 1993 (*Live At Sweet Basil*, Reservoir); and, with Bob Berg sharing frontline duties, on 1997's *A Star For You* (see below) and with Jimmy Cobb on drums for 2001's *The Messenger* (Reservoir). A fine, sensitive trumpeter in the hard-bop mould, Ponomarev is also an accomplished composer of memorable themes in the genre. [CP]

⊙ **Trip To Moscow** (1985; Reservoir). Sinewy but surprisingly subtle playing from Ponomarev, particularly on "For You Only", capably backed by bassist Dennis Irwin and drummer Kenny Washington, and sharing frontline duties with Ralph Moore and pianist Hideki Tadao.

⊙ **Profile** (1991; Reservoir). Considerably abetted by the presence of Joe Henderson and Kenny Barron, Ponomarev mines the hard-bop legacy with fire and sensitivity to produce an entirely unpretentious, enjoyable album.

⊙ **A Star For You** (1997; Reservoir). Steaming set of Blakey-like hard-bop vehicles, with pianist Sid Simmons and bassist Ken Walker supporting hard-driving solos from Bob Berg (tenor saxophone) and Ponomarev, the whole subtly propelled by Billy Hart and perfectly engineered in Rudy Van Gelder's studio.

Jean-Luc Ponty

Acoustic and electric violins, violectra (baritone violin), composer, keyboards.

b. Avranches, France, 29 Sept 1942.

Ponty's father was a violin teacher and his mother a piano teacher. He began studying the violin at five, and at thirteen left regular school to practise six hours a day to become a concert violinist. He studied at the Conservatoire National Supérieur de Musique in Paris, and after two years gained the highest award for violin. He then spent two years with the Lamoureux Symphony Orchestra. From 1961–4 he played with the Jef Gilson jazz group, then, after a big success at the Antibes jazz festival in 1964, he committed himself totally to jazz, freelancing all over Europe. In 1967, at John Lewis's invitation, he participated in the violin workshop at the Monterey jazz festival, making another big impact. In 1969 he went to the USA, recording and working with Frank Zappa and the George Duke trio. From 1970–72, back in France, he worked throughout Europe with his own group. In 1973 he emigrated to the USA, working with Zappa and the Mothers of Invention, then joining John McLaughlin's Mahavishnu Orchestra in 1974. From 1975 onwards he has led his own groups. His early inspirations were first Stephane Grappelli, then Stuff Smith, but he also names Miles Davis, Clifford Brown, Parker, Rollins, Coltrane, Monk, Bill Evans and Ornette Coleman among his favourite musicians. In the early 1960s Stuff Smith said of Ponty, "He is a killer! He plays on violin like Coltrane does on saxophone", and by establishing the instrument as a force in contemporary jazz Ponty paved the way for others such as Jerry Goodman, Zbigniew Seifert and Didier Lockwood.

To be audible in a jazz context he had to be amplified from the very beginning, but from 1969 on, after working with Wolfgang Dauner and George Duke, he began to go deeply into the use of electronics. Ponty has said: "The amplification and the weird sounds I got helped me ... get away from the classical sound and classical aesthetics and forget what the teachers had been teaching me." Yet his residual classicism is a stamp of his identity, and a strain of European romantic lyricism colours the sound of his groups. [IC]

⊙ **King Kong** (1969; Blue Note); **Aurora** (1975; Atlantic); **Imaginary Voyage** (1976; Atlantic). Ponty combines superb violin-playing with fine small-group composing and arranging, though the wayward masterpiece *King Kong* was produced and largely composed by Frank Zappa. After that fiery baptism, Ponty comes into his own, and *Aurora* and *Imaginary Voyage* are full of new ideas and blazing improvisations.

⊙ **No Absolute Time** (1992–3; Fnac). The African/world music elements that had appeared tentatively in Ponty's work in the previous few years are developed on *No Absolute Time*, which is a masterpiece – homogeneous, but full of variety and constantly charged with feeling.

Odean Pope

Tenor saxophone.

b. Ninety Six, South Carolina, 24 Oct 1938.

Philadelphian tenor saxophonist Odean Pope studied with pianist Ray Bryant. In the 60s he gigged with organist Jimmy McGriff and Art Blakey and the Jazz Messengers, and late in the decade he began a long, continuing association with drummer Max Roach. With Roach he has recorded frequently, including *Pictures In A Frame* (1979; Soul Note), *Chattahoochee Red* (1980; Columbia), *In The Light* (1982; Soul Note), *Easy Winners* (1985; Soul Note) and *It's Christmas Again* (1994; Soul Note). Pope was a member of the freewheeling funky group Catalyst in the 70s, and he continued an interest in electric funk in his killer trio, with bassist Gerald Veasley and drummer Cornell Rochester. This trio has made two absolutely great records for the German Moers label, *Almost Like Me* (1990) and *Out For A Walk* (1992); a new trio with drummer Mickey Roker and bassist Tyrone Brown recorded a disc dedicated to Pope's town of birth, *Ninety Six* (1995; Enja) with Brown remaining for *Ebioto* (1999; Knitting Factory) and Craig McIver taking the drum chair. The trio remains Pope's most common live format, but *Changes And Chances* (1999; CIMP) was an abstruse duo album with inquiring pianist Dave Burrell. In 1977, Pope started the Saxophone Choir, a huge saxophone ensemble backed by a rhythm-section. With this group he has explored his sensitive skills as arranger and composer, leading the group through spirituals-influenced choral sounds and deep into the improvised outback on records like *The Saxophone Shop* (1985; Soul Note) and *The Ponderer* (1990; Soul Note). [JC]

⊙ **Epitome** (1994; Soul Note). While my favourite Pope material is unquestionably the Moers trios (both now available on disc), the Saxophone Choir is the best place to hear the bigger picture this wonderful musician paints. *Epitome* includes a nine-saxophone frontline, weaving polyphonic rugs out of Trane's "Coltrane Time", the classic spiritual "Lift Ev'ry Voice", and Pope's own rich compositions.

Michel Portal

Clarinet, saxophone.

b. Bayonne, France, 27 Nov 1935.

Portal studied the clarinet at the Paris Conservatoire. A powerful post-Coltrane player active in all areas of contemporary jazz, he also seems to be equally at home with classical music – avant-garde and otherwise. He played and recorded with John Surman's trio in 1970; from 1976–82 he worked with Albert Mangelsdorff in quartet and quintet formations. Others he has worked with include Sunny Murray, Joachim Kuhn, Jack DeJohnette and Dave Liebman. He has also led his own groups, which have included many leading French and Swiss musicians. His influences include Mingus, Dolphy and Stockhausen. [IC]

⊙ **¡Dejarme Solo!** (1979; Dreyfus Jazz Line); **Arrivederci le Chouartse** (1980; hat Art). *Solo* has Portal playing solo saxophones, clarinets, percussion and accordion, with folky elements and free improvising. On *Arrivederci* he's in trio with bassist Leon Francioli and drummer Pierre Favre, improvising with no prisoners taken.

Joe Poston

Alto saxophone, clarinet, vocals.

b. Alexandria, Louisiana, c.1895; d. May 1942.

Joe Poston, a graduate of Fate Marable's riverboat bands and Doc Cooke's Dreamland Orchestra, is remembered chiefly as the alto saxophonist with Jimmie Noone's Apex Club Orchestra, which set a pace in Chicago (1926–8) and featured the young Earl Hines. "With Poston's lead carrying the melody," says critic Martin Williams, "Noone would improvise complex interweaving counter-themes [and] beneath this Hines provided not only harmony but sometimes a third counter-melody as well." Classic tracks such as "Apex Blues", "Sweet Lorraine" and "I Know That You Know" show Poston at his best. After leaving Noone he returned to Cooke briefly before illness ended his career in his late forties. [DF]

➤➤ **Jimmie Noone** *(The Complete Recordings Vol. 1).*

Chris Potter

Tenor, soprano and alto saxophones, bass clarinet.

b. Chicago, 1 Jan 1971.

Joseph Christopher Potter started playing at age eleven, then studied jazz privately while in high school in Columbia, South Carolina. He moved to New York in 1989, studying for one year at the New School, followed by two years at the Manhattan School of Music. He had also started professional work when he arrived in New York, playing with Red Rodney (1989–93), then with Steely Dan and with the Mingus Big Band from 1993. He has ongoing musical relationships with Paul Motian, Steve Swallow, Jim Hall, Dave Douglas, Billy Hart and Dave Holland. Potter's own debut album was released in 1993, and since then he has released six more, on either Criss Cross or Concord Records. Potter has the makings of a major talent, and is one of the most vital and original saxophone voices on the American scene. [IC]

⦿ **Vertigo** (1998; Concord). Potter leads an all-star quartet with guitarist Kurt Rosenwinkel, bassist Scott Colley and drummer Billy Drummond, with Joe Lovano playing tenor saxophone on three tracks. All nine compositions are by Potter and they show the range and completeness of his talent, plus the sheer passion of his playing. Eastern musical elements in "Shiva", wild free improvisation with Lovano in "Modeen's Mood", introspective saxophone self-communing in "Act III Scene I" (inspired by Hamlet's "To be, or not to be"), humour in "Fishy", and exquisite lyricism in "Wake Up" – it's a feast.

Tommy Potter

Bass.

b. Philadelphia, 21 Sept 1915; d. 5 March 1988.

Potter played piano and guitar before taking up the bass in 1940. He worked with pianist John Malachi in Washington, where he first met Charlie Parker in 1943; all three joined the Billy Eckstine band from 1944–5. In between, Potter worked with the Trummy Young group, and he went on to play with John Hardee and Max Roach. He was the bassist with the classic Parker quintet from 1947–50, and also recorded with Wardell Gray and Bud Powell in 1949, and Stan Getz in 1950. He performed regularly with Count Basie in 1950, Earl Hines from 1952–3, Artie Shaw from 1953–4, Eddie Heywood in 1955, Bud Powell and Rolf Ericson in 1956, Tyree Glenn from 1958–60, Harry Edison from 1960–61, Buck Clayton in 1963, Al Cohn-Zoot Sims in 1965, and Jimmy McPartland and Buddy Tate in the late 1960s. He toured Europe and Japan with a Parker "tribute" package in 1964. He left full-time music for work with hospital recreational facilities, but continued freelance gigging. On the rare occasions when he was heard as a soloist he displayed a melodic intelligence which, amply present in his backing work, made for a particularly fluid partnership with Parker's drummers Max Roach and Roy Haynes. [BP]

➤➤ **Charlie Parker** *(The Dial Masters; Complete Live Performances On Savoy).*

Steve Potts

Soprano and alto saxophones.

b. Columbus, Ohio, 21 Jan 1945.

The cousin of Count Basie's tenor saxophonist Buddy Tate, Steve Potts, inspired in the beginning by Eric Dolphy and Charles Lloyd, played with Ron Carter, Chick Corea, Chico Hamilton, Joe Henderson and Roy Ayers, before moving to Paris in 1972. The bulk of his work in Europe has been in the context of his long-standing musical relationship with Steve Lacy, with whom he has been performing for over twenty years, recording scores of albums and joining him in collaborations with painters, poets, dancers, etc. Potts has also worked in Europe with the Art Ensemble of Chicago, Mal Waldron, Ben Webster, Johnny Griffin and Dexter Gordon, and his own band, the Steve Potts 4, featuring Richard Galliano (accordion), Jean-Jacques Avenel (bass) and Bertrand Renaudin (drums), performs regularly there. A recent quartet comprised guitarist Michael Felberbaum, bassist Stéphane Persiani and drummer Richard Portier and was heard in 2000 on *Wet Spot*, released on Potts's own label. He has also composed music for theatrical projects for the Théâtre du Silence and the Paris Opera Research Group, recorded with Imaran, a group of Touareg musicians, and has given many musical seminars and workshops, but he is celebrated chiefly for his partnership with Lacy, his gutsy, passionate playing providing an excellent contrast with Lacy's more restrained style. [CP]

Steve Potts

⦿ **Pearl** (1990; Caravan). Potts can be heard at full throttle on this album of his own compositions, specially voiced to feature the quintessentially French accordion sound of Galliano.

Misha Mengelberg

The Root Of The Problem (1997; hatOLOGY). An intriguing example of Potts's playing outside a Lacy context in a duo with the pianist, and in trios with him and either percussionist Achim Kremer or serpent/tuba player Michel Godard, in three performances packed with wit and energy. In John Corbett's words, Potts "sends a stream of notes out like target ducks across a fairground shooting range, while Mengelberg picks them off with single-note shots".

➤➤ **Steve Lacy** *(Morning Joy; Vespers).*

Bud Powell

Piano, composer.

b. New York, 27 Sept 1924; d. 31 July 1966.

Bud Powell, whose given names were Earl Rudolph, was one of the most important figures in the history of jazz piano. He studied European music as a child, but was a keen observer of the beginnings of bebop in the early 1940s. Encouraged by Thelonious Monk, he joined the Cootie Williams band from 1943–4 and made his recording debut with them. After touring he became involved in the 52nd Street scene, working (and later recording) with Charlie Parker. He was hospitalized in 1945, allegedly as a result of police brutality, and suffered recurrent mental instability for which he received electro-convulsive therapy in 1947–8. He was active as a trio leader from 1953 onwards, though he was often heavily tranquillized. He took up residence in Paris with his wife and son from 1959–64. Sanatorium treatment for tuberculosis and subsequent recuperation in 1962–3 led to an invitation to work in New York for two months in 1964. Powell failed to return to Paris as planned and, after making concert appearances in early 1965, disappeared from view entirely, although for his funeral more than five thousand people lined the streets of Harlem. The story of Powell's Paris stay and fateful return to the USA formed the basis for the screenplay of the film *Round Midnight*.

Herman Leonard

Bud Powell

Like his painful personal history, Powell's music parallels that of Charlie Parker. In Powell's case, his roots in pianists Teddy Wilson, Nat "King" Cole and his particular favourite, Billy Kyle, are discernible in his earliest recordings and in the famous Massey Hall concert of 1953. His interpretation of ballads was often indebted to Art Tatum, but it was the intensity of his uptempo right-hand lines that was unique. John Stevens once said metaphorically of Powell that "He almost plays off the end of the piano", and there is a sense in which much of what he expressed, especially in the late 1940s, would have seemed more appropriate on a harsh-toned saxophone. Indeed, his glittering personal sound and brilliant percussive attack were the nearest thing to a piano equivalent of Parker's emotional message and instrumental authority. For this reason, his left hand was often most useful when at its most sparse, as was also true of Kyle and Cole, although Powell's rhythmic interaction with bass and drums was seldom understood by antagonists of bebop. Nevertheless, he was the single most influential pianist of the period 1945–60, and has clearly marked the work of most players since then.

It must be said that Powell's command of the instrument was always more or less impaired during the last decade of his life, and only imperfectly reflected in his earlier work. But there is often a subsidiary intensity caused by the diminished means of expression, which results in an even clearer distillation of his melodic gift. Equally, many of his compositions, such as "Dance Of The Infidels" of 1949, or "Hallucinations" (aka "Budo", performed by the Miles Davis band in 1948–9 but only recorded by Powell in 1951), merely crystallize his improvisational style, and these have entered the general repertoire. A few are more ambitious, however: the driving mambo "Un Poco Loco" of 1951 and the macabre and haunting "Glass Enclosure" of 1953 are unlikely to be satisfactorily reproduced by other performers. The same may be said of his improvisation which, for all its wide influence, has an emotional atmosphere impossible to duplicate. [BP]

The Amazing Bud Powell: Vol. 1 (1949–51; Blue Note). Beginning with the session which introduced both "Dance Of The Infidels" and an eighteen-year-old Sonny Rollins (with Fats Navarro too), this includes a bit of Tatum-oriented balladry and concludes with the furious "Un Poco Loco".

The Genius of Bud Powell (1950–1; Verve). Opening with a trio set, this progresses to an exhaustive and exhausting solo session, including "Hallucinations", "Parisian Thoroughfare" (later covered by Max Roach-Clifford Brown) and an impossible "Just One Of Those Things".

The Amazing Bud Powell: Vol. 2 (1953; Blue Note). This is all trio music apart from a couple of unaccompanied ballad items, and (as well as some recently discovered out-takes) it contains the unique, through-composed "Glass Enclosure". It is probably necessary to absorb the above material before the fitful beauty of Powell's later work becomes apparent.

➤➤ **Fats Navarro** *(Bird And Fats – Live At Birdland);* **Charlie Parker** *(Jazz At Massey Hall).*

Mel Powell

Piano, composer.
b. New York, 12 Feb 1923; d. 24 April 1998.

Mel Powell's "underground" reputation in mid-period jazz is gigantic: his short, phenomenal career is remembered with awe and his comparatively few records are constantly reissued. A pianist of limitless and versatile technique, Powell played intermission piano at Nick's club while still in his teens, worked for Muggsy Spanier's big band soon after, and in the summer of 1941 auditioned for Benny Goodman at MCA (at George T. Simon's instigation). "I get more kicks out of Mel's playing than any other pianist in the business," said Simon, and Goodman was soon in agreement. By 1942 Powell was a staffman for Raymond Scott at CBS (along with a second pianist, Sanford Gold), and the year after he joined Glenn Miller; in 1944 he came to Britain with Miller's AEF band, where he featured with Miller's Uptown Hall Gang and broadcast for the BBC on *Piano Party* programmes. When he came back to the USA he spent a brief spell in Hollywood studios, then went to Yale to study composition with Paul Hindemith and piano with Nadia Reisenberg; from there he graduated to teach theory at Queens College and composition at Yale, and by 1959 had been awarded a Guggenheim fellowship. Powell's compositions (including a harpsichord concerto for Ferdinand Valenti) became familiar items on American concert programmes, and in the 1970s he was Dean of Music at the California Institute of Arts. Powell's return to jazz recorded in the mid-1950s produced classic albums with Ruby Braff and Paul Quinichette; ten years on he could be spotted sitting in with Bobby Hackett in Connecticut. In 1986 Powell was heard again, playing for jazz cruises with cornettist Warren Vaché and others; in 1987 he recorded for Chiaroscuro, but by 1994 was inactive through illness. [DF]

Borderline/Thingamagig (1954; Vanguard). Very important Powell sessions, teaming him with Ruby Braff plus Bobby Donaldson on *Thingamagig*, and with Lester Young soundalike Paul Quinichette on *Borderline*. An essential double.

Easy Swing (1955; Vanguard). Less well known than the above but very good nevertheless; the underrated John Glasel is on trumpet in a fine band led by Nat Pierce.

The Return Of Mel Powell (1987; Chiaroscuro). With a quintet completed by Benny Carter, Howard Alden, Milt Hinton and Louie Bellson, this was a second historic return to recording for Powell.

Richie Powell

Piano, arranger.
b. New York, 5 Sept 1931; d. 26 June 1956.

Richie, the younger brother of Bud Powell, began practising with his near neighbour Jackie McLean. He toured with the R&B saxophonist Paul Williams in 1952 and with the Johnny Hodges small band from 1953–4. During the last two years of his life, he began to reach musical maturity as a member of the Max Roach-Clifford Brown quintet. His only featured recordings were with this group, including a last session under Sonny Rollins's name, and, although they demonstrate a certain lack of fluency, this is amply compensated by his interesting ideas and very individual sound. McCoy Tyner said, "I was impressed by the harmonies Richard Powell used to play and by his use of the sustaining pedal on chords." In fact, the chords built up of fourths, which became a Tyner trademark ("quartal harmony" in the language of musical theorists), seem to have originated with Powell, who thus exercised a considerable longterm influence on the following generation. He died in the same car accident as Clifford Brown. [BP]

Sonny Rollins

Plus Four (1956; Prestige/OJC). In an exciting session which introduced Rollins's "Pent Up House" and "Valse Hot", Powell's previously hesitant playing is carried forward on the surging energy of Clifford Brown and Max Roach, especially in the exultant "I Feel A Song Coming On".

Rudy Powell

Alto saxophone, clarinet.
b. New York, 28 Oct 1907; d. 30 Oct 1976.

Rudy (Everard Stephen) Powell was well known around New York by 1928, when he joined Cliff Jackson's Krazy Kats for three years. After that he worked with a variety of bands before starting a regular partnership with Fats Waller, live and on record (1934–7). Much of the next twelve years he spent in big bands: Teddy Wilson (1939–40), Don Redman, Eddie South, Claude Hopkins, Cab Calloway (1945–8) and Lucky Millinder (1948–50). During the 1950s he worked with Jimmy Rushing and Benton Heath before spending years in the 1960s with Ray Charles and latterly the Saints and Sinners, which starred Herman Autrey and Vic Dickenson. In his last years he freelanced around New York. [DF]

Chano Pozo

Percussion, vocals.
b. Havana, Cuba, 7 Jan 1915; d. New York, 2 Dec 1948.

Luciano Pozo y Gonzales derived his musical background and knowledge from Cuban religious cults, and by the early 1940s was a noted player and composer, some of his material being covered by the Machito band. When he moved to New York and was introduced to Dizzy Gillespie in 1947, the latter added him to his big band for a historic fifteen-month collaboration. In works like Gillespie's "Algo Bueno" (aka "Woody'n You") and George Russell's "Afro-Cuban Suite (Cubana Be – Cubana Bop)", the latter a feature for Pozo, his contribution to the ensemble laid the foundation for the development of Latin jazz and for the jazz work of Candido, Mongo Santamaria and others. He was given co-composer credit on Gillespie's jazz standards "Manteca" and "Tin Tin Deo", the latter recorded with James Moody just five weeks before Pozo's murder by shooting in a Harlem bar. [BP]

➤➤ **Dizzy Gillespie** *(Pleyel '48).*

Pérez Prado

Piano, composer.

b. Matanzas, Cuba, 11 Dec 1916; d. Mexico City, 14 Sept 1989.

Starting out as a teenage pianist in Havana's Casino De La Playa band, Prado moved to Mexico in 1948. His simplified recordings of the Cuban mambo were successful throughout Latin America ("Mambo Jambo", "Caballo Negro" and others); released for the US Hispanic market, they crossed over to the pop market. He toured the West Coast in 1951 with a band that included trumpeter Pete Candoli and Mongo Santamaria, and later in the 1950s he worked in Argentina and Spain, adding local brass players to his line-up. From the mid-1950s on, Prado's only hits were the schmaltzy "Cherry Pink" and the nugatory "Patricia", but his early work reached a wide public not yet ready for Machito. [BP]

⊙ **Mambo Mania/Havana 3 a.m.** (1949–56; Bear Family). Beware the compilation of inferior remakes called *King Of Mambo*, and instead look for this two-LPs-on-one-CD beginning with five of Prado's Mexican recordings. One of these contains a direct quote from Gillespie's "Ray's Idea" (unfortunately titled "Mambo A La Kenton"!), while the West Coast material veers from "Cherry Pink" to adaptations of big-band hits to several Latin standards, such as "Besame Mucho", and variable originals.

Pérez Prado

Gerard Presencer

Flugelhorn and trumpet.

b. Watford, Herts, UK, 12 Sept 1972.

His father is a jazz fan, but Presencer had no musical education. He was the youngest trumpet player with NYJO, which he joined at the age of eleven. He began playing professionally at fourteen, and was soon working with Tommy Smith, Stan Tracey, John Dankworth, Julian Joseph and Jason Rebello. Internationally, he played with Johnny Griffin, Phil Woods, Joe Sample and Niels-Henning Ørsted Pedersen. Presencer won the Best Trumpeter category at the British Jazz Awards three times, has recorded four albums with the Charlie Watts quintet, and was featured soloist (and sounding amazingly like Freddie Hubbard) on Blue Note's biggest-selling release, "Cantaloop" by US3. Presencer's own debut album, *Platypus*, was released in 1998.

He is also much in demand as a session musician and has played commercially with Sting, James Brown, Ray Charles, Tina Turner, Incognito, Kula Shaker and the Pet Shop Boys, among others. Teaching has become an important part of his work in recent years, and he is a member of staff at London's Guildhall School and the Royal Academy of Music. He was recently appointed professor in Berlin, at the Hochschule für Musik "Hanns Eisler". His favourites include Tom Harrell, Miles, Kenny Wheeler, Hubbard, Woody Shaw, Herbie Hancock and Coltrane. [IC]

⊙ **Platypus** (1998; Linn). Presencer's group in this impressive debut is a quintet of British young lions – Jason Rebello, John Parricelli, Andrew Cleyndert and drummer Jeremy Stacey. Presencer composed seven of the pieces, which range from fusion outings to straight jazz performances, and he plays flugelhorn throughout with virtuoso skill and artistry. The rhythm-section is magnificent and there are fine solos all round.

André Previn

Piano, conductor.

b. Berlin, 6 April 1929.

Previn's family moved to the USA when he was nine, and his father (Charles Previn) became the musical director for the *Flash Gordon* serial and other Hollywood films. André was frequently active as a jazz pianist, especially in the mid-1940s (he made his recording debut at the age of sixteen) and mid-1950s. He wrote and conducted for films, and for singers including Ella Fitzgerald. From the 1960s he became an internationally celebrated symphonic conductor and television personality, and since the late 1980s he has made several new jazz albums with Ray Brown. [BP]

⊙ **Plays Songs by Vernon Duke** (1958; Contemporary/OJC). As well as a reminder that Duke wrote at least five well-known standards (eg "I Can't Get Started", "April In Paris"), this unaccompanied session is a reminder of the time Previn was a jazz pianist of considerable imagination.

➤➤ **Shelly Manne** *(My Fair Lady).*

Bobby Previte

Drums, composer.

b. Niagara Falls, 16 July 1957.

After moving to New York in 1980, Bobby Previte swiftly established himself as a leading figure in the city's "Downtown" scene, collaborating with the likes of John Zorn, Wayne Horvitz, Bill Frisell and Elliott Sharp on a range of projects. His own music, first recorded by the European label Sound Aspects in the mid-1980s, betrays a lively amalgam of influences, ranging from minimalism to film music, but always contains a bustling, jazz-based energy at its core, whether it be his music for the Moscow Circus (recorded for Gramavision in 1990), more overtly straightahead fare such as his band Weather Clear, Track Fast's eponymous debut album (1991), or his more electronically oriented music for the band Empty Suits. The last group could function as a quintet featuring Jerome Harris (guitar and bass), Michael Cain and Steve Gaboury (keyboards) and trumpeter Herb Robertson, but recorded using various permutations of the pool of musicians with whom Previte works.

Previte himself is not interested in categorization – "I couldn't give two cents whether it's called jazz or anything. Music separates; that's the way of the modern world" – and his later 1990s recordings, particularly *Too Close To The Pole* (1996; Enja), which uses an extraordinary variety of instruments, from Lindsey Horner's tin whistles and Tamie Saft's assorted keyboards to Cuong Vu's trumpet and Curtis Hasselbring's trombone, not to mention the various reeds of Andy Laster and Andrew D'Angelo, to create highly unusual yet compellingly propulsive soundscapes, defy any attempt at neat pigeonholing. Indeed Previte's band Latin For Travelers, which toured extensively in 1997 and made a live album in Australia, *My Man In Sydney* (Enja), was variously described as playing avant-rock and as "a basic bar band". In the same year, Previte started a record label, Depth of Field, and its first two albums documented a series of lightning, duo improvisations with John Zorn (*Euclid's Nightmare*) and a quartet session involving old associates Zorn, keyboard player Wayne Horvitz and guitarist Elliott Sharp. As his prolific output continues into the new century and barely seems to dip in quality, in many ways, Previte is the archetypal millennial jazz musician: open-eared, adventurous, uncategorizable, technically flawless. [CP]

Claude's Late Morning (1988; Gramavision). Featuring Ray Anderson and Bill Frisell, a thoughtful, densely textured album of great controlled power and energy.

Empty Suits (1990; Gramavision). Exuberant, buoyantly optimistic album packed with incident and subtly shifting textures. Guitarists Allan Jafee and Elliott Sharp are strongly featured, and one piece, "Great Wall", is dedicated to composer John Adams.

Hue And Cry (1994; Enja). Subtle, intelligent but highly enjoyable album from the Weather Clear, Track Fast band, featuring reeds players Don Byron and Marty Ehrlich, pianist Anthony Davis and bassist Anthony Cox, among others.

The 23 Constellations Of Joan Miró (2002; Tzadik). Remarkable set of miniatures for jazz group, harp and electronics, inspired by the work of Catalan artist Miró, featuring Lew Soloff and Ralph Alessi on dual trumpets among much else of fascination.

Counterclockwise (2003; Palmetto). A funky, belligerent smorgasbord whose invention and interplay doesn't let up for a moment. Featuring the stellar group of bassist Steve Swallow, tenorist Marty Ehrlich, pianist Wayne Horvitz and trombonist Curtis Fowlkes.

Eddie Prévost

Drums, percussion.

b. Hitchin, Hertfordshire, UK, 22 June 1942.

Prévost began as a teenager in traditional jazz bands, and later worked in "imitation hard-bop groups". In 1965 he co-founded AMM, a free-improvising group, with Lou Gare and Keith Rowe, later to be joined by Cornelius Cardew. AMM has continued to perform over the years and has included at various times Christian Wolff, Christopher Hobbs, John Tilbury and Rohan de Saram. Since the early 1970s Prévost has also led a number of free jazz groups, including Larry Stabbins, Veryan Weston and Marcio Mattos. He is also a member of Supersession with Evan Parker, Keith Rowe and Barry Guy. His main influences are Max Roach and Ed Blackwell, and other inspirations are Sun Ra, Art Blakey, the Gagaku (ancient Japanese court music) and David Tudor. He also writes and lectures on improvisation and related subjects. [IC]

AMM

AMM Music 1966 (Matchless); **The Crypt – 12th June 1968** (Matchless). The late great Cornelius Cardew graced both of these sessions, doubling on piano and transistor radio for the first, and piano and cello for the second. Prévost and saxophonist Lou Gare are the heart and soul of these sessions of pristine improvised music.

Supersession

Supersession (1984; Matchless). Prévost alongside Evan Parker, guitarist Keith Rowe and Barry Guy results in this summit meeting of pioneers.

AMM

The Inexhaustible Document (1987; Matchless). Improvised music of subdued intensity, with cellist Rohan de Saram blending with more regular members Prévost, Rowe and Tilbury, to produce a music that's more a richly textured soundscape than a series of events.

Sammy Price

Piano, leader.

b. Honey Grove, Texas, 6 Oct 1908; d. 14 April 1992.

Price studied piano in Dallas, then joined local revues as a singer/dancer, was a Charleston dancer with Alphonso Trent's mighty band, and toured on the TOBA circuit from 1927–30. That year he arrived in Kansas City and spent three years soaking up the music of Count Basie, Pete Johnson and others, before moving on to Chicago and Detroit. In 1938 he was hired as house pianist for Decca in New York, accompanying singers such as Trixie Smith and Sister Rosetta Tharpe, making boogie sides of his own (unlike many of his contemporaries, Price was versatile enough to survive the boogie phase) and leading his own band: a 1940 Decca date featuring his Texas Bluesicians (including Don Stovall and Emmett Berry) shows where Price was happiest to operate. After studio work slowed he began a busy career on 52nd Street (playing the Famous Door and Café Society), organized the first black-administered jazz festival (Philadelphia, 1946), and visited the Nice festival in 1948 with Mezz Mezzrow, who called him "the finest blues pianist I know". After some years back in Texas, Price returned to New York to work with Henry "Red" Allen at the Metropole (he was also the Metropole's unofficial bouncer) and for the next ten years partnered Allen, while also leading various teams of Bluesicians at home and in Europe. As well as being a premier blues pianist, in his spare time he ran a succession of companies (latterly Down Home Meat Products) and took part in local politics and community policing (as an honorary captain in the New York Police auxiliary); at various times he was also an undertaker, nightclub owner (twice), photographer and PR man. [DF]

⊙ **Sammy Price** (1929–41; Classics). Dating mainly from 1940–41, these tracks feature solo work from Don Stovall, Joe Brown and Lester Young, in addition to the leader.

⊙ **Blues And Boogie** (1955; Vogue). One of Price's best from the mid-1950s, this has the added bonus of the great Emmett Berry on trumpet amid a rolling blues band.

⊙ **Barrelhouse And Blues** (1969; Black Lion). A fine set, produced by Alan Bates and featuring an on-form Keith Smith, the immaculate Roy Williams, and Sandy Brown in one of his later – and most effective – settings.

⊙ **Fire** (1975; Black and Blue). With a hard-hitting and basic blues band – featuring Gene Connors, Ted Buckner and the great Doc Cheatham – this set mixes piano features with band titles in equal measure.

➤➤ **Henry "Red" Allen** *(Feelin' Good).*

Julian Priester

Trombone.

b. Chicago, 29 June 1935.

Priester took piano lessons at the age of ten for a year; he later studied baritone horn and trombone at Du Sable High School. His early influences were J.J. Johnson, Charlie Parker, Sonny Rollins, Thelonious Monk and Dizzy Gillespie. From 1953–8 he worked with Sun Ra, Lionel Hampton, Dinah Washington and others. He moved to New York in the summer of 1958, working with Max Roach and Slide Hampton, and continued with Max Roach in the early 1960s, when the band included Eric Dolphy, Clifford Jordan and Booker Little. He freelanced in New York during the rest of the decade, including a six-month stint with Duke Ellington. From 1970–73 he worked with the Herbie Hancock sextet, touring in the USA and Europe and playing major festivals. He moved to San Francisco in the mid-1970s, freelancing there and experimenting with electronic sounds and effects. In the early 1980s he was playing acoustically with the Dave Holland quintet, which included Kenny Wheeler, touring extensively in the USA and Europe. Priester left the group in 1985, and recorded again with Sun Ra in the late 1980s. [IC]

➤➤ **Billy Harper** *(Capra Black);* **Dave Holland** *(Jumpin' In);* **Booker Little** *(Out Front);* **Max Roach** *(We Insist!: Freedom Now Suite).*

Brian Priestley

Piano, arranger, writer.

b. Manchester, UK, 10 July 1940.

After studying music from the age of eight and modern languages at university, Priestley lived in Oxford from the mid-1960s, accompanying visiting soloists and arranging for the National Youth Jazz Orchestra. In 1970 he moved to London, gigging and broadcasting with bands led by Tony Faulkner and Alan Cohen. He has transcribed Ellington scores for Cohen (including *Black, Brown and Beige*, recorded in 1972, with Priestley on piano), the New York Jazz Repertory Orchestra and Lincoln Center Jazz Orchestra. He has also prepared transcriptions for the Midnite Follies Orchestra, Stan Tracey and classical pianist Katia Labèque, and has

Noel Chay

Brian Priestley

published six anthologies of piano transcriptions (IMP 1982–90). Priestley led his own sextet/septet 1980–1999, plays solo piano and in various duos and formed a new quartet in 2003.

He taught jazz piano at Goldsmiths' College for seventeen years, ran jazz workshops, and acted as jazz history tutor for various universities. A prolific contributor to periodicals since the mid-1960s, Priestley wrote biographies of Mingus, Parker and Coltrane in the 1980s, plus *Jazz On Record* (Elm Tree Books, 1988). From 1971–88 he hosted an influential weekly programme on BBC Radio London and has contributed to Jazz FM and, more recently, BBC Radio 3. [CA]

Brian Priestley

You Taught My Heart To Sing (1994; Spirit Of Jazz). On this largely solo piano album (Don Rendell joins him on saxophones or flute on five tracks), featuring a dozen compositions by other jazz pianists (from Duke Ellington to Bill Evans, Horace Silver and Stan Tracey), Priestley confirms his status as an outstanding, expressive solo performer.

Louise Gibbs and Brian Priestley

Love You Madly (1999; 33 Jazz). A vocal tribute to Ellington, with just voice and piano (abetted by Tony Coe on seven tracks), reveals Priestley's feeling for Ducal textures without direct imitation.

Brian Priestley

Who Knows? (2003; 33 Jazz). The latest and perhaps best offering in Priestley's ongoing preoccupation with Duke, this collection of connoisseurs' Ellington and Strayhorn is a treasure trove. Lesser-known gems (an unheard sketch and a discarded blues from the Far East Suite period, an underscore theme from *Anatomy Of A Murder*) juxtapose original rearrangements of "Lotus Blossom" and "Johnny Come Lately" and the band (Priestley – piano, Frank Griffith – saxes, Bruce Adams – trumpet, Simon Woolf – bass and Steve Brown – drums) perform splendidly.

➤➤ **Alan Cohen** *(Duke Ellington's Black, Brown And Beige).*

Louis Prima

Trumpet, vocals.

b. New Orleans, 7 Dec 1911; d. 24 Aug 1978.

Younger brother of Leon Prima, one of the best New Orleans trumpeters, by 1923 Louis Prima was the natural leader of a New Orleans "kids' band" (it featured a ten-year-old Irving Prestopnik, whom Prima re-christened Fazola) and was making connections all around the French Quarter. An irresistible performer and exuberant frontman, Prima worked in Cleveland, Ohio (with Red Nichols), recorded in Chicago (as the "Hotcha Trio" with pianist David Rose, 1933) and arrived in New York in 1935 to headline at the Famous Door, where his husky vocals and musical partnership with Pee Wee Russell created a sensation: society columnists such as Walter Winchell wrote him up, he had a coast-to-coast radio show, *Swing It* (one of Prima's several catchphrases), and the club became the hub of 52nd Street. After the Mafia moved in on Prima he moved out and opened his own Famous Door in Hollywood with comedian Red Colonna: there his success was just as spectacular and by 1937 he was filming with Alice Faye (*You Can't Have Everything*), writing hits like "Sing Sing Sing", and touring with his own big swing orchestra (featuring Russell and Sal Franzella).

All through the 1940s Prima's big-band success continued: he recorded hits including "There, I've Said It Again", "One Mint Julep" and "Angelina", and with the aid of a shrewd manager, Barbara Belle, weathered the big-band decline until 1954. That year he began his high-powered jazz-cum-rock'n'roll cabaret act with wife Keely Smith, Sam Butera and the Witnesses (featuring James Blounty on trombone). It scored his biggest success yet on the New York, Chicago, Hollywood and Las Vegas circuits, but sometimes made people forget the fine jazz trumpeting (somewhere between Louis Armstrong and Jonah Jones) that adorns all but his very last records. Prima remained highly successful into the 1960s and that "hoarse horny voice of his" (Sam Weiss's description) was teamed with an old 52nd Street crony, Phil Harris, in Walt Disney's *Jungle Book* (1966): Prima's trumpet-playing on the soundtrack, just as much as his singing, is worth the price of a seat. His music was a profound influence on Acker Bilk's Paramount Jazz Band during its hit-making years. [DF]

Louis Prima Vol. 1 (1934–5; JSP). Featuring a mixture of New Orleans men and New York swing musicians, this collection has Prima on top form on early hits including "Let's Swing It", "Let's Have A Jubilee" and "Swing Me With Rhythm"; expert remastering by John R.T. Davies.

The Versatile Mr. Prima – Trumpet, Vocal And Hits (2000; Jasmine). Worthwhile collation of Prima's 1940s work mingling rhythm and blues hits like "Hey!Ba-Ba-Re-Bop" with novelties like "Felicia, No Capicia" and "Josephina, Please No Leana On The Bell!"

Marcus Printup

Trumpet, composer.

b. Conyers, Georgia, 24 Jan 1967.

Strongly influenced by church music as a child, Marcus Printup also played in various marching and concert bands at high school before attending the Georgia State University in Atlanta, subsequently transferring to the University of North Florida in Jacksonville. After winning the National Collegiate Jazz Competition and the Thelonious Monk International Trumpet Competition in 1991, he met up with pianist Marcus Roberts and road managed his US tour in 1992, joining him on stage, and finally becoming a regular member of the band and recording *Blues For The New Millennium* (Columbia) with them in 1997. In addition to studio sideman work with drummer Carl Allen and fellow trumpeter Tim Hagans – a Freddie Hubbard tribute, *Subsongs* (1994; Blue Note) – Printup has also toured and recorded with the Lincoln Center Jazz Orchestra, appearing on Wynton Marsalis's epic *Blood On The Fields* (Columbia) in 1994. His own albums began with *Song For The Beautiful Woman* (see below), and continued with *Unveiled* (1996; Blue Note), featuring Roberts, tenor player Stephen Riley, bassist Reuben Rogers and drummer Jason Marsalis, and *Nocturnal Traces* (1998; Blue Note) with his then-regular quartet of pianist Kevin Bales, bassist Ricky Ravelo and drummer Woody Williams. A bright, agile player with an affecting tone, Printup is also a promising composer, though his latest offering, *The New Boogaloo* (see below), suggests that for all his strengths – and like many of his young lion contemporaries – he will be content with a twist on existing genres rather than stylistic innovation. [CP]

⊙ **Song For The Beautiful Woman** (1995; Blue Note). Sharing frontline duties with tenor player Walter Blanding, Printup brings verve and, occasionally, a burnished romanticism to a lively mix of standards ("I Remember April", "Speak Low") and originals, propelled by a sparky rhythm team: pianist Eric Reed, bassist Reuben Rogers, drummer Brian Blade.

⊙ **The New Boogaloo** (2002; Nagel Heyer). A tough and tidy updating of the soul jazz style on the excellent modern mainstream label, featuring the significant gifts of pianist George Colligan, trombonist Wycliffe Gordon and saxist Walter Blanding.

Bernie Privin

Trumpet.

b. Brooklyn, New York, 12 Feb 1919; d. 9 Oct 1999.

By 1938 Bernie Privin was attracting good reviews in the Tommy Dorsey and Bunny Berigan big bands, and his reputation grew with Artie Shaw, for whom Privin was a featured cornerman (his work can be heard on Shaw tracks such as "One Night Stand" and "My Heart Stood Still"). After a couple of stints with Charlie Barnet's informal and very successful big band, he spent time with Mal Hallett, Benny Goodman and Jerry Wald, before joining Glenn Miller's AEF band in 1943. Miller featured Privin's biting Armstrong-like solos both with the big band and as part of the Uptown Hall Gang, who had their own BBC radio show in Britain, but Privin found Miller's unblinking discipline hard to accept (especially when all band members wearing moustaches were ordered to shave them off) and was probably relieved to move into studio work. He joined NBC in 1946, then in 1950 moved to CBS, where he played for shows including Ed Sullivan's, Garry Moore's and Andy Williams's. From then on Privin's jazz gifts were heard more rarely, but in the 1970s he was a welcome addition to a Kings Of Jazz tour of Europe (with Pee Wee Erwin, Johnny Mince and others), and in the 1980s he was making the rounds of the jazz clubs and festivals. He remained active into the 1990s. [DF]

➤➤ **Kenny Davern** *(A Night With Eddie Condon).*

Glenn Miller

⊙ **Uptown Hall Gang** (1944–5; Esquire). Privin in Miller's peppy small group, with Peanuts Hucko, Mel Powell, Ray McKinley, etc.

Russell Procope

Alto saxophone, clarinet.

b. New York, 11 Aug 1908; d. 21 Jan 1981.

Procope grew up in a San Juan Hill household where records of Ted Lewis and Mamie Smith played, and went to school with Benny Carter. By 1929 he was playing in Carter's band, until his leader joined Fletcher Henderson, whereupon Procope joined Chick Webb: later, in a spectacular swap, their leaders exchanged sidemen and Procope worked for Henderson until 1934. He left (in the same period as Coleman Hawkins) at a time when Henderson's leadership was in question ("I got a bit disgusted"), then worked for Tiny Bradshaw, Teddy Hill and Willie Bryant before joining John Kirby's fleet sextet, replacing Pete Brown. With Kirby's band Procope's perfect playing found both its perfect expression and public recognition. In 1943 he followed Billy Kyle into the army and in 1946 joined Duke Ellington as one-fifth of Ellington's greatest-ever reed section. "Otto Hardwicke had wandered off and got lost and Duke didn't know where he would find him!" remembered Procope: he subbed one night for Ellington in Worcester and stayed 28 years. In Ellington's orchestra he found two congenial qualities: a bandleader he respected musically and professionally, and a featured role he enjoyed. "In Duke's band I could play more in the styles by which I had genuinely been influenced", he said. These included the deep, mellow aged-in-the-wood New Orleans-influenced clarinet sound that Ellington loved and featured on his 1950 "Mood Indigo" recording. "Why did I stay 28 years? Because I loved the music! Besides which it was a chance to go round the world. Besides which it was security. To do what you like and get paid for it – isn't that what everybody wants? So I stayed with Duke until he died." In the 1970s Procope toured with Ellington scholar Brooks Kerr's trio: a living memorial to his late great leader. [DF]

➤➤ **Duke Ellington** *(Ellington At Newport); John Kirby (The John Kirby Sextet).*

Clarence Profit

Piano.

b. New York, 26 June 1912; d. 22 Oct 1944.

Profit was a schoolfriend of Edgar Sampson, with whom he wrote the harmonically adventurous song "Lullaby In Rhythm". He led his own big band during his late teens, and then worked with Teddy Bunn in the Washboard Serenaders from 1930–31. His own trio, continuously employed from 1936 until his death, may have been the first to use the piano-guitar-bass format popularized by Nat "King" Cole. Much admired by pianists of his own generation, but now virtually forgotten, he employed the innovations of Tatum in a less overpowering and more straightahead style. [BP]

⊙ **Solo And Trio Sides Plus** (1930–40; Memoir). This valuable reissue collects all the material from the two 1939–40 sessions Profit recorded with his influential trio, and adds four tracks from his session work with washboard bands. The later work demonstrates why Profit was so highly rated by people such as Teddy Wilson and Oscar Peterson.

"Pucho"

Timbales, percussion.
b. New York, 1 Nov 1938.

Henry Lee Brown acquired his nickname with self-taught imitations of his favourite musician, Tito Puente, and then played timbales professionally from the age of sixteen with bands such as Joe Panama in Harlem and the Bronx. Forming his own group in 1959 with an augmented rhythm-section including vibes, he appeared at venues such as Count Basie's club and a 1966 festival date at Carnegie Hall. From 1966–74 he made several albums for Prestige, who named his band The Latin Soul Brothers because their repertoire went from R&B to boogaloo; during the same period he recorded with George Benson, Lonnie Smith and Gene Ammons. The late 1970s to 1980s were spent with a trio at Catskill Mountain resorts, until the acid-jazz movement in Britain and Japan led to a re-formed band visiting these countries in 1993. Since then, he has made several new albums and his early material has been reissued. [BP]

⊙ **Rip-A-Dip** (1995; Milestone). Pucho's first new US recording in decades reunites former sidemen Al and Ed Pazant on trumpet and reeds, Bill Bivens on vibes and John Spruill on piano and organ. The material includes Latin originals as well as jazz classics such as "Caravan" and "Milestones".

Tito Puente

Percussion, vibes, piano, arranger.
b. New York, 23 April 1920; d. 31 May 2000.

Tito (Ernestito Antonio) Puente, born of Puerto Rican parents, hoped to be a professional dancer until halted by injury. In the navy in World War II, he became interested in big-band music and studied briefly at the Juilliard. From 1945–7 he played with Noro Morales, Machito and others, and then formed his own Piccadilly Boys. Resident at New York's Palladium in the 1950s along with the Machito and Tito Rodriguez groups, the Puente band brought the mambo and later the cha-cha to great artistic heights. He recorded more than a hundred albums, including three jazz-inclined sessions in the 1950s (one with Woody Herman), and after breaking up his big band in 1981, formed a Latin Percussion Jazz Ensemble which continues to tour. His compositions "Para Los Rumberos" and "Oye Como Va", covered by Carlos Santana in the early 1970s, are Latin jazz standards. [BP]

⊙ **Top Percussion/Dance Mania** (1957; Bear Family). Without any obvious attempt to import foreign jazz elements, Puente shows how aware of jazz values his brand of salsa music was. *Dance Mania* is the classic Latin band with flaring brass, while *Top Percussion* is more like a companion piece to Art Blakey's contemporary *Orgy In Rhythm*.

Dudu Pukwana

Alto and soprano saxophones, piano, composer, vocals.
b. Port Elizabeth, South Africa, 18 July 1938; d. London, 28 June 1990.

Pukwana's father was a pianist and vocalist, his mother a singer. Self-taught with the exception of some lessons from his father, Dudu began on the piano at six, then at eighteen started on saxophone. In 1962 he played with his own group, Jazz Giants, at the Johannesburg jazz festival and was awarded the prize for Best Saxophonist of the Year. The white pianist Chris McGregor formed his band the Blue Notes from the best musicians at that festival, with Pukwana on alto, Mongezi Feza (trumpet), Nick Moyake (tenor), Johnny Dyani (bass) and Louis Moholo (drums). Under apartheid, racially mixed groups were illegal and it became impossible for the Blue Notes to work together, so in 1964 they left for Europe, where they played at the Antibes jazz festival, in Paris and in Switzerland, eventually arriving in London, which they made their home after appearing at Ronnie Scott's club. Pukwana began to work with a diversity of British groups, including Keith Tippett's Centipede and the Incredible String Band, while continuing to write and play with the Blue Notes.

In 1970 McGregor enlarged his band, calling it the Brotherhood of Breath, and Pukwana also composed for this ensemble. The Brotherhood toured Britain and Europe, playing many major festivals. They also recorded the soundtrack for the film of Wole Soyinka's *Kongi's Harvest*. In 1969 Dudu started his own kwela band, Spear, and toured in South Africa, where he began a collaboration with trumpeter Hugh Masekela and trombonist Jonas Gwangwa. They played together in the USA and recorded as the African Explosion. Back in the UK, he formed a band called Assagai, featuring black musicians from South Africa and elsewhere, and continued to work with reggae bands, as well as with freer jazz improvisers such as Han Bennink, Misha Mengelberg, John Surman and Mike Osborne. In 1977 he took Spear to Nigeria for Festac, the international festival of black arts held in Lagos. In 1978 he formed a new group, Zila, which toured and played major festivals all over the UK and Europe. Most of the Spear/Zila music was composed by Pukwana, and some of his best compositions were on the album *Blue Notes In Concert Vol. 1*.

Dudu Pukwana and his African associates made an immense contribution to the British (and European) jazz scene, infusing it with a sense of urgency and purpose, reinvigorating the music with fiery improvisation and exultant rhythms beautifully executed, and inspiring successive generations of young British musicians. Pukwana's favourites were Ben Webster, Ornette Coleman and Archie Shepp, and he also gained inspiration from the members of Zila, Chris McGregor, Dave Holland, Count Basie, Dollar Brand (Abdullah Ibrahim), Ahmad Jamal and others. [IC]

SPEAR

⊙ **In The Townships** (1973; Earthworks/Virgin). Pukwana's quintet playing classic Afro/jazz with kwela rhythms, vocals, added percussion and hard-bop overtones.

➤➤ **Johnny Dyani** *(Witchdoctor's Son; Song for Biko); John Stevens (Mbizo Radebe).*

Don Pullen

Piano, organ, composer.

b. Roanoke, Virginia, 25 Dec 1944; d. 22 April 1995.

Pullen came from a musical family, and studied with Muhal Richard Abrams and reedman Giuseppe Logan, with whom he made his recording debut in 1964. He worked with his own groups and in a duo with Milford Graves, producing self-distributed duo albums. During the same period he played in many R&B groups, mostly on the organ, and backed singers such as Big Maybelle and Ruth Brown. He also worked with Nina Simone in 1970–71 and briefly with Art Blakey in 1974. He was a member of the Charles Mingus quintet from 1973–5, and then began touring in his own right, including annual visits to Europe from 1976–9. From 1979–88 he co-led a quartet with George Adams, touring internationally and making several albums. After that he led his own groups again, including his African-Brazilian Connection featuring Carlos Ward, and recorded and toured as a soloist. He also recorded with Kip Hanrahan, the "supergroups" Conjure and Roots, John Scofield, Maceo Parker and David Murray.

As well as his great versatility, Pullen had a comprehensive technique that attracted attention in whatever setting he appeared. Even when playing within relatively conventional structures, he was fond of rapid right-hand clusters which, though less percussive than Cecil Taylor's, were more flowing and equally exciting. [BP]

⊙ **The Sixth Sense** (1985; Black Saint). Fronting a quintet including Donald Harrison and the underrated Olu Dara on trumpet, Pullen's compositions take the group to many different places and his improvisations are invariably the most gripping contribution.

⊙ **Random Thoughts** (1990; Blue Note). Again Pullen's original material covers a lot of ground, from "Andre's Ups And Downs", with its almost Jamalesque rhythms and Tayloresque right hand, to the unaccompanied "Ode To Life", which begins and ends as a piece of pseudo-Brahms.

Colin Purbrook

Piano, double bass, arranger, composer.

b. Seaford, Sussex, UK, 26 Feb 1936; d. 5 Feb 1999.

Purbrook was one of the UK's premier pianists from the 1950s to the 1990s. He learned the piano from the age of six and, after leaving Cambridge in 1957, joined Sandy Brown and Al Fairweather. A stylistically comprehensive musician, Purbrook worked equally effortlessly with players ranging from Brown to Tubby Hayes, appearing in the film *All Night Long* (1961) and leading the trio for the *Beyond The Fringe* review (1963). He also played bass at various times for Dudley Moore and Brian Lemon.

Working regularly as a freelancer thereafter, Purbrook was also musical director for the West End successes *Bubbling Brown Sugar* (1977), *One Mo' Time* (1981), as well as *Lady Day* (1987), and *Rent Party* (1989), while continuing to lead his own trio. As a soloist he was under-recorded, a trio album appearing just before his death. [DF]

⊙ **My ideal** (1996; Trio). A thoroughly overdue showcase for Purbrook's calm, clear playing amid a trio completed by Colin Oxley (guitar) and Andrew Cleyndert (double bass).

Bernard Purdie

Drums.

b. Elkton, Maryland, 11 June 1939.

Purdie started playing from the age of six but didn't possess his own drumset until he was fifteen, when he began leading a country-and-western band in high school. After attending Morgan State College, he moved to New York in 1960 and studied with Sticks Evans, who improved his reading and versatility. He became involved in studio work, recording with such as James Brown (several sessions from 1966–8), and was also favoured by producers such as Bob Thiele, Creed Taylor and Bob Porter. This led to dates with Albert Ayler, Dizzy Gillespie, Louis Armstrong, Oliver Nelson, Hank Crawford, Gato Barbieri and many others, as well as touring with King Curtis in 1970 and becoming Aretha Franklin's musical director (1971–6). He also played live with Gillespie in the 1980s and made annual tours and recordings in Europe in the late 1990s. Nicknamed "Pretty" because of his surname, Purdie laid the groundwork for such studio monsters as Idris Muhammad and Steve Gadd, and his playing is effortlessly inspiring, whatever the context. [BP]

⊙ **Legends Of Acid Jazz** (1971; Prestige). A reissue of the albums *Purdie Good* and *Shaft*, featuring Houston Person on the title track of the latter and keyboardist Neal Creque and bassist Gordon Edwards throughout, with the drummer emphasizing the groove content more than the jazzy horn section.

➤➤ **Jimmy McGriff** *(The Starting Five).*

Flora Purim

Vocals, guitar, percussion.
b. Rio de Janeiro, 6 March 1942.

Purim's father was a violinist, her mother a classical pianist. From 1950–54 she had piano lessons and from 1954–8 guitar lessons, and also studied percussion with Airto Moreira, whom she married. She worked with the Brazilian group Quarteto Novo, which was co-led by Moreira and Hermeto Pascoal. She went to live in the USA in 1967, toured Europe with Stan Getz in 1968, and freelanced from 1969–70. In 1971 she worked regularly with the Gil Evans band, Chick Corea's group, and with Moreira. Both she and Moreira were with Joe Farrell and Stanley Clarke, members of Corea's first Return to Forever band, touring the USA, Europe and Japan with it, and recording two classic albums, *Return To Forever* and *Light As A Feather*. In 1973 Purim and Moreira left in order to start their own group, featuring her as soloist under his leadership, which combined elements from jazz, pop and Brazilian music in a rich mélange. In 1974 she began making her own solo albums. In 1974–5 she was imprisoned for over a year for a drugs charge that was never proven. In 1976 she again started working with Moreira, and has continued to do so, sometimes under her own name, sometimes in the group Fourth World. Her early inspirations were first Erroll Garner and then Miles Davis, Dinah Washington and Ella Fitzgerald. Her vocal range originally covered about three octaves but, under the guidance of Hermeto Pascoal, she has gradually increased it to six octaves. Flora Purim sings her own and others' lyrics, but also performs wordlessly, blending her voice (often aided by electronics) with other instruments. During the late 1980s and the 1990s, she and Moreira had regular residencies at Ronnie Scott's in London. [IC]

Flora Purim

⊙ **The Flight** (1989; B&W); **The Speed Of Light** (1994; B&W). Both these albums feature Purim with Moreira and other Brazilian (or world) musicians. The music is warm and buoyant both emotionally and rhythmically, and Purim is a most dynamic vocalist.

Fourth World

⊙ **Fourth World** (1992; Jazz House). Brazilian vocal and instrumental music which has melodic and rhythmic magic, with aesthetics and athletics in fine balance.

➤➤ **Chick Corea** *(Return To Forever; Light As A Feather).*

Alton Purnell

Piano, vocals.
b. New Orleans, 16 April 1911; d. 14 Jan 1987.

Alton Purnell was the pianist in Bunk Johnson's 1945 band and for the following twelve years was a mainstay of George Lewis's, providing the striding, raggy piano and vocals that Lewis loved to feature. In the late 1950s, after a move to California, he worked with Kid Ory and a variety of other West Coast-based leaders, including Joe Darensbourg, Teddy Buckner and (more surprisingly) Ben Pollack, before beginning a life of solo performing, which brought him to Europe many times (he also toured with packages such as the 1966 New Orleans All Stars). Purnell's industrious piano stride and jingling, jolly right-hand figures are set deep in the New Orleans tradition, his singing likewise. [DF]

⊙ **In Japan** (1976; GHB). A rare live session under Purnell's leadership, with an excellent team of Japanese New Orleans-style men including trumpeter Yoshio Toyama.

➤➤ **George Lewis** *(The George Lewis Ragtime Band of New Orleans: The Oxford Series Vols. 1–10).*

Jack Purvis

Trumpet, trombone, vocals, piano, multi-instrumentalist, composer.
b. Kokomo, Indiana, 11 Dec 1906; d. 30 March 1962.

The most generally remembered fact about Purvis is that in 1929 he had the chutzpah to record, for Tommy Rockwell and OKeh, a direct Louis Armstrong pastiche, "Copyin' Louis". Such a venture (at a period when Armstrong was at his technical best) suggests nerve as well as ability, and Purvis – "the swingin'est white trumpeter I ever heard", according to Rex Stewart – was loaded with both. In the disconnected periods of his life when he was actually involved with music full-time, Purvis repeatedly turns up playing brilliantly in unsurpassable company: sitting in with Fletcher Henderson's band to improvise fourth-trumpet parts (as difficult a task as it was a rare honour); recording a string of his own top-class compositions with an orchestra of his own (including such black heavyweights as Coleman Hawkins and J.C. Higginbotham, as well as Adrian Rollini); playing with Hal Kemp's orchestra (his replacement was Bunny Berigan); and – perhaps most incredibly of all – arranging for George Stoll and Warner Bros (one of his compositions, "Legends Of Haiti", was composed for a 110-piece orchestra). For many musicians any one of these achievements would have been the climax to a life in music: for Purvis, an uncommonly gifted "natural" performer, they were intermittent activities in a life of adventure and crime which involved, at various times, barefoot Alpine climbing (claimed Eddie Condon), smuggling contraband in a light plane, and fighting as a mercenary. In 1937 *Down Beat* published an article titled "What happened to Jack Purvis?"; the next year he was heard broadcasting from Texas State Penitentiary, playing his own compositions with a prison band. Purvis's later years are misty. For a long time it was thought that he was incarcerated in Georgia for second-degree murder and died in jail. Thanks to researcher Paul Larsen we now know that the corpse of an unemployed radio-repair man discovered in a gas-filled room in 1962 was that of Purvis. His life is still insufficiently researched, but it makes a ripping jazz yarn. [DF]

Louis Armstrong and Jack Purvis

Satchmo Style (1929–30; Parlophone). So far there is no Purvis on CD but this old vinyl album has eight of his best recordings.

Wolfgang Puschnig

Alto saxophone, other reeds, flute, piccolo.
b. Klagenfurt, Austria, 21 May 1956.

After beginning his musical life singing in a church choir, and coming into contact with Asian music at twelve, Wolfgang Puschnig gave his first public concert at fourteen, performing thereafter in dance bands, operetta and even circuses, as well as in more conventional jazz settings. Although he is still perhaps best known outside Austria for his work with the Vienna Art Orchestra (which he co-founded), and with Carla Bley's various outfits, Puschnig is a musical polymath, as at home playing freeish funk with bassist Jamaaladeen Tacuma, or exploring the relationship between music and speech with his wife, singer Linda Sharrock, as he is collaborating with Korean drummers Samul Nori, or reformulating Austrian folk forms with like-minded compatriots. His recordings as a sideman include fifteen albums with the VAO, six with Bley and a similar number with Sharrock, plus many dates with the likes of Michael Mantler, Hans Koller, Sigi Finkel and Nguyên Lê. His own albums (all on Amadeo) include the somewhat episodic but wide-ranging *Pieces Of The Dream* (1998), the brass-band-based *Alpine Aspects* (1991), the eclectic, hard-hitting *Mixed Metaphors* (1994), which featured rap from Antoine "Bun" Green alongside Sharrock and Tacuma, and the celebratory *Roots And Fruits* (see below) and the funky *Chants* (see below). Heard latterly in the quartet Grey alongside percussionist Don Alias, Puschnig is a fluent soloist with a sensitive but hard-edged, almost astringent sound. He received Austria's most prestigious jazz award, the Hans Koller Preis, in 1998. [CP]

Roots And Fruits (1996; Amadeo). Recorded during his fortieth birthday celebrations in Klagenfurt, this double CD documents all Puschnig's many, wide-ranging musical interests, from his Alpine Aspects project, through a standards band AM4, to funky trios and Korean band Samul Nori.

Chants (2002; Quinton). Blending Ornette-style jazz with unfolding R&B leanings and featuring the voice of wife Linda Sharrock, Puschnig's stated aim here was "to simplify, concentrate, go beyond concepts and create a peaceful, open space to step into."

Chris Pyne

Trombone, valve-trombone, piano.
b. Bridlington, Yorkshire, UK, 14 Feb 1939; d. 12 April 1995.

Pyne's father was a pianist, his brother Mick plays the piano and trumpet. He had childhood piano lessons, but was self-taught on trombone. In 1960–61 he was in an RAF band with John Stevens, Paul Rutherford and Trevor Watts. In 1963 he came to London, playing with various bands including those of Alexis Korner, Humphrey Lyttelton, John Dankworth, Ronnie Scott, Maynard Ferguson and Tubby Hayes; he did all of Sinatra's UK and Europe tours between 1970–83. Between 1967–79 he was with all Mike Gibbs's UK bands, and was with the John Taylor sextet from 1971–81. He toured with Gordon Beck in 1982. From 1965 he played with many Kenny Wheeler groups and was a member of John Surman's Brass Project from 1984–92. He also did much freelance work. Pyne was a world-class trombonist, a superb section player and outstanding soloist. He recorded with Dizzy Gillespie, Ella Fitzgerald, Sarah Vaughan, Mike Gibbs, Philly Joe Jones and others. His favourite trombonists were J.J. Johnson, Jimmy Knepper, Vic Dickenson, Frank Rosolino and Jack Teagarden. [IC]

➤➤ **John Surman** *(The Brass Project);* **Kenny Wheeler** *(Music For Large And Small Ensembles; Kayak).*

Mick Pyne

Piano, keyboards, trumpet.
b. Thornton-le-Dale, Yorkshire, UK, 2 Sept 1940; d. 24 May 1995.

Mick Pyne was self-taught, with some help from his father. He came to London in 1961 and played with Tony Kinsey's quintet until 1962. In 1965 he worked with Alexis Korner's Blues Incorporated, then from 1966–73 he was with the Tubby Hayes quintet. He joined the Humphrey Lyttelton band in 1972, staying for twelve years. Pyne always led his own groups – trios, quartets and bigger ensembles up to twelve-piece. He also worked with Hank Mobley, Joe Williams, Stan Getz, Philly Joe Jones, Roland Kirk, the Mike Gibbs orchestra, Dexter Gordon, the Ronnie Scott quintet and Georgie Fame's "Stardust Road" show (1983–5). In the late 1980s his trio accompanied the 85-year-old singer Adelaide Hall in some wonderfully dynamic club performances. Pyne recorded with many, including Michael Gibbs, Charles Tolliver, Philly Joe Jones and trumpeter John Eardley. His favourites were Art Tatum and Bill Evans and other influences were Louis Armstrong, Delius and John Coltrane. [IC]

➤➤ **Tubby Hayes** *(For Members Only; Live 1969);* **Humphrey Lyttelton** *(Movin' And Groovin').*

Severi Pyysalo

Vibraphone.
b. Finland, 19 Dec 1967.

Pyysalo started on drums at the age of six, and three years later he began his classical studies at the Conservatory of Turku. While there he discovered

the sonorities of the vibraphone and made it his first instrument. In 1982, he appeared at the Pori jazz festival, and two years later was invited to sit in with both Sarah Vaughan and Paquito D'Rivera, which did wonders for his reputation. In 1987 he began studies at the Sibelius Academy, and also began leading his own groups. His first was modelled largely on Mike Mainieri's Steps Ahead, but in 1989 Pyysalo founded another group, The Front, which leaned more towards Pat Metheny's bands. Eventually Pyysalo concentrated on The Poppoo, the ambitious group which he co-led with saxophonist Jukka Perko. The Poppoo have released three albums and appeared all over the world, including a three-week tour of Australia in 1995. Pyysalo has also performed with McCoy Tyner, Bobby Hutcherson, Frank Foster, Zoot Sims, James Newton, Bobby Bradford and Anders Jormin. In 1998 he released a duo album, *Turn Out The Stars*, with Danish pianist and composer Thomas Clausen. Pyysalo was awarded the annual European Jazz Soloist prize at the 1993 Leverkusener Jazztage, Germany, and the same year he was chosen as Jazz Artist of the Year in Finland. One of the world's leading vibraphonists, Pyysalo has also received commissions for symphonic works and TV music. [IC]

➤➤ **Jukka Perko** *(Varia).*

Ike Quebec

Tenor saxophone.

b. Newark, New Jersey, 17 Aug 1918; d. 16 Jan 1963.

Quebec began on piano, changing to tenor only in 1940. He played with bands such as those of Benny Carter, Coleman Hawkins and Roy Eldridge (in 1943), and then worked with the Cab Calloway band and small group from 1944–51. From "Cab Jiver" to cab-driver (literally), Ike was out of the music business for much of the 1950s. His comeback began in 1959, when he not only made records again, but became assistant musical director for the Blue Note label, responsible for producing Dexter Gordon and new discoveries. This dual career was cut short by lung cancer.

Quebec will be chiefly remembered for his two periods of recording under his own name. In the mid-1940s his Websterish style fronted some beautifully cohesive sessions, including the jukebox hit "Blue Harlem". Fifteen years later, with only a slightly harder edge to his sound, he demonstrated the close connections between his earlier music (by now called "mainstream") and the budding "soul jazz" movement. At his best Quebec was a moving performer, whose posthumous rediscovery has been amply justified. [BP]

⊙ **Blue And Sentimental** (1961; Blue Note). Most of his recordings being now unavailable except as compilation items, this representative album will suffice to win round any listener. With a typical rhythm-section including Grant Green, Quebec's big sound enlivens a couple of medium-bounce tunes and ballads such as "Don't Take Your Love From Me" and the Basie title track.

Paul Quinichette

Tenor saxophone.

b. Denver, Colorado, 17 May 1916; d. 25 May 1983.

Quinichette played with many territory bands, such as those of Nat Towles and Ernie Fields, and toured nationally with Jay McShann from 1942–4, replacing Jimmy Forrest. He worked on the West Coast with Johnny Otis in 1945–7, and then went to New York with the Louis Jordan group. He was a member of the Lucky Millinder band from 1948–9, Henry "Red" Allen's group and the Hot Lips Page septet in 1951, before joining the new Count Basie band for 1952–3. He led his own group for several years, but also worked briefly for Benny Goodman in 1955, Nat Pierce in 1957, and Billie Holiday. He left music in the 1950s, returning in 1973 with Sammy Price and Buddy Tate, before being restricted by ill health. Quinichette became known in the late 1940s and early 1950s as a Lester Young imitator (and sometimes as the "Vice-Pres"), when all the other contenders for this honour were white. Although he had the makings of an individual soloist of the Southwestern school, the reputation for being a clone clung to him too closely. [BP]

Various Artists

⊙ **Six Classic Tenors** (1952; EPM Musique). Like several of his sessions of the period, these four tracks have Quinichette with the Basie rhythm-section of the day plus a pianist (in this case Kenny Drew) in a seemingly casual but stylish brush with two blues and two ballads. The other five tenors are Byas, "Lockjaw" Davis, Hawk, Webster and John Hardee.

R

John Rae

Drums, composer.

b. Edinburgh, 8 June 1966.

Son of bassist Ronnie Rae (who worked with influential Scottish jazz player Alex Welsh during the late 1960s), John has a brother and four sisters who all play music. In 1983, aged sixteen, Rae performed on the debut album of the even younger Tommy Smith, and went on to work at home and abroad with a wide variety of musicians ranging from Martin Taylor to Spike Robinson, and Kenny Wheeler to Maria Schneider. In the late 1980s Rae, along with saxophonist Phil Bancroft, formed the fondly remembered sextet, the John Rae Collective, which recorded The Big If Smiles Again. A founding member of the Scottish Composer's Jazz Ensemble as well as playing for the Scottish National Jazz Orchestra, Rae leads the Power Of Scotland Big Band and in 1999 created the group Celtic Feet. Comprising Phil Bancroft, Brazilian bassist Mario Caribé, Brian Kellock on piano, concertina player Simon Thoumire and traditional fiddle player Eilidh Shaw, the group's exhilarating fusions have struck a chord with many different kinds of listeners. Rae is also the drummer for the Brian Kellock Trio. [BP]

⊙ **Beware The Feet** (2000; Caber). Retaining the distinctive concertina-and-fiddle lead of the first Celtic Feet album, plus saxophone (Phil Bancroft), piano (Brian Kellock), bass and drums, the line-up is used in different groupings and with a couple of guests. But the humorous original material goes from strength to strength.

➤➤ **Brian Kellock** *(Live At Henry's).*

Boyd Raeburn

Tenor, baritone and bass saxophones, leader.

b. Faith, South Dakota, 27 Oct 1913; d. 2 Aug 1966.

After leading dance bands from the age of twenty, Raeburn became interested in advanced swing and bop. In the mid-1940s, based first in New York and then Los Angeles, he employed as sidemen or guest stars Roy Eldridge, Trummy Young, Oscar Pettiford, Shelly Manne, Serge Chaloff, Dizzy Gillespie, Lucky Thompson and Dodo Marmarosa, among others. His key acquisition, perhaps, was pianist-arranger George Handy (b. 17 Jan 1920; d. 8 Jan 1997), who involved other advanced writers – as a result, Raeburn's band was the first to record Gillespie's "Night In Tunisia" – and himself wrote complex scores influenced by twentieth-century European music. Some of Raeburn's ever-changing personnel went on to work with Woody Herman but his popularity never matched theirs and his band reverted after the 1940s to more commercial fare. After recording such material in 1956–7, he retired from the music business. [BP]

⊙ **Boyd Meets Stravinsky** (1945–6; Savoy). A representative programme of Raeburn's key period, including "Night In Tunisia" and ambitious originals such as "Dalvatore Sally" and the title track, alongside a couple of vocal ballads sung against impossibly portentous arrangements.

Ma Rainey

Vocals.

b. Columbus, Georgia, 26 April 1886; d. 22 Dec 1939.

"Ma" Rainey (Gertrude Malissa Nix Pridgett) is appropriately named, for in historical terms she really was the "Mother of the Blues" – the recorded link between the "country" style of early blues performers and such sophisticated later artists as her pupil Bessie Smith. Rainey began her career at twelve and in 1904 married William "Pa" Rainey, with whom she toured for many years as a member of the Rabbit Foot Minstrels. In 1923 she began a sequence of more than one hundred recordings with Lovie Austin's Blues Serenaders (her favourite accompanist was Tommy Ladnier) and their fabulous success helped her to set up her own tent shows, which toured the South throughout the 1920s.

Her show in 1927, *Louisiana Blackbirds*, a 1500-seater which spent a week in each town it visited, may have been the one Mary Lou Williams saw: "Ma was loaded with diamonds, in her ears, round her neck, in a tiara on her head. Both hands were full of rocks, too: her hair was wild and she had gold teeth! What a sight!" Although she was nobody's idea of a good-looking woman, there was beauty in her smile and in the gentle personality that accepted taunts from her audience with great humour, and she was a kindly and much loved employer: "She treated her musicians so wonderfully," says Lionel Hampton, "and she always bought them an instrument."

Her vaudeville material included such showstoppers as "Ma Rainey's Black Bottom". When she retired, after the death of her sister and her mother, in 1933, she could never have envisaged that fifty years on a Broadway show of the same name would

MAX JONES FILES/REDFERNS

Ma Rainey

be highly successful. Rainey spent her last years as an active member of the Friendship Baptist Church in Columbus, Georgia; her daughter, Ma Rainey II, also a blues singer, died in 1985. [DF]

⊙ **Ma Rainey's Black Bottom** (1924–8; Yazoo). Good cross-section of Rainey's classic titles, with Don Redman, Fletcher Henderson, Buster Bailey, Coleman Hawkins, Kid Ory and others.

Gene Ramey

Bass.

b. Austin, Texas, 4 April 1913; d. 8 Dec 1984.

One of the most respected bassists in jazz, Ramey took lessons from Walter Page, spent several years leading his own bands, then joined Jay McShann (1938–43). From 1944, in New York, he worked with a bewildering variety of leaders from Tiny Grimes to Miles Davis, and in the 1950s was heard with Art Blakey as well as with singer Eartha Kitt. In 1959 and 1961 he toured Europe with Buck Clayton's All Stars and in the ensuing two decades worked more regularly with mainstream-Dixieland stylists from Muggsy Spanier and Dick Wellstood to Jimmy Rushing and Peanuts Hucko. By 1979 he was once again a regular partner to Jay McShann. [DF]

Ram Ramirez

Piano, organ.

b. Puerto Rico, 15 Sept 1913; d. New York, 11 Jan 1994.

A professional at thirteen, Ram (Roger) Ramirez played with many bands in New York (including Rex Stewart) before touring Europe with Bobby Martin (1937–9). From there he led groups of his own, then worked with Ella Fitzgerald, Frankie Newton, Charlie Barnet, John Kirby and Sid Catlett (1944). Thereafter he led his own trios at New York clubs and from 1953, inspired by Wild Bill Davis, specialized on Hammond organ. Ramirez toured with T-Bone Walker (1968), with the Harlem Blues and Jazz Band (1979–80) and worked regularly as a soloist in later years. He was the co-composer of "Lover Man, Oh Where Can You Be?" and also wrote "Mad About You". [DF]

Mark Ramsden

Alto and soprano saxophones, flute.

b. Liverpool, UK, 13 July 1956.

A consummate saxophonist and a talented composer, Ramsden spent one year at Leeds College of Music, after which he joined singer/songwriter Tom Robinson, touring and recording with him, and having some success with the hit single "War Baby". He has also played with Jimmy Witherspoon, NYJO, Loose Tubes, Dudu Pukwana and Bert Jansch. Ramsden eventually settled in London, and has since released two well-received albums, *Above The Clouds* and *Tribute To Paul Desmond*. He has also published a novel, *The Dark Magus And The Sacred Whore* (Serpent's Tail). [IC]

MARK RAMSDEN/DAVE CLIFF

⊙ **Tribute To Paul Desmond** (1998; 33 Jazz). Cliff is one of the finest British guitarists and the perfect choice for this elegant tribute album featuring Ramsden's eloquent alto saxophone.

Freddy Randall

Trumpet.

b. London, 6 May 1921; d. 18 May 1999.

Freddy Randall worked first with comedy bandleader Freddy Mirfield's Garbage Men, then quickly formed his own driving Chicago-style band, through which most of the best British Dixielanders of the period passed: Lennie Hastings, Dave Shepherd, Bruce Turner, Roy Crimmins, Harry Smith, Betty Smith, Al Gay, Norman Cave, Eddie Thompson, Pete Hodge and others. A huge-toned trumpeter of exuberant technique, Randall became the figurehead for post-war Chicago jazz buffs, playing in a style which varied from the direct punch of Muggsy Spanier to the more florid creations of Harry James and Charlie Teagarden (late Teagarden and late Randall are nearly interchangeable). His records of the 1950s – for Parlophone's Super Rhythm Style – are great jazz in any language. Later, after a lung disorder, Randall worked more sparingly. In the 1960s' trad boom he briefly re-formed a band with Shepherd and trombonist Jackie Free;

in 1971, with Shepherd again, he led the Randall-Shepherd All Stars (featuring Danny Moss and Brian Lemon), which broadcast in Britain on a near-daily basis, appeared on TV, played the Montreux jazz festival and recorded two excellent albums for Alan Bates and Black Lion. After the All Stars had dispersed, Randall – a sensitive man who disliked the traumas of bandleading and ran an old people's home later in his career – became more of a cult figure than ever, appearing when it suited him (but always brilliantly) in out-of-the-way pubs and clubs, often with less gifted bands, usually around his own East London territory. Randall's appearances became more sparse in the later 1980s, and in 1993 he finally left his London home for retirement in Devon. By 1997 he was inactive through ill health. Randall's admirers still rate him with the trumpet-kings of Britain. Hopefully his later work from the early 1970s (with Dave Shepherd) will soon reappear on CD. [DF]

⊙ **Vintage Freddy Randall 1949-51** (Lake). Six sides for Tempo, four for Decca and Randall's first twelve Parlophone sides are all here and the music (after almost too much excitement on early tracks) regularly re-raises to boiling point with Randall's ecstatic lead and high-octane soloing at its most exhuberant on sides such as "Since My Best Girl Turned Me Down", "South" and "Miss Jenny's Ball". Sidemen include Bruce Turner, Norman Cave, Lennie Hastings et al.

⊙ **Freddy Randall And His Band, Featuring Archie Semple** (1953-5; Lake). More top-drawer Randall including "Way Down Yonder In New Orleans", "Someday Sweetheart" and his own entertaining "Professor Jazz". As of now Randall's trumpeting was comparable to Kenny Baker's for confidence and swing, and his distinguished sidemen include Semple (a near-genius of the genre), Roy Crimmins, Dave Shepherd, Betty and Harry Smith.

Mouse Randolph

Trumpet.

b. St Louis, Missouri, 22 June 1909; d. 10 Dec 1997.

Mouse (Irving) Randolph worked with Fate Marable's riverboat bands and with a variety of territory bands (including Alphonso Trent's) before joining Andy Kirk in Kansas City (1931–3). He moved to New York soon after and joined Fletcher Henderson (1934), Cab Calloway (1935–9), and then Ella Fitzgerald's band (1939–41), which she had taken over from Chick Webb. After a spell with Don Redman came a long stint with Ed Hall's sextet (1944–8), before time with Eddie Barefield (1950), Marcelino Guerra's Latin-American band and, from 1958, Henry "Chick" Morrison's orchestra. A fine Armstrong-style player and versatile all-rounder, Randolph has never received the credit due to him. "He could always play," says Doc Cheatham. "He had studied a lot and he played everything, especially good New Orleans music. He had a good conception and I could never understand how he could give up music, but I think it was just that he got tired and wanted to be more with his family." [DF]

➤➤ **Ed Hall** *(Louis Armstrong All Star Dates 1947–50; With Edmond Hall's All Stars 1947).*

Jimmy Raney

Guitar.

b. Louisville, Kentucky, 20 Aug 1927; d. 10 May 1995.

Raney lived briefly in New York and then in Chicago as a teenager, working with local groups. He joined Woody Herman for nine months in 1948, and then played in New York with Al Haig, Buddy DeFranco, Artie Shaw and Terry Gibbs. He was a member of the Stan Getz quintet from 1951–2, and replaced Tal Farlow in the Red Norvo trio in 1953–4. He recorded regularly under his own name in the mid-1950s, but worked in a supper club with pianist Jimmy Lyon (who had earlier encouraged Farlow) from 1954–60. He rejoined Getz from 1962–3, but, after some work in the studio and backing singers, he returned to Louisville to work outside music. He started making playing trips, some for recording, to New York in 1972, and made a gradual return to his former reputation. From the mid-1970s he toured regularly in Europe, often in the company of his guitarist son Doug Raney (b. 29 Aug 1956), who has been a resident of Copenhagen since the late 1970s.

Raney was one of the few guitarists on whom the inspiration of bebop had a positive effect; he was not only extremely fluent but melodically lyrical as well. His best work usually required the presence of inspiring collaborators, who could bring out all his latent rhythmic strength. A number of interesting original tunes, of which "Signal" gained some currency with European groups, also demonstrate the qualities of which Raney was capable. [BP]

⊙ **But Beautiful** (1990; Criss Cross). Playing with just bass and drums (here the excellent George Mraz and Lewis Nash) is a test of whether any guitarist can hold the attention, and Raney comes up trumps with a programme that may seem a little unambitious but inspires him to great heights.

Ernest Ranglin

Guitar, arranger.

b. Robin's Hall, Manchester, Jamaica, 19 June 1932.

Ernest imitated his guitar-playing uncles and learned from Charlie Christian records. At fourteen he moved to the capital, Kingston, and was soon playing with leading dance bands, touring as far as the Bahamas. First recording with his own group in 1958, he then became busy with studio work, including a collaboration with altoist Bertie King, and was instrumental in creating ska music. As arranger/director he contributed to hit records by Prince Buster, Millie (Small), The Melodians and Bob Marley, while in 1963–4 he played jazz regularly at Ronnie Scott's, London. Back in Jamaica, Ranglin worked with singers Johnny Nash and Jimmy Cliff, with whom he toured internationally. More active in jazz since the mid-1970s, he moved to New York and began a working relationship with Monty Alexander. In 1997 he recorded in Senegal with Baaba Maal, whom he first met in the 70s. Admired by guitarists as different as Les Paul, Kenny Burrell and Charlie Byrd, he was awarded Jamaica's Order of Distinction in 1973 and the Musgrave Medal in 1992. [BP]

Now Is The Time (1974–80; MPS). The guitarist's jazz work recalls Wes Montgomery, not only in his freedom but in his melodic sensibility. All the tracks feature Monty Alexander (some were first issued under his name) and, while early jazz-and-Caribbean crossovers are rather simplistic, the unaccompanied duos are sensational.

Below The Bassline (1996; Island). A convincing combination of Afro-Caribbean rhythms (and some covers of classic reggae) with improvisation by Ranglin and Alexander, backed by Idris Muhammad and bassist Ira Coleman.

➤➤ **Ronnie Scott** *(The Night Is Scott…)*

Bill Rank

Trombone.

b. Lafayette, Indiana, 8 June 1904; d. 20 May 1979.

From 1926 Bill Rank was a regular musical companion to Bix Beiderbecke in Jean Goldkette's orchestra, in Adrian Rollini's short-lived New Yorker band, with Paul Whiteman and in the famous "Gang" records – and listening to Rank's brilliantly agile, full-toned trombone it is hard to understand how his name has never achieved even the familiarity of Miff Mole's. For more than a decade from December 1927 he was with Paul Whiteman, leading his trombone section. It was a plum job for any young player, and Rank was good at it. "Jack Teagarden told me that Bill was a very fine lead player," says Bob Havens, "and he would sort of carry the lead as far as playing in the ensemble work. Bill would tell Jack and the rest of them: 'You don't have to bother to count the bars – I'll let you know when it's time to come in!'" However, after 1933, when Teagarden joined Whiteman as featured soloist, Rank's solo talents were heard less often, and, while (no doubt) working with Teagarden was a trombonist's education, Rank must sometimes have wondered what was happening to his own career. By the end of the war – with bebop in fashion – he was leading his own band in Cincinnati, and in the 1950s he combined music with work as an insurance man. (In this period it was sometimes fashionable to downgrade Rank, after Eddie Condon's off-centre comment that Beiderbecke recorded only with "blood relations".) In 1968 and 1969 Rank came to England to play and record with his most famous Boswell, Dick Sudhalter, and in the 1970s, his talent intact, was a regular senior ambassador at jazz festivals. [DF]

➤➤ **Bix Beiderbecke** *(Bix Beiderbecke Vol. 2: At The Jazz Band Ball).*

Iiro Rantala

Piano.

b. Finland, 19 Jan 1970.

Rantala was first gripped by music at the age of seven, when he was in the children's choir Cantores Minores, and shortly afterwards he began taking piano lessons. In 1983 he began studying at the Pop and Jazz Conservatory, and taking private lessons with superb pianist Seppo Kantonen. Rantala was soon performing with pop groups and dance bands. In 1988, he enrolled at the Sibelius Academy, and with bassist Eerik Siikasaari and drummer Rami Eskelinen founded Trio Toykeat, which was to become one of the most successful Finnish groups. In its first year of existence the trio won first prize at the Hoielaart International jazz concert in Belgium. In 1990, Trio Toykeat released their first album, *Paivaa*, which also featured ex-Miles Davis saxophonist Rick Margitza and included several of Rantala's quirky original pieces. That same year, he and Eskelinen went to study at the Manhattan School of Music. Trio Toykeat had, by this time, the beginnings of an international reputation, which burgeoned after their second album, *Jazzlantis*, was released in 1995. Tours in France, Canada, New Zealand, Singapore, Indonesia and Thailand ensued. In Finland, Rantala received the Georgie Award, and the Trio Toykeat were invited to accompany the Finnish President on his visit to the Czech Republic. They were also the first jazz group ever to play at Finland's official Independence Day festivities. In 1997 the trio released their third album, *Sisu*, which featured two classical violinists. With accordionist Gil Goldstein, Rantala also co-founded the multinational Tango Kings in New York in 1992, and he has worked with the Mingus Workshop Big Band and with pianist Dave Kikoski. [IC]

Sisu (1997; Polygram Finland). This is a brilliant, roistering album, now serious, now jokey, ferociously manic at times (the last half of "Unfinished Tango"), and then sensuous and poetic ("The Lust And The Doom"). The two violinists hang on manfully in this barely classifiable encounter with the jazz daredevils.

Ken Rattenbury

Trumpet, piano, composer.

b. Spilsby, Lincolnshire, UK, 10 Sept 1920.

Rattenbury's paternal grandfather was a virtuoso cornet soloist, touring the world with many brass bands. Rattenbury had several years of piano tuition, but was self-taught in musical theory, orchestration and composition. In 1933 he began as pianist with a blues group specializing in Bessie Smith's repertoire. He also did various other jobs on piano, before switching to trumpet in 1939. He was in the army during World War II, spending the latter half of his service leading a jazz sextet and touring theatres of war as part of an entertainment unit. Demobilized, he freelanced with local Midlands bands from 1947–50, gaining experience in writing and broadcasting, and started leading his own bands in 1951.

In the early 1960s BBC Radio commissioned him to compose two thirty-minute jazz suites which combined words and music – *The Seven Ages Of Man*, based on texts from Shakespeare, and *The Rime Of*

The Ancient Mariner, based on Coleridge's poem. The suites were recorded by an all-star line-up of British musicians, including trumpeter Kenny Baker. The *Seven Ages* suite was rebroadcast worldwide 150 times over the following few years and remains in the BBC archives as a definitive example of the marriage of literature with jazz. He also recorded two albums for EMI.

In 1984 he obtained an MA in musicology from the University of Keele, and his book based on his thesis, *Duke Ellington, Jazz Composer*, was published in 1990 by Yale University Press. Now in his seventies, Rattenbury continues to lead a quartet and compose. His favourites are Clark Terry, Bix Beiderbecke, Bobby Hackett and Louis Armstrong, and Rattenbury's warm-sounding, urbane trumpet style grows out of that tradition. [IC]

Jim Rattigan

French horn, composer, arranger.

b.Houghton Regis, Bedfordshire, 24 July 1960.

The fourth of five musical children, Jim Rattigan and his sister Ann became the all Britain advanced duet champions on piano accordion in 1977. He went on to study at Trinity College of Music (1979–82) and at the Royal Academy of Music (1982–3), specializing in French horn and piano. While still a student he was a member of the European Community Youth Orchestra, and a founder Member of the European Community Youth Jazz Orchestra. This pattern of dividing his playing between classical music and jazz continued, and he cites as equal inspirations the great classical horn player Dennis Brain and the jazz pianist Oscar Peterson. From 1983–9 Rattigan toured extensively and recorded with all the major London orchestras, before becoming a member of the Royal Philharmonic Orchestra (1989–95). During this period he also played with the Bobby Lamb/Ray Premru big band and on Mike Gibbs' album *By The Way*.

In 1995, Rattigan left the RPO to concentrate on jazz and composition. Since then he's played with Mike Gibbs, Django Bates's Delightful Precipice, the Creative Jazz Orchestra, and with Kenny Wheeler on his 70th Birthday concert. He's also worked with the BBC Radio Big Band, the Simon Purcell Octet, and played on Julian Argüelles' latest album. Rattigan has also toured and recorded with Mark Lockheart's Scratch Band, and was a featured soloist on Hans Koller's debut album, *The Magic Mountain*. In 2000 Rattigan formed his own group Pavillon (named after the bell of a French horn), and recorded his debut album *Unfamiliar Guise*. In 2001, he toured in the UK as a member of the McCoyTyner Big Band. [IC]

⊙ **Unfamiliar Guise** (2000; BlackBox). Rattigan's debut album reveals him as a brilliant and versatile jazz soloist on French horn, and already an interesting and questing composer/arranger. Pavillon is an excellent outfit, with Hans Koller on piano, the hugely talented Amy Gamlen on alto sax, plus a fine rhythm section made up of Dave Whitford on bass and Stuart Laurence on drums.

Enrico Rava

Trumpet, flugelhorn.

b. Trieste, Italy, 20 Aug 1943.

Rava's mother was a classical pianist. He is self-taught and started on trombone with traditional jazz groups, and then took up the trumpet. Later he studied with Carmine Caruso in New York. In 1964 he played with the Gato Barbieri quintet and from 1965–8 he played with Steve Lacy groups, touring in Europe, South America and the USA. From 1969–72 he worked with Roswell Rudd's groups, with the Jazz Composers' Orchestra Association and with Bill Dixon. In the early 1970s he divided his time between New York, Italy and Buenos Aires, where his wife Graciela, a film-maker, lived. In 1975 he formed his own group with John Abercrombie, Palle Danielsson and Jon Christensen. He then had his own quartet in 1976–7 with altoist Massimo Urbani, J.-F. Jenny-Clark and Aldo Romano; from 1978–9 the quartet consisted of Roswell Rudd, Giovanni Tommaso and Bruce Ditmas. From 1980–83 he worked with Franco d'Andrea (piano), Furio di Castri (bass) and Aldo Romano (drums). In 1984–5 he had another quartet with Tony Oxley on drums. Rava has also worked with Gil Evans (in 1982), toured with Cecil Taylor in Europe in 1984, and was involved in the festival devoted to Taylor in Berlin in 1988. He has led big bands with special guests such as Rudd, Albert Mangelsdorff and Ray Anderson.

Rava is a fiery and lyrical trumpet player, capable of handling anything from abstraction to conventional song structures and orchestral work. He is influenced by Miles Davis, João Gilberto, Monk, Ellington, Charlie Parker, Chet Baker, Coltrane, Armstrong and "all the greats". He also loves cinema, literature and the visual arts, sometimes working with visual artists such as Michelangelo Pistoletto. In 1980 he collaborated on a project with Pistoletto and composer Morton Feldman in Atlanta, Georgia. Rava is also becoming more and more interested in composition: he has written a big-band suite, *F(rag)ments*, for the Rome Opera, and his albums contain many of his own pieces. [IC]

⊙ **Rava String Band** (1984; Soul Note). *Rava String Band* is an ambitious project bringing together guitarist Augusto Mancinelli, bassist Giovanni Tommaso, Tony Oxley, Nana Vasconcelos and a string quartet.

⊙ **Secrets** (1986; Soul Note); **Enrico Rava Quintet** (1989; Nabel). *Secrets* has Mancinelli and John Taylor, plus bass and drums, providing admirable support; the *Quintet* lacks Taylor, but has some of Rava's most impressive playing.

➤➤ **Abdullah Ibrahim** *(African Space Programme)*; **Steve Lacy** *(The Forest And The Zoo)*; **Rita Marcotulli** *(The Woman Next Door)*.

Alison Rayner

Electric bass.

b. Bromley, Kent, UK, 7 Sept 1952.

From 1957–67 Rayner took piano and singing lessons, and played violin in the school orchestra, but she is self-taught on bass guitar. From 1976–84 she played with various small groups and big bands in the UK. In 1983 she joined the Guest Stars, an all-women fusion band, which toured the US East Coast in September 1984, and the UK in December. In 1985 the Guest Stars were the support group to Jan Garbarek for his London concert; since the early 1990s she has organized weekly events at north London clubs. Her favourites include Jaco Pastorius, Scott LaFaro, Ron Carter, John Entwistle, Charles Mingus, Miles Davis, Joe Zawinul, Pat Metheny and Jimi Hendrix. [IC]

➤➤ **Deirdre Cartwright** *(Debut).*

Casper Reardon

Harp.

b. Little Falls, New York, 15 April 1907; d. 9 March 1941.

While the violin has – however tenuously – managed to survive the swiftly changing times of jazz history, very few harpists easily survived the 1930s. Perhaps because the instrument was impossible to amplify, and because of the practical difficulties of moving it around, only isolated players (Corky Hale and David Snell, for example) still occasionally remind us of the irresistible sound of the harp in jazz. In the 1930s the instrument's most famous practitioner was Casper Reardon, who played first with the Philadelphia Symphony Orchestra and then became principal harpist with the Cincinnati Symphony, while broadcasting regularly in his own time as a jazzman under the pseudonym Arpeggio Glissandi. One of his earliest records with Jack Teagarden, "Junk Man", demonstrates his admirable talent, and by 1936 Reardon was featured with the Three Ts (Jack and Charlie Teagarden and Frank Trumbauer) and as a frequent guest with great orchestras from Paul Whiteman's on down. Reardon worked in Hollywood too, and led his own small groups in New York and Chicago until his premature death. [DF]

➤➤ **Jack Teagarden** *(A Hundred Years From Today).*

Jason Rebello

Piano, keyboards.

b. Surrey, UK, 29 March 1969.

Rebello studied piano to grade eight, attended the jazz workshops at the weekend arts course at Interchange from 1985–6, and graduated from the London Guildhall School of Music. He won the Pat Smythe Award, and in 1988 received *The Wire* magazine's Most Promising Newcomer of the Year award. He has worked with a wide variety of musicians, including Courtney Pine, Tommy Smith, Art Blakey, Branford Marsalis and Gary Burton, as well as accompanying soul singers and R&B vocalists. He was signed by Novus records at the end of the 1980s and became something of a media figure, presenting the BBC2 arts programme *Artrageous* for a time, and appearing on *The Late Show* and *The South Bank Show*.

He also began studying Buddhism at the end of the 1980s, perhaps inspired in this – as he is musically – by Herbie Hancock. Disillusioned with a record industry that didn't seem to know how to handle him or his music, he started his own record label, All That Records, and released the album *Last Dance* in 1995, just before entering a Buddhist monastery. Rebello's is a very great talent: he has brilliant technique, and is familiar with soul, funk, Latin, classical music and jazz. His eclectic style reflects all these and also encompasses stride piano and even Erroll Garner impersonations, but his eclecticism has made him seem unsure of his musical identity. It is to be hoped that his monastic retreat will resemble Sonny Rollins's reclusive practice sessions on Brooklyn Bridge and result in self-renewal and a re-emergence on the jazz scene. [IC]

⊙ **A Clearer View** (1990; Novus). Rebello's debut album, with bass, drums, percussion and saxophone ace Dave O'Higgins, was a promising affair, with some excellent piano and composing from the leader, and sparkling performances by O'Higgins and the rhythm-section.

⊙ **Last Dance** (1995; All That Records). This duo album with singer Joy Rose is a little gem. Rebello plays piano, alternating solo spots with vocal numbers, and his playing is superbly joyful and rhythmic. The material is mostly Rebello originals, but he and Rose also reinterpret some standards including "What Is This Thing Called Love" and "A Foggy Day".

Dewey Redman

Tenor and alto saxophones, musette, clarinet, composer, educator.

b. Fort Worth, Texas, 17 May 1931.

Dewey Redman began playing the clarinet at the age of thirteen. He had some lessons, but is mostly self-taught. He played in his high school marching band, where among his fellow pupils were Ornette Coleman, Charles Moffett and Prince Lasha. In 1949 he attended Prairie View A & M, studying industrial arts, with music as a subsidiary subject, and received his Bachelor's degree in 1953. While there he switched from alto to tenor, playing in the marching band and the swing band. He received his Master's degree in education from North Texas State in 1959. He taught in schools from 1956–9 and then moved to Los Angeles. Shortly afterwards he settled in San Francisco, staying for seven years, leading his own groups and working with Pharoah Sanders, Wes Montgomery and others. He moved to New

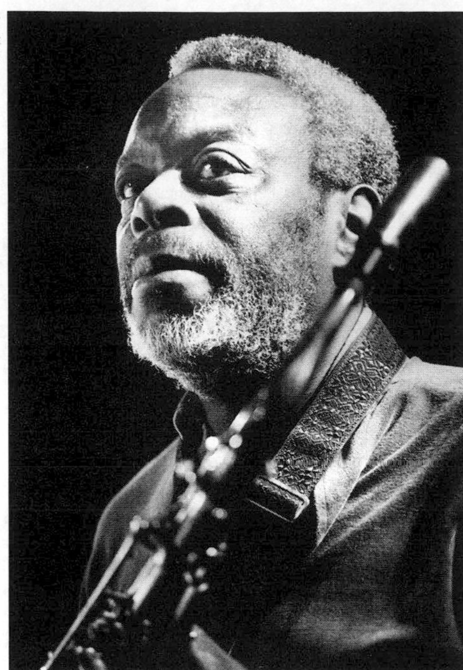

Jak Kilby

Dewey Redman

York in 1967, joining Ornette Coleman and staying with his group until late 1974. He also worked in the early 1970s with Charlie Haden's Liberation Music Orchestra, with Keith Jarrett and with his own groups. Redman recorded several albums with Jarrett, including a small masterpiece, *The Survivors Suite*, in 1976, a year in which he also began working in a quartet with Coleman's old associates Don Cherry, Haden and Ed Blackwell. They toured in the USA and Europe, and took the name Old And New Dreams from an album they recorded in 1979. In 1980 Old And New Dreams recorded a live album in Austria; the same year, Redman played on a studio album with Pat Metheny, in the company of Mike Brecker, Haden and Jack DeJohnette. In 1982 he worked with Haden's re-formed Liberation Music Orchestra, and in the later 80s and 90s recorded with Paul Motian. He has also continued to lead his own groups. Redman is a consummate player who can work with set structures and with semi- or total abstraction; he also incorporates elements from ethnic music into his work, and sometimes features the musette – a double-reed Arabian instrument. [IC]

⊙ **Living On The Edge** (1989; Black Saint); **Choices** (1992; Enja). *Living On The Edge* has a splendid coherence, with Geri Allen on piano and Cameron Brown and Eddie Moore on bass and drums respectively. Brown is also the bassist on *Choices*, with drummer Leon Parker, and the quartet is completed by Joshua Redman on tenor. Sparks fly in this good-natured family cutting contest.

➤➤ **Charlie Haden** *(Liberation Music Orchestra; Old And New Dreams)*; **Keith Jarrett** *(The Survivors Suite)*.

Don Redman

Alto and soprano saxophones, multi-instrumentalist, vocals, arranger, composer.

b. Piedmont, West Virginia, 29 July 1900; d. 30 Nov 1964.

A conservatory-trained multi-instrumentalist, Redman came to New York with Billy Paige's Broadway Syncopators, a Pittsburgh-based band, in 1923; there he met Fletcher Henderson, who was assembling his fledgling band, and joined him at Harlem's Club Alabam as alto saxophonist and staff arranger. Over the next four years Redman transformed the sound of Henderson's band, writing scores that were sometimes simple, always effective and ideal for the dancers at Roseland Ballroom: "No matter how musical he arranges today," said Coleman Hawkins, "Don used to make some very good gut-bucket arrangements! Rock'n'roll with a little music behind it!" After Hawkins and Louis Armstrong had joined the band Redman's arranging took on a new enthusiasm, but in 1927 he was weaned away from Henderson by Jean Goldkette (at $300 a week) to arrange and direct for McKinney's Cotton Pickers. Redman rewrote the book, hired cornermen such as Prince Robinson (tenor) and Ralph Escudero (bass), and in a long residency at the Graystone Ballroom, Detroit, he transformed the Cotton Pickers into one of the best bands of the day; they also recorded in New York (initially without Goldkette's approval), augmenting with New York stars such as Benny Carter, Hawkins and Fats Waller. For the next nine years from 1931 Redman led his own band, recording such classics as "Chant Of The Weed" and "Shakin' The African", and often writing with that same delicious economy. "Some of Don's best arrangements were the simple ones," says Quentin Jackson. "He used to say, 'This is just a little something to get by!' And it would be beautiful!" In 1941 Redman gave up bandleading and opened an arranging office on Broadway, writing for bandleaders from Fred Waring and Paul Whiteman to Harry James and Jimmie Lunceford (he also arranged Jimmy Dorsey's hit "Deep Purple"). In 1946 Redman organized the first band to visit Europe after the war (featuring such as Don Byas, Tyree Glenn and Peanuts Holland) and by 1951 was musical director for Pearl Bailey, as well as arranger for orchestras all over New York. [DF]

⊙ **Chronological Don Redman: 1931–39** (Classics). All Redman's titles are in this three-volume series, featuring sidemen such as Bill Coleman, Henry Allen, Benny Morton and more stars of their stature. Much classic-level music, with generally good-quality sound.

Joshua Redman

Tenor saxophone, composer.

b. Berkeley, Calfornia, 1 Feb 1969.

The son of saxophonist Dewey Redman and a Russian-Jewish dancer, Joshua Redman graduated

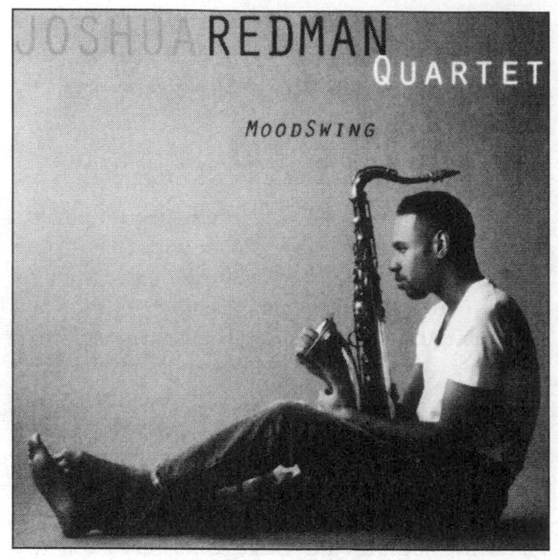

summa cum laude from Harvard and turned down a chance to study law at Yale in order to become a professional musician. After winning the saxophone prize in the 1991 Thelonious Monk competition, he embarked on a hectic but much lauded recording binge, making albums with trombonists Eric Felten and Jimmy Knepper, drummers Elvin Jones and Paul Motian (in his Electric Bebop Band), organist Melvin Rhyne, pianists Kenny Drew Jnr, John Hicks and Mike LeDonne, and fellow tenormen Joe Lovano and Dewey Redman. Much praised for his clear musical affiliation with swing masters as well as with later saxophonists, he cites Sonny Rollins as his main influence, but also admires Dexter Gordon, Coltrane, Stanley Turrentine and Illinois Jacquet. He brought all these influences, plus a refreshingly open-minded approach – he reinterprets everything from The Beatles, Stevie Wonder and Joni Mitchell tunes, through material by Prince, to Rodgers and Hart and Cole Porter, and his originals draw on funk, soul and pop as well as on straightahead jazz – to his 1990s albums as a leader, and consequently established himself with remarkable speed as one of the biggest draws on the live jazz circuit. A pair of intriguingly ambitious if ultimately puzzling albums in *Beyond* (2000; Warner) and *Passage Of Time* (2001; Warner) were followed by a new project featuring organist Sam Yahel and drummer Brian Blade – *Yaya3* – and a Redman album featuring the same players, *Elastic* (see below). One of the most intrepid musical thinkers working in the contemporary mainstream, Redman himself refers to his creative process as "preserving my roots while extending my branches". His musical intelligence, his unerring eye for compatible band-members (pianists Brad Mehldau and Aaron Goldberg, bassists Larry Grenadier and Reuben Rogers, among others), plus an unfailingly modest and engaging stage manner, should ensure his continuing success. [CP]

⊙ **Joshua Redman** (1992; Warner). Covering ground from James Brown through Monk to standards, this debut caused something of a sensation in the jazz world; sidemen include Mike LeDonne and bassist Christian McBride.

⊙ **Wish** (1993; Warner). A stellar band – Pat Metheny, Charlie Haden and Billie Higgins – help Redman swing enjoyably through Stevie Wonder's "Make Sure You're Sure" to Ornette Coleman's "Turnaround", plus a number of band-member originals. Another high-profile, big-selling album.

⊙ **Mood Swing** (1994; Warner). Redman leads his own young quartet – Brad Mehldau (piano), Christian McBride (bass) and Brian Blade (drums) – through a set of pithy self-penned material: a cogent, intelligent and lively programme.

⊙ **Timeless Tales (For Changing Times)** (1998; Warner). Juxtaposing "Love for Sale" with "Eleanor Rigby", and "The Times They Are A-changin'" with "It Might As Well Be Spring", a brave – and mostly successful – stab at "a jazz celebration of twentieth-century Western popular song".

⊙ **Elastic** (2002; Warner). After a somewhat self-conscious period, Redman sounds like he really enjoys himself on this sax-organ-drums plus electronic processing date, released only a few months after the groovy *Yaya3* album which also featured Yahel and Blade.

Dizzy Reece

Trumpet.

b. Kingston, Jamaica, 5 Jan 1931.

Dizzy (Alphonso) Reece took up the trumpet at the age of fourteen; he moved to Europe and worked from 1949–54 with Don Byas and others. He was then based in the UK from 1954–9, recording regularly under his own name, including a 1958 London session with sidemen Donald Byrd and Art Taylor. He settled in New York in 1959, making occasional trips to Europe, such as with the Dizzy Gillespie big band in 1968 and the Paris Reunion Band in 1985. Reece is an extrovert but thoughtful post-bop stylist who, despite his nickname, does not sound like Gillespie, or Navarro or Miles. Aspects of each are hinted at in his playing, but his tone and choice of phraseology are interestingly individual. [BP]

⊙ **Asia Minor** (1962; New Jazz/OJC). One of Reece's few American recordings is restored to circulation, with a Rolls-Royce rhythm-section led by Hank Jones and a frontline completed by Joe Farrell and Cecil Payne. Reece's own bop-to-modal material is balanced by Gershwin's "Summertime".

Eric Reed

Piano, composer.

b. Philadelphia, 21 June 1970.

Having begun to play piano at two, Eric Reed was playing along with jazz records at six and in a Baptist church (his father being a pastor) by the age of seven. When his family moved to Los Angeles, he studied at the Community School there under the dean of the Eastern Music Festival, Joe Thayer, who – on advice from Wynton and Ellis Marsalis – encouraged Reed to study jazz with Harold Battiste. Work with Charlie Haden, Benny Carter, Joshua Redman and others followed, but it was his joining

Wynton Marsalis's band in the early 1990s that put him on the jazz map. Reed has since recorded not only with Marsalis satellites such as alto player Wessell Anderson and trumpeter Marcus Printup, but also with the Lincoln Center Jazz Orchestra and – since the trumpeter's *Citi Movement* (Columbia; 1993) – with Marsalis himself in his various bands. As a leader, Reed made his debut with a 1990 Candid album, *Soldier's Hymn*, a trio outing with Dwayne Burno on bass and drummer Gregory Hutchinson, but after a couple of outings on MoJazz, he signed for Impulse! in the mid-1990s, producing *Musicale* in 1996 (mostly originals and featuring a strong opening track dedicated to one of Reed's chief musical influences, Art Blakey) and *Pure Imagination* (see below). A brief tenure at Verve produced the imposing trio album *Manhattan Melodies* (see below), while his recent concurrent output on Savant (*From My Heart*, 2001, and *Ebop*, 2003 – see below) and Nagel Heyer (*Happiness*, 2001, and *Mercy And Grace*, 2003) has been no less impressive. An exhilarating live performer, Reed is a strong believer in continuous artistic evolution: "Making it different every single time is the goal." [CP]

⊙ **Pure Imagination** (1997; Impulse!). Show tunes such as "Hello, Young Lovers", "Send In The Clowns" and "You'll Never Walk Alone", subjected to Reed's finely honed jazz sensibility, impeccably supported by bassist Reginald Veal and drummer Gregory Hutchinson.

⊙ **Manhattan Melodies** (1999; Verve). Same trio, same quality with perhaps even more authority on a winning set of tunes with a New York theme, including a cunningly reharmonised "59th Street Bridge Song" and a Latinised "Puttin' On The Ritz".

⊙ **Ebop** (2003; Savant). A rigorously executed hard bop quintet date featuring trumpeter Marcus Printup, saxist Walter Blanding Jnr., bassist Rodney Whittaker and drummer Rodney Green. Not the most adventurous of Reed's outings, but hugely enjoyable.

Dianne Reeves

Vocals.

b. Detroit, Michigan, 23 Oct 1956.

Raised in Denver from the age of two, Dianne Reeves sang with her high-school band, through which she was encouraged by Clark Terry at the age of seventeen. She performed with him while a student at the University of Colorado and after moving to Los Angeles in 1976. There she did session work with Lenny White, Stanley Turrentine and pianists Eddie Del Barrio (of Latin jazz group Caldera) and Billy Childs. After studying with Phil Moore, she toured worldwide with Sergio Mendes in 1981 and Harry Belafonte in 1984, and made her first album in 1982. With two late 1980s recordings produced by George Duke (who is her cousin), she achieved considerable success, and she has also recorded for Eddie Henderson, Victor Feldman, Steps Ahead in 1985 and McCoy Tyner in 1991. She appeared at the Montreux festival in 1991 with Quincy Jones, and in 1995 performed there in her own right. Her gift for conviction and communication is well summarized by the comparisons she herself has made: "I love Sarah [Vaughan] and Dinah Washington, but I also grew up listening to Motown and Chick Corea. And you can hear all that in my music." In addition, the content of her own lyrics, such as "Better Days" and "How Long", is markedly original. [BP]

⊙ **Quiet After The Storm** (1994; Blue Note). With George Duke back in the producer's seat Reeves goes from strength to strength, featuring two new originals, covers of standards including "Detour Ahead", and a dedication to Cannonball Adderley, "Country Preacher", on which she sings alongside his recording of the solo.

Reuben Reeves

Trumpet.

b. Evansville, Indiana, 25 Oct 1905; d. Sept 1975.

Reeves was a graduate of Chicago's American Conservatory, teaching music by day at Wendell Phillips High School during the late 1920s. At the same time he was a featured soloist with premier Chicago groups led by Erskine Tate and Dave Peyton. Later he joined Cab Calloway (1931) before returning to Chicago where he led his own touring group, and toured with Connie's *Hot Chocolates* revue. From the late 1930s he served in the US National Guard as a musician, and after demobilization joined Harry Dial's band (1946), continuing to work with Dial regularly after retirement from full-time music in 1952.

Reeves was recorded in 1928 by Vocalion Records as their "answer" to Louis Armstrong. While lacking Armstrong's inimitable genius, his work reveals power, skill and an admirable creativity that led Danny Barker to describe him as "a fantastic trumpeter". [DF]

⊙ **Reuben Reeves – The Complete Vocalions 1928–33** (Timeless). Twenty-one highly enjoyable sides encompassing Reeves's recording career both as a leader and as a featured sideman; included are titles by Fess Williams and the Hollywood Shufflers in addition to his self-led sessions.

Hans Reichel

Guitar.

b. Hagen, Germany, 10 May 1949.

Although he began his musical life as a classical violinist, then a bass guitarist in rock, Hans Reichel has worked in improvised music since the early 1970s. Operating with equal success as both solo performer and recording artist, and in duos with the likes of cellist Tom Cora, accordion/reeds player Rüdiger Carl and fellow guitarist Fred Frith, Reichel contrives to invest his surprisingly accessible free-form playing with wit and intelligence. In addition to his strictly musical talents, he is also an inventor, designing a wide variety of stringed instruments and playing them in unconventional ways, greatly increasing the range of his music's aural possibilities, and drawing from *Guitar Player* magazine the comment: "Reichel has failed to acknowledge what a guitar is supposed to look and sound like." Since the late 1980s he has played the "daxophone", an array of specially shaped wooden tongues animated by the stroke of a double-bass bow, which produces an extraordinary range of sounds startlingly reminiscent of both animal and human voices. In his twenty-year career to date, Reichel has toured in more than thirty countries, including the visit to New York in 1979 that brought him to world attention, a tour of Southeast Asia for the Goethe Institute in 1980, a spell in Tokyo in 1986, during which he played with Japanese musicians Ueno Tenko and Kenichi Takeda, as well as visiting Americans John Zorn and Ned Rothenberg, and a tour of the USA in 1987 with Fred Frith. He has recorded nearly two dozen albums, including 1994's extraordinary "operetta for guitar and daxophone", *Lower Lurum* (BRD), and 2002's impish sequel *Yuxo: A New Daxophone Operetta* (a/l/l), as well as those listed below. [CP]

⊙ **The Death Of The Rare Bird Ymir/Bonobo Beach** (1979/81; FMP). Two solo albums, slightly edited for CD release. Reichel demonstrates a fair range of his skills, from fretless-guitar work to playing two instruments at once.

⊙ **Stop Complaining/Sundown** (1990/91; FMP). Pairs a lengthy duet with Fred Frith and a live set recorded in Kobe, Japan, with another fellow guitarist, Kazuhisa Uchihashi.

⊙ **Shanghaied On Tor Road** (1992; FMP). Wide-ranging exploration of the possibilities of the daxophone, at once solemn and witty, spontaneous and organized, virtuosic and unfussy.

Rufus Reid

Bass.

b. Atlanta, Georgia, 10 Feb 1944.

Growing up in Sacramento, California, Reid began on trumpet, switching to bass while in the air force. Although there was no musical tradition in his family, Reid's subsequent studies were partly financed by his brother. He received an arts degree from Olympic College, Bremerton (near Seattle), and his Bachelor of Music/Performance at Northwestern University, in 1969 and 1971 respectively. His jazz career began in Chicago, where he recorded in concert with Gene Ammons-Dexter Gordon and others in 1970. He then worked with Bobby Hutcherson-Harold Land in 1971, Eddie Harris from 1971–4 and, after moving to New York, Thad Jones-Mel Lewis from 1976–7. He toured widely with Gordon in 1977–9, and then taught at William Paterson College from 1979, where he is still Director of Jazz Studies. In the meantime he has toured abroad regularly, including with Jack DeJohnette's Special Edition, Dizzy Gillespie-Phil Woods, J.J. Johnson and with TanaReid, a group co-led with drummer Akira Tana. In 1992 he recorded with André Previn, and also performed a double bass concerto written for him by Benny Golson. Reid's full sound complements his perfect sense of time in both the rhythm-section and solo roles. [BP]

TanaReid

⊙ **Blue Motion** (1993; Paddle Wheel/Evidence). The third album by Reid and Tana's quintet, with Rob Schneiderman on piano and saxophonists Craig Bailey and Dan Faulk, has excellent playing by the leaders and original material by Tana, including a closing suggestion of free improvisation.

➤➤ **Mel Lewis** *(Thad Jones-Mel Lewis Quartet).*

Django Reinhardt

Guitar.

b. Liverchies, near Charleroi, Belgium, 23 Jan 1910;

d. Fontainebleau, France, 16 May 1953.

Django (Jean Baptiste) Reinhardt was born in a caravan in a shantytown, the son of a gypsy entertainer who worked as "La Belle Laurence" in a travelling show in France and Belgium. He learned the violin first, later the guitar, and, when a caravan fire in 1928 deprived him of the use of two fingers of his left hand, he developed a revolutionary and spellbinding technique based on his limitations. Playing solo in cafés around Montmartre, he was discovered by a young French artist, Emile Savitry from Toulon, who found him work and introduced him to a young French singer, Jean Sablon. For a while Reinhardt played Eddie Lang to Sablon's Crosby (Lang was Reinhardt's primary influence) until in 1934 he formed a quintet with violinist Stephane Grappelli, based on a band led by Louis Vola at Paris's Claridge Hotel, and the intimate little group attracted the attention of members of the Hot Club of France, a record society which occasionally put on concerts. The Hot Club's next presentation – at the Salle Pleyel, starring Coleman Hawkins – also featured the Quintette du Hot Club de France and successfully launched its career.

Within a year, Reinhardt, Grappelli and their group were becoming internationally famous and in the five years up to the war they recorded more than two hundred sides. Most of the records are acknowledged classics (even though at the time critics often downgraded the music as a country-style rehash of Joe Venuti and Eddie Lang's masterworks) and Reinhardt's work on them is as powerful as Louis Armstrong's best. An imposing man, dressed like a gypsy prince and with a powerful air of distinction, Reinhardt was an unpredictable handful. "Ah, what trouble he gave me!" remembers Grappelli, then very much the hard-worked junior partner. "I think now I would rather play with lesser musicians and have a peaceable time than with Django and his monkey-business." But the music Reinhardt produced was worth all the trouble – it was the greatest European jazz so far, and a mystifying revelation to confident American originators: "It was upsetting to hear a man who was a foreigner swing like that!" remembered Doc Cheatham.

William Gottlieb

Django Reinhardt

opments had muted his passionate creativity. Certainly Reinhardt was disillusioned with his reception in the USA and found little to enjoy in the intellectualism of bebop, but his music stayed powerful to the end, which came with a stroke when he was only 43.

"The most creative jazz musician to originate anywhere outside the USA," Mercer Ellington describes him. More than forty years on, and despite the huge upsurge in European creativity in jazz since 1960, there seems little reason to argue. Django Reinhardt's period of creative omnipotence was, in retrospect, brief: within a few years of his appearance the most cataclysmic development in twentieth-century guitar – its electrification – was under way, and by 1942 a younger, more fashionable genius, Charlie Christian, had redefined the guitar's role for a generation. Yet Reinhardt's colossal impact left an impression too deep to be forgotten, and his music has been perpetuated (appropriately in Europe) by a devoted salon of followers from Denny Wright and Diz Disley in Britain to Frenchman Bireli Lagrene. [DF]

The Hot Club quintet lasted until 1939, when Grappelli stayed in London for the duration of the war and Reinhardt once again went his own wandering way. On the road in his caravan, keeping clear of the Germans as he meandered from Switzerland to North Africa, he stopped off to experiment with a big band, then dutifully formed a new quintet (with clarinettist Hubert Rostaing), but devoted a lot of his interest to a new challenge: "He wanted to make it as a writer of serious music," says Gerard Leveque. Reinhardt's planned compositions included a Mass for organ (never completed), a "Bolero" and a symphony (which may have been performed in the eastern bloc by a conductor with whom Reinhardt had planned a performance and who was subsequently abducted by the Nazis); much of the best of this music was retained in a film for which Reinhardt supplied the soundtrack, *Le Village de la colère* (1946).

That year, back in his caravan, he received a cable from Duke Ellington inviting him to play concerts. Despite the unreliability of Reinhardt's travelling methods, he made it to the USA (his first question, stepping off the boat, was reportedly "Where's Dizzy playing?") and played – on amplified guitar for the first time – a set of moderately successful concerts with Ellington, but it was a brief visit. Back home again, Reinhardt – by now playing amplified guitar and leaning towards bop idioms – spent his last years touring and recording with his quintet (sometimes including Grappelli again). But the critical feeling was that jazz fashion had taken the creative edge off him, that his determination to keep up with modern devel-

⊙ **Django Reinhardt 1934–5/1935–6/1937 Vols. 1 & 2/1937–8/1938–9/1939–40/1940/1940–41/1941–2/1942–3/1944–6** (Classics). This twelve-volume set is a masterly collation of Django's chronological recordings and includes in several cases significant recordings made with other leaders. Undoubtedly the best buy for completists.

⊙ **Django Reinhardt Vols. 1–5** (1934–9; JSP). Excellent survey of Reinhardt's recorded career, with production and remastering by Ted Kendall to a very high level. The set is non-chronological but deals with specific areas of Reinhardt's recording in a sensible and practical fashion. Highly recommended.

⊙ **The Chronological Django Reinhardt: 1934–5 & 1935–6** (Classics). All Reinhardt's recordings from the periods specified; good transfers and essential music.

⊙ **Swing In Paris** (1936–40; Affinity). A glorious five-CD boxed set gathering together titles by the Quintette du Hot Club de France, as well as all Reinhardt's recordings from the period – with Coleman Hawkins's All Star Jam Band, Eddie South, Larry Adler, Philippe Brun, Rex Stewart, Dicky Wells and more.

⊙ **The Quintessential Django Reinhardt and Stephane Grappelli** (1934-40/ASV). For those requiring a sampler of this legendary team there could be few better choices than this; excellent sound and twenty-five masterpieces.

⊙ **Django!** (1934–8; Happy Days). A good collection spanning Reinhardt's first recordings with the QHCF through to four fine sides featuring Larry Adler. Once again produced by the indefatigable Ted Kendall.

⊙ **Django's Music** (1940–42; Hep). This valuable set brings together the music from the period after Reinhardt's split from Grappelli, much of it with big bands and frequently featuring Reinhardt's fascinating compositions.

⊙ **Swing Guitar** (1945–6; Jas). Django with the European Division Band of the Air Transport Command, recorded live at Salle Pleyel, on broadcasts and in rehearsal; small group titles are included too. All of great interest; excellent sound.

⊙ **Pêche A La Mouche** (1947 & 53; Verve). Django with the re-formed QHCF, plus titles from Rex Stewart and more from 1953, by which time Reinhardt had assimilated bebop and mastered electric guitar to its full extent. Fascinating music from the last months of Django's life.

⊙ **Indispensable Django Reinhardt 1949–50** (RCA). Later Reinhardt with two formative partners – Grappelli and André Ekyan.

Emily Remler

Guitar.

b. New York, 18 Sept 1957; d. Sydney, Australia, 4 May 1990.

Remler, who was brought up in Englewood Cliffs, New Jersey, studied at Berklee College from 1974–6. She spent three years gigging and teaching in New Orleans from 1976–9, as well as working there and in New York with singers Nancy Wilson and Astrud Gilberto. Encouraged by Herb Ellis, she made her first album under her own name in 1980, and appeared at the Kool and Berlin festivals in 1981. She played in the Los Angeles production of *Sophisticated Ladies* from 1981–2, and then led her own trio and quartet in New York. She formed a duo with Larry Coryell in 1985, and recorded and toured successfully with David Benoit shortly before her fatal heart attack. While strongly marked by her appreciation of Wes Montgomery, Remler was also interested in the directions pursued by Pat Metheny, and with her all-round competence she made an important contribution to consolidating current trends into the mainstream. [BP]

⊙ **East To Wes** (1988; Concord). Though she recorded reasonably prolifically, Remler's final album under her own name remains her best tribute. Conceived in homage to Montgomery, her versions of standards, bop classics, her own originals and even "Sweet Georgie Fame" are a strong reminder of her expertise.

Tony Remy

Guitar, vocoder, composer.

b. London, 13 Aug 1962.

After coming to the UK jazz world's attention with flautist Phillip Bent's band in the mid-1980s, Tony Remy rose to prominence in the highly acclaimed band Desperately Seeking Fusion, a quintet also featuring his long-standing musical partner, bassist Nick Cohen. A fluent but raunchy improviser influenced as much by rock guitarists like Jimi Hendrix as by more jazz-based players such as John Scofield, Remy formed two bands in the late 1980s. The first, Lateral Thinking, a world-music-flavoured outfit, featured steel drums, vibes and vocals; the other, the Tony Remy Band, dispensed exuberant but thoughtful jazz-funk, and attracted a large UK following, leading eventually to Remy's being signed by GRP in the early 1990s. Although *Boof!* (see below) was impressive, both it and Remy's first album for his own label, *Metamorfollow-g* (Alltone; 1997), were criticized for containing too little of what had attracted his many fans: his flowing, inexhaustibly inventive, viscerally exciting guitar playing. Remy, however, is an all-round musician, not just a head-banging guitar soloist, and he proved it by composing the soundtrack to the Spike Leigh film *Career Girls* (Tweed Records; 1998), utilizing a string quartet, Stringology, and by playing with a series of stellar Americans – Pee Wee Ellis, Lenny White, Nelson Rangell – and with UK-based musicians like Steve Williamson, Courtney Pine, Jason Rebello and Jean Toussaint. In 1999, though, Remy delighted his hardcore admirers with *Jammin' At The 12 Bar Club* (see below), and has since appeared on recordings by artists as diverse as funk outfit Down To The Bone, Cuban bassist Cachaito Lopez and pop singer Sheena Easton. [CP]

Nazaire

⊙ **Who's Blues** (1992; Ronnie Scott's Jazz House). Remy joins stellar young UK band (led by US/Caribbean expatriate saxophonist Jean Toussaint), including Jason Rebello and Nick Cohen, writing the title track and providing scorching guitar throughout.

Tony Remy

⊙ **Boof!** (1994; GRP). Remy's acclaimed debut for the US label covers jazz-funk territory, highly accessible and including compositions by Marvin Gaye ("Mercy Mercy Me") and Bruce Smith/Nathaniel Phillips ("Glide") as well as Remy himself. Guests include Courtney Pine and Cleveland Watkiss, and Remy employs vocoder as well as his trademark virtuosic guitar.

⊙ **Jammin' At The 12 Bar Club** (1999; Alltone). Of this live album's 70+ minutes, over an hour is taken up by Remy's blisteringly eloquent guitar-playing on a series of long, bluesy jams. A perfect showcase for one of the UK's most exciting soloists on any instrument.

Kid Rena

Trumpet.

b. New Orleans, 30 Aug 1898; d. 25 April 1949.

Kid Rena (Henry René) played alongside Louis Armstrong in the Colored Waifs' Home brass band and replaced him in Kid Ory's 1919 band. He was a flashy trumpeter with high notes to spare, and his band, featuring brother Joseph (a less than outstanding drummer) and young George Lewis (clarinet), was very popular in New Orleans by the mid-1920s: they played dances, functions and saloons, and featured a mixture of new jazz repertoire and loosely played ragtime from the stock "Red Back Book". Though never the most highly rated New Orleans trumpeter, Rena probably influenced young players such as Sharky Bonano and Louis Prima, and by the 1930s was leading a fashionable big band at the Gypsy Tea Rooms. In 1940 he was spotted by jazz researcher/journalist Heywood Broun, at whose instigation he recorded the first-ever sides (for Delta) to launch the American jazz revival; other players in

Rena's band for this historic date included Louis "Big Eye" Nelson, Alphonse Picou and Ed Garland. Later in the 1940s Kid Rena played the Brown Derby Café with a hung-over jazz band: heavy drinking had dulled his spark and he was inactive for the last two years of his life. [DF]

Prelude To The Revival Vol. 2 (1940 & 42; American Music). Rena's seminal recordings, with additional solo sides by Bunk Johnson.

Henri Renaud

Piano.

b. Villedieu (Indre), France, 10 April 1925; d. 16 Oct 2002.

From 1949–50 Renaud played with Don Byas, Buck Clayton and Roy Eldridge, and then formed his own small group. He performed on, and helped to produce, albums by visiting US musicians in the early 1950s, and produced albums recorded in the USA for release in France in 1954. He worked with the Kenny Clarke quintet in 1961 and, while still active as a player, started introducing a regular radio series in 1962, and later hosted TV jazz spots. In 1964 he became an executive of CBS Records (France), occasionally producing new sessions by musicians such as Jean-Luc Ponty and organizing several important series of jazz reissues. [BP]

The 1954 Paris Sessions (Vogue). These three dates combine Renaud's excellent playing with his nascent role as producer. They include the first recordings under their own name of René Thomas, Frank Foster (visiting Paris with Basie) and almost the first to feature Roy Haynes, then touring with Sarah Vaughan.

➤➤ **Clifford Brown** *(Complete Paris Sessions).*

Don Rendell

Tenor and soprano saxophones, flute, clarinet.

b. Plymouth, UK, 4 March 1926.

Rendell, whose parents were both musicians, took up the alto at fifteen. He worked with American musicians in a backing band for United Services Organization entertainers at US bases in 1944, and then with several local big bands. He was a founder member of the Johnny Dankworth Seven, staying from 1950–53, and also worked with Tony Crombie in 1955 and Ted Heath from 1955–6. He toured Europe with Stan Kenton, taking uncredited solos on the *Live At Albert Hall* album, and with the Woody Herman Anglo-American Herd, in 1956 and 1959 respectively. He first led his own group from 1953–55, and has led one continuously since 1960. During that time he has featured such collaborators as Graham Bond in 1961–2, Michael Garrick from 1965–9, and Barbara Thompson from 1973–6; Ian Carr, who joined in 1962, was co-leader of the Rendell-Carr quintet from 1963–9. He has also worked and recorded for Neil Ardley, Garrick, Thompson and others.

For the last thirty years he has been a prominent teacher of jazz (and Bible studies), including periods at the Royal Academy of Music from 1974–7 and at the Guildhall from 1984 until the present. Specializing on tenor from the mid-1940s, Rendell was initially enamoured of Lester Young and later, though less audibly, John Coltrane. From these and other influences, such as Parker, Gillespie, Ellington, Monk and Holiday, he has forged a style of great strength and resilience that has been an inspiration to many younger UK musicians. [BP]

Space Walk (c.1971; Redial). A surprising choice for reissue, this neglected album from a high-water mark of the British scene spotlights Rendell's regular quintet of the time, with fellow reedman Stan Robinson and vibist Peter Shade (all three play flute at one point) in a stimulating all-original programme.

What Am I Here For? (1993–6; Spotlite). Leading two dissimilar quintets, joined by either Art Themen or trumpeter Steve Waterman (with the bonus of two vocals by Christine Tobin), Rendell answers the Ellingtonian title-question with communicative, highly personal playing on all his horns.

Allan Reuss

Guitar.

b. New York, 15 June 1915.

A pupil of George Van Eps. and one of jazz guitar's most skilled and underrated artists, Reuss is generally remembered as a mainstay of great jazz rhythm-sections, but he was a skilled soloist too. Like his teacher, Reuss began on banjo but studied guitar from the early 1930s and played regularly with Benny Goodman (1935–8), Paul Whiteman, Jack Teagarden (1939), and into the 1940s with Ted Weems and Jimmy Dorsey (1942). In the same year he began studio work for NBC, briefly returning to Goodman (1943–4) before joining Harry James (1944–5). After this he turned freelance and started teaching. Generously represented on record with his various bandleaders, he can also be heard as a studio player with Lionel Hampton, Billie Holiday, Teddy Wilson and many more. [DF]

Jack Teagarden And His Orchestra 1934–9 (Classics). This set contains a (relatively) rare solo feature for Reuss, "Pickin' for Patsie", which beautifully illustrates his chordal facility, comparable to that of his teacher George Van Eps.

Buddy Rich

Drums, vocals, leader.

b. Brooklyn, New York, 30 June 1917; d. 2 April 1987.

Buddy (Bernard) Rich was a performer at eighteen months (he toured as "Baby Traps" in his parents' vaudeville act, Wilson and Rich), danced and drummed on Broadway at four, toured Australia as a single act at six, and by eleven was leading his own band. At 21 he replaced Danny Alvin in Joe Marsala's band and by then was already clearly a super-talent destined for the big bands that were to remain his first love.

HERMAND LEONARD

Buddy Rich

"Bunny Berigan's was my first," he recalled later to Les Tomkins, "and it was a whole different world opened up to me! 'Oh so this is what music's all about!'" A succession of great big bands followed – Harry James's, Artie Shaw's, and, from November 1939, Tommy Dorsey's – and Rich, with his abrasive tongue, fine ear for what was good and bad, and ruthlessly competitive edge, was a match not only for any other drummer within cutting distance but also for his leader. "Dorsey's wasn't a hot band," he coolly remembered later, "it never professed to be. It was a dance band with good musicians. Then he hired Sy Oliver – started getting some jazz arrangements in, and then that band would kick as well as any for that time and period."

With Dorsey's orchestra Rich established a royal reputation and in 1945 (at a time when big bands were in severe decline) he formed his own and doggedly ran it for two years until the money finally ran out: "We suffered! But even finally when there was no money that was a joy because we weren't bending to the big brains who said, 'Big bands are out'." The attitude was typical of Rich, whose flint-hard convictions never allowed others to do his thinking for him. In 1947 he joined Jazz At The Philharmonic and for the next thirteen years he lent his talents to Charlie Ventura, Harry James and Tommy Dorsey again, while cultivating a reputation as a stylish singer and leading his own small groups and bands. By 1959, now slightly out of jazz fashion, he was contemplating a career switch to singing and acting. That year he suffered his first heart attack, but came back fighting – some years later, well into his forties, he achieved a black belt in karate.

For five years from 1961 he worked for Harry James, then in 1966, at the height of Beatlemania, reformed his big band, at a time when the idea seemed ludicrous. "Everybody said, 'Who the hell wants a big band?'" he remembers. "But I said, 'Well, who knows better than me? We don't know if the kids want it yet – they've never been exposed to it!'" Rich's brilliant band – boasting a battalion of fine arrangers (including Bill Holman and Don Sebesky) and *tour de force* drum features, such as a ten-minute *West Side Story* broadside – became an international success, touring Japan, Britain, Australia and elsewhere, playing the best American venues, breaking into TV in 1968 (replacing Jackie Gleason for a season), and recording best sellers. Like Tommy Dorsey, Rich was a ruthless (even cruel) taskmaster, but he got results, and his honest championship of his music values was a necessary reaffirmation of principles in an era of hype and pseudo-intellectualism. After heart bypass surgery in 1983 he unwisely cut his recuperation time from six months to two, but in 1985, back to full strength, he was once again touring nine months out of twelve, recording spectaculars for American TV, and appearing with old friend-cum-sparring-partner Frank Sinatra for concerts. [DF]

⊙ **Buddy Rich And His Legendary Orchestra** (1947–8; Hep). As well as sides, including V-discs, by Rich's big bands of the period (Doug Mettome, Allan Eager and Terry Gibbs are among the featured soloists), this excellent issue has a couple of bonuses: Rich and Ella Fitzgerald singing with Joe Mooney, and Ella plus a Rich small group including Charlie Shavers.

⊙ **Illusion** (1947–71; Sequel). The perfect introduction to Rich's work, spread over three CDs and taking in almost every aspect of his drum supremacy: trios with Nat Cole and Lester Young; sets at JATP; sides with Bud Powell and Charlie Parker; a duet with Gene Krupa; and tracks from his Swinging New Big Band of the 1960s.

⊙ **Krupa And Rich** (1955; Verve). One of the great drum-battle records, with Gillespie, Eldridge, Flip Phillips, Ben Webster and Oscar Peterson in attendance.

⊙ **Swingin' New Big Band** (1966; Pacific). Rich's classic and courageous re-entry into the big band world at a time when all around was rock. Arrangements by Oliver Nelson and Bill Holman frame a band legendary for its strength, excitement and refusal to take prisoners, and there are bonus CD tracks too, amid excellent Pacific production.

⊙ **Big Swing Face** (1967; Pacific Jazz). Another acknowledged classic from Rich's brand-new big band of the time;soloists and sections once again take no prisoners (they wouldn't have been allowed to anyhow!) on the title track and elsewhere.

⊙ **Mercy, Mercy** (1968; Pacific Jazz). Art Pepper and Don Menza shine brightly amid the soloists on this album; proof that Rich was ever up-to-date is his exciting version of Joe Zawinul's title track.

Fred Rich

Piano, composer, leader.

b. Warsaw, Poland, 3 Jan 1898; d. Beverly Hills, California, 8 Sept 1956.

Fred Rich was a capable studio pianist, arranger and bandleader who, in his capacity as musical director for studio orchestras on the Harmony, OKeh and Hit of the Week labels (among others), recorded scores of sides from 1925 on. The records were issued under a bewildering variety of pseudonyms (including The Deauville Syncopators, Chester Leighton and his Sophomores, and The New York Syncopators), and his regular sidemen included the cream of 1920s session and jazz players: a shortlist would include Leo McConville, Bunny Berigan, Tommy and Jimmy Dorsey, Carl Kress, Tony Parenti, Joe Venuti, Frank Signorelli, Dick McDonough, Joe Tarto and Stan King. By the late 1930s he was working mainly in radio: his last recording dates, from 1940, included such as Roy Eldridge, Benny Carter, Clyde Hart and Hayes Alvis. From 1942, Rich worked on the musical staff for United Artists; in 1945 he was partly paralysed as a result of a fall, but he continued his career up to the 1950s. [DF]

Red Richards

Piano, vocals.
b. Brooklyn, New York, 19 Oct 1912; d. 12 March 1998.

Red (Charles) Richards worked early on with players as varied as Tab Smith (for four years), Jimmy McPartland and Roy Eldridge, and by the early 1950s had played for Sidney Bechet, his pupil Bob Wilber and Mezz Mezzrow. After a long stint with Muggsy Spanier (1953–7) he was regularly to be found among Chicago-style jazzmen, including Wild Bill Davison, and as solo pianist at Eddie Condon's. From 1960 (and 1964 full-time) he co-led the successful Saints and Sinners with Vic Dickenson, featuring Herman Autrey. Later, after Dickenson left, Richards reduced to a quartet with clarinettist Herbie Hall, played club residencies including Condon's (solo 1975–7, and with his own trio 1977–8), subbed with The World's Greatest Jazz Band, toured Europe as a soloist, and worked with Panama Francis's Savoy Sultans. In the 1980s and into the 1990s Richards stayed busy, including tours of Spain, Japan and Australia. His fine rolling style, sympathetic backing talent and encyclopedic knowledge of jazz piano history made him one of the most satisfying classic pianists around. [DF]

⦿ **Just Friends** (1981; Sackville). An intimate trio session co-featuring Richards with his longtime friend, trombonist Vic Dickenson, plus bassist Johnny Williams. Outstanding.

Tim Richards

Piano, composer.
b. London, 23 June 1952.

A fluent, lucid but vigorous pianist in (at least initially) the McCoy Tyner mould, Tim Richards first came to public attention when he formed the West Country-based quintet Spirit Level with saxophonist Paul Dunmall in 1979. After recording their first Spotlite album, *Mice In The Wallet*, the quintet won first prize at France's Dunkirk jazz festival in 1982 and toured extensively in Europe before recording their second album, *Proud Owners*, with trumpeter Dave Holdsworth in 1984. Moving to London the following year, Richards led Spirit Level, augmented by US trumpeter Jack Walrath, on a European tour in 1987 and released the album *Killer Bunnies* the same year. In 1988 Richards toured and recorded with US bluesmen Joe Louis Walker and Otis Grand, and in 1989 made a tenth-anniversary tour of Europe with Spirit Level. A new line-up of the band, featuring saxophonist Jerry Underwood, and a trio with bassist Kubryk Townsend and drummer Kenrick Rowe, were Richards's chief musical outlets in the late 1980s and early 1990s, but he also played with fellow pianist Roland Perrin, guitarist Jim Mullen and saxophonists Ed Jones and Jean Toussaint during this period. In 1993 Richards formed the London Blues Band, a quintet featuring guitarist Jon Taylor and tenor player Brian Iddenden, and the following year took Spirit Level on a fifteenth-anniversary tour of the UK. Although Spirit Level play a straightforwardly accessible modern jazz, Richards's own playing is laced with the blues, and he demonstrated his skill in this (and other) forms on a 1998 trio recording *The Other Side* (33 Records), some material from which was also contained in Richards's excellent educational book *Improvising Blues Piano* (Schott Educational, 1997). In 1996, Richards collaborated with Vienna-based saxophonist Sigi Finkel, making a series of recordings for radio and CD (*Dervish Dances*, ORF; 1997) and performing in duo and quartet settings (as Soundscape) with him. In 1999, Spirit Level, with an entirely new line-up, celebrated their twentieth anniversary,though that group was eventually superseded by Great Spirit, which plays Richards's charts for a nine-piece. Of his other current projects, Grooveyard is a funk and soul group while his piano-bass-drums trio gets bluesier with each incarnation. [CP]

Spirit Level

⊙ **On The Level** (1994; 33 Records). Kubryk Townsend (bass) and Kenrick Rowe (drums) form the new rhythm-section, but the mix remains the same: bright, airy modern jazz featuring gutsy saxophone playing (Jerry Underwood) and luminously funky Richards.

⊙ **Great Spirit/Best Of Spirit Level** (1999; 33 Records). A double CD of Richards new nine-piece band(with Denys Baptiste and Gilad Atzmon among others) features the composition "Suite for the Shed" – his most ambitious piece yet. Packaged with highlights of the two earlier Spirit Level albums *Killer Bunnies* (1987) and *New Year* (1991).

Tim Richards Trio

⊙ **Twelve By Three** (2003; 33 Records). Another line-up – bassist Dominic Howles and drummer Matt Home – and a strong one, with Richards displaying his increasingly down-home style on material by Billy Taylor, Gene Harris and Horace Silver.

Trevor Richards

Drums.
b. UK, 1945.

Richards played with groups in Britain and Europe before moving to the USA in 1966 where he studied informally with Zutty Singleton in New York and with Cie Frazier and Louis Barbarin in New Orleans. Here he played with surviving veterans and parade bands as well as researching jazz history at Tulane University. In 1972 he formed his New Orleans Trio, touring internationally for another ten years, before returning to New Orleans to co-lead the Original Camellia Jazz Band. Since 1981 he has also toured annually with the Art Hodes trio and later Ralph Sutton, as well as continuing jazz research, organizing concerts and festivals and working on extended literary projects. In 1993 he was awarded a certificate of merit for outstanding services to the city of New Orleans. [DF]

⊙ **The International Trio** (1995; New Orleans Jazz Productions). Authentic New Orleans trio music featuring Reimer Von Essen (reeds), along with the rolling drums of Richards, and the magnificent piano-playing of Ralph Sutton.

Hannah Richardson

Vocals.
b. Alexandria, Virginia, 16 May 1956.

A singer for over twenty-five years, Richardson has recently gained prominence on the US jazz scene following collaborations with her bass-playing husband Phil Flanigan. Richardson's most noticeable influence is Maxine Sullivan, particularly in the way an unassuming approach is wedded to an effortless swing, and she looks likely to join that highly skilled group of American swing singers which includes Rebecca Kilgore and Daryl Sherman. She has appeared at jazz festivals including the Arbors March of Jazz, Clearwater Florida, the Atlantic Mutual Jazz Fest in New Jersey and most recently the Blackpool Swinging Jazz Party in England. [DF]

⊙ **Something To Remember You By** (2001; Lala). A tribute to Maxine Sullivan featuring relaxed vocal performance by Richardson amid a group including Allan Vaché and Ken Peplowski on reeds and Flanigan on bass.

Jerome Richardson

Alto, tenor, soprano and baritone saxophones, flute.
b. Sealy, Texas, 15 Nov 1920; d. 23 June 2000.

Brought up in Oakland, he played alto professionally with local bands from the age of fourteen, and was in a navy band alongside Marshall Royal during World War II. He toured with Lionel Hampton in 1949–51, adding flute to his arsenal, and with Earl Hines in 1954–5. Settling in New York he began studio work, often on tenor and often for Ernie Wilkins or Quincy Jones, with whose band he played in Paris in 1959–60. A founder member of the Thad Jones-Mel Lewis band in 1966 until moving to Los Angeles in 1971, he created one of its distinctive sounds by leading the saxophone section on soprano. Also a valued sideman for Oliver Nelson and several other West Coast-based leaders, he returned to New York in the 1980s, taking part in the premiere of Mingus's *Epitaph* and other live appearances, as well as continued session work. His popular tune "The Groove Merchant" is heard on the two albums listed below. [BP]

⊙ **Jazz Station Runaway** (1996–7; TCB). Backed by a four-piece rhythm-section including George Mraz and Lewis Nash, Richardson's first solo date in nearly three decades features him on alto, soprano and flute in an interesting set of original pieces and two Ellington ballads.

➤➤ **Thad Jones** *(Central Park North).*

John Richardson

Drums.
b. London, 8 Aug 1932.

John Richardson worked from the 1950s with Alex Welsh, Acker Bilk, the Randall-Shepherd All Stars, Stan Greig's trio, John Picard's sextet and others, as well as freelancing and leading his own small groups. He plays in a high-powered, dynamic style that owes a lot to the most creative and colourful mid-period drummers such as Dave Tough, Cliff Leeman and Sid Catlett. In recent years Richardson has freelanced, working in London pubs and clubs and regularly leading for himself. [DF]

➤➤ **Freddy Randall** *(Freddy Randall-Dave Shepherd Jazz All Stars).*

Boomie Richman

Tenor saxophone, clarinet, flute.
b. Brockton, Massachusetts, 2 April 1921.

A very underrated tenor saxophonist in the style of Eddie Miller, Boomie (Abraham Samuel) Richman played his first dates around Boston and came to New York in 1942 to join longtime colleague Muggsy Spanier's big band. After work with Jerry Wald's, and George Paxton's orchestras, he joined Tommy Dorsey for a six-year stay and became, along with Charlie Shavers, Pee Wee Erwin and Dave Tough, one of Dorsey's most outstanding cornermen, whose work is nicely captured on the 1946 version of "At Sundown". After he left Dorsey in 1952, Richman worked in the studios and regularly for Benny Goodman (whom he met first on a 1946 Dorsey radio show for NBC) until 1958, when Zoot Sims took over his chair. Recorded work from Richman is rarer than it should be: one fine date with Spanier shows off his tasteful swing skills to good advantage. [DF]

➤➤ **Muggsy Spanier** *(Muggsy Spanier).*

Dannie Richmond

Drums; also tenor saxophone.

b. New York, 15 Dec 1931; d. 15 March 1988.

Richmond played tenor from the age of thirteen, and toured with the Paul Williams R&B band around 1955. Six months after taking up the drums seriously, he joined Charles Mingus, with whom, apart from a few interruptions, he was associated for the next 21 years. He also worked in the late 1950s with Chet Baker, in the late 1960s with soul singer Johnny Taylor, and from 1971–3 with Joe Cocker, Elton John and the ex-John Mayall sidemen of the Mark-Almond group. Following his return to jazz, he also did a great deal of freelance recording and gigging with the likes of Duke Jordan, Jimmy Knepper and Bennie Wallace. After Mingus's death, he was the original musical director of Mingus Dynasty in 1980, and played with the George Adams-Don Pullen group from 1980–83 and in 1985. His own quintet with Ricky Ford (or Kenny Garrett) and Jack Walrath made several albums and European tours.

Richmond was typecast for many years as Mingus's drummer, and it is true that the qualities of all-round musicianship that he brought to the task made him ideally suited, as almost any record of them working together will demonstrate. Developing from a profound admiration for Max Roach and Philly Joe Jones, he perfected a style that was responsive both to the needs of a particular soloist at a particular moment and also to the overall structure of a composition. The combination of supportiveness and excitement he created was equally adaptable to a piano trio or a big band, to a conservative mainstream context or a freely organized group improvisation, but this versatility is still underrecognized. [BP]

⊙ **Three Or Four Shades Of Dannie Richmond** (1981; Tutu). A live festival recording of the quintet with Walrath and Kenny Garrett, which re-creates Don Pullen's "Big Alice And John Henry", a passable "Goodbye Pork Pie Hat" and a truly exciting "Cumbia And Jazz Fusion", written by Mingus.

➤➤ **Charles Mingus** *(Mingus Ah Um; Charles Mingus Presents Charles Mingus; The Black Saint And The Sinner Lady).*

Alex Riel

Drums.

b. Copenhagen, 13 Sept 1940.

Riel took lessons in Copenhagen during the 1960s, and spent one term at the Berklee School, Boston, in 1966. During the early 1960s he went deeply into free jazz, working with John Tchicai, Archie Shepp and Gary Peacock among others. In 1965 he was voted Danish Musician of the Year. With trumpeter Palle Mikkelborg, Riel formed a quintet in 1966, and in 1968 it won first prize at the Montreux festival and then played at the Newport festival. While in the USA in 1966, Riel played with many musicians including Roland Kirk and Toshiko Akiyoshi. During the early 1970s he again co-led a group, V8, with Mikkelborg. Since then he has freelanced in Europe. He has recorded with many people, including Mikkelborg, Ben Webster, Gary Bartz, Sahib Shihab, Stuff Smith and Herb Geller. [IC]

➤➤ **Allan Botschinsky** *(The Bench);* **Ben Webster** *(Stormy Weather/Gone With The Wind).*

Barry Ries

Trumpet, flugelhorn, drums.

b. Cincinnati, 16 March 1952.

His father, a drummer, gave Barry Ries drum lessons from the age of seven, and passed on all the dance rhythms of the day. Ries began on trumpet at the age of eleven, and from the age of fourteen began playing dance functions on trumpet and drums. He also heard trumpeter Kenny Dorham on record, and at fifteen heard the Davis album *Miles Smiles*, and Coltrane's *Love Supreme*, which broadened his conception. From 1968, he also played with local rock bands, and for two years (1974–6) was drummer with a Cincinnati piano trio playing week-long engagements with visiting stars such as Milt Jackson, Sonny Stitt and singer Earl Coleman. In 1978, he joined the trumpet section of Woody Herman's band and moved to New York, playing sessions with Joe Lovano, Jeff Hirschfield, Adam Nussbaum and others.

Ries joined Gerry Mulligan's Concert Jazz Band and gained valuable experience. Mulligan introduced him to composer/arranger Don Sebesky, who gave him a lot of studio work, and recruited Ries for the Don Sebesky New York All Stars band. Ries also began working with Lionel Hampton and Horace Silver – with the latter he played all the major jazz clubs in America. Through working with Machito he became more involved with Latin music. He has recorded albums with Mulligan, Hampton and Sebesky, but did not release his own debut CD, *Solitude In The Crowd*, until 1998. Ries was a member of the Steve Swallow all-star quintet with Adam Nussbaum, Mick Goodrick and Chris Potter, which played at London's Ronnie Scott's club in 1999. He currently lives in Boston, where he performs and teaches both trumpet and drums.

Ries is a natural improviser, with a smooth, glowing sound on trumpet and flugelhorn, and a wonderfully wayward sense of harmony and line. His favourites are Miles, Lee Morgan, Cherry and Dorham, among others, and other inspirations include Armstrong, Lester Young, Parker, Coltrane, Ornette Coleman, Mahler and Alban Berg. [IC]

⊙ **Solitude In The Crowd** (1998; Double-Time). This mixture of originals and standards displays Ries's great versatility and maturity. Three of the eight tracks are by his quartet with pianist Michael Cochrane, bassist Dennis Irwin and either Billy Drummond or Yoron Israel on drums. Joe Lovano is added for the other five tracks. Ries's composing is as assured and wide-ranging as his playing, and the material ranges from atmospheric free-ish pieces like his "Akasha", with its spacey sounds and Cherryesque trumpet, to "Hormone Derange", which is hard, angular and full of surprising twists and turns.

Herlin Riley

Drums.

b. New Orleans, 15 Feb 1957.

Born into a New Orleans musical family, the Lasties, Herlin Riley began on drums at three, but also studied trumpet throughout high school and two years of college. Between 1984–7, he played drums with Ahmad Jamal and gained theatre experience in *One Mo' Time* and *Satchmo: America's Musical Legend*. He has recorded with New Orleans singer/pianists Dr John and Harry Connick Jnr, guitarists George Benson, Doug Raney and Mark Whitfield and pianists Monty Alexander, Marcus Roberts and Junko Onishi, and in 2000 released his solo debut (see below). But his fame in the jazz community rests mainly on his work with the Marsalises, Branford and especially Wynton, with whom he has appeared eighteen times on album since joining the trumpeter's septet in spring 1988. A regular performer also with the Lincoln Center Jazz Orchestra, he's nicknamed "Homey" by Marsalis, "because he makes everyone feel at home". Riley has, according to the same source, "a real spiritual connection to the drums ... he grew up playing in the church, so knows that tradition. He can play the tambourine, the washboard; anything you can hit, he can play." [CP]

⊙ **Watch What You're Doing** (2000; Criss Cross). Riley expertly steers a lineup of LCJO alumni (trumpeter Ryan Kisor, saxist Victor Goines and trombonist Wycliffe Gordon among them) through eight originals in a variety of on-the-button grooves, plus a touching tribute to John Lewis written by bassist Rodney Whitaker.

WYNTON MARSALIS

⊙ **Blue Interlude** (1992; Columbia). Marsalis's classic septet in an early outing: fresh, democratic, cultured yet hard-swinging music impeccably driven by Riley.

Howard Riley

Piano.

b. Huddersfield, Yorkshire, UK, 16 Feb 1943.

Son of a semi-pro dance-band pianist, Riley became interested in jazz in the mid-1950s and was self-taught with some paternal help. From 1959 he played in jazz clubs around Yorkshire, then, while studying theory and composition during the 1960s (at the universities of Wales, Indiana and York), he played with his own trios and in 1965 with the Evan Parker quartet, devoting himself almost exclusively to free improvisation. Since 1967 he has played clubs and festivals in Europe, the USA and Canada. He led his own trio from 1967–76, and since then has given many solo performances.

In 1970 he became a founder member of the Musicians' Co-operative in London. He has also played duo with John McLaughlin (1968), Keith Tippett (from 1981), Jaki Byard (from 1982), Eddie Prévost (from 1984) and Elton Dean (from 1984); in quartets with Trevor Watts, Barry Guy, John Stevens (1978–81), Evan Parker, Guy and Stevens (from 1983); and with Tony Oxley groups (from 1972), the London Jazz Composers' Orchestra (from 1970) and the Barbara Thompson-Art Themen quintet (1969–70). Riley has also composed for the LJCO and the New Jazz Orchestra and for his own groups. He is active in education and has taught jazz piano and taken workshops at the Guildhall School of Music (from 1969) and Goldsmiths' College (from 1975) in London. In 1976–7 he was the Creative Associate at the Center of the Creative and Performing Arts, Buffalo, New York. In the 1990s Riley resumed his association with Elton Dean and made three albums with him. More recently he has joined forces with saxophonist Larry Stabbins, bassist Tony Wren and drummer Mark Sanders and produced an outstanding album, *Four In The Afternoon*. His favourite pianists range from Bill Evans and Monk to Richard Twardzik and Art Tatum. [IC]

⊙ **Procession** (1990; Wondrous); **The Heat of Moments** (1991–2; Wondrous); **Beyond Category** (1993; Wondrous). Three fine solo albums, the first two comprising spontaneous improvisations, the third showcasing Riley playing Thelonious Monk and Ellington pieces, straining the themes through the sieve of his own sensibilities.

⊙ **Four In The Afternoon** (2002; Emanem). An outstandingly good quartet gets stuck into some truly mind-blowing improvisation. Riley shows an amazing range of tone colour and harmonic imagination, while Stabbins is at his virtuosic best.

➤➤ **Elton Dean** *(Twos And Threes)*; **Barry Guy** *(Harmos)*.

Sammy Rimington

Clarinet, alto saxophone, leader.

b. London, 29 April 1942.

Of all the "honorary" New Orleans citizens who happen to come from Britain, Sammy Rimington is perhaps the most lyrically musical. A graceful and highly creative master of New Orleans jazz, he came to prominence with Ken Colyer's Jazzmen around 1960 and worked regularly with them thereafter, as well as with like-minded musicians countrywide in Britain, Europe and America. In 1965 he moved to the USA, worked with "Red" Allen, Zutty Singleton, Herman Autrey and others, and soon after moved to New Orleans, where he replaced Butch Thompson in the Hall Brothers' Band, recorded with Kid Thomas (George Lewis shared the sessions) and regularly collaborated with visitors like Don Ewell and Max Morath. After returning to Europe he worked with Barry Martyn, formed his jazz-rock band Armada, and worked around Britain and Europe with, among others, George Webb (1973), Martyn's Legends of Jazz

(1974), Duke Burrell (1974–5) and Chris Barber (1977–9). By 1995 he had played and recorded with every American and European New Orleans-style jazzman of note, and like a small number of other great British reedmen (eg Tubby Hayes and Pete King) his name had become a promise of quality and flair. "It's very difficult to express my feeling for this kind of music," says Rimington, "but I know after years of playing and experience that it's one of the most difficult forms of music to play well, due to its simplicity and relaxed rhythmic feel. I prefer the music to be quite free but controlled ... also not to be restricted and tied down to sounding like a particular band on record." [DF]

Ken Colyer

When I Leave The World Behind (1963; Lake). Colyer's greatest band, with Geoff Cole and Rimington, playing a programme of New Orleans standards, rags and spirituals.

Sammy Rimington

The Exciting Saxophone Of Sammy Rimington (1986–91; Progressive). Working with just a rhythm-section, Rimington's solo powers are captured at length here.

Very Live At Pakefield Rose (1999/RRCD). This date teams him with a worthy set of creative compatriots; the great trumpeter Cuff Billett, trombonist Mike Pointon, and a rhythm section including the outstanding Nick Dawson (piano) plus Louis Lince, Annie Hawkins and entrepreneur-drummer John Petters. In this 'spirited and passionate outing' (Cook/Morton) Rimington shines in the ensemble, in solo and by himself on "Burgundy Street Blues".

Lee Ritenour

Guitar.

b. Los Angeles, 1 Nov 1952.

Ritenour studied privately with Duke Miller, Joe Pass, Howard Roberts and Christopher Parkening, and at the University of Southern California School of Music under Jack Marshall, whom he succeeded as guitar instructor at the age of 21 after Marshall's death. In 1974 he joined Sergio Mendes and Brasil '77, touring extensively. Returning to LA, he became, and remains, one of the busiest session guitarists on account of his excellent musicianship, awareness of contemporary styles and versatility on electric and acoustic guitars. He has recorded with hundreds of leading musicians including Dave Grusin, Herbie Hancock, Oliver Nelson, Sonny Rollins, Gato Barbieri, George Benson, Earl Klugh and Tom Scott, and has accompanied singers Peggy Lee, Aretha Franklin, Barbra Streisand, Stevie Wonder, Ray Charles and Johnny Mathis. Since 1974 he has recorded a series of solo albums and in recent years has been extensively featured on the GRP label and latterly on the Verve imprint. His 2002 offering, *Rit's House*, is archetypal Ritenour. [CA/CI]

Stolen Moments (1990; GRP Records). Any lingering suggestion that Ritenour is a surface player, capable only of lightweight, well-crafted music such as on the commercially aware *Captain Fingers* (1978), is finally dispelled by this performance – mature, passionate and focused playing with more than a nod in the direction of his first inspiration, Wes Montgomery.

Sam Rivers

Tenor and soprano saxophones, piano, flute, bass clarinet, viola, composer.

b. El Reno, Oklahoma, 25 Sept 1923.

Rivers's grandfather, a minister and musician, published *A Collection of Revival Hymns and Plantation Melodies* in 1882. His mother was a pianist; his father, a Fisk University graduate, sang with the Fisk Jubilee Singers and the Silverstone quartet. Rivers heard spirituals and light classics at home; he began on piano at five years old, and then took up the violin and alto saxophone. At twelve he played soprano in a marching band, then took up the tenor saxophone seriously at Jarvis Christian College, Texas. In 1947 he went to the Boston Conservatory, studying composition and viola, and also playing the violin; at night, however, he played the saxophone in a bar. He also worked with Jaki Byard, Joe Gordon and Herb Pomeroy. His early influences were Lester Young, Coleman Hawkins and Eddie Davis, and later ones included John Coltrane, Charlie Parker and Sonny Rollins. From 1955–7 he was in Florida, composing music for lyrics and working for singers and dancers; he also co-led a band with Don Wilkerson and accompanied Billie Holiday on tour. In 1958 he was with the Herb Pomeroy big band in Boston, and also led his own quartet with the thirteen-year-old Tony Williams on drums. At the beginning of the 1960s he was listening to Cecil Taylor and Ornette Coleman, and becoming interested in the abstract music of the avant-garde.

In the early 1960s he was also musical director of a band backing visiting artists such as Maxine Brown, Wilson Pickett and B.B. King, and he toured with T-Bone Walker. In 1964 he spent six months with Miles Davis, touring in the USA and playing in Japan, where they recorded a live album. In 1967 he moved to New York and began teaching at his own studio in Harlem. From 1968–73 he played with Cecil Taylor. In 1971, with his wife Bea, he opened Studio Rivbea as a teaching and music performance centre, presenting his own group with guest artists such as Dewey Redman, Clifford Jordan and Sonny Fortune, and also presenting other groups.

Talking of music teaching, Rivers told Michael Ullman: "I make sure that I'm not imitated. I make sure that my students come up with their own individual approaches to the music. My students write their own exercises. They don't play anything but their own music so how are they going to copy anybody?" As well as teaching at his own loft, Rivers was from 1968 composer in residence for the Harlem Opera Society, lecturer on African-American musical history at Connecticut College in 1972, and artist in residence at Wesleyan University from 1970–73.

In January 1975 he was guest soloist with the San Francisco Symphony Orchestra; in 1978 the Newport in New York festival presented "The World of Sam Rivers" at Carnegie Hall, and in 1979 he presented a piece for 32 musicians at New York's Public Theater. During the later 1970s Rivers was closely associated with Dave Holland in duo and trio formations. The trio toured the USA and Europe, several times playing major festivals, and Rivers began to feature more strongly piano-playing and flute – he also sang the blues spiritedly. Rivers toured with Dizzy Gillespie in the late 1980s, and has continued to lead his own groups.

Rivers is a virtuoso whose style is a compendium of the jazz tradition from the early blues to abstraction. In one sense, however, he is conservative – he has completely ignored the electronic revolution of the 1970s, and confines himself entirely to acoustic music. [IC]

Dave Holland-Sam Rivers (1976; Improvising Artists). Rivers on tenor and soprano saxophones and Holland on bass improvise two long tracks – "Waterfall" and "Cascade" – and create abstract music which is shot through with feeling.

Waves (1978; Tomato). With Holland on bass and cello, drummer Thurman Barker, and Joe Daley on tuba and baritone horn, Rivers delivers his vital brand of controlled freedom.

Colors (1982; Black Saint). Rivers leads ten musicians (the Winds of Manhattan), all doubling on reeds or woodwind or both, without rhythm-section. The leader flits across this landscape of shifting sounds and harmonies.

Lazuli (1989; Timeless). Rivers with guitar, bass and drums, playing in more conventional settings – which he also does exceedingly well.

➤➤ **Dave Holland** *(Conference of the Birds).*

Max Roach

Drums, composer.

b. New Land, North Carolina, 10 Jan 1924.

Roach was brought up from the age of four in New York, and was given a drumkit at twelve. He played with teenage friends, studied theory and composition at the Manhattan School of Music, started sitting in at Minton's and Monroe's, and then replaced Kenny Clarke in the Coleman Hawkins group, making his recording debut with Hawkins in 1943. He worked with Dizzy Gillespie on 52nd Street in 1944, then deputized briefly with Duke Ellington and toured with the Benny Carter band for a year in 1944–5. He did nightclub and recording work with Charlie Parker in 1945, including Parker's first session under his own name, as well as working with Gillespie's big band. The next year he played with Stan Getz, Allen Eager and Hawkins again, and from 1947–9 he was the regular drummer in the classic Parker quintet. This was followed by freelance work (including Jazz At The Philharmonic) and leading his own groups. He became a partner in Charles Mingus's Debut Records, and appeared on several sessions, including the celebrated Massey Hall concert of 1953. He worked in California in 1953–4, and while there formed a new quintet in 1954, featuring Clifford Brown as co-leader.

Despite the tragic death of both Brown and Richie Powell in 1956, Roach has maintained his group continuously to the present day. Among his many collaborators have been Donald Byrd, Kenny Dorham, Booker Little, Freddie Hubbard, Sonny Rollins, Hank Mobley, George Coleman, Stanley Turrentine, Billy Harper, Barry Harris, Ray Bryant, Mal Waldron and George Cables, and his regular 1980s–90s sidemen, trumpeter Cecil Bridgewater and Odean Pope. He has also expanded his interests beyond the conventional horns-and-rhythm grouping for specific projects, incorporating choirs, solo singers such as Andy Bey and Abbey Lincoln (to whom he was married from 1962–70), and string quartets (including, on occasion, his daughter Maxine). In 1972, he formed a regular group combining various drums and tuned percussion, such as vibes and steel-pans, called M'Boom. In the 1970s and 80s he performed duos with Archie Shepp, Anthony Braxton, Cecil Taylor and Abdullah Ibrahim, and in the early 1980s he was one of the first jazzmen to collaborate with rappers.

Although he has collaborated with various composer/arrangers on some of these projects, he has been the composer of the greater part of the material performed by his groups in the last 35 years. It is no exaggeration, however, to say that Roach is composing each time he plays the drums. Not only are his solos models of structured development, but his manner of backing other soloists encourages or reinforces similar tendencies in them. This ability, which first surfaced alongside Parker (and during Rollins's eighteen months with Roach), has become more evident, and perhaps more necessary, in the marathon performances of the post-Coltrane era. It is, however, based on ideas arising from the work of Jo Jones and Kenny Clarke, who not only prompted the soloists but made them sound good within the ensemble. Even Roach's own playing, while displaying extreme independence on each part of the kit (an influence in turn on Elvin Jones), always makes the whole greater than the parts.

Perhaps there is a parallel here with Roach's view of music's reflection of, and responsibility to, society as a whole. He marked the start of the 1960s with his *We Insist: Freedom Now Suite* and, while far from being the first musician to comment on the civil rights struggle, he has been the most consistent in his concern. More importantly, unlike much other politically inspired jazz, Roach's work in this direction always stands up musically, even long after its initial impetus. And, from being a performer who organized protests and lectured audiences from the bandstand, he was able, after 1972, to combine his artistic and educational communication as professor of music at the University of Massachusetts. [BP]

Clifford Brown/Max Roach (1954–5; Verve). Now reissued in expanded form, the first classic album of the jointly led quintet features iconic tunes like Duke Jordan's "Jor-

Max Roach

Du" and Brownie's "Daahoud" and "Joy Spring", on which Roach plays one of his brilliant solos entirely with brushes.

⊙ **Deeds Not Words** (1958; Riverside/OJC). After the departure of Sonny Rollins and bassist George Morrow (survivors of the Brown-Richie Powell tragedy), Roach picked up the pieces by hiring the Memphis team of Booker Little and George Coleman, and wrote striking and demanding originals and arrangements for them.

⊙ **We Insist!: Freedom Now Suite** (1960; Candid). Booker remains, and the combined weight of a guest solo by Coleman Hawkins, the added Afro-Latin percussion, and Abbey Lincoln's wordless duo with Roach on "Triptych" make Roach's composition a political statement that stands up musically.

⊙ **Lift Every Voice And Sing** (1971; Koch). A very different political statement is this marriage of post-Coltrane jazz, featuring Billy Harper and George Cables, with the strength of gospel music and spirituals, dedicated to Paul Robeson.

⊙ **To The Max!** (1990–91; Enja). While showing no signs of diminishing his activity, Roach's double CD is a résumé of his activities of the previous twenty years. The percussion group M'Boom contributes three tracks; Roach plays solo, with his quartet and with the string quartet; and combines them with a chorus on the American Indian-inspired composition "Ghost Dance".

➤➤ **Clifford Brown** *(Brownie; Alone Together);* **Charlie Parker** *(Complete Savoy And Dial Studio Recordings; The Dial Masters; Complete Live Performances On Savoy);* **Sonny Rollins** *(Saxophone Colossus; Freedom Suite).*

Yves Robert

Trombone.

b. Clermont-Ferrand, France, 17 Jan 1958.

Robert studied at music school until the age of eighteen. In 1977 he played with hard-bop groups in the Hot Club de Lyon; in 1979 he joined the Nancy Jazz Action and the free jazz group Agapao. He returned to Lyons in 1982 to work with ARFI (Association de la Recherche d'un Folklore Imaginaire) and the big band La Marmite Infernale. In 1984 he moved to Marseilles and in the mid-1980s was working with GRIM (Groupe de Recherche et d'Improvisation Musicale), La Marmite Infernale, the Didier Levallet quintet, and *Futurities*, a dance show led by Steve Lacy. Robert has also worked with the Brotherhood of Breath, touring the UK and Mozambique with them, and with La Marmite Infernale he appeared at the New jazz festival in Moers. In 1985 he joined the Orchestre National de Jazz, led by François Jeanneau. He has recorded with André Jaume, La Marmite Infernale, Denis Levaillant, Didier Levallet, Company and Louis Sclavis, among others. [IC]

Luckey Roberts

Piano, composer.

b. Philadelphia, 7 Aug 1887; d. 5 Feb 1968.

After early days in vaudeville working as an acrobat and child juggler, Luckey (Charles Luckyeth) Roberts learned his profession in Baltimore's saloons and cabarets. A huge man – his fingers could stretch a record-breaking fourteenth on the piano keys – Roberts was well established in New York by 1913, the year that two of his most famous compositions, "Pork And Beans" and "Junk Man Rag", were published. As with all of Roberts's output, they became test pieces for such young hopefuls as Fats Waller, Duke Ellington and James P.

Johnson (whom Roberts tutored). Besides being one of the most technically dazzling piano soloists of the late ragtime era (his piano rolls, from 1916, are sensational), Roberts led his own band too: it worked on the vaudeville circuit as well as at hotels and high society functions throughout the 1920s and 1930s, and Roberts quickly became a society favourite. Like Eubie Blake (who was a shade jealous of his young rival, whom he accused of being able to cry at will to avert trouble), Roberts was a prolific composer: he had fourteen of his musical comedies successfully produced in the prewar years. In 1939 he was the star of a concert at New York's Carnegie Hall, in 1941 he headlined another at Town Hall, and he was a featured artist on Rudi Blesh's *This Is Jazz* series in 1947, by which time he was writing extended works for his orchestra, as well as hits such as "Moonlight Cocktail". In later years Roberts often played at his own Harlem bar, the Rendezvous. [DF]

The Circle Recordings (1946; Solo Art). Invaluable documentation of this giant of stride piano on just six tracks. The rest are (worthily) devoted to Ralph Sutton, but more Roberts on CD – or anywhere! – would be welcome.

Marcus Roberts

Piano.

b. Jacksonville, Florida, 7 Aug 1963.

Marcus (Marthaniel) Roberts was blind from the age of five, started on piano at the age of eight and studied music formally, including at Florida State University, until 1984. Two years earlier he was heard by Wynton Marsalis, whose band he joined from 1985–91. He won the Great American Jazz Piano Competition held in his home town in 1982 and the first Thelonious Monk Competition in 1987, and signed a contract to record under his own name; he then became the first musician to have his first three albums reach No. 1 in *Billboard*'s jazz chart. Since leaving Marsalis, he has toured as a soloist and with his own groups, and premiered his extended work *Romance, Swing And The Blues* at the Lincoln Center in 1993. The following winter he was musical director of the Lincoln Center Jazz Orchestra on a thirty-city tour, and in 1994 he played Gershwin with the American Symphony Orchestra. An interest in composers, also including Ellington, Monk and Morton (featured on the album *Alone With Three Giants*), has categorized Marcus in some people's eyes as only interested in repertory interpretation. Roberts's intention, however, is clearly to combine his diligent research in this area with his own considerable compositional gifts. [BP]

Deep In The Shed (1989; Novus). As well as marking the first appearance of "E. Dankworth" as a pseudonym for Wynton, this features other members of his current band in sextet/septet performances of Roberts's modal and post-bop compositions, wherein he shows a leaning towards McCoy Tyner.

Gershwin For Lovers (1994; Columbia). Using former Marsalis colleagues Reginald Veal and Herlin Riley on bass and drums, this is Roberts's first conventional trio album and dwells for the most part on Ahmad Jamal-type arrangements and low-key piano-playing.

Herb Robertson

Trumpet, pocket trumpet, cornet, flugelhorn.

b. Plainfield, New Jersey, 21 Feb 1951.

An important, if relatively underrated, member of New York's coterie of creative jazz musicians since the early 1980s, Herb Robertson is memorably described by drummer/composer Bobby Previte as "a wild card ... like a part of yourself that likes to lose control but is a bit nervous about it". Robertson is chiefly famous for his unpredictable, jittery – but always cogent – contributions on his variety of brass instruments on the albums of saxophonist Tim Berne, as part of his band Caos Totale, but he has also been featured on recordings by bassists Mark Helias (in the late 1980s) and Lindsey Horner (1989), David Sanborn and French guitarist Marc Ducret (both 1991). Perhaps his most telling experience, however, because it exploits both his ability to contribute textural density to ensemble work and his highly unusual soloing, has been with Bobby Previte, with whom he has recorded and toured, as a member of his band Empty Suits. In the mid-1990s, Robertson sent tapes of freeish trio music, involving bassist Dominic Duval and drummer/percussionist Jay Rosen, to Cadence, and it subsequently appeared as *Falling In Flat Space* and *Sound Implosion* (both 1996) on the label. He also continued his associations with the more adventurous of contemporary jazz musicians: Anthony Braxton, the Fonda-Stevens group (with whom he has made several albums in the 1990s and 2000s), composer/conductor Klaus Konig, drummer Paul Lytton et al. He cameoed on Joe Lovano's *Viva Caruso* in 2002. [CP]

Tim Berne

Sanctified Dreams (1987; Columbia). Innovative, challenging music infused with almost Ornette Coleman-like intensity and featuring the whole extraordinary range of Robertson's playing on all his brass instruments.

Mark Helias

Desert Blue (1989; Enja). Wonderfully varied album featuring slinky blues through rumbustious funk to semi-abstract improvisation: the perfect setting for Robertson's quirky individuality.

Bobby Previte

Music Of The Moscow Circus (1991; Gramavision). Again an excellent setting for Robertson, being a highly idiosyncratic soundtrack for clowns, high-wire acts, etc.

Zue Robertson

Trombone.

b. New Orleans, 7 March 1891; d. 1943.

Zue (C. Alvin) Robertson was "credited by many with setting the style for all who followed after on the slide trombone," says Orrin Keepnews, "but he was a rambler and irresponsible, which is probably why lasting fame eluded him". Certainly Robertson's credentials are impressive enough: he was working in Kit Carson's Wild West Show by 1910 (his nickname is thought to come from "zoo", a reference to his work in carnivals and travelling circuses), then played with the great New Orleans trumpeter Manuel Perez and others, and by 1917 was in Chicago, where he teamed at various times with King Oliver, Jelly Roll Morton, W.C. Handy's highly drilled band and Dave Peyton's theatre orchestra – jobs requiring skill, musicianship and probably reading ability. From 1929 Robertson was settled in New York, where he played organ and piano at major theatres such as the Lincoln and the Lafayette; after a move to California in 1932 he concentrated on piano and bass. John Chilton's researches indicate a musician to reckon with, but no records exist to prove the point. [DF]

John Robichaux

Violin, bass, drums, accordion, leader.

b. Thibodaux, Louisiana, 16 Jan 1866; d. 1939.

After early years as bass drummer with the Excelsior Brass Band, John Robichaux formed his first band in 1893 and, says the *New Orleans Family Album*, was "the most continuously active dance-band leader in New Orleans history" until he died. Robichaux's group played for the elite of New Orleans society and used many of the city's greatest musicians, including Lorenzo Tio. He tends to be remembered in jazz history as the respectable dance-band leader regularly bested by Buddy Bolden's hotter jazz music, but according to Bud Scott (who joined Robichaux in 1904), the facts were different. "Robichaux had the town sewn up. In about 1908 he had a contest with Bolden in Lincoln Park and Robichaux won. For the contest he added Manuel Perez and Bolden got hot-headed that night, as Robichaux really had his gang out." Despite the obvious error in date (Bolden was out of circulation in 1907), Scott's story sounds plausible. [DF]

Joseph Robichaux

Piano.

b. New Orleans, 8 March 1900; d. 17 Jan 1965.

A nephew of John Robichaux, Joe took lessons from pianist Steve Lewis (a major influence) early on and played for parties before a brief exploratory visit to Chicago in 1918. He soon returned to New Orleans, and worked with Lee Collins, the Black Eagle Band and travelling shows all through the 1920s, as well as taking part in the classic Jones-Collins Astoria Hot Eight sessions in New Orleans in 1929. In the 1930s Robichaux formed a big band and recorded for Vocalion, and through the 1940s worked as a solo pianist in New Orleans clubs, before moving to the West Coast where, during the 1950s, he accompanied blues singer Lizzie Miles, then joined George Lewis, replacing Alton Purnell, for seven years from 1957. [DF]

Jim Robinson

Trombone.

b. Deer Range, Louisiana, 25 Dec 1890; d. 4 May 1976.

Jim Robinson took up trombone late at 25, while serving in France with the US army, after early years as a guitar player. When he came home in 1919 he studied with trombonist Sunny Henry, then worked part-time with bands such as the Golden Leaf Orchestra (featuring Lee Collins) and Tuxedo Band, before joining Isaiah and Sam Morgan's band for over ten years. In the 1930s he worked a long residency at the La Vida Restaurant – really a dime-a-dance ballroom – where the hours were long and the tunes necessarily short. The routine bored Robinson and he took work as a shipyard labourer instead, playing part-time with George Lewis, Kid Howard and others. When the great New Orleans revival began, however, he was quickly back in demand: first for Heywood Broun's records with Kid Rena, then for more records with Bunk Johnson, whose playing he liked and respected ("He had taste," explained Robinson). From the late 1940s his brusque, direct trombone was increasingly associated with George Lewis who, despite occasional criticisms, was partial to the Robinson style that Johnny Wiggs describes to Tom Bethell: "Jim has a good sharp attack and a good crack to his notes, clarity, and he plays well-formed phrases. He's the top old-time trombone player. His solos [though] are nothing but background music – he comes from an era when solos weren't used." In fact, while Robinson was a fine ensemble player, his solos – full of saxophonic riffs and trumpet stabs, as well as standard trombonistics – are often startling. He came to Britain with Lewis in 1959 and continued to work with him and as a freelance throughout the 1960s, producing records of his own and guesting with Billie and Dee Dee Pierce, the Preservation Hall Jazz Band and touring groups. [DF]

>> **George Lewis** *(George Lewis Ragtime Band Of New Orleans: The Oxford Series Vols. 1–10).*

Orphy Robinson

Vibes, marimba, composer.

b. London, 13 Oct 1960.

After playing with the Hackney and Islington Youth Band at 14 and becoming interested in his mid-teens by bands such as Tower of Power and Earth, Wind And Fire, Orphy Robinson was inspired to take up vibes by hearing Roy Ayers. Early playing experience with the funk band Savannah and exposure to jazz through the influence of trumpeter Claude Deppa led to Robinson's interest in improvisation, which he practised initially by playing along with the music provided by TV test transmissions. He was invited by Courtney Pine to play with the mid-1980s big band Jazz Warriors, and subsequently with the saxophonist's own quartet, but Robinson soon attracted audiences leading his own band. A spell with saxophonist Andy Sheppard brought him more exposure, and he was signed to Blue Note in 1990, co-leading the Annavas Project with keyboard player Joe Bashorun. Robinson's music is eclectic, embracing everything from funk to African music, jazz to classical, and he is a frequent collaborator (on marimba) with Shiva Nova, a band whose members are drawn from a wide variety of musical traditions, organized by composer Priti Paintal. He has even collaborated with the free improvisers and visionary composers Simon Fell and Butch Morris. In the late 1990s, Robinson formed a band, Codefive, to dispense what he described as "nouveau jazz swing", a combination of straightahead jazz, New Orleans music, swing and West African influences, all filtered through contemporary jazz. Its members were saxophonist Jean Toussaint, pianist Pat Thomas, bassist Darren Taylor and drummer Kenrick Rowe. Robinson's ambitious composition *Dancing On The Surface Of Nature – Creation* was commissioned by the Jerwood Foundation and was premiered in a former power station in London's East End for the Solo with Light festival in 2002. [CP]

⊙ **When Tomorrow Comes** (1991; Blue Note). Adventurous album with highly unusual line-up – flute, cello and kora in addition to keyboards, vibes, bass and drums – containing some beautiful textures and intriguing rhythms, but not consistently successful due to lack of overall coherence.

⊙ **The Vibes Describes** (1993; Blue Note). Less diffuse, funkier follow-up to the above, replacing diaphanous texture with a more solid, more straightforward approach, but retaining Robinson's trademark eclecticism and adventurousness.

Perry Robinson

Clarinet.

b. New York, 17 Aug 1938.

Robinson, the son of the composer Earl Robinson, attended the High School of Music and Art, New York, graduating in 1956. He then attended the Lenox School of Jazz in 1959, and the Manhattan School of Music in 1960–61. He was associated with the avant-garde movement of the 1960s, playing with Sunny Murray, Paul Bley, Archie Shepp and Bill Dixon. He performed at the World Youth festival, Helsinki, in 1967, and also worked with the Jazz Composers' Orchestra in the mid-1970s. In 1968 he worked with Roswell Rudd's Primordial Quintet, and in a trio with David Izenzon. At the end of the decade he played on Carla Bley's album *Escalator Over The Hill*. In 1972 he started what has been his most important association, with Gunter Hampel's Galaxie Dream Band. From 1973 he was with Dave and Darius Brubeck in their Two Generations band. Then in 1978 he recorded *Kundalini* with Nana Vasconcelos and Indian tabla player Badal Roy. Robinson's influences include Pee Wee Russell, Charlie Parker, Sonny Rollins and Tony Scott, and his approach is a composite of elements from abstraction, rock and all eras of jazz. [IC]

⊙ **Call To The Stars** (1990; West Wind). This recording features Robinson with Russian pianist Simon Nabatov, Ed Schuller (Gunther's son) on bass, and drummer Ernst Bier, and features good clarinet work from Robinson.

➤➤ **Gunter Hampel** *(Spirits)*.

Prince Robinson

Clarinet, tenor saxophone.

b. Portsmouth, near Norfolk, Virginia, 7 June 1902; d. 23 July 1960.

"We used to listen to Prince Robinson in those days. He was the tenor player with McKinney's Cotton Pickers, the one that really made it big on the tenor before anybody – but he was very underrated because he was like an old man when Hawk started playing!" Buddy Tate's description, and Coleman Hawkins's frequent citation of Robinson as a primary influence, have sealed an impression of Robinson as a dinosaur of the saxophone. In fact he was a year younger than Hawkins, led a very successful career until the late 1950s, and is underrated now because the impact of Hawkins was so cataclysmic and because Robinson never recorded under his own name.

After formative years with Elmer Snowden, Duke Ellington and others, Robinson joined McKinney's Cotton Pickers and recorded with them. One famous session, which produced "Four Or Five Times", "Milneburg Joys" and others, is recalled by Cuba Austin: "In those days everybody took off their shoes – so the thud from beating the rhythm didn't ruin things. Now worst of all was Prince Robinson. Don [Redman] hit on the idea of lashing Prince's ankles and knees together with rope to hold him steady ... Things went smoothly till Prince started a solo, then he began to bob up and down with his feet tied together and finally gave up ... but finally we got by with a good one!" After he left McKinney in 1935, Robinson worked with Blanche Calloway, Willie Bryant and for two years with Roy Eldridge, then with Louis Armstrong's big band, with bands led by Lucky Millinder, Benny Morton and Claude Hopkins, as well as with Henry "Red" Allen, his own quartet and the Fletcher Henderson reunion band assembled by Rex Stewart in the 1950s. [DF]

➤➤ **Bill McKinney** *(McKinney's Cotton Pickers)*.

Scott Robinson

Clarinet, saxphones.

b. New Jersey, 27 April 1959.

While in high school Robinson won the Louis Armstrong Award and Best Soloist Award from the National Association of Jazz Educators, and after graduating from Berklee (1981) became the College's youngest faculty member. He moved to New York in 1984 and played with an impressively wide range of musicians from Buck Clayton, Lionel Hampton, Paquito D'Rivera to the New York City Opera and Anthony Braxton.

A respected performer in all styles of jazz as well as on most instruments – though specializing on reeds – Robinson has appeared on over 75 albums in a wide variety of jazz contexts including the orchestras of Toshiko Akiyoshi, Loren Schoenberg, Illinois Jacquet, Mel Lewis, Lionel Hampton, Louie Bellson and Tom Pierson, the Buck Clayton Legacy Band, and with fellow musicians including Peter Ecklund, Dan Barrett, Randy Sandke, Greg Cohen, Marty Grosz, Jon-Erik Kellso, Per Husby and Carol Sloane (a Sinatra tribute for which Robinson arranged several tracks). He also leads his own quartet which tours internationally, and has won four fellowships from the National Endowment for the Arts. [DF]

Thinking Big (1997; Arbors). With an all-star team, this splendid display of Robinson's good-humoured, yet highly refined, art has numerous delights including a cavernous re-creation of Ellington's "Ko-Ko" and the appearance of contrabass sarrusophone on "Mandy Make Up Your Mind".

Melody From The Sky; Scott Robinson Plays C-Melody saxophone (2000/Arbors). Robinson delights in the instrumental eccentricities of jazz and on this album his celebration of the largely-forgotten C-melody saxophone is accompanied by a string quartet on three delightful tracks as well as like-minded contemporaries including Jon-Erik Kellso, James Chirillo, Mark Shane and Marty Grosz.

Spike Robinson

Tenor saxophone.

b. Kenosha, Wisconsin, 16 Jan 1930.

Spike (Henry Berthold) Robinson began on alto at twelve, joined the US navy as a musician in 1948, and by 1950 was part of Britain's bebop revolution at Club Eleven, working with Victor Feldman and others, and recording six titles for Esquire (with Feldman on drums) in July 1951. Returning home, Robinson took a degree in engineering at the University of Colorado, and subsequently got a day job there, returning to playing local clubs for fun, this time on tenor. He next recorded in 1981 for Discovery Records (again with Feldman, but this time on piano) – this fine album brought bookings, and in 1984 Robinson came back to Britain for a tour which produced another recording session for Alistair Robertson's Hep label. Robinson made his New York debut in 1990, and despite a spell of serious illness he then began performing full-time from a UK base. In the mid-1990s Robinson was playing better than ever: his full-toned lyric style (reminiscent of Zoot Sims) flourishes on swing tunes and the great American standards, and is regularly heard at all the best European and American jazz venues. [DF]

Plays Harry Warren (1981 & 93; Hep). This important set contains Robinson's first comeback album, playing Warren tunes with Victor Feldman, plus Warren titles recorded with Pete Jolly.

Spike Robinson At Chesters Vols. 1 & 2 (1984; Hep). Now reissued on two CDs, this set marks Robinson's historic return to Britain, with Eddie Thompson, Len Skeat and Jim Hall.

Plays Gershwin (1987; Hep). One of Robinson's greatest albums, featuring the lush string writing of Jimmy Deuchar and a faultless selection of Gershwin themes.

Just Bit O' Blues Vols. 1 & 2 (1988; Capri). A relaxed title for a relaxed date pairing Robinson with Harry Edison (and both of them on excellent form), with a rhythm-section of Ross Tompkins (piano), Monty Budwig (bass) and Paul Humphrey (drums). Elegant music from intro to coda.

Groovin' High (1992; Concord). This set teams Robinson with Peplowski and Scott Hamilton in a three tenor conversation that's always passionate but never overheated.

Reminiscin' (1992; Capri). Recorded at the Jazz Works in his one-time home town of Denver. Robinson is a scholar of fine tunes and here they include "Dream Dancing", "My Silent Love" and "Yours Is My Heart Alone". Mundell Lowe heads the rhythm-section completed by Jake Hanna and the late Monty Budwig to whom the album is dedicated.

Tenor Madness (1997; Essential Jazz). A short-lived project for Robinson teaming him with two contrasting tenor voices; John Barnes and the great Bobby Wellins. With an A-team rhythm-section (John Pearce, Leon Clayton and Bobby Worth) the saxophones have separate stories to tell in a programme nicely laden with Al Cohn repertoire.

Young Lions, Old Tigers (2000; Jazzizit). A likeable late partnership between old Lion Robinson and young tiger Nash; one of Britain's most forthright, swinging and creatively gifted saxophonists. While Robinson is too wily an old hand to rise to many of Nash's friendly challenges this is an altogether pleasurable record of Robinson's last regular partnership.

Willard Robison

Composer.

b. Shelbina, Missouri, 18 Sept 1894; d. 24 June 1968.

Along with Alec Wilder, Robison is still the most undervalued of American popular songwriters, although jazz musicians from Mildred Bailey to Dick Sudhalter have recorded important Robison tunes such as "Old Pigeon-Toed Joad", "T'Ain't So Honey, T'Ain't So!", "Round My Old Deserted Farm" and his biggest hit, "A Cottage For Sale"; in addition, Charlie Parker's version added "Old Folks" to the modern standard repertoire. While aspects of Johnny Mercer's work – and sometimes Hoagy Carmichael's – recall the scent of cornfields and cotton-blossom clouds, many of Robison's songs are more deeply localized in America's Midwest. "Generally his songs were known only to a few singers and lovers of the off-beat non-urban song," says Alec Wilder. "He, if ever there was one, was the maverick among songwriters." Robison's "Peaceful Valley" was an early theme song for Paul Whiteman in the 1920s (before "Rhapsody In Blue" was written), and at the same time Robison himself recorded a handful of sides playing piano and singing with his own groups: these included, at various times, Alcide "Yellow" Nuñez, Frank Trumbauer, Jack Teagarden and Bix Beiderbecke. [DF]

Jack Teagarden

⊙ **Think Well Of Me** (1962; Verve). This extremely rare album has many of Robison's greatest songs, and they suit Teagarden's folksy delivery to perfection.

Phil Robson

Guitar.
b. Derby, UK, 28 Feb 1970.

From the age of fourteen Phil Robson had lessons with session guitarist John Richards, and played in his home town with his father, clarinettist Trevor Robson, as well as with visiting musicians such as John Etheridge and Bheki Mseleku. After leaving the Guildhall School, he played and toured with many leading UK musicians and groups, including Jean Toussaint, Django Bates's Delightful Precipice, Stan Sulzmann, Martin Speake, Gerard Presencer, The Creative Jazz Orchestra and Iain Ballamy's Acme. He has also played with the American "rare groove" stars Big John Patton and Charles Earland, and recorded extensively with many musicians, including singer Christine Tobin. Robson co-leads the band Partisans with saxophonist Julian Siegel, which has completed three major tours and recorded an eponymous album (1996). In 1997, Robson won the BT Best Soloist of the Year award; the following year he won the Perrier Young Jazz Award for the Instrumentalist of the Year. In July 1998, sponsored by the British Council, he took his own trio to South Africa for a week of engagements, and in November, with Christine Tobin's group, of which he is a regular member, Robson played the Berlin jazz festival. His favourites are Wes Montgomery, Pat Metheny, Kevin Eubanks and Bill Frisell, and other inspirations are Miles Davis, Ornette Coleman and Dave Holland. [IC]

Partisans

⊙ **Partisans** (1996; EFZ). Bassist Steve Watts and drummer Gene Calderazzo are the other two members of this dynamic quartet. Robson wrote five and Siegel four of the ten pieces, and the one standard ballad, "Like Someone In Love", is given a most unusual performance at an exceptionally slow tempo. The originals range from funk to Latin to bravura jazz pieces and moody and rocky ballads.

Phil Robson

Sebastian Rochford

Drums, piano
b. Aberdeen, Scotland, 20 Nov 1973.

Rochford studied classical percussion at school with Ron Forbes, and at Newcastle College of Music with Roger Hempsall. He came to London in 1997 and soon began playing with top musicians like Stan Tracey, Christine Tobin, Andy Sheppard, Damon Brown, Perico Sambeat and Tim Richards. Rochford's solid yet versatile playing has made him an in-demand drummer for recordings, and among the many albums he has appeared on are *Blues On The Run* (2001) and *A Bigger Picture* (2002), both for Damon Brown, the Hendrix tribute album *Acoustic LadyLand* (2002), and singer Juliet Kelly's *Aphrodite's Child* (2003).

In 1999 Rochford founded the group Polar Bear, along with Mark Lockheart and Peter Wareham – both on tenor saxophones – and Tom Herbert on double bass, which soon established a reputation as an exciting cutting-edge ensemble. In 2002 the group toured Holland and Belgium, and recorded its first album, *Dim Lit*, for the Dutch label Rub Recordings (now available in the UK on Babel, see below), featuring guest singer Julia Biel. Rochford also performs with the Damon Brown Quintet, the band Menlo Park, and runs his own trio, Fulbourne Teversham, with Pete Wareham and Ben Hazleton. [IC]

Polar Bear

Dim Lit (2004; Babel). With smouldering drum breaks that amble like an intoxicated mammoth, and sweetly smoked brass, this set finds 'The Bear' in a relaxed, but decidedly groovy mood. Biel's vocals add a haunting, melacholic edge to the more spacious tunes.

Gil Rodin

Saxophones, clarinet, flute.

b. Russia, 9 Dec 1906; d. Palm Springs, California, 17 June 1974.

Although he was never even a competent jazz soloist (*Down Beat* magazine once published a spoof transcription of a Rodin solo: it consisted of one long note), Rodin's name is usually a guarantee of jazz quality. For eight years from 1926 he was alto saxophonist for Ben Pollack, and very much his right-hand man: he acted as talent scout for the band, shared an apartment with Pollack and advised him on key decisions. By 1934, however, after Pollack had ignored him over one or two important policies (including the vexed issue of Doris Robbins, Pollack's new singer and girlfriend), Rodin found himself more in sympathy with the sidemen than with the leader and, to Pollack's surprise, followed them in the ensuing walk-out. To the younger men Rodin was already a father figure and it was he who helped engineer the signing of Bob Crosby to their nominal leadership. For the next seven years Rodin was saxophonist and business adviser to the Bob Crosby orchestra, planned their campaigns and paid their money: despite one or two disagreements over wages (probably inevitable), he remained the well-liked power behind Bob Crosby's throne until the band broke up. In later years Rodin became a successful radio and TV producer, as well as occasionally helping Crosby to re-form bands for special occasions. [DF]

➤➤ **Bob Crosby** *(South Rampart Street Parade).*

Claudio Roditi

Trumpet, flugelhorn.

b. Rio de Janeiro, 28 May 1946.

After studying at Berklee College of Music (1970–71), Claudio Roditi remained in Boston, playing with drummer Alan Dawson, until he moved to New York in 1976. During the late 1970s he played with Charlie Rouse and Herbie Mann, and in the early 1980s formed a lasting musical relationship with Cuban saxophonist Paquito D'Rivera, with whom he shares an interest in a Dizzy Gillespie-type fusion of Latin music and jazz. In the 1980s he established himself as a first-call trumpeter for recording sessions where a bright, lively frontline sound was required, playing with pianists Klaus Ignatzek and Buddy Montgomery and backing singers such as Chris Connor, Michele Hendricks and Mark Murphy. His numerous collaborations with saxophonists – among them Gary Bartz and Greg Abate – and his flaring brilliance in big bands such as those of Jimmy Heath and Dizzy Gillespie mark him out as a sharp, virtuosic soloist of the first rank.

His mid- and late-1990s recordings are to be found mainly on three labels: Reservoir, with Argentinian saxophonist Andres Boiarsky and reedsman Nick Brignola (who both appeared on Roditi's own Lee Morgan tribute album for the label, *Free Wheelin'*, in 1994), Telarc, with singer Jeanie Bryson, trombonist Slide Hampton and guitarist Jim Hall; and Postcards, with saxophonist Jorge Sylvester and drummer Chip White. Roditi also appeared on Horace Silver's *Hardbop Grandpop* (1996; Impulse!), and – in company with a Brazilian band, the Cama de Gato Quartet – on *Claudio, Rio And Friends* (1995; Groovin' High), which explored the common ground between jazz and Brazilian music. This area was further addressed in *Samba – Manhattan Style* (1995; Reservoir), featuring trombonist Jay Ashby and *Brazilian Dreams* (2002; Telarc) featuring old friend D'Rivera and vocal group New York Voices. [CP]

Slow Fire (1989; Milestone). Sharing frontline duties with trombonist Jay Ashby and tenorman Ralph Moore, and supported by drums and percussion, Roditi serves up a rich amalgam of jazz and Latin music.

Two Of Swords (1990; Candid). Heavier than usual on the flugelhorn, but with Roditi's usual mix of lively jazz and Latin, featuring Ashby again.

Milestones (1990; Candid). Superb band (D' Rivera, plus pianist Kenny Barron, bassist Ray Drummond and drummer Ben Riley) in lengthy set of rumbustiously energetic flag-wavers leavened by the ballad feature "Brussels In The Rain".

Red Rodney

Trumpet.

b. Philadelphia, 27 Sept 1927; d. 27 May 1994.

Rodney (originally Robert Chudnick) gained big-band experience as a teenager with leaders such as Gene Krupa in 1946, Claude Thornhill in 1947 and Woody Herman from 1948–9. He made his first small-group recordings under his own name at the age of nineteen. From late 1949 to 1951, with an absence through illness, he was the regular trumpeter with the Charlie Parker quintet. Later absences from the scene were due to his drugs involvement, and were followed by brief returns and regular non-jazz backing work in Las Vegas throughout the 1960s. He re-emerged on the New York jazz scene in 1972, and from then on he continued group playing, including a quintet co-led with Ira Sullivan that was formed in 1980, and his own quintet from the mid-1980s to the early 1990s, which included pianist Garry Dial and, latterly, saxophonist Chris Potter. One of the first white trumpeters to show a grasp of bebop, Rodney was first noticed for brief solos on big-band records, but his exposure alongside Parker was not undeserved. He was a far more complete stylist in later years, still with a bristling bebop edge to his playing. [BP]

⊙ **Bird Lives!** (1973; Muse). An unashamedly bop-oriented programme, featuring two Monk tunes and three credited to Parker ("Donna Lee" is actually by Miles Davis), marked Rodney's return to jazz, with fine playing by Charles McPherson and Barry Harris.

Shorty Rogers

Trumpet, flugelhorn, arranger.

b. Great Barrington, Massachusetts, 14 April 1924; d. 7 Nov 1994.

Rogers (whose given name was Milton Rajonsky) first worked professionally with Will Bradley and Red Norvo. Following his subsequent army service, Rogers found his niche with Woody Herman from 1945–6 and 1947–9, and with Stan Kenton from 1950–51. Having settled in Los Angeles, he became a figurehead of the West Coast period, writing and playing on his own records and those of many others. His involvement in film and television in the 1950s increased further in the next decade, causing him to give up the trumpet altogether. He resumed playing after a tour with Britain's National Youth Jazz Orchestra in 1982, and in the early 1990s formed a new Lighthouse All Stars group with old hands such as Bud Shank, Bill Perkins and Bob Cooper.

A distinctive if limited trumpeter, Rogers was always more influential through his writing. The rather fussy quality of his small-group charts, often a watered-down version of the Miles Davis 1948 band, detracted from the lively performances he elicited from his colleagues. This aspect tends to triumph on the big-band performances and, although none of his originals became standard material, some early items – such as "Keen And Peachy" (for Herman) and "Jolly Rogers" (for Kenton) – and his own big-band albums stand up extremely well. [BP]

⊙ **Short Stops** (1953; Bluebird). This CD, made up of three popular and influential sessions, includes a Shorty's Giants small-group session, another featuring material he arranged for the movie *The Wild One*, and reaches a climax with the big-band *Cool And Crazy* album. Rogers's own solos are overshadowed by contributions from Art Pepper, Jimmy Giuffre and Bill Perkins.

➤➤ **Shelly Manne** *(The Three And The Two).*

Adrian Rollini

Bass saxophone, vibes, multi-instrumentalist.

b. New York, 28 June 1904; d. 15 May 1956.

Rollini's prodigious talent (he played a Chopin concert at four years old, at New York's Waldorf Astoria) may have been obscured by his fascination with such "novelty" instruments as the goofus, hot fountain-pen, vibraphone – then a daring innovation – and bass saxophone, which he took up at manager Ed Kirkeby's suggestion soon after joining the California Ramblers in 1922 when he was eighteen. His newest instrument, which he learned in a week, became the envy of black stars such as Coleman Hawkins, who briefly struggled with one in Fletcher Henderson's orchestra; more successful learners, who listened to Rollini in awe, were Budd Johnson, who said he "used to play everything Rollini played", and Harry Carney, who later remembered: "I actually tried to get a sound as big as Adrian – so I suppose whatever sound I've got goes back to that." After leaving the Ramblers, Rollini became a busy sessionman in New York with Bix Beiderbecke, Red Nichols, Joe Venuti, Frank Trumbauer and others, then, after a brief band-leading disaster at the Hotel New Yorker, travelled to London to work with Fred Elizalde at the Savoy. Here British bandleader Harry Gold saw him: "I used to slip behind the stage with a few pals at the Savoy and watch him. His sound and concept were my biggest influences."

Back in America by 1930, Rollini became a busy studio man, over the next decade recording with giants from Coleman Hawkins to Bunny Berigan and Bobby Hackett. In 1935 he opened his own club, Adrian's Tap Room, in the basement of the Hotel President on West 48th Street – Wingy Manone's quartet played here regularly. From that time on Rollini concentrated on vibes (his four-mallet work uncannily resembles Gary Burton's two generations later) and worked hotels with his smooth trio until 1955. Recent research suggests that the Mafia may have been implicated in his death the following year, by which time he was running his own hotel, and his name was a stranger to top-flight jazz activity. [DF]

⊙ **The Goofus Five** (1926–7; Timeless). Twenty-four titles by this fine little band, featuring Rollini on bass saxophone and goofus; remastering by John R.T. Davies.

⊙ **Bouncin' In Rhythm** (1926–35; Topaz). A good across-the-board selection of Rollini in premier company that avoids much duplication with the above. As many of the tracks are classics, however – including those with Venuti, Trumbauer and Beiderbecke – some collectors may have them already. If not, snap it up.

⊙ **Tap Room Swing** (1927–38; ASV). The best current portrait of Rollini on CD: titles with Red Nichols (1927)

Joe Venuti, Miff Mole, Fred Elizalde (three valuable selections), Bix and his Gang, the Dorsey Brothers, three wonderful tracks by Rollini's Orchestra with Jack Teagarden from 1934 (including 'Davenport Blues') and ending with two tracks from his 1938 session with Bobby Hackett and vocal group The Tune Twisters.

Dennis Rollins

Trombone.

b. Birmingham UK, 11 Nov 1964.

Born to Jamaican parents, Rollins first started playing trombone in 1980 when his elder brother (also a trombonist) passed on an instrument to him. He was soon playing in brass bands, but his jazz education began in earnest the following year at the Doncaster Youth Jazz Association. By 1985 he was a member of the National Youth Jazz Orchestra (NYJO), and in 1986 he joined the all-black big band, Jazz Warriors. As a youngster he had listened to a lot of funk, and when he arrived in London in 1987 he was able to play with such diverse outfits as Steve Williamson, Chris McGregor's Brotherhood of Breath, Jazz Jamaica, Blur, US3, Brand New Heavies and Jamiroquai. From 1995–7 he ran his own seven-piece jazz-funk band DeRoe, and from 1999 to 2002 toured and recorded with Courtney Pine. It was Pine who gave the trombonist the nickname Badbone, and when Rollins formed a new band in February 2000 he named it Dennis Rollins' Badbone & Co. Two albums have been recorded to date, *Badbone* (2001), released on Rollins' own label Raestar Records, and *Make Your Move* (2003). The earlier album has a kind of popular party and dance atmosphere, with some rather repetitive vocals which border on easy listening. But there are also some fine solos by Rollins himself, for instance on the lovely ballad "Can It Be Done?". Undoubtedly one of the most exciting trombonists playing today, Rollins has a brilliant technique and real star quality. Fred Wesley, James Brown's legendary trombonist, is one important influence on his playing, as is jazzman J. J. Johnson. He is also an extremely promising composer and arranger, who is likely to go from strength to strength. [IC]

⊙ **Make Your Move** (2003; Sound Recordings). A highly focused second album that gets down to business straightaway with the funky rhythms of "FreeStyle". "Ujamma" strikes a more poetic note with a fine electric piano solo, more great guitar and some virtuoso trombone playing. There's a lot of wit and intelligence in evidence, and not one weak or slack moment in the ten tracks.

➤➤ **Courtney Pine** *(To The Eyes Of Creation)*.

Sonny Rollins

Tenor; also soprano saxophone.

b. New York, 7 Sept 1930.

Sonny (Theodore) Rollins took up the alto while in high school, and then began gigging on tenor in 1947. His first recordings were with singer Babs

DAVID REDFERN

Sonny Rollins with Ronnie Scott

Gonzales, J.J. Johnson and Bud Powell, all when he was eighteen. During this period he rehearsed and made live appearances with Thelonious Monk, Powell and Art Blakey in 1949, and with Miles Davis and Tadd Dameron in 1950. He made records with Miles Davis from 1951, and with Monk from 1953; he first recorded under his own name in 1951. After living in Chicago for a year in 1954–5, he joined the Max Roach-Clifford Brown quintet from 1955–7. He led his own groups for two years, and then spent two years studying, with no public appearances. Then he formed a quartet, Sonny Rollins & Co., featuring Jim Hall from 1961–2, and Don Cherry and Billy Higgins, with whom he made a European tour, from 1962–3. Thereafter he worked with varying personnel, and also played as a soloist with local rhythm-sections, including in Europe in 1965, 1966 and 1967, and a European tour as guest soloist with Max Roach in 1966. He had a further period of public inactivity from 1968–71, while studying in India and Japan, but since 1972 he has performed regularly with his own quintet. He was a member of a 1978 concert tour by the Milestone All Stars with McCoy Tyner, Ron Carter and drummer Al Foster, and in 1986 he premiered his self-composed saxophone concerto in Japan. After being critical of nightclub conditions for some time, he has virtually abandoned them since the 1980s in favour of concert-hall performances.

Inspired to take up the alto by Louis Jordan, Rollins soon came under the influence of Charlie Parker and, when he switched to tenor, Sonny Stitt and Dexter Gordon. These are all audible in his early work, but it is the rhythmic freedom of Parker which

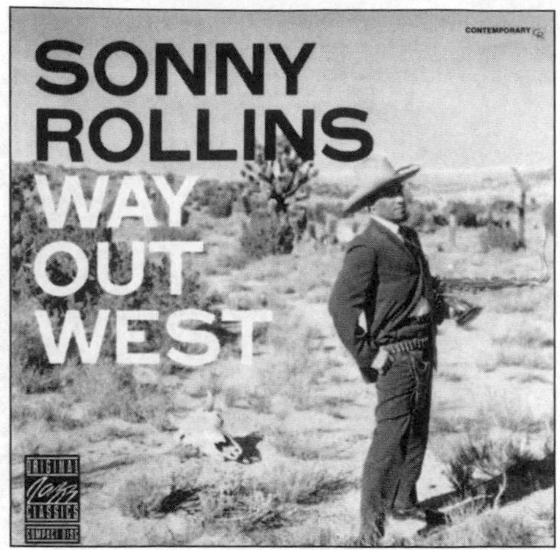

particularly marked Rollins's style, and the one occasion on which they recorded together (Miles Davis, Collectors' Items) showed Sonny on better form than Bird in this respect. By the mid-1950s his partnership with Parker's former drummer Max Roach (producing numerous albums under both their names) revealed total command and total emancipation from the beat; each was able to stay in time while throwing outrageous rhythmic challenges to the other. Sonny's up-ending of other players' clichés and his general indirectness led to critical accusations of being sardonic or cynical, and his tonal distortions also increased the impression that he was impatient with the confines of post-bop.

Sonny never sought compositional solutions, despite having the composer copyright of the traditional calypsos "St Thomas" and "Don't Stop The Carnival", and writing several other minimalist tunes such as "Doxy" and "Oleo". Instead he remained an improviser through and through, and the standard songs he favoured in the 1950s and 1960s were often reduced to melodic skeletons, the better to play with the bare bones. This motivic approach naturally led to a friendly interest in free jazz, but the most beneficial effect of this for Rollins was to vindicate his musical restlessness. Whereas some of his earlier extended solos seemed comparatively neatly structured, he now felt justified in changing direction several times in the course of one improvisation (see, for example, *On The Outside*).

Since the 1970s Sonny has been engaged in what might be considered a sensible compromise. The short, recognizable melodies and the over-obvious rhythm-section are now used more as a reference point for audiences than for the soloist, who still feels free to get up to all his old tricks from time to time. This is frequently unsatisfying, like most compromises, but it allows him (like the later Miles Davis) to display his own playing more or less unchanged to a much younger audience. In doing so, he reminds us that his influence has been extremely widespread, and that he remains one of the most important musicians of the last forty-five years. [BP]

Moving Out (1954; Prestige/OJC). An early session in which Rollins has the benefit of Kenny Dorham and Art Blakey on four of his own deceptively simple hard-bop originals, plus the ballad "More Than You Know" from his date with Thelonious Monk as his "accompanist".

Saxophone Colossus (1956; Prestige/OJC). A high-water mark of the series of albums with Max Roach, this has a quartet including Tommy Flanagan and Doug Watkins exploring "You Don't Know What Love Is" and the then newly rediscovered "Mack The Knife (aka Moritat)", plus the calypso "St Thomas" and Sonny's much praised extended blues "Blue Seven".

Way Out West (1957; Contemporary/OJC). One of the most popular early Rollins albums, with its iconic cover photo, this is his first recording without a piano dictating the chords. Joined by Ray Brown and Shelly Manne, he is magisterial on tunes like "Solitude" and "Come, Gone" (based on the ancient standard "After You've Gone") and wittily inventive on the unlikely "I'm An Old Cowhand".

A Night At The Village Vanguard Vols. 1/2 (1957; Blue Note). This famous set, on two separate CDs, is the result of a quite casual encounter with Elvin Jones and Wilbur Ware, which generated some supremely inventive Sonny, for instance on "Night In Tunisia" and "Old Devil Moon" (both Vol. 1), or the blues "Sonnymoon For Two" and the "Confirmation" improvisation called "Strivers Row" (both Vol. 2).

The Sound Of Sonny/Freedom Suite (1957–8; Riverside). Available as a single CD in the UK (though without the bonus track from each session which graces the separate OJC albums). The first date is the more conventional quartet, with Sonny Clark and Roy Haynes, while the second (and more essential) trio date with Pettiford and Roach is highlighted by the twenty-minute title track.

The Bridge (1962; RCA Victor). Rollins's group with Jim Hall, though short-lived, touched the heights on this set. The interplay of the two frontliners is what Sonny has often sought but infrequently found, and there are a couple of rare out-of-tempo sections by the whole quartet.

On The Outside (1962–3; Bluebird). A few short months after the above sessions, Rollins explored group freedoms more closely, with Don Cherry replacing Hall in the quartet. Not free jazz but quite unpredictable, and containing long, live versions of "Doxy" and "Oleo", first recorded on Miles Davis's *Bags' Groove* reissue.

Don't Stop The Carnival (1978; Milestone). A slightly laboured live set with an off-form Donald Byrd on some tracks and Tony Willliams throughout. Sonny does a great unaccompanied, free-association intro to "Autumn Nocturne" and, almost despite the rhythm-section, a definitive title track.

Dancing In The Dark (1987; Milestone). A favourite later album has Rollins's quintet, with Marvin "Smitty" Smith and guitarist/bassist Jerome Harris, covering pop songs from the 1930s and 1980s (the latter by James Ingram) and introducing a new original titled for the calypsonian "The Duke Of Iron".

>> **Miles Davis** *(Bags' Groove);* **Thelonious Monk** *(Monk/Rollins);* **Bud Powell** *(The Amazing Bud Powell Vol. 1).*

Aldo Romano

Drums, guitar.

b. Sicily, 16 Jan 1941.

Romano moved to France in 1947, and began on guitar while at school, then switched to drums. In 1960 he began playing in clubs with Bud Powell, Jackie McLean, Stan Getz, J.J. Johnson and various French musicians. In 1963 he began playing free jazz with Don Cherry and Gato Barbieri. At the end of 1966 he joined Carla Bley's group, which broke up in 1967. He worked with Joachim Kuhn for two years, playing most major festivals including Newport, and joined Jean-Luc Ponty in 1970, touring throughout Europe. From 1971–3 he led his own rock group in which he played drums and guitar, sang and composed the music. In 1973 he joined Pork Pie, which included Charlie Mariano, Jasper van't Hof, Philip Catherine and J.-F. Jenny-Clark. Romano left after two years, played some concerts with Catherine, and then got back on the French scene, recording his first solo album and playing with the group Eyeball. He has recorded with Steve Lacy, Gordon Beck, Joachim Kuhn and many others. [IC]

⊙ **Il Piacere** (1978; Owl).This is a compelling series of duos and trios with guitarist and bassist Claude Barthelemy and Jean-Francois Jenny-Clark. Romano too plays some guitar.

⊙ **Ritual** (1988; Owl); **To Be Ornette To Be** (1989; Owl).On these two albums Romano investigates his own past – conventional jazz, free jazz and progressive rock – in the company of trumpeter Paolo Fresu, pianist Franco d'Andrea and bassist Furio Di Castri. There's a moving tribute on *Ritual* to the recently deceased Chet Baker, while the excruciatingly titled *To Be Ornette To Be* is a meaty investigation of Coleman territory.

Dom Um Romão

Drums, percussion.

b. Rio de Janeiro, 3 Aug 1925.

Son of an African drummer, Dom Um Romão played drums with the Bossa Rio sextet with Sergio Mendes on keyboards, and with Cannonball Adderley in 1962 at Carnegie Hall, New York, then moved to the USA. In 1965 he worked with Oscar Brown in Chicago. He worked for about a year (1966) in Los Angeles, then in 1967 he toured the world with Sergio Mendes and Brazil '66. He joined Weather Report when Airto Moreira left, playing percussion. He settled in New York in the early 1970s, opening his own rehearsal studio – Black Beans Studio. In 1977 he worked extensively in Europe, playing percussion with the Swiss group Om. [IC]

➤➤ **Joe Zawinul**(*I Sing The Body Electric*).

Wallace Roney

Trumpet.

b. Philadelphia, 25 May 1960.

After studying at both Howard University and the Duke Ellington School, Wallace Roney joined the big band of Abdullah Ibrahim in 1979 and Art Blakey's Jazz Messengers in 1981, establishing himself as a virtuosic but entirely reliable frontline player specializing in fleet, tasteful post-bop. He consolidated this reputation with the drummer-led bands of Cindy Blackman and Tony Williams, and he also recorded in the late 1980s and early 1990s with drummers Marvin "Smitty" Smith and Cody Moffett, pianists Geri Allen, Kenny Barron, Randy Weston and the Finn Jarmo Savolainen, and with saxophonists Kenny Garrett, James Spaulding, Vincent Herring and Christopher Hollyday. At this time he also carved a useful niche for himself in "tribute" bands, touring with Herbie Hancock, Wayne Shorter, Ron Carter and Tony Williams in the Miles Davis tribute quintet; appearing on a "Re-Birth of the Cool" session led by Gerry Mulligan; recording a tribute to Clifford Brown under the leadership of singer Helen Merrill; and playing in the last concerts of both Miles Davis and Dizzy Gillespie. Similar projects by Chick Corea (*Remembering Bud Powell*, 1996; Stretch) and Thelonious's son T.S. Monk (*Monk On Monk*, 1997; N2K Encoded Music,) also featured Roney, as did contemporary albums by saxophonist Bill Evans, pianist/composer Randy Weston and Detroit bassist Rodney Whitaker. Roney himself moved to Warner Bros, and started making characteristically classy albums in stellar company – Michael Brecker, Pharoah Sanders and Chick Corea were among the players on 1996's *Village* – of which the pick is *The Wallace Roney Quintet* (see below). His move to Chick Corea's Stretch label in 2000 produced the well received album *No Room For Argument* (see below), the adventurous approach of which signalled a change of direction for the trumpeter. [CP]

⊙ **Verses** (1987; Muse).Excellent band – Gary Thomas (trumpet); Mulgrew Miller (piano), Charnett Moffett (bass), Tony Williams (drums) – propels Roney through a selection of lively band-member originals, a lengthy blues, "Slaves", and a delicate version of "Blue In Green".

⊙ **Obsession** (1990; Muse).Stand-out album from solid band featuring Thomas and Cindy Blackman, steaming through staples such as "Donna Lee" and "Alone Together".

⊙ **Seth Air** (1991; Muse).Brother Antoine joins the band for an energetic set considerably enlivened by the presence of the quirky but virtuosic pianist Jacky Terrasson.

⊙ **The Wallace Roney Quintet** (1995; Warner Bros). In-house originals impeccably played by a tight band: Antoine Roney (tenor saxophone); Carlos McKinney (piano); Clarence Seay (bass); Eric Allen (drums). The session ends with an original by the leader dedicated to his wife, Geri Allen.

⊙ **No Room For Argument** (2000; Stretch).With cut-up speeches from Malcolm X and Martin Luther King and musical references to 1970s Miles, *Love Supreme*-era Coltrane and the 1980s funk of Prince, Roney produces a genuinely impressive *mélange* of mood and manner in the company once more of his brother and his wife, along with keyboardist Adam Holzman, bassist Buster Williams and drummer Lenny White.

Leon Roppolo

Clarinet, composer.

b. Lutcher, Louisiana, 16 March 1902; d. 14 Oct 1943.

A handsome, high-powered young man who, in Eddie Miller's words, had "a tone all over the instrument", Leon Roppolo was the son of a saloon-owner-cum-clarinettist. Young Leon – often a problem to his father – picked up the sound of jazz from visiting bands and took informal lessons from Eddie Shields (the piano-playing brother of clarinettist Larry) while working in his band at Toro's Club, New Orleans. The Brunies family were also friends, and Roppolo worked with them, too, before travelling upriver to Chicago with Georg Brunis and cornettist Paul Mares in 1921 to form the great new band at Friars Inn – the soon-to-be-headlining New Orleans Rhythm Kings. Today's image of Roppolo comes from then: playing the clarinet with a clear, singing sound all his own, experimentally bouncing that sound off the floors and pillars of Friars Inn (just as Sonny Rollins did forty years later), often pausing to jot new phrases and themes on a shirt-cuff. (Sometimes, the story goes, Roppolo – like Rollins again – would play out of doors, matching his sound to the wind in the wires.) By now he was drinking and smoking marijuana, but he kept working regularly until 1925 when, after bandwork which included a spell with pianist Peck Kelley, he came back to New Orleans to play with the NORK again and to record (for OKeh) with Abbie Brunies's Halfway House Dance Orchestra. That same year he broke down mentally and until his death was confined to an institution. For his last 18 years Roppolo's music was seldom heard outside the walls of the institution (where he led a jazz band): in 1928 he played at the La Vida dance hall in New Orleans ("survivors still talk about his memorable saxophone chase choruses there with the younger Scag Scaglione," says Frank Driggs), and early in the 1940s (says John Chilton) he played a couple of nights with trombonist Santo Pecora and old friend Abbie Brunies. [DF]

Wally Rose

Piano.

b. Oakland, California, 2 Oct 1913; d. 12 Jan 1997.

One of the legends of America's West Coast jazz revival, Rose studied piano at high school (under Elizabeth Simpson) and worked during holidays as a ship's pianist before joining Lu Watters' band from 1939, introducing ragtime into its repertoire. Rose's 1941 recording of "Black And White Rag" brought him international fame and thereafter he worked with Watters (until 1949), at the Balalaika Club (1949–50), with Bob Scobey (1950–51) and Turk Murphy (he also featured with Arthur Fiedler playing Gershwin's "Rhapsody" on a Symphony Pops summer season (1959). In the 1960s he worked at San Francisco nightclubs and hotels (including Fairmont, 1965) and remained busy, playing (sometimes with old Watters colleagues), researching ragtime music, and guesting with scores of bands. It has been suggested that the ragtime renaissance really began with Rose's 1941 recording success, and he was honoured (with clarinettist Bob Helm) at the San Diego jazz festival in 1994. [DF]

⊙ **Ragtime Classics** (1953; Good Time Jazz). A good example of Rose at his best, in the company of Bob Short (tuba) and old boss Turk Murphy on washboard.

Bobby Rosengarden

Drums, percussion.

b. Elgin, Illinois, 23 April 1924.

"We were playing the other night," says British trombonist Roy Williams, "'Bourbon Street Parade', and, you know, Bobby starts with press-rolls. You wouldn't catch a lot of drummers doing that! But Bobby loves everybody from Baby Dodds to Buddy Rich – and it shows. And of course it works!" Rosengarden, who attracted much attention when he joined The World's Greatest Jazz Band (1974–8), came from a highly professional background of studio work, and for five years was MD for the *Dick Cavett Show* (1969–74). "He learned the hard way," says Oliver Jackson, "with the networks, the broadcasting people, CBS and others, in the studio bands." Rosengarden took over the resident band at New York's Rainbow Room, played with Soprano Summit (1975–8) and with Kenny Davern and Dick Wellstood in a highly successful small group, the Blue Three (1981–3), and visited Britain as soloist and leader; he also played for the New York Jazz Repertory Company (from 1974) and with Gerry Mulligan's sextet (from 1976). In the 1980s and 1990s he continued to work in studios on jazz and related projects, his presentation ranging from African talking drums, via Baby Dodds and Sid Catlett, to the high-powered onslaught of a Buddy Rich in full flight. [DF]

➤➤ **World's Greatest Jazz Band** *(Plays Duke Ellington).*

Bernt Røsengren

Tenor saxophone.

b. Stockholm, 24 Dec 1937.

In 1958, when he was already active in Swedish jazz circles, Røsengren was a member of the Newport International Youth Band. He played tenor solos on the soundtrack of Polanski's film *Knife in the Water* (1962), composed by Krzysztof Komeda, and appeared with him at the Polish Jazz Jamboree in 1961. He then led his own quartet and occasional big band. An early figurehead of free jazz on the Swedish scene, he worked and recorded in the late 1960s with George Russell and Don Cherry, and in the early 1970s with Lars Gullin, including a live album. His many unreissued albums include 1980s tentet and big-band sessions, the latter featuring Horace Parlan and (a regular partner) Doug Raney. Seemingly inspired at first by Chicago tenorists such as Gene Ammons, Røsengren then became adept at reproducing the sound of early John Coltrane; later, however, he absorbed a variety of influences into a convincing mature style. [BP]

Summit Meeting

⊙ **Bent's Jump: Summit Meeting Live at Bent J** (1993; Dragon). Røsengren has made two albums with Summit Meeting; this, the second, finds saxophonist Nisse Sandström replaced by Krister Andersson, and this uncombative quintet sounds rather like a post-bop Al-Cohn-and-Zoot-Sims.

Michele Rosewoman

Piano.

b. Oakland, California, 29 March 1953.

Raised in a highly musical and artistic family, Michele Rosewoman began playing piano at the age of six. As a teenager she studied with pianist Ed Kelly. She led her own groups in Oakland before moving to New York in around 1977. In the Big Apple she played with many of the post-free-jazz leading lights, including Oliver Lake and Billy Bang. With Bang she recorded in the early 80s on *Rainbow Gladiator* and *Invitation* (both Soul Note). Around the same time she wrote *New Yor-Uba: A Musical Celebration of Cuba in America*, which integrated Cuban percussion and vocalists with a fourteen-piece jazz ensemble. Influenced by Thelonious Monk and Cecil Taylor, Rosewoman also carries a deeply lyrical line into her playing. She has worked with the members of M-Base, recording as a side(wo)man on Greg Osby's *Greg Osby And Sound Theater* (1987; JMT) and as a leader with saxophonists Osby and Steve Coleman, bassist Anthony Cox, and others on *Quintessence* (1987; Enja), *Contrast High* (1988; Enja) and *Harvest* (1993; Enja). In 1993 she released a solid trio recording with bassist Rufus Reid and drummer Ralph Peterson – a trio with whom she still performs – and recorded for Blue Note on *Spirit* (1994), where she sang a couple of songs and worked out standards and originals with a trio of Gene Jackson on drums and Kenny Davis on bass. That lineup was augmented by sax players Steve Wilson and Craig Handy for *Guardians Of The Light* (2000; Enja), recorded live at New York's Sweet Basil. Active in jazz education, she performs regular concerts and workshops with her Quintessence ensemble (of floating personnel but often featuring saxist Mark Shim), her trio and a nonet version of her New Yor-Uba band. [JC]

⊙ **The Source** (1983; Soul Note). Though her later records are generally worth while, her debut as a leader remains a very fine disc. Under-recognized trumpeter Baikida Carroll blows beautifully on Rosewoman's airy tunes, and drummer Pheeroan Ak Laff shows an early glimpse of what will later develop into one of the best touches in today's music.

Eddie Rosner

Trumpet.

b. Berlin, Germany, 26 May 1910; d. Berlin, 8 Aug 1976.

Dubbed by critics "the white Louis Armstrong", Eddie Rosner (his real first name was Adolph) was one of the most talented and successful European jazz trumpeters of the 1930s and 40s. Unfortunately the ideological turmoil that racked Europe during that period meant that, as a Jew, his career was equally beset by extreme hardship and personal danger. Something of a prodigy, Rosner started as a violinist but took up the trumpet to earn extra money. In 1930 he joined the Weintraub Syncopators, a leading jazz band that regularly toured outside Germany. When the Nazis came to power jazz was denounced as "degenerate Negro music"; Rosner was abroad at the time and decided to move to Poland where he set up his own 13-piece Polish swing band. Enormously popular, the band were regulars at two Warsaw nightclubs, and appeared thoughout Europe including Paris where he shared the bill with Maurice Chevalier, and Italy where he met Louis Armstrong. He also made records for French Columbia with sides including "On The Sentimental Side", "Midnight In Harlem", "Caravan" and "Take Your Pick And Swing".

After the Germans invaded Poland, Rosner and his Polish wife, singer Ruth Kaminska, headed eastwards, eventually fetching up in Lvov. When Rosner's new band was heard by the First Secretary of the Belarussian Communist Party, they were invited to become the State Jazz Orchestra of the Belarus Republic. A concert for Stalin followed shortly afterwards, and his approval meant automatic success. "Stalin's Band" toured across the whole of the Soviet Union, playing for the troops and for party officials, and Rosner became one of the most highly-paid musicians in the country with an apartment close to the Kremlin.

All this changed after World War II ended. As the Soviet Union's cultural policies became ever more restrictive, Rosner found himself denounced for pandering to decadent, capitalist tastes. He was imprisoned in Siberia, but again had a degree of luck in that the camp commander turned out to be a jazz fan who allowed Rosner to form a band from fellow-prisoners. The band eventually began touring the Gulag, entertaining guards and officials, but Rosner was only released following the death of Stalin in 1953. Back in Moscow he formed another big band, and to a large extent regained his popularity as an artist – if not his prestige. He was by now understandably an embittered man and, with anti-Semitism on the rise in the Soviet Union, he decided to return to Berlin in 1973. He died three years later.

A Rosner revival has been underway over the last fifteen years. In 1988 some of his Russian recordings were reissued in Melodiya's Soviet Anthology of Jazz series, and four years later a tribute band performed a memorial concert for him in Moscow's Tchaikovsky Hall, playing music painstakingly transcribed from recordings. The recordings themselves are still pretty hard to get hold of, but an excellent documentary, *A Jazzman From The Gulag* (2002), made by French film-maker Pierre-Henri Salfati is well worth looking out for. [RB]

Renee Rosnes

Piano, composer.

b. Regina, Saskatchewan, 24 March 1962.

Adopted at four months – she traced her birth mother, Mohindar, in 1994 and was inspired to make an album, *Ancestors* (1995; Blue Note), about that experience and the almost simultaneous loss of her adoptive mother Audrey to cancer – Renee Rosnes was brought up in Vancouver, where she took up the piano at three and the violin a few years later. In her teens, she discovered jazz through listening to Oscar Peterson, Cedar Walton and Herbie Hancock, but it was with classical piano that she won awards and a scholarship to the University of Toronto. After gigging with the likes of guitarists Oliver Gannon and Peter Leitch, and visiting artists such as Dave Liebman and Joe Farrell, she received a grant from the Canada Council of the Arts and moved to New York. Work with Joe Henderson and, in 1987, Out of the Blue (where she replaced Harry Pickens) followed, and she toured the USA, Europe and Japan with the latter sextet. Rosnes also freelanced with Jon Faddis, Gary Thomas and Sonny Fortune, and toured extensively with the J.J. Johnson quintet and with Wayne Shorter's double keyboard quintet. In 1988, she made her eponymous Blue Note debut, an album of pieces by modern jazz masters (Monk, Wayne Shorter, Joe Henderson), plus three originals, and featuring Branford Marsalis, tenorman Ralph Bowen, Ron Carter on bass and Lewis Nash on drums, plus guest appearances from Hancock and Shorter. Her follow-up, *For The Moment* (1990; Blue Note), found her in more confident form, fronting a sparky band driven by hushand Billy Drummond on drums, and with a nicely contrasted saxophone pairing of old employer Henderson and Steve Wilson. A with-strings album, *Without Words* (1992; Blue Note), was followed by the above-mentioned, deeply personal *Ancestors*, with saxophonist Chris Potter and trumpeter Nicholas Payton, but it was *As We Are Now* (see below) and *Art And Soul* (1999; Blue Note) that signalled Rosnes's true maturity as composer, performer and leader. *Life On Earth* (see below) marked a decided change in direction, indicating even richer possibilities for the future.[CP]

⊙ **As We Are Now** (1997; Blue Note). Her rapport with Chris Potter and Christian McBride honed live at Bradley's, this quartet album (the band completed by drummer Jack DeJohnette) showcases Rosnes's beguiling combination of delicate lyricism and vigour perfectly, with a piece dedicated to Georgia O'Keeffe, one by the then recently deceased Tony Williams, and the memorable title tune, named after a novel by May Sarton.

⊙ **With A Little Help From My Friends** (2001; Blue Note). With much of her Blue Note catalogue out of print, this collection, taken from her first six albums, is a good place to get an overview of this important pianist/composer. The title track is a gorgeous treatment of the Beatles' tune first heard on 1999's *Art And Soul*.

⊙ **Life On Earth** (2002; Blue Note). A dizzying array of world influences (from India, Bali, Senegal, Spain) makes this Rosnes's most ambitious album to date. It features the exotic percussion effects of Duduka Dafonseca among a large cast.

Frank Rosolino

Trombone, vocals.

b. Detroit, Michigan, 20 Aug 1926; d. 26 Nov 1978.

Rosolino's early big-band experience included Gene Krupa's bop-influenced 1948–9 line-up. He worked with the Georgie Auld quintet in 1951, and then joined one of Stan Kenton's more swinging outfits from 1952–4. Living in Los Angeles, he became a prominent session musician, but was always ready for an opportunity to play jazz, making solo tours from 1973 onwards. He committed suicide after the murder and attempted murder respectively of his two children.

The records under his own name, even those that have been reissued, are with one exception unavailable, but his intriguing fourteen-bar tune "Blue Daniel" was recorded by Cannonball Adderley and others. Although aware of the style of J.J. Johnson, Rosolino's trombone work seemed able to use the harmonic language of bebop with some of the bluster and gusto of Bill Harris. His free-ranging lines and musical humour often succeeded in disguising the immense adroitness of his playing. Though still associated in many people's minds with Kenton, Rosolino was in fact a soloist for all seasons.[BP]

⊙ **Free For All** (c.1957; Specialty/OJC). Apparently unreleased at the time of recording (which remains obscure), this quintet with Harold Land and Victor Feldman finds Rosolino's trombone on blistering form, as it always seemed to be.

➤➤ **Stan Kenton** *(New Concepts Of Artistry In Rhythm)*

Annie Ross

Vocals, songwriter, actress.

b. Surrey, UK, 25 July 1930.

Annie Ross (Annabelle Short Lynch) moved to Los Angeles at the age of three, where she was brought up, then studied drama in New York. In 1947 she returned to the UK, working there and in France as a singer. Back in the USA, she came to prominence in 1952, when she wrote lyrics to a solo by saxophonist Wardell Gray on his tune "Twisted" and recorded her vocalese version. In the mid-1950s she sang with the bands of Jack Parnell and Tony Crombie in the UK, then with American singers Dave Lambert and Jon Hendricks she formed Lambert, Hendricks and Ross, a trio specializing in the technically brilliant vocalizing and verbalizing of jazz instrumental music. This brought her to international notice; the trio toured in the USA and Europe and played festivals, including the Playboy and Monterey jazz festivals in America. By the end of

1959 she was winning readers' polls in jazz magazines. Leonard Feather wrote of her: "technically she is the most remarkable female vocalist since Ella Fitzgerald". Illness forced her to leave the trio in 1962.

She freelanced in the UK from 1962–6, singing on TV shows, with bands and in nightclubs, and ran her own club, Annie's Room, for a while. She also appeared at Ronnie Scott's club and played festivals throughout Europe. From the 1970s she began to take more acting roles, also performing on stage, in TV plays and musicals. She starred in *The Threepenny Opera* with Vanessa Redgrave, appeared with André Previn at the Royal Festival Hall in a concert of Kurt Weill's music, and played in Weill and Brecht's *The Seven Deadly Sins* for the Royal Ballet. In 1985 she returned to the USA and was active in New York as a singer. In 1993 she appeared in Robert Altman's film *Short Cuts*.

Annie Ross is a superb lyricist, combining dexterity, wit and black humour, and a consummate singer, able to handle anything from torch songs and medium-paced swing to breakneck tempos and intricate melodic lines. [IC]

➤➤ **Lambert, Hendricks and Ross** *(Sing A Song Of Basie);* **King Pleasure** *(King Pleasure Sings – Annie Ross Sings).*

Florian Ross

Piano, organ, drums, composer.

b. Pforzheim, Germany, 1 Aug 1972.

Florian Ross started improvising on the piano at the age of four, and began lessons at seven; he took up drums when he was twenty. In 1986 he was invited to the Young Composers' Summit (Jeunesses Musicales) in Weikersheim, Germany, and the following year he won first prize at the Landes Rock Festival, Baden-Württemberg. In 1988 he played a concert at the Internationale Stuttgarter Jazz-Tage, and also won first prize in the Newcomer Competition of the Jazz and Rock School, Freiburg. In 1990 he joined the State Youth Jazz Orchestra (SYJO), Baden-Württemberg, and played concerts with them in Moscow and St Petersburg. A year later, he was a member of the Klaus Graf big band in Stuttgart, and with his own quintet played at the Russian Novokuznetsk international jazz festival. In the 1992 German Orchestra Competition, when he played with the Klaus Graf big band, Ross won first prize as soloist, and that year he began studies at the Cologne Conservatory, with John Taylor (piano) and Michael Kuttner (drums). He also formed his own Florian Ross quintet, which made some radio broadcasts on Westdeutscher Rundfunk and Hessischer Rundfunk. In 1990 Ross was commissioned to write music for the Woody Allen play *Death Or Kleinman's Last Night*, and made such a success of it that he has continued to receive commissions for theatre music.

He attended the London Guildhall School postgraduate jazz course from 1995–6, studying piano with Simon Purcell and composition with Django Bates and Scott Stroman. With the Guildhall Big Band, Ross won the MCPS 1996 Composition Prize at the BBC National Big Band Competition. After yet more studies, commissions and prizes, Ross premiered his hour-long *Suite For Soprano Saxophone & String Orchestra (plus piano trio)* in 1998, with Dave Liebman as soloist; it was later released on CD by Naxos. For his first album on Naxos, *Seasons & Places*, Ross had formed a quintet of German young lions – trombonist Nils Wogram, tenor saxophonist Matthias Erlewein, bassist Diemar Fuhr and drummer Jochen Ruckert – with outstanding results. His favourites include John Taylor, Jarrett, Bobo Stenson, Django Bates, Bill Evans and Herbie Hancock; other inspirations include several classical composers, and jazz composers Brookmeyer, McNeely, Mendoza, Bill Holman, Thad Jones and Gismonti. [IC]

⊙ **Seasons & Places** (1998; Naxos). Ross composed all ten of the excellent compositions here, and his musicians rise to the occasion in a highly original and delightful album.

⊙ **Suite For Soprano Saxophone & String Orchestra** (1999; Naxos). This eight-movement, hour-long suite offers a wealth of musical ideas and emotions. The interplay between rhythm-section, string orchestra and soloist is superbly done, and there are welcome lyrical/romantic moments after the sometimes wild climaxes.

Ronnie Ross

Baritone, alto and tenor saxophones, clarinet, flutes.

b. Calcutta, 2 Oct 1933; d. London, 12 Dec 1991.

After settling in the UK in 1946, Ronnie Ross played with Tony Kinsey, Ted Heath and Don Rendell (who switched him to baritone), before representing Britain in Marshall Brown's International Youth Band at 1958's Newport jazz festival. The same year he formed the Jazz Makers with drummer Allan Ganley, touring America with the band in 1959. That year he also performed with the Modern Jazz Quartet in Europe and played with Woody Herman's Anglo-American Herd. Subsequent collaborations with Maynard Ferguson and Tubby Hayes established him as a distinctive voice on an instrument overshadowed by Gerry Mulligan, and in 1961 Ross formed a quartet which he co-led with Bill Le Sage until 1965. In the 1960s and 1970s, as well as recording with the likes of John Dankworth, Friedrich Gulda and the Clarke-Boland big band, he led his own bands and did a fair amount of session work, most famously for Lou Reed on "Walk On The Wild Side". He toured the UK with his own quartet in 1986, but died five years later. [CP]

John Lewis

⊙ **European Windows** (1958; RCA). Recorded with the John Lewis orchestra in Stuttgart, this was Ross's own favourite recording.

Jazz Makers

⊙ **Cleopatra's Needle** (1968; Fontana). Sextet recording featuring Ross's cultured sound briskly but tastefully propelled by Allan Ganley's drumming in a band they co-led.

Charlie Rouse

Tenor saxophone.

b. Washington, DC, 6 April 1924; d. 30 Nov 1988.

Rouse worked briefly with the Billy Eckstine band in 1944 and the first Dizzy Gillespie big band in 1945, and then worked with Tadd Dameron in 1947. He spent several months each with Duke Ellington in 1949–50 and Count Basie in 1950. Much of the 1950s was spent freelancing, but he also worked with Bennie Green in 1955, Buddy Rich in 1959, and co-led his own group Les Jazz Modes from 1956–8. He was a permanent member of the Thelonious Monk quartet from 1959–70, then did further freelancing, including his own groups, the Mal Waldron quintet in the early 1980s, and the co-operative band Sphere formed in 1979. In the last year of his life he recorded with Stan Tracey, Carmen McRae and Marcus Roberts. Rouse had a very distinctive nasal tone, already discernible in his 1940s recordings with Dameron; so was his choppy rhythmic style which, though compared by some to that of Monk, sounded rather trite alongside him. In other contexts, however, Rouse stood out as a strong, individualistic player. [BP]

⊙ **Takin' Care Of Business** (1960; Jazzland/OJC). From the period before Rouse became stuck in his cameo role with Monk, this lively quintet with Blue Mitchell, Walter Bishop and Art Taylor contains spiky originals and the standard "They Didn't Believe Me".

Rova Saxophone Quartet

San Francisco Bay Area-based saxophonists Jon Raskin, Larry Ochs, Andrew Voigt and Bruce Ackley formed ROVA in 1977. Inspired by the reed musics of restructuralists like Anthony Braxton, Roscoe Mitchell and Steve Lacy, as well as various popular, classical and traditional musics from around the world, they quickly made a series of records for Ochs's own Metalanguage label, including *Cinema Rovaté* (1978), *The Removal Of Secrecy* (1979), *Daredevils* (1979, with free improvising guitarist Henry Kaiser) and *As Was*; they also recorded *This, This, This, This* (1979; Moers) and *The Bay* (1978; Ictus), the latter with Italian drummer Andrea Centazzo. Highly inventive, eclectic and willing to experiment, ROVA is arguably the most exciting of the saxophone quartets to emerge in the format's late 70s boom. They have collaborated with contemporary classical composers Alvin Curran on *Electric Rags II* (1990; New Albion) and Terry Riley on *Chanting The Light Of Foresight* (1994; New Albion); with Braxton they recorded the incredible *The Aggregate* (1986–8; Sound Aspects); and they have done a series of "recital" CDs, including *Bingo* (1998; Victo, with pieces by Lindsay Cooper, Fred Frith and Barry Guy), and three volumes of CDs entitled *The Works*, with pieces by John Carter, Jack DeJohnette, Tim Berne, Fred Ho and Muhal Richard Abrams. In 1983 they made a historic tour behind the Iron Curtain that resulted in *Saxophone Diplomacy* (hat Art), a trip they repeated six years later and documented on *This Time We Are Both* (New Albion).

The prolific quartet gigged and recorded steadily through the 80s and 90s, putting out a set of Steve Lacy tunes, *Favorite Street* (1983; Black Saint), and several records of their own material, including *The Crowd* (1985; hat Art), *Beat Kennel* (1987; Black Saint), *Ptow!* (1995; Victo) and *Morphological Echo* (1996; Rastascan). In 1988 Steve Adams (of Boston's Your Neighborhood Saxophone Quartet) replaced Andrew Voigt, playing primarily alto. The group's members have worked outside of ROVA as well. Baritonist Raskin appears on Braxton's *Eight (+3) Tristano Compositions 1989* (hat Art), and Ochs is a member of the Glenn Spearman Double Trio and Chris Brown's Room, and recorded a nonet piece, *The Secrect Magritte* (1995; Black Saint). Under Ochs's initiative, ROVA was joined by four more reed players – and renamed Figure 8 – for the record *Pipe Dreams* (1994; Black Saint), and another large ensemble with ROVA at its core recorded a new version of John Coltrane's *Ascension* (1996; Black Saint). Ochs has worked increasingly with the trio What We Live, with bassist Lisle Ellis and drummer Donald Robinson, recording for DIW, Black Saint and New World. Ackley made a great all-soprano outing, *The Hearing* (1998; Avant), with drummer Joey Baron and bassist Greg Cohen.

Rova released the album *Resistance* in 2003, continuing their tradition of showcasing their own pieces whilst providing a platform for ambitious quartet music by like-minded souls (in this case, Wadada Leo Smith). The quartet now occasionally mushrooms into the Orchestrova, to play large-group and orchestral compositions, and it continues to tirelessly promote new music on America's left coast. [JC]

⊙ **Long On Logic** (1989; Sound Aspects). ROVA have never let their audience down, and this CD – the first with Adams – is a suitable starter. Compositions include English folkish fun by guitarist Fred Frith and a rhythmic Henry Kaiser piece dedicated to player-piano genius Conlon Nancarrow, as well as two gems from Ochs, Raskin's "Wig Hat Six Step" and Adams's premier for the group, "K/24". Challenging, forward-sounding, but not averse to a deep groove and wistful melody, this should only be the first ROVA record you buy.

Dennis Rowland

Vocals; piano.

b. Detroit, Michigan, 2 March 1948.

First exposed to Duke Ellington, Joe Williams, Handel, show music and soundtrack albums by his parents, Rowland gained his BA in music education at Kentucky State University. The musical environment of his home town involved him in jazz, blues, R&B and soul and, from 1977–84, he toured with the Basie band, performing alongside guests such as Ella Fitzgerald, Sarah Vaughan and Tony Bennett. From the mid-1980s he took part in theatrical productions as varied as *Jesus Christ Superstar* and Kurt Weill's *The Seven Deadly Sins* (with Cleo Laine). As well as making his own albums since 1994, Rowland has also appeared on record with Joe Sample, and live with Wynton Marsalis and with Frank Foster's Loud Minority Band, both in 1997. [BP]

Now Dig This! (1996–7; Concord). The singer's most focused album to date is a recital of tunes associated with Miles Davis, backed by Joe Sample and Rowland's regular drummer/producer Gregg Field. Trumpet solos by Sal Marquez and Wallace Roney highlight the dynamism and expressive delivery of the leader.

Jimmy Rowles

Piano, vocals.

b. Spokane, Washington, 19 Aug 1918; d. 28 May 1996.

Rowles moved to Los Angeles in 1940 and worked with Slim Gaillard, Lester Young, Benny Goodman and Woody Herman (all in 1942) before army service. In the late 1940s he worked with Goodman and Herman again, and with Les Brown and Tommy Dorsey. He was then a busy freelance studio musician in Los Angeles until he moved to New York in 1973, where he became established as a soloist and duettist and recorded (separately) with Stan Getz, Al Cohn and Zoot Sims. From 1981–3 he toured with Ella Fitzgerald, and then returned to California for continued playing and nightclub work.

Known originally as an accompanist with an encyclopedic repertoire, he was valued by other musicians for his fills on records by such as Henry Mancini and Tony Bennett. Rowles also made more obvious contributions in this role, notably to records by Peggy Lee, Billie Holiday and Sarah Vaughan. The solo style revealed on the many later albums under his own name is quirky and totally unclassifiable, its relaxed wit matched by a sure sense of rhythmic brinkmanship, and the mellow content is typified by his composition "The Peacocks", which became a standard thanks to Getz and the film *Round Midnight*. His daughter Stacy (b. 11 Sept 1955) is an excellent trumpeter. [BP]

Jimmy Rowles and Red Mitchell

I'm Glad There Is You (1985; Contemporary). As well as several recent albums under his own name, this reissue restores a splendid trio session, augmented by Stacy Rowles on three tunes, including Billy Strayhorn's "Blood Count" and the title track. A pity that Mitchell sings the latter, and not Rowles, who is an even more unconventional vocalist.

>> **Ray Brown** *(As Good As It Gets)*; **Zoot Sims** *(If I'm Lucky)*; **Norma Winstone** *(Well Kept Secret)*.

Ernie Royal

Trumpet.

b. Los Angeles, 6 Feb 1921; d. 16 March 1983.

A magnificent and much underrated trumpeter (at least outside the profession), Royal was influenced initially by Louis Armstrong and later by Roy Eldridge, Harry Edison and Dizzy Gillespie. He took up trumpet at ten (his teacher was lead trumpeter with the Los Angeles Philharmonic) and began playing professionally at fifteen, quickly gaining a reputation as a high-note specialist. Royal joined Les Hite in 1938 and Lionel Hampton in 1940, in both cases alongside his elder brother Marshall, then after military service worked with Count Basie, Phil Moore and Woody Herman before the end of the 1940s. After that he played with Charlie Barnet, Duke Ellington, Wardell Gray, Stan Kenton, Gil Evans, Quincy Jones and Oliver Nelson, as well as doing much studio work. [DF]

Accent On Trumpet (1953–4; International Jazz Club). Royal's only solo album, with a quintet that includes George Barnes.

Marshall Royal

Clarinet, alto saxophone.

b. Oklahoma, 12 May 1912; d. 5 May 1995.

Royal began his full-time career with Les Hite's band (1931–9), then moved on to Lionel Hampton (1940–42). After military service he played with Eddie Heywood, did studio work, and in 1951 joined Count Basie's septet on clarinet, replacing Buddy DeFranco. The inscrutable Royal remained with the Count after he re-formed his big band until 1970, stamping his mark on Basie's saxophone section, seldom soloing except on ballad features, but leading with a rich creamy tone and drilling his section members into an unbeatable team who phrased, breathed and treated the beat as one. After he left Basie, Royal freelanced, played for big bands led by Bill Berry and Frank Capp-Nat Pierce, and worked with Earl Hines and Duke Ellington. In 1989 he was once again playing lead alto, this time for Frank Wess's big band. [DF]

Count Basie

Count Basie And His Orchestra Live (1956–69; Sequel). This triple-CD set, capturing the Basie band live in four separate concerts, is a clear and well-recorded illustration of Royal's powerful presence as lead altoist.

Basie One More Time (1959; Roulette). This classic collection of Quincy Jones arrangements for Basie has Royal beautifully featured as soloist on a typical ballad feature, "The Midnite Sun Never Sets", as well as leading his section.

Gonzalo Rubalcaba

Piano, keyboards.

b. Havana, Cuba, 27 May 1963.

At five Rubalcaba was joining in on percussion with his father Guilhermo, pianist with the Enrique Jorrin dance orchestra. Soon becoming aware of jazz on record, he studied classical piano from 1971–83, and graduated from the conservatory and from Havana's Institute of Fine Arts. As a teenager he played with Los Van Van, Beny More and others, and jammed with members of Irakere. After touring in France and Africa with the Orquesta Aragón in 1983, he formed his own Grupo Proyecto, which toured Europe regularly from 1985. In 1986 he met and recorded in Cuba with Charlie Haden, who later arranged for Rubalcaba's appearances at the Montreal and Montreux festivals in 1989 and 1990 respectively. The latter was recorded and issued worldwide, as were subsequent trio performances in Toronto and Japan (with Haden or John Patitucci and Jack DeJohnette) and albums of his own quartet. Still based in Cuba, he now spends much time touring abroad. His studies have given Rubalcaba a phenomenal technique and, whether he is demolishing jazz standards or creating his own music, he uses it to interesting ends. [BP]

Rapsodia (1992; Blue Note). Combining the ability shown in his straightahead trio records and his more Afro-Latin and electric bands in earlier albums on Messidor, this high-energy electric quartet with Reynaldo Melian on trumpet concentrates on original compositions apart from an adaptation of Parker's "Moose The Mooche".

Ron Rubin

Piano, double bass.

b. Liverpool, UK, 8 July 1933.

A stylistically adaptable and sensitive player, Rubin began on violin, then changed to piano before army service in Germany, after which he took up double bass. In 1961 he moved to London and worked with a huge variety of fine bands; a shortlist includes Dick Williams, Brian Leake, the Fairweather-Brown All Stars, Mike Taylor trio and quartet, Littlejohn-Milliner, Howard Riley, the Keith Ingham trio with Susannah McCorkle, Bill Coleman, the Alex Welsh Band, John Chilton's Feetwarmers and Phil Franklin, plus solo piano work. [DF]

Susannah McCorkle with the Keith Ingham Quintet

The Quality Of Mercer (1977; Jazz Alliance). Rubin on bass in an excellent early outing for McCorkle, including Mercer's witty "My New Celebrity Is You" and "Harlem Butterfly"; his unobtrusive but faultless musicianship shows up well amid the rhythm-section.

Ellyn Rucker

Piano, vocals.

b. Des Moines, Iowa, 29 July 1937.

Ellyn Rucker first played piano at eight, and was introduced to jazz by her brother during her teens, but took up music as a full-time profession only in 1979, in Denver, Colorado, where she worked regularly as a soloist and with tenorist Spike Robinson (they later toured together). Encouraged by Mark Murphy (who contributed notes to her first album, *Ellyn*, 1987), she made an outstanding appearance at the Northsea jazz festival and quickly moved on to the festival circuits of Europe and America. Two more albums followed, and she consolidated her reputation with solo tours of Britain, as well as continuing to work around Denver. She is a powerful, skilled pianist and an appealingly ingenuous singer whose current recognition is fully deserved if a little overdue; following illness in 2001 she was quickly back to fulltime playing and toured Britain in 2002, playing at clubs and festivals. [DF]

Live In New Orleans (1992; Leisure Jazz). Available on both CD and a well-produced video, this set illustrates Rucker's talents perfectly, in company with Mark Singer (bass) and Jill Fredrickson (drums).

Roswell Rudd

Trombone, composer.

b. Sharon, Connecticut, 17 Nov 1935.

Rudd studied French horn as a child. From 1954–9 he played with traditional jazz groups in New York, but in the early 1960s he began working with the avant-garde. From 1960–62 he was with Herbie Nichols, and from 1961–3 worked with Steve Lacy. From 1964 he was with the New York Art Quartet, which included John Tchicai and Milford Graves, and which visited Europe in 1965 for concerts, radio and TV appearances. Rudd played the Newport festival the same year with the Jazz Composers' Orchestra. He also worked with Karl Berger, Perry Robinson, Charlie Haden and others. In 1966–7 he worked with Archie Shepp, touring in the USA and Europe. In the later 1970s Rudd had a fruitful association with trumpet player Enrico Rava, touring and recording with him in the USA and Europe.

A graduate of Yale University, Rudd worked from 1964 as a musicologist in association with Alan Lomax, and ultimately became professor of music ethnology at the University of Maine. His study of ancient music helped him in his activities as a composer and performer, in which he has consistently striven to make the connection between the jazz tradition, ethnic music and the European classical heritage. He has said: "Vocal techniques I had associated at one time only with the jazz singers of my own country were revealed to be common to the oldest known musical traditions the world over. What I had always considered the epitome of musical expression in America, the blues, could be felt everywhere in the so-called 'folk world'." [IC]

Roswell Rudd, Steve Lacy, Misha Mengelberg, Kent Carter and Han Bennink

Regeneration (1982; Soul Note). A fine tribute album to pianist/composers Herbie Nichols and Thelonious Monk – Rudd had worked with Nichols (who admired Monk) and had also worked with Lacy in a band that played only Monk tunes. This session features three of Nichols's excellent but little-known originals and three of Monk's most famous pieces.

➤➤ **Carla Bley** *(Dinner Music)*; **Steve Lacy** *(Trickles)*; **Cecil Taylor** *(Jumpin' Punkins)*; **John Tchicai** *(The New York Art Quartet)*.

Mathias Rüegg

Composer, piano.

b. Zurich, Switzerland, 8 Dec 1952.

Rüegg studied composition and arranging in Graz and Vienna, while gigging on piano in the 1970s. He settled in Austria, and founded the Vienna Art Orchestra in 1977, which has since recorded many albums. The orchestra appeared at the Berlin festival in 1981, toured Asia, the USA and Canada in 1984, and fifteen European countries in autumn 1985, and recorded in New York in 1993. Rüegg also formed the Vienna Art Choir in 1983 and has written symphonic works. A competent pianist whose favourites include Bud Powell, Chick Corea and VAO member Uli Scherer, Rüegg's reputation rests on his writing. Despite admiration for Carla Bley, Gil Evans, J.S. Bach and Nali Gruber, he seems rather to belong to the theatrically inclined school of writers that also includes Mike Westbrook. Extremely eclectic, equally at home using themes by Mingus or Erik Satie, his arrangements have enough individuality to provide a framework yet allow considerable freedom to soloists such as Herbert Joos. [BP]

Vienna Art Orchestra

⊙ **From No Time To Rag Time** (1982; hat Art). This 13-piece edition of the VAO, including Joos, Scherer and Wolfgang Puschnig (who has also toured with Carla Bley), takes on material from Anthony Braxton to Scott Joplin, with cross-referential titles like "Jelly Roll But Mingus Rolls Better", and almost ends up proving the VAO rolls better than anyone.

⊙ **All That Strauss** (2000; TCB). Long skilled at such cross-over projects, the VAO approaches their programme with the appropriate mixture of grace and ebullience, and with telling contributions from guests including Michel Portal and the returning Puschnig.

Jak Kilby

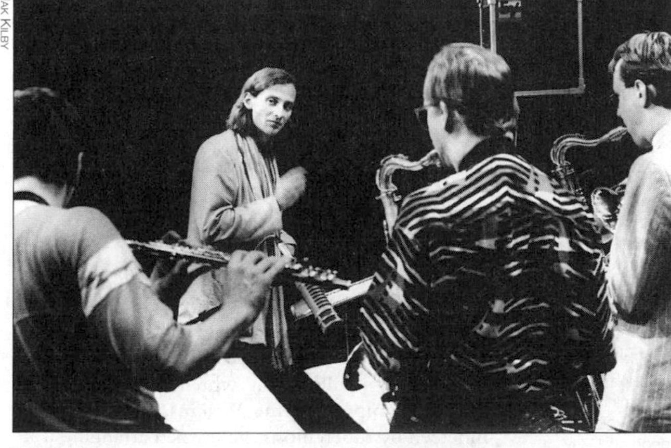

Mathias Rüegg

Hilton Ruiz

Piano.

b. New York, 29 May 1952.

Born of Puerto Rican parents, Ruiz was a child prodigy, appearing on television and at Carnegie Recital Hall at the age of eight. As a teenager he worked with Latin-soul bands, recording with Ray Jay and the East Siders. By the age of twenty he had played with Cal Massey, Joe Newman, Frank Foster, Freddie Hubbard and George Coleman. He then worked for Rahsaan Roland Kirk from 1973–7, toured with Coleman in 1978–9, and studied with Mary Lou Williams. He also played briefly for Mingus, Betty Carter, Archie Shepp and Chico Freeman with whom he visited Europe again in 1999. Since the 1980s he has toured with his own groups, often featuring a piano-bass-drums trio with additional Latin percussionists, including on occasion Daniel Ponce. Ruiz's knowledge of mainstream jazz, fuelled by Kirk and Williams especially, enlivens his already exciting approach to playing Latin material and the rhythmic adaptation of jazz standards. [BP]

⊙ **Heroes** (1993; Telarc). With Tito Puente guesting on two tracks, Ruiz leads a two-horn, four-percussion line-up featuring Steve Turre and trumpeter Charlie Sepulveda in a programme of originals and standards, the latter including "Maiden Voyage", Gillespie's "Con Alma" and Parker's "Little Suede Shoes".

Jimmy Rushing

Vocals, piano.

b. Oklahoma City, 26 Aug 1902; d. 8 June 1972.

Rushing's parents were both musical, his uncle played piano in a sporting-house, and in his early years "little Jimmy" (known universally by his vital statistics as "Mr Five-by-Five") was "official pianist" at Wilberforce University hops. After school he still made a living as a pianist although, as he remembered, "I could only play in three keys. After a time everything began to sound alike to me and it was then they told me to sing." From then on Rushing's voice – high, intense, and with a dramatic, near-operatic vibrato – became familiar all over the Southwest in Walter Page's Blue Devils (he recorded "Blue Devil Blues" with them for Vocalion in 1929), in Bennie Moten's band (which took over most of Page's young stars, including Count Basie and Eddie Durham), and finally, after Moten's death, in Count Basie's ad hoc group at the Reno Club in 1935. He stayed with Basie's band until 1948, by which time he had made films with Basie (including the full-length *Funzapoppin'* in 1943) and recorded with Benny Goodman, Bob Crosby and others, as well as with his leader. When Basie reduced his band Rushing took his own band on tour (it included Buck Clayton and Dicky Wells), then into the Savoy for two years, where he often appeared opposite Basie and created a sensation.

From then on, albeit with frequent returns to his ex-leader for touring and special occasions, Rushing worked freelance, producing a string of great recordings for John Hammond (*Little Jimmy Rushing And The Big Brass, Meets The Smith Girls, Jazz Odyssey Of James Rushing Esq* and others) and singing his blues all around America and beyond. George Melly remembers him on a 1957 trip to England, where he sang with Humphrey Lyttelton's band: "Jimmy's bulk – and its attendant problems, getting in and out of cars for example – soon appeared irrelevant except to give his movements a deliberation, an almost balletic adjustment of weight in relation to gravity which suggested his inner calm." Through the 1960s Rushing remained busy, working with Harry James, Benny Goodman and Eddie Condon, as well as Basie, and later in the decade appearing regularly at the Half Note with compatibles Al Cohn and Zoot Sims. Only occasionally did he find himself out of sympathy with a new generation of accompanists: "I never thought the time would come," he said at this period, echoing Billie Holiday fifteen years earlier, "when I would go up on the bandstand, call this or that familiar number and have some of the cats on the stand say 'I don't know it'." On his last recording, *The You And Me That Used To Be*, Rushing's voice sometimes sounds tired, but the disc was nevertheless first choice for jazz critics in the *Down Beat* poll of 1972, the year Rushing died of leukaemia. [DF]

⊙ **With Count Basie and Bennie Moten** (1930–38; Giants Of Jazz). A budget-label collection of excellence; fourteen tracks of Rushing with Basie (1937–8) and, interestingly, seven more with Moten (1930–32) including "That Too Do" and "New Orleans".

⊙ **Mr Five by Five** (1929-42; Topaz). A perceptive sampler which includes some of Rushing's earliest sides (made with Benny Moten) as well as classics with Basie including the (lyrically intriguing) "Harvard Blues', "Sent For You Yesterday" and more.

⊙ **His Complete Vanguard Recordings** (1954–7; Vanguard). With accompanists including Emmett Berry, Buddy Tate, Lawrence Brown, Vic Dickenson and Freddie Green, these are some of Rushing's finest performances, in a generous collation of three LP sessions.

⊙ **Rushing Lullabies** (1958–9; Columbia). A set that combines the very good *Rushing Lullabies* with the outstanding *Little Jimmy Rushing And The Big Brass* set. Among countless highlights on this are Dicky Wells at his most outrageous, Buddy Tate and Coleman Hawkins side by side on "When You're Smiling" and the superb orchestra arranged by Jimmy Mundy, Buck Clayton and Nat Pierce.

⊙ **The You And Me That Used To Be** (1971; RCA Bluebird). A record that's underrated. Though Rushing was becoming ill, he still sounds impressive: the minimalist arrangements by Dave Frishberg are perfect, and solo contributions from Zoot Sims, Al Cohn, Budd Johnson and Ray Nance are all outstanding.

Joe Rushton

Bass saxophone, clarinet.

b. Evanston, Illinois, 7 Nov 1907; d. 2 March 1964.

The best-known American bass saxophonist after Adrian Rollini, Rushton worked early on with the California Ramblers, then through the 1930s for a variety of American bandleaders, most of them based in the Chicago area, though from 1931 he combined music with a full-time job in the aircraft industry and an intense interest in motorbikes. He combined the two careers in the following decade, when he had stints with Jimmy McPartland (1940), Benny Goodman (1942–3) and Horace Heidt (1944–5). From 1947 he formed his most famous association: with bandleader Red Nichols, who featured him as a cornerman until the year Rushton died. His contributions to Nichols's records – booming-toned, technically assured and smoothly rhythmic – are some of the most likeable sounds on the cornettist's fine late sessions. [DF]

➤➤ **Red Nichols** *(Dixieland Dinner Dance).*

Curley Russell

Bass.

b. Trinidad, 19 March 1917; d. 3 July 1986.

Curley (Dillon) Russell played with the big bands of Don Redman in 1941 and Benny Carter in 1943. He became extremely busy in the early bop period, working and recording with Dizzy Gillespie in 1945 and with Charlie Parker in 1945, 1948 and 1950. He was a regular member of the Tadd Dameron group from 1947–9, and the Buddy DeFranco quartet in 1952–3. He also recorded with, among others, Bud Powell in 1951, Horace Silver in 1952, Thelonious Monk in 1954, and the Art Blakey quintet, which included Clifford Brown, also in 1954. Although an extremely propulsive rhythm player, Russell was not featured as a soloist and was seemingly uninterested in the melodic mobility that came to be expected of bassists. He dropped out of the jazz scene in the late 1950s. [BP]

➤➤ **Art Blakey** *(A Night At Birdland, Vols. 1 & 2).*

George Russell

Composer, piano, educator.

b. Cincinnati, Ohio, 23 June 1923.

Russell's father was professor of music at Oberlin University. Russell started on drums, playing in the Boy Scout Drum and Bugle Corps, and received a scholarship to Wilberforce University where he joined the Collegians, which included saxophonist/composer Ernie Wilkins. Hospitalized at nineteen by tuberculosis, he learned arranging from a fellow patient. He joined the Benny Carter band on drums in Chicago, but was soon replaced by Max Roach, and began to concentrate more on arranging and composing than on playing the drums. After hearing Thelonious Monk's tune "Round Midnight", he moved to New York, where he became part of a coterie of young musicians, including Miles Davis and Gerry Mulligan, who gathered round Gil Evans to discuss their ideas. Russell was again hospitalized for sixteen months, and while incapacitated he conceived the basic idea of his influential theoretical (and practical) work *The Lydian Chromatic Concept of Tonal Organization*, of which he finished writing the first version in 1953, and of which J. E. Berendt has said: "Russell's concept of improvisation, 'Lydian' in terms of medieval church scales, yet chromatic in the modern sense, was the great pathbreaker for Miles Davis's and John Coltrane's modality."

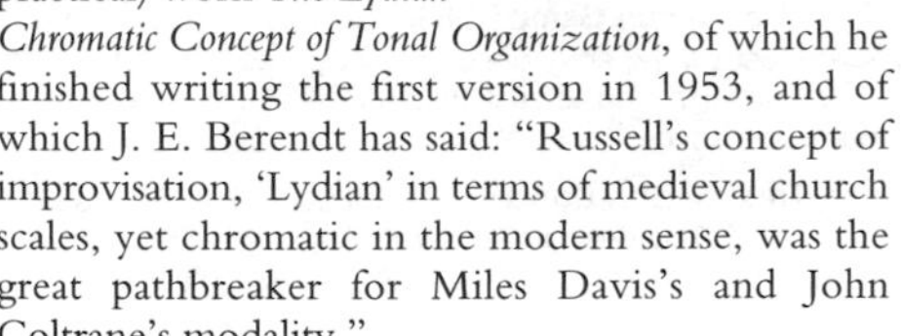

Jak Kilby

George Russell

After leaving hospital he collaborated with Dizzy Gillespie in a composition which combined contemporary jazz with African-Cuban rhythms, "Cubana-Be And Cubana-Bop", and which was first performed by Gillespie's band in September 1947. During the later 1940s he composed and arranged for various others, including Claude Thornhill and Artie Shaw, and in 1949 his composition *A Bird In Igor's Yard*, combining elements from Charlie Parker and Igor Stravinsky, was recorded by Buddy DeFranco's big band. In the mid-1950s Russell became friendly with trumpeter Art Farmer and pianist Bill Evans, who were interested in his Lydian Concept. With them, saxophonist Hal McCusick and guitarist Barry Galbraith, Russell formed a rehearsal sextet whose bass role was filled by either Milt Hinton or Teddy Kotick, and drums by Joe Harris, Osie Johnson or Paul Motian. They were known as the George Russell Smalltet and over a period of months in 1956 they recorded an album of Russell's compositions, *Jazz Workshop*, which is one of the recorded masterpieces of that decade. Russell was also commissioned by Brandeis University to compose a "serious" jazz work and produced his brilliant orchestral suite *All About Rosie*, which featured Bill Evans. In 1958–9 he taught at the School of Jazz at Lenox, Massachusetts.

From 1960 Russell began leading his own sextets around the New York area and at festivals; he also toured throughout the Midwest and played at the Newport festival in 1964. During this time he recorded a series of albums, of which *Ezz-thetics* has been perhaps the most influential. In 1964 Russell toured Europe with his sextet, appearing at the first Berlin jazz festival, and then lived in Sweden for five years. The Swedish Radio director of jazz, a trumpet player called Bosse Broberg, was an admirer of Russell, and during the latter's five-year stay, Broberg recorded everything Russell had ever written, and also provided him with several new commissions, including a Mass, music for a ballet based on *Othello*, and an orchestral suite combining tapes and improvisation with ensemble passages, the *Electronic Sonata For Souls Loved By Nature*. Russell also taught his Lydian Concept in Stockholm, and toured in Europe with a sextet of Scandinavian musicians sometimes augmented with Americans such as Don Cherry. He also taught in Finland, Norway and Denmark, and performed his music with the radio orchestras of Oslo and Copenhagen.

In 1969 he returned to the USA to take up a permanent teaching post at the New England Conservatory in Boston. This post allowed him to continue touring and performing occasionally with his own groups, and in 1978 he led a nineteen-piece band at the Village Vanguard in New York for six weeks; in the 1980s he regularly played the Bottom Line as part of the Newport jazz festival in New York. In 1981 he toured Italy, and in 1983 he toured the West Coast of America. In 1986 he made his first visit to the UK, touring for the Contemporary Music Network with an Anglo-American big band, the Living Time Orchestra, and he has returned several times since. He had other big composing commissions in the late 1980s and early 1990s, which resulted in long works including *Uncommon Ground*, *An American Trilogy*, and the gigantic three-hour *Time Line* for symphony orchestra, jazz ensembles, choirs, rock groups and dancers, composed for the celebration of the 125th anniversary of the Boston New England Conservatory in 1992.

Since the mid-1950s Russell has been an *éminence grise* of modernism and a musical adventurer. In the late 1950s and early 1960s his pupils included Art Farmer, Rahsaan Roland Kirk, Eric Dolphy and Carla Bley, and in the later 1960s his influence was pervasive in Scandinavia; Jan Garbarek, Terje Rypdal and Palle Mikkelborg, among others, worked with him and studied his Lydian Concept. Since 1967 *The Lydian Chromatic Concept* has been an official text at the University of Indiana Music School. The basic point about this concept is that it encourages improvisers to convert chord symbols into the scales that best convey the sound of the chords. The next stage is the idea of the superimposition of one scale on another, which leads to pan-tonality, the presence of more than one key centre, but occurring within a dominant tonality. In other words, the music is not atonal (in no particular key), but it can accommodate some polytonality. Russell has said: "Jazz is a music that is rooted in folk scales, which again are rooted strongly in tonality. Atonality is the complete negation of tonal centres . . . It would not support, therefore, the utterance of a blues scale because this implies a tonic."

Russell's own music synthesizes elements from jazz, blues and gospel music with techniques from serialism and abstraction. He says that he is not a revolutionary but an evolutionary: he does not negate the jazz tradition – he adds dimensions to it. The blues and song structures, however they are seen through his creatively distorting mirrors, are, nevertheless, still structurally present in his work. In particular, his music is always immensely eloquent rhythmically, and his recent performances have shown that he has absorbed and transformed elements from African drumming and rock, integrating them with his own jazz heritage. In the spring of 1998, Russell spent several days in London rehearsing his music with students from the London Guildhall School of Music and from a French academy. This culminated in a highly successful London concert, followed by a Paris concert. During the year, several of his earlier albums were reissued including *New York, New York* (Impulse!), *Jazz In The Space Age* (GRP Records), *Stratusphunk* (Riverside Original Jazz Classics), *Living Time* (CBS/Sony). The latest (1995) George Russell Living Time Orchestra recording, *It's About Time* (Label Bleu), was also released in 1998. [IC]

⊙ **Jazz Workshop** (1956; Bluebird). Twelve marvellously composed pieces plus two alternate takes, and brilliant group and individual playing, make this one of the most dynamic jazz albums of all time. Bill Evans's solos on both takes of "Concerto For Billy The Kid" are superlative.

⊙ **Ezz-thetics** (1961; OJC). Russell's sextets of the early 1960s produced some of the most vital music of the time. *Ezz-thetics,* with the superb Eric Dolphy plus Don Ellis, Dave Baker, Steve Swallow and Joe Hunt, is the seminal masterpiece, including one of the most evocative versions of "Round Midnight" ever recorded – it begins and ends with abstract sounds, but the core is a solo feature for Dolphy on alto saxophone.

⊙ **The Outer View** (1962; OJC). *The Outer View* has the superbly evocative and moving "You Are My Sunshine" in an eleven-minute mini-orchestral version with stunning vocals by Sheila Jordan.

⊙ **Othello Ballet Suite/Electric Organ Sonata No. 1** (1967; Soul Note). *Othello* is a big-band work for a Scandinavian orchestra that includes the young Jan Garbarek and Jon Christensen. There's some excellent orchestral writing, much movement and pan-tonal bravura. *The Electronic Organ Sonata*, improvised on a church organ with the electronics grafted on later, doesn't add much to his opus.

⊙ **Electric Sonata For Souls Loved By Nature** (1969; Soul Note). This album is by Russell's sextet plus taped electronics, creating a vast shifting tableau of sound, straddling passionate free improvisation, rocky elements and echoes of African rhythms. Garbarek is prominently featured and also had a hand in some of the composition. (A 1980 recorded performance with different personnel added little of note.)

⊙ **Trip To Prillargui** (1970; Soul Note). Garbarek again, with Christensen, guitarist Terje Rypdal, bassist Arild Andersen and American trumpeter Stanton Davis. The seven pieces are all composed by either Garbarek or Russell, and the playing – often very free – is excellent.

⊙ **New York Big Band** (1977–8; Soul Note); **Live In An American Time Spiral** (1982; Soul Note). These are two fine big-band albums with a host of jazz stars doing justice to Russell's compositions and the occasional standard.

⊙ **The African Game** (1983; Blue Note). An orchestral masterwork, an enormously disciplined development of motifs with rich elegiac sections, magnificent climaxes and much solo space.

⊙ **The London Concert** (1989; Label Bleu). This is a two-CD recording of Russell's Anglo-American orchestra at Ronnie Scott's, with some new works including "Uncommon Ground" and "Six Aesthetic Gravities", and some older pieces such as "Listen To The Silence".

Hal Russell

Tenor and soprano saxophones, trumpet, drums.

b. Detroit, Michigan, 1926; d. 5 Sep 1992.

Hal Russell (Harold Luttenbacher) picked up drums at the age of four, leading a jazz quartet while at Riverside-Brookfield High School, outside Chicago. In college – where he majored in trumpet – he led a big band and toured during the summers, playing drums with the bands of Woody Herman (with whom Russell made his first recording), Boyd Raeburn and Claude Thornhill. Inspired by bebop, Russell spent the 1950s in Chicago, playing support for a huge range of entertainers and jazz musicians, including Billie Holiday, Benny Goodman, Duke Ellington and John Coltrane. Plagued by drug addiction for ten years, by the end of the decade he had cleaned up and was doing commercial session work. In 1959 he began playing a nascent form of free music in a trio fronted by tenor saxophonist Joe Daley. They recorded *Newport '63* (RCA), a fascinating investigation of post-bop alternatives that desperately needs to be reissued. After the trio disbanded, Russell moved briefly to Florida in 1969, then returned to Chicago, hoping to establish a working group, and by the late 70s the NRG Ensemble was formed with reed player Chuck Burdelik, bassists Brian Sandstrom and Curt Bley, and drummer Steve Hunt. In 1979 Russell picked up the tenor saxophone, on which his prime influence was

Albert Ayler, and returned to the trumpet after a long hiatus. With NRG Russell built a substantial book of original tunes, including extended suites. The group recorded *NRG Ensemble* (1981; Nessa), *Conserving NRG* (1984; Principally Jazz) and *Generation* (1982; Nessa; with saxophonist Charles Tyler). In 1981 Russell recorded *Eftsoons* (Nessa), duets with saxophonist Mars Williams, who eventually replaced Burdelik. Largely under the impetus of writer/producer Steve Lake, Russell got his big break with ECM, for whom he recorded *The Finnish/Swiss Tour* (1990) and the solo overdub record *Hal's Bells* (1991). He can be heard with the self-proclaimed "punk jazz" outfit the Flying Luttenbachers on *Live At WNUR 2–6–92* (1996; Coat-Tail), a group that kept Hal's name against his wishes when he left the band shortly before he died. [JC]

⊙ **The Hal Russell Story** (1992; ECM). Ironically, this record-length autobiography was waxed just five weeks before Russell's tragic, unexpected death. NRG – which Williams has kept afloat since then, recording a number of excellent CDs – is in fine form, ranging between tight, loopy charts and loose, hard blowing, and in between tunes Russell narrates in his inimitable, grumbling-old-guy manner.

Luis Russell

Piano, arranger.

b. Careening Clay, near Bocas Del Toro, Panama, 6 Aug 1902; d. New York, 11 Dec 1963.

Luis Russell used his $3000 winnings from a lottery ticket to settle in New Orleans, where by 1923 he was working for Albert Nicholas at Tom Anderson's Café. By 1927 – after an unsuccessful trip to New York with King Oliver – he had taken over George Howe's band at the Nest Club and was forming his own from it, bringing in keymen such as Henry "Red" Allen, Paul Barbarin and Albert Nicholas (and founding, in the process, a happy New Orleans family). Soon after, amongst other work, he landed "the best job in Harlem" (says Frank Driggs), playing at the Saratoga Club owned by millionaire Casper Holstein, a gambler who ran the premises for his own amusement and subsequently offered the place to the band as a gift. "I enjoyed playing in Luis's band more than any I performed in in those days," says "Red" Allen, and Charlie Holmes agrees: "Luis was the nicest guy in the world. But you know they say nice people don't get nowhere!"

In 1935 Louis Armstrong heard the band – now much improved after seven years of club work and touring – and took it over for two days at the Savoy; Joe Glaser, his young and ruthless manager, promptly signed up the orchestra as Armstrong's backing group. The new discipline, the accompanying role and the mafioso shadow of Glaser took their toll. "I didn't like working with the band then," says Holmes. "It was OK when it was Russell's but afterwards it became very commercial and there was always this one and that one telling you what to do. But you have to be careful when it comes to naming people!" In 1940, on thin excuses, the band was dismissed by Glaser's office ("Jimmy Archey got told he was too short," remembers Pops Foster, "and I was too old!"), but Russell was retained until 1943 as Armstrong's musical director. Then he formed his own band for touring and recording, but by 1948 musical fashion was moving too fast. Russell opened a candy store in Brooklyn, then a gift shop, then worked as a booking agent for the Town Hall Club. He was a chauffeur-cum-piano teacher when he died. [DF]

⊙ **The Luis Russell Story** (1929-34; Retrieval). The best choice; forty eight tracks in admirable sound telling the Russell-on-record story.

⊙ **Luis Russell And His Orchestra** (1929-34; Topaz). Topaz always produces excellent samplers and this is one including most of Russell's most important titles and adding three with Louis Armstrong, including "Mahogany Hall Stomp".

⊙ **Savoy Shout** (1929–30; JSP). An outstanding set, collecting all the best of the Russell band, with superb remastering by John R.T. Davies and scrupulous attention to discographic detail.

➤➤ **Louis Armstrong** *(Louis Armstrong 1937–38).*

Pee Wee Russell

Clarinet, saxophones.

b. Maple Wood, Missouri, 27 March 1906; d. 15 Feb 1969.

"He is no virtuoso, and his tone is breathy and squeaky, but you forget those shortcomings when you hear the bliss and the sadness and the compassion and the humility that are there in the notes he plays" – George Frazier, one of the finest jazz writers, offering a key to the work of one of the greatest and most original jazz clarinettists.

Pee Wee (Charles Ellsworth) Russell spent twenty years working with the best company around St Louis, New York and the Midwest – stars such as Peck Kelley, Red Nichols, Bix Beiderbecke, Frank Trumbauer, Ben Pollack and dozens of others. "I made God knows how many records in New York in the late 1920s and early 1930s," he recalled later, "and at night we lived uptown." A 1929 Vitaphone short, *Red Nichols And His Five Pennies*, shows Russell's face fresh and unlined, but those nights uptown, as well as his huge capacity for liquor, were quickly to effect a change, in more ways than one. "Pee Wee had to change his style, you know," opines Peanuts Hucko. "I've heard some records and it's amazing, the technique he had as a young man. I think the booze just slowed him down completely."

By 1935, when he worked for Louis Prima (who called him "the most fabulous musical mind I've known"), Russell's aharmonic approach and fractured, cliffhanging style were, for whatever reason, fully formed: a brave and revolutionary artistic departure that upended the traditional musicology of clarinet tone and cocked a snook at such fashionable and highly capable contemporaries as Goodman and Shaw. In 1937 he began his permanent resi-

William Gottlieb

Pee Wee Russell

dency in New York's clubland, working with all the best of the New-York-from-Chicago Dixielanders and with their figurehead, Eddie Condon. Condon loved Russell for his musical sincerity, serious approach and anti-commercial leanings, but was canny enough to see that Russell himself was potentially highly marketable. For the next 25 years he featured regularly in Condon's concerts, club dates, recordings and radio and TV appearances – as well as on club flyers and posters, and on the pages of *Life* magazine. He had become a central figure of Chicago jazz.

The composite of Russell's clownish, wrinkle-racked features and eccentric clarinet style made a number of people like him for the wrong reasons. "I'll bet you anything," said critic George T. Simon in 1944, "that Pee Wee's face is far more important to some young fans than what he plays – and commercially I daresay it's far more important to Pee Wee too." Russell's account of this period contradicts him: "I worked at Nick's and Condon's for ten years or more, and there's a sadness about that time. Those guys made a joke of me, a clown, and I let myself be treated that way because I was afraid. I didn't know where else to take refuge!" Russell was often irascible, often unhappy, often drunk, and by the late 1950s he was working in new surroundings such as George Wein's small group. In 1962 the progressive side of Pee Wee Russell came dramatically into view. That year, with trombonist Marshall Brown, he formed a piano-less quartet reminiscent of Gerry Mulligan's, which – with its use of contemporary tunes and album titles such as *New Groove* – announced plainly that Pee Wee Russell, progressive, was making his entry. Other then-revolutionary statements (including an album with Oliver Nelson) were to follow, but by the middle of the decade Russell had returned, willingly or not, to more familiar territory: touring as a soloist with Alex Welsh in England (where a gifted clone, Archie Semple, bemused him), playing again with Wein, Condon and Bobby Hackett, an old friend. He died of a liver complaint that had first laid him low in 1950. [DF]

⊙ **Jazz Original** (1938–45; Commodore). Canny collection of Russell on Commodore with Condon (eight tracks) but also Muggsy Spanier, Wild Bill Davison, the Three Deuces (Russell, Joe Sullivan, Zutty Singleton) and Russell's own Hot Four. Excellent notes by Joe Muranyi.

⊙ **We're In The Money** (1954; Black Lion). An interesting date, teaming Russell with his longtime sidekick Wild Bill Davison, as well Doc Cheatham, Vic Dickenson and George Wein.

⊙ **Swingin' With Pee Wee** (1960; Prestige). Long overdue for CD re-release, this superb date teams Pee Wee with Buck Clayton and Tommy Flanagan's trio; it did much to refocus attention on Russell's talents on its original release.

⊙ **Jazz Reunion** (1961; Candid). Coleman Hawkins and Russell together again with a rhythm-section centred on Jo Jones and a bonus in the presence of a great trumpeter, Emmett Berry.

⊙ **Pee Wee Russell Quartet** (1962; Columbia). Russell's superb late quartet with valve-trombonist Marshall Brown, with Pee Wee tackling bebop material and beyond.

⊙ **With Alex Welsh And His Band** (1964/6; Lake). Recorded at 1960s stronghold the Manchester Sports Guild, Welsh and Russell make a strong team (during Pee Wee's earlier visits he was put out by clarinettist Archie Semple's soundalike devotion). On this brightly recorded set everyone plays well and Russell is audibly invigorated by his surroundings.

⊙ **Over The Rainbow** (1965; Xanadu). Pee Wee is beautifully featured as soloist most of the way here, although Bobby Hackett appears as a welcome guest on one track with Dave Frishberg.

➤➤ **Eddie Condon** *(Chronological Eddie Condon 1942–43);* **Louis Prima** *(Louis Prima Vol. 1).*

Babe Russin

Tenor saxophone, clarinet.

b. Pittsburgh, Pennsylvania, 18 June 1911; d. 4 Aug 1964.

A fine hot tenor soloist, Babe (Irving) Russin is best remembered for a long association with Benny Goodman, which began in 1937 and was regularly renewed over a twenty-year period. He worked first with the California Ramblers in 1926, and for the next ten years for a variety of prominent white bandleaders, including Red Nichols, Roger Wolfe Kahn and Ben Pollack, as well as at CBS as a studio man. All through the big-band years he worked for leaders such as Tommy Dorsey (1938–40) and Jimmy Dorsey (1942–4), and led his own orchestra in between, but after the war he moved into studio work in Hollywood, where he took part in jazz films including *The Glenn Miller Story* (1953) and *The Benny Goodman Story* (1955), as well as numerous sessions for soundtracks, radio and TV. [DF]

Session At Midnight (1955; Dormouse). Overdue for CD release, this five-star jam session has Russin solo alongside fellow tenorist Plas Johnson and two seminal altoists, Benny Carter and Willie Smith, along with a gang of swing champions.

Bill Russo

Arranger, composer, trombone.

b. Chicago, 25 June 1928; ; d. 11 Jan 2003.

After studying with Lennie Tristano in 1943–7, Russo formed his own rehearsal band and in 1950 joined Stan Kenton's Innovations Orchestra. He gave up playing in 1953, continuing to contribute to Kenton's library while studying composition. In 1958 he moved to New York, recording with his own large orchestra, and then did likewise in London from 1962–5. He taught at Columbia College, Chicago, from 1965–75 and again from 1979–90. His compositions, ranging from the avant-garde to the frankly eclectic, have been conducted by Seiji Ozawa and heard on film soundtracks, and his textbooks on jazz composition, though opinionated, were some of the first in the field. [BP]

➤➤ **Stan Kenton** *(Complete Bill Holman And Bill Russo Arrangements).*

Paul Rutherford

Trombone, euphonium.

b. London, 29 Feb 1940.

Rutherford spent five years in an RAF regional band (1958–63), where he met John Stevens, Trevor Watts, Bob Downes, Chris Pyne and other kindred spirits. Then came four years at the Guildhall School of Music (1964–8). In 1964 he joined the New Jazz Orchestra, the next year he founded the Spontaneous Music Ensemble with Stevens and Watts, and from 1967 on he was with Mike Westbrook's various bands. Rutherford has always been an indefatigable experimenter deeply immersed in the more abstract aspects of improvisation, and during the 1960s he was one of a tiny handful of people developing a new language for trombone: new sounds, new intervals, new textures. In 1970 he formed his group Iskra 1903, and also became the principal trombone of the London Jazz Composers' Orchestra. At that time he also became associated with Peter Brötzmann and Alexander von Schlippenbach, playing with the Globe Unity Orchestra until he was sacked in 1981, though he plays on the 1986 *20th Anniversary* record. Since 1973 he has been playing unaccompanied trombone. For such an uncompromising avant-gardist, his taste in trombone players is surprisingly conventional: Jim Robinson, Jack Teagarden, J.J. Johnson, Bob Brookmeyer, Jimmy Knepper and Roy Williams. Rutherford also gets inspiration from musicians right across the modern spectrum, from John Coltrane and Eric Dolphy to Bartók and Varèse. [IC]

➤➤ **Globe Unity Orchestra** *(Rumbling);* **Barry Guy** *(Harmos);* **Kenny Wheeler** *(Music For Large And Small Ensembles).*

Terje Rypdal

Guitar, composer; also flute, soprano saxophone.

b. Oslo, Norway, 23 Aug 1947.

Rypdal's father, Jakop, was a nationally renowned conductor of orchestras and marching bands. Rypdal studied the piano from the age of five, and started the guitar at thirteen. He began as a pop/rock guitarist, then, under the influence of Jimi Hendrix, moved towards improvisation and blues-based rock. In the late 1960s he played with Jan Garbarek's quartet, which included Jon Christensen and Arild Andersen. He also played with the George Russell sextet and big band, and studied Russell's *Lydian Chromatic Concept of Tonal Organization*, which helped him develop his improvisational abilities. At the Baden-Baden free-jazz festival in 1969 he played in a big band led by Lester Bowie, which featured most of the Art Ensemble of Chicago, and this enabled him to make his first real international impact. He played on Garbarek's first two ECM albums and then began recording for the label himself. In 1972 he performed with his own trio at the Berlin jazz festival. In the mid-1970s he led his own group, Odyssey, which toured internationally. From the late 1970s into the 1980s he led a trio with Palle Mikkelborg and Jon Christensen. Rypdal is an important composer both for small groups and for large orchestras, and has also written symphonies, a piano concerto and a composition featuring himself and Mikkelborg improvising with a symphonic group. He has said, "I find that a lot of rock guitarists have a more interesting tone than mellow-type jazz guitarists", and, though he cites Wes Montgomery as an influence, he has more affinity with rock guitarists in his brilliant use of electronic colours and textures. Rypdal is one of that new breed of European musicians who are deeply conversant with western classical music without ever allowing it to undermine their natural sense of rhythm and their ability to improvise. [IC]

Odyssey (1975; ECM); **Waves** (1977; ECM). Two excellent quartet sessions, with trombone, bass and drums on *Odyssey*, and with trumpeter Palle Mikkelborg, bassist Sveinung Hovensjo and Jon Christensen on *Waves*. The small groups get down to business without fuss, and the music mirrors its time, with elements of free jazz and rock, and subtle contrast between electronic and acoustic sounds. Mikkelborg is, as always, impressive.

Terje Rypdal/Miroslav Vitous/Jack DeJohnette (1978; ECM); **Descendere** (1979; ECM); **To Be Continued** (1981; ECM). The 1978 and 1981 albums have the same personnel, whereas *Descendere* has Rypdal with Mikkelborg and Christensen. These three albums, characteristic of Rypdal's echo-laden approach at the time, are worthy of repeated hearings.

Eos (1984; ECM). David Darling on cello (acoustic and electric) matches the evocative sonority of Rypdal in a mainly poetic outing.

Johnny St Cyr

Banjo, guitar.

b. New Orleans, 17 April 1890; d. 17 June 1966.

Johnny St Cyr is remembered as the banjo player who played on Louis Armstrong's Hot Five and Seven recordings, and with Jelly Roll Morton, while he was working for Doc Cooke's Dreamland Orchestra in Chicago. Around 1930 he returned to New Orleans, where he played regularly and worked as a plasterer, and he did not move from his home town again until 1955, when he went to the West Coast at the age of 65 to work with New Orleans-style bands for another ten years. His fascinating story was told in a lengthy *Jazz Journal* serial (Sept–Dec 1966): a fine portrait of a great New Orleans musician. [DF]

➤➤ **Louis Armstrong** *(Louis Armstrong 1925–6 & 1926–7).*

Dino Saluzzi

Bandoneon.

b. Campo Santo, Argentina, 20 May 1935.

Timoteo "Dino" Saluzzi's father played guitar, mandolin and bandoneon, and gave Saluzzi lessons on the bandoneon. By the age of fourteen, Saluzzi knew enough to play in his first band, the Trio Carnaval. He began to play professionally while studying in Buenos Aires and soon became a member of the Symphonic Orquesta Estable at Argentina's first radio station, Radio El Mundo. In 1956 Saluzzi resigned from his radio orchestra job and returned to Salta to work on his compositions, aiming to meld folk-music elements and aspects from other genres into a coherent form that was "vital and real beyond the conventions".

He worked briefly with Gato Barbieri in the early 1970s, helping the saxophonist, who had turned away from free jazz, to rediscover his musical roots, and the collaboration resulted in Barbieri's album, *Chapter One: Latin America.* With pianist and tango expert Mariano Mores, Saluzzi completed many South American tours. He also worked as arranger and soloist for Enrique Mario Francini's Sinfonica de Tango, playing in Japan with the band in 1977. Two years later he formed his first Cuarteto Dino Saluzzi, and co-founded the experimental chamber ensemble Musica Creativa. In the 1980s European and American jazz musicians, fascinated by the musical and emotional richness of his bandoneon-playing, were eager to collaborate with Saluzzi, and in 1982 he began recording for ECM, which further helped the development of his music and his career. The company initiated his collaboration with Charlie Haden, Palle Mikkelborg and Pierre Favre for the album *Once Upon A Time…Far Away In The South,* and later with Enrico Rava for *Volver.* Later on Saluzzi played with Haden's Liberation Music Orchestra, and co-led the Rava/Saluzzi Quintet. Saluzzi has also worked with Louis Sclavis, Edward Vesala, Charlie Mariano, Al Di Meola, David Friedman and Anthony Cox, among many others.

In a *Down Beat* interview, Saluzzi said, "I'm not afraid of anything I create because I know it will be a reflection of myself and my culture. If I play jazz, I play my jazz. It's just a different way of expressing my feelings." In 1991 Saluzzi revisited his roots by

Juan Hitters

Dino Saluzzi

making an ECM album in Argentina together with his brothers Felix and Celso and his son José. The resulting *Mojotoro* explored the many strands of South American music – tango, folk, candina music, candombe, the milonga music of the La Pampa province – and was so successful that the Dino Saluzzi Family Project was subsequently able to tour Europe. [IC]

Kultrum (1982; ECM). With bandoneon, voice, percussion and flutes Saluzzi creates a heartfelt musical evocation of an imaginary return to the towns and villages of his childhood.

Andina (1988; ECM). Saluzzi solo again – the extraordinary virtuoso alone with his bandoneon (and some flute), playing his autobiography. The dance is ever-present but he sometimes seems to be praying or thinking aloud on the instrument.

Cité de la Musique (1996; ECM). This is a ravishing trio album with Saluzzi's son José (a very fine acoustic guitarist), and the great bassist Marc Johnson. Eight of the nine compositions are by Dino and the ninth is Carl Zindars's lovely ballad, "How My Heart Sings". The three instruments blend beautifully, the sound is airy, and the writing consistently lovely.

Dino Saluzzi/Rosamunde Quartett (1998; ECM). Saluzzi's writing for this superb quartet skilfully invests the music with his own essence – the yearning, the melancholy, the flashes of exhilaration. The Rosamunde Quartett must have worked very hard to become familiar with the South American rhythms, and their integration with the bandoneon is a triumph – "Salon de Tango", for example, has great bandoneon-playing accompanied by string rhythms. This is an exquisite album.

Perico Sambeat

Alto saxophone, flute.

b. Valencia, Spain, 13 July 1962.

Having begun his musical education playing piano at the age of six, Perico Sambeat later took up flute and saxophone. In 1982, he moved to Barcelona, where he completed his classical studies and studied harmony with Ze Eduardo before forming his own jazz group, gigging all over Spain and, subsequently, Europe. In 1991, in New York, he was able to play with Jimmy Cobb, Lee Konitz, Joe Chambers and others, and he has also worked with Steve Lacy, Louie Bellson, Daniel Humair, Fred Hersch et al. With his own quartet, he has toured Argentina and Mexico, and with Portuguese pianist Bernardo Sassetti, Angola and Brazil. In 1996, Sambeat joined the international sextet led by UK trumpeter Guy Barker, initially alongside tenorman Dale Barlow, and he appears on two Verve albums under Barker's name, *Timeswing* (1996) and the with-strings recording *What Love Is* (1997), on which he contributes his agile, boppish alto sound to an Ornette Coleman medley. Other leaders for whom Sambeat has recorded include Jack Walrath, Carlos Barretto, Eddie Henderson and Sassetti, and he has also made albums with a quartet co-led with pianist Bruce Barth, and with pianist Brad Mehldau (*New York-Barcelona Crossing*, 1993; Fresh Sound). Sambeat's own albums appear mostly on the EGT label, and include an album made at Ronnie Scott's in 1993 with pianist Steve Melling, bassist Dave Green and drummer Stephen Keogn, *Dual Force* (Jazz House), and one with a band co-led with trumpeter Michael Mossman, *Uptown Dance* (see below), and in 2001, the flamenco-flavoured Perico (see below). Latterly he has been a member of pianist George Colligan's quartet, appearing on *Desire* (2000; Fresh Sound) and *Como La Vida Puede Ser* (2001; Fresh Sound). Sambeat is essentially a regular bop alto player with a stinging attack and great facility, and his fiery playing lifts any band with which he plays. [CP]

Uptown Dance (1992; EGT). Sharing frontline duties with the above-mentioned Mossman, and propelled by a superb rhythm team (pianist Dave Kikoski, bassist Bill Morning and one of the most tasteful – if underrated – drummers in the music, Keith Copeland), Sambeat digs into his co-leader's themes with great brio.

Perico (2001; Lola). Sambeat hints at fusion possibilities by adding flamenco percussion to the work of pianist Sassetti, bassist Javier Collina and drummer Mark Miralta to distinctive effect.

➤➤ **Bernardo Sassetti** *(Salsetti).*

Joe Sample

Piano, composer.

b. Houston, Texas, 1 Feb 1939.

Sample formed a group with schoolfriends, including Hubert Laws, in 1954, which was known, after they moved to Los Angeles in 1960, as the Jazz Crusaders. By this time they consisted of Wayne Henderson (trombone), Wilton Felder (tenor), Stix Hooper (drums) and a succession of bassists. Sample also worked with many other West Coast-based musicians such as the Harold Land-Bobby Hutcherson band in 1967–8, and saxophonist Tom Scott in 1973, and became heavily involved in studio work. In 1972 the Jazz Crusaders became simply the Crusaders, and were highly successful in the instrumental soul/funk field; Felder was now doubling on electric bass, and studio guitarists Arthur Adams, David T. Walker and later Larry Carlton were added for recording and touring. Sample also became involved in album production, and, latterly, songwriting, for Minnie Riperton, Randy Crawford and B.B. King. His solo style with the Crusaders tends towards the superficial, and on his own post-1978 albums it is often also saccharine. His rhythm playing, however, is always on target and his latent ability as a Tyneresque improviser was well demonstrated by some of the early Jazz Crusaders recordings and by the first album below. [BP]

Joe Sample

Fancy Dance (1969; Sonet). Joined by two American expatriates, Red Mitchell and drummer J.C. Moses, Sample here combines attractive post-Tyner themes with alert improvisation.

Crusaders

Finest Hour (1971-81; Verve). On this greatest-hits-by-another-name album, "Street Life" (best known as an edited single) is restored to its full 11 minutes, and the symphonic "Last Call" with B.B. King is a structural mess. But the simple, guitar-led funk of "Put It Where You Want It" is glorious.

>> **Dennis Rowland** *(Now Dig This!)*.

Edgar Sampson

Alto and baritone saxophones, violin, arranger, composer.

b. New York, 31 Aug 1907; d. 16 Jan 1973.

Sampson played with many New York-based bands, including Duke Ellington's (c. 1926), Fletcher Henderson's from 1931–2 and Rex Stewart's short-lived big band in 1933. He led the saxophone section and arranged for the Chick Webb band from 1933–6, when he was replaced by Louis Jordan. He then became a highly successful freelance arranger for Benny Goodman, Artie Shaw, Red Norvo and many others. He took up more regular playing in the late 1940s, and then started writing and playing for the top Latin bands, such as that of Tito Puente, in the 1950s. He also led his own occasional small group, but was incapacitated by illness for some years before his death.

One of the most widely heard and least celebrated writers of the swing era, Sampson was no slouch as a player, although infrequently featured in solo spots. But it was his arranging and his dynamic but light-fingered way with the Webb band which attracted the attention of others, especially Goodman who further spread the popularity of many Sampson charts previously written for Webb. These may seem too genteel for present-day tastes, but his original melodies are destined to remain immortal, and it would be difficult to think of anyone else so overlooked who wrote tunes as good as "Stompin' At The Savoy", "Don't Be That Way", "If (When) Dreams Come True", "Lullaby In Rhythm" (co-written with Clarence Profit) and "Blue Lou". [BP]

>> **Chick Webb** *(Rhythm Man)*.

David Samuels

Vibraphone, marimba.

b. Waukegan, Illinois, 9 Oct 1948.

Samuels started on the drums at the age of six. He began studying mallet instruments at Boston University, from which he graduated with a degree in psychology in 1971, and then taught at Berklee College for two and a half years, where he worked with Pat Metheny and John Scofield. In 1974 he joined Gerry Mulligan's sextet, recording three albums, touring with the group four times in Europe and once in the USA. In 1975, with Gerry Niewood, Rick Laird and Ron Davis, he co-founded the group Timepiece, and also worked and recorded with Frank Zappa. In the later 1970s he was with Double Image until it split up in 1980 when, with Michael Di Pasqua, Paul McCandless and David Darling, he formed the group Gallery. Samuels has been a member of Spyro Gyra since the mid-1980s and is also active as a teacher in schools throughout the USA and Europe. [IC]

David Sanborn

Alto saxophone, flute.

b. Tampa, Florida, 30 July 1945.

Sanborn's family moved to St Louis, where he was brought up, when he was young. He contracted polio as a child, spending some time in an iron lung and was advised to take up a wind instrument as physical therapy. In 1963–4 he studied music at Northwestern University and from 1965–7 he undertook additional studies at the University of Iowa. He moved to the West Coast, playing and recording with the Paul Butterfield band from 1967–71. He was with Stevie Wonder in 1972–3, touring with him in a Rolling Stones concert package, and began a long association with Gil Evans in January 1973, playing on several Evans albums including the classic *Svengali*. He worked with the Brecker Brothers in 1975 and also began leading his own groups that year. During the 1970s and into the 1980s he was perhaps the most in-demand alto session player on the US scene, interpreting melodies and playing solos on dozens of albums, perhaps most famously on David Bowie's *Young Americans*.

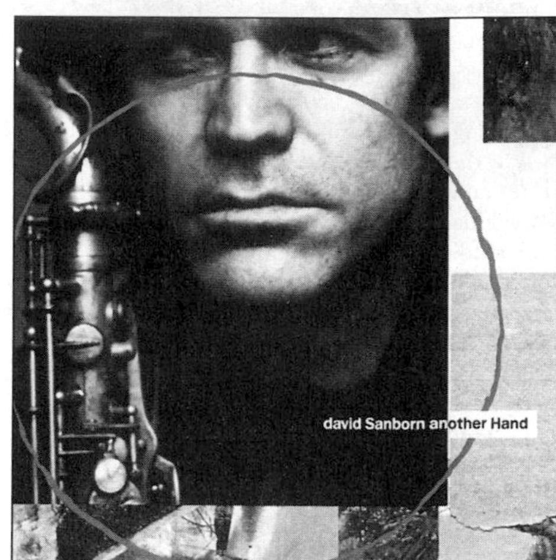

In the 1980s he led his own groups and toured internationally, and has continued to record successfully, as well as hosting his own radio show. Sanborn's influences include Hank Crawford, Jackie McLean and Charlie Parker, and he is steeped in the blues. He is a passionate, eloquent player with a tremendously expressive sound and the ability to make melodies "speak". He has, in addition to his work with Gil Evans, always been involved with electronic fusion music – often in the disco vein – but his recordings in that genre have been among the more forward-looking, and whatever the setting his sound is immediately identifiable. [IC]

Another Hand (1990; Elektra). Sanborn in strangely experimental vein with a disparate pool of players, involving four guitarists including Bill Frisell, three bassists including Marcus Miller (who did not produce this one) and Charlie Haden, three drummers including Jack DeJohnette and Joey Baron, as well as trombone and reeds. Sanborn wanders through this impressionistic landscape sketching occasional viewpoints.

Upfront (1991; Elektra). When Marcus Miller began producing Sanborn's albums the saxophonist thrived on the tuneful and funky contexts. This is perhaps the pick of their collaborations; Ornette Coleman's "Ramblin'" is given a wonderfully steamy funk treatment, and Sanborn's playing benefits from the loose (often organ-led) backings.

➤➤ **Gil Evans** *(Plays The Music Of Jimi Hendrix; Priestess).*

David Sanchez

Tenor and soprano saxophones.

b. Guaynabo, Puerto Rico, 3 Sept 1968.

Trained classically in a Puerto Rican performing arts school in Hato Rey, Sanchez played percussion in salsa and show bands before taking up the saxophone. He came to the mainland in 1988 and studied jazz with Kenny Barron at Rutgers University, absorbing a sense of chordal articulation which enriched Sanchez's concept of arrangement and composition. His percussive experience gave him a cunning grasp of rhythm, and by 1989 he was gigging with Eddie Palmieri and Claudio Roditi. The latter brought him to the attention and encouragement of Dizzy Gillespie, whom Sanchez joined in the United Nation Orchestra from 1991–3. Sanchez then commenced touring under his own name and recorded a series of six increasingly commanding and exotic albums for Columbia/Sony, gaining a Grammy nomination for both *Obsesión* (see below) in 1999 and *Melaza* in 2000. His protean ensembles have included fellow Latins Milton Cardona, Jerry Gonzalez and Danilo Perez, as well as Roy Hargrove, Tom Harrell and Dave Kikoski. [JK]

Obsesión (1998; Columbia). Sanchez makes a spirited sweep through lesser-known compositions of Brazil, Cuba and his native Puerto Rico and across his broadening talents. While drawing his song list, quintet members, and percussion backup from the tropics, Sanchez transcends any stereotype of Latin jazz with a variety of expression, sometimes tender, sometimes dancing, sometimes exuberantly edgy in the manner of his idol Sonny Rollins.

Travesia (2001; Sony). Persuasively exploring the meld of Puerto Rican folk and jazz in the company of his excellent latter day group, featuring Miguel Zenon (alto), Edsel Gomez (piano), Hans Glawischnig (bass) and Antonio Sanchez (drums), an impressive climax to his Columbia/Sony output.

Poncho Sanchez

Congas, timbales, percussion, vocals.

b. Laredo, Texas, 30 Oct 1951.

The young Ildefonso Sanchez was one of eleven siblings, all excellent dancers, but he is the only musician. Basically self-taught, although he studied music at Cerlitos College from 1970–72, he first played guitar before specializing in percussion. He turned professional at New Year 1975 and for the next seven years worked with Cal Tjader, whom he calls "my musical father". He formed his own band after Tjader's death in 1982, and has also appeared alongside Tito Puente, Mongo Santamaria, Clare Fischer (all among his favourite musicians), Willie Bobo and Celia Cruz, as well as Dizzy Gillespie, Eddie Harris, Freddie Hubbard and Dianne Reeves, the last two having guested on his recordings. He has eighteen CDs to his credit and feels proud that his band "has played an important part in the growth of Latin jazz today". [BP]

Afro-Cuban Fantasy (1998; Concord). With his regular group, Sanchez covers various areas of Afro-Latin music from the relatively loose-sounding to highly organized post-bop arrangements. Providing a focus is guest Dianne Reeves, who performs two Clare Fischer songs and a slowly swaying "Darn That Dream".

Pharoah Sanders

Tenor and soprano saxophones, composer.

b. Little Rock, Arkansas, 13 Oct 1940.

Pharoah (Farrell) Sanders had piano lessons from his grandfather, and also studied drums and clarinet. He began on saxophone and flute at sixteen, and played with local R&B bands. In 1959 he went to Oakland, California, on a music scholarship, playing with Dewey Redman, Philly Joe Jones and Vi Redd, among others. He moved to New York in 1962, working with Sun Ra, Rashied Ali, Don Cherry and others of the avant-garde, and came under the influence of Albert Ayler. From 1966–7 he worked with John Coltrane, and after Trane's death continued with Alice Coltrane until 1969. Sanders then began leading his own groups. He has toured and played many festivals in the USA and internationally. [IC]

Pharoah's First (1964; ESP); **Tauhid** (1966; Impulse!); **Welcome To Love** (1990; Timeless). The trajectory of Sanders's career, charted on these three albums, is not

wholly untypical, but Pharoah is perhaps the most extreme case. The ESP disc is a fearsome freak-out under Albert Ayler's influence, while *Tauhid*, made during his association with Coltrane (and featuring an early appearance by Sonny Sharrock), is more thoughtful, though it shares some of the prolixity of Coltrane's later work. Since then Sanders has flirted with African rhythms, dance-floor music and, on *Welcome To Love*, has returned to the jazz mainstream. Subtitled "plays beautiful ballads", it finds the man whose tone once approximated tearing metal tackling "Polka Dots And Moonbeams".

➤➤ **John Coltrane** *(The Major Works)*.

Randy Sandke

Trumpet, flugelhorn.

b. Chicago, 23 May 1949.

Randy Sandke is perhaps the most talented of the new generation of swing trumpeters who followed in the pioneering steps of Warren Vaché Jnr. He grew up in Chicago listening to Bix Beiderbecke and Louis Armstrong, and learned to play trumpet in his high school band, later majoring in music composition at Indiana University. After a brief period of inactivity, he moved to New York to work for ASCAP, but began playing again in 1980, taking lessons from Vince Penzerrella. Soon after, Sandke worked with Peanuts Hucko, Bob Wilber (1983), Benny Goodman (1984–6), Buck Clayton and the Newport Allstars. He also combined playing at functions around New York with writing for the Carnegie Hall Band (including an Armstrong tribute), and appeared with, and wrote for, the Tulsa Philharmonic in Oklahoma. By the 1990s he was becoming an ever-more familiar vistor to Europe, producing a string of hugely skilled recordings which are remarkable for their grasp of jazz tradition (Bix and Louis) and their effortless exploration of contemporary jazz and classical music. A master of his craft, Sandke is also a truly gifted composer and arranger, who arguably should receive the credit more readily accorded to less talented, but more fashionable, contemporaries. His work, in whatever discipline, demands attention and promises an even more exciting future. [DF]

⊙ **The Bix Beiderbecke Era** (1993; Nagel-Heyer). Home territory for Sandke, who not only introduces the concert but blows authoritatively through seventeen Beiderbecke-associated tunes including niceties like "I'll Be A Friend With Pleasure", "My Pretty Girl" and "Changes". His well-conceived arrangements in no way impede the passion of the performance.

⊙ **The Rediscovered Louis And Bix** (1999; Nagel-Heyer). A fine example of Sandke the researcher – unissued/unheard compositions and recorded tunes by Armstrong and Beiderbecke. As George Avakian remarks, the versatility needed to accomplish both roles is challenging, but Sandke is a master craftsman and meets the challenge easily, even recording the album on Armstrong's trumpet and Bix's cornet. His accompanists – Dick Hyman, Scott Robinson, Dan Barrett, Ken Peplowski and their peers – are as great as you'd expect.

⊙ **The Music of Bob Haggart** (2002; Arbors). Most of this CD is given over to Haggart's underrated rescoring of *Porgy and Bess* (1958). Sandke tracked down the music and replays it maginificently here with an all-star cast including Byron Stripling, Wycliffe Gordon, Kellso et al. Seven Haggart standards complete the set.

⊙ **Inside Out** (2002; Nagel Heyer). Or *Mainstream Meets The New Music,* as the secondary title has it. And with regular cohorts Ken Peplowski, Wycliffe Gordon et al playing with the likes of Marty Ehrlich and Uri Caine, that's exactly what happens on a terrific record full of delight and surprise. Sandke's range and versatility are now in danger of making him one of a kind.

⊙ **Celebrating Bix!** (2003; Arbors). This set, though the brainchild of fellow-trumpeter Peter Ecklund, is clearly close to Sandke's heart; he co-wrote the notes, played on all but a couple of tracks and makes telling contributions in both roles. The Bix Centennial All Stars (also including Randy Reinhardt, Dan Barrett, Dick Hyman and others) present Bix's original leads and solos scored in a wide variety of contexts.

Arturo Sandoval

Trumpet, flugelhorn, keyboards, percussion, vocals.

b. Artemisa, Havana, 6 Nov 1949.

Sandoval began studying classical trumpet at the age of twelve and, although attracted at an early age to jazz in general and Dizzy Gillespie in particular, he at first pursued a classical career. He performed with the Orquesta Moderna de Musica Cubana, and was a guest artist with the BBC Symphony Orchestra in London and the Leningrad Symphony Orchestra. His abilities in this field earned him the respect and friendship of classical trumpeters Maurice André and Adolph Herseth.

Back in Cuba, he was a founder member of Chucho Valdes's group Irakere, which fused an explosive mixture of jazz, classical, rock and traditional Cuban music, and soon gained an international reputation. He played in Havana with the group until 1981, when he left to lead his own band, which had much success with audiences and critics all over Europe and South America. Sandoval was voted Cuba's Best Instrumentalist each year from 1982–4.

His main inspiration has always been Dizzy Gillespie, and he played a prominent part in a documentary TV film about Gillespie's visit to Cuba in the 1980s. He was also a featured musician for three years in Gillespie's United Nation Orchestra and on the orchestra's Grammy-winning album *Live At The Royal Festival Hall.* Sandoval, who has been a regular visitor to London since the mid-1980s, defected from Cuba in 1990, and was granted political asylum by the USA, taking up residence in Miami. In the mid-1990s he had a full professorship at Florida International University. He has also played with Billy Cobham, Woody Herman, Herbie Hancock, Michel Legrand, Stan Getz and composer John Williams at the Boston Pops, and worked on film soundtracks including *Havana* and *Mambo Kings* which included his composition "Mambo Caliente".

Sandoval is an extraordinary virtuoso with an exceptional range, a brilliantly fleet technique and almost superhuman stamina, but his playing sometimes seems to have more to do with athletics than aesthetics, with showy technical forays which have little musical depth. His trumpet can blare in the brashest Latin tradition, but he can play pretty and, when in the mood, can touch and enthral listeners with the sheer poetry of his quiet reflections. At a German festival in the later 1980s, after playing a concert with his own group, he sat in with Woody Shaw's band and played some stunning low-register solos in what seemed to be an affectionate homage to Shaw. [IC]

No Problem (1986; Jazz House); **Straight Ahead** (1988; Jazz House). The 1986 album was recorded live at Ronnie Scott's, with Sandoval's Cuban musicians firing him up to voluble frenzies from time to time. *Straight Ahead* has him in the studio with Scott's rhythm-section and Chucho Valdes on piano – a much more considered session with only an occasional trip over the top.

I Remember Clifford (1991; GRP). Sandoval in fast jazz company including Kenny Kirkland, Ernie Watts and Charnett Moffett, in a brilliant and at times moving tribute to Brownie. No over-production here.

Danzon (Dance On) (1994; GRP). Sandoval plays pretty with some nice flugelhorn and harmon mute on many occasions during this rich album which covers the spectrum of his abilities. The brashness is there at times, but there is much fine and creative playing – also some excellent orchestral arrangements and a benign Dizzyesque scat vocal on "Groovin' High".

John Sangster

Composer, arranger, multi-instrumentalist.

b. Melbourne, Australia, 17 Nov 1928; d. 26 Oct 1995.

Sangster began as a drummer/cornettist soon after the war but eventually specialized on vibraphone and marimba, on which his improvised music was beyond reproach. But, as with Ellington, his best instrument was the arranger's pen, which in Sangster's grip, was a flexible and totally imaginative tool. The first of his major works was *The Hobbit Suite*, a combination of irresistible tunes and near-avant-garde sound-poems, which features regular colleagues Bob Barnard (a brilliant all-round trumpeter), his brother Len Barnard (a drummer of similar ability) and clarinettist John McCarthy. A magnificent follow-up, *The Lord Of The Rings*, moves from Ellington to Evan Parker and back with consummate ease. Sangster also wrote numerous film soundtracks and some wholly original tributes to Bix Beiderbecke and Ellington, often mixing washboards with electronic music to great effect. Sangster's writing was among the most eclectic in jazz: he delighted in two-beat as much as in the abstract use of atonal sound, and managed to work in existing disciplines with striking melodic and conceptual originality – his Beiderbecke tribute, for example, applies white 1920s voicing to original themes topped with electronic effects (a typical Sangster conceit). In the 1980s Sangster's position in the Australian jazz hierarchy was unassailable: it's unfortunate that, because of international reluctance to accept that a non-American might make a contribution of real value, his position in world-class jazz circles was never fully established. [DF]

The Hobbit Suite (1973; Swaggie). This work is a classic example of Sangster's witty eclectic writing for a superb small group. His magnum opus, *The Lord Of The Rings*, is now available on CD on the Move label.

Mongo Santamaria

Conga, percussion.

b. Havana, Cuba, 7 April 1922; d. Miami, 1 Feb 2003.

Mongo (derived from Ramón) absorbed African-Cuban music as a child. He studied violin but transferred to the drums and became a sought-after local musician. In the late 1940s he moved to Mexico and played with Perez Prado, also participating in Prado's first US band in 1951. He then worked in New York with Tito Puente for six years, during which time he recorded with Dizzy Gillespie in 1954. Based on the West Coast with Cal Tjader from 1957–60, he began recording his own albums, the second of which included his "Afro-Blue", later recorded by John Coltrane and others. Forming a New York-based group in 1961, he had early success with two singles released in 1963, Herbie Hancock's "Watermelon Man" and "Yeh-Yeh" written by his pianist Rodgers Grant. He had previously hired Brazilian Joao Donato on piano, and later in the 1960s used such people as Pat Patrick, Hubert Laws, Chick Corea and Sonny Fortune. His band has continued to exercise considerable influence on the cusp of Afro-Latin and African-American music, and his own percussion work was a major force in introducing various Latin rhythms to R&B, soul and jazz drummers. [BP]

Afro-Roots (1958–9; Prestige/OJC). Heavily dominated by African percussion and folklore forms, these first recordings include vocalists and fellow Cuban exile Armando

David Redfern

Mongo Santamaria

Peraza, along with Cal Tjader bandmates Willie Bobo and Al McKibbon. One track is titled "For Chano Pozo", and the first version of "Afro-Blue" is one of four tracks with Paul Horn on flute.

⊙ **Mongo Explodes/Watermelon Man** (1962–4; BGP). Another two-LPs-on-one-CD set, this British reissue has the early breakthrough albums with jazz horns leading the way. The short tracks of the 1962–3 sessions include the title track, "Yeh-Yeh" and Mongo's version of "Peanut Vendor", while the later live set has Nat Adderley and Jimmy Cobb for a couple of numbers.

➤➤ **Cal Tjader** *(Monterey Concerts).*

Heikki Sarmanto

Composer, piano.
b. Helsinki, 22 June 1939.

Heikki has three brothers who are also musicians, including bassist Pekka Sarmanto (b. 15 Feb 1945). He studied languages and music at Helskini University and the Sibelius Academy from 1962–4 and then attended the Berklee School in 1968–71, when he also took lessons with Serge Chaloff's mother. Named best pianist at the 1971 Montreux festival, he visited London in 1975 with his own twelve-piece workshop ensemble, which then became the independent big band UMO. Sarmanto went on to write his *New Hope Jazz Mass*, which was premiered in New York, as well as a jazz ballet, jazz opera and several suites. He was chosen by Sonny Rollins to arrange and conduct the latter's saxophone concerto, premiered in Tokyo in 1986, while albums of Sarmanto's songs have been recorded by Helen Merrill and Brazilian vocalist Claudya de Oliviera. [BP]

Helen Merrill

⊙ **Carousel** (1996; Finlandia). Much of Sarmanto's earlier work appears to be unavailable, but his prolific songwriting is here honoured by Merrill, with arrangements by Torrie Zito and solos by Juhani Aaltonen.

Bernardo Sassetti

Piano, composer.
b. Lisbon, 24 July 1970.

Sassetti's first instrument was the guitar, then from the age of nine he studied classical piano and music theory. After hearing Bill Evans, he became interested in jazz and was soon backing visitors such as Al Grey, Eddie Henderson, John Stubblefield, Frank Lacy and Andy Sheppard, and attending workshops by Horace Parlan, Roland Hanna, Dave Liebman, etc. During 1989–90 he taught jazz piano in Lisbon and later in Angola, Mozambique, Madeira and the Azores. Appearing all over Europe from 1991, he performed regularly with Art Farmer, and a major influence, Paquito D'Rivera, who involved him in the United Nation Orchestra in 1993. Based in London in 1994, he worked with Peter King, Jean Toussaint, Guy Barker (with whom he has made three albums) and formed his own trio. He has also recorded with Conrad Herwig, Andy Hamilton and Eddie Henderson, and his large-scale composition, "Echoes Of Africa" (1994), was partly funded by the Gulbenkian Foundation. [BP]

⊙ **Salsetti** (1994; Movieplay/Groove). Despite the album title, this covers a wide range of grooves, leaning not only towards Cuba but Brazil (one of the pianist's two unaccompanied tracks is a tribute to the composer Villa-Lobos). Paquito D'Rivera guests on three tracks, alternating with Perico Sambeat, but the rhythm-section (including drummer Jordi Rossy) is either too laid-back or under-recorded.

➤➤ **Guy Barker** *(Into The Blue).*

Keshav Sathe

Tabla.
b. Bombay, 31 Jan 1928.

Sathe studied privately from 1947–52 with Pandit Joshi, and from 1951–5 was accompanist to the singer Mr Kelkar Bombay. He came to the UK in 1956, playing tabla in Asian Music Circle (1957–9), and also gave lecture recitals in schools and colleges with Bhaskar Chandavarkar (sitar). From 1965–70 he worked with Joe Harriott and John Mayer in their *Indo-Jazz Fusions*. In 1967 the Keshav Sathe trio worked with the Irene Schweizer trio, Barney Wilen and Manfred Schoof, in a "Jazz Meets India" package which toured Germany and recorded an album. Through the 1970s and into the 1980s, he led his own trio and worked with Julie Felix, Danny Thompson, John Renbourn and others. He toured Europe and the USA with John Renbourn and Friends in 1979 and 1981. His favourites are Mahapurush Misra and Zakir Hussain. [IC]

➤➤ **Joe Harriott** *(Indo-Jazz Fusions).*

Tom Saunders

Trumpet, cornet.
b. Detroit, Michigan, 21 April 1938.

Saunders took up cornet at seven, joined his brother's band on second cornet (at nine), and made his first jazz appearance on the Ted Mack Amateur Hour (1950). After leading his own high school band, he was a music graduate of the USN School of Music (1957), then, after military service, he played with Pee Wee Hunt (1962–3) and led his own successful Surf Side Six (1963–85), while also working as an accountant and a safety director. During this period he met and played with many classic figures including Bobby Hackett, Eddie Condon, Louis Armstrong, and, in particular, Wild Bill Davison with whom he formed a lifelong friendship and musical partnership. Saunders' biographical video of Davison *@WBD; His Life, His Times, His Music* (TTT Network Inc) is well worth searching for. He also co-directs the Central Illinois jazz festival, and currently tours nationally and abroad with the Wild Bill Davison Legacy, the Saunders/Hirsch All Stars, the Detroit All Stars as well as playing major festivals like Sacramento, Toronto and Michigan. Despite his personal devotion to Davison, Saunders is an original cornet voice who makes no attempt to copy his idol. His mellow, mid-range approach also recalls Hackett, Pee Wee Erwin and other great players of the classic school. [DF]

⊙ **Call Of The Wild** (1995; Arbors). Five-star tribute to Wild Bill Davison by gifted contemporaries and led by Saunders's polished cornet.

⊙ **Exactly Like You** (1995; Nagel Heyer). An enjoyable Dixieland clambake, recorded in concert in Hamburg and headed by Saunders and Dick Sudhalter but also featuring an all-star team of mainstreamers including Roy Williams, Danny Moss, Chuck Hedges, Bill Allred, Johnny Varro, Marty Grosz et. al. Jeannie Lambe sings on one track.

Eddie Sauter

Trumpet, arranger.

b. New York, 2 Dec 1914; d. 21 April 1981.

One of jazz's most brilliant arrangers, Sauter began as a trumpeter with Red Norvo's band (1935) and quickly moved on to the position of staff arranger – a job for which he was highly qualified, having studied music at Columbia and the Juilliard. In 1939 he became a staff arranger for Benny Goodman, for whom he wrote arrangements including "Benny Rides Again" and "Clarinet A La King". During the 1940s Sauter wrote for other leaders, including Tommy Dorsey and Woody Herman, then after periods of illness teamed up with pianist/arranger Bill Finegan in 1952 to form the Sauter-Finegan orchestra, an exercise in arrangers' ingenuity which gained them hit records like "Midnight Sleigh Ride" and "Doodletown Fifers". In the later 50s Sauter worked in Germany, but returned to America to collaborate with Stan Getz on the *Focus* album, arguably the most dynamic use of strings with a jazz artist on record. Sauter collaborated further with Getz on the film soundtrack of *Mickey One* (1965) and *Tanglewood Concerto* (1966), works which came close to equalling the raw brilliance of *Focus*. [DF]

Sauter-Finegan Orchestra

⊙ **Directions In Music 1952–58** (RCA Bluebird). This zenith of big-band excellence goes well beyond the Sauter-Finegan orchestra hits to encompass lesser-known tone poems like "Two Bats In A Cave".

➤➤ **Stan Getz** *(Focus);* **Benny Goodman** *(Benny Goodman: His Orchestra And His Combos 1941–55).*

Jarmo Savolainen

Piano.

b. Finland, 24 May 1961.

Savolainen started piano at the age of nine, and studied classical piano until he was nineteen years old, during which time he had become inspired by Keith Jarrett and Chick Corea. Then, after making his well-received debut as a piano soloist with the

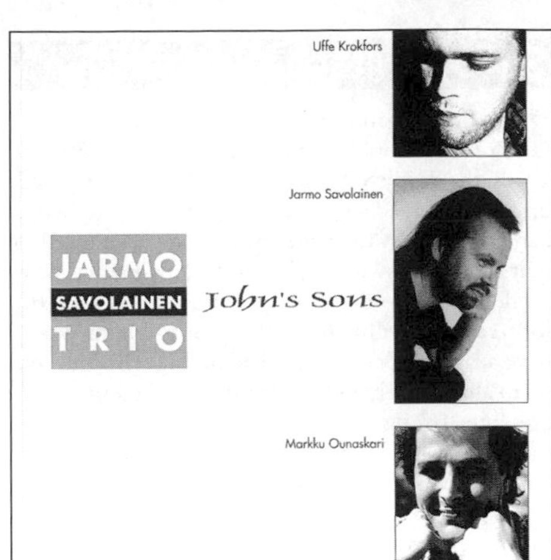

Kuopio Symphony Orchestra, he suddenly decided to abandon a classical career and devote himself to jazz. He went to Berklee College of Music in Boston for two years, immersing himself in jazz and playing with Tom Harrell, Bob Berg and Wallace Roney, among others. He was at Berklee for the practical experience of jazz, rather than its theoretical basis, and left the school before graduating.

He recorded his first album, *Nonet*, in 1985, and two years later released *Blue Dreams*. In 1992 he recorded his first New York album, *First Sight*, with an all-star line-up of Rick Margitza, Wallace Roney, Ron McClure and Billy Hart, but after that began to include more Finns and other Scandinavians on his albums. The personnel for his 1995 album, *True Image*, was McClure and Hart, saxophonists Dave Liebman and Finn Kari Heinila, plus trumpeter Tim Hagans, and his 1997 release, *Another Story*, featured Hagans, and three Scandinavians: bassist Anders Jormin, Heinila, and drummer Markku Ounaskari. Savolainen had also recorded *Songs For Solo Piano* in 1990, and an improvised duo keyboards album, *Phases*, with Seppo Kantonen in 1989. In addition, Savolainen has worked as sideman with other Finnish bands, including the Pekka Pohjola group, 1987–92.

He is a brilliantly accomplished pianist, steeped in jazz piano – yet, like Keith Jarrett, he still keeps in touch with classical music, and has played from time to time with classical ensembles including the Finnish National Opera Orchestra. He has also composed music for the Finnish Radio Symphony Orchestra, the UMO, and for various film projects and theatre companies. Savolainen has played on over forty albums, and in several movies. His most recent trio, John's Sons, an all-Finnish unit with Markku Ounaskari and bassist Uffe Krokfors, released an eponymous album in 1998. [IC]

⊙ **John's Sons** (1998; A-Records). This dynamic album contains three wholly improvised pieces by the trio, and seven compositions by Savolainen, including the two final pieces: the spacey, passionate ballad, "Do I Care?" and the tender afterthoughts of "Another Story", both of which are beautifully conceived and performed. The trio's deconstruction of "Tea For Two" is an exhilarating experience.

Savoy Sultans

The house band at the Savoy Ballroom, New York, for much of the swing-happy 1930s and 1940s, the Savoy Sultans were an efficient eight-piece unit who played simple and effective riff tunes for dancing. "From the time they hit to the time they quit they were swinging!" said Panama Francis who, while he was with Lucky Millinder (1940–46), formed an attachment to the group which was to have a lasting effect. "They had no big stars [but] put them all together, and look out!" The Sultans – who presented strong opposition for any star band visiting the Savoy – included trumpeter Pat Jenkins, bassist Grachan Moncur II and Razz Mitchell, one of the first drummers to introduce a riveted swizzle-cymbal to the jazz band; their two best soloists were Sam Massenberg (trumpet) and Rudy Williams (alto), who was the youngest and (according to Francis) the "most outstanding guy in the band". The group broke up in the 1940s but were re-formed by Francis in the 1970s: they scored an enormous success at the Nice jazz festival in 1979 and 1980, and made a number of uniformly excellent albums. [DF]

⊙ **Al Cooper's Savoy Sultans 1938-41** (Classics). Though these two dozen tracks fail to achieve the live heat of the Sultans at the Savoy, they nevertheless reveal a neat and swinging ensemble. Francis' later recreations are noticeably more dynamic.

➤➤ **Panama Francis** *(Gettin' In The Groove).*

Sax Appeal

➤➤ *see entry on* **Derek Nash**.

Giancarlo Schiaffini

Trombone, euphonium, tuba, electronics.

b. Rome, 1942.

Schiaffini studied physics at the University of Rome, graduating in 1965. An autodidact on trombone, he was at this time also involved in the very first performances of vanguard jazz in Italy, playing with the important ensemble Gruppo Romano Free Jazz; this group has released a very interesting retrospective disc of material from 1967–70 on the Italian Splasc(h) label. In the early 70s, Schiaffini studied at Darmstadt with Karlheinz Stockhausen, György Ligeti and Vinko Globokar, confirming his place in the world of contemporary classical virtuosi. He has continued playing new music, collaborating with Luigi Nono, Giacinto Scelsi and John Cage, and appearing at most of the major festivals; through 1983 he was a member of the Gruppo di Improvvisazione di Nuova Consonanza. His jazz and improvised music endeavours have been varied, as well. He co-founded the Instabile Orchestra and has specialised in trombone-led performances with electronic manipulations, such as the solo *Edula* (1993; Pentaphon) and using electronics, again with his quintet on *Dubs* (1997; ART PURecords), featuring an unorthodox line-up of trombone, voice, violin, bass and Middle-Eastern percussion. He has also used electronics effectively in a trio setting with reed player Gianluigi Trovesi and percussionist Fulvio Maras on *Let* (Splasc(h); 1995), and in frequent duos with fellow trombonist Sebi Tramontana. On the purely improvised acoustic trombone front, Schiaffini has played sporadically with SIC Trio, alongside reedist Eugenio Colombo and percussionist Michele Iannaccone since 1978; they waxed *Passemmezzo* (Splasc(h)) in 1997. For slightly more jazz-oriented outings, check his Monk and Parker tributes *About Monk* (1992; Pentaflowers) and *As A Bird* (1994; Pentaflowers).

Lesser known than many of the Northern figures, less self-consciously "Italian" than some of his countrymen, Schiaffini is nonetheless a very important part of the pan-European free scene. He represents a rare crossover classical improviser, and his soft, melodic, thoughtful music is in its own way very deeply Italian. His fine playing and composing – such as *Litania Sibilante* (2001; Enja) for the Instabile Orchestra – is well worth seeking out. [JC]

Lalo Schifrin

Piano, composer.

b. Buenos Aires, 21 June 1932.

Schifrin had piano lessons from the age of seven, and harmony lessons from sixteen, but studied sociology and law at the University of Buenos Aires. In the early 1950s he studied music in Paris with a disciple of Ravel, and in 1956, back in Argentina, he met Dizzy Gillespie who heard Schifrin's work and admired it. In 1957 Schifrin began writing for films and moved to New York in 1958, leading a trio and writing arrangements for various bands, including Xavier Cugat's. He spent three years, 1960–63, with Gillespie, touring the USA and Europe and coming to international notice. For Dizzy he wrote the suite *Gillespiana* which was premiered at Carnegie Hall in November 1961, and *New Continent* which was performed at the 1962 Monterey jazz festival. He also wrote and did most of the arranging on one of the most delightful Gillespie albums, *Dizzy On The French Riviera*.

After leaving Gillespie, he worked and recorded with Quincy Jones, and then began to concentrate on composing and arranging, writing innumerable film and TV scores. His *Jazz Suite On The Mass Text* was recorded by Paul Horn (RCA), and in 1969 he wrote *Dialogues For Jazz Quintet And Orchestra* for Cannonball Adderley. He taught composition at the University of California from 1968–71, and scored many feature films including *The Cincinnati Kid* (1965), *The Good, The Bad, And The Ugly* (1966), *Bullitt* (1968) and *Dirty Harry* (1971).

Latterly his main interest has been in the classical field, composing and arranging for the likes of the Three Tenors and Daniel Barenboim. Through the 90s and beyond he has also pursued a classical/jazz hybrid on five volumes of *Jazz Meets The Symphony*, most recently featuring Christian McBride, James Morrison and David Sanchez. Schifrin's piano influences include Thelonious Monk, Bill Evans, Oscar Peterson and Bud Powell. Among his composing influences are Gillespie and Stravinsky. [IC]

➤➤ **Dizzy Gillespie** *(Gillespiana/Carnegie Hall Concert).*

Alexander Von Schlippenbach

Piano, composer.

b. Berlin, 7 April 1938.

Schlippenbach studied piano and composition at school, and jazz piano with Francis Coppieters. At thirteen he was playing boogie-woogie and blues, and then became interested in Oscar Peterson, Thelonious Monk and Bud Powell. He became totally involved with free improvisation in the 1960s, working with the Gunter Hampel quintet in 1963, and from 1964–7 with the Manfred Schoof quintet, during which time he started his Globe Unity Orchestra which featured many luminaries of the European free scene. Since 1970 he has led his own quartet and trio featuring Evan Parker, and during the 1970s and 1980s also played in duo with Swedish drummer Sven-Ake Johansson and performed solo piano concerts. With the GUO and in his other capacities he has toured and played major festivals in Europe and the Far East; in 1978 he played solo piano at the first Jazz Yatra in Bombay, and in 1980 the GUO also performed there. Since the late 1980s he has occasionally performed with his partner, pianist Aki Takase. A version of the GUO (with Schoof, Parker, Peter Brötzmann et al) was performing and recording as recently as 2002. Schlippenbach's influences range from Schoenberg to Charlie Parker, Monk and Cecil Taylor, among others. [IC]

Schlippenbach and Sunny Murray

⊙ **Smoke** (1989; FMP). After the furore of 1960s free jazz, we now have *Smoke* drifting over the scene. Schlippenbach and Murray have mellowed and there is a beguiling thoughtfulness and lyricism in this music – they even give a lovely rendition of Monk's "Trinkle Tinkle".

Schlippenbach, Evan Parker and Paul Lovens

⊙ **Elf Bagatellen** (1990; FMP); **Physics** (1991; FMP); Complete Combustion (1999; FMP). These post-avant-garde performances by this long-standing trio also have a poise that comes from slowly achieved wisdom.

➤➤ **Globe Unity Orchestra** *(Rumbling).*

Barak Schmool

Saxes, flutes, percussion, keyboards.

b.London, 7 Feb 1969.

Born into a Jewish family of Mediterranean and East European origin, Schmool had piano and recorder lessons from an early age, before progressing to the flute and saxophone. At school he formed his own sax quartet and big band, but he got in to the Royal Academy of Music on the strength of his classical saxophone, studying composition and sax there from 1988-91, with further studies at London's City University from 1993–4. His enthusiasm for African and Brazilian percussion began when an illness prevented him from playing the sax for six months. Additional education came from, in his own words, "being Django Bates's roadie and hanging out with Loose Tubes." From 1991 Schmool played percussion in various Brazilian bands and with a number of community African drumming and Dance groups. He also became a member of Django Bates's Delightful Precipice, Robert Mitchell's Panacea, and Grupo Sambando with Bosco De Oliveira.

In 1996 Schmool started forming his own groups: Roots Of Unity, a twelve-piece band combining singing, jazz, percussion and dance; Timeline, a group that buries "African music structures in jazz music sounds"; and Méta Méta, a Cuban batafusion band. Schmool is also very active in education, with an especial commitment to communal projects, and as well as teaching at the City University and at RAM, he has founded three community percussion ensembles: Akwaaba Drum Orchestra, Sounds of Senegal, and Rhythms Of the City. These initiatives led to the setting up of F-IRE, a musicians' collective that promotes education in the rhythmic arts, and supports artists and community ventures. Schmool's activities as a sideman include appearances on two Django Bates albums, *Winter Truce (And Homes Blaze)* (1995) and *Summer Fruits (And Unrest)* (1993), and on Robert Mitchell's Panacea album, *Voyager* (2001). [IC]

Timeline

⊙ **Know Hope** (2002; F-IRE CD 01). Timeline's first album is a highly original effort – Ghanaian dance music and bravura jazz-rock are effortlessly refashioned into a startling gestalt. Schmool oversees some rigorously taut unison playing, and whenever the mood gets too comfortable it's routinely punctured by David Okumu's playfully snide guitar.

Maria Schneider

Arranger, piano.

b. Windom, Minnesota, 27 Nov 1960.

Schneider studied piano and music theory from the age of five till eighteen with the same classical and stride pianist, Evelyn Butler. She went on to become a music student at the University of Minnesota, the University of Miami and the Eastman School. Moving to New York in 1985, she studied with Bob Brookmeyer and, from 1985–8, became assistant to Gil Evans, writing film music and vocal backings with him. She also wrote for Woody Herman and Mel Lewis, and has conducted her music with various European radio orchestras. She was commissioned to write for the Carnegie Hall Jazz

Maria Schneider

Orchestra in 1994 and the Monterey festival in 1995, and her own band, formed in 1989, played weekly in Greenwich Village from 1993-9. As well as help from Brookmeyer and Evans, Maria draws inspiration from Ellington, George Russell and Thad Jones and, while these influences may be audible, her music has developed a truly personal sound. [BP]

⊙ **Evanescence** (1993; Enja). A programme of original music, from the delicate to the driving, is performed by an entirely conventional seventeen-piece line-up, but the sound is anything but. Key soloists are saxophonist Rick Margitza (who had a moment of fame with Miles Davis) and trumpeter Tim Hagans. Standout tracks are "My Lament" and the title number dedicated to Gil Evans.

⊙ **Allégresse** (2000; Enja). Airy, gliding themes are intelligently interspersed with perky shuffles, carefully controlled rumbustiousness and the occasionally bluesy climax, making a varied, richly allusive and utterly satisfying whole.

Moe Schneider

Trombone.

b. Bessie, Oklahoma, 24 Dec 1919.

One of the best Dixieland trombonists ever, Moe (Elmer Reuben) Schneider worked most remarkably with a series of "Dixieland academies", including Ben Pollack's band (before the war and after), and with Bob Crosby from 1949. Schneider merged the tone of Jack Teagarden with much of the athletic rangy approach of Abe Lincoln, and some of his best work turns up on the recorded music from *Pete Kelly's Blues* (radio, TV and a full-length feature film), in which he played with Cathcart and Matlock: the records are copybook "white" Dixieland without ever sounding too precise. Later in his career Schneider combined studio work (he also appeared in *The Five Pennies* and *The Gene Krupa Story* in 1959) with part-time accountancy. Though he remains mainly a collector's delight, his work is of the highest standard. [DF]

⊙ **Classic Columbia Condon Mob Sessions** (1940-59; Mosaic). This eight CD set is currently the only source for these classy sides that feature Schneider with Matty Matlock and his Jazz Band from their "Pete Kelly" period. Cuts include "Smiles"/"Sugar" and "I'm Gonna Meet My Sweetie Now!"

➤➤ **Dick Cathcart** *(The Authentic Music From "Pete Kelly's Blues")*.

Loren Schoenberg

Tenor saxophone.

b. Fair Lawn, New Jersey, 23 July 1958.

Schoenberg studied at the Manhattan School of Music (from 1976) while working with Eddie Durham and subsequently Russell Procope, Al Casey, Jo Jones, Harold Ashby and others. He formed his own big band in 1980 in New York while working as archivist and manager for Benny Goodman. Following Goodman's death in 1986, he was appointed curator of the Goodman Archives at Yale University, producing multi-CD reissues of unissued Goodman recordings. Schoenberg's big band appeared with Goodman in the PBS special *Let's Dance* (1985), established an ongoing relationship with the New York Swing Dance Society, and worked at major New York venues (Village Vanguard, Blue Note, Michael's Pub). Between 1986–92 Schoenberg played with the American Jazz Orchestra, directing it for its last two seasons. He is also a seasoned broadcaster who from 1984 co-hosted on WBGO's *Jazz From The Archives*. A regular concert-producer, director and guest conductor (including the Lincoln Center Jazz Orchestra and Smithsonian Jazz Masterworks Orchestra), Schoenberg is also a prolific writer, and in 1995 was awarded a Grammy for best album notes (along with Dan Morgenstern). One of American jazz's most active and gifted jazz polymaths, his contributions to the art are considerable, in particular his saxophone is a lyrical jazz voice located firmly in the classic jazz tradition. [DF]

⊙ **Out Of This World: Loren Schoenberg And His Jazz Orchestra** (1997; TCB). Outstanding collection by a superb orchestra featuring John Eckert, Scott Robinson, Bobby Pring and James Chirillo. The great Barbara Lea guests on several tracks.

Manfred Schoof

Trumpet, flugelhorn, piano, composer.

b. Magdeburg, Germany, 6 April 1936.

Schoof studied at the Musikakademie, Kassel, from 1955–8, and at the Cologne Musikhochschule from 1958–63. He played in student groups with Alexander von Schlippenbach, Gerd Dudek and others; from 1963–5 he worked with Gunter Hampel, and he started leading his own group in 1965. Free jazz was burgeoning in Europe then and Schoof's quintet was one of the most important German groups in the abstract field, becoming, with the Peter Brötzmann trio, the nucleus for Schlippenbach's Globe Unity Orchestra which was formed in 1966. In 1968 he joined the Clarke-Boland international big band, staying until 1972, and from 1969–73 he led the New Jazz Trio with Peter Trunk (bass) and Cees See (drums). His composition "Ode", for the Globe Unity Orchestra, was performed at the Donaueschingen festival in 1970, and "Kontraste und Synthesen", for Globe Unity and choir, was performed in 1974 on North German Radio. In 1975 Schoof's sextet and critic J.E. Berendt toured Asia under the auspices of the Goethe Institute, in a programme combining concerts and lectures. In 1977 his LP *Scales* received the German Record Critics' Prize, and in 1980 he formed the Manfred Schoof Orchestra, a big band. He has also worked with Albert Mangelsdorff, George Russell, Quincey Jones and Mal Waldron, and has performed at festivals all over Europe.

Schoof is a very active composer and arranger, and has written for the Kurt Edelhagen big band at West German Radio. He has collaborated with various contemporary composers, working on a 1966 opera, *Die Soldaten*, and a 1969 trumpet concerto performed by the Berlin Philharmonic. He has also composed for small groups, and for film and TV. His influences are Miles Davis, Booker Little and Kenny Dorham, and also Schoenberg, Anton Bruckner and Gil Evans. Schoof's playing and composing cover the whole spectrum of contemporary music: all forms of jazz from abstract to tightly structured, and areas of European "art" music. He has also given performances of unaccompanied trumpet improvisation. [IC]

⊙ **Shadows And Smiles** (1987–8; Wergo). Schoof in duo with pianist/keyboardist Rainer Brüninghaus in an airily impressionistic session.

➤➤ **Globe Unity Orchestra** *(Rumbling)*; **George Russell** *(Electronic Sonata For Souls Loved By Nature).*

Gene Schroeder

Piano.

b. Madison, Wisconsin, 5 Feb 1915; d. 16 Feb 1975.

Gene Schroeder is well remembered for his lengthy partnership with Eddie Condon, which began at Nick's Club around 1944. Condon liked the sound of Schroeder straight away: he played the right changes for Condon's style of music, knew how to integrate himself into a four-man rhythm-section featuring the straight four-to-the-bar of Condon's rhythm guitar, showed a gratifying lack of interest in the bebop trends that Condon hated and, unlike former colleagues Jess Stacy and Joe Sullivan, was neither committed to a big band nor intent on leading his own show. Schroeder played at the opening of Condon's own club in 1945, and for the next seventeen years played pianistic Harry Carney to Condon's Ellington. "There are few pianists in the business who can equal him," said Condon, "either as soloist or member of the rhythm-section", and this was, no doubt, because Schroeder enjoyed Condon's musicians and their "timeless" jazz concepts. "We had a sort of a huge roving clique of guys that played at a certain level," he explained later, "slightly modern but they knew all the old tunes. Most important, these were guys who knew how to swing." After Schroeder left Condon, he worked freelance and with a like-minded group, the Dukes of Dixieland, for whom he recorded fine albums such as *Now Hear This* and *Breaking It Up On Broadway*, but by the late 1960s ill health had immobilized him. Since his death a school of followers, including pianist Mark Shane, has carried on Schroeder's traditions. [DF]

➤➤ **Eddie Condon** *(Dixieland Jam).*

Matthias Schubert

Tenor saxophone, composer.

b. Kassel, Germany, 18 April 1960.

Having received lessons from saxophonists Andy Scherrer (in Switzerland) and Herb Geller (in Hamburg), and from pianist Walter Morris, Matthias Schubert received prizes at the 1980 Amsterdam jazz festival and subsequently at the 1982 International Jazz Federation competition, thereby establishing himself on the European scene. Work with the Euro Jazz Big Band, Basslab (*Aisha*, 1991; Edition Frankfurt), Jazzartrio (*From Time To Time*, 1987; Splasc(h)) and the Galaxy Dream Band followed, in addition to sideman duties in bands led by Graham Collier, Marty Cook, Albert Mangelsdorff and Klaus König. The latter leader's formal, subtle, yet adventurous music – drawing on influences as diverse as Braxton and Bartók, Mahler and Mingus, and involving a multinational cast of jazz's most original and skilful players (Mark Dresser, Michel Godard, Ray Anderson, Louis Sclavis and Gerry Hemingway among them) – suits Schubert's vigorous, intensely personal playing perfectly. He has also contributed to projects by Frank Gratkowski and Renato Cordovanni (saxophone duos), Simon Nabatov and Holger Mantei (saxophone/piano duos), and led his own quartet (with Nabatov, bassist Lindsey Horner and drummer Tom Rainey) and sextet (with violinist Mark Feldman, clarinettist Claudio Puntin, tuba player Carl Ludwig Hübsch, bassist Drew Gress and Rainey). Schubert's own powerful music is best represented by *Blue And Grey Suite* (see below) and *Momentum* (2000; Jazzline) featuring his own quartet (with Nabatov, bassist Lindsey Horner and Rainey). [CP]

Blue And Grey Suite (1994; Enja). Quartet (see above for personnel) recording of scorching intensity touching bases ranging from Messiaen to Herbie Nichols, but filtering them through the sensibilities of four of the most original musicians currently active. Schubert's rapport with Nabatov is particularly rewarding, but his selfless interplay with the rhythm-section is also deeply impressive.

Gunther Schuller

French horn, composer, conductor, writer.
b. Jackson Heights, New York, 11 Nov 1925.

Schuller studied with the first French horn player of New York's Metropolitan Opera and with Robert Schulze of the Manhattan School of Music. After spending two years with the Eugene Goossens Cincinnati Symphony, he was with the Metropolitan Opera for ten years. Although brought up and educated in classical music, Schuller had from the beginning a greater understanding and appreciation of jazz than possibly anyone else in the classical world. He became friendly with many musicians whom he admired including John Lewis, with whom he has worked closely on numerous occasions, and George Russell who has also been a longtime associate. In 1950 Schuller played French horn on four tracks of Miles Davis's *Birth Of The Cool* recordings and also gave Davis help and advice when he was having embouchure problems.

In the mid-1950s Schuller, in collaboration with Lewis, invented the term "third stream music", which described their attempts to fuse jazz and classical music. Schuller conducted the orchestra they assembled – the Brass Ensemble of the Jazz and Classical Music Society, which in 1956 recorded John Lewis's "Three Little Feelings" and J.J. Johnson's "Poem For Brass", both with solos by Miles Davis.

At Brandeis University in 1957 he started an annual jazz festival, and commissioned compositions from three jazz and three classical composers, to be played by an orchestra which was made up of both jazz and classical musicians. The jazz commissions went to George Russell, Jimmy Giuffre and Charles Mingus – none of whom had ever had a proper commission before. The classical composers were Harold Shapiro, Milton Babbitt and Schuller himself. In 1959 one of Schuller's works, *Conversations*, was performed at New York Town Hall by the Modern Jazz Quartet with the Beaux Arts String Quartet. He and John Lewis also started the Lenox School of Jazz Summer School, which was where, in 1959, Ornette Coleman's career was launched.

In 1961 Schuller was acting musical director at the Monterey jazz festival, and in 1962 he was musical director of the first international jazz festival to be held in Washington, DC. In 1963–4 he continued his long association with John Lewis, conducting their third stream ensemble, Orchestra USA. In 1963 he presented the first fully fledged jazz concert ever held at Tanglewood, Massachusetts, and went on a US State Department-sponsored tour lecturing in Poland, Yugoslavia and Germany on new developments in jazz. In 1967 he became President of the New England Conservatory at Boston, and virtually the first thing he did was to create a jazz department. This was the first to offer a full four-year degree in jazz, and set a model for many music schools including Berklee, which got its own degree course a few years later. Schuller formed the New England Conservatory Jazz Repertory Orchestra, for which he transcribed Ellington works and planned to incorporate arrangements from other famous bands. In 1969 he brought in George Russell as resident composer at the Conservatory. In 1989 Schuller conducted the huge orchestra performing the premiere of Mingus's vast *Epitaph*, the score of which he had reconstructed and edited; he also directed the 1991 international tour of the same work.

Schuller has composed many jazz works including his 1961 jazz ballet *Variants*, *Concertino for Jazz Quartet and Orchestra* (recorded with the MJQ), *Abstraction and Variants on a Theme of Thelonious Monk* (featuring John Lewis), and has written many essays on jazz, and two brilliant books: *Early Jazz* and *The Swing Era, The Development of Jazz 1930–1945.* [IC]

➤➤ **Joe Lovano** *(Rush Hour).*

Arthur Schutt

Piano, arranger.
b. Reading, Pennsylvania, 21 Nov 1902; d. 28 Jan 1965.

One of the finest white pianists of the 1920s – he recorded with all the white stars from Bix Beiderbecke to Benny Goodman – Schutt was a trained musician and skilled reader who specialized in studio work and freelance arranging, and became rich in the process. Always superbly dressed, with a carnation in his buttonhole, Schutt was the very image of a successful society pianist; significantly he was heard less often with the speedy passage of jazz fashion through the 1930s. But he continued to make a comfortable living in the studios, working for MGM, Columbia and others until the early 1960s, when ill health took its toll. [DF]

Irene Schweizer

Piano.
b. Schaffhausen, Switzerland, 2 June 1941.

At the age of eight Schweizer began to play folk songs on the accordion, and at twelve switched to piano. She played hard bop in a student band, and heard Joe Harriott (who was already pioneering his own brand of free jazz) and Tubby Hayes when she visited London in the early 1960s, taking jazz lessons with Eddie Thompson. Back in Switzerland, she moved to Zurich and started her first trio; Bill Evans and Junior Mance had been her early inspirations, but after hearing Cecil Taylor she soon became involved with free improvisation, which was to become her staple interest. In the late 1960s she recorded with Pierre Favre's groups, and then began releasing her own albums on the FMP label, several featuring her in duo with saxophonist Rudiger Carl and others with Louis Moholo, Baby Sommer and Manfred Schoof. She joined the newly formed Feminist Improvising Group in 1978, and in 1983 started the European Women's Improvising Group and later – along similar gender lines – Les Diaboliques with Maggie Nichols and Joelle Leandre. In 1986, she helped to organize the Canaille Festival of Women's Improvised Music in Zurich, and in the mid-1980s was the main inspiration behind Switzerland's annual Taktlos festival of improvised music and its associated label, Intakt, on which many of her later albums have been released. She toured the UK in 1991 and Europe in the mid 90s with the London Jazz Composers Orchestra, and the leader, Barry Guy, composed a piece featuring her, *Theoria*, for her fiftieth birthday. [IC]

⊙ **Irene Schweizer & Pierre Favre** (1990; Intakt); **Piano Solo: Vol. 1** (1990; Intakt); **Piano Solo: Vol. 2** (1990; Intakt); **Chicago Piano Solo** (2001; Intakt). The duos with Pierre Favre are interesting, but the piano solos are very fine indeed – self-communions which ebb and flow with lyricism and wit.

Louis Sclavis

Clarinet, bass-clarinet, soprano and tenor saxophones.
b. Lyon, France, 1953.

Sclavis studied clarinet at the Lyon Conservatoire, and began his professional career at the end of the 1960s. Even at that early stage he was looking for very diverse creative experiences, and began playing music for theatrical productions, while also being a member of the Workshop de Lyon (1975–88), which was dedicated to improvised music. Sclavis toured extensively with the Workshop and under its auspices worked with singer Colette Magny. During this time, he also played with Chris McGregor's Brotherhood Of Breath, the Henry Texier quartet and many other leading musicians. From 1982 onwards he led his own groups.

In 1985 his album *Clarinettes* (IDA), on which he played solo and with percussion, served notice that he was a musician to be reckoned with. His 1987 album, *Chine* (IDA), was recorded by a quintet of Sclavis plus keyboards, violin, bass and drums. In 1988, he founded the Trio de Clarinettes with fellow virtuosi Jacques di Donato and Armand Angster, a group which included in its repertoire free improvisation, pieces written by its members, and also works from contemporary composers such as Pierre Boulez and Brian Ferneyhough. Sclavis has long been incorporating elements from French and other folk musics into his work, but his studies of the modern classical tradition have been as important to his development as his immersion in jazz.

His 1989 album, *Chamber Music* (IDA), features a septet of virtuosi, with trombonist Yves Robert, tuba player Michel Godard, violinist Dominique Pifarely, guitarist Philippe de Schepper, pianist François Raulin and bassist Bruno Chevillon. In 1991, when Sclavis began recording for ECM, it was becoming clear that he was at his best when working with an ongoing group of musical collaborators, as his idol Duke Ellington had done. Sclavis's first album on ECM, *Rouge*, was recorded by the same quintet who had made *Chine* four years earlier – Pifarely, Raulin, Chevillon and Ville. His second ECM album was a Duke Ellington tribute, *Ellington On The Air*, and the personnel was the same as that of *Chamber Music*, except that Schepper was omitted and drummer Francis Lassus added. In 1993, with Pifarely, Chevillon and idiosyncratic guitarist Marc Ducret, Sclavis formed and recorded his Acoustic Quartet.

There seem to be no stylistic limits to Sclavis's music, but he surprised people when he turned to the eighteenth century for his "Rameau project", which he introduced at the Théâtre de la Résistance in Oulins in early 1994. To some of his contemporaries, Rameau's music seemed harsh and subversive, and Sclavis was taken with the "wildness and rawness in the sound". The results were recorded in 1996 by his sextet with the same personnel as *Rouge*, but with Yves Robert (trombone) added and Francis Lassus replacing Ville on drums. In 2000, a new group was heard on *L'Affrontement Des Prétendants* (see below) and the soundtrack to an unearthed silent film, *Dans La Nuit* (2002; ECM). [IC]

⊙ **Les Violences de Rameau** (1996; ECM). Compositionally and instrumentally, this is highly concentrated music which goes some way towards reconciling all the disparate strands of Sclavis's conception. The music is often intensely rhythmic, with stately court music jostling against funky rhythms, and Sclavis is spectacular throughout on soprano, alto and clarinet.

⊙ **Danses et Autres Scènes** (1997; Label Bleu). For this collection of Sclavis's theatre music his sextet is the nucleus of a pool of twelve musicians, from which he draws different instrumental combinations. Sclavis's invention in composition and performance is remarkable. His folk roots are much in evidence, the dance is rarely far away and often centre-stage, and the music is frequently benign and charming.

⊙ **L'Affrontement Des Prétendants** (2000; ECM). Featuring trumpeter Jean Luc Capozzo and cellist Vincent Courtois in a heart-rending tribute to the murdered Algerian political singer Lounes Matoub among other typically unpredictable and rich Sclavisian treasures.

Bob Scobey

Trumpet.
b. Tucumcari, New Mexico, 9 Dec 1916; d. Montreal, 12 June 1963.

Bob Scobey worked his way up through dance orchestras, pit bands and nightclubs in the 1930s, and then in 1938 met Lu Watters. From 1940 for nine years (with a four-year spell in the army) he was second trumpeter to Watters in the great Yerba Buena Jazz Band, but by 1949 was tired of the volume and two-beat concept that Watters loved, and left to form his own band. For the next fourteen years Scobey's career spiralled up. He was a natural leader, bubbling with ideas ("There was always something cooking," remembered Art Hodes, "new arrangements, rehearsals every week, fresh uniforms"), and by the early 1950s his Frisco Jazz Band was recording regularly for Good Time Jazz, as well as headlining at the Dixieland festivals organized by Gene Norman and Frank Bull; they also played a three-year residency at Victor and Roxie's in Oakland. Scobey's ace in the hole all through the 1950s was banjoist Clancy Hayes, whose lazy Southern charm was central to the band's presentation: Hayes was co-billed with Scobey throughout their partnership. By the mid-1950s, augmented on record by stars such as Bing Crosby and superguests including Abe Lincoln, Manny Klein, Matty Matlock, Dick Cathcart and Frank Beach, the band had reached a peak of Dixieland.

In 1959, after a short experiment with a solo act, Scobey opened his Club Bourbon Street in Chicago, playing long sets (10pm to 4am) and making regular trips to Las Vegas, New York and San Francisco in spare weeks. Scobey's band of the period featured ex-Ellington drummer Dave Black, whom he had hired after Black had been incapacitated with polio: it was the generous move of a big man. Scobey finally succumbed to cancer. His wife Jan has kept his memory alive with a biography, an album on which she re-formed the band to sing some blues for her husband, and a regular reissue programme for Scobey albums. [DF]

⊙ **Frisco Band Featuring Vocals By Clancy Hayes** (1950–55; Giants of Jazz). Excellently selected budget CD of Scobey titles, plus Clancy Hayes favourites including "Huggin' And Chalkin'" and "Silver Dollar".

⊙ **Direct From San Francisco** (1956; Good Time Jazz). One of the classic Scobey collections, this has his band on best form plus right-hand man Clancy Hayes in attendance.

John Scofield

Guitar, composer.
b. Ohio, 26 Dec 1951.

Scofield was brought up in Wilton, Connecticut, where he began on guitar at high school, playing in soul bands and R&B groups. At fifteen he studied with a local jazz player and spent the years 1970–73 at Berklee College, also playing around Boston, and recording two live albums with Gerry Mulligan and Chet Baker at Carnegie Hall. In 1974 he replaced John Abercrombie in Billy Cobham's band, staying for two years and recording four albums with it. In 1976 he freelanced around New York, and in 1977 he recorded with Charles Mingus, later joining Gary Burton's quartet. The same year he formed his own quartet with Richie Beirach, George Mraz and Joe La Barbera, touring Europe and playing at the Berlin festival.

From the later 1970s to the early 1980s he was a regular member of the Dave Liebman quintet, touring worldwide with it and playing most major festivals. In 1982 he joined Miles Davis, touring the USA, Europe and Japan in 1983, 1984 and 1985, and playing on three of Davis's albums. By 1984 Scofield was not only playing themes and solos with the band, but also collaborating with Davis in the composition of several of the pieces. Before he joined Davis, Scofield had also played or recorded with Zbigniew Seifert, Tony Williams, Ron Carter, Terumasa Hino and Lee Konitz. His main influences are Jim Hall, George Benson, Pat Martino, and to a lesser extent B.B. King and Otis Rush, but he has totally absorbed all these and arrived at a sound and approach that are all his own. He was always a player of consummate grace and inventiveness, conjuring melodic lines out of thin air, but during his stint with Miles Davis his authority grew perceptibly, his rhythms becoming stronger, the lines more audacious and the emotional power of his work absolutely compelling.

RAFFAELLA CAVALIERI

John Scofield

In the later 1990s, Scofield carried on touring nationally and internationally, but also took part in an unusual contemporary classical project with Mark-Anthony Turnage – a young English classical composer steeped in the blues, black music and the music of Miles Davis. Performed by the German Ensemble Modern, with Scofield on guitar, Peter Erskine on drums and Martin Robertson on saxophone, Turnage's composition, *Blood On the Floor,* was premiered at London's Queen Elizabeth Hall in May 1996 to great acclaim. In 1998, it was performed again in London, this time at the much larger Royal Festival Hall. Again the piece was given an ecstatic reception, as were Scofield and Erskine. A couple of weeks later Scofield was back at the Queen Elizabeth

Hall with his quartet – Bill Stewart on drums, bassist James Genus and Larry Golding on organ, playing the music from his great album *A Go Go*. [IC]

⊙ **Rough House** (1978; Enja). As demonstrated by this set with Hal Galper, bassist Stafford James and the redoubtable Adam Nussbaum, Scofield already had considerable authority before he joined Miles Davis. The rhythm-section boots along and Scofield's unfailing swing and invention enthral.

⊙ **Who's Who?** (1979–80; Novus). *Who's Who?* presents Scofield in different contexts – a quintet with Kenny Kirkland, quartet with Dave Liebman and a trio with Nussbaum and Steve Swallow. A good overview of Scofield's marvellously comprehensive talents.

⊙ **Shinola** (1981; Enja); **Out Like A Light** (1981; Enja). The Scofield-Swallow-Nussbaum trio shines on in these two superb live albums, and the leader plays with telling economy.

⊙ **Still Warm** (1985; Gramavision). Scofield enters his post-Miles Davis phase with Don Grolnick, bassist Darryl Jones from Miles's band and drummer Omar Hakim, who had been a recent member of Weather Report. By now, Scofield's writing was becoming as pointed and fertile as his playing.

⊙ **Flat Out** (1988; Gramavision). There's a pleasing lightness of touch and some humour in the compositions on this delightful album, which has Grolnick again, plus shared drum chores by Terri Lyne Carrington and Johnny Vidacovich. Anthony Cox is the bassist.

⊙ **Time On My Hands** (1989; Blue Note). A superb quartet with Charlie Haden, Jack DeJohnette and tenor saxophonist Joe Lovano is featured on this album. Scofield's composing goes from strength to strength, displaying a gift for catchy rhythms and melodies.

⊙ **Grace Under Pressure** (1991; Blue Note). If anything, Scofield's compositions are even stronger on this set. The basic group has Bill Frisell, Charlie Haden and Joey Baron, but Randy Brecker (flugelhorn), Jim Pugh (trombone) and John Clark (French horn) play backing on a few tracks. Scofield's playing is as fresh and strong as his writing, and his association with the idiosyncratic Frisell is fruitful.

⊙ **A Go Go** (1997; Verve). Scofield seems to go from strength to strength and this light-hearted, funky album is full of compelling music. He recruited the Martin (drums), Medeski (organ) and Wood (bass) trio for the project, and wrote ten pieces all with different rhythmic feels and ways of breathing. The grooves are often ecstatic, and the unhurried emergence of the music is wonderful. Scofield's playing is beautifully paced. He's a master, and the trio bask in his sunshine, sustaining the grooves, with Medeski also contributing some fine solos.

Cecil Scott

Clarinet, saxophones.

b. Springfield, Ohio, 22 Nov 1905; d. 5 Jan 1964.

One of the most driving and creative first-generation saxophonists, Scott led a fine band which by the late 1920s was causing a stir at New York's Savoy Ballroom, where they often made short work of better-known opposition. "They [Cecil and his brother Lloyd Scott] had brought their band to New York from Springfield, Ohio, in 1926", remembered Cab Calloway, whose first band, the Alabamians, could not equal Scott's. "Cecil had developed his own style and was running the band himself. He was a bitch: those guys played gut-bucket, stomping, gutsy New York jazz. Cecil was one of the most exciting and fiery horn blowers in Harlem – and in addition to blowing up a storm they put on a hell of a show." Scott later joined Calloway's new band, the Missourians, then worked with Fletcher Henderson, Vernon Andrade and Teddy Hill (1936–7), and by 1942 had his own band again at the Ubangi Club. The swift passage of jazz fashion in the 1940s made it hard for Scott to maintain his initial impact (he had also suffered a severe leg injury around 1930 which subsequently necessitated amputation) but his big sound and "fiery dynamic style" (Panassié) guaranteed him a steady flow of work all through the 1940s with leaders such as Art Hodes as well as with his own trio. In the 1950s he carried on his club activities around New York, working at Central Plaza, Ryan's and Stuyvesant Casino, and he played at the Great South Bay jazz festival in 1957 and 1958; he continued to work regularly until his death. [DF]

➤➤ **Willie "The Lion" Smith And His Cubs** *(Willie The Lion Smith And His Cubs).*

Little Jimmy Scott

Vocals.

b. Cleveland, Ohio, 17 July 1925.

One of ten children, Scott suffered from Kallman's Syndrome, a hormone disorder preventing adolescent growth and causing, in Scott's case, the retention of a high-pitched voice. After professional work with vocal groups and in provincial tent-shows, he joined Lionel Hampton's band in 1948, contributing the hit ballad "Everybody's Somebody Fool" in 1950. That year he began his single career, sitting in with Charlie Parker (*One Night In Birdland*) and touring with the Paul Gayten band. He recorded steadily in the 50s but, in the following decade, two new albums were blocked by contractual hassles. Scott retired until the mid-1980s, finally achieving cult success in the 90s. A favourite of such diverse performers as Quincy Jones, Liza Minnelli and Lou Reed, he is heard on the soundtracks of *Albino Alligator*, *A Rage In Harlem*, *Glengarry Glen Ross* and *Twin Peaks*, and his falsetto-range, gospel-tinged interpretation of standards is seen as an influence on Nancy Wilson, Stevie Wonder, Marvin Gaye, Michael Jackson and Take 6. [BP]

⊙ **Falling In Love Is Wonderful** (1962; Rhino). Originally withdrawn from sale due to a contractual claim on Scott's services, this was done for the Tangerine label owned by Ray Charles (who plays background keyboard) and finally reissued forty years later. Far superior to Scott's early work with Hampton or various studio bands (also recently reissued), it finds his mature style fully on display.

⊙ **All The Way** (1992; WEA). Scott's comeback album features his heart-stopping versions of nine standard ballads, including "Angel Eyes", "I'll Be Around" and, of course, the title track, with a quintet featuring David "Fathead" Newman and Kenny Barron.

Raymond Scott

Leader, piano.

b. Brooklyn, New York, 10 Sept 1910.

Raymond Scott (Harold Warnow) became well known on CBS radio (1934–8), leading a quintet which played novelties such as "Toy Trumpet", "Dinner Music For A Pack Of Hungry Cannibals" and "War Dance For Wooden Indians". By 1938, Scott had established a strong reputation as an arranger, and a year later formed his own big band, which toured and played residencies from 1938–42; Shelly Manne was his drummer. That year he was asked by CBS to form the first desegregated staff orchestra in history; they recorded a now-legendary series of broadcasts, *Jazz Laboratory*. On the face of it this was a good idea, and Scott's orchestra corralled black musicians such as Charlie Shavers, Ben Webster and Benny Morton alongside white men such as Johnny Guarnieri, Cliff Leeman and Frank Sinatra. But in 1945, after what Frank Driggs calls "devious politicking", the whole ensemble, including Scott, was unceremoniously sacked. Thereafter Scott held a variety of commercial staff posts, ran his own record label (Audivox), and in the 1950s was musical director for Everest Records. He also conducted his orchestra for New York's *Saturday Night Hit Parade* show. By the 1970s Scott (always a keen recording engineer) was running an electronic research firm in New Jersey, and later moved out to Van Nuys, California. His suite *A Yank In Europe* was recorded by Ted Heath's orchestra in Britain in 1957. [DF]

Ronnie Scott

Tenor and soprano saxophones.

b. London, 28 Jan 1927; d. 23 Dec 1996.

Scott began gigging in small clubs at the age of sixteen, and then toured with trumpeter Johnny Claes in 1944–5 and Ted Heath in 1946. He also worked with the Ambrose band, Cab Kaye, Tito Burns and on transatlantic liners. He played at a co-operative musicians' venue, Club 11, between 1948–50, and joined the Jack Parnell band in 1952. From 1953–6 he led his own nine-piece group, and then co-led the Jazz Couriers with Tubby Hayes from 1957–9. He opened a jazz nightclub in 1959, which rapidly became world-renowned (in recent years, a series of documentary recordings made at the club during 1963–5 has been issued on the Ronnie Scott's Jazz House label, while the number of albums done there by other record companies is past counting). He continued to play regularly, leading a quartet including Stan Tracey from 1960–67, an eight-piece band including John Surman and Kenny Wheeler from 1968–9, and a trio with Mike Carr from 1971–5. He was also a member of the Kenny Clarke-Francy Boland band from 1962–73. From the mid-1970s he led quartets, quintets and sextets, usually including John Critchinson and Martin Drew. Having been for longer than he cared to remember an effective figurehead of British jazz ("The establishment", as he ironically described himself), recurrent depression led him to take his own life.

Scott had already established himself as a forthright and committed jazz player long before the success of the pace-setting Jazz Couriers. Given the fact that most British musicians then tended to imitate the letter rather than the spirit of jazz, there was pointed praise in Charles Mingus's 1961 observation of the local scene: "Of the white boys, Ronnie Scott gets closer to the negro blues feeling, the way Zoot Sims does." The influence of Sims and countless others moulded Ronnie's mainstream-modern style, both its phraseology and time-feeling being easily recognizable and effortlessly authoritative. Doubtless this is why he was awarded an OBE in 1981 by the sister of one of his club's celebrity customers. [BP]

⊙ **The Night Is Scott And You're So Swingable** (1964–5; Redial). Despite the awful title, this is a rewarding and somewhat unusual programme for Scott. The blowing-session material heard on Jazz House reissues is hinted at on two short items, but otherwise the focus is on ballads (four tracks have a string section) with either Stan Tracey or Ernest Ranglin in support.

⊙ **Never Pat A Burning Dog** (1990; Jazz House). Recorded appropriately enough in his own club, this is the last representation of the infrequently documented Scott. His own playing is the best thing about his then regular quintet (a sixth player, saxophonist Mornington Lockett, replaces Dick Pearce on one track), and the choice of material is typically varied.

➤➤ **Kenny Clarke** *(Two Originals)*.

Shirley Scott

Organ.

b. Philadelphia, 14 March 1934; d. 10 March 2002.

Scott studied the piano and trumpet as a child, and later played piano in her brother's group. She changed to organ in 1955, the same time as her fellow Philadelphian Jimmy Smith, and became a member of the Eddie Davis trio, staying from 1956–60. She started making records under her own name in 1958, formed her own trio in 1960 and then toured with Stanley Turrentine, whom she married. After ending that association, she led her own groups, and recorded with Dexter Gordon in 1982. While she was not perhaps as original as Smith, and did not so blatantly batter the senses of the listener, Scott was a dynamic performer whose work is rhythmically compelling. [BP]

⊙ **Legends Of Acid Jazz** (1961; Prestige). Combining her albums *Hip Soul* and *Hip Twist*, both featuring Turrentine on tenor, Shirley adds her intelligent touch to conventional blues and standards such as "Out Of This World" and "The Very Thought Of You".

Stephen Scott

Piano, composer.

b. Queens, New York, 13 March 1969.

Having taken up piano at the age of five and been introduced to jazz in high school, Stephen Scott later took private lessons at the Juilliard School before winning the Young Talent Award from the National Association of Jazz Educators in 1986. A year later, he was part of talent-spotter supreme Betty Carter's trio, learning to "be honest", rather than "playing like my idols Wynton Kelly, Thelonious Monk, Kenny Kirkland and Mulgrew Miller", in his words. Work with Joe Henderson (*Lush Life*, 1992; Verve), Roy Hargrove (*Parker's Mood*, 1995; Verve), Sonny Rollins (*+3*, 1995, *Global Warming*, 1998, and *This Is What I Do*, 2000, all on Milestone) and the likes of Bobby Watson, Craig Handy, Victor Lewis and the Harper Brothers firmly established him as one of the music's brightest young stars), but his own albums (four for Verve: 1991's *Something To Consider*, 1992's *Amina's Dream*, 1994's *Renaissance Suite*, and *The Beautiful Thing* from the following year, plus *Vision Quest* – see below) demonstrate most clearly just why Carter called him "a genius". His own writing is imbued with myriad influences of his Queens childhood: reggae, salsa and soul as well as jazz, but he claims: "Monk is the foundation of most of my musical concept – clusters, and space, and all that stuff. And I like Wynton Kelly's swing feel, his ideas and how he deals with the beat." Not heard as a recorded leader since 1998, Scott's recent sidesman duties include three albums for bassist Ron Carter, *Orfeu* (1999; Blue Note), *When Skies Are Grey* (2001; Blue Note) and *Eight Plus* (2003; Dreyfus), and two for trombonist Steve Turre, *In The Spur Of The Moment* (2000; Telarc) and *One4J* (2003; Telarc). [CP]

⊙ **Vision Quest** (1998; Enja). Fronting a dream band – bassist Ron Carter, drummer Victor Lewis and percussionist Steve Kroon – Scott produces his most mature work to date, a mix of originals and material like "Cheek To Cheek", "Round Midnight" and Wayne Shorter's "Virgo", the last given a Brazilian twist.

Tom Scott

Alto, tenor and soprano saxophones, flutes, woodwinds, composer.

b. Los Angeles, 19 May 1948.

Scott's mother was a pianist, his father a composer, and Tom played clarinet at high school, but is self-taught as a composer/arranger. Scott was extraordinarily precocious: his trio won a teenage jazz competition at the Hollywood Bowl, and he played as a teenager with the Don Ellis and Oliver Nelson bands and in orchestras on TV shows. When he was nineteen he recorded as a featured soloist with Roger Kellaway's quartet on *The Spirit Feel* and also as leader (*The Honeysuckle Breeze*), and on both albums it is not his virtuosity which astonishes, but his artistic maturity – nothing is superfluous and every note tells. From his early twenties he wrote prolifically for TV shows and occasionally for feature films. He had a long and fruitful association with Kellaway, John Guerin, Chuck Domanico, Victor Feldman and others, playing clubs and concerts, and was part of the initial jazz-rock-fusion movement, forming his own band, Tom Scott and the L.A. Express, which became one of the most successful groups of the 1970s, touring in the USA and internationally, playing major festivals and winning various awards.

Following a string of Scott solo albums on GRP in the 80s and 90s, which mostly fit nicely into the burgeoning popular smooth jazz genre, the L.A. Express reformed in the mid 90s to tour and record though Scott returned to leading a series of star guests on *New Found Freedom* (2002; Higher Octave).

Scott's influences include John Coltrane, Charlie Parker, Gerry Mulligan, Phil Woods, Cannonball Adderley and King Curtis, and other inspirations include Indian music, the Beatles, Aretha Franklin, Ray Charles and early twentieth-century classical music. [IC]

⊙ **Born Again** (1992; GRP). Scott in a (rare) non-fusion recording with Kenny Kirkland and Randy Brecker combines strong soloing with melodic themes.

Tony Scott

Clarinet, saxophones, piano, composer, arranger, electronics.

b. Morristown, New Jersey, 17 June 1921.

Tony Scott (Anthony Sciacca) studied at the Juilliard from 1940–42. During the next thirteen years, Scott worked as a sideman with Buddy Rich, Ben Webster, Sid Catlett, Trummy Young, Earl Bostic, Charlie Ventura, Claude Thornhill and (for a month) Duke Ellington; he also wrote arrangements for singers, including Billie Holiday and Sarah Vaughan, and did a nine-month stint as musical director for Harry Belafonte. From 1953 he led his own groups, winning polls as a clarinettist and establishing himself as an important new voice on the instrument. In 1957 his group spent seven months touring in Europe and Africa and in 1959 Scott left the USA and spent the next six years travelling and working in the Far East. Explaining his departure from the scene, Scott said: "The clarinet died, and I hate funerals."

His main initial influences were Charlie Parker and Ben Webster, and, although Scott was perfectly at home with mainstream and bebop musicians, his concept and style were, even at that time, beyond pigeonholes. He played the clarinet with immense power and expressiveness (Perry Robinson has called him "the loudest of all clarinettists"), and the whole jazz tradition was evident in his work, but he was also one of the earliest experimenters in free improvisation and atonality. On his 1957 album *Scott's Fling*, two pieces, "Abstraction No. 1" and "Three Short Dances For Clarinet", are abstract improvisations, and he took part in a free collective improvisation on a 1958 programme, *The Subject Is Jazz*.

Scott was the first modern American jazz musician to make such a prolonged visit to the Far East. He visited Japan, Taiwan, Okinawa, Hong Kong, Korea, the Philippines, Indonesia, Bali, Singapore, Malaya, Thailand and Saigon. Throughout the trip he was active as a player and teacher of jazz, but also immersed himself in the music and the culture of the countries in which he stayed. He recorded classical folk music of the Far East, and made concert appearances with indigenous musicians. He played at the first Hong Kong jazz festival in 1961, and the first Japanese festival in 1962. He played with a traditional Balinese orchestra in Bali, and with an Indian classical singer at Hindu and Sikh temples in Hong Kong. In July 1965 Scott returned to the USA, leading a quartet in New York and incorporating elements from ethnic music into his jazz. In 1967, with Collin Walcott on sitar and tabla, Scott gave a concert of Indo-jazz music for the Museum of Modern Art's "Jazz in the Garden" series.

He moved to Italy in the 1970s, living in Rome and working with a group led by pianist Romano Mussolini. In the 1980s and 1990s he remained active, recording (often on the Italian Philology label) and experimenting with electronics, leading his own groups, fronting jam sessions and appearing both with groups and as a soloist at festivals.

Scott is a loner and a musical adventurer, and in a long and fascinating career he has anticipated several major new developments in jazz: the free jazz of the 1960s, Indo-jazz fusions, the gradual absorption by jazz of elements from ethnic musics and the progress towards the idea of "world music". [IC]

⊙ **A Day In New York** (1957; Fresh Sound); **Dedications** (1957–9; Core). Scott had a productive relationship with pianist Bill Evans in the 1950s and *A Day In New York* has Scott's quartet featuring Evans and guests Clark Terry, Jimmy Knepper and Sahib Shihab. They play familiar standards and several originals by Scott and Evans in a dynamic and thrilling session. *Dedications* is a series of moving homages to people ranging from Billie Holiday and Art Tatum to Anne Frank and the bullfighter Manolete. The Evans trio with Scott LaFaro play on some pieces and pianist Horst Jankowski, bassist Peter Witte and drummer Herman Mutschler on others. A koto player is added for some traditionally based Japanese pieces. Scott's massive but relatively unsung originality is much in evidence.

⊙ **Lush Life Vols. 1 & 2** (1981–4; Core). Scott probes kaleidoscopically his lifetime obsession with Billy Strayhorn's classic song. The personnel includes the composer himself, plus Bill Frisell, bassist Ed Schuller, drummer Tony D'Arco and Scott's daughter, vocalist Monica Sciacca. A fascinating and sometimes wayward menu of music.

⊙ **African Bird** (1984; Soul Note). Drawing on a pool of seven instrumentalists, including marimba, kalimba, flutes, alto saxophone and trombone, plus a vocalist, Scott achieves a superb fusion of African and African-American elements in a series of eloquent songs.

⊙ **Astral Meditation: Voyage Into A Black Hole 1** (1988; Core). In total there are three volumes of the *Astral Meditations*, which are created by Scott's solo playing and self-devised electronic treatments, but the first trip is the most interesting. Scott yet again is travelling in fresh fields and the results have all the exhilarations and disappointments of a man in unmapped territory.

Paul Sealey

Guitar, banjo, bass guitar.

b. Watford, Hertfordshire, UK, 9 March 1943.

Paul Sealey's jazz career began in the UK trad boom of the early 1960s, when he worked with Nat Gonella, Bobby Mickleburgh's Confederates and others, but not until the early 1980s did his talents as a fleet acoustic guitarist, nimble banjoist (specializing in single-string solo work) and highly capable bass guitarist first become seriously noticed. At this period Sealey worked for an enormous number of local New Orleans-to-mainstream bands, for American visitors such as George Kelly, Benny Waters and Ruby Braff, and with British talents as varied as traditional saxophonist Eggy Ley's Hotshots and Humphrey Lyttelton's eclectic band (as a regular deputy). From the mid-1980s Sealey worked regularly in groups assembled by Keith Nichols and worked the club and festival circuit as a soloist and with a wide variety of bands, including his own trio. In late 1994 he joined Chris Barber's band full-time. [DF]

Phil Seamen

Drums.

b. Burton-upon-Trent, Staffordshire, UK, 28 Aug 1926;

d. 13 Oct 1972.

A legendary British drummer, Seamen came to prominence with big bands after World War II, playing and recording with the Ken Turner orchestra and Nat Gonella from 1946–7, Tommy Sampson in 1948, Joe Loss, and Jack Parnell in the early 1950s. In 1955 he was with the Ronnie Scott orchestra, and in the later 1950s he played with the Jazz Couriers (co-led by Ronnie Scott and Tubby Hayes), the Tubby Hayes quartet and the Joe Harriott quintet. During the early 1960s he worked with Alexis Korner's Blues Incorporated and did gigs with Georgie Fame. He also did some teaching, one of his most illustrious students being Ginger Baker. From 1964–8 he spent much time as resident drummer at Ronnie Scott's club accompanying many US jazzmen including Johnny Griffin, Stan Getz, Roland Kirk and Freddie Hubbard. From 1969–70 he worked with Ginger Baker's Air Force, recording LPs and touring with the group. The last two years of his life were spent playing in London pubs.

Phil Seamen arrived on the scene with the bebop movement, and he had from the beginning all the basic virtues: beautiful time, energy and an innate musicality, but it was the dynamism of his indelible spirit that made his work so exceptional. His abilities transcended bebop: he was with the glorious Joe

Harriott quintet when it was creating the very first European free jazz from 1959–60; and he was equally at home with the R&B of Alexis Korner or the heavy rock of Air Force. He was also a man of great humour and trenchant wit, but the drug addiction which caused his premature death also blighted a career which had begun with magnificent promise. [IC]

➤➤ **Joe Harriott** *(Abstract).*

Al Sears

Tenor saxophone.

b. Macomb, Illinois, 22 Feb 1910; d. 23 March 1990.

Sears worked in Buffalo before he replaced Johnny Hodges in the Chick Webb band in 1928. He played with Elmer Snowden in 1931 and had spells with other leaders before he started to lead his own band, which he did for most of 1933–43. He also worked with Andy Kirk in 1941–2, Lionel Hampton in 1943–4, and then with Duke Ellington from 1944–9. In 1951, he was a founder member of the Johnny Hodges small group, also recording with this group under his own name. He recorded several R&B dates, founded a music publishing company, and led the house band for Alan Freed's rock'n'roll shows during the 1950s. Thereafter he was inactive as a player. Sears had a distinctive, rather querulous tone and an emphatic style of phrasing which became an important influence in R&B (his feature on Duke's gospellish "A Gathering In A Clearing" of 1946 cleverly used this style: "Anybody can tell it was my riff, because there wasn't no preachers in the Ellington band till I joined," said Sears). His own arrangement, "Castle Rock", with the 1951 Hodges group, was a sizeable jukebox hit and pointed the direction of his future career. [BP]

⊙ **Sear-iously** (1949–56; Bear Family). A compilation of seven quintet-to-big-band sessions, covering the chronological distance from instrumental R&B to R&B-influenced rock'n'roll, closing with a couple of vocals by songwriter "Charles Calhoun" who used to be bandleader Jesse Stone.

Don Sebesky

Piano, accordion, trombone.

b. Perth Amboy, New Jersey, 10 Dec 1937.

Sebesky studied at the Manhattan School of Music, and while there he worked with Claude Thornhill, Kai Winding and Tommy Dorsey. He played trombone and wrote arrangements for Maynard Ferguson and Stan Kenton, but then gave up the trombone to concentrate on composing, arranging and conducting. With Verve records, he recorded as a leader and wrote for Wes Montgomery, Astrud Gilberto and many others. He also arranged material for Buddy Rich, Peggy Lee, Dionne Warwick, Roberta Flack, Sonny Stitt and Freddie Hubbard. Sebesky had perhaps his greatest successes with a series of albums he scored for various artists on the A&M and CTI labels, where his expertise in jazz, classical and rock music enabled him to combine elements of all three genres in a way that made the music of the featured artists accessible to a wider audience. He has also written for fims and TV, and has had twenty Grammy nominations. In recent years he has been leading a band, Don Sebesky's New York All Stars. His most recent albums are fine tributes in memory of pianist Bill Evans, *I Remember Bill* (see below), and Duke Ellington, *Joyful Noise* (1999; BMG). [IC]

⊙ **I Remember Bill** (1997; BMG). Deploying brass and woodwinds, a string section and harp, plus a pool of great jazz soloists and rhythm-section players, Sebesky has come up with a rich, heartfelt tribute to Evans. He arranges some Evans compositions, including "Waltz For Debby" and "Peace Piece", plus pieces associated with the pianist. His title track is a sonorous ballad with a vocal by John Pizzarelli and a great Toots Thielemans harmonica solo. Sebesky's arrangement of "So What" is a gem with a kind of light rock/funk feel, great guitar comping by Larry Coryell and solos by Joe Lovano and Tom Harrell, plus Evans's original piano solo beautifully orchestrated.

Andy Secrest

Trumpet, cornet.

b. Muncie, Indiana, 2 Aug 1907; d. 1977.

Usually remembered as the trumpeter who replaced Bix Beiderbecke in Paul Whiteman's orchestra in 1928, Andy Secrest caught Whiteman's ear playing on a record of "Here Comes The Showboat" with Jean Goldkette's organization – where Secrest was working in a chair vacated by Beiderbecke. While he was never the genius that Bix was, Secrest read quickly and sounded similar in tone and approach. "You could say I was a pupil", Secrest told Dick Sudhalter later. "I idolized the guy – thought his style and tone were way ahead of the times. I started playing that way because it was the style that I wanted to obtain." When Secrest left Whiteman in 1932 he moved into studio work with orchestras such as Victor Young's and John Scott Trotter's (his cornet pops up on records by Bing Crosby from the period), and in the 1950s he was still playing on many of the Hollywood-based Dixieland big-band broadcasts of the period. With the onset of rock'n'roll, however, Secrest left music and worked in real estate until he retired. [DF]

Gene Sedric

Tenor saxophone, clarinet.

b. St Louis, Missouri, 17 June 1907; d. 3 April 1963.

Gene "Honey Bear" Sedric worked in St Louis with trumpeter Charlie Creath's band in the early 1920s, then from 1925–32 was one of the best soloists in Sam Wooding's globetrotting band. After work for Luis Russell and Fletcher Henderson his big break came: the years with Fats Waller and his Rhythm, 1934–43. "I was associated with Fats to the end," he remembered, "and from 1939 to 1943 we travelled all over the country, always on the move. Waller was one of the greatest box-office attractions of all time. The largest crowd we ever played to was at the musical fête held every year in Chicago at Soldier Field. It holds 120,000 people. And the largest dance crowd we ever played to was 20,000 in New Orleans at the Race Track." With Waller, Sedric did radio work and recording almost daily, as well as films and plum concert bookings all round the USA, and he continued his successful career after the pianist died, leading his own bands in New York clubs and on tour. In the 1950s he worked for leaders such as Jimmy McPartland, Bobby Hackett and Mezz Mezzrow as well as Conrad Janis (the trombonist who later became a Hollywood actor and starred in *Happy Days*). But the Sedric most jazz fans remember is the forthright tenor saxophonist and plummy chalumeau clarinettist on those irreplaceable Waller sides of the 1930s and 1940s. [DF]

➤➤ **Fats Waller** *(The Last Years 1940–43).*

Zbigniew Seifert

Violin, alto saxophone.

b. Cracow, Poland, 6 June 1946; d. 15 Feb 1979.

Seifert studied violin and alto saxophone at the Chopin School of Music in Cracow, and graduated from the Cracow Higher School of Music in 1970. His main inspiration was John Coltrane, and he began as a saxophonist, forming his own quartet in 1965. He gained rapid critical acclaim in Europe and won several prizes at jazz festivals – both for his group and as soloist. He played with Swedish trombonist Eje Thelin, from whom he learned something of the art of "free" improvisation. In 1970 he joined Tomasz Stanko's group and played with it at the Berlin festival; it was with Stanko that Seifert began playing violin and gradually phasing out the saxophone. From 1973 on he appeared at many European festivals with Hans Koller and as a soloist. Later he played with Joachim Kuhn and Hamburg Radio commissioned him to write a 25-minute concerto for a violin, orchestra and jazz group. He played and recorded with Ralph Towner's group Oregon, Volker Kriegel, Charlie Mariano and appeared live in duet with Philip Catherine. Seifert once said, "I try to play as Coltrane would if he played the violin", and his playing has much of the passionate intensity and the fleetness of his idol. The last two years of Seifert's life were spent in a heroic battle against the cancer which ultimately killed him at the age of 32. He recorded his final album only three months before he died and yet it was ablaze with energy, passion and great playing from Seifert and the all-star group under his leadership: Jack DeJohnette, John Scofield, Eddie Gomez, Richie Beirach and Nana Vasconcelos. [IC]

Oregon

⊙ **The Essential Oregon** (1973–4; Vanguard). It's sad that the only available Zbigniew Seifert on record are the tracks on this Oregon compilation. However, with his fiery rhythmic playing and flowing angularity he fits in well with the uncharacteristically North American flavour of the bulk of the chosen tracks.

Roger Sellars

Drums, percussion.

b. Melbourne, Australia, 18 July 1939.

Sellars studied percussion in Australia and New Zealand, and later in the USA and UK. In 1959 he met and worked with Dave MacRae and Mike Nock. In 1972 he went to the USA, staying for eighteen months, before moving to the UK. From 1974–80 he worked with Nucleus, with whom he toured extensively in Europe and spent three weeks in India in 1978, playing at the first Jazz Yatra in Bombay. While in Britain he also worked with many other British musicians, including Ronnie Scott and Neil Ardley, and with Americans such as Al Grey, Sonny Stitt, Art Farmer and Ernestine Anderson. In 1981 he moved to New Zealand where he worked with local musicians and visiting Americans. [IC]

Archie Semple

Clarinet.

b. Edinburgh, Scotland, 31 March 1928; d. 26 Jan 1974.

A spiritual son of Ed Hall, then Pee Wee Russell, Semple came south from Edinburgh in 1952 and joined Alex Welsh after year-long stays with Mick Mulligan and Freddy Randall. For the next decade he provided the perfect foil for Welsh's Chicago-style lead, recording British jazz classics such as *It's Right Here For You* (a Semple showcase) and small-group collectors' items such as *Night People* (1961). On his own the clarinettist recorded quartet, trio and duo albums, and a 1962 session with strings, directed by Johnny Scott, which might be the best of its kind ever recorded. By the early 1960s Semple was drinking heavily, though still playing brilliantly: a tour with Pee Wee Russell in 1964 provided almost comedic proof of the similar talents and dispositions of the pair, with Semple nervous of Russell (his inspiration), and Russell agitated by Semple's style, which he mistook for direct copying. A charming man but with a deeply nervous disposition, Semple suffered a breakdown on stage at the 1964 Richmond jazz festival, and never really played again. His departure from Welsh's first great band was a serious blow, and his death from alcoholism ten years later nothing short of tragic. [DF]

⊙ **Night People** (2004; Lake). A recent reissue, combining all of *Night People* with most of *Jazz For Young Lovers* (1960), reveals Semple at his peak. On the latter album he plays with Fred Hunt (piano) and Jack Fallon (bass), while on the former the trio are joined by Alex Welsh. Semple's unique brand of elegant melancholy is heard at its most beguiling on the self-penned "Deep Sleep".

➤➤ **Freddy Randall** *(Freddy Randall & His Band).*

Boyd Senter

Clarinet.

b. Lyons, Nebraska, 30 Nov 1899; d. (unknown).

Known in the 1920s as "Jazzologist Supreme" for his comedic sides played on a diamond-studded clarinet, Senter began on classical piano and turned to jazz after hearing the Original Dixieland Jazz Band. He led a touring band, around 1925, which recorded for Autograph, but in 1927 he transferred to OKeh first with a trio and then, in 1928, with a full band known as the Senterpedes, which included the Dorsey Brothers and trumpeter Mickey Bloom. His 1927–8 records for OKeh, which turned him into an international star, included "Mobile Blues" – issued in England but not in the USA. In 1930 Senter became a RCA Victor artist, and throughout the 1930s worked regularly in Detroit. After the war he continued playing, but also opened his Sports Senter, and pursued other business interests including running a company producing saw blades. [DF]

⊙ **Jazzologist Supreme 1928–30** (Timeless). Twenty-four of Senter's sides, all but three with his Senterpedes. Like Ted Lewis, Senter exploited the comedic side of jazz performance (sometimes relentlessly) but he was also a skilled player and performances like "T'aint Clean" are certainly appealing.

Bud Shank

Alto saxophone, flute and baritone saxophone.

b. Dayton, Ohio, 27 May 1926.

Bud (Clifford) Shank began on clarinet at the age of ten and took up the saxophone at fourteen. He moved to the West Coast in 1947 after university. He joined Charlie Barnet, on tenor, from 1947–8, and was part of Stan Kenton's forty-piece band of 1950–51. He was a regular member of the Lighthouse All Stars group from 1953–6, and then led his own quartet. He started making albums under his own name in 1954, some of which (recorded in the mid-1960s) were of more middle-of-the-road music. He was heavily involved in studio work, but continued to appear regularly on jazz gigs. In 1974 he was a founder member of the LA4, and also toured Europe as a soloist and with Shorty Rogers in the mid-1980s.

Shank's early alto work reflected a polite blend of Charlie Parker and Benny Carter influences, with a touch of the early Art Pepper for flavouring; this was later roughened up considerably in terms of tone-quality and rhythmic emphasis. It is perhaps, however, his flute-playing which is his most important achievement, as the instrument had been hard to take seriously in a bebop context. Yet Bud's phrasing and articulation, and even more so his pliant tone, make the listener aware not of the flute's limitations in jazz but of its real communicative power. [BP]

⊙ **I Told You So!** (1992; Candid). This recent live quartet set, with Kenny Barron and Victor Lewis, shows how Shank's playing has developed steadily since the 1950s, and has gutsy versions of "Limehouse Blues", "Emily" and even "My Funny Valentine".

➤➤ **Barney Kessel** *(Easy Like).*

Lakshminarayana Shankar

Violin, composer.

b. Madras, India, 26 April 1950.

At the age of two Shankar was taught to sing ragas, and at five he began violin lessons with his father, a noted violinist. His primary involvement was with Indian classical music, but he was always aware of Western influences and as a young boy heard many Western classical artists as well as groups such as the Beatles, and singers such as Elvis Presley and Frank Sinatra. In 1969 he moved to the USA in order to play different kinds of music as well as to popularize Indian music in the West. He took a PhD in ethnomusicology at Wesleyan University, and while working as a teaching assistant and concert master of the university chamber orchestra he began meeting jazz musicians such as Ornette Coleman, Jimmy Garrison and John McLaughlin. From 1973 Shankar and McLaughlin studied together: "John gave me a lot of jazz lessons and I gave him a lot of Indian lessons." In 1975, they co-founded and co-wrote the material for the group Shakti, an acoustic group which created a unique synthesis of Indian classical music and Western jazz, recorded three albums and brought Shankar to the notice of a worldwide audience. The original Shakti disbanded

Jak Kilby

Shankar, with Zakir Hussain on tabla

in 1978, and Shankar was uninvolved with McLaughlin's Remember Shakti project of the late 90s.

Shankar is a complete virtuoso with a vision of a pan-cultural musical synthesis – a slowly emerging world music – which he is helping to create and which can be heard in perhaps its most evolved state on his most recent recording, *Eternal Light* (2000; Moment). Chris Doering has written, "Shankar executes the microtonal slurs of Indian music with liquid precision even in the highest octaves where fingering is difficult", and he is completely at home with Eastern secular and religious music and Western jazz and rock. He has also pioneered a new instrument: the ten-string, double-neck violin, a double-bodied instrument conceived and designed by Shankar and built by Stuyvesant Music in New York to his specifications. The necks can be played individually or collectively; when played individually, the strings of the other neck create sympathetic overtones. The double violin can cover the range of a whole string orchestra.

Shankar has also recorded with Frank Zappa, Phil Collins and Peter Gabriel, among others. He performs for two months a year in India where he is a major recording artist, and where many of his albums of Indian classical music top the charts. [IC]

⊙ **Who's To Know** (1980; ECM). Shankar with Indian musicians playing authentic Indian classical music and equally authentic variations of that tradition.

⊙ **Vision** (1983; ECM); **Song For Everyone** (1984; ECM). *Vision* is a trio summit meeting with Jan Garbarek and trumpeter Palle Mikkelborg – a brilliantly focused session with Garbarek also playing bass saxophone. *Song* is similarly intense, but Mikkelborg is replaced by percussionists Zakir Hussain and Trilok Gurtu.

⊙ **M.R.C.S** (1988; ECM). A quartet with Zakir Hussain (tabla), Vikku Vinayakram (ghatam) and Norwegian drummer Jon Christensen in a powerfully percussive session.

➤➤ **John McLaughlin** *(Shakti).*

Art Shapiro

Bass.

b. Denver, Colorado, 15 Jan 1916.

Art Shapiro took up bass at thirteen and came to New York in 1934 with Wingy Manone to work in 52nd Street's clubland. Working with Frank Froeba, Sharkey Bonano, Chu Berry, Paul Whiteman (1938-41), Bud Freeman and others and as a busy studio man he appeared on a huge number of jazz records of the period (including classics such as Eddie Condon's *Commodore Jam Sessions*). Shapiro moved to Hollywood in 1941 and worked with Jack Teagarden, Joe Sullivan and Eddie Miller before army service; afterwards he worked with Charlie Ventura, Artie Shaw and Benny Goodman and was active as an MGM studio musician from the late 40s to the end of the 50s. [DF]

➤➤ **Pee Wee Russell** *(Topaz).*

Sonny Sharrock

Guitar, composer, pedal steel guitar, banjo.

b. Ossining, New York, 27 Aug 1940; d. 25 May 1994.

Sharrock began on guitar at the age of twenty, though he had early experience singing with a doo-wop group. He studied at the Berklee School of Music for four months when he was 21, and studied composition for four months in 1963. From 1965 he worked with Olatunji, Pharoah Sanders, Sunny Murray, Don Cherry and others. He was with Herbie Mann from 1967–73, touring in the USA and internationally, and playing on the 1969 hit album, *Memphis Underground*; the same year he appeared on Wayne Shorter's Blue Note album, *Super Nova*. He played major festivals with Mann, including Montreux and Newport in 1970, and worked on Miles Davis's *Jack Johnson*, creating electronic textures. In 1973 he formed a group with his wife Linda, and they also toured in the USA and Europe. In 1985 he cut his first album in ten years and became a member of Last Exit, with Peter Brötzmann, Ronald Shannon Jackson and bassist Bill Laswell. His last years found him recording more prolifically, and touring with a package of musicians associated with New York's Knitting Factory club.

Sharrock came to prominence on the crest of abstraction and rock. With Mann's group he often played a non-tonal role, "freaking out" with feedback and other sounds, but this was all done in a rhythmically coherent context. Sharrock claimed to be the first guitarist to play free jazz, and so topsy-turvy had values become at the end of the 1960s that he actually boasted of his musical ignorance, saying he could write "but not read music. Do not know any standard tunes or any other musicians' licks." He won the *Down Beat* critics' poll in the category Talent Deserving Wider Recognition in 1970, recognition which was belatedly reaching him just before he died of a heart attack. [IC]

Last Exit

⊙ **Last Exit** (1986; Enemy). Free jazz meets avant-garde rock; the combination of Ronald Shannon Jackson's insistent pulse and Bill Laswell's floor-shaking bass lines provides the impetus for the screeching interplay (or duel) of Peter Brötzmann and Sharrock, who sounds inspired.

Sonny Sharrock

⊙ **Guitar** (1986; Enemy). This is a fine compendium of the electric guitar's scope, ranging from impressionistic sound-poetry to abstract-expressionist blitzkrieg.

➤➤ **Miles Davis** *(Jack Johnson);* **Herbie Mann** *(Memphis Underground);* **Wayne Shorter** *(Super Nova).*

Karen Sharp

Tenor saxophone.

b. Ipswich, Suffolk, 30 Sept 1971.

Sharp studied piano and clarinet and specialized mainly in classical music at school before taking up the tenor saxophone at the Royal Northern College of Music, Manchester, where a primary influence was Dexter Gordon. She played in the RNCM jazz ensemble and other groups before moving to London in 1999 to freelance with Humphrey Lyttelton, Digby Fairweather, Enrico Tomasso and others. In 2003 she worked with Dick Sudhalter and Barbara Lea at London's Pizza on the Park. Inspired by the classic jazz saxophonists, Sharp is currently making a name as a soloist and has been described by Humphrey Lyttelton as "a superb musician fit and ready to take off". [DF]

⊙ **Karen Sharp** (2002; 33 Records). On this album Sharp plays standards and originals revealing the melodic style and big warm tone which have singled her out as a British player of remarkable talent. Her backing group includes pianist Richard Busiakiewicz and bassist John Day whose taut swinging lines propel the rhythm section.

Charlie Shavers

Trumpet, vocals, arranger, composer.

b. New York, 3 Aug 1917; d. 8 July 1971.

Charlie Shavers played the piano well enough to perform at Tilly's Chicken Shack (a Harlem rib-joint) in his teens, and the banjo well enough to play duets with Bobby Hackett later for fun. By the age of eighteen, when he joined Tiny Bradshaw's band in New York, Shavers had mastered the trumpet so completely that he must have brought to near-despair a generation of trumpeters who had just got over worrying about Louis Armstrong and Roy Eldridge. By 1937, when he joined Lucky Millinder, his talent was fully grown and less than a year later – at the ripe age of twenty – he joined John Kirby's new band at the Onyx, replacing Frankie Newton: it was Kirby's luckiest career move. For the next six years Shavers masterminded the Kirby operation, providing hit tunes ("Pastel Blue" and "Undecided"), tiny, faultless arrangements and effortless, flighty trumpet. "I really loved all the guys in that band," he said later, in a monumental downgrading of his own contribution, "and the reason it sounded so good was that we were all personal friends!"

He left Kirby in 1944, by which time a year's work with Raymond Scott's integrated CBS staff orchestra had come and gone; the following year he joined Tommy Dorsey, who guarded his new cornerman jealously and (says Alun Morgan) on one occasion even sent a private detective to find Shavers after the trumpeter had tried to leave. He stayed eleven years, on and off, until Dorsey's death, but Shavers's dynamic talent was heard all over during this period: in the ranks of Jazz At The Philharmonic, where he and Roy Eldridge were best equipped to deal with Granz's crucifying high-note finales; recording with all and sundry from Charlie Parker to Billie Holiday (his bravura introduction to Holiday's "My Man" makes everything after it sound flat); and producing classics of his own, like an immortal "Stardust" from a 1947 Gene Norman concert featuring Lionel Hampton. His trumpet-playing contemporaries held him in awe ("After Charlie," said Billy Butterfield once, "there's nothing left to play!"), and it was left to critics joylessly frozen into the cool school or holed up in austere revivalism to brand his work as "tasteless".

After Dorsey died in 1956, Shavers began leading groups of his own (often he adopted the fashionable shufflebeat Jonah Jones format) and by 1963 was back with a re-formed Tommy Dorsey orchestra, led by saxophonist Sam Donahue and featuring Frank Sinatra Jnr. His act at this time – coming on late from the wrong side of the stage, gag endings, stopping half-way to blow his nose – was the epitome of trumpet cabaret. Later in the decade he was on tour with Sinatra again, regularly leading his own quintet (with Budd Johnson) and touring as a soloist, including a 1969 trip to England, where he was delighted to see hotel-room electric sockets marked "For Shavers Only" ("Wait till Eldridge sees this!"). By 1970, however, the good humour and the trumpet perfection were beginning to slip as throat cancer took hold, and he died the year after, two days after Louis Armstrong – his mouthpiece, at his request, was buried in Armstrong's coffin. Charlie Shavers might just be the best trumpeter the swing era ever produced. Others may have extended the trumpet's capabilities further in one direction (Cat Anderson played higher, Rex Stewart was perhaps more of a half-valve master), but Shavers had the perfect technique for whatever he wanted to do, and he did most things. [DF]

⊙ **Young Shavers** (1937-45; Topaz). As usual a fine cherry-picked selection of Shavers' best early work from Topaz, including ten choice John Kirby selections (1938-42) plus sides by Coleman Hawkins, Billy Kyle, Walter 'Foots' Thomas, Sidney Bechet, Herbie Haymer, and Nat Cole's Quintet.A very good buy.

⊙ **Charlie Shavers And The Blues Singers** (1938-9; Timeless). A fascinating collection though Shavers lovers may want more of him; however he is audible on all tracks and spectacular on some.

⊙ **Charlie Shavers 1944-5** (Classics). Nineteen sides with Shavers in the company of The Keynoters, Linda Keene, Walter 'Foots' Thomas, his own Quintet (six tracks) and a V-Disc All Star jam session with Trummy Young et al. His airy swaggering trumpet is regularly well in evidence and seldom sounds tired.

⊙ **The Most Intimate** (1955; Bethlehem). The flawless Shavers this time with Sy Oliver's strings in a highly under-rated collection, including "Ill Wind", "You're Mine You" and eight more.

⊙ **The Complete Charlie Shavers With Maxine Sullivan** (1957; Avenue). Pleasant mid-period collaboration between Shavers and Sullivan engineered by Leonard Feather (five tracks) plus four more by Shavers' ensemble. Shavers' playing as always is fantastical though his impressions of trumpeters including Armstrong, Eldridge, Dizzy Gillespie sound most like himself; no problem.

⊙ **Live** (1970; Black and Blue). This late set with Budd Johnson occasionally sounds tired, but his superb technique and wonderfully motivic imagination still flash through.

➤➤ **Lionel Hampton** *(Stardust)*; **John Kirby** *(John Kirby Sextet 1939–41)*.

Artie Shaw

Clarinet, saxophones, composer.
b. New York, 23 May 1910.

Artie Shaw (Arthur Jacob Arshawsky) began his New York career as a lead-alto sessionman working for leaders such as Paul Specht, Vincent Lopez and Roger Wolfe Kahn, and on records with such as Fred Rich and Teddy Wilson (his clarinet sides with Billie Holiday, including "Did I Remember" and "A Fine Romance", are some of the best she made). After a concert in 1936 at New York's Imperial Theater, featuring a small string section, Shaw formed his first big band; over the next few years he became a centre of swing-music attention, releasing hit records such as "Frenesi", "Adios Mariquita Linda" and, of course, "Begin The Beguine", with a new high-powered orchestra that featured saxophonist Tony Pastor (a boyhood friend), and such black artists as Billie Holiday, Hot Lips Page and Lena Horne.

In addition to his huge talent as a clarinettist, Shaw made excellent copy (sometimes to his dismay). His career – especially in its early years – was littered with famous wives (including Lana Turner), unexpected disbandments, disillusioned disappearances and frank public announcements proclaiming the inanity of the music industry and even of his young jitterbugging audiences. At the time the musical press found his outbursts mystifying and unsporting: in retrospect they were clearly the outpourings of a sensitive and intelligent musician all too aware that all was not what it could be down Tin Pan Alley.

MAX JONES FILES

Artie Shaw

After disbanding in 1939, Shaw re-formed a year later, his orchestra featuring the much loved small group the Gramercy Five, with Johnny Guarnieri on harpsichord and Billy Butterfield on trumpet. By 1942 he was leading an all-star navy band which toured the Pacific. "They went wild at the mere sight of us", recalls Max Kaminsky. "It was like being back in the Paramount Theater again ... those men went stark raving crazy. Even the fellows in the band were shaken!" From 1944, Shaw's bandleading career was more spasmodic. Jazz fashion was gravitating to bebop and big bands were on the decline, but he carried on recording for another ten years, toured what remained of the big-band circuit, led a small string-based group at Bop City in 1949 and played Carnegie Hall in a classical programme the same year – accomplishing, in short, many of the same aims as Benny Goodman. But where Goodman was a stoical leader and an omnidirectional musician who liked nothing better than to play the clarinet all day, Shaw was a diversifier. By 1950 he had taken up Spanish guitar as a second instrument, gone into psychoanalysis and begun to realize that he was perhaps too bright to be just a jazzman. In 1952 he produced his long, romantic and thoughtful autobiography (*The Trouble With Cinderella*), which is one of the most substantial self-portraits produced by a jazz musician. Shaw was to make his career as a writer from the mid-1950s, publishing an entertaining trio of short stories in the 1960s (*I Love You, I Hate You, Drop Dead*) and writing regularly for the theatre and for films. In the 1980s it was good to welcome him back to bandleading (as frontman for a re-formed orchestra led by Dick Johnson), and to see and hear him commenting on earlier triumphs for documentaries, including a riveting full-length study, *Time Is All You've Got* (1985). In 1992 Shaw visited London, energy undimmed, to conduct performances of Mozart's *Clarinet Concerto* as well as his own concerto for soloist Bob Wilber. In 2003 Shaw was still active and talking as lucidly as ever for a major TV documentary.

Along with Benny Goodman, Shaw was the leading clarinettist of the swing era. Because he achieved his first major success two years after Goodman, and his musical career was intermittent, his contribution is often considered secondary to Goodman's, but many jazz musicians find a warmth and creativity in Shaw's work that they miss in Goodman's, and many of his 1940s recordings ("Stardust" is one classic) stand alongside the best jazz ever recorded. [DF]

⊙ **In The Beginning** (1936; Hep); **The Chant** (1936–7; Hep); **Non-stop Flight** (1937; Hep). The first years of Shaw, available separately and with excellent sound.

⊙ **The Complete Artie Shaw And His Orchestra** (1938; Le Jazz). Fine one-volume collection of Shaw's first great hit-making year; "Begin The Beguine" and "Nightmare" are both here, as well as beauties like "Back Bay Shuffle" and Billie Holiday's glorious "Any Old Time".

Begin The Beguine (1938–41; RCA Bluebird). Taking the story on from the CD listed above, this set has later Shaw hits including "Frenesi" and "Traffic Jam", plus two tracks by his Gramercy Five and – arguably – the greatest-ever version of "Stardust", with Billy Butterfield plus Shaw's incomparable clarinet chorus.

Let's Go For Shaw (1938–41; Avid). A tempting selection of Shaw "lollipops": "Solid Sam", "Concerto For Clarinet", "What Is There To Say", "The Blues" and sixteen more, including Helen Forrest's charming "Someone's Rockin' My Dreamboat".

The Complete Gramercy Five Sessions (1940–45; RCA Bluebird). An essential area of Shaw's discography, sensibly isolated by RCA. There are many high spots – including the best-selling "Summit Ridge Drive/Special Delivery Stomp" coupling; Billy Butterfield and Roy Eldridge are superb and Guarnieri's harpsichord was one of the great original touches of the swing era.

Blues In The Night (1941–5; RCA Bluebird). This fine collection has many gems, including Shaw's wonderful titles with Roy Eldridge and Hot Lips Page (outstanding singing and playing on "Blues In The Night", "St James Infirmary" and "Take Your Shoes Off Baby"), two rough-edged trumpeters who complemented his svelte approach to perfection. The string section is an added delight, and much of the arranging (including work by Eddie Sauter and Ray Conniff) is state-of-the-art for the period.

The Last Recordings (1954; Musicmasters/Limelight). These sides, of which Shaw is exceptionally proud, are perfectly recorded models of jazz clarinet-playing, with superb support from compatible masters like Hank Jones and Tal Farlow.

Arvell Shaw

Bass.

b. St Louis, Missouri, 15 Sept 1923; d. 6 Dec 2002.

If only because of his skilful four bars in "Now You Has Jazz" from the film *High Society* (1956), Arvell Shaw will always be associated with Louis Armstrong's All Stars. But though Shaw (like Trummy Young and other All Stars) was selflessly happy to serve his leader, he was himself an influential and highly progressive player who, just three years after the death of Jimmy Blanton, was already impressing older hands such as Earl Hines with his power, creativity and speed, at a time when most bass players offered much less. Shaw first worked with Armstrong in his big band in 1945, rejoined him when the All Stars were formed and (apart from a two-year break to study at the Geneva Conservatory) was with him up to 1956. His bass solos of the period, such as "Blues For Bass" from the Crescendo sessions, are models of virtuoso performance, right down to their audible in-time gasps for air. After *High Society* he worked with a variety of talents including Teddy Wilson's trio, Benny Goodman and Sidney Bechet, before rejoining Louis Armstrong, with whom he then stayed (with short breaks) until the end. After 1971 he was active as a freelance and teacher, and in the 1980s toured with Keith Smith's Wonderful World of Louis Armstrong, playing the bass as well as ever, singing in a pleasing, plummy baritone, and reminiscing in good-humoured tempo. [DF]

➤➤ **Louis Armstrong** *(The California Concerts).*

Charles "Bobo" Shaw

Drums.

b. Pope, Mississippi, 5 Sept 1947.

Charles "Bobo" Shaw studied drums with a number of people, including Joe Charles, Ben Thigpen and Charles Payne, and he played trombone and bass in passing. He played with blues and R&B artists, like Oliver Sain, Ike and Tina Turner, and Albert King. In St Louis in 1968 he co-founded the artist collective called Black Artists Group (BAG). During the 70s Shaw led the Human Arts Ensemble and played with many prominent creative musicians including saxophonists Julius Hemphill, Oliver Lake and Luther Thomas, and the Bowie brothers (trumpeter Lester and trombonist Joseph). He appeared on many records, including Lester Bowie's *Rope-A-Dope* (1975; Muse) and the St Louis Creative Ensemble's *I Can't Figure Out (Whatcha Doin' To Me)* (1979; Moers), and as a leader on *Streets Of St Louis* (1974; Moers) and *Junk Trap* (1978; Black Saint). As late as 1984, he recorded on violinist Billy Bang's *The Fire From Within* (Soul Note), and in 2000 a vintage concert with Anthony Braxton, *Quintet (Basel) 1977* (hatOLOGY), appeared on CD, but latterly Shaw has largely been absent from the scene. [JC]

Clarence Shaw

Trumpet.

b. Detroit, Michigan, 16 June 1926; d. late 1970s.

Shaw had piano lessons at age four and switched to trombone at six, and later studied classical piano for two years. He became interested in the trumpet after hearing Dizzy Gillespie's record of "Hot House" when he was convalescing in an army hospital in Detroit after his army service. He made such rapid progress on the trumpet that within a few weeks he was playing his first engagement at a Detroit club, and later studied harmony, theory and composition at a Detroit music college. He worked locally, then played with Lester Young, Wardell Gray, Lucky Thompson and worked regularly for a while with Charles Mingus. In 1957 he played on the Mingus albums *East Coasting* and *Tijuana Moods*; in the liner note to the latter, Mingus heaped detailed praise on Shaw, prefacing his remarks with: "Not only does Clarence Shaw have a beautiful sound and ideas, but he is creative and original and plays like no other trumpet man – with the exception that he bears a close relationship soul-wise to Freddie Webster." Shaw recorded two albums in the 1960s as Gene Shaw, and then withdrew from the jazz scene. [IC]

➤➤ **Charles Mingus** *(New Tijuana Moods).*

Ian Shaw

Vocals.

b. St Asaph, Wales, 2 June 1962.

Brought up in North Wales, Ian Shaw began musical life by playing cornet in a brass band. After moving to London to study Messiaen and late Beethoven for a BMus from King's College and training as a classical bass, he met Madeline Bell – from whom he learned a great deal, including microphone technique – and Mel Tormé, and was encouraged in his ambition to become a professional singer. In addition to spells in the chorus of musicals such as *Cats* and *Chess*, Shaw gigged tirelessly, particularly in London, and built up such a following that in 1990 he was voted Best Vocalist in the *Wire* magazine readers' poll. Describing himself as "not strictly a jazz singer – more someone who sings with soul and uses jazz phrasing", Shaw is as indebted to pop/soul singers such as Dusty Springfield and Johnny Mathis as to jazz singers like Sarah Vaughan for his extraordinarily flexible, adventurous vocal style. He is also noted for highlighting gender issues; he himself comments: "Most jazz standards – especially the Billie Holiday repertoire like 'Don't Explain', 'Lover Man', etc – are written from a woman's point of view, which is why I sing them: it's good to turn things round."

In 1997, having established himself as the UK's top jazz singer through constant solo, group and duo appearances (the last with Claire Martin, performing themed sets such as "The Look Of Love", dedicated to the music of Burt Bacharach), Shaw toured America to genuine acclaim, performing material taken not only from the albums below, but also from 1995's *Famous Rainy Day* (33 Records) and another Jazz House recording from Ronnie Scott's (in studio format), *The Echo Of A Song* (1996). The former concentrated on contemporary pop and rock tunes, by the likes of Stevie Wonder and Joni Mitchell, through Todd Rundgren to Lennon and McCartney; the latter was more standards-based, beginning with Cole Porter's "I Concentrate On You" and also including songs by Irving Berlin, Jerome Kern and Rodgers and Hart. A signing to US label Milestone produced two fine albums, *In A New York Minute* (1999), co-led with pianist Cedar Walton, and *Soho Stories* (see below). Shaw's current stature is neatly summed up by the *Hollywood Reporter*: "If Ian Shaw had been around forty years ago, this fine singer would have been maybe bigger than Mel Tormé or Betty Carter." [CP]

Carol Grimes and Ian Shaw

⊙ **Lazy Blue Eyes** (1990; Offbeat Records). Joined by singer Carol Grimes and tastefully backed by guitarist Tony Remy and keyboard player Steve Lodder, Shaw duets on such pieces as "Lover Man" and solos on songs such as "I Love You" and "Misty".

Ian Shaw

⊙ **Ghostsongs** (1992; Ronnie Scott's Jazz House). Fair representation of Shaw's sparky, soulful live act, backed by longtime associate, pianist Adrian York, and band, plus guest saxophonist Iain Ballamy.

⊙ **Taking It To Hart** (1995; Ronnie Scott's Jazz House). Again backed by Adrian York and assorted guests, innovative but respectful versions of classics such as "Where Or When", "My Funny Valentine", "Blue Moon" and many more.

⊙ **Soho Stories** (2001; Milestone). Shaw at his mature best, equally assured and sensitive on his customary range of material, from Arlen and Kern to Janis Ian and Tom Waits, with some notably neat arrangements from bassist Geoff Gascoyne.

Marlena Shaw

Vocals.

b. New Rochelle, New York, 22 Sept 1944.

Shaw learned piano informally with her uncle, becoming a professional vocalist in 1964 with Howard McGhee and playing concerts with Marian McPartland. She recorded albums and singles (including her hit "Go Away Little Boy") from 1966, singing at Playboy Clubs and then working with Count Basie during 1968–70. A series of recordings for the 70s Blue Note label successfully targeted the pop and soul market, often incorporating spoken monologues, but Shaw maintained links with small-group jazz musicians. As well as her own trio-backed appearances, since the mid-1980s she has contributed to albums by Buddy Montgomery, Jimmy Smith, two by Joe Williams, Benny Carter and Ray Brown. In 1998 she fronted an Ella Fitzgerald tribute at US and European festivals, with Frank Foster as musical director, her somewhat Carmen McRae-influenced style sounding fully at home on blues and standards. [BP]

⊙ **Elemental Soul** (1997; Concord). Marlena's second Concord album covers blues and gospel-type repertoire as well as ancient standards like "Love Is Here To Stay" and lightly funkified versions of "My Old Flame" and "How Deep Is The Ocean". The three tracks with commentary by Stanley Turrentine are a highlight.

Woody Shaw

Trumpet, flugelhorn, composer.

b. Laurinburg, North Carolina, 24 Dec 1944; d. 10 May 1989.

Shaw's family moved to Newark, New Jersey, where his father was a member of a gospel group, the Diamond Jubilee Singers. Woody started on bugle, then changed to the trumpet at eleven. His teacher, Jerry Ziering, gave him classical lessons, but introduced him to the work of Dizzy Gillespie, Bix Beiderbecke and Bunny Berigan. He began to sit in locally with visiting guest stars, then at eighteen toured with Rufus Jones, after which he got his first big-time job with Willie Bobo in a Brooklyn club in a band which included Chick Corea, Larry Gales, Joe Farrell and Garnett Brown. Then he joined Eric Dolphy's group until the saxophonist's sudden death in 1964. Shaw said of this period, "Eric helped me

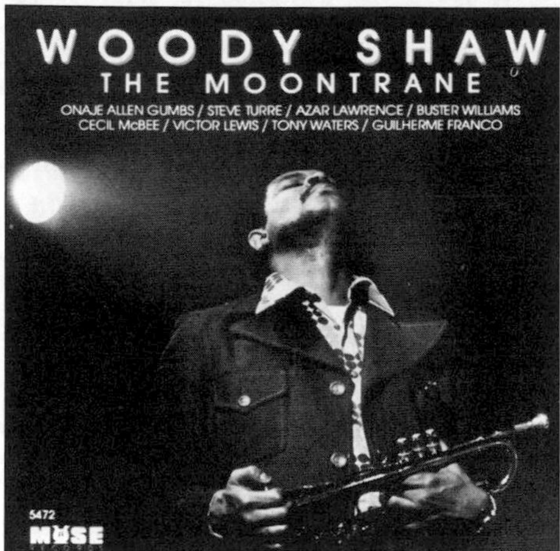

to find my own individual approach to playing trumpet. He taught me to play inside and outside at the same time." In 1964 he went to Paris, working with Bud Powell, Kenny Clarke, Art Taylor, Johnny Griffin and Larry Young. He also played in Belgium and Germany before returning to the USA where in 1965 he joined Horace Silver, and in 1968–9 played on and off with Max Roach, touring the Middle East and performing at a festival in Iran. 1970–72 was a time of little work, though he played with Joe Henderson and Gil Evans, and in 1973 joined Art Blakey before spending some time freelancing on the West Coast with Herbie Hancock and Bobby Hutcherson.

WOODY SHAW
THE MOONTRANE
ONAJE ALLEN GUMBS / STEVE TURRE / AZAR LAWRENCE / BUSTER WILLIAMS
CECIL McBEE / VICTOR LEWIS / TONY WATERS / GUILHERME FRANCO
5472
MUSE

Back in New York in 1974 he recorded the third album under his own name, *The Moontrane*, which got favourable reviews and made enough of an impact to give Shaw the viability to lead his own groups. Shortly afterwards, at Miles Davis's suggestion, Columbia signed him up, and a spate of fine albums ensued. He continued touring and playing festivals internationally with his own groups. In 1985 he played the Camden festival, London, with a quintet that included Joe Farrell and the "young lion" drummer Ronnie Burrage. Shaw's original influences were Gillespie, Miles Davis and Clifford Brown, and later Booker Little, Donald Byrd, Lee Morgan and perhaps most of all Freddie Hubbard. Other influences were McCoy Tyner, with whom he played and recorded in the late 1960s, and classical composers such as Debussy. He was a superb player who had shrugged off most of the Hubbard influence by the mid-1970s, forging a highly individual style compounded of playing "inside" (on the chords) and "outside" (superimposing foreign notes on the chord). He suffered from an eye disease which severely damaged his sight, and fell under a subway train, dying of his injuries three months later. [IC]

⊙ **Cassandranite** (1965–71; Muse). Shaw at his best with an all-star cast in 1965, plus one track (and another all-star group) from 1971.

⊙ **The Moontrane** (1974; Muse). The breakthrough album for Shaw finds him in strong company, particularly trombonist Steve Turre, playing a set of unmodish originals. The leader's unclichéd, full-bodied trumpet is also heard to good advantage.

⊙ **Solid** (1986; Muse). A sextet session with Kenny Garrett, Kenny Barron plus guitar, bass and drums, with fresh renditions of standard songs including "It Might As Well Be Spring".

⊙ **Imagination** (1987; Muse). *Imagination* is a quintet outing with trombonist Steve Turre supporting and challenging Shaw, who responds magnificently.

⊙ **In My Own Sweet Way** (1987; In + Out). *In My Own Sweet Way* has Shaw with piano, bass and drums playing a variety of standards, including a fine version of the beautiful Brubeck title piece.

George Shearing

Piano.

b. London, 13 Aug 1919.

Blind from birth, Shearing began gigging in the late 1930s with the Ambrose dance band. He did hotel, radio and record work with Harry Parry in 1940–41, and played with Stephane Grappelli, who was then resident in London. Shearing visited the USA at the end of 1946 and settled there permanently a year later. He formed an extremely popular quintet, which lasted from 1949–67, and for nearly three decades he has led a trio and then a duo (currently with bassist Neil Swainson). Shearing has made records under his own name since 1939, and in that time has successfully imitated boogie, Earl Hines, Bud Powell, Lennie Tristano, Latin jazz, Milt Buckner, Horace Silver and Bill Evans. In recent years, he has occasionally sung in public as well without denting his popularity, and a series of albums with other stars (including Grammy-award winners with Mel Tormé) has raised his critical profile in the last decade. Of his compositions, "Conception" was recorded by Miles Davis, Bill Evans and others, while "She" was covered by Bud Powell; his 1952 tune, "Lullaby Of Birdland", is one of the most widely known jazz standards. [BP]

⊙ **Verve Jazz Masters** (1949–54; Verve). This compilation of Shearing's famous quintet, with Margie Hyams's vibes and Chuck Wayne's guitar stating themes in unison with the piano, has most of the early hits including the inevitable "Lullaby Of Birdland".

⊙ **That Shearing Sound** (1994; Telarc). Shearing returned to the early quintet's characteristic instrumentation for this session, featuring Louis Stewart, vibist Steve Nelson and drummer Dennis Mackrel, for which he turned in some of his most driving work for ages.

Jack Sheldon

Trumpet.

b. Jacksonville, Florida, 30 Nov 1931.

A professional trumpet player from the age of thirteen, Jack Sheldon moved to Los Angeles in his mid-teens, subsequently joining the air force and playing in military bands in Texas and California. In his twenties, he became a familiar figure in West

Coast jazz circles, playing in the small groups of Jimmy Giuffre, Art Pepper and Curtis Counce and with larger ensembles, including those of Benny Goodman and Stan Kenton. A parallel career as an actor developed in the 1960s, but Sheldon continued to play jazz, contributing to recordings by singers Mel Tormé and Helen Humes, and making a record with Gary Burton in 1963. In the following decades, Sheldon played with Bill Berry's big band (1976), backed June Christy on a late recording (1977) and led his own small groups, singing and playing his underrated, sure-footed trumpet. In the 1980s and 1990s, Sheldon contributed both skills to a Tom Kubis big-band recording, played with Vic Lewis and Rosemary Clooney and continued to play clubs in the LA area with his California Cool Quartet, dispensing his own brand of light-hearted but impeccably performed jazz, laced with humour. [CP]

CURTIS COUNCE

⊙ **You Get More Bounce With Curtis Counce** (1957; OJC). Curtis Counce's albums present West Coast jazz at its best, light, airy, uplifting, and Sheldon's bright trumpet is a vital ingredient of the band's sound.

JACK SHELDON

⊙ **Hollywood Heroes** (1988; Concord). Lively, good-natured jazz, Sheldon having surrounded himself with sympathetic souls to dispense good cheer on numbers like "The Joint Is Jumpin'" and "I Want To Be Happy".

⊙ **On My Own** (1991; Concord). Sheldon joins frequent collaborator, pianist Russ Tompkins, to cover familiar territory.

⊙ **Playing For Change** (1997; Uptown). Recorded with a sparkily responsive band – Jerry Dodgion (alto saxophone); Barry Harris (piano), Rufus Reid (bass), Ben Riley (drums) – in 1986, and engineered by Rudy Van Gelder, this is close to definitive Sheldon: bright, confident trumpet on a varied selection of songs, the whole laced with typically Sheldonian wit.

Dave Shepherd

Clarinet, bandleader.
b. London, 7 Feb 1929.

The most polished jazz clarinettist of post-war Britain, Dave Shepherd is more often than not associated with his highly successful Benny Goodman-style quintet. In fact, Shepherd's terms of reference are much wider (including Irving Fazola, Matty Matlock and Artie Shaw) and over thirty years he has played in a diverse variety of jazz settings: the 1950s Jazz Today unit (with Bert Courtley, Johnny Rogers and others), Freddy Randall's and Joe Daniels's bands, Norman Granz's Jazz At The Philharmonic package for a British tour with Ella Fitzgerald and Oscar Peterson, and with his own Dixieland-style groups. (He also backed Billie Holiday during her visit to England in 1954 and worked in Long Island while resident in New York around the same period.) Since the 1970s Shepherd has toured internationally with Teddy Wilson, appeared solo at numerous festivals, played with Lennie Hastings's band and led Peter Boizot's Pizza All Stars (1979–2002), as well as his own quintet, featuring vibraphonist Roger Nobes. Shepherd's immaculate style was in constant demand for radio and recording work from the 1950s to the 1980s and he remains as busy as ever working with his Quintet, 'The Great British Jazz Band' and freelancing. [DF]

➤➤ **Freddy Randall** *(Freddy Randall & His Band)*; **Pete Strange** *(The Great British Jazz Band)*.

Jim Shepherd

Trombone, bass saxophone.
b. London, 29 March 1936.

Jim Shepherd worked with Steve Lane's Southern Stompers early in his career, then with bands led by Brian White, Dave Keir and Ian Bell. A close associate of clarinettist Alan Cooper, he subbed regularly with the Temperance Seven, played in the house band at Osterley Jazz Club (1963–8), and then joined a great – and much underrated – British-based band, the Anglo-American Alliance (featuring Dick Sudhalter, pianist Henry Francis and singer Chris Ellis). In the 1970s he freelanced, playing with a resident group (including trumpeter Bob Kerr) at the Half Moon, Putney, and with violinist Dick Powell at the Redan, Queensway. After a brief spell of inactivity came work with the newly formed Five-a-Slide trombone group, tours and recordings with a variety of visiting Americans such as Wild Bill Davison, Jimmy McPartland, Yank Lawson and Franc Williams, and in 1985 a short season with the American Harlem Blues and Jazz Band. Into the 1990s Shepherd continued to freelance with a variety of groups, and in 1994 he recorded again with Dick Sudhalter. A fine trombonist with an eye to classic principles, he plays naturally in the style of white Americans such as Miff Mole, Bill Rank and Jack Teagarden. [DF]

➤➤ **Dick Sudhalter** *(After Awhile)*.

Archie Shepp

Tenor, soprano and alto saxophones, piano, vocals, composer, educator.
b. Fort Lauderdale, Florida, 24 May 1937.

Shepp was brought up in Philadelphia, where he started on piano, clarinet and alto, and switched to tenor, playing with R&B bands. He met Lee Morgan, Cal Massey, Jimmy Heath and John Coltrane in Philadelphia, studied drama at Goddard College from 1955–9, and after graduating settled in New York. In 1960 he worked with Cecil Taylor, playing concerts and also appearing in the play *The Connection*. He co-led a group with trumpeter Bill Dixon, then co-led the New York Contemporary Five with John Tchicai and Don Cherry, touring the USSR and Czechoslovakia with it in 1964, and appearing at the Helsinki World Youth Festival.

In 1965 he began an occasional association with John Coltrane, working with him in various clubs, and recordings made by Shepp at the Newport jazz festival that year were coupled with a Coltrane performance in a release on the Impulse! label called *New Thing At Newport*. This exposure, and the endorsement of his abilities by Coltrane, were enormously helpful in establishing Shepp in the USA and internationally. Also in 1965 he began establishing himself as a dramatist, and his play *The Communist* was performed in New York.

From the early 1960s he was closely associated with the avant-garde movement and with its manifestations as an expression of black solidarity. In December 1965, addressing himself to the white readership of *Down Beat* magazine, he wrote: "I am an anti-fascist artist. My music is functional. I play about the death of me by you. I exult in the life of me in spite of you. I give some of that life to you whenever you listen to me, which right now is never. My music is for the people."

Shepp's music has almost always been less abstract than that of the other avant-gardists, and his 1965 Newport concert revealed him to be a deft and highly original composer, as well as a distinctive new voice on tenor saxophone. His music featured rock rhythms, jazz swing, tonalities, harmonic structures, tightly composed passages and occasional texts spoken by Shepp. His gruff tenor sound came out of Hawkins, but it included passionately vocalized tones, with falsetto passages sometimes tender, sometimes brutal, and he also showed an extraordinarily caressing way of handling a romantic melody as if he were savouring and consuming it.

From the mid-1960s Shepp led his own groups, touring and playing festivals internationally. His 1967 octet album *Mama Too Tight* showed a rich eclecticism, with overtones of Ellington and Ben Webster, R&B rhythms, street-band marches, lascivious parodies of popular ballads, non-tonal collective "freak-outs". All these elements were included in the music of his band, which toured Europe that year and in London shared the bill with the Miles Davis quintet.

In 1969 he began collaborating with trumpeter and composer Cal Massey, playing his compositions and taking him on tour in Europe and North Africa, where Shepp appeared at the Pan-African festival, playing a concert with African musicians which was released on record. This attempt to get back to roots was, however, a disaster; Shepp's jazz sensibilities and the musical tradition of the African musicians found no common ground.

Shepp continued to be active in the theatre, collaborating with Cal Massey on *Lady Day: A Musical Tragedy*, which was performed at the Brooklyn Academy of Music in 1972. He also wrote other plays that were performed, including *Junebug Graduates Tonight*. In 1972 he taught a course in playwriting at the University of Buffalo while holding the post of consultant in music, and from 1973 he lectured at the University of Massachusetts.

JAK KILBY

Archie Shepp, with Sati di Brian on bass

Shepp continued to tour and play major international festivals. In 1979 he toured Europe with a group which included Mal Waldron, and at this point in his career Shepp was featuring soprano as well as tenor saxophone. By 1985 when he toured Europe with his group, he was playing post-bebop music – a kind of contemporary mainstream confection with strong roots in the blues; at one point he actually sang blues. Shepp's music always carried a strong sense of jazz history but, as many of his recent recordings show, Shepp has mostly adopted more of a curatorial role than might have been expected of the 1960s firebrand, reaching into the (pre-Coltrane) roots of his music. However, a recent set reuniting several players of similar vintage and persuasion – *Live In New York* (2001; Verve) with Roswell Rudd, Grachan Moncur III, Reggie Workman and Andrew Cyrille – showed that Shepp and his contemporaries can still have much fire to offer. [IC]

Archie Shepp

⊙ **New Thing At Newport** (1965; Impulse!). Shepp was always something of a sheep in wolf's clothing, and under a veneer of avant-gardism this quartet with Bobby Hutcherson, Barre Phillips and Joe Chambers is rooted deep in the jazz tradition.

Yasmina/Poem For Malcolm (1969; Affinity). Shepp with a large pool of players wrestles with tradition and innovation; the two long title pieces explore the further limits of Shepp's 1960s musical radicalism, but remain rooted enough in the jazz tradition for a reading of "Body And Soul" not to seem too incongruous.

Montreux One (1975; Freedom); **A Sea Of Faces** (1975; Black Saint). Both of these sets examine the jazz tradition – blues, gospel, conventional structures, free jazz – through Shepp's customary gruff parody of Ben Webster. The treatment of "Lush Life" on the former album is a fine example of innovation by way of desecration.

Archie Shepp and Max Roach

The Long March (1979; hat Art). Shepp in duo with legendary drummer Max Roach in a live recording made in Switzerland; at two CDs it's too long for most tastes, but full of classy playing.

Archie Shepp and Horace Parlan

Trouble In Mind (Steeplechase; 1980). Parlan has been a frequent (and sympathetic) collaborator with Shepp over the last couple of decades, and here the dynamic duo burrow into the blues.

➤➤ **John Coltrane** *(The Major Works)*; **Karin Krog** *(Hi-Fly)*; **Cecil Taylor** *(Jumpin' Punkins)*.

Andy Sheppard

Tenor and soprano saxophones, flute, composer.
b. Warminster, Wiltshire, UK, 20 Jan 1957.

Sheppard sang in a church choir until he was eleven, discovering in the process that he had perfect pitch, but he had no formal music lessons. At nineteen, he left school and was preparing to go to art college when some friends introduced him to the music of John Coltrane. He stayed up all night listening to Coltrane and the next day sold all his possessions and bought a saxophone. Within three weeks he was in a Bristol-based quartet called Sphere (Thelonious Monk's middle name, and not to be confused with the American group of the same name), and performing in public. He occasionally played with another locally based group, Spirit Level, which was also rooted in acoustic hard bop at a time when that was not fashionable. After four or five years of scuffling and scraping a non-living, he left Sphere and went to live in Paris where he survived as a street busker until he got work teaching saxophone and working with French bands including the big band Lumière and Urban Saxophone.

He returned to the UK in the mid-1980s, made Bristol his adopted home and formed his own quartet, which soon gained a very large local following. Then in 1986 he won the Best Soloist award at the Jazz Services-Schlitz jazz competition which was televised by the BBC. Joe Zawinul was one of the judges and, on television, he praised Sheppard to the skies. As a result of that publicity Sheppard was offered a record contract by Island's Antilles label within a week. Since then he has worked incessantly in a variety of contexts.

In 1987 he worked with Gil Evans in France, and also began playing regularly with George Russell's Anglo-American Living Time Orchestra, and with Carla Bley's band. Sheppard also led his own small band, recording two successful albums and touring. In 1990 he formed his Soft On The Inside big band, which produced an album and a video. Since 1991 he has led an acoustic/electric quintet, In Co-Motion, which includes keyboardist Steve Lodder and South African trumpeter Claude Deppa, and which, when augmented to big-band status, is called Big Co-Motion. Sheppard has also worked with the occasional trio, Inclassifiable, which comprises Lodder and percussionist Nana Vasconcelos. In the early 1990s he began performing in trio with Carla Bley and Steve Swallow and they recorded a CD, *Songs With Legs*, in 1994. Sheppard has also worked in duo with his longtime friend and associate, pianist Keith Tippett.

With Lodder, Sheppard set up Shoddy Music Inc, to handle any composing they do for films or TV. Sheppard has composed music for two BBC TV *Natural World* documentaries, an *Arena* programme about Peter Sellers (released as *Moving Image* on Verve) and also a production of Arthur Miller's play, *The Man Who Had All The Luck*, which ran in Bristol and London. He has also written a chamber piece for pianist Joanne MacGregor. A latterday recording deal with Provocateur records (see below) continues to document Sheppard's increasingly commanding and lyrical playing and writing.

Sheppard's ten years in the wilderness gave him the inner resources necessary to handle his subsequent successes. His writing grows ever stronger and his playing has the authority of a master. He said: "Writing is hard work, practising is hard work, but the moment of playing is wonderful!" [IC]

Andy Sheppard (1987; Antilles); **Introductions In The Dark** (1988; Antilles). Sheppard was fully mature as a soloist when he made his first album and the performances are very assured. *Introductions* is a different statement of intent, serving notice that Sheppard will explore new structures and fresh modes of procedure; for this follow-up album he augments the debut album's quintet with vibist Orphy Robinson, Steve Lodder, guitarist Chris Watson and percussionist Dave Adams. It's a boldly ambitious move.

Soft On The Inside (1989; Antilles). Sheppard's writing for a fifteen-piece band is astonishingly adept – full of variety, incident and personal touches.

Rhythm Method (1993; Blue Note); **Delivery Suite** (1993; Blue Note). For both of these, Sheppard augments his quintet with five more musicians – trumpeter Kevin Robinson, trombonists Ashley Slater and Gary Valente, tenor saxophonist Jerry Underwood and baritone saxophonist Julian Argüelles. There's much invention in the writing, the band playing is immaculate and a lot of thought has gone into these projects – perhaps too much forethought, because there are few surprises, though "Hop Dreams" at the end of *Rhythm Method* is a gloriously elegaic improvised duet.

Learning To Wave (1998; Provocateur); **Dancing Man And Woman** (2000; Provocateur); **P.S.** (2002; Provocateur). Gorgeously, slyly polite records, full of ever wiser musical detail, minimalist wit and memorable themes. *Learning To Wave* and *Dancing Man And Woman* are essentially beautiful chamber quintet records (featuring the ever-present, ever-resourceful Steve Lodder, guitarist John Parricelli, bassists Chris Lawrence or Steve Swallow and drummer Paul Clarvis) plus guest tabla players Shalda Sahai and Kuljit Bhamra. *P.S.* is a superbly understated duet album with Parricelli.

➤➤ **Carla Bley** *(Songs With Legs).*

John Sheridan

Piano, arranger.

b. Columbus, Ohio 20 Jan 1946.

Sheridan took up piano at seven but it was hearing an LP of Benny Goodman's 1938 Carnegie Hall concert that turned him on to jazz. Clarinet lessons followed when he was ten, but the piano remained his main preoccupation and he played in his first band, The Novelaires, during his high school years (1959–64). His piano studies continued at Capital University, Columbus, but he carried on working professionally while still an undergraduate with the Ray Cincione and Howard Everitt orchestras. From 1968–72 he served with the US Navy Band in Washington DC, and then studied for a Master's Degree in Music at North Texas State University. After receiving his degree in 1977, Sheridan worked with Tommy Loy's Upper Dallas Jazz Band before joining Jim Cullum's Jazz Band (1979–2003) as its main arranger. Sheridan has also worked with Brooks Tegler, John Otto, Dan Barrett and Dave Frishberg and singer Banu Gibson and records regularly for the Arbors label with his own Dream Band. As well as his front-rank gifts as a jazz panist, Sheridan is a superb arranger with a connoisseur's ear for repertoire married to an ability to present fine material in witty and always-interesting settings. [DF]

⊙ **Get Rhythm In Your Feet** (2002; Arbors). A particularly fine set by Sheridan's Dream Band featuring a good selection of material ("Humpty Dumpty Heart", "People Like You And Me", "Walkin' By The River" and more) placed in exquisite settings and graced on half the tracks by the always-excellent Rebecca Kilgore. Trumpeter Randy Reinhart is on especially scintillating form.

Daryl Sherman

Vocals, piano.

b. Woonsocket, Rhode Island.

Underrated so far outside of America (though her international reputation is steadily growing), Sherman is a major artist whose bell-clear singing, accomplished piano-playing and encyclopedic knowledge of popular song deserve far wider recognition. Daryl began learning the piano at the age of five, and singing with her father – trombonist Sammy Sherman – from the age of thirteen. Later, via Dave McKenna, she began singing at Michael's Pub (with Bobby Hackett, Milt Hinton, Hank Jones, Red Norvo and others), and received musical guidance from George Duvivier and Sylvia Sims. After recording her first solo album *I'm A Dreamer, Aren't We All?* (1983), she sang with Artie Shaw's revived orchestra, and steadily became a familiar sight and sound at New York clubs and hotels. These included Freddy's Supper Club, Manhattan (where her second solo album *She's A Great Great Girl!* was recorded), the Fortune Garden, Tavern On The Green, Knickerbocker, and Café Pierre, as well as the Firebird Café and the Waldorf Astoria where she is currently resident.

During the 1980s her collaboration with Dick Sudhalter on a variety of projects produced the characterful and delightful albums *Friends With Pleasure* (1981) and *Mr Tram Associates* (1989). Recent career highlights include concerts with Dick Hyman at the Lincoln Center, a tribute to Ira Gershwin in Westport, Connecticut, a further season at the Algonquin (2003), seasons at London's Pizza On The Park (2002/3), guesting at the Blackpool Swinging Jazz Party 2002, and much more solo recording. [DF]

⊙ **Look What I Found** (1996; Arbors). Surrounded by Dan Barrett's summa-cum-laude group (Sandke, Dodgion, Peplowski, Robinson, with typically superb arrangements by the leader), Sherman is in jubilant charge throughout; connoisseurs' selections include an irresistible "Cheek To Cheek", the sensual "Lazy In Love", Shaw's "Any Old Time", a skipping "Many A New Day" and her own very funny "Something Brazilian".

⊙ **A Lady Must Live** (1998; After Nine). Described by Rex Reed as "an inventive tapestry of moods" and by Doug Ramsey as "her pièce de résistance", this collection features an all-star cast with cameos by Tommy Flanagan and Frank Wess, amid an all-star group with Barrett, Jay Leonhart, Ken Peplowski et al; thirteen superb songs.

⊙ **Jubilee** (2000; Arbors). A totally captivating album in which Sherman sings and plays with her own rhythm section (highspots include a latin-esque "Perdido" and hilarious "Swingtime In Honolulu") and sings with old friend Dave McKenna. Repertoire homes in on Noël Coward and Carmichael but all is delightful.

⊙ **A Hundred Million Miracles** (2003; Arbors). "No sobs, no sorrows, no sighs, simply swing!" said authority Max Wilk of this collection of Richard Rogers songs. As usual Sherman is warm, humorous and musically irresistible on fourteen selections (including the seldom-sung title track), and her guests include Houston Person, Bob Dorough and (wonderfully) Ruby Braff.

Shorty Sherock

Trumpet.

b. Minneapolis, Minnesota, 17 Nov 1915; d. 19 Feb 1980.

A student of cornet as a child, Shorty (Clarence Francis) Sherock became a fine swing trumpeter who worked early in his career with Ben Pollack (1936), then with Jimmy Dorsey, Bob Crosby, Gene Krupa, Tommy Dorsey and others before forming his own band in 1945. He rejoined Dorsey, replacing Charlie Teagarden in the Dorseylanders (1950), and then moved into studio work, playing for TV and radio. [DF]

➤➤ **Gene Krupa** *(Drum Boogie).*

Bobby Shew

Trumpet, flugelhorn, slide, piccolo, pocket trumpet, Shew-horn.

b. Albuquerque, New Mexico, 4 March 1941.

Bobby Shew (originally Robert Joratz) is largely self-taught, though he spent one year at the University of New Mexico, studying commercial art with some music classes. From 1959–60 he attended Stan Kenton clinics, then from 1964–9 he worked with the Tommy Dorsey orchestra, Woody Herman, Della Reese, Terry Gibbs, Robert Goulet, as well as in Las Vegas house bands and hotels. In the 1970s he settled in Los Angeles working in the studios, also doing jazz gigs and spending a longish period with the Toshiko Akiyoshi-Lew Tabackin big band and recording several albums with them, including *Kogun* (1974), *Tales Of A Courtesan* (1975) and *Insights* (1976). He toured as lead trumpet with Tom Jones and Paul Anka, and toured Europe and the UK with Louie Bellson's big band, appearing on some of the live recordings – *Dynamite!* (1979) and *London Scene* (1980). He also played with Neal Hefti, Don Menza, Bud Shank and Art Pepper. During the 1980s Shew started to lead his own small groups more frequently, but he also made occasional appearances with youth bands including the UK's Wigan Youth Jazz Orchestra, recording *Aim For The Heart* with them in 1987. He continues to be a busy studio musician, private teacher and conductor of jazz clinics. Influenced by Art Farmer, Dizzy Gillespie, Conte Candoli and Kenny Dorham, Shew is a fine section player and lead trumpet, and remains a gifted straight-ahead soloist, as heard on his collaboration with trombonist Carl Fontana *Heavyweights* (1995; MAMA) and Swiss saxophonist George Robert on *Live In Switzerland* (2003; TCB). He has also invented a double-belled trumpet which he calls the Shew-horn. [IC]

⊙ **Trumpets No End** (1983; Delos). Shew, with fellow trumpeter Chuck Findley and an excellent rhythm-section, glides with impeccable lyricism and invention through a couple of Clifford Brown themes and other pieces.

⊙ **Tributes To The Masters** (1995; Double-Time). Shew and a rhythm-section, along with Jamey Aebersold's exemplary saxophone, run through a programme of jazz standards by such as Gillespie, Parker, Clifford Brown, Horace Silver, Monk and Ellington.

Sahib Shihab

Baritone, alto and soprano saxophones, flute.

b. Savannah, Georgia, 23 June 1925; d. 24 Oct 1989.

Sahib Shihab (whose given name was Edmund Gregory) gained early experience with various territory bands, then studied in Boston in 1941–2. He toured (on alto, as "Eddie Gregory") with Fletcher Henderson in 1944–5 and the Roy Eldridge band in 1946. After working in Boston, he gigged and recorded in New York with Art Blakey in 1947, Thelonious Monk in 1947 and 1951, and the Tadd Dameron ten-piece band in 1949. He was out of music for a few years, then appeared on baritone with Dizzy Gillespie in 1953, Illinois Jacquet in 1954–5 (including a European tour), his own group in 1956, the Oscar Pettiford big band in 1957 and Dakota Staton in the late 1950s. He went to Europe with the Quincy Jones band in 1959–60, and settled there for the next twelve years, working as a freelance soloist and with the Kenny Clarke-Francy Boland band, with whom he played from 1961–72. In 1973 he moved to Los Angeles, and worked again in Europe and New York in the 1980s. Shihab played both flute and soprano with an individual approach, and not just for the sake of doubling. However, it was on baritone that he made his most distinctive contribution. [BP]

⊙ **And All Those Cats** (1964–70; Rearward/Schema). Various small-group sessions with members of the Clarke-Boland band, not only the leaders but Benny Bailey and Aake Persson (Johnny Griffin is mentioned but not heard). Apart from the rather empty flute-and-percussion workout "Om Mani Padme Hum" (a one-time dance-floor hit), there's much absorbing music especially when Shihab plays baritone.

Matthew Shipp

Piano, keyboards.

b. Wilmington, Delaware, 7 Dec 1960.

Shipp started on piano at the age of five, took lessons with a local church organist and learned the bass clarinet in high school. While his father sparked his interest in jazz, it was his mother's childhood friendship with Clifford Brown which led to him having some lessons from Brown's teacher, Ellis Lowery. He then studied at University of Delaware and, from 1982, the New England Conservatory, where he met saxophonist Rob Brown. Moving to New York in 1984, he worked frequently with Brown and began an ongoing musical relationship with William Parker. They have played as a duo and in each other's groups, also appearing together from 1990 into the early 2000s in David S. Ware's high-profile quartet. During the 1990s Shipp also performed with other musicians such as Roscoe Mitchell, Joe Morris and saxist Ivo Perelman, and with his String Trio featuring Parker and Mat Maneri (not to be confused with John Lindberg's String Trio Of New York). Shipp has said in an interview that "...of course Monk, Bud Powell, Andrew Hill, Paul Bley and Cecil Taylor are where I come from, but sometimes all of it feels like a straitjacket and posturing". He began the new millennium by becoming associated with the Thirsty Ear record label, as both performer and producer of their Blue Series. In tandem with this activity, he has become more involved in the use of keyboards and marrying his improvisational approach with hip-hop and electronica. [BP]

⊙ **Multiplication Table** (1997; HatART). One of the best albums in Shipp's large discography, this has William Parker and drummer Susie Ibarra in a programme that pulls in "Take The A Train", "C Jam Blues" and "Autumn Leaves", but is most notable for the leader's originals and all three musicians' improvisation.

⊙ **Equilibrium** (2002; Thirsty Ear). The first part of a trilogy focusing on Shipp's new directions. As well as bass, drums and vibes (Parker, Gerald Cleaver, Khan Jamal), the group includes FLAM on synths and general programming, and the mix is intelligent and fascinating.

➤➤ **David S. Ware** *(Flight Of I).*

Dinah Shore

Vocals.

b. Winchester, Tennesee, 1 March 1917.

Shore sang on radio in Nashville at the start of her career, then moved to New York in 1938. A year later she sang on WNEW Radio and recorded with Xavier Cugat, before attracting attention as resident singer on the *Chamber Music Society Of Lower Basin Street* radio show (1940). Soon after, she became nationally prominent on Eddie Cantor's show, and had a hit record with "Yes My Darling Daughter". In late 1941 she presented her own radio show, and rapidly became America's favourite, later touring in forces shows and appearing in films (including *Thank Your Lucky Stars* and *Up In Arms*). Her own television show carried on very successfully into the early 1960s, but with the arrival of rock'n'roll Shore's career slowed down. A new and successful morning TV show *Dinah's Place* helped re-establish her fame in the early 1970s. She is sometimes overlooked in jazz circles because of her status as an American popular icon, but Shore was first and foremost a jazz person. Even her name was adopted from the Lewis/Young/Akst standard of 1925, and her first big seller, "Blues In The Night", and her early recordings with Henry Levine, both clearly demonstrate her jazz affiliations, which were renewed in the 1950s with artists like André Previn and Red Norvo. [DF]

⊙ **You'd Be So Nice To Come Home To** (1939-42/Flapper). Excellent selection of early Shore audibly celebrating her jazz roots in tracks like "Dinah's Blues", "How Come You Do Me Like You Do" (with Paul Weston) and "Blues In The Night" (with Leonard Joy) amid twenty two more.

⊙ **NBC's Chamber Music Society Of Lower Basin Street** (1940–41; Harlequin). Amid highly crafted and spirited Dixieland surroundings (featuring Levine's splendid trumpet), Shore gently delivers jazz standards including Memphis Blues' "Loveless Love" and "Mood Indigo".

Wayne Shorter

Tenor and soprano saxophones, composer.

b. Newark, New Jersey, 25 Aug 1933.

Shorter studied music at New York University for four years, and then in the army from 1956–8. He freelanced in New York until he joined Art Blakey's Jazz Messengers in 1959, staying with the group until he joined Miles Davis in the summer of 1964. During his four years with Blakey he toured extensively in the USA, Japan and Europe and recorded several albums with the group, establishing himself as one of the most gifted of the younger saxophonists. His influences then were Sonny Rollins, John Coltrane and Coleman Hawkins, but he was already finding his own stylistic synthesis, and was also composing pieces for the Messengers. He was with Davis through six crucial years of the trumpeter's career (1964–70), and it was during this period that Shorter really found his own voice as both a player and composer. Blakey's hard-driving, straightahead rhythms had brought out the muscularity in Shorter's tenor playing, but the greater freedom of the Davis rhythm-section allowed him to explore new emotional and technical dimensions. He said, "With Miles I felt like a cello, I felt viola, I felt liquid, dot-dash . . . and colours really started coming." The muscularity was still there when he wanted it, of course, as were the technique and speed of execution but, particularly on the studio albums with Davis, he began to practise a kind of understatement, often projecting an urbane melancholy and tenderness. Several of his compositions also bore these qualities, and his sound and style had a pervasive influence in the jazz world during the later 1960s and the early 1970s. His influence might have been even greater if the album he recorded with Davis in December 1965, *Live At The Plugged Nickel*, had been released at the time instead of more than ten years after the event. On this his playing is extraordinary; the influences of Coltrane, Rollins and Ornette Coleman have been totally absorbed, and Shorter shows a devastating originality which covers the entire technical and emotional spectrum; on solo after solo he seems to be reappraising the whole current saxophone vocabulary.

His compositions were an important part of the Davis repertoire until 1967, and subsequently several of them became part of the standard jazz repertoire – "ESP", "Footprints", "Dolores", "Nefertiti" and "Pinocchio" among others. Shorter left Davis in the spring of 1970, and later that year, together with Joe Zawinul, formed Weather Report. Shorter is more a player who composes, and Zawinul more a composer who plays, and in its first stages Weather Report's approach was quite open and loose, featuring electronics and much rhythmic and tonal abstraction. But the whole tendency of jazz in the early 1970s was away from the overemphasis on improvisation which had unbalanced the music in the 1960s, and towards a greater emphasis on composition, clear tonalities and coherent rhythms. As Weather Report moved gradually in this direction, Shorter's role became reduced in it, with less solo space and fewer of his compositions in the band's repertoire. Explaining in 1982 why he was writing so little for the band, he said, "Miles used to say that I was a great short story writer, but now we have epics and sagas." Weather Report disbanded in 1985. During his time with Davis in the 1960s, and with Weather Report in the 1970s and 1980s, Shorter also recorded independently under his own name, writing most or all of the music for these albums, which is

Wayne Shorter

generally less radical and more conservative than the music of his two longtime associates, and often tinged with a Brazilian influence. Shorter seems, paradoxically, at his most independent and individual when functioning under the umbrella of a strong leader such as Blakey or Miles Davis. Certainly, his composing and playing flourished with Miles, and Shorter's most productive recording period as leader also coincides with his association with Davis, 1964–70. However, Shorter is incapable of shallowness and, whether as leader or sideman, playing or composing, or both, his music always has the larger view and his recent output – *Footprints Live!* and *Alegria* (see below) – indicates that his story is far from over. He is something of a visionary, with a knowledge of other cultures and other musics, and his striking use of imagery in conversation also points to his unusual sensibilities and viewpoint.

His playing and composing have inspired countless musicians on all instruments. With Davis, Shorter first played soprano saxophone on *In A Silent Way* and *Bitches Brew* (both 1969), producing such an ethereal, seductively forlorn sound that he probably started the whole rise to prominence of the soprano with electronic fusion groups. He has appeared at all major festivals around the world with his various associates, and has won many polls in the USA and internationally. [IC]

⊙ **The VeeJay Years** (1959–60; Affinity). This combination of Shorter's first two albums, *Blues A La Carte* and *Second Genesis*, shows what a fine composer he already was, and that the Coltrane influence on his playing was strong.

⊙ **Night Dreamer** (1964; Blue Note). With Lee Morgan and Coltrane associates McCoy Tyner, Reginald Workman and Elvin Jones, Shorter's writing is more poetic but gets down to basics with "Charcoal Blues" and Coltrane-like balladry on "Virgo". A very fine pre-Miles album.

⊙ **The Best Of Wayne Shorter** (1964–7; Blue Note). This compilation is a useful introduction for newcomers to Shorter's work.

⊙ **Speak No Evil** (1965; Blue Note); **Juju** (1965; Blue Note); **The Soothsayer** (1965; Blue Note). Shorter joined Davis in the late summer of 1964, and his floodgates were opened – 1965 was a bumper year, producing these three fine albums and the deleted *The All-Seeing Eye* and *Etcetera*. *Speak No Evil*, with Freddie Hubbard, Herbie Hancock, Ron Carter and Elvin Jones, is a classic album in terms of both composition and improvisation, and has been inspirational for many musicians.

⊙ **Adam's Apple** (1966; Blue Note). More innovative composing, including Shorter's classic reworking of the blues "Footprints", and other structural and rhythmic novelties that stretch the quartet of Shorter, Hancock, Workman and Joe Chambers.

⊙ **Super Nova** (1969; Blue Note). *Super Nova* was recorded a month after *Bitches Brew* and the residual dynamism hangs over this excellent session, which has John McLaughlin working with the anarchic Sonny Sharrock, plus Jack DeJohnette, Airto Moreira, Chick Corea, Miroslav Vitous and a vocalist. Seeds of Weather Report are evident.

⊙ **Footprints Live!** (2001; Verve); **Alegria** (2003; Verve). The music documented on *Footprints Live!* (featuring the superbly sparky acoustic quartet comprising Shorter with Danilo Perez on piano, John Patitucci on bass and Brian Blade on drums addressing some of Wayne's 60s themes) was received as something of a renaissance for the saxophonist. If the studio follow-up *Alegria* – further reworking of established Shorter music, this time with a multi-ensemble approach – doesn't quite hit the heights of his mid-60s peak, it's not far off. The man has plenty to tell us yet.

➤➤ **Art Blakey** *(Free For All)*; **Miles Davis** *(ESP; In A Silent Way; Bitches Brew)*; **Joe Zawinul** *(Weather Report; I Sing The Body Electric; Black Market; Heavy Weather; Night Passage)*.

Ramesh Shotham

South Indian percussion.

b. Madras, India, 7 May 1948.

Shotham's mother was an amateur violinist. Shotham himself is largely self-taught, but studied for two years at the Karnataka College of Percussion, Bangalore; he also took a BSc in zoology. With his brother, Suresh Shotham, he formed a group called Human Bondage in the late 1960s, which lasted for seven years and won several awards in India. He played at the 1978 and 1980 Jazz Yatras in Bombay with Louis Banks (keyboards) and Braz Gonsalves (reeds), forming the Jazz Yatra septet (later called Sangam) with them. Sangam toured Europe in

1980–81, playing festivals in Prague and Warsaw and recording in Germany, and in 1983 toured with Charlie Mariano. Shotham has lived in Europe since 1981, working with various people including Dutch flautist Chris Hinze, the group Embryo and Norwegian Jon Balke. In the 1990s he was heard on recordings by artists as diverse as saxist Steve Coleman, oud player Rabih Abou-Khalil and pianist Matthias Frey. In 2003 he was part of the acoustic guitar and percussion group Tri Continental. He has conducted workshops all over Germany and was artist in residence at Bayreuth University. His favourites include Tony Williams, Elvin Jones, Billy Hart, Shannon Jackson, and several Indian and South American percussionists. [IC]

➤➤ **Charlie Mariano** *(Live)*.

Don Sickler

Trumpet, arranger, producer.

b. Spokane, Washington, 6 Jan 1944.

Sickler's mother played piano, organ and accordion, and Don started on piano at age four. Studying trumpet from the age of ten, he formed his own group and big band, playing for high-school dances. He attended two Stan Kenton Summer Music Camps, earned a BA at Gonzaga University and, encouraged by Donald Byrd, moved to the Manhattan School of Music for his Master's in 1970, while playing in lofts, shows and rehearsal bands. He worked in music publishing and transcribed solos by Joe Henderson and John Coltrane, setting up his own company in 1979 to copyright and publish jazz classics. With Philly Joe Jones he set up the Dameronia band, also directing retrospective concerts of Gil Evans, Kenny Dorham (both in 1983), the Blue Note label (1985) and Monk (1986–7). Working with T.S. Monk since 1991, Sickler has also arranged, directed and/or co-produced numerous projects by Joe Henderson (earning him four Grammy awards), Clifford Jordan, Jack Walrath, Jackie McLean and J.J. Johnson. Inspired especially by Philly Joe, Dameron, Hank Mobley and Johnny Griffin, he loves all the great trumpeters and feels his own playing is influenced by Dorham, Art Farmer, Freddie Hubbard and Booker Little. [BP]

➤➤ **T.S. Monk** *(Monk On Monk)*.

Ben Sidran

Piano, vocals.

b. Chicago, 14 Aug 1943.

Sidran is an eclectic performer who combines playing and singing with a keen interest in writing and talking about jazz (he has published two books, *Black Talk* and *Talking Jazz*). A member of the Steve Miller band early on, Sidran was in Britain during the late 1960s and worked with British rock players like Charlie Watts and Peter Frampton (both of whom guested on his first album, *Feel Your Groove*, in 1971). Since then he has recorded prolifically, mixing jazz dates like *The Doctor Is In* (1977) with fusion undertakings like *On The Cool Side* (1985), with Steve Miller and Dr John. In 1990 Sidran released a debut album on the Go Jazz label, followed by a multi-CD issue for Bulldog Productions. Other recent albums convey a feeling of artistic arrival, suggesting that Sidran has found exactly where he wants his music to be. [DF]

⊙ **Cool Paradise** (1990; Go Jazz). Featuring Bob Malach, Billy Peterson, Gordy Knudson and Ricky Peterson (Sidran's working band since 1985), this album is a delight, from the cool cocktail of the title track to the ingenious multitracked vocal passages of "She Steps Into A Dream".

⊙ **Go Jazz All Stars** (1991; Go Jazz). Also available on video, this set teams Sidran and his band with kindred spirit Georgie Fame for fun duos as well as solo showcases for both of them; Sidran's hilarious and hard-rocking "Too Hot To Touch" is outstanding.

Julian Siegel

Tenor and soprano saxes, clarinet and bass clarinet, double bass.

b. Nottingham, England, 13 May 1966.

Julian Siegel's interest in jazz was fostered by his father, a professional singer in pre-war Poland who toured the Middle East during World War II entertaining Allied troops. He grew up with a parental record collection which included Count Basie, Duke Ellington, Eddie "Lockjaw" Davis, Ben Webster and Joe Williams, alongside lots of classical music. At school Siegel played in wind bands, orchestras and choirs, before gaining a degree in music at the University of East Anglia, Norwich, in 1987. After graduating, he remained in Norwich playing with a quintet for four years, before moving to London in 1991. In 1996 he formed Partisans, co-led by guitarist Phil Robson with Gene Calderazzo on drums and Thad Kelly on bass. He and Robson write all Partisans' repertoire and the group remain one of the most exciting outfits on the London scene with two well-received albums to its name – Partisans for Efz and *Sourpuss* for Babel in 2001.

Since 2001 Siegel has also run his own quartet featuring pianist Liam Noble, bassist Jeremy Brown and Gary Husband on drums, and in 2002 the group produced their first album, *Close Up*. Siegel's superb musicianship means that he appears regularly with other bands, including Stan Sulzmann's Big Band featuring Kenny Wheeler, the Creative Jazz Orchestra with John Taylor, Django Bates' Delightful Precipice, Colin Town's Mask Orchestra, Julian Argüelles' Octet, Jazz Jamaica big band with Andy Sheppard and Orphy Robinson, and Phil Robson's Beyond the Net Curtains. He has also played with the singers Norma Winstone, Cleo Laine and Jacqui Dankworth, and with pianists such as Kirk Lightsey,

BOB MEYRICK

Julian Siegel with fellow Partisans

Robert Mitchell and Nikki Iles. As well as being a skilled horn player Siegel is a highly proficient bassist, and has worked as such with Bobby Wellins, Iain Ballamy and Christine Tobin among others. [IC]

Partisans

⦿ **Sourpuss** (2001; Babel). Partisans is a hot group whose second album exudes confidence and imagination in equal measures. Siegel really lets rip on the title track, but he is no less effective in more thoughtful moments like his own "Passacaglia". This is very much a collection of equals, however, with Siegel and Robson's inspiration kept in check by the tightness of Calderazzo and Kelly's underpinning.

Julian Siegel

⦿ **Close Up** (2002; Sound). A marvellous album that reveals Siegel for the star that he is. All but two of the nine tracks are his own compositions, beginning with "City Of Dreams", which features some great solo work from Liam Noble and some stylishly forceful drumming from Gary Husband. Other highpoints include an outing for Siegel's quirky bass clarinet playing on "Hero To The New UFO" and a highly sensitive rendition of Dizzy Gillespie's "Con Alma".

➤➤ **Phill Robson** *(Partisans).*

Frank Signorelli

Piano, composer.

b. New York, 24 May 1901; d. 9 Dec 1975.

A close friend and associate of Phil Napoleon for well over thirty years, Frank Signorelli had a comfortably successful career which began when he assembled the Original Memphis Five to play at the Balconnades Ballroom on 66th Street, New York, in 1917. From then on he stayed busy, working with Napoleon, Joe Venuti and Adrian Rollini's New Yorker orchestra, as well as working freelance and in studios. During the 1930s he became a highly successful songwriter: "I'll Never Be The Same", "Stairway To The Stars" and "A Blues Serenade" are all Signorelli tunes. During the swing era and after he was a frequent soloist along 52nd Street, worked with a re-formed Original Dixieland Jazz Band and Paul Whiteman, and by the late 1940s was working Nick's Club with Bobby Hackett and a re-formed Original Memphis Five, which continued to get together for records, radio and TV all through the 1950s. A fine pianist who worked in a style reminiscent of Bob Zurke, Signorelli should be better known than he is. [DF]

Connee Boswell and the Original Memphis Five

⦿ **In Hi-Fi** (1956; RCA). Now rare, this is a worthy example of Signorelli's playing later in his career, amid excellent company including Billy Butterfield, Miff Mole, Jimmy Lytell and the great Connee Boswell.

Eric Silk

Banjo, leader.

b. London, 19 May 1926; d. 17 April 1982.

Silk worked first with John Haim's Jellyroll Kings, then after Haim's death assembled his own Southern Jazz Band in 1949 for a sensational appearance at Cooks Ferry Inn. Hand-picked to play post-Armstrong New Orleans jazz, Silk's first band contained clarinettist Teddy Layton and trumpeter Spencer Dunmore (soon to be replaced by a longterm partner, cornettist Dennis Field, and – for a while – Alan Littlejohn). In 1951 his group began a long residency at the Red Lion, Leytonstone, then played a succession of pioneering Riverboat Shuffles, and through the 1950s produced many records and broadcasts of their scholarly and well-rehearsed repertoire. The last of the determined amateurs ("I'm convinced that to turn professional you have to turn commercial," he said), Silk gained a devoted following and produced at least one classic British LP, *Off The Cuff*. By the end of the 1960s Field had left (replaced by Phil Mason), and in 1973 Silk disbanded; trombonist Alan Dean formed the Gene Allen Jazzmen from former band members, including keymen Arthur Bird and Steve Nice. Silk became ill with pleurisy and died of a heart attack at only 55. [DF]

⊙ **Eric Silk And His Southern Jazz Band** (1956–8; Lake). Silk at the zenith of Britain's Jazz Revival; his band includes the (very) hot cornettist Dennis Field, Ron Weatherburn (piano) and a youthful Pete Strange on his first recording date. Neat and focused classic jazz.

Alan Silva

Bass, violin, cello, piano, synthesizer.

b. Bermuda, 22 Jan 1939.

Alan Treadwell Silva moved from Bermuda to Brooklyn, New York, at the age of five, where he grew up studying violin, piano, drums and trumpet (the latter including lessons with Donald Byrd). He turned to bass in college. Silva was one of the primary bassists in 60s free jazz, participating in the legendary October Revolution In Jazz, playing and recording with Albert Ayler, Sun Ra, Archie Shepp, the Jazz Composers' Orchestra, among others. Perhaps his most notable appearances from this period were on Cecil Taylor's *Unit Structures* and *Conquistador!* (both 1966; Blue Note). Though primarily known as a rough-and-ready, absolutely outré bassist, Silva played violin on Sunny Murray's 1969 record *Big Chief* (Pathé), and his debut as a leader on ESP records found him playing fiddle, cello and piano, no bass. Silva eventually settled in France, which he perceived to be more open to his music. There he recorded with his large Celestrial Communication Orchestra (which included Shepp, Anthony Braxton and Leroy Jenkins) and recorded for the French BYG label. He worked frequently with expressionist saxophonist Frank Wright, future Steve Lacy pianist Bobby Few, and drummer Muhammed Ali (brother of Rashied) in a rotating ex-patriot ensemble that recorded a multivolume series called *Center Of The World* (1975; Sun). In 1980, he played with Taylor on *It Is In The Brewing Luminous* (hat Art). Into the 80s, Silva largely disappeared from the international music scene, popping up in 1986 with the Globe Unity Orchestra on *20th Anniversary* (FMP). But surprisingly enough, he surfaced again in the 90s playing synthesizer – and extremely well at that – and releasing *Sweethearts In A Drugstore* (1996; Ninth World). [JC]

⊙ **In The Tradition** (1996; In Situ). Recorded live in 1993, this trio with British drummer Roger Turner and German trombonist Johannes Bauer (the latter also on *Sweethearts*) finds a rejuvenated Silva playing extremely hot synth – the first cut is a five-minute model of high-intensity interactive free improvisation. Fascinating rebirth on a new axe!

Horace Silver

Piano, composer.

b. Norwalk, Connecticut, 2 Sept 1928.

After gigging locally on tenor as well as piano, Horace Silver and his trio toured with Stan Getz, who became the first person to record Silver tunes in 1950–51. He made appearances in New York, often at Birdland, backing Terry Gibbs, Coleman Hawkins, Getz, Lester Young and others in 1952–3. He started recording under his own name with Art Blakey in 1952–3, and made albums under Blakey and Miles Davis in 1954. Silver's own quintet recording of 1954 led to the formation of the Jazz Messengers, using the same personnel from 1955–6. The departure of Horace, Hank Mobley, Donald Byrd (initially for work with Max Roach) and Doug Watkins enabled Silver to form a regular quintet, replacing Blakey (who kept the group's name) with Louis Hayes. Apart from spending part of the late 1970s and early 1980s in semi-retirement, he has continued to lead a quintet ever since, including, at various times, Art Farmer in 1957–8, Blue Mitchell from 1958–64, Joe Henderson from 1964–6, Woody Shaw from 1965–7, Randy and Michael Brecker in 1973–4, and, on record, Eddie Harris in 1981–2. After recording albums on Blue Note for 28 years, some of which from the mid-1970s had large ensemble backings and/or featured singers, Horace formed his own company, Silveto Records, in 1981, and then signed to Columbia in 1993. Following serious health problems in that year, he resumed performing a limited number of engagements in 1994. Two years later he recorded for Impulse!/Verve with a septet, and for the first time toured with this line-up, including in Europe.

His composing ability is pre-eminently as a stylistic consolidator, although one less academically inclined would be hard to find. In the mid-1950s he created the "hard bop" writing style virtually single-handed, by taking for granted that even a fairly "mainstream" rhythm-section would be heavily bop-influenced and contrasting this with simple swing-era phrasing for the frontline instruments. The rapid acceptance of his "Opus De Funk" (one of the first uses of the word in a tune title) and "Doodlin'" by artists such as Woody Herman and Ray Charles illustrates the extent of this backward-looking fusion.

Horace Silver

The gospel influence of "The Preacher" was achieved subtly (compared to others' later excesses) with a melody and associated riffs which had a natural, built-in back-beat. His equally fine "Sister Sadie" (1959) bore a remarkable resemblance to the 1930s pop song "Do You Wanna Jump, Children?" recorded by Count Basie and Cab Calloway, among others.

This joyously conservative approach stems directly from Horace's piano style (compare, for instance, the trio and quintet versions of "Quicksilver" on the 1953 album below and Art Blakey's *A Night At Birdland*). Even when a tune is voiced in two-part harmony (for example "Ecaroh" or "Silver's Serenade"), it turns out to be just the top two notes of the full two-handed piano chords. Sometimes on record it seems that his improvisations flirt too much with the obvious, but to witness in the flesh their ease of construction – even down to the quotations – is completely captivating. Whether soloing or backing, Horace is first and foremost a rhythm player and has enjoyed excellent partnerships with Kenny Clarke (on records) and with Art Blakey; like Blakey, his accompaniment can be almost overwhelming but its flowing compulsion cushions the soloists and forces them to say what they have to say. [BP]

⊙ **Horace Silver Trio** (1952–3; Blue Note). These earliest recordings under his own name feature dynamically simplified ("hardened") bebop just waiting to influence horn players. Blakey is a key factor in the original versions of "Ecaroh" and "Opus De Funk".

⊙ **Horace Silver And The Jazz Messengers** (1954–5; Blue Note). United for two record dates (though they were already working together) was the first version of the famous group Blakey later took over. Hank Mobley and Kenny Dorham shine on "The Preacher" and "Doodlin'", the latter also having a stunning, medium-slow solo by Blakey.

⊙ **Blowin' The Blues Away** (1959; Blue Note). One of Silver's most famous quintets (featuring Blue Mitchell and Junior Cook) gets into stride with the exhilarating title track, "Sister Sadie" and the now standard ballad "Peace". Providing continuity with earlier work, there are also two trio tracks without Mitchell and Cook.

⊙ **Song For My Father** (1963–4; Blue Note). Augmented with extra material from the period, this CD reissues Silver's most popular tune ever and other modal-influenced numbers such as the fine "Que Pasa". Most tracks introduce the then new quintet with Carmell Jones and the bustling Joe Henderson.

➤➤ **Art Blakey** *(A Night At Birdland, Vols. 1 & 2)*; **Miles Davis** *(Walkin'; Bags' Groove)*.

Omer Simeon

Clarinet.

b. New Orleans, 21 July 1902; d. 17 Sept 1959.

One of the most gifted of Lorenzo Tio's pupils and one of the great classic jazz clarinettists, Simeon worked from 1923–7 with Charlie Elgar's Creole band and in 1926 recorded classic titles with Jelly Roll Morton, including "The Chant" and "Black Bottom Stomp". After more work with Morton, King Oliver, Luis Russell and Erskine Tate, Simeon worked for most of the 1930s with Earl Hines, who remembers him as "a very quiet sort of fellow and serious about his work. But whenever we went to New Orleans his people used to open the doors and we'd have a great time at his house." From Hines he went on to work for Coleman Hawkins and Walter Fuller (1941) before joining Jimmy Lunceford (1942–50). In the 1950s Simeon recorded widely and to great effect with Wilbur de Paris's fine band; he died of throat cancer at 57. [DF]

⊙ **Omer Simeon 1926–29** (Jazz Archives). Excellent collection of Simeon with Morton, King Oliver's Dixie Syncopators, Jabbo Smith, Reuben Reeves, the Dixie Rhythm Kings and Simeon's trio.

Norman Simmons

Piano, arranger.

b. Chicago, 6 Oct 1929.

Norman (Sarney) Simmons had regular work in the 1950s backing soloists visiting Chicago, and this led to touring with singers Dakota Staton, Ernestine Anderson, Carmen McRae (in 1961), Betty Carter and, from 1979, Joe Williams. He arranged three albums for Johnny Griffin and worked with the "Lockjaw" Davis-Griffin group in 1960. He is little known as a piano soloist despite making recordings under his own name, although he is a superior accompanist. His writing contribution to the album below, including superb arrangements such as "Wade In The Water" (which preceded the Ramsey Lewis version), deserves wider recognition. [BP]

Johnny Griffin

⊙ **Big Soul Band** (1960; Riverside/OJC). Earlier and more successful than most of the Oliver-Nelson-backs-big-names-with-big-bands, this is a winning combination of functional but inventive arrangements for a tentet and the ebullient work of master soloist Griffin.

Nina Simone

Vocals, piano.

b. Tryon, North Carolina, 21 Feb 1933; d. 21 April 2003.

A performer of raw power, Nina Simone (Eunice Waymon) studied piano at the Juilliard School before making recordings with Bethlehem Records which showed strong jazz leanings – including an emotional version of "I Loves You Porgy" which became a hit. Later well-known Simone performances included "I Put A Spell On You", "Gin House Blues", "Don't Let Me Be Misunderstood", "Ain't Got No – I Got Life" and a cover of the Bee Gees' "To Love Somebody", a range clearly indicating that Simone chose to draw her inspiration from any source she found suitable. Yet she regularly returned to jazz material over the years, including (for random examples) tracks like "Fine And Mellow", Willard Robison's "Don't Smoke In Bed", "I Want A Little Sugar In My Bowl", "Little Girl Blue" and "My Baby Just Cares For Me", which charted in Britain after its use in a perfume advert in 1987. The determinedly cheerful tone of this last song hints at the hard edge that exists close to the surface of some of Simone's work, an edge which – combined with her strident political militancy – tended to reduce the appeal of her work for some people. She remained however, a striking performer and a star of international standing. Her death was widely mourned in and beyond the jazz community. [DF]

Zoot Sims

Tenor, soprano; also alto saxophone.

b. Inglewood, California, 29 Oct 1925; d. 23 March 1985.

Zoot (John) Sims toured with several big bands during World War II, but also did small-group work with Sid Catlett and with Bill Harris (including his recording debut with Harris's pianist Joe Bushkin) in 1944. After army service he was a member of the Benny Goodman band in 1946–7, together with his trombonist brother Ray Sims (b. 18 Jan 1921). He then joined Woody Herman from 1947–9, establishing a reputation alongside fellow tenorists Stan Getz and Al Cohn, who also worked with him for Artie Shaw in 1949–50. He made several European tours with Goodman (in 1950, 1958, 1962, 1972, 1976), with Stan Kenton in 1953, with the Gerry Mulligan sextet in 1956 and big band in 1960, with the "Jazz From Carnegie Hall" group in 1958, and with Jazz At The Philharmonic in 1967 and 1975. He also took part in reunion concerts with Herman in 1972 and 1978. For the rest of the time, Sims was a freelance soloist, often (from 1957 onwards) in a two-tenor team with Al Cohn. He was the first US performer to play a season at Ronnie Scott's, in 1961, and returned several times between then and 1982. He made his final tour of Scandinavia late in 1984 after hospitalization and diagnosis of his terminal cancer.

Zoot's tenor playing was one of the most delightful outgrowths of Lester Young's influence. While less emotionally ambiguous than Lester, Sims absorbed the rhythmic strengths of the parent style into his own self-propelled lines. Always intensely melodic, he developed over the decades a tone that was superbly sleek though never flamboyant. This transferred well to the soprano, which he took up in the 1970s and which he turned into a much gentler instrument than in the hands of its previous practitioners. During his final years, his already economical approach became more spare and astringent than ever. [BP]

Zoot Sims

⊙ **Zoot!** (1956; Riverside/OJC). Prolifically recorded during the early twelve-inch LP boom, Zoot could just blow a whole album into shape as quickly as Erroll Garner. Joined here by trumpeter Nick Travis and pianist George Handy, Sims takes on a couple of standards and uses his alto on a couple of Handy originals.

⊙ **If I'm Lucky** (1977; Pablo/OJC). From a series of late albums featuring Jimmy Rowles, this is an informal session of mainly standards including the funky "I Wonder Where Our Love Has Gone" to the sprightly but laid-back "I Hear A Rhapsody".

Zoot Sims and Al Cohn

⊙ **Zoot Case** (1982; Sonet). A last stand, as far as recording is concerned, for the 25-year-long duo, which did its cooperative but not combative thing in front of any rhythm-section that could play straight down the middle.

➤➤ **Al Cohn** *(You'N' Me).*

Herman Leonard

Zoot Sims

Frank Sinatra

Vocals.

b. Hoboken, New Jersey, 12 Dec 1915; d. 14 May 1998.

Sinatra first attracted attention when he won a New York radio talent contest for Major Edward Bowes's *Amateur Hour* in 1935, and after radio work (including WNEW's *Dance Parade*) he joined Harry James (1939) and Tommy Dorsey (1940–42) before embarking on a solo career. His first solo hits were made with Axel Stordahl in 1943, the year in which he starred in the musicals *Reveille With Beverly* and *Higher And Higher*; they were followed by *Step Lively* (1944), *Anchors Aweigh* (1945), *It Happened In Brooklyn* (1947), *Take Me Out to the Ball Game* and of course *On The Town* (both 1949). Sinatra's career flagged slightly in the late 1940s and early 1950s, but was revitalized in 1954 by his appearance in *From Here To Eternity*, and from the middle of the decade his teaming with Nelson Riddle produced a string of classic albums for Capitol, including *Songs For Swingin' Lovers*. From the 1960s Sinatra weathered changing musical fashion with a mixture of resignation and inspiration – later hits like "That's Life" and "My Way" revealed that his undimmed talent just needed the material to match it. In the 1980s and 1990s his regular re-emergences proved that although he had done it all, he could do it again wherever necessary.

Frank Sinatra and Bing Crosby are the greatest popular male singers of the twentieth century, and both of them grew up amid the burgeoning culture of jazz, reflecting its approaches and using its material. With both, the jazz element to their performance tends to depend on the musical company they are in – Sinatra, for example, sounds like a jazz singer with Count Basie's orchestra, less so when singing with Axel Stordahl's strings. But whereas Crosby's musical approach was often freshened up when he sang in the surroundings of Dixieland or with Louis Armstrong, Sinatra's chemistry worked differently. Singing with the Metronome All Stars or with Louis on TV shows he sounds as if he is making the best of an ill-fitting suit: Sinatra's immense intensity and tenderness seem wasted in less tailored jazz formats, whereas for Crosby it was that very informality which raised his game.

The best of Sinatra's arrangers, Nelson Riddle, understood the precise science of his singer's approach, weaving arrangements that fitted them to perfection, and adding the odd thread of jazz (such as Harry Edison's muted trumpet) as appropriate, for a dash of colour. The result was that Sinatra's performances lay on the music like jewels on velvet, unimpeded by intrusive solos. When, in "I Get A Kick Out Of You", Sinatra sings the words "and I suddenly turn and see – your fabulous face", the arrangement lets you see the turn as clearly as you could see him perform the action on stage. Such crafted interpretive moments go some way to explain why Sinatra seldom invited jazz musicians into his company to share the spotlight. But for all that, Sinatra was a superlative swing singer whose vocabulary compared with that of some of the greatest jazz musicians. [DF]

HERMAN LEONARD

Frank Sinatra

Tommy Dorsey

⊙ **Learn To Croon** (1940–42; Buddha). Sinatra sings with amazing assurance, and a youthful smoothness of tone, on this collection of radio broadcasts. The influence of Bing Crosby is still apparent – especially on tracks like "Blue Moon" and "East Of The Sun" – but it's all wonderfully fresh and lively with some great playing from a fine Dorsey band, which includes Bunny Berigan and Buddy Rich among the personnel.

Frank Sinatra

⊙ **Songs For Swingin' Lovers** (1955–6; Capitol). That this is most people's candidate for Sinatra's greatest album is due in no small part to Riddle's wonderful arrangements, which are lush but perfectly judged in terms of balance and taste. Frank Edison's keening, echoing trumpet reaches perfection on masterpieces like "You're Getting To Be A Habit With Me", "I've Got You Under My Skin" and "We'll Be Together Again", and Sinatra's phrasing and sheer style are always impeccable.

Count Basie

⊙ **Sinatra-Basie** (1962; Warner). Of the three albums Sinatra made with Count Basie this is easily the best – despite a little vocal roughness around the edges. The two artists sound made for each other, and Sinatra really swings in a collection of brilliantly arranged classics that includes "Pennies From Heaven", "Learnin' The Blues", and a sparkling rendition of "I Won't Dance" that takes the breath away.

Zutty Singleton

Drums.

b. Bunkie, Louisiana, 14 May 1898; d. 14 July 1975.

Zutty (Arthur James) Singleton was one of the most influential of all classic jazz drummers: he may have been the first to develop the idea of extended drum solos; he developed certain percussive effects, for example the clicking temple-blocks and tiny choke cymbals that adorn records such as Louis Armstrong's "My Monday Date" and "West End Blues"; he was the first to introduce brushes to jazz drum vocabulary; and he made a big impact on later drummers such as Cliff Leeman (who copied the "tip" or "ride" cymbal from Singleton) and Stan Greig. As if this were not enough, Singleton was always one of the personalities of the jazz era: "the senior senator of the jazz community" in New Orleans (according to Milt Hinton) and a man who was held in respectful regard by all his fellows, including Louis Armstrong. "Even now," said Hinton in the 1960s, "Louis looks up to Zutty and Zutty looks down to Louis. Even though Zutty isn't doing very well."

Singleton never worked much for Louis Armstrong (once at least he was dropped from a band that Armstrong was leading at Connie's Inn) but this may be because he was – rather like Sid Catlett – too much of a leader for Armstrong. "If you're not in a band with Zutty," said Barney Bigard, significantly, "he's the greatest guy in the world!" Singleton's approach to music strongly resembled Catlett's. He was as happy playing bebop as Dixieland (on Slim Gaillard's "Slim's Jam" he can be heard tapping away alongside Dizzy Gillespie and Charlie Parker), he was a great show drummer and, like Catlett and Baby Dodds, heard drums as musical sounds. But perhaps more than either of them, Singleton was by vocation a leader.

One of his first bands in New Orleans, at the Orchard Club, featured Louis Armstrong and by the early 1930s he had worked with most of the biggest names in New York, too, but later in the decade, for whatever reason, he moved back to Chicago (his career would have fared better in New York) to work with Carroll Dickerson (whose name was ten years out of fashion), as well as with younger lions such as Roy Eldridge.

In 1937 he came back to New York and was often bandleading there until 1943, when he moved out to Los Angeles to take a quartet into Billy Berg's. That year he made the first of three films, *Stormy Weather* with Bill Robinson, Fats Waller and Lena Horne (the others were *New Orleans* with Louis Armstrong and Billie Holiday in 1946, and *Turned-Up Toes* in 1949). Until the 1950s he regularly led bands of his own as well as working for leaders such as Eddie Condon and Nappy Lamare; after that he spent time in Europe with Bill Coleman, Mezz Mezzrow and others, and finally came back to New York, where he worked clubs including Jimmy Ryan's until the late 1960s. [DF]

Bill Coleman

⊙ **Rarities** (1952; Rarities). Hard to find but worth the effort: Singleton with Bill Coleman's band at Salle Pleyel in Paris, featured on his speciality "Drum Face".

>> **Jelly Roll Morton** *(The Last Sessions)*; **Buster Bailey** *(1925–40)*.

Sirone

Bass.

b. Atlanta, Georgia, 28 Sept 1940.

Born Norris Jones (the name he worked under until the early 70s), Sirone played with tenor saxophonist George Adams while still in Atlanta. In 1966, he moved to New York, prompted by John Coltrane, with whom he briefly worked. In his new home, he quickly became one of the most in-demand free-jazz bass players, recording with saxophonist Gato Barbieri on his debut *In Search Of The Mystery* (1967; ESP), saxophonist Noah Howard on *At Judson Hall* (1966; ESP), and guitarist Sonny Sharrock on *Black Woman* (1969; Vortex), among others. As Sirone, he played from 1971–7 with the Revolutionary Ensemble, a ground-breaking trio with Leroy Jenkins on violin and Jerome Cooper on percussion; this group recorded for ESP, Re, India Navigation and A&M. In the late 70s he was a member of the Cecil Taylor Unit, playing all of the classic recordings for New World and hat Art. In the 1980s, Sirone worked once again with Adams, appearing on *Nightingale* (1988; Blue Note) and with the tenorman as a member of James "Blood" Ulmer's group Phalanx. He also recorded with Charles Gayle and Billy Bang in 1988 but his presence in the 90s – a brief reunion with Cecil Taylor in 1993 notwithstanding – was not as significant as it was in the previous 25 years. [JC]

>> **Gato Barbieri** *(In Search Of The Mystery)*; **Marion Brown** *(Why Not?)*.

Original Phalanx (1987; DIW). Sirone has one of the hugest bass sounds in contemporary jazz – well documented on this date with Adams, Ulmer and drummer Rashied Ali. He burbles, soars, generates endless energy, and offers two of his original compositions to boot.

Noble Sissle

Leader, vocals, composer.

b. Indianapolis, Indiana, 10 July 1889; d. 17 Dec 1975.

Noble Lee Sissle is remembered primarily as a bandleader and solo performer of the 1920s (when he recorded prolifically for Victor, OKeh and other companies) and as the highly gifted composer who collaborated with Eubie Blake, most notably in 1921 on the monumentally successful *Shuffle Along*, the first all-black Broadway revue. His orchestras, usually formed as backing groups for his own routines, often contained famous jazzmen: a shortlist includes Buster Bailey, Tommy Ladnier, Frank Goudie, Sidney Bechet, Chauncey Haughton, Wilbert Kirk and singer Billie Banks. Sissle did little recording after the 1920s and consequently tends to remain a shadowy figure; Sidney Bechet said that Sissle became precoccupied more with himself than with his sidemen, and Earle Warren added a possible confirmation – "I didn't care for the way he dominated his men". Sissle remained highly successful, however, until the 1960s, by which time he was running not only a band but his own nightclub and publishing company. [DF]

➤➤ **Eubie Blake** *(Wizard Of The Ragtime Piano Vol. 1).*

Len Skeat

Bass.

b. London, 9 Feb 1937.

Known as "The Time Lord", Len Skeat's career began in the late 1950s and by the early 1960s he was working with Eddie Thompson's trio (a chair he was to occupy continuously until Thompson's death in 1986). Skeat has at times worked with Ted Heath's band, in Stephane Grappelli's trio, and with a formidable list of American visitors, including Ruby Braff, "Lockjaw" Davis, Ben Webster, Harry Edison, Billy Eckstine, Scott Hamilton, Joe Newman, Lou Rawls, Peggy Lee, Bob Wilber, Lionel Hampton and Helen Merrill. Skeat has also been to America to work with Bobby Rosengarden's band (among others), toured Europe with drummer Charlie Antolini and played for Val Wiseman's *Lady Sings The Blues* show, and by the mid-1990s was working regularly for house groups organized by Nagel Heyer Records. A musician who values the traditions perpetuated by his close friend Ray Brown (acoustic-based sound, faultless time and chord changes, and a primarily rhythm-based foundation), Skeat is at last enjoying the respect he deserves. [DF]

➤➤ **Randy Sandke** *(Happy Birthday Jazz Welle Plus).*

Alan Skidmore

Tenor and soprano saxophones, flute, alto flute, drums.

b. London, 21 April 1942.

Skidmore's father, tenor saxophonist Jimmy Skidmore, gave him help and encouragement, and he studied sight-reading with Les Evans. In 1958 he began playing with dance orchestras and pop bands. In 1961 he made his first BBC Jazz Club broadcast. In 1963 he recorded with Eric Delaney and Louie Bellson (*Repercussion*). He joined Alexis Korner's Blues Incorporated in 1964, and recorded with John Mayall and Eric Clapton. In 1965 he worked with the Ronnie Scott quintet. From 1965–9 he took part in several televised jazz workshops at NDR (North German Radio and TV), Hamburg, with Chick Corea, Dave Holland, Albert Mangelsdorff and John Surman among others; he also guested with the Maynard Ferguson orchestra and recorded film soundtrack music with Herbie Hancock. In 1969 he formed his own quintet with Kenny Wheeler, Tony Oxley, Harry Miller and John Taylor, and at the Montreux festival won the International Press Award for best band and the soloist award. He also won a scholarship to Berklee School of Music, Boston, but did not take it up.

In 1970 he joined Georgie Fame and the Blue Flames (with whom Skidmore was still appearing over thirty years on), worked with Weather Report on an NDR televised workshop, and played concerts in Hamburg and Berlin. From 1971–2 he worked with Mike Gibbs, Mike Westbrook and Chris McGregor's Brotherhood of Breath, and toured Italy with Nucleus. With John Surman and Mike Osborne he formed SOS, an innovative three-saxophone group, in 1973, and they toured in Italy, Germany and France. They also co-wrote and performed music for a ballet, *Sablier Prison*, at the Paris Opera House. In 1974 he formed his own trio with Chris Laurence and Tony Oxley. He worked from 1976–82 with the George Gruntz Concert Band which included Joe Henderson, Elvin Jones, Jimmy Knepper and Charlie Mariano. In 1978 he formed SOH (Skidmore, Oxley, Ali Haurand), which toured Europe extensively for six years. From 1981–4 he was guest soloist with the WDR (West German Radio) Orchestra in Cologne, working with Gil Evans, Airto Moreira, Mel Lewis and others. With the WDR band, he toured India and Southeast Asia for the Goethe Institute in 1984, and in 1986 appeared at Ronnie Scott's club with Elvin Jones. He has recorded with Stan Tracey, Westbrook, Gibbs, Volker Kriegel, George Gruntz and many others. His interest in traditional African percussion informed his well-received, latterday releases on Provocateur records (see below).

His favourite saxophonists are John Coltrane (for whom he can often be heard delivering a live tribute show), Sonny Rollins, Dexter Gordon, Michael

Brecker, Gerd Dudek and Ronnie Scott, and perhaps like Brecker most of all, Skidmore is a man for all seasons, a player with immense physical and imaginative stamina, at home in any context, from tight structures to total abstraction, and with any tempo, from breakneck to slow. [IC]

Tribute To Trane (1988; Miles Music). Skidmore's playing has deepened and become even more expressive over the years. *Tribute* is a glorious thanksgiving album to Coltrane, with pianist Jason Rebello, bassist Dave Green and drummer Stephen Keogh (a superb rhythm-section), and Skidmore is sublime.

East To West (1989/92; Miles Music). *East To West* continues the tribute with three live tracks from a 1989 Hong Kong gig with Stan Tracey's trio and three more performances from a 1992 date at Ronnie Scott's, with pianist Steve Melling and rhythm-section. The sound is not so good, but Skidmore's passionate intensity wins through.

The Call (2000; Provocateur); **Ubizo** (2003; Provocateur). This pair of joyous collaborations between Skidmore and members of African percussion group Amampondo represent an unexpected but delightful autumnal left-turn for the saxophonist whose power and ardour show no sign of easing.

»» **Danny Thompson** *(Elemental).*

Jimmy Skidmore

Tenor saxophone.

b. London, 8 Feb 1916; d. 23 April 1998.

One of Britain's greatest and best-loved tenorists, Skidmore began on guitar but switched to saxophone at the age of twenty and joined Jack Wallace's band, making regular appearances at London's Number One Rhythm Club, and thereafter at rhythm clubs across London (including West London), before joining Harry Parry briefly in July 1942. Work with Carlo Krahmer (1943) and Frank Deniz's Spirits of Rhythm (1944) followed, until in 1945 Skidmore joined Vic Lewis's Jazzmen, then Lewis's big band, with which he recorded a memorable version of "Come Back To Sorrento" (après Kenton). He left Lewis in 1947 and the following year appeared with Derek Neville (and Humphrey Lyttelton) at the Nice jazz festival, before working with Ralph Sharon (1949–50), Kenny Baker (1951, with the young Tubby Hayes), trumpeters Eddie Calvert and Terry Brown, and then Eric Delaney (1954–6).

During this time Skidmore continued regular club work, toured with his close friend Bix Curtis's Jazz At The Prom and from 1957–60 (with a break for illness from October 1957 to January 1958) achieved premier profile with Humphrey Lyttelton's band. "Jimmy is for me the finest tenor player in the country", Lyttelton wrote that year, but after his departure from Lyttelton Skidmore's career levelled off. Various reasons could be guessed at – the rise of Tubby Hayes who would later meet Lyttelton's description of Skidmore, the gradual emergence of rock'n'roll and avant-garde jazz, the decline of the club scene, perhaps above all Skidmore's wonderfully easy-going nature and refusal to take anything too seriously. By the 1960s he was guesting at jazz clubs (and briefly worked in a supermarket); in later years, living at Codicote in Hertfordshire he could be heard regularly at the local pub, The Bell, and as President of Panshanger Jazz Club, Welwyn Garden City, could be heard playing regularly and seen to be enjoying the honours he deserved.

"Skid", as he was known, left a legacy of elegant tenor-playing and hilarious personal memories to his many friends. His catch-greeting " 'Ello Darling!", normally followed by a smacking kiss to the cheek, is just one of many fondly recalled (and frequently ribald) trademarks rendering him a unique figure in British Jazz. [DF]

Humph Plays Standards (Pye; 1960). Amid his best-remembered context, Skidmore's powerful version of "Body And Soul" is a fitting climax to a classic Lyttelton collection.

»» **Humphrey Lyttelton** *(Back To The Sixties).*

Tom Skinner

Drums.

b. London, 26 Jan 1980.

Tom Skinner started playing drums aged nine, and attended jazz workshops at the Weekend Arts College in North London from 1993–6. After leaving school at eighteen, he became a professional musician joining Gary Crosby's Youth Jazz project Tomorrow's Warriors. As a member of the band, he performed for four years alongside Soweto Kinch (alto sax), Dave Okumu (guitar), Andrew McCormac (piano) and Tom Herbert (bass), including a three year residency at London's Jazz Café. Because of his versatility and his combination of strength and subtlety, Skinner is much in demand as a drummer. Since 1998 he has been a member of the Denys Baptiste Quartet, and has recorded two albums with the group for Dune Records; the MOBO award-winning *Be Where You Are* (1999) and *Alternating Currents* (2001). He has also performed and recorded with Byron Wallen's Quartet, Ingrid Laubrock's Quartet, Martin Speake's Quartet, and with singer Cleveland Watkiss. Skinner does not regard himself as exclusively a jazz musician: "I see music as one constantly evolving, changing thing … I try not to break it down into genres or categories, and think it's very important to be open to all styles of music from around the globe." [IC]

Ingrid Laubrock

Some Times (2001; Candid). German saxophonist Ingrid Laubrock's second album is a sophisticatedly mellow performance of mostly her own compositions. It features guest spots from Byron Wallen on trumpet, Nikki Iles on piano and Julian Siegel on bass clarinet; while her regular rhythm section of Skinner and bassist Larry Bartley keep the ensemble tight and together.

»» **Byron Wallen Quartet** *(Indigo).*

Nevil Skrimshire

Guitar.

b. Sydenham, Kent, 11 April 1923.

Skrimshire learned guitar while serving with the RAF in Malta (his teacher was Bill Bramwell) and played there with Juice Wilson. After demobilization he played with John Haim, then in the ten years from 1948 played with Humphrey Lyttelton, Freddy Randall, Reg Rigden, Joe Daniels's Jazz Group, the Christie Brothers' Stompers, Alex Welsh, Mick Mulligan and Bob Cort. (During this period Skrimshire often recorded for contractual reasons as "Nigel Sinclair", with Welsh, Mulligan, George Melly, The Saints Jazz Band, the Merseysippi Jazz Band, Cort and others.) After that he worked with Diz Disley's string quintet, Freddy Randall, Johnny Toogood and Dick Sudhalter's Anglo-American Alliance, then in the 1970s formed the group Swinging Strings with guitarist Ray Catling; he also played with Eggy Ley, Cy Laurie, John Petters, and continued working with these and other players through the 1980s. In the 1990s he recorded with Sudhalter's Anglo-American Reunion outfit and played dates with Brian White's Muggsy Remembered band. A dedicated rhythm guitarist, "Skrim" is a skilled musician of exacting standards, and a jazz historian who has contributed liner notes to a wide variety of excellent reissues. He is married to jazz historian/critic Sally Ann Worsfold. [DF]

➤➤ **Dick Sudhalter** *(After Awhile).*

Ashley Slater

Trombone, bass trombone, tuba, vocals.

b. Scuefferville, Quebec, 20 April 1961.

Slater was in an army band from 1977–83, then joined Loose Tubes in 1984, staying with the band until it disbanded at the beginning of the 1990s. He also did various session jobs during his time with Loose Tubes, and toured and recorded with George Russell's Anglo-American Living Time Orchestra, Carla Bley's band and Andy Sheppard, as well as playing with Django Bates's Delightful Precipice, The London Jazz Orchestra and Joe Gallivan. Slater began leading his own groups in the later 1980s, and experimented with "small jazz-oriented groups without traditional rhythm-sections". He formed a funk band, Microgroove, around a tuba bass which eventually led to his succcessful group, Freak Power, in which he is singer and frontman as well as playing trombone with, as he wrote, "several effects processors being used to good effect, particularly overdrive and distortion sounds. This allows me to exorcize my latent 'guitar fiend' tendencies." An association with Fatboy Slim led to Slater singing and co-writing a pair of tracks on the dance DJ's 2000 hit album *Halfway Between The Gutter And The Stars*. After Freak Power folded, Slater's next project was Ashley Slater's Big Lounge, with the largely programmed music pitched somewhere between vintage easy listening and Euro Nu jazz. Slater has a Dadaist wit, and something of Zappa's satiric propensities. He also brings a bizarre theatricality to his extremely inventive performances both live and on record. He has said, "When Freak Power finishes, I intend to get more heavily into trombone again. I still want to make a good *modern* trombone album." His favourites are J.J. Johnson, Gary Valente, Ray Anderson, and other inspirations are George Russell, Sly Stone, Gil Evans and Django Bates. [IC]

MICROGROOVE

⊙ **The Human Groove** (1993; Antilles). Microgroove was the predecessor and prototype of Freak Power with funky, tuba-based rhythms, wild humour in song and rap (by Slater), some jazz soloing by the band or guests and occasional wonderfully bad taste. There's hardly a dull moment in all ten tracks.

Holly Slater

Tenor saxophone, composer.

b. Redhill, UK, 8 Nov 1972.

While attending the Wells Cathedral School, Holly Slater studied classical piano, saxophone and flute before focusing on jazz with a performing arts degree from Middlesex University in 1995, a course involving a year studying jazz and pop music at New Jersey's William Paterson College. After finding her big, rich tenor sound by playing in London-based R&B bands like Inner Vision and with singer Noel McKoy, Slater formed her own quartet and rose to fame by winning the first Royal Sun Alliance UK Young Jazz Musician of the Year award in 1996. This in turn resulted in two high-profile residencies: at Ronnie Scott's in London, recorded for the club's own label (see below), and at New York's Blue Note. Strongly influenced by Dexter Gordon, but also inspired by the likes of Sonny Rollins, Hank Mobley and Stanley Turrentine, Slater is currently resident in the USA – she is married to American saxophonist DeAndre Hampton – but does cross the Atlantic for occasional gigs with UK pianist Nikki Yeoh et al. [CP]

⊙ **The Mood Was There** (1997; Ronnie Scott's Jazz House). Split between two bands – the "house" band of pianist John Critchinson, bassist Leon Clayton and drummer Dave Barry, Slater's own quartet with pianist Mike Gorman, bassist Romain Collard and drummer Richard Lucock – this live album showcases the whole range of Slater's considerable strengths: a warm, blustery, tough yet sensitive sound, and a great communicative gift which makes all she plays instantly accessible.

Slim and Slam

➤➤ *see entry for* **Slim Gaillard** *and* **Slam Stewart**

Cliff Smalls

Piano, trombone, arranger.

b. Charleston, South Carolina, 3 March 1918.

A graduate of Kansas Conservatory, Smalls worked with Earl Hines's big band (1942–6) as relief pianist and trombonist before short stays with Lucky Millinder and Bennie Green. In 1948 he took the first of his jobs as MD/conductor for a singer – Billy Eckstine – and over the next twenty years was to perform the same service for Clyde McPhatter, Brook Benton and Smokey Robinson and the Miracles. Smalls's tastes ran naturally to R&B – he had worked with Earl Bostic during his controversial "Flamingo" period, which helped to usher in rock'n'roll – but by the 1970s he had returned more regularly to his jazz side, working with Sy Oliver and the New York Jazz Repertory Company. In the 1980s he toured Europe regularly with Oliver Jackson's trio. [DF]

Bessie Smith

Vocals.

b. Chattanooga, Tennessee, 15 April 1895; d. 26 Sept 1937.

"She was a wild lady with her blues" – thus Lester Young brought together the two main facets of Bessie Smith, the "Empress of the Blues". First, she was the greatest blues singer ever, a woman whose rich, passionate contralto could fill a hall with the devastation of grief or the celebration of earthly joys from gin to sexual ecstasy. Second, her hard-lived life was a prototype for wild women who sing the blues, right down to Janis Joplin, who lived in her hard-drinking, hard-loving, bisexual image.

A protégée of Ma Rainey, Bessie Smith sang in Rainey's minstrel show and by 1913 – when she was eighteen, strikingly beautiful, very black, with a belling blues cry stronger than her employer's – was stopping shows all around the South. By 1920 she had her own show in Atlantic City, and in 1923 made the big career move to New York, where she lived in Harlem with her ne'er-do-well husband Jack Gee. At first her blues seemed too slow and measured for city audiences ("I'd go to the bathroom, come back and catch the rest of one verse", said bandleader Sam Wooding), but by the end of the year Bessie had signed for Columbia, produced her first issue ("Downhearted Blues" and "Gulf Coast Blues" with pianist Clarence Williams) and begun a long year of club work and touring. Recordings with Fletcher Henderson's small group furthered her reputation, as did a highly paid tour for TOBA (Theatre Owners' Booking Association), and by 1925 she was star of her own summer tent show, *Harlem Frolics*, which travelled the South in its own luxury railcar, thereby avoiding the dual problems of segregation ("We could just live on the train", said Maud Smith) and declining interest in the blues in symphonic jazz-crazy New York. For the next three years *Harlem Frolics* grossed huge sums – 1000 people were turned away from a performance in Kansas City – and Bessie Smith became the highest-salaried black star in the world. Her new show in 1928, *Mississippi Days*, had a cast of 45 and again grossed record amounts on TOBA.

By then she had been recording for three years with such giants as James P. Johnson, Fred Longshaw, Fletcher Henderson, Louis Armstrong, Charlie Green and Joe Smith: the records that resulted – from "St Louis Blues" (with Armstrong's speaking cornet and Longshaw's measured harmonium) to "Backwater Blues" (which coincided with a flood disaster in the Mississippi delta) are required listening. From the late 1920s, however, popular fashion began to reject the matchless Empress of the Blues: talking pictures were drawing public attention from live shows, and the TOBA circuit was suffering like all the rest. Although Bessie appeared in a Broadway musical in 1929, *Pansy* by Maceo Pinkard (it flopped), and made a film short (*St Louis Blues*) the same year, her star was waning, and in 1931 she was dropped by Columbia. In 1932, after a spring tour of

MAX JONES FILES/REDFERNS

Bessie Smith

the South, she found herself back in New York with more clubs closing. But Spike Hughes, on a visit from England a year later, was still able to hear her: "A mountainous woman who sang with pathos, humour and terrifying sincerity: there is little I've heard outside a Verdi opera that was so moving as her six-minute masterpiece called 'Empty Bed Blues'." In November 1933 Bessie made her last classic recordings for John Hammond (with Jack Teagarden, Coleman Hawkins and Benny Goodman) and by 1934 was touring in *Hot From Harlem*, a show built around Ida Cox. In 1935 she played the Apollo, subbing first for Louis Armstrong, then in her own Christmas show; the year after she subbed again – for Billie Holiday this time – in *Stars Over Broadway*. The reviews were ecstatic. By 1937 the Empress of the Blues was touring with the Broadway Rastus troupe, but on 25 September 1937 she was involved in a car crash and died the next day in Clarksdale Hospital, after amputation of her right arm. "If she had lived," says Lionel Hampton, "she would have been right up there with the rest of us – a national figure." Seven thousand people attended her funeral, but her grave went unmarked until Janis Joplin and Juanita Green (once Smith's cleaner) financed a headstone in 1970: "The greatest blues singer in the world", it read, "will never stop singing." [DF]

⊙ **Empty Bed Blues** (1923-33/ASV). Excellent twenty-three track Smith sampler including many classics; "St Louis Blues" (with Armstrong and Longshaw), "Backwater Blues" (with James P. Johnson), "Trombone Cholly" (with Fletcher Henderson and Charlie Green) and two titles from her last recording session with Benny Goodman and Jack Teagarden.

⊙ **Complete Recordings 1923–33** (Columbia). The complete Smith saga on five double CDs; essential listening from the fountainhead of the blues.

Betty Smith

Saxophone, vocals, leader.

b. Sileby, Leicestershire, UK, 6 July 1929.

Betty Smith began her professional career with Freddy Randall's band in 1954, then formed her own quintet (with Brian Lemon) and quickly established a fine reputation as a swing saxophonist. (Her style in the early days came close to Eddie Miller and Bud Freeman; later it broadened and took on a harder swinging edge.) In the 1960s and 1970s she worked regularly alongside Kenny Baker in a quintet, recorded as a soloist (singing as convincingly as she played), and from the mid-1970s was a central feature of the *Best of British Jazz* package (also starring Baker and Don Lusher), which recorded, played concerts and clubs, and appeared on TV. A club entertainer with a nice line in raunchy humour, Betty Smith was still active in 1987, when she appeared as a guest with Eggy Ley's band, but had retired by the mid-1990s. [DF]

➤➤ **Freddy Randall** *(Freddy Randall & His Band).*

Brian Smith

Tenor and soprano saxophones, flute, alto flute.

b. Wellington, New Zealand, 3 Jan 1939.

Smith's family was interested in music and drama and his uncle ran a dance/jazz band in the 1920s. He had four years' piano lessons, but is basically self-taught on clarinet and saxophone. He played in rock'n'roll, jazz and dance bands in New Zealand and Australia before coming to the UK in 1964, where his first job was with Alexis Korner's Blues Incorporated. In 1966–7 he worked at Ronnie Scott's Old Place with various blues and jazz musicians. In 1969 he began working with the Tubby Hayes and Maynard Ferguson big bands, and in the autumn of 1969 was a founder member of Nucleus, staying with the group, except for two brief periods away, until 1982. In 1970, with Nucleus, he played the Montreux festival, where the group won first prize, and then the Newport festival and the Village Gate in New York. He also made extensive tours of Europe, particularly Germany and Italy, with the group. In 1972 and 1974 he toured the USA with Maynard Ferguson and made a trip to Japan. He made tours with Nucleus in Scandinavia and eastern Europe, and went to the first Jazz Yatra in Bombay in 1978, followed by concerts in Delhi and Calcutta. Smith has also worked with Gordon Beck, Annie Ross, Mike Gibbs, Graham Collier, Dave MacRae, Mike Westbrook, John Stevens, Keith Tippett and others. He moved back to New Zealand in 1982, where he plays with his own quartet and with drummer Frank Gibson's Space Case, and also does some teaching and studio work. In 1984 he received the Australian Jazz Record of the Year award for his quartet album *Southern Excursion* and also recorded two platinum-selling easy listening albums, *Moonlight Sax Volumes 1* and *2* in the early 1990s.

His favourite saxophonists are Sonny Rollins, John Coltrane, Charlie Parker, Wayne Shorter, Joe Henderson and Michael Brecker. He names as other influences Herbie Hancock, Miles Davis, Wynton Kelly, Gil Evans, Louis Armstrong and Dizzy Gillespie. Smith is the complete musician – an all-rounder who is perfectly at home with anything from blues to rock, jazz and free improvisation. He also plays, and has recorded on, bamboo flute and percussion. [IC]

⊙ **Rendezvous** (1988; Ode). Smith with the fine drummer Frank Gibson, the pianist Phil Broadhurst and bass chores shared between Andy Brown and Billy Kristian. The mix of standards and originals is familiar territory, but it is beautifully done, with Smith in great form.

Buster Smith

Alto saxophone, clarinet, arranger, guitar.

b. Alfdorf, nr Ennis, Texas, 26 Aug 1904; d. 10 Aug 1991.

Buster (Henry) Smith was a key member of Walter Page's Blue Devils from 1923–33 as lead saxophonist and arranger. He worked for Bennie Moten from 1933–5, before co-leading the Count Basie-Buster Smith Barons of Rhythm at Kansas City's Reno Club in 1935–6. He then led his own bands, one of which had Charlie Parker among the personnel, and moved to New York in 1938 as a freelance arranger, working for Gene Krupa and Hot Lips Page. He also played alto for Don Redman, Page, Eddie Durham and Snub Mosley, with each of whom he also recorded. He returned to bandleading in Kansas City (from 1942 onwards) and later in Texas, where his sidemen included the future Ray Charles saxophonists Leroy Cooper and David "Fathead" Newman.

Smith's arranging contribution to the seminal Blue Devils must be taken on trust, since the band was virtually unrecorded, and likewise with the very early Basie band, although he was the uncredited co-composer of "One O'Clock Jump" and others. On alto his influence may have been even more far-reaching, for both he and Charlie Parker acknowledged the debt Parker owed to him; Jay McShann once said, "When I heard Bird that night [on the radio] I thought I was listening to Buster Smith." The disappointing contents of his one LP (made in 1959) make it all the more frustrating that Smith's early work is so sparsely represented on disc. [BP]

➤➤ **Hot Lips Page** *(Hot Lips Page 1938–40).*

Carrie Smith

Vocals.

b. Fort Gaines, Georgia, 25 Aug 1941.

A powerful blues singer, Carrie Smith began her professional career with Big "Tiny" Little in 1972, but it was her appearance at Dick Hyman's Satchmo Remembered concert at Carnegie Hall (November 1974), in which she played the part of Bessie Smith, which called international attention to her talent. After that she toured with the NYJRC for a year before beginning solo appearances and recording in her own right. Since then she has appeared regularly at jazz festivals and continued to record, as well as making appearances with Yank Lawson and others in America and Europe. [DF]

⊙ **Fine And Mellow** (1976; Audiophile). Excellent Smith recital with Loonis McGlohon's trio.

Clara Smith

Vocals.

b. Spartanburg, South Carolina, 1894; d. Feb 1935.

Clara Smith was no relation to Bessie, but she ran a highly successful career in the shadow of the "Empress of the Blues" all through the 1920s. "Clara was the greatest for me", says Doc Cheatham. "She wasn't an educated kind of person – very rough and mean, and the lower people who came to see her appreciated her because she spoke the language." She had come up the hard way, on Southern vaudeville circuits, and by 1918 was playing big venues such as the Lyric Theater, New Orleans, and the Bijou in Nashville. When she arrived in New York in 1923 she was signed by Columbia (who wanted a second blues-singing Smith on their books), began a recording career which totalled well over one hundred sides and opened her own Theatrical Club, which lasted for nine successful years. Perhaps because Clara's records only ever sold about half as well as Bessie's, Columbia sometimes teamed them on sides such as "Faraway Blues" and "I'm Goin' Back To My Used-To-Be"; the relationship stayed friendly until 1925, when a fist fight in New York put an end to the duo. Clara remained active in the 1930s around New York, Cleveland and Detroit, where she died of a heart attack. [DF]

Colin Smith

Trumpet.

b. London, 20 Nov 1934.

An ex-clarinettist, Colin Ranger Smith began his career in bands led by Cy Laurie and Terry Lightfoot and became well known after joining Acker Bilk, at the height of Britain's "trad boom" in 1960, replacing Ken Sims (the changeover produced storms of correspondence in the *Melody Maker* letter columns of the period). Two long stints with Bilk occupied Smith during the 1960s and 1970s (he also acted as Bilk's in-house musical director), but his musical approach quickly broadened, permitting long interim stints with – among others – John Picard's band (a mainstream-to-avant-garde six-piece featuring Tony Coe), the London Jazz Big Band (for whom he initially played lead as well as solos) and Peter Boizot's Pizza All Stars (from 1983). At the turn of the 1990s Smith rejoined Acker Bilk for the third time and stayed for five years, continuing related commitments including the Pizza All Stars when not with his long-time partner. He works naturally in a Roy Eldridge-based swing style, but can move forward stylistically without noticeably donning a musical hat; his strong technique, harmonic flair and reliability are a musician's delight. Smith is unquestionably one of Britain's greatest ever swing trumpeters who, at any time, could mine new ideas from standard vehicles. He became ill in 2001 and at the time of writing was inactive but hoping to return to fulltime playing. [DF]

➤➤ **Acker Bilk** *(Chalumeau – That's My Home);* **Brian Leake** *(Benign Jazz).*

Hal Smith

Drums.

b. Indianapolis, Indiana, 30 July 1953.

A traditional specialist who particularly admires Fred Higuera from Bob Scobey's band, Smith took up drums in 1963 and was taught briefly by Jake Hanna. Since turning professional in 1978 he has worked with Jim Cullum, the Lawson-Haggart jazz band and Dukes of Dixieland, Grand Dominion Jazz Band and South Frisco Jazz Band; currently leading the Frisco Syncopaters and Down Home Jazz Band, he also plays with Butch Thompson, Bobby Gordon, Marty Grosz's Destiny's Tots, Keith Ingham's trio and the Minstrels of Annie Street. Smith has contributed numerous articles to *Mississippi Rag*, *West Coast Rag* and *Jazz Rambler*, and serves on the board of the George Buck Jazz Foundation. [DF]

⊙ **Music Of The Mauve Decade** (1993; Sackville). In this bass-less trio Smith's marvellous orchestral drumming shows up well in company with Keith Ingham (piano) and Bobby Gordon (clarinet).

➤➤ *see entry on* **Wadada Leo Smith**.

Jabbo Smith

Trumpet, trombone, vocals.

b. Pembroke, Georgia, 24 Dec 1908; d. 16 Jan 1991.

"I remember several occasions when Jabbo came in to the Savoy when Louis was there, and he'd say something like 'Let me play something with you! I'll blow you down!'" – so Milt Hinton recalled the late 1920s. Jabbo (Cladys) Smith never managed to blow Louis down, but he was a considerable talent who early on played the kind of fast-moving, often stratospheric trumpet (he described it himself as "running horn with lots of notes") which was later taken to its limits by Roy Eldridge. By 1929 Smith had worked for top bandleaders such as Charlie Johnson, Duke Ellington (on record) and James P. Johnson, and in that year he replaced Louis Armstrong as featured soloist with Carroll Dickerson's orchestra at the Showboat in Chicago. What happened then, however, was prophetic, and must have secretly pleased Armstrong, who too often found Smith's trumpetistics buzzing round him like a persistent wasp. "They got him the job and he blew it", recalled Hinton. "He didn't show up."

Unreliability, complicated by girls-a-million and hard drinking, was to be the downfall of handsome Jabbo Smith's early career. In 1928 he had been signed by Brunswick as an "alternative" Louis Armstrong and the nineteen resulting sides had been brilliant. But often he would turn up two hours late (if at all) at the Chicago clubs that headlined him, and after the resulting fracas he would use his home town Milwaukee as a bolt hole: "You get in a little trouble in Chicago, you run to Milwaukee. You get in a little trouble in Milwaukee, you run to Chicago!"

By the late 1930s Smith's career had slowed up. In 1941 he was heard at Newark Hot Club by Phil Stearn: "He was kind of down and out. He was sickly and his lip was bad, and he had a miserable room in Milwaukee." From the late 1940s very little more was heard from Jabbo Smith until the 1970s: he worked close to home, took day jobs and recharged his batteries – "If I hadn't laid off twenty years I'd probably be burned out now," he recalled later. In the 1970s he relaunched his career full-time, played at Preservation Hall in New Orleans and then took a leading role in a New York musical, *One More Time*. By the 1980s he was a celebrity again, songwriting (sometimes with British pianist Keith Ingham), appearing in film documentaries and telling his story to writer Whitney Balliett. [DF]

⊙ **Ace Of Rhythm** (1927–38; Topaz). A vivid portrait of Smith in varied contexts – Duke Ellington's orchestra (1927), sixteen of his classic Rhythm Aces sides from 1929 and seven more tracks of comparable value.

⊙ **Jabbo Smith 1929–38** (Classics). Despite some duplication with the above, this is still a worthwhile purchase including all twenty sides by Smith's Rhythm Aces, plus four from a 1938 session with his eight-piece band.

Jimmy Smith

Organ, piano, vocals.

b. Norristown, Pennsylvania, 8 Dec 1925.

Smith won an amateur contest at the age of nine, and later appeared with his entertainer father as a duo. After navy service he studied bass and piano in Philadelphia. He worked with the local Don Gardner group from 1952–5, moving on to electric organ. He formed his own trio, which John Coltrane joined for two weeks, in 1955. The following year he made his New York debut and his first trio albums; their immediate success led, from 1957 onwards, to jam-session albums, with Smith joined by fellow Blue Note artists such as Art Blakey, Lou Donaldson, Lee Morgan and Jackie McLean. In 1960 there were successful quartet dates combining Stanley Turrentine and Kenny Burrell. Recording for the Verve label

DAVID REDFERN

Jimmy Smith

from 1962, he redoubled his popularity with big-band backings arranged by Oliver Nelson and others, even singing on a couple of albums. He toured Europe in 1966, 1972 and 1975 and, settling on the West Coast, gave up touring and opened his own nightclub. He resumed touring in the 1980s, including Japanese and European tours in 1993 and 1995.

It was Smith who defined the still standard approach to jazz organ by his work of the late 1950s and 1960s. Taking the organ/guitar/drums format (with optional saxophone) established by Wild Bill Davis and Milt Buckner, he replaced their big-band-inspired chording and substituted fast-moving bebop lines. With a shrill but punchy sound, he made sure his articulation was well defined at all tempos, so that the excitement of his concept was clearly communicated to audiences. Added to this was a distinct flavouring of blues phrases which was one of the factors feeding the fruition of "soul jazz" in the late 1950s; by the mid-1960s it came to dominate Smith's work to the exclusion of all else, and from this time on he influenced not only former jazz pianists who took up organ but also all those keyboard players in blues and funk bands. There is, however, only one Jimmy Smith. [BP]

JIMMY SMITH

⊙ **The Sermon** (1957–8; Blue Note). A blowing date with Smith and Art Blakey in charge, incorporating Lee Morgan, Lou Donaldson, George Coleman (his jazz recording debut), and Tina Brooks whose solo on the title track made his reputation.

JIMMY SMITH AND WES MONTGOMERY

⊙ **Further Adventures Of Jimmy And Wes** (1966; Verve). Ignoring the big-band work which effectively defined the work of both principals for mass popularity, Smith and Montgomery just go for the jugular in "Milestones", "Call Me" and, less successfully, "King Of The Road".

Joe Smith

Trumpet.

b. Ripley, Ohio, 28 June 1902; d. 2 Dec 1937.

"I used to hate him when he came in, because otherwise I had the joint locked up!" remembered Roy Eldridge, Joe Smith's arch-competitor. "Then he'd come in there and play so pretty!" Joe Smith was a roamer and a wild man (unlike his brother Russell "Pops" Smith), but his music suggested a quite different personality. His speciality was a sweet and low-down plunger-mute style which – devoid of a growl-effect – produced the sound of a gently crooning human voice.

By 1920 Smith was playing in New York, by 1922 he was accompanying Ethel Waters and Mamie Smith, and in 1924 he was musical director for Sissle and Blake's *In Bamville*, appearing on stage at the end of the show to play the "walking-out music": his gentle preaching tone (played into a coconut-shell mute) stopped the departing audience in their tracks, and people became jammed in the doorways. Smith's sensational new style was quickly noted by Fletcher Henderson, whom he joined from 1925–8, a period during which he recorded classics with Bessie Smith and became her favourite accompanist. Then from 1929–30 he worked with McKinney's Cotton Pickers, becoming close friends (a rare event) with singer George "Fathead" Thomas. But one autumn night in 1930, when both were drunk, he drove his friend into a major car accident: Thomas was killed, and Smith never really recovered from the shock. Later details of his career are misty: he worked briefly with Henderson, Moten, McKinney and others, but in 1933 was picked up in Kansas City by Fletcher Henderson's band, who found him rambling and incoherent. They took him back to New York, where he died in a sanatorium after four years of progressive mental decline. [DF]

➤➤ **Fletcher Henderson** *(A Study In Frustration).*

Johnny Smith

Guitar, trumpet.

b. Birmingham, Alabama, 25 June 1922.

Self-taught on both trumpet and guitar, Smith played country music professionally in his teens and, after army service, became a New York studio musician from 1947 onwards. Best-known as a guitarist, he recorded regularly under his own name from 1952, and used Stan Getz on a famous version of "Moonlight In Vermont". His most famous composition, "Walk Don't Run" (later a hit for The Ventures), was written for the 1954 album *In A Sentimental Mood*. All of his 1950s albums were made for the Birdland-associated Roost label, and he played regularly at Birdland while continuing his studio work. He moved to Colorado in 1958 and opened a music store, teaching and performing locally, and making occasional new records. A byword among fellow guitarists, especially of a certain generation, Smith has an innovative approach to harmonizing a line with close-voiced chords that has rarely been emulated, and his velvety tone remains unique. [BP]

⊙ **Moonlight In Vermont** (1952-3; Roost). Sixteen quintet tracks that made Smith's reputation, with Stan Getz (featured on the title-track and seven others) being replaced by Zoot Sims and Paul Quinichette on the remainder.

Keith Smith

Trumpet, vocals, leader.

b. London, 19 March 1940.

Keith Smith has developed steadily from a back-to-the-roots trumpeter into one of Britain's most authoritative mainstream players. After a 1964 trip to New Orleans, where he recorded with George Lewis, followed by a British tour with the New Orleans All Stars (Darnell Howard, Jimmy Archey, etc), Smith returned to the city to live. Later he moved to California and then to New York, where he played at Eddie Condon's before working with Tony Parenti, Zutty Singleton and others, and joining Papa Bue Jensen (1972). In 1981 Smith came back to Britain to front the former Louis Armstrong All Stars, and by this time was also leading his own Hefty Jazz six-piece, which quickly became the centre-point for a variety of well-packaged jazz shows, including *The Stardust Road* (a Carmichael tribute featuring Georgie Fame and female trio Sweet Substitute) and *One Hundred Years Of Dixieland* (featuring George Chisholm). Other Smith enterprises included *The Wonderful World Of Louis Armstrong*, for which he re-assembled five of Armstrong's ex-All Stars to tour Britain, and *One Hundred Years Of American Dixieland*, starring such fine players as Johnny Mince and Johnny Guarnieri. To back up his projects, Smith formed the Hefty Jazz Agency and started his own record label, and by 1985 was heading a highly successful operation. That year he toured the USA with great success and received an award from the Overseas Press Club of America for "creative and outstanding contributions to the international world of jazz". Since then he has continued to tour internationally and to present a variety of package shows: in 1994 he was once again celebrating Louis with guest clarinettist Joe Muranyi in theatres and at festivals around the UK. In 2003, after a sojourn abroad, he was once again playing in Britain with all-star groups that included Dave Shepherd, Roy Williams et al. [DF]

⊙ **Swing Is Here Again** (1978–91; Lake). Smith in deservingly classy company including, on sixteen tracks, Benny Waters, Vic Dickenson, Johnny Mince, Peanuts Hucko, Bob Havens, and fine British players including Al Gay, Bobby Worth, Mick Pyne et al.

Dr Lonnie Smith

Organ, piano, synthesizer.

b. Buffalo, New York, 3 July 1942.

Not to be confused with Lonnie Liston Smith (below), Lonnie was self-taught but had an uncle who played piano, while his mother and her sisters performed as a vocal group in church and on radio. He worked with George Benson's touring group from 1965–7 and Lou Donaldson (1967–8), making his own first album in 1966 and then recording for Blue Note, Kudu and Groove Merchant. During the 1980s' eclipse of organ jazz in the USA, he made albums in Paris (*Lenox & 7th Avenue*, with drummer Alvin Queen) and for Japanese fans, while the 1990s brought a prolific renaissance in his activities. He has performed with the all-star groups Essence All Stars and Chartbusters, and appeared regularly with Lou Donaldson as well as his own band. He cites as favourites Jimmy Smith, Larry Young, Wild Bill Davis, Milt Buckner, Bill Doggett, Don Patterson and Johnny Hammond, while inspired by Tatum, Garner, Monk, Jamal, Newborn, Tyner, Coltrane, Davis, Grant Green, Wes Montgomery, Lou Donaldson and more. [BP]

⊙ **Live At Club Mozambique** (1970; Blue Note). Smith says he prefers live recordings, and this originally unreleased Detroit session has his regular group with saxophonists Dave Hubbard and Ronnie Cuber joined by former colleague George Benson, climaxing with an exciting "Seven Steps To Heaven".

Lonnie Liston Smith

Piano, electronic keyboards, composer.

b. Richmond, Virginia, 28 Dec 1940.

At high school Smith played trumpet in a marching band and sang bass and baritone in choirs. He graduated in music from Morgan State College, where he played tuba in a marching band and piano in the orchestra. He moved to New York and played with Betty Carter from 1963–4, with Roland Kirk from 1964–5, Art Blakey from 1966–7, Joe Williams from 1967–8, Pharoah Sanders and Leon Thomas from 1969–71, Gato Barbieri from 1971–3 and Miles Davis from 1973–4. He then formed his fusion group Cosmic Echoes, and his 1974 album Expansions became a hit, giving him star status overnight. A prolific composer, Smith went on to release over a dozen albums in various crossover styles and remains a solid attraction on the international club circuit. His influences include Fats Waller, Art Tatum, Jelly Roll Morton, Duke Ellington, Miles Davis, Cecil Taylor, John Coltrane and Eubie Blake. With Barbieri and others he has played festivals on both coasts of the USA, and at Berlin, Nice, Milan, Hammerveld, Düsseldorf and Copenhagen. [IC]

⊙ **New World Visions** (1976; RCA). Perhaps the best compilation, giving an overview of Smith's fusion activities, containing two versions of "Expansions".

➤➤ **Rahsaan Roland Kirk** *(Rip, Rig and Panic; Now Please Don't You Cry, Beautiful Edith).*

Mamie Smith

Vocals.

b. Cincinnati, Ohio, 26 May 1883; d. 30 Oct 1946.

Mamie Smith (née Mamie Robinson) occupies a key position in jazz history, as it was her recording of "Crazy Blues" for OKeh in 1920 which began the post-war craze for "negro blues" and opened the floodgates for thousands of "race records" aimed at the black audience. "Crazy Blues" (composed by Perry Bradford, who arranged the session) was her second record; her first, "That Thing Called Love!", accompanied by white musicians, had sold only moderately well. But "Crazy Blues" sold 7500 copies in its first week, and provided the ticket to success that Smith – a very ambitious entertainer and (according to Willie "The Lion" Smith, who played piano on the session) "a pretty bossy gal" who had trouble keeping her musicians – had been waiting for. She formed her Jazz Hounds (including, from time to time, stars such as Joe Smith and Coleman Hawkins) and, with regular appearances in New

York and around the South for TOBA, became a hugely successful entertainer whose shows had "crowds lined up for two blocks" (said Dave Dexter). By the mid-1920s Smith had more money than she knew what to do with. For her stage appearances she wore $3000 feathered gowns and she owned three palatial New York homes, each with luxury furnishings and a brand-new electric player-piano in every room (the proceeds from these properties were later acquired by her manager Ocie Wilson). But although she appeared regularly in and out of New York through the 1930s and early 1940s, public interest in the blues was declining and she was suffering from a progressive arthritic condition: when her illness worsened, financial help from her manager never came. She died in poverty in a boarding house on New York's 8th Avenue after a long hospital stay and was buried on Staten Island. [DF]

Marvin "Smitty" Smith

Drums.

b. Waukegan, Illinois, 24 June 1961.

Encouraged by his elder brother, Smith was already backing Sonny Stitt, Earl Hines and others in a local club at the age of fifteen. He studied at Berklee from 1979–81, and then turned pro with Jon Hendricks from 1981–3. Freelancing since then, he has played with a vast number of musicians of varied styles, such as David Murray, Archie Shepp, Branford Marsalis, Roland Hanna, Art Farmer, Sonny Rollins and Bheki Mseleku. A key relationship has been his work with Dave Holland and Steve Coleman, firstly in Holland's quintet and quartet from 1985 into the 1990s, and during the same period in the M-Base context of Coleman's music. Inspired by Billy Higgins, Max Roach and Jack DeJohnette, Smith's wide experience is typical of players who appeared during the 1980s, but his excellence in all the styles he has touched is only rarely to be found. [BP]

⊙ **Keeper Of The Drums** (1987; Concord). Smith's own two albums seem to pay more attention to his versatility than to the voice of a compelling composer. Maybe this would require more time and a regular group, but meanwhile post-boppers Wallace Roney, Ralph Moore and Mulgrew Miller are well balanced against M-Base-influenced colleagues Robin Eubanks, Lonnie Plaxico and Coleman.

➤➤ **Steve Coleman** *(Black Science)*; **Dave Holland** *(Seeds Of Time; The Razor's Edge)*.

Pine Top Smith

Piano, vocals.

b. Troy, Alabama, 11 June 1904; d. 15 March 1929.

A club and vaudeville entertainer, Pine Top (Clarence) Smith worked on the TOBA circuit in the 1920s. "Pinetop's Boogie-Woogie", recorded in 1928, was a big hit after his death, and he is said to have invented the name for his eight-to-the-bar music. Shot in a Chicago dance-hall brawl over a woman, Smith missed the boogie boom by ten years. [DF]

Various Artists

⊙ **The Boogie-Woogie Masters** (1928–45; Charly). One of the best boogie compilations, with two tracks each by Pine Top, Cow-Cow Davenport, Meade "Lux" Lewis and Albert Ammons, plus the amazing "Chicago Breakdown" by Big Maceo.

Russell Smith

Trumpet.

b. Ripley, Ohio, 1890; d. Los Angeles, 27 March 1966.

Brother of Joe Smith (they came from a brass-playing family), Russell T. "Pops" Smith played for Fletcher Henderson and others from 1925–42. Strictly a trained musician who left the playing of jazz to others, he was a steadying influence on many of the younger men around him (Benny Morton, for one, called him a "father-figure"), seldom drank – it was said that he could make half a pint last a week – and kept regular hours. Consequently he led a long, successful playing life, and after leaving Henderson worked for other respected leaders such as Cab Calloway and Noble Sissle until retiring to teach and play part-time in the 1950s. [DF]

➤➤ **Fletcher Henderson** *(A Study In Frustration)*.

Ruthie Smith

Tenor, alto and soprano saxophones, vocals, cello.

b. Manchester, UK, 24 Nov 1950.

Ruthie Smith had classical lessons as a child, and took a degree in English and music at York University, but is self-taught on saxophone. From 1972–84 she played with various big and small bands including Brian Abrahams's District Six and Annie Whitehead's band. She was a founder member of the Guest Stars, an all-women fusion group. In 1982 she helped to organize the first British women's jazz festival. The Guest Stars' first album received critical acclaim in the UK, and the group toured the US East Coast and the UK in 1984. In the 1990s she remained active in jazz. [IC]

Stuff Smith

Violin, vocals.

b. Portsmouth, Ohio, 14 Aug 1909; d. Munich, 25 Sept 1967.

"The cat that took the apron-strings off the fiddle." Jo Jones's neat summing-up says a lot about Stuff Smith's hard-bowing approach to the violin, which made him the most forceful swing fiddler in jazz history. "It was just Louis who influenced me", Smith remembered later. "I got some Venuti records and they were pretty" (Venuti is still the nearest equivalent to Smith's unbuttoned approach), "but they didn't push me enough. I use my bow the way a horn player uses breath control and I may hit a note like a drummer hits a cymbal!"

Stuff (Hezekiah Leroy Gordon) Smith came up in the 1920s with Alphonso Trent's orchestra, for whom he played a variety of sweet and hot features, including comedy "point" numbers. Later he married and settled in Buffalo, where he teamed with trumpeter Jonah Jones, a life-long friend; agent-bandleader Dick Stabile booked the two of them and their band into the Onyx Club on 52nd Street in 1936. The same year they recorded "I'se A Muggin'" (twice), followed by "If You'se A Viper", and were soon the biggest attraction on Swing Street. But Smith – a temperamental talent who jealously guarded his own interests – could be hard to handle. After Joe Helbock, boss of the Onyx, reluctantly released him to make a Hollywood film, *Swing Street* (1938), Smith was slow to come back, and by the time he did reappear public attention had moved on. From then on his career levelled out: he had regular work with a trio in New York and Chicago (where Smith opened a restaurant) but there was some evidence all through the 1940s of a mercurial temperament at work. "Stuff's trio at the Onyx in 1944 was one of the greatest, most rhythmic trios I ever heard", says Billy Taylor. "Their only records were made for Asch but they didn't show what the trio could do. They'd worked up some things for the session but then Stuff goofed and played some other things instead – as he was likely to do!" In the 1950s, working more often as a soloist, Smith was California-based and often beset by health problems, including pneumonia and ulcers ("The trouble with me and my liver was that I just couldn't stand food while I was drinking!"). By the 1960s he was a familiar face in Europe, touring concert halls, clubs and festivals: his last recordings, as hard-swinging as ever, came from the year he died. [DF]

⊙ **Stuff Smith And His Onyx Club Boys** (1936–9; Classics). All the sides by Smith's Onyx Club Boys in chronology; Jonah Jones co-stars on classics including "You'se A Viper", "Old Joe's Hittin' The Jug" and "I'se A Muggin'".

⊙ **With Dizzy Gillespie And Oscar Peterson** (1956–7; Verve). This excellent double CD contains not just Smith's sessions with the two giants of the title but also other important Smith sessions from the 1950s with Wynton Kelly, Carl Perkins and others.

⊙ **Hot Violins** (1965–7; Storyville). Excellent sides from Smith's later days, also including fellow violinists Poul Olsen and Svend Asmussen.

Tab Smith

Saxophones.

b. Kinston, North Carolina, 11 Jan 1909; d. 17 Aug 1971.

Tab (Talmadge) Smith's lengthy jazz pedigree began in territory bands (starting with Henry Edwards's) and by 1936 he was experienced enough to come to New York to join Lucky Millinder, the new leader of Mills' Blue Rhythm Band, replacing Buster Bailey. He stayed with Millinder for two years, recording over two dozen fine sides, and also worked regularly with top-rankers such as Frankie Newton, Henry "Red" Allen, Teddy Wilson and Eddie Durham before joining Count Basie in 1940 to work alongside Earle Warren. "He was a formidable musician," remembers Warren, "and a nice guy to know, with an even personality, no animosity towards anyone. And he was happy with Basie." In 1942 he returned to Millinder for two more years and from then on led his own small groups, sometimes with singer Wynonie Harris, often recording for small R&B labels: several of his early 1950s sides were best sellers. He continued to be successful until the early 1960s, when he retired to St Louis to develop the property his mother and sister owned; in later years he got involved in real estate, played the organ for fun and taught locally. Like Earl Bostic, guitarist Tiny Grimes and singer Dinah Washington, Smith was – just possibly – born too soon for rock'n'roll. [DF]

⊙ **Jump Time/Ace High** (1951–3; Delmark). Smith is often underrated but this pair of CDs, offering a chronology of his work for United Records, does much to illustrate his high level of performance.

Tommy Smith

Tenor and soprano saxophones, flute.

b. Luton, Bedfordshire, UK, 27 April 1967.

Smith was brought up in Edinburgh, where he took up the saxophone at twelve. He made his national television debut at fifteen, backed by Gordon Beck and Niels-Henning Ørsted Pedersen and, within the next year, recorded two albums for different local labels. He gained a scholarship to Berklee College and began studies there in 1984. He formed the group Forward Motion with fellow students, which made UK and European tours in 1985–6, and he also became a regular member of his tutor Gary Burton's quintet in 1986. Since returning to the UK in 1988, Smith has led his own groups including, on occasion, Jason Rebello and Idris Muhammad. Also in 1988 he became the first UK musician signed to Blue Note, for whom he produced four albums before transferring to the Glasgow-based Linn Records and subsequently forming his own Spartacus label. In 1990 he did some guest spots with the group Hue And Cry, and was the soloist in a saxophone concerto written for him by composer William Sweeney.

Although his earliest recorded work was heavily marked by Coltrane (hence one of his album titles, *Giant Strides*), Smith's style soon transcended this direct influence, recalling players as different as Jan Garbarek and Bobby Wellins. In addition, his own writing of original material has developed considerably in interest since his emergence. Since autumn 1995 he has been musical director of the Scottish National Jazz Orchestra, which has successfully re-created Ellington, Mingus,

Miles Davis/Gil Evans and others, as well as commissioning new work. [BP]

⊙ **Misty Morning And No Time** (1994; Linn). Smith's second album for sextet has the same front line players as 1992's *Paris*, namely Guy Barker and Julian Argüelles. The leader's fourteen varied compositions offer a suitable challenge to them, and his own solo work, only occasionally Garbaresque, is compelling.

Tommy Smith-Brian Kellock

⊙ **Bezique** (2002; Spartacus). This live duo recording, released on Smith's own label, finds both him and pianist Kellock working at the spontaneous extremities of straightahead material, by such as Chick Corea, Steve Swallow, Harold Arlen and Duke Ellington.

Trixie Smith

Vocals.

b. Atlanta, Georgia, 1895; d. 21 Sept 1943.

In the 1920s there seemed to be just too many blues-singing Smiths. One of the most neglected – and also one of the most talented – was Trixie Smith, who brought a new polish to her often vaudeville-based material. After winning Black Swan's blues contest in 1921 she recorded regularly with a wide variety of jazz stars, including Fletcher Henderson and his alumni, as well as Jimmy Blythe, James P. Johnson, Louis Armstrong and Freddie Keppard. One of her most popular blues, "The World's Jazz Crazy, Lawdy, So Am I", turned into a classic of its kind; another that should have done was "Freight Train Blues". "Her record of that is one of the greatest blues records ever made", said Sammy Price. "Trixie had depth, real warmth and appeal. What was she like? She was just like another woman called Smith – but she could sing like hell!" [DF]

Louis Armstrong

⊙ **Louis Armstrong And The Blues Singers** (1924–30; Affinity). This definitive set has Trixie's four sides with Louis, including "The World's Jazz Crazy, Lawdy, So Am I" (1925), plus alternate takes.

Wadada Leo Smith

Trumpet, flugelhorn, mbira, flutes, percussion, vocals.

b. Leland, Mississippi, 18 Dec 1941.

As a child, Smith briefly studied drums, then French horn, before taking up trumpet, on which he received tutelage from his stepfather, blues guitarist Alex "Little Bill" Wallace. After a stint in the military, where he played in an army band, in 1967 Leo Smith moved from Mississippi to Chicago, where he took up with the active Association for the Advancement of Creative Musicians (AACM). In particular, he collaborated with Anthony Braxton, and as a member of Braxton's group he travelled to Europe in 69, recording for BYG and Freedom, and back in Chicago recording Braxton's seminal *Three Compositions Of New Jazz*. His own composition which gave the title to Braxton's *Silence* (1969; Freedom) is as radical an incorporation of blank space into sound construction as any post-free player has made. Smith moved to New Haven, Connecticut, in the early 1970s, where he started Kabell Records, on which he released a string of fine records. His self-published 1973 book *notes (8 pieces) source a new world music: creative music* was a major theoretical statement on improvisation and creative jazz. Among various ongoing groups, Smith worked with multiple reedman Dwight Andrews, bassist Wes Brown and vibes player Bobby Naughton (sometimes as New Dalta Ahkri). He worked in a great trio with German bassist Peter Kowald and percussionist Gunter "Baby" Sommer, and recorded *Budding Of A Rose* (1979; Moers) with a large American-European ensemble. In the 80s, Smith converted to Rastafarianism (assuming the name Wadada), and his work now often contains elements of reggae and nyabingi. For the ECM label he recorded *Divine Love* (1978) and *Kulture Jazz* (1992), while two of his finest records – *Rastafari* (1983; Sackville) and *Mass On The World* (1978; Moers) – are as yet unavailable on CD. In 1993 Smith began teaching in California, at Cal Arts, and at the same time he began performing and recording more actively, participating in the Henry Kaiser-formulated Miles Davis electric tribute *Yo Miles!* (1998; Shanachie) and releasing a string of new discs including *Tao Njia* (1996; Tzadik), *Golden Hearts Remembrance* (1997; Chap Chap), and with multiple reed player Vinny Golia and bass pioneer Bertram Turetzky the trio date *Prataksis* (1997; 9 Winds). [JC]

⊙ **Procession Of The Great Ancestry** (1983; Chief). Strength and serenity characterize Smith's approach to composition and trumpet-playing. This excellent outing with two bassists, tenor saxophone, Kahil El Zabar on percussion, Naughton's vibes, and blues guitarist Louis Myers pays homage to the past with a keen ear to the future.

➤➤ **Susie Ibarra** *(Flower After Flower).*

Willie "The Lion" Smith

Piano, composer, vocals.

b. Goshen, New York, 25 Nov 1897; d. 18 April 1973.

With Jelly Roll Morton, Willie "The Lion" Smith (William Henry Joseph Bonaparte Bertholoff) was the most celebrated braggart of jazz piano, whose sometimes overwhelming gift for self-promotion was somehow at odds with the delicacy of his playing and compositions. But "The Lion" was a vital figure in piano jazz, and a great example of the school of pianists that seems to have originated on America's eastern seaboard and became known – rightly or wrongly – as the Harlem stride school.

Smith grew up musically in the tough New York Jungles between 60th and 63rd Streets – an area full of clubs and dives – and for much of the rest of his life was to remain a New Yorker. He had the natural pizazz to survive in such surroundings: taking his style from the ragtime professors who preceded him, he

dressed immaculately, carried a cane, and always announced his arrival in a club with the warning growl, "The Lion is here!" He quickly became an influence on younger musicians such as Duke Ellington (who later dedicated a tune, "Portrait Of The Lion", to him), and ran regularly with fellow piano-masters James P. Johnson and young Fats Waller. After active service in World War I (according to his story he stayed at the front for 33 days and acquired his nickname for valour) he settled down to a jazzman's lifestyle, including club work, recording and touring with blues singer Mamie Smith (he played on the historic "Crazy Blues" session), acting (he had one line in a Broadway play, *Four Walls*), working with Will Mastin's revue, hanging out at the Rhythm Club and playing rent parties. In the 1930s Smith became well known on record (gentle reflective solos like "Morning Air" and "Echoes Of Spring" are classics), and from the 1940s to the end of his days he led bands, toured Canada and parts of Europe as a soloist, and starred at jazz festivals. In 1965 he published his larger-than-life autobiography.

"The Lion has been the greatest influence on most of the great piano players who have been exposed to his fire, his harmonic lavishness, his stride – what a luxury", said Duke Ellington. "Even the great Art Tatum – and I know he was the the greatest – showed strong patterns of Willie Smith-isms after being exposed to The Lion. I can't think of anything good enough to say about him." [DF]

⊙ **Willie The Lion Smith 1925–37/1937–8/1938–40** (Classics). Beginning with Smith's titles with the Gulf Coast Seven (1925), the three-volume Classics series contains all of his small-band sides (including masterpieces like "Echoes Of Spring"), piano solos from 1938 (including "Passionnette" and "Morning Air"), plus fourteen solos originally recorded for Commodore in just one day. Smith at his greatest.

⊙ **The Lion Roars!** (1934-44; ASV). Smith in a wide variety of settings: the Alabama Jug Band, Mezz Mezzrow, eight tracks with his excellent Cubs (1935-44), four solo tracks (including "Morning Air") plus titles with Sidney Bechet and Max Kaminsky. A good all-round portrait of the Lion.

⊙ **Willie The Lion Smith And His Cubs** (1935–7; Timeless Historical). All the titles by Smith's Cubs, amongst them Ed Allen, Cecil Scott, Buster Bailey, and in 1937 the great Frankie Newton with Buster Bailey, Pete Brown and John Kirby (ie an early version of Kirby's band). Excellent remastering.

⊙ **Pork And Beans** (1966; Black Lion). The Lion reminiscing and playing solo in later years, including talk about stride-pianist Luckey Roberts; invaluable oral history.

Willie Smith

Alto and baritone saxophones, clarinet, vocals.
b. Charleston, South Carolina, 25 Nov 1910; d. 7 March 1967.

A magnificent soloist and faultless section leader, Willie Smith (William McLeish) began on clarinet and later, after graduating in chemistry at Fisk University, joined Jimmie Lunceford's ambitious new band (on alto saxophone) while they were working up country and down for cents. Band morale was high, however, and Smith, who had known Lunceford while the older man was teaching at Fisk, took up his former teacher's cause with enthusiasm. Because he was popular – "one of the warmest guys you could ever meet", said Harry Edison – Smith brought the best out of his saxophone section, which under his leadership became the most balanced, efficient and technically able of its time, playing the high-speed choruses written by pianist Ed Wilcox with spellbinding flair. Smith's awesome solo ability, likeable personality and fine singing were soon spotted by Tommy Dorsey, and one night – on a job when the whole orchestra was playing for expenses – he offered the saxophonist whatever he wanted to move over. Smith refused. "That was the spirit we all had in those days", he told Stanley Dance later. "Nobody would quit, regardless of what happened."

But Lunceford's non-stop touring schedule (almost 365 days a year) laid the foundations of Smith's drink problems, and suspicions were forming that Lunceford was creaming money from his sidemen's salaries. In 1942, shedding tears, Smith left, and two years later (after one year with Charlie Spivak, one in the navy) he joined Harry James; for much of the rest of his life he was to play Johnny Hodges to James's Ellington (in 1951 he did the same for Ellington himself). At that period Smith's driving, cutting-edged alto was also heard with Jazz At The Philharmonic, with Billy May's orchestra, and in the studios, right up to the mid-1960s, by which time his long battle with alcoholism was complicated by cancer. A less-than-perfect latterday Smith can be heard on Ella Fitzgerald's Johnny Mercer collection, but almost all of his recorded work ranks with Benny Carter's or Johnny Hodges'. [DF]

Willie Smith with the Harry James Orchestra

⊙ **Snooty Fruity** (1944–7; Columbia). Now regrettably deleted but worth searching for: Smith's second great partnership, after Lunceford, was with James, forming a team of dazzling virtuosity. This admirably selected set isolates tracks on which both men shine, including "I'm Confessin' " and "Cottontail".

Charlie Parker

Jazz At The Philharmonic 1946 (Verve). Smith live was one of the great saxophone experiences, and here he's teamed with Parker plus Gillespie, Al Killian, Hawkins and more in a set of show-stopping performances.

Willie Smith

A Sound Of Distinction (1947–51; Ocium). Essential – and long overdue – compendium of 20 Smith selections spotlighting his elastic alto playing. Outstanding tracks include "Not So Bop Blues", "Tea For Two" and "Sophisticated Lady", all with Dodo Marmarosa's quartet in 1947, and "Please Be Kind" with Ellington in 1951.

➤➤ **Jimmie Lunceford** *(Jimmie Lunceford 1930–41).*

Paul Smoker

Trumpet.

b. Muncie, Indiana, 1941.

Moving to Davenport, Iowa, at the age of two, Paul Smoker studied piano from the age of six to fourteen, and took up trumpet at ten, inspired by the soaring, vocal sound of Harry James. During high school, he surreptitiously played jazz (against his parents' wishes) in small clubs across the Mississippi river in Rock Island, Illinois. There he played with Dodo Marmarosa in the early 60s, and in 1964 he met Doc Severinsen, with whom he played duets and took informal lessons. As a graduate student at the University of Iowa, he gigged frequently at the Tender Trap in Cedar Rapids, Iowa, where he played with a variety of people including J.R. Montrose, and at the same time he played avant-garde classical music with various Iowa City ensembles. Advised against a career in jazz, Smoker entered academia, teaching at the University of Wisconsin, Oshkosh (1968–71), University of Northern Iowa (1975–6), and finally at Coe College, back in Cedar Rapids (1976–90). In the 70s he had played bop and swing, but at Coe in the 1980s he began playing more out of free jazz and postbop. In 1979 he commenced work with a trio of Ron Rohovit on bass and Phil Haynes on drums.This trio was augmented by Anthony Braxton for Smoker's first record, *QB* (1984; Alvas), and has recorded several excellent dates including *Mississippi River Rat* (1984; Sound Aspects) and *Genuine Fables* (1988; hat Art). A bold, technically brilliant, highly creative player, whose sound often draws comparisons with Louis Armstrong, Smoker continued to work with Braxton – for instance appearing on *Charlie Parker Project 1993* (1995; hat Art) with Dutch pianist Misha Mengelberg and Chicago tenor Ari Brown, and Braxton's examination of Andrew Hill's oeuvre *Nine Compositions (Hill) 2000* (2000; CIMP). He was a member of Joint Venture and Phil Haynes's 4 Horns & What? and has appeared latterly in the groups of Jay Rosen, Lou Grassi and Damon Short. Several records under his own name have appeared of late, including a string of albums with various ensembles for CIMP and an archetypal recording with an all-brass group, *Brass Reality* (2002; Nine Winds). [JC]

Come Rain Or Come Shine (1986; Sound Aspects). This in-the-pocket trio disc tells all about Smoker: nimble, blues-drenched, spaciously free, and full of New Orleans wah mutation and harmolodic motion. Included are the standard that gives the disc its name, cool tunes by Haynes and Smoker, and Joseph Jarman's Art Ensemble classic "Old Time Southside Street Dance".

Pat Smythe

Piano, composer, arranger.

b. Edinburgh, Scotland, 2 May 1923; d. 6 May 1983.

Smythe was a squadron leader in the RAF during World War II. After demobilization he practised as a lawyer in Edinburgh, but his heart was in jazz, and he gave up law at the end of the 1950s, moving to London. He played with trumpeter Dizzy Reece, then joined Joe Harriott's radically innovative quintet, which included Coleridge Goode (bass), Shake Keane (trumpet) and either Phil Seamen or Bobby Orr (drums). Harriott pioneered the European free-jazz movement, and Smythe made a great contribution in helping to formulate and organize the new ideas. He also went on to break other new ground with Harriott with Indo-Jazz Fusions in the mid-1960s. The brilliantly creative work of Harriott's team of players was documented on a series of fine albums – some of which gained the maximum star-rating in *Down Beat*. Smythe also had a long and fruitful association with Kenny Wheeler in big-band and small-group formations. He had a keen ear for outstanding young talent: his own small groups included bassist Dave Holland and guitarists John McLaughlin and Allan Holdsworth.

As well as being an excellent composer and arranger, Pat was a fine soloist and accompanist, conversant with the whole spectrum of contemporary jazz. He worked with Stan Getz and Paul Gonsalves (with whom he recorded), Ben Webster, Zoot Sims, Sonny Stitt and many others. He also accompanied singers Anita O'Day, Blossom Dearie, Tony Bennett, Annie Ross, Elaine Delmar and Mark Murphy.

After his death from cancer, a group of friends established the Pat Smythe Memorial Trust and Award in his memory, to provide an annual award for a young jazz musician. [IC]

➤➤ **Joe Harriott** *(Indo-Jazz Fusions; Abstract).*

Valaida Snow

Trumpet, vocals.

b. Chattanooga, Tennessee, or Washington, DC, 2 June c.1900; d. 30 May 1956.

Coming from a Baltimore family of three girls (her sisters were named Lavaida and Alvaida; her mother was a – presumably eccentric – music teacher), Valaida Snow was headlining at Barron Wilkins's Harlem cabaret by the time she was 22, with an act in which she danced, sang, played the violin and topped off with hot trumpet solos. For the rest of the 1920s she built her reputation around the USA, toured with Will Mastin (Sammy Davis Senior's partner) and his trio, made a trip to the Far East in 1926 to front Jack Carter's band, and in 1928 was top of the bill at Sunset Café, Chicago. There Louis Armstrong was impressed by her ("Boy, I never saw anything that great!" he said) and Earl Hines fell for her: "I thought she was the greatest girl I'd ever seen." Snow – a beautiful woman who loved life and liked the best of everything – kept on the move: she toured Europe, the Middle East and Russia, then took a starring role in Sissle and Blake's review *Rhapsody In Black* and by 1933 was back in Chicago with Hines, producing and starring in shows for Ed Fox at the Grand Terrace Ballroom. (She featured a number of tap routines, including one in everything from tap shoes to Russian clogs, and often danced herself into near insensibility.) "Valaida's shows were big productions like you see on TV, in Hollywood or at the Cotton Club," said Quinn Wilson, "with sixteen chorus girls, eight show girls, besides the acts!"

For the rest of the 1930s Snow enjoyed her stardom, made three films, visited Britain and toured Europe. In 1941 she was interned in Nazi-occupied Copenhagen. "I don't think she ever recovered, physically or mentally, although she kept working until she died", remembered Hines, who did not recognize his former lover when he met her again in 1943. Snow married her manager Earle Edwards, who had helped to nurse her, and carried on fronting bands and singing. She died of a cerebral haemorrhage soon after shows at the Palace Theater, New York, when she was 55. [DF]

Hot Snow (1937–50; Rosetta). Only out on vinyl so far, this excellent portrait has many of Snow's best European sides plus a 1946 film soundtrack and a 1950 track with Jimmy Mundy's orchestra, featuring Jonah Jones.

Elmer Snowden

Guitar, banjo, saxophones, leader.

b. Baltimore, Maryland, 9 Oct 1900; d. 14 May 1973.

A trained banjo player and a smart businessman, Elmer Snowden worked with Eubie Blake in a dance school and first played with Duke Ellington in a Washington trio around 1919. He was, he made it clear later, none too impressed with the aspiring piano player who only seemed to know one tune ("Soda Fountain Rag") and hung around asking to sit in. Ellington's opportunity came when Snowden was asked to take a band to New York, assembled Sonny Greer, Arthur Whetsol and Otto Hardwicke, then got off the train in town only to find that his pianist, Fats Waller, had disappeared. Snowden contacted Ellington, who joined his band at Barron's Club and rapidly impressed Greer, Whetsol and Hardwicke with his charisma and go-ahead ideas. These included bringing new talent such as Charlie Irvis and Bubber Miley into the band – apparent takeover tactics that were probably prompted by a general suspicion that Snowden was short-changing his employees. When the banjoist walked into the club and heard his band talking about getting rid of him, he complied with their wish (although just once, briefly, he came back at the request of Barron's club mafia).

Snowden's future was secure enough without the Washingtonians: he was hiring out five bands a night as an agent, playing in productions such as the 1927 *Rang Tang Show* (featuring 48 banjo players), bandleading in other big clubs such as the Bamville and Small's Paradise, and earning big money. In 1933, after a union dispute, he was barred from playing in New York (things were finally sorted out by John Hammond) and for the next thirty years he led a highly successful career fronting his own groups. In 1963 he moved to California to teach at Berkeley for three years and by 1967 was touring Europe for George Wein. By that time the old rift with Ellington was healed and the greying Duke was even light-heartedly suggesting that Snowden might like to come back in the band. The banjoist – one year younger than Ellington – declined, though in tones that sounded like an indulgent father-figure. "I was very close to Duke's father and he made me promise I would look out for his boy", said Snowden. "And Duke is still holding me to that promise!" [DF]

Martial Solal

Piano, composer.

b. Algiers, 23 Aug 1927.

Born of French parents (not Algerian, as sometimes implied), Solal settled in Paris in the late 1940s. He worked with expatriate US musicians such as Kenny Clarke, Don Byas, and recorded with Sidney Bechet. He started leading his own trio in 1959, including the drummer Daniel Humair. Since a 1963 visit to New York and the Newport festival his reputation has been international, entailing solo and trio appearances all over Europe and occasionally the USA. He has led an occasional big band in recent decades, and written much film music, beginning with Jean-Luc Godard's *Breathless* (1959). In 1999 he was awarded the Jazzpar prize, and performed in concert with the Danish Radio Jazz Orchestra. His daughter, singer Claudia Solal (b. 30 March 1971), recorded her first album in 1997.

Solal's piano style, although capable of sounding momentarily like anyone from Art Tatum to Bill Evans, is unique. Filled with glittering Gallic wit (or, according to his detractors, frigid French intellectualism), it is characterized by a restless abundance of ideas. Naturally enough, the technique required to execute these ideas is abundant too, as is Solal's harmonic knowledge, and both are perhaps best appreciated in his frequent demolition of popular song standards. But, not surprisingly, his original compositions are equally arresting and, as well as being immediately attractive, often have hidden depths. [BP]

The Vogue Recordings: Vol. 2 – Trios And Solos (1954–6; Vogue). In the absence of his 1960 album for EMI, this is the most valuable of his early compilations. The twelve solo standards are the most individualistic, but the trios with Sarah Vaughan's rhythm-section (Joe Benjamin and Roy Haynes) are not far behind.

Martial Solal Big Band (1981; Verve). This reissue of one of Solal's three 1980s albums with the big band gives perhaps a better idea of his originality than his André Hodeir and Monk adaptations, especially on the rhythmic "Tango" and "Valse à Trois Temps".

NY-1 (2001; Blue Note). Solal's first appearance at the Village Vanguard, days after the 11 September attack on New York, finds him with Francois Moutin (bass) and Bill Stewart in a typical demolition of standards mixed with originals by his daughter Claudia.

Lew Soloff

Trumpet, flugelhorn, piccolo, trumpet.

b. New York, 20 Jan 1944.

Soloff's father was a soft-shoe dancer and his mother a vaudeville violinist. He had piano lessons from the age of five until thirteen, and took up the trumpet at school. From 1955–61 he attended the Juilliard Preparatory Department; from 1961–5 he studied at the Eastman School, gaining a BMus in applied trumpet and music education, and undertook further studies at the Juilliard in 1965–6. Until May 1968 he played with many Latin bands and also with Maynard Ferguson, Joe Henderson, Gil Evans, Thad Jones-Mel Lewis, Clark Terry, Chuck Mangione and Duke Pearson among others. From 1968–73 he worked with Blood, Sweat And Tears, touring worldwide. He has also been the featured soloist on classical pieces, including the Concerto for Trumpet and Orchestra by Alexandra Pakhmutova, with the New Orleans Symphony Orchestra.

Soloff was closely associated with Gil Evans from 1973 until the composer's death, doing worldwide tours with him and playing on several albums. With Evans he also played most major jazz festivals, and with Blood, Sweat And Tears he played most of the main rock festivals. In 1975 he formed a quintet with fellow trumpeter, Jon Faddis. In 1977 Soloff was working regularly in a trio with Peter Levin (French horn) and Jeff Berlin (bass). Through the 1980s and 1990s he recorded with the Manhattan Jazz Quintet, cut many sessions with artists as diverse as Duran Duran, Charles Earland and Frank Sinatra and made several albums as leader. Since the late 80s he has been the trumpet soloist in Carla Bley's big bands, a role he still plays.

His influences include Charlie Parker, Dizzy Gillespie, Miles Davis, Hannibal Peterson, Jon Faddis, Clifford Brown, Freddie Hubbard and Clark Terry. Soloff is a virtuoso who can handle any idiom or context; he has a brilliant technique and a magnificent range and some of his most powerful and moving solo work can be heard on the 1993 Carla Bley album, *Big Band Theory* and *Looking For America* (2003; Watt). [IC]

Little Wing (1991; Sweet Basil). Soloff may not reach the heights he achieves with other leaders on his own discs, but he is never less than excellent; *Little Wing* has the volatile Ray Anderson on trombone and several original pieces by members of the band, and is a lively affair.

With A Song In My Heart (1999; Milestone). Mostly classy, low-key standards and originals (with a little Tchaikovsky) featuring Soloff on uncharacteristically muted horn in the stellar company of Mulgrew Miller (piano), George Mraz (bass) and Victor Lewis (drums), with wife Emily Mitchell making a cameo on harp.

➤➤ **Carla Bley** *(Fleur Carnivore; Big Band Theory).*

Arnie Somogyi

Double Bass

b. UK, 7 Sept 1965.

The son of a Hungarian refugee who arrived in the UK in 1956, Arnie Somogyi took up the violin at the age of five, and by fourteen was playing the bass guitar. While at Bristol University, he bought his first double bass, took some lessons with Paul Anstey, and began playing with Tommy Chase and Portishead's Adrian Utley. Further Jazz studies took place at London's Guildhall School of Music with Jeff Clyne.

Somogyi's versatility has led to him working with a diversity of different artists, from acid-jazz to mainstream, and he has appeared on albums by Urban Species, Galliano, and R&B singer Omar. Since 1997 he has regularly appeared in various Alan Skidmore outfits, and features on the Skidmore/Amanpondo album *The Call* (1999; Provocateur Records). He has also played with Herb Ellis, Art Farmer, Randy Brecker and the singers Annie Ross, Claire Martin and Anita Wardell. In 2001 Somogyi featured on drummer Clark Tracey's album *Stability* (Linn Records) alongside several British jazz luminaries, and his playing has graced two movie soundtracks, *Blue Ice* (1993) and *The Talented Mr Ripley* (1999). He is currently the visiting double bass tutor on the Jazz course at the Birmingham Conservatoire.

In 2000 Somogyi travelled to Hungary and Transylvania as part of a jazz quartet put together by Transylvanian guitarist Zsolt Bende. During the journey he visited Segesvar, the town where his great-great-grandfather had been Rabbi over 100 years earlier. The experience was captured in BBC radio documentary, *Cool Roots*, produced by Somogyi, and inspired him to form a quintet, Cold Cherry Soup. He was joined by Bende and Hungarian saxophonist Tony Lakatos alongside Liam Noble on piano and Winston Clifford on drums. The quintet debuted at Ronnie Scott's in August 2000, and a subsequent CD, *Cold Cherry Soup*, was released the following year. [IC]

Cold Cherry Soup (2001; Forged Records). Of the nine pieces on this excellent album, Somogyi contributes five (including two beautiful folk song arrangements) and Lakatos three, while the final piece is a glorious version of the late Jimmy Rowles's famous ballad "The Peacocks".

Eddie South

Violin.

b. Louisiana, Missouri, 27 Nov 1904; d. 25 April 1962.

A child prodigy who was later billed as "the dark angel of the violin", Eddie South was a graduate of Chicago Music College and received special jazz tuition (said Earl Hines) from Darnell Howard. South worked in bands around Chicago and New York before touring Europe with his own group, where he took time out to study in Paris and Budapest; when he got back to the USA in 1931 he formed a big band, for which Milt Hinton – just out of high school – played bass. "It was very good," said Hinton, "but it seemed as though the time wasn't right for a big band with a negro violinist standing in front playing ballads!" So South went back to a small group, played clubs such as the Rubaiyat and Congress Hotel in Chicago and then toured Southern towns on the Keith and RKO circuits, playing chamber jazz that was technically perfect and ahead of its time. Said Hinton: "This country wasn't prepared to accept his kind of continental saloon music. John Kirby's group had class and precision but Eddie's was before his and it was even more delicate." As vaudeville and theatre circuits closed, South's career faltered and he went back to Europe (along the way he met Django Reinhardt and recorded classics with him), finally sailing back home for good with Benny Carter on the SS *Normandie* in 1938. Through the 1940s South's career moved comfortably along: he played clubs such as Kelly's Stables, toured with Billy Taylor, and worked for studio bands in New York, at MGM and elsewhere. As he gradually came into fashion he had his own radio series in the 1940s and regular TV in the 1950s with presenters such as Herb Lyons and Dave Garroway. And yet he never achieved the publicity of Stuff Smith (who was more of a clown) or Stephane Grappelli (who was white). [DF]

⊙ **Eddie South 1923–41** (Classics). Two-volume chronological sequence of South's great recordings, including titles with Reinhardt and Grappelli – "Lady Be Good", "Sweet Georgia Brown", "Eddie's Blues" and others.

Muggsy Spanier

Cornet, trumpet.

b. Chicago, 9 Nov 1906; d. 12 Feb 1967.

All through the 1920s Muggsy (Francis Joseph) Spanier worked in Chicago club bands, soaking up the lessons of Louis Armstrong, King Oliver and Tommy Ladnier, a player who – like Spanier – played economically and often in the middle register, with a big tone. "When old Gabe blows that horn," said Muggsy later, in a fit of Armstrong-esque good humour, "he'll probably use the fingering that Tommy Ladnier taught him". In 1929 Spanier joined Ted Lewis for seven years (the records are treasures), then Ben Pollack for two and, after a near-fatal illness (he was hospitalized for three months in 1938), formed the great band for which he is best remembered, Muggsy Spanier's Ragtime Band, in 1939. During a six-month stay at the Sherman Hotel, Chicago, followed by a brief appearance at Nick's Club, New York, they recorded sixteen Chicago-style Dixieland sides for Bluebird (including "Relaxin' At The Touro", commemorating Spanier's hospital stay) which are still known to jazz fans simply as "The Great Sixteen". But the Ragtimers disbanded soon after (it was the height of the big-band era) and Spanier rejoined Lewis, worked for Bob Crosby, briefly formed his own big band (which recorded just seven sides before the Musicians' Union recording ban bit), then went back to Lewis again in 1944. From then on Spanier played for Miff Mole (often at Nick's in New York), led his own groups for record dates and live appearances, and from 1950 was often on the West Coast, where he moved permanently in 1957, at the same time joining Earl Hines at Club Hangover for a two-year residency. At the end of his life came five more years' bandleading.

DAVID REDFERN

Muggsy Spanier

"The kind of guy Muggsy was? Direct, honest and vital!" said George T. Simon. The description fits Spanier personally and musically. His cornet encapsulates the art of direct musical lead (a quality which King Oliver, one of Spanier's idols, put first) and, while Muggsy was never the most technically startling player, no one knew better how to lead a Dixieland band with perfect economy, power, time and note placement. One of the kindliest and best-loved of Chicago jazzmen, Spanier also made big contributions to jazz trumpet vocabulary. "I don't believe there was any other trumpeter to use a growl mute like he did", said Freddy Goodman. "Muggsy influenced a lot of players. He had a beautiful tone and he played with a kind of natural feeling. Bunny Berigan was the only other white guy with that kind of feeling." [DF]

Muggsy 1924–54 (Avid) An excellent double-CD set, covering Spanier's career from the Bucktown Five (1924) on through the Chicago Rhythm Kings, Ted Lewis, three tracks by his classic Ragtimers, but strong on his later sides (36 of them) from 1942–54 – a neglected period but frequently wonderful. Fine sound from Dave Bennett.

The Great Sixteen (1939; RCA Victor). A jazz classic, remastered from RCA's original analogue tapes and presented with original artwork. Spanier in charge of his Ragtime Band; an ecstatic all-for-one eight-piece and essential listening.

The Ragtime Band Sessions 1939 (RCA Bluebird). Completists may prefer this album, if they can find it. Collectors argued for years about alternate takes of "The Great Sixteen" and here are all eight of them alongside the originals.

Muggsy Spanier 1939–42/1944/1944–6 (Classics). Spanier's Classics chronology including all of "The Great Sixteen" on *(1939–42)* and titles recorded for Commodore thereafter with Miff Mole, Bud Freeman, Peanuts Hucko and more stars.

Little David Play On Your Harp (1941–2; Archives of Jazz). Spanier's big band has been regularly underrated: its Crosby-esque buoyancy is well captured here, on broadcasts from New York's Arcadia Ballroom.

Muggshot (1924-42; ASV). Excellent sampler of Spanier pointing up his essential contributions to a whole variety of historic jazz situations: amongst them Ted Lewis's hottest band, the Bechet-Spanier Big Four, delicate duets with Lee Wiley, and of course his Ragtimers (four tracks). Those who have discovered "The Great Sixteen" should move onto this collection to broaden their view of Spanier.

Tony Spargo

Drums, kazoo.

b. New Orleans, 27 June 1897; d. 30 Oct 1969.

Tony Spargo (Antonio Sbarbaro) was a regular colleague of Eddie Edwards and Nick LaRocca in Papa Jack Laine's bands back in New Orleans and went to Chicago with them in 1916 to form the Original Dixieland Jazz Band. For the next thirty years his name was to be much associated with the ODJB: he was in the 1936 re-creation with LaRocca, which he led from 1938–40, was in another for the Katherine Dunham revue in 1943 (without LaRocca), and then another for Eddie Edwards in 1945–6. Before he retired in the 1960s Spargo worked regularly with Phil Napoleon, and showed that his drumming style had kept up well with the times; he also featured spirited kazoo-playing, a central point of his jazz act. [DF]

➤➤ **Original Dixieland Jazz Band** *(Sensation)*.

Andra Sparks

Voice, Piano.

b. Coleraine, Northern Ireland, 7 Dec 1951.

Andra Sparks grew up surrounded by music of all kinds – classical, folk, show and pop. Her mother played the piano and sang, and she had piano lessons from an early age. Singing was her other passion and while at the University of Kent, where she studied English and American literature, she got involved in several musical productions and began a serious study of classical vocal technique. Because of her enthusiasm for poetry, she was especially drawn to those 20th century classical song-writers who were sensitive verse-setters, in particular Gerald Finzi, Frank Bridge, Madeleine Dring, Claude Debussy, François Poulenc and Samuel Barber.

Sparks was deeply involved with the classical scene for several years, but in the mid-1980s she started to get interested in some of the outstanding popular songwriters of the 20th century – Richard Rodgers, Kurt Weill, Harold Arlen, Cole Porter, Stephen Sondheim – but felt that she didn't have the right technique to perform them. Then in 1992 she attended the Wavendon Summer School where she met jazz musicians and singers, and underwent a real conversion to jazz. After singing with a couple of big bands in Hertfordshire, she attended a jazz workshop in Ireland in 1996 (where she met Norma Winstone), and two years later another workshop at Banff in Canada. Kenny Wheeler was among the tutors in Canada, and Sparks performed in his Sweet Sister Suite. She had already started performing with a trio consisting of pianist Nick Weldon, bassist Jeff Clyne and drummer Trevor Tomkins, and in 1999 the four of them – plus Iain Dixon on sax and clarinet – recorded *People We Once Knew* on Weldon's Verge label. This was followed in 2004 by a second album for Verge, *Your Time*, with Russell van den Berg replacing Dixon on reeds. [IC]

Your Time (2004; Verge). On this second album Sparks's husky, intimate tones are brought to bear on an interestingly varied range of songs in clean but colourful arrangements by Weldon. She's especially strong on the more soulful and introspective numbers, and clearly has a strong affinity with Kenny Wheeler material (his "Sweet Dulcinea Blue" is one of the standout tracks). Well supported by her band, with some particularly edgy sax from van den Berg on "But Beautiful".

James Spaulding

Alto saxophone, flute.

b. Indianapolis, Indiana, 30 July 1937.

After studying at the Chicago Cosmopolitan School of Music from 1957, James Spaulding stayed in the city, playing and recording with Sun Ra, until moving to New York in the early 1960s. Although he did lead his own bands during this period, he established himself mainly as a first-call sideman on both his instruments for Blue Note, contributing his distinctive sound to recordings by Freddie Hubbard, Larry Young, Joe Henderson, Wayne Shorter, Stanley Turrentine, Horace Silver and others. In the 1970s and 1980s, Spaulding continued his sideman activities, playing with Charles

Tolliver, Ricky Ford and Bobby Hutcherson, and forming a strong musical relationship with David Murray, both in his big band and in the World Saxophone Quartet, but a series of Muse recordings with superb bands brought him into the limelight as a leader in the late 1980s and early 1990s. The disappearance of these from the catalogue in the late 1990s, however, again unfairly weighted Spaulding's discography towards his sideman appearances, such as his flute-playing cameo on Bheki Mseleku's *Beauty Of Sunrise* (1997; Verve) and organist/singer Eddie Landsberg's *Remembering Eddie Jefferson* (2002; Berghem). Although he is an extremely valuable contributor to others' ensembles, with both his vibrant alto and his gentler flute, Spaulding is a passionate and highly underrated soloist and leader. [CP]

Plays The Legacy Of Duke Ellington (1976; Storyville). Not entirely successful Duke tribute culminating in "It Don't Mean A Thing ..." and featuring Steve Nelson (vibes) and pianist Cedar Walton.

Brilliant Corners (1988; Muse). Greatly improved leader's album, also a tribute, but to Monk, and showcasing a stellar band – Wallace Roney (trumpet), Mulgrew Miller (piano), Ron Carter (bass), Kenny Washington (drums) – on everything from "Little Willie Leaps" to "Little Rootie Tootie".

Songs Of Courage (1991; Muse). With frontline support from trombonist Tyrone Jefferson and tenor player Roland Alexander and with a rhythm-section of Kenny Barron (piano), Ray Drummond (bass) and Louis Hayes (drums), this is an appealing run-through of standards like "Wee" and Elmo Hope's "Minor Bertha"; a highlight is Spaulding's flute on a threnody to Martin Luther King.

Escapade (1999; High Note). A good hard bop date for quintet, featuring Don Sickler (trumpet), John Hicks (piano), Billy Drummond (bass) and Kenny Washington (drums) in reliable form on Blue Note-era material from Mobley, Dorham, Grant Green and Dexter Gordon.

Martin Speake

Alto saxophone, composer; also soprano, tenor and baritone saxophones.

b. Barnet, Herts, UK, 3 April 1958.

Speake studied saxophone at Trinity College of Music, London, from 1977–81, but learned jazz from records, concerts and other musicians. In the mid-1980s he attended the Banff jazz summer school in Canada, studying with saxophonist Steve Coleman, who had taken over from Dave Holland as course director. Speake became a founder member of the British saxophone quartet, Itchy Fingers, which won the group prize at the 1986 Schlitz Young Jazz Musicians Competition in London. They toured Africa, South America and Europe, played many festivals and broadcasts, and recorded two albums, *Quark* and *Teranga*, before Speake left the group in 1988. After leaving, he concentrated on his own projects, including a quartet with guitarist John Parricelli, bassist Steve Watts and drummer Steve Argüelles, a duo with guitarist Phil Lee, a trio with Indian musicians Dharambir Singh and Sarvar Sabri, a seven-piece group, Fever Pitch, including three percussionists, playing Indian- and Arab-influenced music, and a quartet with trumpeter Ted Emmett, playing Ornette Coleman's music.

Speake was featured on the 1991 recording of Billy Jenkins's *Entertainment USA* and made his own debut album, *In Our Time*, with his quartet in 1994. Since then he has made two albums each with pianist Nikki Iles and guitarist John Parricelli; with Iles a duo record *The Tan T'ien* (1998; FMR) and a quartet album *Secret* (2001; Basho); with Parricelli the quartet outings *Trust* (1997; 33 Records) and *Hullabaloo* (2000; Linn). A recent project featured long-time compatriot Mick Hutton (bass) and Tom Skinner (drums) in the Exploring Standards Trio.

He is involved in jazz education at the Royal Academy of Music in London, and Middlesex University. Speake has also worked with many other people including Loose Tubes, Flora Purim and Airto Moreira, Paul Motian, Django Bates and Ashley Slater's Microgroove. His favourites range from Steve Coleman to Charlie Parker and Johnny Hodges, and other inspirations include Bill Evans (the pianist) and Keith Jarrett, Kenny Wheeler, Monk, Miles and Mingus. Speake's sound is wonderfully unfashionable, harking back to the almost disembodied pure tone of early Lee Konitz. [IC]

In Our Time (1994; The Jazz Label). This is a very refreshing quartet album, with nine excellent compositions by Speake, full of invention and variety, yet with a homogeneous identity so that they seem to make an hour-long suite. His improvisations are lyrical, often understated, but leavened on occasion by harmonically wayward melodic lines. Parricelli and the rhythm-section are also very fine. A sheer delight.

Secret (2001; Basho). Speake's elliptical, highly musical approach requires musical partners of great resource, taste and imagination. Pianist Nikki Iles has all these qualities and more, and composes much of this splendid record, which also features bassist Duncan Hopkins and drummer Anthony Michelli.

Spikes Brothers

A very influential pair of jazz entrepreneurs, the Spikes brothers – Reb (Benjamin) and John – were active on and off for more than half a century. In the mid-1900s they ran a highly successful showband and travelling show (Jelly Roll Morton was in it for a while) and by 1919 had settled in Los Angeles. Here they opened a music store, a nightclub (the Dreamland Café), an agency and a publishing house (which handled their most successful composition, "Someday Sweetheart", and new lyrics to "Wolverine Blues"), and formed a band, the Majors and Minors, featuring singer Ivie Anderson, which played the Follies Theater on Main Street. In 1922 they were the first to record an all-black jazz band (Kid Ory's, on their Sunshine label), in 1924 they wrote a show for Eddie "Rochester" Anderson (*Stepping High*) and in 1927 they made a short sound film, *Reb Spikes And His Follies Entertainers* for Warner Bros, which predated *The Jazz Singer*. Gradually music fashions passed the Spikes Brothers by. John went blind, Reb became ill and by 1962 was an estate agent. But ten years on he was working on a new revue, *The Heart And Soul Of A Slave* (based on the story of Biddy Thomas, a slave who became a pioneer black capitalist): the soon-to-be-popular TV series *Roots* showed that Spikes's judgement was as sharp as ever. [DF]

The Spirits Of Rhythm

Featuring Wilbur and Douglas Daniels (tipples/vocals), Teddy Bunn (guitar), Virgil Scroggins (drums/vocals) and Leo Watson (lead voice), The Spirits of Rhythm were a novelty group who made their name in the 1930s, working first at Chick Groman's Stables, New York, then at the Onyx Club. Charles Fox described their act: "Leo Watson moved his arm in and out just like a trombonist (Benny Morton was his idol) improvising one elaborate scat chorus after another. Teddy Bunn played guitar, there were three instruments called tipples, and Virgil Scroggins drummed on a paper-wrapped suitcase with a pair of whisk brooms." The formula was just right for the Onyx and a country which had taken to novelty acts such as Red McKenzie's Mound City Blue Blowers (McKenzie was a regular colleague of the Spirits), but the Spirits also produced a lot of enduring jazz and their records are frequently reissued. "They were," wrote Max Jones, "a fun group; and they were more than that – creative, and adventurous with it!" [DF]

⊙ **The Spirits Of Rhythm** (1933–4; JSP). Excellent set drawn from six Spirits of Rhythm sessions, showing Teddy Bunn at his best and with the great Red McKenzie on three tracks. Fine sound by John R.T. Davies, and sleevenotes by Max Jones.

Victoria Spivey

Vocals, piano, organ, ukulele, composer.
b. Houston, Texas, 15 Oct 1906; d. 3 Oct 1976.

Victoria "Queen" Spivey had an enormous hit in 1926 with her first recording, "Black Snake Blues", which sold 150,000 copies in that year. From then on she was a big star, appearing at top New York theatres, and in *Hallelujah* (1929), an all-black MGM musical (directed by King Vidor) which also featured Curtis Mosby's orchestra, Nina Mae McKinney and drummer Earl Roach. The success of the film, and Spivey's recordings of the period (including "Funny Feathers", "Make A Country Bird Fly Wild" and "Organ Grinder", featuring such accompanists as Clarence Williams, Louis Armstrong and Henry "Red" Allen), assured her a headlining career in vaudeville. During the 1930s she fronted trumpeter Lloyd Hunter's orchestra on tour and later married tap-dancer Billy Adams, with whom she formed a team. By the late 1940s she was still well enough remembered to join Olsen and Johnson's *Hellzapoppin* show (which they toured in the wake of the 1941 film from Universal) and she returned to prominence again in the 1960s, after a temporary retirement, touring with packages, running her own recording company in New York and appearing with Turk Murphy's band. Spivey's work is first-rank blues, and her neglect is hard to understand. [DF]

Louis Armstrong

⊙ **Louis Armstrong And The Blues Singers** (1924–30; Affinity). This set has Spivey's great "Funny Feathers" plus "How Do You Do It That Way?" from 1929.

Bryan Spring

Drums.
b. London, 24 Aug 1945.

Spring started on drums at six, and is self-taught, apart from some lessons from Philly Joe Jones. He began freelancing in London during the early 1960s, and from the mid-1960s he spent eight years with Stan Tracey's various groups. From 1967–9 he was with the Frank Ricotti quartet, in 1972 he was with Klaus Doldinger's Passport and in 1974 he spent several months with Nucleus. In 1975 he was a co-founder of the Don Weller-Bryan Spring quartet with which trumpeter "Hannibal" Marvin Peterson toured the UK in the 1980s. He has also led bands of his own – his most recent being the Bryan Spring Trio featuring pianist Mark Edwards and bassist Andrew Clyndert – and continued to freelance in the London area. Spring has also worked with Jean-Luc Ponty, Tubby Hayes, Joe Williams, Charlie Shavers, George Coleman and Charlie Rouse among others. His favourites include Philly Joe Jones, Roy Haynes, Max Roach, Elvin Jones, Larry Bunker and Johnny Butts; other inspirations are Sonny Rollins, John Coltrane, Bill Evans, Miles Davis and Cannonball Adderley. A prodigious technician, he can handle any tempo and any area of the music. [IC]

➤➤ **Alan Skidmore** *(East To West)*; **Don Weller** *(Live)*.

Larry Stabbins

Tenor and soprano saxophone.
b.Bristol, UK, 9 Sept 1949.

Larry Stabbins is a consummate saxophonist who has been at the cutting edge of jazz for much of his career, especially in the field of free improvisation. He started off playing in dance bands around Bristol from the age of twelve, and at sixteen joined the Quintet of fellow-Bristolian Keith Tippett. He was subsequently involved in many Tippett projects including Centipede, and the ensuing album *Septober Energy* (1971); Ark in the late 70s; Tippett's Septet in the early 80s; and Tapestry in the late 1990s. He and Tippett also briefly formed a trio with South African drummer Louis Moholo, producing the live album *Tern* in 1982.

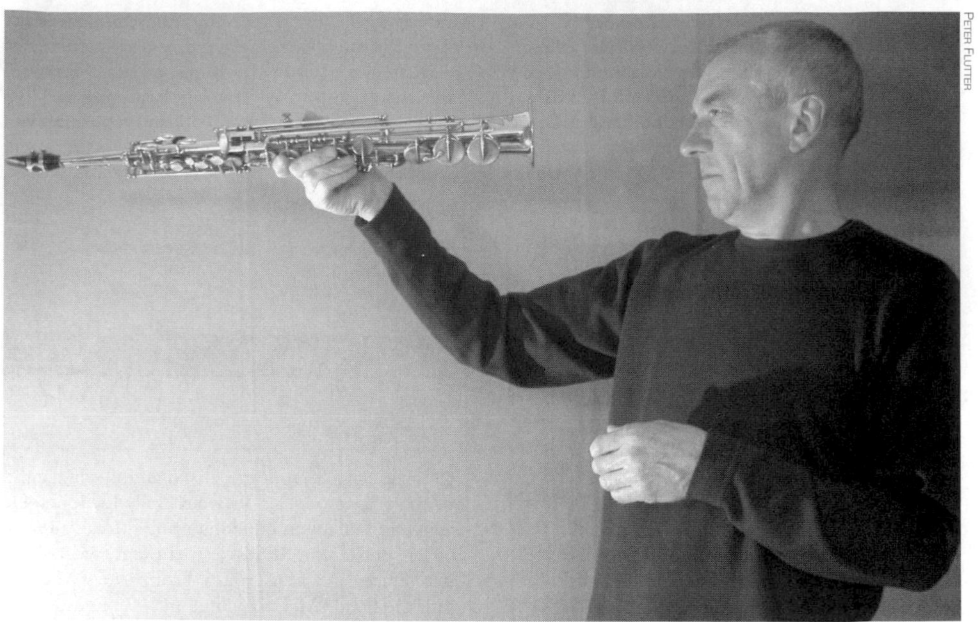

Peter Flutter

Larry Stabbins

As well as his close involvement with Tippett, Stabbins has collaborated with many of the leading figures of the free improv scene. His most experimental music dates from the late 1970s and early 1980s when he formed a duo with percussionist Roy Ashbury, the two recording an album, *Fire Without Bricks*, in 1976. From 1978 he was a member of the Tony Oxley Quintet and the Tony Oxley Celebration Orchestra with whom he recorded *Tomorrow Is Here* (1985; Dossier). He has also played and recorded with the German-based Peter Brötzmann's Alarm Orchestra and März Combo, the London Jazz Composers Orchestra, and the Eddie Prévost Quartet.

Stabbins pursued a different direction through his involvement with Weekend, an indie pop band with soft jazz leanings that was formed in 1980. This was superseded in 1983 by Working Week, a more hard-edged outfit, led by Stabbins and guitarist Simon Booth, that produced a combination of Latin, jazz and dance music. Of the five albums the band made for Virgin, the one that best showcases Stabbins' all-round talents is *Fire In The Mountain* (1989). The group disbanded in 1991; since then Stabbins has worked with the rap-jazz combo QRZ?, and played in a trio with keyboardist Pat Thomas and drummer Mark Sanders, and in pianist Howard Riley's Quartet alongside Sanders and bassist Tony Wren. In 2002 Stabbins recorded the highly impressive solo album *Monadic*. [IC]

Louis Moholo, Larry Stabbins and Keith Tippett

⊙ **Tern** (1982; Atavistic). Recently reissued in Atavistic's Unheard Music series, this is an outstanding example of the creative heights that could be reached in "free music". The three are brilliant improvisers completely in tune with what each is doing.

Larry Stabbins

⊙ **Monadic** (2002; Emanem). Seventy-five minutes of solo saxophone (both soprano and tenor) may sound a challenging prospect, but in the hands of an artist of the calibre of Stabbins it works surprisingly well. Each of the 13 tracks emphasizes a different aspect of playing the instrument ("Breathing", "Singing", "Blowing", etc), and there are subtle allusions to the styles of some of Stabbins' favourites, from Peter Brötzmann to Steve Lacy.

➤➤ **Howard Riley** *(Four In The Afternoon)*.

Jess Stacy

Piano.

b. Bird's Point, Missouri, 11 Aug 1904; d. 5 Jan 1994.

One of the greatest swing pianists, whose sustaining right-hand tremolo was his unmistakable trademark, Jess Stacy began working on Missouri riverboats, where he played piano (and sometimes calliope) with bands such as Tony Catalano's Iowans. By the mid-1920s he had arrived in Chicago, where he worked for numerous leaders in countless speakeasies, clubs and dance halls. Ten years later, at the instigation of John Hammond, he joined Benny Goodman and worked with him intermittently for nine years, in between stints with Bob Crosby, Horace Heidt and Tommy Dorsey. With Goodman, Stacy became a star (an unscheduled solo at the close of Goodman's "Sing, Sing, Sing" routine at Carnegie Hall, 1938, turned him into a legend in two minutes), but his unsuccessful marriage to singer Lee Wiley (which he later referred to as "The Wiley Incident"), his two short-lived big bands (one formed to back his wife) and irregular work made life less satisfactory from the mid-1940s. Though the 1950s produced one late classic – *Tribute To Benny Goodman* by Jess Stacy and the Famous Sidemen (now very rare) – he spent much of his time playing piano bars and clubs and justifiably feeling neglected. In 1963 he retired to become a salesman for Max Factor and not until 1973, when he was persuaded to play soundtrack music for the film *The Great Gatsby*, was Stacy's piano heard again. The following year he played the Newport jazz festival to a standing ovation, and he subsequently appeared regularly at jazz festivals such as Sacramento, on TV and radio, and on record. [DF]

⊙ **Ec-Stacy** (1935–45; ASV). Invaluable and wide-ranging survey of his work, including solos plus sides on which he is featured with Condon, Bob Crosby, Pee Wee Russell, Lionel Hampton and Benny Goodman – his legendary contribution to the 1938 Carnegie Hall concert is here.

⊙ **Jess Stacy And Friends** (1938–44; Commodore). Essential collection of Stacy's best solos and collaborations from the period, including "Complainin'" (which he later did with the Bobcats), Lee Wiley's rare blues outing on "Down To Steamboat Tennessee" (with Muggsy Spanier), and duets with drummer Specs Powell.

⊙ **Stacy Still Swings** (1974–7; Chiaroscuro). A late date for Stacy; though perhaps a little rustier than before, the trademarks are still intact, including the celebrated "Stacy roll", and much of the inspiration is still there.

➤➤ **Benny Goodman** *(Carnegie Hall Concert 1938).*

Tomasz Stanko

Trumpet, flugelhorn, composer.

b. Rzeszow, Poland, 11 July 1942.

Stanko studied violin and piano at school, then studied trumpet at the music high school in Cracow, graduating in 1969. He first heard jazz at a 1958 Dave Brubeck concert. He formed his first group in 1962 with pianist Adam Makowicz, calling it the Jazz Darings. He also worked with Krzysztof Komeda, and from 1965–9 with Andrzej Trzaskowski. Between 1963–5 he did his first major tours in Czechoslovakia, Yugoslavia and Scandinavia. From 1965 he was voted best trumpeter every year in Poland. He took part in Hamburg (NDR) jazz workshops, and also in Manfred Schoof's "Trumpet Summit" in Nuremberg. In 1970 he played with Alex von Schlippenbach's Globe Unity Orchestra and formed the Tomasz Stanko quintet, which included Zbigniew Seifert on alto (it was while he was with Stanko that Seifert switched to violin). In 1971 Stanko played with Don Cherry, Albert Mangelsdorff and Gerd Dudek in the European Free Jazz Orchestra at Donaueschingen. The same year the *Jazz Forum* poll voted him Best European Jazz Musician.

The Tomasz Stanko quintet played all the major European festivals and also toured extensively in Europe in 1972–3. He and Makowicz played with Michal Urbaniak in 1974, and in 1975 he formed the Tomasz Stanko and Adam Makowicz Unit with Czeslaw Bartkowski on drums, touring Germany and receiving ecstatic press notices. In 1985 Stanko formed Freelectronic and was featured in Graham Collier's "Hoarded Dreams" at the Camden festival. Through the 1990s Stanko's international profile steadily increased via remarkable series of albums on ECM (see below). J. E. Berendt has described Stanko as a "white Ornette Coleman", but Stanko's music has developed into a rich compound of all the jazz disciplines – rhythm, harmony, structure, etc, plus the dimension of abstraction. He said in the mid-1970s: "Our music may appear to be atonal and arhythmic, but it is not." As a trumpet player, he is a virtuoso performer with an excellent range. [IC]

Tomasz Stanko

⊙ **Balladyna** (1975; ECM). This was Stanko's breakthrough album, in company with saxophonist Tomasz Szukalski, the Finnish drummer Edward Vesala and the ubiquitous Dave Holland. The music moves between lyrical set structures and freer improvised passages – the Poles and the Finns are probably too steeped in their folk traditions ever to feel totally at ease with complete abstraction.

⊙ **Bluish** (1991; Power Bros); **Bosanossa And Other Ballads** (1993; GOWI). *Bluish* has Stanko in the company of Arild Andersen and Jon Christensen in a dynamic half-structured, half-free session. The trio interacts subtly and powerfully, and Stanko is sonorous, lyrical and nicely unpredictable. He's also in good heart and lip on *Bosanossa And Other Ballads*. His quartet has a conventional piano, bass and drums rhythm-section, but they are all played by unconventional musicians – Bobo Stenson, Anders Jormin and Tony Oxley. The results are superb and deeply affecting. Stanko produces rich sonorities and flowing lyrical phrases which insinuate themselves from the gently evocative themes.

⊙ **Leosia** (1996; ECM); **Litania** (1996; ECM); **From The Green Hill** (1999; ECM); **Soul Of Things** (2002; ECM). A fine run of records which represents the mature distillation of Stanko's art. From the interactive quartet work of Leosia through the gorgeous tribute to composer Krzysztof

Andrzej Tyszko/ECM Records

Tomasz Stanko, right, with the rest of his quartet

Komeda of Litania and the intense, lovely European chamber jazz of *From The Green Hill* (featuring John Surman) and *Soul Of Things*, these resonant albums feature some of the most admired music of the period.

Freelectronic

The Montreux Performance (1987; ITM). Freelectronic was Stanko's drummer-less quartet of the mid-1980s, with Janusz Skowron (piano/synthesizer), Witold E. Szczurek (bass) and Tadeusz Sudnik (electronics). Although leaning towards abstraction the music is controlled, coherent and very much a product of Stanko's unique vision.

Tomasz Stanko and Janusz Skowron

Tales For A Girl, 12/A Shaky Chica (1991; Jam). This duo of Stanko and Skowron is an interesting offshoot from Freelectronic. Stanko's interest in literature and language informs the twelve pieces which comprise *Tales For A Girl* and he creates succinct epigrammatic trumpet phrases to tell his stories.

>> **Krzysztof Komeda** *(Astigmatic).*

Bobby Stark

Trumpet.

b. New York, 6 Jan 1906; d. 29 Dec 1945.

Famous for his fine individual solo powers (and a distinctive off-centre embouchure), Stark was a noted freelance around New York from 1925: he worked in a number of bands (including Chick Webb's), then for Fletcher Henderson (1928–33) and Webb again (1934–9). "No one sounded like Bobby Stark when he came back [to Webb] on trumpet", said Taft Jordan, who did an Armstrong act for the drummer-leader. "His *wasn't* an Armstrong thing. That solo he used to play on 'Squeeze Me' was just Bobby, and no one else." Stark was invalided out of the army in 1943 and worked with Garvin Bushell, Benny Morton and others in New York until his premature death. [DF]

>> **Fletcher Henderson** *(A Study In Frustration).*

Bill Stegmeyer

Clarinet, saxophones, arranger.

b. Detroit, Michigan, 8 Oct 1916; d. 19 Aug 1968.

Bill Stegmeyer was an early colleague of Billy Butterfield: they shared a room at Transylvania College and later worked together in Austin Wylie's band from 1937. From there Stegmeyer made rapid strides: he joined Glenn Miller in 1938 playing saxophone, and then worked with Bob Crosby (1939–40), by which time he was beginning to specialize as an arranger. From then on he continued to play regularly (for Butterfield and others) and to lead his own band at Kelly's Stables, as well as broadening his activities by working for a Detroit radio station (1948–50) and returning to New York to work for TV and (from 1960) conduct at CBS. One of the greatest Dixieland clarinettists, he rates with Matty Matlock, Irving Fazola and Heinie Beau. [DF]

>> **Bob Haggart** *(The Legendary Lawson-Haggart Jazz Band).*

Jeremy Steig

Flute, piccolo, alto flute, bass flute, electronics, composer.

b. New York, 23 Sept 1942.

Son of the well-known artist William Steig, Jeremy Steig began on recorder at the age of six, and took up flute at eleven, having lessons from 1953–6; he then attended the High School of Music and Art. In 1961 he worked with Paul Bley and Gary Peacock. In 1966–7 he was in a jazz-rock group backing Tim Hardin, and in 1967 began leading his own groups, which included Mike Mainieri and Eddie Gomez and, in 1970, Jan Hammer. In 1969 he recorded with Bill Evans but mainly played in his group Jeremy and the Satyrs and played jazz-rock, and during the 1970s he made extensive use of electronics. He played the Berlin jazz festival several times during the 1970s, including with Art Blakey's Orgy in Rhythm in 1972, and Pierre Courbois's Association PC in 1974. Steig has also toured in Europe with his own quartets and quintets and as a soloist. He is a virtuoso with a mastery of the whole flute family, from bass to piccolo, and a wide vocabulary of tonal devices. His work is also notable for his harmonic awareness and the intelligent integration of electronics with acoustic instruments. [IC]

Something Else (1970; LRC). Steig with Eddie Gomez, plus second bassist Gene Perla, percussionist Don Alias and Jan Hammer on electric piano and gongs. Steig was one of the more creative spirits in the jazz-rock movement and this is a genial essay in the genre.

Outlaws (1976; Enja). This lovely duo workout by Steig and Gomez provides a brilliant meeting of sonorities and song structures on some jazz standards. Two virtuosi dancing on common ground.

>> **Eddie Gomez** *(Dedication).*

Bobo Stenson

Piano, composer.

b. Våsterås, Sweden, 4 Aug 1944.

Widely regarded as his country's foremost contemporary jazz pianist, Bobo Stenson established himself, after his move to Stockholm in 1966, by playing both with local musicians – tenor saxophonists Börje Fredriksson and Bernt Røsengren – and with a host of Americans, whether resident (Red Mitchell, Don Cherry, George Russell) or visiting (Sonny Rollins, Stan Getz, Gary Burton). In 1971, Stenson began his long and productive association with ECM, recording *Sart* for the company with Jan Garbarek, Terje Rypdal, Arild Andersen and Jon Christensen, and a trio album, *Underwear*. He also appeared on the enduringly popular Garbarek/Stenson albums *Witchi-Tai-To* (1973; ECM) and *Dansere* (1975; ECM), helping establish a folk-influenced European jazz style in the process. In the late 1970s and early 1980s, Stenson concentrated mainly on his Swedish projects, in particular the cooperative band Rena Rama, which featured saxophonist Lennart Åberg and bassist Palle Danielsson – later replaced by longtime associate Anders Jormin – and produced the celebrated Japo album, *Landscapes*, in 1977. A trio with Jormin and drummer Rune Carlsson produced another highly regarded album for Dragon in 1986, *Very Early*, featuring the eponymous Bill Evans piece, Alex Wilder's "Moon And Sand", the odd standard, plus pieces by Fauré and Coltrane. It was Stenson's lyrical, supremely sympathetic contribution to the recording comeback of Charles Lloyd, however, beginning with *Fish Out Of Water* (1989) and continuing through *Notes From Big Sur* (1991), *The Call* (1993), *All My Relations* (1994) and *Canto* (1996) – all for ECM – that really brought Stenson to international attention, and he consolidated his reputation through more ECM recordings, with Don Cherry (the trumpeter's last session in 1993, *Dona Nostra*) and a series of fine albums with Polish trumpeter Tomasz Stanko, culminating in 1996's *Litania*, dedicated to the music of Krzysztof Komeda. Stenson's own trio, with Jormin and Christensen, also established itself internationally in the late 1990s with two superb albums, *Reflections* (see below) and 1998's *War Orphans*. A mellifluously elegant player with a keen jazz mind, Stenson has done as much as anyone in recent years to put a distinctively European style of jazz on the map. [CP]

Reflections (1996; ECM). Subtly interactive trio music from three musicians who know each other's playing inside out: six band originals, plus Gershwin's "My Man's Gone Now" and Ellington's "Reflections In D".

SSIRUS W PAKZAD/ECM RECORDS

Bobo Stenson

Steps And Steps Ahead

➤➤ *see entry on* **Mike Mainieri**.

Mike Stern

Guitar.

b. Boston, Massachusetts, 10 Jan 1953.

Having grown up with the music of the Beatles, and influenced by Eric Clapton, Jimi Hendrix and blues guitarists such as B.B. King, Mike Stern became interested in jazz in his teens and attended the Berklee School of Music, studying under Pat Metheny and Mick Goodrick. Stern began his professional career with Blood, Sweat And Tears in 1976, but moved into jazz-rock proper two years later with Billy Cobham's band. His big break came in 1981, when he was invited to join Miles Davis's comeback band, appearing on *The Man With The Horn* and touring with the trumpeter until 1983, when he joined Jaco Pastorius's Word of Mouth, subsequently rejoining Davis for his 1985 European tour. Stern is a high-energy electric guitarist, verbose – even garrulous – yet there were signs, manifest in his late 1990s gigs with a supple but punchy band (saxophonist Bob Sheppard, bassist Lincoln Goines, drummer Dave Weckl), that Stern had taken Miles Davis's strictures on his playing to heart ("I thought that if Mike listened to John [Scofield], he might learn something about understatement"). Long, carefully structured lines, perfectly executed, had replaced the screaming rock-based approach of yore, rendering Stern's music a genuine fusion between the immediate accessibility of rock and the rhythmic and harmonic subtlety of jazz, an approach well documented on his late 1990s Atlantic recordings, *Between The Lines* (1996, produced by Jim Beard) and *Give And Take* (1997, produced by Gil Goldstein) and *Play* (see below). His final album for Atlantic, *Voices* (2001), took a particularly expressive turn and effectively blended Stern's increasingly varied approach to the guitar with Elisabeth Kontamanou's vocals. Stern has also contributed to recordings by saxophonists Michael

Brecker and Bob Berg, bassists Bunny Brunel and Harvie Swartz, trumpeter Lew Soloff, drummer Motohiko Hino (brother of trumpeter Terumasa) and has locked axes on the albums of fellow guitarists Jim Hall and Pat Martino. [CP]

⊙ **Odds and Ends** (1991; Atlantic). Powerful, gutsy fusion from Stern, along with frequent associate Bob Berg, drummer Dennis Chambers and percussionist Don Alias.

⊙ **Is What It Is** (1993; Atlantic). Originals, produced by keyboard fusion ace Jim Beard, featuring Michael Brecker and Dennis Chambers; highlight is the lyrical "What I Meant To Say".

⊙ **Play** (1999; Atlantic). From the alluring ambience of "Blue Tone" to the exciting, out-and-out blowing of "Play", Stern blends with his guest guitarists (Bill Frisell on the former, John Scofield on the latter) superbly well, and everyone – not least Lincoln Goines (bass) and Bob Malach (tenor) – plays immaculately.

John Stevens

Drums, percussion, mini trumpet.

b. Brentford, Middlesex, UK, 10 June 1940; d. 13 Sept 1994.

Stevens studied at Ealing Junior Art School and Ealing College of Higher Education. From 1958–64 he was in RAF bands after studying at the RAF School of Music. He had an early interest in skiffle, traditional and modern jazz. He sat in and played occasional gigs with various people including Francy Boland, Tubby Hayes, Derek Humble, Joe Harriott and Shake Keane. From 1964–5 he worked in London with Hayes, Ronnie Scott, Stan Tracey, and in a quartet with John McLaughlin, Jeff Clyne and Ian Carr. In 1965 he began to lead his own groups, with a septet (which included Kenny Wheeler, Alan Skidmore and Ron Mathewson) and the Spontaneous Music Ensemble. With the septet, Stevens explored the jazz language of the day-harmonic structures, set bar-lengths, fixed tempos, composed tunes, and improvisation based on all these factors. With the SME he pursued his growing interest in the current avant-garde music – free or abstract improvisation with no fixed harmonies, bar-lengths or tempos. Stevens and the SME became the focal point for a new generation of British free improvisers which included Evan Parker, Derek Bailey, Trevor Watts, Paul Rutherford, Barry Guy and Howard Riley.

In 1970 he formed the Spontaneous Music Orchestra, a larger ensemble still dealing in abstraction. Then he began to move away from total abstraction and towards more clearly defined rhythms and structures, starting with the group Splinters, which he co-led in 1971 with Phil Seamen, and which included Hayes, Wheeler, Tracey and Clyne. In 1974 he formed the John Stevens Dance Orchestra, in 1975 his jazz-rock group Away, and in 1982 Freebop and Folkus. Stevens also collaborated with Bobby Bradford, Steve Lacy, John Tchicai, Yoko Ono, Dudu Pukwana, Mongezi Feza and Johnny Dyani. Between 1968–85 he developed workshop techniques, and a manual of his workshop pieces was published in 1985. He was musical director of the UK Jazz Centre Society's Outreach Community Music Project after 1983; when the Outreach Project folded, he became the driving force behind Community Music Limited, an independent charity, working with children, schizophrenic patients and devising an improvisation course for teachers. Shortly before his death (from a heart attack), he had completed a major work, *Celebration With Voices*, for a sixty-strong choir, string quartet and jazz octet. His favourites were Kenny Clarke, Phil Seamen and Elvin Jones, and trumpeters Chet Baker, Don Cherry, Louis Armstrong and Bobby Bradford. Other inspirations were Ornette Coleman, Gary Peacock, Bud Powell and Monk. [IC]

Spontaneous Music Ensemble

⊙ **Karyobin** (1968; Chronoscope). Stevens with Kenny Wheeler, Evan Parker, Derek Bailey and Dave Holland – an all-star group, but with each man making himself an ingredient in a collective effort at improvisation with no preconceived structures at all. A classic album mirroring some of the qualities of that optimistic and idealistic decade.

John Stevens

⊙ **Touching On** (1977; Konnex). This has Stevens with seven musicians in a loose jazz-rock session which illustrates one of the drummer's interests. In the mid-1970s he followed his idol Ornette into the rocky wilderness with his group Away: here the freer approach is aided by Allan Holdsworth's guitar, which, even with the most lumpen rock beat, manages to be as free as air.

⊙ **New Cool** (1992; The Jazz Label). This live quartet session is one of the best things Stevens ever did. The

Jak Kilby

John Stevens, with Peter Kowald on bass

excellent Byron Wallen is on trumpet and flugelhorn, Ed Jones, also a fine player, on tenor and soprano saxophones, and Gary Crosby is a tower of strength on bass. Stevens swings quite superbly for three of these four intense performances, culminating with "Dudu's Gone", a powerful, defiant tribute to the memory of the late Pukwana. The music here is rhythmically and melodically excellent, has great clarity and is tremendously uplifting.

➤➤ **Derek Bailey** *(Playing)*; **Evan Parker** *(Corner To Corner)*; **Dudu Pukwana** *(Mbizo Radebe)*.

Bill Stewart

Drums, composer.

b. Des Moines, Iowa, 18 Oct 1966.

Having become interested in the music through exposure to his parents' jazz and R&B records, Bill Stewart played in his school orchestra, and a Top 40 covers band, before attending the University of Northern Iowa in Cedar Falls. He then studied with Dave Samuels, Rufus Reid and Harold Mabern at college in Wayne, New Jersey, and met Joe Lovano there. Recordings with saxophonist Scott Kreitzer and pianist Armen Donelian were followed by gigs (and recordings) with keyboard player Larry Coldings (an ongoing collaborator), JBs alumni Maceo Parker and Fred Wesley, saxophonists Seamus Blake, Marty Ehrlich, Lee Konitz, Jon Gordon, Chris Potter and George Garzone, plus other pianists including Bill Charlap, Andy LaVerne and Steve Kuhn. Perhaps his most celebrated sideman appearances, however, were with guitarist John Scofield's early 1990s band (which also included Lovano), and involved numerous Blue Note recordings beginning with *Meant To Be* (1990) and concluding with 1993's *Hand Jive*, and continued on Verve with 1996's acoustic *Quiet*. Stewart's albums as a leader began with *Think Before You Think* (1990; Jazz City), featuring bassist Dave Holland and pianist Marc Copland, but a move to Blue Note saw him release two further recordings: *Snide Remarks* (1995), featuring trumpeter Eddie Henderson and Lovano, and *Telepathy* (see below). Latterly, Stewart was a valuable member of Pat Metheny's acclaimed trio, heard on the albums *Trio 99>00* and *Trio Live* (both 2000; Warners). [CP]

⊙ **Telepathy** (1996; Blue Note). Sparky, imaginative two-horns (Steve Wilson and Seamus Blake) plus-rhythm (pianist Bill Carrothers, bassist Larry Grenadier) date that visits some bop material (Jackie McLean's "Little Melonae", Monk's "Rhythm-A-Ning") plus a selection of cogent Stewart compositions. As a showcase for Stewart's ability (noted by Lovano) to perform as "a melody player within the concept of rhythm", this would be difficult to beat.

Bob Stewart

Tuba.

b. Sioux Falls, South Dakota, 3 Feb 1945.

Stewart started on the trumpet, gained a scholarship to Philadelphia College of the Performing Arts and switched to tuba, graduating with a teaching degree. In 1968 he moved to New York, teaching at a junior high school as a band director. Howard Johnson showed him the possibilities of the tuba as a solo instrument and he joined Johnson's Substructure, a tuba ensemble. In 1971 he worked with the Collective Black Artists Ensemble. In the early 1970s he worked with Freddie Hubbard, Taj Mahal, Paul Jeffrey and others. In the mid-1970s he began working with three people who opened up even more opportunities for the tuba – Gil Evans, Carla Bley and Arthur Blythe. By the late 1970s he was gaining international recognition and winning polls on tuba. Stewart has also continued to teach, has played with the Globe Unity Orchestra and also co-led, with French horn player John Clark, the Clark-Stewart quartet. From the mid-1980s he worked with Lester Bowie's Brass Fantasy and Henry Threadgill's orchestra, also recording a pair of albums as leader for JMT; *First Line* (1987; JMT) and *Goin' Home* (1988; JMT). In the 1990s he was a regular member of the German tenor saxophonist Christof Lauer's quartet, with drummer Thomas Alkier and alto saxophonist Wolfgang Puschnig, also appearing with David Murray's big band and Howard Johnson's latest all-tuba group, Gravity. [IC]

➤➤ **Carla Bley** *(Dinner Music)*; **Arthur Blythe** *(In Concert)*; **Lester Bowie** *(The Fire This Time)*; **Christof Lauer** *(Bluebells)*.

Louis Stewart

Guitar.

b. Waterford, Ireland, 5 Jan 1944.

A guitarist from the age of fifteen, Louis Stewart gained his initial inspiration from recordings of Barney Kessel and his early professional experience with an Irish showband, with which he visited America in 1961. Working with pianist Noel Kelehan in Dublin in the 1960s, he accompanied Lee Konitz, Gerry Mulligan and other visiting American musicians. In 1968, after winning the Press Award as the outstanding soloist at the Montreux International jazz festival, performing with the Jim Doherty quartet, he joined the Tubby Hayes quartet in London and completed three European tours with the Benny Goodman big band (1969–70). In 1971 he returned to Dublin but, after several return visits to London for concerts arranged by the Jazz Centre Society, he joined the Ronnie Scott quintet (1975–9). Stewart's clear sound, excellent rhythmic control, chordal mastery and articulate, flowing lines have featured on seven albums by George Shearing and on several by the Robert Farnon Orchestra. His recording credits also include albums with Heiner Franz, Martin Taylor, Spike Robinson, and the European Jazz Guitar Orchestra (alongside fellow guitarists Heiner Franz, Doug Raney, Maarten van Der Grinten and Frederic Sylvestre), and as recently as 2002, an album with Irish torch singer Mary Coughlan. Since the early 1980s Stewart has toured extensively in Europe, particularly in Great Britain,

Norway and Germany, has recorded a series of reliable albums for Jardis – a label specializing in jazz guitar releases – and is widely recognized as Ireland's first jazz musician of international stature. In 1998, he received an honorary music doctorate from Trinity College Dublin. [CA/CI]

⊙ **Overdrive** (1994; Hep). Behind his driving swing and articulation at faster tempos and his continuous flow of post-bop ideas lies a sophisticated harmonic thinker, but ultimately Stewart is a teller of tales who leads his attentive audience on this live album through the twists and turns of "Polka Dots And Moonbeams" to the final enigmatic chord.

➤➤ **George Shearing** *(That Shearing Sound).*

Michael "Patches" Stewart

Trumpet, flugelhorn.

b. New Orleans, 31 July 1955.

Michael Kenneth Stewart had little exposure to music in the family, but was surrounded by music in New Orleans. He began on trumpet at the age of eleven, and played in the Lawless Junior High School Band Class, then in the St Augustine High School Band Class and the Purple Knights marching band. During high school summer vacations he went "on the road" with groups, and his first professional recording session happened when he was sixteen and played trumpet on LaBelle's hit, "Lady Marmalade". He said, "I guess all that gave me an appetite for performing on stage ... I made a youthful decision to turn down scholarships I was offered to Berklee and local universities in favour of 'real world' experiences." He worked with the Brothers Johnson, 1979–80, Quincy Jones, 1981–2, Al Jarreau, 1983–90, and Marcus Miller from 1989 to the present. In 1997 he released his own debut album, *Blue Patches*, an acoustic jazz project, and in 1998 followed up with *Penetration*, an electric, highly produced album. Of his nickname, he said, "Back in the hippie days, I had a pair of bell bottom pants with patches all over them ... Peace signs, stuff like that. Some guy said to me, 'If you put another patch on your pants, we're gonna call you "Patches",' and that name followed me from New Orleans to California." Stewart is a virtuoso trumpeter with a full, rounded sound and an excellent range who could often be heard through the 1990s taking the Miles Davis role in the ensembles of late-period Davis arranger Marcus Miller (who produced Stewart's third solo album *Blow* in 2003). His first favourite was Freddie Hubbard, but then he discovered Davis, Clifford Brown and Kenny Dorham. Davis is a special inspiration "because he was constantly renewing himself". [IC]

Michael "Patches" Stewart

⊙ **Blue Patches** (1997; Hip Bop Essence). This is something of a tribute to Miles Davis, and several of the pieces are associated with him. Stewart sounds inhibited by shades of Miles at the outset, but he shakes the influence off in Miles's blues "Pfrancing" with marvellous open-trumpet runs and phrases, and things look up and up thereafter. He plays eight of the nine tracks with a superb, but little-known, piano trio – pianist Shelly Bery, bassist Adrian Rosen and drummer Bob Leatherbarrow.

Rex Stewart

Cornet, trumpet.

b. Philadelphia, 22 Feb 1907; d. 7 Sept 1967.

Stewart's major contribution to jazz trumpet and cornet was to develop the technique of "half-valving" (pushing the trumpet valves halfway down to create quarter-tones and freak sounds) to its limit. Like most of his 1920s contemporaries, Stewart idolized Louis Armstrong – "I tried to walk like him, talk like him, eat like him, sleep like him", he said later – but very early on he recognized the futility of trying to play as Armstrong did. The problem was presented in sharp relief when Stewart – at Armstrong's recommendation – replaced him in Fletcher Henderson's orchestra, and it became clear quite quickly to senior members such as Coleman Hawkins that Stewart was having to mug his way through passages that were beyond him. It may have been in sheer self-defence that Stewart – an unconventional and hard-blowing trumpeter who relied on energy as much as on legitimate training – developed his half-valving technique. Though other jazz trumpeters from Muggsy Spanier to Freddy Randall also used the device, Stewart's abilities were always way ahead.

It was lucky for the cornettist that in Duke Ellington he found an orchestrator capable of framing his original talent to perfection: from 1934–45,

Stewart's weird half-vocal creations and walls-down blowing power were central to Ellington features such as "Trumpet In Spades" and "Boy Meets Horn", both written for him. After he left Ellington, Stewart's "alternative trumpet" talent earned him work as a soloist across America and Europe. In 1957 and 1958 he organized the Fletcher Henderson reunion band at South Bay's jazz festival, before working for Eddie Condon (1958–9): his Condon recordings – often rough and fallible but filled with highly charged energy – are a dramatic contrast to the more familiar sounds of Billy Butterfield, Bobby Hackett or Wild Bill Davison. By the 1960s he was an established broadcaster, and writing marvellous articles for *Down Beat*, but a 1966 tour with Alex Welsh's band in Britain proved that he was finding it harder to deliver the goods. (But a recording with Henri Chaix from the same year, including the eerie "Headshrinker Blues" and "Conversation Piece", is wonderful: unworried by the need to play difficult melodies or hold long notes, he disappears into a fantasy world of sound.) Stewart died of a brain haemorrhage at sixty; his excellent book, *Jazz Masters Of The 1930s* (a collection of his *Down Beat* articles), contains a word-portrait of him by Francis Thorne. [DF]

⊙ **Rexatious** (1926-41). Stewart's first break was with Fletcher Henderson and this set takes him from there to great 1940 sides with Ellington ("Morning Glory"/ "Boy Meets Horn") via important titles with his "52nd Street Stompers" ("Rexatious"/"Back Room Romp" 1936/7) and more with his Feetwarmers (Barney Bigard, Django Reinhardt, Billy Taylor 1939). A fine overview of Stewart's vintage years.

⊙ **Finesse** (1934–40; Affinity). This set from Stewart's peak years has important titles like "Stingaree", "Finesse" and "Cherry" (with its amazing Bix-ish solo), and sides with Jack Teagarden.

⊙ **Chronological Rex Stewart** (1934–46; Classics). Stewart recorded sparingly as a leader in his first years, hence the wide span of this Classics CD. Titles originally on Vocalion, Keynote, Capitol and Parlophone are featured.

⊙ **Rex Meets Horn** (1955–6; Jazz and Jazz). Good set of titles including a session originally issued under Cozy Cole's name; Lawrence Brown, Hilton Jefferson, Coleman Hawkins and Claude Hopkins are amongst the co-stars., and there's a spirited uptempo re-creation of Stewart's "Boy Meets Horn", among other delights.

⊙ **Rendezvous With Rex** (1958; Limelight). Produced by Stanley Dance, this is a fine session with Stewart's sometimes buzzy open-horn sound still in full control; the neglected Hilton Jefferson features on three tracks.

⊙ **Chatter Jazz** (1959; RCA Victor). Both Dicky Wells and Stewart were masters of sound as well as possessing rich senses of musical humour, and this is what this album is about. They converse amicably and spiritedly on suitable selections including "Little Sir Echo", "Side By Side" and "Together", with John Bunch behind them outstanding on piano. A few tracks at a time may be the best way.

Slam Stewart

Bass, vocals.

b. Englewood, New Jersey, 21 Sept 1914; d. 10 Dec 1987.

In the 1930s Slam (Leroy) Stewart studied at Boston Conservatory, where (John Chilton tells us) he heard violinist Ray Perry – later a successful jazzman in his own right – singing in unison with his bowed lines. Stewart borrowed the idea (singing an octave up from the bass), worked on his bowing technique and by the time he joined Peanuts Holland's band in 1936 was in charge of a truly original idea. It appealed to Slim Gaillard (whom Stewart had met at a Harlem club, Jock's Place) and the two formed a duo, Slim and Slam, in 1937. A year later a hit record, "Flat Fleet Floogie" (later universally known as "Flat Foot Floogie"), was one of the hits of 52nd Street.

Stewart stayed on the Street, working Kelly's Stables, the Three Deuces (in a trio with Art Tatum) and other clubs, and often ran his own trio, which later – for three and a half years – featured the young Erroll Garner, who wrote bass features for his leader. The uncanny sound Stewart produced as he played these features marked him out as something special and provided a comedic effect which was to be emulated by fellow bassists Coleridge Goode, Major Holley and countless others. But although his invention had its funny side, Stewart was a great musician, who worked easily with Art Tatum, Benny Goodman and other taskmasters, and became a celebrity (he appeared in the film *Stormy Weather*, 1943, and won the *Metronome* poll in 1946). All through the 1950s and 1960s Slam Stewart continued his career with the likes of Tatum, Garner, pianist Beryl Booker, Roy Eldridge and Rose Murphy, and in the 1970s he featured as soloist with the Indianapolis Symphony Orchestra, gave master classes, played with fellow masters, worked on the *Today* show, wrote instructional tutors and featured with the New York Jazz Repertory Company. In the 1980s Stewart was still just as busy as he wanted to be. [DF]

⊙ **Slam Stewart 1945–6** (Classics). Five early sessions under Stewart's name with Erroll Garner, Red Norvo and others. His bowed-bass and humming trademark is regularly to the fore.

⊙ **Fish Scales** (1972–5; Black and Blue). The accent is on comedy here, but "Willow Weep For Me" is a beautiful performance, and a bonus is the presence of the under-recorded virtuoso Johnny Guarnieri.

➤➤ **Art Tatum** *(I Got Rhythm)*.

Sonny Stitt

Alto, tenor and baritone saxophones.

b. Boston, 2 Feb 1924; d. 22 July 1982.

Sonny (Edward) Stitt toured with the Tiny Bradshaw band (on alto) in 1943–4; during this engagement he met (separately) the young Miles Davis and Charlie Parker, whose style Stitt had already partly assimilated. He settled in New York, working with Dizzy Gillespie in 1945–6, and recording with the Bebop Boys and Kenny Clarke. Sonny then decided to specialize on tenor for the next few years, co-leading a band with Gene Ammons from 1950–52, and then fronting his own groups. Incorporating the alto into his performances again after the death of Parker, he was regularly in demand as a visiting soloist with local rhythm-sections. He also worked with Jazz At The Philharmonic in 1957 and 1959, Gillespie in 1958, Miles Davis in 1960–61, at the Newport festival tributes to Parker in 1964 and 1974, and with the Giants of Jazz in 1971 and 1972.

Stitt was a rewarding and extremely consistent performer, despite his debilitating struggles with narcotics and alcoholism. The question of his musical dependency on the contribution of Parker is a more thorny one; in tone and improvisatory approach he often matched the intensity, though not the intricacy, of his chief model. It was frequently observed that, on tenor, the sound and the lines were much closer to those of Lester Young, but there was much beneficial interaction between his later alto and tenor playing. Although more evenly paced and less individual than either Young or Parker, Sonny was especially authoritative in a jamming context and always instantly recognizable. [BP]

⊙ **Sonny Stitt/Bud Powell/J.J. Johnson** (1949–50; Prestige/OJC). Stitt's re-emergence after his early travails found him concentrating on tenor and carrying all before him, whether the Bud Powell trio on some famously headlong up-tempos, or the more reflective quintet with Johnson and John Lewis, premiering the latter's "Afternoon In Paris".

⊙ **Only The Blues** (1957; Verve). The title of the original album (now supplemented by three standards) is nearly true, with blues at three different tempos plus Stitt's "The String" (aka "The Eternal Triangle") brought to the boil by Stitt, Roy Eldridge and the Oscar Peterson trio.

Kathy Stobart

Tenor, soprano and baritone saxophones.

b. South Shields, Co Durham, UK, 1 April 1925.

Stobart started playing in touring band shows at the age of fourteen, and then had a Newcastle ballroom residency. In 1942 she moved to London, working in nightclubs with players such as Denis Rose, Jimmy Skidmore and visiting American servicemen Peanuts Hucko and Art Pepper; she also made many broadcasts with the British AEF band. Between two stints with the Vic Lewis big band in 1948–9 and 1951–2, she led her own regular group including Derek Humble, Dill Jones and trumpeter Bert Courtley (her second husband from 1951 until his death in 1969). She then did casual gigging and guest spots (plus three months with Humphrey Lyttelton depping for Skidmore in 1957) while raising her family; she later rejoined Humph on a regular basis from 1969–78 and from 1991–present. In 1974 she began leading her own groups, at first with Harry Beckett, then (since 1979) with vibist Lennie Best. She made guest appearances in New York in the early 1980s with Marian McPartland, Zoot Sims and others, and she headlined the first British women's jazz festival in 1982.

Jak Kilby

Kathy Stobart

Always possessed of a robust tone and forthright style, Kathy has progressed from early "modern jazz" to a timeless mainstream approach capable of taking on any musical situation. She has been very influential as a teacher of saxophone classes in London and Exeter and of London's City Lit band. Her position as a pioneer female jazzer was acknowledged by her inclusion in the US-compiled album *Jazz Women: A Feminist Retrospective*. [BP]

➤➤ **Humphrey Lyttelton** *(Movin' And Groovin').*

Ståle Storløkken

Synthesizer, piano, church organ.

b. Lillehammer, Norway, 19 Feb 1969.

Having begun on electronic organ at the age of nine, Ståle Storløkken took lessons on classical piano and church organ at twelve, studied music in high school for three years (1985–8), then spent four years studying jazz and composition at the Music Conservatory in Trondheim (1988–92). During this last period, he also played in several student bands and formed Veslefrekk with Arve Henriksen and Jarle Vespestad, which played all over Norway throughout the 1990s, and – with the addition of Helge Sten to form the quartet Supersilent – won *Wire* magazine's Record of the Year award in 1998 with their mix of jazz, rock and soundscape music. Storløkken also plays with, and composes for, the Weather Report-influenced band Cucumber Slumber and TSTT!, a group specializing in improvised music. Together with Tone Åse, he has arranged Norwegian psalms for vocal and church organ, and, with guitarist Terje Rypdal and drummer Paolo Vinaccia in the group Skywards, has toured Europe, the USA and Canada. Storløkken also plays with Pocket Corner, a Miles Davis-influenced fusion band, and has contributed his multifaceted keyboard work to the music of Jon Balke, Nils Petter Molvær, Anders Jormin, Anders Kjellberg, Jon Christensen and Louis Sclavis. His chief influences are Joe Zawinul and the contemporary classical music of Messiaen, Cage et al, plus that of everyone from Sun Ra to Emerson, Lake and Palmer; his own music attempts to fuse all these disparate influences into a personal voice. [CP]

Pocket Corner

By-Music (1997; Da-Da). Sharing keyboard duties with John Erik Kaada, Storløkken contributes great textural density and variety to this neat jazz-rock, led by trumpeter Didrik Ingvaldsen.

Pete Strange

Trombone, arranger.
b. London, 19 Dec 1938.

Pete Strange joined Eric Silk's Southern Jazz Band in the late 1950s, then Ken Sims, Teddy Layton, and finally replaced John Picard in Bruce Turner's Jump Band. Playing with confident technique in a style that took the best of Dicky Wells, Lawrence Brown and "Tricky Sam" Nanton, Strange made a good showing on Turner's 1963 album *Going Places*. After Turner disbanded, he took a civil service job and freelanced around London's club and pub scene, working with the likes of Lennie Hastings, Stan Greig, Dave Jones and Colin Smith, and in the 1970s appeared regularly with Ron Russell's Dixieland band. In the late 1970s, turning professional again, he joined Keith Nichols's Midnite Follies Orchestra and Digby Fairweather's band (for whom he wrote the library), formed an ambitious five-trombone ensemble Five-a-Slide (for which again he wrote the book), and joined Alan Elsdon's band. In 1983 he joined Humphrey Lyttelton (as a replacement for Roy Williams), where his talent as trombonist and arranger found a perfect outlet and he at last achieved the recognition due to him. In 1995 Strange was still with Lyttelton as well as directing The Great British Jazz Band; he also leads the two-trombone band Slide by Slide and runs an agency that supplies his well-crafted swing arrangements to a variety of bands in Europe and the USA. [DF]

A British Jazz Odyssey (1996; Candid). Strange's exemplary project for his ten-piece Great British Jazz Band spotlighting British composers from George Shearing to Ray Noble to Sandy Brown. He made the selections, wrote the arrangements and directed the session in odd moments away from Humphrey Lyttelton's band.

➤➤ **Humphrey Lyttelton** *(Swing, Sing...Together Again).*

Billy Strayhorn

Composer, arranger, piano.
b. Dayton, Ohio, 29 Nov 1915; d. 31 May 1967.

After high school in Pittsburgh and private musical tuition, Strayhorn started writing for Duke Ellington in 1939. After playing the piano briefly in Mercer Ellington's first band in 1939, he joined Duke's permanent staff and, until his death from cancer, wrote almost exclusively for Ellington's band and associated small groups; a few arrangements for trusted singers such as Carmen McRae and Lena Horne were the chief exceptions. He played on occasional band recordings while Ellington himself directed, and, more frequently, on records by Duke's sidemen. He appeared as the leader of Ellingtonian groups in Florida in 1958 and, at the Chicago Century of Negro Progress exhibition, backing the production *My People* in 1963.

HERMAN LEONARD

Billy Strayhorn with Duke Ellington

Before his Ducal association, Strayhorn had written the music and lyrics of, among others, the remarkable song "Lush Life" (c. 1938) and, in fact, he joined Ellington initially as a lyric writer. Within a year he began arranging songs for the band, and then contributing instrumentals such as "Day Dream", "Chelsea Bridge" and "Take The A-Train" (which, in early 1941, became the band's theme tune). From 1945 onwards, some of Duke's extended works appeared with the credit "Ellington-Strayhorn", which has made it easy for commentators and band members to claim that the two writers' styles were indistinguishable. In fact the pieces credited to Strayhorn alone display clear differences from Duke's writing, whether in choice of rhythm or of texture, and they are somewhat more conventional in technique, though far from uninteresting. The two later became fairly adept at imitating one another, and some serious study is now being undertaken on Strayhorn's individual contribution to Ellingtonia. [BP]

Billy Strayhorn

Lush Life (1964–5; Red Baron). Given that his 1958 *Cue For Saxophone* septet session has been deleted again, this recent first-time issue gives us some of the only other music he recorded in his own right, by a small group featuring Bob Wilber and sundry Ellingtonians. Strayhorn also sings "Lush Life", a rare experience in all senses.

Dutch Jazz Orchestra

Portrait Of A Silk Thread (1995; Dutch Jazz). If ever a vindication of the jazz repertory movement were needed, this recording of twelve Strayhorn scores (eight never heard before in any form, the others substantially different from Ellington's versions) is it. Strayhorn's invention and orchestration easily survive the "ghost band" treatment.

Julian Marc Stringle

Clarinet, alto and tenor saxophones, vocals.
b. Marlow, Bucks 13 June 1961.

Stringle was a musically precocious child who formed his first Dixieland band, Stringle's Swingers (later Julian Stringle's Young Jazz), in 1973, made his TV debut at fifteen (appearing with Acker Bilk and Roy Castle), and was touring Europe with his own quintet at seventeen. From 1983 he combined bandleading with freelance work; playing in Paris with Maxim Saury, and in Manchester with the house band for the shortlived Trombone Club where he appeared alongside Bud Freeman, Wild Bill Davison, George Masso and Peanuts Hucko amng others.

As Stringle-Bannerman he combined with songwriter James Bannerman for rock projects, and in 1995 formed the group Pathfinder producing an album of the same name. Pathfinder supported Barbara Dickson in concerts in 1996 and toured with great success in 2001. More recently Stringle has appeared in Digby Fairweather's Half Dozen and led his own quintet, The Dream Band, consisting of Neil Angilley (keyboards), Dominic Ashworth (guitars), Rufus Philpot (bass) and Mike Bradley (drums). The band have so far produced three albums, *Sundance* (2001), *Blues For The Morning After* (2002) and *The New Voice Of The Clarinet* (2003), all for Merfangle Music.

A highly gifted and eclectic musician, Stringle has also recorded with rock stars, including Meatloaf and the Spice Girls, as well as with an 18-piece big band for a Latin dance album, *Beach Samba* (1996; Pro TV). His clarinet playing has been praised by John Dankworth, who called him "the most gifted British performer to emerge in several generations", but he is equally fluent and convincing on saxophones as well as an appealing singer. [DF]

⊙ **Blues For The Morning After** (2002; Merfangle). Although the material tends to the smooth, there's some superbly controlled and tonally-varied clarinet playing on this album from Stringle, who shows himself to be a complete master of his instrument.

➤➤ **Digby Fairweather** *(Twelve Feet Off The Ground).*

Scott Stroman

Trombone, vocals, composer, educator.
b. Kendallville, Indiana, 3 April 1958.

Stroman graduated from high school in Kendallville in 1976, then studied for his Bachelor of Music degree at Northern Illinois University. He earned his Master of Music degree at the University of Miami in 1982 and his Certificate of Advanced Study at London's Guildhall School in 1983. While a student in the USA, he worked as trombonist and singer with Dizzy Gillespie, Louie Bellson, Frank Rosolino, Marvin Stamm and many others. He also led many professional groups in the USA, and did several years of work with top salsa and Latin bands in Miami, plus several salsa recordings.

Since 1983, he has been a professor at the Guildhall, teaching history and performance of contemporary classical music, co-ordinating the post-graduate jazz studies course, and directing the Guildhall jazz big band and various other ensembles. In 1984 he founded the Guildhall summer school, Britain's largest summer school for jazz, rock and studio music, and in the following year founded the Opus 20 string orchestra, a professional ensemble which performs twentieth-century music.

Stroman and trumpeter Noel Langley were the driving forces behind The London Jazz Orchestra, which had some of the most exciting young (and occasionally older) talents in its ranks. Stroman also co-leads a regular quintet with star saxophonist Bobby Wellins, a group called North by NorthWest with Billy Cobham and Swedish saxophonist Cennet Jönsson and has – with the jazzgroup/choir ensemble Eclectic Voices - released an album of his jazz song cycle *Songs Of The Spirit* (33 Records). Despite the academic conditioning of his long education, Stroman has always retained the spontaneity and open mind necessary for jazz. To quote Duke Ellington, "he never lets his learning get in the way of his understanding". He is a prolific composer – some of his jazz pieces are featured on the two albums made by the Guildhall Jazz Band, *Midnight Oil* and *Walk Softly*. [IC]

THE GUILDHALL JAZZ BAND FEATURING KENNY WHEELER

⊙ **Walk Softly** (1987; Wave). Stroman's charges, although only students, perform like seasoned professionals. the section work is excellent, and Wheeler's contributions make this a magnificent achievement.

John Stubblefield

Tenor and soprano saxophones, flute, clarinet; also piano.
b. Little Rock, Arkansas, 4 Feb 1945.

Starting on piano at the age of nine, John switched to tenor in junior high school, thanks to a friend related by marriage to Don Byas. Weekly R&B gigs at sixteen led to arranging lessons from local trombonist Richard Boone, then to touring with soul singers and session work for Stax. With a music degree from Arkansas University in 1967, he moved to Chicago, joining the AACM and recording with Joseph Jarman and Maurice McIntyre. In New York from 1971, he worked with Charles Mingus and Mary Lou Williams (first of many to record his compositions) and soon made albums and tours with Miles Davis, McCoy Tyner, Gil Evans and, from 1975–7, Nat Adderley. He taught for the Jazzmobile, for Rutgers University and workshops around the USA and abroad. In addition to his own quartet, he deputizes in the World Saxophone Quartet and is a regular member of Tyner's big band, Kenny Barron's quintet, the Mingus Big Band and Jerry Gonzalez's Fort Apache Band. His favourite saxophonists extend from Stump Evans to Frank Trumbauer and Don Byas to Warne Marsh and, as well as writers from Don Redman to Henry Mancini, he cites "Bach, Mozart, Beethoven, etc". [BP]

⊙ **Morning Song** (1993; Enja). A fine quartet record, with Victor Lewis, George Cables and bassist Clint Houston, finds Stubblefield's tenor and soprano investing great interest and authority in a programme that runs from the hoary "Blue Moon" through "So What" to Lewis's "The Shaw Of Newark", dedicated to Woody Shaw.

➤➤ **Kenny Barron** *(What If)*; **Jerry Gonzalez** *(Crossroads)*; **Charles Mingus** *(Live In Time)*.

Fredy Studer

Drums, percussion.

b. Lucerne, Switzerland, 16 June 1948.

Studer, who is self-taught, began on drums at sixteen, playing all kinds of music: folk, rock, jazz-rock, R&B, hard bop, free jazz and experimental music. In 1970 he moved to Rome playing with a rock trio. He is a consultant in the sound development of Paiste cymbals and gongs. From 1972–82 he worked with the electric jazz group Om. From 1982–3 he was a member of the rock group Hand in Hand. From 1981–4 he was the drummer in the trio Brüninghaus-Stockhausen-Studer. He has also played with Joe Henderson, Albert Mangelsdorff, Enrico Rava, Eberhard Weber, Kenny Wheeler, Joachim Kuhn, Tomasz Stanko and Miroslav Vitous. He was a member of the Charlie Mariano-Jasper van't Hof band, and of the group Singing Drums, with Pierre Favre, Paul Motian and Nana Vasconcelos. He has made several adventurous albums including *Hardcore Chamber Music* (1994; Impakt) with Hans Koch and Martin Shütz and has recorded latterly on Swiss label For 4 Ears Records, most recently with DJ M. Singh. His favourites are Elvin Jones, Tony Williams, Jack DeJohnette and Andrew Cyrille; Jimi Hendrix, John Coltrane, Miles Davis and Wayne Shorter are also influences. [IC]

➤➤ **Pierre Favre** *(Singing Drums)*.

L. Subramaniam

Violin.

b. Madras, India, 23 July 1947.

Subramaniam began on violin at five, taught by his father, a renowned violinist and educator; he gave his first concert at the age of eight. At sixteen he received the President's Award, one of the highest musical honours in India. At eleven, with his older brother and his younger brother Lakshminarayana Shankar, he formed the Violin Trio and became famous in India. He later graduated in medicine from Madras Medical College, and then went to the USA and took his Master's degree in music, studying Western music. In 1973–4 he recorded and toured with Ravi Shankar and George Harrison in the USA and Europe to universal critical acclaim. In 1980–81 he worked with John Handy and Ali Akbar Khan in Rainbow. Like his brother Shankar, who played with John McLaughlin's Shakti, Subramaniam has thoroughly immersed himself in Western music. Talking to Lee Underwood, he has described the music on his own album *Fantasy Without Limit* thus: "The goal was to blend East and West in all forms. Some of the rhythms are 4/4, but others are very complex, some of the melodies are romantic and gypsy-like, but others are directly from Indian conceptions. Through it all, I use a wide variety of harmonies which should help the Western listener feel the music much better." Recent acclaimed albums include *From The Ashes* (1999; Waterlily) and *Global Fusion* (1999; Elektra). [IC]

Dick Sudhalter

Cornet, alto horn, flugelhorn; also piano.

b. Boston, 28 Dec 1938.

Having spent his teenage years around Boston's jazz scene, Sudhalter came to England in the 1960s. A cornettist who identified strongly with Bix Beiderbecke but easily opened out into the territory of Bobby Hackett and Ruby Braff, he organized Bix-related ventures such as the Anglo-American Alliance and the New Paul Whiteman Orchestra (a major triumph), led broad-based bands such as Commodore and Jazz Without Walls, toured with Hackett, worked in academic ensembles such as Keith Nichols's Ragtime Orchestra and formed a quintet with fellow cornettist Gerry Salisbury. In addition, Sudhalter (often hidden under the pseudonym "Art Napoleon") soon revealed himself as a jazz writer whose passion, commitment and understanding set him in a class with rare talents such as George Frazier, Alec Wilder and Whitney Balliett. His writing talent and judgement, applied to the researches of Philip R. Evans and William Dean-Myatt, were to produce the first great jazz biography, *Bix: Man And Legend* (1974). Soon after he returned to the USA to play regularly with the New York Jazz Repertory Company, among others, and to write for the *New York Post*. Of his recordings from this period, the album *Friends With Pleasure* by his Primus Inter Pares Jazz Ensemble is just one sample of Sudhalter's bright imagination and strong sense of history at work. He was also heard to advantage in the witty Classic Jazz Quartet (with Grosz, Muranyi and Wellstood) and continues to tour regularly as a soloist. His recent writings include *Lost Chords* (a masterful and extensive reassessment of the white contribution to jazz history 1915–45) and a centenary biography of Hoagy Carmichael. In 2003 Sudhalter revisited Britain for a short season at London's Pizza On The Park with old friend Barbara Lea. [DF]

Dick Sudhalter

The Tuesday Band (1968; Jazzology). All the recordings of Sudhalter's fondly remembered Anglo-American Alliance group (featuring vocalist Chris Ellis) including its once-available LP *Sweet And Hot*.

New Paul Whiteman Orchestra

Runnin' Wild (1974; Argo). A loving re-creation of Whiteman's recordings with Beiderbecke; Sudhalter takes the Bix role, Alan Cohen directs, and there are solos from Keith Nichols and Harry Gold.

Primus Inter Pares Jazz Ensemble

Friends With Pleasure (1981; Audiophile). Now reissued on CD with extra tracks, this excellent collection features Dave Frishberg, Dan Barrett and Howard Alden in fine repertoire, including Carmichael's "Blue River" and Mercer's "Jamboree Jones".

Classic Jazz Quartet

Classic Jazz Quartet: The Complete Recordings (1984–6; Jazzology). Marty Grosz, Dick Wellstood and Joe Muranyi combine with Sudhalter in fine selections from Durante's "Inka Dinka Doo" to Sudhalter's touching "Home No More".

Mr Tram Associates

Getting Some Fun Out Of Life (1988; Audiophile). Delightful collaboration between Sudhalter, Loren Schoenberg and two fine singers – Barbara Lea and the underrated Daryl Sherman.

Dick Sudhalter

After Awhile (1994; Challenge). Sudhalter with two groups of London friends: a classy group including Roy Williams, Al Gay, Mick Pyne and Allan Ganley; and a near-reunion of his Anglo-American Alliance, with Jim Shepherd, John R.T. Davies and Chris Ellis.

Idrees Sulieman

Trumpet, alto saxophone.

b. St Petersburg, Florida, 7 Aug 1923; d. 31 July 2002.

Sulieman (born Leonard Graham) toured with the Carolina Cotton Pickers and name bands such as Earl Hines's in 1943–4. Then the trumpeter, already known by his Muslim name, became an early associate of Thelonious Monk, Mary Lou Williams and the beboppers. He recorded and gigged with Monk in 1947–8, Coleman Hawkins in 1957 and others during an intermittent career, until settling in Stockholm in the 1960s and Copenhagen in the 1970s. He was a regular member of the Clarke-Boland band, and recorded in New York with Randy Weston and Joe Henderson in 1991–2 before returning to Florida. In the 1970s Sulieman also took up the alto saxophone, but his main contributions were made on trumpet and, despite being a variable performer, he sometimes produced inspired and highly individual work. [BP]

Now Is The Time (1976; Steeplechase). In the exposed situation of just trumpet and rhythm-section, but with the extremely supportive Cedar Walton trio backing, Sulieman turns in a convincing performance of original material supplemented by Charlie Parker's "Now's The Time".

Ira Sullivan

Trumpet, flugelhorn, saxophones, flute, composer.

b. Washington, DC, 1 May 1931.

Sullivan's father taught him the trumpet and his mother taught him the saxophone. He moved to Chicago, working with Sonny Stitt, Howard McGhee, Wardell Gray, Lester Young, Roy Eldridge, Charlie Parker and many others. Later he worked with Bill Russo, and then briefly, in 1956, with Art Blakey. He moved to Southern Florida in the early 1960s, working in Fort Lauderdale and Miami. With his own groups, he played concerts and clubs, and also in elementary schools, junior colleges and churches. He was also a member of a large jazz ensemble, Baker's Dozen, in Miami, for which local boy Jaco Pastorius wrote some arrangements. In the late 1970s, he moved to New York and began co-leading a quintet with Red Rodney. He has recorded with Red Rodney, Art Blakey, Roland Kirk, Eddie Harris and others.

Sullivan is a legendary figure; one of the most gifted improvisers in jazz, he has chosen to maintain a low and local profile, rarely straying far from his base in Florida and hardly ever appearing internationally. His favourites on trumpet are Dizzy Gillespie, Miles Davis, Fats Navarro, Harry Edison and Clark Terry, and on saxophone Charlie Parker, Coleman Hawkins, Lester Young and Sonny Rollins. He began in bebop, but has expanded his concept over the years, incorporating elements from John Coltrane abstraction and rock into his performances, though a recent recording – *After Hours* (2001; Go Jazz) – saw Sullivan return to rigorous straight-ahead playing, mostly on soprano sax. [IC]

Blue Stroll (1959; Delmark). A classic album that shows off Sullivan's amazing versatility as an instrumentalist, in partnership with the brilliant tenor sax of Johnny Griffin and some fine piano from Jodie Christian. Vic Sproles (bass) and Wilbur Campbell (drums) complete the formidable lineup.

Joe Sullivan

Piano.

b. Chicago, 4 Nov 1906; d. 13 Oct 1971.

A graduate of Chicago Conservatory, Sullivan was at the heart of the Chicago jazz scene all through the 1920s, recording with the best (including Louis Armstrong and Eddie Condon) and playing with the fly technique and topsy-turvy time-consciousness of the young Earl Hines – though he was far more than just an inspired copy ("I was playing my own way before I heard Earl", he later said flatly). By the 1930s he was in New York with studio and jazz bands and playing solo (records for John Hammond, including his own "Little Rock Getaway", are outstanding), as well as accompanying Bing Crosby. His finest hour should have come in 1936 when he joined Bob Crosby's band, but Sullivan contracted tuberculosis and spent ten months in hospital; Bob Zurke replaced him, and Sullivan in later years bitterly remembered his bad luck. By 1939 he was bandleading again at Café Society (with a strong multiracial group featuring Ed Hall and Benny Morton) and all through the 1940s stayed busy enough with Eddie Condon, Bobby Hackett and others, and playing solo. By the 1950s solo piano had become, against his will, a permanent occupation, often at the Club Hangover in San Francisco, a venue which – filled with noisy diners and expense-account clientele – often rubbed up badly against Sullivan's musical convictions. In 1964 an article in *Down Beat* by Richard Hadlock, "The Return of Joe Sullivan", celebrated his successful 1963 appearance at Monterey's jazz festival and helped to promote a new (listening) residency at the Trident Club, Sausalito, where people gave him the respect he deserved. Yet Sullivan's bitterness by now ran deep: "It's not that I'm neglected," he told Hadlock, "it's more that I'm completely forgotten." [DF]

➤➤ **Eddie Condon** *(Eddie Condon 1927–38 & 1942–43).*

Maxine Sullivan

Vocals, valve-trombone, flugelhorn.

b. Homestead, Pittsburgh, 13 May 1911; d. 7 April 1987.

In 1937, early in her New York career, Maxine Sullivan (born Marietta Williams) was hired by guitarist Carl Kress to sing for intermissions at the Onyx Club. While she was working there, arranger/bandleader Claude Thornhill (who had engineered the Onyx contract) put together arrangements of two Scottish songs, "Annie Laurie" and "Loch Lomond" – "foreign-theme" tunes like Tommy Dorsey's "Song Of India" had set a trend – and after a feature in the *New Yorker* the young singer became a headliner. She joined John Kirby's new band, the main attraction at the Onyx (she also married Kirby), and starred for two years on a CBS radio programme, *Flow Gently Sweet Rhythm*. When that came to an end, along with her marriage, Sullivan pursued a highly successful solo career – with Benny Goodman, Glen Gray and others – and remained a popular act in nightclubs until temporary retirement and a brief period in nursing during the 1950s. From 1958 she began a comeback, and in 1965 Tommy Gwaltney invited her to work at his Washington club, Blues Alley; from then on Sullivan gradually rebuilt her career, appearing at Dick Gibson's Denver parties, with The World's Greatest Jazz Band and with Bobby Hackett. Albums with Bob Wilber received fine reviews, Sullivan featured valve-trombone and flugelhorn in her armoury, and by the 1980s she had become one of the best-loved singers of great jazz repertoire, recording in Europe and back home in America with young kindred spirits such as Scott Hamilton and Keith Ingham. [DF]

⊙ **Maxine Sullivan 1937-8/1938-41/More 1940-41/1941-6** (Classics).Sullivan's early years documented in full by Classics. Although some of the material now sounds tentative and dated there are many highspots to compensate; Sullivan's cheery theme tune "Loch Lomond" and "Annie Laurie" charming forgotten songs like "Down The Old Ox Road" and "I'm Happy About The Whole Thing" (with Claude Thornhill) plus more classics with Kirby including the beauteous "If I Had A Ribbon Bow".

⊙ **Maxine Sullivan Sings** (1955–6; Fresh Sound). Fascinating recordings from a midpoint in Sullivan's career, masterminded by trumpeter Charlie Shavers and produced by Leonard Feather. Shavers and Dick Hyman figure to great effect on most of the titles, and for a couple of tracks the nucleus of the John Kirby band is reassembled as a bonus.

⊙ **Sings The Music Of Burton Lane** (1985; Harbinger). Sullivan made many fine albums in her later years and this one teams her with pianist Keith Ingham for a connoisseurs' set of Lane tunes, including many should-be standards like "Dancing On A Dime" and "How'dja Like To Love Me", along with better-known titles such as "On A Clear Day" and "How About You". Marty Grosz, Glenn Zottola and Al Klink accompany.

⊙ **Great Songs From The Cotton Club** (1984; Mobile Fidelity).Sullivan joins Ingham again (they were a great team) for an award-winning set of songs associated with the Cotton Club reviews.

Stan Sulzmann

Alto and tenor saxophones, flute, alto flute, clarinet.

b. London, 30 Nov 1948.

Sulzmann started playing with blues bands in clubs such as the Flamingo and the Marquee around 1963. In 1964 he joined the first National Youth Jazz Orchestra. After trips to New York on the *Queen Mary*, he went to the Royal Academy of Music as a mature student. Subsequently he played in bands led by Graham Collier, Mike Gibbs and John Dankworth. Playing at Ronnie Scott's club with such bands led to a tour with the Kenny Clarke-Francy Boland band. Sulzmann also did two NDR radio workshops in Hamburg, and recorded for Volker Kriegel in a band which included John Taylor and Eberhard Weber. He was an original member of the John Taylor sextet, and formed a quartet with Taylor, Ron Mathewson and drummer Tony Levin in 1970. The quartet played Sulzmann's compositions and worked for some ten years, broadcasting regularly for BBC radio and representing the BBC at the Molde jazz festival, Norway. He did many broadcasts in the UK with Taylor, Kenny Wheeler, John Warren and numerous small groups. In the mid-1970s he was with Gordon Beck's Gyroscope. In 1987 he was guest soloist with the Hilversum Radio Orchestra, Holland, and the NDR Big Band in Hamburg, and worked with the Hanover Radio Symphony Orchestra, playing the compositions of John Taylor. The Sulzmann-Taylor duo have played in Germany, Sweden and Finland. Latterly, he formed fruitful musical partnerships with pianists Marc Copland (see below) and particularly Nikki Iles, recording *Treasure Trove* with her (1996; FMR) and appearing in her ensembles.

Sulzmann is also a highly gifted composer and arranger, and he currently writes and plays for The London Jazz Orchestra, The European Jazz Ensemble and the Alleric Saxophone Quartet with Evan Parker, Julian Argüelles and Ray Warleigh. An enthusiastic educator, he teaches at various summer schools including those at the Guildhall and Royal Academy of Music. Sulzmann's most recent project is a duo with New York pianist Marc Copland. His favourite saxophonists are Sonny Rollins, Joe Henderson and John Coltrane, and on clarinet he admires Tony Coe; flautists he likes are James Moody, James Spaulding and Ray Warleigh. [IC]

⊙ **Feudal Rabbits** (1990; Ah Um). Left to his own devices, Sulzmann expresses mostly the wistful, melancholic side of his nature. *Feudal Rabbits*, with electric bassist Patrick Bettison, acoustic bassist Mick Hutton and drummer Steve Argüelles, is no exception, but Sulzmann's highly individual melodic flair often shines through the elegiac mood.

⊙ **Never At All** (1992; Future Music). A duo album with pianist Marc Copland, who plays piano and synthesizer. The elegiac mood again prevails, but underneath its sombre and occasionally oppressive weight there are passages of singular beauty.

⊙ **Birthdays, Birthdays** (2000; Village Life). A striking, varied showcase for Sulzman's writing and arranging gifts featuring a big band of top UK pros, including Kenny Wheeler, Derek Watkins, Ray Warleigh, Pete Saberton and Paul Clarvis.

➤➤ **Allan Botschinsky** *(The Bench)*; **Kenny Wheeler** *(Music For Large And Small Ensembles)*; **Nikki Iles** *(Treasure Trove)*.

Sun Ra

Keyboards, composer.

b. Birmingham, Alabama, 22 May 1914; d. 30 May 1993.

Sun Ra was born Herman Poole "Sonny" Blount, and in his teens played with Avery Parrish and Paul Bascomb, both later in the Erskine Hawkins band. He studied music in college and with John "Fess" Whatley, also touring with the latter's band, which briefly appeared under Sonny's own name at Chicago's Savoy Ballroom in 1934. Back in Birmingham, he organized his first regular group which worked sporadically while he furthered his interest in swing music, songwriting, sound recording and early electric keyboards. In 1946 he settled in Chicago, playing all kinds of piano jobs and making his record debut with R&B singer Wynonie Harris, and was involved in arranging for shows while working as the pianist with Fletcher Henderson at Chicago's Club DeLisa in 1946–7. He then played in the band of bassist (and subsequent Brubeck sideman) Gene Wright, and backed performers such as Coleman Hawkins and Stuff Smith. He started his own trio, and gradually built a rehearsal band with longtime associates John Gilmore, saxophonist Pat (Laurdine) Patrick and others in the early 1950s. A self-styled mystic, he renamed himself Sun Ra and called his band the Arkestra. After making several albums (starting in 1956), they moved briefly to Montreal and then New York in 1961, maintaining the organization despite members' occasional outside work (for example Patrick with Mongo Santamaria, and Gilmore with Art Blakey). Sun Ra was involved with the Jazz Composers' Guild in 1964–5. He thereafter gained an international reputation, based partly on his exotic presentation, and made the first of many tours of Europe in 1970, by which time he had moved his base of operations to Philadelphia. In the late 1950s he formed Saturn Records to document his work both new and old; some of this has been reissued by other labels such as Impulse! in the 1970s and Evidence in the 1990s.

Sun Ra's earliest body of recordings, dating from the mid-1950s, show him close to the flavour of Chicago hard bop, but writing attractive and individualistic themes on a similar Monk-Ellington tangent to that of Herbie Nichols, and capable at times of drawing a rich sound reminiscent of Tadd Dameron from his ten-piece ensemble. By the end of the 1950s, however, the band's music was more percussion-oriented, with results which were much more impressionistic and open-ended than in a conventional Afro-Latin band. Around this same period, the leader began to forgo his composed themes and, in one of the earliest responses to the idea of "free jazz" (predating Ornette Coleman and Cecil Taylor in this respect), he allowed the moods which he prescribed to be created entirely through solo and group improvisations. This was the style for which he finally gained widespread recognition, and which enabled him in the late 1960s to increase the size of the Arkestra for a few years. Sun Ra decided in the mid-1970s to crown his own efforts by establishing conscious links with the tradition of composer/bandleaders, and henceforth expanded his repertoire with loose-limbed performances of classics by Jelly Roll Morton, Fletcher Henderson, Duke Ellington and Thelonious Monk.

As a keyboard player, Sun Ra tended to make a strong impression in live appearances, in a style which could veer from Earl Hines to Cecil Taylor with rambling pseudo-European impressionism thrown in. In the 1950s he was a pioneer in the jazz use of

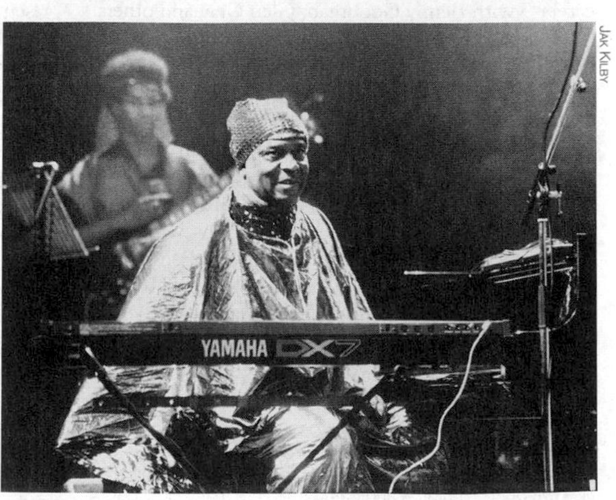

Jak Kilby

Sun Ra

electric keyboards such as the clavioline and what he called his "rocksichord'; later, he gravitated naturally to the early versions of keyboard synthesizer. Again in the 1950s (ages before Ornette tried it) he was regularly using two bassists, one of whom played the then new electric bass. Similarly, his encouragement of the practice of horn men playing additional percussion may have influenced its growing popularity in jazz, especially among the later Chicago avant-garde whose burgeoning in the mid-1960s was partly fuelled by Sun Ra's departure from the city.

The band's continuity enabled his most faithful acolytes to remain longer than any sidemen except Ellington's, but there is also a long list of musicians (such as Von Freeman and Julian Priester) who worked with him briefly and then moved on. Perhaps this is because of Ra's notoriously stern discipline; he himself has said, "I tell my Arkestra that all humanity is in some kind of restricted limitation, but they're in the Ra jail, and it's the best in the world." His reputation in this area is matched by his reputation as an outlandish philosopher/showman, whose costumes and choreography reflect his early experience of Cotton Club-type extravaganzas. Nevertheless, the picturesque side of Sun Ra, like that of Monk, is dwarfed by the strength of his best music. [BP]

⊙ **The Singles** (1954–82; Evidence). For the hard-core jazz fan, this two-CD set may seem a side issue but links usefully with his interest in the entertainment value of black music. Originally released on single 45s, most of the music here is Sun Ra's take on R&B and soul, with "Teenager's Letter Of Promises" lifting some of its backing music from a current Johnny Hodges album.

⊙ **Jazz In Silhouette** (1958; Evidence). The early band's roots in bebop, Ellington and the blues are contrasted with one track "Ancient Ethiopia", whose use of baritone saxophone and flutes is an indication of things to come.

⊙ **The Magic City** (1965; Evidence). The kind of work which influenced late Coltrane and the entire mid-1960s avant-garde encapsulated in a free and extended collective improvisation.

⊙ **Space Is The Place** (1972; Evidence). Only issued in 1993, these soundtrack recordings for the film of the same name include several of Ra's greatest intergalactic hits such as "We Travel The Spaceways", "Planet Earth" and the title track.

⊙ **Space Is The Place** (1972; Impulse!). Not to be confused with the above album, this was probably Ra's best-recorded and best-distributed album to date. The long title track, with vocalist June Tyson, Pat Patrick on electric bass and Sonny on Farfisa organ, bears an interesting relationship to Herbie Hancock's "Ostinato" of two years earlier.

⊙ **Live At The Hackney Empire** (1990; Leo). A two-CD souvenir, but also a decently recorded live album to set alongside many inferior such products. It constitutes a typical programme, with both new and old Ra originals plus versions of standards such as "Prelude To A Kiss" and a couple from the Fletcher Henderson days, "Yeah Man" and "Blue Lou".

⊙ **Mayan Temples** (1990; Black Saint). One of the best late recordings of the classic big band which included John Gilmore and vocalist/dancer June Tyson, this also affords the chance to hear Ra's ensemble keyboard work well reproduced for a change.

Monty Sunshine

Clarinet, leader.

b. London, 8 April 1928.

A founder member of the Crane River Jazz Band in 1949 and later the clarinet star of Chris Barber's 1950s band, Monty Sunshine contributed hugely to Barber's success (with his recordings of clarinet features such as "Hushabye" and "Petite Fleur"), then left in 1960 to form his own strictly New Orleans-style band, which made its debut in 1961. A string of solo albums followed – often featuring large studio groups and ambitious repertoire – and Sunshine built a highly successful career, playing his New Orleans jazz all over Europe, where his reputation soared (a German album sleeve began "Although Humphrey Lyttelton has never reached the stardom achieved by Monty Sunshine ..."). Sidemen who have worked with him regularly include Rod Mason, Ian Hunter-Randall, Alan Gresty, Charlie Galbraith, Eddie Blashfield, John Beecham, Ken Barton, Barry Dew, Mick Ashman, Tony Baghot and Geoff Downs. Sunshine stayed busy with his band throughout much of the 1990s, as well as playing reunion concerts with Barber; they spent much of 1994 on tour, celebrating their fortieth anniversary. Late in the decade Sunshine suffered a stroke however and was inactive by 2003. [DF]

⊙ **Gotta Travel On** (1991; Timeless). Fine live session recorded by Sunshine's six-piece, featuring the sturdy lead trumpet of Alan Gresty and dynamic drummer Geoff Downs.

>> **Chris Barber** *(Forty Years Jubilee).*

John Surman

Baritone and soprano saxophones, bass clarinet, synthesizers.

b. Tavistock, Devon, UK, 30 Aug 1944.

Surman studied at the London College of Music from 1962–5, and then at the London University Institute of Education in 1966. He began on baritone saxophone, joining Mike Westbrook in 1962, and

John Surman

working with Alexis Korner in the early 1960s. His collaboration with Westbrook was particularly fruitful; as well as being the main featured soloist, Surman also composed and arranged pieces for Westbrook's small groups and for the larger orchestral works such as "Marching Song". He developed so fast as an instrumentalist that by the later 1960s he had become a major innovative force on baritone, doing for that instrument what Eric Dolphy had done for the bass clarinet – dramatically increasing its mobility and flexibility, and actually creating, by mastery of the harmonics, an extreme upper register for the first time. In 1968, when the Westbrook band took part in the competition at the Montreux festival, Surman won the Best Soloist award, and his international reputation grew rapidly after that. Between 1964–8 he also worked in the UK with Mike Gibbs, Graham Collier, Chris McGregor, Dave Holland, John McLaughlin and others.

In 1969 he played baritone and soprano on one of the classic albums of the decade, John McLaughlin's *Extrapolation*, with Brian Odges on bass and Tony Oxley on drums, and the same year Surman began leading his own groups, forming The Trio with Barre Phillips (bass) and Stu Martin (drums). One of the most vital and acclaimed groups of its time, for a couple of years it toured and played festivals all over Europe. They were playing high-energy free jazz – abstract and abrasive music – and the inevitable crisis came when Surman became creatively exhausted, and retired from music for a year. Eventually he made his way back, looking for different textures with which to improvise, and longing for some lyricism.

In 1973 Surman formed SOS with fellow saxophonists Alan Skidmore and Mike Osborne. With Surman's use of electronics and synthesizers, and Skidmore doubling on drums and Osborne on percussion, SOS managed to create a huge variety of sounds. Surman also employed synthesizers with the trio, and with Mumps, which was the trio augmented by Albert Mangelsdorff. From 1974–9 he collaborated regularly with the Carolyn Carlson Dance Theatre at the Paris Opera. He made duo recordings with pianist Stan Tracey (*Sonatinas*) and singer (whom he later married) Karin Krog (*Cloudline Blue*) in 1978. From 1979–82, he worked with bassist Miroslav Vitous's quartet. He toured Australia with Vitous in 1983, and with Krog in 1985. In 1984, he collaborated with John Warren in composing and arranging *The Brass Project*, a series of pieces for brass ensemble and rhythm-section featuring Surman on reeds and piano, which finally bore fruit on record in 1992. He often worked in duo with Jack DeJohnette in the 1980s, again playing both reeds and synthesizers. In 1986 he recorded and toured with Paul Bley. Since 1968 Surman has appeared at major festivals all over the world and has won jazz polls and awards in many countries. He has had many commissions for ballet scores and church music – all from outside the UK. His one early British commission resulted in the album *Morning Glory*, for which he collaborated with John Taylor and Terje Rypdal. In latter years he has had a few more British commissions, and in 1994 his fiftieth birthday was celebrated with a concert in Bath Pavilion, for which he performed solo, in duo and with a quartet and also with Brass Project, for which the BBC commissioned him to compose new music. In October 1994 he had three concerts in Japan with his superb English quartet, with John Taylor, bassist Chris Laurence and drummer John Marshall. Despite the inexplicably low profile and rare appearances of the group, when they walked on stage in Tokyo for their first concert they were given a prolonged standing ovation. In December 1993 they recorded *Stranger Than Fiction*, their first album since the 1973 *Morning Glory*. In the next decade or so, Surman produced a run of quietly triumphant records on ECM which cemented his reputation as the most valuable and respected of European jazz musicians.

John Surman is that rare phenomenon in jazz, a musician who was brilliant and innovative at the beginning of his career and has gone on slowly evolving and maturing, so that in mid-career his music has great technical and emotional breadth and depth. Like Albert Mangelsdorff, he is a major figure who chose to remain in Europe. His compositions, and the evocative moods and atmospheres he creates with electronics, derive in part from his European heritage: his experience of church music as a choirboy, his awareness of folk and ethnic music such as Irish jigs, Scottish reels and laments, and his knowledge of European classical music and brass bands. [IC]

John Surman

Upper Reflection (1979; ECM). Surman's solo albums are almost private affairs – a series of soliloquies in which he often uses synthesizers to create the environment he wants. Surman has a lot to say, and this is one of his most personal and poetic musical statements. This fine album deservedly won the 1980 Italian Record Critics' Award.

Road To St Ives (1990; ECM). Surman has recorded several diary-like solo albums in a contemplative and inward-looking vein, and, though some might find the introspective atmosphere oppressive at times, *Road To St Ives* is the masterpiece, rooted in landscapes lodged deep in Surman's memory.

The Brass Project (1992; ECM). This has the superb rhythm-section of Chris Laurence and John Marshall, plus three trumpets and four trombones, playing music by Surman and John Warren. Surman plays all his reeds plus alto clarinet, and there are also fine solos by trumpeters Steve Waterman and Henry Lowther. A rich and emotionally resonant album.

Coruscating (2000; ECM). Chris Lawrence is still a vital presence on perhaps Surman's most acclaimed work of recent times, an elegant, elegiac work for Surman's horns and small string ensemble.

John Surman and Jack DeJohnette

The Amazing Adventures Of Simon Simon (1981; ECM); **Invisible Nature** (2001; ECM); **Free And Equal** (2003; ECM). Surman has had a long, if intermittent, association with DeJohnette, and the interaction of two considerable talents brings a muscularity and greater unpredictability to the music. *Simon Simon* covers a wide spectrum and bristles with incident, and also won several prizes. Twenty-odd years on and *Invisible Nature* and *Free And Equal* create similarly atmospheric improvisations in a live setting. On the latter, the Surman/DeJohnette dialogues intersperse with composed pieces for classical ensemble London Brass.

John Surman, Paul Bley, Gary Peacock and Tony Oxley

Adventure Playground (1991; ECM). This has four compositions by Surman, two by Paul Bley, one each by Peacock and Oxley, plus one by Carla Bley. The approach is looser and rangier, the interplay dynamic, and the standard of playing superlative by four masters of this disciplined freedom.

John Surman, John Taylor, Chris Laurence and John Marshall

Stranger Than Fiction (1993; ECM). Surman's English quartet ended their long silence on record with a stunningly beautiful album which distils their playing experience over the previous twenty years. It ends with a suite in three parts, which is improvised by the quartet. The other seven pieces are all composed by Surman, and range from the icily lyrical freedom of the opening "Canticles With Responses" to the powerful 12/8 feel of "Across The Bridge".

John Surman, Karin Krog, Terje Rypdal and Vigleik Storaas

Nordic Quartet (1994; ECM). The mood here is generally reflective and cool, but on the fourth piece, "Gone To The Dogs", Rypdal works up a wildly rocking lather on guitar and Surman soars and swoops on soprano with searing passion. The quartet is split up into various duos for eight of the nine tracks, but they all convene on the closing track, the strangely beautiful "Wild Bird".

➤➤ **John McLaughlin** *(Extrapolation)*; **Mike Westbrook** *(Citadel; Room315).*

Ralph Sutton

Piano.

b. Hamburg, Missouri, 4 Nov 1922.

"Ralph is without doubt the greatest, and he's just about alone with it now, because he's one of the few left from our finest and most creative piano eras." Thus Milt Hinton talked about Ralph Sutton, who with Dick Wellstood and Keith Ingham is one of the finest exponents of the great piano traditions set down by Fats Waller, Willie "The Lion" Smith and Art Tatum. Though he played with Jack Teagarden while still at college in 1942, Sutton's career got under way post-war, with appearances on Rudi Blesh's *This Is Jazz* show, a trio with Albert Nicholas, and eight years as intermission pianist (usually a thankless job anywhere) at Eddie Condon's. Later he worked for Bob Scobey, then in 1963 was in the first Dick Gibson Jazz Party, which was to pave the way for the formation in 1968 of The World's Greatest Jazz Band (Sutton was a founder member). In the 1970s the process of re-evaluating Sutton's career began in earnest: a biography by James D. Shacter began the operation, followed soon after by a multivolume set of Sutton masterworks for Chaz Jazz (Charlie Baron's label), placing him in every context from solo to band, with such masters as Ruby Braff and Kenny Davern. A gentle bear of a man, albeit with an occasionally explosive temper, Sutton continued to work regularly in the 1980s and 1990s as a soloist, and enjoys his hard-won reputation. [DF]

Last Of The Whorehouse Piano Players: The Original Sessions (1979; Chiaroscuro). Perhaps Sutton's best-known record date, with Jay McShann, Milt Hinton and Gus Johnson.

Partners In Crime (1983; Sackville). A five-star teaming of Sutton with Australian Bob Barnard, one of the great jazz cornettists and the perfect partner.

Eye Opener (1990; J and M). One of Sutton's best latter-day solo recordings, including Waller beauties like "Clothes Line Ballet" and a medley of tunes by the great Willard Robison, a composer who ideally suits Sutton's reflective rural echoes.

Maybeck Recital Hall (1993; Concord). Featuring many of Sutton's favourites, including Waller and Beiderbecke repertoire, this is a great recital, played for people who had come to listen.

Esbjörn Svensson

Piano.

b.Vasteras, Sweden, 16 April 1964.

The son of a jazz-loving father and a piano-playing mother, Svensson played in his first bands at high school where he learnt the piano for three years. After four years at Stockholm University, where he studied music, he soon established himself as a key figure on the burgeoning Scandinavian jazz scene. Important influences from that period were the Swedish pianist, Jan Johansson, Chick Corea, Herbie

Hancock and Keith Jarrett. The current version of the Esbjörn Svensson Trio (EST) was formed in 1993 when bass player Dan Berglund joined Svensson and his childhood friend, drummer Magnus Öström. Their debut album, *When Everyone Has Gone* (Dragon), was released in the same year.

With a growing reputation in Sweden, EST landed a recording contract with the pop label Diesel Music, for whom their first outing was an album of covers entitled *EST Plays Monk* (1995). Another album for Diesel, *Winter In Venice* (1997), revealed Svensson as a composer of great originality and was awarded a Swedish Grammy Award. Two years later they signed for a new label, ACT, and, so far, have made four albums for them: *From Gagarin's Point Of View* (1999), *Good Morning Susie Soho* (2000), *Strange Place For Snow* (2002) and *Seven Days Of Falling* (2003). It was their output for ACT that cemented the group's international reputation, and it now has a fan-base that is virtually unique for including classical and pop, as well as jazz, music lovers. EST perform not just in jazz clubs but also in stadia and rock venues, often with dramatic lighting and other theatrical effects. The trio have also created their very own soundworld, one which combines jazz with drum'n'bass, electronic elements, funky rhythms, as well as elements from pop, rock and European classical music. In so doing they have given a new lease of life to the jazz piano trio. [IC]

EST

⊙ **Winter In Venice** (1999; ACT). Alongside open, airy, hummable themes, Svensson dispenses complex music that draws as much on the eloquent lyricism of Keith Jarrett as on the more overtly robust and interactive style of freely improvised jazz. This ground-breaking Diesel album has now been re-issued by ACT.

⊙ **Strange Place For Snow** (2002; ACT). This is one of the most dynamic and brilliant of EST albums, covering a wide area of music from the luxuriously funky to the elegiac. The trio toured the music on this album for nine months in Europe, hence the amazingly close interplay between the musicians and the coherence of the material.

Steve Swallow

Bass guitar, composer.

b. New York, 4 Oct 1940.

Swallow began on piano and trumpet with private teachers and took up the double bass at eighteen. He joined the Paul Bley trio in 1960, and also worked with George Russell's seminal sextet playing on the classic album *Ezz-thetics*. With Paul Bley, Swallow was also a member of the innovative Jimmy Giuffre trio (1960–62), and the Art Farmer quartet (1962–5). From 1965–7 he worked with Stan Getz and spent 1967–70 with Gary Burton's quartet. Then he spent three years living and writing in Bolinas, California, and playing in San Francisco with pianists Art Lande and Mike Nock. In 1973 he rejoined Burton and has worked with him intermittently ever since.

RAFAELLA CAVALIERI

Steve Swallow

Swallow's original influences were Charles Mingus, Charlie Haden, Wilbur Ware and Red Mitchell, and he had most of their virtues and values. He was involved in the free-jazz scene during the early 1960s and in 1964 he won the *Down Beat* critics' poll as New Star on Bass. During the later 1960s, particularly with the Burton quartet, the music fused elements from jazz, rock and country music in a strongly electronic context, and it required bass guitar, not acoustic bass. Swallow began doubling on bass guitar, and at the beginning of the 1970s he gave up acoustic bass altogether because he discovered that the two techniques were incompatible. Gary Burton told Charles Mitchell: "He reapproached the [electric bass], he plays it with a pick all the time, which few jazz players do, he changed the fingering system around to a more guitar-oriented style. He plays it on its own terms, so it doesn't sound like a plugged-in acoustic bass ... he dropped all preconceived notions, finding his own voice on the instrument."

Since the early 1970s Swallow has also been intermittently associated with Mike Gibbs, recording and touring with him, and since the later 1970s he has been a regular member of partner Carla Bley's various bands and has played on some of her finest albums. In the 1980s he also began producing other people's albums, and in the late 1980s and early 1990s toured and recorded again with Paul Bley in the reunited Giuffre trio, and worked in Carla Bley's trio with Andy Sheppard. An association with increasingly commanding saxophonist Chris Potter and drummer Adam Nussbaum has produced three albums to date under Swallow's name: *Deconstructed* (1996; ECM/XtraWatt) (see below) and two excellent live recordings, the quintet set *Always Pack Your Uniform On Top* (2000; ECM/XtraWatt) and the trio outing *Damaged In Transit* (2003; ECM/XtraWatt).

Swallow is a brilliant bass guitarist with his own sound and style, his concentration and dependability are legendary, and he is a superb soloist. He always plays compositionally, with a comprehensive understanding of the music and his role in it, probably because he is one of the finest and most fertile small-group composers. His pieces have been played and recorded by many musicians, including Gary Burton, Mike Gibbs and Chick Corea – some of his best-known compositions are "Arise Her Eyes", "Chelsea Bells", "Como En Vietnam", "Doin' The Pig", "Domino Biscuit", "Eiderdown", "Falling Grace", "General Mojo's Well Laid Plan", "Green Mountains", "Sweet Henry" and "Hotel Hello". **[IC]**

Home (1979; ECM). Swallow leading a quintet in music to poems by Robert Creeley – a highly sophisticated amalgam, all with Swallow's magic touch.

Carla (1986/7; XtraWatt); **Swallow** (1991; XtraWatt). Featuring Carla Bley on organ, guitarist Hiram Bullock, pianist Larry Willis and drummer Victor Lewis, augmented by violin, viola and cello, *Carla* is Swallow's tribute to his love, not without ups and downs but always interesting. His eponymous album is a stronger family affair with Carla and her daughter Karen on keyboards and harmonica, plus Bullock again and John Scofield in the nine-strong band. Swallow's playing, soloing and writing are impeccable on this well-nigh flawless album.

Real Book (1993; XtraWatt). This is Swallow having some serious fun, writing his own brand of standard tunes for a virtuoso group – Tom Harrell, Joe Lovano, Mulgrew Miller and Jack DeJohnette. The eight pieces range from the fast and aggressive "Bite Your Grandmother", which is a brilliant variation on "I Got Rhythm", to medium-tempo Latin themes.

Deconstructed (1996 XtraWatt). More inscrutable music of a similar playful nature ("Running In The Family" is based on "Basin Street Blues"), this time with trumpeter Ryan Kisor, saxist Chris Potter, guitarist Mick Goodrick and drummer Adam Nussbaum. Irony and intensity in equal measure.

➤➤ **Carla Bley** *(Go Together; Songs With Legs)*; **Gary Burton** *(Hotel Hello)*; **Jimmy Giuffre** *(1961)*; **George Russell** *(Ezz-thetics)*.

Wilbur Sweatman

Clarinet, leader, composer.

b. Brunswick, Missouri, 7 Feb 1882; d. 9 March 1961.

The composer of "Down Home Rag", and one of the pioneer jazz bandleaders, Sweatman formed his first orchestra in 1902 to present a mixture of ragtime, vaudeville and early jazz, and spent a decade touring before settling in New York in 1913. A regular theatre act thereafter (one appearance in March 1923 at the Lafayette in Harlem also featured a youthful Duke Ellington and Sonny Greer), Sweatman usually closed his act with his *pièce de résistance*, playing three clarinets at once, but despite such eccentricities he was a fine musician and a big success. From the 1930s he concentrated on business interests, including administering Scott Joplin's estate, but continued to play on into the 1950s. **[DF]**

Sweet Substitute

A Bristol-based trio of singers, Sweet Substitute – the late Angie Masterson, Teri Leggett and Chris Staples (later replaced by Kate McNab) – began their career in 1975 re-creating the music of "sister acts" such as the Boswells and the Andrews; later their approach broadened to include more contemporary material. A first album, *Something Special* (1978), teamed them with Keith Nichols and a prototype of the Midnite Follies Orchestra; thereafter the trio toured nationally, appeared on radio and TV specials, guested with Nichols's Midnite Follies for live dates and played European jazz festivals. Their MD during this period was guitarist/arranger Andy Leggett; when that association came to an end, Sweet Substitute worked regularly for Chris Barber's agency, and toured and recorded with his band. By the mid-1980s the group was touring for Keith Smith in shows such as *The Stardust Road* (for which they teamed with Georgie Fame as well as Smith's band) as well as appearing in clubs, cabaret and on TV and radio; with occasional line-up adjustments they continued working regularly into the 1990s. **[DF]**

Sophisticated Ladies (1980; Black Lion). Their second album, showing off their widely based repertoire, as well as some witty Leggett originals.

Duncan Swift

Piano, trombone.

b. Rotherham, Yorkshire, UK, 21 Feb 1943; d. 8 Aug 1997.

A musician of prodigious technique and audacious imagination, Swift was classically trained and played piano and trombone with Midlands-based bands including Bill Nile's Delta Jazzmen (his first professional signing) but continued teaching and lecturing in schools and colleges until joining Kenny Ball's Jazzmen (1977 83). Later he worked with groups led by Pete Allen and others and doubled as a landlord in Bewdley while building his solo career. From the mid-1980s this took a notable upturn after Swift signed to Jim Simpson's Big Bear label; for Simpson he recorded two outstanding solo albums, was presented as a premier soloist, and regularly starred in clubs concerts and festivals. Diagnosis of throat cancer in 1995 gradually curtailed Swift's career but by then his reputation was secure as Britain's most audaciously creative stride pianist. **[DF]**

The Broadwood Concert (1991; Big Bear). Recorded live, this set bears testimony to Swift's phenomenal technique and vivid imagination: Jelly Roll Morton, Fats Waller and James P. Johnson mingled with Swift originals and fine standards ("Like Someone In Love" and "Cry Me A River").

The Key Of D Is Daffodil Yellow (1993; Duncan Swift). A thoughtful and often spectacular studio-recorded solo recital based on a quotation from Marian McPartland and containing fine reinterpretations of themes by Waller and Morton, plus originals and standards.

Gabor Szabo

Guitar.

b. Budapest, Hungary, 8 March 1936; d. 26 Feb 1982.

Starting on guitar at the age of fourteen, Szabo was already a skilled player, performing professionally with various groups in Budapest and composing for film and television by the time of the Soviet invasion in 1956. He left Hungary in November 1956 and settled in the USA as a refugee, attending the Berklee School (1957–9). He appeared at the Newport jazz festival in 1958 and was a member of drummer Chico Hamilton's quartet (1961–5) and groups led by arranger Gary McFarland and Charles Lloyd. Named Best New Jazz Guitarist by *Down Beat* in 1964, he toured extensively with his own group (1966–8). His sound and his harmonic approach had always reflected his early immersion in the music of Hungary, but from 1969 his guitar style also featured blues, rock and Eastern music influences. This development was also apparent in the music of his fusion group The Perfect Circle, formed in 1975. In the 1970s Szabo worked as a studio musician in television, but he influenced several younger players including Larry Coryell. He had returned to Hungary at the time of his death. [CA]

⊙ **Spellbinder (1966; Universal).** Szabo brings a restless, questing spirit to this session of standards and originals and is prepared to take risks. It doesn't all work, but when it does the results are exhilarating.

⊙ **Femme Fatale (1979; Hungaroton).** Recorded by Atlantic, who never released it, Szabo's final recording is an eclectic mix of the dynamic and the mellow. His duet with Chick Corea on the latter's "Out Of The Night" is one highlight, as is Szabo's own Flamenco-inspired "A Thousand Times". This moodily atmospheric album deserves to be better known.

T

Lew Tabackin

Tenor saxophone, flute.

b. Philadelphia, 26 May 1940.

Tabackin studied at the Philadelphia Conservatory of Music from 1958–62, taking a BMus and majoring in flute. In 1965 he moved to New York, playing with Maynard Ferguson, Clark Terry, Thad Jones-Mel Lewis and Joe Henderson and in small groups with Donald Byrd, Elvin Jones, Toshiko Akiyoshi and others. From 1968–9 he led his own trio, toured Switzerland, did a jazz workshop in Hamburg and was featured soloist with the Danish Radio Orchestra. He married Toshiko Akiyoshi, touring Japan with her in 1970 and 1971. They moved to Los Angeles in 1972 and the couple ran a workshop big band which evolved into the Toshiko Akiyoshi orchestra. They toured Japan with it several times, visited Europe, and played on the East Coast of the USA, earning worldwide critical acclaim. At the same time Tabackin managed to find the time to play with various trios of his own with, variously, Billy Higgins, John Heard and Charlie Haden; his most consistent partners were Joey Baron and Michael Moore (a trio – without the melodic bedrock of a piano – has always seemed to be his favoured medium). Tabackin has released consistent albums on the Concord label since 1990, recording and touring with various acoustic ensembles. Since 1999, he has played with Muscovite bassist Boris Kozlov and drummer Mark Taylor.

His playing recalls, as Chris Parker put it, "not only the rhapsodic self-absorption of Coleman Hawkins, but also the fierce intensity laced with playfulness that characterizes the solos of Sonny Rollins". A gifted saxophonist, in addition to Rollins, the influences of greats such as Coltrane, Lester Young and Ben Webster are audible in his playing; and he is also one of the finest flute players on the current jazz scene. [IC]

⊙ **Desert Lady** (1989; Concord); **I'll Be Seeing You** (1992; Concord). Two excellent quartet albums, both with superb rhythm-sections – the earlier features Hank Jones, Dave Holland and Victor Lewis; whilst Benny Green, Peter Washington and Lewis Nash contribute to the later – and the leader in fine form.

➤➤ **Toshiko Akiyoshi** *(The Toshiko Akiyoshi-Lew Tabackin Big Band).*

Jamaaladeen Tacuma

Electric bass.

b. Hempstead, New York, 11 June 1956.

Philadelphia-raised bassist Jamaaladeen Tacuma (born Rudy McDaniel) played with organist Charles Earland as a teenager. At nineteen he began playing in Ornette Coleman's electric group Prime Time, appearing under his original name on *Dancing In Your Head* (1975; A&M), and subsequently with his Muslim name on Prime Time records such as *Body Meta* (1975; Artist House) and *Of Human Feelings* (1979; Antilles). His virtuosic incorporation of funk into Coleman's "harmolodic" music system was a key element of the group's sound.

Tacuma plays on several successful, eclectic records produced by Kip Hanrahan, and he's heard to advantage on James "Blood" Ulmer's *Tales Of Captain Black* (1978; Artist House). As a leader, he has recorded several records for Gramavision, including *Renaissance Man* (1984), and a number for the German Moers label, including *The Night Of Chamber Music* (1994), with his bass-centric ensemble Basso Nouveau, and three for the ITM label, *Intense* (1995), *Gemini-Gemini* (1995) and *Journey Into Gemini Territory* (1996). He and drummer Calvin Weston hooked up with Derek Bailey for the disappointing curio *Mirakle* (2000; Tzadik) – a summit that produced some thrilling sounds but evidenced no fluent *lingua franca*. More successfully, Tacuma collaborated with virtuoso of Turkish traditional music Burhan Oçal and singer Natasha Atlas on Oçal's album *Groove Alla Turca* (2003; Doublemoon). [JC]

⊙ **Show Stopper** (1983; Gramavision). Most of Tacuma's best work may have been with Prime Time, but his first Gramavision outing still has some of that feeling – harmonic adventurousness, interesting charts, devastating funk drive – and has the bonus of great players like cornettist Olu Dara, alto saxophonist Julius Hemphill and pianist Anthony Davis. From here on though, Tacuma's music gets much less consistently interesting.

Aki Takase

Piano, Chinese koto, composer.

b. Osaka, Japan, 26 Jan 1948.

Aki Takase's mother, a piano teacher, gave her lessons from the age of three. She also played bass in her school orchestra, and then studied the

Aki Takase

piano at Toho Gakuen University in Tokyo. She heard records of Charles Mingus, Ornette Coleman and John Coltrane, and after hearing a friend improvising on "Autumn Leaves" she began improvising herself. In 1971 she got her first professional engagements and at 25 she began to lead her own groups. In 1978 she made her first album as leader and in 1981 she recorded with Dave Liebman, making her first visit to Europe, performing with her trio at the Berlin festival.

In May 1982 she played in New York with Cecil McBee (bass), Bob Moses and singer Sheila Jordan, and in June her solo piano concert was the high spot of the East-West festival in Nuremberg. She toured Europe with a quartet in 1983 and thereafter worked there extensively, with Alexander von Schlippenbach in particular. In the 1990s she toured with ex-Coltrane players Rashied Ali and Reggie Workman. She has now recorded over a dozen albums to date, ranging from intrepid songbook duets with Rudi Hahall (*Duet For Eric Dolphy* in 1998) and David Murray (see below) to freely improvised solo recitals.

Aki Takase is a brilliant performer who can handle all areas from conventional structures and harmony to semi- or total abstraction. She is steeped in jazz, but also uses elements from the Japanese musical tradition, and often performs on Chinese koto, a 17-string zither. **[IC]**

⊙ **Shima Shoka (1990; Enja).** This solo album is a *tour de force*, with seven of her own highly individual compositions, and bravura performances of "Giant Steps" and Ellington's "Rockin' In Rhythm".

⊙ **Le Cahier Du Bal (2001; Leo).** Another formidable solo work – a series of bewitching, terpsichorean improvisations dedicated to her friend, dancer Anzu Furukawa.

Aki Takase and David Murray

⊙ **Blue Monk (1991; Enja).** This pairing shows just how far Takase has travelled since her record debut in 1981. Here she duets on an equal basis with the formidable saxophonist, on four Monk tunes and other pieces, digging in deep musically and emotionally.

Horace Tapscott

Piano.

b. Houston, Texas, 6 April 1934; d. Los Angeles, 27 Feb 1999.

Son of a jazz musician mother, Horace Tapscott moved from Texas to Fresno and finally Los Angeles at the end of 1943, and there he played trombone in the bands of Dexter Gordon, Wardell Gray and Gerald Wilson, alongside other young players like Eric Dolphy and Frank Morgan. While in the air force in 1953, stationed in Wyoming, he played trombone, baritone saxophone and piano in the band. In the late 50s, he played trombone with Lionel Hampton, but after a severe car accident he focused on piano. In around 1959 he began playing free jazz with his own large group (some 35-strong), the Pan-Afrikan Peoples Arkestra, and he started the associated activist artistic community organization, the Union of God's Musicians and Artists Ascension (UGMAA). Saxophonist Sonny Criss used Tapscott's compositions on his wonderful 1968 record *Sonny's Dream* (Prestige), subtitled "Birth Of The New Cool". The following year, Tapscott recorded *The Giant Is Awakened* (Flying Dutchman) as a leader with young alto saxophonist Arthur Blythe, partially reissued on *West Coast Hot* (Novus). Though his beautiful, highly original music has slowly come into greater recognition, Tapscott's defiant self-determination – he released the bulk of his music on his own Nimbus record label – and community involvement kept him out of the jazz public's attention for the last three decades of his life. On Nimbus he released a series of solo works, *The Tapscott Sessions* (now running, with posthumous releases, at ten volumes), as well as records by the Arkestra and small groups with various personnel. He recorded the excellent two volumes of *The Dark Tree* (1990; hat Art) with a quartet featuring clarinettist John Carter. In 1993, the compositions for *Sonny's Dream* were revived for the Chicago jazz festival, with Blythe in the band.

Tapscott's visibility was rising at the end of his life – he released two fine, critically lauded records on the Arabesque label in the second half of the 90s. In 1998, the tall Texan was diagnosed with cancer and he died early the following year. **[JC]**

⊙ **Aiee! The Phantom (1996; Arabesque).** Along with his final record, a trio titled *Thoughts Of Dar Es Salaam* (1997; Arabesque), this excellent quintet date with trumpeter Marcus Belgrave, alto saxophonist Abraham Burton and elder statesmen Reggie Workman on bass and Andrew Cyrille on drums offers an outstanding perspective on what the pianist had acquired in four decades of jazz-making – an original vision as a composer (all originals) often utilizing odd times, involved sectional charts and thoughtful, but consistently approachable, lines and a uniquely tender, deep touch at the keyboard.

Greg Tardy

Tenor and soprano sax, clarinet, bass clarinet.
b. New Orleans, 3 Feb 1966.

Tardy's parents were both professional opera singers, and his mother also sang jazz, while his brother and sister play trumpet and flute respectively. Studying classical clarinet at University of Wisconsin, Tardy also took jazz theory classes in Milwaukee, and at 19 started playing saxophone with funk-fusion bands. He was in St Louis in 1990, and New Orleans from 1991–3 where he worked with Nicolas Payton, Allen Toussaint and the Neville Brothers among others. During a second spell in St Louis (1993–4), he co-led a band with Russell Gunn before moving to New York, where he has worked with John Hicks, Tom Harrell, Dave Douglas, Andrew Hill and Susie Ibarra, and gigged with many others from Jay McShann to Rashied Ali. Particularly inspired by Harrell and Hill, he admires saxophonists such as Ben Webster, Ornette Coleman, Shorter, Lovano, Marsalis and Parker. Since 1997, he has also played with Christian gospel-jazz groups, a genre he has said he would like to eventually cross over to full-time. [BP]

⊙ **The Hidden Light** (1999; J Curve). Tardy's favourite among his own albums has a quintet featuring Nicolas Payton on some tracks, and definite spiritual overtones that lead towards the closing version of Thomas A. Dorsey's "Take My Hand, Precious Lord".

➤➤ **Tom Harrell** *(The Art Of Rhythm)*; **Andrew Hill** *(Dusk)*.

Buddy Tate

Tenor saxophone.
b. Sherman, Texas, 22 Feb 1913; d. 10 Feb 2001.

One of the great gentlemen of the tenor saxophone, Buddy (George Holmes) Tate learned his craft playing with territory bands around the Southwest in the early 1930s. They included McCloud's Night Owls (for which Booker Ervin Snr played trombone), the St Louis Merrymakers (in which Tate first met Herschel Evans), Terrence Holder (his first big band, later taken over by Andy Kirk), Kirk's own group, and Nat Towles's fine orchestra. In 1939 he was invited by Count Basie to replace Evans, who had died suddenly. "I dreamed he had died," Tate later told Stanley Dance, "and that Basie was going to call me. It happened within a week or two: I still have the telegram!" He stayed with Basie for nine happy years, then worked with Lucky Millinder, Hot Lips Page and Jimmy Rushing's Savoy band before entrepreneur Irving Cohen offered him the residency at the Celebrity Club on 125th Street in Harlem. Tate stayed at the club for 21 straight years "until the clientele began to change: they wanted rock and didn't appreciate what we were doing, so we quit". But he had been canny enough to avoid being buried in this long residency: through the 1950s he had recorded regularly, toured with Buck Clayton and kept himself in the public eye, so when he became a freelance again there were immediate offers for his services. On the European circuit he teamed up with players such as Jim Galloway and Jay McShann and, after the death of Jimmy Forrest, he formed a working duo with trombonist Al Grey. In America he worked the festivals, including Dick Gibson's Jazz Parties, and co-led a band with Bobby Rosengarden at the Rainbow Room. Though seriously hurt when a hotel shower scalded him in 1981, Tate was soon back on the road, playing with the same broad sound, thick vibrato and fine timing; during the 1980s he toured with the Texas Tenors (led by Illinois Jacquet), played as a soloist internationally at clubs and festivals, and appeared regularly at the Grande Parade du Jazz, Nice. A direct musical and spiritual successor to Coleman Hawkins and Herschel Evans, Buddy Tate was a true sax giant. [DF]

⊙ **Buddy Tate 1945-50** (Classics). The later 1940s were uncomfortable times for swing-based musicians who found themselves assailed by the fresh sounds of bebop, and Tate's solo sessions occasionally reflect the temporary malaise, but there is interesting music on this collection, amongst others from Emmett Berry, Tyree Glenn and Jimmy Witherspoon.

⊙ **Swinging Like Tate** (1958; London). Superlative mainstream recordings by Tate with his Celebrity Club and with a Basie-style ensemble co-starring Buck Clayton, Dicky Wells, Earle Warren and Jo Jones. Required listening for Tate followers.

⊙ **Swinging Scorpio** (1974; Black Lion). Humphrey Lyttelton and Tate shared a warm musico-personal relationship from the 1970s and this album is a good example, with arrangements by Buck Clayton.

⊙ **Ballad Artistry Of Buddy Tate** (1981; Sackville). An extremely beautiful record; Tate relaxing on a set of classy ballads amid a trio led by Canadian guitarist Ed Bickert.

Art Tatum

Piano.
b. Toledo, Ohio, 13 Oct 1909; d. 5 Nov 1956.

Virtually blind from birth, Tatum studied piano in early childhood and began gigging as a teenager in Toledo and Cleveland. He was the regular pianist for Adelaide Hall in New York and on tour in 1932–3, and he made his solo recording debut in this period. He had a career as a soloist in clubs in Hollywood, Chicago, New York and briefly (in 1938) in Europe, until forming his own trio in 1943 with Tiny Grimes and Slam Stewart. From then until his death from uraemia, he divided his time between trio and solo work, and between nightclub and concert appearances.

Like no other performer in the history of jazz piano, Tatum summarized everything that had preceded him stylistically, and did so in a supercharged manner which opened doors not only for succeeding generations of pianists but for practitioners of other instruments as well. Initially inspired by Fats Waller

HERMAN LEONARD

Art Tatum

and by "semi-classical" players, he was capable of making complex passages of "stride piano" sound like simple exercises learned by heart, though taken at suicidal speed for the sheer joy of impressing and intimidating would-be competitors. Similarly, although not frequently associated with blues material, when boogie became popular he could produce a boogie speciality full of virtuoso pyrotechnics.

The chief source of Tatum's style, however, was the boundless invention which went into his reworkings of standard material. Like the best of the stride players, he was less of a pure improviser than the kind of flamboyant "arranger" who preferred constantly to hint at the underlying theme while continuously decorating it (even overloading it, in the opinion of some lay listeners). His greatest strength in this area was his incessant rhythmic variation, which took discontinuity to even greater lengths than Earl Hines and, again for the layman, was sometimes just too much to follow. In this respect, he had a greater influence on the embryonic beboppers than on most of his fellow pianists, who attempted to emulate his surface characteristics and missed out on the rhythmic flexibility.

An even greater impact was made by Tatum's harmonic subtlety which, possibly influenced by Ellington's work of the early 1930s, incorporated the upper intervals such as 9ths, 11ths and 13ths, and an overwhelming variety of substitute and passing chords. It is no accident that this interested saxophonists especially, and all the harmonically forward-looking players such as Coleman Hawkins, Don Byas, Charlie Parker and, later, John Coltrane were deeply impressed by Tatum. Yet another facet of his general influence was pinpointed in this comment by Rex Stewart: "One of the most significant aspects of Tatum's artistry stemmed from his constant self-challenge. At the piano, Art seemingly delighted in creating impossible problems from the standpoint of harmonies and chord progressions. Then he would gleefully improvise sequence upon sequence until the phrase emerged as a complete entity within the structure of whatever composition he happened to be playing." [BP]

⊙ **Strange As It Seems** (1932–51; Collectors Items). By far the most interesting selection of miscellaneous Tatum, this has six Decca alternate takes plus a trio broadcast and soundtrack items from *The Fabulous Dorseys*. It also has Tatum's first test recording of "Tiger Rag" and the reissue of his debut recordings behind singer Adelaide Hall.

⊙ **The Standard Transcriptions** (1935–43; Music and Arts). This two-CD collection of radio-studio discs has a more alive sound than other early reissues. Whole swathes of Tatum's vast repertoire are here, including showpieces like "Tiger Rag" and his own "The Shout", plus dozens of standards on which he put his mark.

⊙ **I Got Rhythm** (1935–44; MCA/GRP). This contains most of Tatum's few early band recordings, though sadly not the six titles featuring singer Joe Turner, which were separately reissued under his name. The last batch of ten tracks has the first work of the entertaining trio with Tiny Grimes and Slam Stewart.

⊙ **20th Century Piano Genius** (1950–5; Verve). One of a handful of informal recordings, this has Tatum the soloist entertaining at two private parties and, though sometimes staying with favourites routines, he often elaborates them unexpectedly. A single-CD selection has appeared as *Art Tatum's Finest Hour*.

⊙ **The Complete Capitol Recordings** (1949–52; Capitol). During a comparative lull in Tatum's recording, this adds new solo items such as "Willow Weep For Me", "Nice Work If You Can Get It" and a rare (for Tatum) slow blues "Aunt Hagar's Blues". The trio appears on the later tracks, including the European light classic by Rubinstein, "Melody In F".

⊙ **The Tatum Group Masterpieces Vol. 1** (1954; Pablo). This piano/alto/drums trio is one of two albums from the same session featuring the equally decorative Benny Carter. They run polite and highly complementary rings around each other, while Louie Bellson is a model of supportive swing.

⊙ **The Tatum Group Masterpieces Vol. 8** (1956; Pablo). The final session of Tatum's truncated career finds him alongside the much more simple and direct playing of Ben Webster. The contrast is so extreme, and their mutual admiration and trust so great, that it works like a dream.

Art Taylor

Drums.

b. New York, 6 April 1929; d. 6 Feb 1995.

Taylor gigged with Howard McGhee and Coleman Hawkins in 1950–51, making his record debut with Hawkins. During the early-mid

50s he toured with the Buddy DeFranco quartet, the Bud Powell trio, and the George Wallington trio (and quintet); and he recorded with Art Farmer and with Miles Davis in 1955 and 1957, notably on the *Miles Ahead* album. He also performed and recorded with his own group The Wailers, and with the Donald Byrd-Gigi Gryce group in 1957. During the late 1950s and early 1960s he did copious freelance work: touring Europe with Charlie Byrd; playing with Thelonious Monk at the famous, historic Town Hall concert; and gigging and recording with musicians such as John Coltrane, Jackie McLean, Hank Mobley and Lee Morgan. In 1963 he moved to Europe, working mostly with expatriate Americans such as Dexter Gordon and Johnny Griffin. He also conducted interviews with American musicians in the late 1960s and early 1970s, which were eventually published in book form. Living in New York again from the early 1980s, he became more active as a performer. He organized a concert tribute to Bud Powell, which was repeated and expanded at the Kool festival in 1985. A new edition of The Wailers was active in the early 1990s and, especially after the deaths of Gordon and Art Blakey, he became a figurehead of the post-bop movement. Although his interviews are a significant contribution to the literature of jazz, his most important role was as a dynamic drummer displaying an admiration for both Blakey and Philly Joe Jones, interacting with soloists in the best sense of the word. [BP]

⊙ **Taylor's Wailers** (1957; Prestige/OJC). An excellent illustration of the company he kept, with one track ("C.T.A.") from a quartet session with Coltrane. A couple of weeks earlier, the rest of the material was recorded with Donald Byrd, Jackie McLean, Charlie Rouse and Ray Bryant, including one of several early versions of Bryant's "Cubano Chant".

⊙ **Wailin' At The Vanguard** (1992; Verve). The "documentary" opening apart, this is a typical live set by Taylor's new young band, sporting pianist Jacky Terrasson, altoist Abraham Burton and tenorist Willie Williams.

➤➤ **John Coltrane** *(Giant Steps).*

Billy Taylor

Piano.

b. Greenville, North Carolina, 24 July 1921.

Teenage trips to Harlem acquainted Taylor with pianists such as Art Tatum, Clarence Profit and the young Thelonious Monk. He moved to New York in the early 1940s and worked with Ben Webster, Dizzy Gillespie, Stuff Smith and others. He led the house rhythm-section at Birdland in 1951, and then had his own trio throughout the rest of the 1950s. Taylor then became active (and better known) as a writer, radio disc jockey, television musical director and educator; his book *Jazz Piano* (1982) was based on one of his radio series. He has been a committee member of the National Arts Council and was a co-founder of the Jazzmobile organization, which provides free concerts in Harlem, and recorded a Jazzmobile All Stars album in 1989. Still active as a player, he appeared for the first time ever in the UK in 1997.

Taylor's piano style reflects informal tutoring from Art Tatum plus the rhythmic approach of Nat "King" Cole. While his right-hand lines sometimes seem overloaded, they are very impressive technically, and his close-voiced left-hand inversions may have influenced Ahmad Jamal and therefore countless others. [BP]

⊙ **The Billy Taylor Trio With Candido** (1954; Prestige/OJC). Still sounding fresh after all these years, Taylor's piano style blends with the fairly flamboyant work of the Cuban percussionist, on tunes such as "Love For Sale" and Mario Bauza's "Mambo Inn".

Cecil Taylor

Piano, composer, educator.

b. New York, 15 March 1929.

Taylor's mother was a dancer who also played piano and violin, and who died when he was quite young. He had piano lessons from the age of six, attended the New York College of Music, then spent four years at the New England Conservatory. While there he became influenced by Dave Brubeck's piano style – particularly his thick chords. In later years, Taylor said of Brubeck: "I learned a lot from him. When he's most interesting, he sounds like me." Other initial influences were Bud Powell, Horace Silver, Duke Ellington and Erroll Garner. In the early 1950s he worked with small groups led by Johnny Hodges, Hot Lips Page and Lawrence Brown, and then he began to lead his own group, with Steve Lacy (soprano), Buell Neidlinger (bass) and Dennis Charles (drums). In 1956 this was the first jazz group to play regularly at the Five Spot Cafe, where they had a six-week residency. He was then still using chord changes and the usual jazz structures of 12 or 32 bars, but by the time his group appeared at the Newport jazz festival in 1957 the music had become much more abstract. In fact he was booked there at one of the afternoon "experimental" sessions, having already acquired the reputation of someone working on the frontiers of music. By the early 60s Taylor's music had become totally abstract – non-tonal and without any kind of conventional jazz rhythm.

The whole jazz scene in the late 1950s was ripe for a shake-up, which happened with the advent of free jazz, and Taylor should have played a very prominent role as one of the trailblazers of abstraction, but the arrival in New York of Ornette Coleman, in the autumn of 1959, put Taylor somewhat in the shade. As Thelonious Monk had done the previous decade, Taylor spent much of the 60s at home practising. In 1961 he had a booking at the Five Spot with his quartet, which included Archie Shepp, Neidlinger and Charles; and in 1962 he spent six months in Europe with Jimmy Lyons (alto) and Sunny Murray (drums), playing in Oslo and Stockholm and recording two albums at the Cafe Montmartre, Copenhagen. In Stockholm, Taylor met Albert Ayler, also beginning to find an audience for his music in Europe, and Ayler played with the group at the Montmartre, returning to the USA with them and continuing his association with Taylor until 1963. Back in New York, Taylor did not work again for almost a year. Along with Michael Mantler, he helped organise the Jazz Composers' Guild, which aimed to present the new music without compromise. By 1965, although still working very rarely, he was already an inspirational force in free jazz; pianists were becoming influenced by his style, and his integrity influenced musicians on all instruments.

In 1968 Taylor was a featured soloist on a Jazz Composers' Orchestra recording under the direction of Mantler. The same year, saxophonist Sam Rivers joined Taylor's group, staying with it until 1973, and in this period the pianist began to get more international bookings. The Cecil Taylor Unit toured Europe in 1969; Taylor himself played solo piano concerts at several festivals in the early 1970s, including the Newport jazz festival and Montreux. He also became active in academic circles, first at the University of Wisconsin, where in 1970–71 he taught a course in black music from 1920–70 and directed the Black Music Ensemble. He was awarded a Guggenheim Fellowship in 1973.

Taylor has always been interested in ballet and dance, and once said, "I try to imitate on the piano the leaps in space a dancer makes."; in 1979 he composed and played the music for a twelve-minute ballet, *Tetra Stomp: Eatin' Rain in Space*, featuring Mikhail Baryshnikov and Heather Watts. Opportunities for recording became as plentiful as they were scarce earlier in his career. In 1988 a festival was devoted to Taylor in Berlin, in which he played with many of Europe's leading free improvisors, the results of which were released on ten CDs. His latterday work has found him alternating between performing unaccompanied and group work with a trio (featuring bassist William Parker – or more recently trumpeter William Dixon - and drummer Tony Oxley) and larger units often featuring Harri Sjöström on soprano saxophone. Taylor also sometimes incorporates readings of his poetry into his performances.

Taylor has said that the more he plays, the more he becomes aware of the non-European aspects of the music, and he explained to John Litweiler: "In white music the most admired touch among pianists is light. The same is true among white percussionists. We in black music think of the piano as a percussive instrument: we beat the keyboard, we get inside the instrument. Europeans admire Bill Evans for his touch. But the physical force going into the making of black music – if that is misunderstood, it leads to screaming." As a pianist, Taylor has an exceptionally brilliant technique allied to phenomenal energy and stamina: people often talk about his playing more from a physical than from an aesthetic point of view. He can play the most intricate abstract lines and torrential atonal clusters with a blistering percussive attack, all at high volume, and he can sustain this kind of intensity for anything up to two or three hours. His groups too, reflect his energy, and are relentlessly abstract – it can sometimes seem as if his music has virtually nothing in common with either the European classical tradition or the folk and ethnic musics of the world. [IC]

JAK KILBY

Cecil Taylor

⊙ **Jumpin' Punkins** (1961; Candid). A gentle introduction to Taylor's music; there are two Ellington tunes (one by Duke, and Mercer's title track), Clark Terry on hand for a couple of tracks, and Buell Neidlinger's "OP", a trio tribute to Ellington's bassist Pettiford. This is the outstanding track, though the loose feel of the larger group, with Archie Shepp's raw tenor prominent, has its charm.

⊙ **Student Studies** (1966; Charly). This live recording of the Cecil Taylor Unit has longtime collaborators Andrew Cyrille, Jimmy Lyons and Alan Silva (playing bass). Although the leader's torrents of notes attract the most attention, the level of interaction within the aptly named Unit is impressive, and the highly underrated Lyons is an affecting performer. This is high-energy music, but far from unrelenting.

⊙ **For Olim** (1986; Soul Note). Of the many Taylor solo recordings, this one is recommended not least for the quality of the recording and the piano used. Taylor's habit of taking the simplest thematic material and stretching it to improbable, ground-shaking limits is exemplified here. However, the subtleties of Taylor's keyboard technique are also brought into clear focus.

⊙ **Live In Bologna** (1987; Leo). An exceptional group session, though Taylor's output is remarkably consistent; Carlos Ward's alto gives the set a grounding in jazz (specifically Coltrane) and Thurman Barker is an ideal drummer – the interaction of his marimba and Taylor's piano is one of the disc's highlights.

The Willisau Concert (2002; Intakt). Taylor as septuagenarian, not only showing little sign of easing back, but producing a solo recital that for energy, clarity and passionate exploration, stands with his best work.

John Taylor

Piano.

b. Manchester, UK, 25 Sept 1942.

Taylor, who is self-taught, began working with dance bands in the early 1960s, then in 1964 went to London and was soon playing with the John Surman octet, the Alan Skidmore quintet, and Norma Winstone. He also played with John Warren's band, John Dankworth and Cleo Laine and Marian Montgomery, and led his own trio and sextet in the later 1960s and the 1970s. For a while he was with the Ronnie Scott quintet and in 1977, with Kenny Wheeler and Norma Winstone, he formed the trio Azimuth. In the later 1970s he worked with Jan Garbarek's quintet, Arild Andersen's quartet and the Miroslav Vitous quartet, touring extensively internationally and appearing at many festivals. In the later 1980s he was a member of Kenny Wheeler's touring quintet which included John Abercrombie, Dave Holland and Peter Erskine, and recorded the superb 1990 album *The Widow In The Window*. This quintet was also the nucleus for Wheeler's 1990 magnum opus, *Music For Large And Small Ensembles*. Taylor worked with Wheeler and John Surman throughout the 1990s and was also featured pianist in Peter Erskine's trio, recording three albums for ECM with the drummer's group. A latter day ensemble featured Taylor with singer Maria Pia Da Vito and guitarist Ralph Towner. Since the early 1990s, Taylor has also been teaching regularly at the Cologne music academy.

Taylor has absorbed all his influences (principally Bill Evans) and developed into one of the finest pianists in jazz. The hallmarks of his style are long flowing lyrical lines and sonorous harmonies, and the same qualities are evident in his compositions. He is one of a handful of British musicians with a really solid international reputation. As the driving force behind Azimuth, he composed much of the music, and his piano usually performed the key role of setting up rhythmic or textural terms of reference. His accompaniments too, for instance, on Norma Winstone's solo albums, are exquisite.An influence on his whole approach, he once stated, was that of Mike Gibbs, whose scoring has affected Taylor's attitude to texture and dynamics. [IC]

Blue Glass (1991; Jazz House). A fine British piano trio completed by Mick Hutton (bass) and Steve Argüelles (drums). Recorded live at Ronnie Scott's, there is little in the way of club-pleasing grandstanding with the pianist's pastel gifts much in evidence.

Rosslyn (2003; ECM). Though an established ECM sideman for over 25 years, this is Taylor's debut as leader for the label and it's an archetypically aching, spacious offering, this time in the company of ex-Bill Evans bassist Marc Johnson and New York drummer Joey Baron. Four Taylor originals, a Towner, a Wheeler and the pianist's latest thoughts on a favourite standard, "How Deep Is The Ocean".

Azimuth

Azimuth/The Touchstone/Départ (1977–9; ECM). This three-disc boxed set is a re-release of the first three Azimuth albums. Taylor, Norma Winstone and Kenny Wheeler had already been associated musically for several years, and their rapport was almost transcendental. The hypnotically repeating rhythms, Taylor's luminous melodies and the improvisations of trumpet and voice in this almost chamber-group environment are uniquely attractive. These albums are among the finest examples of a genre Azimuth helped to create.

How It Was Then ... Never Again (1994; ECM). The first new Azimuth release for some time, and it marks a change from long pieces to a variety of short ones. The album opens with a swashbuckling percussion rhythm reminiscent of Big Sid Catlett, created by Taylor using the pedals of the piano and strumming the strings – the result is a funky Azimuth number! A standard is even included – Wheeler plays a sensuous solo trumpet version (with overdubbed parts) of "How Deep Is The Ocean". Norma Winstone handles the wordless singing and the lyrics brilliantly. All in all, a fascinating album.

➤➤ **Peter Erskine** *(Time Being)*; **John Surman** *(Stranger Than Fiction; Proverbs And Songs)*; **Miroslav Vitous** *(Journey's End)*; **Kenny Wheeler** *(The Widow In The Window)*; **Norma Winstone** *(Somewhere Called Home; Like Song Like Weather)*.

Martin Taylor

Guitar.

b. Harlow, Essex, UK, 20 Oct 1956.

A guitarist of virtuoso technique and broad based musical taste, Martin Taylor first picked up a guitar at around four years old. He was being widely noticed in his early teens (one coup was to sit in with Count Basie's orchestra during a jazz cruise), and was soon working with discerning leaders such as Lennie Hastings. In partnership with Ike Isaacs in the late 1970s, Taylor's work showed a maturity beyond his years, and regular work with Peter Ind at the same period indicated that he could move with equal conviction in the contemporary areas occupied by Pat Metheny. His recorded output reflects the same admirable catholicism. Between 1979-90 he partnered Stephane Grappelli; concurrently he toured with Buddy de Franco, and joined the "Great Guitars" package tour with Barney Kessel and Charlie Byrd in 1989 before a contract with Linn Records in 1990 secured him a steady output of solo recordings. Taylor toured internationally as a soloist in the 1990s, by now acknowledged as a talent of international proportions. He possesses a rare, double gift of brilliant musicianship and the ability of keeping a clear eye on the business of making a living at jazz without ever compromising his musical beliefs. Relocated in Scotland in later years (and managed by his son) Taylor now records for the massive Sony label. [DF]

Don't Fret (1990; Linn). With a superb rhythm-section (Dave Newton, Dave Green and Allan Ganley), Taylor here plays an immaculate programme of standards and originals, including his own title track. Gracefully creative playing beautifully recorded.

⊙ **Artistry** (1992; Linn). The best example of Taylor's virtuoso talents on record, this recital has examples of his technique of playing solos accompanied by a simultaneous bass-line on the bottom string(s), a device invented by George Van Eps and duplicated by few others. Taylor's technique, however, never overpowers the music.

⊙ **Spirit of Django** (1994; Linn). A remarkable reapproach to Reinhardt's music, featuring Dave O'Higgins and Jack Emblow (Britain's premier jazz accordionist in a welcome reappearance on record). Taylor's group headlined at Ronnie Scott's during 1994 and provides here, as it did then, a vivid alternative to standard Hot Club formulae.

⊙ **Kiss and Tell** (1999; Columbia). An international line-up (including Randy Brecker, Kirk Whalum and Eddie Gomez and a full string section) showcases Taylor's breadth of skills and musical vision across pop standards (Muldaur's "Midnight at the Oasis"; "Mona Lisa"), movie themes ("The Odd Couple") and even TV themes.

➤➤ **Stephane Grappelli** *(Reunion With Martin Taylor).*

John Tchicai

Alto, tenor and soprano saxophones, bass clarinet.

b. Copenhagen, 28 April 1936.

Born of a Danish mother and Congolese father, Tchicai studied music at conservatory level while playing jazz; he led his own group at the World Youth Festival in Helsinki, and played with the Jørgen Leth quintet at the Warsaw jazz festival (both in 1962). He moved to New York in 1963, and co-led the New York Contemporary Five with Archie Shepp and Bill Dixon (later replaced by Don Cherry). He toured Europe with this group in the autumn of 1963, and then formed the New York Art Quartet with Roswell Rudd and Milford Graves. He joined these musicians and others in the foundation of the Jazz Composers' Guild, and was a member of the augmented John Coltrane group which recorded *Ascension* in 1965. He returned to Europe in 1966, working with Gunter Hampel, Don Cherry and his own seventeen-piece Cadentia Nova Danica. Concentrating more recently on tenor, he has also worked since 1982 with guitarist Pierre Dørge and the New Jungle Orchestra, and with the all-saxophonist sextet De Zes Winden (Six Winds). He also toured Europe with Cecil Taylor and with Johnny Dyani's Witchdoctor's Son. Tchicai was an interesting altoist whose tone, and even phraseology, were most often compared to Lee Konitz, which made a considerable contrast with other saxophonists of the 1960s avant-garde. As a result, he appeared to place less emphasis on the manner of his delivery and more on the content of his lines. [BP]

⊙ **New York Art Quartet** (1964; ESP). Credited to the group rather than Tchicai, this is from the period when he was on the US "free" scene. And this album was one of the first indications that there was a "cooler" approach than Ornette Coleman's available within the freedoms of the new jazz. The closing track with LeRoi Jones's narration forms an alignment with "black power" politics.

Charlie Teagarden

Trumpet.

b. Vernon, Texas, 19 July 1913; d. 10 Dec 1984.

It was probably inevitable that Charlie Teagarden would live his musical life in the shadow of his brother Jack. Although their talents were never dramatically different, Jack Teagarden, in the last analysis, was an innovator and jazz genius; Charlie was simply an outstanding and versatile player. And though Charlie did sing for fun, his voice never had the charm and hint of vulnerability that made his brother's great.

But like Jack he had perfect technique for making the most of what he had: a hot golden tone, the kind of fluid, carefree approach that would have graced a clarinet, and a generous vibrato (like that of the young Harry James) which warmed up everything he played. In the early years, wherever Jack was found – in Ben Pollack's band from 1928, with Whiteman in the 1930s, and later with his own bands – Charlie was often on hand too, which was perhaps unfortunate for the younger man. Charlie worked for Harry James in 1946, then for Jimmy Dorsey (he shared the stage with a tigerish Maynard Ferguson) and by 1948 he had joined the Dorseyland Band: that year Dorsey gave him a picture inscribed to "The most underrated trumpeter in the world". From 1950–58 Teagarden played for Ben Pollack and Bob Crosby in studios, led his own trio with Jess Stacy at Club Hangover, and played and recorded with his brother. By the 60s he was living in Las Vegas, where he did the rounds of the hotel bands ("often six in a week"); then he took a group to the Silver Slipper, where he stayed for three years. In the 1970s he was an officer in the Vegas local of AFM. "My trumpet? Like me it's retired", he told Dave Dexter in 1984. "But I have a jillion memories and I figure life's been good to me." [DF]

➤➤ **Jimmy Dorsey** *(Jimmy Dorsey And His Dorseyland Band).*

Cub Teagarden

Drums.

b. Vernon, Texas, 16 Dec 1915; d. 1969.

The least-known of the Teagarden tribe, Cub (Clois Lee) played drums all round the Midwest in the 1930s before joining his brother Jack's big band (1939–40). In the 1940s he worked with the Oklahoma Symphony Orchestra as well as his own band, but left music in 1948 for a day job at the Long Beach branch of General Telephones. [DF]

Jack Teagarden

Trombone, vocals, leader.

b. Vernon, Texas, 29 Aug 1905; d. 15 Jan 1964.

The greatest jazz trombonist of the music's history, Jack Teagarden first came to local prominence

William Gottlieb

Jack Teagarden

with Peck Kelley's band in 1921 and his talent even then was enough to scare Pee Wee Russell: "Look," said Russell, "I'm a nice guy 1000 miles from home and I'm outclassed! Just send me back to St Louis!" Over the next seven years – with Kelley, then with other leaders such as Willard Robison and "Doc" Ross – Teagarden developed ideas and a technique (including a set of close-to-the-chest slide positions, sadly never written down) which were to complete his armoury. By the time he joined Ben Pollack in 1928 his gifts had matured: a delicately contoured tone in which every note sounded as if it were gift-wrapped, effortless production (he was perhaps the first jazz trombonist to play softly); a startling mobility of approach that used the slide as a means to an end rather than a comedic end in itself; seductive tricks with water-glass mutes; and, above all, an ability to make whatever he played sound intuitively right. Other players, including Miff Mole, Bill Rank and Jimmy Harrison, had helped in the trombone revolution of the 1920s, but Teagarden's work capped theirs.

Teagarden was with Pollack for five years (his arrival hastened Glenn Miller's voluntary departure) and then in 1933 he signed a five-year contract as soloist for Paul Whiteman. Here he became something very close to a household name – through regular network radio from New York, prolific recording for Whiteman, and copious "special material" written for him by his friend Johnny Mercer and later by Bill Conway (whose Modernaires collaborated with Teagarden on later radio shows for Chesterfield cigarettes). But Teagarden found much of Whiteman's material tedious and shared the fashionable desire to lead his own orchestra. In 1939 he formed a big band, backed by MCA, with cornermen such as Charles Spivak (trumpet), Allan Reuss (guitar) and Ernie Caceres (baritone). For the next seven years he led a succession of bands, featuring such gifted soloists as clarinettist Sal Franzella and "Pokey" Carriere (who dubbed the trumpet in the 1940 Bing Crosby film *Birth Of The Blues*, in which Teagarden and his band featured on screen).

But Teagarden's bands came late to the swing fray – his first was formed four years after Benny Goodman was crowned "King of Swing" – and he often found himself at the mercy of dishonest bookers, the US draft or simply his own inability to think fast enough in business. He broke up his band in 1946, after one or two bouts of heavy drinking, and the following year joined Louis Armstrong's All Stars. Armstrong loved Teagarden to the end of his life – "There'll never be another", Louis said – and the early years of their partnership produced fine music and records. But the regimented routines of Armstrong's All Stars, the cavalier management of Joe Glaser (who sometimes worked its bandmembers too hard), plus Teagarden's own memories of being in charge of his music over the previous decade (however tenuously), often led to his finding his role hard-going. (Later partners such as Trummy Young managed to play the support to Armstrong with more verve than Teagarden's talent would allow him.) In 1951 he left, and almost continuously for the last thirteen years of his life led very successful bands of his own, featuring at first sidepersons such as his brother Charlie, his sister Norma, Ed Hall and Jimmy McPartland; from 1955 a contract with Capitol produced classic records with Bobby Hackett (*Coast Concert*), his own studio band (*This Is Teagarden*) and others. In 1957, Teagarden toured Europe with a determined co-leader, Earl Hines, and from 1959 through the early 1960s collaborated in a new and vivacious sextet with trumpeter Don Goldie which toured, broadcast and made a series of wondrous recordings. Teagarden was reunited with brother Charlie and sister Norma (and his mother) at the 1963 Monterey Jazz Festival but a year later he died of bronchial pneumonia brought on by the wear and tear.

The name Jack Teagarden is a two-word definition of jazz trombone. He set a new standard for his instrument in the 1920s and – like Armstrong for the trumpet, and later Parker for alto sax – created a totally new approach. Before him the trombone had provided band harmonies, or raised music-hall laughs: in jazz terms it most often sounded (in Vic Dickenson's words) like "a dying cow in a thunderstorm". After Teagarden, the trombone achieved a status to match the heights being achieved by Armstrong, Bechet and the great masters of the early twentieth century. And more than any other great jazzman he possessed authentic star quality. His lazy Texan singing outcharmed contemporaries from Jimmy Rodgers to Bing Crosby: listening to his early 1930s hits such as "I Ain't Lazy, I'm Just Dreaming", "Aintcha Glad?" and "I Gotta Right To Sing The Blues", right up to later pearls such as "Say It Simple" from 1947 and "Meet Me Where They Play The Blues" from 1954, it is evident that Tin Pan Alley and the star-makers missed gold on their doorstep. [DF]

⊙ **King Of The Blues Trombone** (1928–40; Sony). Once a highly valued vinyl boxed set, this is now a double CD, complete with original cover art and notes by Patrick Scott. still a valuable documentary of Teagarden's early years. There are rare tracks here – Jimmy McHugh's Bostonians (1928), Frank Trumbauer (1934) and more, along with early Teagarden lollipops. Still well worth having.

⊙ **The Indispensable Jack Teagarden** (1928–57; RCA Jazz Tribune). Excellent 2-CD sampler covering a much wider timespan than the above and including some alternate takes, plus extra sides with Paul Whiteman's Three Ts, Ramona And Her Gang, and a delightful vignette by Teagarden's Big Eight, "Say It Simple".

⊙ **That's A Serious Thing** (1929–57; RCA Bluebird). Excellent selection of Teagarden with the likes of Condon's Hot Shots (1929), Roger Wolfe Kahn, Ben Pollack, The Mound City Blue Blowers, Benny Goodman and up through Louis Armstrong's All Stars to superb titles with Bud Freeman ("I Cover The Waterfront").

⊙ **Jack Teagarden And His Orchestra 1930–4/1934–9/1940–1/1941–43/1944–47** (Classics). This has Teagarden's earliest self-led sides – one or two turkeys but getting into gear with Fats Waller's "You Rascal You" and ending with standard-setters like "A Hundred Years From Today". The 1934–39 set starts with two classics, "Junk Man" with harpist Casper Reardon, and "Stars fell on Alabama", but mainly consists of 21 titles from Teagarden's post-Whiteman 1939 big band. 1940–41 is principally the big band again but also has four sides by his Big Eight with Rex Stewart, and 1944–7 reintroduces Teagarden in small group settings including a quartet classic, "Body And Soul", plus titles with Wingy Manone, Max Kaminsky et al.

⊙ **Jack Teagarden Plays And Sings: Stars Fell On Alabama** (1940–57; Giants of Jazz). Excellent budget CD including premier sides with Condon and Armstrong's All Stars, a selection of titles from Teagarden's important *Misery And The Blues* collection (including the enchanting "Meet Me Where They Play The Blues") and titles from his *Jazz Ultimate* set with Bobby Hackett.

⊙ **It's Time For T** (1941; Jass); **Has Anybody Here Seen Jackson?** (1941–4; Jass); **Big T Jump** (1944–5; Jass). On three CDs available separately, the complete Standard Transcription output of Jack Teagarden's big band. Well worth exploring for regular high spots in an underrated period of his career.

⊙ **Complete Capitol Fifties Jack Teagarden Sessions** (1955–8; Mosaic). Indispensable. All the Hackett-Teagarden compilations (including "Jazz Ultimate" and "Coast Concert"), the superb "This Is Teagarden" and rare "Swing Low Sweet Spiritual", "Shades Of Night" with Sid Feller's strings and Big T's Dixieland Band (with trumpeter Dick Oakley). More good music than you could shake a slide at.

⊙ **Jack Teagarden's Sextet Live In Chicago 1960–61** (Jazz Band). Air checks featuring Teagarden's superbly crafted late sextet, including the fantastic trumpet of Don Goldie, whose opening solo on "Riverboat Shuffle" is great improvisation by any standards.

⊙ **Think Well Of Me** (1962; Verve). This is certainly one of Teagarden's greatest; his last but one album, concentrating on the songs of Willard Robison, and set ravishingly amid strings along with Don Goldie's exuberant trumpet. Masterpieces suiting Teagarden's built-in country air include "Round My Old Deserted Farm", "A Cottage For Sale" and "Country Boy Blues".

➤➤ **Bobby Hackett** *(Coast Concert/Jazz Ultimate).*

Norma Teagarden

Piano.

b. Vernon, Texas, 28 April 1911; d. 5 June 1996.

Norma Teagarden's reputation as a pianist unfortunately never emerged from the shadow of her older brother Jack. From her earliest years, learning the ropes with territory bands in the late 1920s, her piano talents were remarkable: a mature echo of solid Dixieland stylists such as Bob Zurke, coupled with a gift for delicate ragtime, learned from her mother. Norma worked all around Texas in the 1930s, led her own band in California from 1942 and, two years later, joined brother Jack's big band until 1946. After commuting between all the best white Dixielanders, from Matty Matlock and Pete Daily to Ben Pollack, she worked for Jack again from 1952–5, then from 1957, after moving back to San Francisco, she played regularly with Turk Murphy, Pete Daily and others. In the 1970s and 1980s Norma Teagarden stayed busy: she was resident at the Washington Bar and Grill from 1975 to the mid-1990s, for example, and in 1986 toured Britain with her own Marin County Band. [DF]

>> Jack Teagarden *(Jack Teagarden Plays And Sings: Stars Fell On Alabama).*

Joe Temperley

Baritone, tenor and soprano saxophones, bass clarinet, flute.

b. Fife, Scotland, 20 Sept 1929.

Temperley worked with London-based dance bands, and also (on tenor) with Harry Parry in 1949, Jack Parnell from 1952–4 and (on baritone) with Tommy Whittle in 1955–6. He then played baritone exclusively while with the Humphrey Lyttelton band from 1958–65. In 1965 he moved to New York, where he was a member of big bands led by Woody Herman, Buddy Rich, Thad Jones-Mel Lewis (also recording with this band under the direction of Charles Mingus), Clark Terry, Duke Pearson and Mercer Ellington. He has done a considerable amount of studio work, including on the soundtrack of the film *The Cotton Club* (1984), performing solos associated with Harry Carney, and has performed and recorded with Buck Clayton, Gerry Mulligan, Freddie Hubbard and Joe Williams. He has been a member of the Lincoln Center Jazz Orchestra since 1990. Beginning with his work for Lyttelton, and increasingly since moving to the USA, Temperley has forged an individual style and has become one of the leading mainstreamers on his demanding instrument. [BP]

⊙ **Concerto For Joe** (1993–4; Hep). A quartet session displaying Ellingtonian leanings precedes the five movements of the title piece, written by Jimmy Deuchar for an eleven-piece band. Temperley plays commandingly throughout, and the album ends with an unaccompanied Scottish folk tune.

Danilo Terenzi

Trombone, composer.

b. Rome, 2 March 1956; d. 4 May 1995.

Terenzi's grandfather was a guitarist, and he himself began on guitar at the age of ten. He studied the trombone at the Santa Cecilia conservatory in Rome from 1969–75, then in 1977 began studying composition there. In 1973 he began his professional career, forming a quartet with Massimo Urbani and playing with Giorgio Gaslini and with Tommaso Vittorini's Living Concert Big Band. Over the years he gigged and recorded with Enrico Rava, Steve Lacy, Paul Rutherford, Kenny Wheeler, Roswell Rudd, Albert Mangelsdorff, Lester Bowie, Archie Shepp, Mel Lewis and others. In 1980 he played with Mike Westbrook's brass band, and in 1984 joined Westbrook's orchestra for performances of *On Duke's Birthday*. All this he balanced with a tenure teaching trombone in the Popular Music School of Testaccio in Rome, where he also conducted a big-band course until his early death from cancer. [IC]

>> Chris Biscoe *(Chris Biscoe Sextet); Mike Westbrook (On Duke's Birthday).*

Jacky Terrasson

Piano, composer.

b. Berlin, 27 Nov 1966.

Born to a French father and an African-American mother, Jacky Terrasson grew up in Paris, and studied classical piano from age five, but became interested in jazz in his early teens through the influence of his mother's record collection. After studying with expatriate American Jeff Gardener, Terrasson enrolled, at 15, at Paris's Lycée Lamartine, a high school dedicated to the performing arts, where he met Francis Paudras's son Stéphane and was thus introduced into the mainstream of the Parisian jazz scene. Paudras *père* encouraged him to study at Berklee, in Boston, and after a brief stint gigging in Chicago, and a year in the French army, Terrasson learned his jazz trade in Paris clubs (backing singer Dee Dee Bridgewater) and at European festivals, playing with Ray Brown's Two Bass Hits. He moved to New York in 1990, was spotted by Arthur Taylor, and gigged and recorded with Cindy Blackman and Betty Carter, winning the prestigious Thelonious Monk Jazz Competition in 1993. Widely regarded as one of the most promising young pianists in the music, he signed with Blue Note in 1994. His debut album for the company (see below) delivered on the promise of his previous album, *What's New*, recorded for the French label Jazz aux Ramparts in 1993. *Reach* (1995; Blue Note) continued the process, confirming the cohesiveness and mutual responsiveness of his rhythm-section, bassist Ugonna Okegwo and drummer Leon Parker, but it was *Alive* (1997; Blue Note) that best represented the trio's musical rapport and vigour. A collaboration with singer Cassandra Wilson the same year, *Rendezvous* (Blue Note), brought out the best in neither participant, but did Terrasson's visibility no harm among the non-jazz fans to whom Wilson's music appeals. Terrasson remains one of the music's brightest young stars, and his live performances can be exhilarating. [CP]

⊙ **Jacky Terrasson** (1995; Blue Note). Astonishingly mature major-label debut as leader of trio featuring bassist Ugonna Okegwo and drummer Leon Parker, crammed with vibrantly original treatments of standards and pungent original blues, combining the eccentricity of Monk or Herbie Nichols with the airy spaciousness of Ahmad Jamal.

>> Cindy Blackman *(Telepathy);* **Art Taylor** *(Wailin' At The Vanguard).*

Clark Terry

Trumpet, flugelhorn, vocals.

b. St Louis, Missouri, 14 Dec 1920.

Terry gained early experience locally with various St Louis bands and then, during World War II, with a famous navy band which included players such as Willie Smith. He worked briefly with Lionel Hampton, and then had a succession of name-band jobs, playing with Charlie Barnet in 1947–8, Count Basie from 1948–51, Duke Ellington from 1951–9 and Quincy Jones in 1959–60. He became one of the first black musicians to be employed in a TV house band (led by former Barnet colleague Doc Severinsen) and during this period (1960–72) he was occasionally featured in his own vocal speciality, "Mumbles". At the same time he was also extremely busy in recording session work, and co-led a part-time quintet with Bob Brookmeyer. Since the late 1960s he has led an occasional big band and, gradually undertaking less studio work, has participated in numerous jazz education clinics.

The creator of an irrepressibly bouncy style, Terry incorporates aspects of predecessors such as Charlie Shavers, Rex Stewart and Dizzy Gillespie, but his rhythmic verve is something entirely his own. His mellifluous tone is said to reflect an earlier school of St Louis players typified by trumpeter Joe Thomas, and is especially noticeable on flugelhorn, an instrument which Terry virtually introduced as a jazz alternative to the trumpet. The very vocal nature of his sound (plus the use of the flugelhorn) was a direct influence on fellow St Louis native Miles Davis, and through him on a whole generation of trumpeters. One of the special effects identified with Terry (heard for instance in "Jim" from the Oscar Peterson album listed below), consists of holding flugelhorn in one hand, muted trumpet in the other and alternating "fours" with himself. His versatility with mutes and, when not muted, with articulation and inflexion turns into affectionate satire when he sings the blues, often employing a personal brand of scat syllables. The good-humoured personality this demonstrates, which also comes across in his bandleading, makes Terry an important propagandist on behalf of jazz, as well as a significant player in his own right. [BP]

⊙ **Serenade To A Bus Seat** (1957; Riverside/OJC). Illustrating the penchant for bebop moulded into Terry's overall style, this hot session with Johnny Griffin opens with a bustling "Donna Lee". The rhythm-section of Wynton Kelly, Paul Chambers and Philly Joe Jones keeps everyone on their toes.

Oscar Peterson

⊙ **Plus One** (1964; Verve). A more laid-back date which has the air of "fun with friends", in this case Oscar's trio including Ray Brown and Ed Thigpen. Terry's contributions to each track include "Jim" described above, and the first recorded outing of "Mumbles", in which the trumpeter merely sings deliberately unintelligible lyrics with the same blues-filled feeling as his playing.

Clark Terry-Bob Brookmeyer

⊙ **Gingerbread** (c. 1966; Mainstream). Any of the three albums by this quintet should be snapped up if found. Terry sings more straight on "I Want A Little Girl", but the meat is his interplay with Brookmeyer, for instance on uptempo tunes such as "Haig And Haig" (aka "Rhythm-A-Ning").

➤➤ **Gary McFarland** *(How To Succeed In Business).*

Frank Teschemacher

Clarinet, alto, violin, arranger.

b. Kansas City, Missouri, 13 March 1906; d. 1 March 1932.

Part of the original Austin High School Gang (in which he played alto, banjo and violin), Frank Teschemacher took up the clarinet in 1925, and by 1928 had moved to New York with his Chicago friends. There he quickly made an impression. "There used to be talk in those days," recalls Max Kaminsky, "that Tesch could play Benny Goodman off the stand." The young clarinettist was certainly good enough to work with Ben Pollack and Sam Lanin in New York and – studious and solemn as he was – probably suited both leaders far better than some other of his rebellious Chicago colleagues. By the end of 1928, however, he was back in Chicago, where he freelanced and played host to musicians such as Kaminsky whenever they found themselves bedless – they usually found him practising hard, talking earnestly about music or tinkering with violin and cornet as a rest from the clarinet. It seems strange that his few recordings are not more remarkable, but, says Kaminsky, "Tesch had a phobia about making records: he'd freeze up in the studio and if he'd recorded more he would have overcome it!" "He never made any records that did him justice", agrees Joe Marsala. Teschemacher died in a crash when he was thrown out of Wild Bill Davison's Packard: "Where," lamented Davison, "will we ever get another clarinet player like Tesch?" [DF]

➤➤ **Eddie Condon** *(Eddie Condon 1927–38).*

Henri Texier

Bass.

b. Paris, 27 Jan 1945.

A self-taught player, Henri Texier acknowledges the influence of the great US bassist Wilbur Ware, but the Frenchman is more interested in the freer end of things than the Chicagoan ever was. Texier came to prominence playing in Paris clubs with stellar US ex-patriates such as Bud Powell, Johnny Griffin and Bill Coleman, but quickly became involved in a wide variety of musical projects, collaborating with Don Cherry in the mid-1960s and joining Phil Woods's European Rhythm Machine in 1968, where he played alongside pianist George Gruntz and drummer Daniel Humair. The latter became a frequent associate of Texier's, both as a leader in big- and small-group contexts and by forming a superb rhythm team with him for such leaders as saxophonist Larry Schneider. In the 1970s, Texier also played with pianist Joachim Kuhn, violinist Didier Lockwood and drummer Aldo Romano, among numerous other European jazz luminaries. In 1982, he formed a quartet with reeds player Louis Sclavis, guitarist Philippe Deschepper and drummer Jacques Mahieux to produce a beguiling mix of popular and ethnic music and jazz, but he also continued to play with visiting Americans, forming the Transatlantik Quartet with Joe Lovano, Steve Swallow and Romano in the mid-1980s.

Film scores, duo improvisations with Michel Portal accompanying Viola Farber's choreography for the Angers ballet, tours with Humair and saxophonist François Jenneau in India, Lebanon, Jordan and Syria were followed by the formation, in 1992, of the Azur Quartet with pianist Bojan Zulfikarparsic, trombonist Glenn Ferris and drummer Tony Rabeson, a unit that made *An Indian's Week* (Label Bleu) the following year, with contributions from Sclavis and Portal. Sclavis, Romano and Texier toured Central and Western Africa in 1990 and 1993 respectively at the instigation of photographer Guy Le Querrec, making a Label Bleu album, *Carnets de Routes*, as a result of the experiences in 1995. Two years later, Texier formed something of a dream band – valve-trombonist Bob Brookmeyer, Lee Konitz on alto, bassist Steve Swallow and drummer Paul Motian – to make the supremely accomplished *Respect*, again on Label Bleu, but Texier's most representative album of the 1990s is *Mad Nomads* (see below) by the Sonjal septet plus Rabeson. [CP]

⊙ **La Companera** (1983; Label Bleu). Texier's own mid-1980s quartet is joined by trumpeter Michel Marre for two tracks, but Sclavis's clarinet and tenor saxophone provide most of the solo interest.

⊙ **Izlaz** (1988; Label Bleu). The Transatlantik Quartet, featuring Steve Swallow on electric bass, frees Texier for solo bass duties, and the band as a whole produce rousing but considered and tasteful jazz.

⊙ **Mad Nomads** (1995; Label Bleu). Interspersing short percussion meditations on world problems with lengthier pieces involving various combinations of reeds players Sebastien Texier, Julien Lourau and François Corneloup, guitarist Noël Akchoté, pianist Bojan Zulfikarparsic and drummer Jacques Mahieux or Tony Rabeson, this is an album touching on all Texier's stylistic bases – free and straightahead jazz, elegant septet pieces, and celebrations of past collaborations with US masters etc.

Sister Rosetta Tharpe

Vocals, guitar.

b. Cotton Plant, Arkansas, 20 March 1915; d. 9 Oct 1973.

Tharpe (née Rosetta Nubin) began singing gospel music in church, and early on became a featured soloist. She was one of the star performers in the Cotton Club revues of 1938–9, backed by the Cab Calloway band. She toured with Calloway and then with Lucky Millinder, recording several singles of gospel and blues material with the latter in 1941–2. After working in nightclubs from 1942–4, she decided to aim her records at the growing gospel market, including duets with Marie Knight and with her mother, Katie Bell Nubin (who later made an album with Dizzy Gillespie's quintet). Rosetta continued to alternate between a religious context and working for jazz audiences, especially on the tours she made of Europe from 1957 onwards.

Tharpe is the only fully fledged gospel singer to cross over into the jazz field. At the time she was starting her rise to stardom it would have been unacceptable to play a guitar in church; and, even in the blues category, only one woman (Memphis Minnie) had attained any prominence as an instrumentalist. Not only did Rosetta play gospel music with jazz groups and in a show-business context, but she effected a new stylistic fusion: many folk-blues guitarists had also been evangelists but she was the first to incorporate the city-blues playing of the 1930s (specifically, it has been suggested, the work of Teddy Bunn) into gospel music. Like most important innovators, she was also a totally convincing and compelling performer. [BP]

➤➤ **Lucky Millinder** *(Lucky Millinder 1941–42).*

Eje Thelin

Trombone, composer.

b. Jönköping, Sweden, 9 Sept 1938; d. 18 May 1990.

Self-taught, Thelin started playing in his teens as a member of a popular Swedish Dixieland group, but soon graduated to more contemporary jazz. His first important gig was with the American drummer Joe Harris from 1958–9. He led his own group from 1961–5, and made extensive tours with it all over Europe, recording the cute album *1966* in its eponymous year with Barney Wilen. He played with George Russell at the Montmartre, Copenhagen, in 1964, and from 1967–72 taught at the Graz Jazz Institute in Austria, a little disillusioned with the Swedish scene. In 1973–4 he worked with John Surman in Europe, then – based again in Sweden – was involved in teaching, playing with his own quartet and various other groups, and experimentation with electronic music. He played on Kenny Wheeler's *Around 6* album on ECM in 1980 and performed at most European festivals, playing with Barney Wilen, Roy Brooks, Palle Danielsson, and Graham Collier's international big band at the 1985 Camden festival. [IC]

⊙ **Raggruppamento** (1989; Phono Suecia). Thelin was terminally ill with cancer and so could not play on the recording of this long suite, his last composition. However, he did conduct it and the Swedish Radio Jazz Group gave him their all.

Art Themen

Tenor, soprano and sopranino saxophones.

b. Manchester, UK, 26 Nov 1939.

Themen taught himself music, starting to play jazz with the Cambridge University Jazz Group which won the UK inter-university jazz contests from 1959–62. On moving to London, he became involved with the early British blues movement, playing with Alexis Korner and Jack Bruce. He also had a brief period with the pop session world, working with Rod Stewart, Joe Cocker, Charlie Watts and Long John Baldry. In 1965 he was chosen to represent the UK in the international Peter Stuyvesant Jazz Orchestra at the Zurich festival. In the late 1960s and early 1970s he played with the Michael Garrick and Graham Collier bands before he began a long and continuing association with Stan Tracey in 1974, playing in all his various groups. He has also toured with Al Haig, Red Rodney and Sal Nistico, and played with Nat Adderley, George Coleman and Billy Mitchell. With Tracey and other groups he has toured India, the Middle East, Greece, South America, Switzerland, Indonesia and the Philippines, and played at most UK festivals. Themen, though a consultant orthopaedic surgeon, is still active on the London scene, and is an immensely gifted saxophonist with a quirky, almost wilful originality. [IC]

➤➤ **Stan Tracey** *(Portraits Plus).*

Toots Thielemans

Harmonica, guitar, whistles, composer.
b. Brussels, 29 April 1922.

Toots (Jean Baptiste) Thielemans started music aged three, playing a homemade accordion, soon graduating to a proper one. He started playing the harmonica at seventeen while studying maths at college. Hearing Django Reinhardt inspired him to take up the guitar. After World War II he gigged at American GI clubs and became interested in bebop. He was befriended by Charlie Parker, with whom he shared the bill at the Paris international jazz festival in May 1949. He had visited the USA in 1947, sitting in with groups on 52nd Street, and in 1950 he toured Europe with the Benny Goodman sextet. He emigrated to the USA in late 1951, and played with Dinah Washington. He joined the George Shearing quintet in early 1953, staying until the autumn of 1959. He then formed his own group, but worked mostly as a freelance and studio musician.

In the early 1960s he began making regular trips to Europe, recorded his composition "Bluesette", which featured him on guitar and whistling, in 1962, and this became a worldwide hit: there have been over 100 recorded versions of it. With this success, Thielemans was "rediscovered" in the USA, and was in constant demand for studio work on guitar and harmonica and whistling. From the mid-1960s he was closely associated with Quincy Jones, playing on the soundtracks of several films including *Midnight Cowboy* (1969) and *The Getaway* (1972), and on Jones's albums.

Since the 1970s he has divided his time between lucrative studio work and jazz gigs at clubs and festivals in the USA and Europe, with his jazz recording career reviving nicely in the late 1980s and into the 90s. His music is known to millions throughout the world via his harmonica playing on – and composition of – the theme music for the children's TV programme *Sesame Street*.

Thielemans is rooted in bebop, but his main inspiration comes from Coltrane, and his work contains many resonances from the whole jazz tradition. He is a compelling performer who projects geniality and passion, and he has brilliantly developed the tonal qualities and expressiveness of the harmonica. Clifford Brown once told him: "Toots, the way you play harmonica, they shouldn't call it a miscellaneous instrument!" [IC]

⊙ **Man Bites Harmonica** (1957; OJC). A great hard-bop workout, with Toots burgeoning in the company of jazz luminaries Pepper Adams, Kenny Drew, Wilbur Ware and Art Taylor.

⊙ **Do Not Leave Me** (1986; Stash). This album was recorded in his home town, Brussels, and seems especially charged with emotion. The group is a quartet with pianist Fred Hersch, Marc Johnson and the exceptional drummer Joey Baron, and they play a mix of standards and originals, with "Stardust" as a tribute to Benny Goodman, Toots's old leader, who had died a few days previously.

⊙ **Only Trust Your Heart** (1988; Concord). Thielemans playing harmonica all the way with virtually the same quartet as on the previous set, in a programme of originals and pieces by Wayne Shorter, Monk and Ellington. Twelve dynamic tracks, most of them first takes.

⊙ **Toots Thielemans and Kenny Werner** (2001; Verve). 79 years old and as nimble and imaginative as ever, Toots responds with brio to the company of pianist/keyboardist Werner on this delightful live set (with no audience noise) of choice standards and jazz tunes which includes a Bill Evans medley and Herbie Hancock's "Dolphin Dance".

➤➤ **Quincy Jones** *(Walking In Space).*

Ed Thigpen

Drums.
b. Chicago, 28 Dec 1930.

Thigpen is the son of another noted drummer, Ben Thigpen, who for sixteen years was a key member of the Andy Kirk band. Ed was brought up in Los Angeles, and toured with Candy Johnson's band and the Cootie Williams group in 1951–2, then, after army service, with Dinah Washington in 1954. In 1955 he worked briefly with Lennie Tristano, the Johnny Hodges band and the Bud Powell trio. He spent long periods with the Billy Taylor trio (from 1956–9) and the Oscar Peterson trio (from 1959–65). In the late 1960s he freelanced in Los Angeles, and toured with Ella Fitzgerald in 1966–7 and from 1968–72. He settled in Copenhagen in 1972, performing with local musicians and visiting Americans and teaching drums. Although extremely versatile, Thigpen is particularly sensitive in a small-group setting, and his work with Taylor and Peterson showed him to be the epitome of a tidy, tasty trio drummer. [BP]

⊙ **Mr Taste** (1991; Justin Time). A trio session with guitarist Tony Purrone (ex-Heath Brothers) and Danish bassist Mads Vinding. Despite their efforts and the fact that Thigpen is officially accompanying most of the time, all interest focuses on the drummer's subtle swinging contributions.

➤➤ **Oscar Peterson** *(The Jazz Soul Of Oscar Peterson).*

Jesper Thilo

Tenor and alto saxophones, clarinet.
b. Copenhagen, 28 Nov 1941.

Thilo studied clarinet as a teenager, and played (sometimes doubling on trombone) in an amateur band. He joined trumpeter Arnvid Meyer's band on tenor from 1960–64, and played in a two-tenor group with Bent Jaedig. From 1966–90 he was a member of the Danish Radio Big Band, adding alto saxophone, and he has led his own small groups, often backing visiting American musicians. During the 1980s he also appeared with Ernie Wilkins's Almost Big Band. Thilo plays superbly confident and idiomatic tenor in a style which covers the ground between Ben Webster, one of his personal heroes, and Dexter Gordon. [BP]

⊙ **Quintet Featuring Hank Jones** (1991; Storyville). Thilo's home group, including local resident Doug Raney on guitar, turn in a beautifully relaxed set including "Shiny Stockings" and "Chelsea Bridge". Hank Jones plays perfectly within his accompanist role, but his solos spark considerable interest.

"Big Charlie" Thomas

Cornet, trumpet.
(Place and date of birth unknown).

Thomas's existence was established by musician and audio-restorer John R.T. Davies, who quizzed blues singer Eva Taylor over the identity of a trumpeter identified only as "Big Charlie" during 1926 recordings by Margaret Johnson. Further evidence from Taylor, plus aural research, aided Davies to isolate 29 tracks featuring Thomas – who previously had been mis-identified by discographers as Louis Armstrong, King Oliver, Jabbo Smith and others. Virtually nothing is known of Thomas's history, although – based on his trumpet-playing technique – Davies was able to surmise that he may also have played reed instruments. Thomas's playing is hugely enjoyable and impressive, and Davies has done jazz history a further service by re-creating a profile for a classic jazzman of importance who would otherwise have been conclusively lost to history. [DF]

⊙ **Big Charlie Thomas** (1925–7; Timeless). Twenty-five of Thomas's known sides, including tracks with Thomas Morris's Seven Hot Babies, Clarence Williams's Blue Five and Rosa Henderson.

Gary Thomas

Tenor saxophone, flute.
b. Baltimore, Maryland, 10 June 1961.

Variously compared with Wayne Shorter, Sonny Rollins and Joe Henderson, Gary Thomas has a grainy, sinewy, dark-toned saxophone sound most readily reminiscent of that of George Coleman, but his uncompromising musical stance – he famously refused to play fusion licks when part of Miles Davis's band in the late 1980s, and one of his avowed musical aims is to "go against the grain of what most people are expecting" – marks him out as very much his own man. Furthermore, his open-eared approach extends to all forms of contemporary music – his albums incorporate rap, standards, dance grooves and synthesized electronics. He first came to prominence in the aforementioned Davis band, but in the late 1980s Thomas was also in great demand as a frontline player for drummers Cecil Brooks III and Tony Reedus, in addition to becoming a vital member of Jack DeJohnette's revamped Special Edition, where he played alongside fellow saxophonist Greg Osby. This partnership can also be heard not only on Osby's own recordings, but also providing a frontline for pianist Michele Rosewoman. In addition to contributing tough, muscular tenor and contrastingly gentle flute to the music of guitarist Christy Doran, playing the Coltrane part in Peter Herborn's *Traces Of Trane*, and forming a fruitful musical relationship with trumpeter Wallace Roney (1987–90), Thomas has made a series of albums as leader for Enja and JMT, but in the mid-1990s signed for the then newly founded Winter & Winter label, making *Found On Sordid Streets* with organist George Colligan, guitarist Paul Bollenback, plus rappers Pork Chop and No Name, in 1996. Two years later, *Pariah's Pariah* followed (see below). [CP]

⊙ **Seventh Quadrant** (1987; Enja). Backed by a superb rhythm-section (bassist Anthony Cox and drummer Jeff Watts) and featuring pianist Renée Rosnes and regular guitarist Paul Bollenback, this is a handy introduction to Thomas.

⊙ **Pariah's Pariah** (1998; Winter & Winter). Frontline duties are shared with Greg Osby, producing some wonderfully garrulous duo improvisations. The whole is propelled by Michael Formanek's lithe bass and the funky drums of John Arnold, and features the leader's gutsy flute as well as his dry, restless tenor, adding up to Thomas's best album for some time.

Joe Thomas

Tenor saxophone, clarinet, vocals.
b. Uniontown, Pennsylvania, 19 June 1909; d. 3 Aug 1986.

Joseph Vankert Thomas began his professional career on alto saxophone with Horace Henderson after time working as a waiter, but changed to tenor after joining Stuff Smith in Buffalo, where Jimmie Lunceford heard and hired him. Working for his new employer improved Thomas's sense of discipline, as did his section leader Willie Smith, who did a lot to improve the young recruit's musicianship. "Joe had a lot of personality," says pianist/arranger Ed Wilcox, "and a lot of tricks on the horn. He had a way of slopping over notes, too, instead of making all the notes in a run. Willie wouldn't settle for that kind of stuff and sitting beside a man like that, Joe naturally got better!" "His solos are always built up in a way which permits the maximum swing," said Hugues Panassié, "but are none the less melodious for that.

He really makes his instrument sing: his playing is full of feeling and his tone very moving." Thomas stayed with Lunceford as featured tenor soloist long after many of his co-stars had left over money disagreements, and after Lunceford's death in 1947 he took over the band with Wilcox for a further year. By the 1950s he had left music and gone back to Kansas City to run a business, but returned to play the 1968 Newport festival with Count Basie, stole the show, and thereafter took up playing and recording again. [DF]

➤➤ **Jimmie Lunceford** *(For Dancers Only)*.

Joe Thomas

Trumpet.

b. Webster Grove, Missouri, 24 July 1909; d. 6 Aug 1984.

Joseph Lewis Thomas played in territory bands in the late 1920s and early 1930s before moving to New York to work at Small's with Ferman Tapp's band. For the rest of the decade he worked with Fletcher Henderson, Benny Carter and others, and throughout the 1940s he was mainly with small bands, establishing a fine reputation with Teddy Wilson (1942–3), Barney Bigard (1943–5), Cozy Cole (1948) and Bud Freeman (1949). In the 1950s he often led his own small groups, as well as working with Eddie Condon in 1964 and Claude Hopkins two years after. "One of the most underrated trumpeters of the swing era," says Leonard Feather, "[with] a fine tone and relaxed style". [DF]

Leone Thomas

Vocals, lyricist, percussion.

b. East St Louis, Illinois, 4 Oct 1937; d. 8 May 1999.

Thomas studied music at Lincoln High School, then in 1959 moved to New York, working in a show at the Apollo Theater with Dakota Staton, Ahmad Jamal, Art Blakey's Jazz Messengers, Randy Weston and Mary Lou Williams. In 1961 he replaced Joe Williams in the Count Basie orchestra, staying, except for a break for army service, until 1965; with Basie he sang at the inaugural balls of Presidents Kennedy and Johnson. From 1969–72 he played with Pharoah Sanders, and wrote lyrics to several of Sanders's tunes; Thomas's cult status of today is largely due to the series of albums he recorded around this time for the Flying Dutchman label. *Spirits Known and Unknown* (1969), *The Leon Thomas Album* (1970) and *Gold Sunrise on Magic Mountain* (1971) showcased his bluesy holler and unique extended vocal techniqes over a soul-jazz backing. (Though he did cut the self-explanatory *In Berlin with Oliver Nelson* (1971), proving his straight jazz credentials.) Bob Thiele produced all of them, and Sanders' presence is almost always palpable.

Thomas added the ultimate "e" to "Leon" in 1976. He continued singing, recording and touring throughout the 1980s (in 1985 he was with the Joe Henderson quintet) and 1990s – his 1995 *U-Turn* album of blues and spirituals, reputedly a masterpiece, remains unreleased. Thomas was a singer in the blues/soul/gospel tradition, but brought his own style and flavour to it. He had perfected a form of yodelling or voice "shaking" which he used to great effect. He supplemented his vocal techniques with off-the-wall practices, such as creating infectious rhythms by blowing into bottles, and was also a tremendously accomplished scat singer. [IC]

René Thomas

Guitar.

b. Liège, Belgium, 25 Feb 1927; d. Santander, Spain, 3 Jan 1975.

Thomas was an active musician in Paris from the early 1950s, playing with visiting American musicians. He then followed the example of his compatriot Bobby Jaspar and emigrated to New York, working with the Toshiko Akiyoshi and Sonny Rollins groups in 1958. He settled in Montreal for two years, recording under his own name in New York in 1960. Busy in Europe again from 1961, he appeared with Jaspar in London in 1962, and performed with Kenny Clarke and others. He was a member of the Stan Getz quartet which included organist Eddie Louiss from 1969–71, and he later recorded a trio album with Louiss and Clarke. Thomas's career, which was terminated by a heart attack, was sadly under-documented on record, but he was highly praised by both Rollins and Getz, and his fresh, unhurried lines amply justify their enthusiasm. [BP]

Stan Getz

⊙ **Dynasty!** (1971; Verve). Partly recorded at the same venue as the Jaspar album mentioned below, this has Getz playing new material mostly contributed by his collaborators, including organist Eddie Louiss. Thomas, however, while appearing to take a back seat, plays with quiet brilliance.

➤➤ **Bobby Jaspar** *(The Bobby Jaspar Quartet At Ronnie Scott's 1962)*.

Barbara Thompson

Alto, tenor and soprano saxophones, flutes.

b. Oxford, UK, 27 July 1944.

It was seeing Johnny Hodges, playing with Duke Ellington, when she was seventeen that had inspired Barbara Thompson to take up the saxophone. She said, "I thought it was the most expressive sound I'd ever heard – like a voice, so I got an alto and practised like mad, trying to play like him." She joined the New Jazz Orchestra in 1965, where she met her future husband, drummer Jon Hiseman. From 1969 onwards she led various groups of her own, but also worked for composers and bandleaders John

Dankworth, Mike Gibbs, Wolfgang Dauner, Don Rendell and Neil Ardley, among others. In 1975 she joined the United Jazz and Rock Ensemble and in 1977 started her own fusion group, Paraphernalia (which Jon Hiseman joined in 1979); she has played with both ever since. In the 1980s, she began leading her own 19-piece big band called Moving Parts, for which she composed and arranged all the music.

She is a prolific composer and has written three long works for a 20-piece jazz orchestra, which have been recorded by the BBC. She also composed *Greek Songs*, a suite for saxophone, percussion, strings and grand piano, which was premiered in Freiburg in 1992. In April 1994, she performed several Kurt Weill songs with the Medici string quartet at London's Purcell Room. She arranged one of the songs, whilst each of the others was arranged by a different composer from a pool which included John Dankworth, Mike Westbrook, Richard Rodney Bennett and Barry Guy. They were subsequently recorded for an album entitled *Barbara Song*. In 1995 she had a commission from BBC Radio 3 to compose a work inspired by Philip Larkin's poetry, featuring The BBC Singers, the Medici quartet, herself on saxophones and flute, and her group Paraphernalia.

In 1999, Thompson's group Paraphernalia toured the UK promoting her new album, *Shifting Sands*. Illness has led Barbara to retire from playing (for now) to concentrate on composition, but not before she completed triumphant farewell tours for Paraphernalia in 2000/2001 and the United Jazz And Rock Ensemble in 2002. [IC]

⊙ **Songs From The Centre Of The Earth** (1990; Black Sun). This is a *tour de force* – 14 pieces of unaccompanied saxophone recorded in the haunting resonance of the abbey of Thoronet in Provence. Thompson worked from midnight to dawn, and her intense self-communing through folk material creates an other-worldly, magnetic atmosphere.

Paraphernalia

⊙ **A Cry From The Heart** (1987; VeraBra). Paraphernalia had just been revamped and keyboardist Pete Lemer had returned to the band after years of absence, so this live recording at London's Riverside studios was a tremendously dynamic session. Paul Dunne was on guitar, so the rock elements were magnified, with the rhythm-section of Phil Mulford and Hiseman snarling and snapping, and Thompson herself sounding inspired all the way.

⊙ **Everlasting Flame** (1993; VeraBra). This is a fascinating synthesis of rock, folk, ethnic, instrumental and vocal music. Paraphernalia are augmented by Thompson's daughter, vocalist Anna Gracey Hiseman, plus the London Community Gospel Singers.

⊙ **Shifting Sands** (1998; Intuition). Barbara Thompson never ceases to grow musically. The title track, which opens the album, evolves so organically and with such subtle dynamics, that it's hypnotic progress is spellbinding. Paraphernalia is a magnificent musical unit now – the long association of Barbara and husband Jon Hiseman with keyboardist Peter Lemer has created a wonderful rapport. The new violinist, Billy Thompson (no relation), is a real find, and bassist Paul Westwood is excellent. Every piece on the album has its own rhythmic feel, its own way of breathing. Lovely textures, sonorities and solos abound.

Danny Thompson

Double bass.

b. Teignmouth, Devon, UK, 4 April 1939.

From an early age Thompson was steeped in black American blues and traditional jazz. Totally self-taught, he worked at music with such dedication that by the mid-1960s he was a key figure on the London scene. He spent three years with Alexis Korner's Blues Incorporated, 1964-6, and during the same period was a member of the Tubby Hayes quartet and several other groups such as those of Ronnie Scott, Stan Tracey, and from America, Josh White, Joe Williams, Art Farmer, Freddie Hubbard, Sonny Terry-Brownie McGhee and others. In 1966 Thompson also led a superb trio with guitarist John McLaughlin and virtuoso saxophonist Tony Roberts – John Dankworth had described it as "the first real emergence in small-group jazz since the Gerry Mulligan Quartet" – but no one was interested in recording it. He was also a founder member of the innovative jazz/folk/fusion band Pentangle which had great international success from 1968–72 and recorded seven albums. During the 1960s, he also emerged as an activist, forming the Fellowship of British Jazz Musicians, which was an attempt to improve their work opportunities.

After Pentangle disbanded, Thompson had a long and productive musical partnership with John Martyn, which he has maintained, albeit more sporadically, ever since. He played on sessions for all sorts of rock and folk musicians over the years, including Julie Felix, Ralph McTell, Donovan and Mary Hopkin, although illness kept him out of music for some years. In the early 80s, however, he started his own group, a trio with saxophonist Tony Roberts and guitarist Bernie Holland, and in 1988 made his first album as leader, *Whatever*, a brilliantly creative fusion of jazz and folk which received tremendous acclaim. Thompson said, "I had an idea to incorporate elements of jazz and folk music to make a melodic instrumental album with a distinct English flavour."

From then on, Thompson continued to lead his own groups and do more session work. However, the activist in him would not be denied and in 1992 he started The Jazz Label to record jazz musicians who were ignored by the major record companies. There were no plans to record his own music on it; the whole venture was very much on a philanthropic, non-profit-making basis, releasing albums such as guitarist John Etheridge's *Ash* and *Frevo* by the eponymous fusion group. Meanwhile, Thompson had converted to Islam in 1990, survived major heart surgery in the late 1990s, and continues to develop as a composer and player; among a dizzying array of session work, he has recorded and toured with singer/songwriter Richard Thompson (no relation) and has been heard latterly with, among many others, The Blind Boys Of Alabama. [IC]

Whatever (1988; Hannibal). An extraordinarily beautiful and unclassifiable masterpiece, with Bernie Holland on guitar, Tony Roberts on tenor and soprano saxophones, alto and bass flute and Northumbrian pipes, and compositions jointly written by all three musicians.

Whatever's Best (1998; Resurgent). A truncated compilation of Thompson's second (*Whatever's Next*; 1989) and third (*Elemental*; 1990) albums. John Etheridge replaces Holland in the group, which now also has Paul Dunmal on reeds, and is augmented by some leading jazz musicians including Stan Tracey, Alan Skidmore and Henry Lowther and others. The bigger ensemble is a bold attempt to find fuller, deeper fusions of jazz and folk elements, and the result is uneven, but full of good things. The tribute to one of his main inspirations, "Musing Mingus", is one of Thompson's best compositions.

Live 1967 (1999; What Disc). Long lost (in Danny's attic) and fascinating archive of Thompson's mid-1960s trio featuring Tony Roberts on flute, tenor and bass clarinet and John McLaughlin on pre-Miles guitar. Surprisingly good recording quality but unsurprisingly well played, the tunes examined include Brubeck's "In Your Own Sweet Way" and Coltrane's "Naima".

Eddie Thompson

Piano.

b. London, 31 May 1925; d. 6 Nov 1986.

An alumnus of the same school for the blind as George Shearing, Thompson soon impressed the British scene in the late 1940s, recording with Victor Feldman and appearing with British jazz musicians at the Paris Jazz Fair in 1949. In the 1950s he worked with Tony Crombie, Ronnie Scott, Vic Ash, Freddy Randall, Tommy Whittle and his own trio, including a spell as house pianist at Ronnie Scott's in 1959–60. He emigrated to the USA in 1962, performing mostly solo, and working steadily until his permanent return to the UK in 1972. Thereafter he took solo and trio engagements, including work backing many American musicians at the Pizza Express, and worked in a duo with Roger Kellaway which led to further appearances together in New York in 1985. An extremely entertaining, if eclectic, improviser, Thompson at one time seemed too gifted for his own good; the earlier effects of undisciplined solo performances were hinted at by the outspoken Ruby Braff, who said in 1976, "The first time I heard him in New York, I didn't think he could play ... He's improved like a thousand per cent." [BP]

Memories Of You (1983; Hep). An excellent example of Thompson's many trio albums, this has, as usual, Len Skeat on bass and a very straightahead repertoire, but what Eddie does with items like "Rosetta" and the title track is exciting stuff. His sessions with Roy Williams or Spike Robinson also bear investigation.

Gail Thompson

Saxophone, flute.

b. London, UK, 15 June 1958.

From a musical family (her mother is a piano teacher and her aunt is an opera singer), Thompson studied the clarinet for six years with Colin Courtney, and by the age of sixteen was playing baritone sax with the National Youth Jazz Orchestra. After leaving school she formed two highly successful bands, The Gail Thompson Approach and Gail Force. A co-founder, with Courtney Pine and Cleveland Watkiss, of the seminal Jazz Warriors, she was also invited to join Art Blakey's Jazz Messengers (making her the only female member it ever had), and also played in Charlie Watts' orchestra. In 1986, while playing with Blakey, Thompson's face muscles failed, making it impossible for to continue playing the sax. She was eventually diagnosed with multiple sclerosis. Her response was to redirect her talents in different directions. As well as composing, she also began working in music education, forming the influential Women in Music, the Brixton community music centre Musicworks, the Sax Council Tuition School, the Richmond Jazz Festival and the Jazz in Women Festival.

In 1988 Thompson made an extended visit to Africa to study African music and culture, travelling overland to thirteen African countries, from Morocco to Kenya. The result was the Jazz Africa Big Band, a dynamic ensemble made up of a combination of British musicians and South African ex-patriates living in London. Jazz Africa have recorded two albums both for the German Enja label: *Gail Thompson's Jazz Africa* (1996) and the Australia-influenced *Jadu* (2001). More recently she founded Noir Femmes, a fifteen-piece, black female touring band (inspired by two similar US bands of the 1940s) for which she also composes. [IC]

Gail Thompson's Jazz Africa (1996; Enja). An exciting album consisting of six Thompson-composed pieces, arranged by Mike Hornet. The poetic opening track, "Long Time In Togo", begins with a lovely flute solo by Thompson, and the rhythm-section creates a wonderfully satisfying groove. There are some outstanding musicians on display here, not least the quicksilver trumpeter Harry Beckett and the talented bassist Mario Castronari.

Lucky Thompson

Tenor and soprano saxophones.

b. Detroit, Michigan, 16 June 1924.

Lucky (Eli) Thompson first toured with the Trenier Twins in the early 1940s. He worked briefly in New York with several bands including Lionel Hampton's and Don Redman's in 1943, and Billy Eckstine's and Lucky Millinder's in 1944. In 1944–5 he joined Count Basie, and then settled on the West Coast, recording separately with Gillespie and Parker in 1946. He also played with Boyd Raeburn, the cooperative band Stars of Swing and many others. Returning first to Detroit in 1947 and then to New York in 1948, he led a band at the Savoy Ballroom and became involved in R&B recording and songwriting, setting up his own publishing company. He was more active in jazz in the mid-1950s, making albums with Oscar Pettiford, Quincy Jones and Milt Jackson in 1956–7. After a visit to France in 1956, where he cut several albums and deputized on tour with Stan Kenton, he settled there for two periods, from 1957–62 and from 1968–71. Though he taught at Dartmouth University in 1973–4 and maintains occasional contact with other musicians, he has been inactive as a player ever since. Meanwhile his son, guitarist Daryl Thompson, has appeared on albums by David Murray, Sam Rivers and saxophonist Robin Kenyatta.

Thompson was one of the earliest and most dedicated of the relatively few Don Byas disciples. But his softer tone, in the mid-1940s especially, made his work quite distinctive and more mellifluous than Byas's. Later, by the period of his longest European stay, his sound had become more aggressive, but his individual time-feeling still made him quite different from anyone else, and his premature retirement represented a considerable loss to the scene. [BP]

⊙ **Tricotism** (1956; Impulse!). Possibly the best representation of Thompson on disc is the material with just Oscar Pettiford and guitarist Skeeter Best, including "Deep Passion", which is Lucky's take on "Body And Soul". Quartet/quintet tracks with Jimmy Cleveland and Hank Jones or Don Abney highlight Thompson's original writing.

⊙ **Lucky Strikes** (1964; Prestige/OJC). Another largely original programme, plus "Invitation" and "In A Sentimental Mood", finds Lucky again backed by Hank Jones in a quartet session which also features his beautifully fragile-sounding soprano.

➤➤ **Miles Davis** *(Walkin'); Milt Jackson (Plenty, Plenty Soul);* **Quincy Jones** *(This Is How I Feel About Jazz).*

Malachi Thompson

Trumpet.

b. Princeton, Kentucky, 21 Aug 1949.

Raised in the Hyde Park area of Chicago, Thompson began playing trumpet at sixteen; he studied with Hobart James and James Mack and took lessons with Freddie Hubbard. In 1967, he became a member of the AACM (after meeting some of the organization's members at Troy Robinson's Jazz Workshop), and he played with Muhal Richard Abrams's big band, with Henry Threadgill and Lester Bowie. He was a member of the Southern Christian Leadership Council's Operation Breadbasket Orchestra (1968), touring the country for four years. Thompson moved to New York for a period starting in 1974, working with a variety of the so-called "loft scene" musicians and forging a longstanding relationship with tenor saxophonist Carter Jefferson (who died in 1993). Before leaving Chicago, Thompson recorded his debut, *The Seventh Son* (1972; Ra), and he also recorded with Archie Shepp, Kalaparusha Maurice McIntyre, and Errol Parker.

While in New York, he was a member of the New York Hot Trumpet Repertory Group, alongside Bowie, Olu Dara, Stanton Davis and Wynton Marsalis (before Marsalis completely denounced such vanguard endeavours), and performed and recorded as a member of Lester Bowie's Brass Fantasy. He left New York in 1983, stopping in Washington, DC, and Austria before returning home to Chicago. Out of the ideas inherent in Brass Fantasy, he formed his own brass-dominated ensemble, Africa Brass, and has also concentrated on a more standard-issue instrumentation with the group he calls the Freebop Band. In 1989, Thompson was diagnosed with a rare blood disease, but he has successfully fought off the ailment and has continued in a very productive mode, recording extensively for the Delmark label in different settings, with his most recent album, the archetypal *Talking Horns* (2002), being a sextet outing featuring Hamiett Bluiett and Oliver Lake.

He has been an active member of the southside Chicago scene, organizing community jazz events and fighting to preserve the historic Sutherland Hotel, an important spot in the topography of the city's jazz legacy. Not a "chops" player by any means, Thompson can nonetheless be extremely musical and has led some strong bands. [JC]

⊙ **New Standards** (1994; Delmark). For such an outspoken "out cat", it's surprising how slick Thompson's brass group sounds, especially on their Delmark releases. His Freebop outings, like this one with the fine Carter Jefferson on saxophone, are a better bet; here he works on standards, Wayne Shorter, Booker Little and John Coltrane tunes, and an appealing "Chicago Soundscapes" portrait of his old stomping grounds.

Sir Charles Thompson

Piano, organ, arranger.

b. Springfield, Ohio, 21 March 1918.

Sir Charles Thompson made his name as a soloist in the 1940s when he worked for Coleman Hawkins, Lucky Millinder and Illinois Jacquet and wrote a hit tune, "Robbins' Nest". In the 1950s Thompson played solo and led trios on the West Coast, produced a set of albums with his trio and bands, and also worked in the very best mainstream company (Jimmy Rushing, Buck Clayton, etc), often for the Vanguard label. He toured Europe with Buck Clayton in 1961, and through the 1960s was regularly around New York piano rooms, jazz clubs and bars, as well as touring in Canada, Puerto Rico and elsewhere. After a period of illness in the 1970s he was active again, touring Furope and working in London for Peter Boizot's Pizza Express chain. A talented arranger who in his formative years worked for Basie, Henderson, Jimmy Dorsey and others, Thompson proved that the old swing and energy are far from gone from his playing on the live album *I Got Rhythm* for Delmark in 2001. [DF]

⊙ **His Personal Vanguard Recordings** (1953–5; Vanguard). Double CD of Thompson's important mainstream sessions from the 1950s, with Coleman Hawkins, Joe Newman, Emmett Berry and other masters. Close to the Clayton *Jam Sessions* in style and almost as important.

Claude Thornhill

Piano, arranger.

b. Terre Haute, Indiana, 10 Aug 1909; d. 1 July 1965.

Thornhill studied at a music conservatory, then played in territory bands before moving to New York in the early 1930s. He worked for various popular bands, including briefly for Paul Whiteman and Benny Goodman in 1934, and played and arranged for Ray Noble's American band in 1935–6. He did prolific session work, including some with Billie Holiday, and also worked as a musical director, his arrangement of "Loch Lomond" for Maxine Sullivan being one example. In 1937–8 he recorded under his own name and toured with Sullivan. He helped singer Skinnay Ennis form a West Coast band by taking over the Gil Evans group in 1938. Thornhill then led his own touring big band from 1940–42, with Evans joining him in 1941. In 1946, after navy service, he re-formed the band, which briefly contained Lee Konitz and Red Rodney and was more highly valued by musicians than by the public. The effects of a nervous breakdown and alcohol consumption slowed his career in the 1950s, but he continued to play for dancing, usually leading small or medium-sized groups.

Though his band was never a fully committed jazz organization, Thornhill's longterm influence was beneficial in a way that was not true of the more flamboyant and more financially successful Stan Kenton. Even viewed as a dance band, Claude's outfit was subtle and intelligent, making a mere slow foxtrot such as his original theme song "Snowfall" into a moody tone poem (his more humorous "Portrait Of A Guinea Farm" was also widely admired). When he added two French horns in 1941 and had all six reedmen play clarinet, Thornhill created some remarkably spacey effects. In 1947–8, when Evans and Gerry Mulligan wrote some of the arrangements, the jazz-oriented instrumentals swung without shouting and hinted at a bebop equivalent of early Basie and Lester Young (without being directly influenced, as Woody Herman was). It was these arrangements that inspired Miles Davis to have Evans and Mulligan create a nine-piece version of the same sound known retrospectively as the Birth of the Cool band. Thornhill is not, however, merely historically significant – the original performances of his band stand up in their own right and are still as fresh as the day they were recorded. [BP]

⊙ **Claude Thornhill 1941 Vol. 1** (Hep). Prior to the influence of Gil Evans, Thornhill was trying to bring added musicianship to the "sweet" band ("Glenn Miller with brains", as Mike Zwerin put it). These early studio sides include Claude's original pieces "Portrait Of A Guinea Farm" and "Snowfall".

⊙ **Transcription Performances 1947**; **1948 Transcription Performances** (Hep). The first set goes from intelligent dance music to bop tunes such as "Anthropology" and "Donna Lee" (with brief Konitz solos) to piano-led ballads where Evans's arrangements forecast his work for Miles Davis. The 1948 follow-up has no Konitz (despite its notes) but includes Evans's amazing adaptations of "La Paloma" and Tchaikovsky's "Arab Dance" and Mulligan's score of "Godchild", also recorded by Davis's *Birth Of The Cool* band.

Henry Threadgill

Saxophones, woodwinds, composer.

b. Chicago, 15 Feb 1944.

Threadgill studied at the American Conservatory of Music, Governor's State University. His first professional job was playing gospel music with travelling church musicians and evangelists, and he later played with blues bands. He joined Richard Abrams's Experimental Band in 1962–3 and became closely associated with the Association for the Advancement of Creative Music. In the 1970s, with Fred Hopkins (bass) and Steve McCall (drums), he formed the group Air which developed into one of the most distinguished offshoots (after the Art Ensemble Of Chicago) of the AACM. Air went through a couple of line-up changes after McCall left in 1982 (replaced by Pheeroan Ak Laff, then Andrew Cyrille), rechristening themselves New Air.

Since 1980 Threadgill has formed a number of groups using unusual instrumentation: X-75 had four bassists; his Sextett, actually of seven musicians, used two drummers and Deidre Murray's cello; Very Very Circus, used tubas, trombones and two guitarists; and Zooid combined Threadgill's alto and flute with acoustic guitar, oud, tuba, cello and drums. Throughout his work Threadgill has been concerned

Jak Kilby

Henry Threadgill

with musical structures, often using early jazz forms like rags, but he has nonetheless always been a fine, raw-toned improviser. [IC]

⊙ **Song Out Of My Trees** (1993; Black Saint). With three guitars, two cellos, bass and two drummers, plus trumpet, piano and organ/harpsichord, Threadgill deploys a brilliant tableau of textures and colours in another fascinating adventure in sound.

⊙ **Carry The Day** (1994; Columbia); **Makin' A Move** (1995; Columbia); **Where's Your Cup** (1996; Columbia). A brief but productive tenure at a major label made no market-driven concessions. As intricate, restless and dense as any Threadgill music, accordions and tubas dominate *Carry The Day*, cellos and guitars abound on *Makin' A Move* while *Where's Your Cup* settles on a near-conventional quintet line-up of guitar, accordion/harmonium, bass and drums – though, the odd recognizable groove notwithstanding, that's where the convention stops.

⊙ **Everybody's Mouth A Book** (2001; PI); **Up Popped The Two Lips** (2001; PI). Following a five-year creative development period away from recording, Threadgill offers two ensembles on two records. Brandon Ross is retained on electric guitar to drive the Make A Move quintet (this time featuring vibes as well as bass and drums) of *Everybody's Mouth A Book*. Cello, oud and tuba return for the group called Zooid performing *Up Popped Two Lips*, a record on which some may discern, as jazz commentator Glenn Astarita did, "a new harmonic palette and a new method of improvisation".

Air

⊙ **Air Lore** (1979; Bluebird). This investigation of ragtime is a classic of restructuralism. The material was actually developed in 1971, when the trio – calling itself Reflection – sat in the pit at a Chicago theatre piece playing the music of Scott Joplin and Jelly Roll Morton. McCall is brilliant, conveying at once bluesy, ragged time, swing-hearty buoyancy, and a sense of unbounded openness.

Henry Threadgill Sextett

⊙ **Rag, Bush And All** (1988; RCA). Threadgill mostly plays alto on this marvellous album where bassist Fred Hopkins also stars as superb time-player and soloist. But almost everything is superlative on this session – Threadgill's greatly varied writing, his organization of the long pieces so that they breathe beautifully, the dramatic changes of pace and space, and his subtle deployment of the powerful rhythm-section (two drummers and bass).

Very Very Circus

⊙ **Spirit Of Nuff ... Nuff** (1990; Black Saint); **Live At Koncepts** (1991; Taylor Made). On *Spirit of Nuff* Threadgill is attempting to move away from the conventional jazz rhythm-section and instrumentation in search of fresh modes. He deploys the unusual line-up of trombone, two tubas, two guitars and drums with considerable skill and invention, and the heartfelt cry of his alto uplifts the bottom-heavy band. The live album, which has French horn instead of trombone, is a powerful session with much of the old jazz spirit reappearing and Threadgill in fine form.

Adrian Tilbrook

Drums.

b. Hartlepool, Co Durham, UK, 20 July 1948.

Tilbrook is best known for his powerful drumming for Back Door, with Ron Aspery (saxophones) and Colin Hodgkinson (bass guitar), which he joined in 1974. The group played a hard, spirited blend of blues and jazz; toured Europe and the UK; and spent two seasons at Ronnie Scott's club, notably supporting Chick Corea's Return to Forever. They were signed to Warner Bros and toured the US, playing huge arenas with ELP and Deep Purple. After their split in late 1975, after recording their last album, *Activate*, Tilbrook joined the All Star Rock Band, with Allan Holdsworth, Jon Anderson and Jack Bruce. Tilbrook has always been active as a percussion teacher, and has also worked with Don Weller, "Lockjaw" Davis, Al Grey, Jimmy Forrest, James Moody, Kai Winding, Al Casey, Jimmy Witherspoon and Stan Tracey. In 1984 he formed a quartet, Full Circle, with trombonist Rick Taylor which toured and recorded an album, *Beauty Of The Unexpected* in 1986. Since then until the present, he has run Jazz Action, a body funded by Yorkshire and Humberside Arts and Northern Arts to promote jazz music in the north east of England, and remains active in that region as a player. [IC]

Martha Tilton

Vocals.

b. 12 Nov 1918.

One of swingdom's most capable, attractive and musical singers, Tilton began her career in 1935, sang briefly with Jimmy Dorsey the following year and with Benny Goodman from 1937–9, with whom she recorded a big hit, "And The Angels Sing". Known appropriately as "The liltin' Miss Tilton", during World War II she toured US bases with Jack Benny, appeared in a string of radio programmes (for Ben Gage, Fibber McGee and Molly, Dick Powell and Milton Berle) and recorded solo for Capitol (including "If I Had A Talking Picture Of You" with Capitol's co-director Johnny Mercer and a big hit, "I'll Walk Alone", 1943). During the later 1940s and early 1950s she remained a regular on radio and television, and appeared in several films from 1941–5 and in the *The Benny Goodman Story* (1956). [DF]

➤➤ **Benny Goodman** *(Benny Goodman On The Air).*

Bobby Timmons

Piano, composer; also vibes.

b. Philadelphia, 19 Dec 1935; d. 1 March 1974.

After work in Philadelphia, Timmons was employed successively from 1956 by Kenny Dorham, Chet Baker, Sonny Stitt and Maynard Ferguson. He came to fame with Art Blakey, with whom he worked in 1958–9 and 1960–61, and with Cannonball Adderley in 1959–60. From 1961 until shortly before his death from cirrhosis of the liver he led his own trio and made regular recordings. Initially very much under the influence of Bud Powell, Timmons became popular by adopting the mannerisms of Red Garland and the phraseology of gospel and blues piano (though in a more mechanical fashion than either Ray Bryant or Junior Mance). In this way he begat players such as Les McCann and Ramsey Lewis, but he is less well remembered for his playing than for his originals such as "Dat Dere" (lyrics added by Oscar Brown Jnr) and "Moanin'". [BP]

⊙ **In Person** (1961; Riverside/OJC). There are still many traces of Powell on standards such as "Autumn Leaves" and "I Didn't Know What Time It Was", along with the already obligatory soul-jazz mannerisms on "So Tired" (a waltz-time follow-up to his Adderley-period hit "Dis Here") and snatches of "Dat Dere", used as a closing theme for each of two sets with Ron Carter and Al Heath.

➤➤ **Art Blakey** *(Moanin')*.

Lorenzo Tio Jnr

Clarinet, tenor saxophone, arranger; also oboe.
b. New Orleans, 21 April 1893; d. 24 Dec 1933.

Lorenzo Tio taught practically all of the great classic jazz clarinettists: a short list would include Barney Bigard, Albert Nicholas, Jimmie Noone and Johnny Dodds. Tio and his family were not just the best, they were the most popular teachers, too: encouraging, honest and ready to give a young pupil his creative head. "They all played clarinets, " Barney Bigard recalls, "the great-grandfather, the grandfather, an uncle and a nephew." (He forgot Tio's father, Lorenzo Snr, a fine trained player.) "Lorenzo and his uncle taught me almost all the rudiments of clarinet – they were straightforward people and very nice. If a guy came to take lessons from them and they didn't see any possibilities in him they'd tell him right off."

Tio worked in orchestras, small chamber groups and brass bands, playing regularly in New Orleans (with Papa Celestin) and Chicago (with Manuel Perez). His most notable leader was Armand J. Piron, with whose orchestra he graduated to New York in the 1920s. He recorded 20 fine titles for Victor in 1921, and worked the Cotton Club and Roseland (where they were later replaced by Fletcher Henderson), as well as back in New Orleans. Tio was a respected bandleader on 52nd Street by 1933 (Sidney Bechet worked alongside him); he died that year and was buried back home. He is remembered also as the composer of "Dreamy Blues", which later became part of Ellington's "Mood Indigo". [DF]

➤➤ **Armand J. Piron** *(Piron's New Orleans Orchestra)*.

Keith Tippett

Piano, composer.
b. Bristol, UK, 25 Aug 1947.

Tippett was a chorister as a boy, and also studied the piano and church organ privately (and also cornet and tenor horn with the Bristol Youth Band). In 1967 he received a scholarship to the Barry (Wales) summer school jazz course, where he met

Keith Tippett

cornettist Marc Charig, saxophonist Elton Dean and trombonist Nick Evans. He formed a sextet which, helped by an Arts Council bursary, performed many broadcasts and played concerts and festivals throughout Britain and Europe. He also recorded with King Crimson and appeared on their hit single "Cat Food". In 1970 he formed a fifty-piece orchestra, Centipede, with an amplified string section to play his two-hour composition, *Septober Energy*. This ensemble, comprising leading musicians from classical, jazz and rock backgrounds, performed in Britain and at festivals in Europe. In 1972 he formed a small, more experimental group, Ovary Lodge, with his wife Julie, Frank Perry and Harry Miller, which featured total improvisation as opposed to the use of pre-composed structures. From 1973–8 he played with Elton Dean's groups and various other ensembles led by Charig, Harry Miller, Louis Moholo and Trevor Watts. He also performed a series of duets with Stan Tracey, under the name TNT. In 1978 he composed *Frames – Music For An Imaginary Film For The Ark*, the Ark being a sprawling 22-piece ensemble of international musicians. It was unmistakably one of the most ambitious albums of British 70s "jazz".

Since then he has occasionally reconvened the Ark; played in septets; in duo with his wife, singer Julie; in duo with Andy Sheppard; with the quartet Mujician (named after his 1981 solo album, the first of a trilogy); with his 21-piece band Tapestry; and solo. An active educator, he is founder of the Rare Music Club, which promotes jazz, new music and roots/ethnic music, often on the same bill. Among his influences are Jaki Byard, Cecil Taylor and Bill Evans, though the sonorities and overtones of Arabic musics inform his playing, particularly in his prepared piano work (which reminds the listener that the piano is both string instrument and percussion too). A fine composer, drawn increasingly to the classical idiom, recent pieces include works for the

Composers' Ensemble, Kokoro, and the Kreutzer String Quartet, whilst *Dance of the Dragonfly* was commissioned and performed in 2002 by percussion group Ensemble Bash. **[IC]**

⊙ **Septober Energy** (1971; BGO). Reissued on different labels at different times, sometimes under Tippett's name, sometimes under Centipede's, it has to be heard to be believed. Overblown solos, Tippett's portentous lyrics (wailed by his wife Julie) and a who's who of the Brit jazz-rock scene – this hubristic behemoth has it all (even some moments of surprising coherence and beauty).

⊙ **Mujician III (August Air)** (1987; FMP). Tippett's solo piano work is not just technically excellent, but is drenched in powerful emotion, ranging from sheer joy, through ironic reflection, to poignant recollection of things past.

⊙ **The Dartington Concert** (1990; Editions EG). Recorded on a Steinway piano which used to belong to Ignacy Paderewski, this even more powerful and resonant performance was dedicated to saxophonist Dudu Pukwana, who had died a few weeks before. It ends with Tippett intoning the name Dudu into the piano strings, which reverberate eerily.

⊙ **Linuckea** (2000; FMR). Hailed by some as a kind of 'future chamber music', Tippett's impressive composed piece for piano and string quartet is like a formalized version of what he has been doing spontaneously for years.

Juan Tizol

Valve-trombone, arranger, composer.

b. San Juan, Puerto Rico, 22 Jan 1900; d. 23 April 1984.

Juan (Vincente Martinez) Tizol came to the USA in 1920 to work at the Howard Theater, Washington, with Marie Lucas's South American-staffed orchestra, and stayed for nine years. Then he joined Duke Ellington (who had become his close friend, and remained so for life), providing Ellington with another challenging new tone colour. "One of the reasons Pop liked Tizol coming into the band was that he would write for him along with the saxophones", remembered Mercer Ellington. "On valve trombone he could move more quickly than Tricky Sam on slide." Tizol was never a strong soloist, but he was one of the best-trained musicians in the orchestra and a gifted composer who, over the years, provided Ellington with highly useable themes including "Caravan", "Perdido", "Conga Brava", "Bakiff", "Pyramid", "Sphinx", "Keb-lah" and "Moonlight Fiesta". He was one of the band's characters: punctilious over time ("He gets everywhere an hour early, rarin' to go", said Willie Smith), drinking little, smoking not at all, and taking a lunatic delight in practical jokes, until someone set off a firecracker under his chair one night. (Another version says that itching powder was the means of revenge.) In 1944, getting tired of travelling, Tizol joined Harry James for seven years, and for the rest of his career commuted between his two leaders before retiring to Los Angeles in 1960, then to Las Vegas. He recorded again with Louie Bellson in 1964 and lived happily for twenty years more. **[DF]**

Nat "King" Cole

⊙ **The Complete After Midnight Sessions** (1956; Capitol). A rare opportunity to hear Tizol in a small-group setting, with Cole's wizardly piano, Harry Edison, and the grand playing of Willie Smith.

Cal Tjader

Vibes; also drums, percussion.

b. St Louis, Missouri, 16 July 1925; d. 5 May 1982.

Born to Swedish-American parents, Tjader was a professional dancer as a child and started to learn the drums as a teenager. He studied music at San Francisco State University, and joined Dave Brubeck's octet on drums in 1948, staying with Brubeck's trio for the next two years and playing drums, vibes and bongos. He was in George Shearing's first Latin-leaning quintet for a year from 1953–4 and then formed his own group, which occasionally borrowed Shearing's percussionist Armando Peraza for recording, and, from 1957–60, included Mongo Santamaria and Willie Bobo. Throughout his career he remained based on the West Coast, though touring widely and recording in New York with Eddie Palmieri's band in 1966. The previous year he had achieved a hit with a simplified version of Dizzy Gillespie's "Guarachi Guaro" (which he had first recorded in 1954, and now retitled "Soul Sauce"). He continued recording successfully in the 1970s, using musicians such as Clare Fischer or Dawili Gonga (aka Herbie Hancock) on keyboards and introducing congero Poncho Sanchez and flautist Roger Glenn, who were the key elements of an award-winning 1979 album *La Onda Va Bien*. Comparable with the equally unlikely Herbie Mann, Tjader's own playing was unexceptional but, as a bandleader, he helped to further an important fusion and to popularize it. **[BP]**

⊙ **Monterey Concerts** (1959; Prestige). Tjader's regular group of the period, in which Bobo and Santamaria are joined by flautist Paul Horn and bassist Al McKibbon, combines straightahead jazz-playing on tracks such as "Doxy" and "Love Me Or Leave Me" with Latin features including Santamaria's newly recorded "Afro-Blue".

Christine Tobin

Vocals.

b. Dublin, 6 Jan 1963.

Tobin started late as a singer. Furthermore, she heard little jazz until 1985 and the revelation that was Joni Mitchell's album *Mingus*, after which she bought some Mingus albums and some Billie Holiday. She began singing around 1986 in Dublin, and set about learning a programme of standards, then moved to London in 1987. There, she sang in a band with pianist Simon Purcell who encouraged her to write her own music. She attended the Guildhall School's postgraduate jazz course (she stopped singing for two years to study anthropology at Goldsmiths' College) before she formed a band with pianist Huw Warren, bassist Steve Watts and drummer Roy Dodds. They recorded two albums, *Aililiu* in 1995, and *Yell Of The Gazelle* in 1996, both on Babel Records and both under Tobin's name. In 1998 she released her third CD, *House Of Women*, which was based around her band of guitarist Phil Robson, Watts and drummer Mike Pickering. Albert Mangelsdorff, after hearing Tobin and her band at the Varna festival, invited them to perform at the 1998 Berlin jazz festival, where they were received with great enthusiasm. She has since regularly appeared on the European festival circuit under her own name and with Django Bates's Delightful Precipice. Continued development, as documented on the Babel label, shows a deepening, darkening fusion of song and atmospheric jazz. [IC]

House Of Women (1998; Babel). Tobin has a group of virtuoso players working on equal musical terms with her, and she has a compositional, as well as a vocal, panache. She can scat-sing with sweet lyricism and with passionate intensity, and the subject matter of her songs often deals with things below the surface. Here, she sings songs by Leonard Cohen, and "Morro Velho" by Milton Nascimento (in Portuguese). With Phil Robson she devises an outrageously wild version of the Hendrix classic "Hey Joe", to conclude this rich and fascinating album.

You Draw The Line (2003; Babel). Robson, guitarist on all Tobin's albums, remains a valuable presence. Here he is joined by pianist Liam Noble, bassist Jeremy Brown and drummers Chris Higginbottom and Steve Argüelles to sensitively and intelligently support the singer through moody, earthy and largely original material; though another Cohen song (and one of the greatest lyrics of all time), "Tower Of Song", also gets the Tobin treatment.

Phil Todd

Saxophones, flutes, clarinets.

b. Borehamwood, Hertfordshire, UK, 6 Aug 1956.

Todd took a two-year music course at Hitchin College, then spent three years at Trinity College of Music, London. From 1973–7 he was with the National Youth Jazz Orchestra, from 1978–82 with Jeff Clyne's Turning Point, from 1982–8 with Nucleus, and from 1989–92 with the Ian Carr group. Todd has also worked as a freelance musician in rock, pop and jazz contexts, and he continues to be much in demand in the studios; he was strongly featured on the soundtrack of the film *Arachnophobia*, on which he played mostly on EWI (electronic wind instrument). He was also a key soloist on the 1988 recording of Ian Carr's *Old Heartland* album, playing soprano saxophone and bass clarinet. In the 1990s he was a regular member of the Colin Towns Mask Orchestra. [IC]

>> **Ian Carr** *(Old Heartland)*; **Mike Westbrook** *(The Cortège)*.

Charles Tolliver

Trumpet, flugelhorn, composer.

b. Jacksonville, Florida, 6 March 1942.

After studying at Washington's Howard University, Charles Tolliver returned to New York, where he had grown up, and played and recorded with Jackie McLean in 1964. His technical gifts, wedded to a clear, unfussy approach modelled on his chief influences Clifford Brown and Freddie Hubbard, led to Tolliver making a considerable name for himself in New York's hard-bop coterie, and in the 1960s he collaborated with a number of leading musicians there, including Art Blakey and Sonny Rollins. Between 1966–7, he played with Gerald Wilson's California-based big band, and subsequently established a fruitful musical relationship with saxophonist Gary Bartz, playing alongside him in Max Roach's small group (1967–8). The following year, Tolliver formed Music, Inc., a cooperative venture involving, at various times, pianists John Hicks and Stanley Cowell, bassists Reggie Workman and Cecil McBee, and drummers Jimmy Hopps and Cliff Barbaro, and in 1971 he and Cowell founded Strata-East Records, in an attempt to allow jazz musicians a greater degree of control over their product. Although under-represented on record in recent years, Tolliver is a passionate but economical player, blessed with the ability to do a great deal with a few simple musical ingredients, and his return to the scene in the late 1980s, after some years away, was marked initially by two live albums recorded with a rhythm-section of pianist Alain Jean-Marie, bassist Ugonna Ukegwo and drummer Ralph Van Duncan in 1988 at Berlin's Quasimodo (Strata-East). The following year saw him grace three albums by drummer Louis Hayes. Two Steeplechase studio sessions, *Light And Lively* and *Una Max*, featured Tolliver alongside, respectively, Bobby Watson and Gerald Hayes and John Stubblefield, and a live Candid album, *The Crawl*, featured him with Stubblefield and alto player Gary Bartz. [CP]

Charles Tolliver And His All Stars (1968; Black Lion). Excellent band featuring Herbie Hancock, Gary Bartz, Ron Carter and Joe Chambers plays cogent Tolliver material, including the memorable bop waltz, "Peace With Myself".

Grand Max (1972; Black Lion). Leading a stellar band – John Hicks (piano), Reggie Workman (bass) and Alvin Queen (drums) – Tolliver applies his intensely lyrical style to simple but effective tunes, including the vigorous title track, dedicated to Max Roach.

Impact (1975; Strata-East). Big band including Jon Faddis, Charles McPherson, James Spaulding, Harold Vick and Stanley Cowell, plus percussionists Big Black and Warren Smith, and strings for good measure, in a highly enjoyable, energetic session.

Tolvan Big Band

The four years that jazz composer and theorist George Russell spent in Scandinavia (1965–9) – chiefly as Composer in Residence with the Danish Radio Big Band in Copenhagen – had a very beneficial effect on the jazz scene of the whole region. At the end of the decade, musicians in the Swedish town of Malmö, across the water from Copenhagen, founded the Tolvan Big Band, and today the enthusiasm for big bands in Sweden is such that, despite having a smaller population than New York City, the country has approximately 500 big bands. A handful of them are of world-class standard, and the Tolvan is perhaps the cream of that crop.

In 1979 Helge Albin, an alto saxophonist and composer/arranger, took over the leadership of the band, which had its first real breakthrough in 1984, with the album *Montreux And More*, recorded partly at the Montreux jazz festival. International tours followed, and several leading Americans worked with the Tolvan, including Dizzy Gillespie, Dave Liebman and Michael Brecker. British pianist and composer Mike Westbrook and his vocalist-wife Kate have also performed their Westbrook-Rossini music with the band. The band remain a touring attraction on the European circuit. [IC]

Tolvan Big Band Plays The Music Of Helge Albin (1998; Naxos). The Tolvan deserves its reputation – the rhythm-section and the brass and reeds are superlative, and the soloists have a lot to say. Albin's writing is often brilliantly fluid and daring: "The Mysterious No. 7", for instance, uses and develops 7/4 time in a highly original way. "Connections" is a mini-concerto for piano, pitting it with superb drama against complex orchestral comments (and silences) – but then, not one of the six performances has a dull moment.

Trevor Tomkins

Drums, percussion.

b. London, 12 May 1941.

At first Tomkins was self-taught, but then studied at the Blackheath Conservatory of Music and the Guildhall School of Music and Drama. His first professional work was with the Rendell-Carr quintet in 1963 (staying with it until its demise in 1969). In the later 60s he also worked with the New Jazz Orchestra. He has worked with many UK musicians – including Keith Tippett, John Taylor, Michael Garrick, Kenny Wheeler, Tony Coe, Mike Westbrook and Barbara Thompson – touring and playing festivals in the UK and Europe – and has been a regular face at Ronnie Scott's club with Americans of the calibre of Phil Woods, Sonny Stitt, Pepper Adams and Art Farmer. In 1985 he toured the UK as a member of the Lee Konitz quartet. Tomkins is also a brilliant teacher and regularly conducts clinics and workshops at the Guildhall School of Music and elsewhere. [ICI

Jim Tomlinson

Tenor, alto and baritone saxophones, clarinet, flute.

b. Sutton Coldfield, West Midlands, UK, 9 Sept 1966.

Tomlinson grew up in Hexham (where he sang from an early age in Hexham Abbey Choir) and studied clarinet and later saxophone at school (he also studied politics, philosophy and economics at University College, Oxford). On graduation he joined the Oxford-based Vile Bodies and took a postgraduate course at London's Guildhall School of Music. Since then he has freelanced, playing with the NYJO, Mike Garrick, Dave Green and Humphrey Lyttelton, and also leads his own groups. He is married to Stacey Kent. A relaxed inventive improviser, whose work reflects the influence of Stan Getz and Lester Young, Tomlinson – like Kent – is a breath of swing air on Britain's jazz scene. [DF]

Only Trust Your Heart (1999; Candid). Excellent Tomlinson showcase featuring Colin Oxley (guitar), John Pearce (piano), and with guest appearances by Guy Barker and Stacey Kent.

Giovanni Tommaso

Bass.

b. Lucca, Italy, 20 Jan 1941.

With his brother, a pianist, Giovanni formed a group called Quartetto di Lucca which was initially influenced by the Modern Jazz Quartet, in his home town of Lucca. It became something of an institution in Italy, and lasted from 1957–66. Tommaso moved to Rome in 1967 and played with many leading musicians including Johnny Griffin, Sonny Rollins, Chet Baker and Barney Kessel. In 1971 he formed a jazz-rock group called Perigeo, which made six albums and toured all over the world. Perigeo broke up in 1977 and Tommaso joined Enrico Rava's quartet, staying with it until 1984, when he formed his own quintet with Massimo Urbani on alto saxophone. An active educator, he has directed Berklee At Umbria Jazz clinics at the Umbria Jazz Festival for many years. He has recorded with Chet Baker, John Lewis, Lee Konitz, Conte Candoli, Frank Rosolino and Quartetto di Lucca, among others. His influences are Paul Chambers, Scott LaFaro, Charlie Parker, Sonny

Rollins, Thelonious Monk, Bill Evans and Miles Davis. Tommaso has also composed over a hundred hours of soundtrack music for silent films. **[IC]**

Via G.T. (1986; Red); **To Chet** (1988; Red). Two fresh if not especially innovative sessions with Tommaso's quintet – trumpeter Danilo Fresu, alto saxophonist Massimo Urbani, pianist Danilo Rea and drummer Roberto Gatto. *Via G.T.* just has the edge, but the tribute to Chet Baker has its good moments – he was imprisoned in Italy for drug offences in the late 1950s, which seems to have lodged him deep into the Italian psyche.

Over The Ocean (1993; Red). With *Over The Ocean*, Flavio Boltro and Pietro Tonolo take over the trumpet and saxophone duties respectively and vocalist Carl Marcotulli is added. There is more solo improvisation in relation to composed sections here, but Tommaso still runs things his way.

La Dolce Vita (2001; Cam Jazz); **Secondo Tempo** (2002; Cam Jazz). Tommaso's albums on the Italian soundtrack label feature interpretations of movie themes by the likes of Ennio Morricone and Nino Rota among others. *La Dolce Vita*, which was voted as among the best jazz albums of the year by Jazziz magazine, features eminent Italians trumpeter Enrico Rava and pianist Stefano Bollini. The follow-up, *Secondo Tempo*, features the international line-up of tenorist Joe Lovano, drummer Terri Lyne Carrington, pianist Antonio Faraò and trombonist Luca Begonia.

Pietro Tonolo

Tenor saxophone.

b. Venice, Italy, 30 May 1959.

Tonolo started piano lessons at seven and at ten he switched to violin, studying it for eight years, and becoming somewhat of a virtuoso. At sixteen he took up the saxophone and taught himself to play it. He came to jazz through jazz-rock, and in 1978 first played with a group in which his brother played piano, sacrificing his promise as a classical violinist for a jazz career. In the summer of 1982 he toured with the Gil Evans orchestra; the same year he began a long-lived association with Enrico Rava and his groups. He has played many European festivals including Nice and Berlin, and has worked with many other leading Italian and international musicians such as pianist Rita Marcotulli, Henri Texier, Dave Holland and Paul Motian. Since 1990 there has been a steady stream of albums under his own name, from the melody-rich duets with pianists – *Simbiosi* (1995; Splasc(h)), *Sotto La Luna* (1999; EGEA) and *Autunno* (2001; EGEA) – to a set of reharmonised classical themes – *Disguise* (1997; Splasc(h)) and a stellar Ellington tribute with Gil Goldstein, Steve Swallow and Paul Motian – *Portrait Of Duke* (1999; Label Bleu). **[IC]**

➤➤ **Giovanni Tommaso** *(Over The Ocean)*.

Mel Tormé

Vocals; also drums, piano.

b. Chicago, 13 Sept 1925; d. 5 June 1999.

Tormé got involved in show business young; he was singing on the radio at the age of four and acting on the radio from the age of nine. He began songwriting at fifteen (enjoying considerable success over the years), and toured as the vocalist with the Chico Marx band in 1942–3. He formed his own vocal group, the Mel-Tones, recording under his own name and with Artie Shaw in 1945–6. After a period of solo hit records, he became a 1950s nightclub attraction, singing and playing with a jazz slant. He then shared billing with many famous big bands including that of Buddy Rich, and later became Rich's biographer. He was a noted songwriter (famous for "The Christmas Song" and others) and, alone among jazz-inclined singers, he scored all his own arrangements, starting in the 1970s. Tormé was, in many ways, the Mark Murphy of an earlier generation, with a light and airy tone and an almost instrumental precision which blended especially well with the West Coast-type backings of Marty Paich. **[BP]**

Mel Tormé Swings Shubert Alley (1960; Verve). One of the series of albums which balanced the light sound of Tormé's voice against the equally weightless Paich Dektette, this is an excellent combination of the approach and the material, including "Too Close For Comfort" and "Just In Time".

Dave Tough

Drums.

b. Oak Park, Illinois, 26 April 1908; d. 6 Dec 1948.

Dave Tough (David Jarvis), the son of a well-to-do physician, was an associate of the Austin High School Gang in Chicago. An intellectual, who read widely and thought intensely about every aspect of life, Tough very early on showed signs of an uncomfortable brilliance in everything he set his hand to, including playing the drums. When not instilling in his young friends a good sense of time and dynamics ("We all got some of that bite from Dave", says Max Kaminsky), Tough was spearheading the Chicagoan campaign against bad commercial music: one night in Chicago he walked off the stand after eight bars with B.A. Rolfe's showband, shaking in anger. He was never slow to make his opinions public.

All through the 1920s he was busy in Chicago, New York and Europe (with George Carhart's band) but in 1936, after at least one serious illness, he moved permanently to New York, where he worked with a string of great bands such as Tommy Dorsey's, Benny Goodman's, Bunny Berigan's, the Summa Cum Laude, and from 1941 Artie Shaw's navy band. By that time Tough – a gaunt, hollow-cheeked man who in khaki fatigues was "a sight to make the blood run cold!" (said Kaminsky) – was recognized as a drummer to set alongside Sid Catlett and ahead of Gene Krupa: a perfectly technical timekeeper and spectacular soloist, capable of working in any surroundings.

When he joined Woody Herman's shouting modern big band in 1944, however, Tough found himself pulled apart by jazz fashion, and instead of being able to weather the verbal rivalries between warring jazz schools by just going along with both (like Sid Catlett), he nearly cracked up. He suffered fits while with Herman, would sometimes burst into tears on the stand, and on one occasion went into print condemning Georg Brunis and Wild Bill Davison respectively as "a clown and a musical gauleiter". In 1948, just after completing a residency with Muggsy Spanier, he fell and fractured his skull after drinking. [DF]

➤➤ **Eddie Condon** *(Eddie Condon 1938–40)*; **Woody Herman** *(The Thundering Herds 1945–47)*.

Jean Toussaint

Tenor and soprano saxophones.

b. St Thomas, Virgin Islands, 27 July 1960.

Toussaint learned saxophone, piano and flute at school in St Thomas, and within six months of joining a local calypso band he became its musical director, steeping himself in the local styles of reggae, salsa and cadence. He then spent five semesters at the Berklee College of Music, where his fellow students incuded Branford Marsalis, Donald Harrison, Jeff Watts, Marvin "Smitty" Smith and Greg Osby. Toussaint joined a Boston R&B band in 1979, playing saxophone, string synthesizer and electric piano, and touring the East Coast, Canada and Europe with them. Back in Boston, Toussaint formed his own jazz quintet which included ex-Jazz Messenger trumpeter Wallace Roney. He was asked to join Art Blakey's Jazz Messengers in 1982, and so moved to New York. He then toured extensively with the Messengers for four and a half years in Europe, Japan, Africa, USA and Canada. Toussaint's own compositions featured regularly in the Messenger repertoire. While he was with Blakey, Toussaint also led the regular jam session at New York's Blue Note jazz club in Greenwich Village.

After leaving the Messengers in 1986, he accepted an invitation to teach on the jazz course at the Guildhall School of Music in London. He formed a quartet and trio whose line-up regularly included pianist Jason Rebello, either Alec Dankworth or Dave Green on bass, with the drum chair being held by Winston Clifford, Brian Abrahams, Bryan Spring or Mark Taylor. Toussaint has also worked with Julian Joseph's quartet and played on two of his albums, as well as appearing with many other leading musicians, including Wynton Marsalis, McCoy Tyner, Sam Rivers's Saxophone Choir, and the Gil Evans orchestra. His recent projects include The Jean Tousaint Orchestra (a 14 piece assembled to play his own works), Nazaire (a fusion band featuring guitarist Tony Remy and other hip young Londoners) and his New York Quartet (featuring big hitters Mulgrew Miller – an old compatriot from the Messengers – also Marsalis alumni bassist Robert Hurst and Jeff 'Tain' Watts). Toussaint has a warm, pliant tone, and is a consummate technician with a fine lyrical flair. [IC]

⊙ **What Goes Around** (1991; World Circuit). Toussaint has gathered most of the British young lions around him for this session, and generously awarded them solo space. The most concentrated performances are three tracks with Julian Joseph and his rhythm-section of Alec Dankworth and the brilliant drummer Mark Mondesir. The other luminaries are guitarist Tony Remy, pianists Jason Rebello and Bheki Mseleku, bassist Wayne Bachelor, drummer Clifford Jarvis and vocalist Cleveland Watkiss.

⊙ **The Street Above The Underground** (2000; All Tones). Some strong instrumental statements from the leader set in the fusion end of Toussaint's range, featuring Remy and Rebello again, but this time joined by trumpeter Byron Wallen and a slew of vocalists, including Noel McCoy.

➤➤ **Julian Joseph** *(The Language Of Truth; Reality)*.

Ralph Towner

Guitars, piano, synthesizer, French horn, composer.

b. Chehalis, Washington, 1 March 1940.

From the age of three the young Ralph Towner would improvise on the piano, and he began to play on trumpet at five; he went on to play in a dance band at thirteen, and later in jazz clubs, while studying theory and composition at the University of Oregon (1958–66). He also studied classical guitar at the Vienna Academy of Music in 1963–4 and

Provocateur Records

Ralph Towner

1967–8, and played lute and guitar with classical chamber groups from 1964–6.

In 1969 he moved to New York, playing with Jimmy Garrison, Jeremy Steig, Paul Winter's Winter Consort, Weather Report and Gary Burton. Towner and three others (Collin Walcott, Glen Moore and Paul McCandless) broke away from Winter Consort to form Oregon in 1971, which was to become one of the key jazz groups of the 1970s and 1980s. At first Towner composed much of the group's material, but, once their identity and scope became clear, the others began to write more, and the band also featured some collective compositions. Oregon extended the whole idea of chamber-group jazz (as championed by the ECM label) by assimilating elements and techniques from folk and ethnic music and classical music both ancient and modern. Walcott died in a road accident in 1984, and the group reformed in 1985 with Indian percussionist Trilok Gurtu, though they have since often played as a trio. Still a working group, Oregon have now produced over 20 albums.

In the later 1970s and the 1980s Towner also toured and recorded in duo with fellow guitarist John Abercrombie, and this association has produced some exceptional music, though he has also worked effectively with Gary Burton, Egberto Gismonti, Larry Coryell, Keith Jarrett, Jan Garbarek and Gary Peacock.Towner is a composer with a recognizable style involving keyboard or guitar ostinati, resonant harmonies, lovely moving bass-lines, and often an organ- or hymn-like sonority in his melodies – good examples are "Icarus", "The Rapids" and "The Juggler's Etude". He told Joachim Berendt: "I wasn't on the jazz scene until I got a classically oriented technique on guitar ... I do find acoustic instruments more sympathetic than electric instruments ... I treat the guitar quite often like a piano trio. If I'm playing alone it's almost like a one-man-band approach." [IC]

⊙ **Diary** (1973; ECM). Towner is a masterful solo player, and this rich and absorbing album has at least two of his most beautiful compositions: the long-structured modal piece "Icarus" and "Silence Of A Candle".

⊙ **Solstice** (1974; ECM). With Garbarek, Weber and Christensen, who are ideally attuned to Towner's music in terms of their sonorities, active rhythms and sculpted phrasing. The romantic "Drifting Petals" also shows that Towner isn't afraid to wear his heart on his sleeve.

⊙ **Old Friends, New Friends** (1979; ECM). Towner's writing is gloriously lyrical, and Kenny Wheeler is on devastating form, playing the demanding themes with ease, and soloing with authority and unfailing invention. "Yesterday And Long Ago" begins elegiacally with Towner prominent on French horn, but evolves into a powerful collective abstract improvisation in which David Darling's cello figures strongly.

⊙ **City Of Eyes** (1990; ECM). A fascinating mix under Towner's direction: Gary Peacock's sensuous bass set against Markus Stockhausen's slightly classical-sounding abstract tendencies, Paul McCandless's haunting oboe and Jerry Granelli's low-key drumming.

⊙ **Anthem** (2001; ECM). A sort of wiser, 28-year-on rerun of the solo musings of *Diary* (which was re-released to coincide with this), it's a fabulous mature summation of Towner's singular gifts; the lovely melodies, the pastel shading, the dramatic nuances.

Oregon

⊙ **Music Of Another Present Era** (1973; Vanguard); **Distant Hills** (1973; Vanguard). *Music From Another Present Era* is Oregon's debut and shows that a rhythmic muscularity underlay the evocative writing and the often ethereal surface of the music right from the beginning. The sheer attractiveness of their music camouflages its scope – from composed and controlled pieces, to collectively improvised performances, and pieces like "Sail" where they hit a powerful groove and follow it through. *Distant Hills* is their second and perhaps their best album.

⊙ **North West Passage** (1997; Intuition). The arrival of percussionists Arto Tuncboyaciyan and Malk Walker into the music of Oregon was welcome and with everyone playing as if happy and stimulated, this is a later-period peak for the group.

➤➤ **Joe Zawinul** *(I Sing The Body Electric).*

Colin Towns

Piano, flute, electronics, composer/arranger.
b. London, 13 May 1948.

Colin Towns was self-taught, and learned by gigging, listening to records and consulting books. He started semi-professional work at the age of 13, playing at weddings and parties in East London and "paid his dues", gigging with dance bands, jazz groups, rehearsal bands and resident trios (writing for and leading a couple of bands too) until well into his twenties. He left his day job in 1975 and became keyboard player with the Ian Gillan Band, recording the jazz-rock album, *Clear Air Turbulence* (Island); he was to stick with them for another nine albums, co-writing most of the material. In 1976, Towns wrote his first film soundtrack, *Full Circle,* and he left Gillan in 1981, to pursue writing work for film and television, his soundtracks earning a cult status among collecors. But it was not until 1991 that he properly addressed his jazz roots, and he put together his own jazz big band. With the aid of Alan Skidmore he recruited some of the finest British jazz musicians to form his Mask Orchestra.

In 1996 Towns founded his own label, Provocateur Records, to release his band's second CD, *Nowhere And Heaven.* As an extremely gifted and prolific composer/arranger, he subsidizes the Mask Orchestra by continuing to write for TV and film, and he has also written orchestral arrangements for its talented members, including Guy Barker's album *What Love Is* (1998; Verve) and Alan Skidmore's *After The Rain*, (1998; Miles Music). In 1998 Towns released a Mask Quintet album, *Still Life*, featuring singer Maria Pia De Vito, and his Mask Symphonic (the orchestra augmented by strings, woodwinds and singers de Vito and Norma Winstone) performed at London's Queen Elizabeth Hall and recorded the album, *Dreaming Man With Blue Suede Shoes.* Towns has twice recorded his music with the NDR Hamburg Radio Orchestra, which has performed some of his pieces on tour and with whom he directed a fine album of Kurt Weill material. IC]

Ssirus W. Pakzad

Colin Towns

Nowhere And Heaven (1996; Provocateur). Some of the straightforward orchestral tracks on this double CD are succinct and delightful, like the two openers, the quasi-African "Skin Treatment", with fine solos from Jamie Talbot (soprano) and Richard Edwards (trombone), and the folky, gospellish "The Sky Is Early", with dynamic sax solos by Nigel Hitchcock and Alan Skidmore. But some of the longer pieces, like the title track, sound like soundtracks in search of a movie. However, the 13-minute "Screech" is a wild and hilarious riot of orchestral writing and scat singing.

Another Think Coming (2001; Provocateur). Not known for its understatement, Towns's music reaches further thunderous heights on his fifth Mask Orchestra album. A highlight is a grotesquely entertaining reworking of the Beatles' "I Am The Walrus" though the quality of dramatic writing and committed playing (from the cream of the UK crop) is tremendous throughout.

Clark Tracey

Drums.

b. London, 5 Feb 1961.

Clark played informally with his father Stan Tracey and studied drums with Bryan Spring. He began working regularly with Stan's various groups as early as 1978, and gradually matured into a forthright and exciting rhythm-section player. He also undertook frequent work with saxophonist Mike Mower and pianist Tony Lee, and has backed (among others) Buddy DeFranco, James Moody, Charlie Rouse, Sal Nistico, Art Farmer, Red Rodney and Benny Waters. From 1984 into the 1990s he led his own quintet, including Guy Barker or Gerard Presencer, altoist Jamie Talbot, Steve Melling and Alec Dankworth. In 1992 he launched a new sextet; he is also a favourite accompanist of vocalist Tina May, his wife, and in the late 1990s, he played regularly with the Echoes Of Ellington big band. From starting out as a raw and relatively unskilled sideman, Clark has moved front-and-centre and is now one of the most experienced and reliable drummers in the UK. [BP]

Full Speed Sideways (1994; 33 Records). A most impressive debut from Tracey's sextet, which features several young bloods, Dave O'Higgins, altoist Nigel Hitchcock and trombonist Mark Nightingale, all of whom feed off the drummer's stimulating and varied writing and playing.

Stan Tracey

Piano, composer, arranger; also accordion, vibes.

b. London, 30 Dec 1926.

Tracey started as a professional musician at the age of sixteen, in groups entertaining armed forces personnel, and then graduated to the dance-band scene. His jazz work in the 1950s included time with Eddie Thompson (on accordion), Kenny Baker, Tony Crombie, Ronnie Scott and Basil Kirchin, and he spent nearly two years, from 1957–9, with Ted Heath (during which he was featured on vibes). He was the house pianist at Ronnie Scott's club from 1960–67, backing soloists such as Zoot Sims and Ben Webster (both of whom he recorded with), Sonny Rollins (cutting the *Alfie* film soundtrack with him in 1966) and many others. He formed his own quartet c. 1964, first with saxophonist Bobby Wellins, then with Peter King, Trevor Watts and, from 1974–95, Art Themen. After the Ronnie Scott's period, his regular drummer was Bryan Spring and then, from 1978, his son Clark. He has also appeared and recorded in solo, duo (with Mike Osborne, John Surman or Tony Coe), trio, sextet, octet, tentet and big band, and has received many composing commissions. In 1993 a concert commemorating his forty years as a professional musician featured his music for several different-sized ensembles. He performed in duo with Jimmy Woode at the 1997 Duke Ellington conference and in 1999 presented an Ellington centenary tribute with his big band.

Although international acceptance was slow in coming, many US players spoke extremely highly of

Stan Tracey (right) with John Surman

Jak Kilby

Tracey (Rollins commented, "Does anyone here realize how good he is?"), though he is now regarded as one of the most original of British musicians. Inspired by Ellington and Monk (in that order), he soon created an idiosyncratic solo style which is instantly recognizable. This also translates into a very stimulating approach to accompaniment (but only for those soloists who relish being stimulated). Equally interesting on standard material and original compositions, Tracey prefers the latter and, while his arranging for larger bands is less individual (occasionally recalling Gerald Wilson or Thad Jones), it mirrors his piano work in its pungent dynamism. [BP]

Under Milk Wood (1965; Jazzizit). The album which made Tracey's name and, amazingly for a British record, continues to sell. An excellent performance by Bobby Wellins and the pianist highlights Tracey's gallery of musical sketches inspired by the Dylan Thomas radio play.

Genesis (1987–9; Steam). The only available record of Tracey's big-band albums, this is another suite (plus two extra tracks) with solo work by Guy Barker and trombonist Malcolm Griffiths, among others. Pitted against this exciting ensemble, the leader's piano is at its most Ellingtonian.

Portraits Plus (1992; Blue Note). Like Ellington, Tracey often hangs his ideas on visual or interpersonal inspirations: this suite of pieces dedicated to Duke, Rollins and others has his writing and his accompaniments drawing the best from such as Guy Barker, Don Weller and Art Themen.

Solo/Trio (1997; Cadillac). Again, this is the only available example of Tracey's less often recorded solo playing which, especially on standards, reveals the full extent of his orchestral approach to the keyboard. His regular rhythm-section of Andy Cleyndert and Clark Tracey join in on several tracks.

>> **Ronnie Scott** *(The Night Is Scott...).*

Theo Travis

Tenor and soprano saxophones, flute, composer.
b. Birmingham, UK, 7 July 1964.

Theo Travis learned classical flute, then studied music at Manchester University, gaining his degree in 1986. There he played with various jazz groups at night, and as a member of NYJO he toured Spain in 1985. In 1987 he performed at New York's Blue Note club, and since 1988 he has led his own groups. Travis was signed to 33 Records in 1993, and that year released his first album under his own name, *2 AM*, which showed an already remarkable sureness of touch in his writing and playing, with an eclectic mix of styles. The album and his constant touring soon established his reputation, and his second album, *View From The Edge* (1994), was voted Best British Jazz CD by the *Jazz On CD* poll. Having been commissioned to write a piece for West Midlands Arts and (with bassist Dave Sturt, with whom he completes the ambient duo Cipher) to compose new music for the 1926 Hitchcock silent film, *The Lodger*, he released his third album on 33 Records, *Secret Island*, which featured guitarist John Etheridge.

Following the album's release, the Theo Travis Band undertook a highly successful UK tour, and then in 1997, with drummer John Marshall and guitarist Mark Wood, Travis formed the free-improvising trio, Marshall Travis Wood, and released an outstanding album, *Bodywork*. In the summer of 1999 he toured with the famous Franco-English psych-rock group Gong (whose prime mover, Daevid Allen, would later guest on *Heart of the Sun*). Travis's distinctive soprano saxophone has featured in films and on albums with other leaders, and Travis was acknowledged by author Nicholas Royle as one of the inspirations for his novel, *Saxophone Dreams*. As well as working with his own quartet – pianist David Gordon, bassist Rob Statham and drummer Marc Parnell – Travis has also played with Bill Bruford, Tony Coe, John Etheridge, Mervyn Africa, Mick Karn, Maggie Nichols and Jim Mullen, among others. His first studio album in five years was *Heart Of The Sun* in 2001 with Palle Mikkelborg and in 2003 he released, on his own label Ether Sounds, a minimalist ambient album for alto flute and loops, *Slow Life*, an area of expression he intends pursuing. [IC]

Secret Island (1996; 33 Records). Travis's Getzian tone and lyricism are much in evidence here, on what is basically a quartet album, with percussion added occasionally and John Etheridge joining in on five of the nine performances. "Lulworth Night" is a calm, lightly rocky lyrical piece, on which Travis's tenor sound is ineffably tender and expressive. "The Crow Road", inspired by Iain Banks's eponymous novel, is ominous and compelling, with excellent writing for the rhythm-section and Travis playing with almost savage passion.

Heart Of The Sun (2001; 33 Records). Rangy, sparky writing and top-drawer playing from Travis, Palle Mikkelborg, pianist David Gordon, bassist Andy Hamill and drummer Marc Parnell. Despite the stylistic restlessness, there's a consistency and intelligence to Travis's output that marks him as one of the more intriguing of the current generation of creative musicians.

Alphonso E. Trent

Piano, leader.

b. Fort Smith, Arkansas, 24 Aug 1905; d. 14 Oct 1959.

Probably the most famous "territory band" of all, Trent's orchestra featured stars such as Snub Mosley, Peanuts Holland and drummer A.C. Godley – who may have been the first-ever drum soloist/showman. Based in the deep South in the 1920s, Trent later played around Texas (his was the first black orchestra to play large hotels like the Adolphus in Dallas for long periods), broadcast concerts over Radio WFAA, Dallas, and by the end of the decade was featuring such budding stars as Sy Oliver and frontman Stuff Smith. Occasionally Trent came in for patronizing publicity in those deep South states, but he was successful enough to organize at least one other orchestra, TNT2, which travelled the circuit simultaneously. [DF]

Lennie Tristano

Piano, composer.

b. Chicago, 19 March 1919; d. 18 Nov 1978.

Tristano, who was blind from childhood, started learning the piano at the age of four and later studied the saxophone, clarinet and cello. He gained a BMus from the American Conservatory in Chicago. He worked in his home town on various commercial gigs (sometimes on tenor) while perfecting his own piano style. After moving to New York in 1946, he formed a trio with Billy Bauer and a succession of bassists, which was later expanded to a sextet from 1949–52 by the addition of various drummers and saxophonists Lee Konitz and Warne Marsh. Both the last-named studied with Tristano when he began formal teaching in 1951, and one or other was usually in attendance on his rare returns to nightclub playing in 1955, 1958–9, 1964 and 1966. He appeared as a soloist at the Berlin festival in 1965 and the Harrogate festival in 1968, but otherwise restricted his activity to teaching.

His educational methods, which give primacy to developing the ear rather than sheer mechanical ability, have been influential through the teaching of his own students such as Konitz and Peter Ind (though, sadly, nowhere near as influential as the kind of big-band apprenticeship that passes for education in most institutions). He was also the first person on record who occasionally persuaded a group of players (the 1949 sextet) to improvise simultaneously without any pre-set limits as to key or duration, and to do so in public rather than merely in a studio. Not surprisingly, this was not the inspiration for the blues-derived "free jazz" which Ornette Coleman and Cecil Taylor introduced in the late 1950s. Tristano may have indirectly encouraged the flirtation with modern European composers that led to "third stream", thanks to the work of temporary Tristano followers Teo Macero, John LaPorta and Charles Mingus. His attempts to make improvisation less predictable and more open-ended certainly influenced European jazz players such as Albert Mangelsdorff and Martial Solal, as well as the 1960 "Blue Note school" including early Wayne Shorter and early Herbie Hancock.

Tristano's longterm influence on jazz piano has been considerable, not so much because of direct disciples like Sal Mosca and Connie Crothers, but through the clear effect he had on the much imitated Bill Evans. But, unlike the romantic Evans, Tristano aspired to a pure dispassionate piano sound (even recording one of his most down-to-earth improvisations, "Requiem", at half-speed so that, when played back, it would have an other-worldly ring to it). He argued equally that his saxophonists should use a flat, uninflected tone so that their lines would stand or fall on the quality of their construction and not on emotional coloration. In furthering his aims, his own playing moved away from the virtuosity of his earliest private recordings, which show fleetingly his roots in Earl Hines and Art Tatum (a progression that parallels Thelonious Monk's withdrawal from the Teddy Wilson style). Instead, he developed a unique approach which strikes many listeners as too cold for comfort but has proved endlessly fascinating for others. [BP]

Live At Birdland 1952 (1945–52; Jazz Records). Despite the title, this usefully closes with four privately cut solos that relate more to earlier jazz piano styles. The very

HERMAN LEONARD

Lennie Tristano

rough recording which opens the live set is calculated to deter anyone but the faithful, but the performance with Warne Marsh and Billy Bauer indicates how far the group differed from the then norm.

⊙ **Lennie Tristano/The New Tristano** (1955–61; Rhino/Atlantic). This combines Tristano's only two LPs that were reasonably well distributed in his lifetime. The first (sometimes issued as *Lines*) includes a few examples of overdubbing, including the remarkable "Requiem", but also has four live tracks with Konitz. The second, not overdubbed despite its technical intensity, is an entirely unaccompanied set of improvisations abstracted from standard chord sequences.

Gianluigi Trovesi

Alto saxophone, clarinets.
b. Nembro, Italy, 1944.

Trovesi received drum lessons from his father – an amateur drummer – at the age of six, then picked up clarinet at fifteen. In 1960 he began studies in the Donizetti Institute in Bergamo, where he first played jazz. In the mid-70s, he played and recorded extensively as a member of Giorgio Gaslini's ensembles, and since then he has quickly risen to the top of the Italian creative music ranks to stand as one of its most important figures.

He issued his own *Baghet* (1978; DDQ), *Cinque Piccole Storie* (1980; DDQ) and *Dances* (1985; Red), leading trios with bassist/cellist Paolo Damiani, and he has collaborated with many of the top European improvisers on the free side of jazz including Misha Mengelberg, Louis Sclavis and Alexander von Schlippenbach. Trovesi's own compositional track has developed in a unique, personal way; he fuses elements of pan-Italian folk musics, classical music (he was attracted by Gaslini's important and under-appreciated meldings of improvisation and twelve-tone technique) and jazz in a distinctive approach to pastiche, particularly well articulated in his octet, which has recorded two discs for Soul Note. "When I play I behave a bit like when I eat", he has said. "I like nibbling here and there." Trovesi is a member of the Italian Instabile Orchestra, which includes his compositions "From G To G" and "Scarlattina" in its repertoire. He is an outstanding clarinettist, as is clear on his lovely duet with accordionist Gianni Coscia, *Radici* (1995; Egea). He has more recently released a suite of rather quaint pieces for chamber orchestra related to his birthplace of Nembro, *Around Small Fairy Tales* (1998; Soul Note), though a latter day pair of albums for ECM – an utterly charming reprise of his duo with Coscia, *In Cerce Di Cibo* (2001) and *Fugace* (2003) – and one recorded with the WDR Big Band, *Dedalo* (2001; Enja), charted his music reaching a new peak. [JC]

⊙ **Les Hommes Armés** (1996; Soul Note). The Trovesi octet in a playful mode – not unlike the best moments of Willem Breuker's Kollektief in basic approach (genre quotation, jokes, tight arranging) but more relaxed and unmistakably Mediterranean. Highlight is "Dance For A King", which effortlessly mixes Eric Dolphy's "Miss Ann" with renaissance and folk motifs. Great fun.

⊙ **Fugace** (2003; ECM). Perhaps the finely-honed culmination of Trovesi's distinctive oeuvre, this expansive but largely restrained octet recording featues an archetypally beguiling blend of early jazz, Italian folk, rock and classical; with wit, sensitivity and sheer musicianship in remarkable balance.

Frankie Trumbauer

C-melody saxophone, multi-instrumentalist, vocals.
b. Carbondale, Illinois, 30 May 1901; d. 11 June 1956.

The most brilliant white saxophonist of the 1920s, Frankie Trumbauer (like Miff Mole) had an incalculable influence on black and white jazzmen alike. "He was the baddest cat back in those days," says Budd Johnson, summing up for his generation, "and everybody was trying to play his stuff. He was boss of the alto like Hawk was boss of the tenor." Trumbauer – "Tram" for short – was spotted early on with the Benson Orchestra of Chicago, by Bix Beiderbecke among others, and soon the pair of them were working for Jean Goldkette's orchestra, where Trumbauer confidently took on the job of musical director and produced super-technical light-toned solos to order ("To say the band was a killer would be putting it mildly", he recalled later). In these years Trumbauer and Bix recorded the greatest white jazz of its period in total harmony ("Singin' The Blues" is only one of many immortal titles) and by 1927 the friends were together again in Paul Whiteman's orchestra. "Trumbauer was a sensation with Whiteman", recalls Earl Hines, and Buddy Tate also remembered him at the period: "The first time I ever spoke to him he said 'Practise! You don't get this overnight!'" Tram flew his own plane to jobs, and Tate remembered, "One night they were opening at some big hotel in St Louis. On the way his plane developed engine trouble and it ended up falling on the hotel they were to play!"

Trumbauer worked for Whiteman from 1927–32 and 1933–6, co-led the Three Ts in 1936 (featuring the Teagarden brothers) and in 1938 co-led a band with Manny Klein. During and after the war he worked for the Civil Aeronautics Authority, but still found time for music, playing with Russ Case and in New York studios from 1945, and producing records of his own. However, little more was heard from this giant in the modern-jazz-crazy 1950s. Benny Carter, another master, reminded us how great Trumbauer was: "My original influence was Frank Trumbauer. I don't think I ever had his facility. He was a great technician but he wasn't an exhibitionist." [DF]

Frankie Trumbauer and Bix Beiderbecke

Bix And Tram Vol. 1 (1927; JSP). Most of Trumbauer's greatest collaborations with Bix are on this set, including "Singin' The Blues", "Clarinet Marmalade" and "For No Reason At All In C".

"Big" Joe Turner

Vocals.

b. Kansas City, Missouri, 18 May 1911; d. 23 Nov 1985.

By the time he was 14, "Big" Joe Turner was singing in the Kingfisher Club, Kansas City, where he worked behind the bar. There he met pianist Pete Johnson and the two of them worked together regularly through the 1940s, usually on the West Coast, and in 1945 they opened their Blue Room club in Los Angeles. Rough, raw, sexually direct, Turner was one of the very first rock'n'roll phenomena, and for a time he looked like becoming a rock star, but his approach was too black and too forceful for a white-dominated commercial music scene, and despite hit records on the Atlantic label, including "Chains Of Love" and "Shake, Rattle And Roll", he never made a permanent crossover. (He was also rather too old: "Imagine Joe, six feet two and weighing 250 lbs, belting out 'Trendsetter' at 46", says Nick Kimberley.) In the 1950s Turner regularly reidentified himself with his jazz roots (not a wise move for a pop star), and albums such as the classic *Boss Of The Blues*, featuring Pete Brown, Lawrence Brown and Pete Johnson, clearly proved he was a jazzman at heart. He moved back to New Orleans in the 1960s, but visited Britain in 1965 to tour with Humphrey Lyttelton, whose account of the tour, *Take It From The Top* (describing Turner's preference for the key of C and liability to set fire to hotel rooms), is a revealing and loving portrait. In the 1970s Big Joe sang at festivals and signed a contract with Norman Granz's Pablo label, which featured him in every context from jazz bands to down-home R&B bands. In 1981 he was hospitalized in Los Angeles with pneumonia and blood clots; by the following year, however, he was back, playing Tramps' Room in New York and singing (said Lee Jeske) in "a voice so rich and clear and strong the walls shake, the plates rattle and the tables roll". In the last year of his life Joe Turner was still appearing with kindred spirit Jimmy Witherspoon. [DF]

Joe Turner's Blues (1938–46; Topaz). Excellent selection of Turner's earlier work in varied surroundings – Pete Johnson, Johnson's Boogie Woogie Boys, Benny Carter, Willie "The Lion" Smith, Bill Moore and six titles from two sessions with Art Tatum in 1941. Highly recommended.

The Boss Of The Blues (1956; Atlantic Jazz). Perhaps Joe's greatest-ever date, with Joe Newman, Lawrence Brown and Pete Brown all on superlative form. Tracks like "How Long Blues" are incredibly moving.

Flip Flop And Fly (1972; Pablo). Turner recorded live in Paris and Frankfurt, with Count Basie and Al Grey amongst a team of latterday Basie regulars.

Stormy Monday (1974–6; Pablo). Turner's colleagues here, on a representative selection of late studio dates, include Dizzy Gillespie, Roy Eldridge and Eddie Vinson.

Bruce Turner

Alto saxophone, clarinet, composer, leader.

b. Saltburn, Yorkshire, UK, 5 July 1922; d. 28 Nov 1993.

Bruce Turner played clarinet for Freddy Randall, then took advice from Lennie Tristano and lessons from Lee Konitz in New York before joining Humphrey Lyttelton on alto saxophone in 1953 (defiant Birmingham traditionalists raised a banner reading "Go home, dirty bopper!"). Turner worked with Lyttelton until 1957 when he formed his first Jump Band, which broadcast, recorded, made a film, *Living Jazz* (1961), and toured the circuit to occasionally hostile receptions from promoters who expected commercial traditional fare. But the band's music had a strong identity of its own, was often gorgeously arranged, and continually drew on the most ambitious repertoire from the late 1930s swing era. Turner carried on with his band until 1966 (by which time they had toured with Americans such as Ben Webster, Bill Coleman,

Don Byas and Ray Nance), when he decided to rest from bandleading and joined Acker Bilk: the records they made together are a logical extension of Turner's own ideas. In 1970 Turner rejoined Humphrey Lyttelton, always his closest ally and best publicist, and fifteen years on was still working regularly with Lyttelton's band. In 1984 he produced a thoughtful autobiography which was a fascinating insight into the character behind the eccentric, cream-cake-loving persona. One of British mainstream jazz's greatest figures, Turner was a highly eclectic alto saxophonist, who moved almost as easily into avant-garde situations (such as Dave Green's Fingers group) as he did into Dixieland. [DF]

⊙ **That's The Blues Dad!** (1955–8; Lake). Overdue collection of Turner sides with Wally Fawkes, the Jazz Today unit with Kenny Baker and Turner's (early) Jump Band. The music is all very good, but we await the issue of Turner's later Jump Band LPs too.

⊙ **Jumpin' For Joy** (1962-3; Lake). Essential portrait of Turner's unique and tailored "Jump Band"; 11 tracks with John Chilton's vivacious and rangey trumpet (including three live) plus a 16 track studio album 'Going places' with Chilton's replacement Ray Crane and Pete Strange on similarly premier form. Some of the best british swing anywhere on record.

⊙ **The Dirty Bopper** (1985; Upbeat). Turner's only fully fledged solo date, with a quartet including Dave Cliff. Featuring delicate examples of his clarinet-playing, this is essential, despite occasionally gritty recording quality. Includes bonus tracks from Humphrey Lyttelton.

➤➤ **Humphrey Lyttelton** *(Jazz At The Royal Festival Hall/Jazz At The Conway Hall; Movin' And Groovin').*

Joe Turner

Piano, vocals.

b. Baltimore, Maryland, 3 Nov 1907; d. Paris, 21 July 1990.

Not to be confused with blues singer "Big" Joe Turner, Joseph H. Turner was a fine pianist/singer who worked steadily around New York in the 1920s, and in the 1930s was accompanist to Adelaide Hall. During the latter decade he spent much time in Europe, and after the war (when he came back to the USA and served in the army) he moved back to Hungary, then to Switzerland and at last to Paris. Most of his activities were European-based after that, though in the 1980s he once again started recording for American labels and appearing in his home country. [DF]

⊙ **Sweet And Lovely** (1952; Vogue). Excellent collection of Turner solos from his Paris heyday, including "Wedding Boogie" and "Hallelujah".

⊙ **I Understand** (1979; Black and Blue). Another good solo set with Turner singing and playing on a varied programme including Willie "The Lion" Smith specials like "Echoes Of Spring", piano-entertainer standbys like "As Time Goes By", and even "I Left My Heart In San Francisco".

⊙ **Stride By Stride Volume 1** (1960; Solo Art). This solo date is a fair representation of his work, including boogie and stride features, all played with commendable control and finesse.

Mark Turner

Tenor and soprano saxophones.

b. Fairborn, Ohio, 10 Nov 1965.

Raised in California from the age of four, Turner learned the clarinet and alto sax, then took up the tenor at around 16. He took a visual arts course before moving to Berklee College, graduating in 1990, and later studied for a year with Ellis Marsalis in New Orleans, after touring and recording with Delfeayo Marsalis from 1991–2. Settling in New York, he worked frequently with guitarist Kurt Rosenwinkel and bassist Rufus Reid's group, and made records with established names such as Jimmy Smith and James Moody. The latter session was a by-product of gaining his own record contract with Warner Brothers, for which he has made four well-received albums: *Mark Turner* (1998), *In This World* (1998), *Ballad Session* (2000) and *Dharma Days* (2001). As well as displaying a great awareness of contemporary saxophone styles, Turner is noted for his long lines and fluid phrasing, which recalls the hitherto unfashionable influence of Warne Marsh, especially in his deliberately flat tone and his fluency in the upper register. [BP]

⊙ **Ballad Session** (1999; Warner). These trio, quartet and quintet settings (including drummer Brian Blade and, on half the tracks, guitarist Kurt Rosenwinkel) shows the musicality behind the leader's technique. As well as items from the American songbook, Turner chooses tunes by Shorter, Hancock, Hutcherson, Paul Desmond and Carla Bley.

⊙ **Dharma Days** (2001; Warner). Turner, plus regular collaborators Kurt Rosenwinkel, bassist Reid Anderson and drummer Nasheet Waits, produces his most mature and inspiring album to date. The overall mood is cool and abstract, but the nine self-penned tracks showcase Turner's elongated lines to perfection.

Norris Turney

Alto and tenor saxophones, flute, clarinet.

b. Wilmington, Ohio 8 Sept 1921; d. 17 Jan 2001.

Turney is principally remembered as the replacement for Johnny Hodges in Duke Ellington's orchestra following the legendary altoist's demise in 1970. His professional career began at 18 in Cincinatti after which he worked with the Jeter-Pillars Orchestra in St Louis, Tiny Bradshaw in Chicago, and Billy Eckstine, on lead alto from 1945–6. A period of retreat in Ohio was followed by work with Elmer Snowden and Ray Charles before Turney regained the spotlight with Ellington (1971-3), playing both alto and flute. From 1973 he worked for ten years in Broadway pit bands before emerging as a freelance soloist with George Wein's Newport All Stars and the Lincoln Center Jazz Orchestra. He was also regularly to be found in big bands led by Clark Terry, Frank Foster, Grover Mitchell, Erskine Hawkins and Machito. Later on Turney relocated to Ohio and also toured with

Claude "Fiddler" Williams and British bassist Dave Green. [DF]

Big Sweet 'N' Blue (Mapleshade; 1995). Turney's first self-led album is a triumph, with his fully-blown alto beautifully recorded in a programme regularly recalling Ellington and Strayhorn but with room for two of his own compositions. Turney is well-supported by Larry Willis on piano, Walter Booker (bass), and the unmistakable cymbal work of Jimmy Cobb on percussion.

Steve Turré

Trombone; also conch-shells, electric bass.

b. Omaha, Nebraska, 12 Sept 1948.

After growing up in California, Turré studied at North Texas State University from 1968–9, later completing a Master's degree at Manhattan School of Music in 1988. He worked in San Francisco with Santana (1970) and Van Morrison (1971) and toured with Ray Charles in 1972. Playing with Woody Shaw for several spells from 1972–83, he also joined Art Blakey, Thad Jones-Mel Lewis, Chico Hamilton, Roland Kirk (1976–7), Slide Hampton, Max Roach and Cedar Walton. He was a frequent member of Lester Bowie's Brass Fantasy (from 1985), McCoy Tyner's big band (from 1988), Dizzy Gillespie's United Nation Orchestra (from 1989) and several New York-based Afro-Latin bands. Their music was one of the influences on his first album in 1987 and, as well as his own groups (often including his wife, cellist Akua Dixon), he has also recorded with the Mingus Big Band, Horace Silver, Tom Harrell and J.J. Johnson. In addition to his versatile trombone work, Turré often obtains sounds by blowing into sea-shells and one of his bands, the Sanctified Shells, has a brass section who all double on such "instruments". [BP]

Lotus Flower (1997; Verve). Setting his fluent and emotive trombone work within a frontline of Regina Carter (violin) and Akua Dixon (cello), Turré produces perhaps his best CD yet, containing mainly original material, although one notable exception is "The Inflated Tear" by ex-employer Roland Kirk.

➤➤ **Don Grolnick** *(Nighttown)*; **Hilton Ruiz** *(Heroes)*; **Woody Shaw** *(The Moontrane; Imagination)*; **McCoy Tyner** *(The Turning Point)*.

Stanley Turrentine

Tenor saxophone.

b. Pittsburgh, Pennsylvania, 5 April 1934; d. 12 Sept 2000.

Stanley's father, Thomas Turrentine, played tenor with the Savoy Sultans in the late 1930s. Stanley began on cello and took up tenor at the age of eleven. He toured with Lowell Fulson in 1950–51, a period which included a recording with the band pianist Ray Charles, then worked with Tadd Dameron in 1952, and, alongside his trumpeter brother, Tommy Jnr (b. 22 April 1928; d. 13 May 1997), with Earl Bostic in 1953–4. After Stanley's three years in the army, the brothers played in the Max Roach quintet in 1959–60. During this period, the first albums under Stanley's own name were made, but he also had a recording partnership with Jimmy Smith, and toured with Shirley Scott, to whom he was married until 1971. Most of his albums in the 1970s were in a heavily arranged pop style, which met with great chart success, but really were quite poor. His reunion with Smith in 1982 and subsequent small-group recording reinforced his jazz credentials, while session work, for instance with vocalist Will Downing, continued to enhance his broad appeal. Turrentine's wide-open, bluesy sound and terse phrasing made him a natural in the role of the "Gene Ammons of the 1970s", but it is his underexposed jazz-playing which is deserving of wider attention. [BP]

Up At Minton's (1961; Blue Note). The legendary Harlem club was still a nightspot in the early 1960s when several live albums were made there. Turrentine is heard stretching out to good effect with Grant Green and the Horace Parlan trio on this two-CD set.

Dick Twardzik

Piano, composer.

b. Danvers, Massachusetts, 30 April 1931; d. 21 Oct 1955.

Twardzik worked in the Boston area, making recordings with Charlie Mariano and Serge Chaloff, with whose mother he first studied the piano. He toured with Lionel Hampton, then in the last months of his life with Chet Baker's quartet; he was in Paris with him when he died of a heroin overdose. As well as writing original material for Chaloff ("The Fable Of Mabel") and Baker, Twardzik recorded one set of piano pieces of a notably individual character. Twardzik's work is related to the Monk "school" of pianist/writers, but is also reminiscent of Jaki Byard, an influence from Boston; his minimal output deserves rediscovery. [BP]

➤➤ **Serge Chaloff** *(The Fable Of Mabel)*; **Russ Freeman** *(Trio)*.

Twenty-Ninth Street Saxophone Quartet

Arising initially from a meeting between baritone saxophonist Jim Hartog and alto player Ed Jackson at Boston's New England Conservatory, the Twenty-Ninth Street Saxophone Quartet took its definitive form with the addition of tenor player Rich Rothenberg in 1982 and the subsequent recruitment of alto saxophonist Bobby Watson, just prior to a tour of Europe. Taking their name from Hartog's address at the time of their first rehearsals, the quartet have always favoured a clean, stridently rhythmic approach, cleverly exploiting the skills and experience of each member (Watson's in hard bop as the Jazz Messengers's musical director; Jackson's in bluesy funk as a former member of the Fatback Band; Rothenberg's in Latin music; and Hartog's in Afro-Cuban bands) to produce an accessible but sophisticatedly eclectic sound which is intriguing on record but best experienced live. Watson describes their approach thus: "We play music that basically has a pulse, a peak and an ending ... we try to use what's inherent in the jazz rhythm even though the bass and drums aren't there. So we use walking bass-lines, waltzes, funk, and all the different modes and then approach it classically – by thinking in counter-point, in order to highlight each individual." Particularly popular on the European festival circuit, the quartet, having made half a dozen albums and established themselves as one of the most influential bands in what was, before their arrival, a relatively unexplored area of jazz, withdrew from the scene, saying goodbye with *Milano New York Bridge* (1993; Red), a collection mostly composed of standards, to remind listeners of their former glories. [CP]

⊙ **Live** (1988; Red). Recorded in Capolinea, a valiant if not entirely successful attempt to capture the quartet's vibrant live sound. Highlights include "The Originator", Wayne Shorter's "Night Dreamer" and Monk's "Pannonica".

⊙ **Underground** (1991; Antilles). Augmented by vocals, Hugh Masekela and a rhythm-section on a couple of tracks, another virtuosic, lively album packed with rhythmic and melodic felicities.

⊙ **Your Move** (1992; Antilles). Three compositions each from Rothenberg and Watson comprise the meat of this album; the quartet have their approach so well worked out now that, as Watson claims, there is no clear division apparent between predetermined structure and improvisation.

Charles Tyler

Baritone and alto saxophone.

b. Cadiz, Kentucky, 20 July 1941; d. 27 June 1992.

Charles Tyler learned piano as a child, taking up clarinet in college. After moving to Cleveland, he played in blues bands, then began to work with free-jazz saxophonist innovator Albert Ayler, whom Tyler had already met when he was 14. Tyler moved to New York to play with Ayler, and he appears on *Bells* and *Spirit's Rejoice* (both 1965; ESP). For the same label, he also made two 60s records as a leader, *Charles Tyler Ensemble* (1966) and *Eastern Man Alone* (1967). He then studied under cellist David Baker at Indiana University (1967-8). In 1969, Tyler moved to Los Angeles and taught for four years in California, before returning to New York and playing with many different ensembles and recording with many of his own groups for small labels: these records include *Voyage From Jericho* (1974; Akba); the particularly strong *Saga Of The Outlaws* (1976; Nessa); *Folk And Mystery Stories* (1980; Sonet); and two volumes of *Definite* (1981; Storyville). His outstanding, long-deleted solo baritone record *Sixty Minute Man* (1979; Adelphi) shows what a powerful personal voice he had on that unwieldy instrument. At the end of the 70s, Tyler's workload dwindled substantially, though he appeared on violinist Billy Bang's *Rainbow Gladiator* (1982; Soul Note) and released his own quartet date *Autumn In Paris* (1988; Silkheart). His largely unremarked-upon passing in his final home, France, in 1992. was at least marked by the band (drummer Dennis Charles, bassist Bernard Santacruz, guitarist Rémi Charmasson) with whom he was meant to make a festival appearance; and they released the grief-stricken set they played only three days after his death as *A Scream For Charles Tyler* (1992; Blue Regard) [JC]

⊙ **Charles Tyler Ensemble** (1966; ESP). Classic old free-jazz album, with Joel Friedman on cello, Henry Grimes on bass, Charles Moffett on orchestral vibes, and a very young Ronald (Shannon) Jackson on drums. Tyler plays alto exclusively here, and his sound reflects both Ayler and reported jam sessions with Ornette Coleman.

McCoy Tyner

Piano, composer.

b. Philadelphia, Pennsylvania, 11 Dec 1938.

Tyner's pianist mother encouraged him, but his main early influences were the famous Powell brothers – Bud and Richie – who were neighbours. At fifteen Tyner was leading his own teenage jazz group, and soon began gigging locally. (A devout Muslim, he took the Islamic name Sulaimon Saud round this time, but has always worked under his original name.) It was in Philadelphia that he first met John Coltrane, playing with him at the Red Rooster. In 1959 Tyner spent six months with the Jazztet, which was co-led by Art Farmer and Benny Golson. From 1960–65 he worked with the John Coltrane quartet, touring in the USA and worldwide and recording intensively. This was perhaps the most influential quartet in jazz history and Tyner played a major role in its artistic success. After leaving Coltrane he led his own trio in New York from 1966, but also worked with Ike and Tina Turner, Jimmy Witherspoon and others. He began recording for Blue Note, and his album *The Real McCoy*, with Joe Henderson, Ron Carter and Elvin Jones, is one of the most perfectly realized albums of the late 1960s.

McCoy Tyner

From 1972, when he signed with Milestone Records and his album *Sahara* was voted Record of the Year by the *Down Beat* critics, Tyner began to tour regularly with his group in the USA, Europe and Japan. For the most part he led a quartet, at first with Sonny Fortune and then Azar Lawrence on reeds, but in the later 1970s he augmented the group with violinist John Blake.

When Blue Note was relaunched in 1985, Tyner was filmed recording a solo piano album for a documentary about the label. Tyner has made more solo recordings for Blue Note since (such as 1991's *Soliloquy*) and continues to work with all-star groups (notably a superb duo with Bobby Hutcherson on *Manhattan Moods* in 1994 and a trio with Stanley Clark and Al Foster in 1999). He also has a regular trio, with Avery Sharpe (bass) and Aaron Scott (drums), and has been leading a big band, reviving some of his compositions from the 1970s.

Tyner's main influences, apart from the Powell brothers (Richie in particular), were Thelonious Monk and Art Tatum, but with the Coltrane quartet he rapidly established his own identity, developing one of the most original piano styles in jazz. Coltrane said of him: "He gets a very personal *sound* from his instrument and because of the clusters he uses and the way he voices them, that sound is brighter than what would normally be expected from most of the chord patterns he plays. In addition, McCoy has an exceptionally well developed sense of form both as a soloist and an accompanist. Invariably in our group, he will take a tune and build his own structure for it." In fact, Tyner has always played compositionally, with an overall view of the music and an unerring instinct for when to improvise uninhibitedly and when to play "within the rhythm-section" in support of a soloist. No matter how wild it gets, his music always "breathes" properly, creating and releasing tension in a way which communicates. He is one of the most dynamic pianists of all, with awesome power and speed, yet he rarely "goes free", preferring to play within tonalities and coherent rhythms which he pushes, with miraculous control, to their limits. He once said of the piano that "After a while it becomes an extension of yourself, and you and your instrument become one"; he has never used synths because his explorations have always been into lines and rhythms rather than texture for its own sake. Talking to J.E. Berendt, Tyner said that for him, all music is "a journey of the soul into new, uncharted territory" yet that, at the same time "all kinds of music are interconnected." Perhaps it is this – Tyner's contrary balance of perpetual curiosity and shrewd apperception – that make his music such an affirmation, an exultation in being alive. [IC]

⊙ **Inception**; **Nights Of Ballads And Blues** (1962; Impulse!). Two trio albums recorded when Tyner was half-way through his epochal five-year stint with Coltrane's group, and they are delightfully warm and optimistic sessions. The first is a mixture of standards and Tyner originals, and the second an album of ballads and blues, all done with the élan of someone on leave of absence.

⊙ **The Real McCoy** (1967; Blue Note). One of the most eloquent albums of the 1960s. The quartet has supreme melodist Joe Henderson on tenor sax, with the Ron Carter and Elvin Jones rhythm-section.

Sahara (1972; Milestone/OJC). Tyner recorded this poll-winning album with Sonny Fortune on saxophones and flute, bassist Calvin Hill and then-fashionable drummer Alphonse Mouzon. His often massive piano sound, complemented by the intensity of Fortune and Mouzon, creates irresistible impetus and fiery passion on a deservedly successful release, which transformed his career.

Enlightenment (1973; Milestone). This double CD was recorded at the Montreux festival with Tyner's quartet, which comprised Mouzon, bassist Joonie Booth and saxophonist Azar Lawrence – a working group functioning at the height of its executive and emotional power. The music has hypnotic intensity but is always utterly coherent. Coltrane's death and passion are not forgotten.

Uptown/Downtown (1988; Milestone). Tyner's big band album is remarkable – his arranging is assuredly in the jazz orchestral tradition and yet the music is completely Tyneresque. His "Passion Dance" sounds even more itself in this powerful version, and three other Tyner originals – including the mighty "Fly With The Wind" and an Ellington tribute, "In A Sentimental Mood" – cover a satisfyingly broad spectrum of music.

Revelations (1988; Blue Note). A much quieter spirituality pervades this solo piano recital at New York's Merkin Hall. Tyner's touch and pedal mastery conjure wonderful subtleties and sonorities in this performance, largely of standards.

Jazz Roots (2000; Telarc). Alone with the giants, Tyner pays full-bodied solo piano tribute to the godfathers of the keys and, as a giant himself, there's little sacrifice of the essential McCoy-ness of his own approach, which makes for a surprisingly well-balanced programme.

➤➤ **John Coltrane** *(My Favorite Things; Live At The Village Vanguard; A Love Supreme).*

U

James "Blood" Ulmer

Guitar, flute, vocals.

b. St Matthews, South Carolina, 2 Feb 1942.

Ulmer sang with a gospel group, the Southern Sons, from the age of seven until thirteen and played guitar from an early age. In 1959 he moved to Pittsburgh, freelancing professionally, and his outlook was broadened by local guitarist Chuck Edwards. From 1964–6 he worked extensively with organ funk groups. From 1967–71 he lived in Detroit where he studied, wrote music and practised regularly for four years with a group that included drums, bass, trombone and alto saxophone. In 1971 he went to New York, playing six nights a week for nine months at Minton's Playhouse. He played briefly with Art Blakey in 1973, and also worked with Paul Bley, Larry Young and Joe Henderson. He met Ornette Coleman and studied with him for a year, and in 1974 they performed at the Ann Arbor jazz and blues festival. In 1977 he played with Coleman's group at the Newport festival, and in 1978 recorded as a leader (*Tales Of Captain Black*) with Coleman as sideman. During the late 1970s he continued to tour with Coleman, playing at major festivals and visiting the UK and Europe. In 1979 and 1980 he also played on two of Arthur Blythe's albums. In 1980 he began working regularly with his own trio, making his first European tour in that year. Through the 80s he worked regularly with George Adams in his band, and toured and recorded with the Music Revelation Ensemble. Though his recordings from 1989 became rather more bland (perhaps the lack of commercial success has pushed him into simpler and more popular funk-based music) there was a distinct return to form in the late 1990s which continues to the present, largely manifest in a series of gritty blues albums.

JAK KILBY

James "Blood" Ulmer

Ulmer is not really an innovator or a revolutionary player, but he has his own distinctive sound and approach. In fact he comes out of the long-established tradition of electric blues-guitar playing with all its tonal distortions, its modally based improvisations and its pitch-bending, which is often so extreme as to imply non-tonality. Ulmer's music is often dissonant and always strongly rhythmic – a kind of abstract funk – and his real identity lies in the emotional climate he projects; playing with an often dry, choked sound, he conveys a claustrophobic feeling of pent-up emotion fighting for expression. [IC]

⊙ **Music Speaks Louder Than Words** (1997; Koch). After a disappointing period, Ulmer produced this striking, dramatic album of Ornette Coleman tunes featuring none other than Rashied Ali guesting on drums.

⊙ **Memphis Blood: The Sun Sessions** (2001; Label M). At the legendary Sun studios in Memphis and with Vernon Reid producing the guitarist on a series of old blues tunes by the likes of Willie Dixon, Sonny Boy Williamson and John Lee Hooker, Ulmer produces some characterful and affecting stuff, up there with the best of his career.

Umo Jazz Orchestra

The Finnish Radio Dance Orchestra was established in 1957, and in 1975 a group of musicians who had occasionally played with it founded the Umo Jazz Orchestra, because they felt it was time their country had a professional jazz big band. The Umo functioned as a part-time orchestra in Helsinki until 1984, when it was made full-time, with the help of the City of Helsinki, the Finnish Broadcasting Company and the Ministry of Education. Since then, it has been a backbone of Finnish jazz, with many of the country's finest jazz musicians honing their art in its ranks. The Umo was conducted from its founding until 1991 by the late Esko Linnavalli, and during his time the orchestra recorded *Umo Plays The Music Of Muhal Richard Abrams* (1988; Umo CD), an adventurous encounter with the avant-garde. The Umo has made successful tours in the USA, Canada, Italy and Germany, and courted the mainstream audience by touring Europe with vocalist Natalie Cole in 1994, and Manhattan Transfer in 1996. Many international jazz soloists, including Dizzy Gillespie and Kenny Wheeler, have worked with the orchestra over the years. In 1996, saxophonist and composer Eero Koivistoinen, who had graduated from the orchestra's saxophone section to being its conductor, was appointed its artistic director. Today the UMO is regarded as one of Europe's leading big bands, and has released over twenty albums. The latest batch, some listed below, are perhaps their most accessible to date. [IC]

⊙ **UMO Jazz Orchestra** (1997; Naxos). The musicianship, section work and writing are exemplary on this adventurous and attractive album. Jarmo Savolainen, one of Finland's leading pianists, contributes "Life Is A Cobra", a wonderfully asymmetrical piece that alternates 7/4, 5/4 and 4/4 in a most artistic and natural manner, while Eero Koivistoinen's two compositions, "What is This?" and "Cuckoo's Nest", show his orchestral virtuosity, and highlight the superb musicianship of the whole ensemble.

⊙ **Electrifying Miles** (1997; A Records); **Ellington Tribute** (1998; Finlandia); **Day Dreamin'** (1998; FSR). A trio of meticulous tribute albums showing the UMO's range, from late-period Miles Davis (with Tim Hagens as guest soloist) through the peppier side of Duke to the reflective side of Strayhorn.

⊙ **One More Time** (2000; Challenge). Kenny Wheeler excels as guest composer and soloist here; vocalist Norma Winstone delivers some charming things too on a suitably attractive and sonorous set.

United Jazz and Rock Ensemble

The UJRE was formed in 1975 in Stuttgart, West Germany, by Wolfgang Dauner, to be the resident band of a TV programme directed by Werner Schretzmeier, the aim of which was to promote social and political awareness among young people. In this programme he presented little-known, talented singer/songwriters as well as the band of leading jazz and rock musicians, hoping that such media exposure of two minority interests might bring them to a wider public. The programme became popular and the band rapidly gained a following. When it began touring and playing live concerts in January 1977, the personnel became fixed: Dauner (keyboards), Eberhard Weber (bass), Volker Kriegel (guitar), Jon Hiseman (drums), Albert Mangelsdorff (trombone), Charlie Mariano and Barbara Thompson (reeds and flutes), Ack Van Rooyen and Ian Carr (trumpets); Kenny Wheeler (trumpet) joined in 1979.

During the later 1970s and the 1980s, the UJRE toured widely in Germany and played major festivals all over Europe, including Sopot and Warsaw in Poland, the North Sea festival and Antibes. In 1984 it toured the UK and one reviewer wrote of "... that international ten-piece band which is so enjoyable to listen to that the serious [British] critics don't like it".

In 1977 Dauner, Kriegel, Mangelsdorff, Van Rooyen and Schretzmeier formed Mood Records to release albums by the band, and by the mid-1980s more than 150,000 had been sold. In the autumn of 1985 a boxed set of the band's six LPs became a best seller in West Germany. Writing in *Down Beat* in the later 1970s, J.E. Berendt called the UJRE "the most successful European band since Django Reinhardt". Mood Records, quite early on in its history, began recording German and other musicians who were not members of the UJRE and who had no other recording outlet. Mood also released a 1978 solo album by Larry Coryell, *Standing Ovation*. The UJRE did a twentieth-anniversary tour of 45 concerts in Germany, Austria and Switzerland in the period September 1994 to January 1995 and a final farewell tour in 2002. Some of the UJRE albums, all on Mood, are as follows: *Live im Schutzenhaus* (1977); *Teamwork* (1978); *The Break-Even Point* (1979); *Live In Berlin* (1981, double); *Opus Sechs* (1984); *Round Seven* (1987); *Na Endlich!* (1992); *Die Neunte Von United* (1996). [IC]

Phil Upchurch

Guitar, bass guitar.
b. Chicago, 19 July 1941.

Switching from ukelele to electric guitar at the age of thirteen, Upchurch gained his early experience playing guitar and electric bass on the R&B circuit in the Chicago area. Work with singer Dee Clark led to recording sessions with Dizzy Gillespie, Stan Getz, Ramsey Lewis, Groove Holmes, Woody Herman, Jimmy Smith, B.B. King, Grover Washington, Cannonball Adderley and the Crusaders. As house guitarist at the Chess label, he recorded with leading blues artists Muddy Waters, Howlin' Wolf and Otis Rush. In 1971 he relocated briefly to California and worked with Quincy Jones, who invited him to tour Japan the following year. A friend of guitarist George Benson since the early 1960s, Upchurch recorded and toured with him (1974–9), and played rhythm guitar on Benson's 1976 Grammy-winning album *Breezin'*. Since 1977 Upchurch has lived in Los Angeles, doing studio work and playing club dates. He worked with Ben Sidran in the 1990s, recording a pair of crossover solo albums for the singer's label (see below), though his 2001 album *Tell The Truth!* (Evidence) exhibited Upchurch perhaps at his most substantial and groovy. [CA]

⊙ **Whatever Happened To The Blues** (1997; Go Jazz). A commercial offering rather than a jazz album, with guests such as Pops Staples and Maceo Parker directing events firmly towards gospel/funk, but Upchurch's precise, pokey rhythm-guitar work and occasional bluesy solo drip with the easy professionalism that keep him in demand for studio assignments straddling jazz and blues.

Michal Urbaniak

Violin, lyricon, composer, soprano and tenor saxophones.
b. Warsaw, 22 Jan 1943.

Urbaniak studied at the Academy of Music in Warsaw. He worked with various Polish groups in the early 1960s, and in 1965 formed his own group which included singer Urszula Dudziak, whom he later married. They toured throughout Europe and Scandinavia during the 1960s. Between 1969–72 they played festivals in Warsaw, Molde (Norway) and in France and Italy. In 1971 he was given the Best Soloist award at the Montreux jazz festival and won a scholarship to the Berklee College of Music. He and Dudziak went to live in the USA in 1973. He formed a new jazz-rock group, Michal Urbaniak Fusion, which toured in the USA and recorded for Columbia. In 1993 he was featured with Barbara Thompson's international group Sans Frontières, which played a London concert and toured the UK, and in the mid-1990s he was leading Urbanator, a fusion group featuring Lenny White (drums), Al McDowell (bass guitar) and John Dryden (keyboards), though by the end of the decade was addressing bop standards with a more-or-less straight ahead rhythm section on *Some Other Blues* (Steeplechase) and *Ask Me Now* (Steeplechase).

Urbaniak plays a custom-made five-string violin and violin synthesizer, and also the lyricon – a saxophone-like wind instrument, the sound of which is treated through a synthesizer. Urbaniak's favourites include John Coltrane, Miles Davis, Zbigniew Namyslowski and Witold Lutoslawski, and he incorporates elements from Polish folk music into his music. Both he and his groups have won various European polls. [IC]

⊙ **Polish Jazz: Vol. 9 – Michal Urbaniak** (1971–3; Polskie Nagrania). This provides a fascinating glimpse into the Polish jazz scene. Urbaniak is playing saxophone at this time and pianist Adam Makowicz and Urszula Dudziak are also members of the sextet.

⊙ **Songbird** (1990; Steeplechase). Urbaniak gives a wholly absorbing performance of a set of his own originals, with pianist Kenny Barron, Peter Washington on bass and Kenny Washington on drums.

⊙ **Live In New York** (1991; L + R). An exploration of standards with a rhythm-section including Ron Carter and Lenny White; begins shakily but gets more rewarding as Urbaniak gets into his stride.

➤➤ **Larry Coryell** *(A Quiet Day In Spring).*

Warren Vaché Jnr

Cornet, flugelhorn.

b. Rahway, New Jersey, 21 Feb 1951.

A student of trumpeters Jim Fitzpatrick and Pee Wee Erwin (a close friend and adviser), Vaché took a degree in music and soon after was playing lead trumpet with Benny Goodman, as well as appearing with Vic Dickenson (at Eddie Condon's), Bob Wilber, his father's group, and as a soloist all over. His first album, *First Time Out* (1976), revealed a cornettist of perfect control, with a singer's vibrato, a mobility around the instrument that recalled Ruby Braff (who loved his work) and, most noticeably, a revolutionary ability to play in high registers at the lowest volume level. Emerging onto the American mainstream scene at a time when it looked like gently winding down for ever, Vaché quickly became a star, and it says much for his strength of character that his performance – under the scrutiny of a hungry but picky generation of mainstream listeners – never faltered once.

With Scott Hamilton he played festivals and toured Europe, then in the late 1970s signed a contract with promoter Carl Jefferson, which led to a string of albums and a regular job with Jefferson's Concord All Stars, who toured worldwide to massive receptions. In the 1980s he consolidated his reputation with more recording, commuting worldwide to jazz venues and festivals, and working clubs in New York and New Jersey with, among others, Bobby Rosengarden's band. Undaunted by an accident in 1984, in which the tendons of his right hand were cut (he played left-handed), Vaché started playing with George Wein's "new" Newport All-Stars, a relationship continued into the 1990s; in mid-decade he signed a new contract with Muse Records and produced an album, *Horn Of Plenty*, which presented him in new company and playing with his accustomed brilliance.

Warren is part of a talented jazz family. His father, the bassist Warren Vaché Snr, was active in the formation of the American Jazz Federation, is director of the New Jersey Jazz Society, leader of a well-respected classic jazz band (which for a long time featured Pee Wee Erwin, replaced after his death by trumpeter Chris Griffin), mastermind of the annual Pee Wee Russell Jazz Stomp, and has produced a wealth of written jazz history, including full-length biographies of Pee Wee and of Sylvester Ahola. Warren Jnr's brother Alan, a highly gifted swing-style clarinettist, works with Jim Cullum's jazz band and has recently branched out with solo touring and recording of his own. [DF]

⊙ **First Time Out** (1976; Audiophile). Vaché's superbly confident first outing; excellent quintet sides with Kenny Davern (including a joyous "Song Of The Wanderer"), plus duos with Bucky Pizzarelli.

⊙ **Midtown Jazz** (1982; Concord). Vaché enjoys playing in a duo or trio situation uncluttered by drums: this set, with John Bunch and Phil Flanigan, has his elegant versions of challenging tunes like "I'm Old Fashioned" plus the breakneck "Rhythm-A-Ning".

⊙ **Warm Evenings** (1989; Concord). Vaché's cornet here sails above Jack Gale's arrangements for the Beaux Arts string quartet with poise and unhurried musicality; this is one of very few jazz records using this format, and Vaché does it proud, especially on delightful creations like "Spike's Waltz" (surprisingly written by Spike Milligan, one of his heroes).

⊙ **Horn Of Plenty** (1994; Muse). Vaché's move to the Muse label brought new colleagues, including tenorist Houston Person, but Vaché plays as he always does – with superb assurance and melodic ingenuity.

⊙ **Warren Plays Warren** (1996; Nagel Heyer). A trumpet-cornet dream; Vaché and Randy Sandke swagger through a programme of Harry Warren's music with undauntable panache. Sandke is his usual flawless self, but Vaché has the edge for stylistic originality, and Kenny Drew Jnr (piano) is formidable too.

➤➤ **Brian Lemon** *(An Affair To Remember).*

Chucho Valdés

Piano, composer.

b. Quivicán, Cuba, 9 Oct 1941.

Jésus "Chucho" Valdés is the son of the famous Cuban pianist Ramón "Bebo" Valdés, whose band performed in the top Havana nightclubs of the pre-Castro era, and whose 1952 "Con Poco Coco" was the first descarga (or jam session) to be recorded in Cuba (for Norman Granz, on the Original *Mambo Kings* compilation, Verve). Chucho himself worked with his father before the latter's defection to Sweden, and then joined the jazz-influenced Orquesta Cubana de Música Moderna in 1967. This group, including trumpeter Arturo Sandoval and Paquito D'Rivera, turned into the famous band Irakere, for which Valdés became the leader and chief composer until the late 1990s. Although they gradually became more pop-oriented and less jazzy, especially after the loss of Sandoval and D'Rivera, Valdés's glittering piano work was always a focal point. Between

1996 and 2000 (coinciding with the Clinton presidency), he developed a solo career involving work in the US, including with the Lincoln Center Jazz Orchestra and Roy Hargrove's band Crisol, and unaccompanied recitals. His playing is aptly summed up as florid and leaning towards 19th-century European piano music, but is nevertheless full of typical Afro-Cuban rhythmic twists. In 2003 he has appeared again as a guest with Irakere, now directed by his son Luís Valdés. [BP]

⊙ **Fantasía Cubana** (2002; Blue Note). Recorded in New York, and with a piano and mike set-up appropriate for classical recitalists, Valdés improvises on Cuban classics and delivers his own rhythmic versions of repertoire by Chopin, Debussy and Ravel.

➤➤ **Irakere** *(La Collección Cubana).*

Kid Thomas Valentine

Trumpet.

b. Reserve, Louisiana, 3 Feb 1896; d. 16 June 1987.

Kid Thomas Valentine worked in the Hall Brothers' band in the early 1920s, then with Elton Theodore's band in Algiers, and from 1926 led his own band, the Algiers Stompers. In later years he was a regular colleague of George Lewis (they worked in one another's bands and recorded together), who said of Valentine: "Thomas just plays the chords, but he's up there all the time, or he's doing something underneath, even just one or two notes you know what he's doing. He has the right idea of this type of music." Valentine was still playing regularly at Preservation Hall, New Orleans, at well over eighty, his trumpet a mercurial mix of growls, note clusters and just plain sound. "You know what I tell 'em?" says Valentine in a film documentary, *Always For Pleasure*, "I tell 'em I'm a hundred! And I say, 'If I knew I was gonna live that long I'd have taken better care of myself!'" [DF]

⊙ **Kid Thomas Valentine And His Algiers Stompers** (1951; American Music). Excellent example of Valentine's highly original style – one of a fine series of American Music albums devoted to his work.

Ken Vandermark

Tenor saxophone, clarinet, bass clarinet.

b. Warwick, Rhode Island, 1964.

Raised in the suburbs of Boston, Vandermark grew up listening to jazz with his father, a fan and writer on the music; he played trumpet until he was sixteen, when he took up tenor saxophone, later adding bass clarinet and finally clarinet. While in college at McGill in Montreal, Vandermark formed his first group, Fourth Stream, which recorded a self-produced album, and back in Boston in the mid-80s he formed the Lombard Street Trio, for which he wrote original music. In 1989 he settled in Chicago, where he has been a major figure in the city's creative music renaissance. With the Vandermark Quartet, he played weekly for several years and recorded two records combining free-jazz energy with sectional compositions and heavy-rock elements, *Big Head Eddie* (1994; Platypus) and *Solid Action* (1994; Platypus). As part of the Steelwool Trio he wrote involved tunes for Lombard Street drummer Curt Newton and Kent Kessler, the superb bassist with whom he has worked continuously since the beginning of the decade; check out this group's *International Front* (1995; Okka Disk) and the Barrage Double Trio's *Utility Hitter* (1996; Quinnah), which adds bassist Nate McBride, multiple reed player Mars Williams and drummer Hamid Drake to Steelwool. Since Vandermark initiated a trio project, *Standards* (Quinnah) in 1995, he has worked steadily with Kessler and Drake in the free-improvising DKV Trio, one of the finest groups to emerge anywhere in this period; their records include *Baraka* (1997; Okka Disk), *DKV Live* (1997; Okka Disk) and an exciting joint session, *Fred Anderson/DKV Trio* (1997; Okka Disk), playing Anderson's compositons.

When legendary bandleader Hal Russell died in 1992, Vandermark took his chair in the NRG Ensemble, and he recorded and performed with the group until 1998; with NRG leader Williams he plays duets as Cinghiale. Outlandishly prolific and hard-working (playing four nights a week), he established the Vandermark 5 in 1996 as his main compositional outlet, exploring the integration of West Coast counterpoint, rock edge, free action and an original approach to arrangement. The group's recordings include *Single Piece Flow* (1997; Atavistic), *Target Or Flag* (1998; Atavistic), and two live discs for Savage Sound Syndicate, *Burn The Incline* (1999; Atavistic) and *Acoustic Machine* (2001; Atavistic). He's also recorded *Straight Lines* (Atavistic; 1999) with his group the Joe Harriott Project in tribute to the Jamaican sax pioneer, *Transatlantic Bridge* (2001; Okkadisk), a nonet album and two albums with his avant-pop outfit, *Spaceways Incorporated; Thirteen Cosmic Standards By Sun Ra And George Clinton* (2001; Atavistic) and *Version Soul* (2002; Atavistic). He has also been heard with Mats Gustafsson (in the groups FJF and AALY Trio), Peter Brötzmann, Joe Morris, Misha Mengelberg, the soul group the Crown Royals, and with various rock bands. [JC]

⊙ **Simpatico** (1999; Atavistic). Perhaps the best release from the Vandermark 5, featuring two reeds of the leader and Dave Rempis, Jeb Bishop on trombone and electric guitar, Kessler on bass and versatile drummer Tim Mulvenna. Aggressive, propulsive post-chord changes jazz, innovative structural ideas, frames for open improvising, swaggering funk lines, refractions through a hard-hitting post-punk lens.

George Van Eps

Guitar.

b. Plainfield, New Jersey, 7 Aug 1913; d. 29 Nov 1998.

Though he never achieved the mass reputation of an Eddie Lang or a Django Reinhardt, George Van Eps has unobtrusively become accepted as a real master, whose gently chorded acoustic guitar is a guarantee of rare beauty. His father, Fred Van Eps, was a well-known banjo virtuoso who recorded often, and – like other guitar players in his style – George studied banjo too before applying the techniques he had learned to the guitar; his teacher later was Carl Kress. After early touring with another great banjo player, Harry Reser, then with the Dutch Master Minstrels, he worked with leaders including Smith Ballew, Freddy Martin, Benny Goodman and Ray Noble before taking up full-time studio work (he rejoined Noble 1940–41). On his later solo work Van Eps introduced the most telling of his many inventions: a seventh bass string on which – by reconceived fingering patterns – he could play his own bass-line to accompany the elegantly chordal solos he played above them. A regular associate of Paul Weston in the 1940s and 1950s, he was featured on albums by Matty Matlock, Dick Cathcart and others, and was staffman all through Cathcart's *Pete Kelly's Blues* successes. In the 1960s and 1970s the old master combined playing the guitar with time devoted to his second love – inventing – and despite occasional bouts of illness was still to be heard live. In 1986 he visited Britain to play the Soho jazz festival and tour nationally, sometimes appearing with clarinettist Peanuts Hucko, and in the later 1980s continued regular appearances with Dick Cathcart's *Pete Kelly* reunions. In 1991 he appeared on record with follower Howard Alden (the first of several collaborations), and continued working (including a 1993 tour with cornettist Ed Polcer saluting Eddie Condon) until very shortly before his death. [DF]

George Van Eps and Howard Alden

⊙ **Hand-Crafted Swing** (1992; Concord). As Stan Dunn of KJAZ San Francisco says on the sleeve, this is "a jazz guitar master-class".

Vanguard Jazz Orchestra

Continuing a tradition of nearly 40 years, the Orchestra is descended from the Thad Jones-Mel Lewis band (1965–78), which became the Mel Lewis band until his death (1990) and then gained its current name in the early 90s. Many generations of band-members and outsiders have written arrangements for its repertoire, but the most significant contributors have been Thad Jones, Bob Brookmeyer and Jim McNeely. [BP]

Fred Van Hove

Piano, accordion, church organ.

b. Antwerp, Belgium, 19 Feb 1937.

Fred Van Hove studied piano, theory and harmony at the Music Academy in Belgium. He played jazz and some commercial dance music before starting to play freely improvised music in the mid-60s, at which point he was one of the most important figures of the emergent music in Europe. In 1966, he began a long-lived creative relationship with German saxophonist Peter Brötzmann, playing on the epochal *Machine Gun* (1968; FMP) octet recordings and the equally seminal LP *Nipples* (1969; Calig), then becoming a permanent member of the important trio with Brötzmann and Dutch drummer Han Bennink; this group lasted for some six years, and toured and recorded extensively for the FMP label. In 1968, his piece *Requiem For Che Guevera* was recorded at the Berlin jazz festival and it was subsequently released as half of an MPS LP. Van Hove began performing solo in 1970, and he has recorded alone a number of times (including two stunning Vogel records, eventually reissued as a single CD on Atavistic), both on piano and on church organ; needless to say, he is one of the very few free-improvisers to perform on the latter. He has worked with virtually every major improviser in Europe, and many Americans and Japanese, often in small-group or duo settings.

In the 1980s, Van Hove began playing and recording with different ensembles with shifting personnel, working under the names MLA (Musica Libera Antverpiae) and MLB (Musica Libera Belgicae). Members have included trumpeter Marc Charig, trombonists Radu Malfatti and Paul Rutherford, violinist Phil Wachsmann, percussionist Günter "Baby" Sommer. The MLB III trio with André Goudbeek on saxophone and longterm partner Ivo Vander Borght on percussion recorded a self-titled LP (1988; BVHAAST). He has also been very active in recent years in trio combination with French vocalist Annick Nozati and German trombonist Johannes Bauer; their disc *Organo Pleno* (1992; FMP) is deserving of anyone's attention. In 1991, Van Hove formed a larger ensemble called 't Nonet, whose outing *Suite For B … City* (1996; FMP) gives a clear sense of his compositional interests, as well as some terrific free playing from trumpeter Axel Dörner and saxophonists Goudbeek and John Butcher.

Van Hove is a tremendous technician and a very powerful musical intellect; he has some of the quickest digits in free music and effortlessly engages in blazing contrapuntal line-swapping with duo partners. While he is one of the oldest elder-statesmen in improvised music, he is also possessed of unsurpassed stamina, so much that his solo performances can be a workout for listeners as well. On top of that, he's a fantastically responsive player and can be one of the most sensitive, delicate pianists in free music. Not the best-known, but one of the all-time best. [JC]

⊙ **Passing Waves** (1998; Nuscope). There are two possible ports of entry into the solo work of Fred Van Hove – this smorgasbord of shorter tracks and more emphasis on variety, or the full-on disc-long track intensity of *Flux* (1998; Potlatch), both of which mark a return to prolific recording that is most welcome.

Ack Van Rooyen

Trumpet, flugelhorn.

b. The Hague, Holland, 1 Jan 1930.

At sixteen Van Rooyen did his first tour with a big band, entertaining troops in Indonesia. After graduating cum laude from The Hague Conservatory in 1949, he was with the Arnhem Symphony Orchestra from 1950–52, and during military service he played with the air force band. Between 1953–6 he toured with various orchestras in Germany, Denmark, Sweden and Belgium, and recorded with Lars Gullin, as well as doing studio work in Hilversum. He lived in France from 1957–9, working in Paris with Kenny Clarke, Lucky Thompson and Barney Wilen. From 1960–66 he lived in West Berlin, joining the SFB Big Band, working in a sextet with Herb Geller, Jerry Van Rooyen and Cees See. He also worked in jazz workshops with Friedrich Gulda, Hans Koller and Ake Persson. He lived in Stuttgart from 1967–78, becoming a regular member of the Erwin Lehn orchestra, Peter Herbolzheimer's Rhythm Combination and Brass, and Wolfgang Dauner's Radio Jazz Group. He did a South American tour with the German All Stars in 1968, and a tour of Asia with them in 1972. In 1975 he was a founder member of the United Jazz and Rock Ensemble. In 1977, with Albert Mangelsdorff, Wolfgang Dauner and Volker Kriegel, he was co-founder of Mood Records. In 1979 he toured with Clark Terry, Gil Evans, Lee Konitz and others, taught at the Musikhochschule in Stuttgart and Mannheim, and took seminars at Remscheid Academy. In 1980 he moved back to Holland where he freelances, leads his own groups and plays with the Skymasters, the Netherlands Concert Jazzband and in duo with pianist Joerg Reiter; he also teaches at The Hague Conservatory and at Hilversum Muzieklyceum. He toured and recorded every year with the UJRE until their 2002 farewell, and has performed at the North Sea jazz festival with Shelly Manne, Dizzy Gillespie and his own groups; he also did a TV show with Gil Evans and Louie Bellson. In 1991 he played in the huge orchestra under the direction of Quincy Jones which accompanied Miles Davis in the performance of his famous Gil Evans arrangements.

Van Rooyen's favourite trumpet players are Clifford Brown, Kenny Dorham, Don Cherry, Tom Harrell and Miles Davis, and other inspirations are Gil Evans, John Coltrane and Bob Brookmeyer. One of the most lyrical soloists, he plays with extraordinary fluidity and flexibility, producing immensely long lines and bubbling streams of triplets. He is all quicksilver and wit, and his solos seem as natural as birdsong. [IC]

Ack van Rooyen

⊙ **Homeward** (1982; Mood). A contemporary hard-bop outing, with Van Rooyen's flugelhorn fluidly incisive with a septet comprising tenor saxophone, trombone, piano, guitar, electric bass and drums. Three of the pieces are by his brother Jerry, two by the band's guitarist Eef Albers, the title track is by Van Rooyen and they also play John Carisi's "Israel" – with Miles Davis's original solo orchestrated and harmonized.

Van Rooyen and Joerg Reiter

⊙ **Music For Piano And Flugelhorn** (1991; Mood). A live performance of three compositions by Reiter, two by Van Rooyen, a couple of standards and Richie Beirach's brightly mournful Spanish tune "Leaving". There's plenty of interplay between Reiter's eloquent piano and Van Rooyen's flugel – working within recognizable ballad and song structures, Van Rooyen comes up with twists of phrase that are all his own.

Van Rooyen and the Metropole Orchestra

⊙ **Colores** (1994; Koala). The Metropole Orchestra has strings, harp, woodwinds, reeds, brass and a six-piece rhythm-section, for which Jerry van Rooyen has arranged some well-known and lesser-known standards ("Django", "The Touch Of Your Lips") and some originals. Ack van Rooyen is the only soloist, and despite this intense exposure is wonderfully sure-footed and unfailingly creative throughout.

➤➤ **Eberhard Weber** *(The Colours of Chloe).*

Jasper Van't Hof

Piano, electric piano, organ, synthesizers, computer.
b. Enschede, Holland, 30 June 1947.

Van't Hof's father was a jazz trumpeter, his mother a classical singer. He had private classical piano lessons for six years, then spent one week studying the piano with Wolfgang Dauner at the Jazzklinik in Remscheid. In 1969 he was a founder member of Association PC, with Pierre Courbois (drums), Toto Blanke (guitar) and Siggi Busch (bass). In 1973 he started his own band Pork Pie, with Philip Catherine, Charlie Mariano, Aldo Romano and J.-F. Jenny-Clark, which lasted some three years, during which time they worked extensively in Europe and made two albums. This was the beginning of his long association with Charlie Mariano, which was still bearing fruit in the late 1980s. Van't Hof has also worked with many other leading musicians such as Jean-Luc Ponty, Stu Martin, Archie Shepp, Alphonse Mouzon, Zbigniew Seifert and Manfred Schoof. Since 1977 he has continued leading various bands of his own: Eyeball, which included Didier Lockwood on violin; Pili-Pili, which comprised African percussion and computer, and several quartets with John Marshall, Bo Stief, or Aldo Romano and J.-F. Jenny-Clark. Since 1978 he has been voted first in jazz polls in the USA and Europe. In 1993 he played in Barbara Thompson's Sans Frontières band, which toured the UK. He has made records with Ernie Watts (*Face To Face*, 1998; Canosa) and Charlie Mariano/Steve Swallow (*Tempo Brutto*, 2001; Intuition); however it may be that the essence of his artistry is best gleaned in his solo recitals (see below). His influences are John Coltrane, Art Blakey, Elvin Jones and Charlie Mariano, and his favourite pianists are Chick Corea, McCoy Tyner, the classical pianist Michelangeli and Irene Schweizer. Van't Hof is an original stylist with an exhilarating speed of thought and execution and a complete mastery of both acoustic piano and electronics. He is also a prolific composer. [IC]

⊙ **Solo Piano** (1987; Timeless). Despite his suave touch and sophisticated harmonic sense Van't Hof is an unpredictable maverick, full of lightning strikes, and the wild creativity that lurks just beneath the surface gives this music its dangerous life.

Un Mondo Illusorio (1998; Challenge). Ditto on this eleven years later. A remarkable solo organ recital; intense, witty and beautifully recorded in a church in Italy.

>> **Philip Catherine** *(Sleep My Love).*

Tom Varner

French horn, composer.

b. New Jersey, 17 June 1957.

After learning the piano from the age of ten, Varner was already playing French horn in school when he turned to jazz at sixteen, and at seventeen he discovered Julius Watkins, his favourite on the instrument. He has a BMus degree from the New England Conservatory, studying from 1977–9 with George Russell, Jaki Byard and Ran Blake, and privately with Dave Liebman and Watkins. He started a quartet in Boston in 1978 including Ed Jackson (of the Twenty-Ninth Street Saxophone Quartet), playing Monk and Coleman pieces and his own compositions. Since moving to New York in 1979, he has led his own groups, including such musicians as Bobby Previte and Lee Konitz (also a favourite), and worked under the leadership of players as varied as Liebman, Bobby Watson, George Gruntz, John Zorn and Steve Lacy, another key inspiration. In addition to admiring soloists such as the above-mentioned and Rollins and Coltrane, Varner is interested in Berg and Webern and the compositional aspects of developing jazz, and his writing is as impressive as his excellent playing. [BP]

Tom Varner

The Mystery Of Compassion (1993; Soul Note). Working with a basic group of himself, bassist Mike Richmond and drummer Tom Rainey, Varner occasionally adds extra brass and evokes the spirit of Mingus along with earlier jazz, in extended original compositions. The violin solo by Mark Feldman on one track, as well as several other moments, pay tribute to Varner's organizational talent.

East Down Septet

Out Of Gridlock (1994; Hep). An excellent example of more straightahead work, with a group containing Rich Rothenberg and Jim Hartog of the Twenty-Ninth Street Saxophone Quartet. The comparison made in the notes with Bob Brookmeyer's playing is relevant, and Varner honours the memory of Julius Watkins with punchy solos on "Three Views Of A Secret" and others.

John Varro

Piano.

b. NewYork, 11 Jan 1930.

Varro began piano at ten, and after discovering jazz at the Commodore Music Shop started playing at jam sessions organized by Jack Crystal (Billy Crystal's father) on New York's lower East Side, sitting in for Joe Sullivan, Willie "The Lion" Smith and others. He then worked for Bobby Hackett's quartet, and at Nick's, from 1954, with Phil Napoleon and Pee Wee Erwin. From 1957 he was intermission pianist at Eddie Condon's, later joining Condon full-time. Between work with Condon he also worked New York jazz rooms including the Embers, Roundtable, Condon's Uptown and the Metropole. From 1965 Varro moved to Miami Beach, working on Jackie Gleason's show and with Flip Phillips, Billy Butterfield and Phil Napoleon, as well as touring with the Dukes of Dixieland, before moving to the West Coast in 1979. After fourteen years in Los Angeles he returned to Florida, and currently plays jazz festivals and parties, as well as touring worldwide, including the LA Classic, Sacramento, Atlanta, San Diego and many more. Since 1986 Varro has toured Europe regularly (with Peanuts Hucko and Wild Bill Davison) and also leads his successful Swing Seven; recently he has recorded prolifically for Arbors and Nagel Heyer, as well as with Napoleon, Erwin and Condon. A pianist of enormous skill, who grew up amid the premier figures of Dixieland-to-swing, Varro is their equal, and his level of expertise is at last being recognized internationally. [DF]

Say Yes (1996; Arbors). Varro's timeless and elegant style captured in a solo recital encompassing fine standards ("You're A Lucky Guy"), jazz piano classics ("Echo Of Spring"), and compositions by Tadd Dameron and John Lewis.

Nana Vasconcelos

Latin percussion, vocals.

b. Recife, Brazil, 2 Aug 1944.

Son of a professional guitarist, Vasconcelos started with his father's band at the age of twelve, playing bongos and maracas. He eventually graduated to a drumkit, playing bossa nova, and in the mid-1960s moved to Rio de Janeiro and worked with the singer

Jak Kilby

Nana Vasconcelos on berimbau

Milton Nascimento. He began to make a big reputation because he was at home with asymmetrical rhythms such as 7/4 and 5/4 which were common in north Brazil, whereas in Rio everything was in 6/8 and 4/4. He learned to play the berimbau, a Brazilian folk instrument which has been described as "resembling an archer's bow stuck on to Edam cheese", the "cheese" being a gourd acting as a sounding box. In 1971 Gato Barbieri brought him to the USA; he played in New York, and then toured Europe with Barbieri. At the end of the tour he stayed in Paris for two years, recording, playing and working intensively with handicapped children, an area of work to which he remains committed. During that period he occasionally played with Don Cherry in Sweden, and also recorded with Egberto Gismonti for ECM (see below). In 1976 he returned to New York. Since then he has toured Europe with Gismonti, played and recorded with Pat Metheny, and with Codona, a cooperative trio consisting of himself with the late Collin Walcott and Don Cherry, and which represents the most regular working association of his career. Among his many activities in the 1980s and 1990s, Vasconcelos was a member of Don Cherry's Nu and recorded with Eliane Elias and Pat Metheny among many others. He also toured and recorded with Jan Garbarek and worked with Arild Anderson, Andy Sheppard and French pianist Jean-Marie Machado as well as leading his own group Bush Dance. In June 1995, he performed in duo with Scottish percussionist Evelyn Glennie at the Bath international music festival. He has composed film soundtracks - highlights of which were gathered in the release *Fragments: Modern Tradition* (1997; Tzadik) – and is often called on to provide some Brazilian "colour" to other people's recordings, e.g. Paul Simon's *Rhythm Of The Saints* (1990; Warners). **[IC]**

⊙ **Saudades** (1979; ECM); **Lester** (1985; Soul Note). Vasconcelos has done much of his best work with fellow Brazilian Egberto Gismonti, who guests on *Saudades*. However, the concept of this album, with its European string writing, and premeditated overdubs by Vasconcelos, is ill-suited to the star's spontaneity and natural musical sense – these are served much better on *Lester*, where Vasconcelos is in duo with guitarist/accordionist/vocalist Antonello Salis, who does not get in his way.

➤➤ **Don Cherry** *(Multi Kulti)*; **Collin Walcott** *(Codona)*.

Sarah Vaughan

Vocals; also piano.

b. Newark, New Jersey, 27 March 1924; d. 3 April 1990.

As a child Vaughan sang in church and studied the piano. After winning an amateur contest at Harlem's Apollo Theater, she joined Earl Hines's band in 1943–4 as vocalist and second pianist. When Hines's colleague Billy Eckstine formed his big band, she became a founder member in 1944–5, and began recording under her own name. Like Eckstine, she had many romantic hit records in the late 1940s and 1950s, which gradually brought a large middle-of-

HERMAN LEONARD

Sarah Vaughan

the-road audience and, at least on disc, accompaniments to match. At her usual public appearances, however, she was backed by piano, bass and drums (including players such as Roy Haynes and Jimmy Cobb), only occasionally augmented by larger bands including, from the 1970s, symphony orchestras.

In terms of vocal equipment and flexibility Vaughan was one of the most gifted of all jazz-associated singers. As Betty Carter once observed, "With training she could have gone as far as Leontyne Price ... But I'm glad she didn't, because otherwise we would have lost what she is now." Her comparatively rare scatting was rhythmically freer in conception than Ella Fitzgerald's and more effortless in execution, an excellent example being her improvisation "Shulie A Bop", based on "Summertime". This rhythmic ease, in fact, underlay everything she did, just as the harmonic ear she acquired from playing the piano enabled her to incorporate the added notes of bebop chords in her melodic lines. And she had a range of tone which changed (sometimes almost too abruptly) from a throaty "hot" sound to a Europeanized head-tone, and the vowels that go with it. All this made a fantastic medium for interpreting songs with an original style which clearly extended the influence of jazz on popular music in general. **[BP]**

⊙ **In Hi-Fi (1949-53; Columbia).** Augmented by alternate takes which afford new glimpses of early Miles Davis, this is Vaughan given her head on several all-star small-group numbers, alongside more conventional arrangements aiming at the pop market of the day.

⊙ **Swingin' Easy** (1954–7; Emarcy). The first, and still perhaps best, album done with her regular accompanying trios, this has the famous "Shulie A Bop" and a "Lover Man" which has been much copied, for instance by Oleta Adams.

⊙ **After Hours** (1961; Roulette). A deservedly famous session with just George Duvivier and Mundell Lowe.

Definitive versions of "My Favourite Things" and "In A Sentimental Mood" are only some of the delights.

⊙ **Crazy And Mixed Up** (1982; Pablo). One late success among a string of them, this has quartet backing led by Roland Hanna, who contributes his own ballad "Seasons". Two songs by Ivan Lins are balanced by extremely well-worn, but burnished-like-new, standards.

Reginald Veal

Bass.

b. Chicago, Illinois, 5 Nov 1963.

Having grown up playing and singing church music with his father, Reginald Veal plays trombone, piano and drums as well as his main instrument, bass. Known by his most celebrated employer, Wynton Marsalis, as "Swing Doom" ("swing for the feeling, doom for the sound"), Veal is famous for preferring to play without an amplifier. He cut his teeth in New Orleans by playing regular weekend gigs with Ellis Marsalis and drummer Noel Kendrick at Tyler's Beer Gardens, but rose to prominence in the jazz world through his association with Ellis's sons, Branford and Wynton, in whose various bands he has been a regular over the years. Wynton says of him: "He has a great pulse, loves to groove, and plays with intelligence. His lines are well heard, logical and melodic." Veal has lent this cultured sound to the music of New Orleans trumpeters Leroy Jones and Nicholas Payton, UK pianist Julian Joseph, Japanese pianist Junko Onishi, Peter Martin, Eric Reed and Marcus Roberts, the Lincoln Center Jazz Orchestra, saxophonist Gregory Tardy and recently, singer Dianne Reeves. [CP]

Wynton Marsalis

⊙ **In This House On This Morning** (1994; Columbia). Septet recording of sweetly swinging Marsalis music, imbued with gospelly feel and driven impeccably by the rhythm team of Veal and his most sympathetic section mate, Herlin Riley.

Charlie Ventura

Tenor and baritone saxophones.

b. Philadelphia, Pennsylvania, 2 Dec 1916; d. 17 Jan 1992.

After gigging locally and jamming with visiting notables, Ventura joined the Gene Krupa band in 1942–3, rejoining from 1944–6 and in 1952. He formed his own big band in 1946–7, re-forming it for 1949–51, and in between led a septet with Kai Winding and then Bennie Green, and in 1951 a quartet with Buddy Rich. He managed a nightclub in the early 1950s, and then continued playing either under his own name or reuniting with Krupa. He was still active in the 1980s. Ventura attained popularity during his first stay with Krupa, thanks to a touch of vulgarity that roughened up his initial Chu Berry-style approach. His late 1940s septet, partly inspired by the early R&B of Illinois Jacquet and others, was billed with some justification as "Bop for the People", but stylistically he was the odd man out in his own group. [BP]

⊙ **Gene Norman Presents A Charlie Ventura Concert** (1949; MCA). A once much loved live album featuring Ventura's septet with Bennie Green, trumpeter Conte Candoli and the bop-vocal duo of Jackie Cain and Roy Kral. Their contributions to "East Of Suez" and "I'm Forever Blowing Bubbles" stand up better perhaps than Ventura's Krupathon on "How High The Moon".

Joe Venuti

Violin.

b. Philadelphia, Pennsylvania, 16 Sept 1903; d. 14 Aug 1978.

There are so many outrageous stories about Joe (Giuseppe) Venuti – pouring flour down the tuba during filming of Paul Whiteman's *King Of Jazz*, eating Whiteman's violin, playing stark naked at a brothel in Philadelphia, pouring liquid Jello into a sleeping Bix Beiderbecke's bath, arranging a plate of salad round his penis to serve at Mildred Bailey's supper party – that simply summarizing his life might seem an anti-climax. Encouragingly, even the story of Venuti's birth (whichever one he told) was usually larger than life: he was born, he said, onboard ship as his parents emigrated from Italy to the USA. He grew up in Philadelphia, a boyhood friend of Eddie Lang, and by 1924 was directing Jean Goldkette's Book-Cadillac orchestra (with Lang); from September 1926 they made a string of recordings (together and apart) co-starring Arthur Schutt, Adrian Rollini, Lennie Hayton, Don Murray and others, and (together and apart) worked for every important white leader of the period, from Red McKenzie to Roger Wolfe Kahn, as well as co-leading bands of their own. In 1929 Venuti joined Paul Whiteman (just in time for the *King Of Jazz*) and stayed a year; after that came four years of session work, including in 1933 the "Blue Four" sessions which produced such classics as "Raggin' The Scale", "Hey Young Fella" and "Satan's Holiday".

In 1935, after a trip to Europe with guitarist Frank Victor, Venuti formed his own big band, which featured at various times the young Barrett Deems (drums) and vocalist Kay Starr: only two sides were

ever recorded, and the band was finally disbanded (after several trial runs) when Venuti was called up. When he had extricated himself from the army, the "Mad Fiddler from Philly" (as he became known) returned to the studios, and by the 1950s was regularly on radio with Bing Crosby's General Electric-sponsored show. By the early 1960s, however, he was an alcoholic, playing music lounges and recording not at all (his only records in the previous decade had been for a Whiteman reunion).

The 1967 Dick Gibson Jazz Party, at which he guested, restored public interest in Venuti; producer Hank O'Neal followed up with albums and Venuti – by this time "a great, squat, square, bustling haystack of a man with a trombone of a voice and a huge Roman head" (Whitney Balliett's definitive description) – was a star for life. He played the 1968 Newport festival, London's Jazz Expo in 1969, and for the next eight years – despite cancer, discovered in 1970 – led quartets at top New York venues such as the Roosevelt Grill and Michael's Pub, worked as guest of honour with the New York Jazz Repertory Company, and recorded with his own quartet and co-stars such as Zoot Sims. Though warned to take things easy, he continued his punishing round until August 1978: the arch-joker of jazz violin died the day he was rebooked at Chicago's Holiday Inn. [DF]

⊙ **Joe Venuti And Eddie Lang Vols. 1 & 2** (1926–31; JSP). The master of swing violin with his greatest partner; fine remasterings, required listening.

⊙ **Wild Cats** (1926–33; ASV). Enjoyable twenty-five track selection of Venuti and Lang together – and apart – but including several of their best sides ("Kickin' The Cat", "Beatin' The Dog"), as well as titles by the Venuti-Lang Blue Five (1933) and Venuti–Lang All Star Orchestra (four classic titles including "Beale Street Blues" and "Farewell Blues" from 1931 feature Teagarden and Goodman).

⊙ **Violin Jazz** (1927–34; Yazoo). Another excellent set, including titles with Trumbauer, Dorsey and Rollini.

⊙ **Joe Venuti And Zoot Sims** (1974–5; Chiaroscuro). One of the more surprising – but nevertheless successful – partnerships of 1970s jazz. Sims's unruffled perfection is a fine contrast with Venuti's constant audaciousness, and the two of them are obviously enjoying each other's company.

⊙ **Alone At The Palace** (1977; Chiaroscuro). Dave McKenna is one of jazz's greatest pianists and (like Dick Hyman) is one of the relatively few who can operate entirely successfully without bass and drums. Venuti loves his company, and sounds as fresh as ever despite the years.

➤➤ **Benny Goodman** *(BG & Big Tea In NYC).*

Ronnie Verrell

Drums.

b. Rochester, Kent, 21 Feb 1926; d. 22 Feb 2002.

Generally regarded as one of Britain's greatest and most powerful drummers (Buddy Rich, who duelled with him on a famous edition of *The Muppet Show*, once said of him "who needs me when you've got Ronnie?"), Verrell was largely self-taught and first worked around Kent with Claude Giddins (1943, 1945–6), later moving to London to work with Cyril Stapleton (1949–51), and the Ted Heath Orchestra (1951–64), with whom he established his premier star-status. Thereafter he was a prolific session player, spending a decade with Jack Parnell's ATV Orchestra. He continued session work throughout the 80s and 90s while also working with Syd Lawrence's Orchestra (1981–2000), Dave Shepherd's Quintet, the Pizza Express All Stars, and his own quintet. In 2000 he replaced Jack Parnell in the Best Of British Jazz ensemble and played with the group until shortly before his death following a fall. [DF]

Edward Vesala

Drums, percussion, multi-instrumentalist, composer.

b. Mantyharju, Finland, 15 Feb 1945; d. Finland, 4 Dec 1999.

Vesala grew up in the remote forests and lakes of Finland where the only available live music was the Nordic tango played in nearby village dance halls. He started on drums at the age of twenty and, after playing for country dances, worked his way through psychedelic rock and free jazz, then spent two years (1972–4) studying at Helsinki's Sibelius Academy, before dropping out to continue his studies in the outside world as a musician and composer. He travelled around Asia in the early 1970s, collecting instruments and absorbing local music in India, Bali and Java, and in 1972 formed a cooperative trio (Triptykon) with Jan Garbarek and bassist Arild Andersen, which brought him some national and international recognition – he was voted Finnish Jazz Musician of the Year in 1972. In 1975 he became co-leader of the Tomasz Stanko-Edward Vesala quartet, one of the most adventurous small groups of that era, and spent most of the rest of the decade on the road as an itinerant jazzman. When not working with the quartet, Vesala accompanied many American musicians, including Paul Bley, Chick Corea, Archie Shepp, Roswell Rudd and Gary Burton.

In June 1980 he and Stanko went to New York to record the album *Heavy Life*, with Chico Freeman, J.D. Parran and James Spaulding on saxophones, Bob Stewart and Joe Daley on tubas and Reggie Workman on bass. In the early 1980s he had intense periods of composing music for all kinds of instrumental combinations, much of which has not yet been recorded. From 1984–6 he conducted clinics and workshops and, for one year, a nine-to-five school to which young players of all levels of ability came to learn his approaches to music-making. After his year at the school, Vesala continued to teach the best students privately and his ensemble, Sound And Fury, was formed from this pool of musicians. This group has developed into one of the outstanding European ensembles, highly disciplined and sharing the leader's vision.

Vesala always contended that the most potent music is rooted in life as it is lived, with all its complexity and gradations of emotion. His own music is shot through with powerful feeling and the sense of his own Finnish heritage, and he was a highly original composer with a palette that included harp, woodwinds, accordion and percussion as well as the more familiar jazz instruments. He wrote impressionist pieces of great beauty, with shimmering woodwinds, soft colours and chords, redolent of Finnish summer landscapes. But his vision could also be internalized and bleak with harsher sounds and dissonance, either with bustling drum rhythm, or with no regular pulse so that the ensemble seems to buck and heave like a wild thing. Vesala and Sound And Fury toured the UK for the Arts Council's Contemporary Music Network in November 1993. He recorded for ECM, but also had his own record label, Leo (not to be confused with the London-based Leo Records). His sudden death in 1999 aged 54 robbed European jazz of a vital and unique musical spirit. [IC]

⊙ **Lumi (1986; ECM).** All of Vesala's currently available output is highly impressive, perfectly integrating improvisation with composition, full of evocative melodies, serious without solemnity. *Lumi* is perhaps the most outstanding in the completeness of its vision and execution – the "long dark nights of the soul" are leavened here by humour and playfulness.

⊙ **Ode To The Death Of Jazz (1989; ECM).** *Ode To The Death Of Jazz* is based on repetitive tango rhythms – echoes from his Nordic youth – and is partly inspired by Vesala's anger at the nostalgic and revivalist mood of much current jazz.

⊙ **Invisible Storm (1991; ECM).** This rivals *Lumi* as the peak of Vesala's output. The opening 33-second track has harsh voices chanting an incomprehensible phrase over and over, a prelude to "Murmuring Morning", which radiates with cello and soft chords. The rest of the album makes dramatic juxtapositions of impressionist pieces with darker sardonic or satiric and witty exercises, all superbly conceived and executed.

Andrea Vicari

Piano, composer.

b. Miami, 16 July 1965.

Although born in the USA, Vicari (family name Vicary) was born to British parents – her father was a jazz pianist who recorded with the Second City Jazzmen in the early 1960s. Vicari had her early education in Birmingham, then studied at University College, Cardiff, before postgraduate work at the London Guildhall School of Music (1988–9), where she studied composition and piano. In the early 1990s she led her own bands and freelanced in London.

In 1992 she was commissioned by the Arts Council to compose music for a ten-piece band, the following year she won the Peter Whittingham Award to enable her to record a CD, and in January 1994 she duly recorded *Andrea Vicari's Suburban Gorillas*. In the summer of 1994, the Suburban Gorillas band toured Britain under the auspices of the Jazz Services National Touring Scheme, and her quintet did a twelve-concert British tour in February 1995. Vicari has also played for several other leading British musicians, including flautist Phillip Bent and saxophonist Mornington Lockett (an ongoing association), and has worked with American Eddie Harris. She is one of the most brilliant young musicians in the UK – an outstanding pianist and superbly fertile composer. In August 1994, she composed the music for a short television film, *Rise Of A New Eve*, shown on Channel 4 in 1994, and also set a poem of A. E. Housman for a Jacqui Dankworth-led ensemble, heard on *New Perspectives* (1995; Spotlite). A second album – *Lunar Spell* (33 Records) – also appeared in 1995, featuring Lockett and guitarist Phil Robson. She is active in jazz education and she remains busy on the London scene, often with her trio featuring bassist Dorian Lockett and drummer Seb Rochford. Her favourites range from Herbie Hancock, Keith Jarrett and John Taylor, to Geri Allen, Monk and Bill Evans. Other inspirations are Django Bates, Vince Mendoza and Hugh Masekela. [IC]

⊙ **Andrea Vicari's Suburban Gorillas (1994; 33 Records).** This is one of the most impressive recording debuts to come from the recent crop of young British jazz musicians. The writing and playing are superlatively assured, and the music covers a vast spectrum, from the elegiac "Awakenings" to the African-inspired "Maibouye", the brittle satire of "Pin Stripe Woman", and the *tour de force* of "L'Orchestre Des Fous", a ten-minute outing in 5/4 time which swings beautifully.

Vienna Art Orchestra and Choir

➤➤ *see entry on* **Matthias Rüegg**.

Vikku Vinayakram

Ghatam (clay pot), mridangam.

b. India, 11 Aug 1942.

Vikku (T.H.) Vinayakram was taught by his father, Sri T.R. Harihara Sarma, a legendary teacher of Carnatic (South Indian classical) percussion. Vinayakram was a child prodigy, taking part in Carnatic music concerts from the age of thirteen, and playing with all the main Indian virtuosi of the 1950s and 1960s. In the mid-1970s he was invited by John McLaughlin to complete the quartet Shakti, and toured the USA and Europe with them. In 1980, with Joel A., he formed the Indian jazz group J.G. Laya. In the mid-1980s Vinayakram was also Principal of Jaya Ganesh Academy of Rhythm in Madras, the leading academy of Carnatic percussion. In the later 80s and 90s he recorded and toured with Lakshminarayana Shankar. He has received several Indian classical music prizes and the formal titles of Nadasudarnava (1980) and Kalaimamani (1982) accorded to legendary musicians. He has done extensive international tours playing Indian music. [IC]

➤➤ **John McLaughlin** *(Shakti)*.

Leroy Vinnegar

Bass.

b. Indianapolis, Indiana, 13 July 1928; d. 2 Aug 1999.

Vinnegar was a school colleague of pianist Carl Perkins, and joined him in Los Angeles in 1954 after working in Chicago behind Charlie Parker, Sonny Stitt and others in 1952. He gigged and recorded with Stan Getz, Barney Kessel and Herb Geller in 1955, and with Shelly Manne in 1955–6, and also had regular work with the Teddy Edwards-Joe Castro band from 1959–61, the Gerald Wilson band in 1961–2, as well as record dates with Sonny Rollins, Phineas Newborn, the Jazz Crusaders and Kenny Dorham. He made festival appearances, including one with Les McCann at Montreux in 1969, and continued freelancing. After severe health problems caused him to move to Portland, Oregon, in the late 1980s, he made several more albums in the 1990s.

Vinnegar was highly valued as a versatile rhythm player with a resilient, almost rubbery tone. Although not reluctant to solo when called upon, Leroy popularized the idea of playing his normal four-to-the-bar walking lines and making them as interesting as more complex solos. Occasional passing notes, unlike those of Mingus or Ray Brown which were played normally, resulted from Vinnegar plucking an open string with his left hand, which he described as: "Like a little flip – actually feeding myself, like a drummer's accent". [BP]

⊙ **Leroy Walks!** (1957; Contemporary/OJC). With a rhythm section including Perkins, and a frontline of Gerald Wilson, Teddy Edwards and Vic Feldman, Vinnegar's best shot at leading his own album triumphs over the "walking bass" concept of tunes like "I'll Walk Alone" and the famous "Walkin'".

>> **Shelly Manne** *(My Fair Lady).*

Eddie "Cleanhead" Vinson

Alto saxophone, vocals, composer.

b. Houston, Texas, 18 Dec 1917; d. 2 July 1988.

Vinson played with the Houston-based Chester Boone band from 1932 and Milt Larkin from 1936. He toured with Larkin's musicians under Floyd Ray in 1940–41, and then was the star singer/saxophonist with Cootie Williams from 1942–5. He led his own sixteen-piece band from 1945–7, and later cut it to a seven-piece, his 1947–8 group containing Johnny Coles, Red Garland and John Coltrane. He continued working under his own name through periods of obscurity and rediscovery. He made his first European tour in 1969 and was featured with the Johnny Otis R&B show at the Monterey festival in 1970. There were recordings made at the Montreux festivals of 1971 and 1974, and he guested with Count Basie in Europe in 1972. He was still undertaking regular solo gigs until shortly before his death.

A unique performer who convincingly straddled the jazz and R&B worlds, Vinson had a forthright alto style less indebted to Louis Jordan than to Charlie Parker, whom he met around 1940. He was the composer of "Tune Up" and "Four", both originally attributed to and recorded by Miles Davis in the 1950s. While his vocal blues hits were usually authored by others, he created some memorable lyrics such as "Alimony Blues" and "Kidney Stew". [BP]

Eddie Vinson and Cannonball Adderley

⊙ **Cleanhead And Cannonball** (1961–2; Landmark). With his one-time protégé Adderley's quintet in attendance, this is the best evidence of Vinson the hot jazz altoist. Vocals include excellent remakes of "Kidney Stew" and others, but a couple of instrumentals have him doing a Sonny Criss to Adderley's Parker.

Eddie Vinson

⊙ **Kidney Stew** (1969–72; Black & Blue). One of his own favourite albums, this was cut in France with the majority of the tracks backed by Jay McShann and T-Bone Walker. They include several early hits remade, including the title tune, while "Alimony" and three others are from later sessions with either Wild Bill Davis or Bill Doggett on organ.

Miroslav Vitous

Bass, guitar, composer.

b. Prague, 6 Dec 1947.

The son of a saxophonist, Vitous studied the violin from the age of six, piano from nine to fourteen, and then started on bass. At Prague Conservatory he played with Jan Hammer (piano) and his brother Alan Vitous (drums) in a junior trio. He won first prize and a scholarship to the Berklee School of Music, Boston, at an international competition in Vienna organized by Friedrich Gulda. Vitous studied at Berklee from August 1966 to April 1967, and then went to New York, working with Art Farmer, Freddie Hubbard and the Bob Brookmeyer-Clark Terry quintet. He worked very briefly with Miles Davis and then joined Herbie Mann, staying with him, apart from one tour with Stan Getz, until the end of 1970. In 1971 he was a founder member of Weather Report, staying with it until late 1973. He moved to Los Angeles in 1974 and, apart from one appearance with Airto Moreira, did not play in public for over a year because he was practising a new instrument custom-made for him – a doublenecked combination guitar and bass. In 1976 he began leading his own groups, and continued doing so into the 1980s, touring worldwide playing major festivals and recording for ECM. For the most part, Vitous's quartet was all European, with John Surman, Jon Christensen and John Taylor, but that particular group broke up in 1983. Through the 1980s he worked again with Corea and formed a bass duo with Stanley Clarke. From 1979 he taught at the New England Conservatory of Music, became head of the jazz department in 1983 but returned to full-time composing and performing in 1988. In the 1990s, Vitous

JAK KILBY

Miroslav Vitous

formed a successful company specializing in high-quality orchestral samples for midi recording. He returned to the jazz scene as recorded leader after an eleven-year hiatus with *Universal Syncopations* (see below).

Vitous is a virtuoso player with a conception that embraces not only his jazz roots but also the folk music of his homeland. His initial influence was Scott LaFaro, and then Ron Carter and Gary Peacock. [IC]

⊙ **First Meeting** (1979; ECM); **Journey's End** (1982; ECM). *First Meeting* was recorded by his working quartet with pianist Kenny Kirkland deputizing very convincingly for John Taylor. Vitous, Surman (playing soprano and bass clarinet) and Christensen are in fine form, and Vitous's writing is beautifully redolent of folk and classical elements, but the almost heart-rending lyricism is often counterbalanced by powerful rhythmic passages. *Journey's End* has more of the same except that Taylor is back at the piano and Surman adds baritone to his armoury.

⊙ **Emergence** (1985; ECM). A superlative solo bass album.

⊙ **Return** (1988; fnac). Vitous with his brother Alan (drums, vocals and recorder) and tenor saxophonist Jan Stolba. Using prerecording and overdubbing, they nostalgically evoke pastoral Czech scenes, though with one aberrant trip to Africa – "B.S.V.Z" (Bedřich Smetana in Zimbabwe) – to break the journey home.

⊙ **Universal Syncopations** (2003; ECM). A very fine return to the spotlight. An imposing all star cast (Jan Garbarek, Chick Corea, John McLaughlin and Jack DeJohnette – the latter two old Herbie Mann compatriots of Vitouss) contribute beautifully to a sensitive, composition-driven album, with archetypical lyricism ("Bamboo Forest", "Sun Flower") juxtaposing edgy swing ("Tramp Blues", "Miro Bop").

➤➤ **Chick Corea** *(Now He Sings, Now He Sobs);* **Herbie Mann** *(Memphis Underground);* **Terje Rypdal** *(To Be Continued);* **Joe Zawinul** *(Weather Report; I Sing The Body Electric).*

Phil Wachsmann

Violin, electronics.
b. Kampala, Uganda, 5 Aug 1944.

Wachsmann came to free improv via modern classical music. In his twenties he won a scholarship to study in Paris with Nadia Boulanger for one year; lectured in contemporary music at Durham University; set up an improvisation workshop; and played with Yggdrasil, a group performing the music of John Cage and Morton Feldman (and integrating multi-media projects into their music). He then formed an improvisation group, Chamberpot, and he has played almost exclusively in free improv ever since. When Derek Bailey left the band Iskra 1903 (with Paul Rutherford and Barry Guy), Wachsmann replaced him, his decorative, elegant playing making the ornery trio a strange and intriguing conjuncture. He has played with the most accomplished and consistently interesting European improvisers: Fred Van Hove, Tony Oxley, Paul Lytton, Derek Bailey, Axel Dörner, Marcio Mattos and vocalist Vanessa Mackness, among others. He continues to be interested in multi-media work, has appeared latterly with drummer Tony Oxley's jazz/electronica ensemble B.I.M.P. quartet and administers his own label, Bead Records.

For a committed free-improviser, Wachsmann is a surprisingly melodic player whose lines sometimes sound more "Viennese School" than contemporary – he is unafraid of pretty trills or full-bodied vibrato (perhaps a legacy of his admiration for Joe Venuti). At the same time he loves a good hypnotic drone (often aided by electronic echo effects) which evokes, by turn, Indian classical, English folk and sometimes American Minimalist music. All these characterful traits lend a resonant anachronism to his collaborations: his assurance and control work best in the least likely situation. [IC]

⊙ **Some Other Season** (1999; ECM). Wachsmann and percussionist Paul Lytton saw, scrape, tap and caress out an extraordinary, electronically-treated panorama of sound. The violinist's pedigree in experimental classical music is evident – quiveringly rebarbative fingerboard runs and charmingly ornery hacking and stabbing – but the pair also explore some beautiful ambient overtones, and what can only be described as a warm, dilapidated industrial folk music.

➤➤ **Barry Guy** *(Harmos).*

Nasheet Waits

Drums.
b. New York, 15 June 1970.

The son of drummer Freddie Waits (1943–1989), who recorded with McCoy Tyner and Andrew Hill among others, Nasheet's playing was encouraged by his father. He first studied psychology and history in Atlanta, then, after his father's death, majored in music at Long Island University, also taking private lessons with Michael Carvin from 1991–5. During this period he worked with Max Roach's ensemble M'Boom, and from 1993–8 performed with Antonio Hart's quintet. Since 2000 he has been closely associated with pianists Hill, Fred Hersch and Jason Moran, making three albums with the latter. Among many favourites, his "big six" drummers are his father Freddie, Tony Williams, Billy Higgins, Elvin Jones, Roach and Michael Carvin, while the Coltrane quartet and Stravinsky are other inspirations. In recording three dozen albums with everyone from Geri Allen to Bojan Zulfikarpasic, his own work has become notably fluid and personal, meeting with widespread enthusiasm. Andrew Hill has said, "I love the way he plays – he brings a certain rhythm dynamic to the music that I haven't heard a drummer use in a decade." [BP]

➤➤ **Jason Moran** *(The Bandwagon).*

Ulf Wakenius

Guitar.
b. Halmstad, Sweden, 16 April 1958.

Initially interested in Spanish guitar, Wakenius then played rock and blues but is equally capable in flamenco, classical and jazz. A member of the Swedish group Mwendo Dawa from 1979–80, and then his own duo Guitars Unlimited, he joined Svend Asmussen's String Swing in 1983. Visiting Brazil in 1984, he recorded part of the album *Aquarela Do Brasil* with local musicians, and toured in 1986 with accordionist Sivuca. He formed an ongoing musical partnership with Niels Lan Doky and, like him, has spent some time working in the USA, gaining experience with the likes of Bob Berg, Randy Brecker, Herbie Hancock, Joe Henderson and Jim Hall. A regular member of Niels-Henning Ørsted Pedersen's trio, with which he played for President Clinton, he

worked with another famous bassist, Ray Brown, recording two albums with him, and more recently he has performed with Oscar Peterson. An outgrowth of both Django Reinhardt and Wes Montgomery, Wakenius's brilliant technique is complemented by a fine rhythmic sense. [BP]

Ray Brown Trio with Ulf Wakenius

Summertime (1997; Telarc). Although perhaps sounding more at home alongside a less mainstream rhythm-section than Brown's trio with Geoff Keezer, Wakenius gets a chance to shine here on several song standards and jazz hits such as Montgomery's "West Coast Blues", "Yours Is My Heart Alone" and, of course, the title track.

Collin Walcott

Sitar, tabla, percussion, vocals.

b. New York, 24 April 1945; d. 8 Nov 1984.

Walcott's mother was a classical pianist, and he learned violin for two years in grammar school. In 1963 he studied percussion at Indiana University, and from 1967 learned sitar with Ravi Shankar and tabla with Alla Rakha. He played with Tony Scott from 1967–9, and Tim Hardin from 1968–9. But it was not until he joined the Paul Winter Consort in 1970 that he began along the musical trajectory for which he is best known – exploring a fragile hinterland between pan-cultural folk musics and jazz. From 1971 until his premature death he worked with Oregon, a splinter group from the Winter Consort that included Ralph Towner, Paul McCandless and Glen Moore, although it is his own albums *Cloud Dance* and *Grazing Dreams* that, as their titles suggest, crystallize his delicate, panoramic musical fusion of east and west. Walcott also worked with dancer, singer and composer Meredith Monk, and he toured and recorded from the late 1970s with Codona, a trio sympathetic to his musical interests, with Don Cherry and Nana Vasconcelos. Shortly before his death in a road accident in East Germany, he toured Europe with his own group, which included Cherry and saxophonist Jim Pepper.

His own groups, and the other groups he worked with, used elements from ethnic music, jazz and occasionally from European art music, and Walcott's presence always gave the groups a very special identity and atmosphere. He not only played sitar in the classical Indian manner, but could also produce walking bass- lines on it, and improvise on jazz changes. [IC]

Cloud Dance (1975; ECM). *Cloud Dance* is a superb album with Walcott in the company of John Abercrombie, Dave Holland and Jack DeJohnette.

Grazing Dreams (1977; ECM). *Grazing Dreams*, with Don Cherry, Abercrombie, Palle Danielsson and Dom Um Romão, is one of Walcott's most beautifully achieved albums – and a dress rehearsal for Codona.

Codona

Codona (1978; ECM). *Codona* was a poetic expression of world music, and the recipient of some of Walcott's best compositions. There were three eponymous albums, all with much to commend them, but the first album is the best.

>> **Ralph Towner** *(Music Of Another Present Era; Distant Hills).*

Myron Walden

Alto saxophone, composer.

b. Miami, Florida, 18 Oct 1972.

Inspired by the sound of Charlie Parker, to which he was exposed at twelve, Myron Walden spent his teens in Harlem attempting to emulate not only Parker himself, but also Cannonball Adderley and Sonny Stitt. He attended LaGuardia High School of Music and Art, where he played in the senior jazz band, and the Harlem School of the Arts, before attending the Jazz Mobile Workshop and the Manhattan School of Music, where he studied with Barry Harris and privately with John Purcell. He has also studied with Yusef Lateef, Vincent Herring and Donald Byrd, among others, and been the recipient of various honours, including being named Saxophonist of the Year by the Harlem School of the Arts. In 1993 he won the Charlie Parker competition at the Lincoln Center's Alice Tully Hall, and subsequently played with Nat Adderley, Lou Donaldson, James Spaulding, Roy Hargrove (in his big band) and Jesse Davis. He had also provided material for Ravi Coltrane and The New Jazz Composers Octet (of which he is a founding member), and so had an already assured pedigree prior to his debut album as a leader, *Hypnosis* from 1996. Its follow-up *Like A Flower Seeking The Sun* (NYC Records) came in 1999, followed by *Higher Ground* in 2003. Walden, a fleet, agile player, has also recorded two albums with drummer Brian Blade and guests on pianist Jason Lindner's *Premonition* (2000; Stretch) and drummer Daniel Freedman's *Trio* (2001; Fresh Sound). [CP]

Hypnosis (1996; NYC Records). All originals, played with a cultured yet gutsy, bustling alto sound by Walden in stellar company: pianists Mulgrew Miller and Kevin Hays, bassist Dwayne Burno and drummers Eric Hartland and Eric McPherson.

Higher Ground (2002; Fresh Sound/New Talent). A new quartet (Marcus Strickland, tenor; Brandon Owens, bass; E.J. Strickland, drums) and increasing authority and gritty distinctiveness from the leader on another impressive set of originals.

>> **Brian Blade** *(Fellowship).*

Mal Waldron

Piano, composer.

b. New York, 16 Aug 1925; d. Brussels, 2 Dec 2002.

After receiving a BA in music and composing for the ballet, Waldron worked with Big Nick Nicholas, Ike Quebec, Della Reese and R&B groups. He was a regular associate of Charles Mingus in 1954–6 and occasionally later, and was the accompanist of Billie Holiday from 1957–9. He also made frequent recordings for which he did all the writing (one tune from these sessions, "Soul Eyes", has become a standard). In 1960 he backed John Coltrane on his first post-Davis gigs and led his own groups, which later featured Eric Dolphy, both live and on record. He wrote three USA film scores and stage background music, then, after film work in Europe in 1965, he settled there. Making occasional trips to Japan and back to the USA, he was resident in Belgium for more than thirty years as an adoptive European.

Elements of Waldron's style can be traced to both Bud Powell and Thelonious Monk, although his sound is less bright and percussive than either. As with some practitioners of later styles, the impact of Mal's playing tends to be cumulative rather than constantly ebbing and flowing, and for this reason he often worked successfully with soloists such as Steve Lacy, who also espoused free jazz only gradually. For this reason too, his original compositions tend to be less memorable in themselves than as an effective stimulus to improvisation. [BP]

Mal Waldron and Eric Dolphy

⊙ **The Quest** (1961; New Jazz/OJC). This quintet session in which Booker Ervin completes the frontline includes the original recordings of Waldron's "Fire Waltz" and "Status Seeking" (redone at Dolphy's *At The Five Spot* sessions), plus other original material such as the ballad "Duquility".

Mal Waldron

⊙ **Soul Eyes** (1997; RCA Victor). An all-star album based around a trio with Reggie Workman and Andrew Cyrille. These are mostly classic Waldron compositions such as the title track, with guest appearances by Steve Coleman, Joe Henderson, singers Jeanne Lee and Abbey Lincoln (on "Straight Ahead", which Mal wrote with her), and they are a worthy celebration of his career.

Bennie Wallace

Tenor saxophone.

b. Chattanooga, Tennessee, 18 Nov 1946.

As a teenager Wallace played jazz and sat in with local country music bands and black R&B combos. He graduated from the University of Tennessee, majoring in clarinet, and moved to New York in the early 1970s, where he worked with the Monty Alexander and Sheila Jordan groups. His record debut was made alongside Flip Phillips and Scott Hamilton in 1977. Appearances at the Berlin festival, as a member of the George Gruntz band in 1979 and fronting the NDR big band in 1981, were among his many appearances in Europe up to the early 1980s. Until 1985 all his own recordings were cut in New York but released by the German label Enja. Living in Hollywood since 1990, he has become a successful writer of music for films such as *White Men Can't Jump*.

Wallace has said, "About 1973, I decided to spend one year totally away from modern music – I listened to all the guys with Duke's band, a lot of Johnny Hodges and Ben Webster, as well as to Don Byas and Coleman Hawkins." This was done against a background of close acquaintance with John Coltrane and, especially, Sonny Rollins, though his most obvious influence is Eric Dolphy. The saxophone style that has emerged from this melting-pot is full of bizarre humour, but is otherwise straightahead and rather intense. Wallace has also allowed his Southern roots in more popular forms to feed into his repertoire and into his improvisation, in an effort to become even more all-embracing. [BP]

⊙ **Bennie Wallace** (1998; AudioQuest). Bennie's latest reveals a new maturity, as he tackles a bunch of mainly slow standards (four of them from Ellington and Strayhorn). With sterling support from Tommy Flanagan, Eddie Gomez and Alvin Queen, Wallace approaches the tone-qualities of Hawkins and Dolphy simultaneously and demonstrates the continuity of the tradition.

Sippie Wallace

Vocals, organ, piano.

b. Houston, Texas, 1 Nov 1898; d. 1 Nov 1986.

Sippie Wallace (Beulah Belle Thomas) came from a musical family and made her first recordings in October 1923, with Eddie Heywood; she then recorded with Clarence Williams (1924) and later in the 1920s with a galaxy of stars, including Louis Armstrong, King Oliver and Perry Bradford's Jazz Phools. She was also active on the TOBA circuit throughout the 1920s but retired to Detroit in the 1930s, recorded again in 1945, and finally recommenced appearances in the mid-1960s. In later years she worked with bandleader/jazz authority James Dapogny, and her 1983 album *Sippie* was nominated for a Grammy. [DF]

Axel Zwingenberger and Sippie Wallace

⊙ **Sippie Wallace And The Friends Of Boogie Woogie** (1983; Vagabond). Marvellous set combining this legend of the blues with Axel Zwingenberger; Wallace sounds remarkably well preserved.

Byron Wallen

Trumpet, flugelhorn, piano.

b. London, 17 July 1969.

As a child, Wallen was surrounded by soul, classical and reggae music. He studied classical piano from the age of twelve, and played euphonium in a brass band. At 16 he took up trumpet, and went to New York to study with Jimmy Owens, Jon Faddis and Terence Blanchard. Wallen also studied Javanese gamelan music in Java and went to Uganda to study its traditional music: early testaments to his ongoing commitment to the fusion of traditional musics with the funk of the day and contemporary classical traditions. He later graduated from Sussex University, UK, with a degree in psy-

Byron Wallen

chology, philosophy and maths, but was active throughout his university career as a jazz trumpeter, working with Mervyn Africa, Courtney Pine, Jean Toussaint and others. In 1995 he composed his *Tarot Suite* for a ten-piece ensemble, and toured England with it early in 1996. Later that year, his regular band, Sound Advice, was invited to the Syrian Anglo-Arabic Festival, where they were enthusiastically received. His first album, *Sound Advice* (1995; B&W), was co-produced by Airto Moreira, and received favourable reviews. His second album, *Earth Roots* (1997), self-produced and inspired by music from the Solomon Islands, Indonesia and the Middle East, was nominated for a MOBO award. Byron's accomplishments – the establishment of his own label, Twilight Jaguar, his third and best-realized album, *Indigo* (2002), a tour with the Andrew Hill Big Band in 2003 and winning the Innovation prize at 2003's BBC Jazz Awards – have cemented his reputation as one of the most intrepid jazz artists on the scene. It is all too easy to pigeonhole Warren in the hip-hop crossover end of jazz (though his contributions to dance acts are always discerning and cogent – Red Snapper's 1998 album *Making Bones* being a case in point). But he has toured with heavyweights such as David Murray, and played with Billy Higgins, Butch Morris and Wynton Marsalis. Wallen is an excellent trumpeter and flugelhornist, with a fleet technique, good range and plenty of imagination. His music grows ever more ambitious, and his profoundly personal synthesis of different music from east and west speaks more and more poetically. [IC]

⊙ **Indigo** (2002; Twilight Jaguar). Perhaps Wallen's horn sound is a little *too* Miles, but its bleached understatement suits *Indigo*'s melancholy mood. There's no disputing the beauty of Wallen's tunes and arrangements, which recall Ellington or Mingus at their most autumnal (with something of the Evans/Davis collaborations about them too). Ghostly Javanese wind and percussion meets the fruity, near-calypso of Tony Kofi's sax and the sandy stoicism of Wallen's trumpet to conjure up a bewitchingly crepuscular funk.

Fats Waller

Piano, organ, vocals, composer.
b. New York, 21 May 1904; d. 15 Dec 1943.

Waller's father (who named him Thomas) was a clergyman who wanted Fats to follow a similar career, and the young Fats played organ in his father's church. After lessons with private piano teachers he became a professional pianist at the age of fifteen. He worked in cabaret clubs and theatres during the 1920s, accompanying Bessie Smith and other blues singers, as well as playing organ and piano solos. During the late 1920s, in collaboration with lyricist Andy Razaf, Waller made a reputation as a composer of popular songs for such shows as *Connie's Hot Chocolates*. He began broadcasting sessions early, and made a brief trip to France in 1932. In May 1934 he began a series of Victor record sessions with six-piece groups known as Fats Waller And His Rhythm, which featured his satirical treatments of current popular songs and gained him a wide, non-jazz audience. The sextets usually featured either Herman Autrey or John "Bugs" Hamilton on trumpets, Gene Sedric on clarinet and tenor, Al Casey on guitar, Cedric Wallace on bass and "Slick" Jones on drums. All these performances are notable for a wonderful sense of time, rhythm and pacing, and some glorious piano-playing; they are also enormous fun. Fats made jazz history by playing the organ in Notre Dame cathedral, Paris, and he recorded on the pipe organ and, from 1940–42, the Hammond organ, on which he recorded his composition "Jitterbug Waltz". Fats appeared in several films, the most successful and influential of which was the all-black *Stormy Weather* (1943). He died of pneumonia on a train returning from Los Angeles to New York, aged just 39.

Waller came out of the James P. Johnson "stride" piano style, but added to it a delicacy, a more powerful rhythmic intensity and a greater speed and deftness. He wore his genius lightly and his lighthearted music had a profound influence on subsequent generations of musicians. He could make an artistic and witty gem out of the tritest popular song; at the same time, his compositions and certain phrases he played vastly enriched the entire jazz repertoire, becoming part of the subconscious of all subsequent players. Among the Waller compositions that have become standards are "Ain't Misbehavin'", and "Blue Turning Grey Over You"; and his "Honeysuckle Rose" is the basis of the harmonic structure of Charlie Parker's bebop composition "Scrapple From The Apple" and many other jazz originals.

Many of the more solemn jazz critics and fans, as they had done in the case of Louis Armstrong, lamented Fats's popularity and humour. They felt he was throwing his gifts away and that he should have devoted himself to more serious musical pursuits. But his occasional attempts at more sober composition (for example his "London Suite") were banal; his genius was for making immortal performances out of ephemeral popular songs. Over fifty years after his death, his biggest record hit, "I'm Going To Sit Right Down And Write Myself A Letter", is played frequently on the radio and sounds as delightfully fresh and humorous as ever. His influence on pianists has been huge; perhaps the most famous of his debtors are Art Tatum, Teddy Wilson, Count Basie (who took lessons from him), Thelonious Monk, Erroll Garner, Bud Powell and Joe Zawinul. [IC]

⦿ **Jazz Classics: Fats Waller 1927–34** (BBC). A well-programmed package in which Waller guests with groups including Ted Lewis and the Little Chocolate Dandies, and plays some solos including the classic "Alligator Crawl".

⦿ **Turn On The Heat** (1927–41; RCA Bluebird). This double CD has all the solo piano sessions Fats recorded for Victor; bad sound but great music, and an essential Waller document.

⦿ **The Joint Is Jumpin'** (1929–43; RCA Bluebird). Several of his hits, including "Your Feet's Too Big", plus ten of Waller's best solos; rich fare, pity about the sound quality.

⦿ **The Definitive Fats Waller, His Rhythm, His Piano** (1935/9; Stash). Nearly eighty minutes of vintage Waller And His Rhythm from broadcasts in 1935 and 1939.

⦿ **The Middle Years Part 1** (1936–8; RCA Bluebird). There are 70 tracks of Waller And His Rhythm on these three CDs – riotous and sometimes over the top, but with nuggets of fine music on most tracks.

⦿ **The Last Years 1940–43** (RCA Bluebird). A wonderful Waller swan song – the final Rhythm tracks on three CDs, full of hot and beautiful jazz, and wild verbal wit.

George Wallington

Piano, composer.

b. Palermo, Sicily, 27 Oct 1923; d. New York, 15 Feb 1993.

Wallington, christened Giacinto Figlia, was brought up in the USA. He gigged as a teenager and participated in Dizzy Gillespie's first 52nd Street group in 1944. He then spent time freelancing and leading his own groups, and made his first recording under his own name in 1949. In 1955–6 he led a regular quintet of young stars-to-be: Donald Byrd, Jackie McLean (later replaced by Phil

BETTMANN/CORBIS

Fats Waller

Woods), Paul Chambers and Art Taylor. In 1957 he left the music business, only re-emerging briefly in the mid-1980s with new recordings and an appearance at the Kool festival in 1985. His piano work is in the typical bebop manner and, though apparently developed independently from that of Bud Powell, differed little from his approach. Wallington wrote the bop standards "Lemon Drop" and "Godchild", as well as numerous other attractive but less well-known tunes. [BP]

Live! At Café Bohemia (1955; Prestige/OJC). From the period when Wallington was still writing important new tunes, this is the quintet referred to above and includes two versions of Jackie McLean's own "Minor March", as well as the club theme "Bohemia After Dark". The pianist's playing and compositions are uniformly excellent.

Bob Wallis

Trumpet, vocals, leader.

b. Bridlington, Yorkshire, UK, 3 June 1934; d. 10 Jan 1991.

Wallis took up the trumpet at twelve, formed his first band at eighteen, and after moving to London played trumpet for Acker Bilk briefly in the 1950s, before forming his own Storyville Jazzmen from members of Hugh Rainey's Storyville Band, including Pete Gresham (piano), Avo Avison (trombone) and Rainey (banjo). His high-pitched singing and powerful trumpet (both influenced by Henry "Red" Allen) achieved commercial success after a hit single, "Come Along Please", and all through the trad boom of the early 1960s his band worked all over Britain and Europe, appearing regularly on radio and TV as well as in two films. After the rock boom bit deeper, Wallis freelanced with various bands (including Monty Sunshine's), then from the early 1970s built a new career in Switzerland, leading at the Casa Bar, Zurich. He worked on into the 1980s with undimmed energy, but contracted cancer late in the decade and returned home in 1990. [DF]

Ol' Man River (1960–61; Lake). Combining one and a half Pye albums (*Ol' Man River* and half of *Travellin' Blues*), this is excellent earlier Wallis with clarinettist Doug Richford, who preceded Al Gay in the ranks. Powerful British trad; excellent illuminative notes by banjoist Hugh Rainey.

Bob Wallis: The Pye Jazz Anthology (1960–62; Castle). All the titles recorded for Pye by the Wallis band including the singles – "Come Along Please" and others – not included in the Lake albums.

The Wallis Collection Vol. 1 (1989; TWC). Studio session by the Wallis band, featuring the leader's driving trumpet and vocals, plus longtime sidemen Forrie Cairns (clarinet), Ian Armit (piano) and Alan Poston (drums).

Jack Walrath

Trumpet, arranger.

b. Stuart, Florida, 5 May 1946.

Raised in Montana, Jack Walrath took up trumpet playing at nine, and studied at the Berklee School of Music from 1964–8. In 1969 he moved to the West Coast, where he led a band called Change with bassist Gary Peacock, and another named Revival with trombonist Glenn Ferris. After touring with Ray Charles (Walrath is a pungent contributor to soul and R&B bands, having played with the Platters, the Drifters and Jackie Wilson), he moved to New York in 1973, where, after a spell playing with Latin bands, he joined Charles Mingus in 1974, an association that was to last until the composer's death in 79. In the 1980s Walrath led his own bands and toured with UK band Spirit Level, recording an album, *Killer Bunnies*, with them in 1986. Continuing his association with Mingus alumni, Walrath recorded and toured with drummer Dannie Richmond in the early 1980s, and with the Mingus Dynasty, a repertoire band organized by Mingus's widow Sue. He is also part of the large pool of musicians upon which the Mingus Big Band draws, appearing on their debut album, *Nostalgia In Times Square* (1993; Dreyfus). Alongside saxophonists Bobby Watson and Steve Grossman, Walrath formed the frontline of a festival band, the Jazz Tribe, and, with French horn player Tom Varner, has contributed to the Manhattan New Music Project. He has also appeared on albums by drummer Mike Clark (alongside fellow Mingus alumnus Ricky Ford), the New York Composers' Orchestra and Canadian saxophonist John Tank. His own albums on the labels Red, Muse and Blue Note are all worth seeking out, despite being out of the current catalogue, and the 1990s recordings *Hipgnosis* with guitarist David Fiuczynski (1995; TCB) and *Solidarity* with saxophonist Ralph Reichert (recorded in his father's Hamburg club and issued on ACT), are characteristically punchy and vigorous. *Sonage* (2000; Rara) was an experimental collaboration with bassist Corrado Canonici while *Invasion Of The Booty Shakers* gave full voice to Walrath's off-beat humour. A witty, fiery trumpeter equally adept at big-band grandstanding (as in his lively work with drummer Charli Persip's Superband), providing cogent contributions to modern, composed music (witness his 1993 work with Muhal Richard Abrams) and leading his own groups, Walrath infuses everything he plays with verve, bite and controlled energy. [CP]

Out Of The Tradition (1990; Muse). Walrath comes in from "outside", along with Benny Green (piano), Larry Coryell (guitar), Anthony Cox (bass) and Ronnie Burrage (drums), to make lively comments on material ranging from "Out Of This World" to "Cabin In The Sky".

Journey, Man! (1996; Evidence). A sharp, gutsy band – Craig Handy (soprano and tenor saxophones), Bubby Watson (alto saxophone), Kenny Drew Jnr (piano), Ray Drummond (bass) and Victor Lewis (drums) – interpret nine typically intelligent Walrath themes drawing on everything from South African reggae through Bo Diddley to Mingus.

Invasion Of the Booty Shakers (2001; Savant). Intrepid, boisterous jazz-rock from Walrath and cohorts (Miles Griffith, vocals; Bill Bickford, bass; Cecil Brooks III, drums), with Walrath's trumpet and Griffith's gruff scat working particularly well together on a Mingus rarity (apparently), "Rats And Moles (Black Bats And Poles)".

➤➤ **Charles Mingus** *(Changes One)*.

John I. Walters

Composer, arranger, synthesizers, soprano saxophone, flutes.
b. Chesterfield, Derbyshire, UK, 16 April 1953.

Whilst a student of maths and physics at King's College, London, Walters played in a university jazz group and attended summer schools with Graham Collier and Mike Gibbs, as well as studying privately with Neil Ardley, Don Rendell and others. In 1974 he formed his own band, Landscape, which a year later became a cooperative five-piece unit with Walters, Peter Thoms, Andy Pask, Chris Heaton and Richard Burgess. The group's music combined the best elements of jazz and rock – a wide variety of perfectly executed rhythms, interesting structures, rich harmonies, strong melodies and quirky improvisation. Their first album, *Landscape* (1979), consisted of pieces they had been playing live for the preceding five years. Their second album, *From the Tea-Rooms of Mars ... To the Hell-Holes of Uranus*, was released in 1981, and two of Walters's songs, "Einstein A Go-Go" and "Norman Bates", came out as singles. Walters's composing and organizing abilities inevitably led him into record production and arranging work on the rock scene, in collaboration with Burgess and others. In 1988 he produced the Mike Gibbs orchestral album *Big Music*, and in 1989 formed the group Zyklus with Neil Ardley and Warren Greveson, using Zyklus computers to compose and play live concerts. Walters is currently an arts critic for *The Guardian* newspaper and also runs the quarterly avant-garde music "magazine", *Unknown Public*, comprising an (audio) CD and a printed magazine on the new music it contains. [IC]

➤➤ **Neil Ardley** *(Virtual Realities).*

Cedar Walton

Piano, composer.
b. Dallas, Texas, 17 Jan 1934.

Walton was taught to play by his mother, and studied from 1951–4 at the University of Denver. He moved to New York in 1955 and then played while in the army in Germany. He worked successively with the sextet of J.J. Johnson from 1958–60, the Benny Golson-Art Farmer Jazztet in 1960–61, and Art Blakey from 1961–4, returning to him in 1973. Freelancing in New York with many different players and singers, Walton was also much in demand for recording, notably on Blue Note and Prestige. Since 1970 he has done much gigging and touring abroad, usually with his own quartet, which has included saxophonists Hank Mobley, George Coleman, Clifford Jordan, Bob Berg and Ralph Moore, and superior rhythm players such as Sam Jones. Walton's work with Billy Higgins has been ongoing since 1966, and is one of the great rhythm-section partnerships of all time. An excellent and stimulating accompanist, Walton is also an interesting writer, some of whose tunes have achieved standard status, for example "Ugetsu" (aka "Polar AC" or "Fantasy in D"), "Mosaic" and "Bolivia". He is a lively soloist whose long lines are the epitome of contemporary neo-bop piano. [BP]

⊙ **First Set** (1977; Steeplechase). The first of three albums recorded on the same night at Copenhagen's Montmartre, this has Walton's popular originals "Holy Land" and "Ojos De Rojo" ("Fantasy In D" and "Bolivia" are on *The Third Set*). Adding the names of Bob Berg, Sam Jones and Billy Higgins says all that needs to be said.

➤➤ **Art Blakey** *(Free For All)*; **Clifford Jordan** *(The Highest Mountain).*

Carlos Ward

Alto saxophone, flute, composer.
b. Ancon, Panama, 1 May 1940.

Ward was raised in Seattle, where he started playing clarinet at thirteen in his school band. He studied clarinet and alto saxophone with John Jessen and, during his tour of duty with the army, attended the Navy School of Music in Washington, DC, and played with military bands in Germany. While there he sat in with many jazz groups, including those of Albert Mangelsdorff and Karl Berger, and in Frankfurt he heard Eric Dolphy, who left an indelible impression on him. Back in Seattle in 1965 he met John Coltrane, whose band was performing at the Penthouse. Ward was invited to play with the band on every night of its engagement there, and he moved to New York that year, to join Coltrane's octet (though he never recorded with the group). There he played with Sunny Murray, Don Cherry, Berger again, Rashied Ali, Dave Izenzon and Paul Motian. He joined the Jazz Composers' Orchestra, where he met Carla Bley, and played in her band for a number of years thereafter.

In the 1970s Ward joined the R&B/funk band that became known as B.T. Express, an outfit that had several hit records. It was also at this time that he began to develop a close association with Abdullah Ibrahim, whom he had met with Don Cherry at the Montmartre Club in Copenhagen back in 64, and from 1973–86 Ward was a significant contributor to Ibrahim's music. In the mid-80s he rekindled his association with Cherry, and became a member of his band NU, a world music tinged cooperative quintet with Ed Blackwell, bassist Mark Helias and Nana Vasconcelos; Ward then played with Cherry's quartet at the 1986 Greenwich Village jazz festival, and on a tour through Central America in 1987. In 1986 he replaced the late Jimmy Lyons in the Cecil Taylor Unit and in 1987 formed his own quartet with trumpeter Charles Sullivan, electric bassist Alex Blake and drummer Ronnie Burrage. He played with Ed Blackwell and Don Pullen through the 1990s and recorded a tribute to his former employers Pullen and Cherry on *Set For Two Dons* (1998; Puell), released on his own label.

Ward has a raw, bluesy tone, and the intelligence and versatility to have made his own distinctive but cogent mark on both Ibrahim's African-oriented Ekaya and Cecil Taylor's turbulent free jazz. He still has not, as yet, been much recorded as a leader. [IC]

Lito (1988; Leo). Ward with Woody Shaw, bassist Walter Schmocker and drummer Alex Deutsch in a session recorded at the North Sea festival. Ward's composing is the basis of an excellent performance, notably from Shaw (this was one of his final recordings).

➤➤ **Abdullah Ibrahim** *(Water From An Ancient Well)*; **Cecil Taylor** *(Live In Bologna)*.

Helen Ward

Vocals.

b. New York, 19 Sept 1916; d. 21 April 1998.

One of the most distinguished swing singers, Ward began her career with Nye Mayhew in 1933 then worked with a variety of leaders including Eddie Duchin, before joining Benny Goodman for most of the decade. From 1937–42 she retired from performing live but recorded prolifically with Teddy Wilson, Gene Krupa and others, returning to Hal McIntyre in 1943 and Harry James briefly in the following year. Later in the 1940s Ward continued radio work and appeared with artists including McIntyre, Peanuts Hucko and Wild Bill Davison (she also worked as radio producer for WGM New York) but apart from occasional recordings was largely retired. However, in the late 1970s she made a comeback, appearing at the Waldorf-Astoria and Rainbow Room, New York, as well as in stage shows, recording *The Helen Ward Songbook* (1981; Lyricon) with an A-team of swing partners (Braff, Pee Wee Erwin, Vic Dickenson, Phil Bodner, Steve Jordan). [DF]

The Queen of Big Band Swing 1935-43 (ASV). Very worthwhile (and overdue) selection of Ward's best sides, 14 with Goodman, plus Teddy Wilson, Gene Krupa, Bob Crosby, Joe Sullivan and Harry James.

Anita Wardell

Vocals.

b. Guildford, UK, 23 Aug 1961.

After emigrating to Australia in 1973, Wardell studied jazz and performance at Adelaide University. Gigging in both Adelaide and Sydney, she twice won the top jazz vocal award in 1984 and 1987, and recorded two albums as a member of the vocal group Adelaide Connection, with Don Burrows and James Morrison. Moving to London in 1989, she studied at the Guildhall School, and began performing and teaching vocal workshops. She has released two duo albums, one with Liam Noble and one with Czech pianist Emil Viklicky, and works with the Michael Garrick big band. She collaborated with Norma Winstone, Kenny Wheeler and John Taylor at the 1998 Berlin festival, and currently leads her own quartet. Inspired by Parker and Coltrane, she names her favourite vocalists as Jon Hendricks, Betty Carter, Mark Murphy and Norma Winstone. [BP]

Why Do You Cry? (1995; FMR/Ultimate Groove). This duo set with Liam Noble, as well as demonstrating a fine rapport, highlights Wardell's control of pitch, tone and content on a mostly standard programme, with her occasional scat improvisations actually enhancing the material.

➤➤ **Michael Garrick** *(Down On Your Knees)*.

David S. Ware

Saxophones.

b. Plainfield, New Jersey, 7 Nov 1949.

Ware began playing saxophone at the age of ten. His father was a saxophone fan with a large record collection and, as a teenager frequenting jazz clubs in New York, Ware was reportedly befriended by Sonny Rollins, who taught him the practice of circular breathing. After high school he briefly went to Berklee School of Music in Boston, but settled in New York in 1973. Ware played with Cecil Taylor at Carnegie Hall a year later and became a full-time member of the Taylor Unit, recording *Dark To Themselves* (1976; Enja) alongside alto saxophonist Jimmy Lyons. He recorded now out-of-print records for hat Hut (solo) and Palm, and appeared on two of the best, criminally underrated records of the period – drummer Andrew Cyrille's *Special People* (1980; Soul Note) and *Metamusicians' Stomp* (1978; Black Saint). as part of Cyrille's stellar quartet that included trumpeter Ted Daniel and bassist Nick DiGeranimo.

The 80s were tough for Ware, and he became a taxi driver for a while, though he continued to play sporadically and toured Europe. In 1988, he roared back into playing with *Passage To Music* (Silkheart), a trio with bassist William Parker and fellow Taylor Unit member Marc Edwards on drums. *Ware's Great Bliss* (1990; Silkheart) was the blueprint for the quartet model he has honed ever since – an expressionistic, at times explosive sound that owes a great deal to the levitational, spiritually motivated music of the late John Coltrane. With young pianist Matthew Shipp, bassist Parker and several different drummers – notably the outstanding Susie Ibarra and latterly Guillermo E. Brown – the David S. Ware quartet has achieved an unusual level of attention for a fiery free-jazz ensemble, garnering rave reviews in the pop and rock press and issuing records on indie rock labels. With his quartet, Ware has amassed an impressive discography, *Third Ear Recitation* (1993; DIW), *Earthquation* (1994; DIW), *Dao* (1996; Homestead) and *Wisdom Of Uncertainty* (1997; Aum Fidelity). The group had an unexpected, short-lived tenure on Columbia records, a result of the unlikely patronage of its A&R man, one Branford Marsalis: *Go And See The World* and *Surrendered* (2000) were its fruits. Ware continues to challenge himself, fanning the flames of his "fire music" in different directions: the electronica-adorned *Corridors And Parallels* (2001) and a reading of Sonny Rollins's epic *Freedom Suite* (2002) on AUM Fidelity, and a late foray into composition for a string ensemble, documented on *Threads* (Thirsty Ear; 2003). [JC]

Flight Of I (1992; DIW/Columbia). An early outing, but this record still finds the flagship 90s free-jazz rebirth band at its best, with dismantled and reconstructed versions of standards –"There Will Never Be Another You", "Sad Eyes" and "Yesterdays" – interspersed with original compositions. Ware's burly sound and pedal-heavy incantations from Shipp give the group weight; on later CDs those factors often just weigh them down.

Wilbur Ware

Bass.

b. Chicago, 8 Sept 1923; d. 9 Sept 1979.

Ware taught himself to play the banjo and a bass homemade by his foster-father. He played in local string bands, and claimed to have recorded with blues singer Big Bill Broonzy in 1936. Later he worked professionally in groups led by Stuff Smith, Roy Eldridge, Sonny Stitt and others in the late 1940s. He led his own groups intermittently from 1953 onwards, and toured with Eddie Vinson in 1954–5, Art Blakey in the summer of 1956, and Buddy DeFranco in 1957. In 1957 and early 1958 he was a member of the classic Thelonious Monk quartet, and played with J.R. Monterose in 1959. He returned to Chicago in 1959, working locally, but then became inactive for a while. Returning to New York in the late 1960s, he gigged with Monk in 1970, and recorded with Clifford Jordan in 1969 and 1976, and with Paul Jeffrey in 1972.

Ware had an instrumental sound redolent of the bop era, similar to certain players who flourished in the 1940s but were gradually left behind by later developments. However, Ware himself influenced those later developments through an idiosyncratic style that may have originated in getting around technical "limitations" (the same allegation, of course, is made about Monk and Miles Davis). Either way, Wilbur's concentration on the lower range of the bass was considerably lightened by his rapid articulation, which – especially though not exclusively while soloing – enabled him to break up the beat in a way that, though rather four-square rhythmically, was totally unexpected from a bassist. Equally, his devotion to the root-notes of chords was varied by his choice of unusual passing tones and substitutions. Taken together, these aspects of Ware's work set an example for Charlie Haden and other players of the 1960s who were diametrically opposed to the Scott LaFaro school. [BP]

➤➤ **Thelonious Monk** *(Thelonious Monk With John Coltrane)*; **Sonny Rollins** *(A Night At The Village Vanguard Vols.1 & 2)*.

Ray Warleigh

Saxophones, flute, clarinet.

b. Sydney, Australia, 28 Sept 1938.

Inspired to take up alto by hearing Paul Desmond, Ray Warleigh started his pro career in 1959, moving to the UK in 1960. In the 1960s he played with a great many UK-based musicians, including Mike Gibbs, Alexis Korner, Tubby Hayes, Ronnie Scott and Mike Westbrook, and in the late 1960s and early 1970s he played with drummer John Stevens's Spontaneous Music Ensemble. In addition to playing with guitarist Allan Holdsworth and drummer Tommy Chase in the 1970s, Warleigh was prominently featured in the pioneering Latin-influenced band Paz, formed by composer/vibraphone player Dick Crouch. His vibrant alto and flute have been a great asset in a number of ambitious larger jazz ensembles, such as those of Kenny Wheeler and Charlie Watts: he contributed to Wheeler's *Music For Large & Small Ensembles* (1990) and composer Gavin Bryars' *After the Requiem* (1991). He is also a very busy studio session musician, having played on albums by artists as diverse as John Mayall, Roy Harper and Ashley Hutchings. In the 1990s and into the new century he continued his extensive freelance activities, playing with big bands – a German radio orchestra in Cologne, the London Jazz Orchestra – and with UK leaders such as Stan Tracey and Derek Wadsworth. He played on the soundtrack to Mike Figgis' *Leaving Las Vegas* and he can also be heard on the Dedication Orchestra's New Year gig at London's 100 Club, caught on *Spirits Rejoice* (1992; Ogun). He continues to lead his own modern-jazz quartet. [CP]

Ray Warleigh's First Album (1968; Philips). An ambitious debut album featuring both a jazz group, including pianist Gordon Beck and guitarist Dave Goldberg, and an orchestra (conductors Jimmy Deuchar and Harry South).

Paz

Look Inside (1983; Paladin). Paz's customary mix of jazz improvisation, Brazilian rhythms and cogent writing, including the disco hit "AC/DC".

➤➤ **Kenny Wheeler** *(Music For Large And Small Ensembles)*.

Earle Warren

Alto saxophone, clarinet, vocals.

b. Springfield, Ohio, 1 July 1914; d. 4 June 1995.

Count Basie's first great lead alto saxophonist – he joined in 1937 in Pittsburgh, replacing Caughey Roberts – Earle Warren was young, highly responsible and a first-class reader, who had already led his own bands around Cleveland, Ohio. After he joined Basie he demonstrated (like Willie Smith) a natural gift for section-leading, a warm plummy voice, and a devotion to Basie's early insecure course that often left him, as he said, "without a nickel to ride the subway". Warren's intense, orange-toned alto was a capable solo voice, but later on – after Basie began to feature his saxophone tandem of Herschel Evans and Lester Young – he was heard more often as a brief shaft of light amid the battling tenors: "I got all the bridges – eight bars in the middle of everything." For the next thirteen years (with occasional absences for band-leading and a bout of lung trouble in 1948)

Warren played and sang with Basie – his vocal features included "Ride On" and "I Struck A Match In The Dark", during which, in a Venuti-esque moment, Lester Young once set fire to Warren's music. In 1950 he struck out for a solo career, working as manager for top acts like Johnny Otis, as an MC, and as bandleader and soloist, with among others Buck Clayton and the vocal group The Platters. In the 1970s and 1980s Warren was as busy as ever, often touring as a soloist and appearing with his own group the Countsmen, featuring swing masters Dicky Wells and Claude Hopkins. [DF]

➤➤ **Count Basie** *(The Original American Decca Recordings).*

Huw Warren

Piano, accordion, cello.

b. Swansea, Wales, 18 May 1962.

Warren studied piano from the age of ten and his earliest musical experiences were as a classical cellist, and as an organist in the working men's clubs of South Wales. Warren moved to London in 1980, studying at Goldsmiths' College and then on the Guildhall School's postgraduate jazz course. He was active in experimental new music, performing with John Cage and John Tilbury, before he began doing jazz gigs. He deputized for Django Bates in Loose Tubes, which brought him into contact with the emerging new British jazz scene. This resulted in work with Mark Lockheart, Steve and Julian Argüelles, Dudley Phillips and Brian Abrahams's District Six. Warren also played with Iranian, African, Brazilian and Indian musicians. In the later 1980s he collaborated with singer June Tabor, recording six albums and touring worldwide with her.

At the beginning of the 1990s he became a member of Perfect Houseplants with Mark Lockheart, Dudley Phillips and Martin France. One of the most creative British groups, they have released four critically acclaimed albums and undertaken adventurous projects with the early music vocal quartet Orlando Consort and with Baroque violinist Andrew Manze. Warren has also had fruitful working relationships with Christine Tobin, Billy Jenkins and singers Billy Bragg and Eddi Reader. With John Parricelli he also leads the Vortex Jazz Quartet, which has performed with leading musicians such as Kenny Wheeler, Iain Ballamy, Norma Winstone and Tim Garland. After over 30 appearances on CD his own debut album, *A Barrel Organ Far From Home*, came quite late in 1997 and was followed four years later with *Infinite Riches In A Little Room*. Warren is a consummate pianist, with an often volatile and quirky imagination, but he can also summon a sonority and emotional eloquence evoking Keith Jarrett, one of his favourite pianists. His aim in music-making on record is, he says, "to explore a larger soundworld than a more conventional jazz record, also getting the right balance between writing, improvisation-experimentalism, and accessibility". [IC]

Huw Warren
A Barrel Organ Far from Home

⊙ **A Barrel Organ Far From Home** (1997; Babel). Melancholia and ecstasy jostle in this highly original confection. Warren deploys a nine-piece pool of musicians, splintering into unusual combinations of his piano and accordion with cello, viola, violin, whistles, saxophone, clarinet and the usual jazz rhythm-section of bass and drums. Warren is a jazz musician with a larger social view, his music fascinating and unclassifiable.

⊙ **Infinite Riches In A Little Room** (2001; Babel). A resonant, typically imaginative solo piano recital, coloured by sensitive use of electronics and ranging from meditations on themes by John Dowland and Charlie Parker to out-and-out avant irreverence.

Dinah Washington

Vocals.

b. Tuscaloosa, Alabama, 29 Aug 1924; d. 14 Dec 1963.

Washington, née Ruth Lee Jones, sang gospel as a member of the Chicago-based Sara Martin Singers while she was a teenager. After winning an amateur contest, she worked in the early 1940s in Chicago nightclubs, then joined the Lionel Hampton band from 1943–6, and began making records under her own name. Although her success in the burgeoning R&B field seldom diminished, from the mid-1950s she also made albums with jazz groups, and others that benefited from a more middle-of-the-road packaging of her distinctive style. Her turbulent private life, involving several marriages and alcoholism, ended in premature death.

The most influential female singer of the last forty years, she achieved what Ray Charles did for male vocalists, making the phrasing and tonal variations of gospel soloists an inescapable part of popular music. As early as the late 1940s her records were being "covered" by white artists such as the derivative Kay Starr, so that her innovations were absorbed extremely rapidly, but it was she who paved the way for Aretha Franklin and Esther Phillips, not to mention gospel-influenced jazz singers who moved on to more popular work, for example Ernestine Anderson and Nancy Wilson. Her most widely known records may

Herman Leonard

Dinah Washington

have seemed rather mannered when the material was not very strong, but her interpretative qualities were at their best against a relaxed jazz backing. [BP]

Dinah Jams (1954; Emarcy). A live set in front of a studio audience, this has relaxed singing from Washington sparked by Clifford Brown, Max Roach, Clark Terry and Maynard Ferguson. The CD reissue also includes her originally unissued, affectionately accurate take-off of Billie Holiday on "Crazy He Calls Me".

The Swinging Miss "D" (1956; Verve). One of Dinah's most vital albums, with big-band backing by Quincy Jones and soloists including Clark Terry, Quentin Jackson and Lucky Thompson, has her putting her stamp on some venerable standards. Seven additional tracks with a similar band were intended as pop singles, but include her version of "Drown In My Own Tears".

Grover Washington Jnr

Saxophones, clarinet, electric bass, piano.
b. Buffalo, New York, 12 Dec 1943; d. 17 Dec 1999.

Washington began on sax at ten, and claims to have been working in clubs by the age of twelve. He studied at the Wurlitzer School of Music and played on baritone in high school bands. From 1959–63 he toured with the Four Clefs; the following two years were spent with organ trios and rock groups, and the years 1965–7 in the army. During the 1970s he achieved enormous success with a series of fusion albums that topped the US charts in all categories – pop, R&B and jazz. At least five of his albums went gold with sales of 500,000 or more, and his double-Grammy-winning *Winelight* went platinum with sales of over a million. Washington has achieved this success without ever having won a poll as an instrumentalist or a composer, and he has been truly savaged by critics on occasion. His brand of fusion – a kind of disco with soul and blues – was really pop music with a jazz tinge. Despite specializing in innocuous MOR, Washington composed some adept pieces and was himself a very fine saxophonist – a technically excellent player with a fine melodic sense and a resonant sound that projected great warmth. His sudden death inspired fulsome tributes to Washington as a Smooth Jazz pioneer though his main influences were, ironically, at the heart of the jazz tradition: Coleman Hawkins, Don Byas, Wardell Gray, Dexter Gordon, Johnny Griffin, Sonny Rollins and Gerry Mulligan. [IC]

Anthology Of Grover Washington Jr (1980–82; Elektra). This set culls its tracks from the albums *Winelight*, *Come Morning* and *The Best Is Yet To Come*, and includes hits such as "East River Drive" and his schmaltzy Grammy-winning ballad, "Just The Two Of Us".

Kenny Washington

Drums.
b. Brooklyn, New York, 29 May 1958.

Encouraged by his father, Washington took lessons with ex-Gillespie drummer Rudy Collins, before studying percussion at the High School of Music and Art. Already an expert drummer in his teens, Washington began gigging with the Lee Konitz nonet in 1977 and was a member of Betty Carter's group in 1978–9. He then continued freelancing with top musicians such as Kenny Burrell, Milt Jackson, George Coleman, Tommy Flanagan, Jay McShann and Benny Goodman, and twice replaced Dannie Richmond in the Mingus Dynasty. From 1980 into the 1990s he was the favoured drummer of Johnny Griffin, and from the late 1980s he also played with Benny Carter, Clark Terry and Dizzy Gillespie. Rather limitingly described elsewhere as "a hard-bop revivalist", Washington is in fact a drummer capable of working sympathetically with anyone, and his contribution invariably enhances any situation without drawing attention to himself. He teaches jazz drums at New York's New School and, an inveterate student of recorded jazz, he also presents a weekly programme of big-band music on WGBO radio. [BP]

>> **Johnny Griffin** *(The Cat)*; **Arturo Sandoval** *(I Remember Clifford)*.

Sadao Watanabe

Alto saxophone, flute, sopranino saxophone, composer.
b. Tochigi, Japan, 1 Feb 1933.

Sadao Watanabe began on clarinet at the age of fifteen in the school band and then took up alto saxophone. In 1953 he joined Toshiko Akiyoshi's quartet, taking over its leadership in 1956 when she left to study at Berklee. In 1962 Watanabe himself went to Berklee, spending three years in the USA and playing and recording with leading US musicians such as Gary McFarland and Chico Hamilton. Returning to Japan in 1965, he started a jazz school for young musicians the following year, eventually becoming one of the strongest musical influences in Japan – he was to be the first Japanese jazz musician to receive a National Award in Japan in 1977 – and his groups brought many fine musicians to prominence. In 68 he made his first appearance at the Newport jazz festival, and in 1970 played at Montreux and Newport. He performed with his quintet at the first Jazz Yatra in Bombay in 1978 and also played there in Clark Terry's international big band. As leader, he recorded regularly through the 1960s–2000s and now has dozens of albums to his credit, divided somewhat schizophrenically between Brazilianesque fusion albums and bebop outings. Primarily influenced by Charlie Parker and Gary McFarland, Watanabe is a virtuoso performer on all his instruments, and a fertile composer. [IC]

⊙ **Bossa Nova Concert** (1967–9; Denon). A Brazilian/fusion record, with Watanabe playing some beautiful flute, an instrument he has latterly abandoned.

⊙ **Round Trip** (1974; Vanguard); **Tokyo Dating** (1985; Elektra); **Remembrance** (1999; Verve). Watanabe in heavy, mightily swinging American company: the first has Chick Corea, Miroslav Vitous and Jack DeJohnette; the second a rhythm-section of pianist James Williams, bassist Charnett Moffett and drummer Jeff Watts; the third matches him with a new generation of young guns including trumpeter Nicholas Payton, pianist Cyrus Chestnut and bassist Christian McBride.

⊙ **Selected** (1983–8; Elektra). A compendium of Brazilianesque fusion tracks from the albums *Good Time For Love*, *Birds Of Passage* and *Elis*, with some excellent examples of Watanabe's sopranino-playing.

Benny Waters

Saxophones, clarinet, arranger.

b. Brighton, Maryland, 23 Jan 1902; d. 11 Aug 1998.

Waters studied at Boston Conservatory in the 1920s before playing with Charlie Johnson's band (1925–32) and recording with Clarence Williams and King Oliver. He worked busily through the 1930s with well-rated bands such as Hot Lips Page's and Fletcher Henderson's, then during and after the war he spent time with Claude Hopkins and Jimmie Lunceford, as well as working as a bandleader. By 1950 he was with the band Jimmy Archey had inherited from Bob Wilber, but soon after left for Europe, joining Jacques Butler's band in Paris in 1955. For the next fifteen years Waters's abilities were a European legend, and in the mid-1970s British promoter Dave Bennett set about remarketing him in Britain. For Bennett, Waters recorded, made festival appearances, and kept up an unrelenting round of European touring, making occasional visits back home to the USA. Short, squat and filled with a bustling energy, he still played with the same creative fire and blistering intensity: his solo performances included high-speed reruns of difficult test pieces like "Cherokee", as well as blues routines and standard swing tunes (on which he played layered solos, full of complex runs, swiftly delivered ideas and altissimo harmonics). [DF]

⊙ **Benny Waters-Freddy Randall Jazz Band** (1982; Jazzology). Waters in a Dixieland context, with the added attraction of Freddy Randall on his last recording date (so far) and veteran Tiny Winters playing slap-bass in the rhythm-section.

⊙ **Hearing Is Convincing** (1987; Muse). A fine quartet date on which Waters plays clarinet, tenor and alto, giving an extended demonstration of his high-energy talents.

⊙ **Swinging Again** (1993; Jazzpoint). Another good quartet session on which Waters sings as well as plays; tidy support from his rhythm-section.

Ethel Waters

Vocals.

b. Chester, Pennsylvania, 31 Oct 1896; d. 1 Sept 1977.

"She sang, man, she really sang," said Jimmy McPartland of Ethel Waters. "We were enthralled with her. We liked Bessie Smith very much, too, but Waters had more polish, I guess you'd say. She phrased so wonderfully, the natural quality of her voice was so fine and she sang the way she felt – that knocked us out always with any artist." A deeply religious woman who used God to keep her own violent demons at bay, during the 1920s Waters toured with Fletcher Henderson's Black Swan Troubadors (her first record for Black Swan, "Oh Daddy'/'Down Home Blues", she said, "got Black Swan out of the red"), appeared at all the best theatres and nightspots, played revue, did the TOBA circuit, and became the first black singer to broadcast in the Deep South. By the end of the decade she was a star as well as a jazz singer. She recorded with Duke Ellington in 1932, Benny Goodman in 1933 ("It was a caper and a delight doing those records with those fellows who could ad lib my music round me"), and toured with her husband, trumpeter Eddie Mallory, for the next six years. After that – with films such as *Cabin in The Sky* (1943), revues such as *Laugh Time* and Broadway plays including *Mamba's Daughter* (1939) – Waters turned into a well-rated actress, and she was seldom out of the public eye for long: until she died at 80, she continued appearing on radio, TV and films, singing and working for religious charities, and putting in live appearances. Her autobiography, deeply disturbing, often violent, is the portrait of a cruelly persecuted black woman determined to succeed, with her fists if necessary. It makes a vivid contrast to Billie Holiday's sad downward run and shows how two underprivileged and talented women of their time found different solutions to the same problem. [DF]

⊙ **Ethel Waters 1923–40** (Classics). It's good that the Classics series saw fit to include Waters in their schedules, and all her sides are in these six volumes; variable quality but first-rate music as a rule, with many of the kings of her generation – Ellington, Goodman and many more.

Matt Wates

Alto sax, flute.

b.London, 7 February 1964.

Wates started playing alto sax at the age of fifteen and later played in the National Youth Jazz Orchestra. After graduating from Berklee College of Music, Boston, in 1988, he returned to London and became a member of several important British groups, including the Latin fusion band Paz, the saxophone quartet Itchy Finger, and Mario Castronari's Roadside Picnic, recording with all three bands. He also played in bands led by Michael Garrick and Humphrey Lyttelton. In 1993 he formed his own group, The Matt Wates Sextet, in order to showcase his own compositions and arrangements, and in the same year recorded an album for Audio-B entitled *Relaxin' At The Cat*. Four years later he won the Rising Star Award, and in 2001 the Matt Wates Sextet won Best Small Group category – both in the BT British Jazz Awards. Apart from Wates, the two members of the sextet who have remained a constant since its inception are the gifted trumpeter and flugelhorn player Martin Shaw and bassist Malcolm Creese. The current lineup is completed by Canadian Steve Kalestad on tenor sax, Leon Greening on piano and Steve Brown on drums. Wates's principal inspirations as a player are Cannonball Adderley and Stan Getz. [IC]

⊙ **The Miller's Tale** (2003; Audio-B). This is the fifth Matt Wates Sextet album and the best so far, consisting of both Wates' own compositions and some standards. As always with Wates, the arrangements are highly original and pack a real punch in their mixture of hard bop and colourful harmonies.

Doug Watkins

Bass.

b. Detroit, Michigan, 2 March 1934; d. 5 Feb 1962.

Watkins left Detroit to tour briefly with James Moody in 1953, and then moved to New York, where in 1954 he gigged separately with Kenny Dorham and the others who became, along with him, the Jazz Messengers in 1955–6. He joined the Horace Silver quintet in 1956–7, recording with them under Silver's name and those of Donald Byrd and Hank Mobley. He was also found on sessions with many others, such as Sonny Rollins, Lee Morgan and Jackie McLean, during the late 1950s. After a hiatus he reappeared in the Charles Mingus group in 1961, while Mingus played piano. He was on his way to reside in San Francisco when a car accident ended his life.

Watkins was one of the important generation of musicians who came out of Detroit in the mid-1950s. He shared many of the characteristics of the great Paul Chambers, who was his cousin by marriage; although more reticent as regards solo work, his time-playing showed the same combination of reliability and resilience. It is to be regretted that he was never in the limelight as much as Chambers and, since his death, his contribution has been largely overlooked. [BP]

➤➤ **Sonny Rollins** *(Saxophone Colossus).*

Julius Watkins

French horn.

b. Detroit, Michigan, 10 Oct 1921; d. 4 April 1977.

Watkins started playing at the age of nine. He worked with the Ernie Fields band on trumpet from 1943–6, but he recorded on French horn for Kenny Clarke (with other Detroiters including Milt Jackson) and for Babs Gonzales in 1949. The same year he was a member of the Milt Buckner big band, and then began three years' study at the Manhattan School of Music. He did much small-group work (including making a recording with Thelonious Monk in 1953) and he co-led his own occasional group, Les Jazz Modes, with Charlie Rouse from 1956–9. He was involved in many short-lived big bands, led by Pete Rugolo, Oscar Pettiford, Johnny Richards and George Shearing and the Quincy Jones touring band from 1959–61. There was also frequent studio work, including appearances on the Miles Davis-Gil Evans albums, and recording and live appearances with Charles Mingus in 1965 and 1971. Watkins was the first musician to show the possibilities of the French horn in bebop improvisation. Thanks to his punchy phrasing and pointed tone, he succeeded where (a few) others unwittingly underlined the difficulties of the instrument itself. [BP]

THELONIOUS MONK

⊙ **Monk** (1953–4; Prestige). Watkins is present on the earlier of two quintet sessions (the other, equally good, featuring Frank Foster). To say that the French horn solos are not anti-climactic alongside Monk and Rollins is sufficient recommendation.

➤➤ **Cal Massey** *(Blues To Coltrane).*

Cleveland Watkiss

Voice, piano, guitar, composer.

b. Hackney, London, 21 Oct 1959.

Watkiss is one of the most talented and versatile British singers around, able to embrace a range of vocal styles with amazing ease – rock, reggae, drum'n'bass as well as jazz. Brought up in Hackney, Watkiss' father was a music enthusiast and both Cleveland and his piano-playing younger brother Trevor were exposed to a lot of different types of music from a very early age. Inspired by Jamaican singers, like Dennis Brown, Bob Marley and Jacob Miller, Watkiss played in local funk and reggae bands during the late 70s. In 1981 he formed his first jazz band, Alumni, and had a three year residency at Blake's Wine Bar in Covent Garden. The following year he joined

Simon Purcell's Jazz Train, an outfit that played in the style of Art Blakey's Jazz Messengers but with vocals. Watkiss also toured with Kenny Wheeler, John Taylor and Norma Winstone.

In 1985 Watkiss was a co-founder with Courtney Pine of Jazz Warriors, a robust and influential big band in which young black musicians could find their feet. Two years later Jazz Warriors won The Wire/Guardian Best Band Award, with Watkiss picking up Best Vocalist Award, and the band recorded the album *Out Of Many, One People* (Antilles) on which Watkiss' scatting made a significant contribution. Watkiss won the same award for the next two years. He has also worked extensively with the London Community Gospel Choir, and recorded a track, "Free", with them for Stevie Wonder's album *Characters* (1990). In 1989 he appeared with The Who on its 25th Anniversary tour of the USA, and he has worked on other projects with Pete Townsend. Two solo albums, *Green Chimneys* (1990; Polydor) and *Blessing In Disguise* (1991; Polydor), were both critically acclaimed, and Watkiss went on to form a drum'n'bass trio, Project 23, with drummer Marque Gilmore and UK garage pioneer DJ Le Rouge. Other projects include working with both Talvin Singh (on his Mercury award winning album *OK*) and a residency as vocalist/MC at London's Blue Note Club. More recently he has recorded a third album, *Victory's Happy Song Book*, which he describes as "a good summation of all that I do," and collaborated with pianist Nikki Yeoh. [IC]

⊙ **Victory's Happy Song Book** (2001; Touch Down Soundz). Not – strictly speaking – a jazz album, but a classy enterprise nevertheless, with Watkiss running the gamut of his brilliant vocal techniques with some splendid support from regular collaborators Byron Wallen (trumpet), Jean Toussaint (sax) and Tom Skinner (drums).

➤➤ **Jazz Warriors** *(Out Of Many, One People)*; **Nikki Yeoh** *(Mutual Serenade)*.

Bill Watrous

Trombone, composer.
b. Middletown, Connecticut, 8 June 1939.

Watrous played in trad jazz bands as a teenager and studied with Herbie Nichols while in the military. He made his debut with Billy Butterfield, going on to play with Roy Eldridge, Kai Winding, Quincy Jones, Woody Herman, Johnny Richards, Count Basie and others. From 1967–70 he worked as a studio musician at CBS and ABC (for the Dick Cavett show). In 1971 he was a member of the jazz-rock band Ten Wheel Drive and then formed his own big band, Manhattan Wildlife Refuge, who were signed to Columbia. Settling in L.A. in the late 1970s, he toured internationally as a soloist with local rhythm-sections throughout the 1980s and beyond, and continued to lead big bands. Watrous is a technically brilliant performer with a flawless tone. His influences include Clifford Brown, Charlie Parker, Carl Fontana, Vic Dickenson and Dizzy Gillespie. [IC]

⊙ **Bill Watrous In London** (1982; Mole). This was recorded with a fine British rhythm-section – pianist Brian Dee, bassist Len Skeat and drummer Martin Drew. Watrous has a great tone and a possibly unsurpassable speed of execution, and both are prominent on this standards and blues session.

⊙ **Bill Watrous And Carl Fontana** (2000; Atlas). Two great trombone virtuosi in an amiable, expert straight-ahead sparring session.

Bobby Watson

Alto and soprano saxophones, clarinet, flute, piano.
b. Lawrence, Kansas, 23 Aug 1953.

Watson began playing the piano at ten, the clarinet at eleven, and saxophone when he was in the eighth grade. He played R&B while at school, and began arranging and composing for the concert band. In 1970 he started private lessons on clarinet with Carlo Minnetti, and in 1975 graduated in theory and composition from the University of Miami. He then left for New York, and from 1977–81 he played with Art Blakey's Jazz Messengers. After leaving Blakey he began a regular association with several groups: from 1981 he was with the George Coleman octet, and played lead alto with Charli Persip and Superband; from 1982 he played with the

Jak Kilby

Bobby Watson, with Curtis Lundy on bass

Louis Hayes quartet; and in 1983 he was a co-founder of the Twenty-Ninth Street Saxophone Quartet. He also worked with Sam Rivers's Winds of Manhattan and Philly Joe Jones.

Since the mid-80s Watson has established himself as an outright leader of small groups. He performed his *Afroism Suite* in 1994 in Vienna and Glasgow and through the 1980s and 1990s recorded for Blue Note, Columbia and latterly Red, among other labels. His wife Pamela, a singer and composer, has sung and performed her songs with him, perhaps most notably on *Quiet As It's Kept* (1999; Red). He is currently the director of jazz studies at the University of Missouri/Kansas City Conservatory of Music. Watson likes any alto players with "a great sound", but particularly Cannonball Adderley, Charlie Parker and Jackie McLean, and he recorded a tribute to Johnny Hodges, *The Year Of The Rabbit*, in 1987. He has absorbed all these influences and arrived at a highly individual, extraordinarily fluid style imbued with powerful feeling. [IC]

⊙ **Love Remains** (1986; Red). This is a superb quartet album with pianist John Hicks, bassist Curtis Lundy and the ubiquitous Marvin "Smitty" Smith. Under Watson's spell, with more than a little compositional help from his wife Pamela, the band ranges from bebop ("Mystery Of Ebop") through funk ("Dark Days") to romantic ballad ("Love Remains").

⊙ **Tailor Made** (1993; Columbia). An excellent big-band album with an almost completely fresh repertoire (Pamela Watson contributes two pieces). The rhythm-section is superb and the whole thing beautifully recorded.

⊙ **Midwest Shuffle** (1993; Columbia). This is a brilliant live session by Watson's quintet, with fine work by young trumpeter Terell Stafford, and stunning work from the Lewis-propelled rhythm-section. Watson's compositions are deft and to the point, and the solos are played in kind.

➤➤ **Art Blakey** *(Straight Ahead)*; **Twenty-Ninth Street Saxophone Quartet** *(Live; Underground; Your Move)*.

Leo Watson

Vocals, drums, trombone, tipple.

b. Kansas City, Missouri, 27 Feb 1898; d. 2 May 1950.

Watson attracted attention after he joined Virgil Scroggins, Wilbur and Douglas Daniels and guitarist Buddy Burton in a novelty act in 1929. Later, at the Onyx Club, New York, they were to find fame as the Spirits of Rhythm (by that time Teddy Bunn had replaced Burton). Watson's scat caused a sensation – he improvised melodies at the same time as lyrics with mind-boggling ease – and he was great to watch as well, miming trombone as he created his whirlwind vocalese. Watson later worked briefly for big bands led by Artie Shaw, Gene Krupa (their version of "Nagasaki" is perhaps the best ever) and Jimmy Mundy, as well as appearing regularly in reincarnations of the highly successful Spirits, and in 1946 he appeared with Slim and Slam around Los Angeles. "He was original," says Slim Gaillard. "Everybody in Hollywood used to come and listen to him. And they'd follow everything he said, because he could sing about anything! He'd start singing about the walls, the rug, the table, ashtrays – he'd just sing!" His act made a deep impression on young singers, including Mel Tormé, who saw Watson's "total improvisation" as the definition of "jazz singing". For the last few years of his life (he died at 52 of pneumonia) Watson worked the cabaret circuit as a solo performer, and sang and played drums for Charlie Raye's band. [DF]

➤➤ **The Spirits Of Rhythm** *(The Spirits Of Rhythm)*.

Lu Watters

Trumpet.

b. Santa Cruz, California, 19 Dec 1911; d. 5 Nov 1990.

After being "most promising bugler" at St Joseph's Military Academy, Sacramento, Lu (Lucious) Watters formed his first jazz band in 1925, and all through the 1930s was working around San Francisco in small groups as well as with his own eleven-piece, formed for a residency at Sweet's Ballroom, Oakland. By 1939 he was rehearsing nightly at the Big Bear in Berkeley Hills with Paul Lingle, Turk Murphy and other kindred spirits, then in December 1939 moved into the Dawn Club every Monday night with his new band, playing back-to-the-roots King Oliver-style jazz. By 1940 his group was so successful that they officially retitled themselves the Yerba Buena Jazz Band, and began a phenomenally successful career as America's first real revivalist band. "It certainly is funny to hear those youngsters trying to play like old men!" said Bobby Hackett, but Watters was unstoppable: his band signed to the Jazz Man label, played and recorded with Bunk Johnson, and packed the Dawn Club nightly with their stomping two-beat sound. From 1942–5 Watters served in the navy (where he led a twenty-piece band in Hawaii), then he regrouped his Yerba Buenans and opened his own Dawn Club on Annie Street in March 1946, to continued success; in June 1947 the whole band moved to Hambone Kelly's Club in El Cerrito, where they remained until the end of 1950. By that time the Yerba Buenans had gone about as far as they could go: the revival had been launched worldwide and they had broadcast and recorded regularly for ten years, but Watters had lost two key-men, Turk Murphy and Bob Scobey, who had gone out on their own. In 1950 he wound up his operation and later studied geology instead. [DF]

⊙ **The Complete Good Time Jazz Recordings 1941–50** (Good Time Jazz). All the classics on four CDs, also containing early recordings by cornettist Bennie Strickland. Packaged with a comprehensive booklet, this is essential for students of West Coast traditional jazz, a school that has maintained its artistic impetus over four and a half decades.

⊙ **Live At Hambone Kelly's 1950** (GHB). Excellent example of the Watters band late in its career, recorded live at its principal stronghold with old hands Bob Helm and Wally Rose still on board.

Charlie Watts

Drums.

b. London, 2 July 1941.

Though best known as superstar drummer with the Rolling Stones, Charlie Watts has always been a committed jazz follower. A childhood friend of British bassist Dave Green, Watts regularly heard Phil Seamen and his drumming compatriots in Britain's clubland at the turn of the 1960s; he also worked with Alexis Korner's seminal R&B group. However, it was not until the 1980s that his jazz preoccupations came strongly to the surface, when he briefly organized a big band (containing double rations of almost every instrument) for recording plus a headlining visit to America. Watts's most notable jazz achievement began in 1991 when he first organized a quintet (completed by Gerard Presencer, Peter King, Brian Lemon and Dave Green) dedicated to Parker and his music. The quintet recorded, toured to sellout crowds in the USA, and continues to work regularly in between Watts's tours with the Stones. [DF]

⊙ **With Strings – A Tribute To Charlie Parker** (1991; Continuum). Recorded live at Ronnie Scott's, Birmingham, this musically admirable package – with narration and vocals by Bernard Fowler, and strings – has tracks from Watts's Parker-style album *From One Charlie*, plus one new original and eight Parker standards.

Ernie Watts

Saxophones.

b. Norfolk, Virginia, 23 Oct 1945.

After studying at Boston's Berklee School of Music, Ernie Watts toured and recorded with Buddy Rich's band in 1966–8 before moving to Los Angeles. On the West Coast he joined the bands of Oliver Nelson (playing on the album Nelson made with Thelonious Monk in 1968) and Gerald Wilson, as well as establishing himself as a staff musician for NBC. In 1969 Watts recorded with violinist Jean-Luc Ponty, and thenceforth collaborated with a number of jazz-rock artists, including Lee Ritenour and Stanley Clarke, forming his own jazz-rock band, the Ernie Watts Quartet. In the 70s, alongside studio session work, Watts recorded with Gerry Mulligan, Cannonball Adderley, Sadao Watanabe, Anita O'Day and George Cables, among many others, but it was for his work on the music for the film *Chariots Of Fire* that he received a Grammy in 1982. In the mid-1980s Watts was recruited by bassist Charlie Haden for his band Quartet West, but it is for his own elegant, thoughtful recordings of the late 1980s and 1990s that he is justly celebrated. These include: an intriguing world-music/ecology album, *Afoxé*, featuring Brazilian singer Gilberto Gil; *The Long Road Home* (1996; JVC), a classy, ruminative album featuring pianist Kenny Barron; and *Classic Moods* (1998; JVC), upon which the supremely cultured and uniquely affecting Watts tone eases movingly through the likes of "In A Sentimental Mood", "Lush Life" and "Good Morning Heartache", backed by pianist Mulgrew Miller, bassist George Mraz and drummer Jimmy Cobb. He is still to be heard on the international jazz circuit. [CP]

⊙ **Ernie Watts Quartet** (1987; JVC). Backed by an unspectacular rhythm-section – Pat Coil (piano), Joel Di Bartolo (bass) and Bob Leatherbarrow (drums) – Watts muscles his way through a pleasant set including "Body And Soul".

⊙ **Reaching Up** (1993; JVC). The most representative Watts jazz album yet, with a superb band – Arturo Sandoval (trumpet), Mulgrew Miller (piano), Charles Fambrough (bass) and Jack DeJohnette (drums) – showing off Watts's highly individual sound to perfection.

Charlie Haden

⊙ **Quartet West** (1987; Verve). A classy album featuring Watts on tenor, alto and soprano alongside Alan Broadbent (piano), Billy Higgins (drums) and Haden himself, on material such as Pat Metheny's "Hermitage", Ornette Coleman's "The Good Life" and Charlie Parker's "Passport".

Jeff "Tain" Watts

Drums.

b. Pittsburgh, Pennsylvania, 20 Jan 1960.

Since he achieved worldwide prominence in the jazz world through his association with the Marsalises – trumpeter Wynton and saxophonist Branford – Jeff Watts has been one of the most in-demand drummers of his generation. His partnership with bassist Robert Hurst in the groups of both Marsalises has been utilized not only by pianists Donald Brown and Geri Allen, but by saxophonists Ricky Ford and Rick Margitza on late 1980s and early 1990s recordings; he has also partnered bassist contemporaries such as Charnett Moffett and Ira Coleman on albums by a wide range of artists, including trombonist Robin Eubanks, singer Betty Carter, pianists McCoy Tyner and Stephen Scott, and saxophonists Gary Thomas, Sadao Watanabe and Jim Snidero. He appears on albums by guitarists Ron Affif and Paul Bollenback. Highlights of the later 1990s included his collaborations with saxophonists Greg Osby (*Art Forum*, 1996, on Blue Note), Kenny Garrett (*Songbook*, 1997, on Warner Bros) and Michael Brecker (*Two Blocks From The Edge*, 1998, on Impulse!), with whom he also toured Europe. Notable among his many latterday sessions include those for vibraphonist Joe Locke and pianists Renee Rosnes, Dave Kikoski and Joey Calderazzo. Though his association with Branford Marsalis continues to produce perhaps his most vibrant performances, his two Columbia albums as leader, *Citizen Tain* (1999) and *Bar Talk* (2002), come close. A hard-swinging, virtuosic drummer who always contrives to temper his bristling assertiveness with subtlety and tastefulness, Watts is one of a handful of drummers whose presence at the heart of a rhythm-section is a guarantee of excellence. [CP]

⊙ **Megawatts** (1991; Sunnyside). Two Watts originals ornament his debut session as a leader; Kenny Kirkland (piano) and Charles Fambrough (bass) – the original Wynton Marsalis rhythm-section – provide excellent support on an album at its best at fast tempos.

Bar Talk (2002; Columbia). The Branford-meets-Brecker burner "Mr J.J." is an obvious highlight, but there's much of consequence on this wide-ranging, nuanced album, featuring Joey Calderazzo (piano), James Genus (bass) and further guests Hiram Bullock (guitar) and Ravi Coltrane (tenor).

➤➤ **Branford Marsalis** *(Trio Jeepy; Crazy People Music).*

Trevor Watts

Alto and soprano saxophones, bass clarinet; also piano.
b. York, UK, 26 Feb 1939.

Watts's parents loved jazz and he heard it from an early age. Largely self-taught, he began on cornet at twelve and took up the saxophone at eighteen. From 1958–63 he played in an RAF band and, when demobilized in 1963, went to London and joined the New Jazz Orchestra. In 1965 he was a founder member of the free-improv Spontaneous Music Ensemble, and formed his first group, Amalgam, in 1967. In 1972–3 he was with the Pierre Jarre group, in 1973 with Bobby Bradford, in 1973–4 with Stan Tracey, and he has been a frequent member of the London Jazz Composers' Orchestra since 1972. In 1976 he formed the Trevor Watts String Ensemble and in 1978 the Universal Music Group. In 1982 he formed Moiré Music and Drum Orchestra, with which he has explored textures made up of overlaid drum patterns, often inspired by African music – touring the world with the group in various forms until 1998. He has played with many of the leading UK improvisers, including Louis Moholo, John Stevens, Harry Miller and Keith Tippett. His current activities include: the Trevor Watts Celebration Band (an eight piece); an improvising duo with long term associate, pianist Veryan Weston; and his membership of the Gibran Cervantes-led Mexican ensemble Enjembre Acustico Urukongolo. [IC]

Trevor Watts And The Celebration Band (2001; Arc). Four saxophones (Watts, Rob Leake, Marcus Cummins and Amy Metcalf) interweave their lines over a polyrhythmic underpinning played on ethnic percussion and a guitar, bass and drums set-up. Alternately fiery and reflective, not to say uniquely inventive, this may be Watts working at the peak of his powers.

Moiré Music

A Wider Embrace (1993; ECM). Watts with bassist Colin Mackenzie and five African percussionists in an exploration of common ground. Although Watts was part of the 1960s avant-garde, he was always steeped in jazz, and over the years his passion has become more informed and his playing richer.

➤➤ **Barry Guy** *(Harmos).*

Teddy Weatherford

Piano.
b. Bluefield, West Virginia, 11 Oct 1903; d. Calcutta, 25 April 1945.

"A great pianist," says Hugues Panassié of Teddy Weatherford, "straightforward, with a powerful left hand. He played blues with a breadth and nostalgia proper to a musician from the South: he could also play good rags." Weatherford, who arrived in Chicago in 1921 from New Orleans, could well have occupied the position in jazz history later taken by Earl Hines, who learnt an incalculable amount from the huge-handed pianist who starred with Erskine Tate's Vendome orchestra. But in 1926, after a trip back to California, Weatherford took up an advantageous offer from bandleader Jack Carter to visit Asia, and stayed to lead his bands all over the Near and Far East. By 1929 he was resident at the Candidrome Club, Shanghai, and in 1934 recruited Buck Clayton's band *en bloc* to play the season there: subsequently he worked in Singapore, Java, and in India at the Taj Mahal Hotel and later the Grand Hotel, Calcutta. He died there of cholera, aged only 41. [DF]

➤➤ **Garnet Clark** *(Piano & Swing).*

Weather Report

➤➤ *see entry on* **Joe Zawinul**

Chick Webb

Drums, leader.
b. Baltimore, Maryland, 10 Feb 1909; d. 16 June 1939.

The greatest drummer-bandleader of the formative swing era, Chick (William Henry) Webb presented a startling image. "He was a tiny man," remembered Buddy Rich, "and with this big face and big stiff shoulders. He sat way up on a kind of throne and used a 28-inch bass drum which had special pedals for his feet, and he had those old gooseneck cymbal holders. Every beat was like a bell." Webb had been bandleading around New York for half a dozen years, usually with his constant friend, guitarist John Trueheart, before he moved into the Savoy in 1931, where he quickly became a fixture. Constantly on the lookout for talent (he was forever swapping good musicians for better with Fletcher Henderson), Webb was highly competitive: "He'd tell you he was the best right quick," said Sandy Williams. He jealously defended his band's reputation at the Savoy – a beautiful ballroom with a sprung floor and a booth full of ten-cent partners – taking on all comers with an onslaught of speciality acts and tightly rehearsed, newly commissioned arrangements. "Chick's was the greatest battling band," says Harry Carney, "and when Charlie Buchanan was at the Savoy he always saw to it that every new band hitting town battled with Chick."

In 1933 Webb hired arranger Edgar Sampson (a coup) and trumpeter Taft Jordan, whose Armstrong impressions were central to his show: by then he could hold off all opposition apart from Duke Ellington and the Casa Lomans. Finally, in 1935, Ella Fitzgerald – Webb's trump card – joined his band. A hit record,

"A-Tisket, A-Tasket", sealed their futures, and from then on "the little giant of the drums" (as Gene Krupa called him) was happy to build his show around his singer – he became her guardian, too, after Ella's mother died. Webb was a great drummer – "the best up to that time", says Eddie Durham – but owing to the limitations of recording techniques he was highly restricted in what he could do in a studio. By the time engineers had learned how to cope with jazz drummers, Webb was ill: tuberculosis of the spine reduced his powers and by 1938 he was using Arnold Bolden to back support acts on theatre engagements. As Webb's condition worsened, Sid Catlett, Bill Beason and Jesse Price, among others, filled in for him. "Just once towards the end," says Sandy Williams, "he was a little pitiful. 'When I was young and playing for peanuts', he said, 'I could eat anything you guys eat, but now I have all this money I can only eat certain things and can't even take a nip when I want to!'" After a major operation in a Baltimore hospital Webb sat up in bed: "I'm sorry, I've got to go," he said, then fell back and died. Ella Fitzgerald, who took over leadership of his band for two years afterwards, sang "My Buddy" at his funeral. [DF]

⊙ **Chick Webb And His Orchestra 1929–34 & 1935–38** (Classics). Webb's saga on two CDs, excluding his sides with Ella Fitzgerald (see below). Webb's orchestra is regularly underrated but was blessed with fine writers, such as Benny Carter and Edgar Sampson, and a roster of impressive soloists, including trumpeter Taft Jordan and trombonist Sandy Williams, as well as the leader. In the second volume Webb features on "Harlem Congo" and "Clap Hands Here Comes Charlie", and the tracks with his Little Chicks (featuring Wayman Carver on flute and Chauncey Haughton on clarinet) are as delicately brilliant as anything by John Kirby's band.

⊙ **Rhythm Man 1931–4** (Hep). Fine selection of Webb's earlier sides, including many of Edgar Sampson's greatest arrangements: "If Dreams Come True", "Let's Get Together", "Stomping At The Savoy" and more. Louis Jordan is generously featured on nine tracks.

⊙ **Stompin' At The Savoy 1934-39** (ASV). Good selection of 19 premier Webb instrumental sides (amongst them "Clap Hands Here Comes Charlie", "Liza" and Edgar Sampson's charming "If dreams come true") and six with Ella, avoiding her more juvenile material but including "A-Tisket, A-Tasket", "Rock It For Me" and "Sing Me A Swing Song".

➤➤ **Ella Fitzgerald** *(The Complete Recordings 1935–39).*

George Webb

Piano, leader.
b. London, 8 Oct 1917.

George Webb is the father of the British post-war jazz revival. His band, featuring Wally Fawkes (clarinet), Ed Harvey (trombone), Reg Rigden and Owen Bryce (trumpets), began playing at the Red Barn, Barnehurst (a London suburb), in 1942, and quickly acquired a dedicated following. After the war Webb's band acquired a regular sitter-in, Humphrey Lyttelton (who subsequently replaced Rigden and Bryce), a manager, Jim Godbolt, and began recording regularly, appearing on radio and playing London clubs and concerts. Playing a stomping two-beat re-creation of Armstrong/Oliver/Henderson/Ellington music, their rough-and-ready approach embodied jazz fans' dissatisfaction with the glossier banalities of swing. A dedicated amateur, Webb worked in 1948 with Humphrey Lyttelton's band (which was formed from ex-Webb musicians), then led for himself again briefly, but during the 1950s and 1960s was equally active as an agent, bringing American stars like Jessie Fuller to Britain. After the failure of a projected Isle of Man jazz festival, which foundered when its venue burnt down, he returned in the early 1970s to lead a band including Dennis Field (cornet), Terry Pitts (trombone) and Sammy Rimington (clarinet), and led bands regularly thereafter. From 1976 he ran a pub in Stansted, Essex, and by then his 1940s recordings were the subject of scholarly reissues; on 4 July 1985 a plaque was unveiled at the Red Barn commemorating Webb's achievements. In the later 1980s and the 1990s he occasionally reassembled his band for festivals and special appearances including annual fundraisers for Britain's National Jazz Archive at 100 Oxford Street. [DF]

⊙ **Dixielanders** (1946; Jazzology). Essential documentation of the band that founded the British revival; rough edges, but spirit enough to change the British jazz world. Humphrey Lyttelton, Wally Fawkes, Ed Harvey and Webb all provide spirited solo moments.

Speed Webb

Leader, drums, vocals.
b. Peru, Indiana, 18 July 1906; d. 4 Nov 1994.

Speed (Lawrence Arthur) Webb led a highly successful territory band for seventeen years from 1925, when he was a founder member of the Hoosier Melody lads, and by 1929 his group included Roy Eldridge, Joe Eldridge, Teddy Wilson, his trombonist brother Gus, and Vic Dickenson. No fewer than five of the band members were excellent arrangers and Wilson often orchestrated Louis Armstrong, Bix Beiderbecke and Johnny Hodges in close harmony for the relevant section: a very early precedent for later groups such as Supersax and the New York Jazz Repertory Company. Webb's band often made short work of bigger visiting names, and after it broke up in 1930 Webb went on to form the Hollywood Blue Devils before leading Jack Johnson's Pullman Porters (featuring Henderson Chambers) and fronting for other leaders including Jean Calloway and Chick Carter. By the late 30s Webb had resumed his original career as an undertaker and went on to direct a chain of successful funeral parlours. [DF]

Eberhard Weber

Bass, cello, composer.
b. Stuttgart, Germany, 22 Jan 1940.

Weber's father, a cello and piano teacher, started teaching him the cello at six, but in the mid-

1950s he switched to the bass after getting into jazz. In the 60s he did a variety of jobs for a company that made TV commercials, and freelanced as a director in theatre and TV, but played a lot of music in his spare time. In 1962 he began playing with pianist Wolfgang Dauner, staying with him until the early 1970s (he didn't actually become a full-time professional musician until 1972). At first they had a trio influenced by Bill Evans and Scott LaFaro, but they soon began to explore the area of free improvisation. In 1970 he spent some time with Dauner's Etcetera, a psychedelic rock-jazz outfit, and in 1972–3 played with the Dave Pike Set, which also included Volker Kriegel, and which toured in Europe and South America. In 1973–4 he worked with Kriegel's Spectrum, another jazz-rock group.

Weber had become one of the best and most experienced bass players in Europe, handling all styles – walking bass-lines, free jazz, jazz-rock – with equal deftness, but he had also begun to evolve into an innovative stylist on his instrument with his own musical identity and sound. He left Spectrum because, while Kriegel was fundamentally into rock rhythms, Weber was moving towards a concept which included spacey, electronic sounds with classical overtones, airy melodies with resonant harmonies and understated rhythms.

The key to his new identity lay in the sound of the instrument he created, which he called an "electrobass": an odd-looking old electric bass with a long neck and small rectangular soundbox, customized (with the help of instrument makers and electronics experts) into a five-string instrument. It was more spacious and had more overtones; its sound was more incisive, yet also more spread and more evocative; and it could sustain notes longer. His new musical persona emerged on his first album as a leader, *The Colours Of Chloe*, recorded in 1973 and released the following year. It received instant critical recognition and popular success. The same year he recorded with Gary Burton (*Ring*), and with Ralph Towner (*Solstice*), touring with Burton in 1975–6, almost certainly the first time that a jazz bass player had toured as a featured soloist and melodist. It was generally recognized that he had made a major contribution to the emancipation of the bass, opening up new dimensions for the instrument. One US critic called him a "Mephisto of the bass, whose overwhelming technique and whose power of invention are awe-inspiring".

He was now able to form his group Colours (1975–82), one of the most important and influential groups of its time, with Charlie Mariano (soprano saxophone/nagaswaram/flutes), Rainer Brüninghaus (keyboards/synthesizers), and at first Jon Christensen, then from 1977 John Marshall, on drums. He was a member of the United Jazz and Rock Ensemble from 1975–87, and in 1982 he joined Jan Garbarek's regular group. playing with it through the 1980s and 1990s. In 1985 Weber began playing solo concerts and was also heard on two Kate Bush albums of that decade. He has recorded for ECM as leader since 1973, though less regularly in latter years.

In his own music, composition is primary and improvised solos are simply a limited and controlled ingredient in his soundscape. The overriding atmosphere of his work is one of reflective melancholy and a warm romanticism, achieved by expansive chords, sustained notes, sonorous bass-lines, hypnotically repeated figures and seductive melodies. [IC]

⊙ **The Colours Of Chloe** (1973; ECM); **Yellow Fields** (1975; ECM). Using his newly designed bass and deploying the cellos of the Stuttgart Radio Symphony Orchestra, Weber created a seductive world of romantic sound colours on *Chloe*, the album that made his reputation. *Yellow Fields* is one of the most beautiful albums of the 1970s, with four superbly evocative compositions performed with an overt or incipient muscularity.

⊙ **Silent Feet** (1977; ECM). Perhaps the best of the Colours albums. Without drums, the muscularity evaporated on *The Following Morning* and *Fluid/Rustle*, but drummer John Marshall rescued *Silent Feet* from the same fate.

⊙ **Pendulum** (1993; ECM). An absolutely superb solo bass album, with prepared synthesized riffs and sonorities complementing Weber's dynamic improvised lines. Colours, lyricism and strength in abundance.

Ben Webster

Tenor saxophone; also arranger, piano.

b. Kansas City, Missouri, 27 March 1909; d. Amsterdam, 20 Sept 1973.

After a grounding on violin, Ben Webster took to the piano naturally – Pete Johnson (a neighbour) taught him how to play blues and soon after Webster was playing for silent movies in Amarillo, Texas. Here, one night, he met Budd Johnson, who showed him the scale of C on the saxophone (Webster had been intrigued with Frankie Trumbauer's "Singin' The Blues"), and soon he was playing saxophone in the Young Family Band (Lester Young and his father both supplied more tips), in Gene Coy's band, then in Jap Allen's group (they specialized in McKinney's Cotton Pickers re-creations) and for Blanche Calloway (where Johnny Hodges heard him first). By the winter of 1931 Webster had joined Bennie Moten as featured soloist and records such as "Lafayette" and "Moten Swing" first helped to get him recognized: for the rest of the 1930s the rough, gruff, sometimes unpredictable saxophonist was with a string of classy big bands (Andy Kirk, Fletcher Henderson, Benny Carter, Willie Bryant, Cab Calloway and Teddy Wilson), as well as doing the rounds of clubs to listen and cut, working on record dates and playing pool.

Until then, Webster was often thought of as a Coleman Hawkins soundalike, but after he joined Duke Ellington in 1940 (the first major tenor saxophonist to do so) his true colours emerged: while Hawkins hustled through chords in the heat of discovery, Webster's approach moved between blustery fundamentalist *tours de force* and a sinuous, breathy sensuality topped with creamy vibrato. The approach

HERMAN LEONARD

Ben Webster

recalled elegant alto saxophonists like Benny Carter and Johnny Hodges (two of Webster's idols), but he replaced their feline grace with a brusque, tender sentiment. His move to Ellington produced new enthusiasm among the saxophones. "Ben brought new life to a section that had been together a long time," says Harry Carney. "He was inspired and he inspired us so that we worked together." Webster – sometimes charming, sometimes curt and rude to his employer – stayed with Ellington for three years, producing such masterpieces as "All Too Soon" and "Cottontail". Later Ellington tenor saxophonists, including Harold Ashby and Paul Gonsalves, knew Webster's solos by heart when they arrived in the band.

Webster left Ellington because one night he had been allowed to play piano with the band, stayed too long at the keyboard, and when Ellington took offence and refused to discuss the matter Webster cut one of Ellington's best suits to bits. In 1944 he began working for other leaders such as Raymond Scott, John Kirby, Sid Catlett and Stuff Smith, then he led his own small groups up and down Swing Street, rejoined Ellington (1948–9), and by the 1950s was working in studios as well as jazz clubs and JATP – for much of the 1950s he lived on the West Coast to be near his mother and sister (all through his career Webster, like Sid Catlett, was devoted to his mother). After their deaths he settled back in New York, playing clubs such as the Half Note, but in 1964, conscious of the tides of jazz fashion, he moved to Copenhagen, and from there toured Europe regularly.

It was now that Webster's unpredictability began to create a body of legend second only to Joe Venuti's. "Ben had a habit of keeping two diaries in which he alternately wrote his bookings up," says journalist Henrik Iversen. "Sometimes this resulted in double bookings – or close. A festival in Italy and a gig in Finland could be placed within a few hours' interval, and since he would only travel by train" (when drunk Webster had been known to fall between the train and the platform) "he could succeed in being several days late for gigs!" Webster also veered between two personae: easy-going, chatty and well behaved when sober, and terrifyingly unpredictable when drunk. "I never forgot," says one British accompanist, "watching Ben with his umbrella and topcoat on, at 3.30am in Trafalgar Square, racketing round and screaming up at the buildings for a whore: 'I know you're there honey! Come on out!'" Regular records showed that Webster's late music had lost none of its passion and intensity. Soon after his death, the Ben Webster Foundation, a philanthropic organization to support jazz music, was set up in Denmark by arranger Billy Moore Jnr. [DF]

Cottontail 1932–46 (RCA Victor). Webster recorded prolifically for RCA but never as a leader, and these intelligently selected sides project important solo work with Benny Moten, Willie Bryant, Lionel Hampton, Benny Carter and of course Duke Ellington.

The Horn (1944; Progressive). Radio transcriptions of Webster with a quintet co-fronted by Hot Lips Page; a fine example of Webster in his formative years.

King Of The Tenors (1953; Verve). Five tracks with Oscar Peterson's quartet, six with Ben plus Peterson's quartet, Benny Carter and Harry Edison, and all of classic status. Ballads including "Danny Boy" and "Tenderly" are outstanding.

Ben Webster Meets Oscar Peterson (1959; Verve). Almost everyone on Verve "met" Oscar Peterson at some stage and Ben makes the most of his meeting, with some ravishingly tender ballads providing the high spot of the record.

Ben And Sweets (1962; CBS). Deservedly reissued in the CBS Jazz Masterpieces series, this set captures the perfectly matched swing masters in classic form; tracks include two wondrous ballads for Ben ("How Long Has This Been Going On?" and "My Romance"), plus one for Edison ("Embraceable You"), and the very funky Webster workout "Did You Call Her Today?"

Stormy Weather/Gone With The Wind (1965; Black Lion). Recorded in Copenhagen on one night, these records are typical of Webster's European phase, working imperturbably with a local rhythm-section and stamping the proceedings with his mixture of tenderness and authority.

No Fool, No Fun (1970; Storyville). A fascinating and funny documentary capturing Webster in rehearsal with the Danish Radio Big Band: a tutorial in basic jazz principles, from which critics – and even some musicians – might learn much.

Freddie Webster

Trumpet.

b. Cleveland, Ohio, 1916; d. 1 April 1947.

An early associate of pianist-arranger Tadd Dameron, Freddie Webster worked with Earl Hines in Cleveland in 1938, then moved to New York around 1940. A year later he was once again with Hines's orchestra, having been noticed by the leader as one of the young bop innovators who "played on a modern kick". For another six years he worked in a string of fine big bands (including Lucky Millinder's, Jimmie Lunceford's and Benny Carter's), and as a regular player at jam sessions at Minton's and elsewhere he was a big influence on younger players such as Kenny Dorham and Miles Davis, who remained his greatest champion. "I used to love what he did to a note," Davis recalled later. "He didn't play a lot of notes, he didn't waste any. I used to try to get his sound. He had a great big tone like Billy Butterfield, but without vibrato." Despite the warm recommendations of Webster's "big pretty sound" (Kenny Dorham), he never achieved the international fame of Gillespie or Davis, never seems to have made much money (Davis taught him the lessons of the Juilliard because "Freddie didn't have any money to go"), and later in his brief career was demonstrating alarming unreliability. "You know when Freddie was supposed to join Count Basie?" says Leon Washington. "When Count asked him what his price was he said, 'After you've paid the rest of those m.f.s you and I split 50–50!' He was serious. He wasn't kidding. He was going down then, though, and he died shortly after that." After brief spells with Dizzy Gillespie and Jazz At The Philharmonic, Webster collapsed and died of a heart attack at no more than 31. [DF]

Dave Weckl

Drums.

b. St Louis, Missouri, 8 Jan 1960.

Chiefly celebrated as Chick Corea's drummer in both his Elektric and Akoustic bands, Dave Weckl is rivalled only by Steve Gadd in his own field, a brand of fusion that is at once fussily virtuosic and immediately accessible. One of the most sought-after drummers in this area, especially in tandem with regular section mate, bassist John Patitucci, Weckl has made albums with a veritable who's who of tasteful fusion, particularly for the chief purveyors of the music, GRP. The label's artists who have employed Weckl's brisk but often surprisingly delicate percussive skills include guitarist Steve Khan, clarinettist/saxophonist Eddie Daniels, Patitucci himself, and expatriate Cuban trumpet maestro Arturo Sandoval. Weckl's skills in more straightforward jazz contexts are less remarkable, but he has made cogent contributions to many albums in this context, most notably with the Manhattan Jazz Quintet, which he and Patitucci joined in 1988, replacing Eddie Gomez and Steve Gadd, but also with pianists Michel Camilo and Andy LaVerne, guitarists Bill Connors and Mike Stern. A string of albums with the Dave Weckl Band on Corea's Stretch label ploughed his favoured fusion furrows with continued panache into the new millennium while 2003 saw him tour with the reformed Elektric Band. [CP]

⊙ **Master Plan** (1990; GRP). Mostly co-written with producer Jay Oliver, tricksy fusion music featuring Corea and Michael Brecker, among others. Highlight is the title track's drum battle with Steve Gadd.

⊙ **Transition** (2000; Stretch). The third Stretch release for Weckl's customarily muscular and highly accomplished electric jazz in the company of regular band members Brandon Fields (sax), Tom Kennedy (bass) and Steve Weingart (keys).

Chick Corea

⊙ **The Elektric Band** (1986; GRP). The Corea-Patitucci-Weckl team is joined by guitarists Scott Henderson and Carlos Rios for this debut Elektric Band album, which is either peerless, sophisticated popular fusion or relentlessly bland commercialism, depending on your point of view.

⊙ **The Akoustic Band** (1990; GRP). Archetypal heart-on-sleeve lush romanticism, with Corea, Patitucci and Weckl gliding with unruffled tastefulness through standards and originals alike.

George Wein

Piano, impresario.

b. Boston, Massachusetts, 3 Oct 1925.

George (Theodore) Wein played piano in high school and while in Boston worked with many celebrated players, including Edmund Hall, Max Kaminsky and Miff Mole. After fixing groups for the Savoy Club in Boston, he opened his own Storyville Club (which played host to many visiting greats) and founded the Storyville record label in 1951. Three years later he began organizing the Newport jazz festival, and thereafter founded festivals in Indiana, Cincinnati, Nice and New Orleans, as well as the Heritage Fair in 1970. Wein's activities as jazz's premier promoter have constantly been combined with his work as a pianist, and as the leader of the Newport All Stars, among others, he has contributed to a long discography of fine mainstream recordings, in company which has featured Ruby Braff, Pee Wee Russell, Bud Freeman, Clark Terry, Warren Vaché and Flip Phillips. [DF]

⊙ **George Wein And The Newport All Stars** (1993; Sony). Regarded by Wein as "maybe the best I ever made", this set includes Terry, Vaché, Phillips, Illinois Jacquet, Al Grey, Howard Alden, Eddie Jones and Kenny Washington; mainstream heaven.

⊙ **Wein, Women And Song And More** (1992; Arbors). A delightful surprise! Wein recorded parts of this album in 1955 singing and playing piano for a 1955 Atlantic release with Ruby Braff and Sam Margolis in attendance; 37 years later he finished it off, this time with Warren Vaché (in premier form throughout, as Wein notes on his sleeve). The twenty-two songs are hand-picked gems (notably "Did I Remember" and "I'm Through With Love") and Wein sings and plays with great charm and jazz feeling.

Nick Weldon

Piano.

b. Cambridge, UK, 19 March 1954.

Nick Weldon's stepfather was a New Orleans-style trumpet player, and his natural father is a folk singer and collector of ballads (his mother is novelist Fay Weldon). Nick's musical pedigree goes right back to his great-grandmother, who was a concert pianist whose career was thwarted by the fall from grace of her father, professor of violin at the Royal College of Music and tutor to Queen Alexandra, after he began sending pamphlets advocating free love to the Archbishop of Canterbury.

Nick did his first professional gigs while living in France, then returned to London in 1979, starting his first trio and becoming part of the London jazz scene. In the 1980s he worked with the Tommy Chase band and the Don Weller/Brian Spring quartet. For a while he returned to Paris and continued playing there. Back in London, he was a member of the resident trio at Peter Ind's Bass Clef (later changed to Tenor Clef), playing with Dewey Redman, Sheila Jordan, Eddie Henderson, Mark Murphy and Bobby Watson, among others. Weldon's own trio has worked with Sonny Stitt, Jimmy Witherspoon and Johnny Griffin. In the 90s he worked increasingly with singers such as Annie Ross, Carol Kidd, Christine Tobin and Trudy Kerr, whose 1998 album *Jazzizit* shows off Weldon's arranging skills.

Weldon is one of the finest pianists and composers on the London scene. He has recorded two excellent trio albums, *Lavender's Blue* and *If I Were A Gong*, both on his own label. He teaches at John Dankworth's Wavendon Summer Schools among others and is a tutor at Trinity College and Head of Jazz Piano at the Royal Academy of Music. [IC]

⊙ **Lavender's Blue** (1994; Verge). This is an all-star trio, with virtuoso bassist Andy Cleyndert and protean drummer/percussionist Paul Clarvis, and their intensity often recalls the Keith Jarrett trio. Nothing is forced, no one overplays and all three feel the time as one man. The material includes several of Weldon's fine compositions, and some exquisite ballads and standards complete the fare.

Don Weller

Tenor, soprano and alto saxophones, clarinet.

b. Croydon, Surrey, UK, 19 Dec 1947.

Weller started playing the clarinet when he was 14, having private lessons, and at 15 he was the soloist in Mozart's Clarinet Concerto at Croydon Town Hall. Inspired by saxophonist Kathy Stobart, he took up the tenor saxophone and played in her rehearsal band. During the 1970s he led his own jazz-rock group, Major Surgery, and worked with Stan Tracey, Harry Beckett, and in quintet with Art Themen. In the 80s he played with the Gil Evans orchestra in the UK, led a quintet with Bobby Wellins, and co-led a quintet with Bryan Spring. Weller continues to freelance as a popular jazz soloist and is active on the London session scene. Though under-represented on CD, his singular tenor work inspires great respect and affection from fellow musicians and audiences alike. A latterday concentration on composition has led to a series of groups including the Don Weller Big Band and regular quartet featuring Dave Newton on piano, Dave Barry on drums and Andrew Cleyndert on bass. Another current group – The Don Weller Electric Jazz Octet, featuring Steve Waterman and Chris Biscoe among others – updates his interest in fusion. [IC]

⊙ **Live** (1997; 33 Jazz). A big band outing featuring a stellar cast of British players (including Gerard Presencer, Pete King, Alan Barnes, David Newton et al) and a clutch of engaging Weller originals. Very fine, very welcome and not before time.

➤➤ **Stan Tracey** *(Portraits Plus).*

Bobby Wellins

Tenor saxophone.

b. Glasgow, Scotland, 24 Jan 1936.

Wellins's mother was a singer, and his father, who played saxophone and clarinet, gave him lessons on alto saxophone and taught him basic harmony on the piano. He was taught clarinet from 1950–52 at the RAF School of Music, Uxbridge. From 1953 on he worked with dance bands in the London area, then in the late 1950s he began to specialize in improvisation and joined Tony Crombie's band Jazz Inc., where he met Stan Tracey. He worked with Tracey's quartet during the early 1960s, playing on the classic album *Under Milk Wood*. Then Wellins's career was blighted by personal problems that kept him off the scene for almost ten years. He resurfaced in 1976, formed a quartet and, with Don Weller, a quintet, and began performing and recording again.

Wellins is, and has always been, an original. He has his own distinctive sound, a reedy keening cry recalling the bagpipes of his native Scotland, and he phrases with immense elegance – every note is meant, none wasted. His taste in saxophonists runs from Charlie Parker, Lester Young and Zoot Sims to John Coltrane, Lee Konitz and Tony Coe, but, while embodying many of their virtues, he sounds like none of them. [IC]

⊙ **Birds Of Brazil** (1989; Sungai). Wellins's quartet of pianist Peter Jacobsen, bassist Kenny Baldock and drummer Spike Wells is here augmented by percussionist Chris Karan, a string quartet, and trumpeter Kenny Wheeler for one spot. The title piece is a suite in three parts, composed by Wellins and orchestrated by Tony Coe. This is quite satisfactorily done, but it is Wellins's playing that keeps things alight.

⊙ **Nomad** (1992; Hot House). This mixture of standards and originals has Claire Martin singing on three of Wellins's compositions. Wellins's rueful quirkiness steals the show.

⊙ **The Satin Album** (1997; Jazzizit). A mature and profound examination of the standards comprising Billie Holiday's controversial – but much loved by Wellins – late album, *Lady In Satin*, the excellent quartet is completed by pianist Colin Purbrook, bassist Dave Green and drummer Clark Tracy.

➤➤ **Stan Tracey** *(Under Milk Wood).*

Dicky Wells

Trombone, vocals, arranger, composer.

b. Centerville, Tennessee, 10 June 1907; d. 12 Nov 1985.

At a time in jazz history when the trombone was just starting not to be an object of comedy, it

was brave of Dicky Wells to put the comedy right back. Often played through a pepperpot mute of his own invention, the trombone in his hands usually sounded more like a voice than an instrument: full of blasé yawns, dismissive grunts and sudden yelps of surprise. It was a sophisticated set of tricks, a million miles from the music-hall humour of trombone features such as "Lassus Trombone", which had only just started to disappear from trombone repertoire by the 1930s, and it took a man of wit to invent them. Wells for most of his life kept a bubbling sense of humour intact: the cover picture of his autobiography shows Count Basie looking up from the piano stool with a delighted grin as Wells solos, and the book itself is one of the funniest jazz autobiographies.

Wells worked his way up through fine New York bands led by Lloyd Scott, Benny Carter, Fletcher Henderson, Charlie Johnson and others; eight years with Count Basie from 1938 established Wells as a trombone stylist who had found an alternative to the approaches of Jimmy Harrison and Jack Teagarden. His account of the troubles encountered by black bands like Basie's in the Deep South (in *The Night People*) is determinedly funny, but the problems he experienced were perhaps to push him into alcoholism. After Basie he worked with Lucky Millinder, Sy Oliver, Willie Bryant and others, and by 1959 was in Europe with Buck Clayton's All Stars, where, just occasionally, he sounded tired. Drink affected his performance badly in the 1960s; a solo tour with Alex Welsh in 1965 in Britain was cut short, and soon after he took a day job on Wall Street. By 1973 his book had been published and he was working with Earle Warren's Countsmen (including Buddy Tate and Paul Quinichette), and in 1978 he toured Europe with Warren and Claude Hopkins. Otherwise the decade was not noticeably kind to Wells – he was ill with pneumonia, was mugged on two occasions, and his wife died – but in the 1980s it was good to hear him on record again, still managing to raise a smile. [DF]

Swingin' In Paris (1937–8; Le Jazz). These are among Wells's greatest recordings – a jazz voice of total originality caught in its prime. Titles with a trio of trumpets (Bill Dillard, Shad Collins, Bill Coleman), including "Between The Devil And The Deep Blue Sea", are classics; so is his "Dicky Wells Blues", recorded with rhythm-section only.

Trombone Four In Hand (1959; Felsted). Wells with a superbly matched trio of compatriots (Vic Dickenson, Benny Morton, George Matthews), plus Skip Hall leading the rhythm-section on piano and organ. This is an essential Wells date and long overdue for CD reissue – keep searching!

Chatter Jazz (1959; RCA Victor). An oddity with Rex Stewart. Not to everyone's taste, but worth sampling as an example of the way that Wells – probably more than any other trombonist – used his trombone as a second voice. Stewart is the perfect partner for such a project.

➤➤ **Count Basie** *(The Original American Decca Recordings);* **Buck Clayton** *(Songs For Swingers).*

Dick Wellstood

Piano.

b. Greenwich, Connecticut, 25 Nov 1927; d. 24 July 1987.

Dick Wellstood came to New York in 1946 in a band led by Bob Wilber, and a year later was working for Sidney Bechet in Chicago: in these two cities he heard most of the great pianists, from James P. Johnson to Bud Powell – on whom he was to model his own approach. Through the 1950s Wellstood worked with an impressive string of older, more established stars, including Bechet, Rex Stewart, Charlie Shavers and Roy Eldridge (a primary influence); in 1953 he was with a band led by actor Conrad Janis, and by 1956 was in the intermission band at Condon's. Later in the decade he was house pianist at the Metropole, New York (an education for Wellstood, who was constantly surrounded by an eclectic parade of jazzmen), then moved to Nick's Club, then into Gene Krupa's quartet. By the late 1960s, Wellstood, now settled in New Jersey, was well established: besides working for classic musicians such as Roy Eldridge, Jimmy McPartland and the Dukes of Dixieland, he was performing solo at prestigious New York rooms, including Michael's Pub, and touring with The World's Greatest Jazz Band. In this period he regularly recorded solo albums, played jazz parties and in odd moments wrote sleevenotes that unobtrusively put him in the class of authors such as George Frazier, Whitney Balliett and Dick Sudhalter. A determined upholder of traditional standards ("All this electric junk's really beaten the shit out of acoustic music", he told *Crescendo* magazine in the 1970s), Wellstood continued to play into the 1980s, touring Europe with, among others, Bobby Rosengarden and Kenny Davern in a reconstituted Blue Three, and working with the Classic Jazz Quartet – and, rather surprisingly, practising as an attorney between times. [DF]

The Blue Three At Hanratty's (1981; Chazz Jazz). One of Wellstood's best showcases, with his longtime partner – and fellow champion of acoustic music – Kenny Davern.

Dick Wellstood And His Famous Orchestra, Featuring Kenny Davern (1981; Chiaroscuro). A duo album (the title is a typical joke) that once again illustrates Wellstood's superb technique and highly original outlook.

Live At The Sticky Wicket (1986; Arbors). A definitive illustration of Wellstood's solo mastery spread over two CDs and spanning eras from "Maple Leaf Rag" to "Giant Steps"; his wonderful Bronx-style announcements are a distinct bonus.

➤➤ **Bob Wilber** *(New Orleans Style Old And New).*

Alex Welsh

Cornet, vocals, leader.

b. Edinburgh, Scotland, 9 July 1929; d. 25 June 1982.

The Alex Welsh band – like many of the Chicagoans that Welsh adored – burned itself out too soon, but is remembered with more affection than almost any other British band, not only because it was arguably, in Bud Freeman's words, "the best small band of its kind in the world", but because its members formed a true "jazz family". Welsh's first band settled down in the 1950s (after a few trial runs) with Archie Semple on clarinet, pianist Fred Hunt, trombonist Roy Crimmins and a top modern drummer of the period, Lennie Hastings, and began broadcasting, playing clubs and concerts, and recording (*Music Of The Mauve Decade*, *Melrose Folio* and *Echoes Of Chicago* are British jazz classics). In the early 1960s, having turned down an offer to join Jack Teagarden in 1957, Welsh had to weather changes: Archie Semple died, Roy Crimmins left to work abroad. Undeterred, Welsh re-formed – with Al Gay, then John Barnes, Roy Williams, Jim Douglas, Ron Mathewson (later replaced by the equally fine Harvey Weston) – and began his busiest period, touring with a stream of US visitors from Earl Hines to Ruby Braff, all of whom praised his new band as world-class. In 1967 they played the Antibes jazz festival to rapturous reviews and produced their first new album for three years, *Strike One*, then appeared at Newport the year after. For the next ten years Welsh continued playing clubs and concerts all over Britain and Europe, recording and perfecting his eclectic programme: mainstream arrangements (by Kenny Graham and others), banjo-based Dixieland, Mulligan-Brookmeyer interludes from Barnes and Williams, and warm solo features for Hunt and his leader. In 1977 Barnes left, the following year Williams followed, and for the last four years of his life Welsh played Dixieland pure and simple, with a variety of sidemen including Campbell Burnap, Mick Cooke and finally Roy Crimmins (back again), Al Gay and pianist Barney Bates. He died after a long debilitating illness. [DF]

Dixieland To Duke/The Melrose Folio (1960; Lake). Two of Welsh's most important records from his first band, co-featuring Roy Crimmins and the great Archie Semple. A very worthwhile compilation from his Condon period.

Classic Concert (1971; Black Lion). Often spoken of as Welsh's best recording (and one that he especially liked), this Dresden concert features his second band, with John Barnes and Roy Williams plus Fred Hunt and Lennie Hastings (from the first band). Welsh's wonderfully varied show – vaudeville features for Williams and Hunt at peak form, plus straightahead Chicago-style jazz – is definitively illustrated.

Doggin' Around (1973; Black Lion). Welsh operated a catholic policy with his later band and favoured his sidemen as generously as himself. These studio recordings again highlight the immense strength and versatility of his team, with everything from features like "You Are The Sunshine Of My Life" (for Williams) to the headlong title track with Barnes's flyaway alto.

➤➤ **Archie Semple** *(Night People).*

Kenny Werner

Piano, composer.

b. Brooklyn, New York, 19 Nov 1951.

Werner joined a children's song-and-dance group at the age of four, started piano lessons at seven and was playing stride piano on television at eleven. He studied classical repertoire at the Manhattan School of Music and at nineteen transferred to Berklee, learning with Madame Chaloff (Serge's mother) from 1971–4. He then worked in Brazil and Bermuda, and on his return began playing and recording with such as Mingus (on his last album), Archie Shepp (with whom he toured in the early 80s) and under his own name. From 1981–95 he led a trio with Ratzo Harris (bass) and Tom Rainey (drums) and from 1984–9 he joined the Mel Lewis band, for which he also wrote. His compositions have been played by various European radio orchestras, and his piano has been sought by numerous hornmen, including frequent associates Joe Lovano and Tom Harrell. Originally inspired by Miles Davis's *In A Silent Way*, and influenced by the philosophy of pianist Joao Assis Brasil, Werner published a well-received book entitled *Effortless Mastery: Liberating The Master Musician Within* in 1997. [BP]

A Delicate Balance (1997; RCA Victor). Werner's first major-label release finds him with Dave Holland and Jack DeJohnette in an absorbing set of original material, augmented by an un-obvious "Work Song". The leader's command of both advanced improvisation and traditional qualities – with even a hint of stride piano – creates a delicate balance.

➤➤ **Tom Harrell** *(Labyrinth);* **Joe Lovano** *(Landmarks).*

Paul Wertico

Drums.

b. Chicago, 5 Jan 1953.

Wertico took up drums at the age of twelve and became a featured soloist with the Illinois High School Band. He was involved in the Chicago musical community for ten years and gained exceptionally wide experience, working with big bands, rock groups and two free-improvising groups, Earwax Control and the Spontaneous Composition Trio. Yet he has also accompanied Larry Coryell, Bunky Green, Jack Bruce and Ellen McIlwaine. He played in Pat Metheny's groups from 1983 to 2001, and the guitarist has said of him: "He can truly play in the variety of styles that we need, but he always sounds like himself, he always plays from the inside out." His solo recordings – *Yin And The Yout* (1993: Intuition) and *Don't Be Scared Anymore* (2000; Premonition) among them – mark him as an intrepid player in the "electric avant fusion" field. After leaving Metheny, Wertico played again with Larry Coryell and joined the European prog-rock and fusion group SBB. Wertico cites Roy Haynes as his main influence, but also finds inspiration in ethnic music, particularly African field recordings. [IC]

Frank Wess

Tenor and alto saxophones, flute, composer.

b. Kansas City, Missouri, 4 Jan 1922.

Wess played locally in Washington, DC, as a teenager, and toured with Blanche Calloway. After army service, he worked in the Billy Eckstine band in 1946, then with Eddie Heywood and Lucky Millinder in 1947–8, and former Millinder singer Bullmoose Jackson in 1948–9. After studying the flute, he joined the Count Basie band from 1953–64, playing tenor (and later alto) but also making use of the flute in solos. He has freelanced in New York since then, including theatre, television and recording work. He played and wrote for Clark Terry's occasional big band from 1969, and was a founder member of the New York Jazz Quartet in 1974. From 1981–5 he worked with Philly Joe Jones's Dameronia group, and co led a quintet with Frank Foster from 1984–6. As Foster moved to lead the Basie band, Wess assembled an occasional competitor, initially in 1989 with Harry Edison, and has continued his session work, including with Harry Connick Jnr.

Wess is a commanding though unflamboyant saxophonist, but is more renowned for his flute work. Using a basically pre-bop phraseology not very far removed from the pioneering efforts of Wayman Carver with the Chick Webb band, Wess helped the instrument to surpass the declining popularity of the clarinet by demonstrating that the flute too could be made to swing. [BP]

⊙ **Entre Nous** (1990; Concord). A big band liberally stocked with Basie alumni of different generations does only one cover version (Frank Foster's "Shiny Stockings") and gives the foreground to the work of Joe Newman and Wess himself.

➤➤ **Milt Jackson** *(Opus De Jazz).*

Bugge Wesseltoft

Piano, keyboards, electronics, composer.

b. Porsgrund, Norway, 1 Feb 1964.

A professional musician since the age of 19, Jens-Christian Bugge Wesseltoft has established himself on the jazz scene, both local and international, with great rapidity. He rose to prominence in Norway with work for the bassist Arild Andersen and the big band run by trombonist Jens Wendleboe, recording *Sagn* (1990; ECM) for the former (alongside saxophonist Bendik Hofseth and percussionist Nana Vasconcelos) and the aptly named *Big Crazy Energy Band* (1991; NOPA/NRK) for the latter, contributing a Hammond organ version of "Abide With Me". Work with Hofseth, tenor player Eero Koivistoinen – he plays synthesizer on *Altered Things* (1991; Timeless) – Jan Garbarek and trumpeter Dennis Gonzalez followed, but it was Wesseltoft's association with singer Sidsel Endresen (he appears on three 1990s albums by her: *Exile*, *Night Song* and *Duplex Ride*) that allowed him to showcase the considerable originality and subtlety of his keyboard work. His own albums as leader, which appear on his own label, Jazzland, and feature what he calls the "new conception of Jazz", began with an eponymous 1996 recording and *It's Snowing On My Piano* the following year, but his third album (see below) marked the beginning of major-label backing from Polygram. Its attendant hype continued for the similar *Moving* (1998) and his profile escalated as a "nu jazz" pioneer. His subtle work on another album with Endresen – *Out Here, In There* (2000; Jazzland) – was impressive, even for those unconvinced by his grander claims for his music elsewhere. [CP]

⊙ **Sharing** (1998; Jazzland/Emarcy). A rich confection of slithering rhythms (scratching and drum'n'bass/Jungle-influenced percussion), softly chanted feel-good injunctions, plus the odd dash of funk and jazz from a horn section often buried deep in the mix, all focused by Wesseltoft's wide-ranging, hypnotic keyboard work.

Kate Westbrook

Vocals, tenor horn, piccolo, bamboo flute.

b. Guildford, Surrey, UK, 18 Sept 1939.

Kate Westbrook (née Barnard) comes from a visual arts background. As a painter, she lived and worked in the USA and had her first major one-person show at the Santa Barbara Museum of Art, California, in 1963. Back in the UK, she taught at Leeds College of Art, before she joined the Mike Westbrook Brass Band in 1974, giving up teaching to concentrate on her dual career of painter and musician. She and Westbrook married, and most of her musical work has been done with him. She joined his orchestra in 1981, and in 1982 formed the trio A Little Westbrook Music with saxophonist Chris Biscoe, a group which has existed for over 20 years.

Apart from collaborations with her husband she was guest soloist with the RAI Orchestra in Rome and with the Zurich Radio Orchestra during the 1970s, and in the 1980s she did several projects with Lindsay Cooper for TV films. In her various projects with Mike Westbrook, she has not only been a soloist and section player, but also a lyricist; she has also worked on scenarios for the Brass Band's jazz/cabaret productions for theatre and TV, and has performed songs in a number of European languages. For *The*

Cortège, she adapted texts by Rimbaud, Lorca, Hermann Hesse, Belli, Blake and Saarikoski. The resulting triple album won the Montreux Grand Prix du Disque in 1982. Her solo recordings include: *Goodbye Peter Lorre* (see below); *Love Or Infatuation* (1997; ASC) based on the Hollywood songs of Fredrich Hollaender and Cuff Clout; a collection of specially commissioned pieces by Barbara Thompson and James McMillan, among others (billed as a "Neoteric Music Hall" and due for release in 2004). She has speculated that: "Perhaps the most important influences on my work have been poets, writers and painters: Goya, Monet, Lorca, Shakespeare, Blake." [IC]

⊙ **Goodbye, Peter Lorre** (1991; Femme Line). Accompanied on piano by John Alley and Mike Westbrook, she performs songs by Brecht (who was a great admirer of the actor Lorre), and compositions by Westbrook. Her high theatricality and vocal flexibility – from husky come-ons to bat-squeaks – appropriately recall the inter-war German cabaret tradition.

⊙ **Love For Sale** (1985; hat Art). A trio album from A Little Westbrook Music, with Kate Westbrook's voice the unifying factor in performances of standard songs, traditional tunes and pieces inspired by William Blake.

⊙ **Platterback** (1998; PAO). With a concentration on theatrical and text-driven effect, in the Westbrooks' by-now customary style, this is one of the more accessible of their latter-day offerings. With John Winfield sharing vocal duties with Kate, and the accompanying accordion and cello textures, this odd travellers' tale is told engagingly and evocatively.

➤➤ **Mike Westbrook** *(The Cortège; Westbrook-Rossini; London Bridge Is Broken Down; Off Abbey Road).*

Mike and Kate Westbrook

Mike Westbrook

Piano, tuba, bandleader, composer, arranger.

b. High Wycombe, Buckinghamshire, UK, 21 March 1936.

Westbrook became seriously interested in music only after hearing jazz records at school – he had a little basic tuition on piano and trumpet but was mainly self-taught. In 1960 he ran a jazz workshop at Plymouth Arts Centre with an eight-piece band that included John Surman. Two years later he moved to London, eventually forming a regular six-piece group that included Surman (which played at the Montreux festival in 1968). He formed the Mike Westbrook Concert Band in 67, which varied in size from 10 to 26 musicians, and which existed to perform the series of long compositions he was beginning to write. In the early 70s, much in the spirit of the times, he branched out in several different directions at once: co-leading (with John Fox of Welfare State Theatre Group) the Cosmic Circus, a multimedia group; leading Solid Gold Cadillac, a rock-oriented group; and forming his Brass Band to perform jazz/cabaret productions for theatre and TV. In 1979 he formed the Mike Westbrook Orchestra for his large-scale work *The Cortège*. With his wife Kate and saxophonist Chris Biscoe he formed the trio The Westbrook Trio in 1982, a group that continues to the present. Again with his wife, in 1984 he formed Westbrook Music Theatre for more mixed-media productions.

Westbrook is not a virtuoso pianist: he says, "I'm a composer really, and an adequate piano player." Over the years he has mastered orchestration, and one of his greatest achievements is to have given jazz wider terms of cultural reference (relating it to poetry, theatre, the visual arts and the European classical music tradition) without in any way diminishing its own identity or vitality. Musically, too, he has enlarged the jazz concept by bringing to it a rich variety of influences: street music, ethnic music, rock, folk and European art music. [IC]

⊙ **Citadel/Room 315** (1975; Novus). Named after the room in Leeds Polytechnic where Westbrook wrote much of the music, this large-scale orchestral work, featuring Surman on sax and bass clarinet, straddles the generic extremes of the time. A driving rock beat underlies much of the performance, but there are two collective improvisations – "Bebop De Rigeur" and, more successfully, "Sleeper Awakening In Sunlight".

⊙ **The Cortège** (1982; Enja). This vast tableau of sounds is Westbrook's masterpiece, in a genre he virtually invented. Kate Westbrook and Phil Minton are in the 17-piece orchestra, setting texts from Lorca, Rimbaud, Hesse and others to structures loosely based on the New Orleans funeral procession.

⊙ **On Duke's Birthday** (1984; hat Art). Westbrook usually has a party at his home every year on Ellington's birthday, and this lovely big-band album is a set of his own original scores in homage to the master.

⊙ **London Bridge Is Broken Down** (1987; Venture). The Westbrooks attempt an evocation of London, Berlin and Prague, using texts ranging from Goethe to the (rewritten) nursery rhyme of the title, and musical forms derived from jazz, cabaret and European art music.

Harvey Weston

Bass.

b. London, 2 March 1940.

A fast-thinking soloist, sympathetic accompanist and excellent teacher, Weston freelanced in London before joining Alex Welsh's great band from 1967–74. From then on he pursued a busy freelance career, working with Kathy Stobart's quintet (1978–81), and with an enormous variety of visiting Americans, including Eddie Vinson, Ruby Braff, Sonny Stitt and Red Holloway, Pepper Adams, Warren Vaché, Scott Hamilton and Roger Kellaway. In the late 1980s and 1990s Weston continued to work in similarly varied contexts, including regular touring with drummer Pete York in a variety of jazz and R&B presentations, featuring Spencer Davis, Chris Farlowe and others, plus a jazz contingent including Roy Williams and Dick Morrissey. [DF]

➤➤ **Alex Welsh** *(Classic Concert).*

Randy Weston

Piano, composer.

b. Brooklyn, New York, 6 April 1926.

Weston began his career in the late 1940s, gigging with R&B bands including Bullmoose Jackson, Frank Culley and Eddie Vinson, and recording with the Clovers vocal group. In 1953 he worked with Kenny Dorham, and in 1954 joined Cecil Payne; he then formed his own trio and quartet. He was active as an educator, then, after visiting Nigeria in 1961 and 1963, and West and North Africa in 1967, he settled in Morocco in 1968. He worked in the USA in 1972–3 and then spent time in Europe, but was based in Morocco again from the mid-1980s, while continuing to make solo, duo and band appearances in Europe and Japan. Beginning in the early 1990s he resumed his career in the USA, collaborating with arranger Melba Liston, who first worked with him in the 1950s, and he has toured in the USA and England with members of Morocco's Gnawa musicians.

Like many pianists initially inspired by Thelonious Monk, Weston often sounds at his best when playing his own compositions. Many of these became standards in the late 1950s, including "Hi-Fly", "Babe's Blues" and "Little Niles", while there are many more worthy of investigation. "Niles" was the nickname of his son Azzedin Weston (b. 12 Aug 1950), who has worked with Dizzy Gillespie, Ahmad Jamal and others. Randy Weston's piano work, perhaps through his interest in West Indian and African music, conveys a particularly dynamic and happy atmosphere, and deserves to be more widely recognized. [BP]

⊙ **Randy Weston** (1957–63; Mosaic Select). As well as conventional but absorbing albums featuring Johnny Griffin and Coleman Hawkins and previously unissued material with Cecil Payne, this three-CD set is the only way to obtain the classic Melba Liston-arranged big-band session *Uhuru Afrika* (with all-star personnel from Clark Terry through to Candido). Equally Afro-oriented is the closing *Highlife* album, featuring Booker Ervin and including two pieces by African composers Ghanaba (Guy Warren) and Bobby Benson.

⊙ **Blues To Africa** (1974; Freedom). This solo performance includes versions of "Uhuru Kwanza" and "Kucheza Blues" from the above big-band album. Typical of his musical fusions is the title and the playing of "African Village Bedford-Stuyvesant".

⊙ **The Spirit Of Our Ancestors** (1991; Verve). A brass-and-percussion-dominated attempt to combine the African music of the Gnawas with US players such as Billy Harper and Dewey Redman. Dizzy Gillespie and Pharoah Sanders also put in extended guest appearances.

George Wettling

Drums.

b. Topeka, Kansas, 28 Nov 1907; d. 6 June 1968.

After working around Chicago for ten years, George Wettling went to New York in 1935 with British bandleader Jack Hylton's specially formed orchestra, and thereafter worked with a string of fine bands (including Artie Shaw's, Bunny Berigan's, Paul Whiteman's, Red Norvo's and Benny Goodman's) before moving into studio work for ABC. Wettling was an intellectual and a diversifier: he frequently led his own bands (a 1939 *Chicago Jazz* album is one of several top-notch recording sessions he organized), wrote hard-hitting pieces for magazines such as *Down Beat*, and was a gifted abstract painter (a close friend of Stuart Davis), who had several exhibitions (a feature in *Collier's Magazine* in 1951 shows pictures of a recording session as well as reproducing a Wettling abstract). For much of the 1950s Wettling was associated with Eddie Condon, as well as with leaders such as Muggsy Spanier; in such surroundings his rattling, sometimes cavernous sound – much influenced by Baby Dodds and Zutty Singleton – produced the very best from his associates: "There are many good kids playing drums today, but none of them has George's flexibility, imagination and virtuosity," said Condon. For the last years of his life, Wettling led his own trio at New York's Gaslight Club and nursed a drink problem: "One or two drinks was all it took to drive him out of his mind," says Bud Freeman. One of the great Chicagoans, he combined aspects of Cliff Leeman and Dave Tough in a single talent. [DF]

⊙ **Dixieland** (1950–66; Giants of Jazz). This budget collection includes all eight titles from a seminal Wettling-led date from 1951 (the one featured in *Collier's*), including "Collier's Climb" and "Collier's Clambake", with Wild Bill Davison, Hall, Cutshall and others. Some of the greatest Dixieland on record.

➤➤ **Eddie Condon** *(Dixieland Jam; Eddie Condon 1938–40).*

Petter Wettre

Soprano and tenor saxophones.
b. Sandefjord, Norway, 11 Aug 1967.

Having taken up piano at the age of seven and saxophone two years later, Petter Wettre was first exposed to jazz in 1977 when he heard a concert involving Oscar Peterson, Niels-Henning Ørsted Pedersen and Louie Bellson. Wettre played with various big bands throughout the 1980s and in 1989 went to Boston to study at Berklee under George Garzone; he has also studied with Joe Viola and David Liebman. After graduating in 1992, Wettre played his first pro gig and quickly established himself on the jazz scene through work with Arild Andersen, Jon Christensen, Alex Riel and Joanna MacGregor, but also backed visiting singers like Shirley Bassey. Recordings as a sideman include *A Touch from Up Above* (1994; Prima Music) with the Stavanger Gospel Choir, *One From the Moon* (1995; Polygram) with Stephen Ackles, and *Live* (1996; Groove Records) with Oslo Groove Company, but the same year Wettre made his debut album as a leader, the quartet recording *Pig Virus* (Curling Legs), involving pianist Håvard Wiik, bassist Terje Gewelt and drummer Per Oddvar Johansen. More sideman work, including contributions to blues bands and gospel choirs, followed, and Wettre also began teaching sax at the Oslo Conservatory, but his own bands, both his quartet and trio (which toured in 1993 playing the music of Ornette Coleman), established him as one of Scandinavia's most sought-after saxophonists. His solo output continued with trio albums *Meet The Locals* (1999; Resonance), *The Mystery Deepens* (2000; BP) and *Live At Copenhagen Jazzhouse* (2003; Household) and a quintet offering *Household Name* (see below). [CP]

⊙ **Household Name** (2003; Household). After an initial period exploring a quasi-free approach, Wettre's oeuvre – at least with this band – is settling into a quirky but rational place, full of striking themes as well as virtuosic excitement. The quintet - pianist Håvard Wiik, guitarist Palle Pesonen, bassist Per Zanussi and drummer Anders Mogensen – is excellent.

Element

⊙ **Shaman** (1999; BP). With a three-saxophone frontline (Wettre joined by soprano/tenor player Gisle W. Johansen and tenorman Vidar Johansen, who also doubles on bass clarinet) and a rhythm-section driven by Paal Nilssen-Love and bassist Ingebrigt Håker Flaten, this is a fierce, ebullient album hovering excitingly on the edge of abstraction at times, but always gutsy, passionate and cogent.

Kenny Wheeler

Trumpet, cornet, flugelhorn, pocket trumpet.
b. Toronto, Canada, 14 Jan 1930.

Wheeler started playing cornet at twelve, and studied harmony and trumpet at Toronto Conservatory before moving in 1952 to the UK, where his

David Redfern

Kenny Wheeler

first professional work was with big bands led by Roy Fox, Vic Lewis and others. While with the John Dankworth orchestra (1959–65) he did his first regular work as a composer/arranger, studied composition with Richard Rodney Bennett for six months, and had some counterpoint lessons with Bill Russo. From the mid-1960s his reputation grew more rapidly and he played with Ronnie Scott, Joe Harriott, Tubby Hayes, Friedrich Gulda and the Clarke-Boland big band. At the same time he became deeply immersed in free improvisation, working first with John Stevens and the Spontaneous Music Ensemble, and later with Tony Oxley's sextet. From 1969 he began to work with the Mike Gibbs orchestra, which used electronic as well as acoustic instruments, often employed rock rhythms and was more formally organized.

Subsequently he has worked with groups that dealt in abstraction, such as (from 1972) the Globe Unity Orchestra and Anthony Braxton's quartet, and also with groups that favoured more formal structures, such as the chamber jazz and folk trio Azimuth (of which he was a founder member with John Taylor and Norma Winstone in 1977) and the United Jazz and Rock Ensemble, which he joined in 1979. Since the 1960s he has also led his own big band and various small groups, becoming more established internationally, and has regularly recorded for ECM since the mid-1970s. From 1983–7 he was a regular member of the Dave Holland quintet, and in the later 1980s began working with an all-star quintet that included Holland, John Abercrombie, John Taylor and Peter Erskine. They toured in the UK and Europe, and formed the nucleus of Wheeler's big band which recorded the 1990 album *Music For Large And Small Ensembles*, and toured Britain for the Arts Council's Contemporary Music Network.

In February 1996, he recorded the beautiful album, *Angel Song*, and the following month he recorded with underground rock star, David Sylvian. 1997 saw him recording with composer Vince Mendoza in an ensemble which included John Taylor, John Abercrombie, Michael Brecker, Joe Lovano, Peter Erskine, Marc Johnson and the London Philharmonic Orchestra. In 1998, Wheeler played on John Abercrombie's ECM recording *Open Land*, and also performed his musical settings of poems for five voices, rhythm-section and himself at the Berlin jazz festival. He continues to be heard at international festivals and concerts, often with the quartet featuring Taylor, Lawrence and Nussbaum.

Although reticent and self-effacing, Wheeler has always had the inner drive and vision of the true artist, perhaps why he went to Europe, which arguably lacks the gladiatorial competitiveness of the American jazz scene. A complete player, he has a technical mastery of trumpets from the lowest to the highest registers, and tremendous stamina. Both his playing and his writing are powerfully individual, possessed of a buoyant, romantic melancholy which has spawned many disciples. Immensely self-critical, he prefers his writing to his playing, and has said, "I don't have any solos of my own that I like completely, only those that are not as bad as other ... perhaps the solos on *Deer Wan* I can live with." [IC]

⊙ **Gnu High** (1975; ECM). Wheeler with Keith Jarrett, Dave Holland and Jack DeJohnette, on one of the classic albums of the 1970s. Three glorious, long compositions by Wheeler, superb solos from him and Jarrett, and a superlative rhythm-section.

⊙ **Deer Wan** (1977; ECM). Another classic, this time with Holland, DeJohnette, Jan Garbarek and John Abercrombie, plus Ralph Towner added for one track – "3/4 in the Afternoon". Wheeler solos at his magnificent best, there are supremely focused contributions from the others, and the atmosphere is highly charged throughout.

⊙ **Double, Double You** (1983; ECM). Wheeler, Holland and DeJohnette are joined here by John Taylor and Michael Brecker in fine compositions by the leader, including the wily "Foxy Trot". Brecker plays the written parts beautifully, but doesn't sound so engaged with the music when he solos.

⊙ **Music For Large And Small Ensembles** (1990; ECM). One of the most impressive jazz documents of recent years. Norma Winstone's voice on top of the 19-piece ensemble reveals Wheeler's grandeur as a composer and improviser, while the trios that end the set show another side of Wheeler – his more abstract adventuring.

⊙ **Angel Song** (1996; ECM). Recorded by a dream quartet of Wheeler leading Lee Konitz (alto saxophone), bassist Dave Holland and guitarist Bill Frisell, this is one of the most exquisite examples of jazz chamber music. It has the unity of a suite, and softly glowing sonorities. The absence of drums emphasizes the role of Holland and Frisell who swing beautifully and subtly colour the sound.

➤➤ **Paul Bley/Kenny Wheeler** *(Touche)*; **Dave Holland** *(Jumpin' In)*; **John Stevens** *(Karyobin)*; **John Taylor** *(Azimuth/The Touchstone/Départ)*.

Artie Whetsol

Trumpet.

b. Punta Gorda, Florida, 1905; d. 5 Jan 1940.

The original trumpeter with Duke Ellington's Washingtonians, Artie (Arthur Parker) Whetsol was a finely trained musician and a consistently reliable performer, rather than a highly creative jazzman. His ability to "sustain notes on the horn ... with a pure sound that was almost violin-like" (Mercer Ellington) was particularly valuable to Ellington for the interpretation of early hits such as "Mood Indigo" (one of the tunes that Whetsol always played better than most of his successors). Apart from a break to study medicine in the 1920s, Whetsol stayed with Ellington until 1937, when a brain disorder caused his premature retirement. Tall, handsome, sophisticated, with a strong sense of correctness that once caused Barney Bigard to call him "prissy", Whetsol featured with Ellington in an award-winning film short, *Black And Tan Fantasy* (1929), although after Bubber Miley's arrival in 1924 less attention was paid to him as a soloist. He remained, however, a vital "lead voice", especially in Ellington's sweeter repertoire. [DF]

➤➤ **Duke Ellington** *(The Early Ellington [MCA])*.

Jiggs Whigham

Trombone, trombonium.

b. Cleveland, Ohio, 20 Aug 1943.

Jiggs (Haydn) Whigham worked from 1961–4 with the Glenn Miller orchestra (under the direction of Ray McKinley) as lead trombonist and soloist, and with Stan Kenton. In 1965 he freelanced in New York, before joining Kurt Edelhagen in Germany, touring Africa with him in 1966. During the 70s he freelanced in Germany, then taught at the Music High School in Cologne where he became head of the jazz faculty, though he still kept active as a player. He was bandleader of the Swiss Radio Band from 1984–86. In 1995 he became Head of Jazz at the Berlin College of Music and in 2000–01 he was visiting professor at Indiana University. From 1995–2000 he was chief conductor and artistic director of the Berlin Radio Orchestra and has conducted the BBC Big Band. [IC]

⊙ **The Jiggs Up** (1989; Capri). With alto saxophonist Bud Shank, pianist George Cables, bassist John Clayton and Jeff Hamilton, Whigham sets the pace in a friendly, competent session, with some nice ballad performances.

Andrew White

Tenor and soprano saxophones, oboe, electric bass.

b. Washington, DC, 6 Sept 1942.

White studied saxophone and theory from 1954–60, playing in a symphony orchestra for the last two years. He played alto with the JFK quintet, including bassist Walter Booker, in Washington from 1961–4. He then moved to Paris, playing tenor with Kenny Clarke in 1964–5, and worked with the New Jazz Trio in Buffalo from 1965–6. After being involved in theatre music in Washington, he played with Otis Redding, Wilson Pickett and Thelma Houston, and toured on electric bass with Stanley Turrentine in 1967, Stevie Wonder from 1968–70, and with the Fifth Dimension vocal group. After working as principal oboe with the American Ballet Theatre in New York, he recorded on oboe and bass with Weather Report in 1971–2. Based in Washington again in the 1970s, he founded the record label Andrew's Music, which released more than forty albums over the next ten years. Andrew's Music also publishes his transcriptions of 642 recorded solos by John Coltrane and 308 by Charlie Parker. White also recorded with McCoy Tyner in 1970 and toured with Elvin Jones occasionally from 1980. Given the excellence and commitment of his saxophone-playing, it is a great pity that only his work with Weather Report is easily available. [BP]

Elvin Jones

Soul Trane (1980; Denon). Jones's quintet on this Tokyo session features the two saxophones of White and Ari Brown (who has also worked with Lester Bowie). Material includes the Japanese folk song "Doll Of The Bride", which was to become standard Elvin repertoire, and White plays commandingly.

➤➤ **Joe Zawinul** *(I Sing The Body Electric).*

Lenny White

Drums, percussion.

b. Jamaica, New York, 19 Dec 1949.

Self-taught musically, White began playing with the Jazz Samaritans and then joined Jackie McLean in 1967-8. He was studying art at the New York Institute of Technology when he appeared on *Bitches Brew*, his first-ever recording, in 1969. He then performed with Freddie Hubbard, Joe Henderson, Woody Shaw and the band Azteca. From 1973–6 he was with Return To Forever, while beginning to make his own albums. During the 1980s he produced sessions such as the two *Echoes Of An Era* (with first Chaka Khan and then Nancy Wilson in a small-group jazz context), various soundtracks and the debut album of singer Rachel Ferrelle. In 1995 he toured with Urbanator (featuring Michal Urbaniak and Tom Browne), recorded under his own name again and appeared live with Geri Allen and Wallace Roney. In 1998 he formed a new band called Vertu with longterm colleague Stanley Clarke, touring Europe in 1999. Describing his favourites as "The Holy 6" (Tony Williams, Elvin and Philly Joe Jones, Blakey, Haynes, Roach), he is also inspired by Miles, Trane, Shorter, Hendrix, James Brown, Ravel and Stravinsky. Combining the energy and volume of rock drummers with the interactive impulse of a jazz player, White sounds good in a variety of contexts. [BP]

Present Tense (1995; Hip Bop). White puts together a heavy programme of original material, performed with a series of all-star groups including Michael Brecker, Stanley Clarke, Chick Corea, Kenny Garrett, Marcus and Mulgrew Miller, John Scofield, Michal Urbaniak and Chaka Khan.

Lenny White

➤➤ **Miles Davis** *(Bitches Brew);* **Michael "Patches" Stewart** *(Blue Patches).*

Michael White

Violin, electric violin.

b. Houston, Texas, 24 May 1933.

White, who was brought up in Oakland, California, began playing violin at the age of nine. He came to prominence with the John Handy quintet, playing an explosive set at the 1965 Monterey festival, and was one of the first violinists to adapt avant-garde techniques and ideas to that instrument. In the late 1960s he pioneered another direction with the group Fourth Way, one of the first jazz-rock outfits. From 1971 he began leading his own groups and recorded five albums for the Impulse! label including *Spirit Dance* (1971) and *The Land Of Spirit And Light* (1973), which bear comparison with Pharoah Sanders' music for the same label: a spiritually uplifting cohesion of post-Coltrane (who White had played with) "fire music" and the soothing, mesmeric facet of jazz-funk. He has also worked with iconoclasts such as Sun Ra, Prince Lasha, Eric Dolphy, Wes Montgomery, Kenny Dorham, Richard Davis and others. He contributed to the Pharoah Sanders album *Message From Home* (1996; Verve) and released a duets album with guitarist Bill Frisell – *Motion Picture* (1997; Intuition) – though unfortunately a reunion with the John Handy Quartet in 2000 went unrecorded. He continues to pursue his singularly spirit-oriented music, combining oriental and classical elements with jazz roots. [IC]

Dr Michael White

Clarinet.

b. New Orleans, 29 Nov 1954.

Perhaps the central figure in the American New Orleans revival scene, in his twenties White played with Doc Paulin (in 1975), the Young Tuxedo Brass Band (in 1979), and with Kid Sheik Cola at Preservation Hall, as well as appearing in the show *One Mo' Time* (1980) and forming his own trio and the Liberty Jazz Band in 1981. Since then White has grown to be recognized as a major authority on New Orleans jazz, and is as efficiently publicized a spokesman for this area of jazz as Wynton Marsalis (who appeared on the recording listed below) is for his. [DF]

⊙ **Crescent City Serenade** (1990; Antilles). White here masterminds some convincing New Orleans music, featuring veterans Teddy Riley, Wendell Brunious and Freddie Lonzo, along with younger players Greg Stafford (leader of the Young Tuxedo Brass Band) and Wynton Marsalis.

Annie Whitehead

Trombone, vocals.

b. Oldham, Lancashire, UK, 16 July 1955.

Whitehead played in brass bands while at school and from 1969 also played in local dance bands. She moved to London in 1981 and played numerous pop, reggae and soul sessions, becoming increasingly involved both in the experimental scene (playing with John Stevens, Maggie Nicols and Evan Parker) and with the ex-pat South African musicans from Brotherhood of Breath. She formed her own group, the Annie Whitehead band, in 1984, releasing her critically acclaimed debut album *Mix Up* that year.

She has since toured with many jazz luminaries, often musicians with a healthy disregard for purism (jazz or otherwise), such as Carla Bley, the Penguin Café Orchestra and Jasper Van't Hof's Dutch/African group Pili Pili; she is also in constant demand as a session player. With the band Rude, she's explored the hinterlands between jazz, rock and reggae (with African influences) alongside bassist Ian Maidman, drummer Liam Genockey and trumpeter Harry Beckett. Her own band, the Annie Whitehead Experience, generally features Genockey and Maidman plus keyboardist Steve Lodder and bassist Steve Lamb. Albums under her own name include *Naked* (1997; EFZ), *The Gathering* (2000; Provocateur) and *Soupsongs: Live* (2000; Jazzprint), a tribute to the songs of Robert Wyatt. [IC]

➤➤ **Carla Bley** *(Big Band Theory).*

Tim Whitehead

Tenor, alto and soprano saxophones, clarinet.

b. Liverpool, UK, 12 Dec 1950.

Tim Whitehead began playing in a folk group while still at school. He went to law school, but quit in 1976 to concentrate on music, forming a quartet called South of the Border which he co-led with guitarist Glenn Cartledge. The same year Whitehead toured Germany with Ian Carr's Nucleus, and the following year he toured with Graham Collier's band. He then played with various London-based bands and in 1980 formed his own quartet, Borderline. In 1984 he joined Loose Tubes, touring and playing on the band's first three albums before leaving in the late 1980s. Throughout that time he had continued to lead his own groups, and this became his overriding interest. In the 1990s he worked frequently with his group at Ronnie Scott's club, and also ran weekly clubs of his own, as well as being active in jazz education.

In 1996, Whitehead was commissioned by Jazz Umbrella (with funding from the Arts Council of England) to compose *Nine Sketches* for solo saxophone. This was performed to critical acclaim later that year at the Purcell Room as part of the London jazz festival. So successful was it that he took the project on tour, performing it at jazz venues and festivals. He won the Andrew Milne Award for Jazz in 1998, allowing him to write, release and tour *Soundtracks*, a project he described as "exploring the words and lives of my mentors and fellow players. I followed their tracks, mostly by instinct, and discovered something of myself as a result." In 1999, he released three CDs – *Nine Sketches*, *Soundtracks* and *New Standards*. In 2001 he formed, with composer Colin Riley, the Homemade Orchestra, an ensemble operating on the boundaries of jazz and contemporary classical. Their first release was *Tides* (see below). Whitehead is one of the most creative, exciting and passionate tenor saxophonists in Europe, and also one of its finest small-group composers. [IC]

⊙ **Authentic** (1991; Jazz House). Whitehead's quartet – pianist Pete Jacobsen, bassist Arnie Somogyi and drummer Dave Barry – caught live at Ronnie Scott's, playing compositions that cover the gamut of swing/bop, funk, rock, expansive ballads and impressionistic pieces, full of subtle harmonies, wonderful melodies and creative rhythms.

⊙ **Silence Between Waves** (1994; Jazz House). This album is still better; the music seems through-composed and yet open to improvisation. Whitehead has heightened the timbral nuances of his playing, and every note is given its full weight. Jacobsen's piano and synthesizer have an eloquence perfectly suited to the music.

⊙ **Tides** (2002; Homemade). A singular ensemble (three wind, three strings, Dick Pearce's trumpet, Liam Noble's piano, bass and percussion), thoughtful compositions and weaving improvisations, the Homemade Orchestra's inaugural attempt at a classical/jazz fusion is a bewitching triumph.

Paul Whiteman

Bandleader, violin.

b. Denver, Colorado, 28 March 1890; d. 29 Dec 1967.

Paul Whiteman was once a figure of enormous controversy in jazz circles, especially after a Universal film in 1930 sealed his publicity campaign for recognition as "The King of Jazz". By then he had been an internationally known show-business figure for ten years. He had promoted the first prestige jazz concert, *An Experiment in Modern Music* at New York's Aeolian Hall in 1924 (featuring George Gershwin playing *Rhapsody In Blue*), and from then on was known for his fast-moving spectacular jazz presentations. Louis Armstrong gives a definitive word picture of the sort of thing that went on at a Whiteman concert: "Mr Whiteman went into the overture by the name of *1812* – and just before the end they started shooting cannons, sirens were howling like mad – and in fact everything was happening in that overture." Not very much of what Whiteman presented ever had much to do with the unbowdlerized creations of more genuine jazzmen of the period, but he did contribute a great deal to the music – he did all he could to make it respectable and to popularize it. He created the idea of a band show: "If you see that picture he made in 1930," says Lawrence Brown, "you can see all the components [of a band show] that are still in use today."

Whiteman was also a generous and discerning employer of the best. "Don't ever make fun of Paul Whiteman," says Joe Venuti. "He took pride in having the finest musicians in the world and paid the highest salaries ever paid." Whiteman's star employees, from a long list, included, as well as Venuti, Bix Beiderbecke, Eddie Lang, Frank Trumbauer and Jack Teagarden. He was a kindly and much loved employer, who kept the sick Beiderbecke's chair open until the end, took a lot from "difficult" bandsmen (like Venuti), and often released artists from their contracts if something good came up (as he did with the Modernaires). Whiteman led a hugely successful band all through the 1930s but gave up regular bandleading in 1944 to become a director of ABC.

Perhaps the most powerful argument for Whiteman is the quality of a lot of his music. The New Paul Whiteman Orchestra, organized by cornettist Dick Sudhalter in the 1970s specifically to play Whiteman's scores, proved the point; so of course do the King of Jazz's original recordings with Bix, Trumbauer, Bing Crosby and the rest, which are charming at least, great at best. [DF]

⊙ **The King of Jazz** (2003; Living Era). Whiteman's output was colossal (and much of it important in jazz terms) but this is a good and perceptive start. His first side of all, "Wang Wang Blues" (1920) is here plus Gershwin's own "Rhapsody in Blue" (1924) ; titles with Beiderbecke, Crosby and the Rhythm Boys, Frank Trumbauer's "Bouncing Ball" and a nine-minute medley, "A night with Paul Whiteman at the Biltmore".

⊙ **Paul Whiteman 1920–28** (Jazz Portraits). A good selection, beginning at the start of Whiteman's career (with his Ambassador Orchestra) and then dipping into a varied menu including three Bix tracks.

⊙ **Bix 'N' Bing 1927–30** (ASV). Excellent selection of Beiderbecke and Crosby's titles with Whiteman; among the leader's best and most jazzy recordings and still fresh today.

⊙ **When Day Is Done 1924–34** (Happy Days). A carefully selected all-round portrait, beginning with *Rhapsody In Blue* (soloist George Gershwin) and moving up through hits of the period (including "When Day Is Done", Whiteman's theme tune), as well as selected tracks with Bix and Hoagy Carmichael ("Washboard Blues").

Mark Whitfield

Guitar.

b. Linden Hurst, Rhode Island, 6 Oct 1966.

Having begun his musical life playing bass in the school orchestra aged seven, Mark Whitfield was introduced to jazz – Coltrane, Basie, Ellington – by his parents. Originally self-taught on guitar, inspired by Charlie Christian, Wes Montgomery, Grant Green and Kenny Burrell, Whitfield studied at the Berklee College of Music (1983–7) before moving to New York and playing with Jack McDuff, an astute judge of guitar talent. Recommended to Warner Bros by George Benson, he made his debut album, *The Marksman*, for them in 1990. In 1991, he toured festivals with George Wein's Jazz Futures band, and established himself as a leader of a trio featuring bassist Roland Guerin and drummer Troy Davis. In addition to studio work with a variety of leaders, including Carl Allen, Teodross Avery, Ernie Watts, Courtney Pine and Christian McBride, he also formed part of a sparky young band put together to welcome the veteran organist Jimmy Smith to Verve. Whitfield's own albums include *True Blue* (1994; Verve), *7th Avenue Stroll* (see below) and *Forever Love* (1997; Verve), which sets his neat guitar against an orchestra arranged and conducted by Dale Ochler. A new deal with Transparent Records began with *Soul Conversation* (2000), a successful smooth jazz/R&B offering in collaboration with producer JK, but swiftly following up with the straightahead *Raw* (see below) indicated that, like his mentor Benson, crossing between genres and audiences would not present a problem. At heart a swinging guitarist with a delicate touch, Whitfield is a fluent improviser with a clear respect for the tradition. [CP]

⊙ **7th Avenue Stroll** (1995; Verve). The album features a stellar cast including pianists Tommy Flanagan and Stephen Scott, bassists Dave Holland and Christian McBride, plus drummers Al Foster and Greg Hutchinson. This is a fine showcase for the guitarist's light, supple swing with Whitfield's own "Headin' To The Wes' Side" a real highlight.

⊙ **Raw** (2000; Transparent). A fine live date with regular group – pianist Robert Glasper, bassist Brandon Owens and drummer Donald Edwards – Whitfield gets to stretch out on five long tunes, including two Edwards' originals and Herbie Hancock's "Tell Me A Bedtime Story".

Tommy Whittle

Tenor saxophone, reeds.
b. Grangemouth, Scotland, 13 Oct 1926.

Tommy Whittle worked early in his career with Claude Giddings's band (including Ronnie Verrell, Pete Chilver, Johnny Claes and Ralph Sharon), then with Johnny Claes's Clay Pigeons, Lew Stone, Carl Barriteau and Harry Hayes. At twenty he joined the great Ted Heath orchestra, but left to develop his solo activities and skills with Tony Kinsey's trio, his own quintet (with Harry Klein), and the BBC Show Band, with whom he was featured soloist. Having topped polls for *Melody Maker* and *New Musical Express*, Whittle formed an eight-piece band which toured for eighteen months, and soon after played solo and with his own small groups in France and the USA, as the "exchange" for Sidney Bechet and Gerry Mulligan's quartet. Then, after a spell of bandleading at the Dorchester Hotel, he joined Jack Parnell's ATV orchestra at the turn of the 60s and remained working in studios regularly thereafter, coming out to play guest spots around the country (often with his wife, singer Barbara Jay), running and sometimes playing at a succession of London jazz clubs, and appearing with the Jazz Journal All Stars (and Barbara Jay) at Nice in 1984. In the late 1980s Whittle joined the Pizza Express All Stars (replacing Danny Moss), and continued freelancing, as well as starring in Ted Heath orchestra reunions; in the 1990s he directed a successful Tribute to Ella Fitzgerald package. Whittle is a polished stylist whose work has proved a shining exception to the view that years of studio work dull the edges of creativity; he remains a great jazz tenor saxophonist by international standards. [DF]

⊙ **Warm Glow** (1992; Teejay). An excellent representation of Whittle's perfectly rounded classic tenor style, in his quartet with Brian Dee, Len Skeat and Bobby Orr.

Peter Whyman

Saxophones, clarinets
b. Leicestershire, England, 14 April 1962.

Whyman first started listening to jazz after his father bought him a Paul Gonsalves album as a present. He went on to study music at London's Guildhall School from 1980–85: clarinet with Yona Ettlinger and Tony Pay, saxophone with Stephen Trier, and jazz with Tony Coe who has remained a mentor and an inspiration ever since. While playing lead alto with the Guildhall Big Band, Whyman was spotted by Mike Westbrook's manager and subsequently played with Westbook on a number of different projects over the following eighteen years (1985–2003). He recorded several albums with him including – a personal favourite – Westbrook's settings of William Blake, *Glad Day* (1997; Enja). At the same time Whyman was a member of the Delta Sax Quartet, co-founded in 1984 with Chris Caldwell, which was dedicated to the performance of avant-garde classical works, including several written specifically for the group. Whyman has also played with the Steve Martland Band (1995–2003), Huw Warren, Peter Fairclough, Barry Adamson, Elvis Costello and Chris Biscoe. His own group, the Pete Whyman Trio, consists of Whyman on clarinet and saxophones, Huw Warren on piano and accordion, and Pete Fairclough on drums and percussion. Very much a group of equals, with each member contributing compositions, the trio recorded an album, *Pulse*, in 1998 which was finally released in 2003 to enthusiastic reviews. Among his favourite saxophone players, he singles out Tony Coe, Cannononball Adderley, Paul Gonsalves, Jimmy Giuffre, Evan Parker and Jan Garbarek. [IC]

⊙ **Pulse** (2003; FMR). A dynamic and highly original album: all three members are virtuosi and their music is full of surprises ranging from a passionate, soaring lyricism to melancholy and even violence. The title track (by Whyman) sets the pace: it begins calmly enough with a quiet piano ostinato followed by long, soothing clarinet phrases which are then broken up by the clarinet's unearthly banshee wails and screams.

➤➤ **Huw Warren** *(A Barrel Organ Far From Home)*; **Mike Westbrook** *(London Bridge Is Broken Down)*.

Johnny Wiggs

Cornet.
b. New Orleans, 25 July 1899; d. 9 Oct 1977.

Initially a violinist, Johnny Wiggs (John Wigginton Hyman) specialized on cornet during the 1920s, and worked with Norman Brownlee from 1924–5, Happy Schilling from 1926 and others, as well as recording with his own band in 1927. He left music to become a schoolmaster in the early 1930s but in 1948 began playing again, and, although he was less active as a player after 1960, he did occasional gigs (including the 1969 New Orleans jazz festival) until 1974. An active member of the New Orleans Jazz Society, Wiggs was a prominent authority on the music as well as a lifelong enthusiast. [DF]

⊙ **Sounds Of New Orleans Vol. 2: Johnny Wiggs 1950–55** (Storyville). Wiggs is featured here with a venerable team of New Orleans players (Raymond Burke, Armand Hug, Doc Souchon and others), as well as playing with just a rhythm-section on five tracks; an excellent cross-section of this versatile player's work.

Bob Wilber

Clarinet, soprano saxophone, arranger, composer.
b. New York, 15 March 1928.

Wilber began as a student clarinettist at Scarsdale High School, New York, where he formed a band with Ed Hubble and Dick Wellstood among others, and sat in at Jimmy Ryan's. When still a teenager he studied under Sidney Bechet, then with Lennie Tristano: the extremes that these two teachers represented clearly indicated the eclecticism of Wilber's ideas (although he recognized the stylistic limitations of bebop very early on). In 1954, after periods leading bands of a Dixieland persuasion with such as Jimmy Archey, he formed The Six. "We wanted to show," he explains, "... that we could use traditional material and modern material and new material: that there was no basic conflict between the old and the new." Such a concept was perhaps overambitious for the period, and when Wilber found the band being compromised into sounding too much like the fashionable modern groups – "That was where the work was" – he broke it up and joined Eddie Condon, with whom he toured England in 1957, then spent a year with Bobby Hackett's band playing clarinet (and a little vibraphone, behind Hackett's wandering ballads).

From then into the 1960s Wilber was a freelance, working on classy recording projects with Ruby Braff, Bud Freeman and others, and studying piano with Sanford Gold; by now he had developed strong new convictions about how jazz should be played. "I have a feeling that jazz has got to be part of the pop music scene to survive," he said in a *Down Beat* interview of the period, "that there are some exciting things going on in the market place in music, more than in the rather introverted jazz scene." In 1968, in the wake of Dick Gibson's jazz parties, he became a founder member of Gibson's cunningly promoted brainchild, The World's Greatest Jazz Band: filled with top-class musicians prepared to play a wide repertoire, the WGJB offered an excitement not always in evidence elsewhere in the jazz world.

When he left in 1973 it was to form Soprano Summit, a quintet co-led with Kenny Davern, which (like all his subsequent groups) presented unusual and well-arranged repertoire with a rare verve. Three years on, after nine albums, Wilber broke up his group again – he and his perceptive wife, Joanne "Pug" Horton, have always been good at knowing when to move on. He formed a trio with Horton and pianist Dave McKenna (which toured widely), retranscribed a set of Jelly Roll Morton titles for recording, worked with the New York Jazz Repertory Company, and by 1981 had embarked on the Bechet Legacy, a six-piece group that set out to recreate music that Bechet had played. Featuring a highly gifted New York trumpeter, Glenn Zottola (later replaced by Randy Sandke), the band was another glittering success for Wilber, whose projects were by now the focus of international jazz attention. He formed his own record company, Bodeswell, and used it to issue more new projects, including *Reflections*, a session with strings on which he played every part in a five-man saxophone section as well as solos, and *The Music Of King Oliver's Jazz Band*, a scholarly transcription of Oliver's 1923 sides. More transcriptions came when Wilber was asked to re-create Duke Ellington's 1927 Washingtonians for a Francis Ford Coppola movie, *The Cotton Club* (1984): his work was uncannily close to the original. After that he continued to re-form his orchestras and small groups for TV, radio, concert and club work in Britain and Europe, and in 1992 was clarinet soloist for Artie Shaw, when Shaw visited London to conduct Mozart's and his own clarinet concertos. In the later 1990s Wilber declared his intention to retire, but his activities since have suggested that the decision was highly (and happily) premature. [DF]

⊙ **Soprano Summit: Live At Concord '77** (Concord). Kenny Davern, Marty Grosz, Mony Budwig and Jake Hanna are co-featured here in the group that turned Wilber into a household name for jazz lovers.

⊙ **On The Road** (1981; Jazzology). A fine collection of tunes by Wilber's Bechet Legacy band: trumpeter Glenn Zottola is impressive in support, as is the British Len Skeat on bass.

⊙ **Summit Reunion** (1990; Chiaroscuro). A welcome reunion for one of the greatest small bands of swing. By this time Davern had renounced soprano saxophone, but in every other way the reunion is wholehearted.

⊙ **Dancing On A Rainbow** (1991; Circle). Wilber with a fine group of New Orleans players, including Wallace Davenport (trumpet) and Danny Barker (guitar), saluting Ellington, Strayhorn and Hodges on many of the tracks. His arrangements are as tasteful and thorough as ever.

⊙ **Reunion At Arbors** (1997; Arbors). The reunion is with Kenny Davern and a stomping rhythm-section headed by Dave Frishberg; the two old reed-compadres lock on immediately in a cohesive session that might persuade you they never broke up to begin with.

⊙ **A Perfect Match** (1997; Arbors). With Dick Hyman on Hammond B-3, a tribute to the collaborations of Johnny Hodges and Wild Bill Davis. Hyman sounds as if he's been playing organ all his life, James Chirillo's funky blues guitar fits the setting, and a bonus is the presence of Britt Woodman who sounds untouched by time in the best sense.

⊙ **You Ain't Heard Nothin' Yet** (1999; Jazzology). A further reunion for Wilber and Davern, this time in a worthy salute to the World's Greatest Entertainer, Al Jolson! Neatly arranged into short tracks it was good to see Wilber and Davern back again though as ever (in later years) the sopranoes stayed in their cases at home.

➤➤ **Eddie Condon** *(Dixieland Jam).*

Alec Wilder

Composer.

b. Rochester, New York, 17 Feb 1907; d. Dec 1980.

Wilder is a songwriter who has always inspired jazz musicians, though compositions such as "It's So Peaceful In The Country", "The Lady Sings The Blues", "The April Age" and "I'll Be Around" are neglected in some quarters. He also wrote many compositions of a classical nature, as well as *American Popular Song*, a highly readable, occasionally contentious but always loving analysis of great songs. The jazz-tinged recordings of the Wilder octet from 1939 onwards are much-sought collectors' items. [DF]

➤➤ **Marian McPartland** *(Plays The Music Of Alec Wilder).*

Joe Wilder

Trumpet.

b. Colwyn, near Philadelphia, 22 Feb 1922.

Now that the first generation of trumpet gods has left the earth, Joe Wilder has begun at last to receive his share of praises. Wilder has always been an outstanding jazz musician, whose poised invention, stylistic wit, originality and shining clear tone mark him out as exceptional. Yet acknowledgement of his gifts has up until recently been too selective. Wilder began his career with Les Hite in 1941 before joining Lionel Hampton until 1946 (with a break for military service). He went on to play with Jimmie Lunceford, Lucky Millinder, Sam Donahue, Herbie Fields and Noble Sissle, before moving into Broadway pit orchestras (three years with *Guys and Dolls*) and then in 1957 onto staff with ABC-TV studios in New York. In 1962 he toured the USSR with Benny Goodman, but continued with ABC until 1973 as well as playing lead for the Symphony Of The New World from 1965–71. Thereafter, he worked with Tony Bennett, Lena Horne and Michel Legrand and kept busy in New York studios (playing, amongst other things, for the Cosby show), and he emerged more regularly to play at Colorado's Jazz Party (from 1972) and jazz situations in general. He recorded with Benny Carter in 1985, and worked for George Wein on major festivals, recording again as a leader from 1991. As a culmination of his 80th birthday celebrations, his third Evening Star album *Among Friends* appeared in 2003. His latter day return to jazz performance has been marked by widespread recognition of his talents, both as an improviser and as one of the pioneers of "crossover". [DF]

⊙ **Wilder 'N' Wilder** (1956; Savoy). One of the rare Wilder solo sessions from the 1950s in company with his lifelong friend and colleague Hank Jones. Both players are masters of control and taste, and listening to the trumpeter's incandescent tone, perfect note-placement and conceptual poise sometimes brings to mind Clifford Brown, though Wilder has always been his own creative voice.

⊙ **Alone With Just My Dreams** (1991; Evening Star). Later Wilder with a trio supplemented by fellow veteran, guitarist Remo Palmieri. The quintessential aspects of Wilder's style are unaltered with time, and the quiet dignity of his ballads is mesmerizing.

Barney Wilen

Tenor and soprano saxophones.

b. Nice, France, 4 March 1937; d. 24 May 1996.

Wilen, a self-taught musician, made a strong impression on the Paris scene in the mid-1950s; he recorded there with both Roy Haynes and John Lewis and made his first album at the age of nineteen. He worked with Miles Davis on the *Lift To The Scaffold* soundtrack and in concert in 1957, and with Art Blakey on the *Les Liaisons Dangereuses* soundtrack and in concert in 1959. Not continuously active as a player, he re-emerged in 1966 as an exponent of free jazz. He appeared at the Berlin festival in 1967 with Indian classical musicians, and acted as the recording engineer for Archie Shepp's live performance in Algiers in 1969, before working as an anthropological film-maker in Africa from 1970–76. A further resurgence on the 1980s Paris scene featured playing that was much nearer to his bop-derived debut years, starting with an album of music inspired by a jazz cartoon, *La Note Bleue*. Wilen's early work absorbed the implications of Americans such as Sonny Rollins, but with a softer tone possibly influenced by Lucky Thompson's first visit to France. As well as demonstrating the maturity of the Paris scene, which was then a Mecca for visiting American players, Wilen himself sounds remarkably fresh and vital in retrospect. [BP]

⊙ **French Ballads** (1987; IDA). A straightahead and even unambitious quartet album with Michel Graillier, this featured exclusively French-written popular songs of the past. Only the internationally known "Autumn Leaves" is a little disappointing.

Lee Wiley

Vocals, composer.

b. Fort Gibson, Oklahoma, 9 Oct 1915; d. 11 Dec 1975.

"Lee Wiley has class ... the best we have," says George Frazier, the singer's most passionate in-print advocate, and most jazz people share at least a fondness for what she did. In her teens she was temporarily blinded in a riding accident, recovered, came to New York around 1930, and by the time she was seventeen was singing with Leo Reisman's orchestra. All through the 1930s she worked constantly on radio, recorded with Victor Young, John Green and the Casa Lomans, and from mid-decade began appearing in clubs with small jazz groups, including Eddie Condon's at the Famous Door (Condon's trumpeter, Bunny Berigan, became her lover). In 1939 and 1940 she recorded albums of songs by Cole Porter and George Gershwin, accompanied by small jazz groups, in which her intimate, veiled voice, precise diction and stroking approach to a note had the power to turn strong men to jelly: "I loved Lee Wiley," said critic Stanley Green, "even before I had any idea who she was, I loved her! She sang to me – just to me!" In June 1943 Wiley married Jess Stacy, a stormy partnership that lasted only five years. Wiley continued to record sporadically during the 1950s but work was thin, and apart from a semi-documentary TV play, *Something About Lee Wiley* (1963), very little more was heard from her until 1971. That year she recorded *Back Home Again* for Monmouth Evergreen, with Rusty Dedrick's band; the album was the last studio recording before her death, but her 1930s sides and broadcasts have never stopped being reissued. [DF]

⊙ **Manhattan Nights 1931–51** (Definitive). A sweep-the-board four-CD compilation covering Wiley's early work with Leo Reisman, Victor Young et al. Contains the complete "Songbook" collections; singles with Crosby, Jess Stacy and Muggsy Spanier; all her titles with Stan Freeman and Cy Walter; and ends up with the great "Night In Manhattan". Perhaps the best collection, if you can find it.

⊙ **Sings The Songs Of George And Ira Gershwin And Cole Porter 1939–40** (Audiophile). The justly famous set has small groups led by Joe Bushkin, Max Kaminsky, Bunny Berigan and Paul Weston, plus Fats Waller on pipe organ, and the great titles include "Sweet And Lowdown", "Looking At You", "Why Shouldn't I" and "Let's Fly Away", with Berigan on magical form.

⊙ **Sings The Songs Of Richard Rodgers, Lorenz Hart And Harold Arlen** (1943; Audiophile). More essential recordings, this time with groups led by Joe Bushkin, Max Kaminsky and Eddie Condon. High spots include the wonderfully bluesy "Moanin' In The Mornin'" and a carefree "Down With Love", with Butterfield and Caceres amid Condon's sextet.

⊙ **Night In Manhattan** (1950; Columbia). Another great Wiley collection, with Joe Bushkin's orchestra and strings plus Bobby Hackett's lyric cornet, on a set of titles including "Manhattan", "Ghost Of A Chance" and Bushkin's own "Oh Look At Me Now". Four extra titles with duo pianists Stan Feeman and Cy Walter are pleasant but less crucial.

⊙ **As Time Goes By** (1956; RCA Bluebird). Very good later material, including five tracks with eight-piece Dixieland bands (featuring Billy Butterfield) plus nine with Butterfield's orchestra from the album *A Touch Of The Blues*. Barbara Lea's perceptive sleevenotes are a welcome bonus.

⊙ **At Carnegie Hall 1972** (Audiophile). A main event, Wiley's return to Carnegie Hall in 1972. There are mistakes and occasional lyric-fluffs but much of the old magic is there.

Dave Wilkins

Trumpet.

b. Barbados, 25 Sept 1914; d. 26 Nov 1990.

Anyone who likes the sides Fats Waller recorded in London in 1938 (eg "Pent Up In A Penthouse" and "Flat Foot Floogie") is bound to like the sound of trumpeter Dave Wilkins. He was born in Barbados, trained in the Salvation Army there, and then played in his family band before joining Richie Keith's Jazz Hounds in Trinidad in 1934. Soon afterwards he joined Ken "Snakehips" Johnson's band in Port of Spain, and in 1938 arrived at the Glasgow Empire: a baptism of fire for the orchestra, which they confidently survived. Johnson's band went on to make a big impact in London, where Wilkins was spotted by Waller and asked to record, but, although he survived the bomb that came down the steps of the Café de Paris in 1941, killing half of Johnson's band, very little more was heard of him after that, apart from recordings with Lord Kitchener and others during the 1950s calypso boom. [DF]

Fats Waller

⊙ **Fats Waller, London Sessions 1938–9** (EMI Pathe). Probably Wilkins's most famous on-record encounter: full-toned and confident, he shines on "Pent Up In A Penthouse" and elsewhere.

Ernie Wilkins

Tenor, alto and soprano saxophones, arranger.

b. St Louis, Missouri, 20 July 1919; d. 5 June 1999.

After university study and navy service, Wilkins played with the Earl Hines band in 1947, and worked in the St Louis area. He joined Count Basie from 1952–5, playing alto and arranging. He left to become a freelance writer for Basie, Dizzy Gillespie (in whose 1956 band he played briefly), Tommy Dorsey and Harry James. He was also the arranger/musical director for countless albums with Sarah Vaughan, Buddy Rich, Oscar Peterson and many others. His career was temporarily halted in the mid-1960s by drug problems, but he returned in 1969 to play and write for the Clark Terry big band and quintet. From 1971–3 he worked for Mainstream Records, arranging and supervising sessions. He then worked in Europe from the mid-1970s, recording with Art Farmer and the Austrian Radio band, writing for other radio orchestras, and, from 1980, also leading his own Copenhagen-based Almost Big Band and touring as a soloist.

Wilkins was an exciting and unfussy writer whose main historical importance lay in his redefining the sound of the 1950s Basie band, which he was then expected to duplicate for his freelance assignments (Basie is alleged to have said to Harry James at a joint appearance, "Who's going to play my arrangements first, me or you?"). This sound would have been widely imitated anyway, and it provided much encouragement for Wilkins's stylistic successor Quincy Jones, but it is a pity that Ernie himself, at least until his expatriate years, was so typecast. [BP]

⊙ **K.a.l.e.i.d.o.d.u.k.e.** (1990; Birdology). A one-off all-star session with a thirteen-piece band featuring soloists such as Art Farmer, Benny Bailey, Alvin Batiste and James Williams, but it is Wilkins's discreet but firm writing that carries the day.

Alan Wilkinson

Saxophones, vocals.

b. London, 22 Aug 1954.

Having started as a painter (he moved to Leeds in 1975 to do a fine arts degree), Wilkinson took up alto in 1978, joining Matthew Coe (aka Xero Slingsby) and drummer Paul Hession, a longtime associate, in the group Crow. In 1979 he formed the band Art, Bart and Fargo with Hession and tenor saxophonist Pete Malham, gradually increasing the range of instruments he played, and starting to mix composition with pure improvisation. A summer school in South Wales in 1982 led to gigs in London with Hession and pianist Akemi Kuniyoshi, and to work in Scandinavia with Welsh expatriate drummer Steve Hubback. In 1983 Wilkinson started the Termite Club in Leeds as a space for experimental music and performing arts, and appeared in Holland and Belgium as a duo with Hession. From the mid-1980s Wilkinson established himself as a regular member of the UK's improvising community, collaborating with drummer Steve Noble and bassist Tony Moore in a trio, touring with guitarist Derek Bailey, and playing regularly in Leeds with both the Quartones and the Sheffield-based improvisers Feetpackets. In 1989 he toured the UK with Alex Maguire's Cat O' Nine Tails, later joining the pianist Willi Kellers and Christoph Winkel in a touring band subsequently known as the Alan Wilkinson quartet, and in the same year formed his long-lived trio with mainstays Hession and bassist Simon Fell. Latterday projects have included Real Time with artist Gina Southgate and drummer Mark Sanders; the London-based band Ya Basta; a duo with guitarist Stefan Jaworzyn captured on an Incus album, *In A Sentimental Mood* (1996); a quartet with Hession, Fell and Boston guitarist Joe Morris (*Registered Firm*, 1998, on Incus again); and cameos on Simon Fell's large ensemble projects. A regular face on the free-improv scene in London and Leeds, Wilkinson is also part of a trio with Noble and bassist Marcio Mattos and has played with younger improvisers such as drummer Tim Goldie and Basque "computer feedback" player Mattin. His most remarkable solo work, *Seedy Boy*, is surely deserving of release on CD, but the two CDs below are excellent showcases. [CP]

Hession-Wilkinson-Fell

⊙ **Foom! Foom!** (1992; Bruce's Fingers). Like their later live CD, *The Horrors of Darmstadt*, this is a great introduction to the Brötzmann-like improvised noisy free-for-all of this trio.

John Law

⊙ **Exploded On Impact** (1992; Slam). One of the freshest and most original talents on the UK improvising scene, Law is more architecturally minded than many free-players; here Wilkinson is heard to great effect on alto and baritone.

Spiegle Willcox

Trombone.

b. Sherburne, New York, 2 May 1903; d. 26 Aug 1999.

After apprenticeship with Bob Causer's Big Four, Willcox stayed with the group when it became Paul Whiteman's Collegians, then played with the California Ramblers, and Jean Goldkette between 1925–7. When most of the Goldkette band were corralled into Whiteman's orchestra, Willcox retired to join his family's coal business. He led a band in Syracuse for many years, and re-emerged almost fifty years later (with the encouragement of Joe Venuti) to play more regularly, including at a 1975 Carnegie Hall tribute to Bix Beiderbecke. Thereafter, he became a regular at clubs and festivals, visited Britain to star at concerts, and continued playing tirelessly into the 1990s. Never a front-rank jazz soloist, Wilcox's polished performance was nevertheless a gracious memory of a bygone era. [DF]

⊙ **Vintage '89** (1992; Timeless). Willcox's schooled trombone amid a friendly Dutch group. While never a world-shaking soloist, he sounds fine on an album produced by the visionary Chris Ellis.

➤➤ **Bill Challis** *(The Goldkette Project).*

Benny Williams

➤➤ *see entry on* **Black Benny.**

Buster Williams

Bass.

b. Camden, New Jersey, 17 April 1942.

Opting to play bass after hearing Oscar Pettiford (his father had taught him both bass and drums), Buster Williams studied at Philadelphia's Combs College of Music in 1959 before launching his career with Jimmy Heath in 1960, juggled with playing in a quintet led by Gene Ammons and Sonny Stitt from 1960–61. He spent most of the 60s in Los Angeles, where he played with the Jazz Crusaders and in a quintet formed by Bobby Hutcherson and Harold Land. Williams backed a number of singers, Dakota Staton, Betty Carter and Nancy Wilson among them. Settling in New York at the end of the 1960s, he played with Herbie Hancock until 1972, with Mary Lou Williams (1973–5), and with Ron Carter (1977–8), simultaneously working as a bandleader. On the day of Thelonious Monk's death (17 Feb 1982), Williams was present at a pre-arranged recording session with two of Monk's sidemen, saxophonist Charlie Rouse and drummer Ben Riley, to celebrate the great pianist's music. With pianist Kenny Barron, they went ahead with what then became the first recorded tribute to Monk, and the band became Sphere, and it recorded and played as such for the next five years, until Rouse's death in 1988. Williams continued his association with Barron (in duo format) and in a trio with Riley for the next ten years. In 1997, with the addition of saxophonist Gary Bartz, Sphere re-formed, making an eponymous album for Verve (see below). In the late 1980s and 1990s Williams established himself as one of the most in-demand bassists in the music, lending his rich, dark tone and supple technique to recordings by, among many others, Frank Morgan, Ralph Moore, Stanley Cowell and Larry Coryell. As well as being among the most frequently-recorded bass players in history, a run of fine albums under his own name for TCB in the late 1990s/early 2000s (among them *Lost In A Memory*, with Geri Allen and vibraphonist Steve Wilson and *Joined At The Hip*, a bebop set featuring Wilson, again and pianist Carlos McKinney) consolidated his credentials as a late-flowering composer and bandleader. [CP]

⊙ **Toku Do** (1978; Denon). Impressive trio recording with Kenny Barron (piano) and Ben Riley (drums), containing Williams originals such as the title track, and a stunning version of "Some Day My Prince Will Come".

Something More (1989; In and Out). Focuses on complex Williams compositions and features an extraordinary band: Shunzu Ono (trumpet), Wayne Shorter (soprano and tenor saxophones), Herbie Hancock (piano) and Al Foster (drums).

Houdini (2000; Sirocco). A side step from his latter day TCB commitments, a delicious trio album featuring pianist Geri Allen and drummer Lenny White on some evocative Williams originals plus Herbie Hancock's "The Sorcerer".

Timeless All-Stars

It's Timeless (1982; Timeless). Standards impeccably performed by a stellar band: Curtis Fuller (trombone), Harold Land (tenor), Bobby Hutcherson (vibes), Cedar Walton (piano) and Billy Higgins (drums), along with Williams.

Sphere

Sphere (1997; Verve). Mixing Monk tunes ("We See", "Hornin' In") with appropriately Monkish originals, plus "Surrey With The Fringe On Top" and Billy Strayhorn's "Isfahan", a classy, elegant album from four masters.

Clarence Williams

Piano, vocals, arranger, composer, leader.

b. Plaquemine Delta, Louisiana, 8 Oct 1898; d. 6 Nov 1965.

Clarence Williams was raised by a hotel-owning family, and quickly acquired a business eye: while playing the field in New Orleans and picking up tips from New Orleans pianists, he ran a suit-cleaning service for the sharp-as-a-tack piano professors. Soon after that he was playing in Storyville as a solo entertainer, keeping an ear out for new material and writing away to New York for the newest hits, as well as managing his own cabaret on the side. During this period he opened a small publishing company with Armand J. Piron (his regular partner), and in 1916, out of the blue, he received a $1600 cheque for a song he had almost forgotten about, "Brownskin, Who You For?", which had been recorded by a New York band for Columbia records. "I believe it was the most money anybody ever made on a song in New Orleans," said Williams, and from then on his course was clear. First he sold songsheets door-to-door around the District music shops (Lizzie Miles often sang the words), then he opened a music store in Chicago, and soon after established a highly successful New York publishing house in which, by 1919, Richard M. Jones was a regular employee.

All through the next decade Williams was organizing record dates (including his classic Blue Five sessions with Louis Armstrong, Sidney Bechet and others), accompanying a string of fine blues singers from Sippie Wallace to Rosetta Crawford and Bessie Smith (he also briefly managed Smith, an arrangement that collapsed suddenly after a royalty dispute), and composing a catalogue of durable hits: "Baby Won't You Please Come Home", "Royal Garden Blues", "Everybody Loves My Baby", "West End Blues" and more. Williams married blues singer Eva Taylor in 1921, and from 1923 was A&R man for the "race" division of OKeh records (a powerful position), as well as regularly leading bands of his own (often including Ed Allen, an underrated trumpeter). As the decade progressed he went on recording (often with bigger bands) and stayed successful until, with the swift passage of jazz fashion, he found himself in less demand than before. In 1943 Williams sold his catalogue to Decca for $50,000 and opened a bargain shop in Harlem. By 1961 his sight was failing; in 1965 he was killed by a taxi. [DF]

Clarence Williams 1921–41 (Classics). This comprehensive fourteen-CD chronology (divided into short, three or four year chunks) s Williams's best testimony, telling his full on-record story, through the legendary Blue Five titles with Armstrong and Bechet, and on through partnerships with blues singer Eva Taylor, cornettist Ed Allen and fellow stars of the era. Volumes available separately as usual.

Baby, Won't You Please Come Home: His 25 Greatest 1923–33 (ASV). For those confused by Williams's prolific discography, this sampler makes a good starting-point to discover his music. Twenty-five tracks, including many hits and a starry collection of sidemen including Red Allen, Louis Armstrong, Buster Bailey, Sidney Bechet, Wilbur de Paris, Eddie Lang, Don Redman, Prince Robinson and others.

Claude "Fiddler" Williams

Violin; also guitar.

b. Muskogee, Oklahoma, 22 Feb 1908.

Williams's full-time musical grounding came with Terrence Holder's band, which later transformed into Andy Kirk's Clouds Of Joy, and soon after he worked with Alphonso Trent in 1932, George E. Lee in 1933), and Chick Stevens from 1934–5. He also played rhythm guitar with Count Basie's orchestra from 1936–7 before being replaced by Freddy Green. After that, Williams worked with a variety of bands in the USA including the Four Shades Of Rhythm, and after years in New York and Chicago moved back to Kansas City (1953) where he played residencies. In the 1970s Williams toured with Jay McShann and also played solo at jazz festivals and parties. A violinist of enormous energy and creative ability, his work is underrated in comparison with figures such as Stuff Smith, but his music rates equally with theirs and, rather amazingly, shows no sign of diminished energy. [DF]

Cootie Williams

Trumpet.

b. Mobile, Alabama, 10 July 1911; d. 14 Sept 1985.

Cootie (Charles Melvin) Williams worked with Alonzo Ross, Chick Webb and Fletcher Henderson before joining Duke Ellington in 1929, where he replaced Bubber Miley. To begin with Williams was never instructed to duplicate Miley's growling *tours de force*. "But," he told Eric Townley later, "I thought as I was taking Bubber's place I'd better learn how to growl ... then one night when I had a solo to play on something I picked up the plunger and

WILLIAM GOTTLIEB

Cootie Williams

surprised the band with a growl solo. When we came off the stand Duke and the boys said, 'That's it, that's it. Keep that in!'" From then on Williams developed Miley's style into a vocabulary of his own ("Carelessly", a side with Billie Holiday from the 1930s, shows how) and featured his powerful horn on specially composed features such as "Concerto For Cootie", which Ellington wrote for him in 1940. That year Williams – amid a blaze of publicity, recrimination and even a Raymond Scott record commemorating the event – left the Duke to join Benny Goodman, a leader he much admired, and stayed a year. After that he led his own big band (Ellington encouraged him to go out on his own when Williams asked to return to the fold), and over the years featured a string of bright young talents, including Charlie Parker, Bud Powell, Eddie "Lockjaw" Davis, Ed Thigpen and Eddie "Cleanhead" Vinson, before cutting down to a R&B-flavoured six-piece at the instigation of Savoy manager Charlie Buchanan in 1948. By the early 1960s, Williams – a trumpeter of unbending standards, strong opinions and inner tensions – was drinking more, developing high blood pressure and feeling the strain of leading. So he rejoined Goodman briefly and, finally, Ellington for good in 1962. From then on his strong, immobile features and masterful trumpet were the centrepoints of Ellington's concerts until his leader's death; Williams carried on with Mercer Ellington's later re-creations, and a very late (unexpected) sample of Williams in 1978 may be heard on the album *Teresa Brewer At Carnegie Hall.* [DF]

⊙ **Duke Ellington's Trumpets 1937–40** (Black and Blue). This CD collects titles by Cootie's fine small groups of the period, with Bigard, Hodges, Hardwicke and others. Cootie played wonderfully all his life but this was his most lissom and urgently creative period; later on he seemed often to play in slow motion.

⊙ **The Big Challenge** (1957; Fresh Sound). A fascinating mainstream date teaming Williams with Rex Stewart (two old champions gradually slowing up), as well as the two-tenor team of Bud Freeman and Coleman Hawkins (another summit meeting) and trombonists Lawrence Brown and J.C. Higginbotham.

James Williams

Piano, composer.
b. Memphis, 8 March 1951.

Williams started playing at the age of thirteen, initially interested in soul and gospel music. While studying theory at Memphis State University, he had the opportunity to play behind George Coleman, Thad Jones and Richard Davis, and became sufficiently expert to begin teaching at Berklee College from 1972–7. Living in Boston, he played regularly with Alan Dawson and backed visiting soloists such as Woody Shaw, Joe Henderson, Milt Jackson and Art Farmer. He joined Art Blakey from 1977–81, contributing many original compositions to the band's repertoire. Since then, he has led his own groups in New York and worked briefly with leaders like Sonny Stitt, Shaw, Henderson, Bobby Hutcherson and Buddy Tate, and he has made some excellent recordings with Farmer, Emily Remler and Tom Harrell. A great one for fostering the talents of others, such as Donald Brown and Geoff Keezer, Williams has often become involved in producing both events and albums, including the Contemporary Piano Ensemble formed in 1993 with Brown, Keezer, Mulgrew Miller and Harold Mabern. His own playing and writing, nurtured by this varied experience, is notably strong and rhythmically alert. [BP]

⊙ **Magical Trio** (1987; Emarcy). Asking for trouble (or, as he put it, "one of the greatest music lessons and experiences"), Williams put together a trio with Blakey and Ray Brown. Needless to say, his playing, from the gospel intro to "Hammerin'" to the modal vamp of "J's Jam Song", was equal to the situation.

➤➤ **Art Blakey** *(Straight Ahead).*

Jessica Williams

Piano, keyboards.
b. Baltimore, Maryland, 17 March 1948.

Williams took piano lessons from the age of four, and was playing jazz professionally at 14. After studying classical music at Peabody Conservatory, she played in Philadelphia in the 1970s with Philly Joe Jones and Joe Morello, and in local rock groups, often on organ. She moved to San Francisco in 1977, becoming the house pianist at the Keystone Korner club and working with Stan Getz, Bobby Hutcherson, Charlie Haden and Tony Williams. Known during this period as Jessica Jennifer Williams, she was involved in the 1980s in synthesizer music, producing numerous albums on her own Quanta and Ear-

Art labels, often overdubbing herself playing bass and drums. She has also recorded acoustic sets, with musicians such as Eddie Harris and Eddie Henderson alongside her, and she appeared on Charlie Rouse's last album. Possessing an eclectic approach in which Thelonious Monk and Bill Evans are only two of her influences, she brings a remarkably fresh touch to standard material and her original compositions are stimulating while seeming inevitably right. [BP]

⊙ **A Song That I Heard** (1994; Hep). This trio set has a clutch of self-composed tunes and an atmospheric Japanese folk song. But there are also standards, both rare and hackneyed, given the Williams treatment and, in the case of "Alone Together", an exciting duo with drummer Dick Berk.

Joe Williams

Vocals.

b. Cordele, Georgia, 12 Dec 1918; d. 29 March 1999.

Williams (whose given name was Joseph Goreed) is not to be confused with the blues singer/guitarist Big Joe Williams (b. 16 Oct 1903; d. 17 Dec 1982). He was brought up in Chicago and sang in nightclubs there with the Jimmie Noone group and others in the late 1930s, and with Coleman Hawkins and Lionel Hampton in the early 1940s. He toured with Andy Kirk in 1946–7, making his first record with him in New York. He worked briefly with the Albert Ammons-Pete Johnson band, then with the Chicago band of Red Saunders, with whom he recorded under the leadership of Hot Lips Page in 1950. He worked in Chicago with the Count Basie septet in 1950, and then built his reputation with the first hit record of "Every Day" (c.1951), backed by the King Kolax band. From 1954–60 he was Basie's regular singer, bringing himself and the band to new popularity. From then on he worked as a soloist, first with the Harry Edison quintet in 1961–2, then with his own trios led by Chicago pianists such as Junior Mance and Norman Simmons. He made regular appearances with all-star jazz groups (including an African tour with the Clark Terry quintet in 1979) and had frequent reunions with the Basie band. Thanks to Bill Cosby, he also had a speaking role on the *Cosby Show* in the 1980s. Williams's distinctive voice, deeper and darker than Billy Eckstine's, was very effective on sophisticated blues performances, but he also showed considerable versatility on jazz and ballad items. [BP]

Count Basie-Joe Williams

⊙ **Count Basie Swings, Joe Williams Sings** (19556; Verve). The classic album, with the remake of "Every Day" plus three extra tracks from the following year, shows the still light-toned Williams taking on the might of the band and coming out ahead.

Joe Williams

⊙ **Ballad And Blues Master** (1987; Verve). A more relaxed latterday Williams is deeper, in all senses of the word, and has both Norman Simmons's trio and the audience in the palm of his hand. Tracks from both these recommendations are on a two-CD set, *Every Day*, issued for Joe's 75th birthday.

Mary Lou Williams

Piano, arranger, composer.

b. Atlanta, Georgia, 8 May 1910; d. 28 May 1981.

Williams, née Mary Elfrieda Scruggs, learned to play by ear as a child, and first performed in public at the age of six. She was brought up in Pittsburgh, where she appeared in talent shows, and from the age of thirteen was working in carnivals and vaudeville. At sixteen she married carnival band member John Williams (who in the 1940s was to play with the Cootie Williams and Earl Hines bands) and moved to Memphis, making her record debut with his Synco Jazzers. When John joined Terrence Holder's band (soon to become Andy Kirk's) she hired Jimmie Lunceford as his replacement and ran the group herself. The Kirk band settled in Kansas City in 1929, where Mary Lou first wrote arrangements for them, then deputized on piano for their initial recording (which was one of her compositions). In 1931 she became the band's regular pianist and chief arranger, writing material that was ahead of its time and, in the case of her 1936 "Walkin' And Swingin'", contained the germ of Thelonious Monk's "Rhythm-A-Ning".

Though also busy as a freelance arranger for Benny Goodman and others from the mid-1930s, she remained with Kirk until 1942. Having divorced and married Shorty Baker, she left to co-lead a sextet with him. When he joined Ellington she led her own group (including Art Blakey in 1942), and then also worked herself for Ellington, as a staff arranger. Settling in New York, she began working regularly under her own name, and performed her *Zodiac Suite* with the New York Philharmonic at the Town Hall in 1945. She lived in England and France from 1952–4, before retiring from music for three years. She made a guest appearance with Dizzy Gillespie at the Newport festival in 1957, followed by further regular playing and composing. She toured Europe in 1968–9 and her subsequent concert appearances included a duo with Cecil Taylor in 1977, the Goodman Carnegie Hall anniversary in 1978, and the Montreux festival in 1979. She was artist in residence at Duke University, North Carolina, from 1977 until shortly before her death from cancer.

In her last years, Mary Lou often gave a recital/demonstration of the history of jazz, most of which she had lived through and influenced. The early Andy Kirk band was a primitive blues-based organization just waiting to be overhauled and modernized by her writing and playing; at the keyboard, she was one of the first anywhere to pick up on the innovations of Earl Hines, whom she first heard before both left Pittsburgh. Always showing an affinity for boogie-woogie (the inspiration for her famous "Roll 'Em", written for Goodman), she also adapted it to more modern patterns and voicings in her own per-

formances of the late 1930s. Then, although she was partly behind the scenes, her friendship in the 1940s with Tadd Dameron, Bud Powell and Thelonious Monk (whom she had met when he visited Kansas City on tour) made her the virtual guru of the bebop movement.

Her interest in astrological titles had few follow-ups until the "Age of Aquarius" suddenly made it acceptable, but her subsequent Christian conversion and writing of religious works from the early 1960s set a precedent for those jazz musicians who then began performing in church, including Duke Ellington; although he only recorded the brilliant "Trumpet No End" of the pieces she wrote for him, she was a close friend in later life and played at his funeral. Rightly revered as the most distinguished forerunner of the present generation of female musicians, she was honoured in 1996 with the first of an annual series of Mary Lou Williams Women In Jazz festivals at the Kennedy Centre in Washington. But, more than with most musicians of historical importance and influence, the sheer enjoyment to be gained from her work is still vastly underrated. [BP]

⊙ **Lady Piano** (1955; Black Bird). This Spanish reissue of Williams's rare Jazztone set with Wendell Marshall and Osie Johnson has variable sound, but shows her interest in jazz history. The first three tracks are an original rag, a slow blues and a boogie originally written for Goodman ("Roll 'Em"), while "Jericho" is a Latin update of the spiritual and "Taurus" is an excerpt from her *Zodiac Suite*.

⊙ **Free Spirits** (1975; Steeplechase). A more expert recording, with Buster Williams and drummer Mickey Roker, is more revealing of Williams's tender but tough piano sound, and includes "All Blues" and "Dat Dere", as well as original compositions and reworked standards.

➤➤ **Andy Kirk** *(The Chronological Andy Kirk 1936–7).*

Richard Williams

Trumpet, piano, saxophone, composer.

b. Galveston, Texas, 4 May 1931.

Richard (Gene) Williams played tenor saxophone in high school and worked with local bands before taking a degree in music at the Manhattan School. After service in the air force he joined Lionel Hampton on trumpet in 1956, touring Europe with him. He also played with Gigi Gryce from 1959–62, and Charles Mingus from 1959–64. In the 60s he played with Lou Donaldson, Quincy Jones, Slide Hampton, Roland Kirk, Eric Dolphy, Duke Ellington and, from 1966–9, Thad Jones-Mel Lewis. He played in the New York premiere of Gunther Schuller's *Journey Into Jazz*, worked in various Broadway musicals, and in the early 70s worked in Europe with local musicians; he was in the trumpet section of Clark Terry's big band in the mid-1970s and played with the Mingus Dynasty in 1982. His early influences were Fats Navarro and Charlie Parker and, right from the start, Williams has always been a sophisticated soloist with a fat, burnished tone, a good harmonic understanding, an excellent range and a lyrical flair. [IC]

⊙ **New Horn In Town** (1960; Candid). The 29-year-old Williams was already a mature player when this album was recorded with Leo Wright (alto saxophone and flute), Richard Wyands (piano), bassist Reggie Workman and drummer Bobby Thomas. Williams's fluency and brilliant technique are to the fore in this mixture of standards ("I Can Dream, Can't I?"), jazz elegy ("I Remember Clifford") and originals.

➤➤ **Charles Mingus** *(The Black Saint And The Sinner Lady).*

Roy Williams

Trombone.

b. Salford, Lancashire, UK, 1 March 1937.

Roy Williams began in Manchester playing tailgate trombone with a local band, Eric Batty's Jazz Aces. Soon after, he joined Mike Peters, then Terry Lightfoot for the duration of the trad boom in Britain, recording widely, appearing in films such as *It's Trad Dad* (1962), and impressing musicians with his rapidly developing technique and fluent ideas. One such was drummer Lennie Hastings who, after Roy Crimmins's departure from Alex Welsh's first band, recommended young Roy Williams as the replacement, and Williams duly joined on 1 April 1965. An Alex Welsh album, *Strike One*, a fanfare for his new band, showed that Williams had turned into a world-class talent, a perfect amalgam of Urbie Green and Jack Teagarden, with a hint of Bob Brookmeyer here and there. For the next thirteen years Williams was a much respected centrepiece of Welsh's great band, but he left in 1978, joined Humphrey Lyttelton for four years, and then became a freelance. By then his reputation was made: a regular poll-winner, he was visiting America to play for Dick Gibson's Colorado Jazz Parties, Don Miller's Phoenix festival, and with Bobby Rosengarden's band at New York's Rainbow Room, as well as recording solo albums and appearing solo around the festival circuit, and playing dates with Peter Boizot's Pizza Express All Stars, the trombone group Five-a-Slide and the Alex Welsh Reunion Band. To the present he has continued to freelance, playing guest dates as a soloist, starring at festivals in Britain and Europe, and touring with Pete York, The World's Greatest Jazz Band, Peanuts Hucko, Thomas Ornberg and Bent Persson, among many others.

Williams is the natural heir to George Chisholm: consistent, perfectly musical and with a pianissimo close-to-the-microphone approach that recalls Jack Teagarden, he has become "first trombone call" for British and many American musicians in his style. [DF]

⊙ **Gruesome Twosome** (1980; Black Lion). Williams's long-time partner in the Alex Welsh band was John Barnes, and this is their on-record meeting with Brian Lemon, Len Skeat and Stan Bourke. Outstanding moments include a lazy reappraisal of the underplayed "When A Woman Loves A Man" and Pete Strange's title track.

⊙ **Something Wonderful** (1981; Hep). One of the albums which helped establish Williams's solo status, with the fleet trio of Eddie Thompson (using string synthesizer here and there), Len Skeat and Jim Hall. A fine showcase with bonus track "It Never Entered My Mind".

⊙ **Shakin' The Blues Away** (1995; Zephyr). With George Masso and the Brian Lemon quartet. Masso and Williams are regular playing-colleagues and the American's approach is sufficiently different from Roy's to make them rewarding co-partners at any time.

⊙ **How Long Has This Been Going On** (1995; Zephyr). They make it sound so easy, but never mundane. Complete with opening chat from the co-leaders Brian Lemon and Williams, this date has Scott Hamilton along with Dave Cliff, Dave Green and Allan Ganley, and the results are flawless swing.

⊙ **Steamers!** (1999; Nagel Heyer). Critics' choice for "Jazz Record of the Year" in Jazz Journal International, a triumph for Williams and partner Danny Moss with their A-team rhythm section: John Pearce, Len Skeat and Charlie Antolini. Both these compatible veterans are on top form and showing the Americans a thing or two!

>> **Pete Strange** *(The Great British Jazz Band)*; **Alex Welsh** *(Classic Concert)*.

Rudy Williams

Alto, tenor and baritone saxophones, clarinet.

b. Newark, New Jersey, 1919; d. Sept 1954.

Williams was the leading soloist with the original Savoy Sultans on his main instrument, the alto, from 1937–43, then worked briefly with Hot Lips Page, Luis Russell and others. He led his own bands in New York and Boston from 1944–51, making tours of Far East army bases in 1945–6 and 1951–2. He also worked with John Kirby in 1945, Babs Gonzales in 1947, Tadd Dameron in 1948, and Illinois Jacquet and Gene Ammons, both in 1951, and was freelancing at the time of his death in a swimming accident. Though not widely recognized, Williams was admired by fellow musicians for his "advanced" work in the early 1940s. Broadly speaking, this can be described as applying the tenor style of Don Byas to the alto, and the link was especially noticeable when Williams played the tenor himself. [BP]

Sandy Williams

Trombone.

b. Summerville, South Carolina, 24 Oct 1906; d. 25 March 1991.

Sandy Williams learned to play in his Delaware school band and began his career working in theatre orchestras. It was then that he first became aware of Jimmy Harrison, the revolutionary trombonist with Fletcher Henderson ("I thought the sun rose and set on him – I had all his records"), and began to get noticed as a stylish jazzman. In 1927 he joined Claude Hopkins for a season in Atlantic City and by 1929 was with Horace Henderson: three years on he was with Fletcher Henderson himself ("It was the height of my ambition to get in that band," he told Stanley Dance later). A natural practical joker, Williams was sacked the following year for setting off a firecracker on stage; he joined Chick Webb and stayed for seven years. He was then briefly with a string of other well-known bands, including Duke Ellington's, but by 1943 the drink was getting to him, and despite a drying-out period he continued to drink heavily until, after work with leaders including Roy Eldridge, Rex Stewart and Art Hodes, he suffered a complete breakdown in health in 1950. When he got back into music in the late 1950s, embouchure problems caused by dental difficulties soon forced him back into inactivity. [DF]

>> **Chick Webb** *(Rhythm Man)*.

Spencer Williams

Composer, piano, vocals.

b. New Orleans, 14 Oct c.1889; d. 14 July 1965.

Spencer Williams was a nephew of bordello owner Lulu White, in whose Mahogany Hall he lived after the death of his mother. In 1907 he worked in Chicago as a pianist, then arrived in New York around 1916, quickly establishing himself with hits including "Squeeze Me" (which he wrote with Fats Waller, a lifelong friend), "I Ain't Got Nobody" (one of a set of tunes for Bert Williams), "Basin Street Blues", "Royal Garden Blues" and "I Found A New Baby". Spencer Williams was a frequent collaborator with Clarence Williams (they were unrelated) and by 1925 was successful enough to travel to Paris to compose material for Josephine Baker at the Folies-Bergère. In 1932, after acquittal on a murder charge, Williams moved to Europe, staying in London for a number of years, then from 1951–7 living comfortably in Stockholm, thanks to his royalties. In 1957 he returned to New York in poor health, and died eight years later. [DF]

Tony Williams

Drums, composer.

b. Chicago, 12 Dec 1945; d. 23 Feb 1997.

Williams was brought up in Boston, where he started playing drums aged ten, studying with

Tony Williams

Alan Dawson. He developed precociously, playing experimental concerts with Sam Rivers and the Boston Improvisational Ensemble in his early teens. In December 1962 he moved to New York, where he played with Jackie McLean. At the age of 17 he joined Miles Davis, staying with him for six years from 1963. With Davis, Williams made an immediate and sensational impact internationally, as both a virtuoso and an original stylist. Technically he had everything: he could play superlative straight jazz in both 4/4 and 3/4 (and that rhythm-section with Ron Carter and Herbie Hancock is widely regarded as one of the greatest of all time-playing units), but he could also play with the utmost freedom, displacing accents, leaving spaces, producing counter-rhythms and polyrhythms, implying the beat and playing on the pulse of the music. After Philly Joe and Elvin Jones, this was another crucial development of the role of the drums, and, during his time with Davis, Williams perfected his approach, building up a whole new vocabulary of rhythmic devices and spawning imitators and disciples all over the globe.

While with Davis he also played with other groups and blossomed as a composer. In 1964 he was a key player on Eric Dolphy's greatest album, the eldritch yet urban *Out To Lunch,* and in the following year recorded his first album as leader, *Life Time*. Frostily *unheimlich*, it is one of Blue Note's oddest and best. However, he was also becoming equally interested in rock rhythms: his comment on Miles Davis in the late 1960s is also true of himself: "He's trying to get further out (more abstract) and yet more basic (funkier) at the same time." In 1969 he left Davis and started his own jazz-rock group, Lifetime (around this time becoming Tony, rather than Anthony), with John McLaughlin, Jack Bruce and Larry Young. This was a wildly exciting and pioneering band, playing loud, extremely complex music. Intricate written passages alternated with brilliant stretches of improvisation. For his part Williams not only kept time, but integrated his drumming in a new way with the rhythms of the melodies, an integration that was to become a cliché of the jazz-rock movement in the later 1970s. Lifetime also offered a rich mixture of techniques and devices: chord-based playing, free improvisation with rock rhythms, modal improvisation and asymmetry in both metre and structure. Although it toured and played festivals in the USA and Europe, the group was dogged by bad luck and mismanagement. McLaughlin left to form his Mahavishnu Orchestra and, after his departure, Williams's personnel changed from year to year – he seemed always to be denied the success and recognition that some of the later jazz-rock groups enjoyed.

In the mid-1970s Williams recorded with the Gil Evans orchestra, and one of his compositions, "There Comes A Time", was the album's title track. In the later 1970s he toured internationally and recorded with VSOP, the reunited Miles Davis quintet (with Hancock, Carter and Shorter) with Freddie Hubbard in place of Davis. In 1982, with the Herbie Hancock quartet (with Carter and Wynton Marsalis), he toured in the USA, Europe and Japan, and recorded a double album. He recorded a series of albums with small groups for Blue Note, working mostly in a post-bop vein; though he revisited Lifetime territory – in a far more fractious and intense way – with Arcana, the trio he formed with Bill Laswell and Derek Bailey.

Tony Williams's vital contribution to jazz has been as a player, not as a bandleader. He made an immense contribution to the music of Miles Davis in the 1960s, playing on about 17 of his albums, several of which are enduring classics. In terms of influence, he and Elvin Jones dominated that decade. Williams seemed to have lost his way in the later 1990s, veering between one musical extreme and another. His death from a heart attack, aged 51, was tragic and premature. His legacy will live on. [IC]

⊙ **Spring** (1965; Blue Note). *Spring*, with two saxophonists (Sam Rivers and Wayne Shorter), Herbie Hancock and Gary Peacock, picks its way with brooding angularity between convention and abstraction.

⊙ **Emergency!** (1969; Polydor). A fascinating glimpse of the pioneering Lifetime, being a session with John McLaughlin and Larry Young, before Jack Bruce joined the band.

⊙ **Foreign Intrigue** (1985; Blue Note). This is a product of a period of general revisionism in jazz, with neo-bop and touches of funk the order of the day. *Foreign Intrigue* is the freshest and best of the latterday Williams discs, with new stars Wallace Roney (trumpet), alto saxophonist Donald Harrison and pianist Mulgrew Miller, and older collaborators Bobby Hutcherson and Ron Carter.

➤➤ **Miles Davis** *(The Complete Concert; ESP; Miles Smiles; In a Silent Way)*; **Eric Dolphy** *(Out To Lunch)*.

Steve Williamson

Tenor, soprano and alto saxophones.

b. London, 28 June 1964.

Williamson began clarinet lessons aged thirteen, at sixteen started on alto saxophone, then switched to tenor saxophone when he heard John Coltrane. He spent one year, 1984–5, on the Guildhall School of Music jazz course; after that, he began gigging with other musicians and eventually leading his own groups. In 1988 he and Courtney Pine accompanied dancers IDJ at the Wembley Nelson Mandela 70th birthday concert. He also played on Louis Moholo's 1988 album *Viva La Black*, worked for a week with Art Blakey at Ronnie Scott's, and played some of his finest solos on a 1989 four-track demo disc with bassist Wayne Bachelor's quartet. Amid the hyped-up UK jazz revival of the late 1980s, he was signed by Verve and made three albums for them; *A Waltz For Grace* (see below), the Steve Coleman-influenced *Rhyme Time (That Fuss Was Us)* (1991) and *Journey To Truth* (1992). In the early 1990s he was also a member of the Brotherhood of Breath. Williamson was one of the young British-born black musicians who, inspired by Courtney Pine and Wynton Marsalis, were the first to turn to jazz rather than to the customary calypso, ska, soul or reggae, though he retreated in the mid-1990s from jazz and even the saxophone itself for several years into the electronic world of hip hop and drum 'n' bass. Heard back on the jazz scene in 2002 in a quartet featuring pianist Robert Mitchell, bassist Robin Mullarky and drummer Daniel Crosby, he remains a virtuoso saxophonist with a beautifully poised sense of time and a compact, dry sound, which is articulated with superb clarity. [IC]

Jak Kilby

Steve Williamson

⊙ **A Waltz For Grace** (1990: Verve). An exciting debut, on which Williamson attempts a fusion of contemporary jazz with West Indian elements. Recorded with a mixture of young American and British black musicians, including Julian Joseph, Mark Mondesir and Gary Crosby, it bustles with vitality and rhythmic variety and seemed to be positing a new approach to the jazz tradition, which, unfortunately, the follow-up didn't pursue.

➤➤ **Louis Moholo** *(Exile)*; *Bheki Mseleku (Celebration)*.

Roy Willox

Alto saxophone, clarinet.

b. Welwyn Garden City, UK, 31 Aug 1929.

Roy Willox has been underrated as a jazz player – largely because of his lengthy studio tenure – but he is a major talent on both his chosen instruments. His fine alto recalls Benny Carter and Cannonball Adderley, while his clarinet playing is a flawless, limpid delight. A pupil of Harry Hayes, he worked with Claude Giddins in 1945, Henry Hall the following year, and, after service in the RAF, joined Ronnie Pleydell in 1950. He was with the Ted Heath Orchestra from 1950–55, Jack Parnell's ATV Band, and the BBC Revue Orchestra from 1958–60. Thereafter his abilities as lead alto won him regular work with visiting American artists such as Frank Sinatra, Benny Goodman, Henry Mancini and Bing Crosby, and he also worked regularly with Harry South's big band in the 60s and 70s. He was also much in demand for TV, radio and recording work as well as West End shows. In the 1990s he worked with Don Lusher's big band, Kenny Baker's re-formed Dozen and joined Baker's Best Of British Jazz ensemble from 1996.

The Best Of British Jazz Live (1999; Merlin). Recorded at the Playhouse Theatre, Norwich, Willox holds his own amid the classic incarnation of this long-travelled outfit (led by Kenny Baker), and his alto is memorably featured on "It Might As Well Be Spring".

Alex Wilson

Piano, keyboards.
b. Belper, Derbyshire, UK, 21 Nov 1971.

The son of an amateur pianist, Alex Wilson had classical guitar lessons from the age of ten, and occasional salsa piano lessons. After graduating in electronics from York University, he spent a postgraduate year in Santa Barbara, California, playing his first piano gigs there. He moved to London in the early 1990s. Wilson is a virtuoso pianist with a rangy, quicksilver imagination and an inclusive view of music (though his predilection is perhaps more for Latin and salsa music than for straight jazz), and he is also a highly skilled composer/arranger. In both these capacities, he has been constantly in demand on the London Latin, salsa, and jazz scenes during the 1990s and beyond, working with Gary Crosby's Jazz Jamaica, Davis Hassel's Apitos, Roberto Pla's Latin Jazz Ensemble and Merengada Salsasorica. Wilson has also performed with several other salsa groups, and with US star saxophonist Bobby Watson, guitarist Ciyo, drummer Frank Tontoh and Larry Adler, as well as playing on over a dozen albums by other leaders. In 1997 he was the pianist on Gary Crosby's Nu Troop's superb sextet album, *Migrations*, though his profile surged with the appearance of his own albums, *Afro-Saxon* (see below) and *Anglo-Cuban* (1999; Candid). After touring the world in Courtney Pine's group in 2000, he released the vocal-oriented pop-salsa album *R&B Latino* (2001; Candid). [IC]

Afro-Saxon (1998; Candid). British-born Wilson is three-quarters English and one-quarter African, via his paternal grandfather. Hence the title. He writes for and plays with ensembles ranging from duos to nine-piece bands in this immensely assured album. The opening "Afro-Saxon (Overture)" sets the tone and pace with bravura changes of tempo and rhythm, pinpoint punctuation, the piano taking the main melody, and the music running the gamut of the emotions – all in less than two minutes. There are magnificent solos from Wilson, trumpeter Paul Jayasinha, tenor saxophonist Paul Booth and alto saxophonist Bobby Watson.

Anthony Wilson

Guitar, composer.
b. Los Angeles, 9 May 1968.

The son of arranger-bandleader Gerald Wilson, Anthony took guitar lessons from the age of seven to 12, and then studied at Tanglewood Music Center and composition at Bennington College. He performed with his father's band from 1984, including European visits in 1986 and 1991, and with Harold Land, bassist Ed Schuller, Dave Pike and Bennie Wallace. Wilson has also played with rock and pop artists, including Lenny Kravitz and Vanessa Paradis. He formed his own nonet in the late 1990s, appearing in Los Angeles and New York, and gained awards for his writing from both the Thelonious Monk Institute (1995) and the Institute of Jazz Educators (1997). *Anthony Wilson* (1997; MAMA), his first album, was nominated for a Grammy Award in the big band category, and his second, *Goat Hill Junket* (1998; MAMA), was no less critically acclaimed. Though Wilson regards himself as a musician firmly rooted in jazz tradition, he is also an innovator who constantly seeks ways of replenishing the tradition: "I listen to old blues and jazz ... and I love swinging music. But even with that as a template, there's something else to get to. I'm trying to let the songs create their own melodic world." As well as a subsequent nonet album, *Adult Themes* (1999; MAMA), Wilson has recorded a trio album, *The Anthony Wilson Trio* (2001; Groove Note), alongside organist Joe Bagg and drummer Mark Ferber. In the early 2000s, he replaced Russell Malone as the guitarist in Diana Krall's trio, and made a major contribution to her live album, *A Night In Paris* (2001; Verve). [BP]

Goat Hill Junket (1998; MAMA). The only one of Wilson's albums so far to be recorded in New York rather than LA, this six-horn ensemble features an excellent reed-section (Ted Nash, Jerry Dodgion, Joe Temperley and guest Bennie Wallace) and the guitarist's arrangements on mainly original material are striking and stimulating.

➤➤ **Gerald Wilson** *(Theme For Monterey).*

Cassandra Wilson

Vocals.
b. Jackson, Mississippi, Dec 1955.

One of the best-known young jazz singers, with a mellow, flexible contralto voice that can harden to an edge on rock material, Wilson began recording widely in the 1980s, initially with Steve Coleman and Henry Threadgill's New Air. By 1993 she had appeared on ten albums on JMT Records, with a wide variety of New York musicians, including Mulgrew Miller and Greg Osby. Using a well-stirred mixture of originals, standards and rock and blues material (Robert Johnson was an influence), she established herself as a singer of great promise, whose style occasionally recalled Nina Simone. In 1993 Wilson signed to Blue Note, a home where she has been given the space to develop as both a singer and writer over several sophisticated albums. [DF]

Live (1991; JMT). Wilson live in Munich, featuring a cohesive rhythm-section of James Weidman (keyboards), Kevin Bruce Harris (electric bass) and Marc Johnson (drums); originals are mixed with standards such as "Round Midnight" (taken unusually and perhaps less comfortably at uptempo) and "Body And Soul".

Cassandra Wilson

She Who Weeps (1991; JMT). Rod Williams on piano and another fine rhythm-section back Wilson on a similarly eclectic selection, including Aretha Franklin's "Angel", an attractively ruminative "Chelsea Bridge" and the effective "New African Blues".

Travelling Miles (1998; Blue Note). Unusually, a highly-successful vocal tribute to the late music of Miles Davis; an area which seems to match Wilson's musical (and possibly personal) attitudes to perfection. She supplies lyrics to "Run The Voodoo Down", "Blue In Green" and revisits "Time After Time"; a song naturally from her generation.

Dick Wilson

Tenor saxophone.

b. Mount Vernon, Illinois, 11 Nov 1911; d. 24 Nov 1941.

One of the brightest-burning of jazz legends, Wilson was a pupil of reedman Joe Darensbourg and worked for territory bands in Portland, Oregon, and his home town before moving to the West Coast and Gene Coy's band. After that he moved to Denver, Colorado, where he worked with Zack Whyte, then finally, in 1936, he joined Andy Kirk's Twelve Clouds of Joy in Kansas City. For the last five years of his life he was the tenor star of Kirk's band, and before tuberculosis killed him at just 30 he had recorded enough to prove that his death – with Jimmy Blanton's and Charlie Christian's – was one of the most bitter blows of the dawning modern-jazz era. [DF]

>> **Andy Kirk** *(The Chronological Andy Kirk: 1936–38).*

Garland Wilson

Piano.

b. Martinsburg, West Virginia, 13 June 1909; d. Paris, 31 May 1954.

Garland Lorenzo Wilson studied at Howard University, Washington, moved to New York around 1930, and by 1931 was working at Covan's, a club close to the Lafayette Theater. At this time John Hammond agreed to finance a recording session for him via Frank Walker of Columbia: the results were reasonably successful and Hammond paid his protégé with an expensive watch. In 1932 Wilson toured Europe as accompanist to Nina Mae McKinney, and all through the 1930s he was a familiar figure in England, playing solo, working with Jack Payne's orchestra (between shows, Wilson would often find a pub with a piano, where he could drink and play contentedly), and recording with Nat Gonella. In 1939 he returned to the USA for nightclub work, returning to Europe in 1951, when he moved to Paris, from where he commuted regularly to London. A modest man, he was inclined to underrate himself. "Garland's best playing was away from the public in some darkened room," says Stewart-Baxter. After hearing the galloping, highly technical work that Wilson recorded, the remark turns into a high compliment. [DF]

The Chronological Garland Wilson 1931–8 (Classics). Overdue collation of Wilson's important work, including breakneck solos plus collaborations with singer Nina Mae McKinney and violinist Michael Warlop. The only gaps are his sides with Gonella, which feature on the disc listed below.

>> **Nat Gonella** *(The Nat Gonella Story Vol. 1: 1931–46).*

Gerald Wilson

Trumpet, arranger.

b. Shelby, Mississippi, 4 Sept 1918.

Wilson began on the piano and learned trumpet while at college in Detroit. He worked there and toured, before joining the Jimmie Lunceford band from 1939–42, for which he played and arranged. He settled in Los Angeles, working with Benny Carter and others before his navy service. In 1944 he formed his own big band, which has continued intermittently until the present day, featuring many important West Coast-based musicians. His freelance arranging work included charts for Duke Ellington from 1947 and for Dizzy Gillespie and Count Basie in the late 1940s; he made occasional recordings on trumpet with all three. He has been the musical director on record and for live appearances for numerous artists, including Al Hirt and singer Nancy Wilson (no relation). He ran his own jazz-based radio show in the mid-1970s, and taught jazz history courses at UCLA. Gerald was never prominent as a player, although he can be heard on albums by Leroy Vinnegar and others, but he has a distinctive style of writing, somewhat similar harmonically to Thad Jones. Even when played by Ellington, Wilson's arrangements are recognizably his own, and are worthy of greater renown. [BP]

Theme For Monterey (1997; MAMA). The meat of this celebratory album is Wilson's suite for the Monterey Festival's 40th anniversary, featuring the same thematic material in five different guises and listing soloists such as trumpeter Oscar Brashear, trombonist George Bohanon and the leader's son, Anthony Wilson.

Matt Wilson

Drums, percussion.

b. Knoxville, Illinois, 27 Sept 1964.

Wilson was inspired to play drums after seeing Buddy Rich on TV, and with his saxophonist brother Mark played in function gigs from the age of fourteen. At both his high school and at Wichita State University, where he studied music, he benefited from teachers who encouraged composition and an entrepreneurial spirit. Living in Boston from 1987–92, he played with the Either/Orchestra, John Medeski and others and, after moving to New York, he began long-term musical relationships with Dewey Redman (from 1994) and Lee Konitz (from 1995). He works with a wide variety of musicians such as Jane Ira Bloom, Ted Nash and pianists Bill Mays and Denny Zeitlin, and has appeared on over 100 albums. He has led four different bands, of which his quartet (formed in 1997) tours internationally. As far as drumming influences go, he professes to find inspiring "...anyone who sings on the instrument". His violinist wife Felicia appears as a guest on his 2003 release, *Humidity*, his fifth album for the Palmetto label. [BP]

Arts And Crafts (2000; Palmetto). Wilson's fourth album is seemingly straightahead in some of its repertoire (Gershwin, Bud Powell, Roland Kirk, a classic bossa), and offers oblique tributes to Ornette Coleman and the recently deceased Lester Bowie. This one-off quartet consists of trumpeter Terell Stafford, bassist Dennis Irwin and Larry Goldings on acoustic piano.

Lee Konitz-Matt Wilson

Gong With Wind Suite (2002; Steeplechase). Though the sound balance could have been more favourable to the drummer, this series of 13 duets shows one of his long-standing partnerships up close.

>> **Ben Allison/Herbie Nichols Project** *(Strange City)*; **Ted Nash** *(Still Evolved)*.

Nancy Wilson

Vocals.

b. Chillicothe, Ohio, 20 Feb 1937.

Nancy Sue Wilson began her career with Rusty Bryant's band (1956–8), but in 1959 sang with Cannonball Adderley, who then persuaded her to come to New York, where she signed with Capitol. Thereafter she recorded with Billy May and Gerald Wilson, but it was her 1961 album with Adderley's quintet that drew her to the attention of jazz lovers, though it followed another fine set for Capitol with George Shearing. Subsequently she enjoyed big success as a pop singer – she had ten Hot 100 singles plus 29 chart LPs between 1962–71. However, in the early 1980s Wilson resumed her jazz connections, touring and recording with Hank Jones, appearing with the Art Farmer-Benny Golson quintet, and recording with Ramsey Lewis and Toots Thielemans. She has appeared on over 60 albums, and only recently retired. [DF]

The Swingin's Mutual (1960; Capitol). Wilson with George Shearing in one of the best-loved jazz dates from her early years.

Nancy Wilson And The Cannonball Adderley Quintet (1961; Capitol). A superb collection pitting Wilson's bluesy voice against Adderley's brilliant group, with outstanding tracks including "A Sleepin' Bee", a very happy "Happy Talk" and a chillingly dramatic version of "The Masquerade Is Over".

Shadow Wilson

Drums.

b. Yonkers, New York, 25 Sept 1919; d. 11 July 1959.

One of jazz's best drummers, Shadow (Rossiere) Wilson joined Lucky Millinder then Jimmy Mundy (1939), and from then into the 1940s worked with a string of bands, large and small, including those of Benny Carter, Lionel Hampton, Earl Hines, Count Basie, Woody Herman, Illinois Jacquet, Georgie Auld and Louis Jordan. In the 1950s Wilson was regularly with Erroll Garner (1950–52), Ella Fitzgerald (1954–5) and Thelonious Monk (1957–8), as well as being a busy freelance, and achieved a reputation as a drummer of great flexibility and musicality. After leaving Monk he continued to take occasional jobs around New York until his death. [DF]

>> **Erroll Garner** *(Body And Soul)*; **Thelonious Monk** *(Thelonious Monk With John Coltrane)*.

Steve Wilson

Alto and soprano saxophones, flutes, clarinet.

b. Hampton, Virginia, 9 Feb 1961.

With a father who sang spirituals in a choir and several cousins who played instruments, Wilson's musical training started at the age of twelve, and during his teens he performed in R&B and funk bands. He studied music at Virginia Commonwealth University and joined the Blue Note Records "house band" Out Of The Blue from 1986–9. Simultaneously he toured for a year with Lionel Hampton and, from 1988, worked for Ralph Peterson, Michele Rosewoman, Renee Rosnes and Buster Williams. From 1991 he taught at William Paterson College in New Jersey and has recorded over seventy albums with such musicians as Louie Bellson, Don Byron, Joe Henderson, Dave Liebman, James Williams and

NINA D'ALESSANDRO

Steve Wilson

various repertory orchestras. As well as leading his own groups, Wilson played with Dave Holland's quintet in 1997–8 and then joined Chick Corea's Origin. Holland said of him: "Steve really impressed me with his instrumental ability and the beautiful sound that he gets, and he's a really strong group player." [BP]

⊙ **Four For Time** (1994; Criss Cross). Recorded by his then regular quartet of pianist Bruce Barth, bassist Larry Grenadier and Leon Parker (with whom he also used to perform as a duo), the collection of originals, cover versions ("Everything Must Change") and bebop ("Perdido", "Woody'n'You") blends into a seamless whole.

➤➤ **Chick Corea** *(Change);* **Dave Holland** *(Points Of View).*

Teddy Wilson

Piano, arranger.

b. Austin, Texas, 24 Nov 1912; d. 31 July 1986.

Teddy (Theodore Shaw) Wilson's father was head of English and his mother chief librarian at Tuskegee University, which might go some way to explain his aura of graceful urbanity. By his teenage years Wilson had fallen in love with records such as Bix Beiderbecke's "Singin' The Blues" and King Oliver's "Snag It", and after a visit to Chicago in 1928 was so inspired by the jazz he heard that he determined to make it his living. The year after, he joined Speed Webb's band, for which he became one of seven staff arrangers, reorchestrating, in close harmony, the solos by Beiderbecke and Hodges that had fascinated him on record (a very early example of the idea). In 1931 he teamed with Art Tatum in a regular duo. "We would go out every night," Wilson recalled later, "and make the rounds of the places, playing on upright pianos until late morning and sometimes early afternoon." Tatum's reputation was already legendary and the bright young pianist keeping up with him was quickly spotted by, among others, Benny Carter and John Hammond. The latter heard Wilson one night in 1933, subbing for Earl Hines in a broadcast from Grand Terrace Ballroom (by then Wilson had been doing the rounds of bands, including Louis Armstrong's, and arranging for Hines). "Hines' substitute, I suddenly realized," said Hammond, "was absolutely unique, with a cleaner and more elegant sound, never flashy but swinging, with an excellent left hand."

It was Hammond – his greatest champion – who recommended Wilson to Benny Carter in New York, sent Carter the $150 needed to get Wilson there, and effectively launched the pianist's career with a recording date for the Chocolate Dandies, led by Carter. From then on Wilson was constantly recording with his own small groups, often featuring a singer about whom Wilson later had mixed feelings: Billie Holiday. But the Wilson-Holiday collaborations are a high-water mark, with Wilson's steady direction, joyful piano and impeccable choice of sidemen setting off the young singer's ingénue genius to perfection. From Hammond came one more introduction, to Benny Goodman, whom Wilson met at a Victor recording date; soon after – following a 1936 concert at Chicago's Hot Club – the pianist became the first black musician to join Goodman's band, a move that caused immense publicity. For the next three years, seated amid the frantic activity of Goodman's frenetic quartet, the cool and dignified Wilson was a perfect ambassador for black music. Soon after, Goodman was to call him "the greatest musician in dance music today, irrespective of instrument", and it was inevitable that Wilson, before long, should have thought about a big band of his own. The one he put together in 1939 caused (like Benny Carter's) a musical sensation ("The most musical and cleanest big band outside of Ellington's," said Billy Strayhorn) but commercially it made little impact (due, said the leader, to a lack of showmanship) and from 1940 he was to confine himself to small groups.

During World War II Wilson led his own highly successful sextet at Café Society (featuring Benny Morton, Jimmy Hamilton and a variety of trumpeters, including Bill Coleman), then rejoined Goodman and afterwards took a studio job at CBS and teaching posts at major colleges such as the Juilliard and Metropolitan schools. In the 1950s he was still working the studios, leading his trio, re-creating swing glories on classic sessions such as *Jazz Giants 1956* and *Prez And Teddy*, playing in Goodman reunions and building his solo reputation. In the 1960s he was more than ever a soloist, visiting Europe, Japan, South America and Australia, as well as holding down local residencies; in the 1970s he was regularly at Michael's Pub, New York, appearing annually at the Newport festival, and still touring abroad. The year before his death, despite severe recent illness, he was playing as impeccably as ever. [DF]

Piano Solos 1934–7 (Affinity). Important piano solos from Wilson's earliest recordings ("Somebody Loves Me" and three more), revealing a talent that was to place him in the pantheon of Earl Hines and Art Tatum.

Teddy Wilson 1934–1945 (Classics). This seven-CD chronology covers everything from Wilson's first solo piano sides, through four classics with Billie Holiday, Webster and Roy Eldridge, and on through seven more years, including his short-lived big band of 1939. Wilson's small groups regularly featured not only Holiday but also virtually every important jazz player of the period, and amid these titles there are dozens of nonpareil swing vignettes.

Gentleman Of The Keyboard 1934–57 (Giants of Jazz). A splendid budget selection, including many of Wilson's best from the 1930s ("Just A Mood" with James, "All My Life" with Fitzgerald, several titles with Billie Holiday), plus titles from his sextet with Charlie Shavers (1944–5), with Benny Goodman (1952) and with his trio.

Teddy Wilson And His Orchestra With Billie Holiday 1935–7 (ASV). This CD combines nine first-class Holiday vocal tracks with one each by "Boots" Castle, Midge Williams, Ella Fitzgerald, Roy Eldridge and Helen Ward and four instrumentals. Wilson's small groups at this period were loaded with stars and there are so many here, they have to be listed by initials only in the track listing!

Stomping At The Savoy (1969; Black Lion). With Dave Shepherd (clarinet), his regular partner over nearly a decade, on some tracks, plus a rhythm-section containing the high-powered drummer John Richardson, this is a classy rerun of standards in swing style.

Masters Of Jazz Vol. 11: Teddy Wilson 1968–80 (Storyville). Some of Wilson's last recordings, with Niels-Henning Ørsted Pedersen and Ed Thigpen among others. As gracefully creative as you'd expect.

➤➤ **Benny Goodman** *(Benny Goodman On The Air).*

Johnny Windhurst

Trumpet.

b. Bronx, New York, 5 Nov 1926; d. 21 Oct 1981.

A hugely undervalued trumpeter, who mixed the delicacy of Bobby Hackett with the mobility of Ruby Braff and a feathery vibrato that was all his own, Windhurst was sitting in at Nick's in New York by the age of fifteen, and just four years on was playing alongside Sidney Bechet (as a late replacement for Bunk Johnson) at the Savoy Café, Boston. Such a talent should quickly have turned into a household name, but somehow Windhurst never did: in the omnipotent shadow of Armstrong, big talents were often underrated. Windhurst did well enough: in the 1940s he played regularly around his home area of Boston, often at the Storyville Club, worked at Gene Norman's Dixieland Jubilee with Louis Armstrong, and spent time with Nappy Lamare's band. In the 1950s he led his Riverboat Five around Boston and Columbus, Ohio, worked and recorded with Eddie Condon (a 1950 Windhurst rerun of "A Hundred Years From Today" is beautiful), played for George Wettling and Jack Teagarden in 1954, and by 1956 had taken a stage role with actor Conrad Janis in an off-Broadway musical, *Joy Ride*. After it closed Windhurst continued to play in New York, as well as touring around his home patch (often with trombonist Eddie Hubble): the odd records he made – with Barbara Lea, Walt Gifford's New Yorkers and his own quartet – indicate a talent comparable at least to Ruby Braff's. But whereas Braff stubbornly stuck to New York, Windhurst was seen there less often, apart from visits to Nick's Club, and by the late 1960s he had moved to Poughkeepsie with his mother. From 1970 he was resident at a local club, Frivolous Sal's Last Chance Saloon (a Victorian theatre), and he was content. "He won't do anything, won't travel, just wants to stay where he is," said Hubble. "He should get out and let people know he's still alive." In November 1981 Windhurst was invited to the Manassas jazz festival, but died of a heart attack shortly before he was due to leave. [DF]

Eddie Condon With Johnny Windurst

Dr. Jazz Vols 1 & 8 (1951–2; Storyville). "There are pitifully few examples of Windhurst available and these may very well be the best" says Jack Sohmer's liner-note and it's true; Windhurst's work (taken from the Dr. Jazz radio series) mingles the elegance of Hackett, the melodic audaciousness of Braff and displays a technical command which compares favourably with Don Goldie. A truly neglected giant of his art.

➤➤ **Barbara Lea** *(With The Johnny Windhurst Quintets; In Love).*

Kai Winding

Trombone.

b. Aarhus, Denmark, 18 May 1922; d. Yonkers, New York, 7 May 1983.

After emigrating to the USA with his family at the age of twelve, Winding began big-band work as a teenager and found fame with Stan Kenton in 1946–7. Then he was active with the small bands of Charlie Ventura in 1947–8, Tadd Dameron in 1948–9, and recorded one session with the Miles Davis band in 1949. He co-led a popular two-trombone quintet with J.J. Johnson from 1954–6, with occasional reunions, followed by his own four-trombone septet from 1956–60. In the 1960s he was the musical director of the Playboy Clubs. Two early 1970s tours with the Giants of Jazz (Gillespie, Monk and others) were followed by semi-retirement in Spain. However, he also toured with Lionel Hampton in 1979, and in a two-trombone group with Curtis Fuller in 1980.

One of the earliest successful trombonists to be influenced by bebop, Winding also allowed some swing-era influences to be retained. Adopting a slightly coarser tone than his contemporaries, he achieved an individual style at a period when the trombone was generally an underrated instrument. [BP]

➤➤ **J.J. Johnson** *(Jay And Kai).*

Norma Winstone

Vocals.

b. London, 23 Sept 1941.

Winstone won a junior exhibition scholarship to Trinity College, London, where she studied piano and organ for three years. In 1965 she began singing with jazz groups and in 1966 joined the New Jazz Orchestra, where she met Michael Garrick, whose group she also joined. She then began working with John Taylor, whom she later married. She has also worked with Neil Ardley, Mike Gibbs, Nucleus, John Surman, John Stevens, Michael Garrick, Kenny Wheeler and John Dankworth, and was in one of Mike Westbrook's groups for a number of years. In 1977, with John Taylor and Kenny Wheeler, she formed the group Azimuth. A beguiling mix of the deadpan, the ruminative and the sentimental, the group's autumnal chamber jazz has been extensively documented by ECM, and it has toured in Europe, appearing at many festivals. Winstone's voice has become an integral sound in the ensemble of Kenny Wheeler's big band, and can be heard on his 1990 album *Music For Large And Small Ensembles*. In 1992, in collaboration with composer/arranger Steve Gray, she created *A French Folk Song Suite* (based on the *Songs Of The Auvergne* by Canteloube), which was commissioned and broadcast by the North German Radio big band. She is also a member of the *a cappella* vocal group Vocal Summit, with Jay Clayton, Urszula Dudziak and Michele Hendricks, which released a live album in the mid-1990s, *Conference Of The Birds*. In the 1990s Winstone also wrote lyrics to some of Steve Swallow's pieces, and in 1994 she performed them with the composer at the London jazz festival. A potent aspect of Winstone's artistry, her lyrics to Swallow's "Ladies In Mercedes" and Jimmy Rowles's "The Peacocks" have made the pieces vocal jazz standards. Though continuing to occasionally perform with old friends, Winstone's groups of the 1990s/2000s have featured next generation virtuosi, including guitarist John Parricelli, vibist Anthony Kerr, saxophonists Iain Ballamy and Julian Siegel and pianists Nikki Iles, Gareth Williams, Robert Mitchell and Fred Hersch. Latter day projects include the Shorter Stories group – performing Wayne Shorter compositions exclusively – and the album *Songs And Lullabies* (2003; Sunnyside), a graceful set of originals composed and performed with Fred Hersch.

Norma Winstone is a singer of brilliant virtuosity and flexibility: she can handle very complex lines and wide intervals, improvise with the fluency of an instrumentalist but also breathe life into a simple song. Her voice is extraordinary: it conveys something of the peculiar balance of fragility and steel you hear in the least compromised of traditional folk music. [IC]

⊙ **Somewhere Called Home** (1986; ECM). Winstone wrote fine lyrics for four tunes on this album: Bill Evans's "Prologue", Egberto Gismonti's "Cafe", Kenny Wheeler's "Sea Lady" and Ralph Towner's "Celeste", which jostle with standards like "Out Of This World", and a tune Bill Evans used to play, "Hi Lili Hi Lo". This is an excellent set with sensitive accompaniment by John Taylor and pithy interjections by Tony Coe.

⊙ **Well Kept Secret** (1993; Hot House). Norma set lyrics to pianist Jimmy Rowles's tune "The Peacocks" – he approved of them, and they decided to make this record, feauring some lovely lesser-known standards, such as Jerome Kern's "I Dream Too Much", as well as familiar pieces. Norma's consummate performance includes "It Amazes Me" accompanied only by bassist George Mraz.

⊙ **Manhattan In The Rain** (1997; ENOCD). Winstone here performs 13 excellent standards, none of them very well known except "People Will Say We're In Love", which is given a brilliantly audacious treatment, with blazing solos from Tony Coe and pianist Steve Gray.

⊙ **Like Song, Like Weather** (1996; ENOCD). Two virtuosi together, singer and pianist John Taylor bring an extraordinary intimacy and rapport to an album of very fresh material. There are pieces from Brubeck, Ellington, Gershwin, Winstone herself, and others, which are all brought to delightful life by the sweet playfulness of two great artists.

➤➤ **John Taylor** *(Azimuth/The Touchstone/Départ; How It Was Then...Never Again).*

Paul Winter

Soprano and alto saxophones, composer.

b. Altoona, Pennsylvania, 31 Aug 1939.

Winter studied the piano from the age of six and then attended Northwestern University in Chicago. While there he organized his own band, which in 1961 won an intercollegiate competition. In 1962 he took his sextet on a US State Department tour of Latin America, visiting 23 countries, and in the same year his was the first jazz group to perform at the White House. In the late 1960s Winter began leading the Winter Consort, which until 1971 included Ralph Towner, Collin Walcott and Glen Moore – all of whom left to form the group Oregon. During the 1970s Winter recorded some interesting albums, including *Common Ground*, which combined his plaintive soprano sound with animal noises and human voices in a series of pieces that ranged from jazz and rock to country and folk. Since then he has made over 20 albums of a similar nature for Living Music records, often attempting to express in musical form his concern with the Earth's spiritual and environmental wellbeing. [IC]

Tiny Winters

Bass, vocals, leader.

b. London, 24 Jan 1909; d. 7 Feb 1996.

Tiny Winters (Frederick Gittens) taught himself bass initially (later he took lessons) and worked from the 1920s with Roy Fox; then as a cornerman in Lew Stone's orchestra during its greatest years; on record for Ray Noble; with Nat Gonella's first Georgians; and later with fine groups such as the short-lived Heralds of Swing. After wartime service in the RAF, his career continued unabated: as a session-man for radio, TV and on records; with a succession of London stage productions including *Annie Get Your Gun* and *West*

Side Story; and with TV's *Black And White Minstrel Show*, as resident bassist and featured comedian with George Chisholm's Jazzers. In the 1970s Winters continued to lead his own trio and orchestra; in 1982 he began touring with a Nat Gonella tribute package, then formed and fronted Kettner's Five (featuring John Barnes, Keith Nichols, John Armatage, Digby Fairweather, Chris Ellis and Liza Lincoln), as well as continuing his South Bank appearances with an aristocratic Palm Court Trio and Café Society Orchestra. Winters carried on appearing until the early 1990s, when – having received the Freedom of the City of London, remarried, and written his autobiography (sadly unpublished so far) – he decided to retire. His career, spanning well over six decades, was a triumph of skill, tenacity and enthusiasm for music-making which ensured his celebrity status until the end. [DF]

⊙ **A tribute to Lew Stone; the legendary Monseigneur Band, London 1932-4** (Claves). Excellent three CD set featuring Winters all the way with the legendary Stone organization – his driving bass is central to proceedings on tracks like "White Jazz", "Blue Jazz" and "Tiger Rag", and he sings too on "I Hate Myself Vol.3"

COLEMAN HAWKINS

⊙ **Coleman Hawkins 1927–39** (BBC). This fine set has two of Winters's most famous sides: "Oh Lady Be Good" and "Lullaby", recorded in London in 1934 with Coleman Hawkins.

Val Wiseman

Vocals.

b. West Bromwich, UK, 15 Aug 1942.

Val Wiseman began her career with Birmingham's Second City Jazzmen and broadcast with Alex Welsh's band (1963), before moving to London to join Monty Sunshine's band. The collapse of the trad boom temporarily slowed her progress, but she continued to broadcast (with Humphrey Lyttelton and others), to work with Rod Mason, Pete Allen and Tommy Burton, and occasionally guest at jazz clubs, while raising a family. From the mid-1980s she also guested regularly with Eggy Ley's Hot Shots, with whom she had great success at the 1986 Birmingham International jazz festival. Subsequently Wiseman resumed work as a solo singer, toured Germany and Canada, broadcast for BBC Radio 2, and from 1987 fronted the acclaimed Billie Holiday tribute package *Lady Sings The Blues*, which toured widely and was voted Jazz Album of the Year by *CD Review*. In the 1990s Wiseman continued to tour with the Holiday show and to work solo with her own band; finally recording her long-awaited first solo album, *Just For A Thrill* (Mainstem) in 2003. An appealingly stylish performer with a connoisseur's ear for repertoire, she is one of Britain's best jazz singers. [DF]

⊙ **Lady Sings The Blues** (1990; Big Bear). Studio recording of Wiseman's successful show, spanning Holiday's on-record career from her first title, "Riffin' The Scotch", to one of her last, "For All We Know". Digby Fairweather, Roy Williams, Al Gay and Brian Lemon all feature in her group.

⊙ **Just For A Thrill** (2003; Mainstem). Excellent and wide-ranging contemporary Wiseman recital that demonstrates her sure approach and catholic tastes, with songs from Rodgers and Hart to James Taylor, Elvis Costello and beyond. The arrangements by Brian Dee spotlight his piano playing as well as the contributions of Jim Mullen on guitar and Bruce Adams on trumpet.

Jimmy Witherspoon

Vocals.

b. Gurdon, Arkansas, 8 Aug 1923; d. 18 Sept 1997.

Witherspoon sang in a church choir as a child, and did his first blues singing during navy service. On demobilization he worked on the West Coast with Jay McShann's band from 1945–7, recording under both McShann's and his own name. He also recorded with backing by the Buddy Tate group, the Roy Milton band and others from 1947–50, and became extremely successful as a solo attraction. The period of obscurity which followed in the mid- and late 1950s was ended by a Monterey festival appearance in 1959 with an all-star jazz line-up. This was followed by frequent tours of Europe, beginning in 1961 with the Buck Clayton group. For a time in the early 1970s Witherspoon was the DJ for a blues radio programme, but then enjoyed another performing comeback thanks to the encouragement of British singer Eric Burdon. Despite serious throat cancer that was successfully treated in England, he made further international tours in the 1980s and 1990s.

His singing, and one or two items of his repertoire, were directly descended from Joe Turner, but Witherspoon's rich baritone foreshadowed the work of Joe Williams. His delivery was earthier, more in the Turner mould, but by the time Spoon was making his mark, jazz-blues was already becoming R&B. This led to many attempts to cross over into the more general popular market, with a lot of ballads and a lot of unsuitable accompaniments, from which he emerged unscathed. Witherspoon's importance derives from a great rapport with jazz players, and the flexibility of both his voice and his timing shows best in this context. [BP]

⊙ **The 'Spoon Concerts** (1959; Fantasy). Also available at one time as *Meets The Jazz Giants* (Charly, with tracks in actual performance order), this has the famous Monterey jam with Hawkins, Eldridge and others, plus a great club set with Gerry Mulligan and Ben Webster.

⊙ **Jimmy Witherspoon And Panama Francis' Savoy Sultans** (1979–80; Black & Blue). Fine singing on the Savoy Sultans album, featuring George Kelly and trumpeter Irv Stokes, and on half an album with an organ trio. An above-average number of cover versions of Jimmy Rushing and others merely proves how inimitable Spoon himself is.

Nils Wogram

Trombone.

b. Braunschweig, Germany, 7 Nov 1972.

Nils Wogram started classical trombone studies at the age of twelve (his father is an amateur trombonist), but at the same time he taught himself to play jazz. His classical education went on until 1992, and between 1989–92 he won several prizes for contemporary classical music and jazz. In 1989 he also became a member of the German Federal Jazz Orchestra, led by trombonist and big-band arranger Peter Herbolzheimer. In 1992, Wogram received a grant from New York City's New School and he studied there until 1994, with leading musicians such as Reggie Workman, Slide Hampton, Conrad Herwig, Kenny Werner, Buster Williams and Maria Schneider. Back in Germany, he studied at the Musikhochschule, Cologne, with Jiggs Whigham from 1995–9. In 1994, he recorded his debut album, *New York Conversations* (Mons), following it with *Round Trip* (Enja), and, in 1998, *Speed Life* (Enja), *Serious Fun* (2000; CIMP) – a freely improvised trombone duet with Conrad Bauer – and *Odd And Awkward* (see below).

Wogram is one of the most remarkable newcomers on the German and European jazz scenes. He is both a virtuoso and an original, whose music cunningly balances the compositional and improvisational elements, while fusing conventional jazz, free jazz and constituents from other genres in a very natural way. As well as leading his own quartet, he appears in several other combos including the Nostalgia Trio (with Florian Ross on Hammond), and an extraordinary duo with pianist Simon Nabotov which released the fine album, *Starting A Story* (2002; ACT). He regularly plays with Gunter Hampel's Next Generation, and he made a major contribution to pianist/composer Florian Ross's debut album, *Seasons & Places* (1998; Naxos) *and Lilacs And Laughter* (2000; Naxos). [IC]

⦿ **Odd And Awkward** (2001; Enja). Previous Wogram albums were often remarkable, but uneven – he may have too much ability and energy for the good of his own art. But this is a rich double CD, with sextet performances on one disc (with no bass or piano), octet performances (with bass and piano) on the other, irrepressibly inventive and consistently impressive: the most satisfying Wogram offering to date.

➤➤ **Florian Ross** *(Seasons & Places).*

The Wolverines

Formed from the remains of a band resident at the Stockton Club, near Hamilton, Cincinnati, by clarinettist Jimmy Hartwell, the Wolverines (so named because of a fondness for Jelly Roll Morton's "Wolverine Blues") are primarily famous as the first band in which cornettist Bix Beiderbecke attracted attention in 1923. The Wolverines, featuring George Johnson (tenor) and Dick Voynow (piano), as well as Beiderbecke, Hartwell and later drummer Vic Berton, recorded a number of titles for Gennett that created a national sensation in 1924 – including Hoagy Carmichael's first tune, "Free Wheeling" (later retitled "Riverboat Shuffle"). After work in the Midwest, they arrived in New York in September 1924 to play the Cinderella Ballroom on 48th and Broadway, and attracted rave reviews. But somehow they lost their impetus after Bix left to join Jean Goldkette's orchestra in 1925 (Jimmy McPartland replaced him) and broke up soon after. [DF]

➤➤ **Bix Beiderbecke** *(Bix Beiderbecke And The Wolverines).*

Mark Wood

Guitar.

b. Newcastle upon Tyne, UK, 29 Aug 1954.

Wood left school at sixteen and was entirely self-taught as a musician. His first professional job was with Joe Harriott. Since then he has toured extensively in Europe, the USA, Scandinavia, Africa and the Far East, and played with Dudu Pukwana, Johnny Dyani, Charlie Mariano, Chris McGregor and Neil Ardley. In 1981 he formed his own band, Sunwind, which won the Greater London Arts Association's Young Musicians Award in 1982, the year he joined Ian Carr's band Nucleus.

Since the mid-1990s, Wood has divided his time between the USA and UK, on various recording and live projects, mainly with cult underground band, The Mystics, whose self-titled album was released on Rotator Records. Through the 1990s he appeared on several of Theo Travis's recordings, including the freely-improvised Marshall/Travis/Wood album *Bodywork*. He also does session work, and writes and produces music for film and TV. His guitar-playing has been influenced by Jimi Hendrix, Eddie Van Halen, Jeff Beck and Joe Zawinul's synthesizer work. [IC]

➤➤ **Ian Carr** *(Old Heartland).*

Jimmy Woode

Bass, vocals, piano.

b. Philadelphia, 23 Sept 1926 or 1927.

Woode is the nephew of arranger Henri Woode (b. 25 Sept 1909; d. 30 May 1994), the co-writer of "Rosetta". Jimmy studied in Philadelphia and Boston, where he returned after navy service. He gigged in the Boston area with Nat Pierce and others through the late 1940s and early 1950s, also touring with Flip Phillips, Sarah Vaughan and Ella Fitzgerald. Then he spent five years with Duke Ellington, from early 1955 to early 1960, after which he relocated to Europe. He was based for several years each in Stockholm, Cologne, Vienna and Munich, and was very successful in studio work. He was a founder member of the Clarke-Boland band, working with it from 1961–73, and has latterly been involved in contracting for and producing studio sessions. Still active as a player, he has appeared at international Duke Ellington conferences in the UK and Sweden. An excellent rhythm-section player, less often heard playing solos, Woode has been an important figurehead on the European scene. As a standard-bearer for the "friendly invasion" by US musicians, his influence has certainly been more helpful than harmful in terms of fostering the maturity of local players. [BP]

>> **Tony Coe** *(Canterbury Song);* **Duke Ellington** *(At Newport);* **Sahib Shihab** *(And All Those Cats).*

Sam Wooding

Piano, arranger.

b. Philadelphia, 17 June 1895; d. 1 Aug 1985.

One of the most important early black bandleaders, Sam Wooding led his Society Syncopators in a variety of New York clubs, as well as for the *Plantation Days* revue, before travelling with his orchestra to Berlin in 1925 to accompany the show *Chocolate Kiddies*. Over the next six years he was to build a huge reputation all over Europe for his orchestra, which at various times featured such stars as Tommy Ladnier, Doc Cheatham, Gene Sedric and Willie Lewis. The orchestra recorded regularly for Pathe-Actuelle (in Paris), Deutsche Grammophon (in Berlin) and Parlophone (in Barcelona), and was heard by the young Hugues Panassié: "They played hot – terrifically hot," he said, "and I was amazed by their dynamism which was so much greater than white bands!"

Wooding played the best venues wherever he went and became a society favourite: problems arose after 1931, however, when his band broke up in Belgium and he came back to the USA to find that, in New York, a host of big bands from Fletcher Henderson's on down were holding sway – and, soon after, that younger white swing kings like Benny Goodman were following in hot pursuit. Wooding re-formed an orchestra, but found it hard to duplicate his European success: by 1935 he had disbanded and left full-time bandleading to study music at Pennsylvania University. From then on he pursued a busy career in teaching, but returned to performing regularly (he led vocal groups from 1937–41 and in 1945), ran his own record company in the 1950s, and in the 1960s formed a duo with singer Rae Harrison that toured the world. In 1968 Wooding, now semi-retired, made his home in Germany, but came back to the USA the year after and visited Europe in the 1970s, prior to retirement. [DF]

Britt Woodman

Trombone.

b. Los Angeles, 4 June 1920; d. 13 Oct 2000.

Woodman's father, William O. Woodman, was a trombonist who recorded with Sonny Clay in 1925–6 and with Teddy Buckner in 1955–6, and Britt's early experience was in the Woodman Brothers' family band. He toured with the West Coast outfits of Phil Moore in 1938, Floyd Turnham in 1938–9, and with Les Hite from 1939–42. This was followed by army service and work with Boyd Raeburn in 1946 and Lionel Hampton in 1946–7. A period of study, and some studio gigs, led to his joining Duke Ellington from 1951–60, after which Woodman specialized in session work, basing himself in New York in the 1960s and 1980s–90s, and in Los Angeles in the 1970s. During the 1990s he was a frequent member of the Lincoln Center Jazz Orchestra and the Mingus Big Band. An admirer of Lawrence Brown, whom he replaced with Ellington, Britt has a more cutting tone, which accords well with his occasionally boppish turn of phrase and excellent command of the extreme upper register. [BP]

>> **Duke Ellington** *(Such Sweet Thunder).*

Phil Woods

Alto saxophone, clarinet.

b. Springfield, Massachusetts, 2 Nov 1931.

After studying at music school, Woods had touring jobs with big bands and then did small-group work with Jimmy Raney in 1955 and with George Wallington in 1956 and 1957. He played with the Dizzy Gillespie big band, including overseas tours, in 1956, and formed a two-alto quintet with Gene Quill in 1957. In 1958–9 he was with the Buddy Rich quintet, and was a founder member of the Quincy Jones big band from 1959–61. He also worked with Benny Goodman in 1962, and did a considerable number of studio sessions in the 1960s. Following a move to Paris with his then wife Chan Richardson (former consort of Charlie Parker), Woods formed his European Rhythm Machine quartet, including Daniel Humair on drums and pianist George Gruntz (later replaced by Gordon Beck), which operated from 1968–72. He returned to the USA, doing some studio work in Los Angeles and later New York, but has been principally active with a new quartet/quintet, which has maintained considerable continuity of personnel over twenty years. Among the members who added to its lustre were

Tom Harrell and pianists Hal Galper and Jim McNeely.

Woods's alto style has helped to define one school of post-Parker players, contemporary with that of Cannonball Adderley. The basic Parker vocabulary was lightened by somewhat broader phrasing, and the full tone occasionally decorated by growls and other bluesy inflections, where appropriate to the melody lines. A frequently exciting and always recognizable performer, Woods has managed to avoid the hysterical edge typical of many post-bop altoists. [BP]

⊙ **Phil And Quill With Prestige** (1957; Prestige/OJC). The exciting pairing of Woods with the late fellow altoist Gene Quill, with a changing rhythm-section, made almost as many albums as gigs. This surviving example is much closer to hard bop than Sims-Cohn of the same vintage.

⊙ **Bouquet** (1987; Concord). At the top of their form, the touring quintet with Tom Harrell and Hal Galper are live in Tokyo, with extended versions of original material plus "Willow Weep For Me" and a bebop approach to "The Theme From Star Trek".

➤➤ **Gary McFarland** *(How To Succeed In Business).*

Sam Woodyard

Drums.

b. Elizabeth, New Jersey, 7 Jan 1925; d. 20 Sept 1988.

Woodyard played locally with the Paul Gayten band in 1950–51 and Joe Holiday in 1951–2, and then worked with Roy Eldridge in 1952 and the Milt Buckner trio from 1953–5. In 1955 he joined Duke Ellington, remaining, apart from short interruptions, for thirteen years. After a period of inactivity he played occasional gigs in the early 1970s and was added (on congas) to the Ellington band in 1973 and the Buddy Rich band in 1974. He moved to France in 1975, working with local musicians and touring Americans such as Buckner and Milt Hinton. He also made appearances in other European countries, including a visit to England in 1979. Woodyard was a somewhat uneven performer who nevertheless assisted the Ellington band through a peak period of its existence. His playing was often quite rudimentary, yet, at its best, swung effortlessly; on other occasions it gave the impression of being laborious and insensitive. His work on Ellington's more subtle compositions drew less comment, simply because it was both effective and self-effacing. [BP]

➤➤ **Duke Ellington** *(At Newport; Such Sweet Thunder).*

Reggie Workman

Bass.

b. Philadelphia, 26 June 1937.

Reggie Workman sang doo-wop at a YMCA, played tuba and euphonium in high school, and bass in R&B bands in his teens. By the early 60s he was working regularly in a panoply of bands led by people like alto saxophonist Gigi Gryce, drummers Roy Haynes and Art Blakey, and Yusef Lateef. A capable swinger, with solid time and facility on changes, Workman was one of a cadre of musicians – like Freddie Hubbard and Art Taylor – who played bop, modal and free jazz. With saxophonist Archie Shepp, he recorded the essential *Four For Trane* (1964; Impulse!), and with John Coltrane he played on *Live At The Village Vanguard* and *Africa/Brass* (both 1961; Impulse!), as well as *Olé* (1961; Atlantic). At the same time, he continued playing hard bop with key figures like Lee Morgan, Booker Ervin and Wayne Shorter.

Since the 1970s, Workman has been a jazz educator, teaching at the New Muse Community Museum of Brooklyn, Manhattan's New School of Social Research and elsewhere. He played in groups led by Charles Tolliver and Max Roach, and recorded with David Murray on *Morning Song* (1983; Black Saint). Latterly, he has played in Trio Three with drummer Andrew Cyrille and alto saxophonist Oliver Lake, performed with groups led by pianists Cecil Taylor and Alexander Von Schlippenbach, and led his own ensembles with line-ups including drummers Rashied Ali and Gerry Hemingway, pianist Marilyn Crispell (who has used Workman in her own trios and quartets), clarinettist Don Byron, violinist Jason Hwang and vocalist Jeanne Lee. Records include *Images* (1989; Music & Arts), *Altered Spaces* (1992; Leo) and the eclectic *Cerebral Caverns* (1995; Postcards) which features pianist Geri Allen as well as tablas, concert harp and electronic drums. A hugely respected statesman of the music, he got a Lifetime Achievement Award from the Jazz Foundation Of America in 1997 and received the Living Legacy Award from the mid-Atlantic Foundation in Washington in 1999. [JC]

⊙ **Summit Conference** (1994; Postcards). Supergroups are often less than the sum of their parts, but this surprise Workman-led session with pianist Andrew Hill, saxophonist Sam Rivers, 'bone man Julian Priester and relative youngster drummer Pheeroan Ak Laff is simply a killer – second only to Workman's 60s free sidework in his catalogue.

➤➤ **John Coltrane** *(Complete Africa/Brass Sessions).*

The World Saxophone Quartet

The World Saxophone Quartet was formed in 1977 by Hamiet Bluiett (baritone saxophone), Julius Hemphill (alto), Oliver Lake (alto) and David Murray (tenor), who all doubled on other instruments, performing mostly without a rhythm-section, although they have recorded with African percussion. The ensemble at times breaks down into trios, duos and unaccompanied solos. Initially they wrote all the music they used, but later recorded tributes to Duke Ellington (*Plays Duke Ellington*) and the soul music of the 1960s (*Rhythm And Blues*). They toured Europe in 1978, and since then have established a strong international reputation. By the mid-1980s they had appeared at most major festivals. After the

World Saxophone Quartet

departure of Hemphill in 1989, the line-up became less stable – his replacements include Arthur Blythe, Eric Person and James Spaulding – and somewhat directionless. However, a string of albums on Justin Time, starting in the late 1990s, featuring Bluitt, Lake, Murray and John Purcell – *Selim Sivad: A Tribute To Miles Davis* (1998), *Requiem For Julius* (see below) and a live concert in Chicago, *Steppenwolf* (2001) – all suggest a revitalized ensemble. [IC]

Point Of No Return (1977; Moers). An exceptional debut – here was a group who could soar and swing, handling dance rhythms, collective improvisation, blues and gospel with passion.

WSQ (1980; Black Saint). Probably the finest of the early albums, with great invention, passionate playing and a long suite combining jazz and popular elements. The group uses a huge armoury of instruments, including alto flute, alto clarinet and bass clarinet.

Plays Duke Ellington (1986; Elektra Musician). This excellent tribute to Duke Ellington was a new departure for the group, and they do terrific performances of several of the best-known pieces.

Dances And Ballads (1987; Elektra Musician). A good combination of physically propulsive pieces like Oliver Lake's "West African Snap" and slower, more sensuous tunes.

Requiem For Julius (2000; Justin Time). A fine tribute to the WSQ's late founder member Hemphill, equally moving and thrilling – perhaps as good as anything they have produced.

World's Greatest Jazz Band

Formed in 1968 by millionaire Dick Gibson after his sixth annual Jazz Party, The World's Greatest Jazz Band numbered among its "charter members" Yank Lawson, Bob Haggart, Bob Wilber, Ralph Sutton and Billy Butterfield, who had previously played at Gibson's parties under the collective title of the Nine Greats of Jazz and worked in Denver for promoter Jack Gurtler. Gibson launched the band under their new name (widely criticized, but excellent American-style hard sell, nevertheless), and after appearances at Manhattan venues such as the Riverboat, Trocadero and Roosevelt Grill, and successful radio and TV, the WGJB was on its way. For the next ten years it toured continuously, and early recordings – such as the live sessions at Massey and Carnegie halls, and studio albums such as *Century Plaza* – show the WGJB in its prime. Later, after fluctuations in line-up and internal strife between co-leaders Lawson and Haggart (later resolved), some of the initial enthusiasm left the project; the contemporary repertoire that had graced early albums was often replaced by ad-lib re-creations of standards, and just occasionally the band sounded too polite, with a tendency sometimes to write in Sammy Kaye-style codas. A great deal of the WGJB's recorded music, however, is seminal, proving them the successor to Bob Crosby's band and the Lawson-Haggart band of the early 1950s. The WGJB broke up in 1978, but in the intervening ten years had done an enormous amount to repopularize jazz and re-present some of its best artists as they deserved. It continued to re-form regularly for tours into the 1990s, incorporating newer members including Warren Vaché Jnr, Brian Lemon and Roy Williams alongside the great originals. [DF]

World's Greatest Jazz Band Live At Massey Hall Vols. 1 & 2 (1972; World Jazz). Magnificent live concert, omitting Butterfield but adding Bobby Hackett and Maxine Sullivan. The Dixieland standards like "ODJB One Step" are as energetic as you could want.

World's Greatest Jazz Band Plays Duke Ellington (1976; World Jazz). Some of the WGJB's later "songbook" albums were marginally less effective, but this one – with Butterfield, Al Klink and Phil Bodner (reeds), plus the driving Bobby Rosengarden (drums) – is superb. Duke would have liked it.

World's Greatest Jazz Band Plays George Gershwin And Rodgers And Hart (1978; Jazzology). Thanks to George Buck the WGJB songbooks are now re-appearing on CD and this collection combines the group's Gershwin celebration with half of its Rodgers and Hart. Bob Haggart's arrangement are tailored perfection, and the soloists – including the soaring Butterfield – masters of their craft. The Rodgers and Hart collection is completed on *Play Cole Porter And Rodgers And Hart* (1975; Jazzology).

Bobby Worth

Drums.

b. London, 7 Jan 1949.

Worth (Robert Dodsworth) was initially inspired by the likes of Mel Lewis and Joe Morello, and at 16 was a founder member of the National Youth Jazz Orchestra, before playing resident (for Bert Rhodes) at London's Talk Of The Town. From 1982 he freelanced in a wide variety of contexts with premier British players (including Pete King, Don Weller and Jim Mullen) and with visiting Americans including Bob Wilber, Buddy Tate, Kenny Davern, Charlie Byrd and Scott Hamilton; he also worked as drummer/MD for Buddy Greco. Worth appears regularly at Ronnie Scott's, as well as all around Britain in a variety of contexts including *Lady Sings The Blues* and with the Alex Welsh Reunion Band. He was winner of the 1998 British Telecom award for Drummer of the Year. and continues to be an invaluable member of the UK's mainstream-modern community. [DF]

At Sundown (1992; Calligraph). With Humphrey Lyttelton and Acker Bilk, Worth's neat, tight-swinging drums lead a relaxed and informed quintet setting with Dave Green and Dave Cliff.

Denny Wright

Guitar, composer, arranger, conductor.
b. Brockley, Kent, UK, 6 May 1924; d. 8 Feb 1992.

Denny Wright (Denys Justin Freeth) turned professional in 1939 and in 1940 joined Cyril "Happy" Blake at London's Jig's Club. In the 1940s his broad-based approach won him studio work (with Phil Green's house band for Decca), big-band dates (with Carl Barriteau and others) and club work (he started London's first bop club, the Fullado, in 1945). In the 1950s Wright played for Kenny Graham's Afro-Cubists and the BBC Show Band (Latin section), founded the Hot Club of London, and was musical director for a variety of nightclubs, before joining Lonnie Donegan and later Johnny Duncan for some pop session years (his was the solo guitar on their records). Later in the 1960s Wright worked in studios full-time (he produced dozens of albums for Music for Pleasure), but in 1973 rejoined Stephane Grappelli, with whom he had first worked in 1944, and stayed with him until 1978. That year he formed Velvet (with Ike Isaacs, Len Skeat and Digby Fairweather), a quartet which toured for four years, recorded and won the *Jazz Journal* small-group poll for 1981. Two years later Wright won the BBC Jazz Society's Musician of the Year award and soon after re-formed both Velvet and his Hot Club of London (with violinist John Van Derrick). A soloist with a quicksilver mind, Wright reflected Django Reinhardt and George Barnes in his work, but his inspirations were all his own. [DF]

Don Harper and Denny Wright

Combo (1977; EMI). A splendid showcase for Wright's pearl-scattering solo style, in tandem with violinist Don Harper, plus eminent sidemen such as Tony Coe, Alan Branscombe and Len Skeat.

Y

Yosuke Yamashita

Piano, composer, author.

b. Tokyo, 26 Feb 1942.

A student at Kunitachi Music University from 1962–7, Yamashita was part of a group, with Terumasa Hino and Masabumi Kikuchi, that met at a jazz club called Gin-Paris in the early 1960s to play and discuss jazz every night. Yamashita formed his own trio in 1969, with Akira Sakata on alto saxophone and Takeo Moriyama on drums, which played a violently abstract music. In 1974 the trio made its first international tour – in Europe – during which it appeared at several festivals in East and West Germany and Yugoslavia. The manic energy of the group earned it the label "The Kamikaze Trio", a title which Yamashita relished. He said later: "They caught on right. We were like kamikaze. We said: OK, let's show them our spirit. And we did just that."

From 1974 the trio visited Europe every year during the 1970s. Then Yamashita disbanded it in 1983, because he felt he had done almost everything he could with the form. He later established a U.S. Trio featuring bassist Cecil McBee and drummer Pheeroan akLaff. He has since led a big band that combined swing music with free jazz, performed his own compositions with the Osaka Philharmonic Orchestra, played with Kodo, the Japanese drum group, performed solo piano concerts, played with the likes of Max Roach, Elvin Jones and Lester Bowie and played his own iconoclastic versions of classical pieces such as Bach's Italian Concerto. As well as producing over 20 albums as leader, he has also written several books and many essays for various magazines.

Although Cecil Taylor was an obvious early influence, Yamashita has arrived at his own concept and style. He has said: "Let's use the words 'in' and 'out'. I always stay 'out' side. Playing solo piano or swing rhythm would be OK as long as I can stay on the 'out' side. An 'out' side approach is what jazz is all about. Jazz started out as 'Africa approaching Europe'. And be careful, it was not 'Europe approaching Africa', but 'Africa approaching Europe'. That was the beginning of jazz – Europe had the system but Africa was alive with feeling. All the material I use belongs to the system, but as long as I can stand on the 'out' side and approach things from the 'out' side, I will never be suffocated." [IC]

Yosuke Yamashita and Akira Sakata

⊙ **Ghosts By Albert Ayler** (1977; West Wind). With Sakata on clarinet and alto saxophone, Yamashita twins his kamikaze "out"-look with the sound and fury of Albert Ayler's legacy. Bracing and not for the faint-hearted.

Yosuke Yamashita

⊙ **It Don't Mean A Thing** (1984; DIW); **Resonant Memories** (2001; Verve). Yamashita's solo piano offers glimpses of his oblique relationship with the mainstream/modern jazz tradition – his originality is a little more user-friendly away from the Dionysian surge of his trio.

⊙ **Kurdish Dance** (1992; Verve); **Dazzling Days** (1993; Verve); **Fragments** (1999; Verve). The former two titles are really exciting quartet albums featuring Joe Lovano with Yashamita's U.S. trio of McBee and akLaff on which the contemporary jazz tradition meets Yamashita head-on and Lovano confirms his status as one of the supreme contemporary jazz saxophonists. *Fragments* features the same trio examining some disguised standards in an archetypically oblique fashion.

Jimmy Yancey

Piano.

b. Chicago, c.1894; d. 17 Sept 1951.

The father of boogie, Jimmy Yancey worked originally as a singing and dancing vaudevillian. A self-taught pianist, he played at rent parties and clubs in Chicago from 1915, and is said to have passed on ideas to Albert Ammons and Meade "Lux" Lewis. In 1925 he became a devoted baseball groundsman, but regained fame on an international scale after boogie came back into fashion in the late 1930s, and played in Chicago and New York, often with his wife, blues singer Mama Yancey. He played at Carnegie Hall as late as 1948. [DF]

Various Artists

⊙ **Barrelhouse Boogie** (1937–41; Bluebird). Compilation including Yancey's eight Bluebird solos, plus nine famous duets by Pete Johnson and Albert Ammons and two tracks from Meade "Lux" Lewis.

Jason Yarde

Soprano and alto saxophones, keyboards.

b. Beckenham, UK, 1 Sept 1970.

Both of Jason Christopher Yarde's parents are from Guyana, South America, and he was the first of their four children to be born in the UK. Yarde first wanted to play soprano saxophone after seeing a picture of Sidney Bechet in his local record shop. He had saxophone lessons at school, studied jazz piano with Brian Priestley at Goldsmiths' College, then attended Middlesex University (1989–93), studying composition with Veryan Weston and saxophone with Alan Barnes and Martin Speake. As part of the latter course, he spent a year in the USA at William Paterson College, New Jersey, studying saxophone with Joe Lovano and others. During this period of study, Yarde had also been playing professionally whenever possible, with Courtney Pine's Jazz Warriors, Mervyn Africa, Louis Moholo's Viva La Black and various other groups. He has also worked with the group Afro Blok since 1992, and two years later was a founder member of the twelve-piece band Rare Mix.

When the first Tomorrow's Warriors workshop group was set up by Gary Crosby in 1993, Jason Yarde led it, and in 1997 the award-winning co-operative band J-Life emerged from that, as a quintet with Yarde, singer Julie Dexter, pianist Robert Mitchell, bassist Darren Taylor and drummer Daniel Crosby. Yarde has also played with Claude Deppa's Frontline, Nikki Yeoh's Infinitum and Jazz Jamaica All Stars. He works extensively as a composer and producer, and has had commissions from Tomorrow's Warriors and the Phoenix Dance Company of Leeds, among others. He performed with a new improvisation group – Out – at London's Freedom Of The City Festival in 2001. His favourites are Wayne Shorter, Branford Marsalis and Johnny Hodges, but he calls Roland Kirk, Courtney Pine, Kenny Garrett, Vincent Harring and Joe Henderson his teachers. [IC]

Tomorrow's Warriors/J-Life

⊙ **Tomorrow's Warriors Presents ... J-Life** (1998; Dune). J-Life are augmented by members of the Warriors on some of the tracks of this magnificently assured debut album. J-Life put new life into well-known pieces – Ellington's "In A Sentimental Mood", for example, is performed in 6/4 time, with Julie Dexter's vocal as sensuous and sultry as Billie Holiday, and Yarde's soprano solo sonorous and superbly lyrical. His composition "Dark Too Bright" is a fast bravura outing with great soprano and sheets of sound from pianist Mitchell.

Nikki Yeoh

Piano, keyboards, composer.
b. London, 24 May 1973.

Yeoh began learning the piano at five years old. At sixteen she started two years of classical lessons at the Centre for Young Musicians in London. She had lessons in jazz for a year, and from 1989–93 attended jazz workshops at Interchange in North London. While there she played with the London Fusion Orchestra, which gave her some exposure in the London area.

By 1992 she was playing in Courtney Pine's jazz and reggae bands, and gigging with soul multi-instrumentalist Don-E. In 1993 she played with Chante Moore, Neneh Cherry, Phillip Bent and Dick Heckstall-Smith. In 1994 she gigged with Steve Williamson and worked with The Roots, a rap group from Philadelphia, and played on *Red Hot And Cool*, an album recorded by The Roots and Roy Ayres plus jazz stars such as Herbie Hancock, Donald Byrd, Ron Carter and Don Cherry. The same year she started her own trio, Infinitum, with Michael Mondesir on bass guitar and American Keith Leblanc on drums, a group rooted in the fusion area of music, but encompassing elements of the whole rich jazz tradition. Yeoh is a superb pianist and composer whose work already has great individuality. Her favourite pianists include Joanne Brackeen, Hermeto Pascoal, Glenn Gould, Herbie Hancock and Keith Jarrett, and other inspirations are Wayne Shorter, Miles Davis and J.S. Bach.

In March 1996, Yeoh and her group, Infinitum, accompanied the American saxophonist Eddie Harris during his two-week residency in a London club and he revelled in their company, though he was terminally ill with cancer at the time. Nikki Yeoh was voted Best Jazz Musician in 1996 by *The Independent* newspaper, and her talent as a composer was also being recognized around this time. She had a commission to compose for a six-piano group called Piano Circus, and the work was premiered in November 1996 at the Place Theatre in London, as part of the Winter Music Festival, alongside the work of other composers such as Brian Eno and John Cage. She was also commissioned by the Bath Festival to write a composition for a twelve-piece band – her group Infinitum plus nine other musicians, and a video called *Speechmik X-ploration*, which was premiered at the festival in May 1997. She has also composed and arranged for the National Youth Jazz Orchestra of Scotland. The classical pianist, Joanna MacGregor, became friendly with Yeoh, and commissioned her to write a collection of short pieces for MacGregor to perform in 1997 at Bridgewater Hall in Manchester. Infinitum and MacGregor worked so well together that they combined to record the tracks for MacGregor's new independent label, Sound Circus. The music was released on a forty-minute long CD, *Piano Language*. Commissions followed for the Norfolk and Norwich Festival (four pieces for piano and cello) and the Scottish NYJO (for whom Yeoh produced the album *Quiet Freedom*) and as the culmination of a London Arts-funded research and development period, Yeoh performed with Infinitum in Cuba in 2000. She has also worked in the hip hop and electronica fields and recently collaborated with vocalist Cleveland Watkiss. [IC]

Nikki Yeoh and Cleveland Watkiss

⊙ **Mutual Serenade** (2003; Watyo). Yeoh's thick and funky piano playing in tandem with Watkiss's polyvocal perversity is always stimulating, and produces moments of sheer improvisatory brilliance. An extraordinary album well-worth investigating.

Larry Young

Organ, piano, electric piano.

b. Newark, New Jersey, 7 Oct 1940; d. 30 March 1978.

Young studied the piano as a child and learned about jazz from Larry Young Snr, a professional organist. When his father opened a nightclub in Newark, Young taught himself to play the house organ, and began gigging with R&B groups at the age of seventeen, eventually touring with Lou Donaldson. He recorded with Jimmy Forrest and under his own name from 1960, and freelanced, often on piano, with Lee Morgan, Hank Mobley and Joe Henderson, among others. In 1964 Young recorded the first of several albums using Elvin Jones, before spending some months in Europe with Woody Shaw. He was a founder member of Tony Williams's Lifetime from 1969–71, and also recorded with John McLaughlin, Jimi Hendrix (an informal jam session) and Miles Davis (*Bitches Brew*). Though he recorded further albums in the 1970s, such as one with Pharoah Sanders and James "Blood" Ulmer, he often worked as a sideman, including with Houston Person in 1977. He died from pneumonia, contracted in hospital while being treated for a stomach infection.

A Sunni Muslim from the early 1960s, Young sometimes worked under the name Khalid Yasin, but was better known as "the Coltrane of the organ", Jack McDuff's description. His sound on the instrument was suitable for incorporating modal jazz and an appropriate rhythmic feel. His partnerships with Elvin and Tony Williams took the organ into a realm with few followers, until the arrival of players like Barbara Dennerlein, and his recognition was unequal to his talents. [BP]

⊙ **Unity** (1965; Blue Note). With a rhythm-section of just Young and Elvin Jones (who take "Monk's Dream" as a duo), the horns riding the waves are Joe Henderson (who contributes "Zoltan" and trumpeter Woody Shaw. Young is at his unbeatable best.

➤➤ **Tony Williams** *(Emergency!)*.

Lee Young

Drums, vocals.

b. New Orleans, 7 March 1917.

Lee (Leonidas Raymond) Young could scarcely have presented a more dramatic contrast to his famous brother Lester. "They were like night and day," says bassist Red Callender, a close friend. "Probably the only thing they shared except their musical family background was their love of sport, particularly baseball. Lee was and is a leader, an extrovert, a consummate businessman, dependable, organized, health-conscious, a terrific golfer, a great drummer!" Apart from the last accolade, Young could scarcely have presented a worse set of qualifications for turning into a jazz legend, and he paid dearly for his thoroughgoing professionalism by being regularly ignored in the media. But in musical terms his career was as great as those of most other drummers of his generation, beginning in the 1930s with such outfits as Mutt Carey's Jeffersonians and Buck Clayton's band, before moving into film work, first as an extra and later as the first black musician to be hired by Columbia for their staff orchestra. In 1941 Young co-led a band with his brother Lester at Billy Berg's Capri Club, then worked in studios for ten years and joined Nat "King" Cole's trio from 1953–62. Then, says Callender, "at the height of his career Lee decided he didn't want anybody saying, 'You should have heard Lee Young in 1954 or whatever year'. So he went into the record business – it's the genius of Lee Young you hear in the Motown Sound and in many of the hit records of the late 1950s, early 1960s and 1970s." [DF]

Lester Young

Tenor saxophone, clarinet.

b. Woodville, Mississippi, 27 Aug 1909; d. 15 March 1959.

"Prez was such a *nice* fellow, a beautiful, beautiful person" says Dicky Wells of Lester Willis Young, the greatest tenor saxophonist (along with Coleman Hawkins) of the classic years. "He was full of jokes, harmless, didn't bother nobody, loved everybody. He was the greatest." "The President" (he acquired the nickname in the 1930s from Billie Holiday) was the first to supply a viable alternative to the tenor saxophone vocabulary that cocksure young Coleman Hawkins had defined by 1930: Young's answer, typically enough, was cool, light-toned, laidback and avuncular, as far away from the charging, full-toned, macho Hawkins as it was possible to be.

The Lester Young formula represented a challenge in the early days of his career with the Blue Devils (1932–3), Bennie Moten (1933–4) and Count Basie's orchestra in 1934 (he had invited himself into the band with a telegram which Basie remembered as "strange and urgent") – and it met with wholesale approval at Kansas City jam sessions. Some months later, however, after he had joined Fletcher Henderson's orchestra, the reaction was very different. Henderson's wife played him records of Hawkins, praising the bigger sound, and even Billie Holiday, with whom Young was a welcome lodger and platonically close friend, tried to help him down an unlooked-for road ("We'll get us a tone!"). Young bore the idiocy with patience and fortitude – "To each his own" was a favoured phrase – but after two more years of wandering, including a failed audition with Earl Hines, with relief he rejoined Basie at Kansas City's Reno Club.

Once again he was accepted on his own terms – "I just know we were all happy, always wanting to go to work and things like that" – and he was soon encouraged by Basie to set his talents against Herschel Evans, a highly gifted Hawkins follower who represented most of the saxophone options against

HERMAN LEONARD

Lester Young

which Young had quietly and determinedly set himself. Against Evans, a musical and personal opposite with whom he established a keen although amicable rivalry, Young could proudly display a kind of music which, until lately, he had been instructed to suppress. He enjoyed girlfriends ("I was tired of looking at chicks running in and out", says Buddy Tate), became the star pitcher in Basie's softball team, played practical jokes (including ringing a bell at any band member who made a mistake on stage), invented a hip nickname for each band member (Harry Edison became "Sweets", Buddy Tate "Moon", the leader "The Holy Main"), and crawled back on the bus at the end of each night to what he called the "sweet music" of rolling dice. And he recorded with Billie Holiday: "She got me little record dates playing behind her, little solos and things like that." Every side is a gem.

In 1940 Young left Basie, due to a flat work patch, depression after the death of Herschel Evans, and the wish to lead for himself. He freelanced and co-led a band with brother Lee before rejoining the Basie band from December 1943 until September 1944. He had just completed a short film for Warner Bros, *Jammin' The Blues* (which was nominated for an Academy Award the following year), when, at the end of a night's work, he was spotted by a plain-clothes army official and summarily conscripted. "It was a nightmare – one mad nightmare," he said later. "They sent me down to Georgia – that was enough to make me blow my top." Young feared his racist captors, and he ended up in a disciplinary centre: when he emerged after an illness in 1945 he bore deep mental scars.

He now had to face the new trend of bebop, fresh recording techniques, and a flock of Young disciples who were achieving fame at his expense and with his ideas: small wonder that at times his music seemed – like him – more heavy-lidded than before. Prez began to withdraw more, developing his own monosyllabic language and a set of speech formulas to cope with the threats of life ("eyes" for wanting, "bells" for approval and so on). But in 1946 he was still a star, and just as creative with Jazz At The Philharmonic, happily playing against his old arch-rival Coleman Hawkins, and for the next ten or more years he appeared regularly with Norman Granz's sometimes hysterical show, as well as leading his own small groups. Poor health (resulting in several hospital visits), heavy smoking and drinking often affected his performance after that: more often, though, his approach was simply and determinedly laid-back. "They say, 'Oh Prez, he don't sound like he used to'," said Jo Jones, "but then when they hear the album he made in 1956 with Roy Eldridge and Teddy Wilson and me they said, 'Wow – that's different'. It was a question of compatibility." (Billie Holiday often sounds worse post-war for the same reason, in part at least, and complained about it in her book *Lady Sings The Blues*.)

In his final years, Lester Young somehow got smaller. One year at Newport, very drunk, he told Buddy Tate: "The other ladies, my imitators, are making the money!" In 1958 he was playing the Blue Note and planning an album with Gil Evans. "He wanted to make the album, but he wanted to die more," Evans recalled. "He came in from his home on Long Island and decided to stay at the Alvin Hotel, just across from Birdland. He never ate a thing. Then he got back from Paris, got in the hotel room again and had a heart attack." Lester Young died; his old friend Billie Holiday followed him within a few months. [DF]

⊙ **The Lester Young Story** (1936–49; Properbox). Probably the best value collection of Young's best years, with excellent sound-restoration and a detailed booklet. Like most Properbox sets, a real bargain though completists will find the odd gap in coverage.

⊙ **Lady Day And Prez** (1930s; Giants of Jazz). This great partnership deserves specific documentation and this CD provides it, including immortal tracks like "Trav'lin' All Alone", "A Sailboat In The Moonlight" and "Foolin' Myself".

⊙ **Lester Young 1943–6/1946–7** (Classics). The 1943–6 disc lists Young's Aladdin sessions, including "Riffin' without Helen" plus sides with Earl Warren and Count Basie's "All-American" rhythm section. The 1946–7 collection has invaluable titles with Nat Cole and Buddy Rich.

⊙ **The Kansas City Sessions** (1938–44; Commodore). Valuable collation of all titles (with alternate takes) by the Kansas City Six groups of 1938 and 44. On the earlier titles Young's clarinet is beautifully featured along with his tenor, opposite Buck Clayton; 1944 has Bill Coleman and Dicky Wells in premier form. Four titles by the Kansas City Five (minus Lester) have been added to complete the set.

⊙ **Lester Young With The Oscar Peterson Trio** (1952; Verve). Important collation of three old 10" LPs on which Young was on vintage form. Fourteen tracks include his wicked (and unique) vocal on "It Takes Two To Tango".

⊙ **Pres And Sweets** (1955; Verve). Eight titles on which, as Stanley Crouch notes, "Lester strips everything down – making each note an event".

⊙ **Pres And Teddy** (1956; Verve). Almost as if to counter the music of the above, Young is frothing with ideas on this quartet set. Proof that Lester – given the best surroundings – still sounded as spontaneously creative as ever.

⊙ **The Jazz Giants** (1956; Verve). Often quoted as some of the last great music made by Young, this session caused a sensation when it was issued. Superbly recorded, and surrounded by compatible spirits – Teddy Wilson again plus Roy Eldridge, Vic Dickenson, Freddy Green, Gene Ramey and Jo Jones – Young sounded almost as good as he ever did on a set of tunes including a glorious "I Guess I'll Have To Change My Plan" and a fighting "Gigantic Blues".

⊙ **Laughin' To Keep From Cryin'** (1958; Verve). With Roy Eldridge and Harry Edison, this date is as appealingly vulnerable as some of Billie Holiday's later recordings. He sounds almost immobilized but every note is still unmistakable Prez. And the cover picture (by Burt Goldblatt) is worth the price alone.

⊙ **Lester Young in Washington 1956, Vols 1–5** (OJC). As on his Jazz Giants session, there's plenty of evidence here of Young at almost full power – extraordinary, as these sides were recorded in the midst of his so-called "decline". More proof that jazz has a way of contradicting its own legend amid the business of a night's creation.

⊙ **The Complete Lester Young Studio Sessions on Verve** (1946–59). This eight-CD box has been written about passionately (and compassionately) in the *Penguin Guide to Jazz on CD* and readers are advised to read that too. There is of course plenty of good music on this set but also evidence of Young's decline – a sound which may either be dismissed simply as sub-standard performance or the honest reflection of a major performer's state of mind. Ultimately you'll have to decide for yourself.

➤➤ **Count Basie** *(The Original American Decca Recordings).*

Snooky Young

Trumpet.

b. Dayton, Ohio, 3 Feb 1919.

Snooky (Eugene Howard) Young took up the trumpet at five years old, and played in the Wilberforce College Band without ever actually attending the college. Then, after time with Clarence "Chic" Carter's territory band in Michigan, he joined Jimmie Lunceford's orchestra in 1939 and stayed for three years: his famous feature was "Uptown Blues". From 1942, when he briefly joined Count Basie, Young worked with Lee Young's band, Les Hite and Benny Carter, Basie again, and Gerald Wilson, before rejoining Basie from 1945–7, where he replaced high-note man Al Killian. For the next ten years, he led his own top-class band, in Dayton, Ohio, featuring players such as Slam Stewart and Booty Wood, before rejoining Basie from 1957–62. From then on he was a busy studio player, and in 1979 produced a long-overdue solo album for Concord. [DF]

⊙ **Snooky And Marshall's Album** (1978; Concord). Young's first album as co-featured artist for Concord, playing alongside Royal, a similarly elusive solo talent. Both are in fine form, and singer-actor Scatman Crothers makes a comparably rare appearance with his old colleagues.

⊙ **Horn Of Plenty** (1979; Concord). Young demonstrates the solo talents that should have been more widely heard, playing trumpet and flugelhorn in a quartet with Ross Tomkins (piano), John Collins (guitar) and Jake Hanna (drums).

Trummy Young

Trombone, vocals, composer.

b. Savannah, Georgia, 12 Jan 1912; d. 10 Sept 1984.

Trummy (James Osborne) Young grew up in Washington, where he studied trumpet first, then made his professional debut in 1928 playing a revolutionary high-noted style of trombone. "People used to say I was crazy," he remembered later, "and ask what I was trying to do." One sympathetic bandleader, however, was Earl Hines, whom Young joined in 1933 and stayed with for four years, perfecting a trumpet style based on Louis Armstrong and a trombone approach based on a musician Young adored, Jimmy Harrison – "I worked very hard on ... a sharper, brilliant sound." But it was after he joined Jimmie Lunceford's orchestra – with its showmanship, strong discipline and regular chances for features – that Young became a figurehead for trombonists everywhere. Says Dicky Wells, "He really brought a modern turn to the trombone and it was unusual for a trombone player to be featured as much as he was." With his jivey voice and supercharged technique, Young was a natural cornerman for his leader, and it was a pity that in 1943 Lunceford's low wages finally forced him to hand in his notice. But he carried on working regularly for four years as bandleader in a variety of other bands (including Norman Granz's Jazz At The Philharmonic) before moving to Hawaii to live and play.

Louis Armstrong heard him in Honolulu in 1952; Young joined Armstrong that year and for the next twelve years played the perfect supporting role, modifying his style accordingly. "A lot of people don't understand what happened to Trummy's style when he joined Louis," says Wells, "but in Dixieland they don't want too many notes anyway. I don't think he ever got enough credit for it. But he had made such a big reputation in his career before that – it was a kind of sacrifice." Young loved his role because he loved Louis. "I try to keep him happy," he said. "Louis's got more soul than anyone I ever met in my life!" He stayed until 1964 ("It was the road that caused me to quit") and then worked back in Hawaii, re-emerging for Dick Gibson's Colorado parties, special events and major jazz festivals such as Nice until his death. [DF]

➤➤ **Louis Armstrong** *(Louis Armstrong Plays W.C. Handy);* **Jimmie Lunceford** *(Jimmie Lunceford 1937–39, 1939–40 & 1940–41).*

Z

Rachel Z

Piano, keyboards.

b. New York, 28 Dec 1962.

Rachel's father Ed Nicolazzo was a visual artist and her mother Mary an opera singer, who together opened their own music and art school. Rachel began voice lessons at age two and piano at the age of seven, but a summer course at Berklee College as a teenager converted her to jazz. She studied with Joanne Brackeen and Richie Beirach, and graduated from the New England Conservatory while working in Boston with such musicians as Bob Moses, Miroslav Vitous and George Garzone. Back in New York from 1988, she toured with her college colleague, saxophonist Najee, and played with Al Di Meola, Larry Coryell and Angela Bofill. She then became a member of Steps Ahead, made her debut album for Columbia, and collaborated on the orchestration of the album *High Life* for Wayne Shorter, with whom she then toured extensively. She performed internationally with Stanley Clarke's band Vertu in 1999, and in 2002 with Peter Gabriel, as well as with her own acoustic trio formed in 2000. In the words of Chick Corea: "Rachel has great harmonies and really swings at the piano." [BP]

⦿ **Room Of One's Own** (1996; NYC Records). Assisted by players such as Garzone, Charnett Moffett, Cindy Blackman and Terri Lyne Carrington (with a wind octet on four tracks and Regina Carter on one), Rachel's absorbing programme of original music has various artistic and literary inspirations, such as Virginia Woolf for the title track and the moving "Trail Of Her Blood In The Snow" from a short story by Gabriel García Márquez.

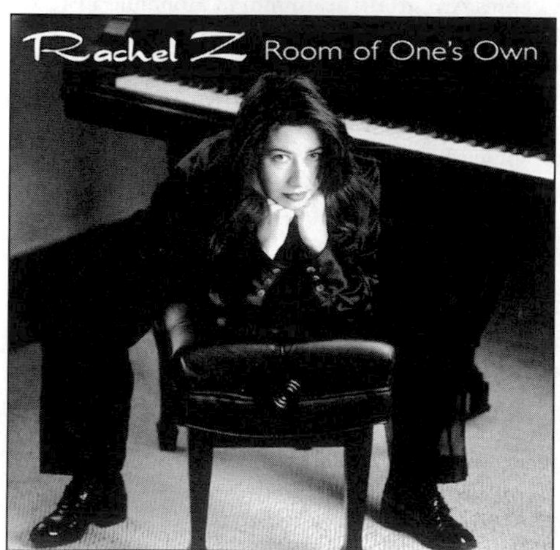

Aziza Mustafa Zadeh

Piano, vocals.

b. Baku, Azerbaijan, 19 Dec 1969.

Aziza Mustafa Zadeh's father Vagif (b. 16 March 1940; d. 17 Dec 1979) was a pioneering jazz pianist, and her mother Eliza was a trained folk singer who turned to jazz and now manages Aziza's career. She began by singing folk songs on radio at the age of three, and she first played piano on stage with her father at the Tiflis jazz festival in 1978. She studied at a school for gifted children and at the State Conservatory of Music, and made her solo debut at the Tbilisi jazz festival in 1986, subsequently appearing throughout eastern Europe. In 1993 her second album was recorded in Los Angeles with John Patitucci and Dave Weckl, and the following year she recorded in New York with Stanley Clarke, Al Di Meola and others. In the mid-1990s she spent more time in Germany, where her first two albums have enjoyed considerable success. Her blend of Jarrett- and Corea-influenced piano with folk-type compositional material, and vocals to match, is more compelling and more far-reaching than many such attempts. [BP]

⦿ **Aziza Mustafa Zadeh** (1991; Columbia). More than her subsequent efforts, this beautiful unaccompanied album rides on the wings of Aziza's expansively lyrical piano, with the occasional vocal as icing on the cake. Anyone who feared that the world-music movement would necessarily bypass keyboard instruments must think again.

Frank Zappa

Guitar, composer.

b. Baltimore, Maryland, 21 Dec 1940; d. 4 Dec 1993.

Although chiefly celebrated as a rock guitarist/composer/leader, and as a pungently intelligent commentator on all aspects of contemporary culture, particularly the excesses of the music world and its press, Frank Zappa produced a good deal of work which could be loosely categorized as jazz, particularly in the late 60s and early 70s. After his family had moved to California in 1950, he took up drums at twelve, and guitar shortly afterwards, leading a high school group, the Blackouts, in his teens. In the early 1960s Zappa joined the Soul Giants, later to become the Mothers, and subsequently the Mothers of Invention under his leadership: a band featuring jazz-rock figures such as saxophonist Ian Underwood and ex-Herbie Mann sideman Don Preston, and, less regularly, George Duke and trombonist Bruce Fowler. Other crossover figures, such as Jean-Luc Ponty, have recorded Zappa's music (*King Kong*, 1969), and Zappa's 1970s sidemen included saxophonist Jay Migliori, bassist David Parlato and multi-reedsman Charles Owens. In the 1980s Zappa's work located itself more in the avant-rock and modern classical genres than in jazz. The legacy of his mix of crude R&B, *musique concrète*, bogus pomp and out-there jazz is poignant in the music and attitude of 1970s-generation art-rockers like Fred Frith and adversarial improvisers of today such as the post-Derek Bailey guitarist Stefan Jaworzyn and the ingenious dictaphone abuser T.H.F. Drenching. [CP]

⊙ **Hot Rats** (1969; WEA). Set the standard for subsequent jazz-rock with its memorably original but immediately accessible tunes, the virtuosity of the soloing from both Zappa and Sugarcane Harris on violin, and the bluesy intensity of the Captain Beefheart vocal on "Willie The Pimp". Has dated far less than similarly legendary 1960s fare.

⊙ **Waka/Jawaka** (1972; WEA). Like its companion album, *The Grand Wazoo*, a definitive Zappa jazz-rock offering with great soloing from Zappa himself, trumpeter Sal Marquez and keyboard player Don Preston, plus deceptively simple horn charts.

⊙ **The Best Band You Never Heard in Your Life** (1991; Zappa Records). Two-CD set documenting the superb Zappa band's 1988 tour (horn section: Bruce Fowler, trombone; Albert Wing, tenor; Paul Carman, alto, baritone), touching all bases from Ravel's *Bolero* through sampling of "Eric Dolphy Memorial Barbecue" to Zappa commentaries on rock staples such as "Purple Haze", "Sunshine Of Your Love" and "Stairway To Heaven".

Zeke Zarchy

Trumpet.
b. New York, 12 June 1915.

Known to friends and jazz critics as "Rubin from Brooklyn", Zarchy was a highly respected lead trumpeter of the swing era and after. Following an initial stint with Joe Haymes's tightly disciplined orchestra in 1935, he worked for Benny Goodman (1936), Artie Shaw (1936–7), with Bob Crosby until he had a fighting disagreement with Irving Fazola (1937–9), Tommy Dorsey (1939–40), Glenn Miller (1940) and others. George T. Simon said in 1939 that he had "a whacky sense of humour ... and he can play pretty fair jazz"; unfortunately Zarchy's talents as a lead player often meant that the jazz was left to others, and after he moved into NBC as a staffman in 1940 there was even less chance to hear what he could do. From 1944–5 he was playing for Glenn Miller's AEF band (Miller appointed him first sergeant and the two men were golfing buddies), but after the war Zarchy moved into TV, radio and recording in Hollywood. Far too little evidence of his abilities was available until the 1980s, when he worked regularly with the Great Pacific Jazz Band and also visited Britain with Ray McKinley and Peanuts Hucko to play for the 1985 VE Day anniversary celebrations with a Miller-style orchestra. [DF]

Joe Zawinul

Piano, keyboards, synthesizers, composer.
b. Vienna, 7 July 1932.

Zawinul was given an accordion at the age of six and played it for a year by ear, playing gypsy melodies and accompanying his family singing folk songs. From the age of seven he studied classical music at the Vienna Conservatory, but was unable to practise at home because his family had no piano. His first opportunity to practise regularly came in 1944, when he and other very gifted students were evacuated from Vienna to a private country estate in Czechoslovakia, where Zawinul had to practise the piano every day. Back in Vienna after the war he became interested in jazz; when the film *Stormy Weather* arrived there he saw it 24 times, and from then on wanted to play jazz with black musicians. In 1952 he worked with the great Austrian saxophonist Hans Koller, which brought Zawinul to the notice of jazz audiences, and from 1953–8 he worked with various leading Austrian musicians, as well as playing at Special Service clubs in France and Germany with his own trio.

In 1959 he won a scholarship to the Berklee School of Music, Boston, and emigrated to the USA, where, after only a week or so at Berklee, he joined Maynard Ferguson and toured with him for eight months. After working briefly with Slide Hampton, Zawinul was accompanist for singer Dinah Washington from October 1959 to March 1961. He played for a month with Harry Edison and Joe Williams, then joined Cannonball Adderley, becoming a key member of his group and staying with him until the autumn of 1970. During that period Zawinul played a major part in the success of the Adderley group as composer of such hits as "Mercy Mercy Mercy", which won a Grammy award for the best instrumental performance. He was also featured on recording sessions with many other leading US jazz musicians. In 1966 he was a judge at the International Jazz Competition in Vienna, and with Friedrich Gulda he recorded Gulda's *Concerto For Two Pianos And Orchestra*.

He also played an important part as both player and composer on four seminal Miles Davis albums between 1969–70: *In A Silent Way* (the title piece is Zawinul's tune), *Bitches Brew*, *Live-Evil* and *Big Fun*. This exposure with Davis brought Zawinul to the attention of a worldwide audience, and in 1971, with ex-Davis saxophonist Wayne Shorter, he co-founded Weather Report. The other original members were Miroslav Vitous, Alphonse Mouzon and Airto Moreira, but throughout Weather Report's existence there were several changes of personnel, Zawinul and Shorter being the only two constant members.

RAFFAELLA CAVALIERI

Joe Zawinul

Weather Report (so named by Shorter after Zawinul's early description of the band's music as "changing from day to day like the weather") rapidly established itself as one of the most vitally creative and influential units in jazz history. The group was a perennial poll-winner, reaching enormous peaks of worldwide popularity without ever diluting its music or lowering its standards, and its fascinating artistic development (from the modish free improvisation plus electronics at the beginning of the 1970s to the more composed structures of its middle and later periods) is minutely documented on record. Its musical scope is huge, ranging from pure abstraction – non-temporal, non-tonal electronic and acoustic sounds – to brilliantly performed rhythms of tremendous variety, rich harmonies, indelible melodies, subtle variations of space and texture, and much improvisation. Its music is always of the heart.

Zawinul's career has reversed the usual jazz musician's pattern; instead of doing his most innovative work when he was young, the whole of his earlier life seems like a prolonged apprenticeship and preparation for the brilliant originality and sustained artistry of Weather Report – begun when he was nearly forty, it was still peaking in his early fifties. Before Weather Report he was an excellent player and composer but perhaps a fairly peripheral figure on the jazz scene: his work with Miles Davis at the end of the 1960s made him a more central figure; then with Weather Report he became, with perhaps John McLaughlin, one of the first Europeans since Django Reinhardt to have a major influence on the course of the music. Since the break-up of Weather Report in 1986 he has tried a number of different contexts: in 1985 he toured in Europe and the USA, playing solo acoustic and electric keyboards, and he has formed the Zawinul Syndicate – the ensemble with which he still tours – and, briefly, Weather Update, an obvious attempt to recapture some of the spirit of Weather Report.

He is generally recognized as being one of the finest composers in jazz, and his work has introduced a huge new vocabulary of compositional devices, new rhythms, new ways of making the music breathe. Zawinul claims Czech, Hungarian and gypsy blood in his ancestry, and his Austrian heritage has had a powerful effect on the nature and quality of his music; all the profound emotion of central and eastern European folk music is present in his work, and his compositions always have something to say about the human condition, conjuring up social scenes – market places, families, gypsy celebrations – and also the inner landscape of solitary individuals. Recalling the genesis of one of his most evocative pieces, he told C. Silvert: "I wrote 'Silent Way' in Vienna, in a hotel room overlooking the park. My kids were off with my parents, and my wife was asleep. The snow was falling down, and I looked out the window to the park, and took out the paper and wrote the whole thing in a few minutes." He is one of the great masters of electronics, and his childhood memories of the accordion make him feel at home with synthesizers; he has likened his synthesized sounds to "native instruments not yet discovered". Among his other important compositions are "74 Miles Away", "Rumpelstiltskin", "Dr Honoris Causa", "Pharoah's Dance", "Badia", "Birdland", "Man In The Green Shirt", "A Remark You Made" and "Experience in E for Symphony Orchestra". [IC]

Weather Report

⊙ **Weather Report** (1971; Columbia). This debut album was a much more cooperative affair than the subsequent Weather Report discs: the composing was shared fairly equally by Zawinul and Shorter, with Vitous contributing one piece. The music comes partly out of the co-leaders' experience with Miles Davis, partly out of psychedelic rock and the distant memory of free jazz. Uneven, but a fascinating document.

⊙ **I Sing The Body Electric** (1972; Columbia). Another document of the times with a sci-fi cover, impressionist pieces, booting rhythms, overdubbed heavenly male voices, heavy electrics, and a liner note of psychedelic gibberish. This is a band in search of its soul, though the performance of Zawinul's "Dr Honoris Causa" has rhythmic and emotional focus.

⊙ **Black Market** (1976; Columbia). Zawinul and Shorter had found their direction by this album. It's varied yet homogeneous, with evocative tone colours, buoyant rhythms and some marvellous compositions, the best of which are Zawinul's title track and Shorter's "Elegant People". Alphonso Johnson is the bass guitarist, but Jaco Pastorius plays bass on his own piece, "Barbary Coast".

⊙ **Heavy Weather** (1976; Columbia). With Pastorius now a regular member, this was their breakthrough album, selling more than 400,000 copies. "Birdland" is one of the most joyfully buoyant pieces in all jazz, with simple but memorable melodic fragments and phenomenally springy rhythms. Zawinul's other great piece, "A Remark You Made", is pure poetry – a deeply affecting conjuncion of romantic and sonorous chords with poignant melody.

Zawinul Syndicate

⊙ **Black Water** (1989; Columbia). This is a rocking live set, very much in the WR mould, but with vocals and narrations. The showmanship in the music's organization dominates (one of the musicians eggs on the crowd to respond), but some of the rhythms are ecstatic – particularly on the title track.

Joe Zawinul

My People (1996; Escapade); **World Tour** (1997; ESC Records); **Faces And Places** (2002; ESC Records). After Weather Report disbanded, Zawinul seemed to become even more interested in ethnic and particularly African music. In the later 1990s, his Zawinul Syndicate reflected his intense love of rhythm and interest in the human voice. At one point in this stage in his career, he did not even want reeds or brass in his band. He coaxed the most affecting human sounds from his synthesizers, sang himself, and the touring band had a basic instrumentation of guitar, bass guitar, drums and percussion, with anyone or everyone liable to double on vocals. If the later studio albums – like *My People* and *Faces And Places* – were sporadically diverting, the concerts – as represented on *World Tour* – were compelling; Zawinul's rhythmic invention is inexhaustible, and his sense of musical drama acute.

➤➤ **Cannonball Adderley** *(The Best of ... The Capitol Years)*; **Miles Davis** *(In A Silent Way)*.

Denny Zeitlin

Piano, synthesizer.

b. Chicago, 10 April 1938.

Zeitlin had piano lessons as a child, which he followed by studies with George Russell and others. He played jazz while in college and recorded his first album in 1964. On qualifying as a psychiatrist he moved to San Francisco, and appeared at the Monterey and Newport festivals in 1965 with a trio including Charlie Haden. He retired from public appearances in the late 1960s, resuming in the mid-1970s. He has continued to perform regularly since then, sometimes reuniting with Haden, and mainly restricting his activities to the West Coast. While his initial fame seemed inflated by his extra-musical profession (there was also a jazz pianist/priest around at the same time), he did produce several attractive pieces, of which "Carole's Garden" was also recorded by other musicians. He can occasionally sound glib and superficial as a soloist, but he has a commanding presence at the keyboard. [BP]

Denny Zeitlin-Charlie Haden

Time Remembers One Time Once (1981; ECM). An interesting choice of standards (including "As Long As There's Music", which Haden also recorded with Hampton Hawes) and originals such as Haden's lovely "Ellen David". Zeitlin's harmonic and melodic freshness comes across well in this exposed setting.

James Zollar

Trumpet.

b. Kansas City, Missouri, 24 July 1959.

Zollar's sister is a dancer/choreographer leading her own group, and his brother is a songwriter, while his mother's collection of jazz records was significant in his development. James started on bugle at the age of ten, soon changing to trumpet, and later studied music for five years in San Diego (at City College and UCSD). After moving to New York in 1984 he took lessons from Woody Shaw, recorded with Bob Stewart and, in the early 1990s, began regular work with David Murray's big band and Mercer Ellington. He also appeared with Mongo Santamaria, Hilton Ruiz and Don Byron, and in 1996 was part of the all-star on-screen band in the film *Kansas City*. His favourites on trumpet are Armstrong, Cootie Williams, Thad Jones and Dizzy Reece as well as Gillespie, Davis, Brown and Hubbard, while other inspirations include Frank Foster, Frank Rosolino, George Benson and Billy Harper. [BP]

Soaring With Bird (1997; Naxos). This is a surprisingly varied tribute, partly because the basic quartet (with Bill Cunliffe on piano) is joined on most tracks by either Pete Christlieb (tenor), Ron Eschete (guitar) or Andy Martin (trombone). Even Zollar's most boppish solos avoid the obvious, while "Parker's Mood" is delivered in Ellingtonian plunger-mute style.

➤➤ **Cecil McBee** *(Unspoken)*.

Attila Zoller

Guitar, bass trumpet.

b. Visegrád, Hungary, 13 June 1927; d. 25 Jan 1998.

Zoller's father, a conductor and music teacher, gave him violin lessons at the age of four, and he took up the trumpet at nine, playing in his school symphony orchestra. After World War II he began to play guitar with jazz groups in Budapest. From 1948–54 he worked in Vienna, and from 1954–9 in Germany, working with Jutta Hipp and Hans Koller, accompanying Bud Shank, Bob Cooper and Tony Scott, and touring with Oscar Pettiford and Kenny Clarke. In the summer of 1959 he studied at the Lenox School of Jazz, Massachusetts. From 1962–5 he worked with Herbie Mann, and then co-led a quartet with pianist Don Friedman. In 1966 he worked with Red Norvo, and in 1967 he was with Benny Goodman and leading his own group. From 1960 into the 1980s he toured Europe extensively every year. He toured Japan with Astrud Gilberto in 1970, and in 1971 he was again in Japan with Jim Hall and Kenny Burrell, as part of the guitar festival. He has also appeared at all the major European festivals, and has been active in jazz education. J.E. Berendt has written: "Zoller is a master of sensitive, romantic restraint, and it is hard to understand why a man of such talent is still known only to insiders." [IC]

Attila Zoller, Hans Koller and Martial Solal

Zo-Ko-So (1965; MPS). This album has absorbing solo performances by all three men, and duos mainly with Zoller accompanying Koller, but the contrapuntal lines he and Solal improvise on "Stella By Starlight" recall the dynamic 1962 duos of Jim Hall and Bill Evans.

Attila Zoller and Wolfgang Lackerschmid

Live Highlights '92 (1991–2; Bhakti). Zoller and vibraphonist Lackerschmid create lovely combinations of timbre, contrapuntal melodic lines and rhythm.

John Zorn

Alto saxophone, clarinet, game calls.
b. New York, 2 Sept 1953.

Reed explorer, eclecticist and cut-up composer John Zorn learned piano as a child, switching to guitar and flute at age ten. Lapping up contemporary classical music on his own, at a precociously young age, he began composing at fourteen, and later, influenced by John Cage, he introduced elements of improvisation into his scores; very early work of his is documented on *First Recordings 1973* (1995; Tzadik). While in college in St Louis, he was introduced to free jazz and creative music, and was especially impressed by Anthony Braxton's solo sax record *For Alto* (1967; Delmark). While in school, he began studying the cartoon music of Carl Stalling and Scott Bradley. After dropping out, he met various American free-improvisers, including guitarists Eugene Chadbourne and Fred Frith, cellist Tom Cora (at that time, Corra), and synthesizer player Bob Ostertag. After settling in New York, Zorn worked extensively with improvisers and the "No Wave" rock bands, whilst both composing and playing free music. His arsenal of instruments included disassembled saxophones and clarinets as well as duck and bird calls, which he sometimes played into buckets of water, and his compositional methods often involved game-like rules that mediated the roles of various musicians. "Cobra" is the most long-lived of Zorn's game-pieces, performed consistently and recorded several times (with and without Zorn) since 1986 – hear *Cobra: Tokyo Operations '94* (1995; Avant) or *Live At The Knitting Factory* (1995; Knitting Factory Works). Records of this period's output – which Zorn has been steadily reissuing – include 1981's *Archery* (available on the seven-disc box set *The Parachute Years*, Tzadik, 1997), two incredible solo LPs called *The Classic Guide To Strategy* (Tzadik, 1996), and a duet with shamisen player Michihiro Sato, *Ganryu Island* (1998; Tzadik). In 1985, Zorn recorded a pastiche-based piece called *Godard* for the French Nato label, and he continued to make cut-up works for the following decade, landing an important deal with Elektra/Nonesuch. This allowed him to release records such as *The Big Gundown* (19845) and *Spillane* (1987) and to start the band Naked City, his free thrash rock band. He has been an active soundtrack composer, with works compiled on a series of *Filmworks* discs on his Tzadik label. Zorn simultaneously developed a number of tribute groups playing the music of Ornette Coleman (merged with thrash punk), Sonny Clark, and great funk jazzers like Hank Mobley, Lee Morgan and Big John Patton (don't miss the two discs with guitarist Bill Frisell and trombonist George Lewis, *News For Lulu* and *More News For Lulu* on hat Art).

Jak Kilby

John Zorn

Never at a loss for projects, he has been involved in Japanese noise bands, played in rock-oriented projects like Painkiller with regular sparring partner Bill Laswell, produced innumerable records for his own labels, Avant and Tzadik, continued to play freely improvised music, composed chamber and orchestral music, and has promoted his liberal ideal of Radical Jewish Culture. Always interested in the collision of things held separate, Zorn's Masada group merges Yiddish music and Ornette Coleman's 1960s quartet. This polymorphous ensemble – extra members gather for the Masada Chamber Ensemble, documented on *Bar Kokhba* (1996; Tzadik) – now has a recorded output truly epic in scope. Indeed, Zorn's prolificacy and multifarious practice have rendered him near-impossible to keep up with, and his various bands and projects now overspill any of the musical categorizations he imposes on them with a bewildering regularity – there simply aren't enough record labels for this man. [JC]

Masada

⊙ **Gimel** (1994; DIW). Zorn's flagship new Judaica outfit, with risen star Dave Douglas on trumpet, Greg Cohen on bass and ever-grooving Joey Baron on drums. The leader's composed hundreds of tunes for this group, which has the fluidity and relaxation of a great 60s free-bop band. For those interested in his more eclectic or extreme work, look elsewhere (say his brutal lament *Kristallnacht* recorded in 1992), but this (or any of the other Masada discs) is a perfect place to hear why Zorn is still one of the most significant alto players in jazz.

Glenn Zottola

Trumpet, alto saxophone.

b. Port Chester, New York, 28 April 1947.

The son of a famous American brass-mouthpiece manufacturer and brother of trumpeter Bob Zottola, Glenn Zottola took up the trumpet at the age of three and played throughout his teens before joining Lionel Hampton in 1970. After that he worked with a range of bands and singers, including Mel Tormé, Tony Martin and Patti Page, then joined Tex Beneke and toured with Benny Goodman's sextet. In the 1980s his all-round skills as a trumpeter took him into pitwork for Broadway shows, touring with Bob Wilber's Bechet Legacy, and hotel dates, leading bands most notably at the Rainbow Room and Hyatt Regency in New York. In 1988 he featured as soloist in Wilber's re-creation of Goodman's 1938 Carnegie Hall concert, and in 1991 toured Europe with Peanuts Hucko. Zottola plays trumpet in a warm and commanding style which takes in influences from Armstrong to Harry James and beyond; his alto-playing is a fluent amalgam of Benny Carter and Charlie Parker. [DF]

➤➤ **Bob Wilber** *(On The Road).*

Bob Zurke

Piano, composer.

b. Detroit, Michigan, 17 Jan 1912; d. 16 Feb 1944.

Bob Zurke (Boguslaw Albert Zukowski) achieved international fame after he joined Bob Crosby's orchestra, replacing Joe Sullivan in 1936. For three years he was central to Crosby's orchestra at the peak of its career, recording such classics as "Old Spinning Wheel", "Gin Mill Blues", "At The Jazz Band Ball", "Big Foot Jump" and "Honky Tonk Train Blues" (his most famous feature). Zurke was a highly trained musician – he had played for Paderewski at the age of ten and, according to Bob Haggart, "could read like a snake" – but a portrait in John Chilton's history of Crosby's orchestra reveals him as a less than prepossessing man: overweight, a heavy drinker and a practised borrower of money. He was probably far from an ideal bandleader too, which might explain why, from 1939, his own big band foundered in just 21 months. Zurke returned to solo piano work: his last date was at San Francisco's Hangover Club, where he collapsed and died soon after. [DF]

Bob Crosby

⊙ **The Big Noise Vol. 7** (1938; Halcyon). Zurke plays on all but one track here, and is featured on his version of "Honky Tonk Train Blues".

Mike Zwerin

Trombone, bass trumpet, author.

b. New York, 18 May 1930.

Zwerin studied the violin in 1936, and later attended the New York High School of Music and Art. In 1948 he played trombone with Miles Davis's nine-piece Birth of the Cool band during its residency at the Royal Roost. Zwerin then spent several years in Paris, returning to the USA in 1958. He worked with Claude Thornhill, Maynard Ferguson and Bill Russo, and from 1962–5 he played with Orchestra USA and was musical director and arranger for a sextet drawn from the orchestra. He also played with small groups around New York. In 1966 he toured the USSR with Earl Hines. He was also very active as a journalist in the 1960s, writing for the *Village Voice*, *Rolling Stone* and *Down Beat*. From 1960 Zwerin was also involved with the family steel business, Capitol Steel Corporation, and in 1969 gave up regular playing and moved to the South of France to write novels and non-fiction works. In the late 1970s he moved to Paris where he still lives, working as a journalist and author – his most recent book being *Swing Under The Nazis* (2000; Cooper Square Press) – and occasionally playing trombone. In 1988 he toured and recorded with Big Band Charlie Mingus, but his main occupation remains literary. "No other writer has a better understanding of jazz music and its place in international waters," said Peter Erskine. "He is fresh, he is literate, he is a player, he is informed and he is trusted by the musical community." [IC]

Axel Zwingenberger

Piano.

b. Hamburg, Germany, 7 May 1955.

A trained classical pianist, Zwingenberger took up boogie-woogie in 1973 and quickly forged a high reputation in Germany with club appearances, concerts and a successful album. By the early 1980s he had begun appearing internationally as a soloist, going on to work with Sippie Wallace, Joe Newman, Joe Turner and a variety of other American stars, several of whom have recorded for his own label, Vagabond. Zwingenberger's achievement is to have revitalized a well-played corner of jazz piano music. [DF]

⊙ **Axel Zwingenberger And The Friends Of Boogie Woogie: Vol. 6** (1982–3; Vagabond). Among Zwingenberger's most interesting activities are his collaborations with older blues masters – here he plays with "Big" Joe Turner plus Joe Newman (Turner's old recording colleague from *The Boss Of The Blues*) on trumpet.

➤➤ **Sippie Wallace** *(Sippie Wallace And The Friends Of Boogie Woogie).*

Glossary

A & R (Artists & Repertoire)
An A & R person is the talent scout for a recording company. He or she discovers and signs up artists, and also monitors the kind of material they record. [IC]

AACM
AACM is the acronym for the Association for the Advancement of Creative Musicians, founded in 1965 under the presidency of Muhal Richard Abrams. For more, see the entry on Abrams.

Abstraction
See "Free jazz".

A cappella
"A cappella" (or "acappella") is a term borrowed from European church music, and is used to describe unaccompanied gospel singing and unaccompanied R&B vocal groups. Sometimes applied by extension to instrumental work which is completely solo. [BP]

Acid jazz
The phrase "acid jazz" was the first jazz term to be coined by a disc jockey rather than by a musician. It is much more a marketing phenomenon than a coherent musical style, even more so than "trad" – and as with trad, acid jazz is very much the commercialization of a revival movement. Just like earlier revivals, it was inspired initially by listening to records rather than to live musicians. In this case the original style is that of late 1960s' and early 1970s' jazz-funk, the sort of music that wasn't heavy enough to be free jazz or early fusion but was more jazz-oriented than the average soul record. At the time, this found a ready response among black listeners and a few white aficionados, and then, after the usual twenty-year gap, a new generation of aficionados succeeded in promoting the music to a much wider crossover audience. Most of the creative musicians who have flirted with the acid-jazz market have found it too restricting and have moved on, exactly as with other revivals, and they have taken some of their listeners with them. [BP]

Africa
In one sense, Africa is the source of all jazz, since the early creators and most of the subsequent innovators were descended from people forcibly removed from Africa, mainly by British slave traders. Such research as there has been (and that is not much) does appear to corroborate the notion that the rhythmic complexity implicit in all jazz (and explicit in Afro-Caribbean and Afro-Latin musics) is the same complexity as is found in various African traditional styles.

The idea of African heritage has inspired jazz performers differently at different periods. In the 1920s Duke Ellington was taking the tourist-attraction exotica of the Cotton Club shows and using it as inspiration for genuine musical advances. The 1940s saw Dizzy Gillespie (consciously) and Charlie Parker (intuitively) effecting a musical rapprochement with actual Afro-Caribbean styles, while in the 1960s, at the height of the US civil rights movement, there was conscious musical and spiritual identification with Africa on the part of North American musicians, with Duke Ellington, Randy Weston, Archie Shepp and others even playing in Africa.

But jazz is not an African music. Indeed, it has never been popular there and, since independence, most African countries have evolved their own contemporary styles, borrowing freely from Western music and now feeding back into it. The main exception is in Southern Africa where urbanized workers were encouraged to listen to and imitate American popular music. As the apartheid regime became increasingly repressive, a local version of jazz came to express the feelings of the majority group and some white sympathizers. Ironically, none of this music was officially exported, so that the work of performers such as Dollar Brand (Abdullah Ibrahim), Hugh Masekela, Dudu Pukwana and Chris McGregor only became known as they emigrated to Europe and the USA. [BP]

Afro-Latin
The term "Afro-Latin" covers a huge variety of music, resulting from the combination of elements of African styles with the Spanish, Portuguese and even French cultures transplanted to South and Central America. The blend was achieved earlier and more thoroughly than any such hybrid in North American music before the 1970s – indeed, watered-down South American music was being successfully exported to the USA (and Europe) from the time of the tango in the 1910s.

However, there were of course hints of African polyrhythms in ragtime and early New Orleans jazz, not to mention occasional borrowings from South American rhythms such as the habanera. So it was only to be expected that, by the 1930s, jazzmen including Duke Ellington were becoming interested in new Latin imports like the rumba, and that bands from those countries who settled in the USA began incorporating jazz-influenced improvisation. In this way, the stage was set for the first real collaborations, joining the innovators of bebop such as Dizzy Gillespie and Charlie Parker with the innovators of the mambo such as Machito.

For a while, progress in this direction was sporadic, but since the early 1960s, with the introduction of the bugalu (and its soft-core contemporary, the bossa nova), there has been a continuous interchange in the USA between jazz and Afro-Latin musicians. As with any fusion, the lowest common denominator often seems to predominate, but it's increasingly the case that the creative performers who have emerged on each side have real knowledge of both fields. What may be even more significant in the long run is that in the last three decades, especially in Paris and London, musicians from Africa have been collaborating with players of a jazz/Afro-Latin background, and the latest fusions from various African countries have achieved some success in the USA.

Africa and Latin America are vast areas, and both still produce distinct regional styles in the way that North America used to before it became so homogenized. Possibilities for interaction are therefore endless, and it has even been suggested that Latin-jazz will eventually become the mainstream. John Storm Roberts's book *The Latin Tinge* gives some idea of the ground covered so far. [BP]

Airshot (or aircheck)

An airshot is a recording taken from a live music broadcast. Extremely significant in the radio industry of the 1930s and 1940s, and of great importance to the bands who benefited from the exposure, these broadcasts were initially taken down by individual listeners (as compared to transcription recordings, performed by the musicians specifically for radio use). Later they came to be exchanged between collectors and, from the 1960s onwards, provided a valuable source of vintage material for albums, though usually without remuneration to those who took part. Without them, most of us would never have heard Ellington playing for dancers or Parker at Birdland. [BP]

Arrangement

The word "arrangement" covers a multitude of musical operations. A new arrangement may amount to a slight redistribution of instruments (as on one of Ellington's many reorchestrations of "Mood Indigo"), or to the conversion of a simple popular melody into the basis of an elaborate composition (such as Duke's arrangement of "Sidewalks Of New York"), or to the alteration of the rhythmic pattern – as in the several greatly different versions of Gillespie's "Night In Tunisia". Naturally, there is a considerable overlap between arrangement and composition in jazz, the question of quality in both areas often being determined by whether or not the result stimulates high-grade improvisation. [BP]

Atonality

Atonality – the absence of a key signature or tonal centre – has been attempted in some composed jazz but rarely with success. The only unforced development of atonality in jazz has taken place in some instances of "free jazz", especially the collective improvisations of large groups, but even then such structural signposts as occur spontaneously often consist of hints at a common tonality. Certainly, in smaller "free" groups, greater rhythmic freedom and freedom from predetermined structures have been sought, but atonality is not high on the agenda. Composers who have striven to achieve atonal jazz even complain that Ornette Coleman is not "advanced" enough in this respect but, of course, he has been far more influential than the atonalists. [BP]

Australian jazz

Australian jazz first made an impact abroad in post-war Britain, notably through the collaborations of British trumpeter Humphrey Lyttelton with Australian pianist Graeme Bell, and the almost disturbingly original contributions of such Bell sidemen as Ade Monsbourgh. Later Australians to make a mark in Europe included singer Judith Durham and saxophonist Bob Bertles (from Ian Carr's Nucleus), but such musicians represent only the tip of a flourishing scene. Top-rated performers include Bob Barnard (a trumpeter who plays in the Hackett-Braff area but regularly works studios as a lead player too), his brother Len Barnard (a drummer of comparable ability), Don Burrows (reeds and flute, who leads his own quartet) and Errol Buddle (a saxophonic equivalent to Britain's Tubby Hayes), as well as leader/arrangers John Sangster and Dave Dallwitz. Other Australian originals include Alan Nash, Eric Holroyd, Roger Bell (trumpets), Ken Herron, Bob McIvor, John Costelloe (trombones), John McCarthy, Graeme Lyall, Tony Buchanan, Paul Furniss (reeds), Col Nolan, Tony Gould, Chris Taperell (piano), and Tom Baker, an ex-trumpeter who, within a matter of months, turned into a saxophonist of scary ability.

Perhaps the most famous centre of activity for Australian jazz is the Sydney Jazz Club (opened in 1953), which published its own magazine, *The Quarterly Rag*, from 1955–70, and still flourishes. A host of other clubs ran in its shadow, and equivalent jazz centres may be found in Perth, Melbourne, Brisbane and elsewhere. One of the most enjoyable Australian jazz institutions is the annual convention, a huge meeting of Australian (and sometimes international) musicians which chooses a new location every year and confines itself primarily to the classic end of jazz. But modern jazz flourishes in Australia too, notably the rock-based jazz band, Galapagos Duck, which achieved huge success in the early 1980s.

Since then, two Australian artists have moved into the international spotlight: singer/trumpeter Vince Jones, whose considerable talents as a performer and songwriter are displayed on solo albums such as *Trustworthy Little Sweethearts* (1991; Intuition), and multi-instrumentalist James Morrison, who specializes on trumpet and trombone but plays almost all instruments with comparable ability. [DF]

Avant-garde
See "Free jazz".

Axe
A now outdated term for a musical instrument, used especially for brass or horns which performers can carry in one hand. Presumably dating from the era of "cutting contests", when you used your axe to mow down the opposition. [BP]

Ballad
A ballad is a slowish popular song, or an original jazz composition in that style or at least that tempo. As instrumental virtuosity has increased and with it the range of tempos used, "ballad tempo" has become slower and slower. When Louis Armstrong recorded the first jazz version of "Body And Soul" in 1930, it moved along at 120 beats per minute, but when Freddie Hubbard did the millionth version of the same tune in 1981 the acceptable tempo had dropped to 48 bpm. A slow ballad and a slow blues played at exactly the same tempo will not feel the same, the blues having more pent-up power and the ballad having a more relaxed lyricism. [BP]

Beat
1. In European terminology, beats are individual pulses within a bar; the time signature 4/4 indicates 4 beats, each a 1/4-note in value. These beats can be either a "down-beat" or an "up-beat" (see "Down" and "Up").

2. "The beat", however, also describes the quality of the overall flow of a performance. The phrase "So long as it's got the beat" (or "a beat") gives the over-simplified impression that the main pulse is the chief thing to listen for. But, in all African-American music influenced by jazz, the time-signature is only the basis for a continuous interplay of counter-rhythms. It is in this sense that "the beat" is usually understood. [BP]

Bebop (or bop)
1. Bebop was the classic style which came to fruition in New York in the early 1940s, masterminded by Dizzy Gillespie and Kenny Clarke and brought to life by Charlie Parker. Its emergence was the result of much open-ended jamming (at after-hours clubs such as Minton's and Monroe's) and some theoretical discussion with like-minded souls including Thelonious Monk, Tadd Dameron and Mary Lou Williams. Its arrival was somewhat masked by the wartime popularity of increasingly formularized big-band swing, but, on the other hand, the 1942–3 musicians' union strike against recordings (often cited as a delaying factor) actually encouraged the formation of small specialist labels which, from 1944, put bebop on record at an earlier stage of development than most previous jazz styles.

Although the new style created consternation and hostility among many established musicians, it was a direct outgrowth of later 1930s jazz. Contributory factors included the harmonic elaboration of Coleman Hawkins, Art Tatum and Duke Ellington, the melodic freedom of such contrasting players as Lester Young and Roy Eldridge, and the airtight looseness of the Basie band rhythm-section with Jo Jones. The work of more truly transitional figures such as Charlie Christian, Jimmy Blanton and the John Kirby sextet (especially Charlie Shavers and Billy Kyle) needs to be set beside the increasing importance of USA-based Afro-Latin bands, for a full appreciation of mature bebop's expansion of jazz vocabulary. And, although bebop's chordal extensions and the angular lines caused the strongest reaction at the time, it has become clear in retrospect that bebop's greater feel for polyrhythms was the most lasting contribution of its exponents.

Bebop was the first kind of jazz whose performers were, to some extent, artistic elitists – but this has to be seen in context with the short-lived social gains of black Americans during World War II, as a musical attempt to establish greater respect for black contributions to US society. Initially the attempt seemed doomed to total failure, and yet not only has every subsequent jazz style been indelibly marked by bebop, but the combined influence of these jazz styles on more popular music of the last twenty years has been enormous.

2. Inevitably, but somewhat confusingly, "bebop" has also been associated with various styles of dancing. There is no particular connection with any one kind of jazz, or indeed of rock, for "bopping" used in this sense tends to drift in and out of fashion. [BP]

B flat
On the main brass instruments, trumpet and trombone, B flat is the home key: in other words, the key in which the most important notes of the major scale can be produced without use of the valves or slide, and where a minimum use of these produces the remainder of the scale. Thus, brass players usually learn to play in this key first, and then in F, which is almost as easy, and many of them go through life feeling that even a complex music such as jazz is somehow less demanding in these two keys.

Although the mechanics are different, B flat is also the home key on tenor and soprano saxophone and on clarinet, while on alto and baritone saxophone B flat is in the same relationship to their home key as F is for trumpet and trombone.

The crucial role of these instruments in early jazz, and their general dominance in later periods, explains the huge number of blues in B flat (some of them even called that, for want of any more inspired title) and the equally huge number of "I Got Rhythm" variants in the same key (see "Rhythm"). Hence also the expression, "Not your standard B-flat gig/person etc." [BP]

Big band
One of the most popular formats for the propagation of jazz, the big band now stands somewhat apart from

the majority of small-group performances. But it was not always so: the earliest big bands, such as those of Fletcher Henderson and Duke Ellington, were only slightly larger than King Oliver's eight-piece Creole Jazz Band. The discovery that reed instruments in particular sounded more impressive playing in pre-arranged harmony led the 3 saxophones/3 brass (plus 4 rhythm) line-up of mid-1920s Henderson and Ellington to become 4 saxophones/6 brass by the late 1930s. In the bands of the swing era improvised solos tended to be seen as enhancing the ensemble, rather than the reverse (which was also true, at least at the time). As the size of big bands increased still further (to 5 saxophones/8–10 brass by the mid-1940s) they lagged behind the stylistic developments in small-group jazz, which they often helped to popularize subsequently.

The occasional "large small-groups" such as Count Basie's in the mid-1930s or Lionel Hampton's in the 1940s, whose comparative simplicity and excitement seemed to arise from the sheer joy of playing together, only emphasized the norm of big bands as vehicles principally either for one leading soloist or for an arranger or composer. Either way, the possible delights are so inviting that, despite the daunting economics of getting twenty or so musicians to work together, the big-band idea seems destined never to die. [BP]

Blue Note Records

Given the huge number of specialist jazz record labels, it is perhaps surprising how few have been sufficiently long-lived or single-minded to have become a definition of the music they purvey. Blue Note, founded in 1939, is one of the exceptions and, although there are alternative descriptions of the style concerned, the phrase "Blue Note jazz" immediately conjures up a specific sound.

The company recorded boogie, small-group swing and bebop for several years before becoming, in the early 1950s, the contractual home of many of the most important post-boppers such as Horace Silver and Art Blakey. As these musicians and the company's owners (Alfred Lion and Francis Wolff) actively sought out younger performers in the same mould, they played a large part in helping to develop what was then becoming known as "hard bop". But the combination of hard-boppers with the "soul jazz" of organist Jimmy Smith and his followers was also a part of the Blue Note sound from around 1956 to 1966.

In the mid-1960s a somewhat different style, associated with Miles Davis alumni such as Jackie McLean, Herbie Hancock and Wayne Shorter, was also described as the Blue Note "school", to distinguish their kind of modal-based "free jazz" from the more thorough going changes wrought by the simultaneous work of Albert Ayler and others. But though this music is still very influential its identification with Blue Note Records was short-lived compared to the earlier style. Their renewed recording activity from 1985 onwards (after a hiatus of several years) has not so far produced a new definition of Blue Note jazz. [BP]

Blue notes

Blue notes are usually defined as the flattened third and flattened seventh of the scale in any particular key. (The flattened fifth is also heard as a blue note when used as a melodic replacement or variation of the normal fifth, but not when it is a harmonic colouring in dense chordal textures.)

It is the melodic context which highlights the impact of these notes, and historically they are not so much an exact note as audibly bent or slurred; if played on an instrument rather than sung, they are usually underlined by a squeezed, growled or otherwise vocalized tone. Their use not only predated the appearance of "blues" music as such, but also occurs in gospel, soul and rock, as well as in jazz of all periods, whether in the 12-bar blues format or not. While they stand out clearly against the major chords typical of most vocal blues and jazz-blues, they are not dependent on the major; the later development of minor-key blues sequences in no way lessens their use or their effectiveness.

For this reason, it is misleading to talk of *the* "blues scale". In a major-key blues, the blue notes exist alongside and in addition to the notes of the major scale, whereas in a minor blues they duplicate some of the notes already included in the minor scale. The mathematically minded will observe that the former situation gives a 10-note scale (9 or 8, if not all the blue notes are used), while the latter could be a 7-note scale or less, since a scale with 6 notes or only 5 (such as the pentatonic minor) can equally sound like a blues scale.

At the other end of the spectrum, in more contemporary chromatic jazz any one of the twelve divisions of a scale can be made to appear in context as a blue note, given the necessary prominence and vocalized articulation. [BP]

Blues

1. Blues is a traditional African-American music which first coalesced in the early 1900s and continues to develop. Originally a predominantly vocal expression accompanied, if at all, by the singer's guitar or piano (its immediate predecessors were totally unaccompanied vocals), it has gradually admitted more and more instrumental work over the decades. Nevertheless, a blues band's instrumental-only numbers are merely a prelude or an interlude to the vocals, a situation that is reversed in most jazz performances.

Although the development of blues has been parallel to, rather than closely interlinked with, that of jazz, they have frequently interacted. For instance, when the blues groups of the 1930s added the occasional trumpet and saxophone solos, the influence of Kansas City jazz led to the formation of "rhythm and blues". Conversely, most significant changes in jazz have been accompanied by a new influx of blues influence: Louis Armstrong's innovations and those of Charlie Parker and Ornette Coleman would have meant less if they had not also instinctively incorporated elements of blues style in their playing.

In this sense, blues is a feeling, but not merely one narrow emotional area. Blues phraseology, either vocal or instrumental, being more honest and realistic than more popular music, expresses ambiguous emotions, as implied by titles such as "Laughing To Keep From Crying" (Lester Young). It is the combination of openness and ambiguity which is the unique quality of the blues and the reason for its worldwide influence.

2. A blues, on the other hand, is not a particular tune but a specific chorus structure of 12 bars continually repeated, which was borrowed initially from folk blues. It was, in fact, the input of early jazz instrumentalists that was responsible for its length becoming fixed at 12 bars.

Because of its short repetitive form (and also because of the emotional climate associated with vocal blues), it has always been regarded as a test of the jazz improviser's creativity and/or authenticity. The form has been so pervasive, however, that already by the 1930s it had moved beyond any necessary connection with the traditional style and become a form adaptable to harmonic improvisations just like any other. A comparison of two pieces such as "Chasin' The Trane" and "Tunji", both by John Coltrane, shows the range of response available to one player within the blues form. For this reason, any example of an instrumental blues is often referred to by jazz musicians as "a 12-bar" rather than "a blues".

A couple of standard sequences have sometimes been referred to, mainly by traditional jazz players, as a 16-bar blues (the sequence of "How Come You Do Me?" or "Doxy") or a 32-bar blues, simply because they were used so frequently at one period, but otherwise they have nothing in common with a blues. There is, however, such a thing as a 24-bar blues, which occurs when the tempo is doubled but the rate of the chord changes is not: Coltrane's "Tunji" is an example of this.

When someone talks about *the* blues, either of the above meanings could apply, according to the context. Jazz musicians saying "Let's play the blues" do not mean, "Let's play some traditional folk music", but rather, "Let's play a 12-bar". (Although, of course, if they actually say "the blues", it may come out more bluesy than if they had said "a 12-bar".) Incidentally, tune titles can be misleading. Especially in the 1920s, when blues were first acknowledged by the music industry, the word was used by numerous items which were blues in neither of the above senses. [BP]

Boogie-woogie (or boogie)

Boogie-woogie was originally a jazz-related solo piano form, featuring round and round bass (often eight-to-the-bar) in the left hand, punctuated by rhythmic, often repetitive, right-hand figures. Repeated bass was a frequent device of early ragtime professors who sometimes called it "the sixteens"; early ragtime compositions like Joplin's "Solace Rag" feature a repeated bass, and (says Clarence Williams) music like boogie-woogie was played around the turn of the century in the lumber and railroad camps of the American Midwest. By the 1920s boogie-woogie had become formalized due in part to the efforts of Albert Ammons and Meade "Lux" Lewis, and in 1928 the first important boogie records were issued – Lewis's "Honky-Tonk Train Blues" and Pine Top Smith's "Pinetop's Boogie-Woogie".

But it was not until ten years later, after a 1938 Carnegie Hall concert which teamed Ammons, Lewis and Pete Johnson, that the international craze for eight-to-the-bar began. Over the next fifteen years boogie became a commercial hit: artists from the Andrews Sisters ("Boogie-Woogie Bugle Boy") to Will Bradley ("Down The Road Apiece") re-created the music with everything from a solo piano to a big band. Most important though, boogie was to supply several fundamental elements to rock'n'roll. The use of a straight-quaver rhythm feel (as, for example, Albert Ammons used it) replaced the concept of "jazz-swing" with a kind of shuffling rock rhythm later "introduced" by rock artists like Frankie Ford and Huey Smith, one of whose first hits was "Rockin' Pneumonia And Boogie-Woogie Flu". By then artists such as Louis Jordan and Lips Page had naturally identified with boogie, and they had been using its devices for ten years before "Rock Around The Clock" was even thought of. Boogie remained popular for twenty years more: Humphrey Lyttelton's "Bad Penny Blues", a hit in 1956, and "Lady Madonna", a hit for the Beatles in 1967, showed how the form survived unaltered; and the rock and roll revival of the 1970s preserved it securely once again.

"Boogie-woogie" was simultaneously (or perhaps first) applied to various forms of dancing. As with the word "bebop" in this connection, it covers virtually any style that moves the whole body and not just the feet. [DF]

Bop

See "Bebop".

Bossa nova

Bossa nova is a style of Brazilian popular song that was most successful in the early 1960s. Strangely cool by comparison with other exportable Afro-Latin rhythms, and distantly influenced by the harmonic language of US West Coast jazz, it soon acquired a permanent place in international middle-of-the-road music. It has also repaid its debt to the West Coast by entering the repertoire of all easy-listening jazz players everywhere. [BP]

Brass

Most generations of jazz musicians have followed the European terminology in using the word "brass" to describe only trumpets, trombones, tubas, etc, excluding the saxophone family, despite their construction. To most rock or post-rock musicians, however, "brass" covers virtually everything that is not a stringed or rhythm instrument. Therefore the phrase "brass section" has different connotations, according to who uses it. [BP]

Breaks

Breaks are an essential ingredient of good jazz, according to Jelly Roll Morton, and, although he exaggerated, it is perhaps a pity they are not used more. A break consists of the rhythm-section marking the first beat of a bar and then remaining silent for the rest of the bar (or longer), while the soloist fills the space alone. Equally, the "break" describes what the soloist plays during the gap, which acquires an inevitable charge of tension which is then resolved as the rhythm-section piles in again. Instances abound in early jazz, while the four-bar break following the interlude of "Night In Tunisia" is the most famous later example.

The idea more or less died out with the democratization of "free jazz", but surfaced again in the 1974–5 Miles Davis bands, on albums such as *Agartha*, where Davis would stop the rhythm-section briefly during someone else's solo. This was done on a totally random basis, unlike the obviously programmed breaks in earlier jazz, where the anticipation of the break by both soloist and audience is part of the fun. [BP]

Changes

The only changes described by that word alone are harmonic ones (tempo changes would have to be spelled out with both words). But "the changes" means specifically the exact series of chords which makes up the required sequence for a particular piece. Whereas rhythm-section instrumentalists have to "play the changes", the frontline soloists may feel free to ignore them to a certain extent, although they at least need to "know the changes" in order to ignore them. [BP]

Chase chorus

See "Fours".

Chicago

Chicago has at least three distinct musical connotations, even leaving aside the fact that most of what we regard as classic New Orleans jazz was actually recorded in Chicago, by musicians who moved there in the 1910s and 1920s. This, however, is not what is meant by "Chicago jazz", but rather the closely related style played by the first generation of white musicians to pick up on the New Orleans innovations. Often considered to be more solo-oriented and less relaxed rhythmically, the music of Jimmy McPartland and others (and of the later Eddie Condon groups) became sufficiently influential, even on the 1950s Armstrong All Stars, to have more adherents worldwide than the "authentic" New Orleans style.

Though seldom acknowledged, Chicago was also in the 1930s the home of a particular jump-band music (typified by the Harlem Hamfats) which combined jazz horns and drums with blues singer/guitarists. This style, influencing the output of even Big Bill Broonzy, led to the post-war outcropping of "Chicago blues" which, through the work of its guitarists and bassists, had a considerable impact on later rock and jazz-rock.

While it is true that Chicago had a thriving bebop scene, particularly strong in tenor players such as Gene Ammons, it is not known for a regional accent in bebop. In the free-jazz area, however, Chicago has made another celebrated contribution. Horn players who worked in blues bands also had an effect on "free jazz", as did the freedom and power of vocalists like Muddy Waters, and during the second half of the 1960s, Anthony Braxton, Muhal Richard Abrams and the members of the Art Ensemble were putting things together in a way that was not being done elsewhere. Now, however, the Chicago style is so widely imitated that it has become virtually the main thread of American free jazz. [BP]

Chorus

In jazz parlance, "a chorus" means once through the entire tune, whether this is 12 bars, 32 bars or longer. This use of the term dates from the days when every popular song was published with a verse (usually of a throwaway nature and usually omitted) followed by "the chorus". The word also became an abbreviation for solo chorus, as in "X's brilliant chorus on Y's otherwise boring version of 'Z'." As soon as this usage was established, it was applied to any length of solo, so that X's chorus might in fact last for several choruses. [BP]

Chromatic

Chromatic is the opposite of diatonic, in which only the notes of a specific major or minor scale are used. In diatonic music, therefore, the appearance of notes outside the starting scale entails modulation to another key, as in a song like "All The Things You Are", whereas chromatic chords allow the use of non-scale notes without changing key.

Chromatic chords (especially the diminished chord) were part of jazz as early as the 1920s. In fundamentally diatonic chord sequences, most of the passing chords in the original version and the substitute chords inserted by jazz musicians are liable to be chromatic. Their use, however, has been less than essential in jazz, although more fashionable at some periods than others, and late

1940s' examples such as Bud Powell's "Dance Of The Infidels" (or even John Coltrane's late 1950s pieces of the "Giant Steps" vintage) are far more complex chromatically than the average jazz material of the period.

What is important to note is the frequent independence of melodic improvisation from the underlying chords. As early as the 1920s Louis Armstrong implied passing chords which were not used by the rhythm-section at hand, whereas King Oliver would diatonically ignore a passing chord if he felt like it. Broadly speaking, Armstrong led to Hawkins, Parker and Coltrane, while Oliver inspired Lester Young, Ornette Coleman, etc, and neither school plays "on the chords" in the way we have been brought up to believe. In fact, both of these different tendencies are present in the free chromatic playing (and chromatic free playing) of more recent times, which is a forcible reminder that the root meaning of the word "chromatic" is not to do with rules but with colouring. [BP]

Circular breathing

Circular breathing is a technique used by some players of wind instruments, usually reed players, but also occasionally brass players. It consists of breathing in through the nose while the cheeks push air out through the instrument thus enabling the player to produce an unbroken column of air. This means that a note can be held indefinitely, because a player need not pause in order to breathe. The technique has only a limited artistic use, because most music needs "breathing" pauses in order to come fully alive. [IC]

Classic (or classical)

"Classic" often simply means "generally acknowledged as great", but the term is also applied retrospectively to specific styles. In some people's usage, "classic jazz" refers only to music of the 1920s, while to many others it covers all music not influenced by bebop and its aftermath. However, the broader term "black classical music" was coined in the 1960s to include everything from ragtime to the avant-garde, in order to distinguish this "serious" music from more popular forms of black music. The distinction may perhaps be tainted with the elitism attached to the classical music of other continents, but it may also be a necessary antidote to the stereotypes of the US music industry. [BP]

Commercial

Commercial is a state of mind, not a style of music. In the mouths of musicians, the word is usually negative (and in the mouths of jazz fans, always), for it seldom refers to the useful ability to understand a royalty statement or count the heads of a paying audience. On the contrary, it describes a person or music deliberately geared to maximizing royalties and audiences, and therefore usually requiring conscious exaggeration of characteristics thought to be successful. Popular fashion being what it is, many performers are more commercial at some periods than at others. But it is also worth pointing out that jazz (like most other music) is capable of operating on several levels at once, so that some music which is obviously commercial in intent can still be worth listening to for its own sake many decades later. [BP]

Commodore

The Commodore record label occupied a pioneering position in jazz history. It was founded by Milton "Milt" Gabler in 1935 and named after the Commodore Music Shop, a New York radio-cum-novelty store that Gabler's father had opened in 1926 and subsequently handed on to his son. The label set out to fill a gap in commercial recorded production by recording only hot small-band jazz rather than the commercial swing fare with which larger record companies were becoming preoccupied. Gabler's first recording session on 18 January 1938, featuring Eddie Condon's band, was in part a result of his knowledge that a small specialist public existed for such music: in 1935 he had begun to reissue a series of hot jazz classics under the logo "United Hot Clubs of America" from a huge purchase of 20,000 OKeh deletions which he had bought as a job lot from Columbia. By 1940 Gabler's dual operation (reissues and new recordings) had won him a huge reputation and in 1941 he was signed by Decca Records as a stock coordinator and A&R man. This enabled him to help major artists like Billie Holiday to record for Decca, but he kept his interest in the Commodore Music Shop, working there every evening and Saturdays, as well as enlarging his activities as a jazz promoter – from 1940 for five years he was the organizer for Jimmy Ryan's weekly jam sessions. Early classics on Commodore included sessions by Condon, Bud Freeman and numerous others, as well as masterpieces by Billie Holiday, including "Strange Fruit" from 1939 with Frankie Newton's band. By the 1950s Gabler's Commodore label had broadened its sights to include more contemporary performers (Frank Wess was one) and from the 1960s valuable earlier material recorded on the label was regularly the subject of reissue programmes: in the 1970s the Atlantic label launched a brief series, and in the 1980s there were more successful reissues on American Columbia and Germany's Teldec. [DF]

Composition

The term "composition" is used indiscriminately in jazz circles to cover anything from a complex original tune to a simple but memorable riff. There are also works which show more obvious compositional effort, some of symphonic length, but few of them worth the paper they are written on.

Very often the most effective jazz writers may appear to be merely rearranging familiar materials, and there is a sense in which the really successful jazz composition is one where the written matter and the improvised content blend into a seamless whole. Few composers have come within touching distance of this holy grail, except for Duke

Ellington, Charles Mingus, George Russell and one or two younger writer/performers. For this concept to work it seems to require the active presence of the writer directing the performers, and to have been created with specific collaborators in mind: the European definition of a composition as something put down on paper in order that anyone will be able to play it is turned on its head in jazz practice.

Historically, the few important figures in this category often appear (in retrospect) to have summarized what is best about the jazz of a certain period, and at the same time to have predicted certain subsequent developments.

How far they actually inspire the next round of improvised innovation is debatable, and certainly it seems that new developments in jazz have to be improvisational, not compositional, to achieve any widespread application. However, it can be argued that the thought processes of, say, Count Basie or Miles Davis make them significant composers, just as much as Ellington or Russell, even though the former organized their bands through their own playing and not on paper. They are at least more important than those would-be composers of various periods who have taken snapshots of what they like about jazz and pasted them together with European compositional techniques. [BP]

Contrapuntal

See "Counterpoint".

Cool

Cool describes the ability of certain jazz improvisers to sound more detached and less "hot" than their colleagues. This is partly a question of tone-colour, and the veiled enthusiasm of Bix Beiderbecke or Lester Young is a far cry from Armstrong's and Hawkins's extrovert declamations, even in their most reflective moments. With or without a particularly cool tone, however, the same impression can be created by drifting behind the beat, which not only sounds "laid-back" but is probably also the source of that expression. Because of its appropriateness to much 1950s jazz, "cool" then became a general term of approval, unrelated to music.

It is possible, though less easily achieved, for an entire ensemble to have this quality – as in the Gil Evans arrangements for the Miles Davis 1948 band, described (nearly 25 years after the arrival of Bix Beiderbecke) as "The Birth of the Cool" – but much of what followed in the West Coast movement almost caused the death of the cool. Nevertheless, the approach constantly resurfaces, for instance in the work of Wayne Shorter, and as in his case many of the most successful jazz performances present a subtle and continually shifting blend of both hot and cool elements. [BP]

Corny

A pretty corny word by now, though not totally lost from everyday conversation, the normal usage of "corny" was created by white jazzmen of the 1920s. Just as corn-fed chickens are supposed to be healthier and therefore better for those who consume them, so corn-fed music (later shortened to corny) was totally innocuous and devoid of the "unhealthy" associations of jazz. Of course, it was its supposed depravity that attracted most of the young white audience to the music in the first place, and the generation gap which was evident after World War I assured jazz of its status as something to shock the bourgeoisie. So, in the eyes of bright young things who danced to jazz and drank Prohibition booze, the older generation (or youngsters pure enough to remain above temptation) were corn-fed; but, to the few dedicated musicians who entered the emotional depths of jazz, it was the fans who were themselves corny. [BP]

Counterpoint

Sometimes referred to in connection with jazz, "counterpoint" means the interweaving of different musical lines. Another European musical term, "polyphonic", describes this kind of overall texture, while "contrapuntal" draws attention to the detail of the interweaving. Although present in many styles, including New Orleans and free jazz, melodic counterpoint is not essential to jazz. Rhythmic counterpoint is, on the other hand, and can be savoured in all jazz. [BP]

Cross-rhythm

See "Polyrhythm".

Cut

1. The verb "to cut" meant to make a recording, as in the pre-tape days when a disc was engraved at the same time as the musicians played. Apart from the brief renaissance of direct-cut recordings in the late 1970s, the terminology has been outdated for forty years, yet it survives in the language, often in conjunction with another archaic term in the phrase "We're cutting some sides" (which implies that each tune occupies one whole side of a disc, as when jazz was recorded for 78 rpm or 45 rpm singles).

2. In jazz circles the term also means "to demonstrate superiority over other players of the same instrument". So-called "cutting contests" developed spontaneously out of the more friendly jamming situation. Two legendary instances involved Coleman Hawkins, in December 1933 at the Cherry Blossom, Kansas City (which he lost), and in July 1939 at Puss Johnson's in Harlem (which he won). Sometimes, however, they were not so spontaneous. Both Roy Eldridge and Chu Berry in the mid-1930s, and Dizzy Gillespie and friends in the early 1940s, were known to go out after their paid gigs looking for bands to ambush with their superior musicianship. And, because the genuinely competitive nature of these encounters refined players' skills to a remarkable degree, the virtuosity of the best soloists of this period was cultivated to such an extent that it went over the heads of most of their potential audience. Producer Norman Granz, however, in his Jazz At The Philharmonic packages from the mid-1940s to the mid-1950s, managed to emphasize the excitement rather than the musicianship, and replaced the spontaneity with twice-nightly exhibition matches. [BP]

Dance bands

Although jazz and dancing were regularly linked until the flowering of rock and roll, dance bands occupy their own echelon in jazz history. From the 1920s such bands, organized to provide copybook replays of popular material at the correct tempo for dancers (not necessarily jazz fans), were a necessary part of America's and Europe's social scene. What they played was functional music with strong emphasis on a singable re-creation of the melody, and jazz – particularly early on – was often heard as an anti-social irrelevance. However, American bandleaders such as Paul Specht, Roger Wolfe Kahn and dozens of others (as well as such studio bands as Fred Rich's, the California Ramblers and the multifarious Denza Dance Bands) often staffed their orchestras with top-rank jazzmen such as Mannie Klein, Sylvester Ahola, Red Nichols, Jack Teagarden, Frank Signorelli and the Dorseys. Hunting down these great musicians' short solo contributions to otherwise mediocre records, as well as records of dance bands that reveal overall jazz feeling and arranging flair, has become a study in itself: in Europe the VJM label has regularly issued examples of the genre known collectively as "hot dance".

Up to World War II, the story in Europe – and particularly in Britain – was much the same. Jazz by and large remained a specialist music played by musicians who made their living working for dance bands, then let their hair down in the small hours playing clubs. Records of British bands of the period (Ambrose, Lew Stone, Ray Noble, Roy Fox and others), like their American counterparts, are often spiced with jazz solos and some are magnificent jazz in their own right. A dramatic and regrettable development in Britain post-war was the wholesale discarding of the pre-war musicians, who, in the wake of crusading revivalism (which condemned commercially based music of any kind) and bebop (which set store by modernism above all), found themselves prematurely consigned to retirement. A highly selective list of British talents who found their careers faltering as a result of jazz trends could include: trumpeters Nat Gonella, Max Goldberg, Norman Payne, Arthur Mouncey and Jack Jackson; saxophone and clarinet players Harry Hayes, Buddy Featherstonhaugh, Derek Neville, Freddy Gardner, Benny Winestone, Don Barrigo, Pat Smuts, Philip Buchel, Andy McDevitt and Joe Crossman; trombonists Lew Davis, Don Macaffer and Joe Ferrie; pianists Eddie Carroll, Harold Hood, Stanley Black and Jack Penn; bassists Dick Ball, Tommy Bromley and Dick Escott; and drummers Sid Heager, Max Bacon and Jock Jacobson. Many such pre-war stars changed their career direction from choice (Buchel became a choreographer, Jackson a broadcaster, Black an orchestral conductor of light music), but many others were consigned to pit-work or forced into alternative careers. The 1970s were to bring about a late reappraisal: American cornettist Dick Sudhalter corralled veterans such as Harry Gold, Pat Dodd, Tommy McQuater, George Elliot and Jock Cummings into his New Paul Whiteman Orchestra and wrote revealingly about the injustice of the two previous decades. In the 1980s late renewed interest was focused on such gifted veterans as Harry Gold, Nat Gonella and Tiny Winters, but British jazz fans certainly missed some good music in the interim. [DF]

Dance Music

Originally, nearly all jazz could function as dance music, and much of the inspiration of even the most creative performers derived from the simultaneous performance of social dancing. Bebop crystallized the move away from entertainment values (and danceable tempos) towards the idea of jazz as an art music, so that the new dance music became R&B, followed by funk, soul, disco, hip-hop and other more contemporary forms – many of which nevertheless owe a musical debt to jazz. [BP]

Dirty

In early jazz, "dirty" describes a style incorporating particular tonal effects which are the opposite of a so-called pure tone. A "hot" tone is not pure either, being especially bright and vibrant, but a dirty tone, on the other hand, includes growls and squeezed notes (and combinations of the two), liable to evoke a gut reaction from the listener, and are often used as a brief contrast to the player's normal style. The implication of earthiness, and the rural roots that go with it, compares interestingly with the later, more citified term "funky" in its musical connotations. [BP]

Dixieland

1. "Dixie's Land" – a song written by Dan Emmett in 1859 – immortalized the Manhattan Island estates of slave-trader Jonathan Dixie, who often sold his slaves to the South; later the song was taken up by the Confederates in the Civil War. Coincidentally "Dixie's line", drawn by two British astronomers Mason and Dixon, came to represent the dividing line between the northern American states, where slaves had been emancipated, and the southern ones that still practised slavery. Between them the two nicknames supplied another for America's South, which in turn passed into jazz lore. [DF]

2. More than most, Dixie is a musical term which has different shades of meaning according to who is using it. Basically, it denotes the standardized and internationalized version of Chicago-style jazz of the 1920s, with extrovert, even brash ensemble improvisations framing solo statements that are far more prevalent than in the New Orleans style typified by the King Oliver Creole Band or even by the contrarily named Original Dixieland Band. In American terminology, Dixieland is also a blanket description for anything descended from early New Orleans jazz and, in the mouths of Americans who earn their living playing it, it is not a disparaging term. It only becomes that when spoken by adherents of the revival of "genuine" New Orleans and by fans of the later generations of New Orleans-born players who benefited from the revival. The same ambiguities surround the use of the word "trad", which is the European term for European Dixieland. [BP]

Double tempo (or double time)

See "Tempo".

Down

1. A slow tempo. Possibly the expression is linked to the use of "down" or "lowdown" to indicate depression or degradation.

2. The down-beat is the first beat of a performance, or else the first beat of each bar (sometimes referred to as the "one"). There is a non-musical usage of this connotation too, as in the dated expression "a down cat", meaning a person sufficiently aware and reliable to know where "one" is. [BP]

Downtown

The term has become attached in the 1990s to the music emerging from various New York venues, especially the Knitting Factory at its original SoHo address and now in the equally downtown Tribeca area. A large contingent of young New York musicians, typified by John Zorn and Don Byron, play what's sometimes described as "post-modern" jazz, mingling a huge variety of influences such as 1960s free jazz, ethnic styles and soundtrack music from action films and cartoons, often switching from one to the other at a bewildering pace. A lack of preconceived ideas about the superiority of particular musics, or about the suitability of juxtaposing them, is a prerequisite for performers and listeners. [BP]

Dubbing

See "Overdubbing".

Electronics

Electricity was first used in jazz to amplify the sound of acoustic instruments through public address systems and, by means of electrical recording in the later 1920s, to reproduce acoustic music on 78 rpm discs. But the very acts of amplifying and recording also involve the electrical modification of acoustic sound, and the electronic treatment of acoustic instruments has grown steadily in sophistication since the 1920s. For example, the metal harmon mute made famous by Miles Davis is played acoustically, but it gains its full tonal expressiveness only when it is placed very close to a sensitive microphone and amplified. Without that electronic treatment the harmon has virtually no tonal interest or expressivity.

From the 1930s, with the invention of the electric guitar, followed by the electric bass and electric piano, instruments began to be amplified by the direct use of electrical power. The first all-electric instrument was the electric organ, which was a kind of primitive synthesizer, in that its sound was created electronically and then amplified. With electric instruments, players began to have more and more control over their own sound, and since the 1950s an enormous number of devices have been invented for the direct treatment of instrumental sound: fuzz boxes, wah-wah pedals, phasers, echoplexes, octave-dividers, etc. Since the 1960s synthesizers have developed from their first primitive manifestations into enormously sophisticated instruments. A recent introduction is the electronic wind instrument (EWI), which is blown like a saxophone and the naturally produced sound is treated to give a range of over nine octaves. With synthesizers a small group can have all the resources of a full orchestra at its disposal (the soundtrack to the film *Arachnophobia* was produced almost entirely on an EWI by Phil Todd), as well as a vast array of other sounds which the players can discover for themselves. Joe Zawinul has discovered many original ways of creating synthesized sounds, which he thinks of as "native instruments not yet discovered".

The conservatism of many jazz musicians made them attack and reject the use of electronics in music – just as, earlier in the century, the introduction of the saxophone into jazz groups had caused an outcry. But synthesizers are a resource to be used just like any other, and the quality of the music they produce depends entirely on the quality of the musician who uses them.

With the jazz-rock-fusion movement of the 1970s, electronics were established as a major ingredient and a massive tonal resource, and the often magnificent results can be heard in the music of Miles Davis, Weather Report, Herbie Hancock, Return to Forever, the Mahavishnu Orchestra and, using an EWI, Michael Brecker. [IC]

Energy (or high-energy) music

During the 1960s, with the rise of free improvisation, the word "energy" began to be used as a term of approbation: a performance with energy was "good", and a high-energy performance was "very good". This usage has carried on into the post-abstract period of jazz, even though inferior performances and inferior music may have a high energy level, while exquisite music has often been produced with little apparent expenditure of energy. [IC]

Europe

1. Continental Europe has always been vitally important to jazz – indeed, the first serious critical appraisals of jazz were made by Europeans. In 1919 the Swiss conductor Ernest Ansermet heard Sidney Bechet in London, recognized his genius immediately and wrote an ecstatic review in the Swiss *Revue Romande*. The first book on jazz was written by a Belgian, Robert Goffin, in 1932, and the first jazz magazine was started in France during the late 1920s, edited by Hugues Panassié. The first jazz discography was compiled by another Frenchman, Charles Delaunay, in 1936. This general tendency – Europeans pointing out the quality of American music to Americans – has continued to varying degrees in subsequent decades. In a 1954 review, for example, the French critic André Hodeir was the first to proclaim in print the quality of Gil Evans, who at that time was living and working in total obscurity in the USA.

From the 1950s onwards many American musicians, encouraged in part by public and critical responsiveness, went to live in Europe, following the pre-war example of Coleman Hawkins. Don Byas, Kenny Clarke, Sidney Bechet and Dexter Gordon, among many others, spent productive years in Europe, and the Art Ensemble Of Chicago first came to prominence in France in 1969 before they had made any impact in America. Since the beginning of the 1970s the visionary German producer Manfred Eicher and his ECM record label have also helped to shift the centre of gravity from the USA to Europe. At a time when the major record companies in America were recording and releasing only jazz-rock-fusion, Eicher had a programme of releases which ranged from the avant-garde to acoustic groups. When Keith Jarrett's contract was terminated by Columbia he was signed up by ECM, and many other US musicians have followed his example, including Ralph Towner, John Abercrombie, the Art Ensemble Of Chicago, Pat Metheny, Sam Rivers, Chick Corea and Gary Burton. Other European labels, such as Black Saint and Leo, have supported American avant-gardists like David Murray and Anthony Braxton, when no large American label would record them.

Since about 1960, moreover, Europe has produced numerous musicians who have become key figures in modern jazz – though the first European of this stature was, of course, Django Reinhardt. By the 1990s the list was long and distinguished: Albert Mangelsdorff and Eberhard Weber from Germany; John McLaughlin, John Surman, John Taylor and Kenny Wheeler from the UK; Joe Zawinul from Austria; Jan Garbarek from Norway; Jean-Luc Ponty from France; and Zbigniew Seifert from Poland. Although influenced and inspired by US musicians, these Europeans have produced music which is very different in identity from the usual American jazz, and one of the reasons is that Europe offers a very different aesthetic climate. The gladiatorial competitiveness of the American scene, where musicians must "fight for their space", does not exist in Europe. Instead, the atmosphere is more expansive and reflective, the struggle is not with other musicians but with received ideas, and the whole continent is steeped in the emotional resonance of folk music and classical music. When John McLaughlin was asked in 1975 why he had moved back from the USA to live in Europe again, he said that in America jazz was often regarded as a commodity by the big companies, whereas in Europe it was regarded as an art. With the exception perhaps of the UK where jazz seems to be regarded as the Cinderella of the arts, the European media in general are generous with their coverage, and even in the UK, the Arts Council has made much brilliant contemporary jazz available to the British public. As a result of this sympathetic climate, some of the finest and most influential groups since the 1970s have been based in Europe, and they have often had mixed European and American personnel: as well as Keith Jarrett's Belonging band, there have been Eberhard Weber's Colours, the Jan Garbarek quartet, and various line-ups led by Albert Mangelsdorff and by John Surman.

2. Many jazz musicians, particularly pianists, have received some form of European classical training, and this has influenced their work. Bix Beiderbecke and Duke Ellington were familiar with the music of Debussy and Ravel, and a strain of romantic impressionism has remained prevalent in jazz since. Wholesale attempts to fuse jazz and the classical tradition (see "Third stream") have not always been successful, nor indeed have many attempts to use jazz elements in classical music, though Milhaud's *La Création du Monde* (1923) and, more recently, Mark-Anthony Turnage's *Three Screaming Popes* (1992) come closest to capturing its rhythmic vitality and emotional resonance. A number of jazz musicians, from Benny Goodman to Wynton Marsalis, have made successful parallel careers as classical musicians. [IC]

Film

Film is an invaluable source of reference for watching performers not easily (or no longer) accessible in the flesh. Its apparent superiority to records, however, has to be balanced against the terrible scarcity of earlier jazz on film. The entire history of jazz exists on disc apart from one or two holes, and even when the records are not available in the marketplace they are preserved in archives and frequently reappear for the benefit of new generations of listeners. But even the comparatively large amount of jazz on film that has found its way onto video in the last decade is a mere drop in the ocean. Pending any further discoveries, Charlie Parker playing on screen consists of just three numbers; for Art Tatum there's a mere twelve bars; while Bix Beiderbecke exists on film only in a silent home movie.

Another small disadvantage is that, for most Hollywood feature films, musicians' work had to be recorded first and then mimed for the cameras, sometimes even by different players. The most reliable and exhaustive documentation of this medium is to be found in David Meeker's *Jazz In The Movies*, which lists everything of the slightest relevance, whether available or not. [BP]

Folk

Once upon a time all music was folk music, in the sense of being made by the community for the community without a thought for monetary or artistic considerations. This is how jazz started, but it started to stop being solely that as soon as it was born, or at least as soon as it was employed in bordellos to put customers in the mood.

The folk revival, which began in the USA in the 1930s, not only had a significant impact on the subsequent appreciation of blues but played a small part in encouraging the 1940s New Orleans jazz revival (although, in both cases, the emphasis was on the sociology of these art forms rather than on the unique African-American music itself). Since that period, contact has been fairly minimal, although one or two musicians originally from the folk field have shown some affinity for jazz, such as mandolinist David Grisman and the singer (and former violinist) Maria Muldaur.

Beginning in the 1960s, however, jazz musicians have taken a new interest in folk music, either of European countries or of more exotic cultures usually classified as "world music". [BP]

Fours

"Fours" refers to the practice of breaking up an improvised chorus into a mere four bars of solo by one instrument followed by four bars by another and so on. This takes place usually, if at all, at medium to up-tempo and usually after each player has had a full-length solo earlier in the same piece.

Until 1950 or so this was always called a "chase chorus", which gave a pleasing picture of horn-men chasing each other's tails melodically (and was a useful expression because it covered the less usual "eights" and "twos" as well as fours). However, Lester Young and Charlie Parker led the way in the late 1940s to the now standard practice of "taking fours" with first a horn player, then the drummer, then horn player, then drummer, etc. As a result the chase image is less apt and has been replaced by a call-and-response pattern in which the drums are the constant factor. [BP]

Free jazz

The term "free jazz" refers to improvisation not based on a predetermined, underlying harmonic structure, and with no predetermined structural length. There are other variable factors. Firstly it may be tonal (occurring in a particular key), or non-tonal (in no particular key and sometimes simply noise, ie non-musical sound), or polytonal (in several keys simultaneously). Secondly, it may be in a regular time with recurring rhythmic patterns and/or a fixed pulse, or it may be out-of-time, with a "free" and irregular temporal momentum. Thirdly, there may or may not be composed themes and/or predetermined textural and spatial considerations for the improvisation.

After the tight structures and the strongly harmonic basis of bebop, a feeling grew during the 1950s that the current jazz language had exhausted itself, and musicians began seeking new approaches to improvisation and music-making. As early as 1949, pianist Lennie Tristano's sextet had recorded a wholly improvised piece, "Intuition", which began in total abstraction, then slowly evolved into a key centre and tempo. During the 1950s Charles Mingus, pianist Cecil Taylor and others began experimenting in this direction. The free-jazz movement in the USA was eventually launched in 1959 by Ornette Coleman, who arrived in New York with a conception that was fully realized and a quartet which thoroughly understood the new idiom.

The founder of European free jazz was the West Indian alto saxophonist Joe Harriott, who worked out his ideas in 1959, recorded his album *Free Form* in 1960, and played his new music at European festivals in the early 1960s. Harriott's music was different from Coleman's in several important respects. Coleman's grew out of the African-American tradition: though harmonically abstract, it was imbued with the feeling of the blues and gospel music, and it usually took place in regular time, swinging beautifully. Harriott's was often totally abstract: it had no regular rhythm; it sometimes featured silence as an integral part of the music; it fused Afro-Caribbean elements with the angularity and dissonance of twentieth-century avant-garde classical music; and occasionally it included unaccompanied solo improvisation by any one of the members of his quintet.

In the USA the more extreme variants of free jazz became known as "Black music" (even though some white musicians were involved) and was identified with the radical protest of the black community against white oppression. This, too, resulted in violent collective improvisations. Val Wilmer has written, "The dominant factor in most Black music is that the performer be aggressive." The spokesman of this movement was the writer LeRoi Jones (Amiri Baraka), and some of the leading exponents were Cecil Taylor, Archie Shepp, Albert Ayler and drummers Milford Graves and Sunny Murray.

Though Europe had its followers of Ornette Coleman, European free jazz in the 1960s tended to follow the road of total abstraction, and some practitioners disassociated themselves from jazz altogether, calling their activity "free improvisation" and its results "improvised music". The results have been varied, from the aggressive anarchism of, for example, Peter Brötzmann and his associates, which expressed itself in violent non-tonal collective improvisation, to the gentler iconoclastic humour of Derek Bailey and Evan Parker, or the irreverent clowning of theatrical performers such as Wolfgang Dauner.

By the late 1960s free jazz had established its own mannerisms and clichés, and, because of the absence of clear rules and the lack of criteria for judging performances, it attracted a number of charlatans and inferior players. By the end of the decade Coltrane and Ayler were dead, and many of its other exponents, including Harriott, Carla Bley, Paul Bley, Abdullah Ibrahim (Dollar Brand), Gato Barbieri and Dauner, had turned away from abstraction to seek other modes of expression. However, many of the key figures in free music continued to develop their conception, and abstraction forced musicians of all ages and all styles to re-examine themselves and their music. Free jazz enriched the existing jazz language with a new dimension which has become a part of the vocabulary of most musicians. [IC]

Frontline

The frontline of a small group consists of those players not in the rhythm-section. In a jam-session situation, the frontline could run to ten or more musicians; but even eight horns, if working from organized arrangements, would no longer be a frontline but the horn section of a small big-band. [BP]

Funk/funky

Possibly derived from an obsolete English word meaning smoke, steam or stench, in jazz and rock the term "funky" signifies music which is extremely physical and "dirty" – the rhythms are strong, clear and hypnotic, and the phrasing of the melodic and chordal instruments is bluesy and very vocalized. The whole musical idea of funk derives from the blues, and from blue notes in particular, which are bent and slurred expressively, so that the notes take on something of the sheer physicality of human experience.

"Funk" and "funky" first came into real prominence during the 1950s when, as a reaction against the "straight" and European sound of much "cool" jazz, musicians turned once more to the vernacular roots of the music, incorporating elements from the blues, gospel and work songs. Horace Silver, in his work with Art Blakey and Miles Davis in the early 1950s as both player and composer, was one of the prime movers of this reinvigoration of jazz, and one of his compositions was actually called "Opus De Funk". By the end of that decade, however, everyone was trying to be funky, and the result was a lot of stale music which had all the mannerisms of funk without any of the substance. Since then, funk has reappeared in various forms, and the word is now usually applied to a form of soul music exemplified by James Brown. The jazz-funk of the 1970s, which enjoys occasional revivals of popularity, is derived from that, and while it is sometimes good dance music the amount of improvisation is often small. However, with great artists – Miles Davis, Joe Zawinul, Herbie Hancock, among others – funk, of whatever form, has often been an integral part of great music. [IC]

Fusion

See "Jazz-rock-fusion".

Gig

A gig is an engagement or a job. It may be "a one-off gig" or "a regular gig" or even a residency (the same band being employed at least one night every week at the same venue). It may be "a money gig" or "a jazz gig", and rarely do the twain ever meet.

Worst of all, from many musicians' point of view, would be having to take "a day gig" (which does not mean playing jazz in the daytime but, on the contrary, living the nine-to-five life) in order to support their musical activities. However, as more and more established performers undertake music teaching to a greater or lesser extent, the great divide has become a little blurred. [BP]

Gospel

One of the central expressions of African-American music, gospel has a longer continuous history than either jazz or blues. Though not under the same name, it can trace its roots back to the pre-ragtime spirituals such as "Walk All Over God's Heaven", and to eighteenth-century English Protestant hymns including "Amazing Grace". What is more remarkable is that both these forms of material continued to evolve well into the second half of the twentieth century, unlike the minstrel-show music which was their secular equivalent. Obviously, the consciousness underlying black secular music has had to reflect greater changes than the eternal message of religious music, yet the latter has never been unaffected by the society it serves and there has been a constant cross-fertilization between what became gospel and what became jazz and blues. This is a vast subject which has yet to be studied in any depth, but it is worth remarking, for instance, the place of spirituals in the repertoire of early New Orleans marching bands, the jazz-blues background of gospel "founder" Thomas A.(Andrew) Dorsey (b. 1 July 1899; d. 23 Jan 1993) and the jazz-blues awareness of great soloists such as Mahalia Jackson, as well as the call-and-response patterns which ensemble jazz borrowed from choral gospel music. Indeed, the whole tension between ensemble and soloist (and the question of whether the latter becomes a superstar at the expense of the former) is another way in which gospel runs parallel to jazz; it also provides a way past the lyrics and into the musical beauties of gospel. [BP]

Hard bop

The term "hard bop" was coined in the late 1950s for the current consolidation of bop, after its more effete tendencies had been effectively hived off by the "cool" West Coast musicians and by East Coasters such as the Modern Jazz Quartet.

The positive aspects of hard bop involved its exaggeration of early bop's polyrhythmic vitality, especially in the accompaniments of bandleaders Art Blakey, Max Roach and Horace Silver, and the resilience of soloists such as Sonny Rollins and Lee Morgan. This was more palatable than the 1940s' style partly because of the apparent simplicity of much of the original material written for these groups. Heard alongside the occasional Parker tune which they retained in their repertoire, a typical hard-bop composition sounded closer to R&B (but with post-bop improvisation), while some even harked back directly to the "jump bands" of the 1930s. This, incidentally, is why it became fashionable in the 1980s for a new generation of listeners to dance to hard-bop records made as much as 25 years earlier, a fashion which began in London and later spread to the rest of the jazz world. [BP]

Harmolodics

The theory of harmolodics was formulated by Ornette Coleman and derived from his practice as an improvising musician. In essence, each instrument in an ensemble is both a melody and a rhythm instrument; players abandon their traditional roles, and instruments that normally accompany now share as lead voices in creating the music. The result is that harmonic consonance and resolution become irrelevant, the emphasis being on creating interacting lines. [IC]

Harmonics

Apart from being founded on the same laws of physics, harmonics have nothing to do with considerations of harmony (see below). The principles are most easily understood in connection with stringed instruments where the act of lightly touching a string at its midpoint sets both halves vibrating at twice the frequency, ie exactly one octave higher than its normal pitch. Used only for special effects, these harmonics created on guitar, violin or bass (even on piano, by playing the strings themselves "under the lid") have a veiled but ringing tone when compared to the normal method of note production on such instruments.

Harmonics are an everyday fact of life for brass players, who blow down tubes with valves or slides attached. For the valves and slides only change the instruments' pitch by half an octave at most, and all other variations of pitch are made by manipulation of the mouthpiece. The lowest available notes (used occasionally by cornettists Rex Stewart and Nat Adderley, and more frequently by trombonists but mostly in big-band arrangements) are rather flatulent sounds called fundamentals; everything else from the low register to the extreme high register is achieved by using the lips to double and redouble the frequency of vibrations, thereby producing a series of harmonics of the fundamental note.

The term is most often employed in connection with the reeds, such as clarinet or saxophones. Here, producing harmonics by accidentally overblowing is heard simply as a squeak, but the controlled use of overblowing (absolutely forbidden in European technique) has become one of the joys of jazz saxophone. Again it involves a different tone-quality, thinner and more urgent, as can be heard in the occasional extra-high notes of Charlie Parker, Paul Desmond or Eric Dolphy. Particularly on tenor saxophone, where their production is easier, extending the upper range with harmonics has become almost mandatory. Illinois Jacquet first made them a speciality in the 1940s, since when they have gone into the vocabulary of funk saxophonists everywhere, but quite different expressive use has been made of them by both John Coltrane and Stan Getz.

Beginning in the 1930s, Lester Young also introduced the harmonics derived from his very lowest notes, which came out not extremely high but in the middle range of his instrument. He, and others who picked up the idea from him, including Sonny Rollins, exploited the difference of tone from the normal middle-range sound of the instrument. (See also "Multiphonics".) [BP]

Harmony

The idea of selected notes sounding together to form chords is the great European additive to African-American music. It may have been less than essential to blues although, by the time they were first recorded, a succession of accompanying chords was fairly standard. The style that came to be known as gospel, on the other hand, had since its beginnings a harmonic content, but treated it with increasing freedom as time went on.

Jazz has always had something of an ambivalent relationship to harmony. For the first fifty-odd years of the century, rhythm-section instruments scrupulously observed the chord changes of a particular piece, while the horns often played with an independence inspired by the blues singers. During the same period, most of the major innovators from Armstrong onwards showed an increasing sophistication in their handling of harmony but, in various ways, avoided being dominated by this concern; Lester Young, in fact, used his harmonic sophistication to work against the chords at times, just as blues-based riffs had often done. However, in the wake of bebop, many lesser players of the 1950s (it is hard now to remember their names, and they have not earned a place elsewhere in this book) seemed over-worried by chordal correctness which is no doubt one reason why the new styles of the late 1950s (free and modal jazz) attempted to abandon harmony altogether.

It is interesting to note, however, that harmony has made several comebacks since then, and to set that fact alongside George Russell's suggestion that jazz improvisation has always been more scale-based than chord-based. Perhaps the truth is that the use of harmony in jazz is less of a guiding light than in most European music, and more a matter of texture. [BP]

Head

1. "A head" is short for "head arrangement", that is an arrangement worked out collectively (or dictated by one band member) and then memorized. There are also spontaneous head arrangements but, unless at least some parts are retained in later performance, only one audience will ever hear them. And, of course, there may be head-arranged riffs or interludes incorporated into a previously written arrangement.

2. Where a performance consists of theme/solos/theme, in that order, the opening section (perhaps including an arranged introduction as well as the theme) is referred to as "the head", and for the final section the performers "go back to the head" (in European classical music, *da capo*). [BP]

Hip

Hip is the opposite of square, just as an earlier form of the word, "hep", was the opposite of what was corny. Claimed by some to derive from the Oriental habit of balancing opium on that part of the anatomy, "hip" is actually more likely to be a rhythmic exclamation related to scat-singing – "hip, hip", "hey, hey", etc. Since it came into use in the jazz world of the 1940s, it has designated the musicality and/or attitudes most desirable in the inner circle of currently fashionable players. Equally, it can be applied to suitably aware fans, especially when talking among themselves.

However, like all complimentary adjectives, it has a double edge. The only difference between hip as a sincere description, and hip meaning "would-be hip", lies in the intonation and authority of the person speaking. The noun "hipster" acquired a fairly negative connotation early on, and was usually applied to non-musicians. The lyric of Dave Frishberg's song says it all: "When it was hip to be hep, I was hep." [BP]

Horn

Centuries ago, "horn" was a generic term for simple brass instruments without valves or slide, such as the posthorn or the alphorn. It is applied by jazz people, however, to any instrument that can be blown (including, but not very often, the so-called French horn and English horn). The players of wind instruments in a jazz group are referred to as "the hornmen" or "the horns". [BP]

Hot

The ability to "play hot" was a vital, but not indispensable, part of the early jazzmen's equipment. An important factor consists of emphatic rhythmic phrasing with the use of relatively obvious syncopation. In addition, for horn players, certain instrumental tone-colours (usually with a brilliant edge, but also including the ability to play "dirty") sounded automatically hot when combined with the necessary phrasing. Of course, since this produced an enthusiastic response from listeners, musicians who did not instinctively play hot often learned how to "get hot" for their featured solos; on the other hand, the tone and timing of some players sounds hot from their very first notes, even when they try to be "cool".

Although the expression is usually confined to traditional styles, the description applies equally to much R&B and "modern-mainstream" playing. But the term has fallen into disuse, largely because in the last thirty years the tonal and dynamic range has become so wide: the more frenetic avant-garde players have been hotter-than-hot, while ECM cool has almost reached absolute zero. [BP]

Hot lick

See "Licks".

Improvisation

Improvisation is the art of playing without premeditation, rather than necessarily "making it up as you go along". It has been responsible for many of the innovations within jazz, from early jazzmen departing from a given melody to decorate it or distort it, through the 1960s' players who developed the art of "free" improvisation. Nevertheless, most jazz performances are less than 100 percent improvised, and some may be less than 5 percent improvised and still be good jazz: it is the spirit (or illusion) of spontaneity which communicates. Even if they are aware of quoting from their earlier efforts, good musicians manage to convince the listener of their spontaneity – and, of course, unconscious quotation is often genuinely spontaneous.

Despite the mystique attached to improvisation, it is perfectly possible to learn playing without premeditation. Just like improvisation in comedy (or, indeed, in conversation) it requires a knowledge of the language; and it requires having something to say or, at least, a point of view (and, in performance involving two or more people, it requires a responsiveness to others' points of view). Above all, it is necessary to have a conviction that the act of improvisation is in some ways superior to making prepared statements, and that is something not easily acquired in Western societies – except by listening to jazz, which is also how the musical language is learned.

Whether it is possible to assimilate what is needed by following any particular teaching method is, however, highly debatable. Like other physical activities, it is only learned by example and practice. Given the magical aura of a satisfying group improvisation, it is somewhat ironic that in the USA "improv" is now an academic subject. [BP]

Improvised music

See "Free jazz".

Jam

Although its origin is rather mysterious, "jam" was probably a verb before it was a noun. In the 1930s and 1940s, "jamming" often appeared to mean cramming as many musicians as possible into one room, but perhaps the concept of cramming the maximum number of ideas into each solo comes closer.

A "jam" was the musicians' term for the occasion where such informal extended playing took place, away from the demands of the regular job; Duke Ellington's title "Dinah's In A Jam" refers to a succession of solos on one of the favourite vehicles for jamming. As well as "Dinah", other material regularly used included "I Got Rhythm", "Honeysuckle Rose", "Lady Be Good" and the 12-bar blues. The phrase "jam session", though doubtless uttered at some stage by a musician, was the description picked up by journalists and favoured by the fans.

The heyday of jamming came to an end in the USA when the musicians' union (the AFM), worried about falling employment in the late 1940s, began to discourage members from doing informal unpaid sessions in front of even an invited audience. However, as recent attempts to revive this institution indicate, it served a valuable purpose in raising performance standards; young players were given the chance to match themselves against the best musicians of their area, and the best local players tried their luck against those with national reputations as they came through on tour. Only rarely did these occasions turn into real "cutting contests" and, even then, they were characterized by a marvellous combination of competition and camaraderie.

Though several rock bands, such as the Grateful Dead and Cream, were including long improvised solos in the 1960s, the term "jam band" to describe such activities has only become popular more recently. As a result, a scene has opened up in which groups of jazzers appeal to a rock audience (e.g. Medeski, Martin and Wood) or rockers such as Phish find an audience among jazz fans. [BP]

Japan

Jazz was banned in Japan during World War II, but after peace was declared the jazz scene there grew with astonishing vigour. Records of bebop and earlier jazz were available in the later 1940s, Norman Granz's Jazz At The Philharmonic toured Japan in the 1950s and from the 1960s US jazz musicians visited regularly: Art Blakey first toured there in 1961, Miles Davis in 1964 and John Coltrane in 1966.

Pianist Toshiko Akiyoshi went to the Berklee School in Boston, in the 1950s, the first of many Japanese musicians to study there. A roster of brilliant Japanese musicians who have established international reputations since then would include: trumpeters Terumasa Hino and Tiger Okoshi; pianists Toshiko Akiyoshi, Aki Takase, Haruko Nara, Yosuke Yamashita and Masabumi Kikuchi; saxophonist Sadao Watanabe; and many excellent rhythm-section players.

By the mid-1990s the Japanese audience for live and recorded jazz was probably the world's largest, and *Swing Journal* is certainly the largest monthly jazz magazine in the world. From the early 1970s the Japanese market featured reissues (in their original covers) of American LPs which were unavailable in the USA and Europe, and such was their success that in the mid-1980s the USA followed suit, and in the later 1980s the Japanese DIW label started recording and distributing the music of a number of top American musicians. [IC]

Jazz-rock-fusion

Towards the end of the 1960s the jazz scene in the USA and Europe found itself in a state of deep crisis. The more conventional forms – bebop, hard bop, modal jazz etc – seemed played out, the avant-garde music of the day (free jazz) had not gained a new audience of any significant size, and rock had established itself as the ascendant vernacular music. Jazz record sales slumped, clubs closed, and the music itself was undergoing a severe identity crisis – was jazz more closely related to the great ethnic musics of the world, or was it now related more to the music of the twentieth-century classical avant-garde, too "serious" to accommodate the comfort of tonality? It was imperative to find a new identity and a fresh approach.

Jazz and rock both came from the same roots: the blues, gospel, worksongs and R&B. Nearly all American jazz musicians had started out with R&B bands, and in the 1960s many younger musicians had grown up with rock and roll, the Beatles and other rock groups. So it was perfectly natural that, throughout the decade, jazz musicians began to use and develop rock rhythms. Miles Davis's young rhythm-section with Tony Williams had played both spontaneous and premeditated rock rhythms in 1964 and 1965, and from the mid-1960s many people, including Gary Burton, Larry Coryell, Herbie Hancock, Keith Jarrett, Freddie Hubbard, Charles Lloyd, Don Ellis and Bob Moses, had made extensive and sometimes very subtle use of them.

The whole jazz-rock movement was crystallized and given its full momentum by three Miles Davis albums, *Filles De Kilimanjaro* (1968), *In A Silent Way* and *Bitches Brew* (both 1969), which produced an astonishingly fresh sound, combining rocky drum rhythms and bass riffs with electric keyboards and guitar, projecting the mysteriously sensuous and evocative atmosphere of the trumpeter's best music. The ensembles which recorded these albums included Herbie Hancock, Chick Corea, Joe Zawinul, Wayne Shorter, John McLaughlin, Tony Williams and Larry Young, all of whom afterwards led their own fusion groups.

Many of the leading practitioners of jazz-rock also looked beyond the confines of either jazz or rock; thus John McLaughlin's Mahavishnu Orchestra often employed the scales and asymmetrical rhythms of Indian music, but also used amplified violin and rich chords which were redolent of the romantic melancholy of the European tradition. Zawinul's Austrian heritage – the wild spirit of gypsy music and the intense emotion of mid-European folk music – could be heard in Weather Report. Chick Corea's Return To Forever had strong influences from Latin music, and African influences were apparent in the work of Miles Davis and others.

Jazz-rock-fusion had its most intense period of creativity from 1969–75, although later in the decade one or two other peaks were reached by various groups, and other encounters between jazz and rock, in the work of musicians such as John Zorn, have taken place without, as yet at least, producing a recognizable new hybrid. Its inevitable dilutions became a kind of musical wallpaper in films and on television, yet the movement vastly enriched the jazz language: whereas abstraction had tended to overemphasize the importance of improvisation at the expense of composition, fusion restored the balance by reinstating composition as a vital factor. More was written for bass than ever before: in a sense, the bass was liberated from "walking" – always playing four steady beats to the bar – without destroying the rhythmic coherence of the music, and even began in some cases (with Eberhard Weber and Jaco Pastorius, for example) to function as a melodic and featured solo instrument.

There were also radical structural and rhythmical innovations. The whole point of rock rhythm is that it works off a slow pulse, and the subdivisions of the pulse gave rise to an enormous number of asymmetrical rhythms – most of them new to jazz. The Mahavishnu Orchestra, and many other groups, began to function not only in common time (3/4 and 4/4), but in 5/4, 10/8, 7/8, 15/8, 19/8, and many other subdivisions, and this asymmetry also extended to whole structures, which might include bars of unequal length and/or irregular groupings of bars. The use of electronics also gave rise to a huge new vocabulary of sounds, textures and colours. [IC]

Jive

1. "Jive" is a word that has carried many different shades of meaning, the common factor seeming to be "something not entirely serious". Therefore, "jive talk" originally covered both harmless tall-storytelling and deliberate attempts to mislead, while "jiving" meant the use of jive talk. A "jive" person, though, was at least untrustworthy (or unjustifiably egomaniacal), while a "jive-ass m-f" is still the ultimate to be avoided. The white journalists and fans who borrowed hip vocabulary and called it "jive talk" fell into the latter category.

2. It follows that no style of jazz was ever described by its players as "jive music". The term is used, however, by fans of a certain age to mean any music suitable for "jive dancing" (also abbreviated to "jiving"). This activity, still popular in some European circles, derives from the Lindy Hop and other dances associated with Harlem's Savoy Ballroom in the 1930s, and was presumably so named because the originators of these styles took such brazen (and humorous) liberties with the underlying rhythm. [BP]

Jump band

A jump band was a small group, especially of the late 1930s, which combined the verve of jazz with the compulsive repetition associated with blues. Bands such as the Harlem Hamfats, Stuff Smith's Onyx Club Boys and the somewhat slicker Louis Jordan Tympany Five shared a similar audience. They were the first small groups to imitate the power and directness of the newly popular big bands, and the first to start emphasizing the up-beat, both factors which were more pronounced in what became R&B. [BP]

Kansas City

A commercial centre of the southwestern USA, Kansas City was also an important musical centre in the 1920s and especially the 1930s. While the Depression decimated the entertainment industry except for radio, the corrupt municipal regime of Kansas City ensured a thriving nightlife and a constant demand for music. Therefore the city attracted all the best jazz players in the entire Southwest, and succeeded in incubating a new style of big-band music.

Early eastern bands such as Fletcher Henderson, Duke Ellington and even McKinney's in Detroit attempted an extrovert but neatly organized version of jazz, justified in hindsight by the inclusion of hot solos, and so at first did Bennie Moten. But the "territory bands" on which he drew for his sidemen had a rougher and more primitive blues-based style that gave the ensemble work more spontaneity, and eventually even introduced head arrangements. The fact that these were little more than riffs, and that opening themes were often interchangeable with backings for soloists, actually gave Kansas City bands (especially Count Basie's) greater stylistic unity and freedom. It is no coincidence that rhythmically repetitive riff-making was so central, for, in rhythm-section work too, the relaxed cohesion of the New Orleans style found a new home in Kansas City.

It is no coincidence either that, by the late 1930s, exports from Kansas City had set the standard rhythmically for everyone else in the country to emulate and, in the innovations of Lester Young and Charlie Parker, they had an incalculable influence on developments in the 1940s and afterwards. [BP]

Latin jazz

See "Afro-Latin".

Licks

Jazz musicians usually begin by copying the phrases of players they like and admire. When a phrase is either copied and learned or habitually repeated, it becomes a lick. The finest musicians build up a vocabulary of their own rhythmic and melodic phrases – their own licks – and when inspired they can escape from the tyranny of their old licks and create new phrases, which of course may turn into licks. On uninspired occasions, they will of necessity fall back on their store of remembered licks, and this memory bank of phrases is part of every musician's identity, without which it would be impossible to function. "Hot licks" was a racy term to describe some of the musical clichés of the "hot" jazz of the 1920s and 1930s. [IC]

Mainstream

1. "Mainstream" was a term coined in the 1950s to describe the small-group swing still being produced by greats such as Coleman Hawkins and Ben Webster. These and other players were perceived as maintaining the same virtues they had displayed in the 1930s and early 1940s, before they were pushed aside in the enmity between the beboppers and the revivalists. Rhythmically and tonally, these "mainstreamers" had changed little, although some had been at least touched by bebop, and mainstream rhythm-sections, especially pianists and bassists, were often irretrievably bop-influenced. Similarly, swing revivalists of a younger generation such as Scott Hamilton have imported more "modern" influences including that of R&B, but these tributaries inevitably become part of the mainstream as it flows ever on.

2. Another "mainstream" has been identified within the last two decades, sometimes called "mainstream-modern" or "modern-mainstream". Broadly speaking, this consists of beboppers still active and bebop revivalists who, whether they realize it or not, play things that could not have been played thirty years ago, for the simple reason that they have absorbed influences from modal and free jazz. Nothing ever stays in the same place, but perhaps the lesson of the mainstream concept is that the more jazz changes, the more it's the same thing. [BP]

Marching bands

The history of marching bands predates jazz by many years, but they have remained up to the present day an integral part of jazz's culture. By the mid-1800s big brass ensembles were common all over America, and they were quick to embrace the ragtime repertoire that was popular by the century's end. Pianist Eubie Blake remembers such highly trained bands "raggin' the hell out of the music" in Baltimore by the 1890s, and New Orleans-based brass bands of the period often reached a standard which jazz listeners more accustomed to the sound of later ear-based groups (the Eureka and many others) might find surprising. An undated early recording by the New Orleans Military Band (on *Thesaurus Of Classic Jazz*), probably staffed by Creole musicians, sets a standard that would be envied by any champion brass band in Britain's Midlands and North, and reflects the fact that back in jazz's early days senior New Orleans players such as Lorenzo Tio and Manuel Perez had received thorough classical training.

Such later New Orleans brass bands as the Tuxedo, Eagle and Magnolia – all packed with young stars from Henry "Red" Allen to Louis Armstrong and King Oliver – achieved a legendary folk-status, playing marches, dirges and upbeat selections by ear for a variety of functions, but most usually for funerals: lodge members who had died would be buried with all the dignity of a full marching band playing a dirge en route to the burial and happy, faster selections on the way back. (New Orleans religious beliefs complied then – and still do, in theory at least – with the Old Testament philosophy "Rejoice at the death and weep at the birth".)

Similar bands have been organized in Europe by such New Orleans figureheads as Ken Colyer, and, broadly speaking, little has changed in the way they play. But in the 1980s a new-generation marching band, the Dirty Dozen Brass Band, achieved widespread publicity playing rock'n'roll and modern jazz repertoire, including Charlie Parker tunes. The Dirty Dozen, despite their huge success (and possibly because of it), had a mixed reception among diehard lovers of New Orleans jazz, but most other people will find their music a rewarding extension of an honourable jazz tradition. [DF]

M-Base

A New York-based music movement (the letters stand for Macro-Basic Array of Structured Extemporization), M-Base is, in the words of its leading light, saxophonist Steve Coleman, "an attempt to develop a modern musical language based on a certain balance of structure and improvisation, incorporating all our members' shared experiences". Coleman readily acknowledges that, at heart, this is not an entirely new idea, but in part it was a reaction against the mid-1980s fashion for what became known as "retro-jazz", where sharp-suited young neo-classicists were seen as merely interested in pushing an audience's nostalgia buttons with polished music based in the modern mainstream. M-Base adherents – among them saxophonist Greg Osby, pianist Geri Allen, trombonist Robin Eubanks and vocalist Cassandra Wilson, though they never constituted a formal grouping – on the other hand, wove street sounds (funk, rap, soul, etc) into jazz structures, and incorporated contemporary references to everything from computerese (hence the name) to kung-fu movies into their art, producing funky, hip music of fearsome technical proficiency, best experienced, as Steve Coleman's exhilarating concerts proved, live in a club setting. By the late 1990s, many of M-Base's original adherents had become famous. Geri Allen received jazz's Nobel Prize, the Jazzpar, in 1996; Cassandra Wilson crossed over into the pop world with a string of eclectic, classy albums for Blue Note; Greg Osby established himself with a series of intense, thoughtful albums for the same company; Steve Coleman remained one of jazz's most effective proselytizers, a spark plug for a whole generation of young musicians. [CP]

Modal jazz

"Modal jazz" implies improvisation on a series of scales instead of a sequence of chords. In practice there is an overlap between the two approaches, but the term describes specifically the style established in the late 1950s and early 1960s by Miles Davis's *Kind Of Blue* and the John Coltrane quartet.

The themes used for modal jazz, although based on chords sounded by the keyboard accompaniment, deliberately avoided the amount of harmonic *movement* and harmonic *direction* of bebop sequences. Ample precedents existed for this, going back to the rather static harmonies of "rhythm changes" and most 12-bar blues, while early Latin-jazz numbers such as "Night In Tunisia" or Bud Powell's "Un Poco Loco" also gave lower priority to chordal improvisation; certain pieces by Thelonious Monk ("Well You Needn't", "Locomotive", etc) and many by Charles Mingus had incorporated sections with no more than two chords continually alternating. The effect of this is to direct the soloist's attention towards melodic creativity and away from chord-derived "filler" material, a trend that had been evident in Davis's own playing long before he gave birth to the modal "school". Interestingly, however, whereas the first modal recordings stimulated soloists by restricting them to the notes found in particular scales, Coltrane's quartet work found him reintroducing a kind of harmonic interest by making passing reference to other scales (a technique known as side-slipping), in order to create tension which would be resolved by a return to the home scale.

The word "modal" came into jazz terminology thanks to composer/theoretician George Russell, and derives from the seven seven-note scales (modes) used in ancient Greece and which, together with certain five- and six-note scales, are the basis of all European music (the Ionian mode is identical to the so-called major scale, the Aeolian mode is one of the possible minor scales). It is a pity that widespread misapplication of Russell's theory by jazz educators has entrenched the belief that for every chord there is a scale and that knowledge of these is essential for improvising. The pathetic results of this kind of teaching tell their own story: as the old blues song put it, "You've got the right key, but the wrong keyhole." [BP]

Modern jazz

The built-in obsolescence of the phrase "modern jazz" did not prevent it gaining currency in the 1950s to describe bebop and post-bop. Chiefly used at the time by writers and fans who found the onomatopoeic word "bebop" childish and demeaning, "modern jazz" is now mainly heard from diehard followers of swing and New Orleans; in their opinion, the term "modernist" sounds equally demeaning, and covers indiscriminately anyone who arrived on the scene after 1940. [BP]

Multiphonics

Multiphonics is the art of producing two or three notes simultaneously on an instrument not designed with this use in mind. Whereas it is child's play on all the keyboards and not much harder on stringed instruments, on horns it requires hard work and is at best a "special effect".

The construction of brass and reeds is intended for playing one note at a time. But the accidental sounds of inexpert players, and the deliberately "dirty" tones of some jazz players, actually consist of two harmonics (or the fundamental note and a harmonic) sounding together (see "Harmonics"). These instances, however, create one main note plus a subsidiary "impure" note, whereas, with sufficient practice, it is possible to produce two adjacent harmonics sounding equally strongly (though less strongly than a single "pure" note), forming a two-note chord as in the later work of John Coltrane and his followers.

As a further refinement, Albert Mangelsdorff, Howard Johnson and others have shown that, by vocalizing their air-column (ie humming a note into the instrument rather than just blowing), additional harmonics can be activated to form three- and four-note chords. [BP]

Mutes

Mutes are devices placed in the bell of a trumpet, trombone or other brass instrument to modify the sound it makes. The commercial production of mutes was stimulated in the 1920s by jazz musicians who regularly used makeshift devices to produce revolutionary new effects: trumpeter Joe Smith used half a coconut, trombonist "Tricky Sam" Nanton employed half a yo-yo, and anything else that came to hand – from water glasses to tin cans – was put to use. By the 1920s American manufacturers such as the Harmon Company had begun designing and marketing a range of mutes to meet this demand: later European entrepreneurs such as British trombonist Lew Davis were to produce their own highly successful variants. In 1934 Nat Gonella was able to write: "There was a time when a trumpet player was judged wholly by the variety and extensiveness of his mutes", but – as his statement implied – by then the demand had reached its height. In addition to the ubiquitous "derby" mute (originally often made from a real hat, usually with a hole punched in the centre), the aspiring brassman could buy "solotone" mutes, "special effects" mutes, as well as the more standard "cup", "harmon" and "straight" designs. It was the last three that were to survive World War II most happily, along with the "plunger" (really simply a rubber sink plunger, the marketed alternative to Joe Smith's coconut shell) and "pixie" (a tiny straight mute used in conjunction with the plunger to produce a sour, choked sound). Post-war jazzmen such as Miles Davis and Harry Edison were to establish the harmon mute (often with its central tube pulled out) as the most popular effect of its kind at the period. American companies including Humes and Berg continued to market full ranges of mutes into the 1980s, but examples of attempts to find new sounds (eg by Peter Gane and bandleader George Evans) seem to have slowed down in the wake of developments in electronic music. [DF]

Muzak

Muzak was the name of a commercial company specializing in taped background music for restaurants, supermarkets, lifts, aircraft, etc. When this venture was still in its infancy (1935) they actually recorded Fats Waller but, since then, any jazz associations have been minimal.

With a small "m", muzak is now the general term for music intended not to be listened to. Calling something muzak which was intended as jazz is, therefore, a deadly insult. [BP]

Neo-bop

Neo-bop is the musician's term for the kind of bebop played from the late 1970s onwards, following the revival of interest in the challenges bebop offers. Whether or not it reworks specific themes written in the 1940s, it differs considerably from early bop because later stylistic influences such as modal and free jazz (plus better amplification) affect the way the players relate to one another. [BP]

Neo-classical

A term from the European arts vocabulary, referring to the approach prevalent in jazz of the 1980s and in the 90s, of using repertory performance as the inspiration for new material. [BP]

New Age

New Age is the generic term for the brand of easy-listening instrumental music identified with the American record company, Windham Hill. Associations with upwardly mobile lifestyles and alternative therapies cannot completely disguise its origins in the open-ended European-influenced improvisation popularized by Keith Jarrett and his ilk. As with other jazz-derived muzak, it may assist in opening the ears of some listeners in the right musical direction. [BP]

New Orleans

New Orleans will be for ever associated with the crystallization of the first classic style of jazz in the early years of the twentieth century. The favourable conditions for this development have often been linked to the French colonization of Louisiana, which only formally ended in 1820; as in the Catholic Caribbean and South America, racial intermixing and mutual musical tolerance (especially in the seaport of New Orleans) were more a feature here than in the predominantly Protestant USA.

The repertoire of the earliest New Orleans jazz bands is a matter for speculation: nothing was put on disc until the white Original Dixieland Jazz Band in 1917. But, as with later bands that were recorded, it seems likely to have consisted of "swinging" versions of European-style marches and dance tunes, the latter often requiring the use of a violin. Through lack of volume, the violin was soon dropped in favour of a frontline of one or more trumpets (or cornets), trombones and clarinets, with a rhythm-section including various combinations of guitar (or banjo), bass, drums and piano. But what was remarkable – and what took the white bands a long time to learn – was the improvised interweaving of simultaneous frontline melodies and the equally interlocking flow of rhythm-section instruments, as exemplified by the King Oliver Creole Jazz Band. This loose polyrhythmic flow tended to be minimized in later Chicago-style jazz and Dixieland, which is probably why they introduced more frontline solo work, whereas the classic New Orleans style is an ensemble style *par excellence*.

New Orleans is also the home of particular regional styles in both R&B and funk, the local recordings of which have often included jazzmen working as session musicians. In fact, even these days there is probably more interchange between players of different styles in New Orleans, and certainly less snobbishness between them than in most other comparable centres of musical activity. [BP]

New York

Despite claims to the contrary, New York still has some cause to consider itself the jazz capital of the world and, although reputations are no longer made and unmade there solely, they are often reinforced by New York's acceptance.

"New York jazz" originally denoted 1920s bands which had not yet felt the impact of New Orleans music. And yet, what Charlie Parker once described as "that fast New York style" undoubtedly existed in the late 1930s and early 1940s. It was typified by players such as Roy Eldridge and Don Byas, whose technical and conceptual brilliance had outstripped their provincial upbringing so comprehensively that they had to "make it" in the Big Apple.

This was the style that rapidly evolved into bebop and, since that time, most of the important schools of jazz have come to fruition there. Even styles pursued more persistently elsewhere (West Coast, European improvised music, ECM jazz) have taken their initial cue from New York trends. [BP]

Original

Original is what most jazz musicians would like to be, although it's easier said than done. "An original" is a composition written by the same person who performs it, as opposed to "a standard" which is something that anyone and everyone plays. Similarly, an "original arrangement" is originated by a member of the group using it, as opposed to a "stock arrangement" that could be bought off the shelf from a publisher. Neither an original nor an original arrangement has to be very original. [BP]

Overdubbing

The technique of overdubbing was a by-product of the introduction of sound films, where music was only one of the elements along with the dialogue, sound effects, and the possibility of replacing an actor's speaking or singing voice with one more desirable (an example of the latter is Joe Turner's soundtrack appearance in the short film *Low Down Dog*).

Only gradually did the record industry take any interest, although Sidney Bechet's recording of five instruments in turn to make a "one-man band" disc in 1941 was an early example. After Les Paul followed suit and then invented the multi-track tape machine, the industry never looked back. Even jazz musicians found uses for it, so that, while in the early 1950s it was possible to add on an instrument that was originally missing or inaudible (eg Eddie Safranski in the 1946 album by Sonny Berman), by the early 1960s overdubbing could be a compositional tool (as in Charles Mingus's *Black Saint And The Sinner Lady*).

From there it was but a short step to the late 1960s' habit (also known as "tracking") of recording an ensemble arrangement first and then taping the improvised solos, several times if necessary; likewise, the early 1970s' practice of "layering", which built up a rhythm-section arrangement or a whole band by recording each instrument in turn, so that what was heard as simultaneous was perfected bit by bit. Though these technological facilities undoubtedly have their positive side, they are so far removed from live performance (even of synthesized sounds) that they encouraged the late 1970s' swing of the pendulum back to acoustic post-bop played in real-time. [BP]

Piano rolls

Piano rolls, an early form of passive home entertainment, offer the first mechanical reproduction of jazz musicians. Gramophone records only caught up with jazz from 1917 onwards (and not in any depth until the mid-1920s), but throughout the 1910s and 1920s performances were being cut by players such as James P. Johnson, Eubie Blake, Luckey Roberts, Fats Waller and Jelly Roll Morton – in each case, piano rolls constituted their earliest solo recordings, while Scott Joplin's were the only records he made.

The barrel-organ-like process of cutting rolls provided a less faithful reproduction of the pianist's individual sound than disc recording (and sometimes they were overdubbed, as it were, with additional "orchestration"), yet they not only entertained but educated other up-and-coming musicians like Duke Ellington. And, since the 1950s, they have been played back and re-recorded on albums, notably on the Biograph label, adding considerably to our overall picture of the period. [BP]

Pick-up group

A pick-up group is one put together for a specific appearance or recording. At worst it may sound like a bunch of strolling players (as Eddie Condon used to call them) picked up off the street, or at least out of the phone book. But if several of the members have worked together under other circumstances, it may have the benefits of a regular gigging group together with an added spontaneity. [BP]

Polyrhythm

"Polyrhythm" means the use of different rhythms simultaneously, and it is far more prevalent in jazz than the average listener (or even player) would readily admit. It covers not only the repetition of explicit patterns which interlock with one another (as in Afro-Latin and traditional African music) but the continual hinting at such patterns in jazz, even in unaccompanied solos.

In most ensemble jazz the polyrhythmic element is fairly pronounced, although not explicit. For instance, the interplay between a single soloist and an apparently straightforward rhythm-section will be filled with all kinds of metrical juggling, including different accents from different members of the rhythm-section. But what transpires in an ensemble improvisation such as a traditional New Orleans band is considerably more complex, as a graph showing the accentuation patterns of all the instruments would demonstrate. Perhaps this is why many listeners choose to miss some of the details and concentrate on the underlying pulse as if they were dancing to it (though dancers introduce cross-rhythms with different parts of the body).

The polyrhythmic sound within the jazz rhythm-section was already implicit in the New Orleans style, where the solid 4/4 beat of each of the rhythm instruments was sometimes supplemented by ragtime figures from the piano or similar double-tempo drum figures, usually on the wood-blocks. But its proliferation can be said to date from the late 1930s Basie band which, alongside the supple but single-minded bass and guitar, included the pianist's and the drummer's reactions to, and complications of, polyrhythms implied by the soloists. These developments were, of course, taken further by bebop and, yet again, in free jazz. If, in some respects, the average fusion or Latin-jazz rhythm-section seems more easily comprehended, it is still far looser and less regimented than the way "authentic" Afro-Latin music is organized, and also far more interactive in a jazz sense than is granted by detractors of these developments. [BP]

Polytonality

Polytonality is the sound of different tonal areas (in other words, key-signatures) being used at once. This happens relatively rarely in arranged jazz and, apart from a few passages of Charles Mingus, examples worth remembering are even rarer. Bitonality, implying two simultaneous keys, has been more common in improvisation when the soloist departs temporarily from the tonal centre being used by the rest of the band; since this happens on a random basis, George Russell's term "pantonality" is more accurate, but has not caught on. But whether arranged or improvised, polytonality is only ever used for brief moments and only makes an impact by contrast with the predominantly tonal nature of jazz. [BP]

Progressive jazz

The label "progressive jazz" was first promulgated by Stan Kenton (to describe his own work, of course) and later applied by journalists and fans to such as Brubeck, the MJQ and 1950s "cool jazz" in general. This usage is now outdated but, perhaps because progress is a phenomenon of fashion and because jazz was next fashionable when it became funky, "progressive jazz" resurfaced in the 1970s as a term to describe jazz-funk-fusion. [BP]

Pseudonyms

Pseudonyms used to provide endless guessing games for dedicated record collectors, until the standard discographies (by Rust, Jepsen and Bruynincx) and reissued albums began giving away all the correct answers. The use of such disguises, incidentally, should be distinguished from the cases of whites of continental European extraction anglicizing their names (Terry Gibbs, Shorty Rogers) or black Americans adopting Islam: it is regrettably still possible to come across writers stating, for instance, that Yusef Lateef's "real" name is William Evans. The only actual pseudonym apparently inspired by racial considerations was that of Eddie Lang (itself an adopted Anglo name), whose more funky records with Lonnie Johnson and King Oliver were credited to "Blind Willie Dunn".

Usually the fictitious names were concocted to cover a record session from which the participant should have been barred by an exclusive contract with another company. No sooner had Duke Ellington's manager/producer sold his services to one label (in 1929) than the band started appearing on other labels as "The Jungle Band", "The Harlem Footwarmers" and "Mills' Ten Black Berries". From the 1930s onwards, contracts tended to be a little more watertight, and the few pseudonyms that were required usually referred to a big-band leader doing a bit of small-group slumming, such as "Shoeless John Jackson" (Benny Goodman) or "Chicago Flash" (Gene Krupa). Often, however, the names reflected more mundane inspirations, as when Nat "King" Cole (who also recorded as "Shorty Nadine" and as "A. Guy") appeared under the name "Eddie Laguna", actually that of the session producer; Bobby Hackett once adopted the persona of "Pete Pesci", owner of the club where he was working at the time. Some pseudonyms were devastatingly prosaic, Cannonball Adderley becoming "Ronnie Peters" and Eric Dolphy "George Lane", each for one session only; but sometimes the musicians could not resist giving clues, such as the West-Coast-based altoist "Art Salt" or the high-note trumpeter "Buddy Maynard".

The fun really started to go out of the name game in the 1960s, when it became more common to negotiate extra-contractual engagements "by permission of So-and-So Records". Ironically, now that it is the fashion to reissue albums in their original sleeves, it is once again important to know that, for instance, both of the two recordings of "Charlie Chan" were actually done by Charlie Parker. [BP]

Quotation

Quotation from another melody during an improvisation is an art whose value has frequently been disputed. It can arise for a variety of reasons, often indicating sheer high spirits (an early example: Louis Armstrong quoting *Rhapsody In Blue* in his original record of "Ain't Misbehavin'"). Or the musical logic of a solo can suggest surprising similarities, as in some of Charlie Parker's more obscure quotations. Quite often there are traces of irony, even deliberate absurdity (such as Art Tatum employed) or the tone can be sardonic or sarcastic, sending up either the basic material or the passing reference or both (eg Dexter Gordon or Sonny Rollins).

Many soloists would say that the most pleasing quotations arise spontaneously and, even for the improviser, unexpectedly. Planned quotations have their place, but can easily sound boring, though then again many of the early jazz soloists did not always improvise, and made self-quotation their stock-in-trade (see "Improvisation"). Of course, written arrangements can also incorporate specific material from elsewhere, or can anthologize memorable phrases originally improvised on the same tune. But the transcription of whole solos (such as Leon Roppolo's in the McKinney version of "Milenberg Joys" or Thelonious Monk's "Little

Rootie Tootie" solo on his big-band Town Hall concert) has been done to death by groups such as Supersax.

Don't assume that such possibilities are limited to harmonically oriented jazz. Ray Smith has noted that one of Evan Parker's solo albums includes an accidental quotation from a recording of African tribal music. And the use of African musicians in performances by Archie Shepp and Ornette Coleman also provides instances of quoting from an outside source (or were Shepp and Coleman being quoted by the Africans?). [BP]

Ragtime

The origins of ragtime, the wildly popular syncopated music that predated jazz but also ran alongside its early history, lie, like those of jazz itself, in a complex set of roots that include (among other elements) black and white folk dance, and brass band music. Its most notable characteristics were, firstly, deliberate use of syncopation in the right hand, often set against a simple, rhythmic bass in 2/4 or 4/4 (playing a tune this way was called "ragging" it), and secondly, a set of related themes in each piece, often linked by modulation (a direct link with band music). By the late nineteenth century ragtime was played by bands and solo pianists alike, but the greatest ragtime exponents were perhaps the high-toned "piano professors" of the period. Eubie Blake recalled one such: "One Leg" Willie Joseph, a virtuoso black pianist from Boston Conservatory who, because he was unable to succeed in the white man's musical world, devoted his colossal talents to playing ragtime in saloons. Willie's music was a spectacular rhythmic *tour de force*, probably nearly as complex as a Max Roach drum solo. "Ragtime is syncopation – and improvising – and accents", said Blake, "and if you could have heard those old fellas play you would have heard ad lib – *and those accents*."

It seems possible that the creations of Joseph and his many contemporaries may have been simplified – even bowdlerized – in their later formalization by Scott Joplin and others. But such formalization was inevitable: by the turn of the century ragtime had created a huge demand for itself, and began to be published, sometimes in "easy to read" versions for America's parlour fixture, the piano. The first rag to be published, Tom Turpin's "Harlem Rag" in 1897, was quickly followed by a string of others from ragtime composers such as Joseph Lamb, James Scott and Scott Joplin. Joplin, possibly the most trained of the three (he studied with a German professor who may have been sent South under the USA's reconstruction policy), was one of the first who, in Eubie Blake's words, "had the nerve to put ragtime down on paper", and his first composition, "Maple Leaf Rag", published in 1899 by John Stark, sold 75,000 copies. It opened the floodgates for a deluge of ragtime piano publications (some good, some not) which in many cases usurped the place rightfully occupied by Joplin and his peers.

By the dawn of the twentieth century ragtime was being played by younger jazz musicians: New Orleans bands such as John Robichaux's and Papa Jack Laine's took most of their repertoire from popular ragtimes published, in stock orchestrations, in the famous "Red Back Book". Within a few years, popular composers such as Irving Berlin were producing songs like "Alexander's Ragtime Band" which owed little to true ragtime, and with the dawn of the jazz age a new, younger music was to catch the public fancy (Joseph Stark's house significantly discontinued publishing in 1922). For the next four decades ragtime was handled best of all by a small coterie of authorities such as pianist Wally Rose in post-World War II America, and in the 1960s and after by Europeans such as Keith Nichols and Ron Weatherburn, as well as Americans such as Dick Hyman. Not every treatment of ragtime by jazz bands was a respectful one, but it can be said that scholarly re-creations by such bands as Chris Barber's and Ken Colyer's helped to refocus attention on the music in the 1950s, and the revival of the late 1960s (consolidated by a Hollywood film, *The Sting*, which used Joplin's "The Entertainer" as a theme tune) fully repositioned the music in the public consciousness. The reworkings of Joshua Rifkin, Dick Hyman, Nichols and others thereafter at last restored ragtime to its rightful place in the music establishment. [DF]

Rebop

An early version of the word "bebop", "rebop" derived from imitating drum patterns as in the 1940 song "Wham, Rebop, Boom, Bam". Now a deliberately antiquated usage, it was already going out of favour by the time of Dizzy Gillespie's 1946 recording "Ol' Man Rebop". [BP]

Records

It would be hard to exaggerate the importance of records in spreading and cultivating the appreciation of jazz. Even musicians, who always prefer to check out fellow performers by playing with them or at least hearing them live, cannot catch up with all those who specifically interest them; and for finding out about the greats now deceased, records are the only solution.

It should be remembered, however, that the process of making records is very different from playing live, whether for paying customers or for the performers' own pleasure. The clinical atmosphere of the studio is not necessarily inhibiting, but the purpose (and the cost) of the venture is usually on somebody's mind and may inhibit everybody. Various strategies have been tried, from switching off all the lights to keeping the tape running continuously – even recording in front of an invited audience – but these do little to solve the basic dilemma of trying to document something that is usually at its most relaxed when not under such scrutiny. There is also the fact that artists invited to record often do not have control over the choice of material, and the company (in the shape of the producer) has the final say over what is released. Small wonder that a long list of musicians, from Fletcher Henderson onwards, have been described by their colleagues as being nowhere near their best on their records.

Some have, of course, learned to use the constraints of recording (eg careful sound balancing and, until the end of the 78 rpm era, enforced brevity) for artistic ends; some have even found good uses for facilities such as editing, overdubbing and sampling. Another technical consideration has provided, for those companies with large archives, a source of interesting historic material in the form of "out-takes" (unused sequences) or "alternate takes" (so-called from the pre-tape habit of keeping two master versions of each piece recorded, as a precaution against manufacturing problems). It has often been claimed that comparisons of these alternates show how a given performer thought about the process of improvisation – but they show still more how the performer thought about trying to make a satisfactory record. [BP]

Reeds

The reed instruments normally employed in jazz are the clarinet and the saxophones – alto and tenor are the principal solo saxophones, followed by baritone and soprano, while occasional use has also been made of bass, contrabass, sopranino saxophones and bass clarinet. Some players of the aforementioned have often "doubled" on other reeds such as oboe and bassoon, and (to a much greater extent, although it does not have a reed mouthpiece) on flute.

Because of the hybrid construction of the saxophone, it is also technically correct to call it a brass instrument. So, when one or more saxophones function in a section with trumpets and/or trombones, the "horns" together are often referred to as a "brass section". [BP]

Repertory bands

The jazz repertory movement gained momentum in the early 1970s. Its inspiration was the realization that popular revivals of earlier jazz styles usually leave the most interesting examples of those styles untouched. Therefore, although for instance the lowest-common-denominator "trad" lives on, the music of (say) Luis Russell would never again be played live unless special efforts were made. The bands assembled and the scores re-created (often with considerable care and expertise) have helped the transmission of dying skills to younger musicians and, especially in the USA, have sometimes attracted subsidizing funds. This has usefully distinguished them from the category of "ghost bands" attempting to pay their way by playing the greatest hits of someone like Glenn Miller or Tommy Dorsey. Ignoring commercial imperatives, repertory bands have played concerts and made recordings investigating everything from the compositions of Sonny Clark to the more obscure works of Duke Ellington. [BP]

Revival

1. In the USA, consciousness of the need to re-explore the fundamentals of classic jazz was detectable no more than six years after Louis Armstrong's Hot Five and Seven sessions had been recorded. The commercial aims of dance and swing band music in the mid-1930s were already leading young players such as Bob Haggart (bassist with Bob Crosby's orchestra) to assert: "We play jazz, not swing. We always hated riff tunes and avoided them whenever possible." The Crosby band's revivals of Hot Five vehicles such as "Savoy Blues" and "Come Back, Sweet Papa" were an early indication of one need to "get back to the roots", but his orchestral formula – highly arranged, played with trained precision and a sophisticated tonal approach – was still closer to swing than to New Orleans jazz, and the same could be applied to his small group, the Bobcats, from two years later. Other revivalist whispers in the breeze came in 1936. That year an article by J.S. Moynahan in the *Saturday Evening Post* pointed out that the re-formed Original Dixieland Jazz Band (they came together for a radio show) played more "authentic" jazz than Benny Goodman; again, in 1939, the Summa Cum Laude band (led by Bud Freeman), Muggsy Spanier's Ragtimers and others made conscious efforts on record to revive older repertoire and steer clear of the blander aspects of American swing.

All these bands, however, reinterpreted old material in their own way, rather than studiously re-creating the original: that breakthrough belonged to the true figureheads of US revivalism, Lu Watters's Yerba Buena Jazz Band, which in 1940 set out to re-create faithfully the two-trumpet format, rhythmic approach and repertoire of King Oliver's Creole Jazz Band. The emergence of the Yerba Buena band coincided with the researches of young missionary revivalists such as Heywood Broun, Frederick Ramsey and William Russell, who created an interest in the whereabouts of such forgotten New Orleans figures as Bunk Johnson, George Lewis and Kid Ory and then satisfied that interest by locating, interviewing, promoting and recording their subjects. The efforts of Broun, Ramsey, Russell, Eugene Williams and others created enormous controversy in a jazz world already split by fashion and faction, and their determined championing of primitive musicians such as Johnson caused bewilderment to ears more attuned to the sophisticated and rapid developments of Goodman, Hawkins and the swing era in general. But they initiated, and followed through, a highly necessary re-evaluation of jazz values at a time when the music had sometimes acquired a facile quality.

The revival – in which "authenticity" was the emotive keyword – set up rules which were to prove too restrictive for many of its early protagonists: leaders such as Bob Scobey (Watters's early crusading trumpet partner) and Turk Murphy (his trombonist) subsequently found themselves working a jazz formula which, whether for business or musical reasons, dispensed with the most austere demands of revivalism. But because of the movement, a whole generation of New Orleans players were restored in the 1940s to glories greater than they ever achieved previously, and an area of jazz which might otherwise have been forgotten was rightfully set back high in the music's hierarchy. Early recordings of revivalists such as Watters, and their originals such as Johnson and Lewis, possess a driving fervour which – set against most of Benny Goodman's 1944 records, for example – still clearly reveal how vital was the need for a jazz revival.

2. The post-war British jazz revival (which, as with most British jazz history, echoed the American original) began for much the same reasons as did the American version. By 1944 British popular music, often commercially based to begin with, was ten years on from its most exciting innovations and was being conveyed by a BBC whose starched-collar presentation offered little to the young generation. In terms of jazz activity too, Britain had reached a level and none-too-exciting plane. Nightclubs, rhythm clubs and record societies offered skilled dance-band musicians playing stylized choruses on chord sequences well established by ten years of jam sessions ("Sweet Sue", "Honeysuckle Rose" and "The Blues" were frequent choices). There was a lack of fervour in the music, and the first re-explorations of New Orleans and its jazz by early revivalists promised fresh repertoire, an intriguing sense of discovery, a tempting permissiveness (well away from the coy *double entendres* of Tin Pan Alley) and, above all, a rejection of the older, less bold generation, in favour of music of superior quality and "authenticity".

A great deal of debate has gone on as to who formed the first revivalist jazz band in Britain (Belfast's Ken Smiley band, which played Chicago-style jazz as early as 1938, is one contender), but the figurehead of the British jazz revival was pianist George Webb, whose band – playing material by King Oliver and other New Orleans giants in the accepted two-trumpet format – was active in South London by 1944. The Webb band – which later included trumpeter Humphrey Lyttelton as well as clarinettist Wally Fawkes and trombonist Eddie Harvey – established the principle of revivalism in Britain, but what exactly was being revived needed further definition. By 1950 three separate factions of British revivalism were clearly apparent: Freddy Randall was playing Chicago-style jazz at a North London venue, Cooks Ferry Inn; Humphrey Lyttelton was playing the Armstrong/Bechet areas of jazz at the London Jazz Club; and – most intriguing of all – Ken Colyer was playing strict New Orleans jazz, slightly to the dismay of Armstrong-based revivalists ("to ears attuned to Morton's Red Hot Peppers", says George Melly, "it was a horrible sound"). It was Colyer, however, who was to make the most important longterm contribution to British New Orleans revivalism. Much as George Lewis and Bunk Johnson had done in the USA, Colyer created – and maintained for over forty years – a climate in which New Orleans jazz could function in Britain as an independent entity. For most other revivalists, including Lyttelton, as well as hundreds of semi-professional bands around the country such as the excellent Merseysippi (Liverpool) and Avon Cities (Bristol) groups, the confines of revivalism pure and simple were too much of a straitjacket. By 1960 most of them, apart from Colyer and one or two kindred spirits like Eric Silk, had moved on to wider terms of reference, although many, notably Chris Barber, saw the re-creation of true New Orleans jazz as a continuing part of their brief. "The battle had been won and therefore lost!" observed George Melly: New Orleans jazz had been thoroughly re-established in jazz's music spectrum and there was no longer any focus for a crusade. [DF]

Revivalism

The term "revivalism" is most generally applied to the re-adoption of New Orleans jazz (either in its sophisticated Oliver/Armstrong incarnation or in the more basic styles of George Lewis and Bunk Johnson) by young musicians in the late 1930s in the USA and in the early 1940s in Great Britain and Europe, but has been used to refer to the bebop revival of the 1970s (see "Neo-bop"). [DF]

Rhythm

1. It seems an understatement to say that the use of rhythm in jazz is its most distinctive feature, and also its most subtle attribute by contrast with music in other ways comparable to jazz. For further discussion, see "Afro-Latin", "Beat", "Polyrhythm", "Stop-time", "Swing", "Syncopation", "Tempo", "Time", "Two-beat".

2. "Rhythm" is also an abbreviation for the song title "I Got Rhythm", since George Gershwin's chord sequence was for many years the second most popular framework for improvisation (after the 12-bar blues). Therefore, the phrase "Rhythm changes" does not mean changes in the rhythm of a performance, but rather the chord changes of the Gershwin song as used in hundreds of jazz pieces such as "Lester Leaps In", "Anthropology", "Rhythm-a-ning", etc.

3. "The rhythm" are the rhythm-section players, as in the phrase "brass, reeds and rhythm". In the early New Orleans days, the rhythm often consisted of only guitar and bass, or only piano and drums, and, in much later periods, if the group's volume level was modest (eg the Benny Goodman trio or Bechet-Spanier Big Four), these duos were sufficient.

The first big bands of the 1920s, and indeed most small groups from the Armstrong Hot Seven onwards, had four rhythm (with banjo and brass bass for a while more popular than guitar or string bass, the situation being reversed from the early 1930s onwards). From the 1940s, the guitar became more marginal, as did the piano from the 1950s although, if they are in the group as soloists, they function as part of the rhythm when not soloing.

From the 1960s it became more common to add one or more Afro-Latin percussionists, and in the 1970s to include more than one keyboard player and/or more than one guitarist. The largest rhythm-section on disc, outside of Archie Shepp's and Ornette Coleman's recordings in North Africa, may well be that on Miles Davis's *On The Corner*, reportedly eleven strong. [BP]

Rhythm-and-blues

Rhythm-and-blues was originally a term for black popular music adopted by the US record industry in the late 1940s to replace demeaning descriptions such as "race records" (1920s) and "sepia series" (1930s). These names had, of course, covered nearly all of the early jazz issues which, it was assumed, were only worth marketing for black listeners.

A lot of what is now thought of as R&B actually predated the term, and was a direct outgrowth of the blues groups and "jump bands" of the late 1930s. But the rhythmic bounce and the saxophone-dominated instrumentation remained a constant thread at least up to the work of Earl Bostic, Fats Domino and Little Richard, although more electric guitar sounds were gradually absorbed (via West Coast blues) in the evolution of R&B into rock'n'roll. Much of the vocal work of the period was more influenced by gospel than by blues, which is one reason why such a thorough going mix made R&B the basis of all pop music since, in the same way that bebop simultaneously laid the foundation for all later jazz.

More than that, R&B has continued to interact with post-bebop jazz: not only had R&B been influenced by jazz, but most of the important jazz players of the hard-bop and free-jazz generation served their apprenticeship in R&B bands, even the great saxophone innovators John Coltrane and Ornette Coleman. [BP]

Riff

A riff is a repeated phrase of pronounced rhythmic character, often not strikingly melodic, usually two bars in length (eg Basie's "Swinging The Blues") or four bars (as in "One O'Clock Jump").

Riffs can be found in solo work, especially from certain players who habitually think along such lines (such as Horace Silver or Illinois Jacquet), and even King Oliver's famous "Dippermouth Blues" cornet solo begins with two riffs. But riffs really found their logical home in the big bands of the late 1920s and 1930s, especially when one section of a band harmonized riffs as a cushion and a catalyst for someone else's solo. The Kansas City bands such as Bennie Moten's, Andy Kirk's and particularly Count Basie's were quite capable of creating new riffs on the spot, thus encouraging the soloist to continue for longer than was ever possible on records of the time, and this practice was readily incorporated into their off-duty "jamming". It even became so habitual that a jamming devotee such as Lester Young can be heard breaking out into one-man riffs behind others' solos even on quintet and sextet recordings.

The move to include riffs in bass-lines dates back at least as far as "Night In Tunisia" (and even Chu Berry's "Christopher Columbus" from 1936 is just a bass riff used as the main melody). Thanks to the gradually increasing Afro-Latin influence on black popular music, and their combined influence on jazz, it was possible by 1970 for Miles Davis's *Jack Johnson* to contain three main themes, each of which consisted solely of a bass riff. And, especially since jazz bassists started to be properly amplified in the late 1960s, the relationship between the bass riff, the rest of the rhythm-section and the soloist is very similar to that created with section riffs in the big bands of forty years earlier. [BP]

Rock

For most non-rock musicians, the word "rock" is now used indiscriminately as a shorthand term for all pop music since the arrival of rock'n'roll in the mid-1950s.

The latter was by and large a continuation of R&B, with a distinct flavour of country music (itself influenced by swing and vocal blues since the 1930s) in the work of leading performers such as Chuck Berry. However, as soon as rock'n'roll was assimilated and anaesthetized by the music industry, the 1960s saw the twin phenomena of the first R&B revival and the emergence of so-called progressive rock; the situation paralleled that of jazz when, after the popularization of swing, there was a split between revivalists and beboppers. It was progressive rock, with its incorporation of extended improvisation in the work of groups such as Cream or the Grateful Dead, which was first shortened to "rock"; from there, it was only a short step to the various hyphenated forms including, of course, "jazz-rock".

There are a couple of generations of jazz fans for whom rock represents the absolute antithesis of what they thought jazz was all about, and yet all the forms of African-American music are closely related. This is hardly surprising when you consider that the musicians who created the swing style all had a background of listening to traditional jazz, the beboppers had their background in swing and early R&B, and all the young jazz players of the last two decades (not merely the jazz-rock and fusion musicians) were brought up on the pop music of their youth, ie rock. [BP]

Russian jazz

During the 1920s jazz was welcomed in the young Soviet Union. In 1926 Sam Wooding's band, with Tommy Ladnier on trumpet, and Benny Payton's Jazz Kings (featuring Sidney Bechet) both played in Moscow, and that same year pianist Leopold Teplitsky sailed to America with an instruction from the Commissariat of Public Enlightenment to: "Master the techniques of American jazz, buy up stock arrangements and all the necessary musical instruments and then put all to use in a new jazz orchestra for the city of Lenin's Revolution." Teplitsky returned to Leningrad in 1927 with crates of recordings, more than twenty Paul Whiteman arrangements and more than forty instruments. Russian jazz musicians soon began to appear and some gained considerable reputations in the Soviet Union: one in particular, Berlin-born trumpeter Eddie Rosner, has been described as "possibly the greatest of Soviet jazzmen".

The subsequent history of jazz in the Soviet Union is the story of successive periods of repression followed by grudging relaxations according to the predominant ideology. Was it a proletarian "people's music" or a bourgeois and elitist phenomenon? Was it subversive or was it ideologically sound? There was no consistent party line on the matter. During one official campaign against jazz, Teplitsky was arrested and exiled. Eventually Rosner and his wife were arrested and tortured; he was exiled to Siberia and made a non-person – rehabilitated only after Stalin's death.

In the 1950s Charlie Parker's influence percolated through, spawning a generation of Russian bebop musicians, and when more than sixty well-established Soviet jazz musicians emigrated between 1971–80, their technical competence astonished Western audiences. Trumpeter Valery Ponomarev, for example, spent three years with Art Blakey's Jazz Messengers, and saxophonist Anatole Gerasimov recorded with Mercer Ellington. But neither Ponomarev nor Gerasimov, nor any other expatriate Russian, made any significant mark on the international jazz scene.

At the beginning of the 1970s, however, free jazz, which had begun a decade earlier in the USA and Europe, began to find its disciples in the Soviet Union. The first wave of free improvisers were schooled classical players and included Anatoly Vapirov (saxophones), Sergey Kuryokhin (piano), and the three members of the Ganelin Trio – Vyacheslav Ganelin (piano), Vladimir Tarasov (drums) and Vladimir Chekasin (saxophones).

Because of the general insulation of Soviet cultural life from that of the West, free improvisation began to thrive there at a time when the international jazz scene was in its post-abstract and post-jazz-rock phase. Whereas in the rest of the world abstraction had become a dimension of a jazz language in which rhythm, swing, tonality, harmony and so forth had been reinstated and transformed, the Russians regarded these factors as "characteristic features of light entertainment". This high seriousness was mirrored in the grotesquely academic jargon of Soviet jazz criticism which was so abstruse that it seemed a secret language. However, jazz had another crucial role in the old Soviet Union: it became an underground phenomenon and the performances rallying-points for those wishing to express their aversion to the regime. Though it was all done by word of mouth, huge audiences attended most concerts, in which the music was usually combined with the language and theatre of satire and protest. Even before the demise of communism, there were many festivals all over the Soviet Union, covering a wide spectrum from swing and bebop to free improvisation and jazz-rock.

One of the most dramatic changes since the collapse of communism has been the increasing two-way traffic of Russian and foreign musicians. Vyacheslav Ganelin now lives in Israel, and the Moscow Composers Orchestra (MCO) – formed in the mid-1980s and initially inspired by Carla Bley's example and Barry Guy's London Jazz Composers' Orchestra – is led by pianist and composer Vladimir Miller, a British subject born to Russian parents, who lives in London and commutes to Moscow.

Miller said, "Although the more famous Russian musicians often play in Europe, the problem is that most Russian musicians get very few chances to play abroad because there isn't the sponsorship. ... Many musicians from Europe are playing in Russia and like doing so because they get huge audiences who take the music very seriously." However, as with so many aspects of society in the former Soviet Union, the future of indigenous jazz and improvising musicians in Russia and its satellite countries is by no means clear. [IC]

Salsa

Salsa is a 1970s development of Afro-Latin music particularly associated with Hispanic New Yorkers. Because of its geographical origin, this style initially had a tougher sound than some earlier Latin music and betrayed the influence of bebop and modal jazz. But, as used by non-specialists, the word has now become virtually a generic term for all Afro-Latin styles. [BP]

Sampling

Sampling is the technological process of isolating certain sounds from a recording and playing them back, often but not necessarily in a repeating loop. Most sampling is funk-oriented, since repeated rhythms seem to survive the transition best. Jazz-related instances have included large chunks of Herbie Hancock's "Canteloupe Island" used as the basis for the US3 hit record "Cantaloop", and Branford Marsalis's "The Blackwidow Blues" (from the album *Buckshot La Fonque*), which borrows a cymbal pattern from Elvin Jones (on Coltrane's "India"). The technique is similar to the borrowing of Charlie Parker's saxophone-playing for the soundtrack of *Bird* while removing and replacing the other sounds of the original recordings.

The popular end of the spectrum sees sampling now linked with re-mixing in a sometimes unholy alliance, the most dire "jazz" example being the post-Miles Davis, post-Bill Laswell album co-credited to "Miles Davis/Various DJs" entitled *Panthalassa: The Remixes*. But rapidly developing technology has also made it possible for musicians to include real-time samples while performing live, as in John Scofield's *Up All Night*. This latter approach is likely to prove more fruitful for jazz than the ministrations of deejays. [BP]

Scat

Scat is the art of creating an instrumental-style improvisation vocally. This requires a vocabulary of vowels and consonants related less to identifiable words and more to the tone and articulation of jazz instrumentalists, as in the trumpet-like "Oop-Pop-a-Da" by Babs Gonzales or Sarah Vaughan's saxophonic "Shulie-a-Bop". First done on records by Louis Armstrong (Fletcher Henderson's "Everybody Loves My Baby" and then Louis's own "Heebie Jeebies"), it is most closely associated by the general public with Ella Fitzgerald and her many imitators. Brought to an early peak of perfection by Leo Watson who, by introducing occasional real words, inspired the development of vocalese (see below), scat has scaled new heights of virtuosity with Bobby McFerrin. [BP]

Section

A group of instruments that functions together as a unit within a larger group is called a "section". The "rhythm-section", for example, can vary enormously in size and make-up – piano, banjo, tuba and drums; two guitars and bass; bass and drums, with or without piano; several keyboard and guitar players; several percussionists and a couple of bassists – but they will always think of themselves, and be thought of, as a section. Similarly, any organized (ie not "jamming") group with four or five horns will have a sufficient ensemble power for them to be heard as the "horn section". Anything larger, say with two trumpets, two trombones and two reeds, will tend to function at least part of the time as a separate "brass section" and "reed section"; whether the brass also subdivide may depend on the nature of the music. In standard big-band formats, even if the arrangers persist in using them together all the time, the trumpets and trombones are located in separate rows called the "trumpet section" and the "trombone section". [BP]

Session musicians

Session musicians are those who earn the greater part of their living working in record, radio, television and film studios. Each of the cities where these activities take place supports a pool of such players, who form a financial, and in some respects a musical, elite. Not all the music involved is necessarily "commercial" in the derogatory sense: it can range from clever advertising jingles to complex pseudo-symphonic soundtracks. The great demands made on the players' skills, however, are often outweighed by the crucifying boredom of much of the work they have to carry out.

Since the 1920s, it has gradually become easier for musicians with a jazz background to gain entry into the exclusive ranks of the "sessionmen" or "sessionists" (the ranks are slowly opening up to women musicians). Many of the players listed in this book have spent at least some of their career specializing in "session work" but, for every Phil Woods or Bud Shank who returned to revitalized jazz playing, there are many who have been swallowed up and whose jazz reputation (and, indeed, jazz ability) has suffered as a result. [BP]

Sideman

A sideman is anyone who is not the group leader on a particular gig. In a big band, they may be sectionmen or soloists (who also play in a section, of course), but they are all sidemen.

There seems to be no non-sexist version of the term, largely because, in the present era of fewer and fewer full-time groups, the syndrome of "always the sideman and never the leader" hardly exists any more, and, where everyone is a potential leader, no one is a sideman. Therefore, the term is now only heard on the lips of people who like jazz of a certain age. [BP]

Skiffle

A name apparently used only a couple of times in the whole history of American blues recording, "skiffle group" was adopted by Ken Colyer as the description of his band-within-a-band. This specialized in the early 1950s in imitating early folk-blues, drawn mainly from the recorded repertoire of Huddie Ledbetter and from the first European visit of Big Bill Broonzy.

The popularity of this music rapidly spread far wider than the world of traditional jazz and, by a freak of history, formed a bridge for British youth to cross over into rock'n'roll. Furthermore, the attempt of Alexis Korner's successive groups to build a serious minority audience in the UK for the full range of blues and R&B actually succeeded; even more remarkably, it created a hybrid called "British blues" which fed back into American rock music via the Rolling Stones, but also laid the groundwork for the late 1960s development in the USA of jazz-rock-fusion. [BP]

Small group

A "small group" is anything that is not a big band or an unaccompanied solo. The smallest groups are usually not thought of as groups but are referred to as duos or trios. The borderline between a large small group and a small big band varies somewhat according to fashion and according to the attitude of the players involved. [BP]

Smooth jazz

This catchphrase, like "bebop" and "fusion" before it, has often been used as a term of abuse. In this case the abuse is largely justified for, unlike bebop or fusion which arose out of the experiments of the musicians involved, "smooth jazz" is a marketing concept above all. At least in the US, where its arch-instigator Ken Gorelick (cutely renamed Kenny G) set hearts a-flutter and accountants' eyes a-bulging. Smooth derives its intellectual justification from the need to make jazz more palatable to the masses (we have been here before, not least during the swing era) and it inherits its historical antecedents from the heavily manipulated productions of the 1970s CTI label, featuring such performers as Grover Washington. Editing, overdubbing and equalization are freely employed to make the result as bland and uneventful as possible, and the most successful tracks in terms of their target audience are those which don't disturb the heart-rate, or even the ear-drums. [BP]

Solo

1. In one sense, a "solo" is any performance which is totally unaccompanied, the first non-keyboard example in jazz being Coleman Hawkins's "Picasso". There have been a multitude of other solo performances, especially in the last three decades, and in the piano jazz of all periods.

2. A solo can also refer to the passage where one person is engaged in prominent melodic improvisation, with some or all other members of the group providing a (usually partly improvised) accompaniment. Where (as is most often the case) the backing is by musicians who are equally capable of taking the lead, they may all take a solo in turn. Earlier generations of players used the phrases "to take off" or "to get off" before the European terminology was turned into a verb, "to solo". [BP]

Soul

1. Soul was a quality first identified by jazz musicians, and which crept into writing about the music in the mid-50s, around the time that Milt Jackson appeared on a 1956 Quincy Jones album under the pseudonym "Brother Soul". It was important that he was a "Brother", because being black was a necessary condition of having soul; whereas "hard bop" was being adopted by whites as well as blacks in reaction to "West Coast jazz", "soul jazz" of the late 1950s and early 1960s was exclusively black. Musically, it implied a direct knowledge of gospel music and of its importance to the black community, and the ability to translate its phraseology into convincing instrumental jazz. In addition to Jackson, players as varied as Horace Silver and Jimmy Smith were thought of as part of this movement.

2. Almost simultaneously, the word was applied to black popular music, as it began increasingly to reflect the influence of gospel. While this had already been a part of R&B vocals by such as Dinah Washington and Ray Charles, the blues element became in the 1960s the province of white "folk" musicians sympathizing with the past travails of black people; but, as the civil rights movement gained strength, blacks rejected the connotations of blues and adopted the much more affirmative sound of gospel. Popular "soul music" became so much like a straight transplant of secularized gospel that the music industry had to coin the expression "blue-eyed soul" to cover would-be white exponents. The term "soul" has now become a vast category encompassing virtually anything by black artists, whereas in jazz usage it is no longer a style but has reverted to being a quality, as in "X has soul" or "is soulful". [BP]

Square

"Square" is one of the many jazz musicians' words to have gone into general usage. Before its application to virtually anyone lacking in awareness, "a square" referred particularly to somebody unable to appreciate jazz. It has a specific rhythmic connotation, in that "square music" lacks the complex polyrhythms of African-American styles and deals in what even European-trained musicians describe as four-square structures. Examples of square music are non-improvising marching bands and most pop of the pre-rock'n'roll era. [BP]

Standard

"Standard" was originally applied to popular songs of the twentieth century whose popularity lasted beyond the period of their initial publication. Just sometimes, tunes have survived solely because of jazz treatments, eg "What A Little Moonlight Can Do" or "On Green Dolphin Street". Certain instrumental items written by jazz musicians have achieved a life far beyond the circumstances and personnel of their original performances, such as "Perdido" or "In A Mellotone", and have therefore become "jazz standards". [BP]

Stop-time

Stop-time consists of a lengthy series of breaks, so that the rhythm-section marks only the start of every bar (or every other bar) for a chorus or more, remaining silent between each of the stop-chords; the soloist has to carry on regardless, however, and the effect is of an unaccompanied solo with marker-posts. The demands placed on the soloist's sense of time, not to mention invention, are of course considerable. Two of the most famous examples on records are Louis Armstrong's "Potato Head Blues" and Sonny Rollins's contribution to the Dizzy Gillespie version of "I Know That You Know". [BP]

Straight music

"Straight music" is still the preferred term among jazz and jazz-influenced performers to describe European-style composed music. Straight music is not the same as "square music" but, like that term, "straight" conveys a clear visual image of starched-shirt rectitude and no seductive polyrhythms. On the other hand, "straightahead" can be a term of approval in a jazz context, implying the ability to incorporate the necessary polyrhythms and still convey a clear sense of direction in one's performance. [BP]

Strings

The only stringed instruments regularly used in jazz are the guitar, bass guitar and acoustic bass (sometimes known as "bass fiddle"). The first-named was replaced in New Orleans bands from around the 1910s by the somewhat louder banjo. In addition, a number of jazz soloists have specialized on violin, a few on cello and a couple on harp.

Occasional use of "the strings" (in the European orchestral sense) dates back to the pretensions of Paul Whiteman. Others such as Artie Shaw, Tommy Dorsey and Earl Hines later enlarged their big bands for brief periods with a "string section", usually in a typically European configuration (ie two groups of violins, and far fewer violas or cellos) and usually with imitation European scoring. This is also the situation that has been foisted on those jazzmen (from Charlie Parker to Wynton Marsalis) who have appeared "with strings" for specific recordings. The results, though attractive, have done little for the soloists concerned, and the whole field of activity amounts to less than a footnote in the history of jazz. [BP]

Studio group (or band)

A studio group may be one of two rather different things. It may be a group which only worked together for the purpose of recording: eg the Louis Armstrong Hot Five and Hot Seven, whose members were regularly employed with various other leaders, or the Ornette Coleman Double Quartet, which made the album *Free Jazz*.

The term can also refer to a group assembled to record accompaniments for a star soloist, which may include his own group augmented (eg John Coltrane's *Africa/Brass*) or may consist entirely of session musicians. As is the way with session musicians, some of them may have jazz credentials but, in the phrase "Wes Montgomery playing with a studio group", they are merely there for backing purposes – or indeed, they may not be there at all, having recorded their parts previously or afterwards. [BP]

Studio musicians

See "Session musicians".

Swing

1. Although the word "swing" was popularized as a noun (in Duke Ellington's "It Don't Mean A Thing If It Ain't Got That Swing"), it was undoubtedly a verb first of all: a performance swings, a performer or a group or a tune swings, and even a less obvious tune can be swung. We all think we can recognize it when we hear it, but describing it is another matter entirely.

Most definitions of swing lay emphasis on the regularity of a pulse, despite the fact that a metronome or a ticking clock conveys no sensation of swing. The latter in fact make compulsive listening only for people unable to hear them without superimposing melodies in their head, which actually provides a clue to the nature of the sensation. Music only starts to swing when there is regularity *combined with* complex variation of the pulse, and when the listener participates mentally in maintaining the tension between the two. (This is indeed why the music of Bach is said to swing; Beethoven and Brahms do not swing, nor does Chopin, for they are too monorhythmic, but there are enough different things going on rhythmically in some of Bach for listeners to experience swing.)

Virtually all African-American music has the same quality to a greater or lesser extent, whether it be jazz, blues, gospel or soul (the only exceptions are pieces, or parts of pieces, which are out-of-tempo or free-tempo). What is endlessly and delightfully variable is the amount of polyrhythmic interplay between members of a rhythm-section, and the amount that takes place between the frontline and the rhythm-section. This has not only varied in the different historical styles of jazz, but changes considerably in different performances within the same style, and indeed from bar to bar of a single performance. As a result of this, and of listeners' and performers' personal preferences, there is no objective standard as to what style of performance swings the most.

2. "Swing" is also the name given to the style of big-band music formulated by Fletcher Henderson and Don Redman and popularized by the Casa Loma Orchestra, the Dorsey Brothers and Benny Goodman. Following Goodman's success in 1935 and until around 1945, more jazz-influenced music was more popular than at any time since. The "swing era", however, did not have a monopoly on swinging; indeed, some of what was played then had as little to do with it as most music of the 1920s "jazz age" had to do with jazz.

3. What has proved more lasting, but was also referred to at the time as swing, was the small-group jazz typified by the clubs on New York's 52nd Street from the mid-1930s to the late 1940s. Hence the street was then known as (and has since been officially named) "Swing Street". Because of the way in which big-band music soon became equated with pure nostalgia, however, the continuing vitality of the small-group style in the 1950s led to the adoption of the term "mainstream" instead. [BP]

Syncopation

Syncopation is a European term describing a European concept, namely a simple and steady pulse disrupted by an anticipated or delayed accent (the accent being called the syncope, which rhymes with "hiccuppy"). This is rather misleading if applied to jazz playing, somewhat similar to describing New Orleans as polyphonic (ie employing simultaneous sounds) without mentioning that it is also polyrhythmic.

It is the least polyrhythmic African-American music, ragtime, which sounds the most syncopated; here the cross-accentuation, and the notes phrased in groups of three over a rhythm in two, are most easily heard as deviations from a European-style march beat. The same principles are also at work in nearly all later jazz, but the cross-rhythms have become an integral part of the natural polyrhythmic flow of jazz. What a European-trained musician would see as syncopation if written down is usually not heard as such, except in the case of an extremely exaggerated example, for it is the flow rather than its constant disruption which is most valued by jazz lovers. [BP]

Tag

A tag is a brief addition to the normal eight-bar sections of a "chorus". For example, the song "I Got Rhythm" has a written two-bar tag (listen to Benny Goodman's version), which is, however, usually dropped in most other jazz versions and certainly in jazz "originals" based on "Rhythm changes". On the other hand, songs like "My Funny Valentine" and "All The Things You Are" have a four-bar tag built into the melody and the chord sequence, and which is therefore retained in each improvised chorus.

The earliest usage in jazz (and probably, in fact, the inspiration for the ending of "I Got Rhythm") was the New Orleans practice of adding an improvised tag to the very last chorus of a long performance; this was expanded in the work of the first Chicago generation to a concluding series of four-bar solos each followed by four-bar ensemble tags. Such instances of tags at the very end of a piece correspond to the European term "coda", but the 1950s–60s Miles Davis quintet borrowed the idea when playing standards and added a series of tags at the end of each individual solo. [BP]

Tempo

Tempo is the basic speed of a given piece, and can vary between different jazz performances more widely than is possible in most other music. The range is not merely from "down tempo" (slow) to "up tempo" (fast) but from "way down" to "way up" to "ridiculous". However, as much of the best jazz is polyrhythmic, there are often parallel tempos occurring simultaneously, so that an obviously slow tempo as defined by the rhythm-section may have the same tempo doubled or quadrupled by a soloist, or else different members of a rhythm-section may appear to be in different tempos.

"Out of tempo" covers everything from a slight relaxation of a previously fixed pulse, for instance just before the end of a ballad performance, to completely free rhapsodizing as in a long introduction (the European term "rubato" is sometimes used loosely for all these situations) – either way, it only has meaning if preceded or followed by an in-tempo passage. On the other hand, "free tempo" playing is very clearly in-tempo with a definite pulse, but 1-1-1-1 rather than 1-2-3, in other words without the need for regular spacing of bars or adhering to specific numbers of bars. [BP]

Theme

1. The theme is the initial melody and chord sequence of a jazz performance. This may be borrowed wholesale from a popular song, or a new-written melody based on someone else's chords, or, in more recent jazz, it could be just a rhythmic figure of a few notes – a "motif", according to European terminology. The theme will be what the soloists improvise "on" or against, or else veer away from totally; either way, it will be a point of reference or at the very least something to start (and possibly end) the piece.

2. The theme or theme song of a particular group is the one used for identification at the start and/or end of each appearance. These were particularly prevalent when bands did a lot of broadcasting. One or two such pieces were identified with venues or eras rather than one group, such as "Lullaby Of Birdland" (written by George Shearing) or Thelonious Monk's "52nd Street Theme". The piece called simply "The Theme" was used for thirty years by both the Art Blakey and Miles Davis bands, and is of indeterminate authorship. [BP]

Third stream

"Third stream" describes the theoretical merging of two souls into one, those of jazz and European composed music. The unrequited love on both sides for the most incompatible characteristics of the other has resulted in many illicit encounters, and quite a few bastard offspring such as Paul Whiteman's "Symphonic Jazz" and Stan Kenton's "Innovations In Modern Music". It is significant that this was no continuous lineage, growing in strength and numbers, for the "third stream" was at the best of times never more than a trickle. As Billie Holiday said about love, "Sometimes when you think it's on, baby, it has turned off and gone." Occasionally the liaison has been less fraught and one could point to a few near successes (eg Charles Mingus's "Revelations"), but, quantitatively, these are hardly enough to encourage further negotiations, let alone regular summit meetings.

Initially the problem was that, more often than not, the development was seen as a collaboration between two parties divided by a very real fence. In fact, more often than not the catalyst for the development was not a jazz player but a European-trained writer such as composer/conductor/critic Gunther Schuller (who coined the phrase "third stream"). Since the late 1960s, however, the consolidation of avant-garde jazz has helped to remove any lingering sense of inferiority about the structural aspects of jazz, as compared to European composed music. Moreover, with so much contemporary European-style writing being elaborately worked out, only to end up sounding like random improvisation, the jazz world has taken cognizance of its own comparative superiority and spontaneity. Perhaps as a result, a more regular flow of music has started to appear (from writer/performers such as Anthony Braxton, Anthony Davis and James Newton) which fulfils the conditions of the elusive third stream but, perhaps fortunately in view of the rather risible reputation of the terminology, it is not usually called by that name.

Latterly also, an attempt has been made by Ran Blake to broaden the definition of the term by incorporating fusions with other music, often of an ethnic nature; this still arises from an academic impulse, however, as opposed to the more spontaneous development of "world music". [BP]

Time

1. "Time" signifies the time-signature or metre of a piece, as in "5/4 time", "6/8 time" or "common time" (ie 4/4).

2. "Time" can also refer to the ability to play "in time" to the nearest microsecond, as used in the phrase "X has good time" or "Kenny Clarke had perfect time". Nothing shows up an inexperienced or rusty musician so much as having lousy time; out-of-tune may be acceptable on occasion, but losing the time, never. Just to complicate matters, it is possible for two musicians to have good time but to have a different "time feel". In a big band this is not a problem, because individual players should defer to section leaders and play according to the leaders' time feel, not their own; but in a pick-up group, or in an ill-chosen rhythm-section, there are often irreconcilable conflicts, and the more "all-star" sessions you attend, the more often you can witness these conflicts between the time feel of different contributors. [BP]

Tonality

Tonal music is music that is in a particular key at a given time, which applies to much the greater part of Western music, including jazz, and to much non-Western music, although the performers may not think of it in that way. (NB: "tonal" is also the adjective deriving from "tone", and it is important to distinguish between the two uses.)

Tonal music may proceed from one tonality (key-signature) to another, or may change quite frequently; for example, the standard song "All The Things You Are" passes through five keys in 24 bars but is nonetheless quite clearly an example of tonality, rather than atonality (ie in no key at all). There is a certain area of post-1960 jazz material, inspired by Coltrane's "Giant Steps", where no one key is retained long enough to be heard as the main key-centre of the piece, but the music is still tonal in nature. This is because of the predominant position given to harmony ("changes") in setting the direction of the performance, whereas in "polytonality" the role of harmony is weakened and in atonality it is negligible. [BP]

Tone

One of the key resources in all eras and styles of jazz has been the variety of instrumental tones employed. It has also been consistently underrated by commentators and educators, perhaps because there is no handy way of describing a performer's tone except with some rather emotive adjectives, and they, of course, are frustratingly vague.

At best, the situation has been oversimplified by statements such as, "The tone used by jazz instrumentalists differs markedly from the sound required in European composed music because it imitates the vocal tones of blues and gospel singers." This is only true of some players: others imitate the tones and rhythms of African-American speech patterns, while some produce a relatively Europeanized tone, especially on certain instruments – compare, say, Bill Evans and Thelonious Monk, and decide which one sounds closer to the European "ideal" tone and which one more like West Indian steel drums. Even this is too much of a generalization, for (as in the vocal comparisons) a jazz instrumentalist will change or distort his tone on certain notes (syllables) for expressive effect, which though common in European folk music is forbidden in nearly all academic music.

Listeners, fortunately, tend to respond directly and without premeditation to the tone produced by an instrumentalist (or vocalist), whether it is somewhat Europeanized or not. The chief outcome of the variations of tone allowable in jazz, and the related variations of articulation and inflection, is the extremely personal nature of each performer's tonal repertoire. Not only do players from different eras, such as Johnny Hodges, Charlie Parker, Ornette Coleman and David Sanborn, sound quite different from one another on the same instrument, but so do performers who are stylistically much closer, for instance Hodges and Willie Smith, or Lee Konitz and Paul Desmond. Any listener familiar with one player from these pairs would not long mistake them for the other player concerned.

Sceptics may object that Hodges and Smith (or Konitz and Desmond) are, after all, trying to be different from each other and that their choice of notes is what is mainly responsible for their being easily distinguished. And yet a player may find it plain sailing to remember and reproduce whole series of phrases once chosen by Parker or Coltrane, but be immediately recognizable as an imitator because of the impossibility of recapturing the exact instrumental tone. A proviso, though, should be added about records: while the varying fashions in studio sound seldom betray a player's tone too seriously, it is certainly possible for an inferior bootleg album of Parker or Coltrane to sound like one of their imitators rather than the real thing. [BP]

Trad

"Trad" is an abbreviation of "traditional jazz" and a curtailment of most of its essential virtues. This peculiarly European form of deviant Dixieland was mainly influenced by British bands, though it might be said to include the more commercial side of the Dutch Swing College Band and several French and German groups.

The negative side of trad came about after the success of skiffle, when there were a few hit-parade singles by such as Chris Barber, Kenny Ball and Acker Bilk. As a result the music industry signed up all the potentially money-making groups, and the gigs which they had been filling were immediately taken over by decidedly inferior musicians all hoping to reach the big time. Nothing like it had happened in the jazz world since the height of the swing era.

The positive side was that some of the leading musicians of the movement, by dint of constant work, eventually evolved from the tight-lipped Europeanized sound of early trad to something more like the relaxation of the real thing. And, perhaps inevitably because of its all-pervading presence, several young players came up through trad who went on to quite other things, such as Ginger Baker, Jack Bruce, Klaus Doldinger, Dave Holland, Ron Mathewson and Roy Williams. [BP]

Transcription

1. A transcription recording is one made specifically for a radio station and then copied for other member stations of the same network. The peak period of their use was the 1930s and 1940s (although such transcription services still exist today) and the material from that period has more recently provided many recordings that are now available publicly. It has to be said that, depending on the demands of the radio stations originally involved, the performances are often less jazz-oriented than the same band's commercial records of the same time, but they can offer insights into their repertoire that would otherwise be lost.

2. Transcription can also refer to the act of copying down a solo previously improvised either by the transcriber or (more likely) by someone better. These too may be used for group performance, but are of limited application, since the original nuances of timing, tone and articulation are all ironed out in such a performance, while the linear and harmonic aspects assume an exaggerated importance. Many solo transcriptions, however, have been published with a view to private study and may have greater value if used intelligently. Some of the greatest jazz soloists, at least from the second generation onwards, have made their own transcriptions from records as a learning process; but, since the main benefit lies in training the ears rather than the fingers, some have simply learned recorded solos directly on their instruments, thus eliminating the tedious task of writing them down.

3. Transcription also denotes the practice of arranging a composition for different instruments, eg a Joplin or Beiderbecke piano solo as played by a band, or an Ellington or other big-band work scaled down for a small group. Again, this is of limited application in a jazz context. [BP]

Two-beat

"Two-beat" is a description of the rhythmic feel created by emphasizing the first and third beats of a 4/4 metre. Originally this was the usual feel prescribed for the European-style marches which went into the early New Orleans repertoire, and it was the feel borrowed for the strongly European-influenced compositions of early ragtime. As the more even marking of all four beats became the norm, thanks to the example of the mature New Orleans style, the occasional use of a two-beat feel by some bassists in the late 1920s and early 1930s created pleasant polyrhythmic tensions, soon to be superseded by more complex factors in the work of the Count Basie band. Because the two-beat idea was then only associated with Dixieland bands seeking a deliberately antique style, the description "two-beat" became a term of abuse used by those who found it quaint and stilted.

But a good idea is hard to keep down. Already it had found a welcome in the Jimmie Lunceford band, and it often proved a highly suitable accompaniment to the complex simplicity of Erroll Garner. Both of these had imitators who reduced it to a one-dimensional "businessmen's bounce", but Garner's follower Ahmad Jamal inspired the 1950s Miles Davis quintet to rehabilitate the idea so successfully that it is still part of the standard rhythm-section arsenal to be able to play "in two". [BP]

Up

1. An "up" tempo is a fast tempo – related to the same image as the use of the word "uppers" in connection with amphetamines, though whether they help up-tempo playing is another matter.

2. The up-beat is the second beat of a piece (and the 4th, 6th, 8th, etc if the time-signature is 2/2 or 4/4 – in 3/4 or 6/4, the up-beat is the 2nd, 5th, 8th, 11th, etc). Contrary to European musical practice, the up-beat in jazz is often felt to be stronger than the down-beat, hence the use of "up-beat" as an adjective to mean affirmative or resilient. The up-beat is also sometimes described as the "off-beat" ("down-beat" being replaced by "on-beat") or as the "after-beat" or, more picturesquely, as the "back-beat": the last name conveys an image of bouncing back either spatially or psychologically, as indeed does the term "up-beat". [BP]

Vocalese

In jazz terminology, vocalese consists of singing lyrics to a previously existing instrumental tune or recorded solo. This extremely circumscribed exercise, which places great demands on the lyric-writer and even more so on the performer, is believed to have been developed as a serious diversion by Eddie Jefferson in the early 1940s, though there was already a precedent in a 1934 Marion Harris record of "Singing The Blues", in which she sings words (writer unknown) to the Trumbauer and Beiderbecke improvisations. It was first popularized in the early 1950s by King Pleasure's recordings of "Moody's Mood For Love" and "Parker's Mood"; other noted exponents include Annie Ross, with her version of Wardell Gray's "Twisted", and Jon Hendricks, who seems to have versions of everything else ever recorded.

In writings about European music, the French term *vocalise* (pronounced the same as "vocalese") denotes the opposite – ie, wordless singing comparable to scat. [BP]

West Coast

The West Coast (or "The Coast") was an established jazz centre by the 1920s, and the first black New Orleans-style band to make records, Kid Ory's, did so in Los Angeles in 1922. But what is usually meant by "West Coast jazz" is a particular type of mutant modernism which became popular in the early 1950s.

Its most typical sounds were associated with former sidemen of the Stan Kenton and Woody Herman bands (often of both, in fact), such as Shorty Rogers and Shelly Manne, who specialized in a brand of easily palatable, filleted bebop. The melodic, and especially rhythmic, predictability of much of their material was sometimes outweighed (as had been true of swing-era material) by superior soloists, in this case people like Bud Shank and Art Pepper, but the occasional use of European-style counterpoint and of instruments such as flute and oboe was greeted with more enthusiasm than seems justified in retrospect. Other, more distinctive, sounds from the groups of Gerry Mulligan and Dave Brubeck were classified for geographical reasons as West Coast jazz, but the movement as a whole is associated with a watering-down of 1940s bebop, just as European trad of the 1950s diluted the 1940s New Orleans revival.

Probably more significant in terms of historical impact was the "West Coast blues" movement of the late 1940s and early 1950s. Groups such as those of Roy Milton and Joe Liggins provided a considerable input into the newly defined field of R&B, while leaders such as T-Bone Walker incorporated the style of amplified guitar work that was to become so crucial in the development of rock'n'roll. [BP]

World music

The phrase "world music" connotes the philosophy that all the "folk" musics of the world are connected at a fundamental level, and is associated with the more or less conscious attempts from the 1960s onwards to prove that jazz, with its improvisatory directness, is best placed to bring out these fundamental connections.

After all, the earlier interest of both North and South American players in various kinds of African music was perhaps only to be expected, although the compatibility of these styles had not been a foregone conclusion. But for jazz musicians to assume that they had any reason or any right to start playing with musicians of other cultures implied a new self-confidence on the part of the jazz community, and could probably only have happened thanks to the 1960s climax of the civil rights movement.

John Coltrane may be said to have heralded this new pan-cultural approach, but it was Don Cherry who put the philosophy continually into practice. As well as being one of the first US musicians to collaborate with the South African pianist Dollar Brand (Abdullah Ibrahim), he was the first to play regularly with totally non-jazz musicians from several continents. But like many vital, or at least interesting, developments in jazz, this was rapidly turned into something more soft-centred and commercial, by groups such as the Paul Winter Consort and Oregon. [BP]

ROUGH GUIDES TRAVEL...

UK & Ireland
Britain
Devon & Cornwall
Dublin
Edinburgh
England
Ireland
Lake District
London
London mini guide
London Restaurants
London & SE England, Walks in
Scotland
Scottish Highlands & Islands
Wales

Europe
Algarve
Amsterdam
Andalucía
Austria
Baltic States
Barcelona
Belgium & Luxembourg
Berlin
Brittany & Normandy
Bruges & Ghent
Brussels
Budapest
Bulgaria
Copenhagen
Corfu
Corsica
Costa Brava
Crete
Croatia
Cyprus
Czech & Slovak Republics
Dodecanese & East Aegean
Dordogne & The Lot
Europe
First-Time Europe
Florence
France
Germany
Greece
Greek Islands
Hungary
Ibiza & Formentera
Iceland
Ionian Islands
Italy
Languedoc & Roussillon
Lisbon
The Loire
Madeira
Madrid
Mallorca
Malta & Gozo
Menorca
Moscow
Netherlands
Norway
Paris
Paris Mini Guide
Poland
Portugal
Prague
Provence & the Côte d'Azur
Pyrenees
Romania
Rome
Sardinia
Scandinavia
Sicily
Slovenia
Spain
St Petersburg
Sweden
Switzerland
Tenerife & La Gomera
Turkey
Tuscany & Umbria
Venice & The Veneto
Vienna

Asia
Bali & Lombok
Bangkok
Beijing
Cambodia
China
First-Time Asia
Goa
Hong Kong & Macau
India
Indonesia
Japan
Laos
Malaysia, Singapore & Brunei
Nepal
Philippines
Singapore
South India
Southeast Asia
Thailand
Thailand Beaches & Islands
Tokyo
Vietnam

Australasia
Australia
Gay & Lesbian Australia
Melbourne
New Zealand
Sydney

North America
Alaska
Baltic States
Big Island of Hawaii
Boston
California
Canada
Chicago
Florida
Grand Canyon
Hawaii
Honolulu
Las Vegas
Los Angeles
Maui
Miami & the Florida Keys
Montréal
New England
New Orleans
New York City
New York City Mini Guide
New York Restaurants
Pacific Northwest
Rocky Mountains
San Francisco
San Francisco Restaurants
Seattle
Skiing & Snowboarding in North America
Southwest USA
Toronto
USA
Vancouver
Washington DC
Yosemite

Caribbean & Latin America
Antigua & Barbuda
Argentina
Bahamas
Barbados
Belize
Bolivia
Brazil
Caribbean
Central America
Chile
Costa Rica
Cuba
Dominican Republic
Ecuador
First-Time Latin America
Guatemala
Jamaica
Maya World
Mexico
Peru
St Lucia
South America
Trinidad & Tobago

...MUSIC & REFERENCE

Africa & Middle East
Cape Town
Egypt
The Gambia
Jerusalem
Jordan
Kenya
Morocco
South Africa, Lesotho & Swaziland
Syria
Tanzania
Tunisia
West Africa
Zanzibar
Zimbabwe

Travel Theme guides
First-Time Around the World
First-Time Asia
First-Time Europe
First-Time Latin America
Gay & Lesbian Australia
Skiing & Snowboarding in North America
Travel Online
Travel Health
Walks in London & SE England
Women Travel

Restaurant guides
French Hotels & Restaurants
London
New York
San Francisco

Maps
Algarve
Amsterdam
Andalucia & Costa del Sol
Argentina
Athens
Australia
Baja California
Barcelona
Boston
Brittany
Brussels
Chicago
Crete
Croatia
Cuba
Cyprus
Czech Republic
Dominican Republic
Dublin
Egypt
Florence & Siena
Frankfurt
Greece
Guatemala & Belize
Iceland
Ireland
Lisbon
London
Los Angeles
Mexico
Miami & Key West
Morocco
New York City
New Zealand
Northern Spain
Paris
Portugal
Prague
Rome
San Francisco
Sicily
South Africa
Sri Lanka
Tenerife
Thailand
Toronto
Trinidad & Tobago
Tuscany
Venice
Washington DC
Yucatán Peninsula

Dictionary Phrasebooks
Czech
Dutch
Egyptian Arabic
European
French
German
Greek
Hindi & Urdu
Hungarian
Indonesian
Italian
Japanese
Mandarin Chinese
Mexican Spanish
Polish
Portuguese
Russian
Spanish
Swahili
Thai
Turkish
Vietnamese

Music Guides
The Beatles
Cult Pop
Classical Music
Country Music
Cuban Music
Drum'n'bass
Elvis
House
Irish Music
Jazz
Music USA
Opera
Reggae
Rock
Techno
World Music (2 vols)

100 Essential CDs series
Country
Latin
Opera
Rock
Soul
World Music

History Guides
China
Egypt
England
France
Greece
India
Ireland
Islam
Italy
Spain
USA

Reference Guides
Books for Teenagers
Children's Books, 0–5
Children's Books, 5–11
Cult Football
Cult Movies
Cult TV
Digital Stuff
Formula 1
The Internet
Internet Radio
James Bond
Lord of the Rings
Man Utd
Personal Computers
Pregnancy & Birth
Shopping Online
Travel Health
Travel Online
Unexplained Phenomena
The Universe
Videogaming
Weather
Website Directory

Also! More than 120 Rough Guide music CDs are available from all good book and record stores. Listen in at www.worldmusic.net

NOTES

NOTES

NOTES

NOTES

NOTES

NOTES

NOTES

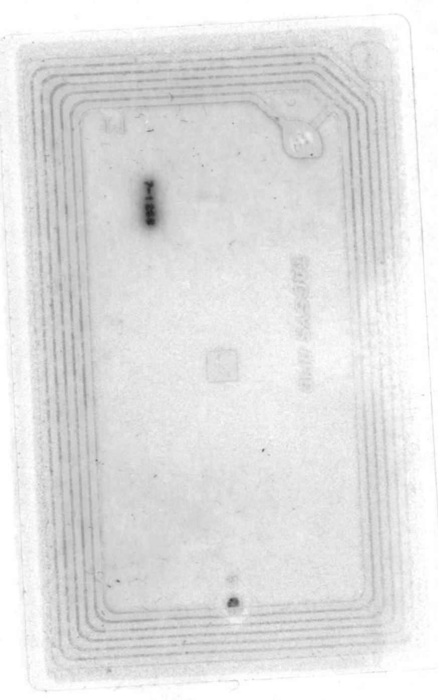